# THE SPORT AMERICANA ®

# PRICE GUIDE
## NO. 9

By
### DR. JAMES BECKETT

ISBN 0-937424-33-1

# About the Author

Jim Beckett, the leading authority on sport card values in the United States, maintains a wide range of activities in the world of sports. He possesses one of the finest collections of sports cards and autographs in the world, has made numerous appearances on radio and television, and has been frequently cited in many national publications. He was awarded the first "Special Achievement Award" for Contributions to the Hobby by the National Sports Collectors Convention in 1980 and the "Jock-Jasperson Award" for Hobby Dedication in 1983.

Dr. Beckett is the author of The Sport Americana Football, Hockey, Basketball and Boxing Price Guide, The Official Price Guide to Football Cards, The Sport Americana Baseball Card Price Guide, The Official Price Guide to Baseball Cards, The Sport Americana Price Guide to Baseball Collectibles, The Sport Americana Baseball Memorabilia and Autograph Price Guide, and The Sport Americana Alphabetical Baseball Card Checklist. In addition, he is the founder, author, and editor of Beckett Baseball Card Monthly, a magazine dedicated to advancing the card collecting hobby.

Jim Beckett received his Ph.D. in Statistics from Southern Methodist University in 1975. He resides in Dallas with his wife Patti and their daughters, Christina and Rebecca, while actively pursuing his writing and consultancy careers.

# Acknowledgements

This edition of the Price Guide contains new sets and, of course, completely revised prices on all the cards. A great deal of hard work went into this volume, and it could not have been done without a considerable amount of help from many people. Our thanks are extended to each and every one of you.

First, we owe a special acknowledgement to Dennis W. Eckes, "Mr. Sport Americana." The success of the Beckett Price Guides has been the result of a team effort. Although Denny has chosen no longer to be a co-author on price guides -- in order to devote more time to his business, Den's Collector's Den -- he is still on board as a special consultant.

Those who have worked closely with us on this and many other books, have again proven themselves invaluable -- Frank and Vivian Barning (Baseball Hobby News), Joe Brown, Cartophilium (Andrew Pywowarczuk), Mike Cramer (Pacific Trading Cards), Bill and Diane Dodge, Gervise Ford, Larry and Jeff Fritsch, Tony Galovich, Mike and Howard Gordon, John Greenwald, Wayne Grove, Bill Haber, Bill Henderson, Danny Hitt, Alan Kaye (Baseball Card News), Ralph Nozaki, Jack Pollard, Gavin Riley, Alan Rosen (Mr. Mint), John Rumierz, San Diego Sport Collectibles (Bill Goepner and Nacho Arredondo), John Spalding, Frank Steele, Murvin Sterling, Lee Temanson, Ed Twombly (New England Bullpen), and Kit Young.

Special mention goes to three people this year. Brian Morris, who has broad collecting and dealing interests, put his experience in writing by marking up and sending us his old (last year's) copy of the Price Guide. This is my favorite way to receive a maximum amount of input from a very knowledgeable person. Others have done this besides Brian -- but Brian did the best job this year.

Lew Lipset has done much to further the knowledge of cards and collecting; most advanced collectors are familiar with his three Encyclopedic volumes covering N, T, and E cards. However we thank him this year for the development of his "Old Judge" newsletter and the popularization of the "break factor". Lew, with help from his son Rob, has analyzed the relationship between the sum of the individual prices and the complete set price. The resulting ratio is the "break factor". This year's edition herein shows that knowledgeable collectors and dealers are increasingly aware of the "break factor" as set prices have risen markedly on most older issues.

Press Pins have always been an interesting sub-area of the card collecting hobby. This year we have a major section in the back of this Price Guide giving the most definitive treatment to date on Press Pins. Thanks primarily to the extensive and laborious contributions of Jim Johnston, one of the top collector/dealers in those attractive and valuable items. We thank him for his labor of love.

All three have my thanks as well as a lifetime subscription to Beckett Monthly.

Special thanks are extended to the Donruss Company, the Fleer Corporation, Sportflics, and the Topps Chewing Gum Company, who have consistently provided checklists and visual materials in order that the Price Guide could be complete.

Many other people have provided price input, illustrative material, checklist verifications, errata, and/or background information. We should like to individually thank Ab D Cards (Dale Wesolewski), Jerry Adamic, A.J.'s Sport Stop, Bob Alexander, Dennis Anderson, Eric Anderson, Lee Anderson, Thomas D. Anderson, Mark Angle, Rick Apter, Mark Argo (Olde South Cards), Jerry Baldwin, Ball Four Cards, Ed Barry (Ed's Collectibles), Bob Bartosz, Baseball Card Shop, Bay State Cards (Lenny DeAngelico), Chris Benjamin, Eric Bechtel, Beulah Sports, Big Andy's, John Blank, Levi Bleam, Bob Boffa, Tim Bond, Gary Borofsky, Joe Borte, Bill Bossert (Mid-Atlantic Coin Exchange), Major Charles Botello, Scott Bowery, Jeffery Brandon, Greg Brown, Kevin Brown, Shanan Brown, Eric Burch, Larry Calder, Murray Calder, California Card Co., Cards and Comics, Louis Centolanza, Ira Cetron, Charles Champ, Sandy Chan, Don Chandler, Dwight Chapin, Chriss Christiansen, Dick Cianciotta, Barry Colla, Collection de Sport AZ, Ben Contorno, Kenny Conyers, Ron Coons, Paul Cords, Kevin Cormier, Taylor Crane, William Craven, James Critzer, John Curtis, Alan Custer, Dave Dame, Donna Davis, James Dickson, Greg Diehl, Dixie Dugout, George Dolence, Serge Donikian, George Dougherty, Bill Downes, John Dorsey, Charles Dugre, Ruston Eastman, Larry Eccles, Jason Egge, Doak Ewing, David and Mark Federman, John Ferer, David Festberg, Bill Finneran, Stewart Flate, Leo Font Jr., Frank Fox (The Card Shop), Steve Freedman, Jeff Freyer, Hank Friedman, Jason Galla, General Hobbies, Willie George, Joe Gering, Mark Gibson, Bob Gilbert (Brewer Sports Collectibles), Dick Goddard, Steve Gold (AU Sports), Greg Goldstein (Dragon's Den), Jeff Goldstein, Rich Gove (Central Coast Baseball Cards), Todd Grady, Grand Slam Sports Collectibles, Ron Gulledge, Dave Hadeler, Dean Haley, Ronald Haley, Charley Hall, Hall's Nostalgia, John Halpin, Ernie Hammond, Hershell Hanks, Phil Haseltine, Mark Hausner, P. Hawkins, Joel Hellman (JJ's Budget Baseball Cards), Jeffrey Hewitt, Janet Hock, Eric Hook, Paul Hundrieser, Ryan Hurba, Tom Hutchinson, Chad Irwin, Richard L. Johnson, Steve Johnson, Rosie Jones, Stewart Jones, Dave Jurgensmeier, John Kagawa, Dr. Neil Katz, Jim Kelley, Rick Keplinger, Ted Kern, Ray Kessler, Tom Kiecker, Robert Lee King, Jim Knowler, John Kolodziej, Thomas Kunnecke, Wayne Larned, Dan Lavin, Leo LeClair, Morley Leeking, Charles Leinberry, Irv Lerner, Kathie Liles, LNW Sports, Chris Lockwood, Mike London, Chad Long, Jeff Long, Steve Ludwiski, John Machacek, Jim Macie, Paul Marchant, Bob May, Raymond May, Dr. William McAvoy, Mike McDonald (Sports Page), Gail McEldowney, J. McElroy, Brian McNeil, Dan McReynolds, Mendal Mearkle (Chariots Inc.), John Mehlin, Blake Meyer (Lone Star Sportscards), Joe Michalowicz, Sean Millar, David "Otis" Miller, Wayne Miller, Dick Millerd, Ashby Milstead, Andy Minton, Ilan Mochari, Mike Moloney, Matthew Morgan, Dick Mueller, Ray Murphy, Gary Nagle, Mark Natale, Edward Nazzaro (The Collector), Chip Nelson, Eddie Nelson, Murry Nelson, Tony Niemann (ADC Sports), Mike Nolde, North Conway Baseball Card Shop, Mike O'Brien, Keith Olbermann, Carl Olsen (Baseball Card Express), Bruce Parker, Jack Parsons, Clay Pasternack, Bill Pekarik (Pastime Hobbies), Michael Perrotta, Gerald Perry, Tom Pfirrmann, Pine Tree Stamps, Charles M. Placek, Michael Poynter, Mickey Rabinowitz, Michael Raduenz, Troy Rambo, Rick Rapa and Barry Sanders (Atlanta Sports Cards), Steve Rateike, Trey Rees, Gordon Reid, Tom Reid, Pat Reiter, Paul Richman, Owen Ricker, Rick's Coin Shop, Ken Rinehart, Dave Ring, Nathan Roach, Norman Rodriguez, Clifton Rouse, George Rusnak, Tom Ryan, Terry Sack, Steve St.Peter, Joe Sak, Jennifer Salems, Ang Savelli, Gary Sawatzki, Robert Scagnelli, Matt Schindler, Don Schlaff, F.C. Schlauch, Shawn Schuetz,

Michele Scott, Sue Scott, David Shannon, Gerry Shebib, Scott Shepherd, Chris and Kelly Shore, Barry Sloate, Darren Smith, Stuart Smith, Robert Sochacki, Southern Sports (Roy Young), State Video and Comics, Dave Steckling, Don Steinbach, Mark Stewart (Blue Chip), Rick Stineman, Raymond Strawn, Strikeout Sports Cards, Richard Strobino, Barrie Sullivan, Hugh Sullivan, Fred Suzman, Swamp Fox Collectibles, David Taylor, Ian Taylor, Lyle Telfer, Scott Thompson, Charles Thorpe, Richard Thurman, Triple Play Cards, Ralph Triplette, 20th Century Collectibles, Rich Unruh, Charles Usher, John Vanden Beek, John Vangen, Trent Vich, Pokie Villalon, Brad Walker, Tom Wamble, Christopher Waters, Bill Wesslund, Richard West, Bob Wilke (The Shoe Box), Jeff Williams, Joe Willis, Eddie Wolfe, World Series Cards (Neil Armstrong), Steve Wozniak, Kit Young, Ted Zanidakis, and Robert Zanze.

We have appreciated all of the help we have received over the years from collectors across the country and, indeed, throughout the world. Every year we make active solicitations to individuals and groups for input to that year's edition and we are particularly appreciative of help (large and small) provided for this volume. While we receive many inquiries, comments, and questions regarding material within this book -- and, in fact, each and every one is read and digested -- time constraints prevent us from personally replying to all but a few such letters. We hope that the letters will continue, and that even though no reply is received, you will feel that you are making significant contributions to the hobby through your interest and comments.

Special thanks go the staff of Beckett Publications for their help on many of the little things that added up to making this book possible. Assistant editors, Fred Reed and Pepper Hastings, were most helpful with the introduction and advertising, respectively. Lou Cather and Edna Harless cheerfully helped with the paste-up and layout. The overall operations of our ongoing commitment to the hobby through Beckett Monthly were skillfully directed by Claire Backus, my sister. Thanks also go to Dale Backus, my new brother-in-law, who was very understanding about Claire's overtime during this period as well as his contributing directly to our success in the past year on the magazine; Claire has been ably assisted by Anne Lowe (our subscription manager), Mary Gregory, Julie Grove, and Nancy Paterson. Thanks also go to James and Sandy Beane, who performed several major system programming jobs for us this year, in order to help us accomplish our work faster and more accurately. The whole Beckett Publications team has my thanks for jobs well done. Thank you, everyone.

Last year I acknowledged my loving family by saying, "Writing this book would have been a very unpleasant experience without the understanding and cooperation of my wife, Patti, and daughters, Christina and Rebecca. I thank them and promise them that I will pay them back for all those hours." This year I must admit that their patience is wearing thin and I don't blame them as they have not been paid back for those many hundreds of missing hours. Writing this book IS an unpleasant experience for someone who really wants to be a good husband and father. My daughters do not understand why Daddy comes home when they are waking up ... Patti isn't too keen on that either. At any rate I am committed to correcting my priorities in the next year, without jeopardizing the high standards my readers have come to expect.

# The Sport Americana
# Baseball Card
# Price Guide
# Table Of Contents

# Preface

Isn't it great? Every year this book gets bigger and bigger with all the new sets coming out. But even more exciting is that every year there are more collectors, more shows, more stores, and ... more interest in the cards we love so much. This edition has been enhanced and expanded from the previous edition. The cards you collect -- who they are, what they look like, where they are from, and (most importantly to many of you) what their current values are -- are enumerated within. Many of the features contained in the other Beckett Price Guides have been incorporated into this volume since condition grading, nomenclature, and many other aspects of collecting are common to the card hobby in general. We hope you find the book both interesting and useful in your collecting pursuits.

The Beckett Guide has been successful where other attempts have failed because it is complete, current, and valid. This Price Guide contains not just one, but three, prices by condition for all the baseball cards in the issues listed. These account for almost all the baseball cards in existence. The prices were added to the card lists just prior to printing and reflect not the author's opinions or desires but the going retail prices for each card, based on the marketplace (sports memorabilia conventions and shows, hobby papers, current mail order catalogs, local club meetings, auction results, and other firsthand reportings of actually realized prices).

To facilitate your use of this book, read the complete introductory section in the pages following before going to the pricing pages. Every collectible field has its own terminology; we've tried to capture most of these terms and definitions in our glossary. Please read carefully the section on grading and the condition of your cards as you will not be able to determine which price column is appropriate for a given card without first knowing its condition.

Welcome to the world of baseball cards.

Sincerely, Dr. James Beckett

# Introduction

Welcome to the exciting world of baseball card collecting, America's fastest-growing avocation. You have made a good choice in buying this book, since it will open up to you the entire panorama of this field in the simplest, most concise way.

It is estimated that nearly a quarter of a million different baseball cards have been issued during the past century. And the number of total cards put out by all manufacturers last year has been estimated at over two billion. With all that cardboard available in the marketplace, it should be no surprise that several million sports fans like you collect baseball cards today, and that number is growing by hundreds of thousands each year.

The growth of Beckett Baseball Card Monthly is another indication of this rising crescendo of popularity for baseball cards. Founded less than three years ago by Dr. James Beckett, the author of this Price Guide, Beckett Monthly has grown to the pinnacle of the baseball card hobby with more than a quarter of a million readers anxiously awaiting each enjoyable issue.

So collecting baseball cards -- while still pursued as a hobby with youthful exuberance by kids in the neighborhood -- has also taken on the trappings of an industry, with thousands of full and parttime card dealers, as well as vendors of supplies, clubs and conventions. Each year since 1980, in fact, thousands of hobbyists have assembled for a National Sports Collectors Convention, at which hundreds of dealers have displayed their wares, seminars have been conducted, autographs penned by sports notables, and millions of cards changed hands. These colossal affairs have been staged in Los Angeles, Detroit, St. Louis, Chicago, New York, Anaheim, Arlington, TX, and this year in San Francisco. So baseball card collecting is really national in scope!

This increasing interest has been reflected in card values. As more collectors compete for available supplies, card prices rise. A national publication indicated a "very strong advance" in baseball card prices during the past decade, and a quick perusal of prices in this book compared to the figures in earlier editions of this Price Guide will quickly confirm this. Which brings us back around again to the book you have in your hands. It is the best annual guide available to this exciting world of baseball cards. Read it and use it. May your enjoyment and your card collection increase in the coming months and years.

# BILL HENDERSON'S CARDS
## "King of the Commons"

"ALWAYS BUYING"
Call or Write
for Quote

2320 RUGER AVE. - PG9
JANESVILLE, WISCONSIN 53545
1-608-755-0922

"ALWAYS BUYING"
Call or Write
for Quote

| | HI NOS. | COMMONS EACH | | EX/MT TO MINT CONDITION | GROUP LOTS FOR SALE | | | VG Condition | | |
|---|---|---|---|---|---|---|---|---|---|---|
| | | | | 50 Diff. | 100 Diff. | 300 Asst. | 500 Asst. | 50 | 100 | 200 Different |
| 1948 BOWMAN | | 4.00 | | | | | | | | |
| 1949 BOWMAN | | 4.00 | | | | | | | | |
| 50-51 BOWMAN | 12.00 | 3.50 | 51 (2-72) 4.00 | 165. | | | | 100. | | |
| 1952 TOPPS | 75.00 | 7.00 | (2-80) 10.00 | 315. | | | | 190. | | |
| 1952 BOWMAN | 7.00 | 3.50 | (2-72) 3.75 | 165. | | | | 100. | | |
| 1953 TOPPS | 14.00 | 4.00 | | 185. | | | | 110. | | |
| 1953 BOWMAN | 10.00 | 7.50 | (113-128) 18.00 | 340. | | | | 200. | | |
| 1954 TOPPS | | 2.00 | (51-75) 4.00 | 95. | 180. | | | 58. | | |
| 1954 BOWMAN | | 1.50 | (129-224) 2.00 | 70. | 135. | | | 45. | | |
| 1955 TOPPS | 4.50 | 1.50 | (151-160) 3.50 | 70. | 135. | 390. | | 45. | | |
| 1955 BOWMAN | 4.00-6. Umps | .75 | (2-96) 1.00 | 35. | 68. | 200. | | 20. | 40. | |
| 1956 TOPPS | | 1.50 | (181-260) 2.50 | 70. | 135. | 390. | | 40. | 75. | |
| 1957 TOPPS | 4.50 | 1.00 | (353-407) 1.25 | 45. | 85. | 245. | | 28. | 50. | |
| 1958 TOPPS | | .65 | (1-110) .85 | 30. | 58. | 170. | | 40. | | |
| 1959 TOPPS | 2.50 | .45 | (1-110) .60 | 20. | 40. | 115. | 185. | 24. | 46. | |
| 1960 TOPPS | (553-572 2.50) 2.00 | .40 | (441-506) .60 | 20. | 38. | 110. | 175. | 24. | 46. | |
| 1961 TOPPS | 6.50-8.50 S.N. | .40 | (371-522) .40 | 17. | 32. | 92. | 150. | 20. | 38. | |
| 1962 TOPPS | 2.00-5.00 RKS. | .60 | (371-522) .60 | 17. | 32. | 92. | 150. | 20. | 38. | |
| 1963 TOPPS | 2.00 | .30 | (197-446) .50 | 14. | 28. | 80. | | 20. | | |
| 1964 TOPPS | 1.00 | .30 | (371-522) .50 | 14. | 28. | 80. | 130. | 18. | 35. | |
| 1965 TOPPS | (447-522 .50) .85 | .30 | (199-446) .35 | 14. | 28. | 80. | 130. | 18. | 35. | |
| 1966 TOPPS | 5.00 | .30 | (447-522) .60 | 14. | 28. | 80. | 130. | 18. | 35. | |
| 1967 TOPPS | 3.00 | .30 | (458-533) 1.00 | 14. | 28. | 80. | 130. | 18. | 35. | |
| 1968 TOPPS | (13-110 .25) .40 | .25 | (458-533) .30 | 12. | 24. | *70. | 110. | 15. | 28. | |
| 1969 TOPPS | | .25 | (219-327) .40 | | 24. | *70. | 110. | 15. | 28. | |
| 1970 TOPPS | 1.00 | .25 | (553-636) .50 | | 24. | *70. | 110. | 15. | 28. | |
| 1971 TOPPS | 1.00 | .25 | (524-643) .50 | | 24. | *70. | 110. | 15. | 28. | |
| 1972 TOPPS | (395-525 .25) 1.00 | .25 | (526-656) .50 | | 24. | *70. | 110. | 15. | 28. | |
| 1973 TOPPS | .75 | .20 | (397-528) .25 | | 18. | *52. | 85. | 10. | 19. | |
| 1974 TOPPS | | .20 | | | 18. | *52. | *85. | 10. | 19. | |
| 1975 TOPPS | (8-132 .25) | .20 | | | 18. | *52. | *85. | 10. | 19. | |
| 1976-77 | | .15 | | | 14. | *42. | *68. | 9. | 16. | |
| 1978-1980 | | .10 | | | 8. | *22. | *35. | 5. | 9. | |
| 1981 thru 1987 Topps, Fleer or Donrus | | .10 | | | 5. | *14. | *20. | 3. | 6. | |
| Specify Year & Company | | | | | Per Yr. | Per Yr. | Per Yr. | | | |
| 1984 DONRUS | | .25 | | 12. | 24. | *70. | *110. | | | |

SPECIAL IN VG
CONDITION-POSTPAID

| 250 | 58-62 | 60.00 |
|---|---|---|
| 500 | 58-62 | 115.00 |
| 250 | 60-69 | 45.00 |
| 500 | 60-69 | 90.00 |
| 1000 | 60-69 | 175.00 |
| 250 | 70-79 | 20.00 |
| 500 | 70-79 | 40.00 |
| 1000 | 70-79 | 75.00 |
| 250 | 80-84 | 10.00 |
| 500 | 80-84 | 17.00 |
| 1000 | 80-84 | 30.00 |

*These lots are all different.
Special 1 Different from each year 1950-86 from above $30.00 postpaid.
Special 100 Different from each year 1956-86 from above $725.00 postpaid.
Special 10 Different from each year 1956-86 from above $75.00 postpaid.
All lot groups are my choice only.

All assorted lots will contain as many different as possible.
Please list alternates whenever possible.
Send your want list and I will fill them at the above price for commons. High numbers, specials, scarce series, and stars extra.

Minimum order $7.50 - Postage and handling .50 per 100 cards (minimum $1.75)

Have thousands of star and super star cards. Call or send for star list.
Also interested in purchasing your collection.
*Groups include various years of my choice.

SETS AVAILABLE
POSTAGE 2.50 PER SET

| 1979 Topps | $95.00 |
|---|---|
| 1980 Topps | 90.00 |
| 1981 Topps | 55.00 |
| 1981 Donrus | 17.00 |
| 1981 Fleer | 14.00 |
| 1982 Topps | 55.00 |
| 1982 Donrus | 14.00 |
| 1983 Topps | 55.00 |
| 1984 Topps | 55.00 |
| 1985 Topps | 55.00 |
| 1986 Topps | 25.00 |
| 1987 Topps | 18.00 |

# How to Collect

Each collection is personal and reflects the individuality of its owner. There are no set rules on how to collect cards. Since card collecting is a hobby or leisure pastime, what you collect, how much you collect, and how much time and money you spend collecting are entirely up to you. The funds you have available for collecting, and your own personal taste should determine how you collect. Information and ideas presented here are intended to help you get the most enjoyment from this hobby.

It is impossible to collect every card ever produced. Therefore, beginners as well as intermediate and advanced collectors usually specialize in some way. One of the reasons this hobby is popular is that individual collectors can define and tailor their collecting methods to match their own tastes. To give you some ideas of the various approaches to collecting, we will list some of the more popular areas of specialization.

Many collectors select complete sets from particular years. For example, they may concentrate on assembling complete sets from all the years since their birth or since they became avid sports fans. They may try to collect a card for every player during that specified period of time.

Many others wish to acquire only certain players. Usually such players are the superstars of the sport, but occasionally collectors will specialize in all the cards of players who attended certain colleges or came from certain towns. Some collectors are only interested in the first cards or rookie cards of certain players.

Another fun way to collect cards is by team. Most fans have a favorite team, and it is natural for that loyalty to be translated into a desire for cards of the players on that favorite team. For most of the recent years, team sets (all the cards from a given team for that year) are readily available at a reasonable price.

## Obtaining Cards

Several avenues are open to card collectors. Cards can be purchased in the traditional way at the local candy, grocery, or drug stores, with the bubble gum or other products included. In recent years, it has also become possible to purchase complete sets of baseball cards through mail order advertisers found in traditional sports media publications, such as The Sporting News, Baseball Digest, Street & Smith's Yearbooks, and others. These sets are also advertised in the card collecting periodicals. Many collectors will begin by subscribing to at least one of the monthly hobby publications, all with good up-to-date information. In fact, subscription offers can be found in the advertising section of this book.

Most serious card collectors obtain old (and new) cards from one or more of several main sources: (1) trading or buying from other collectors or dealers; (2) responding to sale or auction ads in the monthly hobby publications; and/or (3) attending sports collectibles shows or conventions. We advise that you try all three methods since each has its own distinct advantages: (1) trading is a great way to make new friends; (2) monthly hobby periodicals help you keep up with what's going on in the hobby (including when and where the conventions are happening); and (3) shows provide enjoyment and the opportunity to view millions of collectibles under one roof,

in addition to meeting some of the hundreds or even thousands of other collectors with similar interests who also attend the shows.

## Preserving Your Cards

Cards are fragile. They must be handled properly in order to retain their value. Careless handling can easily result in creased or bent cards. It is, however, not recommended that tweezers or tongs be used to pick up your cards since such utensils might mar or indent card surfaces and thus reduce those cards' conditions and values. In general, your cards should be handled directly as little as possible. This is sometimes easier to say than to do. Although there are still many who use custom boxes, storage trays, or even shoe boxes, plastic sheets are the preferred method of storing cards. A collection stored in plastic pages in a three ring album allows you to view your collection at any time without the need to touch the card itself. For a large collection, some collectors may use a combination of the above methods.

When purchasing plastic sheets for your cards, be sure that you find the pocket size that fits the cards snugly. Don't put your 1951 Bowmans in a sheet designed to fit 1981 Topps. Most hobby and collectibles shops, and virtually all collectors' conventions will have these plastic pages available in quantity for the various sizes offered or you can purchase them directly from the advertisers in this book.

Damp, sunny and/or hot conditions -- no, this is not a weather forecast -- are three elements to avoid in extremes if you are interested in preserving your collection. Too much (or too little) humidity can cause gradual deterioration of a card. Direct, bright sun (or flourescent light) over time will bleach out the color of a card. Extreme heat accelerates the decomposition of the card. On the other hand, many cards have lasted more than 50 years without much scientific intervention. So be cautious, even if the above factors typically present a problem only when present in the extreme. It never hurts to be prudent.

## Collecting/Investing

Collecting individual players and collecting complete sets are both popular vehicles for investment and speculation. Most investors and speculators stock up on complete sets or on quantities of players they think have good investment potential. There is obviously no guarantee in this book, or anywhere else for that matter, that cards will outperform the stock market or other investment alternatives in the future. After all, baseball cards do not pay quarterly dividends. Nevertheless, investors have noticed a favorable trend in the past performance of baseball and other sports collectibles, and certain cards and sets have outperformed just about any other investment in some years.

Some of the obvious questions are: Which cards? When to buy? When to sell? The best investment you can make is in your own education. The more you know about your collection and the hobby, the more informed the decisions you will be able to make. We're not selling investment tips. We're selling information about the current value of baseball cards. It's up to you to use that information to your best advantage.

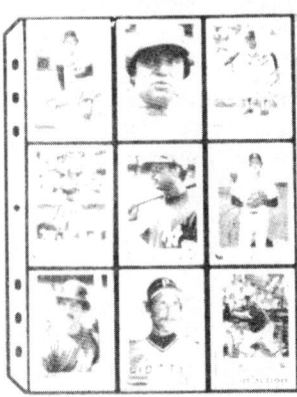

# Nomenclature

Each hobby has its own language to describe its area of interest. The nomenclature traditionally used for trading cards is derived from the American Card Catalog, published in 1960 by Nostalgia Press. That catalog, written by Jefferson Burdick (who is called the "Father of Card Collecting" for his pioneering work), uses letter and number designations for each separate set of cards.

The letter used in the ACC designation refers to the generic type of card. While both sport and non-sport issues are classified in the ACC, we shall confine ourselves to the sport issues. The following list defines the letters and their meanings as used by the American Card Catalog.

(none) or N - 19th Century U.S. Tobacco

B - Blankets

D - Bakery Inserts Including Bread

E - Early Candy and Gum

F - Food Inserts

H - Advertising

M - Periodicals

PC - Postcards

R - Candy and Gum Cards 1930 to Present

T - 20th Century U.S. Tobacco

UO - Gas and Oil Inserts

V - Canadian Candy

W - Exhibits, Strip Cards, Team Issues

Following the letter prefix and an optional hyphen are one, two, or three digit numbers, 1-999. These typically represent the company or entity issuing the cards. In several cases, the ACC number is extended by an additional hyphen and another one or two digit numerical suffix. For example, the 1957 Topps regular series baseball card issue carries an ACC designation of R414-11. The "R" indicates a Candy or Gum Card produced since 1930. The "414" is the ACC designation for Topps Chewing Gum baseball card issues, and the "11" is the ACC designation for the 1957 regular issue (Topps' eleventh baseball set).

Like other traditional methods of identification, this system provides order to the process of cataloguing cards; however, most serious collectors learn the ACC designation of the popular sets by repetition and familiarity, rather than by attempting to "figure out" what they might or should be.

From 1948 forward, collectors and dealers commonly refer to all sets by their year, maker, type of issue, and any other distinguishing characteristic. For example

such a characteristic could be an unusual issue or one of several regular issues put out by a specific maker in a single year. Regional issues are usually referred to by year, maker, and sometimes by title or theme of the set.

# Glossary/Legend

Our glossary defines terms frequently used in the card collecting hobby. Many of these terms are also common to other types of sports memorabilia collecting. Some terms may have several meanings depending on use.

AAS - Action All Stars, a postcard sized set issued by the Donruss Company.

ACC - Acronym for American Card Catalog.

AD CARD - See Display Card.

AL - Abbreviation for American League or American Leaguer.

ALL STAR CARD - A card portraying an All Star Player of the previous year that says "All Star" on its face.

ALPH - Alphabetical.

AS - Abbreviation for All Star (card).

ATG - All Time Great card.

AUTOGRAPHED CARD - A card that has been signed (usually on its face) by the player(s) portrayed on the card with a fountain pen, felt tip, magic marker, or ball-point pen. This term does not include stamped or facsimile signature cards.

BLANKET - A felt square (normally 5" to 6") portraying a baseball player.

BOX - Card issued on a box or a card depicting a Boxer.

BRICK - A group of cards, usually 50 or more having common characteristics, that is intended to be bought, sold or traded as a unit.

C - Abbreviation for Catcher.

CABINETS - Very popular and highly valuable photographs on thick card stock produced in the 19th and early 20th century.

CF - Abbreviation for Center Fielder.

CHECKLIST - A list of the cards contained in a particular set. The list is always in numerical order if the cards are numbered. Some unnumbered sets are artificially numbered in alphabetical order, or by team and alphabetically within the team for convenience.

CHECKLIST CARD - A card which lists in order the cards and players in the set or series. Older checklist cards in Mint condition which have not been checked off are very desirable.

CL - Abbreviation for Checklist.

COA - Abbreviation for Coach.

COIN - A small disc of metal or plastic portraying a player in its center.

COLLECTOR - A person who engages in the hobby of collecting cards primarily for his own enjoyment, with any profit motive being secondary.

COLLECTOR ISSUE - A set produced for the sake of the card itself with no product or service sponsor. It derives its name from the fact that most of these sets are produced for sale directly to the hobby market.

COMBINATION CARD - A single card depicting two or more players (but not a team card).

COMMON CARD - The typical card of any set; it has no premium value accruing from subject matter, numerical scarcity, popular demand, or anomaly.

COMP - Card issued by the Post Cereal Company through their mail in offer.

CONVENTION - A large weekend gathering of dealers and collectors at a single location for the purpose of buying, selling and sometimes trading sports memorabilia items. Conventions are open to the public and sometimes feature celebrities, door prizes, films, contests, etc.

CONVENTION ISSUE - A set produced in conjunction with a sports collectibles convention to commemorate or promote the show.

COR - Correct or corrected card.

COUPON - See Tab.

CREASE - A wrinkle on the card, usually caused by bending the card. Creases are a common defect from careless handling.

CY - Cy Young Award.

DEALER - A person who engages in buying, selling, and trading sports collectibles or supplies. A dealer may also be a collector, but as a dealer, he anticipates a profit.

DH - Double Header (1955 Topps) or Designated Hitter.

DIE-CUT - A card with part of its stock partially cut, allowing one or more parts to be folded or removed. After removal or appropriate folding, the remaining part of the card can frequently be made to stand up.

DISC - A circular shaped card.

DISPLAY CARD - A sheet, usually containing three to nine cards, that is printed and used by the manufacturer to advertise and/or display the packages containing his products and cards. The backs of display cards are blank or contain advertisements.

DK - Diamond King (artwork produced by Perez-Steele for Donruss).

DP - Double Print (a card which was printed in double the quantity compared to the other cards in the same series).

E CARD - A candy or gum card produced and issued prior to 1930.

ERA - Earned Run Average.

ERR - Error card (see also COR).

ERROR CARD - A card with erroneous information, spelling or depiction on either side of the card. Not all errors are corrected by the producing card company.

EXHIBIT - The generic name given to thick stock, postcard sized cards with single color obverse pictures. The name is derived from the Exhibit Supply Co. of Chicago, the principal manufacturer of this type of card. These are also known as Arcade cards since they were found in many arcades.

FDP - First Draft Pick (see 1985 Topps Baseball).

FULL SHEET - A complete sheet of cards that has not been cut up into individual cards by the manufacturer. Also called an uncut sheet.

HALL OF FAMER - (HOF'er) A card which portrays a player who has been inducted into the Hall of Fame.

HIGH NUMBER - The cards in the last series of numbers in a year in which such higher numbered cards were printed or distributed in significantly lesser amounts than the lower numbered cards. The high number designation refers to a scarcity of the high numbered cards. Not all years have high numbers in terms of this definition.

HL - Highlight card.

HOC - House of Collectibles.

HOF - Acronym for Hall of Fame.

HOR - Horizontal pose on card as opposed to the standard vertical orientation found on most cards.

HR - Abbreviation for Home Run.

IA - In Action (type of card).

INF - Abbreviation for Infielder.

INSERT - A card of a different type, e.g., a poster, or any other sports collectible contained and sold in the same package along with a card or cards of a major set.

ISSUE - Synonymous with set, but usually used in conjunction with a manufacturer, e.g., a Topps issue.

KP - Kid Picture (a sub-series issued in the Topps Baseball sets of 1972 and 1973).

LAYERING - The separation or peeling of one or more layers of the card stock, usually at the corner of the card.

LEGITIMATE ISSUE - A set produced to promote or boost sales of a product or service, e.g., bubble gum, cereal, cigarettes, etc. Most collector issues are not legitimate issues in this sense.

LHP - Left Handed Pitcher.

LID - A circular shaped card (possibly with tab) that forms the top of the container for the product being promoted.

LL - Living Legends (Donruss 1984) or large letters.

MAJOR SET - A set produced by a national manufacturer of cards containing a large number of cards. Usually 100 or more different cards comprise the set.

MGR - Abbreviation for Manager.

MINI - A small card; specifically, a Topps baseball card of identical design but smaller dimensions than the regular Topps issue of 1975.

MISCUT - A card that has been cut particularly unevenly at the manufacturer's cutting stage.

ML - Major League.

MVP - Most Valuable Player.

N CARD - A tobacco card produced and issued during the 19th Century.

NL - National League.

NNOF - No Name on Front (see 1949 Bowman).

NOF - Name on Front (see 1949 Bowman).

NON-SPORT CARD - A card from a set whose major theme is a subject other than a sports subject. A card of a sports figure or event that is part of a non-sport set is still a non-sport card, e.g., while the "Look 'N' See" non-sport card set contains a card of Babe Ruth, a sports figure, that card is a non-sport card.

NOTCHING - The grooving of the card, usually caused by fingernails, rubber bands, or bumping card edges against other objects.

NY - New York.

OBVERSE - The front, face, or pictured side of the card.

OF - Outfielder.

OLY - Olympics (see 1985 Topps Baseball; the members of the 1984 U.S. Olympic Baseball team were a featured sub-series).

OPT - Option.

P - Pitcher or Pitching pose.

P1 - First Printing.

P2 - Second Printing.

P3 - Third Printing.

PANEL - An extended card that is composed of two or more individual cards. Often the panel forms the back part of the container for the product being promoted, e.g., a Hostess panel, a Bazooka panel, an Esskay Meat panel.

PCL - Pacific Coast League.

PG - Price Guide.

PLASTIC SHEET - A clear, plastic page which is punched for insertion into a binder (with standard 3-ring spacing) containing pockets for displaying cards. Many different styles of sheets exist with pockets of varying sizes to hold the many differing card formats.

PREMIUM - A card, sometimes on photographic stock, that is purchased or obtained in conjunction with/or redemption for another card or product. The premium is not packaged in the same unit as the primary item.

PUZZLE CARD - A card whose back contains a part of a picture which, when joined correctly with other puzzle cards, forms the completed picture.

PUZZLE PIECE - An die-cut piece designed to interlock with similar pieces.

R CARD - A candy or gum card produced and issued since 1930.

RARE - A card or series of cards of very limited availability. Unfortunately, "rare" is a subjective term sometimes used indiscriminately. Rare cards are harder to obtain than scarce cards.

RB - Record Breaker card.

RBI - Abbreviation for Runs Batted In.

REGIONAL - A card issued and distributed only in a limited geographical area of the country. The producer is not a major, national producer of trading cards.

REPRINT - A reproduction of an original card, usually produced by a maker other than the original manufacturer from a source other than the original artwork or negative.

REVERSE - The back or narrative side of the card.

RHP - Right Handed Pitcher.

ROOKIE CARD - The first regular card of a particular player or a card which portrays one or more players with the notation on the card that those players are Rookies.

ROY - Acronym for Rookie of the Year.

RR - Rated Rookies (a subset featured in the Donruss Baseball sets).

SA - Super Action or Sport Americana.

SASE - Self-Addressed, Stamped Envelope.

SB - Stolen Bases.

SCARCE - A card or series of cards of limited availability. This subjective term is sometimes used indiscriminately to promote or hype value. Scarce cards are not as difficult to obtain as rare cards.

SCR - Script name on Back (see 1949 Bowman Baseball).

SEMI-HIGH - A card from the next to last series of a sequentially issued set. It has more value than an average card and generally less value than a high number. A card is not called a semi-high unless the next to last series in which it exists has an additional premium attached to it.

SERIES - The entire set of cards issued by a particular producer in a particular year, e.g., the 1971 Topps series. Also, within a particular set, series can refer to a group of (consecutively numbered) cards printed at the same time, e.g., the first series of the 1957 Topps issue (numbers 1 through 88).

SET - One each of the entire run of cards of the same type produced by a particular manufacturer during a single year. In other words, if you have a (complete) set of 1976 Topps then you have every card from number 1 up through and including number 660, i.e., all the different cards that were produced.

SF - San Francisco.

SKIP-NUMBERED - A set that has many unissued card numbers between the lowest number in the set and the highest number in the set, e.g., the 1948 Leaf baseball set contains 98 cards skip-numbered from number 1 to number 168. A major set in which a few numbers were not printed is not considered to be skip-numbered.

SO - Strikeouts.

SP - Single or Short Print (a card which was printed in lesser quantity compared to the other cards in the same series; see also DP and TP).

SPECIAL CARD - A card that portrays something other than a single player or team, for example, a card that portrays the previous year's statistical leaders or the results from the previous year's post season action.

SS - Abbreviation for Shortstop.

STAMP - Adhesive backed papers depicting a player. The stamp may be individual or in a sheet of many stamps. Moisture must be applied to the adhesive in order for the stamp to be attached to another surface.

STAR CARD - A card that portrays a player of some repute, usually determined by his ability; however, sometimes referring to sheer popularity.

STICKER - A card with a removable layer that can be affixed to (stuck onto) another surface.

STOCK - The cardboard or paper on which the card is printed.

STRIP CARDS - A sheet or strip of cards, particularly popular in the 1920s and 1930s, with the individual cards usually separated by broken or dotted lines.

SUPERSTAR CARD - A card that portrays a superstar, e.g., a Hall of Fame member or a Hall of Fame prospect.

SV - Super Veteran.

T CARD - A tobacco card produced and issued during the 20th Century.

TAB - A card portion set off from the rest of the card, usually with perforations, that may be removed without damaging the central character or event depicted by the card.

TBC - Turn Back the Clock cards.

TEAM CARD - A card which depicts an entire team.

TEST SET - A set, usually containing a small number of cards, issued by a national card producer and distributed in a limited section or sections of the country. Presumably, the purpose of a test set is to test market appeal for a particular type of card.

TL - Team Leader card.

TP - Triple Print (a card which was printed in triple the quantity compared to the other cards in the same series).

TR - Trade or Traded.

TRIMMED - A card cut down from its original size. Trimmed cards are undesirable to most collectors.

UMP - Umpire (see 1955 Bowman Baseball last series).

VARIATION - One of two or more cards from the same series with the same number (or player with identical pose if the series is unnumbered) differing from one another by some aspect, the different feature stemming from the printing or stock of the card. This can be caused when the manufacturer of the cards notices an error in one (or more) of the cards, makes the changes, and then resumes the print run. In this case there will be two versions or variations of the same card. Sometimes one of the variations is relatively scarce.

VERT - Vertical pose on card.

W CARD - A card grouped within a general miscellaneous category by the ACC. Included in this category are Exhibits, strip cards, team issues, and those issues which do not conveniently fall into other established categories.

WASH - Washington.

WL - White Letters (see 1969 Topps Baseball).

WS - World Series card.

YL - Yellow Letters (see 1958 Topps Baseball).

YT - Yellow Team (see 1958 Topps Baseball).

1B - First Base or First Baseman.

2B - Second Base or Second Baseman.

3B - Third Base or Third Baseman.

# History of Baseball Cards

Today's version of the baseball card, with its colorful front and statistical back, is a far cry from its earliest predecessors. The issue remains cloudy as to which was the very first baseball card ever produced, but the institution of baseball cards dates from the latter half of the 19th century, more than 100 years ago. Early issues, generally printed on heavy cardboard, were of poor quality, with photographs, drawings and printing far short of today's standards.

Goodwin & Co., of New York, makers of Gypsy Queen, Old Judge, and other cigarette brands, is considered by many to be the first issuer of baseball and other sports cards. Their issues, predominantly in the 1 1/2" by 2 1/2" size, generally consisted of photographs of baseball players, boxers, wrestlers, and other subjects mounted on stiff cardboard. More than 2,000 different photos of baseball players alone have been identified. These "Old Judges," a collective name commonly used for the Goodwin & Co. cards, were issued from 1886 to 1890 and are treasured parts of many collections today.

Among the other cigarette companies which issued baseball cards that still attract attention today are Allen & Ginter, D. Buchner & Co. (Gold Coin Chewing Tobacco), and P.H. Mayo & Brother. Cards from the first two companies bore colored line drawings, while the Mayos are sepia photographs on black cardboard.

In addition to the small sized cards from this era, several tobacco companies issued cabinet sized baseball cards. These "cabinets" were considerably larger than the small cards, usually about 4 1/4" by 6 1/2", and were printed on heavy stock. Goodwin & Co.'s Old Judge cabinets and the National Tobacco Works' "Newsboy" baseball photos are two that remain popular today.

By 1895 the American Tobacco Company began to dominate its competition. They discontinued baseball card inserts in their cigarette packages (actually slide boxes in those days). The lack of competition in the cigarette market had made these inserts unnecessary. This marked the end of the first era of the baseball card.

At the dawn of the 20th century, few baseball cards were being issued. But once again it was the cigarette companies -- particularly, the American Tobacco Company -- followed to a lesser extent by the candy and gum makers that revived the practice of including baseball cards with their products. The bulk of these cards, identified in the American Card Catalog (designated hereafter as ACC) as T or E cards for 20th century "Tobacco" or "Early Candy and Gum" issues respectively, were released from 1909 to 1915.

This romantic and popular era of baseball card collecting produced many desirable items. The most outstanding is the fabled T-206 Honus Wagner card. Other perennial favorites among collectors are the T-206 Eddie Plank card, and the T-206 Magee error card. The former was once the second most valuable card and only recently relinquished that position to a more distinctive and aesthetically pleasing Napoleon Lajoie card from the 1933/34 Goudey Gum series. The latter misspells the player's name as "Magie," the most famous and valuable blooper card.

The ingenuity and distinctiveness of this era has yet to be surpassed. Highlights include the T-202 Hassan triple-folders, one of the best looking and the most distinctive cards ever issued; the durable T-201 Mecca double-folders, one of the first sets with players' records on the reverse; the T-3 Turkey Reds, the hobby's most popular cabinet card; the E-145 Cracker Jacks, the only major set containing Federal League player cards; and the T-204 Ramlys, with their distinctive black and white oval photos and ornate gold borders. These are but a few of the varieties issued during this period.

While the American Tobacco Company dominated the field, several other tobacco companies, as well as clothing manufacturers, newspapers and periodicals, game makers, and companies whose identities remain anonymous, also issued cards during this period. In fact, the Collins-McCarthy Candy Company, makers of Zeenuts Pacific Coast League baseball cards, issued cards yearly from 1911 to 1938. Their record for continuous annual card production has been exceeded only by the Topps Chewing Gum Company. The era of the tobacco card issues closed with the onset of World War I, with the exception of the Red Man chewing tobacco sets produced from 1952-1955.

The next flurry of card issues broke out in the roaring and prosperous 1920s, the era of the E card. The caramel companies (National Caramel, American Caramel, York Caramel) were the leading distributors of these E cards. In addition, the strip card, a continous strip with several cards divided by dotted lines or other sectioning features, flourished during this time. While the E cards and the strip cards are generally considered less imaginative than the T cards or the recent candy and gum issues, they are still sought after by many advanced collectors.

Another significant event of the 1920s was the introduction of the arcade card. Taking its designation from its issuer, the Exhibit Supply Company of Chicago, it is usually known as the "Exhibit" card. Once a trademark of the penny arcades, amusement parks, and county fairs across the country, Exhibit machines dispensed nearly post card sized photos on thick stock for one penny. These picture cards bore likenesses of a favorite cowboy, actor, actress or baseball player. Exhibit Supply and its associated companies produced baseball cards during a longer time span, although discontinuous, than any other manufacturer. Its first cards appeared in 1921, while its last issue was in 1966. In 1979, the Exhibit Supply Company was bought and somewhat revived by a collector/dealer who has since reprinted Exhibit photos of the past.

If the T card period, from 1909 to 1915, can be said to be the "Golden Age" of baseball card collecting, then perhaps the "Silver Age" commenced with the introduction of the Big League Gum series of 239 cards in 1933 (a 240th card was added in 1934). These are the forerunners of today's baseball gum cards, and the Goudey Gum Company of Boston is responsible for their success. This era spanned the period from the Depression days of 1933 to America's formal involvement in World War II in 1941.

Goudey's attractive designs, with full color line drawings on thick card stock, influenced greatly other cards being issued at that time. As a result, the most attractive and popular cards in collecting history were produced in this "Silver Age." The 1933

Goudey Big League Gum series also owes its popularity to the more than 40 Hall of Fame players in the set. These include four cards of Babe Ruth and two of Lou Gehrig. Goudey's reign continued in 1934 when it issued a 96 card set in color, together with the single remaining card from the 1933 series, #106, the Napoleon Lajoie card.

In addition to Goudey, several other bubble gum manufacturers issued baseball cards during this era. DeLong Gum Company issued an extremely attractive set in 1933. National Chicle Company's 192 card "Batter-Up" series of 1934-1936 became the largest die-cut set in card history. In addition, that company offered the popular "Diamond Stars" series during the same period. Other popular sets included the "Tattoo Orbit" set of 60 color cards issued in 1933 and Gum Products' 75 card "Double Play" set, featuring sepia depictions of two players per card.

In 1939 Gum Inc., which later became Bowman Gum, replaced Goudey Gum as the leading baseball card producer. In 1939 and the following year, it issued two important sets of black and white cards. In 1939 its "Play Ball America" set consisted of 162 cards. The larger, 240 card "Play Ball" set of 1940 is still considered by many to be the most attractive black and white cards ever produced. That firm introduced its only color set in 1941, consisting of 72 cards entitled "Play Ball Sports Hall of Fame." Many of these were colored repeats of poses from the black and white 1940 series.

In addition to regular gum cards, many manufacturers distributed premium issues during the 1930s. These premiums were printed on paper or photographic stock, rather than card stock. They were much larger than the regular cards and were sold for a penny across the counter with gum (which was packaged separately from the premium). They were often redeemed at the store or through the mail in exchange for the wrappers of previously purchased gum cards, a la proof-of-purchase box-top premiums today. The gum premiums are scarcer than the card issues of the 1930s and in most cases no manufacturer's name is present.

World War II brought an end to this popular era of card collecting when paper and rubber shortages curtailed the production of bubble gum baseball cards. They were resurrected again in 1948 by the Bowman Gum Company (the direct descendant of Gum, Inc.). This marked the beginning of the modern era of card collecting.

In 1948, Bowman Gum issued a 48 card set in black and white consisting of one card and one slab of gum in every one-cent pack. That same year, the Leaf Gum Company also issued a set of cards. Although rather poor in quality, these cards were issued in color. A squabble over the rights to use players' pictures developed between Bowman and Leaf. Eventually Leaf dropped out of the card market, but not before it had left a lasting heritage to the hobby by issuing some of the rarest cards now in existence. Leaf's baseball card series of 1948-49 contained 98 cards, skip numbered to #168 (not all numbers were printed). Of these 98 cards, 49 are relatively plentiful; however, the other 49 are rare and quite valuable.

Bowman continued its production of cards in 1949 with a color series of 240 cards. Because there are many scarce "high numbers" this series remains the most difficult Bowman regular issue to complete. Although the set was printed in color and commands great interest due to its scarcity, it is considered aesthetically inferior to the

Goudey and National Chicle issues of the 1930s. In addition to the regular issue of 1949, Bowman also produced a set of 36 Pacific Coast League players. While this was not a regular issue, it is still prized by collectors. In fact, it has become the most valuable Bowman series.

In 1950 (Bowman's one year monopoly of the baseball card market), the company began a string of top quality cards which continued until its demise in 1955. The 1950 series was itself something of an oddity because the "low" numbers, rather than the traditional high numbers, were the more difficult cards to obtain.

The year 1951 marked the beginning of the most competitive and perhaps the highest quality period of baseball card production. In that year that Topps Chewing Gum Company of Brooklyn entered the market. Topps' 1951 series consisted of two sets of 52 cards each, one set with red backs and the other with blue backs. In addition, Topps also issued 31 insert cards, three of which remain the rarest Topps cards ("Current All-Stars" Konstanty, Roberts, and Stanky). The 1951 Topps cards were unattractive and paled in comparison to the 1951 Bowman issues. However they were successful, and Topps has continued to produce cards ever since.

Topps issued a larger and much more attractive card in 1952. This larger size became standard for the next five years. (Bowman followed with larger size baseball cards in 1953.) This 1952 Topps set has become, like the 1933 Goudey series and the T-206 white border series, the classic set of its era. The 407 card set is a collector's dream of scarcities, rarities, errors and variations. It also contains the first Topps issues of Mickey Mantle and Willie Mays.

As with Bowman and Leaf in the late 1940s, competition over player rights arose. Ensuing court battles occurred between Topps and Bowman. The market split due to stiff competition, and in January, 1956, Topps bought out Bowman. Topps remained relatively unchallenged as the primary producer of baseball cards through 1980. So, the story of major baseball card sets from 1956 through 1980 is by and large the story of Topps' issues with few exceptions. Fleer Gum produced small sets in 1959, 1960, 1961 and 1963, and several cartoon sets in the 1970s, and more recently Kelloggs Cereal and Hostess Cakes issued baseball cards to promote their products.

A court decision in 1980 paved the way for two other large gum companies to enter, or reenter, the baseball card arena. The Fleer Corporation, which had last made photo cards in 1963, and the Donruss Company (a division of General Mills) secured rights to produce baseball cards of current players breaking Topps' monopoly. Each company issued major card sets in 1981 with bubble gum products. Then a higher court decision in that year overturned the lower court ruling against Topps. It appeared that Topps had regained its sole position as a producer of baseball cards. Undaunted by the revocation ruling, Fleer and Donruss continued to issue cards in 1982 but without bubble gum or any other edible product. Fleer issued its current player baseball cards with "team logo stickers," while Donruss issued its cards with a piece of a baseball jigsaw puzzle.

Since 1981, these three major baseball card producers have all thrived, sharing relatively equal recognition. Each has steadily increased its involvement in terms of numbers of issues per year. To the delight of collectors, their competition has generated novel, and in some cases exceptional, issues of current major league baseball players. These major producers have become increasingly aware of the organized collecting market. While the corner candy store remains the major marketplace for card sales, an increasing number of issues have been directed to this organized hobby marketplace. In fact, many of these issues have been distributed exclusively through hobby channels. Although no one can ever say what the future will bring, one can only surmise that the hobby market will play a significant role in future plans of all the major baseball card producers.

The above has been a thumbnail sketch of card collecting from its inception in the 1880s to the present. It is difficult to tell the whole story in just a few pages -- there are several other good sources of information. Serious collectors should subscribe to at least one of the excellent hobby periodicals. We also suggest that collectors attend a sports collectibles convention in their area. Card collecting is still a young and informal hobby. Chances are good that you will run into one or more of the "experts" at such a show. They are usually more than happy to share their knowledge with you.

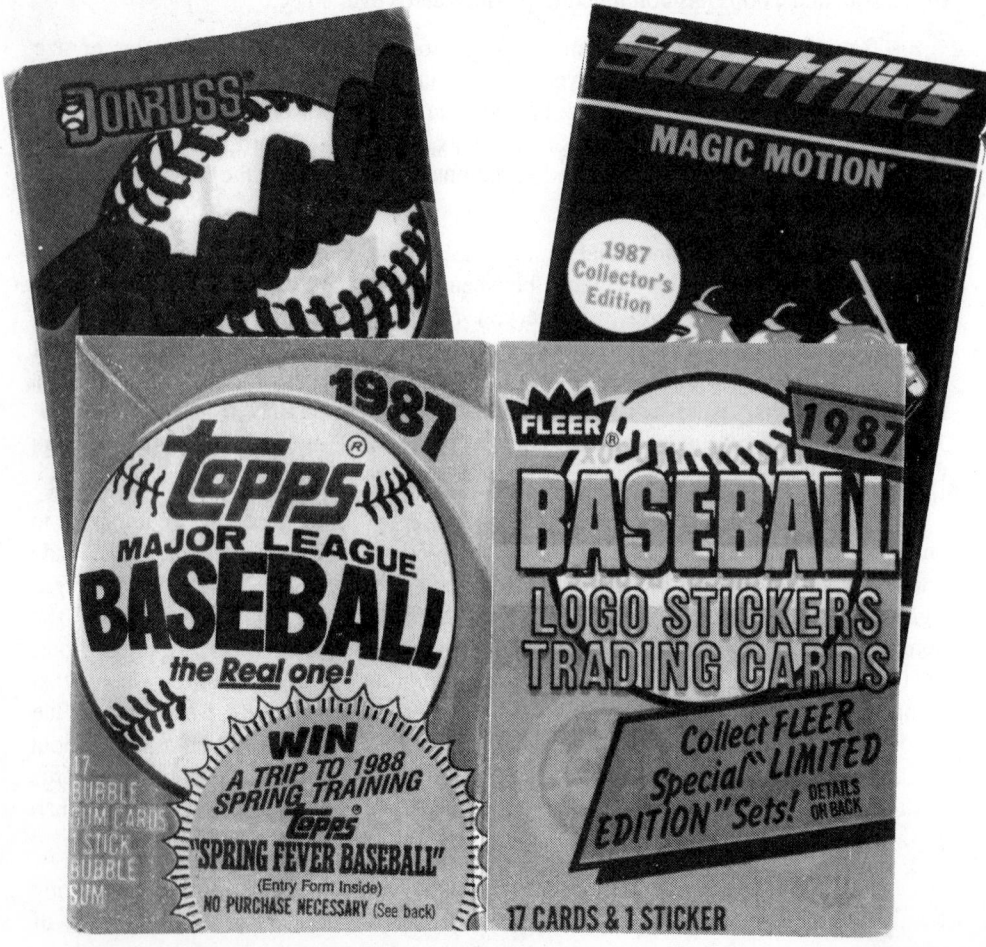

# Business of Baseball Card Collecting

## Determining Value

Why are some cards more valuable than others? Obviously, the economic law of supply and demand is applicable to card collecting just as it is to any other field where a commodity is bought, sold or traded.

Supply (the number of cards available on the market) is less than the total number of cards originally produced since attrition diminishes that original quantity. Each year a percentage of cards are typically thrown away, destroyed or otherwise lost to collectors. This percentage is smaller today than it was in the past because more and more people have become increasingly aware of the value of their cards. For those who collect only "Mint" condition cards, the supply of older cards can be quite small indeed. Until recently, collectors were not so conscious of the need to preserve the condition of their cards. For this reason, it is difficult to know exactly how many 1953 Topps are currently available, Mint or otherwise. It is generally accepted that there are fewer 1953 Topps available than 1963, 1973, or 1983 Topps cards. If demand were equal for each of these sets, the law of supply and demand would increase the price for the least available sets. Demand, however, is not equal for all sets, so price correlations can be complicated.

The demand for a card is influenced by many factors. These include: (1) the age of the card; (2) the number of cards printed; (3) the player(s) portrayed on the card; (4) the attractiveness and popularity of the set; and perhaps most importantly, (5) the physical condition of the card.

In general, (1) the older the card, (2) the fewer the number of the cards printed, (3) the more famous the player, (4) the more attractive and popular the set, or (5) the better the condition of the card, the higher the value of the card will be. There are exceptions to all but one of these factors: the condition of the card. Given two cards similar in all respects except condition, the one in the best condition will always be valued higher.

While there are certain guidelines that help to establish the value of a card, the exceptions and peculiarities make any simple, direct mathematical formula to determine card values impossible.

## Regional Variation

Two types of price variations exist among the sections of the country where a card is bought or sold. The first is the general price variation on all cards bought and sold in one geographical area as compared to another. Card prices are slightly higher on the East and West coasts, and slightly lower in the middle of the country. Although prices may vary from the East to the West, or from the Southwest to the Midwest, the prices listed in this guide are none the less presented as a consensus of all sections of this large and diverse country.

Still prices for a particular player's cards may well be higher in his home team's area than in other regions. This exhibits the second type of regional price variation in which local players are favored over those from distant areas. For example, an Al

Kaline card would be valued higher in Detroit than in Cincinnati because Kaline played in Detroit; therefore, the demand there for Al Kaline cards is higher than it is in Cincinnati. On the other hand, a Johnny Bench card would be priced higher in Cincinnati where he played than in Detroit for similar reasons. Sometimes even common player cards command such a premium from hometown collectors.

## Set Prices

A somewhat paradoxical situation exists in the price of a complete set versus the combined cost of the individual cards in the set. In nearly every case, the sum of the prices for the individual cards is higher than the cost for the complete set. This is especially prevalent in the cards of the past few years. The reasons for this apparent anomaly stem from the habits of collectors and from the carrying costs to dealers. Today each card in a set is normally produced in the same quantity as all others in its set. However, many collectors pick up only stars, superstars and particular teams. As a result, the dealer is left with a shortage of certain player cards and an abundance of others. He therefore incurs an expense in simply "carrying" these less desirable cards in stock. On the other hand, if he sells a complete set, he gets rid of large numbers of cards at one time. For this reason, he is often willing to receive less money for a complete set. By doing this, he recovers all of his costs and also receives some profit.

The disparity between the price of the complete set and that for the sum of the individual cards has also been influenced by the fact that the major manufacturers are now pre-collating card sets. Since "pulling" individual cards from the sets of all three manufacturers involves a specific type of labor (and cost), the singles or star card market is not affected significantly by pre-collation.

Set prices also do not include rare card varieties, unless specifically stated. Of course, the prices for sets do include one example of each type for the given set, but this is the least expensive variety.

## Scarce Series

Scarce series occur because cards issued before 1974 were made available to the public each year in several series of finite numbers of cards, rather than all cards of the set being available for purchase at one time. At some point during the year, usually toward the end of the baseball season, interest in current year baseball cards waned. Consequently, the manufacturers produced smaller numbers of these later series of cards. Nearly all nationwide issues from post-World War II manufacturers (1948 to 1973) exhibit these series variations. Topps, for example, issued series comprised of many different numbers of cards, including 55, 66, 80, 88, and others. Recently Topps has settled on what is now their standard sheet size of 132 cards.

While the number of cards within a given series is usually the same as the number of cards on one printed sheet, this is not always the case. For example, Bowman used 36 cards on its standard printed sheets, but in 1948 substituted 12 cards during later print runs of that year's baseball cards. Twelve of the cards from the initial sheet of 36 cards were removed and replaced by 12 different cards giving, in effect, a first series of 36 cards and a second series of 12 new cards. This replacement produced a scarcity of 24 cards -- the 12 cards removed from the original sheet and the 12 new cards added to the sheet. A full sheet of 1948 Bowman cards (second printing) shows that card numbers 37 through 48 have replaced 12 of the cards on the first printing sheet.

The Topps Gum Company has also created scarcities and/or excesses of certain cards in many of their sets. Topps, however, has most frequently gone the other direction by double printing some of the cards. Double printing causes an abundance of cards of the players who are on the same sheet more than one time. During the years from 1978 to 1981, Topps double printed 66 cards out of their large 726 card set. The Topps practice of double printing cards in earlier years is the most logical explanation for the known scarcities of particular cards in some of these Topps sets.

# Grading Your Cards

Each hobby has its own grading terminology -- stamps, coins, comic books, beer cans, right down the line. Collectors of sports cards are no exception. The one invariable criterion for determining the value of a card is its condition: the better the condition of the card, the more valuable it is. However, condition grading is very subjective. Individual card dealers and collectors differ in the strictness of their grading, but the stated condition of a card should be determined without regard to whether it is being bought or sold.

The physical defects which lower the condition of a card are usually quite apparent, but each individual places his own estimation (negative value in this case) on these defects. We present the condition guide for use in determining values listed in this price guide.

The defects listed in the condition guide below are those either placed in the card at the time of printing -- uneven borders, focus -- or those defects that occur to a card under normal handling -- corner sharpness, gloss, edge wear -- and finally, environmental conditions -- browning. Other defects to cards are caused by human carelessness and in all cases should be noted separately and in addition to the condition grade. Among the more common alterations are tape, tape stains, rubber band marks, water damage, smoke damage, trimming, paste, tears, writing, pin or tack holes, any back damage, and missing parts (tabs, tops, coupons, backgrounds).

# Condition Guide

**MINT (M OR MT)** - A card with no defects. The card has sharp corners, even borders, original gloss or shine on the surface, sharp focus of the picture, smooth edges, no signs of wear, and white borders. There is no allowance made for the age of the card.

**EXCELLENT (EX OR E)** - A card with very minor defects. Any of the following would be sufficient to lower the grade of a card from mint to the excellent category: very slight rounding or layering at some of the corners, a very small amount of the original gloss lost, minor wear on the edges, slight unevenness of the borders, slight wear visible only on close inspection; slight off-whiteness of the borders.

**VERY GOOD (VG)** - A card that has been handled but not abused. Some rounding at all corners, slight layering or scuffing at one or two corners, slight notching on edges, gloss lost from the surface but not scuffed, borders might be somewhat uneven but some white is visible on all borders, noticeable yellowing or browning of borders, pictures may be slightly off focus.

**GOOD (G)** - A well handled card, rounding and some layering at the corners, scuffing at the corners and minor scuffing on the face, borders noticeably uneven and browning, loss of gloss on the face, notching on the edges.

**FAIR (F)** - Round and layering corners, brown and dirty borders, frayed edges, noticeable scuffing on the face, white not visible on one or more borders, cloudy focus.

**POOR (P)** - An abused card, the lowest grade of card, frequently some major physical alteration has been performed on the card, collectible only as a filler until a better condition replacement can be obtained.

Categories between these major condition grades are frequently used, such as, very good to excellent (VG-E), fair to good (F-G), etc. Such grades indicate a card with all qualities at least in the lower of the two categories, but with several qualities in the higher of the two categories.

The most common physical defect in a trading card is the crease or wrinkle. The crease may vary from a slight crease barely noticeable at one corner of the card to a major crease across the entire card. Therefore, the degree that creasing lowers the value of the card depends on the type and number of creases. On giving the condition of a card, creases should be noted separately. If the crease is noticeable only upon close inspection under bright light, an otherwise mint card could be called excellent; whereas noticeable but light creases would lower most otherwise mint cards into the VG category. A heavily creased card could be classified as fair at best.

## Selling Your Cards

Just about every collector sells cards or will sell cards eventually. Someday you may be interested in selling your duplicates or maybe even your whole collection. You may sell to other collectors, friends, or dealers. You may even sell cards you purchased from a certain dealer back to that same dealer. In any event, it helps to know some of the mechanics of the typical transaction between buyer and seller.

Dealers will buy cards in order to resell them to other collectors who are interested in the cards. Dealers will always pay a higher percentage for items which (in their opinion) can be resold quickly, and a much lower percentage for those items which are perceived as having low demand and hence are slow moving. In either case, dealers must buy at a price that allows for the expense of doing business and a fair margin for profit. Virtually all dealers are interested in older complete sets and superstar cards in excellent condition.

If you have cards for sale, the best advice we can give is that you get three offers for your cards and take the best offer, all things considered. Note, the "best" offer may not be the one for the highest amount. And remember, if a dealer really wants your cards, he won't let you get away without making his best competitive offer. Another alternative is to take your cards to a nearby convention and either auction them off in the show auction or offer them for sale to some of the dealers present.

Many people think nothing of going into a department store and paying $15 for an item of clothing for which the store paid $5. But, if you were selling your $15 card to a dealer and he offered you only $5 for it, you might think his mark-up unreasonable. To complete the analogy: most department stores (and card dealers) that pay $10 for $15 items eventually go out of business. An exception to this is when the dealer knows that a willing buyer for the merchandise you are attempting to sell is only a phone call away. Then an offer of 2/3 or maybe 70% of the book value will still allow him to make a reasonable profit due to the short time he will need to hold the merchandise. Nevertheless most cards and collections will bring offers in the range of 25% to 50% of retail price. Material from the past five to ten years or so is very plentiful. Don't be surprised if your best offer is only 20% of the book value for these recent years.

# Other Helpful Hints

## Interesting Notes

The numerically first card of an issue is the single card most likely to obtain excessive wear. Consequently, you will typically find the price on the number one card (in Mint condition) somewhat higher than might otherwise be the case. Similarly, but to a lesser extent (because normally the less important, reverse side of the card is the one exposed), the numerically last card in an issue is also prone to abnormal wear. This extra wear and tear occurs because the first and last cards are exposed to the elements (human element included) more than any other cards. They are generally end cards in any brick formations, rubber bandings, stackings on wet surfaces, and like activities.

Sports cards have no intrinsic value. The value of a card, as the value of other collectibles, can only be determined by you and your enjoyment in viewing and possessing these cardboard swatches.

Remember, the buyer ultimately determines the price of each baseball card. You are the determining price factor because you have the ability to say "No" to the price of any card by not exchanging your hard-earned money for a given card. When the cost of a trading card exceeds the enjoyment you will receive from it, your answer should be "No." We assess and report the prices. You set them!

We are always interested in receiving the price input of collectors and dealers from around the country. We happily credit major contributors. We welcome your opinions, since your contributions assist us in ensuring a better guide each year. If you would like to join our survey list for the next editions of this book and others authored by Dr. Beckett, please send your name and address to Dr. James Beckett, 3410 MidCourt, Suite 110, Carrollton, Texas 75006.

# Advertising

Within this price guide you will find advertisements for sports memorabilia material, mail order and retail sports collectibles establishments. All advertisements were accepted in good faith based on the reputation of the advertiser; however, neither the author, the publisher, the distributors, nor the other advertisers in the price guide accept any responsibility for any particular advertiser not complying with the terms of his or her ad.

Readers should also be aware that prices in advertisements are subject to change over the annual period before a new edition of this volume is issued each spring. When replying to an advertisement late in the baseball year, the reader should take this into account, and contact the dealer by phone or in writing for up-to-date price information. Should you come into contact with any of the advertisers in this guide as a result of their advertisement herein, please mention to them this source as your contact.

# Additional Reading

Other literature on the collecting hobby can be divided into two principal categories: books and periodicals. We have furnished a listing for both that we feel would further advance your knowledge and enjoyment.

## Books Available

**The Sport Americana Price Guide to Baseball Collectibles** by Dr. James Beckett (First Edition, $9.95, released 1986, published by Edgewater Book Company) - - the complete guide/checklist with up to date values for box cards, coins, decals, labels, Canadian cards, stamps, stickers, pins, etc.

**The Sport Americana Football, Hockey, Basketball and Boxing Card Price Guide** by Dr. James Beckett (Fourth Edition, $11.95, released 1985, published by Edgewater Book Company) -- the most comprehensive price guide/checklist ever issued on football and other non-baseball sports cards. No serious hobbyist should be without it.

**The Official Price Guide to Football Cards** by Dr. James Beckett (Sixth Edition, $4.95, released 1986, published by House of Collectibles, Inc.) -- an abridgement of the Sport Americana Price Guide listed above in a convenient and economical pocket size format providing Dr. Beckett's pricing of the major football sets since 1948.

**The Sport Americana Baseball Memorabilia and Autograph Price Guide** by Dr. James Beckett and Dennis W. Eckes (First Edition, $9.95, released 1982, co-published by Den's Collectors Den and Edgewater Book Company) -- the most complete book ever produced on baseball memorabilia other than baseball cards. This book presents in an illustrated, logical fashion information on baseball memorabilia and autographs which had been heretofore unavailable to the collector.

**The Sport Americana Alphabetical Baseball Card Checklist** by Dr. James Beckett and Dennis W. Eckes (Second Edition, $8.95, released 1983, co-published by Den's Collectors Den and Edgewater Book Company) -- an illustrated, alphabetical listing, by the last name of the player portrayed on the card, of virtually all baseball cards produced up to 1983.

**The Sport Americana Price Guide to the Non-Sports Cards** by Christopher Benjamin and Dennis W. Eckes (Second Edition, $8.95, released 1983, co-published by Den's Collector's Den and Edgewater Book Company) -- the definitive guide to all popular non-sports American tobacco and bubble gum cards. In addition to cards, illustrations and prices for wrappers are also included.

**The Sport Americana Baseball Address List** by Jack Smalling and Dennis W. Eckes (Fourth Edition, $9.95, released 1986, co-published by Den's Collector's Den and Edgewater Book Company) -- the definitive guide for autograph hunters giving addresses and deceased information for virtually all major league baseball players past and present.

**The Sport Americana Baseball Card Team Checklist** by Jeff Fritsch and Dennis W. Eckes (Second Edition, $8.95, released 1985, co-published by Den's Collectors Den and Edgewater Book Company) -- includes all Topps, Bowman, Fleer, Play Ball, Goudey, and Donruss cards, with the players portrayed on the cards listed with the teams for whom they played. The book is invaluable to the collector who specializes in an individual team because it is the most complete baseball card team checklist available.

**Hockey Card Checklist and Price Guide** by Andrew Pywowarczuk (Sixth Edition, publisher: Cartophilium) -- contains the most complete list of hockey card checklists ever assembled including a listing of Bee Hive photos.

**The Encyclopedia of Baseball Cards,, Volume I: 19th Century Cards** by Lew Lipset ($9.95, released 1983, published by the author) -- everything you ever wanted to know about 19th century cards.

**The Encyclopedia of Baseball Cards, Volume II: Early Gum and Candy Cards** by Lew Lipset ($10.95, released 1984, published by the author) -- everything you ever wanted to know about Early Candy and Gum cards.

**The Encyclopedia of Baseball Cards, Volume III: 20th Century Tobacco Cards, 1909-1932** by Lew Lipset ($12.95, released 1986, published by the author) -- everything you ever wanted to know about old tobacco cards.

# Periodicals

Several magazines and periodicals about the card collecting hobby are published on monthly, bimonthly, or weekly bases. One (or more) of those listed below should be just right for you.

**Beckett Baseball Card Monthly** authored and edited by Dr. James Beckett -- contains the most extensive and accepted monthly price guide, feature articles, "who's hot and who's not" section, convention calendar, and numerous letters to and responses from the editor. Published 10 times annually, it is the hobby's largest circulation periodical.

**Baseball Hobby News** published by Frank and Vivian Barning -- monthly tabloid newspaper format with good mix of news, editorials, features, and ads.

**The Old Judge** published by Lew Lipset -- bimonthly newsletter with in-depth information about older card issues and memorabilia.

**Sports Collectors Digest** published by Krause Publications -- weekly tabloid issues loaded with ads.

**Baseball Card News** published by Krause Publications -- monthly tabloid format with good mix of editorials, features, and ads.

**Baseball Cards** published by Krause Publications -- monthly magazine with interior color and mix of features and ads.

# Errata

There are thousands of names, more than 100,000 prices, and untold other words in this book. There are going to be a few typographical errors, a few misspellings, and possibly, a number or two out of place. If you catch a blooper, drop me a note directly or in care of the publisher, and we will fix it up in the next year's edition.

# Prices in this Price Guide

Prices found in this guide reflect current retail rates just prior to the printing of this book. They do not reflect the FOR SALE prices of the author, the publisher, the distributors, the advertisers, or any card dealers associated with this guide. No one is obligated in any way to buy, sell, or trade his or her cards based on these prices. The price listings were compiled by the author from actual buy/sell transactions at sports conventions, buy/sell advertisements in the hobby papers, for sale prices from dealer catalogs and price lists, and discussions with leading hobbyists in the U.S. and Canada. All prices are in U.S. dollars.

## 1948 Babe Ruth Story

 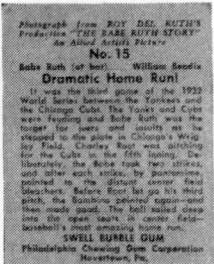

The 1948 Babe Ruth Story set of 28 black and white numbered cards (measuring 2" by 2 1/2") was issued by the Philadelphia Chewing Gum Company to commemorate the 1949 movie of the same name starring William Bendix, Claire Trevor, and Charles Bickford. Babe Ruth himself appears on several cards. The last 12 cards (17 to 28) are more difficult to obtain than other cards in the set and are more desirable in that most picture actual players as well as actors. The ACC designation is R421.

|  | MINT | VG-E | F-G |
|---|---|---|---|
| COMPLETE SET .......................... | 450.00 | 180.00 | 45.00 |
| COMMON PLAYER (1-16) .......... | 7.00 | 2.80 | .70 |
| COMMON PLAYER (17-28) ........ | 21.00 | 8.50 | 2.10 |
| ☐ 1 The Babe Ruth Story ........ In the Making | 25.00 | 5.00 | 1.00 |
| ☐ 2 Bat Boy Becomes ............. the Babe | 7.00 | 2.80 | .70 |
| ☐ 3 Claire Hodgson played ...... by Claire Trevor | 7.00 | 2.80 | .70 |
| ☐ 4 Babe Ruth played by ........ William Bendix; Claire Hodgson played by Claire Trevor | 7.00 | 2.80 | .70 |
| ☐ 5 Brother Matthias played ... by Charles Bickford | 7.00 | 2.80 | .70 |
| ☐ 6 Phil Conrad played .......... by Sam Levene | 7.00 | 2.80 | .70 |
| ☐ 7 Night Club Singer play- ..... ed by Gertrude Niesen | 7.00 | 2.80 | .70 |
| ☐ 8 Baseball's Famous Deal .... | 7.00 | 2.80 | .70 |
| ☐ 9 Babe Ruth played by ........ William Bendix; Mrs. Babe Ruth played by Claire Trevor | 7.00 | 2.80 | .70 |
| ☐ 10 Actors for Babe Ruth, ...... Mrs. Babe Ruth, and Brother Matthias | 7.00 | 2.80 | .70 |
| ☐ 11 Babe Ruth played by ........ William Bendix; Miller Huggins played by Fred Lightner | 7.00 | 2.80 | .70 |
| ☐ 12 Babe Ruth played by ........ William Bendix; Johnny Sylvester played by George Marshall | 7.00 | 2.80 | .70 |
| ☐ 13 Actors for Mr., Mrs. .......... and Johnny Sylvester | 7.00 | 2.80 | .70 |
| ☐ 14 When A Feller Needs ........ A Friend | 7.00 | 2.80 | .70 |
| ☐ 15 Dramatic Home Run ......... | 7.00 | 2.80 | .70 |
| ☐ 16 The Homer That Set ........ the Record | 7.00 | 2.80 | .70 |
| ☐ 17 The Slap That Started ...... Baseball's Most Famous Career | 21.00 | 8.50 | 2.10 |
| ☐ 18 The Babe Plays ................. Santa Claus | 21.00 | 8.50 | 2.10 |
| ☐ 19 Actors for Ed Barrow, ...... Jacob Ruppert, and Miller Huggins | 21.00 | 8.50 | 2.10 |
| ☐ 20 Broken Window Paid Off ... | 21.00 | 8.50 | 2.10 |
| ☐ 21 Regardless of the Gen- ..... eration/ Babe Ruth | 21.00 | 8.50 | 2.10 |
| ☐ 22 Charley Grimm and .......... William Bendix | 21.00 | 8.50 | 2.10 |
| ☐ 23 Ted Lyons and .................. William Bendix | 25.00 | 10.00 | 2.50 |
| ☐ 24 Lefty Gomez, William ........ Bendix, and Bucky Harris | 30.00 | 12.00 | 3.00 |
| ☐ 25 Babe Ruth and ................. William Bendix | 50.00 | 20.00 | 5.00 |
| ☐ 26 Babe Ruth and ................. William Bendix | 50.00 | 20.00 | 5.00 |
| ☐ 27 Babe Ruth and ................. Claire Trevor | 50.00 | 20.00 | 5.00 |
| ☐ 28 William Bendix, Babe ........ Ruth, Claire Trevor | 50.00 | 20.00 | 5.00 |

## 1934-36 Batter-Up

The 1934-36 Batter-Up set issued by National Chicle contains 192 blank-backed die-cut cards. Numbers 1 to 80 are 2 3/8" by 3 1/4" in size while 81 to 192 are 2 3/8" by 3". The latter are more difficult to find than the former. The pictures come in basic black and white or in tints of blue, brown, green, purple, red, or sepia. There are three combination cards (each featuring two players per card) in the high series (98, 111, and 115). The ACC designation for the set is R318. Cards with back s removed are graded fair at best.

|  | MINT | VG-E | F-G |
|---|---|---|---|
| COMPLETE SET ........................ | 7500.00 | 3000.00 | 750.00 |
| COMMON PLAYER (1-80) .......... | 18.00 | 7.25 | 1.80 |
| COMMON PLAYER (81-192) ...... | 40.00 | 16.00 | 4.00 |
| ☐ 1 Wally Berger ..................... | 30.00 | 10.00 | 2.00 |
| ☐ 2 Ed Brandt ........................ | 18.00 | 7.25 | 1.80 |
| ☐ 3 Al Lopez .......................... | 30.00 | 12.00 | 3.00 |
| ☐ 4 Dick Bartell ...................... | 18.00 | 7.25 | 1.80 |
| ☐ 5 Carl Hubbell .................... | 45.00 | 18.00 | 4.50 |
| ☐ 6 Bill Terry ......................... | 45.00 | 18.00 | 4.50 |
| ☐ 7 Pepper Martin ................. | 21.00 | 8.50 | 2.10 |
| ☐ 8 Jim Bottomley ................. | 30.00 | 12.00 | 3.00 |
| ☐ 9 Tom Bridges .................... | 18.00 | 7.25 | 1.80 |
| ☐ 10 Rick Ferrell .................... | 30.00 | 12.00 | 3.00 |
| ☐ 11 Ray Benge ..................... | 18.00 | 7.25 | 1.80 |
| ☐ 12 Wes Ferrell .................... | 21.00 | 8.50 | 2.10 |
| ☐ 13 Chalmer Cissell .............. | 18.00 | 7.25 | 1.80 |
| ☐ 14 Pie Traynor .................... | 35.00 | 14.00 | 3.50 |
| ☐ 15 Leroy Mahaffey .............. | 18.00 | 7.25 | 1.80 |
| ☐ 16 Chick Hafey ................... | 30.00 | 12.00 | 3.00 |
| ☐ 17 Lloyd Waner .................. | 30.00 | 12.00 | 3.00 |
| ☐ 18 Jack Burns ..................... | 18.00 | 7.25 | 1.80 |
| ☐ 19 Buddy Myer ................... | 18.00 | 7.25 | 1.80 |
| ☐ 20 Bob Johnson .................. | 21.00 | 8.50 | 2.10 |
| ☐ 21 Arky Vaughan ................ | 30.00 | 12.00 | 3.00 |
| ☐ 22 Red Rolfe ...................... | 18.00 | 7.25 | 1.80 |
| ☐ 23 Lefty Gomez .................. | 45.00 | 18.00 | 4.50 |
| ☐ 24 Earl Averill ..................... | 30.00 | 12.00 | 3.00 |
| ☐ 25 Mickey Cochrane ........... | 45.00 | 18.00 | 4.50 |
| ☐ 26 Van Lingle Mungo .......... | 18.00 | 7.25 | 1.80 |
| ☐ 27 Mel Ott ......................... | 60.00 | 24.00 | 6.00 |
| ☐ 28 Jimmy Foxx ................... | 70.00 | 28.00 | 7.00 |

| | | | | |
|---|---|---|---|---|
| ☐ | 29 | Jimmy Dykes | 21.00 | 8.50 | 2.10 |
| ☐ | 30 | Bill Dickey | 60.00 | 24.00 | 6.00 |
| ☐ | 31 | Lefty Grove | 60.00 | 24.00 | 6.00 |
| ☐ | 32 | Joe Cronin | 45.00 | 18.00 | 4.50 |
| ☐ | 33 | Frank Frisch | 45.00 | 18.00 | 4.50 |
| ☐ | 34 | Al Simmons | 35.00 | 14.00 | 3.50 |
| ☐ | 35 | Rogers Hornsby | 70.00 | 28.00 | 7.00 |
| ☐ | 36 | Ted Lyons | 30.00 | 12.00 | 3.00 |
| ☐ | 37 | Rabbit Maranville | 30.00 | 12.00 | 3.00 |
| ☐ | 38 | Jimmy Wilson | 18.00 | 7.25 | 1.80 |
| ☐ | 39 | Willie Kamm | 18.00 | 7.25 | 1.80 |
| ☐ | 40 | Bill Hallahan | 18.00 | 7.25 | 1.80 |
| ☐ | 41 | Gus Suhr | 18.00 | 7.25 | 1.80 |
| ☐ | 42 | Charlie Gehringer | 45.00 | 18.00 | 4.50 |
| ☐ | 43 | Joe Heving | 18.00 | 7.25 | 1.80 |
| ☐ | 44 | Adam Comorosky | 18.00 | 7.25 | 1.80 |
| ☐ | 45 | Tony Lazzeri | 21.00 | 8.50 | 2.10 |
| ☐ | 46 | Sam Leslie | 18.00 | 7.25 | 1.80 |
| ☐ | 47 | Bob Smith | 18.00 | 7.25 | 1.80 |
| ☐ | 48 | Willis Hudlin | 18.00 | 7.25 | 1.80 |
| ☐ | 49 | Carl Reynolds | 18.00 | 7.25 | 1.80 |
| ☐ | 50 | Fred Schulte | 18.00 | 7.25 | 1.80 |
| ☐ | 51 | Cookie Lavagetto | 18.00 | 7.25 | 1.80 |
| ☐ | 52 | Hal Schumacher | 18.00 | 7.25 | 1.80 |
| ☐ | 53 | Roger Cramer | 21.00 | 8.50 | 2.10 |
| ☐ | 54 | Sylvester Johnson | 18.00 | 7.25 | 1.80 |
| ☐ | 55 | Ollie Bejma | 18.00 | 7.25 | 1.80 |
| ☐ | 56 | Sam Byrd | 18.00 | 7.25 | 1.80 |
| ☐ | 57 | Hank Greenberg | 60.00 | 24.00 | 6.00 |
| ☐ | 58 | Bill Knickerbocker | 18.00 | 7.25 | 1.80 |
| ☐ | 59 | Bill Urbanski | 18.00 | 7.25 | 1.80 |
| ☐ | 60 | Eddie Morgan | 18.00 | 7.25 | 1.80 |
| ☐ | 61 | Rabbit McNair | 18.00 | 7.25 | 1.80 |
| ☐ | 62 | Ben Chapman | 18.00 | 7.25 | 1.80 |
| ☐ | 63 | Roy Johnson | 18.00 | 7.25 | 1.80 |
| ☐ | 64 | Dizzy Dean | 150.00 | 60.00 | 15.00 |
| ☐ | 65 | Zeke Bonura | 18.00 | 7.25 | 1.80 |
| ☐ | 66 | Fred Marberry | 18.00 | 7.25 | 1.80 |
| ☐ | 67 | Gus Mancuso | 18.00 | 7.25 | 1.80 |
| ☐ | 68 | Joe Vosmik | 18.00 | 7.25 | 1.80 |
| ☐ | 69 | Earl Grace | 18.00 | 7.25 | 1.80 |
| ☐ | 70 | Tony Piet | 18.00 | 7.25 | 1.80 |
| ☐ | 71 | Rollie Hemsley | 18.00 | 7.25 | 1.80 |
| ☐ | 72 | Fred Fitzsimmons | 18.00 | 7.25 | 1.80 |
| ☐ | 73 | Hack Wilson | 45.00 | 18.00 | 4.50 |
| ☐ | 74 | Chick Fullis | 18.00 | 7.25 | 1.80 |
| ☐ | 75 | Fred Frankhouse | 18.00 | 7.25 | 1.80 |
| ☐ | 76 | Ethan Allen | 18.00 | 7.25 | 1.80 |
| ☐ | 77 | Heine Manush | 30.00 | 12.00 | 3.00 |
| ☐ | 78 | Rip Collins | 18.00 | 7.25 | 1.80 |
| ☐ | 79 | Tony Cuccinello | 18.00 | 7.25 | 1.80 |
| ☐ | 80 | Joe Kuhel | 18.00 | 7.25 | 1.80 |
| ☐ | 81 | Tom Bridges | 40.00 | 16.00 | 4.00 |
| ☐ | 82 | Clint Brown | 40.00 | 16.00 | 4.00 |
| ☐ | 83 | Albert Blanche | 40.00 | 16.00 | 4.00 |
| ☐ | 84 | Boze Berger | 40.00 | 16.00 | 4.00 |
| ☐ | 85 | Goose Goslin | 75.00 | 30.00 | 7.50 |
| ☐ | 86 | Lefty Gomez | 100.00 | 40.00 | 10.00 |
| ☐ | 87 | Joe Glenn | 40.00 | 16.00 | 4.00 |
| ☐ | 88 | Cy Blanton | 40.00 | 16.00 | 4.00 |
| ☐ | 89 | Tom Carey | 40.00 | 16.00 | 4.00 |
| ☐ | 90 | Ralph Birkofer | 40.00 | 16.00 | 4.00 |
| ☐ | 91 | Fred Gabler | 40.00 | 16.00 | 4.00 |
| ☐ | 92 | Dick Coffman | 40.00 | 16.00 | 4.00 |
| ☐ | 93 | Ollie Bejma | 40.00 | 16.00 | 4.00 |
| ☐ | 94 | Leroy Parmelee | 40.00 | 16.00 | 4.00 |
| ☐ | 95 | Carl Reynolds | 40.00 | 16.00 | 4.00 |
| ☐ | 96 | Ben Cantwell | 40.00 | 16.00 | 4.00 |
| ☐ | 97 | Curtis Davis | 40.00 | 16.00 | 4.00 |
| ☐ | 98 | Webb and Wally Moses | 50.00 | 20.00 | 5.00 |
| ☐ | 99 | Ray Benge | 40.00 | 16.00 | 4.00 |
| ☐ | 100 | Pie Traynor | 90.00 | 36.00 | 9.00 |
| ☐ | 101 | Phil Cavarretta | 45.00 | 18.00 | 4.50 |
| ☐ | 102 | Pep Young | 40.00 | 16.00 | 4.00 |
| ☐ | 103 | Willis Hudlin | 40.00 | 16.00 | 4.00 |
| ☐ | 104 | Mickey Haslin | 40.00 | 16.00 | 4.00 |
| ☐ | 105 | Oswald Bluege | 40.00 | 16.00 | 4.00 |
| ☐ | 106 | Paul Andrews | 40.00 | 16.00 | 4.00 |
| ☐ | 107 | Ed Brandt | 40.00 | 16.00 | 4.00 |
| ☐ | 108 | Don Taylor | 40.00 | 16.00 | 4.00 |
| ☐ | 109 | Thornton Lee | 40.00 | 16.00 | 4.00 |
| ☐ | 110 | Hal Schumacher | 40.00 | 16.00 | 4.00 |
| ☐ | 111 | Hayes and Ted Lyons | 75.00 | 30.00 | 7.50 |
| ☐ | 112 | Odell Hale | 40.00 | 16.00 | 4.00 |
| ☐ | 113 | Earl Averill | 75.00 | 30.00 | 7.50 |
| ☐ | 114 | Italo Chelini | 40.00 | 16.00 | 4.00 |
| ☐ | 115 | Andrews and Bottomley | 75.00 | 30.00 | 7.50 |
| ☐ | 116 | Bill Walker | 40.00 | 16.00 | 4.00 |
| ☐ | 117 | Bill Dickey | 125.00 | 50.00 | 12.50 |
| ☐ | 118 | Gerald Walker | 40.00 | 16.00 | 4.00 |
| ☐ | 119 | Ted Lyons | 75.00 | 30.00 | 7.50 |
| ☐ | 120 | Eldon Auker | 40.00 | 16.00 | 4.00 |
| ☐ | 121 | Bill Hallahan | 40.00 | 16.00 | 4.00 |
| ☐ | 122 | Fred Lindstrom | 75.00 | 30.00 | 7.50 |
| ☐ | 123 | Oral Hildebrand | 40.00 | 16.00 | 4.00 |
| ☐ | 124 | Luke Appling | 75.00 | 30.00 | 7.50 |
| ☐ | 125 | Pepper Martin | 50.00 | 20.00 | 5.00 |
| ☐ | 126 | Rick Ferrell | 75.00 | 30.00 | 7.50 |
| ☐ | 127 | Ival Goodman | 40.00 | 16.00 | 4.00 |
| ☐ | 128 | Joe Kuhel | 40.00 | 16.00 | 4.00 |
| ☐ | 129 | Ernie Lombardi | 75.00 | 30.00 | 7.50 |
| ☐ | 130 | Charlie Gehringer | 100.00 | 40.00 | 10.00 |
| ☐ | 131 | Van Lingle Mungo | 40.00 | 16.00 | 4.00 |
| ☐ | 132 | Larry French | 40.00 | 16.00 | 4.00 |
| ☐ | 133 | Buddy Myer | 40.00 | 16.00 | 4.00 |
| ☐ | 134 | Mel Harder | 45.00 | 18.00 | 4.50 |
| ☐ | 135 | Augie Galan | 40.00 | 16.00 | 4.00 |
| ☐ | 136 | Gabby Hartnett | 75.00 | 30.00 | 7.50 |
| ☐ | 137 | Stan Hack | 45.00 | 18.00 | 4.50 |
| ☐ | 138 | Billy Herman | 75.00 | 30.00 | 7.50 |
| ☐ | 139 | Bill Jurges | 40.00 | 16.00 | 4.00 |
| ☐ | 140 | Bill Lee | 40.00 | 16.00 | 4.00 |
| ☐ | 141 | Zeke Bonura | 40.00 | 16.00 | 4.00 |
| ☐ | 142 | Tony Piet | 40.00 | 16.00 | 4.00 |
| ☐ | 143 | Paul Dean | 50.00 | 20.00 | 5.00 |
| ☐ | 144 | Jimmy Foxx | 150.00 | 60.00 | 15.00 |
| ☐ | 145 | Joe Medwick | 90.00 | 36.00 | 9.00 |
| ☐ | 146 | Rip Collins | 40.00 | 16.00 | 4.00 |
| ☐ | 147 | Mel Almada | 40.00 | 16.00 | 4.00 |
| ☐ | 148 | Allan Cooke | 40.00 | 16.00 | 4.00 |
| ☐ | 149 | Moe Berg | 50.00 | 20.00 | 5.00 |
| ☐ | 150 | Dolph Camilli | 40.00 | 16.00 | 4.00 |
| ☐ | 151 | Oscar Melillo | 40.00 | 16.00 | 4.00 |
| ☐ | 152 | Bruce Campbell | 40.00 | 16.00 | 4.00 |
| ☐ | 153 | Lefty Grove | 125.00 | 50.00 | 12.50 |
| ☐ | 154 | Johnny Murphy | 45.00 | 18.00 | 4.50 |
| ☐ | 155 | Luke Sewell | 45.00 | 18.00 | 4.50 |
| ☐ | 156 | Leo Durocher | 75.00 | 30.00 | 7.50 |
| ☐ | 157 | Lloyd Waner | 75.00 | 30.00 | 7.50 |
| ☐ | 158 | Gus Bush | 40.00 | 16.00 | 4.00 |
| ☐ | 159 | Jimmy Dykes | 45.00 | 18.00 | 4.50 |
| ☐ | 160 | Steve O'Neill | 40.00 | 16.00 | 4.00 |
| ☐ | 161 | General Crowder | 40.00 | 16.00 | 4.00 |
| ☐ | 162 | Joe Cascarella | 40.00 | 16.00 | 4.00 |
| ☐ | 163 | Daniel (Bud) Hafey | 40.00 | 16.00 | 4.00 |
| ☐ | 164 | Gilly Campbell | 40.00 | 16.00 | 4.00 |
| ☐ | 165 | Ray Hayworth | 40.00 | 16.00 | 4.00 |
| ☐ | 166 | Frank Demaree | 40.00 | 16.00 | 4.00 |
| ☐ | 167 | John Babich | 40.00 | 16.00 | 4.00 |
| ☐ | 168 | Marvin Owen | 40.00 | 16.00 | 4.00 |
| ☐ | 169 | Ralph Kress | 40.00 | 16.00 | 4.00 |
| ☐ | 170 | Mule Haas | 40.00 | 16.00 | 4.00 |
| ☐ | 171 | Frank Higgins | 40.00 | 16.00 | 4.00 |
| ☐ | 172 | Wally Berger | 40.00 | 16.00 | 4.00 |
| ☐ | 173 | Frank Frisch | 90.00 | 36.00 | 9.00 |
| ☐ | 174 | Wes Ferrell | 50.00 | 20.00 | 5.00 |
| ☐ | 175 | Pete Fox | 40.00 | 16.00 | 4.00 |
| ☐ | 176 | John Vergez | 40.00 | 16.00 | 4.00 |
| ☐ | 177 | Billy Rogell | 40.00 | 16.00 | 4.00 |
| ☐ | 178 | Don Brennan | 40.00 | 16.00 | 4.00 |
| ☐ | 179 | Jim Bottomley | 75.00 | 30.00 | 7.50 |
| ☐ | 180 | Travis Jackson | 75.00 | 30.00 | 7.50 |
| ☐ | 181 | Red Rolfe | 45.00 | 18.00 | 4.50 |
| ☐ | 182 | Frank Crosetti | 50.00 | 20.00 | 5.00 |
| ☐ | 183 | Joe Cronin | 75.00 | 30.00 | 7.50 |
| ☐ | 184 | Schoolboy Rowe | 50.00 | 20.00 | 5.00 |
| ☐ | 185 | Chuck Klein | 75.00 | 30.00 | 7.50 |
| ☐ | 186 | Lon Warneke | 40.00 | 16.00 | 4.00 |
| ☐ | 187 | Gus Suhr | 40.00 | 16.00 | 4.00 |
| ☐ | 188 | Ben Chapman | 40.00 | 16.00 | 4.00 |
| ☐ | 189 | Clint Brown | 40.00 | 16.00 | 4.00 |
| ☐ | 190 | Paul Derringer | 50.00 | 20.00 | 5.00 |
| ☐ | 191 | John Burns | 40.00 | 16.00 | 4.00 |
| ☐ | 192 | John Broaca | 50.00 | 20.00 | 5.00 |

# 1959 Bazooka

The 23 full color, unnumbered cards comprising the 1959 Bazooka set were cut from the bottom of the boxes of gum marketed nationally that year by Topps. Bazooka was the brand name which Topps had been using to sell its one cent bubblegum; this year Topps decided to distribute 25 pieces of Bazooka gum in a box. The cards themselves measure 2 13/16" by 4 15/16". Only nine cards were originally issued; 14 more were added to the set at a later date (these are marked with SP in the

HANK AARON
OUTFIELD    MILWAUKEE BRAVES

checklist). The latter are less plentiful and hence more valuable than the original nine. All the cards are blank backed, and the ACC designation is R414-15. The prices below are for the cards cut from the box; complete boxes intact would be worth about 50% more.

|  | MINT | VG-E | F-G |
|---|---|---|---|
| COMPLETE SET | 2500.00 | 900.00 | 250.00 |
| COMMON PLAYER | 30.00 | 12.00 | 3.00 |
| COMMON PLAYER SP | 100.00 | 40.00 | 10.00 |
| ☐ 1 Hank Aaron | 200.00 | 80.00 | 20.00 |
| ☐ 2 Richie Ashburn SP | 150.00 | 60.00 | 15.00 |
| ☐ 3 Ernie Banks SP | 225.00 | 90.00 | 22.00 |
| ☐ 4 Ken Boyer SP | 125.00 | 50.00 | 12.50 |
| ☐ 5 Orlando Cepeda | 35.00 | 14.00 | 3.50 |
| ☐ 6 Bob Cerv SP | 100.00 | 40.00 | 10.00 |
| ☐ 7 Rocco Colavito SP | 125.00 | 50.00 | 12.50 |
| ☐ 8 Del Crandall | 30.00 | 12.00 | 3.00 |
| ☐ 9 Jim Davenport | 30.00 | 12.00 | 3.00 |
| ☐ 10 Don Drysdale SP | 175.00 | 70.00 | 18.00 |
| ☐ 11 Nellie Fox SP | 150.00 | 60.00 | 15.00 |
| ☐ 12 Jackie Jensen SP | 125.00 | 50.00 | 12.50 |
| ☐ 13 Harvey Kuenn SP | 125.00 | 50.00 | 12.50 |
| ☐ 14 Mickey Mantle | 400.00 | 160.00 | 40.00 |
| ☐ 15 Willie Mays | 200.00 | 80.00 | 20.00 |
| ☐ 16 Bill Mazeroski | 40.00 | 16.00 | 4.00 |
| ☐ 17 Roy McMillan | 30.00 | 12.00 | 3.00 |
| ☐ 18 Billy Pierce SP | 100.00 | 40.00 | 10.00 |
| ☐ 19 Roy Sievers SP | 100.00 | 40.00 | 10.00 |
| ☐ 20 Duke Snider SP | 250.00 | 100.00 | 25.00 |
| ☐ 21 Gus Triandos SP | 100.00 | 40.00 | 10.00 |
| ☐ 22 Bob Turley | 30.00 | 12.00 | 3.00 |
| ☐ 23 Vic Wertz SP | 100.00 | 40.00 | 10.00 |

## 1960 Bazooka

In 1960 Topps introduced a 36 card baseball player set in three card panels on the bottom of Bazooka gum boxes. The cards measure 1 13/16"" by 2 3/4" and the panels measure 2 3/4" by 5 1/2". The cards carried full color pictures and were numbered at the bottom underneath the team position. The checklist below contains prices for individual cards. Complete panels of three would have a value of 30% more than the sum of the individual cards (prices) on the panel

and complete boxes would command a premium of another 30% above those prices.

|  | MINT | VG-E | F-G |
|---|---|---|---|
| COMPLETE INDIV. SET | 500.00 | 200.00 | 50.00 |
| COMMON PLAYER | 7.00 | 2.80 | .70 |
| ☐ 1 Ernie Banks | 30.00 | 12.00 | 3.00 |
| ☐ 2 Bud Daley | 7.00 | 2.80 | .70 |
| ☐ 3 Wally Moon | 7.00 | 2.80 | .70 |
| ☐ 4 Hank Aaron | 50.00 | 20.00 | 5.00 |
| ☐ 5 Milt Pappas | 7.00 | 2.80 | .70 |
| ☐ 6 Dick Stuart | 7.00 | 2.80 | .70 |
| ☐ 7 Bob Clemente | 45.00 | 18.00 | 4.50 |
| ☐ 8 Yogi Berra | 35.00 | 14.00 | 3.50 |
| ☐ 9 Ken Boyer | 9.00 | 3.75 | .90 |
| ☐ 10 Orlando Cepeda | 9.00 | 3.75 | .90 |
| ☐ 11 Gus Triandos | 7.00 | 2.80 | .70 |
| ☐ 12 Frank Malzone | 7.00 | 2.80 | .70 |
| ☐ 13 Willie Mays | 50.00 | 20.00 | 5.00 |
| ☐ 14 Camilo Pascual | 7.00 | 2.80 | .70 |
| ☐ 15 Bob Cerv | 7.00 | 2.80 | .70 |
| ☐ 16 Vic Power | 7.00 | 2.80 | .70 |
| ☐ 17 Larry Sherry | 7.00 | 2.80 | .70 |
| ☐ 18 Al Kaline | 30.00 | 12.00 | 3.00 |
| ☐ 19 Warren Spahn | 25.00 | 10.00 | 2.50 |
| ☐ 20 Harmon Killebrew | 25.00 | 10.00 | 2.50 |
| ☐ 21 Jackie Jensen | 9.00 | 3.75 | .90 |
| ☐ 22 Luis Aparicio | 20.00 | 8.00 | 2.00 |
| ☐ 23 Gil Hodges | 20.00 | 8.00 | 2.00 |
| ☐ 24 Richie Ashburn | 12.00 | 5.00 | 1.20 |
| ☐ 25 Nellie Fox | 12.00 | 5.00 | 1.20 |
| ☐ 26 Robin Roberts | 20.00 | 8.00 | 2.00 |
| ☐ 27 Joe Cunningham | 7.00 | 2.80 | .70 |
| ☐ 28 Early Wynn | 20.00 | 8.00 | 2.00 |
| ☐ 29 Frank Robinson | 25.00 | 10.00 | 2.50 |
| ☐ 30 Rocky Colavito | 9.00 | 3.75 | .90 |
| ☐ 31 Mickey Mantle | 100.00 | 40.00 | 10.00 |
| ☐ 32 Glen Hobbie | 7.00 | 2.80 | .70 |
| ☐ 33 Roy McMillan | 7.00 | 2.80 | .70 |
| ☐ 34 Harvey Kuenn | 9.00 | 3.75 | .90 |
| ☐ 35 Johnny Antonelli | 7.00 | 2.80 | .70 |
| ☐ 36 Del Crandall | 7.00 | 2.80 | .70 |

## 1961 Bazooka

The 36 card set issued by Bazooka in 1961 follows the format established in 1960; three full color, numbered cards to each panel found on a Bazooka gum box. The individual cards measure 1 13/16" by 2 3/4" whereas the panels measure 2 3/4" by 5 1/2". The cards of 1960 and 1961 are similar in design but are easily distinguished from one another by their numbers. Complete panels of three would have a value of 30% more than the sum of the individual cards (prices) on the panel and complete boxes would command a premium of another 30% above those prices.

|  | MINT | VG-E | F-G |
|---|---|---|---|
| COMPLETE INDIV. SET | 450.00 | 180.00 | 45.00 |
| COMMON PLAYER | 7.00 | 2.80 | .70 |
| ☐ 1 Art Mahaffey | 7.00 | 2.80 | .70 |
| ☐ 2 Mickey Mantle | 100.00 | 40.00 | 10.00 |
| ☐ 3 Ron Santo | 9.00 | 3.75 | .90 |
| ☐ 4 Bud Daley | 7.00 | 2.80 | .70 |
| ☐ 5 Roger Maris | 40.00 | 16.00 | 4.00 |
| ☐ 6 Eddie Yost | 7.00 | 2.80 | .70 |
| ☐ 7 Minnie Minoso | 9.00 | 3.75 | .90 |
| ☐ 8 Dick Groat | 9.00 | 3.75 | .90 |
| ☐ 9 Frank Malzone | 7.00 | 2.80 | .70 |
| ☐ 10 Dick Donovan | 7.00 | 2.80 | .70 |
| ☐ 11 Ed Mathews | 25.00 | 10.00 | 2.50 |
| ☐ 12 Jim Lemon | 7.00 | 2.80 | .70 |
| ☐ 13 Chuck Estrada | 7.00 | 2.80 | .70 |
| ☐ 14 Ken Boyer | 9.00 | 3.75 | .90 |
| ☐ 15 Harvey Kuenn | 9.00 | 3.75 | .90 |
| ☐ 16 Ernie Broglio | 7.00 | 2.80 | .70 |
| ☐ 17 Rocky Colavito | 9.00 | 3.75 | .90 |
| ☐ 18 Ted Kluszewski | 9.00 | 3.75 | .90 |
| ☐ 19 Ernie Banks | 30.00 | 12.00 | 3.00 |
| ☐ 20 Al Kaline | 30.00 | 12.00 | 3.00 |

| | | MINT | VG-E | F-G |
|---|---|---|---|---|
| ☐ 21 | Ed Bailey | 7.00 | 2.80 | .70 |
| ☐ 22 | Jim Perry | 9.00 | 3.75 | .90 |
| ☐ 23 | Willie Mays | 50.00 | 20.00 | 5.00 |
| ☐ 24 | Bill Mazeroski | 9.00 | 3.75 | .90 |
| ☐ 25 | Gus Triandos | 7.00 | 2.80 | .70 |
| ☐ 26 | Don Drysdale | 20.00 | 8.00 | 2.00 |
| ☐ 27 | Frank Herrera | 7.00 | 2.80 | .70 |
| ☐ 28 | Earl Battey | 7.00 | 2.80 | .70 |
| ☐ 29 | Warren Spahn | 25.00 | 10.00 | 2.50 |
| ☐ 30 | Gene Woodling | 7.00 | 2.80 | .70 |
| ☐ 31 | Frank Robinson | 25.00 | 10.00 | 2.50 |
| ☐ 32 | Pete Runnels | 7.00 | 2.80 | .70 |
| ☐ 33 | Woodie Held | 7.00 | 2.80 | .70 |
| ☐ 34 | Norm Larker | 7.00 | 2.80 | .70 |
| ☐ 35 | Luis Aparicio | 20.00 | 8.00 | 2.00 |
| ☐ 36 | Bill Tuttle | 7.00 | 2.80 | .70 |

## 1962 Bazooka

The 1962 Bazooka set of 45 full color, blank backed, unnumbered cards was issued in panels of three on Bazooka bubble gum boxes. The individual cards measure 1 13/16" by 2 3/4" whereas the panels measure 2 3/4" by 5 1/2". The cards below are numbered by panel alphabetically based on the last name of the player pictured on the far left card of the panel. The cards with SP in the checklist below are more difficult to obtain than other cards in the set as they were printed in shorter supply. Complete panels of three would have a value of 30% more than the sum of the individual cards (prices) on the panel and complete boxes would command a premium of another 30% above those prices.

| | | MINT | VG-E | F-G |
|---|---|---|---|---|
| COMPLETE INDIV. SET | | 800.00 | 320.00 | 80.00 |
| COMMON PLAYER | | 7.00 | 2.80 | .70 |
| ☐ 1 | Bob Allison SP | 15.00 | 6.00 | 1.50 |
| ☐ 2 | Ed Mathews SP | 100.00 | 40.00 | 10.00 |
| ☐ 3 | Vada Pinson SP | 15.00 | 6.00 | 1.50 |
| ☐ 4 | Earl Battey | 7.00 | 2.80 | .70 |
| ☐ 5 | Warren Spahn | 25.00 | 10.00 | 2.50 |
| ☐ 6 | Lee Thomas | 7.00 | 2.80 | .70 |
| ☐ 7 | Orlando Cepeda | 9.00 | 3.75 | .90 |
| ☐ 8 | Woodie Held | 7.00 | 2.80 | .70 |
| ☐ 9 | Bob Aspromonte | 7.00 | 2.80 | .70 |
| ☐ 10 | Dick Howser | 9.00 | 3.75 | .90 |
| ☐ 11 | Bob Clemente | 45.00 | 18.00 | 4.50 |
| ☐ 12 | Al Kaline | 30.00 | 12.00 | 3.00 |
| ☐ 13 | Joe Jay | 7.00 | 2.80 | .70 |
| ☐ 14 | Roger Maris | 35.00 | 14.00 | 3.50 |
| ☐ 15 | Frank Howard | 9.00 | 3.75 | .90 |
| ☐ 16 | Sandy Koufax | 35.00 | 14.00 | 3.50 |
| ☐ 17 | Jim Gentile | 7.00 | 2.80 | .70 |
| ☐ 18 | Johnny Callison | 7.00 | 2.80 | .70 |
| ☐ 19 | Jim Landis | 7.00 | 2.80 | .70 |
| ☐ 20 | Ken Boyer | 9.00 | 3.75 | .90 |
| ☐ 21 | Chuck Schilling | 7.00 | 2.80 | .70 |
| ☐ 22 | Art Mahaffey | 7.00 | 2.80 | .70 |
| ☐ 23 | Mickey Mantle | 100.00 | 40.00 | 10.00 |
| ☐ 24 | Dick Stuart | 7.00 | 2.80 | .70 |
| ☐ 25 | Ken McBride | 7.00 | 2.80 | .70 |
| ☐ 26 | Frank Robinson | 25.00 | 10.00 | 2.50 |
| ☐ 27 | Gil Hodges | 20.00 | 8.00 | 2.00 |
| ☐ 28 | Milt Pappas | 7.00 | 2.80 | .70 |
| ☐ 29 | Hank Aaron | 50.00 | 20.00 | 5.00 |
| ☐ 30 | Luis Aparicio | 20.00 | 8.00 | 2.00 |
| ☐ 31 | Johnny Romano SP | 15.00 | 6.00 | 1.50 |
| ☐ 32 | Ernie Banks SP | 125.00 | 50.00 | 12.50 |
| ☐ 33 | Norm Siebern SP | 15.00 | 6.00 | 1.50 |
| ☐ 34 | Ron Santo | 9.00 | 3.75 | .90 |
| ☐ 35 | Norm Cash | 9.00 | 3.75 | .90 |
| ☐ 36 | Jim Piersall | 9.00 | 3.75 | .90 |
| ☐ 37 | Don Schwall | 7.00 | 2.80 | .70 |
| ☐ 38 | Willie Mays | 50.00 | 20.00 | 5.00 |
| ☐ 39 | Norm Larker | 7.00 | 2.80 | .70 |
| ☐ 40 | Bill White | 9.00 | 3.75 | .90 |
| ☐ 41 | Whitey Ford | 25.00 | 10.00 | 2.50 |
| ☐ 42 | Rocky Colavito | 9.00 | 3.75 | .90 |
| ☐ 43 | Don Zimmer SP | 15.00 | 6.00 | 1.50 |
| ☐ 44 | Harmon Killebrew SP | 100.00 | 40.00 | 10.00 |
| ☐ 45 | Gene Woodling SP | 15.00 | 6.00 | 1.50 |

## 1963 Bazooka

The 1963 Bazooka set of 36 full color, blank backed, numbered cards was issued on Bazooka bubble gum boxes. This year marked a change in format from previous Bazooka issues with a smaller sized card being issued. The individual cards measure 1 9/16" by 2 1/2" whereas the panels measure 2 1/2" by 4 11/16". The card features a white strip with the player's name printed in red and the team position printed in black on the card. The number appears in the white border at the bottom of the card. Three cards were issued per panel. Complete panels of three would have a value of 30% more than the sum of the individual cards (prices) on the panel and complete boxes would command a premium of another 30% above those prices.

| | | MINT | VG-E | F-G |
|---|---|---|---|---|
| COMPLETE INDIV. SET | | 400.00 | 160.00 | 40.00 |
| COMMON PLAYER | | 4.00 | 1.60 | .40 |
| ☐ 1 | Mickey Mantle | 80.00 | 32.00 | 8.00 |
| ☐ 2 | Bob Rodgers | 4.00 | 1.60 | .40 |
| ☐ 3 | Ernie Banks | 25.00 | 10.00 | 2.50 |
| ☐ 4 | Norm Siebern | 4.00 | 1.60 | .40 |
| ☐ 5 | Warren Spahn | 20.00 | 8.00 | 2.00 |
| ☐ 6 | Bill Mazeroski | 6.00 | 2.40 | .60 |
| ☐ 7 | Harmon Killebrew | 20.00 | 8.00 | 2.00 |
| ☐ 8 | Dick Farrell | 4.00 | 1.60 | .40 |
| ☐ 9 | Hank Aaron | 40.00 | 16.00 | 4.00 |
| ☐ 10 | Dick Donovan | 4.00 | 1.60 | .40 |
| ☐ 11 | Jim Gentile | 4.00 | 1.60 | .40 |
| ☐ 12 | Willie Mays | 40.00 | 16.00 | 4.00 |
| ☐ 13 | Camilo Pascual | 4.00 | 1.60 | .40 |
| ☐ 14 | Bob Clemente | 35.00 | 14.00 | 3.50 |
| ☐ 15 | Johnny Callison | 4.00 | 1.60 | .40 |
| ☐ 16 | Carl Yastrzemski | 50.00 | 20.00 | 5.00 |
| ☐ 17 | Don Drysdale | 20.00 | 8.00 | 2.00 |
| ☐ 18 | Johnny Romano | 4.00 | 1.60 | .40 |
| ☐ 19 | Al Jackson | 4.00 | 1.60 | .40 |
| ☐ 20 | Ralph Terry | 4.00 | 1.60 | .40 |
| ☐ 21 | Bill Monbouquette | 4.00 | 1.60 | .40 |
| ☐ 22 | Orlando Cepeda | 6.00 | 2.40 | .60 |
| ☐ 23 | Stan Musial | 35.00 | 14.00 | 3.50 |
| ☐ 24 | Floyd Robinson | 4.00 | 1.60 | .40 |
| ☐ 25 | Chuck Hinton | 4.00 | 1.60 | .40 |
| ☐ 26 | Bob Purkey | 4.00 | 1.60 | .40 |
| ☐ 27 | Ken Hubbs | 6.00 | 2.40 | .60 |
| ☐ 28 | Bill White | 6.00 | 2.40 | .60 |
| ☐ 29 | Ray Herbert | 4.00 | 1.60 | .40 |
| ☐ 30 | Brooks Robinson | 30.00 | 12.00 | 3.00 |
| ☐ 31 | Frank Robinson | 20.00 | 8.00 | 2.00 |
| ☐ 32 | Lee Thomas | 4.00 | 1.60 | .40 |
| ☐ 33 | Rocky Colavito | 6.00 | 2.40 | .60 |
| ☐ 34 | Al Kaline | 25.00 | 10.00 | 2.50 |
| ☐ 35 | Art Mahaffey | 4.00 | 1.60 | .40 |
| ☐ 36 | Tommy Davis | 6.00 | 2.40 | .60 |

## 1963 Bazooka ATG

The 1963 Bazooka All Time Greats set contains 41 black and white numbered cards issued as inserts in boxes of Bazooka Bubble gum. The cards feature bust shots with gold trim and measure 1 9/16" by 2 1/2". The backs are yellow with black print containing vital information and a biography of the player. Many of the players are pictured not as they looked during their playing careers but as they looked many years after their playing days were through. The cards also exist in a scarcer variety with silver trim instead of gold; the silver trim variety

**EDDIE COLLINS**
2B  *Phila.-Chicago*

**BORN: MAY 2, 1887**

**HOME: MILLERTOWN, NEW YORK**

Eddie first joined the Athletics in 1906, but he didn't become a big star until 1909 when he batted .346. Then the second baseman batted over .300 for eight consecutive seasons. Eddie was traded to the White Sox in 1915 and had his best year in the majors in 1920 when he hit .369. At the end of the 1926 season, the lefthanded hitter was dealt back to the Philadelphia Athletics. An exciting ballplayer, Eddie obtained a lifetime batting mark of .333.

©T.C.G. PRINTED IN U.S.A.

cards are worth approximately double the prices listed below. Cards are numbered on the back.

| | | MINT | VG-E | F-G |
|---|---|---|---|---|
| | COMPLETE SET | 150.00 | 60.00 | 15.00 |
| | COMMON PLAYER | 2.50 | 1.00 | .25 |
| ☐ 1 | Joe Tinker | 2.50 | 1.00 | .25 |
| ☐ 2 | Harry Heilmann | 2.50 | 1.00 | .25 |
| ☐ 3 | Jack Chesbro | 2.50 | 1.00 | .25 |
| ☐ 4 | Christy Mathewson | 6.50 | 2.60 | .65 |
| ☐ 5 | Herb Pennock | 2.50 | 1.00 | .25 |
| ☐ 6 | Cy Young | 4.50 | 1.80 | .45 |
| ☐ 7 | Ed Walsh | 2.50 | 1.00 | .25 |
| ☐ 8 | Nap Lajoie | 3.50 | 1.40 | .35 |
| ☐ 9 | Eddie Plank | 3.00 | 1.20 | .30 |
| ☐ 10 | Honus Wagner | 6.50 | 2.60 | .65 |
| ☐ 11 | Chief Bender | 2.50 | 1.00 | .25 |
| ☐ 12 | Walter Johnson | 6.50 | 2.60 | .65 |
| ☐ 13 | Mordecai Brown | 2.50 | 1.00 | .25 |
| ☐ 14 | Rabbit Maranville | 2.50 | 1.00 | .25 |
| ☐ 15 | Lou Gehrig | 14.00 | 5.75 | 1.40 |
| ☐ 16 | Ban Johnson | 2.50 | 1.00 | .25 |
| ☐ 17 | Babe Ruth | 24.00 | 10.00 | 2.40 |
| ☐ 18 | Connie Mack | 3.00 | 1.20 | .30 |
| ☐ 19 | Hank Greenberg | 3.00 | 1.20 | .30 |
| ☐ 20 | John McGraw | 3.00 | 1.20 | .30 |
| ☐ 21 | Al Simmons | 2.50 | 1.00 | .25 |
| ☐ 23 | Jimmy Collins | 2.50 | 1.00 | .25 |
| ☐ 24 | Tris Speaker | 3.50 | 1.40 | .35 |
| ☐ 25 | Frank Chance | 2.50 | 1.00 | .25 |
| ☐ 26 | Fred Clarke | 2.50 | 1.00 | .25 |
| ☐ 27 | Wilbert Robinson | 2.50 | 1.00 | .25 |
| ☐ 28 | Dazzy Vance | 2.50 | 1.00 | .25 |
| ☐ 29 | Pete Alexander | 3.50 | 1.40 | .35 |
| ☐ 30 | Judge Landis | 2.50 | 1.00 | .25 |
| ☐ 31 | Willie Keeler | 2.50 | 1.00 | .25 |
| ☐ 32 | Rogers Hornsby | 4.50 | 1.80 | .45 |
| ☐ 33 | Hugh Duffy | 2.50 | 1.00 | .25 |
| ☐ 34 | Mickey Cochrane | 3.00 | 1.20 | .30 |
| ☐ 35 | Ty Cobb | 16.00 | 6.50 | 1.60 |
| ☐ 36 | Mel Ott | 4.00 | 1.60 | .40 |
| ☐ 37 | Clark Griffith | 2.50 | 1.00 | .25 |
| ☐ 38 | Ted Lyons | 2.50 | 1.00 | .25 |
| ☐ 39 | Cap Anson | 3.00 | 1.20 | .30 |
| ☐ 40 | Bill Dickey | 3.00 | 1.20 | .30 |
| ☐ 41 | Eddie Collins | 2.50 | 1.00 | .25 |

## 1964 Bazooka

The 1964 Bazooka set of 36 full color, blank backed, numbered cards were issued in panels of three on the backs of Bazooka bubble gum boxes. The individual cards measure 1 9/16" by 2 1/2" whereas the panels measure 2 1/2" by 4 11/16". Many players from the 1963 set have the same numbers; however the pictures are different. Complete panels of three would have a value of 30% more than the sum of the individual cards (prices) on the panel and complete boxes would command a premium of another 30% above those prices.

| | | MINT | VG-E | F-G |
|---|---|---|---|---|
| | COMPLETE INDIV. SET | 350.00 | 140.00 | 35.00 |
| | COMMON PLAYER | 3.50 | 1.40 | .35 |
| ☐ 1 | Mickey Mantle | 75.00 | 30.00 | 7.50 |
| ☐ 2 | Dick Groat | 5.00 | 2.00 | .50 |
| ☐ 3 | Steve Barber | 3.50 | 1.40 | .35 |
| ☐ 4 | Ken McBride | 3.50 | 1.40 | .35 |
| ☐ 5 | Warren Spahn | 15.00 | 6.00 | 1.50 |
| ☐ 6 | Bob Friend | 3.50 | 1.40 | .35 |
| ☐ 7 | Harmon Killebrew | 15.00 | 6.00 | 1.50 |
| ☐ 8 | Dick Farrell | 3.50 | 1.40 | .35 |
| ☐ 9 | Hank Aaron | 35.00 | 14.00 | 3.50 |
| ☐ 10 | Rich Rollins | 3.50 | 1.40 | .35 |
| ☐ 11 | Jim Gentile | 3.50 | 1.40 | .35 |
| ☐ 12 | Willie Mays | 35.00 | 14.00 | 3.50 |
| ☐ 13 | Camilo Pascual | 3.50 | 1.40 | .35 |
| ☐ 14 | Bob Clemente | 30.00 | 12.00 | 3.00 |
| ☐ 15 | Johnny Callison | 3.50 | 1.40 | .35 |
| ☐ 16 | Carl Yastrzemski | 40.00 | 16.00 | 4.00 |
| ☐ 17 | Billy Williams | 12.00 | 5.00 | 1.20 |
| ☐ 18 | Johnny Romano | 3.50 | 1.40 | .35 |
| ☐ 19 | Jim Maloney | 5.00 | 2.00 | .50 |
| ☐ 20 | Norm Cash | 5.00 | 2.00 | .50 |
| ☐ 21 | Willie McCovey | 18.00 | 7.25 | 1.80 |
| ☐ 22 | Jim Fregosi | 5.00 | 2.00 | .50 |
| ☐ 23 | George Altman | 3.50 | 1.40 | .35 |
| ☐ 24 | Floyd Robinson | 3.50 | 1.40 | .35 |
| ☐ 25 | Chuck Hinton | 3.50 | 1.40 | .35 |
| ☐ 26 | Ron Hunt | 3.50 | 1.40 | .35 |
| ☐ 27 | Gary Peters | 3.50 | 1.40 | .35 |
| ☐ 28 | Dick Ellsworth | 3.50 | 1.40 | .35 |
| ☐ 29 | Elston Howard | 5.00 | 2.00 | .50 |
| ☐ 30 | Brooks Robinson | 24.00 | 10.00 | 2.40 |
| ☐ 31 | Frank Robinson | 18.00 | 7.25 | 1.80 |
| ☐ 32 | Sandy Koufax | 30.00 | 12.00 | 3.00 |
| ☐ 33 | Rocky Colavito | 5.00 | 2.00 | .50 |
| ☐ 34 | Al Kaline | 24.00 | 10.00 | 2.40 |
| ☐ 35 | Ken Boyer | 5.00 | 2.00 | .50 |
| ☐ 36 | Tommy Davis | 5.00 | 2.00 | .50 |

## 1965 Bazooka

The 1965 Bazooka set of 36 full color, blank backed, numbered cards was issued in panels of three on the backs of Bazooka bubble gum boxes. The individual cards measure 1 9/16" by 2 1/2" whereas the panels measure 2 1/2" by 4 11/16". As in the previous two years some of the players have the same numbers on their cards; however all pictures are different from the previous two years. Complete panels of three would have a value of 30% more than the sum of the individual cards (prices) on the panel and complete boxes would command a premium of another 30% above those prices.

| | | MINT | VG-E | F-G |
|---|---|---|---|---|
| | COMPLETE INDIV. SET | 300.00 | 120.00 | 30.00 |
| | COMMON PLAYER | 3.50 | 1.40 | .35 |
| ☐ 1 | Mickey Mantle | 70.00 | 28.00 | 7.00 |
| ☐ 2 | Larry Jackson | 3.50 | 1.40 | .35 |
| ☐ 3 | Chuck Hinton | 3.50 | 1.40 | .35 |
| ☐ 4 | Tony Oliva | 6.00 | 2.40 | .60 |
| ☐ 5 | Dean Chance | 3.50 | 1.40 | .35 |
| ☐ 6 | Jim O'Toole | 3.50 | 1.40 | .35 |
| ☐ 7 | Harmon Killebrew | 15.00 | 6.00 | 1.50 |
| ☐ 8 | Pete Ward | 3.50 | 1.40 | .35 |
| ☐ 9 | Hank Aaron | 30.00 | 12.00 | 3.00 |
| ☐ 10 | Dick Radatz | 3.50 | 1.40 | .35 |
| ☐ 11 | Boog Powell | 5.00 | 2.00 | .50 |
| ☐ 12 | Willie Mays | 30.00 | 12.00 | 3.00 |
| ☐ 13 | Bob Veale | 3.50 | 1.40 | .35 |
| ☐ 14 | Bob Clemente | 27.00 | 11.00 | 2.70 |
| ☐ 15 | Johnny Callison | 3.50 | 1.40 | .35 |
| ☐ 16 | Joe Torre | 5.00 | 2.00 | .50 |
| ☐ 17 | Billy Williams | 12.00 | 5.00 | 1.20 |
| ☐ 18 | Bob Chance | 3.50 | 1.40 | .35 |
| ☐ 19 | Bob Aspromonte | 3.50 | 1.40 | .35 |
| ☐ 20 | Joe Christopher | 3.50 | 1.40 | .35 |
| ☐ 21 | Jim Bunning | 7.50 | 3.00 | .75 |

| | | MINT | VG-E | F-G |
|---|---|---|---|---|
| ☐ 22 | Jim Fregosi | 5.00 | 2.00 | .50 |
| ☐ 23 | Bob Gibson | 15.00 | 6.00 | 1.50 |
| ☐ 24 | Juan Marichal | 15.00 | 6.00 | 1.50 |
| ☐ 25 | Dave Wickersham | 3.50 | 1.40 | .35 |
| ☐ 26 | Ron Hunt | 3.50 | 1.40 | .35 |
| ☐ 27 | Gary Peters | 3.50 | 1.40 | .35 |
| ☐ 28 | Ron Santo | 5.00 | 2.00 | .50 |
| ☐ 29 | Elston Howard | 5.00 | 2.00 | .50 |
| ☐ 30 | Brooks Robinson | 20.00 | 8.00 | 2.00 |
| ☐ 31 | Frank Robinson | 15.00 | 6.00 | 1.50 |
| ☐ 32 | Sandy Koufax | 25.00 | 10.00 | 2.50 |
| ☐ 33 | Rocky Colavito | 5.00 | 2.00 | .50 |
| ☐ 34 | Al Kaline | 20.00 | 8.00 | 2.00 |
| ☐ 35 | Ken Boyer | 5.00 | 2.00 | .50 |
| ☐ 36 | Tommy Davis | 4.00 | 1.60 | .40 |

## 1966 Bazooka

The 1966 Bazooka set of 48 full color, blank backed, numbered cards was issued in panels of three on the backs of Bazooka bubble gum boxes. The individual cards measure 1 9/16" by 2 1/2" whereas the complete panels measure 2 1/2" by 4 11/16". The set is distinguishable from the previous years by mention of "48 card set" at the bottom of the card. Complete panels of three would have a value of 30% more than the sum of the individual cards (prices) on the panel and complete boxes would command a premium of another 30% above those prices.

| | | MINT | VG-E | F-G |
|---|---|---|---|---|
| COMPLETE INDIV. SET | | 400.00 | 160.00 | 40.00 |
| COMMON PLAYER | | 3.50 | 1.40 | .35 |
| ☐ 1 | Sandy Koufax | 25.00 | 10.00 | 2.50 |
| ☐ 2 | Willie Horton | 3.50 | 1.40 | .35 |
| ☐ 3 | Frank Howard | 4.00 | 1.60 | .40 |
| ☐ 4 | Richie Allen | 5.00 | 2.00 | .50 |
| ☐ 5 | Mel Stottlemyre | 4.00 | 1.60 | .40 |
| ☐ 6 | Tony Conigliaro | 5.00 | 2.00 | .50 |
| ☐ 7 | Mickey Mantle | 70.00 | 28.00 | 7.00 |
| ☐ 8 | Leon Wagner | 3.50 | 1.40 | .35 |
| ☐ 9 | Ed Kranepool | 3.50 | 1.40 | .35 |
| ☐ 10 | Juan Marichal | 15.00 | 6.00 | 1.50 |
| ☐ 11 | Harmon Killebrew | 15.00 | 6.00 | 1.50 |
| ☐ 12 | Johnny Callison | 3.50 | 1.40 | .35 |
| ☐ 13 | Roy McMillan | 3.50 | 1.40 | .35 |
| ☐ 14 | Willie McCovey | 18.00 | 7.25 | 1.80 |
| ☐ 15 | Rocky Colavito | 5.00 | 2.00 | .50 |
| ☐ 16 | Willie Mays | 30.00 | 12.00 | 3.00 |
| ☐ 17 | Sam McDowell | 4.00 | 1.60 | .40 |
| ☐ 18 | Vern Law | 3.50 | 1.40 | .35 |
| ☐ 19 | Jim Fregosi | 5.00 | 2.00 | .50 |
| ☐ 20 | Ron Fairly | 3.50 | 1.40 | .35 |
| ☐ 21 | Bob Gibson | 15.00 | 6.00 | 1.50 |
| ☐ 22 | Carl Yastrzemski | 35.00 | 14.00 | 3.50 |
| ☐ 23 | Bill White | 4.00 | 1.60 | .40 |
| ☐ 24 | Bob Aspromonte | 3.50 | 1.40 | .35 |
| ☐ 25 | Dean Chance | 3.50 | 1.40 | .35 |
| ☐ 26 | Bob Clemente | 27.00 | 11.00 | 2.70 |
| ☐ 27 | Tony Cloninger | 3.50 | 1.40 | .35 |
| ☐ 28 | Curt Blefary | 3.50 | 1.40 | .35 |
| ☐ 29 | Milt Pappas | 4.00 | 1.60 | .40 |
| ☐ 30 | Hank Aaron | 30.00 | 12.00 | 3.00 |
| ☐ 31 | Jim Bunning | 7.50 | 3.00 | .75 |
| ☐ 32 | Frank Robinson | 15.00 | 6.00 | 1.50 |
| ☐ 33 | Bill Skowron | 4.00 | 1.60 | .40 |
| ☐ 34 | Brooks Robinson | 20.00 | 8.00 | 2.00 |
| ☐ 35 | Jim Wynn | 4.00 | 1.60 | .40 |
| ☐ 36 | Joe Torre | 5.00 | 2.00 | .50 |
| ☐ 37 | Jim Grant | 3.50 | 1.40 | .35 |
| ☐ 38 | Pete Rose | 70.00 | 28.00 | 7.00 |
| ☐ 39 | Ron Santo | 4.00 | 1.60 | .40 |
| ☐ 40 | Tom Tresh | 4.00 | 1.60 | .40 |
| ☐ 41 | Tony Oliva | 5.00 | 2.00 | .50 |
| ☐ 42 | Don Drysdale | 12.00 | 5.00 | 1.20 |
| ☐ 43 | Pete Richert | 3.50 | 1.40 | .35 |
| ☐ 44 | Bert Campaneris | 4.00 | 1.60 | .40 |
| ☐ 45 | Jim Maloney | 4.00 | 1.60 | .40 |
| ☐ 46 | Al Kaline | 20.00 | 8.00 | 2.00 |
| ☐ 47 | Eddie Fisher | 3.50 | 1.40 | .35 |
| ☐ 48 | Billy Williams | 12.00 | 5.00 | 1.20 |

## 1967 Bazooka

The 1967 Bazooka set of 48 full color, blank backed, numbered cards was issued in panels of three on the backs of Bazooka bubble gum boxes. The individual cards measure 1 9/16" by 2 1/2" whereas the complete panels measure 2 1/2" by 4 11/16". This set is virtually identical to the 1966 set with the exception of ten new cards as replacements for ten 1966 cards. The remaining 38 cards are identical in both pose and number. The replacement cards are listed in the checklist below with an asterisk. Complete panels of three would have a value of 30% more than the sum of the individual cards (prices) on the panel and complete boxes would command a premium of another 30% above those prices.

| | | MINT | VG-E | F-G |
|---|---|---|---|---|
| COMPLETE INDIV. SET | | 400.00 | 160.00 | 40.00 |
| COMMON PLAYER | | 3.50 | 1.40 | .35 |
| ☐ 1 | Rick Reichardt * | 3.50 | 1.40 | .35 |
| ☐ 2 | Tommy Agee * | 3.50 | 1.40 | .35 |
| ☐ 3 | Frank Howard * | 4.00 | 1.60 | .40 |
| ☐ 4 | Richie Allen | 5.00 | 2.00 | .50 |
| ☐ 5 | Mel Stottlemyre | 4.00 | 1.60 | .40 |
| ☐ 6 | Tony Conigliaro | 5.00 | 2.00 | .50 |
| ☐ 7 | Mickey Mantle | 70.00 | 28.00 | 7.00 |
| ☐ 8 | Leon Wagner | 3.50 | 1.40 | .35 |
| ☐ 9 | Gary Peters * | 3.50 | 1.40 | .35 |
| ☐ 10 | Juan Marichal | 12.00 | 5.00 | 1.20 |
| ☐ 11 | Harmon Killebrew | 12.00 | 5.00 | 1.20 |
| ☐ 12 | Johnny Callison | 3.50 | 1.40 | .35 |
| ☐ 13 | Denny McLain * | 5.00 | 2.00 | .50 |
| ☐ 14 | Willie McCovey | 15.00 | 6.00 | 1.50 |
| ☐ 15 | Rocky Colavito | 5.00 | 2.00 | .50 |
| ☐ 16 | Willie Mays | 30.00 | 12.00 | 3.00 |
| ☐ 17 | Sam McDowell | 4.00 | 1.60 | .40 |
| ☐ 18 | Jim Kaat * | 6.00 | 2.40 | .60 |
| ☐ 19 | Jim Fregosi | 5.00 | 2.00 | .50 |
| ☐ 20 | Ron Fairly | 3.50 | 1.40 | .35 |
| ☐ 21 | Bob Gibson | 12.00 | 5.00 | 1.20 |
| ☐ 22 | Carl Yastrzemski | 35.00 | 14.00 | 3.50 |
| ☐ 23 | Bob White | 4.00 | 1.60 | .40 |
| ☐ 24 | Bob Aspromonte | 3.50 | 1.40 | .35 |
| ☐ 25 | Dean Chance | 3.50 | 1.40 | .35 |
| ☐ 26 | Bob Clemente | 27.00 | 11.00 | 2.70 |
| ☐ 27 | Tony Cloninger | 3.50 | 1.40 | .35 |
| ☐ 28 | Curt Blefary | 3.50 | 1.40 | .35 |
| ☐ 29 | Phil Regan * | 3.50 | 1.40 | .35 |
| ☐ 30 | Hank Aaron | 30.00 | 12.00 | 3.00 |
| ☐ 31 | Jim Bunning | 7.50 | 3.00 | .75 |
| ☐ 32 | Frank Robinson | 15.00 | 6.00 | 1.50 |
| ☐ 33 | Ken Boyer * | 5.00 | 2.00 | .50 |
| ☐ 34 | Brooks Robinson | 20.00 | 8.00 | 2.00 |
| ☐ 35 | Jim Wynn | 4.00 | 1.60 | .40 |
| ☐ 36 | Joe Torre | 5.00 | 2.00 | .50 |
| ☐ 37 | Tommy Davis * | 4.00 | 1.60 | .40 |
| ☐ 38 | Pete Rose | 70.00 | 28.00 | 7.00 |
| ☐ 39 | Ron Santo | 5.00 | 2.00 | .50 |
| ☐ 40 | Tom Tresh | 4.00 | 1.60 | .40 |
| ☐ 41 | Tony Oliva | 6.00 | 2.40 | .60 |
| ☐ 42 | Don Drysdale | 12.00 | 5.00 | 1.20 |
| ☐ 43 | Pete Richert | 3.50 | 1.40 | .35 |
| ☐ 44 | Bert Campaneris | 4.00 | 1.60 | .40 |
| ☐ 45 | Jim Maloney | 4.00 | 1.60 | .40 |
| ☐ 46 | Al Kaline | 20.00 | 8.00 | 2.00 |
| ☐ 47 | Matty Alou * | 4.00 | 1.60 | .40 |
| ☐ 48 | Billy Williams | 12.00 | 5.00 | 1.20 |

## 1968 Bazooka

The 1968 Bazooka Tipps from the Topps is a set of 15 numbered boxes (measuring 5 1/2" by 6 1/4" when detached), each containing on the back panel (measuring 3" by 6 1/4") a baseball playing tip from a star, and on the side panels four mini cards, two per side, in full color, measuring 1 1/4" by 3 1/8".

Although the set contains a total of 60 of these small cards, 4 are repeated; therefore there are only 56 different small cards. Some collectors cut the panels into individual cards; however most collectors retain entire panels or boxes. The prices in the checklist below therefore reflect only the values of the complete boxes.

|                          | MINT   | VG-E   | F-G   |
|--------------------------|--------|--------|-------|
| COMPLETE BOX SET ........ | 900.00 | 360.00 | 90.00 |
| COMMON BOX ............... | 40.00  | 16.00  | 4.00  |
| COMMON INDIV. PLAYER ..... | 2.00   | .80    | .20   |

| | | | MINT | VG-E | F-G |
|---|---|---|---|---|---|
| ☐ | 1 | Maury Wills: Bunting ........<br>Al Kaline/P.Casanova<br>Clete Boyer/Tom Seaver | 50.00 | 20.00 | 5.00 |
| ☐ | 2 | C.Yastrzemski: Batting .....<br>Jim Hunter/B.Freehan<br>Matty Alou/J.Lefebvre | 100.00 | 40.00 | 10.00 |
| ☐ | 3 | B.Campaneris: Stealing .....<br>T.McCarver/Bob Veale<br>Frank Robinson/Knoop | 40.00 | 16.00 | 4.00 |
| ☐ | 4 | Maury Wills: Sliding ........<br>Ken Holtzman/J.Azcue<br>T.Conigliaro/B.White | 40.00 | 16.00 | 4.00 |
| ☐ | 5 | J.Javier: Double Play ........<br>J.Marichal/Petrocelli<br>J.Pepitone/Hank Aaron | 50.00 | 20.00 | 5.00 |
| ☐ | 6 | O.Cepeda: 1st Base ..........<br>R.Santo/Don Drysdale<br>Pete Rose/Tommy Agee | 100.00 | 40.00 | 10.00 |
| ☐ | 7 | B.Mazeroski: 2nd Base .....<br>J.Roseboro/Jim Bunning<br>Frank Howard/G.Scott | 40.00 | 16.00 | 4.00 |
| ☐ | 8 | B.Robinson: 3rd Base .......<br>T.Gonzalez/J.McGlothlin<br>W.Horton/H.Killebrew | 60.00 | 24.00 | 6.00 |
| ☐ | 9 | Jim Fregosi: Shortstop .....<br>Max Alvis/Bob Gibson<br>Tony Oliva/V.Pinson | 40.00 | 16.00 | 4.00 |
| ☐ | 10 | Joe Torre: Catching ..........<br>Dean Chance/F.Jenkins<br>T.Davis/Rick Monday | 40.00 | 16.00 | 4.00 |
| ☐ | 11 | Jim Lonborg: Pitching .......<br>Joel Horlen/Jim Wynn<br>C.Flood/Mickey Mantle | 125.00 | 50.00 | 12.50 |
| ☐ | 12 | Mike McCormick: ..............<br>Fielding Pitcher<br>D.Mincher/Tony Perez<br>R.Clemente/Al Downing | 60.00 | 24.00 | 6.00 |
| ☐ | 13 | F.Crosetti: Coaching .........<br>Rod Carew/Don Wilson<br>R.Swoboda/W.McCovey | 50.00 | 20.00 | 5.00 |
| ☐ | 14 | Willie Mays: Outfield .........<br>R.Allen/Gary Peters<br>B.Williams/R.Staub | 80.00 | 32.00 | 8.00 |
| ☐ | 15 | L.Brock: Base Running .....<br>Tommy Agee/Pete Rose<br>R.Santo/Don Drysdale | 150.00 | 60.00 | 15.00 |

## 1969-70 Bazooka

The 1969-1970 Bazooka Baseball Extra News set contains 12 complete panels, each comprising a large action shot of a significant event in baseball history and four small cards, comparable to those in the Tipps from the Topps set of 1968, of Hall of Fame baseball players. Although some collectors cut the panels into individual cards (measuring 3" by 6 1/4" or 1 1/4" by 3 1/8"), most collectors retain the entire panel, or box (measuring 5 1/2" by 6 1/4"). The prices in the checklist below reflect the value for the entire box, as these cards are more widely seen and collected as complete panels or boxes.

|                          | MINT   | VG-E  | F-G   |
|--------------------------|--------|-------|-------|
| COMPLETE PANEL SET ...... | 100.00 | 40.00 | 10.00 |
| COMMON PANEL ........... | 7.00   | 2.80  | .70   |
| COMMON INDIV. PLAYER ..... | .50    | .20   | .05   |

| | | | MINT | VG-E | F-G |
|---|---|---|---|---|---|
| ☐ | 1 | No-Hit Duel by ..................<br>Toney and Vaughn:<br>Ty Cobb<br>Willie Keeler<br>Mordecai Brown<br>Eddie Plank | 9.00 | 3.75 | .90 |
| ☐ | 2 | Alexander Conquers .........<br>Yankees:<br>Al Simmons<br>Ban Johnson<br>Walter Johnson<br>Rogers Hornsby | 7.00 | 2.80 | .70 |
| ☐ | 3 | Yanks' Lazzeri Sets ...........<br>AL Record:<br>Christy Mathewson<br>Chief Bender<br>Grover Alexander<br>Cy Young | 7.00 | 2.80 | .70 |
| ☐ | 4 | Homerun Almost Hit .........<br>Out of Stadium:<br>Lou Gehrig<br>Hugh Duffy<br>Tris Speaker<br>Joe Tinker | 10.00 | 4.00 | 1.00 |
| ☐ | 5 | Four Consecutive .............<br>Homers by Lou:<br>John McGraw<br>Frank Chance<br>Babe Ruth<br>Mickey Cochrane | 18.00 | 7.25 | 1.80 |
| ☐ | 6 | No-Hit Game by ................<br>Walter Johnson:<br>Cy Young<br>Walter Johnson<br>Johnny Evers<br>John McGraw | 7.00 | 2.80 | .70 |
| ☐ | 7 | Twelve RBIs by .................<br>Bottomley:<br>Johnny Evers<br>Eddie Collins<br>Lou Gehrig<br>Ty Cobb | 12.00 | 5.00 | 1.20 |
| ☐ | 8 | Ty Ties Record: ...............<br>Honus Wagner<br>Mickey Cochrane<br>Eddie Collins<br>Mel Ott | 10.00 | 4.00 | 1.00 |
| ☐ | 9 | Babe Ruth Hits Three .......<br>Homers in Game:<br>Cap Anson<br>Tris Speaker<br>Jack Chesbro<br>Al Simmons | 12.00 | 5.00 | 1.20 |
| ☐ | 10 | Calls Shot in .....................<br>Series Game:<br>Rabbit Maranville<br>Ed Walsh<br>Nap Lajoie<br>Connie Mack | 12.00 | 5.00 | 1.20 |
| ☐ | 11 | Ruth's 60th Homer ..........<br>Sets New Record:<br>Joe Tinker<br>Nap Lajoie<br>Mel Ott<br>Frank Chance | 12.00 | 5.00 | 1.20 |
| ☐ | 12 | Double Shutout by ............<br>Ed Reulbach:<br>Rogers Hornsby<br>Rabbit Maranville<br>Christy Mathewson<br>Honus Wagner | 7.00 | 2.80 | .70 |

## 1971 Bazooka

The 1971 Bazooka set of 36 full color, unnumbered cards was issued in 12 panels of three cards each on the backs of boxes containing one cent Bazooka bubble gum. Individual cards measure 2 5/8" by 2 5/8" whereas the panels measure 2 5/8" by 5 5/16". The panels are numbered in the checklist alphabetically by the player's last name on the left most card of the panel. Complete panels of three would have a value of 30% more than the sum of the individual cards (prices) on the panel and complete boxes

would command a premium of another 30% above
those prices.

| | | MINT | VG-E | F-G |
|---|---|---|---|---|
| | COMPLETE INDIV. SET | 150.00 | 60.00 | 15.00 |
| | COMMON PLAYER | 1.50 | .60 | .15 |
| ☐ 1 | Tommie Agee | 1.50 | .60 | .15 |
| ☐ 2 | Harmon Killebrew | 6.00 | 2.40 | .60 |
| ☐ 3 | Reggie Jackson | 18.00 | 7.25 | 1.80 |
| ☐ 4 | Bert Campaneris | 1.50 | .60 | .15 |
| ☐ 5 | Pete Rose | 30.00 | 12.00 | 3.00 |
| ☐ 6 | Orlando Cepeda | 2.00 | .80 | .20 |
| ☐ 7 | Rico Carty | 1.50 | .60 | .15 |
| ☐ 8 | Johnny Bench | 18.00 | 7.25 | 1.80 |
| ☐ 9 | Tommy Harper | 1.50 | .60 | .15 |
| ☐ 10 | Bill Freehan | 1.50 | .60 | .15 |
| ☐ 11 | Roberto Clemente | 18.00 | 7.25 | 1.80 |
| ☐ 12 | Claude Osteen | 1.50 | .60 | .15 |
| ☐ 13 | Jim Fregosi | 2.00 | .80 | .20 |
| ☐ 14 | Billy Williams | 7.50 | 3.00 | .75 |
| ☐ 15 | Dave McNally | 2.00 | .80 | .20 |
| ☐ 16 | Randy Hundley | 1.50 | .60 | .15 |
| ☐ 17 | Willie Mays | 18.00 | 7.25 | 1.80 |
| ☐ 18 | Jim Hunter | 7.50 | 3.00 | .75 |
| ☐ 19 | Juan Marichal | 9.00 | 3.75 | .90 |
| ☐ 20 | Frank Howard | 2.00 | .80 | .20 |
| ☐ 21 | Bill Melton | 1.50 | .60 | .15 |
| ☐ 22 | Willie McCovey | 10.00 | 4.00 | 1.00 |
| ☐ 23 | Carl Yastrzemski | 21.00 | 8.50 | 2.10 |
| ☐ 24 | Clyde Wright | 1.50 | .60 | .15 |
| ☐ 25 | Jim Merritt | 1.50 | .60 | .15 |
| ☐ 26 | Luis Aparicio | 7.50 | 3.00 | .75 |
| ☐ 27 | Bobby Murcer | 2.00 | .80 | .20 |
| ☐ 28 | Rico Petrocelli | 1.50 | .60 | .15 |
| ☐ 29 | Sam McDowell | 1.50 | .60 | .15 |
| ☐ 30 | Clarence Gaston | 1.50 | .60 | .15 |
| ☐ 31 | Brooks Robinson | 14.00 | 5.75 | 1.40 |
| ☐ 32 | Hank Aaron | 18.00 | 7.25 | 1.80 |
| ☐ 33 | Larry Dierker | 1.50 | .60 | .15 |
| ☐ 34 | Rusty Staub | 2.00 | .80 | .20 |
| ☐ 35 | Bob Gibson | 9.00 | 3.75 | .90 |
| ☐ 36 | Amos Otis | 2.00 | .80 | .20 |

## 1958 Bell Brand

The 1958 Bell Brand Potato Chips set of 10
unnumbered cards features members of the Los
Angeles Dodgers exclusively. Each card has a 1/4"
dark green border, and the Gino Cimoli, Johnny
Podres, and Duke Snider cards are more difficult to
find; they are marked with an asterisk in the
checklist below. The cards measure 3" by 4". This
set marks the first year for the Dodgers in Los
Angeles and includes a Campanella card despite the
fact that he never played for the team in California.
The ACC designation is F339-1.

| | | MINT | VG-E | F-G |
|---|---|---|---|---|
| | COMPLETE SET | 750.00 | 300.00 | 75.00 |
| | COMMON PLAYER (1-10) | 30.00 | 12.00 | 3.00 |
| ☐ 1 | Roy Campanella | 75.00 | 30.00 | 7.50 |
| ☐ 2 | Gino Cimoli * | 120.00 | 50.00 | 12.00 |
| ☐ 3 | Don Drysdale | 60.00 | 24.00 | 6.00 |
| ☐ 4 | Jim Gilliam | 30.00 | 12.00 | 3.00 |
| ☐ 5 | Gil Hodges | 60.00 | 24.00 | 6.00 |
| ☐ 6 | Sandy Koufax | 75.00 | 30.00 | 7.50 |
| ☐ 7 | Johnny Podres * | 120.00 | 50.00 | 12.00 |
| ☐ 8 | Pee Wee Reese | 60.00 | 24.00 | 6.00 |
| ☐ 9 | Duke Snider * | 200.00 | 80.00 | 20.00 |
| ☐ 10 | Don Zimmer | 30.00 | 12.00 | 3.00 |

**YOU CAN HELP:** Your input is
solicited for future editions of this guide.
Write the author at 3410 MidCourt
Suite 110, Carrollton, TX 75006.

## 1960 Bell Brand

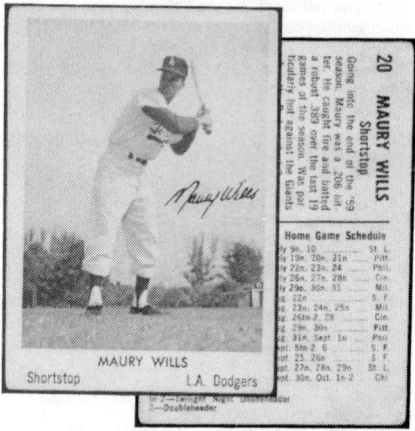

Shortstop — L.A. Dodgers
MAURY WILLS

The 1960 Bell Brand Potato Chips set of 20 full color,
numbered cards features Los Angeles Dodgers only.
Because these cards, measuring 2 1/2" by 3 1/2",
were issued in packages of potato chips, many cards
suffered from stains. Clem Labine, Johnny
Klippstein, and Walter Alston are somewhat more
difficult to obtain than other cards in the set; they
are marked with an asterisk in the checklist below.
The ACC designation is F339- 2.

| | | MINT | VG-E | F-G |
|---|---|---|---|---|
| | COMPLETE SET | 400.00 | 160.00 | 40.00 |
| | COMMON PLAYER (1-20) | 12.00 | 5.00 | 1.20 |
| ☐ 1 | Norm Larker | 12.00 | 5.00 | 1.20 |
| ☐ 2 | Duke Snider | 30.00 | 12.00 | 3.00 |
| ☐ 3 | Danny McDevitt | 12.00 | 5.00 | 1.20 |
| ☐ 4 | Jim Gilliam | 15.00 | 6.00 | 1.50 |
| ☐ 5 | Rip Repulski | 12.00 | 5.00 | 1.20 |
| ☐ 6 | Clem Labine * | 60.00 | 24.00 | 6.00 |
| ☐ 7 | John Roseboro | 12.00 | 5.00 | 1.20 |
| ☐ 8 | Carl Furillo | 15.00 | 6.00 | 1.50 |
| ☐ 9 | Sandy Koufax | 35.00 | 14.00 | 3.50 |
| ☐ 10 | Joe Pignatano | 12.00 | 5.00 | 1.20 |
| ☐ 11 | Chuck Essegian | 12.00 | 5.00 | 1.20 |
| ☐ 12 | John Klippstein * | 80.00 | 32.00 | 8.00 |
| ☐ 13 | Ed Roebuck | 12.00 | 5.00 | 1.20 |
| ☐ 14 | Don Demeter | 12.00 | 5.00 | 1.20 |
| ☐ 15 | Roger Craig | 15.00 | 6.00 | 1.50 |
| ☐ 16 | Stan Williams | 12.00 | 5.00 | 1.20 |
| ☐ 17 | Don Zimmer | 12.00 | 5.00 | 1.20 |
| ☐ 18 | Walt Alston * | 80.00 | 32.00 | 8.00 |
| ☐ 19 | Johnny Podres | 15.00 | 6.00 | 1.50 |
| ☐ 20 | Maury Wills | 20.00 | 8.00 | 2.00 |

## 1961 Bell Brand

The 1961 Bell Brand Potato Chips set of 20 full color
cards features Los Angeles Dodger players only and
is numbered by the uniform numbers of the players.
The cards are slightly smaller than the 1960 cards,
measuring only 2 7/16" by 3 1/2", and are on
thinner paper stock. The ACC designation is F339-3.

| | | MINT | VG-E | F-G |
|---|---|---|---|---|
| | COMPLETE SET | 250.00 | 100.00 | 25.00 |
| | COMMON PLAYER (1-51) | 9.00 | 3.75 | .90 |
| ☐ 3 | Willie Davis | 10.00 | 4.00 | 1.00 |
| ☐ 4 | Duke Snider | 27.00 | 11.00 | 2.70 |
| ☐ 5 | Norm Larker | 9.00 | 3.75 | .90 |
| ☐ 8 | John Roseboro | 9.00 | 3.75 | .90 |

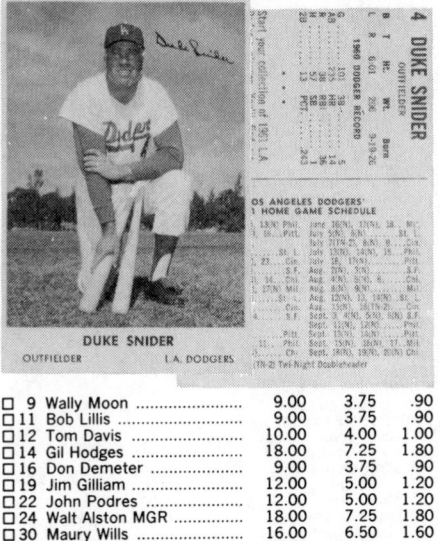

**DUKE SNIDER**
OUTFIELDER      L.A. DODGERS

| | | MINT | VG-E | F-G |
|---|---|---|---|---|
| ☐ | 9 Wally Moon | 9.00 | 3.75 | .90 |
| ☐ | 11 Bob Lillis | 9.00 | 3.75 | .90 |
| ☐ | 12 Tom Davis | 10.00 | 4.00 | 1.00 |
| ☐ | 14 Gil Hodges | 18.00 | 7.25 | 1.80 |
| ☐ | 16 Don Demeter | 9.00 | 3.75 | .90 |
| ☐ | 19 Jim Gilliam | 12.00 | 5.00 | 1.20 |
| ☐ | 22 John Podres | 12.00 | 5.00 | 1.20 |
| ☐ | 24 Walt Alston MGR | 18.00 | 7.25 | 1.80 |
| ☐ | 30 Maury Wills | 16.00 | 6.50 | 1.60 |
| ☐ | 32 Sandy Koufax | 32.00 | 13.00 | 3.20 |
| ☐ | 34 Norm Sherry | 9.00 | 3.75 | .90 |
| ☐ | 37 Ed Roebuck | 9.00 | 3.75 | .90 |
| ☐ | 38 Roger Craig | 12.00 | 5.00 | 1.20 |
| ☐ | 40 Stan Williams | 9.00 | 3.75 | .90 |
| ☐ | 43 Charlie Neal | 9.00 | 3.75 | .90 |
| ☐ | 51 Larry Sherry | 9.00 | 3.75 | .90 |

## 1962 Bell Brand

**DON DRYSDALE**
PITCHER      L.A. DODGERS

The 1962 Bell Brand Potato Chips set of 20 full color cards features Los Angeles Dodger players only and is numbered by the uniform numbers of the players. These cards were printed on a high quality glossy paper, much better than the previous two years, virtually eliminating the grease stains. This set is distinguished by a 1962 Home schedule on the backs of the cards. The cards measure 2 7/16" by 3 1/2", the same size as the year before. The ACC designation is F339-4.

| | MINT | VG-E | F-G |
|---|---|---|---|
| COMPLETE SET | 200.00 | 80.00 | 20.00 |
| COMMON PLAYER (1-56) | 8.00 | 3.25 | .80 |

| | | MINT | VG-E | F-G |
|---|---|---|---|---|
| ☐ | 3 Willie Davis | 9.00 | 3.75 | .90 |
| ☐ | 4 Duke Snider | 21.00 | 8.50 | 2.10 |
| ☐ | 6 Ron Fairly | 8.00 | 3.25 | .80 |
| ☐ | 8 John Roseboro | 8.00 | 3.25 | .80 |
| ☐ | 9 Wally Moon | 8.00 | 3.25 | .80 |
| ☐ | 12 Tom Davis | 9.00 | 3.75 | .90 |
| ☐ | 16 Ron Perranoski | 8.00 | 3.25 | .80 |
| ☐ | 19 Jim Gilliam | 10.00 | 4.00 | 1.00 |
| ☐ | 20 Daryl Spencer | 8.00 | 3.25 | .80 |
| ☐ | 22 John Podres | 9.00 | 3.75 | .90 |
| ☐ | 24 Walt Alston | 16.00 | 6.50 | 1.60 |
| ☐ | 25 Frank Howard | 10.00 | 4.00 | 1.00 |
| ☐ | 30 Maury Wills | 15.00 | 6.00 | 1.50 |
| ☐ | 32 Sandy Koufax | 27.00 | 11.00 | 2.70 |
| ☐ | 34 Norm Sherry | 8.00 | 3.25 | .80 |
| ☐ | 37 Ed Roebuck | 8.00 | 3.25 | .80 |
| ☐ | 40 Stan Williams | 8.00 | 3.25 | .80 |
| ☐ | 51 Larry Sherry | 8.00 | 3.25 | .80 |
| ☐ | 53 Don Drysdale | 20.00 | 8.00 | 2.00 |
| ☐ | 56 Lee Walls | 8.00 | 3.25 | .80 |

## 1951 Berk Ross

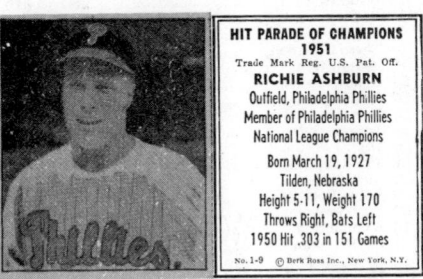

The 1951 Berk Ross set consists of 72 cards (each measuring 2 1/16" by 2 1/2") with tinted photographs, divided evenly into four series (designated in the checklist as A, B, C and D). The cards were marketed in boxes containing two card panels, without gum, and the set includes stars of other sports as well as baseball players. Intact panels are worth 20% more than the sum of the individual cards. The ACC designation is W532-1. In every series the first ten cards are baseball players; the set has a heavy emphasis on Yankees and Phillies players as they were in the World Series the year before.

| | | MINT | VG-E | F-G |
|---|---|---|---|---|
| COMPLETE SET | | 225.00 | 90.00 | 22.00 |
| COMMON BASEBALL | | 3.00 | 1.20 | .30 |
| COMMON FOOTBALL | | 2.50 | 1.00 | .25 |
| COMMON OTHERS | | 1.50 | .60 | .15 |
| ☐ | A1 Al Rosen | 4.50 | 1.80 | .45 |
| ☐ | A2 Bob Lemon | 7.50 | 3.00 | .75 |
| ☐ | A3 Phil Rizzuto | 9.00 | 3.75 | .90 |
| ☐ | A4 Hank Bauer | 4.50 | 1.80 | .45 |
| ☐ | A5 Billy Johnson | 3.00 | 1.20 | .30 |
| ☐ | A6 Jerry Coleman | 3.00 | 1.20 | .30 |
| ☐ | A7 Johnny Mize | 7.50 | 3.00 | .75 |
| ☐ | A8 Dom DiMaggio | 5.00 | 2.00 | .50 |
| ☐ | A9 Richie Ashburn | 6.00 | 2.40 | .60 |
| ☐ | A10 Del Ennis | 3.00 | 1.20 | .30 |
| ☐ | A11 Bob Cousy | 5.00 | 2.00 | .50 |
| ☐ | A12 Dick Schnittker | 1.50 | .60 | .15 |
| ☐ | A13 Ezzard Charles | 2.50 | 1.00 | .25 |
| ☐ | A14 Leon Hart | 2.50 | 1.00 | .25 |
| ☐ | A15 James Martin | 2.50 | 1.00 | .25 |
| ☐ | A16 Ben Hogan | 2.50 | 1.00 | .25 |
| ☐ | A17 Bill Durnan | 2.50 | 1.00 | .25 |
| ☐ | A18 Bill Quackenbush | 1.50 | .60 | .15 |
| ☐ | B1 Stan Musial | 27.00 | 11.00 | 2.70 |
| ☐ | B2 Warren Spahn | 9.00 | 3.75 | .90 |
| ☐ | B3 Tom Henrich | 4.00 | 1.60 | .40 |

| | | | | |
|---|---|---|---|---|
| ☐ | B4 Yogi Berra | 15.00 | 6.00 | 1.50 |
| ☐ | B5 Joe DiMaggio | 45.00 | 18.00 | 4.50 |
| ☐ | B6 Bobby Brown | 5.00 | 2.00 | .50 |
| ☐ | B7 Granny Hamner | 3.00 | 1.20 | .30 |
| ☐ | B8 Willie Jones | 3.00 | 1.20 | .30 |
| ☐ | B9 Stan Lopata | 3.00 | 1.20 | .30 |
| ☐ | B10 Mike Goliat | 3.00 | 1.20 | .30 |
| ☐ | B11 Sherman White | 1.50 | .60 | .15 |
| ☐ | B12 Joe Maxim | 1.50 | .60 | .15 |
| ☐ | B13 Ray Robinson | 3.00 | 1.20 | .30 |
| ☐ | B14 Doak Walker | 5.00 | 2.00 | .50 |
| ☐ | B15 Emil Sitko | 1.50 | .60 | .15 |
| ☐ | B16 Jack Stewart | 1.50 | .60 | .15 |
| ☐ | B17 Dick Button | 1.50 | .60 | .15 |
| ☐ | B18 Melvin Patton | 1.50 | .60 | .15 |
| ☐ | C1 Ralph Kiner | 7.50 | 3.00 | .75 |
| ☐ | C2 Bill Goodman | 3.00 | 1.20 | .30 |
| ☐ | C3 Allie Reynolds | 4.50 | 1.80 | .45 |
| ☐ | C4 Vic Raschi | 4.00 | 1.60 | .40 |
| ☐ | C5 Joe Page | 3.00 | 1.20 | .30 |
| ☐ | C6 Eddie Lopat | 4.50 | 1.80 | .45 |
| ☐ | C7 Andy Seminick | 3.00 | 1.20 | .30 |
| ☐ | C8 Dick Sisler | 3.00 | 1.20 | .30 |
| ☐ | C9 Eddie Waitkus | 3.00 | 1.20 | .30 |
| ☐ | C10 Ken Heintzelman | 3.00 | 1.20 | .30 |
| ☐ | C11 Paul Unruh | 1.50 | .60 | .15 |
| ☐ | C12 Jake LaMotta | 3.00 | 1.20 | .30 |
| ☐ | C13 Ike Williams | 1.50 | .60 | .15 |
| ☐ | C14 Wade Walker | 1.50 | .60 | .15 |
| ☐ | C15 Rodney Franz | 1.50 | .60 | .15 |
| ☐ | C16 Sid Abel | 2.50 | 1.00 | .25 |
| ☐ | C17 Claire Sherman | 1.50 | .60 | .15 |
| ☐ | C18 Jesse Owens | 4.00 | 1.60 | .40 |
| ☐ | D1 Gene Woodling | 3.00 | 1.20 | .30 |
| ☐ | D2 Cliff Mapes | 3.00 | 1.20 | .30 |
| ☐ | D3 Fred Sontort | 3.00 | 1.20 | .30 |
| ☐ | D4 Tommy Byrne | 3.00 | 1.20 | .30 |
| ☐ | D5 Whitey Ford | 10.00 | 4.00 | 1.00 |
| ☐ | D6 Jim Konstanty | 4.00 | 1.60 | .40 |
| ☐ | D7 Russ Meyer | 3.00 | 1.20 | .30 |
| ☐ | D8 Robin Roberts | 9.00 | 3.75 | .90 |
| ☐ | D9 Curt Simmons | 4.00 | 1.60 | .40 |
| ☐ | D10 Sam Jethroe | 3.00 | 1.20 | .30 |
| ☐ | D11 Bill Sharman | 3.00 | 1.20 | .30 |
| ☐ | D12 Sandy Saddler | 1.50 | .60 | .15 |
| ☐ | D13 Margaret DuPont | 1.50 | .60 | .15 |
| ☐ | D14 Arnold Galiffa | 2.50 | 1.00 | .25 |
| ☐ | D15 Charlie Justice | 3.00 | 1.20 | .30 |
| ☐ | D16 Glen Cunningham | 2.00 | .80 | .20 |
| ☐ | D17 Gregory Rice | 1.50 | .60 | .15 |
| ☐ | D18 Harrison Dillard | 1.50 | .60 | .15 |

## 1952 Berk Ross

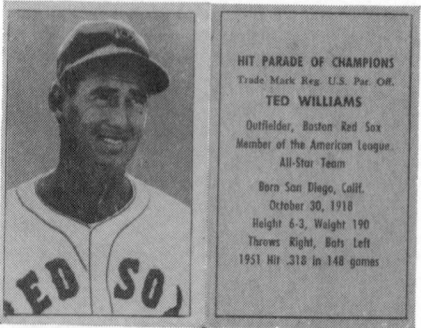

HIT PARADE OF CHAMPIONS
Trade Mark Reg. U.S. Pat. Off.
**TED WILLIAMS**
Outfielder, Boston Red Sox
Member of the American League
All-Star Team
Born San Diego, Calif.
October 30, 1918
Height 6-3, Weight 190
Throws Right, Bats Left
1951 Hit .318 in 148 games

The 1952 Berk Ross set of 72 unnumbered, tinted photocards, each measuring 2" by 3", seems to have been patterned after the highly successful 1951 Bowman set. The reverses of Ewell Blackwell and Nellie Fox are transposed while Phil Rizzuto comes with two different poses. There is a card of Joe DiMaggio even though he retired after the 1951 season. The ACC designation for this set is W532-2, and the cards have been assigned numbers in the alphabetical checklist below.

| | | MINT | VG-E | F-G |
|---|---|---|---|---|
| | COMPLETE SET | 1500.00 | 200.00 | 50.00 |
| | COMMON PLAYER (1-72) | 6.50 | 2.60 | .65 |
| ☐ 1 | Richie Ashburn | 14.00 | 5.75 | 1.40 |
| ☐ 2 | Hank Bauer | 9.00 | 3.75 | .90 |
| ☐ 3 | Yogi Berra | 40.00 | 16.00 | 4.00 |
| ☐ 4 | Ewell Blackwell (photo actually Nellie Fox) | 10.00 | 4.00 | 1.00 |
| ☐ 5 | Bobby Brown | 9.00 | 3.75 | .90 |
| ☐ 6 | Jim Busby | 6.50 | 2.60 | .65 |
| ☐ 7 | Roy Campanella | 65.00 | 26.00 | 6.50 |
| ☐ 8 | Chico Carrasquel | 6.50 | 2.60 | .65 |
| ☐ 9 | Jerry Coleman | 7.50 | 3.00 | .75 |
| ☐ 10 | Joe Collins | 6.50 | 2.60 | .65 |
| ☐ 11 | Alvin Dark | 8.00 | 3.25 | .80 |
| ☐ 12 | Dom DiMaggio | 11.00 | 4.50 | 1.10 |
| ☐ 13 | Joe DiMaggio | 250.00 | 100.00 | 25.00 |
| ☐ 14 | Larry Doby | 9.00 | 3.75 | .90 |
| ☐ 15 | Bobby Doerr | 16.00 | 6.50 | 1.60 |
| ☐ 16 | Bob Elliott | 9.00 | 3.75 | .90 |
| ☐ 17 | Del Ennis | 7.50 | 3.00 | .75 |
| ☐ 18 | Ferris Fain | 7.50 | 3.00 | .75 |
| ☐ 19 | Bob Feller | 35.00 | 14.00 | 3.50 |
| ☐ 20 | Nellie Fox (photo actually Ewell Blackwell) | 10.00 | 4.00 | 1.00 |
| ☐ 21 | Ned Garver | 6.50 | 2.60 | .65 |
| ☐ 22 | Clint Hartung | 6.50 | 2.60 | .65 |
| ☐ 23 | Jim Hearn | 6.50 | 2.60 | .65 |
| ☐ 24 | Gil Hodges | 24.00 | 10.00 | 2.40 |
| ☐ 25 | Monte Irvin | 16.00 | 6.50 | 1.60 |
| ☐ 26 | Larry Jansen | 6.50 | 2.60 | .65 |
| ☐ 27 | Sheldon Jones | 6.50 | 2.60 | .65 |
| ☐ 28 | George Kell | 16.00 | 6.50 | 1.60 |
| ☐ 29 | Monte Kennedy | 6.50 | 2.60 | .65 |
| ☐ 30 | Ralph Kiner | 16.00 | 6.50 | 1.60 |
| ☐ 31 | Dave Koslo | 6.50 | 2.60 | .65 |
| ☐ 32 | Bob Kuzava | 6.50 | 2.60 | .65 |
| ☐ 33 | Bob Lemon | 16.00 | 6.50 | 1.60 |
| ☐ 34 | Whitey Lockman | 7.50 | 3.00 | .75 |
| ☐ 35 | Ed Lopat | 10.00 | 4.00 | 1.00 |
| ☐ 36 | Sal Maglie | 9.00 | 3.75 | .90 |
| ☐ 37 | Mickey Mantle | 350.00 | 140.00 | 35.00 |
| ☐ 38 | Billy Martin | 20.00 | 8.00 | 2.00 |
| ☐ 39 | Willie Mays | 150.00 | 60.00 | 15.00 |
| ☐ 40 | Gil McDougald | 9.00 | 3.75 | .90 |
| ☐ 41 | Minnie Minoso | 9.00 | 3.75 | .90 |
| ☐ 42 | Johnny Mize | 16.00 | 6.50 | 1.60 |
| ☐ 43 | Tom Morgan | 6.50 | 2.60 | .65 |
| ☐ 44 | Don Mueller | 7.50 | 3.00 | .75 |
| ☐ 45 | Stan Musial | 100.00 | 40.00 | 10.00 |
| ☐ 46 | Don Newcombe | 10.00 | 4.00 | 1.00 |
| ☐ 47 | Ray Noble | 6.50 | 2.60 | .65 |
| ☐ 48 | Joe Ostrowski | 6.50 | 2.60 | .65 |
| ☐ 49 | Mel Parnell | 7.50 | 3.00 | .75 |
| ☐ 50 | Vic Raschi | 8.00 | 3.25 | .80 |
| ☐ 51 | Pee Wee Reese | 25.00 | 10.00 | 2.50 |
| ☐ 52 | Allie Reynolds | 10.00 | 4.00 | 1.00 |
| ☐ 53 | Bill Rigney | 6.50 | 2.60 | .65 |
| ☐ 54A | Phil Rizzuto (bunting) | 25.00 | 10.00 | 2.50 |
| ☐ 54B | Phil Rizzuto (swinging) | 25.00 | 10.00 | 2.50 |
| ☐ 55 | Robin Roberts | 16.00 | 6.50 | 1.60 |
| ☐ 56 | Eddie Robinson | 6.50 | 2.60 | .65 |
| ☐ 57 | Jackie Robinson | 100.00 | 40.00 | 10.00 |
| ☐ 58 | Preacher Roe | 10.00 | 4.00 | 1.00 |
| ☐ 59 | Johnny Sain | 10.00 | 4.00 | 1.00 |
| ☐ 60 | Red Schoendienst | 9.00 | 3.75 | .90 |
| ☐ 61 | Duke Snider | 65.00 | 26.00 | 6.50 |
| ☐ 62 | George Spencer | 6.50 | 2.60 | .65 |
| ☐ 63 | Eddie Stanky | 9.00 | 3.75 | .90 |
| ☐ 64 | Hank Thompson | 7.50 | 3.00 | .75 |
| ☐ 65 | Bobby Thomson | 10.00 | 4.00 | 1.00 |
| ☐ 66 | Vic Wertz | 7.50 | 3.00 | .75 |
| ☐ 67 | Wally Westlake | 6.50 | 2.60 | .65 |
| ☐ 68 | Wes Westrum | 6.50 | 2.60 | .65 |
| ☐ 69 | Ted Williams | 150.00 | 60.00 | 15.00 |
| ☐ 70 | Gene Woodling | 6.50 | 2.60 | .65 |
| ☐ 71 | Gus Zernial | 6.50 | 2.60 | .65 |

## 1947 Bond Bread

The 1947 Bond Bread Jackie Robinson set features 13 unnumbered cards of Jackie in different action or portrait poses; each card measures 2 1/4" by 3 1/2". Card number 7, which is the only card in the set to contain a facsimile autograph, was apparently issued in greater quantity than other cards in the set. Several of the cards have a horizontal format; these are marked in the checklist below by HOR. The ACC designation is D302.

| | | MINT | VG-E | F-G |
|---|---|---|---|---|
| COMPLETE SET | | 3000.00 | 1200.00 | 350.00 |
| COMMON PLAYER (1-13) | | 250.00 | 100.00 | 25.00 |
| ☐ 1 | Sliding into base, cap, ump in photo, HOR | 250.00 | 100.00 | 25.00 |
| ☐ 2 | Running down 3rd base line | 250.00 | 100.00 | 25.00 |
| ☐ 3 | Batting, bat behind head, facing camera | 250.00 | 100.00 | 25.00 |
| ☐ 4 | Moving towards second, throw almost to glove, HOR | 250.00 | 100.00 | 25.00 |
| ☐ 5 | Taking throw at first, HOR | 250.00 | 100.00 | 25.00 |
| ☐ 6 | Jumping high in the air for ball | 250.00 | 100.00 | 25.00 |
| ☐ 7 | Profile with glove in front of head (auto) | 150.00 | 60.00 | 15.00 |
| ☐ 8 | Leaping over 2nd base ready to throw | 250.00 | 100.00 | 25.00 |
| ☐ 9 | Portrait, holding glove over head | 250.00 | 100.00 | 25.00 |
| ☐ 10 | Portrait, holding bat perpendicular to body | 250.00 | 100.00 | 25.00 |
| ☐ 11 | Reaching for throw, glove near ankle | 250.00 | 100.00 | 25.00 |
| ☐ 12 | Leaping for throw, no scoreboard background | 250.00 | 100.00 | 25.00 |
| ☐ 13 | Portrait, holding bat parallel to body | 250.00 | 100.00 | 25.00 |

## 1948 Bowman

The 48 card Bowman set of 1948 was the first major set of the post-war period. Each 2 1/16" by 2 1/2" card had a black and white photo of a current player, with his biographical information printed in black ink on a gray back. Due to the printing process and the 36 card sheet size upon which Bowman was then printing, the 12 cards marked with an SP in the checklist are scarcer numerically, as they were

removed from the printing sheet in order to make room for the 12 high numbers (37-48). Many cards are found with over-printed, transposed, or blank backs.

| | | MINT | VG-E | F-G |
|---|---|---|---|---|
| COMPLETE SET | | 700.00 | 280.00 | 70.00 |
| COMMON PLAYER (1-36) | | 5.00 | 2.00 | .50 |
| COMMON PLAYER (37-48) | | 9.00 | 3.75 | .90 |
| COMMON PLAYER SP | | 12.50 | 5.00 | 1.25 |
| ☐ 1 | Bob Elliott | 20.00 | 5.00 | 1.00 |
| ☐ 2 | Ewell Blackwell | 6.50 | 2.60 | .65 |
| ☐ 3 | Ralph Kiner | 20.00 | 8.00 | 2.00 |
| ☐ 4 | Johnny Mize | 16.00 | 6.50 | 1.60 |
| ☐ 5 | Bob Feller | 35.00 | 14.00 | 3.50 |
| ☐ 6 | Yogi Berra | 75.00 | 30.00 | 7.50 |
| ☐ 7 | Peter Reiser SP | 15.00 | 6.00 | 1.50 |
| ☐ 8 | Phil Rizzuto SP | 50.00 | 20.00 | 5.00 |
| ☐ 9 | Walker Cooper | 5.00 | 2.00 | .50 |
| ☐ 10 | Buddy Rosar | 5.00 | 2.00 | .50 |
| ☐ 11 | Johnny Lindell | 5.00 | 2.00 | .50 |
| ☐ 12 | Johnny Sain | 9.00 | 3.75 | .90 |
| ☐ 13 | Willard Marshall SP | 12.50 | 5.00 | 1.25 |
| ☐ 14 | Allie Reynolds | 9.00 | 3.75 | .90 |
| ☐ 15 | Eddie Joost | 5.00 | 2.00 | .50 |
| ☐ 16 | Jack Lohrke SP | 12.50 | 5.00 | 1.25 |
| ☐ 17 | Enos Slaughter | 16.00 | 6.50 | 1.60 |
| ☐ 18 | Warren Spahn | 35.00 | 14.00 | 3.50 |
| ☐ 19 | Tommy Henrich | 7.00 | 2.80 | .70 |
| ☐ 20 | Buddy Kerr SP | 12.50 | 5.00 | 1.25 |
| ☐ 21 | Ferris Fain | 6.00 | 2.40 | .60 |
| ☐ 22 | Floyd Bevens SP | 12.50 | 5.00 | 1.25 |
| ☐ 23 | Larry Jansen | 5.00 | 2.00 | .50 |
| ☐ 24 | Dutch Leonard SP | 12.50 | 5.00 | 1.25 |
| ☐ 25 | Barney McCosky | 5.00 | 2.00 | .50 |
| ☐ 26 | Frank Shea SP | 12.50 | 5.00 | 1.25 |
| ☐ 27 | Sid Gordon | 5.00 | 2.00 | .50 |
| ☐ 28 | Emil Verban SP | 12.50 | 5.00 | 1.25 |
| ☐ 29 | Joe Page SP | 13.50 | 5.50 | 1.00 |
| ☐ 30 | Whitey Lockman SP | 12.50 | 5.00 | 1.25 |
| ☐ 31 | Bill McCahan | 5.00 | 2.00 | .50 |
| ☐ 32 | Bill Rigney | 5.00 | 2.00 | .50 |
| ☐ 33 | Bill Johnson | 5.00 | 2.00 | .50 |
| ☐ 34 | Sheldon Jones SP | 12.50 | 5.00 | 1.25 |
| ☐ 35 | Snuffy Stirnweiss | 5.00 | 2.00 | .50 |
| ☐ 36 | Stan Musial | 150.00 | 60.00 | 15.00 |
| ☐ 37 | Clint Hartung | 9.00 | 3.75 | .90 |
| ☐ 38 | Red Schoendienst | 12.00 | 5.00 | 1.20 |
| ☐ 39 | Augie Galan | 9.00 | 3.75 | .90 |
| ☐ 40 | Marty Marion | 12.00 | 5.00 | 1.20 |
| ☐ 41 | Rex Barney | 9.00 | 3.75 | .90 |
| ☐ 42 | Ray Poat | 9.00 | 3.75 | .90 |
| ☐ 43 | Bruce Edwards | 9.00 | 3.75 | .90 |
| ☐ 44 | Johnny Wyrostek | 9.00 | 3.75 | .90 |
| ☐ 45 | Hank Sauer | 10.00 | 4.00 | 1.00 |
| ☐ 46 | Herman Wehmeier | 9.00 | 3.75 | .90 |
| ☐ 47 | Bobby Thomson | 12.00 | 5.00 | 1.20 |
| ☐ 48 | Dave Koslo | 12.00 | 4.00 | .80 |

## 1949 Bowman

The cards in this 240 card set measure 2 1/16" by 2 1/2". In 1949 Bowman took an intermediate step between black and white and full color with this set of tinted photos on colored backgrounds. Collectors should note the series price variations which reflect

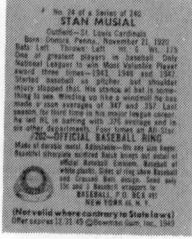

some inconsistencies in the printing process. There are four major varieties in name printing which are noted in the checklist below: NOF: name on front; NNOF: no name on front; PR: printed name on back; and SCR: script name on back. These variations resulted when Bowman used twelve of the lower numbers to fill out the last press sheet of 36 cards adding to numbers 217-240.

|  | MINT | VG-E | F-G |
|---|---|---|---|
| COMPLETE SET | 4000.00 | 1600.00 | 500.00 |
| COMMON CARD (1-3/5-36/73) | | | |
|  | 5.50 | 2.20 | .55 |
| COMMON CARD (4/74-108) | 4.50 | 1.80 | .45 |
| COMMON CARD (109-144) | 3.50 | 1.40 | .35 |
| COMMON CARD (145-180) | 27.00 | 11.00 | 2.70 |
| COMMON CARD (181-216) | 22.00 | 9.00 | 2.20 |
| COMMON CARD (217-240) | 22.00 | 9.00 | 2.20 |

| # | Player | MINT | VG-E | F-G |
|---|---|---|---|---|
| ☐ 1 | Vern Bickford | 20.00 | 3.00 | .60 |
| ☐ 2 | Whitey Lockman | 5.00 | 2.00 | .50 |
| ☐ 3 | Bob Porterfield | 5.00 | 2.00 | .50 |
| ☐ 4A | Jerry Priddy NNOF | 5.00 | 2.00 | .50 |
| ☐ 4B | Jerry Priddy NOF | 18.00 | 7.25 | 1.80 |
| ☐ 5 | Hank Sauer | 6.00 | 2.40 | .60 |
| ☐ 6 | Phil Cavarretta | 6.00 | 2.40 | .60 |
| ☐ 7 | Joe Dobson | 5.00 | 2.00 | .50 |
| ☐ 8 | Murray Dickson | 5.00 | 2.00 | .50 |
| ☐ 9 | Ferris Fain | 6.00 | 2.40 | .60 |
| ☐ 10 | Ted Gray | 5.00 | 2.00 | .50 |
| ☐ 11 | Lou Boudreau | 12.50 | 5.00 | 1.25 |
| ☐ 12 | Cass Michaels | 5.00 | 2.00 | .50 |
| ☐ 13 | Bob Chesnes | 5.00 | 2.00 | .50 |
| ☐ 14 | Curt Simmons | 7.50 | 3.00 | .75 |
| ☐ 15 | Ned Garver | 5.00 | 2.00 | .50 |
| ☐ 16 | Al Kozar | 5.00 | 2.00 | .50 |
| ☐ 17 | Earl Torgeson | 5.00 | 2.00 | .50 |
| ☐ 18 | Bobby Thomson | 6.00 | 2.40 | .60 |
| ☐ 19 | Bobby Brown | 9.00 | 3.75 | .90 |
| ☐ 20 | Gene Hermanski | 5.00 | 2.00 | .50 |
| ☐ 21 | Frank Baumholtz | 5.00 | 2.00 | .50 |
| ☐ 22 | Peanuts Lowrey | 5.00 | 2.00 | .50 |
| ☐ 23 | Bobby Doerr | 12.50 | 5.00 | 1.25 |
| ☐ 24 | Stan Musial | 120.00 | 50.00 | 12.00 |
| ☐ 25 | Carl Scheib | 5.00 | 2.00 | .50 |
| ☐ 26 | George Kell | 12.50 | 5.00 | 1.25 |
| ☐ 27 | Bob Feller | 32.00 | 13.00 | 3.20 |
| ☐ 28 | Don Kolloway | 5.00 | 2.00 | .50 |
| ☐ 29 | Ralph Kiner | 15.00 | 6.00 | 1.50 |
| ☐ 30 | Andy Seminick | 5.00 | 2.00 | .50 |
| ☐ 31 | Dick Kokos | 5.00 | 2.00 | .50 |
| ☐ 32 | Eddie Yost | 5.00 | 2.00 | .50 |
| ☐ 33 | Warren Spahn | 27.00 | 11.00 | 2.70 |
| ☐ 34 | Dave Koslo | 5.00 | 2.00 | .50 |
| ☐ 35 | Vic Raschi | 7.00 | 2.80 | .70 |
| ☐ 36 | Pee Wee Reese | 27.00 | 11.00 | 2.70 |
| ☐ 37 | John Wyrostek | 5.50 | 2.20 | .55 |
| ☐ 38 | Emil Verban | 5.50 | 2.20 | .55 |
| ☐ 39 | Billy Goodman | 6.50 | 2.60 | .65 |
| ☐ 40 | Red Munger | 5.50 | 2.20 | .55 |
| ☐ 41 | Lou Brissie | 5.50 | 2.20 | .55 |
| ☐ 42 | Hoot Evers | 5.50 | 2.20 | .55 |
| ☐ 43 | Dale Mitchell | 6.50 | 2.60 | .65 |
| ☐ 44 | Dave Philley | 5.50 | 2.20 | .55 |
| ☐ 45 | Wally Westlake | 5.50 | 2.20 | .55 |
| ☐ 46 | Robin Roberts | 40.00 | 16.00 | 4.00 |
| ☐ 47 | Johnny Sain | 7.00 | 2.80 | .70 |
| ☐ 48 | Willard Marshall | 5.50 | 2.20 | .55 |
| ☐ 49 | Frank Shea | 5.50 | 2.20 | .55 |
| ☐ 50 | Jackie Robinson | 120.00 | 50.00 | 12.00 |
| ☐ 51 | Herman Wehmeier | 5.50 | 2.20 | .55 |
| ☐ 52 | Johnny Schmitz | 5.50 | 2.20 | .55 |
| ☐ 53 | Jack Kramer | 5.50 | 2.20 | .55 |
| ☐ 54 | Marty Marion | 7.50 | 3.00 | .75 |

| # | Player | MINT | VG-E | F-G |
|---|---|---|---|---|
| ☐ 55 | Eddie Joost | 5.50 | 2.20 | .55 |
| ☐ 56 | Pat Mullin | 5.50 | 2.20 | .55 |
| ☐ 57 | Gene Bearden | 5.50 | 2.20 | .55 |
| ☐ 58 | Bob Elliott | 6.50 | 2.60 | .65 |
| ☐ 59 | Jack Lohrke | 5.50 | 2.20 | .55 |
| ☐ 60 | Yogi Berra | 50.00 | 20.00 | 5.00 |
| ☐ 61 | Rex Barney | 5.50 | 2.20 | .55 |
| ☐ 62 | Grady Hatton | 5.50 | 2.20 | .55 |
| ☐ 63 | Andy Pafko | 5.50 | 2.20 | .55 |
| ☐ 64 | Dom DiMaggio | 7.50 | 3.00 | .75 |
| ☐ 65 | Enos Slaughter | 12.50 | 5.00 | 1.25 |
| ☐ 66 | Elmer Valo | 5.50 | 2.20 | .55 |
| ☐ 67 | Alvin Dark | 7.50 | 3.00 | .75 |
| ☐ 68 | Sheldon Jones | 5.50 | 2.20 | .55 |
| ☐ 69 | Tommy Henrich | 7.50 | 3.00 | .75 |
| ☐ 70 | Carl Furillo | 10.00 | 4.00 | 1.00 |
| ☐ 71 | Vern Stephens | 6.50 | 2.60 | .65 |
| ☐ 72 | Tommy Holmes | 6.50 | 2.60 | .65 |
| ☐ 73 | Billy Cox | 6.50 | 2.60 | .65 |
| ☐ 74 | Tom McBride | 4.50 | 1.80 | .45 |
| ☐ 75 | Eddie Mayo | 4.50 | 1.80 | .45 |
| ☐ 76 | Bill Nicholson | 4.50 | 1.80 | .45 |
| ☐ 77 | Ernie Bonham | 4.50 | 1.80 | .45 |
| ☐ 78A | Sam Zoldak NNOF | 4.50 | 1.80 | .45 |
| ☐ 78B | Sam Zoldak NOF | 18.00 | 7.25 | 1.80 |
| ☐ 79 | Ron Northey | 4.50 | 1.80 | .45 |
| ☐ 80 | Bill McCahan | 4.50 | 1.80 | .45 |
| ☐ 81 | Virgil Stallcup | 4.50 | 1.80 | .45 |
| ☐ 82 | Joe Page | 6.50 | 2.60 | .65 |
| ☐ 83A | Bob Scheffing NNOF | 4.50 | 1.80 | .45 |
| ☐ 83B | Bob Scheffing NOF | 18.00 | 7.25 | 1.80 |
| ☐ 84 | Roy Campanella | 100.00 | 40.00 | 10.00 |
| ☐ 85A | Johnny Mize NNOF | 16.00 | 6.50 | 1.60 |
| ☐ 85B | Johnny Mize NOF | 40.00 | 16.00 | 4.00 |
| ☐ 86 | Johnny Pesky | 5.00 | 2.00 | .50 |
| ☐ 87 | Randy Gumpert | 4.50 | 1.80 | .45 |
| ☐ 88A | Bill Salkeld NNOF | 4.50 | 1.80 | .45 |
| ☐ 88B | Bill Salkeld NOF | 18.00 | 7.25 | 1.80 |
| ☐ 89 | Mizell Platt | 4.50 | 1.80 | .45 |
| ☐ 90 | Gil Coan | 4.50 | 1.80 | .45 |
| ☐ 91 | Dick Wakefield | 4.50 | 1.80 | .45 |
| ☐ 92 | Willie Jones | 4.50 | 1.80 | .45 |
| ☐ 93 | Ed Stevens | 4.50 | 1.80 | .45 |
| ☐ 94 | Mickey Vernon | 7.50 | 3.00 | .75 |
| ☐ 95 | Howie Pollet | 4.50 | 1.80 | .45 |
| ☐ 96 | Taft Wright | 4.50 | 1.80 | .45 |
| ☐ 97 | Danny Litwhiler | 4.50 | 1.80 | .45 |
| ☐ 98A | Phil Rizzuto NNOF | 18.00 | 7.25 | 1.80 |
| ☐ 98B | Phil Rizzuto NOF | 40.00 | 16.00 | 4.00 |
| ☐ 99 | Frank Gustine | 4.50 | 1.80 | .45 |
| ☐ 100 | Gil Hodges | 35.00 | 14.00 | 3.50 |
| ☐ 101 | Sid Gordon | 4.50 | 1.80 | .45 |
| ☐ 102 | Stan Spence | 4.50 | 1.80 | .45 |
| ☐ 103 | Joe Tipton | 4.50 | 1.80 | .45 |
| ☐ 104 | Ed Stanky | 5.50 | 2.20 | .55 |
| ☐ 105 | Bill Kennedy | 4.50 | 1.80 | .45 |
| ☐ 106 | Jake Early | 4.50 | 1.80 | .45 |
| ☐ 107 | Eddie Lake | 4.50 | 1.80 | .45 |
| ☐ 108 | Ken Heintzelman | 4.50 | 1.80 | .45 |
| ☐ 109A | Ed Fitzgerald SCR | 4.00 | 1.60 | .40 |
| ☐ 109B | Ed Fitzgerald PR | 15.00 | 6.00 | 1.50 |
| ☐ 110 | Early Wynn | 30.00 | 12.00 | 3.00 |
| ☐ 111 | Red Schoendienst | 6.00 | 2.40 | .60 |
| ☐ 112 | Sam Chapman | 3.50 | 1.40 | .35 |
| ☐ 113 | Ray LaManno | 3.50 | 1.40 | .35 |
| ☐ 114 | Allie Reynolds | 7.50 | 3.00 | .75 |
| ☐ 115 | Dutch Leonard | 3.50 | 1.40 | .35 |
| ☐ 116 | Joe Hatton | 3.50 | 1.40 | .35 |
| ☐ 117 | Walker Cooper | 3.50 | 1.40 | .35 |
| ☐ 118 | Sam Mele | 3.50 | 1.40 | .35 |
| ☐ 119 | Floyd Baker | 3.50 | 1.40 | .35 |
| ☐ 120 | Cliff Fannin | 3.50 | 1.40 | .35 |
| ☐ 121 | Mark Christman | 3.50 | 1.40 | .35 |
| ☐ 122 | George Vico | 3.50 | 1.40 | .35 |
| ☐ 123 | Johnny Blatnick | 3.50 | 1.40 | .35 |
| ☐ 124A | Danny Murtaugh SCR | 4.00 | 1.60 | .40 |
| ☐ 124B | Danny Murtaugh PR | 15.00 | 6.00 | 1.50 |
| ☐ 125 | Ken Keltner | 4.00 | 1.60 | .40 |
| ☐ 126A | Al Brazle SCR | 4.00 | 1.60 | .40 |
| ☐ 126B | Al Brazle PR | 15.00 | 6.00 | 1.50 |
| ☐ 127A | Hank Majeski SCR | 4.00 | 1.60 | .40 |
| ☐ 127B | Hank Majeski PR | 15.00 | 6.00 | 1.50 |
| ☐ 128 | Johnny VanderMeer | 6.00 | 2.40 | .60 |
| ☐ 129 | Bill Johnson | 4.00 | 1.60 | .40 |
| ☐ 130 | Harry Walker | 4.00 | 1.60 | .40 |
| ☐ 131 | Paul Lehner | 3.50 | 1.40 | .35 |
| ☐ 132A | Al Evans SCR | 4.00 | 1.60 | .40 |
| ☐ 132B | Al Evans PR | 15.00 | 6.00 | 1.50 |
| ☐ 133 | Aaron Robinson | 3.50 | 1.40 | .35 |
| ☐ 134 | Hank Borowy | 3.50 | 1.40 | .35 |
| ☐ 135 | Stan Rojek | 3.50 | 1.40 | .35 |
| ☐ 136 | Hank Edwards | 3.50 | 1.40 | .35 |
| ☐ 137 | Ted Wilks | 3.50 | 1.40 | .35 |

| | | | | |
|---|---|---|---|---|
| ☐ 138 | Buddy Rosar | 3.50 | 1.40 | .35 |
| ☐ 139 | Hank Arft | 3.50 | 1.40 | .35 |
| ☐ 140 | Ray Scarborough | 3.50 | 1.40 | .35 |
| ☐ 141 | Ulysses Lupien | 3.50 | 1.40 | .35 |
| ☐ 142 | Eddie Waitkus | 3.50 | 1.40 | .35 |
| ☐ 143A | Bob Dillinger SCR | 4.00 | 1.60 | .40 |
| ☐ 143B | Bob Dillinger PR | 15.00 | 6.00 | 1.50 |
| ☐ 144 | Mickey Haefner | 3.50 | 1.40 | .35 |
| ☐ 145 | Sylvester Donnelly | 27.00 | 11.00 | 2.70 |
| ☐ 146 | Mike McCormick | 27.00 | 11.00 | 2.70 |
| ☐ 147 | Bert Singleton | 27.00 | 11.00 | 2.70 |
| ☐ 148 | Bob Swift | 27.00 | 11.00 | 2.70 |
| ☐ 149 | Roy Partee | 27.00 | 11.00 | 2.70 |
| ☐ 150 | Allie Clark | 27.00 | 11.00 | 2.70 |
| ☐ 151 | Mickey Harris | 27.00 | 11.00 | 2.70 |
| ☐ 152 | Clarence Maddern | 27.00 | 11.00 | 2.70 |
| ☐ 153 | Phil Masi | 27.00 | 11.00 | 2.70 |
| ☐ 154 | Clint Hartung | 27.00 | 11.00 | 2.70 |
| ☐ 155 | Mickey Guerra | 27.00 | 11.00 | 2.70 |
| ☐ 156 | Al Zarilla | 27.00 | 11.00 | 2.70 |
| ☐ 157 | Walt Masterson | 27.00 | 11.00 | 2.70 |
| ☐ 158 | Harry Brecheen | 30.00 | 12.00 | 3.00 |
| ☐ 159 | Glen Moulder | 27.00 | 11.00 | 2.70 |
| ☐ 160 | Jim Blackburn | 27.00 | 11.00 | 2.70 |
| ☐ 161 | Jocko Thompson | 27.00 | 11.00 | 2.70 |
| ☐ 162 | Preacher Roe | 36.00 | 15.00 | 3.60 |
| ☐ 163 | Clyde McCullough | 27.00 | 11.00 | 2.70 |
| ☐ 164 | Vic Wertz | 30.00 | 12.00 | 3.00 |
| ☐ 165 | Snuffy Stirnweiss | 30.00 | 12.00 | 3.00 |
| ☐ 166 | Mike Tresh | 27.00 | 11.00 | 2.70 |
| ☐ 167 | Babe Martin | 27.00 | 11.00 | 2.70 |
| ☐ 168 | Doyle Lade | 27.00 | 11.00 | 2.70 |
| ☐ 169 | Jeff Heath | 27.00 | 11.00 | 2.70 |
| ☐ 170 | Bill Rigney | 27.00 | 11.00 | 2.70 |
| ☐ 171 | Dick Fowler | 27.00 | 11.00 | 2.70 |
| ☐ 172 | Eddie Pellagrini | 27.00 | 11.00 | 2.70 |
| ☐ 173 | Eddie Stewart | 27.00 | 11.00 | 2.70 |
| ☐ 174 | Terry Moore | 30.00 | 12.00 | 3.00 |
| ☐ 175 | Luke Appling | 40.00 | 16.00 | 4.00 |
| ☐ 176 | Ken Raffensberger | 27.00 | 11.00 | 2.70 |
| ☐ 177 | Stan Lopata | 27.00 | 11.00 | 2.70 |
| ☐ 178 | Tom Brown | 27.00 | 11.00 | 2.70 |
| ☐ 179 | Hugh Casey | 30.00 | 12.00 | 3.00 |
| ☐ 180 | Connie Berry | 27.00 | 11.00 | 2.70 |
| ☐ 181 | Gus Niarhos | 22.00 | 9.00 | 2.20 |
| ☐ 182 | Hall Peck | 22.00 | 9.00 | 2.20 |
| ☐ 183 | Lou Stringer | 22.00 | 9.00 | 2.20 |
| ☐ 184 | Bob Chipman | 22.00 | 9.00 | 2.20 |
| ☐ 185 | Pete Reiser | 25.00 | 10.00 | 2.50 |
| ☐ 186 | Buddy Kerr | 22.00 | 9.00 | 2.20 |
| ☐ 187 | Phil Marchildon | 22.00 | 9.00 | 2.20 |
| ☐ 188 | Karl Drews | 22.00 | 9.00 | 2.20 |
| ☐ 189 | Earl Wooten | 22.00 | 9.00 | 2.20 |
| ☐ 190 | Jim Hearn | 22.00 | 9.00 | 2.20 |
| ☐ 191 | Joe Haynes | 22.00 | 9.00 | 2.20 |
| ☐ 192 | Harry Gumbert | 22.00 | 9.00 | 2.20 |
| ☐ 193 | Ken Trinkle | 22.00 | 9.00 | 2.20 |
| ☐ 194 | Ralph Branca | 25.00 | 10.00 | 2.50 |
| ☐ 195 | Eddie Bockman | 22.00 | 9.00 | 2.20 |
| ☐ 196 | Fred Hutchinson | 25.00 | 10.00 | 2.50 |
| ☐ 197 | Johnny Lindell | 22.00 | 9.00 | 2.20 |
| ☐ 198 | Steve Gromek | 22.00 | 9.00 | 2.20 |
| ☐ 199 | Tex Hughson | 22.00 | 9.00 | 2.20 |
| ☐ 200 | Jess Dobernic | 22.00 | 9.00 | 2.20 |
| ☐ 201 | Sibby Sisti | 22.00 | 9.00 | 2.20 |
| ☐ 202 | Larry Jansen | 22.00 | 9.00 | 2.20 |
| ☐ 203 | Barney McCosky | 22.00 | 9.00 | 2.20 |
| ☐ 204 | Bob Savage | 22.00 | 9.00 | 2.20 |
| ☐ 205 | Dick Sisler | 22.00 | 9.00 | 2.20 |
| ☐ 206 | Bruce Edwards | 22.00 | 9.00 | 2.20 |
| ☐ 207 | Johnny Hopp | 25.00 | 10.00 | 2.50 |
| ☐ 208 | Dizzy Trout | 25.00 | 10.00 | 2.50 |
| ☐ 209 | Charlie Keller | 30.00 | 12.00 | 3.00 |
| ☐ 210 | Joe Gordon | 30.00 | 12.00 | 3.00 |
| ☐ 211 | Boo Ferriss | 22.00 | 9.00 | 2.20 |
| ☐ 212 | Ralph Hamner | 22.00 | 9.00 | 2.20 |
| ☐ 213 | Red Barrett | 22.00 | 9.00 | 2.20 |
| ☐ 214 | Richie Ashburn | 75.00 | 30.00 | 7.50 |
| ☐ 215 | Kirby Higbe | 22.00 | 9.00 | 2.20 |
| ☐ 216 | Schoolboy Rowe | 25.00 | 10.00 | 2.50 |
| ☐ 217 | Marino Pieretti | 22.00 | 9.00 | 2.20 |
| ☐ 218 | Dick Kryhoski | 22.00 | 9.00 | 2.20 |
| ☐ 219 | Virgil "Fire" Trucks | 25.00 | 10.00 | 2.50 |
| ☐ 220 | Johnny McCarthy | 22.00 | 9.00 | 2.20 |
| ☐ 221 | Bob Muncrief | 22.00 | 9.00 | 2.20 |
| ☐ 222 | Alex Kellner | 22.00 | 9.00 | 2.20 |
| ☐ 223 | Bobby Hofman | 22.00 | 9.00 | 2.20 |
| ☐ 224 | Satchell Paige | 500.00 | 200.00 | 50.00 |
| ☐ 225 | Gerry Coleman | 30.00 | 12.00 | 3.00 |
| ☐ 226 | Duke Snider | 325.00 | 130.00 | 32.00 |
| ☐ 227 | Fritz Ostermueller | 22.00 | 9.00 | 2.20 |
| ☐ 228 | Jackie Mayo | 22.00 | 9.00 | 2.20 |
| ☐ 229 | Ed Lopat | 40.00 | 16.00 | 4.00 |

| | | | | |
|---|---|---|---|---|
| ☐ 230 | Augie Galan | 22.00 | 9.00 | 2.20 |
| ☐ 231 | Earl Johnson | 22.00 | 9.00 | 2.20 |
| ☐ 232 | George McQuinn | 22.00 | 9.00 | 2.20 |
| ☐ 233 | Larry Doby | 40.00 | 16.00 | 4.00 |
| ☐ 234 | Rip Sewell | 22.00 | 9.00 | 2.20 |
| ☐ 235 | Jim Russell | 22.00 | 9.00 | 2.20 |
| ☐ 236 | Fred Sanford | 22.00 | 9.00 | 2.20 |
| ☐ 237 | Monte Kennedy | 22.00 | 9.00 | 2.20 |
| ☐ 238 | Bob Lemon | 90.00 | 36.00 | 9.00 |
| ☐ 239 | Frank McCormick | 22.00 | 9.00 | 2.20 |
| ☐ 240 | Babe Young | 30.00 | 12.00 | 3.00 |
| | (photo actually Bobby Young) | | | |

# 1950 Bowman

 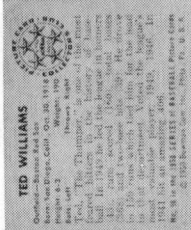

The cards in this 252 card set measure 2 1/16" by 2 1/2". This set, marketed in 1950 by Bowman, represented a major improvement in terms of quality over their previous efforts. Each card was a beautifully colored line drawing developed from a simple photograph. The first 72 cards are the scarcest in the set while the final 72 cards may be found with or without the copyright line. This was the only Bowman sports set to carry the famous "5-Star" logo.

| | | MINT | VG-E | F-G |
|---|---|---|---|---|
| COMPLETE SET | | 2000.00 | 800.00 | 250.00 |
| COMMON PLAYER (1-72) | | 10.00 | 4.00 | 1.00 |
| COMMON PLAYER (73-252) | | 4.00 | 1.60 | .40 |
| ☐ | 1 Mel Parnell | 36.00 | 6.00 | 1.00 |
| ☐ | 2 Vern Stephens | 11.00 | 4.50 | 1.10 |
| ☐ | 3 Dom DiMaggio | 15.00 | 6.00 | 1.50 |
| ☐ | 4 Gus Zernial | 12.00 | 5.00 | 1.20 |
| ☐ | 5 Bob Kuzava | 10.00 | 4.00 | 1.00 |
| ☐ | 6 Bob Feller | 45.00 | 18.00 | 4.50 |
| ☐ | 7 Jim Hegan | 11.00 | 4.50 | 1.10 |
| ☐ | 8 George Kell | 20.00 | 8.00 | 2.00 |
| ☐ | 9 Vic Wertz | 11.00 | 4.50 | 1.10 |
| ☐ | 10 Tommy Henrich | 12.00 | 5.00 | 1.20 |
| ☐ | 11 Phil Rizzuto | 35.00 | 14.00 | 3.50 |
| ☐ | 12 Joe Page | 12.00 | 5.00 | 1.20 |
| ☐ | 13 Ferris Fain | 12.00 | 5.00 | 1.20 |
| ☐ | 14 Alex Kellner | 10.00 | 4.00 | 1.00 |
| ☐ | 15 Al Kozar | 10.00 | 4.00 | 1.00 |
| ☐ | 16 Roy Sievers | 12.00 | 5.00 | 1.20 |
| ☐ | 17 Sid Hudson | 10.00 | 4.00 | 1.00 |
| ☐ | 18 Eddie Robinson | 10.00 | 4.00 | 1.00 |
| ☐ | 19 Warren Spahn | 40.00 | 16.00 | 4.00 |
| ☐ | 20 Bob Elliott | 12.00 | 5.00 | 1.20 |
| ☐ | 21 Pee Wee Reese | 35.00 | 14.00 | 3.50 |
| ☐ | 22 Jackie Robinson | 120.00 | 50.00 | 12.00 |
| ☐ | 23 Don Newcombe | 16.00 | 6.50 | 1.60 |
| ☐ | 24 Johnny Schmitz | 10.00 | 4.00 | 1.00 |
| ☐ | 25 Hank Sauer | 11.00 | 4.50 | 1.10 |
| ☐ | 26 Grady Hatton | 10.00 | 4.00 | 1.00 |
| ☐ | 27 Herman Wehmeier | 10.00 | 4.00 | 1.00 |
| ☐ | 28 Bobby Thomson | 12.00 | 5.00 | 1.20 |
| ☐ | 29 Eddie Stanky | 11.00 | 4.50 | 1.10 |
| ☐ | 30 Eddie Waitkus | 10.00 | 4.00 | 1.00 |
| ☐ | 31 Del Ennis | 11.00 | 4.50 | 1.10 |
| ☐ | 32 Robin Roberts | 25.00 | 10.00 | 2.50 |
| ☐ | 33 Ralph Kiner | 20.00 | 8.00 | 2.00 |
| ☐ | 34 Murry Dickson | 10.00 | 4.00 | 1.00 |
| ☐ | 35 Enos Slaughter | 20.00 | 8.00 | 2.00 |
| ☐ | 36 Eddie Kazak | 10.00 | 4.00 | 1.00 |

| | | | | | | | | | | |
|---|---|---|---|---|---|---|---|---|---|---|
| ☐ 37 | Luke Appling | 16.00 | 6.50 | 1.60 | | ☐ 130 | Dale Mitchell | 4.50 | 1.80 | .45 |
| ☐ 38 | Bill Wight | 10.00 | 4.00 | 1.00 | | ☐ 131 | Steve Gromek | 4.00 | 1.60 | .40 |
| ☐ 39 | Larry Doby | 12.00 | 5.00 | 1.20 | | ☐ 132 | James"Mickey" Vernon | 5.50 | 2.20 | .55 |
| ☐ 40 | Bob Lemon | 20.00 | 8.00 | 2.00 | | ☐ 133 | Don Kolloway | 4.00 | 1.60 | .40 |
| ☐ 41 | Hoot Evers | 10.00 | 4.00 | 1.00 | | ☐ 134 | Paul Trout | 4.00 | 1.60 | .40 |
| ☐ 42 | Art Houtteman | 10.00 | 4.00 | 1.00 | | ☐ 135 | Pat Mullin | 4.00 | 1.60 | .40 |
| ☐ 43 | Bobby Doerr | 20.00 | 8.00 | 2.00 | | ☐ 136 | Warren Rosar | 4.00 | 1.60 | .40 |
| ☐ 44 | Joe Dobson | 10.00 | 4.00 | 1.00 | | ☐ 137 | Johnny Pesky | 4.50 | 1.80 | .45 |
| ☐ 45 | Al Zarilla | 10.00 | 4.00 | 1.00 | | ☐ 138 | Allie Reynolds | 6.50 | 2.60 | .65 |
| ☐ 46 | Yogi Berra | 80.00 | 32.00 | 8.00 | | ☐ 139 | Johnny Mize | 12.00 | 5.00 | 1.20 |
| ☐ 47 | Jerry Coleman | 12.00 | 5.00 | 1.20 | | ☐ 140 | Pete Suder | 4.00 | 1.60 | .40 |
| ☐ 48 | Lou Brissie | 10.00 | 4.00 | 1.00 | | ☐ 141 | Joe Coleman | 4.00 | 1.60 | .40 |
| ☐ 49 | Elmer Valo | 10.00 | 4.00 | 1.00 | | ☐ 142 | Sherman Lollar | 5.00 | 2.00 | .50 |
| ☐ 50 | Dick Kokos | 10.00 | 4.00 | 1.00 | | ☐ 143 | Eddie Stewart | 4.00 | 1.60 | .40 |
| ☐ 51 | Ned Garver | 10.00 | 4.00 | 1.00 | | ☐ 144 | Al Evans | 4.00 | 1.60 | .40 |
| ☐ 52 | Sam Mele | 10.00 | 4.00 | 1.00 | | ☐ 145 | Jack Graham | 4.00 | 1.60 | .40 |
| ☐ 53 | Clyde Vollmer | 10.00 | 4.00 | 1.00 | | ☐ 146 | Floyd Baker | 4.00 | 1.60 | .40 |
| ☐ 54 | Gil Coan | 10.00 | 4.00 | 1.00 | | ☐ 147 | Mike Garcia | 5.00 | 2.00 | .50 |
| ☐ 55 | Buddy Kerr | 10.00 | 4.00 | 1.00 | | ☐ 148 | Early Wynn | 12.00 | 5.00 | 1.20 |
| ☐ 56 | Del Crandall | 12.00 | 5.00 | 1.20 | | ☐ 149 | Bob Swift | 4.00 | 1.60 | .40 |
| ☐ 57 | Vern Bickford | 10.00 | 4.00 | 1.00 | | ☐ 150 | George Vico | 4.00 | 1.60 | .40 |
| ☐ 58 | Carl Furillo | 15.00 | 6.00 | 1.50 | | ☐ 151 | Fred Hutchinson | 5.00 | 2.00 | .50 |
| ☐ 59 | Ralph Branca | 12.00 | 5.00 | 1.20 | | ☐ 152 | Ellis Kinder | 4.00 | 1.60 | .40 |
| ☐ 60 | Andy Pafko | 10.00 | 4.00 | 1.00 | | ☐ 153 | Walt Masterson | 4.00 | 1.60 | .40 |
| ☐ 61 | Bob Rush | 10.00 | 4.00 | 1.00 | | ☐ 154 | Gus Niarhos | 4.00 | 1.60 | .40 |
| ☐ 62 | Ted Kluszewski | 15.00 | 6.00 | 1.50 | | ☐ 155 | Frank Shea | 4.00 | 1.60 | .40 |
| ☐ 63 | Ewell Blackwell | 11.00 | 4.50 | 1.10 | | ☐ 156 | Fred Sanford | 4.00 | 1.60 | .40 |
| ☐ 64 | Al Dark | 12.00 | 5.00 | 1.20 | | ☐ 157 | Mike Guerra | 4.00 | 1.60 | .40 |
| ☐ 65 | Dave Koslo | 10.00 | 4.00 | 1.00 | | ☐ 158 | Paul Lehner | 4.00 | 1.60 | .40 |
| ☐ 66 | Larry Jansen | 10.00 | 4.00 | 1.00 | | ☐ 159 | Joe Tipton | 4.00 | 1.60 | .40 |
| ☐ 67 | Willie Jones | 10.00 | 4.00 | 1.00 | | ☐ 160 | Mickey Harris | 4.00 | 1.60 | .40 |
| ☐ 68 | Curt Simmons | 11.00 | 4.50 | 1.10 | | ☐ 161 | Sherry Robertson | 4.00 | 1.60 | .40 |
| ☐ 69 | Wally Westlake | 10.00 | 4.00 | 1.00 | | ☐ 162 | Eddie Yost | 4.00 | 1.60 | .40 |
| ☐ 70 | Bob Chesnes | 10.00 | 4.00 | 1.00 | | ☐ 163 | Earl Torgeson | 4.00 | 1.60 | .40 |
| ☐ 71 | Red Schoendienst | 12.00 | 5.00 | 1.20 | | ☐ 164 | Sibby Sisti | 4.00 | 1.60 | .40 |
| ☐ 72 | Howie Pollet | 10.00 | 4.00 | 1.00 | | ☐ 165 | Bruce Edwards | 4.00 | 1.60 | .40 |
| ☐ 73 | Willard Marshall | 4.00 | 1.60 | .40 | | ☐ 166 | Joe Hatton | 4.00 | 1.60 | .40 |
| ☐ 74 | Johnny Antonelli | 5.00 | 2.00 | .50 | | ☐ 167 | Preacher Roe | 6.00 | 2.40 | .60 |
| ☐ 75 | Roy Campanella | 65.00 | 26.00 | 6.50 | | ☐ 168 | Bob Scheffing | 4.00 | 1.60 | .40 |
| ☐ 76 | Rex Barney | 4.00 | 1.60 | .40 | | ☐ 169 | Hank Edwards | 4.00 | 1.60 | .40 |
| ☐ 77 | Duke Snider | 50.00 | 20.00 | 5.00 | | ☐ 170 | Dutch Leonard | 4.00 | 1.60 | .40 |
| ☐ 78 | Mickey Owen | 4.00 | 1.60 | .40 | | ☐ 171 | Harry Gumbert | 4.00 | 1.60 | .40 |
| ☐ 79 | Johnny VanderMeer | 5.00 | 2.00 | .50 | | ☐ 172 | Peanuts Lowrey | 4.00 | 1.60 | .40 |
| ☐ 80 | Howard Fox | 4.00 | 1.60 | .40 | | ☐ 173 | Lloyd Merriman | 4.00 | 1.60 | .40 |
| ☐ 81 | Ron Northey | 4.00 | 1.60 | .40 | | ☐ 174 | Hank Thompson | 4.50 | 1.80 | .45 |
| ☐ 82 | Whitey Lockman | 4.00 | 1.60 | .40 | | ☐ 175 | Monte Kennedy | 4.00 | 1.60 | .40 |
| ☐ 83 | Sheldon Jones | 4.00 | 1.60 | .40 | | ☐ 176 | Sylvester Donnelly | 4.00 | 1.60 | .40 |
| ☐ 84 | Richie Ashburn | 12.00 | 5.00 | 1.20 | | ☐ 177 | Hank Borowy | 4.00 | 1.60 | .40 |
| ☐ 85 | Ken Heintzelman | 4.00 | 1.60 | .40 | | ☐ 178 | Eddie Fitzgerald | 4.00 | 1.60 | .40 |
| ☐ 86 | Stan Rojek | 4.00 | 1.60 | .40 | | ☐ 179 | Chuck Diering | 4.00 | 1.60 | .40 |
| ☐ 87 | Bill Werle | 4.00 | 1.60 | .40 | | ☐ 180 | Harry Walker | 4.00 | 1.60 | .40 |
| ☐ 88 | Marty Marion | 6.00 | 2.40 | .60 | | ☐ 181 | Marino Pieretti | 4.00 | 1.60 | .40 |
| ☐ 89 | Red Munger | 4.00 | 1.60 | .40 | | ☐ 182 | Sam Zoldak | 4.00 | 1.60 | .40 |
| ☐ 90 | Harry Brecheen | 4.00 | 1.60 | .40 | | ☐ 183 | Mickey Haefner | 4.00 | 1.60 | .40 |
| ☐ 91 | Cass Michaels | 4.00 | 1.60 | .40 | | ☐ 184 | Randy Gumpert | 4.00 | 1.60 | .40 |
| ☐ 92 | Hank Majeski | 4.00 | 1.60 | .40 | | ☐ 185 | Howie Judson | 4.00 | 1.60 | .40 |
| ☐ 93 | Gene Bearden | 4.00 | 1.60 | .40 | | ☐ 186 | Ken Keltner | 4.50 | 1.80 | .45 |
| ☐ 94 | Lou Boudreau | 11.00 | 4.50 | 1.10 | | ☐ 187 | Lou Stringer | 4.00 | 1.60 | .40 |
| ☐ 95 | Aaron Robinson | 4.00 | 1.60 | .40 | | ☐ 188 | Earl Johnson | 4.00 | 1.60 | .40 |
| ☐ 96 | Virgil Trucks | 4.00 | 1.60 | .40 | | ☐ 189 | Owen Friend | 4.00 | 1.60 | .40 |
| ☐ 97 | Maurice McDermott | 4.00 | 1.60 | .40 | | ☐ 190 | Ken Wood | 4.00 | 1.60 | .40 |
| ☐ 98 | Ted Williams | 150.00 | 60.00 | 15.00 | | ☐ 191 | Dick Starr | 4.00 | 1.60 | .40 |
| ☐ 99 | Billy Goodman | 4.50 | 1.80 | .45 | | ☐ 192 | Bob Chipman | 4.00 | 1.60 | .40 |
| ☐ 100 | Vic Raschi | 5.50 | 2.20 | .55 | | ☐ 193 | Pete Reiser | 5.00 | 2.00 | .50 |
| ☐ 101 | Bobby Brown | 6.50 | 2.60 | .65 | | ☐ 194 | Billy Cox | 4.50 | 1.80 | .45 |
| ☐ 102 | Billy Johnson | 4.50 | 1.80 | .45 | | ☐ 195 | Phil Cavarretta | 4.50 | 1.80 | .45 |
| ☐ 103 | Eddie Joost | 4.00 | 1.60 | .40 | | ☐ 196 | Doyle Lade | 4.00 | 1.60 | .40 |
| ☐ 104 | Sam Chapman | 4.00 | 1.60 | .40 | | ☐ 197 | Johnny Wyrostek | 4.00 | 1.60 | .40 |
| ☐ 105 | Bob Dillinger | 4.00 | 1.60 | .40 | | ☐ 198 | Danny Litwhiler | 4.00 | 1.60 | .40 |
| ☐ 106 | Cliff Fannin | 4.00 | 1.60 | .40 | | ☐ 199 | Jack Kramer | 4.00 | 1.60 | .40 |
| ☐ 107 | Sam Dente | 4.00 | 1.60 | .40 | | ☐ 200 | Kirby Higbe | 4.00 | 1.60 | .40 |
| ☐ 108 | Ray Scarborough | 4.00 | 1.60 | .40 | | ☐ 201 | Pete Castiglione | 4.00 | 1.60 | .40 |
| ☐ 109 | Sid Gordon | 4.00 | 1.60 | .40 | | ☐ 202 | Cliff Chambers | 4.00 | 1.60 | .40 |
| ☐ 110 | Tommy Holmes | 5.00 | 2.00 | .50 | | ☐ 203 | Danny Murtaugh | 4.50 | 1.80 | .45 |
| ☐ 111 | Walker Cooper | 4.00 | 1.60 | .40 | | ☐ 204 | Granny Hamner | 4.00 | 1.60 | .40 |
| ☐ 112 | Gil Hodges | 20.00 | 8.00 | 2.00 | | ☐ 205 | Mike Goliat | 4.00 | 1.60 | .40 |
| ☐ 113 | Gene Hermanski | 4.00 | 1.60 | .40 | | ☐ 206 | Stan Lopata | 4.00 | 1.60 | .40 |
| ☐ 114 | Wayne Terwilliger | 4.00 | 1.60 | .40 | | ☐ 207 | Max Lanier | 4.00 | 1.60 | .40 |
| ☐ 115 | Roy Smalley | 4.00 | 1.60 | .40 | | ☐ 208 | Jim Hearn | 4.00 | 1.60 | .40 |
| ☐ 116 | Virgil Stallcup | 4.00 | 1.60 | .40 | | ☐ 209 | Johnny Lindell | 4.00 | 1.60 | .40 |
| ☐ 117 | Bill Rigney | 4.00 | 1.60 | .40 | | ☐ 210 | Ted Gray | 4.00 | 1.60 | .40 |
| ☐ 118 | Clint Hartung | 4.00 | 1.60 | .40 | | ☐ 211 | Charley Keller | 4.50 | 1.80 | .45 |
| ☐ 119 | Dick Sisler | 4.00 | 1.60 | .40 | | ☐ 212 | Gerry Priddy | 4.00 | 1.60 | .40 |
| ☐ 120 | John Thompson | 4.00 | 1.60 | .40 | | ☐ 213 | Carl Scheib | 4.00 | 1.60 | .40 |
| ☐ 121 | Andy Seminick | 4.00 | 1.60 | .40 | | ☐ 214 | Dick Fowler | 4.00 | 1.60 | .40 |
| ☐ 122 | Johnny Hopp | 4.50 | 1.80 | .45 | | ☐ 215 | Ed Lopat | 6.50 | 2.60 | .65 |
| ☐ 123 | Dino Restelli | 4.00 | 1.60 | .40 | | ☐ 216 | Bob Porterfield | 4.00 | 1.60 | .40 |
| ☐ 124 | Clyde McCullough | 4.00 | 1.60 | .40 | | ☐ 217 | Casey Stengel MGR | 32.00 | 13.00 | 3.20 |
| ☐ 125 | Del Rice | 4.00 | 1.60 | .40 | | ☐ 218 | Cliff Mapes | 4.00 | 1.60 | .40 |
| ☐ 126 | Al Brazle | 4.00 | 1.60 | .40 | | ☐ 219 | Hank Bauer | 12.00 | 5.00 | 1.20 |
| ☐ 127 | Dave Philley | 4.00 | 1.60 | .40 | | ☐ 220 | Leo Durocher MGR | 12.00 | 5.00 | 1.20 |
| ☐ 128 | Phil Masi | 4.00 | 1.60 | .40 | | ☐ 221 | Don Mueller | 5.00 | 2.00 | .50 |
| ☐ 129 | Joe Gordon | 5.00 | 2.00 | .50 | | ☐ 222 | Bobby Morgan | 4.00 | 1.60 | .40 |

| | | | | |
|---|---|---|---|---|
| ☐ 223 | Jim Russell | 4.00 | 1.60 | .40 |
| ☐ 224 | Jack Banta | 4.00 | 1.60 | .40 |
| ☐ 225 | Eddie Sawyer MGR | 4.00 | 1.60 | .40 |
| ☐ 226 | Jim Konstanty | 7.00 | 2.80 | .70 |
| ☐ 227 | Bob Miller | 4.00 | 1.60 | .40 |
| ☐ 228 | Bill Nicholson | 4.00 | 1.60 | .40 |
| ☐ 229 | Frank Frisch | 15.00 | 6.00 | 1.50 |
| ☐ 230 | Bill Serena | 4.00 | 1.60 | .40 |
| ☐ 231 | Preston Ward | 4.00 | 1.60 | .40 |
| ☐ 232 | Al Rosen | 12.00 | 5.00 | 1.20 |
| ☐ 233 | Allie Clark | 4.00 | 1.60 | .40 |
| ☐ 234 | Bobby Shantz | 7.50 | 3.00 | .75 |
| ☐ 235 | Harold Gilbert | 4.00 | 1.60 | .40 |
| ☐ 236 | Bob Cain | 4.00 | 1.60 | .40 |
| ☐ 237 | Bill Salkeld | 4.00 | 1.60 | .40 |
| ☐ 238 | Vernal Jones | 4.00 | 1.60 | .40 |
| ☐ 239 | Bill Howerton | 4.00 | 1.60 | .40 |
| ☐ 240 | Eddie Lake | 4.00 | 1.60 | .40 |
| ☐ 241 | Neil Berry | 4.00 | 1.60 | .40 |
| ☐ 242 | Dick Kryhoski | 4.00 | 1.60 | .40 |
| ☐ 243 | Johnny Groth | 4.00 | 1.60 | .40 |
| ☐ 244 | Dale Coogan | 4.00 | 1.60 | .40 |
| ☐ 245 | Al Papai | 4.00 | 1.60 | .40 |
| ☐ 246 | Walt Dropo | 5.00 | 2.00 | .50 |
| ☐ 247 | Irv Noren | 4.50 | 1.80 | .45 |
| ☐ 248 | Sam Jethroe | 4.50 | 1.80 | .45 |
| ☐ 249 | Snuffy Stirnweiss | 4.00 | 1.60 | .40 |
| ☐ 250 | Ray Coleman | 4.00 | 1.60 | .40 |
| ☐ 251 | John Moss | 4.00 | 1.60 | .40 |
| ☐ 252 | Billy DeMars | 12.50 | 2.00 | .40 |

## 1951 Bowman

PHIL RIZZUTO
Shortstop—New York Yankees
Born: New York, N. Y. Sept. 25, 1918
Height: 5-6        Weight: 160
Bats: Right        Throws: Right
Little Phil was named the most valuable player in the American League in 1950. This was his best among several very good seasons with the Yankees. Led League in fielding at short. Batted .324. Was second highest in total hits (200). His 19 sacrifice hits were tops in their department. He scored 128 runs, drove in 66. Joined Yanks from their farm system, 1941. Spent 3 years in service.

No. 26 in the 1951 SERIES
**BASEBALL**
PICTURE CARDS
©1951 Bowman Gum, Inc., Phila., Pa. U.S.A.

The cards in this 324 card set measure 2 1/16" by 3 1/8". Many of the obverses of the cards appearing in the 1951 Bowman set are enlargements of those appearing in the previous year. The high number series (253-324) is highly valued and contains the rookie cards of Mickey Mantle and Willie Mays. Card number 195 depicts Paul Richards in caricature. George Kell's card (#46) incorrectly lists him as being in the "1941" Bowman series. Player names are found printed in a panel on the front of the card. These cards were also sold in sheets in variety stores in the Philadelphia area.

| | MINT | VG-E | F-G |
|---|---|---|---|
| COMPLETE SET | 3300.00 | 1500.00 | 350.00 |
| COMMON PLAYER (1-36) | 5.00 | 2.00 | .50 |
| COMMON PLAYER (37-72) | 4.50 | 1.80 | .45 |
| COMMON PLAYER (73-252) | 4.00 | 1.60 | .40 |
| COMMON PLAYER (253-324) | 12.50 | 5.00 | 1.25 |

| | | | | |
|---|---|---|---|---|
| ☐ 1 | Whitey Ford | 200.00 | 20.00 | 4.00 |
| ☐ 2 | Yogi Berra | 65.00 | 26.00 | 6.50 |
| ☐ 3 | Robin Roberts | 16.00 | 6.50 | 1.60 |
| ☐ 4 | Del Ennis | 5.50 | 2.20 | .55 |
| ☐ 5 | Dale Mitchell | 5.50 | 2.20 | .55 |
| ☐ 6 | Don Newcombe | 7.50 | 3.00 | .75 |
| ☐ 7 | Gil Hodges | 18.00 | 7.25 | 1.80 |
| ☐ 8 | Paul Lehner | 5.00 | 2.00 | .50 |
| ☐ 9 | Sam Chapman | 5.00 | 2.00 | .50 |
| ☐ 10 | Red Schoendienst | 6.50 | 2.60 | .65 |
| ☐ 11 | Red Munger | 5.00 | 2.00 | .50 |

| | | | | |
|---|---|---|---|---|
| ☐ 12 | Hank Majeski | 5.00 | 2.00 | .50 |
| ☐ 13 | Eddie Stanky | 5.50 | 2.20 | .55 |
| ☐ 14 | Al Dark | 6.00 | 2.40 | .60 |
| ☐ 15 | Johnny Pesky | 5.50 | 2.20 | .55 |
| ☐ 16 | Maurice McDermott | 5.00 | 2.00 | .50 |
| ☐ 17 | Pete Castiglione | 5.00 | 2.00 | .50 |
| ☐ 18 | Gil Coan | 5.00 | 2.00 | .50 |
| ☐ 19 | Sid Gordon | 5.00 | 2.00 | .50 |
| ☐ 20 | Del Crandell | 5.50 | 2.20 | .55 |
| | (sic, Crandall) | | | |
| ☐ 21 | Snuffy Stirnweiss | 5.00 | 2.00 | .50 |
| ☐ 22 | Hank Sauer | 5.50 | 2.20 | .55 |
| ☐ 23 | Hoot Evers | 5.00 | 2.00 | .50 |
| ☐ 24 | Ewell Blackwell | 5.50 | 2.20 | .55 |
| ☐ 25 | Vic Raschi | 6.00 | 2.40 | .60 |
| ☐ 26 | Phil Rizzuto | 18.00 | 7.25 | 1.80 |
| ☐ 27 | Jim Konstanty | 5.50 | 2.20 | .55 |
| ☐ 28 | Eddie Waitkus | 5.00 | 2.00 | .50 |
| ☐ 29 | Allie Clark | 5.00 | 2.00 | .50 |
| ☐ 30 | Bob Feller | 27.00 | 11.00 | 2.70 |
| ☐ 31 | Roy Campanella | 50.00 | 20.00 | 5.00 |
| ☐ 32 | Duke Snider | 36.00 | 15.00 | 3.60 |
| ☐ 33 | Bob Hooper | 5.00 | 2.00 | .50 |
| ☐ 34 | Marty Marion | 6.00 | 2.40 | .60 |
| ☐ 35 | Al Zarilla | 5.00 | 2.00 | .50 |
| ☐ 36 | Joe Dobson | 5.00 | 2.00 | .50 |
| ☐ 37 | Whitey Lockman | 4.50 | 1.80 | .45 |
| ☐ 38 | Al Evans | 4.50 | 1.80 | .45 |
| ☐ 39 | Ray Scarborough | 4.50 | 1.80 | .45 |
| ☐ 40 | Gus Bell | 5.50 | 2.20 | .55 |
| ☐ 41 | Eddie Yost | 4.50 | 1.80 | .45 |
| ☐ 42 | Vern Bickford | 4.50 | 1.80 | .45 |
| ☐ 43 | Billy DeMars | 4.50 | 1.80 | .45 |
| ☐ 44 | Roy Smalley | 4.50 | 1.80 | .45 |
| ☐ 45 | Art Houtteman | 4.50 | 1.80 | .45 |
| ☐ 46 | George Kell 1941 | 14.00 | 5.75 | 1.40 |
| ☐ 47 | Grady Hatton | 4.50 | 1.80 | .45 |
| ☐ 48 | Ken Raffensberger | 4.50 | 1.80 | .45 |
| ☐ 49 | Jerry Coleman | 5.00 | 2.00 | .50 |
| ☐ 50 | Johnny Mize | 12.00 | 5.00 | 1.20 |
| ☐ 51 | Andy Seminick | 4.50 | 1.80 | .45 |
| ☐ 52 | Dick Sisler | 4.50 | 1.80 | .45 |
| ☐ 53 | Bob Lemon | 12.00 | 5.00 | 1.20 |
| ☐ 54 | Ray Boone | 5.00 | 2.00 | .50 |
| ☐ 55 | Gene Hermanski | 4.50 | 1.80 | .45 |
| ☐ 56 | Ralph Branca | 5.00 | 2.00 | .50 |
| ☐ 57 | Alex Kellner | 4.50 | 1.80 | .45 |
| ☐ 58 | Enos Slaughter | 12.00 | 5.00 | 1.20 |
| ☐ 59 | Randy Gumpert | 4.50 | 1.80 | .45 |
| ☐ 60 | Chico Carrasquel | 4.50 | 1.80 | .45 |
| ☐ 61 | Jim Hearn | 4.50 | 1.80 | .45 |
| ☐ 62 | Lou Boudreau | 10.00 | 4.00 | 1.00 |
| ☐ 63 | Bob Dillinger | 4.50 | 1.80 | .45 |
| ☐ 64 | Bill Werle | 4.50 | 1.80 | .45 |
| ☐ 65 | Mickey Vernon | 5.00 | 2.00 | .50 |
| ☐ 66 | Bob Elliott | 5.00 | 2.00 | .50 |
| ☐ 67 | Roy Sievers | 5.00 | 2.00 | .50 |
| ☐ 68 | Dick Kokos | 4.50 | 1.80 | .45 |
| ☐ 69 | Johnny Schmitz | 4.50 | 1.80 | .45 |
| ☐ 70 | Ron Northey | 4.50 | 1.80 | .45 |
| ☐ 71 | Jerry Priddy | 4.50 | 1.80 | .45 |
| ☐ 72 | Lloyd Merriman | 4.50 | 1.80 | .45 |
| ☐ 73 | Tommy Byrne | 4.50 | 1.80 | .45 |
| ☐ 74 | Billy Johnson | 4.50 | 1.80 | .45 |
| ☐ 75 | Russ Meyer | 4.00 | 1.60 | .40 |
| ☐ 76 | Stan Lopata | 4.00 | 1.60 | .40 |
| ☐ 77 | Mike Goliat | 4.00 | 1.60 | .40 |
| ☐ 78 | Early Wynn | 12.00 | 5.00 | 1.20 |
| ☐ 79 | Jim Hegan | 4.00 | 1.60 | .40 |
| ☐ 80 | Pee Wee Reese | 20.00 | 8.00 | 2.00 |
| ☐ 81 | Carl Furillo | 7.00 | 2.80 | .70 |
| ☐ 82 | Joe Tipton | 4.00 | 1.60 | .40 |
| ☐ 83 | Carl Scheib | 4.00 | 1.60 | .40 |
| ☐ 84 | Barney McCosky | 4.00 | 1.60 | .40 |
| ☐ 85 | Eddie Kazak | 4.00 | 1.60 | .40 |
| ☐ 86 | Harry Brecheen | 4.00 | 1.60 | .40 |
| ☐ 87 | Floyd Baker | 4.00 | 1.60 | .40 |
| ☐ 88 | Eddie Robinson | 4.00 | 1.60 | .40 |
| ☐ 89 | Hank Thompson | 4.50 | 1.80 | .45 |
| ☐ 90 | Dave Koslo | 4.00 | 1.60 | .40 |
| ☐ 91 | Clyde Vollmer | 4.00 | 1.60 | .40 |
| ☐ 92 | Vern Stephens | 4.50 | 1.80 | .45 |
| ☐ 93 | Danny O'Connell | 4.00 | 1.60 | .40 |
| ☐ 94 | Clyde McCullough | 4.00 | 1.60 | .40 |
| ☐ 95 | Sherry Robertson | 4.00 | 1.60 | .40 |
| ☐ 96 | Sandy Consuegra | 4.00 | 1.60 | .40 |
| ☐ 97 | Bob Kuzava | 4.00 | 1.60 | .40 |
| ☐ 98 | Willard Marshall | 4.00 | 1.60 | .40 |
| ☐ 99 | Earl Torgeson | 4.00 | 1.60 | .40 |
| ☐ 100 | Sherm Lollar | 4.50 | 1.80 | .45 |
| ☐ 101 | Owen Friend | 4.00 | 1.60 | .40 |
| ☐ 102 | Dutch Leonard | 4.00 | 1.60 | .40 |
| ☐ 103 | Andy Pafko | 4.00 | 1.60 | .40 |

| No. | Player | | | |
|---|---|---|---|---|
| ☐ 104 | Virgil Trucks | 4.00 | 1.60 | .40 |
| ☐ 105 | Don Kolloway | 4.00 | 1.60 | .40 |
| ☐ 106 | Pat Mullin | 4.00 | 1.60 | .40 |
| ☐ 107 | Johnny Wyrostek | 4.00 | 1.60 | .40 |
| ☐ 108 | Virgil Stallcup | 4.00 | 1.60 | .40 |
| ☐ 109 | Allie Reynolds | 6.50 | 2.60 | .65 |
| ☐ 110 | Bobby Brown | 6.00 | 2.40 | .60 |
| ☐ 111 | Curt Simmons | 5.00 | 2.00 | .50 |
| ☐ 112 | Willie Jones | 4.00 | 1.60 | .40 |
| ☐ 113 | Bill Nicholson | 4.00 | 1.60 | .40 |
| ☐ 114 | Sam Zoldak | 4.00 | 1.60 | .40 |
| ☐ 115 | Steve Gromek | 4.00 | 1.60 | .40 |
| ☐ 116 | Bruce Edwards | 4.00 | 1.60 | .40 |
| ☐ 117 | Eddie Miksis | 4.00 | 1.60 | .40 |
| ☐ 118 | Preacher Roe | 6.00 | 2.40 | .60 |
| ☐ 119 | Eddie Joost | 4.00 | 1.60 | .40 |
| ☐ 120 | Joe Coleman | 4.00 | 1.60 | .40 |
| ☐ 121 | Gerry Staley | 4.00 | 1.60 | .40 |
| ☐ 122 | Joe Garagiola | 20.00 | 8.00 | 2.00 |
| ☐ 123 | Howie Judson | 4.00 | 1.60 | .40 |
| ☐ 124 | Gus Niarhos | 4.00 | 1.60 | .40 |
| ☐ 125 | Bill Rigney | 4.00 | 1.60 | .40 |
| ☐ 126 | Bobby Thomson | 6.00 | 2.40 | .60 |
| ☐ 127 | Sal Maglie | 7.50 | 3.00 | .75 |
| ☐ 128 | Ellis Kinder | 4.00 | 1.60 | .40 |
| ☐ 129 | Matt Batts | 4.00 | 1.60 | .40 |
| ☐ 130 | Tom Saffell | 4.00 | 1.60 | .40 |
| ☐ 131 | Cliff Chambers | 4.00 | 1.60 | .40 |
| ☐ 132 | Cass Michaels | 4.00 | 1.60 | .40 |
| ☐ 133 | Sam Dente | 4.00 | 1.60 | .40 |
| ☐ 134 | Warren Spahn | 21.00 | 8.50 | 2.10 |
| ☐ 135 | Walker Cooper | 4.00 | 1.60 | .40 |
| ☐ 136 | Ray Coleman | 4.00 | 1.60 | .40 |
| ☐ 137 | Dick Starr | 4.00 | 1.60 | .40 |
| ☐ 138 | Phil Cavarretta | 4.50 | 1.80 | .45 |
| ☐ 139 | Doyle Lade | 4.00 | 1.60 | .40 |
| ☐ 140 | Eddie Lake | 4.00 | 1.60 | .40 |
| ☐ 141 | Fred Hutchinson | 4.50 | 1.80 | .45 |
| ☐ 142 | Aaron Robinson | 4.00 | 1.60 | .40 |
| ☐ 143 | Ted Kluszewski | 6.50 | 2.60 | .65 |
| ☐ 144 | Herman Wehmeier | 4.00 | 1.60 | .40 |
| ☐ 145 | Fred Sanford | 4.00 | 1.60 | .40 |
| ☐ 146 | Johnny Hopp | 4.00 | 1.60 | .40 |
| ☐ 147 | Ken Heintzelman | 4.00 | 1.60 | .40 |
| ☐ 148 | Granny Hamner | 4.00 | 1.60 | .40 |
| ☐ 149 | Bubba Church | 4.00 | 1.60 | .40 |
| ☐ 150 | Mike Garcia | 5.00 | 2.00 | .50 |
| ☐ 151 | Larry Doby | 6.50 | 2.60 | .65 |
| ☐ 152 | Cal Abrams | 4.00 | 1.60 | .40 |
| ☐ 153 | Rex Barney | 4.00 | 1.60 | .40 |
| ☐ 154 | Pete Suder | 4.00 | 1.60 | .40 |
| ☐ 155 | Lou Brissie | 4.00 | 1.60 | .40 |
| ☐ 156 | Del Rice | 4.00 | 1.60 | .40 |
| ☐ 157 | Al Brazle | 4.00 | 1.60 | .40 |
| ☐ 158 | Chuck Diering | 4.00 | 1.60 | .40 |
| ☐ 159 | Eddie Stewart | 4.00 | 1.60 | .40 |
| ☐ 160 | Phil Masi | 4.00 | 1.60 | .40 |
| ☐ 161 | Wes Westrum | 4.00 | 1.60 | .40 |
| ☐ 162 | Larry Jansen | 4.00 | 1.60 | .40 |
| ☐ 163 | Monte Kennedy | 4.00 | 1.60 | .40 |
| ☐ 164 | Bill Wight | 4.00 | 1.60 | .40 |
| ☐ 165 | Ted Williams | 120.00 | 50.00 | 12.00 |
| ☐ 166 | Stan Rojek | 4.00 | 1.60 | .40 |
| ☐ 167 | Murry Dickson | 4.00 | 1.60 | .40 |
| ☐ 168 | Sam Mele | 4.00 | 1.60 | .40 |
| ☐ 169 | Sid Hudson | 4.00 | 1.60 | .40 |
| ☐ 170 | Sibby Sisti | 4.00 | 1.60 | .40 |
| ☐ 171 | Buddy Kerr | 4.00 | 1.60 | .40 |
| ☐ 172 | Ned Garver | 4.00 | 1.60 | .40 |
| ☐ 173 | Hank Arft | 4.00 | 1.60 | .40 |
| ☐ 174 | Mickey Owen | 4.00 | 1.60 | .40 |
| ☐ 175 | Wayne Terwilliger | 4.00 | 1.60 | .40 |
| ☐ 176 | Vic Wertz | 4.00 | 1.60 | .40 |
| ☐ 177 | Charlie Keller | 4.50 | 1.80 | .45 |
| ☐ 178 | Ted Gray | 4.00 | 1.60 | .40 |
| ☐ 179 | Danny Litwhiler | 4.00 | 1.60 | .40 |
| ☐ 180 | Howie Fox | 4.00 | 1.60 | .40 |
| ☐ 181 | Casey Stengel | 25.00 | 10.00 | 2.50 |
| ☐ 182 | Tom Ferrick | 4.00 | 1.60 | .40 |
| ☐ 183 | Hank Bauer | 6.00 | 2.40 | .60 |
| ☐ 184 | Eddie Sawyer | 4.00 | 1.60 | .40 |
| ☐ 185 | Jimmy Bloodworth | 4.00 | 1.60 | .40 |
| ☐ 186 | Richie Ashburn | 8.00 | 3.25 | .80 |
| ☐ 187 | Al Rosen | 6.50 | 2.60 | .65 |
| ☐ 188 | Bobby Avila | 4.50 | 1.80 | .45 |
| ☐ 189 | Erv Palica | 4.00 | 1.60 | .40 |
| ☐ 190 | Joe Hatton | 4.00 | 1.60 | .40 |
| ☐ 191 | Billy Hitchcock | 4.00 | 1.60 | .40 |
| ☐ 192 | Hank Wyse | 4.00 | 1.60 | .40 |
| ☐ 193 | Ted Wilks | 4.00 | 1.60 | .40 |
| ☐ 194 | Peanuts Lowrey | 4.00 | 1.60 | .40 |
| ☐ 195 | Paul Richards (caricature) | 6.00 | 2.40 | .60 |
| ☐ 196 | Billy Pierce | 6.50 | 2.60 | .65 |
| ☐ 197 | Bob Cain | 4.00 | 1.60 | .40 |
| ☐ 198 | Monte Irvin | 21.00 | 8.50 | 2.10 |
| ☐ 199 | Sheldon Jones | 4.00 | 1.60 | .40 |
| ☐ 200 | Jack Kramer | 4.00 | 1.60 | .40 |
| ☐ 201 | Steve O'Neill | 4.00 | 1.60 | .40 |
| ☐ 202 | Mike Guerra | 4.00 | 1.60 | .40 |
| ☐ 203 | Vernon Law | 6.00 | 2.40 | .60 |
| ☐ 204 | Vic Lombardi | 4.00 | 1.60 | .40 |
| ☐ 205 | Mickey Grasso | 4.00 | 1.60 | .40 |
| ☐ 206 | Conrado Marrero | 4.00 | 1.60 | .40 |
| ☐ 207 | Billy Southworth | 4.00 | 1.60 | .40 |
| ☐ 208 | Blix Donnelly | 4.00 | 1.60 | .40 |
| ☐ 209 | Ken Wood | 4.00 | 1.60 | .40 |
| ☐ 210 | Les Moss | 4.00 | 1.60 | .40 |
| ☐ 211 | Hal Jeffcoat | 4.00 | 1.60 | .40 |
| ☐ 212 | Bob Rush | 4.00 | 1.60 | .40 |
| ☐ 213 | Neil Berry | 4.00 | 1.60 | .40 |
| ☐ 214 | Bob Swift | 4.00 | 1.60 | .40 |
| ☐ 215 | Ken Peterson | 4.00 | 1.60 | .40 |
| ☐ 216 | Connie Ryan | 4.00 | 1.60 | .40 |
| ☐ 217 | Joe Page | 5.00 | 2.00 | .50 |
| ☐ 218 | Ed Lopat | 6.00 | 2.40 | .60 |
| ☐ 219 | Gene Woodling | 6.00 | 2.40 | .60 |
| ☐ 220 | Bob Miller | 4.00 | 1.60 | .40 |
| ☐ 221 | Dick Whitman | 4.00 | 1.60 | .40 |
| ☐ 222 | Thurman Tucker | 4.00 | 1.60 | .40 |
| ☐ 223 | Johnny VanderMeer | 5.00 | 2.00 | .50 |
| ☐ 224 | Billy Cox | 4.50 | 1.80 | .45 |
| ☐ 225 | Dan Bankhead | 4.00 | 1.60 | .40 |
| ☐ 226 | Jimmy Dykes | 4.00 | 1.60 | .40 |
| ☐ 227 | Bobby Schantz (sic, Shantz) | 5.00 | 2.00 | .50 |
| ☐ 228 | Cloyd Boyer | 4.50 | 1.80 | .45 |
| ☐ 229 | Bill Howerton | 4.00 | 1.60 | .40 |
| ☐ 230 | Max Lanier | 4.00 | 1.60 | .40 |
| ☐ 231 | Luis Aloma | 4.00 | 1.60 | .40 |
| ☐ 232 | Nelson Fox | 18.00 | 7.25 | 1.80 |
| ☐ 233 | Leo Durocher MGR | 10.00 | 4.00 | 1.00 |
| ☐ 234 | Clint Hartung | 4.00 | 1.60 | .40 |
| ☐ 235 | Jack Lohrke | 4.00 | 1.60 | .40 |
| ☐ 236 | Warren Rosar | 4.00 | 1.60 | .40 |
| ☐ 237 | Billy Goodman | 4.50 | 1.80 | .45 |
| ☐ 238 | Peter Reiser | 5.00 | 2.00 | .50 |
| ☐ 239 | Bill MacDonald | 4.00 | 1.60 | .40 |
| ☐ 240 | Joe Haynes | 4.00 | 1.60 | .40 |
| ☐ 241 | Irv Noren | 4.00 | 1.60 | .40 |
| ☐ 242 | Sam Jethroe | 4.00 | 1.60 | .40 |
| ☐ 243 | Johnny Antonelli | 4.50 | 1.80 | .45 |
| ☐ 244 | Cliff Fannin | 4.00 | 1.60 | .40 |
| ☐ 245 | John Berardino | 4.50 | 1.80 | .45 |
| ☐ 246 | Bill Serena | 4.00 | 1.60 | .40 |
| ☐ 247 | Bob Ramazotti | 4.00 | 1.60 | .40 |
| ☐ 248 | Johnny Klippstein | 4.00 | 1.60 | .40 |
| ☐ 249 | Johnny Groth | 4.00 | 1.60 | .40 |
| ☐ 250 | Hank Borowy | 4.00 | 1.60 | .40 |
| ☐ 251 | Willard Ramsdell | 4.00 | 1.60 | .40 |
| ☐ 252 | Dixie Howell | 4.00 | 1.60 | .40 |
| ☐ 253 | Mickey Mantle | 800.00 | 320.00 | 80.00 |
| ☐ 254 | Jackie Jensen | 21.00 | 8.50 | 2.10 |
| ☐ 255 | Milo Candini | 12.50 | 5.00 | 1.25 |
| ☐ 256 | Ken Sylvestri | 12.50 | 5.00 | 1.25 |
| ☐ 257 | Birdie Tebbetts | 12.50 | 5.00 | 1.25 |
| ☐ 258 | Luke Easter | 14.00 | 5.75 | 1.40 |
| ☐ 259 | Chuck Dressen MGR | 14.00 | 5.75 | 1.40 |
| ☐ 260 | Carl Erskine | 21.00 | 8.50 | 2.10 |
| ☐ 261 | Wally Moses | 12.50 | 5.00 | 1.25 |
| ☐ 262 | Gus Zernial | 12.50 | 5.00 | 1.25 |
| ☐ 263 | Howie Pollet | 12.50 | 5.00 | 1.25 |
| ☐ 264 | Don Richmond | 12.50 | 5.00 | 1.25 |
| ☐ 265 | Steve Bilko | 12.50 | 5.00 | 1.25 |
| ☐ 266 | Harry Dorish | 12.50 | 5.00 | 1.25 |
| ☐ 267 | Ken Holcomb | 12.50 | 5.00 | 1.25 |
| ☐ 268 | Don Mueller | 14.00 | 5.75 | 1.40 |
| ☐ 269 | Ray Noble | 12.50 | 5.00 | 1.25 |
| ☐ 270 | Willard Nixon | 12.50 | 5.00 | 1.25 |
| ☐ 271 | Tommy Wright | 12.50 | 5.00 | 1.25 |
| ☐ 272 | Billy Meyer MGR | 12.50 | 5.00 | 1.25 |
| ☐ 273 | Danny Murtaugh | 12.50 | 5.00 | 1.25 |
| ☐ 274 | George Metkovich | 12.50 | 5.00 | 1.25 |
| ☐ 275 | Bucky Harris MGR | 18.00 | 7.25 | 1.80 |
| ☐ 276 | Frank Quinn | 12.50 | 5.00 | 1.25 |
| ☐ 277 | Roy Hartsfield | 12.50 | 5.00 | 1.25 |
| ☐ 278 | Norman Roy | 12.50 | 5.00 | 1.25 |
| ☐ 279 | Jim Delsing | 12.50 | 5.00 | 1.25 |
| ☐ 280 | Frank Overmire | 12.50 | 5.00 | 1.25 |
| ☐ 281 | Al Widmar | 12.50 | 5.00 | 1.25 |
| ☐ 282 | Frank Frisch | 21.00 | 8.50 | 2.10 |
| ☐ 283 | Walt Dubiel | 12.50 | 5.00 | 1.25 |
| ☐ 284 | Gene Bearden | 12.50 | 5.00 | 1.25 |
| ☐ 285 | Johnny Lipon | 12.50 | 5.00 | 1.25 |
| ☐ 286 | Bob Usher | 12.50 | 5.00 | 1.25 |
| ☐ 287 | Jim Blackburn | 12.50 | 5.00 | 1.25 |

# 1951 Bowman Reprint Set

## 1951 Bowman Reprint Set

- Complete set of 324 cards.
- Set includes Mickey Mantle rookie, Willie Mays rookie, Whitey Ford rookie, Joe Garagiola rookie and MVP's Yogi Berra and Roy Campanella.
- All cards the same size as the original Bowman 51's.
- The set captures the beautiful artwork and detail of each card.

- All cards are made by the STATE OF THE ART "Diamond Vue" process. There are only four printing presses in the United States that can produce these cards.
- The final product is awesome and something that you will be proud to add to your collection. All cards in full color with a rich lacquer finish. You will be impressed.
- Each set comes in a special collectors box.

Orders will be filled on a first come, first served basis.

Prices:

1 set $29.95

10 sets $225.00 plus $8.00 postage

25 sets $510.00 no postage

## THE MAGNIFICENT MICKEY MANTLE

### Free Advertising Card Giveaway!!

For every $10.00 worth of merchandise that you purchase, you will receive a Free Mickey Mantle Advertising Card. There are ten different advertisement cards. We will give you a different advertising card for every $10.00 worth of merchandise you order. For every $100.00 worth of merchandise that you purchase, we will send you a complete set of 10. All cards our choice.

### NOTICE!! These cards are NOT FOR SALE.

These advertising cards are made by a state of the art "Diamond Vue" process. There are only four printing presses in the United States that can produce these cards. Each card measures a standard 2½"x3½".

The final product is awesome and something that you will be proud to add to your collection. All cards in full color with a rich lacquer finish. You will be impressed.

## OTHER REPRINT SETS AVAILABLE

1885 Mayo Cut Plug (40 cards) includes Anson, Rusie and 8 other Hall of Famers ................. $5.00

1910 T-206 (523 "cards" on 2 posters) includes rare Wagner, Ty Cobb, Cy Young, etc .................... 7.00

1910 T-3 (100 cards) includes Cobb, Young, Mathewson, Lajoie and many other greats ...... 10.00

1915 Crackerjack (176 cards) includes Cobb, Connie Mack, etc. .......................................... 15.00

1933 Sport Kings (48 cards) includes Babe Ruth, Ty Cobb, Red Grange, Jack Dempsey, Johnny Weismuller, and many other legends .............. 7.00

1933 Goudey (240 cards) includes 4 Babe Ruths, 2 Lou Gehrigs, Tris Speaker, Joe Cronin, rare #106 Lajoie and a whole host of other Baseball Giants .. 15.00

1934 Goudey (96 cards) includes J. Foxx, Gehrig, Dizzy Dean, Grove and eleven other Hall of Famers ................................................................. 10.00

1934-1936 Diamond Stars (108 cards) including over 25 Hall of Famers .................................. 10.0

1935 Goudey 4-1 Puzzle Backs (36 cards, 144 players) includes Ruth, Dean, Foxx, Klein and many other Hall of Famer included ........................... 5.00

1935 National Chicle Football (36 cards) includes Knute Rockne and Bronco Nagurski ................. 5.00

1938 Goudey Heads-Up (48 cards) includes 2 Joe DiMaggio, Bob Feller, etc ............................ 7.00

1940 Play Ball Series #1 (45 cards) includes Joe DiMaggio, Bill Dickey, Hank Greenberg ............ 5.00

1953 Bowman Baseball (224 cards - 160 full color, 64 black & white) includes Mantle, Musial, Reese, Hodges, Berra, Ford .................................. 15.00

1941 Play Ball (2 uncut sheets) (72 cards plus 12 unissued cards for a total of 84 cards) includes Joe DiMaggio, T. Williams, "Pee Wee" Reese rookie ....... 6.00

---

### *Also Available:* 1952 TOPPS REPRINT SET (402 cards)
including **Mantle, Mays, Berra, Mathews Rookie, etc. $40.00**

**1940 Playball :** (series #2 — #s 46-90) **$5.00**

---

**POSTAGE & HANDLING:** Please add $3.00 per order unless otherwise noted.

**SATISFACTION GUARANTEED!**

## RICHARD GELMAN

c/o Card Collectors Co.
494 Hudson Street, New York, NY 10014
212-206-0492
*Since 1951*
Visit our store open 7 days 12-7 P.M.
CALL TOLL FREE Outside New York State for orders only
1-800-225-0015 or 1-800-822-0028

64-page catalog $1 or free with every order

| | | | | |
|---|---|---|---|---|
| ☐ 288 | Bobby Adams | 12.50 | 5.00 | 1.25 |
| ☐ 289 | Cliff Mapes | 12.50 | 5.00 | 1.25 |
| ☐ 290 | Bill Dickey | 45.00 | 18.00 | 4.50 |
| ☐ 291 | Tommy Henrich | 18.00 | 7.25 | 1.80 |
| ☐ 292 | Eddie Pellegrini | 12.50 | 5.00 | 1.25 |
| ☐ 293 | Ken Johnson | 12.50 | 5.00 | 1.25 |
| ☐ 294 | Jocko Thompson | 12.50 | 5.00 | 1.25 |
| ☐ 295 | Al Lopez MGR | 25.00 | 10.00 | 2.50 |
| ☐ 296 | Bob Kennedy | 12.50 | 5.00 | 1.25 |
| ☐ 297 | Dave Philley | 12.50 | 5.00 | 1.25 |
| ☐ 298 | Joe Astroth | 12.50 | 5.00 | 1.25 |
| ☐ 299 | Clyde King | 12.50 | 5.00 | 1.25 |
| ☐ 300 | Hal Rice | 12.50 | 5.00 | 1.25 |
| ☐ 301 | Tommy Glaviano | 12.50 | 5.00 | 1.25 |
| ☐ 302 | Jim Busby | 12.50 | 5.00 | 1.25 |
| ☐ 303 | Marv Rotblatt | 12.50 | 5.00 | 1.25 |
| ☐ 304 | Al Gettell | 12.50 | 5.00 | 1.25 |
| ☐ 305 | Willie Mays | 500.00 | 200.00 | 50.00 |
| ☐ 306 | Jim Piersall | 21.00 | 8.50 | 2.10 |
| ☐ 307 | Walt Masterson | 12.50 | 5.00 | 1.25 |
| ☐ 308 | Ted Beard | 12.50 | 5.00 | 1.25 |
| ☐ 309 | Mel Queen | 12.50 | 5.00 | 1.25 |
| ☐ 310 | Erv Dusak | 12.50 | 5.00 | 1.25 |
| ☐ 311 | Mickey Harris | 12.50 | 5.00 | 1.25 |
| ☐ 312 | Gene Mauch | 18.00 | 7.25 | 1.80 |
| ☐ 313 | Ray Mueller | 12.50 | 5.00 | 1.25 |
| ☐ 314 | Johnny Sain | 18.00 | 7.25 | 1.80 |
| ☐ 315 | Zack Taylor | 12.50 | 5.00 | 1.25 |
| ☐ 316 | Duane Pillette | 12.50 | 5.00 | 1.25 |
| ☐ 317 | Smokey Burgess | 15.00 | 6.00 | 1.50 |
| ☐ 318 | Warren Hacker | 12.50 | 5.00 | 1.25 |
| ☐ 319 | Red Rolfe | 14.00 | 5.75 | 1.40 |
| ☐ 320 | Hal White | 12.50 | 5.00 | 1.25 |
| ☐ 321 | Earl Johnson | 12.50 | 5.00 | 1.25 |
| ☐ 322 | Luke Sewell | 14.00 | 5.75 | 1.40 |
| ☐ 323 | Joe Adcock | 18.00 | 7.25 | 1.80 |
| ☐ 324 | Johnny Pramesa | 20.00 | 6.00 | 1.00 |

## 1952 Bowman

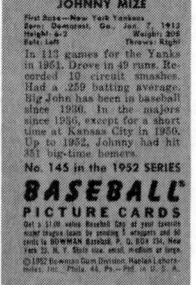

The cards in this 252 card set measure 2 1/16" by
3 1/8". While the Bowman set of 1952 retained the
card size introduced in 1951, it employed a
modification of color tones from the two preceding
years. The cards also appeared with a facsimile
autograph on the front and, for the first time since
1949, premium advertising on the back. The 1952
set was sold in sheets as well as in gum packs.
Artwork for 15 cards that were never issued was
recently discovered.

| | MINT | VG-E | F-G |
|---|---|---|---|
| COMPLETE SET | 2000.00 | 800.00 | 250.00 |
| COMMON PLAYER (1-36) | 4.50 | 1.80 | .45 |
| COMMON PLAYER (37-180) | 4.00 | 1.60 | .40 |
| COMMON PLAYER (181-216) | 3.50 | 1.40 | .35 |
| COMMON PLAYER (217-252) | 7.00 | 2.80 | .70 |

| | | | | |
|---|---|---|---|---|
| ☐ 1 | Yogi Berra | 125.00 | 20.00 | 4.00 |
| ☐ 2 | Bobby Thomson | 6.00 | 2.40 | .60 |
| ☐ 3 | Fred Hutchinson | 5.00 | 2.00 | .50 |
| ☐ 4 | Robin Roberts | 16.00 | 6.50 | 1.60 |
| ☐ 5 | Minnie Minoso | 9.00 | 3.75 | .90 |
| ☐ 6 | Virgil Stallcup | 4.50 | 1.80 | .45 |
| ☐ 7 | Mike Garcia | 5.00 | 2.00 | .50 |

| | | | | |
|---|---|---|---|---|
| ☐ 8 | Pee Wee Reese | 20.00 | 8.00 | 2.00 |
| ☐ 9 | Vern Stephens | 5.00 | 2.00 | .50 |
| ☐ 10 | Bob Hooper | 4.50 | 1.80 | .45 |
| ☐ 11 | Ralph Kiner | 16.00 | 6.50 | 1.60 |
| ☐ 12 | Max Surkont | 4.50 | 1.80 | .45 |
| ☐ 13 | Cliff Mapes | 4.50 | 1.80 | .45 |
| ☐ 14 | Cliff Chambers | 4.50 | 1.80 | .45 |
| ☐ 15 | Sam Mele | 4.50 | 1.80 | .45 |
| ☐ 16 | Turk Lown | 4.50 | 1.80 | .45 |
| ☐ 17 | Ed Lopat | 6.50 | 2.60 | .65 |
| ☐ 18 | Don Mueller | 5.00 | 2.00 | .50 |
| ☐ 19 | Bob Cain | 4.50 | 1.80 | .45 |
| ☐ 20 | Willie Jones | 4.50 | 1.80 | .45 |
| ☐ 21 | Nelson Fox | 7.50 | 3.00 | .75 |
| ☐ 22 | Willard Ramsdell | 4.50 | 1.80 | .45 |
| ☐ 23 | Bob Lemon | 12.50 | 5.00 | 1.25 |
| ☐ 24 | Carl Furillo | 6.50 | 2.60 | .65 |
| ☐ 25 | Mickey McDermott | 4.50 | 1.80 | .45 |
| ☐ 26 | Eddie Joost | 4.50 | 1.80 | .45 |
| ☐ 27 | Joe Garagiola | 15.00 | 6.00 | 1.50 |
| ☐ 28 | Ray Hartsfield | 4.50 | 1.80 | .45 |
| ☐ 29 | Ned Garver | 4.50 | 1.80 | .45 |
| ☐ 30 | Red Schoendienst | 6.00 | 2.40 | .60 |
| ☐ 31 | Eddie Yost | 4.50 | 1.80 | .45 |
| ☐ 32 | Eddie Miksis | 4.50 | 1.80 | .45 |
| ☐ 33 | Gil McDougald | 9.00 | 3.75 | .90 |
| ☐ 34 | Alvin Dark | 5.50 | 2.20 | .55 |
| ☐ 35 | Granny Hamner | 4.50 | 1.80 | .45 |
| ☐ 36 | Cass Michaels | 4.50 | 1.80 | .45 |
| ☐ 37 | Vic Raschi | 5.50 | 2.20 | .55 |
| ☐ 38 | Whitey Lockman | 4.50 | 1.80 | .45 |
| ☐ 39 | Vic Wertz | 4.50 | 1.80 | .45 |
| ☐ 40 | Bubba Church | 4.00 | 1.60 | .40 |
| ☐ 41 | Chico Carrasquel | 4.00 | 1.60 | .40 |
| ☐ 42 | Johnny Wyrostek | 4.00 | 1.60 | .40 |
| ☐ 43 | Bob Feller | 27.00 | 11.00 | 2.70 |
| ☐ 44 | Roy Campanella | 50.00 | 20.00 | 5.00 |
| ☐ 45 | Johnny Pesky | 4.50 | 1.80 | .45 |
| ☐ 46 | Carl Scheib | 4.00 | 1.60 | .40 |
| ☐ 47 | Pete Castiglione | 4.00 | 1.60 | .40 |
| ☐ 48 | Vern Bickford | 4.00 | 1.60 | .40 |
| ☐ 49 | Jim Hearn | 4.00 | 1.60 | .40 |
| ☐ 50 | Gerry Staley | 4.00 | 1.60 | .40 |
| ☐ 51 | Gil Coan | 4.00 | 1.60 | .40 |
| ☐ 52 | Phil Rizzuto | 18.00 | 7.25 | 1.80 |
| ☐ 53 | Richie Ashburn | 8.00 | 3.25 | .80 |
| ☐ 54 | Billy Pierce | 5.00 | 2.00 | .50 |
| ☐ 55 | Ken Raffensberger | 4.00 | 1.60 | .40 |
| ☐ 56 | Clyde King | 4.00 | 1.60 | .40 |
| ☐ 57 | Clyde Vollmer | 4.00 | 1.60 | .40 |
| ☐ 58 | Hank Majeski | 4.00 | 1.60 | .40 |
| ☐ 59 | Murry Dickson | 4.00 | 1.60 | .40 |
| ☐ 60 | Sid Gordon | 4.00 | 1.60 | .40 |
| ☐ 61 | Tommy Byrne | 4.00 | 1.60 | .40 |
| ☐ 62 | Joe Presko | 4.00 | 1.60 | .40 |
| ☐ 63 | Irv Noren | 4.00 | 1.60 | .40 |
| ☐ 64 | Roy Smalley | 4.00 | 1.60 | .40 |
| ☐ 65 | Hank Bauer | 6.00 | 2.40 | .60 |
| ☐ 66 | Sal Maglie | 6.00 | 2.40 | .60 |
| ☐ 67 | Johnny Groth | 4.00 | 1.60 | .40 |
| ☐ 68 | Jim Busby | 4.00 | 1.60 | .40 |
| ☐ 69 | Joe Adcock | 5.00 | 2.00 | .50 |
| ☐ 70 | Carl Erskine | 6.00 | 2.40 | .60 |
| ☐ 71 | Vernon Law | 5.00 | 2.00 | .50 |
| ☐ 72 | Earl Torgeson | 4.00 | 1.60 | .40 |
| ☐ 73 | Gerry Coleman | 4.50 | 1.80 | .45 |
| ☐ 74 | Wes Westrum | 4.00 | 1.60 | .40 |
| ☐ 75 | George Kell | 10.00 | 4.00 | 1.00 |
| ☐ 76 | Del Ennis | 4.50 | 1.80 | .45 |
| ☐ 77 | Eddie Robinson | 4.00 | 1.60 | .40 |
| ☐ 78 | Lloyd Merriman | 4.00 | 1.60 | .40 |
| ☐ 79 | Lou Brissie | 4.00 | 1.60 | .40 |
| ☐ 80 | Gil Hodges | 15.00 | 6.00 | 1.50 |
| ☐ 81 | Billy Goodman | 4.50 | 1.80 | .45 |
| ☐ 82 | Gus Zernial | 4.00 | 1.60 | .40 |
| ☐ 83 | Howie Pollet | 4.00 | 1.60 | .40 |
| ☐ 84 | Sam Jethroe | 4.00 | 1.60 | .40 |
| ☐ 85 | Marty Marion | 5.00 | 2.00 | .50 |
| ☐ 86 | Cal Abrams | 4.00 | 1.60 | .40 |
| ☐ 87 | Mickey Vernon | 4.50 | 1.80 | .45 |
| ☐ 88 | Bruce Edwards | 4.00 | 1.60 | .40 |
| ☐ 89 | Billy Hitchcock | 4.00 | 1.60 | .40 |
| ☐ 90 | Larry Jansen | 4.00 | 1.60 | .40 |
| ☐ 91 | Don Kolloway | 4.00 | 1.60 | .40 |
| ☐ 92 | Eddie Waitkus | 4.00 | 1.60 | .40 |
| ☐ 93 | Paul Richards | 4.00 | 1.60 | .40 |
| ☐ 94 | Luke Sewell | 4.00 | 1.60 | .40 |
| ☐ 95 | Luke Easter | 4.00 | 1.60 | .40 |
| ☐ 96 | Ralph Branca | 4.50 | 1.80 | .45 |
| ☐ 97 | Willard Marshall | 4.00 | 1.60 | .40 |
| ☐ 98 | Jimmy Dykes | 4.00 | 1.60 | .40 |
| ☐ 99 | Clyde McCullough | 4.00 | 1.60 | .40 |
| ☐ 100 | Sibby Sisti | 4.00 | 1.60 | .40 |

| | | | | |
|---|---|---:|---:|---:|
| ☐ 101 | Mickey Mantle | 400.00 | 160.00 | 40.00 |
| ☐ 102 | Peanuts Lowrey | 4.00 | 1.60 | .40 |
| ☐ 103 | Joe Haynes | 4.00 | 1.60 | .40 |
| ☐ 104 | Hal Jeffcoat | 4.00 | 1.60 | .40 |
| ☐ 105 | Bobby Brown | 6.00 | 2.40 | .60 |
| ☐ 106 | Randy Gumpert | 4.00 | 1.60 | .40 |
| ☐ 107 | Del Rice | 4.00 | 1.60 | .40 |
| ☐ 108 | George Metkovich | 4.00 | 1.60 | .40 |
| ☐ 109 | Tom Morgan | 4.00 | 1.60 | .40 |
| ☐ 110 | Max Lanier | 4.00 | 1.60 | .40 |
| ☐ 111 | Hoot Evers | 4.00 | 1.60 | .40 |
| ☐ 112 | Smokey Burgess | 4.50 | 1.80 | .45 |
| ☐ 113 | Al Zarilla | 4.00 | 1.60 | .40 |
| ☐ 114 | Frank Hiller | 4.00 | 1.60 | .40 |
| ☐ 115 | Larry Doby | 6.00 | 2.40 | .60 |
| ☐ 116 | Duke Snider | 36.00 | 15.00 | 3.60 |
| ☐ 117 | Bill Wight | 4.00 | 1.60 | .40 |
| ☐ 118 | Ray Murray | 4.00 | 1.60 | .40 |
| ☐ 119 | Bill Howerton | 4.00 | 1.60 | .40 |
| ☐ 120 | Chet Nichols | 4.00 | 1.60 | .40 |
| ☐ 121 | Al Corwin | 4.00 | 1.60 | .40 |
| ☐ 122 | Billy Johnson | 4.00 | 1.60 | .40 |
| ☐ 123 | Sid Hudson | 4.00 | 1.60 | .40 |
| ☐ 124 | Birdie Tebbetts | 4.00 | 1.60 | .40 |
| ☐ 125 | Howie Fox | 4.00 | 1.60 | .40 |
| ☐ 126 | Phil Cavarretta | 4.50 | 1.80 | .45 |
| ☐ 127 | Dick Sisler | 4.00 | 1.60 | .40 |
| ☐ 128 | Don Newcombe | 6.00 | 2.40 | .60 |
| ☐ 129 | Gus Niarhos | 4.00 | 1.60 | .40 |
| ☐ 130 | Allie Clark | 4.00 | 1.60 | .40 |
| ☐ 131 | Bob Swift | 4.00 | 1.60 | .40 |
| ☐ 132 | Dave Cole | 4.00 | 1.60 | .40 |
| ☐ 133 | Dick Kryhoski | 4.00 | 1.60 | .40 |
| ☐ 134 | Al Brazle | 4.00 | 1.60 | .40 |
| ☐ 135 | Mickey Harris | 4.00 | 1.60 | .40 |
| ☐ 136 | Gene Hermanski | 4.00 | 1.60 | .40 |
| ☐ 137 | Stan Rojek | 4.00 | 1.60 | .40 |
| ☐ 138 | Ted Wilks | 4.00 | 1.60 | .40 |
| ☐ 139 | Jerry Priddy | 4.00 | 1.60 | .40 |
| ☐ 140 | Ray Scarborough | 4.00 | 1.60 | .40 |
| ☐ 141 | Hank Edwards | 4.00 | 1.60 | .40 |
| ☐ 142 | Early Wynn | 11.00 | 4.50 | 1.10 |
| ☐ 143 | Sandy Consuegra | 4.00 | 1.60 | .40 |
| ☐ 144 | Joe Hatton | 4.00 | 1.60 | .40 |
| ☐ 145 | Johnny Mize | 12.00 | 5.00 | 1.20 |
| ☐ 146 | Leo Durocher MGR | 9.00 | 3.75 | .90 |
| ☐ 147 | Marlin Stuart | 4.00 | 1.60 | .40 |
| ☐ 148 | Ken Heintzelman | 4.00 | 1.60 | .40 |
| ☐ 149 | Howie Judson | 4.00 | 1.60 | .40 |
| ☐ 150 | Herman Wehmeier | 4.00 | 1.60 | .40 |
| ☐ 151 | Al Rosen | 6.50 | 2.60 | .65 |
| ☐ 152 | Billy Cox | 4.50 | 1.80 | .45 |
| ☐ 153 | Fred Hatfield | 4.00 | 1.60 | .40 |
| ☐ 154 | Ferris Fain | 4.50 | 1.80 | .45 |
| ☐ 155 | Billy Meyer | 4.00 | 1.60 | .40 |
| ☐ 156 | Warren Spahn | 18.00 | 7.25 | 1.80 |
| ☐ 157 | Jim Delsing | 4.00 | 1.60 | .40 |
| ☐ 158 | Bucky Harris MGR | 7.50 | 3.00 | .75 |
| ☐ 159 | Dutch Leonard | 4.00 | 1.60 | .40 |
| ☐ 160 | Eddie Stanky | 4.50 | 1.80 | .45 |
| ☐ 161 | Jackie Jensen | 6.00 | 2.40 | .60 |
| ☐ 162 | Monte Irvin | 10.00 | 4.00 | 1.00 |
| ☐ 163 | Johnny Lipon | 4.00 | 1.60 | .40 |
| ☐ 164 | Connie Ryan | 4.00 | 1.60 | .40 |
| ☐ 165 | Saul Rogovin | 4.00 | 1.60 | .40 |
| ☐ 166 | Bobby Adams | 4.00 | 1.60 | .40 |
| ☐ 167 | Bobby Avila | 4.50 | 1.80 | .45 |
| ☐ 168 | Preacher Roe | 6.00 | 2.40 | .60 |
| ☐ 169 | Walt Dropo | 4.00 | 1.60 | .40 |
| ☐ 170 | Joe Astroth | 4.00 | 1.60 | .40 |
| ☐ 171 | Mel Queen | 4.00 | 1.60 | .40 |
| ☐ 172 | Ebba St.Claire | 4.00 | 1.60 | .40 |
| ☐ 173 | Gene Bearden | 4.00 | 1.60 | .40 |
| ☐ 174 | Mickey Grasso | 4.00 | 1.60 | .40 |
| ☐ 175 | Ransom Jackson | 4.00 | 1.60 | .40 |
| ☐ 176 | Harry Brecheen | 4.00 | 1.60 | .40 |
| ☐ 177 | Gene Woodling | 5.00 | 2.00 | .50 |
| ☐ 178 | Dave Williams | 4.50 | 1.80 | .45 |
| ☐ 179 | Pete Suder | 4.00 | 1.60 | .40 |
| ☐ 180 | Eddie Fitzgerald | 4.00 | 1.60 | .40 |
| ☐ 181 | Joe Collins | 4.00 | 1.60 | .40 |
| ☐ 182 | Dave Koslo | 3.50 | 1.40 | .35 |
| ☐ 183 | Pat Mullin | 3.50 | 1.40 | .35 |
| ☐ 184 | Curt Simmons | 4.00 | 1.60 | .40 |
| ☐ 185 | Eddie Stewart | 3.50 | 1.40 | .35 |
| ☐ 186 | Frank Smith | 3.50 | 1.40 | .35 |
| ☐ 187 | Jim Hegan | 3.50 | 1.40 | .35 |
| ☐ 188 | Charlie Dressen MGR | 4.00 | 1.60 | .40 |
| ☐ 189 | Jim Piersall | 5.00 | 2.00 | .50 |
| ☐ 190 | Dick Fowler | 3.50 | 1.40 | .35 |
| ☐ 191 | Bob Friend | 5.00 | 2.00 | .50 |
| ☐ 192 | John Cusick | 3.50 | 1.40 | .35 |
| ☐ 193 | Bobby Young | 3.50 | 1.40 | .35 |
| ☐ 194 | Bob Porterfield | 3.50 | 1.40 | .35 |
| ☐ 195 | Frank Baumholtz | 3.50 | 1.40 | .35 |
| ☐ 196 | Stan Musial | 125.00 | 50.00 | 12.50 |
| ☐ 197 | Charlie Silvera | 3.50 | 1.40 | .35 |
| ☐ 198 | Chuck Diering | 3.50 | 1.40 | .35 |
| ☐ 199 | Ted Gray | 3.50 | 1.40 | .35 |
| ☐ 200 | Ken Silvestri | 3.50 | 1.40 | .35 |
| ☐ 201 | Ray Coleman | 3.50 | 1.40 | .35 |
| ☐ 202 | Harry Perkowski | 3.50 | 1.40 | .35 |
| ☐ 203 | Steve Gromek | 3.50 | 1.40 | .35 |
| ☐ 204 | Andy Pafko | 3.50 | 1.40 | .35 |
| ☐ 205 | Walt Masterson | 3.50 | 1.40 | .35 |
| ☐ 206 | Elmer Valo | 3.50 | 1.40 | .35 |
| ☐ 207 | George Strickland | 3.50 | 1.40 | .35 |
| ☐ 208 | Walker Cooper | 3.50 | 1.40 | .35 |
| ☐ 209 | Dick Littlefield | 3.50 | 1.40 | .35 |
| ☐ 210 | Archie Wilson | 3.50 | 1.40 | .35 |
| ☐ 211 | Paul Minner | 3.50 | 1.40 | .35 |
| ☐ 212 | Solly Hemus | 3.50 | 1.40 | .35 |
| ☐ 213 | Monte Kennedy | 3.50 | 1.40 | .35 |
| ☐ 214 | Ray Boone | 3.50 | 1.40 | .35 |
| ☐ 215 | Sheldon Jones | 3.50 | 1.40 | .35 |
| ☐ 216 | Matt Batts | 3.50 | 1.40 | .35 |
| ☐ 217 | Casey Stengel | 30.00 | 12.00 | 3.00 |
| ☐ 218 | Willie Mays | 300.00 | 120.00 | 30.00 |
| ☐ 219 | Neil Berry | 7.00 | 2.80 | .70 |
| ☐ 220 | Russ Meyer | 7.00 | 2.80 | .70 |
| ☐ 221 | Lou Kretlow | 7.00 | 2.80 | .70 |
| ☐ 222 | Dixie Howell | 7.00 | 2.80 | .70 |
| ☐ 223 | Harry Simpson | 7.00 | 2.80 | .70 |
| ☐ 224 | Johnny Schmitz | 7.00 | 2.80 | .70 |
| ☐ 225 | Del Wilber | 7.00 | 2.80 | .70 |
| ☐ 226 | Alex Kellner | 7.00 | 2.80 | .70 |
| ☐ 227 | Clyde Sukeforth | 7.00 | 2.80 | .70 |
| ☐ 228 | Bob Chipman | 7.00 | 2.80 | .70 |
| ☐ 229 | Hank Arft | 7.00 | 2.80 | .70 |
| ☐ 230 | Frank Shea | 7.00 | 2.80 | .70 |
| ☐ 231 | Dee Fondy | 7.00 | 2.80 | .70 |
| ☐ 232 | Enos Slaughter | 21.00 | 8.50 | 2.10 |
| ☐ 233 | Bob Kuzava | 7.00 | 2.80 | .70 |
| ☐ 234 | Fred Fitzsimmons | 7.00 | 2.80 | .70 |
| ☐ 235 | Steve Souchock | 7.00 | 2.80 | .70 |
| ☐ 236 | Tommy Brown | 7.00 | 2.80 | .70 |
| ☐ 237 | Sherman Lollar | 8.00 | 3.25 | .80 |
| ☐ 238 | Roy McMillan | 7.00 | 2.80 | .70 |
| ☐ 239 | Dale Mitchell | 8.00 | 3.25 | .80 |
| ☐ 240 | Billy Loes | 8.00 | 3.25 | .80 |
| ☐ 241 | Mel Parnell | 8.00 | 3.25 | .80 |
| ☐ 242 | Everett Kell | 7.00 | 2.80 | .70 |
| ☐ 243 | Red Munger | 7.00 | 2.80 | .70 |
| ☐ 244 | Lew Burdette | 16.00 | 6.50 | 1.60 |
| ☐ 245 | George Schmees | 7.00 | 2.80 | .70 |
| ☐ 246 | Jerry Snyder | 7.00 | 2.80 | .70 |
| ☐ 247 | John Pramesa | 7.00 | 2.80 | .70 |
| ☐ 248 | Bill Werle | 7.00 | 2.80 | .70 |
| ☐ 249 | Hank Thompson | 8.00 | 3.25 | .80 |
| ☐ 250 | Ivan Delock | 7.00 | 2.80 | .70 |
| ☐ 251 | Jack Lohrke | 7.00 | 2.80 | .70 |
| ☐ 252 | Frank Crosetti | 30.00 | 5.00 | 1.00 |

## 1953 Bowman Color

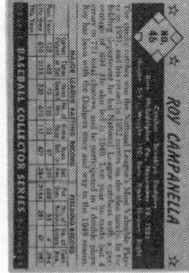

The cards in this 160 card set measure 2 1/2" by
3 3/4". The 1953 Bowman Color set, considered by
many to be the best looking set of the modern era,

contains Kodachrome photographs with no names or facsimile autographs on the face. Numbers 113 to 160 are somewhat more difficult to obtain. There are two cards of Al Corwin (126 and 149). Card number 159 is actually a picture of Floyd Baker.

|  | MINT | VG-E | F-G |
|---|---|---|---|
| COMPLETE SET ..................... | 2750.00 | 1200.00 | 300.00 |
| COMMON PLAYER (1-96) .......... | 7.00 | 2.80 | .70 |
| COMMON PLAYER (97-112) ...... | 8.00 | 3.25 | .80 |
| COMMON PLAYER (113-128) .... | 18.00 | 7.25 | 1.80 |
| COMMON PLAYER (129-160) .... | 12.00 | 5.00 | 1.20 |

| | | MINT | VG-E | F-G |
|---|---|---|---|---|
| ☐ | 1 Dave Williams .................. | 30.00 | 4.00 | .80 |
| ☐ | 2 Vic Wertz ...................... | 7.00 | 2.80 | .70 |
| ☐ | 3 Sam Jethroe .................. | 7.00 | 2.80 | .70 |
| ☐ | 4 Art Houtteman ................ | 7.00 | 2.80 | .70 |
| ☐ | 5 Sid Gordon ................... | 7.00 | 2.80 | .70 |
| ☐ | 6 Joe Ginsberg ................. | 7.00 | 2.80 | .70 |
| ☐ | 7 Harry Chiti .................... | 7.00 | 2.80 | .70 |
| ☐ | 8 Al Rosen ...................... | 10.00 | 4.00 | 1.00 |
| ☐ | 9 Phil Rizzuto .................. | 27.00 | 11.00 | 2.70 |
| ☐ | 10 Richie Ashburn .............. | 12.50 | 5.00 | 1.25 |
| ☐ | 11 Bobby Shantz ................ | 8.00 | 3.25 | .80 |
| ☐ | 12 Carl Erskine ................. | 10.00 | 4.00 | 1.00 |
| ☐ | 13 Gus Zernial .................. | 7.00 | 2.80 | .70 |
| ☐ | 14 Billy Loes ................... | 8.00 | 3.25 | .80 |
| ☐ | 15 Jim Busby .................... | 7.00 | 2.80 | .70 |
| ☐ | 16 Bob Friend ................... | 8.00 | 3.25 | .80 |
| ☐ | 17 Jerry Staley ................. | 7.00 | 2.80 | .70 |
| ☐ | 18 Nelson Fox ................... | 12.50 | 5.00 | 1.25 |
| ☐ | 19 Alvin Dark ................... | 8.00 | 3.25 | .80 |
| ☐ | 20 Don Lenhardt ................ | 7.00 | 2.80 | .70 |
| ☐ | 21 Joe Garagiola ............... | 18.00 | 7.25 | 1.80 |
| ☐ | 22 Bob Porterfield ............. | 7.00 | 2.80 | .70 |
| ☐ | 23 Herman Wehmeier .......... | 7.00 | 2.80 | .70 |
| ☐ | 24 Jackie Jensen ............... | 9.00 | 3.75 | .90 |
| ☐ | 25 Hoot Evers ................... | 7.00 | 2.80 | .70 |
| ☐ | 26 Roy McMillan ................ | 7.00 | 2.80 | .70 |
| ☐ | 27 Vic Raschi ................... | 9.00 | 3.75 | .90 |
| ☐ | 28 Smokey Burgess ............ | 8.00 | 3.25 | .80 |
| ☐ | 29 Bobby Avila .................. | 8.00 | 3.25 | .80 |
| ☐ | 30 Phil Cavarretta ............. | 8.00 | 3.25 | .80 |
| ☐ | 31 Jimmy Dykes ................ | 8.00 | 3.25 | .80 |
| ☐ | 32 Stan Musial .................. | 150.00 | 60.00 | 15.00 |
| ☐ | 33 Pee Wee Reese HOR ....... | 40.00 | 16.00 | 4.00 |
| ☐ | 34 Gil Coan ..................... | 7.00 | 2.80 | .70 |
| ☐ | 35 Maurice McDermott ........ | 7.00 | 2.80 | .70 |
| ☐ | 36 Minnie Minoso ............... | 10.00 | 4.00 | 1.00 |
| ☐ | 37 Jim Wilson ................... | 7.00 | 2.80 | .70 |
| ☐ | 38 Harry Byrd ................... | 7.00 | 2.80 | .70 |
| ☐ | 39 Paul Richards MGR ........ | 7.00 | 2.80 | .70 |
| ☐ | 40 Larry Doby ................... | 9.00 | 3.75 | .90 |
| ☐ | 41 Sammy White ................ | 7.00 | 2.80 | .70 |
| ☐ | 42 Tommy Brown ................ | 7.00 | 2.80 | .70 |
| ☐ | 43 Mike Garcia .................. | 8.00 | 3.25 | .80 |
| ☐ | 44 Berra/Bauer/Mantle ...... | 120.00 | 50.00 | 12.00 |
| ☐ | 45 Walt Dropo .................. | 7.00 | 2.80 | .70 |
| ☐ | 46 Roy Campanella ............ | 80.00 | 32.00 | 8.00 |
| ☐ | 47 Ned Garver .................. | 7.00 | 2.80 | .70 |
| ☐ | 48 Hank Sauer .................. | 8.00 | 3.25 | .80 |
| ☐ | 49 Eddie Stanky ................ | 8.00 | 3.25 | .80 |
| ☐ | 50 Lou Kretlow ................. | 7.00 | 2.80 | .70 |
| ☐ | 51 Monte Irvin .................. | 15.00 | 6.00 | 1.50 |
| ☐ | 52 Marty Marion ................ | 9.00 | 3.75 | .90 |
| ☐ | 53 Del Rice ..................... | 7.00 | 2.80 | .70 |
| ☐ | 54 Chico Carrasquel ........... | 7.00 | 2.80 | .70 |
| ☐ | 55 Leo Durocher MGR ......... | 11.00 | 4.50 | 1.10 |
| ☐ | 56 Bob Cain ..................... | 7.00 | 2.80 | .70 |
| ☐ | 57 Lou Boudreau MGR ........ | 14.00 | 5.75 | 1.40 |
| ☐ | 58 Willard Marshall ............ | 7.00 | 2.80 | .70 |
| ☐ | 59 Mickey Mantle ............... | 400.00 | 160.00 | 40.00 |
| ☐ | 60 Granny Hamner .............. | 7.00 | 2.80 | .70 |
| ☐ | 61 George Kell .................. | 16.00 | 6.50 | 1.60 |
| ☐ | 62 Ted Kluszewski ............. | 11.00 | 4.50 | 1.10 |
| ☐ | 63 Gil McDougald ............... | 10.00 | 4.00 | 1.00 |
| ☐ | 64 Curt Simmons ............... | 8.00 | 3.25 | .80 |
| ☐ | 65 Robin Roberts ............... | 20.00 | 8.00 | 2.00 |
| ☐ | 66 Mel Parnell .................. | 7.00 | 2.80 | .70 |
| ☐ | 67 Mel Clark .................... | 7.00 | 2.80 | .70 |
| ☐ | 68 Allie Reynolds ............... | 11.00 | 4.50 | 1.10 |
| ☐ | 69 Charley Grimm MGR ...... | 7.00 | 2.80 | .70 |
| ☐ | 70 Clint Courtney ............... | 7.00 | 2.80 | .70 |
| ☐ | 71 Paul Minner .................. | 7.00 | 2.80 | .70 |
| ☐ | 72 Ted Gray ..................... | 7.00 | 2.80 | .70 |
| ☐ | 73 Billy Pierce .................. | 9.00 | 3.75 | .90 |
| ☐ | 74 Don Mueller .................. | 7.00 | 2.80 | .70 |
| ☐ | 75 Saul Rogovin ................ | 7.00 | 2.80 | .70 |
| ☐ | 76 Jim Hearn .................... | 7.00 | 2.80 | .70 |
| ☐ | 77 Mickey Grasso .............. | 7.00 | 2.80 | .70 |
| ☐ | 78 Carl Furillo ................... | 11.00 | 4.50 | 1.10 |

| | | MINT | VG-E | F-G |
|---|---|---|---|---|
| ☐ | 79 Ray Boone ................... | 7.00 | 2.80 | .70 |
| ☐ | 80 Ralph Kiner .................. | 16.00 | 6.50 | 1.60 |
| ☐ | 81 Enos Slaughter .............. | 16.00 | 6.50 | 1.60 |
| ☐ | 82 Joe Astroth .................. | 7.00 | 2.80 | .70 |
| ☐ | 83 Jack Daniels ................. | 7.00 | 2.80 | .70 |
| ☐ | 84 Hank Bauer .................. | 9.00 | 3.75 | .90 |
| ☐ | 85 Solly Hemus ................. | 7.00 | 2.80 | .70 |
| ☐ | 86 Harry Simpson .............. | 7.00 | 2.80 | .70 |
| ☐ | 87 Harry Perkowski ............ | 7.00 | 2.80 | .70 |
| ☐ | 88 Joe Dobson .................. | 7.00 | 2.80 | .70 |
| ☐ | 89 Sandy Consuegra ........... | 7.00 | 2.80 | .70 |
| ☐ | 90 Joe Nuxhall ................. | 8.00 | 3.25 | .80 |
| ☐ | 91 Steve Souchock ............. | 7.00 | 2.80 | .70 |
| ☐ | 92 Gil Hodges .................. | 27.00 | 11.00 | 2.70 |
| ☐ | 93 Phil Rizzuto and ........... | 65.00 | 26.00 | 6.50 |
| | Billy Martin | | | |
| ☐ | 94 Bob Addis ................... | 7.00 | 2.80 | .70 |
| ☐ | 95 Wally Moses ................. | 7.00 | 2.80 | .70 |
| ☐ | 96 Sal Maglie ................... | 10.00 | 4.00 | 1.00 |
| ☐ | 97 Ed Mathews ................. | 30.00 | 12.00 | 3.00 |
| ☐ | 98 Hector Rodriguez ........... | 8.00 | 3.25 | .80 |
| ☐ | 99 Warren Spahn ............... | 30.00 | 12.00 | 3.00 |
| ☐ | 100 Bill Wight .................. | 8.00 | 3.25 | .80 |
| ☐ | 101 Red Schoendienst .......... | 12.00 | 5.00 | 1.20 |
| ☐ | 102 Jim Hegan .................. | 8.00 | 3.25 | .80 |
| ☐ | 103 Del Ennis ................... | 9.00 | 3.75 | .90 |
| ☐ | 104 Luke Easter ................ | 9.00 | 3.75 | .90 |
| ☐ | 105 Eddie Joost ................ | 8.00 | 3.25 | .80 |
| ☐ | 106 Ken Raffensberger ......... | 8.00 | 3.25 | .80 |
| ☐ | 107 Alex Kellner ................ | 8.00 | 3.25 | .80 |
| ☐ | 108 Bobby Adams ............... | 8.00 | 3.25 | .80 |
| ☐ | 109 Ken Wood ................... | 8.00 | 3.25 | .80 |
| ☐ | 110 Bob Rush ................... | 8.00 | 3.25 | .80 |
| ☐ | 111 Jim Dyck ................... | 8.00 | 3.25 | .80 |
| ☐ | 112 Toby Atwell ................ | 8.00 | 3.25 | .80 |
| ☐ | 113 Karl Drews ................. | 18.00 | 7.25 | 1.80 |
| ☐ | 114 Bob Feller .................. | 120.00 | 50.00 | 12.00 |
| ☐ | 115 Cloyd Boyer ................ | 21.00 | 8.50 | 2.10 |
| ☐ | 116 Eddie Yost ................. | 18.00 | 7.25 | 1.80 |
| ☐ | 117 Duke Snider ................ | 250.00 | 100.00 | 25.00 |
| ☐ | 118 Billy Martin ................ | 90.00 | 36.00 | 9.00 |
| ☐ | 119 Dale Mitchell ............... | 21.00 | 8.50 | 2.10 |
| ☐ | 120 Marlin Stuart .............. | 18.00 | 7.25 | 1.80 |
| ☐ | 121 Yogi Berra .................. | 200.00 | 80.00 | 20.00 |
| ☐ | 122 Bill Serena ................. | 18.00 | 7.25 | 1.80 |
| ☐ | 123 Johnny Lipon ............... | 18.00 | 7.25 | 1.80 |
| ☐ | 124 Charlie Dressen MGR ..... | 21.00 | 8.50 | 2.10 |
| ☐ | 125 Fred Hatfield ............... | 18.00 | 7.25 | 1.80 |
| ☐ | 126 Al Corwin ................... | 18.00 | 7.25 | 1.80 |
| ☐ | 127 Dick Kryhoski .............. | 18.00 | 7.25 | 1.80 |
| ☐ | 128 Whitey Lockman ........... | 18.00 | 7.25 | 1.80 |
| ☐ | 129 Russ Meyer ................. | 12.00 | 5.00 | 1.20 |
| ☐ | 130 Cass Michaels .............. | 12.00 | 5.00 | 1.20 |
| ☐ | 131 Connie Ryan ................ | 12.00 | 5.00 | 1.20 |
| ☐ | 132 Fred Hutchinson ........... | 16.00 | 6.50 | 1.60 |
| ☐ | 133 Willie Jones ................ | 12.00 | 5.00 | 1.20 |
| ☐ | 134 Johnny Pesky .............. | 12.00 | 5.00 | 1.20 |
| ☐ | 135 Bobby Morgan .............. | 12.00 | 5.00 | 1.20 |
| ☐ | 136 Jim Brideweser ............ | 12.00 | 5.00 | 1.20 |
| ☐ | 137 Sam Dente .................. | 12.00 | 5.00 | 1.20 |
| ☐ | 138 Bubba Church .............. | 12.00 | 5.00 | 1.20 |
| ☐ | 139 Pete Runnels ............... | 16.00 | 6.50 | 1.60 |
| ☐ | 140 Al Brazle ................... | 12.00 | 5.00 | 1.20 |
| ☐ | 141 Frank Shea ................. | 12.00 | 5.00 | 1.20 |
| ☐ | 142 Larry Miggins .............. | 12.00 | 5.00 | 1.20 |
| ☐ | 143 Al Lopez MGR .............. | 21.00 | 8.50 | 2.10 |
| ☐ | 144 Warren Hacker ............. | 12.00 | 5.00 | 1.20 |
| ☐ | 145 George Shuba .............. | 12.00 | 5.00 | 1.20 |
| ☐ | 146 Early Wynn ................. | 50.00 | 20.00 | 5.00 |
| ☐ | 147 Clem Koshorek ............. | 12.00 | 5.00 | 1.20 |
| ☐ | 148 Billy Goodman ............. | 12.00 | 5.00 | 1.20 |
| ☐ | 149 Al Corwin ................... | 12.00 | 5.00 | 1.20 |
| ☐ | 150 Carl Scheib ................ | 12.00 | 5.00 | 1.20 |
| ☐ | 151 Joe Adcock ................. | 15.00 | 6.00 | 1.50 |
| ☐ | 152 Clyde Vollmer .............. | 12.00 | 5.00 | 1.20 |
| ☐ | 153 Whitey Ford ................ | 150.00 | 60.00 | 15.00 |
| ☐ | 154 Turk Lown .................. | 12.00 | 5.00 | 1.20 |
| ☐ | 155 Allie Clark .................. | 12.00 | 5.00 | 1.20 |
| ☐ | 156 Max Surkont ............... | 12.00 | 5.00 | 1.20 |
| ☐ | 157 Sherman Lollar ............ | 12.00 | 5.00 | 1.20 |
| ☐ | 158 Howard Fox ................ | 12.00 | 5.00 | 1.20 |
| ☐ | 159 Mickey Vernon ............. | 16.00 | 6.50 | 1.60 |
| | (photo actually Floyd Baker) | | | |
| ☐ | 160 Cal Abrams ................. | 18.00 | 6.00 | 1.00 |

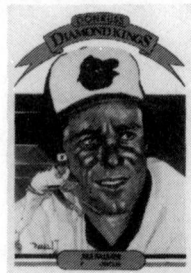
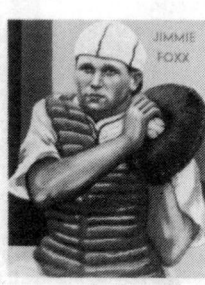
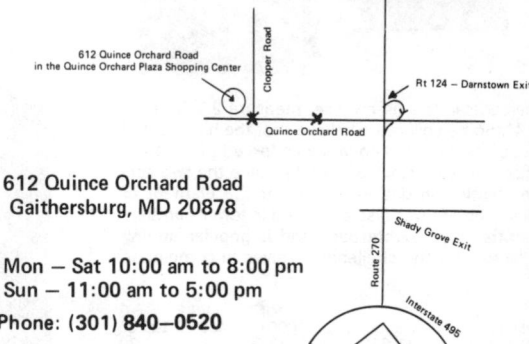

## 1953 Bowman BW

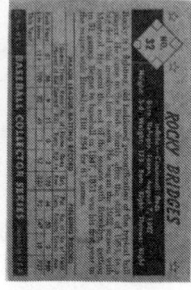

The cards in this 64 card set measure 2 1/2" by 3 3/4". Some collectors believe that the high cost of producing the 1953 color series forced Bowman to issue this set in black and white, since the two sets are identical in design except for the element of color. This set was also produced in fewer numbers than its color counterpart, and is popular among collectors for the challenge involved in completing it.

|  | | MINT | VG-E | F-G |
|---|---|---|---|---|
| COMPLETE SET | | 1000.00 | 400.00 | 125.00 |
| COMMON PLAYER (1-64) | | 13.00 | 5.25 | 1.30 |
| ☐ | 1 Gus Bell | 40.00 | 8.00 | 1.50 |
| ☐ | 2 Willard Nixon | 13.00 | 5.25 | 1.30 |
| ☐ | 3 Bill Rigney | 13.00 | 5.25 | 1.30 |
| ☐ | 4 Pat Mullin | 13.00 | 5.25 | 1.30 |
| ☐ | 5 Dee Fondy | 13.00 | 5.25 | 1.30 |
| ☐ | 6 Ray Murray | 13.00 | 5.25 | 1.30 |
| ☐ | 7 Andy Seminick | 13.00 | 5.25 | 1.30 |
| ☐ | 8 Pete Suder | 13.00 | 5.25 | 1.30 |
| ☐ | 9 Walt Masterson | 13.00 | 5.25 | 1.30 |
| ☐ | 10 Dick Sisler | 13.00 | 5.25 | 1.30 |
| ☐ | 11 Dick Gernert | 13.00 | 5.25 | 1.30 |
| ☐ | 12 Randy Jackson | 13.00 | 5.25 | 1.30 |
| ☐ | 13 Joe Tipton | 13.00 | 5.25 | 1.30 |
| ☐ | 14 Bill Nicholson | 13.00 | 5.25 | 1.30 |
| ☐ | 15 Johnny Mize | 45.00 | 18.00 | 4.50 |
| ☐ | 16 Stu Miller | 13.00 | 5.25 | 1.30 |
| ☐ | 17 Virgil Trucks | 15.00 | 6.00 | 1.50 |
| ☐ | 18 Billy Hoeft | 13.00 | 5.25 | 1.30 |
| ☐ | 19 Paul LaPalme | 13.00 | 5.25 | 1.30 |
| ☐ | 20 Eddie Robinson | 13.00 | 5.25 | 1.30 |
| ☐ | 21 Clarence Podbielan | 13.00 | 5.25 | 1.30 |
| ☐ | 22 Matt Batts | 13.00 | 5.25 | 1.30 |
| ☐ | 23 Wilmer Mizell | 15.00 | 6.00 | 1.50 |
| ☐ | 24 Del Wilber | 13.00 | 5.25 | 1.30 |
| ☐ | 25 Johnny Sain | 25.00 | 10.00 | 2.50 |
| ☐ | 26 Preacher Roe | 25.00 | 10.00 | 2.50 |
| ☐ | 27 Bob Lemon | 45.00 | 18.00 | 4.50 |
| ☐ | 28 Hoyt Wilhelm | 45.00 | 18.00 | 4.50 |
| ☐ | 29 Sid Hudson | 13.00 | 5.25 | 1.30 |
| ☐ | 30 Walker Cooper | 13.00 | 5.25 | 1.30 |
| ☐ | 31 Gene Woodling | 18.00 | 7.25 | 1.80 |
| ☐ | 32 Rocky Bridges | 13.00 | 5.25 | 1.30 |
| ☐ | 33 Bob Kuzava | 13.00 | 5.25 | 1.30 |
| ☐ | 34 Ebba St.Claire | 13.00 | 5.25 | 1.30 |
| ☐ | 35 Johnny Wyrostek | 13.00 | 5.25 | 1.30 |
| ☐ | 36 Jim Piersall | 21.00 | 8.50 | 2.10 |
| ☐ | 37 Hal Jeffcoat | 13.00 | 5.25 | 1.30 |
| ☐ | 38 Dave Cole | 13.00 | 5.25 | 1.30 |
| ☐ | 39 Casey Stengel | 150.00 | 60.00 | 15.00 |
| ☐ | 40 Larry Jansen | 13.00 | 5.25 | 1.30 |
| ☐ | 41 Bob Ramazotti | 13.00 | 5.25 | 1.30 |
| ☐ | 42 Howie Judson | 13.00 | 5.25 | 1.30 |
| ☐ | 43 Hal Bevan | 13.00 | 5.25 | 1.30 |
| ☐ | 44 Jim Delsing | 13.00 | 5.25 | 1.30 |
| ☐ | 45 Irv Noren | 13.00 | 5.25 | 1.30 |
| ☐ | 46 Bucky Harris | 25.00 | 10.00 | 2.50 |
| ☐ | 47 Jack Lohrke | 13.00 | 5.25 | 1.30 |
| ☐ | 48 Steve Ridzik | 13.00 | 5.25 | 1.30 |
| ☐ | 49 Floyd Baker | 13.00 | 5.25 | 1.30 |
| ☐ | 50 Dutch Leonard | 13.00 | 5.25 | 1.30 |
| ☐ | 51 Lou Burdette | 20.00 | 8.00 | 2.00 |
| ☐ | 52 Ralph Branca | 16.00 | 6.50 | 1.60 |
| ☐ | 53 Morris Martin | 13.00 | 5.25 | 1.30 |
| ☐ | 54 Bill Miller | 13.00 | 5.25 | 1.30 |
| ☐ | 55 Don Johnson | 13.00 | 5.25 | 1.30 |
| ☐ | 56 Roy Smalley | 13.00 | 5.25 | 1.30 |
| ☐ | 57 Andy Pafko | 13.00 | 5.25 | 1.30 |
| ☐ | 58 Jim Konstanty | 15.00 | 6.00 | 1.50 |
| ☐ | 59 Duane Pillette | 13.00 | 5.25 | 1.30 |
| ☐ | 60 Billy Cox | 15.00 | 6.00 | 1.50 |
| ☐ | 61 Tom Gorman | 13.00 | 5.25 | 1.30 |
| ☐ | 62 Keith Thomas | 13.00 | 5.25 | 1.30 |
| ☐ | 63 Steve Gromek | 13.00 | 5.25 | 1.30 |
| ☐ | 64 Andy Hansen | 18.00 | 6.00 | 1.25 |

## 1954 Bowman

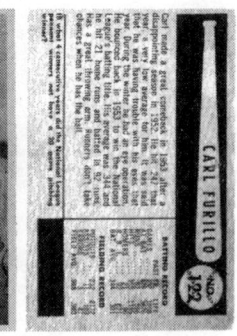

The cards in this 224 card set measure 2 1/2" by 3 3/4". A contractual problem apparently resulted in the deletion of the number 66 Ted Williams card from this Bowman set, thereby creating a scarcity which is highly valued among collectors. The set price below does NOT include number 66 Williams. Many errors in players' statistics exist (and some were corrected) while a few players' names were printed on the front, instead of appearing as a facsimile autograph.

|  | | MINT | VG-E | F-G |
|---|---|---|---|---|
| COMPLETE SET | | 950.00 | 400.00 | 95.00 |
| COMMON PLAYER (1-128) | | 1.75 | .70 | .17 |
| COMMON PLAYER (129-224) | | 2.25 | .90 | .22 |
| ☐ | 1 Phil Rizzuto | 60.00 | 10.00 | 2.50 |
| ☐ | 2 Jackie Jensen | 3.00 | 1.20 | .30 |
| ☐ | 3 Marion Fricano | 1.75 | .70 | .17 |
| ☐ | 4 Bob Hooper | 1.75 | .70 | .17 |
| ☐ | 5 Bill Hunter | 1.75 | .70 | .17 |
| ☐ | 6 Nelson Fox | 4.50 | 1.80 | .45 |
| ☐ | 7 Walt Dropo | 1.75 | .70 | .17 |
| ☐ | 8 Jim Busby | 1.75 | .70 | .17 |
| ☐ | 9 Davey Williams | 2.25 | .90 | .22 |
| ☐ | 10 Carl Erskine | 3.50 | 1.40 | .35 |
| ☐ | 11 Sid Gordon | 1.75 | .70 | .17 |
| ☐ | 12 Roy McMillan | 1.75 | .70 | .17 |
| ☐ | 13 Paul Minner | 1.75 | .70 | .17 |
| ☐ | 14 Gerry Staley | 1.75 | .70 | .17 |
| ☐ | 15 Richie Ashburn | 5.00 | 2.00 | .50 |
| ☐ | 16 Jim Wilson | 1.75 | .70 | .17 |
| ☐ | 17 Tom Gorman | 1.75 | .70 | .17 |
| ☐ | 18 Hoot Evers | 1.75 | .70 | .17 |
| ☐ | 19 Bobby Shantz | 2.25 | .90 | .22 |
| ☐ | 20 Art Houtteman | 1.75 | .70 | .17 |
| ☐ | 21 Vic Wertz | 1.75 | .70 | .17 |
| ☐ | 22 Sam Mele | 1.75 | .70 | .17 |
| ☐ | 23 Harvey Kuenn | 6.00 | 2.40 | .60 |
| ☐ | 24 Bob Porterfield | 1.75 | .70 | .17 |
| ☐ | 25 Wes Westrum | 1.75 | .70 | .17 |
| ☐ | 26 Billy Cox | 2.25 | .90 | .22 |
| ☐ | 27 Dick Cole | 1.75 | .70 | .17 |
| ☐ | 28 Jim Greengrass | 1.75 | .70 | .17 |
| ☐ | 29 Johnny Klippstein | 1.75 | .70 | .17 |
| ☐ | 30 Del Rice | 1.75 | .70 | .17 |

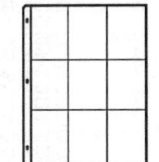

| | # | Name | | | |
|---|---|---|---|---|---|
| ☐ | 31 | Smoky Burgess | 2.25 | .90 | .22 |
| ☐ | 32 | Del Crandall | 2.25 | .90 | .22 |
| ☐ | 33A | Vic Raschi (no mention of trade on back) | 2.75 | 1.10 | .27 |
| ☐ | 33B | Vic Raschi (traded to St.Louis) | 12.00 | 5.00 | 1.20 |
| ☐ | 34 | Sammy White | 1.75 | .70 | .17 |
| ☐ | 35 | Eddie Joost | 1.75 | .70 | .17 |
| ☐ | 36 | George Strickland | 1.75 | .70 | .17 |
| ☐ | 37 | Dick Kokos | 1.75 | .70 | .17 |
| ☐ | 38 | Minnie Minoso | 3.50 | 1.40 | .35 |
| ☐ | 39 | Ned Garver | 1.75 | .70 | .17 |
| ☐ | 40 | Gil Coan | 1.75 | .70 | .17 |
| ☐ | 41 | Alvin Dark | 2.25 | .90 | .22 |
| ☐ | 42 | Billy Loes | 1.75 | .70 | .17 |
| ☐ | 43 | Bob Friend | 2.25 | .90 | .22 |
| ☐ | 44 | Harry Perkowski | 1.75 | .70 | .17 |
| ☐ | 45 | Ralph Kiner | 11.00 | 4.50 | 1.10 |
| ☐ | 46 | Rip Repulski | 1.75 | .70 | .17 |
| ☐ | 47 | Granny Hamner | 1.75 | .70 | .17 |
| ☐ | 48 | Jack Dittmer | 1.75 | .70 | .17 |
| ☐ | 49 | Harry Byrd | 1.75 | .70 | .17 |
| ☐ | 50 | George Kell | 8.00 | 3.25 | .80 |
| ☐ | 51 | Alex Kellner | 1.75 | .70 | .17 |
| ☐ | 52 | Joe Ginsberg | 1.75 | .70 | .17 |
| ☐ | 53 | Don Lenhardt | 1.75 | .70 | .17 |
| ☐ | 54 | Chico Carrasquel | 1.75 | .70 | .17 |
| ☐ | 55 | Jim Delsing | 1.75 | .70 | .17 |
| ☐ | 56 | Maurice McDermott | 1.75 | .70 | .17 |
| ☐ | 57 | Hoyt Wilhelm | 8.00 | 3.25 | .80 |
| ☐ | 58 | Pee Wee Reese | 14.00 | 5.75 | 1.40 |
| ☐ | 59 | Bob Schultz | 1.75 | .70 | .17 |
| ☐ | 60 | Fred Baczewski | 1.75 | .70 | .17 |
| ☐ | 61 | Eddie Miksis | 1.75 | .70 | .17 |
| ☐ | 62 | Enos Slaughter | 8.00 | 3.25 | .80 |
| ☐ | 63 | Earl Torgeson | 1.75 | .70 | .17 |
| ☐ | 64 | Eddie Mathews | 11.00 | 4.50 | 1.10 |
| ☐ | 65 | Mickey Mantle | 200.00 | 80.00 | 20.00 |
| ☐ | 66A | Jim Piersall | 60.00 | 24.00 | 6.00 |
| ☐ | 66B | Ted Williams | 900.00 | 360.00 | 90.00 |
| ☐ | 67 | Carl Scheib | 1.75 | .70 | .17 |
| ☐ | 68 | Bobby Avila | 1.75 | .70 | .17 |
| ☐ | 69 | Clint Courtney | 1.75 | .70 | .17 |
| ☐ | 70 | Willard Marshall | 1.75 | .70 | .17 |
| ☐ | 71 | Ted Gray | 1.75 | .70 | .17 |
| ☐ | 72 | Eddie Yost | 1.75 | .70 | .17 |
| ☐ | 73 | Don Mueller | 2.25 | .90 | .22 |
| ☐ | 74 | Jim Gilliam | 3.50 | 1.40 | .35 |
| ☐ | 75 | Max Surkont | 1.75 | .70 | .17 |
| ☐ | 76 | Joe Nuxhall | 2.25 | .90 | .22 |
| ☐ | 77 | Bob Rush | 1.75 | .70 | .17 |
| ☐ | 78 | Sal Yvars | 1.75 | .70 | .17 |
| ☐ | 79 | Curt Simmons | 2.25 | .90 | .22 |
| ☐ | 80 | Johnny Logan | 2.25 | .90 | .22 |
| ☐ | 81 | Jerry Coleman | 2.25 | .90 | .22 |
| ☐ | 82 | Billy Goodman | 1.75 | .70 | .17 |
| ☐ | 83 | Ray Murray | 1.75 | .70 | .17 |
| ☐ | 84 | Larry Doby | 3.50 | 1.40 | .35 |
| ☐ | 85 | Jim Dyck | 1.75 | .70 | .17 |
| ☐ | 86 | Harry Dorish | 1.75 | .70 | .17 |
| ☐ | 87 | Don Lund | 1.75 | .70 | .17 |
| ☐ | 88 | Tom Umphlett | 1.75 | .70 | .17 |
| ☐ | 89 | Willie Mays | 100.00 | 40.00 | 10.00 |
| ☐ | 90 | Roy Campanella | 36.00 | 15.00 | 3.60 |
| ☐ | 91 | Cal Abrams | 1.75 | .70 | .17 |
| ☐ | 92 | Ken Raffensberger | 1.75 | .70 | .17 |
| ☐ | 93 | Bill Serena | 1.75 | .70 | .17 |
| ☐ | 94 | Solly Hemus | 1.75 | .70 | .17 |
| ☐ | 95 | Robin Roberts | 9.00 | 3.75 | .90 |
| ☐ | 96 | Joe Adcock | 2.25 | .90 | .22 |
| ☐ | 97 | Gil McDougald | 3.00 | 1.20 | .30 |
| ☐ | 98 | Ellis Kinder | 1.75 | .70 | .17 |
| ☐ | 99 | Pete Suder | 1.75 | .70 | .17 |
| ☐ | 100 | Mike Garcia | 2.25 | .90 | .22 |
| ☐ | 101 | Don Larsen | 5.00 | 2.00 | .50 |
| ☐ | 102 | Billy Pierce | 2.50 | 1.00 | .25 |
| ☐ | 103 | Steve Souchock | 1.75 | .70 | .17 |
| ☐ | 104 | Frank Shea | 1.75 | .70 | .17 |
| ☐ | 105 | Sal Maglie | 2.75 | 1.10 | .27 |
| ☐ | 106 | Clem Labine | 2.25 | .90 | .22 |
| ☐ | 107 | Paul LaPalme | 1.75 | .70 | .17 |
| ☐ | 108 | Bobby Adams | 1.75 | .70 | .17 |
| ☐ | 109 | Roy Smalley | 1.75 | .70 | .17 |
| ☐ | 110 | Red Schoendienst | 2.75 | 1.10 | .27 |
| ☐ | 111 | Murry Dickson | 1.75 | .70 | .17 |
| ☐ | 112 | Andy Pafko | 1.75 | .70 | .17 |
| ☐ | 113 | Allie Reynolds | 3.50 | 1.40 | .35 |
| ☐ | 114 | Willard Nixon | 1.75 | .70 | .17 |
| ☐ | 115 | Don Bollweg | 1.75 | .70 | .17 |
| ☐ | 116 | Luke Easter | 1.75 | .70 | .17 |
| ☐ | 117 | Dick Kryhoski | 1.75 | .70 | .17 |
| ☐ | 118 | Bob Boyd | 1.75 | .70 | .17 |
| ☐ | 119 | Fred Hatfield | 1.75 | .70 | .17 |
| ☐ | 120 | Mel Hoderlein | 1.75 | .70 | .17 |
| ☐ | 121 | Ray Katt | 1.75 | .70 | .17 |
| ☐ | 122 | Carl Furillo | 3.50 | 1.40 | .35 |
| ☐ | 123 | Toby Atwell | 1.75 | .70 | .17 |
| ☐ | 124 | Gus Bell | 1.75 | .70 | .17 |
| ☐ | 125 | Warren Hacker | 1.75 | .70 | .17 |
| ☐ | 126 | Cliff Chambers | 1.75 | .70 | .17 |
| ☐ | 127 | Del Ennis | 1.75 | .70 | .17 |
| ☐ | 128 | Ebba St.Claire | 2.25 | .90 | .22 |
| ☐ | 129 | Hank Bauer | 3.50 | 1.40 | .35 |
| ☐ | 130 | Milt Bolling | 2.25 | .90 | .22 |
| ☐ | 131 | Joe Astroth | 2.25 | .90 | .22 |
| ☐ | 132 | Bob Feller | 20.00 | 8.00 | 2.00 |
| ☐ | 133 | Duane Pillette | 2.25 | .90 | .22 |
| ☐ | 134 | Luis Aloma | 2.25 | .90 | .22 |
| ☐ | 135 | Johnny Pesky | 2.25 | .90 | .22 |
| ☐ | 136 | Clyde Vollmer | 2.25 | .90 | .22 |
| ☐ | 137 | Al Corwin | 2.25 | .90 | .22 |
| ☐ | 138 | Gil Hodges | 14.00 | 5.75 | 1.40 |
| ☐ | 139 | Preston Ward | 2.25 | .90 | .22 |
| ☐ | 140 | Saul Rogovin | 2.25 | .90 | .22 |
| ☐ | 141 | Joe Garagiola | 12.50 | 5.00 | 1.25 |
| ☐ | 142 | Al Brazle | 2.25 | .90 | .22 |
| ☐ | 143 | Willie Jones | 2.25 | .90 | .22 |
| ☐ | 144 | Ernie Johnson | 2.25 | .90 | .22 |
| ☐ | 145 | Billy Martin | 15.00 | 6.00 | 1.50 |
| ☐ | 146 | Dick Gernert | 2.25 | .90 | .22 |
| ☐ | 147 | Joe DeMaestri | 2.25 | .90 | .22 |
| ☐ | 148 | Dale Mitchell | 2.75 | 1.10 | .27 |
| ☐ | 149 | Bob Young | 2.25 | .90 | .22 |
| ☐ | 150 | Cass Michaels | 2.25 | .90 | .22 |
| ☐ | 151 | Pat Mullin | 2.25 | .90 | .22 |
| ☐ | 152 | Mickey Vernon | 2.75 | 1.10 | .27 |
| ☐ | 153 | Whitey Lockman | 2.25 | .90 | .22 |
| ☐ | 154 | Don Newcombe | 3.50 | 1.40 | .35 |
| ☐ | 155 | Frank Thomas | 2.75 | 1.10 | .27 |
| ☐ | 156 | Rocky Bridges | 2.25 | .90 | .22 |
| ☐ | 157 | Turk Lown | 2.25 | .90 | .22 |
| ☐ | 158 | Stu Miller | 2.25 | .90 | .22 |
| ☐ | 159 | Johnny Lindell | 2.25 | .90 | .22 |
| ☐ | 160 | Danny O'Connell | 2.25 | .90 | .22 |
| ☐ | 161 | Yogi Berra | 35.00 | 14.00 | 3.50 |
| ☐ | 162 | Ted Lepcio | 2.25 | .90 | .22 |
| ☐ | 163A | Dave Philley (no mention of trade on back) | 2.75 | 1.10 | .27 |
| ☐ | 163B | Dave Philley (traded to Cleveland) | 12.00 | 5.00 | 1.20 |
| ☐ | 164 | Early Wynn | 10.00 | 4.00 | 1.00 |
| ☐ | 165 | Johnny Groth | 2.25 | .90 | .22 |
| ☐ | 166 | Sandy Consuegra | 2.25 | .90 | .22 |
| ☐ | 167 | Billy Hoeft | 2.25 | .90 | .22 |
| ☐ | 168 | Ed Fitzgerald | 2.25 | .90 | .22 |
| ☐ | 169 | Larry Jansen | 2.25 | .90 | .22 |
| ☐ | 170 | Duke Snider | 35.00 | 14.00 | 3.50 |
| ☐ | 171 | Carlos Bernier | 2.25 | .90 | .22 |
| ☐ | 172 | Andy Seminick | 2.25 | .90 | .22 |
| ☐ | 173 | Dee Fondy | 2.25 | .90 | .22 |
| ☐ | 174 | Pete Castiglione | 2.25 | .90 | .22 |
| ☐ | 175 | Mel Clark | 2.25 | .90 | .22 |
| ☐ | 176 | Vern Bickford | 2.25 | .90 | .22 |
| ☐ | 177 | Whitey Ford | 21.00 | 8.50 | 2.10 |
| ☐ | 178 | Del Wilber | 2.25 | .90 | .22 |
| ☐ | 179 | Morris Martin | 2.25 | .90 | .22 |
| ☐ | 180 | Joe Tipton | 2.25 | .90 | .22 |
| ☐ | 181 | Les Moss | 2.25 | .90 | .22 |
| ☐ | 182 | Sherman Lollar | 2.75 | 1.10 | .27 |
| ☐ | 183 | Matt Batts | 2.25 | .90 | .22 |
| ☐ | 184 | Mickey Grasso | 2.25 | .90 | .22 |
| ☐ | 185 | Daryl Spencer | 2.25 | .90 | .22 |
| ☐ | 186 | Russ Meyer | 2.25 | .90 | .22 |
| ☐ | 187 | Vernon Law | 2.75 | 1.10 | .27 |
| ☐ | 188 | Frank Smith | 2.25 | .90 | .22 |
| ☐ | 189 | Randy Jackson | 2.25 | .90 | .22 |
| ☐ | 190 | Joe Presko | 2.25 | .90 | .22 |
| ☐ | 191 | Karl Drews | 2.25 | .90 | .22 |
| ☐ | 192 | Lou Burdette | 3.50 | 1.40 | .35 |
| ☐ | 193 | Eddie Robinson | 2.25 | .90 | .22 |
| ☐ | 194 | Sid Hudson | 2.25 | .90 | .22 |
| ☐ | 195 | Bob Cain | 2.25 | .90 | .22 |
| ☐ | 196 | Bob Lemon | 10.00 | 4.00 | 1.00 |
| ☐ | 197 | Lou Kretlow | 2.25 | .90 | .22 |
| ☐ | 198 | Virgil Trucks | 2.75 | 1.10 | .27 |
| ☐ | 199 | Steve Gromek | 2.25 | .90 | .22 |
| ☐ | 200 | Conrado Marrero | 2.25 | .90 | .22 |
| ☐ | 201 | Bobby Thomson | 3.50 | 1.40 | .35 |
| ☐ | 202 | George Shuba | 2.75 | 1.10 | .27 |
| ☐ | 203 | Vic Janowicz | 2.75 | 1.10 | .27 |
| ☐ | 204 | Jackie Collum | 2.25 | .90 | .22 |
| ☐ | 205 | Hal Jeffcoat | 2.25 | .90 | .22 |
| ☐ | 206 | Steve Bilko | 2.25 | .90 | .22 |

| | | MINT | VG-E | F-G |
|---|---|---|---|---|
| ☐ 207 | Stan Lopata | 2.25 | .90 | .22 |
| ☐ 208 | Johnny Antonelli | 2.75 | 1.10 | .27 |
| ☐ 209 | Gene Woodling | 3.00 | 1.20 | .30 |
| ☐ 210 | Jim Piersall | 3.50 | 1.40 | .35 |
| ☐ 211 | Al Robertson | 2.25 | .90 | .22 |
| ☐ 212 | Owen Friend | 2.25 | .90 | .22 |
| ☐ 213 | Dick Littlefield | 2.25 | .90 | .22 |
| ☐ 214 | Ferris Fain | 2.75 | 1.10 | .27 |
| ☐ 215 | Johnny Bucha | 2.25 | .90 | .22 |
| ☐ 216 | Jerry Snyder | 2.25 | .90 | .22 |
| ☐ 217 | Henry Thompson | 2.75 | 1.10 | .27 |
| ☐ 218 | Preacher Roe | 3.50 | 1.40 | .35 |
| ☐ 219 | Hal Rice | 2.25 | .90 | .22 |
| ☐ 220 | Hobie Landrith | 2.25 | .90 | .22 |
| ☐ 221 | Frank Baumholtz | 2.25 | .90 | .22 |
| ☐ 222 | Memo Luna | 2.25 | .90 | .22 |
| ☐ 223 | Steve Ridzik | 2.25 | .90 | .22 |
| ☐ 224 | Bill Bruton | 4.00 | 1.00 | .20 |

## 1955 Bowman

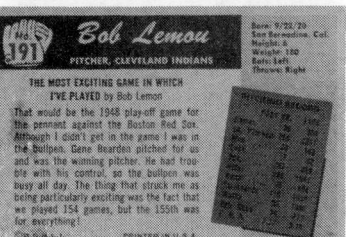

The cards in this 320 card set measure 2 1/2" by 3 3/4". The Bowman set of 1955 is known as the "TV set" because each player photograph is cleverly shown within a television set design. The set contains umpire cards, some transposed pictures (e.g., Johnsons and Bollings), an incorrect spelling for Harvey Kuenn, and a traded line for Palica (all of which are noted in the checklist below). Some three-card advertising strips exist.

| | MINT | VG-E | F-G |
|---|---|---|---|
| COMPLETE SET | 1000.00 | 400.00 | 125.00 |
| COMMON PLAYER (1-96) | 1.25 | .50 | .12 |
| COMMON PLAYER (97-224) | .90 | .36 | .09 |
| COMMON PLAYER (225-320) | 3.50 | 1.40 | .35 |
| COMMON UMPIRES (225-320) | 6.00 | 2.40 | .60 |

| | | MINT | VG-E | F-G |
|---|---|---|---|---|
| ☐ | 1 Hoyt Wilhelm | 30.00 | 5.00 | 1.00 |
| ☐ | 2 Alvin Dark | 1.75 | .70 | .17 |
| ☐ | 3 Joe Coleman | 1.25 | .50 | .12 |
| ☐ | 4 Eddie Waitkus | 1.25 | .50 | .12 |
| ☐ | 5 Jim Robertson | 1.25 | .50 | .12 |
| ☐ | 6 Pete Suder | 1.25 | .50 | .12 |
| ☐ | 7 Gene Baker | 1.25 | .50 | .12 |
| ☐ | 8 Warren Hacker | 1.25 | .50 | .12 |
| ☐ | 9 Gil McDougald | 2.50 | 1.00 | .25 |
| ☐ | 10 Phil Rizzuto | 13.00 | 5.25 | 1.30 |
| ☐ | 11 Billy Bruton | 1.25 | .50 | .12 |
| ☐ | 12 Andy Pafko | 1.25 | .50 | .12 |
| ☐ | 13 Clyde Vollmer | 1.25 | .50 | .12 |
| ☐ | 14 Gus Keriazakos | 1.25 | .50 | .12 |
| ☐ | 15 Frank Sullivan | 1.25 | .50 | .12 |
| ☐ | 16 Jim Piersall | 2.00 | .80 | .20 |
| ☐ | 17 Del Ennis | 1.50 | .60 | .15 |
| ☐ | 18 Stan Lopata | 1.25 | .50 | .12 |
| ☐ | 19 Bobby Avila | 1.25 | .50 | .12 |
| ☐ | 20 Al Smith | 1.25 | .50 | .12 |
| ☐ | 21 Don Hoak | 1.25 | .50 | .12 |
| ☐ | 22 Roy Campanella | 27.00 | 11.00 | 2.70 |
| ☐ | 23 Al Kaline | 16.00 | 6.50 | 1.60 |
| ☐ | 24 Al Aber | 1.25 | .50 | .12 |
| ☐ | 25 Minnie Minoso | 2.50 | 1.00 | .25 |
| ☐ | 26 Virgil Trucks | 1.25 | .50 | .12 |
| ☐ | 27 Preston Ward | 1.25 | .50 | .12 |
| ☐ | 28 Dick Cole | 1.25 | .50 | .12 |
| ☐ | 29 Red Schoendienst | 2.00 | .80 | .20 |
| ☐ | 30 Bill Sarni | 1.25 | .50 | .12 |
| ☐ | 31 Johnny Temple | 1.50 | .60 | .15 |
| ☐ | 32 Wally Post | 1.25 | .50 | .12 |
| ☐ | 33 Nelson Fox | 3.50 | 1.40 | .35 |
| ☐ | 34 Clint Courtney | 1.25 | .50 | .12 |
| ☐ | 35 Bill Tuttle | 1.25 | .50 | .12 |
| ☐ | 36 Wayne Belardi | 1.25 | .50 | .12 |
| ☐ | 37 Pee Wee Reese | 16.00 | 6.50 | 1.60 |
| ☐ | 38 Early Wynn | 7.50 | 3.00 | .75 |
| ☐ | 39 Bob Darnell | 1.25 | .50 | .12 |
| ☐ | 40 Vic Wertz | 1.25 | .50 | .12 |
| ☐ | 41 Mel Clark | 1.25 | .50 | .12 |
| ☐ | 42 Bob Greenwood | 1.25 | .50 | .12 |
| ☐ | 43 Bob Buhl | 1.25 | .50 | .12 |
| ☐ | 44 Danny O'Connell | 1.25 | .50 | .12 |
| ☐ | 45 Tom Umphlett | 1.25 | .50 | .12 |
| ☐ | 46 Mickey Vernon | 1.50 | .60 | .15 |
| ☐ | 47 Sammy White | 1.25 | .50 | .12 |
| ☐ | 48A Milt Bolling ERR (photo actually Frank Bolling) | 1.50 | .60 | .15 |
| ☐ | 48B Milt Bolling COR | 6.00 | 2.40 | .60 |
| ☐ | 49 Jim Greengrass | 1.25 | .50 | .12 |
| ☐ | 50 Hobie Landrith | 1.25 | .50 | .12 |
| ☐ | 51 Elvin Tappe | 1.25 | .50 | .12 |
| ☐ | 52 Hal Rice | 1.25 | .50 | .12 |
| ☐ | 53 Alex Kellner | 1.25 | .50 | .12 |
| ☐ | 54 Don Bollweg | 1.25 | .50 | .12 |
| ☐ | 55 Cal Abrams | 1.25 | .50 | .12 |
| ☐ | 56 Billy Cox | 1.50 | .60 | .15 |
| ☐ | 57 Bob Friend | 1.50 | .60 | .15 |
| ☐ | 58 Frank Thomas | 1.50 | .60 | .15 |
| ☐ | 59 Whitey Ford | 14.00 | 5.75 | 1.40 |
| ☐ | 60 Enos Slaughter | 7.50 | 3.00 | .75 |
| ☐ | 61 Paul LaPalme | 1.25 | .50 | .12 |
| ☐ | 62 Royce Lint | 1.25 | .50 | .12 |
| ☐ | 63 Irv Noren | 1.25 | .50 | .12 |
| ☐ | 64 Curt Simmons | 1.50 | .60 | .15 |
| ☐ | 65 Don Zimmer | 2.00 | .80 | .20 |
| ☐ | 66 George Shuba | 1.50 | .60 | .15 |
| ☐ | 67 Don Larsen | 2.50 | 1.00 | .25 |
| ☐ | 68 Elston Howard | 6.00 | 2.40 | .60 |
| ☐ | 69 Bill Hunter | 1.25 | .50 | .12 |
| ☐ | 70 Lou Burdette | 2.00 | .80 | .20 |
| ☐ | 71 Dave Jolly | 1.25 | .50 | .12 |
| ☐ | 72 Chet Nichols | 1.25 | .50 | .12 |
| ☐ | 73 Eddie Yost | 1.25 | .50 | .12 |
| ☐ | 74 Jerry Snyder | 1.25 | .50 | .12 |
| ☐ | 75 Brooks Lawrence | 1.25 | .50 | .12 |
| ☐ | 76 Tom Poholsky | 1.25 | .50 | .12 |
| ☐ | 77 Jim McDonald | 1.25 | .50 | .12 |
| ☐ | 78 Gil Coan | 1.25 | .50 | .12 |
| ☐ | 79 Willie Miranda | 1.25 | .50 | .12 |
| ☐ | 80 Lou Limmer | 1.25 | .50 | .12 |
| ☐ | 81 Bob Morgan | 1.25 | .50 | .12 |
| ☐ | 82 Lee Walls | 1.25 | .50 | .12 |
| ☐ | 83 Max Surkont | 1.25 | .50 | .12 |
| ☐ | 84 George Freese | 1.25 | .50 | .12 |
| ☐ | 85 Cass Michaels | 1.25 | .50 | .12 |
| ☐ | 86 Ted Gray | 1.25 | .50 | .12 |
| ☐ | 87 Randy Jackson | 1.25 | .50 | .12 |
| ☐ | 88 Steve Bilko | 1.25 | .50 | .12 |
| ☐ | 89 Lou Boudreau MGR | 7.00 | 2.80 | .70 |
| ☐ | 90 Art Dittmar | 1.25 | .50 | .12 |
| ☐ | 91 Dick Marlowe | 1.25 | .50 | .12 |
| ☐ | 92 George Zuverink | 1.25 | .50 | .12 |
| ☐ | 93 Andy Seminick | 1.25 | .50 | .12 |
| ☐ | 94 Hank Thompson | 1.50 | .60 | .15 |
| ☐ | 95 Sal Maglie | 2.00 | .80 | .20 |
| ☐ | 96 Ray Narleski | 1.25 | .50 | .12 |
| ☐ | 97 Johnny Podres | 2.50 | 1.00 | .25 |
| ☐ | 98 Jim Gilliam | 2.50 | 1.00 | .25 |
| ☐ | 99 Jerry Coleman | 1.25 | .50 | .12 |
| ☐ | 100 Tom Morgan | .90 | .36 | .09 |
| ☐ | 101A Don Johnson ERR (photo actually Ernie Johnson) | 1.00 | .40 | .10 |
| ☐ | 101B Don Johnson COR | 4.50 | 1.80 | .45 |
| ☐ | 102 Bobby Thomson | 2.50 | 1.00 | .25 |

| | | | | |
|---|---|---|---|---|
| ☐ 103 | Eddie Mathews | 8.50 | 3.50 | .85 |
| ☐ 104 | Bob Porterfield | .90 | .36 | .09 |
| ☐ 105 | Johnny Schmitz | .90 | .36 | .09 |
| ☐ 106 | Del Rice | .90 | .36 | .09 |
| ☐ 107 | Solly Hemus | .90 | .36 | .09 |
| ☐ 108 | Lou Kretlow | .90 | .36 | .09 |
| ☐ 109 | Vern Stephens | 1.00 | .40 | .10 |
| ☐ 110 | Bob Miller | .90 | .36 | .09 |
| ☐ 111 | Steve Ridzik | .90 | .36 | .09 |
| ☐ 112 | Granny Hamner | .90 | .36 | .09 |
| ☐ 113 | Bob Hall | .90 | .36 | .09 |
| ☐ 114 | Vic Janowicz | 1.00 | .40 | .10 |
| ☐ 115 | Roger Bowman | .90 | .36 | .09 |
| ☐ 116 | Sandy Consuegra | .90 | .36 | .09 |
| ☐ 117 | Johnny Groth | .90 | .36 | .09 |
| ☐ 118 | Bobby Adams | .90 | .36 | .09 |
| ☐ 119 | Joe Astroth | .90 | .36 | .09 |
| ☐ 120 | Ed Burtschy | .90 | .36 | .09 |
| ☐ 121 | Rufus Crawford | .90 | .36 | .09 |
| ☐ 122 | Al Corwin | .90 | .36 | .09 |
| ☐ 123 | Marv Grissom | .90 | .36 | .09 |
| ☐ 124 | Johnny Antonelli | 1.00 | .40 | .10 |
| ☐ 125 | Paul Giel | .90 | .36 | .09 |
| ☐ 126 | Billy Goodman | 1.00 | .40 | .10 |
| ☐ 127 | Hank Majeski | .90 | .36 | .09 |
| ☐ 128 | Mike Garcia | 1.00 | .40 | .10 |
| ☐ 129 | Hal Naragon | .90 | .36 | .09 |
| ☐ 130 | Richie Ashburn | 3.50 | 1.40 | .35 |
| ☐ 131 | Willard Marshall | .90 | .36 | .09 |
| ☐ 132A | Harvey Kueen ERR (sic, Kuenn) | 2.00 | .80 | .20 |
| ☐ 132B | Harvey Kuenn COR | 6.00 | 2.40 | .60 |
| ☐ 133 | Charles King | .90 | .36 | .09 |
| ☐ 134 | Bob Feller | 18.00 | 7.25 | 1.80 |
| ☐ 135 | Lloyd Merriman | .90 | .36 | .09 |
| ☐ 136 | Rocky Bridges | .90 | .36 | .09 |
| ☐ 137 | Bob Talbot | .90 | .36 | .09 |
| ☐ 138 | Davey Williams | 1.00 | .40 | .10 |
| ☐ 139 | Shantz Brothers Wilmer and Bobby | 1.75 | .70 | .17 |
| ☐ 140 | Bobby Shantz | 1.50 | .60 | .15 |
| ☐ 141 | Wes Westrum | .90 | .36 | .09 |
| ☐ 142 | Rudy Regalado | .90 | .36 | .09 |
| ☐ 143 | Don Newcombe | 3.50 | 1.40 | .35 |
| ☐ 144 | Art Houtteman | .90 | .36 | .09 |
| ☐ 145 | Bob Nieman | .90 | .36 | .09 |
| ☐ 146 | Don Liddle | .90 | .36 | .09 |
| ☐ 147 | Sam Mele | .90 | .36 | .09 |
| ☐ 148 | Bob Chakales | .90 | .36 | .09 |
| ☐ 149 | Cloyd Boyer | 1.00 | .40 | .10 |
| ☐ 150 | Bill Klaus | .90 | .36 | .09 |
| ☐ 151 | Jim Brideweser | .90 | .36 | .09 |
| ☐ 152 | Johnny Klippstein | .90 | .36 | .09 |
| ☐ 153 | Eddie Robinson | .90 | .36 | .09 |
| ☐ 154 | Frank Lary | 1.25 | .50 | .12 |
| ☐ 155 | Gerry Staley | .90 | .36 | .09 |
| ☐ 156 | Jim Hughes | .90 | .36 | .09 |
| ☐ 157A | Ernie Johnson ERR (photo actually Don Johnson) | 1.00 | .40 | .10 |
| ☐ 157B | Ernie Johnson COR | 4.50 | 1.80 | .45 |
| ☐ 158 | Gil Hodges | 9.00 | 3.75 | .90 |
| ☐ 159 | Harry Byrd | .90 | .36 | .09 |
| ☐ 160 | Bill Skowron | 2.50 | 1.00 | .25 |
| ☐ 161 | Matt Batts | .90 | .36 | .09 |
| ☐ 162 | Charlie Maxwell | .90 | .36 | .09 |
| ☐ 163 | Sid Gordon | .90 | .36 | .09 |
| ☐ 164 | Toby Atwell | .90 | .36 | .09 |
| ☐ 165 | Maurice McDermott | .90 | .36 | .09 |
| ☐ 166 | Jim Busby | .90 | .36 | .09 |
| ☐ 167 | Bob Grim | 1.25 | .50 | .12 |
| ☐ 168 | Yogi Berra | 25.00 | 10.00 | 2.50 |
| ☐ 169 | Carl Furillo | 3.00 | 1.20 | .30 |
| ☐ 170 | Carl Erskine | 2.50 | 1.00 | .25 |
| ☐ 171 | Robin Roberts | 7.00 | 2.80 | .70 |
| ☐ 172 | Willie Jones | .90 | .36 | .09 |
| ☐ 173 | Chico Carrasquel | .90 | .36 | .09 |
| ☐ 174 | Sherman Lollar | 1.00 | .40 | .10 |
| ☐ 175 | Wilmer Shantz | .90 | .36 | .09 |
| ☐ 176 | Joe DeMaestri | .90 | .36 | .09 |
| ☐ 177 | Willard Nixon | .90 | .36 | .09 |
| ☐ 178 | Tom Brewer | .90 | .36 | .09 |
| ☐ 179 | Hank Aaron | 50.00 | 20.00 | 5.00 |
| ☐ 180 | Johnny Logan | 1.00 | .40 | .10 |
| ☐ 181 | Eddie Miksis | .90 | .36 | .09 |
| ☐ 182 | Bob Rush | .90 | .36 | .09 |
| ☐ 183 | Ray Katt | .90 | .36 | .09 |
| ☐ 184 | Willie Mays | 50.00 | 20.00 | 5.00 |
| ☐ 185 | Vic Raschi | 1.50 | .60 | .15 |
| ☐ 186 | Alex Grammas | .90 | .36 | .09 |
| ☐ 187 | Fred Hatfield | .90 | .36 | .09 |
| ☐ 188 | Ned Garver | .90 | .36 | .09 |
| ☐ 189 | Jack Collum | .90 | .36 | .09 |
| ☐ 190 | Fred Baczewski | .90 | .36 | .09 |
| ☐ 191 | Bob Lemon | 7.50 | 3.00 | .75 |
| ☐ 192 | George Strickland | .90 | .36 | .09 |
| ☐ 193 | Howie Judson | .90 | .36 | .09 |
| ☐ 194 | Joe Nuxhall | 1.00 | .40 | .10 |
| ☐ 195A | Erv Palica (without trade) | 1.00 | .40 | .10 |
| ☐ 195B | Erv Palica (with trade) | 8.00 | 3.25 | .80 |
| ☐ 196 | Russ Meyer | .90 | .36 | .09 |
| ☐ 197 | Ralph Kiner | 8.00 | 3.25 | .80 |
| ☐ 198 | Dave Pope | .90 | .36 | .09 |
| ☐ 199 | Vernon Law | 1.00 | .40 | .10 |
| ☐ 200 | Dick Littlefield | .90 | .36 | .09 |
| ☐ 201 | Allie Reynolds | 3.00 | 1.20 | .30 |
| ☐ 202 | Mickey Mantle | 120.00 | 50.00 | 12.00 |
| ☐ 203 | Steve Gromek | .90 | .36 | .09 |
| ☐ 204A | Frank Bolling ERR (photo actually Milt Bolling) | 1.00 | .40 | .10 |
| ☐ 204B | Frank Bolling COR | 4.50 | 1.80 | .45 |
| ☐ 205 | Rip Repulski | .90 | .36 | .09 |
| ☐ 206 | Ralph Beard | .90 | .36 | .09 |
| ☐ 207 | Frank Shea | .90 | .36 | .09 |
| ☐ 208 | Eddy Fitzgerald | .90 | .36 | .09 |
| ☐ 209 | Smokey Burgess | 1.00 | .40 | .10 |
| ☐ 210 | Earl Torgeson | .90 | .36 | .09 |
| ☐ 211 | Sonny Dixon | .90 | .36 | .09 |
| ☐ 212 | Jack Dittmer | .90 | .36 | .09 |
| ☐ 213 | George Kell | 6.50 | 2.60 | .65 |
| ☐ 214 | Billy Pierce | 1.50 | .60 | .15 |
| ☐ 215 | Bob Kuzava | .90 | .36 | .09 |
| ☐ 216 | Preacher Roe | 2.00 | .80 | .20 |
| ☐ 217 | Del Crandall | 1.00 | .40 | .10 |
| ☐ 218 | Joe Adcock | 1.50 | .60 | .15 |
| ☐ 219 | Whitey Lockman | 1.00 | .40 | .10 |
| ☐ 220 | Jim Hearn | .90 | .36 | .09 |
| ☐ 221 | Hector Brown | .90 | .36 | .09 |
| ☐ 222 | Russ Kemmerer | .90 | .36 | .09 |
| ☐ 223 | Hal Jeffcoat | .90 | .36 | .09 |
| ☐ 224 | Dee Fondy | .90 | .36 | .09 |
| ☐ 225 | Paul Richards | 4.00 | 1.60 | .40 |
| ☐ 226 | W. McKinley UMP | 6.00 | 2.40 | .60 |
| ☐ 227 | Frank Baumholtz | 3.50 | 1.40 | .35 |
| ☐ 228 | John Phillips | 3.50 | 1.40 | .35 |
| ☐ 229 | Jim Brosnan | 4.00 | 1.60 | .40 |
| ☐ 230 | Al Brazle | 3.50 | 1.40 | .35 |
| ☐ 231 | Jim Konstanty | 4.00 | 1.60 | .40 |
| ☐ 232 | Birdie Tebbetts | 4.00 | 1.60 | .40 |
| ☐ 233 | Bill Serena | 3.50 | 1.40 | .35 |
| ☐ 234 | Dick Bartell | 3.50 | 1.40 | .35 |
| ☐ 235 | J. Paparella UMP | 6.00 | 2.40 | .60 |
| ☐ 236 | Murry Dickson | 3.50 | 1.40 | .35 |
| ☐ 237 | Johnny Wyrostek | 3.50 | 1.40 | .35 |
| ☐ 238 | Eddie Stanky | 5.00 | 2.00 | .50 |
| ☐ 239 | Edwin Rommel UMP | 6.00 | 2.40 | .60 |
| ☐ 240 | Billy Loes | 5.00 | 2.00 | .50 |
| ☐ 241 | Johnny Pesky | 4.00 | 1.60 | .40 |
| ☐ 242 | Ernie Banks | 80.00 | 32.00 | 8.00 |
| ☐ 243 | Gus Bell | 4.00 | 1.60 | .40 |
| ☐ 244 | Duane Pillette | 3.50 | 1.40 | .35 |
| ☐ 245 | Bill Miller | 3.50 | 1.40 | .35 |
| ☐ 246 | Hank Bauer | 8.50 | 3.50 | .85 |
| ☐ 247 | Dutch Leonard | 3.50 | 1.40 | .35 |
| ☐ 248 | Harry Dorish | 3.50 | 1.40 | .35 |
| ☐ 249 | Billy Gardner | 4.50 | 1.80 | .45 |
| ☐ 250 | Larry Napp UMP | 6.00 | 2.40 | .60 |
| ☐ 251 | Stan Jok | 3.50 | 1.40 | .35 |
| ☐ 252 | Roy Smalley | 3.50 | 1.40 | .35 |
| ☐ 253 | Jim Wilson | 3.50 | 1.40 | .35 |
| ☐ 254 | Bennett Flowers | 3.50 | 1.40 | .35 |
| ☐ 255 | Pete Runnels | 4.00 | 1.60 | .40 |
| ☐ 256 | Owen Friend | 3.50 | 1.40 | .35 |
| ☐ 257 | Tom Alston | 3.50 | 1.40 | .35 |
| ☐ 258 | John Stevens UMP | 6.00 | 2.40 | .60 |
| ☐ 259 | Don Mossi | 5.00 | 2.00 | .50 |
| ☐ 260 | Edwin Hurley UMP | 6.00 | 2.40 | .60 |
| ☐ 261 | Walt Moryn | 3.50 | 1.40 | .35 |
| ☐ 262 | Jim Lemon | 4.00 | 1.60 | .40 |
| ☐ 263 | Eddie Joost | 3.50 | 1.40 | .35 |
| ☐ 264 | Bill Henry | 3.50 | 1.40 | .35 |
| ☐ 265 | Albert Barlick UMP | 6.00 | 2.40 | .60 |
| ☐ 266 | Mike Fornieles | 3.50 | 1.40 | .35 |
| ☐ 267 | Jim Honochick UMP | 18.00 | 7.25 | 1.80 |
| ☐ 268 | Roy Lee Hawes | 3.50 | 1.40 | .35 |
| ☐ 269 | Joe Amalfitano | 3.50 | 1.40 | .35 |
| ☐ 270 | Chico Fernandez | 3.50 | 1.40 | .35 |
| ☐ 271 | Bob Hooper | 3.50 | 1.40 | .35 |
| ☐ 272 | John Flaherty UMP | 6.00 | 2.40 | .60 |
| ☐ 273 | Bubba Church | 3.50 | 1.40 | .35 |
| ☐ 274 | Jim Delsing | 3.50 | 1.40 | .35 |
| ☐ 275 | William Grieve UMP | 6.00 | 2.40 | .60 |
| ☐ 276 | Ike Delock | 3.50 | 1.40 | .35 |

| | | | |
|---|---|---|---|
| ☐ 277 Ed Runge UMP | 6.00 | 2.40 | .60 |
| ☐ 278 Charles Neal | 4.50 | 1.80 | .45 |
| ☐ 279 Hank Soar UMP | 6.00 | 2.40 | .60 |
| ☐ 280 Clyde McCullough | 3.50 | 1.40 | .35 |
| ☐ 281 Charles Berry UMP | 6.00 | 2.40 | .60 |
| ☐ 282 Phil Cavarretta | 4.00 | 1.60 | .40 |
| ☐ 283 Nestor Chylak UMP | 6.00 | 2.40 | .60 |
| ☐ 284 Bill Jackowski UMP | 6.00 | 2.40 | .60 |
| ☐ 285 Walt Dropo | 4.00 | 1.60 | .40 |
| ☐ 286 Frank Secory UMP | 6.00 | 2.40 | .60 |
| ☐ 287 Ron Mrozinski | 3.50 | 1.40 | .35 |
| ☐ 288 Dick Smith | 3.50 | 1.40 | .35 |
| ☐ 289 Arthur Gore UMP | 6.00 | 2.40 | .60 |
| ☐ 290 Hershell Freeman | 3.50 | 1.40 | .35 |
| ☐ 291 Frank Dascoli UMP | 6.00 | 2.40 | .60 |
| ☐ 292 Marv Blaylock | 3.50 | 1.40 | .35 |
| ☐ 293 Thomas Gorman UMP | 6.00 | 2.40 | .60 |
| ☐ 294 Wally Moses | 4.00 | 1.60 | .40 |
| ☐ 295 Lee Ballanfant UMP | 6.00 | 2.40 | .60 |
| ☐ 296 Bill Virdon | 12.00 | 5.00 | 1.20 |
| ☐ 297 Dusty Boggess UMP | 6.00 | 2.40 | .60 |
| ☐ 298 Charlie Grimm | 4.50 | 1.80 | .45 |
| ☐ 299 Lon Warneke UMP | 6.00 | 2.40 | .60 |
| ☐ 300 Tommy Byrne | 4.00 | 1.60 | .40 |
| ☐ 301 William Engeln UMP | 6.00 | 2.40 | .60 |
| ☐ 302 Frank Malzone | 5.00 | 2.00 | .50 |
| ☐ 303 Jocko Conlan UMP | 18.00 | 7.25 | 1.80 |
| ☐ 304 Harry Chiti | 3.50 | 1.40 | .35 |
| ☐ 305 Frank Umont UMP | 6.00 | 2.40 | .60 |
| ☐ 306 Bob Cerv | 4.50 | 1.80 | .45 |
| ☐ 307 Babe Pinelli UMP | 7.50 | 3.00 | .75 |
| ☐ 308 Al Lopez MGR | 12.00 | 5.00 | 1.20 |
| ☐ 309 Hal Dixon UMP | 6.00 | 2.40 | .60 |
| ☐ 310 Ken Lehman | 3.50 | 1.40 | .35 |
| ☐ 311 Lawrence Goetz UMP | 6.00 | 2.40 | .60 |
| ☐ 312 Bill Wight | 3.50 | 1.40 | .35 |
| ☐ 313 Augie Donatelli UMP | 9.00 | 3.75 | .90 |
| ☐ 314 Dale Mitchell | 4.50 | 1.80 | .45 |
| ☐ 315 Cal Hubbard UMP | 18.00 | 7.25 | 1.80 |
| ☐ 316 Marion Fricano | 3.50 | 1.40 | .35 |
| ☐ 317 William Summers UMP | 6.00 | 2.40 | .60 |
| ☐ 318 Sid Hudson | 3.50 | 1.40 | .35 |
| ☐ 319 Albert Schroll | 3.50 | 1.40 | .35 |
| ☐ 320 George Susce Jr. | 6.00 | 1.50 | .30 |

alphabetically by name and the New York players are numbered 26-37 similarly.

| | | MINT | VG-E | F-G |
|---|---|---|---|---|
| COMPLETE SET | | 4400.00 | 1800.00 | 450.00 |
| COMMON PLAYERS | | 70.00 | 28.00 | 7.00 |
| ☐ 1 | Jim Busby | 70.00 | 28.00 | 7.00 |
| ☐ 2 | Tommy Byrne | 70.00 | 28.00 | 7.00 |
| ☐ 3 | Sonny Dixon | 70.00 | 28.00 | 7.00 |
| ☐ 4 | Ed Fitzgerald | 70.00 | 28.00 | 7.00 |
| ☐ 5 | Mickey Grasso | 70.00 | 28.00 | 7.00 |
| ☐ 6 | Mel Hoderlein | 70.00 | 28.00 | 7.00 |
| ☐ 7 | Jackie Jensen | 120.00 | 50.00 | 12.00 |
| ☐ 8 | Connie Marrero | 70.00 | 28.00 | 7.00 |
| ☐ 9 | Carmen Mauro | 70.00 | 28.00 | 7.00 |
| ☐ 10 | Walt Masterson | 70.00 | 28.00 | 7.00 |
| ☐ 11 | Mickey McDermott | 70.00 | 28.00 | 7.00 |
| ☐ 12 | Bob Oldis | 70.00 | 28.00 | 7.00 |
| ☐ 13 | Bob Porterfield | 70.00 | 28.00 | 7.00 |
| ☐ 14 | Pete Runnels | 100.00 | 40.00 | 10.00 |
| ☐ 15 | Johnny Schmitz | 70.00 | 28.00 | 7.00 |
| ☐ 16 | Angel Scull | 70.00 | 28.00 | 7.00 |
| ☐ 17 | Spec Shea | 70.00 | 28.00 | 7.00 |
| ☐ 18 | Chuck Stobbs | 70.00 | 28.00 | 7.00 |
| ☐ 19 | Wayne Terwilliger | 70.00 | 28.00 | 7.00 |
| ☐ 20 | Joe Tipton | 70.00 | 28.00 | 7.00 |
| ☐ 21 | Tom Umphlett | 70.00 | 28.00 | 7.00 |
| ☐ 22 | Mickey Vernon | 100.00 | 40.00 | 10.00 |
| ☐ 23 | Clyde Vollmer | 70.00 | 28.00 | 7.00 |
| ☐ 24 | Gene Werbil | 70.00 | 28.00 | 7.00 |
| ☐ 25 | Eddie Yost | 70.00 | 28.00 | 7.00 |
| ☐ 26 | Hank Bauer | 90.00 | 36.00 | 9.00 |
| ☐ 27 | Carl Erskine | 90.00 | 36.00 | 9.00 |
| ☐ 28 | Gil Hodges | 150.00 | 60.00 | 15.00 |
| ☐ 29 | Monte Irvin | 125.00 | 50.00 | 12.50 |
| ☐ 30 | Whitey Lockman | 70.00 | 28.00 | 7.00 |
| ☐ 31 | Mickey Mantle | 1000.00 | 400.00 | 100.00 |
| ☐ 32 | Willie Mays | 650.00 | 260.00 | 65.00 |
| ☐ 33 | Gil McDougald | 90.00 | 36.00 | 9.00 |
| ☐ 34 | Don Mueller | 70.00 | 28.00 | 7.00 |
| ☐ 35 | Don Newcombe | 90.00 | 36.00 | 9.00 |
| ☐ 36 | Phil Rizzuto | 150.00 | 60.00 | 15.00 |
| ☐ 37 | Duke Snider | 275.00 | 110.00 | 27.00 |

## 1953-54 Briggs

GIL HODGES

## 1977 Burger King Yankees

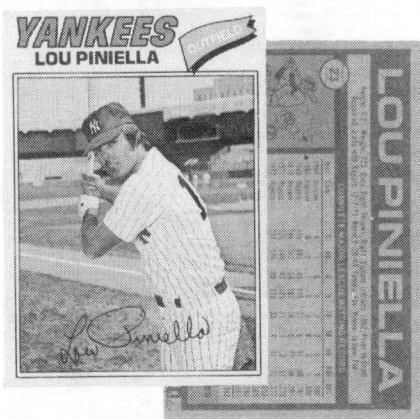

The cards in this 37 card set measure 2 1/4" by 3 1/2". The 1953-54 Briggs Hot Dog set of color cards contains 25 Senators and 12 known players from the Dodgers, Yankees, and Giants. They were issued in two card panels in the Washington, D.C. area as part of the hot dog package itself. The cards are unnumbered and are printed on waxed cardboard, and the style of the Senator cards differs from that of the Ney York players. The latter appear in poses which also exist in the Dan Dee and Stahl Meyer card sets. The ACC designation is F154. In the checklist below the Washington players are numbered 1-25

The cards in this 24 card set measure 2 1/2" by 3 1/2". The cards in this set marked with an asterisk have different poses than those cards in the regular 1977 Topps set. The checklist card is unnumbered and the Piniella card was issued subsequent to the original printing.

| | MINT | VG-E | F-G |
|---|---|---|---|
| COMPLETE SET | 26.00 | 10.00 | 2.50 |
| COMMON PLAYER (1-24) | .30 | .12 | .03 |
| ☐ 1 Yankees Team Billy Martin MGR | .75 | .30 | .07 |

| | | MINT | VG-E | F-G |
|---|---|---|---|---|
| ☐ 2 | Thurman Munson * .......... | 3.00 | 1.20 | .30 |
| ☐ 3 | Fran Healy ...................... | .30 | .12 | .03 |
| ☐ 4 | Jim Hunter ...................... | 1.50 | .60 | .15 |
| ☐ 5 | Ed Figueroa .................... | .30 | .12 | .03 |
| ☐ 6 | Don Gullett * .................. | .40 | .16 | .04 |
| ☐ 7 | Mike Torrez * .................. | .40 | .16 | .04 |
| ☐ 8 | Ken Holtzman .................. | .30 | .12 | .03 |
| ☐ 9 | Dick Tidrow .................... | .30 | .12 | .03 |
| ☐ 10 | Sparky Lyle .................... | .50 | .20 | .05 |
| ☐ 11 | Ron Guidry ...................... | 1.50 | .60 | .15 |
| ☐ 12 | Chris Chambliss ............ | .40 | .16 | .04 |
| ☐ 13 | Willie Randolph * .......... | .60 | .24 | .06 |
| ☐ 14 | Bucky Dent * .................. | .40 | .16 | .04 |
| ☐ 15 | Graig Nettles * .............. | 1.00 | .40 | .10 |
| ☐ 16 | Fred Stanley .................. | .30 | .12 | .03 |
| ☐ 17 | Reggie Jackson .............. | 3.00 | 1.20 | .30 |
| ☐ 18 | Mickey Rivers ................ | .40 | .16 | .04 |
| ☐ 19 | Roy White ...................... | .30 | .12 | .03 |
| ☐ 20 | Jim Wynn ........................ | .30 | .12 | .03 |
| ☐ 21 | Paul Blair * .................... | .40 | .16 | .04 |
| ☐ 22 | Carlos May * .................. | .30 | .12 | .03 |
| ☐ 23 | Lou Piniella .................... | 16.00 | 6.50 | 1.60 |
| ☐ 24 | Checklist card ................ (unnumbered) | .10 | .01 | .00 |

## 1978 Burger King Astros

JESUS ALOU

The cards in this 23 card set measure 2 1/2" by 3 1/2". Released in local Houston Burger King outlets during the 1978 season, this Houston Astros series contains the standard 22 numbered player cards and one unnumbered checklist. The player poses found to differ from the regular Topps issue are marked with astericks.

| | | MINT | VG-E | F-G |
|---|---|---|---|---|
| COMPLETE SET ...................... | | 10.00 | 4.00 | 1.00 |
| COMMON PLAYER (1-23) .......... | | .30 | .12 | .03 |
| ☐ 1 | Bill Virdon MGR .............. | .75 | .30 | .07 |
| ☐ 2 | Joe Ferguson .................. | .30 | .12 | .03 |
| ☐ 3 | Ed Herrmann .................. | .30 | .12 | .03 |
| ☐ 4 | J.R. Richard .................... | 1.00 | .40 | .10 |
| ☐ 5 | Joe Niekro ...................... | 1.00 | .40 | .10 |
| ☐ 6 | Floyd Bannister .............. | 1.00 | .40 | .10 |
| ☐ 7 | Joaquin Andujar ............ | 1.00 | .40 | .10 |
| ☐ 8 | Ken Forsch ...................... | .40 | .16 | .04 |
| ☐ 9 | Mark Lemongello ............ | .30 | .12 | .03 |
| ☐ 10 | Joe Sambito .................... | .50 | .20 | .05 |
| ☐ 11 | Gene Pentz ...................... | .30 | .12 | .03 |
| ☐ 12 | Bob Watson .................... | .50 | .20 | .05 |
| ☐ 13 | Julio Gonzales ................ | .30 | .12 | .03 |
| ☐ 14 | Enos Cabell .................... | .40 | .16 | .04 |
| ☐ 15 | Roger Metzger ................ | .30 | .12 | .03 |
| ☐ 16 | Art Howe ........................ | .30 | .12 | .03 |
| ☐ 17 | Jose Cruz ........................ | 1.00 | .40 | .10 |
| ☐ 18 | Cesar Cedeno .................. | .75 | .30 | .07 |
| ☐ 19 | Terry Puhl ...................... | .40 | .16 | .04 |
| ☐ 20 | Wilbur Howard ................ | .30 | .12 | .03 |
| ☐ 21 | Dave Bergman * ............ | .40 | .16 | .04 |
| ☐ 22 | Jesus Alou * .................. | .40 | .16 | .04 |
| ☐ 23 | Checklist card .................. (unnumbered) | .05 | .01 | .00 |

## 1978 Burger King Rangers

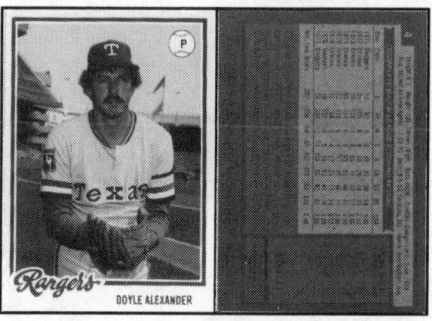

DOYLE ALEXANDER

The cards in this 23 card set measure 2 1/2" by 3 1/2". This set of 22 numbered player cards (featuring the Texas Rangers) and one unnumbered checklist was issued regionally by Burger King in 1978. Astericks denote poses different from those found in the regular Topps cards of this year.

| | | MINT | VG-E | F-G |
|---|---|---|---|---|
| COMPLETE SET ...................... | | 10.00 | 4.00 | 1.00 |
| COMMON PLAYER (1-23) .......... | | .30 | .12 | .03 |
| ☐ 1 | Billy Hunter MGR .............. | .30 | .12 | .03 |
| ☐ 2 | Jim Sundberg .................... | .60 | .24 | .06 |
| ☐ 3 | John Ellis ........................ | .30 | .12 | .03 |
| ☐ 4 | Doyle Alexander ................ | .50 | .20 | .05 |
| ☐ 5 | Jon Matlack * .................. | .60 | .24 | .06 |
| ☐ 6 | Dock Ellis ........................ | .30 | .12 | .03 |
| ☐ 7 | Doc Medich ...................... | .30 | .12 | .03 |
| ☐ 8 | Fergie Jenkins * .............. | 1.50 | .60 | .15 |
| ☐ 9 | Len Barker ...................... | .40 | .16 | .04 |
| ☐ 10 | Reggie Cleveland * .......... | .30 | .12 | .03 |
| ☐ 11 | Mike Hargrove .................. | .50 | .20 | .05 |
| ☐ 12 | Bump Wills ...................... | .40 | .16 | .04 |
| ☐ 13 | Toby Harrah .................... | .75 | .30 | .07 |
| ☐ 14 | Bert Campaneris .............. | .50 | .20 | .05 |
| ☐ 15 | Sandy Alomar .................. | .30 | .12 | .03 |
| ☐ 16 | Kurt Bevacqua ................ | .30 | .12 | .03 |
| ☐ 17 | Al Oliver * ...................... | 1.00 | .40 | .10 |
| ☐ 18 | Juan Beniquez ................ | .40 | .16 | .04 |
| ☐ 19 | Claudell Washington ........ | .75 | .30 | .07 |
| ☐ 20 | Richie Zisk ...................... | .50 | .20 | .05 |
| ☐ 21 | John Lowenstein * .......... | .40 | .16 | .04 |
| ☐ 22 | Bobby Thompson * .......... | .30 | .12 | .03 |
| ☐ 23 | Checklist card .................. (unnumbered) | .05 | .01 | .00 |

## 1978 Burger King Tigers

The cards in this 23 card set measure 2 1/2" by 3 1/2". Twenty-three color cards, 22 players and one numbered checklist, comprise the 1978 Burger King Tigers set issued in the Detroit area. The cards marked with an asterisk contain photos different from those appearing on the Topps regular issue cards of that year.

| | | MINT | VG-E | F-G |
|---|---|---|---|---|
| COMPLETE SET ...................... | | 25.00 | 10.00 | 2.50 |
| COMMON PLAYER (1-23) .......... | | .30 | .12 | .03 |
| ☐ 1 | Ralph Houk MGR .............. | .50 | .20 | .05 |
| ☐ 2 | Milt May ........................ | .30 | .12 | .03 |
| ☐ 3 | John Wockenfuss .............. | .30 | .12 | .03 |
| ☐ 4 | Mark Fidrych .................. | .75 | .30 | .07 |
| ☐ 5 | Dave Rozema .................. | .30 | .12 | .03 |
| ☐ 6 | Jack Billingham * ............ | .30 | .12 | .03 |
| ☐ 7 | Jim Slaton * .................... | .30 | .12 | .03 |
| ☐ 8 | Jack Morris * .................. | 8.00 | 3.00 | .75 |

MICKEY STANLEY

| | | | MINT | VG-E | F-G |
|---|---|---|---|---|---|
| ☐ | 9 | John Hiller | .50 | .20 | .05 |
| ☐ | 10 | Steve Foucault | .30 | .12 | .03 |
| ☐ | 11 | Milt Wilcox | .30 | .12 | .03 |
| ☐ | 12 | Jason Thompson | .75 | .30 | .07 |
| ☐ | 13 | Lou Whitaker * | 6.00 | 2.40 | .60 |
| ☐ | 14 | Aurelio Rodriguez | .30 | .12 | .03 |
| ☐ | 15 | Alan Trammell * | 6.00 | 2.40 | .60 |
| ☐ | 16 | Steve Dillard * | .30 | .12 | .03 |
| ☐ | 17 | Phil Mankowski | .30 | .12 | .03 |
| ☐ | 18 | Steve Kemp | .75 | .30 | .07 |
| ☐ | 19 | Ron LeFlore | .40 | .16 | .04 |
| ☐ | 20 | Tim Corcoran | .30 | .12 | .03 |
| ☐ | 21 | Mickey Stanley | .40 | .16 | .04 |
| ☐ | 22 | Rusty Staub | .75 | .30 | .07 |
| ☐ | 23 | Checklist card (unnumbered) | .05 | .01 | .00 |

## 1978 Burger King Yankees

CLIFF JOHNSON

The cards in this 23 card set measure 2 1/2" by 3 1/2". These cards were distributed in packs of three players plus a checklist at Burger King's New York area outlets. Cards with an asterisk have different poses than those in the Topps regular issue.

| | | | MINT | VG-E | F-G |
|---|---|---|---|---|---|
| | COMPLETE SET | | 7.50 | 3.00 | .75 |
| | COMMON PLAYER (1-23) | | .15 | .06 | .01 |
| ☐ | 1 | Billy Martin MGR | .40 | .16 | .04 |
| ☐ | 2 | Thurman Munson | 2.00 | .80 | .20 |
| ☐ | 3 | Cliff Johnson | .15 | .06 | .01 |
| ☐ | 4 | Ron Guidry | 1.50 | .60 | .15 |
| ☐ | 5 | Ed Figueroa | .15 | .06 | .01 |
| ☐ | 6 | Dick Tidrow | .15 | .06 | .01 |
| ☐ | 7 | Jim Hunter | 1.50 | .60 | .15 |
| ☐ | 8 | Don Gullett | .15 | .06 | .01 |
| ☐ | 9 | Sparky Lyle | .40 | .16 | .04 |
| ☐ | 10 | Rich Gossage * | 1.00 | .40 | .10 |
| ☐ | 11 | Rawly Eastwick * | .15 | .06 | .01 |

| | | | | | |
|---|---|---|---|---|---|
| ☐ | 12 | Chris Chambliss | .20 | .08 | .02 |
| ☐ | 13 | Willie Randolph | .30 | .12 | .03 |
| ☐ | 14 | Graig Nettles | .60 | .24 | .06 |
| ☐ | 15 | Bucky Dent | .20 | .08 | .02 |
| ☐ | 16 | Jim Spencer * | .15 | .06 | .01 |
| ☐ | 17 | Fred Stanley | .15 | .06 | .01 |
| ☐ | 18 | Lou Piniella | .30 | .12 | .03 |
| ☐ | 19 | Roy White | .20 | .08 | .02 |
| ☐ | 20 | Mickey Rivers | .20 | .08 | .02 |
| ☐ | 21 | Reggie Jackson | 2.00 | .80 | .20 |
| ☐ | 22 | Paul Blair | .15 | .06 | .01 |
| ☐ | 23 | Checklist card (unnumbered) | .05 | .01 | .00 |

## 1979 Burger King Phillies

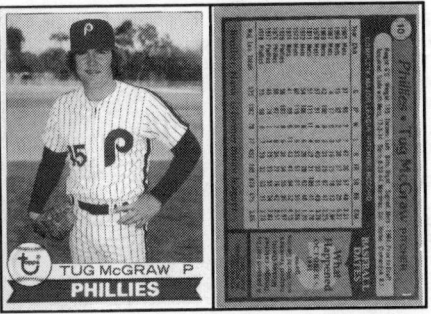

TUG McGRAW P
PHILLIES

The cards in this 23 card set measure 2 1/2" by 3 1/2". The 1979 Burger King Phillies set follows the regular format of 22 player cards and one unnumbered checklist card. The asterisk indicates where the pose differs from the Topps card of that year.

| | | | MINT | VG-E | F-G |
|---|---|---|---|---|---|
| | COMPLETE SET | | 5.00 | 2.00 | .50 |
| | COMMON PLAYER (1-23) | | .10 | .04 | .01 |
| ☐ | 1 | Danny Ozark MGR * | .10 | .04 | .01 |
| ☐ | 2 | Bob Boone | .15 | .06 | .01 |
| ☐ | 3 | Tim McCarver | .20 | .08 | .02 |
| ☐ | 4 | Steve Carlton | 1.50 | .60 | .15 |
| ☐ | 5 | Larry Christenson | .10 | .04 | .01 |
| ☐ | 6 | Dick Ruthven | .10 | .04 | .01 |
| ☐ | 7 | Ron Reed | .10 | .04 | .01 |
| ☐ | 8 | Randy Lerch | .10 | .04 | .01 |
| ☐ | 9 | Warren Brusstar | .10 | .04 | .01 |
| ☐ | 10 | Tug McGraw | .25 | .10 | .02 |
| ☐ | 11 | Nino Espinosa * | .10 | .04 | .01 |
| ☐ | 12 | Doug Bird * | .10 | .04 | .01 |
| ☐ | 13 | Pete Rose * | 2.50 | 1.00 | .25 |
| ☐ | 14 | Manny Trillo * | .15 | .06 | .01 |
| ☐ | 15 | Larry Bowa | .30 | .12 | .03 |
| ☐ | 16 | Mike Schmidt | 1.50 | .60 | .15 |
| ☐ | 17 | Pete Mackanin * | .10 | .04 | .01 |
| ☐ | 18 | Jose Cardenal | .10 | .04 | .01 |
| ☐ | 19 | Greg Luzinski | .30 | .12 | .03 |
| ☐ | 20 | Garry Maddox | .15 | .06 | .01 |
| ☐ | 21 | Bake McBride | .10 | .04 | .01 |
| ☐ | 22 | Greg Gross * | .10 | .04 | .01 |
| ☐ | 23 | Checklist card (unnumbered) | .05 | .01 | .00 |

## 1979 Burger King Yankees

The cards in this 23 card set measure 2 1/2" X 3 1/2". There are 22 numbered cards and one unnumbered checklist in the 1979 Burger King Yankee set. The poses of Guidry, Tiant, John and

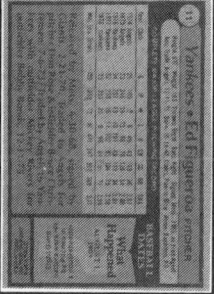

was the first Burger King set to carry the Burger King logo and hence does not generate the same confusion that the three previous years do for collectors trying to distinguish Burger King cards from the very similar Topps cards of the same years.

|  |  | MINT | VG-E | F-G |
|---|---|---|---|---|
| COMPLETE SET | | 4.50 | 1.80 | .45 |
| COMMON PLAYER (1-23) | | .10 | .04 | .01 |
| ☐ 1 | Dallas Green MGR * | .15 | .06 | .01 |
| ☐ 2 | Bob Boone | .10 | .04 | .01 |
| ☐ 3 | Keith Moreland * | .75 | .30 | .07 |
| ☐ 4 | Pete Rose | 2.50 | 1.00 | .25 |
| ☐ 5 | Manny Trillo | .15 | .06 | .01 |
| ☐ 6 | Mike Schmidt | 1.50 | .60 | .15 |
| ☐ 7 | Larry Bowa | .30 | .12 | .03 |
| ☐ 8 | John Vukovich * | .10 | .04 | .01 |
| ☐ 9 | Bake McBride | .10 | .04 | .01 |
| ☐ 10 | Garry Maddox | .15 | .06 | .01 |
| ☐ 11 | Greg Luzinski | .25 | .10 | .02 |
| ☐ 12 | Greg Gross | .10 | .04 | .01 |
| ☐ 13 | Del Unser | .10 | .04 | .01 |
| ☐ 14 | Lonnie Smith * | .15 | .06 | .01 |
| ☐ 15 | Steve Carlton | 1.25 | .50 | .12 |
| ☐ 16 | Larry Christenson | .10 | .04 | .01 |
| ☐ 17 | Nino Espinosa | .10 | .04 | .01 |
| ☐ 18 | Randy Lerch | .10 | .04 | .01 |
| ☐ 19 | Dick Ruthven | .10 | .04 | .01 |
| ☐ 20 | Tug McGraw | .20 | .08 | .02 |
| ☐ 21 | Ron Reed | .10 | .04 | .01 |
| ☐ 22 | Kevin Saucier * | .10 | .04 | .01 |
| ☐ 23 | Checklist card (unnumbered) | .05 | .01 | .00 |

Beniquez, each marked with an asterisk below, are different from their poses appearing in the regular Topps issue. The team card has a picture of Lemon rather than Martin.

|  |  | MINT | VG-E | F-G |
|---|---|---|---|---|
| COMPLETE SET | | 5.00 | 2.00 | .50 |
| COMMON PLAYER (1-23) | | .10 | .04 | .01 |
| ☐ 1 | Yankees Team: Bob Lemon MGR * | .30 | .12 | .03 |
| ☐ 2 | Thurman Munson | 1.50 | .60 | .15 |
| ☐ 3 | Cliff Johnson | .10 | .04 | .01 |
| ☐ 4 | Ron Guidry * | 1.00 | .40 | .10 |
| ☐ 5 | Jay Johnstone | .15 | .06 | .01 |
| ☐ 6 | Jim Hunter | 1.00 | .40 | .10 |
| ☐ 7 | Jim Beattie | .10 | .04 | .01 |
| ☐ 8 | Luis Tiant * | .20 | .08 | .02 |
| ☐ 9 | Tommy John * | .40 | .16 | .04 |
| ☐ 10 | Rich Gossage | .60 | .24 | .06 |
| ☐ 11 | Ed Figueroa | .10 | .04 | .01 |
| ☐ 12 | Chris Chambliss | .15 | .06 | .01 |
| ☐ 13 | Willie Randolph | .20 | .08 | .02 |
| ☐ 14 | Bucky Dent | .15 | .06 | .01 |
| ☐ 15 | Graig Nettles | .40 | .16 | .04 |
| ☐ 16 | Fred Stanley | .10 | .04 | .01 |
| ☐ 17 | Jim Spencer | .10 | .04 | .01 |
| ☐ 18 | Lou Piniella | .30 | .12 | .03 |
| ☐ 19 | Roy White | .15 | .06 | .01 |
| ☐ 20 | Mickey Rivers | .15 | .06 | .01 |
| ☐ 21 | Reggie Jackson | 1.75 | .70 | .17 |
| ☐ 22 | Juan Beniquez * | .15 | .06 | .01 |
| ☐ 23 | Checklist card (unnumbered) | .05 | .01 | .00 |

## 1980 Burger King Pitch/Hit/Run

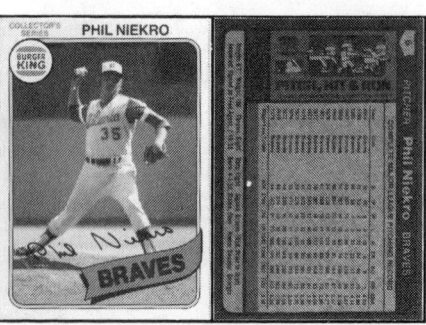

The cards in this 34 card set measure 2 1/2" by 3 1/2". The "Pitch, Hit, and Run" set was a promotion introduced by Burger King in 1980. The cards carry a Burger King logo on the front and those marked by an asterisk in the checklist contain a different photo from that found in the regularly issued Topps series. Cards 1-11 are pitchers, 12-22 are hitters, and 23-33 are speedsters. Within each subgroup, the players are numbered corresponding to the alphabetical order of their names. The unnumbered checklist card was triple printed and is the least valuable card in the set.

## 1980 Burger King Phillies

The cards in this 23 card set measure 2 1/2" by 3 1/2". The 1980 edition of Burger King Phillies follows the established pattern of 22 numbered player cards and one unnumbered checklist. Cards marked with astericks contain poses different from those found in the regular 1980 Topps cards. This

|  |  | MINT | VG-E | F-G |
|---|---|---|---|---|
| COMPLETE SET | | 9.00 | 3.75 | .90 |
| COMMON PLAYER (1-34) | | .10 | .04 | .01 |
| ☐ 1 | Vida Blue * | .15 | .06 | .01 |
| ☐ 2 | Steve Carlton | 1.00 | .40 | .10 |
| ☐ 3 | Rollie Fingers | .30 | .12 | .03 |
| ☐ 4 | Ron Guidry * | .40 | .16 | .04 |
| ☐ 5 | Jerry Koosman * | .15 | .06 | .01 |
| ☐ 6 | Phil Niekro | .40 | .16 | .04 |
| ☐ 7 | Jim Palmer * | .75 | .30 | .07 |
| ☐ 8 | J.R. Richard | .15 | .06 | .01 |

| | | MINT | VG-E | F-G |
|---|---|---|---|---|
| ☐ 9 | Nolan Ryan * | 1.00 | .40 | .10 |
| ☐ 10 | Tom Seaver * | 1.00 | .40 | .10 |
| ☐ 11 | Bruce Sutter | .25 | .10 | .02 |
| ☐ 12 | Don Baylor | .15 | .06 | .01 |
| ☐ 13 | George Brett | 1.00 | .40 | .10 |
| ☐ 14 | Rod Carew | .75 | .30 | .07 |
| ☐ 15 | George Foster | .15 | .06 | .01 |
| ☐ 16 | Keith Hernandez * | .75 | .30 | .07 |
| ☐ 17 | Reggie Jackson * | 1.25 | .50 | .12 |
| ☐ 18 | Fred Lynn * | .25 | .10 | .02 |
| ☐ 19 | Dave Parker | .30 | .12 | .03 |
| ☐ 20 | Jim Rice | .75 | .30 | .07 |
| ☐ 21 | Pete Rose | 2.00 | .80 | .20 |
| ☐ 22 | Dave Winfield * | 1.00 | .40 | .10 |
| ☐ 23 | Bobby Bonds * | .15 | .06 | .01 |
| ☐ 24 | Enos Cabell | .10 | .04 | .01 |
| ☐ 25 | Cesar Cedeno | .15 | .06 | .01 |
| ☐ 26 | Julio Cruz | .10 | .04 | .01 |
| ☐ 27 | Ron LeFlore * | .10 | .04 | .01 |
| ☐ 28 | Dave Lopes * | .15 | .06 | .01 |
| ☐ 29 | Omar Moreno * | .10 | .04 | .01 |
| ☐ 30 | Joe Morgan * | .75 | .30 | .07 |
| ☐ 31 | Bill North | .10 | .04 | .01 |
| ☐ 32 | Frank Taveras | .10 | .04 | .01 |
| ☐ 33 | Willie Wilson | .25 | .10 | .02 |
| ☐ 34 | Unnumbered Checklist | .05 | .01 | .00 |

## 1982 Burger King Indians

Dave Garcia
MANAGER

BE IN THE GAME

When our base runner gets to first base our coaches tell him right away: check the scoreboard, check the outfielder, make a line drive go through, check the third base coach. You have to be alert at all times.

TIPS FROM THE DUGOUT

Burger King — Reg. U.S. Pat. & TM Off. © 1982 Burger King Corporation

The cards in this 12 card set measure 3" by 5". Tips From The Dugout is the series title of this set issued on a one card per week basis by the Burger King chain in the Cleveland area. Each card contains a black and white photo of manager Dave Garcia or coaches Goryl, McCraw, Queen and Sommers, under whom appears a paragraph explaining some aspect of inside baseball. The photo and "Tip" are set upon a large yellow area surrounded by green borders. The cards are not numbered and are blank-backed. The logos of Burger King and WUAB-TV appear at the base of the card.

| | | MINT | VG-E | F-G |
|---|---|---|---|---|
| | COMPLETE SET | 4.00 | 1.60 | .40 |
| | COMMON PLAYER | .40 | .16 | .04 |
| ☐ 1 | Dave Garcia: | .40 | .16 | .04 |
| | Be in the Game | | | |
| ☐ 2 | Dave Garcia: | .40 | .16 | .04 |

| | | MINT | VG-E | F-G |
|---|---|---|---|---|
| | Sportsmanship | | | |
| ☐ 3 | Johnny Goryl: | .40 | .16 | .04 |
| | Rounding Bases | | | |
| ☐ 4 | Johnny Goryl: | .40 | .16 | .04 |
| | 3B Running | | | |
| ☐ 5 | Tom McCraw: | .40 | .16 | .04 |
| | Follow Thru | | | |
| ☐ 6 | Tom McCraw: | .40 | .16 | .04 |
| | Selecting a Bat | | | |
| ☐ 7 | Tom McCraw: | .40 | .16 | .04 |
| | Watch the Ball | | | |
| ☐ 8 | Mel Queen: | .40 | .16 | .04 |
| | Master One Pitch | | | |
| ☐ 9 | Mel Queen: | .40 | .16 | .04 |
| | Warm Up | | | |
| ☐ 10 | Dennis Sommers: | .40 | .16 | .04 |
| | Protect Fingers | | | |
| ☐ 11 | Dennis Sommers: | .40 | .16 | .04 |
| | Tagging 1st Base | | | |
| ☐ 12 | Dennis Sommers | .40 | .16 | .04 |

## 1986 Burger King All Pro

This 20 card set was distributed in Burger King restaurants across the country. They were produced as panels of three where the middle card was actually a special discount coupon card. The folded panel was given with the purchase of a Whopper. Each individual card measures 2 1/2" by 3 1/2". The team logos have been airbrushed from the pictures. The cards are numbered on the front at the top.

| | | MINT | VG-E | F-G |
|---|---|---|---|---|
| | COMPLETE SET | 7.00 | 2.50 | .60 |
| | COMMON PLAYER | .20 | .08 | .02 |
| ☐ 1 | Tony Pena | .20 | .08 | .02 |
| ☐ 2 | Dave Winfield | .40 | .16 | .04 |
| ☐ 3 | Fernando Valenzuela | .40 | .16 | .04 |
| ☐ 4 | Pete Rose | .80 | .32 | .08 |
| ☐ 5 | Mike Schmidt | .60 | .24 | .06 |
| ☐ 6 | Steve Carlton | .40 | .16 | .04 |
| ☐ 7 | Glenn Wilson | .20 | .08 | .02 |
| ☐ 8 | Jim Rice | .40 | .16 | .04 |
| ☐ 9 | Wade Boggs | .80 | .32 | .08 |
| ☐ 10 | Juan Samuel | .20 | .08 | .02 |
| ☐ 11 | Dale Murphy | .60 | .24 | .06 |
| ☐ 12 | Reggie Jackson | .60 | .24 | .06 |
| ☐ 13 | Kirk Gibson | .40 | .16 | .04 |
| ☐ 14 | Eddie Murray | .50 | .20 | .05 |
| ☐ 15 | Cal Ripken | .50 | .20 | .05 |
| ☐ 16 | Willie McGee | .30 | .12 | .03 |
| ☐ 17 | Dwight Gooden | .80 | .32 | .08 |
| ☐ 18 | Steve Garvey | .50 | .20 | .05 |
| ☐ 19 | Don Mattingly | 1.00 | .40 | .10 |
| ☐ 20 | George Brett | .50 | .20 | .05 |

# 1933 Butter Cream R306

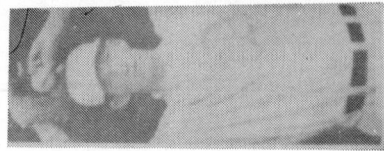

The small, elongated (measuring 1 1/4" by 3 1/2") cards of this 29 card set are unnumbered and contain many cut-down, blurry black and white photos. The producer's name is sometimes printed on the reverse. Despite their limitations, Butter Cream cards are highly prized by collectors, and carry the ACC designation R306. The cards have been alphabetized and numbered for reference in the checklist below.

|  |  | MINT | VG-E | F-G |
|---|---|---|---|---|
| COMPLETE SET | | 5500.00 | 2400.00 | 600.00 |
| COMMON PLAYER (1-29) | | 150.00 | 60.00 | 15.00 |
| ☐ 1 | Earl Averill | 200.00 | 80.00 | 20.00 |
| ☐ 2 | Ed Brandt | 150.00 | 60.00 | 15.00 |
| ☐ 3 | Guy T. Bush | 150.00 | 60.00 | 15.00 |
| ☐ 4 | Gordon Cochrane | 250.00 | 100.00 | 25.00 |
| ☐ 5 | Joe Cronin | 250.00 | 100.00 | 25.00 |
| ☐ 6 | George Earnshaw | 150.00 | 60.00 | 15.00 |
| ☐ 7 | Wesley Ferrell | 150.00 | 60.00 | 15.00 |
| ☐ 8 | Jimmy E. Foxx | 375.00 | 150.00 | 37.00 |
| ☐ 9 | Frank C. Frisch | 250.00 | 100.00 | 25.00 |
| ☐ 10 | Charles M. Gelbert | 150.00 | 60.00 | 15.00 |
| ☐ 11 | Lefty Grove | 300.00 | 120.00 | 30.00 |
| ☐ 12 | Leo Hartnett | 225.00 | 90.00 | 22.00 |
| ☐ 13 | Babe Herman | 175.00 | 70.00 | 18.00 |
| ☐ 14 | Charles Klein | 250.00 | 100.00 | 25.00 |
| ☐ 15 | Ray Kremer | 150.00 | 60.00 | 15.00 |
| ☐ 16 | Fred C. Lindstrom | 200.00 | 80.00 | 20.00 |
| ☐ 17 | Ted A. Lyons | 200.00 | 80.00 | 20.00 |
| ☐ 18 | Pepper Martin | 175.00 | 70.00 | 18.00 |
| ☐ 19 | Robert O'Farrell | 150.00 | 60.00 | 15.00 |
| ☐ 20 | Ed A. Rommell | 150.00 | 60.00 | 15.00 |
| ☐ 21 | Charles Root | 150.00 | 60.00 | 15.00 |
| ☐ 22 | Harold Ruel | 150.00 | 60.00 | 15.00 |
| ☐ 23 | Al Simmons | 225.00 | 90.00 | 22.00 |
| ☐ 24 | Bill N. Terry | 250.00 | 100.00 | 25.00 |
| ☐ 25 | George Uhle | 150.00 | 60.00 | 15.00 |
| ☐ 26 | Lloyd J. Waner | 200.00 | 80.00 | 20.00 |
| ☐ 27 | Paul C. Waner | 225.00 | 90.00 | 22.00 |
| ☐ 28 | Hack Wilson | 250.00 | 100.00 | 25.00 |
| ☐ 29 | Glenn Wright | 150.00 | 60.00 | 15.00 |

# 1950-56 Callahan HOF

 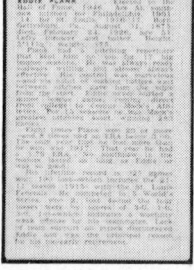

The cards in this 82 card set measure 1 3/4" by 2 1/2". The 1950-56 Callahan Hall of Fame set was issued over a number of years at the Baseball Hall of Fame museum in Cooperstown, New York. New cards were added to the set each year when new members were inducted into the Hall of Fame. The cards with (2) in the checklist exist with two different biographies. The year of each card's first inclusion in the set is also given in parentheses; those not listed parenthetically below were issued in 1950 as well as in all the succeeding years and are hence the most common. Naturally the supply of cards is directly related to how many years a player was included in the set; cards that were not issued until 1955 are much scarcer than those printed all the years between 1950 and 1956. The ACC designation is W576. One frequently finds "complete" sets in the original box; take care to investigate the year of issue, the set may be complete in the sense of all the cards issued up to a certain year, but not all 82 cards below. For example, a "complete" 1950 set would obviously not include any of the cards marked below with ('52), ('54), or ('55) as none of those cards existed in 1950 since those respective players had not yet been inducted. The complete set price below refers to a set including all 82 cards below with variations. Since the cards are unnumbered, they are numbered below for reference alphabetically by player's name.

|  |  | MINT | VG-E | F-G |
|---|---|---|---|---|
| COMPLETE SET | | 225.00 | 90.00 | 22.00 |
| COMMON PLAYER ('50) | | .80 | .32 | .08 |
| COMMON PLAYER ('52) | | 1.75 | .70 | .17 |
| COMMON PLAYER ('54) | | 3.00 | 1.20 | .30 |
| COMMON PLAYER ('55) | | 4.50 | 1.80 | .45 |
| ☐ 1 | Grover Alexander | 1.75 | .70 | .17 |
| ☐ 2 | Cap Anson | 1.25 | .50 | .12 |
| ☐ 3 | Frank Baker ('55) | 4.50 | 1.80 | .45 |
| ☐ 4 | Edward Barrow ('54) | 3.00 | 1.20 | .30 |
| ☐ 5 | Chief Bender(2)('54) | 3.00 | 1.20 | .30 |
| ☐ 6 | Roger Bresnahan | .80 | .32 | .08 |
| ☐ 7 | Dan Brouthers | .80 | .32 | .08 |
| ☐ 8 | Mordecai Brown | .80 | .32 | .08 |
| ☐ 9 | Morgan Bulkeley | .80 | .32 | .08 |
| ☐ 10 | Jesse Burkett | .80 | .32 | .08 |
| ☐ 11 | Alexander Cartwright | .80 | .32 | .08 |
| ☐ 12 | Henry Chadwick | .80 | .32 | .08 |
| ☐ 13 | Frank Chance | .80 | .32 | .08 |
| ☐ 14 | Happy Chandler ('52) | 20.00 | 8.00 | 2.00 |
| ☐ 15 | Jack Chesbro | .80 | .32 | .08 |
| ☐ 16 | Fred Clarke | .80 | .32 | .08 |
| ☐ 17 | Ty Cobb | 15.00 | 6.00 | 1.50 |
| ☐ 18A | Mickey Cochran ERR (sic, Cochrane) | 7.50 | 3.00 | .75 |
| ☐ 18B | Mickey Cochrane COR | 1.50 | .60 | .15 |
| ☐ 19 | Eddie Collins (2) | 1.00 | .40 | .10 |
| ☐ 20 | Jimmie Collins | .80 | .32 | .08 |
| ☐ 21 | Charles Comiskey | .80 | .32 | .08 |
| ☐ 22 | Tom Connolly ('54) | 3.00 | 1.20 | .30 |
| ☐ 23 | Candy Cummings | .80 | .32 | .08 |
| ☐ 24 | Dizzy Dean ('54) | 9.00 | 3.75 | .90 |
| ☐ 25 | Ed Delahanty | .80 | .32 | .08 |
| ☐ 26 | Bill Dickey ('54)(2) | 6.00 | 2.40 | .60 |
| ☐ 27 | Joe DiMaggio ('55) | 35.00 | 14.00 | 3.50 |
| ☐ 28 | Hugh Duffy | .80 | .32 | .08 |
| ☐ 29 | Johnny Evers | .80 | .32 | .08 |
| ☐ 30 | Buck Ewing | .80 | .32 | .08 |
| ☐ 31 | Jimmie Foxx | 3.50 | 1.40 | .35 |
| ☐ 32 | Frank Frisch | 1.25 | .50 | .12 |
| ☐ 33 | Lou Gehrig | 15.00 | 6.00 | 1.50 |
| ☐ 34 | Charles Gehringer | 1.25 | .50 | .12 |
| ☐ 35 | Clark Griffith | .80 | .32 | .08 |
| ☐ 36 | Lefty Grove | 1.75 | .70 | .17 |
| ☐ 37 | Gabby Hartnett ('55) | 4.50 | 1.80 | .45 |
| ☐ 38 | Harry Heilmann ('52) | 2.00 | .80 | .20 |
| ☐ 39 | Rogers Hornsby | 3.00 | 1.20 | .30 |
| ☐ 40 | Carl Hubbell | 1.25 | .50 | .12 |
| ☐ 41 | Hughey Jennings | .80 | .32 | .08 |
| ☐ 42 | Ban Johnson | .80 | .32 | .08 |
| ☐ 43 | Walter Johnson | 5.00 | 2.00 | .50 |
| ☐ 44 | Willie Keeler | .80 | .32 | .08 |
| ☐ 45 | Mike Kelly | 1.25 | .50 | .12 |
| ☐ 46 | Bill Klem ('54) | 3.00 | 1.20 | .30 |
| ☐ 47 | Napoleon Lajoie | 1.50 | .60 | .15 |
| ☐ 48 | Kenesaw Landis | .80 | .32 | .08 |

| | | | | |
|---|---|---|---|---|
| ☐ 49 | Ted Lyons ('55) | 4.50 | 1.80 | .45 |
| ☐ 50 | Connie Mack | 1.00 | .40 | .10 |
| ☐ 51 | Walter Maranville ('54) | 3.00 | 1.20 | .30 |
| ☐ 52 | Christy Mathewson | 5.00 | 2.00 | .50 |
| ☐ 53 | Tommy McCarthy | .80 | .32 | .08 |
| ☐ 54 | Joe McGinnity | .80 | .32 | .08 |
| ☐ 55 | John McGraw | 1.00 | .40 | .10 |
| ☐ 56 | Charles Nicholls | .80 | .32 | .08 |
| ☐ 57 | Jim O'Rourke | .80 | .32 | .08 |
| ☐ 58 | Mel Ott | 1.75 | .70 | .17 |
| ☐ 59 | Herb Pennock | .80 | .32 | .08 |
| ☐ 60 | Eddie Plank | 1.00 | .40 | .10 |
| ☐ 61 | Charles Radbourne | .80 | .32 | .08 |
| ☐ 62 | Wilbert Robinson | .80 | .32 | .08 |
| ☐ 63 | Babe Ruth | 25.00 | 10.00 | 2.50 |
| ☐ 64 | Ray Schalk ('55) | 4.50 | 1.80 | .45 |
| ☐ 65 | Al Simmons ('54) | 3.00 | 1.20 | .30 |
| ☐ 66 | George Sisler (2) | 1.25 | .50 | .12 |
| ☐ 67 | A.G. Spalding | .80 | .32 | .08 |
| ☐ 68 | Tris Speaker | 2.50 | 1.00 | .25 |
| ☐ 69 | Bill Terry ('54) | 4.00 | 1.60 | .40 |
| ☐ 70 | Joe Tinker | .80 | .32 | .08 |
| ☐ 71 | Pie Traynor | 1.25 | .50 | .12 |
| ☐ 72 | Dazzy Vance ('55) | 4.00 | 1.60 | .40 |
| ☐ 73 | Rube Waddell | .80 | .32 | .08 |
| ☐ 74 | Hans Wagner | 5.00 | 2.00 | .50 |
| ☐ 75 | Bobby Wallace ('54) | 3.00 | 1.20 | .30 |
| ☐ 76 | Ed Walsh | .80 | .32 | .08 |
| ☐ 77 | Paul Waner ('52) | 2.00 | .80 | .20 |
| ☐ 78 | George Wright | .80 | .32 | .08 |
| ☐ 79 | Harry Wright ('54) | 3.00 | 1.20 | .30 |
| ☐ 80 | Cy Young | 3.00 | 1.20 | .30 |
| ☐ 81 | Museum Interior ('54) (2) | 3.00 | 1.20 | .30 |
| ☐ 82 | Museum Exterior ('54) (2) | 3.00 | 1.20 | .30 |

## 1985 CIGNA Phillies

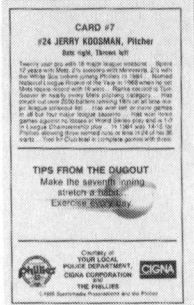

This colorful 16 card set (measuring 2 5/8" by 4 1/8") features the Philadelphia Phillies and was also sponsored by CIGNA Corporation. Cards are numbered on the back and contain a safety tip as such the set is frequently categorized and referenced as a safety set. Cards are also numbered by uniform number on the front.

| | | MINT | VG-E | F-G |
|---|---|---|---|---|
| | COMPLETE SET | 4.50 | 1.80 | .45 |
| | COMMON PLAYER | .20 | .08 | .02 |
| ☐ 1 | Juan Samuel | .50 | .20 | .05 |
| ☐ 2 | Von Hayes | .60 | .24 | .06 |
| ☐ 3 | Ozzie Virgil | .25 | .10 | .02 |
| ☐ 4 | Mike Schmidt | 1.00 | .40 | .10 |
| ☐ 5 | Greg Gross | .20 | .08 | .02 |
| ☐ 6 | Tim Corcoran | .20 | .08 | .02 |
| ☐ 7 | Jerry Koosman | .25 | .10 | .02 |
| ☐ 8 | Jeff Stone | .25 | .10 | .02 |
| ☐ 9 | Glenn Wilson | .50 | .20 | .05 |
| ☐ 10 | Steve Jeltz | .20 | .08 | .02 |
| ☐ 11 | Garry Maddox | .20 | .08 | .02 |

| | | | | |
|---|---|---|---|---|
| ☐ 12 | Steve Carlton | .75 | .30 | .07 |
| ☐ 13 | John Denny | .25 | .10 | .02 |
| ☐ 14 | Kevin Gross | .20 | .08 | .02 |
| ☐ 15 | Shane Rawley | .25 | .10 | .02 |
| ☐ 16 | Charlie Hudson | .20 | .08 | .02 |

## 1986 CIGNA Phillies

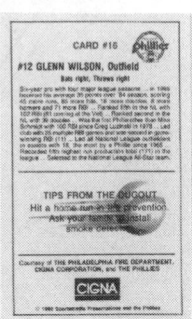

This 16 card set was sponsored by CIGNA Corp. and was given away by the Philadelphia area Fire Departments. Cards measure 2 3/4" by 4 1/8" and feature full color fronts. The card backs are printed in maroon and black on white card stock. Although the uniform numbers are given on the front of the card, the cards are numbered on the back in the order listed below.

| | | MINT | VG-E | F-G |
|---|---|---|---|---|
| | COMPLETE SET | 4.00 | 1.60 | .40 |
| | COMMON PLAYER | .20 | .08 | .02 |
| ☐ 1 | Juan Samuel | .40 | .16 | .04 |
| ☐ 2 | Don Carman | .30 | .12 | .03 |
| ☐ 3 | Von Hayes | .50 | .20 | .05 |
| ☐ 4 | Kent Tekulve | .30 | .12 | .03 |
| ☐ 5 | Greg Gross | .20 | .08 | .02 |
| ☐ 6 | Shane Rawley | .30 | .12 | .03 |
| ☐ 7 | Darren Daulton | .30 | .12 | .03 |
| ☐ 8 | Kevin Gross | .20 | .08 | .02 |
| ☐ 9 | Steve Jeltz | .20 | .08 | .02 |
| ☐ 10 | Mike Schmidt | .75 | .30 | .07 |
| ☐ 11 | Steve Bedrosian | .20 | .08 | .02 |
| ☐ 12 | Gary Redus | .30 | .12 | .03 |
| ☐ 13 | Charles Hudson | .20 | .08 | .02 |
| ☐ 14 | John Russell | .20 | .08 | .02 |
| ☐ 15 | Fred Toliver | .20 | .08 | .02 |
| ☐ 16 | Glenn Wilson | .30 | .12 | .03 |

## 1985 Circle K

The cards in this 33 card set measure 2 1/2" by 3 1/2" and were issued with accompanying box. In 1985, Topps produced this set for Circle K; cards were printed in Ireland. Cards are numbered on the back according to each player's rank on the all-time career Home Run list. The backs are printed in blue and red on white card stock. The card fronts are glossy and each player is named in the lower left corner. Most of the obverses are in color, although the older vintage players are pictured in black and white. Joe DiMaggio was not included in the set.

| | | MINT | VG-E | F-G |
|---|---|---|---|---|
| | COMPLETE SET | 3.50 | 1.60 | .40 |

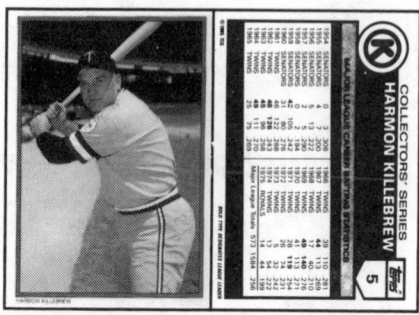

Although the cards are numbered in the upper right corner of the back from 1 to 11, they are re-numbered below within team, i.e., Boston Red Sox (1-12), Chicago Cubs (13-24), Chicago White Sox (25-36), Cincinnati Reds (37-48), Detroit Tigers (49-60), Houston Astros (61-72), Kansas City Royals (73- 84), New York Mets (85-96), Philadelphia Phillies (97-108), Pittsburgh Pirates (109-120), and St. Louis Cardinals (121-132). Within each team the player actually numbered #1 (on the card back) is the first player below and the player numbered #11 is the last in that team's list. These player cards are quite similar to the 1981 Topps issue but feature a Coca-Cola logo on both the front and the back. The advertising card for each team features, on its back, an offer for obtaining an uncut sheet of 1981 Topps cards. These promotional cards were actually issued by Coke in only a few of the cities, and most of these cards have reached collectors hands through dealers who have purchased the cards through suppliers.

| COMMON PLAYER | .10 | .04 | .01 |
|---|---|---|---|
| ☐ 1 Hank Aaron | .35 | .14 | .03 |
| ☐ 2 Babe Ruth | .70 | .28 | .07 |
| ☐ 3 Willie Mays | .35 | .14 | .03 |
| ☐ 4 Frank Robinson | .15 | .06 | .01 |
| ☐ 5 Harmon Killebrew | .15 | .06 | .01 |
| ☐ 6 Mickey Mantle | .70 | .28 | .07 |
| ☐ 7 Jimmie Foxx | .20 | .08 | .02 |
| ☐ 8 Willie McCovey | .20 | .08 | .02 |
| ☐ 9 Ted Williams | .30 | .12 | .03 |
| ☐ 10 Ernie Banks | .20 | .08 | .02 |
| ☐ 11 Eddie Mathews | .15 | .06 | .01 |
| ☐ 12 Mel Ott | .20 | .08 | .02 |
| ☐ 13 Reggie Jackson | .35 | .14 | .03 |
| ☐ 14 Lou Gehrig | .35 | .14 | .03 |
| ☐ 15 Stan Musial | .25 | .10 | .02 |
| ☐ 16 Willie Stargell | .20 | .08 | .02 |
| ☐ 17 Carl Yastrzemski | .40 | .16 | .04 |
| ☐ 18 Billy Williams | .15 | .06 | .01 |
| ☐ 19 Mike Schmidt | .35 | .14 | .03 |
| ☐ 20 Duke Snider | .30 | .12 | .03 |
| ☐ 21 Al Kaline | .20 | .08 | .02 |
| ☐ 22 Johnny Bench | .20 | .08 | .02 |
| ☐ 23 Frank Howard | .10 | .04 | .01 |
| ☐ 24 Orlando Cepeda | .10 | .04 | .01 |
| ☐ 25 Norm Cash | .10 | .04 | .01 |
| ☐ 26 Dave Kingman | .10 | .04 | .01 |
| ☐ 27 Rocky Colavito | .10 | .04 | .01 |
| ☐ 28 Tony Perez | .10 | .04 | .01 |
| ☐ 29 Gil Hodges | .10 | .04 | .01 |
| ☐ 30 Ralph Kiner | .10 | .04 | .01 |
| ☐ 31 Joe DiMaggio | .00 | .00 | .00 |
| (not included in set) | | | |
| ☐ 32 Johnny Mize | .15 | .06 | .01 |
| ☐ 33 Yogi Berra | .20 | .08 | .02 |
| ☐ 34 Lee May | .10 | .04 | .01 |

## 1981 Coke

The cards in this 132 card set measure 2 1/2" by 3 1/2". In 1981, Topps produced 11 sets of 12 cards each for the Coca-Cola Company. Each set features 11 star players for a particular team plus an advertising card with the team name on the front.

| | | | MINT | VG-E | F-G |
|---|---|---|---|---|---|
| COMPLETE SET | | | 14.00 | 5.75 | 1.40 |
| COMMON PLAYER | | | .05 | .02 | .00 |
| COMMON CHECKLIST | | | .03 | .00 | .00 |
| ☐ | 1 | Tom Burgmeier | .05 | .02 | .00 |
| ☐ | 2 | Dennis Eckersley | .10 | .04 | .01 |
| ☐ | 3 | Dwight Evans | .30 | .12 | .03 |
| ☐ | 4 | Bob Stanley | .10 | .04 | .01 |
| ☐ | 5 | Glenn Hoffman | .05 | .02 | .00 |
| ☐ | 6 | Carney Lansford | .30 | .12 | .03 |
| ☐ | 7 | Frank Tanana | .10 | .04 | .01 |
| ☐ | 8 | Tony Perez | .20 | .08 | .02 |
| ☐ | 9 | Jim Rice | 1.00 | .40 | .10 |
| ☐ | 10 | Dave Stapleton | .10 | .04 | .01 |
| ☐ | 11 | Carl Yastrzemski | 1.50 | .60 | .15 |
| ☐ | 12 | Red Sox Checklist | .03 | .00 | .00 |
| | | (unnumbered) | | | |
| ☐ | 13 | Tim Blackwell | .05 | .02 | .00 |
| ☐ | 14 | Bill Buckner | .20 | .08 | .02 |
| ☐ | 15 | Ivan DeJesus | .05 | .02 | .00 |
| ☐ | 16 | Leon Durham | .35 | .14 | .03 |
| ☐ | 17 | Steve Henderson | .05 | .02 | .00 |
| ☐ | 18 | Mike Krukow | .15 | .06 | .01 |
| ☐ | 19 | Ken Reitz | .05 | .02 | .00 |
| ☐ | 20 | Rick Reuschel | .10 | .04 | .01 |
| ☐ | 21 | Scot Thompson | .05 | .02 | .00 |
| ☐ | 22 | Dick Tidrow | .05 | .02 | .00 |
| ☐ | 23 | Mike Tyson | .05 | .02 | .00 |
| ☐ | 24 | Cubs Checklist | .03 | .00 | .00 |
| | | (unnumbered) | | | |
| ☐ | 25 | Britt Burns | .25 | .10 | .02 |
| ☐ | 26 | Todd Cruz | .05 | .02 | .00 |
| ☐ | 27 | Rich Dotson | .25 | .10 | .02 |
| ☐ | 28 | Jim Essian | .05 | .02 | .00 |
| ☐ | 29 | Ed Farmer | .05 | .02 | .00 |
| ☐ | 30 | Lamar Johnson | .05 | .02 | .00 |
| ☐ | 31 | Ron LeFlore | .10 | .04 | .01 |
| ☐ | 32 | Chet Lemon | .10 | .04 | .01 |
| ☐ | 33 | Bob Molinaro | .05 | .02 | .00 |
| ☐ | 34 | Jim Morrison | .05 | .02 | .00 |
| ☐ | 35 | Wayne Nordhagen | .05 | .02 | .00 |
| ☐ | 36 | White Sox Checklist | .03 | .00 | .00 |
| | | (unnumbered) | | | |
| ☐ | 37 | Johnny Bench | 1.00 | .40 | .10 |
| ☐ | 38 | Dave Collins | .10 | .04 | .01 |
| ☐ | 39 | Dave Concepcion | .20 | .08 | .02 |
| ☐ | 40 | Dan Driessen | .05 | .02 | .00 |
| ☐ | 41 | George Foster | .30 | .12 | .03 |
| ☐ | 42 | Ken Griffey | .10 | .04 | .01 |
| ☐ | 43 | Tom Hume | .05 | .02 | .00 |
| ☐ | 44 | Ray Knight | .25 | .10 | .02 |
| ☐ | 45 | Ron Oester | .10 | .04 | .01 |
| ☐ | 46 | Tom Seaver | 1.00 | .40 | .10 |
| ☐ | 47 | Mario Soto | .20 | .08 | .02 |
| ☐ | 48 | Reds Checklist | .03 | .00 | .00 |
| | | (unnumbered) | | | |
| ☐ | 49 | Champ Summers | .05 | .02 | .00 |
| ☐ | 50 | Al Cowens | .05 | .02 | .00 |
| ☐ | 51 | Rich Hebner | .05 | .02 | .00 |
| ☐ | 52 | Steve Kemp | .15 | .06 | .01 |
| ☐ | 53 | Aurelio Lopez | .05 | .02 | .00 |
| ☐ | 54 | Jack Morris | .75 | .30 | .07 |
| ☐ | 55 | Lance Parrish | .75 | .30 | .07 |

| | | | | |
|---|---|---|---|---|
| ☐ 56 | Johnny Wockenfuss | .05 | .02 | .00 |
| ☐ 57 | Alan Trammell | .60 | .24 | .06 |
| ☐ 58 | Lou Whitaker | .60 | .24 | .06 |
| ☐ 59 | Kirk Gibson | 1.25 | .50 | .12 |
| ☐ 60 | Tigers Checklist | .03 | .00 | .00 |
| | (unnumbered) | | | |
| ☐ 61 | Alan Ashby | .05 | .02 | .00 |
| ☐ 62 | Cesar Cedeno | .10 | .04 | .01 |
| ☐ 63 | Jose Cruz | .25 | .10 | .02 |
| ☐ 64 | Art Howe | .05 | .02 | .00 |
| ☐ 65 | Rafael Landestoy | .05 | .02 | .00 |
| ☐ 66 | Joe Niekro | .15 | .06 | .01 |
| ☐ 67 | Terry Puhl | .10 | .04 | .01 |
| ☐ 68 | J.R. Richard | .20 | .08 | .02 |
| ☐ 69 | Nolan Ryan | 1.00 | .40 | .10 |
| ☐ 70 | Joe Sambito | .10 | .04 | .01 |
| ☐ 71 | Don Sutton | .60 | .24 | .06 |
| ☐ 72 | Astros Checklist | .03 | .00 | .00 |
| | (unnumbered) | | | |
| ☐ 73 | Willie Aikens | .10 | .04 | .01 |
| ☐ 74 | George Brett | 1.25 | .50 | .12 |
| ☐ 75 | Larry Gura | .10 | .04 | .01 |
| ☐ 76 | Dennis Leonard | .10 | .04 | .01 |
| ☐ 77 | Hal McRae | .10 | .04 | .01 |
| ☐ 78 | Amos Otis | .10 | .04 | .01 |
| ☐ 79 | Dan Quisenberry | .30 | .12 | .03 |
| ☐ 80 | U.L. Washington | .05 | .02 | .00 |
| ☐ 81 | John Wathan | .05 | .02 | .00 |
| ☐ 82 | Frank White | .20 | .08 | .02 |
| ☐ 83 | Willie Wilson | .30 | .12 | .03 |
| ☐ 84 | Royals Checklist | .03 | .00 | .00 |
| | (unnumbered) | | | |
| ☐ 85 | Neil Allen | .10 | .04 | .01 |
| ☐ 86 | Doug Flynn | .05 | .02 | .00 |
| ☐ 87 | Dave Kingman | .25 | .10 | .02 |
| ☐ 88 | Randy Jones | .05 | .02 | .00 |
| ☐ 89 | Pat Zachry | .05 | .02 | .00 |
| ☐ 90 | Lee Mazzilli | .10 | .04 | .01 |
| ☐ 91 | Rusty Staub | .15 | .06 | .01 |
| ☐ 92 | Craig Swan | .05 | .02 | .00 |
| ☐ 93 | Frank Taveras | .05 | .02 | .00 |
| ☐ 94 | Alex Trevino | .05 | .02 | .00 |
| ☐ 95 | Joel Youngblood | .05 | .02 | .00 |
| ☐ 96 | Mets Checklist | .03 | .00 | .00 |
| | (unnumbered) | | | |
| ☐ 97 | Bob Boone | .10 | .04 | .01 |
| ☐ 98 | Larry Bowa | .20 | .08 | .02 |
| ☐ 99 | Steve Carlton | 1.00 | .40 | .10 |
| ☐ 100 | Greg Luzinski | .20 | .08 | .02 |
| ☐ 101 | Garry Maddox | .10 | .04 | .01 |
| ☐ 102 | Bake McBride | .05 | .02 | .00 |
| ☐ 103 | Tug McGraw | .15 | .06 | .01 |
| ☐ 104 | Pete Rose | 1.75 | .70 | .17 |
| ☐ 105 | Mike Schmidt | 1.25 | .50 | .12 |
| ☐ 106 | Lonnie Smith | .10 | .04 | .01 |
| ☐ 107 | Manny Trillo | .05 | .02 | .00 |
| ☐ 108 | Phillies Checklist | .03 | .00 | .00 |
| | (unnumbered) | | | |
| ☐ 109 | Jim Bibby | .05 | .02 | .00 |
| ☐ 110 | John Candelaria | .10 | .04 | .01 |
| ☐ 111 | Mike Easler | .10 | .04 | .01 |
| ☐ 112 | Tim Foli | .05 | .02 | .00 |
| ☐ 113 | Phil Garner | .10 | .04 | .01 |
| ☐ 114 | Bill Madlock | .30 | .12 | .03 |
| ☐ 115 | Omar Moreno | .05 | .02 | .00 |
| ☐ 116 | Ed Ott | .05 | .02 | .00 |
| ☐ 117 | Dave Parker | .60 | .24 | .06 |
| ☐ 118 | Willie Stargell | .60 | .24 | .06 |
| ☐ 119 | Kent Tekulve | .10 | .04 | .01 |
| ☐ 120 | Pirates Checklist | .03 | .00 | .00 |
| | (unnumbered) | | | |
| ☐ 121 | Bob Forsch | .10 | .04 | .01 |
| ☐ 122 | George Hendrick | .10 | .04 | .01 |
| ☐ 123 | Keith Hernandez | .60 | .24 | .06 |
| ☐ 124 | Tom Herr | .10 | .04 | .01 |
| ☐ 125 | Sixto Lezcano | .05 | .02 | .00 |
| ☐ 126 | Ken Oberkfell | .05 | .02 | .00 |
| ☐ 127 | Darrell Porter | .10 | .04 | .01 |
| ☐ 128 | Tony Scott | .05 | .02 | .00 |
| ☐ 129 | Lary Sorensen | .05 | .02 | .00 |
| ☐ 130 | Bruce Sutter | .25 | .10 | .02 |
| ☐ 131 | Garry Templeton | .10 | .04 | .01 |
| ☐ 132 | Cardinals Checklist | .03 | .00 | .00 |
| | (unnumbered) | | | |

---

**FAMILY FUN:** Have fun with all members of your family. Take them along to a sports collectibles convention in your area.

---

## 1982 Coke Red Sox

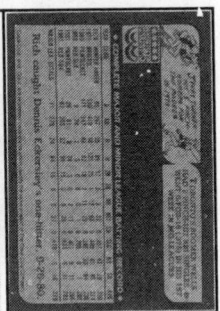

The cards in this 22 card set measure 2 1/2" by 3 1/2". This set of Boston Red Sox ballplayers was issued locally in the Boston area as a joint promotion by Brigham's Ice Cream Stores and Coca-Cola. The pictures are identical to those in the Topps regular 1982 issue, except that the colors are brighter and the Brigham and Coke logos appear inside the frame line. The reverses are done in red, black and gray, in contrast to the Topps set, and the number appears to the right of the position listing. The cards were initally distributed in three-card cello packs with an ice cream or Coca-Cola purchase but later became available as sets within the hobby. The unnumbered title or advertising card carries a premium offer on the reverse.

| | | MINT | VG-E | F-G |
|---|---|---|---|---|
| COMPLETE SET | | 3.50 | 1.40 | .35 |
| COMMON PLAYER | | .05 | .02 | .00 |
| ☐ 1 | Gary Allenson | .05 | .02 | .00 |
| ☐ 2 | Tom Burgmeier | .05 | .02 | .00 |
| ☐ 3 | Mark Clear | .05 | .02 | .00 |
| ☐ 4 | Steve Crawford | .05 | .02 | .00 |
| ☐ 5 | Dennis Eckersley | .10 | .04 | .01 |
| ☐ 6 | Dwight Evans | .60 | .24 | .06 |
| ☐ 7 | Rich Gedman | 1.00 | .40 | .10 |
| ☐ 8 | Garry Hancock | .05 | .02 | .00 |
| ☐ 9 | Glen Hoffman | .05 | .02 | .00 |
| ☐ 10 | Carney Lansford | .20 | .08 | .02 |
| ☐ 11 | Rick Miller | .05 | .02 | .00 |
| ☐ 12 | Reid Nichols | .05 | .02 | .00 |
| ☐ 13 | Bob Ojeda | .30 | .12 | .03 |
| ☐ 14 | Tony Perez | .30 | .12 | .03 |
| ☐ 15 | Chuck Rainey | .05 | .02 | .00 |
| ☐ 16 | Jerry Remy | .05 | .02 | .00 |
| ☐ 17 | Jim Rice | 1.00 | .40 | .10 |
| ☐ 18 | Bob Stanley | .15 | .06 | .01 |
| ☐ 19 | Dave Stapleton | .05 | .02 | .00 |
| ☐ 20 | Mike Torrez | .10 | .04 | .01 |
| ☐ 21 | John Tudor | .30 | .12 | .03 |
| ☐ 22 | Carl Yastrzemski | 1.50 | .60 | .15 |
| ☐ 23 | Title Card | .03 | .00 | .00 |
| | (unnumbered) | | | |

## 1982 Coke Reds

The cards in this 22 card set measure 2 1/2" by 3 1/2". The 1982 Coca-Cola Cincinnati Reds set, issued in conjunction with Topps, contains 22 cards of current Reds players. Although the cards of 15 players feature the exact photo used in the Topps' regular issue, the Coke photos have better coloration and appear sharper than their Topps counterparts. Six players, Cedeno, Harris, Hurdle,

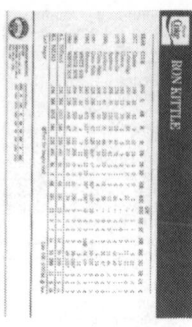

Kern, Krenchicki, and Trevino are new to the Redleg uniform via trades, while Joel Householder had formerly appeared on the Reds' 1982 Topps "Future Stars" card. The cards are numbered 1 to 22 on the red and gray reverse, and the Coke logo appears on both sides of the card. There is an unnumbered title card which contains a premium offer on the reverse.

|  | MINT | VG-E | F-G |
|---|---|---|---|
| COMPLETE SET | 3.50 | 1.40 | .35 |
| COMMON PLAYER | .05 | .02 | .00 |

| | | MINT | VG-E | F-G |
|---|---|---|---|---|
| ☐ 1 | Johnny Bench | 1.25 | .50 | .12 |
| ☐ 2 | Bruce Berenyi | .05 | .02 | .00 |
| ☐ 3 | Larry Biittner | .05 | .02 | .00 |
| ☐ 4 | Cesar Cedeno | .10 | .04 | .01 |
| ☐ 5 | Dave Concepcion | .25 | .10 | .02 |
| ☐ 6 | Dan Driessen | .10 | .04 | .01 |
| ☐ 7 | Greg Harris | .15 | .06 | .01 |
| ☐ 8 | Paul Householder | .05 | .02 | .00 |
| ☐ 9 | Tom Hume | .05 | .02 | .00 |
| ☐ 10 | Clint Hurdle | .05 | .02 | .00 |
| ☐ 11 | Jim Kern | .05 | .02 | .00 |
| ☐ 12 | Wayne Krenchicki | .05 | .02 | .00 |
| ☐ 13 | Rafael Landestoy | .05 | .02 | .00 |
| ☐ 14 | Charlie Leibrandt | .15 | .06 | .01 |
| ☐ 15 | Mike O'Berry | .05 | .02 | .00 |
| ☐ 16 | Ron Oester | .10 | .04 | .01 |
| ☐ 17 | Frank Pastore | .05 | .02 | .00 |
| ☐ 18 | Joe Price | .05 | .02 | .00 |
| ☐ 19 | Tom Seaver | 1.25 | .50 | .12 |
| ☐ 20 | Mario Soto | .30 | .12 | .03 |
| ☐ 21 | Alex Trevino | .05 | .02 | .00 |
| ☐ 22 | Mike Vail | .05 | .02 | .00 |
| ☐ 23 | Title Card (unnumbered) | .03 | .00 | .00 |

## 1985 Coke White Sox

This 30 card set features present and past Chicago White Sox players and personnel. Cards measure 2 5/8" by 4 1/8" and feature a red band at the bottom of the card. Within the red band are the White Sox logo, the player's name, position, uniform number, and a small oval portrait of an all-time White Sox Great at a similar position. the cards were available two at a time at Tuesday night White Sox home games or as a complete set through membership in the Coca-Cola White Sox Fan Club. The cards below are numbered by uniform number; the last three cards are unnumbered.

|  | MINT | VG-E | F-G |
|---|---|---|---|
| COMPLETE SET | 9.00 | 3.75 | .90 |
| COMMON PLAYER | .25 | .10 | .02 |

| | | MINT | VG-E | F-G |
|---|---|---|---|---|
| ☐ 0 | Oscar Gamble Zeke Bonura | .25 | .10 | .02 |

| | | MINT | VG-E | F-G |
|---|---|---|---|---|
| ☐ 1 | Scott Fletcher Luke Appling | .50 | .20 | .05 |
| ☐ 3 | Harold Baines Bill Melton | .60 | .24 | .06 |
| ☐ 5 | Luis Salazar Chico Carrasquel | .25 | .10 | .02 |
| ☐ 7 | Marc Hill Sherm Lollar | .25 | .10 | .02 |
| ☐ 8 | Daryl Boston Jim Landis | .25 | .10 | .02 |
| ☐ 10 | Tony LaRussa Al Lopez | .35 | .14 | .03 |
| ☐ 12 | Julio Cruz Nellie Fox | .35 | .14 | .03 |
| ☐ 13 | Ozzie Guillen Luis Aparicio | .90 | .36 | .09 |
| ☐ 17 | Jerry Hairston Smoky Burgess | .25 | .10 | .02 |
| ☐ 20 | Joe DeSa Carlos May | .25 | .10 | .02 |
| ☐ 22 | Joel Skinner J.C. Martin | .25 | .10 | .02 |
| ☐ 23 | Rudy Law Bill Skowron | .25 | .10 | .02 |
| ☐ 24 | Floyd Bannister Red Faber | .35 | .14 | .03 |
| ☐ 29 | Greg Walker Dick Allen | .60 | .24 | .06 |
| ☐ 30 | Gene Nelson Early Wynn | .35 | .14 | .03 |
| ☐ 32 | Tim Hulett Pete Ward | .25 | .10 | .02 |
| ☐ 34 | Richard Dotson Ed Walsh | .35 | .14 | .03 |
| ☐ 37 | Dan Spillner Thornton Lee | .25 | .10 | .02 |
| ☐ 40 | Britt Burns Gary Peters | .30 | .12 | .03 |
| ☐ 41 | Tom Seaver Ted Lyons | 1.25 | .50 | .12 |
| ☐ 40 | Ron Kittle Minnie Minoso | .40 | .16 | .04 |
| ☐ 43 | Bob James Hoyt Wilhelm | .50 | .20 | .05 |
| ☐ 44 | Tom Paciorek Eddie Collins | .35 | .14 | .03 |
| ☐ 46 | Tim Lollar Billy Pierce | .25 | .10 | .02 |
| ☐ 50 | Juan Agosto Wilbur Wood | .25 | .10 | .02 |
| ☐ 72 | Carlton Fisk Ray Schalk | .50 | .20 | .05 |
| ☐ xx | Comiskey Park (unnumbered) | .25 | .10 | .02 |
| ☐ xx | Nancy Faust (park organist) (unnumbered) | .25 | .10 | .02 |
| ☐ xx | Ribbie and Roobarb (unnumbered) | .25 | .10 | .02 |

## 1986 Coke White Sox

This colorful 30-card set features a borderless photo on top of a blue-on-white name, postion, and uniform number. Card backs provide complete

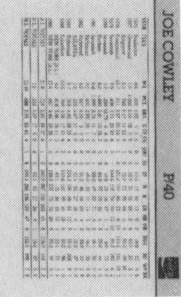

major and minor season-by-season career statistical information. Since the cards are unnumbered, they are numbered below according to uniform number. The cards measure approximately 2 5/8" by 4". The five unnumbered non-player cards are listed at the end.

|  |  | MINT | VG-E | F-G |
|---|---|---|---|---|
| COMPLETE SET | | 8.00 | 3.25 | .80 |
| COMMON PLAYER | | .20 | .08 | .02 |
| ☐ | 1 Wayne Tolleson | .20 | .08 | .02 |
| ☐ | 3 Harold Baines | .90 | .36 | .09 |
| ☐ | 7 Marc Hill | .20 | .08 | .02 |
| ☐ | 8 Daryl Boston | .30 | .12 | .03 |
| ☐ | 12 Julio Cruz | .20 | .08 | .02 |
| ☐ | 13 Ozzie Guillen | .50 | .20 | .05 |
| ☐ | 17 Jerry Hairston | .20 | .08 | .02 |
| ☐ | 19 Floyd Bannister | .30 | .12 | .03 |
| ☐ | 20 Reid Nichols | .20 | .08 | .02 |
| ☐ | 22 Joel Skinner | .30 | .12 | .03 |
| ☐ | 24 Dave Schmidt | .20 | .08 | .02 |
| ☐ | 26 Bobby Bonilla | .30 | .12 | .03 |
| ☐ | 29 Greg Walker | .50 | .20 | .05 |
| ☐ | 30 Gene Nelson | .20 | .08 | .02 |
| ☐ | 32 Tim Hulett | .20 | .08 | .02 |
| ☐ | 33 Neil Allen | .30 | .12 | .03 |
| ☐ | 34 Richard Dotson | .30 | .12 | .03 |
| ☐ | 40 Joe Cowley | .30 | .12 | .03 |
| ☐ | 41 Tom Seaver | .90 | .36 | .09 |
| ☐ | 42 Ron Kittle | .30 | .12 | .03 |
| ☐ | 43 Bob James | .20 | .08 | .02 |
| ☐ | 44 John Cangelosi | .50 | .20 | .05 |
| ☐ | 50 Juan Agosto | .20 | .08 | .02 |
| ☐ | 52 Joel Davis | .30 | .12 | .03 |
| ☐ | 72 Carlton Fisk | .50 | .20 | .05 |
| ☐ | xx Nancy Faust (Organist) (unnumbered) | .20 | .08 | .02 |
| ☐ | xx Ken"Hawk" Harrelson (unnumbered) | .20 | .08 | .02 |
| ☐ | xx Tony LaRussa MGR (unnumbered) | .20 | .08 | .02 |
| ☐ | xx Minnie Minoso COA (unnumbered) | .20 | .08 | .02 |
| ☐ | xx Ribbie and Roobarb (unnumbered) | .20 | .08 | .02 |

## 1914 Cracker Jack

The cards in this 144 card set measure 2 1/4" by 3". This "Series of colored pictures of Famous Ball Players and Managers" was issued in packages of Cracker Jack in 1914. The cards have tinted photos set against red backgrounds and many are found with caramel stains. The set also contains Federal League players. The company claims to have printed 15 million cards. The 1914 series can be distinguished from the 1915 issue by the advertising found on the back of the cards. The ACC catalog number is E145-1.

|  |  | MINT | VG-E | F-G |
|---|---|---|---|---|
| COMPLETE SET | | 8000.00 | 3500.00 | 900.00 |
| COMMON PLAYER (1-144) | | 40.00 | 16.00 | 4.00 |
| ☐ | 1 Otto Knabe | 40.00 | 16.00 | 4.00 |
| ☐ | 2 Frank Baker | 80.00 | 32.00 | 8.00 |
| ☐ | 3 Joe Tinker | 80.00 | 32.00 | 8.00 |
| ☐ | 4 Larry Doyle | 40.00 | 16.00 | 4.00 |
| ☐ | 5 Ward Miller | 40.00 | 16.00 | 4.00 |
| ☐ | 6 Eddie Plank (Phila. AL) | 100.00 | 40.00 | 10.00 |
| ☐ | 7 Eddie Collins (Phila. AL) | 100.00 | 40.00 | 10.00 |
| ☐ | 8 Rube Oldring | 40.00 | 16.00 | 4.00 |
| ☐ | 9 Artie Hoffman | 40.00 | 16.00 | 4.00 |
| ☐ | 10 John McInnis | 45.00 | 18.00 | 4.50 |
| ☐ | 11 George Stovall | 40.00 | 16.00 | 4.00 |
| ☐ | 12 Connie Mack | 125.00 | 50.00 | 12.50 |
| ☐ | 13 Art Wilson | 40.00 | 16.00 | 4.00 |
| ☐ | 14 Sam Crawford | 80.00 | 32.00 | 8.00 |
| ☐ | 15 Reb Russell | 40.00 | 16.00 | 4.00 |
| ☐ | 16 Howie Camnitz | 40.00 | 16.00 | 4.00 |
| ☐ | 17 Roger Bresnahan (Catcher) | 80.00 | 32.00 | 8.00 |
| ☐ | 18 Johnny Evers | 80.00 | 32.00 | 8.00 |
| ☐ | 19 Chief Bender (Phila. AL) | 100.00 | 40.00 | 10.00 |
| ☐ | 20 Cy Falkenberg | 40.00 | 16.00 | 4.00 |
| ☐ | 21 Heine Zimmerman | 40.00 | 16.00 | 4.00 |
| ☐ | 22 Joe Wood | 50.00 | 20.00 | 5.00 |
| ☐ | 23 Charles Comiskey | 100.00 | 40.00 | 10.00 |
| ☐ | 24 George Mullen | 40.00 | 16.00 | 4.00 |
| ☐ | 25 Michael Simon | 40.00 | 16.00 | 4.00 |
| ☐ | 26 James Scott | 40.00 | 16.00 | 4.00 |
| ☐ | 27 Bill Carrigan | 40.00 | 16.00 | 4.00 |
| ☐ | 28 Jack Barry | 40.00 | 16.00 | 4.00 |
| ☐ | 29 Vean Gregg (Cleve) | 50.00 | 20.00 | 5.00 |
| ☐ | 30 Ty Cobb | 800.00 | 320.00 | 80.00 |
| ☐ | 31 Heine Wagner | 40.00 | 16.00 | 4.00 |
| ☐ | 32 Mordecai Brown | 80.00 | 32.00 | 8.00 |
| ☐ | 33 Amos Strunk | 40.00 | 16.00 | 4.00 |
| ☐ | 34 Ira Thomas | 40.00 | 16.00 | 4.00 |
| ☐ | 35 Harry Hooper | 80.00 | 32.00 | 8.00 |
| ☐ | 36 Ed Walsh | 80.00 | 32.00 | 8.00 |
| ☐ | 37 Grover Alexander | 125.00 | 50.00 | 12.50 |
| ☐ | 38 Red Dooin (Phila. NL) | 50.00 | 20.00 | 5.00 |
| ☐ | 39 Chick Gandil | 40.00 | 16.00 | 4.00 |
| ☐ | 40 Jimmy Austin (St.L. AL) | 50.00 | 20.00 | 5.00 |
| ☐ | 41 Tommy Leach | 40.00 | 16.00 | 4.00 |
| ☐ | 42 Al Bridwell | 40.00 | 16.00 | 4.00 |
| ☐ | 43 Rube Marquard (NY NL) | 100.00 | 40.00 | 10.00 |
| ☐ | 44 Charles Tesreau | 40.00 | 16.00 | 4.00 |
| ☐ | 45 Fred Luderus | 40.00 | 16.00 | 4.00 |
| ☐ | 46 Bob Groom | 40.00 | 16.00 | 4.00 |
| ☐ | 47 Josh Devore (Phila. NL) | 50.00 | 20.00 | 5.00 |
| ☐ | 48 Harry Lord | 100.00 | 40.00 | 10.00 |
| ☐ | 49 John Miller | 40.00 | 16.00 | 4.00 |
| ☐ | 50 John Hummell | 40.00 | 16.00 | 4.00 |
| ☐ | 51 Nap Rucker | 40.00 | 16.00 | 4.00 |
| ☐ | 52 Zach Wheat | 80.00 | 32.00 | 8.00 |
| ☐ | 53 Otto Miller | 40.00 | 16.00 | 4.00 |
| ☐ | 54 Marty O'Toole | 40.00 | 16.00 | 4.00 |
| ☐ | 55 Dick Hoblitzel(Cinc.) | 50.00 | 20.00 | 5.00 |
| ☐ | 56 Clyde Milan | 40.00 | 16.00 | 4.00 |
| ☐ | 57 Walter Johnson | 400.00 | 160.00 | 40.00 |
| ☐ | 58 Wally Schang | 40.00 | 16.00 | 4.00 |
| ☐ | 59 Harry Gessler | 40.00 | 16.00 | 4.00 |

| | | | | |
|---|---|---|---|---|
| ☐ | 60 | Rollie Zeider | 100.00 | 40.00 | 10.00 |
| ☐ | 61 | Ray Schalk | 80.00 | 32.00 | 8.00 |
| ☐ | 62 | Jay Cashion | 100.00 | 40.00 | 10.00 |
| ☐ | 63 | Babe Adams | 40.00 | 16.00 | 4.00 |
| ☐ | 64 | Jimmy Archer | 40.00 | 16.00 | 4.00 |
| ☐ | 65 | Tris Speaker | 225.00 | 90.00 | 22.00 |
| ☐ | 66 | Napoleon Lajoie (Cleve.) | 225.00 | 90.00 | 22.00 |
| ☐ | 67 | Otis Crandall | 40.00 | 16.00 | 4.00 |
| ☐ | 68 | Honus Wagner | 350.00 | 140.00 | 35.00 |
| ☐ | 69 | John McGraw | 100.00 | 40.00 | 10.00 |
| ☐ | 70 | Fred Clarke | 80.00 | 32.00 | 8.00 |
| ☐ | 71 | Chief Meyers | 40.00 | 16.00 | 4.00 |
| ☐ | 72 | John Boehling | 40.00 | 16.00 | 4.00 |
| ☐ | 73 | Max Carey | 80.00 | 32.00 | 8.00 |
| ☐ | 74 | Frank Owens | 40.00 | 16.00 | 4.00 |
| ☐ | 75 | Miller Huggins | 80.00 | 32.00 | 8.00 |
| ☐ | 76 | Claude Hendrix | 40.00 | 16.00 | 4.00 |
| ☐ | 77 | Hugh Jennings | 80.00 | 32.00 | 8.00 |
| ☐ | 78 | Fred Merkle | 45.00 | 18.00 | 4.50 |
| ☐ | 79 | Ping Bodie | 40.00 | 16.00 | 4.00 |
| ☐ | 80 | Ed Ruelbach | 40.00 | 16.00 | 4.00 |
| ☐ | 81 | J.C. Delehanty | 40.00 | 16.00 | 4.00 |
| ☐ | 82 | Gavvy Cravath | 45.00 | 18.00 | 4.50 |
| ☐ | 83 | Russ Ford | 40.00 | 16.00 | 4.00 |
| ☐ | 84 | E.E. Knetzer | 40.00 | 16.00 | 4.00 |
| ☐ | 85 | Buck Herzog | 40.00 | 16.00 | 4.00 |
| ☐ | 86 | Burt Shotten | 40.00 | 16.00 | 4.00 |
| ☐ | 87 | Forrest Cady | 40.00 | 16.00 | 4.00 |
| ☐ | 88 | Christy Mathewson (Pitching) | 450.00 | 180.00 | 45.00 |
| ☐ | 89 | Lawrence Cheney | 40.00 | 16.00 | 4.00 |
| ☐ | 90 | Frank Smith | 40.00 | 16.00 | 4.00 |
| ☐ | 91 | Roger Peckinpaugh | 45.00 | 18.00 | 4.50 |
| ☐ | 92 | Al Demaree (N.Y. NL) | 50.00 | 20.00 | 5.00 |
| ☐ | 93 | Derrill Pratt (Throwing) | 100.00 | 40.00 | 10.00 |
| ☐ | 94 | Eddie Cicotte | 50.00 | 20.00 | 5.00 |
| ☐ | 95 | Ray Keating | 40.00 | 16.00 | 4.00 |
| ☐ | 96 | Beals Becker | 40.00 | 16.00 | 4.00 |
| ☐ | 97 | John (Rube) Benton | 40.00 | 16.00 | 4.00 |
| ☐ | 98 | Frank LaPorte | 40.00 | 16.00 | 4.00 |
| ☐ | 99 | Frank Chance | 300.00 | 120.00 | 30.00 |
| ☐ | 100 | Thomas Seaton | 40.00 | 16.00 | 4.00 |
| ☐ | 101 | Frank Schulte | 40.00 | 16.00 | 4.00 |
| ☐ | 102 | Ray Fisher | 40.00 | 16.00 | 4.00 |
| ☐ | 103 | Joe Jackson | 600.00 | 240.00 | 60.00 |
| ☐ | 104 | Vic Saier | 40.00 | 16.00 | 4.00 |
| ☐ | 105 | James Lavender | 40.00 | 16.00 | 4.00 |
| ☐ | 106 | Joe Birmingham | 40.00 | 16.00 | 4.00 |
| ☐ | 107 | Tom Downey | 40.00 | 16.00 | 4.00 |
| ☐ | 108 | Sherwood Magee (Phila. NL) | 50.00 | 20.00 | 5.00 |
| ☐ | 109 | Fred Blanding | 40.00 | 16.00 | 4.00 |
| ☐ | 110 | Bob Bescher | 40.00 | 16.00 | 4.00 |
| ☐ | 111 | Jim Callahan | 100.00 | 40.00 | 10.00 |
| ☐ | 112 | Ed Sweeney | 40.00 | 16.00 | 4.00 |
| ☐ | 113 | George Suggs | 40.00 | 16.00 | 4.00 |
| ☐ | 114 | Geo. J. Moriarty | 40.00 | 16.00 | 4.00 |
| ☐ | 115 | Addison Brennan | 40.00 | 16.00 | 4.00 |
| ☐ | 116 | Rollie Zeider | 40.00 | 16.00 | 4.00 |
| ☐ | 117 | Ted Easterly | 40.00 | 16.00 | 4.00 |
| ☐ | 118 | Ed Konetchy (Pitts.) | 50.00 | 20.00 | 5.00 |
| ☐ | 119 | George Perring | 40.00 | 16.00 | 4.00 |
| ☐ | 120 | Mike Doolan | 40.00 | 16.00 | 4.00 |
| ☐ | 121 | Perdue (Boston NL) | 50.00 | 20.00 | 5.00 |
| ☐ | 122 | Owen Bush | 40.00 | 16.00 | 4.00 |
| ☐ | 123 | Slim Sallee | 40.00 | 16.00 | 4.00 |
| ☐ | 124 | Earl Moore | 40.00 | 16.00 | 4.00 |
| ☐ | 125 | Bert Niehoff | 40.00 | 16.00 | 4.00 |
| ☐ | 126 | Walter Blair | 40.00 | 16.00 | 4.00 |
| ☐ | 127 | Butch Schmidt | 40.00 | 16.00 | 4.00 |
| ☐ | 128 | Steve Evans | 40.00 | 16.00 | 4.00 |
| ☐ | 129 | Ray Caldwell | 40.00 | 16.00 | 4.00 |
| ☐ | 130 | Ivy Wingo | 40.00 | 16.00 | 4.00 |
| ☐ | 131 | George Baumgardner | 40.00 | 16.00 | 4.00 |
| ☐ | 132 | Les Nunamaker | 40.00 | 16.00 | 4.00 |
| ☐ | 133 | Branch Rickey | 100.00 | 40.00 | 10.00 |
| ☐ | 134 | Armando Marsans (Cincinnati) | 50.00 | 20.00 | 5.00 |
| ☐ | 135 | Bill Killefer | 40.00 | 16.00 | 4.00 |
| ☐ | 136 | Rabbit Maranville | 80.00 | 32.00 | 8.00 |
| ☐ | 137 | William Rariden | 40.00 | 16.00 | 4.00 |
| ☐ | 138 | Hank Gowdy | 45.00 | 18.00 | 4.50 |
| ☐ | 139 | Rebel Oakes | 40.00 | 16.00 | 4.00 |
| ☐ | 140 | Danny Murphy | 40.00 | 16.00 | 4.00 |
| ☐ | 141 | Cy Barger | 40.00 | 16.00 | 4.00 |
| ☐ | 142 | Eugene Packard | 40.00 | 16.00 | 4.00 |
| ☐ | 143 | Jake Daubert | 45.00 | 18.00 | 4.50 |
| ☐ | 144 | James C. Walsh | 45.00 | 18.00 | 4.50 |

## 1915 Cracker Jack

FRANK SMITH, BALTIMORE · FEDERALS

The cards in this 176 card set measure 2 1/4" by 3". When turned over in a lateral motion, a 1915 "series of 176" Cracker Jack card shows the back printing upside-down. Cards were available in boxes of Cracker Jack or from the company for "100 Cracker Jack coupons, or one coupon and 25 cents." An album was available for "50 coupons or one coupon and 10 cents." The set essentially duplicates E145-1 (1914 Cracker Jack) except for some additional cards and new poses. Players in the Federal League are indicated by FED in the checklist below. The ACC designation is E145-2.

| | | | MINT | VG-E | F-G |
|---|---|---|---|---|---|
| | COMPLETE SET | | 8000.00 | 3500.00 | 900.00 |
| | COMMON PLAYER (1-144) | | 30.00 | 12.00 | 3.00 |
| | COMMON PLAYER (145-176) | | 40.00 | 16.00 | 4.00 |
| ☐ | 1 | Otto Knabe | 30.00 | 12.00 | 3.00 |
| ☐ | 2 | Frank Baker | 70.00 | 28.00 | 7.00 |
| ☐ | 3 | Joe Tinker | 70.00 | 28.00 | 7.00 |
| ☐ | 4 | Larry Doyle | 30.00 | 12.00 | 3.00 |
| ☐ | 5 | Ward Miller | 30.00 | 12.00 | 3.00 |
| ☐ | 6 | Eddie Plank (St.L. FED) | 90.00 | 36.00 | 9.00 |
| ☐ | 7 | Eddie Collins (Chicago AL) | 90.00 | 36.00 | 9.00 |
| ☐ | 8 | Rube Oldring | 30.00 | 12.00 | 3.00 |
| ☐ | 9 | Artie Hoffman | 30.00 | 12.00 | 3.00 |
| ☐ | 10 | John McInnis | 35.00 | 14.00 | 3.50 |
| ☐ | 11 | George Stovall | 30.00 | 12.00 | 3.00 |
| ☐ | 12 | Connie Mack | 120.00 | 50.00 | 12.00 |
| ☐ | 13 | Art Wilson | 30.00 | 12.00 | 3.00 |
| ☐ | 14 | Sam Crawford | 70.00 | 28.00 | 7.00 |
| ☐ | 15 | Reb Russell | 30.00 | 12.00 | 3.00 |
| ☐ | 16 | Howie Camnitz | 30.00 | 12.00 | 3.00 |
| ☐ | 17 | Roger Bresnahan | 70.00 | 28.00 | 7.00 |
| ☐ | 18 | Johnny Evers | 70.00 | 28.00 | 7.00 |
| ☐ | 19 | Chief Bender (Baltimore FED) | 90.00 | 36.00 | 9.00 |
| ☐ | 20 | Cy Falkenberg | 30.00 | 12.00 | 3.00 |
| ☐ | 21 | Heine Zimmerman | 30.00 | 12.00 | 3.00 |
| ☐ | 22 | Joe Wood | 40.00 | 16.00 | 4.00 |
| ☐ | 23 | Charles Comiskey | 90.00 | 36.00 | 9.00 |
| ☐ | 24 | George Mullen | 30.00 | 12.00 | 3.00 |
| ☐ | 25 | Michael Simon | 30.00 | 12.00 | 3.00 |
| ☐ | 26 | James Scott | 30.00 | 12.00 | 3.00 |
| ☐ | 27 | Bill Carrigan | 30.00 | 12.00 | 3.00 |
| ☐ | 28 | Jack Barry | 30.00 | 12.00 | 3.00 |
| ☐ | 29 | Vean Gregg (Boston AL) | 35.00 | 14.00 | 3.50 |
| ☐ | 30 | Ty Cobb | 700.00 | 280.00 | 70.00 |
| ☐ | 31 | Heine Wagner | 30.00 | 12.00 | 3.00 |
| ☐ | 32 | Mordecai Brown | 70.00 | 28.00 | 7.00 |
| ☐ | 33 | Amos Strunk | 30.00 | 12.00 | 3.00 |
| ☐ | 34 | Ira Thomas | 30.00 | 12.00 | 3.00 |
| ☐ | 35 | Harry Hooper | 70.00 | 28.00 | 7.00 |
| ☐ | 36 | Ed Walsh | 70.00 | 28.00 | 7.00 |
| ☐ | 37 | Grover C. Alexander | 120.00 | 50.00 | 12.00 |
| ☐ | 38 | Red Dooin (Cinc.) | 35.00 | 14.00 | 3.50 |
| ☐ | 39 | Chick Gandil | 30.00 | 12.00 | 3.00 |
| ☐ | 40 | Jimmy Austin (Pitts. FED) | 40.00 | 16.00 | 4.00 |

| | | | | |
|---|---|---|---|---|
| ☐ 41 | Tommy Leach | 30.00 | 12.00 | 3.00 |
| ☐ 42 | Al Bridwell | 30.00 | 12.00 | 3.00 |
| ☐ 43 | Rube Marquard | 90.00 | 36.00 | 9.00 |
| | (Brooklyn FED) | | | |
| ☐ 44 | Charles Tesreau | 30.00 | 12.00 | 3.00 |
| ☐ 45 | Fred Luderus | 30.00 | 12.00 | 3.00 |
| ☐ 46 | Bob Groom | 30.00 | 12.00 | 3.00 |
| ☐ 47 | Josh Devore | 35.00 | 14.00 | 3.50 |
| | (Boston NL) | | | |
| ☐ 48 | Steve O'Neill | 45.00 | 18.00 | 4.50 |
| ☐ 49 | John Miller | 30.00 | 12.00 | 3.00 |
| ☐ 50 | John Hummell | 30.00 | 12.00 | 3.00 |
| ☐ 51 | Nap Rucker | 30.00 | 12.00 | 3.00 |
| ☐ 52 | Zach Wheat | 70.00 | 28.00 | 7.00 |
| ☐ 53 | Otto Miller | 30.00 | 12.00 | 3.00 |
| ☐ 54 | Marty O'Toole | 30.00 | 12.00 | 3.00 |
| ☐ 55 | Dick Hoblitzel | 35.00 | 14.00 | 3.50 |
| | (Boston AL) | | | |
| ☐ 56 | Clyde Milan | 30.00 | 12.00 | 3.00 |
| ☐ 57 | Walter Johnson | 375.00 | 150.00 | 37.00 |
| ☐ 58 | Wally Schang | 30.00 | 12.00 | 3.00 |
| ☐ 59 | Harry Gessler | 30.00 | 12.00 | 3.00 |
| ☐ 60 | Oscar Dugey | 35.00 | 14.00 | 3.50 |
| ☐ 61 | Ray Schalk | 70.00 | 28.00 | 7.00 |
| ☐ 62 | Willie Mitchell | 45.00 | 18.00 | 4.50 |
| ☐ 63 | Babe Adams | 30.00 | 12.00 | 3.00 |
| ☐ 64 | Jimmy Archer | 30.00 | 12.00 | 3.00 |
| ☐ 65 | Tris Speaker | 200.00 | 80.00 | 20.00 |
| ☐ 66 | Napoleon Lajoie | 200.00 | 80.00 | 20.00 |
| | (Phila. AL) | | | |
| ☐ 67 | Otis Crandall | 30.00 | 12.00 | 3.00 |
| ☐ 68 | Honus Wagner | 325.00 | 130.00 | 32.00 |
| ☐ 69 | John McGraw | 90.00 | 36.00 | 9.00 |
| ☐ 70 | Fred Clarke | 70.00 | 28.00 | 7.00 |
| ☐ 71 | Chief Meyers | 30.00 | 12.00 | 3.00 |
| ☐ 72 | John Boehling | 30.00 | 12.00 | 3.00 |
| ☐ 73 | Max Carey | 70.00 | 28.00 | 7.00 |
| ☐ 74 | Frank Owens | 30.00 | 12.00 | 3.00 |
| ☐ 75 | Miller Huggins | 70.00 | 28.00 | 7.00 |
| ☐ 76 | Claude Hendrix | 30.00 | 12.00 | 3.00 |
| ☐ 77 | Hugh Jennings | 70.00 | 28.00 | 7.00 |
| ☐ 78 | Fred Merkle | 35.00 | 14.00 | 3.50 |
| ☐ 79 | Ping Bodie | 30.00 | 12.00 | 3.00 |
| ☐ 80 | Ed Ruelbach | 30.00 | 12.00 | 3.00 |
| ☐ 81 | J.C. Delehanty | 30.00 | 12.00 | 3.00 |
| ☐ 82 | Gavvy Cravath | 35.00 | 14.00 | 3.50 |
| ☐ 83 | Russ Ford | 30.00 | 12.00 | 3.00 |
| ☐ 84 | E.E. Knetzer | 30.00 | 12.00 | 3.00 |
| ☐ 85 | Buck Herzog | 30.00 | 12.00 | 3.00 |
| ☐ 86 | Burt Shotten | 30.00 | 12.00 | 3.00 |
| ☐ 87 | Forrest Cady | 30.00 | 12.00 | 3.00 |
| ☐ 88 | Christy Mathewson | 325.00 | 130.00 | 32.00 |
| | (Portrait) | | | |
| ☐ 89 | Lawrence Cheney | 30.00 | 12.00 | 3.00 |
| ☐ 90 | Frank Smith | 30.00 | 12.00 | 3.00 |
| ☐ 91 | Roger Peckinpaugh | 35.00 | 14.00 | 3.50 |
| ☐ 92 | Al Demaree | 35.00 | 14.00 | 3.50 |
| | (Phila. NL) | | | |
| ☐ 93 | Derrill Pratt | 45.00 | 18.00 | 4.50 |
| | (Portrait) | | | |
| ☐ 94 | Eddie Cicotte | 35.00 | 14.00 | 3.50 |
| ☐ 95 | Ray Keating | 30.00 | 12.00 | 3.00 |
| ☐ 96 | Beals Becker | 30.00 | 12.00 | 3.00 |
| ☐ 97 | John (Rube) Benton | 30.00 | 12.00 | 3.00 |
| ☐ 98 | Frank LaPorte | 30.00 | 12.00 | 3.00 |
| ☐ 99 | Hal Chase | 80.00 | 32.00 | 8.00 |
| ☐ 100 | Thomas Seaton | 30.00 | 12.00 | 3.00 |
| ☐ 101 | Frank Schulte | 30.00 | 12.00 | 3.00 |
| ☐ 102 | Ray Fisher | 30.00 | 12.00 | 3.00 |
| ☐ 103 | Joe Jackson | 550.00 | 220.00 | 55.00 |
| ☐ 104 | Vic Saier | 30.00 | 12.00 | 3.00 |
| ☐ 105 | James Lavender | 30.00 | 12.00 | 3.00 |
| ☐ 106 | Joe Birmingham | 30.00 | 12.00 | 3.00 |
| ☐ 107 | Thomas Downey | 30.00 | 12.00 | 3.00 |
| ☐ 108 | Sherwood Magee | 35.00 | 14.00 | 3.50 |
| | (Boston NL) | | | |
| ☐ 109 | Fred Blanding | 30.00 | 12.00 | 3.00 |
| ☐ 110 | Bob Bescher | 30.00 | 12.00 | 3.00 |
| ☐ 111 | Herbie Moran | 45.00 | 18.00 | 4.50 |
| ☐ 112 | Ed Sweeney | 30.00 | 12.00 | 3.00 |
| ☐ 113 | George Suggs | 30.00 | 12.00 | 3.00 |
| ☐ 114 | Geo. J. Moriarty | 30.00 | 12.00 | 3.00 |
| ☐ 115 | Addison Brennan | 30.00 | 12.00 | 3.00 |
| ☐ 116 | Rollie Zeider | 30.00 | 12.00 | 3.00 |
| ☐ 117 | Ted Easterly | 30.00 | 12.00 | 3.00 |
| ☐ 118 | Ed Konetchy | 40.00 | 16.00 | 4.00 |
| | (Pitts. FED) | | | |
| ☐ 119 | George Perring | 30.00 | 12.00 | 3.00 |
| ☐ 120 | Mike Doolan | 30.00 | 12.00 | 3.00 |
| ☐ 121 | Perdue (St.L. NL) | 35.00 | 14.00 | 3.50 |
| ☐ 122 | Owen Bush | 30.00 | 12.00 | 3.00 |
| ☐ 123 | Slim Sallee | 30.00 | 12.00 | 3.00 |
| ☐ 124 | Earl Moore | 30.00 | 12.00 | 3.00 |
| ☐ 125 | Bert Niehoff | 35.00 | 14.00 | 3.50 |
| | (Phila. NL) | | | |
| ☐ 126 | Walter Blair | 30.00 | 12.00 | 3.00 |
| ☐ 127 | Butch Schmidt | 30.00 | 12.00 | 3.00 |
| ☐ 128 | Steve Evans | 30.00 | 12.00 | 3.00 |
| ☐ 129 | Ray Caldwell | 30.00 | 12.00 | 3.00 |
| ☐ 130 | Ivy Wingo | 30.00 | 12.00 | 3.00 |
| ☐ 131 | Geo. Baumgardner | 30.00 | 12.00 | 3.00 |
| ☐ 132 | Les Nunamaker | 30.00 | 12.00 | 3.00 |
| ☐ 133 | Branch Rickey | 90.00 | 36.00 | 9.00 |
| ☐ 134 | Armando Marsans | 40.00 | 16.00 | 4.00 |
| | (St.L. FED) | | | |
| ☐ 135 | William Killefer | 30.00 | 12.00 | 3.00 |
| ☐ 136 | Rabbit Maranville | 70.00 | 28.00 | 7.00 |
| ☐ 137 | William Rariden | 30.00 | 12.00 | 3.00 |
| ☐ 138 | Hank Gowdy | 35.00 | 14.00 | 3.50 |
| ☐ 139 | Rebel Oakes | 30.00 | 12.00 | 3.00 |
| ☐ 140 | Danny Murphy | 30.00 | 12.00 | 3.00 |
| ☐ 141 | Cy Barger | 30.00 | 12.00 | 3.00 |
| ☐ 142 | Eugene Packard | 30.00 | 12.00 | 3.00 |
| ☐ 143 | Jake Daubert | 35.00 | 14.00 | 3.50 |
| ☐ 144 | James C. Walsh | 30.00 | 12.00 | 3.00 |
| ☐ 145 | Ted Cather | 40.00 | 16.00 | 4.00 |
| ☐ 146 | George Tyler | 40.00 | 16.00 | 4.00 |
| ☐ 147 | Lee Magee | 40.00 | 16.00 | 4.00 |
| ☐ 148 | Owen Wilson | 40.00 | 16.00 | 4.00 |
| ☐ 149 | Hal Janvrin | 40.00 | 16.00 | 4.00 |
| ☐ 150 | Doc Johnston | 40.00 | 16.00 | 4.00 |
| ☐ 151 | George Whitted | 40.00 | 16.00 | 4.00 |
| ☐ 152 | George McQuillen | 40.00 | 16.00 | 4.00 |
| ☐ 153 | Bill James | 40.00 | 16.00 | 4.00 |
| ☐ 154 | Dick Rudolph | 40.00 | 16.00 | 4.00 |
| ☐ 155 | Joe Connolly | 40.00 | 16.00 | 4.00 |
| ☐ 156 | Jean Dubuc | 40.00 | 16.00 | 4.00 |
| ☐ 157 | George Kaiserling | 40.00 | 16.00 | 4.00 |
| ☐ 158 | Fritz Maisel | 40.00 | 16.00 | 4.00 |
| ☐ 159 | Heine Groh | 45.00 | 18.00 | 4.50 |
| ☐ 160 | Benny Kauff | 40.00 | 16.00 | 4.00 |
| ☐ 161 | Ed Rousch | 90.00 | 36.00 | 9.00 |
| ☐ 162 | George Stallings | 40.00 | 16.00 | 4.00 |
| ☐ 163 | Bert Whaling | 40.00 | 16.00 | 4.00 |
| ☐ 164 | Bob Shawkey | 45.00 | 18.00 | 4.50 |
| ☐ 165 | Eddie Murphy | 40.00 | 16.00 | 4.00 |
| ☐ 166 | Joe Bush | 40.00 | 16.00 | 4.00 |
| ☐ 167 | Clark Griffith | 90.00 | 36.00 | 9.00 |
| ☐ 168 | Vin Campbell | 40.00 | 16.00 | 4.00 |
| ☐ 169 | Raymond Collins | 40.00 | 16.00 | 4.00 |
| ☐ 170 | Hans Lobert | 40.00 | 16.00 | 4.00 |
| ☐ 171 | Earl Hamilton | 40.00 | 16.00 | 4.00 |
| ☐ 172 | Erskine Mayer | 40.00 | 16.00 | 4.00 |
| ☐ 173 | Tilly Walker | 40.00 | 16.00 | 4.00 |
| ☐ 174 | Robert Veach | 40.00 | 16.00 | 4.00 |
| ☐ 175 | Joseph Benz | 40.00 | 16.00 | 4.00 |
| ☐ 176 | Jim Vaughn | 40.00 | 16.00 | 4.00 |

## 1982 Cracker Jack

The cards in this 16 card set measure 2 1/2" by 3 1/2"; cards came in two sheets of 8 cards, plus an advertising card with a title in the center, which measured 7 1/2" by 10 1/2". Cracker Jack reentered the baseball card market for the first time since 1915 to promote the first "Old Timers Baseball Classic" held July 19, 1982. The color player photos have a Cracker Jack border and have either green (NL) or red (AL) frame lines and name panels. The Cracker Jack logo appears on both sides of each card, with AL players numbered 1-8 and NL players numbered 9-16. Of the 16 ballplayers pictured, five did not appear at the game. At first, the two sheets were available only through the mail but are now commonly found in hobby circles. The set was prepared for Cracker Jack by Topps.

|  | MINT | VG-E | F-G |
|---|---|---|---|
| COMPLETE SET | 5.00 | 2.00 | .50 |
| COMMON PLAYER | .15 | .06 | .01 |

| | | | MINT | VG-E | F-G |
|---|---|---|---|---|---|
| ☐ | 1 | Larry Doby | .15 | .06 | .01 |
| ☐ | 2 | Bob Feller | .50 | .20 | .05 |
| ☐ | 3 | Whitey Ford | .50 | .20 | .05 |
| ☐ | 4 | Al Kaline | .50 | .20 | .05 |
| ☐ | 5 | Harmon Killebrew | .30 | .12 | .03 |
| ☐ | 6 | Mickey Mantle | 1.50 | .60 | .15 |
| ☐ | 7 | Tony Oliva | .15 | .06 | .01 |
| ☐ | 8 | Brooks Robinson | .50 | .20 | .05 |
| ☐ | 9 | Hank Aaron | .75 | .30 | .07 |
| ☐ | 10 | Ernie Banks | .40 | .16 | .04 |
| ☐ | 11 | Ralph Kiner | .30 | .12 | .03 |
| ☐ | 12 | Ed Mathews | .30 | .12 | .03 |
| ☐ | 13 | Willie Mays | .75 | .30 | .07 |
| ☐ | 14 | Robin Roberts | .30 | .12 | .03 |
| ☐ | 15 | Duke Snider | .60 | .24 | .06 |
| ☐ | 16 | Warren Spahn | .40 | .16 | .04 |

## 1954 Dan Dee

BOB LEMON — CLEVELAND INDIANS — DAN·DEE POTATO CHIPS

The cards in this 29 card set measure 2 1/2" by 3 5/8". Most of the cards marketed by Dan Dee in bags of potato chips in 1954 depict players from the Indians or Pirates. The pictures used for Yankee players were also employed in the Briggs and Stahl-Meyer sets. Dan Dee cards have a waxed surface, but are commonly found with product stains. Smith and Cooper are the known scarcities. The ACC designation is F342.

|  | MINT | VG-E | F-G |
|---|---|---|---|
| COMPLETE SET | 2100.00 | 40.00 | 10.00 |
| COMMON PLAYER (1-29) | 30.00 | 12.00 | 3.00 |

| | | | MINT | VG-E | F-G |
|---|---|---|---|---|---|
| ☐ | 1 | Bobby Avila | 30.00 | 12.00 | 3.00 |
| ☐ | 2 | Hank Bauer | 35.00 | 14.00 | 3.50 |
| ☐ | 3 | Walker Cooper | 200.00 | 80.00 | 20.00 |
| ☐ | 4 | Larry Doby | 35.00 | 14.00 | 3.50 |
| ☐ | 5 | Luke Easter | 30.00 | 12.00 | 3.00 |
| ☐ | 6 | Bob Feller | 100.00 | 40.00 | 10.00 |
| ☐ | 7 | Bob Friend | 40.00 | 16.00 | 4.00 |
| ☐ | 8 | Mike Garcia | 35.00 | 14.00 | 3.50 |
| ☐ | 9 | Sid Gordon | 35.00 | 14.00 | 3.50 |
| ☐ | 10 | Jim Hegan | 30.00 | 12.00 | 3.00 |
| ☐ | 11 | Gil Hodges | 75.00 | 30.00 | 7.50 |
| ☐ | 12 | Art Houtteman | 30.00 | 12.00 | 3.00 |
| ☐ | 13 | Monte Irvin | 60.00 | 24.00 | 6.00 |
| ☐ | 14 | Paul LaPalme | 35.00 | 14.00 | 3.50 |
| ☐ | 15 | Bob Lemon | 60.00 | 24.00 | 6.00 |

| | | | MINT | VG-E | F-G |
|---|---|---|---|---|---|
| ☐ | 16 | Al Lopez | 60.00 | 24.00 | 6.00 |
| ☐ | 17 | Mickey Mantle | 500.00 | 200.00 | 50.00 |
| ☐ | 18 | Dale Mitchell | 30.00 | 12.00 | 3.00 |
| ☐ | 19 | Phil Rizzuto | 75.00 | 30.00 | 7.50 |
| ☐ | 20 | Curt Roberts | 40.00 | 16.00 | 4.00 |
| ☐ | 21 | Al Rosen | 35.00 | 14.00 | 3.50 |
| ☐ | 22 | Red Schoendienst | 35.00 | 14.00 | 3.50 |
| ☐ | 23 | Paul Smith | 300.00 | 120.00 | 30.00 |
| ☐ | 24 | Duke Snider | 100.00 | 40.00 | 10.00 |
| ☐ | 25 | George Strickland | 30.00 | 12.00 | 3.00 |
| ☐ | 26 | Max Surkont | 35.00 | 14.00 | 3.50 |
| ☐ | 27 | Frank Thomas | 75.00 | 30.00 | 7.50 |
| ☐ | 28 | Wally Westlake | 30.00 | 12.00 | 3.00 |
| ☐ | 29 | Early Wynn | 60.00 | 24.00 | 6.00 |

## 1933 Delong

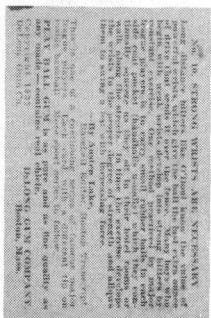

FRANK J. (LEFTY) O'DOUL
BROOKLYN DODGERS

The cards in this 24 card set measures 2" by 3". The 1933 Delong Gum set of 24 multi-colored cards was, along with the 1933 Goudey Big League series, one of the first baseball card sets issued with chewing gum. It was the only card set issued by this company. The reverse text was written by Austen Lake, who also wrote the sports tips found on the Diamond Stars series which began in 1934, leading to speculation that Delong was bought out by National Chicle. The ACC designation is R333.

|  | MINT | VG-E | F-G |
|---|---|---|---|
| COMPLETE SET | 3750.00 | 1600.00 | 450.00 |
| COMMON PLAYER (1-24) | 90.00 | 36.00 | 9.00 |

| | | | MINT | VG-E | F-G |
|---|---|---|---|---|---|
| ☐ | 1 | Marty McManus | 90.00 | 36.00 | 9.00 |
| ☐ | 2 | Al Simmons | 150.00 | 60.00 | 15.00 |
| ☐ | 3 | Oscar Melillo | 90.00 | 36.00 | 9.00 |
| ☐ | 4 | William Terry | 175.00 | 70.00 | 18.00 |
| ☐ | 5 | Charlie Gehringer | 175.00 | 70.00 | 18.00 |
| ☐ | 6 | Mickey Cochrane | 200.00 | 80.00 | 20.00 |
| ☐ | 7 | Lou Gehrig | 1200.00 | 500.00 | 125.00 |
| ☐ | 8 | Kiki Cuyler | 150.00 | 60.00 | 15.00 |
| ☐ | 9 | Bill Urbanski | 90.00 | 36.00 | 9.00 |
| ☐ | 10 | Lefty O'Doul | 90.00 | 36.00 | 9.00 |
| ☐ | 11 | Fred Lindstrom | 150.00 | 60.00 | 15.00 |
| ☐ | 12 | Pie Traynor | 175.00 | 70.00 | 18.00 |
| ☐ | 13 | Rabbit Maranville | 150.00 | 60.00 | 15.00 |
| ☐ | 14 | Lefty Gomez | 200.00 | 80.00 | 20.00 |
| ☐ | 15 | Riggs Stephenson | 100.00 | 40.00 | 10.00 |
| ☐ | 16 | Lon Warneke | 90.00 | 36.00 | 9.00 |
| ☐ | 17 | Pepper Martin | 100.00 | 40.00 | 10.00 |
| ☐ | 18 | Jim Dykes | 90.00 | 36.00 | 9.00 |
| ☐ | 19 | Chick Hafey | 150.00 | 60.00 | 15.00 |
| ☐ | 20 | Joe Vosmik | 90.00 | 36.00 | 9.00 |
| ☐ | 21 | Jimmie Foxx | 325.00 | 130.00 | 32.00 |
| ☐ | 22 | Chuck Klein | 175.00 | 70.00 | 18.00 |
| ☐ | 23 | Lefty Grove | 250.00 | 100.00 | 25.00 |
| ☐ | 24 | Goose Goslin | 150.00 | 60.00 | 15.00 |

# 1934-36 Diamond Stars

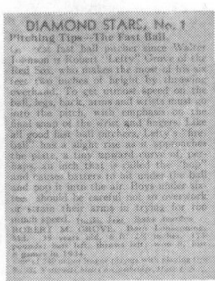

The cards in this 108 card set measure 2 3/8" by 2 7/8". The Diamond Stars set produced by National Chicle from 1934-36 is also commonly known as R327 (ACC). The year of production can be determined by the statistics contained on the back of the card. There are at least 168 possible front/back combinations counting blue (B) and green (G) backs over all three years. The last twelve cards are repeat players and are quite scarce. A blank backed proof sheet of 12 additional cards was recently discovered and has been reproduced from this original artwork and assigned numbers and text by Sport Americana. The checklist below lists the year(s) and back color(s) for the cards. Cards 32 through 72 were issued only in 1935 with green ink on back. Cards 73 through 84 were issued three ways: 35B, 35G, and 36B. Card numbers 85 through 108 were issued only in 1936 with blue ink on back.

|  | MINT | VG-E | F-G |
|---|---|---|---|
| COMPLETE SET | 3750.00 | 1600.00 | 450.00 |
| COMMON PLAYER (1-72) | 20.00 | 8.00 | 2.00 |
| COMMON PLAYER (73-84) | 24.00 | 10.00 | 2.40 |
| COMMON PLAYER (85-96) | 35.00 | 14.00 | 3.50 |
| COMMON PLAYER (97-108) | 90.00 | 36.00 | 9.00 |

| | | | | |
|---|---|---|---|---|
| ☐ | 1 Lefty Grove | 150.00 | 25.00 | 5.00 |
| | (34G, 35G) | | | |
| ☐ | 2A Al Simmons | 40.00 | 16.00 | 4.00 |
| | (34G, 35G) (Sox on uniform) | | | |
| ☐ | 2B Al Simmons | 60.00 | 24.00 | 6.00 |
| | (36B) (No name on uniform) | | | |
| ☐ | 3 Rabbit Maranville | 30.00 | 12.00 | 3.00 |
| | (34G, 35G) | | | |
| ☐ | 4 Buddy Myer | 20.00 | 8.00 | 2.00 |
| | (34G, 35G, 36B) | | | |
| ☐ | 5 Tommy Bridges | 20.00 | 8.00 | 2.00 |
| | (34G, 35G, 36B) | | | |
| ☐ | 6 Max Bishop | 20.00 | 8.00 | 2.00 |
| | (34G, 35G) | | | |
| ☐ | 7 Lew Fonseca | 20.00 | 8.00 | 2.00 |
| | (34G, 35G) | | | |
| ☐ | 8 Joe Vosmik | 20.00 | 8.00 | 2.00 |
| | (34G, 35G) | | | |
| ☐ | 9 Mickey Cochrane | 45.00 | 18.00 | 4.50 |
| | (34G, 35G, 36B) | | | |
| ☐ | 10A Leroy Mahaffey | 20.00 | 8.00 | 2.00 |
| | (34G, 35G) (A's on uniform) | | | |
| ☐ | 10B Leroy Mahaffey | 30.00 | 12.00 | 3.00 |
| | (36B) (No name on uniform) | | | |
| ☐ | 11 Bill Dickey | 60.00 | 24.00 | 6.00 |
| | (34G, 35G) | | | |
| ☐ | 12 F. Walker | 20.00 | 8.00 | 2.00 |
| | 34G, 35G) | | | |
| ☐ | 13 George Blaeholder | 20.00 | 8.00 | 2.00 |
| | (34G, 35G) | | | |
| ☐ | 14 Bill Terry | 45.00 | 18.00 | 4.50 |
| | (34G, 35G) | | | |
| ☐ | 15 Dick Bartell | 20.00 | 8.00 | 2.00 |
| | (34G, 35G) | | | |
| ☐ | 16 Lloyd Waner | 30.00 | 12.00 | 3.00 |

| | | | | |
|---|---|---|---|---|
| | (34G, 35G, 36B) | | | |
| ☐ | 17 Frank Frisch | 40.00 | 16.00 | 4.00 |
| | (34G, 35G) | | | |
| ☐ | 18 Chick Hafey | 35.00 | 14.00 | 3.50 |
| | (34G, 35G) | | | |
| ☐ | 19 Van Lingle Mungo | 20.00 | 8.00 | 2.00 |
| | (34G, 35G) | | | |
| ☐ | 20 Frank Hogan | 20.00 | 8.00 | 2.00 |
| | (34G, 35G) | | | |
| ☐ | 21 Johnny Vergez | 20.00 | 8.00 | 2.00 |
| | (34G, 35G) | | | |
| ☐ | 22 J. Wilson | 20.00 | 8.00 | 2.00 |
| | (34G, 35G, 36B) | | | |
| ☐ | 23 Bill Hallahan | 20.00 | 8.00 | 2.00 |
| | (34G, 35G) | | | |
| ☐ | 24 Earl Adams | 20.00 | 8.00 | 2.00 |
| | (34G, 35G) | | | |
| ☐ | 25 Wally Berger | 20.00 | 8.00 | 2.00 |
| | (35G) | | | |
| ☐ | 26 Pepper Martin | 24.00 | 10.00 | 2.40 |
| | 35G, 36B) | | | |
| ☐ | 27 Pie Traynor (35G) | 40.00 | 16.00 | 4.00 |
| ☐ | 28 Al Lopez (35G) | 35.00 | 14.00 | 3.50 |
| ☐ | 29 Red Rolfe (35G) | 20.00 | 8.00 | 2.00 |
| ☐ | 30A Heine Manush | 40.00 | 16.00 | 4.00 |
| | (35G) (W on sleeve) | | | |
| ☐ | 30B Heine Manush | 60.00 | 24.00 | 6.00 |
| | (36B) (No W on sleeve) | | | |
| ☐ | 31 Kiki Cuyler | 35.00 | 14.00 | 3.50 |
| | (35G, 36B) | | | |
| ☐ | 32 Sam Rice | 35.00 | 14.00 | 3.50 |
| ☐ | 33 Schoolboy Rowe | 20.00 | 8.00 | 2.00 |
| ☐ | 34 Stan Hack | 20.00 | 8.00 | 2.00 |
| ☐ | 35 Earl Averill | 35.00 | 14.00 | 3.50 |
| ☐ | 36A "Earnie" Lombardi | 40.00 | 16.00 | 4.00 |
| | (sic, Ernie) | | | |
| ☐ | 36B "Ernie" Lombardi | 40.00 | 16.00 | 4.00 |
| ☐ | 37 Billy Urbanski | 20.00 | 8.00 | 2.00 |
| ☐ | 38 Ben Chapman | 20.00 | 8.00 | 2.00 |
| ☐ | 39 Carl Hubbell | 45.00 | 18.00 | 4.50 |
| ☐ | 40 Blondy Ryan | 20.00 | 8.00 | 2.00 |
| ☐ | 41 Harvey Hendrick | 20.00 | 8.00 | 2.00 |
| ☐ | 42 Jimmy Dykes | 20.00 | 8.00 | 2.00 |
| ☐ | 43 Ted Lyons | 35.00 | 14.00 | 3.50 |
| ☐ | 44 Rogers Hornsby | 90.00 | 36.00 | 9.00 |
| ☐ | 45 Jo Jo White | 20.00 | 8.00 | 2.00 |
| ☐ | 46 Red Lucas | 20.00 | 8.00 | 2.00 |
| ☐ | 47 Bob Bolton | 20.00 | 8.00 | 2.00 |
| ☐ | 48 Rick Ferrell | 30.00 | 12.00 | 3.00 |
| ☐ | 49 Buck Jordan | 20.00 | 8.00 | 2.00 |
| ☐ | 50 Mel Ott | 60.00 | 24.00 | 6.00 |
| ☐ | 51 Burgess Whitehead | 20.00 | 8.00 | 2.00 |
| ☐ | 52 Tuck Stainback | 20.00 | 8.00 | 2.00 |
| ☐ | 53 Oscar Melillo | 20.00 | 8.00 | 2.00 |
| ☐ | 54A "Hank" Greenburg | 75.00 | 30.00 | 7.50 |
| | (sic, Greenberg) | | | |
| ☐ | 54B "Hank" Greenberg | 75.00 | 30.00 | 7.50 |
| ☐ | 55 Tony Cuccinello | 20.00 | 8.00 | 2.00 |
| ☐ | 56 Gus Suhr | 20.00 | 8.00 | 2.00 |
| ☐ | 57 Cy Blanton | 20.00 | 8.00 | 2.00 |
| ☐ | 58 Glenn Myatt | 20.00 | 8.00 | 2.00 |
| ☐ | 59 Jim Bottomley | 40.00 | 16.00 | 4.00 |
| ☐ | 60 Red Ruffing | 40.00 | 16.00 | 4.00 |
| ☐ | 61 Bill Werber | 20.00 | 8.00 | 2.00 |
| ☐ | 62 Fred Frankhouse | 20.00 | 8.00 | 2.00 |
| ☐ | 63 Travis Jackson | 40.00 | 16.00 | 4.00 |
| ☐ | 64 Jimmy Foxx | 90.00 | 36.00 | 9.00 |
| ☐ | 65 Zeke Bonura | 20.00 | 8.00 | 2.00 |
| ☐ | 66 Ducky Medwick | 40.00 | 16.00 | 4.00 |
| ☐ | 67 Marvin Owen | 20.00 | 8.00 | 2.00 |
| ☐ | 68 Sam Leslie | 20.00 | 8.00 | 2.00 |
| ☐ | 69 Earl Grace | 20.00 | 8.00 | 2.00 |
| ☐ | 70 Hal Trosky | 20.00 | 8.00 | 2.00 |
| ☐ | 71 Ossie Bluege | 20.00 | 8.00 | 2.00 |
| ☐ | 72 Tony Piet | 20.00 | 8.00 | 2.00 |
| ☐ | 73 Fritz Ostermueller | 24.00 | 10.00 | 2.40 |
| ☐ | 74 Tony Lazzeri | 35.00 | 14.00 | 3.50 |
| ☐ | 75 Jack Burns | 24.00 | 10.00 | 2.40 |
| ☐ | 76 Billy Rogell | 24.00 | 10.00 | 2.40 |
| ☐ | 77 Charlie Gehringer | 45.00 | 18.00 | 4.50 |
| ☐ | 78 Joe Kuhel | 24.00 | 10.00 | 2.40 |
| ☐ | 79 Willis Hudlin | 24.00 | 10.00 | 2.40 |
| ☐ | 80 Lou Chiozza | 24.00 | 10.00 | 2.40 |
| ☐ | 81 Bill Delancey | 24.00 | 10.00 | 2.40 |
| ☐ | 82A Johnny Babich | 30.00 | 12.00 | 3.00 |
| | (Dodgers on uniform) | | | |
| ☐ | 82B Johnny Babich | 30.00 | 12.00 | 3.00 |
| | (No name on uniform) | | | |
| ☐ | 83 Paul Waner | 40.00 | 16.00 | 4.00 |
| ☐ | 84 Sam Byrd | 24.00 | 10.00 | 2.40 |
| ☐ | 85 Moose Solters | 35.00 | 14.00 | 3.50 |

| | | | | |
|---|---|---|---|---|
| ☐ | 86 Frank Crosetti | 45.00 | 18.00 | 4.50 |
| ☐ | 87 Steve O'Neill | 35.00 | 14.00 | 3.50 |
| ☐ | 88 George Selkirk | 40.00 | 16.00 | 4.00 |
| ☐ | 89 Joe Stripp | 35.00 | 14.00 | 3.50 |
| ☐ | 90 Ray Hayworth | 35.00 | 14.00 | 3.50 |
| ☐ | 91 Bucky Harris | 45.00 | 18.00 | 4.50 |
| ☐ | 92 Ethan Allen | 35.00 | 14.00 | 3.50 |
| ☐ | 93 General Crowder | 35.00 | 14.00 | 3.50 |
| ☐ | 94 Wes Ferrell | 35.00 | 14.00 | 3.50 |
| ☐ | 95 Luke Appling | 50.00 | 20.00 | 5.00 |
| ☐ | 96 Lew Riggs | 35.00 | 14.00 | 3.50 |
| ☐ | 97 Al Lopez | 150.00 | 60.00 | 15.00 |
| ☐ | 98 Schoolboy Rowe | 100.00 | 40.00 | 10.00 |
| ☐ | 99 Pie Traynor | 200.00 | 80.00 | 20.00 |
| ☐ | 100 Earl Averill | 150.00 | 60.00 | 15.00 |
| ☐ | 101 Dick Bartell | 90.00 | 36.00 | 9.00 |
| ☐ | 102 Van Lingle Mungo | 90.00 | 36.00 | 9.00 |
| ☐ | 103 Bill Dickey | 250.00 | 100.00 | 25.00 |
| ☐ | 104 Red Rolfe | 90.00 | 36.00 | 9.00 |
| ☐ | 105 Ernie Lombardi | 150.00 | 60.00 | 15.00 |
| ☐ | 106 Red Lucas | 90.00 | 36.00 | 9.00 |
| ☐ | 107 Stan Hack | 90.00 | 36.00 | 9.00 |
| ☐ | 108 Wally Berger | 100.00 | 40.00 | 10.00 |

## 1981 Donruss

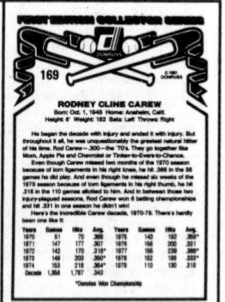

RODNEY CLINE CAREW
ROD CAREW FIRST BASE

The cards in this 605 set measure 2 1/2" by 3 1/2". In 1981 Donruss launched itself into the baseball card market with a set containing 600 numbered cards and five unnumbered checklists. Even though the five checklist cards are unnumbered they are numbered below (601-605) for convenience in reference. The cards are printed on thin stock and more than one pose exists for several popular players. The numerous errors of the first print run were later corrected by the company. These are marked P1 and P2 in the checklist.

| | | MINT | VG-E | F-G |
|---|---|---|---|---|
| | COMPLETE SET | 22.00 | 9.00 | 2.20 |
| | COMMON PLAYER (1-605) | .03 | .01 | .00 |
| ☐ | 1 Ozzie Smith | .35 | .14 | .03 |
| ☐ | 2 Rollie Fingers | .30 | .12 | .03 |
| ☐ | 3 Rick Wise | .06 | .02 | .00 |
| ☐ | 4 Gene Richards | .03 | .01 | .00 |
| ☐ | 5 Alan Trammell | .30 | .12 | .03 |
| ☐ | 6 Tom Brookens | .03 | .01 | .00 |
| ☐ | 7A Duffy Dyer P1 | .06 | .02 | .00 |
| | 1980 batting average has decimal point | | | |
| ☐ | 7B Duffy Dyer P2 | .06 | .02 | .00 |
| | 1980 batting average has no decimal point | | | |
| ☐ | 8 Mark Fidrych | .10 | .04 | .01 |
| ☐ | 9 Dave Rozema | .03 | .01 | .00 |
| ☐ | 10 Ricky Peters | .03 | .01 | .00 |
| ☐ | 11 Mike Schmidt | 1.00 | .40 | .10 |
| ☐ | 12 Willie Stargell | .30 | .12 | .03 |
| ☐ | 13 Tim Foli | .03 | .01 | .00 |
| ☐ | 14 Manny Sanguillen | .06 | .02 | .00 |
| ☐ | 15 Grant Jackson | .03 | .01 | .00 |
| ☐ | 16 Eddie Solomon | .03 | .01 | .00 |
| ☐ | 17 Omar Moreno | .03 | .01 | .00 |

| | | | | |
|---|---|---|---|---|
| ☐ | 18 Joe Morgan | .30 | .12 | .03 |
| ☐ | 19 Rafael Landestoy | .03 | .01 | .00 |
| ☐ | 20 Bruce Bochy | .03 | .01 | .00 |
| ☐ | 21 Joe Sambito | .06 | .02 | .00 |
| ☐ | 22 Manny Trillo | .06 | .02 | .00 |
| ☐ | 23A Dave Smith P1 | .25 | .10 | .02 |
| | Line box around stats is not complete | | | |
| ☐ | 23B Dave Smith P2 | .25 | .10 | .02 |
| | Box totally encloses stats at top | | | |
| ☐ | 24 Terry Puhl | .06 | .02 | .00 |
| ☐ | 25 Bump Wills | .03 | .01 | .00 |
| ☐ | 26A John Ellis P1 ERR | .50 | .20 | .05 |
| | Photo on front shows Danny Walton | | | |
| ☐ | 26B John Ellis P2 COR | .10 | .04 | .01 |
| ☐ | 27 Jim Kern | .03 | .01 | .00 |
| ☐ | 28 Richie Zisk | .06 | .02 | .00 |
| ☐ | 29 John Mayberry | .06 | .02 | .00 |
| ☐ | 30 Bob Davis | .03 | .01 | .00 |
| ☐ | 31 Jackson Todd | .03 | .01 | .00 |
| ☐ | 32 Al Woods | .03 | .01 | .00 |
| ☐ | 33 Steve Carlton | .60 | .24 | .06 |
| ☐ | 34 Lee Mazzilli | .06 | .02 | .00 |
| ☐ | 35 John Stearns | .03 | .01 | .00 |
| ☐ | 36 Roy Lee Jackson | .06 | .02 | .00 |
| ☐ | 37 Mike Scott | .30 | .12 | .03 |
| ☐ | 38 Lamar Johnson | .03 | .01 | .00 |
| ☐ | 39 Kevin Bell | .03 | .01 | .00 |
| ☐ | 40 Ed Farmer | .03 | .01 | .00 |
| ☐ | 41 Ross Baumgarten | .03 | .01 | .00 |
| ☐ | 42 Leo Sutherland | .03 | .01 | .00 |
| ☐ | 43 Dan Meyer | .03 | .01 | .00 |
| ☐ | 44 Ron Reed | .03 | .01 | .00 |
| ☐ | 45 Mario Mendoza | .03 | .01 | .00 |
| ☐ | 46 Rick Honeycutt | .06 | .02 | .00 |
| ☐ | 47 Glenn Abbott | .03 | .01 | .00 |
| ☐ | 48 Leon Roberts | .03 | .01 | .00 |
| ☐ | 49 Rod Carew | .60 | .24 | .06 |
| ☐ | 50 Bert Campaneris | .06 | .02 | .00 |
| ☐ | 51A Tom Donahue P1 ERR | .10 | .04 | .01 |
| | Name on front misspelled Donahue | | | |
| ☐ | 51B Tom Donohue P2 COR | .10 | .04 | .01 |
| ☐ | 52 Dave Frost | .03 | .01 | .00 |
| ☐ | 53 Ed Halicki | .03 | .01 | .00 |
| ☐ | 54 Dan Ford | .06 | .02 | .00 |
| ☐ | 55 Garry Maddox | .06 | .02 | .00 |
| ☐ | 56A Steve Garvey P1 | .60 | .24 | .06 |
| | "Surpassed 25 HR" | | | |
| ☐ | 56B Steve Garvey P2 | .60 | .24 | .06 |
| | "Surpassed 21 HR" | | | |
| ☐ | 57 Bill Russell | .06 | .02 | .00 |
| ☐ | 58 Don Sutton | .30 | .12 | .03 |
| ☐ | 59 Reggie Smith | .10 | .04 | .01 |
| ☐ | 60 Rick Monday | .06 | .02 | .00 |
| ☐ | 61 Ray Knight | .10 | .04 | .01 |
| ☐ | 62 Johnny Bench | .50 | .20 | .05 |
| ☐ | 63 Mario Soto | .10 | .04 | .01 |
| ☐ | 64 Doug Bair | .03 | .01 | .00 |
| ☐ | 65 George Foster | .20 | .08 | .02 |
| ☐ | 66 Jeff Burroughs | .06 | .02 | .00 |
| ☐ | 67 Keith Hernandez | .35 | .14 | .03 |
| ☐ | 68 Tom Herr | .10 | .04 | .01 |
| ☐ | 69 Bob Forsch | .06 | .02 | .00 |
| ☐ | 70 John Fulgham | .03 | .01 | .00 |
| ☐ | 71A Bobby Bonds P1 ERR | .25 | .10 | .02 |
| | 986 lifetime HR | | | |
| ☐ | 71B Bobby Bonds P2 COR | .10 | .04 | .01 |
| | 326 lifetime HR | | | |
| ☐ | 72A Rennie Stennett P1 | .06 | .02 | .00 |
| | "breaking broke leg" | | | |
| ☐ | 72B Rennie Stennett P2 | .06 | .02 | .00 |
| | Word "broke" deleted | | | |
| ☐ | 73 Joe Strain | .03 | .01 | .00 |
| ☐ | 74 Ed Whitson | .06 | .02 | .00 |
| ☐ | 75 Tom Griffin | .03 | .01 | .00 |
| ☐ | 76 Billy North | .03 | .01 | .00 |
| ☐ | 77 Gene Garber | .03 | .01 | .00 |
| ☐ | 78 Mike Hargrove | .06 | .02 | .00 |
| ☐ | 79 Dave Rosello | .03 | .01 | .00 |
| ☐ | 80 Ron Hassey | .03 | .01 | .00 |
| ☐ | 81 Sid Monge | .03 | .01 | .00 |
| ☐ | 82A Joe Charboneau P1 | .15 | .06 | .01 |
| | '78 highlights, "For some reason" | | | |
| ☐ | 82B Joe Charboneau P2 | .10 | .04 | .01 |
| | phrase "For some reason" deleted | | | |
| ☐ | 83 Cecil Cooper | .18 | .08 | .01 |
| ☐ | 84 Sal Bando | .06 | .02 | .00 |
| ☐ | 85 Moose Haas | .06 | .02 | .00 |

| | | | | |
|---|---|---|---|---|
| ☐ 86 | Mike Caldwell | .06 | .02 | .00 |
| ☐ 87A | Larry Hisle P1 | .12 | .05 | .01 |
| | '77 highlights, line | | | |
| | ends with "28 RBI" | | | |
| ☐ 87B | Larry Hisle P2 | .10 | .04 | .01 |
| | correct line "28 HR" | | | |
| ☐ 88 | Luis Gomez | .03 | .01 | .00 |
| ☐ 89 | Larry Parrish | .06 | .02 | .00 |
| ☐ 90 | Gary Carter | .60 | .24 | .06 |
| ☐ 91 | Bill Gullickson | .25 | .10 | .02 |
| ☐ 92 | Fred Norman | .03 | .01 | .00 |
| ☐ 93 | Tommy Hutton | .03 | .01 | .00 |
| ☐ 94 | Carl Yastrzemski | .80 | .32 | .08 |
| ☐ 95 | Glenn Hoffman | .06 | .02 | .00 |
| ☐ 96 | Dennis Eckersley | .06 | .02 | .00 |
| ☐ 97A | Tom Burgmeier P1 | .06 | .02 | .00 |
| | ERR Throws: Right | | | |
| ☐ 97B | Tom Burgmeier P2 | .06 | .02 | .00 |
| | COR Throws: Left | | | |
| ☐ 98 | Win Remmerswaal | .03 | .01 | .00 |
| ☐ 99 | Bob Horner | .25 | .10 | .02 |
| ☐ 100 | George Brett | .80 | .32 | .08 |
| ☐ 101 | Dave Chalk | .03 | .01 | .00 |
| ☐ 102 | Dennis Leonard | .06 | .02 | .00 |
| ☐ 103 | Renie Martin | .03 | .01 | .00 |
| ☐ 104 | Amos Otis | .06 | .02 | .00 |
| ☐ 105 | Graig Nettles | .15 | .06 | .01 |
| ☐ 106 | Eric Soderholm | .03 | .01 | .00 |
| ☐ 107 | Tommy John | .15 | .06 | .01 |
| ☐ 108 | Tom Underwood | .03 | .01 | .00 |
| ☐ 109 | Lou Piniella | .12 | .05 | .01 |
| ☐ 110 | Mickey Klutts | .03 | .01 | .00 |
| ☐ 111 | Bobby Murcer | .10 | .04 | .01 |
| ☐ 112 | Eddie Murray | .80 | .32 | .08 |
| ☐ 113 | Rick Dempsey | .06 | .02 | .00 |
| ☐ 114 | Scott McGregor | .10 | .04 | .01 |
| ☐ 115 | Ken Singleton | .10 | .04 | .01 |
| ☐ 116 | Gary Roenicke | .06 | .02 | .00 |
| ☐ 117 | Dave Revering | .03 | .01 | .00 |
| ☐ 118 | Mike Norris | .03 | .01 | .00 |
| ☐ 119 | Rickey Henderson | .70 | .28 | .07 |
| ☐ 120 | Mike Heath | .03 | .01 | .00 |
| ☐ 121 | Dave Cash | .03 | .01 | .00 |
| ☐ 122 | Randy Jones | .06 | .02 | .00 |
| ☐ 123 | Eric Rasmussen | .03 | .01 | .00 |
| ☐ 124 | Jerry Mumphrey | .06 | .02 | .00 |
| ☐ 125 | Richie Hebner | .03 | .01 | .00 |
| ☐ 126 | Mark Wagner | .03 | .01 | .00 |
| ☐ 127 | Jack Morris | .30 | .12 | .03 |
| ☐ 128 | Dan Petry | .15 | .06 | .01 |
| ☐ 129 | Bruce Robbins | .03 | .01 | .00 |
| ☐ 130 | Champ Summers | .03 | .01 | .00 |
| ☐ 131A | Pete Rose P1 | 1.25 | .50 | .12 |
| | last line ends with | | | |
| | "see card 251" | | | |
| ☐ 131B | Pete Rose P2 | 1.25 | .50 | .12 |
| | last line corrected | | | |
| | "see card 371" | | | |
| ☐ 132 | Willie Stargell | .30 | .12 | .03 |
| ☐ 133 | Ed Ott | .03 | .01 | .00 |
| ☐ 134 | Jim Bibby | .06 | .02 | .00 |
| ☐ 135 | Bert Blyleven | .15 | .06 | .01 |
| ☐ 136 | Dave Parker | .30 | .12 | .03 |
| ☐ 137 | Bill Robinson | .03 | .01 | .00 |
| ☐ 138 | Enos Cabell | .03 | .01 | .00 |
| ☐ 139 | Dave Bergman | .03 | .01 | .00 |
| ☐ 140 | J.R. Richard | .10 | .04 | .01 |
| ☐ 141 | Ken Forsch | .06 | .02 | .00 |
| ☐ 142 | Larry Bowa | .12 | .05 | .01 |
| ☐ 143 | Frank LaCorte | .03 | .01 | .00 |
| ☐ 144 | Dennis Walling | .03 | .01 | .00 |
| ☐ 145 | Buddy Bell | .15 | .06 | .01 |
| ☐ 146 | Ferguson Jenkins | .18 | .08 | .01 |
| ☐ 147 | Danny Darwin | .06 | .02 | .00 |
| ☐ 148 | John Grubb | .03 | .01 | .00 |
| ☐ 149 | Alfredo Griffin | .10 | .04 | .01 |
| ☐ 150 | Jerry Garvin | .03 | .01 | .00 |
| ☐ 151 | Paul Mirabella | .03 | .01 | .00 |
| ☐ 152 | Rick Bosetti | .03 | .01 | .00 |
| ☐ 153 | Dick Ruthven | .03 | .01 | .00 |
| ☐ 154 | Frank Taveras | .03 | .01 | .00 |
| ☐ 155 | Craig Swan | .03 | .01 | .00 |
| ☐ 156 | Jeff Reardon | .40 | .16 | .04 |
| ☐ 157 | Steve Henderson | .03 | .01 | .00 |
| ☐ 158 | Jim Morrison | .03 | .01 | .00 |
| ☐ 159 | Glenn Borgmann | .03 | .01 | .00 |
| ☐ 160 | LaMarr Hoyt | .40 | .16 | .04 |
| ☐ 161 | Rich Wortham | .03 | .01 | .00 |
| ☐ 162 | Thad Bosley | .03 | .01 | .00 |
| ☐ 163 | Julio Cruz | .03 | .01 | .00 |
| ☐ 164A | Del Unser P1 | .06 | .02 | .00 |
| | no "3B" heading | | | |
| ☐ 164B | Del Unser P2 | .06 | .02 | .00 |

| | | | | |
|---|---|---|---|---|
| | Batting record on back | | | |
| | corrected ("3B") | | | |
| ☐ 165 | Jim Anderson | .03 | .01 | .00 |
| ☐ 166 | Jim Beattie | .03 | .01 | .00 |
| ☐ 167 | Shane Rawley | .10 | .04 | .01 |
| ☐ 168 | Joe Simpson | .03 | .01 | .00 |
| ☐ 169 | Rod Carew | .60 | .24 | .06 |
| ☐ 170 | Fred Patek | .03 | .01 | .00 |
| ☐ 171 | Frank Tanana | .06 | .02 | .00 |
| ☐ 172 | Alfredo Martinez | .03 | .01 | .00 |
| ☐ 173 | Chris Knapp | .03 | .01 | .00 |
| ☐ 174 | Joe Rudi | .06 | .02 | .00 |
| ☐ 175 | Greg Luzinski | .15 | .06 | .01 |
| ☐ 176 | Steve Garvey | .60 | .24 | .06 |
| ☐ 177 | Joe Ferguson | .03 | .01 | .00 |
| ☐ 178 | Bob Welch | .10 | .04 | .01 |
| ☐ 179 | Dusty Baker | .10 | .04 | .01 |
| ☐ 180 | Rudy Law | .03 | .01 | .00 |
| ☐ 181 | Dave Concepcion | .15 | .06 | .01 |
| ☐ 182 | Johnny Bench | .50 | .20 | .05 |
| ☐ 183 | Mike LaCoss | .03 | .01 | .00 |
| ☐ 184 | Ken Griffey | .10 | .04 | .01 |
| ☐ 185 | Dave Collins | .06 | .02 | .00 |
| ☐ 186 | Brian Asselstine | .03 | .01 | .00 |
| ☐ 187 | Garry Templeton | .10 | .04 | .01 |
| ☐ 188 | Mike Phillips | .03 | .01 | .00 |
| ☐ 189 | Pete Vuckovich | .06 | .02 | .00 |
| ☐ 190 | John Urrea | .03 | .01 | .00 |
| ☐ 191 | Tony Scott | .03 | .01 | .00 |
| ☐ 192 | Darrell Evans | .12 | .05 | .01 |
| ☐ 193 | Milt May | .03 | .01 | .00 |
| ☐ 194 | Bob Knepper | .12 | .05 | .01 |
| ☐ 195 | Randy Moffitt | .03 | .01 | .00 |
| ☐ 196 | Larry Herndon | .03 | .01 | .00 |
| ☐ 197 | Rick Camp | .03 | .01 | .00 |
| ☐ 198 | Andre Thornton | .10 | .04 | .01 |
| ☐ 199 | Tom Veryzer | .03 | .01 | .00 |
| ☐ 200 | Gary Alexander | .03 | .01 | .00 |
| ☐ 201 | Rick Waits | .03 | .01 | .00 |
| ☐ 202 | Rick Manning | .03 | .01 | .00 |
| ☐ 203 | Paul Molitor | .15 | .06 | .01 |
| ☐ 204 | Jim Gantner | .06 | .02 | .00 |
| ☐ 205 | Paul Mitchell | .03 | .01 | .00 |
| ☐ 206 | Reggie Cleveland | .03 | .01 | .00 |
| ☐ 207 | Sixto Lezcano | .03 | .01 | .00 |
| ☐ 208 | Bruce Benedict | .03 | .01 | .00 |
| ☐ 209 | Rodney Scott | .03 | .01 | .00 |
| ☐ 210 | John Tamargo | .03 | .01 | .00 |
| ☐ 211 | Bill Lee | .06 | .02 | .00 |
| ☐ 212 | Andre Dawson | .25 | .10 | .02 |
| ☐ 213 | Rowland Office | .03 | .01 | .00 |
| ☐ 214 | Carl Yastrzemski | .80 | .32 | .08 |
| ☐ 215 | Jerry Remy | .06 | .02 | .00 |
| ☐ 216 | Mike Torrez | .06 | .02 | .00 |
| ☐ 217 | Skip Lockwood | .03 | .01 | .00 |
| ☐ 218 | Fred Lynn | .25 | .10 | .02 |
| ☐ 219 | Chris Chambliss | .06 | .02 | .00 |
| ☐ 220 | Willie Aikens | .06 | .02 | .00 |
| ☐ 221 | John Wathan | .03 | .01 | .00 |
| ☐ 222 | Dan Quisenberry | .25 | .10 | .02 |
| ☐ 223 | Willie Wilson | .20 | .08 | .02 |
| ☐ 224 | Clint Hurdle | .03 | .01 | .00 |
| ☐ 225 | Bob Watson | .06 | .02 | .00 |
| ☐ 226 | Jim Spencer | .03 | .01 | .00 |
| ☐ 227 | Ron Guidry | .30 | .12 | .03 |
| ☐ 228 | Reggie Jackson | .80 | .32 | .08 |
| ☐ 229 | Oscar Gamble | .06 | .02 | .00 |
| ☐ 230 | Jeff Cox | .03 | .01 | .00 |
| ☐ 231 | Luis Tiant | .10 | .04 | .01 |
| ☐ 232 | Rich Dauer | .03 | .01 | .00 |
| ☐ 233 | Dan Graham | .03 | .01 | .00 |
| ☐ 234 | Mike Flanagan | .10 | .04 | .01 |
| ☐ 235 | John Lowenstein | .03 | .01 | .00 |
| ☐ 236 | Benny Ayala | .03 | .01 | .00 |
| ☐ 237 | Wayne Gross | .03 | .01 | .00 |
| ☐ 238 | Rick Langford | .03 | .01 | .00 |
| ☐ 239 | Tony Armas | .12 | .05 | .01 |
| ☐ 240A | Bob Lacy P1 ERR | .12 | .05 | .01 |
| | Name misspelled | | | |
| | Bob "Lacy" | | | |
| ☐ 240B | Bob Lacey P2 COR | .08 | .03 | .01 |
| ☐ 241 | Gene Tenace | .03 | .01 | .00 |
| ☐ 242 | Bob Shirley | .03 | .01 | .00 |
| ☐ 243 | Gary Lucas | .10 | .04 | .01 |
| ☐ 244 | Jerry Turner | .03 | .01 | .00 |
| ☐ 245 | John Wockenfuss | .03 | .01 | .00 |
| ☐ 246 | Stan Papi | .03 | .01 | .00 |
| ☐ 247 | Milt Wilcox | .03 | .01 | .00 |
| ☐ 248 | Dan Schatzeder | .03 | .01 | .00 |
| ☐ 249 | Steve Kemp | .10 | .04 | .01 |
| ☐ 250 | Jim Lentine | .03 | .01 | .00 |
| ☐ 251 | Pete Rose | 1.25 | .50 | .12 |
| ☐ 252 | Bill Madlock | .20 | .08 | .02 |

| | | | | |
|---|---|---|---|---|
| ☐ 253 | Dale Berra | .06 | .02 | .00 |
| ☐ 254 | Kent Tekulve | .06 | .02 | .00 |
| ☐ 255 | Enrique Romo | .03 | .01 | .00 |
| ☐ 256 | Mike Easler | .06 | .02 | .00 |
| ☐ 257 | Chuck Tanner MGR | .06 | .02 | .00 |
| ☐ 258 | Art Howe | .03 | .01 | .00 |
| ☐ 259 | Alan Ashby | .03 | .01 | .00 |
| ☐ 260 | Nolan Ryan | .50 | .20 | .05 |
| ☐ 261A | Vern Ruhle P1 ERR Photo on front actually Ken Forsch | .50 | .20 | .05 |
| ☐ 261B | Vern Ruhle P2 COR | .10 | .04 | .01 |
| ☐ 262 | Bob Boone | .06 | .02 | .00 |
| ☐ 263 | Cesar Cedeno | .10 | .04 | .01 |
| ☐ 264 | Jeff Leonard | .10 | .04 | .01 |
| ☐ 265 | Pat Putnam | .03 | .01 | .00 |
| ☐ 266 | Jon Matlack | .06 | .02 | .00 |
| ☐ 267 | Dave Rajsich | .03 | .01 | .00 |
| ☐ 268 | Bill Sample | .03 | .01 | .00 |
| ☐ 269 | Damaso Garcia | .50 | .20 | .05 |
| ☐ 270 | Tom Buskey | .03 | .01 | .00 |
| ☐ 271 | Joey McLaughlin | .03 | .01 | .00 |
| ☐ 272 | Barry Bonnell | .03 | .01 | .00 |
| ☐ 273 | Tug McGraw | .10 | .04 | .01 |
| ☐ 274 | Mike Jorgensen | .03 | .01 | .00 |
| ☐ 275 | Pat Zachry | .03 | .01 | .00 |
| ☐ 276 | Neil Allen | .06 | .02 | .00 |
| ☐ 277 | Joel Youngblood | .03 | .01 | .00 |
| ☐ 278 | Greg Pryor | .03 | .01 | .00 |
| ☐ 279 | Britt Burns | .30 | .12 | .03 |
| ☐ 280 | Rich Dotson | .25 | .10 | .02 |
| ☐ 281 | Chet Lemon | .10 | .04 | .01 |
| ☐ 282 | Rusty Kuntz | .03 | .01 | .00 |
| ☐ 283 | Ted Cox | .03 | .01 | .00 |
| ☐ 284 | Sparky Lyle | .12 | .05 | .01 |
| ☐ 285 | Larry Cox | .03 | .01 | .00 |
| ☐ 286 | Floyd Bannister | .06 | .02 | .00 |
| ☐ 287 | Byron McLaughlin | .03 | .01 | .00 |
| ☐ 288 | Rodney Craig | .03 | .01 | .00 |
| ☐ 289 | Bobby Grich | .10 | .04 | .01 |
| ☐ 290 | Dickie Thon | .10 | .04 | .01 |
| ☐ 291 | Mark Clear | .06 | .02 | .00 |
| ☐ 292 | Dave Lemanczyk | .03 | .01 | .00 |
| ☐ 293 | Jason Thompson | .06 | .02 | .00 |
| ☐ 294 | Rick Miller | .03 | .01 | .00 |
| ☐ 295 | Lonnie Smith | .06 | .02 | .00 |
| ☐ 296 | Ron Cey | .15 | .06 | .01 |
| ☐ 297 | Steve Yeager | .06 | .02 | .00 |
| ☐ 298 | Bobby Castillo | .03 | .01 | .00 |
| ☐ 299 | Manny Mota | .06 | .02 | .00 |
| ☐ 300 | Jay Johnstone | .06 | .02 | .00 |
| ☐ 301 | Dan Driessen | .06 | .02 | .00 |
| ☐ 302 | Joe Nolan | .03 | .01 | .00 |
| ☐ 303 | Paul Householder | .06 | .02 | .00 |
| ☐ 304 | Harry Spilman | .03 | .01 | .00 |
| ☐ 305 | Cesar Geronimo | .03 | .01 | .00 |
| ☐ 306A | Gary Mathews P1 ERR . Name misspelled | .15 | .06 | .01 |
| ☐ 306B | Gary Matthews P2 COR | .10 | .04 | .01 |
| ☐ 307 | Ken Reitz | .03 | .01 | .00 |
| ☐ 308 | Ted Simmons | .15 | .06 | .01 |
| ☐ 309 | John Littlefield | .06 | .02 | .00 |
| ☐ 310 | George Frazier | .03 | .01 | .00 |
| ☐ 311 | Dane Iorg | .03 | .01 | .00 |
| ☐ 312 | Mike Ivie | .03 | .01 | .00 |
| ☐ 313 | Dennis Littlejohn | .03 | .01 | .00 |
| ☐ 314 | Gary Lavelle | .06 | .02 | .00 |
| ☐ 315 | Jack Clark | .15 | .06 | .01 |
| ☐ 316 | Jim Wohlford | .03 | .01 | .00 |
| ☐ 317 | Rick Matula | .03 | .01 | .00 |
| ☐ 318 | Toby Harrah | .06 | .02 | .00 |
| ☐ 319A | Dwane Kuiper P1 ERR .. Name misspelled | .12 | .05 | .01 |
| ☐ 319B | Duane Kuiper P2 COR .. | .08 | .03 | .01 |
| ☐ 320 | Len Barker | .06 | .02 | .00 |
| ☐ 321 | Victor Cruz | .03 | .01 | .00 |
| ☐ 322 | Dell Alston | .03 | .01 | .00 |
| ☐ 323 | Robin Yount | .50 | .20 | .05 |
| ☐ 324 | Charlie Moore | .03 | .01 | .00 |
| ☐ 325 | Lary Sorensen | .03 | .01 | .00 |
| ☐ 326A | Gorman Thomas P1 2nd line on back: "30 HR mark 4th" | .15 | .06 | .01 |
| ☐ 326B | Gorman Thomas P2 "30 HR mark 3rd" | .10 | .04 | .01 |
| ☐ 327 | Bob Rodgers MGR | .03 | .01 | .00 |
| ☐ 328 | Phil Niekro | .25 | .10 | .02 |
| ☐ 329 | Chris Speier | .03 | .01 | .00 |
| ☐ 330A | Steve Rodgers P1 ERR . Name misspelled | .15 | .06 | .01 |
| ☐ 330B | Steve Rogers P2 COR | .10 | .04 | .01 |
| ☐ 331 | Woodie Fryman | .03 | .01 | .00 |
| ☐ 332 | Warren Cromartie | .03 | .01 | .00 |
| ☐ 333 | Jerry White | .03 | .01 | .00 |
| ☐ 334 | Tony Perez | .15 | .06 | .01 |
| ☐ 335 | Carlton Fisk | .20 | .08 | .02 |
| ☐ 336 | Dick Drago | .03 | .01 | .00 |
| ☐ 337 | Steve Renko | .03 | .01 | .00 |
| ☐ 338 | Jim Rice | .60 | .24 | .06 |
| ☐ 339 | Jerry Royster | .03 | .01 | .00 |
| ☐ 340 | Frank White | .10 | .04 | .01 |
| ☐ 341 | Jamie Quirk | .03 | .01 | .00 |
| ☐ 342A | Paul Spittorff P1 ERR ... Name misspelled | .10 | .04 | .01 |
| ☐ 342B | Paul Splittorff P2 COR | .08 | .03 | .01 |
| ☐ 343 | Marty Pattin | .03 | .01 | .00 |
| ☐ 344 | Pete LaCock | .03 | .01 | .00 |
| ☐ 345 | Willie Randolph | .10 | .04 | .01 |
| ☐ 346 | Rick Cerone | .06 | .02 | .00 |
| ☐ 347 | Rich Gossage | .20 | .08 | .02 |
| ☐ 348 | Reggie Jackson | .75 | .30 | .07 |
| ☐ 349 | Ruppert Jones | .06 | .02 | .00 |
| ☐ 350 | Dave McKay | .03 | .01 | .00 |
| ☐ 351 | Yogi Berra MGR | .20 | .08 | .02 |
| ☐ 352 | Doug DeCinces | .10 | .04 | .01 |
| ☐ 353 | Jim Palmer | .35 | .14 | .03 |
| ☐ 354 | Tippy Martinez | .06 | .02 | .00 |
| ☐ 355 | Al Bumbry | .03 | .01 | .00 |
| ☐ 356 | Earl Weaver MGR | .10 | .04 | .01 |
| ☐ 357A | Bob Picciolo P1 ERR .... Name misspelled | .06 | .02 | .00 |
| ☐ 357B | Rob Picciolo P2 COR .... | .06 | .02 | .00 |
| ☐ 358 | Matt Keough | .03 | .01 | .00 |
| ☐ 359 | Dwayne Murphy | .06 | .02 | .00 |
| ☐ 360 | Brian Kingman | .03 | .01 | .00 |
| ☐ 361 | Bill Fahey | .03 | .01 | .00 |
| ☐ 362 | Steve Mura | .03 | .01 | .00 |
| ☐ 363 | Dennis Kinney | .03 | .01 | .00 |
| ☐ 364 | Dave Winfield | .50 | .20 | .05 |
| ☐ 365 | Lou Whitaker | .20 | .08 | .02 |
| ☐ 366 | Lance Parrish | .35 | .14 | .03 |
| ☐ 367 | Tim Corcoran | .03 | .01 | .00 |
| ☐ 368 | Pat Underwood | .03 | .01 | .00 |
| ☐ 369 | Al Cowens | .06 | .02 | .00 |
| ☐ 370 | Sparky Anderson MGR .... | .06 | .02 | .00 |
| ☐ 371 | Pete Rose | 1.25 | .50 | .12 |
| ☐ 372 | Phil Garner | .06 | .02 | .00 |
| ☐ 373 | Steve Nicosia | .03 | .01 | .00 |
| ☐ 374 | John Candelaria | .06 | .02 | .00 |
| ☐ 375 | Don Robinson | .06 | .02 | .00 |
| ☐ 376 | Lee Lacy | .06 | .02 | .00 |
| ☐ 377 | Lee Milner | .03 | .01 | .00 |
| ☐ 378 | Craig Reynolds | .03 | .01 | .00 |
| ☐ 379A | Luis Pujois P1 ERR Name misspelled | .10 | .04 | .01 |
| ☐ 379B | Luis Pujols P2 COR | .06 | .02 | .00 |
| ☐ 380 | Joe Niekro | .06 | .02 | .00 |
| ☐ 381 | Joaquin Andujar | .15 | .06 | .01 |
| ☐ 382 | Keith Moreland | .45 | .18 | .04 |
| ☐ 383 | Jose Cruz | .15 | .06 | .01 |
| ☐ 384 | Bill Virdon MGR | .06 | .02 | .00 |
| ☐ 385 | Jim Sundberg | .06 | .02 | .00 |
| ☐ 386 | Doc Medich | .03 | .01 | .00 |
| ☐ 387 | Al Oliver | .15 | .06 | .01 |
| ☐ 388 | Jim Norris | .03 | .01 | .00 |
| ☐ 389 | Bob Bailor | .03 | .01 | .00 |
| ☐ 390 | Ernie Whitt | .03 | .01 | .00 |
| ☐ 391 | Otto Velez | .03 | .01 | .00 |
| ☐ 392 | Roy Howell | .03 | .01 | .00 |
| ☐ 393 | Bob Walk | .06 | .02 | .00 |
| ☐ 394 | Doug Flynn | .03 | .01 | .00 |
| ☐ 395 | Pete Falcone | .03 | .01 | .00 |
| ☐ 396 | Tom Hausman | .03 | .01 | .00 |
| ☐ 397 | Elliott Maddox | .03 | .01 | .00 |
| ☐ 398 | Mike Squires | .03 | .01 | .00 |
| ☐ 399 | Marvis Foley | .03 | .01 | .00 |
| ☐ 400 | Steve Trout | .06 | .02 | .00 |
| ☐ 401 | Wayne Nordhagen | .03 | .01 | .00 |
| ☐ 402 | Tony LaRussa MGR | .06 | .02 | .00 |
| ☐ 403 | Bruce Bochte | .06 | .02 | .00 |
| ☐ 404 | Bake McBride | .06 | .02 | .00 |
| ☐ 405 | Jerry Narron | .03 | .01 | .00 |
| ☐ 406 | Rob Dressler | .03 | .01 | .00 |
| ☐ 407 | Dave Heaverlo | .03 | .01 | .00 |
| ☐ 408 | Tom Paciorek | .03 | .01 | .00 |
| ☐ 409 | Carney Lansford | .15 | .06 | .01 |
| ☐ 410 | Brian Downing | .06 | .02 | .00 |
| ☐ 411 | Don Aase | .06 | .02 | .00 |
| ☐ 412 | Jim Barr | .03 | .01 | .00 |
| ☐ 413 | Don Baylor | .20 | .08 | .02 |
| ☐ 414 | Jim Fregosi | .06 | .02 | .00 |
| ☐ 415 | Dallas Green MGR | .06 | .02 | .00 |
| ☐ 416 | Dave Lopes | .10 | .04 | .01 |
| ☐ 417 | Jerry Reuss | .06 | .02 | .00 |

| No. | Player | | | |
|---|---|---|---|---|
| ☐ 418 | Rick Sutcliffe | .15 | .06 | .01 |
| ☐ 419 | Derrel Thomas | .03 | .01 | .00 |
| ☐ 420 | Tommy Lasorda MGR | .10 | .04 | .01 |
| ☐ 421 | Charles Leibrandt | .35 | .14 | .03 |
| ☐ 422 | Tom Seaver | .50 | .20 | .05 |
| ☐ 423 | Ron Oester | .06 | .02 | .00 |
| ☐ 424 | Junior Kennedy | .03 | .01 | .00 |
| ☐ 425 | Tom Seaver | .50 | .20 | .05 |
| ☐ 426 | Bobby Cox MGR | .03 | .01 | .00 |
| ☐ 427 | Leon Durham | .50 | .20 | .05 |
| ☐ 428 | Terry Kennedy | .12 | .05 | .01 |
| ☐ 429 | Silvio Martinez | .03 | .01 | .00 |
| ☐ 430 | George Hendrick | .10 | .04 | .01 |
| ☐ 431 | Red Schoendienst MGR | .06 | .02 | .00 |
| ☐ 432 | Johnnie LeMaster | .03 | .01 | .00 |
| ☐ 433 | Vida Blue | .10 | .04 | .01 |
| ☐ 434 | John Montefusco | .06 | .02 | .00 |
| ☐ 435 | Terry Whitfield | .03 | .01 | .00 |
| ☐ 436 | Dave Bristol MGR | .03 | .01 | .00 |
| ☐ 437 | Dale Murphy | 1.25 | .50 | .12 |
| ☐ 438 | Jerry Dybzinski | .03 | .01 | .00 |
| ☐ 439 | Jorge Orta | .03 | .01 | .00 |
| ☐ 440 | Wayne Garland | .03 | .01 | .00 |
| ☐ 441 | Miguel Dilone | .03 | .01 | .00 |
| ☐ 442 | Dave Garcia MGR | .03 | .01 | .00 |
| ☐ 443 | Don Money | .03 | .01 | .00 |
| ☐ 444A | Buck Martinez P1 ERR reverse negative | .12 | .05 | .01 |
| ☐ 444B | Buck Martinez P2 COR | .08 | .03 | .01 |
| ☐ 445 | Jerry Augustine | .03 | .01 | .00 |
| ☐ 446 | Ben Oglivie | .06 | .02 | .00 |
| ☐ 447 | Jim Slaton | .06 | .02 | .00 |
| ☐ 448 | Doyle Alexander | .06 | .02 | .00 |
| ☐ 449 | Tony Bernazard | .06 | .02 | .00 |
| ☐ 450 | Scott Sanderson | .03 | .01 | .00 |
| ☐ 451 | Dave Palmer | .06 | .02 | .00 |
| ☐ 452 | Stan Bahnsen | .03 | .01 | .00 |
| ☐ 453 | Dick Williams MGR | .06 | .02 | .00 |
| ☐ 454 | Rick Burleson | .06 | .02 | .00 |
| ☐ 455 | Gary Allenson | .03 | .01 | .00 |
| ☐ 456 | Bob Stanley | .06 | .02 | .00 |
| ☐ 457A | John Tudor P1 ERR lifetime W-L "9.7" | 1.00 | .40 | .10 |
| ☐ 457B | John Tudor P2 COR corrected "9-7" | 1.00 | .40 | .10 |
| ☐ 458 | Dwight Evans | .15 | .06 | .01 |
| ☐ 459 | Glenn Hubbard | .03 | .01 | .00 |
| ☐ 460 | U.L. Washington | .03 | .01 | .00 |
| ☐ 461 | Larry Gura | .06 | .02 | .00 |
| ☐ 462 | Rich Gale | .06 | .02 | .00 |
| ☐ 463 | Hal McRae | .06 | .02 | .00 |
| ☐ 464 | Jim Frey MGR | .03 | .01 | .00 |
| ☐ 465 | Bucky Dent | .10 | .04 | .01 |
| ☐ 466 | Dennis Werth | .03 | .01 | .00 |
| ☐ 467 | Ron Davis | .03 | .01 | .00 |
| ☐ 468 | Reggie Jackson | .75 | .30 | .07 |
| ☐ 469 | Bobby Brown | .03 | .01 | .00 |
| ☐ 470 | Mike Davis | .30 | .12 | .03 |
| ☐ 471 | Gaylord Perry | .30 | .12 | .03 |
| ☐ 472 | Mark Belanger | .06 | .02 | .00 |
| ☐ 473 | Jim Palmer | .35 | .14 | .03 |
| ☐ 474 | Sammy Stewart | .03 | .01 | .00 |
| ☐ 475 | Tim Stoddard | .03 | .01 | .00 |
| ☐ 476 | Steve Stone | .06 | .02 | .00 |
| ☐ 477 | Jeff Newman | .03 | .01 | .00 |
| ☐ 478 | Steve McCatty | .03 | .01 | .00 |
| ☐ 479 | Billy Martin MGR | .15 | .06 | .01 |
| ☐ 480 | Mitchell Page | .03 | .01 | .00 |
| ☐ 481 | Cy Young Winner 1980 Steve Carlton | .30 | .12 | .03 |
| ☐ 482 | Bill Buckner | .15 | .06 | .01 |
| ☐ 483A | Ivan DeJesus P1 ERR lifetime hits "702" | .06 | .02 | .00 |
| ☐ 483B | Ivan DeJesus P2 COR lifetime hits "642" | .06 | .02 | .00 |
| ☐ 484 | Cliff Johnson | .03 | .01 | .00 |
| ☐ 485 | Lenny Randle | .03 | .01 | .00 |
| ☐ 486 | Larry Milbourne | .03 | .01 | .00 |
| ☐ 487 | Roy Smalley | .06 | .02 | .00 |
| ☐ 488 | John Castino | .06 | .02 | .00 |
| ☐ 489 | Ron Jackson | .03 | .01 | .00 |
| ☐ 490A | Dave Roberts P1 "Showed pop in" | .06 | .02 | .00 |
| ☐ 490B | Dave Roberts P2 "Declared himself" | .06 | .02 | .00 |
| ☐ 491 | MVP: George Brett | .50 | .20 | .05 |
| ☐ 492 | Mike Cubbage | .03 | .01 | .00 |
| ☐ 493 | Rob Wilfong | .03 | .01 | .00 |
| ☐ 494 | Danny Goodwin | .03 | .01 | .00 |
| ☐ 495 | Jose Morales | .03 | .01 | .00 |
| ☐ 496 | Mickey Rivers | .06 | .02 | .00 |
| ☐ 497 | Mike Edwards | .03 | .01 | .00 |
| ☐ 498 | Mike Sadek | .03 | .01 | .00 |
| ☐ 499 | Lenn Sakata | .03 | .01 | .00 |
| ☐ 500 | Gene Michael MGR | .06 | .02 | .00 |
| ☐ 501 | Dave Roberts | .03 | .01 | .00 |
| ☐ 502 | Steve Dillard | .03 | .01 | .00 |
| ☐ 503 | Jim Essian | .03 | .01 | .00 |
| ☐ 504 | Rance Mulliniks | .03 | .01 | .00 |
| ☐ 505 | Darrell Porter | .06 | .02 | .00 |
| ☐ 506 | Joe Torre MGR | .10 | .04 | .01 |
| ☐ 507 | Terry Crowley | .03 | .01 | .00 |
| ☐ 508 | Bill Travers | .03 | .01 | .00 |
| ☐ 509 | Nelson Norman | .03 | .01 | .00 |
| ☐ 510 | Bob McClure | .03 | .01 | .00 |
| ☐ 511 | Steve Howe | .15 | .06 | .01 |
| ☐ 512 | Dave Rader | .03 | .01 | .00 |
| ☐ 513 | Mick Kelleher | .03 | .01 | .00 |
| ☐ 514 | Kiko Garcia | .03 | .01 | .00 |
| ☐ 515 | Larry Biittner | .03 | .01 | .00 |
| ☐ 516A | Willie Norwood P1 Career Highlights "Spent most of" | .06 | .02 | .00 |
| ☐ 516B | Willie Norwood P2 "Traded to Seattle" | .06 | .02 | .00 |
| ☐ 517 | Bo Diaz | .06 | .02 | .00 |
| ☐ 518 | Juan Beniquez | .06 | .02 | .00 |
| ☐ 519 | Scot Thompson | .03 | .01 | .00 |
| ☐ 520 | Jim Tracy | .03 | .01 | .00 |
| ☐ 521 | Carlos Lezcano | .03 | .01 | .00 |
| ☐ 522 | Joe Amalfitano MGR | .03 | .01 | .00 |
| ☐ 523 | Preston Hanna | .03 | .01 | .00 |
| ☐ 524A | Ray Burris P1 Career Highlights: "Went on ..." | .06 | .02 | .00 |
| ☐ 524B | Ray Burris P2 "Drafted by ..." | .06 | .02 | .00 |
| ☐ 525 | Broderick Perkins | .03 | .01 | .00 |
| ☐ 526 | Mickey Hatcher | .03 | .01 | .00 |
| ☐ 527 | John Goryl MGR | .03 | .01 | .00 |
| ☐ 528 | Dick Davis | .03 | .01 | .00 |
| ☐ 529 | Butch Wynegar | .06 | .02 | .00 |
| ☐ 530 | Sal Butera | .03 | .01 | .00 |
| ☐ 531 | Jerry Koosman | .10 | .04 | .01 |
| ☐ 532A | Geoff Zahn P1 Career Highlights: "Was 2nd in" | .06 | .02 | .00 |
| ☐ 532B | Geoff Zahn P2 "Signed a 3 year" | .06 | .02 | .00 |
| ☐ 533 | Dennis Martinez | .03 | .01 | .00 |
| ☐ 534 | Gary Thomasson | .03 | .01 | .00 |
| ☐ 535 | Steve Macko | .03 | .01 | .00 |
| ☐ 536 | Jim Kaat | .15 | .06 | .01 |
| ☐ 537 | Best Hitters: George Brett Rod Carew | 1.00 | .40 | .10 |
| ☐ 538 | Tim Raines | 4.00 | 1.60 | .40 |
| ☐ 539 | Keith Smith | .03 | .01 | .00 |
| ☐ 540 | Ken Macha | .03 | .01 | .00 |
| ☐ 541 | Burt Hooton | .03 | .01 | .00 |
| ☐ 542 | Butch Hobson | .03 | .01 | .00 |
| ☐ 543 | Bill Stein | .03 | .01 | .00 |
| ☐ 544 | Dave Stapleton | .06 | .02 | .00 |
| ☐ 545 | Bob Pate | .03 | .01 | .00 |
| ☐ 546 | Doug Corbett | .10 | .04 | .01 |
| ☐ 547 | Darrell Jackson | .03 | .01 | .00 |
| ☐ 548 | Pete Redfern | .03 | .01 | .00 |
| ☐ 549 | Roger Erickson | .03 | .01 | .00 |
| ☐ 550 | Al Hrabosky | .06 | .02 | .00 |
| ☐ 551 | Dick Tidrow | .03 | .01 | .00 |
| ☐ 552 | Dave Ford | .03 | .01 | .00 |
| ☐ 553 | Dave Kingman | .15 | .06 | .01 |
| ☐ 554A | Mike Vail P1 Career Highlights: "After two ..." | .06 | .02 | .00 |
| ☐ 554B | Mike Vail P2 "Traded to ..." | .06 | .02 | .00 |
| ☐ 555A | Jerry Martin P1 Career Highlights: "Overcame a ..." | .06 | .02 | .00 |
| ☐ 555B | Jerry Martin P2 "Traded to ..." | .06 | .02 | .00 |
| ☐ 556A | Jesus Figueroa P1 Career Highlights: "Had an ..." | .06 | .02 | .00 |
| ☐ 556B | Jesus Figueroa P2 "Traded to ..." | .06 | .02 | .00 |
| ☐ 557 | Don Stanhouse | .03 | .01 | .00 |
| ☐ 558 | Barry Foote | .03 | .01 | .00 |
| ☐ 559 | Tim Blackwell | .03 | .01 | .00 |
| ☐ 560 | Bruce Sutter | .20 | .08 | .02 |
| ☐ 561 | Rick Reuschel | .06 | .02 | .00 |
| ☐ 562 | Lynn McGlothen | .03 | .01 | .00 |
| ☐ 563A | Bob Owchinko P1 Career Highlights: "Traded to ..." | .06 | .02 | .00 |

| | | | |
|---|---|---|---|
| ☐ 563B Bob Owchinko P2 ......... "Involved in a ..." | .06 | .02 | .00 |
| ☐ 564 John Verhoeven ............. | .03 | .01 | .00 |
| ☐ 565 Ken Landreaux ............. | .06 | .02 | .00 |
| ☐ 566A Glen Adams P1 ERR ..... Name misspelled | .10 | .04 | .01 |
| ☐ 566B Glenn Adams P2 COR ... | .06 | .02 | .00 |
| ☐ 567 Hosken Powell ............. | .03 | .01 | .00 |
| ☐ 568 Dick Noles ................. | .03 | .01 | .00 |
| ☐ 569 Danny Ainge .............. | .25 | .10 | .02 |
| ☐ 570 Bobby Mattick MGR ....... | .03 | .01 | .00 |
| ☐ 571 Joe Lefebvre ............. | .06 | .02 | .00 |
| ☐ 572 Bobby Clark .............. | .03 | .01 | .00 |
| ☐ 573 Dennis Lamp ............. | .03 | .01 | .00 |
| ☐ 574 Randy Lerch .............. | .03 | .01 | .00 |
| ☐ 575 Mookie Wilson ........... | .35 | .14 | .03 |
| ☐ 576 Ron LeFlore .............. | .06 | .02 | .00 |
| ☐ 577 Jim Dwyer ................. | .03 | .01 | .00 |
| ☐ 578 Bill Castro ................ | .03 | .01 | .00 |
| ☐ 579 Greg Minton .............. | .06 | .02 | .00 |
| ☐ 580 Mark Littell .............. | .03 | .01 | .00 |
| ☐ 581 Andy Hassler ............. | .03 | .01 | .00 |
| ☐ 582 Dave Stieb ............... | .30 | .12 | .03 |
| ☐ 583 Ken Oberkfell ............ | .06 | .02 | .00 |
| ☐ 584 Larry Bradford ........... | .03 | .01 | .00 |
| ☐ 585 Fred Stanley ............. | .03 | .01 | .00 |
| ☐ 586 Bill Caudill .............. | .06 | .02 | .00 |
| ☐ 587 Doug Capilla ............. | .03 | .01 | .00 |
| ☐ 588 George Riley ............. | .03 | .01 | .00 |
| ☐ 589 Willie Hernandez ........ | .15 | .06 | .01 |
| ☐ 590 MVP: Mike Schmidt ........ | .45 | .18 | .04 |
| ☐ 591 Cy Young Winner 1980: .. Steve Stone | .06 | .02 | .00 |
| ☐ 592 Rick Sofield ............. | .03 | .01 | .00 |
| ☐ 593 Bombo Rivera ............. | .03 | .01 | .00 |
| ☐ 594 Gary Ward ................ | .10 | .04 | .01 |
| ☐ 595A Dave Edwards P1 ........ Career Highlights: "Sidelined the" | .06 | .02 | .00 |
| ☐ 595B Dave Edwards P2 ........ "Traded to ..." | .06 | .02 | .00 |
| ☐ 596 Mike Proly ............... | .03 | .01 | .00 |
| ☐ 597 Tommy Boggs ............. | .03 | .01 | .00 |
| ☐ 598 Greg Gross ............... | .03 | .01 | .00 |
| ☐ 599 Elias Sosa ............... | .03 | .01 | .00 |
| ☐ 600 Pat Kelly ................ | .03 | .01 | .00 |
| ☐ 601A Checklist 1 P1 ERR ...... unnumbered (51 Donahue) | .10 | .01 | .00 |
| ☐ 601B Checklist 1 P2 COR ...... unnumbered (51 Donohue) | .75 | .07 | .00 |
| ☐ 602 Checklist 2 ............... unnumbered | .10 | .01 | .00 |
| ☐ 603A Checklist 3 P1 ERR ...... unnumbered (306 Mathews) | .10 | .01 | .00 |
| ☐ 603B Checklist 3 P2 COR ...... unnumbered (306 Matthews) | .10 | .01 | .00 |
| ☐ 604A Checklist 4 P1 ERR ...... unnumbered (379 Pujois) | .10 | .01 | .00 |
| ☐ 604B Checklist 4 P2 COR ...... unnumbered (379 Pujols) | .10 | .01 | .00 |
| ☐ 605A Checklist 5 P1 ERR ...... unnumbered (566 Glen Adams) | .10 | .01 | .00 |
| ☐ 605B Checklist 5 P2 COR ...... unnumbered (566 Glenn Adams) | .10 | .01 | .00 |

# 1982 Donruss

The 1982 Donruss set contains 653 numbered cards and the seven unnumbered checklists; each card measures 2 1/2" by 3 1/2". The first 26 cards of this set are entitled Donruss Diamond Kings (DK) and feature the artwork of Dick Perez of Perez-Steele Galleries. The set was marketed with puzzle pieces rather than with bubble gum. There are 63 pieces to the puzzle, which when put together make

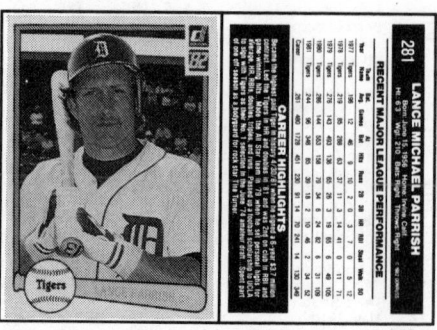

a collage of Babe Ruth entitled "Hall of Fame Diamond King." The card stock in this year's Donruss cards is considerably thicker than that of the 1981 cards. The seven unnumbered checklist cards are arbitrarily assigned numbers 654 through 660 and are listed at the end of the list below.

| | | MINT | VG-E | F-G |
|---|---|---|---|---|
| COMPLETE SET .......................... | | 22.00 | 9.00 | 2.20 |
| COMMON PLAYER (1-660) ........ | | .03 | .01 | .00 |
| ☐ | 1 Pete Rose DK ................ | 1.50 | .60 | .15 |
| ☐ | 2 Gary Carter DK ............. | .50 | .20 | .05 |
| ☐ | 3 Steve Garvey DK ............ | .50 | .20 | .05 |
| ☐ | 4 Vida Blue DK ................ | .10 | .04 | .01 |
| ☐ | 5A Alan Trammel DK ERR .. (name misspelled) | .60 | .24 | .06 |
| ☐ | 5B Alan Trammell DK ........ COR | .30 | .12 | .03 |
| ☐ | 6 Len Barker DK .............. | .06 | .02 | .00 |
| ☐ | 7 Dwight Evans DK ........... | .12 | .05 | .01 |
| ☐ | 8 Rod Carew DK .............. | .50 | .20 | .05 |
| ☐ | 9 George Hendrick DK ....... | .08 | .03 | .01 |
| ☐ | 10 Phil Niekro DK .............. | .30 | .12 | .03 |
| ☐ | 11 Richie Zisk DK ............. | .06 | .02 | .00 |
| ☐ | 12 Dave Parker DK ............ | .30 | .12 | .03 |
| ☐ | 13 Nolan Ryan DK ............. | .50 | .20 | .05 |
| ☐ | 14 Ivan DeJesus DK ........... | .06 | .02 | .00 |
| ☐ | 15 George Brett DK ........... | .75 | .30 | .07 |
| ☐ | 16 Tom Seaver DK ............ | .50 | .20 | .05 |
| ☐ | 17 Dave Kingman DK .......... | .12 | .05 | .01 |
| ☐ | 18 Mike Norris DK ............. | .45 | .18 | .04 |
| ☐ | 19 Mike Norris DK ............. | .06 | .02 | .00 |
| ☐ | 20 Carlton Fisk DK ............ | .20 | .08 | .02 |
| ☐ | 21 Ozzie Smith DK ............ | .15 | .06 | .01 |
| ☐ | 22 Roy Smalley DK ............ | .06 | .02 | .00 |
| ☐ | 23 Buddy Bell DK .............. | .10 | .04 | .01 |
| ☐ | 24 Ken Singleton DK .......... | .10 | .04 | .01 |
| ☐ | 25 John Mayberry DK .......... | .06 | .02 | .00 |
| ☐ | 26 Gorman Thomas DK ........ | .10 | .04 | .01 |
| ☐ | 27 Earl Weaver MGR ........... | .08 | .03 | .01 |
| ☐ | 28 Rollie Fingers ............. | .20 | .08 | .02 |
| ☐ | 29 Sparky Anderson MGR .... | .08 | .03 | .01 |
| ☐ | 30 Dennis Eckersley .......... | .06 | .02 | .00 |
| ☐ | 31 Dave Winfield ............. | .45 | .18 | .04 |
| ☐ | 32 Burt Hooton ............... | .03 | .01 | .00 |
| ☐ | 33 Rick Waits ................. | .03 | .01 | .00 |
| ☐ | 34 George Brett .............. | .65 | .26 | .06 |
| ☐ | 35 Steve McCatty ............. | .03 | .01 | .00 |
| ☐ | 36 Steve Rogers .............. | .06 | .02 | .00 |
| ☐ | 37 Bill Stein ................. | .03 | .01 | .00 |
| ☐ | 38 Steve Renko ............... | .03 | .01 | .00 |
| ☐ | 39 Mike Squires .............. | .03 | .01 | .00 |
| ☐ | 40 George Hendrick ........... | .08 | .03 | .01 |
| ☐ | 41 Bob Knepper ............... | .10 | .04 | .01 |
| ☐ | 42 Steve Carlton ............. | .50 | .20 | .05 |
| ☐ | 43 Larry Biittner ............. | .03 | .01 | .00 |
| ☐ | 44 Chris Welsh ............... | .06 | .02 | .00 |
| ☐ | 45 Steve Nicosia ............. | .03 | .01 | .00 |
| ☐ | 46 Jack Clark ................. | .15 | .06 | .01 |
| ☐ | 47 Chris Chambliss ........... | .06 | .02 | .00 |
| ☐ | 48 Ivan DeJesus .............. | .03 | .01 | .00 |
| ☐ | 49 Lee Mazzilli ............... | .06 | .02 | .00 |
| ☐ | 50 Julio Cruz ................. | .03 | .01 | .00 |
| ☐ | 51 Pete Redfern .............. | .03 | .01 | .00 |
| ☐ | 52 Dave Stieb ................ | .20 | .08 | .02 |
| ☐ | 53 Doug Corbett .............. | .03 | .01 | .00 |
| ☐ | 54 Jorge Bell ................. | 1.50 | .60 | .15 |
| ☐ | 55 Joe Simpson ............... | .03 | .01 | .00 |
| ☐ | 56 Rusty Staub ............... | .10 | .04 | .01 |

| # | Player | | | |
|---|--------|---|---|---|
| 57 | Hector Cruz | .03 | .01 | .00 |
| 58 | Claudell Washington | .08 | .03 | .01 |
| 59 | Enrique Romo | .03 | .01 | .00 |
| 60 | Gary Lavelle | .06 | .02 | .00 |
| 61 | Tim Flannery | .03 | .01 | .00 |
| 62 | Joe Nolan | .03 | .01 | .00 |
| 63 | Larry Bowa | .12 | .05 | .01 |
| 64 | Sixto Lezcano | .03 | .01 | .00 |
| 65 | Joe Sambito | .06 | .02 | .00 |
| 66 | Bruce Kison | .03 | .01 | .00 |
| 67 | Wayne Nordhagen | .03 | .01 | .00 |
| 68 | Woodie Fryman | .03 | .01 | .00 |
| 69 | Billy Sample | .03 | .01 | .00 |
| 70 | Amos Otis | .08 | .03 | .01 |
| 71 | Matt Keough | .03 | .01 | .00 |
| 72 | Toby Harrah | .06 | .02 | .00 |
| 73 | Dave Righetti | 1.25 | .50 | .12 |
| 74 | Carl Yastrzemski | .70 | .28 | .07 |
| 75 | Bob Welch | .08 | .03 | .01 |
| 76A | Alan Trammel ERR (name misspelled) | .60 | .24 | .06 |
| 76B | Alan Trammell CORR | .25 | .10 | .02 |
| 77 | Rick Dempsey | .06 | .02 | .00 |
| 78 | Paul Molitor | .12 | .05 | .01 |
| 79 | Dennis Martinez | .03 | .01 | .00 |
| 80 | Jim Slaton | .03 | .01 | .00 |
| 81 | Champ Summers | .03 | .01 | .00 |
| 82 | Carney Lansford | .12 | .05 | .01 |
| 83 | Barry Foote | .03 | .01 | .00 |
| 84 | Steve Garvey | .50 | .20 | .05 |
| 85 | Rick Manning | .03 | .01 | .00 |
| 86 | John Wathan | .03 | .01 | .00 |
| 87 | Brian Kingman | .03 | .01 | .00 |
| 88 | Andre Dawson | .25 | .10 | .02 |
| 89 | Jim Kern | .03 | .01 | .00 |
| 90 | Bobby Grich | .08 | .03 | .01 |
| 91 | Bob Forsch | .06 | .02 | .00 |
| 92 | Art Howe | .03 | .01 | .00 |
| 93 | Marty Bystrom | .03 | .01 | .00 |
| 94 | Ozzie Smith | .15 | .06 | .01 |
| 95 | Dave Parker | .25 | .10 | .02 |
| 96 | Doyle Alexander | .06 | .02 | .00 |
| 97 | Al Hrabosky | .06 | .02 | .00 |
| 98 | Frank Taveras | .03 | .01 | .00 |
| 99 | Tim Blackwell | .03 | .01 | .00 |
| 100 | Floyd Bannister | .06 | .02 | .00 |
| 101 | Alfredo Griffin | .06 | .02 | .00 |
| 102 | Dave Engle | .03 | .01 | .00 |
| 103 | Mario Soto | .10 | .04 | .01 |
| 104 | Ross Baumgarten | .03 | .01 | .00 |
| 105 | Ken Singleton | .10 | .04 | .01 |
| 106 | Ted Simmons | .15 | .06 | .01 |
| 107 | Jack Morris | .25 | .10 | .02 |
| 108 | Bob Watson | .06 | .02 | .00 |
| 109 | Dwight Evans | .15 | .06 | .01 |
| 110 | Tom Lasorda MGR | .10 | .04 | .01 |
| 111 | Bert Blyleven | .15 | .06 | .01 |
| 112 | Dan Quisenberry | .20 | .08 | .02 |
| 113 | Rickey Henderson | .60 | .24 | .06 |
| 114 | Gary Carter | .50 | .20 | .05 |
| 115 | Brian Downing | .06 | .02 | .00 |
| 116 | Al Oliver | .15 | .06 | .01 |
| 117 | LaMarr Hoyt | .10 | .04 | .01 |
| 118 | Cesar Cedeno | .08 | .03 | .01 |
| 119 | Keith Moreland | .08 | .03 | .01 |
| 120 | Bob Shirley | .03 | .01 | .00 |
| 121 | Terry Kennedy | .08 | .03 | .01 |
| 122 | Frank Pastore | .03 | .01 | .00 |
| 123 | Gene Garber | .03 | .01 | .00 |
| 124 | Tony Pena | .15 | .06 | .01 |
| 125 | Allen Ripley | .03 | .01 | .00 |
| 126 | Randy Martz | .03 | .01 | .00 |
| 127 | Richie Zisk | .06 | .02 | .00 |
| 128 | Mike Scott | .25 | .10 | .02 |
| 129 | Lloyd Moseby | .15 | .06 | .01 |
| 130 | Rob Wilfong | .03 | .01 | .00 |
| 131 | Tim Stoddard | .03 | .01 | .00 |
| 132 | Gorman Thomas | .12 | .05 | .01 |
| 133 | Dan Petry | .15 | .06 | .01 |
| 134 | Bob Stanley | .06 | .02 | .00 |
| 135 | Lou Piniella | .10 | .04 | .01 |
| 136 | Pedro Guerrero | .35 | .14 | .03 |
| 137 | Len Barker | .06 | .02 | .00 |
| 138 | Rich Gale | .03 | .01 | .00 |
| 139 | Wayne Gross | .03 | .01 | .00 |
| 140 | Tim Wallach | .45 | .18 | .04 |
| 141 | Gene Mauch MGR | .06 | .02 | .00 |
| 142 | Doc Medich | .03 | .01 | .00 |
| 143 | Tony Bernazard | .06 | .02 | .00 |
| 144 | Bill Virdon MGR | .06 | .02 | .00 |
| 145 | John Littlefield | .03 | .01 | .00 |
| 146 | Dave Bergman | .03 | .01 | .00 |
| 147 | Dick Davis | .03 | .01 | .00 |
| 148 | Tom Seaver | .40 | .16 | .04 |
| 149 | Matt Sinatro | .03 | .01 | .00 |
| 150 | Chuck Tanner MGR | .06 | .02 | .00 |
| 151 | Leon Durham | .15 | .06 | .01 |
| 152 | Gene Tenace | .03 | .01 | .00 |
| 153 | Al Bumbry | .03 | .01 | .00 |
| 154 | Mark Brouhard | .03 | .01 | .00 |
| 155 | Rick Peters | .03 | .01 | .00 |
| 156 | Jerry Remy | .03 | .01 | .00 |
| 157 | Rick Reuschel | .06 | .02 | .00 |
| 158 | Steve Howe | .06 | .02 | .00 |
| 159 | Alan Bannister | .03 | .01 | .00 |
| 160 | U.L. Washington | .03 | .01 | .00 |
| 161 | Rick Langford | .03 | .01 | .00 |
| 162 | Bill Gullickson | .06 | .02 | .00 |
| 163 | Mark Wagner | .03 | .01 | .00 |
| 164 | Geoff Zahn | .03 | .01 | .00 |
| 165 | Ron LeFlore | .06 | .02 | .00 |
| 166 | Dane Iorg | .03 | .01 | .00 |
| 167 | Joe Niekro | .08 | .03 | .01 |
| 168 | Pete Rose | 1.25 | .50 | .12 |
| 169 | Dave Collins | .06 | .02 | .00 |
| 170 | Rick Wise | .06 | .02 | .00 |
| 171 | Jim Bibby | .06 | .02 | .00 |
| 172 | Larry Herndon | .06 | .02 | .00 |
| 173 | Bob Horner | .25 | .10 | .02 |
| 174 | Steve Dillard | .03 | .01 | .00 |
| 175 | Mookie Wilson | .10 | .04 | .01 |
| 176 | Dan Meyer | .03 | .01 | .00 |
| 177 | Fernando Arroyo | .03 | .01 | .00 |
| 178 | Jackson Todd | .03 | .01 | .00 |
| 179 | Darrell Jackson | .03 | .01 | .00 |
| 180 | Al Woods | .03 | .01 | .00 |
| 181 | Jim Anderson | .03 | .01 | .00 |
| 182 | Dave Kingman | .15 | .06 | .01 |
| 183 | Steve Henderson | .03 | .01 | .00 |
| 184 | Brian Asselstine | .03 | .01 | .00 |
| 185 | Rod Scurry | .03 | .01 | .00 |
| 186 | Fred Breining | .08 | .03 | .01 |
| 187 | Danny Boone | .03 | .01 | .00 |
| 188 | Junior Kennedy | .03 | .01 | .00 |
| 189 | Sparky Lyle | .12 | .05 | .01 |
| 190 | Whitey Herzog MGR | .06 | .02 | .00 |
| 191 | Dave Smith | .06 | .02 | .00 |
| 192 | Ed Ott | .03 | .01 | .00 |
| 193 | Greg Luzinski | .12 | .05 | .01 |
| 194 | Bill Lee | .06 | .02 | .00 |
| 195 | Don Zimmer MGR | .06 | .02 | .00 |
| 196 | Hal McRae | .06 | .02 | .00 |
| 197 | Mike Norris | .03 | .01 | .00 |
| 198 | Duane Kuiper | .03 | .01 | .00 |
| 199 | Rick Cerone | .03 | .01 | .00 |
| 200 | Jim Rice | .45 | .18 | .04 |
| 201 | Steve Yeager | .06 | .02 | .00 |
| 202 | Tom Brookens | .03 | .01 | .00 |
| 203 | Jose Morales | .03 | .01 | .00 |
| 204 | Roy Howell | .03 | .01 | .00 |
| 205 | Tippy Martinez | .03 | .01 | .00 |
| 206 | Moose Haas | .06 | .02 | .00 |
| 207 | Al Cowens | .06 | .02 | .00 |
| 208 | Dave Stapleton | .03 | .01 | .00 |
| 209 | Bucky Dent | .08 | .03 | .01 |
| 210 | Ron Cey | .10 | .04 | .01 |
| 211 | Jorge Orta | .03 | .01 | .00 |
| 212 | Jamie Quirk | .03 | .01 | .00 |
| 213 | Jeff Jones | .03 | .01 | .00 |
| 214 | Tim Raines | .50 | .20 | .05 |
| 215 | Jon Matlack | .06 | .02 | .00 |
| 216 | Rod Carew | .50 | .20 | .05 |
| 217 | Jim Kaat | .15 | .06 | .01 |
| 218 | Joe Pittman | .03 | .01 | .00 |
| 219 | Larry Christenson | .03 | .01 | .00 |
| 220 | Juan Bonilla | .06 | .02 | .00 |
| 221 | Mike Easler | .08 | .03 | .01 |
| 222 | Vida Blue | .08 | .03 | .01 |
| 223 | Rick Camp | .03 | .01 | .00 |
| 224 | Mike Jorgensen | .03 | .01 | .00 |
| 225 | Jody Davis | .50 | .20 | .05 |
| 226 | Mike Parrott | .03 | .01 | .00 |
| 227 | Jim Clancy | .06 | .02 | .00 |
| 228 | Hosken Powell | .03 | .01 | .00 |
| 229 | Tom Hume | .03 | .01 | .00 |
| 230 | Britt Burns | .08 | .03 | .01 |
| 231 | Jim Palmer | .30 | .12 | .03 |
| 232 | Bob Rodgers MGR | .03 | .01 | .00 |
| 233 | Milt Wilcox | .03 | .01 | .00 |
| 234 | Dave Revering | .03 | .01 | .00 |
| 235 | Mike Torrez | .06 | .02 | .00 |
| 236 | Robert Castillo | .03 | .01 | .00 |
| 237 | Von Hayes | 1.00 | .40 | .10 |
| 238 | Renie Martin | .03 | .01 | .00 |
| 239 | Dwayne Murphy | .06 | .02 | .00 |
| 240 | Rodney Scott | .03 | .01 | .00 |

| | | | | |
|---|---|---|---|---|
| ☐ 241 | Fred Patek | .03 | .01 | .00 |
| ☐ 242 | Mickey Rivers | .06 | .02 | .00 |
| ☐ 243 | Steve Trout | .06 | .02 | .00 |
| ☐ 244 | Jose Cruz | .12 | .05 | .01 |
| ☐ 245 | Manny Trillo | .06 | .02 | .00 |
| ☐ 246 | Lary Sorensen | .03 | .01 | .00 |
| ☐ 247 | Dave Edwards | .03 | .01 | .00 |
| ☐ 248 | Dan Driessen | .03 | .01 | .00 |
| ☐ 249 | Tommy Boggs | .03 | .01 | .00 |
| ☐ 250 | Dale Berra | .06 | .02 | .00 |
| ☐ 251 | Ed Whitson | .06 | .02 | .00 |
| ☐ 252 | Lee Smith | .50 | .20 | .05 |
| ☐ 253 | Tom Paciorek | .03 | .01 | .00 |
| ☐ 254 | Pat Zachry | .03 | .01 | .00 |
| ☐ 255 | Luis Leal | .03 | .01 | .00 |
| ☐ 256 | John Castino | .03 | .01 | .00 |
| ☐ 257 | Rich Dauer | .03 | .01 | .00 |
| ☐ 258 | Cecil Cooper | .15 | .06 | .01 |
| ☐ 259 | Dave Rozema | .03 | .01 | .00 |
| ☐ 260 | John Tudor | .15 | .06 | .01 |
| ☐ 261 | Jerry Mumphrey | .06 | .02 | .00 |
| ☐ 262 | Jay Johnstone | .06 | .02 | .00 |
| ☐ 263 | Bo Diaz | .06 | .02 | .00 |
| ☐ 264 | Dennis Leonard | .06 | .02 | .00 |
| ☐ 265 | Jim Spencer | .03 | .01 | .00 |
| ☐ 266 | John Milner | .03 | .01 | .00 |
| ☐ 267 | Don Aase | .06 | .02 | .00 |
| ☐ 268 | Jim Sundberg | .06 | .02 | .00 |
| ☐ 269 | Lamar Johnson | .03 | .01 | .00 |
| ☐ 270 | Frank LaCorte | .03 | .01 | .00 |
| ☐ 271 | Barry Evans | .03 | .01 | .00 |
| ☐ 272 | Enos Cabell | .03 | .01 | .00 |
| ☐ 273 | Del Unser | .03 | .01 | .00 |
| ☐ 274 | George Foster | .15 | .06 | .01 |
| ☐ 275 | Brett Butler | .60 | .24 | .06 |
| ☐ 276 | Lee Lacy | .06 | .02 | .00 |
| ☐ 277 | Ken Reitz | .03 | .01 | .00 |
| ☐ 278 | Keith Hernandez | .30 | .12 | .03 |
| ☐ 279 | Doug DeCinces | .10 | .04 | .01 |
| ☐ 280 | Charlie Moore | .03 | .01 | .00 |
| ☐ 281 | Lance Parrish | .30 | .12 | .03 |
| ☐ 282 | Ralph Houk MGR | .06 | .02 | .00 |
| ☐ 283 | Rich Gossage | .20 | .08 | .02 |
| ☐ 284 | Jerry Reuss | .06 | .02 | .00 |
| ☐ 285 | Mike Stanton | .03 | .01 | .00 |
| ☐ 286 | Frank White | .08 | .03 | .01 |
| ☐ 287 | Bob Owchinko | .03 | .01 | .00 |
| ☐ 288 | Scott Sanderson | .03 | .01 | .00 |
| ☐ 289 | Bump Wills | .03 | .01 | .00 |
| ☐ 290 | Dave Frost | .03 | .01 | .00 |
| ☐ 291 | Chet Lemon | .06 | .02 | .00 |
| ☐ 292 | Tito Landrum | .03 | .01 | .00 |
| ☐ 293 | Vern Ruhle | .03 | .01 | .00 |
| ☐ 294 | Mike Schmidt | .60 | .24 | .06 |
| ☐ 295 | Sam Mejias | .03 | .01 | .00 |
| ☐ 296 | Gary Lucas | .03 | .01 | .00 |
| ☐ 297 | John Candelaria | .08 | .03 | .01 |
| ☐ 298 | Jerry Martin | .03 | .01 | .00 |
| ☐ 299 | Dale Murphy | .90 | .36 | .09 |
| ☐ 300 | Mike Lum | .03 | .01 | .00 |
| ☐ 301 | Tom Hausman | .03 | .01 | .00 |
| ☐ 302 | Glenn Abbott | .03 | .01 | .00 |
| ☐ 303 | Roger Erickson | .03 | .01 | .00 |
| ☐ 304 | Otto Velez | .03 | .01 | .00 |
| ☐ 305 | Danny Goodwin | .03 | .01 | .00 |
| ☐ 306 | John Mayberry | .06 | .02 | .00 |
| ☐ 307 | Lenny Randle | .03 | .01 | .00 |
| ☐ 308 | Bob Bailor | .03 | .01 | .00 |
| ☐ 309 | Jerry Morales | .03 | .01 | .00 |
| ☐ 310 | Rufino Linares | .03 | .01 | .00 |
| ☐ 311 | Kent Tekulve | .06 | .02 | .00 |
| ☐ 312 | Joe Morgan | .25 | .10 | .02 |
| ☐ 313 | John Urrea | .03 | .01 | .00 |
| ☐ 314 | Paul Householder | .03 | .01 | .00 |
| ☐ 315 | Garry Maddox | .06 | .02 | .00 |
| ☐ 316 | Mike Ramsey | .03 | .01 | .00 |
| ☐ 317 | Alan Ashby | .03 | .01 | .00 |
| ☐ 318 | Bob Clark | .03 | .01 | .00 |
| ☐ 319 | Tony LaRussa MGR | .06 | .02 | .00 |
| ☐ 320 | Charlie Lea | .06 | .02 | .00 |
| ☐ 321 | Danny Darwin | .03 | .01 | .00 |
| ☐ 322 | Cesar Geronimo | .03 | .01 | .00 |
| ☐ 323 | Tom Underwood | .03 | .01 | .00 |
| ☐ 324 | Andre Thornton | .08 | .03 | .01 |
| ☐ 325 | Rudy May | .03 | .01 | .00 |
| ☐ 326 | Frank Tanana | .06 | .02 | .00 |
| ☐ 327 | Davey Lopes | .08 | .03 | .01 |
| ☐ 328 | Richie Hebner | .03 | .01 | .00 |
| ☐ 329 | Mike Flanagan | .08 | .03 | .01 |
| ☐ 330 | Mike Caldwell | .06 | .02 | .00 |
| ☐ 331 | Scott McGregor | .08 | .03 | .01 |
| ☐ 332 | Jerry Augustine | .03 | .01 | .00 |
| ☐ 333 | Stan Papi | .03 | .01 | .00 |
| ☐ 334 | Rick Miller | .03 | .01 | .00 |
| ☐ 335 | Graig Nettles | .15 | .06 | .01 |
| ☐ 336 | Dusty Baker | .08 | .03 | .01 |
| ☐ 337 | Dave Garcia MGR | .03 | .01 | .00 |
| ☐ 338 | Larry Gura | .06 | .02 | .00 |
| ☐ 339 | Cliff Johnson | .03 | .01 | .00 |
| ☐ 340 | Warren Cromartie | .03 | .01 | .00 |
| ☐ 341 | Steve Comer | .03 | .01 | .00 |
| ☐ 342 | Rick Burleson | .06 | .02 | .00 |
| ☐ 343 | John Martin | .03 | .01 | .00 |
| ☐ 344 | Craig Reynolds | .03 | .01 | .00 |
| ☐ 345 | Mike Proly | .03 | .01 | .00 |
| ☐ 346 | Ruppert Jones | .03 | .01 | .00 |
| ☐ 347 | Omar Moreno | .03 | .01 | .00 |
| ☐ 348 | Greg Minton | .06 | .02 | .00 |
| ☐ 349 | Rick Mahler | .20 | .08 | .02 |
| ☐ 350 | Alex Trevino | .03 | .01 | .00 |
| ☐ 351 | Mike Krukow | .08 | .03 | .01 |
| ☐ 352A | Shane Rawley ERR (photo actually Jim Anderson) | .60 | .24 | .06 |
| ☐ 352B | Shane Rawley COR | .10 | .04 | .01 |
| ☐ 353 | Garth Iorg | .03 | .01 | .00 |
| ☐ 354 | Pete Mackanin | .03 | .01 | .00 |
| ☐ 355 | Paul Moskau | .03 | .01 | .00 |
| ☐ 356 | Richard Dotson | .08 | .03 | .01 |
| ☐ 357 | Steve Stone | .06 | .02 | .00 |
| ☐ 358 | Larry Hisle | .06 | .02 | .00 |
| ☐ 359 | Aurelio Lopez | .03 | .01 | .00 |
| ☐ 360 | Oscar Gamble | .06 | .02 | .00 |
| ☐ 361 | Tom Burgmeier | .03 | 01 | .00 |
| ☐ 362 | Terry Forster | .08 | .03 | .01 |
| ☐ 363 | Joe Charboneau | .06 | .02 | .00 |
| ☐ 364 | Ken Brett | .03 | .01 | .00 |
| ☐ 365 | Tony Armas | .12 | .05 | .01 |
| ☐ 366 | Chris Speier | .03 | .01 | .00 |
| ☐ 367 | Fred Lynn | .20 | .08 | .02 |
| ☐ 368 | Buddy Bell | .12 | .05 | .01 |
| ☐ 369 | Jim Essian | .03 | .01 | .00 |
| ☐ 370 | Terry Puhl | .06 | .02 | .00 |
| ☐ 371 | Greg Gross | .03 | .01 | .00 |
| ☐ 372 | Bruce Sutter | .20 | .08 | .02 |
| ☐ 373 | Joe Lefebvre | .03 | .01 | .00 |
| ☐ 374 | Ray Knight | .08 | .03 | .01 |
| ☐ 375 | Bruce Benedict | .03 | .01 | .00 |
| ☐ 376 | Tim Foli | .03 | .01 | .00 |
| ☐ 377 | Al Holland | .06 | .02 | .00 |
| ☐ 378 | Ken Kravec | .03 | .01 | .00 |
| ☐ 379 | Jeff Burroughs | .06 | .02 | .00 |
| ☐ 380 | Pete Falcone | .03 | .01 | .00 |
| ☐ 381 | Ernie Whitt | .03 | .01 | .00 |
| ☐ 382 | Brad Havens | .06 | .02 | .00 |
| ☐ 383 | Terry Crowley | .03 | .01 | .00 |
| ☐ 384 | Don Money | .03 | .01 | .00 |
| ☐ 385 | Dan Schatzeder | .03 | .01 | .00 |
| ☐ 386 | Gary Allenson | .03 | .01 | .00 |
| ☐ 387 | Yogi Berra MGR | .15 | .06 | .01 |
| ☐ 388 | Ken Landreaux | .06 | .02 | .00 |
| ☐ 389 | Mike Hargrove | .06 | .02 | .00 |
| ☐ 390 | Darryl Motley | .12 | .05 | .01 |
| ☐ 391 | Dave McKay | .03 | .01 | .00 |
| ☐ 392 | Stan Bahnsen | .03 | .01 | .00 |
| ☐ 393 | Ken Forsch | .03 | .01 | .00 |
| ☐ 394 | Mario Mendoza | .03 | .01 | .00 |
| ☐ 395 | Jim Morrison | .03 | .01 | .00 |
| ☐ 396 | Mike Ivie | .03 | .01 | .00 |
| ☐ 397 | Broderick Perkins | .03 | .01 | .00 |
| ☐ 398 | Darrell Evans | .12 | .05 | .01 |
| ☐ 399 | Ron Reed | .03 | .01 | .00 |
| ☐ 400 | Johnny Bench | .40 | .16 | .04 |
| ☐ 401 | Steve Bedrosian | .30 | .12 | .03 |
| ☐ 402 | Bill Robinson | .03 | .01 | .00 |
| ☐ 403 | Bill Buckner | .12 | .05 | .01 |
| ☐ 404 | Ken Oberkfell | .03 | .01 | .00 |
| ☐ 405 | Cal Ripken Jr. | 5.00 | 2.00 | .50 |
| ☐ 406 | Jim Gantner | .06 | .02 | .00 |
| ☐ 407 | Kirk Gibson | .35 | .14 | .03 |
| ☐ 408 | Tony Perez | .15 | .06 | .01 |
| ☐ 409 | Tommy John | .18 | .08 | .01 |
| ☐ 410 | Dave Stewart | .15 | .06 | .01 |
| ☐ 411 | Dan Spillner | .03 | .01 | .00 |
| ☐ 412 | Willie Aikens | .06 | .02 | .00 |
| ☐ 413 | Mike Heath | .03 | .01 | .00 |
| ☐ 414 | Ray Burris | .03 | .01 | .00 |
| ☐ 415 | Leon Roberts | .03 | .01 | .00 |
| ☐ 416 | Mike Witt | 1.00 | .40 | .10 |
| ☐ 417 | Bob Molinaro | .03 | .01 | .00 |
| ☐ 418 | Steve Braun | .03 | .01 | .00 |
| ☐ 419 | Nolan Ryan | .40 | .16 | .04 |
| ☐ 420 | Tug McGraw | .10 | .04 | .01 |
| ☐ 421 | Dave Concepcion | .12 | .05 | .01 |
| ☐ 422A | Juan Eichelberger ERR (photo actually | .60 | .24 | .06 |

| | | | | |
|---|---|---|---|---|
| | Gary Lucas) | | | |
| ☐ 422B | Juan Eichelberger | .08 | .03 | .01 |
| | COR | | | |
| ☐ 423 | Rick Rhoden | .08 | .03 | .01 |
| ☐ 424 | Frank Robinson MGR | .15 | .06 | .01 |
| ☐ 425 | Eddie Miller | .03 | .01 | .00 |
| ☐ 426 | Bill Caudill | .06 | .02 | .00 |
| ☐ 427 | Doug Flynn | .03 | .01 | .00 |
| ☐ 428 | Larry Andersen | .03 | .01 | .00 |
| ☐ 429 | Al Williams | .03 | .01 | .00 |
| ☐ 430 | Jerry Garvin | .03 | .01 | .00 |
| ☐ 431 | Glenn Adams | .03 | .01 | .00 |
| ☐ 432 | Barry Bonnell | .03 | .01 | .00 |
| ☐ 433 | Jerry Narron | .03 | .01 | .00 |
| ☐ 434 | John Stearns | .03 | .01 | .00 |
| ☐ 435 | Mike Tyson | .03 | .01 | .00 |
| ☐ 436 | Glenn Hubbard | .03 | .01 | .00 |
| ☐ 437 | Eddie Solomon | .03 | .01 | .00 |
| ☐ 438 | Jeff Leonard | .06 | .02 | .00 |
| ☐ 439 | Randy Bass | .03 | .01 | .00 |
| ☐ 440 | Mike LaCoss | .03 | .01 | .00 |
| ☐ 441 | Gary Matthews | .08 | .03 | .01 |
| ☐ 442 | Mark Littell | .03 | .01 | .00 |
| ☐ 443 | Don Sutton | .25 | .10 | .02 |
| ☐ 444 | John Harris | .03 | .01 | .00 |
| ☐ 445 | Vada Pinson CO | .08 | .03 | .01 |
| ☐ 446 | Elias Sosa | .03 | .01 | .00 |
| ☐ 447 | Charlie Hough | .08 | .03 | .01 |
| ☐ 448 | Willie Wilson | .20 | .08 | .02 |
| ☐ 449 | Fred Stanley | .03 | .01 | .00 |
| ☐ 450 | Tom Veryzer | .03 | .01 | .00 |
| ☐ 451 | Ron Davis | .03 | .01 | .00 |
| ☐ 452 | Mark Clear | .03 | .01 | .00 |
| ☐ 453 | Bill Russell | .06 | .02 | .00 |
| ☐ 454 | Lou Whitaker | .15 | .06 | .01 |
| ☐ 455 | Dan Graham | .03 | .01 | .00 |
| ☐ 456 | Reggie Cleveland | .03 | .01 | .00 |
| ☐ 457 | Sammy Stewart | .03 | .01 | .00 |
| ☐ 458 | Pete Vuckovich | .10 | .04 | .01 |
| ☐ 459 | John Wockenfuss | .03 | .01 | .00 |
| ☐ 460 | Glen Hoffman | .03 | .01 | .00 |
| ☐ 461 | Willie Randolph | .08 | .03 | .01 |
| ☐ 462 | Fernando Valenzuela | .50 | .20 | .05 |
| ☐ 463 | Ron Hassey | .03 | .01 | .00 |
| ☐ 464 | Paul Splittorff | .06 | .02 | .00 |
| ☐ 465 | Rob Picciolo | .03 | .01 | .00 |
| ☐ 466 | Larry Parrish | .06 | .02 | .00 |
| ☐ 467 | Johnny Grubb | .03 | .01 | .00 |
| ☐ 468 | Dan Ford | .03 | .01 | .00 |
| ☐ 469 | Silvio Martinez | .03 | .01 | .00 |
| ☐ 470 | Kiko Garcia | .03 | .01 | .00 |
| ☐ 471 | Bob Boone | .06 | .02 | .00 |
| ☐ 472 | Luis Salazar | .03 | .01 | .00 |
| ☐ 473 | Randy Niemann | .03 | .01 | .00 |
| ☐ 474 | Tom Griffin | .03 | .01 | .00 |
| ☐ 475 | Phil Niekro | .20 | .08 | .02 |
| ☐ 476 | Hubie Brooks | .15 | .06 | .01 |
| ☐ 477 | Dick Tidrow | .03 | .01 | .00 |
| ☐ 478 | Jim Beattie | .03 | .01 | .00 |
| ☐ 479 | Damaso Garcia | .10 | .04 | .01 |
| ☐ 480 | Mickey Hatcher | .03 | .01 | .00 |
| ☐ 481 | Joe Price | .03 | .01 | .00 |
| ☐ 482 | Ed Farmer | .03 | .01 | .00 |
| ☐ 483 | Eddie Murray | .65 | .26 | .06 |
| ☐ 484 | Ben Oglivie | .08 | .03 | .01 |
| ☐ 485 | Kevin Saucier | .03 | .01 | .00 |
| ☐ 486 | Bobby Murcer | .10 | .04 | .01 |
| ☐ 487 | Bill Campbell | .06 | .02 | .00 |
| ☐ 488 | Reggie Smith | .10 | .04 | .01 |
| ☐ 489 | Wayne Garland | .03 | .01 | .00 |
| ☐ 490 | Jim Wright | .03 | .01 | .00 |
| ☐ 491 | Billy Martin MGR | .15 | .06 | .01 |
| ☐ 492 | Jim Fanning MGR | .03 | .01 | .00 |
| ☐ 493 | Don Baylor | .15 | .06 | .01 |
| ☐ 494 | Rick Honeycutt | .06 | .02 | .00 |
| ☐ 495 | Carlton Fisk | .18 | .08 | .01 |
| ☐ 496 | Denny Walling | .03 | .01 | .00 |
| ☐ 497 | Bake McBride | .03 | .01 | .00 |
| ☐ 498 | Darrell Porter | .06 | .02 | .00 |
| ☐ 499 | Gene Richards | .03 | .01 | .00 |
| ☐ 500 | Ron Oester | .06 | .02 | .00 |
| ☐ 501 | Ken Dayley | .20 | .08 | .02 |
| ☐ 502 | Jason Thompson | .06 | .02 | .00 |
| ☐ 503 | Milt May | .03 | .01 | .00 |
| ☐ 504 | Doug Bird | .03 | .01 | .00 |
| ☐ 505 | Bruce Bochte | .06 | .02 | .00 |
| ☐ 506 | Neil Allen | .06 | .02 | .00 |
| ☐ 507 | Joey McLaughlin | .03 | .01 | .00 |
| ☐ 508 | Butch Wynegar | .06 | .02 | .00 |
| ☐ 509 | Gary Roenicke | .06 | .02 | .00 |
| ☐ 510 | Robin Yount | .50 | .20 | .05 |
| ☐ 511 | Dave Tobik | .03 | .01 | .00 |
| ☐ 512 | Rich Gedman | .75 | .30 | .07 |

| | | | | |
|---|---|---|---|---|
| ☐ 513 | Gene Nelson | .10 | .04 | .01 |
| ☐ 514 | Rick Monday | .06 | .02 | .00 |
| ☐ 515 | Miguel Dilone | .03 | .01 | .00 |
| ☐ 516 | Clint Hurdle | .03 | .01 | .00 |
| ☐ 517 | Jeff Newman | .03 | .01 | .00 |
| ☐ 518 | Grant Jackson | .03 | .01 | .00 |
| ☐ 519 | Andy Hassler | .03 | .01 | .00 |
| ☐ 520 | Pat Putnam | .03 | .01 | .00 |
| ☐ 521 | Greg Pryor | .03 | .01 | .00 |
| ☐ 522 | Tony Scott | .03 | .01 | .00 |
| ☐ 523 | Steve Mura | .03 | .01 | .00 |
| ☐ 524 | Johnnie LeMaster | .03 | .01 | .00 |
| ☐ 525 | Dick Ruthven | .03 | .01 | .00 |
| ☐ 526 | John McNamara MGR | .03 | .01 | .00 |
| ☐ 527 | Larry McWilliams | .06 | .02 | .00 |
| ☐ 528 | Johnny Ray | .75 | .30 | .07 |
| ☐ 529 | Pat Tabler | .75 | .30 | .07 |
| ☐ 530 | Tom Herr | .10 | .04 | .01 |
| ☐ 531A | San Diego Chicken | .90 | .36 | .09 |
| | (with TM) | | | |
| ☐ 531B | San Diego Chicken | .90 | .36 | .09 |
| | (without TM) | | | |
| ☐ 532 | Sal Butera | .03 | .01 | .00 |
| ☐ 533 | Mike Griffin | .03 | .01 | .00 |
| ☐ 534 | Kelvin Moore | .06 | .02 | .00 |
| ☐ 535 | Reggie Jackson | .50 | .20 | .05 |
| ☐ 536 | Ed Romero | .03 | .01 | .00 |
| ☐ 537 | Derrel Thomas | .03 | .01 | .00 |
| ☐ 538 | Mike O'Berry | .03 | .01 | .00 |
| ☐ 539 | Jack O'Connor | .03 | .01 | .00 |
| ☐ 540 | Bob Ojeda | .75 | .30 | .07 |
| ☐ 541 | Roy Lee Jackson | .03 | .01 | .00 |
| ☐ 542 | Lynn Jones | .03 | .01 | .00 |
| ☐ 543 | Gaylord Perry | .25 | .10 | .02 |
| ☐ 544A | Phil Garner ERR | .50 | .20 | .05 |
| | (reverse negative) | | | |
| ☐ 544B | Phil Garner COR | .08 | .03 | .01 |
| ☐ 545 | Garry Templeton | .10 | .04 | .01 |
| ☐ 546 | Rafael Ramirez | .03 | .01 | .00 |
| ☐ 547 | Jeff Reardon | .08 | .03 | .01 |
| ☐ 548 | Ron Guidry | .20 | .08 | .02 |
| ☐ 549 | Tim Laudner | .08 | .03 | .01 |
| ☐ 550 | John Henry Johnson | .03 | .01 | .00 |
| ☐ 551 | Chris Bando | .03 | .01 | .00 |
| ☐ 552 | Bobby Brown | .03 | .01 | .00 |
| ☐ 553 | Larry Bradford | .03 | .01 | .00 |
| ☐ 554 | Scott Fletcher | .30 | .12 | .03 |
| ☐ 555 | Jerry Royster | .03 | .01 | .00 |
| ☐ 556 | Shooty Babitt | .03 | .01 | .00 |
| ☐ 557 | Kent Hrbek | 2.50 | 1.00 | .25 |
| ☐ 558 | Yankee Winners | .15 | .06 | .01 |
| | Ron Guidry | | | |
| | Tommy John | | | |
| ☐ 559 | Mark Bomback | .03 | .01 | .00 |
| ☐ 560 | Julio Valdez | .03 | .01 | .00 |
| ☐ 561 | Buck Martinez | .03 | .01 | .00 |
| ☐ 562 | Mike Marshall | 1.25 | .50 | .12 |
| | (Dodger hitter) | | | |
| ☐ 563 | Rennie Stennett | .03 | .01 | .00 |
| ☐ 564 | Steve Crawford | .06 | .02 | .00 |
| ☐ 565 | Bob Babcock | .03 | .01 | .00 |
| ☐ 566 | Johnny Podres CO | .06 | .02 | .00 |
| ☐ 567 | Paul Serna | .06 | .02 | .00 |
| ☐ 568 | Harold Baines | .35 | .14 | .03 |
| ☐ 569 | Dave LaRoche | .03 | .01 | .00 |
| ☐ 570 | Lee May | .06 | .02 | .00 |
| ☐ 571 | Gary Ward | .06 | .02 | .00 |
| ☐ 572 | John Denny | .08 | .03 | .01 |
| ☐ 573 | Roy Smalley | .06 | .02 | .00 |
| ☐ 574 | Bob Brenly | .35 | .14 | .03 |
| ☐ 575 | Bronx Bombers: | .40 | .16 | .04 |
| | Reggie Jackson | | | |
| | Dave Winfield | | | |
| ☐ 576 | Luis Pujols | .03 | .01 | .00 |
| ☐ 577 | Butch Hobson | .03 | .01 | .00 |
| ☐ 578 | Harvey Kuenn MGR | .06 | .02 | .00 |
| ☐ 579 | Cal Ripken Sr. | .10 | .04 | .01 |
| | (Orioles coach) | | | |
| ☐ 580 | Juan Berenguer | .03 | .01 | .00 |
| ☐ 581 | Benny Ayala | .03 | .01 | .00 |
| ☐ 582 | Vance Law | .03 | .01 | .00 |
| ☐ 583 | Rick Leach | .06 | .02 | .00 |
| ☐ 584 | George Frazier | .03 | .01 | .00 |
| ☐ 585 | Phillies Finest | .75 | .30 | .07 |
| | Pete Rose | | | |
| | Mike Schmidt | | | |
| ☐ 586 | Joe Rudi | .06 | .02 | .00 |
| ☐ 587 | Juan Beniquez | .06 | .02 | .00 |
| ☐ 588 | Luis DeLeon | .10 | .04 | .01 |
| ☐ 589 | Craig Swan | .03 | .01 | .00 |
| ☐ 590 | Dave Chalk | .03 | .01 | .00 |
| ☐ 591 | Billy Gardner | .03 | .01 | .00 |
| ☐ 592 | Sal Bando | .06 | .02 | .00 |

| | | | | |
|---|---|---|---|---|
| ☐ 593 | Bert Campaneris | .08 | .03 | .01 |
| ☐ 594 | Steve Kemp | .08 | .03 | .01 |
| ☐ 595A | Randy Lerch ERR (Braves) | .50 | .20 | .05 |
| ☐ 595B | Randy Lerch COR (Brewers) | .08 | .03 | .01 |
| ☐ 596 | Bryan Clark | .03 | .01 | .00 |
| ☐ 597 | David Ford | .03 | .01 | .00 |
| ☐ 598 | Mike Scioscia | .06 | .02 | .00 |
| ☐ 599 | John Lowenstein | .03 | .01 | .00 |
| ☐ 600 | Rene Lachemann MGR | .03 | .01 | .00 |
| ☐ 601 | Mick Kelleher | .03 | .01 | .00 |
| ☐ 602 | Ron Jackson | .03 | .01 | .00 |
| ☐ 603 | Jerry Koosman | .08 | .03 | .01 |
| ☐ 604 | Dave Goltz | .03 | .01 | .00 |
| ☐ 605 | Ellis Valentine | .03 | .01 | .00 |
| ☐ 606 | Lonnie Smith | .08 | .03 | .01 |
| ☐ 607 | Joaquin Andujar | .12 | .05 | .01 |
| ☐ 608 | Garry Hancock | .03 | .01 | .00 |
| ☐ 609 | Jerry Turner | .03 | .01 | .00 |
| ☐ 610 | Bob Bonner | .03 | .01 | .00 |
| ☐ 611 | Jim Dwyer | .03 | .01 | .00 |
| ☐ 612 | Terry Bulling | .03 | .01 | .00 |
| ☐ 613 | Joel Youngblood | .03 | .01 | .00 |
| ☐ 614 | Larry Milbourne | .03 | .01 | .00 |
| ☐ 615 | Gene Roof (name on front is Phil Roof) | .10 | .04 | .01 |
| ☐ 616 | Keith Drumright | .03 | .01 | .00 |
| ☐ 617 | Dave Rosello | .03 | .01 | .00 |
| ☐ 618 | Rickey Keeton | .03 | .01 | .00 |
| ☐ 619 | Dennis Lamp | .03 | .01 | .00 |
| ☐ 620 | Sid Monge | .03 | .01 | .00 |
| ☐ 621 | Jerry White | .03 | .01 | .00 |
| ☐ 622 | Luis Aguayo | .03 | .01 | .00 |
| ☐ 623 | Jamie Easterly | .03 | .01 | .00 |
| ☐ 624 | Steve Sax | 1.25 | .50 | .12 |
| ☐ 625 | Dave Roberts | .03 | .01 | .00 |
| ☐ 626 | Rick Bosetti | .03 | .01 | .00 |
| ☐ 627 | Terry Francona | .20 | .08 | .02 |
| ☐ 628 | Pride of Reds: Tom Seaver Johnny Bench | .35 | .14 | .03 |
| ☐ 629 | Paul Mirabella | .03 | .01 | .00 |
| ☐ 630 | Rance Mulliniks | .03 | .01 | .00 |
| ☐ 631 | Kevin Hickey | .06 | .02 | .00 |
| ☐ 632 | Reid Nichols | .03 | .01 | .00 |
| ☐ 633 | Dave Geisel | .03 | .01 | .00 |
| ☐ 634 | Ken Griffey | .08 | .03 | .01 |
| ☐ 635 | Bob Lemon MGR | .10 | .04 | .01 |
| ☐ 636 | Orlando Sanchez | .03 | .01 | .00 |
| ☐ 637 | Bill Almon | .03 | .01 | .00 |
| ☐ 638 | Danny Ainge | .08 | .03 | .01 |
| ☐ 639 | Willie Stargell | .25 | .10 | .02 |
| ☐ 640 | Bob Sykes | .03 | .01 | .00 |
| ☐ 641 | Ed Lynch | .10 | .04 | .01 |
| ☐ 642 | John Ellis | .03 | .01 | .00 |
| ☐ 643 | Ferguson Jenkins | .15 | .06 | .01 |
| ☐ 644 | Lenn Sakata | .03 | .01 | .00 |
| ☐ 645 | Julio Gonzalez | .03 | .01 | .00 |
| ☐ 646 | Jesse Orosco | .08 | .03 | .01 |
| ☐ 647 | Jerry Dybzinski | .03 | .01 | .00 |
| ☐ 648 | Tommy Davis | .06 | .02 | .00 |
| ☐ 649 | Ron Gardenhire | .08 | .03 | .01 |
| ☐ 650 | Felipe Alou | .06 | .02 | .00 |
| ☐ 651 | Harvey Haddix | .06 | .02 | .00 |
| ☐ 652 | Willie Upshaw | .08 | .03 | .01 |
| ☐ 653 | Bill Madlock | .15 | .06 | .01 |
| ☐ 654A | DK Checklist (unnumbered) (with Trammel) | .15 | .02 | .00 |
| ☐ 654B | DK Checklist (unnumbered) (with Trammell) | .12 | .02 | .00 |
| ☐ 655 | Checklist 1 (unnumbered) | .07 | .01 | .00 |
| ☐ 656 | Checklist 2 (unnumbered) | .07 | .01 | .00 |
| ☐ 657 | Checklist 3 (unnumbered) | .07 | .01 | .00 |
| ☐ 658 | Checklist 4 (unnumbered) | .07 | .01 | .00 |
| ☐ 659 | Checklist 5 (unnumbered) | .07 | .01 | .00 |
| ☐ 660 | Checklist 6 (unnumbered) | .07 | .01 | .00 |

## 1983 Donruss

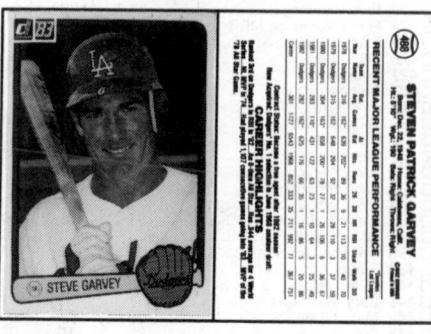

The cards in this 660 card set measure 2 1/2" by 3 1/2". The 1983 Donruss baseball set, issued with a 63 piece Diamond King puzzle, again leads off with a 26 card Diamond Kings (DK) series. Of the remaining 634 cards, two are combination cards, one portrays the San Diego Chicken, one shows the completed Ty Cobb puzzle, and seven are unnumbered checklist cards. The seven unnumbered checklist cards are arbitrarily assigned numbers 654 through 660 and are listed at the end of the list below. The Donruss logo and the year of issue are shown in the upper left corner of the obverse. The card backs have black print on yellow and white and are numbered on a small ball design. The complete set price below includes only the more common of each variation pair.

| | | MINT | VG-E | F-G |
|---|---|---|---|---|
| COMPLETE SET (660) | | 27.00 | 11.00 | 2.70 |
| COMMON PLAYER (1-660) | | .03 | .01 | .00 |
| ☐ | 1 Fernando Valenzuela DK | .50 | .20 | .05 |
| ☐ | 2 Rollie Fingers DK | .25 | .10 | .02 |
| ☐ | 3 Reggie Jackson DK | .50 | .20 | .05 |
| ☐ | 4 Jim Palmer DK | .35 | .14 | .03 |
| ☐ | 5 Jack Morris DK | .30 | .12 | .03 |
| ☐ | 6 George Foster DK | .15 | .06 | .01 |
| ☐ | 7 Jim Sundberg DK | .06 | .02 | .00 |
| ☐ | 8 Willie Stargell DK | .25 | .10 | .02 |
| ☐ | 9 Dave Stieb DK | .20 | .08 | .02 |
| ☐ | 10 Joe Niekro DK | .08 | .03 | .01 |
| ☐ | 11 Rickey Henderson DK | .50 | .20 | .05 |
| ☐ | 12 Dale Murphy DK | .75 | .30 | .07 |
| ☐ | 13 Toby Harrah DK | .06 | .02 | .00 |
| ☐ | 14 Bill Buckner DK | .12 | .05 | .01 |
| ☐ | 15 Willie Wilson DK | .20 | .08 | .02 |
| ☐ | 16 Steve Carlton DK | .40 | .16 | .04 |
| ☐ | 17 Ron Guidry DK | .25 | .10 | .02 |
| ☐ | 18 Steve Rogers DK | .06 | .02 | .00 |
| ☐ | 19 Kent Hrbek DK | .30 | .12 | .03 |
| ☐ | 20 Keith Hernandez DK | .30 | .12 | .03 |
| ☐ | 21 Floyd Bannister DK | .06 | .02 | .00 |
| ☐ | 22 John Bench DK | .40 | .16 | .04 |
| ☐ | 23 Britt Burns DK | .06 | .02 | .00 |
| ☐ | 24 Joe Morgan DK | .25 | .10 | .02 |
| ☐ | 25 Carl Yastrzemski DK | .75 | .30 | .07 |
| ☐ | 26 Terry Kennedy DK | .08 | .03 | .01 |
| ☐ | 27 Gary Roenicke | .06 | .02 | .00 |
| ☐ | 28 Dwight Bernard | .03 | .01 | .00 |
| ☐ | 29 Pat Underwood | .03 | .01 | .00 |
| ☐ | 30 Gary Allenson | .03 | .01 | .00 |
| ☐ | 31 Ron Guidry | .20 | .08 | .02 |
| ☐ | 32 Burt Hooton | .03 | .01 | .00 |
| ☐ | 33 Chris Bando | .03 | .01 | .00 |
| ☐ | 34 Vida Blue | .08 | .03 | .01 |
| ☐ | 35 Rickey Henderson | .45 | .18 | .04 |
| ☐ | 36 Ray Burris | .03 | .01 | .00 |
| ☐ | 37 John Butcher | .03 | .01 | .00 |
| ☐ | 38 Don Aase | .05 | .02 | .00 |
| ☐ | 39 Jerry Koosman | .07 | .03 | .01 |
| ☐ | 40 Bruce Sutter | .15 | .06 | .01 |
| ☐ | 41 Jose Cruz | .10 | .04 | .01 |
| ☐ | 42 Pete Rose | 1.00 | .40 | .10 |

| # | Name | | | |
|---|------|---|---|---|
| ☐ 43 | Cesar Cedeno | .07 | .03 | .01 |
| ☐ 44 | Floyd Chiffer | .05 | .02 | .00 |
| ☐ 45 | Larry McWilliams | .03 | .01 | .00 |
| ☐ 46 | Alan Fowlkes | .03 | .01 | .00 |
| ☐ 47 | Dale Murphy | .75 | .30 | .07 |
| ☐ 48 | Doug Bird | .03 | .01 | .00 |
| ☐ 49 | Hubie Brooks | .10 | .04 | .01 |
| ☐ 50 | Floyd Bannister | .06 | .02 | .00 |
| ☐ 51 | Jack O'Connor | .03 | .01 | .00 |
| ☐ 52 | Steve Senteney | .03 | .01 | .00 |
| ☐ 53 | Gary Gaetti | .75 | .30 | .07 |
| ☐ 54 | Damaso Garcia | .09 | .04 | .01 |
| ☐ 55 | Gene Nelson | .03 | .01 | .00 |
| ☐ 56 | Mookie Wilson | .08 | .03 | .01 |
| ☐ 57 | Allen Ripley | .03 | .01 | .00 |
| ☐ 58 | Bob Horner | .20 | .08 | .02 |
| ☐ 59 | Tony Pena | .15 | .06 | .01 |
| ☐ 60 | Gary Lavelle | .05 | .02 | .00 |
| ☐ 61 | Tim Lollar | .03 | .01 | .00 |
| ☐ 62 | Frank Pastore | .03 | .01 | .00 |
| ☐ 63 | Garry Maddox | .05 | .02 | .00 |
| ☐ 64 | Bob Forsch | .05 | .02 | .00 |
| ☐ 65 | Harry Spilman | .03 | .01 | .00 |
| ☐ 66 | Geoff Zahn | .03 | .01 | .00 |
| ☐ 67 | Salome Barojas | .03 | .01 | .00 |
| ☐ 68 | David Palmer | .05 | .02 | .00 |
| ☐ 69 | Charlie Hough | .07 | .03 | .01 |
| ☐ 70 | Dan Quisenberry | .18 | .08 | .01 |
| ☐ 71 | Tony Armas | .10 | .04 | .01 |
| ☐ 72 | Rick Sutcliffe | .15 | .06 | .01 |
| ☐ 73 | Steve Balboni | .07 | .03 | .01 |
| ☐ 74 | Jerry Remy | .03 | .01 | .00 |
| ☐ 75 | Mike Scioscia | .05 | .02 | .00 |
| ☐ 76 | John Wockenfuss | .03 | .01 | .00 |
| ☐ 77 | Jim Palmer | .25 | .10 | .02 |
| ☐ 78 | Rollie Fingers | .20 | .08 | .02 |
| ☐ 79 | Joe Nolan | .03 | .01 | .00 |
| ☐ 80 | Pete Vuckovich | .07 | .03 | .01 |
| ☐ 81 | Rick Leach | .03 | .01 | .00 |
| ☐ 82 | Rick Miller | .03 | .01 | .00 |
| ☐ 83 | Graig Nettles | .14 | .06 | .01 |
| ☐ 84 | Ron Cey | .10 | .04 | .01 |
| ☐ 85 | Miguel Dilone | .03 | .01 | .00 |
| ☐ 86 | John Wathan | .03 | .01 | .00 |
| ☐ 87 | Kelvin Moore | .03 | .01 | .00 |
| ☐ 88A | Byrn Smith ERR | .15 | .06 | .01 |
| | (sic, Bryn) | | | |
| ☐ 88B | Bryn Smith COR | .75 | .30 | .07 |
| ☐ 89 | Dave Hostetler | .05 | .02 | .00 |
| ☐ 90 | Rod Carew | .40 | .16 | .04 |
| ☐ 91 | Lonnie Smith | .07 | .03 | .01 |
| ☐ 92 | Bob Knepper | .09 | .04 | .01 |
| ☐ 93 | Marty Bystrom | .03 | .01 | .00 |
| ☐ 94 | Chris Welsh | .03 | .01 | .00 |
| ☐ 95 | Jason Thompson | .05 | .02 | .00 |
| ☐ 96 | Tom O'Malley | .05 | .02 | .00 |
| ☐ 97 | Phil Niekro | .20 | .08 | .02 |
| ☐ 98 | Neil Allen | .05 | .02 | .00 |
| ☐ 99 | Bill Buckner | .10 | .04 | .01 |
| ☐ 100 | Ed VandeBerg | .08 | .03 | .01 |
| ☐ 101 | Jim Clancy | .03 | .01 | .00 |
| ☐ 102 | Robert Castillo | .03 | .01 | .00 |
| ☐ 103 | Bruce Berenyi | .03 | .01 | .00 |
| ☐ 104 | Carlton Fisk | .15 | .06 | .01 |
| ☐ 105 | Mike Flanagan | .07 | .03 | .01 |
| ☐ 106 | Cecil Cooper | .15 | .06 | .01 |
| ☐ 107 | Jack Morris | .20 | .08 | .02 |
| ☐ 108 | Mike Morgan | .03 | .01 | .00 |
| ☐ 109 | Luis Aponte | .05 | .02 | .00 |
| ☐ 110 | Pedro Guerrero | .30 | .12 | .03 |
| ☐ 111 | Len Barker | .05 | .02 | .00 |
| ☐ 112 | Willie Wilson | .20 | .08 | .02 |
| ☐ 113 | Dave Beard | .03 | .01 | .00 |
| ☐ 114 | Mike Gates | .03 | .01 | .00 |
| ☐ 115 | Reggie Jackson | .40 | .16 | .04 |
| ☐ 116 | George Wright | .08 | .03 | .01 |
| ☐ 117 | Vance Law | .03 | .01 | .00 |
| ☐ 118 | Nolan Ryan | .35 | .14 | .03 |
| ☐ 119 | Mike Krukow | .08 | .03 | .01 |
| ☐ 120 | Ozzie Smith | .15 | .06 | .01 |
| ☐ 121 | Broderick Perkins | .03 | .01 | .00 |
| ☐ 122 | Tom Seaver | .35 | .14 | .03 |
| ☐ 123 | Chris Chambliss | .05 | .02 | .00 |
| ☐ 124 | Chuck Tanner MGR | .03 | .01 | .00 |
| ☐ 125 | Johnnie LeMaster | .03 | .01 | .00 |
| ☐ 126 | Mel Hall | .75 | .30 | .07 |
| ☐ 127 | Bruce Bochte | .05 | .02 | .00 |
| ☐ 128 | Charlie Puleo | .03 | .01 | .00 |
| ☐ 129 | Luis Leal | .03 | .01 | .00 |
| ☐ 130 | John Pacella | .03 | .01 | .00 |
| ☐ 131 | Glenn Gulliver | .03 | .01 | .00 |
| ☐ 132 | Don Money | .03 | .01 | .00 |
| ☐ 133 | Dave Rozema | .03 | .01 | .00 |
| ☐ 134 | Bruce Hurst | .09 | .04 | .01 |
| ☐ 135 | Rudy May | .03 | .01 | .00 |
| ☐ 136 | Tom Lasorda MGR | .07 | .03 | .01 |
| ☐ 137 | Dan Spillner | .10 | .04 | .01 |
| | (photo actually | | | |
| | Ed Whitson) | | | |
| ☐ 138 | Jerry Martin | .03 | .01 | .00 |
| ☐ 139 | Mike Norris | .05 | .02 | .00 |
| ☐ 140 | Al Oliver | .12 | .05 | .01 |
| ☐ 141 | Daryl Sconiers | .03 | .01 | .00 |
| ☐ 142 | Lamar Johnson | .03 | .01 | .00 |
| ☐ 143 | Harold Baines | .25 | .10 | .02 |
| ☐ 144 | Alan Ashby | .03 | .01 | .00 |
| ☐ 145 | Garry Templeton | .10 | .04 | .01 |
| ☐ 146 | Al Holland | .05 | .02 | .00 |
| ☐ 147 | Bo Diaz | .05 | .02 | .00 |
| ☐ 148 | Dave Concepcion | .10 | .04 | .01 |
| ☐ 149 | Rick Camp | .03 | .01 | .00 |
| ☐ 150 | Jim Morrison | .03 | .01 | .00 |
| ☐ 151 | Randy Martz | .03 | .01 | .00 |
| ☐ 152 | Keith Hernandez | .30 | .12 | .03 |
| ☐ 153 | John Lowenstein | .03 | .01 | .00 |
| ☐ 154 | Mike Caldwell | .05 | .02 | .00 |
| ☐ 155 | Milt Wilcox | .03 | .01 | .00 |
| ☐ 156 | Rich Gedman | .12 | .05 | .01 |
| ☐ 157 | Rich Gossage | .18 | .08 | .01 |
| ☐ 158 | Jerry Reuss | .06 | .02 | .00 |
| ☐ 159 | Ron Hassey | .03 | .01 | .00 |
| ☐ 160 | Larry Gura | .05 | .02 | .00 |
| ☐ 161 | Dwayne Murphy | .06 | .02 | .00 |
| ☐ 162 | Woodie Fryman | .03 | .01 | .00 |
| ☐ 163 | Steve Comer | .03 | .01 | .00 |
| ☐ 164 | Ken Forsch | .03 | .01 | .00 |
| ☐ 165 | Dennis Lamp | .03 | .01 | .00 |
| ☐ 166 | David Green | .08 | .03 | .01 |
| ☐ 167 | Terry Puhl | .05 | .02 | .00 |
| ☐ 168 | Mike Schmidt | .50 | .20 | .05 |
| ☐ 169 | Eddie Milner | .15 | .06 | .01 |
| ☐ 170 | John Curtis | .03 | .01 | .00 |
| ☐ 171 | Don Robinson | .03 | .01 | .00 |
| ☐ 172 | Rich Gale | .03 | .01 | .00 |
| ☐ 173 | Steve Bedrosian | .07 | .03 | .01 |
| ☐ 174 | Willie Hernandez | .15 | .06 | .01 |
| ☐ 175 | Ron Gardenhire | .03 | .01 | .00 |
| ☐ 176 | Jim Beattie | .03 | .01 | .00 |
| ☐ 177 | Tim Laudner | .03 | .01 | .00 |
| ☐ 178 | Buck Martinez | .03 | .01 | .00 |
| ☐ 179 | Kent Hrbek | .35 | .14 | .03 |
| ☐ 180 | Alfredo Griffin | .05 | .02 | .00 |
| ☐ 181 | Larry Andersen | .03 | .01 | .00 |
| ☐ 182 | Pete Falcone | .03 | .01 | .00 |
| ☐ 183 | Jody Davis | .08 | .03 | .01 |
| ☐ 184 | Glen Hubbard | .03 | .01 | .00 |
| ☐ 185 | Dale Berra | .05 | .02 | .00 |
| ☐ 186 | Greg Minton | .05 | .02 | .00 |
| ☐ 187 | Gary Lucas | .03 | .01 | .00 |
| ☐ 188 | Dave Van Gorder | .05 | .02 | .00 |
| ☐ 189 | Bob Dernier | .06 | .02 | .00 |
| ☐ 190 | Willie McGee | 1.25 | .50 | .12 |
| ☐ 191 | Dickie Thon | .05 | .02 | .00 |
| ☐ 192 | Bob Boone | .05 | .02 | .00 |
| ☐ 193 | Britt Burns | .05 | .02 | .00 |
| ☐ 194 | Jeff Reardon | .07 | .03 | .01 |
| ☐ 195 | Jon Matlack | .05 | .02 | .00 |
| ☐ 196 | Don Slaught | .25 | .10 | .02 |
| ☐ 197 | Fred Stanley | .03 | .01 | .00 |
| ☐ 198 | Rick Manning | .03 | .01 | .00 |
| ☐ 199 | Dave Righetti | .15 | .06 | .01 |
| ☐ 200 | Dave Stapleton | .03 | .01 | .00 |
| ☐ 201 | Steve Yeager | .03 | .01 | .00 |
| ☐ 202 | Enos Cabell | .03 | .01 | .00 |
| ☐ 203 | Sammy Stewart | .03 | .01 | .00 |
| ☐ 204 | Moose Haas | .03 | .01 | .00 |
| ☐ 205 | Lenn Sakata | .03 | .01 | .00 |
| ☐ 206 | Charlie Moore | .03 | .01 | .00 |
| ☐ 207 | Alan Trammell | .15 | .06 | .01 |
| ☐ 208 | Jim Rice | .35 | .14 | .03 |
| ☐ 209 | Roy Smalley | .05 | .02 | .00 |
| ☐ 210 | Bill Russell | .05 | .02 | .00 |
| ☐ 211 | Andre Thornton | .07 | .03 | .01 |
| ☐ 212 | Willie Aikens | .05 | .02 | .00 |
| ☐ 213 | Dave McKay | .03 | .01 | .00 |
| ☐ 214 | Tim Blackwell | .03 | .01 | .00 |
| ☐ 215 | Buddy Bell | .10 | .04 | .01 |
| ☐ 216 | Doug DeCinces | .10 | .04 | .01 |
| ☐ 217 | Tom Herr | .08 | .03 | .01 |
| ☐ 218 | Frank LaCorte | .03 | .01 | .00 |
| ☐ 219 | Steve Carlton | .35 | .14 | .03 |
| ☐ 220 | Terry Kennedy | .08 | .03 | .01 |
| ☐ 221 | Mike Easler | .06 | .02 | .00 |
| ☐ 222 | Jack Clark | .14 | .06 | .01 |
| ☐ 223 | Gene Garber | .03 | .01 | .00 |
| ☐ 224 | Scott Holman | .05 | .02 | .00 |

| # | Player | | | |
|---|---|---|---|---|
| ☐ 225 | Mike Proly | .03 | .01 | .00 |
| ☐ 226 | Terry Bulling | .03 | .01 | .00 |
| ☐ 227 | Jerry Garvin | .03 | .01 | .00 |
| ☐ 228 | Ron Davis | .03 | .01 | .00 |
| ☐ 229 | Tom Hume | .03 | .01 | .00 |
| ☐ 230 | Marc Hill | .03 | .01 | .00 |
| ☐ 231 | Dennis Martinez | .03 | .01 | .00 |
| ☐ 232 | Jim Gantner | .05 | .02 | .00 |
| ☐ 233 | Larry Pashnick | .03 | .01 | .00 |
| ☐ 234 | Dave Collins | .05 | .02 | .00 |
| ☐ 235 | Tom Burgmeier | .03 | .01 | .00 |
| ☐ 236 | Ken Landreaux | .05 | .02 | .00 |
| ☐ 237 | John Denny | .08 | .03 | .01 |
| ☐ 238 | Hal McRae | .06 | .02 | .00 |
| ☐ 239 | Matt Keough | .03 | .01 | .00 |
| ☐ 240 | Doug Flynn | .03 | .01 | .00 |
| ☐ 241 | Fred Lynn | .20 | .08 | .02 |
| ☐ 242 | Billy Sample | .03 | .01 | .00 |
| ☐ 243 | Tom Paciorek | .03 | .01 | .00 |
| ☐ 244 | Joe Sambito | .05 | .02 | .00 |
| ☐ 245 | Sid Monge | .03 | .01 | .00 |
| ☐ 246 | Ken Oberkfell | .03 | .01 | .00 |
| ☐ 247 | Joe Pittman (photo actually Juan Eichelberger) | .10 | .04 | .01 |
| ☐ 248 | Mario Soto | .07 | .03 | .01 |
| ☐ 249 | Claudell Washington | .07 | .03 | .01 |
| ☐ 250 | Rick Rhoden | .07 | .03 | .01 |
| ☐ 251 | Darrell Evans | .09 | .04 | .01 |
| ☐ 252 | Steve Henderson | .03 | .01 | .00 |
| ☐ 253 | Manny Castillo | .03 | .01 | .00 |
| ☐ 254 | Craig Swan | .03 | .01 | .00 |
| ☐ 255 | Joey McLaughlin | .03 | .01 | .00 |
| ☐ 256 | Pete Redfern | .03 | .01 | .00 |
| ☐ 257 | Ken Singleton | .08 | .03 | .01 |
| ☐ 258 | Robin Yount | .30 | .12 | .03 |
| ☐ 259 | Elias Sosa | .03 | .01 | .00 |
| ☐ 260 | Bob Ojeda | .12 | .05 | .01 |
| ☐ 261 | Bobby Murcer | .09 | .04 | .01 |
| ☐ 262 | Candy Maldonado | .35 | .14 | .03 |
| ☐ 263 | Rick Waits | .03 | .01 | .00 |
| ☐ 264 | Greg Pryor | .03 | .01 | .00 |
| ☐ 265 | Bob Owchinko | .03 | .01 | .00 |
| ☐ 266 | Chris Speier | .03 | .01 | .00 |
| ☐ 267 | Bruce Kison | .03 | .01 | .00 |
| ☐ 268 | Mark Wagner | .03 | .01 | .00 |
| ☐ 269 | Steve Kemp | .07 | .03 | .01 |
| ☐ 270 | Phil Garner | .05 | .02 | .00 |
| ☐ 271 | Gene Richards | .03 | .01 | .00 |
| ☐ 272 | Renie Martin | .03 | .01 | .00 |
| ☐ 273 | Dave Roberts | .03 | .01 | .00 |
| ☐ 274 | Dan Driessen | .05 | .02 | .00 |
| ☐ 275 | Rufino Linares | .03 | .01 | .00 |
| ☐ 276 | Lee Lacy | .05 | .02 | .00 |
| ☐ 277 | Ryne Sandberg | 3.50 | 1.40 | .35 |
| ☐ 278 | Darrell Porter | .05 | .02 | .00 |
| ☐ 279 | Cal Ripken | .75 | .30 | .07 |
| ☐ 280 | Jamie Easterly | .03 | .01 | .00 |
| ☐ 281 | Bill Fahey | .03 | .01 | .00 |
| ☐ 282 | Glenn Hoffman | .03 | .01 | .00 |
| ☐ 283 | Willie Randolph | .06 | .02 | .00 |
| ☐ 284 | Fernando Valenzuela | .35 | .14 | .03 |
| ☐ 285 | Alan Bannister | .03 | .01 | .00 |
| ☐ 286 | Paul Splittorff | .03 | .01 | .00 |
| ☐ 287 | Joe Rudi | .05 | .02 | .00 |
| ☐ 288 | Bill Gullickson | .03 | .01 | .00 |
| ☐ 289 | Danny Darwin | .03 | .01 | .00 |
| ☐ 290 | Andy Hassler | .03 | .01 | .00 |
| ☐ 291 | Ernesto Escarrega | .03 | .01 | .00 |
| ☐ 292 | Steve Mura | .03 | .01 | .00 |
| ☐ 293 | Tony Scott | .03 | .01 | .00 |
| ☐ 294 | Manny Trillo | .05 | .02 | .00 |
| ☐ 295 | Greg Harris | .05 | .02 | .00 |
| ☐ 296 | Luis DeLeon | .03 | .01 | .00 |
| ☐ 297 | Kent Tekulve | .07 | .03 | .01 |
| ☐ 298 | Atlee Hammaker | .05 | .02 | .00 |
| ☐ 299 | Bruce Benedict | .03 | .01 | .00 |
| ☐ 300 | Fergie Jenkins | .12 | .05 | .01 |
| ☐ 301 | Dave Kingman | .12 | .05 | .01 |
| ☐ 302 | Bill Caudill | .05 | .02 | .00 |
| ☐ 303 | John Castino | .03 | .01 | .00 |
| ☐ 304 | Ernie Whitt | .03 | .01 | .00 |
| ☐ 305 | Randy Johnson | .05 | .02 | .00 |
| ☐ 306 | Garth Iorg | .03 | .01 | .00 |
| ☐ 307 | Gaylord Perry | .20 | .08 | .02 |
| ☐ 308 | Ed Lynch | .03 | .01 | .00 |
| ☐ 309 | Keith Moreland | .07 | .03 | .01 |
| ☐ 310 | Rafael Ramirez | .03 | .01 | .00 |
| ☐ 311 | Bill Madlock | .15 | .06 | .01 |
| ☐ 312 | Milt May | .03 | .01 | .00 |
| ☐ 313 | John Montefusco | .05 | .02 | .00 |
| ☐ 314 | Wayne Krenchicki | .03 | .01 | .00 |
| ☐ 315 | George Vukovich | .03 | .01 | .00 |
| ☐ 316 | Joaquin Andujar | .10 | .04 | .01 |
| ☐ 317 | Craig Reynolds | .03 | .01 | .00 |
| ☐ 318 | Rick Burleson | .06 | .02 | .00 |
| ☐ 319 | Richard Dotson | .06 | .02 | .00 |
| ☐ 320 | Steve Rogers | .06 | .02 | .00 |
| ☐ 321 | Dave Schmidt | .03 | .01 | .00 |
| ☐ 322 | Bud Black | .20 | .08 | .02 |
| ☐ 323 | Jeff Burroughs | .05 | .02 | .00 |
| ☐ 324 | Von Hayes | .18 | .08 | .01 |
| ☐ 325 | Butch Wynegar | .05 | .02 | .00 |
| ☐ 326 | Carl Yastrzemski | .50 | .20 | .05 |
| ☐ 327 | Ron Roenicke | .03 | .01 | .00 |
| ☐ 328 | Howard Johnson | .12 | .05 | .01 |
| ☐ 329 | Rick Dempsey | .05 | .02 | .00 |
| ☐ 330A | Jim Slaton (bio printed black on white) | .07 | .03 | .01 |
| ☐ 330B | Jim Slaton (bio printed black on yellow) | .07 | .03 | .01 |
| ☐ 331 | Benny Ayala | .03 | .01 | .00 |
| ☐ 332 | Ted Simmons | .12 | .05 | .01 |
| ☐ 333 | Lou Whitaker | .15 | .06 | .01 |
| ☐ 334 | Chuck Rainey | .03 | .01 | .00 |
| ☐ 335 | Lou Piniella | .10 | .04 | .01 |
| ☐ 336 | Steve Sax | .18 | .08 | .01 |
| ☐ 337 | Toby Harrah | .06 | .02 | .00 |
| ☐ 338 | George Brett | .45 | .18 | .04 |
| ☐ 339 | Davey Lopes | .07 | .03 | .01 |
| ☐ 340 | Gary Carter | .35 | .14 | .03 |
| ☐ 341 | John Grubb | .03 | .01 | .00 |
| ☐ 342 | Tim Foli | .03 | .01 | .00 |
| ☐ 343 | Jim Kaat | .10 | .04 | .01 |
| ☐ 344 | Mike LaCoss | .03 | .01 | .00 |
| ☐ 345 | Larry Christenson | .03 | .01 | .00 |
| ☐ 346 | Juan Bonilla | .03 | .01 | .00 |
| ☐ 347 | Omar Moreno | .03 | .01 | .00 |
| ☐ 348 | Chili Davis | .12 | .05 | .01 |
| ☐ 349 | Tommy Boggs | .03 | .01 | .00 |
| ☐ 350 | Rusty Staub | .10 | .04 | .01 |
| ☐ 351 | Bump Wills | .03 | .01 | .00 |
| ☐ 352 | Rick Sweet | .03 | .01 | .00 |
| ☐ 353 | Jim Gott | .09 | .04 | .01 |
| ☐ 354 | Terry Felton | .03 | .01 | .00 |
| ☐ 355 | Jim Kern | .03 | .01 | .00 |
| ☐ 356 | Bill Almon | .03 | .01 | .00 |
| ☐ 357 | Tippy Martinez | .03 | .01 | .00 |
| ☐ 358 | Roy Howell | .03 | .01 | .00 |
| ☐ 359 | Dan Petry | .12 | .05 | .01 |
| ☐ 360 | Jerry Mumphrey | .05 | .02 | .00 |
| ☐ 361 | Mark Clear | .03 | .01 | .00 |
| ☐ 362 | Mike Marshall | .20 | .08 | .02 |
| ☐ 363 | Lary Sorensen | .03 | .01 | .00 |
| ☐ 364 | Amos Otis | .07 | .03 | .01 |
| ☐ 365 | Rick Langford | .03 | .01 | .00 |
| ☐ 366 | Brad Mills | .03 | .01 | .00 |
| ☐ 367 | Brian Downing | .03 | .01 | .00 |
| ☐ 368 | Mike Richardt | .03 | .01 | .00 |
| ☐ 369 | Aurelio Rodriguez | .03 | .01 | .00 |
| ☐ 370 | Dave Smith | .06 | .02 | .00 |
| ☐ 371 | Tug McGraw | .09 | .04 | .01 |
| ☐ 372 | Doug Bair | .03 | .01 | .00 |
| ☐ 373 | Ruppert Jones | .03 | .01 | .00 |
| ☐ 374 | Alex Trevino | .03 | .01 | .00 |
| ☐ 375 | Ken Dayley | .03 | .01 | .00 |
| ☐ 376 | Rod Scurry | .03 | .01 | .00 |
| ☐ 377 | Bob Brenly | .07 | .03 | .01 |
| ☐ 378 | Scot Thompson | .03 | .01 | .00 |
| ☐ 379 | Julio Cruz | .03 | .01 | .00 |
| ☐ 380 | John Stearns | .03 | .01 | .00 |
| ☐ 381 | Dale Murray | .03 | .01 | .00 |
| ☐ 382 | Frank Viola | .45 | .18 | .04 |
| ☐ 383 | Al Bumbry | .03 | .01 | .00 |
| ☐ 384 | Ben Oglivie | .07 | .03 | .01 |
| ☐ 385 | Dave Tobik | .03 | .01 | .00 |
| ☐ 386 | Bob Stanley | .05 | .02 | .00 |
| ☐ 387 | Andre Robertson | .03 | .01 | .00 |
| ☐ 388 | Jorge Orta | .03 | .01 | .00 |
| ☐ 389 | Ed Whitson | .05 | .02 | .00 |
| ☐ 390 | Don Hood | .03 | .01 | .00 |
| ☐ 391 | Tom Underwood | .03 | .01 | .00 |
| ☐ 392 | Tim Wallach | .08 | .03 | .01 |
| ☐ 393 | Steve Renko | .03 | .01 | .00 |
| ☐ 394 | Mickey Rivers | .06 | .02 | .00 |
| ☐ 395 | Greg Luzinski | .10 | .04 | .01 |
| ☐ 396 | Art Howe | .03 | .01 | .00 |
| ☐ 397 | Alan Wiggins | .15 | .06 | .01 |
| ☐ 398 | Jim Barr | .03 | .01 | .00 |
| ☐ 399 | Ivan DeJesus | .03 | .01 | .00 |
| ☐ 400 | Tom Lawless | .05 | .02 | .00 |
| ☐ 401 | Bob Walk | .03 | .01 | .00 |
| ☐ 402 | Jimmy Smith | .03 | .01 | .00 |
| ☐ 403 | Lee Smith | .09 | .04 | .01 |

| | | | | |
|---|---|---|---|---|
| ☐ 404 | George Hendrick | .07 | .03 | .01 |
| ☐ 405 | Eddie Murray | .50 | .20 | .05 |
| ☐ 406 | Marshall Edwards | .03 | .01 | .00 |
| ☐ 407 | Lance Parrish | .30 | .12 | .03 |
| ☐ 408 | Carney Lansford | .10 | .04 | .01 |
| ☐ 409 | Dave Winfield | .35 | .14 | .03 |
| ☐ 410 | Bob Welch | .07 | .03 | .01 |
| ☐ 411 | Larry Milbourne | .03 | .01 | .00 |
| ☐ 412 | Dennis Leonard | .05 | .02 | .00 |
| ☐ 413 | Dan Meyer | .03 | .01 | .00 |
| ☐ 414 | Charlie Lea | .05 | .02 | .00 |
| ☐ 415 | Rick Honeycutt | .05 | .02 | .00 |
| ☐ 416 | Mike Witt | .10 | .04 | .01 |
| ☐ 417 | Steve Trout | .05 | .02 | .00 |
| ☐ 418 | Glenn Brummer | .03 | .01 | .00 |
| ☐ 419 | Denny Walling | .03 | .01 | .00 |
| ☐ 420 | Gary Matthews | .08 | .03 | .01 |
| ☐ 421 | Charlie Leibrandt (Liebrandt on front of card) | .06 | .02 | .00 |
| ☐ 422 | Juan Eichelberger (photo actually Joe Pittman) | .07 | .03 | .01 |
| ☐ 423 | Matt Guante | .10 | .04 | .01 |
| ☐ 424 | Bill Laskey | .10 | .04 | .01 |
| ☐ 425 | Jerry Royster | .03 | .01 | .00 |
| ☐ 426 | Dickie Noles | .03 | .01 | .00 |
| ☐ 427 | George Foster | .15 | .06 | .01 |
| ☐ 428 | Mike Moore | .25 | .10 | .02 |
| ☐ 429 | Gary Ward | .06 | .02 | .00 |
| ☐ 430 | Barry Bonnell | .05 | .02 | .00 |
| ☐ 431 | Ron Washington | .05 | .02 | .00 |
| ☐ 432 | Rance Mulliniks | .03 | .01 | .00 |
| ☐ 433 | Mike Stanton | .03 | .01 | .00 |
| ☐ 434 | Jesse Orosco | .08 | .03 | .01 |
| ☐ 435 | Larry Bowa | .10 | .04 | .01 |
| ☐ 436 | Biff Pocoroba | .03 | .01 | .00 |
| ☐ 437 | Johnny Ray | .12 | .05 | .01 |
| ☐ 438 | Joe Morgan | .25 | .10 | .02 |
| ☐ 439 | Eric Show | .12 | .05 | .01 |
| ☐ 440 | Larry Biittner | .03 | .01 | .00 |
| ☐ 441 | Greg Gross | .03 | .01 | .00 |
| ☐ 442 | Gene Tenace | .03 | .01 | .00 |
| ☐ 443 | Danny Heep | .03 | .01 | .00 |
| ☐ 444 | Bobby Clark | .03 | .01 | .00 |
| ☐ 445 | Kevin Hickey | .03 | .01 | .00 |
| ☐ 446 | Scott Sanderson | .03 | .01 | .00 |
| ☐ 447 | Frank Tanana | .06 | .02 | .00 |
| ☐ 448 | Cesar Geronimo | .03 | .01 | .00 |
| ☐ 449 | Jimmy Sexton | .03 | .01 | .00 |
| ☐ 450 | Mike Hargrove | .05 | .02 | .00 |
| ☐ 451 | Doyle Alexander | .05 | .02 | .00 |
| ☐ 452 | Dwight Evans | .12 | .05 | .01 |
| ☐ 453 | Terry Forster | .07 | .03 | .01 |
| ☐ 454 | Tom Brookens | .03 | .01 | .00 |
| ☐ 455 | Rich Dauer | .03 | .01 | .00 |
| ☐ 456 | Rob Picciolo | .03 | .01 | .00 |
| ☐ 457 | Terry Crowley | .03 | .01 | .00 |
| ☐ 458 | Ned Yost | .03 | .01 | .00 |
| ☐ 459 | Kirk Gibson | .25 | .10 | .02 |
| ☐ 460 | Reid Nichols | .03 | .01 | .00 |
| ☐ 461 | Oscar Gamble | .06 | .02 | .00 |
| ☐ 462 | Dusty Baker | .07 | .03 | .01 |
| ☐ 463 | Jack Perconte | .03 | .01 | .00 |
| ☐ 464 | Frank White | .07 | .03 | .01 |
| ☐ 465 | Mickey Klutts | .03 | .01 | .00 |
| ☐ 466 | Warren Cromartie | .03 | .01 | .00 |
| ☐ 467 | Larry Parrish | .06 | .02 | .00 |
| ☐ 468 | Bobby Grich | .08 | .03 | .01 |
| ☐ 469 | Dane Iorg | .03 | .01 | .00 |
| ☐ 470 | Joe Niekro | .08 | .03 | .01 |
| ☐ 471 | Ed Farmer | .03 | .01 | .00 |
| ☐ 472 | Tim Flannery | .03 | .01 | .00 |
| ☐ 473 | Dave Parker | .25 | .10 | .02 |
| ☐ 474 | Jeff Leonard | .07 | .03 | .01 |
| ☐ 475 | Al Hrabosky | .05 | .02 | .00 |
| ☐ 476 | Ron Hodges | .03 | .01 | .00 |
| ☐ 477 | Leon Durham | .09 | .04 | .01 |
| ☐ 478 | Jim Essian | .03 | .01 | .00 |
| ☐ 479 | Roy Lee Jackson | .03 | .01 | .00 |
| ☐ 480 | Brad Havens | .03 | .01 | .00 |
| ☐ 481 | Joe Price | .03 | .01 | .00 |
| ☐ 482 | Tony Bernazard | .05 | .02 | .00 |
| ☐ 483 | Scott McGregor | .08 | .03 | .01 |
| ☐ 484 | Paul Molitor | .12 | .05 | .01 |
| ☐ 485 | Mike Ivie | .03 | .01 | .00 |
| ☐ 486 | Ken Griffey | .09 | .04 | .01 |
| ☐ 487 | Dennis Eckersley | .06 | .02 | .00 |
| ☐ 488 | Steve Garvey | .40 | .16 | .04 |
| ☐ 489 | Mike Fischlin | .03 | .01 | .00 |
| ☐ 490 | U.L. Washington | .03 | .01 | .00 |
| ☐ 491 | Steve McCatty | .03 | .01 | .00 |
| ☐ 492 | Roy Johnson | .03 | .01 | .00 |
| ☐ 493 | Don Baylor | .12 | .05 | .01 |
| ☐ 494 | Bobby Johnson | .03 | .01 | .00 |
| ☐ 495 | Mike Squires | .03 | .01 | .00 |
| ☐ 496 | Bert Roberge | .03 | .01 | .00 |
| ☐ 497 | Dick Ruthven | .03 | .01 | .00 |
| ☐ 498 | Tito Landrum | .03 | .01 | .00 |
| ☐ 499 | Sixto Lezcano | .03 | .01 | .00 |
| ☐ 500 | Johnny Bench | .35 | .14 | .03 |
| ☐ 501 | Larry Whisenton | .03 | .01 | .00 |
| ☐ 502 | Manny Sarmiento | .03 | .01 | .00 |
| ☐ 503 | Fred Breining | .03 | .01 | .00 |
| ☐ 504 | Bill Campbell | .03 | .01 | .00 |
| ☐ 505 | Todd Cruz | .03 | .01 | .00 |
| ☐ 506 | Bob Bailor | .03 | .01 | .00 |
| ☐ 507 | Dave Stieb | .18 | .08 | .01 |
| ☐ 508 | Al Williams | .03 | .01 | .00 |
| ☐ 509 | Dan Ford | .03 | .01 | .00 |
| ☐ 510 | Gorman Thomas | .10 | .04 | .01 |
| ☐ 511 | Chet Lemon | .06 | .02 | .00 |
| ☐ 512 | Mike Torrez | .05 | .02 | .00 |
| ☐ 513 | Shane Rawley | .06 | .02 | .00 |
| ☐ 514 | Mark Belanger | .05 | .02 | .00 |
| ☐ 515 | Rodney Craig | .03 | .01 | .00 |
| ☐ 516 | Onix Concepcion | .05 | .02 | .00 |
| ☐ 517 | Mike Heath | .03 | .01 | .00 |
| ☐ 518 | Andre Dawson | .20 | .08 | .02 |
| ☐ 519 | Luis Sanchez | .03 | .01 | .00 |
| ☐ 520 | Terry Bogener | .03 | .01 | .00 |
| ☐ 521 | Rudy Law | .03 | .01 | .00 |
| ☐ 522 | Ray Knight | .08 | .03 | .01 |
| ☐ 523 | Joe Lefebvre | .03 | .01 | .00 |
| ☐ 524 | Jim Wohlford | .03 | .01 | .00 |
| ☐ 525 | Julio Franco | 1.25 | .50 | .12 |
| ☐ 526 | Ron Oester | .05 | .02 | .00 |
| ☐ 527 | Rick Mahler | .05 | .02 | .00 |
| ☐ 528 | Steve Nicosia | .03 | .01 | .00 |
| ☐ 529 | Junior Kennedy | .03 | .01 | .00 |
| ☐ 530A | Whitey Herzog MGR (bio printed black on white) | .10 | .04 | .01 |
| ☐ 530B | Whitey Herzog MGR (bio printed black on yellow) | .10 | .04 | .01 |
| ☐ 531A | Don Sutton (blue border on photo) | .35 | .14 | .03 |
| ☐ 531B | Don Sutton (green border on photo) | .35 | .14 | .03 |
| ☐ 532 | Mark Brouhard | .03 | .01 | .00 |
| ☐ 533A | Sparky Anderson MGR (bio printed black on white) | .10 | .04 | .01 |
| ☐ 533B | Sparky Anderson MGR (bio printed black on yellow) | .10 | .04 | .01 |
| ☐ 534 | Roger LaFrancois | .03 | .01 | .00 |
| ☐ 535 | George Frazier | .03 | .01 | .00 |
| ☐ 536 | Tom Niedenfuer | .08 | .03 | .01 |
| ☐ 537 | Ed Glynn | .03 | .01 | .00 |
| ☐ 538 | Lee May | .06 | .02 | .00 |
| ☐ 539 | Bob Kearney | .08 | .03 | .01 |
| ☐ 540 | Tim Raines | .30 | .12 | .03 |
| ☐ 541 | Paul Mirabella | .03 | .01 | .00 |
| ☐ 542 | Luis Tiant | .08 | .03 | .01 |
| ☐ 543 | Ron LeFlore | .05 | .02 | .00 |
| ☐ 544 | Dave LaPoint | .12 | .05 | .01 |
| ☐ 545 | Randy Moffitt | .03 | .01 | .00 |
| ☐ 546 | Luis Aguayo | .03 | .01 | .00 |
| ☐ 547 | Brad Lesley | .06 | .02 | .00 |
| ☐ 548 | Luis Salazar | .03 | .01 | .00 |
| ☐ 549 | John Candelaria | .08 | .03 | .01 |
| ☐ 550 | Dave Bergman | .03 | .01 | .00 |
| ☐ 551 | Bob Watson | .06 | .02 | .00 |
| ☐ 552 | Pat Tabler | .12 | .05 | .01 |
| ☐ 553 | Brent Gaff | .03 | .01 | .00 |
| ☐ 554 | Al Cowens | .03 | .01 | .00 |
| ☐ 555 | Tom Brunansky | .20 | .08 | .02 |
| ☐ 556 | Lloyd Moseby | .14 | .06 | .01 |
| ☐ 557A | Pascual Perez ERR (Twins in glove) | 2.00 | .80 | .20 |
| ☐ 557B | Pascual Perez COR (Braves in glove) | .10 | .04 | .01 |
| ☐ 558 | Willie Upshaw | .08 | .03 | .01 |
| ☐ 559 | Richie Zisk | .05 | .02 | .00 |
| ☐ 560 | Pat Zachry | .03 | .01 | .00 |
| ☐ 561 | Jay Johnstone | .05 | .02 | .00 |
| ☐ 562 | Carlos Diaz | .10 | .04 | .01 |
| ☐ 563 | John Tudor | .12 | .05 | .01 |
| ☐ 564 | Frank Robinson MGR | .14 | .06 | .01 |
| ☐ 565 | Dave Edwards | .03 | .01 | .00 |
| ☐ 566 | Paul Householder | .03 | .01 | .00 |
| ☐ 567 | Ron Reed | .03 | .01 | .00 |

| | | | | |
|---|---|---|---|---|
| ☐ 568 | Mike Ramsey | .03 | .01 | .00 |
| ☐ 569 | Kiko Garcia | .03 | .01 | .00 |
| ☐ 570 | Tommy John | .12 | .05 | .01 |
| ☐ 571 | Tony LaRussa MGR | .05 | .02 | .00 |
| ☐ 572 | Joel Youngblood | .03 | .01 | .00 |
| ☐ 573 | Wayne Tolleson | .06 | .02 | .00 |
| ☐ 574 | Keith Creel | .03 | .01 | .00 |
| ☐ 575 | Billy Martin MGR | .12 | .05 | .01 |
| ☐ 576 | Jerry Dybzinski | .03 | .01 | .00 |
| ☐ 577 | Rick Cerone | .03 | .01 | .00 |
| ☐ 578 | Tony Perez | .12 | .05 | .01 |
| ☐ 579 | Greg Brock | .35 | .14 | .03 |
| ☐ 580 | Glen Wilson | .60 | .24 | .06 |
| ☐ 581 | Tim Stoddard | .03 | .01 | .00 |
| ☐ 582 | Bob McClure | .03 | .01 | .00 |
| ☐ 583 | Jim Dwyer | .03 | .01 | .00 |
| ☐ 584 | Ed Romero | .03 | .01 | .00 |
| ☐ 585 | Larry Herndon | .03 | .01 | .00 |
| ☐ 586 | Wade Boggs | 12.00 | 5.00 | 1.20 |
| ☐ 587 | Jay Howell | .06 | .02 | .00 |
| ☐ 588 | Dave Stewart | .03 | .01 | .00 |
| ☐ 589 | Bert Blyleven | .12 | .05 | .01 |
| ☐ 590 | Dick Howser MGR | .05 | .02 | .00 |
| ☐ 591 | Wayne Gross | .03 | .01 | .00 |
| ☐ 592 | Terry Francona | .05 | .02 | .00 |
| ☐ 593 | Don Werner | .03 | .01 | .00 |
| ☐ 594 | Bill Stein | .03 | .01 | .00 |
| ☐ 595 | Jesse Barfield | .25 | .10 | .02 |
| ☐ 596 | Bobby Molinaro | .03 | .01 | .00 |
| ☐ 597 | Mike Vail | .03 | .01 | .00 |
| ☐ 598 | Tony Gwynn | 4.50 | 1.80 | .45 |
| ☐ 599 | Gary Rajsich | .05 | .02 | .00 |
| ☐ 600 | Jerry Ujdur | .03 | .01 | .00 |
| ☐ 601 | Cliff Johnson | .03 | .01 | .00 |
| ☐ 602 | Jerry White | .03 | .01 | .00 |
| ☐ 603 | Bryan Clark | .03 | .01 | .00 |
| ☐ 604 | Joe Ferguson | .03 | .01 | .00 |
| ☐ 605 | Guy Sularz | .03 | .01 | .00 |
| ☐ 606A | Ozzie Virgil (green border on photo) | .10 | .04 | .01 |
| ☐ 606B | Ozzie Virgil (orange border on photo) | .10 | .04 | .01 |
| ☐ 607 | Terry Harper | .03 | .01 | .00 |
| ☐ 608 | Harvey Kuenn MGR | .05 | .02 | .00 |
| ☐ 609 | Jim Sundberg | .05 | .02 | .00 |
| ☐ 610 | Willie Stargell | .20 | .08 | .02 |
| ☐ 611 | Reggie Smith | .08 | .03 | .01 |
| ☐ 612 | Rob Wilfong | .03 | .01 | .00 |
| ☐ 613 | The Niekro Brothers: Joe Niekro Phil Niekro | .12 | .05 | .01 |
| ☐ 614 | Lee Elia MGR | .03 | .01 | .00 |
| ☐ 615 | Mickey Hatcher | .03 | .01 | .00 |
| ☐ 616 | Jerry Hairston | .03 | .01 | .00 |
| ☐ 617 | John Martin | .03 | .01 | .00 |
| ☐ 618 | Wally Backman | .08 | .03 | .01 |
| ☐ 619 | Storm Davis | .45 | .18 | .04 |
| ☐ 620 | Alan Knicely | .03 | .01 | .00 |
| ☐ 621 | John Stuper | .08 | .03 | .01 |
| ☐ 622 | Matt Sinatro | .03 | .01 | .00 |
| ☐ 623 | Gene Petralli | .03 | .01 | .00 |
| ☐ 624 | Duane Walker | .06 | .02 | .00 |
| ☐ 625 | Dick Williams MGR | .03 | .01 | .00 |
| ☐ 626 | Pat Corrales MGR | .03 | .01 | .00 |
| ☐ 627 | Vern Ruhle | .03 | .01 | .00 |
| ☐ 628 | Joe Torre MGR | .07 | .03 | .01 |
| ☐ 629 | Anthony Johnson | .05 | .02 | .00 |
| ☐ 630 | Steve Howe | .05 | .02 | .00 |
| ☐ 631 | Gary Woods | .03 | .01 | .00 |
| ☐ 632 | LaMarr Hoyt | .07 | .03 | .01 |
| ☐ 633 | Steve Swisher | .03 | .01 | .00 |
| ☐ 634 | Terry Leach | .03 | .01 | .00 |
| ☐ 635 | Jeff Newman | .03 | .01 | .00 |
| ☐ 636 | Brett Butler | .10 | .04 | .01 |
| ☐ 637 | Gary Gray | .03 | .01 | .00 |
| ☐ 638 | Lee Mazzilli | .05 | .02 | .00 |
| ☐ 639A | Ron Jackson ERR (A's in glove) | 10.00 | 4.00 | 1.00 |
| ☐ 639B | Ron Jackson COR (Angels in glove, red border on photo) | .15 | .06 | .01 |
| ☐ 639C | Ron Jackson COR (Angels in glove, green border on photo) | .50 | .20 | .05 |
| ☐ 640 | Juan Beniquez | .05 | .02 | .00 |
| ☐ 641 | Dave Rucker | .03 | .01 | .00 |
| ☐ 642 | Luis Pujols | .03 | .01 | .00 |
| ☐ 643 | Rick Monday | .05 | .02 | .00 |
| ☐ 644 | Hosken Powell | .03 | .01 | .00 |

| | | | | |
|---|---|---|---|---|
| ☐ 645 | The Chicken | .25 | .10 | .02 |
| ☐ 646 | Dave Engle | .03 | .01 | .00 |
| ☐ 647 | Dick Davis | .03 | .01 | .00 |
| ☐ 648 | Frank Robinson Vida Blue Joe Morgan | .12 | .05 | .01 |
| ☐ 649 | Al Chambers | .08 | .03 | .01 |
| ☐ 650 | Jesus Vega | .05 | .02 | .00 |
| ☐ 651 | Jeff Jones | .03 | .01 | .00 |
| ☐ 652 | Marvis Foley | .03 | .01 | .00 |
| ☐ 653 | Ty Cobb Puzzle Card | .05 | .02 | .00 |
| ☐ 654A | Dick Perez/Diamond King Checklist (unnumbered) (word "checklist" omitted from back) | .15 | .02 | .00 |
| ☐ 654B | Dick Perez/Diamond King Checklist (unnumbered) (word "checklist" is on back) | .15 | .02 | .00 |
| ☐ 655 | Checklist 1 (unnumbered) | .07 | .01 | .00 |
| ☐ 656 | Checklist 2 (unnumbered) | .07 | .01 | .00 |
| ☐ 657 | Checklist 3 (unnumbered) | .07 | .01 | .00 |
| ☐ 658 | Checklist 4 (unnumbered) | .07 | .01 | .00 |
| ☐ 659 | Checklist 5 (unnumbered) | .07 | .01 | .00 |
| ☐ 660 | Checklist 6 (unnumbered) | .07 | .01 | .00 |

## 1983 Donruss Action All-Stars

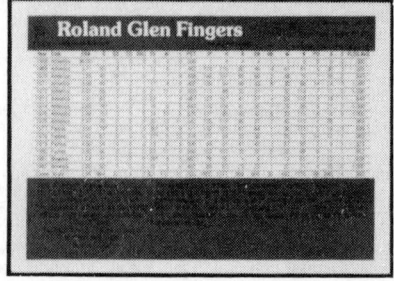

The cards in this 60 card set measure 3 1/2" by 5". The 1983 Action All Stars series depicts 60 major leaguers in a distinctive new style. Each card contains a large close-up on the left and an action photo on the right. Team affiliations appear as part of the background design, and the cards have cranberry color borders. The backs contain the card number, the player's major league line record, and biographical material. A 63 piece Mickey Mantle puzzle (three pieces on one card per pack) was marketed as an insert premium.

|  | | MINT | VG-E | F-G |
|---|---|---|---|---|
| COMPLETE SET | | 5.50 | 2.00 | .50 |
| COMMON PLAYER | | .05 | .02 | .00 |
| ☐ | 1 Eddie Murray | .40 | .16 | .04 |
| ☐ | 2 Dwight Evans | .10 | .04 | .01 |
| ☐ | 3 Reggie Jackson | .40 | .16 | .04 |
| ☐ | 4 Greg Luzinski | .10 | .04 | .01 |
| ☐ | 5 Larry Herndon | .05 | .02 | .00 |
| ☐ | 6 Al Oliver | .10 | .04 | .01 |
| ☐ | 7 Bill Buckner | .10 | .04 | .01 |
| ☐ | 8 Jason Thompson | .05 | .02 | .00 |
| ☐ | 9 Andre Dawson | .20 | .08 | .02 |
| ☐ | 10 Greg Minton | .05 | .02 | .00 |
| ☐ | 11 Terry Kennedy | .05 | .02 | .00 |
| ☐ | 12 Phil Niekro | .15 | .06 | .01 |
| ☐ | 13 Willie Wilson | .15 | .06 | .01 |
| ☐ | 14 Johnny Bench | .25 | .10 | .02 |
| ☐ | 15 Ron Guidry | .15 | .06 | .01 |
| ☐ | 16 Hal McRae | .05 | .02 | .00 |
| ☐ | 17 Damaso Garcia | .05 | .02 | .00 |
| ☐ | 18 Gary Ward | .05 | .02 | .00 |
| ☐ | 19 Cecil Cooper | .15 | .06 | .01 |
| ☐ | 20 Keith Hernandez | .20 | .08 | .02 |
| ☐ | 21 Ron Cey | .05 | .02 | .00 |
| ☐ | 22 Rickey Henderson | .40 | .16 | .04 |
| ☐ | 23 Nolan Ryan | .30 | .12 | .03 |
| ☐ | 24 Steve Carlton | .30 | .12 | .03 |
| ☐ | 25 John Stearns | .05 | .02 | .00 |
| ☐ | 26 Jim Sundberg | .05 | .02 | .00 |
| ☐ | 27 Joaquin Andujar | .10 | .04 | .01 |
| ☐ | 28 Gaylord Perry | .20 | .08 | .02 |
| ☐ | 29 Jack Clark | .10 | .04 | .01 |
| ☐ | 30 Bill Madlock | .10 | .04 | .01 |
| ☐ | 31 Pete Rose | .60 | .24 | .06 |
| ☐ | 32 Mookie Wilson | .05 | .02 | .00 |
| ☐ | 33 Rollie Fingers | .15 | .06 | .01 |
| ☐ | 34 Lonnie Smith | .05 | .02 | .00 |
| ☐ | 35 Tony Pena | .10 | .04 | .01 |
| ☐ | 36 Dave Winfield | .25 | .10 | .02 |
| ☐ | 37 Tim Lollar | .05 | .02 | .00 |
| ☐ | 38 Rod Carew | .30 | .12 | .03 |
| ☐ | 39 Toby Harrah | .05 | .02 | .00 |
| ☐ | 40 Buddy Bell | .08 | .03 | .01 |
| ☐ | 41 Bruce Sutter | .10 | .04 | .01 |
| ☐ | 42 George Brett | .50 | .20 | .05 |
| ☐ | 43 Carlton Fisk | .10 | .04 | .01 |
| ☐ | 44 Carl Yastrzemski | .50 | .20 | .05 |
| ☐ | 45 Dale Murphy | .50 | .20 | .05 |
| ☐ | 46 Bob Horner | .15 | .06 | .01 |
| ☐ | 47 Dave Concepcion | .10 | .04 | .01 |
| ☐ | 48 Dave Stieb | .15 | .06 | .01 |
| ☐ | 49 Kent Hrbek | .20 | .08 | .02 |
| ☐ | 50 Lance Parrish | .20 | .08 | .02 |
| ☐ | 51 Joe Niekro | .08 | .03 | .01 |
| ☐ | 52 Cal Ripken | .40 | .16 | .04 |
| ☐ | 53 Fernando Valenzuela | .30 | .12 | .03 |
| ☐ | 54 Richie Zisk | .05 | .02 | .00 |
| ☐ | 55 Leon Durham | .05 | .02 | .00 |
| ☐ | 56 Robin Yount | .30 | .12 | .03 |
| ☐ | 57 Mike Schmidt | .50 | .20 | .05 |
| ☐ | 58 Gary Carter | .50 | .20 | .05 |
| ☐ | 59 Fred Lynn | .15 | .06 | .01 |
| ☐ | 60 Checklist card | .10 | .01 | .00 |

## 1983 Donruss HOF Heroes

The cards in this 44 card set measure 2 1/2" by 3 1/2". Although it was issued with the same Mantle puzzle as the Action All Stars set, the Donruss Hall of Fame Heroes set is completely different in content and design. Of the 44 cards in the set, 42 are Dick Perez artwork portraying Hall of Fame members, while one card depicts the completed Mantle puzzle and the last card is a checklist. The red, white, and blue backs contain the card number and a short player biography. The cards were packaged 8 cards plus one puzzle card (3 pieces) for 30 cents in the summer of 1983.

|  | MINT | VG-E | F-G |
|---|---|---|---|
| COMPLETE SET | 3.50 | 1.40 | .35 |
| COMMON PLAYER | .03 | .01 | .00 |

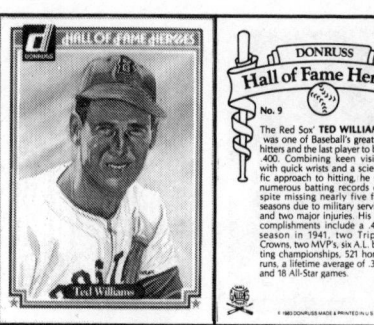

| ☐ | 1 Ty Cobb | .35 | .14 | .03 |
|---|---|---|---|---|
| ☐ | 2 Walter Johnson | .15 | .06 | .01 |
| ☐ | 3 Christy Mathewson | .15 | .06 | .01 |
| ☐ | 4 Josh Gibson | .15 | .06 | .01 |
| ☐ | 5 Honus Wagner | .15 | .06 | .01 |
| ☐ | 6 Jackie Robinson | .15 | .06 | .01 |
| ☐ | 7 Mickey Mantle | .50 | .20 | .05 |
| ☐ | 8 Luke Appling | .05 | .02 | .00 |
| ☐ | 9 Ted Williams | .15 | .06 | .01 |
| ☐ | 10 Johnny Mize | .05 | .02 | .00 |
| ☐ | 11 Satchel Paige | .05 | .02 | .00 |
| ☐ | 12 Lou Boudreau | .03 | .01 | .00 |
| ☐ | 13 Jimmie Foxx | .07 | .03 | .01 |
| ☐ | 14 Duke Snider | .12 | .05 | .01 |
| ☐ | 15 Monte Irvin | .03 | .01 | .00 |
| ☐ | 16 Hank Greenberg | .05 | .02 | .00 |
| ☐ | 17 Roberto Clemente | .12 | .05 | .01 |
| ☐ | 18 Al Kaline | .12 | .05 | .01 |
| ☐ | 19 Frank Robinson | .12 | .05 | .01 |
| ☐ | 20 Joe Cronin | .05 | .02 | .00 |
| ☐ | 21 Burleigh Grimes | .03 | .01 | .00 |
| ☐ | 22 The Waner Brothers: Paul Waner Lloyd Waner | .03 | .01 | .00 |
| ☐ | 23 Grover Alexander | .07 | .03 | .01 |
| ☐ | 24 Yogi Berra | .12 | .05 | .01 |
| ☐ | 25 Cool Papa Bell | .05 | .02 | .00 |
| ☐ | 26 Bill Dickey | .05 | .02 | .00 |
| ☐ | 27 Cy Young | .10 | .04 | .01 |
| ☐ | 28 Charlie Gehringer | .05 | .02 | .00 |
| ☐ | 29 Dizzy Dean | .15 | .06 | .01 |
| ☐ | 30 Bob Lemon | .08 | .03 | .01 |
| ☐ | 31 Red Ruffing | .03 | .01 | .00 |
| ☐ | 32 Stan Musial | .15 | .06 | .01 |
| ☐ | 33 Hank Hubbell | .07 | .03 | .01 |
| ☐ | 34 Hank Aaron | .15 | .06 | .01 |
| ☐ | 35 John McGraw | .05 | .02 | .00 |
| ☐ | 36 Bob Feller | .12 | .05 | .01 |
| ☐ | 37 Casey Stengel | .07 | .03 | .01 |
| ☐ | 38 Ralph Kiner | .08 | .03 | .01 |
| ☐ | 39 Roy Campanella | .15 | .06 | .01 |
| ☐ | 40 Mel Ott | .07 | .03 | .01 |
| ☐ | 41 Robin Roberts | .08 | .03 | .01 |
| ☐ | 42 Early Wynn | .08 | .03 | .01 |
| ☐ | 43 Mantle Puzzle card | .05 | .02 | .00 |
| ☐ | 44 Checklist card | .05 | .01 | .00 |

## 1984 Donruss

The 1984 Donruss set contains a total of 660 cards, each measuring 2 1/2" by 3 1/2"; however, only 658 are numbered. The first 26 cards in the set are again Diamond Kings (DK) although the drawings this year were styled differently and are easily differentiated from other DK issues. A new feature, Rated Rookies (RR), was introduced with this set with Bill Madden's 20 selections comprising numbers 27 through 46. Two "Living Legend" cards designated A (featuring Gaylord Perry and Rollie Fingers) and B (featuring Johnny Bench and Carl Yastrzemski) were issued as bonus cards in wax packs, but were not issued in the vending sets sold

to hobby dealers. The seven unnumbered checklist cards are arbitrarily assigned numbers 652 through 658 and are listed at the end of the list below. The designs on the fronts of the Donruss cards changed considerably from the past two years. The backs contain statistics and are printed in green and black ink. The cards were distributed with a 63 piece puzzle of Duke Snider.

|  | MINT | VG-E | F-G |
|---|---|---|---|
| COMPLETE SET (658) | 225.00 | 90.00 | 22.00 |
| COMMON PLAYER (1-660) | .07 | .03 | .01 |

| | | | MINT | VG-E | F-G |
|---|---|---|---|---|---|
| ☐ | 1 | Robin Yount DK | .75 | .30 | .07 |
| ☐ | 2 | Dave Concepcion DK | .12 | .05 | .01 |
| ☐ | 3 | Dwayne Murphy DK | .09 | .04 | .01 |
| ☐ | 4 | John Castino DK | .09 | .04 | .01 |
| ☐ | 5 | Leon Durham DK | .12 | .05 | .01 |
| ☐ | 6 | Rusty Staub DK | .12 | .05 | .01 |
| ☐ | 7 | Jack Clark DK | .15 | .06 | .01 |
| ☐ | 8 | Dave Dravecky DK | .09 | .04 | .01 |
| ☐ | 9 | Al Oliver DK | .15 | .06 | .01 |
| ☐ | 10 | Dave Righetti DK | .20 | .08 | .02 |
| ☐ | 11 | Hal McRae DK | .09 | .04 | .01 |
| ☐ | 12 | Ray Knight DK | .12 | .05 | .01 |
| ☐ | 13 | Bruce Sutter DK | .15 | .06 | .01 |
| ☐ | 14 | Bob Horner DK | .25 | .10 | .02 |
| ☐ | 15 | Lance Parrish DK | .30 | .12 | .03 |
| ☐ | 16 | Matt Young DK | .09 | .04 | .01 |
| ☐ | 17 | Fred Lynn DK | .20 | .08 | .02 |
| ☐ | 18 | Ron Kittle DK | .20 | .08 | .02 |
| ☐ | 19 | Jim Clancy DK | .09 | .04 | .01 |
| ☐ | 20 | Bill Madlock DK | .15 | .06 | .01 |
| ☐ | 21 | Larry Parrish DK | .12 | .05 | .01 |
| ☐ | 22 | Eddie Murray DK | .75 | .30 | .07 |
| ☐ | 23 | Mike Schmidt DK | .90 | .36 | .09 |
| ☐ | 24 | Pedro Guerrero DK | .35 | .14 | .03 |
| ☐ | 25 | Andre Thornton DK | .12 | .05 | .01 |
| ☐ | 26 | Wade Boggs DK | 2.50 | 1.00 | .25 |
| ☐ | 27 | Joel Skinner DK | .20 | .08 | .02 |
| ☐ | 28 | Tommy Dunbar RR | .10 | .04 | .01 |
| ☐ | 29A | Mike Stenhouse RR ERR (no back number) | .20 | .08 | .02 |
| ☐ | 29B | Mike Stenhouse RR COR | 1.50 | .60 | .15 |
| ☐ | 30A | Ron Darling RR ERR (no number on back) | 6.00 | 2.40 | .60 |
| ☐ | 30B | Ron Darling RR COR | 9.00 | 3.75 | .90 |
| ☐ | 31 | Dion James RR | .25 | .10 | .02 |
| ☐ | 32 | Tony Fernandez RR | 3.00 | 1.20 | .30 |
| ☐ | 33 | Angel Salazar RR | .10 | .04 | .01 |
| ☐ | 34 | Kevin McReynolds RR | 4.00 | 1.60 | .40 |
| ☐ | 35 | Dick Schofield RR | 1.25 | .50 | .12 |
| ☐ | 36 | Brad Komminsk RR | .25 | .10 | .02 |
| ☐ | 37 | Tim Teufel RR | .50 | .20 | .05 |
| ☐ | 38 | Doug Frobel RR | .15 | .06 | .01 |
| ☐ | 39 | Greg Gagne RR | .35 | .14 | .03 |
| ☐ | 40 | Mike Fuentes RR | .10 | .04 | .01 |
| ☐ | 41 | Joe Carter RR | 6.00 | 2.40 | .60 |
| ☐ | 42 | Mike Brown RR OF | .35 | .14 | .03 |
| ☐ | 43 | Mike Jeffcoat RR | .15 | .06 | .01 |
| ☐ | 44 | Sid Fernandez RR | 6.00 | 2.40 | .60 |
| ☐ | 45 | Brian Dayett RR | .15 | .06 | .01 |
| ☐ | 46 | Chris Smith RR | .10 | .04 | .01 |
| ☐ | 47 | Eddie Murray | .75 | .30 | .07 |
| ☐ | 48 | Robin Yount | .50 | .20 | .05 |
| ☐ | 49 | Lance Parrish | .35 | .14 | .03 |
| ☐ | 50 | Jim Rice | .60 | .24 | .06 |
| ☐ | 51 | Dave Winfield | .45 | .18 | .04 |

| | | | MINT | VG-E | F-G |
|---|---|---|---|---|---|
| ☐ | 52 | Fernando Valenzuela | .45 | .18 | .04 |
| ☐ | 53 | George Brett | .75 | .30 | .07 |
| ☐ | 54 | Rickey Henderson | .70 | .28 | .07 |
| ☐ | 55 | Gary Carter | .60 | .24 | .06 |
| ☐ | 56 | Buddy Bell | .12 | .05 | .01 |
| ☐ | 57 | Reggie Jackson | .75 | .30 | .07 |
| ☐ | 58 | Harold Baines | .25 | .10 | .02 |
| ☐ | 59 | Ozzie Smith | .20 | .08 | .02 |
| ☐ | 60 | Nolan Ryan | .60 | .24 | .06 |
| ☐ | 61 | Pete Rose | 2.00 | .80 | .20 |
| ☐ | 62 | Ron Oester | .07 | .03 | .01 |
| ☐ | 63 | Steve Garvey | .55 | .22 | .05 |
| ☐ | 64 | Jason Thompson | .09 | .04 | .01 |
| ☐ | 65 | Jack Clark | .15 | .06 | .01 |
| ☐ | 66 | Dale Murphy | 1.25 | .50 | .12 |
| ☐ | 67 | Leon Durham | .20 | .08 | .02 |
| ☐ | 68 | Darryl Strawberry | 10.00 | 4.00 | 1.00 |
| ☐ | 69 | Richie Zisk | .07 | .03 | .01 |
| ☐ | 70 | Kent Hrbek | .40 | .16 | .04 |
| ☐ | 71 | Dave Stieb | .25 | .10 | .02 |
| ☐ | 72 | Ken Schrom | .10 | .04 | .01 |
| ☐ | 73 | George Bell | .25 | .10 | .02 |
| ☐ | 74 | John Moses | .10 | .04 | .01 |
| ☐ | 75 | Ed Lynch | .07 | .03 | .01 |
| ☐ | 76 | Chuck Rainey | .07 | .03 | .01 |
| ☐ | 77 | Biff Pocoroba | .07 | .03 | .01 |
| ☐ | 78 | Cecilio Guante | .07 | .03 | .01 |
| ☐ | 79 | Jim Barr | .07 | .03 | .01 |
| ☐ | 80 | Kurt Bevacqua | .07 | .03 | .01 |
| ☐ | 81 | Tom Foley | .08 | .03 | .01 |
| ☐ | 82 | Joe Lefebvre | .07 | .03 | .01 |
| ☐ | 83 | Andy Van Slyke | .50 | .20 | .05 |
| ☐ | 84 | Bob Lillis MGR | .07 | .03 | .01 |
| ☐ | 85 | Rick Adams | .09 | .04 | .01 |
| ☐ | 86 | Jerry Hairston | .07 | .03 | .01 |
| ☐ | 87 | Bob James | .20 | .08 | .02 |
| ☐ | 88 | Joe Altobelli MGR | .07 | .03 | .01 |
| ☐ | 89 | Ed Romero | .07 | .03 | .01 |
| ☐ | 90 | John Grubb | .07 | .03 | .01 |
| ☐ | 91 | John Henry Johnson | .07 | .03 | .01 |
| ☐ | 92 | Juan Espino | .08 | .03 | .01 |
| ☐ | 93 | Candy Maldonado | .10 | .04 | .01 |
| ☐ | 94 | Andre Thornton | .10 | .04 | .01 |
| ☐ | 95 | Onix Concepcion | .07 | .03 | .01 |
| ☐ | 96 | Don Hill | .10 | .04 | .01 |
| ☐ | 97 | Andre Dawson | .25 | .10 | .02 |
| ☐ | 98 | Frank Tanana | .10 | .04 | .01 |
| ☐ | 99 | Curt Wilkerson | .10 | .04 | .01 |
| ☐ | 100 | Larry Gura | .10 | .04 | .01 |
| ☐ | 101 | Dwayne Murphy | .10 | .04 | .01 |
| ☐ | 102 | Tom Brennan | .07 | .03 | .01 |
| ☐ | 103 | Dave Righetti | .25 | .10 | .02 |
| ☐ | 104 | Steve Sax | .25 | .10 | .02 |
| ☐ | 105 | Dan Petry | .20 | .08 | .02 |
| ☐ | 106 | Cal Ripken | .75 | .30 | .07 |
| ☐ | 107 | Paul Molitor | .15 | .06 | .01 |
| ☐ | 108 | Fred Lynn | .25 | .10 | .02 |
| ☐ | 109 | Neil Allen | .10 | .04 | .01 |
| ☐ | 110 | Joe Niekro | .10 | .04 | .01 |
| ☐ | 111 | Steve Carlton | .50 | .20 | .05 |
| ☐ | 112 | Terry Kennedy | .10 | .04 | .01 |
| ☐ | 113 | Bill Madlock | .15 | .06 | .01 |
| ☐ | 114 | Chili Davis | .10 | .04 | .01 |
| ☐ | 115 | Jim Gantner | .10 | .04 | .01 |
| ☐ | 116 | Tom Seaver | .50 | .20 | .05 |
| ☐ | 117 | Bill Buckner | .15 | .06 | .01 |
| ☐ | 118 | Bill Caudill | .10 | .04 | .01 |
| ☐ | 119 | Jim Clancy | .07 | .03 | .01 |
| ☐ | 120 | John Castino | .07 | .03 | .01 |
| ☐ | 121 | Dave Concepcion | .10 | .04 | .01 |
| ☐ | 122 | Greg Luzinski | .15 | .06 | .01 |
| ☐ | 123 | Mike Boddicker | .15 | .06 | .01 |
| ☐ | 124 | Pete Ladd | .07 | .03 | .01 |
| ☐ | 125 | Juan Berenguer | .07 | .03 | .01 |
| ☐ | 126 | John Montefusco | .07 | .03 | .01 |
| ☐ | 127 | Ed Jurak | .07 | .03 | .01 |
| ☐ | 128 | Tom Niedenfuer | .10 | .04 | .01 |
| ☐ | 129 | Bert Blyleven | .15 | .06 | .01 |
| ☐ | 130 | Bud Black | .07 | .03 | .01 |
| ☐ | 131 | Gorman Heimueller | .07 | .03 | .01 |
| ☐ | 132 | Dan Schatzeder | .07 | .03 | .01 |
| ☐ | 133 | Ron Jackson | .07 | .03 | .01 |
| ☐ | 134 | Tom Henke | .50 | .20 | .05 |
| ☐ | 135 | Kevin Hickey | .07 | .03 | .01 |
| ☐ | 136 | Mike Scott | .30 | .12 | .03 |
| ☐ | 137 | Bo Diaz | .10 | .04 | .01 |
| ☐ | 138 | Glenn Brummer | .07 | .03 | .01 |
| ☐ | 139 | Sid Monge | .07 | .03 | .01 |
| ☐ | 140 | Rich Gale | .07 | .03 | .01 |
| ☐ | 141 | Brett Butler | .15 | .06 | .01 |
| ☐ | 142 | Brian Harper | .10 | .04 | .01 |
| ☐ | 143 | John Rabb | .10 | .04 | .01 |
| ☐ | 144 | Gary Woods | .07 | .03 | .01 |

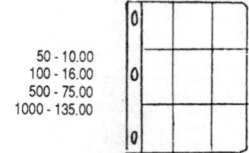

| □ | | | | |
|---|---|---|---|---|
| □ 145 | Pat Putnam | .07 | .03 | .01 |
| □ 146 | Jim Acker | .20 | .08 | .02 |
| □ 147 | Mickey Hatcher | .07 | .03 | .01 |
| □ 148 | Todd Cruz | .07 | .03 | .01 |
| □ 149 | Tom Tellmann | .07 | .03 | .01 |
| □ 150 | John Wockenfuss | .07 | .03 | .01 |
| □ 151 | Wade Boggs | 8.00 | 3.25 | .80 |
| □ 152 | Don Baylor | .15 | .06 | .01 |
| □ 153 | Bob Welch | .10 | .04 | .01 |
| □ 154 | Alan Bannister | .07 | .03 | .01 |
| □ 155 | Willie Aikens | .10 | .04 | .01 |
| □ 156 | Jeff Burroughs | .07 | .03 | .01 |
| □ 157 | Bryan Little | .07 | .03 | .01 |
| □ 158 | Bob Boone | .10 | .04 | .01 |
| □ 159 | Dave Hostetler | .07 | .03 | .01 |
| □ 160 | Jerry Dybzinski | .07 | .03 | .01 |
| □ 161 | Mike Madden | .15 | .06 | .01 |
| □ 162 | Luis DeLeon | .07 | .03 | .01 |
| □ 163 | Willie Hernandez | .30 | .12 | .03 |
| □ 164 | Frank Pastore | .07 | .03 | .01 |
| □ 165 | Rick Camp | .07 | .03 | .01 |
| □ 166 | Lee Mazzilli | .20 | .08 | .02 |
| □ 167 | Scot Thompson | .07 | .03 | .01 |
| □ 168 | Bob Forsch | .10 | .04 | .01 |
| □ 169 | Mike Flanagan | .10 | .04 | .01 |
| □ 170 | Rick Manning | .07 | .03 | .01 |
| □ 171 | Chet Lemon | .10 | .04 | .01 |
| □ 172 | Jerry Remy | .07 | .03 | .01 |
| □ 173 | Ron Guidry | .25 | .10 | .02 |
| □ 174 | Pedro Guerrero | .40 | .16 | .04 |
| □ 175 | Willie Wilson | .25 | .10 | .02 |
| □ 176 | Carney Lansford | .15 | .06 | .01 |
| □ 177 | Al Oliver | .20 | .08 | .02 |
| □ 178 | Jim Sundberg | .10 | .04 | .01 |
| □ 179 | Bobby Grich | .12 | .05 | .01 |
| □ 180 | Rich Dotson | .10 | .04 | .01 |
| □ 181 | Joaquin Andujar | .15 | .06 | .01 |
| □ 182 | Jose Cruz | .15 | .06 | .01 |
| □ 183 | Mike Schmidt | 1.00 | .40 | .10 |
| □ 184 | Gary Redus | .35 | .14 | .03 |
| □ 185 | Garry Templeton | .15 | .06 | .01 |
| □ 186 | Tony Pena | .20 | .08 | .02 |
| □ 187 | Greg Minton | .10 | .04 | .01 |
| □ 188 | Phil Niekro | .30 | .12 | .03 |
| □ 189 | Ferguson Jenkins | .20 | .08 | .02 |
| □ 190 | Mookie Wilson | .10 | .04 | .01 |
| □ 191 | Jim Beattie | .07 | .03 | .01 |
| □ 192 | Gary Ward | .10 | .04 | .01 |
| □ 193 | Jesse Barfield | .30 | .12 | .03 |
| □ 194 | Pete Filson | .07 | .03 | .01 |
| □ 195 | Roy Lee Jackson | .07 | .03 | .01 |
| □ 196 | Rick Sweet | .07 | .03 | .01 |
| □ 197 | Jesse Orosco | .10 | .04 | .01 |
| □ 198 | Steve Lake | .07 | .03 | .01 |
| □ 199 | Ken Dayley | .07 | .03 | .01 |
| □ 200 | Manny Sarmiento | .07 | .03 | .01 |
| □ 201 | Mark Davis | .07 | .03 | .01 |
| □ 202 | Tim Flannery | .07 | .03 | .01 |
| □ 203 | Bill Scherrer | .10 | .04 | .01 |
| □ 204 | Al Holland | .07 | .03 | .01 |
| □ 205 | Dave Von Ohlen | .07 | .03 | .01 |
| □ 206 | Mike LaCoss | .07 | .03 | .01 |
| □ 207 | Juan Beniquez | .07 | .03 | .01 |
| □ 208 | Juan Agosto | .07 | .03 | .01 |
| □ 209 | Bobby Ramos | .07 | .03 | .01 |
| □ 210 | Al Bumbry | .07 | .03 | .01 |
| □ 211 | Mark Brouhard | .07 | .03 | .01 |
| □ 212 | Howard Bailey | .07 | .03 | .01 |
| □ 213 | Bruce Hurst | .15 | .06 | .01 |
| □ 214 | Bob Shirley | .07 | .03 | .01 |
| □ 215 | Pat Zachry | .07 | .03 | .01 |
| □ 216 | Julio Franco | .20 | .08 | .02 |
| □ 217 | Mike Armstrong | .07 | .03 | .01 |
| □ 218 | Dave Beard | .07 | .03 | .01 |
| □ 219 | Steve Rogers | .10 | .04 | .01 |
| □ 220 | John Butcher | .07 | .03 | .01 |
| □ 221 | Mike Smithson | .15 | .06 | .01 |
| □ 222 | Frank White | .15 | .06 | .01 |
| □ 223 | Mike Heath | .07 | .03 | .01 |
| □ 224 | Chris Bando | .07 | .03 | .01 |
| □ 225 | Roy Smalley | .10 | .04 | .01 |
| □ 226 | Dusty Baker | .10 | .04 | .01 |
| □ 227 | Lou Whitaker | .25 | .10 | .02 |
| □ 228 | John Lowenstein | .07 | .03 | .01 |
| □ 229 | Ben Oglivie | .10 | .04 | .01 |
| □ 230 | Doug DeCinces | .15 | .06 | .01 |
| □ 231 | Lonnie Smith | .10 | .04 | .01 |
| □ 232 | Ray Knight | .15 | .06 | .01 |
| □ 233 | Gary Matthews | .10 | .04 | .01 |
| □ 234 | Juan Bonilla | .07 | .03 | .01 |
| □ 235 | Rod Scurry | .07 | .03 | .01 |
| □ 236 | Atlee Hammaker | .07 | .03 | .01 |
| □ 237 | Mike Caldwell | .07 | .03 | .01 |
| □ 238 | Keith Hernandez | .35 | .14 | .03 |
| □ 239 | Larry Bowa | .15 | .06 | .01 |
| □ 240 | Tony Bernazard | .10 | .04 | .01 |
| □ 241 | Damaso Garcia | .15 | .06 | .01 |
| □ 242 | Tom Brunansky | .25 | .10 | .02 |
| □ 243 | Dan Driessen | .07 | .03 | .01 |
| □ 244 | Ron Kittle | .25 | .10 | .02 |
| □ 245 | Tim Stoddard | .07 | .03 | .01 |
| □ 246 | Bob L. Gibson | .10 | .04 | .01 |
| | (Brewers Pitcher) | | | |
| □ 247 | Marty Castillo | .07 | .03 | .01 |
| □ 248 | Don Mattingly | 90.00 | 30.00 | 6.00 |
| □ 249 | Jeff Newman | .07 | .03 | .01 |
| □ 250 | Alejandro Pena | .25 | .10 | .02 |
| □ 251 | Toby Harrah | .07 | .03 | .01 |
| □ 252 | Cesar Geronimo | .07 | .03 | .01 |
| □ 253 | Tom Underwood | .07 | .03 | .01 |
| □ 254 | Doug Flynn | .07 | .03 | .01 |
| □ 255 | Andy Hassler | .07 | .03 | .01 |
| □ 256 | Odell Jones | .07 | .03 | .01 |
| □ 257 | Rudy Law | .07 | .03 | .01 |
| □ 258 | Harry Spilman | .07 | .03 | .01 |
| □ 259 | Marty Bystrom | .07 | .03 | .01 |
| □ 260 | Dave Rucker | .07 | .03 | .01 |
| □ 261 | Ruppert Jones | .07 | .03 | .01 |
| □ 262 | Jeff R. Jones | .10 | .04 | .01 |
| | (Reds OF) | | | |
| □ 263 | Gerald Perry | .25 | .10 | .02 |
| □ 264 | Gene Tenace | .07 | .03 | .01 |
| □ 265 | Brad Wellman | .10 | .04 | .01 |
| □ 266 | Dickie Noles | .07 | .03 | .01 |
| □ 267 | Jamie Allen | .10 | .04 | .01 |
| □ 268 | Jim Gott | .07 | .03 | .01 |
| □ 269 | Ron Davis | .07 | .03 | .01 |
| □ 270 | Benny Ayala | .07 | .03 | .01 |
| □ 271 | Ned Yost | .07 | .03 | .01 |
| □ 272 | Dave Rozema | .07 | .03 | .01 |
| □ 273 | Dave Stapleton | .07 | .03 | .01 |
| □ 274 | Lou Piniella | .10 | .04 | .01 |
| □ 275 | Jose Morales | .07 | .03 | .01 |
| □ 276 | Brod Perkins | .07 | .03 | .01 |
| □ 277 | Butch Davis | .10 | .04 | .01 |
| □ 278 | Tony Phillips | .10 | .04 | .01 |
| □ 279 | Jeff Reardon | .10 | .04 | .01 |
| □ 280 | Ken Forsch | .07 | .03 | .01 |
| □ 281 | Pete O'Brien | 1.50 | .60 | .15 |
| □ 282 | Tom Paciorek | .07 | .03 | .01 |
| □ 283 | Frank LaCorte | .07 | .03 | .01 |
| □ 284 | Tim Lollar | .07 | .03 | .01 |
| □ 285 | Greg Gross | .07 | .03 | .01 |
| □ 286 | Alex Trevino | .07 | .03 | .01 |
| □ 287 | Gene Garber | .07 | .03 | .01 |
| □ 288 | Dave Parker | .30 | .12 | .03 |
| □ 289 | Lee Smith | .15 | .06 | .01 |
| □ 290 | Dave LaPoint | .07 | .03 | .01 |
| □ 291 | John Shelby | .10 | .04 | .01 |
| □ 292 | Charlie Moore | .07 | .03 | .01 |
| □ 293 | Alan Trammell | .25 | .10 | .02 |
| □ 294 | Tony Armas | .15 | .06 | .01 |
| □ 295 | Shane Rawley | .10 | .04 | .01 |
| □ 296 | Greg Brock | .10 | .04 | .01 |
| □ 297 | Hal McRae | .10 | .04 | .01 |
| □ 298 | Mike Davis | .15 | .06 | .01 |
| □ 299 | Tim Raines | .35 | .14 | .03 |
| □ 300 | Bucky Dent | .10 | .04 | .01 |
| □ 301 | Tommy John | .20 | .08 | .02 |
| □ 302 | Carlton Fisk | .20 | .08 | .02 |
| □ 303 | Darrell Porter | .10 | .04 | .01 |
| □ 304 | Dickie Thon | .10 | .04 | .01 |
| □ 305 | Garry Maddox | .10 | .04 | .01 |
| □ 306 | Cesar Cedeno | .10 | .04 | .01 |
| □ 307 | Gary Lucas | .07 | .03 | .01 |
| □ 308 | Johnny Ray | .15 | .06 | .01 |
| □ 309 | Andy McGaffigan | .07 | .03 | .01 |
| □ 310 | Claudell Washington | .10 | .04 | .01 |
| □ 311 | Ryne Sandberg | 1.75 | .70 | .17 |
| □ 312 | George Foster | .25 | .10 | .02 |
| □ 313 | Spike Owen | .35 | .14 | .03 |
| □ 314 | Gary Gaetti | .15 | .06 | .01 |
| □ 315 | Willie Upshaw | .15 | .06 | .01 |
| □ 316 | Al Williams | .07 | .03 | .01 |
| □ 317 | Jorge Orta | .07 | .03 | .01 |
| □ 318 | Orlando Mercado | .07 | .03 | .01 |
| □ 319 | Junior Ortiz | .07 | .03 | .01 |
| □ 320 | Mike Proly | .07 | .03 | .01 |
| □ 321 | Randy Johnson | .07 | .03 | .01 |
| □ 322 | Jim Morrison | .07 | .03 | .01 |
| □ 323 | Max Venable | .07 | .03 | .01 |
| □ 324 | Tony Gwynn | 1.75 | .70 | .17 |
| □ 325 | Duane Walker | .07 | .03 | .01 |
| □ 326 | Ozzie Virgil | .07 | .03 | .01 |
| □ 327 | Jeff Lahti | .07 | .03 | .01 |
| □ 328 | Bill Dawley | .15 | .06 | .01 |

| # | Player | | | |
|---|---|---|---|---|
| ☐ 329 | Rob Wilfong | .07 | .03 | .01 |
| ☐ 330 | Marc Hill | .07 | .03 | .01 |
| ☐ 331 | Ray Burris | .07 | .03 | .01 |
| ☐ 332 | Allan Ramirez | .10 | .04 | .01 |
| ☐ 333 | Chuck Porter | .07 | .03 | .01 |
| ☐ 334 | Wayne Krenchicki | .07 | .03 | .01 |
| ☐ 335 | Gary Allenson | .07 | .03 | .01 |
| ☐ 336 | Bobby Meacham | .25 | .10 | .02 |
| ☐ 337 | Joe Beckwith | .07 | .03 | .01 |
| ☐ 338 | Rick Sutcliffe | .20 | .08 | .02 |
| ☐ 339 | Mark Huismann | .15 | .06 | .01 |
| ☐ 340 | Tim Conroy | .15 | .06 | .01 |
| ☐ 341 | Scott Sanderson | .07 | .03 | .01 |
| ☐ 342 | Larry Biittner | .07 | .03 | .01 |
| ☐ 343 | Dave Stewart | .07 | .03 | .01 |
| ☐ 344 | Darryl Motley | .07 | .03 | .01 |
| ☐ 345 | Chris Codiroli | .10 | .04 | .01 |
| ☐ 346 | Rich Behenna | .10 | .04 | .01 |
| ☐ 347 | Andre Robertson | .07 | .03 | .01 |
| ☐ 348 | Mike Marshall | .20 | .08 | .02 |
| ☐ 349 | Larry Herndon | .07 | .03 | .01 |
| ☐ 350 | Rich Dauer | .07 | .03 | .01 |
| ☐ 351 | Cecil Cooper | .20 | .08 | .02 |
| ☐ 352 | Rod Carew | .50 | .20 | .05 |
| ☐ 353 | Willie McGee | .30 | .12 | .03 |
| ☐ 354 | Phil Garner | .10 | .04 | .01 |
| ☐ 355 | Joe Morgan | .25 | .10 | .02 |
| ☐ 356 | Luis Salazar | .07 | .03 | .01 |
| ☐ 357 | John Candelaria | .10 | .04 | .01 |
| ☐ 358 | Bill Laskey | .07 | .03 | .01 |
| ☐ 359 | Bob McClure | .07 | .03 | .01 |
| ☐ 360 | Dave Kingman | .20 | .08 | .02 |
| ☐ 361 | Ron Cey | .15 | .06 | .01 |
| ☐ 362 | Matt Young | .15 | .06 | .01 |
| ☐ 363 | Lloyd Moseby | .20 | .08 | .02 |
| ☐ 364 | Frank Viola | .15 | .06 | .01 |
| ☐ 365 | Eddie Milner | .10 | .04 | .01 |
| ☐ 366 | Floyd Bannister | .10 | .04 | .01 |
| ☐ 367 | Dan Ford | .07 | .03 | .01 |
| ☐ 368 | Moose Haas | .07 | .03 | .01 |
| ☐ 369 | Doug Bair | .07 | .03 | .01 |
| ☐ 370 | Ray Fontenot | .10 | .04 | .01 |
| ☐ 371 | Luis Aponte | .07 | .03 | .01 |
| ☐ 372 | Jack Fimple | .07 | .03 | .01 |
| ☐ 373 | Neal Heaton | .15 | .06 | .01 |
| ☐ 374 | Greg Pryor | .07 | .03 | .01 |
| ☐ 375 | Wayne Gross | .07 | .03 | .01 |
| ☐ 376 | Charlie Lea | .07 | .03 | .01 |
| ☐ 377 | Steve Lubratich | .07 | .03 | .01 |
| ☐ 378 | Jon Matlack | .10 | .04 | .01 |
| ☐ 379 | Julio Cruz | .07 | .03 | .01 |
| ☐ 380 | John Mizerock | .07 | .03 | .01 |
| ☐ 381 | Kevin Gross | .25 | .10 | .02 |
| ☐ 382 | Mike Ramsey | .07 | .03 | .01 |
| ☐ 383 | Doug Gwosdz | .07 | .03 | .01 |
| ☐ 384 | Kelly Paris | .10 | .04 | .01 |
| ☐ 385 | Pete Falcone | .07 | .03 | .01 |
| ☐ 386 | Milt May | .07 | .03 | .01 |
| ☐ 387 | Fred Breining | .07 | .03 | .01 |
| ☐ 388 | Craig Lefferts | .15 | .06 | .01 |
| ☐ 389 | Steve Henderson | .07 | .03 | .01 |
| ☐ 390 | Randy Moffitt | .07 | .03 | .01 |
| ☐ 391 | Ron Washington | .07 | .03 | .01 |
| ☐ 392 | Gary Roenicke | .07 | .03 | .01 |
| ☐ 393 | Tom Candiotti | .25 | .10 | .02 |
| ☐ 394 | Larry Pashnick | .07 | .03 | .01 |
| ☐ 395 | Dwight Evans | .15 | .06 | .01 |
| ☐ 396 | Goose Gossage | .20 | .08 | .02 |
| ☐ 397 | Derrel Thomas | .07 | .03 | .01 |
| ☐ 398 | Juan Eichelberger | .07 | .03 | .01 |
| ☐ 399 | Leon Roberts | .07 | .03 | .01 |
| ☐ 400 | Davey Lopes | .10 | .04 | .01 |
| ☐ 401 | Bill Gullickson | .10 | .04 | .01 |
| ☐ 402 | Geoff Zahn | .07 | .03 | .01 |
| ☐ 403 | Billy Sample | .07 | .03 | .01 |
| ☐ 404 | Mike Squires | .07 | .03 | .01 |
| ☐ 405 | Craig Reynolds | .07 | .03 | .01 |
| ☐ 406 | Eric Show | .07 | .03 | .01 |
| ☐ 407 | John Denny | .10 | .04 | .01 |
| ☐ 408 | Dann Bilardello | .07 | .03 | .01 |
| ☐ 409 | Bruce Benedict | .07 | .03 | .01 |
| ☐ 410 | Kent Tekulve | .10 | .04 | .01 |
| ☐ 411 | Mel Hall | .15 | .06 | .01 |
| ☐ 412 | John Stuper | .07 | .03 | .01 |
| ☐ 413 | Rick Dempsey | .10 | .04 | .01 |
| ☐ 414 | Don Sutton | .30 | .12 | .03 |
| ☐ 415 | Jack Morris | .30 | .12 | .03 |
| ☐ 416 | John Tudor | .20 | .08 | .02 |
| ☐ 417 | Willie Randolph | .10 | .04 | .01 |
| ☐ 418 | Jerry Reuss | .10 | .04 | .01 |
| ☐ 419 | Don Slaught | .10 | .04 | .01 |
| ☐ 420 | Steve McCatty | .07 | .03 | .01 |
| ☐ 421 | Tim Wallach | .15 | .06 | .01 |
| ☐ 422 | Larry Parrish | .10 | .04 | .01 |
| ☐ 423 | Brian Downing | .10 | .04 | .01 |
| ☐ 424 | Britt Burns | .10 | .04 | .01 |
| ☐ 425 | David Green | .10 | .04 | .01 |
| ☐ 426 | Jerry Mumphrey | .10 | .04 | .01 |
| ☐ 427 | Ivan DeJesus | .07 | .03 | .01 |
| ☐ 428 | Mario Soto | .10 | .04 | .01 |
| ☐ 429 | Gene Richards | .07 | .03 | .01 |
| ☐ 430 | Dale Berra | .10 | .04 | .01 |
| ☐ 431 | Darrell Evans | .15 | .06 | .01 |
| ☐ 432 | Glenn Hubbard | .07 | .03 | .01 |
| ☐ 433 | Jody Davis | .15 | .06 | .01 |
| ☐ 434 | Danny Heep | .07 | .03 | .01 |
| ☐ 435 | Ed Nunez | .30 | .12 | .03 |
| ☐ 436 | Bobby Castillo | .07 | .03 | .01 |
| ☐ 437 | Ernie Whitt | .07 | .03 | .01 |
| ☐ 438 | Scott Ullger | .07 | .03 | .01 |
| ☐ 439 | Doyle Alexander | .07 | .03 | .01 |
| ☐ 440 | Domingo Ramos | .07 | .03 | .01 |
| ☐ 441 | Craig Swan | .07 | .03 | .01 |
| ☐ 442 | Warren Brusstar | .07 | .03 | .01 |
| ☐ 443 | Len Barker | .07 | .03 | .01 |
| ☐ 444 | Mike Easler | .10 | .04 | .01 |
| ☐ 445 | Renie Martin | .07 | .03 | .01 |
| ☐ 446 | Dennis Rasmussen | .75 | .30 | .07 |
| ☐ 447 | Ted Power | .15 | .06 | .01 |
| ☐ 448 | Charlie Hudson | .15 | .06 | .01 |
| ☐ 449 | Danny Cox | .40 | .16 | .04 |
| ☐ 450 | Kevin Bass | .15 | .06 | .01 |
| ☐ 451 | Daryl Sconiers | .07 | .03 | .01 |
| ☐ 452 | Scott Fletcher | .10 | .04 | .01 |
| ☐ 453 | Bryn Smith | .07 | .03 | .01 |
| ☐ 454 | Jim Dwyer | .07 | .03 | .01 |
| ☐ 455 | Rob Picciolo | .07 | .03 | .01 |
| ☐ 456 | Enos Cabell | .07 | .03 | .01 |
| ☐ 457 | Dennis Boyd | 1.50 | .60 | .15 |
| ☐ 458 | Butch Wynegar | .07 | .03 | .01 |
| ☐ 459 | Burt Hooton | .07 | .03 | .01 |
| ☐ 460 | Ron Hassey | .07 | .03 | .01 |
| ☐ 461 | Danny Jackson | .75 | .30 | .07 |
| ☐ 462 | Bob Kearney | .07 | .03 | .01 |
| ☐ 463 | Terry Francona | .10 | .04 | .01 |
| ☐ 464 | Wayne Tolleson | .07 | .03 | .01 |
| ☐ 465 | Mickey Rivers | .10 | .04 | .01 |
| ☐ 466 | John Wathan | .07 | .03 | .01 |
| ☐ 467 | Bill Almon | .07 | .03 | .01 |
| ☐ 468 | George Vukovich | .07 | .03 | .01 |
| ☐ 469 | Steve Kemp | .10 | .04 | .01 |
| ☐ 470 | Ken Landreaux | .07 | .03 | .01 |
| ☐ 471 | Milt Wilcox | .07 | .03 | .01 |
| ☐ 472 | Tippy Martinez | .07 | .03 | .01 |
| ☐ 473 | Ted Simmons | .15 | .06 | .01 |
| ☐ 474 | Tim Foli | .07 | .03 | .01 |
| ☐ 475 | George Hendrick | .10 | .04 | .01 |
| ☐ 476 | Terry Puhl | .10 | .04 | .01 |
| ☐ 477 | Von Hayes | .25 | .10 | .02 |
| ☐ 478 | Bobby Brown | .07 | .03 | .01 |
| ☐ 479 | Lee Lacy | .10 | .04 | .01 |
| ☐ 480 | Joel Youngblood | .07 | .03 | .01 |
| ☐ 481 | Jim Slaton | .07 | .03 | .01 |
| ☐ 482 | Mike Fitzgerald | .10 | .04 | .01 |
| ☐ 483 | Keith Moreland | .15 | .06 | .01 |
| ☐ 484 | Ron Roenicke | .07 | .03 | .01 |
| ☐ 485 | Luis Leal | .07 | .03 | .01 |
| ☐ 486 | Bryan Oelkers | .10 | .04 | .01 |
| ☐ 487 | Bruce Berenyi | .07 | .03 | .01 |
| ☐ 488 | LaMarr Hoyt | .15 | .06 | .01 |
| ☐ 489 | Joe Nolan | .07 | .03 | .01 |
| ☐ 490 | Marshall Edwards | .07 | .03 | .01 |
| ☐ 491 | Mike Laga | .10 | .04 | .01 |
| ☐ 492 | Rick Cerone | .07 | .03 | .01 |
| ☐ 493 | Rick Miller (listed as Mike on card front) | .10 | .04 | .01 |
| ☐ 494 | Rick Honeycutt | .10 | .04 | .01 |
| ☐ 495 | Mike Hargrove | .10 | .04 | .01 |
| ☐ 496 | Joe Simpson | .07 | .03 | .01 |
| ☐ 497 | Keith Atherton | .07 | .03 | .01 |
| ☐ 498 | Chris Welsh | .07 | .03 | .01 |
| ☐ 499 | Bruce Kison | .07 | .03 | .01 |
| ☐ 500 | Bobby Johnson | .07 | .03 | .01 |
| ☐ 501 | Jerry Koosman | .10 | .04 | .01 |
| ☐ 502 | Frank DiPino | .07 | .03 | .01 |
| ☐ 503 | Tony Perez | .15 | .06 | .01 |
| ☐ 504 | Ken Oberkfell | .07 | .03 | .01 |
| ☐ 505 | Mark Thurmond | .20 | .08 | .02 |
| ☐ 506 | Joe Price | .07 | .03 | .01 |
| ☐ 507 | Pascual Perez | .07 | .03 | .01 |
| ☐ 508 | Marvell Wynne | .15 | .06 | .01 |
| ☐ 509 | Mike Krukow | .15 | .06 | .01 |
| ☐ 510 | Dick Ruthven | .07 | .03 | .01 |
| ☐ 511 | Al Cowens | .07 | .03 | .01 |
| ☐ 512 | Cliff Johnson | .07 | .03 | .01 |

| | | | | |
|---|---|---|---|---|
| ☐ 513 | Randy Bush .............. | .07 | .03 | .01 |
| ☐ 514 | Sammy Stewart ........... | .07 | .03 | .01 |
| ☐ 515 | Bill Schroeder .............. | .20 | .08 | .02 |
| ☐ 516 | Aurelio Lopez ............... | .07 | .03 | .01 |
| ☐ 517 | Mike Brown ............... | .10 | .04 | .01 |
| | (Red Sox pitcher) | | | |
| ☐ 518 | Graig Nettles ............... | .15 | .06 | .01 |
| ☐ 519 | Dave Sax ............... | .07 | .03 | .01 |
| ☐ 520 | Gerry Willard .............. | .15 | .06 | .01 |
| ☐ 521 | Paul Splittorff ............... | .07 | .03 | .01 |
| ☐ 522 | Tom Burgmeier .............. | .07 | .03 | .01 |
| ☐ 523 | Chris Speier ............... | .07 | .03 | .01 |
| ☐ 524 | Bobby Clark ............... | .07 | .03 | .01 |
| ☐ 525 | George Wright ............... | .07 | .03 | .01 |
| ☐ 526 | Dennis Lamp ............... | .07 | .03 | .01 |
| ☐ 527 | Tony Scott ............... | .07 | .03 | .01 |
| ☐ 528 | Ed Whitson ............... | .10 | .04 | .01 |
| ☐ 529 | Ron Reed ............... | .07 | .03 | .01 |
| ☐ 530 | Charlie Puleo ............... | .07 | .03 | .01 |
| ☐ 531 | Jerry Royster ............... | .07 | .03 | .01 |
| ☐ 532 | Don Robinson ............... | .07 | .03 | .01 |
| ☐ 533 | Steve Trout ............... | .07 | .03 | .01 |
| ☐ 534 | Bruce Sutter ............... | .20 | .08 | .02 |
| ☐ 535 | Bob Horner ............... | .25 | .10 | .02 |
| ☐ 536 | Pat Tabler ............... | .15 | .06 | .01 |
| ☐ 537 | Chris Chambliss .............. | .10 | .04 | .01 |
| ☐ 538 | Bob Ojeda ............... | .15 | .06 | .01 |
| ☐ 539 | Alan Ashby ............... | .07 | .03 | .01 |
| ☐ 540 | Jay Johnstone ............... | .10 | .04 | .01 |
| ☐ 541 | Bob Dernier ............... | .10 | .04 | .01 |
| ☐ 542 | Brook Jacoby ............... | 2.00 | .80 | .20 |
| ☐ 543 | U.L. Washington .............. | .07 | .03 | .01 |
| ☐ 544 | Danny Darwin ............... | .07 | .03 | .01 |
| ☐ 545 | Kiko Garcia ............... | .07 | .03 | .01 |
| ☐ 546 | Vance Law ............... | .07 | .03 | .01 |
| ☐ 547 | Tug McGraw ............... | .15 | .06 | .01 |
| ☐ 548 | Dave Smith ............... | .10 | .04 | .01 |
| ☐ 549 | Len Matuszek ............... | .07 | .03 | .01 |
| ☐ 550 | Tom Hume ............... | .07 | .03 | .01 |
| ☐ 551 | Dave Dravecky ............... | .10 | .04 | .01 |
| ☐ 552 | Rick Rhoden ............... | .10 | .04 | .01 |
| ☐ 553 | Duane Kuiper ............... | .07 | .03 | .01 |
| ☐ 554 | Rusty Staub ............... | .10 | .04 | .01 |
| ☐ 555 | Bill Campbell ............... | .07 | .03 | .01 |
| ☐ 556 | Mike Torrez ............... | .10 | .04 | .01 |
| ☐ 557 | Dave Henderson ........... | .10 | .04 | .01 |
| ☐ 558 | Len Whitehouse ........... | .10 | .04 | .01 |
| ☐ 559 | Barry Bonnell ............... | .07 | .03 | .01 |
| ☐ 560 | Rick Lysander ............... | .07 | .03 | .01 |
| ☐ 561 | Garth Iorg ............... | .07 | .03 | .01 |
| ☐ 562 | Bryan Clark ............... | .07 | .03 | .01 |
| ☐ 563 | Brian Giles ............... | .07 | .03 | .01 |
| ☐ 564 | Vern Ruhle ............... | .07 | .03 | .01 |
| ☐ 565 | Steve Bedrosian ........... | .07 | .03 | .01 |
| ☐ 566 | Larry McWilliams ........... | .07 | .03 | .01 |
| ☐ 567 | Jeff Leonard ............... | .07 | .03 | .01 |
| ☐ 568 | Alan Wiggins ............... | .10 | .04 | .01 |
| ☐ 569 | Jeff Russell ............... | .10 | .04 | .01 |
| ☐ 570 | Salome Barojas ........... | .07 | .03 | .01 |
| ☐ 571 | Dane Iorg ............... | .07 | .03 | .01 |
| ☐ 572 | Bob Knepper ............... | .15 | .06 | .01 |
| ☐ 573 | Gary Lavelle ............... | .10 | .04 | .01 |
| ☐ 574 | Gorman Thomas ........... | .15 | .06 | .01 |
| ☐ 575 | Manny Trillo ............... | .10 | .04 | .01 |
| ☐ 576 | Jim Palmer ............... | .35 | .14 | .03 |
| ☐ 577 | Dale Murray ............... | .07 | .03 | .01 |
| ☐ 578 | Tom Brookens ............... | .07 | .03 | .01 |
| ☐ 579 | Rich Gedman ............... | .15 | .06 | .01 |
| ☐ 580 | Bill Doran ............... | .30 | .12 | .03 |
| ☐ 581 | Steve Yeager ............... | .07 | .03 | .01 |
| ☐ 582 | Dan Spillner ............... | .07 | .03 | .01 |
| ☐ 583 | Dan Quisenberry ........... | .20 | .08 | .02 |
| ☐ 584 | Rance Mulliniks ........... | .07 | .03 | .01 |
| ☐ 585 | Storm Davis ............... | .15 | .06 | .01 |
| ☐ 586 | Dave Schmidt ............... | .07 | .03 | .01 |
| ☐ 587 | Bill Russell ............... | .10 | .04 | .01 |
| ☐ 588 | Pat Sheridan ............... | .15 | .06 | .01 |
| ☐ 589 | Rafael Ramirez ............... | .07 | .03 | .01 |
| | (A's on front) | | | |
| ☐ 590 | Bud Anderson ............... | .07 | .03 | .01 |
| ☐ 591 | George Frazier ............... | .07 | .03 | .01 |
| ☐ 592 | Lee Tunnell ............... | .10 | .04 | .01 |
| ☐ 593 | Kirk Gibson ............... | .30 | .12 | .03 |
| ☐ 594 | Scott McGregor ............... | .10 | .04 | .01 |
| ☐ 595 | Bob Bailor ............... | .07 | .03 | .01 |
| ☐ 596 | Tommy Herr ............... | .10 | .04 | .01 |
| ☐ 597 | Luis Sanchez ............... | .07 | .03 | .01 |
| ☐ 598 | Dave Engle ............... | .07 | .03 | .01 |
| ☐ 599 | Craig McMurtry ............... | .10 | .04 | .01 |
| ☐ 600 | Carlos Diaz ............... | .07 | .03 | .01 |
| ☐ 601 | Tom O'Malley ............... | .07 | .03 | .01 |
| ☐ 602 | Nick Esasky ............... | .30 | .12 | .03 |
| ☐ 603 | Ron Hodges ............... | .07 | .03 | .01 |

| | | | | |
|---|---|---|---|---|
| ☐ 604 | Ed VandeBerg ............... | .07 | .03 | .01 |
| ☐ 605 | Alfredo Griffin ............... | .07 | .03 | .01 |
| ☐ 606 | Glen Hoffman ............... | .07 | .03 | .01 |
| ☐ 607 | Hubie Brooks ............... | .15 | .06 | .01 |
| ☐ 608 | Richard Barnes ............... | .07 | .03 | .01 |
| ☐ 609 | Greg Walker ............... | 1.25 | .50 | .12 |
| ☐ 610 | Ken Singleton ............... | .10 | .04 | .01 |
| ☐ 611 | Mark Clear ............... | .07 | .03 | .01 |
| ☐ 612 | Buck Martinez ............... | .07 | .03 | .01 |
| ☐ 613 | Ken Griffey ............... | .10 | .04 | .01 |
| ☐ 614 | Reid Nichols ............... | .07 | .03 | .01 |
| ☐ 615 | Doug Sisk ............... | .10 | .04 | .01 |
| ☐ 616 | Bob Brenly ............... | .10 | .04 | .01 |
| ☐ 617 | Joey McLaughlin ........... | .07 | .03 | .01 |
| ☐ 618 | Glenn Wilson ............... | .15 | .06 | .01 |
| ☐ 619 | Bob Stoddard ............... | .07 | .03 | .01 |
| ☐ 620 | Lenn Sakata ............... | .07 | .03 | .01 |
| ☐ 621 | Mike Young ............... | 1.00 | .40 | .10 |
| ☐ 622 | John Stefero ............... | .10 | .04 | .01 |
| ☐ 623 | Carmelo Martinez ........... | .30 | .12 | .03 |
| ☐ 624 | Dave Bergman ............... | .07 | .03 | .01 |
| ☐ 625 | Runnin' Reds ............... | .20 | .08 | .02 |
| | (sic, Redbirds) | | | |
| | David Green | | | |
| | Willie McGee | | | |
| | Lonnie Smith | | | |
| | Ozzie Smith | | | |
| ☐ 626 | Rudy May ............... | .07 | .03 | .01 |
| ☐ 627 | Matt Keough ............... | .07 | .03 | .01 |
| ☐ 628 | Jose DeLeon ............... | .25 | .10 | .02 |
| ☐ 629 | Jim Essian ............... | .07 | .03 | .01 |
| ☐ 630 | Darnell Coles ............... | 1.00 | .40 | .10 |
| ☐ 631 | Mike Warren ............... | .15 | .06 | .01 |
| ☐ 632 | Del Crandall MGR ........... | .07 | .03 | .01 |
| ☐ 633 | Dennis Martinez ............... | .07 | .03 | .01 |
| ☐ 634 | Mike Moore ............... | .10 | .04 | .01 |
| ☐ 635 | Lary Sorensen ............... | .07 | .03 | .01 |
| ☐ 636 | Rick Nelson ............... | .10 | .04 | .01 |
| ☐ 637 | Omar Moreno ............... | .07 | .03 | .01 |
| ☐ 638 | Charlie Hough ............... | .10 | .04 | .01 |
| ☐ 639 | Dennis Eckersley ........... | .10 | .04 | .01 |
| ☐ 640 | Walt Terrell ............... | .35 | .14 | .03 |
| ☐ 641 | Denny Walling ............... | .07 | .03 | .01 |
| ☐ 642 | Dave Anderson ............... | .15 | .06 | .01 |
| ☐ 643 | Jose Oquendo ............... | .10 | .04 | .01 |
| ☐ 644 | Bob Stanley ............... | .10 | .04 | .01 |
| ☐ 645 | Dave Geisel ............... | .07 | .03 | .01 |
| ☐ 646 | Scott Garrelts ............... | .50 | .20 | .05 |
| ☐ 647 | Gary Pettis ............... | 1.00 | .40 | .10 |
| ☐ 648 | Duke Snider ............... | .07 | .03 | .01 |
| | Puzzle Card | | | |
| ☐ 649 | Johnnie LeMaster ............... | .07 | .03 | .01 |
| ☐ 650 | Dave Collins ............... | .10 | .04 | .01 |
| ☐ 651 | The Chicken ............... | .25 | .10 | .02 |
| ☐ 652 | DK Checklist ............... | .10 | .01 | .00 |
| | (unnumbered) | | | |
| ☐ 653 | Checklist 1-130 ............... | .08 | .01 | .00 |
| | (unnumbered) | | | |
| ☐ 654 | Checklist 131-234 ........... | .08 | .01 | .00 |
| | (unnumbered) | | | |
| ☐ 655 | Checklist 235-338 ........... | .08 | .01 | .00 |
| | (unnumbered) | | | |
| ☐ 656 | Checklist 339-442 ........... | .08 | .01 | .00 |
| | (unnumbered) | | | |
| ☐ 657 | Checklist 443-546 ........... | .08 | .01 | .00 |
| | (unnumbered) | | | |
| ☐ 658 | Checklist 547-651 ........... | .08 | .01 | .00 |
| | (unnumbered) | | | |
| ☐ A | Living Legends A: | 2.50 | 1.00 | .25 |
| | Gaylord Perry | | | |
| | Rollie Fingers | | | |
| ☐ B | Living Legends B: .............. | 3.50 | 1.40 | .35 |
| | Carl Yastrzemski | | | |
| | Johnny Bench | | | |

# 1984 Donruss Action All-Stars

The cards in this 60 card set measure 3 1/2" X 5". For the second year in a row Donruss issued a postcard size card set. The set was distributed with a 63 piece Ted Williams puzzle. Unlike last year, when the fronts of the cards contained both an action and a portrait shot of the player, the fronts of this year's cards contain only an action photo. On the backs, the top section contains the card number

| | | | MINT | VG-E | F-G |
|---|---|---|---|---|---|
| ☐ | 58 | Ted Simmons | .10 | .04 | .01 |
| ☐ | 59 | Dave Righetti | .15 | .06 | .01 |
| ☐ | 60 | Checklist card | .10 | .01 | .00 |

## 1984 Donruss Champions

and a full color portrait of the player pictured on the front. The bottom half features the player's career statistics.

| | | | MINT | VG-E | F-G |
|---|---|---|---|---|---|
| | | COMPLETE SET | 5.50 | 2.00 | .50 |
| | | COMMON PLAYER | .05 | .02 | .00 |
| ☐ | 1 | Gary Lavelle | .05 | .02 | .00 |
| ☐ | 2 | Willie McGee | .15 | .06 | .01 |
| ☐ | 3 | Tony Pena | .10 | .04 | .01 |
| ☐ | 4 | Lou Whitaker | .15 | .06 | .01 |
| ☐ | 5 | Robin Yount | .25 | .10 | .02 |
| ☐ | 6 | Doug DeCinces | .10 | .04 | .01 |
| ☐ | 7 | John Castino | .05 | .02 | .00 |
| ☐ | 8 | Terry Kennedy | .10 | .04 | .01 |
| ☐ | 9 | Rickey Henderson | .40 | .16 | .04 |
| ☐ | 10 | Bob Horner | .20 | .08 | .02 |
| ☐ | 11 | Harold Baines | .20 | .08 | .02 |
| ☐ | 12 | Buddy Bell | .10 | .04 | .01 |
| ☐ | 13 | Fernando Valenzuela | .30 | .12 | .03 |
| ☐ | 14 | Nolan Ryan | .30 | .12 | .03 |
| ☐ | 15 | Andre Thornton | .10 | .04 | .01 |
| ☐ | 16 | Gary Redus | .10 | .04 | .01 |
| ☐ | 17 | Pedro Guerrero | .25 | .10 | .02 |
| ☐ | 18 | Andre Dawson | .20 | .08 | .02 |
| ☐ | 19 | Dave Stieb | .15 | .06 | .01 |
| ☐ | 20 | Cal Ripken | .40 | .16 | .04 |
| ☐ | 21 | Ken Griffey | .05 | .02 | .00 |
| ☐ | 22 | Wade Boggs | 1.00 | .40 | .10 |
| ☐ | 23 | Keith Hernandez | .25 | .10 | .02 |
| ☐ | 24 | Steve Carlton | .35 | .14 | .03 |
| ☐ | 25 | Hal McRae | .05 | .02 | .00 |
| ☐ | 26 | John Lowenstein | .05 | .02 | .00 |
| ☐ | 27 | Fred Lynn | .15 | .06 | .01 |
| ☐ | 28 | Bill Buckner | .10 | .04 | .01 |
| ☐ | 29 | Chris Chambliss | .05 | .02 | .00 |
| ☐ | 30 | Richie Zisk | .05 | .02 | .00 |
| ☐ | 31 | Jack Clark | .10 | .04 | .01 |
| ☐ | 32 | George Hendrick | .05 | .02 | .00 |
| ☐ | 33 | Bill Madlock | .15 | .06 | .01 |
| ☐ | 34 | Lance Parrish | .20 | .08 | .02 |
| ☐ | 35 | Paul Molitor | .10 | .04 | .01 |
| ☐ | 36 | Reggie Jackson | .50 | .20 | .05 |
| ☐ | 37 | Kent Hrbek | .25 | .10 | .02 |
| ☐ | 38 | Steve Garvey | .40 | .16 | .04 |
| ☐ | 39 | Carney Lansford | .10 | .04 | .01 |
| ☐ | 40 | Dale Murphy | .60 | .24 | .06 |
| ☐ | 41 | Greg Luzinski | .10 | .04 | .01 |
| ☐ | 42 | Larry Parrish | .05 | .02 | .00 |
| ☐ | 43 | Ryne Sandberg | .50 | .20 | .05 |
| ☐ | 44 | Dickie Thon | .05 | .02 | .00 |
| ☐ | 45 | Bert Blyleven | .10 | .04 | .01 |
| ☐ | 46 | Ron Oester | .05 | .02 | .00 |
| ☐ | 47 | Dusty Baker | .05 | .02 | .00 |
| ☐ | 48 | Steve Rogers | .05 | .02 | .00 |
| ☐ | 49 | Jim Clancy | .05 | .02 | .00 |
| ☐ | 50 | Eddie Murray | .45 | .18 | .04 |
| ☐ | 51 | Ron Guidry | .20 | .08 | .02 |
| ☐ | 52 | Jim Rice | .30 | .12 | .03 |
| ☐ | 53 | Tom Seaver | .30 | .12 | .03 |
| ☐ | 54 | Pete Rose | .75 | .30 | .07 |
| ☐ | 55 | George Brett | .50 | .20 | .05 |
| ☐ | 56 | Dan Quisenberry | .15 | .06 | .01 |
| ☐ | 57 | Mike Schmidt | .50 | .20 | .05 |

The cards in this 60 card set measure 3 1/2" by 5". The 1984 Donruss Champions set is a hybrid photo/artwork issue. Grand Champions, listed GC in the checklist below, feature the artwork of Dick Perez of Perez-Steele Galleries. Current players in the set feature photographs. The theme of this post card-sized set features a Grand Champion and those current players that are directly behind him in a baseball statistical category, for example, Season Home Runs (1-7), Career Home Runs (8-13), Season Batting Average (14-19), Career Batting Average (20-25), Career Hits (26-30), Career Victories (31-36), Career Strikeouts (37-42), Most Valuable Players (43-49), World Series stars (50-54), and All Star heroes (55-59). The cards were issued in cello packs with pieces of the Duke Snider puzzle.

| | | | MINT | VG-E | F-G |
|---|---|---|---|---|---|
| | | COMPLETE SET | 5.50 | 2.00 | .50 |
| | | COMMON PLAYER | .05 | .02 | .00 |
| ☐ | 1 | Babe Ruth GC | .60 | .24 | .06 |
| ☐ | 2 | George Foster | .10 | .04 | .01 |
| ☐ | 3 | Dave Kingman | .10 | .04 | .01 |
| ☐ | 4 | Jim Rice | .30 | .12 | .03 |
| ☐ | 5 | Gorman Thomas | .05 | .02 | .00 |
| ☐ | 6 | Ben Oglivie | .05 | .02 | .00 |
| ☐ | 7 | Jeff Burroughs | .05 | .02 | .00 |
| ☐ | 8 | Hank Aaron GC | .30 | .12 | .03 |
| ☐ | 9 | Reggie Jackson | .40 | .16 | .04 |
| ☐ | 10 | Carl Yastrzemski | .40 | .16 | .04 |
| ☐ | 11 | Mike Schmidt | .40 | .16 | .04 |
| ☐ | 12 | Graig Nettles | .10 | .04 | .01 |
| ☐ | 13 | Greg Luzinski | .05 | .02 | .00 |
| ☐ | 14 | Ted Williams GC | .35 | .14 | .03 |
| ☐ | 15 | George Brett | .40 | .16 | .04 |
| ☐ | 16 | Wade Boggs | .75 | .30 | .07 |
| ☐ | 17 | Hal McRae | .05 | .02 | .00 |
| ☐ | 18 | Bill Buckner | .10 | .04 | .01 |
| ☐ | 19 | Eddie Murray | .35 | .14 | .03 |
| ☐ | 20 | Rogers Hornsby GC | .15 | .06 | .01 |
| ☐ | 21 | Rod Carew | .30 | .12 | .03 |
| ☐ | 22 | Bill Madlock | .10 | .04 | .01 |
| ☐ | 23 | Lonnie Smith | .05 | .02 | .00 |
| ☐ | 24 | Cecil Cooper | .10 | .04 | .01 |
| ☐ | 25 | Ken Griffey | .05 | .02 | .00 |
| ☐ | 26 | Ty Cobb GC | .50 | .20 | .05 |
| ☐ | 27 | Pete Rose | .60 | .24 | .06 |
| ☐ | 28 | Rusty Staub | .05 | .02 | .00 |

| | | MINT | VG-E | F-G |
|---|---|---|---|---|
| ☐ | 29 Tony Perez | .10 | .04 | .01 |
| ☐ | 30 Al Oliver | .10 | .04 | .01 |
| ☐ | 31 Cy Young GC | .15 | .06 | .01 |
| ☐ | 32 Gaylord Perry | .15 | .06 | .01 |
| ☐ | 33 Ferguson Jenkins | .10 | .04 | .01 |
| ☐ | 34 Phil Niekro | .20 | .08 | .02 |
| ☐ | 35 Jim Palmer | .20 | .08 | .02 |
| ☐ | 36 Tommy John | .10 | .04 | .01 |
| ☐ | 37 Walter Johnson GC | .20 | .08 | .02 |
| ☐ | 38 Steve Carlton | .30 | .12 | .03 |
| ☐ | 39 Nolan Ryan | .30 | .12 | .03 |
| ☐ | 40 Tom Seaver | .30 | .12 | .03 |
| ☐ | 41 Don Sutton | .15 | .06 | .01 |
| ☐ | 42 Bert Blyleven | .10 | .04 | .01 |
| ☐ | 43 Frank Robinson GC | .20 | .08 | .02 |
| ☐ | 44 Joe Morgan | .15 | .06 | .01 |
| ☐ | 45 Rollie Fingers | .15 | .06 | .01 |
| ☐ | 46 Keith Hernandez | .20 | .08 | .02 |
| ☐ | 47 Robin Yount | .25 | .10 | .02 |
| ☐ | 48 Cal Ripken | .30 | .12 | .03 |
| ☐ | 49 Dale Murphy | .50 | .20 | .05 |
| ☐ | 50 Mickey Mantle GC | .60 | .24 | .06 |
| ☐ | 51 Johnny Bench | .30 | .12 | .03 |
| ☐ | 52 Carlton Fisk | .10 | .04 | .01 |
| ☐ | 53 Tug McGraw | .05 | .02 | .00 |
| ☐ | 54 Paul Molitor | .05 | .02 | .00 |
| ☐ | 55 Carl Hubbell GC | .10 | .04 | .01 |
| ☐ | 56 Steve Garvey | .30 | .12 | .03 |
| ☐ | 57 Dave Parker | .20 | .08 | .02 |
| ☐ | 58 Gary Carter | .30 | .12 | .03 |
| ☐ | 59 Fred Lynn | .15 | .06 | .01 |
| ☐ | 60 Checklist card | .10 | .01 | .00 |

## 1985 Donruss

The cards in this 660 card set measure 2 1/2" by 3 1/2". The 1985 Donruss regular issue cards have fronts that feature jet black borders on which orange lines have been placed. The fronts contain the standard team logo, player's name, position, and Donruss logo. The cards were distributed with puzzle pieces from a Dick Perez rendition of Lou Gehrig. The first 26 cards of the set feature Diamond Kings (DK), for the fourth year in a row; the artwork on the Diamond Kings was again produced by the Perez-Steele Galleries. Cards 27-46 feature Rated Rookies (RR). The unnumbered checklist cards are arbitrarily numbered below as numbers 654 through 660. The boxes in which the wax packs were contained feature four baseball cards, with backs. The price of the set below does not include these cards; however, these cards are priced at the end of the set below.

| | | MINT | VG-E | F-G |
|---|---|---|---|---|
| | COMPLETE SET | 80.00 | 32.00 | 8.00 |
| | COMMON PLAYER | .04 | .02 | .00 |
| ☐ | 1 Ryne Sandberg DK | .50 | .20 | .05 |
| ☐ | 2 Doug DeCinces DK | .08 | .03 | .01 |
| ☐ | 3 Richard Dotson DK | .06 | .02 | .00 |

| | | MINT | VG-E | F-G |
|---|---|---|---|---|
| ☐ | 4 Bert Blyleven DK | .10 | .04 | .01 |
| ☐ | 5 Lou Whitaker DK | .15 | .06 | .01 |
| ☐ | 6 Dan Quisenberry DK | .15 | .06 | .01 |
| ☐ | 7 Don Mattingly DK | 4.00 | 1.60 | .40 |
| ☐ | 8 Carney Lansford DK | .08 | .03 | .01 |
| ☐ | 9 Frank Tanana DK | .06 | .02 | .00 |
| ☐ | 10 Willie Upshaw DK | .08 | .03 | .01 |
| ☐ | 11 Claudell Washington DK | .08 | .03 | .01 |
| ☐ | 12 Mike Marshall DK | .15 | .06 | .01 |
| ☐ | 13 Joaquin Andujar DK | .10 | .04 | .01 |
| ☐ | 14 Cal Ripken DK | .45 | .18 | .04 |
| ☐ | 15 Jim Rice DK | .35 | .14 | .03 |
| ☐ | 16 Don Sutton DK | .15 | .06 | .01 |
| ☐ | 17 Frank Viola DK | .08 | .03 | .01 |
| ☐ | 18 Alvin Davis DK | .50 | .20 | .05 |
| ☐ | 19 Mario Soto DK | .08 | .03 | .01 |
| ☐ | 20 Jose Cruz DK | .10 | .04 | .01 |
| ☐ | 21 Charlie Lea DK | .06 | .02 | .00 |
| ☐ | 22 Jesse Orosco DK | .08 | .03 | .01 |
| ☐ | 23 Juan Samuel DK | .20 | .08 | .02 |
| ☐ | 24 Tony Pena DK | .12 | .05 | .01 |
| ☐ | 25 Tony Gwynn DK | .45 | .18 | .04 |
| ☐ | 26 Bob Brenly DK | .08 | .03 | .01 |
| ☐ | 27 Danny Tartabull RR | 3.50 | 1.40 | .35 |
| ☐ | 28 Mike Bielecki RR | .10 | .04 | .01 |
| ☐ | 29 Steve Lyons RR | .15 | .06 | .01 |
| ☐ | 30 Jeff Reed RR | .10 | .04 | .01 |
| ☐ | 31 Tony Brewer RR | .10 | .04 | .01 |
| ☐ | 32 John Morris RR | .15 | .06 | .01 |
| ☐ | 33 Daryl Boston RR | .35 | .14 | .03 |
| ☐ | 34 Alfonso Pulido RR | .10 | .04 | .01 |
| ☐ | 35 Steve Kiefer RR | .10 | .04 | .01 |
| ☐ | 36 Larry Sheets RR | .50 | .20 | .05 |
| ☐ | 37 Scott Bradley RR | .30 | .12 | .03 |
| ☐ | 38 Calvin Schiraldi RR | 1.00 | .40 | .10 |
| ☐ | 39 Shawon Dunston RR | 1.50 | .60 | .15 |
| ☐ | 40 Charlie Mitchell RR | .10 | .04 | .01 |
| ☐ | 41 Billy Hatcher RR | .35 | .14 | .03 |
| ☐ | 42 Russ Stephans RR | .10 | .04 | .01 |
| ☐ | 43 Alejandro Sanchez RR | .10 | .04 | .01 |
| ☐ | 44 Steve Jeltz RR | .15 | .06 | .01 |
| ☐ | 45 Jim Traber RR | 1.00 | .40 | .10 |
| ☐ | 46 Doug Loman RR | .20 | .08 | .02 |
| ☐ | 47 Eddie Murray | .40 | .16 | .04 |
| ☐ | 48 Robin Yount | .25 | .10 | .02 |
| ☐ | 49 Lance Parrish | .20 | .08 | .02 |
| ☐ | 50 Jim Rice | .35 | .14 | .03 |
| ☐ | 51 Dave Winfield | .30 | .12 | .03 |
| ☐ | 52 Fernando Valenzuela | .30 | .12 | .03 |
| ☐ | 53 George Brett | .50 | .20 | .05 |
| ☐ | 54 Dave Kingman | .12 | .05 | .01 |
| ☐ | 55 Gary Carter | .35 | .14 | .03 |
| ☐ | 56 Buddy Bell | .10 | .04 | .01 |
| ☐ | 57 Reggie Jackson | .40 | .16 | .04 |
| ☐ | 58 Harold Baines | .20 | .08 | .02 |
| ☐ | 59 Ozzie Smith | .10 | .04 | .01 |
| ☐ | 60 Nolan Ryan | .35 | .14 | .03 |
| ☐ | 61 Mike Schmidt | .45 | .18 | .04 |
| ☐ | 62 Dave Parker | .20 | .08 | .02 |
| ☐ | 63 Tony Gwynn | .45 | .18 | .04 |
| ☐ | 64 Tony Pena | .12 | .05 | .01 |
| ☐ | 65 Jack Clark | .12 | .05 | .01 |
| ☐ | 66 Dale Murphy | .60 | .24 | .06 |
| ☐ | 67 Ryne Sandberg | .45 | .18 | .04 |
| ☐ | 68 Keith Hernandez | .25 | .10 | .02 |
| ☐ | 69 Alvin Davis | 2.25 | .90 | .22 |
| ☐ | 70 Kent Hrbek | .30 | .12 | .03 |
| ☐ | 71 Willie Upshaw | .10 | .04 | .01 |
| ☐ | 72 Dave Engle | .04 | .02 | .00 |
| ☐ | 73 Alfredo Griffin | .06 | .02 | .00 |
| ☐ | 74A Jack Perconte (Career Highlights four lines) | .15 | .06 | .01 |
| ☐ | 74B Jack Perconte (Career Highlights three lines) | .15 | .06 | .01 |
| ☐ | 75 Jesse Orosco | .08 | .03 | .01 |
| ☐ | 76 Jody Davis | .10 | .04 | .01 |
| ☐ | 77 Bob Horner | .15 | .06 | .01 |
| ☐ | 78 Larry McWilliams | .04 | .02 | .00 |
| ☐ | 79 Joel Youngblood | .04 | .02 | .00 |
| ☐ | 80 Alan Wiggins | .08 | .03 | .01 |
| ☐ | 81 Ron Oester | .04 | .02 | .00 |
| ☐ | 82 Ozzie Virgil | .04 | .02 | .00 |
| ☐ | 83 Ricky Horton | .15 | .06 | .01 |
| ☐ | 84 Bill Doran | .08 | .03 | .01 |
| ☐ | 85 Rod Carew | .35 | .14 | .03 |
| ☐ | 86 LaMarr Hoyt | .10 | .04 | .01 |
| ☐ | 87 Tim Wallach | .08 | .03 | .01 |
| ☐ | 88 Mike Flanagan | .08 | .03 | .01 |
| ☐ | 89 Jim Sundberg | .06 | .02 | .00 |
| ☐ | 90 Chet Lemon | .06 | .02 | .00 |
| ☐ | 91 Bob Stanley | .06 | .02 | .00 |

# COMPLETE SETS FOR SALE (NR MT-MT)

1983 Donruss Action All-Stars (60) . . . . . . . . .$4.95
1983 Donruss HOF Heroes (44) . . . . . . . . . .$3.50
1984 Donruss Action All-Stars (60) . . . . . . . .$4.95
1984 Donruss Champions (60) . . . . . . . . $5.50
1986 Donruss Highlights (56) . . . . . . . . . . .$9.95
1986 Donruss Rookies (56) . . . . . . . . . . $24.95
1986 Burger King (20) . . . . . . . . . . . . . .$9.95
1981 Drakes (33) . . . . . . . . . . . . . . . . $2.95
1983 Drakes (33) . . . . . . . . . . . . . . . . $4.95
1985 Drakes (44) . . . . . . . . . . . . . . . . $7.95
1985 Fleer Limited (44) . . . . . . . . . . . . .$5.95
1986 Fleer Future Hall of Fame (6) . . . . . . . .$4.95
1982 K mart (44) . . . . . . . . . . . . . . . . $ .95
1984 Milton Bradley (30) . . . . . . . . . . . . $8.95
1986 Mother's Cookies Jose Canseco (1) . . . . .$9.95
1986 Atlanta Braves Police (30) . . . . . . . . .$9.95
1984 Nestle (22) . . . . . . . . . . . . . . . $14.95
1984 Ralston-Purina (33) . . . . . . . . . . . .$3.95
1986 Sportflics Decade Greats (75) . . . . . . .$18.95
1986 Sportflics Rookies (50) . . . . . . . . . .$16.95
1987 Sportflics (200) . . . . . . . . . . . . .$35.95
1986 Topps Traded (132) . . . . . . . . . . . .$14.95
1985 Hostess Braves (22) . . . . . . . . . . . .$9.95
1986 Conlin Smithsonian (60) . . . . . . . . . .$15.95
1984 Topps Rubdowns . . . . . . . . . . . . .$4.95
1985 Topps Rubdowns . . . . . . . . . . . . .$5.95
1986 Topps 'Minis' (66) . . . . . . . . . . . . .$5.95
1986 Fleer Classic Miniatures (120) . . . . . . .$12.95
1986 Fleer Limited Sluggers v. Pitchers (44) . . . . $6.95
1985 Huntsville Stars (Canseco) (25) . . . . . . .$9.95
1985 Big Apple (8) . . . . . . . . . . . . . . .$5.95
1986 Big Apple Yankees-Mets (12) . . . . . . . .$4.95
1985 Big Apple Rookies (12) . . . . . . . . . . .$4.95

$ $ $ $ $ $ $ $ $

## NEED TO BUY BASEBALL CARDS
## MOST WANTED PRE-1960
## INCLUDING: GOUDY, TOPPS,
## BOWMAN, TOBACCO

Send Cards or Description for Offer

$ $ $ $ $ $ $ $ $

## Dalton Stamp and Coin
### 102 W. Waugh St., Dept P
### Dalton, GA 30720
### PHONE: (404) 278-2321

STEVE GOLDBERG
JUAN LAMA
DAVID FENSTER
*SE HABLA ESPANOL*

MasterCard
VISA

## SETS BY THE "STAR" COMPANY

Murphy . . . . . . . . . . . . . . . . . $8.95
Yaz . . . . . . . . . . . . . . . . . . $11.95
Schmidt . . . . . . . . . . . . . . . . $19.95
Boggs . . . . . . . . . . . . . . . . . $8.95
Canseco . . . . . . . . . . . . . . . . $8.95
Joyner . . . . . . . . . . . . . . . . . $7.95
Clemens . . . . . . . . . . . . . . . . $6.95
Raines . . . . . . . . . . . . . . . . . $6.95
Garvey . . . . . . . . . . . . . . . . . $8.95
Brett . . . . . . . . . . . . . . . . . $9.95
Jackson . . . . . . . . . . . . . . . . $10.95
Ryan . . . . . . . . . . . . . . . . . . $7.95
Seaver . . . . . . . . . . . . . . . . . $7.95
Carew . . . . . . . . . . . . . . . . . $7.95
Rice . . . . . . . . . . . . . . . . . . $7.95
Mattingly . . . . . . . . . . . . . . . . $9.95

## CLOSEOUT SPECIAL
### Topps Football Sets

1982 (528) . . . . . . . . . . . . . . . .$13.95
1983 (396) . . . . . . . . . . . . . . . .$12.95
1984 (396) . . . . . . . . . . . . . . . .$12.95

### * Special - One of Each *
### $34.95

### MVP Top Quality Plastic Sheets

| | | | | |
|---|---|---|---|---|
| 25 | $6.00 | #1A | 8x10 or Yearbooks |
| 50 | $10.00 | #2 | 5x7 |
| 100 | $18.50 | #4 | 4x6 |
| 500 | $74.50 | #8 | early Topps |
| | | #9TL | standard |

### * Mix and Match *
Postage on Sheets, add 10%

### Plastic Boxes
### good for team sets,
### storage of cards

| | 1 | 20 | 50 |
|---|---|---|---|
| #1 (10-12 cards) | .25 | .22ea | .21ea |
| #2 (35 cards) | .35 | .32ea | .30ea |
| #3 (55 cards) | .45 | .41ea | .36ea |
| #4 (100 cards) | .60 | .55ea | .48ea |

### ORDERING INSTRUCTIONS:

1. NO MINIMUM
2. POSTAGE
Up to $10 . . . . . . . . . . . . . . . . . add $2.00
$10.01 to $20.00 . . . . . . . . . . . . . .add $2.50
$20.01 to $30 . . . . . . . . . . . . . . . add $3.00
over $30.00 . . . . . . . . . . . . . . . . add $3.50
3. Canada, Hawaii, Alaska, add sufficient postage.
4. Georgia residents add 4% sales tax
5. No P.O. Box (UPS will not deliver)

| | | | | | | | | | |
|---|---|---|---|---|---|---|---|---|---|
| ☐ | 92 | Willie Randolph | .06 | .02 | .00 | | | | |
| ☐ | 93 | Bill Russell | .06 | .02 | .00 | | | | |
| ☐ | 94 | Julio Franco | .12 | .05 | .01 | | | | |
| ☐ | 95 | Dan Quisenberry | .15 | .06 | .01 | | | | |
| ☐ | 96 | Bill Caudill | .06 | .02 | .00 | | | | |
| ☐ | 97 | Bill Gullickson | .06 | .02 | .00 | | | | |
| ☐ | 98 | Danny Darwin | .04 | .02 | .00 | | | | |
| ☐ | 99 | Curtis Wilkerson | .04 | .02 | .00 | | | | |
| ☐ | 100 | Bud Black | .04 | .02 | .00 | | | | |
| ☐ | 101 | Tony Phillips | .04 | .02 | .00 | | | | |
| ☐ | 102 | Tony Bernazard | .06 | .02 | .00 | | | | |
| ☐ | 103 | Jay Howell | .06 | .02 | .00 | | | | |
| ☐ | 104 | Burt Hooton | .04 | .02 | .00 | | | | |
| ☐ | 105 | Milt Wilcox | .04 | .02 | .00 | | | | |
| ☐ | 106 | Rich Dauer | .04 | .02 | .00 | | | | |
| ☐ | 107 | Don Sutton | .15 | .06 | .01 | | | | |
| ☐ | 108 | Mike Witt | .12 | .05 | .01 | | | | |
| ☐ | 109 | Bruce Sutter | .15 | .06 | .01 | | | | |
| ☐ | 110 | Enos Cabell | .04 | .02 | .00 | | | | |
| ☐ | 111 | John Denny | .06 | .02 | .00 | | | | |
| ☐ | 112 | Dave Dravecky | .06 | .02 | .00 | | | | |
| ☐ | 113 | Marvell Wynne | .04 | .02 | .00 | | | | |
| ☐ | 114 | Johnnie LeMaster | .04 | .02 | .00 | | | | |
| ☐ | 115 | Chuck Porter | .04 | .02 | .00 | | | | |
| ☐ | 116 | John Gibbons | .08 | .03 | .01 | | | | |
| ☐ | 117 | Keith Moreland | .06 | .02 | .00 | | | | |
| ☐ | 118 | Darnell Coles | .10 | .04 | .01 | | | | |
| ☐ | 119 | Dennis Lamp | .04 | .02 | .00 | | | | |
| ☐ | 120 | Ron Davis | .04 | .02 | .00 | | | | |
| ☐ | 121 | Nick Esasky | .06 | .02 | .00 | | | | |
| ☐ | 122 | Vance Law | .04 | .02 | .00 | | | | |
| ☐ | 123 | Gary Roenicke | .04 | .02 | .00 | | | | |
| ☐ | 124 | Bill Schroeder | .04 | .02 | .00 | | | | |
| ☐ | 125 | Dave Rozema | .04 | .02 | .00 | | | | |
| ☐ | 126 | Bobby Meacham | .04 | .02 | .00 | | | | |
| ☐ | 127 | Marty Barrett | .12 | .05 | .01 | | | | |
| ☐ | 128 | R.J. Reynolds | .30 | .12 | .03 | | | | |
| ☐ | 129 | Ernie Camacho (photo actually Rich Thompson) | .06 | .02 | .00 | | | | |
| ☐ | 130 | Jorge Orta | .04 | .02 | .00 | | | | |
| ☐ | 131 | Lary Sorensen | .04 | .02 | .00 | | | | |
| ☐ | 132 | Terry Francona | .06 | .02 | .00 | | | | |
| ☐ | 133 | Fred Lynn | .15 | .06 | .01 | | | | |
| ☐ | 134 | Bob Jones | .04 | .02 | .00 | | | | |
| ☐ | 135 | Jerry Hairston | .04 | .02 | .00 | | | | |
| ☐ | 136 | Kevin Bass | .08 | .03 | .01 | | | | |
| ☐ | 137 | Garry Maddox | .06 | .02 | .00 | | | | |
| ☐ | 138 | Dave LaPoint | .04 | .02 | .00 | | | | |
| ☐ | 139 | Kevin McReynolds | .15 | .06 | .01 | | | | |
| ☐ | 140 | Wayne Krenchicki | .04 | .02 | .00 | | | | |
| ☐ | 141 | Rafael Ramirez | .04 | .02 | .00 | | | | |
| ☐ | 142 | Rod Scurry | .04 | .02 | .00 | | | | |
| ☐ | 143 | Greg Minton | .06 | .02 | .00 | | | | |
| ☐ | 144 | Tim Stoddard | .04 | .02 | .00 | | | | |
| ☐ | 145 | Steve Henderson | .04 | .02 | .00 | | | | |
| ☐ | 146 | George Bell | .15 | .06 | .01 | | | | |
| ☐ | 147 | Dave Meier | .15 | .06 | .01 | | | | |
| ☐ | 148 | Sammy Stewart | .04 | .02 | .00 | | | | |
| ☐ | 149 | Mark Brouhard | .04 | .02 | .00 | | | | |
| ☐ | 150 | Larry Herndon | .04 | .02 | .00 | | | | |
| ☐ | 151 | Oil Can Boyd | .12 | .05 | .01 | | | | |
| ☐ | 152 | Brian Dayett | .04 | .02 | .00 | | | | |
| ☐ | 153 | Tom Niedenfuer | .06 | .02 | .00 | | | | |
| ☐ | 154 | Brook Jacoby | .10 | .04 | .01 | | | | |
| ☐ | 155 | Onix Concepcion | .04 | .02 | .00 | | | | |
| ☐ | 156 | Tim Conroy | .04 | .02 | .00 | | | | |
| ☐ | 157 | Joe Hesketh | .25 | .10 | .02 | | | | |
| ☐ | 158 | Brian Downing | .06 | .02 | .00 | | | | |
| ☐ | 159 | Tommy Dunbar | .04 | .02 | .00 | | | | |
| ☐ | 160 | Marc Hill | .04 | .02 | .00 | | | | |
| ☐ | 161 | Phil Garner | .04 | .02 | .00 | | | | |
| ☐ | 162 | Jerry Davis | .10 | .04 | .01 | | | | |
| ☐ | 163 | Bill Campbell | .04 | .02 | .00 | | | | |
| ☐ | 164 | John Franco | .35 | .14 | .03 | | | | |
| ☐ | 165 | Len Barker | .06 | .02 | .00 | | | | |
| ☐ | 166 | Benny Distefano | .10 | .04 | .01 | | | | |
| ☐ | 167 | George Frazier | .04 | .02 | .00 | | | | |
| ☐ | 168 | Tito Landrum | .04 | .02 | .00 | | | | |
| ☐ | 169 | Cal Ripken | .40 | .16 | .04 | | | | |
| ☐ | 170 | Cecil Cooper | .12 | .05 | .01 | | | | |
| ☐ | 171 | Alan Trammell | .15 | .06 | .01 | | | | |
| ☐ | 172 | Wade Boggs | 4.00 | 1.60 | .40 | | | | |
| ☐ | 173 | Don Baylor | .12 | .05 | .01 | | | | |
| ☐ | 174 | Pedro Guerrero | .25 | .10 | .02 | | | | |
| ☐ | 175 | Frank White | .08 | .03 | .01 | | | | |
| ☐ | 176 | Rickey Henderson | .45 | .18 | .04 | | | | |
| ☐ | 177 | Charlie Lea | .06 | .02 | .00 | | | | |
| ☐ | 178 | Pete O'Brien | .08 | .03 | .01 | | | | |
| ☐ | 179 | Doug DeCinces | .08 | .03 | .01 | | | | |
| ☐ | 180 | Ron Kittle | .15 | .06 | .01 | | | | |
| ☐ | 181 | George Hendrick | .06 | .02 | .00 | | | | |
| ☐ | 182 | Joe Niekro | .08 | .03 | .01 | | | | |

| | | | | | |
|---|---|---|---|---|---|
| ☐ | 183 | Juan Samuel | .20 | .08 | .02 |
| ☐ | 184 | Mario Soto | .08 | .03 | .01 |
| ☐ | 185 | Goose Gossage | .15 | .06 | .01 |
| ☐ | 186 | Johnny Ray | .10 | .04 | .01 |
| ☐ | 187 | Bob Brenly | .08 | .03 | .01 |
| ☐ | 188 | Craig McMurtry | .04 | .02 | .00 |
| ☐ | 189 | Leon Durham | .10 | .04 | .01 |
| ☐ | 190 | Dwight Gooden | 10.00 | 4.00 | 1.00 |
| ☐ | 191 | Barry Bonnell | .04 | .02 | .00 |
| ☐ | 192 | Tim Teufel | .06 | .02 | .00 |
| ☐ | 193 | Dave Stieb | .15 | .06 | .01 |
| ☐ | 194 | Mickey Hatcher | .04 | .02 | .00 |
| ☐ | 195 | Jesse Barfield | .15 | .06 | .01 |
| ☐ | 196 | Al Cowens | .04 | .02 | .00 |
| ☐ | 197 | Hubie Brooks | .10 | .04 | .01 |
| ☐ | 198 | Steve Trout | .04 | .02 | .00 |
| ☐ | 199 | Glenn Hubbard | .04 | .02 | .00 |
| ☐ | 200 | Bill Madlock | .10 | .04 | .01 |
| ☐ | 201 | Jeff Robinson | .10 | .04 | .01 |
| ☐ | 202 | Eric Show | .04 | .02 | .00 |
| ☐ | 203 | Dave Concepcion | .08 | .03 | .01 |
| ☐ | 204 | Ivan DeJesus | .04 | .02 | .00 |
| ☐ | 205 | Neil Allen | .06 | .02 | .00 |
| ☐ | 206 | Jerry Mumphrey | .06 | .02 | .00 |
| ☐ | 207 | Mike Brown (Angels OF) | .06 | .02 | .00 |
| ☐ | 208 | Carlton Fisk | .15 | .06 | .01 |
| ☐ | 209 | Bryn Smith | .06 | .02 | .00 |
| ☐ | 210 | Tippy Martinez | .04 | .02 | .00 |
| ☐ | 211 | Dion James | .06 | .02 | .00 |
| ☐ | 212 | Willie Hernandez | .12 | .05 | .01 |
| ☐ | 213 | Mike Easler | .06 | .02 | .00 |
| ☐ | 214 | Ron Guidry | .20 | .08 | .02 |
| ☐ | 215 | Rick Honeycutt | .06 | .02 | .00 |
| ☐ | 216 | Brett Butler | .10 | .04 | .01 |
| ☐ | 217 | Larry Gura | .06 | .02 | .00 |
| ☐ | 218 | Ray Burris | .04 | .02 | .00 |
| ☐ | 219 | Steve Rogers | .06 | .02 | .00 |
| ☐ | 220 | Frank Tanana | .06 | .02 | .00 |
| ☐ | 221 | Ned Yost | .04 | .02 | .00 |
| ☐ | 222 | Bret Saberhagen | 1.50 | .60 | .15 |
| ☐ | 223 | Mike Davis | .06 | .02 | .00 |
| ☐ | 224 | Bert Blyleven | .10 | .04 | .01 |
| ☐ | 225 | Steve Kemp | .08 | .03 | .01 |
| ☐ | 226 | Jerry Reuss | .06 | .02 | .00 |
| ☐ | 227 | Darrell Evans | .10 | .04 | .01 |
| ☐ | 228 | Wayne Gross | .04 | .02 | .00 |
| ☐ | 229 | Jim Gantner | .06 | .02 | .00 |
| ☐ | 230 | Bob Boone | .06 | .02 | .00 |
| ☐ | 231 | Lonnie Smith | .06 | .02 | .00 |
| ☐ | 232 | Frank DiPino | .04 | .02 | .00 |
| ☐ | 233 | Jerry Koosman | .06 | .02 | .00 |
| ☐ | 234 | Graig Nettles | .12 | .05 | .01 |
| ☐ | 235 | John Tudor | .12 | .05 | .01 |
| ☐ | 236 | John Rabb | .06 | .02 | .00 |
| ☐ | 237 | Rick Manning | .04 | .02 | .00 |
| ☐ | 238 | Mike Fitzgerald | .06 | .02 | .00 |
| ☐ | 239 | Gary Matthews | .06 | .02 | .00 |
| ☐ | 240 | Jim Presley | 2.00 | .80 | .20 |
| ☐ | 241 | Dave Collins | .06 | .02 | .00 |
| ☐ | 242 | Gary Gaetti | .10 | .04 | .01 |
| ☐ | 243 | Dann Bilardello | .04 | .02 | .00 |
| ☐ | 244 | Rudy Law | .04 | .02 | .00 |
| ☐ | 245 | John Lowenstein | .04 | .02 | .00 |
| ☐ | 246 | Tom Tellman | .04 | .02 | .00 |
| ☐ | 247 | Howard Johnson | .04 | .02 | .00 |
| ☐ | 248 | Ray Fontenot | .04 | .02 | .00 |
| ☐ | 249 | Tony Armas | .10 | .04 | .01 |
| ☐ | 250 | Candy Maldonado | .08 | .03 | .01 |
| ☐ | 251 | Mike Jeffcoat | .06 | .02 | .00 |
| ☐ | 252 | Dane Iorg | .04 | .02 | .00 |
| ☐ | 253 | Bruce Bochte | .06 | .02 | .00 |
| ☐ | 254 | Pete Rose | 1.50 | .60 | .15 |
| ☐ | 255 | Don Aase | .06 | .02 | .00 |
| ☐ | 256 | George Wright | .04 | .02 | .00 |
| ☐ | 257 | Britt Burns | .06 | .02 | .00 |
| ☐ | 258 | Mike Scott | .15 | .06 | .01 |
| ☐ | 259 | Len Matuszek | .04 | .02 | .00 |
| ☐ | 260 | Dave Rucker | .04 | .02 | .00 |
| ☐ | 261 | Craig Lefferts | .04 | .02 | .00 |
| ☐ | 262 | Jay Tibbs | .20 | .08 | .02 |
| ☐ | 263 | Bruce Benedict | .04 | .02 | .00 |
| ☐ | 264 | Don Robinson | .06 | .02 | .00 |
| ☐ | 265 | Gary Lavelle | .06 | .02 | .00 |
| ☐ | 266 | Scott Sanderson | .04 | .02 | .00 |
| ☐ | 267 | Matt Young | .04 | .02 | .00 |
| ☐ | 268 | Ernie Whitt | .04 | .02 | .00 |
| ☐ | 269 | Houston Jimenez | .04 | .02 | .00 |
| ☐ | 270 | Ken Dixon | .25 | .10 | .02 |
| ☐ | 271 | Peter Ladd | .04 | .02 | .00 |
| ☐ | 272 | Juan Berenguer | .04 | .02 | .00 |
| ☐ | 273 | Roger Clemens | 10.00 | 4.00 | 1.00 |
| ☐ | 274 | Rick Cerone | .04 | .02 | .00 |

| □ 275 | Dave Anderson | .04 | .02 | .00 |
|---|---|---|---|---|
| □ 276 | George Vukovich | .04 | .02 | .00 |
| □ 277 | Greg Pryor | .04 | .02 | .00 |
| □ 278 | Mike Warren | .04 | .02 | .00 |
| □ 279 | Bob James | .04 | .02 | .00 |
| □ 280 | Bobby Grich | .08 | .03 | .01 |
| □ 281 | Mike Mason | .10 | .04 | .01 |
| □ 282 | Ron Reed | .04 | .02 | .00 |
| □ 283 | Alan Ashby | .04 | .02 | .00 |
| □ 284 | Mark Thurmond | .06 | .02 | .00 |
| □ 285 | Joe Lefebvre | .04 | .02 | .00 |
| □ 286 | Ted Power | .08 | .03 | .01 |
| □ 287 | Chris Chambliss | .06 | .02 | .00 |
| □ 288 | Lee Tunnell | .04 | .02 | .00 |
| □ 289 | Rich Bordi | .04 | .02 | .00 |
| □ 290 | Glenn Brummer | .04 | .02 | .00 |
| □ 291 | Mike Boddicker | .10 | .04 | .01 |
| □ 292 | Rollie Fingers | .15 | .06 | .01 |
| □ 293 | Lou Whitaker | .15 | .06 | .01 |
| □ 294 | Dwight Evans | .10 | .04 | .01 |
| □ 295 | Don Mattingly | 12.50 | 5.00 | 1.25 |
| □ 296 | Mike Marshall | .15 | .06 | .01 |
| □ 297 | Willie Wilson | .15 | .06 | .01 |
| □ 298 | Mike Heath | .04 | .02 | .00 |
| □ 299 | Tim Raines | .25 | .10 | .02 |
| □ 300 | Larry Parrish | .06 | .02 | .00 |
| □ 301 | Geoff Zahn | .04 | .02 | .00 |
| □ 302 | Rich Dotson | .06 | .02 | .00 |
| □ 303 | David Green | .04 | .02 | .00 |
| □ 304 | Jose Cruz | .10 | .04 | .01 |
| □ 305 | Steve Carlton | .35 | .14 | .03 |
| □ 306 | Gary Redus | .06 | .02 | .00 |
| □ 307 | Steve Garvey | .35 | .14 | .03 |
| □ 308 | Jose DeLeon | .06 | .02 | .00 |
| □ 309 | Randy Lerch | .04 | .02 | .00 |
| □ 310 | Claudell Washington | .06 | .02 | .00 |
| □ 311 | Lee Smith | .08 | .03 | .01 |
| □ 312 | Darryl Strawberry | 1.50 | .60 | .15 |
| □ 313 | Jim Beattie | .04 | .02 | .00 |
| □ 314 | John Butcher | .04 | .02 | .00 |
| □ 315 | Damaso Garcia | .08 | .03 | .01 |
| □ 316 | Mike Smithson | .04 | .02 | .00 |
| □ 317 | Luis Leal | .04 | .02 | .00 |
| □ 318 | Ken Phelps | .06 | .02 | .00 |
| □ 319 | Wally Backman | .08 | .03 | .01 |
| □ 320 | Ron Cey | .10 | .04 | .01 |
| □ 321 | Brad Komminsk | .08 | .03 | .01 |
| □ 322 | Jason Thompson | .06 | .02 | .00 |
| □ 323 | Frank Williams | .10 | .04 | .01 |
| □ 324 | Tim Lollar | .04 | .02 | .00 |
| □ 325 | Eric Davis | 8.00 | 3.25 | .80 |
| □ 326 | Von Hayes | .12 | .05 | .01 |
| □ 327 | Andy Van Slyke | .08 | .03 | .01 |
| □ 328 | Craig Reynolds | .04 | .02 | .00 |
| □ 329 | Dick Schofield | .08 | .03 | .01 |
| □ 330 | Scott Fletcher | .06 | .02 | .00 |
| □ 331 | Jeff Reardon | .08 | .03 | .01 |
| □ 332 | Rick Dempsey | .06 | .02 | .00 |
| □ 333 | Ben Oglivie | .06 | .02 | .00 |
| □ 334 | Dan Petry | .12 | .05 | .01 |
| □ 335 | Jackie Gutierrez | .08 | .03 | .01 |
| □ 336 | Dave Righetti | .15 | .06 | .01 |
| □ 337 | Alejandro Pena | .06 | .02 | .00 |
| □ 338 | Mel Hall | .08 | .03 | .01 |
| □ 339 | Pat Sheridan | .04 | .02 | .00 |
| □ 340 | Keith Atherton | .04 | .02 | .00 |
| □ 341 | David Palmer | .06 | .02 | .00 |
| □ 342 | Gary Ward | .06 | .02 | .00 |
| □ 343 | Dave Stewart | .04 | .02 | .00 |
| □ 344 | Mark Gubicza | .35 | .14 | .03 |
| □ 345 | Carney Lansford | .10 | .04 | .01 |
| □ 346 | Jerry Willard | .04 | .02 | .00 |
| □ 347 | Ken Griffey | .08 | .03 | .01 |
| □ 348 | Franklin Stubbs | 1.00 | .40 | .10 |
| □ 349 | Aurelio Lopez | .04 | .02 | .00 |
| □ 350 | Al Bumbry | .04 | .02 | .00 |
| □ 351 | Charlie Moore | .04 | .02 | .00 |
| □ 352 | Luis Sanchez | .04 | .02 | .00 |
| □ 353 | Darrell Porter | .06 | .02 | .00 |
| □ 354 | Bill Dawley | .04 | .02 | .00 |
| □ 355 | Charles Hudson | .06 | .02 | .00 |
| □ 356 | Garry Templeton | .10 | .04 | .01 |
| □ 357 | Cecilio Guante | .04 | .02 | .00 |
| □ 358 | Jeff Leonard | .06 | .02 | .00 |
| □ 359 | Paul Molitor | .10 | .04 | .01 |
| □ 360 | Ron Gardenhire | .04 | .02 | .00 |
| □ 361 | Larry Bowa | .08 | .03 | .01 |
| □ 362 | Bob Kearney | .04 | .02 | .00 |
| □ 363 | Garth Iorg | .04 | .02 | .00 |
| □ 364 | Tom Brunansky | .12 | .05 | .01 |
| □ 365 | Brad Gulden | .04 | .02 | .00 |
| □ 366 | Greg Walker | .10 | .04 | .01 |
| □ 367 | Mike Young | .12 | .05 | .01 |
| □ 368 | Rick Waits | .04 | .02 | .00 |
| □ 369 | Doug Bair | .04 | .02 | .00 |
| □ 370 | Bob Shirley | .04 | .02 | .00 |
| □ 371 | Bob Ojeda | .08 | .03 | .01 |
| □ 372 | Bob Welch | .08 | .03 | .01 |
| □ 373 | Neal Heaton | .06 | .02 | .00 |
| □ 374 | Danny Jackson | .08 | .03 | .01 |
| □ 375 | Donnie Hill | .04 | .02 | .00 |
| □ 376 | Mike Stenhouse | .06 | .02 | .00 |
| □ 377 | Bruce Kison | .04 | .02 | .00 |
| □ 378 | Wayne Tolleson | .04 | .02 | .00 |
| □ 379 | Floyd Bannister | .06 | .02 | .00 |
| □ 380 | Vern Ruhle | .04 | .02 | .00 |
| □ 381 | Tim Corcoran | .04 | .02 | .00 |
| □ 382 | Kurt Kepshire | .08 | .03 | .01 |
| □ 383 | Bobby Brown | .04 | .02 | .00 |
| □ 384 | Dave Van Gorder | .04 | .02 | .00 |
| □ 385 | Rick Mahler | .04 | .02 | .00 |
| □ 386 | Lee Mazzilli | .06 | .02 | .00 |
| □ 387 | Bill Laskey | .04 | .02 | .00 |
| □ 388 | Thad Bosley | .04 | .02 | .00 |
| □ 389 | Al Chambers | .04 | .02 | .00 |
| □ 390 | Tony Fernandez | .12 | .05 | .01 |
| □ 391 | Ron Washington | .04 | .02 | .00 |
| □ 392 | Bill Swaggerty | .10 | .04 | .01 |
| □ 393 | Bob L. Gibson | .04 | .02 | .00 |
| □ 394 | Marty Castillo | .04 | .02 | .00 |
| □ 395 | Steve Crawford | .04 | .02 | .00 |
| □ 396 | Clay Christiansen | .12 | .05 | .01 |
| □ 397 | Bob Bailor | .04 | .02 | .00 |
| □ 398 | Mike Hargrove | .06 | .02 | .00 |
| □ 399 | Charlie Leibrandt | .06 | .02 | .00 |
| □ 400 | Tom Burgmeier | .04 | .02 | .00 |
| □ 401 | Razor Shines | .10 | .04 | .01 |
| □ 402 | Rob Wilfong | .04 | .02 | .00 |
| □ 403 | Tom Henke | .08 | .03 | .01 |
| □ 404 | Al Jones | .10 | .04 | .01 |
| □ 405 | Mike LaCoss | .04 | .02 | .00 |
| □ 406 | Luis DeLeon | .04 | .02 | .00 |
| □ 407 | Greg Gross | .04 | .02 | .00 |
| □ 408 | Tom Hume | .04 | .02 | .00 |
| □ 409 | Rick Camp | .04 | .02 | .00 |
| □ 410 | Milt May | .04 | .02 | .00 |
| □ 411 | Henry Cotto | .08 | .03 | .01 |
| □ 412 | David Von Ohlen | .04 | .02 | .00 |
| □ 413 | Scott McGregor | .08 | .03 | .01 |
| □ 414 | Ted Simmons | .10 | .04 | .01 |
| □ 415 | Jack Morris | .15 | .06 | .01 |
| □ 416 | Bill Buckner | .08 | .03 | .01 |
| □ 417 | Butch Wynegar | .06 | .02 | .00 |
| □ 418 | Steve Sax | .12 | .05 | .01 |
| □ 419 | Steve Balboni | .06 | .02 | .00 |
| □ 420 | Dwayne Murphy | .06 | .02 | .00 |
| □ 421 | Andre Dawson | .20 | .08 | .02 |
| □ 422 | Charlie Hough | .08 | .03 | .01 |
| □ 423 | Tommy John | .12 | .05 | .01 |
| □ 424A | Tom Seaver ERR (photo actually Floyd Bannister) | 1.25 | .50 | .12 |
| □ 424B | Tom Seaver COR | 6.00 | 2.40 | .60 |
| □ 425 | Tommy Herr | .10 | .04 | .01 |
| □ 426 | Terry Puhl | .06 | .02 | .00 |
| □ 427 | Al Holland | .04 | .02 | .00 |
| □ 428 | Eddie Milner | .04 | .02 | .00 |
| □ 429 | Terry Kennedy | .08 | .03 | .01 |
| □ 430 | John Candelaria | .08 | .03 | .01 |
| □ 431 | Manny Trillo | .06 | .02 | .00 |
| □ 432 | Ken Oberkfell | .04 | .02 | .00 |
| □ 433 | Rick Sutcliffe | .10 | .04 | .01 |
| □ 434 | Ron Darling | 1.00 | .40 | .10 |
| □ 435 | Spike Owen | .06 | .02 | .00 |
| □ 436 | Frank Viola | .08 | .03 | .01 |
| □ 437 | Lloyd Moseby | .10 | .04 | .01 |
| □ 438 | Kirby Puckett | 6.50 | 2.60 | .65 |
| □ 439 | Jim Clancy | .04 | .02 | .00 |
| □ 440 | Mike Moore | .06 | .02 | .00 |
| □ 441 | Doug Sisk | .06 | .02 | .00 |
| □ 442 | Dennis Eckersley | .06 | .02 | .00 |
| □ 443 | Gerald Perry | .06 | .02 | .00 |
| □ 444 | Dale Berra | .06 | .02 | .00 |
| □ 445 | Dusty Baker | .06 | .02 | .00 |
| □ 446 | Ed Whitson | .06 | .02 | .00 |
| □ 447 | Cesar Cedeno | .08 | .03 | .01 |
| □ 448 | Rick Schu | .20 | .08 | .02 |
| □ 449 | Joaquin Andujar | .10 | .04 | .01 |
| □ 450 | Mark Bailey | .10 | .04 | .01 |
| □ 451 | Ron Romanick | .20 | .08 | .02 |
| □ 452 | Julio Cruz | .04 | .02 | .00 |
| □ 453 | Miguel Dilone | .04 | .02 | .00 |
| □ 454 | Storm Davis | .08 | .03 | .01 |
| □ 455 | Jaime Cocanower | .08 | .03 | .01 |
| □ 456 | Barbaro Garbey | .08 | .03 | .01 |
| □ 457 | Rich Gedman | .08 | .03 | .01 |

| # | Player | | | |
|---|---|---|---|---|
| 458 | Phil Niekro | .15 | .06 | .01 |
| 459 | Mike Scioscia | .06 | .02 | .00 |
| 460 | Pat Tabler | .08 | .03 | .01 |
| 461 | Darryl Motley | .04 | .02 | .00 |
| 462 | Chris Codiroli | .04 | .02 | .00 |
| 463 | Doug Flynn | .04 | .02 | .00 |
| 464 | Billy Sample | .04 | .02 | .00 |
| 465 | Mickey Rivers | .06 | .02 | .00 |
| 466 | John Wathan | .04 | .02 | .00 |
| 467 | Bill Krueger | .04 | .02 | .00 |
| 468 | Andre Thornton | .06 | .02 | .00 |
| 469 | Rex Hudler | .10 | .04 | .01 |
| 470 | Sid Bream | .35 | .14 | .03 |
| 471 | Kirk Gibson | .20 | .08 | .02 |
| 472 | John Shelby | .04 | .02 | .00 |
| 473 | Moose Haas | .06 | .02 | .00 |
| 474 | Doug Corbett | .04 | .02 | .00 |
| 475 | Willie McGee | .35 | .14 | .03 |
| 476 | Bob Knepper | .08 | .03 | .01 |
| 477 | Kevin Gross | .04 | .02 | .00 |
| 478 | Carmelo Martinez | .08 | .03 | .01 |
| 479 | Kent Tekulve | .06 | .02 | .00 |
| 480 | Chili Davis | .08 | .03 | .01 |
| 481 | Bobby Clark | .04 | .02 | .00 |
| 482 | Mookie Wilson | .06 | .02 | .00 |
| 483 | Dave Owen | .08 | .03 | .01 |
| 484 | Ed Nunez | .06 | .02 | .00 |
| 485 | Rance Mulliniks | .04 | .02 | .00 |
| 486 | Ken Schrom | .06 | .02 | .00 |
| 487 | Jeff Russell | .04 | .02 | .00 |
| 488 | Tom Paciorek | .04 | .02 | .00 |
| 489 | Dan Ford | .04 | .02 | .00 |
| 490 | Mike Caldwell | .06 | .02 | .00 |
| 491 | Scottie Earl | .08 | .03 | .01 |
| 492 | Jose Rijo | .30 | .12 | .03 |
| 493 | Bruce Hurst | .08 | .03 | .01 |
| 494 | Ken Landreaux | .06 | .02 | .00 |
| 495 | Mike Fischlin | .04 | .02 | .00 |
| 496 | Don Slaught | .04 | .02 | .00 |
| 497 | Steve McCatty | .04 | .02 | .00 |
| 498 | Gary Lucas | .04 | .02 | .00 |
| 499 | Gary Pettis | .08 | .03 | .01 |
| 500 | Marvis Foley | .04 | .02 | .00 |
| 501 | Mike Squires | .04 | .02 | .00 |
| 502 | Jim Pankovitz | .08 | .03 | .01 |
| 503 | Luis Aguayo | .04 | .02 | .00 |
| 504 | Ralph Citarella | .08 | .03 | .01 |
| 505 | Bruce Bochy | .04 | .02 | .00 |
| 506 | Bob Owchinko | .04 | .02 | .00 |
| 507 | Pascual Perez | .04 | .02 | .00 |
| 508 | Lee Lacy | .06 | .02 | .00 |
| 509 | Atlee Hammaker | .06 | .02 | .00 |
| 510 | Bob Dernier | .06 | .02 | .00 |
| 511 | Ed VandeBerg | .04 | .02 | .00 |
| 512 | Cliff Johnson | .04 | .02 | .00 |
| 513 | Len Whitehouse | .04 | .02 | .00 |
| 514 | Dennis Martinez | .04 | .02 | .00 |
| 515 | Ed Romero | .04 | .02 | .00 |
| 516 | Rusty Kuntz | .04 | .02 | .00 |
| 517 | Rick Miller | .04 | .02 | .00 |
| 518 | Dennis Rasmussen | .08 | .03 | .01 |
| 519 | Steve Yeager | .06 | .02 | .00 |
| 520 | Chris Bando | .04 | .02 | .00 |
| 521 | U.L. Washington | .04 | .02 | .00 |
| 522 | Curt Young | .08 | .03 | .01 |
| 523 | Angel Salazar | .06 | .02 | .00 |
| 524 | Curt Kaufman | .08 | .03 | .01 |
| 525 | Odell Jones | .04 | .02 | .00 |
| 526 | Juan Agosto | .04 | .02 | .00 |
| 527 | Denny Walling | .04 | .02 | .00 |
| 528 | Andy Hawkins | .06 | .02 | .00 |
| 529 | Sixto Lezcano | .04 | .02 | .00 |
| 530 | Skeeter Barnes | .06 | .02 | .00 |
| 531 | Randy Johnson | .04 | .02 | .00 |
| 532 | Jim Morrison | .04 | .02 | .00 |
| 533 | Warren Brusstar | .04 | .02 | .00 |
| 534A | Jeff Pendleton ERR (wrong first name) | .30 | .12 | .03 |
| 534B | Terry Pendleton COR | 2.25 | .90 | .22 |
| 535 | Vic Rodriguez | .10 | .04 | .01 |
| 536 | Bob McClure | .04 | .02 | .00 |
| 537 | Dave Bergman | .04 | .02 | .00 |
| 538 | Mark Clear | .04 | .02 | .00 |
| 539 | Mike Pagliarulo | 2.00 | .80 | .20 |
| 540 | Terry Whitfield | .04 | .02 | .00 |
| 541 | Joe Beckwith | .04 | .02 | .00 |
| 542 | Jeff Burroughs | .04 | .02 | .00 |
| 543 | Dan Schatzeder | .04 | .02 | .00 |
| 544 | Donnie Scott | .06 | .02 | .00 |
| 545 | Jim Slaton | .04 | .02 | .00 |
| 546 | Greg Luzinski | .10 | .04 | .01 |
| 547 | Mark Salas | .25 | .10 | .02 |
| 548 | Dave Smith | .08 | .03 | .01 |
| 549 | John Wockenfuss | .04 | .02 | .00 |
| 550 | Frank Pastore | .04 | .02 | .00 |
| 551 | Tim Flannery | .04 | .02 | .00 |
| 552 | Rick Rhoden | .08 | .03 | .01 |
| 553 | Mark Davis | .06 | .02 | .00 |
| 554 | Jeff Dedmon | .08 | .03 | .01 |
| 555 | Gary Woods | .04 | .02 | .00 |
| 556 | Danny Heep | .04 | .02 | .00 |
| 557 | Mark Langston | .45 | .18 | .04 |
| 558 | Darrell Brown | .04 | .02 | .00 |
| 559 | Jimmy Key | .45 | .18 | .04 |
| 560 | Rick Lysander | .04 | .02 | .00 |
| 561 | Doyle Alexander | .06 | .02 | .00 |
| 562 | Mike Stanton | .04 | .02 | .00 |
| 563 | Sid Fernandez | 1.00 | .40 | .10 |
| 564 | Richie Hebner | .04 | .02 | .00 |
| 565 | Alex Trevino | .04 | .02 | .00 |
| 566 | Brian Harper | .04 | .02 | .00 |
| 567 | Dan Gladden | .25 | .10 | .02 |
| 568 | Luis Salazar | .04 | .02 | .00 |
| 569 | Tom Foley | .04 | .02 | .00 |
| 570 | Larry Andersen | .04 | .02 | .00 |
| 571 | Danny Cox | .08 | .03 | .01 |
| 572 | Joe Sambito | .06 | .02 | .00 |
| 573 | Juan Beniquez | .06 | .02 | .00 |
| 574 | Joel Skinner | .06 | .02 | .00 |
| 575 | Randy St.Claire | .10 | .04 | .01 |
| 576 | Floyd Rayford | .04 | .02 | .00 |
| 577 | Roy Howell | .04 | .02 | .00 |
| 578 | John Grubb | .04 | .02 | .00 |
| 579 | Ed Jurak | .04 | .02 | .00 |
| 580 | John Montefusco | .06 | .02 | .00 |
| 581 | Orel Hershiser | 2.50 | 1.00 | .25 |
| 582 | Tom Waddell | .10 | .04 | .01 |
| 583 | Mark Huismann | .04 | .02 | .00 |
| 584 | Joe Morgan | .15 | .06 | .01 |
| 585 | Jim Wohlford | .04 | .02 | .00 |
| 586 | Dave Schmidt | .04 | .02 | .00 |
| 587 | Jeff Kunkel | .08 | .03 | .01 |
| 588 | Hal McRae | .06 | .02 | .00 |
| 589 | Bill Almon | .04 | .02 | .00 |
| 590 | Carmen Castillo | .04 | .02 | .00 |
| 591 | Omar Moreno | .04 | .02 | .00 |
| 592 | Ken Howell | .25 | .10 | .02 |
| 593 | Tom Brookens | .04 | .02 | .00 |
| 594 | Joe Nolan | .04 | .02 | .00 |
| 595 | Willie Lozado | .10 | .04 | .01 |
| 596 | Tom Nieto | .06 | .02 | .00 |
| 597 | Walt Terrell | .04 | .02 | .00 |
| 598 | Al Oliver | .10 | .04 | .01 |
| 599 | Shane Rawley | .06 | .02 | .00 |
| 600 | Denny Gonzalez | .08 | .03 | .01 |
| 601 | Mark Grant | .08 | .03 | .01 |
| 602 | Mike Armstrong | .04 | .02 | .00 |
| 603 | George Foster | .12 | .05 | .01 |
| 604 | Davey Lopes | .06 | .02 | .00 |
| 605 | Salome Barojas | .04 | .02 | .00 |
| 606 | Roy Lee Jackson | .04 | .02 | .00 |
| 607 | Pete Filson | .04 | .02 | .00 |
| 608 | Duane Walker | .04 | .02 | .00 |
| 609 | Glenn Wilson | .08 | .03 | .01 |
| 610 | Rafael Santana | .08 | .03 | .01 |
| 611 | Roy Smith | .08 | .03 | .01 |
| 612 | Ruppert Jones | .04 | .02 | .00 |
| 613 | Joe Cowley | .06 | .02 | .00 |
| 614 | Al Nipper (photo actually Mike Brown) | .25 | .10 | .02 |
| 615 | Gene Nelson | .04 | .02 | .00 |
| 616 | Joe Carter | .75 | .30 | .07 |
| 617 | Ray Knight | .10 | .04 | .01 |
| 618 | Chuck Rainey | .04 | .02 | .00 |
| 619 | Dan Driessen | .04 | .02 | .00 |
| 620 | Daryl Sconiers | .04 | .02 | .00 |
| 621 | Bill Stein | .04 | .02 | .00 |
| 622 | Roy Smalley | .06 | .02 | .00 |
| 623 | Ed Lynch | .04 | .02 | .00 |
| 624 | Jeff Stone | .25 | .10 | .02 |
| 625 | Bruce Berenyi | .04 | .02 | .00 |
| 626 | Kelvin Chapman | .08 | .03 | .01 |
| 627 | Joe Price | .04 | .02 | .00 |
| 628 | Steve Bedrosian | .06 | .02 | .00 |
| 629 | Vic Mata | .10 | .04 | .01 |
| 630 | Mike Krukow | .08 | .03 | .01 |
| 631 | Phil Bradley | 1.75 | .70 | .17 |
| 632 | Jim Gott | .04 | .02 | .00 |
| 633 | Randy Bush | .04 | .02 | .00 |
| 634 | Tom Browning | 1.00 | .40 | .10 |
| 635 | Lou Gehrig Puzzle Card | .06 | .02 | .00 |
| 636 | Reid Nichols | .04 | .02 | .00 |
| 637 | Dan Pasqua | 2.50 | 1.00 | .25 |
| 638 | German Rivera | .10 | .04 | .01 |

| | | MINT | VG-E | F-G |
|---|---|---|---|---|
| ☐ 639 | Don Schulze | .08 | .03 | .01 |
| ☐ 640A | Mike Jones (Career Highlights, five lines) | .15 | .06 | .01 |
| ☐ 640B | Mike Jones (Career Highlights, four lines) | .15 | .06 | .01 |
| ☐ 641 | Pete Rose | 1.00 | .40 | .10 |
| ☐ 642 | Wade Rowdon | .10 | .04 | .01 |
| ☐ 643 | Jerry Narron | .04 | .02 | .00 |
| ☐ 644 | Darrell Miller | .15 | .06 | .01 |
| ☐ 645 | Tim Hulett | .20 | .08 | .02 |
| ☐ 646 | Andy McGaffigan | .04 | .02 | .00 |
| ☐ 647 | Kurt Bevacqua | .04 | .02 | .00 |
| ☐ 648 | John Russell | .20 | .08 | .02 |
| ☐ 649 | Ron Robinson | .20 | .08 | .02 |
| ☐ 650 | Donnie Moore | .06 | .02 | .00 |
| ☐ 651A | Two for the Title Dave Winfield Don Mattingly (yellow letters) | 2.50 | 1.00 | .25 |
| ☐ 651B | Two for the Title Dave Winfield Don Mattingly (white letters) | 6.00 | 2.40 | .60 |
| ☐ 652 | Tim Laudner | .04 | .02 | .00 |
| ☐ 653 | Steve Farr | .10 | .04 | .01 |
| ☐ 654 | DK Checklist 1-26 (unnumbered) | .09 | .01 | .00 |
| ☐ 655 | Checklist 27-130 (unnumbered) | .07 | .01 | .00 |
| ☐ 656 | Checklist 131-234 (unnumbered) | .07 | .01 | .00 |
| ☐ 657 | Checklist 235-338 (unnumbered) | .07 | .01 | .00 |
| ☐ 658 | Checklist 339-442 (unnumbered) | .07 | .01 | .00 |
| ☐ 659 | Checklist 443-546 (unnumbered) | .07 | .01 | .00 |
| ☐ 660 | Checklist 547-653 (unnumbered) | .07 | .01 | .00 |
| ☐ PC1 | Dwight Gooden (wax pack box card) | 4.00 | 1.60 | .40 |
| ☐ PC2 | Ryne Sandberg (wax pack box card) | .50 | .20 | .05 |
| ☐ PC3 | Ron Kittle (wax pack box card) | .20 | .08 | .02 |
| ☐ PUZ | Lou Gehrig Puzzle Card (wax pack box card) | .06 | .02 | .00 |

## 1985 Donruss Super DK's

The cards in this 28 card set measure 4 15/16 by 6 3/4". The 1985 Donruss Diamond Kings Supers set contains enlarged cards of the first 26 cards of the Donruss regular set of this year. In addition, the Diamond Kings checklist card, a card of artist Dick Perez, and a Lou Gehrig puzzle card are included in the set. The set was the brain-child of the Perez-Steele Galleries and could be obtained via a write-in offer on the wrappers of the Donruss regular cards of this year. The Gehrig puzzle card is actually a 12-piece jigsaw puzzle. The back of the checklist card is blank; however, the Dick Perez card back gives a short history of Dick Perez and the Perez-Steele Galleries. The offer for obtaining this set was detailed on the wax pack wrappers; three wrappers plus 9.00 was required for this mail-in offer.

| | | MINT | VG-E | F-G |
|---|---|---|---|---|
| COMPLETE SET (28) | | 10.00 | 4.00 | 1.00 |
| COMMON PLAYER (1-26) | | .20 | .08 | .02 |
| ☐ 1 | Ryne Sandberg | .90 | .36 | .09 |
| ☐ 2 | Doug DeCinces | .20 | .08 | .02 |
| ☐ 3 | Richard Dotson | .20 | .08 | .02 |
| ☐ 4 | Bert Blyleven | .30 | .12 | .03 |
| ☐ 5 | Lou Whitaker | .30 | .12 | .03 |
| ☐ 6 | Dan Quisenberry | .30 | .12 | .03 |
| ☐ 7 | Don Mattingly | 4.00 | 1.60 | .40 |
| ☐ 8 | Carney Lansford | .30 | .12 | .03 |

| | | MINT | VG-E | F-G |
|---|---|---|---|---|
| ☐ 9 | Frank Tanana | .20 | .08 | .02 |
| ☐ 10 | Willie Upshaw | .20 | .08 | .02 |
| ☐ 11 | Claudell Washington | .20 | .08 | .02 |
| ☐ 12 | Mike Marshall | .25 | .10 | .02 |
| ☐ 13 | Joaquin Andujar | .20 | .08 | .02 |
| ☐ 14 | Cal Ripken | 1.25 | .50 | .12 |
| ☐ 15 | Jim Rice | .75 | .30 | .07 |
| ☐ 16 | Don Sutton | .40 | .16 | .04 |
| ☐ 17 | Frank Viola | .20 | .08 | .02 |
| ☐ 18 | Alvin Davis | .75 | .30 | .07 |
| ☐ 19 | Mario Soto | .20 | .08 | .02 |
| ☐ 20 | Jose Cruz | .20 | .08 | .02 |
| ☐ 21 | Charlie Lea | .20 | .08 | .02 |
| ☐ 22 | Jesse Orosco | .20 | .08 | .02 |
| ☐ 23 | Juan Samuel | .45 | .18 | .04 |
| ☐ 24 | Tony Pena | .25 | .10 | .02 |
| ☐ 25 | Tony Gwynn | 1.00 | .40 | .10 |
| ☐ 26 | Bob Brenly | .20 | .08 | .02 |
| ☐ 27 | Checklist card (unnumbered) | .10 | .01 | .00 |
| ☐ 28 | Dick Perez (unnumbered) (History of DK's) | .10 | .04 | .01 |

## 1985 Donruss Action All Stars

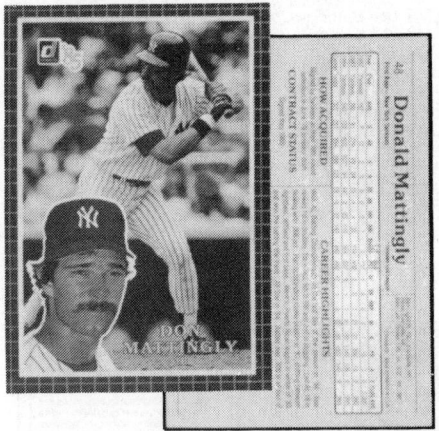

The cards in this 60 card set measure 3 1/2" by 5". For the third year in a row, Donruss issued a set of Action All-Stars. This set features action photos on the obverse which also contains a portrait inset of the player. The backs, unlike the year before, do not contain a full color picture of the player but list, if space is available, full statistical data, biographical data, career highlights, and acquisition and contract status. The cards were issued with a Lou Gehrig puzzle card.

| | | MINT | VG-E | F-G |
|---|---|---|---|---|
| COMPLETE SET | | 5.50 | 2.00 | .50 |
| COMMON PLAYER | | .05 | .02 | .00 |
| ☐ 1 | Tim Raines | .30 | .12 | .03 |
| ☐ 2 | Jim Gantner | .05 | .02 | .00 |
| ☐ 3 | Mario Soto | .05 | .02 | .00 |
| ☐ 4 | Spike Owen | .05 | .02 | .00 |
| ☐ 5 | Lloyd Moseby | .10 | .04 | .01 |
| ☐ 6 | Damaso Garcia | .05 | .02 | .00 |
| ☐ 7 | Cal Ripken | .35 | .14 | .03 |
| ☐ 8 | Dan Quisenberry | .15 | .06 | .01 |
| ☐ 9 | Eddie Murray | .40 | .16 | .04 |
| ☐ 10 | Tony Pena | .10 | .04 | .01 |
| ☐ 11 | Buddy Bell | .10 | .04 | .01 |
| ☐ 12 | Dave Winfield | .30 | .12 | .03 |
| ☐ 13 | Ron Kittle | .20 | .08 | .02 |
| ☐ 14 | Rich Gossage | .15 | .06 | .01 |
| ☐ 15 | Dwight Evans | .10 | .04 | .01 |
| ☐ 16 | Alvin Davis | .20 | .08 | .02 |
| ☐ 17 | Mike Schmidt | .50 | .20 | .05 |
| ☐ 18 | Pascual Perez | .05 | .02 | .00 |

| | | MINT | VG-E | F-G |
|---|---|---|---|---|
| ☐ 19 | Tony Gwynn | .40 | .16 | .04 |
| ☐ 20 | Nolan Ryan | .35 | .14 | .03 |
| ☐ 21 | Robin Yount | .25 | .10 | .02 |
| ☐ 22 | Mike Marshall | .15 | .06 | .01 |
| ☐ 23 | Brett Butler | .10 | .04 | .01 |
| ☐ 24 | Ryne Sandberg | .35 | .14 | .03 |
| ☐ 25 | Dale Murphy | .60 | .24 | .06 |
| ☐ 26 | George Brett | .50 | .20 | .05 |
| ☐ 27 | Jim Rice | .35 | .14 | .03 |
| ☐ 28 | Ozzie Smith | .15 | .06 | .01 |
| ☐ 29 | Larry Parrish | .05 | .02 | .00 |
| ☐ 30 | Jack Clark | .10 | .04 | .01 |
| ☐ 31 | Manny Trillo | .05 | .02 | .00 |
| ☐ 32 | Dave Kingman | .10 | .04 | .01 |
| ☐ 33 | Geoff Zahn | .05 | .02 | .00 |
| ☐ 34 | Pedro Guerrero | .20 | .08 | .02 |
| ☐ 35 | Dave Parker | .20 | .08 | .02 |
| ☐ 36 | Rollie Fingers | .15 | .06 | .01 |
| ☐ 37 | Fernando Valenzuela | .25 | .10 | .02 |
| ☐ 38 | Wade Boggs | .90 | .36 | .09 |
| ☐ 39 | Reggie Jackson | .60 | .24 | .06 |
| ☐ 40 | Kent Hrbek | .25 | .10 | .02 |
| ☐ 41 | Keith Hernandez | .20 | .08 | .02 |
| ☐ 42 | Lou Whitaker | .15 | .06 | .01 |
| ☐ 43 | Tom Herr | .05 | .02 | .00 |
| ☐ 44 | Alan Trammell | .15 | .06 | .01 |
| ☐ 45 | Butch Wynegar | .05 | .02 | .00 |
| ☐ 46 | Leon Durham | .05 | .02 | .00 |
| ☐ 47 | Dwight Gooden | 1.25 | .50 | .12 |
| ☐ 48 | Don Mattingly | 1.50 | .60 | .15 |
| ☐ 49 | Phil Niekro | .20 | .08 | .02 |
| ☐ 50 | Johnny Ray | .10 | .04 | .01 |
| ☐ 51 | Doug DeCinces | .10 | .04 | .01 |
| ☐ 52 | Willie Upshaw | .07 | .03 | .01 |
| ☐ 53 | Lance Parrish | .20 | .08 | .02 |
| ☐ 54 | Jody Davis | .07 | .03 | .01 |
| ☐ 55 | Steve Carlton | .35 | .14 | .03 |
| ☐ 56 | Juan Samuel | .15 | .06 | .01 |
| ☐ 57 | Gary Carter | .35 | .14 | .03 |
| ☐ 58 | Harold Baines | .20 | .08 | .02 |
| ☐ 59 | Eric Show | .05 | .02 | .00 |
| ☐ 60 | Checklist card | .10 | .01 | .00 |

## 1985 Donruss Highlights

**Dale Murphy**

**National League Player of the Month April**

Before the '85 National League season was even one month old, fans were fitting Dale Murphy for a place in the record books alongside Hack Wilson who, in '30 set National League records of 56 homers and 190 RBI. The reason for such lofty comparisons was obvious. Murphy tied a major league record for most RBI in one month with 29 in April of '85. In addition, the Atlanta Braves' perennial All-Star centerfielder and two-time winner of the Most Valuable Player Award, hit nine homers. His batting average for the month was .380, including 8 doubles, 62 total bases and 17 runs scored in just 19 games. Along with his offensive stats, Murphy kept his consecutive games playing streak going through 515 entering May.

DALE MURPHY
PLAYER OF THE MONTH—APRIL

NO. 5

© 1985 LEAF-DONRUSS          MADE & PRINTED IN U.S.A.

This 56 card set features the players and pitchers of the month for each league as well as a number of highlight cards commemorating the 1985 season. The Donruss Company dedicated the last two cards to their own selections for Rookies of the Year (ROY). This set proved to be much more popular than the Donruss Company had predicted as their first and only print run was exhausted even before card dealers' initial orders were filled.

| | | MINT | VG-E | F-G |
|---|---|---|---|---|
| COMPLETE SET | | 20.00 | 8.00 | 2.00 |
| COMMON PLAYER | | .10 | .04 | .01 |
| ☐ 1 | Tom Seaver: Sets Opening Day Record | .50 | .20 | .05 |
| ☐ 2 | Rollie Fingers: Sets AL Save Mark | .20 | .08 | .02 |
| ☐ 3 | Mike Davis: AL Player April | .10 | .04 | .01 |

| | | MINT | VG-E | F-G |
|---|---|---|---|---|
| ☐ 4 | Charlie Leibrandt: AL Pitcher April | .10 | .04 | .01 |
| ☐ 5 | Dale Murphy: NL Player April | 1.00 | .40 | .10 |
| ☐ 6 | Fernando Valenzuela: NL Pitcher April | .50 | .20 | .05 |
| ☐ 7 | Larry Bowa: NL Shortstop Record | .15 | .06 | .01 |
| ☐ 8 | Dave Concepcion: Joins Reds' 2000 Hit Club | .10 | .04 | .01 |
| ☐ 9 | Tony Perez: Eldest Grand Slammer | .20 | .08 | .02 |
| ☐ 10 | Pete Rose: NL Career Run Leader | 2.00 | .80 | .20 |
| ☐ 11 | George Brett: AL Player May | 1.00 | .40 | .10 |
| ☐ 12 | Dave Stieb: AL Pitcher May | .20 | .08 | .02 |
| ☐ 13 | Dave Parker: NL Player May | .30 | .12 | .03 |
| ☐ 14 | Andy Hawkins: NL Pitcher May | .10 | .04 | .01 |
| ☐ 15 | Andy Hawkins: Records 11th Straight Win | .10 | .04 | .01 |
| ☐ 16 | Von Hayes: Two Homers in First Inning | .20 | .08 | .02 |
| ☐ 17 | Rickey Henderson: AL Player June | 1.00 | .40 | .10 |
| ☐ 18 | Jay Howell: AL Pitcher June | .10 | .04 | .01 |
| ☐ 19 | Pedro Guerrero: NL Player June | .30 | .12 | .03 |
| ☐ 20 | John Tudor: NL Pitcher June | .20 | .08 | .02 |
| ☐ 21 | Hernandez/Carter: Marathon Game Iron Men | .50 | .20 | .05 |
| ☐ 22 | Nolan Ryan: Records 4000th K | .60 | .24 | .06 |
| ☐ 23 | LaMarr Hoyt: All-Star Game MVP | .10 | .04 | .01 |
| ☐ 24 | Oddibe McDowell: 1st Ranger to Hit for Cycle | .90 | .36 | .09 |
| ☐ 25 | George Brett: AL Player July | 1.00 | .40 | .10 |
| ☐ 26 | Bret Saberhagen: AL Pitcher July | .60 | .24 | .06 |
| ☐ 27 | Keith Hernandez: NL Player July | .40 | .16 | .04 |
| ☐ 28 | Fernando Valenzuela: NL Pitcher July | .50 | .20 | .05 |
| ☐ 29 | McGee/Coleman: Record Setting Base Stealers | 1.25 | .50 | .12 |
| ☐ 30 | Tom Seaver: Notches 300th Career Win | .50 | .20 | .05 |
| ☐ 31 | Rod Carew: Strokes 3000th Hit | .50 | .20 | .05 |
| ☐ 32 | Dwight Gooden: Establishes Met Record | 2.50 | 1.00 | .25 |
| ☐ 33 | Dwight Gooden: Achieves Strikeout Milestone | 2.50 | 1.00 | .25 |
| ☐ 34 | Eddie Murray: Explodes for 9 RBI | 1.00 | .40 | .10 |
| ☐ 35 | Don Baylor: AL Career HBP Leader | .20 | .08 | .02 |
| ☐ 36 | Don Mattingly: AL Player August | 3.00 | 1.20 | .30 |
| ☐ 37 | Dave Righetti: AL Pitcher August | .20 | .08 | .02 |
| ☐ 38 | Willie McGee: NL Player August | .30 | .12 | .03 |
| ☐ 39 | Shane Rawley: NL Pitcher August | .10 | .04 | .01 |
| ☐ 40 | Pete Rose: Ty-Breaking Hit | 2.00 | .80 | .20 |
| ☐ 41 | Andre Dawson: Hits 3 HR's Drives in 8 Runs | .30 | .12 | .03 |
| ☐ 42 | Rickey Henderson: Sets Yankee Theft Mark | 1.00 | .40 | .10 |
| ☐ 43 | Tom Browning: 20 Wins in Rookie Season | .30 | .12 | .03 |
| ☐ 44 | Don Mattingly: Yankee Milestone for Hits | 3.00 | 1.20 | .30 |
| ☐ 45 | Don Mattingly: AL Player September | 3.00 | 1.20 | .30 |
| ☐ 46 | Charlie Leibrandt: AL Pitcher September | .10 | .04 | .01 |
| ☐ 47 | Gary Carter: NL Player September | .50 | .20 | .05 |
| ☐ 48 | Dwight Gooden: NL Pitcher for September | 2.50 | 1.00 | .25 |
| ☐ 49 | Wade Boggs: Major League Record Setter | 2.50 | 1.00 | .25 |

| | | | | |
|---|---|---|---|---|
| ☐ 50 | Phil Niekro: Hurls .............. Shutout for 300th Win | .30 | .12 | .03 |
| ☐ 51 | Darrell Evans: .................. Venerable HR King | .10 | .04 | .01 |
| ☐ 52 | Willie McGee: NL ............... Switch-Hitting Record | .30 | .12 | .03 |
| ☐ 53 | Dave Winfield: ................. Equals DiMaggio Feat | .50 | .20 | .05 |
| ☐ 54 | Vince Coleman: ................ Donruss NL ROY | 3.00 | 1.20 | .30 |
| ☐ 55 | Ozzie Guillen: .................. Donruss AL ROY | .50 | .20 | .05 |
| ☐ 56 | Checklist card ................... (unnumbered) | .10 | .01 | .00 |

## 1986 Donruss

ROBIN YOUNT SS

The cards in this 660 card set measure 2 1/2" by 3 1/2". The 1986 Donruss regular issue cards have fronts that feature blue borders. The fronts contain the standard team logo, player's name, position, and Donruss logo. The cards were distributed with puzzle pieces from a Dick Perez rendition of Hank Aaron. The first 26 cards of the set are Diamond Kings (DK), for the fifth year in a row; the artwork on the Diamond Kings was again produced by the Perez-Steele Galleries. Cards 27-46 again feature Rated Rookies (RR); Danny Tartabull is included in this subset for the second year in a row. The unnumbered checklist cards are arbitrarily numbered below as numbers 654 through 660. The boxes in which the wax packs were contained feature four baseball cards, with backs. The price of the set below does not include these cards; however, these cards are priced at the end of the set below.

| | | MINT | VG-E | F-G |
|---|---|---|---|---|
| | COMPLETE SET ........................ | 40.00 | 16.00 | 4.00 |
| | COMMON PLAYER ...................... | .03 | .01 | .00 |

| | | | | |
|---|---|---|---|---|
| ☐ 1 | Kirk Gibson DK ............... | .25 | .10 | .02 |
| ☐ 2 | Goose Gossage DK ......... | .15 | .06 | .01 |
| ☐ 3 | Willie McGee DK .............. | .20 | .08 | .02 |
| ☐ 4 | George Bell DK ............... | .15 | .06 | .01 |
| ☐ 5 | Tony Armas DK ............... | .10 | .04 | .01 |
| ☐ 6 | Chili Davis DK ................ | .08 | .03 | .01 |
| ☐ 7 | Cecil Cooper DK ............. | .12 | .05 | .01 |
| ☐ 8 | Mike Boddicker DK .......... | .10 | .04 | .01 |
| ☐ 9 | Davey Lopes DK ............. | .08 | .03 | .01 |
| ☐ 10 | Bill Doran DK ................. | .10 | .04 | .01 |
| ☐ 11 | Bret Saberhagen DK ....... | .25 | .10 | .02 |
| ☐ 12 | Brett Butler DK .............. | .10 | .04 | .01 |
| ☐ 13 | Harold Baines DK ........... | .20 | .08 | .02 |
| ☐ 14 | Mike Davis DK ............... | .10 | .04 | .01 |
| ☐ 15 | Tony Perez DK ............... | .12 | .05 | .01 |
| ☐ 16 | Willie Randolph DK ......... | .08 | .03 | .01 |
| ☐ 17 | Bob Boone DK ............... | .08 | .03 | .01 |
| ☐ 18 | Orel Hershiser DK ........... | .30 | .12 | .03 |
| ☐ 19 | Johnny Ray DK ............... | .10 | .04 | .01 |

| | | | | |
|---|---|---|---|---|
| ☐ 20 | Gary Ward DK ................. | .08 | .03 | .01 |
| ☐ 21 | Rick Mahler DK ............... | .06 | .02 | .00 |
| ☐ 22 | Phil Bradley DK .............. | .25 | .10 | .02 |
| ☐ 23 | Jerry Koosman DK ......... | .08 | .03 | .01 |
| ☐ 24 | Tom Brunansky DK .......... | .12 | .05 | .01 |
| ☐ 25 | Andre Dawson DK ........... | .20 | .08 | .02 |
| ☐ 26 | Dwight Gooden DK ......... | 1.25 | .50 | .12 |
| ☐ 27 | Kal Daniels RR ............... | .50 | .20 | .05 |
| ☐ 28 | Fred McGriff RR ............. | .10 | .04 | .01 |
| ☐ 29 | Cory Snyder RR .............. | 2.00 | .80 | .20 |
| ☐ 30 | Jose Guzman RR .............. | .25 | .10 | .02 |
| ☐ 31 | Ty Gainey RR .................. | .20 | .08 | .02 |
| ☐ 32 | Johnny Abrego RR ........... | .10 | .04 | .01 |
| ☐ 33 | Andres Galarraga RR ...... | .35 | .14 | .03 |
| ☐ 34 | Dave Shipanoff RR ........... | .15 | .06 | .01 |
| ☐ 35 | Mark McLemore RR ....... | .15 | .06 | .01 |
| ☐ 36 | Marty Clary RR .............. | .10 | .04 | .01 |
| ☐ 37 | Paul O'Neill RR .............. | .20 | .08 | .02 |
| ☐ 38 | Danny Tartabull RR ........ | .60 | .24 | .06 |
| ☐ 39 | Jose Canseco RR .......... | 9.00 | 3.75 | .90 |
| ☐ 40 | Juan Nieves RR .............. | .35 | .14 | .03 |
| ☐ 41 | Lance McCullers RR ....... | .25 | .10 | .02 |
| ☐ 42 | Rick Surhoff RR .............. | .10 | .04 | .01 |
| ☐ 43 | Todd Worrell RR ............. | 1.25 | .50 | .12 |
| ☐ 44 | Bob Kipper RR ............... | .20 | .08 | .02 |
| ☐ 45 | John Habyan RR ............. | .15 | .06 | .01 |
| ☐ 46 | Mike Woodard RR ........... | .10 | .04 | .01 |
| ☐ 47 | Mike Boddicker ............... | .08 | .03 | .01 |
| ☐ 48 | Robin Yount ................... | .25 | .10 | .02 |
| ☐ 49 | Lou Whitaker ................. | .15 | .06 | .01 |
| ☐ 50 | Oil Can Boyd ................. | .08 | .03 | .01 |
| ☐ 51 | Rickey Henderson .......... | .35 | .14 | .03 |
| ☐ 52 | Mike Marshall ................ | .12 | .05 | .01 |
| ☐ 53 | George Brett ................. | .40 | .16 | .04 |
| ☐ 54 | Dave Kingman ............... | .12 | .05 | .01 |
| ☐ 55 | Hubie Brooks ................. | .10 | .04 | .01 |
| ☐ 56 | Oddibe McDowell ............ | .45 | .18 | .04 |
| ☐ 57 | Doug DeCinces ............... | .08 | .03 | .01 |
| ☐ 58 | Britt Burns ................... | .06 | .02 | .00 |
| ☐ 59 | Ozzie Smith ................... | .10 | .04 | .01 |
| ☐ 60 | Jose Cruz ...................... | .10 | .04 | .01 |
| ☐ 61 | Mike Schmidt ................. | 1.00 | .40 | .10 |
| ☐ 62 | Pete Rose ...................... | 1.00 | .40 | .10 |
| ☐ 63 | Steve Garvey ................. | .35 | .14 | .03 |
| ☐ 64 | Tony Pena ...................... | .10 | .04 | .01 |
| ☐ 65 | Chili Davis ..................... | .08 | .03 | .01 |
| ☐ 66 | Dale Murphy ................... | .60 | .24 | .06 |
| ☐ 67 | Ryne Sandberg ............... | .35 | .14 | .03 |
| ☐ 68 | Gary Carter ................... | .30 | .12 | .03 |
| ☐ 69 | Alvin Davis .................... | .12 | .05 | .01 |
| ☐ 70 | Kent Hrbek .................... | .15 | .06 | .01 |
| ☐ 71 | George Bell ................... | .15 | .06 | .01 |
| ☐ 72 | Kirby Puckett ................. | .60 | .24 | .06 |
| ☐ 73 | Lloyd Moseby ................. | .12 | .05 | .01 |
| ☐ 74 | Bob Kearney ................. | .03 | .01 | .00 |
| ☐ 75 | Dwight Gooden ............... | 2.50 | 1.00 | .25 |
| ☐ 76 | Gary Matthews ............... | .06 | .02 | .00 |
| ☐ 77 | Rick Mahler ................... | .03 | .01 | .00 |
| ☐ 78 | Benny Distefano ............. | .03 | .01 | .00 |
| ☐ 79 | Jeff Leonard ................. | .05 | .02 | .00 |
| ☐ 80 | Kevin McReynolds .......... | .10 | .04 | .01 |
| ☐ 81 | Ron Oester .................... | .05 | .02 | .00 |
| ☐ 82 | John Russell ................. | .03 | .01 | .00 |
| ☐ 83 | Tommy Herr ................... | .07 | .03 | .01 |
| ☐ 84 | Jerry Mumphrey ............. | .05 | .02 | .00 |
| ☐ 85 | Ron Romanick ................ | .05 | .02 | .00 |
| ☐ 86 | Daryl Boston ................. | .05 | .02 | .00 |
| ☐ 87 | Andre Dawson ............... | .20 | .08 | .02 |
| ☐ 88 | Eddie Murray ................. | .40 | .16 | .04 |
| ☐ 89 | Dion James ................... | .05 | .02 | .00 |
| ☐ 90 | Chet Lemon ................... | .05 | .02 | .00 |
| ☐ 91 | Bob Stanley ................... | .05 | .02 | .00 |
| ☐ 92 | Willie Randolph .............. | .05 | .02 | .00 |
| ☐ 93 | Mike Scioscia ................ | .05 | .02 | .00 |
| ☐ 94 | Tom Waddell .................. | .03 | .01 | .00 |
| ☐ 95 | Danny Jackson ............... | .06 | .02 | .00 |
| ☐ 96 | Mike Davis ..................... | .07 | .03 | .01 |
| ☐ 97 | Mike Fitzgerald .............. | .03 | .01 | .00 |
| ☐ 98 | Gary Ward ..................... | .05 | .02 | .00 |
| ☐ 99 | Pete O'Brien ................. | .08 | .03 | .01 |
| ☐ 100 | Bret Saberhagen ........... | .25 | .10 | .02 |
| ☐ 101 | Alfredo Griffin .............. | .05 | .02 | .00 |
| ☐ 102 | Brett Butler ................. | .08 | .03 | .01 |
| ☐ 103 | Ron Guidry .................... | .15 | .06 | .01 |
| ☐ 104 | Jerry Reuss .................. | .05 | .02 | .00 |
| ☐ 105 | Jack Morris ................... | .15 | .06 | .01 |
| ☐ 106 | Rick Dempsey ................ | .05 | .02 | .00 |
| ☐ 107 | Ray Burris ..................... | .03 | .01 | .00 |
| ☐ 108 | Brian Downing ............... | .05 | .02 | .00 |
| ☐ 109 | Willie McGee ................. | .15 | .06 | .01 |
| ☐ 110 | Bill Doran ..................... | .08 | .03 | .01 |
| ☐ 111 | Kent Tekulve ................. | .05 | .02 | .00 |
| ☐ 112 | Tony Gwynn ................... | .25 | .10 | .02 |

| | | | | | | | | |
|---|---|---|---|---|---|---|---|---|
| ☐ 113 | Marvell Wynne | .03 | .01 | .00 | ☐ 205 | Terry Pendleton | .06 | .02 | .00 |
| ☐ 114 | David Green | .03 | .01 | .00 | ☐ 206 | Terry Puhl | .05 | .02 | .00 |
| ☐ 115 | Jim Gantner | .05 | .02 | .00 | ☐ 207 | Bobby Grich | .06 | .02 | .00 |
| ☐ 116 | George Foster | .12 | .05 | .01 | ☐ 208 | Ozzie Guillen | .50 | .20 | .05 |
| ☐ 117 | Steve Trout | .03 | .01 | .00 | ☐ 209 | Jeff Reardon | .07 | .03 | .01 |
| ☐ 118 | Mark Langston | .07 | .03 | .01 | ☐ 210 | Cal Ripken | .35 | .14 | .03 |
| ☐ 119 | Tony Fernandez | .10 | .04 | .01 | ☐ 211 | Bill Schroeder | .05 | .02 | .00 |
| ☐ 120 | John Butcher | .03 | .01 | .00 | ☐ 212 | Dan Petry | .10 | .04 | .01 |
| ☐ 121 | Ron Robinson | .03 | .01 | .00 | ☐ 213 | Jim Rice | .35 | .14 | .03 |
| ☐ 122 | Dan Spillner | .03 | .01 | .00 | ☐ 214 | Dave Righetti | .14 | .06 | .01 |
| ☐ 123 | Mike Young | .10 | .04 | .01 | ☐ 215 | Fernando Valenzuela | .30 | .12 | .03 |
| ☐ 124 | Paul Molitor | .10 | .04 | .01 | ☐ 216 | Julio Franco | .10 | .04 | .01 |
| ☐ 125 | Kirk Gibson | .15 | .06 | .01 | ☐ 217 | Darryl Motley | .03 | .01 | .00 |
| ☐ 126 | Ken Griffey | .05 | .02 | .00 | ☐ 218 | Dave Collins | .05 | .02 | .00 |
| ☐ 127 | Tony Armas | .09 | .04 | .01 | ☐ 219 | Tim Wallach | .07 | .03 | .01 |
| ☐ 128 | Mariano Duncan | .40 | .16 | .04 | ☐ 220 | George Wright | .03 | .01 | .00 |
| ☐ 129 | Pat Tabler | .08 | .03 | .01 | ☐ 221 | Tommy Dunbar | .03 | .01 | .00 |
| ☐ 130 | Frank White | .06 | .02 | .00 | ☐ 222 | Steve Balboni | .05 | .02 | .00 |
| ☐ 131 | Carney Lansford | .09 | .04 | .01 | ☐ 223 | Jay Howell | .05 | .02 | .00 |
| ☐ 132 | Vance Law | .03 | .01 | .00 | ☐ 224 | Joe Carter | .30 | .12 | .03 |
| ☐ 133 | Dick Schofield | .06 | .02 | .00 | ☐ 225 | Ed Whitson | .05 | .02 | .00 |
| ☐ 134 | Wayne Tolleson | .03 | .01 | .00 | ☐ 226 | Orel Hershiser | .30 | .12 | .03 |
| ☐ 135 | Greg Walker | .10 | .04 | .01 | ☐ 227 | Willie Hernandez | .12 | .05 | .01 |
| ☐ 136 | Denny Walling | .03 | .01 | .00 | ☐ 228 | Lee Lacy | .05 | .02 | .00 |
| ☐ 137 | Ozzie Virgil | .03 | .01 | .00 | ☐ 229 | Rollie Fingers | .15 | .06 | .01 |
| ☐ 138 | Ricky Horton | .03 | .01 | .00 | ☐ 230 | Bob Boone | .05 | .02 | .00 |
| ☐ 139 | LaMarr Hoyt | .07 | .03 | .01 | ☐ 231 | Joaquin Andujar | .08 | .03 | .01 |
| ☐ 140 | Wayne Krenchicki | .03 | .01 | .00 | ☐ 232 | Craig Reynolds | .03 | .01 | .00 |
| ☐ 141 | Glenn Hubbard | .03 | .01 | .00 | ☐ 233 | Shane Rawley | .06 | .02 | .00 |
| ☐ 142 | Cecilio Guante | .03 | .01 | .00 | ☐ 234 | Eric Show | .05 | .02 | .00 |
| ☐ 143 | Mike Krukow | .07 | .03 | .01 | ☐ 235 | Jose DeLeon | .05 | .02 | .00 |
| ☐ 144 | Lee Smith | .08 | .03 | .01 | ☐ 236 | Jose Uribe | .08 | .03 | .01 |
| ☐ 145 | Edwin Nunez | .05 | .02 | .00 | ☐ 237 | Moose Haas | .05 | .02 | .00 |
| ☐ 146 | Dave Stieb | .12 | .05 | .01 | ☐ 238 | Wally Backman | .07 | .03 | .01 |
| ☐ 147 | Mike Smithson | .03 | .01 | .00 | ☐ 239 | Dennis Eckersley | .05 | .02 | .00 |
| ☐ 148 | Ken Dixon | .05 | .02 | .00 | ☐ 240 | Mike Moore | .06 | .02 | .00 |
| ☐ 149 | Danny Darwin | .03 | .01 | .00 | ☐ 241 | Damaso Garcia | .06 | .02 | .00 |
| ☐ 150 | Chris Pittaro | .08 | .03 | .01 | ☐ 242 | Tim Teufel | .06 | .02 | .00 |
| ☐ 151 | Bill Buckner | .08 | .03 | .01 | ☐ 243 | Dave Concepcion | .08 | .03 | .01 |
| ☐ 152 | Mike Pagliarulo | .25 | .10 | .02 | ☐ 244 | Floyd Bannister | .06 | .02 | .00 |
| ☐ 153 | Bill Russell | .05 | .02 | .00 | ☐ 245 | Fred Lynn | .15 | .06 | .01 |
| ☐ 154 | Brook Jacoby | .10 | .04 | .01 | ☐ 246 | Charlie Moore | .03 | .01 | .00 |
| ☐ 155 | Pat Sheridan | .03 | .01 | .00 | ☐ 247 | Walt Terrell | .03 | .01 | .00 |
| ☐ 156 | Mike Gallego | .08 | .03 | .01 | ☐ 248 | Dave Winfield | .25 | .10 | .02 |
| ☐ 157 | Jim Wohlford | .03 | .01 | .00 | ☐ 249 | Dwight Evans | .10 | .04 | .01 |
| ☐ 158 | Gary Pettis | .08 | .03 | .01 | ☐ 250 | Dennis Powell | .12 | .05 | .01 |
| ☐ 159 | Toby Harrah | .05 | .02 | .00 | ☐ 251 | Andre Thornton | .06 | .02 | .00 |
| ☐ 160 | Richard Dotson | .05 | .02 | .00 | ☐ 252 | Onix Concepcion | .03 | .01 | .00 |
| ☐ 161 | Bob Knepper | .08 | .03 | .01 | ☐ 253 | Mike Heath | .03 | .01 | .00 |
| ☐ 162 | Dave Dravecky | .06 | .02 | .00 | ☐ 254A | David Palmer ERR | .10 | .04 | .01 |
| ☐ 163 | Greg Gross | .03 | .01 | .00 | | (position 2B) | | | |
| ☐ 164 | Eric Davis | 1.25 | .50 | .12 | ☐ 254B | David Palmer COR | .50 | .20 | .05 |
| ☐ 165 | Gerald Perry | .05 | .02 | .00 | | (position P) | | | |
| ☐ 166 | Rick Rhoden | .07 | .03 | .01 | ☐ 255 | Donnie Moore | .05 | .02 | .00 |
| ☐ 167 | Keith Moreland | .06 | .02 | .00 | ☐ 256 | Curtis Wilkerson | .03 | .01 | .00 |
| ☐ 168 | Jack Clark | .12 | .05 | .01 | ☐ 257 | Julio Cruz | .03 | .01 | .00 |
| ☐ 169 | Storm Davis | .07 | .03 | .01 | ☐ 258 | Nolan Ryan | .30 | .12 | .03 |
| ☐ 170 | Cecil Cooper | .12 | .05 | .01 | ☐ 259 | Jeff Stone | .06 | .02 | .00 |
| ☐ 171 | Alan Trammell | .15 | .06 | .01 | ☐ 260 | John Tudor | .12 | .05 | .01 |
| ☐ 172 | Roger Clemens | 2.50 | 1.00 | .25 | ☐ 261 | Mark Thurmond | .05 | .02 | .00 |
| ☐ 173 | Don Mattingly | 5.00 | 2.00 | .50 | ☐ 262 | Jay Tibbs | .03 | .01 | .00 |
| ☐ 174 | Pedro Guerrero | .25 | .10 | .02 | ☐ 263 | Rafael Ramirez | .03 | .01 | .00 |
| ☐ 175 | Willie Wilson | .15 | .06 | .01 | ☐ 264 | Larry McWilliams | .03 | .01 | .00 |
| ☐ 176 | Dwayne Murphy | .06 | .02 | .00 | ☐ 265 | Mark Davis | .03 | .01 | .00 |
| ☐ 177 | Tim Raines | .20 | .08 | .02 | ☐ 266 | Bob Dernier | .03 | .01 | .00 |
| ☐ 178 | Larry Parrish | .06 | .02 | .00 | ☐ 267 | Matt Young | .03 | .01 | .00 |
| ☐ 179 | Mike Witt | .10 | .04 | .01 | ☐ 268 | Jim Clancy | .03 | .01 | .00 |
| ☐ 180 | Harold Baines | .20 | .08 | .02 | ☐ 269 | Mickey Hatcher | .03 | .01 | .00 |
| ☐ 181 | Vince Coleman | 2.50 | 1.00 | .25 | ☐ 270 | Sammy Stewart | .03 | .01 | .00 |
| | (BA 2.67 on back) | | | | ☐ 271 | Bob L. Gibson | .03 | .01 | .00 |
| ☐ 182 | Jeff Heathcock | .08 | .03 | .01 | ☐ 272 | Nelson Simmons | .15 | .06 | .01 |
| ☐ 183 | Steve Carlton | .30 | .12 | .03 | ☐ 273 | Rich Gedman | .09 | .04 | .01 |
| ☐ 184 | Mario Soto | .08 | .03 | .01 | ☐ 274 | Butch Wynegar | .05 | .02 | .00 |
| ☐ 185 | Goose Gossage | .14 | .06 | .01 | ☐ 275 | Ken Howell | .06 | .02 | .00 |
| ☐ 186 | Johnny Ray | .10 | .04 | .01 | ☐ 276 | Mel Hall | .08 | .03 | .01 |
| ☐ 187 | Dan Gladden | .06 | .02 | .00 | ☐ 277 | Jim Sundberg | .05 | .02 | .00 |
| ☐ 188 | Bob Horner | .15 | .06 | .01 | ☐ 278 | Chris Codiroli | .03 | .01 | .00 |
| ☐ 189 | Rick Sutcliffe | .10 | .04 | .01 | ☐ 279 | Herman Winningham | .15 | .06 | .01 |
| ☐ 190 | Keith Hernandez | .25 | .10 | .02 | ☐ 280 | Rod Carew | .30 | .12 | .03 |
| ☐ 191 | Phil Bradley | .20 | .08 | .02 | ☐ 281 | Don Slaught | .03 | .01 | .00 |
| ☐ 192 | Tom Brunansky | .10 | .04 | .01 | ☐ 282 | Scott Fletcher | .05 | .02 | .00 |
| ☐ 193 | Jesse Barfield | .15 | .06 | .01 | ☐ 283 | Bill Dawley | .03 | .01 | .00 |
| ☐ 194 | Frank Viola | .07 | .03 | .01 | ☐ 284 | Andy Hawkins | .06 | .02 | .00 |
| ☐ 195 | Willie Upshaw | .08 | .03 | .01 | ☐ 285 | Glenn Wilson | .10 | .04 | .01 |
| ☐ 196 | Jim Beattie | .03 | .01 | .00 | ☐ 286 | Nick Esasky | .06 | .02 | .00 |
| ☐ 197 | Darryl Strawberry | .60 | .24 | .06 | ☐ 287 | Claudell Washington | .06 | .02 | .00 |
| ☐ 198 | Ron Cey | .08 | .03 | .01 | ☐ 288 | Lee Mazzilli | .05 | .02 | .00 |
| ☐ 199 | Steve Bedrosian | .05 | .02 | .00 | ☐ 289 | Jody Davis | .08 | .03 | .01 |
| ☐ 200 | Steve Kemp | .06 | .02 | .00 | ☐ 290 | Darrell Porter | .05 | .02 | .00 |
| ☐ 201 | Manny Trillo | .05 | .02 | .00 | ☐ 291 | Scott McGregor | .07 | .03 | .01 |
| ☐ 202 | Garry Templeton | .08 | .03 | .01 | ☐ 292 | Ted Simmons | .10 | .04 | .01 |
| ☐ 203 | Dave Parker | .18 | .08 | .01 | ☐ 293 | Aurelio Lopez | .03 | .01 | .00 |
| ☐ 204 | John Denny | .06 | .02 | .00 | ☐ 294 | Marty Barrett | .12 | .05 | .01 |

| | | | | |
|---|---|---|---|---|
| ☐ 295 | Dale Berra | .05 | .02 | .00 |
| ☐ 296 | Greg Brock | .06 | .02 | .00 |
| ☐ 297 | Charlie Leibrandt | .06 | .02 | .00 |
| ☐ 298 | Bill Krueger | .03 | .01 | .00 |
| ☐ 299 | Bryn Smith | .05 | .02 | .00 |
| ☐ 300 | Burt Hooton | .03 | .01 | .00 |
| ☐ 301 | Stu Cliburn | .15 | .06 | .01 |
| ☐ 302 | Luis Salazar | .03 | .01 | .00 |
| ☐ 303 | Ken Dayley | .03 | .01 | .00 |
| ☐ 304 | Frank DiPino | .03 | .01 | .00 |
| ☐ 305 | Von Hayes | .12 | .05 | .01 |
| ☐ 306 | Gary Redus | .05 | .02 | .00 |
| ☐ 307 | Craig Lefferts | .03 | .01 | .00 |
| ☐ 308 | Sammy Khalifa | .09 | .04 | .01 |
| ☐ 309 | Scott Garrelts | .05 | .02 | .00 |
| ☐ 310 | Rick Cerone | .03 | .01 | .00 |
| ☐ 311 | Shawon Dunston | .10 | .04 | .01 |
| ☐ 312 | Howard Johnson | .03 | .01 | .00 |
| ☐ 313 | Jim Presley | .50 | .20 | .05 |
| ☐ 314 | Gary Gaetti | .10 | .04 | .01 |
| ☐ 315 | Luis Leal | .03 | .01 | .00 |
| ☐ 316 | Mark Salas | .06 | .02 | .00 |
| ☐ 317 | Bill Caudill | .05 | .02 | .00 |
| ☐ 318 | Dave Henderson | .06 | .02 | .00 |
| ☐ 319 | Rafael Santana | .03 | .01 | .00 |
| ☐ 320 | Leon Durham | .08 | .03 | .01 |
| ☐ 321 | Bruce Sutter | .12 | .05 | .01 |
| ☐ 322 | Jason Thompson | .05 | .02 | .00 |
| ☐ 323 | Bob Brenly | .05 | .02 | .00 |
| ☐ 324 | Carmelo Martinez | .05 | .02 | .00 |
| ☐ 325 | Eddie Milner | .05 | .02 | .00 |
| ☐ 326 | Juan Samuel | .12 | .05 | .01 |
| ☐ 327 | Tom Nieto | .03 | .01 | .00 |
| ☐ 328 | Dave Smith | .06 | .02 | .00 |
| ☐ 329 | Urbano Lugo | .08 | .03 | .01 |
| ☐ 330 | Joel Skinner | .05 | .02 | .00 |
| ☐ 331 | Bill Gullickson | .05 | .02 | .00 |
| ☐ 332 | Floyd Rayford | .03 | .01 | .00 |
| ☐ 333 | Ben Oglivie | .05 | .02 | .00 |
| ☐ 334 | Lance Parrish | .18 | .08 | .01 |
| ☐ 335 | Jackie Gutierrez | .03 | .01 | .00 |
| ☐ 336 | Dennis Rasmussen | .06 | .02 | .00 |
| ☐ 337 | Terry Whitfield | .03 | .01 | .00 |
| ☐ 338 | Neal Heaton | .03 | .01 | .00 |
| ☐ 339 | Jorge Orta | .03 | .01 | .00 |
| ☐ 340 | Donnie Hill | .03 | .01 | .00 |
| ☐ 341 | Joe Hesketh | .07 | .03 | .01 |
| ☐ 342 | Charlie Hough | .06 | .02 | .00 |
| ☐ 343 | Dave Rozema | .03 | .01 | .00 |
| ☐ 344 | Greg Pryor | .03 | .01 | .00 |
| ☐ 345 | Mickey Tettleton | .07 | .03 | .01 |
| ☐ 346 | George Vukovich | .03 | .01 | .00 |
| ☐ 347 | Don Baylor | .10 | .04 | .01 |
| ☐ 348 | Carlos Diaz | .03 | .01 | .00 |
| ☐ 349 | Barbaro Garbey | .03 | .01 | .00 |
| ☐ 350 | Larry Sheets | .10 | .04 | .01 |
| ☐ 351 | Ted Higuera | 1.00 | .40 | .10 |
| ☐ 352 | Juan Beniquez | .05 | .02 | .00 |
| ☐ 353 | Bob Forsch | .06 | .02 | .00 |
| ☐ 354 | Mark Bailey | .03 | .01 | .00 |
| ☐ 355 | Larry Andersen | .03 | .01 | .00 |
| ☐ 356 | Terry Kennedy | .07 | .03 | .01 |
| ☐ 357 | Don Robinson | .03 | .01 | .00 |
| ☐ 358 | Jim Gott | .03 | .01 | .00 |
| ☐ 359 | Earnie Riles | .50 | .20 | .05 |
| ☐ 360 | John Christensen | .07 | .03 | .01 |
| ☐ 361 | Ray Fontenot | .03 | .01 | .00 |
| ☐ 362 | Spike Owen | .06 | .02 | .00 |
| ☐ 363 | Jim Acker | .03 | .01 | .00 |
| ☐ 364 | Ron Davis | .03 | .01 | .00 |
| ☐ 365 | Tom Hume | .03 | .01 | .00 |
| ☐ 366 | Carlton Fisk | .15 | .06 | .01 |
| ☐ 367 | Nate Snell | .10 | .04 | .01 |
| ☐ 368 | Rick Manning | .03 | .01 | .00 |
| ☐ 369 | Darrell Evans | .10 | .04 | .01 |
| ☐ 370 | Ron Hassey | .03 | .01 | .00 |
| ☐ 371 | Wade Boggs | 2.00 | .80 | .20 |
| ☐ 372 | Rick Honeycutt | .05 | .02 | .00 |
| ☐ 373 | Chris Bando | .03 | .01 | .00 |
| ☐ 374 | Bud Black | .03 | .01 | .00 |
| ☐ 375 | Steve Henderson | .03 | .01 | .00 |
| ☐ 376 | Charlie Lea | .03 | .01 | .00 |
| ☐ 377 | Reggie Jackson | .35 | .14 | .03 |
| ☐ 378 | Dave Schmidt | .03 | .01 | .00 |
| ☐ 379 | Bob James | .03 | .01 | .00 |
| ☐ 380 | Glenn Davis | 1.50 | .60 | .15 |
| ☐ 381 | Tim Corcoran | .03 | .01 | .00 |
| ☐ 382 | Danny Cox | .07 | .03 | .01 |
| ☐ 383 | Tim Flannery | .03 | .01 | .00 |
| ☐ 384 | Tom Browning | .15 | .06 | .01 |
| ☐ 385 | Rick Camp | .03 | .01 | .00 |
| ☐ 386 | Jim Morrison | .03 | .01 | .00 |
| ☐ 387 | Dave LaPoint | .03 | .01 | .00 |
| ☐ 388 | Davey Lopes | .06 | .02 | .00 |
| ☐ 389 | Al Cowens | .05 | .02 | .00 |
| ☐ 390 | Doyle Alexander | .05 | .02 | .00 |
| ☐ 391 | Tim Laudner | .03 | .01 | .00 |
| ☐ 392 | Don Aase | .05 | .02 | .00 |
| ☐ 393 | Jaime Cocanower | .03 | .01 | .00 |
| ☐ 394 | Randy O'Neal | .05 | .02 | .00 |
| ☐ 395 | Mike Easler | .05 | .02 | .00 |
| ☐ 396 | Scott Bradley | .05 | .02 | .00 |
| ☐ 397 | Tom Niedenfuer | .06 | .02 | .00 |
| ☐ 398 | Jerry Willard | .03 | .01 | .00 |
| ☐ 399 | Lonnie Smith | .06 | .02 | .00 |
| ☐ 400 | Bruce Bochte | .05 | .02 | .00 |
| ☐ 401 | Terry Francona | .05 | .02 | .00 |
| ☐ 402 | Jim Slaton | .03 | .01 | .00 |
| ☐ 403 | Bill Stein | .03 | .01 | .00 |
| ☐ 404 | Tim Hulett | .06 | .02 | .00 |
| ☐ 405 | Alan Ashby | .03 | .01 | .00 |
| ☐ 406 | Tim Stoddard | .03 | .01 | .00 |
| ☐ 407 | Garry Maddox | .05 | .02 | .00 |
| ☐ 408 | Ted Power | .07 | .03 | .01 |
| ☐ 409 | Len Barker | .06 | .02 | .00 |
| ☐ 410 | Denny Gonzalez | .05 | .02 | .00 |
| ☐ 411 | George Frazier | .03 | .01 | .00 |
| ☐ 412 | Andy Van Slyke | .06 | .02 | .00 |
| ☐ 413 | Jim Dwyer | .03 | .01 | .00 |
| ☐ 414 | Paul Householder | .03 | .01 | .00 |
| ☐ 415 | Alejandro Sanchez | .05 | .02 | .00 |
| ☐ 416 | Steve Crawford | .03 | .01 | .00 |
| ☐ 417 | Dan Pasqua | .20 | .08 | .02 |
| ☐ 418 | Enos Cabell | .03 | .01 | .00 |
| ☐ 419 | Mike Jones | .03 | .01 | .00 |
| ☐ 420 | Steve Kiefer | .03 | .01 | .00 |
| ☐ 421 | Tim Burke | .25 | .10 | .02 |
| ☐ 422 | Mike Mason | .03 | .01 | .00 |
| ☐ 423 | Ruppert Jones | .03 | .01 | .00 |
| ☐ 424 | Jerry Hairston | .03 | .01 | .00 |
| ☐ 425 | Tito Landrum | .03 | .01 | .00 |
| ☐ 426 | Jeff Calhoun | .08 | .03 | .01 |
| ☐ 427 | Don Carman | .25 | .10 | .02 |
| ☐ 428 | Tony Perez | .12 | .05 | .01 |
| ☐ 429 | Jerry Davis | .03 | .01 | .00 |
| ☐ 430 | Bob Walk | .03 | .01 | .00 |
| ☐ 431 | Brad Wellman | .03 | .01 | .00 |
| ☐ 432 | Terry Forster | .06 | .02 | .00 |
| ☐ 433 | Billy Hatcher | .06 | .02 | .00 |
| ☐ 434 | Clint Hurdle | .03 | .01 | .00 |
| ☐ 435 | Ivan Calderon | .25 | .10 | .02 |
| ☐ 436 | Pete Filson | .03 | .01 | .00 |
| ☐ 437 | Tom Henke | .07 | .03 | .01 |
| ☐ 438 | Dave Engle | .03 | .01 | .00 |
| ☐ 439 | Tom Filer | .05 | .02 | .00 |
| ☐ 440 | Gorman Thomas | .08 | .03 | .01 |
| ☐ 441 | Rick Aguilera | .25 | .10 | .02 |
| ☐ 442 | Scott Sanderson | .03 | .01 | .00 |
| ☐ 443 | Jeff Dedmon | .03 | .01 | .00 |
| ☐ 444 | Joe Orsulak | .25 | .10 | .02 |
| ☐ 445 | Atlee Hammaker | .05 | .02 | .00 |
| ☐ 446 | Jerry Royster | .03 | .01 | .00 |
| ☐ 447 | Buddy Bell | .09 | .04 | .01 |
| ☐ 448 | Dave Rucker | .03 | .01 | .00 |
| ☐ 449 | Ivan DeJesus | .03 | .01 | .00 |
| ☐ 450 | Jim Pankovits | .03 | .01 | .00 |
| ☐ 451 | Jerry Narron | .03 | .01 | .00 |
| ☐ 452 | Bryan Little | .03 | .01 | .00 |
| ☐ 453 | Gary Lucas | .03 | .01 | .00 |
| ☐ 454 | Dennis Martinez | .03 | .01 | .00 |
| ☐ 455 | Ed Romero | .03 | .01 | .00 |
| ☐ 456 | Bob Melvin | .08 | .03 | .01 |
| ☐ 457 | Glenn Hoffman | .03 | .01 | .00 |
| ☐ 458 | Bob Shirley | .03 | .01 | .00 |
| ☐ 459 | Bob Welch | .06 | .02 | .00 |
| ☐ 460 | Carmen Castillo | .03 | .01 | .00 |
| ☐ 461 | Dave Leiper | .08 | .03 | .01 |
| ☐ 462 | Tim Birtsas | .15 | .06 | .01 |
| ☐ 463 | Randy St.Claire | .03 | .01 | .00 |
| ☐ 464 | Chris Welsh | .03 | .01 | .00 |
| ☐ 465 | Greg Harris | .05 | .02 | .00 |
| ☐ 466 | Lynn Jones | .03 | .01 | .00 |
| ☐ 467 | Dusty Baker | .06 | .02 | .00 |
| ☐ 468 | Roy Smith | .03 | .01 | .00 |
| ☐ 469 | Andre Robertson | .03 | .01 | .00 |
| ☐ 470 | Ken Landreaux | .05 | .02 | .00 |
| ☐ 471 | Dave Bergman | .03 | .01 | .00 |
| ☐ 472 | Gary Roenicke | .05 | .02 | .00 |
| ☐ 473 | Pete Vuckovich | .05 | .02 | .00 |
| ☐ 474 | Kirk McCaskill | 1.00 | .40 | .10 |
| ☐ 475 | Jeff Lahti | .03 | .01 | .00 |
| ☐ 476 | Mike Scott | .25 | .10 | .02 |
| ☐ 477 | Darren Daulton | .25 | .10 | .02 |
| ☐ 478 | Graig Nettles | .12 | .05 | .01 |
| ☐ 479 | Bill Almon | .03 | .01 | .00 |
| ☐ 480 | Greg Minton | .05 | .02 | .00 |

| # | Player | | | |
|---|--------|---|---|---|
| □ 481 | Randy Ready | .03 | .01 | .00 |
| □ 482 | Lenny Dykstra | 1.50 | .60 | .15 |
| □ 483 | Thad Bosley | .03 | .01 | .00 |
| □ 484 | Harold Reynolds | .15 | .06 | .01 |
| □ 485 | Al Oliver | .10 | .04 | .01 |
| □ 486 | Roy Smalley | .05 | .02 | .00 |
| □ 487 | John Franco | .10 | .04 | .01 |
| □ 488 | Juan Agosto | .03 | .01 | .00 |
| □ 489 | Al Pardo | .10 | .04 | .01 |
| □ 490 | Bill Wegman | .15 | .06 | .01 |
| □ 491 | Frank Tanana | .06 | .02 | .00 |
| □ 492 | Brian Fisher | .30 | .12 | .03 |
| □ 493 | Mark Clear | .03 | .01 | .00 |
| □ 494 | Len Matuszek | .03 | .01 | .00 |
| □ 495 | Ramon Romero | .08 | .03 | .01 |
| □ 496 | John Wathan | .03 | .01 | .00 |
| □ 497 | Rob Picciolo | .03 | .01 | .00 |
| □ 498 | U.L. Washington | .03 | .01 | .00 |
| □ 499 | John Candelaria | .07 | .03 | .01 |
| □ 500 | Duane Walker | .03 | .01 | .00 |
| □ 501 | Gene Nelson | .03 | .01 | .00 |
| □ 502 | John Mizerock | .03 | .01 | .00 |
| □ 503 | Luis Aguayo | .03 | .01 | .00 |
| □ 504 | Kurt Kepshire | .03 | .01 | .00 |
| □ 505 | Ed Wojna | .10 | .04 | .01 |
| □ 506 | Joe Price | .03 | .01 | .00 |
| □ 507 | Milt Thompson | .20 | .08 | .02 |
| □ 508 | Junior Ortiz | .03 | .01 | .00 |
| □ 509 | Vida Blue | .07 | .03 | .01 |
| □ 510 | Steve Engel | .08 | .03 | .01 |
| □ 511 | Karl Best | .08 | .03 | .01 |
| □ 512 | Cecil Fielder | .25 | .10 | .02 |
| □ 513 | Frank Eufemia | .10 | .04 | .01 |
| □ 514 | Tippy Martinez | .03 | .01 | .00 |
| □ 515 | Billy Robidoux | .35 | .14 | .03 |
| □ 516 | Bill Scherrer | .03 | .01 | .00 |
| □ 517 | Bruce Hurst | .07 | .03 | .01 |
| □ 518 | Rich Bordi | .03 | .01 | .00 |
| □ 519 | Steve Yeager | .05 | .02 | .00 |
| □ 520 | Tony Bernazard | .05 | .02 | .00 |
| □ 521 | Hal McRae | .06 | .02 | .00 |
| □ 522 | Jose Rijo | .08 | .03 | .01 |
| □ 523 | Mitch Webster | .75 | .30 | .07 |
| □ 524 | Jack Howell | .35 | .14 | .03 |
| □ 525 | Alan Bannister | .03 | .01 | .00 |
| □ 526 | Ron Kittle | .10 | .04 | .01 |
| □ 527 | Phil Garner | .05 | .02 | .00 |
| □ 528 | Kurt Bevacqua | .03 | .01 | .00 |
| □ 529 | Kevin Gross | .03 | .01 | .00 |
| □ 530 | Bo Diaz | .05 | .02 | .00 |
| □ 531 | Ken Oberkfell | .03 | .01 | .00 |
| □ 532 | Rick Reuschel | .05 | .02 | .00 |
| □ 533 | Ron Meridith | .10 | .04 | .01 |
| □ 534 | Steve Braun | .03 | .01 | .00 |
| □ 535 | Wayne Gross | .03 | .01 | .00 |
| □ 536 | Ray Searage | .03 | .01 | .00 |
| □ 537 | Tom Brookens | .03 | .01 | .00 |
| □ 538 | Al Nipper | .05 | .02 | .00 |
| □ 539 | Billy Sample | .03 | .01 | .00 |
| □ 540 | Steve Sax | .12 | .05 | .01 |
| □ 541 | Dan Quisenberry | .12 | .05 | .01 |
| □ 542 | Tony Phillips | .03 | .01 | .00 |
| □ 543 | Floyd Youmans | 1.00 | .40 | .10 |
| □ 544 | Steve Buechele | .25 | .10 | .02 |
| □ 545 | Craig Gerber | .08 | .03 | .01 |
| □ 546 | Joe DeSa | .07 | .03 | .01 |
| □ 547 | Brian Harper | .03 | .01 | .00 |
| □ 548 | Kevin Bass | .07 | .03 | .01 |
| □ 549 | Tom Foley | .03 | .01 | .00 |
| □ 550 | Dave Van Gorder | .03 | .01 | .00 |
| □ 551 | Bruce Bochy | .03 | .01 | .00 |
| □ 552 | R.J. Reynolds | .05 | .02 | .00 |
| □ 553 | Chris Brown | 1.25 | .50 | .12 |
| □ 554 | Bruce Benedict | .03 | .01 | .00 |
| □ 555 | Warren Brusstar | .03 | .01 | .00 |
| □ 556 | Danny Heep | .03 | .01 | .00 |
| □ 557 | Darnell Coles | .08 | .03 | .01 |
| □ 558 | Greg Gagne | .05 | .02 | .00 |
| □ 559 | Ernie Whitt | .03 | .01 | .00 |
| □ 560 | Ron Washington | .03 | .01 | .00 |
| □ 561 | Jimmy Key | .10 | .04 | .01 |
| □ 562 | Billy Swift | .06 | .02 | .00 |
| □ 563 | Ron Darling | .25 | .10 | .02 |
| □ 564 | Dick Ruthven | .03 | .01 | .00 |
| □ 565 | Zane Smith | .06 | .02 | .00 |
| □ 566 | Sid Bream | .06 | .02 | .00 |
| □ 567A | Joel Youngblood ERR (position P) | .10 | .04 | .01 |
| □ 567B | Joel Youngblood COR (position IF) | .50 | .20 | .05 |
| □ 568 | Mario Ramirez | .03 | .01 | .00 |
| □ 569 | Tom Runnels | .10 | .04 | .01 |
| □ 570 | Rick Schu | .06 | .02 | .00 |

| # | Player | | | |
|---|--------|---|---|---|
| □ 571 | Bill Campbell | .03 | .01 | .00 |
| □ 572 | Dickie Thon | .05 | .02 | .00 |
| □ 573 | Al Holland | .03 | .01 | .00 |
| □ 574 | Reid Nichols | .03 | .01 | .00 |
| □ 575 | Bert Roberge | .03 | .01 | .00 |
| □ 576 | Mike Flanagan | .07 | .03 | .01 |
| □ 577 | Tim Leary | .03 | .01 | .00 |
| □ 578 | Mike Laga | .05 | .02 | .00 |
| □ 579 | Steve Lyons | .05 | .02 | .00 |
| □ 580 | Phil Niekro | .15 | .06 | .01 |
| □ 581 | Gilberto Reyes | .15 | .06 | .01 |
| □ 582 | Jamie Easterly | .03 | .01 | .00 |
| □ 583 | Mark Gubicza | .07 | .03 | .01 |
| □ 584 | Stan Javier | .20 | .08 | .02 |
| □ 585 | Bill Laskey | .03 | .01 | .00 |
| □ 586 | Jeff Russell | .03 | .01 | .00 |
| □ 587 | Dickie Noles | .03 | .01 | .00 |
| □ 588 | Steve Farr | .03 | .01 | .00 |
| □ 589 | Steve Ontiveros | .20 | .08 | .02 |
| □ 590 | Mike Hargrove | .05 | .02 | .00 |
| □ 591 | Marty Bystrom | .03 | .01 | .00 |
| □ 592 | Franklin Stubbs | .10 | .04 | .01 |
| □ 593 | Larry Herndon | .03 | .01 | .00 |
| □ 594 | Bill Swaggerty | .03 | .01 | .00 |
| □ 595 | Carlos Ponce | .07 | .03 | .01 |
| □ 596 | Pat Perry | .07 | .03 | .01 |
| □ 597 | Ray Knight | .08 | .03 | .01 |
| □ 598 | Steve Lombardozzi | .15 | .06 | .01 |
| □ 599 | Brad Havens | .03 | .01 | .00 |
| □ 600 | Pat Clements | .15 | .06 | .01 |
| □ 601 | Joe Niekro | .08 | .03 | .01 |
| □ 602 | Hank Aaron Puzzle Card | .10 | .04 | .01 |
| □ 603 | Dwayne Henry | .08 | .03 | .01 |
| □ 604 | Mookie Wilson | .06 | .02 | .00 |
| □ 605 | Buddy Biancalana | .05 | .02 | .00 |
| □ 606 | Rance Mulliniks | .03 | .01 | .00 |
| □ 607 | Alan Wiggins | .06 | .02 | .00 |
| □ 608 | Joe Cowley | .05 | .02 | .00 |
| □ 609A | Tom Seaver (green borders on name) | .35 | .14 | .03 |
| □ 609B | Tom Seaver (yellow borders on name) | 1.00 | .40 | .10 |
| □ 610 | Neil Allen | .05 | .02 | .00 |
| □ 611 | Don Sutton | .18 | .08 | .01 |
| □ 612 | Fred Toliver | .15 | .06 | .01 |
| □ 613 | Jay Baller | .10 | .04 | .01 |
| □ 614 | Marc Sullivan | .08 | .03 | .01 |
| □ 615 | John Grubb | .03 | .01 | .00 |
| □ 616 | Bruce Kison | .03 | .01 | .00 |
| □ 617 | Bill Madlock | .10 | .04 | .01 |
| □ 618 | Chris Chambliss | .06 | .02 | .00 |
| □ 619 | Dave Stewart | .03 | .01 | .00 |
| □ 620 | Tim Lollar | .03 | .01 | .00 |
| □ 621 | Gary Lavelle | .05 | .02 | .00 |
| □ 622 | Charlie Hudson | .05 | .02 | .00 |
| □ 623 | Joel Davis | .20 | .08 | .02 |
| □ 624 | Joe Johnson | .20 | .08 | .02 |
| □ 625 | Sid Fernandez | .20 | .08 | .02 |
| □ 626 | Dennis Lamp | .03 | .01 | .00 |
| □ 627 | Terry Harper | .03 | .01 | .00 |
| □ 628 | Jack Lazorko | .03 | .01 | .00 |
| □ 629 | Roger McDowell | .50 | .20 | .05 |
| □ 630 | Mark Funderburk | .15 | .06 | .01 |
| □ 631 | Ed Lynch | .03 | .01 | .00 |
| □ 632 | Rudy Law | .03 | .01 | .00 |
| □ 633 | Roger Mason | .15 | .06 | .01 |
| □ 634 | Mike Felder | .20 | .08 | .02 |
| □ 635 | Ken Schrom | .05 | .02 | .00 |
| □ 636 | Bob Ojeda | .08 | .03 | .01 |
| □ 637 | Ed VandeBerg | .03 | .01 | .00 |
| □ 638 | Bobby Meacham | .03 | .01 | .00 |
| □ 639 | Cliff Johnson | .03 | .01 | .00 |
| □ 640 | Garth Iorg | .03 | .01 | .00 |
| □ 641 | Dan Driessen | .03 | .01 | .00 |
| □ 642 | Mike Brown OF | .05 | .02 | .00 |
| □ 643 | John Shelby | .03 | .01 | .00 |
| □ 644 | Pete Rose (Ty-Breaking) | .30 | .12 | .03 |
| □ 645 | The Knuckle Brothers: Phil Niekro Joe Niekro | .10 | .04 | .01 |
| □ 646 | Jesse Orosco | .06 | .02 | .00 |
| □ 647 | Billy Beane | .20 | .08 | .02 |
| □ 648 | Cesar Cedeno | .06 | .02 | .00 |
| □ 649 | Bert Blyleven | .10 | .04 | .01 |
| □ 650 | Max Venable | .03 | .01 | .00 |
| □ 651 | Fleet Feet: Vince Coleman Willie McGee | .30 | .12 | .03 |
| □ 652 | Calvin Schiraldi | .09 | .04 | .01 |

| | | | MINT | VG-E | F-G |
|---|---|---|---|---|---|
| ☐ 653 | King of Kings: Pete Rose | | .75 | .30 | .07 |
| ☐ 654 | CL: Diamond Kings (unnumbered) | | .08 | .01 | .00 |
| ☐ 655A | CL 1: 27-130 (unnumbered) (45 Beane ERR) | | .10 | .01 | .00 |
| ☐ 655B | CL 1: 27-130 (unnumbered) (45 Habyan COR) | | .50 | .05 | .01 |
| ☐ 656 | CL 2: 131-234 (unnumbered) | | .06 | .01 | .00 |
| ☐ 657 | CL 3: 235-338 (unnumbered) | | .06 | .01 | .00 |
| ☐ 658 | CL 4: 339-442 (unnumbered) | | .06 | .01 | .00 |
| ☐ 659 | CL 5: 443-546 (unnumbered) | | .06 | .01 | .00 |
| ☐ 660 | CL 6: 547-653 (unnumbered) | | .06 | .01 | .00 |
| ☐ PC4 | Kirk Gibson (wax pack box card) | | .35 | .14 | .03 |
| ☐ PC5 | Willie Hernandez (wax pack box card) | | .15 | .06 | .01 |
| ☐ PC6 | Doug DeCinces (wax pack box card) | | .10 | .04 | .01 |
| ☐ PUZ | Hank Aaron Puzzle Card (wax pack box card) | | .06 | .02 | .00 |
| ☐ PC7 | Wade Boggs (all star box card) | | 2.00 | .80 | .20 |
| ☐ PC8 | Lee Smith (all star box card) | | .10 | .04 | .01 |
| ☐ PC9 | Cecil Cooper (all star box card) | | .10 | .04 | .01 |
| ☐ PUZ | Hank Aaron Puzzle Card (all star box card) | | .06 | .02 | .00 |

## 1986 Donruss All-Stars

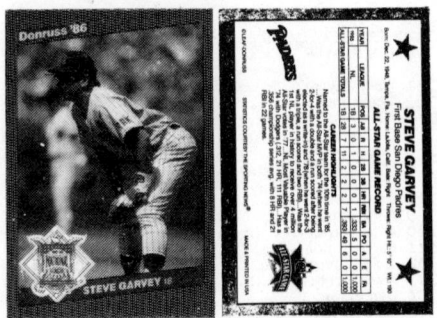

The cards in this 60 card set measure 3 1/2" by 5". Players featured were involved in the 1985 All-Star game played in Minnesota. Cards are very similar in design to the 1986 Donruss regular issue set. The backs give each player's All-Star game statistics and have an orange-yellow border. Wax pack boxes contained cards on the bottom; these four cards (PC7 to PC9 plus a Hank Aaron puzzle card) are listed at the end of the 1986 Donruss regular issue above.

| | | MINT | VG-E | F-G |
|---|---|---|---|---|
| COMPLETE SET | | 5.50 | 2.00 | .50 |
| COMMON PLAYERS | | .05 | .02 | .00 |
| ☐ 1 | Tony Gwynn | .30 | .12 | .03 |
| ☐ 2 | Tommy Herr | .05 | .02 | .00 |
| ☐ 3 | Steve Garvey | .30 | .12 | .03 |
| ☐ 4 | Dale Murphy | .50 | .20 | .05 |
| ☐ 5 | Darryl Strawberry | .40 | .16 | .04 |
| ☐ 6 | Graig Nettles | .10 | .04 | .01 |
| ☐ 7 | Terry Kennedy | .05 | .02 | .00 |
| ☐ 8 | Ozzie Smith | .10 | .04 | .01 |

| ☐ 9 | LaMarr Hoyt | .05 | .02 | .00 |
|---|---|---|---|---|
| ☐ 10 | Rickey Henderson | .40 | .16 | .04 |
| ☐ 11 | Lou Whitaker | .10 | .04 | .01 |
| ☐ 12 | George Brett | .40 | .16 | .04 |
| ☐ 13 | Eddie Murray | .35 | .14 | .03 |
| ☐ 14 | Cal Ripken | .30 | .12 | .03 |
| ☐ 15 | Dave Winfield | .25 | .10 | .02 |
| ☐ 16 | Jim Rice | .25 | .10 | .02 |
| ☐ 17 | Carlton Fisk | .10 | .04 | .01 |
| ☐ 18 | Jack Morris | .10 | .04 | .01 |
| ☐ 19 | Jose Cruz | .05 | .02 | .00 |
| ☐ 20 | Tim Raines | .20 | .08 | .02 |
| ☐ 21 | Nolan Ryan | .30 | .12 | .03 |
| ☐ 22 | Tony Pena | .10 | .04 | .01 |
| ☐ 23 | Jack Clark | .10 | .04 | .01 |
| ☐ 24 | Dave Parker | .15 | .06 | .01 |
| ☐ 25 | Tim Wallach | .05 | .02 | .00 |
| ☐ 26 | Ozzie Virgil | .05 | .02 | .00 |
| ☐ 27 | Fernando Valenzuela | .25 | .10 | .02 |
| ☐ 28 | Dwight Gooden | .90 | .36 | .09 |
| ☐ 29 | Glenn Wilson | .10 | .04 | .01 |
| ☐ 30 | Garry Templeton | .05 | .02 | .00 |
| ☐ 31 | Goose Gossage | .10 | .04 | .01 |
| ☐ 32 | Ryne Sandberg | .30 | .12 | .03 |
| ☐ 33 | Jeff Reardon | .05 | .02 | .00 |
| ☐ 34 | Pete Rose | .90 | .36 | .09 |
| ☐ 35 | Scott Garrelts | .05 | .02 | .00 |
| ☐ 36 | Willie McGee | .15 | .06 | .01 |
| ☐ 37 | Ron Darling | .20 | .08 | .02 |
| ☐ 38 | Dick Williams MGR | .05 | .02 | .00 |
| ☐ 39 | Paul Molitor | .10 | .04 | .01 |
| ☐ 40 | Damaso Garcia | .05 | .02 | .00 |
| ☐ 41 | Phil Bradley | .15 | .06 | .01 |
| ☐ 42 | Dan Petry | .10 | .04 | .01 |
| ☐ 43 | Willie Hernandez | .10 | .04 | .01 |
| ☐ 44 | Tom Brunansky | .10 | .04 | .01 |
| ☐ 45 | Alan Trammell | .15 | .06 | .01 |
| ☐ 46 | Donnie Moore | .05 | .02 | .00 |
| ☐ 47 | Wade Boggs | .90 | .36 | .09 |
| ☐ 48 | Ernie Whitt | .05 | .02 | .00 |
| ☐ 49 | Harold Baines | .15 | .06 | .01 |
| ☐ 50 | Don Mattingly | 1.50 | .60 | .15 |
| ☐ 51 | Gary Ward | .05 | .02 | .00 |
| ☐ 52 | Bert Blyleven | .10 | .04 | .01 |
| ☐ 53 | Jimmy Key | .10 | .04 | .01 |
| ☐ 54 | Cecil Cooper | .10 | .04 | .01 |
| ☐ 55 | Dave Stieb | .10 | .04 | .01 |
| ☐ 56 | Rich Gedman | .10 | .04 | .01 |
| ☐ 57 | Jay Howell | .05 | .02 | .00 |
| ☐ 58 | Sparky Anderson MGR | .05 | .02 | .00 |
| ☐ 59 | Minneapolis Metrodome | .05 | .02 | .00 |
| ☐ 60 | Checklist card (unnumbered) | .05 | .01 | .00 |

## 1986 Donruss Pop-Ups

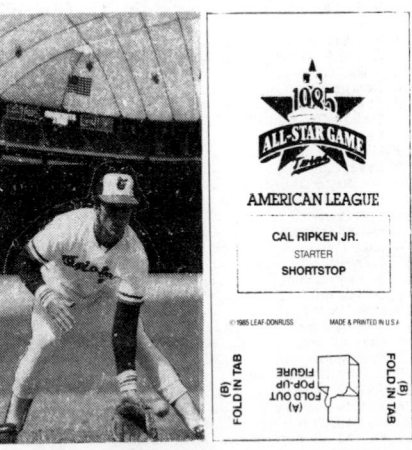

This set is the companion of the 1986 Donruss All-Star (60) set; as such it features the first 18 cards of that set (the All-Star starting line-ups) in a pop-up, die-cut type of card. These cards (measuring (2 1/2" by 5") can be "popped up" to feature a standing card showing the player in action in front of the Metrodome ballpark background. Although this set is unnumbered it is numbered in the same order as its companion set, presumably according to the respective batting orders of the starting line-ups. The first nine numbers below are National Leaguers and the last nine are American Leaguers. See also the Donruss All-Star checklist card which contains a checklist for the Pop-Ups as well.

|  | | MINT | VG-E | F-G |
|---|---|---|---|---|
| COMPLETE SET | | 4.50 | 1.75 | .40 |
| COMMON PLAYERS | | .15 | .06 | .01 |
| ☐ 1 | Tony Gwynn | .40 | .16 | .04 |
| ☐ 2 | Tommy Herr | .15 | .06 | .01 |
| ☐ 3 | Steve Garvey | .60 | .24 | .06 |
| ☐ 4 | Dale Murphy | .80 | .32 | .08 |
| ☐ 5 | Darryl Strawberry | .60 | .24 | .06 |
| ☐ 6 | Graig Nettles | .20 | .08 | .02 |
| ☐ 7 | Terry Kennedy | .15 | .06 | .01 |
| ☐ 8 | Ozzie Smith | .20 | .08 | .02 |
| ☐ 9 | LaMarr Hoyt | .15 | .06 | .01 |
| ☐ 10 | Rickey Henderson | .60 | .24 | .06 |
| ☐ 11 | Lou Whitaker | .20 | .08 | .02 |
| ☐ 12 | George Brett | .60 | .24 | .06 |
| ☐ 13 | Eddie Murray | .60 | .24 | .06 |
| ☐ 14 | Cal Ripken | .50 | .20 | .05 |
| ☐ 15 | Dave Winfield | .40 | .16 | .04 |
| ☐ 16 | Jim Rice | .40 | .16 | .04 |
| ☐ 17 | Carlton Fisk | .25 | .10 | .02 |
| ☐ 18 | Jack Morris | .25 | .10 | .02 |

## 1986 Donruss Super DK's

This 29 card set of large Diamond Kings features the full- color artwork of Dick Perez. The set could be obtained from Perez-Steele Galleries by sending three Donruss wrappers and 9.00. The cards measure 4 7/8" by 6 13/16" and are identical in design to the Diamond King cards in the Donruss regular issue.

|  | | MINT | VG-E | F-G |
|---|---|---|---|---|
| COMPLETE SET | | 9.00 | 3.75 | .90 |
| COMMON PLAYER | | .20 | .08 | .02 |
| ☐ 1 | Kirk Gibson | .30 | .12 | .03 |
| ☐ 2 | Goose Gossage | .30 | .12 | .03 |
| ☐ 3 | Willie McGee | .30 | .12 | .03 |
| ☐ 4 | George Bell | .30 | .12 | .03 |
| ☐ 5 | Tony Armas | .20 | .08 | .02 |
| ☐ 6 | Chili Davis | .20 | .08 | .02 |
| ☐ 7 | Cecil Cooper | .30 | .12 | .03 |
| ☐ 8 | Mike Boddicker | .30 | .12 | .03 |
| ☐ 9 | Davey Lopes | .20 | .08 | .02 |
| ☐ 10 | Bill Doran | .30 | .12 | .03 |
| ☐ 11 | Bret Saberhagen | .30 | .12 | .03 |
| ☐ 12 | Brett Butler | .30 | .12 | .03 |
| ☐ 13 | Harold Baines | .50 | .20 | .05 |
| ☐ 14 | Mike Davis | .20 | .08 | .02 |
| ☐ 15 | Tony Perez | .30 | .12 | .03 |
| ☐ 16 | Willie Randolph | .20 | .08 | .02 |
| ☐ 17 | Bob Boone | .20 | .08 | .02 |
| ☐ 18 | Orel Hershiser | .30 | .12 | .03 |
| ☐ 19 | Johnny Ray | .30 | .12 | .03 |
| ☐ 20 | Gary Ward | .20 | .08 | .02 |
| ☐ 21 | Rick Mahler | .20 | .08 | .02 |
| ☐ 22 | Phil Bradley | .40 | .16 | .04 |
| ☐ 23 | Jerry Koosman | .30 | .12 | .03 |
| ☐ 24 | Tom Brunansky | .30 | .12 | .03 |
| ☐ 25 | Andre Dawson | .50 | .20 | .05 |
| ☐ 26 | Dwight Gooden | 1.25 | .50 | .12 |
| ☐ 27 | Pete Rose | 1.25 | .50 | .12 |
| | King of Kings | | | |
| ☐ 28 | Checklist card | .20 | .02 | .00 |
| | (unnumbered) | | | |

| ☐ 29 | Aaron Puzzle | .20 | .08 | .02 |
|---|---|---|---|---|
| | (unnumbered) | | | |

## 1986 Donruss Rookies

The 1986 Donruss "The Rookies" set features 56 cards plus a 15-piece puzzle of Hank Aaron. Cards are in full color and are standard size, 2 1/2" by 3 1/2". The set was distributed in a small green box with gold lettering. Although the set was wrapped in cellophane, the top card was #1 Joyner resulting in a percentage of (Joyner) cards arriving in less than perfect condition. Card fronts are similar in design to the 1986 Donruss regular issue except for the presence of "The Rookies" logo in the lower left corner and a bluish green border instead of a blue border.

|  | | MINT | VG-E | F-G |
|---|---|---|---|---|
| COMPLETE SET | | 21.00 | 7.50 | 1.75 |
| COMMON PLAYER | | .06 | .02 | .00 |
| ☐ 1 | Wally Joyner | 5.00 | 1.50 | .30 |
| ☐ 2 | Tracy Jones | .40 | .16 | .04 |
| ☐ 3 | Allan Anderson | .20 | .08 | .02 |
| ☐ 4 | Ed Correa | .40 | .16 | .04 |
| ☐ 5 | Reggie Williams | .25 | .10 | .02 |
| ☐ 6 | Charlie Kerfeld | .30 | .12 | .03 |
| ☐ 7 | Andres Galarraga | .20 | .08 | .02 |
| ☐ 8 | Bob Tewksbury | .30 | .12 | .03 |
| ☐ 9 | Al Newman | .20 | .08 | .02 |
| ☐ 10 | Andres Thomas | .40 | .16 | .04 |
| ☐ 11 | Barry Bonds | .90 | .36 | .09 |
| ☐ 12 | Juan Nieves | .10 | .04 | .01 |
| ☐ 13 | Mark Eichhorn | .60 | .24 | .06 |
| ☐ 14 | Dan Plesac | .25 | .10 | .02 |
| ☐ 15 | Cory Snyder | 1.75 | .70 | .17 |
| ☐ 16 | Kelly Gruber | .20 | .08 | .02 |
| ☐ 17 | Kevin Mitchell | .75 | .30 | .07 |
| ☐ 18 | Steve Lombardozzi | .10 | .04 | .01 |
| ☐ 19 | Mitch Williams | .35 | .14 | .03 |
| ☐ 20 | John Cerutti | .35 | .14 | .03 |
| ☐ 21 | Todd Worrell | .75 | .30 | .07 |
| ☐ 22 | Jose Canseco | 3.50 | 1.40 | .35 |
| ☐ 23 | Pete Incaviglia | 2.25 | .90 | .22 |
| ☐ 24 | Jose Guzman | .10 | .04 | .01 |
| ☐ 25 | Scott Bailes | .20 | .08 | .02 |
| ☐ 26 | Greg Mathews | .50 | .20 | .05 |
| ☐ 27 | Eric King | .50 | .20 | .05 |
| ☐ 28 | Paul Assenmacher | .20 | .08 | .02 |
| ☐ 29 | Jeff Sellers | .20 | .08 | .02 |
| ☐ 30 | Bobby Bonilla | .20 | .08 | .02 |
| ☐ 31 | Doug Drabek | .20 | .08 | .02 |
| ☐ 32 | Will Clark | 1.25 | .50 | .12 |
| ☐ 33 | Leon"Bip" Roberts | .20 | .08 | .02 |
| ☐ 34 | Jim Deshaies | .60 | .24 | .06 |
| ☐ 35 | Mike Lavalliere | .20 | .08 | .02 |
| ☐ 36 | Scott Bankhead | .20 | .08 | .02 |
| ☐ 37 | Dale Sveum | .20 | .08 | .02 |
| ☐ 38 | Bo Jackson | 2.25 | .90 | .22 |
| ☐ 39 | Rob Thompson | .50 | .20 | .05 |
| ☐ 40 | Eric Plunk | .20 | .08 | .02 |
| ☐ 41 | Bill Bathe | .20 | .08 | .02 |
| ☐ 42 | John Kruk | .40 | .16 | .04 |

| | | MINT | VG-E | F-G |
|---|---|---|---|---|
| ☐ 43 | Andy Allanson | .20 | .08 | .02 |
| ☐ 44 | Mark Portugal | .20 | .08 | .02 |
| ☐ 45 | Danny Tartabull | .75 | .30 | .07 |
| ☐ 46 | Bob Kipper | .06 | .02 | .00 |
| ☐ 47 | Gene Walter | .20 | .08 | .02 |
| ☐ 48 | Rey Quinones | .20 | .08 | .02 |
| ☐ 49 | Bobby Witt | .60 | .24 | .06 |
| ☐ 50 | Bill Mooneyham | .20 | .08 | .02 |
| ☐ 51 | John Cangelosi | .50 | .20 | .05 |
| ☐ 52 | Ruben Sierra | 1.75 | .70 | .17 |
| ☐ 53 | Rob Woodward | .20 | .08 | .02 |
| ☐ 54 | Ed Hearn | .20 | .08 | .02 |
| ☐ 55 | Joel McKeon | .20 | .08 | .02 |
| ☐ 56 | Checklist card | .20 | .02 | .00 |

## 1986 Donruss Highlights

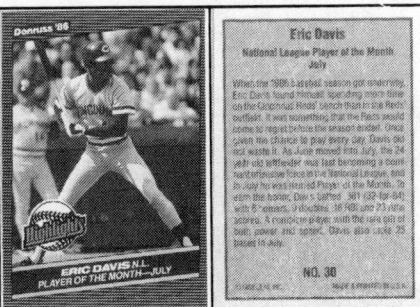

Donruss' second edition of Highlights was released late in 1986. The cards are standard size measuring 2 1/2" by 3 1/2" and are glossy in appearance. Cards commemorate events during the 1986 season as well as players and pitchers of the month from each league. The set was distributed in its own red, white, blue, and gold box along with a small Hank Aaron puzzle. Card fronts are similar to the regular 1986 Donruss issue except that the Highlights logo is positioned in the lower left hand corner and the borders are in gold instead of blue. The blacks are printed in black and gold on white card stock.

| | | MINT | VG-E | F-G |
|---|---|---|---|---|
| | COMPLETE SET | 9.00 | 3.00 | .75 |
| | COMMON PLAYER | .06 | .02 | .00 |
| ☐ 1 | Will Clark Homers in First At-Bat | .35 | .14 | .03 |
| ☐ 2 | Jose Rijo Oakland Milestone for Strikeouts | .10 | .04 | .01 |
| ☐ 3 | George Brett Royals' All-Time Hit Man | .35 | .14 | .03 |
| ☐ 4 | Mike Schmidt Phillies RBI Leader | .45 | .18 | .04 |
| ☐ 5 | Roger Clemens KKKKKKKKKK KKKKKKKKKK | .75 | .30 | .07 |
| ☐ 6 | Roger Clemens AL Pitcher April | .75 | .30 | .07 |
| ☐ 7 | Kirby Puckett AL Player April | .30 | .12 | .03 |
| ☐ 8 | Dwight Gooden NL Pitcher April | .75 | .30 | .07 |
| ☐ 9 | Johnny Ray NL Player April | .06 | .02 | .00 |
| ☐ 10 | Reggie Jackson Eclipses Mantle HR Record | .50 | .20 | .05 |
| ☐ 11 | Wade Boggs First Five Hit Game of Career | .75 | .30 | .07 |
| ☐ 12 | Don Aase AL Pitcher May | .05 | .02 | .00 |
| ☐ 13 | Wade Boggs AL Player May | .75 | .30 | .07 |
| ☐ 14 | Jeff Reardon NL Pitcher May | .05 | .02 | .00 |
| ☐ 15 | Hubie Brooks NL Player May | .10 | .04 | .01 |
| ☐ 16 | Don Sutton Notches 300th | .20 | .08 | .02 |
| ☐ 17 | Roger Clemens Starts 14-0 | .75 | .30 | .07 |
| ☐ 18 | Roger Clemens AL Pitcher June | .75 | .30 | .07 |
| ☐ 19 | Kent Hrbek AL Player June | .20 | .08 | .02 |
| ☐ 20 | Rick Rhoden NL Pitcher June | .05 | .02 | .00 |
| ☐ 21 | Kevin Bass NL Player June | .15 | .06 | .01 |
| ☐ 22 | Bob Horner Blasts 4 HRs in 1 Game | .15 | .06 | .01 |
| ☐ 23 | Wally Joyner Starting All Star Rookie | .75 | .30 | .07 |
| ☐ 24 | Darryl Strawberry Starts 3rd Straight All Star Game | .45 | .18 | .04 |
| ☐ 25 | Fernando Valenzuela Ties All Star Game Record | .30 | .12 | .03 |
| ☐ 26 | Roger Clemens All Star Game MVP | .75 | .30 | .07 |
| ☐ 27 | Jack Morris AL Pitcher July | .15 | .06 | .01 |
| ☐ 28 | Scott Fletcher AL Player July | .05 | .02 | .00 |
| ☐ 29 | Todd Worrell NL Pitcher July | .20 | .08 | .02 |
| ☐ 30 | Eric Davis NL Player July | .40 | .16 | .04 |
| ☐ 31 | Bert Blyleven Records 3000th Strikeout | .10 | .04 | .01 |
| ☐ 32 | Bobby Doerr '86 HOF Inductee | .15 | .06 | .01 |
| ☐ 33 | Ernie Lombardi '86 HOF Inductee | .15 | .06 | .01 |
| ☐ 34 | Willie McCovey '86 HOF Inductee | .20 | .08 | .02 |
| ☐ 35 | Steve Carlton Notches 4000th K | .30 | .12 | .03 |
| ☐ 36 | Mike Schmidt Surpasses DiMaggio Record | .45 | .18 | .04 |
| ☐ 37 | Juan Samuel Records 3rd "Quadruple Double" | .10 | .04 | .01 |
| ☐ 38 | Mike Witt AL Pitcher August | .10 | .04 | .01 |
| ☐ 39 | Doug DeCinces AL Player August | .05 | .02 | .00 |
| ☐ 40 | Bill Gullickson NL Pitcher August | .05 | .02 | .00 |
| ☐ 41 | Dale Murphy NL Player August | .40 | .16 | .04 |
| ☐ 42 | Joe Carter Sets Tribe Offensive Record | .20 | .08 | .02 |
| ☐ 43 | Bo Jackson Longest HR in Royals Stadium | .40 | .16 | .04 |
| ☐ 44 | Joe Cowley Majors 1st No-Hitter in 2 Years | .05 | .02 | .00 |
| ☐ 45 | Jim Deshaies Sets ML Strikeout Record | .15 | .06 | .01 |
| ☐ 46 | Mike Scott No Hitter Clinches Division | .20 | .08 | .02 |
| ☐ 47 | Bruce Hurst AL Pitcher September | .10 | .04 | .01 |
| ☐ 48 | Don Mattingly AL Player September | 1.00 | .40 | .10 |
| ☐ 49 | Mike Krukow NL Pitcher September | .10 | .04 | .01 |
| ☐ 50 | Steve Sax NL Player September | .20 | .08 | .02 |
| ☐ 51 | John Cangelosi AL Rookie Steals Record | .20 | .08 | .02 |

| | | MINT | VG-E | F-G |
|---|---|---|---|---|
| ☐ 52 | Dave Righetti ML Save Mark | .15 | .06 | .01 |
| ☐ 53 | Don Mattingly Yankee Record for Hits and Doubles | 1.00 | .40 | .10 |
| ☐ 54 | Todd Worrell Donruss NL ROY | .30 | .12 | .03 |
| ☐ 55 | Jose Canseco Donruss AL ROY | 1.00 | .40 | .10 |
| ☐ 56 | Checklist card | .10 | .01 | .00 |

## 1987 Donruss

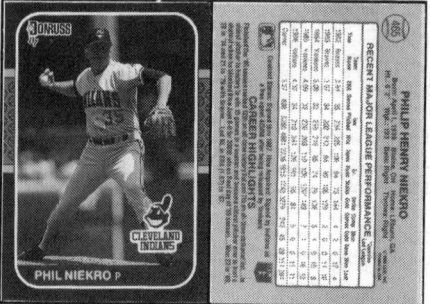

This 660 card set was distributed along with a puzzle of Roberto Clemente. The checklist cards are numbered throughout the set as multiples of 100. The wax pack boxes contain four cards printed on the bottom of the box. Cards measure 2 1/2" by 3 1/2" and feature a black and gold border on the front; the backs are also done in black and gold on white card stock. The popular Diamond King subset returns for the sixth consecutive year. Some of the Diamond King selections are repeats from prior years; Perez-Steele Galleries has indicated that a five year rotation will be maintained in order to avoid depleting the pool of available worthy "kings" on some of the teams.

| | | MINT | VG-E | F-G |
|---|---|---|---|---|
| | COMPLETE SET | 25.00 | 10.00 | 2.50 |
| | COMMON PLAYER | .03 | .01 | .00 |
| ☐ 1 | Wally Joyner DK | 1.25 | .30 | .06 |
| ☐ 2 | Roger Clemens DK | .60 | .24 | .06 |
| ☐ 3 | Dale Murphy DK | .40 | .16 | .04 |
| ☐ 4 | Darryl Strawberry DK | .40 | .16 | .04 |
| ☐ 5 | Ozzie Smith DK | .10 | .04 | .01 |
| ☐ 6 | Jose Canseco DK | 1.00 | .40 | .10 |
| ☐ 7 | Charlie Hough DK | .06 | .02 | .00 |
| ☐ 8 | Brook Jacoby DK | .09 | .04 | .01 |
| ☐ 9 | Fred Lynn DK | .15 | .06 | .01 |
| ☐ 10 | Rick Rhoden DK | .06 | .02 | .00 |
| ☐ 11 | Chris Brown DK | .15 | .06 | .01 |
| ☐ 12 | Von Hayes DK | .12 | .05 | .01 |
| ☐ 13 | Jack Morris DK | .15 | .06 | .01 |
| ☐ 14 | Kevin McReynolds DK | .12 | .05 | .01 |
| ☐ 15 | George Brett DK | .35 | .14 | .03 |
| ☐ 16 | Ted Higuera DK | .15 | .06 | .01 |
| ☐ 17 | Hubie Brooks DK | .10 | .04 | .01 |
| ☐ 18 | Mike Scott DK | .18 | .08 | .01 |
| ☐ 19 | Kirby Puckett DK | .25 | .10 | .02 |
| ☐ 20 | Dave Winfield DK | .25 | .10 | .02 |
| ☐ 21 | Lloyd Moseby DK | .10 | .04 | .01 |
| ☐ 22 | Eric Davis DK | .50 | .20 | .05 |
| ☐ 23 | Jim Presley DK | .25 | .10 | .02 |
| ☐ 24 | Keith Moreland DK | .08 | .03 | .01 |
| ☐ 25 | Greg Walker DK | .10 | .04 | .01 |
| ☐ 26 | Steve Sax DK | .15 | .06 | .01 |
| ☐ 27 | DK Checklist 1-26 | .06 | .01 | .00 |
| ☐ 28 | B.J. Surhoff RR | .60 | .24 | .06 |
| ☐ 29 | Randy Myers RR | .45 | .18 | .04 |
| ☐ 30 | Ken Gerhart RR | .25 | .10 | .02 |
| ☐ 31 | Benito Santiago RR | .25 | .10 | .02 |
| ☐ 32 | Greg Swindell RR | .45 | .18 | .04 |
| ☐ 33 | Mike Birkbeck RR | .12 | .05 | .01 |
| ☐ 34 | Terry Steinbach RR | .35 | .14 | .03 |
| ☐ 35 | Bo Jackson RR | 1.25 | .50 | .12 |
| ☐ 36 | Greg Maddux RR | .10 | .04 | .01 |
| ☐ 37 | Jim Lindeman RR | .20 | .08 | .02 |
| ☐ 38 | Devon White RR | .30 | .12 | .03 |
| ☐ 39 | Eric Bell RR | .25 | .10 | .02 |
| ☐ 40 | Will Fraser RR | .12 | .05 | .01 |
| ☐ 41 | Jerry Browne RR | .12 | .05 | .01 |
| ☐ 42 | Chris James RR | .20 | .08 | .02 |
| ☐ 43 | Rafael Palmeiro RR | .40 | .12 | .03 |
| ☐ 44 | Pat Dodson RR | .25 | .10 | .02 |
| ☐ 45 | Duane Ward RR | .10 | .04 | .01 |
| ☐ 46 | Mark McGwire RR | .10 | .04 | .01 |
| ☐ 47 | Bruce Fields RR | .10 | .04 | .01 |
| ☐ 48 | Eddie Murray | .25 | .10 | .02 |
| ☐ 49 | Ted Higuera | .15 | .06 | .01 |
| ☐ 50 | Kirk Gibson | .20 | .08 | .02 |
| ☐ 51 | Oil Can Boyd | .08 | .03 | .01 |
| ☐ 52 | Don Mattingly | 2.00 | .80 | .20 |
| ☐ 53 | Pedro Guerrero | .20 | .08 | .02 |
| ☐ 54 | George Brett | .30 | .12 | .03 |
| ☐ 55 | Jose Rijo | .08 | .03 | .01 |
| ☐ 56 | Tim Raines | .25 | .10 | .02 |
| ☐ 57 | Ed Correa | .35 | .14 | .03 |
| ☐ 58 | Mike Witt | .10 | .04 | .01 |
| ☐ 59 | Greg Walker | .10 | .04 | .01 |
| ☐ 60 | Ozzie Smith | .10 | .04 | .01 |
| ☐ 61 | Glenn Davis | .25 | .10 | .02 |
| ☐ 62 | Glenn Wilson | .10 | .04 | .01 |
| ☐ 63 | Tom Browning | .10 | .04 | .01 |
| ☐ 64 | Tony Gwynn | .30 | .12 | .03 |
| ☐ 65 | R.J. Reynolds | .06 | .02 | .00 |
| ☐ 66 | Will Clark | .60 | .24 | .06 |
| ☐ 67 | Ozzie Virgil | .05 | .02 | .00 |
| ☐ 68 | Rick Sutcliffe | .10 | .04 | .01 |
| ☐ 69 | Gary Carter | .25 | .10 | .02 |
| ☐ 70 | Mike Moore | .05 | .02 | .00 |
| ☐ 71 | Bert Blyleven | .08 | .03 | .01 |
| ☐ 72 | Tony Fernandez | .09 | .04 | .01 |
| ☐ 73 | Kent Hrbek | .15 | .06 | .01 |
| ☐ 74 | Lloyd Moseby | .10 | .04 | .01 |
| ☐ 75 | Alvin Davis | .10 | .04 | .01 |
| ☐ 76 | Keith Hernandez | .20 | .08 | .02 |
| ☐ 77 | Ryne Sandberg | .25 | .10 | .02 |
| ☐ 78 | Dale Murphy | .40 | .16 | .04 |
| ☐ 79 | Sid Bream | .06 | .02 | .00 |
| ☐ 80 | Chris Brown | .15 | .06 | .01 |
| ☐ 81 | Steve Garvey | .30 | .12 | .03 |
| ☐ 82 | Mario Soto | .08 | .03 | .01 |
| ☐ 83 | Shane Rawley | .07 | .03 | .01 |
| ☐ 84 | Willie McGee | .15 | .06 | .01 |
| ☐ 85 | Jose Cruz | .09 | .04 | .01 |
| ☐ 86 | Brian Downing | .05 | .02 | .00 |
| ☐ 87 | Ozzie Guillen | .10 | .04 | .01 |
| ☐ 88 | Hubie Brooks | .10 | .04 | .01 |
| ☐ 89 | Cal Ripken | .25 | .10 | .02 |
| ☐ 90 | Juan Nieves | .07 | .03 | .01 |
| ☐ 91 | Lance Parrish | .20 | .08 | .02 |
| ☐ 92 | Jim Rice | .25 | .10 | .02 |
| ☐ 93 | Ron Guidry | .15 | .06 | .01 |
| ☐ 94 | Fernando Valenzuela | .25 | .10 | .02 |
| ☐ 95 | Andy Allanson | .12 | .05 | .01 |
| ☐ 96 | Willie Wilson | .12 | .05 | .01 |
| ☐ 97 | Jose Canseco | 1.25 | .50 | .12 |
| ☐ 98 | Jeff Reardon | .06 | .02 | .00 |
| ☐ 99 | Bobby Witt | .40 | .16 | .04 |
| ☐ 100 | Checklist | .06 | .01 | .00 |
| ☐ 101 | Jose Guzman | .06 | .02 | .00 |
| ☐ 102 | Steve Balboni | .05 | .02 | .00 |
| ☐ 103 | Tony Phillips | .03 | .01 | .00 |
| ☐ 104 | Brook Jacoby | .08 | .03 | .01 |
| ☐ 105 | Dave Winfield | .25 | .10 | .02 |
| ☐ 106 | Orel Hershiser | .15 | .06 | .01 |
| ☐ 107 | Lou Whitaker | .10 | .04 | .01 |
| ☐ 108 | Fred Lynn | .15 | .06 | .01 |
| ☐ 109 | Bill Wegman | .03 | .01 | .00 |
| ☐ 110 | Donnie Moore | .05 | .02 | .00 |
| ☐ 111 | Jack Clark | .09 | .04 | .01 |
| ☐ 112 | Bob Knepper | .08 | .03 | .01 |
| ☐ 113 | Von Hayes | .12 | .05 | .01 |
| ☐ 114 | Leon "Bip" Roberts | .09 | .04 | .01 |
| ☐ 115 | Tony Pena | .09 | .04 | .01 |
| ☐ 116 | Scott Garrelts | .05 | .02 | .00 |
| ☐ 117 | Paul Molitor | .08 | .03 | .01 |
| ☐ 118 | Darryl Strawberry | .30 | .12 | .03 |
| ☐ 119 | Shawon Dunston | .09 | .04 | .01 |
| ☐ 120 | Jim Presley | .18 | .08 | .01 |
| ☐ 121 | Jesse Barfield | .15 | .06 | .01 |
| ☐ 122 | Gary Gaetti | .09 | .04 | .01 |
| ☐ 123 | Kurt Stillwell | .12 | .05 | .01 |

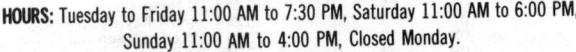
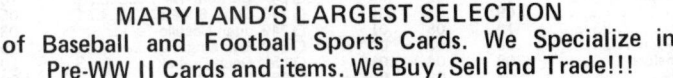

| | | | |
|---|---|---|---|
| ☐ 124 Joel Davis | .12 | .05 | .01 |
| ☐ 125 Mike Boddicker | .08 | .03 | .01 |
| ☐ 126 Robin Yount | .25 | .10 | .02 |
| ☐ 127 Alan Trammell | .15 | .06 | .01 |
| ☐ 128 Dave Righetti | .12 | .05 | .01 |
| ☐ 129 Dwight Evans | .09 | .04 | .01 |
| ☐ 130 Mike Scioscia | .05 | .02 | .00 |
| ☐ 131 Julio Franco | .09 | .04 | .01 |
| ☐ 132 Bret Saberhagen | .15 | .06 | .01 |
| ☐ 133 Mike Davis | .06 | .02 | .00 |
| ☐ 134 Joe Hesketh | .05 | .02 | .00 |
| ☐ 135 Wally Joyner | 2.00 | .80 | .20 |
| ☐ 136 Don Slaught | .03 | .01 | .00 |
| ☐ 137 Daryl Boston | .05 | .02 | .00 |
| ☐ 138 Nolan Ryan | .30 | .12 | .03 |
| ☐ 139 Mike Schmidt | .35 | .14 | .03 |
| ☐ 140 Tommy Herr | .08 | .03 | .01 |
| ☐ 141 Garry Templeton | .07 | .03 | .01 |
| ☐ 142 Kal Daniels | .12 | .05 | .01 |
| ☐ 143 Billy Sample | .03 | .01 | .00 |
| ☐ 144 Johnny Ray | .09 | .04 | .01 |
| ☐ 145 Rob Thompson | .30 | .12 | .03 |
| ☐ 146 Bob Dernier | .05 | .02 | .00 |
| ☐ 147 Danny Tartabull | .25 | .10 | .02 |
| ☐ 148 Ernie Whitt | .03 | .01 | .00 |
| ☐ 149 Kirby Puckett | .25 | .10 | .02 |
| ☐ 150 Mike Young | .09 | .04 | .01 |
| ☐ 151 Ernest Riles | .07 | .03 | .01 |
| ☐ 152 Frank Tanana | .05 | .02 | .00 |
| ☐ 153 Rich Gedman | .08 | .03 | .01 |
| ☐ 154 Willie Randolph | .06 | .02 | .00 |
| ☐ 155 Bill Madlock | .09 | .04 | .01 |
| ☐ 156 Joe Carter | .18 | .08 | .01 |
| ☐ 157 Danny Jackson | .06 | .02 | .00 |
| ☐ 158 Carney Lansford | .09 | .04 | .01 |
| ☐ 159 Bryn Smith | .05 | .02 | .00 |
| ☐ 160 Gary Pettis | .07 | .03 | .01 |
| ☐ 161 Oddibe McDowell | .20 | .08 | .02 |
| ☐ 162 John Cangelosi | .25 | .10 | .02 |
| ☐ 163 Mike Scott | .15 | .06 | .01 |
| ☐ 164 Eric Show | .03 | .01 | .00 |
| ☐ 165 Juan Samuel | .10 | .04 | .01 |
| ☐ 166 Nick Esasky | .03 | .01 | .00 |
| ☐ 167 Zane Smith | .03 | .01 | .00 |
| ☐ 168 Mike Brown | .03 | .01 | .00 |
| ☐ 169 Keith Moreland | .05 | .02 | .00 |
| ☐ 170 John Tudor | .08 | .03 | .01 |
| ☐ 171 Ken Dixon | .05 | .02 | .00 |
| ☐ 172 Jim Gantner | .05 | .02 | .00 |
| ☐ 173 Jack Morris | .15 | .06 | .01 |
| ☐ 174 Bruce Hurst | .08 | .03 | .01 |
| ☐ 175 Dennis Rasmussen | .06 | .02 | .00 |
| ☐ 176 Mike Marshall | .10 | .04 | .01 |
| ☐ 177 Dan Quisenberry | .12 | .05 | .01 |
| ☐ 178 Eric Plunk | .10 | .04 | .01 |
| ☐ 179 Tim Wallach | .08 | .03 | .01 |
| ☐ 180 Steve Buechele | .05 | .02 | .00 |
| ☐ 181 Don Sutton | .12 | .05 | .01 |
| ☐ 182 Dave Schmidt | .03 | .01 | .00 |
| ☐ 183 Terry Pendleton | .05 | .02 | .00 |
| ☐ 184 Jim Deshaies | .20 | .08 | .02 |
| ☐ 185 Steve Bedrosian | .05 | .02 | .00 |
| ☐ 186 Pete Rose | .60 | .24 | .06 |
| ☐ 187 Dave Dravecky | .06 | .02 | .00 |
| ☐ 188 Rick Reuschel | .05 | .02 | .00 |
| ☐ 189 Dan Gladden | .05 | .02 | .00 |
| ☐ 190 Rick Mahler | .03 | .01 | .00 |
| ☐ 191 Thad Bosley | .03 | .01 | .00 |
| ☐ 192 Ron Darling | .20 | .08 | .02 |
| ☐ 193 Matt Young | .03 | .01 | .00 |
| ☐ 194 Tom Brunansky | .09 | .04 | .01 |
| ☐ 195 Dave Stieb | .10 | .04 | .01 |
| ☐ 196 Frank Viola | .05 | .02 | .00 |
| ☐ 197 Tom Henke | .05 | .02 | .00 |
| ☐ 198 Karl Best | .03 | .01 | .00 |
| ☐ 199 Dwight Gooden | 1.00 | .40 | .10 |
| ☐ 200 Checklist | .06 | .01 | .00 |
| ☐ 201 Steve Trout | .03 | .01 | .00 |
| ☐ 202 Rafael Ramirez | .03 | .01 | .00 |
| ☐ 203 Bob Walk | .03 | .01 | .00 |
| ☐ 204 Roger Mason | .05 | .02 | .00 |
| ☐ 205 Terry Kennedy | .06 | .02 | .00 |
| ☐ 206 Ron Oester | .05 | .02 | .00 |
| ☐ 207 John Russell | .03 | .01 | .00 |
| ☐ 208 Greg Mathews | .20 | .08 | .02 |
| ☐ 209 Charlie Kerfeld | .10 | .04 | .01 |
| ☐ 210 Reggie Jackson | .30 | .12 | .03 |
| ☐ 211 Floyd Bannister | .05 | .02 | .00 |
| ☐ 212 Vance Law | .03 | .01 | .00 |
| ☐ 213 Rich Bordi | .03 | .01 | .00 |
| ☐ 214 Dan Plesac | .20 | .08 | .02 |
| ☐ 215 Dave Collins | .05 | .02 | .00 |
| ☐ 216 Bob Stanley | .05 | .02 | .00 |

| | | | |
|---|---|---|---|
| ☐ 217 Joe Niekro | .07 | .03 | .01 |
| ☐ 218 Tom Niedenfuer | .06 | .02 | .00 |
| ☐ 219 Brett Butler | .08 | .03 | .01 |
| ☐ 220 Charlie Leibrandt | .05 | .02 | .00 |
| ☐ 221 Steve Ontiveros | .05 | .02 | .00 |
| ☐ 222 Tim Burke | .05 | .02 | .00 |
| ☐ 223 Curtis Wilkerson | .03 | .01 | .00 |
| ☐ 224 Pete Incaviglia | 1.00 | .40 | .10 |
| ☐ 225 Lonnie Smith | .06 | .02 | .00 |
| ☐ 226 Chris Codiroli | .03 | .01 | .00 |
| ☐ 227 Scott Bailes | .10 | .04 | .01 |
| ☐ 228 Rickey Henderson | .30 | .12 | .03 |
| ☐ 229 Ken Howell | .06 | .02 | .00 |
| ☐ 230 Darnell Coles | .10 | .04 | .01 |
| ☐ 231 Don Aase | .05 | .02 | .00 |
| ☐ 232 Tim Leary | .03 | .01 | .00 |
| ☐ 233 Bob Boone | .05 | .02 | .00 |
| ☐ 234 Ricky Horton | .03 | .01 | .00 |
| ☐ 235 Mark Bailey | .03 | .01 | .00 |
| ☐ 236 Kevin Gross | .03 | .01 | .00 |
| ☐ 237 Lance McCullers | .05 | .02 | .00 |
| ☐ 238 Cecilio Guante | .03 | .01 | .00 |
| ☐ 239 Bob Melvin | .03 | .01 | .00 |
| ☐ 240 Billy Jo Robidoux | .05 | .02 | .00 |
| ☐ 241 Roger McDowell | .10 | .04 | .01 |
| ☐ 242 Leon Durham | .08 | .03 | .01 |
| ☐ 243 Ed Nunez | .03 | .01 | .00 |
| ☐ 244 Jimmy Key | .08 | .03 | .01 |
| ☐ 245 Mike Smithson | .03 | .01 | .00 |
| ☐ 246 Bo Diaz | .05 | .02 | .00 |
| ☐ 247 Carlton Fisk | .10 | .04 | .01 |
| ☐ 248 Larry Sheets | .05 | .02 | .00 |
| ☐ 249 Juan Castillo | .03 | .01 | .00 |
| ☐ 250 Eric King | .25 | .10 | .02 |
| ☐ 251 Doug Drabek | .20 | .08 | .02 |
| ☐ 252 Wade Boggs | 1.00 | .40 | .10 |
| ☐ 253 Mariano Duncan | .08 | .03 | .01 |
| ☐ 254 Pat Tabler | .08 | .03 | .01 |
| ☐ 255 Frank White | .06 | .02 | .00 |
| ☐ 256 Alfredo Griffin | .05 | .02 | .00 |
| ☐ 257 Floyd Youmans | .10 | .04 | .01 |
| ☐ 258 Rob Wilfong | .03 | .01 | .00 |
| ☐ 259 Pete O'Brien | .08 | .03 | .01 |
| ☐ 260 Tim Hulett | .05 | .02 | .00 |
| ☐ 261 Dickie Thon | .05 | .02 | .00 |
| ☐ 262 Darren Daulton | .05 | .02 | .00 |
| ☐ 263 Vince Coleman | .30 | .12 | .03 |
| ☐ 264 Andy Hawkins | .03 | .01 | .00 |
| ☐ 265 Eric Davis | .50 | .20 | .05 |
| ☐ 266 Andres Thomas | .30 | .12 | .03 |
| ☐ 267 Mike Diaz | .25 | .10 | .02 |
| ☐ 268 Chili Davis | .08 | .03 | .01 |
| ☐ 269 Jody Davis | .07 | .03 | .01 |
| ☐ 270 Phil Bradley | .15 | .06 | .01 |
| ☐ 271 George Bell | .15 | .06 | .01 |
| ☐ 272 Keith Atherton | .03 | .01 | .00 |
| ☐ 273 Storm Davis | .07 | .03 | .01 |
| ☐ 274 Rob Deer | .15 | .06 | .01 |
| ☐ 275 Walt Terrell | .03 | .01 | .00 |
| ☐ 276 Roger Clemens | 1.00 | .40 | .10 |
| ☐ 277 Mike Easler | .06 | .02 | .00 |
| ☐ 278 Steve Sax | .12 | .05 | .01 |
| ☐ 279 Andre Thornton | .06 | .02 | .00 |
| ☐ 280 Jim Sundberg | .05 | .02 | .00 |
| ☐ 281 Bill Bathe | .10 | .04 | .01 |
| ☐ 282 Jay Tibbs | .03 | .01 | .00 |
| ☐ 283 Dick Schofield | .05 | .02 | .00 |
| ☐ 284 Mike Mason | .03 | .01 | .00 |
| ☐ 285 Jerry Hairston | .03 | .01 | .00 |
| ☐ 286 Bill Doran | .07 | .03 | .01 |
| ☐ 287 Tim Flannery | .03 | .01 | .00 |
| ☐ 288 Gary Redus | .05 | .02 | .00 |
| ☐ 289 John Franco | .09 | .04 | .01 |
| ☐ 290 Paul Assenmacher | .10 | .04 | .01 |
| ☐ 291 Joe Orsulak | .03 | .01 | .00 |
| ☐ 292 Lee Smith | .07 | .03 | .01 |
| ☐ 293 Mike Laga | .03 | .01 | .00 |
| ☐ 294 Rick Dempsey | .05 | .02 | .00 |
| ☐ 295 Mike Felder | .06 | .02 | .00 |
| ☐ 296 Tom Brookens | .03 | .01 | .00 |
| ☐ 297 Al Nipper | .03 | .01 | .00 |
| ☐ 298 Mike Pagliarulo | .15 | .06 | .01 |
| ☐ 299 Franklin Stubbs | .10 | .04 | .01 |
| ☐ 300 Checklist | .06 | .01 | .00 |
| ☐ 301 Steve Farr | .03 | .01 | .00 |
| ☐ 302 Bill Mooneyham | .10 | .04 | .01 |
| ☐ 303 Andres Galarraga | .08 | .03 | .01 |
| ☐ 304 Scott Fletcher | .05 | .02 | .00 |
| ☐ 305 Jack Howell | .05 | .02 | .00 |
| ☐ 306 Russ Morman | .25 | .10 | .02 |
| ☐ 307 Todd Worrell | .20 | .08 | .02 |
| ☐ 308 Dave Smith | .06 | .02 | .00 |
| ☐ 309 Jeff Stone | .05 | .02 | .00 |

| | | | |
|---|---|---|---|
| ☐ 310 Ron Robinson | .03 | .01 | .00 |
| ☐ 311 Bruce Bochy | .03 | .01 | .00 |
| ☐ 312 Jim Winn | .03 | .01 | .00 |
| ☐ 313 Mark Davis | .03 | .01 | .00 |
| ☐ 314 Jeff Dedmon | .03 | .01 | .00 |
| ☐ 315 Jamie Moyer | .15 | .06 | .01 |
| ☐ 316 Wally Backman | .07 | .03 | .01 |
| ☐ 317 Ken Phelps | .05 | .02 | .00 |
| ☐ 318 Steve Lombardozzi | .06 | .02 | .00 |
| ☐ 319 Rance Mulliniks | .03 | .01 | .00 |
| ☐ 320 Tim Laudner | .03 | .01 | .00 |
| ☐ 321 Mark Eichhorn | .30 | .12 | .03 |
| ☐ 322 Lee Guetterman | .12 | .05 | .01 |
| ☐ 323 Sid Fernandez | .18 | .08 | .01 |
| ☐ 324 Jerry Mumphrey | .05 | .02 | .00 |
| ☐ 325 David Palmer | .05 | .02 | .00 |
| ☐ 326 Bill Almon | .03 | .01 | .00 |
| ☐ 327 Candy Maldonado | .06 | .02 | .00 |
| ☐ 328 John Kruk | .25 | .10 | .02 |
| ☐ 329 John Denny | .06 | .02 | .00 |
| ☐ 330 Milt Thompson | .05 | .02 | .00 |
| ☐ 331 Mike Lavalliere | .10 | .04 | .01 |
| ☐ 332 Alan Ashby | .03 | .01 | .00 |
| ☐ 333 Doug Corbett | .03 | .01 | .00 |
| ☐ 334 Ron Karkovice | .25 | .10 | .02 |
| ☐ 335 Mitch Webster | .08 | .03 | .01 |
| ☐ 336 Lee Lacy | .05 | .02 | .00 |
| ☐ 337 Glenn Braggs | .45 | .18 | .04 |
| ☐ 338 Dwight Lowry | .15 | .06 | .01 |
| ☐ 339 Don Baylor | .10 | .04 | .01 |
| ☐ 340 Brian Fisher | .05 | .02 | .00 |
| ☐ 341 Reggie Williams | .20 | .08 | .02 |
| ☐ 342 Tom Candiotti | .05 | .02 | .00 |
| ☐ 343 Rudy Law | .03 | .01 | .00 |
| ☐ 344 Curt Young | .03 | .01 | .00 |
| ☐ 345 Mike Fitzgerald | .03 | .01 | .00 |
| ☐ 346 Ruben Sierra | 1.00 | .40 | .10 |
| ☐ 347 Mitch Williams | .25 | .10 | .02 |
| ☐ 348 Jorge Orta | .03 | .01 | .00 |
| ☐ 349 Mickey Tettleton | .03 | .01 | .00 |
| ☐ 350 Ernie Camacho | .03 | .01 | .00 |
| ☐ 351 Ron Kittle | .08 | .03 | .01 |
| ☐ 352 Ken Landreaux | .03 | .01 | .00 |
| ☐ 353 Chet Lemon | .05 | .02 | .00 |
| ☐ 354 John Shelby | .03 | .01 | .00 |
| ☐ 355 Mark Clear | .03 | .01 | .00 |
| ☐ 356 Doug DeCinces | .07 | .03 | .01 |
| ☐ 357 Ken Dayley | .03 | .01 | .00 |
| ☐ 358 Phil Garner | .05 | .02 | .00 |
| ☐ 359 Steve Jeltz | .03 | .01 | .00 |
| ☐ 360 Ed Whitson | .03 | .01 | .00 |
| ☐ 361 Barry Bonds | .35 | .14 | .03 |
| ☐ 362 Vida Blue | .07 | .03 | .01 |
| ☐ 363 Cecil Cooper | .09 | .04 | .01 |
| ☐ 364 Bob Ojeda | .08 | .03 | .01 |
| ☐ 365 Dennis Eckersley | .05 | .02 | .00 |
| ☐ 366 Mike Morgan | .03 | .01 | .00 |
| ☐ 367 Willie Upshaw | .07 | .03 | .01 |
| ☐ 368 Allan Anderson | .15 | .06 | .01 |
| ☐ 369 Bob Gullickson | .05 | .02 | .00 |
| ☐ 370 Bobby Thigpen | .18 | .08 | .01 |
| ☐ 371 Juan Beniquez | .05 | .02 | .00 |
| ☐ 372 Charlie Moore | .03 | .01 | .00 |
| ☐ 373 Dan Petry | .09 | .04 | .01 |
| ☐ 374 Rod Scurry | .03 | .01 | .00 |
| ☐ 375 Tom Seaver | .25 | .10 | .02 |
| ☐ 376 Ed VandeBerg | .03 | .01 | .00 |
| ☐ 377 Tony Bernazard | .05 | .02 | .00 |
| ☐ 378 Greg Pryor | .03 | .01 | .00 |
| ☐ 379 Dwayne Murphy | .05 | .02 | .00 |
| ☐ 380 Andy McGaffigan | .03 | .01 | .00 |
| ☐ 381 Kirk McCaskill | .10 | .04 | .01 |
| ☐ 382 Greg Harris | .05 | .02 | .00 |
| ☐ 383 Rich Dotson | .05 | .02 | .00 |
| ☐ 384 Craig Reynolds | .03 | .01 | .00 |
| ☐ 385 Greg Gross | .03 | .01 | .00 |
| ☐ 386 Tito Landrum | .03 | .01 | .00 |
| ☐ 387 Craig Lefferts | .03 | .01 | .00 |
| ☐ 388 Dave Parker | .15 | .06 | .01 |
| ☐ 389 Bob Horner | .15 | .06 | .01 |
| ☐ 390 Pat Clements | .05 | .02 | .00 |
| ☐ 391 Jeff Leonard | .06 | .02 | .00 |
| ☐ 392 Chris Speier | .03 | .01 | .00 |
| ☐ 393 John Moses | .15 | .06 | .01 |
| ☐ 394 Garth Iorg | .03 | .01 | .00 |
| ☐ 395 Greg Gagne | .05 | .02 | .00 |
| ☐ 396 Nate Snell | .03 | .01 | .00 |
| ☐ 397 Bryan Clutterbuck | .10 | .04 | .01 |
| ☐ 398 Darrell Evans | .08 | .03 | .01 |
| ☐ 399 Steve Crawford | .03 | .01 | .00 |
| ☐ 400 Checklist | .06 | .01 | .00 |
| ☐ 401 Phil Lombardi | .25 | .10 | .02 |
| ☐ 402 Rick Honeycutt | .05 | .02 | .00 |
| ☐ 403 Ken Schrom | .05 | .02 | .00 |
| ☐ 404 Bud Black | .03 | .01 | .00 |
| ☐ 405 Donnie Hill | .03 | .01 | .00 |
| ☐ 406 Wayne Krenchicki | .03 | .01 | .00 |
| ☐ 407 Chuck Finley | .10 | .04 | .01 |
| ☐ 408 Toby Harrah | .05 | .02 | .00 |
| ☐ 409 Steve Lyons | .03 | .01 | .00 |
| ☐ 410 Kevin Bass | .07 | .03 | .01 |
| ☐ 411 Marvell Wynne | .03 | .01 | .00 |
| ☐ 412 Ron Roenicke | .03 | .01 | .00 |
| ☐ 413 Tracy Jones | .25 | .10 | .02 |
| ☐ 414 Gene Garber | .03 | .01 | .00 |
| ☐ 415 Mike Bielecki | .03 | .01 | .00 |
| ☐ 416 Frank DiPino | .03 | .01 | .00 |
| ☐ 417 Andy Van Slyke | .05 | .02 | .00 |
| ☐ 418 Jim Dwyer | .03 | .01 | .00 |
| ☐ 419 Ben Oglivie | .06 | .02 | .00 |
| ☐ 420 Dave Bergman | .03 | .01 | .00 |
| ☐ 421 Joe Sambito | .05 | .02 | .00 |
| ☐ 422 Bob Tewksbury | .20 | .08 | .02 |
| ☐ 423 Len Matuszek | .03 | .01 | .00 |
| ☐ 424 Mike Kingery | .15 | .06 | .01 |
| ☐ 425 Dave Kingman | .10 | .04 | .01 |
| ☐ 426 Al Newman | .10 | .04 | .01 |
| ☐ 427 Gary Ward | .06 | .02 | .00 |
| ☐ 428 Ruppert Jones | .03 | .01 | .00 |
| ☐ 429 Harold Baines | .15 | .06 | .01 |
| ☐ 430 Pat Perry | .03 | .01 | .00 |
| ☐ 431 Terry Puhl | .05 | .02 | .00 |
| ☐ 432 Don Carman | .05 | .02 | .00 |
| ☐ 433 Eddie Milner | .05 | .02 | .00 |
| ☐ 434 LaMarr Hoyt | .05 | .02 | .00 |
| ☐ 435 Rick Rhoden | .06 | .02 | .00 |
| ☐ 436 Jose Uribe | .03 | .01 | .00 |
| ☐ 437 Ken Oberkfell | .03 | .01 | .00 |
| ☐ 438 Ron Davis | .03 | .01 | .00 |
| ☐ 439 Jesse Orosco | .05 | .02 | .00 |
| ☐ 440 Scott Bradley | .06 | .02 | .00 |
| ☐ 441 Randy Bush | .03 | .01 | .00 |
| ☐ 442 John Cerutti | .20 | .08 | .02 |
| ☐ 443 Roy Smalley | .05 | .02 | .00 |
| ☐ 444 Kelly Gruber | .03 | .01 | .00 |
| ☐ 445 Bob Kearney | .03 | .01 | .00 |
| ☐ 446 Ed Hearn | .10 | .04 | .01 |
| ☐ 447 Scott Sanderson | .03 | .01 | .00 |
| ☐ 448 Bruce Benedict | .03 | .01 | .00 |
| ☐ 449 Junior Ortiz | .03 | .01 | .00 |
| ☐ 450 Mike Aldrete | .12 | .05 | .01 |
| ☐ 451 Kevin McReynolds | .12 | .05 | .01 |
| ☐ 452 Rob Murphy | .15 | .06 | .01 |
| ☐ 453 Kent Tekulve | .05 | .02 | .00 |
| ☐ 454 Curt Ford | .25 | .10 | .02 |
| ☐ 455 Davey Lopes | .06 | .02 | .00 |
| ☐ 456 Bobby Grich | .06 | .02 | .00 |
| ☐ 457 Jose DeLeon | .05 | .02 | .00 |
| ☐ 458 Andre Dawson | .15 | .06 | .01 |
| ☐ 459 Mike Flanagan | .07 | .03 | .01 |
| ☐ 460 Joey Meyer | .25 | .10 | .02 |
| ☐ 461 Chuck Cary | .20 | .08 | .02 |
| ☐ 462 Bill Buckner | .08 | .03 | .01 |
| ☐ 463 Bob Shirley | .03 | .01 | .00 |
| ☐ 464 Jeff Hamilton | .15 | .06 | .01 |
| ☐ 465 Phil Niekro | .15 | .06 | .01 |
| ☐ 466 Mark Gubicza | .06 | .02 | .00 |
| ☐ 467 Jerry Willard | .03 | .01 | .00 |
| ☐ 468 Bob Sebra | .10 | .04 | .01 |
| ☐ 469 Larry Parrish | .05 | .02 | .00 |
| ☐ 470 Charlie Hough | .06 | .02 | .00 |
| ☐ 471 Hal McRae | .05 | .02 | .00 |
| ☐ 472 Dave Leiper | .05 | .02 | .00 |
| ☐ 473 Mel Hall | .07 | .03 | .01 |
| ☐ 474 Dan Pasqua | .12 | .05 | .01 |
| ☐ 475 Bob Welch | .06 | .02 | .00 |
| ☐ 476 Johnny Grubb | .03 | .01 | .00 |
| ☐ 477 Jim Traber | .09 | .04 | .01 |
| ☐ 478 Chris Bosio | .10 | .04 | .01 |
| ☐ 479 Mark McLemore | .06 | .02 | .00 |
| ☐ 480 John Morris | .03 | .01 | .00 |
| ☐ 481 Billy Hatcher | .05 | .02 | .00 |
| ☐ 482 Dan Schatzeder | .03 | .01 | .00 |
| ☐ 483 Rich Gossage | .12 | .05 | .01 |
| ☐ 484 Jim Morrison | .03 | .01 | .00 |
| ☐ 485 Bob Brenly | .05 | .02 | .00 |
| ☐ 486 Bill Schroeder | .03 | .01 | .00 |
| ☐ 487 Mookie Wilson | .06 | .02 | .00 |
| ☐ 488 Dave Martinez | .18 | .08 | .01 |
| ☐ 489 Harold Reynolds | .03 | .01 | .00 |
| ☐ 490 Jeff Hearron | .10 | .04 | .01 |
| ☐ 491 Mickey Hatcher | .03 | .01 | .00 |
| ☐ 492 Barry Larkin | .50 | .20 | .05 |
| ☐ 493 Bob James | .03 | .01 | .00 |
| ☐ 494 John Habyan | .03 | .01 | .00 |
| ☐ 495 Jim Adduci | .15 | .06 | .01 |

| | | | |
|---|---|---|---|
| ☐ 496 Mike Heath | .03 | .01 | .00 |
| ☐ 497 Tim Stoddard | .03 | .01 | .00 |
| ☐ 498 Tony Armas | .08 | .03 | .01 |
| ☐ 499 Dennis Powell | .10 | .04 | .01 |
| ☐ 500 Checklist | .06 | .01 | .00 |
| ☐ 501 Chris Bando | .03 | .01 | .00 |
| ☐ 502 Dave Cone | .10 | .04 | .01 |
| ☐ 503 Jay Howell | .05 | .02 | .00 |
| ☐ 504 Tom Foley | .03 | .01 | .00 |
| ☐ 505 Ray Chadwick | .10 | .04 | .01 |
| ☐ 506 Mike Loynd | .25 | .10 | .02 |
| ☐ 507 Neil Allen | .05 | .02 | .00 |
| ☐ 508 Danny Darwin | .03 | .01 | .00 |
| ☐ 509 Rick Schu | .03 | .01 | .00 |
| ☐ 510 Jose Oquendo | .03 | .01 | .00 |
| ☐ 511 Gene Walter | .05 | .02 | .00 |
| ☐ 512 Terry McGriff | .10 | .04 | .01 |
| ☐ 513 Ken Griffey | .06 | .02 | .00 |
| ☐ 514 Benny Distefano | .03 | .01 | .00 |
| ☐ 515 Terry Mulholland | .10 | .04 | .01 |
| ☐ 516 Ed Lynch | .03 | .01 | .00 |
| ☐ 517 Bill Swift | .03 | .01 | .00 |
| ☐ 518 Manny Lee | .05 | .02 | .00 |
| ☐ 519 Andre David | .03 | .01 | .00 |
| ☐ 520 Scott McGregor | .07 | .03 | .01 |
| ☐ 521 Rick Manning | .03 | .01 | .00 |
| ☐ 522 Willie Hernandez | .09 | .04 | .01 |
| ☐ 523 Marty Barrett | .10 | .04 | .01 |
| ☐ 524 Wayne Tolleson | .03 | .01 | .00 |
| ☐ 525 Jose Gonzalez | .30 | .12 | .03 |
| ☐ 526 Cory Snyder | .60 | .24 | .06 |
| ☐ 527 Buddy Biancalana | .03 | .01 | .00 |
| ☐ 528 Moose Haas | .03 | .01 | .00 |
| ☐ 529 Wilfredo Tejada | .10 | .04 | .01 |
| ☐ 530 Stu Cliburn | .03 | .01 | .00 |
| ☐ 531 Dale Mohorcic | .15 | .06 | .01 |
| ☐ 532 Ron Hassey | .03 | .01 | .00 |
| ☐ 533 Ty Gainey | .03 | .01 | .00 |
| ☐ 534 Jerry Royster | .03 | .01 | .00 |
| ☐ 535 Mike Maddux | .07 | .03 | .01 |
| ☐ 536 Ted Power | .07 | .03 | .01 |
| ☐ 537 Ted Simmons | .09 | .04 | .01 |
| ☐ 538 Rafael Belliard | .10 | .04 | .01 |
| ☐ 539 Chico Walker | .15 | .06 | .01 |
| ☐ 540 Bob Forsch | .05 | .02 | .00 |
| ☐ 541 John Stefero | .03 | .01 | .00 |
| ☐ 542 Dale Sveum | .12 | .05 | .01 |
| ☐ 543 Mark Thurmond | .03 | .01 | .00 |
| ☐ 544 Jeff Sellers | .12 | .05 | .01 |
| ☐ 545 Joel Skinner | .05 | .02 | .00 |
| ☐ 546 Alex Trevino | .03 | .01 | .00 |
| ☐ 547 Randy Kutcher | .10 | .04 | .01 |
| ☐ 548 Joaquin Andujar | .08 | .03 | .01 |
| ☐ 549 Casey Candaele | .10 | .04 | .01 |
| ☐ 550 Jeff Russell | .03 | .01 | .00 |
| ☐ 551 John Candelaria | .07 | .03 | .01 |
| ☐ 552 Joe Cowley | .05 | .02 | .00 |
| ☐ 553 Danny Cox | .05 | .02 | .00 |
| ☐ 554 Denny Walling | .03 | .01 | .00 |
| ☐ 555 Bruce Ruffin | .30 | .12 | .03 |
| ☐ 556 Buddy Bell | .09 | .04 | .01 |
| ☐ 557 Jimmy Jones | .20 | .08 | .02 |
| ☐ 558 Bobby Bonilla | .15 | .06 | .01 |
| ☐ 559 Jeff Robinson | .03 | .01 | .00 |
| ☐ 560 Ed Olwine | .10 | .04 | .01 |
| ☐ 561 Glenallen Hill | .35 | .14 | .03 |
| ☐ 562 Lee Mazzilli | .05 | .02 | .00 |
| ☐ 563 Mike Brown | .03 | .01 | .00 |
| ☐ 564 George Frazier | .03 | .01 | .00 |
| ☐ 565 Mike Sharperson | .10 | .04 | .01 |
| ☐ 566 Mark Portugal | .10 | .04 | .01 |
| ☐ 567 Rick Leach | .03 | .01 | .00 |
| ☐ 568 Mark Langston | .07 | .03 | .01 |
| ☐ 569 Rafael Santana | .03 | .01 | .00 |
| ☐ 570 Manny Trillo | .05 | .02 | .00 |
| ☐ 571 Cliff Speck | .09 | .04 | .01 |
| ☐ 572 Bob Kipper | .03 | .01 | .00 |
| ☐ 573 Kelly Downs | .10 | .04 | .01 |
| ☐ 574 Randy Asadoor | .15 | .06 | .01 |
| ☐ 575 Dave Magadan | .50 | .20 | .05 |
| ☐ 576 Marvin Freeman | .25 | .10 | .02 |
| ☐ 577 Jeff Lahti | .03 | .01 | .00 |
| ☐ 578 Jeff Calhoun | .05 | .02 | .00 |
| ☐ 579 Gus Polidor | .08 | .03 | .01 |
| ☐ 580 Gene Nelson | .03 | .01 | .00 |
| ☐ 581 Tim Teufel | .05 | .02 | .00 |
| ☐ 582 Odell Jones | .03 | .01 | .00 |
| ☐ 583 Mark Ryal | .10 | .04 | .01 |
| ☐ 584 Randy O'Neal | .03 | .01 | .00 |
| ☐ 585 Mike Greenwell | .15 | .06 | .01 |
| ☐ 586 Ray Knight | .07 | .03 | .01 |
| ☐ 587 Ralph Bryant | .25 | .10 | .02 |
| ☐ 588 Carmen Castillo | .03 | .01 | .00 |

| | | | |
|---|---|---|---|
| ☐ 589 Ed Wojna | .03 | .01 | .00 |
| ☐ 590 Stan Javier | .05 | .02 | .00 |
| ☐ 591 Jeff Musselman | .10 | .04 | .01 |
| ☐ 592 Mike Stanley | .10 | .04 | .01 |
| ☐ 593 Darrell Porter | .05 | .02 | .00 |
| ☐ 594 Drew Hall | .12 | .05 | .01 |
| ☐ 595 Rob Nelson | .15 | .06 | .01 |
| ☐ 596 Bryan Oelkers | .03 | .01 | .00 |
| ☐ 597 Scott Nielsen | .15 | .06 | .01 |
| ☐ 598 Brian Holton | .10 | .04 | .01 |
| ☐ 599 Kevin Mitchell | .35 | .14 | .03 |
| ☐ 600 Checklist | .06 | .01 | .00 |
| ☐ 601 Jackie Gutierrez | .03 | .01 | .00 |
| ☐ 602 Barry Jones | .12 | .05 | .01 |
| ☐ 603 Jerry Narron | .03 | .01 | .00 |
| ☐ 604 Steve Lake | .03 | .01 | .00 |
| ☐ 605 Jim Pankovits | .03 | .01 | .00 |
| ☐ 606 Ed Romero | .03 | .01 | .00 |
| ☐ 607 Dave LaPoint | .03 | .01 | .00 |
| ☐ 608 Don Robinson | .03 | .01 | .00 |
| ☐ 609 Mike Krukow | .07 | .03 | .01 |
| ☐ 610 Dave Valle | .03 | .01 | .00 |
| ☐ 611 Len Dykstra | .20 | .08 | .02 |
| ☐ 612 Roberto Clemente Puzzle Card | .07 | .03 | .01 |
| ☐ 613 Mike Trujillo | .05 | .02 | .00 |
| ☐ 614 Damaso Garcia | .06 | .02 | .00 |
| ☐ 615 Neal Heaton | .03 | .01 | .00 |
| ☐ 616 Juan Berenguer | .03 | .01 | .00 |
| ☐ 617 Steve Carlton | .25 | .10 | .02 |
| ☐ 618 Gary Lucas | .03 | .01 | .00 |
| ☐ 619 Geno Petralli | .03 | .01 | .00 |
| ☐ 620 Rick Aguilera | .05 | .02 | .00 |
| ☐ 621 Fred McGriff | .10 | .04 | .01 |
| ☐ 622 Dave Henderson | .06 | .02 | .00 |
| ☐ 623 Dave Clark | .20 | .08 | .02 |
| ☐ 624 Angel Salazar | .03 | .01 | .00 |
| ☐ 625 Randy Hunt | .03 | .01 | .00 |
| ☐ 626 John Gibbons | .03 | .01 | .00 |
| ☐ 627 Kevin Brown | .20 | .08 | .02 |
| ☐ 628 Bill Dawley | .03 | .01 | .00 |
| ☐ 629 Aurelio Lopez | .03 | .01 | .00 |
| ☐ 630 Charlie Hudson | .05 | .02 | .00 |
| ☐ 631 Ray Soff | .09 | .04 | .01 |
| ☐ 632 Ray Hayward | .10 | .04 | .01 |
| ☐ 633 Spike Owen | .05 | .02 | .00 |
| ☐ 634 Glenn Hubbard | .03 | .01 | .00 |
| ☐ 635 Kevin Elster | .20 | .08 | .02 |
| ☐ 636 Mike LaCoss | .03 | .01 | .00 |
| ☐ 637 Dwayne Henry | .10 | .04 | .01 |
| ☐ 638 Rey Quinones | .10 | .04 | .01 |
| ☐ 639 Jim Clancy | .03 | .01 | .00 |
| ☐ 640 Larry Andersen | .03 | .01 | .00 |
| ☐ 641 Calvin Schiraldi | .08 | .03 | .01 |
| ☐ 642 Stan Jefferson | .15 | .06 | .01 |
| ☐ 643 Marc Sullivan | .03 | .01 | .00 |
| ☐ 644 Mark Grant | .03 | .01 | .00 |
| ☐ 645 Cliff Johnson | .03 | .01 | .00 |
| ☐ 646 Howard Johnson | .03 | .01 | .00 |
| ☐ 647 Dave Sax | .03 | .01 | .00 |
| ☐ 648 Dave Stewart | .03 | .01 | .00 |
| ☐ 649 Danny Heep | .03 | .01 | .00 |
| ☐ 650 Joe Johnson | .03 | .01 | .00 |
| ☐ 651 Bob Brower | .25 | .10 | .02 |
| ☐ 652 Rob Woodward | .05 | .02 | .00 |
| ☐ 653 John Mizerock | .03 | .01 | .00 |
| ☐ 654 Tim Pyznarski | .18 | .08 | .01 |
| ☐ 655 Luis Aquino | .09 | .04 | .01 |
| ☐ 656 Mickey Brantley | .12 | .05 | .01 |
| ☐ 657 Doyle Alexander | .05 | .02 | .00 |
| ☐ 658 Sammy Stewart | .03 | .01 | .00 |
| ☐ 659 Jim Acker | .03 | .01 | .00 |
| ☐ 660 Pete Ladd | .03 | .01 | .00 |
| ☐ PC10 Dale Murphy (wax box card) | .50 | .20 | .05 |
| ☐ PC11 Jeff Reardon (wax box card) | .10 | .04 | .01 |
| ☐ PC12 Jose Canseco (wax box card) | .75 | .30 | .07 |
| ☐ PUZ Clemente Puzzle (wax box card) | .08 | .03 | .01 |

**PICTURE GALLERY:** Any set in this Price Guide not illustrated below its respective set title is pictured in the Picture Gallery section in the back of the book. Those pages are arranged in the same order as the overall book.

## 1987 Donruss Super DK's

This 28 card set was available through a mail-in offer detailed on the wax packs. The set was sent in return for 8.00 and three wrappers plus 1.50 postage and handling. The set features the popular Diamond King sub-series in large (approximately 4 7/8" by 6 13/16") form. Dick Perez of Perez-Steele Galleries did another outstanding job on the artwork. The cards are essentially a large version of the Donruss regular issue Diamond Kings.

|  | | MINT | VG-E | F-G |
|---|---|---|---|---|
| | COMPLETE SET | 10.00 | 4.00 | 1.00 |
| | COMMON PLAYER | .15 | .06 | .01 |
| ☐ 1 | Wally Joyner | 1.50 | .50 | .10 |
| ☐ 2 | Roger Clemens | 1.00 | .40 | .10 |
| ☐ 3 | Dale Murphy | .75 | .30 | .07 |
| ☐ 4 | Darryl Strawberry | .75 | .30 | .07 |
| ☐ 5 | Ozzie Smith | .20 | .08 | .02 |
| ☐ 6 | Jose Canseco | 1.50 | .60 | .15 |
| ☐ 7 | Charlie Hough | .15 | .06 | .01 |
| ☐ 8 | Brook Jacoby | .20 | .08 | .02 |
| ☐ 9 | Fred Lynn | .25 | .10 | .02 |
| ☐ 10 | Rick Rhoden | .15 | .06 | .01 |
| ☐ 11 | Chris Brown | .25 | .10 | .02 |
| ☐ 12 | Von Hayes | .30 | .12 | .03 |
| ☐ 13 | Jack Morris | .25 | .10 | .02 |
| ☐ 14 | Kevin McReynolds | .25 | .10 | .02 |
| ☐ 15 | George Brett | .75 | .30 | .07 |
| ☐ 16 | Ted Higuera | .25 | .10 | .02 |
| ☐ 17 | Hubie Brooks | .25 | .10 | .02 |
| ☐ 18 | Mike Scott | .30 | .12 | .03 |
| ☐ 19 | Kirby Puckett | .60 | .24 | .06 |
| ☐ 20 | Dave Winfield | .60 | .24 | .06 |
| ☐ 21 | Lloyd Moseby | .25 | .10 | .02 |
| ☐ 22 | Eric Davis | .75 | .30 | .07 |
| ☐ 23 | Jim Presley | .35 | .14 | .03 |
| ☐ 24 | Keith Moreland | .15 | .06 | .01 |
| ☐ 25 | Greg Walker | .20 | .08 | .02 |
| ☐ 26 | Steve Sax | .25 | .10 | .02 |
| ☐ 27 | DK Checklist 1-26 | .15 | .01 | .00 |
| ☐ 28 | Roberto Clemente Large Puzzle (unnumbered) | .15 | .01 | .00 |

## 1987 Donruss All Stars

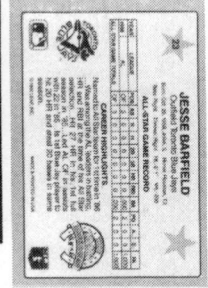

This 60 card set features cards measuring 3 1/2" by 5". Card fronts are in full color with a black border. The card backs are printed in black and blue on white card stock. Cards are numbered on the back. Card backs feature statistical information about the player's performance in past All-Star games. The set was distributed in packs which also contained a Pop-Up.

|  | | MINT | VG-E | F-G |
|---|---|---|---|---|
| | COMPLETE SET | 5.50 | 2.20 | .55 |
| | COMMON PLAYER | .05 | .02 | .00 |
| ☐ 1 | Wally Joyner | .75 | .30 | .07 |
| ☐ 2 | Dave Winfield | .25 | .10 | .02 |
| ☐ 3 | Lou Whitaker | .15 | .06 | .01 |
| ☐ 4 | Kirby Puckett | .25 | .10 | .02 |
| ☐ 5 | Cal Ripken | .35 | .14 | .03 |
| ☐ 6 | Rickey Henderson | .45 | .18 | .04 |
| ☐ 7 | Wade Boggs | .75 | .30 | .07 |
| ☐ 8 | Roger Clemens | .75 | .30 | .07 |
| ☐ 9 | Lance Parrish | .15 | .06 | .01 |
| ☐ 10 | Dick Howser MGR | .05 | .02 | .00 |
| ☐ 11 | Keith Hernandez | .25 | .10 | .02 |
| ☐ 12 | Darryl Strawberry | .35 | .14 | .03 |
| ☐ 13 | Ryne Sandberg | .35 | .14 | .03 |
| ☐ 14 | Dale Murphy | .45 | .18 | .04 |
| ☐ 15 | Ozzie Smith | .15 | .06 | .01 |
| ☐ 16 | Tony Gwynn | .35 | .14 | .03 |
| ☐ 17 | Mike Schmidt | .45 | .18 | .04 |
| ☐ 18 | Dwight Gooden | .75 | .30 | .07 |
| ☐ 19 | Gary Carter | .35 | .14 | .03 |
| ☐ 20 | Whitey Herzog MGR | .05 | .02 | .00 |
| ☐ 21 | Jose Canseco | .75 | .30 | .07 |
| ☐ 22 | John Franco | .10 | .04 | .01 |
| ☐ 23 | Jesse Barfield | .15 | .06 | .01 |
| ☐ 24 | Rick Rhoden | .05 | .02 | .00 |
| ☐ 25 | Harold Baines | .15 | .06 | .01 |
| ☐ 26 | Sid Fernandez | .15 | .06 | .01 |
| ☐ 27 | George Brett | .45 | .18 | .04 |
| ☐ 28 | Steve Sax | .15 | .06 | .01 |
| ☐ 29 | Jim Presley | .15 | .06 | .01 |
| ☐ 30 | Dave Smith | .05 | .02 | .00 |
| ☐ 31 | Eddie Murray | .35 | .14 | .03 |
| ☐ 32 | Mike Scott | .15 | .06 | .01 |
| ☐ 33 | Don Mattingly | .90 | .36 | .09 |
| ☐ 34 | Dave Parker | .25 | .10 | .02 |
| ☐ 35 | Tony Fernandez | .15 | .06 | .01 |
| ☐ 36 | Tim Raines | .25 | .10 | .02 |
| ☐ 37 | Brook Jacoby | .15 | .06 | .01 |
| ☐ 38 | Chili Davis | .10 | .04 | .01 |
| ☐ 39 | Rich Gedman | .10 | .04 | .01 |
| ☐ 40 | Kevin Bass | .10 | .04 | .01 |
| ☐ 41 | Frank White | .10 | .04 | .01 |
| ☐ 42 | Glenn Davis | .25 | .10 | .02 |
| ☐ 43 | Willie Hernandez | .15 | .06 | .01 |
| ☐ 44 | Chris Brown | .15 | .06 | .01 |
| ☐ 45 | Jim Rice | .25 | .10 | .02 |
| ☐ 46 | Tony Pena | .15 | .06 | .01 |
| ☐ 47 | Don Aase | .05 | .02 | .00 |
| ☐ 48 | Hubie Brooks | .10 | .04 | .01 |
| ☐ 49 | Charlie Hough | .05 | .02 | .00 |
| ☐ 50 | Jody Davis | .10 | .04 | .01 |
| ☐ 51 | Mike Witt | .15 | .06 | .01 |
| ☐ 52 | Jeff Reardon | .10 | .04 | .01 |
| ☐ 53 | Ken Schrom | .05 | .02 | .00 |
| ☐ 54 | Fernando Valenzuela | .25 | .10 | .02 |
| ☐ 55 | Dave Righetti | .15 | .06 | .01 |
| ☐ 56 | Shane Rawley | .10 | .04 | .01 |
| ☐ 57 | Ted Higuera | .15 | .06 | .01 |
| ☐ 58 | Mike Krukow | .05 | .02 | .00 |
| ☐ 59 | Lloyd Moseby | .10 | .04 | .01 |
| ☐ 60 | Checklist card | .10 | .01 | .00 |

## 1987 Donruss Pop-Ups

This 20 card set features "fold-out" cards measuring 2 1/2" by 5". Card fronts are in full color. Cards are unnumbered but are listed in the same order as the Donruss All Stars on the All Star checklist card. Card backs present essentially no information about the player. The set was distributed in packs which also contained All Star cards (3 1/2" by 5").

|  | | MINT | VG-E | F-G |
|---|---|---|---|---|
| | COMPLETE SET | 4.50 | 1.80 | .45 |
| | COMMON PLAYER | .10 | .04 | .01 |
| ☐ 1 | Wally Joyner | .75 | .30 | .07 |
| ☐ 2 | Dave Winfield | .25 | .10 | .02 |
| ☐ 3 | Lou Whitaker | .15 | .06 | .01 |
| ☐ 4 | Kirby Puckett | .35 | .14 | .03 |
| ☐ 5 | Cal Ripken | .35 | .14 | .03 |
| ☐ 6 | Rickey Henderson | .45 | .18 | .04 |
| ☐ 7 | Wade Boggs | .75 | .30 | .07 |

| | | | | |
|---|---|---|---|---|
| ☐ 8 | Roger Clemens ................. | .75 | .30 | .07 |
| ☐ 9 | Lance Parrish ................... | .25 | .10 | .02 |
| ☐ 10 | Dick Howser MGR ............. | .10 | .04 | .01 |
| ☐ 11 | Keith Hernandez ............... | .25 | .10 | .02 |
| ☐ 12 | Darryl Strawberry ............. | .35 | .14 | .03 |
| ☐ 13 | Ryne Sandberg ................. | .35 | .14 | .03 |
| ☐ 14 | Dale Murphy ..................... | .45 | .18 | .04 |
| ☐ 15 | Ozzie Smith ..................... | .15 | .06 | .01 |
| ☐ 16 | Tony Gwynn ..................... | .35 | .14 | .03 |
| ☐ 17 | Mike Schmidt ................... | .45 | .18 | .04 |
| ☐ 18 | Dwight Gooden ................. | .75 | .30 | .07 |
| ☐ 19 | Gary Carter ..................... | .35 | .14 | .03 |
| ☐ 20 | Whitey Herzog MGR ......... | .10 | .04 | .01 |

## 1941 Double Play

The cards in this 75 card set measure 2 1/2" by 3 1/8". The 1941 Double Play set, listed as R330 in the American Card Catalog, was a blank backed issue distributed by Gum Products. It consists of 75 numbered cards (two consecutive numbers per card), each depicting two players in sepia tone photographs. Cards 81-100 contain action poses, and the last 50 numbers of the set are slightly harder to find. Cards that have been cut in half to form "singles" have a greatly reduced value.

| | | MINT | VG-E | F-G |
|---|---|---|---|---|
| COMPLETE SET | ........................ | 1350.00 | 600.00 | 150.00 |
| COMMON PAIRS (1-100) | ........... | 11.00 | 4.50 | 1.10 |
| COMMON PAIRS (101-150) | ...... | 13.00 | 5.25 | 1.30 |
| ☐ 1 | Larry French and ............. <br> 2 Vance Page | 11.00 | 4.50 | 1.10 |
| ☐ 3 | Billy Herman and ............. <br> 4 Stan Hack | 15.00 | 6.00 | 1.50 |
| ☐ 5 | Lonnie Frey and .............. <br> 6 Johnny vanderMeer | 13.00 | 5.25 | 1.30 |

| | | | | |
|---|---|---|---|---|
| ☐ 7 | Paul Derringer and ......... <br> 8 Bucky Walters | 13.00 | 5.25 | 1.30 |
| ☐ 9 | Frank McCormick and .... <br> 10 Bill Werber | 11.00 | 4.50 | 1.10 |
| ☐ 11 | Jimmy Ripple and ........... <br> 12 Ernie Lombardi | 15.00 | 6.00 | 1.50 |
| ☐ 13 | Alex Kampouris and ........ <br> 14 Whitlow Wyatt | 11.00 | 4.50 | 1.10 |
| ☐ 15 | Mickey Owen and ........... <br> 16 Paul Waner | 15.00 | 6.00 | 1.50 |
| ☐ 17 | Cookie Lavagetto and ..... <br> 18 Pete Reiser | 13.00 | 5.25 | 1.30 |
| ☐ 19 | James Wasdell and ......... <br> 20 Dolf Camilli | 11.00 | 4.50 | 1.10 |
| ☐ 21 | Dixie Walker and ............ <br> 22 Joe Medwick | 15.00 | 6.00 | 1.50 |
| ☐ 23 | Pee Wee Reese and ....... <br> 24 Kirby Higbe | 40.00 | 16.00 | 4.00 |
| ☐ 25 | Harry Danning and .......... <br> 26 Cliff Melton | 11.00 | 4.50 | 1.10 |
| ☐ 27 | Harry Gumbert and .......... <br> 28 Burgess Whitehead | 11.00 | 4.50 | 1.10 |
| ☐ 29 | Joe Orengo and ............. <br> 30 Joe Moore | 11.00 | 4.50 | 1.10 |
| ☐ 31 | Mel Ott and .................... <br> 32 Norman Young | 30.00 | 12.00 | 3.00 |
| ☐ 33 | Lee Handley and ............ <br> 34 Arky Vaughan | 15.00 | 6.00 | 1.50 |
| ☐ 35 | Bob Klinger and ............. <br> 36 Stanley Brown | 11.00 | 4.50 | 1.10 |
| ☐ 37 | Terry Moore and ............. <br> 38 Gus Mancuso | 11.00 | 4.50 | 1.10 |
| ☐ 39 | Johnny Mize and ............ <br> 40 Enos Slaughter | 40.00 | 16.00 | 4.00 |
| ☐ 41 | Johnny Cooney and ........ <br> 42 Sibby Sisti | 11.00 | 4.50 | 1.10 |
| ☐ 43 | Max West and ................ <br> 44 Carvel Rowell | 11.00 | 4.50 | 1.10 |
| ☐ 45 | Danny Litwhiler and ........ <br> 46 Merrill May | 11.00 | 4.50 | 1.10 |
| ☐ 47 | Frank Hayes and ............ <br> 48 Al Brancato | 11.00 | 4.50 | 1.10 |
| ☐ 49 | Bob Johnson and ............ <br> 50 Bill Nagel | 11.00 | 4.50 | 1.10 |
| ☐ 51 | Buck Newsom and .......... <br> 52 Hank Greenberg | 20.00 | 8.00 | 2.00 |
| ☐ 53 | Barney McCosky and ...... <br> 54 Charlie Gehringer | 20.00 | 8.00 | 2.00 |
| ☐ 55 | Mike Higgins and ........... <br> 56 Dick Bartell | 11.00 | 4.50 | 1.10 |
| ☐ 57 | Ted Williams and ............ <br> 58 Jim Tabor | 125.00 | 50.00 | 12.50 |
| ☐ 59 | Joe Cronin and ............... <br> 60 Jimmie Foxx | 75.00 | 30.00 | 7.50 |
| ☐ 61 | Lefty Gomez and ............ <br> 62 Phil Rizzuto | 75.00 | 30.00 | 7.50 |
| ☐ 63 | Joe DiMaggio and ........... <br> 64 Charlie Keller | 175.00 | 70.00 | 18.00 |
| ☐ 65 | Red Rolfe and ................. <br> 66 Bill Dickey | 35.00 | 14.00 | 3.50 |
| ☐ 67 | Joe Gordon and ............. <br> 68 Red Ruffing | 25.00 | 10.00 | 2.50 |
| ☐ 69 | Mike Tresh and .............. <br> 70 Luke Appling | 15.00 | 6.00 | 1.50 |
| ☐ 71 | Moose Solters and .......... <br> 72 Johnny Rigney | 11.00 | 4.50 | 1.10 |
| ☐ 73 | Buddy Myer and ............. <br> 74 Ben Chapman | 11.00 | 4.50 | 1.10 |
| ☐ 75 | Cecil Travis and ............. <br> 76 George Case | 11.00 | 4.50 | 1.10 |
| ☐ 77 | Joe Krakauskas and ....... <br> 78 Bob Feller | 40.00 | 16.00 | 4.00 |
| ☐ 79 | Ken Keltner and ............. <br> 80 Hal Trosky | 11.00 | 4.50 | 1.10 |
| ☐ 81 | Ted Williams and ............ <br> 82 Joe Cronin | 150.00 | 60.00 | 15.00 |
| ☐ 83 | Joe Gordon and ............. <br> 84 Charlie Keller | 15.00 | 6.00 | 1.50 |
| ☐ 85 | Hank Greenberg and ...... <br> 86 Red Ruffing | 60.00 | 24.00 | 6.00 |
| ☐ 87 | Hal Trosky and ............... <br> 88 George Case | 11.00 | 4.50 | 1.10 |
| ☐ 89 | Mel Ott and .................... <br> 90 Burgess Whitehead | 30.00 | 12.00 | 3.00 |
| ☐ 91 | Harry Danning and ......... <br> 92 Harry Gumbert | 11.00 | 4.50 | 1.10 |
| ☐ 93 | Norman Young and ......... <br> 94 Cliff Melton | 11.00 | 4.50 | 1.10 |
| ☐ 95 | Jimmy Ripple and ........... <br> 96 Bucky Walters | 11.00 | 4.50 | 1.10 |
| ☐ 97 | Stanley Jack and ............ <br> 98 Bob Klinger | 11.00 | 4.50 | 1.10 |

| | | | | |
|---|---|---|---|---|
| ☐ 99 | Johnny Mize and ........... 100 Dan Litwhiler | 20.00 | 8.00 | 2.00 |
| ☐ 101 | Dom Dallesandro and ..... 102 Augie Galan | 13.00 | 5.25 | 1.30 |
| ☐ 103 | Bill Lee and ................ 104 Phil Cavarretta | 13.00 | 5.25 | 1.30 |
| ☐ 105 | Lefty Grove and ............ 106 Bobby Doerr | 60.00 | 24.00 | 6.00 |
| ☐ 107 | Frank Pytlak and ........... 108 Dom DiMaggio | 15.00 | 6.00 | 1.50 |
| ☐ 109 | Jerry Priddy and ............ 110 Johnny Murphy | 13.00 | 5.25 | 1.30 |
| ☐ 111 | Tommy Henrich and ....... 112 Marius Russo | 15.00 | 6.00 | 1.50 |
| ☐ 113 | Frank Crosetti and ......... 114 John Sturm | 15.00 | 6.00 | 1.50 |
| ☐ 115 | Ival Goodman and .......... 116 Myron McCormick | 13.00 | 5.25 | 1.30 |
| ☐ 117 | Eddie Joost and ............ 118 Ernie Koy | 13.00 | 5.25 | 1.30 |
| ☐ 119 | Lloyd Waner and ............ 120 Hank Majeski | 18.00 | 7.25 | 1.80 |
| ☐ 121 | Buddy Hassett and ........ 122 Eugene Moore | 13.00 | 5.25 | 1.30 |
| ☐ 123 | Nick Etten and ............... 124 John Rizzo | 13.00 | 5.25 | 1.30 |
| ☐ 125 | Sam Chapman and ........ 126 Wally Moses | 13.00 | 5.25 | 1.30 |
| ☐ 127 | Johnny Babich and ........ 128 Dick Siebert | 13.00 | 5.25 | 1.30 |
| ☐ 129 | Nelson Potter and .......... 130 Benny McCoy | 13.00 | 5.25 | 1.30 |
| ☐ 131 | Clarence Campbell and ... 132 Lou Boudreau | 20.00 | 8.00 | 2.00 |
| ☐ 133 | Rollie Hemsley and ........ 134 Mel Harder | 13.00 | 5.25 | 1.30 |
| ☐ 135 | Gerald Walker and ......... 136 Joe Heving | 13.00 | 5.25 | 1.30 |
| ☐ 137 | Johnny Rucker and ........ 138 Ace Adams | 13.00 | 5.25 | 1.30 |
| ☐ 139 | Morris Arnovich and ....... 140 Carl Hubbell | 30.00 | 12.00 | 3.00 |
| ☐ 141 | Lew Riggs and ................ 142 Leo Durocher | 20.00 | 8.00 | 2.00 |
| ☐ 143 | Fred Fitzsimmons and .... 144 Joe Vosmik | 13.00 | 5.25 | 1.30 |
| ☐ 145 | Frank Crespi and ........... 146 Jim Brown | 13.00 | 5.25 | 1.30 |
| ☐ 147 | Don Heffner and ............ 148 Harland Clift | 13.00 | 5.25 | 1.30 |
| ☐ 149 | Debs Garms and ............ 150 Elbert Fletcher | 13.00 | 5.25 | 1.30 |

## 1950 Drake's

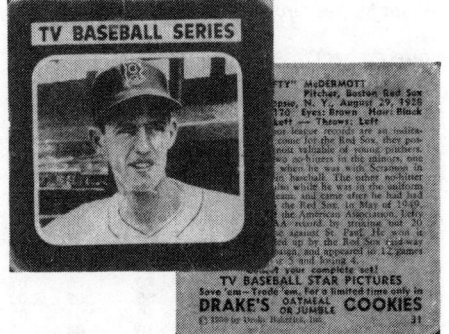

The cards in this 36 card set measure 2 1/2" by 2 1/2". The 1950 Drake's Cookies set contains numbered black and white cards. The players are pictured inside a simulated television screen and the caption "TV Baseball Series" appears on the cards. The ACC designation is D358.

| | MINT | VG-E | F-G |
|---|---|---|---|
| COMPLETE SET ........................ | 1350.00 | 600.00 | 150.00 |

| | | | | |
|---|---|---|---|---|
| COMMON PLAYER (1-36) .......... | 25.00 | 10.00 | 2.50 |
| ☐ 1 Preacher Roe ................. | 35.00 | 14.00 | 3.50 |
| ☐ 2 Clint Hartung ................. | 25.00 | 10.00 | 2.50 |
| ☐ 3 Earl Torgeson ................ | 25.00 | 10.00 | 2.50 |
| ☐ 4 Lou Brissie ..................... | 25.00 | 10.00 | 2.50 |
| ☐ 5 Duke Snider .................. | 120.00 | 50.00 | 12.00 |
| ☐ 6 Roy Campanella ............. | 150.00 | 60.00 | 15.00 |
| ☐ 7 Sheldon Jones .............. | 25.00 | 10.00 | 2.50 |
| ☐ 8 Whitey Lockman ............ | 25.00 | 10.00 | 2.50 |
| ☐ 9 Bobby Thomson ............ | 35.00 | 14.00 | 3.50 |
| ☐ 10 Dick Sisler ................... | 25.00 | 10.00 | 2.50 |
| ☐ 11 Gil Hodges .................... | 75.00 | 30.00 | 7.50 |
| ☐ 12 Eddie Waitkus ............... | 25.00 | 10.00 | 2.50 |
| ☐ 13 Bobby Kerr ................... | 25.00 | 10.00 | 2.50 |
| ☐ 14 Warren Spahn ............... | 90.00 | 36.00 | 9.00 |
| ☐ 15 Buddy Kerr ................... | 25.00 | 10.00 | 2.50 |
| ☐ 16 Sid Gordon ................... | 25.00 | 10.00 | 2.50 |
| ☐ 17 Willard Marshall ............ | 25.00 | 10.00 | 2.50 |
| ☐ 18 Carl Furillo .................. | 35.00 | 14.00 | 3.50 |
| ☐ 19 Pee Wee Reese ............. | 75.00 | 30.00 | 7.50 |
| ☐ 20 Alvin Dark .................... | 35.00 | 14.00 | 3.50 |
| ☐ 21 Del Ennis .................... | 30.00 | 12.00 | 3.00 |
| ☐ 22 Ed Stanky ................... | 30.00 | 12.00 | 3.00 |
| ☐ 23 Tom Henrich ................ | 35.00 | 14.00 | 3.50 |
| ☐ 24 Yogi Berra ................... | 120.00 | 50.00 | 12.00 |
| ☐ 25 Phil Rizzuto ................. | 75.00 | 30.00 | 7.50 |
| ☐ 26 Jerry Coleman .............. | 30.00 | 12.00 | 3.00 |
| ☐ 27 Joe Page ..................... | 30.00 | 12.00 | 3.00 |
| ☐ 28 Allie Reynolds .............. | 35.00 | 14.00 | 3.50 |
| ☐ 29 Ray Scarborough .......... | 25.00 | 10.00 | 2.50 |
| ☐ 30 Birdie Tebbetts ............. | 25.00 | 10.00 | 2.50 |
| ☐ 31 Maurice McDermott ....... | 25.00 | 10.00 | 2.50 |
| ☐ 32 Johnny Pesky ............... | 30.00 | 12.00 | 3.00 |
| ☐ 33 Dom DiMaggio ............. | 35.00 | 14.00 | 3.50 |
| ☐ 34 Vern Stephens ............. | 30.00 | 12.00 | 3.00 |
| ☐ 35 Bob Elliott ................... | 35.00 | 14.00 | 3.50 |
| ☐ 36 Enos Slaughter ............. | 75.00 | 30.00 | 7.50 |

## 1981 Drake's

The cards in this 33 card set measure 2 1/2" by 3 1/2". The 1981 Drake's Bakeries set contains National and American League stars. Produced in conjunction with Topps and released to the public in Drake's Cakes, this set features red frames for American League players and blue frames for National League players. A Drake's Cakes logo with the words "Big Hitters" appears on the lower front of each card. The backs are quite similar to the 1981 Topps backs but contain the Drake's logo, a different card number, and a short paragraph entitled "What Makes a Big Hitter?" at the top of the card.

| | MINT | VG-E | F-G |
|---|---|---|---|
| COMPLETE SET ......................... | 5.00 | 2.00 | .50 |
| COMMON PLAYER ................... | .05 | .02 | .00 |
| ☐ 1 Carl Yastrzemski ............. | .75 | .30 | .07 |
| ☐ 2 Rod Carew .................... | .50 | .20 | .05 |
| ☐ 3 Pete Rose .................... | 1.00 | .40 | .10 |
| ☐ 4 Dave Parker .................. | .25 | .10 | .02 |
| ☐ 5 George Brett ................. | .75 | .30 | .07 |

| | | | | | |
|---|---|---|---|---|---|
| ☐ | 6 | Eddie Murray | .75 | .30 | .07 |
| ☐ | 7 | Mike Schmidt | .75 | .30 | .07 |
| ☐ | 8 | Jim Rice | .35 | .14 | .03 |
| ☐ | 9 | Fred Lynn | .20 | .08 | .02 |
| ☐ | 10 | Reggie Jackson | .75 | .30 | .07 |
| ☐ | 11 | Steve Garvey | .55 | .22 | .05 |
| ☐ | 12 | Ken Singleton | .05 | .02 | .00 |
| ☐ | 13 | Bill Buckner | .05 | .02 | .00 |
| ☐ | 14 | Dave Winfield | .40 | .16 | .04 |
| ☐ | 15 | Jack Clark | .10 | .04 | .01 |
| ☐ | 16 | Cecil Cooper | .10 | .04 | .01 |
| ☐ | 17 | Bob Horner | .25 | .10 | .02 |
| ☐ | 18 | George Foster | .10 | .04 | .01 |
| ☐ | 19 | Dave Kingman | .10 | .04 | .01 |
| ☐ | 20 | Cesar Cedeno | .05 | .02 | .00 |
| ☐ | 21 | Joe Charboneau | .05 | .02 | .00 |
| ☐ | 22 | George Hendrick | .05 | .02 | .00 |
| ☐ | 23 | Gary Carter | .50 | .20 | .05 |
| ☐ | 24 | Al Oliver | .15 | .06 | .01 |
| ☐ | 25 | Bruce Bochte | .05 | .02 | .00 |
| ☐ | 26 | Jerry Mumphrey | .05 | .02 | .00 |
| ☐ | 27 | Steve Kemp | .10 | .04 | .01 |
| ☐ | 28 | Bob Watson | .05 | .02 | .00 |
| ☐ | 29 | John Castino | .05 | .02 | .00 |
| ☐ | 30 | Tony Armas | .10 | .04 | .01 |
| ☐ | 31 | John Mayberry | .05 | .02 | .00 |
| ☐ | 32 | Carlton Fisk | .15 | .06 | .01 |
| ☐ | 33 | Lee Mazzilli | .05 | .02 | .00 |

| | | | | | |
|---|---|---|---|---|---|
| ☐ | 12 | Carlton Fisk | .15 | .06 | .01 |
| ☐ | 13 | George Foster | .10 | .04 | .01 |
| ☐ | 14 | Steve Garvey | .50 | .20 | .05 |
| ☐ | 15 | Kirk Gibson | .30 | .12 | .03 |
| ☐ | 16 | Mike Hargrove | .05 | .02 | .00 |
| ☐ | 17 | George Hendrick | .05 | .02 | .00 |
| ☐ | 18 | Bob Horner | .20 | .08 | .02 |
| ☐ | 19 | Reggie Jackson | .75 | .30 | .07 |
| ☐ | 20 | Terry Kennedy | .05 | .02 | .00 |
| ☐ | 21 | Dave Kingman | .10 | .04 | .01 |
| ☐ | 22 | Greg Luzinski | .10 | .04 | .01 |
| ☐ | 23 | Bill Madlock | .10 | .04 | .01 |
| ☐ | 24 | John Mayberry | .05 | .02 | .00 |
| ☐ | 25 | Eddie Murray | .70 | .28 | .07 |
| ☐ | 26 | Graig Nettles | .15 | .06 | .01 |
| ☐ | 27 | Jim Rice | .35 | .14 | .03 |
| ☐ | 28 | Pete Rose | 1.00 | .40 | .10 |
| ☐ | 29 | Mike Schmidt | .75 | .30 | .07 |
| ☐ | 30 | Ken Singleton | .05 | .02 | .00 |
| ☐ | 31 | Dave Winfield | .40 | .16 | .04 |
| ☐ | 32 | Butch Wynegar | .05 | .02 | .00 |
| ☐ | 33 | Richie Zisk | .05 | .02 | .00 |

## 1983 Drake's

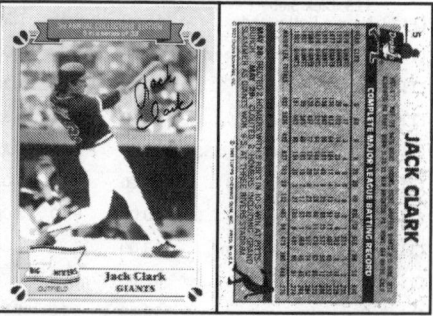

The cards in this 33 card series measure 2 1/2" by 3 1/2". For the third year in a row, Drake's Cakes, in conjunction with Topps, issued a set entitled Big Hitters. The fronts appear very similar to those of the previous two years with slight variations on the framelines and player identification sections. The backs are the same as the Topps backs of this year except for the card number and the Drake's logo.

| | | | MINT | VG-E | F-G |
|---|---|---|---|---|---|
| | COMPLETE SET | | 5.00 | 2.00 | .50 |
| | COMMON PLAYER | | .05 | .02 | .00 |
| ☐ | 1 | Don Baylor | .15 | .06 | .01 |
| ☐ | 2 | Bill Buckner | .10 | .04 | .01 |
| ☐ | 3 | Rod Carew | .50 | .20 | .05 |
| ☐ | 4 | Gary Carter | .50 | .20 | .05 |
| ☐ | 5 | Jack Clark | .10 | .04 | .01 |
| ☐ | 6 | Cecil Cooper | .10 | .04 | .01 |
| ☐ | 7 | Dwight Evans | .10 | .04 | .01 |
| ☐ | 8 | George Foster | .10 | .04 | .01 |
| ☐ | 9 | Pedro Guerrero | .35 | .14 | .03 |
| ☐ | 10 | George Hendrick | .05 | .02 | .00 |
| ☐ | 11 | Bob Horner | .20 | .08 | .02 |
| ☐ | 12 | Reggie Jackson | .70 | .28 | .07 |
| ☐ | 13 | Steve Kemp | .05 | .02 | .00 |
| ☐ | 14 | Dave Kingman | .10 | .04 | .01 |
| ☐ | 15 | Bill Madlock | .10 | .04 | .01 |
| ☐ | 16 | Gary Matthews | .05 | .02 | .00 |
| ☐ | 17 | Hal McRae | .05 | .02 | .00 |
| ☐ | 18 | Dale Murphy | .75 | .30 | .07 |
| ☐ | 19 | Eddie Murray | .70 | .28 | .07 |
| ☐ | 20 | Ben Oglivie | .05 | .02 | .00 |
| ☐ | 21 | Al Oliver | .10 | .04 | .01 |
| ☐ | 22 | Jim Rice | .35 | .14 | .03 |
| ☐ | 23 | Cal Ripken | .50 | .20 | .05 |
| ☐ | 24 | Pete Rose | 1.00 | .40 | .10 |
| ☐ | 25 | Mike Schmidt | .75 | .30 | .07 |
| ☐ | 26 | Ken Singleton | .05 | .02 | .00 |
| ☐ | 27 | Gorman Thomas | .05 | .02 | .00 |

## 1982 Drake's

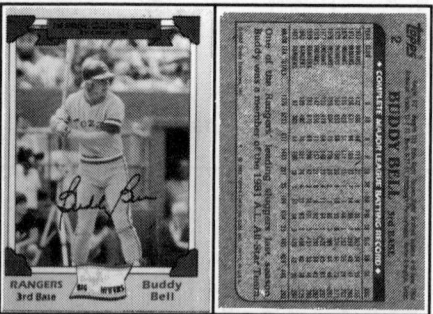

The cards in this 33 card set measure 2 1/2" by 3 1/2". The 1982 Drake's Big Hitters series cards each has the title "2nd Annual Collectors' Edition" in a ribbon design at the top of the picture area. Each color player photo has "photo mount" designs in the corners, red for the AL and green for the NL. The reverses are green and blue, the same as the regular 1982 Topps format, and the photos are larger than those of the previous year. Of the 33 hitters featured, 19 represent the National League. There are 21 returnees from the 1981 set and only one photo, that of Kennedy, is the same as that appearing in the regular Topps issue. The Drake's logo appears centered in the bottom border on the obverse.

| | | | MINT | VG-E | F-G |
|---|---|---|---|---|---|
| | COMPLETE SET | | 5.00 | 2.00 | .50 |
| | COMMON PLAYER | | .05 | .02 | .00 |
| ☐ | 1 | Tony Armas | .10 | .04 | .01 |
| ☐ | 2 | Buddy Bell | .10 | .04 | .01 |
| ☐ | 3 | Johnny Bench | .35 | .14 | .03 |
| ☐ | 4 | George Brett | .75 | .30 | .07 |
| ☐ | 5 | Bill Buckner | .05 | .02 | .00 |
| ☐ | 6 | Rod Carew | .50 | .20 | .05 |
| ☐ | 7 | Gary Carter | .50 | .20 | .05 |
| ☐ | 8 | Jack Clark | .10 | .04 | .01 |
| ☐ | 9 | Cecil Cooper | .15 | .06 | .01 |
| ☐ | 10 | Jose Cruz | .10 | .04 | .01 |
| ☐ | 11 | Dwight Evans | .10 | .04 | .01 |

| | | | MINT | VG-E | F-G |
|---|---|---|---|---|---|
| ☐ | 28 | Jason Thompson ............ | .05 | .02 | .00 |
| ☐ | 29 | Mookie Wilson ................ | .05 | .02 | .00 |
| ☐ | 30 | Willie Wilson .................... | .10 | .04 | .01 |
| ☐ | 31 | Dave Winfield ................. | .40 | .16 | .04 |
| ☐ | 32 | Carl Yastrzemski ............. | .75 | .30 | .07 |
| ☐ | 33 | Robin Yount .................... | .35 | .14 | .03 |

## 1984 Drake's

The cards in this 33 card set measure 2 1/2" by 3 1/2". The Fourth Annual Collectors Edition of baseball cards produced by Drake's Cakes in conjunction with Topps continued this now annual set entitled Big Hitters. As in previous years, the front contains a frameline in which the title of the set, the Drake's logo, and the player's name, his team, and position appear. The cards all feature the player in a batting action pose. While the cards fronts are different from the Topps fronts of this year, the backs differ only in the card number and the use of the Drake's logo instead of the Topps logo.

| | | | MINT | VG-E | F-G |
|---|---|---|---|---|---|
| | | COMPLETE SET ........................ | 5.00 | 2.00 | .50 |
| | | COMMON PLAYER .................... | .05 | .02 | .00 |
| ☐ | 1 | Don Baylor .................. | .15 | .06 | .01 |
| ☐ | 2 | Wade Boggs ................. | .90 | .36 | .09 |
| ☐ | 3 | George Brett ................. | .75 | .30 | .07 |
| ☐ | 4 | Bill Buckner ................. | .05 | .02 | .00 |
| ☐ | 5 | Rod Carew .................. | .50 | .20 | .05 |
| ☐ | 6 | Gary Carter .................. | .50 | .20 | .05 |
| ☐ | 7 | Ron Cey ...................... | .05 | .02 | .00 |
| ☐ | 8 | Cecil Cooper ................. | .10 | .04 | .01 |
| ☐ | 9 | Andre Dawson .............. | .20 | .08 | .02 |
| ☐ | 10 | Steve Garvey ............... | .50 | .20 | .05 |
| ☐ | 11 | Pedro Guerrero ............. | .30 | .12 | .03 |
| ☐ | 12 | George Hendrick ............ | .05 | .02 | .00 |
| ☐ | 13 | Keith Hernandez ............ | .35 | .14 | .03 |
| ☐ | 14 | Bob Horner .................. | .20 | .08 | .02 |
| ☐ | 15 | Reggie Jackson ............. | .70 | .28 | .07 |
| ☐ | 16 | Steve Kemp .................. | .05 | .02 | .00 |
| ☐ | 17 | Ron Kittle ................... | .10 | .04 | .01 |
| ☐ | 18 | Greg Luzinski ............... | .10 | .04 | .01 |
| ☐ | 19 | Fred Lynn .................... | .15 | .06 | .01 |
| ☐ | 20 | Bill Madlock ................. | .10 | .04 | .01 |
| ☐ | 21 | Gary Matthews .............. | .05 | .02 | .00 |
| ☐ | 22 | Dale Murphy ................. | .75 | .30 | .07 |
| ☐ | 23 | Eddie Murray ................ | .60 | .24 | .06 |
| ☐ | 24 | Al Oliver ..................... | .10 | .04 | .01 |
| ☐ | 25 | Jim Rice ...................... | .30 | .12 | .03 |
| ☐ | 26 | Cal Ripken ................... | .50 | .20 | .05 |
| ☐ | 27 | Pete Rose .................... | .90 | .36 | .09 |
| ☐ | 28 | Mike Schmidt ................ | .75 | .30 | .07 |
| ☐ | 29 | Darryl Strawberry .......... | 1.00 | .40 | .10 |
| ☐ | 30 | Alan Trammell ............... | .15 | .06 | .01 |
| ☐ | 31 | Mookie Wilson ............... | .05 | .02 | .00 |
| ☐ | 32 | Dave Winfield ............... | .40 | .16 | .04 |
| ☐ | 33 | Robin Yount .................. | .30 | .12 | .03 |

## 1985 Drake's

The cards in this 44 card set measure 2 1/2" by 3 1/2". The Fifth Annual Collectors Edition of baseball cards produced by Drake's Cakes in conjunction with Topps continued this apparently annual set with a new twist, for the first time, 11 pitchers were included. The "Big Hitters" are numbered 1-33 and the pitchers are numbered 34-44; each subgroup is ordered alphabetically. The cards are numbered in the upper right corner of the backs of the cards. The complete set could be obtained directly from the company by sending 2.95 with four proofs of purchase.

| | | | MINT | VG-E | F-G |
|---|---|---|---|---|---|
| | | COMPLETE SET ........................ | 8.00 | 3.25 | .80 |
| | | COMMON PLAYER .................... | .05 | .02 | .00 |
| ☐ | 1 | Tony Armas .................... | .10 | .04 | .01 |
| ☐ | 2 | Harold Baines ................ | .20 | .08 | .02 |
| ☐ | 3 | Don Baylor ................... | .15 | .06 | .01 |
| ☐ | 4 | George Brett ................. | .75 | .30 | .07 |
| ☐ | 5 | Gary Carter .................. | .50 | .20 | .05 |
| ☐ | 6 | Ron Cey ...................... | .05 | .02 | .00 |
| ☐ | 7 | Jose Cruz ..................... | .05 | .02 | .00 |
| ☐ | 8 | Alvin Davis .................. | .15 | .06 | .01 |
| ☐ | 9 | Chili Davis ................... | .05 | .02 | .00 |
| ☐ | 10 | Dwight Evans ................ | .10 | .04 | .01 |
| ☐ | 11 | Steve Garvey ............... | .35 | .14 | .03 |
| ☐ | 12 | Kirk Gibson .................. | .20 | .08 | .02 |
| ☐ | 13 | Pedro Guerrero ............. | .20 | .08 | .02 |
| ☐ | 14 | Tony Gwynn .................. | .35 | .14 | .03 |
| ☐ | 15 | Keith Hernandez ............ | .25 | .10 | .02 |
| ☐ | 16 | Kent Hrbek ................... | .20 | .08 | .02 |
| ☐ | 17 | Reggie Jackson ............. | .70 | .28 | .07 |
| ☐ | 18 | Gary Matthews .............. | .05 | .02 | .00 |
| ☐ | 19 | Don Mattingly ................ | 1.50 | .60 | .15 |
| ☐ | 20 | Dale Murphy ................. | .75 | .30 | .07 |
| ☐ | 21 | Eddie Murray ................ | .60 | .24 | .06 |
| ☐ | 22 | Dave Parker ................. | .25 | .10 | .02 |
| ☐ | 23 | Lance Parrish ............... | .25 | .10 | .02 |
| ☐ | 24 | Tim Raines ................... | .25 | .10 | .02 |
| ☐ | 25 | Jim Rice ...................... | .30 | .12 | .03 |
| ☐ | 26 | Cal Ripken ................... | .50 | .20 | .05 |
| ☐ | 27 | Juan Samuel ................. | .15 | .06 | .01 |
| ☐ | 28 | Ryne Sandberg .............. | .30 | .12 | .03 |
| ☐ | 29 | Mike Schmidt ................ | .60 | .24 | .06 |
| ☐ | 30 | Darryl Strawberry .......... | .60 | .24 | .06 |
| ☐ | 31 | Alan Trammell ............... | .15 | .06 | .01 |
| ☐ | 32 | Dave Winfield ............... | .30 | .12 | .03 |
| ☐ | 33 | Robin Yount .................. | .30 | .12 | .03 |
| ☐ | 34 | Mike Boddicker ............. | .05 | .02 | .00 |
| ☐ | 35 | Steve Carlton ............... | .30 | .12 | .03 |
| ☐ | 36 | Dwight Gooden .............. | 1.00 | .40 | .10 |
| ☐ | 37 | Willie Hernandez ........... | .10 | .04 | .01 |
| ☐ | 38 | Mark Langston ............... | .10 | .04 | .01 |
| ☐ | 39 | Dan Quisenberry ............ | .15 | .06 | .01 |
| ☐ | 40 | Dave Righetti ............... | .15 | .06 | .01 |
| ☐ | 41 | Tom Seaver .................. | .30 | .12 | .03 |
| ☐ | 42 | Bob Stanley ................. | .05 | .02 | .00 |
| ☐ | 43 | Rick Sutcliffe ............... | .10 | .04 | .01 |
| ☐ | 44 | Bruce Sutter ................. | .10 | .04 | .01 |

## 1986 Drake's

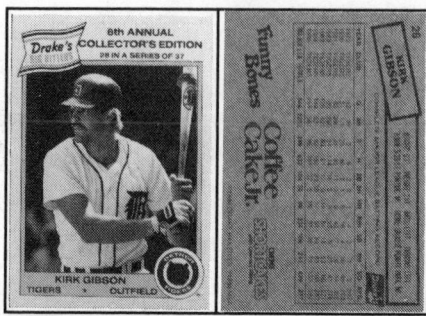

This set of 37 cards was distributed as back panels of various Drake's snack products. Each individual card measures 2 1/2" by 3 1/2". Each specially marked package features two, three, or four cards on the back. Each player appeared on only one type of snack package. The set is easily recognized by the Drake's logo and "6th Annual Collector's Edition" at the top of the obverse. Cards are numbered on the front and the back. Cards below are coded based on the product upon which they appeared, for example, Apple Pies (AP), Cherry Pies (CP), Chocolate Donut Delites (CDD), Coffee Cake Jr. (CCJ), Creme Shortcakes (CS), Devil Dogs (DD), Funny Bones (FB), Peanut Butter Squares (PBS), Powdered Sugar Donut Delites (PSDD), Ring Ding Jr. (RDJ), Sunny Doodles (SD), Swiss Rolls (SR), Yankee Doodles (YD), and Yodels (Y). The last nine cards are pitchers.

|  | MINT | VG-E | F-G |
|---|---|---|---|
| COMPLETE SET | 24.00 | 9.00 | 2.20 |
| COMMON PLAYER (1-37) | .30 | .12 | .03 |
| 1 Gary Carter Y | .80 | .30 | .07 |
| 2 Dwight Evans Y | .30 | .12 | .03 |
| 3 Reggie Jackson SR | 1.00 | .40 | .10 |
| 4 Dave Parker SR | .40 | .16 | .04 |
| 5 Rickey Henderson FB | 1.00 | .40 | .10 |
| 6 Pedro Guerrero FB | .40 | .16 | .04 |
| 7 Don Mattingly YD | 3.00 | 1.00 | .25 |
| 8 Mike Marshall YD | .40 | .16 | .04 |
| 9 Keith Moreland YD | .30 | .12 | .03 |
| 10 Keith Hernandez CS | .60 | .24 | .06 |
| 11 Cal Ripken CS | .60 | .24 | .06 |
| 12 Dale Murphy RDJ | 1.25 | .50 | .12 |
| 13 Jim Rice RDJ | .60 | .24 | .06 |
| 14 George Brett CCJ | .75 | .30 | .07 |
| 15 Tim Raines CCJ | .50 | .20 | .05 |
| 16 Darryl Strawberry DD | 1.25 | .50 | .12 |
| 17 Bill Buckner DD | .30 | .12 | .03 |
| 18 Dave Winfield AP | .50 | .20 | .05 |
| 19 Ryne Sandberg AP | .50 | .20 | .05 |
| 20 Steve Balboni AP | .30 | .12 | .03 |
| 21 Tom Herr AP | .30 | .12 | .03 |
| 22 Pete Rose CP | 1.50 | .60 | .15 |
| 23 Willie McGee CP | .50 | .20 | .05 |
| 24 Harold Baines CP | .50 | .20 | .05 |
| 25 Eddie Murray CP | .75 | .30 | .07 |
| 26 Mike Schmidt SD | 1.25 | .50 | .12 |
| 27 Wade Boggs SD | 1.75 | .70 | .17 |
| 28 Kirk Gibson SD | .50 | .20 | .05 |
| 29 Bret Saberhagen PBS | .40 | .16 | .04 |
| 30 John Tudor PBS | .30 | .12 | .03 |
| 31 Orel Hershiser PBS | .40 | .16 | .04 |
| 32 Ron Guidry CDD | .50 | .20 | .05 |
| 33 Nolan Ryan CDD | .60 | .24 | .06 |
| 34 Dave Stieb CDD | .40 | .16 | .04 |
| 35 Dwight Gooden SDD | 1.00 | .40 | .10 |
| 36 Fernando Valenzuela SDD | .50 | .20 | .05 |
| 37 Tom Browning SDD | .30 | .12 | .03 |

## East Hills Pirates

BOB VEALE          (Pitcher)          #39

The 1966 East Hills Pirates set consists of 25 large (3 1/4" by 4 1/4"), full color photos of Pittsburgh Pirate ballplayers. These blank-backed cards are numbered in the lower right corner according to the uniform number of the individual depicted. The set was distributed by various stores located in the East Hills Shopping Center. The ACC catalog number is F405.

|  | MINT | VG-E | F-G |
|---|---|---|---|
| COMPLETE SET | 18.00 | 7.25 | 1.80 |
| COMMON PLAYER (1-45) | .35 | .14 | .03 |
| 3 Harry Walker MGR | .50 | .20 | .05 |
| 7 Bob Bailey | .35 | .14 | .03 |
| 8 Willie Stargell | 3.50 | 1.40 | .35 |
| 9 Bill Mazeroski | 1.25 | .50 | .12 |
| 10 Jim Pagliaroni | .35 | .14 | .03 |
| 11 Jose Pagan | .35 | .14 | .03 |
| 12 Jerry May | .35 | .14 | .03 |
| 14 Gene Alley | .50 | .20 | .05 |
| 15 Manny Mota | .60 | .24 | .06 |
| 16 Andy Rodgers | .35 | .14 | .03 |
| 17 Donn Clendenon | .50 | .20 | .05 |
| 18 Matty Alou | .50 | .20 | .05 |
| 19 Pete Mikkelsen | .35 | .14 | .03 |
| 20 Jesse Gonder | .35 | .14 | .03 |
| 21 Bob Clemente | 7.50 | 3.00 | .75 |
| 22 Woody Fryman | .40 | .16 | .04 |
| 24 Jerry Lynch | .35 | .14 | .03 |
| 25 Tommie Sisk | .35 | .14 | .03 |
| 26 Roy Face | .80 | .32 | .08 |
| 28 Steve Blass | .50 | .20 | .05 |
| 32 Vernon Law | .80 | .32 | .08 |
| 34 Al McBean | .35 | .14 | .03 |
| 39 Bob Veale | .40 | .16 | .04 |
| 43 Don Cardwell | .35 | .14 | .03 |
| 45 Gene Michael | .50 | .20 | .05 |

## 1954 Esskay

The cards in this 36 card set measure 2 1/4" by 3 1/2". The 1954 Esskay Meats set contains color, unnumbered cards featuring Baltimore Orioles only.

ROBERT L. TURLEY, Pitcher
Born Sept. 19, 1930
Hometown: Troy, Illinois
Throws Right — Bats Right

ROBERT L. KUZAVA, Pitcher
Born May 28, 1923
Hometown: Wyandotte, Mich.
Throws Left — Bats Right

Collect and Save ESSKAY Trading Cards.
Dealer or write to address in coupon.

The cards were issued in panels of two on boxes of Esskay hot dogs; consequently, many have grease stains on the cards and are quite difficult to obtain in mint condition. The 1954 Esskay set can be distinguished from the 1955 Esskay set supposedly by the white or off-white (the 1955 set) backs of the cards. The backs of the 1954 cards are also supposedly "waxed" to a greater degree than the 1955 cards. The ACC designation is F181-1. Since the cards are unnumbered, they are ordered below in alphabetical order for convenience.

|  |  |  | MINT | VG-E | F-G |
|---|---|---|---|---|---|
| COMPLETE SET |  |  | 2500.00 | 1000.00 | 300.00 |
| COMMON PLAYER (1-36) |  |  | 70.00 | 28.00 | 7.00 |
| ☐ | 1 | Cal Abrams | 80.00 | 32.00 | 8.00 |
| ☐ | 2 | Neil Berry | 70.00 | 28.00 | 7.00 |
| ☐ | 3 | Michael Blyzka | 70.00 | 28.00 | 7.00 |
| ☐ | 4 | Harry Brecheen | 80.00 | 32.00 | 8.00 |
| ☐ | 5 | Gil Coan | 70.00 | 28.00 | 7.00 |
| ☐ | 6 | Joe Coleman | 70.00 | 28.00 | 7.00 |
| ☐ | 7 | Clint Courtney | 80.00 | 32.00 | 8.00 |
| ☐ | 8 | Charles E. Diering | 70.00 | 28.00 | 7.00 |
| ☐ | 9 | Jimmie Dykes | 80.00 | 32.00 | 8.00 |
| ☐ | 10 | Frank Fanovich | 70.00 | 28.00 | 7.00 |
| ☐ | 11 | Howard Fox | 70.00 | 28.00 | 7.00 |
| ☐ | 12 | Jim Fridley | 70.00 | 28.00 | 7.00 |
| ☐ | 13 | Chico Garcia | 70.00 | 28.00 | 7.00 |
| ☐ | 14 | Jehosie Heard | 70.00 | 28.00 | 7.00 |
| ☐ | 15 | Darrell Johnson | 80.00 | 32.00 | 8.00 |
| ☐ | 16 | Robert D. Kennedy | 80.00 | 32.00 | 8.00 |
| ☐ | 17 | Dick Kokos | 70.00 | 28.00 | 7.00 |
| ☐ | 18 | Dave Koslo | 70.00 | 28.00 | 7.00 |
| ☐ | 19 | Lou Kretlow | 70.00 | 28.00 | 7.00 |
| ☐ | 20 | Richard D. Kryhoski | 70.00 | 28.00 | 7.00 |
| ☐ | 21 | Robert Kuzava | 70.00 | 28.00 | 7.00 |
| ☐ | 22 | Don Larsen | 150.00 | 60.00 | 15.00 |
| ☐ | 23 | Don Lenhardt | 70.00 | 28.00 | 7.00 |
| ☐ | 24 | Dick Littlefield | 70.00 | 28.00 | 7.00 |
| ☐ | 25 | Sam Mele | 80.00 | 32.00 | 8.00 |
| ☐ | 26 | John Lester Moss | 80.00 | 32.00 | 8.00 |
| ☐ | 27 | Ray L. Murray | 70.00 | 28.00 | 7.00 |
| ☐ | 28 | Bobo Newsom | 80.00 | 32.00 | 8.00 |
| ☐ | 29 | Tom Oliver | 70.00 | 28.00 | 7.00 |
| ☐ | 30 | Duane Pillette | 70.00 | 28.00 | 7.00 |
| ☐ | 31 | Francis M. Skaff | 70.00 | 28.00 | 7.00 |
| ☐ | 32 | Marlin Stuart | 70.00 | 28.00 | 7.00 |
| ☐ | 33 | Robert L. Turley | 150.00 | 60.00 | 15.00 |
| ☐ | 34 | Eddie Waitkus | 80.00 | 32.00 | 8.00 |
| ☐ | 35 | Vic Wertz | 100.00 | 40.00 | 10.00 |
| ☐ | 36 | Robert G. Young | 70.00 | 28.00 | 7.00 |

## 1955 Esskay

The cards in this 27 card set measure 2 1/4" by 3 1/2". The 1955 Esskay Meats set was issued in panels of two on boxes of Esskay hot dogs. This set of full color, blank back, unnumbered cards features Baltimore Orioles only. Many of the players in the

1954 Esskay set were also issued in this set. The ACC designation is F181-2. Since the cards are unnumbered, they are ordered below in alphabetical order for convenience. The 1955 set is supposedly somewhat more difficult to find than the 1954 set.

|  |  |  | MINT | VG-E | F-G |
|---|---|---|---|---|---|
| COMPLETE SET |  |  | 2400.00 | 1000.00 | 300.00 |
| COMMON PLAYER (1-27) |  |  | 90.00 | 36.00 | 9.00 |
| ☐ | 1 | Cal Abrams | 100.00 | 40.00 | 10.00 |
| ☐ | 2 | Robert Alexander | 90.00 | 36.00 | 9.00 |
| ☐ | 3 | Harry Brecheen | 100.00 | 40.00 | 10.00 |
| ☐ | 4 | Harry Byrd | 90.00 | 36.00 | 9.00 |
| ☐ | 5 | Gil Coan | 90.00 | 36.00 | 9.00 |
| ☐ | 6 | Joe Coleman | 90.00 | 36.00 | 9.00 |
| ☐ | 7 | William Cox | 100.00 | 40.00 | 10.00 |
| ☐ | 8 | Charles E. Diering | 90.00 | 36.00 | 9.00 |
| ☐ | 9 | Walter Evers | 100.00 | 40.00 | 10.00 |
| ☐ | 10 | Don Johnson | 90.00 | 36.00 | 9.00 |
| ☐ | 11 | Robert D. Kennedy | 100.00 | 40.00 | 10.00 |
| ☐ | 12 | Lou Kretlow | 90.00 | 36.00 | 9.00 |
| ☐ | 13 | Robert Kuzava | 90.00 | 36.00 | 9.00 |
| ☐ | 14 | Fred Marsh | 90.00 | 36.00 | 9.00 |
| ☐ | 15 | Charles Maxwell | 100.00 | 40.00 | 10.00 |
| ☐ | 16 | Jim McDonald | 90.00 | 36.00 | 9.00 |
| ☐ | 17 | Bill Miller | 90.00 | 36.00 | 9.00 |
| ☐ | 18 | Willie Miranda | 100.00 | 40.00 | 10.00 |
| ☐ | 19 | Raymond L. Moore | 90.00 | 36.00 | 9.00 |
| ☐ | 20 | John Lester Moss | 100.00 | 40.00 | 10.00 |
| ☐ | 21 | Bobo Newsom | 100.00 | 40.00 | 10.00 |
| ☐ | 22 | Duane Pillette | 90.00 | 36.00 | 9.00 |
| ☐ | 23 | Harold W. Smith | 90.00 | 36.00 | 9.00 |
| ☐ | 24 | Gus Triandos | 100.00 | 40.00 | 10.00 |
| ☐ | 25 | Eddie Waitkus | 100.00 | 40.00 | 10.00 |
| ☐ | 26 | Gene Woodling | 125.00 | 50.00 | 12.50 |
| ☐ | 27 | Robert G. Young | 90.00 | 36.00 | 9.00 |

## 1959 Fleer

The cards in this 80 card set measure 2 1/2" by 3 1/2". The 1959 Fleer set, designated as R418-1 in the ACC, portrays the life of Ted Williams. The wording of the wrapper, "Baseball's Greatest Series," has led to speculation that Fleer contemplated similar sets honoring other baseball immortals, but chose to develop instead the format of the 1960 and 1961 issues. Card number 68, which was withdrawn early in production, is considered scarce and has even been counterfeited; the fake has a rosey coloration and a cross-hatch pattern visible over the picture area.

|  | MINT | VG-E | F-G |
|---|---|---|---|
| COMPLETE SET | 175.00 | 70.00 | 18.00 |
| COMMON CARDS | .90 | .36 | .09 |

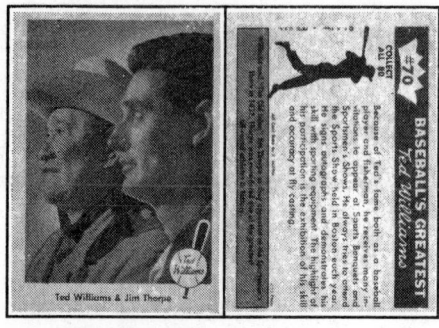

Ted Williams & Jim Thorpe

| | | | |
|---|---|---|---|
| ☐ 1 | The Early Years | 5.00 | 1.00 | .20 |
| ☐ 2 | Ted's Idol Babe Ruth | 3.00 | 1.20 | .30 |
| ☐ 3 | Practice Makes Perfect | .90 | .36 | .09 |
| ☐ 4 | Learns Fine Points | .90 | .36 | .09 |
| ☐ 5 | Ted's Fame Spreads | .90 | .36 | .09 |
| ☐ 6 | Ted Turns Pro | .90 | .36 | .09 |
| ☐ 7 | From Mound to Plate | .90 | .36 | .09 |
| ☐ 8 | 1937 First Full Season | .90 | .36 | .09 |
| ☐ 9 | First Step to Majors | .90 | .36 | .09 |
| ☐ 10 | Gunning as Pasttime | .90 | .36 | .09 |
| ☐ 11 | First Spring Training (with Jimmie Foxx) | 1.50 | .60 | .15 |
| ☐ 12 | Burning Up Minors | .90 | .36 | .09 |
| ☐ 13 | 1939 Shows Will Stay | .90 | .36 | .09 |
| ☐ 14 | Outstanding Rookie '39 | .90 | .36 | .09 |
| ☐ 15 | Licks Sophomore Jinx | .90 | .36 | .09 |
| ☐ 16 | 1941 Greatest Year | .90 | .36 | .09 |
| ☐ 17 | How Ted Hit .400 | .90 | .36 | .09 |
| ☐ 18 | 1941 All Star Hero | .90 | .36 | .09 |
| ☐ 19 | Ted Wins Triple Crown | .90 | .36 | .09 |
| ☐ 20 | On to Naval Training | .90 | .36 | .09 |
| ☐ 21 | Honors for Williams | .90 | .36 | .09 |
| ☐ 22 | 1944 Ted Solos | .90 | .36 | .09 |
| ☐ 23 | Williams Wins Wings | .90 | .36 | .09 |
| ☐ 24 | 1945 Sharpshooter | .90 | .36 | .09 |
| ☐ 25 | 1945 Ted Discharged | .90 | .36 | .09 |
| ☐ 26 | Off to Flying Start | .90 | .36 | .09 |
| ☐ 27 | 7/9/46 One Man Show | .90 | .36 | .09 |
| ☐ 28 | The Williams Shift | .90 | .36 | .09 |
| ☐ 29 | Ted Hits for Cycle | .90 | .36 | .09 |
| ☐ 30 | Beating Williams Shift | .90 | .36 | .09 |
| ☐ 31 | Sox Lose Series | .90 | .36 | .09 |
| ☐ 32 | Most Valuable Player | .90 | .36 | .09 |
| ☐ 33 | Another Triple Crown | .90 | .36 | .09 |
| ☐ 34 | Runs Scored Record | .90 | .36 | .09 |
| ☐ 35 | Sox Miss Pennant | .90 | .36 | .09 |
| ☐ 36 | Banner Year for Ted | .90 | .36 | .09 |
| ☐ 37 | 1949 Sox Miss Again | .90 | .36 | .09 |
| ☐ 38 | 1949 Power Rampage | .90 | .36 | .09 |
| ☐ 39 | 1950 Great Start | .90 | .36 | .09 |
| ☐ 40 | Ted Crashes into Wall | .90 | .36 | .09 |
| ☐ 41 | 1950 Ted Recovers | .90 | .36 | .09 |
| ☐ 42 | Slowed by Injury | .90 | .36 | .09 |
| ☐ 43 | Double Play Lead | .90 | .36 | .09 |
| ☐ 44 | Back to Marines | .90 | .36 | .09 |
| ☐ 45 | Farewell to Baseball? | .90 | .36 | .09 |
| ☐ 46 | Ready for Combat | .90 | .36 | .09 |
| ☐ 47 | Ted Crash Lands Jet | .90 | .36 | .09 |
| ☐ 48 | 1953 Ted Returns | .90 | .36 | .09 |
| ☐ 49 | Smash Return | .90 | .36 | .09 |
| ☐ 50 | 1954 Spring Injury | .90 | .36 | .09 |
| ☐ 51 | Ted is Patched Up | .90 | .36 | .09 |
| ☐ 52 | 1954 Ted's Comeback | .90 | .36 | .09 |
| ☐ 53 | Comeback is Success | .90 | .36 | .09 |
| ☐ 54 | Ted Hooks Big One | .90 | .36 | .09 |
| ☐ 55 | Retirement "No Go" | .90 | .36 | .09 |
| ☐ 56 | 2000th Hit | .90 | .36 | .09 |
| ☐ 57 | 400th Homer | .90 | .36 | .09 |
| ☐ 58 | Williams Hits .388 | .90 | .36 | .09 |
| ☐ 59 | Hot September for Ted | .90 | .36 | .09 |
| ☐ 60 | More Records for Ted | .90 | .36 | .09 |
| ☐ 61 | 1957 Outfielder Ted | .90 | .36 | .09 |
| ☐ 62 | 1958 6th Batting Title | .90 | .36 | .09 |
| ☐ 63 | Ted's All-Star Record | .90 | .36 | .09 |
| ☐ 64 | Daughter and Daddy | .90 | .36 | .09 |
| ☐ 65 | 1958 August 30 | .90 | .36 | .09 |
| ☐ 66 | 1958 Powerhouse | .90 | .36 | .09 |
| ☐ 67 | Two Famous Fishermen | 1.50 | .60 | .15 |
| ☐ 68 | Ted Signs for 1959 | 120.00 | 50.00 | 12.00 |
| ☐ 69 | A Future Ted Williams? | .90 | .36 | .09 |
| ☐ 70 | Williams and Thorpe | 2.00 | .80 | .20 |
| ☐ 71 | Hitting Fund. 1 | .90 | .36 | .09 |
| ☐ 72 | Hitting Fund. 2 | .90 | .36 | .09 |
| ☐ 73 | Hitting Fund. 3 | .90 | .36 | .09 |
| ☐ 74 | Here's How | .90 | .36 | .09 |
| ☐ 75 | Williams' Value to Sox | .90 | .36 | .09 |
| ☐ 76 | On Base Record | .90 | .36 | .09 |
| ☐ 77 | Ted Relaxes | .90 | .36 | .09 |
| ☐ 78 | Honors for Williams | .90 | .36 | .09 |
| ☐ 79 | Where Ted Stands | .90 | .36 | .09 |
| ☐ 80 | Ted's Goals for 1959 | 1.50 | .50 | .10 |

# 1960 Fleer

The cards in this 79 card set measure 2 1/2" by 3 1/2". The cards from the 1960 Fleer series of Baseball Greats are sometimes mistaken for 1930's cards by collectors not familiar with this set. The cards each contain a tinted photo of a baseball immortal, and were issued in one series. There are no known scarcities, although a number 80 card (Pepper Martin reverse with either a Tinker, Collins, or Grove obverse) exists (this is not considered part of the set). The catalog designation for 1960 Fleer is R418-2.

| | | MINT | VG-E | F-G |
|---|---|---|---|---|
| COMPLETE SET (79) | | 120.00 | 50.00 | 12.00 |
| COMMON PLAYER (1-79) | | .80 | .32 | .08 |
| ☐ 1 | Napoleon Lajoie | 5.00 | .60 | .10 |
| ☐ 2 | Christy Mathewson | 2.50 | 1.00 | .25 |
| ☐ 3 | George H. Ruth | 15.00 | 6.00 | 1.50 |
| ☐ 4 | Carl Hubbell | 1.25 | .50 | .12 |
| ☐ 5 | Grover Alexander | 1.50 | .60 | .15 |
| ☐ 6 | Walter P. Johnson | 3.00 | 1.20 | .30 |
| ☐ 7 | Charles A. Bender | .80 | .32 | .08 |
| ☐ 8 | Roger P. Bresnahan | .80 | .32 | .08 |
| ☐ 9 | Mordecai P. Brown | .80 | .32 | .08 |
| ☐ 10 | Tristram Speaker | 1.50 | .60 | .15 |
| ☐ 11 | Joseph (Arky) Vaughan | .80 | .32 | .08 |
| ☐ 12 | Zachariah Wheat | .80 | .32 | .08 |
| ☐ 13 | George Sisler | 1.00 | .40 | .10 |
| ☐ 14 | Connie Mack | 1.25 | .50 | .12 |
| ☐ 15 | Clark C. Griffith | .80 | .32 | .08 |
| ☐ 16 | Louis Boudreau | 1.25 | .50 | .12 |
| ☐ 17 | Ernest Lombardi | .80 | .32 | .08 |
| ☐ 18 | Henry Manush | .80 | .32 | .08 |
| ☐ 19 | Martin Marion | .80 | .32 | .08 |
| ☐ 20 | Edward Collins | .80 | .32 | .08 |
| ☐ 21 | James Maranville | .80 | .32 | .08 |
| ☐ 22 | Joseph Medwick | .80 | .32 | .08 |
| ☐ 23 | Edward Barrow | .80 | .32 | .08 |
| ☐ 24 | Gordon Cochrane | 1.00 | .40 | .10 |
| ☐ 25 | James J. Collins | .80 | .32 | .08 |
| ☐ 26 | Robert Feller | 3.50 | 1.40 | .35 |
| ☐ 27 | Lucius Appling | 1.25 | .50 | .12 |
| ☐ 28 | Lou Gehrig | 8.00 | 3.25 | .80 |
| ☐ 29 | Charles Hartnett | .80 | .32 | .08 |
| ☐ 30 | Charles Klein | .80 | .32 | .08 |
| ☐ 31 | Anthony Lazzeri | .80 | .32 | .08 |
| ☐ 32 | Aloysius Simmons | .80 | .32 | .08 |
| ☐ 33 | Wilbert Robinson | .80 | .32 | .08 |
| ☐ 34 | Edgar Rice | .80 | .32 | .08 |
| ☐ 35 | Herbert Pennock | .80 | .32 | .08 |

| □ 36 | Melvin Ott | 1.25 | .50 | .12 |
|---|---|---|---|---|
| □ 37 | Frank O'Doul | .80 | .32 | .08 |
| □ 38 | John Mize | 1.25 | .50 | .12 |
| □ 39 | Edmund Miller | .80 | .32 | .08 |
| □ 40 | Joseph Tinker | .80 | .32 | .08 |
| □ 41 | John Baker | .80 | .32 | .08 |
| □ 42 | Tyrus Cobb | 9.00 | 3.75 | .90 |
| □ 43 | Paul Derringer | .80 | .32 | .08 |
| □ 44 | Adrian Anson | 1.00 | .40 | .10 |
| □ 45 | James Bottomley | .80 | .32 | .08 |
| □ 46 | Edward S. Plank | 1.00 | .40 | .10 |
| □ 47 | Denton (Cy) Young | 2.00 | .80 | .20 |
| □ 48 | Hack Wilson | 1.00 | .40 | .10 |
| □ 49 | Edward Walsh | .80 | .32 | .08 |
| □ 50 | Frank Chance | .80 | .32 | .08 |
| □ 51 | Arthur Vance | .80 | .32 | .08 |
| □ 52 | William Terry | 1.00 | .40 | .10 |
| □ 53 | James Foxx | 2.00 | .80 | .20 |
| □ 54 | Vernon Gomez | 1.25 | .50 | .12 |
| □ 55 | Branch Rickey | .80 | .32 | .08 |
| □ 56 | Raymond Schalk | .80 | .32 | .08 |
| □ 57 | John Evers | .80 | .32 | .08 |
| □ 58 | Charles Gehringer | 1.00 | .40 | .10 |
| □ 59 | Burleigh Grimes | .80 | .32 | .08 |
| □ 60 | Robert (Lefty) Grove | 1.50 | .60 | .15 |
| □ 61 | George Waddell | .80 | .32 | .08 |
| □ 62 | John (Honus) Wagner | 3.00 | 1.20 | .30 |
| □ 63 | Charles (Red) Ruffing | .80 | .32 | .08 |
| □ 64 | Kenesaw M. Landis | .80 | .32 | .08 |
| □ 65 | Harry Heilmann | .80 | .32 | .08 |
| □ 66 | John McGraw | 1.00 | .40 | .10 |
| □ 67 | Hugh Jennings | .80 | .32 | .08 |
| □ 68 | Harold Newhouser | .80 | .32 | .08 |
| □ 69 | Waite Hoyt | .80 | .32 | .08 |
| □ 70 | Louis (Bobo) Newsom | .80 | .32 | .08 |
| □ 71 | Howard (Earl) Averill | .80 | .32 | .08 |
| □ 72 | Theodore Williams | 9.00 | 3.75 | .90 |
| □ 73 | Warren Giles | .80 | .32 | .08 |
| □ 74 | Ford Frick | .80 | .32 | .08 |
| □ 75 | Hazen (Kiki) Cuyler | .80 | .32 | .08 |
| □ 76 | Paul Waner | .80 | .32 | .08 |
| □ 77 | Harold Pie) Traynor | 1.00 | .40 | .10 |
| □ 78 | Lloyd Waner | .80 | .32 | .08 |
| □ 79 | Ralph Kiner | 1.50 | .60 | .15 |
| □ 80 | Pepper Martin * | 75.00 | 30.00 | 7.50 |
|  | (Collins, Tinker, |  |  |  |
|  | or Grove pictured) |  |  |  |

## 1961 Fleer

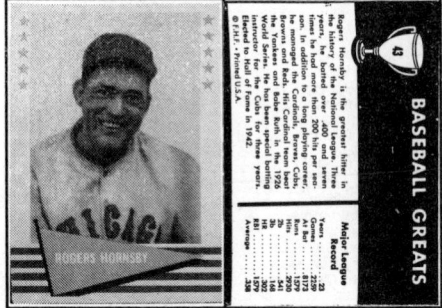

The cards in this 154 card set measure 2 1/2" by 3 1/2". In 1961, Fleer continued its Baseball Greats format by issuing this series of cards. The set was released in two distinct series, 1-88 and 89-154 (of which the last is more difficult to obtain). The players within each series are conveniently numbered in alphabetical order. It appears that this set continued to be issued the following year by Fleer. The catalog number is F418-3.

|  | MINT | VG-E | F-G |
|---|---|---|---|
| COMPLETE SET | 275.00 | 110.00 | 27.00 |
| COMMON PLAYER (1-88) | .80 | .32 | .08 |
| COMMON PLAYER (89-154) | 2.00 | .80 | .20 |

| □ 1 | Baker/Cobb/Wheat | 7.50 | 1.00 | .20 |
|---|---|---|---|---|
|  | (checklist back) |  |  |  |
| □ 2 | Grover C. Alexander | 1.25 | .50 | .12 |
| □ 3 | Nick Altrock | .80 | .32 | .08 |
| □ 4 | Cap Anson | 1.00 | .40 | .10 |
| □ 5 | Earl Averill | .80 | .32 | .08 |
| □ 6 | Frank Baker | .80 | .32 | .08 |
| □ 7 | Dave Bancroft | .80 | .32 | .08 |
| □ 8 | Chief Bender | .80 | .32 | .08 |
| □ 9 | Jim Bottomley | .80 | .32 | .08 |
| □ 10 | Roger Bresnahan | .80 | .32 | .08 |
| □ 11 | Mordecai Brown | .80 | .32 | .08 |
| □ 12 | Max Carey | .80 | .32 | .08 |
| □ 13 | Jack Chesbro | .80 | .32 | .08 |
| □ 14 | Ty Cobb | 9.00 | 3.75 | .90 |
| □ 15 | Mickey Cochrane | 1.00 | .40 | .10 |
| □ 16 | Eddie Collins | .80 | .32 | .08 |
| □ 17 | Earle Combs | .80 | .32 | .08 |
| □ 18 | Charles Comiskey | .80 | .32 | .08 |
| □ 19 | Kiki Cuyler | .80 | .32 | .08 |
| □ 20 | Paul Derringer | .80 | .32 | .08 |
| □ 21 | Howard Ehmke | .80 | .32 | .08 |
| □ 22 | W. Evans | .80 | .32 | .08 |
| □ 23 | Johnny Evers | .80 | .32 | .08 |
| □ 24 | Urban Faber | .80 | .32 | .08 |
| □ 25 | Bob Feller | 3.50 | 1.40 | .35 |
| □ 26 | Wes Ferrell | .80 | .32 | .08 |
| □ 27 | Lew Fonseca | .80 | .32 | .08 |
| □ 28 | Jimmy Foxx | 2.00 | .80 | .20 |
| □ 29 | Ford Frick | .80 | .32 | .08 |
| □ 30 | Frank Frisch | 1.00 | .40 | .10 |
| □ 31 | Lou Gehrig | 8.00 | 3.25 | .80 |
| □ 32 | Charlie Gehringer | 1.00 | .40 | .10 |
| □ 33 | Warren Giles | .80 | .32 | .08 |
| □ 34 | Lefty Gomez | 1.25 | .50 | .12 |
| □ 35 | Goose Goslin | .80 | .32 | .08 |
| □ 36 | Clark Griffith | .80 | .32 | .08 |
| □ 37 | Burleigh Grimes | .80 | .32 | .08 |
| □ 38 | Lefty Grove | 1.50 | .60 | .15 |
| □ 39 | Chick Hafey | .80 | .32 | .08 |
| □ 40 | Jesse Haines | .80 | .32 | .08 |
| □ 41 | Gabby Hartnett | .80 | .32 | .08 |
| □ 42 | Harry Heilmann | .80 | .32 | .08 |
| □ 43 | Rogers Hornsby | 2.00 | .80 | .20 |
| □ 44 | Waite Hoyt | .80 | .32 | .08 |
| □ 45 | Carl Hubbell | 1.25 | .50 | .12 |
| □ 46 | Miller Huggins | .80 | .32 | .08 |
| □ 47 | Hugh Jennings | .80 | .32 | .08 |
| □ 48 | Ban Johnson | .80 | .32 | .08 |
| □ 49 | Walter Johnson | 3.00 | 1.20 | .30 |
| □ 50 | Ralph Kiner | 1.50 | .60 | .15 |
| □ 51 | Chuck Klein | .80 | .32 | .08 |
| □ 52 | Johnny Kling | .80 | .32 | .08 |
| □ 53 | K.M. Landis | .80 | .32 | .08 |
| □ 54 | Tony Lazzeri | .80 | .32 | .08 |
| □ 55 | Ernie Lombardi | .80 | .32 | .08 |
| □ 56 | Dolf Luque | .80 | .32 | .08 |
| □ 57 | Heine Manush | .80 | .32 | .08 |
| □ 58 | Marty Marion | .80 | .32 | .08 |
| □ 59 | Christy Mathewson | 2.50 | 1.00 | .25 |
| □ 60 | John McGraw | 1.00 | .40 | .10 |
| □ 61 | Joe Medwick | .80 | .32 | .08 |
| □ 62 | E. (Bing) Miller | .80 | .32 | .08 |
| □ 63 | Johnny Mize | 1.50 | .60 | .15 |
| □ 64 | John Mostil | .80 | .32 | .08 |
| □ 65 | Art Nehf | .80 | .32 | .08 |
| □ 66 | Hal Newhouser | .80 | .32 | .08 |
| □ 67 | D. (Bobo) Newsom | .80 | .32 | .08 |
| □ 68 | Mel Ott | 1.25 | .50 | .12 |
| □ 69 | Allie Reynolds | .80 | .32 | .08 |
| □ 70 | Sam Rice | .80 | .32 | .08 |
| □ 71 | Eppa Rixey | .80 | .32 | .08 |
| □ 72 | Edd Roush | .80 | .32 | .08 |
| □ 73 | Schoolboy Rowe | .80 | .32 | .08 |
| □ 74 | Red Ruffing | .80 | .32 | .08 |
| □ 75 | Babe Ruth | 15.00 | 6.00 | 1.50 |
| □ 76 | Joe Sewell | .80 | .32 | .08 |
| □ 77 | Al Simmons | .80 | .32 | .08 |
| □ 78 | George Sisler | 1.00 | .40 | .10 |
| □ 79 | Tris Speaker | 1.50 | .60 | .15 |
| □ 80 | Fred Toney | .80 | .32 | .08 |
| □ 81 | Dazzy Vance | .80 | .32 | .08 |
| □ 82 | Jim Vaughn | .80 | .32 | .08 |
| □ 83 | Ed Walsh | .80 | .32 | .08 |
| □ 84 | Lloyd Waner | .80 | .32 | .08 |
| □ 85 | Paul Waner | .80 | .32 | .08 |
| □ 86 | Zack Wheat | .80 | .32 | .08 |
| □ 87 | Hack Wilson | 1.00 | .40 | .10 |
| □ 88 | Jimmy Wilson | .80 | .32 | .08 |
| □ 89 | Sisler and Traynor | 7.50 | 1.00 | .20 |
|  | (checklist back) |  |  |  |
| □ 90 | Babe Adams | 2.00 | .80 | .20 |

| | | | | |
|---|---|---|---|---|
| ☐ 91 | Dale Alexander | 2.00 | .80 | .20 |
| ☐ 92 | Jim Bagby | 2.00 | .80 | .20 |
| ☐ 93 | Ossie Bluege | 2.00 | .80 | .20 |
| ☐ 94 | Lou Boudreau | 3.50 | 1.40 | .35 |
| ☐ 95 | Tom Bridges | 2.00 | .80 | .20 |
| ☐ 96 | Donie Bush | 2.00 | .80 | .20 |
| ☐ 97 | Dolph Camilli | 2.00 | .80 | .20 |
| ☐ 98 | Frank Chance | 3.00 | 1.20 | .30 |
| ☐ 99 | Jimmy Collins | 3.00 | 1.20 | .30 |
| ☐ 100 | Stan Coveleskie | 3.00 | 1.20 | .30 |
| ☐ 101 | Hugh Critz | 2.00 | .80 | .20 |
| ☐ 102 | Alvin Crowder | 2.00 | .80 | .20 |
| ☐ 103 | Joe Dugan | 2.00 | .80 | .20 |
| ☐ 104 | Bibb Falk | 2.00 | .80 | .20 |
| ☐ 105 | Rick Ferrell | 3.00 | 1.20 | .30 |
| ☐ 106 | Art Fletcher | 2.00 | .80 | .20 |
| ☐ 107 | Dennis Galehouse | 2.00 | .80 | .20 |
| ☐ 108 | Chick Galloway | 2.00 | .80 | .20 |
| ☐ 109 | Mule Haas | 2.00 | .80 | .20 |
| ☐ 110 | Stan Hack | 2.00 | .80 | .20 |
| ☐ 111 | Bump Hadley | 2.00 | .80 | .20 |
| ☐ 112 | Billy B. Hamilton | 3.00 | 1.20 | .30 |
| ☐ 113 | Joe Hauser | 2.00 | .80 | .20 |
| ☐ 114 | Babe Herman | 2.00 | .80 | .20 |
| ☐ 115 | Travis Jackson | 3.00 | 1.20 | .30 |
| ☐ 116 | Eddie Joost | 2.00 | .80 | .20 |
| ☐ 117 | Addie Joss | 3.50 | 1.40 | .35 |
| ☐ 118 | Joe Judge | 2.00 | .80 | .20 |
| ☐ 119 | Joe Kuhel | 2.00 | .80 | .20 |
| ☐ 120 | Napoleon Lajoie | 6.00 | 2.40 | .60 |
| ☐ 121 | Dutch Leonard | 2.00 | .80 | .20 |
| ☐ 122 | Ted Lyons | 3.00 | 1.20 | .30 |
| ☐ 123 | Connie Mack | 6.00 | 2.40 | .60 |
| ☐ 124 | Rabbit Maranville | 3.00 | 1.20 | .30 |
| ☐ 125 | Fred Marberry | 2.00 | .80 | .20 |
| ☐ 126 | Joe McGinnity | 4.00 | 1.60 | .40 |
| ☐ 127 | Oscar Melillo | 2.00 | .80 | .20 |
| ☐ 128 | Ray Mueller | 2.00 | .80 | .20 |
| ☐ 129 | Kid Nichols | 3.50 | 1.40 | .35 |
| ☐ 130 | Lefty O'Doul | 2.00 | .80 | .20 |
| ☐ 131 | Bob O'Farrell | 2.00 | .80 | .20 |
| ☐ 132 | Roger Peckinpaugh | 2.00 | .80 | .20 |
| ☐ 133 | Herb Pennock | 3.00 | 1.20 | .30 |
| ☐ 134 | George Pipgras | 2.00 | .80 | .20 |
| ☐ 135 | Eddie Plank | 3.50 | 1.40 | .35 |
| ☐ 136 | Ray Schalk | 3.00 | 1.20 | .30 |
| ☐ 137 | Hal Schumacher | 2.00 | .80 | .20 |
| ☐ 138 | Luke Sewell | 2.00 | .80 | .20 |
| ☐ 139 | Bob Shawkey | 2.00 | .80 | .20 |
| ☐ 140 | Riggs Stephenson | 2.00 | .80 | .20 |
| ☐ 141 | Billy Sullivan | 2.00 | .80 | .20 |
| ☐ 142 | Bill Terry | 5.00 | 2.00 | .50 |
| ☐ 143 | Joe Tinker | 3.00 | 1.20 | .30 |
| ☐ 144 | Pie Traynor | 4.00 | 1.60 | .40 |
| ☐ 145 | Hal Trosky | 2.00 | .80 | .20 |
| ☐ 146 | George Uhle | 2.00 | .80 | .20 |
| ☐ 147 | Johnny VanderMeer | 2.50 | 1.00 | .25 |
| ☐ 148 | Arky Vaughan | 3.00 | 1.20 | .30 |
| ☐ 149 | Rube Waddell | 3.00 | 1.20 | .30 |
| ☐ 150 | Honus Wagner | 9.00 | 3.75 | .90 |
| ☐ 151 | Dixie Walker | 2.00 | .80 | .20 |
| ☐ 152 | Ted Williams | 15.00 | 6.00 | 1.50 |
| ☐ 153 | Cy Young | 7.50 | 3.00 | .75 |
| ☐ 154 | Ross Young | 4.00 | 1.60 | .40 |

## 1963 Fleer

The cards in this 66 card set measure 2 1/2" by 3 1/2". The Fleer set of current baseball players was marketed in 1963 in a gum card style waxed wrapper package which contained a cherry cookie instead of gum. The cards were printed in sheets of 66 with the scarce card of Adcock apparently being replaced by the unnumbered checklist card for the final press run. The complete set price includes the checklist card. The catalog designation is R418-4.

| | | MINT | VG-E | F-G |
|---|---|---|---|---|
| COMPLETE SET | | 200.00 | 80.00 | 20.00 |
| COMMON PLAYER (1-66) | | .90 | .36 | .09 |
| ☐ 1 | Steve Barber | 2.00 | .50 | .10 |
| ☐ 2 | Ron Hansen | .90 | .36 | .09 |
| ☐ 3 | Milt Pappas | 1.25 | .50 | .12 |

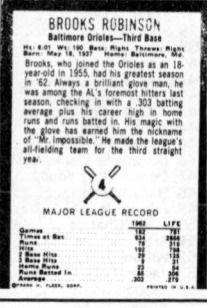

| | | | | |
|---|---|---|---|---|
| ☐ 4 | Brooks Robinson | 9.00 | 3.75 | .90 |
| ☐ 5 | Willie Mays | 15.00 | 6.00 | 1.50 |
| ☐ 6 | Lou Clinton | .90 | .36 | .09 |
| ☐ 7 | Bill Monbouquette | .90 | .36 | .09 |
| ☐ 8 | Carl Yastrzemski | 18.00 | 7.25 | 1.80 |
| ☐ 9 | Ray Herbert | .90 | .36 | .09 |
| ☐ 10 | Jim Landis | .90 | .36 | .09 |
| ☐ 11 | Dick Donovan | .90 | .36 | .09 |
| ☐ 12 | Tito Francona | .90 | .36 | .09 |
| ☐ 13 | Jerry Kindall | .90 | .36 | .09 |
| ☐ 14 | Frank Lary | 1.25 | .50 | .12 |
| ☐ 15 | Dick Howser | 1.25 | .50 | .12 |
| ☐ 16 | Jerry Lumpe | .90 | .36 | .09 |
| ☐ 17 | Norm Siebern | .90 | .36 | .09 |
| ☐ 18 | Don Lee | .90 | .36 | .09 |
| ☐ 19 | Albie Pearson | .90 | .36 | .09 |
| ☐ 20 | Bob Rodgers | .90 | .36 | .09 |
| ☐ 21 | Leon Wagner | .90 | .36 | .09 |
| ☐ 22 | Jim Kaat | 2.50 | 1.00 | .25 |
| ☐ 23 | Vic Power | .90 | .36 | .09 |
| ☐ 24 | Rich Rollins | .90 | .36 | .09 |
| ☐ 25 | Bobby Richardson | 1.75 | .70 | .17 |
| ☐ 26 | Ralph Terry | 1.25 | .50 | .12 |
| ☐ 27 | Tom Cheney | .90 | .36 | .09 |
| ☐ 28 | Chuck Cottier | .90 | .36 | .09 |
| ☐ 29 | Jim Piersall | 1.25 | .50 | .12 |
| ☐ 30 | Dave Stenhouse | .90 | .36 | .09 |
| ☐ 31 | Glen Hobbie | .90 | .36 | .09 |
| ☐ 32 | Ron Santo | 1.50 | .60 | .15 |
| ☐ 33 | Gene Freese | .90 | .36 | .09 |
| ☐ 34 | Vada Pinson | 1.50 | .60 | .15 |
| ☐ 35 | Bob Purkey | .90 | .36 | .09 |
| ☐ 36 | Joe Amalfitano | .90 | .36 | .09 |
| ☐ 37 | Bob Aspromonte | .90 | .36 | .09 |
| ☐ 38 | Dick Farrell | .90 | .36 | .09 |
| ☐ 39 | Al Spangler | .90 | .36 | .09 |
| ☐ 40 | Tommy Davis | 1.25 | .50 | .12 |
| ☐ 41 | Don Drysdale | 6.00 | 2.40 | .60 |
| ☐ 42 | Sandy Koufax | 15.00 | 6.00 | 1.50 |
| ☐ 43 | Maury Wills | 12.50 | 5.00 | 1.25 |
| ☐ 44 | Frank Bolling | .90 | .36 | .09 |
| ☐ 45 | Warren Spahn | 6.00 | 2.40 | .60 |
| ☐ 46 | Joe Adcock SP | 40.00 | 16.00 | 4.00 |
| ☐ 47 | Roger Craig | 1.50 | .60 | .15 |
| ☐ 48 | Al Jackson | .90 | .36 | .09 |
| ☐ 49 | Rod Kanehl | .90 | .36 | .09 |
| ☐ 50 | Ruben Amaro | .90 | .36 | .09 |
| ☐ 51 | John Callison | 1.25 | .50 | .12 |
| ☐ 52 | Clay Dalrymple | .90 | .36 | .09 |
| ☐ 53 | Don Demeter | .90 | .36 | .09 |
| ☐ 54 | Art Mahaffey | .90 | .36 | .09 |
| ☐ 55 | Smokey Burgess | 1.25 | .50 | .12 |
| ☐ 56 | Roberto Clemente | 15.00 | 6.00 | 1.50 |
| ☐ 57 | Roy Face | 1.25 | .50 | .12 |
| ☐ 58 | Vernon Law | 1.25 | .50 | .12 |
| ☐ 59 | Bill Mazeroski | 1.75 | .70 | .17 |
| ☐ 60 | Ken Boyer | 1.75 | .70 | .17 |
| ☐ 61 | Bob Gibson | 6.00 | 2.40 | .60 |
| ☐ 62 | Gene Oliver | .90 | .36 | .09 |
| ☐ 63 | Bill White | 1.25 | .50 | .12 |
| ☐ 64 | Orlando Cepeda | 1.75 | .70 | .12 |
| ☐ 65 | Jim Davenport | 1.25 | .50 | .12 |
| ☐ 66 | Bill O'Dell | 1.50 | .50 | .10 |
| ☐ 67 | Checklist card (unnumbered) | 50.00 | 10.00 | 2.00 |

# 1981 Fleer

The cards in this 660 card set measure 2 1/2" by 3 1/2". This issue of cards marks Fleer's first entry into the current player baseball card market since 1963. Players from the same team are conveniently grouped together by number in the set. The teams are ordered (by 1980 standings) as follows: Philadelphia (1-27), Kansas City (28-50), Houston (51-78), New York Yankees (79-109), Los Angeles (110-141), Montreal (142-168), Baltimore (169-195), Cincinnati (196-220), Boston (221-241), Atlanta (242-257), California (258-290), Chicago Cubs (291-315), New York Mets (316-338), Chicago White Sox (339-359), Pittsburgh (360-386), Cleveland (387-408), Toronto (409-431), San Francisco (432-458), Detroit (459-483), San Diego (484-506), Milwaukee (507-527), St. Louis (528-550), Minnesota (551-571), Oakland (572-594), Seattle (595-616), and Texas (617-637). Cards 638-660 feature specials and checklists There were three distinct printings: the two following the primary run were designed to correct numerous errors. The variations caused by these multiple printings are noted in the checklist below (P1, P2 or P3).

| | MINT | VG-E | F-G |
|---|---|---|---|
| COMPLETE SET (660) | 22.00 | 9.00 | 2.20 |
| COMMON PLAYER (1-660) | .03 | .01 | .00 |

| | | MINT | VG-E | F-G |
|---|---|---|---|---|
| ☐ | 1 Pete Rose | 1.75 | .70 | .17 |
| ☐ | 2 Larry Bowa | .12 | .05 | .01 |
| ☐ | 3 Manny Trillo | .06 | .02 | .00 |
| ☐ | 4 Bob Boone | .06 | .02 | .00 |
| ☐ | 5 Mike Schmidt | .80 | .32 | .08 |
| | See 640A | | | |
| ☐ | 6A Steve Carlton P1 | .60 | .24 | .06 |
| | Pitcher of Year | | | |
| | See also 660A | | | |
| | Back "1066 Cardinals" | | | |
| ☐ | 6B Steve Carlton P2 | .60 | .24 | .06 |
| | Pitcher of Year | | | |
| | Back "1066 Cardinals" | | | |
| ☐ | 6C Steve Carlton P3 | 1.75 | .70 | .17 |
| | "1966 Cardinals" | | | |
| ☐ | 7 Tug McGraw | .10 | .04 | .01 |
| | See 657A | | | |
| ☐ | 8 Larry Christenson | .03 | .01 | .00 |
| ☐ | 9 Bake McBride | .06 | .02 | .00 |
| ☐ | 10 Greg Luzinski | .12 | .05 | .01 |
| ☐ | 11 Ron Reed | .03 | .01 | .00 |
| ☐ | 12 Dickie Noles | .03 | .01 | .00 |
| ☐ | 13 Keith Moreland | .45 | .18 | .04 |
| ☐ | 14 Bob Walk | .06 | .02 | .00 |
| ☐ | 15 Lonnie Smith | .08 | .03 | .01 |
| ☐ | 16 Dick Ruthven | .03 | .01 | .00 |
| ☐ | 17 Sparky Lyle | .12 | .05 | .01 |
| ☐ | 18 Greg Gross | .03 | .01 | .00 |
| ☐ | 19 Garry Maddox | .06 | .02 | .00 |
| ☐ | 20 Nino Espinosa | .03 | .01 | .00 |
| ☐ | 21 George Vukovich | .03 | .01 | .00 |
| ☐ | 22 John Vukovich | .03 | .01 | .00 |
| ☐ | 23 Ramon Aviles | .03 | .01 | .00 |
| ☐ | 24A Ken Saucier P1 | .06 | .02 | .00 |
| | Name on front "Ken" | | | |
| ☐ | 24B Ken Saucier P2 | .06 | .02 | .00 |
| | Name on front "Ken" | | | |
| ☐ | 24C Kevin Saucier P3 | .35 | .14 | .03 |
| | Name on front "Kevin" | | | |
| ☐ | 25 Randy Lerch | .03 | .01 | .00 |
| ☐ | 26 Del Unser | .03 | .01 | .00 |
| ☐ | 27 Tim McCarver | .06 | .02 | .00 |
| ☐ | 28 George Brett | .80 | .32 | .08 |
| | See 655A | | | |
| ☐ | 29 Willie Wilson | .20 | .08 | .02 |
| | See 653A | | | |
| ☐ | 30 Paul Splittorff | .06 | .02 | .00 |
| ☐ | 31 Dan Quisenberry | .20 | .08 | .02 |
| ☐ | 32A Amos Otis P1 | .10 | .04 | .01 |
| | Batting Pose | | | |
| | "Outfield" | | | |
| | (32 on back) | | | |
| ☐ | 32B Amos Otis P2 | .10 | .04 | .01 |
| | "Series Starter" | | | |
| | (483 on back) | | | |
| ☐ | 33 Steve Busby | .06 | .02 | .00 |
| ☐ | 34 U.L. Washington | .03 | .01 | .00 |
| ☐ | 35 Dave Chalk | .03 | .01 | .00 |
| ☐ | 36 Darrell Porter | .06 | .02 | .00 |
| ☐ | 37 Marty Pattin | .03 | .01 | .00 |
| ☐ | 38 Larry Gura | .06 | .02 | .00 |
| ☐ | 39 Renie Martin | .03 | .01 | .00 |
| ☐ | 40 Rich Gale | .03 | .01 | .00 |
| ☐ | 41A Hal McRae P1 | .50 | .20 | .05 |
| | "Royals" on front | | | |
| | in black letters | | | |
| ☐ | 41B Hal McRae P2 | .10 | .04 | .01 |
| | "Royals" on front | | | |
| | in blue letters | | | |
| ☐ | 42 Dennis Leonard | .06 | .02 | .00 |
| ☐ | 43 Willie Aikens | .06 | .02 | .00 |
| ☐ | 44 Frank White | .10 | .04 | .01 |
| ☐ | 45 Clint Hurdle | .03 | .01 | .00 |
| ☐ | 46 John Wathan | .03 | .01 | .00 |
| ☐ | 47 Pete LaCock | .03 | .01 | .00 |
| ☐ | 48 Rance Mulliniks | .03 | .01 | .00 |
| ☐ | 49 Jeff Twitty | .03 | .01 | .00 |
| ☐ | 50 Jamie Quirk | .03 | .01 | .00 |
| ☐ | 51 Art Howe | .03 | .01 | .00 |
| ☐ | 52 Ken Forsch | .03 | .01 | .00 |
| ☐ | 53 Vern Ruhle | .03 | .01 | .00 |
| ☐ | 54 Joe Niekro | .10 | .04 | .01 |
| ☐ | 55 Frank LaCorte | .03 | .01 | .00 |
| ☐ | 56 J.R. Richard | .10 | .04 | .01 |
| ☐ | 57 Nolan Ryan | .45 | .18 | .04 |
| ☐ | 58 Enos Cabell | .03 | .01 | .00 |
| ☐ | 59 Cesar Cedeno | .10 | .04 | .01 |
| ☐ | 60 Jose Cruz | .15 | .06 | .01 |
| ☐ | 61 Bill Virdon MGR | .06 | .02 | .00 |
| ☐ | 62 Terry Puhl | .06 | .02 | .00 |
| ☐ | 63 Joaquin Andujar | .12 | .05 | .01 |
| ☐ | 64 Alan Ashby | .03 | .01 | .00 |
| ☐ | 65 Joe Sambito | .06 | .02 | .00 |
| ☐ | 66 Denny Walling | .03 | .01 | .00 |
| ☐ | 67 Jeff Leonard | .10 | .04 | .01 |
| ☐ | 68 Luis Pujols | .03 | .01 | .00 |
| ☐ | 69 Bruce Bochy | .03 | .01 | .00 |
| ☐ | 70 Rafael Landestoy | .03 | .01 | .00 |
| ☐ | 71 Dave Smith | .25 | .10 | .02 |
| ☐ | 72 Danny Heep | .15 | .06 | .01 |
| ☐ | 73 Julio Gonzalez | .03 | .01 | .00 |
| ☐ | 74 Craig Reynolds | .03 | .01 | .00 |
| ☐ | 75 Gary Woods | .03 | .01 | .00 |
| ☐ | 76 Dave Bergman | .03 | .01 | .00 |
| ☐ | 77 Randy Niemann | .03 | .01 | .00 |
| ☐ | 78 Joe Morgan | .30 | .12 | .03 |
| ☐ | 79 Reggie Jackson | .75 | .30 | .07 |
| | See 650A | | | |
| ☐ | 80 Bucky Dent | .10 | .04 | .01 |
| ☐ | 81 Tommy John | .15 | .06 | .01 |
| ☐ | 82 Luis Tiant | .10 | .04 | .01 |
| ☐ | 83 Rick Cerone | .06 | .02 | .00 |
| ☐ | 84 Dick Howser MGR | .10 | .04 | .01 |
| ☐ | 85 Lou Piniella | .10 | .04 | .01 |
| ☐ | 86 Ron Davis | .03 | .01 | .00 |
| ☐ | 87A Craig Nettles P1 ERR | 11.00 | 4.50 | 1.10 |
| | Name on back | | | |
| | misspelled "Craig" | | | |
| ☐ | 87B Graig Nettles P2 COR | .30 | .12 | .03 |
| | "Graig" | | | |
| ☐ | 88 Ron Guidry | .25 | .10 | .02 |
| ☐ | 89 Rich Gossage | .20 | .08 | .02 |
| ☐ | 90 Rudy May | .03 | .01 | .00 |
| ☐ | 91 Gaylord Perry | .25 | .10 | .02 |

| | | | | | |
|---|---|---|---|---|---|
| ☐ 92 Eric Soderholm | .03 | .01 | .00 | | |
| ☐ 93 Bob Watson | .06 | .02 | .00 | | |
| ☐ 94 Bobby Murcer | .10 | .04 | .01 | | |
| ☐ 95 Bobby Brown | .03 | .01 | .00 | | |
| ☐ 96 Jim Spencer | .03 | .01 | .00 | | |
| ☐ 97 Tom Underwood | .03 | .01 | .00 | | |
| ☐ 98 Oscar Gamble | .06 | .02 | .00 | | |
| ☐ 99 Johnny Oates | .03 | .01 | .00 | | |
| ☐ 100 Fred Stanley | .03 | .01 | .00 | | |
| ☐ 101 Ruppert Jones | .03 | .01 | .00 | | |
| ☐ 102 Dennis Werth | .03 | .01 | .00 | | |
| ☐ 103 Joe Lefebvre | .06 | .02 | .00 | | |
| ☐ 104 Brian Doyle | .06 | .02 | .00 | | |
| ☐ 105 Aurelio Rodriguez | .03 | .01 | .00 | | |
| ☐ 106 Doug Bird | .03 | .01 | .00 | | |
| ☐ 107 Mike Griffin | .03 | .01 | .00 | | |
| ☐ 108 Tim Lollar | .10 | .04 | .01 | | |
| ☐ 109 Willie Randolph | .10 | .04 | .01 | | |
| ☐ 110 Steve Garvey | .50 | .20 | .05 | | |
| ☐ 111 Reggie Smith | .10 | .04 | .01 | | |
| ☐ 112 Don Sutton | .25 | .10 | .02 | | |
| ☐ 113 Burt Hooton | .03 | .01 | .00 | | |
| ☐ 114A Dave Lopes P1 | .50 | .20 | .05 | | |
| small hand on back | | | | | |
| ☐ 114B Dave Lopes P2 | .10 | .04 | .01 | | |
| no hand | | | | | |
| ☐ 115 Dusty Baker | .08 | .03 | .01 | | |
| ☐ 116 Tom Lasorda MGR | .08 | .03 | .01 | | |
| ☐ 117 Bill Russell | .06 | .02 | .00 | | |
| ☐ 118 Jerry Reuss | .06 | .02 | .00 | | |
| ☐ 119 Terry Forster | .06 | .02 | .00 | | |
| ☐ 120A Bob Welch P1 | .15 | .06 | .01 | | |
| Name on back Bob | | | | | |
| ☐ 120B Bob Welch P2 | .15 | .06 | .01 | | |
| Name on back Robert | | | | | |
| ☐ 121 Don Stanhouse | .03 | .01 | .00 | | |
| ☐ 122 Rick Monday | .06 | .02 | .00 | | |
| ☐ 123 Derrel Thomas | .03 | .01 | .00 | | |
| ☐ 124 Joe Ferguson | .03 | .01 | .00 | | |
| ☐ 125 Rick Sutcliffe | .15 | .06 | .01 | | |
| ☐ 126A Ron Cey P1 | .50 | .20 | .05 | | |
| small hand on back | | | | | |
| ☐ 126B Ron Cey P2 | .15 | .06 | .01 | | |
| no hand | | | | | |
| ☐ 127 Dave Goltz | .03 | .01 | .00 | | |
| ☐ 128 Jay Johnstone | .06 | .02 | .00 | | |
| ☐ 129 Steve Yeager | .03 | .01 | .00 | | |
| ☐ 130 Gary Weiss | .03 | .01 | .00 | | |
| ☐ 131 Mike Scioscia | .35 | .14 | .03 | | |
| ☐ 132 Vic Davalillo | .03 | .01 | .00 | | |
| ☐ 133 Doug Rau | .03 | .01 | .00 | | |
| ☐ 134 Pepe Frias | .03 | .01 | .00 | | |
| ☐ 135 Mickey Hatcher | .03 | .01 | .00 | | |
| ☐ 136 Steve Howe | .15 | .06 | .01 | | |
| ☐ 137 Robert Castillo | .03 | .01 | .00 | | |
| ☐ 138 Gary Thomasson | .03 | .01 | .00 | | |
| ☐ 139 Rudy Law | .03 | .01 | .00 | | |
| ☐ 140 Fernand Valenzuela | 5.00 | 2.00 | .50 | | |
| (sic, Fernando) | | | | | |
| ☐ 141 Manny Mota | .06 | .02 | .00 | | |
| ☐ 142 Gary Carter | .50 | .20 | .05 | | |
| ☐ 143 Steve Rogers | .08 | .03 | .01 | | |
| ☐ 144 Warren Cromartie | .03 | .01 | .00 | | |
| ☐ 145 Andre Dawson | .25 | .10 | .02 | | |
| ☐ 146 Larry Parrish | .06 | .02 | .00 | | |
| ☐ 147 Rowland Office | .03 | .01 | .00 | | |
| ☐ 148 Ellis Valentine | .06 | .02 | .00 | | |
| ☐ 149 Dick Williams MGR | .03 | .01 | .00 | | |
| ☐ 150 Bill Gullickson | .25 | .10 | .02 | | |
| ☐ 151 Elias Sosa | .03 | .01 | .00 | | |
| ☐ 152 John Tamargo | .03 | .01 | .00 | | |
| ☐ 153 Chris Speier | .03 | .01 | .00 | | |
| ☐ 154 Ron LeFlore | .06 | .02 | .00 | | |
| ☐ 155 Rodney Scott | .03 | .01 | .00 | | |
| ☐ 156 Stan Bahnsen | .03 | .01 | .00 | | |
| ☐ 157 Bill Lee | .06 | .02 | .00 | | |
| ☐ 158 Fred Norman | .03 | .01 | .00 | | |
| ☐ 159 Woodie Fryman | .03 | .01 | .00 | | |
| ☐ 160 Dave Palmer | .06 | .02 | .00 | | |
| ☐ 161 Jerry White | .03 | .01 | .00 | | |
| ☐ 162 Roberto Ramos | .03 | .01 | .00 | | |
| ☐ 163 John D'Acquisto | .03 | .01 | .00 | | |
| ☐ 164 Tommy Hutton | .03 | .01 | .00 | | |
| ☐ 165 Charlie Lea | .20 | .08 | .02 | | |
| ☐ 166 Scott Sanderson | .03 | .01 | .00 | | |
| ☐ 167 Ken Macha | .03 | .01 | .00 | | |
| ☐ 168 Tony Bernazard | .06 | .02 | .00 | | |
| ☐ 169 Jim Palmer | .30 | .12 | .03 | | |
| ☐ 170 Steve Stone | .06 | .02 | .00 | | |
| ☐ 171 Mike Flanagan | .10 | .04 | .01 | | |
| ☐ 172 Al Bumbry | .03 | .01 | .00 | | |
| ☐ 173 Doug DeCinces | .10 | .04 | .01 | | |
| ☐ 174 Scott McGregor | .10 | .04 | .01 | | |

| | | | |
|---|---|---|---|
| ☐ 175 Mark Belanger | .06 | .02 | .00 |
| ☐ 176 Tim Stoddard | .03 | .01 | .00 |
| ☐ 177A Rick Dempsey P1 | .50 | .20 | .05 |
| small hand on front | | | |
| ☐ 177B Rick Dempsey P2 | .10 | .04 | .01 |
| no hand | | | |
| ☐ 178 Earl Weaver MGR | .08 | .03 | .01 |
| ☐ 179 Tippy Martinez | .06 | .02 | .00 |
| ☐ 180 Dennis Martinez | .03 | .01 | .00 |
| ☐ 181 Sammy Stewart | .03 | .01 | .00 |
| ☐ 182 Rich Dauer | .03 | .01 | .00 |
| ☐ 183 Lee May | .06 | .02 | .00 |
| ☐ 184 Eddie Murray | .75 | .30 | .07 |
| ☐ 185 Benny Ayala | .03 | .01 | .00 |
| ☐ 186 John Lowenstein | .03 | .01 | .00 |
| ☐ 187 Gary Roenicke | .06 | .02 | .00 |
| ☐ 188 Ken Singleton | .10 | .04 | .01 |
| ☐ 189 Dan Graham | .03 | .01 | .00 |
| ☐ 190 Terry Crowley | .03 | .01 | .00 |
| ☐ 191 Kiko Garcia | .03 | .01 | .00 |
| ☐ 192 Dave Ford | .03 | .01 | .00 |
| ☐ 193 Mark Corey | .03 | .01 | .00 |
| ☐ 194 Lenn Sakata | .03 | .01 | .00 |
| ☐ 195 Doug DeCinces | .10 | .04 | .01 |
| ☐ 196 Johnny Bench | .50 | .20 | .05 |
| ☐ 197 Dave Concepcion | .12 | .05 | .01 |
| ☐ 198 Ray Knight | .10 | .04 | .01 |
| ☐ 199 Ken Griffey | .08 | .03 | .01 |
| ☐ 200 Tom Seaver | .50 | .20 | .05 |
| ☐ 201 Dave Collins | .06 | .02 | .00 |
| ☐ 202A George Foster P1 | .20 | .08 | .02 |
| Slugger | | | |
| number on back 216 | | | |
| ☐ 202B George Foster P2 | .20 | .08 | .02 |
| Slugger | | | |
| number on back 202 | | | |
| ☐ 203 Junior Kennedy | .03 | .01 | .00 |
| ☐ 204 Frank Pastore | .03 | .01 | .00 |
| ☐ 205 Dan Driessen | .06 | .02 | .00 |
| ☐ 206 Hector Cruz | .03 | .01 | .00 |
| ☐ 207 Paul Moskau | .03 | .01 | .00 |
| ☐ 208 Charlie Leibrandt | .30 | .12 | .03 |
| ☐ 209 Harry Spilman | .03 | .01 | .00 |
| ☐ 210 Joe Price | .06 | .02 | .00 |
| ☐ 211 Tom Hume | .03 | .01 | .00 |
| ☐ 212 Joe Nolan | .03 | .01 | .00 |
| ☐ 213 Doug Bair | .03 | .01 | .00 |
| ☐ 214 Mario Soto | .10 | .04 | .01 |
| ☐ 215A Bill Bonham P1 | .50 | .20 | .05 |
| small hand on back | | | |
| ☐ 215B Bill Bonham P2 | .06 | .02 | .00 |
| no hand | | | |
| ☐ 216 George Foster | .20 | .08 | .02 |
| See 202 | | | |
| ☐ 217 Paul Householder | .08 | .03 | .01 |
| ☐ 218 Ron Oester | .06 | .02 | .00 |
| ☐ 219 Sam Mejias | .03 | .01 | .00 |
| ☐ 220 Sheldon Burnside | .03 | .01 | .00 |
| ☐ 221 Carl Yastrzemski | .75 | .30 | .07 |
| ☐ 222 Jim Rice | .50 | .20 | .05 |
| ☐ 223 Fred Lynn | .25 | .10 | .02 |
| ☐ 224 Carlton Fisk | .20 | .08 | .02 |
| ☐ 225 Rick Burleson | .06 | .02 | .00 |
| ☐ 226 Dennis Eckersley | .06 | .02 | .00 |
| ☐ 227 Butch Hobson | .03 | .01 | .00 |
| ☐ 228 Tom Burgmeier | .03 | .01 | .00 |
| ☐ 229 Garry Hancock | .03 | .01 | .00 |
| ☐ 230 Don Zimmer MGR | .03 | .01 | .00 |
| ☐ 231 Steve Renko | .03 | .01 | .00 |
| ☐ 232 Dwight Evans | .12 | .05 | .01 |
| ☐ 233 Mike Torrez | .06 | .02 | .00 |
| ☐ 234 Bob Stanley | .06 | .02 | .00 |
| ☐ 235 Jim Dwyer | .03 | .01 | .00 |
| ☐ 236 Dave Stapleton | .06 | .02 | .00 |
| ☐ 237 Glen Hoffman | .06 | .02 | .00 |
| ☐ 238 Jerry Remy | .06 | .02 | .00 |
| ☐ 239 Dick Drago | .03 | .01 | .00 |
| ☐ 240 Bill Campbell | .06 | .02 | .00 |
| ☐ 241 Tony Perez | .15 | .06 | .01 |
| ☐ 242 Phil Niekro | .25 | .10 | .02 |
| ☐ 243 Dale Murphy | 1.25 | .50 | .12 |
| ☐ 244 Bob Horner | .25 | .10 | .02 |
| ☐ 245 Jeff Burroughs | .06 | .02 | .00 |
| ☐ 246 Rick Camp | .03 | .01 | .00 |
| ☐ 247 Bob Cox MGR | .03 | .01 | .00 |
| ☐ 248 Bruce Benedict | .03 | .01 | .00 |
| ☐ 249 Gene Garber | .03 | .01 | .00 |
| ☐ 250 Jerry Royster | .03 | .01 | .00 |
| ☐ 251A Gary Matthews P1 | .50 | .20 | .05 |
| small hand on back | | | |
| ☐ 251B Gary Matthews P2 | .10 | .04 | .01 |
| no hand | | | |
| ☐ 252 Chris Chambliss | .06 | .02 | .00 |

| | | | | |
|---|---|---|---|---|
| ☐ 253 | Luis Gomez | .03 | .01 | .00 |
| ☐ 254 | Bill Nahorodny | .03 | .01 | .00 |
| ☐ 255 | Doyle Alexander | .06 | .02 | .00 |
| ☐ 256 | Brian Asselstine | .03 | .01 | .00 |
| ☐ 257 | Biff Pocoroba | .03 | .01 | .00 |
| ☐ 258 | Mike Lum | .03 | .01 | .00 |
| ☐ 259 | Charlie Spikes | .03 | .01 | .00 |
| ☐ 260 | Glen Hubbard | .03 | .01 | .00 |
| ☐ 261 | Tommy Boggs | .03 | .01 | .00 |
| ☐ 262 | Al Hrabosky | .06 | .02 | .00 |
| ☐ 263 | Rick Matula | .03 | .01 | .00 |
| ☐ 264 | Preston Hanna | .03 | .01 | .00 |
| ☐ 265 | Larry Bradford | .03 | .01 | .00 |
| ☐ 266 | Rafael Ramirez | .20 | .08 | .02 |
| ☐ 267 | Larry McWilliams | .03 | .01 | .00 |
| ☐ 268 | Rod Carew | .50 | .20 | .05 |
| ☐ 269 | Bobby Grich | .10 | .04 | .01 |
| ☐ 270 | Carney Lansford | .15 | .06 | .01 |
| ☐ 271 | Don Baylor | .20 | .08 | .02 |
| ☐ 272 | Joe Rudi | .06 | .02 | .00 |
| ☐ 273 | Dan Ford | .03 | .01 | .00 |
| ☐ 274 | Jim Fregosi | .06 | .02 | .00 |
| ☐ 275 | Dave Frost | .03 | .01 | .00 |
| ☐ 276 | Frank Tanana | .06 | .02 | .00 |
| ☐ 277 | Dickie Thon | .08 | .03 | .01 |
| ☐ 278 | Jason Thompson | .06 | .02 | .00 |
| ☐ 279 | Rick Miller | .03 | .01 | .00 |
| ☐ 280 | Bert Campaneris | .08 | .03 | .01 |
| ☐ 281 | Tom Donohue | .03 | .01 | .00 |
| ☐ 282 | Brian Downing | .06 | .02 | .00 |
| ☐ 283 | Fred Patek | .03 | .01 | .00 |
| ☐ 284 | Bruce Kison | .03 | .01 | .00 |
| ☐ 285 | Dave LaRoche | .03 | .01 | .00 |
| ☐ 286 | Don Aase | .06 | .02 | .00 |
| ☐ 287 | Jim Barr | .03 | .01 | .00 |
| ☐ 288 | Alfredo Martinez | .03 | .01 | .00 |
| ☐ 289 | Larry Harlow | .03 | .01 | .00 |
| ☐ 290 | Andy Hassler | .03 | .01 | .00 |
| ☐ 291 | Dave Kingman | .15 | .06 | .01 |
| ☐ 292 | Bill Buckner | .12 | .05 | .01 |
| ☐ 293 | Rick Reuschel | .06 | .02 | .00 |
| ☐ 294 | Bruce Sutter | .20 | .08 | .02 |
| ☐ 295 | Jerry Martin | .03 | .01 | .00 |
| ☐ 296 | Scot Thompson | .03 | .01 | .00 |
| ☐ 297 | Ivan DeJesus | .03 | .01 | .00 |
| ☐ 298 | Steve Dillard | .03 | .01 | .00 |
| ☐ 299 | Dick Tidrow | .03 | .01 | .00 |
| ☐ 300 | Randy Martz | .03 | .01 | .00 |
| ☐ 301 | Lenny Randle | .03 | .01 | .00 |
| ☐ 302 | Lynn McGlothen | .03 | .01 | .00 |
| ☐ 303 | Cliff Johnson | .03 | .01 | .00 |
| ☐ 304 | Tim Blackwell | .03 | .01 | .00 |
| ☐ 305 | Dennis Lamp | .03 | .01 | .00 |
| ☐ 306 | Bill Caudill | .06 | .02 | .00 |
| ☐ 307 | Carlos Lezcano | .03 | .01 | .00 |
| ☐ 308 | Jim Tracy | .03 | .01 | .00 |
| ☐ 309 | Doug Capilla | .03 | .01 | .00 |
| ☐ 310 | Willie Hernandez | .15 | .06 | .01 |
| ☐ 311 | Mike Vail | .03 | .01 | .00 |
| ☐ 312 | Mike Krukow | .10 | .04 | .01 |
| ☐ 313 | Barry Foote | .03 | .01 | .00 |
| ☐ 314 | Larry Biittner | .03 | .01 | .00 |
| ☐ 315 | Mike Tyson | .03 | .01 | .00 |
| ☐ 316 | Lee Mazzilli | .06 | .02 | .00 |
| ☐ 317 | John Stearns | .03 | .01 | .00 |
| ☐ 318 | Alex Trevino | .03 | .01 | .00 |
| ☐ 319 | Craig Swan | .03 | .01 | .00 |
| ☐ 320 | Frank Taveras | .03 | .01 | .00 |
| ☐ 321 | Steve Henderson | .03 | .01 | .00 |
| ☐ 322 | Neil Allen | .06 | .02 | .00 |
| ☐ 323 | Mark Bomback | .03 | .01 | .00 |
| ☐ 324 | Mike Jorgensen | .03 | .01 | .00 |
| ☐ 325 | Joe Torre MGR | .10 | .04 | .01 |
| ☐ 326 | Elliott Maddox | .03 | .01 | .00 |
| ☐ 327 | Pete Falcone | .03 | .01 | .00 |
| ☐ 328 | Ray Burris | .03 | .01 | .00 |
| ☐ 329 | Claudell Washington | .06 | .02 | .00 |
| ☐ 330 | Doug Flynn | .03 | .01 | .00 |
| ☐ 331 | Joel Youngblood | .03 | .01 | .00 |
| ☐ 332 | Bill Almon | .03 | .01 | .00 |
| ☐ 333 | Tom Hausman | .03 | .01 | .00 |
| ☐ 334 | Pat Zachry | .03 | .01 | .00 |
| ☐ 335 | Jeff Reardon | .35 | .14 | .03 |
| ☐ 336 | Wally Backman | .50 | .20 | .05 |
| ☐ 337 | Dan Norman | .03 | .01 | .00 |
| ☐ 338 | Jerry Morales | .03 | .01 | .00 |
| ☐ 339 | Ed Farmer | .03 | .01 | .00 |
| ☐ 340 | Bob Molinaro | .03 | .01 | .00 |
| ☐ 341 | Todd Cruz | .03 | .01 | .00 |
| ☐ 342A | Britt Burns P1 small hand on front | .50 | .20 | .05 |
| ☐ 342B | Britt Burns P2 no hand | .30 | .12 | .03 |

| | | | | |
|---|---|---|---|---|
| ☐ 343 | Kevin Bell | .03 | .01 | .00 |
| ☐ 344 | Tony LaRussa MGR | .06 | .02 | .00 |
| ☐ 345 | Steve Trout | .06 | .02 | .00 |
| ☐ 346 | Harold Baines | 2.00 | .80 | .20 |
| ☐ 347 | Richard Wortham | .03 | .01 | .00 |
| ☐ 348 | Wayne Nordhagen | .03 | .01 | .00 |
| ☐ 349 | Mike Squires | .03 | .01 | .00 |
| ☐ 350 | Lamar Johnson | .03 | .01 | .00 |
| ☐ 351 | Rickey Henderson | .70 | .28 | .07 |
| ☐ 352 | Francisco Barrios | .03 | .01 | .00 |
| ☐ 353 | Thad Bosley | .03 | .01 | .00 |
| ☐ 354 | Chet Lemon | .06 | .02 | .00 |
| ☐ 355 | Bruce Kimm | .03 | .01 | .00 |
| ☐ 356 | Richard Dotson | .25 | .10 | .02 |
| ☐ 357 | Jim Morrison | .03 | .01 | .00 |
| ☐ 358 | Mike Proly | .03 | .01 | .00 |
| ☐ 359 | Greg Pryor | .03 | .01 | .00 |
| ☐ 360 | Dave Parker | .30 | .12 | .03 |
| ☐ 361 | Omar Moreno | .03 | .01 | .00 |
| ☐ 362A | Kent Tekulve P1 Back "1071 Waterbury and "1078 Pirates" | .12 | .05 | .01 |
| ☐ 362B | Kent Tekulve P2 "1971 Waterbury" and "1978 Pirates" | .08 | .03 | .01 |
| ☐ 363 | Willie Stargell | .30 | .12 | .03 |
| ☐ 364 | Phil Garner | .06 | .02 | .00 |
| ☐ 365 | Ed Ott | .03 | .01 | .00 |
| ☐ 366 | Don Robinson | .03 | .01 | .00 |
| ☐ 367 | Chuck Tanner MGR | .03 | .01 | .00 |
| ☐ 368 | Jim Rooker | .03 | .01 | .00 |
| ☐ 369 | Dale Berra | .06 | .02 | .00 |
| ☐ 370 | Jim Bibby | .03 | .01 | .00 |
| ☐ 371 | Steve Nicosia | .03 | .01 | .00 |
| ☐ 372 | Mike Easler | .08 | .03 | .01 |
| ☐ 373 | Bill Robinson | .03 | .01 | .00 |
| ☐ 374 | Lee Lacy | .06 | .02 | .00 |
| ☐ 375 | John Candelaria | .08 | .03 | .01 |
| ☐ 376 | Manny Sanguillen | .06 | .02 | .00 |
| ☐ 377 | Rick Rhoden | .08 | .03 | .01 |
| ☐ 378 | Grant Jackson | .03 | .01 | .00 |
| ☐ 379 | Tim Foli | .03 | .01 | .00 |
| ☐ 380 | Rod Scurry | .12 | .05 | .01 |
| ☐ 381 | Bill Madlock | .15 | .06 | .01 |
| ☐ 382A | Kurt Bevacqua P1 ERR P on cap backwards | .20 | .08 | .02 |
| ☐ 382B | Kurt Bevacqua P2 COR | .06 | .02 | .00 |
| ☐ 383 | Bert Blyleven | .12 | .05 | .01 |
| ☐ 384 | Eddie Solomon | .03 | .01 | .00 |
| ☐ 385 | Enrique Romo | .03 | .01 | .00 |
| ☐ 386 | John Milner | .03 | .01 | .00 |
| ☐ 387 | Mike Hargrove | .06 | .02 | .00 |
| ☐ 388 | Jorge Orta | .03 | .01 | .00 |
| ☐ 389 | Toby Harrah | .06 | .02 | .00 |
| ☐ 390 | Tom Veryzer | .03 | .01 | .00 |
| ☐ 391 | Miguel Dilone | .03 | .01 | .00 |
| ☐ 392 | Dan Spillner | .03 | .01 | .00 |
| ☐ 393 | Jack Brohamer | .03 | .01 | .00 |
| ☐ 394 | Wayne Garland | .03 | .01 | .00 |
| ☐ 395 | Sid Monge | .03 | .01 | .00 |
| ☐ 396 | Rick Waits | .03 | .01 | .00 |
| ☐ 397 | Joe Charboneau | .10 | .04 | .01 |
| ☐ 398 | Gary Alexander | .03 | .01 | .00 |
| ☐ 399 | Jerry Dybzinski | .03 | .01 | .00 |
| ☐ 400 | Mike Stanton | .03 | .01 | .00 |
| ☐ 401 | Mike Paxton | .03 | .01 | .00 |
| ☐ 402 | Gary Gray | .06 | .02 | .00 |
| ☐ 403 | Rick Manning | .03 | .01 | .00 |
| ☐ 404 | Bo Diaz | .06 | .02 | .00 |
| ☐ 405 | Ron Hassey | .03 | .01 | .00 |
| ☐ 406 | Ross Grimsley | .03 | .01 | .00 |
| ☐ 407 | Victor Cruz | .03 | .01 | .00 |
| ☐ 408 | Len Barker | .06 | .02 | .00 |
| ☐ 409 | Bob Bailor | .03 | .01 | .00 |
| ☐ 410 | Otto Velez | .03 | .01 | .00 |
| ☐ 411 | Ernie Whitt | .03 | .01 | .00 |
| ☐ 412 | Jim Clancy | .03 | .01 | .00 |
| ☐ 413 | Barry Bonnell | .03 | .01 | .00 |
| ☐ 414 | Dave Stieb | .20 | .08 | .02 |
| ☐ 415 | Damaso Garcia | .45 | .18 | .04 |
| ☐ 416 | John Mayberry | .06 | .02 | .00 |
| ☐ 417 | Roy Howell | .03 | .01 | .00 |
| ☐ 418 | Dan Ainge | .20 | .08 | .02 |
| ☐ 419A | Jesse Jefferson P1 Back says Pirates | .06 | .02 | .00 |
| ☐ 419B | Jesse Jefferson P2 Back says Pirates | .06 | .02 | .00 |
| ☐ 419C | Jesse Jefferson P3 Back says Blue Jays | .35 | .14 | .03 |
| ☐ 420 | Joey McLaughlin | .03 | .01 | .00 |
| ☐ 421 | Lloyd Moseby | 1.00 | .40 | .10 |
| ☐ 422 | Al Woods | .03 | .01 | .00 |

| | | | | |
|---|---|---|---|---|
| ☐ 423 | Garth Iorg | .03 | .01 | .00 |
| ☐ 424 | Doug Ault | .03 | .01 | .00 |
| ☐ 425 | Ken Schrom | .15 | .06 | .01 |
| ☐ 426 | Mike Willis | .03 | .01 | .00 |
| ☐ 427 | Steve Braun | .03 | .01 | .00 |
| ☐ 428 | Bob Davis | .03 | .01 | .00 |
| ☐ 429 | Jerry Garvin | .03 | .01 | .00 |
| ☐ 430 | Alfredo Griffin | .06 | .02 | .00 |
| ☐ 431 | Bob Mattick MGR | .03 | .01 | .00 |
| ☐ 432 | Vida Blue | .08 | .03 | .01 |
| ☐ 433 | Jack Clark | .12 | .05 | .01 |
| ☐ 434 | Willie McCovey | .30 | .12 | .03 |
| ☐ 435 | Mike Ivie | .03 | .01 | .00 |
| ☐ 436A | Darrel Evans P1 ERR | .30 | .12 | .03 |
| | Name on front "Darrel" | | | |
| ☐ 436B | Darrell Evans P2 | .12 | .05 | .01 |
| | Name on front "Darrell" | | | |
| ☐ 437 | Terry Whitfield | .03 | .01 | .00 |
| ☐ 438 | Rennie Stennett | .03 | .01 | .00 |
| ☐ 439 | John Montefusco | .06 | .02 | .00 |
| ☐ 440 | Jim Wohlford | .03 | .01 | .00 |
| ☐ 441 | Bill North | .03 | .01 | .00 |
| ☐ 442 | Milt May | .03 | .01 | .00 |
| ☐ 443 | Max Venable | .03 | .01 | .00 |
| ☐ 444 | Ed Whitson | .06 | .02 | .00 |
| ☐ 445 | Al Holland | .12 | .05 | .01 |
| ☐ 446 | Randy Moffitt | .03 | .01 | .00 |
| ☐ 447 | Bob Knepper | .12 | .05 | .01 |
| ☐ 448 | Gary Lavelle | .06 | .02 | .00 |
| ☐ 449 | Greg Minton | .06 | .02 | .00 |
| ☐ 450 | Johnnie LeMaster | .03 | .01 | .00 |
| ☐ 451 | Larry Herndon | .03 | .01 | .00 |
| ☐ 452 | Rich Murray | .03 | .01 | .00 |
| ☐ 453 | Joe Pettini | .03 | .01 | .00 |
| ☐ 454 | Allen Ripley | .03 | .01 | .00 |
| ☐ 455 | Dennis Littlejohn | .03 | .01 | .00 |
| ☐ 456 | Tom Griffin | .03 | .01 | .00 |
| ☐ 457 | Alan Hargesheimer | .03 | .01 | .00 |
| ☐ 458 | Joe Strain | .03 | .01 | .00 |
| ☐ 459 | Steve Kemp | .08 | .03 | .01 |
| ☐ 460 | Sparky Anderson MGR | .08 | .03 | .01 |
| ☐ 461 | Alan Trammell | .20 | .08 | .02 |
| ☐ 462 | Mark Fidrych | .10 | .04 | .01 |
| ☐ 463 | Lou Whitaker | .15 | .06 | .01 |
| ☐ 464 | Dave Rozema | .03 | .01 | .00 |
| ☐ 465 | Milt Wilcox | .03 | .01 | .00 |
| ☐ 466 | Champ Summers | .03 | .01 | .00 |
| ☐ 467 | Lance Parrish | .35 | .14 | .03 |
| ☐ 468 | Dan Petry | .12 | .05 | .01 |
| ☐ 469 | Pat Underwood | .03 | .01 | .00 |
| ☐ 470 | Rick Peters | .03 | .01 | .00 |
| ☐ 471 | Al Cowens | .03 | .01 | .00 |
| ☐ 472 | John Wockenfuss | .03 | .01 | .00 |
| ☐ 473 | Tom Brookens | .03 | .01 | .00 |
| ☐ 474 | Richie Hebner | .03 | .01 | .00 |
| ☐ 475 | Jack Morris | .35 | .14 | .03 |
| ☐ 476 | Jim Lentine | .03 | .01 | .00 |
| ☐ 477 | Bruce Robbins | .03 | .01 | .00 |
| ☐ 478 | Mark Wagner | .03 | .01 | .00 |
| ☐ 479 | Tim Corcoran | .03 | .01 | .00 |
| ☐ 480A | Stan Papi P1 | .15 | .06 | .01 |
| | Front as Pitcher | | | |
| ☐ 480B | Stan Papi P2 | .10 | .04 | .01 |
| | Front as Shortstop | | | |
| ☐ 481 | Kirk Gibson | 2.00 | .80 | .20 |
| ☐ 482 | Dan Schatzeder | .03 | .01 | .00 |
| ☐ 483A | Amos Otis P1 | .10 | .04 | .01 |
| | See card 32 | | | |
| ☐ 483B | Amos Otis P2 | .10 | .04 | .01 |
| | See card 32 | | | |
| ☐ 484 | Dave Winfield | .45 | .18 | .04 |
| ☐ 485 | Rollie Fingers | .25 | .10 | .02 |
| ☐ 486 | Gene Richards | .03 | .01 | .00 |
| ☐ 487 | Randy Jones | .06 | .02 | .00 |
| ☐ 488 | Ozzie Smith | .25 | .10 | .02 |
| ☐ 489 | Gene Tenace | .03 | .01 | .00 |
| ☐ 490 | Bill Fahey | .03 | .01 | .00 |
| ☐ 491 | John Curtis | .03 | .01 | .00 |
| ☐ 492 | Dave Cash | .03 | .01 | .00 |
| ☐ 493A | Tim Flannery P1 | .12 | .05 | .01 |
| | Batting right | | | |
| ☐ 493B | Tim Flannery P2 | .08 | .03 | .01 |
| | Batting left | | | |
| ☐ 494 | Jerry Mumphrey | .06 | .02 | .00 |
| ☐ 495 | Bob Shirley | .03 | .01 | .00 |
| ☐ 496 | Steve Mura | .03 | .01 | .00 |
| ☐ 497 | Eric Rasmussen | .03 | .01 | .00 |
| ☐ 498 | Broderick Perkins | .03 | .01 | .00 |
| ☐ 499 | Barry Evans | .03 | .01 | .00 |
| ☐ 500 | Chuck Baker | .03 | .01 | .00 |
| ☐ 501 | Luis Salazar | .06 | .02 | .00 |
| ☐ 502 | Gary Lucas | .10 | .04 | .01 |
| ☐ 503 | Mike Armstrong | .10 | .04 | .01 |

| | | | | |
|---|---|---|---|---|
| ☐ 504 | Jerry Turner | .03 | .01 | .00 |
| ☐ 505 | Dennis Kinney | .03 | .01 | .00 |
| ☐ 506 | Willie Montanez | .03 | .01 | .00 |
| ☐ 507 | Gorman Thomas | .10 | .04 | .01 |
| ☐ 508 | Ben Oglivie | .08 | .03 | .01 |
| ☐ 509 | Larry Hisle | .06 | .02 | .00 |
| ☐ 510 | Sal Bando | .06 | .02 | .00 |
| ☐ 511 | Robin Yount | .45 | .18 | .04 |
| ☐ 512 | Mike Caldwell | .06 | .02 | .00 |
| ☐ 513 | Sixto Lezcano | .03 | .01 | .00 |
| ☐ 514A | Bill Travers P1 ERR | .15 | .06 | .01 |
| | "Jerry Augustine" | | | |
| | with Augustine back | | | |
| ☐ 514B | Bill Travers P2 COR | .10 | .04 | .01 |
| ☐ 515 | Paul Molitor | .12 | .05 | .01 |
| ☐ 516 | Moose Haas | .06 | .02 | .00 |
| ☐ 517 | Bill Castro | .03 | .01 | .00 |
| ☐ 518 | Jim Slaton | .06 | .02 | .00 |
| ☐ 519 | Lary Sorensen | .03 | .01 | .00 |
| ☐ 520 | Bob McClure | .03 | .01 | .00 |
| ☐ 521 | Charlie Moore | .03 | .01 | .00 |
| ☐ 522 | Jim Gantner | .06 | .02 | .00 |
| ☐ 523 | Reggie Cleveland | .03 | .01 | .00 |
| ☐ 524 | Don Money | .03 | .01 | .00 |
| ☐ 525 | Bill Travers | .03 | .01 | .00 |
| ☐ 526 | Buck Martinez | .03 | .01 | .00 |
| ☐ 527 | Dick Davis | .03 | .01 | .00 |
| ☐ 528 | Ted Simmons | .15 | .06 | .01 |
| ☐ 529 | Garry Templeton | .10 | .04 | .01 |
| ☐ 530 | Ken Reitz | .03 | .01 | .00 |
| ☐ 531 | Tony Scott | .03 | .01 | .00 |
| ☐ 532 | Ken Oberkfell | .03 | .01 | .00 |
| ☐ 533 | Bob Sykes | .03 | .01 | .00 |
| ☐ 534 | Keith Smith | .03 | .01 | .00 |
| ☐ 535 | John Littlefield | .03 | .01 | .00 |
| ☐ 536 | Jim Kaat | .15 | .06 | .01 |
| ☐ 537 | Bob Forsch | .06 | .02 | .00 |
| ☐ 538 | Mike Phillips | .03 | .01 | .00 |
| ☐ 539 | Terry Landrum | .08 | .03 | .01 |
| ☐ 540 | Leon Durham | .50 | .20 | .05 |
| ☐ 541 | Terry Kennedy | .10 | .04 | .01 |
| ☐ 542 | George Hendrick | .08 | .03 | .01 |
| ☐ 543 | Dane Iorg | .03 | .01 | .00 |
| ☐ 544 | Mark Littell | .03 | .01 | .00 |
| ☐ 545 | Keith Hernandez | .30 | .12 | .03 |
| ☐ 546 | Silvio Martinez | .03 | .01 | .00 |
| ☐ 547A | Don Hood P1 ERR | .20 | .08 | .02 |
| | "Pete Vuckovich" | | | |
| | with Vuckovich back | | | |
| ☐ 547B | Don Hood P2 COR | .10 | .04 | .01 |
| ☐ 548 | Bobby Bonds | .10 | .04 | .01 |
| ☐ 549 | Mike Ramsey | .03 | .01 | .00 |
| ☐ 550 | Tom Herr | .10 | .04 | .01 |
| ☐ 551 | Roy Smalley | .06 | .02 | .00 |
| ☐ 552 | Jerry Koosman | .08 | .03 | .01 |
| ☐ 553 | Ken Landreaux | .06 | .02 | .00 |
| ☐ 554 | John Castino | .06 | .02 | .00 |
| ☐ 555 | Doug Corbett | .08 | .03 | .01 |
| ☐ 556 | Bombo Rivera | .03 | .01 | .00 |
| ☐ 557 | Ron Jackson | .03 | .01 | .00 |
| ☐ 558 | Butch Wynegar | .06 | .02 | .00 |
| ☐ 559 | Hosken Powell | .03 | .01 | .00 |
| ☐ 560 | Pete Redfern | .03 | .01 | .00 |
| ☐ 561 | Roger Erickson | .03 | .01 | .00 |
| ☐ 562 | Glenn Adams | .03 | .01 | .00 |
| ☐ 563 | Rick Sofield | .03 | .01 | .00 |
| ☐ 564 | Geoff Zahn | .03 | .01 | .00 |
| ☐ 565 | Pete Mackanin | .03 | .01 | .00 |
| ☐ 566 | Mike Cubbage | .03 | .01 | .00 |
| ☐ 567 | Darrell Jackson | .03 | .01 | .00 |
| ☐ 568 | Dave Edwards | .03 | .01 | .00 |
| ☐ 569 | Rob Wilfong | .03 | .01 | .00 |
| ☐ 570 | Sal Butera | .03 | .01 | .00 |
| ☐ 571 | Jose Morales | .03 | .01 | .00 |
| ☐ 572 | Rick Langford | .03 | .01 | .00 |
| ☐ 573 | Mike Norris | .06 | .02 | .00 |
| ☐ 574 | Rickey Henderson | .70 | .28 | .07 |
| ☐ 575 | Tony Armas | .10 | .04 | .01 |
| ☐ 576 | Dave Revering | .03 | .01 | .00 |
| ☐ 577 | Jeff Newman | .03 | .01 | .00 |
| ☐ 578 | Bob Lacey | .03 | .01 | .00 |
| ☐ 579 | Brian Kingman | .03 | .01 | .00 |
| ☐ 580 | Mitchell Page | .03 | .01 | .00 |
| ☐ 581 | Billy Martin MGR | .10 | .04 | .01 |
| ☐ 582 | Rob Picciolo | .03 | .01 | .00 |
| ☐ 583 | Mike Heath | .03 | .01 | .00 |
| ☐ 584 | Mickey Klutts | .03 | .01 | .00 |
| ☐ 585 | Orlando Gonzalez | .03 | .01 | .00 |
| ☐ 586 | Mike Davis | .30 | .12 | .03 |
| ☐ 587 | Wayne Gross | .03 | .01 | .00 |
| ☐ 588 | Matt Keough | .03 | .01 | .00 |
| ☐ 589 | Steve McCatty | .03 | .01 | .00 |
| ☐ 590 | Dwayne Murphy | .06 | .02 | .00 |

| | | | | |
|---|---|---|---|---|
| ☐ 591 | Mario Guerrero | .03 | .01 | .00 |
| ☐ 592 | Dave McKay | .03 | .01 | .00 |
| ☐ 593 | Jim Essian | .03 | .01 | .00 |
| ☐ 594 | Dave Heaverlo | .03 | .01 | .00 |
| ☐ 595 | Maury Wills MGR | .08 | .03 | .01 |
| ☐ 596 | Juan Beniquez | .06 | .02 | .00 |
| ☐ 597 | Rodney Craig | .03 | .01 | .00 |
| ☐ 598 | Jim Anderson | .03 | .01 | .00 |
| ☐ 599 | Floyd Bannister | .06 | .02 | .00 |
| ☐ 600 | Bruce Bochte | .06 | .02 | .00 |
| ☐ 601 | Julio Cruz | .06 | .02 | .00 |
| ☐ 602 | Ted Cox | .03 | .01 | .00 |
| ☐ 603 | Dan Meyer | .03 | .01 | .00 |
| ☐ 604 | Larry Cox | .03 | .01 | .00 |
| ☐ 605 | Bill Stein | .03 | .01 | .00 |
| ☐ 606 | Steve Garvey | .50 | .20 | .05 |
| ☐ 607 | Dave Roberts | .03 | .01 | .00 |
| ☐ 608 | Leon Roberts | .03 | .01 | .00 |
| ☐ 609 | Reggie Walton | .03 | .01 | .00 |
| ☐ 610 | Dave Edler | .03 | .01 | .00 |
| ☐ 611 | Larry Milbourne | .03 | .01 | .00 |
| ☐ 612 | Kim Allen | .03 | .01 | .00 |
| ☐ 613 | Mario Mendoza | .03 | .01 | .00 |
| ☐ 614 | Tom Paciorek | .03 | .01 | .00 |
| ☐ 615 | Glenn Abbott | .03 | .01 | .00 |
| ☐ 616 | Joe Simpson | .03 | .01 | .00 |
| ☐ 617 | Mickey Rivers | .06 | .02 | .00 |
| ☐ 618 | Jim Kern | .03 | .01 | .00 |
| ☐ 619 | Jim Sundberg | .06 | .02 | .00 |
| ☐ 620 | Richie Zisk | .06 | .02 | .00 |
| ☐ 621 | Jon Matlack | .06 | .02 | .00 |
| ☐ 622 | Ferguson Jenkins | .15 | .06 | .01 |
| ☐ 623 | Pat Corrales MGR | .06 | .02 | .00 |
| ☐ 624 | Ed Figueroa | .03 | .01 | .00 |
| ☐ 625 | Buddy Bell | .12 | .05 | .01 |
| ☐ 626 | Al Oliver | .12 | .05 | .01 |
| ☐ 627 | Doc Medich | .03 | .01 | .00 |
| ☐ 628 | Bump Wills | .03 | .01 | .00 |
| ☐ 629 | Rusty Staub | .10 | .04 | .01 |
| ☐ 630 | Pat Putnam | .03 | .01 | .00 |
| ☐ 631 | John Grubb | .03 | .01 | .00 |
| ☐ 632 | Danny Darwin | .03 | .01 | .00 |
| ☐ 633 | Ken Clay | .03 | .01 | .00 |
| ☐ 634 | Jim Norris | .03 | .01 | .00 |
| ☐ 635 | John Butcher | .15 | .06 | .01 |
| ☐ 636 | Dave Roberts | .03 | .01 | .00 |
| ☐ 637 | Billy Sample | .03 | .01 | .00 |
| ☐ 638 | Carl Yastrzemski | .75 | .30 | .07 |
| ☐ 639 | Cecil Cooper | .18 | .08 | .01 |
| ☐ 640A | Mike Schmidt P1 (Portrait) "Third Base" (number on back 5) | 1.00 | .40 | .10 |
| ☐ 640B | Mike Schmidt P2 "1980 Home Run King" (640 on back) | 1.00 | .40 | .10 |
| ☐ 641A | CL: Phils/Royals P1 41 is Hal McRae | .07 | .01 | .00 |
| ☐ 641B | CL: Phils/Royals P2 41 is Hal McRae, Double Threat | .07 | .01 | .00 |
| ☐ 642 | CL: Astros/Yankees | .07 | .01 | .00 |
| ☐ 643 | CL: Expos/Dodgers | .07 | .01 | .00 |
| ☐ 644A | CL: Reds/Orioles P1 202 is George Foster | .07 | .01 | .00 |
| ☐ 644B | CL: Reds/Orioles P2 202 is Foster Slugger | .07 | .01 | .00 |
| ☐ 645A | Rose/Bowa/Schmidt Triple Threat P1 (No number on back) | 2.00 | .80 | .20 |
| ☐ 645B | Rose/Bowa/Schmidt Triple Threat P2 (Back numbered 645) | 1.00 | .40 | .10 |
| ☐ 646 | CL: Braves/Red Sox | .07 | .01 | .00 |
| ☐ 647 | CL: Cubs/Angels | .07 | .01 | .00 |
| ☐ 648 | CL: Mets/White Sox | .07 | .01 | .00 |
| ☐ 649 | CL: Indians/Pirates | .07 | .01 | .00 |
| ☐ 650A | Reggie Jackson Mr. Baseball P1 Number on back 79 | .80 | .32 | .08 |
| ☐ 650B | Reggie Jackson Mr. Baseball P2 Number on back 650 | .70 | .28 | .07 |
| ☐ 651 | CL: Giants/Blue Jays | .07 | .01 | .00 |
| ☐ 652A | CL: Tigers/Padres P1 483 is listed | .07 | .01 | .00 |
| ☐ 652B | CL: Tigers/Padres P2 483 is deleted | .07 | .01 | .00 |
| ☐ 653A | Willie Wilson P1 Most Hits Most Runs Number on back 29 | .25 | .10 | .02 |
| ☐ 653B | Willie Wilson P2 Most Hits Most Runs Number on back 653 | .25 | .10 | .02 |

| | | | | |
|---|---|---|---|---|
| ☐ 654A | CL: Brewers/Cards P1 514 Jerry Augustine 547 Pete Vuckovich | .07 | .01 | .00 |
| ☐ 654B | CL: Brewers/Cards P2 514 Billy Travers 547 Don Hood | .07 | .01 | .00 |
| ☐ 655A | George Brett P1 .390 Average Number on back 28 | .75 | .30 | .07 |
| ☐ 655B | George Brett P2 .390 Average Number on back 655 | .75 | .30 | .07 |
| ☐ 656 | CL: Twins/Oakland A's | .07 | .01 | .00 |
| ☐ 657A | Tug McGraw P1 Game Saver Number on back 7 | .10 | .04 | .01 |
| ☐ 657B | Tug McGraw P2 Game Saver Number on back 657 | .10 | .04 | .01 |
| ☐ 658 | CL: Rangers/Mariners | .07 | .01 | .00 |
| ☐ 659A | Checklist P1 of Special Cards Last lines on front Wilson Most Hits | .07 | .01 | .00 |
| ☐ 659B | Checklist P2 of Special Cards Last lines on front Otis Series Starter | .07 | .01 | .00 |
| ☐ 660A | Steve Carlton P1 Golden Arm Back "1066 Cardinals" Number on back 6 | .60 | .24 | .06 |
| ☐ 660B | Steve Carlton P2 Golden Arm Number on back 660 Back "1066 Cardinals" | .60 | .24 | .06 |
| ☐ 660C | Steve Carlton P3 Golden Arm "1966 Cardinals" | 2.00 | .80 | .20 |

# 1982 Fleer

The cards in this 660 card set measure 2 1/2" by 3 1/2". The 1982 Fleer set is again ordered by teams; in fact the players within each team are listed in alphabetical order. The teams are ordered (by 1981 standings) as follows: Los Angeles (1- 29), New York Yankees (30-56), Cincinnati (57-84), Oakland (85- 109), St. Louis (110-132), Milwaukee (133-156), Baltimore (157- 182), Montreal (183-211), Houston (212-237), Philadelphia (238- 262), Detroit (263-286), Boston (287-312), Texas (313-334), Chicago White Sox (335-358), Cleveland (359-382), San Francisco (383-403), Kansas City (404-427), Atlanta (428-449), California (450-474), Pittsburgh (475-501), Seattle (502-519), New York Mets (520-544), Minnesota (545-565), San Diego (566-585), Chicago Cubs (586-607), and Toronto (608-627). Cards numbered 628 through 646 are special cards highlighting some of the stars and leaders of the

1981 season. The last 14 cards in the set (647-660) are checklist cards. The backs feature player statistics and a full color team logo in the upper right hand corner of each card.

|  | MINT | VG-E | F-G |
|---|---|---|---|
| COMPLETE SET .................. | 21.00 | 8.50 | 2.10 |
| COMMON PLAYER (1-660) ........ | .03 | .01 | .00 |

| | | MINT | VG-E | F-G |
|---|---|---|---|---|
| ☐ | 1 Dusty Baker ................ | .12 | .05 | .01 |
| ☐ | 2 Robert Castillo .............. | .03 | .01 | .00 |
| ☐ | 3 Ron Cey .................... | .10 | .04 | .01 |
| ☐ | 4 Terry Forster ............... | .06 | .02 | .00 |
| ☐ | 5 Steve Garvey ............... | .40 | .16 | .04 |
| ☐ | 6 Dave Goltz ................. | .03 | .01 | .00 |
| ☐ | 7 Pedro Guerrero ............. | .30 | .12 | .03 |
| ☐ | 8 Burt Hooton ................ | .03 | .01 | .00 |
| ☐ | 9 Steve Howe ................ | .06 | .02 | .00 |
| ☐ | 10 Jay Johnstone ............. | .06 | .02 | .00 |
| ☐ | 11 Ken Landreaux ............. | .06 | .02 | .00 |
| ☐ | 12 Davey Lopes ............... | .08 | .03 | .01 |
| ☐ | 13 Mike Marshall ............. | 1.25 | .50 | .12 |
| ☐ | 14 Bobby Mitchell ............ | .06 | .02 | .00 |
| ☐ | 15 Rick Monday .............. | .06 | .02 | .00 |
| ☐ | 16 Tom Niedenfuer ........... | .45 | .18 | .04 |
| ☐ | 17 Ted Power ................ | .40 | .16 | .04 |
| ☐ | 18 Jerry Reuss ............... | .06 | .02 | .00 |
| ☐ | 19 Ron Roenicke ............. | .06 | .02 | .00 |
| ☐ | 20 Bill Russell ............... | .06 | .02 | .00 |
| ☐ | 21 Steve Sax ................. | 1.25 | .50 | .12 |
| ☐ | 22 Mike Scioscia ............. | .03 | .01 | .00 |
| ☐ | 23 Reggie Smith .............. | .08 | .03 | .01 |
| ☐ | 24 Dave Stewart ............. | .15 | .06 | .01 |
| ☐ | 25 Rick Sutcliffe ............. | .15 | .06 | .01 |
| ☐ | 26 Derrel Thomas ............ | .03 | .01 | .00 |
| ☐ | 27 Fernando Valenzuela ...... | .50 | .20 | .05 |
| ☐ | 28 Bob Welch ................ | .08 | .03 | .01 |
| ☐ | 29 Steve Yeager ............. | .06 | .02 | .00 |
| ☐ | 30 Bobby Brown .............. | .03 | .01 | .00 |
| ☐ | 31 Rick Cerone ............... | .03 | .01 | .00 |
| ☐ | 32 Ron Davis ................. | .03 | .01 | .00 |
| ☐ | 33 Bucky Dent ............... | .08 | .03 | .01 |
| ☐ | 34 Barry Foote ............... | .03 | .01 | .00 |
| ☐ | 35 George Frazier ............ | .03 | .01 | .00 |
| ☐ | 36 Oscar Gamble ............. | .06 | .02 | .00 |
| ☐ | 37 Rich Gossage ............. | .20 | .08 | .02 |
| ☐ | 38 Ron Guidry ............... | .20 | .08 | .02 |
| ☐ | 39 Reggie Jackson ........... | .50 | .20 | .05 |
| ☐ | 40 Tommy John ............... | .15 | .06 | .01 |
| ☐ | 41 Rudy May ................. | .03 | .01 | .00 |
| ☐ | 42 Larry Milbourne ........... | .03 | .01 | .00 |
| ☐ | 43 Jerry Mumphrey ........... | .06 | .02 | .00 |
| ☐ | 44 Bobby Murcer ............. | .10 | .04 | .01 |
| ☐ | 45 Gene Nelson .............. | .10 | .04 | .01 |
| ☐ | 46 Graig Nettles ............. | .15 | .06 | .01 |
| ☐ | 47 Johnny Oates ............. | .03 | .01 | .00 |
| ☐ | 48 Lou Piniella .............. | .10 | .04 | .01 |
| ☐ | 49 Willie Randolph ........... | .08 | .03 | .01 |
| ☐ | 50 Rick Reuschel ............. | .06 | .02 | .00 |
| ☐ | 51 Dave Revering ............ | .03 | .01 | .00 |
| ☐ | 52 Dave Righetti ............. | 1.25 | .50 | .12 |
| ☐ | 53 Aurelio Rodriguez ......... | .03 | .01 | .00 |
| ☐ | 54 Bob Watson ............... | .06 | .02 | .00 |
| ☐ | 55 Dennis Werth ............. | .03 | .01 | .00 |
| ☐ | 56 Dave Winfield ............. | .40 | .16 | .04 |
| ☐ | 57 Johnny Bench ............. | .40 | .16 | .04 |
| ☐ | 58 Bruce Berenyi ............. | .03 | .01 | .00 |
| ☐ | 59 Larry Biittner ............. | .03 | .01 | .00 |
| ☐ | 60 Scott Brown ............... | .03 | .01 | .00 |
| ☐ | 61 Dave Collins .............. | .06 | .02 | .00 |
| ☐ | 62 Geoff Combe .............. | .03 | .01 | .00 |
| ☐ | 63 Dave Concepcion .......... | .10 | .04 | .01 |
| ☐ | 64 Dan Driessen ............. | .03 | .01 | .00 |
| ☐ | 65 Joe Edelen ............... | .03 | .01 | .00 |
| ☐ | 66 George Foster ............. | .15 | .06 | .01 |
| ☐ | 67 Ken Griffey ............... | .10 | .04 | .01 |
| ☐ | 68 Paul Householder .......... | .03 | .01 | .00 |
| ☐ | 69 Tom Hume ................ | .03 | .01 | .00 |
| ☐ | 70 Junior Kennedy ........... | .03 | .01 | .00 |
| ☐ | 71 Ray Knight ................ | .10 | .04 | .01 |
| ☐ | 72 Mike LaCoss .............. | .03 | .01 | .00 |
| ☐ | 73 Rafael Landestoy .......... | .03 | .01 | .00 |
| ☐ | 74 Charlie Leibrandt .......... | .06 | .02 | .00 |
| ☐ | 75 Sam Mejias ............... | .03 | .01 | .00 |
| ☐ | 76 Paul Moskau .............. | .03 | .01 | .00 |
| ☐ | 77 Joe Nolan ................ | .03 | .01 | .00 |
| ☐ | 78 Mike O'Berry ............. | .03 | .01 | .00 |
| ☐ | 79 Ron Oester ............... | .06 | .02 | .00 |
| ☐ | 80 Frank Pastore ............. | .03 | .01 | .00 |
| ☐ | 81 Joe Price ................. | .03 | .01 | .00 |
| ☐ | 82 Tom Seaver ............... | .40 | .16 | .04 |
| ☐ | 83 Mario Soto ............... | .10 | .04 | .01 |
| ☐ | 84 Mike Vail ................. | .03 | .01 | .00 |
| ☐ | 85 Tony Armas ............... | .10 | .04 | .01 |
| ☐ | 86 Shooty Babitt ............. | .03 | .01 | .00 |
| ☐ | 87 Dave Beard ............... | .03 | .01 | .00 |
| ☐ | 88 Rick Bosetti .............. | .03 | .01 | .00 |
| ☐ | 89 Keith Drumright ........... | .03 | .01 | .00 |
| ☐ | 90 Wayne Gross .............. | .03 | .01 | .00 |
| ☐ | 91 Mike Heath ............... | .03 | .01 | .00 |
| ☐ | 92 Rickey Henderson ......... | .50 | .20 | .05 |
| ☐ | 93 Cliff Johnson ............. | .03 | .01 | .00 |
| ☐ | 94 Jeff Jones ................ | .03 | .01 | .00 |
| ☐ | 95 Matt Keough .............. | .03 | .01 | .00 |
| ☐ | 96 Brian Kingman ............ | .03 | .01 | .00 |
| ☐ | 97 Mickey Klutts ............. | .03 | .01 | .00 |
| ☐ | 98 Rick Langford ............. | .03 | .01 | .00 |
| ☐ | 99 Steve McCatty ............ | .03 | .01 | .00 |
| ☐ | 100 Dave McKay .............. | .03 | .01 | .00 |
| ☐ | 101 Dwayne Murphy .......... | .06 | .02 | .00 |
| ☐ | 102 Jeff Newman ............. | .03 | .01 | .00 |
| ☐ | 103 Mike Norris .............. | .06 | .02 | .00 |
| ☐ | 104 Bob Owchinko ............ | .03 | .01 | .00 |
| ☐ | 105 Mitchell Page ............ | .03 | .01 | .00 |
| ☐ | 106 Rob Picciolo ............. | .03 | .01 | .00 |
| ☐ | 107 Jim Spencer ............. | .03 | .01 | .00 |
| ☐ | 108 Fred Stanley ............. | .03 | .01 | .00 |
| ☐ | 109 Tom Underwood ......... | .03 | .01 | .00 |
| ☐ | 110 Joaquin Andujar .......... | .12 | .05 | .01 |
| ☐ | 111 Steve Braun ............. | .03 | .01 | .00 |
| ☐ | 112 Bob Forsch .............. | .06 | .02 | .00 |
| ☐ | 113 George Hendrick ......... | .08 | .03 | .01 |
| ☐ | 114 Keith Hernandez ......... | .30 | .12 | .03 |
| ☐ | 115 Tom Herr ................ | .08 | .03 | .01 |
| ☐ | 116 Dane Iorg ............... | .03 | .01 | .00 |
| ☐ | 117 Jim Kaat ................ | .15 | .06 | .01 |
| ☐ | 118 Tito Landrum ............ | .03 | .01 | .00 |
| ☐ | 119 Sixto Lezcano ........... | .03 | .01 | .00 |
| ☐ | 120 Mark Littell ............. | .03 | .01 | .00 |
| ☐ | 121 John Martin ............. | .03 | .01 | .00 |
| ☐ | 122 Silvio Martinez .......... | .03 | .01 | .00 |
| ☐ | 123 Ken Oberkfell ........... | .03 | .01 | .00 |
| ☐ | 124 Darrell Porter ........... | .06 | .02 | .00 |
| ☐ | 125 Mike Ramsey ............ | .03 | .01 | .00 |
| ☐ | 126 Orlando Sanchez ........ | .03 | .01 | .00 |
| ☐ | 127 Bob Shirley ............. | .03 | .01 | .00 |
| ☐ | 128 Lary Sorensen ........... | .03 | .01 | .00 |
| ☐ | 129 Bruce Sutter ............ | .20 | .08 | .02 |
| ☐ | 130 Bob Sykes .............. | .03 | .01 | .00 |
| ☐ | 131 Garry Templeton ........ | .10 | .04 | .01 |
| ☐ | 132 Gene Tenace ............ | .03 | .01 | .00 |
| ☐ | 133 Jerry Augustine ......... | .03 | .01 | .00 |
| ☐ | 134 Sal Bando ............... | .06 | .02 | .00 |
| ☐ | 135 Mark Brouhard .......... | .03 | .01 | .00 |
| ☐ | 136 Mike Caldwell ........... | .03 | .01 | .00 |
| ☐ | 137 Reggie Cleveland ........ | .03 | .01 | .00 |
| ☐ | 138 Cecil Cooper ............ | .15 | .06 | .01 |
| ☐ | 139 Jamie Easterly .......... | .03 | .01 | .00 |
| ☐ | 140 Marshall Edwards ........ | .03 | .01 | .00 |
| ☐ | 141 Rollie Fingers ........... | .20 | .08 | .02 |
| ☐ | 142 Jim Gantner ............. | .06 | .02 | .00 |
| ☐ | 143 Moose Haas ............. | .06 | .02 | .00 |
| ☐ | 144 Larry Hisle .............. | .06 | .02 | .00 |
| ☐ | 145 Roy Howell ............. | .03 | .01 | .00 |
| ☐ | 146 Rickey Keeton .......... | .03 | .01 | .00 |
| ☐ | 147 Randy Lerch ............ | .03 | .01 | .00 |
| ☐ | 148 Paul Molitor ............. | .10 | .04 | .01 |
| ☐ | 149 Don Money .............. | .03 | .01 | .00 |
| ☐ | 150 Charlie Moore ........... | .03 | .01 | .00 |
| ☐ | 151 Ben Oglivie ............. | .06 | .02 | .00 |
| ☐ | 152 Ted Simmons ............ | .12 | .05 | .01 |
| ☐ | 153 Jim Slaton .............. | .06 | .02 | .00 |
| ☐ | 154 Gorman Thomas ......... | .10 | .04 | .01 |
| ☐ | 155 Robin Yount ............. | .50 | .20 | .05 |
| ☐ | 156 Pete Vuckovich ......... | .10 | .04 | .01 |
| ☐ | 157 Benny Ayala ............ | .03 | .01 | .00 |
| ☐ | 158 Mark Belanger .......... | .06 | .02 | .00 |
| ☐ | 159 Al Bumbry ............... | .03 | .01 | .00 |
| ☐ | 160 Terry Crowley ........... | .03 | .01 | .00 |
| ☐ | 161 Rich Dauer .............. | .03 | .01 | .00 |
| ☐ | 162 Doug DeCinces .......... | .10 | .04 | .01 |
| ☐ | 163 Rick Dempsey ........... | .06 | .02 | .00 |
| ☐ | 164 Jim Dwyer .............. | .03 | .01 | .00 |
| ☐ | 165 Mike Flanagan ........... | .08 | .03 | .01 |
| ☐ | 166 Dave Ford .............. | .03 | .01 | .00 |
| ☐ | 167 Dan Graham ............. | .03 | .01 | .00 |
| ☐ | 168 Wayne Krenchicki ....... | .03 | .01 | .00 |
| ☐ | 169 John Lowenstein ........ | .03 | .01 | .00 |
| ☐ | 170 Dennis Martinez ......... | .03 | .01 | .00 |
| ☐ | 171 Tippy Martinez .......... | .03 | .01 | .00 |
| ☐ | 172 Scott McGregor ......... | .08 | .03 | .01 |
| ☐ | 173 Jose Morales ............ | .03 | .01 | .00 |
| ☐ | 174 Eddie Murray ............ | .60 | .24 | .06 |
| ☐ | 175 Jim Palmer .............. | .30 | .12 | .03 |
| ☐ | 176 Cal Ripken .............. | 5.00 | 2.00 | .50 |

| | | | | |
|---|---|---|---|---|
| ☐ 177 Gary Roenicke | .03 | .01 | .00 | |
| ☐ 178 Lenn Sakata | .03 | .01 | .00 | |
| ☐ 179 Ken Singleton | .10 | .04 | .01 | |
| ☐ 180 Sammy Stewart | .03 | .01 | .00 | |
| ☐ 181 Tim Stoddard | .03 | .01 | .00 | |
| ☐ 182 Steve Stone | .06 | .02 | .00 | |
| ☐ 183 Stan Bahnsen | .03 | .01 | .00 | |
| ☐ 184 Ray Burris | .03 | .01 | .00 | |
| ☐ 185 Gary Carter | .50 | .20 | .05 | |
| ☐ 186 Warren Cromartie | .03 | .01 | .00 | |
| ☐ 187 Andre Dawson | .25 | .10 | .02 | |
| ☐ 188 Terry Francona | .20 | .08 | .02 | |
| ☐ 189 Woodie Fryman | .03 | .01 | .00 | |
| ☐ 190 Bill Gullickson | .06 | .02 | .00 | |
| ☐ 191 Grant Jackson | .03 | .01 | .00 | |
| ☐ 192 Wallace Johnson | .06 | .02 | .00 | |
| ☐ 193 Charlie Lea | .06 | .02 | .00 | |
| ☐ 194 Bill Lee | .06 | .02 | .00 | |
| ☐ 195 Jerry Manuel | .03 | .01 | .00 | |
| ☐ 196 Brad Mills | .06 | .02 | .00 | |
| ☐ 197 John Milner | .03 | .01 | .00 | |
| ☐ 198 Rowland Office | .03 | .01 | .00 | |
| ☐ 199 David Palmer | .06 | .02 | .00 | |
| ☐ 200 Larry Parrish | .06 | .02 | .00 | |
| ☐ 201 Mike Phillips | .03 | .01 | .00 | |
| ☐ 202 Tim Raines | .50 | .20 | .05 | |
| ☐ 203 Bobby Ramos | .03 | .01 | .00 | |
| ☐ 204 Jeff Reardon | .10 | .04 | .01 | |
| ☐ 205 Steve Rogers | .08 | .03 | .01 | |
| ☐ 206 Scott Sanderson | .03 | .01 | .00 | |
| ☐ 207 Rodney Scott | .03 | .01 | .00 | |
| ☐ 208 Elias Sosa | .03 | .01 | .00 | |
| ☐ 209 Chris Speier | .03 | .01 | .00 | |
| ☐ 210 Tim Wallach | .45 | .18 | .04 | |
| ☐ 211 Jerry White | .03 | .01 | .00 | |
| ☐ 212 Alan Ashby | .03 | .01 | .00 | |
| ☐ 213 Cesar Cedeno | .08 | .03 | .01 | |
| ☐ 214 Jose Cruz | .12 | .05 | .01 | |
| ☐ 215 Kiko Garcia | .03 | .01 | .00 | |
| ☐ 216 Phil Garner | .06 | .02 | .00 | |
| ☐ 217 Danny Heep | .03 | .01 | .00 | |
| ☐ 218 Art Howe | .03 | .01 | .00 | |
| ☐ 219 Bob Knepper | .10 | .04 | .01 | |
| ☐ 220 Frank LaCorte | .03 | .01 | .00 | |
| ☐ 221 Joe Niekro | .10 | .04 | .01 | |
| ☐ 222 Joe Pittman | .03 | .01 | .00 | |
| ☐ 223 Terry Puhl | .06 | .02 | .00 | |
| ☐ 224 Luis Pujols | .03 | .01 | .00 | |
| ☐ 225 Craig Reynolds | .03 | .01 | .00 | |
| ☐ 226 J.R. Richard | .10 | .04 | .01 | |
| ☐ 227 Dave Roberts | .03 | .01 | .00 | |
| ☐ 228 Vern Ruhle | .03 | .01 | .00 | |
| ☐ 229 Nolan Ryan | .45 | .18 | .04 | |
| ☐ 230 Joe Sambito | .06 | .02 | .00 | |
| ☐ 231 Tony Scott | .03 | .01 | .00 | |
| ☐ 232 Dave Smith | .06 | .02 | .00 | |
| ☐ 233 Harry Spilman | .03 | .01 | .00 | |
| ☐ 234 Don Sutton | .30 | .12 | .03 | |
| ☐ 235 Dickie Thon | .08 | .03 | .01 | |
| ☐ 236 Denny Walling | .03 | .01 | .00 | |
| ☐ 237 Gary Woods | .03 | .01 | .00 | |
| ☐ 238 Luis Aguayo | .03 | .01 | .00 | |
| ☐ 239 Ramon Aviles | .03 | .01 | .00 | |
| ☐ 240 Bob Boone | .06 | .02 | .00 | |
| ☐ 241 Larry Bowa | .12 | .05 | .01 | |
| ☐ 242 Warren Brusstar | .03 | .01 | .00 | |
| ☐ 243 Steve Carlton | .50 | .20 | .05 | |
| ☐ 244 Larry Christenson | .03 | .01 | .00 | |
| ☐ 245 Dick Davis | .03 | .01 | .00 | |
| ☐ 246 Greg Gross | .03 | .01 | .00 | |
| ☐ 247 Sparky Lyle | .12 | .05 | .01 | |
| ☐ 248 Garry Maddox | .06 | .02 | .00 | |
| ☐ 249 Gary Matthews | .08 | .03 | .01 | |
| ☐ 250 Bake McBride | .06 | .02 | .00 | |
| ☐ 251 Tug McGraw | .10 | .04 | .01 | |
| ☐ 252 Keith Moreland | .08 | .03 | .01 | |
| ☐ 253 Dickie Noles | .03 | .01 | .00 | |
| ☐ 254 Mike Proly | .03 | .01 | .00 | |
| ☐ 255 Ron Reed | .03 | .01 | .00 | |
| ☐ 256 Pete Rose | 1.25 | .50 | .12 | |
| ☐ 257 Dick Ruthven | .03 | .01 | .00 | |
| ☐ 258 Mike Schmidt | .70 | .28 | .07 | |
| ☐ 259 Lonnie Smith | .08 | .03 | .01 | |
| ☐ 260 Manny Trillo | .06 | .02 | .00 | |
| ☐ 261 Del Unser | .03 | .01 | .00 | |
| ☐ 262 George Vukovich | .03 | .01 | .00 | |
| ☐ 263 Tom Brookens | .03 | .01 | .00 | |
| ☐ 264 George Cappuzzello | .03 | .01 | .00 | |
| ☐ 265 Marty Castillo | .06 | .02 | .00 | |
| ☐ 266 Al Cowens | .03 | .01 | .00 | |
| ☐ 267 Kirk Gibson | .40 | .16 | .04 | |
| ☐ 268 Richie Hebner | .03 | .01 | .00 | |
| ☐ 269 Ron Jackson | .03 | .01 | .00 | |
| ☐ 270 Lynn Jones | .03 | .01 | .00 | |
| ☐ 271 Steve Kemp | .08 | .03 | .01 | |
| ☐ 272 Rick Leach | .06 | .02 | .00 | |
| ☐ 273 Aurelio Lopez | .03 | .01 | .00 | |
| ☐ 274 Jack Morris | .30 | .12 | .03 | |
| ☐ 275 Kevin Saucier | .03 | .01 | .00 | |
| ☐ 276 Lance Parrish | .35 | .14 | .03 | |
| ☐ 277 Rick Peters | .03 | .01 | .00 | |
| ☐ 278 Dan Petry | .12 | .05 | .01 | |
| ☐ 279 David Rozema | .03 | .01 | .00 | |
| ☐ 280 Stan Papi | .03 | .01 | .00 | |
| ☐ 281 Dan Schatzeder | .03 | .01 | .00 | |
| ☐ 282 Champ Summers | .03 | .01 | .00 | |
| ☐ 283 Alan Trammell | .20 | .08 | .02 | |
| ☐ 284 Lou Whitaker | .15 | .06 | .01 | |
| ☐ 285 Milt Wilcox | .03 | .01 | .00 | |
| ☐ 286 John Wockenfuss | .03 | .01 | .00 | |
| ☐ 287 Gary Allenson | .03 | .01 | .00 | |
| ☐ 288 Tom Burgmeier | .03 | .01 | .00 | |
| ☐ 289 Bill Campbell | .03 | .01 | .00 | |
| ☐ 290 Mark Clear | .03 | .01 | .00 | |
| ☐ 291 Steve Crawford | .06 | .02 | .00 | |
| ☐ 292 Dennis Eckersley | .06 | .02 | .00 | |
| ☐ 293 Dwight Evans | .12 | .05 | .01 | |
| ☐ 294 Rich Gedman | .75 | .30 | .07 | |
| ☐ 295 Garry Hancock | .03 | .01 | .00 | |
| ☐ 296 Glenn Hoffman | .03 | .01 | .00 | |
| ☐ 297 Bruce Hurst | .10 | .04 | .01 | |
| ☐ 298 Carney Lansford | .12 | .05 | .01 | |
| ☐ 299 Rick Miller | .03 | .01 | .00 | |
| ☐ 300 Reid Nichols | .03 | .01 | .00 | |
| ☐ 301 Bob Ojeda | .75 | .30 | .07 | |
| ☐ 302 Tony Perez | .15 | .06 | .01 | |
| ☐ 303 Chuck Rainey | .03 | .01 | .00 | |
| ☐ 304 Jerry Remy | .05 | .02 | .00 | |
| ☐ 305 Jim Rice | .50 | .20 | .05 | |
| ☐ 306 Joe Rudi | .06 | .02 | .00 | |
| ☐ 307 Bob Stanley | .06 | .02 | .00 | |
| ☐ 308 Dave Stapleton | .03 | .01 | .00 | |
| ☐ 309 Frank Tanana | .06 | .02 | .00 | |
| ☐ 310 Mike Torrez | .06 | .02 | .00 | |
| ☐ 311 John Tudor | .15 | .06 | .01 | |
| ☐ 312 Carl Yastrzemski | .70 | .28 | .07 | |
| ☐ 313 Buddy Bell | .12 | .05 | .01 | |
| ☐ 314 Steve Comer | .03 | .01 | .00 | |
| ☐ 315 Danny Darwin | .03 | .01 | .00 | |
| ☐ 316 John Ellis | .03 | .01 | .00 | |
| ☐ 317 John Grubb | .03 | .01 | .00 | |
| ☐ 318 Rick Honeycutt | .06 | .02 | .00 | |
| ☐ 319 Charlie Hough | .08 | .03 | .01 | |
| ☐ 320 Ferguson Jenkins | .15 | .06 | .01 | |
| ☐ 321 John Henry Johnson | .03 | .01 | .00 | |
| ☐ 322 Jim Kern | .03 | .01 | .00 | |
| ☐ 323 Jon Matlack | .06 | .02 | .00 | |
| ☐ 324 Doc Medich | .03 | .01 | .00 | |
| ☐ 325 Mario Mendoza | .03 | .01 | .00 | |
| ☐ 326 Al Oliver | .15 | .06 | .01 | |
| ☐ 327 Pat Putnam | .03 | .01 | .00 | |
| ☐ 328 Mickey Rivers | .06 | .02 | .00 | |
| ☐ 329 Leon Roberts | .03 | .01 | .00 | |
| ☐ 330 Billy Sample | .03 | .01 | .00 | |
| ☐ 331 Bill Stein | .03 | .01 | .00 | |
| ☐ 332 Jim Sundberg | .06 | .02 | .00 | |
| ☐ 333 Mark Wagner | .03 | .01 | .00 | |
| ☐ 334 Bump Wills | .03 | .01 | .00 | |
| ☐ 335 Bill Almon | .03 | .01 | .00 | |
| ☐ 336 Harold Baines | .35 | .14 | .03 | |
| ☐ 337 Ross Baumgarten | .03 | .01 | .00 | |
| ☐ 338 Tony Bernazard | .06 | .02 | .00 | |
| ☐ 339 Britt Burns | .08 | .03 | .01 | |
| ☐ 340 Richard Dotson | .08 | .03 | .01 | |
| ☐ 341 Jim Essian | .03 | .01 | .00 | |
| ☐ 342 Ed Farmer | .03 | .01 | .00 | |
| ☐ 343 Carlton Fisk | .18 | .08 | .01 | |
| ☐ 344 Kevin Hickey | .06 | .02 | .00 | |
| ☐ 345 LaMarr Hoyt | .10 | .04 | .01 | |
| ☐ 346 Lamar Johnson | .03 | .01 | .00 | |
| ☐ 347 Jerry Koosman | .08 | .03 | .01 | |
| ☐ 348 Rusty Kuntz | .03 | .01 | .00 | |
| ☐ 349 Dennis Lamp | .03 | .01 | .00 | |
| ☐ 350 Ron LeFlore | .06 | .02 | .00 | |
| ☐ 351 Chet Lemon | .08 | .03 | .01 | |
| ☐ 352 Greg Luzinski | .12 | .05 | .01 | |
| ☐ 353 Bob Molinaro | .03 | .01 | .00 | |
| ☐ 354 Jim Morrison | .03 | .01 | .00 | |
| ☐ 355 Wayne Nordhagen | .03 | .01 | .00 | |
| ☐ 356 Greg Pryor | .03 | .01 | .00 | |
| ☐ 357 Mike Squires | .03 | .01 | .00 | |
| ☐ 358 Steve Trout | .06 | .02 | .00 | |
| ☐ 359 Alan Bannister | .03 | .01 | .00 | |
| ☐ 360 Len Barker | .08 | .03 | .01 | |
| ☐ 361 Bert Blyleven | .12 | .05 | .01 | |
| ☐ 362 Joe Charboneau | .06 | .02 | .00 | |

| | | | |
|---|---|---|---|
| ☐ 363 John Denny | .10 | .04 | .01 |
| ☐ 364 Bo Diaz | .06 | .02 | .00 |
| ☐ 365 Miguel Dilone | .03 | .01 | .00 |
| ☐ 366 Jerry Dybzinski | .03 | .01 | .00 |
| ☐ 367 Wayne Garland | .03 | .01 | .00 |
| ☐ 368 Mike Hargrove | .06 | .02 | .00 |
| ☐ 369 Toby Harrah | .06 | .02 | .00 |
| ☐ 370 Ron Hassey | .03 | .01 | .00 |
| ☐ 371 Von Hayes | 1.00 | .40 | .10 |
| ☐ 372 Pat Kelly | .03 | .01 | .00 |
| ☐ 373 Duane Kuiper | .03 | .01 | .00 |
| ☐ 374 Rick Manning | .03 | .01 | .00 |
| ☐ 375 Sid Monge | .03 | .01 | .00 |
| ☐ 376 Jorge Orta | .03 | .01 | .00 |
| ☐ 377 Dave Rosello | .03 | .01 | .00 |
| ☐ 378 Dan Spillner | .03 | .01 | .00 |
| ☐ 379 Mike Stanton | .03 | .01 | .00 |
| ☐ 380 Andre Thornton | .08 | .03 | .01 |
| ☐ 381 Tom Veryzer | .03 | .01 | .00 |
| ☐ 382 Rick Waits | .03 | .01 | .00 |
| ☐ 383 Doyle Alexander | .06 | .02 | .00 |
| ☐ 384 Vida Blue | .08 | .03 | .01 |
| ☐ 385 Fred Breining | .08 | .03 | .01 |
| ☐ 386 Enos Cabell | .03 | .01 | .00 |
| ☐ 387 Jack Clark | .12 | .05 | .01 |
| ☐ 388 Darrell Evans | .10 | .04 | .01 |
| ☐ 389 Tom Griffin | .03 | .01 | .00 |
| ☐ 390 Larry Herndon | .03 | .01 | .00 |
| ☐ 391 Al Holland | .06 | .02 | .00 |
| ☐ 392 Gary Lavelle | .06 | .02 | .00 |
| ☐ 393 Johnnie LeMaster | .03 | .01 | .00 |
| ☐ 394 Jerry Martin | .03 | .01 | .00 |
| ☐ 395 Milt May | .03 | .01 | .00 |
| ☐ 396 Greg Minton | .06 | .02 | .00 |
| ☐ 397 Joe Morgan | .25 | .10 | .02 |
| ☐ 398 Joe Pettini | .03 | .01 | .00 |
| ☐ 399 Alan Ripley | .03 | .01 | .00 |
| ☐ 400 Billy Smith | .03 | .01 | .00 |
| ☐ 401 Rennie Stennett | .03 | .01 | .00 |
| ☐ 402 Ed Whitson | .06 | .02 | .00 |
| ☐ 403 Jim Wohlford | .03 | .01 | .00 |
| ☐ 404 Willie Aikens | .06 | .02 | .00 |
| ☐ 405 George Brett | .70 | .28 | .07 |
| ☐ 406 Ken Brett | .06 | .02 | .00 |
| ☐ 407 Dave Chalk | .03 | .01 | .00 |
| ☐ 408 Rich Gale | .03 | .01 | .00 |
| ☐ 409 Cesar Geronimo | .03 | .01 | .00 |
| ☐ 410 Larry Gura | .06 | .02 | .00 |
| ☐ 411 Clint Hurdle | .03 | .01 | .00 |
| ☐ 412 Mike Jones | .03 | .01 | .00 |
| ☐ 413 Dennis Leonard | .06 | .02 | .00 |
| ☐ 414 Renie Martin | .03 | .01 | .00 |
| ☐ 415 Lee May | .06 | .02 | .00 |
| ☐ 416 Hal McRae | .06 | .02 | .00 |
| ☐ 417 Darryl Motley | .12 | .05 | .01 |
| ☐ 418 Rance Mulliniks | .03 | .01 | .00 |
| ☐ 419 Amos Otis | .08 | .03 | .01 |
| ☐ 420 Ken Phelps | .30 | .12 | .03 |
| ☐ 421 Jamie Quirk | .03 | .01 | .00 |
| ☐ 422 Dan Quisenberry | .20 | .08 | .02 |
| ☐ 423 Paul Splittorff | .06 | .02 | .00 |
| ☐ 424 U.L. Washington | .03 | .01 | .00 |
| ☐ 425 John Wathan | .03 | .01 | .00 |
| ☐ 426 Frank White | .08 | .03 | .01 |
| ☐ 427 Willie Wilson | .20 | .08 | .02 |
| ☐ 428 Brian Asselstine | .03 | .01 | .00 |
| ☐ 429 Bruce Benedict | .03 | .01 | .00 |
| ☐ 430 Tom Boggs | .03 | .01 | .00 |
| ☐ 431 Larry Bradford | .03 | .01 | .00 |
| ☐ 432 Rick Camp | .03 | .01 | .00 |
| ☐ 433 Chris Chambliss | .06 | .02 | .00 |
| ☐ 434 Gene Garber | .03 | .01 | .00 |
| ☐ 435 Preston Hanna | .03 | .01 | .00 |
| ☐ 436 Bob Horner | .25 | .10 | .02 |
| ☐ 437 Glenn Hubbard | .03 | .01 | .00 |
| ☐ 438A Al Hrabosky (height 5'1") | 15.00 | 6.00 | 1.50 |
| ☐ 438B Al Hrabosky (height 5'1") | .75 | .30 | .07 |
| ☐ 438C Al Hrabosky (height 5'10") | .10 | .04 | .01 |
| ☐ 439 Rufino Linares | .05 | .02 | .00 |
| ☐ 440 Rick Mahler | .20 | .08 | .02 |
| ☐ 441 Ed Miller | .03 | .01 | .00 |
| ☐ 442 John Montefusco | .06 | .02 | .00 |
| ☐ 443 Dale Murphy | .90 | .36 | .09 |
| ☐ 444 Phil Niekro | .20 | .08 | .02 |
| ☐ 445 Gaylord Perry | .20 | .08 | .02 |
| ☐ 446 Biff Pocoroba | .03 | .01 | .00 |
| ☐ 447 Rafael Ramirez | .03 | .01 | .00 |
| ☐ 448 Jerry Royster | .03 | .01 | .00 |
| ☐ 449 Claudell Washington | .08 | .03 | .01 |
| ☐ 450 Don Aase | .06 | .02 | .00 |

| | | | |
|---|---|---|---|
| ☐ 451 Don Baylor | .15 | .06 | .01 |
| ☐ 452 Juan Beniquez | .06 | .02 | .00 |
| ☐ 453 Rick Burleson | .06 | .02 | .00 |
| ☐ 454 Bert Campaneris | .08 | .03 | .01 |
| ☐ 455 Rod Carew | .50 | .20 | .05 |
| ☐ 456 Bob Clark | .03 | .01 | .00 |
| ☐ 457 Brian Downing | .06 | .02 | .00 |
| ☐ 458 Dan Ford | .03 | .01 | .00 |
| ☐ 459 Ken Forsch | .03 | .01 | .00 |
| ☐ 460A Dave Frost (5 mm space before ERA) | .35 | .14 | .03 |
| ☐ 460B Dave Frost (1 mm space) | .05 | .02 | .00 |
| ☐ 461 Bobby Grich | .08 | .03 | .01 |
| ☐ 462 Larry Harlow | .03 | .01 | .00 |
| ☐ 463 John Harris | .03 | .01 | .00 |
| ☐ 464 Andy Hassler | .03 | .01 | .00 |
| ☐ 465 Butch Hobson | .03 | .01 | .00 |
| ☐ 466 Jesse Jefferson | .03 | .01 | .00 |
| ☐ 467 Bruce Kison | .03 | .01 | .00 |
| ☐ 468 Fred Lynn | .25 | .10 | .02 |
| ☐ 469 Angel Moreno | .03 | .01 | .00 |
| ☐ 470 Ed Ott | .03 | .01 | .00 |
| ☐ 471 Fred Patek | .03 | .01 | .00 |
| ☐ 472 Steve Renko | .03 | .01 | .00 |
| ☐ 473 Mike Witt | 1.00 | .40 | .10 |
| ☐ 474 Geoff Zahn | .03 | .01 | .00 |
| ☐ 475 Gary Alexander | .03 | .01 | .00 |
| ☐ 476 Dale Berra | .06 | .02 | .00 |
| ☐ 477 Kurt Bevacqua | .03 | .01 | .00 |
| ☐ 478 Jim Bibby | .06 | .02 | .00 |
| ☐ 479 John Candelaria | .08 | .03 | .01 |
| ☐ 480 Victor Cruz | .03 | .01 | .00 |
| ☐ 481 Mike Easler | .08 | .03 | .01 |
| ☐ 482 Tim Foli | .03 | .01 | .00 |
| ☐ 483 Lee Lacy | .08 | .03 | .01 |
| ☐ 484 Vance Law | .03 | .01 | .00 |
| ☐ 485 Bill Madlock | .15 | .06 | .01 |
| ☐ 486 Willie Montanez | .03 | .01 | .00 |
| ☐ 487 Omar Moreno | .03 | .01 | .00 |
| ☐ 488 Steve Nicosia | .03 | .01 | .00 |
| ☐ 489 Dave Parker | .25 | .10 | .02 |
| ☐ 490 Tony Pena | .15 | .06 | .01 |
| ☐ 491 Pascual Perez | .06 | .02 | .00 |
| ☐ 492 Johnny Ray | .60 | .24 | .06 |
| ☐ 493 Rick Rhoden | .08 | .03 | .01 |
| ☐ 494 Bill Robinson | .03 | .01 | .00 |
| ☐ 495 Don Robinson | .03 | .01 | .00 |
| ☐ 496 Enrique Romo | .03 | .01 | .00 |
| ☐ 497 Rod Scurry | .03 | .01 | .00 |
| ☐ 498 Eddie Solomon | .03 | .01 | .00 |
| ☐ 499 Willie Stargell | .25 | .10 | .02 |
| ☐ 500 Kent Tekulve | .08 | .03 | .01 |
| ☐ 501 Jason Thompson | .06 | .02 | .00 |
| ☐ 502 Glenn Abbott | .03 | .01 | .00 |
| ☐ 503 Jim Anderson | .03 | .01 | .00 |
| ☐ 504 Floyd Bannister | .06 | .02 | .00 |
| ☐ 505 Bruce Bochte | .06 | .02 | .00 |
| ☐ 506 Jeff Burroughs | .06 | .02 | .00 |
| ☐ 507 Bryan Clark | .03 | .01 | .00 |
| ☐ 508 Ken Clay | .03 | .01 | .00 |
| ☐ 509 Julio Cruz | .03 | .01 | .00 |
| ☐ 510 Dick Drago | .03 | .01 | .00 |
| ☐ 511 Gary Gray | .03 | .01 | .00 |
| ☐ 512 Dan Meyer | .03 | .01 | .00 |
| ☐ 513 Jerry Narron | .03 | .01 | .00 |
| ☐ 514 Tom Paciorek | .03 | .01 | .00 |
| ☐ 515 Casey Parsons | .03 | .01 | .00 |
| ☐ 516 Lenny Randle | .03 | .01 | .00 |
| ☐ 517 Shane Rawley | .08 | .03 | .01 |
| ☐ 518 Joe Simpson | .03 | .01 | .00 |
| ☐ 519 Richie Zisk | .06 | .02 | .00 |
| ☐ 520 Neil Allen | .06 | .02 | .00 |
| ☐ 521 Bob Bailor | .03 | .01 | .00 |
| ☐ 522 Hubie Brooks | .15 | .06 | .01 |
| ☐ 523 Mike Cubbage | .03 | .01 | .00 |
| ☐ 524 Pete Falcone | .03 | .01 | .00 |
| ☐ 525 Doug Flynn | .03 | .01 | .00 |
| ☐ 526 Tom Hausman | .03 | .01 | .00 |
| ☐ 527 Ron Hodges | .03 | .01 | .00 |
| ☐ 528 Randy Jones | .06 | .02 | .00 |
| ☐ 529 Mike Jorgensen | .03 | .01 | .00 |
| ☐ 530 Dave Kingman | .15 | .06 | .01 |
| ☐ 531 Ed Lynch | .10 | .04 | .01 |
| ☐ 532 Mike Marshall (screwball pitcher) | .06 | .02 | .00 |
| ☐ 533 Lee Mazzilli | .06 | .02 | .00 |
| ☐ 534 Dyar Miller | .03 | .01 | .00 |
| ☐ 535 Mike Scott | .25 | .10 | .02 |
| ☐ 536 Rusty Staub | .10 | .04 | .01 |
| ☐ 537 John Stearns | .03 | .01 | .00 |
| ☐ 538 Craig Swan | .03 | .01 | .00 |
| ☐ 539 Frank Taveras | .03 | .01 | .00 |

| | | | | |
|---|---|---|---|---|
| ☐ 540 | Alex Trevino | .03 | .01 | .00 |
| ☐ 541 | Ellis Valentine | .03 | .01 | .00 |
| ☐ 542 | Mookie Wilson | .08 | .03 | .01 |
| ☐ 543 | Joel Youngblood | .03 | .01 | .00 |
| ☐ 544 | Pat Zachry | .03 | .01 | .00 |
| ☐ 545 | Glenn Adams | .03 | .01 | .00 |
| ☐ 546 | Fernando Arroyo | .03 | .01 | .00 |
| ☐ 547 | John Verhoeven | .03 | .01 | .00 |
| ☐ 548 | Sal Butera | .03 | .01 | .00 |
| ☐ 549 | John Castino | .03 | .01 | .00 |
| ☐ 550 | Don Cooper | .03 | .01 | .00 |
| ☐ 551 | Doug Corbett | .03 | .01 | .00 |
| ☐ 552 | Dave Engle | .03 | .01 | .00 |
| ☐ 553 | Roger Erickson | .03 | .01 | .00 |
| ☐ 554 | Danny Goodwin | .03 | .01 | .00 |
| ☐ 555A | Darrell Jackson (black hat) | 1.25 | .50 | .12 |
| ☐ 555B | Darrell Jackson (red hat) | .08 | .03 | .01 |
| ☐ 556 | Pete Mackanin | .03 | .01 | .00 |
| ☐ 557 | Jack O'Connor | .03 | .01 | .00 |
| ☐ 558 | Hosken Powell | .03 | .01 | .00 |
| ☐ 559 | Pete Redfern | .03 | .01 | .00 |
| ☐ 560 | Roy Smalley | .06 | .02 | .00 |
| ☐ 561 | Chuck Baker | .03 | .01 | .00 |
| ☐ 562 | Gary Ward | .06 | .02 | .00 |
| ☐ 563 | Rob Wilfong | .03 | .01 | .00 |
| ☐ 564 | Al Williams | .03 | .01 | .00 |
| ☐ 565 | Butch Wynegar | .06 | .02 | .00 |
| ☐ 566 | Randy Bass | .03 | .01 | .00 |
| ☐ 567 | Juan Bonilla | .03 | .01 | .00 |
| ☐ 568 | Danny Boone | .03 | .01 | .00 |
| ☐ 569 | John Curtis | .03 | .01 | .00 |
| ☐ 570 | Juan Eichelberger | .03 | .01 | .00 |
| ☐ 571 | Barry Evans | .03 | .01 | .00 |
| ☐ 572 | Tim Flannery | .03 | .01 | .00 |
| ☐ 573 | Ruppert Jones | .03 | .01 | .00 |
| ☐ 574 | Terry Kennedy | .08 | .03 | .01 |
| ☐ 575 | Joe Lefebvre | .03 | .01 | .00 |
| ☐ 576A | John Littlefield ERR (left handed) | 50.00 | 20.00 | 5.00 |
| ☐ 576B | John Littlefield COR (right handed) | .08 | .03 | .01 |
| ☐ 577 | Gary Lucas | .03 | .01 | .00 |
| ☐ 578 | Steve Mura | .03 | .01 | .00 |
| ☐ 579 | Broderick Perkins | .03 | .01 | .00 |
| ☐ 580 | Gene Richards | .03 | .01 | .00 |
| ☐ 581 | Luis Salazar | .03 | .01 | .00 |
| ☐ 582 | Ozzie Smith | .18 | .08 | .01 |
| ☐ 583 | John Urrea | .03 | .01 | .00 |
| ☐ 584 | Chris Welsh | .06 | .02 | .00 |
| ☐ 585 | Rick Wise | .06 | .02 | .00 |
| ☐ 586 | Doug Bird | .03 | .01 | .00 |
| ☐ 587 | Tim Blackwell | .03 | .01 | .00 |
| ☐ 588 | Bobby Bonds | .08 | .03 | .01 |
| ☐ 589 | Bill Buckner | .12 | .05 | .01 |
| ☐ 590 | Bill Caudill | .06 | .02 | .00 |
| ☐ 591 | Hector Cruz | .03 | .01 | .00 |
| ☐ 592 | Jody Davis | .45 | .18 | .04 |
| ☐ 593 | Ivan DeJesus | .03 | .01 | .00 |
| ☐ 594 | Steve Dillard | .03 | .01 | .00 |
| ☐ 595 | Leon Durham | .10 | .04 | .01 |
| ☐ 596 | Rawly Eastwick | .03 | .01 | .00 |
| ☐ 597 | Steve Henderson | .03 | .01 | .00 |
| ☐ 598 | Mike Krukow | .08 | .03 | .01 |
| ☐ 599 | Mike Lum | .03 | .01 | .00 |
| ☐ 600 | Randy Martz | .03 | .01 | .00 |
| ☐ 601 | Jerry Morales | .03 | .01 | .00 |
| ☐ 602 | Ken Reitz | .03 | .01 | .00 |
| ☐ 603A | Lee Smith ERR (Cubs logo reversed) | .90 | .36 | .09 |
| ☐ 603B | Lee Smith COR | .60 | .24 | .06 |
| ☐ 604 | Dick Tidrow | .03 | .01 | .00 |
| ☐ 605 | Jim Tracy | .03 | .01 | .00 |
| ☐ 606 | Mike Tyson | .03 | .01 | .00 |
| ☐ 607 | Ty Waller | .06 | .02 | .00 |
| ☐ 608 | Danny Ainge | .08 | .03 | .01 |
| ☐ 609 | Jorge Bell | 1.50 | .60 | .15 |
| ☐ 610 | Mark Bomback | .03 | .01 | .00 |
| ☐ 611 | Barry Bonnell | .03 | .01 | .00 |
| ☐ 612 | Jim Clancy | .06 | .02 | .00 |
| ☐ 613 | Damaso Garcia | .10 | .04 | .01 |
| ☐ 614 | Jerry Garvin | .03 | .01 | .00 |
| ☐ 615 | Alfredo Griffin | .06 | .02 | .00 |
| ☐ 616 | Garth Iorg | .03 | .01 | .00 |
| ☐ 617 | Luis Leal | .03 | .01 | .00 |
| ☐ 618 | Ken Macha | .03 | .01 | .00 |
| ☐ 619 | John Mayberry | .06 | .02 | .00 |
| ☐ 620 | Joey McLaughlin | .03 | .01 | .00 |
| ☐ 621 | Lloyd Moseby | .15 | .06 | .01 |
| ☐ 622 | Dave Stieb | .15 | .06 | .01 |
| ☐ 623 | Jackson Todd | .03 | .01 | .00 |
| ☐ 624 | Willie Upshaw | .08 | .03 | .01 |
| ☐ 625 | Otto Velez | .03 | .01 | .00 |
| ☐ 626 | Ernie Whitt | .03 | .01 | .00 |
| ☐ 627 | Al Woods | .03 | .01 | .00 |
| ☐ 628 | All Star Game Cleveland, Ohio | .06 | .02 | .00 |
| ☐ 629 | All Star Infielders Frank White and Bucky Dent | .06 | .02 | .00 |
| ☐ 630 | Big Red Machine Dan Driessen Dave Concepcion George Foster | .08 | .03 | .01 |
| ☐ 631 | Bruce Sutter Top NL Relief Pitcher | .10 | .04 | .01 |
| ☐ 632 | "Steve and Carlton" Steve Carlton and Carlton Fisk | .20 | .08 | .02 |
| ☐ 633 | Carl Yastrzemski 3000th Game | .30 | .12 | .03 |
| ☐ 634 | Dynamic Duo Johnny Bench and Tom Seaver | .25 | .10 | .02 |
| ☐ 635 | West Meets East Fernando Valenzuela and Gary Carter | .30 | .12 | .03 |
| ☐ 636A | Fernando Valenzuela: NL SO King ("he" NL) | .35 | .14 | .03 |
| ☐ 636B | Fernando Valenzuela: NL SO King ("the" NL) | .30 | .12 | .03 |
| ☐ 637 | Mike Schmidt Home Run King | .35 | .14 | .03 |
| ☐ 638 | NL All Stars Gary Carter and Dave Parker | .20 | .08 | .02 |
| ☐ 639 | Perfect Game Len Barker and Bo Diaz (catcher actually Ron Hassey) | .08 | .03 | .01 |
| ☐ 640 | Pete and Re-Pete Pete Rose and Son | 1.25 | .50 | .12 |
| ☐ 641 | Phillies Finest Lonnie Smith Mike Schmidt Steve Carlton | .30 | .12 | .03 |
| ☐ 642 | Red Sox Reunion Fred Lynn and Dwight Evans | .10 | .04 | .01 |
| ☐ 643 | Rickey Henderson Most Hits and Runs | .30 | .12 | .03 |
| ☐ 644 | Rollie Fingers Most Saves AL | .10 | .04 | .01 |
| ☐ 645 | Tom Seaver Most 1981 Wins | .20 | .08 | .02 |
| ☐ 646A | Yankee Powerhouse Reggie Jackson and Dave Winfield (comma on back after outfielder) | .50 | .20 | .05 |
| ☐ 646B | Yankee Powerhouse Reggie Jackson and Dave Winfield (no comma) | .40 | .16 | .04 |
| ☐ 647 | CL: Yankees/Dodgers | .08 | .01 | .00 |
| ☐ 648 | CL: A's/Reds | .07 | .01 | .00 |
| ☐ 649 | CL: Cards/Brewers | .07 | .01 | .00 |
| ☐ 650 | CL: Expos/Orioles | .07 | .01 | .00 |
| ☐ 651 | CL: Astros/Phillies | .07 | .01 | .00 |
| ☐ 652 | CL: Tigers/Red Sox | .07 | .01 | .00 |
| ☐ 653 | CL: Rangers/White Sox | .07 | .01 | .00 |
| ☐ 654 | CL: Giants/Indians | .07 | .01 | .00 |
| ☐ 655 | CL: Royals/Braves | .07 | .01 | .00 |
| ☐ 656 | CL: Angels/Pirates | .07 | .01 | .00 |
| ☐ 657 | CL: Mariners/Mets | .07 | .01 | .00 |
| ☐ 658 | CL: Padres/Twins | .07 | .01 | .00 |
| ☐ 659 | CL: Blue Jays/Cubs | .07 | .01 | .00 |
| ☐ 660 | Specials Checklist | .10 | .01 | .00 |

# 1983 Fleer

The cards in this 660 card set measure 2 1/2" by 3 1/2". In 1983, for the third straight year, Fleer has produced a baseball series numbering 660 cards. Of these, 1-628 are player cards, 629-646 are special cards, and 647-660 are checklist cards. The player

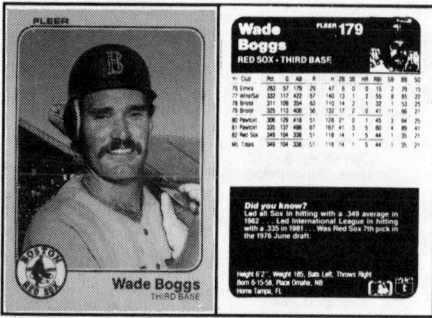

cards are again ordered alphabetically within team. The team order relates back to each team's on-field performance during the previous year, i.e., World Champion Cardinals (1-25), AL Champion Brewers (26-51), Baltimore (52-75), California (76-103), Kansas City (104-128), Atlanta (129-152), Philadelphia (153-176), Boston (177-200), Los Angeles (201-227), Chicago White Sox (228-251), San Francisco (252-276), Montreal (277-301), Pittsburgh (302-326), Detroit (327-351), San Diego (352-375), New York Yankees (376-399), Cleveland (400-423), Toronto (424-444), Houston (445-469), Seattle (470-489), Chicago Cubs (490-512), Oakland (513-535), New York Mets (536-561), Texas (562-583), Cincinnati (584-606), and Minnesota (607-628). The front of each card has a colorful team logo at bottom left and the player's name and position at lower right. The reverses are done in shades of brown on white. The cards are numbered on the back next to a small black and white photo of the player.

|  | MINT | VG-E | F-G |
|---|---|---|---|
| COMPLETE SET | 25.00 | 10.00 | 2.50 |
| COMMON PLAYER (1-660) | .03 | .01 | .00 |

|  |  |  | MINT | VG-E | F-G |
|---|---|---|---|---|---|
| ☐ | 1 | Joaquin Andujar | .12 | .05 | .01 |
| ☐ | 2 | Doug Bair | .03 | .01 | .00 |
| ☐ | 3 | Steve Braun | .03 | .01 | .00 |
| ☐ | 4 | Glenn Brummer | .03 | .01 | .00 |
| ☐ | 5 | Bob Forsch | .06 | .02 | .00 |
| ☐ | 6 | David Green | .08 | .03 | .01 |
| ☐ | 7 | George Hendrick | .07 | .03 | .01 |
| ☐ | 8 | Keith Hernandez | .30 | .12 | .03 |
| ☐ | 9 | Tom Herr | .08 | .03 | .01 |
| ☐ | 10 | Dane Iorg | .03 | .01 | .00 |
| ☐ | 11 | Jim Kaat | .12 | .05 | .01 |
| ☐ | 12 | Jeff Lahti | .06 | .02 | .00 |
| ☐ | 13 | Tito Landrum | .03 | .01 | .00 |
| ☐ | 14 | Dave LaPoint | .12 | .05 | .01 |
| ☐ | 15 | Willie McGee | 1.25 | .50 | .12 |
| ☐ | 16 | Steve Mura | .03 | .01 | .00 |
| ☐ | 17 | Ken Oberkfell | .03 | .01 | .00 |
| ☐ | 18 | Darrell Porter | .05 | .02 | .00 |
| ☐ | 19 | Mike Ramsey | .03 | .01 | .00 |
| ☐ | 20 | Gene Roof | .05 | .02 | .00 |
| ☐ | 21 | Lonnie Smith | .07 | .03 | .01 |
| ☐ | 22 | Ozzie Smith | .15 | .06 | .01 |
| ☐ | 23 | John Stuper | .07 | .03 | .01 |
| ☐ | 24 | Bruce Sutter | .15 | .06 | .01 |
| ☐ | 25 | Gene Tenace | .03 | .01 | .00 |
| ☐ | 26 | Jerry Augustine | .03 | .01 | .00 |
| ☐ | 27 | Dwight Bernard | .03 | .01 | .00 |
| ☐ | 28 | Mark Brouhard | .03 | .01 | .00 |
| ☐ | 29 | Mike Caldwell | .05 | .02 | .00 |
| ☐ | 30 | Cecil Cooper | .14 | .06 | .01 |
| ☐ | 31 | Jamie Easterly | .03 | .01 | .00 |
| ☐ | 32 | Marshall Edwards | .03 | .01 | .00 |
| ☐ | 33 | Rollie Fingers | .18 | .08 | .01 |
| ☐ | 34 | Jim Gantner | .05 | .02 | .00 |
| ☐ | 35 | Moose Haas | .03 | .01 | .00 |
| ☐ | 36 | Roy Howell | .03 | .01 | .00 |
| ☐ | 37 | Peter Ladd | .03 | .01 | .00 |
| ☐ | 38 | Bob McClure | .03 | .01 | .00 |
| ☐ | 39 | Doc Medich | .03 | .01 | .00 |

| ☐ | 40 | Paul Molitor | .10 | .04 | .01 |
|---|---|---|---|---|---|
| ☐ | 41 | Don Money | .03 | .01 | .00 |
| ☐ | 42 | Charlie Moore | .03 | .01 | .00 |
| ☐ | 43 | Ben Oglivie | .07 | .03 | .01 |
| ☐ | 44 | Ed Romero | .03 | .01 | .00 |
| ☐ | 45 | Ted Simmons | .12 | .05 | .01 |
| ☐ | 46 | Jim Slaton | .03 | .01 | .00 |
| ☐ | 47 | Don Sutton | .25 | .10 | .02 |
| ☐ | 48 | Gorman Thomas | .10 | .04 | .01 |
| ☐ | 49 | Pete Vuckovich | .07 | .03 | .01 |
| ☐ | 50 | Ned Yost | .03 | .01 | .00 |
| ☐ | 51 | Robin Yount | .30 | .12 | .03 |
| ☐ | 52 | Benny Ayala | .03 | .01 | .00 |
| ☐ | 53 | Bob Bonner | .03 | .01 | .00 |
| ☐ | 54 | Al Bumbry | .03 | .01 | .00 |
| ☐ | 55 | Terry Crowley | .03 | .01 | .00 |
| ☐ | 56 | Storm Davis | .45 | .18 | .04 |
| ☐ | 57 | Rich Dauer | .03 | .01 | .00 |
| ☐ | 58 | Rick Dempsey | .05 | .02 | .00 |
| ☐ | 59 | Jim Dwyer | .03 | .01 | .00 |
| ☐ | 60 | Mike Flanagan | .08 | .03 | .01 |
| ☐ | 61 | Dan Ford | .03 | .01 | .00 |
| ☐ | 62 | Glenn Gulliver | .03 | .01 | .00 |
| ☐ | 63 | John Lowenstein | .03 | .01 | .00 |
| ☐ | 64 | Dennis Martinez | .03 | .01 | .00 |
| ☐ | 65 | Tippy Martinez | .03 | .01 | .00 |
| ☐ | 66 | Scott McGregor | .08 | .03 | .01 |
| ☐ | 67 | Eddie Murray | .55 | .22 | .05 |
| ☐ | 68 | Joe Nolan | .03 | .01 | .00 |
| ☐ | 69 | Jim Palmer | .30 | .12 | .03 |
| ☐ | 70 | Cal Ripken Jr. | .70 | .28 | .07 |
| ☐ | 71 | Gary Roenicke | .05 | .02 | .00 |
| ☐ | 72 | Lenn Sakata | .03 | .01 | .00 |
| ☐ | 73 | Ken Singleton | .08 | .03 | .01 |
| ☐ | 74 | Sammy Stewart | .03 | .01 | .00 |
| ☐ | 75 | Tim Stoddard | .03 | .01 | .00 |
| ☐ | 76 | Don Aase | .05 | .02 | .00 |
| ☐ | 77 | Don Baylor | .12 | .05 | .01 |
| ☐ | 78 | Juan Beniquez | .05 | .02 | .00 |
| ☐ | 79 | Bob Boone | .05 | .02 | .00 |
| ☐ | 80 | Rick Burleson | .06 | .02 | .00 |
| ☐ | 81 | Rod Carew | .40 | .16 | .04 |
| ☐ | 82 | Bobby Clark | .03 | .01 | .00 |
| ☐ | 83 | Doug Corbett | .03 | .01 | .00 |
| ☐ | 84 | John Curtis | .03 | .01 | .00 |
| ☐ | 85 | Doug DeCinces | .09 | .04 | .01 |
| ☐ | 86 | Brian Downing | .05 | .02 | .00 |
| ☐ | 87 | Joe Ferguson | .03 | .01 | .00 |
| ☐ | 88 | Tim Foli | .03 | .01 | .00 |
| ☐ | 89 | Ken Forsch | .03 | .01 | .00 |
| ☐ | 90 | Dave Goltz | .03 | .01 | .00 |
| ☐ | 91 | Bobby Grich | .07 | .03 | .01 |
| ☐ | 92 | Andy Hassler | .03 | .01 | .00 |
| ☐ | 93 | Reggie Jackson | .45 | .18 | .04 |
| ☐ | 94 | Ron Jackson | .03 | .01 | .00 |
| ☐ | 95 | Tommy John | .15 | .06 | .01 |
| ☐ | 96 | Bruce Kison | .03 | .01 | .00 |
| ☐ | 97 | Fred Lynn | .18 | .08 | .01 |
| ☐ | 98 | Ed Ott | .03 | .01 | .00 |
| ☐ | 99 | Steve Renko | .03 | .01 | .00 |
| ☐ | 100 | Luis Sanchez | .03 | .01 | .00 |
| ☐ | 101 | Rob Wilfong | .03 | .01 | .00 |
| ☐ | 102 | Mike Witt | .12 | .05 | .01 |
| ☐ | 103 | Geoff Zahn | .03 | .01 | .00 |
| ☐ | 104 | Willie Aikens | .03 | .01 | .00 |
| ☐ | 105 | Mike Armstrong | .03 | .01 | .00 |
| ☐ | 106 | Vida Blue | .08 | .03 | .01 |
| ☐ | 107 | Bud Black | .20 | .08 | .02 |
| ☐ | 108 | George Brett | .50 | .20 | .05 |
| ☐ | 109 | Bill Castro | .03 | .01 | .00 |
| ☐ | 110 | Onix Concepcion | .06 | .02 | .00 |
| ☐ | 111 | Dave Frost | .03 | .01 | .00 |
| ☐ | 112 | Cesar Geronimo | .03 | .01 | .00 |
| ☐ | 113 | Larry Gura | .05 | .02 | .00 |
| ☐ | 114 | Steve Hammond | .05 | .02 | .00 |
| ☐ | 115 | Don Hood | .03 | .01 | .00 |
| ☐ | 116 | Dennis Leonard | .05 | .02 | .00 |
| ☐ | 117 | Jerry Martin | .03 | .01 | .00 |
| ☐ | 118 | Lee May | .05 | .02 | .00 |
| ☐ | 119 | Hal McRae | .06 | .02 | .00 |
| ☐ | 120 | Amos Otis | .06 | .02 | .00 |
| ☐ | 121 | Greg Pryor | .03 | .01 | .00 |
| ☐ | 122 | Dan Quisenberry | .15 | .06 | .01 |
| ☐ | 123 | Don Slaught | .20 | .08 | .02 |
| ☐ | 124 | Paul Splittorff | .05 | .02 | .00 |
| ☐ | 125 | U.L. Washington | .03 | .01 | .00 |
| ☐ | 126 | John Wathan | .03 | .01 | .00 |
| ☐ | 127 | Frank White | .07 | .03 | .01 |
| ☐ | 128 | Willie Wilson | .18 | .08 | .01 |
| ☐ | 129 | Steve Bedrosian | .06 | .02 | .00 |
| ☐ | 130 | Bruce Benedict | .03 | .01 | .00 |
| ☐ | 131 | Tommy Boggs | .03 | .01 | .00 |
| ☐ | 132 | Brett Butler | .09 | .04 | .01 |

| # | Player | | | |
|---|--------|------|------|------|
| ☐ 133 | Rick Camp | .03 | .01 | .00 |
| ☐ 134 | Chris Chambliss | .05 | .02 | .00 |
| ☐ 135 | Ken Dayley | .03 | .01 | .00 |
| ☐ 136 | Gene Garber | .03 | .01 | .00 |
| ☐ 137 | Terry Harper | .03 | .01 | .00 |
| ☐ 138 | Bob Horner | .20 | .08 | .02 |
| ☐ 139 | Glenn Hubbard | .03 | .01 | .00 |
| ☐ 140 | Rufino Linares | .03 | .01 | .00 |
| ☐ 141 | Rick Mahler | .05 | .02 | .00 |
| ☐ 142 | Dale Murphy | .75 | .30 | .07 |
| ☐ 143 | Phil Niekro | .20 | .08 | .02 |
| ☐ 144 | Pascual Perez | .05 | .02 | .00 |
| ☐ 145 | Biff Pocoroba | .03 | .01 | .00 |
| ☐ 146 | Rafael Ramirez | .03 | .01 | .00 |
| ☐ 147 | Jerry Royster | .03 | .01 | .00 |
| ☐ 148 | Ken Smith | .03 | .01 | .00 |
| ☐ 149 | Bob Walk | .03 | .01 | .00 |
| ☐ 150 | Claudell Washington | .06 | .02 | .00 |
| ☐ 151 | Bob Watson | .06 | .02 | .00 |
| ☐ 152 | Larry Whisenton | .03 | .01 | .00 |
| ☐ 153 | Porfirio Altamirano | .03 | .01 | .00 |
| ☐ 154 | Marty Bystrom | .03 | .01 | .00 |
| ☐ 155 | Steve Carlton | .35 | .14 | .03 |
| ☐ 156 | Larry Christenson | .03 | .01 | .00 |
| ☐ 157 | Ivan DeJesus | .03 | .01 | .00 |
| ☐ 158 | John Denny | .08 | .03 | .01 |
| ☐ 159 | Bob Dernier | .07 | .03 | .01 |
| ☐ 160 | Bo Diaz | .05 | .02 | .00 |
| ☐ 161 | Ed Farmer | .03 | .01 | .00 |
| ☐ 162 | Greg Gross | .03 | .01 | .00 |
| ☐ 163 | Mike Krukow | .08 | .03 | .01 |
| ☐ 164 | Garry Maddox | .05 | .02 | .00 |
| ☐ 165 | Gary Matthews | .08 | .03 | .01 |
| ☐ 166 | Tug McGraw | .09 | .04 | .01 |
| ☐ 167 | Bob Molinaro | .03 | .01 | .00 |
| ☐ 168 | Sid Monge | .03 | .01 | .00 |
| ☐ 169 | Ron Reed | .03 | .01 | .00 |
| ☐ 170 | Bill Robinson | .03 | .01 | .00 |
| ☐ 171 | Pete Rose | 1.00 | .40 | .10 |
| ☐ 172 | Dick Ruthven | .03 | .01 | .00 |
| ☐ 173 | Mike Schmidt | .50 | .20 | .05 |
| ☐ 174 | Manny Trillo | .05 | .02 | .00 |
| ☐ 175 | Ozzie Virgil | .06 | .02 | .00 |
| ☐ 176 | George Vuckovich | .03 | .01 | .00 |
| ☐ 177 | Gary Allenson | .03 | .01 | .00 |
| ☐ 178 | Luis Aponte | .05 | .02 | .00 |
| ☐ 179 | Wade Boggs | 12.00 | 5.00 | 1.20 |
| ☐ 180 | Tom Burgmeier | .03 | .01 | .00 |
| ☐ 181 | Mark Clear | .03 | .01 | .00 |
| ☐ 182 | Dennis Eckersley | .05 | .02 | .00 |
| ☐ 183 | Dwight Evans | .12 | .05 | .01 |
| ☐ 184 | Rich Gedman | .10 | .04 | .01 |
| ☐ 185 | Glenn Hoffman | .03 | .01 | .00 |
| ☐ 186 | Bruce Hurst | .09 | .04 | .01 |
| ☐ 187 | Carney Lansford | .10 | .04 | .01 |
| ☐ 188 | Rick Miller | .03 | .01 | .00 |
| ☐ 189 | Reid Nichols | .03 | .01 | .00 |
| ☐ 190 | Bob Ojeda | .09 | .04 | .01 |
| ☐ 191 | Tony Perez | .12 | .05 | .01 |
| ☐ 192 | Chuck Rainey | .03 | .01 | .00 |
| ☐ 193 | Jerry Remy | .03 | .01 | .00 |
| ☐ 194 | Jim Rice | .30 | .12 | .03 |
| ☐ 195 | Bob Stanley | .05 | .02 | .00 |
| ☐ 196 | Dave Stapleton | .03 | .01 | .00 |
| ☐ 197 | Mike Torrez | .05 | .02 | .00 |
| ☐ 198 | John Tudor | .12 | .05 | .01 |
| ☐ 199 | Julio Valdez | .03 | .01 | .00 |
| ☐ 200 | Carl Yastrzemski | .55 | .22 | .05 |
| ☐ 201 | Dusty Baker | .07 | .03 | .01 |
| ☐ 202 | Joe Beckwith | .03 | .01 | .00 |
| ☐ 203 | Greg Brock | .35 | .14 | .03 |
| ☐ 204 | Ron Cey | .10 | .04 | .01 |
| ☐ 205 | Terry Forster | .07 | .03 | .01 |
| ☐ 206 | Steve Garvey | .40 | .16 | .04 |
| ☐ 207 | Pedro Guerrero | .30 | .12 | .03 |
| ☐ 208 | Burt Hooton | .03 | .01 | .00 |
| ☐ 209 | Steve Howe | .05 | .02 | .00 |
| ☐ 210 | Ken Landreaux | .05 | .02 | .00 |
| ☐ 211 | Mike Marshall | .20 | .08 | .02 |
| ☐ 212 | Candy Maldonado | .35 | .14 | .03 |
| ☐ 213 | Rick Monday | .05 | .02 | .00 |
| ☐ 214 | Tom Niedenfuer | .07 | .03 | .01 |
| ☐ 215 | Jorge Orta | .03 | .01 | .00 |
| ☐ 216 | Jerry Reuss | .06 | .02 | .00 |
| ☐ 217 | Ron Roenicke | .03 | .01 | .00 |
| ☐ 218 | Vicente Romo | .03 | .01 | .00 |
| ☐ 219 | Bill Russell | .05 | .02 | .00 |
| ☐ 220 | Steve Sax | .18 | .08 | .01 |
| ☐ 221 | Mike Scioscia | .05 | .02 | .00 |
| ☐ 222 | Dave Stewart | .03 | .01 | .00 |
| ☐ 223 | Derrel Thomas | .03 | .01 | .00 |
| ☐ 224 | Fernando Valenzuela | .35 | .14 | .03 |
| ☐ 225 | Bob Welch | .07 | .03 | .01 |
| ☐ 226 | Ricky Wright | .06 | .02 | .00 |
| ☐ 227 | Steve Yeager | .05 | .02 | .00 |
| ☐ 228 | Bill Almon | .03 | .01 | .00 |
| ☐ 229 | Harold Baines | .25 | .10 | .02 |
| ☐ 230 | Salome Barojas | .03 | .01 | .00 |
| ☐ 231 | Tony Bernazard | .05 | .02 | .00 |
| ☐ 232 | Britt Burns | .07 | .03 | .01 |
| ☐ 233 | Richard Dotson | .07 | .03 | .01 |
| ☐ 234 | Ernesto Escarrega | .03 | .01 | .00 |
| ☐ 235 | Carlton Fisk | .15 | .06 | .01 |
| ☐ 236 | Jerry Hairston | .03 | .01 | .00 |
| ☐ 237 | Kevin Hickey | .03 | .01 | .00 |
| ☐ 238 | LaMarr Hoyt | .08 | .03 | .01 |
| ☐ 239 | Steve Kemp | .08 | .03 | .01 |
| ☐ 240 | Jim Kern | .03 | .01 | .00 |
| ☐ 241 | Ron Kittle | .70 | .28 | .07 |
| ☐ 242 | Jerry Koosman | .07 | .03 | .01 |
| ☐ 243 | Dennis Lamp | .03 | .01 | .00 |
| ☐ 244 | Rudy Law | .03 | .01 | .00 |
| ☐ 245 | Vance Law | .03 | .01 | .00 |
| ☐ 246 | Ron LeFlore | .05 | .02 | .00 |
| ☐ 247 | Greg Luzinski | .10 | .04 | .01 |
| ☐ 248 | Tom Paciorek | .03 | .01 | .00 |
| ☐ 249 | Aurelio Rodriguez | .03 | .01 | .00 |
| ☐ 250 | Mike Squires | .03 | .01 | .00 |
| ☐ 251 | Steve Trout | .05 | .02 | .00 |
| ☐ 252 | Jim Barr | .03 | .01 | .00 |
| ☐ 253 | Dave Bergman | .03 | .01 | .00 |
| ☐ 254 | Fred Breining | .03 | .01 | .00 |
| ☐ 255 | Bob Brenly | .07 | .03 | .01 |
| ☐ 256 | Jack Clark | .14 | .06 | .01 |
| ☐ 257 | Chili Davis | .12 | .05 | .01 |
| ☐ 258 | Darrell Evans | .09 | .04 | .01 |
| ☐ 259 | Alan Fowlkes | .03 | .01 | .00 |
| ☐ 260 | Rich Gale | .03 | .01 | .00 |
| ☐ 261 | Atlee Hammaker | .05 | .02 | .00 |
| ☐ 262 | Al Holland | .05 | .02 | .00 |
| ☐ 263 | Duane Kuiper | .03 | .01 | .00 |
| ☐ 264 | Bill Laskey | .08 | .03 | .01 |
| ☐ 265 | Gary Lavelle | .05 | .02 | .00 |
| ☐ 266 | Johnnie LeMaster | .03 | .01 | .00 |
| ☐ 267 | Renie Martin | .03 | .01 | .00 |
| ☐ 268 | Milt May | .03 | .01 | .00 |
| ☐ 269 | Greg Minton | .05 | .02 | .00 |
| ☐ 270 | Joe Morgan | .20 | .08 | .02 |
| ☐ 271 | Tom O'Malley | .06 | .02 | .00 |
| ☐ 272 | Reggie Smith | .09 | .04 | .01 |
| ☐ 273 | Guy Sularz | .03 | .01 | .00 |
| ☐ 274 | Champ Summers | .03 | .01 | .00 |
| ☐ 275 | Max Venable | .03 | .01 | .00 |
| ☐ 276 | Jim Wohlford | .03 | .01 | .00 |
| ☐ 277 | Ray Burris | .03 | .01 | .00 |
| ☐ 278 | Gary Carter | .40 | .16 | .04 |
| ☐ 279 | Warren Cromartie | .03 | .01 | .00 |
| ☐ 280 | Andre Dawson | .25 | .10 | .02 |
| ☐ 281 | Terry Francona | .05 | .02 | .00 |
| ☐ 282 | Doug Flynn | .03 | .01 | .00 |
| ☐ 283 | Woody Fryman | .03 | .01 | .00 |
| ☐ 284 | Bill Gullickson | .05 | .02 | .00 |
| ☐ 285 | Wallace Johnson | .05 | .02 | .00 |
| ☐ 286 | Charlie Lea | .05 | .02 | .00 |
| ☐ 287 | Randy Lerch | .03 | .01 | .00 |
| ☐ 288 | Brad Mills | .03 | .01 | .00 |
| ☐ 289 | Dan Norman | .03 | .01 | .00 |
| ☐ 290 | Al Oliver | .10 | .04 | .01 |
| ☐ 291 | David Palmer | .06 | .02 | .00 |
| ☐ 292 | Tim Raines | .30 | .12 | .03 |
| ☐ 293 | Jeff Reardon | .09 | .04 | .01 |
| ☐ 294 | Steve Rogers | .07 | .03 | .01 |
| ☐ 295 | Scott Sanderson | .03 | .01 | .00 |
| ☐ 296 | Dan Schatzeder | .03 | .01 | .00 |
| ☐ 297 | Bryn Smith | .05 | .02 | .00 |
| ☐ 298 | Chris Speier | .03 | .01 | .00 |
| ☐ 299 | Tim Wallach | .08 | .03 | .01 |
| ☐ 300 | Jerry White | .03 | .01 | .00 |
| ☐ 301 | Joel Youngblood | .03 | .01 | .00 |
| ☐ 302 | Ross Baumgarten | .03 | .01 | .00 |
| ☐ 303 | Dale Berra | .05 | .02 | .00 |
| ☐ 304 | John Candelaria | .07 | .03 | .01 |
| ☐ 305 | Dick Davis | .03 | .01 | .00 |
| ☐ 306 | Mike Easler | .07 | .03 | .01 |
| ☐ 307 | Richie Hebner | .03 | .01 | .00 |
| ☐ 308 | Lee Lacy | .06 | .02 | .00 |
| ☐ 309 | Bill Madlock | .14 | .06 | .01 |
| ☐ 310 | Larry McWilliams | .03 | .01 | .00 |
| ☐ 311 | John Milner | .03 | .01 | .00 |
| ☐ 312 | Omar Moreno | .03 | .01 | .00 |
| ☐ 313 | Jim Morrison | .03 | .01 | .00 |
| ☐ 314 | Steve Nicosia | .03 | .01 | .00 |
| ☐ 315 | Dave Parker | .20 | .08 | .02 |
| ☐ 316 | Tony Pena | .14 | .06 | .01 |
| ☐ 317 | Johnny Ray | .12 | .05 | .01 |
| ☐ 318 | Rick Rhoden | .08 | .03 | .01 |

| | | | | |
|---|---|---|---|---|
| ☐ 319 Don Robinson | .03 | .01 | .00 |
| ☐ 320 Enrique Romo | .03 | .01 | .00 |
| ☐ 321 Manny Sarmiento | .03 | .01 | .00 |
| ☐ 322 Rod Scurry | .03 | .01 | .00 |
| ☐ 323 Jim Smith | .03 | .01 | .00 |
| ☐ 324 Willie Stargell | .20 | .08 | .02 |
| ☐ 325 Jason Thompson | .06 | .02 | .00 |
| ☐ 326 Kent Tekulve | .07 | .03 | .01 |
| ☐ 327 Tom Brookens | .03 | .01 | .00 |
| ☐ 328 Enos Cabell | .03 | .01 | .00 |
| ☐ 329 Kirk Gibson | .25 | .10 | .02 |
| ☐ 330 Larry Herndon | .03 | .01 | .00 |
| ☐ 331 Mike Ivie | .03 | .01 | .00 |
| ☐ 332 Howard Johnson | .12 | .05 | .01 |
| ☐ 333 Lynn Jones | .03 | .01 | .00 |
| ☐ 334 Rick Leach | .03 | .01 | .00 |
| ☐ 335 Chet Lemon | .06 | .02 | .00 |
| ☐ 336 Jack Morris | .20 | .08 | .02 |
| ☐ 337 Lance Parrish | .25 | .10 | .02 |
| ☐ 338 Larry Pashnick | .03 | .01 | .00 |
| ☐ 339 Dan Petry | .12 | .05 | .01 |
| ☐ 340 Dave Rozema | .03 | .01 | .00 |
| ☐ 341 Dave Rucker | .03 | .01 | .00 |
| ☐ 342 Elias Sosa | .03 | .01 | .00 |
| ☐ 343 Dave Tobik | .03 | .01 | .00 |
| ☐ 344 Alan Trammell | .20 | .08 | .02 |
| ☐ 345 Jerry Turner | .03 | .01 | .00 |
| ☐ 346 Jerry Ujdur | .03 | .01 | .00 |
| ☐ 347 Pat Underwood | .03 | .01 | .00 |
| ☐ 348 Lou Whitaker | .15 | .06 | .01 |
| ☐ 349 Milt Wilcox | .03 | .01 | .00 |
| ☐ 350 Glenn Wilson | .60 | .24 | .06 |
| ☐ 351 John Wockenfuss | .03 | .01 | .00 |
| ☐ 352 Kurt Bevacqua | .03 | .01 | .00 |
| ☐ 353 Juan Bonilla | .03 | .01 | .00 |
| ☐ 354 Floyd Chiffer | .03 | .01 | .00 |
| ☐ 355 Luis DeLeon | .03 | .01 | .00 |
| ☐ 356 Dave Dravecky | .40 | .16 | .04 |
| ☐ 357 Dave Edwards | .03 | .01 | .00 |
| ☐ 358 Juan Eichelberger | .03 | .01 | .00 |
| ☐ 359 Tim Flannery | .03 | .01 | .00 |
| ☐ 360 Tony Gwynn | 4.50 | 1.80 | .45 |
| ☐ 361 Ruppert Jones | .03 | .01 | .00 |
| ☐ 362 Terry Kennedy | .07 | .03 | .01 |
| ☐ 363 Joe Lefebvre | .03 | .01 | .00 |
| ☐ 364 Sixto Lezcano | .03 | .01 | .00 |
| ☐ 365 Tim Lollar | .03 | .01 | .00 |
| ☐ 366 Gary Lucas | .03 | .01 | .00 |
| ☐ 367 John Montefusco | .05 | .02 | .00 |
| ☐ 368 Broderick Perkins | .03 | .01 | .00 |
| ☐ 369 Joe Pittman | .03 | .01 | .00 |
| ☐ 370 Gene Richards | .03 | .01 | .00 |
| ☐ 371 Luis Salazar | .03 | .01 | .00 |
| ☐ 372 Eric Show | .12 | .05 | .01 |
| ☐ 373 Garry Templeton | .10 | .04 | .01 |
| ☐ 374 Chris Welsh | .03 | .01 | .00 |
| ☐ 375 Alan Wiggins | .20 | .08 | .02 |
| ☐ 376 Rick Cerone | .03 | .01 | .00 |
| ☐ 377 Dave Collins | .05 | .02 | .00 |
| ☐ 378 Roger Erickson | .03 | .01 | .00 |
| ☐ 379 George Frazier | .03 | .01 | .00 |
| ☐ 380 Oscar Gamble | .05 | .02 | .00 |
| ☐ 381 Goose Gossage | .18 | .08 | .01 |
| ☐ 382 Ken Griffey | .08 | .03 | .01 |
| ☐ 383 Ron Guidry | .20 | .08 | .02 |
| ☐ 384 Dave LaRoche | .03 | .01 | .00 |
| ☐ 385 Rudy May | .03 | .01 | .00 |
| ☐ 386 John Mayberry | .05 | .02 | .00 |
| ☐ 387 Lee Mazzilli | .05 | .02 | .00 |
| ☐ 388 Mike Morgan | .03 | .01 | .00 |
| ☐ 389 Jerry Mumphrey | .05 | .02 | .00 |
| ☐ 390 Bobby Murcer | .09 | .04 | .01 |
| ☐ 391 Graig Nettles | .14 | .06 | .01 |
| ☐ 392 Lou Piniella | .10 | .04 | .01 |
| ☐ 393 Willie Randolph | .06 | .02 | .00 |
| ☐ 394 Shane Rawley | .06 | .02 | .00 |
| ☐ 395 Dave Righetti | .15 | .06 | .01 |
| ☐ 396 Andre Robertson | .03 | .01 | .00 |
| ☐ 397 Roy Smalley | .05 | .02 | .00 |
| ☐ 398 Dave Winfield | .35 | .14 | .03 |
| ☐ 399 Butch Wynegar | .05 | .02 | .00 |
| ☐ 400 Chris Bando | .03 | .01 | .00 |
| ☐ 401 Alan Bannister | .03 | .01 | .00 |
| ☐ 402 Len Barker | .05 | .02 | .00 |
| ☐ 403 Tom Brennan | .03 | .01 | .00 |
| ☐ 404 Carmelo Castillo | .06 | .02 | .00 |
| ☐ 405 Miguel Dilone | .03 | .01 | .00 |
| ☐ 406 Jerry Dybzinski | .03 | .01 | .00 |
| ☐ 407 Mike Fischlin | .03 | .01 | .00 |
| ☐ 408 Ed Glynn | .06 | .02 | .00 |
| (photo actually Bud Anderson) | | | |
| ☐ 409 Mike Hargrove | .05 | .02 | .00 |

| | | | | |
|---|---|---|---|---|
| ☐ 410 Toby Harrah | .05 | .02 | .00 |
| ☐ 411 Ron Hassey | .03 | .01 | .00 |
| ☐ 412 Von Hayes | .15 | .06 | .01 |
| ☐ 413 Rick Manning | .03 | .01 | .00 |
| ☐ 414 Bake McBride | .05 | .02 | .00 |
| ☐ 415 Larry Milbourne | .03 | .01 | .00 |
| ☐ 416 Bill Nahorodny | .03 | .01 | .00 |
| ☐ 417 Jack Perconte | .03 | .01 | .00 |
| ☐ 418 Lary Sorensen | .03 | .01 | .00 |
| ☐ 419 Dan Spillner | .03 | .01 | .00 |
| ☐ 420 Rick Sutcliffe | .15 | .06 | .01 |
| ☐ 421 Andre Thornton | .07 | .03 | .01 |
| ☐ 422 Rick Waits | .03 | .01 | .00 |
| ☐ 423 Eddie Whitson | .06 | .02 | .00 |
| ☐ 424 Jesse Barfield | .20 | .08 | .02 |
| ☐ 425 Barry Bonnell | .03 | .01 | .00 |
| ☐ 426 Jim Clancy | .03 | .01 | .00 |
| ☐ 427 Damaso Garcia | .08 | .03 | .01 |
| ☐ 428 Jerry Garvin | .03 | .01 | .00 |
| ☐ 429 Alfredo Griffin | .05 | .02 | .00 |
| ☐ 430 Garth Iorg | .03 | .01 | .00 |
| ☐ 431 Roy Lee Jackson | .03 | .01 | .00 |
| ☐ 432 Luis Leal | .03 | .01 | .00 |
| ☐ 433 Buck Martinez | .03 | .01 | .00 |
| ☐ 434 Joey McLaughlin | .03 | .01 | .00 |
| ☐ 435 Lloyd Moseby | .12 | .05 | .01 |
| ☐ 436 Rance Mulliniks | .03 | .01 | .00 |
| ☐ 437 Dale Murray | .03 | .01 | .00 |
| ☐ 438 Wayne Nordhagen | .03 | .01 | .00 |
| ☐ 439 Gene Petralli | .03 | .01 | .00 |
| ☐ 440 Hosken Powell | .03 | .01 | .00 |
| ☐ 441 Dave Stieb | .15 | .06 | .01 |
| ☐ 442 Willie Upshaw | .08 | .03 | .01 |
| ☐ 443 Ernie Whitt | .03 | .01 | .00 |
| ☐ 444 Al Woods | .03 | .01 | .00 |
| ☐ 445 Alan Ashby | .03 | .01 | .00 |
| ☐ 446 Jose Cruz | .10 | .04 | .01 |
| ☐ 447 Kiko Garcia | .03 | .01 | .00 |
| ☐ 448 Phil Garner | .05 | .02 | .00 |
| ☐ 449 Danny Heep | .03 | .01 | .00 |
| ☐ 450 Art Howe | .03 | .01 | .00 |
| ☐ 451 Bob Knepper | .09 | .04 | .01 |
| ☐ 452 Alan Knicely | .03 | .01 | .00 |
| ☐ 453 Ray Knight | .09 | .04 | .01 |
| ☐ 454 Frank LaCorte | .03 | .01 | .00 |
| ☐ 455 Mike LaCoss | .03 | .01 | .00 |
| ☐ 456 Randy Moffitt | .03 | .01 | .00 |
| ☐ 457 Joe Niekro | .08 | .03 | .01 |
| ☐ 458 Terry Puhl | .05 | .02 | .00 |
| ☐ 459 Luis Pujols | .03 | .01 | .00 |
| ☐ 460 Craig Reynolds | .03 | .01 | .00 |
| ☐ 461 Bert Roberge | .03 | .01 | .00 |
| ☐ 462 Vern Ruhle | .03 | .01 | .00 |
| ☐ 463 Nolan Ryan | .30 | .12 | .03 |
| ☐ 464 Joe Sambito | .05 | .02 | .00 |
| ☐ 465 Tony Scott | .03 | .01 | .00 |
| ☐ 466 Dave Smith | .07 | .03 | .01 |
| ☐ 467 Harry Spilman | .03 | .01 | .00 |
| ☐ 468 Dickie Thon | .06 | .02 | .00 |
| ☐ 469 Denny Walling | .03 | .01 | .00 |
| ☐ 470 Larry Andersen | .03 | .01 | .00 |
| ☐ 471 Floyd Bannister | .07 | .03 | .01 |
| ☐ 472 Jim Beattie | .03 | .01 | .00 |
| ☐ 473 Bruce Bochte | .05 | .02 | .00 |
| ☐ 474 Manny Castillo | .03 | .01 | .00 |
| ☐ 475 Bill Caudill | .05 | .02 | .00 |
| ☐ 476 Bryan Clark | .03 | .01 | .00 |
| ☐ 477 Al Cowens | .05 | .02 | .00 |
| ☐ 478 Julio Cruz | .03 | .01 | .00 |
| ☐ 479 Todd Cruz | .03 | .01 | .00 |
| ☐ 480 Gary Gray | .03 | .01 | .00 |
| ☐ 481 Dave Henderson | .08 | .03 | .01 |
| ☐ 482 Mike Moore | .25 | .10 | .02 |
| ☐ 483 Gaylord Perry | .20 | .08 | .02 |
| ☐ 484 Dave Revering | .03 | .01 | .00 |
| ☐ 485 Joe Simpson | .03 | .01 | .00 |
| ☐ 486 Mike Stanton | .03 | .01 | .00 |
| ☐ 487 Rick Sweet | .03 | .01 | .00 |
| ☐ 488 Ed VandeBerg | .08 | .03 | .01 |
| ☐ 489 Richie Zisk | .05 | .02 | .00 |
| ☐ 490 Doug Bird | .03 | .01 | .00 |
| ☐ 491 Larry Bowa | .10 | .04 | .01 |
| ☐ 492 Bill Buckner | .10 | .04 | .01 |
| ☐ 493 Bill Campbell | .03 | .01 | .00 |
| ☐ 494 Jody Davis | .08 | .03 | .01 |
| ☐ 495 Leon Durham | .08 | .03 | .01 |
| ☐ 496 Steve Henderson | .03 | .01 | .00 |
| ☐ 497 Willie Hernandez | .12 | .05 | .01 |
| ☐ 498 Ferguson Jenkins | .15 | .06 | .01 |
| ☐ 499 Jay Johnstone | .05 | .02 | .00 |
| ☐ 500 Junior Kennedy | .03 | .01 | .00 |
| ☐ 501 Randy Martz | .03 | .01 | .00 |
| ☐ 502 Jerry Morales | .03 | .01 | .00 |

| | | | |
|---|---|---|---|
| ☐ 503 Keith Moreland | .08 | .03 | .01 |
| ☐ 504 Dickie Noles | .03 | .01 | .00 |
| ☐ 505 Mike Proly | .03 | .01 | .00 |
| ☐ 506 Allen Ripley | .03 | .01 | .00 |
| ☐ 507 Ryne Sandberg | 3.50 | 1.40 | .35 |
| ☐ 508 Lee Smith | .10 | .04 | .01 |
| ☐ 509 Pat Tabler | .10 | .04 | .01 |
| ☐ 510 Dick Tidrow | .03 | .01 | .00 |
| ☐ 511 Bump Wills | .03 | .01 | .00 |
| ☐ 512 Gary Woods | .03 | .01 | .00 |
| ☐ 513 Tony Armas | .10 | .04 | .01 |
| ☐ 514 Dave Beard | .03 | .01 | .00 |
| ☐ 515 Jeff Burroughs | .05 | .02 | .00 |
| ☐ 516 John D'Acquisto | .03 | .01 | .00 |
| ☐ 517 Wayne Gross | .03 | .01 | .00 |
| ☐ 518 Mike Heath | .03 | .01 | .00 |
| ☐ 519 Rickey Henderson | .50 | .20 | .05 |
| ☐ 520 Cliff Johnson | .03 | .01 | .00 |
| ☐ 521 Matt Keough | .03 | .01 | .00 |
| ☐ 522 Brian Kingman | .03 | .01 | .00 |
| ☐ 523 Rick Langford | .03 | .01 | .00 |
| ☐ 524 Davey Lopes | .06 | .02 | .00 |
| ☐ 525 Steve McCatty | .03 | .01 | .00 |
| ☐ 526 Dave McKay | .03 | .01 | .00 |
| ☐ 527 Dan Meyer | .03 | .01 | .00 |
| ☐ 528 Dwayne Murphy | .06 | .02 | .00 |
| ☐ 529 Jeff Newman | .03 | .01 | .00 |
| ☐ 530 Mike Norris | .05 | .02 | .00 |
| ☐ 531 Bob Owchinko | .03 | .01 | .00 |
| ☐ 532 Joe Rudi | .06 | .02 | .00 |
| ☐ 533 Jimmy Sexton | .03 | .01 | .00 |
| ☐ 534 Fred Stanley | .03 | .01 | .00 |
| ☐ 535 Tom Underwood | .03 | .01 | .00 |
| ☐ 536 Neil Allen | .06 | .02 | .00 |
| ☐ 537 Wally Backman | .07 | .03 | .01 |
| ☐ 538 Bob Bailor | .03 | .01 | .00 |
| ☐ 539 Hubie Brooks | .12 | .05 | .01 |
| ☐ 540 Carlos Diaz | .10 | .04 | .01 |
| ☐ 541 Pete Falcone | .03 | .01 | .00 |
| ☐ 542 George Foster | .14 | .06 | .01 |
| ☐ 543 Ron Gardenhire | .03 | .01 | .00 |
| ☐ 544 Brian Giles | .03 | .01 | .00 |
| ☐ 545 Ron Hodges | .03 | .01 | .00 |
| ☐ 546 Randy Jones | .05 | .02 | .00 |
| ☐ 547 Mike Jorgensen | .03 | .01 | .00 |
| ☐ 548 Dave Kingman | .14 | .06 | .01 |
| ☐ 549 Ed Lynch | .03 | .01 | .00 |
| ☐ 550 Jesse Orosco | .07 | .03 | .01 |
| ☐ 551 Rick Ownbey | .06 | .02 | .00 |
| ☐ 552 Charlie Puleo | .03 | .01 | .00 |
| ☐ 553 Gary Rajsich | .03 | .01 | .00 |
| ☐ 554 Mike Scott | .20 | .08 | .02 |
| ☐ 555 Rusty Staub | .10 | .04 | .01 |
| ☐ 556 John Stearns | .03 | .01 | .00 |
| ☐ 557 Craig Swan | .03 | .01 | .00 |
| ☐ 558 Ellis Valentine | .03 | .01 | .00 |
| ☐ 559 Tom Veryzer | .03 | .01 | .00 |
| ☐ 560 Mookie Wilson | .07 | .03 | .01 |
| ☐ 561 Pat Zachry | .03 | .01 | .00 |
| ☐ 562 Buddy Bell | .10 | .04 | .01 |
| ☐ 563 John Butcher | .03 | .01 | .00 |
| ☐ 564 Steve Comer | .03 | .01 | .00 |
| ☐ 565 Danny Darwin | .03 | .01 | .00 |
| ☐ 566 Bucky Dent | .06 | .02 | .00 |
| ☐ 567 John Grubb | .03 | .01 | .00 |
| ☐ 568 Rick Honeycutt | .05 | .02 | .00 |
| ☐ 569 Dave Hostetler | .05 | .02 | .00 |
| ☐ 570 Charlie Hough | .06 | .02 | .00 |
| ☐ 571 Lamar Johnson | .03 | .01 | .00 |
| ☐ 572 Jon Matlack | .05 | .02 | .00 |
| ☐ 573 Paul Mirabella | .03 | .01 | .00 |
| ☐ 574 Larry Parrish | .06 | .02 | .00 |
| ☐ 575 Mike Richardt | .03 | .01 | .00 |
| ☐ 576 Mickey Rivers | .05 | .02 | .00 |
| ☐ 577 Billy Sample | .03 | .01 | .00 |
| ☐ 578 Dave Schmidt | .03 | .01 | .00 |
| ☐ 579 Bill Stein | .03 | .01 | .00 |
| ☐ 580 Jim Sundberg | .05 | .02 | .00 |
| ☐ 581 Frank Tanana | .06 | .02 | .00 |
| ☐ 582 Mark Wagner | .03 | .01 | .00 |
| ☐ 583 George Wright | .07 | .03 | .01 |
| ☐ 584 Johnny Bench | .35 | .14 | .03 |
| ☐ 585 Bruce Berenyi | .03 | .01 | .00 |
| ☐ 586 Larry Biittner | .03 | .01 | .00 |
| ☐ 587 Cesar Cedeno | .07 | .03 | .01 |
| ☐ 588 Dave Concepcion | .09 | .04 | .01 |
| ☐ 589 Dan Driessen | .05 | .02 | .00 |
| ☐ 590 Greg Harris | .06 | .02 | .00 |
| ☐ 591 Ben Hayes | .03 | .01 | .00 |
| ☐ 592 Paul Householder | .03 | .01 | .00 |
| ☐ 593 Tom Hume | .03 | .01 | .00 |
| ☐ 594 Wayne Krenchicki | .03 | .01 | .00 |
| ☐ 595 Rafael Landestoy | .03 | .01 | .00 |

| | | | |
|---|---|---|---|
| ☐ 596 Charlie Leibrandt | .06 | .02 | .00 |
| ☐ 597 Eddie Milner | .15 | .06 | .01 |
| ☐ 598 Ron Oester | .05 | .02 | .00 |
| ☐ 599 Frank Pastore | .03 | .01 | .00 |
| ☐ 600 Joe Price | .03 | .01 | .00 |
| ☐ 601 Tom Seaver | .35 | .14 | .03 |
| ☐ 602 Bob Shirley | .03 | .01 | .00 |
| ☐ 603 Mario Soto | .08 | .03 | .01 |
| ☐ 604 Alex Trevino | .03 | .01 | .00 |
| ☐ 605 Mike Vail | .03 | .01 | .00 |
| ☐ 606 Duane Walker | .06 | .02 | .00 |
| ☐ 607 Tom Brunansky | .15 | .06 | .01 |
| ☐ 608 Bobby Castillo | .03 | .01 | .00 |
| ☐ 609 John Castino | .03 | .01 | .00 |
| ☐ 610 Ron Davis | .03 | .01 | .00 |
| ☐ 611 Lenny Faedo | .03 | .01 | .00 |
| ☐ 612 Terry Felton | .03 | .01 | .00 |
| ☐ 613 Gary Gaetti | .60 | .24 | .06 |
| ☐ 614 Mickey Hatcher | .03 | .01 | .00 |
| ☐ 615 Brad Havens | .03 | .01 | .00 |
| ☐ 616 Kent Hrbek | .30 | .12 | .03 |
| ☐ 617 Randy Johnson | .03 | .01 | .00 |
| ☐ 618 Tim Laudner | .03 | .01 | .00 |
| ☐ 619 Jeff Little | .03 | .01 | .00 |
| ☐ 620 Bob Mitchell | .03 | .01 | .00 |
| ☐ 621 Jack O'Connor | .03 | .01 | .00 |
| ☐ 622 John Pacella | .03 | .01 | .00 |
| ☐ 623 Pete Redfern | .03 | .01 | .00 |
| ☐ 624 Jesus Vega | .03 | .01 | .00 |
| ☐ 625 Frank Viola | .45 | .18 | .04 |
| ☐ 626 Ron Washington | .05 | .02 | .00 |
| ☐ 627 Gary Ward | .06 | .02 | .00 |
| ☐ 628 Al Williams | .03 | .01 | .00 |
| ☐ 629 Red Sox All-Stars: Carl Yastrzemski Dennis Eckersley Mark Clear | .18 | .08 | .01 |
| ☐ 630 "300 Career Wins" Gaylord Perry and Terry Bulling 5/6/82 | .12 | .05 | .01 |
| ☐ 631 Pride of Venezuela Dave Concepcion and Manny Trillo | .06 | .02 | .00 |
| ☐ 632 All-Star Infielders Robin Yount and Buddy Bell | .15 | .06 | .01 |
| ☐ 633 Mr.Vet and Mr.Rookie: Dave Winfield and Kent Hrbek | .20 | .08 | .02 |
| ☐ 634 Fountain of Youth: Willie Stargell and Pete Rose | .60 | .24 | .06 |
| ☐ 635 Big Chiefs: Toby Harrah and Andre Thornton | .06 | .02 | .00 |
| ☐ 636 Smith Brothers: Ozzie and Lonnie | .08 | .03 | .01 |
| ☐ 637 Base Stealers' Threat Bo Diaz and Gary Carter | .12 | .05 | .01 |
| ☐ 638 All-Star Catchers: Carlton Fisk and Gary Carter | .15 | .06 | .01 |
| ☐ 639 The Silver Shoe: Rickey Henderson | .30 | .12 | .03 |
| ☐ 640 Home Run Threats: Ben Oglivie and Reggie Jackson | .18 | .08 | .01 |
| ☐ 641 Two Teams Same Day: Joel Youngblood August 4, 1982 | .06 | .02 | .00 |
| ☐ 642 Last Perfect Game: Ron Hassey and Len Barker | .06 | .02 | .00 |
| ☐ 643 Black and Blue: Bud Black | .06 | .02 | .00 |
| ☐ 644 Black and Blue: Vida Blue | .06 | .02 | .00 |
| ☐ 645 Speed and Power: Reggie Jackson | .30 | .12 | .03 |
| ☐ 646 Speed and Power: Rickey Henderson | .30 | .12 | .03 |
| ☐ 647 CL: Cards/Brewers | .07 | .01 | .00 |
| ☐ 648 CL: Orioles/Angels | .07 | .01 | .00 |
| ☐ 649 CL: Royals/Braves | .07 | .01 | .00 |
| ☐ 650 CL: Phillies/Red Sox | .07 | .01 | .00 |
| ☐ 651 CL: Dodgers/White Sox | .07 | .01 | .00 |
| ☐ 652 CL: Giants/Expos | .07 | .01 | .00 |
| ☐ 653 CL: Pirates/Tigers | .07 | .01 | .00 |
| ☐ 654 CL: Padres/Yankees | .07 | .01 | .00 |
| ☐ 655 CL: Indians/Blue Jays | .07 | .01 | .00 |
| ☐ 656 CL: Astros/Mariners | .07 | .01 | .00 |
| ☐ 657 CL: Cubs/A's | .07 | .01 | .00 |

☐ 658 CL: Mets/Rangers .......... .07 .01 .00
☐ 659 CL: Reds/Twins .............. .07 .01 .00
☐ 660 CL: Specials/Teams ....... .09 .01 .00

# 1984 Fleer

Kent Hrbek

FIRST BASE

The cards in this 660 card set measure 2 1/2" by 3 1/2". The 1984 Fleer card set featured fronts with full color team logos along with the player's name and position and the Fleer identification. The set features many imaginative photos, several multi-player cards, and many more action shots than the 1983 card set. The backs are quite similar to the 1983 backs except that blue rather than brown ink is used. The player cards are alphabetized within team and the teams are ordered by their 1983 season finish and won-lost record, e.g., Baltimore (1-23), Philadelphia (24-49), Chicago White Sox (50-73), Detroit (74-95), Los Angeles (96-118), New York Yankees (119-144), Toronto (145- 169), Atlanta (170-193), Milwaukee (194-219), Houston (220-244), Pittsburgh (245-269), Montreal (270-293), San Diego (294-317), St. Louis (318-340), Kansas City (341-364), San Francisco (365- 387), Boston (388-412), Texas (413-435), Oakland (436-461), Cincinnati (462-485), Chicago (486-507), California (508-532), Cleveland (533-555), Minnesota (556-579), New York Mets (580- 603), and Seattle (604-625). Specials (626-646) and checklist cards (647-660) make up the end of the set.

|  | MINT | VG-E | F-G |
|---|---|---|---|
| COMPLETE SET ...................... | 48.00 | 18.00 | 4.50 |
| COMMON PLAYER (1-660) ........ | .03 | .01 | .00 |

| | | | | |
|---|---|---|---|---|
| ☐ | 1 | Mike Boddicker .............. | .12 | .05 | .01 |
| ☐ | 2 | Al Bumbry ...................... | .03 | .01 | .00 |
| ☐ | 3 | Todd Cruz ...................... | .03 | .01 | .00 |
| ☐ | 4 | Rich Dauer ..................... | .03 | .01 | .00 |
| ☐ | 5 | Storm Davis ................... | .07 | .03 | .01 |
| ☐ | 6 | Rick Dempsey ................ | .05 | .02 | .00 |
| ☐ | 7 | Jim Dwyer ...................... | .03 | .01 | .00 |
| ☐ | 8 | Mike Flanagan ............... | .07 | .03 | .01 |
| ☐ | 9 | Dan Ford ........................ | .03 | .01 | .00 |
| ☐ | 10 | John Lowenstein ........... | .03 | .01 | .00 |
| ☐ | 11 | Dennis Martinez ............ | .03 | .01 | .00 |
| ☐ | 12 | Tippy Martinez .............. | .03 | .01 | .00 |
| ☐ | 13 | Scott McGregor ............. | .07 | .03 | .01 |
| ☐ | 14 | Eddie Murray ................. | .50 | .20 | .05 |
| ☐ | 15 | Joe Nolan ...................... | .03 | .01 | .00 |
| ☐ | 16 | Jim Palmer .................... | .25 | .10 | .02 |
| ☐ | 17 | Cal Ripken ..................... | .60 | .24 | .06 |
| ☐ | 18 | Gary Roenicke ............... | .05 | .02 | .00 |
| ☐ | 19 | Lenn Sakata .................. | .03 | .01 | .00 |
| ☐ | 20 | John Shelby ................... | .07 | .03 | .01 |
| ☐ | 21 | Ken Singleton ................ | .09 | .04 | .01 |
| ☐ | 22 | Sammy Stewart .............. | .03 | .01 | .00 |
| ☐ | 23 | Tim Stoddard ................ | .03 | .01 | .00 |

| | | | | |
|---|---|---|---|---|
| ☐ | 24 | Marty Bystrom ............... | .03 | .01 | .00 |
| ☐ | 25 | Steve Carlton ................ | .30 | .12 | .03 |
| ☐ | 26 | Ivan DeJesus ................. | .03 | .01 | .00 |
| ☐ | 27 | John Denny .................... | .07 | .03 | .01 |
| ☐ | 28 | Bob Dernier ................... | .05 | .02 | .00 |
| ☐ | 29 | Bo Diaz ......................... | .05 | .02 | .00 |
| ☐ | 30 | Kiko Garcia .................... | .03 | .01 | .00 |
| ☐ | 31 | Greg Gross .................... | .03 | .01 | .00 |
| ☐ | 32 | Kevin Gross ................... | .20 | .08 | .02 |
| ☐ | 33 | Von Hayes ..................... | .12 | .05 | .01 |
| ☐ | 34 | Willie Hernandez ............ | .20 | .08 | .02 |
| ☐ | 35 | Al Holland ..................... | .05 | .02 | .00 |
| ☐ | 36 | Charles Hudson ............. | .12 | .05 | .01 |
| ☐ | 37 | Joe Lefebvre .................. | .03 | .01 | .00 |
| ☐ | 38 | Sixto Lezcano ................ | .03 | .01 | .00 |
| ☐ | 39 | Garry Maddox ................ | .05 | .02 | .00 |
| ☐ | 40 | Gary Matthews .............. | .08 | .03 | .01 |
| ☐ | 41 | Len Matuszek ................ | .03 | .01 | .00 |
| ☐ | 42 | Tug McGraw ................... | .09 | .04 | .01 |
| ☐ | 43 | Joe Morgan .................... | .18 | .08 | .01 |
| ☐ | 44 | Tony Perez ..................... | .12 | .05 | .01 |
| ☐ | 45 | Ron Reed ....................... | .03 | .01 | .00 |
| ☐ | 46 | Pete Rose ...................... | .75 | .30 | .07 |
| ☐ | 47 | Juan Samuel .................. | 1.50 | .60 | .15 |
| ☐ | 48 | Mike Schmidt ................. | .40 | .16 | .04 |
| ☐ | 49 | Ozzie Virgil ................... | .03 | .01 | .00 |
| ☐ | 50 | Juan Agosto ................... | .05 | .02 | .00 |
| ☐ | 51 | Harold Baines ................ | .20 | .08 | .02 |
| ☐ | 52 | Floyd Bannister .............. | .06 | .02 | .00 |
| ☐ | 53 | Salome Barojas .............. | .03 | .01 | .00 |
| ☐ | 54 | Britt Burns .................... | .06 | .02 | .00 |
| ☐ | 55 | Julio Cruz ...................... | .03 | .01 | .00 |
| ☐ | 56 | Richard Dotson .............. | .06 | .02 | .00 |
| ☐ | 57 | Jerry Dybzinski .............. | .03 | .01 | .00 |
| ☐ | 58 | Carlton Fisk .................. | .14 | .06 | .01 |
| ☐ | 59 | Scott Fletcher ............... | .05 | .02 | .00 |
| ☐ | 60 | Jerry Hairston ............... | .03 | .01 | .00 |
| ☐ | 61 | Kevin Hickey .................. | .03 | .01 | .00 |
| ☐ | 62 | Marc Hill ....................... | .03 | .01 | .00 |
| ☐ | 63 | LaMarr Hoyt ................... | .08 | .03 | .01 |
| ☐ | 64 | Ron Kittle ...................... | .15 | .06 | .01 |
| ☐ | 65 | Jerry Koosman .............. | .07 | .03 | .01 |
| ☐ | 66 | Dennis Lamp .................. | .03 | .01 | .00 |
| ☐ | 67 | Rudy Law ....................... | .03 | .01 | .00 |
| ☐ | 68 | Vance Law ..................... | .03 | .01 | .00 |
| ☐ | 69 | Greg Luzinski ................. | .10 | .04 | .01 |
| ☐ | 70 | Tom Paciorek ................. | .03 | .01 | .00 |
| ☐ | 71 | Mike Squires .................. | .03 | .01 | .00 |
| ☐ | 72 | Dick Tidrow ................... | .03 | .01 | .00 |
| ☐ | 73 | Greg Walker ................... | .50 | .20 | .05 |
| ☐ | 74 | Glenn Abbott .................. | .03 | .01 | .00 |
| ☐ | 75 | Howard Bailey ................ | .03 | .01 | .00 |
| ☐ | 76 | Doug Bair ....................... | .03 | .01 | .00 |
| ☐ | 77 | Juan Berenguer .............. | .03 | .01 | .00 |
| ☐ | 78 | Tom Brookens ................ | .03 | .01 | .00 |
| ☐ | 79 | Enos Cabell ................... | .03 | .01 | .00 |
| ☐ | 80 | Kirk Gibson ................... | .25 | .10 | .02 |
| ☐ | 81 | John Grubb .................... | .03 | .01 | .00 |
| ☐ | 82 | Larry Herndon ............... | .03 | .01 | .00 |
| ☐ | 83 | Wayne Krenchicki ........... | .03 | .01 | .00 |
| ☐ | 84 | Rick Leach ..................... | .03 | .01 | .00 |
| ☐ | 85 | Chet Lemon .................... | .05 | .02 | .00 |
| ☐ | 86 | Aurelio Lopez ................. | .03 | .01 | .00 |
| ☐ | 87 | Jack Morris .................... | .20 | .08 | .02 |
| ☐ | 88 | Lance Parrish ................ | .25 | .10 | .02 |
| ☐ | 89 | Dan Petry ...................... | .12 | .05 | .01 |
| ☐ | 90 | Dave Rozema .................. | .03 | .01 | .00 |
| ☐ | 91 | Alan Trammell ................ | .18 | .08 | .01 |
| ☐ | 92 | Lou Whitaker .................. | .15 | .06 | .01 |
| ☐ | 93 | Milt Wilcox .................... | .03 | .01 | .00 |
| ☐ | 94 | Glenn Wilson .................. | .10 | .04 | .01 |
| ☐ | 95 | John Wockenfuss ............ | .03 | .01 | .00 |
| ☐ | 96 | Dusty Baker ................... | .05 | .02 | .00 |
| ☐ | 97 | Joe Beckwith .................. | .03 | .01 | .00 |
| ☐ | 98 | Greg Brock ..................... | .05 | .02 | .00 |
| ☐ | 99 | Jack Fimple .................... | .05 | .02 | .00 |
| ☐ | 100 | Pedro Guerrero .............. | .25 | .10 | .02 |
| ☐ | 101 | Rick Honeycutt .............. | .05 | .02 | .00 |
| ☐ | 102 | Burt Hooton ................... | .03 | .01 | .00 |
| ☐ | 103 | Steve Howe .................... | .05 | .02 | .00 |
| ☐ | 104 | Ken Landreaux ............... | .05 | .02 | .00 |
| ☐ | 105 | Mike Marshall ................ | .15 | .06 | .01 |
| ☐ | 106 | Rick Monday .................. | .05 | .02 | .00 |
| ☐ | 107 | Jose Morales .................. | .03 | .01 | .00 |
| ☐ | 108 | Tom Niedenfuer .............. | .05 | .02 | .00 |
| ☐ | 109 | Alejandro Pena .............. | .20 | .08 | .02 |
| ☐ | 110 | Jerry Reuss .................... | .05 | .02 | .00 |
| ☐ | 111 | Bill Russell .................... | .05 | .02 | .00 |
| ☐ | 112 | Steve Sax ...................... | .15 | .06 | .01 |
| ☐ | 113 | Mike Scioscia ................ | .05 | .02 | .00 |
| ☐ | 114 | Derrel Thomas ................ | .03 | .01 | .00 |
| ☐ | 115 | Fernando Valenzuela ...... | .30 | .12 | .03 |
| ☐ | 116 | Bob Welch ..................... | .07 | .03 | .01 |

| □ | # | Name | | | |
|---|---|---|---|---|---|
| □ | 117 | Steve Yeager | .05 | .02 | .00 |
| □ | 118 | Pat Zachry | .03 | .01 | .00 |
| □ | 119 | Don Baylor | .12 | .05 | .01 |
| □ | 120 | Bert Campaneris | .06 | .02 | .00 |
| □ | 121 | Rick Cerone | .03 | .01 | .00 |
| □ | 122 | Ray Fontenot | .07 | .03 | .01 |
| □ | 123 | George Frazier | .03 | .01 | .00 |
| □ | 124 | Oscar Gamble | .05 | .02 | .00 |
| □ | 125 | Goose Gossage | .14 | .06 | .01 |
| □ | 126 | Ken Griffey | .07 | .03 | .01 |
| □ | 127 | Ron Guidry | .14 | .06 | .01 |
| □ | 128 | Jay Howell | .06 | .02 | .00 |
| □ | 129 | Steve Kemp | .06 | .02 | .00 |
| □ | 130 | Matt Keough | .03 | .01 | .00 |
| □ | 131 | Don Mattingly | 30.00 | 12.00 | 3.00 |
| □ | 132 | John Montefusco | .05 | .02 | .00 |
| □ | 133 | Omar Moreno | .03 | .01 | .00 |
| □ | 134 | Dale Murray | .03 | .01 | .00 |
| □ | 135 | Graig Nettles | .12 | .05 | .01 |
| □ | 136 | Lou Piniella | .09 | .04 | .01 |
| □ | 137 | Willie Randolph | .06 | .02 | .00 |
| □ | 138 | Shane Rawley | .06 | .02 | .00 |
| □ | 139 | Dave Righetti | .15 | .06 | .01 |
| □ | 140 | Andre Robertson | .03 | .01 | .00 |
| □ | 141 | Bob Shirley | .03 | .01 | .00 |
| □ | 142 | Roy Smalley | .05 | .02 | .00 |
| □ | 143 | Dave Winfield | .30 | .12 | .03 |
| □ | 144 | Butch Wynegar | .05 | .02 | .00 |
| □ | 145 | Jim Acker | .10 | .04 | .01 |
| □ | 146 | Doyle Alexander | .05 | .02 | .00 |
| □ | 147 | Jesse Barfield | .18 | .08 | .01 |
| □ | 148 | Jorge Bell | .15 | .06 | .01 |
| □ | 149 | Barry Bonnell | .03 | .01 | .00 |
| □ | 150 | Jim Clancy | .03 | .01 | .00 |
| □ | 151 | Dave Collins | .05 | .02 | .00 |
| □ | 152 | Tony Fernandez | 1.50 | .60 | .15 |
| □ | 153 | Damaso Garcia | .08 | .03 | .01 |
| □ | 154 | Dave Geisel | .03 | .01 | .00 |
| □ | 155 | Jim Gott | .03 | .01 | .00 |
| □ | 156 | Alfredo Griffin | .05 | .02 | .00 |
| □ | 157 | Garth Iorg | .03 | .01 | .00 |
| □ | 158 | Roy Lee Jackson | .03 | .01 | .00 |
| □ | 159 | Cliff Johnson | .03 | .01 | .00 |
| □ | 160 | Luis Leal | .03 | .01 | .00 |
| □ | 161 | Buck Martinez | .03 | .01 | .00 |
| □ | 162 | Joey McLaughlin | .03 | .01 | .00 |
| □ | 163 | Randy Moffitt | .03 | .01 | .00 |
| □ | 164 | Lloyd Moseby | .12 | .05 | .01 |
| □ | 165 | Rance Mulliniks | .03 | .01 | .00 |
| □ | 166 | Jorge Orta | .03 | .01 | .00 |
| □ | 167 | Dave Stieb | .15 | .06 | .01 |
| □ | 168 | Willie Upshaw | .08 | .03 | .01 |
| □ | 169 | Ernie Whitt | .03 | .01 | .00 |
| □ | 170 | Len Barker | .05 | .02 | .00 |
| □ | 171 | Steve Bedrosian | .05 | .02 | .00 |
| □ | 172 | Bruce Benedict | .03 | .01 | .00 |
| □ | 173 | Brett Butler | .09 | .04 | .01 |
| □ | 174 | Rick Camp | .03 | .01 | .00 |
| □ | 175 | Chris Chambliss | .05 | .02 | .00 |
| □ | 176 | Ken Dayley | .03 | .01 | .00 |
| □ | 177 | Pete Falcone | .03 | .01 | .00 |
| □ | 178 | Terry Forster | .07 | .03 | .01 |
| □ | 179 | Gene Garber | .03 | .01 | .00 |
| □ | 180 | Terry Harper | .03 | .01 | .00 |
| □ | 181 | Bob Horner | .20 | .08 | .02 |
| □ | 182 | Glenn Hubbard | .03 | .01 | .00 |
| □ | 183 | Randy Johnson | .03 | .01 | .00 |
| □ | 184 | Craig McMurtry | .08 | .03 | .01 |
| □ | 185 | Donnie Moore | .06 | .02 | .00 |
| □ | 186 | Dale Murphy | .60 | .24 | .06 |
| □ | 187 | Phil Niekro | .15 | .06 | .01 |
| □ | 188 | Pascual Perez | .05 | .02 | .00 |
| □ | 189 | Biff Pocoroba | .03 | .01 | .00 |
| □ | 190 | Rafael Ramirez | .03 | .01 | .00 |
| □ | 191 | Jerry Royster | .03 | .01 | .00 |
| □ | 192 | Claudell Washington | .05 | .02 | .00 |
| □ | 193 | Bob Watson | .05 | .02 | .00 |
| □ | 194 | Jerry Augustine | .03 | .01 | .00 |
| □ | 195 | Mark Brouhard | .03 | .01 | .00 |
| □ | 196 | Mike Caldwell | .05 | .02 | .00 |
| □ | 197 | Tom Candiotti | .15 | .06 | .01 |
| □ | 198 | Cecil Cooper | .14 | .06 | .01 |
| □ | 199 | Rollie Fingers | .15 | .06 | .01 |
| □ | 200 | Jim Gantner | .05 | .02 | .00 |
| □ | 201 | Bob L. Gibson | .06 | .02 | .00 |
| □ | 202 | Moose Haas | .05 | .02 | .00 |
| □ | 203 | Roy Howell | .03 | .01 | .00 |
| □ | 204 | Pete Ladd | .03 | .01 | .00 |
| □ | 205 | Rick Manning | .03 | .01 | .00 |
| □ | 206 | Bob McClure | .03 | .01 | .00 |
| □ | 207 | Paul Molitor | .10 | .04 | .01 |
| □ | 208 | Don Money | .03 | .01 | .00 |
| □ | 209 | Charlie Moore | .03 | .01 | .00 |
| □ | 210 | Ben Oglivie | .06 | .02 | .00 |
| □ | 211 | Chuck Porter | .03 | .01 | .00 |
| □ | 212 | Ed Romero | .03 | .01 | .00 |
| □ | 213 | Ted Simmons | .10 | .04 | .01 |
| □ | 214 | Jim Slaton | .03 | .01 | .00 |
| □ | 215 | Don Sutton | .18 | .08 | .01 |
| □ | 216 | Tom Tellmann | .03 | .01 | .00 |
| □ | 217 | Pete Vuckovich | .07 | .03 | .01 |
| □ | 218 | Ned Yost | .03 | .01 | .00 |
| □ | 219 | Robin Yount | .30 | .12 | .03 |
| □ | 220 | Alan Ashby | .03 | .01 | .00 |
| □ | 221 | Kevin Bass | .09 | .04 | .01 |
| □ | 222 | Jose Cruz | .09 | .04 | .01 |
| □ | 223 | Bill Dawley | .09 | .04 | .01 |
| □ | 224 | Frank DiPino | .05 | .02 | .00 |
| □ | 225 | Bill Doran | .50 | .20 | .05 |
| □ | 226 | Phil Garner | .05 | .02 | .00 |
| □ | 227 | Art Howe | .03 | .01 | .00 |
| □ | 228 | Bob Knepper | .08 | .03 | .01 |
| □ | 229 | Ray Knight | .08 | .03 | .01 |
| □ | 230 | Frank LaCorte | .03 | .01 | .00 |
| □ | 231 | Mike LaCoss | .03 | .01 | .00 |
| □ | 232 | Mike Madden | .09 | .04 | .01 |
| □ | 233 | Jerry Mumphrey | .05 | .02 | .00 |
| □ | 234 | Joe Niekro | .08 | .03 | .01 |
| □ | 235 | Terry Puhl | .05 | .02 | .00 |
| □ | 236 | Luis Pujols | .03 | .01 | .00 |
| □ | 237 | Craig Reynolds | .03 | .01 | .00 |
| □ | 238 | Vern Ruhle | .03 | .01 | .00 |
| □ | 239 | Nolan Ryan | .25 | .10 | .02 |
| □ | 240 | Mike Scott | .18 | .08 | .01 |
| □ | 241 | Tony Scott | .03 | .01 | .00 |
| □ | 242 | Dave Smith | .07 | .03 | .01 |
| □ | 243 | Dickie Thon | .06 | .02 | .00 |
| □ | 244 | Denny Walling | .03 | .01 | .00 |
| □ | 245 | Dale Berra | .05 | .02 | .00 |
| □ | 246 | Jim Bibby | .05 | .02 | .00 |
| □ | 247 | John Candelaria | .08 | .03 | .01 |
| □ | 248 | Jose DeLeon | .20 | .08 | .02 |
| □ | 249 | Mike Easler | .07 | .03 | .01 |
| □ | 250 | Cecilio Guante | .03 | .01 | .00 |
| □ | 251 | Richie Hebner | .03 | .01 | .00 |
| □ | 252 | Lee Lacy | .06 | .02 | .00 |
| □ | 253 | Bill Madlock | .12 | .05 | .01 |
| □ | 254 | Milt May | .03 | .01 | .00 |
| □ | 255 | Lee Mazzilli | .05 | .02 | .00 |
| □ | 256 | Larry McWilliams | .03 | .01 | .00 |
| □ | 257 | Jim Morrison | .03 | .01 | .00 |
| □ | 258 | Dave Parker | .20 | .08 | .02 |
| □ | 259 | Tony Pena | .14 | .06 | .01 |
| □ | 260 | Johnny Ray | .10 | .04 | .01 |
| □ | 261 | Rick Rhoden | .08 | .03 | .01 |
| □ | 262 | Don Robinson | .03 | .01 | .00 |
| □ | 263 | Manny Sarmiento | .03 | .01 | .00 |
| □ | 264 | Rod Scurry | .03 | .01 | .00 |
| □ | 265 | Kent Tekulve | .06 | .02 | .00 |
| □ | 266 | Gene Tenace | .03 | .01 | .00 |
| □ | 267 | Jason Thompson | .06 | .02 | .00 |
| □ | 268 | Lee Tunnell | .06 | .02 | .00 |
| □ | 269 | Marvell Wynne | .10 | .04 | .01 |
| □ | 270 | Ray Burris | .03 | .01 | .00 |
| □ | 271 | Gary Carter | .35 | .14 | .03 |
| □ | 272 | Warren Cromartie | .03 | .01 | .00 |
| □ | 273 | Andre Dawson | .20 | .08 | .02 |
| □ | 274 | Doug Flynn | .03 | .01 | .00 |
| □ | 275 | Terry Francona | .05 | .02 | .00 |
| □ | 276 | Bill Gullickson | .05 | .02 | .00 |
| □ | 277 | Bob James | .12 | .05 | .01 |
| □ | 278 | Charlie Lea | .05 | .02 | .00 |
| □ | 279 | Bryan Little | .03 | .01 | .00 |
| □ | 280 | Al Oliver | .10 | .04 | .01 |
| □ | 281 | Tim Raines | .25 | .10 | .02 |
| □ | 282 | Bobby Ramos | .03 | .01 | .00 |
| □ | 283 | Jeff Reardon | .08 | .03 | .01 |
| □ | 284 | Steve Rogers | .06 | .02 | .00 |
| □ | 285 | Scott Sanderson | .03 | .01 | .00 |
| □ | 286 | Dan Schatzeder | .03 | .01 | .00 |
| □ | 287 | Bryn Smith | .03 | .01 | .00 |
| □ | 288 | Chris Speier | .03 | .01 | .00 |
| □ | 289 | Manny Trillo | .05 | .02 | .00 |
| □ | 290 | Mike Vail | .03 | .01 | .00 |
| □ | 291 | Tim Wallach | .08 | .03 | .01 |
| □ | 292 | Chris Welsh | .03 | .01 | .00 |
| □ | 293 | Jim Wohlford | .03 | .01 | .00 |
| □ | 294 | Kurt Bevacqua | .03 | .01 | .00 |
| □ | 295 | Juan Bonilla | .03 | .01 | .00 |
| □ | 296 | Bobby Brown | .03 | .01 | .00 |
| □ | 297 | Luis DeLeon | .03 | .01 | .00 |
| □ | 298 | Dave Dravecky | .08 | .03 | .01 |
| □ | 299 | Tim Flannery | .03 | .01 | .00 |
| □ | 300 | Steve Garvey | .40 | .16 | .04 |
| □ | 301 | Tony Gwynn | .90 | .36 | .09 |
| □ | 302 | Andy Hawkins | .20 | .08 | .02 |

| No. | Player | | | | No. | Player | | | |
|---|---|---|---|---|---|---|---|---|---|
| ☐ 303 | Ruppert Jones | .03 | .01 | .00 | ☐ 396 | Dennis Eckersley | .05 | .02 | .00 |
| ☐ 304 | Terry Kennedy | .07 | .03 | .01 | ☐ 397 | Dwight Evans | .10 | .04 | .01 |
| ☐ 305 | Tim Lollar | .03 | .01 | .00 | ☐ 398 | Rich Gedman | .09 | .04 | .01 |
| ☐ 306 | Gary Lucas | .03 | .01 | .00 | ☐ 399 | Glenn Hoffman | .03 | .01 | .00 |
| ☐ 307 | Kevin McReynolds | 1.50 | .60 | .15 | ☐ 400 | Bruce Hurst | .08 | .03 | .01 |
| ☐ 308 | Sid Monge | .03 | .01 | .00 | ☐ 401 | John Henry Johnson | .03 | .01 | .00 |
| ☐ 309 | Mario Ramirez | .05 | .02 | .00 | ☐ 402 | Ed Jurak | .03 | .01 | .00 |
| ☐ 310 | Gene Richards | .03 | .01 | .00 | ☐ 403 | Rick Miller | .03 | .01 | .00 |
| ☐ 311 | Luis Salazar | .03 | .01 | .00 | ☐ 404 | Jeff Newman | .03 | .01 | .00 |
| ☐ 312 | Eric Show | .05 | .02 | .00 | ☐ 405 | Reid Nichols | .03 | .01 | .00 |
| ☐ 313 | Elias Sosa | .03 | .01 | .00 | ☐ 406 | Bob Ojeda | .09 | .04 | .01 |
| ☐ 314 | Garry Templeton | .08 | .03 | .01 | ☐ 407 | Jerry Remy | .03 | .01 | .00 |
| ☐ 315 | Mark Thurmond | .12 | .05 | .01 | ☐ 408 | Jim Rice | .35 | .14 | .03 |
| ☐ 316 | Ed Whitson | .06 | .02 | .00 | ☐ 409 | Bob Stanley | .05 | .02 | .00 |
| ☐ 317 | Alan Wiggins | .06 | .02 | .00 | ☐ 410 | Dave Stapleton | .03 | .01 | .00 |
| ☐ 318 | Neil Allen | .06 | .02 | .00 | ☐ 411 | John Tudor | .15 | .06 | .01 |
| ☐ 319 | Joaquin Andujar | .10 | .04 | .01 | ☐ 412 | Carl Yastrzemski | .45 | .18 | .04 |
| ☐ 320 | Steve Braun | .03 | .01 | .00 | ☐ 413 | Buddy Bell | .10 | .04 | .01 |
| ☐ 321 | Glenn Brummer | .03 | .01 | .00 | ☐ 414 | Larry Biittner | .03 | .01 | .00 |
| ☐ 322 | Bob Forsch | .05 | .02 | .00 | ☐ 415 | John Butcher | .03 | .01 | .00 |
| ☐ 323 | David Green | .05 | .02 | .00 | ☐ 416 | Danny Darwin | .03 | .01 | .00 |
| ☐ 324 | George Hendrick | .07 | .03 | .01 | ☐ 417 | Bucky Dent | .06 | .02 | .00 |
| ☐ 325 | Tom Herr | .08 | .03 | .01 | ☐ 418 | Dave Hostetler | .03 | .01 | .00 |
| ☐ 326 | Dane Iorg | .03 | .01 | .00 | ☐ 419 | Charlie Hough | .06 | .02 | .00 |
| ☐ 327 | Jeff Lahti | .03 | .01 | .00 | ☐ 420 | Bobby Johnson | .03 | .01 | .00 |
| ☐ 328 | Dave LaPoint | .05 | .02 | .00 | ☐ 421 | Odell Jones | .03 | .01 | .00 |
| ☐ 329 | Willie McGee | .25 | .10 | .02 | ☐ 422 | Jon Matlack | .05 | .02 | .00 |
| ☐ 330 | Ken Oberkfell | .03 | .01 | .00 | ☐ 423 | Pete O'Brien | .50 | .20 | .05 |
| ☐ 331 | Darrell Porter | .05 | .02 | .00 | ☐ 424 | Larry Parrish | .06 | .02 | .00 |
| ☐ 332 | Jamie Quirk | .03 | .01 | .00 | ☐ 425 | Mickey Rivers | .05 | .02 | .00 |
| ☐ 333 | Mike Ramsey | .03 | .01 | .00 | ☐ 426 | Billy Sample | .03 | .01 | .00 |
| ☐ 334 | Floyd Rayford | .03 | .01 | .00 | ☐ 427 | Dave Schmidt | .03 | .01 | .00 |
| ☐ 335 | Lonnie Smith | .07 | .03 | .01 | ☐ 428 | Mike Smithson | .10 | .04 | .01 |
| ☐ 336 | Ozzie Smith | .14 | .06 | .01 | ☐ 429 | Bill Stein | .03 | .01 | .00 |
| ☐ 337 | John Stuper | .03 | .01 | .00 | ☐ 430 | Dave Stewart | .03 | .01 | .00 |
| ☐ 338 | Bruce Sutter | .14 | .06 | .01 | ☐ 431 | Jim Sundberg | .05 | .02 | .00 |
| ☐ 339 | Andy Van Slyke | .35 | .14 | .03 | ☐ 432 | Frank Tanana | .06 | .02 | .00 |
| ☐ 340 | Dave Von Ohlen | .05 | .02 | .00 | ☐ 433 | Dave Tobik | .03 | .01 | .00 |
| ☐ 341 | Willie Aikens | .05 | .02 | .00 | ☐ 434 | Wayne Tolleson | .03 | .01 | .00 |
| ☐ 342 | Mike Armstrong | .03 | .01 | .00 | ☐ 435 | George Wright | .03 | .01 | .00 |
| ☐ 343 | Bud Black | .05 | .02 | .00 | ☐ 436 | Bill Almon | .03 | .01 | .00 |
| ☐ 344 | George Brett | .45 | .18 | .04 | ☐ 437 | Keith Atherton | .05 | .02 | .00 |
| ☐ 345 | Onix Concepcion | .03 | .01 | .00 | ☐ 438 | Dave Beard | .03 | .01 | .00 |
| ☐ 346 | Keith Creel | .03 | .01 | .00 | ☐ 439 | Tom Burgmeier | .03 | .01 | .00 |
| ☐ 347 | Larry Gura | .05 | .02 | .00 | ☐ 440 | Jeff Burroughs | .05 | .02 | .00 |
| ☐ 348 | Don Hood | .03 | .01 | .00 | ☐ 441 | Chris Codiroli | .07 | .03 | .01 |
| ☐ 349 | Dennis Leonard | .06 | .02 | .00 | ☐ 442 | Tim Conroy | .07 | .03 | .01 |
| ☐ 350 | Hal McRae | .06 | .02 | .00 | ☐ 443 | Mike Davis | .08 | .03 | .01 |
| ☐ 351 | Amos Otis | .07 | .03 | .01 | ☐ 444 | Wayne Gross | .03 | .01 | .00 |
| ☐ 352 | Gaylord Perry | .15 | .06 | .01 | ☐ 445 | Garry Hancock | .03 | .01 | .00 |
| ☐ 353 | Greg Pryor | .03 | .01 | .00 | ☐ 446 | Mike Heath | .03 | .01 | .00 |
| ☐ 354 | Dan Quisenberry | .15 | .06 | .01 | ☐ 447 | Rickey Henderson | .45 | .18 | .04 |
| ☐ 355 | Steve Renko | .03 | .01 | .00 | ☐ 448 | Donnie Hill | .07 | .03 | .01 |
| ☐ 356 | Leon Roberts | .03 | .01 | .00 | ☐ 449 | Bob Kearney | .03 | .01 | .00 |
| ☐ 357 | Pat Sheridan | .10 | .04 | .01 | ☐ 450 | Bill Krueger | .07 | .03 | .01 |
| ☐ 358 | Joe Simpson | .03 | .01 | .00 | ☐ 451 | Rick Langford | .03 | .01 | .00 |
| ☐ 359 | Don Slaught | .05 | .02 | .00 | ☐ 452 | Carney Lansford | .09 | .04 | .01 |
| ☐ 360 | Paul Splittorff | .05 | .02 | .00 | ☐ 453 | Davey Lopes | .07 | .03 | .01 |
| ☐ 361 | U.L. Washington | .03 | .01 | .00 | ☐ 454 | Steve McCatty | .03 | .01 | .00 |
| ☐ 362 | John Wathan | .03 | .01 | .00 | ☐ 455 | Dan Meyer | .03 | .01 | .00 |
| ☐ 363 | Frank White | .07 | .03 | .01 | ☐ 456 | Dwayne Murphy | .06 | .02 | .00 |
| ☐ 364 | Willie Wilson | .15 | .06 | .01 | ☐ 457 | Mike Norris | .05 | .02 | .00 |
| ☐ 365 | Jim Barr | .03 | .01 | .00 | ☐ 458 | Ricky Peters | .03 | .01 | .00 |
| ☐ 366 | Dave Bergman | .03 | .01 | .00 | ☐ 459 | Tony Phillips | .07 | .03 | .01 |
| ☐ 367 | Fred Breining | .03 | .01 | .00 | ☐ 460 | Tom Underwood | .03 | .01 | .00 |
| ☐ 368 | Bob Brenly | .07 | .03 | .01 | ☐ 461 | Mike Warren | .10 | .04 | .01 |
| ☐ 369 | Jack Clark | .12 | .05 | .01 | ☐ 462 | Johnny Bench | .40 | .16 | .04 |
| ☐ 370 | Chili Davis | .10 | .04 | .01 | ☐ 463 | Bruce Berenyi | .03 | .01 | .00 |
| ☐ 371 | Mark Davis | .03 | .01 | .00 | ☐ 464 | Dann Bilardello | .03 | .01 | .00 |
| ☐ 372 | Darrell Evans | .09 | .04 | .01 | ☐ 465 | Cesar Cedeno | .07 | .03 | .01 |
| ☐ 373 | Atlee Hammaker | .05 | .02 | .00 | ☐ 466 | Dave Concepcion | .09 | .04 | .01 |
| ☐ 374 | Mike Krukow | .07 | .03 | .01 | ☐ 467 | Dan Driessen | .05 | .02 | .00 |
| ☐ 375 | Duane Kuiper | .03 | .01 | .00 | ☐ 468 | Nick Esasky | .25 | .10 | .02 |
| ☐ 376 | Bill Laskey | .03 | .01 | .00 | ☐ 469 | Rich Gale | .03 | .01 | .00 |
| ☐ 377 | Gary Lavelle | .05 | .02 | .00 | ☐ 470 | Ben Hayes | .03 | .01 | .00 |
| ☐ 378 | Johnnie LeMaster | .03 | .01 | .00 | ☐ 471 | Paul Householder | .03 | .01 | .00 |
| ☐ 379 | Jeff Leonard | .08 | .03 | .01 | ☐ 472 | Tom Hume | .03 | .01 | .00 |
| ☐ 380 | Randy Lerch | .03 | .01 | .00 | ☐ 473 | Alan Knicely | .03 | .01 | .00 |
| ☐ 381 | Renie Martin | .03 | .01 | .00 | ☐ 474 | Eddie Milner | .03 | .01 | .00 |
| ☐ 382 | Andy McGaffigan | .03 | .01 | .00 | ☐ 475 | Ron Oester | .05 | .02 | .00 |
| ☐ 383 | Greg Minton | .05 | .02 | .00 | ☐ 476 | Kelly Paris | .07 | .03 | .01 |
| ☐ 384 | Tom O'Malley | .03 | .01 | .00 | ☐ 477 | Frank Pastore | .03 | .01 | .00 |
| ☐ 385 | Max Venable | .03 | .01 | .00 | ☐ 478 | Ted Power | .07 | .03 | .01 |
| ☐ 386 | Brad Wellman | .05 | .02 | .00 | ☐ 479 | Joe Price | .03 | .01 | .00 |
| ☐ 387 | Joel Youngblood | .03 | .01 | .00 | ☐ 480 | Charlie Puleo | .03 | .01 | .00 |
| ☐ 388 | Gary Allenson | .03 | .01 | .00 | ☐ 481 | Gary Redus | .25 | .10 | .02 |
| ☐ 389 | Luis Aponte | .03 | .01 | .00 | ☐ 482 | Bill Scherrer | .07 | .03 | .01 |
| ☐ 390 | Tony Armas | .09 | .04 | .01 | ☐ 483 | Mario Soto | .08 | .03 | .01 |
| ☐ 391 | Doug Bird | .03 | .01 | .00 | ☐ 484 | Alex Trevino | .03 | .01 | .00 |
| ☐ 392 | Wade Boggs | 4.00 | 1.60 | .40 | ☐ 485 | Duane Walker | .03 | .01 | .00 |
| ☐ 393 | Dennis Boyd | .75 | .30 | .07 | ☐ 486 | Larry Bowa | .09 | .04 | .01 |
| ☐ 394 | Mike Brown | .05 | .02 | .00 | ☐ 487 | Warren Brusstar | .03 | .01 | .00 |
| ☐ 395 | Mark Clear | .03 | .01 | .00 | ☐ 488 | Bill Buckner | .09 | .04 | .01 |

| | | | |
|---|---|---|---|
| ☐ 489 Bill Campbell | .03 | .01 | .00 |
| ☐ 490 Ron Cey | .09 | .04 | .01 |
| ☐ 491 Jody Davis | .09 | .04 | .01 |
| ☐ 492 Leon Durham | .08 | .03 | .01 |
| ☐ 493 Mel Hall | .10 | .04 | .01 |
| ☐ 494 Ferguson Jenkins | .14 | .06 | .01 |
| ☐ 495 Jay Johnstone | .05 | .02 | .00 |
| ☐ 496 Craig Lefferts | .09 | .04 | .01 |
| ☐ 497 Carmelo Martinez | .20 | .08 | .02 |
| ☐ 498 Jerry Morales | .03 | .01 | .00 |
| ☐ 499 Keith Moreland | .07 | .03 | .01 |
| ☐ 500 Dickie Noles | .03 | .01 | .00 |
| ☐ 501 Mike Proly | .03 | .01 | .00 |
| ☐ 502 Chuck Rainey | .03 | .01 | .00 |
| ☐ 503 Dick Ruthven | .03 | .01 | .00 |
| ☐ 504 Ryne Sandberg | .75 | .30 | .07 |
| ☐ 505 Lee Smith | .09 | .04 | .01 |
| ☐ 506 Steve Trout | .05 | .02 | .00 |
| ☐ 507 Gary Woods | .03 | .01 | .00 |
| ☐ 508 Juan Beniquez | .05 | .02 | .00 |
| ☐ 509 Bob Boone | .06 | .02 | .00 |
| ☐ 510 Rick Burleson | .06 | .02 | .00 |
| ☐ 511 Rod Carew | .35 | .14 | .03 |
| ☐ 512 Bobby Clark | .03 | .01 | .00 |
| ☐ 513 John Curtis | .03 | .01 | .00 |
| ☐ 514 Doug DeCinces | .10 | .04 | .01 |
| ☐ 515 Brian Downing | .05 | .02 | .00 |
| ☐ 516 Tim Foli | .03 | .01 | .00 |
| ☐ 517 Ken Forsch | .03 | .01 | .00 |
| ☐ 518 Bobby Grich | .07 | .03 | .01 |
| ☐ 519 Andy Hassler | .03 | .01 | .00 |
| ☐ 520 Reggie Jackson | .45 | .18 | .04 |
| ☐ 521 Ron Jackson | .03 | .01 | .00 |
| ☐ 522 Tommy John | .15 | .06 | .01 |
| ☐ 523 Bruce Kison | .03 | .01 | .00 |
| ☐ 524 Steve Lubratich | .05 | .02 | .00 |
| ☐ 525 Fred Lynn | .18 | .08 | .01 |
| ☐ 526 Gary Pettis | .45 | .18 | .04 |
| ☐ 527 Luis Sanchez | .03 | .01 | .00 |
| ☐ 528 Daryl Sconiers | .03 | .01 | .00 |
| ☐ 529 Ellis Valentine | .03 | .01 | .00 |
| ☐ 530 Rob Wilfong | .03 | .01 | .00 |
| ☐ 531 Mike Witt | .10 | .04 | .01 |
| ☐ 532 Geoff Zahn | .03 | .01 | .00 |
| ☐ 533 Bud Anderson | .03 | .01 | .00 |
| ☐ 534 Chris Bando | .03 | .01 | .00 |
| ☐ 535 Alan Bannister | .03 | .01 | .00 |
| ☐ 536 Bert Blyleven | .11 | .05 | .01 |
| ☐ 537 Tom Brennan | .03 | .01 | .00 |
| ☐ 538 Jamie Easterly | .03 | .01 | .00 |
| ☐ 539 Juan Eichelberger | .03 | .01 | .00 |
| ☐ 540 Jim Essian | .03 | .01 | .00 |
| ☐ 541 Mike Fischlin | .03 | .01 | .00 |
| ☐ 542 Julio Franco | .12 | .05 | .01 |
| ☐ 543 Mike Hargrove | .05 | .02 | .00 |
| ☐ 544 Toby Harrah | .05 | .02 | .00 |
| ☐ 545 Ron Hassey | .03 | .01 | .00 |
| ☐ 546 Neal Heaton | .10 | .04 | .01 |
| ☐ 547 Bake McBride | .03 | .01 | .00 |
| ☐ 548 Broderick Perkins | .03 | .01 | .00 |
| ☐ 549 Lary Sorensen | .03 | .01 | .00 |
| ☐ 550 Dan Spillner | .03 | .01 | .00 |
| ☐ 551 Rick Sutcliffe | .12 | .05 | .01 |
| ☐ 552 Pat Tabler | .09 | .04 | .01 |
| ☐ 553 Gorman Thomas | .09 | .04 | .01 |
| ☐ 554 Andre Thornton | .07 | .03 | .01 |
| ☐ 555 George Vukovich | .03 | .01 | .00 |
| ☐ 556 Darrell Brown | .05 | .02 | .00 |
| ☐ 557 Tom Brunansky | .14 | .06 | .01 |
| ☐ 558 Randy Bush | .03 | .01 | .00 |
| ☐ 559 Bobby Castillo | .03 | .01 | .00 |
| ☐ 560 John Castino | .03 | .01 | .00 |
| ☐ 561 Ron Davis | .03 | .01 | .00 |
| ☐ 562 Dave Engle | .03 | .01 | .00 |
| ☐ 563 Lenny Faedo | .03 | .01 | .00 |
| ☐ 564 Pete Filson | .03 | .01 | .00 |
| ☐ 565 Gary Gaetti | .10 | .04 | .01 |
| ☐ 566 Mickey Hatcher | .03 | .01 | .00 |
| ☐ 567 Kent Hrbek | .30 | .12 | .03 |
| ☐ 568 Rusty Kuntz | .03 | .01 | .00 |
| ☐ 569 Tim Laudner | .03 | .01 | .00 |
| ☐ 570 Rick Lysander | .03 | .01 | .00 |
| ☐ 571 Bobby Mitchell | .03 | .01 | .00 |
| ☐ 572 Ken Schrom | .06 | .02 | .00 |
| ☐ 573 Ray Smith | .03 | .01 | .00 |
| ☐ 574 Tim Teufel | .35 | .14 | .03 |
| ☐ 575 Frank Viola | .07 | .03 | .01 |
| ☐ 576 Gary Ward | .06 | .02 | .00 |
| ☐ 577 Ron Washington | .03 | .01 | .00 |
| ☐ 578 Len Whitehouse | .03 | .01 | .00 |
| ☐ 579 Al Williams | .03 | .01 | .00 |
| ☐ 580 Bob Bailor | .03 | .01 | .00 |
| ☐ 581 Mark Bradley | .09 | .04 | .01 |

| | | | |
|---|---|---|---|
| ☐ 582 Hubie Brooks | .10 | .04 | .01 |
| ☐ 583 Carlos Diaz | .03 | .01 | .00 |
| ☐ 584 George Foster | .12 | .05 | .01 |
| ☐ 585 Brian Giles | .03 | .01 | .00 |
| ☐ 586 Danny Heep | .03 | .01 | .00 |
| ☐ 587 Keith Hernandez | .25 | .10 | .02 |
| ☐ 588 Ron Hodges | .03 | .01 | .00 |
| ☐ 589 Scott Holman | .03 | .01 | .00 |
| ☐ 590 Dave Kingman | .14 | .06 | .01 |
| ☐ 591 Ed Lynch | .03 | .01 | .00 |
| ☐ 592 Jose Oquendo | .06 | .02 | .00 |
| ☐ 593 Jesse Orosco | .07 | .03 | .01 |
| ☐ 594 Junior Ortiz | .05 | .02 | .00 |
| ☐ 595 Tom Seaver | .30 | .12 | .03 |
| ☐ 596 Doug Sisk | .10 | .04 | .01 |
| ☐ 597 Rusty Staub | .09 | .04 | .01 |
| ☐ 598 John Stearns | .03 | .01 | .00 |
| ☐ 599 Darryl Strawberry | 7.50 | 3.00 | .75 |
| ☐ 600 Craig Swan | .03 | .01 | .00 |
| ☐ 601 Walt Terrell | .25 | .10 | .02 |
| ☐ 602 Mike Torrez | .06 | .02 | .00 |
| ☐ 603 Mookie Wilson | .07 | .03 | .01 |
| ☐ 604 Jamie Allen | .07 | .03 | .01 |
| ☐ 605 Jim Beattie | .03 | .01 | .00 |
| ☐ 606 Tony Bernazard | .05 | .02 | .00 |
| ☐ 607 Manny Castillo | .03 | .01 | .00 |
| ☐ 608 Bill Caudill | .05 | .02 | .00 |
| ☐ 609 Bryan Clark | .03 | .01 | .00 |
| ☐ 610 Al Cowens | .05 | .02 | .00 |
| ☐ 611 Dave Henderson | .07 | .03 | .01 |
| ☐ 612 Steve Henderson | .03 | .01 | .00 |
| ☐ 613 Orlando Mercado | .05 | .02 | .00 |
| ☐ 614 Mike Moore | .07 | .03 | .01 |
| ☐ 615 Ricky Nelson | .07 | .03 | .01 |
| ☐ 616 Spike Owen | .20 | .08 | .02 |
| ☐ 617 Pat Putnam | .03 | .01 | .00 |
| ☐ 618 Ron Roenicke | .03 | .01 | .00 |
| ☐ 619 Mike Stanton | .03 | .01 | .00 |
| ☐ 620 Bob Stoddard | .03 | .01 | .00 |
| ☐ 621 Rick Sweet | .03 | .01 | .00 |
| ☐ 622 Roy Thomas | .05 | .02 | .00 |
| ☐ 623 Ed VandeBerg | .03 | .01 | .00 |
| ☐ 624 Matt Young | .12 | .05 | .01 |
| ☐ 625 Richie Zisk | .05 | .02 | .00 |
| ☐ 626 Fred Lynn: 1982 AS Game RB | .10 | .04 | .01 |
| ☐ 627 Manny Trillo: 1983 AS Game RB | .06 | .02 | .00 |
| ☐ 628 Steve Garvey: NL Iron Man | .20 | .08 | .02 |
| ☐ 629 Rod Carew: AL Batting Runner-Up | .20 | .08 | .02 |
| ☐ 630 Wade Boggs: AL Batting Champion | .40 | .16 | .04 |
| ☐ 631 Tim Raines: Letting Go Of The Raines | .16 | .07 | .01 |
| ☐ 632 Al Oliver: Double Trouble | .10 | .04 | .01 |
| ☐ 633 Steve Sax: AS Second Base | .10 | .04 | .01 |
| ☐ 634 Dickie Thon: AS Shortstop | .06 | .02 | .00 |
| ☐ 635 Ace Firemen: Dan Quisenberry and Tippy Martinez | .06 | .02 | .00 |
| ☐ 636 Reds Reunited: Joe Morgan Pete Rose Tony Perez | .40 | .16 | .04 |
| ☐ 637 Backstop Stars: Lance Parrish Bob Boone | .08 | .03 | .01 |
| ☐ 638 Geo.Brett and G.Perry: Pine Tar 7/24/83 | .25 | .10 | .02 |
| ☐ 639 1983 No Hitters: Dave Righetti Mike Warren Bob Forsch | .08 | .03 | .01 |
| ☐ 640 Bench and Yaz: Retiring Superstars | .25 | .10 | .02 |
| ☐ 641 Gaylord Perry: Going Out In Style | .10 | .04 | .01 |
| ☐ 642 Steve Carlton: 300 Club and Strikeout Record | .20 | .08 | .02 |
| ☐ 643 Altobelli and Owens: WS Managers | .05 | .02 | .00 |
| ☐ 644 Rick Dempsey: World Series MVP | .05 | .02 | .00 |
| ☐ 645 Mike Boddicker: WS Rookie Winner | .07 | .03 | .01 |
| ☐ 646 Scott McGregor: WS Clincher | .05 | .02 | .00 |

| | | | | |
|---|---|---|---|---|
| ☐ 647 | CL: Orioles/Royals ......... | .08 | .01 | .00 |
| ☐ 648 | CL: Phillies/Giants ......... | .07 | .01 | .00 |
| ☐ 649 | CL: White Sox/Red Sox .. | .07 | .01 | .00 |
| ☐ 650 | CL: Tigers/Rangers ......... | .07 | .01 | .00 |
| ☐ 651 | CL: Dodgers/A's ............. | .07 | .01 | .00 |
| ☐ 652 | CL: Yankees/Reds .......... | .07 | .01 | .00 |
| ☐ 653 | CL: Blue Jays/Cubs ........ | .07 | .01 | .00 |
| ☐ 654 | CL: Braves/Angels .......... | .07 | .01 | .00 |
| ☐ 655 | CL: Brewers/Indians ....... | .07 | .01 | .00 |
| ☐ 656 | CL: Astros/Twins ............ | .07 | .01 | .00 |
| ☐ 657 | CL: Pirates/Mets ............ | .07 | .01 | .00 |
| ☐ 658 | CL: Expos/Mariners ........ | .07 | .01 | .00 |
| ☐ 659 | CL: Padres/Specials ....... | .07 | .01 | .00 |
| ☐ 660 | CL: Cardinals/Teams ..... | .08 | .01 | .00 |

## 1984 Fleer Update

The cards in this 132 card set measure 2 1/2" by 3 1/2". For the first time, the Fleer Gum Company issued a traded, extended, or update set. The purpose of the set was the same as the traded sets issued by Topps over the past four years, i.e., to portray players with their proper team for the current year and to portray rookies who were not in their regular issue. Like the Topps Traded sets of the past four years, the Fleer Update sets were distributed through hobby channels only. The set was quite popular with collectors, and apparently, the print run was relatively short, as the set was quickly in short supply and exhibited a rapid and dramatic price increase. The cards are numbered on the back with a U prefix; the order corresponds to the alphabetical order of the subjects' names.

| | MINT | VG-E | F-G |
|---|---|---|---|
| COMPLETE SET ......................... | 250.00 | 100.00 | 25.00 |
| COMMON PLAYER ..................... | .20 | .08 | .02 |

| | | | | |
|---|---|---|---|---|
| ☐ 1U | Willie Aikens .................. | .25 | .10 | .02 |
| ☐ 2U | Luis Aponte ................... | .20 | .08 | .02 |
| ☐ 3U | Mark Bailey ................... | .25 | .10 | .02 |
| ☐ 4U | Bob Bailor ..................... | .20 | .08 | .02 |
| ☐ 5U | Dusty Baker ................... | .25 | .10 | .02 |
| ☐ 6U | Steve Balboni ................. | .25 | .10 | .02 |
| ☐ 7U | Alan Bannister ............... | .20 | .08 | .02 |
| ☐ 8U | Marty Barrett ................. | 4.00 | 1.60 | .40 |
| ☐ 9U | Dave Beard .................... | .20 | .08 | .02 |
| ☐ 10U | Joe Beckwith ................. | .20 | .08 | .02 |
| ☐ 11U | Dave Bergman ............... | .20 | .08 | .02 |
| ☐ 12U | Tony Bernazard ............. | .25 | .10 | .02 |
| ☐ 13U | Bruce Bochte ................. | .25 | .10 | .02 |
| ☐ 14U | Barry Bonnell ................. | .20 | .08 | .02 |
| ☐ 15U | Phil Bradley .................. | 9.00 | 3.75 | .90 |
| ☐ 16U | Fred Breining ................. | .20 | .08 | .02 |
| ☐ 17U | Mike Brown ................... | .25 | .10 | .02 |
| ☐ 18U | Bill Buckner .................. | .35 | .14 | .03 |
| ☐ 19U | Ray Burris .................... | .20 | .08 | .02 |
| ☐ 20U | John Butcher ................. | .20 | .08 | .02 |
| ☐ 21U | Brett Butler .................. | .35 | .14 | .03 |
| ☐ 22U | Enos Cabell .................. | .20 | .08 | .02 |
| ☐ 23U | Bill Campbell ................. | .20 | .08 | .02 |
| ☐ 24U | Bill Caudill ................... | .25 | .10 | .02 |

| | | | | |
|---|---|---|---|---|
| ☐ 25U | Bobby Clark .................. | .20 | .08 | .02 |
| ☐ 26U | Bryan Clark .................. | .20 | .08 | .02 |
| ☐ 27U | Roger Clemens .............. | 75.00 | 30.00 | 7.50 |
| ☐ 28U | Jaime Cocanower ........... | .25 | .10 | .02 |
| ☐ 29U | Ron Darling .................. | 12.00 | 5.00 | 1.20 |
| ☐ 30U | Alvin Davis ................... | 8.00 | 3.25 | .80 |
| ☐ 31U | Bob Dernier .................. | .25 | .10 | .02 |
| ☐ 32U | Carlos Diaz .................. | .20 | .08 | .02 |
| ☐ 33U | Mike Easler .................. | .25 | .10 | .02 |
| ☐ 34U | Dennis Eckersley ........... | .25 | .10 | .02 |
| ☐ 35U | Jim Essian ................... | .20 | .08 | .02 |
| ☐ 36U | Darrell Evans ................ | .35 | .14 | .03 |
| ☐ 37U | Mike Fitzgerald ............. | .25 | .10 | .02 |
| ☐ 38U | Tim Foli ...................... | .20 | .08 | .02 |
| ☐ 39U | John Franco .................. | 2.00 | .80 | .20 |
| ☐ 40U | George Frazier .............. | .20 | .08 | .02 |
| ☐ 41U | Rich Gale ..................... | .20 | .08 | .02 |
| ☐ 42U | Barbaro Garbey ............. | .35 | .14 | .03 |
| ☐ 43U | Dwight Gooden .............. | 75.00 | 30.00 | 6.00 |
| ☐ 44U | Goose Gossage ............. | 1.00 | .40 | .10 |
| ☐ 45U | Wayne Gross ................ | .20 | .08 | .02 |
| ☐ 46U | Mark Gubicza ............... | 1.00 | .40 | .10 |
| ☐ 47U | Jackie Gutierrez ............ | .35 | .14 | .03 |
| ☐ 48U | Toby Harrah ................. | .25 | .10 | .02 |
| ☐ 49U | Ron Hassey .................. | .20 | .08 | .02 |
| ☐ 50U | Richie Hebner ............... | .20 | .08 | .02 |
| ☐ 51U | Willie Hernandez ............ | .75 | .30 | .07 |
| ☐ 52U | Ed Hodge ..................... | .25 | .10 | .02 |
| ☐ 53U | Ricky Horton ................. | .60 | .24 | .06 |
| ☐ 54U | Art Howe ..................... | .20 | .08 | .02 |
| ☐ 55U | Dane Iorg .................... | .20 | .08 | .02 |
| ☐ 56U | Brook Jacoby ................ | 4.00 | 1.60 | .40 |
| ☐ 57U | Dion James .................. | .60 | .24 | .06 |
| ☐ 58U | Mike Jeffcoat ................ | .25 | .10 | .02 |
| ☐ 59U | Ruppert Jones .............. | .25 | .10 | .02 |
| ☐ 60U | Bob Kearney ................. | .20 | .08 | .02 |
| ☐ 61U | Jimmy Key ................... | 2.00 | .80 | .20 |
| ☐ 62U | Dave Kingman ............... | .50 | .20 | .05 |
| ☐ 63U | Brad Komminsk ............. | .50 | .20 | .05 |
| ☐ 64U | Jerry Koosman .............. | .25 | .10 | .02 |
| ☐ 65U | Wayne Krenchicki ......... | .20 | .08 | .02 |
| ☐ 66U | Rusty Kuntz ................. | .20 | .08 | .02 |
| ☐ 67U | Frank LaCorte ............... | .20 | .08 | .02 |
| ☐ 68U | Dennis Lamp ................. | .20 | .08 | .02 |
| ☐ 69U | Tito Landrum ................ | .20 | .08 | .02 |
| ☐ 70U | Mark Langston .............. | 3.00 | 1.20 | .30 |
| ☐ 71U | Rick Leach ................... | .20 | .08 | .02 |
| ☐ 72U | Craig Lefferts ............... | .20 | .08 | .02 |
| ☐ 73U | Gary Lucas ................... | .20 | .08 | .02 |
| ☐ 74U | Jerry Martin ................. | .20 | .08 | .02 |
| ☐ 75U | Carmelo Martinez .......... | .25 | .10 | .02 |
| ☐ 76U | Mike Mason .................. | .50 | .20 | .05 |
| ☐ 77U | Gary Matthews .............. | .25 | .10 | .02 |
| ☐ 78U | Andy McGaffigan ........... | .20 | .08 | .02 |
| ☐ 79U | Joey McLaughlin ............ | .20 | .08 | .02 |
| ☐ 80U | Joe Morgan .................. | 3.00 | 1.20 | .30 |
| ☐ 81U | Darryl Motley ................ | .25 | .10 | .02 |
| ☐ 82U | Graig Nettles ................ | 1.00 | .40 | .10 |
| ☐ 83U | Phil Niekro .................. | 3.00 | 1.20 | .30 |
| ☐ 84U | Ken Oberkfell ................ | .20 | .08 | .02 |
| ☐ 85U | Al Oliver ...................... | .50 | .20 | .05 |
| ☐ 86U | Jorge Orta ................... | .20 | .08 | .02 |
| ☐ 87U | Amos Otis .................... | .25 | .10 | .02 |
| ☐ 88U | Bob Owchinko ............... | .20 | .08 | .02 |
| ☐ 89U | Dave Parker .................. | 3.00 | 1.20 | .30 |
| ☐ 90U | Jack Perconte ............... | .20 | .08 | .02 |
| ☐ 91U | Tony Perez ................... | .75 | .30 | .07 |
| ☐ 92U | Gerald Perry ................. | .35 | .14 | .03 |
| ☐ 93U | Kirby Puckett ................ | 40.00 | 16.00 | 4.00 |
| ☐ 94U | Shane Rawley ................ | .35 | .14 | .03 |
| ☐ 95U | Floyd Rayford ................ | .25 | .10 | .02 |
| ☐ 96U | Ron Reed ..................... | .20 | .08 | .02 |
| ☐ 97U | R.J. Reynolds ................ | 1.50 | .60 | .15 |
| ☐ 98U | Gene Richards ............... | .20 | .08 | .02 |
| ☐ 99U | Jose Rijo ..................... | 1.00 | .40 | .10 |
| ☐ 100U | Jeff Robinson ................ | .25 | .10 | .02 |
| ☐ 101U | Ron Romanick ............... | 1.50 | .60 | .15 |
| ☐ 102U | Pete Rose .................... | 25.00 | 10.00 | 2.50 |
| ☐ 103U | Bret Saberhagen ........... | 6.00 | 2.40 | .60 |
| ☐ 104U | Scott Sanderson ............ | .25 | .10 | .02 |
| ☐ 105U | Dick Schofield .............. | 2.00 | .80 | .20 |
| ☐ 106U | Tom Seaver ................... | 8.00 | 3.25 | .80 |
| ☐ 107U | Jim Slaton ................... | .25 | .10 | .02 |
| ☐ 108U | Mike Smithson .............. | .20 | .08 | .02 |
| ☐ 109U | Lary Sorensen ............... | .20 | .08 | .02 |
| ☐ 110U | Tim Stoddard ............... | .20 | .08 | .02 |
| ☐ 111U | Jeff Stone ................... | 1.00 | .40 | .10 |
| ☐ 112U | Champ Summers ........... | .20 | .08 | .02 |
| ☐ 113U | Jim Sundberg ............... | .25 | .10 | .02 |
| ☐ 114U | Rick Sutcliffe ............... | .75 | .30 | .07 |
| ☐ 115U | Craig Swan ................... | .20 | .08 | .02 |
| ☐ 116U | Derrel Thomas .............. | .20 | .08 | .02 |
| ☐ 117U | Gorman Thomas ........... | .30 | .12 | .03 |

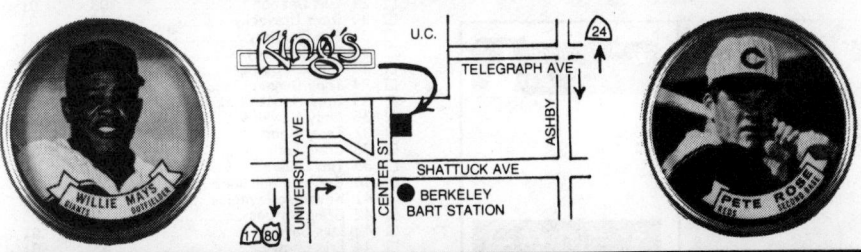

| | | | | |
|---|---|---|---|---|
| ☐ 118U | Alex Trevino | .20 | .08 | .02 |
| ☐ 119U | Manny Trillo | .25 | .10 | .02 |
| ☐ 120U | John Tudor | .50 | .20 | .05 |
| ☐ 121U | Tom Underwood | .20 | .08 | .02 |
| ☐ 122U | Mike Vail | .20 | .08 | .02 |
| ☐ 123U | Tom Waddell | .25 | .10 | .02 |
| ☐ 124U | Gary Ward | .25 | .10 | .02 |
| ☐ 125U | Terry Whitfield | .20 | .08 | .02 |
| ☐ 126U | Curtis Wilkerson | .25 | .10 | .02 |
| ☐ 127U | Frank Williams | .35 | .14 | .03 |
| ☐ 128U | Glenn Wilson | .35 | .14 | .03 |
| ☐ 129U | John Wockenfuss | .20 | .08 | .02 |
| ☐ 130U | Ned Yost | .20 | .08 | .02 |
| ☐ 131U | Mike Young | 2.00 | .80 | .20 |
| ☐ 132U | Checklist: 1-132 | .25 | .02 | .00 |

## 1985 Fleer

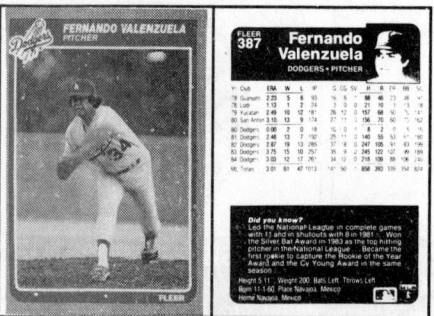

The cards in this 660 card set measure 2 1/2" by 3 1/2". The 1985 Fleer set features fronts which contain the team logo along with the players name and position. The borders enclosing the photo are color coded to correspond to the player's team. In each case, the color is one of the standard colors of that team, e.g., orange for Baltimore, red for St. Louis, etc. The backs feature the same name, number, and statistics format that Fleer has been using over the past few years. The cards are ordered alphabetically within team. The teams are ordered based on their respective performance during the prior year, e.g., World Champion Detroit Tigers (1-25), NL Champion San Diego (26- 48), Chicago Cubs (49-71), New York Mets (72-95), Toronto (96- 119), New York Yankees (120-147), Boston (148-169), Baltimore (170-195), Kansas City (196-218), St. Louis (219-243), Philadelphia (244-269), Minnesota (270-292), California (293- 317), Atlanta (318-342), Houston (343-365), Los Angeles (366- 391), Montreal (392-413), Oakland (414-436), Cleveland (437-460), Pittsburgh (461-481), Seattle (482-505), Chicago White Sox (506- 530), Cincinnati (531-554), Texas (555-575), Milwaukee (576-601), and San Francisco (602-625). Specials (626-643), Rookie pairs (644-653), and checklist cards (654-660) complete the set. The black and white photo on the reverse is included for the third straight year.

| | MINT | VG-E | F-G |
|---|---|---|---|
| COMPLETE SET | 45.00 | 18.00 | 4.50 |
| COMMON PLAYER (1-660) | .03 | .01 | .00 |

| | | | | |
|---|---|---|---|---|
| ☐ 1 | Doug Bair | .05 | .02 | .00 |
| ☐ 2 | Juan Berenguer | .03 | .01 | .00 |
| ☐ 3 | Dave Bergman | .03 | .01 | .00 |
| ☐ 4 | Tom Brookens | .03 | .01 | .00 |
| ☐ 5 | Marty Castillo | .03 | .01 | .00 |
| ☐ 6 | Darrell Evans | .08 | .03 | .01 |
| ☐ 7 | Barbaro Garbey | .08 | .03 | .01 |

| | | | | |
|---|---|---|---|---|
| ☐ 8 | Kirk Gibson | .20 | .08 | .02 |
| ☐ 9 | John Grubb | .03 | .01 | .00 |
| ☐ 10 | Willie Hernandez | .15 | .06 | .01 |
| ☐ 11 | Larry Herndon | .03 | .01 | .00 |
| ☐ 12 | Howard Johnson | .03 | .01 | .00 |
| ☐ 13 | Ruppert Jones | .03 | .01 | .00 |
| ☐ 14 | Rusty Kuntz | .03 | .01 | .00 |
| ☐ 15 | Chet Lemon | .05 | .02 | .00 |
| ☐ 16 | Aurelio Lopez | .03 | .01 | .00 |
| ☐ 17 | Sid Monge | .03 | .01 | .00 |
| ☐ 18 | Jack Morris | .15 | .06 | .01 |
| ☐ 19 | Lance Parrish | .20 | .08 | .02 |
| ☐ 20 | Dan Petry | .10 | .04 | .01 |
| ☐ 21 | Dave Rozema | .03 | .01 | .00 |
| ☐ 22 | Bill Scherrer | .03 | .01 | .00 |
| ☐ 23 | Alan Trammell | .15 | .06 | .01 |
| ☐ 24 | Lou Whitaker | .12 | .05 | .01 |
| ☐ 25 | Milt Wilcox | .03 | .01 | .00 |
| ☐ 26 | Kurt Bevacqua | .03 | .01 | .00 |
| ☐ 27 | Greg Booker | .05 | .02 | .00 |
| ☐ 28 | Bobby Brown | .03 | .01 | .00 |
| ☐ 29 | Luis DeLeon | .03 | .01 | .00 |
| ☐ 30 | Dave Dravecky | .05 | .02 | .00 |
| ☐ 31 | Tim Flannery | .03 | .01 | .00 |
| ☐ 32 | Steve Garvey | .35 | .14 | .03 |
| ☐ 33 | Goose Gossage | .12 | .05 | .01 |
| ☐ 34 | Tony Gwynn | .40 | .16 | .04 |
| ☐ 35 | Greg Harris | .05 | .02 | .00 |
| ☐ 36 | Andy Hawkins | .05 | .02 | .00 |
| ☐ 37 | Terry Kennedy | .07 | .03 | .01 |
| ☐ 38 | Craig Lefferts | .03 | .01 | .00 |
| ☐ 39 | Tim Lollar | .03 | .01 | .00 |
| ☐ 40 | Carmelo Martinez | .05 | .02 | .00 |
| ☐ 41 | Kevin McReynolds | .15 | .06 | .01 |
| ☐ 42 | Graig Nettles | .12 | .05 | .01 |
| ☐ 43 | Luis Salazar | .03 | .01 | .00 |
| ☐ 44 | Eric Show | .03 | .01 | .00 |
| ☐ 45 | Garry Templeton | .07 | .03 | .01 |
| ☐ 46 | Mark Thurmond | .05 | .02 | .00 |
| ☐ 47 | Ed Whitson | .05 | .02 | .00 |
| ☐ 48 | Alan Wiggins | .06 | .02 | .00 |
| ☐ 49 | Rich Bordi | .03 | .01 | .00 |
| ☐ 50 | Larry Bowa | .07 | .03 | .01 |
| ☐ 51 | Warren Brusstar | .03 | .01 | .00 |
| ☐ 52 | Ron Cey | .09 | .04 | .01 |
| ☐ 53 | Henry Cotto | .09 | .04 | .01 |
| ☐ 54 | Jody Davis | .08 | .03 | .01 |
| ☐ 55 | Bob Dernier | .05 | .02 | .00 |
| ☐ 56 | Leon Durham | .08 | .03 | .01 |
| ☐ 57 | Dennis Eckersley | .05 | .02 | .00 |
| ☐ 58 | George Frazier | .03 | .01 | .00 |
| ☐ 59 | Richie Hebner | .03 | .01 | .00 |
| ☐ 60 | Dave Lopes | .06 | .02 | .00 |
| ☐ 61 | Gary Matthews | .07 | .03 | .01 |
| ☐ 62 | Keith Moreland | .08 | .03 | .01 |
| ☐ 63 | Rick Reuschel | .05 | .02 | .00 |
| ☐ 64 | Dick Ruthven | .03 | .01 | .00 |
| ☐ 65 | Ryne Sandberg | .40 | .16 | .04 |
| ☐ 66 | Scott Sanderson | .03 | .01 | .00 |
| ☐ 67 | Lee Smith | .07 | .03 | .01 |
| ☐ 68 | Tim Stoddard | .03 | .01 | .00 |
| ☐ 69 | Rick Sutcliffe | .10 | .04 | .01 |
| ☐ 70 | Steve Trout | .03 | .01 | .00 |
| ☐ 71 | Gary Woods | .03 | .01 | .00 |
| ☐ 72 | Wally Backman | .07 | .03 | .01 |
| ☐ 73 | Bruce Berenyi | .03 | .01 | .00 |
| ☐ 74 | Hubie Brooks | .10 | .04 | .01 |
| ☐ 75 | Kelvin Chapman | .09 | .04 | .01 |
| ☐ 76 | Ron Darling | .50 | .20 | .05 |
| ☐ 77 | Sid Fernandez | .50 | .20 | .05 |
| ☐ 78 | Mike Fitzgerald | .03 | .01 | .00 |
| ☐ 79 | George Foster | .12 | .05 | .01 |
| ☐ 80 | Brent Gaff | .03 | .01 | .00 |
| ☐ 81 | Ron Gardenhire | .03 | .01 | .00 |
| ☐ 82 | Dwight Gooden | 7.50 | 3.00 | .75 |
| ☐ 83 | Tom Gorman | .03 | .01 | .00 |
| ☐ 84 | Danny Heep | .03 | .01 | .00 |
| ☐ 85 | Keith Hernandez | .25 | .10 | .02 |
| ☐ 86 | Ray Knight | .07 | .03 | .01 |
| ☐ 87 | Ed Lynch | .03 | .01 | .00 |
| ☐ 88 | Jose Oquendo | .03 | .01 | .00 |
| ☐ 89 | Jesse Orosco | .05 | .02 | .00 |
| ☐ 90 | Rafael Santana | .08 | .03 | .01 |
| ☐ 91 | Doug Sisk | .03 | .01 | .00 |
| ☐ 92 | Rusty Staub | .07 | .03 | .01 |
| ☐ 93 | Darryl Strawberry | .90 | .36 | .09 |
| ☐ 94 | Walt Terrell | .05 | .02 | .00 |
| ☐ 95 | Mookie Wilson | .07 | .03 | .01 |
| ☐ 96 | Jim Acker | .03 | .01 | .00 |
| ☐ 97 | Willie Aikens | .05 | .02 | .00 |
| ☐ 98 | Doyle Alexander | .05 | .02 | .00 |
| ☐ 99 | Jesse Barfield | .15 | .06 | .01 |
| ☐ 100 | George Bell | .15 | .06 | .01 |

| □ | # | Player | | | |
|---|---|---|---|---|---|
| □ | 101 | Jim Clancy | .05 | .02 | .00 |
| □ | 102 | Dave Collins | .05 | .02 | .00 |
| □ | 103 | Tony Fernandez | .10 | .04 | .01 |
| □ | 104 | Damaso Garcia | .08 | .03 | .01 |
| □ | 105 | Jim Gott | .03 | .01 | .00 |
| □ | 106 | Alfredo Griffin | .05 | .02 | .00 |
| □ | 107 | Garth Iorg | .03 | .01 | .00 |
| □ | 108 | Roy Lee Jackson | .03 | .01 | .00 |
| □ | 109 | Cliff Johnson | .03 | .01 | .00 |
| □ | 110 | Jimmy Key | .35 | .14 | .03 |
| □ | 111 | Dennis Lamp | .03 | .01 | .00 |
| □ | 112 | Rick Leach | .03 | .01 | .00 |
| □ | 113 | Luis Leal | .03 | .01 | .00 |
| □ | 114 | Buck Martinez | .03 | .01 | .00 |
| □ | 115 | Lloyd Moseby | .10 | .04 | .01 |
| □ | 116 | Rance Mulliniks | .03 | .01 | .00 |
| □ | 117 | Dave Stieb | .12 | .05 | .01 |
| □ | 118 | Willie Upshaw | .08 | .03 | .01 |
| □ | 119 | Ernie Whitt | .03 | .01 | .00 |
| □ | 120 | Mike Armstrong | .03 | .01 | .00 |
| □ | 121 | Don Baylor | .12 | .05 | .01 |
| □ | 122 | Marty Bystrom | .03 | .01 | .00 |
| □ | 123 | Rick Cerone | .03 | .01 | .00 |
| □ | 124 | Joe Cowley | .03 | .01 | .00 |
| □ | 125 | Brian Dayett | .03 | .01 | .00 |
| □ | 126 | Tim Foli | .03 | .01 | .00 |
| □ | 127 | Ray Fontenot | .03 | .01 | .00 |
| □ | 128 | Ken Griffey | .07 | .03 | .01 |
| □ | 129 | Ron Guidry | .15 | .06 | .01 |
| □ | 130 | Toby Harrah | .05 | .02 | .00 |
| □ | 131 | Jay Howell | .06 | .02 | .00 |
| □ | 132 | Steve Kemp | .08 | .03 | .01 |
| □ | 133 | Don Mattingly | 7.50 | 3.00 | .75 |
| □ | 134 | Bobby Meacham | .03 | .01 | .00 |
| □ | 135 | John Montefusco | .05 | .02 | .00 |
| □ | 136 | Omar Moreno | .03 | .01 | .00 |
| □ | 137 | Dale Murray | .03 | .01 | .00 |
| □ | 138 | Phil Niekro | .15 | .06 | .01 |
| □ | 139 | Mike Pagliarulo | 1.25 | .50 | .12 |
| □ | 140 | Willie Randolph | .06 | .02 | .00 |
| □ | 141 | Dennis Rasmussen | .07 | .03 | .01 |
| □ | 142 | Dave Righetti | .15 | .06 | .01 |
| □ | 143 | Jose Rijo | .30 | .12 | .03 |
| □ | 144 | Andre Robertson | .03 | .01 | .00 |
| □ | 145 | Bob Shirley | .03 | .01 | .00 |
| □ | 146 | Dave Winfield | .35 | .14 | .03 |
| □ | 147 | Butch Wynegar | .05 | .02 | .00 |
| □ | 148 | Gary Allenson | .03 | .01 | .00 |
| □ | 149 | Tony Armas | .09 | .04 | .01 |
| □ | 150 | Marty Barrett | .12 | .05 | .01 |
| □ | 151 | Wade Boggs | 2.50 | 1.00 | .25 |
| □ | 152 | Dennis Boyd | .08 | .03 | .01 |
| □ | 153 | Bill Buckner | .08 | .03 | .01 |
| □ | 154 | Mark Clear | .03 | .01 | .00 |
| □ | 155 | Roger Clemens | 7.50 | 3.00 | .75 |
| □ | 156 | Steve Crawford | .03 | .01 | .00 |
| □ | 157 | Mike Easler | .06 | .02 | .00 |
| □ | 158 | Dwight Evans | .10 | .04 | .01 |
| □ | 159 | Rich Gedman | .09 | .04 | .01 |
| □ | 160 | Jackie Gutierrez | .07 | .03 | .01 |
| □ | 161 | Bruce Hurst | .07 | .03 | .01 |
| □ | 162 | John Henry Johnson | .03 | .01 | .00 |
| □ | 163 | Rick Miller | .03 | .01 | .00 |
| □ | 164 | Reid Nichols | .03 | .01 | .00 |
| □ | 165 | Al Nipper | .15 | .06 | .01 |
| □ | 166 | Bob Ojeda | .09 | .04 | .01 |
| □ | 167 | Jerry Remy | .03 | .01 | .00 |
| □ | 168 | Jim Rice | .35 | .14 | .03 |
| □ | 169 | Bob Stanley | .05 | .02 | .00 |
| □ | 170 | Mike Boddicker | .09 | .04 | .01 |
| □ | 171 | Al Bumbry | .03 | .01 | .00 |
| □ | 172 | Todd Cruz | .03 | .01 | .00 |
| □ | 173 | Rich Dauer | .03 | .01 | .00 |
| □ | 174 | Storm Davis | .07 | .03 | .01 |
| □ | 175 | Rick Dempsey | .05 | .02 | .00 |
| □ | 176 | Jim Dwyer | .03 | .01 | .00 |
| □ | 177 | Mike Flanagan | .06 | .02 | .00 |
| □ | 178 | Dan Ford | .03 | .01 | .00 |
| □ | 179 | Wayne Gross | .03 | .01 | .00 |
| □ | 180 | John Lowenstein | .03 | .01 | .00 |
| □ | 181 | Dennis Martinez | .03 | .01 | .00 |
| □ | 182 | Tippy Martinez | .03 | .01 | .00 |
| □ | 183 | Scott McGregor | .07 | .03 | .01 |
| □ | 184 | Eddie Murray | .40 | .16 | .04 |
| □ | 185 | Joe Nolan | .03 | .01 | .00 |
| □ | 186 | Floyd Rayford | .03 | .01 | .00 |
| □ | 187 | Cal Ripken | .40 | .16 | .04 |
| □ | 188 | Gary Roenicke | .05 | .02 | .00 |
| □ | 189 | Lenn Sakata | .03 | .01 | .00 |
| □ | 190 | John Shelby | .03 | .01 | .00 |
| □ | 191 | Ken Singleton | .07 | .03 | .01 |
| □ | 192 | Sammy Stewart | .03 | .01 | .00 |
| □ | 193 | Bill Swaggerty | .09 | .04 | .01 |
| □ | 194 | Tom Underwood | .03 | .01 | .00 |
| □ | 195 | Mike Young | .15 | .06 | .01 |
| □ | 196 | Steve Balboni | .07 | .03 | .01 |
| □ | 197 | Joe Beckwith | .03 | .01 | .00 |
| □ | 198 | Bud Black | .03 | .01 | .00 |
| □ | 199 | George Brett | .40 | .16 | .04 |
| □ | 200 | Onix Concepcion | .03 | .01 | .00 |
| □ | 201 | Mark Gubicza | .25 | .10 | .02 |
| □ | 202 | Larry Gura | .05 | .02 | .00 |
| □ | 203 | Mark Huismann | .05 | .02 | .00 |
| □ | 204 | Dane Iorg | .03 | .01 | .00 |
| □ | 205 | Danny Jackson | .06 | .02 | .00 |
| □ | 206 | Charlie Leibrandt | .06 | .02 | .00 |
| □ | 207 | Hal McRae | .06 | .02 | .00 |
| □ | 208 | Darryl Motley | .03 | .01 | .00 |
| □ | 209 | Jorge Orta | .03 | .01 | .00 |
| □ | 210 | Greg Pryor | .03 | .01 | .00 |
| □ | 211 | Dan Quisenberry | .12 | .05 | .01 |
| □ | 212 | Bret Saberhagen | 1.00 | .40 | .10 |
| □ | 213 | Pat Sheridan | .03 | .01 | .00 |
| □ | 214 | Don Slaught | .03 | .01 | .00 |
| □ | 215 | U.L. Washington | .03 | .01 | .00 |
| □ | 216 | John Wathan | .03 | .01 | .00 |
| □ | 217 | Frank White | .06 | .02 | .00 |
| □ | 218 | Willie Wilson | .12 | .05 | .01 |
| □ | 219 | Neil Allen | .05 | .02 | .00 |
| □ | 220 | Joaquin Andujar | .08 | .03 | .01 |
| □ | 221 | Steve Braun | .03 | .01 | .00 |
| □ | 222 | Danny Cox | .08 | .03 | .01 |
| □ | 223 | Bob Forsch | .06 | .02 | .00 |
| □ | 224 | David Green | .05 | .02 | .00 |
| □ | 225 | George Hendrick | .06 | .02 | .00 |
| □ | 226 | Tom Herr | .08 | .03 | .01 |
| □ | 227 | Ricky Horton | .15 | .06 | .01 |
| □ | 228 | Art Howe | .03 | .01 | .00 |
| □ | 229 | Mike Jorgensen | .03 | .01 | .00 |
| □ | 230 | Kurt Kepshire | .08 | .03 | .01 |
| □ | 231 | Jeff Lahti | .03 | .01 | .00 |
| □ | 232 | Tito Landrum | .03 | .01 | .00 |
| □ | 233 | Dave LaPoint | .03 | .01 | .00 |
| □ | 234 | Willie McGee | .25 | .10 | .02 |
| □ | 235 | Tom Nieto | .05 | .02 | .00 |
| □ | 236 | Terry Pendleton | .35 | .14 | .03 |
| □ | 237 | Darrell Porter | .05 | .02 | .00 |
| □ | 238 | Dave Rucker | .03 | .01 | .00 |
| □ | 239 | Lonnie Smith | .06 | .02 | .00 |
| □ | 240 | Ozzie Smith | .10 | .04 | .01 |
| □ | 241 | Bruce Sutter | .12 | .05 | .01 |
| □ | 242 | Andy Van Slyke | .07 | .03 | .01 |
| □ | 243 | Dave Von Ohlen | .03 | .01 | .00 |
| □ | 244 | Larry Andersen | .03 | .01 | .00 |
| □ | 245 | Bill Campbell | .03 | .01 | .00 |
| □ | 246 | Steve Carlton | .30 | .12 | .03 |
| □ | 247 | Tim Corcoran | .03 | .01 | .00 |
| □ | 248 | Ivan DeJesus | .03 | .01 | .00 |
| □ | 249 | John Denny | .06 | .02 | .00 |
| □ | 250 | Bo Diaz | .05 | .02 | .00 |
| □ | 251 | Greg Gross | .03 | .01 | .00 |
| □ | 252 | Kevin Gross | .03 | .01 | .00 |
| □ | 253 | Von Hayes | .12 | .05 | .01 |
| □ | 254 | Al Holland | .03 | .01 | .00 |
| □ | 255 | Charles Hudson | .05 | .02 | .00 |
| □ | 256 | Jerry Koosman | .07 | .03 | .01 |
| □ | 257 | Joe Lefebvre | .03 | .01 | .00 |
| □ | 258 | Sixto Lezcano | .03 | .01 | .00 |
| □ | 259 | Garry Maddox | .05 | .02 | .00 |
| □ | 260 | Len Matuszek | .03 | .01 | .00 |
| □ | 261 | Tug McGraw | .08 | .03 | .01 |
| □ | 262 | Al Oliver | .10 | .04 | .01 |
| □ | 263 | Shane Rawley | .07 | .03 | .01 |
| □ | 264 | Juan Samuel | .20 | .08 | .02 |
| □ | 265 | Mike Schmidt | .35 | .14 | .03 |
| □ | 266 | Jeff Stone | .20 | .08 | .02 |
| □ | 267 | Ozzie Virgil | .06 | .02 | .00 |
| □ | 268 | Glenn Wilson | .08 | .03 | .01 |
| □ | 269 | John Wockenfuss | .03 | .01 | .00 |
| □ | 270 | Darrell Brown | .03 | .01 | .00 |
| □ | 271 | Tom Brunansky | .10 | .04 | .01 |
| □ | 272 | Randy Bush | .03 | .01 | .00 |
| □ | 273 | John Butcher | .03 | .01 | .00 |
| □ | 274 | Bobby Castillo | .03 | .01 | .00 |
| □ | 275 | Ron Davis | .03 | .01 | .00 |
| □ | 276 | Dave Engle | .03 | .01 | .00 |
| □ | 277 | Pete Filson | .03 | .01 | .00 |
| □ | 278 | Gary Gaetti | .09 | .04 | .01 |
| □ | 279 | Mickey Hatcher | .03 | .01 | .00 |
| □ | 280 | Ed Hodge | .06 | .02 | .00 |
| □ | 281 | Kent Hrbek | .25 | .10 | .02 |
| □ | 282 | Houston Jimenez | .03 | .01 | .00 |
| □ | 283 | Tim Laudner | .03 | .01 | .00 |
| □ | 284 | Rick Lysander | .03 | .01 | .00 |
| □ | 285 | Dave Meier | .09 | .04 | .01 |
| □ | 286 | Kirby Puckett | 5.00 | 2.00 | .50 |

| # | Player | | | |
|---|---|---|---|---|
| ☐ 287 | Pat Putnam | .03 | .01 | .00 |
| ☐ 288 | Ken Schrom | .06 | .02 | .00 |
| ☐ 289 | Mike Smithson | .05 | .02 | .00 |
| ☐ 290 | Tim Teufel | .06 | .02 | .00 |
| ☐ 291 | Frank Viola | .08 | .03 | .01 |
| ☐ 292 | Ron Washington | .03 | .01 | .00 |
| ☐ 293 | Don Aase | .05 | .02 | .00 |
| ☐ 294 | Juan Beniquez | .05 | .02 | .00 |
| ☐ 295 | Bob Boone | .05 | .02 | .00 |
| ☐ 296 | Mike Brown (Angels OF) | .05 | .02 | .00 |
| ☐ 297 | Rod Carew | .30 | .12 | .03 |
| ☐ 298 | Doug Corbett | .03 | .01 | .00 |
| ☐ 299 | Doug DeCinces | .08 | .03 | .01 |
| ☐ 300 | Brian Downing | .05 | .02 | .00 |
| ☐ 301 | Ken Forsch | .03 | .01 | .00 |
| ☐ 302 | Bobby Grich | .06 | .02 | .00 |
| ☐ 303 | Reggie Jackson | .35 | .14 | .03 |
| ☐ 304 | Tommy John | .10 | .04 | .01 |
| ☐ 305 | Curt Kaufman | .08 | .03 | .01 |
| ☐ 306 | Bruce Kison | .03 | .01 | .00 |
| ☐ 307 | Fred Lynn | .15 | .06 | .01 |
| ☐ 308 | Gary Pettis | .08 | .03 | .01 |
| ☐ 309 | Ron Romanick | .25 | .10 | .02 |
| ☐ 310 | Luis Sanchez | .03 | .01 | .00 |
| ☐ 311 | Dick Schofield | .07 | .03 | .01 |
| ☐ 312 | Daryl Sconiers | .03 | .01 | .00 |
| ☐ 313 | Jim Slaton | .03 | .01 | .00 |
| ☐ 314 | Derrel Thomas | .03 | .01 | .00 |
| ☐ 315 | Rob Wilfong | .03 | .01 | .00 |
| ☐ 316 | Mike Witt | .10 | .04 | .01 |
| ☐ 317 | Geoff Zahn | .03 | .01 | .00 |
| ☐ 318 | Len Barker | .03 | .01 | .00 |
| ☐ 319 | Steve Bedrosian | .06 | .02 | .00 |
| ☐ 320 | Bruce Benedict | .03 | .01 | .00 |
| ☐ 321 | Rick Camp | .03 | .01 | .00 |
| ☐ 322 | Chris Chambliss | .05 | .02 | .00 |
| ☐ 323 | Jeff Dedmon | .07 | .03 | .01 |
| ☐ 324 | Terry Forster | .06 | .02 | .00 |
| ☐ 325 | Gene Garber | .03 | .01 | .00 |
| ☐ 326 | Albert Hall | .08 | .03 | .01 |
| ☐ 327 | Terry Harper | .03 | .01 | .00 |
| ☐ 328 | Bob Horner | .15 | .06 | .01 |
| ☐ 329 | Glenn Hubbard | .03 | .01 | .00 |
| ☐ 330 | Randy Johnson | .03 | .01 | .00 |
| ☐ 331 | Brad Komminsk | .06 | .02 | .00 |
| ☐ 332 | Rick Mahler | .03 | .01 | .00 |
| ☐ 333 | Craig McMurtry | .03 | .01 | .00 |
| ☐ 334 | Donnie Moore | .05 | .02 | .00 |
| ☐ 335 | Dale Murphy | .50 | .20 | .05 |
| ☐ 336 | Ken Oberkfell | .03 | .01 | .00 |
| ☐ 337 | Pascual Perez | .03 | .01 | .00 |
| ☐ 338 | Gerald Perry | .03 | .01 | .00 |
| ☐ 339 | Rafael Ramirez | .03 | .01 | .00 |
| ☐ 340 | Jerry Royster | .03 | .01 | .00 |
| ☐ 341 | Alex Trevino | .03 | .01 | .00 |
| ☐ 342 | Claudell Washington | .06 | .02 | .00 |
| ☐ 343 | Alan Ashby | .03 | .01 | .00 |
| ☐ 344 | Mark Bailey | .07 | .03 | .01 |
| ☐ 345 | Kevin Bass | .07 | .03 | .01 |
| ☐ 346 | Enos Cabell | .03 | .01 | .00 |
| ☐ 347 | Jose Cruz | .10 | .04 | .01 |
| ☐ 348 | Bill Dawley | .03 | .01 | .00 |
| ☐ 349 | Frank DiPino | .03 | .01 | .00 |
| ☐ 350 | Bill Doran | .07 | .03 | .01 |
| ☐ 351 | Phil Garner | .05 | .02 | .00 |
| ☐ 352 | Bob Knepper | .08 | .03 | .01 |
| ☐ 353 | Mike LaCoss | .03 | .01 | .00 |
| ☐ 354 | Jerry Mumphrey | .05 | .02 | .00 |
| ☐ 355 | Joe Niekro | .08 | .03 | .01 |
| ☐ 356 | Terry Puhl | .05 | .02 | .00 |
| ☐ 357 | Craig Reynolds | .03 | .01 | .00 |
| ☐ 358 | Vern Ruhle | .03 | .01 | .00 |
| ☐ 359 | Nolan Ryan | .30 | .12 | .03 |
| ☐ 360 | Joe Sambito | .05 | .02 | .00 |
| ☐ 361 | Mike Scott | .15 | .06 | .01 |
| ☐ 362 | Dave Smith | .07 | .03 | .01 |
| ☐ 363 | Julio Solano | .07 | .03 | .01 |
| ☐ 364 | Dickie Thon | .05 | .02 | .00 |
| ☐ 365 | Denny Walling | .03 | .01 | .00 |
| ☐ 366 | Dave Anderson | .03 | .01 | .00 |
| ☐ 367 | Bob Bailor | .03 | .01 | .00 |
| ☐ 368 | Greg Brock | .05 | .02 | .00 |
| ☐ 369 | Carlos Diaz | .03 | .01 | .00 |
| ☐ 370 | Pedro Guerrero | .25 | .10 | .02 |
| ☐ 371 | Orel Hershiser | 1.50 | .60 | .15 |
| ☐ 372 | Rick Honeycutt | .05 | .02 | .00 |
| ☐ 373 | Burt Hooton | .03 | .01 | .00 |
| ☐ 374 | Ken Howell | .20 | .08 | .02 |
| ☐ 375 | Ken Landreaux | .05 | .02 | .00 |
| ☐ 376 | Candy Maldonado | .06 | .02 | .00 |
| ☐ 377 | Mike Marshall | .12 | .05 | .01 |
| ☐ 378 | Tom Niedenfuer | .06 | .02 | .00 |
| ☐ 379 | Alejandro Pena | .05 | .02 | .00 |
| ☐ 380 | Jerry Reuss | .05 | .02 | .00 |
| ☐ 381 | R.J. Reynolds | .25 | .10 | .02 |
| ☐ 382 | German Rivera | .10 | .04 | .01 |
| ☐ 383 | Bill Russell | .05 | .02 | .00 |
| ☐ 384 | Steve Sax | .15 | .06 | .01 |
| ☐ 385 | Mike Scioscia | .05 | .02 | .00 |
| ☐ 386 | Franklin Stubbs | .60 | .24 | .06 |
| ☐ 387 | Fernando Valenzuela | .30 | .12 | .03 |
| ☐ 388 | Bob Welch | .06 | .02 | .00 |
| ☐ 389 | Terry Whitfield | .03 | .01 | .00 |
| ☐ 390 | Steve Yeager | .05 | .02 | .00 |
| ☐ 391 | Pat Zachry | .03 | .01 | .00 |
| ☐ 392 | Fred Breining | .03 | .01 | .00 |
| ☐ 393 | Gary Carter | .30 | .12 | .03 |
| ☐ 394 | Andre Dawson | .20 | .08 | .02 |
| ☐ 395 | Miguel Dilone | .03 | .01 | .00 |
| ☐ 396 | Dan Driessen | .05 | .02 | .00 |
| ☐ 397 | Doug Flynn | .03 | .01 | .00 |
| ☐ 398 | Terry Francona | .05 | .02 | .00 |
| ☐ 399 | Bill Gullickson | .05 | .02 | .00 |
| ☐ 400 | Bob James | .05 | .02 | .00 |
| ☐ 401 | Charlie Lea | .05 | .02 | .00 |
| ☐ 402 | Bryan Little | .03 | .01 | .00 |
| ☐ 403 | Gary Lucas | .03 | .01 | .00 |
| ☐ 404 | David Palmer | .05 | .02 | .00 |
| ☐ 405 | Tim Raines | .20 | .08 | .02 |
| ☐ 406 | Mike Ramsey | .03 | .01 | .00 |
| ☐ 407 | Jeff Reardon | .06 | .02 | .00 |
| ☐ 408 | Steve Rogers | .06 | .02 | .00 |
| ☐ 409 | Dan Schatzeder | .03 | .01 | .00 |
| ☐ 410 | Bryn Smith | .05 | .02 | .00 |
| ☐ 411 | Mike Stenhouse | .05 | .02 | .00 |
| ☐ 412 | Tim Wallach | .08 | .03 | .01 |
| ☐ 413 | Jim Wohlford | .03 | .01 | .00 |
| ☐ 414 | Bill Almon | .03 | .01 | .00 |
| ☐ 415 | Keith Atherton | .03 | .01 | .00 |
| ☐ 416 | Bruce Bochte | .05 | .02 | .00 |
| ☐ 417 | Tom Burgmeier | .03 | .01 | .00 |
| ☐ 418 | Ray Burris | .03 | .01 | .00 |
| ☐ 419 | Bill Caudill | .05 | .02 | .00 |
| ☐ 420 | Chris Codiroli | .03 | .01 | .00 |
| ☐ 421 | Tim Conroy | .03 | .01 | .00 |
| ☐ 422 | Mike Heath | .03 | .01 | .00 |
| ☐ 423 | Jim Essian | .03 | .01 | .00 |
| ☐ 424 | Mike Heath | .03 | .01 | .00 |
| ☐ 425 | Rickey Henderson | .40 | .16 | .04 |
| ☐ 426 | Donnie Hill | .03 | .01 | .00 |
| ☐ 427 | Dave Kingman | .09 | .04 | .01 |
| ☐ 428 | Bill Krueger | .03 | .01 | .00 |
| ☐ 429 | Carney Lansford | .08 | .03 | .01 |
| ☐ 430 | Steve McCatty | .03 | .01 | .00 |
| ☐ 431 | Joe Morgan | .15 | .06 | .01 |
| ☐ 432 | Dwayne Murphy | .06 | .02 | .00 |
| ☐ 433 | Tony Phillips | .03 | .01 | .00 |
| ☐ 434 | Lary Sorensen | .03 | .01 | .00 |
| ☐ 435 | Mike Warren | .05 | .02 | .00 |
| ☐ 436 | Curt Young | .09 | .04 | .01 |
| ☐ 437 | Luis Aponte | .03 | .01 | .00 |
| ☐ 438 | Chris Bando | .03 | .01 | .00 |
| ☐ 439 | Tony Bernazard | .05 | .02 | .00 |
| ☐ 440 | Bert Blyleven | .09 | .04 | .01 |
| ☐ 441 | Brett Butler | .09 | .04 | .01 |
| ☐ 442 | Ernie Camacho | .03 | .01 | .00 |
| ☐ 443 | Joe Carter | .25 | .10 | .02 |
| ☐ 444 | Carmelo Castillo | .03 | .01 | .00 |
| ☐ 445 | Jamie Easterly | .03 | .01 | .00 |
| ☐ 446 | Steve Farr | .09 | .04 | .01 |
| ☐ 447 | Mike Fischlin | .03 | .01 | .00 |
| ☐ 448 | Julio Franco | .10 | .04 | .01 |
| ☐ 449 | Mel Hall | .08 | .03 | .01 |
| ☐ 450 | Mike Hargrove | .05 | .02 | .00 |
| ☐ 451 | Neal Heaton | .05 | .02 | .00 |
| ☐ 452 | Brook Jacoby | .12 | .05 | .01 |
| ☐ 453 | Mike Jeffcoat | .05 | .02 | .00 |
| ☐ 454 | Don Schulze | .07 | .03 | .01 |
| ☐ 455 | Roy Smith | .07 | .03 | .01 |
| ☐ 456 | Pat Tabler | .08 | .03 | .01 |
| ☐ 457 | Andre Thornton | .07 | .03 | .01 |
| ☐ 458 | George Vukovich | .03 | .01 | .00 |
| ☐ 459 | Tom Waddell | .10 | .04 | .01 |
| ☐ 460 | Jerry Willard | .03 | .01 | .00 |
| ☐ 461 | Dale Berra | .05 | .02 | .00 |
| ☐ 462 | John Candelaria | .07 | .03 | .01 |
| ☐ 463 | Jose DeLeon | .05 | .02 | .00 |
| ☐ 464 | Doug Frobel | .03 | .01 | .00 |
| ☐ 465 | Cecilio Guante | .03 | .01 | .00 |
| ☐ 466 | Brian Harper | .03 | .01 | .00 |
| ☐ 467 | Lee Lacy | .05 | .02 | .00 |
| ☐ 468 | Bill Madlock | .12 | .05 | .01 |
| ☐ 469 | Lee Mazzilli | .05 | .02 | .00 |
| ☐ 470 | Larry McWilliams | .05 | .02 | .00 |
| ☐ 471 | Jim Morrison | .03 | .01 | .00 |

| | | | | | |
|---|---|---|---|---|---|
| ☐ 472 | Tony Pena | .12 | .05 | .01 |
| ☐ 473 | Johnny Ray | .09 | .04 | .01 |
| ☐ 474 | Rick Rhoden | .07 | .03 | .01 |
| ☐ 475 | Don Robinson | .03 | .01 | .00 |
| ☐ 476 | Rod Scurry | .03 | .01 | .00 |
| ☐ 477 | Kent Tekulve | .06 | .02 | .00 |
| ☐ 478 | Jason Thompson | .06 | .02 | .00 |
| ☐ 479 | John Tudor | .15 | .06 | .01 |
| ☐ 480 | Lee Tunnell | .03 | .01 | .00 |
| ☐ 481 | Marvell Wynne | .05 | .02 | .00 |
| ☐ 482 | Salome Barojas | .03 | .01 | .00 |
| ☐ 483 | Dave Beard | .03 | .01 | .00 |
| ☐ 484 | Jim Beattie | .03 | .01 | .00 |
| ☐ 485 | Barry Bonnell | .03 | .01 | .00 |
| ☐ 486 | Phil Bradley | 1.25 | .50 | .12 |
| ☐ 487 | Al Cowens | .05 | .02 | .00 |
| ☐ 488 | Alvin Davis | 1.25 | .50 | .12 |
| ☐ 489 | Dave Henderson | .07 | .03 | .01 |
| ☐ 490 | Steve Henderson | .03 | .01 | .00 |
| ☐ 491 | Bob Kearney | .03 | .01 | .00 |
| ☐ 492 | Mark Langston | .50 | .20 | .05 |
| ☐ 493 | Larry Milbourne | .03 | .01 | .00 |
| ☐ 494 | Paul Mirabella | .03 | .01 | .00 |
| ☐ 495 | Mike Moore | .06 | .02 | .00 |
| ☐ 496 | Edwin Nunez | .05 | .02 | .00 |
| ☐ 497 | Spike Owen | .05 | .02 | .00 |
| ☐ 498 | Jack Perconte | .03 | .01 | .00 |
| ☐ 499 | Ken Phelps | .05 | .02 | .00 |
| ☐ 500 | Jim Presley | 1.50 | .60 | .15 |
| ☐ 501 | Mike Stanton | .03 | .01 | .00 |
| ☐ 502 | Bob Stoddard | .03 | .01 | .00 |
| ☐ 503 | Gorman Thomas | .09 | .04 | .01 |
| ☐ 504 | Ed VandeBerg | .03 | .01 | .00 |
| ☐ 505 | Matt Young | .03 | .01 | .00 |
| ☐ 506 | Juan Agosto | .03 | .01 | .00 |
| ☐ 507 | Harold Baines | .20 | .08 | .02 |
| ☐ 508 | Floyd Bannister | .05 | .02 | .00 |
| ☐ 509 | Britt Burns | .06 | .02 | .00 |
| ☐ 510 | Julio Cruz | .03 | .01 | .00 |
| ☐ 511 | Richard Dotson | .06 | .02 | .00 |
| ☐ 512 | Jerry Dybzinski | .03 | .01 | .00 |
| ☐ 513 | Carlton Fisk | .12 | .05 | .01 |
| ☐ 514 | Scott Fletcher | .05 | .02 | .00 |
| ☐ 515 | Jerry Hairston | .03 | .01 | .00 |
| ☐ 516 | Marc Hill | .03 | .01 | .00 |
| ☐ 517 | LaMarr Hoyt | .06 | .02 | .00 |
| ☐ 518 | Ron Kittle | .12 | .05 | .01 |
| ☐ 519 | Rudy Law | .03 | .01 | .00 |
| ☐ 520 | Vance Law | .03 | .01 | .00 |
| ☐ 521 | Greg Luzinski | .09 | .04 | .01 |
| ☐ 522 | Gene Nelson | .03 | .01 | .00 |
| ☐ 523 | Tom Paciorek | .03 | .01 | .00 |
| ☐ 524 | Ron Reed | .03 | .01 | .00 |
| ☐ 525 | Bert Roberge | .03 | .01 | .00 |
| ☐ 526 | Tom Seaver | .25 | .10 | .02 |
| ☐ 527 | Roy Smalley | .05 | .02 | .00 |
| ☐ 528 | Dan Spillner | .03 | .01 | .00 |
| ☐ 529 | Mike Squires | .03 | .01 | .00 |
| ☐ 530 | Greg Walker | .12 | .05 | .01 |
| ☐ 531 | Cesar Cedeno | .07 | .03 | .01 |
| ☐ 532 | Dave Concepcion | .08 | .03 | .01 |
| ☐ 533 | Eric Davis | 6.00 | 2.40 | .60 |
| ☐ 534 | Nick Esasky | .05 | .02 | .00 |
| ☐ 535 | Tom Foley | .03 | .01 | .00 |
| ☐ 536 | John Franco | .40 | .16 | .04 |
| ☐ 537 | Brad Gulden | .03 | .01 | .00 |
| ☐ 538 | Tom Hume | .03 | .01 | .00 |
| ☐ 539 | Wayne Krenchicki | .03 | .01 | .00 |
| ☐ 540 | Andy McGaffigan | .03 | .01 | .00 |
| ☐ 541 | Eddie Milner | .05 | .02 | .00 |
| ☐ 542 | Ron Oester | .05 | .02 | .00 |
| ☐ 543 | Bob Owchinko | .03 | .01 | .00 |
| ☐ 544 | Dave Parker | .15 | .06 | .01 |
| ☐ 545 | Frank Pastore | .03 | .01 | .00 |
| ☐ 546 | Tony Perez | .12 | .05 | .01 |
| ☐ 547 | Ted Power | .07 | .03 | .01 |
| ☐ 548 | Joe Price | .03 | .01 | .00 |
| ☐ 549 | Gary Redus | .06 | .02 | .00 |
| ☐ 550 | Pete Rose | .75 | .30 | .07 |
| ☐ 551 | Jeff Russell | .03 | .01 | .00 |
| ☐ 552 | Mario Soto | .06 | .02 | .00 |
| ☐ 553 | Jay Tibbs | .15 | .06 | .01 |
| ☐ 554 | Duane Walker | .03 | .01 | .00 |
| ☐ 555 | Alan Bannister | .03 | .01 | .00 |
| ☐ 556 | Buddy Bell | .09 | .04 | .01 |
| ☐ 557 | Danny Darwin | .03 | .01 | .00 |
| ☐ 558 | Charlie Hough | .07 | .03 | .01 |
| ☐ 559 | Bobby Jones | .03 | .01 | .00 |
| ☐ 560 | Odell Jones | .03 | .01 | .00 |
| ☐ 561 | Jeff Kunkel | .09 | .04 | .01 |
| ☐ 562 | Mike Mason | .09 | .04 | .01 |
| ☐ 563 | Pete O'Brien | .08 | .03 | .01 |
| ☐ 564 | Larry Parrish | .06 | .02 | .00 |

| | | | | | |
|---|---|---|---|---|---|
| ☐ 565 | Mickey Rivers | .05 | .02 | .00 |
| ☐ 566 | Billy Sample | .03 | .01 | .00 |
| ☐ 567 | Dave Schmidt | .03 | .01 | .00 |
| ☐ 568 | Donnie Scott | .05 | .02 | .00 |
| ☐ 569 | Dave Stewart | .03 | .01 | .00 |
| ☐ 570 | Frank Tanana | .05 | .02 | .00 |
| ☐ 571 | Wayne Tolleson | .03 | .01 | .00 |
| ☐ 572 | Gary Ward | .06 | .02 | .00 |
| ☐ 573 | Curtis Wilkerson | .05 | .02 | .00 |
| ☐ 574 | George Wright | .03 | .01 | .00 |
| ☐ 575 | Ned Yost | .03 | .01 | .00 |
| ☐ 576 | Mark Brouhard | .03 | .01 | .00 |
| ☐ 577 | Mike Caldwell | .05 | .02 | .00 |
| ☐ 578 | Bobby Clark | .03 | .01 | .00 |
| ☐ 579 | Jaime Cocanower | .05 | .02 | .00 |
| ☐ 580 | Cecil Cooper | .10 | .04 | .01 |
| ☐ 581 | Rollie Fingers | .15 | .06 | .01 |
| ☐ 582 | Jim Gantner | .05 | .02 | .00 |
| ☐ 583 | Moose Haas | .05 | .02 | .00 |
| ☐ 584 | Dion James | .06 | .02 | .00 |
| ☐ 585 | Pete Ladd | .03 | .01 | .00 |
| ☐ 586 | Rick Manning | .03 | .01 | .00 |
| ☐ 587 | Bob McClure | .03 | .01 | .00 |
| ☐ 588 | Paul Molitor | .09 | .04 | .01 |
| ☐ 589 | Charlie Moore | .03 | .01 | .00 |
| ☐ 590 | Ben Oglivie | .06 | .02 | .00 |
| ☐ 591 | Chuck Porter | .03 | .01 | .00 |
| ☐ 592 | Randy Ready | .10 | .04 | .01 |
| ☐ 593 | Ed Romero | .03 | .01 | .00 |
| ☐ 594 | Bill Schroeder | .03 | .01 | .00 |
| ☐ 595 | Ray Searage | .03 | .01 | .00 |
| ☐ 596 | Ted Simmons | .09 | .04 | .01 |
| ☐ 597 | Jim Sundberg | .05 | .02 | .00 |
| ☐ 598 | Don Sutton | .15 | .06 | .01 |
| ☐ 599 | Tom Tellmann | .03 | .01 | .00 |
| ☐ 600 | Rick Waits | .03 | .01 | .00 |
| ☐ 601 | Robin Yount | .25 | .10 | .02 |
| ☐ 602 | Dusty Baker | .05 | .02 | .00 |
| ☐ 603 | Bob Brenly | .07 | .03 | .01 |
| ☐ 604 | Jack Clark | .09 | .04 | .01 |
| ☐ 605 | Chili Davis | .07 | .03 | .01 |
| ☐ 606 | Mark Davis | .03 | .01 | .00 |
| ☐ 607 | Dan Gladden | .20 | .08 | .02 |
| ☐ 608 | Atlee Hammaker | .05 | .02 | .00 |
| ☐ 609 | Mike Krukow | .07 | .03 | .01 |
| ☐ 610 | Duane Kuiper | .03 | .01 | .00 |
| ☐ 611 | Bob Lacey | .03 | .01 | .00 |
| ☐ 612 | Bill Laskey | .03 | .01 | .00 |
| ☐ 613 | Gary Lavelle | .05 | .02 | .00 |
| ☐ 614 | Johnnie LeMaster | .03 | .01 | .00 |
| ☐ 615 | Jeff Leonard | .06 | .02 | .00 |
| ☐ 616 | Randy Lerch | .03 | .01 | .00 |
| ☐ 617 | Greg Minton | .05 | .02 | .00 |
| ☐ 618 | Steve Nicosia | .03 | .01 | .00 |
| ☐ 619 | Gene Richards | .03 | .01 | .00 |
| ☐ 620 | Jeff Robinson | .10 | .04 | .01 |
| ☐ 621 | Scot Thompson | .03 | .01 | .00 |
| ☐ 622 | Manny Trillo | .05 | .02 | .00 |
| ☐ 623 | Brad Wellman | .03 | .01 | .00 |
| ☐ 624 | Frank Williams | .10 | .04 | .01 |
| ☐ 625 | Joel Youngblood | .03 | .01 | .00 |
| ☐ 626 | Cal Ripken IA | .25 | .10 | .02 |
| ☐ 627 | Mike Schmidt IA | .25 | .10 | .02 |
| ☐ 628 | Giving The Signs: Sparky Anderson | .05 | .02 | .00 |
| ☐ 629 | AL Pitcher's Nightmare .. Dave Winfield Rickey Henderson | .25 | .10 | .02 |
| ☐ 630 | NL Pitcher's Nightmare .. Mike Schmidt Ryne Sandberg | .25 | .10 | .02 |
| ☐ 631 | NL All-Stars: Darryl Strawberry Gary Carter Steve Garvey Ozzie Smith | .25 | .10 | .02 |
| ☐ 632 | A-S Winning Battery: Gary Carter Charlie Lea | .08 | .03 | .01 |
| ☐ 633 | NL Pennant Clinchers: Steve Garvey Goose Gossage | .12 | .05 | .01 |
| ☐ 634 | NL Rookie Phenoms: Dwight Gooden Juan Samuel | 1.00 | .40 | .10 |
| ☐ 635 | Toronto's Big Guns: Willie Upshaw | .07 | .03 | .01 |
| ☐ 636 | Toronto's Big Guns: Lloyd Moseby | .07 | .03 | .01 |
| ☐ 637 | HOLLAND: Al Holland | .05 | .02 | .00 |
| ☐ 638 | TUNNELL: Lee Tunnell | .05 | .02 | .00 |
| ☐ 639 | 500th Homer: Reggie Jackson | .25 | .10 | .02 |

| | | MINT | VG-E | F-G |
|---|---|---|---|---|
| ☐ 640 | 4000th Hit: Pete Rose | .35 | .14 | .03 |
| ☐ 641 | Father and Son: Cal Ripken Jr. and Sr. | .25 | .10 | .02 |
| ☐ 642 | Cubs: Division Champs ... | .05 | .02 | .00 |
| ☐ 643 | Two Perfect Games and . One No-Hitter: Mike Witt David Palmer Jack Morris | .07 | .03 | .01 |
| ☐ 644 | Willie Lozado and Vic Mata | .10 | .04 | .01 |
| ☐ 645 | Kelly Gruber and Randy O'Neal | .15 | .06 | .01 |
| ☐ 646 | Jose Roman and Joel Skinner | .12 | .05 | .01 |
| ☐ 647 | Steve Kiefer and Danny Tartabull | 2.25 | .90 | .22 |
| ☐ 648 | Rob Deer and Alejandro Sanchez | 1.50 | .60 | .15 |
| ☐ 649 | Bill Hatcher and Shawon Dunston | 1.00 | .40 | .10 |
| ☐ 650 | Ron Robinson and Mike Bielecki | .15 | .06 | .01 |
| ☐ 651 | Zane Smith and Paul Zuvella | .15 | .06 | .01 |
| ☐ 652 | Joe Hesketh and Glenn Davis | 4.50 | 1.80 | .45 |
| ☐ 653 | John Russell and Steve Jeltz | .20 | .08 | .02 |
| ☐ 654 | CL: Tigers/Padres and Cubs/Mets | .07 | .01 | .00 |
| ☐ 655 | CL: Blue Jays/Yankees .. and Red Sox/Orioles | .07 | .01 | .00 |
| ☐ 656 | CL: Royals/Cardinals ..... and Phillies/Twins | .07 | .01 | .00 |
| ☐ 657 | CL: Angels/Braves and Astros/Dodgers | .07 | .01 | .00 |
| ☐ 658 | CL: Expos/A's and Indians/Pirates | .07 | .01 | .00 |
| ☐ 659 | CL: Mariners/White Sox . and Reds/Rangers | .07 | .01 | .00 |
| ☐ 660 | CL: Brewers/Giants and Special Cards | .07 | .01 | .00 |

| | | MINT | VG-E | F-G |
|---|---|---|---|---|
| ☐ 6 | Steve Carlton | .30 | .12 | .03 |
| ☐ 7 | Alvin Davis | .15 | .06 | .01 |
| ☐ 8 | Andre Dawson | .15 | .06 | .01 |
| ☐ 9 | Steve Garvey | .30 | .12 | .03 |
| ☐ 10 | Goose Gossage | .15 | .06 | .01 |
| ☐ 11 | Tony Gwynn | .30 | .12 | .03 |
| ☐ 12 | Keith Hernandez | .20 | .08 | .02 |
| ☐ 13 | Kent Hrbek | .20 | .08 | .02 |
| ☐ 14 | Reggie Jackson | .50 | .20 | .05 |
| ☐ 15 | Dave Kingman | .07 | .03 | .01 |
| ☐ 16 | Ron Kittle | .09 | .04 | .01 |
| ☐ 17 | Mark Langston | .07 | .03 | .01 |
| ☐ 18 | Jeff Leonard | .05 | .02 | .00 |
| ☐ 19 | Bill Madlock | .07 | .03 | .01 |
| ☐ 20 | Don Mattingly | 1.25 | .50 | .12 |
| ☐ 21 | Jack Morris | .10 | .04 | .01 |
| ☐ 22 | Dale Murphy | .60 | .24 | .06 |
| ☐ 23 | Eddie Murray | .40 | .16 | .04 |
| ☐ 24 | Tony Pena | .07 | .03 | .01 |
| ☐ 25 | Dan Quisenberry | .10 | .04 | .01 |
| ☐ 26 | Tim Raines | .25 | .10 | .02 |
| ☐ 27 | Jim Rice | .25 | .10 | .02 |
| ☐ 28 | Cal Ripken | .35 | .14 | .03 |
| ☐ 29 | Pete Rose | .80 | .32 | .08 |
| ☐ 30 | Nolan Ryan | .35 | .14 | .03 |
| ☐ 31 | Ryne Sandberg | .35 | .14 | .03 |
| ☐ 32 | Steve Sax | .10 | .04 | .01 |
| ☐ 33 | Mike Schmidt | .50 | .20 | .05 |
| ☐ 34 | Tom Seaver | .30 | .12 | .03 |
| ☐ 35 | Ozzie Smith | .10 | .04 | .01 |
| ☐ 36 | Mario Soto | .07 | .03 | .01 |
| ☐ 37 | Dave Stieb | .10 | .04 | .01 |
| ☐ 38 | Darryl Strawberry | .50 | .20 | .05 |
| ☐ 39 | Rick Sutcliffe | .10 | .04 | .01 |
| ☐ 40 | Alan Trammell | .15 | .06 | .01 |
| ☐ 41 | Willie Upshaw | .07 | .03 | .01 |
| ☐ 42 | Fernando Valenzuela | .25 | .10 | .02 |
| ☐ 43 | Dave Winfield | .25 | .10 | .02 |
| ☐ 44 | Robin Yount | .25 | .10 | .02 |

## 1985 Fleer Update

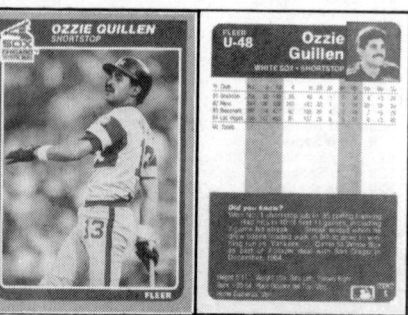

This 132 card set was issued late in the collecting year and features new players and players on new teams compared to the 1985 Fleer regular issue cards. Cards measure 2 1/2" by 3 1/2" and were distributed together as a complete set within a special box. The cards are numbered with a U prefix and are ordered alphabetically by the player's name.

| | | MINT | VG-E | F-G |
|---|---|---|---|---|
| | COMPLETE SET | 15.00 | 6.00 | 1.50 |
| | COMMON PLAYER (1-132) | .05 | .02 | .00 |
| ☐ | U1 Don Aase | .10 | .04 | .01 |
| ☐ | U2 Bill Almon | .05 | .02 | .00 |
| ☐ | U3 Dusty Baker | .10 | .04 | .01 |
| ☐ | U4 Dale Berra | .10 | .04 | .01 |
| ☐ | U5 Karl Best | .15 | .06 | .01 |
| ☐ | U6 Tim Birtsas | .35 | .14 | .03 |
| ☐ | U7 Vida Blue | .10 | .04 | .01 |
| ☐ | U8 Rich Bordi | .05 | .02 | .00 |
| ☐ | U9 Daryl Boston | .25 | .10 | .02 |
| ☐ | U10 Hubie Brooks | .25 | .10 | .02 |

## 1985 Fleer Limited Edition

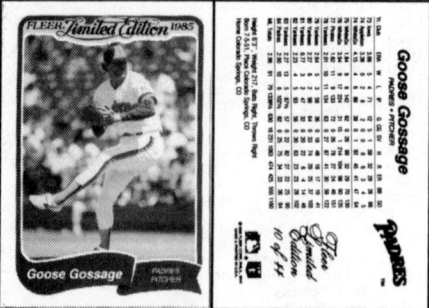

This 44 card set features standard size cards (2 1/2" by 3 1/2") which were distributed in a colorful box as a complete set. The back of the box gives a complete checklist of the cards in the set. The cards are ordered alphabetically by the player's name. Backs of the cards are yellow and white whereas the fronts show a picture of the player inside a red banner-type border.

| | | MINT | VG-E | F-G |
|---|---|---|---|---|
| | COMPLETE SET | 4.50 | 1.50 | .40 |
| | COMMON PLAYER (1-44) | .05 | .02 | .00 |
| ☐ 1 | Buddy Bell | .07 | .03 | .01 |
| ☐ 2 | Bert Blyleven | .07 | .03 | .01 |
| ☐ 3 | Wade Boggs | .80 | .32 | .08 |
| ☐ 4 | George Brett | .50 | .20 | .05 |
| ☐ 5 | Rod Carew | .30 | .12 | .03 |

| | | | | |
|---|---|---|---|---|
| ☐ U11 | Chris Brown | 2.25 | .90 | .22 |
| ☐ U12 | Tom Browning | .75 | .30 | .07 |
| ☐ U13 | Al Bumbry | .05 | .02 | .00 |
| ☐ U14 | Tim Burke | .35 | .14 | .03 |
| ☐ U15 | Ray Burris | .05 | .02 | .00 |
| ☐ U16 | Jeff Burroughs | .05 | .02 | .00 |
| ☐ U17 | Ivan Calderon | .25 | .10 | .02 |
| ☐ U18 | Jeff Calhoun | .15 | .06 | .01 |
| ☐ U19 | Bill Campbell | .05 | .02 | .00 |
| ☐ U20 | Don Carman | .35 | .14 | .03 |
| ☐ U21 | Gary Carter | .75 | .30 | .07 |
| ☐ U22 | Bobby Castillo | .05 | .02 | .00 |
| ☐ U23 | Bill Caudill | .10 | .04 | .01 |
| ☐ U24 | Rick Cerone | .05 | .02 | .00 |
| ☐ U25 | Jack Clark | .25 | .10 | .02 |
| ☐ U26 | Pat Clements | .25 | .10 | .02 |
| ☐ U27 | Stewart Cliburn | .25 | .10 | .02 |
| ☐ U28 | Vince Coleman | 4.50 | 1.80 | .45 |
| ☐ U29 | Dave Collins | .10 | .04 | .01 |
| ☐ U30 | Fritz Connally | .15 | .06 | .01 |
| ☐ U31 | Henry Cotto | .05 | .02 | .00 |
| ☐ U32 | Danny Darwin | .05 | .02 | .00 |
| ☐ U33 | Darren Daulton | .25 | .10 | .02 |
| ☐ U34 | Jerry Davis | .15 | .06 | .01 |
| ☐ U35 | Brian Dayett | .10 | .04 | .01 |
| ☐ U36 | Ken Dixon | .20 | .08 | .02 |
| ☐ U37 | Tommy Dunbar | .10 | .04 | .01 |
| ☐ U38 | Mariano Duncan | .75 | .30 | .07 |
| ☐ U39 | Bob Fallon | .10 | .04 | .01 |
| ☐ U40 | Brian Fisher | .35 | .14 | .03 |
| ☐ U41 | Mike Fitzgerald | .05 | .02 | .00 |
| ☐ U42 | Ray Fontenot | .05 | .02 | .00 |
| ☐ U43 | Greg Gagne | .10 | .04 | .01 |
| ☐ U44 | Oscar Gamble | .10 | .04 | .01 |
| ☐ U45 | Jim Gott | .05 | .02 | .00 |
| ☐ U46 | David Green | .05 | .02 | .00 |
| ☐ U47 | Alfredo Griffin | .05 | .02 | .00 |
| ☐ U48 | Ozzie Guillen | .75 | .30 | .07 |
| ☐ U49 | Toby Harrah | .10 | .04 | .01 |
| ☐ U50 | Ron Hassey | .05 | .02 | .00 |
| ☐ U51 | Rickey Henderson | 1.00 | .40 | .10 |
| ☐ U52 | Steve Henderson | .05 | .02 | .00 |
| ☐ U53 | George Hendrick | .10 | .04 | .01 |
| ☐ U54 | Teddy Higuera | 2.00 | .80 | .20 |
| ☐ U55 | Al Holland | .10 | .04 | .01 |
| ☐ U56 | Burt Hooton | .05 | .02 | .00 |
| ☐ U57 | Jay Howell | .15 | .06 | .01 |
| ☐ U58 | LaMarr Hoyt | .15 | .06 | .01 |
| ☐ U59 | Tim Hulett | .15 | .06 | .01 |
| ☐ U60 | Bob James | .10 | .04 | .01 |
| ☐ U61 | Cliff Johnson | .05 | .02 | .00 |
| ☐ U62 | Howard Johnson | .10 | .04 | .01 |
| ☐ U63 | Ruppert Jones | .10 | .04 | .01 |
| ☐ U64 | Steve Kemp | .10 | .04 | .01 |
| ☐ U65 | Bruce Kison | .05 | .02 | .00 |
| ☐ U66 | Mike LaCoss | .05 | .02 | .00 |
| ☐ U67 | Lee Lacy | .10 | .04 | .01 |
| ☐ U68 | Dave LaPoint | .05 | .02 | .00 |
| ☐ U69 | Gary Lavelle | .10 | .04 | .01 |
| ☐ U70 | Vance Law | .05 | .02 | .00 |
| ☐ U71 | Manny Lee | .15 | .06 | .01 |
| ☐ U72 | Sixto Lezcano | .05 | .02 | .00 |
| ☐ U73 | Tim Lollar | .05 | .02 | .00 |
| ☐ U74 | Urbano Lugo | .10 | .04 | .01 |
| ☐ U75 | Fred Lynn | .25 | .10 | .02 |
| ☐ U76 | Steve Lyons | .25 | .10 | .02 |
| ☐ U77 | Mickey Mahler | .05 | .02 | .00 |
| ☐ U78 | Ron Mathis | .15 | .06 | .01 |
| ☐ U79 | Len Matuszek | .10 | .04 | .01 |
| ☐ U80 | Oddibe McDowell | 1.50 | .60 | .15 |
| | (part of bio | | | |
| | actually Roger's) | | | |
| ☐ U81 | Roger McDowell | 1.00 | .40 | .10 |
| ☐ U82 | Donnie Moore | .10 | .04 | .01 |
| ☐ U83 | Ron Musselman | .10 | .04 | .01 |
| ☐ U84 | Al Oliver | .25 | .10 | .02 |
| ☐ U85 | Joe Orsulak | .25 | .10 | .02 |
| ☐ U86 | Dan Pasqua | 1.50 | .60 | .15 |
| ☐ U87 | Chris Pittaro | .15 | .06 | .01 |
| ☐ U88 | Rick Reuschel | .10 | .04 | .01 |
| ☐ U89 | Earnie Riles | .75 | .30 | .07 |
| ☐ U90 | Jerry Royster | .05 | .02 | .00 |
| ☐ U91 | Dave Rozema | .05 | .02 | .00 |
| ☐ U92 | Dave Rucker | .05 | .02 | .00 |
| ☐ U93 | Vern Ruhle | .05 | .02 | .00 |
| ☐ U94 | Mark Salas | .35 | .14 | .03 |
| ☐ U95 | Luis Salazar | .05 | .02 | .00 |
| ☐ U96 | Joe Sambito | .10 | .04 | .01 |
| ☐ U97 | Billy Sample | .05 | .02 | .00 |
| ☐ U98 | Alex Sanchez | .10 | .04 | .01 |
| ☐ U99 | Calvin Schiraldi | .75 | .30 | .07 |
| ☐ U100 | Rick Schu | .25 | .10 | .02 |
| ☐ U101 | Larry Sheets | .50 | .20 | .05 |

| | | | | |
|---|---|---|---|---|
| ☐ U102 | Ron Shephard | .10 | .04 | .01 |
| ☐ U103 | Nelson Simmons | .15 | .06 | .01 |
| ☐ U104 | Don Slaught | .10 | .04 | .01 |
| ☐ U105 | Roy Smalley | .10 | .04 | .01 |
| ☐ U106 | Lonnie Smith | .10 | .04 | .01 |
| ☐ U107 | Nate Snell | .15 | .06 | .01 |
| ☐ U108 | Lary Sorensen | .05 | .02 | .00 |
| ☐ U109 | Chris Speier | .05 | .02 | .00 |
| ☐ U110 | Mike Stenhouse | .10 | .04 | .01 |
| ☐ U111 | Tim Stoddard | .05 | .02 | .00 |
| ☐ U112 | John Stuper | .05 | .02 | .00 |
| ☐ U113 | Jim Sundberg | .10 | .04 | .01 |
| ☐ U114 | Bruce Sutter | .25 | .10 | .02 |
| ☐ U115 | Don Sutton | .50 | .20 | .05 |
| ☐ U116 | Bruce Tanner | .15 | .06 | .01 |
| ☐ U117 | Kent Tekulve | .10 | .04 | .01 |
| ☐ U118 | Walt Terrell | .10 | .04 | .01 |
| ☐ U119 | Mickey Tettleton | .10 | .04 | .01 |
| ☐ U120 | Rich Thompson | .10 | .04 | .01 |
| ☐ U121 | Louis Thornton | .10 | .04 | .01 |
| ☐ U122 | Alex Trevino | .05 | .02 | .00 |
| ☐ U123 | John Tudor | .20 | .08 | .02 |
| ☐ U124 | Jose Uribe | .10 | .04 | .01 |
| ☐ U125 | Dave Valle | .10 | .04 | .01 |
| ☐ U126 | Dave Von Ohlen | .05 | .02 | .00 |
| ☐ U127 | Curt Wardle | .10 | .04 | .01 |
| ☐ U128 | U.L. Washington | .05 | .02 | .00 |
| ☐ U129 | Ed Whitson | .10 | .04 | .01 |
| ☐ U130 | Herm Winningham | .20 | .08 | .02 |
| ☐ U131 | Rich Yett | .10 | .04 | .01 |
| ☐ U132 | Checklist U1-U132 | .05 | .01 | .00 |

## 1986 Fleer

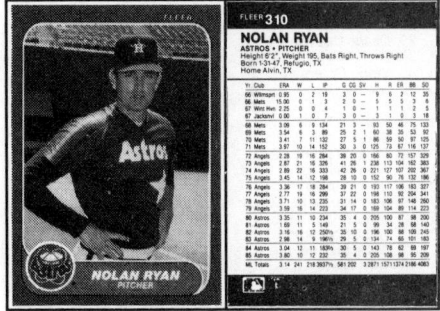

The cards in this 660 card set measure 2 1/2" by 3 1/2". The 1986 Fleer set features fronts which contain the team logo along with the players name and position. The player cards are alphabetized within team and the teams are ordered by their 1985 season finish and won-lost record, e.g., Kansas City (1-25), St. Louis (26-49), Toronto (50-73), New York Mets (74-97), New York Yankees (98-122), Los Angeles (123-147), California (148-171), Cincinnati (172-196), Chicago White Sox (197-220), Detroit (221-243), Montreal (244-267), Baltimore (268-291), Houston (292-314), San Diego (315-338), Boston (339-360), Chicago Cubs (361-385), Minnesota (386-409), Oakland (410-432), Philadelphia (433-457), Seattle (458-481), Milwaukee (482-506), Atlanta (507-532), San Francisco (533-555), Texas (556-578), Cleveland (579-601), and Pittsburgh (602-625). Specials (626-643), Rookie pairs (644-653), and checklist cards (654-660) complete the set. The Dennis and Tippy Martinez cards were apparently switched in the set numbering as their adjacent numbers (279 and 280) were reversed on the Orioles checklist card. The border enclosing the photo is dark blue. The backs feature the same name, number, and statistics format that Fleer has been using over the past few years. Wax pack and cello pack boxes contained a four card panel on the bottom; these cards were numbered C-1 through C-8 and are listed at the end of the list of regular issue cards below. The set is considered complete without the box bottom cards.

|  | | MINT | VG-E | F-G |
|---|---|---|---|---|
| | COMPLETE SET | 27.00 | 11.00 | 2.70 |
| | COMMON PLAYER | .03 | .01 | .00 |

| | | MINT | VG-E | F-G |
|---|---|---|---|---|
| ☐ | 1 Steve Balboni | .05 | .02 | .00 |
| ☐ | 2 Joe Beckwith | .03 | .01 | .00 |
| ☐ | 3 Buddy Biancalana | .03 | .01 | .00 |
| ☐ | 4 Bud Black | .03 | .01 | .00 |
| ☐ | 5 George Brett | .35 | .14 | .03 |
| ☐ | 6 Onix Concepcion | .03 | .01 | .00 |
| ☐ | 7 Steve Farr | .03 | .01 | .00 |
| ☐ | 8 Mark Gubicza | .06 | .02 | .00 |
| ☐ | 9 Dane Iorg | .03 | .01 | .00 |
| ☐ | 10 Danny Jackson | .06 | .02 | .00 |
| ☐ | 11 Lynn Jones | .03 | .01 | .00 |
| ☐ | 12 Mike Jones | .03 | .01 | .00 |
| ☐ | 13 Charlie Leibrandt | .05 | .02 | .00 |
| ☐ | 14 Hal McRae | .05 | .02 | .00 |
| ☐ | 15 Omar Moreno | .03 | .01 | .00 |
| ☐ | 16 Darryl Motley | .03 | .01 | .00 |
| ☐ | 17 Jorge Orta | .03 | .01 | .00 |
| ☐ | 18 Dan Quisenberry | .12 | .05 | .01 |
| ☐ | 19 Bret Saberhagen | .25 | .10 | .02 |
| ☐ | 20 Pat Sheridan | .03 | .01 | .00 |
| ☐ | 21 Lonnie Smith | .06 | .02 | .00 |
| ☐ | 22 Jim Sundberg | .05 | .02 | .00 |
| ☐ | 23 John Wathan | .03 | .01 | .00 |
| ☐ | 24 Frank White | .06 | .02 | .00 |
| ☐ | 25 Willie Wilson | .15 | .06 | .01 |
| ☐ | 26 Joaquin Andujar | .08 | .03 | .01 |
| ☐ | 27 Steve Braun | .03 | .01 | .00 |
| ☐ | 28 Bill Campbell | .03 | .01 | .00 |
| ☐ | 29 Cesar Cedeno | .06 | .02 | .00 |
| ☐ | 30 Jack Clark | .12 | .05 | .01 |
| ☐ | 31 Vince Coleman | 1.50 | .60 | .15 |
| ☐ | 32 Danny Cox | .07 | .03 | .01 |
| ☐ | 33 Ken Dayley | .03 | .01 | .00 |
| ☐ | 34 Ivan DeJesus | .03 | .01 | .00 |
| ☐ | 35 Bob Forsch | .05 | .02 | .00 |
| ☐ | 36 Brian Harper | .03 | .01 | .00 |
| ☐ | 37 Tom Herr | .08 | .03 | .01 |
| ☐ | 38 Ricky Horton | .05 | .02 | .00 |
| ☐ | 39 Kurt Kepshire | .03 | .01 | .00 |
| ☐ | 40 Jeff Lahti | .03 | .01 | .00 |
| ☐ | 41 Tito Landrum | .03 | .01 | .00 |
| ☐ | 42 Willie McGee | .15 | .06 | .01 |
| ☐ | 43 Tom Nieto | .03 | .01 | .00 |
| ☐ | 44 Terry Pendleton | .05 | .02 | .00 |
| ☐ | 45 Darrell Porter | .05 | .02 | .00 |
| ☐ | 46 Ozzie Smith | .10 | .04 | .01 |
| ☐ | 47 John Tudor | .10 | .04 | .01 |
| ☐ | 48 Andy Van Slyke | .06 | .02 | .00 |
| ☐ | 49 Todd Worrell | 1.00 | .40 | .10 |
| ☐ | 50 Jim Acker | .03 | .01 | .00 |
| ☐ | 51 Doyle Alexander | .05 | .02 | .00 |
| ☐ | 52 Jesse Barfield | .15 | .06 | .01 |
| ☐ | 53 George Bell | .15 | .06 | .01 |
| ☐ | 54 Jeff Burroughs | .03 | .01 | .00 |
| ☐ | 55 Bill Caudill | .05 | .02 | .00 |
| ☐ | 56 Jim Clancy | .03 | .01 | .00 |
| ☐ | 57 Tony Fernandez | .10 | .04 | .01 |
| ☐ | 58 Tom Filer | .05 | .02 | .00 |
| ☐ | 59 Damaso Garcia | .07 | .03 | .01 |
| ☐ | 60 Tom Henke | .06 | .02 | .00 |
| ☐ | 61 Garth Iorg | .03 | .01 | .00 |
| ☐ | 62 Cliff Johnson | .03 | .01 | .00 |
| ☐ | 63 Jimmy Key | .08 | .03 | .01 |
| ☐ | 64 Dennis Lamp | .03 | .01 | .00 |
| ☐ | 65 Gary Lavelle | .05 | .02 | .00 |
| ☐ | 66 Buck Martinez | .03 | .01 | .00 |
| ☐ | 67 Lloyd Moseby | .10 | .04 | .01 |
| ☐ | 68 Rance Mulliniks | .03 | .01 | .00 |
| ☐ | 69 Al Oliver | .10 | .04 | .01 |
| ☐ | 70 Dave Stieb | .10 | .04 | .01 |
| ☐ | 71 Louis Thornton | .10 | .04 | .01 |
| ☐ | 72 Willie Upshaw | .07 | .03 | .01 |
| ☐ | 73 Ernie Whitt | .03 | .01 | .00 |
| ☐ | 74 Rick Aguilera | .25 | .10 | .02 |
| ☐ | 75 Wally Backman | .07 | .03 | .01 |
| ☐ | 76 Gary Carter | .35 | .14 | .03 |
| ☐ | 77 Ron Darling | .20 | .08 | .02 |
| ☐ | 78 Len Dykstra | 1.00 | .40 | .10 |
| ☐ | 79 Sid Fernandez | .20 | .08 | .02 |
| ☐ | 80 George Foster | .12 | .05 | .01 |
| ☐ | 81 Dwight Gooden | 2.00 | .80 | .20 |
| ☐ | 82 Tom Gorman | .03 | .01 | .00 |
| ☐ | 83 Danny Heep | .03 | .01 | .00 |
| ☐ | 84 Keith Hernandez | .25 | .10 | .02 |
| ☐ | 85 Howard Johnson | .03 | .01 | .00 |
| ☐ | 86 Ray Knight | .07 | .03 | .01 |
| ☐ | 87 Terry Leach | .03 | .01 | .00 |
| ☐ | 88 Ed Lynch | .03 | .01 | .00 |
| ☐ | 89 Roger McDowell | .50 | .20 | .05 |
| ☐ | 90 Jesse Orosco | .06 | .02 | .00 |
| ☐ | 91 Tom Paciorek | .03 | .01 | .00 |
| ☐ | 92 Ronn Reynolds | .08 | .03 | .01 |
| ☐ | 93 Rafael Santana | .03 | .01 | .00 |
| ☐ | 94 Doug Sisk | .03 | .01 | .00 |
| ☐ | 95 Rusty Staub | .07 | .03 | .01 |
| ☐ | 96 Darryl Strawberry | .35 | .14 | .03 |
| ☐ | 97 Mookie Wilson | .06 | .02 | .00 |
| ☐ | 98 Neil Allen | .05 | .02 | .00 |
| ☐ | 99 Don Baylor | .10 | .04 | .01 |
| ☐ | 100 Dale Berra | .05 | .02 | .00 |
| ☐ | 101 Rich Bordi | .03 | .01 | .00 |
| ☐ | 102 Marty Bystrom | .03 | .01 | .00 |
| ☐ | 103 Joe Cowley | .03 | .01 | .00 |
| ☐ | 104 Brian Fisher | .25 | .10 | .02 |
| ☐ | 105 Ken Griffey | .06 | .02 | .00 |
| ☐ | 106 Ron Guidry | .15 | .06 | .01 |
| ☐ | 107 Ron Hassey | .03 | .01 | .00 |
| ☐ | 108 Rickey Henderson | .35 | .14 | .03 |
| ☐ | 109 Don Mattingly | 3.50 | 1.40 | .35 |
| ☐ | 110 Bobby Meacham | .03 | .01 | .00 |
| ☐ | 111 John Montefusco | .05 | .02 | .00 |
| ☐ | 112 Phil Niekro | .15 | .06 | .01 |
| ☐ | 113 Mike Pagliarulo | .25 | .10 | .02 |
| ☐ | 114 Dan Pasqua | .20 | .08 | .02 |
| ☐ | 115 Willie Randolph | .06 | .02 | .00 |
| ☐ | 116 Dave Righetti | .15 | .06 | .01 |
| ☐ | 117 Andre Robertson | .03 | .01 | .00 |
| ☐ | 118 Billy Sample | .03 | .01 | .00 |
| ☐ | 119 Bob Shirley | .03 | .01 | .00 |
| ☐ | 120 Ed Whitson | .05 | .02 | .00 |
| ☐ | 121 Dave Winfield | .30 | .12 | .03 |
| ☐ | 122 Butch Wynegar | .05 | .02 | .00 |
| ☐ | 123 Dave Anderson | .03 | .01 | .00 |
| ☐ | 124 Bob Bailor | .03 | .01 | .00 |
| ☐ | 125 Greg Brock | .05 | .02 | .00 |
| ☐ | 126 Enos Cabell | .03 | .01 | .00 |
| ☐ | 127 Bobby Castillo | .03 | .01 | .00 |
| ☐ | 128 Carlos Diaz | .03 | .01 | .00 |
| ☐ | 129 Mariano Duncan | .35 | .14 | .03 |
| ☐ | 130 Pedro Guerrero | .25 | .10 | .02 |
| ☐ | 131 Orel Hershiser | .30 | .12 | .03 |
| ☐ | 132 Rick Honeycutt | .05 | .02 | .00 |
| ☐ | 133 Ken Howell | .05 | .02 | .00 |
| ☐ | 134 Ken Landreaux | .05 | .02 | .00 |
| ☐ | 135 Bill Madlock | .10 | .04 | .01 |
| ☐ | 136 Candy Maldonado | .06 | .02 | .00 |
| ☐ | 137 Mike Marshall | .12 | .05 | .01 |
| ☐ | 138 Len Matuszek | .03 | .01 | .00 |
| ☐ | 139 Tom Niedenfuer | .06 | .02 | .00 |
| ☐ | 140 Alejandro Pena | .05 | .02 | .00 |
| ☐ | 141 Jerry Reuss | .06 | .02 | .00 |
| ☐ | 142 Bill Russell | .05 | .02 | .00 |
| ☐ | 143 Steve Sax | .12 | .05 | .01 |
| ☐ | 144 Mike Scioscia | .05 | .02 | .00 |
| ☐ | 145 Fernando Valenzuela | .30 | .12 | .03 |
| ☐ | 146 Bob Welch | .06 | .02 | .00 |
| ☐ | 147 Terry Whitfield | .03 | .01 | .00 |
| ☐ | 148 Juan Beniquez | .05 | .02 | .00 |
| ☐ | 149 Bob Boone | .05 | .02 | .00 |
| ☐ | 150 John Candelaria | .07 | .03 | .01 |
| ☐ | 151 Rod Carew | .30 | .12 | .03 |
| ☐ | 152 Stewart Cliburn | .15 | .06 | .01 |
| ☐ | 153 Doug DeCinces | .08 | .03 | .01 |
| ☐ | 154 Brian Downing | .05 | .02 | .00 |
| ☐ | 155 Ken Forsch | .03 | .01 | .00 |
| ☐ | 156 Craig Gerber | .08 | .03 | .01 |
| ☐ | 157 Bobby Grich | .07 | .03 | .01 |
| ☐ | 158 George Hendrick | .06 | .02 | .00 |
| ☐ | 159 Al Holland | .03 | .01 | .00 |
| ☐ | 160 Reggie Jackson | .35 | .14 | .03 |
| ☐ | 161 Ruppert Jones | .05 | .02 | .00 |
| ☐ | 162 Urbano Lugo | .08 | .03 | .01 |
| ☐ | 163 Kirk McCaskill | .60 | .24 | .06 |
| ☐ | 164 Donnie Moore | .05 | .02 | .00 |
| ☐ | 165 Gary Pettis | .08 | .03 | .01 |
| ☐ | 166 Ron Romanick | .05 | .02 | .00 |
| ☐ | 167 Dick Schofield | .07 | .03 | .01 |
| ☐ | 168 Daryl Sconiers | .03 | .01 | .00 |
| ☐ | 169 Jim Slaton | .03 | .01 | .00 |
| ☐ | 170 Don Sutton | .15 | .06 | .01 |
| ☐ | 171 Mike Witt | .10 | .04 | .01 |
| ☐ | 172 Buddy Bell | .09 | .04 | .01 |
| ☐ | 173 Tom Browning | .15 | .06 | .01 |

| | | | |
|---|---|---|---|
| ☐ 174 Dave Concepcion | .08 | .03 | .01 |
| ☐ 175 Eric Davis | 1.00 | .40 | .10 |
| ☐ 176 Bo Diaz | .05 | .02 | .00 |
| ☐ 177 Nick Esasky | .06 | .02 | .00 |
| ☐ 178 John Franco | .10 | .04 | .01 |
| ☐ 179 Tom Hume | .03 | .01 | .00 |
| ☐ 180 Wayne Krenchicki | .03 | .01 | .00 |
| ☐ 181 Andy McGaffigan | .03 | .01 | .00 |
| ☐ 182 Eddie Milner | .05 | .02 | .00 |
| ☐ 183 Ron Oester | .05 | .02 | .00 |
| ☐ 184 Dave Parker | .15 | .06 | .01 |
| ☐ 185 Frank Pastore | .03 | .01 | .00 |
| ☐ 186 Tony Perez | .10 | .04 | .01 |
| ☐ 187 Ted Power | .07 | .03 | .01 |
| ☐ 188 Joe Price | .03 | .01 | .00 |
| ☐ 189 Gary Redus | .05 | .02 | .00 |
| ☐ 190 Ron Robinson | .03 | .01 | .00 |
| ☐ 191 Pete Rose | .60 | .24 | .06 |
| ☐ 192 Mario Soto | .08 | .03 | .01 |
| ☐ 193 John Stuper | .03 | .01 | .00 |
| ☐ 194 Jay Tibbs | .03 | .01 | .00 |
| ☐ 195 Dave Van Gorder | .03 | .01 | .00 |
| ☐ 196 Max Venable | .03 | .01 | .00 |
| ☐ 197 Juan Agosto | .03 | .01 | .00 |
| ☐ 198 Harold Baines | .15 | .06 | .01 |
| ☐ 199 Floyd Bannister | .05 | .02 | .00 |
| ☐ 200 Britt Burns | .05 | .02 | .00 |
| ☐ 201 Julio Cruz | .03 | .01 | .00 |
| ☐ 202 Joel Davis | .20 | .08 | .02 |
| ☐ 203 Richard Dotson | .05 | .02 | .00 |
| ☐ 204 Carlton Fisk | .12 | .05 | .01 |
| ☐ 205 Scott Fletcher | .05 | .02 | .00 |
| ☐ 206 Ozzie Guillen | .40 | .16 | .04 |
| ☐ 207 Jerry Hairston | .03 | .01 | .00 |
| ☐ 208 Tim Hulett | .05 | .02 | .00 |
| ☐ 209 Bob James | .05 | .02 | .00 |
| ☐ 210 Ron Kittle | .10 | .04 | .01 |
| ☐ 211 Rudy Law | .03 | .01 | .00 |
| ☐ 212 Bryan Little | .03 | .01 | .00 |
| ☐ 213 Gene Nelson | .03 | .01 | .00 |
| ☐ 214 Reid Nichols | .03 | .01 | .00 |
| ☐ 215 Luis Salazar | .03 | .01 | .00 |
| ☐ 216 Tom Seaver | .25 | .10 | .02 |
| ☐ 217 Dan Spillner | .03 | .01 | .00 |
| ☐ 218 Bruce Tanner | .10 | .04 | .01 |
| ☐ 219 Greg Walker | .10 | .04 | .01 |
| ☐ 220 Dave Wehrmeister | .03 | .01 | .00 |
| ☐ 221 Juan Berenguer | .03 | .01 | .00 |
| ☐ 222 Dave Bergman | .03 | .01 | .00 |
| ☐ 223 Tom Brookens | .03 | .01 | .00 |
| ☐ 224 Darrell Evans | .09 | .04 | .01 |
| ☐ 225 Barbaro Garbey | .03 | .01 | .00 |
| ☐ 226 Kirk Gibson | .15 | .06 | .01 |
| ☐ 227 John Grubb | .03 | .01 | .00 |
| ☐ 228 Willie Hernandez | .12 | .05 | .01 |
| ☐ 229 Larry Herndon | .03 | .01 | .00 |
| ☐ 230 Chet Lemon | .05 | .02 | .00 |
| ☐ 231 Aurelio Lopez | .03 | .01 | .00 |
| ☐ 232 Jack Morris | .15 | .06 | .01 |
| ☐ 233 Randy O'Neal | .03 | .01 | .00 |
| ☐ 234 Lance Parrish | .18 | .08 | .01 |
| ☐ 235 Dan Petry | .10 | .04 | .01 |
| ☐ 236 Alex Sanchez | .03 | .01 | .00 |
| ☐ 237 Bill Scherrer | .03 | .01 | .00 |
| ☐ 238 Nelson Simmons | .15 | .06 | .01 |
| ☐ 239 Frank Tanana | .05 | .02 | .00 |
| ☐ 240 Walt Terrell | .03 | .01 | .00 |
| ☐ 241 Alan Trammell | .15 | .06 | .01 |
| ☐ 242 Lou Whitaker | .12 | .05 | .01 |
| ☐ 243 Milt Wilcox | .03 | .01 | .00 |
| ☐ 244 Hubie Brooks | .10 | .04 | .01 |
| ☐ 245 Tim Burke | .20 | .08 | .02 |
| ☐ 246 Andre Dawson | .20 | .08 | .02 |
| ☐ 247 Mike Fitzgerald | .03 | .01 | .00 |
| ☐ 248 Terry Francona | .05 | .02 | .00 |
| ☐ 249 Bill Gullickson | .05 | .02 | .00 |
| ☐ 250 Joe Hesketh | .07 | .03 | .01 |
| ☐ 251 Bill Laskey | .03 | .01 | .00 |
| ☐ 252 Vance Law | .03 | .01 | .00 |
| ☐ 253 Charlie Lea | .03 | .01 | .00 |
| ☐ 254 Gary Lucas | .03 | .01 | .00 |
| ☐ 255 David Palmer | .05 | .02 | .00 |
| ☐ 256 Tim Raines | .20 | .08 | .02 |
| ☐ 257 Jeff Reardon | .07 | .03 | .01 |
| ☐ 258 Bert Roberge | .03 | .01 | .00 |
| ☐ 259 Dan Schatzeder | .03 | .01 | .00 |
| ☐ 260 Bryn Smith | .05 | .02 | .00 |
| ☐ 261 Randy St.Claire | .03 | .01 | .00 |
| ☐ 262 Scot Thompson | .03 | .01 | .00 |
| ☐ 263 Tim Wallach | .08 | .03 | .01 |
| ☐ 264 U.L. Washington | .03 | .01 | .00 |
| ☐ 265 Mitch Webster | .50 | .20 | .05 |
| ☐ 266 Herm Winningham | .15 | .06 | .01 |
| ☐ 267 Floyd Youmans | .65 | .26 | .06 |
| ☐ 268 Don Aase | .05 | .02 | .00 |
| ☐ 269 Mike Boddicker | .08 | .03 | .01 |
| ☐ 270 Rich Dauer | .03 | .01 | .00 |
| ☐ 271 Storm Davis | .07 | .03 | .01 |
| ☐ 272 Rick Dempsey | .05 | .02 | .00 |
| ☐ 273 Ken Dixon | .06 | .02 | .00 |
| ☐ 274 Jim Dwyer | .03 | .01 | .00 |
| ☐ 275 Mike Flanagan | .07 | .03 | .01 |
| ☐ 276 Wayne Gross | .03 | .01 | .00 |
| ☐ 277 Lee Lacy | .06 | .02 | .00 |
| ☐ 278 Fred Lynn | .15 | .06 | .01 |
| ☐ 279 Tippy Martinez | .05 | .01 | .00 |
| ☐ 280 Dennis Martinez | .05 | .01 | .00 |
| ☐ 281 Scott McGregor | .07 | .03 | .01 |
| ☐ 282 Eddie Murray | .35 | .14 | .03 |
| ☐ 283 Floyd Rayford | .03 | .01 | .00 |
| ☐ 284 Cal Ripken | .35 | .14 | .03 |
| ☐ 285 Gary Roenicke | .05 | .02 | .00 |
| ☐ 286 Larry Sheets | .08 | .03 | .01 |
| ☐ 287 John Shelby | .03 | .01 | .00 |
| ☐ 288 Nate Snell | .10 | .04 | .01 |
| ☐ 289 Sammy Stewart | .03 | .01 | .00 |
| ☐ 290 Alan Wiggins | .06 | .02 | .00 |
| ☐ 291 Mike Young | .10 | .04 | .01 |
| ☐ 292 Alan Ashby | .03 | .01 | .00 |
| ☐ 293 Mark Bailey | .03 | .01 | .00 |
| ☐ 294 Kevin Bass | .07 | .03 | .01 |
| ☐ 295 Jeff Calhoun | .08 | .03 | .01 |
| ☐ 296 Jose Cruz | .10 | .04 | .01 |
| ☐ 297 Glenn Davis | .75 | .30 | .07 |
| ☐ 298 Bill Dawley | .03 | .01 | .00 |
| ☐ 299 Frank DiPino | .03 | .01 | .00 |
| ☐ 300 Bill Doran | .07 | .03 | .01 |
| ☐ 301 Phil Garner | .05 | .02 | .00 |
| ☐ 302 Jeff Heathcock | .08 | .03 | .01 |
| ☐ 303 Charlie Kerfeld | .30 | .12 | .03 |
| ☐ 304 Bob Knepper | .07 | .03 | .01 |
| ☐ 305 Ron Mathis | .10 | .04 | .01 |
| ☐ 306 Jerry Mumphrey | .05 | .02 | .00 |
| ☐ 307 Jim Pankovits | .03 | .01 | .00 |
| ☐ 308 Terry Puhl | .05 | .02 | .00 |
| ☐ 309 Craig Reynolds | .03 | .01 | .00 |
| ☐ 310 Nolan Ryan | .30 | .12 | .03 |
| ☐ 311 Mike Scott | .20 | .08 | .02 |
| ☐ 312 Dave Smith | .07 | .03 | .01 |
| ☐ 313 Dickie Thon | .05 | .02 | .00 |
| ☐ 314 Denny Walling | .03 | .01 | .00 |
| ☐ 315 Kurt Bevacqua | .03 | .01 | .00 |
| ☐ 316 Al Bumbry | .03 | .01 | .00 |
| ☐ 317 Jerry Davis | .03 | .01 | .00 |
| ☐ 318 Luis DeLeon | .03 | .01 | .00 |
| ☐ 319 Dave Dravecky | .06 | .02 | .00 |
| ☐ 320 Tim Flannery | .03 | .01 | .00 |
| ☐ 321 Steve Garvey | .35 | .14 | .03 |
| ☐ 322 Goose Gossage | .14 | .06 | .01 |
| ☐ 323 Tony Gwynn | .30 | .12 | .03 |
| ☐ 324 Andy Hawkins | .06 | .02 | .00 |
| ☐ 325 LaMarr Hoyt | .07 | .03 | .01 |
| ☐ 326 Roy Lee Jackson | .03 | .01 | .00 |
| ☐ 327 Terry Kennedy | .07 | .03 | .01 |
| ☐ 328 Craig Lefferts | .03 | .01 | .00 |
| ☐ 329 Carmelo Martinez | .05 | .02 | .00 |
| ☐ 330 Lance McCullers | .25 | .10 | .02 |
| ☐ 331 Kevin McReynolds | .10 | .04 | .01 |
| ☐ 332 Graig Nettles | .12 | .05 | .01 |
| ☐ 333 Jerry Royster | .03 | .01 | .00 |
| ☐ 334 Eric Show | .03 | .01 | .00 |
| ☐ 335 Tim Stoddard | .03 | .01 | .00 |
| ☐ 336 Garry Templeton | .07 | .03 | .01 |
| ☐ 337 Mark Thurmond | .05 | .02 | .00 |
| ☐ 338 Ed Wojna | .10 | .04 | .01 |
| ☐ 339 Tony Armas | .09 | .04 | .01 |
| ☐ 340 Marty Barrett | .12 | .05 | .01 |
| ☐ 341 Wade Boggs | 1.50 | .60 | .15 |
| ☐ 342 Dennis Boyd | .08 | .03 | .01 |
| ☐ 343 Bill Buckner | .08 | .03 | .01 |
| ☐ 344 Mark Clear | .03 | .01 | .00 |
| ☐ 345 Roger Clemens | 1.50 | .60 | .15 |
| ☐ 346 Steve Crawford | .03 | .01 | .00 |
| ☐ 347 Mike Easler | .05 | .02 | .00 |
| ☐ 348 Dwight Evans | .10 | .04 | .01 |
| ☐ 349 Rich Gedman | .09 | .04 | .01 |
| ☐ 350 Jackie Gutierrez | .03 | .01 | .00 |
| ☐ 351 Glenn Hoffman | .03 | .01 | .00 |
| ☐ 352 Bruce Hurst | .07 | .03 | .01 |
| ☐ 353 Bruce Kison | .03 | .01 | .00 |
| ☐ 354 Tim Lollar | .03 | .01 | .00 |
| ☐ 355 Steve Lyons | .03 | .01 | .00 |
| ☐ 356 Al Nipper | .03 | .01 | .00 |
| ☐ 357 Bob Ojeda | .08 | .03 | .01 |
| ☐ 358 Jim Rice | .30 | .12 | .03 |
| ☐ 359 Bob Stanley | .05 | .02 | .00 |

| | | | | |
|---|---|---|---|---|
| ☐ 360 Mike Trujillo | .08 | .03 | .01 |
| ☐ 361 Thad Bosley | .03 | .01 | .00 |
| ☐ 362 Warren Brusstar | .03 | .01 | .00 |
| ☐ 363 Ron Cey | .08 | .03 | .01 |
| ☐ 364 Jody Davis | .08 | .03 | .01 |
| ☐ 365 Bob Dernier | .03 | .01 | .00 |
| ☐ 366 Shawon Dunston | .09 | .04 | .01 |
| ☐ 367 Leon Durham | .08 | .03 | .01 |
| ☐ 368 Dennis Eckersley | .05 | .02 | .00 |
| ☐ 369 Ray Fontenot | .03 | .01 | .00 |
| ☐ 370 George Frazier | .03 | .01 | .00 |
| ☐ 371 Bill Hatcher | .06 | .02 | .00 |
| ☐ 372 Dave Lopes | .06 | .02 | .00 |
| ☐ 373 Gary Matthews | .06 | .02 | .00 |
| ☐ 374 Ron Meredith | .09 | .04 | .01 |
| ☐ 375 Keith Moreland | .06 | .02 | .00 |
| ☐ 376 Reggie Patterson | .03 | .01 | .00 |
| ☐ 377 Dick Ruthven | .03 | .01 | .00 |
| ☐ 378 Ryne Sandberg | .30 | .12 | .03 |
| ☐ 379 Scott Sanderson | .03 | .01 | .00 |
| ☐ 380 Lee Smith | .07 | .03 | .01 |
| ☐ 381 Lary Sorensen | .03 | .01 | .00 |
| ☐ 382 Chris Speier | .03 | .01 | .00 |
| ☐ 383 Rick Sutcliffe | .10 | .04 | .01 |
| ☐ 384 Steve Trout | .03 | .01 | .00 |
| ☐ 385 Gary Woods | .03 | .01 | .00 |
| ☐ 386 Bert Blyleven | .10 | .04 | .01 |
| ☐ 387 Tom Brunansky | .10 | .04 | .01 |
| ☐ 388 Randy Bush | .03 | .01 | .00 |
| ☐ 389 John Butcher | .03 | .01 | .00 |
| ☐ 390 Ron Davis | .03 | .01 | .00 |
| ☐ 391 Dave Engle | .03 | .01 | .00 |
| ☐ 392 Frank Eufemia | .10 | .04 | .01 |
| ☐ 393 Pete Filson | .03 | .01 | .00 |
| ☐ 394 Gary Gaetti | .09 | .04 | .01 |
| ☐ 395 Greg Gagne | .05 | .02 | .00 |
| ☐ 396 Mickey Hatcher | .03 | .01 | .00 |
| ☐ 397 Kent Hrbek | .15 | .06 | .01 |
| ☐ 398 Tim Laudner | .03 | .01 | .00 |
| ☐ 399 Rick Lysander | .03 | .01 | .00 |
| ☐ 400 Dave Meier | .03 | .01 | .00 |
| ☐ 401 Kirby Puckett | .60 | .24 | .06 |
| ☐ 402 Mark Salas | .06 | .02 | .00 |
| ☐ 403 Ken Schrom | .05 | .02 | .00 |
| ☐ 404 Roy Smalley | .05 | .02 | .00 |
| ☐ 405 Mike Smithson | .05 | .02 | .00 |
| ☐ 406 Mike Stenhouse | .05 | .02 | .00 |
| ☐ 407 Tim Teufel | .06 | .02 | .00 |
| ☐ 408 Frank Viola | .07 | .03 | .01 |
| ☐ 409 Ron Washington | .03 | .01 | .00 |
| ☐ 410 Keith Atherton | .03 | .01 | .00 |
| ☐ 411 Dusty Baker | .06 | .02 | .00 |
| ☐ 412 Tim Birtsas | .20 | .08 | .02 |
| ☐ 413 Bruce Bochte | .05 | .02 | .00 |
| ☐ 414 Chris Codiroli | .03 | .01 | .00 |
| ☐ 415 Dave Collins | .05 | .02 | .00 |
| ☐ 416 Mike Davis | .06 | .02 | .00 |
| ☐ 417 Alfredo Griffin | .05 | .02 | .00 |
| ☐ 418 Mike Heath | .03 | .01 | .00 |
| ☐ 419 Steve Henderson | .03 | .01 | .00 |
| ☐ 420 Donnie Hill | .03 | .01 | .00 |
| ☐ 421 Jay Howell | .05 | .02 | .00 |
| ☐ 422 Tommy John | .10 | .04 | .01 |
| ☐ 423 Dave Kingman | .10 | .04 | .01 |
| ☐ 424 Bill Krueger | .03 | .01 | .00 |
| ☐ 425 Rick Langford | .03 | .01 | .00 |
| ☐ 426 Carney Lansford | .08 | .03 | .01 |
| ☐ 427 Steve McCatty | .03 | .01 | .00 |
| ☐ 428 Dwayne Murphy | .06 | .02 | .00 |
| ☐ 429 Steve Ontiveros | .20 | .08 | .02 |
| ☐ 430 Tony Phillips | .03 | .01 | .00 |
| ☐ 431 Jose Rijo | .08 | .03 | .01 |
| ☐ 432 Mickey Tettleton | .10 | .04 | .01 |
| ☐ 433 Luis Aguayo | .03 | .01 | .00 |
| ☐ 434 Larry Andersen | .03 | .01 | .00 |
| ☐ 435 Steve Carlton | .30 | .12 | .03 |
| ☐ 436 Don Carman | .25 | .10 | .02 |
| ☐ 437 Tim Corcoran | .03 | .01 | .00 |
| ☐ 438 Darren Daulton | .20 | .08 | .02 |
| ☐ 439 John Denny | .06 | .02 | .00 |
| ☐ 440 Tom Foley | .03 | .01 | .00 |
| ☐ 441 Greg Gross | .03 | .01 | .00 |
| ☐ 442 Kevin Gross | .03 | .01 | .00 |
| ☐ 443 Von Hayes | .12 | .05 | .01 |
| ☐ 444 Charles Hudson | .05 | .02 | .00 |
| ☐ 445 Garry Maddox | .05 | .02 | .00 |
| ☐ 446 Shane Rawley | .06 | .02 | .00 |
| ☐ 447 Dave Rucker | .03 | .01 | .00 |
| ☐ 448 John Russell | .05 | .02 | .00 |
| ☐ 449 Juan Samuel | .10 | .04 | .01 |
| ☐ 450 Mike Schmidt | .40 | .16 | .04 |
| ☐ 451 Rick Schu | .06 | .02 | .00 |
| ☐ 452 Dave Shipanoff | .15 | .06 | .01 |

| | | | | |
|---|---|---|---|---|
| ☐ 453 Dave Stewart | .03 | .01 | .00 |
| ☐ 454 Jeff Stone | .05 | .02 | .00 |
| ☐ 455 Kent Tekulve | .05 | .02 | .00 |
| ☐ 456 Ozzie Virgil | .06 | .02 | .00 |
| ☐ 457 Glenn Wilson | .10 | .04 | .01 |
| ☐ 458 Jim Beattie | .03 | .01 | .00 |
| ☐ 459 Karl Best | .08 | .03 | .01 |
| ☐ 460 Barry Bonnell | .03 | .01 | .00 |
| ☐ 461 Phil Bradley | .20 | .08 | .02 |
| ☐ 462 Ivan Calderon | .20 | .08 | .02 |
| ☐ 463 Al Cowens | .05 | .02 | .00 |
| ☐ 464 Alvin Davis | .20 | .08 | .02 |
| ☐ 465 Dave Henderson | .06 | .02 | .00 |
| ☐ 466 Bob Kearney | .03 | .01 | .00 |
| ☐ 467 Mark Langston | .07 | .03 | .01 |
| ☐ 468 Bob Long | .03 | .01 | .00 |
| ☐ 469 Mike Moore | .06 | .02 | .00 |
| ☐ 470 Edwin Nunez | .05 | .02 | .00 |
| ☐ 471 Spike Owen | .06 | .02 | .00 |
| ☐ 472 Jack Perconte | .03 | .01 | .00 |
| ☐ 473 Jim Presley | .30 | .12 | .03 |
| ☐ 474 Donnie Scott | .03 | .01 | .00 |
| ☐ 475 Bill Swift | .05 | .02 | .00 |
| ☐ 476 Danny Tartabull | .25 | .10 | .02 |
| ☐ 477 Gorman Thomas | .08 | .03 | .01 |
| ☐ 478 Roy Thomas | .03 | .01 | .00 |
| ☐ 479 Ed VandeBerg | .03 | .01 | .00 |
| ☐ 480 Frank Wills | .10 | .04 | .01 |
| ☐ 481 Matt Young | .03 | .01 | .00 |
| ☐ 482 Ray Burris | .03 | .01 | .00 |
| ☐ 483 Jaime Cocanower | .03 | .01 | .00 |
| ☐ 484 Cecil Cooper | .10 | .04 | .01 |
| ☐ 485 Danny Darwin | .03 | .01 | .00 |
| ☐ 486 Rollie Fingers | .15 | .06 | .01 |
| ☐ 487 Jim Gantner | .05 | .02 | .00 |
| ☐ 488 Bob L. Gibson | .03 | .01 | .00 |
| ☐ 489 Moose Haas | .05 | .02 | .00 |
| ☐ 490 Teddy Higuera | .65 | .26 | .06 |
| ☐ 491 Paul Householder | .03 | .01 | .00 |
| ☐ 492 Pete Ladd | .03 | .01 | .00 |
| ☐ 493 Rick Manning | .03 | .01 | .00 |
| ☐ 494 Bob McClure | .03 | .01 | .00 |
| ☐ 495 Paul Molitor | .09 | .04 | .01 |
| ☐ 496 Charlie Moore | .03 | .01 | .00 |
| ☐ 497 Ben Oglivie | .06 | .02 | .00 |
| ☐ 498 Randy Ready | .05 | .02 | .00 |
| ☐ 499 Earnie Riles | .35 | .14 | .03 |
| ☐ 500 Ed Romero | .03 | .01 | .00 |
| ☐ 501 Bill Schroeder | .03 | .01 | .00 |
| ☐ 502 Ray Searage | .03 | .01 | .00 |
| ☐ 503 Ted Simmons | .10 | .04 | .01 |
| ☐ 504 Pete Vuckovich | .05 | .02 | .00 |
| ☐ 505 Rick Waits | .03 | .01 | .00 |
| ☐ 506 Robin Yount | .25 | .10 | .02 |
| ☐ 507 Len Barker | .05 | .02 | .00 |
| ☐ 508 Steve Bedrosian | .05 | .02 | .00 |
| ☐ 509 Bruce Benedict | .03 | .01 | .00 |
| ☐ 510 Rick Camp | .03 | .01 | .00 |
| ☐ 511 Rick Cerone | .03 | .01 | .00 |
| ☐ 512 Chris Chambliss | .05 | .02 | .00 |
| ☐ 513 Jeff Dedmon | .03 | .01 | .00 |
| ☐ 514 Terry Forster | .06 | .02 | .00 |
| ☐ 515 Gene Garber | .03 | .01 | .00 |
| ☐ 516 Terry Harper | .03 | .01 | .00 |
| ☐ 517 Bob Horner | .15 | .06 | .01 |
| ☐ 518 Glenn Hubbard | .03 | .01 | .00 |
| ☐ 519 Joe Johnson | .20 | .08 | .02 |
| ☐ 520 Brad Komminsk | .06 | .02 | .00 |
| ☐ 521 Rick Mahler | .03 | .01 | .00 |
| ☐ 522 Dale Murphy | .45 | .18 | .04 |
| ☐ 523 Ken Oberkfell | .03 | .01 | .00 |
| ☐ 524 Pascual Perez | .03 | .01 | .00 |
| ☐ 525 Gerald Perry | .03 | .01 | .00 |
| ☐ 526 Rafael Ramirez | .03 | .01 | .00 |
| ☐ 527 Steve Shields | .08 | .03 | .01 |
| ☐ 528 Zane Smith | .05 | .02 | .00 |
| ☐ 529 Bruce Sutter | .12 | .05 | .01 |
| ☐ 530 Milt Thompson | .20 | .08 | .02 |
| ☐ 531 Claudell Washington | .06 | .02 | .00 |
| ☐ 532 Paul Zuvella | .05 | .02 | .00 |
| ☐ 533 Vida Blue | .07 | .03 | .01 |
| ☐ 534 Bob Brenly | .05 | .02 | .00 |
| ☐ 535 Chris Brown | .90 | .36 | .09 |
| ☐ 536 Chili Davis | .08 | .03 | .01 |
| ☐ 537 Mark Davis | .03 | .01 | .00 |
| ☐ 538 Rob Deer | .25 | .10 | .02 |
| ☐ 539 Dan Driessen | .03 | .01 | .00 |
| ☐ 540 Scott Garrelts | .06 | .02 | .00 |
| ☐ 541 Dan Gladden | .06 | .02 | .00 |
| ☐ 542 Jim Gott | .03 | .01 | .00 |
| ☐ 543 David Green | .05 | .02 | .00 |
| ☐ 544 Atlee Hammaker | .05 | .02 | .00 |
| ☐ 545 Mike Jeffcoat | .03 | .01 | .00 |

| | | | | |
|---|---|---|---|---|
| ☐ 546 | Mike Krukow | .07 | .03 | .01 |
| ☐ 547 | Dave LaPoint | .03 | .01 | .00 |
| ☐ 548 | Jeff Leonard | .05 | .02 | .00 |
| ☐ 549 | Greg Minton | .05 | .02 | .00 |
| ☐ 550 | Alex Trevino | .03 | .01 | .00 |
| ☐ 551 | Manny Trillo | .05 | .02 | .00 |
| ☐ 552 | Jose Uribe | .08 | .03 | .01 |
| ☐ 553 | Brad Wellman | .03 | .01 | .00 |
| ☐ 554 | Frank Williams | .03 | .01 | .00 |
| ☐ 555 | Joel Youngblood | .03 | .01 | .00 |
| ☐ 556 | Alan Bannister | .03 | .01 | .00 |
| ☐ 557 | Glenn Brummer | .03 | .01 | .00 |
| ☐ 558 | Steve Buechele | .25 | .10 | .02 |
| ☐ 559 | Jose Guzman | .25 | .10 | .02 |
| ☐ 560 | Toby Harrah | .05 | .02 | .00 |
| ☐ 561 | Greg Harris | .05 | .02 | .00 |
| ☐ 562 | Dwayne Henry | .10 | .04 | .01 |
| ☐ 563 | Burt Hooton | .03 | .01 | .00 |
| ☐ 564 | Charlie Hough | .06 | .02 | .00 |
| ☐ 565 | Mike Mason | .03 | .01 | .00 |
| ☐ 566 | Oddibe McDowell | .30 | .12 | .03 |
| ☐ 567 | Dickie Noles | .03 | .01 | .00 |
| ☐ 568 | Pete O'Brien | .08 | .03 | .01 |
| ☐ 569 | Larry Parrish | .06 | .02 | .00 |
| ☐ 570 | Dave Rozema | .03 | .01 | .00 |
| ☐ 571 | Dave Schmidt | .03 | .01 | .00 |
| ☐ 572 | Don Slaught | .03 | .01 | .00 |
| ☐ 573 | Wayne Tolleson | .03 | .01 | .00 |
| ☐ 574 | Duane Walker | .03 | .01 | .00 |
| ☐ 575 | Gary Ward | .06 | .02 | .00 |
| ☐ 576 | Chris Welsh | .03 | .01 | .00 |
| ☐ 577 | Curtis Wilkerson | .03 | .01 | .00 |
| ☐ 578 | George Wright | .03 | .01 | .00 |
| ☐ 579 | Chris Bando | .03 | .01 | .00 |
| ☐ 580 | Tony Bernazard | .05 | .02 | .00 |
| ☐ 581 | Brett Butler | .08 | .03 | .01 |
| ☐ 582 | Ernie Camacho | .03 | .01 | .00 |
| ☐ 583 | Joe Carter | .25 | .10 | .02 |
| ☐ 584 | Carmen Castillo | .03 | .01 | .00 |
| ☐ 585 | Jamie Easterly | .03 | .01 | .00 |
| ☐ 586 | Julio Franco | .10 | .04 | .01 |
| ☐ 587 | Mel Hall | .08 | .03 | .01 |
| ☐ 588 | Mike Hargrove | .05 | .02 | .00 |
| ☐ 589 | Neal Heaton | .03 | .01 | .00 |
| ☐ 590 | Brook Jacoby | .10 | .04 | .01 |
| ☐ 591 | Otis Nixon | .20 | .08 | .02 |
| ☐ 592 | Jerry Reed | .08 | .03 | .01 |
| ☐ 593 | Vern Ruhle | .03 | .01 | .00 |
| ☐ 594 | Pat Tabler | .08 | .03 | .01 |
| ☐ 595 | Rich Thompson | .07 | .03 | .01 |
| ☐ 596 | Andre Thornton | .06 | .02 | .00 |
| ☐ 597 | Dave Von Ohlen | .03 | .01 | .00 |
| ☐ 598 | George Vukovich | .03 | .01 | .00 |
| ☐ 599 | Tom Waddell | .03 | .01 | .00 |
| ☐ 600 | Curt Wardle | .08 | .03 | .01 |
| ☐ 601 | Jerry Willard | .03 | .01 | .00 |
| ☐ 602 | Bill Almon | .03 | .01 | .00 |
| ☐ 603 | Mike Bielecki | .05 | .02 | .00 |
| ☐ 604 | Sid Bream | .07 | .03 | .01 |
| ☐ 605 | Mike Brown | .05 | .02 | .00 |
| ☐ 606 | Pat Clements | .20 | .08 | .02 |
| ☐ 607 | Jose DeLeon | .05 | .02 | .00 |
| ☐ 608 | Denny Gonzalez | .05 | .02 | .00 |
| ☐ 609 | Cecilio Guante | .03 | .01 | .00 |
| ☐ 610 | Steve Kemp | .06 | .02 | .00 |
| ☐ 611 | Sam Khalifa | .10 | .04 | .01 |
| ☐ 612 | Lee Mazzilli | .05 | .02 | .00 |
| ☐ 613 | Larry McWilliams | .03 | .01 | .00 |
| ☐ 614 | Jim Morrison | .03 | .01 | .00 |
| ☐ 615 | Joe Orsulak | .25 | .10 | .02 |
| ☐ 616 | Tony Pena | .12 | .05 | .01 |
| ☐ 617 | Johnny Ray | .10 | .04 | .01 |
| ☐ 618 | Rick Reuschel | .05 | .02 | .00 |
| ☐ 619 | R.J. Reynolds | .06 | .02 | .00 |
| ☐ 620 | Rick Rhoden | .06 | .02 | .00 |
| ☐ 621 | Don Robinson | .03 | .01 | .00 |
| ☐ 622 | Jason Thompson | .06 | .02 | .00 |
| ☐ 623 | Lee Tunnell | .03 | .01 | .00 |
| ☐ 624 | Jim Winn | .03 | .01 | .00 |
| ☐ 625 | Marvell Wynne | .03 | .01 | .00 |
| ☐ 626 | Dwight Gooden IA | .50 | .20 | .05 |
| ☐ 627 | Don Mattingly IA | .90 | .36 | .09 |
| ☐ 628 | 4192 (Pete Rose) | .40 | .16 | .04 |
| ☐ 629 | 3000 Career Hits | .20 | .08 | .02 |
| | Rod Carew | | | |
| ☐ 630 | 300 Career Wins | .15 | .06 | .01 |
| | Tom Seaver | | | |
| | Phil Niekro | | | |
| ☐ 631 | Ouch (Don Baylor) | .07 | .03 | .01 |
| ☐ 632 | Instant Offense | .20 | .08 | .02 |
| | Darryl Strawberry | | | |
| | Tim Raines | | | |
| ☐ 633 | Shortstops Supreme | .15 | .06 | .01 |
| | Cal Ripken | | | |
| | Alan Trammell | | | |
| ☐ 634 | Boggs and "Hero" | .50 | .20 | .05 |
| | Wade Boggs | | | |
| | George Brett | | | |
| ☐ 635 | Braves Dynamic Duo | .25 | .10 | .02 |
| | Bob Horner | | | |
| | Dale Murphy | | | |
| ☐ 636 | Cardinal Ignitors | .35 | .14 | .03 |
| | Willie McGee | | | |
| | Vince Coleman | | | |
| ☐ 637 | Terror on Basepaths | .35 | .14 | .03 |
| | Vince Coleman | | | |
| ☐ 638 | Charlie Hustle / Dr.K | 1.00 | .40 | .10 |
| | Pete Rose | | | |
| | Dwight Gooden | | | |
| ☐ 639 | 1984 and 1985 AL | 1.50 | .60 | .15 |
| | Batting Champs | | | |
| | Wade Boggs | | | |
| | Don Mattingly | | | |
| ☐ 640 | NL West Sluggers | .25 | .10 | .02 |
| | Dale Murphy | | | |
| | Steve Garvey | | | |
| | Dave Parker | | | |
| ☐ 641 | Staff Aces | .50 | .20 | .05 |
| | Fernando Valenzuela | | | |
| | Dwight Gooden | | | |
| ☐ 642 | Blue Jay Stoppers | .07 | .03 | .01 |
| | Jimmy Key | | | |
| | Dave Stieb | | | |
| ☐ 643 | AL All-Star Backstops | .07 | .03 | .01 |
| | Carlton Fisk | | | |
| | Rich Gedman | | | |
| ☐ 644 | Gene Walter and | .25 | .10 | .02 |
| | Benito Santiago | | | |
| ☐ 645 | Mike Woodard and | .12 | .05 | .01 |
| | Collin Ward | | | |
| ☐ 646 | Kal Daniels and | .40 | .16 | .04 |
| | Paul O'Neill | | | |
| ☐ 647 | Andres Galarraga and | .35 | .14 | .03 |
| | Fred Toliver | | | |
| ☐ 648 | Bob Kipper and | .20 | .08 | .02 |
| | Curt Ford | | | |
| ☐ 649 | Jose Canseco and | 6.50 | 2.60 | .65 |
| | Eric Plunk | | | |
| ☐ 650 | Mark McLemore and | .15 | .06 | .01 |
| | Gus Polidor | | | |
| ☐ 651 | Rob Woodward and | .25 | .10 | .02 |
| | Mickey Brantley | | | |
| ☐ 652 | Billy Jo Robidoux and | .25 | .10 | .02 |
| | Mark Funderburk | | | |
| ☐ 653 | Cecil Fielder and | 2.00 | .80 | .20 |
| | Cory Snyder | | | |
| ☐ 654 | CL: Royals/Cardinals | .07 | .01 | .00 |
| | Blue Jays/Mets | | | |
| ☐ 655 | CL: Yankees/Dodgers | .07 | .01 | .00 |
| | Angels/Reds | | | |
| ☐ 656 | CL: White Sox/Tigers | .07 | .01 | .00 |
| | Expos/Orioles | | | |
| | (279 Dennis, | | | |
| | 280 Tippy) | | | |
| ☐ 657 | CL: Astros/Padres | .07 | .01 | .00 |
| | Red Sox/Cubs | | | |
| ☐ 658 | CL: Twins/A's | .07 | .01 | .00 |
| | Phillies/Mariners | | | |
| ☐ 659 | CL: Brewers/Braves | .07 | .01 | .00 |
| | Giants/Rangers | | | |
| ☐ 660 | CL: Indians/Pirates | .07 | .01 | .00 |
| | Special Cards | | | |
| ☐ C1 | Royals Logo | .05 | .02 | .00 |
| | (wax pack box card) | | | |
| ☐ C2 | George Brett | .60 | .24 | .06 |
| | (wax pack box card) | | | |
| ☐ C3 | Ozzie Guillen | .25 | .10 | .02 |
| | (wax pack box card) | | | |
| ☐ C4 | Dale Murphy | .90 | .36 | .09 |
| | (wax pack box card) | | | |
| ☐ C5 | Cardinals Logo | .05 | .02 | .00 |
| | (wax pack box card) | | | |
| ☐ C6 | Tom Browning | .15 | .06 | .01 |
| | (wax pack box card) | | | |
| ☐ C7 | Gary Carter | .35 | .14 | .03 |
| | (wax pack box card) | | | |
| ☐ C8 | Carlton Fisk | .15 | .06 | .01 |
| | (wax pack box card) | | | |

## 1986 Fleer Future HOF

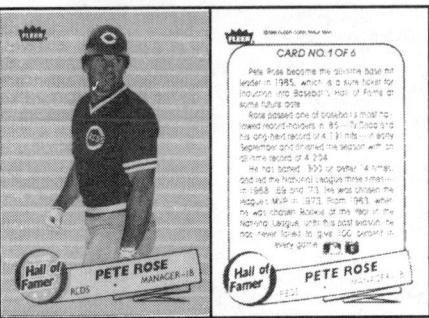

These attractive cards were issued as inserts with the Fleer three-packs. They are the same size as the regular issue (2 1/2" by 3 1/2") and feature players that Fleer predicts will be "Future Hall of Famers." The card backs describe career highlights, records, and honors won by the player. The cards are numbered on the back; Pete Rose is given the honor of being card #1.

|  | MINT | VG-E | F-G |
|---|---|---|---|
| COMPLETE SET | 6.00 | 2.00 | .50 |
| COMMON PLAYER (1-6) | .75 | .30 | .07 |

| | | MINT | VG-E | F-G |
|---|---|---|---|---|
| ☐ 1 | Pete Rose | 2.25 | .80 | .20 |
| ☐ 2 | Steve Carlton | .80 | .30 | .07 |
| ☐ 3 | Tom Seaver | 1.00 | .30 | .07 |
| ☐ 4 | Rod Carew | .80 | .30 | .07 |
| ☐ 5 | Nolan Ryan | 1.00 | .30 | .07 |
| ☐ 6 | Reggie Jackson | 1.25 | .40 | .10 |

## 1986 Fleer All-Stars

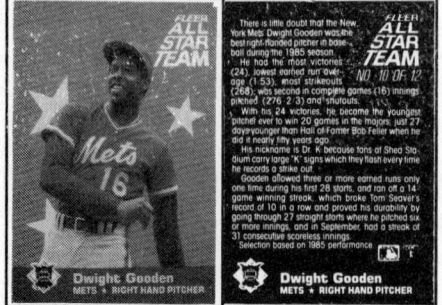

Fleer selected a 12 card (Major League) All-Star team to be included as inserts in their 39 cent wax packs and 59 cent cello packs. However they were randomly inserted in such a way that not all wax packs contain the insert. Cards measure 2 1/2" by 3 1/2" and feature attractive red backgrounds (American Leaguers) and blue backgrounds (National Leaguers). The 12 selections cover each position, left and right-handed starting pitchers, a reliever, and a designated hitter.

|  | MINT | VG-E | F-G |
|---|---|---|---|
| COMPLETE SET | 12.00 | 4.00 | 1.00 |
| COMMON PLAYER | .20 | .08 | .02 |

| | | MINT | VG-E | F-G |
|---|---|---|---|---|
| ☐ 1 | Don Mattingly First Base | 4.50 | 1.60 | .40 |
| ☐ 2 | Tom Herr Second Base | .25 | .08 | .02 |
| ☐ 3 | George Brett Third Base | 1.25 | .40 | .10 |
| ☐ 4 | Gary Carter Catcher | .90 | .30 | .07 |
| ☐ 5 | Cal Ripken Shortstop | .90 | .30 | .07 |
| ☐ 6 | Dave Parker Outfield | .45 | .16 | .04 |
| ☐ 7 | Rickey Henderson Outfield | 1.25 | .40 | .10 |
| ☐ 8 | Pedro Guerrero Outfield | .45 | .16 | .04 |
| ☐ 9 | Dan Quisenberry Relief Pitcher | .25 | .10 | .02 |
| ☐ 10 | Dwight Gooden Right-Hand Pitcher | 3.00 | 1.00 | .25 |
| ☐ 11 | Gorman Thomas Designated Hitter | .25 | .08 | .02 |
| ☐ 12 | John Tudor Left-Hand Pitcher | .25 | .10 | .02 |

## 1986 Fleer League Leaders

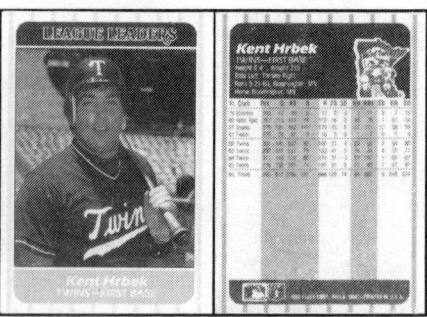

This 44 card set is also sometimes referred to as the Walgreen's set. Although the set was distributed through Walgreen's, there is no mention on the cards or box of that fact. The cards are easily recognizable by the fact that they contain the phrase "Fleer League Leaders" at the top of the obverse. Both sides of the cards are designed with a blue stripe on white pattern. The checklist for the set is given on the outside of the red, white, blue, and gold box in which the set was packaged. Cards are numbered on the back and measure the standard 2 1/2" by 3 1/2".

|  | MINT | VG-E | F-G |
|---|---|---|---|
| COMPLETE SET | 5.00 | 1.50 | .40 |
| COMMON PLAYER | .10 | .04 | .01 |

| | | MINT | VG-E | F-G |
|---|---|---|---|---|
| ☐ 1 | Wade Boggs | .60 | .24 | .06 |
| ☐ 2 | George Brett | .40 | .16 | .04 |
| ☐ 3 | Jose Canseco | .75 | .30 | .07 |
| ☐ 4 | Rod Carew | .30 | .12 | .03 |
| ☐ 5 | Gary Carter | .30 | .12 | .03 |
| ☐ 6 | Jack Clark | .10 | .04 | .01 |
| ☐ 7 | Vince Coleman | .60 | .24 | .06 |
| ☐ 8 | Jose Cruz | .10 | .04 | .01 |
| ☐ 9 | Alvin Davis | .15 | .06 | .01 |
| ☐ 10 | Mariano Duncan | .15 | .06 | .01 |
| ☐ 11 | Leon Durham | .10 | .04 | .01 |
| ☐ 12 | Carlton Fisk | .20 | .08 | .02 |
| ☐ 13 | Julio Franco | .10 | .04 | .01 |
| ☐ 14 | Scott Garrelts | .10 | .04 | .01 |
| ☐ 15 | Steve Garvey | .40 | .16 | .04 |
| ☐ 16 | Dwight Gooden | .60 | .24 | .06 |
| ☐ 17 | Ozzie Guillen | .20 | .08 | .02 |
| ☐ 18 | Willie Hernandez | .10 | .04 | .01 |
| ☐ 19 | Bob Horner | .20 | .08 | .02 |

| | | MINT | VG-E | F-G |
|---|---|---|---|---|
| ☐ 20 | Kent Hrbek | .20 | .08 | .02 |
| ☐ 21 | Charlie Leibrandt | .10 | .04 | .01 |
| ☐ 22 | Don Mattingly | .75 | .30 | .07 |
| ☐ 23 | Oddibe McDowell | .25 | .10 | .02 |
| ☐ 24 | Willie McGee | .20 | .08 | .02 |
| ☐ 25 | Keith Moreland | .10 | .04 | .01 |
| ☐ 26 | Lloyd Moseby | .15 | .06 | .01 |
| ☐ 27 | Dale Murphy | .50 | .20 | .05 |
| ☐ 28 | Phil Niekro | .20 | .08 | .02 |
| ☐ 29 | Joe Orsulak | .10 | .04 | .01 |
| ☐ 30 | Dave Parker | .20 | .08 | .02 |
| ☐ 31 | Lance Parrish | .25 | .10 | .02 |
| ☐ 32 | Kirby Puckett | .25 | .10 | .02 |
| ☐ 33 | Tim Raines | .25 | .10 | .02 |
| ☐ 34 | Earnie Riles | .15 | .06 | .01 |
| ☐ 35 | Cal Ripken, Jr. | .40 | .16 | .04 |
| ☐ 36 | Pete Rose | .60 | .24 | .06 |
| ☐ 37 | Bret Saberhagen | .20 | .08 | .02 |
| ☐ 38 | Juan Samuel | .15 | .06 | .01 |
| ☐ 39 | Ryne Sandberg | .35 | .14 | .03 |
| ☐ 40 | Tom Seaver | .30 | .12 | .03 |
| ☐ 41 | Lee Smith | .10 | .04 | .01 |
| ☐ 42 | Ozzie Smith | .20 | .08 | .02 |
| ☐ 43 | Dave Stieb | .15 | .06 | .01 |
| ☐ 44 | Robin Yount | .30 | .12 | .03 |

| | | MINT | VG-E | F-G |
|---|---|---|---|---|
| ☐ 25 | LaMarr Hoyt | .10 | .04 | .01 |
| ☐ 26 | Reggie Jackson | .50 | .20 | .05 |
| ☐ 27 | Don Mattingly | .75 | .30 | .07 |
| ☐ 28 | Oddibe McDowell | .25 | .10 | .02 |
| ☐ 29 | Willie McGee | .20 | .08 | .02 |
| ☐ 30 | Paul Molitor | .15 | .06 | .01 |
| ☐ 31 | Dale Murphy | .50 | .20 | .05 |
| ☐ 32 | Eddie Murray | .40 | .16 | .04 |
| ☐ 33 | Dave Parker | .30 | .12 | .03 |
| ☐ 34 | Tony Pena | .15 | .06 | .01 |
| ☐ 35 | Jeff Reardon | .10 | .04 | .01 |
| ☐ 36 | Cal Ripken, Jr. | .40 | .16 | .04 |
| ☐ 37 | Pete Rose | .60 | .24 | .06 |
| ☐ 38 | Bret Saberhagen | .20 | .08 | .02 |
| ☐ 39 | Juan Samuel | .15 | .06 | .01 |
| ☐ 40 | Ryne Sandberg | .35 | .14 | .03 |
| ☐ 41 | Mike Schmidt | .50 | .20 | .05 |
| ☐ 42 | Lee Smith | .10 | .04 | .01 |
| ☐ 43 | Don Sutton | .20 | .08 | .02 |
| ☐ 44 | Lou Whitaker | .15 | .06 | .01 |

## 1986 Fleer Limited Edition

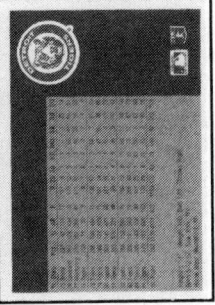

The 44 card boxed set was produced by Fleer for McCrory's. The cards are standard size 2 1/2" by 3 1/2" and have green and yellow borders. Card backs are printed in red and black on white card stock. Cards are numbered on the back; the back of the original box gives a complete checklist of the players in the set. The box also contains six logo stickers.

| | | MINT | VG-E | F-G |
|---|---|---|---|---|
| | COMPLETE SET | 4.50 | 1.50 | .40 |
| | COMMON PLAYER | .10 | .04 | .01 |
| ☐ 1 | Doyle Alexander | .10 | .04 | .01 |
| ☐ 2 | Joaquin Andujar | .15 | .06 | .01 |
| ☐ 3 | Harold Baines | .25 | .10 | .02 |
| ☐ 4 | Wade Boggs | .60 | .24 | .06 |
| ☐ 5 | Phil Bradley | .20 | .08 | .02 |
| ☐ 6 | George Brett | .40 | .16 | .04 |
| ☐ 7 | Hubie Brooks | .15 | .06 | .01 |
| ☐ 8 | Chris Brown | .20 | .08 | .02 |
| ☐ 9 | Tom Brunansky | .15 | .06 | .01 |
| ☐ 10 | Gary Carter | .35 | .14 | .03 |
| ☐ 11 | Vince Coleman | .40 | .16 | .04 |
| ☐ 12 | Cecil Cooper | .15 | .06 | .01 |
| ☐ 13 | Jose Cruz | .10 | .04 | .01 |
| ☐ 14 | Mike Davis | .10 | .04 | .01 |
| ☐ 15 | Carlton Fisk | .20 | .08 | .02 |
| ☐ 16 | Julio Franco | .10 | .04 | .01 |
| ☐ 17 | Damaso Garcia | .10 | .04 | .01 |
| ☐ 18 | Rich Gedman | .15 | .06 | .01 |
| ☐ 19 | Kirk Gibson | .25 | .10 | .02 |
| ☐ 20 | Dwight Gooden | .60 | .24 | .06 |
| ☐ 21 | Pedro Guerrero | .25 | .10 | .02 |
| ☐ 22 | Tony Gwynn | .30 | .12 | .03 |
| ☐ 23 | Rickey Henderson | .50 | .20 | .05 |
| ☐ 24 | Orel Hershiser | .20 | .08 | .02 |

## 1986 Fleer Mini

The Fleer "Classic Miniatures" set consists of 120 small cards with all new pictures of the players as compared to the 1986 Fleer regular issue. The cards are only 1 13/16" by 2 9/16", making them one of the smallest (in size) produced in recent memory. Card backs provide career year-by-year statistics. The complete set was distributed in a red, white, and silver box along with 18 logo stickers. The card numbering is done in team order as is the usual Fleer style.

| | | MINT | VG-E | F-G |
|---|---|---|---|---|
| | COMPLETE SET | 12.50 | 5.00 | 1.25 |
| | COMMON PLAYER | .05 | .02 | .00 |
| ☐ 1 | George Brett | .25 | .10 | .02 |
| ☐ 2 | Dan Quisenberry | .10 | .04 | .01 |
| ☐ 3 | Bret Saberhagen | .15 | .06 | .01 |
| ☐ 4 | Lonnie Smith | .05 | .02 | .00 |
| ☐ 5 | Willie Wilson | .10 | .04 | .01 |
| ☐ 6 | Jack Clark | .10 | .04 | .01 |
| ☐ 7 | Vince Coleman | .25 | .10 | .02 |
| ☐ 8 | Tom Herr | .05 | .02 | .00 |
| ☐ 9 | Willie McGee | .15 | .06 | .01 |
| ☐ 10 | Ozzie Smith | .10 | .04 | .01 |
| ☐ 11 | John Tudor | .10 | .04 | .01 |
| ☐ 12 | Jesse Barfield | .15 | .06 | .01 |
| ☐ 13 | George Bell | .15 | .06 | .01 |
| ☐ 14 | Tony Fernandez | .10 | .04 | .01 |
| ☐ 15 | Damaso Garcia | .05 | .02 | .00 |
| ☐ 16 | Dave Stieb | .10 | .04 | .01 |
| ☐ 17 | Gary Carter | .20 | .08 | .02 |
| ☐ 18 | Ron Darling | .15 | .06 | .01 |
| ☐ 19A | Dwight Gooden (R on Mets logo) | 1.00 | .40 | .10 |
| ☐ 19B | Dwight Gooden (no R on Mets logo) | 1.50 | .60 | .15 |
| ☐ 20 | Keith Hernandez | .15 | .06 | .01 |
| ☐ 21 | Darryl Strawberry | .30 | .12 | .03 |
| ☐ 22 | Ron Guidry | .15 | .06 | .01 |
| ☐ 23 | Rickey Henderson | .25 | .10 | .02 |

| | | | | |
|---|---|---|---|---|
| ☐ 24 | Don Mattingly | 2.00 | .80 | .20 |
| ☐ 25 | Dave Righetti | .15 | .06 | .01 |
| ☐ 26 | Dave Winfield | .20 | .08 | .02 |
| ☐ 27 | Mariano Duncan | .10 | .04 | .01 |
| ☐ 28 | Pedro Guerrero | .15 | .06 | .01 |
| ☐ 29 | Bill Madlock | .10 | .04 | .01 |
| ☐ 30 | Mike Marshall | .10 | .04 | .01 |
| ☐ 31 | Fernando Valenzuela | .20 | .08 | .02 |
| ☐ 32 | Reggie Jackson | .25 | .10 | .02 |
| ☐ 33 | Gary Pettis | .10 | .04 | .01 |
| ☐ 34 | Ron Romanick | .10 | .04 | .01 |
| ☐ 35 | Don Sutton | .10 | .04 | .01 |
| ☐ 36 | Mike Witt | .10 | .04 | .01 |
| ☐ 37 | Buddy Bell | .10 | .04 | .01 |
| ☐ 38 | Tom Browning | .10 | .04 | .01 |
| ☐ 39 | Dave Parker | .15 | .06 | .01 |
| ☐ 40 | Pete Rose | .75 | .30 | .07 |
| ☐ 41 | Mario Soto | .05 | .02 | .00 |
| ☐ 42 | Harold Baines | .15 | .06 | .01 |
| ☐ 43 | Carlton Fisk | .15 | .06 | .01 |
| ☐ 44 | Ozzie Guillen | .15 | .06 | .01 |
| ☐ 45 | Ron Kittle | .10 | .04 | .01 |
| ☐ 46 | Tom Seaver | .20 | .08 | .02 |
| ☐ 47 | Kirk Gibson | .15 | .06 | .01 |
| ☐ 48 | Jack Morris | .15 | .06 | .01 |
| ☐ 49 | Lance Parrish | .15 | .06 | .01 |
| ☐ 50 | Alan Trammell | .10 | .04 | .01 |
| ☐ 51 | Lou Whitaker | .10 | .04 | .01 |
| ☐ 52 | Hubie Brooks | .10 | .04 | .01 |
| ☐ 53 | Andre Dawson | .15 | .06 | .01 |
| ☐ 54 | Tim Raines | .20 | .08 | .02 |
| ☐ 55 | Bryn Smith | .05 | .02 | .00 |
| ☐ 56 | Tim Wallach | .05 | .02 | .00 |
| ☐ 57 | Mike Boddicker | .10 | .04 | .01 |
| ☐ 58 | Eddie Murray | .25 | .10 | .02 |
| ☐ 59 | Cal Ripken, Jr. | .25 | .10 | .02 |
| ☐ 60 | John Shelby | .05 | .02 | .00 |
| ☐ 61 | Mike Young | .10 | .04 | .01 |
| ☐ 62 | Jose Cruz | .10 | .04 | .01 |
| ☐ 63 | Glenn Davis | .25 | .10 | .02 |
| ☐ 64 | Phil Garner | .05 | .02 | .00 |
| ☐ 65 | Nolan Ryan | .20 | .08 | .02 |
| ☐ 66 | Mike Scott | .15 | .06 | .01 |
| ☐ 67 | Steve Garvey | .20 | .08 | .02 |
| ☐ 68 | Goose Gossage | .10 | .04 | .01 |
| ☐ 69 | Tony Gwynn | .25 | .10 | .02 |
| ☐ 70 | Andy Hawkins | .05 | .02 | .00 |
| ☐ 71 | Garry Templeton | .05 | .02 | .00 |
| ☐ 72 | Wade Boggs | .75 | .30 | .07 |
| ☐ 73 | Roger Clemens | .75 | .30 | .07 |
| ☐ 74 | Dwight Evans | .10 | .04 | .01 |
| ☐ 75 | Rich Gedman | .10 | .04 | .01 |
| ☐ 76 | Jim Rice | .20 | .08 | .02 |
| ☐ 77 | Shawon Dunston | .10 | .04 | .01 |
| ☐ 78 | Leon Durham | .10 | .04 | .01 |
| ☐ 79 | Keith Moreland | .10 | .04 | .01 |
| ☐ 80 | Ryne Sandberg | .20 | .08 | .02 |
| ☐ 81 | Rick Sutcliffe | .10 | .04 | .01 |
| ☐ 82 | Bert Blyleven | .10 | .04 | .01 |
| ☐ 83 | Tom Brunansky | .10 | .04 | .01 |
| ☐ 84 | Kent Hrbek | .15 | .06 | .01 |
| ☐ 85 | Kirby Puckett | .20 | .08 | .02 |
| ☐ 86 | Bruce Bochte | .05 | .02 | .00 |
| ☐ 87 | Jose Canseco | 1.25 | .50 | .12 |
| ☐ 88 | Mike Davis | .05 | .02 | .00 |
| ☐ 89 | Jay Howell | .05 | .02 | .00 |
| ☐ 90 | Dwayne Murphy | .05 | .02 | .00 |
| ☐ 91 | Steve Carlton | .20 | .08 | .02 |
| ☐ 92 | Von Hayes | .15 | .06 | .01 |
| ☐ 93 | Juan Samuel | .10 | .04 | .01 |
| ☐ 94 | Mike Schmidt | .35 | .14 | .03 |
| ☐ 95 | Glenn Wilson | .10 | .04 | .01 |
| ☐ 96 | Phil Bradley | .15 | .06 | .01 |
| ☐ 97 | Alvin Davis | .15 | .06 | .01 |
| ☐ 98 | Jim Presley | .15 | .06 | .01 |
| ☐ 99 | Danny Tartabull | .20 | .08 | .02 |
| ☐ 100 | Cecil Cooper | .10 | .04 | .01 |
| ☐ 101 | Paul Molitor | .10 | .04 | .01 |
| ☐ 102 | Ernie Riles | .10 | .04 | .01 |
| ☐ 103 | Robin Yount | .20 | .08 | .02 |
| ☐ 104 | Bob Horner | .15 | .06 | .01 |
| ☐ 105 | Dale Murphy | .35 | .14 | .03 |
| ☐ 106 | Bruce Sutter | .10 | .04 | .01 |
| ☐ 107 | Claudell Washington | .05 | .02 | .00 |
| ☐ 108 | Chris Brown | .20 | .08 | .02 |
| ☐ 109 | Chili Davis | .05 | .02 | .00 |
| ☐ 110 | Scott Garrelts | .05 | .02 | .00 |
| ☐ 111 | Oddibe McDowell | .20 | .08 | .02 |
| ☐ 112 | Pete O'Brien | .10 | .04 | .01 |
| ☐ 113 | Gary Ward | .05 | .02 | .00 |
| ☐ 114 | Brett Butler | .10 | .04 | .01 |
| ☐ 115 | Julio Franco | .10 | .04 | .01 |
| ☐ 116 | Brook Jacoby | .10 | .04 | .01 |

| | | | | |
|---|---|---|---|---|
| ☐ 117 | Mike Brown OF | .05 | .02 | .00 |
| ☐ 118 | Joe Orsulak | .10 | .04 | .01 |
| ☐ 119 | Tony Pena | .10 | .04 | .01 |
| ☐ 120 | R.J. Reynolds | .10 | .04 | .01 |

## 1986 Fleer Sluggers/Pitchers

Fleer produced this 44 card boxed set although it was primarily distributed by Kress, McCrory, Newberry, T.G.Y., and other similar stores. The set features 22 sluggers and 22 pitchers and is subtitled "Baseball's Best". Card are standard size, 2 1/2" by 3 1/2", and was packed in its own red, white, blue, and yellow custom box along with six logo stickers. The set checklist is given on the back of the box.

| | | MINT | VG-E | F-G |
|---|---|---|---|---|
| COMPLETE SET | | 5.00 | 2.00 | .40 |
| COMMON PLAYER | | .10 | .04 | .01 |

| | | | | |
|---|---|---|---|---|
| ☐ 1 | Bert Blyleven | .15 | .06 | .01 |
| ☐ 2 | Wade Boggs | .60 | .24 | .06 |
| ☐ 3 | George Brett | .40 | .16 | .04 |
| ☐ 4 | Tom Browning | .15 | .06 | .01 |
| ☐ 5 | Jose Canseco | .75 | .30 | .07 |
| ☐ 6 | Will Clark | .35 | .14 | .03 |
| ☐ 7 | Roger Clemens | .60 | .24 | .06 |
| ☐ 8 | Alvin Davis | .15 | .06 | .01 |
| ☐ 9 | Julio Franco | .15 | .06 | .01 |
| ☐ 10 | Kirk Gibson | .20 | .08 | .02 |
| ☐ 11 | Dwight Gooden | .60 | .24 | .06 |
| ☐ 12 | Goose Gossage | .15 | .06 | .01 |
| ☐ 13 | Pedro Guerrero | .20 | .08 | .02 |
| ☐ 14 | Ron Guidry | .20 | .08 | .02 |
| ☐ 15 | Tony Gwynn | .35 | .14 | .03 |
| ☐ 16 | Orel Hershiser | .20 | .08 | .02 |
| ☐ 17 | Kent Hrbek | .20 | .08 | .02 |
| ☐ 18 | Reggie Jackson | .40 | .16 | .04 |
| ☐ 19 | Wally Joyner | 1.25 | .50 | .12 |
| ☐ 20 | Charlie Leibrandt | .10 | .04 | .01 |
| ☐ 21 | Don Mattingly | 1.00 | .40 | .10 |
| ☐ 22 | Willie McGee | .20 | .08 | .02 |
| ☐ 23 | Jack Morris | .20 | .08 | .02 |
| ☐ 24 | Dale Murphy | .50 | .20 | .05 |
| ☐ 25 | Eddie Murray | .35 | .14 | .03 |
| ☐ 26 | Jeff Reardon | .10 | .04 | .01 |
| ☐ 27 | Rick Reuschel | .10 | .04 | .01 |
| ☐ 28 | Cal Ripken, Jr. | .35 | .14 | .03 |
| ☐ 29 | Pete Rose | .60 | .24 | .06 |
| ☐ 30 | Nolan Ryan | .35 | .14 | .03 |
| ☐ 31 | Bret Saberhagen | .20 | .08 | .02 |
| ☐ 32 | Ryne Sandberg | .30 | .12 | .03 |
| ☐ 33 | Mike Schmidt | .50 | .20 | .05 |
| ☐ 34 | Tom Seaver | .30 | .12 | .03 |
| ☐ 36 | Mario Soto | .10 | .04 | .01 |
| ☐ 37 | Dave Stieb | .15 | .06 | .01 |
| ☐ 38 | Darryl Strawberry | .50 | .20 | .05 |
| ☐ 39 | Rick Sutcliffe | .15 | .06 | .01 |
| ☐ 40 | John Tudor | .15 | .06 | .01 |
| ☐ 41 | Fernando Valenzuela | .30 | .12 | .03 |
| ☐ 42 | Bobby Witt | .25 | .10 | .02 |
| ☐ 43 | Mike Witt | .15 | .06 | .01 |
| ☐ 44 | Robin Yount | .30 | .12 | .03 |

# 1986 Fleer Update

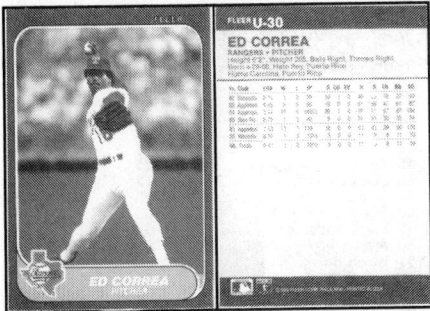

This 132 card set was distributed by Fleer to dealers as a complete set within a custom box. In addition to the complete set of 132 cards, the box also contains 25 Team Logo Stickers.The card fronts look very similar to the 1986 Fleer regular issue. The cards are numbered (with a U prefix) alphabetically according to player's last name. Cards measure the standard size, 2 1/2" by 3 1/2".

|  | MINT | VG-E | F-G |
|---|---|---|---|
| COMPLETE SET | 15.00 | 6.00 | 1.50 |
| COMMON PLAYER | .06 | .02 | .00 |

| | | MINT | VG-E | F-G |
|---|---|---|---|---|
| ☐ | U1 Mike Aldrete | .20 | .08 | .02 |
| ☐ | U2 Andy Allanson | .20 | .08 | .02 |
| ☐ | U3 Neil Allen | .06 | .02 | .00 |
| ☐ | U4 Joaquin Andujar | .10 | .04 | .01 |
| ☐ | U5 Paul Assenmacher | .20 | .08 | .02 |
| ☐ | U6 Scott Bailes | .20 | .08 | .02 |
| ☐ | U7 Jay Baller | .10 | .04 | .01 |
| ☐ | U8 Scott Bankhead | .20 | .08 | .02 |
| ☐ | U9 Bill Bathe | .15 | .06 | .01 |
| ☐ | U10 Don Baylor | .15 | .06 | .01 |
| ☐ | U11 Billy Beane | .15 | .06 | .01 |
| ☐ | U12 Steve Bedrosian | .10 | .04 | .01 |
| ☐ | U13 Juan Beniquez | .10 | .04 | .01 |
| ☐ | U14 Barry Bonds | .75 | .30 | .07 |
| ☐ | U15 Bobby Bonilla | .20 | .08 | .02 |
| ☐ | U16 Rich Bordi | .06 | .02 | .00 |
| ☐ | U17 Bill Campbell | .06 | .02 | .00 |
| ☐ | U18 Tom Candiotti | .10 | .04 | .01 |
| ☐ | U19 John Cangelosi | .35 | .14 | .03 |
| ☐ | U20 Jose Canseco | 3.00 | 1.20 | .30 |
| | (headings on back for a pitcher) | | | |
| ☐ | U21 Chuck Cary | .20 | .08 | .02 |
| ☐ | U22 Juan Castillo | .15 | .06 | .01 |
| ☐ | U23 Rick Cerone | .06 | .02 | .00 |
| ☐ | U24 John Cerutti | .30 | .12 | .03 |
| ☐ | U25 Will Clark | 1.25 | .50 | .12 |
| ☐ | U26 Mark Clear | .06 | .02 | .00 |
| ☐ | U27 Darnell Coles | .20 | .08 | .02 |
| ☐ | U28 Dave Collins | .06 | .02 | .00 |
| ☐ | U29 Tim Conroy | .06 | .02 | .00 |
| ☐ | U30 Ed Correa | .35 | .14 | .03 |
| ☐ | U31 Joe Cowley | .10 | .04 | .01 |
| ☐ | U32 Bill Dawley | .06 | .02 | .00 |
| ☐ | U33 Rob Deer | .40 | .16 | .04 |
| ☐ | U34 John Denny | .10 | .04 | .01 |
| ☐ | U35 Jim Deshaies | .50 | .20 | .05 |
| ☐ | U36 Doug Drabek | .20 | .08 | .02 |
| ☐ | U37 Mike Easler | .10 | .04 | .01 |
| ☐ | U38 Mark Eichhorn | .50 | .20 | .05 |
| ☐ | U39 Dave Engle | .06 | .02 | .00 |
| ☐ | U40 Mike Fischlin | .06 | .02 | .00 |
| ☐ | U41 Scott Fletcher | .10 | .04 | .01 |
| ☐ | U42 Terry Forster | .10 | .04 | .01 |
| ☐ | U43 Terry Francona | .06 | .02 | .00 |
| ☐ | U44 Andres Galarraga | .20 | .08 | .02 |
| ☐ | U45 Lee Guetterman | .20 | .08 | .02 |
| ☐ | U46 Bill Gullickson | .10 | .04 | .01 |
| ☐ | U47 Jackie Gutierrez | .06 | .02 | .00 |
| ☐ | U48 Moose Haas | .10 | .04 | .01 |
| ☐ | U49 Billy Hatcher | .10 | .04 | .01 |
| ☐ | U50 Mike Heath | .06 | .02 | .00 |
| ☐ | U51 Guy Hoffman | .06 | .02 | .00 |
| ☐ | U52 Tom Hume | .06 | .02 | .00 |
| ☐ | U53 Pete Incaviglia | 2.00 | .80 | .20 |
| ☐ | U54 Dane Iorg | .06 | .02 | .00 |
| ☐ | U55 Chris James | .35 | .14 | .03 |
| ☐ | U56 Stan Javier | .20 | .08 | .02 |
| ☐ | U57 Tommy John | .15 | .06 | .01 |
| ☐ | U58 Tracy Jones | .30 | .12 | .03 |
| ☐ | U59 Wally Joyner | 3.50 | 1.40 | .35 |
| ☐ | U60 Wayne Krenchicki | .06 | .02 | .00 |
| ☐ | U61 John Kruk | .30 | .12 | .03 |
| ☐ | U62 Mike LaCoss | .06 | .02 | .00 |
| ☐ | U63 Pete Ladd | .06 | .02 | .00 |
| ☐ | U64 Dave LaPoint | .06 | .02 | .00 |
| ☐ | U65 Mike Lavalliere | .15 | .06 | .01 |
| ☐ | U66 Rudy Law | .06 | .02 | .00 |
| ☐ | U67 Dennis Leonard | .10 | .04 | .01 |
| ☐ | U68 Steve Lombardozzi | .15 | .06 | .01 |
| ☐ | U69 Aurelio Lopez | .06 | .02 | .00 |
| ☐ | U70 Mickey Mahler | .06 | .02 | .00 |
| ☐ | U71 Candy Maldonado | .10 | .04 | .01 |
| ☐ | U72 Roger Mason | .15 | .06 | .01 |
| ☐ | U73 Greg Mathews | .35 | .14 | .03 |
| ☐ | U74 Andy McGaffigan | .06 | .02 | .00 |
| ☐ | U75 Joel McKeon | .20 | .08 | .02 |
| ☐ | U76 Kevin Mitchell | .60 | .24 | .06 |
| ☐ | U77 Bill Mooneyham | .15 | .06 | .01 |
| ☐ | U78 Omar Moreno | .06 | .02 | .00 |
| ☐ | U79 Jerry Mumphrey | .06 | .02 | .00 |
| ☐ | U80 Al Newman | .15 | .06 | .01 |
| ☐ | U81 Phil Niekro | .25 | .10 | .02 |
| ☐ | U82 Randy Niemann | .06 | .02 | .00 |
| ☐ | U83 Juan Nieves | .10 | .04 | .01 |
| ☐ | U84 Bob Ojeda | .15 | .06 | .01 |
| ☐ | U85 Rick Ownbey | .06 | .02 | .00 |
| ☐ | U86 Tom Paciorek | .06 | .02 | .00 |
| ☐ | U87 David Palmer | .06 | .02 | .00 |
| ☐ | U88 Jeff Parrett | .15 | .06 | .01 |
| ☐ | U89 Pat Perry | .15 | .06 | .01 |
| ☐ | U90 Dan Plesac | .20 | .08 | .02 |
| ☐ | U91 Darrell Porter | .10 | .04 | .01 |
| ☐ | U92 Luis Quinones | .15 | .06 | .01 |
| ☐ | U93 Rey Quinones | .20 | .08 | .02 |
| ☐ | U94 Gary Redus | .10 | .04 | .01 |
| ☐ | U95 Jeff Reed | .15 | .06 | .01 |
| ☐ | U96 Bip Roberts | .15 | .06 | .01 |
| ☐ | U97 Billy Joe Robidoux | .20 | .08 | .02 |
| ☐ | U98 Gary Roenicke | .10 | .04 | .01 |
| ☐ | U99 Ron Roenicke | .06 | .02 | .00 |
| ☐ | U100 Angel Salazar | .06 | .02 | .00 |
| ☐ | U101 Joe Sambito | .10 | .04 | .01 |
| ☐ | U102 Billy Sample | .06 | .02 | .00 |
| ☐ | U103 Dave Schmidt | .06 | .02 | .00 |
| ☐ | U104 Ken Schrom | .10 | .04 | .01 |
| ☐ | U105 Ruben Sierra | 1.50 | .60 | .15 |
| ☐ | U106 Ted Simmons | .15 | .06 | .01 |
| ☐ | U107 Sammy Stewart | .06 | .02 | .00 |
| ☐ | U108 Kurt Stillwell | .15 | .06 | .01 |
| ☐ | U109 Dale Sveum | .15 | .06 | .01 |
| ☐ | U110 Tim Teufel | .10 | .04 | .01 |
| ☐ | U111 Bob Tewksbury | .35 | .14 | .03 |
| ☐ | U112 Andres Thomas | .35 | .14 | .03 |
| ☐ | U113 Jason Thompson | .10 | .04 | .01 |
| ☐ | U114 Milt Thompson | .10 | .04 | .01 |
| ☐ | U115 Rob Thompson | .40 | .16 | .04 |
| ☐ | U116 Jay Tibbs | .06 | .02 | .00 |
| ☐ | U117 Fred Toliver | .10 | .04 | .01 |
| ☐ | U118 Wayne Tolleson | .06 | .02 | .00 |
| ☐ | U119 Alex Trevino | .06 | .02 | .00 |
| ☐ | U120 Manny Trillo | .06 | .02 | .00 |
| ☐ | U121 Ed VandeBerg | .06 | .02 | .00 |
| ☐ | U122 Ozzie Virgil | .06 | .02 | .00 |
| ☐ | U123 Tony Walker | .25 | .10 | .02 |
| ☐ | U124 Gene Walter | .10 | .04 | .01 |
| ☐ | U125 Duane Ward | .20 | .08 | .02 |
| ☐ | U126 Jerry Willard | .06 | .02 | .00 |
| ☐ | U127 Mitch Williams | .30 | .12 | .03 |
| ☐ | U128 Reggie Williams | .30 | .12 | .03 |
| ☐ | U129 Bobby Witt | .45 | .18 | .04 |
| ☐ | U130 Marvell Wynne | .06 | .02 | .00 |
| ☐ | U131 Steve Yeager | .06 | .02 | .00 |
| ☐ | U132 Checklist card | .10 | .01 | .00 |

# 1987 Fleer

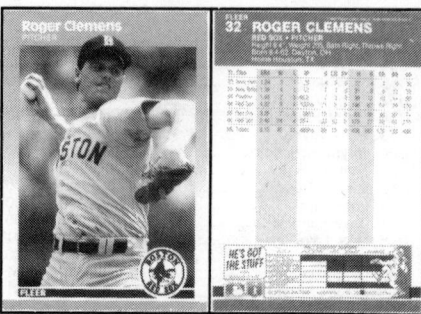

This 660 card set features a distinctive blue border which fades to white on the card fronts. The backs are printed in blue, red, and pink on white card stock. The bottom of the card back shows an innovative graph of the player's ability, e.g., "He's got the stuff" for pitchers and "How he's hitting 'em", for hitters. Cards are numbered on the back and are again the standard 2 1/2" by 3 1/2". Cards are again organized numerically by teams, i.e., World Champion Mets (1-25), Boston Red Sox (26-48), Houston Astros (49-72), California Angels (73-95), New York Yankees (96-120), Texas Rangers (121-143), Detroit Tigers (144-168), Philadelphia Phillies (169-192), Cincinnati Reds (193-218), Toronto Blue Jays (219-240), Cleveland Indians (241-263), San Francisco Giants (264-288), St. Louis Cardinals (289-312), Montreal Expos (313-337), Milwaukee Brewers (338-361), Kansas City Royals (362-384), Oakland A's (385-410), San Diego Padres (411-435), Los Angeles Dodgers (436-460), Baltimore Orioles (461-483), Chicago White Sox (484-508), Atlanta Braves (509-532), Minnesota Twins (533-554), Chicago Cubs (555-578), Seattle Mariners (579-600), and Pittsburgh Pirates (601-624). The last 36 cards in the set consist of Specials (625-643), Rookie Pairs (644-653), and Checklists (654-660).

|  | MINT | VG-E | F-G |
|---|---|---|---|
| COMPLETE SET | 25.00 | 10.00 | 2.50 |
| COMMON PLAYER | .03 | .01 | .00 |

| | | MINT | VG-E | F-G |
|---|---|---|---|---|
| ☐ | 1 Rick Aguilera | .06 | .02 | .00 |
| ☐ | 2 Richard Anderson | .03 | .01 | .00 |
| ☐ | 3 Wally Backman | .06 | .02 | .00 |
| ☐ | 4 Gary Carter | .25 | .10 | .02 |
| ☐ | 5 Ron Darling | .20 | .08 | .02 |
| ☐ | 6 Len Dykstra | .20 | .08 | .02 |
| ☐ | 7 Kevin Elster | .20 | .08 | .02 |
| ☐ | 8 Sid Fernandez | .18 | .08 | .01 |
| ☐ | 9 Dwight Gooden | 1.00 | .40 | .10 |
| ☐ | 10 Ed Hearn | .10 | .04 | .01 |
| ☐ | 11 Danny Heep | .03 | .01 | .00 |
| ☐ | 12 Keith Hernandez | .20 | .08 | .02 |
| ☐ | 13 Howard Johnson | .03 | .01 | .00 |
| ☐ | 14 Ray Knight | .07 | .03 | .01 |
| ☐ | 15 Lee Mazzilli | .05 | .02 | .00 |
| ☐ | 16 Roger McDowell | .10 | .04 | .01 |
| ☐ | 17 Kevin Mitchell | .35 | .14 | .03 |
| ☐ | 18 Randy Niemann | .03 | .01 | .00 |
| ☐ | 19 Bob Ojeda | .08 | .03 | .01 |
| ☐ | 20 Jesse Orosco | .05 | .02 | .00 |
| ☐ | 21 Rafael Santana | .03 | .01 | .00 |
| ☐ | 22 Doug Sisk | .03 | .01 | .00 |
| ☐ | 23 Darryl Strawberry | .30 | .12 | .03 |
| ☐ | 24 Tim Teufel | .05 | .02 | .00 |
| ☐ | 25 Mookie Wilson | .05 | .02 | .00 |
| ☐ | 26 Tony Armas | .08 | .03 | .01 |
| ☐ | 27 Marty Barrett | .10 | .04 | .01 |

| | | MINT | VG-E | F-G |
|---|---|---|---|---|
| ☐ | 28 Don Baylor | .10 | .04 | .01 |
| ☐ | 29 Wade Boggs | 1.00 | .40 | .10 |
| ☐ | 30 Oil Can Boyd | .08 | .03 | .01 |
| ☐ | 31 Bill Buckner | .08 | .03 | .01 |
| ☐ | 32 Roger Clemens | 1.00 | .40 | .10 |
| ☐ | 33 Steve Crawford | .03 | .01 | .00 |
| ☐ | 34 Dwight Evans | .08 | .03 | .01 |
| ☐ | 35 Rich Gedman | .08 | .03 | .01 |
| ☐ | 36 Dave Henderson | .06 | .02 | .00 |
| ☐ | 37 Bruce Hurst | .08 | .03 | .01 |
| ☐ | 38 Tim Lollar | .03 | .01 | .00 |
| ☐ | 39 Al Nipper | .03 | .01 | .00 |
| ☐ | 40 Spike Owen | .05 | .02 | .00 |
| ☐ | 41 Jim Rice | .25 | .10 | .02 |
| ☐ | 42 Ed Romero | .03 | .01 | .00 |
| ☐ | 43 Joe Sambito | .05 | .02 | .00 |
| ☐ | 44 Calvin Schiraldi | .08 | .03 | .01 |
| ☐ | 45 Tom Seaver | .25 | .10 | .02 |
| ☐ | 46 Jeff Sellers | .12 | .05 | .01 |
| ☐ | 47 Bob Stanley | .05 | .02 | .00 |
| ☐ | 48 Sammy Stewart | .03 | .01 | .00 |
| ☐ | 49 Larry Andersen | .03 | .01 | .00 |
| ☐ | 50 Alan Ashby | .03 | .01 | .00 |
| ☐ | 51 Kevin Bass | .07 | .03 | .01 |
| ☐ | 52 Jeff Calhoun | .05 | .02 | .00 |
| ☐ | 53 Jose Cruz | .09 | .04 | .01 |
| ☐ | 54 Danny Darwin | .03 | .01 | .00 |
| ☐ | 55 Glenn Davis | .25 | .10 | .02 |
| ☐ | 56 Jim Deshaies | .25 | .10 | .02 |
| ☐ | 57 Bill Doran | .08 | .03 | .01 |
| ☐ | 58 Phil Garner | .05 | .02 | .00 |
| ☐ | 59 Billy Hatcher | .05 | .02 | .00 |
| ☐ | 60 Charlie Kerfeld | .08 | .03 | .01 |
| ☐ | 61 Bob Knepper | .08 | .03 | .01 |
| ☐ | 62 Dave Lopes | .06 | .02 | .00 |
| ☐ | 63 Aurelio Lopez | .03 | .01 | .00 |
| ☐ | 64 Jim Pankovits | .03 | .01 | .00 |
| ☐ | 65 Terry Puhl | .05 | .02 | .00 |
| ☐ | 66 Craig Reynolds | .03 | .01 | .00 |
| ☐ | 67 Nolan Ryan | .30 | .12 | .03 |
| ☐ | 68 Mike Scott | .16 | .07 | .01 |
| ☐ | 69 Dave Smith | .06 | .02 | .00 |
| ☐ | 70 Dickie Thon | .05 | .02 | .00 |
| ☐ | 71 Tony Walker | .15 | .06 | .01 |
| ☐ | 72 Denny Walling | .03 | .01 | .00 |
| ☐ | 73 Bob Boone | .05 | .02 | .00 |
| ☐ | 74 Rick Burleson | .06 | .02 | .00 |
| ☐ | 75 John Candelaria | .07 | .03 | .01 |
| ☐ | 76 Doug Corbett | .03 | .01 | .00 |
| ☐ | 77 Doug DeCinces | .07 | .03 | .01 |
| ☐ | 78 Brian Downing | .05 | .02 | .00 |
| ☐ | 79 Chuck Finley | .10 | .04 | .01 |
| ☐ | 80 Terry Forster | .06 | .02 | .00 |
| ☐ | 81 Bob Grich | .06 | .02 | .00 |
| ☐ | 82 George Hendrick | .06 | .02 | .00 |
| ☐ | 83 Jack Howell | .05 | .02 | .00 |
| ☐ | 84 Reggie Jackson | .30 | .12 | .03 |
| ☐ | 85 Ruppert Jones | .03 | .01 | .00 |
| ☐ | 86 Wally Joyner | 2.00 | .80 | .20 |
| ☐ | 87 Gary Lucas | .03 | .01 | .00 |
| ☐ | 88 Kirk McCaskill | .10 | .04 | .01 |
| ☐ | 89 Donnie Moore | .05 | .02 | .00 |
| ☐ | 90 Gary Pettis | .07 | .03 | .01 |
| ☐ | 91 Vern Ruhle | .03 | .01 | .00 |
| ☐ | 92 Dick Schofield | .05 | .02 | .00 |
| ☐ | 93 Don Sutton | .12 | .05 | .01 |
| ☐ | 94 Rob Wilfong | .03 | .01 | .00 |
| ☐ | 95 Mike Witt | .10 | .04 | .01 |
| ☐ | 96 Doug Drabek | .20 | .08 | .02 |
| ☐ | 97 Mike Easler | .06 | .02 | .00 |
| ☐ | 98 Mike Fischlin | .03 | .01 | .00 |
| ☐ | 99 Brian Fisher | .05 | .02 | .00 |
| ☐ | 100 Ron Guidry | .15 | .06 | .01 |
| ☐ | 101 Rickey Henderson | .30 | .12 | .03 |
| ☐ | 102 Tommy John | .10 | .04 | .01 |
| ☐ | 103 Ron Kittle | .09 | .04 | .01 |
| ☐ | 104 Don Mattingly | 2.00 | .80 | .20 |
| ☐ | 105 Bobby Meacham | .03 | .01 | .00 |
| ☐ | 106 Joe Niekro | .07 | .03 | .01 |
| ☐ | 107 Mike Pagliarulo | .15 | .06 | .01 |
| ☐ | 108 Dan Pasqua | .12 | .05 | .01 |
| ☐ | 109 Willie Randolph | .06 | .02 | .00 |
| ☐ | 110 Dennis Rasmussen | .07 | .03 | .01 |
| ☐ | 111 Dave Righetti | .12 | .05 | .01 |
| ☐ | 112 Gary Roenicke | .05 | .02 | .00 |
| ☐ | 113 Rod Scurry | .03 | .01 | .00 |
| ☐ | 114 Bob Shirley | .03 | .01 | .00 |
| ☐ | 115 Joel Skinner | .05 | .02 | .00 |
| ☐ | 116 Tim Stoddard | .03 | .01 | .00 |
| ☐ | 117 Bob Tewksbury | .20 | .08 | .02 |
| ☐ | 118 Wayne Tolleson | .03 | .01 | .00 |
| ☐ | 119 Claudell Washington | .05 | .02 | .00 |
| ☐ | 120 Dave Winfield | .25 | .10 | .02 |

# McCarty Cards 800-228-2028 Ext. 2

## *The Hobby's Choice for Highest Quality Supplies*

---

## MORGAN COLLECTORS BOXES

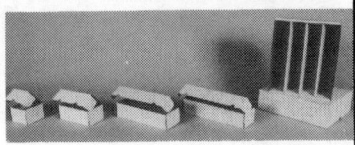

*Our Morgan Boxes are rated #1 by collectors and dealers. Built for maximum protection, they will not crack or split like inferior brands. Available in six convenient sizes, each with a specific capacity, these boxes are a must for the serious collector.*

| DESCRIPTION | STOCK # | Quantity | Price | Quantity | Price |
|---|---|---|---|---|---|
| 3200 Count, (2-Piece Organizer) | 10-607 | **Stock #10-607** | | **All other stock #s:** | |
| 800 Count | 10-608 | 1-4 | $4.50 ea. | 50 (min. order) | $18.00 |
| 660 Count | 10-609 | 5-9 | 3.75 ea. | 100 | .32 ea. |
| 550 Count | 10-612 | 10-24 | 3.25 ea. | 250 | .30 ea. |
| 400 Count | 10-613 | | | 500 | .28 ea. |
| 200 Count | 10-614 | Mix and match permitted in groups of 25 only, e.g. 25, 50, 75, 100, etc. | | | |

---

## ROTMAN DISPLAY SHEETS

*The Rotman Display Sheets are of the highest quality and carry a lifetime guarantee. The 9 pocket sheets are available in either top or side load, while the eight, four, two and single pocket sheets come in top load only. A Quality Vue single pocket sleeve is also available and measures 2⅝" x 3⅝".*

| DESCRIPTION | STOCK # | Quantity | Price | Quantity | Price |
|---|---|---|---|---|---|
| **Top Load** | | **Stock #10-625** | | **All other stock #s:** | |
| 9 Pocket | 10-615 | 1,000 | $ 9.95 | 25 | 25.0¢ ea. |
| 8 Pocket | 10-617 | 5,000 | 39.00 | 50 | 22.0¢ ea. |
| 4 Pocket | 10-618 | 10,000 | 69.00 | 100 | 18.0¢ ea. |
| 2 Pocket | 10-620 | Standard hobby size, fits | | 500 | 13.5¢ ea. |
| 1 Pocket | 10-621 | all Topps cards 1957 to | | 1000 | 12.5¢ ea. |
| **Side Load** | | present | | | |
| 9 Pocket | 10-622 | | | | |
| **Quality Vue** | | | | | |
| Single Pocket Sleeve | 10-625 | | | | |

---

## REMINGTON D RING CARD ALBUMS

*The Remington D Ring Card Album is the perfect choice for the individual who wants the opportunity to display his collection, while at the same time giving it the protection it deserves. Each album has a ⅛" padded cover and comes in two sizes. The large album holds 110 pages, while the small one holds 70 pages. Both are available in one of three distinctive colors.*

| DESCRIPTION | STOCK # | Quantity | Price | Quantity | Price |
|---|---|---|---|---|---|
| 2" Brown Album | 10-627 | **1½", any color:** | | **2", any color:** | |
| 2" Blue Album | 10-628 | 1 | $ 6.95 | 1 | $ 7.95 |
| 2" Burgundy Album | 10-629 | 2 | 12.95 | 2 | 14.95 |
| 1½" Brown Album | 10-630 | 5 | 29.95 | 5 | 34.95 |
| 1½" Blue Album | 10-631 | Full Case | 49.00 | Full Case | 59.00 |
| 1½" Burgundy Album | 10-632 | (12 binders) | | (12 binders) | |

---

**McCarty Cards** • P.O. Box 13067, Dept. PG2 • Lexington, KY 40583

MasterCard

A 02

VISA

**Ordering Information:**

1. Write down the **stock numbers** of the items you want.
2. Have your **credit card** and expiration date handy.
3. **Call toll-free 800-228-2028.** Ask for **Ext. 2** and give our operator your order.
4. Add a $1.95 **processing fee** for all orders.
5. KY residents add 5% sales tax.
6. All orders shipped **postpaid** within continental U.S. Allow

7-10 days for delivery.
7. **COD orders** will include a **$2.50 UPS COD charge** per carton.
8. A **telephone number required** on all orders. Sorry, we cannot ship to a P.O. box.
9. **Mail orders** include check or money order made out to McCarty Cards.

| # | Player | | | |
|---|--------|-----|-----|-----|
| ☐ 121 | Steve Buechele | .05 | .02 | .00 |
| ☐ 122 | Ed Correa | .35 | .14 | .03 |
| ☐ 123 | Scott Fletcher | .05 | .02 | .00 |
| ☐ 124 | Jose Guzman | .06 | .02 | .00 |
| ☐ 125 | Toby Harrah | .05 | .02 | .00 |
| ☐ 126 | Greg Harris | .05 | .02 | .00 |
| ☐ 127 | Charlie Hough | .05 | .02 | .00 |
| ☐ 128 | Pete Incaviglia | 1.00 | .40 | .10 |
| ☐ 129 | Mike Mason | .05 | .02 | .00 |
| ☐ 130 | Oddibe McDowell | .20 | .08 | .02 |
| ☐ 131 | Dave Mohorcic | .15 | .06 | .01 |
| ☐ 132 | Pete O'Brien | .09 | .04 | .01 |
| ☐ 133 | Tom Paciorek | .03 | .01 | .00 |
| ☐ 134 | Larry Parrish | .05 | .02 | .00 |
| ☐ 135 | Geno Petralli | .03 | .01 | .00 |
| ☐ 136 | Darrell Porter | .05 | .02 | .00 |
| ☐ 137 | Jeff Russell | .03 | .01 | .00 |
| ☐ 138 | Ruben Sierra | 1.00 | .40 | .10 |
| ☐ 139 | Don Slaught | .03 | .01 | .00 |
| ☐ 140 | Gary Ward | .05 | .02 | .00 |
| ☐ 141 | Curtis Wilkerson | .03 | .01 | .00 |
| ☐ 142 | Mitch Williams | .25 | .10 | .02 |
| ☐ 143 | Bobby Witt | .40 | .16 | .04 |
| ☐ 144 | Dave Bergman | .03 | .01 | .00 |
| ☐ 145 | Tom Brookens | .03 | .01 | .00 |
| ☐ 146 | Bill Campbell | .03 | .01 | .00 |
| ☐ 147 | Chuck Cary | .20 | .08 | .02 |
| ☐ 148 | Darnell Coles | .09 | .04 | .01 |
| ☐ 149 | Dave Collins | .05 | .02 | .00 |
| ☐ 150 | Darrell Evans | .08 | .03 | .01 |
| ☐ 151 | Kirk Gibson | .20 | .08 | .02 |
| ☐ 152 | John Grubb | .03 | .01 | .00 |
| ☐ 153 | Willie Hernandez | .09 | .04 | .01 |
| ☐ 154 | Larry Herndon | .03 | .01 | .00 |
| ☐ 155 | Eric King | .25 | .10 | .02 |
| ☐ 156 | Chet Lemon | .05 | .02 | .00 |
| ☐ 157 | Dwight Lowry | .15 | .06 | .01 |
| ☐ 158 | Jack Morris | .15 | .06 | .01 |
| ☐ 159 | Randy O'Neal | .03 | .01 | .00 |
| ☐ 160 | Lance Parrish | .20 | .08 | .02 |
| ☐ 161 | Dan Petry | .09 | .04 | .01 |
| ☐ 162 | Pat Sheridan | .03 | .01 | .00 |
| ☐ 163 | Jim Slaton | .03 | .01 | .00 |
| ☐ 164 | Frank Tanana | .05 | .02 | .00 |
| ☐ 165 | Walt Terrell | .03 | .01 | .00 |
| ☐ 166 | Mark Thurmond | .03 | .01 | .00 |
| ☐ 167 | Alan Trammell | .12 | .05 | .01 |
| ☐ 168 | Lou Whitaker | .10 | .04 | .01 |
| ☐ 169 | Luis Aguayo | .03 | .01 | .00 |
| ☐ 170 | Steve Bedrosian | .05 | .02 | .00 |
| ☐ 171 | Don Carman | .05 | .02 | .00 |
| ☐ 172 | Darren Daulton | .03 | .01 | .00 |
| ☐ 173 | Greg Gross | .03 | .01 | .00 |
| ☐ 174 | Kevin Gross | .03 | .01 | .00 |
| ☐ 175 | Von Hayes | .12 | .05 | .01 |
| ☐ 176 | Charles Hudson | .05 | .02 | .00 |
| ☐ 177 | Tom Hume | .03 | .01 | .00 |
| ☐ 178 | Steve Jeltz | .03 | .01 | .00 |
| ☐ 179 | Mike Maddux | .09 | .04 | .01 |
| ☐ 180 | Shane Rawley | .07 | .03 | .01 |
| ☐ 181 | Gary Redus | .05 | .02 | .00 |
| ☐ 182 | Ron Roenicke | .03 | .01 | .00 |
| ☐ 183 | Bruce Ruffin | .30 | .12 | .03 |
| ☐ 184 | John Russell | .03 | .01 | .00 |
| ☐ 185 | Juan Samuel | .10 | .04 | .01 |
| ☐ 186 | Dan Schatzeder | .03 | .01 | .00 |
| ☐ 187 | Mike Schmidt | .30 | .12 | .03 |
| ☐ 188 | Rick Schu | .03 | .01 | .00 |
| ☐ 189 | Jeff Stone | .05 | .02 | .00 |
| ☐ 190 | Kent Tekulve | .05 | .02 | .00 |
| ☐ 191 | Milt Thompson | .05 | .02 | .00 |
| ☐ 192 | Glenn Wilson | .09 | .04 | .01 |
| ☐ 193 | Buddy Bell | .09 | .04 | .01 |
| ☐ 194 | Tom Browning | .09 | .04 | .01 |
| ☐ 195 | Sal Butera | .03 | .01 | .00 |
| ☐ 196 | Dave Concepcion | .08 | .03 | .01 |
| ☐ 197 | Kal Daniels | .12 | .05 | .01 |
| ☐ 198 | Eric Davis | .45 | .18 | .04 |
| ☐ 199 | John Denny | .06 | .02 | .00 |
| ☐ 200 | Bo Diaz | .05 | .02 | .00 |
| ☐ 201 | Nick Esasky | .03 | .01 | .00 |
| ☐ 202 | John Franco | .08 | .03 | .01 |
| ☐ 203 | Bill Gullickson | .05 | .02 | .00 |
| ☐ 204 | Barry Larkin | .45 | .18 | .04 |
| ☐ 205 | Eddie Milner | .05 | .02 | .00 |
| ☐ 206 | Rob Murphy | .15 | .06 | .01 |
| ☐ 207 | Ron Oester | .05 | .02 | .00 |
| ☐ 208 | Dave Parker | .15 | .06 | .01 |
| ☐ 209 | Tony Perez | .10 | .04 | .01 |
| ☐ 210 | Ted Power | .07 | .03 | .01 |
| ☐ 211 | Joe Price | .03 | .01 | .00 |
| ☐ 212 | Ron Robinson | .03 | .01 | .00 |
| ☐ 213 | Pete Rose | .60 | .24 | .06 |
| ☐ 214 | Mario Soto | .08 | .03 | .01 |
| ☐ 215 | Kurt Stillwell | .15 | .06 | .01 |
| ☐ 216 | Max Venable | .03 | .01 | .00 |
| ☐ 217 | Chris Welsh | .03 | .01 | .00 |
| ☐ 218 | Carl Willis | .12 | .05 | .01 |
| ☐ 219 | Jesse Barfield | .15 | .06 | .01 |
| ☐ 220 | George Bell | .15 | .06 | .01 |
| ☐ 221 | Bill Caudill | .05 | .02 | .00 |
| ☐ 222 | John Cerutti | .25 | .10 | .02 |
| ☐ 223 | Jim Clancy | .03 | .01 | .00 |
| ☐ 224 | Mark Eichhorn | .30 | .12 | .03 |
| ☐ 225 | Tony Fernandez | .09 | .04 | .01 |
| ☐ 226 | Damaso Garcia | .07 | .03 | .01 |
| ☐ 227 | Kelly Gruber | .03 | .01 | .00 |
| ☐ 228 | Tom Henke | .05 | .02 | .00 |
| ☐ 229 | Garth Iorg | .03 | .01 | .00 |
| ☐ 230 | Cliff Johnson | .03 | .01 | .00 |
| ☐ 231 | Joe Johnson | .03 | .01 | .00 |
| ☐ 232 | Jimmy Key | .08 | .03 | .01 |
| ☐ 233 | Dennis Lamp | .03 | .01 | .00 |
| ☐ 234 | Rick Leach | .03 | .01 | .00 |
| ☐ 235 | Buck Martinez | .03 | .01 | .00 |
| ☐ 236 | Lloyd Moseby | .10 | .04 | .01 |
| ☐ 237 | Rance Mulliniks | .03 | .01 | .00 |
| ☐ 238 | Dave Stieb | .10 | .04 | .01 |
| ☐ 239 | Willie Upshaw | .07 | .03 | .01 |
| ☐ 240 | Ernie Whitt | .03 | .01 | .00 |
| ☐ 241 | Andy Allanson | .12 | .05 | .01 |
| ☐ 242 | Scott Bailes | .10 | .04 | .01 |
| ☐ 243 | Chris Bando | .03 | .01 | .00 |
| ☐ 244 | Tony Bernazard | .05 | .02 | .00 |
| ☐ 245 | John Butcher | .03 | .01 | .00 |
| ☐ 246 | Brett Butler | .08 | .03 | .01 |
| ☐ 247 | Ernie Camacho | .03 | .01 | .00 |
| ☐ 248 | Tom Candiotti | .03 | .01 | .00 |
| ☐ 249 | Joe Carter | .18 | .08 | .01 |
| ☐ 250 | Carmen Castillo | .03 | .01 | .00 |
| ☐ 251 | Julio Franco | .08 | .03 | .01 |
| ☐ 252 | Mel Hall | .08 | .03 | .01 |
| ☐ 253 | Brook Jacoby | .08 | .03 | .01 |
| ☐ 254 | Phil Niekro | .15 | .06 | .01 |
| ☐ 255 | Otis Nixon | .15 | .06 | .01 |
| ☐ 256 | Dickie Noles | .03 | .01 | .00 |
| ☐ 257 | Bryan Oelkers | .03 | .01 | .00 |
| ☐ 258 | Ken Schrom | .05 | .02 | .00 |
| ☐ 259 | Don Schulze | .03 | .01 | .00 |
| ☐ 260 | Cory Snyder | .60 | .24 | .06 |
| ☐ 261 | Pat Tabler | .08 | .03 | .01 |
| ☐ 262 | Andre Thornton | .06 | .02 | .00 |
| ☐ 263 | Rich Yett | .03 | .01 | .00 |
| ☐ 264 | Mike Aldrete | .12 | .05 | .01 |
| ☐ 265 | Juan Berenguer | .03 | .01 | .00 |
| ☐ 266 | Vida Blue | .07 | .03 | .01 |
| ☐ 267 | Bob Brenly | .05 | .02 | .00 |
| ☐ 268 | Chris Brown | .15 | .06 | .01 |
| ☐ 269 | Will Clark | .60 | .24 | .06 |
| ☐ 270 | Chili Davis | .08 | .03 | .01 |
| ☐ 271 | Mark Davis | .03 | .01 | .00 |
| ☐ 272 | Kelly Downs | .10 | .04 | .01 |
| ☐ 273 | Scott Garrelts | .05 | .02 | .00 |
| ☐ 274 | Dan Gladden | .05 | .02 | .00 |
| ☐ 275 | Mike Krukow | .07 | .03 | .01 |
| ☐ 276 | Randy Kutcher | .15 | .06 | .01 |
| ☐ 277 | Mike LaCoss | .03 | .01 | .00 |
| ☐ 278 | Jeff Leonard | .05 | .02 | .00 |
| ☐ 279 | Candy Maldonado | .06 | .02 | .00 |
| ☐ 280 | Roger Mason | .05 | .02 | .00 |
| ☐ 281 | Bob Melvin | .03 | .01 | .00 |
| ☐ 282 | Greg Minton | .05 | .02 | .00 |
| ☐ 283 | Jeff Robinson | .03 | .01 | .00 |
| ☐ 284 | Harry Spilman | .03 | .01 | .00 |
| ☐ 285 | Robby Thompson | .30 | .12 | .03 |
| ☐ 286 | Jose Uribe | .03 | .01 | .00 |
| ☐ 287 | Frank Williams | .03 | .01 | .00 |
| ☐ 288 | Joel Youngblood | .03 | .01 | .00 |
| ☐ 289 | Jack Clark | .10 | .04 | .01 |
| ☐ 290 | Vince Coleman | .35 | .14 | .03 |
| ☐ 291 | Tom Conroy | .03 | .01 | .00 |
| ☐ 292 | Danny Cox | .05 | .02 | .00 |
| ☐ 293 | Ken Dayley | .03 | .01 | .00 |
| ☐ 294 | Curt Ford | .25 | .10 | .02 |
| ☐ 295 | Bob Forsch | .05 | .02 | .00 |
| ☐ 296 | Tom Herr | .07 | .03 | .01 |
| ☐ 297 | Ricky Horton | .03 | .01 | .00 |
| ☐ 298 | Clint Hurdle | .03 | .01 | .00 |
| ☐ 299 | Jeff Lahti | .03 | .01 | .00 |
| ☐ 300 | Steve Lake | .03 | .01 | .00 |
| ☐ 301 | Tito Landrum | .03 | .01 | .00 |
| ☐ 302 | Mike Lavalliere | .03 | .01 | .00 |
| ☐ 303 | Greg Mathews | .20 | .08 | .02 |
| ☐ 304 | Willie McGee | .15 | .06 | .01 |
| ☐ 305 | Jose Oquendo | .03 | .01 | .00 |
| ☐ 306 | Terry Pendleton | .05 | .02 | .00 |

| | | | |
|---|---|---|---|
| ☐ 307 Pat Perry | .07 | .03 | .01 |
| ☐ 308 Ozzie Smith | .12 | .05 | .01 |
| ☐ 309 Ray Soff | .09 | .04 | .01 |
| ☐ 310 John Tudor | .09 | .04 | .01 |
| ☐ 311 Andy Van Slyke | .06 | .02 | .00 |
| ☐ 312 Todd Worrell | .20 | .08 | .02 |
| ☐ 313 Dann Bilardello | .03 | .01 | .00 |
| ☐ 314 Hubie Brooks | .09 | .04 | .01 |
| ☐ 315 Tim Burke | .05 | .02 | .00 |
| ☐ 316 Andre Dawson | .16 | .07 | .01 |
| ☐ 317 Mike Fitzgerald | .03 | .01 | .00 |
| ☐ 318 Tom Foley | .03 | .01 | .00 |
| ☐ 319 Andres Galarraga | .08 | .03 | .01 |
| ☐ 320 Joe Hesketh | .05 | .02 | .00 |
| ☐ 321 Wallace Johnson | .03 | .01 | .00 |
| ☐ 322 Wayne Krenchicki | .03 | .01 | .00 |
| ☐ 323 Vance Law | .03 | .01 | .00 |
| ☐ 324 Dennis Martinez | .03 | .01 | .00 |
| ☐ 325 Bob McClure | .03 | .01 | .00 |
| ☐ 326 Andy McGaffigan | .03 | .01 | .00 |
| ☐ 327 Al Newman | .10 | .04 | .01 |
| ☐ 328 Tim Raines | .25 | .10 | .02 |
| ☐ 329 Jeff Reardon | .06 | .02 | .00 |
| ☐ 330 Luis Rivera | .10 | .04 | .01 |
| ☐ 331 Bob Sebra | .10 | .04 | .01 |
| ☐ 332 Bryn Smith | .05 | .02 | .00 |
| ☐ 333 Jay Tibbs | .03 | .01 | .00 |
| ☐ 334 Tim Wallach | .08 | .03 | .01 |
| ☐ 335 Mitch Webster | .07 | .03 | .01 |
| ☐ 336 Jim Wohlford | .03 | .01 | .00 |
| ☐ 337 Floyd Youmans | .16 | .07 | .01 |
| ☐ 338 Chris Bosio | .10 | .04 | .01 |
| ☐ 339 Glenn Braggs | .40 | .16 | .04 |
| ☐ 340 Rick Cerone | .03 | .01 | .00 |
| ☐ 341 Mark Clear | .03 | .01 | .00 |
| ☐ 342 Bryan Clutterbuck | .10 | .04 | .01 |
| ☐ 343 Cecil Cooper | .09 | .04 | .01 |
| ☐ 344 Rob Deer | .15 | .06 | .01 |
| ☐ 345 Jim Gantner | .05 | .02 | .00 |
| ☐ 346 Ted Higuera | .15 | .06 | .01 |
| ☐ 347 John H. Johnson | .03 | .01 | .00 |
| ☐ 348 Tim Leary | .03 | .01 | .00 |
| ☐ 349 Rick Manning | .03 | .01 | .00 |
| ☐ 350 Paul Molitor | .08 | .03 | .01 |
| ☐ 351 Charlie Moore | .03 | .01 | .00 |
| ☐ 352 Juan Nieves | .07 | .03 | .01 |
| ☐ 353 Ben Oglivie | .06 | .02 | .00 |
| ☐ 354 Dan Plesac | .20 | .08 | .02 |
| ☐ 355 Ernest Riles | .07 | .03 | .01 |
| ☐ 356 Billy Joe Robidoux | .09 | .04 | .01 |
| ☐ 357 Bill Schroeder | .03 | .01 | .00 |
| ☐ 358 Dale Sveum | .10 | .04 | .01 |
| ☐ 359 Gorman Thomas | .08 | .03 | .01 |
| ☐ 360 Bill Wegman | .06 | .02 | .00 |
| ☐ 361 Robin Yount | .25 | .10 | .02 |
| ☐ 362 Steve Balboni | .05 | .02 | .00 |
| ☐ 363 Scott Bankhead | .06 | .02 | .00 |
| ☐ 364 Buddy Biancalana | .03 | .01 | .00 |
| ☐ 365 Bud Black | .03 | .01 | .00 |
| ☐ 366 George Brett | .30 | .12 | .03 |
| ☐ 367 Steve Farr | .03 | .01 | .00 |
| ☐ 368 Mark Gubicza | .06 | .02 | .00 |
| ☐ 369 Bo Jackson | 1.00 | .40 | .10 |
| ☐ 370 Danny Jackson | .06 | .02 | .00 |
| ☐ 371 Mike Kingery | .20 | .08 | .02 |
| ☐ 372 Rudy Law | .03 | .01 | .00 |
| ☐ 373 Charlie Leibrandt | .05 | .02 | .00 |
| ☐ 374 Dennis Leonard | .05 | .02 | .00 |
| ☐ 375 Hal McRae | .05 | .02 | .00 |
| ☐ 376 Jorge Orta | .03 | .01 | .00 |
| ☐ 377 Jamie Quirk | .03 | .01 | .00 |
| ☐ 378 Dan Quisenberry | .12 | .05 | .01 |
| ☐ 379 Bret Saberhagen | .15 | .06 | .01 |
| ☐ 380 Angel Salazar | .03 | .01 | .00 |
| ☐ 381 Lonnie Smith | .05 | .02 | .00 |
| ☐ 382 Jim Sundberg | .05 | .02 | .00 |
| ☐ 383 Frank White | .06 | .02 | .00 |
| ☐ 384 Willie Wilson | .12 | .05 | .01 |
| ☐ 385 Joaquin Andujar | .08 | .03 | .01 |
| ☐ 386 Doug Bair | .05 | .02 | .00 |
| ☐ 387 Dusty Baker | .06 | .02 | .00 |
| ☐ 388 Bruce Bochte | .05 | .02 | .00 |
| ☐ 389 Jose Canseco | 1.25 | .50 | .12 |
| ☐ 390 Chris Codiroli | .03 | .01 | .00 |
| ☐ 391 Mike Davis | .05 | .02 | .00 |
| ☐ 392 Alfredo Griffin | .05 | .02 | .00 |
| ☐ 393 Moose Haas | .03 | .01 | .00 |
| ☐ 394 Donnie Hill | .03 | .01 | .00 |
| ☐ 395 Jay Howell | .05 | .02 | .00 |
| ☐ 396 Dave Kingman | .10 | .04 | .01 |
| ☐ 397 Carney Lansford | .09 | .04 | .01 |
| ☐ 398 Dave Leiper | .07 | .03 | .01 |
| ☐ 399 Bill Mooneyham | .10 | .04 | .01 |
| ☐ 400 Dwayne Murphy | .05 | .02 | .00 |
| ☐ 401 Steve Ontiveros | .05 | .02 | .00 |
| ☐ 402 Tony Phillips | .03 | .01 | .00 |
| ☐ 403 Eric Plunk | .05 | .02 | .00 |
| ☐ 404 Jose Rijo | .08 | .03 | .01 |
| ☐ 405 Terry Steinbach | .35 | .14 | .03 |
| ☐ 406 Dave Stewart | .03 | .01 | .00 |
| ☐ 407 Mickey Tettleton | .03 | .01 | .00 |
| ☐ 408 Dave Von Ohlen | .03 | .01 | .00 |
| ☐ 409 Jerry Willard | .03 | .01 | .00 |
| ☐ 410 Curt Young | .03 | .01 | .00 |
| ☐ 411 Bruce Bochy | .03 | .01 | .00 |
| ☐ 412 Dave Dravecky | .05 | .02 | .00 |
| ☐ 413 Tim Flannery | .03 | .01 | .00 |
| ☐ 414 Steve Garvey | .25 | .10 | .02 |
| ☐ 415 Goose Gossage | .12 | .05 | .01 |
| ☐ 416 Tony Gwynn | .25 | .10 | .02 |
| ☐ 417 Andy Hawkins | .05 | .02 | .00 |
| ☐ 418 LaMarr Hoyt | .06 | .02 | .00 |
| ☐ 419 Terry Kennedy | .06 | .02 | .00 |
| ☐ 420 John Kruk | .25 | .10 | .02 |
| ☐ 421 Dave LaPoint | .03 | .01 | .00 |
| ☐ 422 Craig Lefferts | .03 | .01 | .00 |
| ☐ 423 Carmelo Martinez | .05 | .02 | .00 |
| ☐ 424 Lance McCullers | .05 | .02 | .00 |
| ☐ 425 Kevin McReynolds | .12 | .05 | .01 |
| ☐ 426 Graig Nettles | .12 | .05 | .01 |
| ☐ 427 Bip Roberts | .09 | .04 | .01 |
| ☐ 428 Jerry Royster | .03 | .01 | .00 |
| ☐ 429 Benito Santiago | .25 | .10 | .02 |
| ☐ 430 Eric Show | .03 | .01 | .00 |
| ☐ 431 Bob Stoddard | .03 | .01 | .00 |
| ☐ 432 Garry Templeton | .07 | .03 | .01 |
| ☐ 433 Gene Walter | .05 | .02 | .00 |
| ☐ 434 Ed Whitson | .03 | .01 | .00 |
| ☐ 435 Marvell Wynne | .03 | .01 | .00 |
| ☐ 436 Dave Anderson | .03 | .01 | .00 |
| ☐ 437 Greg Brock | .05 | .02 | .00 |
| ☐ 438 Enos Cabell | .03 | .01 | .00 |
| ☐ 439 Mariano Duncan | .08 | .03 | .01 |
| ☐ 440 Pedro Guerrero | .20 | .08 | .02 |
| ☐ 441 Orel Hershiser | .16 | .07 | .01 |
| ☐ 442 Rick Honeycutt | .03 | .01 | .00 |
| ☐ 443 Ken Howell | .05 | .02 | .00 |
| ☐ 444 Ken Landreaux | .03 | .01 | .00 |
| ☐ 445 Bill Madlock | .09 | .04 | .01 |
| ☐ 446 Mike Marshall | .12 | .05 | .01 |
| ☐ 447 Len Matuszek | .03 | .01 | .00 |
| ☐ 448 Tom Niedenfuer | .06 | .02 | .00 |
| ☐ 449 Alejandro Pena | .05 | .02 | .00 |
| ☐ 450 Dennis Powell | .09 | .04 | .01 |
| ☐ 451 Jerry Reuss | .05 | .02 | .00 |
| ☐ 452 Bill Russell | .05 | .02 | .00 |
| ☐ 453 Steve Sax | .12 | .05 | .01 |
| ☐ 454 Mike Scioscia | .05 | .02 | .00 |
| ☐ 455 Franklin Stubbs | .09 | .04 | .01 |
| ☐ 456 Alex Trevino | .03 | .01 | .00 |
| ☐ 457 Fernando Valenzuela | .25 | .10 | .02 |
| ☐ 458 Ed VandeBerg | .03 | .01 | .00 |
| ☐ 459 Bob Welch | .06 | .02 | .00 |
| ☐ 460 Reggie Williams | .18 | .08 | .01 |
| ☐ 461 Don Aase | .05 | .02 | .00 |
| ☐ 462 Juan Beniquez | .05 | .02 | .00 |
| ☐ 463 Mike Boddicker | .07 | .03 | .01 |
| ☐ 464 Juan Bonilla | .03 | .01 | .00 |
| ☐ 465 Rich Bordi | .03 | .01 | .00 |
| ☐ 466 Storm Davis | .07 | .03 | .01 |
| ☐ 467 Rick Dempsey | .05 | .02 | .00 |
| ☐ 468 Ken Dixon | .05 | .02 | .00 |
| ☐ 469 Jim Dwyer | .03 | .01 | .00 |
| ☐ 470 Mike Flanagan | .07 | .03 | .01 |
| ☐ 471 Jackie Gutierrez | .03 | .01 | .00 |
| ☐ 472 Brad Havens | .03 | .01 | .00 |
| ☐ 473 Lee Lacy | .05 | .02 | .00 |
| ☐ 474 Fred Lynn | .15 | .06 | .01 |
| ☐ 475 Scott McGregor | .07 | .03 | .01 |
| ☐ 476 Eddie Murray | .25 | .10 | .02 |
| ☐ 477 Tom O'Malley | .03 | .01 | .00 |
| ☐ 478 Cal Ripken Jr. | .25 | .10 | .02 |
| ☐ 479 Larry Sheets | .06 | .02 | .00 |
| ☐ 480 John Shelby | .03 | .01 | .00 |
| ☐ 481 Nate Snell | .03 | .01 | .00 |
| ☐ 482 Jim Traber | .09 | .04 | .01 |
| ☐ 483 Mike Young | .07 | .03 | .01 |
| ☐ 484 Neil Allen | .05 | .02 | .00 |
| ☐ 485 Harold Baines | .15 | .06 | .01 |
| ☐ 486 Floyd Bannister | .05 | .02 | .00 |
| ☐ 487 Daryl Boston | .05 | .02 | .00 |
| ☐ 488 Ivan Calderon | .15 | .06 | .01 |
| ☐ 489 John Cangelosi | .25 | .10 | .02 |
| ☐ 490 Steve Carlton | .25 | .10 | .02 |
| ☐ 491 Joe Cowley | .05 | .02 | .00 |
| ☐ 492 Julio Cruz | .03 | .01 | .00 |

| | | | | |
|---|---|---|---|---|
| ☐ 493 | Bill Dawley | .03 | .01 | .00 |
| ☐ 494 | Jose DeLeon | .05 | .02 | .00 |
| ☐ 495 | Richard Dotson | .05 | .02 | .00 |
| ☐ 496 | Carlton Fisk | .12 | .05 | .01 |
| ☐ 497 | Ozzie Guillen | .10 | .04 | .01 |
| ☐ 498 | Jerry Hairston | .03 | .01 | .00 |
| ☐ 499 | Ron Hassey | .03 | .01 | .00 |
| ☐ 500 | Tim Hulett | .05 | .02 | .00 |
| ☐ 501 | Bob James | .03 | .01 | .00 |
| ☐ 502 | Steve Lyons | .03 | .01 | .00 |
| ☐ 503 | Joel McKeon | .20 | .08 | .02 |
| ☐ 504 | Gene Nelson | .03 | .01 | .00 |
| ☐ 505 | Dave Schmidt | .03 | .01 | .00 |
| ☐ 506 | Ray Searage | .03 | .01 | .00 |
| ☐ 507 | Bobby Thigpen | .18 | .08 | .01 |
| ☐ 508 | Greg Walker | .10 | .04 | .01 |
| ☐ 509 | Jim Acker | .03 | .01 | .00 |
| ☐ 510 | Doyle Alexander | .05 | .02 | .00 |
| ☐ 511 | Paul Assenmacher | .10 | .04 | .01 |
| ☐ 512 | Bruce Benedict | .03 | .01 | .00 |
| ☐ 513 | Chris Chambliss | .05 | .02 | .00 |
| ☐ 514 | Jeff Dedmon | .03 | .01 | .00 |
| ☐ 515 | Gene Garber | .03 | .01 | .00 |
| ☐ 516 | Ken Griffey | .06 | .02 | .00 |
| ☐ 517 | Terry Harper | .03 | .01 | .00 |
| ☐ 518 | Bob Horner | .15 | .06 | .01 |
| ☐ 519 | Glenn Hubbard | .03 | .01 | .00 |
| ☐ 520 | Rick Mahler | .03 | .01 | .00 |
| ☐ 521 | Omar Moreno | .03 | .01 | .00 |
| ☐ 522 | Dale Murphy | .45 | .18 | .04 |
| ☐ 523 | Ken Oberkfell | .03 | .01 | .00 |
| ☐ 524 | Ed Olwine | .10 | .04 | .01 |
| ☐ 525 | David Palmer | .05 | .02 | .00 |
| ☐ 526 | Rafael Ramirez | .03 | .01 | .00 |
| ☐ 527 | Billy Sample | .03 | .01 | .00 |
| ☐ 528 | Ted Simmons | .09 | .04 | .01 |
| ☐ 529 | Zane Smith | .03 | .01 | .00 |
| ☐ 530 | Bruce Sutter | .10 | .04 | .01 |
| ☐ 531 | Andres Thomas | .25 | .10 | .02 |
| ☐ 532 | Ozzie Virgil | .05 | .02 | .00 |
| ☐ 533 | Allan Anderson | .15 | .06 | .01 |
| ☐ 534 | Keith Atherton | .03 | .01 | .00 |
| ☐ 535 | Billy Beane | .06 | .02 | .00 |
| ☐ 536 | Bert Blyleven | .09 | .04 | .01 |
| ☐ 537 | Tom Brunansky | .09 | .04 | .01 |
| ☐ 538 | Randy Bush | .03 | .01 | .00 |
| ☐ 539 | George Frazier | .03 | .01 | .00 |
| ☐ 540 | Gary Gaetti | .08 | .03 | .01 |
| ☐ 541 | Greg Gagne | .05 | .02 | .00 |
| ☐ 542 | Mickey Hatcher | .03 | .01 | .00 |
| ☐ 543 | Neal Heaton | .03 | .01 | .00 |
| ☐ 544 | Kent Hrbek | .15 | .06 | .01 |
| ☐ 545 | Roy Lee Jackson | .03 | .01 | .00 |
| ☐ 546 | Tim Laudner | .03 | .01 | .00 |
| ☐ 547 | Steve Lombardozzi | .07 | .03 | .01 |
| ☐ 548 | Mark Portugal | .10 | .04 | .01 |
| ☐ 549 | Kirby Puckett | .25 | .10 | .02 |
| ☐ 550 | Jeff Reed | .03 | .01 | .00 |
| ☐ 551 | Mark Salas | .03 | .01 | .00 |
| ☐ 552 | Roy Smalley | .05 | .02 | .00 |
| ☐ 553 | Mike Smithson | .03 | .01 | .00 |
| ☐ 554 | Frank Viola | .05 | .02 | .00 |
| ☐ 555 | Thad Bosley | .03 | .01 | .00 |
| ☐ 556 | Ron Cey | .07 | .03 | .01 |
| ☐ 557 | Jody Davis | .07 | .03 | .01 |
| ☐ 558 | Ron Davis | .03 | .01 | .00 |
| ☐ 559 | Bob Dernier | .05 | .02 | .00 |
| ☐ 560 | Frank DiPino | .03 | .01 | .00 |
| ☐ 561 | Shawon Dunston | .09 | .04 | .01 |
| ☐ 562 | Leon Durham | .08 | .03 | .01 |
| ☐ 563 | Dennis Eckersley | .05 | .02 | .00 |
| ☐ 564 | Terry Francona | .03 | .01 | .00 |
| ☐ 565 | Dave Gumpert | .03 | .01 | .00 |
| ☐ 566 | Guy Hoffman | .03 | .01 | .00 |
| ☐ 567 | Ed Lynch | .03 | .01 | .00 |
| ☐ 568 | Gary Matthews | .05 | .02 | .00 |
| ☐ 569 | Keith Moreland | .07 | .03 | .01 |
| ☐ 570 | Jamie Moyer | .15 | .06 | .01 |
| ☐ 571 | Jerry Mumphrey | .05 | .02 | .00 |
| ☐ 572 | Ryne Sandberg | .25 | .10 | .02 |
| ☐ 573 | Scott Sanderson | .03 | .01 | .00 |
| ☐ 574 | Lee Smith | .07 | .03 | .01 |
| ☐ 575 | Chris Speier | .03 | .01 | .00 |
| ☐ 576 | Rick Sutcliffe | .10 | .04 | .01 |
| ☐ 577 | Manny Trillo | .05 | .02 | .00 |
| ☐ 578 | Steve Trout | .05 | .02 | .00 |
| ☐ 579 | Karl Best | .03 | .01 | .00 |
| ☐ 580 | Phil Bradley | .20 | .08 | .02 |
| ☐ 581 | Scott Bradley | .06 | .02 | .00 |
| ☐ 582 | Mickey Brantley | .20 | .08 | .02 |
| ☐ 583 | Mike Brown | .03 | .01 | .00 |
| ☐ 584 | Alvin Davis | .10 | .04 | .01 |
| ☐ 585 | Lee Guetterman | .12 | .05 | .01 |

| | | | | |
|---|---|---|---|---|
| ☐ 586 | Mark Huismann | .05 | .02 | .00 |
| ☐ 587 | Bob Kearney | .03 | .01 | .00 |
| ☐ 588 | Pete Ladd | .03 | .01 | .00 |
| ☐ 589 | Mark Langston | .07 | .03 | .01 |
| ☐ 590 | Mike Moore | .06 | .02 | .00 |
| ☐ 591 | Mike Morgan | .03 | .01 | .00 |
| ☐ 592 | John Moses | .10 | .04 | .01 |
| ☐ 593 | Ken Phelps | .05 | .02 | .00 |
| ☐ 594 | Jim Presley | .15 | .06 | .01 |
| ☐ 595 | Rey Quinones | .10 | .04 | .01 |
| ☐ 596 | Harold Reynolds | .03 | .01 | .00 |
| ☐ 597 | Billy Swift | .03 | .01 | .00 |
| ☐ 598 | Danny Tartabull | .25 | .10 | .02 |
| ☐ 599 | Steve Yeager | .05 | .02 | .00 |
| ☐ 600 | Matt Young | .03 | .01 | .00 |
| ☐ 601 | Bill Almon | .03 | .01 | .00 |
| ☐ 602 | Rafael Belliard | .10 | .04 | .01 |
| ☐ 603 | Mike Bielecki | .03 | .01 | .00 |
| ☐ 604 | Barry Bonds | .35 | .14 | .03 |
| ☐ 605 | Bobby Bonilla | .15 | .06 | .01 |
| ☐ 606 | Sid Bream | .05 | .02 | .00 |
| ☐ 607 | Mike Brown | .03 | .01 | .00 |
| ☐ 608 | Pat Clements | .05 | .02 | .00 |
| ☐ 609 | Mike Diaz | .25 | .10 | .02 |
| ☐ 610 | Cecilio Guante | .03 | .01 | .00 |
| ☐ 611 | Barry Jones | .15 | .06 | .01 |
| ☐ 612 | Bob Kipper | .03 | .01 | .00 |
| ☐ 613 | Larry McWilliams | .03 | .01 | .00 |
| ☐ 614 | Jim Morrison | .03 | .01 | .00 |
| ☐ 615 | Joe Orsulak | .03 | .01 | .00 |
| ☐ 616 | Junior Ortiz | .03 | .01 | .00 |
| ☐ 617 | Tony Pena | .10 | .04 | .01 |
| ☐ 618 | Johnny Ray | .09 | .04 | .01 |
| ☐ 619 | Rick Reuschel | .05 | .02 | .00 |
| ☐ 620 | R.J. Reynolds | .06 | .02 | .00 |
| ☐ 621 | Rick Rhoden | .06 | .02 | .00 |
| ☐ 622 | Don Robinson | .03 | .01 | .00 |
| ☐ 623 | Bob Walk | .03 | .01 | .00 |
| ☐ 624 | Jim Winn | .03 | .01 | .00 |
| ☐ 625 | Youthful Power | .40 | .16 | .04 |
| | Pete Incaviglia | | | |
| | Jose Canseco | | | |
| ☐ 626 | 300 Game Winners | .10 | .04 | .01 |
| | Don Sutton | | | |
| | Phil Niekro | | | |
| ☐ 627 | A.L. Firemen | .08 | .03 | .01 |
| | Dave Righetti | | | |
| | Don Aase | | | |
| ☐ 628 | Rookie All-Stars | .90 | .36 | .09 |
| | Wally Joyner | | | |
| | Jose Canseco | | | |
| ☐ 629 | Magic Mets | .75 | .30 | .07 |
| | Gary Carter | | | |
| | Sid Fernandez | | | |
| | Dwight Gooden | | | |
| | Keith Hernandez | | | |
| | Darryl Strawberry | | | |
| ☐ 630 | NL Best Righties | .08 | .03 | .01 |
| | Mike Scott | | | |
| | Mike Krukow | | | |
| ☐ 631 | Sensational Southpaws | .12 | .05 | .01 |
| | Fernando Valenzuela | | | |
| | John Franco | | | |
| ☐ 632 | Count'Em | .08 | .03 | .01 |
| | Bob Horner | | | |
| ☐ 633 | AL Pitcher's Nightmare | .40 | .16 | .04 |
| | Jose Canseco | | | |
| | Jim Rice | | | |
| | Kirby Puckett | | | |
| ☐ 634 | All Star Battery | .75 | .30 | .07 |
| | Gary Carter | | | |
| | Roger Clemens | | | |
| ☐ 635 | 4000 Strikeouts | .15 | .06 | .01 |
| | Steve Carlton | | | |
| ☐ 636 | Big Bats at First | .15 | .06 | .01 |
| | Glenn Davis | | | |
| | Eddie Murray | | | |
| ☐ 637 | On Base | .40 | .16 | .04 |
| | Wade Boggs | | | |
| | Keith Hernandez | | | |
| ☐ 638 | Sluggers Left Side | .90 | .36 | .09 |
| | Don Mattingly | | | |
| | Darryl Strawberry | | | |
| ☐ 639 | Former MVP's | .15 | .06 | .01 |
| | Dave Parker | | | |
| | Ryne Sandberg | | | |
| ☐ 640 | Dr. K , Super K | .90 | .36 | .09 |
| | Dwight Gooden | | | |
| | Roger Clemens | | | |
| ☐ 641 | AL West Stoppers | .08 | .03 | .01 |
| | Mike Witt | | | |
| | Charlie Hough | | | |
| ☐ 642 | Doubles and Triples | .08 | .03 | .01 |

| | | | |
|---|---|---|---|
| | Juan Samuel | | | |
| | Tim Raines | | | |
| ☐ 643 | Outfielders with Punch ... | .08 | .03 | .01 |
| | Harold Baines | | | |
| | Jesse Barfield | | | |
| ☐ 644 | Dave Clark and ............... | .60 | .24 | .06 |
| | Greg Swindell | | | |
| ☐ 645 | Ron Karkovice and ......... | .35 | .14 | .03 |
| | Russ Morman | | | |
| ☐ 646 | Devon White and ............ | .35 | .14 | .03 |
| | Willie Fraser | | | |
| ☐ 647 | Mike Stanley and ............ | .25 | .10 | .02 |
| | Jerry Browne | | | |
| ☐ 648 | Dave Magadan and ......... | .75 | .30 | .07 |
| | Phil Lombardi | | | |
| ☐ 649 | Jose Gonzalez and .......... | .60 | .24 | .06 |
| | Ralph Bryant | | | |
| ☐ 650 | Jimmy Jones and ............ | .35 | .14 | .03 |
| | Randy Asadoor | | | |
| ☐ 651 | Tracy Jones and ............. | .35 | .14 | .03 |
| | Marvin Freeman | | | |
| ☐ 652 | John Stefero and ............ | .20 | .08 | .02 |
| | Kevin Seitzer | | | |
| ☐ 653 | Rob Nelson and .............. | .20 | .08 | .02 |
| | Steve Fireovid | | | |
| ☐ 654 | CL: Mets/Red Sox .......... | .06 | .01 | .00 |
| | Astros/Angels | | | |
| ☐ 655 | CL: Yankees/Rangers ..... | .06 | .01 | .00 |
| | Tigers/Phillies | | | |
| ☐ 656 | CL: Reds/Blue Jays ........ | .06 | .01 | .00 |
| | Indians/Giants | | | |
| ☐ 657 | CL: Cardinals/Expos ....... | .06 | .01 | .00 |
| | Brewers/Royals | | | |
| ☐ 658 | CL: A's/Padres ............... | .06 | .01 | .00 |
| | Dodgers/Orioles | | | |
| ☐ 659 | CL: White Sox/Braves .... | .06 | .01 | .00 |
| | Twins/Cubs | | | |
| ☐ 660 | CL: Mariners/Pirates ...... | .06 | .01 | .00 |
| | Special Cards | | | |
| ☐ C1 | Mets Logo ...................... | .08 | .03 | .01 |
| | (wax box card) | | | |
| ☐ C2 | Jesse Barfield ................ | .15 | .06 | .01 |
| | (wax box card) | | | |
| ☐ C3 | George Brett ................... | .50 | .20 | .05 |
| | (wax box card) | | | |
| ☐ C4 | Dwight Gooden ............... | .75 | .30 | .07 |
| | (wax box card) | | | |
| ☐ C5 | Boston Logo ................... | .08 | .03 | .01 |
| | (wax box card) | | | |
| ☐ C6 | Keith Hernandez ............ | .25 | .10 | .02 |
| | (wax box card) | | | |
| ☐ C7 | Wally Joyner ................... | 1.00 | .40 | .10 |
| | (wax box card) | | | |
| ☐ C8 | Dale Murphy ................... | .60 | .24 | .06 |
| | (wax box card) | | | |
| ☐ C9 | Astros Logo .................... | .08 | .03 | .01 |
| | (wax box card) | | | |
| ☐ C10 | Dave Parker .................... | .20 | .08 | .02 |
| | (wax box card) | | | |
| ☐ C11 | Kirby Puckett ................. | .40 | .16 | .04 |
| | (wax box card) | | | |
| ☐ C12 | Dave Righetti ................. | .20 | .08 | .02 |
| | (wax box card) | | | |
| ☐ C13 | Angels Logo ................... | .08 | .03 | .01 |
| | (wax box card) | | | |
| ☐ C14 | Ryne Sandberg .............. | .30 | .12 | .03 |
| | (wax box card) | | | |
| ☐ C15 | Mike Schmidt ................. | .50 | .20 | .05 |
| | (wax box card) | | | |
| ☐ C16 | Robin Yount ................... | .30 | .12 | .03 |
| | (wax box card) | | | |

## 1987 Fleer All Stars

This 12- card set was distributed as an insert in packs of the Fleer regular issue. The cards are 2 1/2" by 3 1/2" and designed with a color player photo superimposed on a gray or black background with yellow stars. The player's name, team, and position are printed in orange on black or gray at the bottom of the obverse. The card backs are done predominantly in gray, red, and black. Cards are numbered on the back in the upper right hand corner.

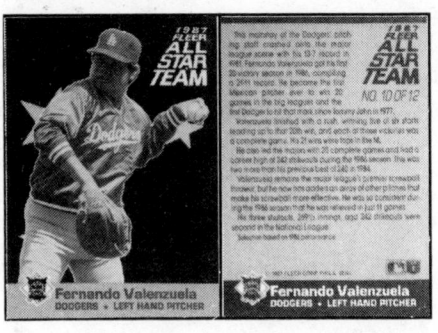

| | | MINT | VG-E | F-G |
|---|---|---|---|---|
| | COMPLETE SET ......... | 10.00 | 4.00 | 1.00 |
| | COMMON PLAYER ................ | .25 | .10 | .02 |
| ☐ 1 | Don Mattingly ................ | 4.00 | 1.60 | .40 |
| | First Base | | | |
| ☐ 2 | Gary Carter .................... | 1.00 | .40 | .10 |
| | Catcher | | | |
| ☐ 3 | Tony Fernandez .............. | .50 | .20 | .05 |
| | Shortstop | | | |
| ☐ 4 | Steve Sax ...................... | .50 | .20 | .05 |
| | Second Base | | | |
| ☐ 5 | Kirby Puckett ................. | 1.00 | .40 | .10 |
| | Outfield | | | |
| ☐ 6 | Mike Schmidt ................. | 1.25 | .50 | .12 |
| | Third Base | | | |
| ☐ 7 | Mike Easler .................... | .25 | .10 | .02 |
| | Designated Hitter | | | |
| ☐ 8 | Todd Worrell ................... | .50 | .20 | .05 |
| | Relief Pitcher | | | |
| ☐ 9 | George Bell .................... | .50 | .20 | .05 |
| | Outfield | | | |
| ☐ 10 | Fernando Valenzuela ........ | .75 | .30 | .07 |
| | Left Hand Starter | | | |
| ☐ 11 | Roger Clemens ................. | 1.50 | .60 | .15 |
| | Right Hand Starter | | | |
| ☐ 12 | Tim Raines ..................... | .75 | .30 | .07 |
| | Outfield | | | |

## 1987 Fleer Headliners

This six card set was distributed as a special insert in rack packs. The obverse features the player photo against a beige background with irregular red stripes. Cards are 2 1/2" by 3 1/2". The cards are numbered on the back.

| | | MINT | VG-E | F-G |
|---|---|---|---|---|
| | COMPLETE SET ......................... | 6.00 | 2.40 | .60 |
| | COMMON PLAYER .................... | .50 | .20 | .05 |
| ☐ 1 | Wade Boggs .......................... | 2.00 | .80 | .20 |

| | | | MINT | VG-E | F-G |
|---|---|---|---|---|---|
| ☐ 2 | Jose Canseco | | 1.50 | .60 | .15 |
| ☐ 3 | Dwight Gooden | | 1.50 | .60 | .15 |
| ☐ 4 | Rickey Henderson | | 1.00 | .40 | .10 |
| ☐ 5 | Keith Hernandez | | .75 | .30 | .07 |
| ☐ 6 | Jim Rice | | .75 | .30 | .07 |

## 1987 Fleer Record Setters

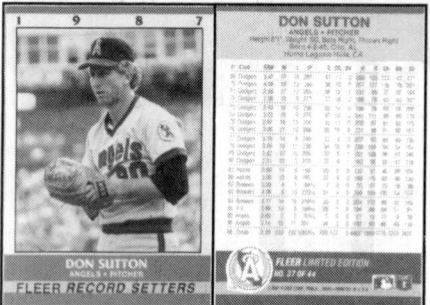

This 44-card boxed set was produced by Fleer for distribution by Eckerd's Drug Stores and is sometimes referred to as the Eckerd's set. Six team logo stickers are included in the box with the complete set. The numerical checklist on the back of the box shows that the set is numbered alphabetically. The cards measure 2 1/2" by 3 1/2".

| | | MINT | VG-E | F-G |
|---|---|---|---|---|
| COMPLETE SET | | 4.50 | 1.80 | .45 |
| COMMON PLAYER | | .05 | .02 | .00 |
| ☐ 1 | George Brett | .35 | .14 | .03 |
| ☐ 2 | Chris Brown | .15 | .06 | .01 |
| ☐ 3 | Jose Canseco | .60 | .24 | .06 |
| ☐ 4 | Roger Clemens | .60 | .24 | .06 |
| ☐ 5 | Alvin Davis | .15 | .06 | .01 |
| ☐ 6 | Shawon Dunston | .15 | .06 | .01 |
| ☐ 7 | Tony Fernandez | .15 | .06 | .01 |
| ☐ 8 | Carlton Fisk | .15 | .06 | .01 |
| ☐ 9 | Gary Gaetti | .10 | .04 | .01 |
| ☐10 | Gene Garber | .05 | .02 | .00 |
| ☐11 | Rich Gedman | .10 | .04 | .01 |
| ☐12 | Dwight Gooden | .60 | .24 | .06 |
| ☐13 | Ozzie Guillen | .15 | .06 | .01 |
| ☐14 | Bill Gullickson | .05 | .02 | .00 |
| ☐15 | Billy Hatcher | .05 | .02 | .00 |
| ☐16 | Orel Hershiser | .15 | .06 | .01 |
| ☐17 | Wally Joyner | .60 | .24 | .06 |
| ☐18 | Ray Knight | .10 | .04 | .01 |
| ☐19 | Craig Lefferts | .05 | .02 | .00 |
| ☐20 | Don Mattingly | .75 | .30 | .07 |
| ☐21 | Kevin Mitchell | .15 | .06 | .01 |
| ☐22 | Lloyd Moseby | .10 | .04 | .01 |
| ☐23 | Dale Murphy | .45 | .18 | .04 |
| ☐24 | Eddie Murray | .35 | .14 | .03 |
| ☐25 | Phil Niekro | .15 | .06 | .01 |
| ☐26 | Ben Oglivie | .05 | .02 | .00 |
| ☐27 | Jesse Orosco | .05 | .02 | .00 |
| ☐28 | Joe Orsulak | .05 | .02 | .00 |
| ☐29 | Larry Parrish | .05 | .02 | .00 |
| ☐30 | Tim Raines | .25 | .10 | .02 |
| ☐31 | Shane Rawley | .05 | .02 | .00 |
| ☐32 | Dave Righetti | .15 | .06 | .01 |
| ☐33 | Pete Rose | .60 | .24 | .06 |
| ☐34 | Steve Sax | .15 | .06 | .01 |
| ☐35 | Mike Schmidt | .35 | .14 | .03 |
| ☐36 | Mike Scott | .15 | .06 | .01 |
| ☐37 | Don Sutton | .15 | .06 | .01 |
| ☐38 | Alan Trammell | .15 | .06 | .01 |
| ☐39 | John Tudor | .10 | .04 | .01 |
| ☐40 | Gary Ward | .05 | .02 | .00 |
| ☐41 | Lou Whitaker | .10 | .04 | .01 |
| ☐42 | Willie Wilson | .15 | .06 | .01 |
| ☐43 | Todd Worrell | .15 | .06 | .01 |
| ☐44 | Floyd Youmans | .15 | .06 | .01 |

## 1987 Fleer Superstars

This 44-card boxed set was produced by Fleer for distribution by McCrory's and is sometimes referred to as the McCrory's set. The numerical checklist on the back of the box shows that the set is numbered alphabetically. The cards measure 2 1/2" by 3 1/2".

| | | MINT | VG-E | F-G |
|---|---|---|---|---|
| COMPLETE SET | | 4.50 | 1.80 | .45 |
| COMMON PLAYER | | .05 | .02 | .00 |
| ☐ 1 | Floyd Bannister | .05 | .02 | .00 |
| ☐ 2 | Marty Barrett | .10 | .04 | .01 |
| ☐ 3 | Steve Bedrosian | .05 | .02 | .00 |
| ☐ 4 | George Bell | .15 | .06 | .01 |
| ☐ 5 | George Brett | .35 | .14 | .03 |
| ☐ 6 | Jose Canseco | .60 | .24 | .06 |
| ☐ 7 | Joe Carter | .15 | .06 | .01 |
| ☐ 8 | Will Clark | .15 | .06 | .01 |
| ☐ 9 | Roger Clemens | .60 | .24 | .06 |
| ☐10 | Vince Coleman | .35 | .14 | .03 |
| ☐11 | Glenn Davis | .25 | .10 | .02 |
| ☐12 | Mike Davis | .05 | .02 | .00 |
| ☐13 | Len Dykstra | .15 | .06 | .01 |
| ☐14 | John Franco | .10 | .04 | .01 |
| ☐15 | Julio Franco | .10 | .04 | .01 |
| ☐16 | Steve Garvey | .35 | .14 | .03 |
| ☐17 | Kirk Gibson | .25 | .10 | .02 |
| ☐18 | Dwight Gooden | .60 | .24 | .06 |
| ☐19 | Tony Gwynn | .35 | .14 | .03 |
| ☐20 | Keith Hernandez | .25 | .10 | .02 |
| ☐21 | Teddy Higuera | .15 | .06 | .01 |
| ☐22 | Kent Hrbek | .15 | .06 | .01 |
| ☐23 | Wally Joyner | .60 | .24 | .06 |
| ☐24 | Mike Krukow | .05 | .02 | .00 |
| ☐25 | Mike Marshall | .10 | .04 | .01 |
| ☐26 | Don Mattingly | .75 | .30 | .07 |
| ☐27 | Oddibe McDowell | .15 | .06 | .01 |
| ☐28 | Jack Morris | .15 | .06 | .01 |
| ☐29 | Lloyd Moseby | .10 | .04 | .01 |
| ☐30 | Dale Murphy | .45 | .18 | .04 |
| ☐31 | Eddie Murray | .35 | .14 | .03 |
| ☐32 | Tony Pena | .10 | .04 | .01 |
| ☐33 | Jim Presley | .15 | .06 | .01 |
| ☐34 | Jeff Reardon | .05 | .02 | .00 |
| ☐35 | Jim Rice | .25 | .10 | .02 |
| ☐36 | Pete Rose | .60 | .24 | .06 |
| ☐37 | Mike Schmidt | .35 | .14 | .03 |
| ☐38 | Mike Scott | .15 | .06 | .01 |
| ☐39 | Lee Smith | .05 | .02 | .00 |
| ☐40 | Lonnie Smith | .05 | .02 | .00 |
| ☐41 | Gary Ward | .05 | .02 | .00 |
| ☐42 | Dave Winfield | .25 | .10 | .02 |
| ☐43 | Todd Worrell | .15 | .06 | .01 |
| ☐44 | Robin Yount | .25 | .10 | .02 |

## 1983 Gardner's Brewers

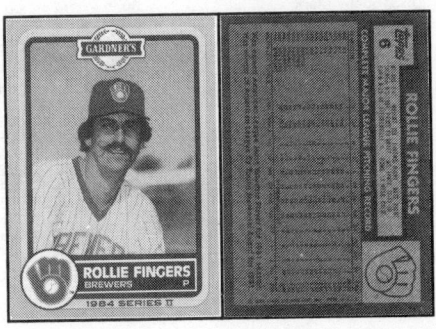

The cards in this 22 card set measure 2 1/2" by 3 1/2". The 1983 Gardner's Brewers set features Milwaukee Brewer players and manager Harvey Kuenn. Topps printed the set for the Madison (Wisconsin) bakery, hence, the backs are identical to the 1983 Topps backs except for the card number. The fronts of the cards, however, feature all new photos and include the Gardner's logo and the Brewers' logo. Many of the cards are grease laden, as they were issued with packages of bread and hamburger and hot- dog buns.

|  | MINT | VG-E | F-G |
|---|---|---|---|
| COMPLETE SET | 18.00 | 7.25 | 1.80 |
| COMMON PLAYER | .40 | .16 | .04 |

| | | MINT | VG-E | F-G |
|---|---|---|---|---|
| ☐ 1 | Harvey Kuenn MGR | 1.00 | .40 | .10 |
| ☐ 2 | Dwight Bernard | .40 | .16 | .04 |
| ☐ 3 | Mark Brouhard | .40 | .16 | .04 |
| ☐ 4 | Mike Caldwell | .60 | .24 | .06 |
| ☐ 5 | Cecil Cooper | 1.50 | .60 | .15 |
| ☐ 6 | Marshall Edwards | .40 | .16 | .04 |
| ☐ 7 | Rollie Fingers | 2.50 | 1.00 | .25 |
| ☐ 8 | Jim Gantner | .80 | .32 | .08 |
| ☐ 9 | Moose Haas | .60 | .24 | .06 |
| ☐ 10 | Bob McClure | .40 | .16 | .04 |
| ☐ 11 | Paul Molitor | 2.00 | .80 | .20 |
| ☐ 12 | Don Money | .60 | .24 | .06 |
| ☐ 13 | Charlie Moore | .60 | .24 | .06 |
| ☐ 14 | Ben Oglivie | .80 | .32 | .08 |
| ☐ 15 | Ed Romero | .40 | .16 | .04 |
| ☐ 16 | Ted Simmons | 1.50 | .60 | .15 |
| ☐ 17 | Jim Slaton | .60 | .24 | .06 |
| ☐ 18 | Don Sutton | 2.50 | 1.00 | .25 |
| ☐ 19 | Gorman Thomas | 1.00 | .40 | .10 |
| ☐ 20 | Pete Vuckovich | .80 | .32 | .08 |
| ☐ 21 | Ned Yost | .40 | .16 | .04 |
| ☐ 22 | Robin Yount | 4.00 | 1.60 | .40 |

| | | MINT | VG-E | F-G |
|---|---|---|---|---|
| ☐ 1 | Rene Lachemann MGR | .40 | .16 | .04 |
| ☐ 2 | Mark Brouhard | .30 | .12 | .03 |
| ☐ 3 | Mike Caldwell | .50 | .20 | .05 |
| ☐ 4 | Bobby Clark | .30 | .12 | .03 |
| ☐ 5 | Cecil Cooper | 1.00 | .40 | .10 |
| ☐ 6 | Rollie Fingers | 1.50 | .60 | .15 |
| ☐ 7 | Jim Gantner | .60 | .24 | .06 |
| ☐ 8 | Moose Haas | .40 | .16 | .04 |
| ☐ 9 | Roy Howell | .30 | .12 | .03 |
| ☐ 10 | Pete Ladd | .30 | .12 | .03 |
| ☐ 11 | Rick Manning | .30 | .12 | .03 |
| ☐ 12 | Bob McClure | .30 | .12 | .03 |
| ☐ 13 | Paul Molitor | 1.25 | .50 | .12 |
| ☐ 14 | Charlie Moore | .40 | .16 | .04 |
| ☐ 15 | Ben Oglivie | .60 | .24 | .06 |
| ☐ 16 | Ed Romero | .30 | .12 | .03 |
| ☐ 17 | Ted Simmons | 1.00 | .40 | .10 |
| ☐ 18 | Jim Sundberg | .50 | .20 | .05 |
| ☐ 19 | Don Sutton | 1.50 | .60 | .15 |
| ☐ 20 | Tom Tellman | .30 | .12 | .03 |
| ☐ 21 | Pete Vuckovich | .60 | .24 | .06 |
| ☐ 22 | Robin Yount | 2.50 | 1.00 | .25 |

## 1985 Gardner's Brewers

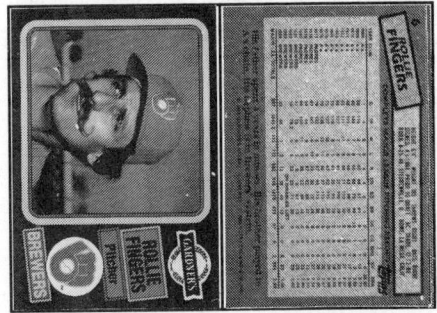

The cards in this 22 card set measure 2 1/2" by 3 1/2". For the third year in a row, the Gardner Bakery Company issued a set of cards available in packages of Gardner Bakery products. The set was manufactured by Topps, and the backs of the cards are identical to the Topps cards of this year except for the card numbers and copyright information. The Gardner logo appears on the fronts of the cards with the player's name, position abbreviation, and the name Brewers.

|  | MINT | VG-E | F-G |
|---|---|---|---|
| COMPLETE SET | 9.00 | 3.75 | .90 |
| COMMON PLAYER | .30 | .12 | .03 |

| | | MINT | VG-E | F-G |
|---|---|---|---|---|
| ☐ 1 | George Bamberger MGR | .40 | .16 | .04 |
| ☐ 2 | Mark Brouhard | .30 | .12 | .03 |

## 1984 Gardner's Brewers

The cards in this 22 card set measure 2 1/2" by 3 1/2". For the second year in a row, the Gardner Bakery Company issued a set of cards available in packages of Gardner Bakery products. The set was manufactured by Topps, and the backs of the cards are identical to the Topps cards of this year except for the numbers. The Gardner logo appears on the fronts of the cards with the player's name, position abbreviation, the name Brewers, and the words 1984 Series II.

|  | MINT | VG-E | F-G |
|---|---|---|---|
| COMPLETE SET (22) | 10.00 | 4.00 | 1.00 |
| COMMON PLAYER | .30 | .12 | .03 |

| | | | MINT | VG-E | F-G |
|---|---|---|---|---|---|
| ☐ | 3 | Bobby Clark | .30 | .12 | .03 |
| ☐ | 4 | Jaime Cocanower | .30 | .12 | .03 |
| ☐ | 5 | Cecil Cooper | 1.00 | .40 | .10 |
| ☐ | 6 | Rollie Fingers | 1.50 | .60 | .15 |
| ☐ | 7 | Jim Gantner | .50 | .20 | .05 |
| ☐ | 8 | Moose Haas | .40 | .16 | .04 |
| ☐ | 9 | Dion James | .40 | .16 | .04 |
| ☐ | 10 | Pete Ladd | .30 | .12 | .03 |
| ☐ | 11 | Rick Manning | .30 | .12 | .03 |
| ☐ | 12 | Bob McClure | .30 | .12 | .03 |
| ☐ | 13 | Paul Molitor | 1.25 | .50 | .12 |
| ☐ | 14 | Charlie Moore | .40 | .16 | .04 |
| ☐ | 15 | Ben Oglivie | .50 | .20 | .05 |
| ☐ | 16 | Chuck Porter | .30 | .12 | .03 |
| ☐ | 17 | Ed Romero | .30 | .12 | .03 |
| ☐ | 18 | Bill Schroeder | .40 | .16 | .04 |
| ☐ | 19 | Ted Simmons | 1.00 | .40 | .10 |
| ☐ | 20 | Tom Tellman | .30 | .12 | .03 |
| ☐ | 21 | Pete Vuckovich | .50 | .20 | .05 |
| ☐ | 22 | Robin Yount | 2.50 | 1.00 | .25 |

## 1986 Gatorade Cubs

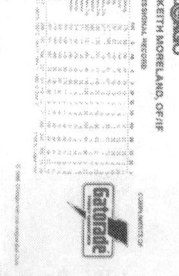

(6)  KEITH MORELAND, OF/IF

This 28 card set was given out at Wrigley Field on the Cubs' special "baseball card" promotion held July 17th for the game against the Giants. The set was sponsored by Gatorade. The cards are unnumbered except for uniform number. Card backs feature blue print on white card stock. The cards measure 2 7/8" by 4 1/4" and are in full color.

| | | | MINT | VG-E | F-G |
|---|---|---|---|---|---|
| | | COMPLETE SET | 5.00 | 2.00 | .50 |
| | | COMMON PLAYER | .10 | .04 | .01 |
| ☐ | 4 | Gene Michael MGR | .15 | .06 | .01 |
| ☐ | 6 | Keith Moreland | .30 | .12 | .03 |
| ☐ | 7 | Jody Davis | .30 | .12 | .03 |
| ☐ | 10 | Leon Durham | .30 | .12 | .03 |
| ☐ | 11 | Ron Cey | .30 | .12 | .03 |
| ☐ | 12 | Shawon Dunston | .50 | .20 | .05 |
| ☐ | 15 | Davey Lopes | .20 | .08 | .02 |
| ☐ | 16 | Terry Francona | .10 | .04 | .01 |
| ☐ | 18 | Steve Christmas | .20 | .08 | .02 |
| ☐ | 19 | Manny Trillo | .15 | .06 | .01 |
| ☐ | 20 | Bob Dernier | .15 | .06 | .01 |
| ☐ | 21 | Scott Sanderson | .10 | .04 | .01 |
| ☐ | 22 | Jerry Mumphrey | .15 | .06 | .01 |
| ☐ | 23 | Ryne Sandberg | 1.00 | .40 | .10 |
| ☐ | 27 | Thad Bosley | .10 | .04 | .01 |
| ☐ | 28 | Chris Speier | .10 | .04 | .01 |
| ☐ | 29 | Steve Lake | .10 | .04 | .01 |
| ☐ | 31 | Ray Fontenot | .10 | .04 | .01 |
| ☐ | 34 | Steve Trout | .15 | .06 | .01 |
| ☐ | 36 | Gary Matthews | .20 | .08 | .02 |
| ☐ | 39 | George Frazier | .10 | .04 | .01 |
| ☐ | 40 | Rick Sutcliffe | .20 | .08 | .02 |
| ☐ | 43 | Dennis Eckersley | .15 | .06 | .01 |
| ☐ | 46 | Lee Smith | .20 | .08 | .02 |
| ☐ | 48 | Jay Baller | .10 | .04 | .01 |
| ☐ | 49 | Jamie Moyer | .20 | .08 | .02 |
| ☐ | 50 | Guy Hoffman | .10 | .04 | .01 |
| ☐ | xx | Coaches Card (unnumbered) | .10 | .04 | .01 |

## 1953 Glendale

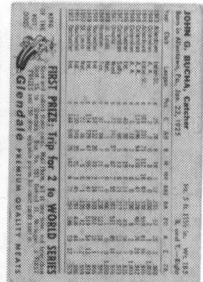

The cards in this 28 card set measure 2 5/8" by 3 3/4". The 1953 Glendale Meats set of full-color, unnumbered cards features Detroit Tiger ballplayers exclusively and was distributed one per package of Glendale Meats in the Detroit area. The back contains the complete major and minor league record through the 1952 season. The scarcer cards of the set command higher prices, with the Houtteman card being the most difficult to find. There is an album associated with the set (which also is quite scarce now). The ACC designation for this scarce regional set is F151. Since the cards are unnumbered, they are ordered below alphabetically.

| | | | MINT | VG-E | F-G |
|---|---|---|---|---|---|
| | | COMPLETE SET | 3000.00 | 1200.00 | 350.00 |
| | | COMMON PLAYER (1-28) | 75.00 | 30.00 | 7.50 |
| ☐ | 1 | Matt Batts | 75.00 | 30.00 | 7.50 |
| ☐ | 2 | Johnny Bucha | 75.00 | 30.00 | 7.50 |
| ☐ | 3 | Frank Carswell | 75.00 | 30.00 | 7.50 |
| ☐ | 4 | Jim Delsing | 75.00 | 30.00 | 7.50 |
| ☐ | 5 | Walt Dropo | 75.00 | 30.00 | 7.50 |
| ☐ | 6 | Hal Erickson | 75.00 | 30.00 | 7.50 |
| ☐ | 7 | Paul Foytack | 75.00 | 30.00 | 7.50 |
| ☐ | 8 | Owen Friend | 75.00 | 30.00 | 7.50 |
| ☐ | 9 | Ned Garver | 75.00 | 30.00 | 7.50 |
| ☐ | 10 | Joe Ginsberg | 250.00 | 100.00 | 25.00 |
| ☐ | 11 | Ted Gray | 90.00 | 36.00 | 9.00 |
| ☐ | 12 | Fred Hatfield | 75.00 | 30.00 | 7.50 |
| ☐ | 13 | Ray Herbert | 75.00 | 30.00 | 7.50 |
| ☐ | 14 | Bill Hitchcock | 75.00 | 30.00 | 7.50 |
| ☐ | 15 | Bill Hoeft | 150.00 | 60.00 | 15.00 |
| ☐ | 16 | Art Houtteman | 1200.00 | 500.00 | 125.00 |
| ☐ | 17 | Milt Jordan | 90.00 | 36.00 | 9.00 |
| ☐ | 18 | Harvey Kuenn | 150.00 | 60.00 | 15.00 |
| ☐ | 19 | Don Lund | 75.00 | 30.00 | 7.50 |
| ☐ | 20 | Dave Madison | 75.00 | 30.00 | 7.50 |
| ☐ | 21 | Dick Marlowe | 75.00 | 30.00 | 7.50 |
| ☐ | 22 | Pat Mullin | 75.00 | 30.00 | 7.50 |
| ☐ | 23 | Bob Nieman | 75.00 | 30.00 | 7.50 |
| ☐ | 24 | Johnny Pesky | 75.00 | 30.00 | 7.50 |
| ☐ | 25 | Jerry Priddy | 75.00 | 30.00 | 7.50 |
| ☐ | 26 | Steve Souchock | 75.00 | 30.00 | 7.50 |
| ☐ | 27 | Russ Sullivan | 75.00 | 30.00 | 7.50 |
| ☐ | 28 | Bill Wight | 90.00 | 36.00 | 9.00 |

**NEED HELP:** Special terms and abbreviations are listed in glossary.

**MAKE FRIENDS:** By attending a sports collectibles convention, you'll pick up items for your collection, and likely see your friends there, too.

## 1961 Golden Press

DAZZY VANCE
pitcher

The cards in this 33 card set measure 2 1/2" by 3 1/2". The 1961 Golden Press set of full color cards features members of Baseball's Hall of Fame. The cards came in a booklet with perforations for punching the cards out of the book. The catalog designation is W524. The price for the full book intact is 25% higher than the complete set price listed.

|  | | MINT | VG-E | F-G |
|---|---|---|---|---|
| COMPLETE SET ................... | | 40.00 | 16.00 | 4.00 |
| COMMON PLAYER (1-33) .......... | | .50 | .20 | .05 |
| ☐ 1 | Mel Ott ............................ | 1.50 | .60 | .15 |
| ☐ 2 | Grover C. Alexander ......... | 1.00 | .40 | .10 |
| ☐ 3 | Babe Ruth ....................... | 7.50 | 3.00 | .75 |
| ☐ 4 | Hank Greenberg ............... | .75 | .30 | .07 |
| ☐ 5 | Bill Terry ........................ | .75 | .30 | .07 |
| ☐ 6 | Carl Hubbell .................... | .75 | .30 | .07 |
| ☐ 7 | Rogers Hornsby ................ | 2.00 | .80 | .20 |
| ☐ 8 | Dizzy Dean ...................... | 3.00 | 1.20 | .30 |
| ☐ 9 | Joe DiMaggio ................... | 5.00 | 2.00 | .50 |
| ☐ 10 | Charlie Gehringer ............. | .75 | .30 | .07 |
| ☐ 11 | Gabby Hartnett ................ | .50 | .20 | .05 |
| ☐ 12 | Mickey Cochrane ............... | .75 | .30 | .07 |
| ☐ 13 | George Sisler .................. | .75 | .30 | .07 |
| ☐ 14 | Joe Cronin ...................... | .65 | .26 | .06 |
| ☐ 15 | Pie Traynor ..................... | .65 | .26 | .06 |
| ☐ 16 | Lou Gehrig ...................... | 5.00 | 2.00 | .50 |
| ☐ 17 | Lefty Grove ..................... | 1.25 | .50 | .12 |
| ☐ 18 | Chief Bender .................... | .50 | .20 | .05 |
| ☐ 19 | Frankie Frisch .................. | .65 | .26 | .06 |
| ☐ 20 | Al Simmons ..................... | .50 | .20 | .05 |
| ☐ 21 | Home Run Baker ............... | .50 | .20 | .05 |
| ☐ 22 | Jimmy Foxx ..................... | 1.50 | .60 | .15 |
| ☐ 23 | John McGraw ................... | .75 | .30 | .07 |
| ☐ 24 | Christy Mathewson ........... | 2.50 | 1.00 | .25 |
| ☐ 25 | Ty Cobb ......................... | 5.00 | 2.00 | .50 |
| ☐ 26 | Dazzy Vance .................... | .50 | .20 | .05 |
| ☐ 27 | Bill Dickey ...................... | .75 | .30 | .07 |
| ☐ 28 | Eddie Collins ................... | .50 | .20 | .05 |
| ☐ 29 | Walter Johnson ................ | 2.50 | 1.00 | .25 |
| ☐ 30 | Tris Speaker .................... | 1.25 | .50 | .12 |
| ☐ 31 | Nap Lajoie ...................... | 1.25 | .50 | .12 |
| ☐ 32 | Honus Wagner .................. | 2.50 | 1.00 | .25 |
| ☐ 33 | Cy Young ........................ | 1.50 | .60 | .15 |

## 1933 Goudey

The cards in this 240 card set measure 2 3/8" by 2 7/8". The 1933 Goudey set, designated R319 by the ACC, was that company's first baseball issue. The four Babe Ruth and two Lou Gehrig cards in the set are extremely popular with collectors. Card number 106, Napoleon Lajoie, was not printed in 1933, and was circulated to a limited number of collectors in 1934 upon request (it was printed along

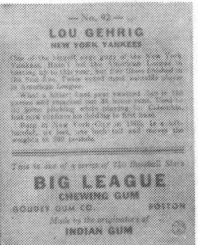

with the 1934 Goudey cards). An album was offered to house the 1933 set. Several minor leaguers are depicted. Card number 1 (Bengough) is very rarely found in mint condition; in fact, as a general rule all the first series cards are more difficult to find in Mint condition. Players with more than one card are also sometimes differentiated below by their pose: BAT (Batting), FIELD (Fielding), PIT (Pitching), THROW (Throwing). One of the Babe Ruth cards was double printed (DP) apparently in place of the Lajoie and hence is easier to obtain than the others. Due to the scarcity of the Lajoie card, the set is considered complete at 239 cards and is priced as such below.

|  | | MINT | VG-E | F-G |
|---|---|---|---|---|
| COMPLETE SET (239) ................ | | 9000.00 | 4000.00 | 950.00 |
| COMMON PLAYER (1-40) .......... | | 27.00 | 11.00 | 2.70 |
| COMMON PLAYER (41-44) ........ | | 22.00 | 9.00 | 2.20 |
| COMMON PLAYER (45-52) ........ | | 27.00 | 11.00 | 2.70 |
| COMMON PLAYER (53-240) ...... | | 22.00 | 9.00 | 2.20 |
| ☐ 1 | Benny Bengough ............ | 400.00 | 20.00 | 4.00 |
| ☐ 2 | Dazzy Vance ................... | 45.00 | 18.00 | 4.50 |
| ☐ 3 | Hugh Critz ...................... | 27.00 | 11.00 | 2.70 |
| ☐ 4 | Heine Schuble ................. | 27.00 | 11.00 | 2.70 |
| ☐ 5 | Babe Herman ................... | 30.00 | 12.00 | 3.00 |
| ☐ 6 | Jimmy Dykes ................... | 30.00 | 12.00 | 3.00 |
| ☐ 7 | Ted Lyons ....................... | 45.00 | 18.00 | 4.50 |
| ☐ 8 | Roy Johnson .................... | 27.00 | 11.00 | 2.70 |
| ☐ 9 | Dave Harris ..................... | 27.00 | 11.00 | 2.70 |
| ☐ 10 | Glenn Myatt ................... | 27.00 | 11.00 | 2.70 |
| ☐ 11 | Billy Rogell ..................... | 27.00 | 11.00 | 2.70 |
| ☐ 12 | George Pipgras ................ | 27.00 | 11.00 | 2.70 |
| ☐ 13 | Lafayette Thompson ....... | 27.00 | 11.00 | 2.70 |
| ☐ 14 | Henry Johnson ................ | 27.00 | 11.00 | 2.70 |
| ☐ 15 | Victor Sorrell .................. | 27.00 | 11.00 | 2.70 |
| ☐ 16 | George Blaeholder ........... | 27.00 | 11.00 | 2.70 |
| ☐ 17 | Watson Clark .................. | 27.00 | 11.00 | 2.70 |
| ☐ 18 | Muddy Ruel .................... | 27.00 | 11.00 | 2.70 |
| ☐ 19 | Bill Dickey ...................... | 80.00 | 32.00 | 8.00 |
| ☐ 20 | Bill Terry THROW ............ | 65.00 | 26.00 | 6.50 |
| ☐ 21 | Phil Collins .................... | 27.00 | 11.00 | 2.70 |
| ☐ 22 | Pie Traynor .................... | 65.00 | 26.00 | 6.50 |
| ☐ 23 | Kiki Cuyler ..................... | 45.00 | 18.00 | 4.50 |
| ☐ 24 | Horace Ford .................... | 27.00 | 11.00 | 2.70 |
| ☐ 25 | Paul Waner ..................... | 45.00 | 18.00 | 4.50 |
| ☐ 26 | Chalmer Cissell ............... | 27.00 | 11.00 | 2.70 |
| ☐ 27 | George Connally .............. | 27.00 | 11.00 | 2.70 |
| ☐ 28 | Dick Bartell .................... | 27.00 | 11.00 | 2.70 |
| ☐ 29 | Jimmy Foxx ..................... | 100.00 | 40.00 | 10.00 |
| ☐ 30 | Frank Hogan ................... | 27.00 | 11.00 | 2.70 |
| ☐ 31 | Tony Lazzeri .................... | 40.00 | 16.00 | 4.00 |
| ☐ 32 | Bud Clancy ..................... | 27.00 | 11.00 | 2.70 |
| ☐ 33 | Ralph Kress .................... | 27.00 | 11.00 | 2.70 |
| ☐ 34 | Bob O'Farrell .................. | 27.00 | 11.00 | 2.70 |
| ☐ 35 | Al Simmons ..................... | 65.00 | 26.00 | 6.50 |
| ☐ 36 | Tommy Thevenow ............ | 27.00 | 11.00 | 2.70 |
| ☐ 37 | Jimmy Wilson .................. | 27.00 | 11.00 | 2.70 |
| ☐ 38 | Fred Bickell .................... | 27.00 | 11.00 | 2.70 |
| ☐ 39 | Mark Koenig ................... | 27.00 | 11.00 | 2.70 |
| ☐ 40 | Taylor Douthit ................ | 27.00 | 11.00 | 2.70 |
| ☐ 41 | Gus Mancuso ................... | 22.00 | 9.00 | 2.20 |
| ☐ 42 | Eddie Collins ................... | 45.00 | 18.00 | 4.50 |
| ☐ 43 | Lew Fonseca ................... | 22.00 | 9.00 | 2.20 |
| ☐ 44 | Jim Bottomley ................. | 40.00 | 16.00 | 4.00 |
| ☐ 45 | Larry Benton ................... | 27.00 | 11.00 | 2.70 |
| ☐ 46 | Ethan Allen .................... | 27.00 | 11.00 | 2.70 |
| ☐ 47 | Heine Manush BAT ......... | 45.00 | 18.00 | 4.50 |
| ☐ 48 | Marty McManus ............... | 27.00 | 11.00 | 2.70 |
| ☐ 49 | Frank Frisch ................... | 60.00 | 24.00 | 6.00 |
| ☐ 50 | Ed Brandt ...................... | 27.00 | 11.00 | 2.70 |

| | | | | |
|---|---|---|---|---|
| □ 51 | Charlie Grimm | 30.00 | 12.00 | 3.00 |
| □ 52 | Andy Cohen | 27.00 | 11.00 | 2.70 |
| □ 53 | Babe Ruth | 900.00 | 360.00 | 90.00 |
| □ 54 | Ray Kremer | 22.00 | 9.00 | 2.20 |
| □ 55 | Pat Malone | 22.00 | 9.00 | 2.20 |
| □ 56 | Charlie Ruffing | 45.00 | 18.00 | 4.50 |
| □ 57 | Earl Clark | 22.00 | 9.00 | 2.20 |
| □ 58 | Lefty O'Doul | 25.00 | 10.00 | 2.50 |
| □ 59 | Bing Miller | 22.00 | 9.00 | 2.20 |
| □ 60 | Waite Hoyt | 40.00 | 16.00 | 4.00 |
| □ 61 | Max Bishop | 22.00 | 9.00 | 2.20 |
| □ 62 | Pepper Martin | 25.00 | 10.00 | 2.50 |
| □ 63 | Joe Cronin BAT | 40.00 | 16.00 | 4.00 |
| □ 64 | Burleigh Grimes | 40.00 | 16.00 | 4.00 |
| □ 65 | Milt Gaston | 22.00 | 9.00 | 2.20 |
| □ 66 | George Grantham | 22.00 | 9.00 | 2.20 |
| □ 67 | Guy Bush | 22.00 | 9.00 | 2.20 |
| □ 68 | Horace Lisenbee | 22.00 | 9.00 | 2.20 |
| □ 69 | Randy Moore | 22.00 | 9.00 | 2.20 |
| □ 70 | Floyd (Pete) Scott | 22.00 | 9.00 | 2.20 |
| □ 71 | Robert J. Burke | 22.00 | 9.00 | 2.20 |
| □ 72 | Owen Carroll | 22.00 | 9.00 | 2.20 |
| □ 73 | Jess Haines | 40.00 | 16.00 | 4.00 |
| □ 74 | Eppa Rixey | 40.00 | 16.00 | 4.00 |
| □ 75 | Willie Kamm | 22.00 | 9.00 | 2.20 |
| □ 76 | Mickey Cochrane | 50.00 | 20.00 | 5.00 |
| □ 77 | Adam Comorosky | 22.00 | 9.00 | 2.20 |
| □ 78 | Jack Quinn | 22.00 | 9.00 | 2.20 |
| □ 79 | Red Faber | 40.00 | 16.00 | 4.00 |
| □ 80 | Clyde Manion | 22.00 | 9.00 | 2.20 |
| □ 81 | Sam Jones | 22.00 | 9.00 | 2.20 |
| □ 82 | Dibrell Williams | 22.00 | 9.00 | 2.20 |
| □ 83 | Pete Jablonowski | 22.00 | 9.00 | 2.20 |
| □ 84 | Glenn Spencer | 22.00 | 9.00 | 2.20 |
| □ 85 | Heine Sand | 22.00 | 9.00 | 2.20 |
| □ 86 | Phil Todt | 22.00 | 9.00 | 2.20 |
| □ 87 | Frank O'Rourke | 22.00 | 9.00 | 2.20 |
| □ 88 | Russell Rollings | 22.00 | 9.00 | 2.20 |
| □ 89 | Tris Speaker | 100.00 | 40.00 | 10.00 |
| □ 90 | Jess Petty | 22.00 | 9.00 | 2.20 |
| □ 91 | Tom Zachary | 22.00 | 9.00 | 2.20 |
| □ 92 | Lou Gehrig | 500.00 | 200.00 | 50.00 |
| □ 93 | John Welch | 22.00 | 9.00 | 2.20 |
| □ 94 | Bill Walker | 22.00 | 9.00 | 2.20 |
| □ 95 | Alvin Crowder | 22.00 | 9.00 | 2.20 |
| □ 96 | Willis Hudlin | 22.00 | 9.00 | 2.20 |
| □ 97 | Joe Morrissey | 22.00 | 9.00 | 2.20 |
| □ 98 | Walter Berger | 22.00 | 9.00 | 2.20 |
| □ 99 | Tony Cuccinello | 22.00 | 9.00 | 2.20 |
| □ 100 | George Uhle | 22.00 | 9.00 | 2.20 |
| □ 101 | Richard Coffman | 22.00 | 9.00 | 2.20 |
| □ 102 | Travis Jackson | 40.00 | 16.00 | 4.00 |
| □ 103 | Earl Combs | 40.00 | 16.00 | 4.00 |
| □ 104 | Fred Marberry | 22.00 | 9.00 | 2.20 |
| □ 105 | Bernie Friberg | 22.00 | 9.00 | 2.20 |
| □ 106 | Napoleon Lajoie (not issued until 1934) | 7000.00 | 2800.00 | 700.00 |
| □ 107 | Heine Manush | 40.00 | 16.00 | 4.00 |
| □ 108 | Joe Kuhel | 22.00 | 9.00 | 2.20 |
| □ 109 | Joe Cronin | 40.00 | 16.00 | 4.00 |
| □ 110 | Goose Goslin | 40.00 | 16.00 | 4.00 |
| □ 111 | Monte Weaver | 22.00 | 9.00 | 2.20 |
| □ 112 | Fred Schulte | 22.00 | 9.00 | 2.20 |
| □ 113 | Oswald Bluege | 22.00 | 9.00 | 2.20 |
| □ 114 | Luke Sewell | 22.00 | 9.00 | 2.20 |
| □ 115 | Cliff Heathcote | 22.00 | 9.00 | 2.20 |
| □ 116 | Eddie Morgan | 22.00 | 9.00 | 2.20 |
| □ 117 | Rabbit Maranville | 40.00 | 16.00 | 4.00 |
| □ 118 | Val Picinich | 22.00 | 9.00 | 2.20 |
| □ 119 | Rogers Hornsby FIELD | 100.00 | 40.00 | 10.00 |
| □ 120 | Carl Reynolds | 22.00 | 9.00 | 2.20 |
| □ 121 | Walter Stewart | 22.00 | 9.00 | 2.20 |
| □ 122 | Alvin Crowder | 22.00 | 9.00 | 2.20 |
| □ 123 | Jack Russell | 22.00 | 9.00 | 2.20 |
| □ 124 | Earl Whitehill | 22.00 | 9.00 | 2.20 |
| □ 125 | Bill Terry | 65.00 | 26.00 | 6.50 |
| □ 126 | Joe Moore | 22.00 | 9.00 | 2.20 |
| □ 127 | Mel Ott | 80.00 | 32.00 | 8.00 |
| □ 128 | Chuck Klein | 45.00 | 18.00 | 4.50 |
| □ 129 | Hal Schumacher PIT | 22.00 | 9.00 | 2.20 |
| □ 130 | Fred Fitzsimmons | 22.00 | 9.00 | 2.20 |
| □ 131 | Fred Frankhouse | 22.00 | 9.00 | 2.20 |
| □ 132 | Jim Elliott | 22.00 | 9.00 | 2.20 |
| □ 133 | Fred Lindstrom | 40.00 | 16.00 | 4.00 |
| □ 134 | Sam Rice | 40.00 | 16.00 | 4.00 |
| □ 135 | Woody English | 22.00 | 9.00 | 2.20 |
| □ 136 | Flint Rhem | 22.00 | 9.00 | 2.20 |
| □ 137 | Fred (Red) Lucas | 22.00 | 9.00 | 2.20 |
| □ 138 | Herb Pennock | 40.00 | 16.00 | 4.00 |
| □ 139 | Ben Cantwell | 22.00 | 9.00 | 2.20 |
| □ 140 | Bump Hadley | 22.00 | 9.00 | 2.20 |
| □ 141 | Ray Benge | 22.00 | 9.00 | 2.20 |
| □ 142 | Paul Richards | 25.00 | 10.00 | 2.50 |
| □ 143 | Glenn Wright | 22.00 | 9.00 | 2.20 |
| □ 144 | Babe Ruth BAT DP | 750.00 | 300.00 | 75.00 |
| □ 145 | George Walberg | 22.00 | 9.00 | 2.20 |
| □ 146 | Walter Stewart PIT | 22.00 | 9.00 | 2.20 |
| □ 147 | Leo Durocher | 35.00 | 14.00 | 3.50 |
| □ 148 | Eddie Farrell | 22.00 | 9.00 | 2.20 |
| □ 149 | Babe Ruth | 900.00 | 360.00 | 90.00 |
| □ 150 | Ray Kolp | 22.00 | 9.00 | 2.20 |
| □ 151 | Jake Flowers | 22.00 | 9.00 | 2.20 |
| □ 152 | Zack Taylor | 22.00 | 9.00 | 2.20 |
| □ 153 | Buddy Myer | 22.00 | 9.00 | 2.20 |
| □ 154 | Jimmy Foxx | 100.00 | 40.00 | 10.00 |
| □ 155 | Joe Judge | 22.00 | 9.00 | 2.20 |
| □ 156 | Danny MacFayden | 22.00 | 9.00 | 2.20 |
| □ 157 | Sam Byrd | 22.00 | 9.00 | 2.20 |
| □ 158 | Moe Berg | 25.00 | 10.00 | 2.50 |
| □ 159 | Oswald Bluege | 22.00 | 9.00 | 2.20 |
| □ 160 | Lou Gehrig | 500.00 | 200.00 | 50.00 |
| □ 161 | Al Spohrer | 22.00 | 9.00 | 2.20 |
| □ 162 | Leo Mangum | 22.00 | 9.00 | 2.20 |
| □ 163 | Luke Sewell | 22.00 | 9.00 | 2.20 |
| □ 164 | Lloyd Waner | 40.00 | 16.00 | 4.00 |
| □ 165 | Joe Sewell | 40.00 | 16.00 | 4.00 |
| □ 166 | Sam West | 22.00 | 9.00 | 2.20 |
| □ 167 | Jack Russell | 22.00 | 9.00 | 2.20 |
| □ 168 | Goose Goslin | 40.00 | 16.00 | 4.00 |
| □ 169 | Al Thomas | 22.00 | 9.00 | 2.20 |
| □ 170 | Harry McCurdy | 22.00 | 9.00 | 2.20 |
| □ 171 | Charlie Jamieson | 22.00 | 9.00 | 2.20 |
| □ 172 | Billy Hargrave | 22.00 | 9.00 | 2.20 |
| □ 173 | Roscoe Holm | 22.00 | 9.00 | 2.20 |
| □ 174 | Warren (Curly) Ogden | 22.00 | 9.00 | 2.20 |
| □ 175 | Dan Howley | 22.00 | 9.00 | 2.20 |
| □ 176 | John Ogden | 22.00 | 9.00 | 2.20 |
| □ 177 | Walter French | 22.00 | 9.00 | 2.20 |
| □ 178 | Jackie Warner | 22.00 | 9.00 | 2.20 |
| □ 179 | Fred Leach | 22.00 | 9.00 | 2.20 |
| □ 180 | Eddie Moore | 22.00 | 9.00 | 2.20 |
| □ 181 | Babe Ruth | 1000.00 | 400.00 | 100.00 |
| □ 182 | Andy High | 22.00 | 9.00 | 2.20 |
| □ 183 | George Walberg | 22.00 | 9.00 | 2.20 |
| □ 184 | Charley Berry | 22.00 | 9.00 | 2.20 |
| □ 185 | Bob Smith | 22.00 | 9.00 | 2.20 |
| □ 186 | John Schulte | 22.00 | 9.00 | 2.20 |
| □ 187 | Heine Manush | 40.00 | 16.00 | 4.00 |
| □ 188 | Rogers Hornsby | 100.00 | 40.00 | 10.00 |
| □ 189 | Joe Cronin | 40.00 | 16.00 | 4.00 |
| □ 190 | Fred Schulte | 22.00 | 9.00 | 2.20 |
| □ 191 | Ben Chapman | 22.00 | 9.00 | 2.20 |
| □ 192 | Walter Brown | 22.00 | 9.00 | 2.20 |
| □ 193 | Lynford Lary | 22.00 | 9.00 | 2.20 |
| □ 194 | Earl Averill | 40.00 | 16.00 | 4.00 |
| □ 195 | Evar Swanson | 22.00 | 9.00 | 2.20 |
| □ 196 | Leroy Mahaffey | 22.00 | 9.00 | 2.20 |
| □ 197 | Rick Ferrell | 40.00 | 16.00 | 4.00 |
| □ 198 | Jack Burns | 22.00 | 9.00 | 2.20 |
| □ 199 | Tom Bridges | 22.00 | 9.00 | 2.20 |
| □ 200 | Bill Hallahan | 22.00 | 9.00 | 2.20 |
| □ 201 | Ernie Orsatti | 22.00 | 9.00 | 2.20 |
| □ 202 | Gabby Hartnett | 40.00 | 16.00 | 4.00 |
| □ 203 | Lon Warneke | 22.00 | 9.00 | 2.20 |
| □ 204 | Riggs Stephenson | 25.00 | 10.00 | 2.50 |
| □ 205 | Heine Meine | 22.00 | 9.00 | 2.20 |
| □ 206 | Gus Suhr | 22.00 | 9.00 | 2.20 |
| □ 207 | Mel Ott BAT | 80.00 | 32.00 | 8.00 |
| □ 208 | Bernie James | 22.00 | 9.00 | 2.20 |
| □ 209 | Adolfo Luque | 22.00 | 9.00 | 2.20 |
| □ 210 | Virgil Davis | 22.00 | 9.00 | 2.20 |
| □ 211 | Hack Wilson | 65.00 | 26.00 | 6.50 |
| □ 212 | Billy Urbanski | 22.00 | 9.00 | 2.20 |
| □ 213 | Earl Adams | 22.00 | 9.00 | 2.20 |
| □ 214 | John Kerr | 22.00 | 9.00 | 2.20 |
| □ 215 | Russ Van Atta | 22.00 | 9.00 | 2.20 |
| □ 216 | Vernon Gomez | 80.00 | 32.00 | 8.00 |
| □ 217 | Frank Crosetti | 30.00 | 12.00 | 3.00 |
| □ 218 | Wes Ferrell | 25.00 | 10.00 | 2.50 |
| □ 219 | Mule Haas | 22.00 | 9.00 | 2.20 |
| □ 220 | Lefty Grove | 100.00 | 40.00 | 10.00 |
| □ 221 | Dale Alexander | 22.00 | 9.00 | 2.20 |
| □ 222 | Charley Gehringer | 65.00 | 26.00 | 6.50 |
| □ 223 | Dizzy Dean | 250.00 | 100.00 | 25.00 |
| □ 224 | Frank Demaree | 22.00 | 9.00 | 2.20 |
| □ 225 | Bill Jurges | 22.00 | 9.00 | 2.20 |
| □ 226 | Charley Root | 22.00 | 9.00 | 2.20 |
| □ 227 | Billy Herman | 40.00 | 16.00 | 4.00 |
| □ 228 | Tony Piet | 22.00 | 9.00 | 2.20 |
| □ 229 | Floyd (Arky) Vaughan | 40.00 | 16.00 | 4.00 |
| □ 230 | Carl Hubbell PIT | 60.00 | 24.00 | 6.00 |
| □ 231 | Joe Moore FIELD | 22.00 | 9.00 | 2.20 |
| □ 232 | Lefty O'Doul | 25.00 | 10.00 | 2.50 |
| □ 233 | Johnny Vergez | 22.00 | 9.00 | 2.20 |
| □ 234 | Carl Hubbell | 60.00 | 24.00 | 6.00 |

| | | MINT | VG-E | F-G |
|---|---|---|---|---|
| ☐ 235 | Fred Fitzsimmons | 22.00 | 9.00 | 2.20 |
| ☐ 236 | George Davis | 22.00 | 9.00 | 2.20 |
| ☐ 237 | Gus Mancuso | 22.00 | 9.00 | 2.20 |
| ☐ 238 | Hugh Critz | 22.00 | 9.00 | 2.20 |
| ☐ 239 | Leroy Parmelee | 22.00 | 9.00 | 2.20 |
| ☐ 240 | Hal Schumacher | 30.00 | 10.00 | 2.00 |

## 1934 Goudey

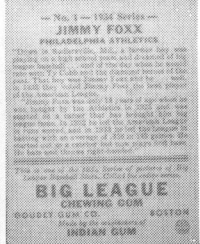

The cards in this 96 card set measure 2 3/8" by 2 7/8". The 1934 Goudey set of color cards carries the ACC catalog number R320. Cards 1-48 are considered to be the easiest to find (although card number 1, Foxx, is very scarce in mint condition) while 73-96 are much more difficult to find. Cards of this 1934 Goudey series are slightly less abundant than cards of the 1933 Goudey set. Of the 96 cards, 84 contain a "Lou Gehrig Says" line on the front in a blue design, while 12 of the high series contain a "Chuck Klein Says" line in a red design.

| | MINT | VG-E | F-G |
|---|---|---|---|
| COMPLETE SET | 4500.00 | 200.00 | 50.00 |
| COMMON PLAYER (1-48) | 21.00 | 8.50 | 2.10 |
| COMMON PLAYER (49-72) | 28.00 | 11.50 | 2.80 |
| COMMON PLAYER (73-96) | 80.00 | 32.00 | 8.00 |

| | | | | |
|---|---|---|---|---|
| ☐ 1 | Jimmy Foxx | 250.00 | 50.00 | 10.00 |
| ☐ 2 | Mickey Cochrane | 50.00 | 20.00 | 5.00 |
| ☐ 3 | Charlie Grimm | 25.00 | 10.00 | 2.50 |
| ☐ 4 | Woody English | 21.00 | 8.50 | 2.10 |
| ☐ 5 | Ed Brandt | 21.00 | 8.50 | 2.10 |
| ☐ 6 | Dizzy Dean | 250.00 | 100.00 | 25.00 |
| ☐ 7 | Leo Durocher | 30.00 | 12.00 | 3.00 |
| ☐ 8 | Tony Piet | 21.00 | 8.50 | 2.10 |
| ☐ 9 | Ben Chapman | 21.00 | 8.50 | 2.10 |
| ☐ 10 | Chuck Klein | 45.00 | 18.00 | 4.50 |
| ☐ 11 | Paul Waner | 40.00 | 16.00 | 4.00 |
| ☐ 12 | Carl Hubbell | 45.00 | 18.00 | 4.50 |
| ☐ 13 | Frank Frisch | 45.00 | 18.00 | 4.50 |
| ☐ 14 | Willie Kamm | 21.00 | 8.50 | 2.10 |
| ☐ 15 | Alvin Crowder | 21.00 | 8.50 | 2.10 |
| ☐ 16 | Joe Kuhel | 21.00 | 8.50 | 2.10 |
| ☐ 17 | Hugh Critz | 21.00 | 8.50 | 2.10 |
| ☐ 18 | Heinie Manush | 40.00 | 16.00 | 4.00 |
| ☐ 19 | Lefty Grove | 65.00 | 26.00 | 6.50 |
| ☐ 20 | Frank Hogan | 21.00 | 8.50 | 2.10 |
| ☐ 21 | Bill Terry | 50.00 | 20.00 | 5.00 |
| ☐ 22 | Arky Vaughan | 40.00 | 16.00 | 4.00 |
| ☐ 23 | Charlie Gehringer | 50.00 | 20.00 | 5.00 |
| ☐ 24 | Ray Benge | 21.00 | 8.50 | 2.10 |
| ☐ 25 | Roger Cramer | 25.00 | 10.00 | 2.50 |
| ☐ 26 | Gerald Walker | 21.00 | 8.50 | 2.10 |
| ☐ 27 | Luke Appling | 40.00 | 16.00 | 4.00 |
| ☐ 28 | Ed Coleman | 21.00 | 8.50 | 2.10 |
| ☐ 29 | Larry French | 21.00 | 8.50 | 2.10 |
| ☐ 30 | Julius Solters | 21.00 | 8.50 | 2.10 |
| ☐ 31 | Buck Jordan | 21.00 | 8.50 | 2.10 |
| ☐ 32 | Blondy Ryan | 21.00 | 8.50 | 2.10 |
| ☐ 33 | Frank Hurst | 21.00 | 8.50 | 2.10 |
| ☐ 34 | Chick Hafey | 40.00 | 16.00 | 4.00 |
| ☐ 35 | Ernie Lombardi | 40.00 | 16.00 | 4.00 |
| ☐ 36 | Walter Betts | 21.00 | 8.50 | 2.10 |
| ☐ 37 | Lou Gehrig | 600.00 | 240.00 | 60.00 |
| ☐ 38 | Oral Hildebrand | 21.00 | 8.50 | 2.10 |
| ☐ 39 | Fred Walker | 21.00 | 8.50 | 2.10 |
| ☐ 40 | John Stone | 21.00 | 8.50 | 2.10 |

| | | | | |
|---|---|---|---|---|
| ☐ 41 | George Earnshaw | 21.00 | 8.50 | 2.10 |
| ☐ 42 | John Allen | 21.00 | 8.50 | 2.10 |
| ☐ 43 | Dick Porter | 21.00 | 8.50 | 2.10 |
| ☐ 44 | Tom Bridges | 21.00 | 8.50 | 2.10 |
| ☐ 45 | Oscar Melillo | 21.00 | 8.50 | 2.10 |
| ☐ 46 | Joe Stripp | 21.00 | 8.50 | 2.10 |
| ☐ 47 | John Frederick | 21.00 | 8.50 | 2.10 |
| ☐ 48 | Tex Carleton | 21.00 | 8.50 | 2.10 |
| ☐ 49 | Sam Leslie | 28.00 | 11.50 | 2.80 |
| ☐ 50 | Walter Beck | 28.00 | 11.50 | 2.80 |
| ☐ 51 | Rip Collins | 28.00 | 11.50 | 2.80 |
| ☐ 52 | Herman Bell | 28.00 | 11.50 | 2.80 |
| ☐ 53 | George Watkins | 28.00 | 11.50 | 2.80 |
| ☐ 54 | Wesley Schulmerich | 28.00 | 11.50 | 2.80 |
| ☐ 55 | Ed Holley | 28.00 | 11.50 | 2.80 |
| ☐ 56 | Mark Koenig | 28.00 | 11.50 | 2.80 |
| ☐ 57 | Bill Swift | 28.00 | 11.50 | 2.80 |
| ☐ 58 | Earl Grace | 28.00 | 11.50 | 2.80 |
| ☐ 59 | Joe Mowry | 28.00 | 11.50 | 2.80 |
| ☐ 60 | Lynn Nelson | 28.00 | 11.50 | 2.80 |
| ☐ 61 | Lou Gehrig | 650.00 | 260.00 | 65.00 |
| ☐ 62 | Hank Greenberg | 80.00 | 32.00 | 8.00 |
| ☐ 63 | Minter Hayes | 28.00 | 11.50 | 2.80 |
| ☐ 64 | Frank Grube | 28.00 | 11.50 | 2.80 |
| ☐ 65 | Cliff Bolton | 28.00 | 11.50 | 2.80 |
| ☐ 66 | Mel Harder | 30.00 | 12.00 | 3.00 |
| ☐ 67 | Bob Weiland | 28.00 | 11.50 | 2.80 |
| ☐ 68 | Bob Johnson | 30.00 | 12.00 | 3.00 |
| ☐ 69 | John Marcum | 28.00 | 11.50 | 2.80 |
| ☐ 70 | Pete Fox | 28.00 | 11.50 | 2.80 |
| ☐ 71 | Lyle Tinning | 28.00 | 11.50 | 2.80 |
| ☐ 72 | Arndt Jorgens | 28.00 | 11.50 | 2.80 |
| ☐ 73 | Ed Wells | 80.00 | 32.00 | 8.00 |
| ☐ 74 | Bob Boken | 80.00 | 32.00 | 8.00 |
| ☐ 75 | Bill Werber | 80.00 | 32.00 | 8.00 |
| ☐ 76 | Hal Trosky | 80.00 | 32.00 | 8.00 |
| ☐ 77 | Joe Vosmik | 80.00 | 32.00 | 8.00 |
| ☐ 78 | Pinky Higgins | 80.00 | 32.00 | 8.00 |
| ☐ 79 | Ed Durham | 80.00 | 32.00 | 8.00 |
| ☐ 80 | Marty McManus | 80.00 | 32.00 | 8.00 |
| ☐ 81 | Bob Brown | 80.00 | 32.00 | 8.00 |
| ☐ 82 | Bill Hallahan | 80.00 | 32.00 | 8.00 |
| ☐ 83 | Jim Mooney | 80.00 | 32.00 | 8.00 |
| ☐ 84 | Paul Derringer | 100.00 | 40.00 | 10.00 |
| ☐ 85 | Adam Comorosky | 80.00 | 32.00 | 8.00 |
| ☐ 86 | Lloyd Johnson | 80.00 | 32.00 | 8.00 |
| ☐ 87 | George Darrow | 80.00 | 32.00 | 8.00 |
| ☐ 88 | Homer Peel | 80.00 | 32.00 | 8.00 |
| ☐ 89 | Linus Frey | 80.00 | 32.00 | 8.00 |
| ☐ 90 | Ki-Ki Cuyler | 150.00 | 60.00 | 15.00 |
| ☐ 91 | Dolph Camilli | 80.00 | 32.00 | 8.00 |
| ☐ 92 | Steve Larkin | 80.00 | 32.00 | 8.00 |
| ☐ 93 | Fred Ostermueller | 80.00 | 32.00 | 8.00 |
| ☐ 94 | Red Rolfe | 80.00 | 32.00 | 8.00 |
| ☐ 95 | Myril Hoag | 80.00 | 32.00 | 8.00 |
| ☐ 96 | James DeShong | 100.00 | 40.00 | 8.00 |

## 1935 Goudey

The cards in this 36 card set (the number of different front pictures) measure 2 3/8" by 2 7/8". The 1935 Goudey set is sometimes called the Goudey Puzzle Set, the Goudey 4 in 1's, or R321 (ACC). There are 36 different card fronts but 114 different front/back combinations. The card number in the checklist refers to the back puzzle number, as the backs can be arranged to form a puzzle picturing a player or team. To avoid the confusion caused by two different fronts having the same back number, the rarer cards have been arbitrarily given a "1" prefix. The scarcer puzzle cards are hence all listed at the numerical end of the list below, i.e. rare puzzle 1 is listed as number 11, rare puzzle 2 is listed as 12, etc. The BLUE in the checklist refers to a card with a blue border, as most cards have a red border. The set price below includes only the 36 different fronts, making no distinction as to which backs are present. The following is the list of the puzzle back pictures: 1) Detroit Tigers; 2) Chuck Klein; 3) Frankie Frisch; 4) Mickey Cochrane; 5) Joe Cronin; 6) Jimmy Foxx; 7) Al Simmons; 8) Cleveland Indians; and 9) Washington Senators.

|  | MINT | VG-E | F-G |
|---|---|---|---|
| COMPLETE SET (36) | 1250.00 | 550.00 | 150.00 |
| COMMON CARDS (1-9) | 20.00 | 8.00 | 2.00 |
| STARRED CARDS (11-17) | 30.00 | 12.00 | 3.00 |

| | | | | |
|---|---|---|---|---|
| ☐ 1A | F.Frisch/Dizzy Dean Orsatti/Carleton | 60.00 | 24.00 | 6.00 |
| ☐ 1B | Mahaffey/Jimmie Foxx Williams/Higgins | 40.00 | 16.00 | 4.00 |
| ☐ 1C | Heine Manush/Lary Weaver/Hadley | 25.00 | 10.00 | 2.50 |
| ☐ 1D | Cochrane/C.Gehringer Bridges/Rogell | 40.00 | 16.00 | 4.00 |
| ☐ 1E | Paul Waner/Bush W.Hoyt/Lloyd Waner | 40.00 | 16.00 | 4.00 |
| ☐ 1F | B.Grimes/Chuck Klein K.Cuyler/English | 40.00 | 16.00 | 4.00 |
| ☐ 1G | Leslie/Frey Joe Stripp/Clark | 20.00 | 8.00 | 2.00 |
| ☐ 1H | Piet/Comorosky Bottomley/Adams | 25.00 | 10.00 | 2.50 |
| ☐ 1I | Earnshaw/Dykes Luke Sewell/Appling | 25.00 | 10.00 | 2.50 |
| ☐ 1J | Babe Ruth/McManus Brandt/Maranville | 250.00 | 100.00 | 25.00 |
| ☐ 1K | Bill Terry/Schumacher Mancuso/Jackson | 40.00 | 16.00 | 4.00 |
| ☐ 1L | Kamm/Hildebrand Averill/Trosky | 25.00 | 10.00 | 2.50 |
| ☐ 2A | F.Frisch/Dizzy Dean Orsatti/Carleton | 60.00 | 24.00 | 6.00 |
| ☐ 2B | Mahaffey/Jimmie Foxx Williams/Higgins | 40.00 | 16.00 | 4.00 |
| ☐ 2C | Heine Manush/Lary Weaver/Hadley | 25.00 | 10.00 | 2.50 |
| ☐ 2D | Cochrane/C.Gehringer Bridges/Rogell | 40.00 | 16.00 | 4.00 |
| ☐ 2E | Kamm/Hildebrand Earl Averill/Trosky | 25.00 | 10.00 | 2.50 |
| ☐ 2F | Earnshaw/Dykes Luke Sewell/Appling | 25.00 | 10.00 | 2.50 |
| ☐ 3A | Babe Ruth/McManus Brandt/Maranville | 250.00 | 100.00 | 25.00 |
| ☐ 3B | Bill Terry/Schumacher Mancuso/T.Jackson | 40.00 | 16.00 | 4.00 |
| ☐ 3C | Paul Waner/Bush W.Hoyt/Lloyd Waner | 40.00 | 16.00 | 4.00 |
| ☐ 3D | B.Grimes/Chuck Klein K.Cuyler/English | 40.00 | 16.00 | 4.00 |
| ☐ 3E | Leslie/Frey Joe Stripp/Clark | 20.00 | 8.00 | 2.00 |
| ☐ 3F | Piet/Comorosky Jim Bottomley/Adams | 25.00 | 10.00 | 2.50 |
| ☐ 4A | Critz/D.Bartell BLUE Mel Ott/Mancuso | 40.00 | 16.00 | 4.00 |
| ☐ 4B | Pie Traynor/Lucas BLUE Tom Thevenow/Wright | 25.00 | 10.00 | 2.50 |
| ☐ 4C | Berry/Burke BLUE Kress/Dazzy Vance | 25.00 | 10.00 | 2.50 |
| ☐ 4D | R.Ruffing/Malone BLUE Lazzeri/Bill Dickey | 60.00 | 24.00 | 6.00 |
| ☐ 4E | Moore/Hogan BLUE Frankhouse/Brandt | 20.00 | 8.00 | 2.00 |
| ☐ 4F | Martin/O'Farrell BLUE Byrd/MacFayden | 20.00 | 8.00 | 2.00 |
| ☐ 5A | Ruel/Al Simmons Kamm/M.Cochrane | 40.00 | 16.00 | 4.00 |
| ☐ 5B | Willis Hudlin/Myatt Comorosky/Bottomley | 25.00 | 10.00 | 2.50 |
| ☐ 5C | Paul Waner/Bush W.Hoyt/Lloyd Waner | 40.00 | 16.00 | 4.00 |

| | | | | |
|---|---|---|---|---|
| ☐ 5D | West/Oscar Melillo Blaeholder/Coffman | 20.00 | 8.00 | 2.00 |
| ☐ 5E | Leslie/Frey Joe Stripp/Clark | 20.00 | 8.00 | 2.00 |
| ☐ 5F | Schuble/Marberry Goose Goslin/Crowder | 25.00 | 10.00 | 2.50 |
| ☐ 6A | Ruel/Al Simmons Kamm/M.Cochrane | 40.00 | 16.00 | 4.00 |
| ☐ 6B | Willis Hudlin/Myatt Comorosky/Bottomley | 25.00 | 10.00 | 2.50 |
| ☐ 6C | Wilson/Allen Jonnard/Brickell | 20.00 | 8.00 | 2.00 |
| ☐ 6D | West/Oscar Melillo Blaeholder/Coffman | 20.00 | 8.00 | 2.00 |
| ☐ 6E | Joe Cronin/Reynolds Bishop/Cissell | 25.00 | 10.00 | 2.50 |
| ☐ 6F | Schuble/Marberry Goose Goslin/Crowder | 25.00 | 10.00 | 2.50 |
| ☐ 7A | Critz/Bartell BLUE Mel Ott/Mancuso | 35.00 | 14.00 | 3.50 |
| ☐ 7B | Pie Traynor/Lucas BLUE Tom Thevenow/Wright | 25.00 | 10.00 | 2.50 |
| ☐ 7C | Berry/Burke BLUE Kress/Dazzy Vance | 25.00 | 10.00 | 2.50 |
| ☐ 7D | R.Ruffing/Malone BLUE Lazzeri/Bill Dickey | 60.00 | 24.00 | 6.00 |
| ☐ 7E | Moore/Hogan BLUE Frankhouse/Brandt | 20.00 | 8.00 | 2.00 |
| ☐ 7F | Martin/O'Farrell BLUE Byrd/MacFayden | 20.00 | 8.00 | 2.00 |
| ☐ 8A | M.Koenig/Fitzsimmons Benge/Zachary | 20.00 | 8.00 | 2.00 |
| ☐ 8B | Hayes/Ted Lyons Haas/Zeke Bonura | 25.00 | 10.00 | 2.50 |
| ☐ 8C | Burns/Rollie Hemsley Grube/Weiland | 20.00 | 8.00 | 2.00 |
| ☐ 8D | Campbell/Meyers Goodman/Kampouris | 20.00 | 8.00 | 2.00 |
| ☐ 8E | DeShong/Allen Red Rolfe/Walker | 20.00 | 8.00 | 2.00 |
| ☐ 8F | P.Fox/Hank Greenberg Walker/Rowe | 30.00 | 12.00 | 3.00 |
| ☐ 8G | Werber/Rick Ferrell W.Ferrell/Ostermueller | 25.00 | 10.00 | 2.50 |
| ☐ 8H | Joe Kuhel/Whitehill Meyer/Stone | 20.00 | 8.00 | 2.00 |
| ☐ 8I | J.Vosmik/Knickerbocker Mel Harder/Stewart | 20.00 | 8.00 | 2.00 |
| ☐ 8J | Johnson/Coleman Marcum/Cramer | 20.00 | 8.00 | 2.00 |
| ☐ 8K | Herman/Suhr Padden/Blanton | 20.00 | 8.00 | 2.00 |
| ☐ 8L | Spohrer/Rhem Cantwell/Benton | 20.00 | 8.00 | 2.00 |
| ☐ 8M | M.Koenig/Fitzsimmons Benge/Zachary | 20.00 | 8.00 | 2.00 |
| ☐ 9B | Hayes/Ted Lyons Haas/Zeke Bonura | 25.00 | 10.00 | 2.50 |
| ☐ 9C | Burns/Rollie Hemsley Grube/Weiland | 20.00 | 8.00 | 2.00 |
| ☐ 9D | Campbell/Meyers Goodman/Kampouris | 20.00 | 8.00 | 2.00 |
| ☐ 9E | DeShong/Allen Red Rolfe/Walker | 20.00 | 8.00 | 2.00 |
| ☐ 9F | P.Fox/Hank Greenberg Walker/Rowe | 30.00 | 12.00 | 3.00 |
| ☐ 9G | Werber/Rick Ferrell W.Ferrell/Ostermueller | 25.00 | 10.00 | 2.50 |
| ☐ 9H | Joe Kuhel/Whitehill Meyer/Stone | 20.00 | 8.00 | 2.00 |
| ☐ 9I | J.Vosmik/Knickerbocker Mel Harder/Stewart | 20.00 | 8.00 | 2.00 |
| ☐ 9J | Johnson/Coleman Marcum/Cramer | 20.00 | 8.00 | 2.00 |
| ☐ 9K | Herman/Suhr Padden/Blanton | 20.00 | 8.00 | 2.00 |
| ☐ 9L | Spohrer/Rhem Cantwell/Benton | 20.00 | 8.00 | 2.00 |
| ☐ 11E | Wilson/Allen Jonnard/Brickell | 30.00 | 12.00 | 3.00 |
| ☐ 11F | West/Melillo Blaeholder/Coffman | 30.00 | 12.00 | 3.00 |
| ☐ 11G | Joe Cronin/Reynolds Bishop/Cissell | 35.00 | 14.00 | 3.50 |
| ☐ 11H | Schuble/Marberry Goose Goslin/Crowder | 35.00 | 14.00 | 3.50 |
| ☐ 11J | Ruel/Al Simmons Kamm/M.Cochrane | 60.00 | 24.00 | 6.00 |
| ☐ 11K | Hudlin/Myatt Comorosky/Bottomley | 35.00 | 14.00 | 3.50 |
| ☐ 12A | Critz/Bartell BLUE Mel Ott/Mancuso | 50.00 | 20.00 | 5.00 |
| ☐ 12B | P.Traynor/Lucas BLUE Thevenow/Wright | 35.00 | 14.00 | 3.50 |

| | | | | |
|---|---|---|---|---|
| ☐ 12C | Berry/Burke BLUE ......... Kress/D.Vance | 35.00 | 14.00 | 3.50 |
| ☐ 12D | R.Ruffing/Malone BLUE . Lazzeri/Bill Dickey | 75.00 | 30.00 | 7.50 |
| ☐ 12E | Moore/Hogan BLUE ....... Frankhouse/Brandt | 30.00 | 12.00 | 3.00 |
| ☐ 12F | Martin/O'Farrell BLUE .... Byrd/MacFayden | 30.00 | 12.00 | 3.00 |
| ☐ 13A | Ruel/Al Simmons .......... Kamm/M.Cochrane | 60.00 | 24.00 | 6.00 |
| ☐ 13B | Hudlin/Myatt ................ Comorosky/Bottomley | 35.00 | 14.00 | 3.50 |
| ☐ 13C | Wilson/Allen ................. Jonnard/Brickell | 30.00 | 12.00 | 3.00 |
| ☐ 13D | West/Oscar Melillo ........ Blaeholder/Coffman | 30.00 | 12.00 | 3.00 |
| ☐ 13E | Joe Cronin/Reynolds ..... Bishop/Cissell | 35.00 | 14.00 | 3.50 |
| ☐ 13F | Schuble/Marberry ......... Goose Goslin/Crowder | 35.00 | 14.00 | 3.50 |
| ☐ 14A | Babe Ruth/McManus ..... Brandt/Maranville | 450.00 | 180.00 | 45.00 |
| ☐ 14B | Bill Terry/Schumacher .. Mancuso/Jackson | 60.00 | 24.00 | 6.00 |
| ☐ 14C | Paul Waner/Bush .......... W.Hoyt/Lloyd Waner | 60.00 | 24.00 | 6.00 |
| ☐ 14D | B.Grimes/Chuck Klein ... K.Cuyler/English | 60.00 | 24.00 | 6.00 |
| ☐ 14E | Leslie/Frey ................... Joe Stripp/Clark | 30.00 | 12.00 | 3.00 |
| ☐ 14F | Piet/Comorosky ............ Jim Bottomley/Adams | 35.00 | 14.00 | 3.50 |
| ☐ 15A | Babe Ruth/McManus ..... Brandt/Maranville | 450.00 | 180.00 | 45.00 |
| ☐ 15B | Bill Terry/Schumacher .. Mancuso/T.Jackson | 60.00 | 24.00 | 6.00 |
| ☐ 15C | Wilson/Allen ................. Jonnard/Brickell | 30.00 | 12.00 | 3.00 |
| ☐ 15D | B.Grimes/Chuck Klein ... K.Cuyler/English | 60.00 | 24.00 | 6.00 |
| ☐ 15E | Joe Cronin/Reynolds ..... Bishop/Cissell | 35.00 | 14.00 | 3.50 |
| ☐ 15F | Piet/Comorosky ............ Jim Bottomley/Adams | 35.00 | 14.00 | 3.50 |
| ☐ 16A | F.Frisch/Dizzy Dean ...... E.Orsatti/Carleton | 80.00 | 32.00 | 8.00 |
| ☐ 16B | Mahaffey/Jimmie Foxx .. Williams/Higgins | 60.00 | 24.00 | 6.00 |
| ☐ 16C | Heine Manush/Lary ....... Weaver/Hadley | 35.00 | 14.00 | 3.50 |
| ☐ 16D | Cochrane/C.Gehringer .. Tom Bridges/Rogell | 60.00 | 24.00 | 6.00 |
| ☐ 16E | Kamm/Hildebrand ......... Earl Averill/Trosky | 35.00 | 14.00 | 3.50 |
| ☐ 16F | G.Earnshaw/Dykes ........ Luke Sewell/Appling | 35.00 | 14.00 | 3.50 |
| ☐ 17A | F.Frisch/Dizzy Dean ...... E.Orsatti/Carleton | 80.00 | 32.00 | 8.00 |
| ☐ 17B | Mahaffey/Jimmie Foxx .. Williams/Higgins | 60.00 | 24.00 | 6.00 |
| ☐ 17C | Heine Manush/Lary ....... Weaver/Hadley | 35.00 | 14.00 | 3.50 |
| ☐ 17D | Cochrane/C.Gehringer .. Tom Bridges/Rogell | 60.00 | 24.00 | 6.00 |
| ☐ 17E | Kamm/Hildebrand ......... Earl Averill/Trosky | 35.00 | 14.00 | 3.50 |
| ☐ 17F | G.Earnshaw/Dykes ......... Luke Sewell/Appling | 35.00 | 14.00 | 3.50 |

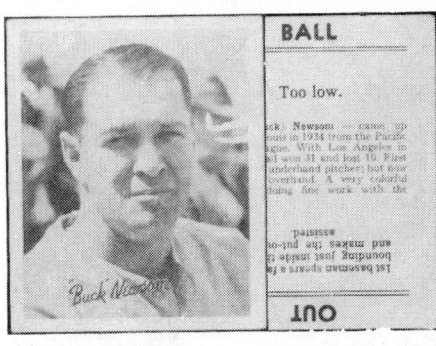

| | | | | |
|---|---|---|---|---|
| ☐ 1 | Wally Berger ..................... | 18.00 | 7.25 | 1.80 |
| ☐ 2 | Zeke Bonura ..................... | 18.00 | 7.25 | 1.80 |
| ☐ 3 | Stan Bordagaray .............. | 18.00 | 7.25 | 1.80 |
| ☐ 4 | Bill Brubaker ................... | 18.00 | 7.25 | 1.80 |
| ☐ 5 | Dolph Camilli ................... | 18.00 | 7.25 | 1.80 |
| ☐ 6 | Clyde Castleman .............. | 18.00 | 7.25 | 1.80 |
| ☐ 7 | Mickey Cochrane ............. | 50.00 | 20.00 | 5.00 |
| ☐ 8 | Joe Coscarart ................... | 18.00 | 7.25 | 1.80 |
| ☐ 9 | Frank Crosetti .................. | 21.00 | 8.50 | 2.10 |
| ☐ 10 | Kiki Cuyler ..................... | 35.00 | 14.00 | 3.50 |
| ☐ 11 | Paul Derringer ................. | 21.00 | 8.50 | 2.10 |
| ☐ 12 | Jimmy Dykes ................... | 21.00 | 8.50 | 2.10 |
| ☐ 13 | Rick Ferrell ..................... | 35.00 | 14.00 | 3.50 |
| ☐ 14 | Lefty Gomez ................... | 50.00 | 20.00 | 5.00 |
| ☐ 15 | Hank Greenberg .............. | 50.00 | 20.00 | 5.00 |
| ☐ 16 | Bucky Harris ................... | 30.00 | 12.00 | 3.00 |
| ☐ 17 | Rollie Hemsley ................ | 18.00 | 7.25 | 1.80 |
| ☐ 18 | Pinky Higgins .................. | 18.00 | 7.25 | 1.80 |
| ☐ 19 | Oral Hildbrand ................. | 18.00 | 7.25 | 1.80 |
| ☐ 20 | Chuck Klein ..................... | 40.00 | 16.00 | 4.00 |
| ☐ 21 | Pepper Martin .................. | 21.00 | 8.50 | 2.10 |
| ☐ 22 | Bobo Newsom .................. | 18.00 | 7.25 | 1.80 |
| ☐ 23 | Joe Vosmik ..................... | 18.00 | 7.25 | 1.80 |
| ☐ 24 | Paul Waner ..................... | 40.00 | 16.00 | 4.00 |
| ☐ 25 | Bill Werber ..................... | 21.00 | 8.50 | 2.10 |

## 1938 Goudey Heads Up

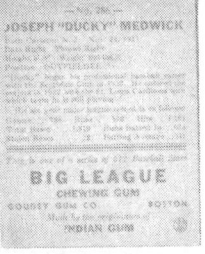

The cards in this 48 card set measure 2 3/8" by 2 7/8". The 1938 Goudey set is commonly referred to as the Heads-Up set, or R323 (ACC). These very popular but difficult to obtain cards came in two series of the same 24 players. The first series, numbers 241-264, is distinguished from the second series, numbers 265-288, in that the second contains etched cartoons and comments surrounding the player picture. Although the set starts with number 241, it is not a continuation of the 1933 Goudey set, but a separate set in its own right.

| | MINT | VG-E | F-G |
|---|---|---|---|
| COMPLETE SET ........................ | 4250.00 | 1900.00 | 500.00 |
| COMMON PLAYER (241-264) .... | 40.00 | 16.00 | 4.00 |
| COMMON PLAYER (265-288) .... | 50.00 | 20.00 | 5.00 |
| ☐ 241 Charlie Gehringer ........... | 125.00 | 50.00 | 12.50 |
| ☐ 242 Pete Fox ......................... | 40.00 | 16.00 | 4.00 |

## 1936 Goudey

The cards in this 25 card black and white set measure 2 3/8" by 2 7/8". In contrast to the color artwork of its previous sets, the 1936 Goudey set contained a simple black and white player photograph. A facsimile autograph appeared within the picture area. Each card was issued with a number of different "game situation" backs, and there may be as many as 200 different front/back combinations. The ACC designation is R322.

| | MINT | VG-E | F-G |
|---|---|---|---|
| COMPLETE SET ...................... | 525.00 | 225.00 | 55.00 |
| COMMON PLAYER (1-25) .......... | 18.00 | 7.25 | 1.80 |

| | | | | |
|---|---|---|---|---|
| ☐ 243 | Joe Kuhel | 40.00 | 16.00 | 4.00 |
| ☐ 244 | Frank Demaree | 40.00 | 16.00 | 4.00 |
| ☐ 245 | Frank Pytlak | 40.00 | 16.00 | 4.00 |
| ☐ 246 | Ernie Lombardi | 75.00 | 30.00 | 7.50 |
| ☐ 247 | Joe Vosmik | 40.00 | 16.00 | 4.00 |
| ☐ 248 | Dick Bartell | 40.00 | 16.00 | 4.00 |
| ☐ 249 | Jimmie Foxx | 200.00 | 80.00 | 20.00 |
| ☐ 250 | Joe DiMaggio | 750.00 | 300.00 | 75.00 |
| ☐ 251 | Bump Hadley | 40.00 | 16.00 | 4.00 |
| ☐ 252 | Zeke Bonura | 40.00 | 16.00 | 4.00 |
| ☐ 253 | Hank Greenberg | 125.00 | 50.00 | 12.50 |
| ☐ 254 | Van Lingle Mungo | 40.00 | 16.00 | 4.00 |
| ☐ 255 | Moose Solters | 40.00 | 16.00 | 4.00 |
| ☐ 256 | Vernon Kennedy | 40.00 | 16.00 | 4.00 |
| ☐ 257 | Al Lopez | 75.00 | 30.00 | 7.50 |
| ☐ 258 | Bobby Doerr | 100.00 | 40.00 | 10.00 |
| ☐ 259 | Billy Werber | 40.00 | 16.00 | 4.00 |
| ☐ 260 | Rudy York | 40.00 | 16.00 | 4.00 |
| ☐ 261 | Rip Radcliff | 40.00 | 16.00 | 4.00 |
| ☐ 262 | Joe Medwick | 100.00 | 40.00 | 10.00 |
| ☐ 263 | Marvin Owen | 40.00 | 16.00 | 4.00 |
| ☐ 264 | Bob Feller | 250.00 | 100.00 | 25.00 |
| ☐ 265 | Charlie Gehringer | 150.00 | 60.00 | 15.00 |
| ☐ 266 | Pete Fox | 50.00 | 20.00 | 5.00 |
| ☐ 267 | Joe Kuhel | 50.00 | 20.00 | 5.00 |
| ☐ 268 | Frank Demaree | 50.00 | 20.00 | 5.00 |
| ☐ 269 | Frank Pytlak | 50.00 | 20.00 | 5.00 |
| ☐ 270 | Ernie Lombardi | 85.00 | 34.00 | 8.50 |
| ☐ 271 | Joe Vosmik | 50.00 | 20.00 | 5.00 |
| ☐ 272 | Dick Bartell | 50.00 | 20.00 | 5.00 |
| ☐ 273 | Jimmie Foxx | 225.00 | 90.00 | 22.00 |
| ☐ 274 | Joe DiMaggio | 900.00 | 360.00 | 90.00 |
| ☐ 275 | Bump Hadley | 50.00 | 20.00 | 5.00 |
| ☐ 276 | Zeke Bonura | 50.00 | 20.00 | 5.00 |
| ☐ 277 | Hank Greenberg | 150.00 | 60.00 | 15.00 |
| ☐ 278 | Van Lingle Mungo | 50.00 | 20.00 | 5.00 |
| ☐ 279 | Moose Solters | 50.00 | 20.00 | 5.00 |
| ☐ 280 | Vernon Kennedy | 50.00 | 20.00 | 5.00 |
| ☐ 281 | Al Lopez | 85.00 | 34.00 | 8.50 |
| ☐ 282 | Bobby Doerr | 120.00 | 50.00 | 12.00 |
| ☐ 283 | Billy Werber | 50.00 | 20.00 | 5.00 |
| ☐ 284 | Rudy York | 50.00 | 20.00 | 5.00 |
| ☐ 285 | Rip Radcliff | 50.00 | 20.00 | 5.00 |
| ☐ 286 | Joe Medwick | 120.00 | 50.00 | 12.00 |
| ☐ 287 | Marvin Owen | 50.00 | 20.00 | 5.00 |
| ☐ 288 | Bob Feller | 300.00 | 120.00 | 30.00 |

| | | | | |
|---|---|---|---|---|
| ☐ 1 | Hugh Mulcahy | 20.00 | 8.00 | 2.00 |
| ☐ 2 | Harland Clift | 20.00 | 8.00 | 2.00 |
| ☐ 3 | Louis Chiozza | 20.00 | 8.00 | 2.00 |
| ☐ 4 | Warren Rosar | 20.00 | 8.00 | 2.00 |
| ☐ 5 | George McQuinn | 20.00 | 8.00 | 2.00 |
| ☐ 6 | George Dickman | 20.00 | 8.00 | 2.00 |
| ☐ 7 | Wayne Ambler | 20.00 | 8.00 | 2.00 |
| ☐ 8 | Bob Muncrief | 20.00 | 8.00 | 2.00 |
| ☐ 9 | Bill Dietrich | 20.00 | 8.00 | 2.00 |
| ☐ 10 | Taft Wright | 20.00 | 8.00 | 2.00 |
| ☐ 11 | Don Heffner | 20.00 | 8.00 | 2.00 |
| ☐ 12 | Fritz Ostermueller | 20.00 | 8.00 | 2.00 |
| ☐ 13 | Frank Hayes | 20.00 | 8.00 | 2.00 |
| ☐ 14 | John Kramer | 20.00 | 8.00 | 2.00 |
| ☐ 15 | Dario Lodigiani | 20.00 | 8.00 | 2.00 |
| ☐ 16 | George Case | 20.00 | 8.00 | 2.00 |
| ☐ 17 | Vito Tamulis | 20.00 | 8.00 | 2.00 |
| ☐ 18 | Whitlow Wyatt | 20.00 | 8.00 | 2.00 |
| ☐ 19 | Bill Posedel | 20.00 | 8.00 | 2.00 |
| ☐ 20 | Carl Hubbell | 80.00 | 32.00 | 8.00 |
| ☐ 21 | Harold Warstler | 80.00 | 32.00 | 8.00 |
| ☐ 22 | Joe Sullivan | 200.00 | 80.00 | 20.00 |
| ☐ 23 | Norman Young | 100.00 | 40.00 | 10.00 |
| ☐ 24 | John Andrews | 175.00 | 70.00 | 18.00 |
| ☐ 25 | Morris Arnovich | 80.00 | 32.00 | 8.00 |
| ☐ 26 | Elbert Fletcher | 20.00 | 8.00 | 2.00 |
| ☐ 27 | Bill Crough | 20.00 | 8.00 | 2.00 |
| ☐ 28 | Al Todd | 20.00 | 8.00 | 2.00 |
| ☐ 29 | Debs Garms | 20.00 | 8.00 | 2.00 |
| ☐ 30 | Jim Tobin | 20.00 | 8.00 | 2.00 |
| ☐ 31 | Chester Ross | 20.00 | 8.00 | 2.00 |
| ☐ 32 | George Coffman | 20.00 | 8.00 | 2.00 |
| ☐ 33 | Mel Ott | 100.00 | 40.00 | 10.00 |

## Robert Gould W605

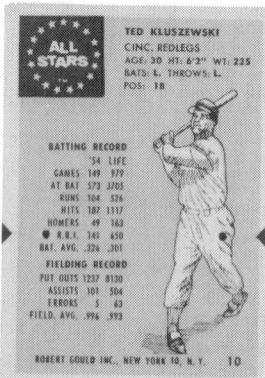

The cards in this 28 card set measure 2 1/2" by 3 1/2". The 1955 Robert F. Gould set of black and white on green cards were toy store cardboard holders for small plastic statues. The statues were attached to the card by a rubber band through two holes on the side of the card. The ACC designation is W605. The cards are numbered in the bottom right corner of the obverse and are blank-backed.

| | | MINT | VG-E | F-G |
|---|---|---|---|---|
| COMPLETE SET | | 750.00 | 300.00 | 75.00 |
| COMMON PLAYER | | 16.00 | 6.50 | 1.60 |
| ☐ 1 | Willie Mays | 200.00 | 80.00 | 20.00 |
| ☐ 2 | Gus Zernial | 16.00 | 6.50 | 1.60 |
| ☐ 3 | Red Schoendienst | 24.00 | 10.00 | 2.40 |
| ☐ 4 | Chico Carrasquel | 16.00 | 6.50 | 1.60 |
| ☐ 5 | Jim Hegan | 16.00 | 6.50 | 1.60 |
| ☐ 6 | Curt Simmons | 18.00 | 7.25 | 1.80 |
| ☐ 7 | Bob Porterfield | 16.00 | 6.50 | 1.60 |
| ☐ 8 | Jim Busby | 16.00 | 6.50 | 1.60 |
| ☐ 9 | Don Mueller | 18.00 | 7.25 | 1.80 |
| ☐ 10 | Ted Kluszewski | 30.00 | 12.00 | 3.00 |

## 1941 Goudey

The cards in this 33 card set measure 2 3/8" by 2 7/8". The 1941 Series of blank backed baseball cards was the last baseball issue marketed by Goudey before the war closed the door on that company for good. Each black and white player photo comes with four color backgrounds (blue, green, red, or yellow). Cards without numbers are probably miscut, while cards 21-25 are scarce in relation to the rest of the set. The ACC catalog number is R324.

| | MINT | VG-E | F-G |
|---|---|---|---|
| COMPLETE SET | 1200.00 | 500.00 | 125.00 |
| COMMON PLAYER (1-33) | 20.00 | 8.00 | 2.00 |

| | | | MINT | VG-E | F-G |
|---|---|---|---|---|---|
| ☐ | 11 | Ray Boone | 16.00 | 6.50 | 1.60 |
| ☐ | 12 | Smokey Burgess | 18.00 | 7.25 | 1.80 |
| ☐ | 13 | Bob Rush | 16.00 | 6.50 | 1.60 |
| ☐ | 14 | Early Wynn | 50.00 | 20.00 | 5.00 |
| ☐ | 15 | Bill Bruton | 16.00 | 6.50 | 1.60 |
| ☐ | 16 | Gus Bell | 16.00 | 6.50 | 1.60 |
| ☐ | 17 | Jim Finigan | 16.00 | 6.50 | 1.60 |
| ☐ | 18 | Granny Hamner | 16.00 | 6.50 | 1.60 |
| ☐ | 19 | Hank Thompson | 18.00 | 7.25 | 1.80 |
| ☐ | 20 | Joe Coleman | 16.00 | 6.50 | 1.60 |
| ☐ | 21 | Don Newcombe | 30.00 | 12.00 | 3.00 |
| ☐ | 22 | Richie Ashburn | 40.00 | 16.00 | 4.00 |
| ☐ | 23 | Bobby Thomson | 24.00 | 10.00 | 2.40 |
| ☐ | 24 | Sid Gordon | 16.00 | 6.50 | 1.60 |
| ☐ | 25 | Gerry Coleman | 18.00 | 7.25 | 1.80 |
| ☐ | 26 | Ernie Banks | 100.00 | 40.00 | 10.00 |
| ☐ | 27 | Billy Pierce | 24.00 | 10.00 | 2.40 |
| ☐ | 28 | Mel Parnell | 18.00 | 7.25 | 1.80 |

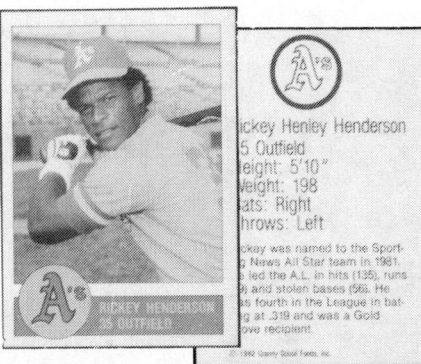

## 1981 Granny Goose

Rickey Henley Henderson
35 Outfield
Height: 5'10"
Weight: 198
Bats: Right
Throws: Left

In 1980 Rickey became the first American Leaguer and the 3rd in baseball history to steal 100 bases in a season. Rickey was 2nd in the league in walks with 117, and led the A's with 179 hits.

© 1981 East West Promotions, Inc.

This set is the hardest to obtain of the three years Granny Goose issued cards of the Oakland A's. The Revering card was supposedly destroyed by the printer soon after he was traded away and hence is in shorter supply than the other 14 cards in the set. Wayne Gross is also supposedly available in lesser quantity compared to the other players. Cards are standard size (2 1/2" by 3 1/2") and were issued in bags of potato chips. Cards are numbered on the front and back by the player's uniform number.

| | | | MINT | VG-E | F-G |
|---|---|---|---|---|---|
| | | COMPLETE SET | 60.00 | 24.00 | 6.00 |
| | | COMMON PLAYER | 1.00 | .40 | .10 |
| ☐ | 1 | Billy Martin MGR | 4.00 | 1.60 | .40 |
| ☐ | 2 | Mike Heath | 1.00 | .40 | .10 |
| ☐ | 5 | Jeff Newman | 1.00 | .40 | .10 |
| ☐ | 6 | Mitchell Page | 1.00 | .40 | .10 |
| ☐ | 8 | Rob Picciolo | 1.00 | .40 | .10 |
| ☐ | 10 | Wayne Gross | 6.00 | 2.40 | .60 |
| ☐ | 13 | Dave Revering SP | 30.00 | 12.00 | 3.00 |
| ☐ | 17 | Mike Norris | 1.00 | .40 | .10 |
| ☐ | 20 | Tony Armas | 3.00 | 1.20 | .30 |
| ☐ | 21 | Dwayne Murphy | 3.00 | 1.20 | .30 |
| ☐ | 22 | Rick Langford | 1.00 | .40 | .10 |
| ☐ | 27 | Matt Keough | 1.00 | .40 | .10 |
| ☐ | 35 | Rickey Henderson | 18.00 | 7.25 | 1.80 |
| ☐ | 39 | Dave McKay | 1.00 | .40 | .10 |
| ☐ | 54 | Steve McCatty | 1.00 | .40 | .10 |

## 1982 Granny Goose

The cards in this 15 card set measure 2 1/2" by 3 1/2". Granny Goose Foods, Inc., a California based company, repeated its successful promotional idea of 1981 by issuing a new set of Oakland A's baseball cards for 1982. Each color player picture is surrounded by white borders and has trim and lettering done in Oakland's green and yellow colors. The cards are numbered according to the uniform number of the player, and the backs carry vital statistics done in black print on a white background. The cards were distributed in packages of potato chips and were also handed out on Fan Appreciation Day at the stadium. Although Picciolo was traded, his card was not withdrawn (as was Revering last year) and, therefore, its value is no greater than other cards in the set.

| | | | MINT | VG-E | F-G |
|---|---|---|---|---|---|
| | | COMPLETE SET | 12.00 | 5.00 | 1.20 |
| | | COMMON PLAYER | .40 | .16 | .04 |
| ☐ | 1 | Tony Armas | 1.00 | .40 | .10 |
| ☐ | 2 | Wayne Gross | .40 | .16 | .04 |
| ☐ | 3 | Mike Heath | .40 | .16 | .04 |
| ☐ | 4 | Rickey Henderson | 6.00 | 2.40 | .60 |
| ☐ | 5 | Cliff Johnson | .40 | .16 | .04 |
| ☐ | 6 | Matt Keough | .40 | .16 | .04 |
| ☐ | 7 | Rick Langford | .40 | .16 | .04 |
| ☐ | 8 | Davey Lopes | .75 | .30 | .07 |
| ☐ | 9 | Billy Martin MGR | 1.50 | .60 | .15 |
| ☐ | 10 | Steve McCatty | .40 | .16 | .04 |
| ☐ | 11 | Dwayne Murphy | 1.00 | .40 | .10 |
| ☐ | 12 | Jeff Newman | .40 | .16 | .04 |
| ☐ | 13 | Mike Norris | .40 | .16 | .04 |
| ☐ | 14 | Rob Picciolo | .40 | .16 | .04 |
| ☐ | 15 | Fred Stanley | .40 | .16 | .04 |

## 1983 Granny Goose

The cards in this 15 card set measure 2 1/2" by 4 1/4". The 1983 Granny Goose Potato Chips set again features Oakland A's players. The cards that were issued in bags of potato chips have a tear off coupon on the bottom with a scratch off section featuring prizes. In addition to their release in bags of potato chips, the Granny Goose cards were also given away to fans attending the Oakland game of July 3, 1983. These give away cards did not contain the coupon on the bottom. Prices listed below are for cards without the detachable tabs that came on the bottom of the cards; cards with tabs intact are valued 50% higher than the prices listed below.

| | | | MINT | VG-E | F-G |
|---|---|---|---|---|---|
| | | COMPLETE SET | 8.00 | 3.25 | .80 |
| | | COMMON PLAYER | .40 | .16 | .04 |
| ☐ | 2 | Mike Heath | .40 | .16 | .04 |

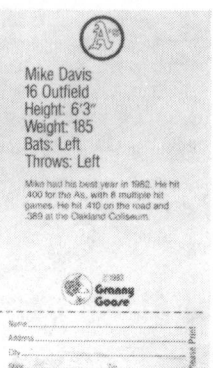

Mike Davis
16 Outfield
Height: 6'3"
Weight: 185
Bats: Left
Throws: Left

Mike had his best year in 1982. He hit
400 for the A's, with 6 multiple hit
games. He hit .410 on the road and
.389 at the Oakland Coliseum.

Granny GRAND SLAM Goose Instant-Winner Game

| | | | | |
|---|---|---|---|---|
| ☐ 4 | Carney Lansford | 1.00 | .40 | .10 |
| ☐ 10 | Wayne Gross | .40 | .16 | .04 |
| ☐ 14 | Steve Boros MGR | .40 | .16 | .04 |
| ☐ 15 | Davey Lopes | .75 | .30 | .07 |
| ☐ 16 | Mike Davis | .75 | .30 | .07 |
| ☐ 17 | Mike Norris | .50 | .20 | .05 |
| ☐ 21 | Dwayne Murphy | 1.00 | .40 | .10 |
| ☐ 22 | Rick Langford | .40 | .16 | .04 |
| ☐ 27 | Matt Keough | .40 | .16 | .04 |
| ☐ 31 | Tom Underwood | .40 | .16 | .04 |
| ☐ 33 | Dave Beard | .40 | .16 | .04 |
| ☐ 35 | Rickey Henderson | 4.50 | 1.80 | .45 |
| ☐ 39 | Tom Burgmeier | .40 | .16 | .04 |
| ☐ 54 | Steve McCatty | .40 | .16 | .04 |

## 1958 Hires

The cards in this 66 card set measure 2 5/16" by
3 1/2" or 2 5/16" by 7" with tabs. The 1958 Hires
Root Beer set of numbered, colored cards was
issued with detachable coupons as inserts with Hires
Root Beer cartons. Cards with the coupon still intact
are worth double the prices listed below. The card
front picture is surrounded by a wood grain effect
which makes it look like the player is seen through
a knot hole. The numbering of this set is rather
strange in that it begins with 10 and skips 69.

| | MINT | VG-E | F-G |
|---|---|---|---|
| COMPLETE SET | 500.00 | 200.00 | 50.00 |
| COMMON PLAYER (10-76) | 5.00 | 2.00 | .50 |
| | | | |
| ☐ 10 Richie Ashburn | 15.00 | 6.00 | 1.50 |
| ☐ 11 Chico Carrasquel | 5.00 | 2.00 | .50 |
| ☐ 12 Dave Philley | 5.00 | 2.00 | .50 |
| ☐ 13 Don Newcombe | 8.00 | 3.25 | .80 |
| ☐ 14 Wally Post | 5.00 | 2.00 | .50 |
| ☐ 15 Rip Repulski | 5.00 | 2.00 | .50 |
| ☐ 16 Chico Fernandez | 5.00 | 2.00 | .50 |
| ☐ 17 Larry Doby | 8.00 | 3.25 | .80 |
| ☐ 18 Hector Brown | 5.00 | 2.00 | .50 |
| ☐ 19 Danny O'Connell | 5.00 | 2.00 | .50 |
| ☐ 20 Granny Hamner | 5.00 | 2.00 | .50 |
| ☐ 21 Dick Groat | 7.00 | 2.80 | .70 |
| ☐ 22 Ray Narleski | 5.00 | 2.00 | .50 |
| ☐ 23 Pee Wee Reese | 25.00 | 10.00 | 2.50 |
| ☐ 24 Bob Friend | 6.00 | 2.40 | .60 |
| ☐ 25 Willie Mays | 100.00 | 40.00 | 10.00 |
| ☐ 26 Bob Nieman | 5.00 | 2.00 | .50 |
| ☐ 27 Frank Thomas | 6.00 | 2.40 | .60 |
| ☐ 28 Curt Simmons | 6.00 | 2.40 | .60 |
| ☐ 29 Stan Lopata | 5.00 | 2.00 | .50 |
| ☐ 30 Bob Skinner | 5.00 | 2.00 | .50 |
| ☐ 31 Ron Kline | 5.00 | 2.00 | .50 |
| ☐ 32 Willie Miranda | 5.00 | 2.00 | .50 |
| ☐ 33 Bobby Avila | 5.00 | 2.00 | .50 |
| ☐ 34 Clem Labine | 6.00 | 2.40 | .60 |
| ☐ 35 Ray Jablonski | 5.00 | 2.00 | .50 |
| ☐ 36 Bill Mazeroski | 8.00 | 3.25 | .80 |

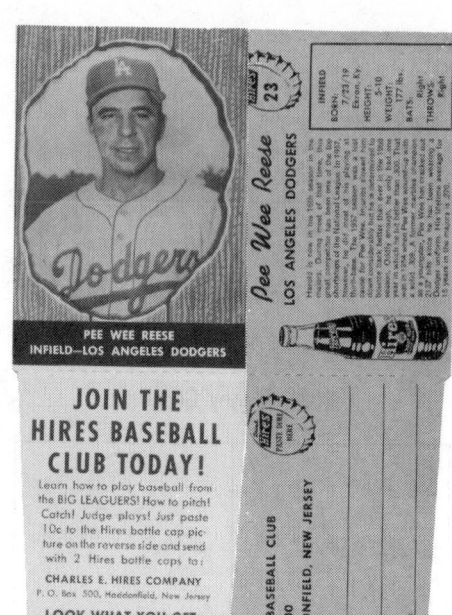

PEE WEE REESE
INFIELD—LOS ANGELES DODGERS

### JOIN THE HIRES BASEBALL CLUB TODAY!

Learn how to play baseball from
the BIG LEAGUERS! How to pitch!
Catch! Judge plays! Just paste
10c to the Hires bottle cap picture on the reverse side and send
with 2 Hires bottle caps to:

CHARLES E. HIRES COMPANY
P. O. Box 500, Haddonfield, New Jersey

**LOOK WHAT YOU GET:**

**1** Hires "How To Play
Baseball Book.

**2** Valuable membership card.

Printed in U. S. A.

| | | | |
|---|---|---|---|
| ☐ 37 Billy Gardner | 5.00 | 2.00 | .50 |
| ☐ 38 Pete Runnels | 6.00 | 2.40 | .60 |
| ☐ 39 Jack Sanford | 5.00 | 2.00 | .50 |
| ☐ 40 Dave Sisler | 5.00 | 2.00 | .50 |
| ☐ 41 Don Zimmer | 6.00 | 2.40 | .60 |
| ☐ 42 Johnny Podres | 7.00 | 2.80 | .70 |
| ☐ 43 Dick Farrell | 5.00 | 2.00 | .50 |
| ☐ 44 Hank Aaron | 100.00 | 40.00 | 10.00 |
| ☐ 45 Bill Virdon | 7.00 | 2.80 | .70 |
| ☐ 46 Bobby Thomson | 7.00 | 2.80 | .70 |
| ☐ 47 Willard Nixon | 5.00 | 2.00 | .50 |
| ☐ 48 Billy Loes | 5.00 | 2.00 | .50 |
| ☐ 49 Hank Sauer | 6.00 | 2.40 | .60 |
| ☐ 50 Johnny Antonelli | 6.00 | 2.40 | .60 |
| ☐ 51 Daryl Spencer | 5.00 | 2.00 | .50 |
| ☐ 52 Ken Lehman | 5.00 | 2.00 | .50 |
| ☐ 53 Sammy White | 5.00 | 2.00 | .50 |
| ☐ 54 Charley Neal | 5.00 | 2.00 | .50 |
| ☐ 55 Don Drysdale | 20.00 | 8.00 | 2.00 |
| ☐ 56 Jackie Jensen | 7.00 | 2.80 | .70 |
| ☐ 57 Ray Katt | 5.00 | 2.00 | .50 |
| ☐ 58 Frank Sullivan | 5.00 | 2.00 | .50 |
| ☐ 59 Roy Face | 6.00 | 2.40 | .60 |
| ☐ 60 Willie Jones | 5.00 | 2.00 | .50 |
| ☐ 61 Duke Snider | 45.00 | 18.00 | 4.50 |
| ☐ 62 Whitey Lockman | 6.00 | 2.40 | .60 |
| ☐ 63 Gino Cimoli | 5.00 | 2.00 | .50 |
| ☐ 64 Marv Grissom | 5.00 | 2.00 | .50 |
| ☐ 65 Gene Baker | 5.00 | 2.00 | .50 |
| ☐ 66 George Zuverink | 5.00 | 2.00 | .50 |
| ☐ 67 Ted Kluszewski | 8.00 | 3.25 | .80 |
| ☐ 68 Jim Busby | 5.00 | 2.00 | .50 |
| ☐ 69 Not Issued | .00 | .00 | .00 |
| ☐ 70 Curt Barclay | 5.00 | 2.00 | .50 |
| ☐ 71 Hank Foiles | 5.00 | 2.00 | .50 |
| ☐ 72 Gene Stephens | 5.00 | 2.00 | .50 |
| ☐ 73 Al Worthington | 5.00 | 2.00 | .50 |
| ☐ 74 Al Walker | 5.00 | 2.00 | .50 |
| ☐ 75 Bob Boyd | 5.00 | 2.00 | .50 |
| ☐ 76 Al Pilarcik | 5.00 | 2.00 | .50 |

## 1958 Hires Test

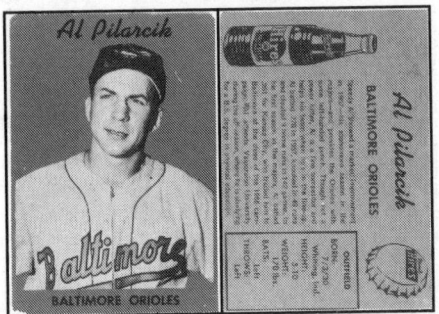

The cards in this 8 card test set measure 2 5/16" by 3 1/2" or 2 5/16" by 7" with tabs. The 1958 Hires Root Beer test set features unnumbered, color cards. The card front photos are shown on a yellow or orange back ground instead of the wood grain background used in the Hires regular set. The cards contain a detachable coupon just as the regular Hires issue does. Cards were test marketed on a very limited basis in a few cities. Cards with the coupon still intact are worth double the prices in the checklist below. The checklist below is ordered alphabetically.

|  | MINT | VG-E | F-G |
|---|---|---|---|
| COMPLETE SET | 500.00 | 200.00 | 50.00 |
| COMMON PLAYER (1-8) | 50.00 | 20.00 | 5.00 |

| | | MINT | VG-E | F-G |
|---|---|---|---|---|
| ☐ 1 | Johnny Antonelli | 60.00 | 24.00 | 6.00 |
| ☐ 2 | Jim Busby | 50.00 | 20.00 | 5.00 |
| ☐ 3 | Chico Fernandez | 50.00 | 20.00 | 5.00 |
| ☐ 4 | Bob Friend | 60.00 | 24.00 | 6.00 |
| ☐ 5 | Vern Law | 60.00 | 24.00 | 6.00 |
| ☐ 6 | Stan Lopata | 50.00 | 20.00 | 5.00 |
| ☐ 7 | Willie Mays | 200.00 | 80.00 | 20.00 |
| ☐ 8 | Al Pilarcik | 50.00 | 20.00 | 5.00 |

## 1947 Homogenized Bond

The cards in this 48 card set measure 2 1/4" by 3 1/2". The 1947 W571/D305 Homogenized Bread are sets of unnumbered cards containing 44 baseball players and four boxers. The W571 set exists in two styles. Style one is identical to the D305 set except for the back printing while style two has perforated edges and movie stars depicted on the backs. The second style of W571 cards contains only 13 cards. The four boxers in the checklist below are indicated by BOX. The checklist below is ordered alphabetically.

|  | MINT | VG-E | F-G |
|---|---|---|---|
| COMPLETE SET | 300.00 | 120.00 | 30.00 |
| COMMON PLAYER (1-48) | 4.00 | 1.60 | .40 |
| COMMON BOXER | 2.00 | .80 | .20 |

| | | MINT | VG-E | F-G |
|---|---|---|---|---|
| ☐ 1 | Rex Barney | 4.00 | 1.60 | .40 |
| ☐ 2 | Larry Berra | 15.00 | 6.00 | 1.50 |
| ☐ 3 | Ewell Blackwell | 4.00 | 1.60 | .40 |
| ☐ 4 | Lou Boudreau | 8.00 | 3.25 | .80 |

| | | MINT | VG-E | F-G |
|---|---|---|---|---|
| ☐ 5 | Ralph Branca | 5.00 | 2.00 | .50 |
| ☐ 6 | Harry Brecheen | 4.00 | 1.60 | .40 |
| ☐ 7 | Primo Carnera BOX | 2.00 | .80 | .20 |
| ☐ 8 | Marcel Cerdan BOX | 2.00 | .80 | .20 |
| ☐ 9 | Dom DiMaggio | 6.00 | 2.40 | .60 |
| ☐ 10 | Joe DiMaggio | 50.00 | 20.00 | 5.00 |
| ☐ 11 | Bobbie Doerr | 8.00 | 3.25 | .80 |
| ☐ 12 | Bruce Edwards | 4.00 | 1.60 | .40 |
| ☐ 13 | Bob Elliott | 5.00 | 2.00 | .50 |
| ☐ 14 | Del Ennis | 5.00 | 2.00 | .50 |
| ☐ 15 | Bob Feller | 15.00 | 6.00 | 1.50 |
| ☐ 16 | Carl Furillo | 6.00 | 2.40 | .60 |
| ☐ 17 | Joe Gordon | 5.00 | 2.00 | .50 |
| ☐ 18 | Sid Gordon | 4.00 | 1.60 | .40 |
| ☐ 19 | Joe Hatten | 4.00 | 1.60 | .40 |
| ☐ 20 | Gil Hodges | 12.00 | 5.00 | 1.20 |
| ☐ 21 | Tommy Holmes | 5.00 | 2.00 | .50 |
| ☐ 22 | Larry Jansen | 4.00 | 1.60 | .40 |
| ☐ 23 | Sheldon Jones | 4.00 | 1.60 | .40 |
| ☐ 24 | Edwin Joost | 4.00 | 1.60 | .40 |
| ☐ 25 | Charlie Keller | 5.00 | 2.00 | .50 |
| ☐ 26 | Ken Keltner | 4.00 | 1.60 | .40 |
| ☐ 27 | Buddy Kerr | 4.00 | 1.60 | .40 |
| ☐ 28 | Ralph Kiner | 10.00 | 4.00 | 1.00 |
| ☐ 29 | Jake LaMotta BOX | 4.00 | 1.60 | .40 |
| ☐ 30 | John Lindell | 4.00 | 1.60 | .40 |
| ☐ 31 | Whitey Lockman | 4.00 | 1.60 | .40 |
| ☐ 32 | Joe Louis BOX | 8.00 | 3.25 | .80 |
| ☐ 33 | Willard Marshall | 4.00 | 1.60 | .40 |
| ☐ 34 | Johnny Mize | 10.00 | 4.00 | 1.00 |
| ☐ 35 | Stan Musial | 25.00 | 10.00 | 2.50 |
| ☐ 36 | Andy Pafko | 4.00 | 1.60 | .40 |
| ☐ 37 | Johnny Pesky | 4.00 | 1.60 | .40 |
| ☐ 38 | Pee Wee Reese | 15.00 | 6.00 | 1.50 |
| ☐ 39 | Phil Rizzuto | 12.00 | 5.00 | 1.20 |
| ☐ 40 | Aaron Robinson | 4.00 | 1.60 | .40 |
| ☐ 41 | Jackie Robinson | 25.00 | 10.00 | 2.50 |
| ☐ 42 | John Sain | 6.00 | 2.40 | .60 |
| ☐ 43 | Enos Slaughter | 8.00 | 3.25 | .80 |
| ☐ 44 | Vern Stephens | 5.00 | 2.00 | .50 |
| ☐ 45 | George Tebbetts | 4.00 | 1.60 | .40 |
| ☐ 46 | Bobby Thomson | 6.00 | 2.40 | .60 |
| ☐ 47 | Johnny VanderMeer | 5.00 | 2.00 | .50 |
| ☐ 48 | Ted Williams | 30.00 | 12.00 | 3.00 |

## 1975 Hostess

The cards in this 150 card set measure 2 1/4" by 3 1/4" individually or 3 1/4" by 7 1/4" as panels of three. The 1975 Hostess set was issued in panels of three cards each on the backs of family sized packages of Hostess cakes. Card number 125, Bill Madlock, was listed correctly as an infielder and incorrectly as a pitcher. Number 11, Burt Hooton, and number 89, Doug Rader, are spelled two different ways. Some panels are more scarce than others as they were issued only on the backs of less popular Hostess products. These scarcer panels are

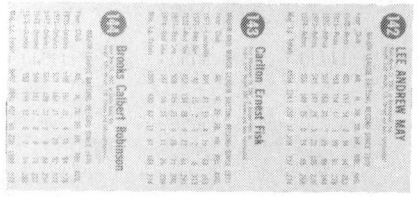

shown with asterisks in the checklist. Although complete panel prices are not explicitly listed, they would generally have a value 25% greater than the sum of the values of the individual players on that panel.

| | | MINT | VG-E | F-G |
|---|---|---|---|---|
| | COMPLETE INDIV. SET | 120.00 | 50.00 | 12.00 |
| | COMMON PLAYER | .30 | .12 | .03 |
| ☐ | 1 Bob Tolan | .30 | .12 | .03 |
| ☐ | 2 Cookie Rojas | .30 | .12 | .03 |
| ☐ | 3 Darrell Evans | .50 | .20 | .05 |
| ☐ | 4 Sal Bando | .40 | .16 | .04 |
| ☐ | 5 Joe Morgan | 2.00 | .80 | .20 |
| ☐ | 6 Mickey Lolich | .50 | .20 | .05 |
| ☐ | 7 Don Sutton | 1.50 | .60 | .15 |
| ☐ | 8 Bill Melton | .30 | .12 | .03 |
| ☐ | 9 Tim Foli | .30 | .12 | .03 |
| ☐ | 10 Joe LaHoud | .30 | .12 | .03 |
| ☐ | 11A Bert Hooten (sic) | 1.00 | .40 | .10 |
| ☐ | 11B Burt Hooton | 1.00 | .40 | .10 |
| ☐ | 12 Paul Blair | .30 | .12 | .03 |
| ☐ | 13 Jim Barr | .30 | .12 | .03 |
| ☐ | 14 Toby Harrah | .40 | .16 | .04 |
| ☐ | 15 John Milner | .30 | .12 | .03 |
| ☐ | 16 Ken Holtzman | .40 | .16 | .04 |
| ☐ | 17 Cesar Cedeno | .40 | .16 | .04 |
| ☐ | 18 Dwight Evans | .60 | .24 | .06 |
| ☐ | 19 Willie McCovey | 2.50 | 1.00 | .25 |
| ☐ | 20 Tony Oliva | .60 | .24 | .06 |
| ☐ | 21 Manny Sanguillen | .40 | .16 | .04 |
| ☐ | 22 Mickey Rivers | .40 | .16 | .04 |
| ☐ | 23 Lou Brock | 2.50 | 1.00 | .25 |
| ☐ | 24 Graig Nettles (Craig on front) | 1.50 | .60 | .15 |
| ☐ | 25 Jim Wynn | .40 | .16 | .04 |
| ☐ | 26 George Scott | .30 | .12 | .03 |
| ☐ | 27 Greg Luzinski | .50 | .20 | .05 |
| ☐ | 28 Bert Campaneris | .40 | .16 | .04 |
| ☐ | 29 Pete Rose | 9.00 | 3.75 | .90 |
| ☐ | 30 Buddy Bell | .50 | .20 | .05 |
| ☐ | 31 Gary Matthews | .40 | .16 | .04 |
| ☐ | 32 Freddie Patek | .30 | .12 | .03 |
| ☐ | 33 Mike Lum | .30 | .12 | .03 |
| ☐ | 34 Ellie Rodriguez | .30 | .12 | .03 |
| ☐ | 35 Milt May (photo actually Lee May) | .50 | .20 | .05 |
| ☐ | 36 Willie Horton | .40 | .16 | .04 |
| ☐ | 37 Dave Winfield | 3.00 | 1.20 | .30 |
| ☐ | 38 Tom Grieve | .40 | .16 | .04 |
| ☐ | 39 Barry Foote | .30 | .12 | .03 |
| ☐ | 40 Joe Rudi | .40 | .16 | .04 |
| ☐ | 41 Bake McBride | .30 | .12 | .03 |
| ☐ | 42 Mike Cuellar | .40 | .16 | .04 |
| ☐ | 43 Garry Maddox | .40 | .16 | .04 |
| ☐ | 44 Carlos May | .30 | .12 | .03 |
| ☐ | 45 Bud Harrelson | .30 | .12 | .03 |
| ☐ | 46 Dave Chalk | .30 | .12 | .03 |
| ☐ | 47 Dave Concepcion | .50 | .20 | .05 |
| ☐ | 48 Carl Yastrzemski | 6.00 | 2.40 | .60 |
| ☐ | 49 Steve Garvey | 4.00 | 1.60 | .40 |
| ☐ | 50 Amos Otis | .40 | .16 | .04 |
| ☐ | 51 Rick Reuschel | .40 | .16 | .04 |
| ☐ | 52 Rollie Fingers | 1.00 | .40 | .10 |
| ☐ | 53 Bob Watson | .40 | .16 | .04 |
| ☐ | 54 John Ellis | .30 | .12 | .03 |
| ☐ | 55 Bob Bailey | .30 | .12 | .03 |
| ☐ | 56 Rod Carew | 4.00 | 1.60 | .40 |
| ☐ | 57 Rich Hebner | .30 | .12 | .03 |
| ☐ | 58 Nolan Ryan | 4.00 | 1.60 | .40 |
| ☐ | 59 Reggie Smith | .50 | .20 | .05 |
| ☐ | 60 Joe Coleman | .30 | .12 | .03 |
| ☐ | 61 Ron Cey | .50 | .20 | .05 |
| ☐ | 62 Darrell Porter | .40 | .16 | .04 |
| ☐ | 63 Steve Carlton | 4.00 | 1.60 | .40 |
| ☐ | 64 Gene Tenace | .30 | .12 | .03 |
| ☐ | 65 Jose Cardenal | .30 | .12 | .03 |
| ☐ | 66 Bill Lee | .30 | .12 | .03 |
| ☐ | 67 Dave Lopes | .40 | .16 | .04 |
| ☐ | 68 Wilbur Wood | .40 | .16 | .04 |
| ☐ | 69 Steve Renko | .30 | .12 | .03 |
| ☐ | 70 Joe Torre | .50 | .20 | .05 |
| ☐ | 71 Ted Sizemore | .30 | .12 | .03 |
| ☐ | 72 Bobby Grich | .40 | .16 | .04 |
| ☐ | 73 Chris Speier | .30 | .12 | .03 |
| ☐ | 74 Bert Blyleven | .60 | .24 | .06 |
| ☐ | 75 Tom Seaver | 4.00 | 1.60 | .40 |
| ☐ | 76 Nate Colbert | .30 | .12 | .03 |
| ☐ | 77 Don Kessinger | .40 | .16 | .04 |
| ☐ | 78 George Medich | .30 | .12 | .03 |
| ☐ | 79 Andy Messersmith * | .50 | .20 | .05 |
| ☐ | 80 Robin Yount * | 7.50 | 3.00 | .75 |
| ☐ | 81 Al Oliver * | 1.00 | .40 | .10 |
| ☐ | 82 Bill Singer * | .40 | .16 | .04 |
| ☐ | 83 Johnny Bench * | 4.00 | 1.60 | .40 |
| ☐ | 84 Gaylord Perry * | 2.00 | .80 | .20 |
| ☐ | 85 Dave Kingman * | 1.00 | .40 | .10 |
| ☐ | 86 Ed Herrmann * | .40 | .16 | .04 |
| ☐ | 87 Ralph Garr * | .40 | .16 | .04 |
| ☐ | 88 Reggie Jackson * | 6.00 | 2.40 | .60 |
| ☐ | 89A Doug Radar ERR * (sic, Rader) | 1.00 | .40 | .10 |
| ☐ | 89B Doug Rader COR * | 2.00 | .80 | .20 |
| ☐ | 90 Elliott Maddox * | .40 | .16 | .04 |
| ☐ | 91 Bill Russell * | .50 | .20 | .05 |
| ☐ | 92 John Mayberry * | .40 | .16 | .04 |
| ☐ | 93 Dave Cash * | .40 | .16 | .04 |
| ☐ | 94 Jeff Burroughs * | .40 | .16 | .04 |
| ☐ | 95 Ted Simmons * | 1.00 | .40 | .10 |
| ☐ | 96 Joe Decker * | .40 | .16 | .04 |
| ☐ | 97 Bill Buckner * | 1.00 | .40 | .10 |
| ☐ | 98 Bobby Darwin * | .40 | .16 | .04 |
| ☐ | 99 Phil Niekro * | 2.50 | 1.00 | .25 |
| ☐ | 100 Jim Sundberg | .40 | .16 | .04 |
| ☐ | 101 Greg Gross | .30 | .12 | .03 |
| ☐ | 102 Luis Tiant | .50 | .20 | .05 |
| ☐ | 103 Glenn Beckert | .30 | .12 | .03 |
| ☐ | 104 Hal McRae | .40 | .16 | .04 |
| ☐ | 105 Mike Jorgensen | .30 | .12 | .03 |
| ☐ | 106 Mike Hargrove | .40 | .16 | .04 |
| ☐ | 107 Don Gullett | .40 | .16 | .04 |
| ☐ | 108 Tito Fuentes | .30 | .12 | .03 |
| ☐ | 109 John Grubb | .30 | .12 | .03 |
| ☐ | 110 Jim Kaat | .75 | .30 | .07 |
| ☐ | 111 Felix Millan | .30 | .12 | .03 |
| ☐ | 112 Don Money | .30 | .12 | .03 |
| ☐ | 113 Rick Monday | .40 | .16 | .04 |
| ☐ | 114 Dick Bosman | .30 | .12 | .03 |
| ☐ | 115 Roger Metzger | .30 | .12 | .03 |
| ☐ | 116 Fergie Jenkins | .75 | .30 | .07 |
| ☐ | 117 Dusty Baker | .50 | .20 | .05 |
| ☐ | 118 Billy Champion * | .40 | .16 | .04 |
| ☐ | 119 Bob Gibson * | 3.00 | 1.20 | .30 |
| ☐ | 120 Bill Freehan * | .50 | .20 | .05 |
| ☐ | 121 Cesar Geronimo | .30 | .12 | .03 |
| ☐ | 122 Jorge Orta | .30 | .12 | .03 |
| ☐ | 123 Cleon Jones | .30 | .12 | .03 |
| ☐ | 124 Steve Busby | .40 | .16 | .04 |
| ☐ | 125A Bill Madlock ERR (pitcher) | 1.50 | .60 | .15 |
| ☐ | 125B Bill Madlock COR (infielder) | 1.50 | .60 | .15 |
| ☐ | 126 Jim Palmer | 2.50 | 1.00 | .25 |
| ☐ | 127 Tony Perez | .75 | .30 | .07 |
| ☐ | 128 Larry Hisle | .40 | .16 | .04 |
| ☐ | 129 Rusty Staub | .50 | .20 | .05 |
| ☐ | 130 Hank Aaron * | 6.00 | 2.40 | .60 |
| ☐ | 131 Rennie Stennett * | .40 | .16 | .04 |
| ☐ | 132 Rico Petrocelli * | .50 | .20 | .05 |
| ☐ | 133 Mike Schmidt * | 5.00 | 2.00 | .50 |
| ☐ | 134 Sparky Lyle | .50 | .20 | .05 |
| ☐ | 135 Willie Stargell | 2.00 | .80 | .20 |
| ☐ | 136 Ken Henderson | .30 | .12 | .03 |
| ☐ | 137 Willie Montanez | .30 | .12 | .03 |
| ☐ | 138 Thurman Munson | 3.00 | 1.20 | .30 |
| ☐ | 139 Richie Zisk | .40 | .16 | .04 |

| | | | | MINT | VG-E | F-G |
|---|---|---|---|---|---|---|
| ☐ 140 | George Hendrick | | | .40 | .16 | .04 |
| ☐ 141 | Bobby Murcer | | | .50 | .20 | .05 |
| ☐ 142 | Lee May | | | .40 | .16 | .04 |
| ☐ 143 | Carlton Fisk | | | .75 | .30 | .07 |
| ☐ 144 | Brooks Robinson | | | 3.00 | 1.20 | .30 |
| ☐ 145 | Bobby Bonds | | | .40 | .16 | .04 |
| ☐ 146 | Gary Sutherland | | | .30 | .12 | .03 |
| ☐ 147 | Oscar Gamble | | | .30 | .12 | .03 |
| ☐ 148 | Jim Hunter | | | 2.00 | .80 | .20 |
| ☐ 149 | Tug McGraw | | | .50 | .20 | .05 |
| ☐ 150 | Dave McNally | | | .40 | .16 | .04 |

## 1975 Hostess Twinkie

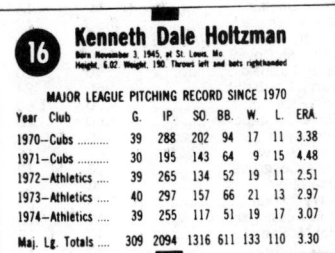

| | | | | MINT | VG-E | F-G |
|---|---|---|---|---|---|---|
| ☐ 36 | Willie Horton | | | .75 | .30 | .07 |
| ☐ 40 | Joe Rudi | | | .75 | .30 | .07 |
| ☐ 43 | Garry Maddox | | | .75 | .30 | .07 |
| ☐ 46 | Dave Chalk | | | .60 | .24 | .06 |
| ☐ 49 | Steve Garvey | | | 4.00 | 1.60 | .40 |
| ☐ 52 | Rollie Fingers | | | 1.00 | .40 | .10 |
| ☐ 58 | Nolan Ryan | | | 4.00 | 1.60 | .40 |
| ☐ 61 | Ron Cey | | | .90 | .36 | .09 |
| ☐ 64 | Gene Tenace | | | .60 | .24 | .06 |
| ☐ 65 | Jose Cardenal | | | .60 | .24 | .06 |
| ☐ 67 | Dave Lopes | | | .75 | .30 | .07 |
| ☐ 68 | Wilbur Wood | | | .75 | .30 | .07 |
| ☐ 73 | Chris Speier | | | .60 | .24 | .06 |
| ☐ 77 | Don Kessinger | | | .75 | .30 | .07 |
| ☐ 79 | Andy Messersmith | | | .75 | .30 | .07 |
| ☐ 80 | Robin Yount | | | 7.50 | 3.00 | .75 |
| ☐ 82 | Bill Singer | | | .60 | .24 | .06 |
| ☐ 103 | Glenn Beckert | | | .60 | .24 | .06 |
| ☐ 110 | Jim Kaat | | | 1.00 | .40 | .10 |
| ☐ 112 | Don Money | | | .60 | .24 | .06 |
| ☐ 113 | Rick Monday | | | .75 | .30 | .07 |
| ☐ 122 | Jorge Orta | | | .60 | .24 | .06 |
| ☐ 125 | Bill Madlock | | | 1.25 | .50 | .12 |
| ☐ 130 | Hank Aaron | | | 6.00 | 2.40 | .60 |
| ☐ 136 | Ken Henderson | | | .60 | .24 | .06 |

The cards in this 60 card set measure 2 1/4" by 3 1/4". The 1975 Hostess Twinkie set was issued on a limited basis in the far western part of the country. The set contains the same numbers as the regular set to number 36; however, the set is skip numbered after number 36. The cards were issued as the backs for 25 cent Twinkies packs. The fronts are indistinguishable from the regular Hostess cards; however the card backs are different in that the Twinkie cards have a thick black bar in the middle of the reverse.

## 1976 Hostess

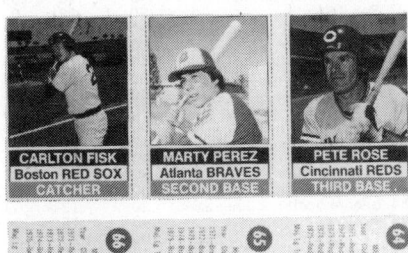

The cards in this 150 card set measure 2 1/4" by 3 1/4" individually or 3 1/4" by 7 1/4" as panels of three. The 1976 Hostess set contains color, numbered cards issued in panels of three cards each on family sized packages of Hostess cakes. Scarcer panels (those only found on less popular Hostess products) are listed in the checklist below with asterisks. Complete panels of three have a value 25% more than the sum of the individual cards on the panel. Ten additional numbers (151-160) were apparently planned but never actually issued. These exist as proof cards and are quite scarce, e.g., 151 Ferguson Jenkins, 152 Mike Cuellar, 153 Tom Murphy, 155 Barry Foote, 157 Richie Zisk, 158 Ken Holtzman, and 159 Cliff Johnson.

| | MINT | VG-E | F-G |
|---|---|---|---|
| COMPLETE SET | 60.00 | 24.00 | 6.00 |
| COMMON PLAYER | .60 | .24 | .06 |

| | | | | MINT | VG-E | F-G |
|---|---|---|---|---|---|---|
| ☐ | 1 | Bob Tolan | | .60 | .24 | .06 |
| ☐ | 2 | Cookie Rojas | | .60 | .24 | .06 |
| ☐ | 3 | Darrell Evans | | .90 | .36 | .09 |
| ☐ | 4 | Sal Bando | | .75 | .30 | .07 |
| ☐ | 5 | Joe Morgan | | 2.00 | .80 | .20 |
| ☐ | 6 | Mickey Lolich | | .90 | .36 | .09 |
| ☐ | 7 | Don Sutton | | 1.50 | .60 | .15 |
| ☐ | 8 | Bill Melton | | .60 | .24 | .06 |
| ☐ | 9 | Tim Foli | | .60 | .24 | .06 |
| ☐ | 10 | Joe LaHoud | | .60 | .24 | .06 |
| ☐ | 11 | Bert Hooten (sic) | | 1.00 | .40 | .10 |
| ☐ | 12 | Paul Blair | | .60 | .24 | .06 |
| ☐ | 13 | Jim Barr | | .60 | .24 | .06 |
| ☐ | 14 | Toby Harrah | | .75 | .30 | .07 |
| ☐ | 15 | John Milner | | .60 | .24 | .06 |
| ☐ | 16 | Ken Holtzman | | .75 | .30 | .07 |
| ☐ | 17 | Cesar Cedeno | | .75 | .30 | .07 |
| ☐ | 18 | Dwight Evans | | .90 | .36 | .09 |
| ☐ | 19 | Willie McCovey | | 2.50 | 1.00 | .25 |
| ☐ | 20 | Tony Oliva | | .90 | .36 | .09 |
| ☐ | 21 | Manny Sanguillen | | .75 | .30 | .07 |
| ☐ | 22 | Mickey Rivers | | .75 | .30 | .07 |
| ☐ | 23 | Lou Brock | | 2.50 | 1.00 | .25 |
| ☐ | 24 | Graig Nettles | | 1.50 | .60 | .15 |
| | | (Craig on front) | | | | |
| ☐ | 25 | Jim Wynn | | .75 | .30 | .07 |
| ☐ | 26 | George Scott | | .60 | .24 | .06 |
| ☐ | 27 | Greg Luzinski | | .90 | .36 | .09 |
| ☐ | 28 | Bert Campaneris | | .75 | .30 | .07 |
| ☐ | 29 | Pete Rose | | 9.00 | 3.75 | .90 |
| ☐ | 30 | Buddy Bell | | .90 | .36 | .09 |
| ☐ | 31 | Gary Matthews | | .75 | .30 | .07 |
| ☐ | 32 | Freddie Patek | | .60 | .24 | .06 |
| ☐ | 33 | Mike Lum | | .60 | .24 | .06 |
| ☐ | 34 | Ellie Rodriguez | | .60 | .24 | .06 |
| ☐ | 35 | Milt May | | .90 | .36 | .09 |
| | | (Lee May picture) | | | | |

| | MINT | VG-E | F-G |
|---|---|---|---|
| COMPLETE INDIV. SET (150) | 120.00 | 50.00 | 12.00 |
| COMMON PLAYER (1-150) | .30 | .12 | .03 |

| | | | | MINT | VG-E | F-G |
|---|---|---|---|---|---|---|
| ☐ | 1 | Fred Lynn | | 1.50 | .60 | .15 |
| ☐ | 2 | Joe Morgan | | 2.00 | .80 | .20 |
| ☐ | 3 | Phil Niekro | | 2.00 | .80 | .20 |
| ☐ | 4 | Gaylord Perry | | 1.50 | .60 | .15 |
| ☐ | 5 | Bob Watson | | .40 | .16 | .04 |
| ☐ | 6 | Bill Freehan | | .40 | .16 | .04 |
| ☐ | 7 | Lou Brock | | 2.50 | 1.00 | .25 |
| ☐ | 8 | Al Fitzmorris | | .30 | .12 | .03 |
| ☐ | 9 | Rennie Stennett | | .30 | .12 | .03 |

| | | | | |
|---|---|---|---|---|
| ☐ 10 | Tony Oliva | .60 | .24 | .06 |
| ☐ 11 | Robin Yount | 3.00 | 1.20 | .30 |
| ☐ 12 | Rick Manning | .30 | .12 | .03 |
| ☐ 13 | Bobby Grich | .40 | .16 | .04 |
| ☐ 14 | Terry Forster | .40 | .16 | .04 |
| ☐ 15 | Dave Kingman | .60 | .24 | .06 |
| ☐ 16 | Thurman Munson | 3.00 | 1.20 | .30 |
| ☐ 17 | Rick Reuschel | .40 | .16 | .04 |
| ☐ 18 | Bobby Bonds | .40 | .16 | .04 |
| ☐ 19 | Steve Garvey | 4.00 | 1.60 | .40 |
| ☐ 20 | Vida Blue | .40 | .16 | .04 |
| ☐ 21 | Dave Rader | .30 | .12 | .03 |
| ☐ 22 | Johnny Bench | 3.00 | 1.20 | .30 |
| ☐ 23 | Luis Tiant | .50 | .20 | .05 |
| ☐ 24 | Darrell Evans | .50 | .20 | .05 |
| ☐ 25 | Larry Dierker | .30 | .12 | .03 |
| ☐ 26 | Willie Horton | .40 | .16 | .04 |
| ☐ 27 | John Ellis | .30 | .12 | .03 |
| ☐ 28 | Al Cowens | .40 | .16 | .04 |
| ☐ 29 | Jerry Reuss | .40 | .16 | .04 |
| ☐ 30 | Reggie Smith | .50 | .20 | .05 |
| ☐ 31 | Bobby Darwin * | .40 | .16 | .04 |
| ☐ 32 | Fritz Peterson * | .40 | .16 | .04 |
| ☐ 33 | Rod Carew * | 4.00 | 1.60 | .40 |
| ☐ 34 | Carlos May * | .40 | .16 | .04 |
| ☐ 35 | Tom Seaver * | 4.00 | 1.60 | .40 |
| ☐ 36 | Brooks Robinson * | 4.00 | 1.60 | .40 |
| ☐ 37 | Jose Cardenal | .30 | .12 | .03 |
| ☐ 38 | Ron Blomberg | .30 | .12 | .03 |
| ☐ 39 | Leroy Stanton | .30 | .12 | .03 |
| ☐ 40 | Dave Cash | .30 | .12 | .03 |
| ☐ 41 | John Montefusco | .40 | .16 | .04 |
| ☐ 42 | Bob Tolan | .30 | .12 | .03 |
| ☐ 43 | Carl Morton | .30 | .12 | .03 |
| ☐ 44 | Rick Burleson | .50 | .20 | .05 |
| ☐ 45 | Don Gullett | .40 | .16 | .04 |
| ☐ 46 | Vern Ruhle | .30 | .12 | .03 |
| ☐ 47 | Cesar Cedeno | .40 | .16 | .04 |
| ☐ 48 | Toby Harrah | .40 | .16 | .04 |
| ☐ 49 | Willie Stargell | 2.00 | .80 | .20 |
| ☐ 50 | Al Hrabosky | .40 | .16 | .04 |
| ☐ 51 | Amos Otis | .40 | .16 | .04 |
| ☐ 52 | Bud Harrelson | .30 | .12 | .03 |
| ☐ 53 | Jim Hughes | .30 | .12 | .03 |
| ☐ 54 | George Scott | .30 | .12 | .03 |
| ☐ 55 | Mike Vail * | .40 | .16 | .04 |
| ☐ 56 | Jim Palmer * | 3.00 | 1.20 | .30 |
| ☐ 57 | Jorge Orta * | .40 | .16 | .04 |
| ☐ 58 | Chris Chambliss * | .50 | .20 | .05 |
| ☐ 59 | Dave Chalk * | .40 | .16 | .04 |
| ☐ 60 | Ray Burris * | .40 | .16 | .04 |
| ☐ 61 | Bert Campaneris * | .50 | .20 | .05 |
| ☐ 62 | Gary Carter * | 5.00 | 2.00 | .50 |
| ☐ 63 | Ron Cey * | .75 | .30 | .07 |
| ☐ 64 | Carlton Fisk * | 1.00 | .40 | .10 |
| ☐ 65 | Marty Perez * | .40 | .16 | .04 |
| ☐ 66 | Pete Rose * | 9.00 | 3.75 | .90 |
| ☐ 67 | Roger Metzger * | .40 | .16 | .04 |
| ☐ 68 | Jim Sundberg * | .40 | .16 | .04 |
| ☐ 69 | Ron LeFlore * | .40 | .16 | .04 |
| ☐ 70 | Ted Sizemore * | .40 | .16 | .04 |
| ☐ 71 | Steve Busby * | .50 | .20 | .05 |
| ☐ 72 | Manny Sanguillen * | .50 | .20 | .05 |
| ☐ 73 | Larry Hisle * | .40 | .16 | .04 |
| ☐ 74 | Pete Broberg * | .40 | .16 | .04 |
| ☐ 75 | Boog Powell * | .75 | .30 | .07 |
| ☐ 76 | Ken Singleton * | .75 | .30 | .07 |
| ☐ 77 | Rich Gossage * | 1.50 | .60 | .15 |
| ☐ 78 | Jerry Grote * | .40 | .16 | .04 |
| ☐ 79 | Nolan Ryan * | 4.00 | 1.60 | .40 |
| ☐ 80 | Rick Monday * | .50 | .20 | .05 |
| ☐ 81 | Graig Nettles * | .75 | .30 | .07 |
| ☐ 82 | Chris Speier * | .30 | .12 | .03 |
| ☐ 83 | Dave Winfield * | 3.00 | 1.20 | .30 |
| ☐ 84 | Mike Schmidt * | 5.00 | 2.00 | .50 |
| ☐ 85 | Buzz Capra | .30 | .12 | .03 |
| ☐ 86 | Tony Perez | .75 | .30 | .07 |
| ☐ 87 | Dwight Evans | .60 | .24 | .06 |
| ☐ 88 | Mike Hargrove | .30 | .12 | .03 |
| ☐ 89 | Joe Coleman | .30 | .12 | .03 |
| ☐ 90 | Greg Gross | .30 | .12 | .03 |
| ☐ 91 | John Mayberry | .40 | .16 | .04 |
| ☐ 92 | John Candelaria | .50 | .20 | .05 |
| ☐ 93 | Bake McBride | .30 | .12 | .03 |
| ☐ 94 | Hank Aaron | 5.00 | 2.00 | .50 |
| ☐ 95 | Buddy Bell | .50 | .20 | .05 |
| ☐ 96 | Steve Braun | .30 | .12 | .03 |
| ☐ 97 | Jon Matlack | .40 | .16 | .04 |
| ☐ 98 | Lee May | .40 | .16 | .04 |
| ☐ 99 | Wilbur Wood | .40 | .16 | .04 |
| ☐ 100 | Bill Madlock | .75 | .30 | .07 |
| ☐ 101 | Frank Tanana | .40 | .16 | .04 |
| ☐ 102 | Mickey Rivers | .40 | .16 | .04 |

| | | | | |
|---|---|---|---|---|
| ☐ 103 | Mike Ivie | .30 | .12 | .03 |
| ☐ 104 | Rollie Fingers | 1.00 | .40 | .10 |
| ☐ 105 | Dave Lopes | .40 | .16 | .04 |
| ☐ 106 | George Foster | 1.00 | .40 | .10 |
| ☐ 107 | Denny Doyle | .30 | .12 | .03 |
| ☐ 108 | Earl Williams | .30 | .12 | .03 |
| ☐ 109 | Tom Veryzer | .30 | .12 | .03 |
| ☐ 110 | J.R. Richard | .40 | .16 | .04 |
| ☐ 111 | Jeff Burroughs | .30 | .12 | .03 |
| ☐ 112 | Al Oliver | .80 | .32 | .08 |
| ☐ 113 | Ted Simmons | .75 | .30 | .07 |
| ☐ 114 | George Brett | 6.00 | 2.40 | .60 |
| ☐ 115 | Frank Duffy | .30 | .12 | .03 |
| ☐ 116 | Bert Blyleven | .50 | .20 | .05 |
| ☐ 117 | Darrell Porter | .30 | .12 | .03 |
| ☐ 118 | Don Baylor | .50 | .20 | .05 |
| ☐ 119 | Bucky Dent | .40 | .16 | .04 |
| ☐ 120 | Felix Millan | .30 | .12 | .03 |
| ☐ 121 | Mike Cuellar | .40 | .16 | .04 |
| ☐ 122 | Gene Tenace | .30 | .12 | .03 |
| ☐ 123 | Bobby Murcer | .50 | .20 | .05 |
| ☐ 124 | Willie McCovey | 2.00 | .80 | .20 |
| ☐ 125 | Greg Luzinski | .50 | .20 | .05 |
| ☐ 126 | Larry Parrish | .60 | .24 | .06 |
| ☐ 127 | Jim Rice | 4.00 | 1.60 | .40 |
| ☐ 128 | Dave Concepcion | .50 | .20 | .05 |
| ☐ 129 | Jim Wynn | .40 | .16 | .04 |
| ☐ 130 | Tom Grieve | .40 | .16 | .04 |
| ☐ 131 | Mike Cosgrove | .30 | .12 | .03 |
| ☐ 132 | Dan Meyer | .30 | .12 | .03 |
| ☐ 133 | Dave Parker | 2.00 | .80 | .20 |
| ☐ 134 | Don Kessinger | .40 | .16 | .04 |
| ☐ 135 | Hal McRae | .40 | .16 | .04 |
| ☐ 136 | Don Money | .30 | .12 | .03 |
| ☐ 137 | Dennis Eckersley | .40 | .16 | .04 |
| ☐ 138 | Fergie Jenkins | .60 | .24 | .06 |
| ☐ 139 | Mike Torrez | .40 | .16 | .04 |
| ☐ 140 | Jerry Morales | .30 | .12 | .03 |
| ☐ 141 | Jim Hunter | 2.00 | .80 | .20 |
| ☐ 142 | Gary Matthews | .40 | .16 | .04 |
| ☐ 143 | Randy Jones | .40 | .16 | .04 |
| ☐ 144 | Mike Jorgensen | .30 | .12 | .03 |
| ☐ 145 | Larry Bowa | .40 | .16 | .04 |
| ☐ 146 | Reggie Jackson | 4.00 | 1.60 | .40 |
| ☐ 147 | Steve Yeager | .30 | .12 | .03 |
| ☐ 148 | Dave May | .30 | .12 | .03 |
| ☐ 149 | Carl Yastrzemski | 5.00 | 2.00 | .50 |
| ☐ 150 | Cesar Geronimo | .30 | .12 | .03 |

## 1976 Hostess Twinkie

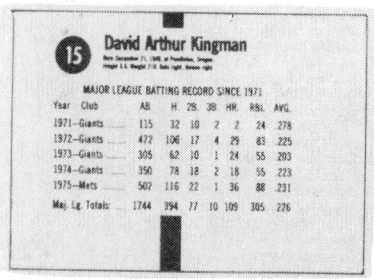

The cards in this 60 card set measure 2 1/4" by 3 1/4". The 1976 Hostess Twinkies set contains the first 60 cards of the 1976 Hostess set. These cards were issued as backs on 25 cent Twinkie packages as in the 1975 Twinkies set. The fronts are indistinguishable from the regular Hostess cards; however the card backs are different in that the Twinkie cards have a thick black bar in the middle of the reverse.

| | MINT | VG-E | F-G |
|---|---|---|---|
| COMPLETE SET | 60.00 | 24.00 | 6.00 |
| COMMON PLAYER | .60 | .24 | .06 |
| ☐ 1 Fred Lynn | 1.50 | .60 | .15 |

| | | | MINT | VG-E | F-G |
|---|---|---|---|---|---|
| ☐ | 2 | Joe Morgan | 2.00 | .80 | .20 |
| ☐ | 3 | Phil Niekro | 2.00 | .80 | .20 |
| ☐ | 4 | Gaylord Perry | 1.50 | .60 | .15 |
| ☐ | 5 | Bob Watson | .75 | .30 | .07 |
| ☐ | 6 | Bill Freehan | .75 | .30 | .07 |
| ☐ | 7 | Lou Brock | 2.50 | 1.00 | .25 |
| ☐ | 8 | Al Fitzmorris | .60 | .24 | .06 |
| ☐ | 9 | Rennie Stennett | .60 | .24 | .06 |
| ☐ | 10 | Tony Oliva | .90 | .36 | .09 |
| ☐ | 11 | Robin Yount | 3.00 | 1.20 | .30 |
| ☐ | 12 | Rick Manning | .60 | .24 | .06 |
| ☐ | 13 | Bobby Grich | .75 | .30 | .07 |
| ☐ | 14 | Terry Forster | .75 | .30 | .07 |
| ☐ | 15 | Dave Kingman | .90 | .36 | .09 |
| ☐ | 16 | Thurman Munson | 3.00 | 1.20 | .30 |
| ☐ | 17 | Rick Reuschel | .75 | .30 | .07 |
| ☐ | 18 | Bobby Bonds | .75 | .30 | .07 |
| ☐ | 19 | Steve Garvey | 4.00 | 1.60 | .40 |
| ☐ | 20 | Vida Blue | .75 | .30 | .07 |
| ☐ | 21 | Dave Rader | .60 | .24 | .06 |
| ☐ | 22 | Johnny Bench | 3.00 | 1.20 | .30 |
| ☐ | 23 | Luis Tiant | .75 | .30 | .07 |
| ☐ | 24 | Darrell Evans | .90 | .36 | .09 |
| ☐ | 25 | Larry Dierker | .60 | .24 | .06 |
| ☐ | 26 | Willie Horton | .75 | .30 | .07 |
| ☐ | 27 | John Ellis | .60 | .24 | .06 |
| ☐ | 28 | Al Cowens | .75 | .30 | .07 |
| ☐ | 29 | Jerry Reuss | .75 | .30 | .07 |
| ☐ | 30 | Reggie Smith | .90 | .36 | .09 |
| ☐ | 31 | Bobby Darwin | .60 | .24 | .06 |
| ☐ | 32 | Fritz Peterson | .60 | .24 | .06 |
| ☐ | 33 | Rod Carew | 4.00 | 1.60 | .40 |
| ☐ | 34 | Carlos May | .60 | .24 | .06 |
| ☐ | 35 | Tom Seaver | 4.00 | 1.60 | .40 |
| ☐ | 36 | Brooks Robinson | 4.00 | 1.60 | .40 |
| ☐ | 37 | Jose Cardenal | .60 | .24 | .06 |
| ☐ | 38 | Ron Blomberg | .60 | .24 | .06 |
| ☐ | 39 | Leroy Stanton | .60 | .24 | .06 |
| ☐ | 40 | Dave Cash | .60 | .24 | .06 |
| ☐ | 41 | John Montefusco | .75 | .30 | .07 |
| ☐ | 42 | Bob Tolan | .60 | .24 | .06 |
| ☐ | 43 | Carl Morton | .60 | .24 | .06 |
| ☐ | 44 | Rick Burleson | .90 | .36 | .09 |
| ☐ | 45 | Don Gullett | .75 | .30 | .07 |
| ☐ | 46 | Vern Ruhle | .60 | .24 | .06 |
| ☐ | 47 | Cesar Cedeno | .75 | .30 | .07 |
| ☐ | 48 | Toby Harrah | .75 | .30 | .07 |
| ☐ | 49 | Willie Stargell | 2.00 | .80 | .20 |
| ☐ | 50 | Al Hrabosky | .75 | .30 | .07 |
| ☐ | 51 | Amos Otis | .75 | .30 | .07 |
| ☐ | 52 | Bud Harrelson | .60 | .24 | .06 |
| ☐ | 53 | Jim Hughes | .60 | .24 | .06 |
| ☐ | 54 | George Scott | .60 | .24 | .06 |
| ☐ | 55 | Mike Vail | .60 | .24 | .06 |
| ☐ | 56 | Jim Palmer | 3.00 | 1.20 | .30 |
| ☐ | 57 | Jorge Orta | .60 | .24 | .06 |
| ☐ | 58 | Chris Chambliss | .75 | .30 | .07 |
| ☐ | 59 | Dave Chalk | .60 | .24 | .06 |
| ☐ | 60 | Ray Burris | .60 | .24 | .06 |

## 1977 Hostess

The cards in this 150 card set measure 2 1/4" by 3 1/4" individually or 3 1/4" by 7 1/4" as panels of three. The 1977 Hostess set contains color, numbered cards issued in panels of three cards each with Hostess family sized caked products. Scarcer panels are listed in the checklist below with asterisks. Although complete panel prices are not explicitly listed below, they would generally have a value 25% greater than the sum of the individual players on the panel.

| | | | MINT | VG-E | F-G |
|---|---|---|---|---|---|
| | | COMPLETE INDIV. SET | 120.00 | 50.00 | 12.00 |
| | | COMMON PLAYER | .30 | .12 | .03 |
| ☐ | 1 | Jim Palmer | 2.50 | 1.00 | .25 |
| ☐ | 2 | Joe Morgan | 2.00 | .80 | .20 |
| ☐ | 3 | Reggie Jackson | 4.00 | 1.60 | .40 |
| ☐ | 4 | Carl Yastrzemski | 5.00 | 2.00 | .50 |
| ☐ | 5 | Thurman Munson | 3.00 | 1.20 | .30 |
| ☐ | 6 | Johnny Bench | 3.00 | 1.20 | .30 |
| ☐ | 7 | Tom Seaver | 3.50 | 1.40 | .35 |

BILL STEIN
Seattle MARINERS
SECOND BASE

ROLLIE FINGERS
San Diego PADRES
PITCHER

BRIAN DOWNING
Chicago WHITE SOX
CATCHER

| | | | MINT | VG-E | F-G |
|---|---|---|---|---|---|
| ☐ | 8 | Pete Rose | 8.00 | 3.25 | .80 |
| ☐ | 9 | Rod Carew | 3.50 | 1.40 | .35 |
| ☐ | 10 | Luis Tiant | .40 | .16 | .04 |
| ☐ | 11 | Phil Garner | .30 | .12 | .03 |
| ☐ | 12 | Sixto Lezcano | .30 | .12 | .03 |
| ☐ | 13 | Mike Torrez | .30 | .12 | .03 |
| ☐ | 14 | Dave Lopes | .40 | .16 | .04 |
| ☐ | 15 | Doug DeCinces | .50 | .20 | .05 |
| ☐ | 16 | Jim Spencer | .30 | .12 | .03 |
| ☐ | 17 | Hal McRae | .40 | .16 | .04 |
| ☐ | 18 | Mike Hargrove | .30 | .12 | .03 |
| ☐ | 19 | Willie Montanez * | .40 | .16 | .04 |
| ☐ | 20 | Roger Metzger * | .40 | .16 | .04 |
| ☐ | 21 | Dwight Evans * | 1.00 | .40 | .10 |
| ☐ | 22 | Steve Rogers * | 1.00 | .40 | .10 |
| ☐ | 23 | Jim Rice * | 4.00 | 1.60 | .40 |
| ☐ | 24 | Pete Falcone * | .40 | .16 | .04 |
| ☐ | 25 | Greg Luzinski * | 1.00 | .40 | .10 |
| ☐ | 26 | Randy Jones * | .50 | .20 | .05 |
| ☐ | 27 | Willie Stargell * | 2.00 | .80 | .20 |
| ☐ | 28 | John Hiller * | .40 | .16 | .04 |
| ☐ | 29 | Bobby Murcer * | .50 | .20 | .05 |
| ☐ | 30 | Rick Monday * | .50 | .20 | .05 |
| ☐ | 31 | John Montefusco * | .40 | .16 | .04 |
| ☐ | 32 | Lou Brock * | 3.00 | 1.20 | .30 |
| ☐ | 33 | Bill North * | .40 | .16 | .04 |
| ☐ | 34 | Robin Yount * | 3.00 | 1.20 | .30 |
| ☐ | 35 | Steve Garvey * | 5.00 | 2.00 | .50 |
| ☐ | 36 | George Brett * | 6.00 | 2.40 | .60 |
| ☐ | 37 | Toby Harrah * | .50 | .20 | .05 |
| ☐ | 38 | Jerry Royster * | .40 | .16 | .04 |
| ☐ | 39 | Bob Watson * | .40 | .16 | .04 |
| ☐ | 40 | George Foster | 1.00 | .40 | .10 |
| ☐ | 41 | Gary Carter | 3.50 | 1.40 | .35 |
| ☐ | 42 | John Denny | .50 | .20 | .05 |
| ☐ | 43 | Mike Schmidt | 4.50 | 1.80 | .45 |
| ☐ | 44 | Dave Winfield | 3.00 | 1.20 | .30 |
| ☐ | 45 | Al Oliver | .80 | .32 | .08 |
| ☐ | 46 | Mark Fidrych | .50 | .20 | .05 |
| ☐ | 47 | Larry Herndon | .30 | .12 | .03 |
| ☐ | 48 | Dave Goltz | .30 | .12 | .03 |
| ☐ | 49 | Jerry Morales | .30 | .12 | .03 |
| ☐ | 50 | Ron LeFlore | .40 | .16 | .04 |
| ☐ | 51 | Fred Lynn | 1.50 | .60 | .15 |
| ☐ | 52 | Vida Blue | .40 | .16 | .04 |
| ☐ | 53 | Rick Manning | .30 | .12 | .03 |
| ☐ | 54 | Bill Buckner | .60 | .24 | .06 |
| ☐ | 55 | Lee May | .40 | .16 | .04 |
| ☐ | 56 | John Mayberry | .40 | .16 | .04 |
| ☐ | 57 | Darrell Chaney | .30 | .12 | .03 |
| ☐ | 58 | Cesar Cedeno | .40 | .16 | .04 |
| ☐ | 59 | Ken Griffey | .40 | .16 | .04 |
| ☐ | 60 | Dave Kingman | .60 | .24 | .06 |
| ☐ | 61 | Ted Simmons | .75 | .30 | .07 |
| ☐ | 62 | Larry Bowa | .50 | .20 | .05 |
| ☐ | 63 | Frank Tanana | .40 | .16 | .04 |
| ☐ | 64 | Jason Thompson | .40 | .16 | .04 |
| ☐ | 65 | Ken Brett | .30 | .12 | .03 |
| ☐ | 66 | Roy Smalley | .40 | .16 | .04 |
| ☐ | 67 | Ray Burris | .30 | .12 | .03 |
| ☐ | 68 | Rick Burleson | .50 | .20 | .05 |
| ☐ | 69 | Buddy Bell | .50 | .20 | .05 |
| ☐ | 70 | Don Sutton | 1.50 | .60 | .15 |
| ☐ | 71 | Mark Belanger | .40 | .16 | .04 |
| ☐ | 72 | Dennis Leonard | .40 | .16 | .04 |
| ☐ | 73 | Gaylord Perry | 1.50 | .60 | .15 |

| ☐ | 74 | Dick Ruthven | .30 | .12 | .03 |
|---|----|------------|-----|-----|-----|
| ☐ | 75 | Jose Cruz | .50 | .20 | .05 |
| ☐ | 76 | Cesar Geronimo | .30 | .12 | .03 |
| ☐ | 77 | Jerry Koosman | .50 | .20 | .05 |
| ☐ | 78 | Garry Templeton | 1.00 | .40 | .10 |
| ☐ | 79 | Jim Hunter | 2.00 | .80 | .20 |
| ☐ | 80 | John Candelaria | .50 | .20 | .05 |
| ☐ | 81 | Nolan Ryan | 3.50 | 1.40 | .35 |
| ☐ | 82 | Rusty Staub | .50 | .20 | .05 |
| ☐ | 83 | Jim Barr | .30 | .12 | .03 |
| ☐ | 84 | Butch Wynegar | .40 | .16 | .04 |
| ☐ | 85 | Jose Cardenal | .30 | .12 | .03 |
| ☐ | 86 | Claudell Washington | .40 | .16 | .04 |
| ☐ | 87 | Bill Travers | .30 | .12 | .03 |
| ☐ | 88 | Rick Waits | .30 | .12 | .03 |
| ☐ | 89 | Ron Cey | .50 | .20 | .05 |
| ☐ | 90 | Al Bumbry | .30 | .12 | .03 |
| ☐ | 91 | Bucky Dent | .40 | .16 | .04 |
| ☐ | 92 | Amos Otis | .40 | .16 | .04 |
| ☐ | 93 | Tom Grieve | .40 | .16 | .04 |
| ☐ | 94 | Enos Cabell | .30 | .12 | .03 |
| ☐ | 95 | Dave Concepcion | .40 | .16 | .04 |
| ☐ | 96 | Felix Millan | .30 | .12 | .03 |
| ☐ | 97 | Bake McBride | .30 | .12 | .03 |
| ☐ | 98 | Chris Chambliss | .40 | .16 | .04 |
| ☐ | 99 | Butch Metzger | .30 | .12 | .03 |
| ☐ | 100 | Rennie Stennett | .30 | .12 | .03 |
| ☐ | 101 | Dave Roberts | .30 | .12 | .03 |
| ☐ | 102 | Lyman Bostock | .40 | .16 | .04 |
| ☐ | 103 | Rick Reuschel | .40 | .16 | .04 |
| ☐ | 104 | Carlton Fisk | .75 | .30 | .07 |
| ☐ | 105 | Jim Slaton | .30 | .12 | .03 |
| ☐ | 106 | Dennis Eckersley | .40 | .16 | .04 |
| ☐ | 107 | Ken Singleton | .50 | .20 | .05 |
| ☐ | 108 | Ralph Garr | .30 | .12 | .03 |
| ☐ | 109 | Freddie Patek * | .40 | .16 | .04 |
| ☐ | 110 | Jim Sundberg * | .40 | .16 | .04 |
| ☐ | 111 | Phil Niekro * | 2.00 | .80 | .20 |
| ☐ | 112 | J.R. Richard * | .50 | .20 | .05 |
| ☐ | 113 | Gary Nolan * | .40 | .16 | .04 |
| ☐ | 114 | Jon Matlack * | .50 | .20 | .05 |
| ☐ | 115 | Keith Hernandez * | 3.00 | 1.20 | .30 |
| ☐ | 116 | Graig Nettles * | 1.00 | .40 | .10 |
| ☐ | 117 | Steve Carlton * | 3.50 | 1.40 | .35 |
| ☐ | 118 | Bill Madlock * | 1.50 | .60 | .15 |
| ☐ | 119 | Jerry Reuss * | .60 | .24 | .06 |
| ☐ | 120 | Aurelio Rodriguez * | .40 | .16 | .04 |
| ☐ | 121 | Dan Ford * | .40 | .16 | .04 |
| ☐ | 122 | Ray Fosse * | .40 | .16 | .04 |
| ☐ | 123 | George Hendrick * | .50 | .20 | .05 |
| ☐ | 124 | Alan Ashby | .30 | .12 | .03 |
| ☐ | 125 | Joe Lis | .30 | .12 | .03 |
| ☐ | 126 | Sal Bando | .40 | .16 | .04 |
| ☐ | 127 | Richie Zisk | .40 | .16 | .04 |
| ☐ | 128 | Rich Gossage | .80 | .32 | .08 |
| ☐ | 129 | Don Baylor | .50 | .20 | .05 |
| ☐ | 130 | Dave McKay | .30 | .12 | .03 |
| ☐ | 131 | Bob Grich | .40 | .16 | .04 |
| ☐ | 132 | Dave Pagan | .30 | .12 | .03 |
| ☐ | 133 | Dave Cash | .30 | .12 | .03 |
| ☐ | 123 | Steve Braun | .30 | .12 | .03 |
| ☐ | 135 | Dan Meyer | .30 | .12 | .03 |
| ☐ | 136 | Bill Stein | .30 | .12 | .03 |
| ☐ | 137 | Rollie Fingers | 1.25 | .50 | .12 |
| ☐ | 138 | Brian Downing | .50 | .20 | .05 |
| ☐ | 139 | Bill Singer | .30 | .12 | .03 |
| ☐ | 140 | Doyle Alexander | .40 | .16 | .04 |
| ☐ | 141 | Gene Tenace | .30 | .12 | .03 |
| ☐ | 142 | Gary Matthews | .40 | .16 | .04 |
| ☐ | 143 | Don Gullett | .40 | .16 | .04 |
| ☐ | 144 | Wayne Garland | .30 | .12 | .03 |
| ☐ | 145 | Pete Broberg | .30 | .12 | .03 |
| ☐ | 146 | Joe Rudi | .40 | .16 | .04 |
| ☐ | 147 | Glenn Abbott | .30 | .12 | .03 |
| ☐ | 148 | George Scott | .30 | .12 | .03 |
| ☐ | 149 | Bert Campaneris | .40 | .16 | .04 |
| ☐ | 150 | Andy Messersmith | .40 | .16 | .04 |

# 1978 Hostess

The cards in this 150 card set measure 2 1/4" by 3 1/4" individually or 3 1/4" by 7 1/4" as panels of three. The 1978 Hostess set contains full color, numbered cards issued in panels of three cards each on family packages of Hostess cake products.

TOMMY JOHN — LOS ANGELES DODGERS
GREG LUZINSKI — PHILADELPHIA PHILLIES
ENOS CABELL — HOUSTON ASTROS

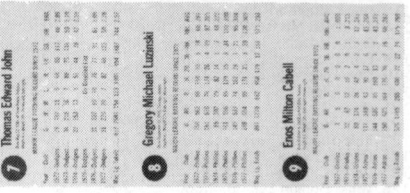

Scarcer panels are listed in the checklist with asterisks. The 1978 Hostess panels are considered by some collectors to be somewhat more difficult to obtain than Hostess panels of other years. Although complete panel prices are not explicitly listed below, they would generally have a value 25% greater than the sum of the individual players on the panel.

| | | | MINT | VG-E | F-G |
|---|---|---|------|------|-----|
| | | COMPLETE INDIV. SET | 120.00 | 50.00 | 12.00 |
| | | COMMON PLAYER | .30 | .12 | .03 |
| ☐ | 1 | Butch Hobson | .30 | .12 | .03 |
| ☐ | 2 | George Foster | 1.00 | .40 | .10 |
| ☐ | 3 | Bob Forsch | .40 | .16 | .04 |
| ☐ | 4 | Tony Perez | .75 | .30 | .07 |
| ☐ | 5 | Bruce Sutter | 1.00 | .40 | .10 |
| ☐ | 6 | Hal McRae | .40 | .16 | .04 |
| ☐ | 7 | Tommy John | .75 | .30 | .07 |
| ☐ | 8 | Greg Luzinski | .50 | .20 | .05 |
| ☐ | 9 | Enos Cabell | .30 | .12 | .03 |
| ☐ | 10 | Doug DeCinces | .50 | .20 | .05 |
| ☐ | 11 | Willie Stargell | 1.50 | .60 | .15 |
| ☐ | 12 | Ed Halicki | .30 | .12 | .03 |
| ☐ | 13 | Larry Hisle | .40 | .16 | .04 |
| ☐ | 14 | Jim Slaton | .30 | .12 | .03 |
| ☐ | 15 | Buddy Bell | .50 | .20 | .05 |
| ☐ | 16 | Earl Williams | .30 | .12 | .03 |
| ☐ | 17 | Glenn Abbott | .30 | .12 | .03 |
| ☐ | 18 | Dan Ford | .30 | .12 | .03 |
| ☐ | 19 | Gary Matthews | .40 | .16 | .04 |
| ☐ | 20 | Eric Soderholm | .30 | .12 | .03 |
| ☐ | 21 | Bump Wills | .30 | .12 | .03 |
| ☐ | 22 | Keith Hernandez | 2.50 | 1.00 | .25 |
| ☐ | 23 | Dave Cash | .30 | .12 | .03 |
| ☐ | 24 | George Scott | .30 | .12 | .03 |
| ☐ | 25 | Ron Guidry | 1.50 | .60 | .15 |
| ☐ | 26 | Dave Kingman | .60 | .24 | .06 |
| ☐ | 27 | George Brett | 5.00 | 2.00 | .50 |
| ☐ | 28 | Bob Watson * | .40 | .16 | .04 |
| ☐ | 29 | Bob Boone * | .50 | .20 | .05 |
| ☐ | 30 | Reggie Smith * | .60 | .24 | .06 |
| ☐ | 31 | Eddie Murray * | 9.00 | 3.75 | .90 |
| ☐ | 32 | Gary Lavelle * | .40 | .16 | .04 |
| ☐ | 33 | Rennie Stennett * | .40 | .16 | .04 |
| ☐ | 34 | Duane Kuiper * | .40 | .16 | .04 |
| ☐ | 35 | Sixto Lezcano * | .40 | .16 | .04 |
| ☐ | 36 | Dave Rozema * | .40 | .16 | .04 |
| ☐ | 37 | Butch Wynegar * | .50 | .20 | .05 |
| ☐ | 38 | Mitchell Page * | .40 | .16 | .04 |
| ☐ | 39 | Bill Stein * | .40 | .16 | .04 |
| ☐ | 40 | Elliott Maddox | .30 | .12 | .03 |
| ☐ | 41 | Mike Hargrove | .40 | .16 | .04 |
| ☐ | 42 | Bobby Bonds | .50 | .20 | .05 |
| ☐ | 43 | Garry Templeton | .60 | .24 | .06 |
| ☐ | 44 | Johnny Bench | 3.50 | 1.40 | .35 |
| ☐ | 45 | Jim Rice | 3.50 | 1.40 | .35 |
| ☐ | 46 | Bill Buckner | .60 | .24 | .06 |
| ☐ | 47 | Reggie Jackson | 4.00 | 1.60 | .40 |
| ☐ | 48 | Freddie Patek | .30 | .12 | .03 |
| ☐ | 49 | Steve Carlton | 3.50 | 1.40 | .35 |
| ☐ | 50 | Cesar Cedeno | .40 | .16 | .04 |
| ☐ | 51 | Steve Yeager | .30 | .12 | .03 |

| | | | | | |
|---|---|---|---|---|---|
| ☐ | 52 | Phil Garner | .30 | .12 | .03 |
| ☐ | 53 | Lee May | .40 | .16 | .04 |
| ☐ | 54 | Darrell Evans | .50 | .20 | .05 |
| ☐ | 55 | Steve Kemp | .50 | .20 | .05 |
| ☐ | 56 | Dusty Baker | .50 | .20 | .05 |
| ☐ | 57 | Ray Fosse | .30 | .12 | .03 |
| ☐ | 58 | Manny Sanguillen | .40 | .16 | .04 |
| ☐ | 59 | Tom Johnson | .30 | .12 | .03 |
| ☐ | 60 | Lee Stanton | .30 | .12 | .03 |
| ☐ | 61 | Jeff Burroughs | .40 | .16 | .04 |
| ☐ | 62 | Bobby Grich | .40 | .16 | .04 |
| ☐ | 63 | Dave Winfield | 3.00 | 1.20 | .30 |
| ☐ | 64 | Dan Driessen | .30 | .12 | .03 |
| ☐ | 65 | Ted Simmons | .75 | .30 | .07 |
| ☐ | 66 | Jerry Remy | .30 | .12 | .03 |
| ☐ | 67 | Al Cowens | .40 | .16 | .04 |
| ☐ | 68 | Sparky Lyle | .60 | .24 | .06 |
| ☐ | 69 | Manny Trillo | .40 | .16 | .04 |
| ☐ | 70 | Don Sutton | 1.50 | .60 | .15 |
| ☐ | 71 | Larry Bowa | .50 | .20 | .05 |
| ☐ | 72 | Jose Cruz | .50 | .20 | .05 |
| ☐ | 73 | Willie McCovey | 2.00 | .80 | .20 |
| ☐ | 74 | Bert Blyleven | .60 | .24 | .06 |
| ☐ | 75 | Ken Singleton | .50 | .20 | .05 |
| ☐ | 76 | Bill North | .30 | .12 | .03 |
| ☐ | 77 | Jason Thompson | .40 | .16 | .04 |
| ☐ | 78 | Dennis Eckersley | .40 | .16 | .04 |
| ☐ | 79 | Jim Sundberg | .40 | .16 | .04 |
| ☐ | 80 | Jerry Koosman | .50 | .20 | .05 |
| ☐ | 81 | Bruce Bochte | .30 | .12 | .03 |
| ☐ | 82 | George Hendrick | .40 | .16 | .04 |
| ☐ | 83 | Nolan Ryan | 3.00 | 1.20 | .30 |
| ☐ | 84 | Roy Howell | .30 | .12 | .03 |
| ☐ | 85 | Roger Metzger | .30 | .12 | .03 |
| ☐ | 86 | Doc Medich | .30 | .12 | .03 |
| ☐ | 87 | Joe Morgan | 2.00 | .80 | .20 |
| ☐ | 88 | Dennis Leonard | .40 | .16 | .04 |
| ☐ | 89 | Willie Randolph | .40 | .16 | .04 |
| ☐ | 90 | Bobby Murcer | .50 | .20 | .05 |
| ☐ | 91 | Rick Manning | .30 | .12 | .03 |
| ☐ | 92 | J.R. Richard | .40 | .16 | .04 |
| ☐ | 93 | Ron Cey | .50 | .20 | .05 |
| ☐ | 94 | Sal Bando | .40 | .16 | .04 |
| ☐ | 95 | Ron LeFlore | .40 | .16 | .04 |
| ☐ | 96 | Dave Goltz | .30 | .12 | .03 |
| ☐ | 97 | Dan Meyer | .30 | .12 | .03 |
| ☐ | 98 | Chris Chambliss | .40 | .16 | .04 |
| ☐ | 99 | Biff Pocoroba | .30 | .12 | .03 |
| ☐ | 100 | Oscar Gamble | .40 | .16 | .04 |
| ☐ | 101 | Frank Tanana | .40 | .16 | .04 |
| ☐ | 102 | Len Randle | .30 | .12 | .03 |
| ☐ | 103 | Tommy Hutton | .30 | .12 | .03 |
| ☐ | 104 | John Candelaria | .50 | .20 | .05 |
| ☐ | 105 | George Orta | .30 | .12 | .03 |
| ☐ | 106 | Ken Reitz | .30 | .12 | .03 |
| ☐ | 107 | Bill Campbell | .30 | .12 | .03 |
| ☐ | 108 | Dave Concepcion | .50 | .20 | .05 |
| ☐ | 109 | Joe Ferguson | .30 | .12 | .03 |
| ☐ | 110 | Mickey Rivers | .40 | .16 | .04 |
| ☐ | 111 | Paul Splittorff | .30 | .12 | .03 |
| ☐ | 112 | Dave Lopes | .40 | .16 | .04 |
| ☐ | 113 | Mike Schmidt | 4.50 | 1.80 | .45 |
| ☐ | 114 | Joe Rudi | .40 | .16 | .04 |
| ☐ | 115 | Milt May | .30 | .12 | .03 |
| ☐ | 116 | Jim Palmer | 2.00 | .80 | .20 |
| ☐ | 117 | Bill Madlock | 1.00 | .40 | .10 |
| ☐ | 118 | Roy Smalley | .40 | .16 | .04 |
| ☐ | 119 | Cecil Cooper | .90 | .36 | .09 |
| ☐ | 120 | Rick Langford | .30 | .12 | .03 |
| ☐ | 121 | Ruppert Jones | .40 | .16 | .04 |
| ☐ | 122 | Phil Niekro | 1.50 | .60 | .15 |
| ☐ | 123 | Toby Harrah | .40 | .16 | .04 |
| ☐ | 124 | Chet Lemon | .40 | .16 | .04 |
| ☐ | 125 | Gene Tenace | .30 | .12 | .03 |
| ☐ | 126 | Steve Henderson | .30 | .12 | .03 |
| ☐ | 127 | Mike Torrez | .30 | .12 | .03 |
| ☐ | 128 | Pete Rose | 8.00 | 3.25 | .80 |
| ☐ | 129 | John Denny | .50 | .20 | .05 |
| ☐ | 130 | Darrell Porter | .40 | .16 | .04 |
| ☐ | 131 | Rick Reuschel | .40 | .16 | .04 |
| ☐ | 132 | Graig Nettles | .75 | .30 | .07 |
| ☐ | 133 | Garry Maddox | .40 | .16 | .04 |
| ☐ | 134 | Mike Flanagan | .40 | .16 | .04 |
| ☐ | 135 | Dave Parker | 2.00 | .80 | .20 |
| ☐ | 136 | Terry Whitfield | .30 | .12 | .03 |
| ☐ | 137 | Wayne Garland | .30 | .12 | .03 |
| ☐ | 138 | Robin Yount | 3.00 | 1.20 | .30 |
| ☐ | 139 | Gaylord Perry | 1.50 | .60 | .15 |
| ☐ | 140 | Rod Carew | 3.00 | 1.20 | .30 |
| ☐ | 141 | Greg Gross | .30 | .12 | .03 |
| ☐ | 142 | Barry Bonnell | .30 | .12 | .03 |
| ☐ | 143 | Willie Montanez | .30 | .12 | .03 |
| ☐ | 144 | Rollie Fingers | 1.25 | .50 | .12 |
| ☐ | 145 | Lyman Bostock | .40 | .16 | .04 |
| ☐ | 146 | Gary Carter | 3.50 | 1.40 | .35 |
| ☐ | 147 | Ron Blomberg | .30 | .12 | .03 |
| ☐ | 148 | Bob Bailor | .30 | .12 | .03 |
| ☐ | 149 | Tom Seaver | 3.50 | 1.40 | .35 |
| ☐ | 150 | Thurman Munson | 3.00 | 1.20 | .30 |

## 1979 Hostess

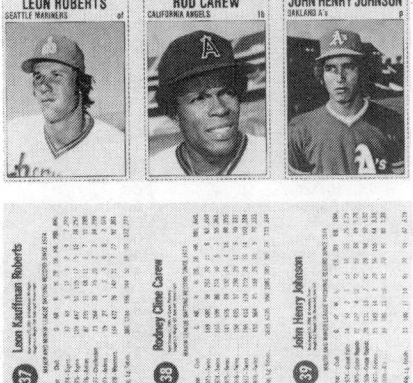

The cards in this 150 card set measure 3 1/4" by 7 1/4" as panels of three. The 1979 Hostess set contains full color, numbered cards issued in panels of three cards each on the backs of family sized Hostess cake products. Scarcer panels are listed in the checklist below with asterisks. Although complete panel prices are not explicitly listed below they would generally have a value 25% greater than the sum of the individual players on the panel.

| | | | MINT | VG-E | F-G |
|---|---|---|---|---|---|
| | COMPLETE INDIV. SET | | 120.00 | 50.00 | 12.00 |
| | COMMON PLAYER | | .30 | .12 | .03 |
| | | | | | |
| ☐ | 1 | John Denny | .40 | .16 | .04 |
| ☐ | 2 | Jim Rice | 3.50 | 1.40 | .35 |
| ☐ | 3 | Doug Bair | .30 | .12 | .03 |
| ☐ | 4 | Darrell Porter | .40 | .16 | .04 |
| ☐ | 5 | Ross Grimsley | .30 | .12 | .03 |
| ☐ | 6 | Bobby Murcer | .50 | .20 | .05 |
| ☐ | 7 | Lee Mazzilli | .30 | .12 | .03 |
| ☐ | 8 | Steve Garvey | 3.50 | 1.40 | .35 |
| ☐ | 9 | Mike Schmidt | 4.50 | 1.80 | .45 |
| ☐ | 10 | Terry Whitfield | .30 | .12 | .03 |
| ☐ | 11 | Jim Palmer | 2.50 | 1.00 | .25 |
| ☐ | 12 | Omar Moreno | .30 | .12 | .03 |
| ☐ | 13 | Duane Kuiper | .30 | .12 | .03 |
| ☐ | 14 | Mike Caldwell | .40 | .16 | .04 |
| ☐ | 15 | Steve Kemp | .50 | .20 | .05 |
| ☐ | 16 | Dave Goltz | .30 | .12 | .03 |
| ☐ | 17 | Mitchell Page | .30 | .12 | .03 |
| ☐ | 18 | Bill Stein | .30 | .12 | .03 |
| ☐ | 19 | Gene Tenace | .30 | .12 | .03 |
| ☐ | 20 | Jeff Burroughs | .40 | .16 | .04 |
| ☐ | 21 | Francisco Barrios | .30 | .12 | .03 |
| ☐ | 22 | Mike Torrez | .30 | .12 | .03 |
| ☐ | 23 | Ken Reitz | .30 | .12 | .03 |
| ☐ | 24 | Gary Carter | 3.50 | 1.40 | .35 |
| ☐ | 25 | Al Hrabosky | .40 | .16 | .04 |
| ☐ | 26 | Thurman Munson | 3.00 | 1.20 | .30 |
| ☐ | 27 | Bill Buckner | .60 | .24 | .06 |
| ☐ | 28 | Ron Cey * | .60 | .24 | .06 |
| ☐ | 29 | J.R. Richard * | .50 | .20 | .05 |
| ☐ | 30 | Greg Luzinski * | 1.00 | .40 | .10 |
| ☐ | 31 | Ed Ott * | .40 | .16 | .04 |
| ☐ | 32 | Dennis Martinez * | .40 | .16 | .04 |
| ☐ | 33 | Darrell Evans * | .60 | .24 | .06 |
| ☐ | 34 | Ron LeFlore | .40 | .16 | .04 |
| ☐ | 35 | Rick Waits | .30 | .12 | .03 |
| ☐ | 36 | Cecil Cooper | .80 | .32 | .08 |

| | | | | |
|---|---|---|---|---|
| ☐ 37 | Leon Roberts | .30 | .12 | .03 |
| ☐ 38 | Rod Carew | 3.00 | 1.20 | .30 |
| ☐ 39 | John Henry Johnson | .30 | .12 | .03 |
| ☐ 40 | Chet Lemon | .40 | .16 | .04 |
| ☐ 41 | Craig Swan | .30 | .12 | .03 |
| ☐ 42 | Gary Matthews | .40 | .16 | .04 |
| ☐ 43 | Lamar Johnson | .30 | .12 | .03 |
| ☐ 44 | Ted Simmons | .75 | .30 | .07 |
| ☐ 45 | Ken Griffey | .50 | .20 | .05 |
| ☐ 46 | Fred Patek | .30 | .12 | .03 |
| ☐ 47 | Frank Tanana | .40 | .16 | .04 |
| ☐ 48 | Goose Gossage | 1.00 | .40 | .10 |
| ☐ 49 | Burt Hooton | .30 | .12 | .03 |
| ☐ 50 | Ellis Valentine | .30 | .12 | .03 |
| ☐ 51 | Ken Forsch | .30 | .12 | .03 |
| ☐ 52 | Bob Knepper | .60 | .24 | .06 |
| ☐ 53 | Dave Parker | 2.00 | .80 | .20 |
| ☐ 54 | Doug DeCinces | .50 | .20 | .05 |
| ☐ 55 | Robin Yount | 3.00 | 1.20 | .30 |
| ☐ 56 | Rusty Staub | .50 | .20 | .05 |
| ☐ 57 | Gary Alexander | .30 | .12 | .03 |
| ☐ 58 | Julio Cruz | .30 | .12 | .03 |
| ☐ 59 | Matt Keough | .30 | .12 | .03 |
| ☐ 60 | Roy Smalley | .40 | .16 | .04 |
| ☐ 61 | Joe Morgan | 2.00 | .80 | .20 |
| ☐ 62 | Phil Niekro | 2.00 | .80 | .20 |
| ☐ 63 | Don Baylor | .50 | .20 | .05 |
| ☐ 64 | Dwight Evans | .50 | .20 | .05 |
| ☐ 65 | Tom Seaver | 3.00 | 1.20 | .30 |
| ☐ 66 | George Hendrick | .40 | .16 | .04 |
| ☐ 67 | Rick Reuschel | .40 | .16 | .04 |
| ☐ 68 | George Brett | 5.00 | 2.00 | .50 |
| ☐ 69 | Lou Piniella | .50 | .20 | .05 |
| ☐ 70 | Enos Cabell | .30 | .12 | .03 |
| ☐ 71 | Steve Carlton | 3.00 | 1.20 | .30 |
| ☐ 72 | Reggie Smith | .50 | .20 | .05 |
| ☐ 73 | Rick Dempsey * | .50 | .20 | .05 |
| ☐ 74 | Vida Blue * | .50 | .20 | .05 |
| ☐ 75 | Phil Garner * | .40 | .16 | .04 |
| ☐ 76 | Rick Manning * | .40 | .16 | .04 |
| ☐ 77 | Mark Fidrych * | .50 | .20 | .05 |
| ☐ 78 | Mario Guerrero * | .40 | .16 | .04 |
| ☐ 79 | Bob Stinson * | .40 | .16 | .04 |
| ☐ 80 | Al Oliver * | 1.00 | .40 | .10 |
| ☐ 81 | Doug Flynn * | .40 | .16 | .04 |
| ☐ 82 | John Mayberry * | .40 | .16 | .04 |
| ☐ 83 | Gaylord Perry | 1.50 | .60 | .15 |
| ☐ 84 | Joe Rudi | .40 | .16 | .04 |
| ☐ 85 | Dave Concepcion | .50 | .20 | .05 |
| ☐ 86 | John Candelaria | .40 | .16 | .04 |
| ☐ 87 | Pete Vuckovich | .40 | .16 | .04 |
| ☐ 88 | Ivan DeJesus | .30 | .12 | .03 |
| ☐ 89 | Ron Guidry | 1.50 | .60 | .15 |
| ☐ 90 | Hal McRae | .40 | .16 | .04 |
| ☐ 91 | Cesar Cedeno | .40 | .16 | .04 |
| ☐ 92 | Don Sutton | 1.50 | .60 | .15 |
| ☐ 93 | Andre Thornton | .50 | .20 | .05 |
| ☐ 94 | Roger Erickson | .30 | .12 | .03 |
| ☐ 95 | Larry Hisle | .40 | .16 | .04 |
| ☐ 96 | Jason Thompson | .40 | .16 | .04 |
| ☐ 97 | Jim Sundberg | .40 | .16 | .04 |
| ☐ 98 | Bob Horner | 3.00 | 1.20 | .30 |
| ☐ 99 | Ruppert Jones | .40 | .16 | .04 |
| ☐ 100 | Willie Montanez | .30 | .12 | .03 |
| ☐ 101 | Nolan Ryan | 3.00 | 1.20 | .30 |
| ☐ 102 | Ozzie Smith | 1.00 | .40 | .10 |
| ☐ 103 | Eric Soderholm | .30 | .12 | .03 |
| ☐ 104 | Willie Stargell | 1.50 | .60 | .15 |
| ☐ 105A | Bob Bailor ERR (reverse negative) | .50 | .20 | .05 |
| ☐ 105B | Bob Bailor COR | .75 | .30 | .07 |
| ☐ 106 | Carlton Fisk | .90 | .36 | .09 |
| ☐ 107 | George Foster | 1.00 | .40 | .10 |
| ☐ 108 | Keith Hernandez | 2.50 | 1.00 | .25 |
| ☐ 109 | Dennis Leonard | .40 | .16 | .04 |
| ☐ 110 | Graig Nettles | .80 | .32 | .08 |
| ☐ 111 | Jose Cruz | .50 | .20 | .05 |
| ☐ 112 | Bobby Grich | .40 | .16 | .04 |
| ☐ 113 | Bob Boone | .40 | .16 | .04 |
| ☐ 114 | Dave Lopes | .40 | .16 | .04 |
| ☐ 115 | Eddie Murray | 4.50 | 1.80 | .45 |
| ☐ 116 | Jack Clark | 1.25 | .50 | .12 |
| ☐ 117 | Lou Whitaker | 1.00 | .40 | .10 |
| ☐ 118 | Miguel Dilone | .30 | .12 | .03 |
| ☐ 119 | Sal Bando | .40 | .16 | .04 |
| ☐ 120 | Reggie Jackson | 4.00 | 1.60 | .40 |
| ☐ 121 | Dale Murphy | 8.00 | 3.25 | .80 |
| ☐ 122 | Jon Matlack | .40 | .16 | .04 |
| ☐ 123 | Bruce Bochte | .30 | .12 | .03 |
| ☐ 124 | John Stearns | .30 | .12 | .03 |
| ☐ 125 | Dave Winfield | 3.00 | 1.20 | .30 |
| ☐ 126 | Jorge Orta | .30 | .12 | .03 |
| ☐ 127 | Garry Templeton | .50 | .20 | .05 |

| | | | | |
|---|---|---|---|---|
| ☐ 128 | Johnny Bench | 3.00 | 1.20 | .30 |
| ☐ 129 | Butch Hobson | .30 | .12 | .03 |
| ☐ 130 | Bruce Sutter | 1.00 | .40 | .10 |
| ☐ 131 | Bucky Dent | .40 | .16 | .04 |
| ☐ 132 | Amos Otis | .40 | .16 | .04 |
| ☐ 133 | Bert Blyleven | .50 | .20 | .05 |
| ☐ 134 | Larry Bowa | .50 | .20 | .05 |
| ☐ 135 | Ken Singleton | .50 | .20 | .05 |
| ☐ 136 | Sixto Lezcano | .30 | .12 | .03 |
| ☐ 137 | Roy Howell | .30 | .12 | .03 |
| ☐ 138 | Bill Madlock | .90 | .36 | .09 |
| ☐ 139 | Dave Revering | .30 | .12 | .03 |
| ☐ 140 | Richie Zisk | .40 | .16 | .04 |
| ☐ 141 | Butch Wynegar | .40 | .16 | .04 |
| ☐ 142 | Alan Ashby | .30 | .12 | .03 |
| ☐ 143 | Sparky Lyle | .50 | .20 | .05 |
| ☐ 144 | Pete Rose | 8.00 | 3.25 | .80 |
| ☐ 145 | Dennis Eckersley | .40 | .16 | .04 |
| ☐ 146 | Dave Kingman | .60 | .24 | .06 |
| ☐ 147 | Buddy Bell | .50 | .20 | .05 |
| ☐ 148 | Mike Hargrove | .40 | .16 | .04 |
| ☐ 149 | Jerry Koosman | .50 | .20 | .05 |
| ☐ 150 | Toby Harrah | .40 | .16 | .04 |

## 1985 Hostess Braves

The cards in this 22 card set measure 2 1/2" by 3 1/2" and feature players of the Atlanta Braves. Cards were produced by Topps for Hostess (Continental Baking Co.) and are quite attractive. The card backs are similar in design to the 1985 Topps regular issue; however all photos are different from those that Topps used as these were apparently taken during Spring Training. Cards were available in boxes of Hostess products in packs of four (three players and a contest card).

| | | MINT | VG-E | F-G |
|---|---|---|---|---|
| COMPLETE SET | | 7.50 | 3.00 | .75 |
| COMMON PLAYER (1-22) | | .25 | .10 | .02 |
| ☐ 1 | Eddie Haas MGR | .25 | .10 | .02 |
| ☐ 2 | Len Barker | .25 | .10 | .02 |
| ☐ 3 | Steve Bedrosian | .25 | .10 | .02 |
| ☐ 4 | Bruce Benedict | .25 | .10 | .02 |
| ☐ 5 | Rick Camp | .25 | .10 | .02 |
| ☐ 6 | Rick Cerone | .25 | .10 | .02 |
| ☐ 7 | Chris Chambliss | .35 | .14 | .03 |
| ☐ 8 | Terry Forster | .50 | .20 | .05 |
| ☐ 9 | Gene Garber | .25 | .10 | .02 |
| ☐ 10 | Albert Hall | .25 | .10 | .02 |
| ☐ 11 | Bob Horner | .75 | .30 | .07 |
| ☐ 12 | Glenn Hubbard | .35 | .14 | .03 |
| ☐ 13 | Brad Komminsk | .35 | .14 | .03 |
| ☐ 14 | Rick Mahler | .35 | .14 | .03 |
| ☐ 15 | Craig McMurtry | .25 | .10 | .02 |
| ☐ 16 | Dale Murphy | 3.00 | 1.20 | .30 |
| ☐ 17 | Ken Oberkfell | .25 | .10 | .02 |
| ☐ 18 | Pascual Perez | .25 | .10 | .02 |
| ☐ 19 | Gerald Perry | .25 | .10 | .02 |
| ☐ 20 | Rafael Ramirez | .25 | .10 | .02 |
| ☐ 21 | Bruce Sutter | .65 | .26 | .06 |
| ☐ 22 | Claudell Washington | .35 | .14 | .03 |

# 1953 Hunters

The cards in this 26 card set measure 2 1/4" by 3 1/2". The 1953 Hunter's Wieners set of full color, blank backed unnumbered cards feature St. Louis Cardinal players only. The cards have red borders and were issued in panels of two on hot dog packages. The ACC designation is F153-1. The list below is numbered according to alphabetical order.

|  |  | MINT | VG-E | F-G |
|---|---|---|---|---|
|  | COMPLETE SET | 2000.00 | 900.00 | 225.00 |
|  | COMMON PLAYER (1-26) | 50.00 | 20.00 | 5.00 |
| ☐ 1 | Steve Bilko | 50.00 | 20.00 | 5.00 |
| ☐ 2 | Alpha Brazle | 50.00 | 20.00 | 5.00 |
| ☐ 3 | Cloyd Boyer | 60.00 | 24.00 | 6.00 |
| ☐ 4 | Cliff Chambers | 50.00 | 20.00 | 5.00 |
| ☐ 5 | Mike Clark | 50.00 | 20.00 | 5.00 |
| ☐ 6 | Jack Crimian | 50.00 | 20.00 | 5.00 |
| ☐ 7 | Les Fusselman | 50.00 | 20.00 | 5.00 |
| ☐ 8 | Harvey Haddix | 75.00 | 30.00 | 7.50 |
| ☐ 9 | Solly Hemus | 50.00 | 20.00 | 5.00 |
| ☐ 10 | Ray Jablonski | 50.00 | 20.00 | 5.00 |
| ☐ 11 | Will Johnson | 50.00 | 20.00 | 5.00 |
| ☐ 12 | Harry Lowrey | 50.00 | 20.00 | 5.00 |
| ☐ 13 | Larry Miggins | 50.00 | 20.00 | 5.00 |
| ☐ 14 | Stuart Miller | 60.00 | 24.00 | 6.00 |
| ☐ 15 | Wilmer Mizell | 60.00 | 24.00 | 6.00 |
| ☐ 16 | Stan Musial | 650.00 | 260.00 | 65.00 |
| ☐ 17 | Joe Presko | 50.00 | 20.00 | 5.00 |
| ☐ 18 | Del Rice | 50.00 | 20.00 | 5.00 |
| ☐ 19 | Hal Rice | 50.00 | 20.00 | 5.00 |
| ☐ 20 | Willard Schmidt | 50.00 | 20.00 | 5.00 |
| ☐ 21 | Al Schoendienst | 100.00 | 40.00 | 10.00 |
| ☐ 22 | Dick Sisler | 50.00 | 20.00 | 5.00 |
| ☐ 23 | Enos Slaughter | 150.00 | 60.00 | 15.00 |
| ☐ 24 | Gerry Staley | 50.00 | 20.00 | 5.00 |
| ☐ 25 | Ed Stanky | 75.00 | 30.00 | 7.50 |
| ☐ 26 | John Yuhas | 50.00 | 20.00 | 5.00 |

# 1954 Hunters

The cards in this 30 card set measure 2 1/4" by 3 1/2". The 1954 Hunter's Wieners set of full color, blank backed, unnumbered cards features St. Louis Cardinals only. They were issued in pairs on the backs of hot dog packages as in 1953; however one of the cards is a statistical record of the player's career. The poses are very similar to those used in the 1953 set; however, there are captions which read "What's My Name" and "What's My Record." The ACC designation is F153-2.

|  |  | MINT | VG-E | F-G |
|---|---|---|---|---|
|  | COMPLETE SET | 2700.00 | 1250.00 | 300.00 |
|  | COMMON PLAYER (1-30) | 75.00 | 30.00 | 7.50 |
| ☐ 1 | Tom Alston | 75.00 | 30.00 | 7.50 |
| ☐ 2 | Steve Bilko | 75.00 | 30.00 | 7.50 |
| ☐ 3 | Alpha Brazle | 75.00 | 30.00 | 7.50 |
| ☐ 4 | Tom Burgess | 75.00 | 30.00 | 7.50 |
| ☐ 5 | Cot Deal | 75.00 | 30.00 | 7.50 |
| ☐ 6 | Alex Grammas | 75.00 | 30.00 | 7.50 |
| ☐ 7 | Harvey Haddix | 90.00 | 36.00 | 9.00 |
| ☐ 8 | Solly Hemus | 75.00 | 30.00 | 7.50 |
| ☐ 9 | Ray Jablonski | 75.00 | 30.00 | 7.50 |
| ☐ 10 | Royce Lint | 75.00 | 30.00 | 7.50 |
| ☐ 11 | Harry Lowrey | 75.00 | 30.00 | 7.50 |
| ☐ 12 | Memo Luna | 75.00 | 30.00 | 7.50 |
| ☐ 13 | Stu Miller | 90.00 | 36.00 | 9.00 |
| ☐ 14 | Stan Musial | 800.00 | 320.00 | 80.00 |
| ☐ 15 | Tom Poholsky | 75.00 | 30.00 | 7.50 |
| ☐ 16 | Bill Posedel | 75.00 | 30.00 | 7.50 |
| ☐ 17 | Joe Presko | 75.00 | 30.00 | 7.50 |
| ☐ 18 | Vic Raschi | 100.00 | 40.00 | 10.00 |
| ☐ 19 | Dick Rand | 75.00 | 30.00 | 7.50 |
| ☐ 20 | Rip Repulski | 75.00 | 30.00 | 7.50 |
| ☐ 21 | Del Rice | 75.00 | 30.00 | 7.50 |

| ☐ 22 | John Riddle | 75.00 | 30.00 | 7.50 |
|---|---|---|---|---|
| ☐ 23 | Mike Ryba | 75.00 | 30.00 | 7.50 |
| ☐ 24 | Al Schoendienst | 125.00 | 50.00 | 12.50 |
| ☐ 25 | Dick Schofield | 90.00 | 36.00 | 9.00 |
| ☐ 26 | Enos Slaughter | 175.00 | 70.00 | 18.00 |
| ☐ 27 | Gerry Staley | 75.00 | 30.00 | 7.50 |
| ☐ 28 | Ed Stanky | 90.00 | 36.00 | 9.00 |
| ☐ 29 | Ed Yuhas | 75.00 | 30.00 | 7.50 |
| ☐ 30 | Sal Yvars | 75.00 | 30.00 | 7.50 |

# 1955 Hunters

The cards in this 30 card set measure 2" by 4 3/4". The 1955 Hunter's Wieners set of full color, blank back, unnumbered cards features St. Louis Cardinals only. This year presented a different format from the previous two years in that there are two pictures on the front of each card, one full figure shot and a close up bust shot. The card was actually the side panel of the hot dog package rather than the back as in the previous two years. The ACC designation of this scarce regional issue is F153-3.

|  |  | MINT | VG-E | F-G |
|---|---|---|---|---|
|  | COMPLETE SET | 2700.00 | 1250.00 | 300.00 |
|  | COMMON PLAYER (1-30) | 75.00 | 30.00 | 7.50 |
| ☐ 1 | Tom Alston | 75.00 | 30.00 | 7.50 |
| ☐ 2 | Ken Boyer | 150.00 | 60.00 | 15.00 |
| ☐ 3 | Harry Elliott | 75.00 | 30.00 | 7.50 |
| ☐ 4 | Jack Faszholz | 75.00 | 30.00 | 7.50 |
| ☐ 5 | Joe Frazier | 75.00 | 30.00 | 7.50 |
| ☐ 6 | Alex Grammas | 75.00 | 30.00 | 7.50 |
| ☐ 7 | Harvey Haddix | 90.00 | 36.00 | 9.00 |
| ☐ 8 | Solly Hemus | 75.00 | 30.00 | 7.50 |
| ☐ 9 | Larry Jackson | 75.00 | 30.00 | 7.50 |
| ☐ 10 | Tony Jacobs | 75.00 | 30.00 | 7.50 |
| ☐ 11 | Gordon Jones | 75.00 | 30.00 | 7.50 |
| ☐ 12 | Paul LaPalme | 75.00 | 30.00 | 7.50 |
| ☐ 13 | Brooks Lawrence | 75.00 | 30.00 | 7.50 |
| ☐ 14 | Wally Moon | 90.00 | 36.00 | 9.00 |
| ☐ 15 | Stan Musial | 850.00 | 340.00 | 85.00 |
| ☐ 16 | Tom Poholsky | 75.00 | 30.00 | 7.50 |
| ☐ 17 | Bill Posedel | 75.00 | 30.00 | 7.50 |
| ☐ 18 | Vic Raschi | 100.00 | 40.00 | 10.00 |
| ☐ 19 | Rip Repulski | 75.00 | 30.00 | 7.50 |
| ☐ 20 | Del Rice | 75.00 | 30.00 | 7.50 |
| ☐ 21 | John Riddle | 75.00 | 30.00 | 7.50 |
| ☐ 22 | Bill Sarni | 75.00 | 30.00 | 7.50 |
| ☐ 23 | Al Schoendienst | 125.00 | 50.00 | 12.50 |
| ☐ 24 | Dick Schofield | 90.00 | 36.00 | 9.00 |
| ☐ 25 | Frank Smith | 75.00 | 30.00 | 7.50 |
| ☐ 26 | Ed Stanky | 90.00 | 36.00 | 9.00 |
| ☐ 27 | Bob Tiefenauer | 75.00 | 30.00 | 7.50 |
| ☐ 28 | Bill Virdon | 125.00 | 50.00 | 12.50 |
| ☐ 29 | Fred Walker | 75.00 | 30.00 | 7.50 |
| ☐ 30 | Floyd Woolridge | 75.00 | 30.00 | 7.50 |

# 1962 Jello

The cards in this 200 card (only 197 were ever issued) set measure 2 1/2" by 3 3/8". The 1962 Jello set has the same checklist as the Post Cereal set of the same year, but is considered by some to be a test issue. The cards are grouped numerically by team, for example, New York Yankees (1-13), Detroit (14-26), Baltimore (27-36), Cleveland (37-45), Chicago White Sox (46-55), Boston (56-64), Washington (65-73), Los Angeles Angels (74-82), Minnesota (83-91), Kansas City (92-100), Los Angeles Dodgers (101-115), Cincinnati (116-130), San Francisco (131-144), Milwaukee (145-157), St. Louis (158-168), Pittsburgh (169-181), Chicago

Cubs (182-191), and Philadelphia (192-200). Although the players and numbers are identical in both sets, the Jello series has its own list of scarce and difficult cards. Numbers 29, 82 and 176 were never issued. A Jello card is easily distinguished from its counterpart in Post by the absence of the Post logo. The catalog designation is F229-1.

| | | MINT | VG-E | F-G |
|---|---|---|---|---|
| COMPLETE SET | | 2500.00 | 1000.00 | 300.00 |
| COMMON PLAYER (1-200) | | 3.50 | 1.40 | .35 |

| | | MINT | VG-E | F-G |
|---|---|---|---|---|
| ☐ 1 | Bill Skowron | 15.00 | 6.00 | 1.50 |
| ☐ 2 | Bobby Richardson | 15.00 | 6.00 | 1.50 |
| ☐ 3 | Cletis Boyer | 6.00 | 2.40 | .60 |
| ☐ 4 | Tony Kubek | 9.00 | 3.75 | .90 |
| ☐ 5 | Mickey Mantle | 200.00 | 80.00 | 20.00 |
| ☐ 6 | Roger Maris | 30.00 | 12.00 | 3.00 |
| ☐ 7 | Yogi Berra | 30.00 | 12.00 | 3.00 |
| ☐ 8 | Elston Howard | 6.00 | 2.40 | .60 |
| ☐ 9 | Whitey Ford | 25.00 | 10.00 | 2.50 |
| ☐ 10 | Ralph Terry | 5.00 | 2.00 | .50 |
| ☐ 11 | John Blanchard | 5.00 | 2.00 | .50 |
| ☐ 12 | Luis Arroyo | 5.00 | 2.00 | .50 |
| ☐ 13 | Bill Stafford | 10.00 | 4.00 | 1.00 |
| ☐ 14 | Norm Cash | 4.50 | 1.80 | .45 |
| ☐ 15 | Jake Wood | 3.50 | 1.40 | .35 |
| ☐ 16 | Steve Boros | 3.50 | 1.40 | .35 |
| ☐ 17 | Chico Fernandez | 3.50 | 1.40 | .35 |
| ☐ 18 | Bill Bruton | 3.50 | 1.40 | .35 |
| ☐ 19 | Ken Aspromonte | 3.50 | 1.40 | .35 |
| ☐ 20 | Al Kaline | 25.00 | 10.00 | 2.50 |
| ☐ 21 | Dick Brown | 3.50 | 1.40 | .35 |
| ☐ 22 | Frank Lary | 4.50 | 1.80 | .45 |
| ☐ 23 | Don Mossi | 4.50 | 1.80 | .45 |
| ☐ 24 | Phil Regan | 3.50 | 1.40 | .35 |
| ☐ 25 | Charley Maxwell | 3.50 | 1.40 | .35 |
| ☐ 26 | Jim Bunning | 12.00 | 5.00 | 1.20 |
| ☐ 27 | Jim Gentile | 4.50 | 1.80 | .45 |
| ☐ 28 | Marv Breeding | 4.50 | 1.80 | .45 |
| ☐ 29 | Not issued | .00 | .00 | .00 |
| ☐ 30 | Ron Hansen | 4.50 | 1.80 | .45 |
| ☐ 31 | Jackie Brandt | 12.00 | 5.00 | 1.20 |
| ☐ 32 | Dick Williams | 4.50 | 1.80 | .45 |
| ☐ 33 | Gus Triandos | 4.50 | 1.80 | .45 |
| ☐ 34 | Milt Pappas | 4.50 | 1.80 | .45 |
| ☐ 35 | Hoyt Wilhelm | 20.00 | 8.00 | 2.00 |
| ☐ 36 | Chuck Estrada | 4.50 | 1.80 | .45 |
| ☐ 37 | Vic Power | 3.50 | 1.40 | .35 |
| ☐ 38 | Johnny Temple | 3.50 | 1.40 | .35 |
| ☐ 39 | Bubba Phillips | 15.00 | 6.00 | 1.50 |
| ☐ 40 | Tito Francona | 4.50 | 1.80 | .45 |
| ☐ 41 | Willie Kirkland | 3.50 | 1.40 | .35 |
| ☐ 42 | John Romano | 3.50 | 1.40 | .35 |
| ☐ 43 | Jim Perry | 4.50 | 1.80 | .45 |
| ☐ 44 | Woodie Held | 3.50 | 1.40 | .35 |
| ☐ 45 | Chuck Essegian | 3.50 | 1.40 | .35 |
| ☐ 46 | Roy Sievers | 4.50 | 1.80 | .45 |
| ☐ 47 | Nellie Fox | 8.00 | 3.25 | .80 |
| ☐ 48 | Al Smith | 3.50 | 1.40 | .35 |
| ☐ 49 | Luis Aparicio | 15.00 | 6.00 | 1.50 |
| ☐ 50 | Jim Landis | 3.50 | 1.40 | .35 |
| ☐ 51 | Minnie Minoso | 6.00 | 2.40 | .60 |
| ☐ 52 | Andy Carey | 12.00 | 5.00 | 1.20 |
| ☐ 53 | Sherman Lollar | 3.50 | 1.40 | .35 |
| ☐ 54 | Bill Pierce | 4.50 | 1.80 | .45 |
| ☐ 55 | Early Wynn | 12.00 | 5.00 | 1.20 |
| ☐ 56 | Chuck Schilling | 15.00 | 6.00 | 1.50 |
| ☐ 57 | Pete Runnels | 6.00 | 2.40 | .60 |
| ☐ 58 | Frank Malzone | 6.00 | 2.40 | .60 |
| ☐ 59 | Don Buddin | 7.00 | 2.80 | .70 |
| ☐ 60 | Gary Geiger | 15.00 | 6.00 | 1.50 |
| ☐ 61 | Carl Yastrzemski | 150.00 | 60.00 | 15.00 |
| ☐ 62 | Jackie Jensen | 15.00 | 6.00 | 1.50 |
| ☐ 63 | Jim Pagliaroni | 15.00 | 6.00 | 1.50 |
| ☐ 64 | Don Schwall | 6.00 | 2.40 | .60 |
| ☐ 65 | Dale Long | 6.00 | 2.40 | .60 |
| ☐ 66 | Chuck Cottier | 6.00 | 2.40 | .60 |
| ☐ 67 | Billy Klaus | 12.00 | 5.00 | 1.20 |
| ☐ 68 | Coot Veal | 6.00 | 2.40 | .60 |
| ☐ 69 | Marty Keough | 20.00 | 8.00 | 2.00 |
| ☐ 70 | Willie Tasby | 20.00 | 8.00 | 2.00 |
| ☐ 71 | Gene Woodling | 6.00 | 2.40 | .60 |
| ☐ 72 | Gene Green | 20.00 | 8.00 | 2.00 |
| ☐ 73 | Dick Donovan | 6.00 | 2.40 | .60 |
| ☐ 74 | Steve Bilko | 6.00 | 2.40 | .60 |
| ☐ 75 | Rocky Bridges | 15.00 | 6.00 | 1.50 |
| ☐ 76 | Eddie Yost | 8.00 | 3.25 | .80 |
| ☐ 77 | Leon Wagner | 8.00 | 3.25 | .80 |
| ☐ 78 | Albie Pearson | 6.00 | 2.40 | .60 |
| ☐ 79 | Ken Hunt | 8.00 | 3.25 | .80 |
| ☐ 80 | Earl Averill | 20.00 | 8.00 | 2.00 |
| ☐ 81 | Ryne Duren | 6.00 | 2.40 | .60 |
| ☐ 82 | Not issued | .00 | .00 | .00 |
| ☐ 83 | Bob Allison | 3.50 | 1.40 | .35 |
| ☐ 84 | Billy Martin | 9.00 | 3.75 | .90 |
| ☐ 85 | Harmon Killebrew | 20.00 | 8.00 | 2.00 |
| ☐ 86 | Zoilo Versalles | 4.50 | 1.80 | .45 |
| ☐ 87 | Lenny Green | 15.00 | 6.00 | 1.50 |
| ☐ 88 | Bill Tuttle | 4.50 | 1.80 | .45 |
| ☐ 89 | Jim Lemon | 3.50 | 1.40 | .35 |
| ☐ 90 | Earl Battey | 12.00 | 5.00 | 1.20 |
| ☐ 91 | Camilo Pascual | 4.50 | 1.80 | .45 |
| ☐ 92 | Norm Sieburn | 6.00 | 2.40 | .60 |
| ☐ 93 | Jerry Lumpe | 6.00 | 2.40 | .60 |
| ☐ 94 | Dick Howser | 7.00 | 2.80 | .70 |
| ☐ 95 | Gene Stephens | 20.00 | 8.00 | 2.00 |
| ☐ 96 | Leo Posada | 8.00 | 3.25 | .80 |
| ☐ 97 | Joe Pignatano | 6.00 | 2.40 | .60 |
| ☐ 98 | Jim Archer | 6.00 | 2.40 | .60 |
| ☐ 99 | Haywood Sullivan | 15.00 | 6.00 | 1.50 |
| ☐ 100 | Art Ditmar | 6.00 | 2.40 | .60 |
| ☐ 101 | Gil Hodges | 20.00 | 8.00 | 2.00 |
| ☐ 102 | Charlie Neal | 6.00 | 2.40 | .60 |
| ☐ 103 | Daryl Spencer | 6.00 | 2.40 | .60 |
| ☐ 104 | Maury Wills | 12.00 | 5.00 | 1.20 |
| ☐ 105 | Tommy Davis | 8.00 | 3.25 | .80 |
| ☐ 106 | Willie Davis | 8.00 | 3.25 | .80 |
| ☐ 107 | John Roseboro | 20.00 | 8.00 | 2.00 |
| ☐ 108 | John Podres | 8.00 | 3.25 | .80 |
| ☐ 109 | Sandy Koufax | 40.00 | 16.00 | 4.00 |
| ☐ 110 | Don Drysdale | 30.00 | 12.00 | 3.00 |
| ☐ 111 | Larry Sherry | 12.00 | 5.00 | 1.20 |
| ☐ 112 | Jim Gilliam | 15.00 | 6.00 | 1.50 |
| ☐ 113 | Norm Larker | 30.00 | 12.00 | 3.00 |
| ☐ 114 | Duke Snider | 40.00 | 16.00 | 4.00 |
| ☐ 115 | Stan Williams | 15.00 | 6.00 | 1.50 |
| ☐ 116 | Gordy Coleman | 40.00 | 16.00 | 4.00 |
| ☐ 117 | Don Blasingame | 15.00 | 6.00 | 1.50 |
| ☐ 118 | Gene Freese | 30.00 | 12.00 | 3.00 |
| ☐ 119 | Ed Kasko | 30.00 | 12.00 | 3.00 |
| ☐ 120 | Gus Bell | 15.00 | 6.00 | 1.50 |
| ☐ 121 | Vada Pinson | 8.00 | 3.25 | .80 |
| ☐ 122 | Frank Robinson | 15.00 | 6.00 | 1.50 |
| ☐ 123 | Bob Purkey | 6.00 | 2.40 | .60 |
| ☐ 124 | Joey Jay | 6.00 | 2.40 | .60 |
| ☐ 125 | Jim Brosnan | 6.00 | 2.40 | .60 |
| ☐ 126 | Jim O'Toole | 6.00 | 2.40 | .60 |
| ☐ 127 | Jerry Lynch | 6.00 | 2.40 | .60 |
| ☐ 128 | Wally Post | 6.00 | 2.40 | .60 |
| ☐ 129 | Ken Hunt | 6.00 | 2.40 | .60 |
| ☐ 130 | Jerry Zimmerman | 6.00 | 2.40 | .60 |
| ☐ 131 | Willie McCovey | 25.00 | 10.00 | 2.50 |
| ☐ 132 | Jose Pagan | 15.00 | 6.00 | 1.50 |
| ☐ 133 | Felipe Alou | 7.00 | 2.80 | .70 |
| ☐ 134 | Jim Davenport | 8.00 | 3.25 | .80 |
| ☐ 135 | Harvey Kuenn | 8.00 | 3.25 | .80 |
| ☐ 136 | Orlando Cepeda | 10.00 | 4.00 | 1.00 |
| ☐ 137 | Ed Bailey | 7.00 | 2.80 | .70 |
| ☐ 138 | Sam Jones | 7.00 | 2.80 | .70 |
| ☐ 139 | Mike McCormick | 7.00 | 2.80 | .70 |
| ☐ 140 | Juan Marichal | 25.00 | 10.00 | 2.50 |
| ☐ 141 | Jack Sanford | 6.00 | 2.40 | .60 |
| ☐ 142 | Willie Mays | 75.00 | 30.00 | 7.50 |
| ☐ 143 | Stu Miller | 45.00 | 18.00 | 4.50 |
| ☐ 144 | Joe Amalfitano | 6.00 | 2.40 | .60 |
| ☐ 145 | Joe Adcock | 4.50 | 1.80 | .45 |
| ☐ 146 | Frank Bolling | 4.50 | 1.80 | .45 |
| ☐ 147 | Ed Mathews | 15.00 | 6.00 | 1.50 |
| ☐ 148 | Roy McMillan | 3.50 | 1.40 | .35 |
| ☐ 149 | Hank Aaron | 75.00 | 30.00 | 7.50 |
| ☐ 150 | Gino Cimoli | 12.00 | 5.00 | 1.20 |
| ☐ 151 | Frank Thomas | 4.50 | 1.80 | .45 |
| ☐ 152 | Joe Torre | 7.00 | 2.80 | .70 |
| ☐ 153 | Lew Burdette | 7.00 | 2.80 | .70 |
| ☐ 154 | Bob Buhl | 3.50 | 1.40 | .35 |

| | | | | |
|---|---|---|---|---|
| ☐ 155 | Carlton Willey | 3.50 | 1.40 | .35 |
| ☐ 156 | Lee Maye | 12.00 | 5.00 | 1.20 |
| ☐ 157 | Al Spangler | 25.00 | 10.00 | 2.50 |
| ☐ 158 | Bill White | 25.00 | 10.00 | 2.50 |
| ☐ 159 | Ken Boyer | 10.00 | 4.00 | 1.00 |
| ☐ 160 | Joe Cunningham | 6.00 | 2.40 | .60 |
| ☐ 161 | Carl Warwick | 7.00 | 2.80 | .70 |
| ☐ 162 | Carl Sawatski | 4.50 | 1.80 | .45 |
| ☐ 163 | Lindy McDaniel | 4.50 | 1.80 | .45 |
| ☐ 164 | Ernie Broglio | 7.00 | 2.80 | .70 |
| ☐ 165 | Larry Jackson | 4.50 | 1.80 | .45 |
| ☐ 166 | Curt Flood | 10.00 | 4.00 | 1.00 |
| ☐ 167 | Curt Simmons | 20.00 | 8.00 | 2.00 |
| ☐ 168 | Alex Grammas | 15.00 | 6.00 | 1.50 |
| ☐ 169 | Dick Stuart | 4.50 | 1.80 | .45 |
| ☐ 170 | Bill Mazeroski | 15.00 | 6.00 | 1.50 |
| ☐ 171 | Don Hoak | 7.00 | 2.80 | .70 |
| ☐ 172 | Dick Groat | 8.00 | 3.25 | .80 |
| ☐ 173 | Roberto Clemente | 75.00 | 30.00 | 7.50 |
| ☐ 174 | Bob Skinner | 15.00 | 6.00 | 1.50 |
| ☐ 175 | Bill Virdon | 20.00 | 8.00 | 2.00 |
| ☐ 176 | Not issued | 0.00 | .00 | .00 |
| ☐ 177 | Elroy Face | 7.00 | 2.80 | .70 |
| ☐ 178 | Bob Friend | 4.50 | 1.80 | .45 |
| ☐ 179 | Vernon Law | 15.00 | 6.00 | 1.50 |
| ☐ 180 | Harvey Haddix | 20.00 | 8.00 | 2.00 |
| ☐ 181 | Hal Smith | 15.00 | 6.00 | 1.50 |
| ☐ 182 | Ed Bouchee | 15.00 | 6.00 | 1.50 |
| ☐ 183 | Don Zimmer | 4.50 | 1.80 | .45 |
| ☐ 184 | Ron Santo | 6.00 | 2.40 | .60 |
| ☐ 185 | Andre Rodgers | 3.50 | 1.40 | .35 |
| ☐ 186 | Richie Ashburn | 10.00 | 4.00 | 1.00 |
| ☐ 187 | George Altman | 3.50 | 1.40 | .35 |
| ☐ 188 | Ernie Banks | 15.00 | 6.00 | 1.50 |
| ☐ 189 | Sam Taylor | 4.50 | 1.80 | .45 |
| ☐ 190 | Don Elston | 3.50 | 1.40 | .35 |
| ☐ 191 | Jerry Kindall | 12.00 | 5.00 | 1.20 |
| ☐ 192 | Pancho Herrera | 3.50 | 1.40 | .35 |
| ☐ 193 | Tony Taylor | 3.50 | 1.40 | .35 |
| ☐ 194 | Ruben Amaro | 12.00 | 5.00 | 1.20 |
| ☐ 195 | Don Demeter | 3.50 | 1.40 | .35 |
| ☐ 196 | Bobby Gene Smith | 3.50 | 1.40 | .35 |
| ☐ 197 | Clay Dalrymple | 3.50 | 1.40 | .35 |
| ☐ 198 | Robin Roberts | 12.00 | 5.00 | 1.20 |
| ☐ 199 | Art Mahaffey | 3.50 | 1.40 | .35 |
| ☐ 200 | John Buzhardt | 3.50 | 1.40 | .35 |

## 1963 Jello

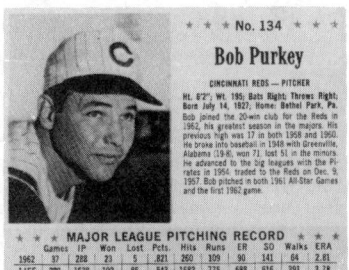

★ ★ ★ No. 134 ★ ★ ★
### Bob Purkey
CINCINNATI REDS — PITCHER
Ht. 6'2"; Wt. 195; Bats Right; Throws Right;
Born July 14, 1927; Home: Bethel Park, Pa.
Bob joined the 20-win club for the Reds in
1962, his greatest season in the majors. His
previous high was 17 in both 1958 and 1960.
He broke into baseball in 1948 with Greenville,
Alabama (19-8), won 21, lost 51 in the minors.
He advanced to the big leagues with the Pi-
rates in 1954 traded to the Reds on Dec. 9,
1957. Bob pitched in both 1961 All-Star Games
and the first 1962 game.

★ ★ ★ MAJOR LEAGUE PITCHING RECORD ★ ★ ★

| | Games | IP | Won | Lost | Pct's. | Hits | Runs | ER | SO | Walks | ERA |
|---|---|---|---|---|---|---|---|---|---|---|---|
| 1962 | 37 | 288 | 23 | 5 | .821 | 260 | 109 | 90 | 141 | 64 | 2.81 |
| LIFE | 289 | 1638 | 102 | 85 | .543 | 1682 | 775 | 688 | 816 | 391 | 3.78 |

The cards in this 200 card set measure 2 1/2" by
3 3/8". The 1963 Jello set contains the same
players and numbers as the Post Cereal set of the
same year. The players are grouped by team with
American Leaguers comprising 1-100 and National
Leaguers 101-200. The ordering of teams is as
follows: Minnesota (1-11), New York Yankees, Los
Angeles Angels (24-34), Chicago White Sox (35-45),
Detroit (46-56), Baltimore (57-66), Cleveland (67-
76), Boston (77-84), Kansas City (85-92),
Washington (93-100), San Francisco (101-112), Los
Angeles Dodgers (113-124), Cincinnati (125-136),
Pittsburgh (137-147), Milwaukee (148-157), St.
Louis (158-168), Chicago Cubs (169-176),
Philadelphia (177- 184), Houston (185-192), and

New York Mets (193-200). As in 1962, the Jello
series has its own list of scarcities (many resulting
from an unpopular package size) and these are
marked with an asterisk in the checklist. Since the
Post Cereal logo was removed from the 1963 cereal
set, Jello cards are primarily distinguishable by (1)
smaller card size and (2) smaller print. The catalog
designation is F229-2.

| | | MINT | VG-E | F-G |
|---|---|---|---|---|
| COMPLETE SET | | 1500.00 | 650.00 | 175.00 |
| COMMON PLAYER (1-200) | | 1.00 | .40 | .10 |
| ☐ | 1 Vic Power | 1.00 | .40 | .10 |
| ☐ | 2 Bernie Allen * | 12.00 | 5.00 | 1.20 |
| ☐ | 3 Zoilo Versalles * | 16.00 | 6.50 | 1.60 |
| ☐ | 4 Rich Rollins | 1.00 | .40 | .10 |
| ☐ | 5 Harmon Killebrew | 4.00 | 1.60 | .40 |
| ☐ | 6 Lenny Green * | 16.00 | 6.50 | 1.60 |
| ☐ | 7 Bob Allison | 1.25 | .50 | .12 |
| ☐ | 8 Earl Battey * | 9.00 | 3.75 | .90 |
| ☐ | 9 Camilo Pascual | 1.25 | .50 | .12 |
| ☐ | 10 Jim Kaat * | 25.00 | 10.00 | 2.50 |
| ☐ | 11 Jack Kralick | 1.00 | .40 | .10 |
| ☐ | 12 Bill Skowron * | 12.00 | 5.00 | 1.20 |
| ☐ | 13 Bobby Richardson | 1.50 | .60 | .15 |
| ☐ | 14 Cletis Boyer | 1.25 | .50 | .12 |
| ☐ | 15 Mickey Mantle | 75.00 | 30.00 | 7.50 |
| ☐ | 16 Roger Maris | 8.00 | 3.25 | .80 |
| ☐ | 17 Yogi Berra | 8.00 | 3.25 | .80 |
| ☐ | 18 Elston Howard * | 16.00 | 6.50 | 1.60 |
| ☐ | 19 Whitey Ford | 4.00 | 1.60 | .40 |
| ☐ | 20 Ralph Terry | 1.00 | .40 | .10 |
| ☐ | 21 John Blanchard * | 9.00 | 3.75 | .90 |
| ☐ | 22 Bill Stafford * | 16.00 | 6.50 | 1.60 |
| ☐ | 23 Tom Tresh | 1.25 | .50 | .12 |
| ☐ | 24 Steve Bilko | 1.00 | .40 | .10 |
| ☐ | 25 Bill Moran | 1.00 | .40 | .10 |
| ☐ | 26 Joe Koppe | 1.00 | .40 | .10 |
| ☐ | 27 Felix Torres | 1.00 | .40 | .10 |
| ☐ | 28 Leon Wagner | 1.00 | .40 | .10 |
| ☐ | 29 Albie Pearson | 1.00 | .40 | .10 |
| ☐ | 30 Lee Thomas | 1.00 | .40 | .10 |
| ☐ | 31 Bob Rodgers * | 16.00 | 6.50 | 1.60 |
| ☐ | 32 Dean Chance | 1.25 | .50 | .12 |
| ☐ | 33 Ken McBride * | 16.00 | 6.50 | 1.60 |
| ☐ | 34 George Thomas * | 16.00 | 6.50 | 1.60 |
| ☐ | 35 Joe Cunningham * | 16.00 | 6.50 | 1.60 |
| ☐ | 36 Nelson Fox | 2.00 | .80 | .20 |
| ☐ | 37 Luis Aparicio | 3.00 | 1.20 | .30 |
| ☐ | 38 Al Smith | 1.00 | .40 | .10 |
| ☐ | 39 Floyd Robinson | 1.00 | .40 | .10 |
| ☐ | 40 Jim Landis | 1.00 | .40 | .10 |
| ☐ | 41 Charlie Maxwell | 1.00 | .40 | .10 |
| ☐ | 42 Sherman Lollar | 1.25 | .50 | .12 |
| ☐ | 43 Early Wynn | 2.50 | 1.00 | .25 |
| ☐ | 44 Juan Pizarro * | 12.00 | 5.00 | 1.20 |
| ☐ | 45 Ray Herbert * | 16.00 | 6.50 | 1.60 |
| ☐ | 46 Norm Cash | 1.50 | .60 | .15 |
| ☐ | 47 Steve Boros * | 20.00 | 8.00 | 2.00 |
| ☐ | 48 Dick McAuliffe | 1.00 | .40 | .10 |
| ☐ | 49 Bill Bruton * | 12.00 | 5.00 | 1.20 |
| ☐ | 50 Rocky Colavito | 2.00 | .80 | .20 |
| ☐ | 51 Al Kaline | 8.00 | 3.25 | .80 |
| ☐ | 52 Dick Brown * | 16.00 | 6.50 | 1.60 |
| ☐ | 53 Jim Bunning | 2.00 | .80 | .20 |
| ☐ | 54 Hank Aguirre | 1.00 | .40 | .10 |
| ☐ | 55 Frank Lary * | 16.00 | 6.50 | 1.60 |
| ☐ | 56 Don Mossi * | 16.00 | 6.50 | 1.60 |
| ☐ | 57 Jim Gentile | 1.25 | .50 | .12 |
| ☐ | 58 Jackie Brandt | 1.00 | .40 | .10 |
| ☐ | 59 Brooks Robinson | 8.00 | 3.25 | .80 |
| ☐ | 60 Ron Hanson | 1.00 | .40 | .10 |
| ☐ | 61 Jerry Adair * | 30.00 | 12.00 | 3.00 |
| ☐ | 62 John"Boog" Powell | 2.00 | .80 | .20 |
| ☐ | 63 Russ Snyder * | 16.00 | 6.50 | 1.60 |
| ☐ | 64 Steve Barber | 1.00 | .40 | .10 |
| ☐ | 65 Milt Pappas * | 12.00 | 5.00 | 1.20 |
| ☐ | 66 Robin Roberts | 3.50 | 1.40 | .35 |
| ☐ | 67 Tito Francona | 1.00 | .40 | .10 |
| ☐ | 68 Jerry Kindall * | 16.00 | 6.50 | 1.60 |
| ☐ | 69 Woody Held | 1.00 | .40 | .10 |
| ☐ | 70 Bubba Phillips | 1.00 | .40 | .10 |
| ☐ | 71 Chuck Essegian | 1.00 | .40 | .10 |
| ☐ | 72 Willie Kirkland * | 16.00 | 6.50 | 1.60 |
| ☐ | 73 Al Luplow | 1.00 | .40 | .10 |
| ☐ | 74 Ty Cline * | 16.00 | 6.50 | 1.60 |
| ☐ | 75 Dick Donovan | 1.00 | .40 | .10 |
| ☐ | 76 John Romano | 1.00 | .40 | .10 |
| ☐ | 77 Pete Runnels | 1.25 | .50 | .12 |

| | | | | | |
|---|---|---|---|---|---|
| ☐ 78 | Ed Bressoud * | 12.00 | 5.00 | 1.20 |
| ☐ 79 | Frank Malzone | 1.25 | .50 | .12 |
| ☐ 80 | Carl Yastrzemski | 40.00 | 16.00 | 4.00 |
| ☐ 81 | Gary Geiger | 1.00 | .40 | .10 |
| ☐ 82 | Lou Clinton * | 12.00 | 5.00 | 1.20 |
| ☐ 83 | Earl Wilson | 1.00 | .40 | .10 |
| ☐ 84 | Bill Monbouquette | 1.00 | .40 | .10 |
| ☐ 85 | Norm Sieburn | 1.00 | .40 | .10 |
| ☐ 86 | Jerry Lumpe | 1.00 | .40 | .10 |
| ☐ 87 | Manny Jimenez | 1.00 | .40 | .10 |
| ☐ 88 | Gino Cimoli | 1.00 | .40 | .10 |
| ☐ 89 | Ed Charles * | 30.00 | 12.00 | 3.00 |
| ☐ 90 | Ed Rakow | 1.00 | .40 | .10 |
| ☐ 91 | Bob DelGreco * | 16.00 | 6.50 | 1.60 |
| ☐ 92 | Haywood Sullivan * | 16.00 | 6.50 | 1.60 |
| ☐ 93 | Chuck Hinton | 1.00 | .40 | .10 |
| ☐ 94 | Ken Retzer * | 16.00 | 6.50 | 1.60 |
| ☐ 95 | Harry Bright * | 16.00 | 6.50 | 1.60 |
| ☐ 96 | Bob Johnson | 1.00 | .40 | .10 |
| ☐ 97 | Dave Stenhouse * | 12.00 | 5.00 | 1.20 |
| ☐ 98 | Chuck Cottier | 1.00 | .40 | .10 |
| ☐ 99 | Tom Cheney | 1.00 | .40 | .10 |
| ☐ 100 | Claude Osteen * | 20.00 | 8.00 | 2.00 |
| ☐ 101 | Orlando Cepeda * | 1.50 | .60 | .15 |
| ☐ 102 | Chuck Hiller * | 12.00 | 5.00 | 1.20 |
| ☐ 103 | Jose Pagan * | 12.00 | 5.00 | 1.20 |
| ☐ 104 | Jim Davenport | 1.25 | .50 | .12 |
| ☐ 105 | Harvey Kuenn | 1.50 | .60 | .15 |
| ☐ 106 | Willie Mays | 35.00 | 14.00 | 3.50 |
| ☐ 107 | Felipe Alou | 1.25 | .50 | .12 |
| ☐ 108 | Tom Haller | 1.25 | .50 | .12 |
| ☐ 109 | Juan Marichal | 3.00 | 1.20 | .30 |
| ☐ 110 | Jack Sanford | 1.00 | .40 | .10 |
| ☐ 111 | Bill O'Dell | 1.00 | .40 | .10 |
| ☐ 112 | Willie McCovey * | 50.00 | 20.00 | 5.00 |
| ☐ 113 | Lee Walls * | 12.00 | 5.00 | 1.20 |
| ☐ 114 | Jim Gilliam * | 12.00 | 5.00 | 1.20 |
| ☐ 115 | Maury Wills | 2.00 | .80 | .20 |
| ☐ 116 | Ron Fairly | 1.00 | .40 | .10 |
| ☐ 117 | Tommy Davis | 1.25 | .50 | .12 |
| ☐ 118 | Duke Snider | 4.00 | 1.60 | .40 |
| ☐ 119 | Willie Davis | 1.50 | .60 | .15 |
| ☐ 120 | John Roseboro | 1.00 | .40 | .10 |
| ☐ 121 | Sandy Koufax | 12.00 | 5.00 | 1.20 |
| ☐ 122 | Stan Williams * | 16.00 | 6.50 | 1.60 |
| ☐ 123 | Don Drysdale | 3.50 | 1.40 | .35 |
| ☐ 124 | Daryl Spencer | 1.00 | .40 | .10 |
| ☐ 125 | Gordy Coleman | 1.00 | .40 | .10 |
| ☐ 126 | Don Blasingame * | 16.00 | 6.50 | 1.60 |
| ☐ 127 | Leo Cardenas | 1.00 | .40 | .10 |
| ☐ 128 | Eddie Kasko * | 12.00 | 5.00 | 1.20 |
| ☐ 129 | Jerry Lynch | 1.00 | .40 | .10 |
| ☐ 130 | Vada Pinson | 1.50 | .60 | .15 |
| ☐ 131 | Frank Robinson | 3.50 | 1.40 | .35 |
| ☐ 132 | John Edwards * | 16.00 | 6.50 | 1.60 |
| ☐ 133 | Joey Jay | 1.00 | .40 | .10 |
| ☐ 134 | Bob Purkey | 1.00 | .40 | .10 |
| ☐ 135 | Marty Keough * | 30.00 | 12.00 | 3.00 |
| ☐ 136 | Jim O'Toole * | 16.00 | 6.50 | 1.60 |
| ☐ 137 | Dick Stuart | 1.00 | .40 | .10 |
| ☐ 138 | Bill Mazeroski | 1.50 | .60 | .15 |
| ☐ 139 | Dick Groat | 1.25 | .50 | .12 |
| ☐ 140 | Don Hoak | 1.00 | .40 | .10 |
| ☐ 141 | Bob Skinner | 1.25 | .50 | .12 |
| ☐ 142 | Bill Virdon | 1.50 | .60 | .15 |
| ☐ 143 | Roberto Clemente | 25.00 | 10.00 | 2.50 |
| ☐ 144 | Smokey Burgess | 1.50 | .60 | .15 |
| ☐ 145 | Bob Friend | 1.25 | .50 | .12 |
| ☐ 146 | Al McBean * | 16.00 | 6.50 | 1.60 |
| ☐ 147 | Elroy Face | 1.25 | .50 | .12 |
| ☐ 148 | Joe Adcock | 1.25 | .50 | .12 |
| ☐ 149 | Frank Bolling | 1.00 | .40 | .10 |
| ☐ 150 | Roy McMillan | 1.00 | .40 | .10 |
| ☐ 151 | Eddie Mathews | 4.00 | 1.60 | .40 |
| ☐ 152 | Hank Aaron | 35.00 | 14.00 | 3.50 |
| ☐ 153 | Del Crandall * | 16.00 | 6.50 | 1.60 |
| ☐ 154 | Bob Shaw | 1.00 | .40 | .10 |
| ☐ 155 | Lew Burdette | 1.25 | .50 | .12 |
| ☐ 156 | Joe Torre * | 20.00 | 8.00 | 2.00 |
| ☐ 157 | Tony Cloninger * | 20.00 | 8.00 | 2.00 |
| ☐ 158 | Bill White | 1.25 | .50 | .12 |
| ☐ 159 | Julian Javier * | 16.00 | 6.50 | 1.60 |
| ☐ 160 | Ken Boyer | 1.50 | .60 | .15 |
| ☐ 161 | Julio Gotay * | 16.00 | 6.50 | 1.60 |
| ☐ 162 | Curt Flood | 1.25 | .50 | .12 |
| ☐ 163 | Charlie James * | 20.00 | 8.00 | 2.00 |
| ☐ 164 | Gene Oliver * | 16.00 | 6.50 | 1.60 |
| ☐ 165 | Ernie Broglio | 1.00 | .40 | .10 |
| ☐ 166 | Bob Gibson * | 35.00 | 14.00 | 3.50 |
| ☐ 167 | Lindy McDaniel * | 12.00 | 5.00 | 1.20 |
| ☐ 168 | Ray Washburn | 1.00 | .40 | .10 |
| ☐ 169 | Ernie Banks | 8.00 | 3.25 | .80 |
| ☐ 170 | Ron Santo | 1.50 | .60 | .15 |

| | | | | | |
|---|---|---|---|---|---|
| ☐ 171 | George Altman | 1.00 | .40 | .10 |
| ☐ 172 | Billy Williams * | 35.00 | 14.00 | 3.50 |
| ☐ 173 | Andre Rodgers * | 16.00 | 6.50 | 1.60 |
| ☐ 174 | Ken Hubbs | 1.50 | .60 | .15 |
| ☐ 175 | Don Landrum * | 16.00 | 6.50 | 1.60 |
| ☐ 176 | Dick Bertell * | 16.00 | 6.50 | 1.60 |
| ☐ 177 | Roy Sievers | 1.25 | .50 | .12 |
| ☐ 178 | Tony Taylor * | 16.00 | 6.50 | 1.60 |
| ☐ 179 | John Callison | 1.00 | .40 | .10 |
| ☐ 180 | Don Demeter | 1.00 | .40 | .10 |
| ☐ 181 | Tony Gonzalez * | 16.00 | 6.50 | 1.60 |
| ☐ 182 | Wes Covington * | 16.00 | 6.50 | 1.60 |
| ☐ 183 | Art Mahaffey | 1.00 | .40 | .10 |
| ☐ 184 | Clay Dalrymple | 1.00 | .40 | .10 |
| ☐ 185 | Al Spangler | 1.00 | .40 | .10 |
| ☐ 186 | Roman Mejias | 1.00 | .40 | .10 |
| ☐ 187 | Bob Aspromonte * | 25.00 | 10.00 | 2.50 |
| ☐ 188 | Norm Larker | 1.00 | .40 | .10 |
| ☐ 189 | Johnny Temple | 1.00 | .40 | .10 |
| ☐ 190 | Carl Warwick * | 16.00 | 6.50 | 1.60 |
| ☐ 191 | Bob Lillis * | 12.00 | 5.00 | 1.20 |
| ☐ 192 | Dick Farrell * | 25.00 | 10.00 | 2.50 |
| ☐ 193 | Gil Hodges | 3.50 | 1.40 | .35 |
| ☐ 194 | Marv Throneberry | 1.25 | .50 | .12 |
| ☐ 195 | Charlie Neal * | 16.00 | 6.50 | 1.60 |
| ☐ 196 | Frank Thomas | 1.50 | .60 | .15 |
| ☐ 197 | Richie Ashburn | 1.50 | .60 | .15 |
| ☐ 198 | Felix Mantilla * | 12.00 | 5.00 | 1.20 |
| ☐ 199 | Rod Kanehl * | 12.00 | 5.00 | 1.20 |
| ☐ 200 | Roger Craig * | 20.00 | 8.00 | 2.00 |

## 1953 Johnston Cookies

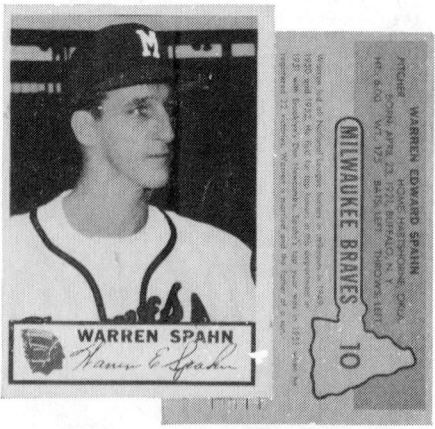

The cards in this 25 card set measure 2 9/16" by 3 5/16". The 1953 Johnston's Cookies set of numbered cards features Milwaukee Braves players only. This set is the most plentiful of the three Johnston's Cookies sets and no known scarcities exist. The ACC designation is D356-1.

| | | MINT | VG-E | F-G |
|---|---|---|---|---|
| COMPLETE SET | | 120.00 | 50.00 | 12.00 |
| COMMON PLAYER (1-25) | | 4.00 | 1.60 | .40 |
| | | | | |
| ☐ 1 | Charlie Grimm MGR | 5.00 | 2.00 | .50 |
| ☐ 2 | John Antonelli | 5.00 | 2.00 | .50 |
| ☐ 3 | Vern Bickford | 4.00 | 1.60 | .40 |
| ☐ 4 | Bob Buhl | 4.00 | 1.60 | .40 |
| ☐ 5 | Lew Burdette | 8.00 | 3.25 | .80 |
| ☐ 6 | Dave Cole | 4.00 | 1.60 | .40 |
| ☐ 7 | Ernie Johnson | 4.00 | 1.60 | .40 |
| ☐ 8 | Dave Jolly | 4.00 | 1.60 | .40 |
| ☐ 9 | Don Liddle | 4.00 | 1.60 | .40 |
| ☐ 10 | Warren Spahn | 21.00 | 8.50 | 2.10 |
| ☐ 11 | Max Surkont | 4.00 | 1.60 | .40 |
| ☐ 12 | Jim Wilson | 4.00 | 1.60 | .40 |
| ☐ 13 | Sibbi Sisti | 4.00 | 1.60 | .40 |
| ☐ 14 | Walker Cooper | 4.00 | 1.60 | .40 |
| ☐ 15 | Del Crandall | 5.00 | 2.00 | .50 |
| ☐ 16 | Ebba St.Claire | 4.00 | 1.60 | .40 |

| | | | MINT | VG-E | F-G |
|---|---|---|---|---|---|
| ☐ 17 | Joe Adcock | | 5.00 | 2.00 | .50 |
| ☐ 18 | George Crowe | | 4.00 | 1.60 | .40 |
| ☐ 19 | Jack Dittmer | | 4.00 | 1.60 | .40 |
| ☐ 20 | Johnny Logan | | 5.00 | 2.00 | .50 |
| ☐ 21 | Ed Mathews | | 21.00 | 8.50 | 2.10 |
| ☐ 22 | Bill Bruton | | 5.00 | 2.00 | .50 |
| ☐ 23 | Sid Gordon | | 4.00 | 1.60 | .40 |
| ☐ 24 | Andy Pafko | | 4.00 | 1.60 | .40 |
| ☐ 25 | Jim Pendleton | | 4.00 | 1.60 | .40 |

| | | | MINT | VG-E | F-G |
|---|---|---|---|---|---|
| ☐ 48 | Andy Pafko | | 6.00 | 2.40 | .60 |
| ☐ 49 | Dr. Charles Lacks | | 6.00 | 2.40 | .60 |
| | (unnumbered) | | | | |
| ☐ 50 | Joseph F. Taylor | | 6.00 | 2.40 | .60 |
| | (unnumbered) | | | | |

## 1954 Johnston Cookies

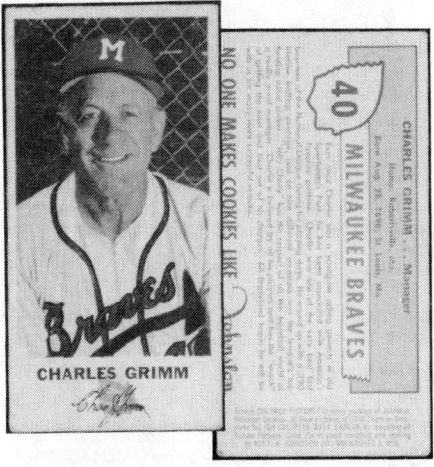

CHARLES GRIMM

The cards in this 35 card set measure 2" by 3 7/8". The 1954 Johnston's Cookies set of color cards of Milwaukee Braves are numbered according to the player's uniform number, except for the non-players, Lacks and Taylor, who are found at the end of the set. The Bobby Thomson card was withdrawn early in the year after his injury and is scarce. The ACC catalog number for this set is D356-2.

| | | | MINT | VG-E | F-G |
|---|---|---|---|---|---|
| COMPLETE SET | | | 450.00 | 180.00 | 45.00 |
| COMMON PLAYER (1-50) | | | 6.00 | 2.40 | .60 |
| ☐ | 1 | Del Crandall | 7.50 | 3.00 | .75 |
| ☐ | 3 | Jim Pendleton | 6.00 | 2.40 | .60 |
| ☐ | 4 | Danny O'Connell | 6.00 | 2.40 | .60 |
| ☐ | 5 | Hank Aaron | 125.00 | 50.00 | 12.50 |
| ☐ | 6 | Jack Dittmer | 6.00 | 2.40 | .60 |
| ☐ | 9 | Joe Adcock | 7.50 | 3.00 | .75 |
| ☐ | 10 | Bob Buhl | 6.00 | 2.40 | .60 |
| ☐ | 11 | Phil Paine | 6.00 | 2.40 | .60 |
| ☐ | 12 | Ben Johnson | 6.00 | 2.40 | .60 |
| ☐ | 13 | Sibbi Sisti | 6.00 | 2.40 | .60 |
| ☐ | 15 | Charles Gorin | 6.00 | 2.40 | .60 |
| ☐ | 16 | Chet Nichols | 6.00 | 2.40 | .60 |
| ☐ | 17 | Dave Jolly | 6.00 | 2.40 | .60 |
| ☐ | 19 | Jim Wilson | 6.00 | 2.40 | .60 |
| ☐ | 20 | Ray Crone | 6.00 | 2.40 | .60 |
| ☐ | 21 | Warren Spahn | 25.00 | 10.00 | 2.50 |
| ☐ | 22 | Gene Conley | 6.00 | 2.40 | .60 |
| ☐ | 23 | Johnny Logan | 7.50 | 3.00 | .75 |
| ☐ | 24 | Charlie White | 6.00 | 2.40 | .60 |
| ☐ | 27 | George Metkovich | 6.00 | 2.40 | .60 |
| ☐ | 28 | Johnny Cooney | 6.00 | 2.40 | .60 |
| ☐ | 29 | Paul Burris | 6.00 | 2.40 | .60 |
| ☐ | 31 | Bucky Walters | 7.50 | 3.00 | .75 |
| ☐ | 32 | Ernie Johnson | 6.00 | 2.40 | .60 |
| ☐ | 33 | Lou Burdette | 10.00 | 4.00 | 1.00 |
| ☐ | 34 | Bob Thomson | 125.00 | 50.00 | 12.50 |
| ☐ | 35 | Bob Keely | 6.00 | 2.40 | .60 |
| ☐ | 38 | Bill Bruton | 7.50 | 3.00 | .75 |
| ☐ | 40 | Charlie Grimm MGR | 7.50 | 3.00 | .75 |
| ☐ | 41 | Eddie Mathews | 25.00 | 10.00 | 2.50 |
| ☐ | 42 | Sam Calderone | 6.00 | 2.40 | .60 |
| ☐ | 47 | Joey Jay | 6.00 | 2.40 | .60 |

## 1955 Johnston Cookies

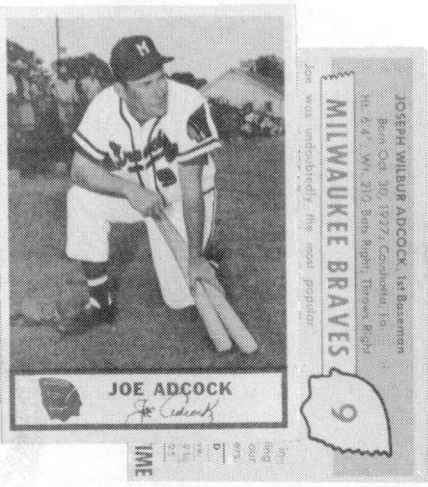

JOE ADCOCK

The cards in this 35 card set measure 2 3/4" by 4". This set of Milwaukee Braves issued in 1955 by Johnston Cookies are numbered by the uniform number of the player depicted, except for non-players Lacks, Lewis and Taylor. The cards were issued in strips of six which accounts for the rouletted edges found on single cards. They are larger in size than the two previous sets but are printed on thinner cardboard. Each player in the checklist has been marked to show on which panel or strip he appeared (Pafko appears twice). A complete panel of six cards is worth 25% more than the sum of the individual players. The ACC designation is D356-3.

| | | | MINT | VG-E | F-G |
|---|---|---|---|---|---|
| COMPLETE SET | | | 500.00 | 200.00 | 50.00 |
| COMMON PLAYER (1-51) | | | 10.00 | 4.00 | 1.00 |
| ☐ | 1 | Del Crandall P1 | 12.50 | 5.00 | 1.25 |
| ☐ | 3 | Jim Pendleton P3 | 10.00 | 4.00 | 1.00 |
| ☐ | 4 | Danny O'Connell P1 | 10.00 | 4.00 | 1.00 |
| ☐ | 6 | Jack Dittmer P6 | 10.00 | 4.00 | 1.00 |
| ☐ | 9 | Joe Adcock P2 | 12.50 | 5.00 | 1.25 |
| ☐ | 10 | Bob Buhl P6 | 10.00 | 4.00 | 1.00 |
| ☐ | 11 | Phil Paine P5 | 10.00 | 4.00 | 1.00 |
| ☐ | 12 | Ray Crone P5 | 10.00 | 4.00 | 1.00 |
| ☐ | 15 | Charlie Gorin P1 | 10.00 | 4.00 | 1.00 |
| ☐ | 16 | Dave Jolly P4 | 10.00 | 4.00 | 1.00 |
| ☐ | 17 | Chet Nichols P2 | 10.00 | 4.00 | 1.00 |
| ☐ | 18 | Chuck Tanner P5 | 15.00 | 6.00 | 1.50 |
| ☐ | 19 | Jim Wilson P6 | 10.00 | 4.00 | 1.00 |
| ☐ | 20 | Dave Koslo P4 | 10.00 | 4.00 | 1.00 |
| ☐ | 21 | Warren Spahn P3 | 40.00 | 16.00 | 4.00 |
| ☐ | 22 | Gene Conley P3 | 10.00 | 4.00 | 1.00 |
| ☐ | 23 | Johnny Logan P4 | 12.50 | 5.00 | 1.25 |
| ☐ | 24 | Charlie White P2 | 10.00 | 4.00 | 1.00 |
| ☐ | 28 | Johnny Cooney P4 | 10.00 | 4.00 | 1.00 |
| ☐ | 30 | Roy Smalley P3 | 10.00 | 4.00 | 1.00 |
| ☐ | 31 | Bucky Walters P6 | 12.50 | 5.00 | 1.25 |
| ☐ | 32 | Ernie Johnson P5 | 10.00 | 4.00 | 1.00 |
| ☐ | 33 | Lou Burdette P1 | 20.00 | 8.00 | 2.00 |
| ☐ | 34 | Bobby Thomson P6 | 15.00 | 6.00 | 1.50 |
| ☐ | 35 | Bob Keely P1 | 10.00 | 4.00 | 1.00 |
| ☐ | 38 | Bill Bruton P4 | 12.50 | 5.00 | 1.25 |
| ☐ | 39 | George Crowe P3 | 10.00 | 4.00 | 1.00 |

| | | MINT | VG-E | F-G |
|---|---|---|---|---|
| ☐ 40 | Charlie Grimm MGR P6 .... | 12.50 | 5.00 | 1.25 |
| ☐ 41 | Eddie Mathews P5 ........... | 40.00 | 16.00 | 4.00 |
| ☐ 44 | Hank Aaron P1 ................. | 150.00 | 60.00 | 15.00 |
| ☐ 47 | Joey Jay P2 ..................... | 10.00 | 4.00 | 1.00 |
| ☐ 48 | Andy Pafko P2 P4 ............ | 10.00 | 4.00 | 1.00 |
| ☐ 49 | Dr. Charles Leaks P2 ........ (unnumbered) | 10.00 | 4.00 | 1.00 |
| ☐ 50 | Duffy Lewis P5 .................. (unnumbered) | 10.00 | 4.00 | 1.00 |
| ☐ 51 | Joe Taylor P3 ................... (unnumbered) | 10.00 | 4.00 | 1.00 |

## 1955 Kahn's

Compliments of Kahn's Wieners
"THE WIENER THE WORLD AWAITED"

The cards in this 6 card set measure 3 1/4" by 4". The 1955 Kahn's Wieners set received very limited distribution. The cards were supposedly given away at an amusement park. The set portrays the players in street clothes rather than in uniform and hence are sometimes referred to as "street clothes" Kahn's. All Kahn's sets from 1955 through 1963 are black and white and contain a 1/2" tab. Cards with the tab still intact are worth approximately 50% more than cards without the tab. Cards feature a facsimile autograph of the player on the front. Cards are blank-backed. Cincinnati Redlegs players only are featured.

| | | MINT | VG-E | F-G |
|---|---|---|---|---|
| COMPLETE SET | ......................... | 1700.00 | 750.00 | 200.00 |
| COMMON PLAYER (1-6) | ........... | 250.00 | 100.00 | 25.00 |
| ☐ 1 | Gus Bell ............................. | 450.00 | 180.00 | 45.00 |
| ☐ 2 | Ted Kluszewski ................... | 300.00 | 120.00 | 30.00 |
| ☐ 3 | Roy McMillan ..................... | 250.00 | 100.00 | 25.00 |
| ☐ 4 | Joe Nuxhall ........................ | 250.00 | 100.00 | 25.00 |
| ☐ 5 | Wally Post .......................... | 250.00 | 100.00 | 25.00 |
| ☐ 6 | Johnny Temple ................... | 250.00 | 100.00 | 25.00 |

## 1956 Kahn's

The cards in this 15 card set measure 3 1/4" by 4". The 1956 Kahn's set was the first set to be issued with Kahn's meat products. The cards are blank backed. The set is distinguished by the old style, short sleeve shirts on the players and the existence of backgounds (Kahn's cards of later years utilize a

Compliments of Kahn's Wieners
"THE WIENER THE WORLD AWAITED"

blank background). Cards which have the tab still intact are worth approximately 50% more than cards without the tab. Cincinnati Redlegs players only are featured.

| | | MINT | VG-E | F-G |
|---|---|---|---|---|
| COMPLETE SET | ......................... | 700.00 | 280.00 | 70.00 |
| COMMON PLAYER (1-15) | .......... | 40.00 | 16.00 | 4.00 |
| ☐ 1 | Ed Bailey .......................... | 40.00 | 16.00 | 4.00 |
| ☐ 2 | Gus Bell ............................ | 45.00 | 18.00 | 4.50 |
| ☐ 3 | Joe Black .......................... | 45.00 | 18.00 | 4.50 |
| ☐ 4 | Smoky Burgess ................. | 45.00 | 18.00 | 4.50 |
| ☐ 5 | Art Fowler ......................... | 40.00 | 16.00 | 4.00 |
| ☐ 6 | Hershel Freeman .............. | 40.00 | 16.00 | 4.00 |
| ☐ 7 | Ray Jablonski .................... | 40.00 | 16.00 | 4.00 |
| ☐ 8 | John Klippstein ................. | 40.00 | 16.00 | 4.00 |
| ☐ 9 | Ted Kluszewski ................. | 80.00 | 32.00 | 8.00 |
| ☐ 10 | Brooks Lawrence .............. | 40.00 | 16.00 | 4.00 |
| ☐ 11 | Roy McMillan .................... | 40.00 | 16.00 | 4.00 |
| ☐ 12 | Joe Nuxhall ....................... | 45.00 | 18.00 | 4.50 |
| ☐ 13 | Wally Post ......................... | 40.00 | 16.00 | 4.00 |
| ☐ 14 | Frank Robinson ................ | 150.00 | 60.00 | 15.00 |
| ☐ 15 | Johnny Temple .................. | 40.00 | 16.00 | 4.00 |

## 1957 Kahn's

Compliments of Kahn's Wieners
"THE WIENER THE WORLD AWAITED"

The cards in this 29 card set measure 3 1/4" by 4". The 1957 Kahn's Wieners set contains black and white, blank backed, unnumbered cards. The set features the Cincinnati Redlegs and Pittsburgh

Pirates only. The cards feature a light background. Each card features a facsimile autograph of the player on the front. The Groat card exists with a "Richard Groat" autograph and also exists with the printed name "Dick Groat" on the card. The ACC designation is D155-3.

| | | MINT | VG-E | F-G |
|---|---|---|---|---|
| COMPLETE SET | | 1250.00 | 550.00 | 150.00 |
| COMMON PLAYER | | 30.00 | 12.00 | 3.00 |
| ☐ 1 | Tom Acker | 30.00 | 12.00 | 3.00 |
| ☐ 2 | Ed Bailey | 30.00 | 12.00 | 3.00 |
| ☐ 3 | Gus Bell | 35.00 | 14.00 | 3.50 |
| ☐ 4 | Smoky Burgess | 35.00 | 14.00 | 3.50 |
| ☐ 5 | Robert Clemente | 300.00 | 120.00 | 30.00 |
| ☐ 6 | George Crowe | 30.00 | 12.00 | 3.00 |
| ☐ 7 | Elroy Face | 35.00 | 14.00 | 3.50 |
| ☐ 8 | Hershel Freeman | 30.00 | 12.00 | 3.00 |
| ☐ 9 | Bob Friend | 35.00 | 14.00 | 3.50 |
| ☐ 10 | Dick Groat | 50.00 | 20.00 | 5.00 |
| ☐ 11 | Richard Groat | 100.00 | 40.00 | 10.00 |
| ☐ 12 | Don Gross | 30.00 | 12.00 | 3.00 |
| ☐ 13 | Warren Hacker | 30.00 | 12.00 | 3.00 |
| ☐ 14 | Don Hoak | 30.00 | 12.00 | 3.00 |
| ☐ 15 | Hal Jeffcoat | 30.00 | 12.00 | 3.00 |
| ☐ 16 | Ron Kline | 30.00 | 12.00 | 3.00 |
| ☐ 17 | John Klippstein | 30.00 | 12.00 | 3.00 |
| ☐ 18 | Ted Kluszewski | 60.00 | 24.00 | 6.00 |
| ☐ 19 | Brooks Lawrence | 30.00 | 12.00 | 3.00 |
| ☐ 20 | Dale Long | 30.00 | 12.00 | 3.00 |
| ☐ 21 | Bill Mazeroski | 75.00 | 30.00 | 7.50 |
| ☐ 22 | Roy McMillan | 30.00 | 12.00 | 3.00 |
| ☐ 23 | Joe Nuxhall | 35.00 | 14.00 | 3.50 |
| ☐ 24 | Wally Post | 30.00 | 12.00 | 3.00 |
| ☐ 25 | Frank Robinson | 125.00 | 50.00 | 12.50 |
| ☐ 26 | John Temple | 35.00 | 14.00 | 3.50 |
| ☐ 27 | Frank Thomas | 35.00 | 14.00 | 3.50 |
| ☐ 28 | Bob Thurman | 30.00 | 12.00 | 3.00 |
| ☐ 29 | Lee Walls | 30.00 | 12.00 | 3.00 |

but not on the front of the 1959 cards. Cards of Wally Post, Charlie Rabe, and Frank Thomas are somewhat more difficult to find and are marked with an asterisk in the checklist below.

| | | MINT | VG-E | F-G |
|---|---|---|---|---|
| COMPLETE SET | | 1500.00 | 200.00 | 50.00 |
| COMMON PLAYER (1-29) | | 30.00 | 12.00 | 3.00 |
| ☐ 1 | Ed Bailey | 30.00 | 12.00 | 3.00 |
| ☐ 2 | Gene Baker | 30.00 | 12.00 | 3.00 |
| ☐ 3 | Gus Bell | 35.00 | 14.00 | 3.50 |
| ☐ 4 | Smoky Burgess | 35.00 | 14.00 | 3.50 |
| ☐ 5 | Roberto Clemente | 250.00 | 100.00 | 25.00 |
| ☐ 6 | George Crowe | 30.00 | 12.00 | 3.00 |
| ☐ 7 | Elroy Face | 35.00 | 14.00 | 3.50 |
| ☐ 8 | Hank Foiles | 30.00 | 12.00 | 3.00 |
| ☐ 9 | Dee Fondy | 30.00 | 12.00 | 3.00 |
| ☐ 10 | Bob Friend | 35.00 | 14.00 | 3.50 |
| ☐ 11 | Dick Groat | 45.00 | 18.00 | 4.50 |
| ☐ 12 | Harvey Haddix | 35.00 | 14.00 | 3.50 |
| ☐ 13 | Don Hoak | 30.00 | 12.00 | 3.00 |
| ☐ 14 | Hal Jeffcoat | 30.00 | 12.00 | 3.00 |
| ☐ 15 | Ron Kline | 30.00 | 12.00 | 3.00 |
| ☐ 16 | Ted Kluszewski | 60.00 | 24.00 | 6.00 |
| ☐ 17 | Vernon Law | 35.00 | 14.00 | 3.50 |
| ☐ 18 | Brooks Lawrence | 30.00 | 12.00 | 3.00 |
| ☐ 19 | Bill Mazeroski | 60.00 | 24.00 | 6.00 |
| ☐ 20 | Roy McMillan | 30.00 | 12.00 | 3.00 |
| ☐ 21 | Joe Nuxhall | 35.00 | 14.00 | 3.50 |
| ☐ 22 | Wally Post * | 150.00 | 60.00 | 15.00 |
| ☐ 23 | John Powers | 30.00 | 12.00 | 3.00 |
| ☐ 24 | Bob Purkey | 30.00 | 12.00 | 3.00 |
| ☐ 25 | Charlie Rabe * | 150.00 | 60.00 | 15.00 |
| ☐ 26 | Frank Robinson | 120.00 | 50.00 | 12.00 |
| ☐ 27 | Bob Skinner | 30.00 | 12.00 | 3.00 |
| ☐ 28 | Johnny Temple | 30.00 | 12.00 | 3.00 |
| ☐ 29 | Frank Thomas * | 150.00 | 60.00 | 15.00 |

## 1958 Kahn's

Compliments of Kahn's Wieners
"THE WIENER THE WORLD AWAITED"

## 1959 Kahn's

Compliments of Kahn's
"THE WIENER THE WORLD AWAITED"

The cards in this 29 card set measure 3 1/4" by 4". The 1958 Kahn's Wieners set of unnumbered, black and white cards features Cincinnati Redlegs, Philadelphia Phillies, and Pittsburgh Pirates. The backs present a story for each player entitled "My Greatest Thrill in Baseball". A method of distinguishing 1958 Kahn's from 1959 Kahn's is that the word Wieners is found on the front of the 1958

The cards in this 38 card set measure 3 1/4" by 4". The 1959 Kahn's set features Cincinnati, Cleveland, and Pittsburgh players. The backs feature stories entitled "The Toughest Play I have to Make," or "The Toughest Batter I Have To Face." The Brodowski card is very scarce while Haddix, Held and McLish are considered quite difficult to obtain; these scarcities are the asterisked cards in the checklist below.

|  | MINT | VG-E | F-G |
|---|---|---|---|
| COMPLETE SET ....................... | 1900.00 | 800.00 | 225.00 |
| COMMON PLAYER (1-38) .......... | 25.00 | 10.00 | 2.50 |

| | | MINT | VG-E | F-G |
|---|---|---|---|---|
| ☐ | 1 Ed Bailey ......................... | 25.00 | 10.00 | 2.50 |
| ☐ | 2 Gary Bell .......................... | 25.00 | 10.00 | 2.50 |
| ☐ | 3 Gus Bell ........................... | 30.00 | 12.00 | 3.00 |
| ☐ | 4 Dick Brodowski * ............. | 250.00 | 100.00 | 25.00 |
| ☐ | 5 Smoky Burgess ................. | 30.00 | 12.00 | 3.00 |
| ☐ | 6 Roberto Clemente ............ | 225.00 | 90.00 | 22.00 |
| ☐ | 7 Rocky Colavito ................. | 50.00 | 20.00 | 5.00 |
| ☐ | 8 Elroy Face ........................ | 30.00 | 12.00 | 3.00 |
| ☐ | 9 Bob Friend ....................... | 30.00 | 12.00 | 3.00 |
| ☐ | 10 Joe Gordon ...................... | 30.00 | 12.00 | 3.00 |
| ☐ | 11 Jim Grant ........................ | 25.00 | 10.00 | 2.50 |
| ☐ | 12 Dick Groat ...................... | 35.00 | 14.00 | 3.50 |
| ☐ | 13 Harvey Haddix * ............... | 150.00 | 60.00 | 15.00 |
| | (blank back) | | | |
| ☐ | 14 Woodie Held * ................. | 150.00 | 60.00 | 15.00 |
| ☐ | 15 Don Hoak ........................ | 25.00 | 10.00 | 2.50 |
| ☐ | 16 Ron Kline ........................ | 25.00 | 10.00 | 2.50 |
| ☐ | 17 Ted Kluszewski ................ | 50.00 | 20.00 | 5.00 |
| ☐ | 18 Vernon Law ..................... | 30.00 | 12.00 | 3.00 |
| ☐ | 19 Jerry Lynch ..................... | 25.00 | 10.00 | 2.50 |
| ☐ | 20 Billy Martin ..................... | 60.00 | 24.00 | 6.00 |
| ☐ | 21 Bill Mazeroski ................. | 50.00 | 20.00 | 5.00 |
| ☐ | 22 Cal McLish * .................... | 150.00 | 60.00 | 15.00 |
| ☐ | 23 Roy McMillan .................. | 25.00 | 10.00 | 2.50 |
| ☐ | 24 Minnie Minoso ................ | 40.00 | 16.00 | 4.00 |
| ☐ | 25 Russ Nixon ...................... | 25.00 | 10.00 | 2.50 |
| ☐ | 26 Joe Nuxhall ..................... | 30.00 | 12.00 | 3.00 |
| ☐ | 27 Jim Perry ........................ | 30.00 | 12.00 | 3.00 |
| ☐ | 28 Vada Pinson .................... | 35.00 | 14.00 | 3.50 |
| ☐ | 29 Vic Power ........................ | 25.00 | 10.00 | 2.50 |
| ☐ | 30 Bob Purkey ..................... | 25.00 | 10.00 | 2.50 |
| ☐ | 31 Frank Robinson ............... | 100.00 | 40.00 | 10.00 |
| ☐ | 32 Herb Score ..................... | 35.00 | 14.00 | 3.50 |
| ☐ | 33 Bob Skinner .................... | 25.00 | 10.00 | 2.50 |
| ☐ | 34 George Strickland ........... | 25.00 | 10.00 | 2.50 |
| ☐ | 35 Dick Stuart ..................... | 30.00 | 12.00 | 3.00 |
| ☐ | 36 Johnny Temple ................ | 25.00 | 10.00 | 2.50 |
| ☐ | 37 Frank Thomas .................. | 25.00 | 10.00 | 2.50 |
| ☐ | 38 George Witt ..................... | 25.00 | 10.00 | 2.50 |

## 1960 Kahn's

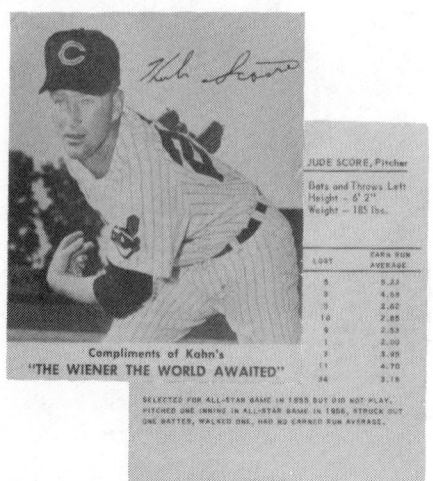

Compliments of Kahn's

"THE WIENER THE WORLD AWAITED"

The cards in this 42 card set measure 3 1/4" by 4". The 1960 Kahn's set features players of the Chicago Cubs, Chicago White Sox, Cincinnati Redlegs, Cleveland Indians, Pittsburgh Pirates, and St. Louis Cardinals. The backs give vital player information and records through the 1959 season. Kline appears with either St. Louis or Pittsburgh. The Harvey Kuenn card (asterisked below) appears with a blank back, and is scarce.

|  | MINT | VG-E | F-G |
|---|---|---|---|
| COMPLETE SET ....................... | 1000.00 | 450.00 | 125.00 |
| COMMON PLAYER (1-42) .......... | 15.00 | 6.00 | 1.50 |

| | | MINT | VG-E | F-G |
|---|---|---|---|---|
| ☐ | 1 Ed Bailey ......................... | 15.00 | 6.00 | 1.50 |
| ☐ | 2 Gary Bell .......................... | 15.00 | 6.00 | 1.50 |
| ☐ | 3 Gus Bell ........................... | 18.00 | 7.25 | 1.80 |
| ☐ | 4 Smoky Burgess ................. | 18.00 | 7.25 | 1.80 |
| ☐ | 5 Gino Cimoli ...................... | 15.00 | 6.00 | 1.50 |
| ☐ | 6 Roberto Clemente ............ | 150.00 | 60.00 | 15.00 |
| ☐ | 7 Roy Face .......................... | 18.00 | 7.25 | 1.80 |
| ☐ | 8 Tito Francona .................. | 15.00 | 6.00 | 1.50 |
| ☐ | 9 Bob Friend ....................... | 18.00 | 7.25 | 1.80 |
| ☐ | 10 Jim Grant ........................ | 15.00 | 6.00 | 1.50 |
| ☐ | 11 Dick Groat ...................... | 20.00 | 8.00 | 2.00 |
| ☐ | 12 Harvey Haddix ................. | 18.00 | 7.25 | 1.80 |
| ☐ | 13 Woodie Held ................... | 15.00 | 6.00 | 1.50 |
| ☐ | 14 Bill Henry ....................... | 15.00 | 6.00 | 1.50 |
| ☐ | 15 Don Hoak ........................ | 15.00 | 6.00 | 1.50 |
| ☐ | 16 Jay Hook ......................... | 15.00 | 6.00 | 1.50 |
| ☐ | 17 Eddie Kasko .................... | 15.00 | 6.00 | 1.50 |
| ☐ | 18A Ron Kline ...................... | 30.00 | 12.00 | 3.00 |
| | (Pittsburgh) | | | |
| ☐ | 18B Ron Kline ...................... | 30.00 | 12.00 | 3.00 |
| | (St. Louis) | | | |
| ☐ | 19 Ted Kluszewski ................ | 30.00 | 12.00 | 3.00 |
| ☐ | 20 Harvey Kuenn .................. | 150.00 | 60.00 | 15.00 |
| | (blank back) | | | |
| ☐ | 21 Vernon Law ..................... | 18.00 | 7.25 | 1.80 |
| ☐ | 22 Brooks Lawrence ............. | 15.00 | 6.00 | 1.50 |
| ☐ | 23 Jerry Lynch ..................... | 15.00 | 6.00 | 1.50 |
| ☐ | 24 Billy Martin ..................... | 35.00 | 14.00 | 3.50 |
| ☐ | 25 Bill Mazeroski ................. | 25.00 | 10.00 | 2.50 |
| ☐ | 26 Cal McLish ...................... | 15.00 | 6.00 | 1.50 |
| ☐ | 27 Roy McMillan .................. | 15.00 | 6.00 | 1.50 |
| ☐ | 28 Don Newcombe ................ | 20.00 | 8.00 | 2.00 |
| ☐ | 29 Russ Nixon ...................... | 15.00 | 6.00 | 1.50 |
| ☐ | 30 Joe Nuxhall ..................... | 18.00 | 7.25 | 1.80 |
| ☐ | 31 Jim O'Toole .................... | 15.00 | 6.00 | 1.50 |
| ☐ | 32 Jim Perry ........................ | 18.00 | 7.25 | 1.80 |
| ☐ | 33 Vada Pinson .................... | 20.00 | 8.00 | 2.00 |
| ☐ | 34 Vic Power ........................ | 15.00 | 6.00 | 1.50 |
| ☐ | 35 Bob Purkey ..................... | 15.00 | 6.00 | 1.50 |
| ☐ | 36 Frank Robinson ............... | 75.00 | 30.00 | 7.50 |
| ☐ | 37 Herb Score ..................... | 20.00 | 8.00 | 2.00 |
| ☐ | 38 Bob Skinner .................... | 15.00 | 6.00 | 1.50 |
| ☐ | 39 Dick Stuart ..................... | 18.00 | 7.25 | 1.80 |
| ☐ | 40 Johnny Temple ................ | 15.00 | 6.00 | 1.50 |
| ☐ | 41 Frank Thomas .................. | 15.00 | 6.00 | 1.50 |
| ☐ | 42 Lee Walls ........................ | 15.00 | 6.00 | 1.50 |

## 1961 Kahn's

The cards in this 43 card set measure 3 1/4" by 4". The 1961 Kahn's Wieners set of black and white, unnumbered cards features players from Cincinnati, Cleveland, and Pittsburgh. This year was the first year Kahn's made complete sets available to the public; hence they are more available, especially in the better condition grades, than the Kahn's of the previous years. The backs give vital player information and year by year career statistics through 1960. The ACC designation is F155-7.

|  | MINT | VG-E | F-G |
|---|---|---|---|
| COMPLETE SET ....................... | 450.00 | 180.00 | 45.00 |
| COMMON PLAYER (1-43) .......... | 8.00 | 3.25 | .80 |

| | | MINT | VG-E | F-G |
|---|---|---|---|---|
| ☐ | 1 John Antonelli .................. | 9.00 | 3.75 | .90 |
| ☐ | 2 Ed Bailey ......................... | 8.00 | 3.25 | .80 |
| ☐ | 3 Gary Bell .......................... | 8.00 | 3.25 | .80 |
| ☐ | 4 Gus Bell ........................... | 9.00 | 3.75 | .90 |
| ☐ | 5 Jim Brosnan ..................... | 9.00 | 3.75 | .90 |
| ☐ | 6 Smoky Burgess ................. | 9.00 | 3.75 | .90 |
| ☐ | 7 Gino Cimoli ...................... | 8.00 | 3.25 | .80 |
| ☐ | 8 Roberto Clemente ............ | 125.00 | 50.00 | 12.50 |
| ☐ | 9 Gordie Coleman ............... | 8.00 | 3.25 | .80 |
| ☐ | 10 Jimmy Dykes ................... | 9.00 | 3.75 | .90 |
| ☐ | 11 Roy Face ......................... | 9.00 | 3.75 | .90 |
| ☐ | 12 Tito Francona .................. | 9.00 | 3.75 | .90 |
| ☐ | 13 Gene Freese .................... | 8.00 | 3.25 | .80 |
| ☐ | 14 Bob Friend ...................... | 9.00 | 3.75 | .90 |

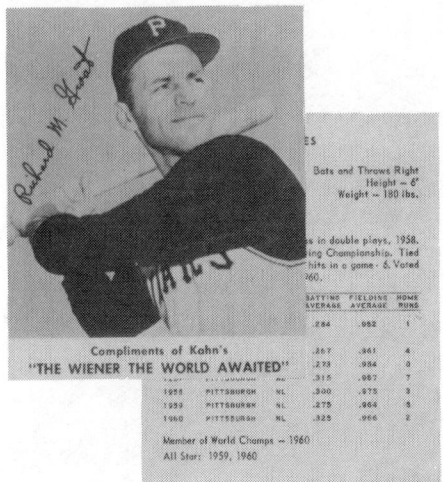

Compliments of Kahn's
"THE WIENER THE WORLD AWAITED"

Compliments of Kahn's
"THE WIENER THE WORLD AWAITED"

| | | | | |
|---|---|---|---|---|
| ☐ 15 | Jim Grant | 8.00 | 3.25 | .80 |
| ☐ 16 | Dick Groat | 12.00 | 5.00 | 1.20 |
| ☐ 17 | Harvey Haddix | 9.00 | 3.75 | .90 |
| ☐ 18 | Woodie Held | 8.00 | 3.25 | .80 |
| ☐ 19 | Don Hoak | 8.00 | 3.25 | .80 |
| ☐ 20 | Jay Hook | 8.00 | 3.25 | .80 |
| ☐ 21 | Joey Jay | 8.00 | 3.25 | .80 |
| ☐ 22 | Eddie Kasko | 8.00 | 3.25 | .80 |
| ☐ 23 | Willie Kirkland | 8.00 | 3.25 | .80 |
| ☐ 24 | Vernon Law | 9.00 | 3.75 | .90 |
| ☐ 25 | Jerry Lynch | 8.00 | 3.25 | .80 |
| ☐ 26 | Jim Maloney | 9.00 | 3.75 | .90 |
| ☐ 27 | Bill Mazeroski | 15.00 | 6.00 | 1.50 |
| ☐ 28 | Wilmer Mizell | 8.00 | 3.25 | .80 |
| ☐ 29 | Rocky Nelson | 8.00 | 3.25 | .80 |
| ☐ 30 | Jim O'Toole | 8.00 | 3.25 | .80 |
| ☐ 31 | Jim Perry | 9.00 | 3.75 | .90 |
| ☐ 32 | Bubba Phillips | 8.00 | 3.25 | .80 |
| ☐ 33 | Vada Pinson | 12.00 | 5.00 | 1.20 |
| ☐ 34 | Wally Post | 8.00 | 3.25 | .80 |
| ☐ 35 | Vic Power | 8.00 | 3.25 | .80 |
| ☐ 36 | Bob Purkey | 8.00 | 3.25 | .80 |
| ☐ 37 | Frank Robinson | 50.00 | 20.00 | 5.00 |
| ☐ 38 | John Romano | 8.00 | 3.25 | .80 |
| ☐ 39 | Dick Schofield | 8.00 | 3.25 | .80 |
| ☐ 40 | Bob Skinner | 8.00 | 3.25 | .80 |
| ☐ 41 | Hal Smith | 8.00 | 3.25 | .80 |
| ☐ 42 | Dick Stuart | 9.00 | 3.75 | .90 |
| ☐ 43 | Johnny Temple | 8.00 | 3.25 | .80 |

## 1962 Kahn's

The cards in this 38 card set measure 3 1/4" by 4". The 1962 Kahn's Wieners set of black and white, unnumbered cards features Cincinnati, Cleveland, Minnesota, and Pittsburgh players. Card numbers 1 Bell, 33 Power, and 34 Purkey exist in two different forms; these variations are listed in the checklist below. The backs of the cards contain career information. The ACC designation is F155-8. The set price below includes the set with all variation cards.

| | | MINT | VG-E | F-G |
|---|---|---|---|---|
| | COMPLETE SET | 725.00 | 325.00 | 75.00 |
| | COMMON PLAYER | 7.00 | 2.80 | .70 |
| ☐ 1A | Gary Bell (with fat man) | 75.00 | 30.00 | 7.50 |
| ☐ 1B | Gary Bell (no fat man) | 25.00 | 10.00 | 2.50 |
| ☐ 2 | Jim Brosnan | 8.00 | 3.25 | .80 |
| ☐ 3 | Smoky Burgess | 8.00 | 3.25 | .80 |

| | | | | |
|---|---|---|---|---|
| ☐ 4 | Chico Cardenas | 7.00 | 2.80 | .70 |
| ☐ 5 | Roberto Clemente | 100.00 | 40.00 | 10.00 |
| ☐ 6 | Ty Cline | 7.00 | 2.80 | .70 |
| ☐ 7 | Gordon Coleman | 7.00 | 2.80 | .70 |
| ☐ 8 | Dick Donovan | 10.00 | 4.00 | 1.00 |
| ☐ 9 | John Edwards | 7.00 | 2.80 | .70 |
| ☐ 10 | Tito Francona | 8.00 | 3.25 | .80 |
| ☐ 11 | Gene Freese | 7.00 | 2.80 | .70 |
| ☐ 12 | Bob Friend | 8.00 | 3.25 | .80 |
| ☐ 13 | Joe Gibbon | 75.00 | 30.00 | 7.50 |
| ☐ 14 | Jim Grant | 7.00 | 2.80 | .70 |
| ☐ 15 | Dick Groat | 10.00 | 4.00 | 1.00 |
| ☐ 16 | Harvey Haddix | 8.00 | 3.25 | .80 |
| ☐ 17 | Woodie Held | 7.00 | 2.80 | .70 |
| ☐ 18 | Bill Henry | 7.00 | 2.80 | .70 |
| ☐ 19 | Don Hoak | 7.00 | 2.80 | .70 |
| ☐ 20 | Ken Hunt | 7.00 | 2.80 | .70 |
| ☐ 21 | Joey Jay | 7.00 | 2.80 | .70 |
| ☐ 22 | Eddie Kasko | 7.00 | 2.80 | .70 |
| ☐ 23 | Willie Kirkland | 7.00 | 2.80 | .70 |
| ☐ 24 | Barry Latman | 7.00 | 2.80 | .70 |
| ☐ 25 | Jerry Lynch | 7.00 | 2.80 | .70 |
| ☐ 26 | Jim Maloney | 8.00 | 3.25 | .80 |
| ☐ 27 | Bill Mazeroski | 12.00 | 5.00 | 1.20 |
| ☐ 28 | Jim O'Toole | 7.00 | 2.80 | .70 |
| ☐ 29 | Jim Perry | 8.00 | 3.25 | .80 |
| ☐ 30 | Bubba Phillips | 7.00 | 2.80 | .70 |
| ☐ 31 | Vada Pinson | 10.00 | 4.00 | 1.00 |
| ☐ 32 | Wally Post | 7.00 | 2.80 | .70 |
| ☐ 33A | Vic Power (Indians) | 25.00 | 10.00 | 2.50 |
| ☐ 33B | Vic Power (Twins) | 75.00 | 30.00 | 7.50 |
| ☐ 34A | Bob Purkey (with autograph) | 25.00 | 10.00 | 2.50 |
| ☐ 34B | Bob Purkey (no autograph) | 75.00 | 30.00 | 7.50 |
| ☐ 35 | Frank Robinson | 45.00 | 18.00 | 4.50 |
| ☐ 36 | John Romano | 7.00 | 2.80 | .70 |
| ☐ 37 | Dick Stuart | 8.00 | 3.25 | .80 |
| ☐ 38 | Bill Virdon | 10.00 | 4.00 | 1.00 |

## 1962 Kahn's Atlanta

The cards in this 24 card set measure 3 1/4" by 4". The 1962 Kahn's Wieners Atlanta set features unnumbered, black and white cards of the Atlanta Crackers of the International League. The backs contain player statistical information as well as instructions on how to obtain free tickets. The ACC designation is F155-9.

| | MINT | VG-E | F-G |
|---|---|---|---|
| COMPLETE SET | 225.00 | 90.00 | 22.00 |
| COMMON PLAYER | 9.00 | 3.75 | .90 |

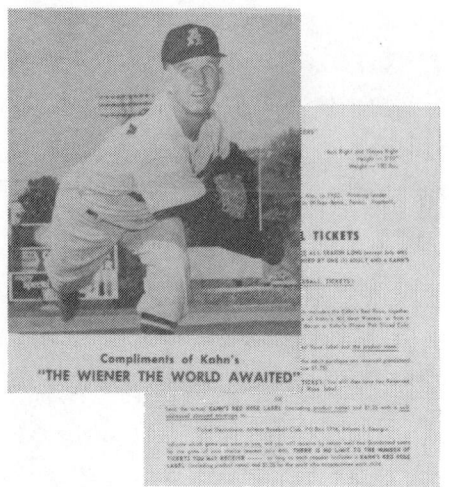

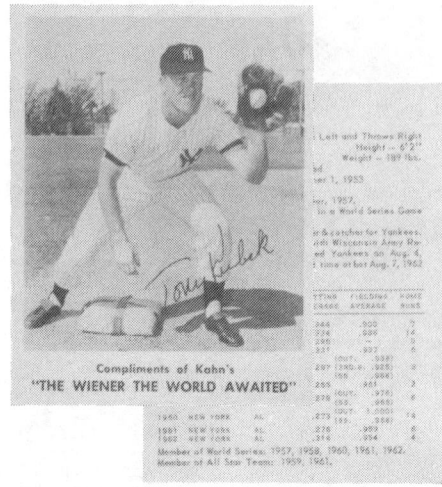

| | | | MINT | VG-E | F-G |
|---|---|---|---|---|---|
| ☐ | 1 | Jim Beauchamp | 10.00 | 4.00 | 1.00 |
| ☐ | 2 | Gerry Buchek | 9.00 | 3.75 | .90 |
| ☐ | 3 | Bob Burda | 9.00 | 3.75 | .90 |
| ☐ | 4 | Dick Dietz | 9.00 | 3.75 | .90 |
| ☐ | 5 | Bob Duliba | 9.00 | 3.75 | .90 |
| ☐ | 6 | Harry Fanok | 9.00 | 3.75 | .90 |
| ☐ | 7 | Phil Gagliano | 10.00 | 4.00 | 1.00 |
| ☐ | 8 | John Glenn | 9.00 | 3.75 | .90 |
| ☐ | 9 | Leroy Gregory | 9.00 | 3.75 | .90 |
| ☐ | 10 | Dick Hughes | 9.00 | 3.75 | .90 |
| ☐ | 11 | Johnny Kucks | 10.00 | 4.00 | 1.00 |
| ☐ | 12 | Johnny Lewis | 9.00 | 3.75 | .90 |
| ☐ | 13 | Tim McCarver | 25.00 | 10.00 | 2.50 |
| ☐ | 14 | Bob Milliken | 9.00 | 3.75 | .90 |
| ☐ | 15 | Joe Morgan | 9.00 | 3.75 | .90 |
| ☐ | 16 | Ron Plaza | 9.00 | 3.75 | .90 |
| ☐ | 17 | Bob Sadowski | 9.00 | 3.75 | .90 |
| ☐ | 18 | Jim Saul | 9.00 | 3.75 | .90 |
| ☐ | 19 | Willard Schmidt | 9.00 | 3.75 | .90 |
| ☐ | 20 | Joe Schultz | 9.00 | 3.75 | .90 |
| ☐ | 21 | Mike Shannon | 20.00 | 8.00 | 2.00 |
| ☐ | 22 | Paul Toth | 9.00 | 3.75 | .90 |
| ☐ | 23 | Lou Vickery | 9.00 | 3.75 | .90 |
| ☐ | 24 | Fred Whitfield | 10.00 | 4.00 | 1.00 |

| | | | MINT | VG-E | F-G |
|---|---|---|---|---|---|
| ☐ | 14 | Harvey Haddix | 8.00 | 3.25 | .80 |
| ☐ | 15 | Elston Howard | 12.00 | 5.00 | 1.20 |
| ☐ | 16 | Joey Jay | 7.00 | 2.80 | .70 |
| ☐ | 17 | Eddie Kasko | 7.00 | 2.80 | .70 |
| ☐ | 18 | Tony Kubek | 12.00 | 5.00 | 1.20 |
| ☐ | 19 | Jerry Lynch | 7.00 | 2.80 | .70 |
| ☐ | 20 | Jim Maloney | 8.00 | 3.25 | .80 |
| ☐ | 21 | Bill Mazeroski | 12.00 | 5.00 | 1.20 |
| ☐ | 22 | Joe Nuxhall | 8.00 | 3.25 | .80 |
| ☐ | 23 | Jim O'Toole | 7.00 | 2.80 | .70 |
| ☐ | 24 | Vada Pinson | 10.00 | 4.00 | 1.00 |
| ☐ | 25 | Bob Purkey | 7.00 | 2.80 | .70 |
| ☐ | 26 | Bobby Richardson | 12.00 | 5.00 | 1.20 |
| ☐ | 27 | Frank Robinson | 40.00 | 16.00 | 4.00 |
| ☐ | 28 | Bill Stafford | 7.00 | 2.80 | .70 |
| ☐ | 29 | Ralph Terry | 8.00 | 3.25 | .80 |
| ☐ | 30 | Bill Virdon | 10.00 | 4.00 | 1.00 |

## 1964 Kahn's

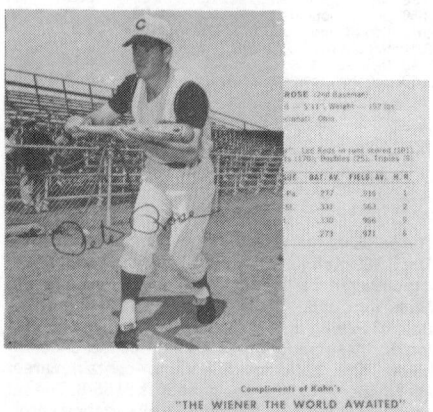

## 1963 Kahn's

The cards in this 30 card set measure 3 1/4" by 4". The 1963 Kahn's Wieners set of black and white, unnumbered cards features players from Cincinnati, Cleveland, St. Louis, Pittsburgh and the New York Yankees. The cards feature a white border around the picture of the players. The backs contain career information. The ACC designation is F155-10.

| | | | MINT | VG-E | F-G |
|---|---|---|---|---|---|
| COMPLETE SET | | | 325.00 | 130.00 | 32.00 |
| COMMON PLAYER | | | 7.00 | 2.80 | .70 |
| ☐ | 1 | Bob Bailey | 7.00 | 2.80 | .70 |
| ☐ | 2 | Don Blasingame | 7.00 | 2.80 | .70 |
| ☐ | 3 | Clete Boyer | 8.00 | 3.25 | .80 |
| ☐ | 4 | Smoky Burgess | 8.00 | 3.25 | .80 |
| ☐ | 5 | Chico Cardenas | 7.00 | 2.80 | .70 |
| ☐ | 6 | Roberto Clemente | 100.00 | 40.00 | 10.00 |
| ☐ | 7 | Donn Clendenon | 7.00 | 2.80 | .70 |
| ☐ | 8 | Gordon Coleman | 7.00 | 2.80 | .70 |
| ☐ | 9 | John Edwards | 7.00 | 2.80 | .70 |
| ☐ | 10 | Gene Freese | 7.00 | 2.80 | .70 |
| ☐ | 11 | Bob Friend | 8.00 | 3.25 | .80 |
| ☐ | 12 | Joe Gibbon | 7.00 | 2.80 | .70 |
| ☐ | 13 | Dick Groat | 10.00 | 4.00 | 1.00 |

The cards in this 31 card set measure 3" by 3 1/2". The 1964 Kahn's set marks the beginning of the full color cards and the elimination of the tabs which existed on previous Kahn's cards. The set of unnumbered cards contains player information through the 1963 season on the backs. The set features Cincinnati, Cleveland and Pittsburgh players.

|  | | MINT | VG-E | F-G |
|---|---|---|---|---|
| COMPLETE SET | | 550.00 | 220.00 | 55.00 |
| COMMON PLAYER (1-31) | | 7.00 | 2.80 | .70 |
| ☐ 1 | Max Alvis | 7.00 | 2.80 | .70 |
| ☐ 2 | Bob Bailey | 7.00 | 2.80 | .70 |
| ☐ 3 | Chico Cardenas | 7.00 | 2.80 | .70 |
| ☐ 4 | Roberto Clemente | 100.00 | 40.00 | 10.00 |
| ☐ 5 | Donn Clendenon | 8.00 | 3.25 | .80 |
| ☐ 6 | Vic Davalillo | 7.00 | 2.80 | .70 |
| ☐ 7 | Dick Donovan | 7.00 | 2.80 | .70 |
| ☐ 8 | John Edwards | 7.00 | 2.80 | .70 |
| ☐ 9 | Bob Friend | 8.00 | 3.25 | .80 |
| ☐ 10 | Jim Grant | 7.00 | 2.80 | .70 |
| ☐ 11 | Tommy Harper | 7.00 | 2.80 | .70 |
| ☐ 12 | Woodie Held | 7.00 | 2.80 | .70 |
| ☐ 13 | Joey Jay | 7.00 | 2.80 | .70 |
| ☐ 14 | Jack Kralick | 7.00 | 2.80 | .70 |
| ☐ 15 | Jerry Lynch | 7.00 | 2.80 | .70 |
| ☐ 16 | Jim Maloney | 8.00 | 3.25 | .80 |
| ☐ 17 | Bill Mazeroski | 12.00 | 5.00 | 1.20 |
| ☐ 18 | Alvin McBean | 7.00 | 2.80 | .70 |
| ☐ 19 | Joe Nuxhall | 8.00 | 3.25 | .80 |
| ☐ 20 | Jim Pagliaroni | 7.00 | 2.80 | .70 |
| ☐ 21 | Vada Pinson | 10.00 | 4.00 | 1.00 |
| ☐ 22 | Bob Purkey | 7.00 | 2.80 | .70 |
| ☐ 23 | Pedro Ramos | 7.00 | 2.80 | .70 |
| ☐ 24 | Frank Robinson | 40.00 | 16.00 | 4.00 |
| ☐ 25 | John Romano | 7.00 | 2.80 | .70 |
| ☐ 26 | Pete Rose | 250.00 | 100.00 | 25.00 |
| ☐ 27 | John Tsitouris | 7.00 | 2.80 | .70 |
| ☐ 28 | Bob Veale | 7.00 | 2.80 | .70 |
| ☐ 29 | Bill Virdon | 10.00 | 4.00 | 1.00 |
| ☐ 30 | Leon Wagner | 7.00 | 2.80 | .70 |
| ☐ 31 | Fred Whitfield | 7.00 | 2.80 | .70 |

| | | MINT | VG-E | F-G |
|---|---|---|---|---|
| ☐ 9 | Tony Cloninger | 7.00 | 2.80 | .70 |
| ☐ 10 | Gordon Coleman | 7.00 | 2.80 | .70 |
| ☐ 11 | Vic Davalillo | 7.00 | 2.80 | .70 |
| ☐ 12 | John Edwards | 7.00 | 2.80 | .70 |
| ☐ 13 | Sammy Ellis | 7.00 | 2.80 | .70 |
| ☐ 14 | Bob Friend | 8.00 | 3.25 | .80 |
| ☐ 15 | Tommy Harper | 7.00 | 2.80 | .70 |
| ☐ 16 | Chuck Hinton | 7.00 | 2.80 | .70 |
| ☐ 17 | Dick Howser | 10.00 | 4.00 | 1.00 |
| ☐ 18 | Joey Jay | 7.00 | 2.80 | .70 |
| ☐ 19 | Deron Johnson | 7.00 | 2.80 | .70 |
| ☐ 20 | Jack Kralick | 7.00 | 2.80 | .70 |
| ☐ 21 | Denver LeMaster | 7.00 | 2.80 | .70 |
| ☐ 22 | Jerry Lynch | 7.00 | 2.80 | .70 |
| ☐ 23 | Jim Maloney | 8.00 | 3.25 | .80 |
| ☐ 24 | Lee Maye | 7.00 | 2.80 | .70 |
| ☐ 25 | Bill Mazeroski | 12.00 | 5.00 | 1.20 |
| ☐ 26 | Alvin McBean | 7.00 | 2.80 | .70 |
| ☐ 27 | Bill McCool | 7.00 | 2.80 | .70 |
| ☐ 28 | Sam McDowell | 8.00 | 3.25 | .80 |
| ☐ 29 | Don McMahon | 7.00 | 2.80 | .70 |
| ☐ 30 | Denis Menke | 7.00 | 2.80 | .70 |
| ☐ 31 | Joe Nuxhall | 8.00 | 3.25 | .80 |
| ☐ 32 | Gene Oliver | 7.00 | 2.80 | .70 |
| ☐ 33 | Jim O'Toole | 7.00 | 2.80 | .70 |
| ☐ 34 | Jim Pagliaroni | 7.00 | 2.80 | .70 |
| ☐ 35 | Vada Pinson | 10.00 | 4.00 | 1.00 |
| ☐ 36 | Frank Robinson | 35.00 | 14.00 | 3.50 |
| ☐ 37 | Pete Rose | 175.00 | 70.00 | 18.00 |
| ☐ 38 | Willie Stargell | 40.00 | 16.00 | 4.00 |
| ☐ 39 | Ralph Terry | 8.00 | 3.25 | .80 |
| ☐ 40 | Luis Tiant | 10.00 | 4.00 | 1.00 |
| ☐ 41 | Joe Torre | 12.00 | 5.00 | 1.20 |
| ☐ 42 | John Tsitouris | 7.00 | 2.80 | .70 |
| ☐ 43 | Bob Veale | 8.00 | 3.25 | .80 |
| ☐ 44 | Bill Virdon | 10.00 | 4.00 | 1.00 |
| ☐ 45 | Leon Wagner | 7.00 | 2.80 | .70 |

## 1965 Kahn's

Compliments of Kahn's
"THE WIENER THE WORLD AWAITED"

The cards in this 45 card set measure 3" by 3 1/2". The 1965 Kahn's set contains full color, unnumbered cards. The set features Cincinnati, Cleveland, Pittsburgh, and Milwaukee players. Backs contain statistical information through the 1964 season.

| | | MINT | VG-E | F-G |
|---|---|---|---|---|
| COMPLETE SET | | 550.00 | 220.00 | 55.00 |
| COMMON PLAYER (1-45) | | 7.00 | 2.80 | .70 |
| ☐ 1 | Henry Aaron | 90.00 | 36.00 | 9.00 |
| ☐ 2 | Max Alvis | 7.00 | 2.80 | .70 |
| ☐ 3 | Joe Azcue | 7.00 | 2.80 | .70 |
| ☐ 4 | Bob Bailey | 7.00 | 2.80 | .70 |
| ☐ 5 | Frank Bolling | 7.00 | 2.80 | .70 |
| ☐ 6 | Chico Cardenas | 7.00 | 2.80 | .70 |
| ☐ 7 | Rico Carty | 10.00 | 4.00 | 1.00 |
| ☐ 8 | Donn Clendenon | 8.00 | 3.25 | .80 |

## 1966 Kahn's

The cards in this 32 card set measure 2 13/16" by 4". 1966 Kahn's full color, unnumbered set features players from Atlanta, Cincinnati, Cleveland, and Pittsburgh. The set is identified by yellow and white vertical stripes and the name Kahn's written in red across a red rose at the top. The cards contain a 1 5/16" ad in the form of a tab. Cards with the ad (tab) are worth twice as much as cards without the ad, i.e., double the prices below.

| | | MINT | VG-E | F-G |
|---|---|---|---|---|
| COMPLETE SET | | 300.00 | 120.00 | 30.00 |
| COMMON PLAYER (1-32) | | 4.00 | 1.60 | .40 |
| ☐ 1 | Henry Aaron (portrait, no windbreaker under jersey | 50.00 | 20.00 | 5.00 |
| ☐ 2 | Felipe Alou: Braves (full pose, batting screen in background) | 5.00 | 2.00 | .50 |

| | | MINT | VG-E | F-G |
|---|---|---|---|---|
| ☐ 3 | Max Alvis: Indians ............. (kneeling, full pose, with bat, no patch on jersey) | 4.00 | 1.60 | .40 |
| ☐ 4 | Bob Bailey ........................ | 4.00 | 1.60 | .40 |
| ☐ 5 | Wade Blasingame ............. | 4.00 | 1.60 | .40 |
| ☐ 6 | Frank Bolling .................... | 4.00 | 1.60 | .40 |
| ☐ 7 | Chico Cardenas: Reds ...... (fielding, feet at base) | 4.00 | 1.60 | .40 |
| ☐ 8 | Roberto Clemente ............ | 50.00 | 20.00 | 5.00 |
| ☐ 9 | Tony Cloninger: Braves ..... (pitching, foulpole in background) | 4.00 | 1.60 | .40 |
| ☐ 10 | Vic Davalillo ..................... | 4.00 | 1.60 | .40 |
| ☐ 11 | John Edwards: Reds ......... (catching) | 4.00 | 1.60 | .40 |
| ☐ 12 | Sam Ellis: Reds ................ (white hat) | 4.00 | 1.60 | .40 |
| ☐ 13 | Pedro Gonzalez ................ | 4.00 | 1.60 | .40 |
| ☐ 14 | Tommy Harper: Reds ....... (arm cocked) | 4.00 | 1.60 | .40 |
| ☐ 15 | Deron Johnson: Reds ....... (batting with batting cage in background) | 4.00 | 1.60 | .40 |
| ☐ 16 | Mack Jones ...................... | 4.00 | 1.60 | .40 |
| ☐ 17 | Denver Lemaster .............. | 4.00 | 1.60 | .40 |
| ☐ 18 | Jim Maloney: Reds ........... (pitching, white hat) | 5.00 | 2.00 | .50 |
| ☐ 19 | Bill Mazeroski: Pirates ...... (throwing) | 7.50 | 3.00 | .75 |
| ☐ 20 | Bill McCool: Reds ............. (white hat) | 4.00 | 1.60 | .40 |
| ☐ 21 | Sam McDowell: Indians ..... (kneeling) | 5.00 | 2.00 | .50 |
| ☐ 22 | Denis Menke: Braves ........ (white windbreaker under jersey) | 4.00 | 1.60 | .40 |
| ☐ 23 | Joe Nuxhall ...................... | 5.00 | 2.00 | .50 |
| ☐ 24 | Jim Pagliaroni: Pirates ...... (catching) | 4.00 | 1.60 | .40 |
| ☐ 25 | Milt Pappas ...................... | 5.00 | 2.00 | .50 |
| ☐ 26 | Vada Pinson: Reds ............ (fielding, ball on ground) | 7.50 | 3.00 | .75 |
| ☐ 27 | Pete Rose: Reds ............... (with glove) | 100.00 | 40.00 | 10.00 |
| ☐ 28 | Sonny Siebert: Indians ..... (pitching, signature at feet) | 4.00 | 1.60 | .40 |
| ☐ 29 | Willie Stargell: ................... Pirates (batting, clouds in sky) | 25.00 | 10.00 | 2.50 |
| ☐ 30 | Joe Torre: Braves ............. (catching with hand on mask) | 9.00 | 3.75 | .90 |
| ☐ 31 | Bob Veale: Pirates ............ (hands at knee with glasses) | 5.00 | 2.00 | .50 |
| ☐ 32 | Fred Whitfield ................... | 4.00 | 1.60 | .40 |

## 1967 Kahn's

The cards in this 41 card set measure 2 13/16" by 4". The 1967 Kahn's set of full color, unnumbered cards is almost identical in style to the 1966 issue. Different meat products had different background colors (yellow and white stripes, red and white stripes, etc.). The set features players from Atlanta, Cincinnati, Cleveland, New York Mets and Pittsburgh. Cards with the ads (see 1966 set) are worth twice as much as cards without the ad, i.e., double the prices below.

| | | MINT | VG-E | F-G |
|---|---|---|---|---|
| COMPLETE SET | ......................... | 325.00 | 130.00 | 32.00 |
| COMMON PLAYER (1-41) | .......... | 4.00 | 1.60 | .40 |
| ☐ 1 | Henry Aaron: Braves ........ (swinging pose, batting glove, ball, and hat on ground) | 50.00 | 20.00 | 5.00 |
| ☐ 2 | Gene Alley: Pirates ........... (portrait) | 5.00 | 2.00 | .50 |

| | | | | |
|---|---|---|---|---|
| ☐ 3 | Felipe Alou: Braves ........... (full pose, bat on shoulder) | 5.00 | 2.00 | .50 |
| ☐ 4 | Matty Alou: Pirates ........... (portrait with bat, "Matio Rojas Alou") | 5.00 | 2.00 | .50 |
| ☐ 5 | Max Alvis: Indians ............. (fielding, hands on knees) | 4.00 | 1.60 | .40 |
| ☐ 6 | Ken Boyer ......................... | 8.00 | 3.25 | .80 |
| ☐ 7 | Chico Cardenas: Reds ...... (fielding, hand on knee) | 4.00 | 1.60 | .40 |
| ☐ 8 | Rico Carty ........................ | 6.00 | 2.40 | .60 |
| ☐ 9 | Tony Cloninger: Braves ..... (pitching, no foulpole in background) | 4.00 | 1.60 | .40 |
| ☐ 10 | Tommy Davis ..................... | 6.00 | 2.40 | .60 |
| ☐ 11 | John Edwards: Reds ......... (kneeling with bat) | 4.00 | 1.60 | .40 |
| ☐ 12 | Sam Ellis: Reds ................ (all red hat) | 4.00 | 1.60 | .40 |
| ☐ 13 | Jack Fisher ...................... | 4.00 | 1.60 | .40 |
| ☐ 14 | Steve Hargan: Indians ....... (pitching, no clouds, blue sky) | 4.00 | 1.60 | .40 |
| ☐ 15 | Tommy Harper: Reds ....... (fielding, glove on ground) | 4.00 | 1.60 | .40 |
| ☐ 16 | Tommy Helms ................... | 4.00 | 1.60 | .40 |
| ☐ 17 | Deron Johnson: Reds ....... (batting, blue sky) | 4.00 | 1.60 | .40 |
| ☐ 18 | Ken Johnson .................... | 4.00 | 1.60 | .40 |
| ☐ 19 | Cleon Jones ..................... | 4.00 | 1.60 | .40 |
| ☐ 20 | Ed Kranepool .................... | 5.00 | 2.00 | .50 |
| ☐ 21 | Jim Maloney: Reds ........... (pitching, red hat, follow thru delivery) | 5.00 | 2.00 | .50 |
| ☐ 22 | Lee May: Reds .................. (hands on knee) | 5.00 | 2.00 | .50 |
| ☐ 23 | Bill Mazeroski: Pirates ...... (portrait) | 7.50 | 3.00 | .75 |
| ☐ 24 | Bill McCool: Reds (red ...... hat, left hand out) | 4.00 | 1.60 | .40 |
| ☐ 25 | Sam McDowell: Indians .... (pitching, left hand under glove) | 5.00 | 2.00 | .50 |
| ☐ 26 | Denis Menke: Braves ........ (blue sleeves) | 4.00 | 1.60 | .40 |
| ☐ 27 | Jim Pagliaroni: Pirates ...... (catching, no chest protector) | 4.00 | 1.60 | .40 |
| ☐ 28 | Don Pavletich ................... | 4.00 | 1.60 | .40 |
| ☐ 29 | Tony Perez: Reds ............. (throwing) | 10.00 | 4.00 | 1.00 |
| ☐ 30 | Vada Pinson: Reds ............ (ready to throw) | 7.50 | 3.00 | .75 |
| ☐ 31 | Dennis Ribant ................... | 4.00 | 1.60 | .40 |
| ☐ 32 | Pete Rose: Reds ............... (batting) | 100.00 | 40.00 | 10.00 |
| ☐ 33 | Art Shamsky: Reds ........... | 4.00 | 1.60 | .40 |
| ☐ 34 | Bob Shaw ........................ | 4.00 | 1.60 | .40 |
| ☐ 35 | Sonny Siebert: Indians ...... (pitching, signature at knees) | 4.00 | 1.60 | .40 |
| ☐ 36 | Willie Stargell: ................... Pirates (batting, | 25.00 | 10.00 | 2.50 |

| | | MINT | VG-E | F-G |
|---|---|---|---|---|
| | no clouds) | | | |
| ☐ 37 | Joe Torre: Braves ............ (catching, mask on ground) | 9.00 | 3.75 | .90 |
| ☐ 38 | Bob Veale: Pirates ............ (portrait, hands not shown) | 5.00 | 2.00 | .50 |
| ☐ 39 | Leon Wagner: Indians ....... (fielding) | 4.00 | 1.60 | .40 |
| ☐ 40 | Fred Whitfield ................... | 4.00 | 1.60 | .40 |
| ☐ 41 | Woody Woodward ............. | 4.00 | 1.60 | .40 |

## 1968 Kahn's

The cards in this 50 card set contain two different sizes. The smaller of the two sizes, which contains 12 cards, is 2 13/16" by 3 1/4" with the ad tab and 2 13/16" by 1 7/8" without the ad tab. The larger size, which contains 38 cards, measures 2 13/16" by 3 7/8" with the ad tab and 2 13/16" by 2 11/16" without the ad tab. The 1968 Kahn's set of full color, blank backed, unnumbered cards features players from Atlanta, Chicago Cubs, Chicago White Sox, Cincinnati, Cleveland, Detroit, New York Mets and Pittsburgh. In the set of 12, listed with the letter A in the checklist, Maloney exists with either yellow or yellow and green stripes at the top of the card. The large set of 38, listed with a letter B in the checklist, contains five cards which exist in two variations. The variations in this large set have either yellow or red stripes at the top of the cards, with Maloney being an exception. Maloney has either a yellow stripe or a Blue Mountain ad at the top. Cards with the ad tabs (see other Kahn's sets) are worth twice as much as cards without the ad, i.e., double the prices below.

| | | MINT | VG-E | F-G |
|---|---|---|---|---|
| COMPLETE SET | ..................... | 400.00 | 160.00 | 40.00 |
| COMMON PLAYER | ................ | 4.00 | 1.60 | .40 |
| ☐ A1 | Hank Aaron .................... | 50.00 | 20.00 | 5.00 |
| ☐ A2 | Gene Alley ...................... | 5.00 | 2.00 | .50 |
| ☐ A3 | Max Alvis ....................... | 4.00 | 1.60 | .40 |
| ☐ A4 | Clete Boyer .................... | 5.00 | 2.00 | .50 |
| ☐ A5 | Chico Cardenas ............... | 4.00 | 1.60 | .40 |
| ☐ A6 | Bill Freehan ................... | 5.00 | 2.00 | .50 |
| ☐ A7 | Jim Maloney (2) ............. | 5.00 | 2.00 | .50 |
| ☐ A8 | Lee May ......................... | 5.00 | 2.00 | .50 |
| ☐ A9 | Bill Mazeroski ................ | 7.50 | 3.00 | .75 |
| ☐ A10 | Vada Pinson ................... | 7.50 | 3.00 | .75 |
| ☐ A11 | Joe Torre ....................... | 9.00 | 3.75 | .90 |
| ☐ A12 | Bob Veale ...................... | 5.00 | 2.00 | .50 |
| ☐ B1 | Hank Aaron: Braves ........ (full pose, batting bat cocked) | 50.00 | 20.00 | 5.00 |
| ☐ B2 | Tommy Agee ................... | 4.00 | 1.60 | .40 |

| | | MINT | VG-E | F-G |
|---|---|---|---|---|
| ☐ B3 | Gene Alley: Pirates ......... (fielding, full pose) | 5.00 | 2.00 | .50 |
| ☐ B4 | Felipe Alou(full pose, ...... batting, swinging, player in background) | 5.00 | 2.00 | .50 |
| ☐ B5 | Matty Alou: Pirates ......... (portrait with bat, "Matio Alou" (2) | 5.00 | 2.00 | .50 |
| ☐ B6 | Max Alvis (fielding, ......... glove on ground) | 4.00 | 1.60 | .40 |
| ☐ B7 | Gerry Arrigo: Reds ......... (pitching, follow thru delivery) | 4.00 | 1.60 | .40 |
| ☐ B8 | John Bench .................... | 150.00 | 60.00 | 15.00 |
| ☐ B9 | Clete Boyer .................... | 5.00 | 2.00 | .50 |
| ☐ B10 | Larry Brown ................... | 4.00 | 1.60 | .40 |
| ☐ B11 | Leo Cardenas: Reds ....... (leaping in the air) | 4.00 | 1.60 | .40 |
| ☐ B12 | Bill Freehan ................... | 5.00 | 2.00 | .50 |
| ☐ B13 | Steve Hargan: Indians .... (pitching, clouds in background) | 4.00 | 1.60 | .40 |
| ☐ B14 | Joel Horlen: White Sox ... (portrait) | 4.00 | 1.60 | .40 |
| ☐ B15 | Tony Horton: Indians ...... (portrait, signed Anthony) | 4.00 | 1.60 | .40 |
| ☐ B16 | Willie Horton .................. | 5.00 | 2.00 | .50 |
| ☐ B17 | Ferguson Jenkins ............ | 10.00 | 4.00 | 1.00 |
| ☐ B18 | Deron Johnson: Braves .. | 4.00 | 1.60 | .40 |
| ☐ B19 | Mack Jones: Reds .......... | 4.00 | 1.60 | .40 |
| ☐ B20 | Bob Lee ......................... | 4.00 | 1.60 | .40 |
| ☐ B21 | Jim Maloney: Reds ......... (red hat, pitching hands up) (2) | 5.00 | 2.00 | .50 |
| ☐ B22 | Lee May: Reds ............... (batting) | 5.00 | 2.00 | .50 |
| ☐ B23 | Bill Mazeroski: ............... Pirates (fielding, hands in front of body) | 7.50 | 3.00 | .75 |
| ☐ B24 | Dick McAuliffe ................ | 4.00 | 1.60 | .40 |
| ☐ B25 | Bill McCool (red hat, ...... left hand down) | 4.00 | 1.60 | .40 |
| ☐ B26 | Sam McDowell: Indians .. (pitching, left hand over glove) (2) | 5.00 | 2.00 | .50 |
| ☐ B27 | Tony Perez (fielding ........ ball in glove (2) | 10.00 | 4.00 | 1.00 |
| ☐ B28 | Gary Peters: White Sox .. (portrait) | 4.00 | 1.60 | .40 |
| ☐ B29 | Vada Pinson: Reds ......... (batting) | 7.50 | 3.00 | .75 |
| ☐ B30 | Chico Ruiz ..................... | 4.00 | 1.60 | .40 |
| ☐ B31 | Ron Santo: Cubs ............ (batting, follow thru (2) | 7.50 | 3.00 | .75 |
| ☐ B32 | Art Shamsky: Mets ......... | 4.00 | 1.60 | .40 |
| ☐ B33 | Luis Tiant: Indians .......... (hands over head) | 6.00 | 2.40 | .60 |
| ☐ B34 | Joe Torre: Braves ........... (batting) | 9.00 | 3.75 | .90 |
| ☐ B35 | Bob Veale: Pirates .......... (hands chest high) | 5.00 | 2.00 | .50 |
| ☐ B36 | Leon Wagner: Indians ..... (batting) | 4.00 | 1.60 | .40 |
| ☐ B37 | Billy Williams: Cubs ......... (bat behind back) | 20.00 | 8.00 | 2.00 |
| ☐ B38 | Earl Wilson ..................... | 4.00 | 1.60 | .40 |

## 1969 Kahn's

The cards in this 25 card set contain two different sizes. The three small cards (see 1968 description) measure 2 13/16" by 3 1/4" and the 22 large cards (see 1968 description) measure 2 13/16" by 3 15/16". The 1969 Kahn's Wieners set of full color, unnumbered cards features players from Atlanta, Chicago Cubs, Chicago White Sox, Cincinnati, Cleveland, Pittsburgh, and St. Louis. The small cards have the letter A in the checklist while the large cards have the letter B in the checklist. Four of the larger cards exist in two variations (red or yellow

color stripes at the top of the card). These variations are identified in the checklist below. Cards with the ad tabs (see other Kahn's sets) are worth twice as much as cards without the ad, i.e., double the prices below.

|  | MINT | VG-E | F-G |
|---|---|---|---|
| COMPLETE SET ............... | 200.00 | 80.00 | 20.00 |
| COMMON PLAYER ............. | 4.00 | 1.60 | .40 |

| | | MINT | VG-E | F-G |
|---|---|---|---|---|
| ☐ | A1 Hank Aaron (portrait) ..... | 50.00 | 20.00 | 5.00 |
| ☐ | A2 Jim Maloney (pitching .... hands at side) | 5.00 | 2.00 | .50 |
| ☐ | A3 Tony Perez (glove on) .... | 10.00 | 4.00 | 1.00 |
| ☐ | B1 Hank Aaron ................... | 50.00 | 20.00 | 5.00 |
| ☐ | B2 Matty Alou (batting) ....... | 5.00 | 2.00 | .50 |
| ☐ | B3 Max Alvis ('69 patch) ..... | 4.00 | 1.60 | .40 |
| ☐ | B4 Gerry Arrigo (leg up) ...... | 4.00 | 1.60 | .40 |
| ☐ | B5 Steve Blass .................. | 4.00 | 1.60 | .40 |
| ☐ | B6 Clay Carroll ................. | 4.00 | 1.60 | .40 |
| ☐ | B7 Tony Cloninger: Reds ..... | 4.00 | 1.60 | .40 |
| ☐ | B8 George Culver .............. | 4.00 | 1.60 | .40 |
| ☐ | B9 Joel Horlen (pitching) ..... | 4.00 | 1.60 | .40 |
| ☐ | B10 Tony Horton (batting) .... | 4.00 | 1.60 | .40 |
| ☐ | B11 Alex Johnson .............. | 4.00 | 1.60 | .40 |
| ☐ | B12 Jim Maloney .............. | 5.00 | 2.00 | .50 |
| ☐ | B13 Lee May (foot on ........... bag) (2) | 5.00 | 2.00 | .50 |
| ☐ | B14 Bill Mazeroski ............. (hands on knees) (2) | 7.50 | 3.00 | .75 |
| ☐ | B15 Sam McDowell .............. (leg up) (2) | 5.00 | 2.00 | .50 |
| ☐ | B16 Tony Perez ................. | 10.00 | 4.00 | 1.00 |
| ☐ | B17 Gary Peters (pitching) .... | 4.00 | 1.60 | .40 |
| ☐ | B18 Ron Santo (emblem 2) ... | 7.50 | 3.00 | .75 |
| ☐ | B19 Luis Tiant (glove at ......... knee) | 6.00 | 2.40 | .60 |
| ☐ | B20 Joe Torre: Cardinals ....... | 9.00 | 3.75 | .90 |
| ☐ | B21 Bob Veale (hands at ....... knees, no glasses) | 5.00 | 2.00 | .50 |
| ☐ | B22 Billy Williams (bat ........... behind head) | 20.00 | 8.00 | 2.00 |

# 1986 Kay-Bee Young Stars

This 33-card, standard-sized (2 1/2" by 3 1/2") set was produced by Topps, although manufactured in Northern Ireland. This boxed set retailed in Kay-Bee stores for 1.99; the checklist was listed on the back of the box. The set is subtitled "Young Superstars of Baseball" and does indeed feature many young players. The cards are numbered on the back.

| | MINT | VG-E | F-G |
|---|---|---|---|
| COMPLETE SET .......................... | 4.00 | 1.25 | .30 |
| COMMON PLAYER .................... | .10 | .04 | .01 |

| | | MINT | VG-E | F-G |
|---|---|---|---|---|
| ☐ | 1 Rick Aguilera ...................... | .15 | .06 | .01 |
| ☐ | 2 Chris Brown ...................... | .25 | .10 | .02 |
| ☐ | 3 Tom Browning ................. | .15 | .06 | .01 |
| ☐ | 4 Tom Brunansky ............... | .15 | .06 | .01 |
| ☐ | 5 Vince Coleman ................ | .35 | .14 | .03 |
| ☐ | 6 Ron Darling ...................... | .20 | .08 | .02 |
| ☐ | 7 Alvin Davis ...................... | .20 | .08 | .02 |
| ☐ | 8 Mariano Duncan ............... | .15 | .06 | .01 |
| ☐ | 9 Shawon Dunston .............. | .20 | .08 | .02 |
| ☐ | 10 Sid Fernandez ................. | .20 | .08 | .02 |
| ☐ | 11 Tony Fernandez .............. | .15 | .06 | .01 |
| ☐ | 12 Brian Fisher ................... | .15 | .06 | .01 |
| ☐ | 13 John Franco ................... | .15 | .06 | .01 |
| ☐ | 14 Julio Franco .................. | .15 | .06 | .01 |
| ☐ | 16 Dwight Gooden ................. | .75 | .30 | .07 |
| ☐ | 16 Ozzie Guillen ................. | .20 | .08 | .02 |
| ☐ | 17 Tony Gwynn ................... | .35 | .14 | .03 |
| ☐ | 18 Jimmy Key .................... | .15 | .06 | .01 |
| ☐ | 19 Don Mattingly ................ | 1.00 | .40 | .10 |
| ☐ | 20 Oddibe McDowell ............. | .20 | .08 | .02 |
| ☐ | 21 Roger McDowell .............. | .15 | .06 | .01 |
| ☐ | 22 Dan Pasqua ................... | .25 | .10 | .02 |
| ☐ | 23 Terry Pendleton .............. | .10 | .04 | .01 |
| ☐ | 24 Jim Presley ................... | .25 | .10 | .02 |
| ☐ | 25 Kirby Puckett ................. | .35 | .14 | .03 |
| ☐ | 26 Earnie Riles .................. | .10 | .04 | .01 |
| ☐ | 27 Bret Saberhagen ............. | .20 | .08 | .02 |
| ☐ | 28 Mark Salas ................... | .10 | .04 | .01 |
| ☐ | 29 Juan Samuel ................. | .15 | .06 | .01 |
| ☐ | 30 Jeff Stone .................... | .10 | .04 | .01 |
| ☐ | 31 Darryl Strawberry ............ | .50 | .20 | .05 |
| ☐ | 32 Andy Van Slyke .............. | .10 | .04 | .01 |
| ☐ | 33 Frank Viola ................... | .10 | .04 | .01 |

# 1970 Kellogg's

The cards in this 75 card set measure 2 1/4" by 3 1/2". The 1970 Kellogg's set was Kellogg's first venture into the baseball card producing field. The design incorporates a brilliant color photo of the player set against an indistinct background, which is then covered with a layer of plastic to simulate a 3-D look. Cards 16-30 seem to be in shorter supply than the other cards in the set.

|  | MINT | VG-E | F-G |
|---|---|---|---|
| COMPLETE SET .................. | 65.00 | 25.00 | 6.00 |
| COMMON PLAYER (1-15) .......... | .60 | .24 | .06 |
| COMMON PLAYER (16-30) ........ | .75 | .30 | .07 |
| COMMON PLAYER (31-75) ........ | .60 | .24 | .06 |

| | | | MINT | VG-E | F-G |
|---|---|---|---|---|---|
| ☐ | 1 | Ed Kranepool ..................... | .60 | .24 | .06 |
| ☐ | 2 | Pete Rose ......................... | 10.00 | 4.00 | 1.00 |
| ☐ | 3 | Cleon Jones ....................... | .60 | .24 | .06 |
| ☐ | 4 | Willie McCovey ................... | 2.50 | 1.00 | .25 |
| ☐ | 5 | Mel Stottlemyre ................. | .75 | .30 | .07 |
| ☐ | 6 | Frank Howard .................... | .75 | .30 | .07 |
| ☐ | 7 | Tom Seaver ....................... | 4.00 | 1.60 | .40 |
| ☐ | 8 | Don Sutton ....................... | 1.50 | .60 | .15 |
| ☐ | 9 | Jim Wynn ......................... | .75 | .30 | .07 |
| ☐ | 10 | Jim Maloney ...................... | .75 | .30 | .07 |
| ☐ | 11 | Tommie Agee ..................... | .60 | .24 | .06 |
| ☐ | 12 | Willie Mays ....................... | 5.00 | 2.00 | .50 |
| ☐ | 13 | Juan Marichal .................... | 2.50 | 1.00 | .25 |
| ☐ | 14 | Dave McNally .................... | .75 | .30 | .07 |
| ☐ | 15 | Frank Robinson ................. | 3.00 | 1.20 | .30 |
| ☐ | 16 | Carlos May ....................... | .75 | .30 | .07 |
| ☐ | 17 | Bill Singer ........................ | .75 | .30 | .07 |
| ☐ | 18 | Rick Reichardt ................... | .75 | .30 | .07 |
| ☐ | 19 | Boog Powell ..................... | 1.00 | .40 | .10 |
| ☐ | 20 | Gaylord Perry .................... | 2.50 | 1.00 | .25 |
| ☐ | 21 | Brooks Robinson ............... | 4.00 | 1.60 | .40 |
| ☐ | 22 | Luis Aparicio ..................... | 3.00 | 1.20 | .30 |
| ☐ | 23 | Joel Horlen ....................... | .75 | .30 | .07 |
| ☐ | 24 | Mike Epstein ..................... | .75 | .30 | .07 |
| ☐ | 25 | Tom Haller ........................ | .75 | .30 | .07 |
| ☐ | 26 | Willie Crawford .................. | .75 | .30 | .07 |
| ☐ | 27 | Roberto Clemente .............. | 6.00 | 2.40 | .60 |
| ☐ | 28 | Matty Alou ........................ | .75 | .30 | .07 |
| ☐ | 29 | Willie Stargell ................... | 2.50 | 1.00 | .25 |
| ☐ | 30 | Tim Cullen ........................ | .75 | .30 | .07 |
| ☐ | 31 | Randy Hundley ................... | .50 | .20 | .05 |
| ☐ | 32 | Reggie Jackson .................. | 5.00 | 2.00 | .50 |
| ☐ | 33 | Rich Allen ......................... | .75 | .30 | .07 |
| ☐ | 34 | Tim McCarver .................... | .75 | .30 | .07 |
| ☐ | 35 | Ray Culp .......................... | .50 | .20 | .05 |
| ☐ | 36 | Jim Fregosi ....................... | .75 | .30 | .07 |
| ☐ | 37 | Billy Williams .................... | 2.50 | 1.00 | .25 |
| ☐ | 38 | Johnny Odom .................... | .60 | .24 | .06 |
| ☐ | 39 | Bert Campaneris ............... | .75 | .30 | .07 |
| ☐ | 40 | Ernie Banks ...................... | 3.00 | 1.20 | .30 |
| ☐ | 41 | Chris Short ....................... | .60 | .24 | .06 |
| ☐ | 42 | Ron Santo ........................ | .90 | .36 | .09 |
| ☐ | 43 | Glenn Beckert .................... | .60 | .24 | .06 |
| ☐ | 44 | Lou Brock ......................... | 3.00 | 1.20 | .30 |
| ☐ | 45 | Larry Hisle ........................ | .75 | .30 | .07 |
| ☐ | 46 | Reggie Smith ..................... | .75 | .30 | .07 |
| ☐ | 47 | Rod Carew ........................ | 3.00 | 1.20 | .30 |
| ☐ | 48 | Curt Flood ........................ | .75 | .30 | .07 |
| ☐ | 49 | Jim Lonborg ...................... | .75 | .30 | .07 |
| ☐ | 50 | Sam McDowell ................... | .75 | .30 | .07 |
| ☐ | 51 | Sal Bando ......................... | .75 | .30 | .07 |
| ☐ | 52 | Al Kaline .......................... | 3.00 | 1.20 | .30 |
| ☐ | 53 | Gary Nolan ....................... | .60 | .24 | .06 |
| ☐ | 54 | Rico Petrocelli ................... | .60 | .24 | .06 |
| ☐ | 55 | Ollie Brown ....................... | .60 | .24 | .06 |
| ☐ | 56 | Luis Tiant ......................... | .75 | .30 | .07 |
| ☐ | 57 | Bill Freehan ...................... | .75 | .30 | .07 |
| ☐ | 58 | Johnny Bench .................... | 3.50 | 1.40 | .35 |
| ☐ | 59 | Joe Pepitone ..................... | .75 | .30 | .07 |
| ☐ | 60 | Bobby Murcer .................... | .90 | .36 | .09 |
| ☐ | 61 | Harmon Killebrew .............. | 2.50 | 1.00 | .25 |
| ☐ | 62 | Don Wilson ....................... | .60 | .24 | .06 |
| ☐ | 63 | Tony Oliva ........................ | .90 | .36 | .09 |
| ☐ | 64 | Jim Perry ......................... | .75 | .30 | .07 |
| ☐ | 65 | Mickey Lolich .................... | .90 | .36 | .09 |
| ☐ | 66 | Jose Laboy ....................... | .60 | .24 | .06 |
| ☐ | 67 | Dean Chance ..................... | .60 | .24 | .06 |
| ☐ | 68 | Bud Harrelson ................... | .60 | .24 | .06 |
| ☐ | 69 | Willie Horton ..................... | .75 | .30 | .07 |
| ☐ | 70 | Wally Bunker ..................... | .60 | .24 | .06 |
| ☐ | 71 | Bob Gibson ....................... | 2.50 | 1.00 | .25 |
| ☐ | 72 | Joe Morgan ....................... | 2.50 | 1.00 | .25 |
| ☐ | 73 | Denny McLain .................... | .90 | .36 | .09 |
| ☐ | 74 | Tommy Harper ................... | .60 | .24 | .06 |
| ☐ | 75 | Don Mincher ..................... | .60 | .24 | .06 |

> **PLEASE NOTE:** Prices in advertising are subject to change, as is the availability of items listed for sale. If you are responding to an ad late in the baseball season, write or phone ahead for current availability and prices.

## 1971 Kellogg's

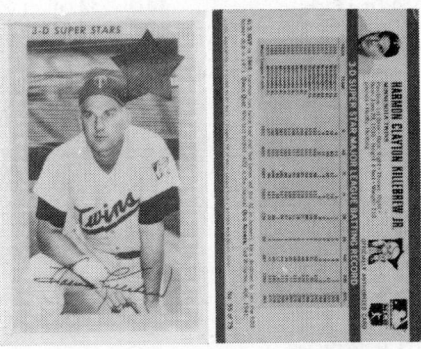

The cards in this 75 card set measure 2 1/4" by 3 1/2". The 1971 set of 3-D cards marketed by the Kellogg Company is the scarcest of all that company's issues. It was distributed as single cards, one in each package of cereal, without the usual complete set mail in offer. In addition, card dealers were unable to obtain this set in quantity, as they have in other years. All the cards are available with and without the copyright notice on the back; the version without carries a slight premium for most numbers. Prices listed below are for the more common variety with copyright.

| | | | MINT | VG-E | F-G |
|---|---|---|---|---|---|
| | COMPLETE SET ...................... | | 400.00 | 160.00 | 40.00 |
| | COMMON PLAYER (1-75) .......... | | 3.25 | 1.30 | .32 |
| ☐ | 1 | Wayne Simpson ................ | 3.25 | 1.30 | .32 |
| ☐ | 2 | Tom Seaver ...................... | 15.00 | 6.00 | 1.50 |
| ☐ | 3 | Jim Perry ......................... | 3.75 | 1.50 | .37 |
| ☐ | 4 | Bob Robertson ................. | 3.25 | 1.30 | .32 |
| ☐ | 5 | Roberto Clemente ............ | 18.00 | 7.25 | 1.80 |
| ☐ | 6 | Gaylord Perry ................... | 7.50 | 3.00 | .75 |
| ☐ | 7 | Felipe Alou ....................... | 3.75 | 1.50 | .37 |
| ☐ | 8 | Denis Menke ..................... | 3.25 | 1.30 | .32 |
| ☐ | 9 | Don Kessinger ................... | 3.25 | 1.30 | .32 |
| ☐ | 10 | Willie Mays ....................... | 18.00 | 7.25 | 1.80 |
| ☐ | 11 | Jim Hickman ..................... | 3.25 | 1.30 | .32 |
| ☐ | 12 | Tony Oliva ........................ | 5.00 | 2.00 | .50 |
| ☐ | 13 | Manny Sanguillen .............. | 3.75 | 1.50 | .37 |
| ☐ | 14 | Frank Howard .................... | 3.75 | 1.50 | .37 |
| ☐ | 15 | Frank Robinson ................. | 9.00 | 3.75 | .90 |
| ☐ | 16 | Willie Davis ...................... | 3.75 | 1.50 | .37 |
| ☐ | 17 | Lou Brock ......................... | 10.00 | 4.00 | 1.00 |
| ☐ | 18 | Cesar Tovar ...................... | 3.25 | 1.30 | .32 |
| ☐ | 19 | Luis Aparicio ..................... | 7.50 | 3.00 | .75 |
| ☐ | 20 | Boog Powell ..................... | 5.00 | 2.00 | .50 |
| ☐ | 21 | Dick Selma ....................... | 3.25 | 1.30 | .32 |
| ☐ | 22 | Danny Walton .................... | 3.25 | 1.30 | .32 |
| ☐ | 23 | Carl Morton ...................... | 3.25 | 1.30 | .32 |
| ☐ | 24 | Sonny Siebert ................... | 3.25 | 1.30 | .32 |
| ☐ | 25 | Jim Merritt ....................... | 3.25 | 1.30 | .32 |
| ☐ | 26 | Jose Cardenal ................... | 3.25 | 1.30 | .32 |
| ☐ | 27 | Don Mincher ..................... | 3.25 | 1.30 | .32 |
| ☐ | 28 | Clyde Wright ..................... | 3.25 | 1.30 | .32 |
| ☐ | 29 | Les Cain .......................... | 3.25 | 1.30 | .32 |
| ☐ | 30 | Danny Cater ..................... | 3.25 | 1.30 | .32 |
| ☐ | 31 | Don Sutton ....................... | 7.50 | 3.00 | .75 |
| ☐ | 32 | Chuck Dobson ................... | 3.25 | 1.30 | .32 |
| ☐ | 33 | Willie McCovey .................. | 10.00 | 4.00 | 1.00 |
| ☐ | 34 | Mike Epstein ..................... | 3.25 | 1.30 | .32 |
| ☐ | 35 | Paul Blair ......................... | 3.75 | 1.50 | .37 |
| ☐ | 36 | Gary Nolan ....................... | 3.25 | 1.30 | .32 |
| ☐ | 37 | Sam McDowell ................... | 3.75 | 1.50 | .37 |
| ☐ | 38 | Amos Otis ........................ | 3.25 | 1.30 | .32 |
| ☐ | 39 | Ray Fosse ........................ | 3.25 | 1.30 | .32 |
| ☐ | 40 | Mel Stottlemyre ................. | 3.75 | 1.50 | .37 |
| ☐ | 41 | Clarence Gaston ................ | 3.25 | 1.30 | .32 |
| ☐ | 42 | Dick Dietz ........................ | 3.25 | 1.30 | .32 |
| ☐ | 43 | Roy White ......................... | 3.75 | 1.50 | .37 |
| ☐ | 44 | Al Kaline .......................... | 12.00 | 5.00 | 1.20 |
| ☐ | 45 | Carlos May ....................... | 3.25 | 1.30 | .32 |

| | | | |
|---|---|---|---|
| ☐ 46 Tommie Agee | 3.25 | 1.30 | .32 |
| ☐ 47 Tommy Harper | 3.25 | 1.30 | .32 |
| ☐ 48 Larry Dierker | 3.25 | 1.30 | .32 |
| ☐ 49 Mike Cuellar | 3.75 | 1.50 | .37 |
| ☐ 50 Ernie Banks | 10.00 | 4.00 | 1.00 |
| ☐ 51 Bob Gibson | 9.00 | 3.75 | .90 |
| ☐ 52 Reggie Smith | 3.75 | 1.50 | .37 |
| ☐ 53 Matty Alou | 3.75 | 1.50 | .37 |
| ☐ 54 Alex Johnson | 3.25 | 1.30 | .32 |
| ☐ 55 Harmon Killebrew | 9.00 | 3.75 | .90 |
| ☐ 56 Bill Grabarkewitz | 3.25 | 1.30 | .32 |
| ☐ 57 Richie Allen | 5.00 | 2.00 | .50 |
| ☐ 58 Tony Perez | 6.00 | 2.40 | .60 |
| ☐ 59 Dave McNally | 3.75 | 1.50 | .37 |
| ☐ 60 Jim Palmer | 9.00 | 3.75 | .90 |
| ☐ 61 Billy Williams | 9.00 | 3.75 | .90 |
| ☐ 62 Joe Torre | 5.00 | 2.00 | .50 |
| ☐ 63 Jim Northrup | 3.25 | 1.30 | .32 |
| ☐ 64 Jim Fregosi | 3.75 | 1.50 | .37 |
| ☐ 65 Pete Rose | 40.00 | 16.00 | 4.00 |
| ☐ 66 Bud Harrelson | 3.25 | 1.30 | .32 |
| ☐ 67 Tony Taylor | 3.25 | 1.30 | .32 |
| ☐ 68 Willie Stargell | 9.00 | 3.75 | .90 |
| ☐ 69 Tony Horton | 3.25 | 1.30 | .32 |
| ☐ 70 Claude Osteen | 3.25 | 1.30 | .32 |
| ☐ 71 Glenn Beckert | 3.25 | 1.30 | .32 |
| ☐ 72 Nate Colbert | 3.25 | 1.30 | .32 |
| ☐ 73 Rick Monday | 3.75 | 1.50 | .37 |
| ☐ 74 Tommy John | 6.00 | 2.40 | .60 |
| ☐ 75 Chris Short | 3.25 | 1.30 | .32 |

| | | | |
|---|---|---|---|
| ☐ 19 Manny Sanguillen | .50 | .20 | .05 |
| ☐ 20 Reggie Jackson | 4.50 | 1.80 | .45 |
| ☐ 21 Ralph Garr | .40 | .16 | .04 |
| ☐ 22 Jim Hunter | 2.00 | .80 | .20 |
| ☐ 23 Rick Wise | .40 | .16 | .04 |
| ☐ 24 Glenn Beckert | .40 | .16 | .04 |
| ☐ 25 Tony Oliva | .75 | .30 | .07 |
| ☐ 26 Bob Gibson | 2.00 | .80 | .20 |
| ☐ 27 Mike Cuellar | .50 | .20 | .05 |
| ☐ 28 Chris Speier | .40 | .16 | .04 |
| ☐ 29 Dave McNally | .50 | .20 | .05 |
| ☐ 30 Leo Cardenas | .40 | .16 | .04 |
| ☐ 31 Bill Freehan | .50 | .20 | .05 |
| ☐ 32 Bud Harrelson | .40 | .16 | .04 |
| ☐ 33 Sam McDowell | .50 | .20 | .05 |
| ☐ 34 Claude Osteen | .50 | .20 | .05 |
| ☐ 35 Reggie Smith | .50 | .20 | .05 |
| ☐ 36 Sonny Siebert | .40 | .16 | .04 |
| ☐ 37 Lee May | .50 | .20 | .05 |
| ☐ 38 Mickey Lolich | .60 | .24 | .06 |
| ☐ 39 Cookie Rojas | .40 | .16 | .04 |
| ☐ 40 Dick Drago | .40 | .16 | .04 |
| ☐ 41 Nate Colbert | .40 | .16 | .04 |
| ☐ 42 Andy Messersmith | .50 | .20 | .05 |
| ☐ 43 Dave Johnson | .50 | .20 | .05 |
| ☐ 44 Steve Blass | .40 | .16 | .04 |
| ☐ 45 Bob Robertson | .40 | .16 | .04 |
| ☐ 46 Billy Williams | 2.00 | .80 | .20 |
| ☐ 47 Juan Marichal | 2.00 | .80 | .20 |
| ☐ 48 Lou Brock | 2.50 | 1.00 | .25 |
| ☐ 49 Roberto Clemente | 4.50 | 1.80 | .45 |
| ☐ 50 Mel Stottlemyre | .50 | .20 | .05 |
| ☐ 51 Don Wilson | .40 | .16 | .04 |
| ☐ 52 Sal Bando | .50 | .20 | .05 |
| ☐ 53 Willie Stargell | 2.00 | .80 | .20 |
| ☐ 54 Willie Mays | 4.50 | 1.80 | .45 |

## 1972 Kellogg's

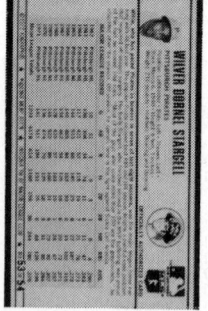

The cards in this 54 card set measure 2 1/8" by 3 1/4". The dimensions of the cards in the 1972 Kellogg's set were reduced in comparison to those of the 1971 series. In addition, the length of the set was set at 54 cards rather than the 75 of the previous year. The cards of this Kellogg's set are characterized by the diagonal bands found on the obverse.

| | MINT | VG-E | F-G |
|---|---|---|---|
| COMPLETE SET | 40.00 | 16.00 | 4.00 |
| COMMON PLAYER (1-54) | .40 | .16 | .04 |
| ☐ 1 Tom Seaver | 4.00 | 1.60 | .40 |
| ☐ 2 Amos Otis | .60 | .24 | .06 |
| ☐ 3 Willie Davis | .50 | .20 | .05 |
| ☐ 4 Wilbur Wood | .50 | .20 | .05 |
| ☐ 5 Bill Parsons | .40 | .16 | .04 |
| ☐ 6 Pete Rose | 9.00 | 3.75 | .90 |
| ☐ 7 Willie McCovey | 2.50 | 1.00 | .25 |
| ☐ 8 Ferguson Jenkins | .75 | .30 | .07 |
| ☐ 9 Vida Blue | .50 | .20 | .05 |
| ☐ 10 Joe Torre | .75 | .30 | .07 |
| ☐ 11 Merv Rettenmund | .40 | .16 | .04 |
| ☐ 12 Bill Melton | .40 | .16 | .04 |
| ☐ 13 Jim Palmer | 2.50 | 1.00 | .25 |
| ☐ 14 Doug Rader | .40 | .16 | .04 |
| ☐ 15 Dave Roberts | .40 | .16 | .04 |
| ☐ 16 Bobby Murcer | .50 | .20 | .05 |
| ☐ 17 Wes Parker | .40 | .16 | .04 |
| ☐ 18 Joe Coleman | .40 | .16 | .04 |

## 1972 Kellogg's ATG

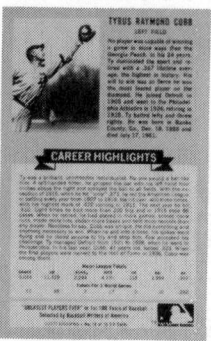

The cards in this 15 card set measure 2 1/4" by 3 1/2". The 1972 All-Time Greats 3-D set was issued with Kellogg's Danish Go Rounds. The set is a reissue of a 1970 set issued by Rold Gold Pretzels to commemorate baseball's first 100 years. The set contains two different cards of Babe Ruth.

| | MINT | VG-E | F-G |
|---|---|---|---|
| COMPLETE SET | 10.00 | 4.00 | 1.00 |
| COMMON PLAYER (1-15) | .40 | .16 | .04 |
| ☐ 1 Walter Johnson | 1.00 | .40 | .10 |
| ☐ 2 Rogers Hornsby | .60 | .24 | .06 |
| ☐ 3 John McGraw | .40 | .16 | .04 |
| ☐ 4 Mickey Cochrane | .50 | .20 | .05 |
| ☐ 5 George Sisler | .50 | .20 | .05 |
| ☐ 6 Babe Ruth | 2.00 | .80 | .20 |
| ☐ 7 Lefty Grove | .60 | .24 | .06 |
| ☐ 8 Pie Traynor | .40 | .16 | .04 |
| ☐ 9 Honus Wagner | 1.00 | .40 | .10 |
| ☐ 10 Eddie Collins | .40 | .16 | .04 |
| ☐ 11 Tris Speaker | .60 | .24 | .06 |
| ☐ 12 Cy Young | .60 | .24 | .06 |
| ☐ 13 Lou Gehrig | 1.25 | .50 | .12 |

| | | MINT | VG-E | F-G |
|---|---|---|---|---|
| ☐ 14 | Babe Ruth | 2.00 | .80 | .20 |
| ☐ 15 | Ty Cobb | 1.25 | .50 | .12 |

| | | | | |
|---|---|---|---|---|
| ☐ 45 | Carlos May | .40 | .16 | .04 |
| ☐ 46 | Tom Seaver | 3.00 | 1.20 | .30 |
| ☐ 47 | Mike Cuellar | .50 | .20 | .05 |
| ☐ 48 | Joe Coleman | .40 | .16 | .04 |
| ☐ 49 | Claude Osteen | .50 | .20 | .05 |
| ☐ 50 | Steve Kline | .40 | .16 | .04 |
| ☐ 51 | Rod Carew | 3.00 | 1.20 | .30 |
| ☐ 52 | Al Kaline | 2.50 | 1.00 | .25 |
| ☐ 53 | Larry Dierker | .40 | .16 | .04 |
| ☐ 54 | Ron Santo | .60 | .24 | .06 |

# 1973 Kellogg's 2D

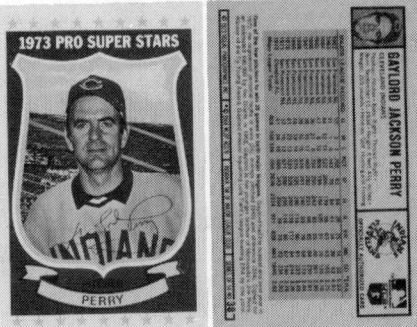

The cards in this 54 card set measure 2 1/4" by 3 1/2". The 1973 Kellogg's set is the only non 3-D set produced by the Kellogg Company. Apparently Kellogg's decided to have the cards produced through Visual Panographics rather than by Xograph as in the other years. The complete set could be obtained from the company through a box top redemption procedure. The card size is slightly larger than the previous year.

| | | MINT | VG-E | F-G |
|---|---|---|---|---|
| COMPLETE SET | | 35.00 | 14.00 | 3.50 |
| COMMON PLAYER (1-54) | | .40 | .16 | .04 |
| ☐ 1 | Amos Otis | .60 | .24 | .06 |
| ☐ 2 | Ellie Rodriguez | .40 | .16 | .04 |
| ☐ 3 | Mickey Lolich | .60 | .24 | .06 |
| ☐ 4 | Tony Oliva | .60 | .24 | .06 |
| ☐ 5 | Don Sutton | 1.50 | .60 | .15 |
| ☐ 6 | Pete Rose | 9.00 | 3.75 | .90 |
| ☐ 7 | Steve Carlton | 3.50 | 1.40 | .35 |
| ☐ 8 | Bobby Bonds | .60 | .24 | .06 |
| ☐ 9 | Wilbur Wood | .50 | .20 | .05 |
| ☐ 10 | Billy Williams | 2.00 | .80 | .20 |
| ☐ 11 | Steve Blass | .40 | .16 | .04 |
| ☐ 12 | Jon Matlack | .50 | .20 | .05 |
| ☐ 13 | Cesar Cedeno | .50 | .20 | .05 |
| ☐ 14 | Bob Gibson | 2.00 | .80 | .20 |
| ☐ 15 | Sparky Lyle | .60 | .24 | .06 |
| ☐ 16 | Nolan Ryan | 3.00 | 1.20 | .30 |
| ☐ 17 | Jim Palmer | 2.00 | .80 | .20 |
| ☐ 18 | Ray Fosse | .40 | .16 | .04 |
| ☐ 19 | Bobby Murcer | .60 | .24 | .06 |
| ☐ 20 | Jim Hunter | 2.00 | .80 | .20 |
| ☐ 21 | Tom McCraw | .40 | .16 | .04 |
| ☐ 22 | Reggie Jackson | 4.00 | 1.60 | .40 |
| ☐ 23 | Bill Stoneman | .40 | .16 | .04 |
| ☐ 24 | Lou Piniella | .60 | .24 | .06 |
| ☐ 25 | Willie Stargell | 2.00 | .80 | .20 |
| ☐ 26 | Dick Allen | .60 | .24 | .06 |
| ☐ 27 | Carlton Fisk | 1.25 | .50 | .12 |
| ☐ 28 | Ferguson Jenkins | .75 | .30 | .07 |
| ☐ 29 | Phil Niekro | 2.00 | .80 | .20 |
| ☐ 30 | Gary Nolan | .40 | .16 | .04 |
| ☐ 31 | Joe Torre | .60 | .24 | .06 |
| ☐ 32 | Bobby Tolan | .40 | .16 | .04 |
| ☐ 33 | Nate Colbert | .40 | .16 | .04 |
| ☐ 34 | Joe Morgan | 2.00 | .80 | .20 |
| ☐ 35 | Bert Blyleven | .60 | .24 | .06 |
| ☐ 36 | Joe Rudi | .50 | .20 | .05 |
| ☐ 37 | Ralph Garr | .40 | .16 | .04 |
| ☐ 38 | Gaylord Perry | 1.50 | .60 | .15 |
| ☐ 39 | Bobby Grich | .50 | .20 | .05 |
| ☐ 40 | Lou Brock | 2.00 | .80 | .20 |
| ☐ 41 | Pete Broberg | .40 | .16 | .04 |
| ☐ 42 | Manny Sanguillen | .50 | .20 | .05 |
| ☐ 43 | Willie Davis | .50 | .20 | .05 |
| ☐ 44 | Dave Kingman | .75 | .30 | .07 |

# 1974 Kellogg's

The cards in this 54 card set measure 2 1/8" by 3 1/4". In 1974 the Kellogg's set returned to its 3-D format; it also returned to the smaller sized card. Complete sets could be obtained from the company through a box top offer.

| | | MINT | VG-E | F-G |
|---|---|---|---|---|
| COMPLETE SET | | 35.00 | 14.00 | 3.50 |
| COMMON PLAYER (1-54) | | .30 | .12 | .03 |
| ☐ 1 | Bob Gibson | 2.00 | .80 | .20 |
| ☐ 2 | Rick Monday | .40 | .16 | .04 |
| ☐ 3 | Joe Coleman | .30 | .12 | .03 |
| ☐ 4 | Bert Campaneris | .40 | .16 | .04 |
| ☐ 5 | Carlton Fisk | .90 | .36 | .09 |
| ☐ 6 | Jim Palmer | 2.00 | .80 | .20 |
| ☐ 7 | Ron Santo | .50 | .20 | .05 |
| ☐ 8 | Nolan Ryan | 3.00 | 1.20 | .30 |
| ☐ 9 | Greg Luzinski | .60 | .24 | .06 |
| ☐ 10 | Buddy Bell | .60 | .24 | .06 |
| ☐ 11 | Bob Watson | .40 | .16 | .04 |
| ☐ 12 | Bill Singer | .30 | .12 | .03 |
| ☐ 13 | Dave May | .30 | .12 | .03 |
| ☐ 14 | Jim Brewer | .30 | .12 | .03 |
| ☐ 15 | Manny Sanguillen | .40 | .16 | .04 |
| ☐ 16 | Jeff Burroughs | .40 | .16 | .04 |
| ☐ 17 | Amos Otis | .40 | .16 | .04 |
| ☐ 18 | Ed Goodson | .30 | .12 | .03 |
| ☐ 19 | Nate Colbert | .30 | .12 | .03 |
| ☐ 20 | Reggie Jackson | 4.00 | 1.60 | .40 |
| ☐ 21 | Ted Simmons | .75 | .30 | .07 |
| ☐ 22 | Bobby Murcer | .50 | .20 | .05 |
| ☐ 23 | Willie Horton | .40 | .16 | .04 |
| ☐ 24 | Orlando Cepeda | .60 | .24 | .06 |
| ☐ 25 | Ron Hunt | .30 | .12 | .03 |
| ☐ 26 | Wayne Twitchell | .30 | .12 | .03 |
| ☐ 27 | Ron Fairly | .30 | .12 | .03 |
| ☐ 28 | Johnny Bench | 3.00 | 1.20 | .30 |
| ☐ 29 | John Mayberry | .30 | .12 | .03 |
| ☐ 30 | Rod Carew | 3.00 | 1.20 | .30 |
| ☐ 31 | Ken Holtzman | .40 | .16 | .04 |
| ☐ 32 | Billy Williams | 1.50 | .60 | .15 |
| ☐ 33 | Dick Allen | .60 | .24 | .06 |
| ☐ 34 | Wilbur Wood | .40 | .16 | .04 |
| ☐ 35 | Danny Thompson | .30 | .12 | .03 |
| ☐ 36 | Joe Morgan | 2.00 | .80 | .20 |
| ☐ 37 | Willie Stargell | 1.50 | .60 | .15 |
| ☐ 38 | Pete Rose | 8.00 | 3.25 | .80 |
| ☐ 39 | Bobby Bonds | .50 | .20 | .05 |
| ☐ 40 | Chris Speier | .30 | .12 | .03 |
| ☐ 41 | Sparky Lyle | .50 | .20 | .05 |
| ☐ 42 | Cookie Rojas | .30 | .12 | .03 |

| | | | | | |
|---|---|---|---|---|---|
| ☐ 43 | Tommy Davis | .40 | .16 | .04 |
| ☐ 44 | Jim Hunter | 1.50 | .60 | .15 |
| ☐ 45 | Willie Davis | .40 | .16 | .04 |
| ☐ 46 | Bert Blyleven | .50 | .20 | .05 |
| ☐ 47 | Pat Kelly | .30 | .12 | .03 |
| ☐ 48 | Ken Singleton | .40 | .16 | .04 |
| ☐ 49 | Manny Mota | .40 | .16 | .04 |
| ☐ 50 | Dave Johnson | .40 | .16 | .04 |
| ☐ 51 | Sal Bando | .40 | .16 | .04 |
| ☐ 52 | Tom Seaver | 3.00 | 1.20 | .30 |
| ☐ 53 | Felix Millan | .30 | .12 | .03 |
| ☐ 54 | Ron Blomberg | .30 | .12 | .03 |

| | | | | | |
|---|---|---|---|---|---|
| ☐ 40 | Ken Singleton | .80 | .32 | .08 |
| ☐ 41 | Steve Braun | .50 | .20 | .05 |
| ☐ 42 | Rich Allen | .90 | .36 | .09 |
| ☐ 43 | John Grubb | .50 | .20 | .05 |
| ☐ 44 | Jim Hunter (2) | 3.00 | 1.20 | .30 |
| ☐ 45 | Gaylord Perry | 2.00 | .80 | .20 |
| ☐ 46 | George Hendrick | .80 | .32 | .08 |
| ☐ 47 | Sparky Lyle | .90 | .36 | .09 |
| ☐ 48 | Dave Cash | .50 | .20 | .05 |
| ☐ 49 | Luis Tiant | .75 | .30 | .07 |
| ☐ 50 | Cesar Geronimo | .50 | .20 | .05 |
| ☐ 51 | Carl Yastrzemski | 8.00 | 3.25 | .80 |
| ☐ 52 | Ken Brett | .50 | .20 | .05 |
| ☐ 53 | Hal McRae | .80 | .32 | .08 |
| ☐ 54 | Reggie Jackson | 6.00 | 2.40 | .60 |
| ☐ 55 | Rollie Fingers | 2.00 | .80 | .20 |
| ☐ 56 | Mike Schmidt | 8.00 | 3.25 | .80 |
| ☐ 57 | Richie Hebner | .50 | .20 | .05 |

## 1975 Kellogg's

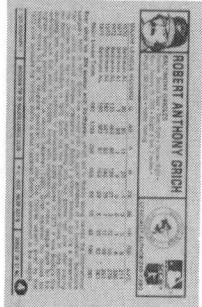

The cards in this 57 card set measure 2 1/8" by 3 1/4". The 1975 Kellogg's 3-D set could be obtained card by card in cereal boxes or as a set from a box top offer from the company. Card number 44 Jim Hunter exists with the A's emblem or the Yankee's emblem on the back of the card.

| | MINT | VG-E | F-G |
|---|---|---|---|
| COMPLETE SET | 90.00 | 36.00 | 9.00 |
| COMMON PLAYER (1-57) | .50 | .20 | .05 |

| | | | | | |
|---|---|---|---|---|---|
| ☐ | 1 | Roy White | .60 | .24 | .06 |
| ☐ | 2 | Ross Grimsley | .50 | .20 | .05 |
| ☐ | 3 | Reggie Smith | .60 | .24 | .06 |
| ☐ | 4 | Bob Grich | .60 | .24 | .06 |
| ☐ | 5 | Greg Gross | .50 | .20 | .05 |
| ☐ | 6 | Bob Watson | .60 | .24 | .06 |
| ☐ | 7 | Johnny Bench | 5.00 | 2.00 | .50 |
| ☐ | 8 | Jeff Burroughs | .60 | .24 | .06 |
| ☐ | 9 | Elliott Maddox | .50 | .20 | .05 |
| ☐ | 10 | Jon Matlack | .60 | .24 | .06 |
| ☐ | 11 | Pete Rose | 12.50 | 5.00 | 1.25 |
| ☐ | 12 | Lee Stanton | .50 | .20 | .05 |
| ☐ | 13 | Bake McBride | .50 | .20 | .05 |
| ☐ | 14 | Jorge Orta | .50 | .20 | .05 |
| ☐ | 15 | Al Oliver | 1.25 | .50 | .12 |
| ☐ | 16 | John Briggs | .50 | .20 | .05 |
| ☐ | 17 | Steve Garvey | 5.00 | 2.00 | .50 |
| ☐ | 18 | Brooks Robinson | 4.00 | 1.60 | .40 |
| ☐ | 19 | John Hiller | .60 | .24 | .06 |
| ☐ | 20 | Lynn McGlothen | .50 | .20 | .05 |
| ☐ | 21 | Cleon Jones | .50 | .20 | .05 |
| ☐ | 22 | Fergie Jenkins | 1.00 | .40 | .10 |
| ☐ | 23 | Bill North | .50 | .20 | .05 |
| ☐ | 24 | Steve Busby | .60 | .24 | .06 |
| ☐ | 25 | Richie Zisk | .60 | .24 | .06 |
| ☐ | 26 | Nolan Ryan | 5.00 | 2.00 | .50 |
| ☐ | 27 | Joe Morgan | 3.00 | 1.20 | .30 |
| ☐ | 28 | Joe Rudi | .60 | .24 | .06 |
| ☐ | 29 | Jose Cardenal | .50 | .20 | .05 |
| ☐ | 30 | Andy Messersmith | .60 | .24 | .06 |
| ☐ | 31 | Willie Montanez | .50 | .20 | .05 |
| ☐ | 32 | Bill Buckner | .90 | .36 | .09 |
| ☐ | 33 | Rod Carew | 5.00 | 2.00 | .50 |
| ☐ | 34 | Lou Piniella | .75 | .30 | .07 |
| ☐ | 35 | Ralph Garr | .60 | .24 | .06 |
| ☐ | 36 | Mike Marshall | .60 | .24 | .06 |
| ☐ | 37 | Garry Maddox | .60 | .24 | .06 |
| ☐ | 38 | Dwight Evans | 1.00 | .40 | .10 |
| ☐ | 39 | Lou Brock | 4.00 | 1.60 | .40 |

## 1976 Kellogg's

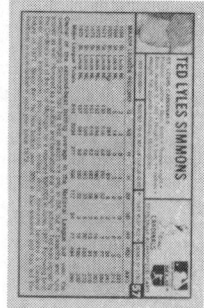

The cards in this 57 card set measure 2 1/8" by 3 1/4". The 1976 Kellogg's 3-D set could be obtained card by card in cereal boxes or as a set from the company for box tops. Card number 6, that of Clay Carroll, exists with both a Reds or White Sox emblem on the back. Cards 1-3 (marked in the checklist below with SP) were apparently printed apart from the other 54 and are in shorter supply.

| | MINT | VG-E | F-G |
|---|---|---|---|
| COMPLETE SET | 45.00 | 18.00 | 4.50 |
| COMMON PLAYER (1-3) SP | 6.00 | 2.40 | .60 |
| COMMON PLAYER (4-57) | .30 | .12 | .03 |

| | | | | | |
|---|---|---|---|---|---|
| ☐ | 1 | Steve Hargan SP | 6.00 | 2.40 | .60 |
| ☐ | 2 | Claudell Washington SP | 6.00 | 2.40 | .60 |
| ☐ | 3 | Don Gullett SP | 6.00 | 2.40 | .60 |
| ☐ | 4 | Randy Jones | .40 | .16 | .04 |
| ☐ | 5 | Jim Hunter | 1.50 | .60 | .15 |
| ☐ | 6 | Clay Carroll (2) | .60 | .24 | .06 |
| ☐ | 7 | Joe Rudi | .40 | .16 | .04 |
| ☐ | 8 | Reggie Jackson | 3.50 | 1.40 | .35 |
| ☐ | 9 | Felix Millan | .30 | .12 | .03 |
| ☐ | 10 | Jim Rice | 2.50 | 1.00 | .25 |
| ☐ | 11 | Bert Blyleven | .50 | .20 | .05 |
| ☐ | 12 | Ken Singleton | .40 | .16 | .04 |
| ☐ | 13 | Don Sutton | 1.25 | .50 | .12 |
| ☐ | 14 | Joe Morgan | 2.00 | .80 | .20 |
| ☐ | 15 | Dave Parker | 1.50 | .60 | .15 |
| ☐ | 16 | Dave Cash | .30 | .12 | .03 |
| ☐ | 17 | Ron LeFlore | .40 | .16 | .04 |
| ☐ | 18 | Greg Luzinski | .60 | .24 | .06 |
| ☐ | 19 | Dennis Eckersley | .40 | .16 | .04 |
| ☐ | 20 | Bill Madlock | .90 | .36 | .09 |
| ☐ | 21 | George Scott | .30 | .12 | .03 |
| ☐ | 22 | Willie Stargell | 1.25 | .50 | .12 |
| ☐ | 23 | Al Hrabosky | .40 | .16 | .04 |
| ☐ | 24 | Carl Yastrzemski | 4.00 | 1.60 | .40 |
| ☐ | 25 | Jim Kaat | .75 | .30 | .07 |
| ☐ | 26 | Marty Perez | .30 | .12 | .03 |
| ☐ | 27 | Bob Watson | .30 | .12 | .03 |
| ☐ | 28 | Eric Soderholm | .30 | .12 | .03 |
| ☐ | 29 | Bill Lee | .30 | .12 | .03 |

| | | MINT | VG-E | F-G |
|---|---|---|---|---|
| ☐ 30 | Frank Tanana | .40 | .16 | .04 |
| ☐ 31 | Fred Lynn | 1.50 | .60 | .15 |
| ☐ 32 | Tom Seaver | 3.00 | 1.20 | .30 |
| ☐ 33 | Steve Busby | .40 | .16 | .04 |
| ☐ 34 | Gary Carter | 3.50 | 1.40 | .35 |
| ☐ 35 | Rick Wise | .30 | .12 | .03 |
| ☐ 36 | Johnny Bench | 2.50 | 1.00 | .25 |
| ☐ 37 | Jim Palmer | 1.50 | .60 | .15 |
| ☐ 38 | Bobby Murcer | .50 | .20 | .05 |
| ☐ 39 | Von Joshua | .30 | .12 | .03 |
| ☐ 40 | Lou Brock | 2.00 | .80 | .20 |
| ☐ 41 | Mickey Rivers (2) | .40 | .16 | .04 |
| ☐ 42 | Manny Sanguillen | .40 | .16 | .04 |
| ☐ 43 | Jerry Reuss | .40 | .16 | .04 |
| ☐ 44 | Ken Griffey | .40 | .16 | .04 |
| ☐ 45 | Jorge Orta | .30 | .12 | .03 |
| ☐ 46 | John Mayberry | .30 | .12 | .03 |
| ☐ 47 | Vida Blue (2) | .40 | .16 | .04 |
| ☐ 48 | Rod Carew | 2.50 | 1.00 | .25 |
| ☐ 49 | Jon Matlack | .40 | .16 | .04 |
| ☐ 50 | Boog Powell | .50 | .20 | .05 |
| ☐ 51 | Mike Hargrove | .50 | .20 | .05 |
| ☐ 52 | Paul Lindblad | .30 | .12 | .03 |
| ☐ 53 | Thurman Munson | 2.50 | 1.00 | .25 |
| ☐ 54 | Steve Garvey | 3.00 | 1.20 | .30 |
| ☐ 55 | Pete Rose | 7.50 | 3.00 | .75 |
| ☐ 56 | Greg Gross | .30 | .12 | .03 |
| ☐ 57 | Ted Simmons | .75 | .30 | .07 |

| | | MINT | VG-E | F-G |
|---|---|---|---|---|
| ☐ 21 | Wayne Garland | .25 | .10 | .02 |
| ☐ 22 | Bill North | .25 | .10 | .02 |
| ☐ 23 | Thurman Munson | 2.00 | .80 | .20 |
| ☐ 24 | Tom Poquette | .25 | .10 | .02 |
| ☐ 25 | Ron LeFlore | .30 | .12 | .03 |
| ☐ 26 | Mark Fidrych | .35 | .14 | .03 |
| ☐ 27 | Sixto Lezcano | .25 | .10 | .02 |
| ☐ 28 | Dave Winfield | 2.50 | 1.00 | .25 |
| ☐ 29 | Jerry Koosman | .35 | .14 | .03 |
| ☐ 30 | Mike Hargrove | .30 | .12 | .03 |
| ☐ 31 | Willie Montanez | .25 | .10 | .02 |
| ☐ 32 | Don Stanhouse | .25 | .10 | .02 |
| ☐ 33 | Jay Johnstone | .25 | .10 | .02 |
| ☐ 34 | Bake McBride | .25 | .10 | .02 |
| ☐ 35 | Dave Kingman | .60 | .24 | .06 |
| ☐ 36 | Fred Patek | .25 | .10 | .02 |
| ☐ 37 | Garry Maddox | .30 | .12 | .03 |
| ☐ 38 | Ken Reitz | .25 | .10 | .02 |
| ☐ 39 | Bobby Grich | .30 | .12 | .03 |
| ☐ 40 | Cesar Geronimo | .25 | .10 | .02 |
| ☐ 41 | Jim Lonborg | .30 | .12 | .03 |
| ☐ 42 | Ed Figueroa | .25 | .10 | .02 |
| ☐ 43 | Bill Madlock | .80 | .32 | .08 |
| ☐ 44 | Jerry Remy | .25 | .10 | .02 |
| ☐ 45 | Paul Tanana | .30 | .12 | .03 |
| ☐ 46 | Al Oliver | .80 | .32 | .08 |
| ☐ 47 | Charlie Hough | .35 | .14 | .03 |
| ☐ 48 | Lou Piniella | .50 | .20 | .05 |
| ☐ 49 | Ken Griffey | .35 | .14 | .03 |
| ☐ 50 | Jose Cruz | .60 | .24 | .06 |
| ☐ 51 | Rollie Fingers | 1.00 | .40 | .10 |
| ☐ 52 | Chris Chambliss | .30 | .12 | .03 |
| ☐ 53 | Rod Carew | 2.50 | 1.00 | .25 |
| ☐ 54 | Andy Messersmith | .35 | .14 | .03 |
| ☐ 55 | Mickey Rivers | .30 | .12 | .03 |
| ☐ 56 | Butch Wynegar | .30 | .12 | .03 |
| ☐ 57 | Steve Carlton | 2.50 | 1.00 | .25 |

## 1977 Kellogg's

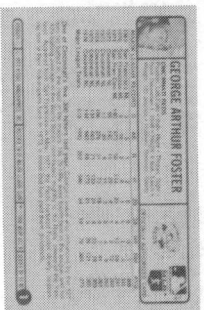

The cards in this 57 card set measure 2 1/8" by 3 1/4". The 1977 Kellogg's series of 3-D Baseball player cards could be obtained card by card from cereal boxes or by sending in box tops and money. Each player's picture appears in miniature form on the reverse, an idea begun in 1971 and replaced in subsequent years by the use of a picture of the Kellogg mascot.

| | | MINT | VG-E | F-G |
|---|---|---|---|---|
| COMPLETE SET | | 32.00 | 13.00 | 3.20 |
| COMMON PLAYER (1-57) | | .25 | .10 | .02 |
| ☐ 1 | George Foster | .90 | .36 | .09 |
| ☐ 2 | Bert Campaneris | .30 | .12 | .03 |
| ☐ 3 | Fergie Jenkins | .60 | .24 | .06 |
| ☐ 4 | Dock Ellis | .25 | .10 | .02 |
| ☐ 5 | John Montefusco | .25 | .10 | .02 |
| ☐ 6 | George Brett | 5.00 | 2.00 | .50 |
| ☐ 7 | John Candelaria | .35 | .14 | .03 |
| ☐ 8 | Fred Norman | .25 | .10 | .02 |
| ☐ 9 | Bill Travers | .25 | .10 | .02 |
| ☐ 10 | Hal McRae | .30 | .12 | .03 |
| ☐ 11 | Doug Rau | .25 | .10 | .02 |
| ☐ 12 | Greg Luzinski | .60 | .24 | .06 |
| ☐ 13 | Ralph Garr | .30 | .12 | .03 |
| ☐ 14 | Steve Garvey | 3.00 | 1.20 | .30 |
| ☐ 15 | Rick Manning | .25 | .10 | .02 |
| ☐ 16 | Lyman Bostock | .35 | .14 | .03 |
| ☐ 17 | Randy Jones | .30 | .12 | .03 |
| ☐ 18 | Ron Cey | .50 | .20 | .05 |
| ☐ 19 | Dave Parker | 1.00 | .40 | .10 |
| ☐ 20 | Pete Rose | 6.50 | 2.60 | .65 |

## 1978 Kellogg's

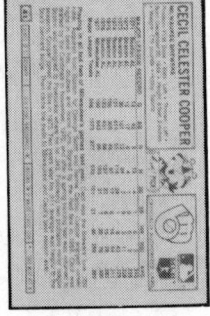

The cards in this 57 card set measure 2 1/8" by 3 1/4". This 1978 3-D Kellogg's series marks the first year in which Tony the Tiger appears on the reverse of each card next to the team and MLB logos. Once again the set could be obtained as individually wrapped cards in cereal boxes or as a set via a mail in offer.

| | | MINT | VG-E | F-G |
|---|---|---|---|---|
| COMPLETE SET | | 25.00 | 10.00 | 2.50 |
| COMMON PLAYER (1-57) | | .20 | .08 | .02 |
| ☐ 1 | Steve Carlton | 2.00 | .80 | .20 |
| ☐ 2 | Bucky Dent | .25 | .10 | .02 |
| ☐ 3 | Mike Schmidt | 3.00 | 1.20 | .30 |
| ☐ 4 | Ken Griffey | .25 | .10 | .02 |
| ☐ 5 | Al Cowens | .20 | .08 | .02 |
| ☐ 6 | George Brett | 3.00 | 1.20 | .30 |
| ☐ 7 | Lou Brock | 1.50 | .60 | .15 |
| ☐ 8 | Rich Gossage | .65 | .26 | .06 |
| ☐ 9 | Tom Johnson | .20 | .08 | .02 |
| ☐ 10 | George Foster | .65 | .26 | .06 |
| ☐ 11 | Dave Winfield | 2.00 | .80 | .20 |
| ☐ 12 | Dan Meyer | .20 | .08 | .02 |

| | | | | |
|---|---|---|---|---|
| ☐ 13 | Chris Chambliss | .25 | .10 | .02 |
| ☐ 14 | Paul Dade | .20 | .08 | .02 |
| ☐ 15 | Jeff Burroughs | .25 | .10 | .02 |
| ☐ 16 | Jose Cruz | .35 | .14 | .03 |
| ☐ 17 | Mickey Rivers | .25 | .10 | .02 |
| ☐ 18 | John Candelaria | .25 | .10 | .02 |
| ☐ 19 | Ellis Valentine | .20 | .08 | .02 |
| ☐ 20 | Hal McRae | .25 | .10 | .02 |
| ☐ 21 | Dave Rozema | .20 | .08 | .02 |
| ☐ 22 | Lenny Randle | .20 | .08 | .02 |
| ☐ 23 | Willie McCovey | 1.50 | .60 | .15 |
| ☐ 24 | Ron Cey | .50 | .20 | .05 |
| ☐ 25 | Eddie Murray | 5.00 | 2.00 | .50 |
| ☐ 26 | Larry Bowa | .35 | .14 | .03 |
| ☐ 27 | Tom Seaver | 2.00 | .80 | .20 |
| ☐ 28 | Garry Maddox | .25 | .10 | .02 |
| ☐ 29 | Rod Carew | 2.00 | .80 | .20 |
| ☐ 30 | Thurman Munson | 1.50 | .60 | .15 |
| ☐ 31 | Gary Templeton | .50 | .20 | .05 |
| ☐ 32 | Eric Soderholm | .20 | .08 | .02 |
| ☐ 33 | Greg Luzinski | .50 | .20 | .05 |
| ☐ 34 | Reggie Smith | .25 | .10 | .02 |
| ☐ 35 | Dave Goltz | .20 | .08 | .02 |
| ☐ 36 | Tommy John | .60 | .24 | .06 |
| ☐ 37 | Ralph Garr | .25 | .10 | .02 |
| ☐ 38 | Alan Bannister | .20 | .08 | .02 |
| ☐ 39 | Bob Bailor | .20 | .08 | .02 |
| ☐ 40 | Reggie Jackson | 3.00 | 1.20 | .30 |
| ☐ 41 | Cecil Cooper | .60 | .24 | .06 |
| ☐ 42 | Burt Hooton | .20 | .08 | .02 |
| ☐ 43 | Sparky Lyle | .40 | .16 | .04 |
| ☐ 44 | Steve Ontiveros | .20 | .08 | .02 |
| ☐ 45 | Rick Reuschel | .25 | .10 | .02 |
| ☐ 46 | Lyman Bostock | .25 | .10 | .02 |
| ☐ 47 | Mitchell Page | .20 | .08 | .02 |
| ☐ 48 | Bruce Sutter | .75 | .30 | .07 |
| ☐ 49 | Jim Rice | 2.00 | .80 | .20 |
| ☐ 50 | Ken Forsch | .25 | .10 | .02 |
| ☐ 51 | Nolan Ryan | 2.00 | .80 | .20 |
| ☐ 52 | Dave Parker | 1.00 | .40 | .10 |
| ☐ 53 | Bert Blyleven | .40 | .16 | .04 |
| ☐ 54 | Frank Tanana | .25 | .10 | .02 |
| ☐ 55 | Ken Singleton | .35 | .14 | .03 |
| ☐ 56 | Mike Hargrove | .25 | .10 | .02 |
| ☐ 57 | Don Sutton | 1.00 | .40 | .10 |

| | | | | |
|---|---|---|---|---|
| ☐ 5 | Jim Palmer | 1.25 | .50 | .12 |
| ☐ 6 | John Henry Johnson | .15 | .06 | .01 |
| ☐ 7 | Jason Thompson | .25 | .10 | .02 |
| ☐ 8 | Pat Zachry | .15 | .06 | .01 |
| ☐ 9 | Dennis Eckersley | .20 | .08 | .02 |
| ☐ 10 | Paul Splittorff | .15 | .06 | .01 |
| ☐ 11 | Ron Guidry | 1.00 | .40 | .10 |
| ☐ 12 | Jeff Burroughs | .15 | .06 | .01 |
| ☐ 13 | Rod Carew | 2.00 | .80 | .20 |
| ☐ 14 | Buddy Bell | .30 | .12 | .03 |
| ☐ 15 | Jim Rice | 2.00 | .80 | .20 |
| ☐ 16 | Garry Maddox | .20 | .08 | .02 |
| ☐ 17 | Willie McCovey | 1.50 | .60 | .15 |
| ☐ 18 | Steve Carlton | 2.00 | .80 | .20 |
| ☐ 19 | J.R. Richard | .25 | .10 | .02 |
| ☐ 20 | Paul Molitor | .40 | .16 | .04 |
| ☐ 21 | Dave Parker | .75 | .30 | .07 |
| ☐ 22 | Pete Rose | 5.00 | 2.00 | .50 |
| ☐ 23 | Vida Blue | .25 | .10 | .02 |
| ☐ 24 | Richie Zisk | .20 | .08 | .02 |
| ☐ 25 | Darrell Porter | .15 | .06 | .01 |
| ☐ 26 | Dan Driessen | .15 | .06 | .01 |
| ☐ 27 | Geoff Zahn | .15 | .06 | .01 |
| ☐ 28 | Phil Niekro | 1.00 | .40 | .10 |
| ☐ 29 | Tom Seaver | 2.00 | .80 | .20 |
| ☐ 30 | Fred Lynn | .75 | .30 | .07 |
| ☐ 31 | Bill Bonham | .15 | .06 | .01 |
| ☐ 32 | George Foster | .60 | .24 | .06 |
| ☐ 33 | Terry Puhl | .20 | .08 | .02 |
| ☐ 34 | John Candelaria | .20 | .08 | .02 |
| ☐ 35 | Bob Knepper | .30 | .12 | .03 |
| ☐ 36 | Fred Patek | .15 | .06 | .01 |
| ☐ 37 | Chris Chambliss | .20 | .08 | .02 |
| ☐ 38 | Bob Forsch | .20 | .08 | .02 |
| ☐ 39 | Ken Griffey | .25 | .10 | .02 |
| ☐ 40 | Jack Clark | .75 | .30 | .07 |
| ☐ 41 | Dwight Evans | .50 | .20 | .05 |
| ☐ 42 | Lee Mazzilli | .20 | .08 | .02 |
| ☐ 43 | Mario Guerrero | .15 | .06 | .01 |
| ☐ 44 | Larry Bowa | .35 | .14 | .03 |
| ☐ 45 | Carl Yastrzemski | 3.00 | 1.20 | .30 |
| ☐ 46 | Reggie Jackson | 2.50 | 1.00 | .25 |
| ☐ 47 | Rick Reuschel | .20 | .08 | .02 |
| ☐ 48 | Mike Flanagan | .25 | .10 | .02 |
| ☐ 49 | Gaylord Perry | .75 | .30 | .07 |
| ☐ 50 | George Brett | 3.00 | 1.20 | .30 |
| ☐ 51 | Craig Reynolds | .15 | .06 | .01 |
| ☐ 52 | Dave Lopes | .25 | .10 | .02 |
| ☐ 53 | Bill Almon | .15 | .06 | .01 |
| ☐ 54 | Roy Howell | .15 | .06 | .01 |
| ☐ 55 | Frank Tanana | .20 | .08 | .02 |
| ☐ 56 | Doug Rau | .15 | .06 | .01 |
| ☐ 57 | Rick Monday | .20 | .08 | .02 |
| ☐ 58 | Jon Matlack | .20 | .08 | .02 |
| ☐ 59 | Ron Jackson | .15 | .06 | .01 |
| ☐ 60 | Jim Sundberg | .20 | .08 | .02 |

## 1979 Kellogg's

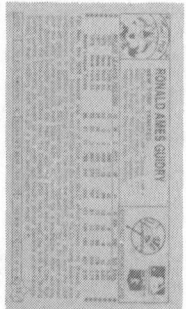

The cards in this 60 card set measure 1 15/16" by 3 1/4". The 1979 edition of Kellogg's 3-D baseball cards have a 3/16" reduced width from the previous year; a nicely designed curved panel above the picture gives this set a distinctive appearance. The set contains the largest number of cards issued in a Kellogg's set since the 1971 series.

| | MINT | VG-E | F-G |
|---|---|---|---|
| COMPLETE SET | 20.00 | 8.00 | 2.00 |
| COMMON PLAYER (1-60) | .15 | .06 | .01 |

| | | | | |
|---|---|---|---|---|
| ☐ 1 | Bruce Sutter | .60 | .24 | .06 |
| ☐ 2 | Ted Simmons | .40 | .16 | .04 |
| ☐ 3 | Ross Grimsley | .15 | .06 | .01 |
| ☐ 4 | Wayne Nordhagen | .15 | .06 | .01 |

## 1980 Kellogg's

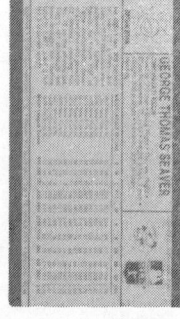

The cards in this 60 card set measure 1 7/8" by 3 1/4". The 1980 Kellogg's 3-D set is quite similar to, but smaller (narrower) than, the other recent Kellogg's issues. Sets could be obtained card by card from cereal boxes or as a set from a box top offer from the company.

|  | MINT | VG-E | F-G |
|---|---|---|---|
| COMPLETE SET | 16.00 | 6.50 | 1.60 |
| COMMON PLAYER (1-60) | .15 | .06 | .01 |

| | | MINT | VG-E | F-G |
|---|---|---|---|---|
| ☐ 1 | Ross Grimsley | .15 | .06 | .01 |
| ☐ 2 | Mike Schmidt | 2.00 | .80 | .20 |
| ☐ 3 | Mike Flanagan | .20 | .08 | .02 |
| ☐ 4 | Ron Guidry | .80 | .32 | .08 |
| ☐ 5 | Bert Blyleven | .30 | .12 | .03 |
| ☐ 6 | Dave Kingman | .35 | .14 | .03 |
| ☐ 7 | Jeff Newman | .15 | .06 | .01 |
| ☐ 8 | Steve Rogers | .25 | .10 | .02 |
| ☐ 9 | George Brett | 2.00 | .80 | .20 |
| ☐ 10 | Bruce Sutter | .60 | .24 | .06 |
| ☐ 11 | Gorman Thomas | .30 | .12 | .03 |
| ☐ 12 | Darrell Porter | .15 | .06 | .01 |
| ☐ 13 | Roy Smalley | .15 | .06 | .01 |
| ☐ 14 | Steve Carlton | 1.50 | .60 | .15 |
| ☐ 15 | Jim Palmer | 1.00 | .40 | .10 |
| ☐ 16 | Bob Bailor | .15 | .06 | .01 |
| ☐ 17 | Jason Thompson | .15 | .06 | .01 |
| ☐ 18 | Graig Nettles | .35 | .14 | .03 |
| ☐ 19 | Ron Cey | .30 | .12 | .03 |
| ☐ 20 | Nolan Ryan | 1.50 | .60 | .15 |
| ☐ 21 | Ellis Valentine | .15 | .06 | .01 |
| ☐ 22 | Larry Hisle | .20 | .08 | .02 |
| ☐ 23 | Dave Parker | .75 | .30 | .07 |
| ☐ 24 | Eddie Murray | 2.00 | .80 | .20 |
| ☐ 25 | Willie Stargell | .75 | .30 | .07 |
| ☐ 26 | Reggie Jackson | 2.00 | .80 | .20 |
| ☐ 27 | Carl Yastrzemski | 2.00 | .80 | .20 |
| ☐ 28 | Andre Thorton | .25 | .10 | .02 |
| ☐ 29 | Dave Lopes | .20 | .08 | .02 |
| ☐ 30 | Ken Singleton | .25 | .10 | .02 |
| ☐ 31 | Steve Garvey | 1.50 | .60 | .15 |
| ☐ 32 | Dave Winfield | 1.50 | .60 | .15 |
| ☐ 33 | Steve Kemp | .20 | .08 | .02 |
| ☐ 34 | Claudell Washington | .20 | .08 | .02 |
| ☐ 35 | Pete Rose | 4.00 | 1.60 | .40 |
| ☐ 36 | Cesar Cedeno | .20 | .08 | .02 |
| ☐ 37 | John Stearns | .15 | .06 | .01 |
| ☐ 38 | Lee Mazzilli | .15 | .06 | .01 |
| ☐ 39 | Larry Bowa | .30 | .12 | .03 |
| ☐ 40 | Fred Lynn | .60 | .24 | .06 |
| ☐ 41 | Carlton Fisk | .60 | .24 | .06 |
| ☐ 42 | Vida Blue | .25 | .10 | .02 |
| ☐ 43 | Keith Hernandez | 1.00 | .40 | .10 |
| ☐ 44 | Ted Simmons | .40 | .16 | .04 |
| ☐ 45 | Chet Lemon | .20 | .08 | .02 |
| ☐ 46 | Jim Rice | 1.50 | .60 | .15 |
| ☐ 47 | Ferguson Jenkins | .35 | .14 | .03 |
| ☐ 48 | Gary Matthews | .20 | .08 | .02 |
| ☐ 49 | Tom Seaver | 1.50 | .60 | .15 |
| ☐ 50 | George Foster | .60 | .24 | .06 |
| ☐ 51 | Phil Niekro | 1.00 | .40 | .10 |
| ☐ 52 | Johnny Bench | 1.50 | .60 | .15 |
| ☐ 53 | Buddy Bell | .30 | .12 | .03 |
| ☐ 54 | Lance Parrish | 1.00 | .40 | .10 |
| ☐ 55 | Joaquin Andujar | .25 | .10 | .02 |
| ☐ 56 | Don Baylor | .35 | .14 | .03 |
| ☐ 57 | Jack Clark | .60 | .24 | .06 |
| ☐ 58 | J.R. Richard | .25 | .10 | .02 |
| ☐ 59 | Bruce Bochte | .20 | .08 | .02 |
| ☐ 60 | Rod Carew | 1.50 | .60 | .15 |

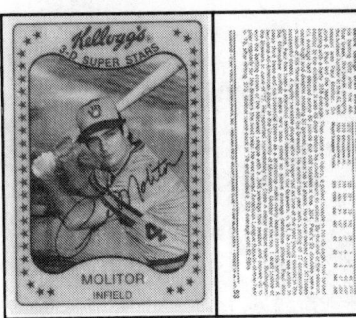

## 1981 Kellogg's

The cards in this 66 card set measure 2 1/2" by 3 1/2". The 1981 Kellogg's set witnessed an increase in both the size of the card and the size of the set. For the first time, cards were not packed in cereal sizes but available only by mail- in procedure. The offer for the card set was advertised on boxes of Kellogg's Corn Flakes. The cards were printed on a different stock than in previous years, presumably to prevent the cracking problem which has plagued all Kellogg's 3-D issues. At the end of the promotion, the remainder of the sets not distributed (to cereal-eaters), were "sold" into the organized hobby, thus creating a situation where the set is relatively plentiful compared to other years of Kellogg's.

|  | MINT | VG-E | F-G |
|---|---|---|---|
| COMPLETE SET | 5.00 | 2.00 | .50 |
| COMMON PLAYER | .06 | .02 | .00 |

| | | MINT | VG-E | F-G |
|---|---|---|---|---|
| ☐ 1 | George Foster | .15 | .06 | .01 |
| ☐ 2 | Jim Palmer | .25 | .10 | .02 |
| ☐ 3 | Reggie Jackson | .75 | .30 | .07 |
| ☐ 4 | Al Oliver | .10 | .04 | .01 |
| ☐ 5 | Mike Schmidt | .75 | .30 | .07 |
| ☐ 6 | Nolan Ryan | .35 | .14 | .03 |
| ☐ 7 | Bucky Dent | .07 | .03 | .01 |
| ☐ 8 | George Brett | .75 | .30 | .07 |
| ☐ 9 | Jim Rice | .35 | .14 | .03 |
| ☐ 10 | Steve Garvey | .45 | .18 | .04 |
| ☐ 11 | Willie Stargell | .25 | .10 | .02 |
| ☐ 12 | Phil Niekro | .25 | .10 | .02 |
| ☐ 13 | Dave Parker | .25 | .10 | .02 |
| ☐ 14 | Cesar Cedeno | .07 | .03 | .01 |
| ☐ 15 | Don Baylor | .08 | .03 | .01 |
| ☐ 16 | J.R. Richard | .07 | .03 | .01 |
| ☐ 17 | Tony Perez | .10 | .04 | .01 |
| ☐ 18 | Eddie Murray | .75 | .30 | .07 |
| ☐ 19 | Chet Lemon | .08 | .03 | .01 |
| ☐ 20 | Ben Oglivie | .07 | .03 | .01 |
| ☐ 21 | Dave Winfield | .45 | .18 | .04 |
| ☐ 22 | Joe Morgan | .25 | .10 | .02 |
| ☐ 23 | Vida Blue | .07 | .03 | .01 |
| ☐ 24 | Willie Wilson | .10 | .04 | .01 |
| ☐ 25 | Steve Henderson | .06 | .02 | .00 |
| ☐ 26 | Rod Carew | .45 | .18 | .04 |
| ☐ 27 | Garry Templeton | .10 | .04 | .01 |
| ☐ 28 | Dave Concepcion | .10 | .04 | .01 |
| ☐ 29 | Dave Lopes | .07 | .03 | .01 |
| ☐ 30 | Ken Landreaux | .06 | .02 | .00 |
| ☐ 31 | Keith Hernandez | .30 | .12 | .03 |
| ☐ 32 | Cecil Cooper | .10 | .04 | .01 |
| ☐ 33 | Rickey Henderson | .50 | .20 | .05 |
| ☐ 34 | Frank White | .08 | .03 | .01 |
| ☐ 35 | George Hendrick | .08 | .03 | .01 |
| ☐ 36 | Reggie Smith | .07 | .03 | .01 |
| ☐ 37 | Tug McGraw | .06 | .02 | .00 |
| ☐ 38 | Tom Seaver | .45 | .18 | .04 |
| ☐ 39 | Ken Singleton | .09 | .04 | .01 |
| ☐ 40 | Fred Lynn | .15 | .06 | .01 |
| ☐ 41 | Rich Gossage | .15 | .06 | .01 |
| ☐ 42 | Terry Puhl | .06 | .02 | .00 |
| ☐ 43 | Larry Bowa | .10 | .04 | .01 |
| ☐ 44 | Phil Garner | .06 | .02 | .00 |
| ☐ 45 | Ron Guidry | .20 | .08 | .02 |
| ☐ 46 | Lee Mazzilli | .06 | .02 | .00 |
| ☐ 47 | Dave Kingman | .10 | .04 | .01 |
| ☐ 48 | Carl Yastrzemski | .75 | .30 | .07 |
| ☐ 49 | Rick Burleson | .07 | .03 | .01 |
| ☐ 50 | Steve Carlton | .45 | .18 | .04 |
| ☐ 51 | Alan Trammell | .20 | .08 | .02 |
| ☐ 52 | Tommy John | .15 | .06 | .01 |
| ☐ 53 | Paul Molitor | .10 | .04 | .01 |
| ☐ 54 | Joe Charbonneau | .06 | .02 | .00 |
| ☐ 55 | Rick Langford | .06 | .02 | .00 |
| ☐ 56 | Bruce Sutter | .10 | .04 | .01 |
| ☐ 57 | Robin Yount | .25 | .10 | .02 |
| ☐ 58 | Steve Stone | .06 | .02 | .00 |
| ☐ 59 | Larry Gura | .06 | .02 | .00 |
| ☐ 60 | Mike Flanagan | .07 | .03 | .01 |
| ☐ 61 | Bob Horner | .25 | .10 | .02 |
| ☐ 62 | Bruce Bochte | .06 | .02 | .00 |
| ☐ 63 | Pete Rose | 1.00 | .40 | .10 |
| ☐ 64 | Buddy Bell | .10 | .04 | .01 |
| ☐ 65 | Johnny Bench | .35 | .14 | .03 |
| ☐ 66 | Mike Hargrove | .06 | .02 | .00 |

## 1982 Kellogg's

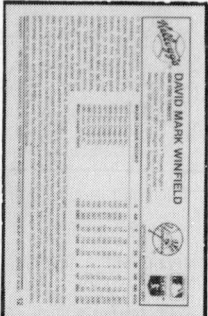

The cards in this 64 card set measure 2 1/8" by 3 1/4". The 1982 version of 3-D cards prepared for the Kellogg Company by Visual Panographics, Inc., is not only smaller in physical dimensions from the 1981 series (which was standard card size at 2 1/2 by 3 1/2) but is also two cards shorter in length (64 in '82 and 66 in '81). In addition, while retaining the policy of not inserting single cards into cereal packages and offering the sets through box top mail ins only, the Kellogg Company accepted box tops from four types of cereals, as opposed to only one type the previous year. Each card features a color 3-D ballplayer picture with a vertical line of white stars on each side set upon a blue background. The player's name and the word Kellogg's are printed in red on the obverse, and the card number is found on the bottom right of the reverse.

| | MINT | VG-E | F-G |
|---|---|---|---|
| COMPLETE SET | 10.00 | 4.00 | 1.00 |
| COMMON PLAYER | .06 | .02 | .00 |

| | | MINT | VG-E | F-G |
|---|---|---|---|---|
| ☐ 1 | Richie Zisk | .06 | .02 | .00 |
| ☐ 2 | Bill Buckner | .10 | .04 | .01 |
| ☐ 3 | George Brett | .75 | .30 | .07 |
| ☐ 4 | Rickey Henderson | .60 | .24 | .06 |
| ☐ 5 | Jack Morris | .15 | .06 | .01 |
| ☐ 6 | Ozzie Smith | .15 | .06 | .01 |
| ☐ 7 | Rollie Fingers | .15 | .06 | .01 |
| ☐ 8 | Tom Seaver | .45 | .18 | .04 |
| ☐ 9 | Fernando Valuenzuela | .45 | .18 | .04 |
| ☐ 10 | Hubie Brooks | .10 | .04 | .01 |
| ☐ 11 | Nolan Ryan | .45 | .18 | .04 |
| ☐ 12 | Dave Winfield | .35 | .14 | .03 |
| ☐ 13 | Bob Horner | .20 | .08 | .02 |
| ☐ 14 | Reggie Jackson | .60 | .24 | .06 |
| ☐ 15 | Burt Hooton | .06 | .02 | .00 |
| ☐ 16 | Mike Schmidt | .75 | .30 | .07 |
| ☐ 17 | Bruce Sutter | .15 | .06 | .01 |
| ☐ 18 | Pete Rose | 1.00 | .40 | .10 |
| ☐ 19 | Dave Kingman | .12 | .05 | .01 |
| ☐ 20 | Neil Allen | .06 | .02 | .00 |
| ☐ 21 | Don Sutton | .25 | .10 | .02 |
| ☐ 22 | Dave Concepcion | .10 | .04 | .01 |
| ☐ 23 | Keith Hernandez | .25 | .10 | .02 |
| ☐ 24 | Gary Carter | .45 | .18 | .04 |
| ☐ 25 | Carlton Fisk | .20 | .08 | .02 |
| ☐ 26 | Ron Guidry | .20 | .08 | .02 |
| ☐ 27 | Steve Carlton | .35 | .14 | .03 |
| ☐ 28 | Robin Yount | .35 | .14 | .03 |
| ☐ 29 | John Castino | .07 | .03 | .01 |
| ☐ 30 | Johnny Bench | .35 | .14 | .03 |
| ☐ 31 | Bob Knepper | .10 | .04 | .01 |
| ☐ 32 | Rich Gossage | .15 | .06 | .01 |
| ☐ 33 | Buddy Bell | .10 | .04 | .01 |
| ☐ 34 | Art Howe | .06 | .02 | .00 |
| ☐ 35 | Tony Armas | .10 | .04 | .01 |
| ☐ 36 | Phil Niekro | .25 | .10 | .02 |

| | | MINT | VG-E | F-G |
|---|---|---|---|---|
| ☐ 37 | Len Barker | .08 | .03 | .01 |
| ☐ 38 | Bob Grich | .09 | .04 | .01 |
| ☐ 39 | Steve Kemp | .08 | .03 | .01 |
| ☐ 40 | Kirk Gibson | .25 | .10 | .02 |
| ☐ 41 | Carney Lansford | .10 | .04 | .01 |
| ☐ 42 | Jim Palmer | .25 | .10 | .02 |
| ☐ 43 | Carl Yastrzemski | .60 | .24 | .06 |
| ☐ 44 | Rick Burleson | .07 | .03 | .01 |
| ☐ 45 | Dwight Evans | .10 | .04 | .01 |
| ☐ 46 | Ron Cey | .10 | .04 | .01 |
| ☐ 47 | Steve Garvey | .45 | .18 | .04 |
| ☐ 48 | Dave Parker | .20 | .08 | .02 |
| ☐ 49 | Mike Easler | .07 | .03 | .01 |
| ☐ 50 | Dusty Baker | .08 | .03 | .01 |
| ☐ 51 | Rod Carew | .40 | .16 | .04 |
| ☐ 52 | Chris Chambliss | .07 | .03 | .01 |
| ☐ 53 | Tim Raines | .35 | .14 | .03 |
| ☐ 54 | Chet Lemon | .08 | .03 | .01 |
| ☐ 55 | Bill Madlock | .15 | .06 | .01 |
| ☐ 56 | George Foster | .15 | .06 | .01 |
| ☐ 57 | Dwayne Murphy | .07 | .03 | .01 |
| ☐ 58 | Ken Singleton | .10 | .04 | .01 |
| ☐ 59 | Mike Norris | .06 | .02 | .00 |
| ☐ 60 | Cecil Cooper | .12 | .05 | .01 |
| ☐ 61 | Al Oliver | .15 | .06 | .01 |
| ☐ 62 | Willie Wilson | .12 | .05 | .01 |
| ☐ 63 | Vida Blue | .08 | .03 | .01 |
| ☐ 64 | Eddie Murray | .60 | .24 | .06 |

## 1983 Kellogg's

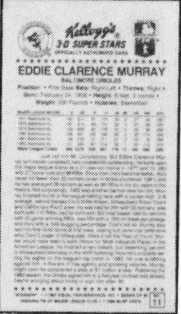

The cards in this 60 card set measure 1 7/8" by 3 1/4". For the 14th year in a row, the Kellogg Company issued a card set of Major League players. The set of 3-D cards contains the photo, player's autograph, Kellogg's logo, and name and position of the player on the front of the card. The backs feature the player's team logo, career statistics, player biography, and a narrative on the player's career.

| | MINT | VG-E | F-G |
|---|---|---|---|
| COMPLETE SET | 10.00 | 4.00 | 1.00 |
| COMMON PLAYER | .06 | .02 | .00 |

| | | MINT | VG-E | F-G |
|---|---|---|---|---|
| ☐ 1 | Rod Carew | .40 | .16 | .04 |
| ☐ 2 | Rollie Fingers | .20 | .08 | .02 |
| ☐ 3 | Reggie Jackson | .60 | .24 | .06 |
| ☐ 4 | George Brett | .75 | .30 | .07 |
| ☐ 5 | Hal McRae | .08 | .03 | .01 |
| ☐ 6 | Pete Rose | 1.00 | .40 | .10 |
| ☐ 7 | Fernando Valenzuela | .35 | .14 | .03 |
| ☐ 8 | Rickey Henderson | .60 | .24 | .06 |
| ☐ 9 | Carl Yastrzemski | .60 | .24 | .06 |
| ☐ 10 | Rich Gossage | .15 | .06 | .01 |
| ☐ 11 | Eddie Murray | .60 | .24 | .06 |
| ☐ 12 | Buddy Bell | .10 | .04 | .01 |
| ☐ 13 | Jim Rice | .45 | .18 | .04 |
| ☐ 14 | Robin Yount | .35 | .14 | .03 |
| ☐ 15 | Dave Winfield | .35 | .14 | .03 |
| ☐ 16 | Harold Baines | .25 | .10 | .02 |
| ☐ 17 | Garry Templeton | .08 | .03 | .01 |
| ☐ 18 | Bill Madlock | .15 | .06 | .01 |
| ☐ 19 | Pete Vuckovich | .08 | .03 | .01 |

| | | | | |
|---|---|---|---|---|
| ☐ 20 | Pedro Guerrero | .25 | .10 | .02 |
| ☐ 21 | Ozzie Smith | .15 | .06 | .01 |
| ☐ 22 | George Foster | .12 | .05 | .01 |
| ☐ 23 | Willie Wilson | .12 | .05 | .01 |
| ☐ 24 | Johnny Ray | .10 | .04 | .01 |
| ☐ 25 | George Hendrick | .08 | .03 | .01 |
| ☐ 26 | Andre Thornton | .10 | .04 | .01 |
| ☐ 27 | Leon Durham | .10 | .04 | .01 |
| ☐ 28 | Cecil Cooper | .12 | .05 | .01 |
| ☐ 29 | Don Baylor | .10 | .04 | .01 |
| ☐ 30 | Lonnie Smith | .08 | .03 | .01 |
| ☐ 31 | Nolan Ryan | .35 | .14 | .03 |
| ☐ 32 | Dan Quisenberry | .12 | .05 | .01 |
| ☐ 33 | Len Barker | .08 | .03 | .01 |
| ☐ 34 | Neil Allen | .08 | .03 | .01 |
| ☐ 35 | Jack Morris | .25 | .10 | .02 |
| ☐ 36 | Dave Stieb | .12 | .05 | .01 |
| ☐ 37 | Bruce Sutter | .12 | .05 | .01 |
| ☐ 38 | Jim Sundberg | .06 | .02 | .00 |
| ☐ 39 | Jim Palmer | .25 | .10 | .02 |
| ☐ 40 | Lance Parrish | .25 | .10 | .02 |
| ☐ 41 | Floyd Bannister | .08 | .03 | .01 |
| ☐ 42 | Larry Gura | .06 | .02 | .00 |
| ☐ 43 | Britt Burns | .08 | .03 | .01 |
| ☐ 44 | Toby Harrah | .08 | .03 | .01 |
| ☐ 45 | Steve Carlton | .35 | .14 | .03 |
| ☐ 46 | Greg Minton | .06 | .02 | .00 |
| ☐ 47 | Gorman Thomas | .08 | .03 | .01 |
| ☐ 48 | Jack Clark | .15 | .06 | .01 |
| ☐ 49 | Keith Hernandez | .25 | .10 | .02 |
| ☐ 50 | Greg Luzinski | .10 | .04 | .01 |
| ☐ 51 | Fred Lynn | .15 | .06 | .01 |
| ☐ 52 | Dale Murphy | .75 | .30 | .07 |
| ☐ 53 | Kent Hrbek | .35 | .14 | .03 |
| ☐ 54 | Bob Horner | .20 | .08 | .02 |
| ☐ 55 | Gary Carter | .45 | .18 | .04 |
| ☐ 56 | Carlton Fisk | .15 | .06 | .01 |
| ☐ 57 | Dave Concepcion | .10 | .04 | .01 |
| ☐ 58 | Mike Schmidt | .75 | .30 | .07 |
| ☐ 59 | Bill Buckner | .10 | .04 | .01 |
| ☐ 60 | Bob Grich | .08 | .03 | .01 |

## 1982 K-Mart

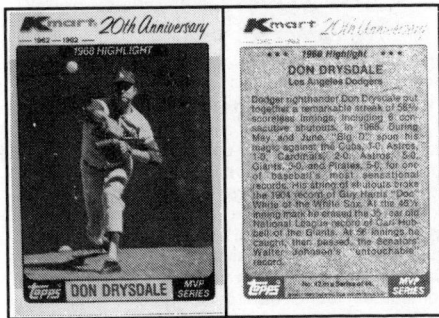

The cards in this 44 card set measure 2 1/2" by 3 1/2". This set was produced by Topps for K Mart's 20th Anniversary Celebration. The set features Topps cards of National and American League MVP's from 1962 through 1981. The backs highlight individual MVP winning performances. The dual National League MVP winners of 1979 and special cards commemorating the accomplishments of Drysdale (scoreless consecutive innings pitched streak), Aaron (home run record), and Rose (National League most hits lifetime record) round out the set. The 1975 Fred Lynn card is an original construction from the multi-player "Rookie Outfielders" card of Lynn of 1975. The Maury Wills card #2, similarly, was created after the fact as Maury was not originally included in the 1962 Topps set. The set was "mass" produced for K-Mart

distribution as a complete set in a box. Some collectors consider this to be one of the most plentiful sets ever produced.

| | | | MINT | VG-E | F-G |
|---|---|---|---|---|---|
| | COMPLETE SET | | .60 | .24 | .06 |
| | COMMON PLAYER | | .01 | .00 | .00 |
| ☐ | 1 | Mickey Mantle: 62AL | .12 | .05 | .01 |
| ☐ | 2 | Maury Wills: 62NL | .02 | .01 | .00 |
| ☐ | 3 | Elston Howard: 63AL | .01 | .00 | .00 |
| ☐ | 4 | Sandy Koufax: 63NL | .04 | .02 | .00 |
| ☐ | 5 | Brooks Robinson: 64AL | .04 | .02 | .00 |
| ☐ | 6 | Ken Boyer: 64NL | .01 | .00 | .00 |
| ☐ | 7 | Zoilo Versalles: 65AL | .01 | .00 | .00 |
| ☐ | 8 | Willie Mays: 65NL | .06 | .02 | .00 |
| ☐ | 9 | Frank Robinson: 66AL | .03 | .01 | .00 |
| ☐ | 10 | Bob Clemente: 66NL | .05 | .02 | .00 |
| ☐ | 11 | Carl Yastrzemski: 67AL | .06 | .02 | .00 |
| ☐ | 12 | Orlando Cepeda: 67NL | .01 | .00 | .00 |
| ☐ | 13 | Denny McLain: 68AL | .01 | .00 | .00 |
| ☐ | 14 | Bob Gibson: 68NL | .03 | .01 | .00 |
| ☐ | 15 | Harmon Killebrew: 69AL | .02 | .01 | .00 |
| ☐ | 16 | Willie McCovey: 69NL | .03 | .01 | .00 |
| ☐ | 17 | Boog Powell: 70AL | .01 | .00 | .00 |
| ☐ | 18 | Johnny Bench: 70NL | .04 | .02 | .00 |
| ☐ | 19 | Vida Blue: 71AL | .01 | .00 | .00 |
| ☐ | 20 | Joe Torre: 71NL | .01 | .00 | .00 |
| ☐ | 21 | Rich Allen: 72AL | .01 | .00 | .00 |
| ☐ | 22 | Johnny Bench: 72NL | .04 | .02 | .00 |
| ☐ | 23 | Reggie Jackson: 73AL | .05 | .02 | .00 |
| ☐ | 24 | Pete Rose: 73NL | .10 | .04 | .01 |
| ☐ | 25 | Jeff Burroughs: 74AL | .01 | .00 | .00 |
| ☐ | 26 | Steve Garvey: 74NL | .04 | .02 | .00 |
| ☐ | 27 | Fred Lynn: 75AL | .03 | .01 | .00 |
| ☐ | 28 | Joe Morgan: 75NL | .02 | .01 | .00 |
| ☐ | 29 | Thurman Munson: 76AL | .04 | .02 | .00 |
| ☐ | 30 | Joe Morgan: 76NL | .02 | .01 | .00 |
| ☐ | 31 | Rod Carew: 77AL | .04 | .02 | .00 |
| ☐ | 32 | George Foster: 77NL | .02 | .01 | .00 |
| ☐ | 33 | Jim Rice: 78AL | .03 | .01 | .00 |
| ☐ | 34 | Dave Parker: 78NL | .02 | .01 | .00 |
| ☐ | 35 | Don Baylor: 79AL | .01 | .00 | .00 |
| ☐ | 36 | Keith Hernandez: 79NL | .01 | .00 | .00 |
| ☐ | 37 | Willie Stargell: 79NL | .02 | .01 | .00 |
| ☐ | 38 | George Brett: 80AL | .05 | .02 | .00 |
| ☐ | 39 | Mike Schmidt: 80NL | .06 | .02 | .00 |
| ☐ | 40 | Rollie Fingers: 81AL | .02 | .01 | .00 |
| ☐ | 41 | Mike Schmidt: 81NL | .06 | .02 | .00 |
| ☐ | 42 | '68 HL: Don Drysdale (scoreless innings) | .02 | .01 | .00 |
| ☐ | 43 | '74 HL: Hank Aaron (home run record) | .06 | .02 | .00 |
| ☐ | 44 | '81 HL: Pete Rose (NL most hits) | .10 | .04 | .01 |

## 1987 K-Mart

Topps produced this 33-card boxed set for K-Mart. The set celebrates K-Mart's 25th anniversary and is subtitled, "Stars of the Decades." Card fronts feature a color photo of the player oriented diagonally. Cards measure 2 1/2" by 3 1/2" and are numbered on the back. Card backs provide statistics for the player's best decade.

|  | MINT | VG-E | F-G |
|---|---|---|---|
| COMPLETE SET ..................... | 4.00 | 1.60 | .40 |
| COMMON PLAYER ..................... | .10 | .04 | .01 |

| | | MINT | VG-E | F-G |
|---|---|---|---|---|
| ☐ | 1 Hank Aaron ..................... | .25 | .10 | .02 |
| ☐ | 2 Roberto Clemente ............ | .15 | .06 | .01 |
| ☐ | 3 Bob Gibson ..................... | .10 | .04 | .01 |
| ☐ | 4 Harmon Killebrew ............ | .10 | .04 | .01 |
| ☐ | 5 Mickey Mantle ................. | .50 | .20 | .05 |
| ☐ | 6 Juan Marichal ................. | .10 | .04 | .01 |
| ☐ | 7 Roger Maris ..................... | .15 | .06 | .01 |
| ☐ | 8 Willie Mays ..................... | .25 | .10 | .02 |
| ☐ | 9 Brooks Robinson ............. | .15 | .06 | .01 |
| ☐ | 10 Frank Robinson ............. | .10 | .04 | .01 |
| ☐ | 11 Carl Yastrzemski ............ | .25 | .10 | .02 |
| ☐ | 12 Johnny Bench ................. | .15 | .06 | .01 |
| ☐ | 13 Lou Brock ..................... | .15 | .06 | .01 |
| ☐ | 14 Rod Carew ..................... | .15 | .06 | .01 |
| ☐ | 15 Steve Carlton ................. | .15 | .06 | .01 |
| ☐ | 16 Reggie Jackson ............. | .25 | .10 | .02 |
| ☐ | 17 Jim Palmer ..................... | .10 | .04 | .01 |
| ☐ | 18 Jim Rice ..................... | .15 | .06 | .01 |
| ☐ | 19 Pete Rose ..................... | .50 | .20 | .05 |
| ☐ | 20 Nolan Ryan ..................... | .25 | .10 | .02 |
| ☐ | 21 Tom Seaver ..................... | .25 | .10 | .02 |
| ☐ | 22 Willie Stargell ............... | .10 | .04 | .01 |
| ☐ | 23 Wade Boggs ................. | .50 | .20 | .05 |
| ☐ | 24 George Brett ................. | .25 | .10 | .02 |
| ☐ | 25 Gary Carter ................. | .15 | .06 | .01 |
| ☐ | 26 Dwight Gooden ............. | .50 | .20 | .05 |
| ☐ | 27 Rickey Henderson ............ | .25 | .10 | .02 |
| ☐ | 28 Don Mattingly ................. | .60 | .24 | .06 |
| ☐ | 29 Dale Murphy ................. | .25 | .10 | .02 |
| ☐ | 30 Eddie Murray ................. | .25 | .10 | .02 |
| ☐ | 31 Mike Schmidt ................. | .25 | .10 | .02 |
| ☐ | 32 Darryl Strawberry ............ | .25 | .10 | .02 |
| ☐ | 33 Fernando Valenzuela ........ | .15 | .06 | .01 |

| | | MINT | VG-E | F-G |
|---|---|---|---|---|
| ☐ | 1 Hank Aaron ..................... | 125.00 | 50.00 | 12.50 |
| ☐ | 2 Joe Adcock ..................... | 6.00 | 2.40 | .60 |
| ☐ | 3 Ray Boone ..................... | 60.00 | 24.00 | 6.00 |
| ☐ | 4 Bill Bruton ..................... | 125.00 | 50.00 | 12.50 |
| ☐ | 5 Bob Buhl ..................... | 5.00 | 2.00 | .50 |
| ☐ | 6 Lew Burdette ................. | 8.00 | 3.25 | .80 |
| ☐ | 7 Chuck Cottier ................. | 5.00 | 2.00 | .50 |
| ☐ | 8 Wes Covington ............... | 5.00 | 2.00 | .50 |
| ☐ | 9 Del Crandall ................. | 6.00 | 2.40 | .60 |
| ☐ | 10 Chuck Dressen ............. | 5.00 | 2.00 | .50 |
| ☐ | 11 Bob Giggie ..................... | 5.00 | 2.00 | .50 |
| ☐ | 12 Joey Jay ..................... | 5.00 | 2.00 | .50 |
| ☐ | 13 Johnny Logan ................. | 6.00 | 2.40 | .60 |
| ☐ | 14 Felix Mantilla ................. | 5.00 | 2.00 | .50 |
| ☐ | 15 Lee Maye ..................... | 5.00 | 2.00 | .50 |
| ☐ | 16 Don McMahon ................. | 5.00 | 2.00 | .50 |
| ☐ | 17 George Myatt ................. | 5.00 | 2.00 | .50 |
| ☐ | 18 Andy Pafko ..................... | 5.00 | 2.00 | .50 |
| ☐ | 19 Juan Pizarro ................. | 5.00 | 2.00 | .50 |
| ☐ | 20 Mel Roach ..................... | 5.00 | 2.00 | .50 |
| ☐ | 21 Bob Rush ..................... | 5.00 | 2.00 | .50 |
| ☐ | 22 Bob Scheffing ................. | 5.00 | 2.00 | .50 |
| ☐ | 23 Red Schoendienst ............ | 8.00 | 3.25 | .80 |
| ☐ | 24 Warren Spahn ................. | 25.00 | 10.00 | 2.50 |
| ☐ | 25 Al Spangler ................. | 5.00 | 2.00 | .50 |
| ☐ | 26 Frank Torre ................. | 5.00 | 2.00 | .50 |
| ☐ | 27 Carlton Willey ................. | 5.00 | 2.00 | .50 |
| ☐ | 28 Whit Wyatt ..................... | 5.00 | 2.00 | .50 |

## 1948-49 Leaf

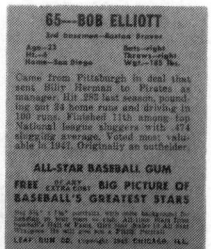

The cards in this 98 card set measure 2 3/8" by 2 7/8". The 1948-49 Leaf set was the first post-war baseball series issued in color. This effort was not entirely successful due to a lack of refinement which resulted in many color variations and cards out of register. In addition, the set was skip numbered from 1-168, with 49 of the 98 cards printed in limited quantities (marked with an asterisk in the checklist). Cards 102 and 136 have variations, and cards are sometimes found with overprinted or incorrect backs.

|  | MINT | VG-E | F-G |
|---|---|---|---|
| COMPLETE SET ......................... | 8000.00 | 3500.00 | 900.00 |
| COMMON NUMBERS ................. | 11.00 | 4.50 | 1.10 |
| RARE NUMBERS ................................ | 110.00 | 45.00 | 11.00 |

| | | MINT | VG-E | F-G |
|---|---|---|---|---|
| ☐ | 1 Joe DiMaggio ................. | 375.00 | 100.00 | 20.00 |
| ☐ | 3 Babe Ruth ..................... | 400.00 | 160.00 | 40.00 |
| ☐ | 4 Stan Musial ................. | 125.00 | 50.00 | 12.50 |
| ☐ | 5 Virgil Trucks * ............... | 110.00 | 45.00 | 11.00 |
| ☐ | 6 Satchel Paige * ............... | 650.00 | 260.00 | 65.00 |
| ☐ | 10 Dizzy Trout ................. | 11.00 | 4.50 | 1.10 |
| ☐ | 11 Phil Rizzuto ................. | 40.00 | 16.00 | 4.00 |
| ☐ | 13 Cass Michaels * ............. | 110.00 | 45.00 | 11.00 |
| ☐ | 14 Billy Johnson ................. | 11.00 | 4.50 | 1.10 |
| ☐ | 17 Frank Overmire ............. | 11.00 | 4.50 | 1.10 |
| ☐ | 19 Johnny Wyrostek * ......... | 110.00 | 45.00 | 11.00 |
| ☐ | 20 Hank Sauer * ............... | 110.00 | 45.00 | 11.00 |
| ☐ | 22 Al Evans ..................... | 11.00 | 4.50 | 1.10 |
| ☐ | 26 Sam Chapman ................. | 11.00 | 4.50 | 1.10 |
| ☐ | 27 Mickey Harris ................. | 11.00 | 4.50 | 1.10 |
| ☐ | 28 Jim Hegan ..................... | 11.00 | 4.50 | 1.10 |
| ☐ | 29 Elmer Valo ................. | 11.00 | 4.50 | 1.10 |

## 1960 Lake to Lake

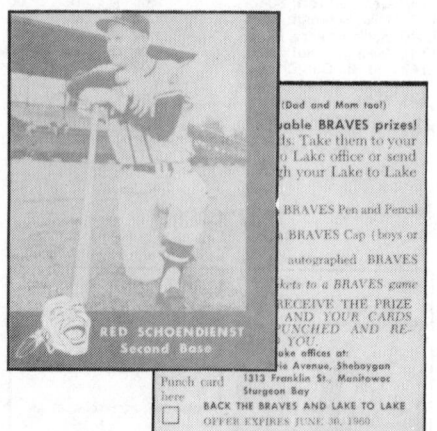

The cards in this 28 card set measure 2 1/2" by 3 1/4". The 1960 Lake to Lake set of unnumbered, blue tinted cards features Milwaukee Braves players only. The cards were issued on milk cartons by Lake to Lake Dairy. Most cards have staple holes in the upper right corner. The backs are in red and give details and prizes associated with the card promotion. Cards with staple holes can be considered very good to excellent at best. The ACC designation is F102-1.

|  | MINT | VG-E | F-G |
|---|---|---|---|
| COMPLETE SET ......................... | 400.00 | 160.00 | 40.00 |
| COMMON PLAYER (1-28) .......... | 5.00 | 2.00 | .50 |

| | | | | |
|---|---|---|---|---|
| ☐ | 30 | Billy Goodman * | 110.00 | 45.00 | 11.00 |
| ☐ | 31 | Lou Brissie | 11.00 | 4.50 | 1.10 |
| ☐ | 32 | Warren Spahn | 50.00 | 20.00 | 5.00 |
| ☐ | 33 | Peanuts Lowrey * | 110.00 | 45.00 | 11.00 |
| ☐ | 36 | Al Zarilla * | 110.00 | 45.00 | 11.00 |
| ☐ | 38 | Ted Kluszewski | 16.00 | 6.50 | 1.60 |
| ☐ | 39 | Ewell Blackwell | 11.00 | 4.50 | 1.10 |
| ☐ | 42 | Kent Peterson | 11.00 | 4.50 | 1.10 |
| ☐ | 43 | Ed Stevens * | 110.00 | 45.00 | 11.00 |
| ☐ | 45 | Ken Keltner * | 110.00 | 45.00 | 11.00 |
| ☐ | 46 | Johnny Mize | 35.00 | 14.00 | 3.50 |
| ☐ | 47 | George Vico | 11.00 | 4.50 | 1.10 |
| ☐ | 48 | Johnny Schmitz * | 110.00 | 45.00 | 11.00 |
| ☐ | 49 | Del Ennis | 11.00 | 4.50 | 1.10 |
| ☐ | 50 | Dick Wakefield | 11.00 | 4.50 | 1.10 |
| ☐ | 51 | Al Dark * | 150.00 | 60.00 | 15.00 |
| ☐ | 53 | Johnny VanderMeer | 12.50 | 5.00 | 1.25 |
| ☐ | 54 | Bobby Adams * | 110.00 | 45.00 | 11.00 |
| ☐ | 55 | Tommy Henrich * | 125.00 | 50.00 | 12.50 |
| ☐ | 56 | Larry Jansen | 11.00 | 4.50 | 1.10 |
| ☐ | 57 | Bob McCall | 11.00 | 4.50 | 1.10 |
| ☐ | 59 | Luke Appling | 20.00 | 8.00 | 2.00 |
| ☐ | 61 | Jake Early | 11.00 | 4.50 | 1.10 |
| ☐ | 62 | Eddie Joost * | 110.00 | 45.00 | 11.00 |
| ☐ | 73 | Barney McCosky * | 110.00 | 45.00 | 11.00 |
| ☐ | 75 | Robert Elliott | 12.50 | 5.00 | 1.25 |
| ☐ | 66 | Orval Grove * | 110.00 | 45.00 | 11.00 |
| ☐ | 68 | Eddie Miller * | 110.00 | 45.00 | 11.00 |
| ☐ | 70 | Honus Wagner * | 90.00 | 36.00 | 9.00 |
| ☐ | 72 | Hank Edwards | 11.00 | 4.50 | 1.10 |
| ☐ | 73 | Pat Seerey | 11.00 | 4.50 | 1.10 |
| ☐ | 75 | Dom DiMaggio * | 150.00 | 60.00 | 15.00 |
| ☐ | 76 | Ted Williams * | 175.00 | 70.00 | 18.00 |
| ☐ | 77 | Roy Smalley | 11.00 | 4.50 | 1.10 |
| ☐ | 78 | Hoot Evers * | 110.00 | 45.00 | 11.00 |
| ☐ | 79 | Jackie Robinson | 125.00 | 50.00 | 12.50 |
| ☐ | 81 | Whitey Kurowski * | 110.00 | 45.00 | 11.00 |
| ☐ | 82 | Johnny Lindell | 11.00 | 4.50 | 1.10 |
| ☐ | 83 | Bobby Doerr | 40.00 | 16.00 | 4.00 |
| ☐ | 84 | Sid Hudson | 11.00 | 4.50 | 1.10 |
| ☐ | 85 | Dave Philley * | 110.00 | 45.00 | 11.00 |
| ☐ | 86 | Ralph Weigel | 11.00 | 4.50 | 1.10 |
| ☐ | 88 | Frank Gustine * | 110.00 | 45.00 | 11.00 |
| ☐ | 91 | Ralph Kiner | 35.00 | 14.00 | 3.50 |
| ☐ | 93 | Bob Feller * | 450.00 | 180.00 | 45.00 |
| ☐ | 95 | George Stirnweiss | 11.00 | 4.50 | 1.10 |
| ☐ | 97 | Marty Marion | 12.50 | 5.00 | 1.25 |
| ☐ | 98 | Hal Newhouser * | 150.00 | 60.00 | 15.00 |
| ☐ | 102A | Gene Hermansk (sic) | 100.00 | 40.00 | 10.00 |
| ☐ | 102B | Gene Hermanski | 12.50 | 5.00 | 1.25 |
| ☐ | 104 | Eddie Stewart * | 110.00 | 45.00 | 11.00 |
| ☐ | 106 | Lou Boudreau * | 35.00 | 14.00 | 3.50 |
| ☐ | 108 | Matt Batts * | 110.00 | 45.00 | 11.00 |
| ☐ | 111 | Jerry Priddy | 11.00 | 4.50 | 1.10 |
| ☐ | 113 | Dutch Leonard * | 110.00 | 45.00 | 11.00 |
| ☐ | 117 | Joe Gordon | 12.50 | 5.00 | 1.25 |
| ☐ | 120 | George Kell * | 250.00 | 100.00 | 25.00 |
| ☐ | 121 | Johnny Pesky * | 125.00 | 50.00 | 12.50 |
| ☐ | 123 | Cliff Fannin * | 110.00 | 45.00 | 11.00 |
| ☐ | 125 | Andy Pafko | 11.00 | 4.50 | 1.10 |
| ☐ | 127 | Enos Slaughter * | 250.00 | 100.00 | 25.00 |
| ☐ | 128 | Buddy Rosar | 11.00 | 4.50 | 1.10 |
| ☐ | 129 | Kirby Higbe * | 110.00 | 45.00 | 11.00 |
| ☐ | 131 | Sid Gordon * | 110.00 | 45.00 | 11.00 |
| ☐ | 133 | Tommy Holmes * | 125.00 | 50.00 | 12.50 |
| ☐ | 136A | Cliff Aberson (full sleeve) | 11.00 | 4.50 | 1.10 |
| ☐ | 136B | Cliff Aberson (short sleeve) | 40.00 | 16.00 | 4.00 |
| ☐ | 137 | Harry Walker * | 125.00 | 50.00 | 12.50 |
| ☐ | 138 | Larry Doby * | 150.00 | 60.00 | 15.00 |
| ☐ | 139 | Johnny Hopp | 12.50 | 5.00 | 1.25 |
| ☐ | 142 | Danny Murtaugh * | 125.00 | 50.00 | 12.50 |
| ☐ | 143 | Dick Sisler * | 110.00 | 45.00 | 11.00 |
| ☐ | 144 | Bob Dillinger * | 110.00 | 45.00 | 11.00 |
| ☐ | 146 | Pete Reiser * | 125.00 | 50.00 | 12.50 |
| ☐ | 149 | Hank Majeski * | 110.00 | 45.00 | 11.00 |
| ☐ | 153 | Floyd Baker * | 110.00 | 45.00 | 11.00 |
| ☐ | 158 | Harry Brecheen * | 125.00 | 50.00 | 12.50 |
| ☐ | 159 | Mizell Platt | 11.00 | 4.50 | 1.10 |
| ☐ | 160 | Bob Scheffing * | 110.00 | 45.00 | 11.00 |
| ☐ | 161 | Vern Stephens * | 125.00 | 50.00 | 12.50 |
| ☐ | 163 | Fred Hutchinson * | 125.00 | 50.00 | 12.50 |
| ☐ | 165 | Dale Mitchell * | 125.00 | 50.00 | 12.50 |
| ☐ | 168 | Phil Cavarretta * | 125.00 | 50.00 | 12.50 |

# 1960 Leaf

The cards in this 144 card set measure 2 1/2" by 3 1/2". The 1960 Leaf set was issued in a regular gum package style but with a marble instead of gum. The series was a joint production by Sports Novelties, Inc., and Leaf, two Chicago based companies. Cards 73-144 are more difficult to find than the lower numbers. Photo variations exist for the seven cards listed with an asterisk and there is a well-known error card, number 25 showing Brooks Lawrence (in a Reds uniform) with Jim Grant's name on front, and Grant's biography and record on back. The corrected version with Grant's photo is the more difficult variety.

| | | | MINT | VG-E | F-G |
|---|---|---|---|---|---|
| | COMPLETE SET | | 650.00 | 260.00 | 65.00 |
| | COMMON PLAYER (1-72) | | .75 | .30 | .07 |
| | COMMON PLAYER (73-144) | | 7.50 | 3.00 | .75 |
| ☐ | 1 | Luis Aparicio * | 4.00 | 1.00 | .20 |
| ☐ | 2 | Woodson Held | .75 | .30 | .07 |
| ☐ | 3 | Frank Lary | .90 | .36 | .09 |
| ☐ | 4 | Camilo Pascual | .90 | .36 | .09 |
| ☐ | 5 | Juan Herrera | .75 | .30 | .07 |
| ☐ | 6 | Felipe Alou | .90 | .36 | .09 |
| ☐ | 7 | Benjamin Daniels | .75 | .30 | .07 |
| ☐ | 8 | Roger Craig | 1.25 | .50 | .12 |
| ☐ | 9 | Edward Kasko | .75 | .30 | .07 |
| ☐ | 10 | Robert Anton Grim | .90 | .36 | .09 |
| ☐ | 11 | James Busby | .75 | .30 | .07 |
| ☐ | 12 | Kenton Boyer | 2.00 | .80 | .20 |
| ☐ | 13 | Robert Boyd | .75 | .30 | .07 |
| ☐ | 14 | Samuel Jones | .90 | .36 | .09 |
| ☐ | 15 | Lawence Jackson | .75 | .30 | .07 |
| ☐ | 16 | Elroy Face | .90 | .36 | .09 |
| ☐ | 17 | Walter Moryn * | .90 | .36 | .09 |
| ☐ | 18 | James Gilliam | 1.50 | .60 | .15 |
| ☐ | 19 | Donald Newcombe | 1.00 | .40 | .10 |
| ☐ | 20 | Glen Hobbie | .75 | .30 | .07 |
| ☐ | 21 | Pedro Ramos | .75 | .30 | .07 |
| ☐ | 22 | Rinold Duren | 1.00 | .40 | .10 |
| ☐ | 23 | Joseph Jay * | .90 | .36 | .09 |
| ☐ | 24 | Louis Berberet | .75 | .30 | .07 |
| ☐ | 25A | Jim Grant COR | 15.00 | 6.00 | 1.50 |
| ☐ | 25B | Jim Grant ERR (photo actually Brooks Lawrence) | 10.00 | 4.00 | 1.00 |
| ☐ | 26 | Thomas Borland | .75 | .30 | .07 |
| ☐ | 27 | Brooks Robinson | 9.00 | 3.75 | .90 |
| ☐ | 28 | Jerry Adair | .75 | .30 | .07 |
| ☐ | 29 | Ronald Jackson | .75 | .30 | .07 |
| ☐ | 30 | George Strickland | .75 | .30 | .07 |
| ☐ | 31 | Everett Rocky Bridges | .75 | .30 | .07 |
| ☐ | 32 | William Tuttle | .75 | .30 | .07 |
| ☐ | 33 | Kenneth Hunt | .75 | .30 | .07 |
| ☐ | 34 | Harold Griggs | .75 | .30 | .07 |
| ☐ | 35 | James Coates * | .90 | .36 | .09 |
| ☐ | 36 | Brooks Lawrence | .90 | .36 | .09 |
| ☐ | 37 | Edwin (Duke) Snider | 9.00 | 3.75 | .90 |
| ☐ | 38 | Albert Spangler | .75 | .30 | .07 |
| ☐ | 39 | James Owens | .75 | .30 | .07 |
| ☐ | 40 | William Virdon | 1.00 | .40 | .10 |
| ☐ | 41 | Ernest Broglio | .75 | .30 | .07 |
| ☐ | 42 | Andre Rodgers | .75 | .30 | .07 |

| | | | | |
|---|---|---|---|---|
| ☐ 43 | Julio Becquer | .75 | .30 | .07 |
| ☐ 44 | Antonio (Tony) Taylor | .75 | .30 | .07 |
| ☐ 45 | Gerald Lynch | .75 | .30 | .07 |
| ☐ 46 | Cletis Boyer | .90 | .36 | .09 |
| ☐ 47 | Jerry Lumpe | .75 | .30 | .07 |
| ☐ 48 | Charles Maxwell | .75 | .30 | .07 |
| ☐ 49 | James Perry | .90 | .36 | .09 |
| ☐ 50 | Daniel McDevitt | .75 | .30 | .07 |
| ☐ 51 | Juan Pizarro | .75 | .30 | .07 |
| ☐ 52 | Dallas Green | 1.25 | .50 | .12 |
| ☐ 53 | Robert Friend | .90 | .36 | .09 |
| ☐ 54 | Jack Sanford | .75 | .30 | .07 |
| ☐ 55 | Manuel (Jim) Rivera | .75 | .30 | .07 |
| ☐ 56 | Theodore Wills | .75 | .30 | .07 |
| ☐ 57 | Milton Pappas | .90 | .36 | .09 |
| ☐ 58 | Harold Smith * | .90 | .36 | .09 |
| ☐ 59 | Roberto Avila | .90 | .36 | .09 |
| ☐ 60 | Clement Labine | .90 | .36 | .09 |
| ☐ 61 | Norman Rehm * | .90 | .36 | .09 |
| ☐ 62 | John Gabler | .75 | .30 | .07 |
| ☐ 63 | John Tsitouris | .75 | .30 | .07 |
| ☐ 64 | David Sisler | .75 | .30 | .07 |
| ☐ 65 | Victor Power | .75 | .30 | .07 |
| ☐ 66 | Earl Battey | .90 | .36 | .09 |
| ☐ 67 | Robert Purkey | .75 | .30 | .07 |
| ☐ 68 | Myron(Moe) Drabowsky | .75 | .30 | .07 |
| ☐ 69 | James (Hoyt) Wilhelm | 3.50 | 1.40 | .35 |
| ☐ 70 | Humberto Robinson | .75 | .30 | .07 |
| ☐ 71 | Dorrel (Whitey) Herzog | 1.25 | .50 | .12 |
| ☐ 72 | Richard Donovan * | .90 | .36 | .09 |
| ☐ 73 | Gordon Jones | 7.50 | 3.00 | .75 |
| ☐ 74 | Joe Hicks | 7.50 | 3.00 | .75 |
| ☐ 75 | Ray Culp | 7.50 | 3.00 | .75 |
| ☐ 76 | Dick Drott | 7.50 | 3.00 | .75 |
| ☐ 77 | Bob Duliba | 7.50 | 3.00 | .75 |
| ☐ 78 | Art Ditmar | 7.50 | 3.00 | .75 |
| ☐ 79 | Steve Korcheck | 7.50 | 3.00 | .75 |
| ☐ 80 | Henry Mason | 7.50 | 3.00 | .75 |
| ☐ 81 | Harry Simpson | 7.50 | 3.00 | .75 |
| ☐ 82 | Gene Green | 7.50 | 3.00 | .75 |
| ☐ 83 | Bob Shaw | 7.50 | 3.00 | .75 |
| ☐ 84 | Howard Reed | 7.50 | 3.00 | .75 |
| ☐ 85 | Dick Stigman | 7.50 | 3.00 | .75 |
| ☐ 86 | Rip Repulski | 7.50 | 3.00 | .75 |
| ☐ 87 | Seth Morehead | 7.50 | 3.00 | .75 |
| ☐ 88 | Camilo Carreon | 7.50 | 3.00 | .75 |
| ☐ 89 | John Blanchard | 9.00 | 3.75 | .90 |
| ☐ 90 | Billy Hoeft | 7.50 | 3.00 | .75 |
| ☐ 91 | Fred Hopke | 7.50 | 3.00 | .75 |
| ☐ 92 | Joe Martin | 7.50 | 3.00 | .75 |
| ☐ 93 | Wally Shannon | 7.50 | 3.00 | .75 |
| ☐ 94 | Two Hal Smith's | 11.00 | 4.50 | 1.10 |
| | Hal R. Smith | | | |
| | Hal W. Smith | | | |
| ☐ 95 | Al Schroll | 7.50 | 3.00 | .75 |
| ☐ 96 | John Kucks | 7.50 | 3.00 | .75 |
| ☐ 97 | Tom Morgan | 7.50 | 3.00 | .75 |
| ☐ 98 | Willie Jones | 7.50 | 3.00 | .75 |
| ☐ 99 | Marshall Renfroe | 7.50 | 3.00 | .75 |
| ☐ 100 | Willie Tasby | 7.50 | 3.00 | .75 |
| ☐ 101 | Irv Noren | 7.50 | 3.00 | .75 |
| ☐ 102 | Russ Snyder | 7.50 | 3.00 | .75 |
| ☐ 103 | Bob Turley | 11.00 | 4.50 | 1.10 |
| ☐ 104 | Jim Woods | 7.50 | 3.00 | .75 |
| ☐ 105 | Ronnie Kline | 7.50 | 3.00 | .75 |
| ☐ 106 | Steve Bilko | 7.50 | 3.00 | .75 |
| ☐ 107 | Elmer Valo | 7.50 | 3.00 | .75 |
| ☐ 108 | Tom McAvoy | 7.50 | 3.00 | .75 |
| ☐ 109 | Stan Williams | 9.00 | 3.75 | .90 |
| ☐ 110 | Earl Averill Jr. | 7.50 | 3.00 | .75 |
| ☐ 111 | Lee Walls | 7.50 | 3.00 | .75 |
| ☐ 112 | Paul Richards MGR | 9.00 | 3.75 | .90 |
| ☐ 113 | Ed Sadowski | 7.50 | 3.00 | .75 |
| ☐ 114 | Stover McIlwain | 7.50 | 3.00 | .75 |
| ☐ 115 | Chuck Tanner | 11.00 | 4.50 | 1.10 |
| ☐ 116 | Lou Klimchock | 7.50 | 3.00 | .75 |
| ☐ 117 | Neil Chrisley | 7.50 | 3.00 | .75 |
| ☐ 118 | John Callison | 9.00 | 3.75 | .90 |
| ☐ 119 | Hal Smith | 7.50 | 3.00 | .75 |
| ☐ 120 | Carl Sawatski | 7.50 | 3.00 | .75 |
| ☐ 121 | Frank Leja | 7.50 | 3.00 | .75 |
| ☐ 122 | Earl Torgeson | 7.50 | 3.00 | .75 |
| ☐ 123 | Art Schult | 7.50 | 3.00 | .75 |
| ☐ 124 | Jim Brosnan | 9.00 | 3.75 | .90 |
| ☐ 125 | George Anderson | 12.50 | 5.00 | 1.25 |
| ☐ 126 | Joe Pignatano | 7.50 | 3.00 | .75 |
| ☐ 127 | Rocky Nelson | 7.50 | 3.00 | .75 |
| ☐ 128 | Orlando Cepeda | 18.00 | 7.25 | 1.80 |
| ☐ 129 | Daryl Spencer | 7.50 | 3.00 | .75 |
| ☐ 130 | Ralph Lumenti | 7.50 | 3.00 | .75 |
| ☐ 131 | Sam Taylor | 7.50 | 3.00 | .75 |
| ☐ 132 | Harry Brecheen | 7.50 | 3.00 | .75 |
| ☐ 133 | Johnny Groth | 7.50 | 3.00 | .75 |
| ☐ 134 | Wayne Terwilliger | 7.50 | 3.00 | .75 |
| ☐ 135 | Kent Hadley | 7.50 | 3.00 | .75 |
| ☐ 136 | Faye Throneberry | 7.50 | 3.00 | .75 |
| ☐ 137 | Jack Meyer | 7.50 | 3.00 | .75 |
| ☐ 138 | Chuck Cottier | 9.00 | 3.75 | .90 |
| ☐ 139 | Joe DeMaestri | 7.50 | 3.00 | .75 |
| ☐ 140 | Gene Freese | 7.50 | 3.00 | .75 |
| ☐ 141 | Curt Flood | 12.50 | 5.00 | 1.25 |
| ☐ 142 | Gino Cimoli | 7.50 | 3.00 | .75 |
| ☐ 143 | Clay Dalrymple | 7.50 | 3.00 | .75 |
| ☐ 144 | Jim Bunning | 20.00 | 6.00 | 1.00 |

# 1933 Geo. C. Miller

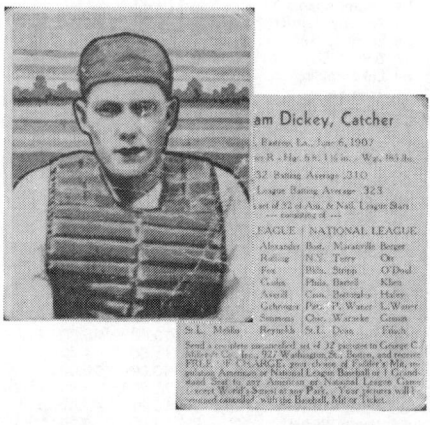

The cards in this 32 card set measure 2 1/2" by 3". This set of soft tone color baseball cards issued in 1933 by the George C. Miller Company consists of 16 players from each league. The bottom portion of the reverse contained a premium offer and many cards are found with this section cut off. Cards without the coupon are considered fair to good condition at best. The Andrews card (with coupon intact) is considered scarce in relation to all other common players. The ACC catalog number is R300.

| | | MINT | VG-E | F-G |
|---|---|---|---|---|
| COMPLETE SET | | 8500.00 | 3200.00 | 750.00 |
| COMMON PLAYER (1-32) | | 200.00 | 80.00 | 20.00 |
| ☐ 1 | Dale Alexander | 200.00 | 80.00 | 20.00 |
| ☐ 2 | Ivy Andrews | 1200.00 | 250.00 | 50.00 |
| ☐ 3 | Earl Averill | 300.00 | 120.00 | 30.00 |
| ☐ 4 | Dick Bartell | 200.00 | 80.00 | 20.00 |
| ☐ 5 | Wally Berger | 200.00 | 80.00 | 20.00 |
| ☐ 6 | Jim Bottomley | 300.00 | 120.00 | 30.00 |
| ☐ 7 | Joe Cronin | 350.00 | 140.00 | 35.00 |
| ☐ 8 | Dizzy Dean | 600.00 | 240.00 | 60.00 |
| ☐ 9 | Bill Dickey | 400.00 | 160.00 | 40.00 |
| ☐ 10 | Jimmy Dykes | 200.00 | 80.00 | 20.00 |
| ☐ 11 | Wes Ferrell | 200.00 | 80.00 | 20.00 |
| ☐ 12 | Jimmy Foxx | 450.00 | 180.00 | 45.00 |
| ☐ 13 | Frank Frisch | 350.00 | 140.00 | 35.00 |
| ☐ 14 | Charlie Gehringer | 350.00 | 140.00 | 35.00 |
| ☐ 15 | Goose Goslin | 300.00 | 120.00 | 30.00 |
| ☐ 16 | Charlie Grimm | 200.00 | 80.00 | 20.00 |
| ☐ 17 | Lefty Grove | 400.00 | 160.00 | 40.00 |
| ☐ 18 | Chick Hafey | 300.00 | 120.00 | 30.00 |
| ☐ 19 | Ray Hayworth | 200.00 | 80.00 | 20.00 |
| ☐ 20 | Chuck Klein | 350.00 | 140.00 | 35.00 |
| ☐ 21 | Rabbit Maranville | 300.00 | 120.00 | 30.00 |
| ☐ 22 | Oscar Melillo | 200.00 | 80.00 | 20.00 |
| ☐ 23 | Lefty O'Doul | 200.00 | 80.00 | 20.00 |
| ☐ 24 | Mel Ott | 400.00 | 160.00 | 40.00 |
| ☐ 25 | Carl Reynolds | 200.00 | 80.00 | 20.00 |
| ☐ 26 | Red Ruffing | 300.00 | 120.00 | 30.00 |
| ☐ 27 | Al Simmons | 300.00 | 120.00 | 30.00 |
| ☐ 28 | Joe Stripp | 200.00 | 80.00 | 20.00 |
| ☐ 29 | Bill Terry | 350.00 | 140.00 | 35.00 |

| | | MINT | VG-E | F-G |
|---|---|---|---|---|
| ☐ 30 | Lloyd Waner | 300.00 | 120.00 | 30.00 |
| ☐ 31 | Paul Waner | 300.00 | 120.00 | 30.00 |
| ☐ 32 | Lon Warneke | 200.00 | 80.00 | 20.00 |

## 1984 Milton Bradley

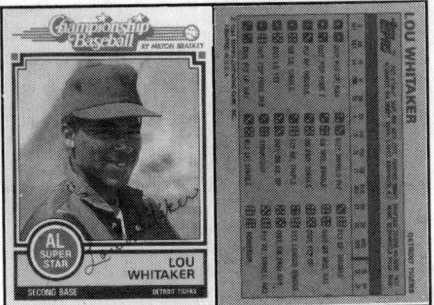

The cards in this 30 card set measure 2 1/2" by 3 1/2". This set of full color cards was produced by Topps for the Milton Bradley Co. The set was included in a board game entitled Championship Baseball. The fronts feature portraits of the players and the name, Championship Baseball, by Milton Bradley. The backs feature the Topps logo, statistics for the past year (pitchers' cards have career statistics), and dice rolls which are part of the board game. Pitcher cards have no dice roll charts. There are 15 players from each league. These unnumbered cards are listed below in alphabetical order. The cap logos and uniforms have been airbrushed to remove all team references.

| | | MINT | VG-E | F-G |
|---|---|---|---|---|
| | COMPLETE SET | 7.00 | 2.80 | .70 |
| | COMMON PLAYER | .15 | .06 | .01 |
| ☐ 1 | Wade Boggs | 1.00 | .40 | .10 |
| ☐ 2 | George Brett | .60 | .24 | .06 |
| ☐ 3 | Rod Carew | .35 | .14 | .03 |
| ☐ 4 | Steve Carlton | .35 | .14 | .03 |
| ☐ 5 | Gary Carter | .35 | .14 | .03 |
| ☐ 6 | Dave Concepcion | .15 | .06 | .01 |
| ☐ 7 | Cecil Cooper | .15 | .06 | .01 |
| ☐ 8 | Andre Dawson | .20 | .08 | .02 |
| ☐ 9 | Carlton Fisk | .15 | .06 | .01 |
| ☐ 10 | Steve Garvey | .35 | .14 | .03 |
| ☐ 11 | Pedro Guerrero | .20 | .08 | .02 |
| ☐ 12 | Ron Guidry | .20 | .08 | .02 |
| ☐ 13 | Rickey Henderson | .60 | .24 | .06 |
| ☐ 14 | Reggie Jackson | .60 | .24 | .06 |
| ☐ 15 | Ron Kittle | .15 | .06 | .01 |
| ☐ 16 | Bill Madlock | .15 | .06 | .01 |
| ☐ 17 | Dale Murphy | .75 | .30 | .07 |
| ☐ 18 | Al Oliver | .15 | .06 | .01 |
| ☐ 19 | Darrell Porter | .15 | .06 | .01 |
| ☐ 20 | Cal Ripken | 1.00 | .40 | .10 |
| ☐ 21 | Pete Rose | 1.00 | .40 | .10 |
| ☐ 22 | Steve Sax | .20 | .08 | .02 |
| ☐ 23 | Mike Schmidt | .75 | .30 | .07 |
| ☐ 24 | Ted Simmons | .20 | .08 | .02 |
| ☐ 25 | Ozzie Smith | .20 | .08 | .02 |
| ☐ 26 | Dave Stieb | .20 | .08 | .02 |
| ☐ 27 | Fernando Valenzuela | .30 | .12 | .03 |
| ☐ 28 | Lou Whitaker | .15 | .06 | .01 |
| ☐ 29 | Dave Winfield | .35 | .14 | .03 |
| ☐ 30 | Robin Yount | .35 | .14 | .03 |

## 1959 Morrell

The cards in this 12 card set measure 2 1/2" by 3 1/2". The 1959 Morrell Meats set of full color, unnumbered cards features Los Angeles Dodger players only. The photos used are the same as those selected for the Dodger team issue postcards in 1959. The Morrell Meats logo is on the backs of the cards. The Clem Labine card actually features a picture of Stan Williams and the Norm Larker card actually features a picture of Joe Pignatano. The ACC designation is F172-1.

| | | MINT | VG-E | F-G |
|---|---|---|---|---|
| | COMPLETE SET | 700.00 | 280.00 | 70.00 |
| | COMMON PLAYER (1-12) | 40.00 | 16.00 | 4.00 |
| ☐ 1 | Don Drysdale | 80.00 | 32.00 | 8.00 |
| ☐ 2 | Carl Furillo | 50.00 | 20.00 | 5.00 |
| ☐ 3 | Jim Gilliam | 50.00 | 20.00 | 5.00 |
| ☐ 4 | Gil Hodges | 80.00 | 32.00 | 8.00 |
| ☐ 5 | Sandy Koufax | 125.00 | 50.00 | 12.50 |
| ☐ 6 | Clem Labine (photo actually Stan Williams) | 40.00 | 16.00 | 4.00 |
| ☐ 7 | Norm Larker (photo actually Joe Pignatano) | 40.00 | 16.00 | 4.00 |
| ☐ 8 | Charlie Neal | 40.00 | 16.00 | 4.00 |
| ☐ 9 | Johnny Podres | 50.00 | 20.00 | 5.00 |
| ☐ 10 | John Roseboro | 40.00 | 16.00 | 4.00 |
| ☐ 11 | Duke Snider | 125.00 | 50.00 | 12.50 |
| ☐ 12 | Don Zimmer | 40.00 | 16.00 | 4.00 |

## 1960 Morrell

The cards in this 12 card set measure 2 1/2" by 3 1/2". The 1960 Morrell Meats set of full color, unnumbered cards is similar in format to the 1959 Morrell set but can be distinguished from the 1959 set by a red heart which appears in the Morrell logo on the back. The photos used are the same as those selected for the Dodger team issue postcards in 1960. The Furillo, Hodges, and Snider cards received limited distribution and are hence more scarce. The ACC designation is F172-2. The cards were printed in Japan.

| | | MINT | VG-E | F-G |
|---|---|---|---|---|
| | COMPLETE SET | 400.00 | 160.00 | 40.00 |
| | COMMON PLAYER (1-12) | 12.00 | 5.00 | 1.20 |
| ☐ 1 | Walt Alston MGR | 20.00 | 8.00 | 2.00 |
| ☐ 2 | Roger Craig | 15.00 | 6.00 | 1.50 |
| ☐ 3 | Don Drysdale | 30.00 | 12.00 | 3.00 |
| ☐ 4 | Carl Furillo SP | 60.00 | 24.00 | 6.00 |
| ☐ 5 | Gil Hodges SP | 90.00 | 36.00 | 9.00 |
| ☐ 6 | Sandy Koufax | 50.00 | 20.00 | 5.00 |
| ☐ 7 | Wally Moon | 12.00 | 5.00 | 1.20 |
| ☐ 8 | Charlie Neal | 12.00 | 5.00 | 1.20 |
| ☐ 9 | Johnny Podres | 15.00 | 6.00 | 1.50 |
| ☐ 10 | John Roseboro | 12.00 | 5.00 | 1.20 |
| ☐ 11 | Larry Sherry | 12.00 | 5.00 | 1.20 |
| ☐ 12 | Duke Snider SP | 120.00 | 50.00 | 12.00 |

## 1961 Morrell

The cards in this 6 card set measure 2 1/2" by 3 1/2". The 1961 Morrell Meats set of full color, unnumbered cards features Los Angeles Dodger players only and contains statistical information on the backs of the cards in brown print. The ACC designation is F172-3.

| | MINT | VG-E | F-G |
|---|---|---|---|
| COMPLETE SET ........................ | 120.00 | 50.00 | 12.00 |
| COMMON PLAYER (1-6) ............ | 12.00 | 5.00 | 1.20 |
| ☐ 1 Tommy Davis ..................... | 15.00 | 6.00 | 1.50 |
| ☐ 2 Don Drysdale .................... | 30.00 | 12.00 | 3.00 |
| ☐ 3 Frank Howard .................... | 15.00 | 6.00 | 1.50 |
| ☐ 4 Sandy Koufax .................... | 50.00 | 20.00 | 5.00 |
| ☐ 5 Norm Larker ..................... | 12.00 | 5.00 | 1.20 |
| ☐ 6 Maury Wills ...................... | 20.00 | 8.00 | 2.00 |

## 1983 Mother's Giants

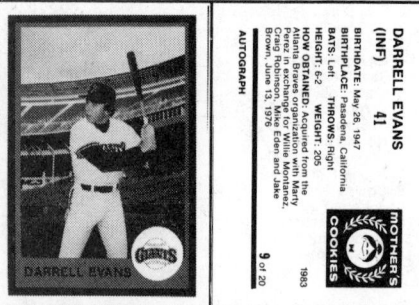

The cards in this 20 card set measure 2 1/2" by 3 1/2". For the first time in 30 years, Mother's Cookies issued a baseball card set. The full color set, produced by hobbyist Barry Colla, features San Francisco Giants players only. Fifteen cards were issued at the Astros vs. Giants game of August 7, 1983. Five of the cards were redeemable by sending in a coupon. The five additional cards received from redemption of the coupon were not guaranteed to be the five needed to complete the set. The fronts feature the player's photo, his name, and the Giants' logo, while the backs feature player biographies and the Mother's Cookies logo. The backs also contain a space in which to obtain the player's autograph.

| | MINT | VG-E | F-G |
|---|---|---|---|
| COMPLETE SET ........................ | 12.50 | 5.00 | 1.25 |
| COMMON PLAYER .................... | .50 | .20 | .05 |
| ☐ 1 Frank Robinson MGR ........ | 1.50 | .60 | .15 |
| ☐ 2 Jack Clark ....................... | 1.50 | .60 | .15 |
| ☐ 3 Chili Davis ....................... | 1.50 | .60 | .15 |
| ☐ 4 Johnnie LeMaster ............. | .50 | .20 | .05 |
| ☐ 5 Greg Minton ..................... | .60 | .24 | .06 |
| ☐ 6 Bob Brenly ....................... | .75 | .30 | .07 |
| ☐ 7 Fred Breining .................... | .50 | .20 | .05 |
| ☐ 8 Jeff Leonard ..................... | .75 | .30 | .07 |
| ☐ 9 Darrell Evans .................... | 1.00 | .40 | .10 |
| ☐ 10 Tom O'Malley .................. | .50 | .20 | .05 |
| ☐ 11 Duane Kuiper .................. | .50 | .20 | .05 |
| ☐ 12 Mike Krukow ................... | .75 | .30 | .07 |
| ☐ 13 Atlee Hammaker .............. | .60 | .24 | .06 |
| ☐ 14 Gary Lavelle ................... | .60 | .24 | .06 |
| ☐ 15 Bill Laskey ..................... | .50 | .20 | .05 |
| ☐ 16 Max Venable ................... | .50 | .20 | .05 |
| ☐ 17 Joel Youngblood .............. | .50 | .20 | .05 |
| ☐ 18 Dave Bergman ................. | .50 | .20 | .05 |
| ☐ 19 Mike Vail ........................ | .50 | .20 | .05 |
| ☐ 20 Andy McGaffigan .............. | .50 | .20 | .05 |

## 1984 Mother's A's

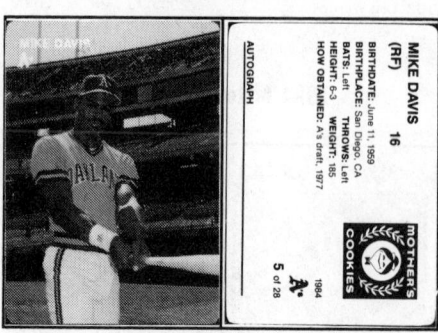

The cards in this 28 card set measure 2 1/2" by 3 1/2". In 1984, the Los Angeles based Mother's Cookies Co. issued five sets of cards featuring players from major league teams. The Oakland A's set features current players depicted by photos. Similar to their 1952 and 1953 issues, the cards have rounded corners. The backs of the cards contain the Mother's Cookies logo. The cards were distributed in partial sets to fans at the respective stadiums of the teams involved. Whereas 20 cards were given to each patron, a redemption card, redeemable for eight more cards was included. Unfortunately, the eight cards received by redeeming the coupon were not necessarily the eight cards needed to complete a set. Hobbyist Barry Colla was involved in the production of these sets.

| | MINT | VG-E | F-G |
|---|---|---|---|
| COMPLETE SET ........................ | 12.50 | 5.00 | 1.25 |
| COMMON PLAYER .................... | .40 | .16 | .04 |
| ☐ 1 Steve Boros MGR ............. | .40 | .16 | .04 |
| ☐ 2 Rickey Henderson ............. | 3.00 | 1.20 | .30 |
| ☐ 3 Joe Morgan ...................... | 1.50 | .60 | .15 |
| ☐ 4 Dwayne Murphy ................. | .75 | .30 | .07 |
| ☐ 5 Mike Davis ....................... | .50 | .20 | .05 |
| ☐ 6 Bruce Bochte .................... | .40 | .16 | .04 |
| ☐ 7 Carney Lansford ................ | .75 | .30 | .07 |
| ☐ 8 Steve McCatty .................. | .40 | .16 | .04 |
| ☐ 9 Mike Heath ...................... | .40 | .16 | .04 |
| ☐ 10 Chris Codiroli .................. | .40 | .16 | .04 |
| ☐ 11 Bill Almon ...................... | .40 | .16 | .04 |
| ☐ 12 Bill Caudill ..................... | .50 | .20 | .05 |
| ☐ 13 Donnie Hill ..................... | .40 | .16 | .04 |
| ☐ 14 Lary Sorensen ................. | .40 | .16 | .04 |
| ☐ 15 Dave Kingman ................. | .75 | .30 | .07 |
| ☐ 16 Garry Hancock ................. | .40 | .16 | .04 |
| ☐ 17 Jeff Burroughs ................. | .40 | .16 | .04 |
| ☐ 18 Tom Burgmeier ................ | .40 | .16 | .04 |
| ☐ 19 Jim Essian ..................... | .40 | .16 | .04 |
| ☐ 20 Mike Warren ................... | .40 | .16 | .04 |
| ☐ 21 Davey Lopes ................... | .50 | .20 | .05 |
| ☐ 22 Ray Burris ...................... | .40 | .16 | .04 |
| ☐ 23 Tony Phillips ................... | .40 | .16 | .04 |
| ☐ 24 Tim Conroy ..................... | .40 | .16 | .04 |
| ☐ 25 Jeff Bettendorf ................ | .40 | .16 | .04 |
| ☐ 26 Keith Atherton ................. | .40 | .16 | .04 |
| ☐ 27 A's Coaches .................... | .40 | .16 | .04 |
| ☐ 28 A's Checklist ................... | .40 | .05 | .01 |

## 1984 Mother's Astros

The cards in this 28 card set measure 2 1/2" by 3 1/2". In 1984, the Los Angeles based Mother's Cookies Co. issued five sets of cards featuring players from major league teams. The Houston

Astros set features current players depicted by photos. Similar to their 1952 and 1953 issues, the cards have rounded corners. The backs of the cards contain the Mother's Cookies logo. The cards were distributed in partial sets to fans at the respective stadiums of the teams involved. Whereas 20 cards were given to each patron, a redemption card, redeemable for eight more cards was included. Unfortunately, the eight cards received by redeeming the coupon were not necessarily the eight needed to complete a set. Hobbyist Barry Colla was involved in the production of these sets.

|  | MINT | VG-E | F-G |
|---|---|---|---|
| COMPLETE SET | 10.00 | 4.00 | 1.00 |
| COMMON PLAYER | .30 | .12 | .03 |

| | | MINT | VG-E | F-G |
|---|---|---|---|---|
| ☐ 1 | Nolan Ryan | 2.50 | 1.00 | .25 |
| ☐ 2 | Joe Niekro | .60 | .24 | .06 |
| ☐ 3 | Alan Ashby | .30 | .12 | .03 |
| ☐ 4 | Bill Doran | 1.00 | .40 | .10 |
| ☐ 5 | Phil Garner | .40 | .16 | .04 |
| ☐ 6 | Ray Knight | .50 | .20 | .05 |
| ☐ 7 | Dickie Thon | .50 | .20 | .05 |
| ☐ 8 | Jose Cruz | .75 | .30 | .07 |
| ☐ 9 | Jerry Mumphrey | .40 | .16 | .04 |
| ☐ 10 | Terry Puhl | .40 | .16 | .04 |
| ☐ 11 | Enos Cabell | .30 | .12 | .03 |
| ☐ 12 | Harry Spilman | .30 | .12 | .03 |
| ☐ 13 | Dave Smith | .40 | .16 | .04 |
| ☐ 14 | Mike Scott | 1.00 | .40 | .10 |
| ☐ 15 | Bob Lillis MGR | .30 | .12 | .03 |
| ☐ 16 | Bob Knepper | .50 | .20 | .05 |
| ☐ 17 | Frank DiPino | .40 | .16 | .04 |
| ☐ 18 | Tom Wieghaus | .30 | .12 | .03 |
| ☐ 19 | Denny Walling | .30 | .12 | .03 |
| ☐ 20 | Tony Scott | .30 | .12 | .03 |
| ☐ 21 | Alan Bannister | .30 | .12 | .03 |
| ☐ 22 | Bill Dawley | .30 | .12 | .03 |
| ☐ 23 | Vern Ruhle | .30 | .12 | .03 |
| ☐ 24 | Mike LaCoss | .30 | .12 | .03 |
| ☐ 25 | Mike Madden | .30 | .12 | .03 |
| ☐ 26 | Craig Reynolds | .40 | .16 | .04 |
| ☐ 27 | Astros' Coaches | .30 | .12 | .03 |
| ☐ 28 | Astros' Checklist | .30 | .05 | .01 |

# 1984 Mother's Giants

The cards in this 28 card set measure 2 1/2" by 3 1/2". In 1984, the Los Angeles based Mother's Cookies Co. issued five sets of cards featuring players from major league teams. The San Francisco Giants set features previous Giant All-Star selections depicted by drawings. Similar to their 1952 and 1953 issues, the cards have rounded corners. The backs of the cards contain the Mother's Cookies logo. The cards were distributed in partial sets to fans at the respective stadiums of the teams involved. Whereas 20 cards were given to each

patron, a redemption card, redeemable for eight more cards was included. Unfortunately, the eight cards received by redeeming the coupon were not necessarily the eight needed to complete a set. Hobbyist Barry Colla was involved in the production of these sets.

| | | MINT | VG-E | F-G |
|---|---|---|---|---|
| COMPLETE SET | | 12.50 | 5.00 | 1.25 |
| COMMON PLAYER | | .40 | .16 | .04 |

| | | MINT | VG-E | F-G |
|---|---|---|---|---|
| ☐ 1 | Willie Mays | 2.00 | .80 | .20 |
| ☐ 2 | Willie McCovey | 1.50 | .60 | .15 |
| ☐ 3 | Juan Marichal | 1.50 | .60 | .15 |
| ☐ 4 | Gaylord Perry | 1.00 | .40 | .10 |
| ☐ 5 | Tom Haller | .40 | .16 | .04 |
| ☐ 6 | Jim Davenport | .50 | .20 | .05 |
| ☐ 7 | Jack Clark | .75 | .30 | .07 |
| ☐ 8 | Greg Minton | .40 | .16 | .04 |
| ☐ 9 | Atlee Hammaker | .50 | .20 | .05 |
| ☐ 10 | Gary Lavelle | .50 | .20 | .05 |
| ☐ 11 | Orlando Cepeda | .75 | .30 | .07 |
| ☐ 12 | Bobby Bonds | .60 | .24 | .06 |
| ☐ 13 | John Antonelli | .40 | .16 | .04 |
| ☐ 14 | Bob Schmidt | .40 | .16 | .04 |
| ☐ 15 | Sam Jones | .40 | .16 | .04 |
| ☐ 16 | Mike McCormick | .40 | .16 | .04 |
| ☐ 17 | Ed Bailey | .40 | .16 | .04 |
| ☐ 18 | Stu Miller | .40 | .16 | .04 |
| ☐ 19 | Felipe Alou | .50 | .20 | .05 |
| ☐ 20 | Jim Ray Hart | .40 | .16 | .04 |
| ☐ 21 | Dick Dietz | .40 | .16 | .04 |
| ☐ 22 | Chris Speier | .40 | .16 | .04 |
| ☐ 23 | Bobby Murcer | .60 | .24 | .06 |
| ☐ 24 | John Montefusco | .40 | .16 | .04 |
| ☐ 25 | Vida Blue | .50 | .20 | .05 |
| ☐ 26 | Ed Whitson | .50 | .20 | .05 |
| ☐ 27 | Darrell Evans | .60 | .24 | .06 |
| ☐ 28 | Checklist | .40 | .05 | .01 |

# 1984 Mother's Mariners

The cards in this 28 card set measure 2 1/2" by 3 1/2". In 1984, The Los Angeles-based Mother's Cookies Co. issued five sets of cards featuring players from major league teams. The Seattle Mariners set features current players depicted by photos. Similar to their 1952 and 1953 issues, the cards have rounded corners. The backs of the cards contain the Mother's Cookies logo. The cards were distributed in partial sets to fans at the respective stadiums of the teams involved. Whereas 20 cards were given to each patron, a redemption card, redeemable for eight more cards was included. Unfortunately, the eight cards received by redeeming the coupon were not necessarily the eight needed to complete a set. Hobbyist Barry Colla was involved in the production of these sets.

contain the Mother's Cookies logo. The cards were distributed in partial sets to fans at the respective stadiums of the teams involved. Whereas 20 cards were given to each patron, a redemption card, redeemable for eight more cards was included. Unfortunately, the eight cards received by redeeming the coupon were not necessarily the eight needed to complete a set. Hobbyist Barry Colla was involved in the production of these sets.

|  | | MINT | VG-E | F-G |
|---|---|---|---|---|
| COMPLETE SET | | 15.00 | 6.00 | 1.50 |
| COMMON PLAYER | | .50 | .20 | .05 |
| ☐ 1 | Dick Williams MGR | .50 | .20 | .05 |
| ☐ 2 | Rich Gossage | 1.00 | .40 | .10 |
| ☐ 3 | Tim Lollar | .50 | .20 | .05 |
| ☐ 4 | Eric Show | .50 | .20 | .05 |
| ☐ 5 | Terry Kennedy | .60 | .24 | .06 |
| ☐ 6 | Kurt Bevacqua | .50 | .20 | .05 |
| ☐ 7 | Steve Garvey | 2.00 | .80 | .20 |
| ☐ 8 | Garry Templeton | .60 | .24 | .06 |
| ☐ 9 | Tony Gwynn | 2.00 | .80 | .20 |
| ☐ 10 | Alan Wiggins | .60 | .24 | .06 |
| ☐ 11 | Dave Dravecky | .60 | .24 | .06 |
| ☐ 12 | Tim Flannery | .50 | .20 | .05 |
| ☐ 13 | Kevin McReynolds | 1.50 | .60 | .15 |
| ☐ 14 | Bobby Brown | .50 | .20 | .05 |
| ☐ 15 | Ed Whitson | .60 | .24 | .06 |
| ☐ 16 | Doug Gwosdz | .50 | .20 | .05 |
| ☐ 17 | Luis DeLeon | .50 | .20 | .05 |
| ☐ 18 | Andy Hawkins | .60 | .24 | .06 |
| ☐ 19 | Craig Lefferts | .50 | .20 | .05 |
| ☐ 20 | Carmelo Martinez | .60 | .24 | .06 |
| ☐ 21 | Sid Monge | .50 | .20 | .05 |
| ☐ 22 | Graig Nettles | .75 | .30 | .07 |
| ☐ 23 | Mario Ramirez | .50 | .20 | .05 |
| ☐ 24 | Luis Salazar | .50 | .20 | .05 |
| ☐ 25 | Champ Summers | .50 | .20 | .05 |
| ☐ 26 | Mark Thurmond | .60 | .24 | .06 |
| ☐ 27 | Padres' Coaches | .50 | .20 | .05 |
| ☐ 28 | Padres' Checklist | .50 | .05 | .01 |

|  | | MINT | VG-E | F-G |
|---|---|---|---|---|
| COMPLETE SET | | 12.50 | 5.00 | 1.25 |
| COMMON PLAYER | | .40 | .16 | .04 |
| ☐ 1 | Del Crandall MGR | .50 | .20 | .05 |
| ☐ 2 | Barry Bonnell | .40 | .16 | .04 |
| ☐ 3 | Dave Henderson | .50 | .20 | .05 |
| ☐ 4 | Bob Kearney | .40 | .16 | .04 |
| ☐ 5 | Mike Moore | .60 | .24 | .06 |
| ☐ 6 | Spike Owen | .50 | .20 | .05 |
| ☐ 7 | Gorman Thomas | .60 | .24 | .06 |
| ☐ 8 | Ed VandeBerg | .50 | .20 | .05 |
| ☐ 9 | Matt Young | .50 | .20 | .05 |
| ☐ 10 | Larry Milbourne | .40 | .16 | .04 |
| ☐ 11 | Dave Beard | .40 | .16 | .04 |
| ☐ 12 | Jim Beattie | .40 | .16 | .04 |
| ☐ 13 | Mark Langston | 1.00 | .40 | .10 |
| ☐ 14 | Orlando Mercado | .40 | .16 | .04 |
| ☐ 15 | Jack Perconte | .40 | .16 | .04 |
| ☐ 16 | Pat Putnam | .40 | .16 | .04 |
| ☐ 17 | Paul Mirabella | .40 | .16 | .04 |
| ☐ 18 | Domingo Ramos | .40 | .16 | .04 |
| ☐ 19 | Al Cowens | .50 | .20 | .05 |
| ☐ 20 | Mike Stanton | .40 | .16 | .04 |
| ☐ 21 | Steve Henderson | .40 | .16 | .04 |
| ☐ 22 | Bob Stoddard | .40 | .16 | .04 |
| ☐ 23 | Alvin Davis | 2.00 | .80 | .20 |
| ☐ 24 | Phil Bradley | 2.00 | .80 | .20 |
| ☐ 25 | Roy Thomas | .40 | .16 | .04 |
| ☐ 26 | Darnell Coles | .75 | .30 | .07 |
| ☐ 27 | Mariners' Coaches | .40 | .16 | .04 |
| ☐ 28 | Mariners' Checklist | .40 | .05 | .01 |

## 1984 Mother's Padres

The cards in this 28 card set measure 2 1/2" by 3 1/2". In 1984, the Los Angeles based Mother's Cookies Co. issued five sets of cards featuring players from major league teams. The San Diego Padres set features current players depicted by photos. Similar to their 1952 and 1953 issues, the cards have rounded corners. The backs of the cards

## 1985 Mother's A's

The cards in this 28 card set measure 2 1/2" by 3 1/2". In 1985, the Los Angeles based Mother's Cookies Co. again issued five sets of cards featuring players from major league teams. The Oakland A's set features current players depicted by photos on cards with rounded corners. The backs of the cards contain the Mother's Cookies logo. Cards were passed out at the stadium on July 6.

|  | | MINT | VG-E | F-G |
|---|---|---|---|---|
| COMPLETE SET | | 8.00 | 3.25 | .80 |
| COMMON PLAYER | | .30 | .12 | .03 |
| ☐ 1 | Jackie Moore MGR | .30 | .12 | .03 |
| ☐ 2 | Dave Kingman | .60 | .24 | .06 |
| ☐ 3 | Don Sutton | 1.00 | .40 | .10 |
| ☐ 4 | Mike Heath | .30 | .12 | .03 |

| | | | | | |
|---|---|---|---|---|---|
| ☐ | 5 | Alfredo Griffin | .50 | .20 | .05 |
| ☐ | 6 | Dwayne Murphy | .50 | .20 | .05 |
| ☐ | 7 | Mike Davis | .50 | .20 | .05 |
| ☐ | 8 | Carney Lansford | .60 | .24 | .06 |
| ☐ | 9 | Chris Codiroli | .30 | .12 | .03 |
| ☐ | 10 | Bruce Bochte | .30 | .12 | .03 |
| ☐ | 11 | Mickey Tettleton | .30 | .12 | .03 |
| ☐ | 12 | Donnie Hill | .30 | .12 | .03 |
| ☐ | 13 | Rob Picciolo | .30 | .12 | .03 |
| ☐ | 14 | Dave Collins | .40 | .16 | .04 |
| ☐ | 15 | Dusty Baker | .40 | .16 | .04 |
| ☐ | 16 | Tim Conroy | .30 | .12 | .03 |
| ☐ | 17 | Keith Atherton | .30 | .12 | .03 |
| ☐ | 18 | Jay Howell | .50 | .20 | .05 |
| ☐ | 19 | Mike Warren | .30 | .12 | .03 |
| ☐ | 20 | Steve McCatty | .30 | .12 | .03 |
| ☐ | 21 | Bill Krueger | .30 | .12 | .03 |
| ☐ | 22 | Curt Young | .30 | .12 | .03 |
| ☐ | 23 | Dan Meyer | .30 | .12 | .03 |
| ☐ | 24 | Mike Gallego | .30 | .12 | .03 |
| ☐ | 25 | Jeff Kaiser | .30 | .12 | .03 |
| ☐ | 26 | Steve Henderson | .30 | .12 | .03 |
| ☐ | 27 | A's Coaches | .30 | .12 | .03 |
| ☐ | 28 | A's Checklist | .30 | .05 | .01 |

| | | | | | |
|---|---|---|---|---|---|
| ☐ | 23 | Tim Tolman | .30 | .12 | .03 |
| ☐ | 24 | Jeff Calhoun | .30 | .12 | .03 |
| ☐ | 25 | Jim Pankovits | .30 | .12 | .03 |
| ☐ | 26 | Ron Mathis | .30 | .12 | .03 |
| ☐ | 27 | Astros' Coaches | .30 | .12 | .03 |
| ☐ | 28 | Astros' Checklist | .30 | .05 | .01 |

# 1985 Mother's Giants

The cards in this 28 card set measure 2 1/2" by 3 1/2". In 1985, the Los Angeles based Mother's Cookies Co. again issued five sets of cards featuring players from major league teams. The San Francisco Giants set features current players depicted by photos on cards with rounded corners. The backs of the cards contain the Mother's Cookies logo. Cards were passed out at the stadium on June 30.

| | | | MINT | VG-E | F-G |
|---|---|---|---|---|---|
| | COMPLETE SET | | 8.00 | 3.25 | .80 |
| | COMMON PLAYER | | .30 | .12 | .03 |
| | | | | | |
| ☐ | 1 | Jim Davenport MGR | .30 | .12 | .03 |
| ☐ | 2 | Chili Davis | .60 | .24 | .06 |
| ☐ | 3 | Dan Gladden | .50 | .20 | .05 |
| ☐ | 4 | Jeff Leonard | .40 | .16 | .04 |
| ☐ | 5 | Manny Trillo | .30 | .12 | .03 |
| ☐ | 6 | Atlee Hammaker | .30 | .12 | .03 |
| ☐ | 7 | Bob Brenly | .50 | .20 | .05 |
| ☐ | 8 | Greg Minton | .40 | .16 | .04 |
| ☐ | 9 | Bill Laskey | .30 | .12 | .03 |
| ☐ | 10 | Vida Blue | .40 | .16 | .04 |
| ☐ | 11 | Mike Krukow | .50 | .20 | .05 |
| ☐ | 12 | Frank Williams | .30 | .12 | .03 |
| ☐ | 13 | Jose Uribe | .30 | .12 | .03 |
| ☐ | 14 | Johnnie LeMaster | .30 | .12 | .03 |
| ☐ | 15 | Scot Thompson | .30 | .12 | .03 |
| ☐ | 16 | Dave LaPoint | .30 | .12 | .03 |
| ☐ | 17 | David Green | .40 | .16 | .04 |
| ☐ | 18 | Chris Brown | .90 | .36 | .09 |
| ☐ | 19 | Joel Youngblood | .30 | .12 | .03 |
| ☐ | 20 | Mark Davis | .40 | .16 | .04 |
| ☐ | 21 | Jim Gott | .30 | .12 | .03 |
| ☐ | 22 | Doug Gwosdz | .30 | .12 | .03 |
| ☐ | 23 | Scott Garrelts | .50 | .20 | .05 |
| ☐ | 24 | Gary Rajsich | .30 | .12 | .03 |
| ☐ | 25 | Rob Deer | .75 | .30 | .07 |
| ☐ | 26 | Brad Wellman | .30 | .12 | .03 |
| ☐ | 27 | Giants' Coaches | .30 | .12 | .03 |
| ☐ | 28 | Giants' Checklist | .30 | .05 | .01 |

# 1985 Mother's Astros

The cards in this 28 card set measure 2 1/2" by 3 1/2". In 1985, the Los Angeles-based Mother's Cookies Co. again issued five sets of cards featuring players from major league teams. The Houston Astros set features current players depicted by photos on cards with rounded corners. The backs of the cards contain the Mother's Cookies logo. Cards were passed out at the stadium on July 13. The checklist card features the Astros logo on the obverse.

| | | | MINT | VG-E | F-G |
|---|---|---|---|---|---|
| | COMPLETE SET | | 9.00 | 3.75 | .90 |
| | COMMON PLAYER | | .30 | .12 | .03 |
| | | | | | |
| ☐ | 1 | Bob Lillis MGR | .30 | .12 | .03 |
| ☐ | 2 | Nolan Ryan | 2.00 | .80 | .20 |
| ☐ | 3 | Phil Garner | .40 | .16 | .04 |
| ☐ | 4 | Jose Cruz | .60 | .24 | .06 |
| ☐ | 5 | Denny Walling | .30 | .12 | .03 |
| ☐ | 6 | Joe Niekro | .60 | .24 | .06 |
| ☐ | 7 | Terry Puhl | .40 | .16 | .04 |
| ☐ | 8 | Bill Doran | .60 | .24 | .06 |
| ☐ | 9 | Dickie Thon | .40 | .16 | .04 |
| ☐ | 10 | Enos Cabell | .30 | .12 | .03 |
| ☐ | 11 | Frank DiPino | .30 | .12 | .03 |
| ☐ | 12 | Julio Solano | .30 | .12 | .03 |
| ☐ | 13 | Alan Ashby | .30 | .12 | .03 |
| ☐ | 14 | Craig Reynolds | .30 | .12 | .03 |
| ☐ | 15 | Jerry Mumphrey | .30 | .12 | .03 |
| ☐ | 16 | Bill Dawley | .30 | .12 | .03 |
| ☐ | 17 | Mark Bailey | .30 | .12 | .03 |
| ☐ | 18 | Mike Scott | 1.00 | .40 | .10 |
| ☐ | 19 | Harry Spilman | .30 | .12 | .03 |
| ☐ | 20 | Bob Knepper | .50 | .20 | .05 |
| ☐ | 21 | Dave Smith | .40 | .16 | .04 |
| ☐ | 22 | Kevin Bass | .60 | .24 | .06 |

# 1985 Mother's Mariners

The cards in this 28 card set measure 2 1/2" by 3 1/2". In 1985, the Los Angeles based Mother's Cookies Co. again issued five sets of cards featuring players from major league teams. The Seattle

Mariners set features current players depicted by photos on cards with rounded corners. The backs of the cards contain the Mother's Cookies logo. Cards were passed out at the stadium on August 10.

| | | MINT | VG-E | F-G |
|---|---|---|---|---|
| COMPLETE SET | | 10.00 | 4.00 | 1.00 |
| COMMON PLAYER | | .30 | .12 | .03 |
| ☐ 1 | Chuck Cottier MGR | .30 | .12 | .03 |
| ☐ 2 | Alvin Davis | 1.00 | .40 | .10 |
| ☐ 3 | Mark Langston | .50 | .20 | .05 |
| ☐ 4 | Dave Henderson | .40 | .16 | .04 |
| ☐ 5 | Ed VandeBerg | .40 | .16 | .04 |
| ☐ 6 | Al Cowens | .40 | .16 | .04 |
| ☐ 7 | Spike Owen | .40 | .16 | .04 |
| ☐ 8 | Mike Moore | .50 | .20 | .05 |
| ☐ 9 | Gorman Thomas | .50 | .20 | .05 |
| ☐ 10 | Barry Bonnell | .30 | .12 | .03 |
| ☐ 11 | Jack Perconte | .30 | .12 | .03 |
| ☐ 12 | Domingo Ramos | .30 | .12 | .03 |
| ☐ 13 | Bob Kearney | .30 | .12 | .03 |
| ☐ 14 | Matt Young | .40 | .16 | .04 |
| ☐ 15 | Jim Beattie | .30 | .12 | .03 |
| ☐ 16 | Mike Stanton | .30 | .12 | .03 |
| ☐ 17 | David Valle | .30 | .12 | .03 |
| ☐ 18 | Ken Phelps | .40 | .16 | .04 |
| ☐ 19 | Salome Barojas | .30 | .12 | .03 |
| ☐ 20 | Jim Presley | 2.00 | .80 | .20 |
| ☐ 21 | Phil Bradley | 1.00 | .40 | .10 |
| ☐ 22 | Dave Geisel | .30 | .12 | .03 |
| ☐ 23 | Harold Reynolds | .40 | .16 | .04 |
| ☐ 24 | Ed Nunez | .40 | .16 | .04 |
| ☐ 25 | Mike Morgan | .30 | .12 | .03 |
| ☐ 26 | Ivan Calderon | .40 | .16 | .04 |
| ☐ 27 | Mariners Coaches | .30 | .12 | .03 |
| ☐ 28 | Checklist | .30 | .05 | .01 |

## 1985 Mother's Padres

The cards in this 28 card set measure 2 1/2" by 3 1/2". In 1985, the Los Angeles based Mother's Cookies Co. again issued five sets of cards featuring players from major league teams. The San Diego

Padres set features current players depicted by photos on cards with rounded corners. The backs of the cards contain the Mother's Cookies logo. Cards were passed out at the stadium on August 11.

| | | MINT | VG-E | F-G |
|---|---|---|---|---|
| COMPLETE SET | | 10.00 | 4.00 | 1.00 |
| COMMON PLAYER | | .30 | .12 | .03 |
| ☐ 1 | Dick Williams MGR | .40 | .16 | .04 |
| ☐ 2 | Tony Gwynn | 1.50 | .60 | .15 |
| ☐ 3 | Kevin McReynolds | .75 | .30 | .07 |
| ☐ 4 | Graig Nettles | .75 | .30 | .07 |
| ☐ 5 | Rich Gossage | .75 | .30 | .07 |
| ☐ 6 | Steve Garvey | 1.50 | .60 | .15 |
| ☐ 7 | Garry Templeton | .40 | .16 | .04 |
| ☐ 8 | Dave Dravecky | .40 | .16 | .04 |
| ☐ 9 | Eric Show | .30 | .12 | .03 |
| ☐ 10 | Terry Kennedy | .40 | .16 | .04 |
| ☐ 11 | Luis DeLeon | .30 | .12 | .03 |
| ☐ 12 | Bruce Bochy | .30 | .12 | .03 |
| ☐ 13 | Andy Hawkins | .40 | .16 | .04 |
| ☐ 14 | Kurt Bevacqua | .30 | .12 | .03 |
| ☐ 15 | Craig Lefferts | .30 | .12 | .03 |
| ☐ 16 | Mario Ramirez | .30 | .12 | .03 |
| ☐ 17 | LaMarr Hoyt | .40 | .16 | .04 |
| ☐ 18 | Jerry Royster | .30 | .12 | .03 |
| ☐ 19 | Tim Stoddard | .30 | .12 | .03 |
| ☐ 20 | Tim Flannery | .30 | .12 | .03 |
| ☐ 21 | Mark Thurmond | .40 | .16 | .04 |
| ☐ 22 | Greg Booker | .30 | .12 | .03 |
| ☐ 23 | Bobby Brown | .30 | .12 | .03 |
| ☐ 24 | Carmelo Martinez | .40 | .16 | .04 |
| ☐ 25 | Al Bumbry | .30 | .12 | .03 |
| ☐ 26 | Jerry Davis | .30 | .12 | .03 |
| ☐ 27 | Padres' Coaches | .30 | .12 | .03 |
| ☐ 28 | Padres' Checklist | .30 | .05 | .01 |

## 1986 Mother's A's

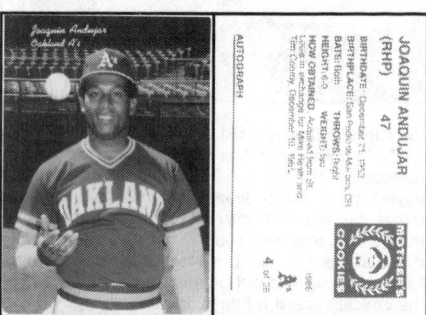

This set consists of 28 full-color, rounded-corner cards each measuring 2 1/2" by 3 1/2". Starter sets (only 20 cards but also including a certificate for eight more cards) were given out at the ballpark and collectors were encouraged to trade to fill in the rest of their set. The cards were originally given away on July 20th at Oakland Coliseum.

| | | MINT | VG-E | F-G |
|---|---|---|---|---|
| COMPLETE SET | | 12.00 | 5.00 | 1.20 |
| COMMON PLAYER | | .30 | .12 | .03 |
| ☐ 1 | Jackie Moore MGR | .30 | .12 | .03 |
| ☐ 2 | Dave Kingman | .60 | .24 | .06 |
| ☐ 3 | Dusty Baker | .40 | .16 | .04 |
| ☐ 4 | Joaquin Andujar | .50 | .20 | .05 |
| ☐ 5 | Alfredo Griffin | .40 | .16 | .04 |
| ☐ 6 | Dwayne Murphy | .50 | .20 | .05 |
| ☐ 7 | Mike Davis | .40 | .16 | .04 |
| ☐ 8 | Carney Lansford | .50 | .20 | .05 |
| ☐ 9 | Jose Canseco | 3.50 | 1.40 | .35 |
| ☐ 10 | Bruce Bochte | .40 | .16 | .04 |
| ☐ 11 | Mickey Tettleton | .40 | .16 | .04 |
| ☐ 12 | Donnie Hill | .30 | .12 | .03 |

| | | MINT | VG-E | F-G |
|---|---|---|---|---|
| ☐ 13 | Jose Rijo | .40 | .16 | .04 |
| ☐ 14 | Rick Langford | .30 | .12 | .03 |
| ☐ 15 | Chris Codiroli | .30 | .12 | .03 |
| ☐ 16 | Moose Haas | .30 | .12 | .03 |
| ☐ 17 | Keith Atherton | .30 | .12 | .03 |
| ☐ 18 | Jay Howell | .40 | .16 | .04 |
| ☐ 19 | Tony Phillips | .30 | .12 | .03 |
| ☐ 20 | Steve Henderson | .30 | .12 | .03 |
| ☐ 21 | Bill Krueger | .30 | .12 | .03 |
| ☐ 22 | Steve Ontiveros | .30 | .12 | .03 |
| ☐ 23 | Bill Bathe | .40 | .16 | .04 |
| ☐ 24 | Ricky Peters | .30 | .12 | .03 |
| ☐ 25 | Tim Birtsas | .40 | .16 | .04 |
| ☐ 26 | A's Trainers and Equipment Mgrs | .30 | .12 | .03 |
| ☐ 27 | A's Coaches | .30 | .12 | .03 |
| ☐ 28 | Checklist card | .30 | .03 | .00 |

# 1986 Mother's Astros

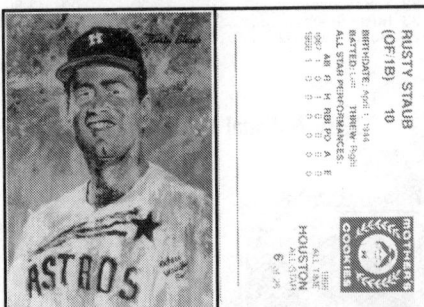

This set consists of 28 full-color, rounded- corner cards each measuring 2 1/2" by 3 1/2". Starter sets (only 20 cards but also including a certificate for eight more cards) were given out at the ballpark and collectors were encouraged to trade to fill in the rest of their set. Cards were originally given out at the Astrodome on July 10th. Since the 1986 All-Star Game was held in Houston, the set features Astro All-Stars since 1962 as painted by artist Richard Wallich.

| | | MINT | VG-E | F-G |
|---|---|---|---|---|
| COMPLETE SET | | 8.00 | 3.25 | .80 |
| COMMON PLAYER | | .30 | .12 | .03 |
| ☐ 1 | Dick Farrell | .30 | .12 | .03 |
| ☐ 2 | Hal Woodeshick | .30 | .12 | .03 |
| ☐ 3 | Joe Morgan | .75 | .30 | .07 |
| ☐ 4 | Claude Raymond | .30 | .12 | .03 |
| ☐ 5 | Mike Cuellar | .40 | .16 | .04 |
| ☐ 6 | Rusty Staub | .50 | .20 | .05 |
| ☐ 7 | Jimmy Wynn | .40 | .16 | .04 |
| ☐ 8 | Larry Dierker | .40 | .16 | .04 |
| ☐ 9 | Denis Menke | .30 | .12 | .03 |
| ☐ 10 | Don Wilson | .30 | .12 | .03 |
| ☐ 11 | Cesar Cedeno | .40 | .16 | .04 |
| ☐ 12 | Lee May | .40 | .16 | .04 |
| ☐ 13 | Bob Watson | .40 | .16 | .04 |
| ☐ 14 | Ken Forsch | .30 | .12 | .03 |
| ☐ 15 | Joaquin Andujar | .40 | .16 | .04 |
| ☐ 16 | Terry Puhl | .40 | .16 | .04 |
| ☐ 17 | Joe Niekro | .40 | .16 | .04 |
| ☐ 18 | Craig Reynolds | .30 | .12 | .03 |
| ☐ 19 | Joe Sambito | .30 | .12 | .03 |
| ☐ 20 | Jose Cruz | .50 | .20 | .05 |
| ☐ 21 | J.R. Richard | .50 | .20 | .05 |
| ☐ 22 | Bob Knepper | .50 | .20 | .05 |
| ☐ 23 | Nolan Ryan | 1.00 | .40 | .10 |
| ☐ 24 | Ray Knight | .40 | .16 | .04 |
| ☐ 25 | Bill Dawley | .30 | .12 | .03 |
| ☐ 26 | Dickie Thon | .30 | .12 | .03 |
| ☐ 27 | Jerry Mumphrey | .30 | .12 | .03 |
| ☐ 28 | Checklist card | .30 | .03 | .00 |

# 1986 Mother's Giants

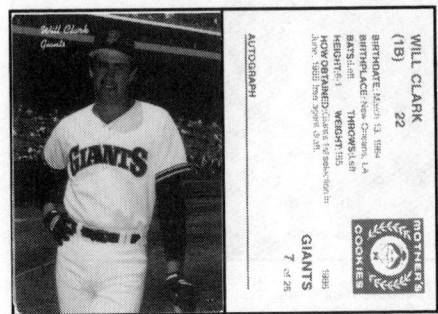

This set consists of 28 full-color, rounded- corner cards each measuring 2 1/2" by 3 1/2". Starter sets (only 20 cards but also including a certificate for eight more cards) were given out at the ballpark and collectors were encouraged to trade to fill in the rest of their set. Cards were originally given out at Candlestick Park on July 13th.

| | | MINT | VG-E | F-G |
|---|---|---|---|---|
| COMPLETE SET | | 9.00 | 3.75 | .90 |
| COMMON PLAYER | | .30 | .12 | .03 |
| ☐ 1 | Roger Craig MGR | .40 | .16 | .04 |
| ☐ 2 | Chili Davis | .50 | .20 | .05 |
| ☐ 3 | Dan Gladden | .30 | .12 | .03 |
| ☐ 4 | Jeff Leonard | .40 | .16 | .04 |
| ☐ 5 | Bob Brenly | .40 | .16 | .04 |
| ☐ 6 | Atlee Hammaker | .30 | .12 | .03 |
| ☐ 7 | Will Clark | .75 | .30 | .07 |
| ☐ 8 | Greg Minton | .40 | .16 | .04 |
| ☐ 9 | Candy Maldonado | .40 | .16 | .04 |
| ☐ 10 | Vida Blue | .40 | .16 | .04 |
| ☐ 11 | Mike Krukow | .50 | .20 | .05 |
| ☐ 12 | Bob Melvin | .40 | .16 | .04 |
| ☐ 13 | Jose Uribe | .40 | .16 | .04 |
| ☐ 14 | Dan Driessen | .30 | .12 | .03 |
| ☐ 15 | Jeff Robinson | .30 | .12 | .03 |
| ☐ 16 | Rob Thompson | .60 | .24 | .06 |
| ☐ 17 | Mike LaCoss | .30 | .12 | .03 |
| ☐ 18 | Chris Brown | .60 | .24 | .06 |
| ☐ 19 | Scott Garrelts | .40 | .16 | .04 |
| ☐ 20 | Mark Davis | .40 | .16 | .04 |
| ☐ 21 | Jim Gott | .30 | .12 | .03 |
| ☐ 22 | Brad Wellman | .30 | .12 | .03 |
| ☐ 23 | Roger Mason | .40 | .16 | .04 |
| ☐ 24 | Bill Laskey | .30 | .12 | .03 |
| ☐ 25 | Brad Gulden | .30 | .12 | .03 |
| ☐ 26 | Joel Youngblood | .30 | .12 | .03 |
| ☐ 27 | Juan Berenguer | .30 | .12 | .03 |
| ☐ 28 | Checklist card | .30 | .03 | .00 |

# 1986 Mother's Mariners

This set consists of 28 full-color, rounded- corner cards each measuring 2 1/2" by 3 1/2". Starter sets (only 20 cards but also including a certificate for eight more cards) were given out at the ballpark and collectors were encouraged to trade to fill in the rest of their set. Cards were originally given out on July 27th at the Seattle Kingdome.

| | | MINT | VG-E | F-G |
|---|---|---|---|---|
| COMPLETE SET | | 9.00 | 3.75 | .90 |
| COMMON PLAYER | | .30 | .12 | .03 |
| ☐ 1 | Dick Williams MGR | .30 | .12 | .03 |
| ☐ 2 | Alvin Davis | .60 | .24 | .06 |
| ☐ 3 | Mark Langston | .50 | .20 | .05 |

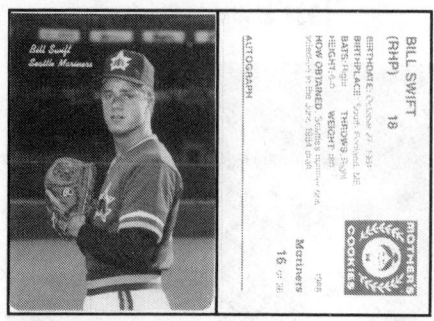

|  |  | MINT | VG-E | F-G |
|---|---|---|---|---|
| COMPLETE SET | | 250.00 | 100.00 | 25.00 |
| COMMON PLAYER (1-24) | | 3.50 | 1.40 | .35 |
| ☐ 1 | Hank Aaron | 30.00 | 12.00 | 3.00 |
| ☐ 2 | Richie Allen | 4.50 | 1.80 | .45 |
| ☐ 3 | Lou Brock | 20.00 | 8.00 | 2.00 |
| ☐ 4 | Paul Casanova | 3.50 | 1.40 | .35 |
| ☐ 5 | Roberto Clemente | 30.00 | 12.00 | 3.00 |
| ☐ 6 | Al Ferrara | 3.50 | 1.40 | .35 |
| ☐ 7 | Bill Freehan | 4.00 | 1.60 | .40 |
| ☐ 8 | Jim Fregosi | 4.00 | 1.60 | .40 |
| ☐ 9 | Bob Gibson | 15.00 | 6.00 | 1.50 |
| ☐ 10 | Tony Horton | 3.50 | 1.40 | .35 |
| ☐ 11 | Tommy John | 6.00 | 2.40 | .60 |
| ☐ 12 | Al Kaline | 20.00 | 8.00 | 2.00 |
| ☐ 13 | Jim Lonborg | 3.50 | 1.40 | .35 |
| ☐ 14 | Juan Marichal | 15.00 | 6.00 | 1.50 |
| ☐ 15 | Willie Mays | 30.00 | 12.00 | 3.00 |
| ☐ 16 | Rick Monday | 3.50 | 1.40 | .35 |
| ☐ 17 | Tony Oliva | 6.00 | 2.40 | .60 |
| ☐ 18 | Brooks Robinson | 20.00 | 8.00 | 2.00 |
| ☐ 19 | Frank Robinson | 18.00 | 7.25 | 1.80 |
| ☐ 20 | Pete Rose | 50.00 | 20.00 | 5.00 |
| ☐ 21 | Ron Santo | 4.50 | 1.80 | .45 |
| ☐ 22 | Tom Seaver | 25.00 | 10.00 | 2.50 |
| ☐ 23 | Rusty Staub | 5.00 | 2.00 | .50 |
| ☐ 24 | Mel Stottlemyre | 4.00 | 1.60 | .40 |

| ☐ 4 | Dave Henderson | .40 | .16 | .04 |
|---|---|---|---|---|
| ☐ 5 | Steve Yeager | .40 | .16 | .04 |
| ☐ 6 | Al Cowens | .40 | .16 | .04 |
| ☐ 7 | Jim Presley | .75 | .30 | .07 |
| ☐ 8 | Phil Bradley | .75 | .30 | .07 |
| ☐ 9 | Gorman Thomas | .50 | .20 | .05 |
| ☐ 10 | Barry Bonnell | .30 | .12 | .03 |
| ☐ 11 | Milt Wilcox | .30 | .12 | .03 |
| ☐ 12 | Domingo Ramos | .30 | .12 | .03 |
| ☐ 13 | Paul Mirabella | .30 | .12 | .03 |
| ☐ 14 | Matt Young | .30 | .12 | .03 |
| ☐ 15 | Ivan Calderon | .40 | .16 | .04 |
| ☐ 16 | Bill Swift | .30 | .12 | .03 |
| ☐ 17 | Pete Ladd | .30 | .12 | .03 |
| ☐ 18 | Ken Phelps | .30 | .12 | .03 |
| ☐ 19 | Karl Best | .30 | .12 | .03 |
| ☐ 20 | Spike Owen | .40 | .16 | .04 |
| ☐ 21 | Mike Moore | .40 | .16 | .04 |
| ☐ 22 | Danny Tartabull | .75 | .30 | .07 |
| ☐ 23 | Bob Kearney | .30 | .12 | .03 |
| ☐ 24 | Edwin Nunez | .30 | .12 | .03 |
| ☐ 25 | Mike Morgan | .30 | .12 | .03 |
| ☐ 26 | Roy Thomas | .30 | .12 | .03 |
| ☐ 27 | Jim Beattie | .30 | .12 | .03 |
| ☐ 28 | Checklist card | .30 | .03 | .00 |

## 1986 National Photo Royals

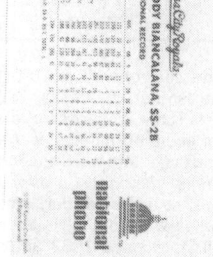

(1) BUDDY BIANCALANA, SS-2B

## 1969 Nabisco Team Flakes

Frank Robinson—OF
Baltimore Orioles

Frank Robinson—OF
Baltimore Orioles

The cards in this 24 card set measure either 1 15/16" by 3" or 1 3/4" by 2 15/16" depending on the amount of yellow border area provided between the "cut lines." The 1969 Nabisco Team Flakes set of full color, blank-backed and unnumbered cards was issued on the backs of Team Flakes cereal boxes. The cards are numbered in the checklist below in alphabetical order. There were three different panels or box backs containing eight cards each. The cards have yellow borders and are devoid of team insignias. The catalog designation is F275-34.

The set contains 24 cards which are numbered only by uniform number except for the checklist card and discount card, which entitles the bearer to a 40% discount at National Photo. Cards measure 2 7/8" by 4 1/4". Cards were distributed at the stadium on August 14th. The set was supposedly later available for 3.00 directly from the Royals.

|  |  | MINT | VG-E | F-G |
|---|---|---|---|---|
| COMPLETE SET | | 9.00 | 3.75 | .90 |
| COMMON PLAYER | | .30 | .12 | .03 |
| ☐ 1 | Buddy Biancalana | .30 | .12 | .03 |
| ☐ 3 | Jorge Orta | .30 | .12 | .03 |
| ☐ 4 | Greg Pryor | .30 | .12 | .03 |
| ☐ 5 | George Brett | 1.00 | .40 | .10 |
| ☐ 6 | Willie Wilson | .50 | .20 | .05 |
| ☐ 8 | Jim Sundberg | .30 | .12 | .03 |
| ☐ 10 | Dick Howser MGR | .40 | .16 | .04 |
| ☐ 11 | Hal McRae | .40 | .16 | .04 |
| ☐ 20 | Frank White | .50 | .20 | .05 |
| ☐ 21 | Lonnie Smith | .40 | .16 | .04 |
| ☐ 22 | Dennis Leonard | .40 | .16 | .04 |
| ☐ 23 | Mark Gubicza | .40 | .16 | .04 |
| ☐ 24 | Darryl Motley | .30 | .12 | .03 |
| ☐ 25 | Danny Jackson | .40 | .16 | .04 |
| ☐ 26 | Steve Farr | .30 | .12 | .03 |
| ☐ 29 | Dan Quisenberry | .50 | .20 | .05 |
| ☐ 31 | Bret Saberhagen | .50 | .20 | .05 |
| ☐ 35 | Lynn Jones | .30 | .12 | .03 |
| ☐ 37 | Charlie Leibrandt | .40 | .16 | .04 |

| | | | | |
|---|---|---|---|---|
| ☐ 38 | Mark Huismann | .30 | .12 | .03 |
| ☐ 40 | Buddy Black | .30 | .12 | .03 |
| ☐ 45 | Steve Balboni | .40 | .16 | .04 |
| ☐ xx | Discount card (unnumbered) | .30 | .12 | .03 |
| ☐ xx | Checklist card (unnumbered) | .30 | .03 | .00 |

## 1984 Nestle Dream Team

The cards in this 22 card set measure 2 1/2" by 3 1/2". In conjunction with Topps, the Nestle Company issued this set entitled the Dream Team. The fronts have the Nestle trademark in the upper frameline, and the backs are identical to the Topps cards of this year except for the number and the Nestle's logo. Cards 1-11 feature stars of the American League while cards 12-22 show National League stars. Each league's "Dream team" consists of eight position players and three pitchers. The cards were included with the Nestle chocolate bars as a pack of four (three player cards and a checklist header card). This set should not be confused with the Nestle 792 card (same player-number correspondence as 1984 Topps 792) set. That set was (as detailed on the back of the checklist card) originally available from the Nestle Company in full sheets of 132 cards, 24" by 48", for ▲4.95 plus five Nestle candy wrappers per sheet.

| | | MINT | VG-E | F-G |
|---|---|---|---|---|
| | COMPLETE SET | 12.50 | 5.00 | 1.25 |
| | COMMON PLAYER | .35 | .14 | .03 |
| ☐ 1 | Eddie Murray | 1.50 | .60 | .15 |
| ☐ 2 | Lou Whitaker | .35 | .14 | .03 |
| ☐ 3 | George Brett | 1.50 | .60 | .15 |
| ☐ 4 | Cal Ripken | 1.25 | .50 | .12 |
| ☐ 5 | Jim Rice | .90 | .36 | .09 |
| ☐ 6 | Dave Winfield | .90 | .36 | .09 |
| ☐ 7 | Lloyd Moseby | .35 | .14 | .03 |
| ☐ 8 | Lance Parrish | .75 | .30 | .07 |
| ☐ 9 | LaMarr Hoyt | .35 | .14 | .03 |
| ☐ 10 | Ron Guidry | .50 | .20 | .05 |
| ☐ 11 | Dan Quisenberry | .45 | .18 | .04 |
| ☐ 12 | Steve Garvey | 1.25 | .50 | .12 |
| ☐ 13 | Johnny Ray | .35 | .14 | .03 |
| ☐ 14 | Mike Schmidt | 1.50 | .60 | .15 |
| ☐ 15 | Ozzie Smith | .35 | .14 | .03 |
| ☐ 16 | Andre Dawson | .45 | .18 | .04 |
| ☐ 17 | Tim Raines | .75 | .30 | .07 |
| ☐ 18 | Dale Murphy | 1.50 | .60 | .15 |
| ☐ 19 | Tony Pena | .35 | .14 | .03 |
| ☐ 20 | John Denny | .35 | .14 | .03 |
| ☐ 21 | Steve Carlton | .90 | .36 | .09 |
| ☐ 22 | Al Holland | .35 | .14 | .03 |
| ☐ 23 | Checklist card (unnumbered) | .35 | .05 | .01 |

## 1954 N.Y. Journal American

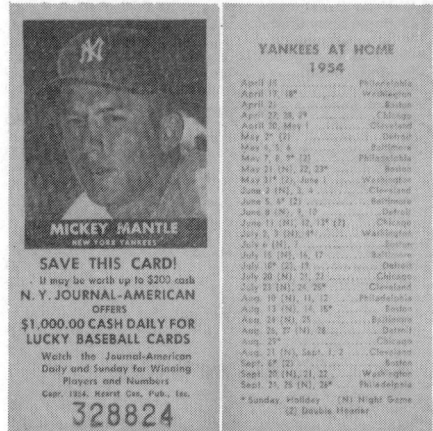

The cards in this 59 card set measure 2" by 4". The 1954 New York Journal American set contains black and white, unnumbered cards issued in conjunction with the newspaper. News stands were given boxes of cards to be distributed with purchases and each card had a serial number for redemption in the contest. The set spotlights New York teams only and carries game schedules on the reverse. The cards have been assigned numbers in the listing below alphabetically within team so that Brooklyn Dodgers are 1-19, New York Giants are 20-39, and New York Yankees are 40- 59. There is speculation that a 20th Dodger card may exist. The ACC designation for this set is M127.

| | | MINT | VG-E | F-G |
|---|---|---|---|---|
| | COMPLETE SET | 700.00 | 280.00 | 70.00 |
| | COMMON PLAYER | 5.00 | 2.00 | .50 |
| ☐ 1 | Joe Black | 6.00 | 2.40 | .60 |
| ☐ 2 | Roy Campanella | 40.00 | 16.00 | 4.00 |
| ☐ 3 | Billy Cox | 6.00 | 2.40 | .60 |
| ☐ 4 | Carl Erskine | 8.00 | 3.25 | .80 |
| ☐ 5 | Carl Furillo | 9.00 | 3.75 | .90 |
| ☐ 6 | Junior Gilliam | 8.00 | 3.25 | .80 |
| ☐ 7 | Gil Hodges | 16.00 | 6.50 | 1.60 |
| ☐ 8 | Jim Hughes | 5.00 | 2.00 | .50 |
| ☐ 9 | Clem Labine | 6.00 | 2.40 | .60 |
| ☐ 10 | Billy Loes | 5.00 | 2.00 | .50 |
| ☐ 11 | Russ Meyer | 5.00 | 2.00 | .50 |
| ☐ 12 | Don Newcombe | 9.00 | 3.75 | .90 |
| ☐ 13 | Ervin Palica | 20.00 | 8.00 | 2.00 |
| ☐ 14 | PeeWee Reese | 20.00 | 8.00 | 2.00 |
| ☐ 15 | Jackie Robinson | 60.00 | 24.00 | 6.00 |
| ☐ 16 | Preacher Roe | 9.00 | 3.75 | .90 |
| ☐ 17 | George Shuba | 5.00 | 2.00 | .50 |
| ☐ 18 | Duke Snider | 40.00 | 16.00 | 4.00 |
| ☐ 19 | Dick Williams | 7.00 | 2.80 | .70 |
| ☐ 20 | John Antonelli | 6.00 | 2.40 | .60 |
| ☐ 21 | Alvin Dark | 7.00 | 2.80 | .70 |
| ☐ 22 | Marv Grissom | 5.00 | 2.00 | .50 |
| ☐ 23 | Ruben Gomez | 5.00 | 2.00 | .50 |
| ☐ 24 | Jim Hearn | 5.00 | 2.00 | .50 |
| ☐ 25 | Bobby Hofman | 5.00 | 2.00 | .50 |
| ☐ 26 | Monte Irvin | 12.50 | 5.00 | 1.25 |
| ☐ 27 | Larry Jansen | 5.00 | 2.00 | .50 |
| ☐ 28 | Ray Katt | 5.00 | 2.00 | .50 |
| ☐ 29 | Don Liddle | 5.00 | 2.00 | .50 |
| ☐ 30 | Whitey Lockman | 6.00 | 2.40 | .60 |
| ☐ 31 | Sal Maglie | 8.00 | 3.25 | .80 |
| ☐ 32 | Willie Mays | 120.00 | 50.00 | 12.00 |
| ☐ 33 | Don Mueller | 6.00 | 2.40 | .60 |
| ☐ 34 | Dusty Rhodes | 5.00 | 2.00 | .50 |
| ☐ 35 | Hank Thompson | 6.00 | 2.40 | .60 |
| ☐ 36 | Wes Westrum | 5.00 | 2.00 | .50 |
| ☐ 37 | Hoyt Wilhelm | 15.00 | 6.00 | 1.50 |

| | | MINT | VG-E | F-G |
|---|---|---|---|---|
| ☐ 38 | Davey Williams | 6.00 | 2.40 | .60 |
| ☐ 39 | Al Worthington | 5.00 | 2.00 | .50 |
| ☐ 40 | Hank Bauer | 8.00 | 3.25 | .80 |
| ☐ 41 | Yogi Berra | 40.00 | 16.00 | 4.00 |
| ☐ 42 | Harry Byrd | 5.00 | 2.00 | .50 |
| ☐ 43 | Andy Carey | 5.00 | 2.00 | .50 |
| ☐ 44 | Jerry Coleman | 6.00 | 2.40 | .60 |
| ☐ 45 | Joe Collins | 5.00 | 2.00 | .50 |
| ☐ 46 | Whitey Ford | 20.00 | 8.00 | 2.00 |
| ☐ 47 | Steve Kraly | 5.00 | 2.00 | .50 |
| ☐ 48 | Bob Kuzava | 5.00 | 2.00 | .50 |
| ☐ 49 | Frank Leja | 5.00 | 2.00 | .50 |
| ☐ 50 | Ed Lopat | 9.00 | 3.75 | .90 |
| ☐ 51 | Mickey Mantle | 200.00 | 80.00 | 20.00 |
| ☐ 52 | Gil McDougald | 8.00 | 3.25 | .80 |
| ☐ 53 | Bill Miller | 5.00 | 2.00 | .50 |
| ☐ 54 | Tom Morgan | 5.00 | 2.00 | .50 |
| ☐ 55 | Irv Noren | 5.00 | 2.00 | .50 |
| ☐ 56 | Allie Reynolds | 9.00 | 3.75 | .90 |
| ☐ 57 | Phil Rizzuto | 16.00 | 6.50 | 1.60 |
| ☐ 58 | Eddie Robinson | 5.00 | 2.00 | .50 |
| ☐ 59 | Gene Woodling | 6.00 | 2.40 | .60 |

## 1960 Nu-Card Hi-Lites

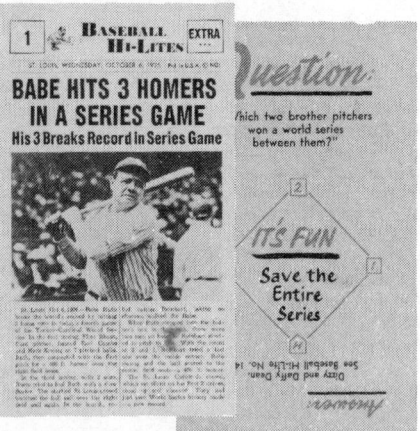

The cards in this 72 card set measure 3 1/4" by 5 3/8". In 1960, the Nu-Card Company introduced its Baseball Hi-Lites set of newspaper style cards. Each card singled out an individual baseball achievement with a picture and story. The reverses contain a baseball quiz. Cards 1-18 are more valuable if found printed totally in black on the front; these are copyrighted CVC as opposed to the NCI designation found on the red and black printed fronts.

| | | MINT | VG-E | F-G |
|---|---|---|---|---|
| COMPLETE SET | | 100.00 | 40.00 | 10.00 |
| COMMON PLAYER (1-72) | | 1.00 | .40 | .10 |
| ☐ 1 | Babe Hits 3 Homers In A Series Game | 6.00 | 2.40 | .60 |
| ☐ 2 | Podres Pitching Wins Series | 1.00 | .40 | .10 |
| ☐ 3 | Bevans Pitches No Hitter, Almost | 1.00 | .40 | .10 |
| ☐ 4 | Box Score Devised By Reporter | 1.00 | .40 | .10 |
| ☐ 5 | VanderMeer Pitches Two No Hitters | 1.25 | .50 | .12 |
| ☐ 6 | Indians Take Bums | 1.00 | .40 | .10 |
| ☐ 7 | DiMag Comes Thru | 5.00 | 2.00 | .50 |
| ☐ 8 | Mathewson Pitches Three WS Shutouts | 1.50 | .60 | .15 |
| ☐ 9 | Haddix Pitches 12 Perfect Innings | 1.00 | .40 | .10 |
| ☐ 10 | Thomson's Homer Sinks Dodgers | 1.25 | .50 | .12 |
| ☐ 11 | Hubbell Strikes Out | 1.25 | .50 | .12 |
| | Five A.L. Stars | | | |
| ☐ 12 | Pickoff Ends Series | 1.00 | .40 | .10 |
| ☐ 13 | Cards Take Series From Yanks | 1.00 | .40 | .10 |
| ☐ 14 | Dizzy And Daffy Dean Win Series | 2.50 | 1.00 | .25 |
| ☐ 15 | Owen Drops 3rd Strike | 1.00 | .40 | .10 |
| ☐ 16 | Ruth Calls Shot | 6.00 | 2.40 | .60 |
| ☐ 17 | Merkle Pulls Boner | 1.00 | .40 | .10 |
| ☐ 18 | Larsen Hurls Perfect World Series Game | 1.50 | .60 | .15 |
| ☐ 19 | Bean Ball Ends Career of Mickey Cochrane | 1.25 | .50 | .12 |
| ☐ 20 | Banks Belts 47 Homers Earns MVP | 2.50 | 1.00 | .25 |
| ☐ 21 | Stan Musial Hits Five Homers in One Day | 3.50 | 1.40 | .35 |
| ☐ 22 | Mickey Mantle Hits Longest Homer | 6.00 | 2.40 | .60 |
| ☐ 23 | Sievers Captures Home Run Title | 1.00 | .40 | .10 |
| ☐ 24 | Gehrig 2130 Consecutive Game Record Ends | 4.50 | 1.80 | .45 |
| ☐ 25 | Red Schoendienst Key Player Braves Pennant | 1.00 | .40 | .10 |
| ☐ 26 | Midget Pinch-Hits For St. Louis | 2.50 | 1.00 | .25 |
| ☐ 27 | Willie Mays Makes Greatest Catch | 3.50 | 1.40 | .35 |
| ☐ 28 | Homer by Yogi Berra Puts Yanks In 1st | 2.50 | 1.00 | .25 |
| ☐ 29 | Campy NL MVP | 3.50 | 1.40 | .35 |
| ☐ 30 | Bob Turley Hurls Yanks To WS Champions | 1.00 | .40 | .10 |
| ☐ 31 | Dodgers Take Series From Sox in Six | 1.00 | .40 | .10 |
| ☐ 32 | Furillo Hero as Dodgers Beat Chicago in 3rd World Series Game | 1.00 | .40 | .10 |
| ☐ 33 | Adcock Gets 4 Homers And A Double | 1.00 | .40 | .10 |
| ☐ 34 | Dickey Chosen All-Star Catcher | 1.50 | .60 | .15 |
| ☐ 35 | Burdette Beats Yanks In Three WS Games | 1.25 | .50 | .12 |
| ☐ 36 | Umpires Clear White Sox Bench | 1.00 | .40 | .10 |
| ☐ 37 | Reese Honored As Greatest Dodger SS | 2.50 | 1.00 | .25 |
| ☐ 38 | Joe DiMaggio Hits In 56 Straight | 5.00 | 2.00 | .50 |
| ☐ 39 | Ted Williams Hits .406 For Season | 4.00 | 1.60 | .40 |
| ☐ 40 | Walter Johnson Pitches 56 Straight | 2.50 | 1.00 | .25 |
| ☐ 41 | Hodges Hits 4 Home Runs In Nite Game | 1.50 | .60 | .15 |
| ☐ 42 | Greenberg Returns to Tigers From Army | 1.50 | .60 | .15 |
| ☐ 43 | Ty Cobb Named Best Player Of All Time | 6.00 | 2.40 | .60 |
| ☐ 44 | Robin Roberts Wins 28 Games | 1.50 | .60 | .15 |
| ☐ 45 | Rizzuto's Two Runs Save 1st Place | 1.50 | .60 | .15 |
| ☐ 46 | Tigers Beat Out Senators For Pennant | 1.00 | .40 | .10 |
| ☐ 47 | Babe Ruth Hits 60th Home Run | 6.00 | 2.40 | .60 |
| ☐ 48 | Cy Young Honored | 2.00 | .80 | .20 |
| ☐ 49 | Killebrew Starts Spring Training | 2.00 | .80 | .20 |
| ☐ 50 | Mantle Hits Longest Homer at Stadium | 6.00 | 2.40 | .60 |
| ☐ 51 | Braves Take Pennant | 1.00 | .40 | .10 |
| ☐ 52 | Ted Williams Hero Of All-Star Game | 3.50 | 1.40 | .35 |
| ☐ 53 | Robinson Saves Dodgers For Play-off Series | 3.50 | 1.40 | .35 |
| ☐ 54 | Snodgrass Muffs Fly | 1.00 | .40 | .10 |
| ☐ 55 | Snider Belts 2 Homers Ties Homer Record | 2.50 | 1.00 | .25 |
| ☐ 56 | Giants Win 26 Straight | 1.00 | .40 | .10 |
| ☐ 57 | Ted Kluszewski Stars In 1st Series Win | 1.25 | .50 | .12 |
| ☐ 58 | Ott Walks 5 Times In Single Game | 1.50 | .60 | .15 |
| ☐ 59 | Harvey Kuenn Takes A.L. Batting Title | 1.00 | .40 | .10 |
| ☐ 60 | Bob Feller Hurls 3rd No-Hitter of Career | 2.50 | 1.00 | .25 |
| ☐ 61 | Yanks Champs Again | 1.25 | .50 | .12 |
| ☐ 62 | Aaron's Bat Beats | 3.50 | 1.40 | .35 |

|   |   |   |   |
|---|---|---|---|
| | Yankees In Series | | |
| ☐ 63 | Warren Spahn Beats | 2.00 | .80 | .20 |
| | Yanks in W.S. | | |
| ☐ 64 | Ump's Wrong Call Helps ... | 1.00 | .40 | .10 |
| | Dodgers Beat Yanks | | |
| ☐ 65 | Kaline Hits 3 Homers | 2.50 | 1.00 | .25 |
| | Two In Same Inning | | |
| ☐ 66 | Bob Allison Named AL | 1.00 | .40 | .10 |
| | Rookie of the Year | | |
| ☐ 67 | McCovey Blasts Way | 2.50 | 1.00 | .25 |
| | Into Giant Lineup | | |
| ☐ 68 | Colavito Hits Four | 1.25 | .50 | .12 |
| | Homers in One Game | | |
| ☐ 69 | Erskine Sets Strike Out | 1.00 | .40 | .10 |
| | Record in World Series | | |
| ☐ 70 | Sal Maglie Pitches | 1.25 | .50 | .12 |
| | No-Hit Game | | |
| ☐ 71 | Early Wynn Victory | 1.50 | .60 | .15 |
| | Crushes Yanks | | |
| ☐ 72 | Nellie Fox AL MVP | 1.50 | .60 | .15 |

## 1961 Nu-Card Scoops

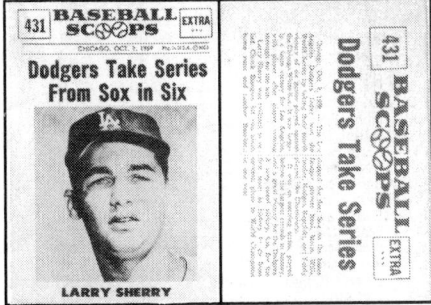

LARRY SHERRY

The cards in this 80 card set measure 2 1/2" by 3 1/2". This series depicts great moments in the history of individual ballplayers. Each card is designed as a miniature newspaper front-page, complete with data and picture. Both the number (401-480) and title are printed in red on the obverse, and the story is found on the back. An album was issued to hold the set. The set has apparently been reprinted, which has served to suppress the demand for the originals as well as the reprints.

|   | MINT | VG-E | F-G |
|---|---|---|---|
| COMPLETE SET | 65.00 | 26.00 | 6.50 |
| COMMON PLAYER (401-480) | .40 | .16 | .04 |

|   |   |   |   |   |
|---|---|---|---|---|
| ☐ 401 | Jim Gentile | .40 | .16 | .04 |
| ☐ 402 | Warren Spahn | 1.25 | .50 | .12 |
| | (No-hitter) | | | |
| ☐ 403 | Bill Mazeroski | .60 | .24 | .06 |
| ☐ 404 | Willie Mays: | 3.00 | 1.20 | .30 |
| | (three triples) | | | |
| ☐ 405 | Woodie Held | .40 | .16 | .04 |
| ☐ 406 | Vern Law | .40 | .16 | .04 |
| ☐ 407 | Pete Runnels | .40 | .16 | .04 |
| ☐ 408 | Lew Burdette | .50 | .20 | .05 |
| | (No-hitter) | | | |
| ☐ 409 | Dick Stuart | .40 | .16 | .04 |
| ☐ 410 | Don Cardwell | .40 | .16 | .04 |
| ☐ 411 | Camilo Pascual | .40 | .16 | .04 |
| ☐ 412 | Ed Mathews | 1.25 | .50 | .12 |
| ☐ 413 | Dick Groat | .60 | .24 | .06 |
| ☐ 414 | Gene Autry | 1.50 | .60 | .15 |
| ☐ 415 | Bobby Richardson | .60 | .24 | .06 |
| ☐ 416 | Roger Maris | 2.00 | .80 | .20 |
| ☐ 417 | Fred Merkle | .40 | .16 | .04 |
| ☐ 418 | Don Larson | .50 | .20 | .05 |
| ☐ 419 | Mickey Cochrane | .75 | .30 | .07 |
| ☐ 420 | Ernie Banks | 1.50 | .60 | .15 |
| ☐ 421 | Stan Musial | 2.50 | 1.00 | .25 |
| ☐ 422 | Mickey Mantle | 5.00 | 2.00 | .50 |
| | (longest homer) | | | |

|   |   |   |   |   |
|---|---|---|---|---|
| ☐ 423 | Roy Sievers | .40 | .16 | .04 |
| ☐ 424 | Lou Gehrig | 3.50 | 1.40 | .35 |
| ☐ 425 | Red Schoendienst | .50 | .20 | .05 |
| ☐ 426 | Eddie Gaedel | 1.50 | .60 | .15 |
| ☐ 427 | Willie Mays | 3.00 | 1.20 | .30 |
| | (greatest catch) | | | |
| ☐ 428 | Jackie Robinson | 3.00 | 1.20 | .30 |
| ☐ 429 | Roy Campanella | 3.00 | 1.20 | .30 |
| ☐ 430 | Bob Turley | .40 | .16 | .04 |
| ☐ 431 | Larry Sherry | .40 | .16 | .04 |
| ☐ 432 | Carl Furillo | .50 | .20 | .05 |
| ☐ 433 | Joe Adcock | .50 | .20 | .05 |
| ☐ 434 | Bill Dickey | .75 | .30 | .07 |
| ☐ 435 | Burdette 3 wins | .50 | .20 | .05 |
| ☐ 436 | Umpire Clears Bench | .40 | .16 | .04 |
| ☐ 437 | Pee Wee Reese | 1.50 | .60 | .15 |
| ☐ 438 | Joe DiMaggio | 4.50 | 1.80 | .45 |
| | (56 Game Hit Streak) | | | |
| ☐ 439 | Ted Williams | 3.50 | 1.40 | .35 |
| | Hits .406 | | | |
| ☐ 440 | Walter Johnson | 2.00 | .80 | .20 |
| ☐ 441 | Gil Hodges | 1.50 | .60 | .15 |
| ☐ 442 | Hank Greenberg | 1.00 | .40 | .10 |
| ☐ 443 | Ty Cobb | 4.50 | 1.80 | .45 |
| ☐ 444 | Robin Roberts | 1.50 | .60 | .15 |
| ☐ 445 | Phil Rizzuto | 1.25 | .50 | .12 |
| ☐ 446 | Hal Newhouser | .60 | .24 | .06 |
| ☐ 447 | Babe Ruth 60th Homer | 5.00 | 2.00 | .50 |
| ☐ 448 | Cy Young | 1.50 | .60 | .15 |
| ☐ 449 | Harmon Killebrew | 1.50 | .60 | .15 |
| ☐ 450 | Mickey Mantle | 5.00 | 2.00 | .50 |
| | (longest homer) | | | |
| ☐ 451 | Braves Take Pennant | .40 | .16 | .04 |
| ☐ 452 | Ted Williams | 3.50 | 1.40 | .35 |
| | (All-Star Hero) | | | |
| ☐ 453 | Yogi Berra | 2.00 | .80 | .20 |
| ☐ 454 | Fred Snodgrass | .40 | .16 | .04 |
| ☐ 455 | Ruth 3 Homers | 5.00 | 2.00 | .50 |
| ☐ 456 | Giants 26 Game Streak | .40 | .16 | .04 |
| ☐ 457 | Ted Kluszewski | .50 | .20 | .05 |
| ☐ 458 | Mel Ott | 1.00 | .40 | .10 |
| ☐ 459 | Harvey Kuenn | .60 | .24 | .06 |
| ☐ 460 | Bob Feller | 2.00 | .80 | .20 |
| ☐ 461 | Casey Stengel | 1.50 | .60 | .15 |
| ☐ 462 | Hank Aaron | 3.00 | 1.20 | .30 |
| ☐ 463 | Spahn Beats Yanks | 1.00 | .40 | .10 |
| ☐ 464 | Ump's Wrong Call | .40 | .16 | .04 |
| ☐ 465 | Al Kaline | 1.50 | .60 | .15 |
| ☐ 466 | Bob Allison | .40 | .16 | .04 |
| ☐ 467 | Joe DiMaggio | 4.50 | 1.80 | .45 |
| | (Four Homers) | | | |
| ☐ 468 | Rocky Colavito | .60 | .24 | .06 |
| ☐ 469 | Carl Erskine | .50 | .20 | .05 |
| ☐ 470 | Sal Maglie | .50 | .20 | .05 |
| ☐ 471 | Early Wynn | 1.00 | .40 | .10 |
| ☐ 472 | Nellie Fox | .75 | .30 | .07 |
| ☐ 473 | Marty Marion | .60 | .24 | .06 |
| ☐ 474 | Johnny Podres | .50 | .20 | .05 |
| ☐ 475 | Mickey Owen | .40 | .16 | .04 |
| ☐ 476 | Dean Brothers | 2.00 | .80 | .20 |
| | (Dizzy and Daffy) | | | |
| ☐ 477 | Christy Mathewson | 2.00 | .80 | .20 |
| ☐ 478 | Harvey Haddix | .40 | .16 | .04 |
| ☐ 479 | Carl Hubbell | .75 | .30 | .07 |
| ☐ 480 | Bobby Thomson | .60 | .24 | .06 |

## 1952 Num Num

The cards in this 20 card set measure 3 1/2" by 4 1/2". The 1952 Num Num Potato Chips issue features black and white, numbered cards of the Cleveland Indians. Cards came with and without coupons (tabs). The cards were issued without coupons directly by the Cleveland baseball club. When the complete set was obtained the tabs were cut off and exchanged for an autographed baseball. Card Number 16, Kennedy, is rather scarce. Cards with the tabs still intact are worth approximately 25% more than the values listed below. The ACC designation is F337- 2.

|   | MINT | VG-E | F-G |
|---|---|---|---|
| COMPLETE SET | 500.00 | 200.00 | 50.00 |

| COMMON PLAYER (1-20) | ......... | 15.00 | 6.00 | 1.50 |
|---|---|---|---|---|
| ☐ 1 | Lou Brissie | 15.00 | 6.00 | 1.50 |
| ☐ 2 | Jim Hegan | 15.00 | 6.00 | 1.50 |
| ☐ 3 | Birdie Tebbetts | 15.00 | 6.00 | 1.50 |
| ☐ 4 | Bob Lemon | 35.00 | 14.00 | 3.50 |
| ☐ 5 | Bob Feller | 50.00 | 20.00 | 5.00 |
| ☐ 6 | Early Wynn | 35.00 | 14.00 | 3.50 |
| ☐ 7 | Mike Garcia | 18.00 | 7.25 | 1.80 |
| ☐ 8 | Steve Gromek | 15.00 | 6.00 | 1.50 |
| ☐ 9 | Bob Chakales | 15.00 | 6.00 | 1.50 |
| ☐ 10 | Al Rosen | 25.00 | 10.00 | 2.50 |
| ☐ 11 | Dick Rozek | 15.00 | 6.00 | 1.50 |
| ☐ 12 | Luke Easter | 15.00 | 6.00 | 1.50 |
| ☐ 13 | Ray Boone | 15.00 | 6.00 | 1.50 |
| ☐ 14 | Bobby Avila | 15.00 | 6.00 | 1.50 |
| ☐ 15 | Dale Mitchell | 18.00 | 7.25 | 1.80 |
| ☐ 16 | Bob Kennedy | 200.00 | 80.00 | 20.00 |
| ☐ 17 | Harry Simpson | 15.00 | 6.00 | 1.50 |
| ☐ 18 | Larry Doby | 25.00 | 10.00 | 2.50 |
| ☐ 19 | Sam Jones | 15.00 | 6.00 | 1.50 |
| ☐ 20 | Al Lopez MGR | 30.00 | 12.00 | 3.00 |

## 1939 Playball

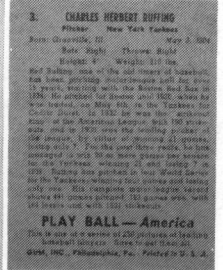

The cards in this 162 card set measure 2 1/2" by 3 1/8". Gum Incorporated introduced a brief (war-shortened) but innovative era of baseball card production with its set of 1939. The combination of actual player photos (black and white), large card size, and extensive biography proved extremely popular. Player names are found either entirely capitalized or with initial caps only, and a "sample card" overprint is not uncommon. Card number 126 was never issued, and cards 116-162 were produced in lesser quantities than 1-115. The ACC designation for this set is R334.

| | | MINT | VG-E | F-G |
|---|---|---|---|---|
| COMPLETE SET | ...................... | 2700.00 | 1200.00 | 300.00 |
| COMMON PLAYER (1-115) | ........ | 5.00 | 2.00 | .50 |
| COMMON PLAYER (116-162) | .... | 30.00 | 12.00 | 3.00 |
| ☐ 1 | Jake Powell | 25.00 | 4.00 | .80 |
| ☐ 2 | Lee Grissom | 5.00 | 2.00 | .50 |
| ☐ 3 | Red Ruffing | 30.00 | 12.00 | 3.00 |
| ☐ 4 | Eldon Auker | 5.00 | 2.00 | .50 |
| ☐ 5 | Luke Sewell | 6.00 | 2.40 | .60 |
| ☐ 6 | Leo Durocher | 18.00 | 7.25 | 1.80 |
| ☐ 7 | Bobby Doerr | 25.00 | 10.00 | 2.50 |
| ☐ 8 | Henry Pippen | 5.00 | 2.00 | .50 |
| ☐ 9 | James Tobin | 5.00 | 2.00 | .50 |
| ☐ 10 | James DeShong | 5.00 | 2.00 | .50 |
| ☐ 11 | Johnny Rizzo | 5.00 | 2.00 | .50 |
| ☐ 12 | Hershel Martin | 5.00 | 2.00 | .50 |
| ☐ 13 | Luke Hamlin | 5.00 | 2.00 | .50 |
| ☐ 14 | Jim Tabor | 5.00 | 2.00 | .50 |
| ☐ 15 | Paul Derringer | 7.50 | 3.00 | .75 |
| ☐ 16 | John Peacock | 5.00 | 2.00 | .50 |
| ☐ 17 | Emerson Dickman | 5.00 | 2.00 | .50 |
| ☐ 18 | Harry Danning | 5.00 | 2.00 | .50 |
| ☐ 19 | Paul Dean | 10.00 | 4.00 | 1.00 |
| ☐ 20 | Joe Heving | 5.00 | 2.00 | .50 |

| ☐ 21 | Dutch Leonard | 6.00 | 2.40 | .60 |
|---|---|---|---|---|
| ☐ 22 | Bucky Walters | 6.00 | 2.40 | .60 |
| ☐ 23 | Burgess Whitehead | 5.00 | 2.00 | .50 |
| ☐ 24 | Richard Coffman | 5.00 | 2.00 | .50 |
| ☐ 25 | George Selkirk | 6.00 | 2.40 | .60 |
| ☐ 26 | Joe DiMaggio | 375.00 | 150.00 | 37.00 |
| ☐ 27 | Fred Ostermueller | 5.00 | 2.00 | .50 |
| ☐ 28 | Sylvester Johnson | 5.00 | 2.00 | .50 |
| ☐ 29 | John (Jack) Wilson | 5.00 | 2.00 | .50 |
| ☐ 30 | Bill Dickey | 60.00 | 24.00 | 6.00 |
| ☐ 31 | Sam West | 5.00 | 2.00 | .50 |
| ☐ 32 | Bob Seeds | 5.00 | 2.00 | .50 |
| ☐ 33 | Del Young | 5.00 | 2.00 | .50 |
| ☐ 34 | Frank Demaree | 5.00 | 2.00 | .50 |
| ☐ 35 | Bill Jurges | 5.00 | 2.00 | .50 |
| ☐ 36 | Frank McCormick | 6.00 | 2.40 | .60 |
| ☐ 37 | Virgil Davis | 5.00 | 2.00 | .50 |
| ☐ 38 | Billy Myers | 5.00 | 2.00 | .50 |
| ☐ 39 | Rick Ferrell | 24.00 | 10.00 | 2.40 |
| ☐ 40 | James Bagby Jr. | 5.00 | 2.00 | .50 |
| ☐ 41 | Lon Warneke | 5.00 | 2.00 | .50 |
| ☐ 42 | Arndt Jorgens | 5.00 | 2.00 | .50 |
| ☐ 43 | Melo Almada | 5.00 | 2.00 | .50 |
| ☐ 44 | Don Heffner | 5.00 | 2.00 | .50 |
| ☐ 45 | Merrill May | 5.00 | 2.00 | .50 |
| ☐ 46 | Morris Arnovich | 5.00 | 2.00 | .50 |
| ☐ 47 | Buddy Lewis | 5.00 | 2.00 | .50 |
| ☐ 48 | Lefty Gomez | 45.00 | 18.00 | 4.50 |
| ☐ 49 | Eddie Miller | 5.00 | 2.00 | .50 |
| ☐ 50 | Charlie Gehringer | 45.00 | 18.00 | 4.50 |
| ☐ 51 | Mel Ott | 60.00 | 24.00 | 6.00 |
| ☐ 52 | Tommy Henrich | 10.00 | 4.00 | 1.00 |
| ☐ 53 | Carl Hubbell | 45.00 | 18.00 | 4.50 |
| ☐ 54 | Harry Gumpert | 5.00 | 2.00 | .50 |
| ☐ 55 | Arky Vaughan | 24.00 | 10.00 | 2.40 |
| ☐ 56 | Hank Greenberg | 60.00 | 24.00 | 6.00 |
| ☐ 57 | Buddy Hassett | 5.00 | 2.00 | .50 |
| ☐ 58 | Lou Chiozza | 5.00 | 2.00 | .50 |
| ☐ 59 | Ken Chase | 5.00 | 2.00 | .50 |
| ☐ 60 | Schoolboy Rowe | 6.00 | 2.40 | .60 |
| ☐ 61 | Tony Cuccinello | 5.00 | 2.00 | .50 |
| ☐ 62 | Tom Carey | 5.00 | 2.00 | .50 |
| ☐ 63 | Emmett Mueller | 5.00 | 2.00 | .50 |
| ☐ 64 | Wally Moses | 6.00 | 2.40 | .60 |
| ☐ 65 | Harry Craft | 5.00 | 2.00 | .50 |
| ☐ 66 | Jimmy Ripple | 5.00 | 2.00 | .50 |
| ☐ 67 | Ed Joost | 5.00 | 2.00 | .50 |
| ☐ 68 | Fred Sington | 5.00 | 2.00 | .50 |
| ☐ 69 | Elbie Fletcher | 5.00 | 2.00 | .50 |
| ☐ 70 | Fred Frankhouse | 5.00 | 2.00 | .50 |
| ☐ 71 | Monte Pearson | 5.00 | 2.00 | .50 |
| ☐ 72 | Debs Garms | 5.00 | 2.00 | .50 |
| ☐ 73 | Hal Schumacher | 5.00 | 2.00 | .50 |
| ☐ 74 | Cookie Lavagetto | 6.00 | 2.40 | .60 |
| ☐ 75 | Stan Bordagaray | 5.00 | 2.00 | .50 |
| ☐ 76 | Goody Rosen | 5.00 | 2.00 | .50 |
| ☐ 77 | Lew Riggs | 5.00 | 2.00 | .50 |
| ☐ 78 | Julius Solters | 5.00 | 2.00 | .50 |
| ☐ 79 | Jo Jo Moore | 5.00 | 2.00 | .50 |
| ☐ 80 | Pete Fox | 5.00 | 2.00 | .50 |
| ☐ 81 | Babe Dahlgren | 6.00 | 2.40 | .60 |
| ☐ 82 | Chuck Klein | 35.00 | 14.00 | 3.50 |
| ☐ 83 | Gus Suhr | 5.00 | 2.00 | .50 |
| ☐ 84 | Skeeter Newsom | 5.00 | 2.00 | .50 |
| ☐ 85 | Johnny Cooney | 5.00 | 2.00 | .50 |
| ☐ 86 | Dolph Camilli | 5.00 | 2.00 | .50 |
| ☐ 87 | Milburn Schoffner | 5.00 | 2.00 | .50 |
| ☐ 88 | Charlie Keller | 10.00 | 4.00 | 1.00 |
| ☐ 89 | Lloyd Waner | 24.00 | 10.00 | 2.40 |
| ☐ 90 | Robert Klinger | 5.00 | 2.00 | .50 |
| ☐ 91 | John Knott | 5.00 | 2.00 | .50 |
| ☐ 92 | Ted Williams | 300.00 | 120.00 | 30.00 |
| ☐ 93 | Charles Gelbert | 5.00 | 2.00 | .50 |
| ☐ 94 | Heinie Manush | 24.00 | 10.00 | 2.40 |
| ☐ 95 | Whit Wyatt | 6.00 | 2.40 | .60 |
| ☐ 96 | Babe Phelps | 5.00 | 2.00 | .50 |
| ☐ 97 | Bob Johnson | 6.00 | 2.40 | .60 |
| ☐ 98 | Pinky Whitney | 5.00 | 2.00 | .50 |
| ☐ 99 | Wally Berger | 6.00 | 2.40 | .60 |
| ☐ 100 | Charles Myer | 5.00 | 2.00 | .50 |
| ☐ 101 | Roger Cramer | 6.00 | 2.40 | .60 |
| ☐ 102 | Lem Young | 5.00 | 2.00 | .50 |
| ☐ 103 | Moe Berg | 6.00 | 2.40 | .60 |
| ☐ 104 | Tom Bridges | 6.00 | 2.40 | .60 |
| ☐ 105 | Rabbit McNair | 5.00 | 2.00 | .50 |
| ☐ 106 | Dolly Stark | 6.00 | 2.40 | .60 |
| ☐ 107 | Joe Vosmik | 5.00 | 2.00 | .50 |
| ☐ 108 | Frank Hayes | 5.00 | 2.00 | .50 |
| ☐ 109 | Myril Hoag | 5.00 | 2.00 | .50 |
| ☐ 110 | Fred Fitzsimmons | 5.00 | 2.00 | .50 |
| ☐ 111 | Van Lingle Mungo | 6.00 | 2.40 | .60 |
| ☐ 112 | Paul Waner | 30.00 | 12.00 | 3.00 |
| ☐ 113 | Al Schacht | 6.00 | 2.40 | .60 |

| | | | | |
|---|---|---|---|---|
| ☐ 114 | Cecil Travis | 5.00 | 2.00 | .50 |
| ☐ 115 | Ralph Kress | 5.00 | 2.00 | .50 |
| ☐ 116 | Gene Desautels | 30.00 | 12.00 | 3.00 |
| ☐ 117 | Wayne Ambler | 30.00 | 12.00 | 3.00 |
| ☐ 118 | Lynn Nelson | 30.00 | 12.00 | 3.00 |
| ☐ 119 | Will Hershberger | 30.00 | 12.00 | 3.00 |
| ☐ 120 | Rabbit Warstler | 30.00 | 12.00 | 3.00 |
| ☐ 121 | Bill Posedel | 30.00 | 12.00 | 3.00 |
| ☐ 122 | George McQuinn | 30.00 | 12.00 | 3.00 |
| ☐ 123 | Ray T. Davis | 30.00 | 12.00 | 3.00 |
| ☐ 124 | Walter Brown | 30.00 | 12.00 | 3.00 |
| ☐ 125 | Cliff Melton | 30.00 | 12.00 | 3.00 |
| ☐ 126 | Not issued | 0.00 | 0.00 | 0.00 |
| ☐ 127 | Gil Brack | 30.00 | 12.00 | 3.00 |
| ☐ 128 | Joe Bowman | 30.00 | 12.00 | 3.00 |
| ☐ 129 | Bill Swift | 30.00 | 12.00 | 3.00 |
| ☐ 130 | Bill Brubaker | 30.00 | 12.00 | 3.00 |
| ☐ 131 | Mort Cooper | 30.00 | 12.00 | 3.00 |
| ☐ 132 | Jim Brown | 30.00 | 12.00 | 3.00 |
| ☐ 133 | Lynn Myers | 30.00 | 12.00 | 3.00 |
| ☐ 134 | Tot Presnell | 30.00 | 12.00 | 3.00 |
| ☐ 135 | Mickey Owen | 30.00 | 12.00 | 3.00 |
| ☐ 136 | Roy Bell | 30.00 | 12.00 | 3.00 |
| ☐ 137 | Pete Appleton | 30.00 | 12.00 | 3.00 |
| ☐ 138 | George Case | 30.00 | 12.00 | 3.00 |
| ☐ 139 | Vito Tamulis | 30.00 | 12.00 | 3.00 |
| ☐ 140 | Ray Hayworth | 30.00 | 12.00 | 3.00 |
| ☐ 141 | Pete Coscarart | 30.00 | 12.00 | 3.00 |
| ☐ 142 | Ira Hutchinson | 30.00 | 12.00 | 3.00 |
| ☐ 143 | Earl Averill | 90.00 | 36.00 | 9.00 |
| ☐ 144 | Zeke Bonura | 30.00 | 12.00 | 3.00 |
| ☐ 145 | Hugh Mulcahy | 30.00 | 12.00 | 3.00 |
| ☐ 146 | Tom Sunkel | 30.00 | 12.00 | 3.00 |
| ☐ 147 | George Coffman | 30.00 | 12.00 | 3.00 |
| ☐ 148 | Bill Trotter | 30.00 | 12.00 | 3.00 |
| ☐ 149 | Max West | 30.00 | 12.00 | 3.00 |
| ☐ 150 | James Walkup | 30.00 | 12.00 | 3.00 |
| ☐ 151 | Hugh Casey | 30.00 | 12.00 | 3.00 |
| ☐ 152 | Roy Weatherly | 30.00 | 12.00 | 3.00 |
| ☐ 153 | Paul Trout | 30.00 | 12.00 | 3.00 |
| ☐ 154 | Johnny Hudson | 30.00 | 12.00 | 3.00 |
| ☐ 155 | Jimmy Outlaw | 30.00 | 12.00 | 3.00 |
| ☐ 156 | Ray Berres | 30.00 | 12.00 | 3.00 |
| ☐ 157 | Don Padgett | 30.00 | 12.00 | 3.00 |
| ☐ 158 | Bud Thomas | 30.00 | 12.00 | 3.00 |
| ☐ 159 | Red Evans | 30.00 | 12.00 | 3.00 |
| ☐ 160 | Gene Moore | 30.00 | 12.00 | 3.00 |
| ☐ 161 | Lonnie Frey | 30.00 | 12.00 | 3.00 |
| ☐ 162 | Whitey Moore | 35.00 | 14.00 | 3.50 |

## 1940 Playball

88. MELVIN THOMAS OTT
Outfielder    New York Giants

PLAY BALL

The cards in this 240 card series measure 2 1/2" by 3 1/8". Gum Inc. improved upon its 1939 design by enclosing the 1940 black and white player photo with a frame line and printing the player's name in a panel below the picture (often using a nickname). The set included many Hall of Famers and Old Timers. Cards 181-240 are scarcer than cards 1-180. The backs contain an extensive biography and a dated copyright line. The ACC catalog number is R335.

| | MINT | VG-E | F-G |
|---|---|---|---|
| COMPLETE SET | 4000.00 | 1600.00 | 400.00 |
| COMMON PLAYER (1-120) | 6.00 | 2.40 | .60 |

| | | | | |
|---|---|---|---|---|
| COMMON PLAYER (121-180) | 7.00 | 2.80 | .70 |
| COMMON PLAYER (181-240) | 20.00 | 8.00 | 2.00 |
| ☐ 1 | Joe DiMaggio | 600.00 | 150.00 | 30.00 |
| ☐ 2 | Art Jorgens | 6.00 | 2.40 | .60 |
| ☐ 3 | Babe Dahlgren | 7.00 | 2.80 | .70 |
| ☐ 4 | Tommy Henrich | 10.00 | 4.00 | 1.00 |
| ☐ 5 | Monte Pearson | 6.00 | 2.40 | .60 |
| ☐ 6 | Lefty Gomez | 45.00 | 18.00 | 4.50 |
| ☐ 7 | Bill Dickey | 60.00 | 24.00 | 6.00 |
| ☐ 8 | George Selkirk | 7.00 | 2.80 | .70 |
| ☐ 9 | Charlie Keller | 10.00 | 4.00 | 1.00 |
| ☐ 10 | Red Ruffing | 30.00 | 12.00 | 3.00 |
| ☐ 11 | Jake Powell | 6.00 | 2.40 | .60 |
| ☐ 12 | Johnny Schulte | 6.00 | 2.40 | .60 |
| ☐ 13 | Jack Knott | 6.00 | 2.40 | .60 |
| ☐ 14 | Rabbit McNair | 6.00 | 2.40 | .60 |
| ☐ 15 | George Case | 6.00 | 2.40 | .60 |
| ☐ 16 | Cecil Travis | 6.00 | 2.40 | .60 |
| ☐ 17 | Buddy Myer | 6.00 | 2.40 | .60 |
| ☐ 18 | Charlie Gelbert | 6.00 | 2.40 | .60 |
| ☐ 19 | Ken Chase | 6.00 | 2.40 | .60 |
| ☐ 20 | Buddy Lewis | 6.00 | 2.40 | .60 |
| ☐ 21 | Rick Ferrell | 25.00 | 10.00 | 2.50 |
| ☐ 22 | Sammy West | 6.00 | 2.40 | .60 |
| ☐ 23 | Dutch Leonard | 7.00 | 2.80 | .70 |
| ☐ 24 | Frank Hayes | 6.00 | 2.40 | .60 |
| ☐ 25 | Bob Johnson | 7.00 | 2.80 | .70 |
| ☐ 26 | Wally Moses | 7.00 | 2.80 | .70 |
| ☐ 27 | Ted Williams | 300.00 | 120.00 | 30.00 |
| ☐ 28 | Gene Desautels | 6.00 | 2.40 | .60 |
| ☐ 29 | Doc Cramer | 7.00 | 2.80 | .70 |
| ☐ 30 | Moe Berg | 7.00 | 2.80 | .70 |
| ☐ 31 | Jack Wilson | 6.00 | 2.40 | .60 |
| ☐ 32 | Jim Bagby | 6.00 | 2.40 | .60 |
| ☐ 33 | Fritz Ostermueller | 6.00 | 2.40 | .60 |
| ☐ 34 | John Peacock | 6.00 | 2.40 | .60 |
| ☐ 35 | Joe Heving | 6.00 | 2.40 | .60 |
| ☐ 36 | Jim Tabor | 6.00 | 2.40 | .60 |
| ☐ 37 | Emerson Dickman | 6.00 | 2.40 | .60 |
| ☐ 38 | Bobby Doerr | 25.00 | 10.00 | 2.50 |
| ☐ 39 | Tom Carey | 6.00 | 2.40 | .60 |
| ☐ 40 | Hank Greenberg | 60.00 | 24.00 | 6.00 |
| ☐ 41 | Charley Gehringer | 45.00 | 18.00 | 4.50 |
| ☐ 42 | Bud Thomas | 6.00 | 2.40 | .60 |
| ☐ 43 | Pete Fox | 6.00 | 2.40 | .60 |
| ☐ 44 | Dizzy Trout | 7.00 | 2.80 | .70 |
| ☐ 45 | Red Kress | 6.00 | 2.40 | .60 |
| ☐ 46 | Earl Averill | 30.00 | 12.00 | 3.00 |
| ☐ 47 | Ol' Os Vitt | 6.00 | 2.40 | .60 |
| ☐ 48 | Luke Sewell | 7.00 | 2.80 | .70 |
| ☐ 49 | Stormy Weatherly | 6.00 | 2.40 | .60 |
| ☐ 50 | Hal Trosky | 7.00 | 2.80 | .70 |
| ☐ 51 | Don Heffner | 6.00 | 2.40 | .60 |
| ☐ 52 | Myril Hoag | 6.00 | 2.40 | .60 |
| ☐ 53 | Mac McQuinn | 6.00 | 2.40 | .60 |
| ☐ 54 | Bill Trotter | 6.00 | 2.40 | .60 |
| ☐ 55 | Slick Coffman | 6.00 | 2.40 | .60 |
| ☐ 56 | Eddie Miller | 6.00 | 2.40 | .60 |
| ☐ 57 | Max West | 6.00 | 2.40 | .60 |
| ☐ 58 | Bill Posedel | 6.00 | 2.40 | .60 |
| ☐ 59 | Rabbit Warstler | 6.00 | 2.40 | .60 |
| ☐ 60 | John Cooney | 6.00 | 2.40 | .60 |
| ☐ 61 | Tony Cuccinello | 6.00 | 2.40 | .60 |
| ☐ 62 | Buddy Hassett | 6.00 | 2.40 | .60 |
| ☐ 63 | Pete Coscarart | 6.00 | 2.40 | .60 |
| ☐ 64 | Van Lingle Mungo | 7.00 | 2.80 | .70 |
| ☐ 65 | Fitz Fitzsimmons | 6.00 | 2.40 | .60 |
| ☐ 66 | Babe Phelps | 6.00 | 2.40 | .60 |
| ☐ 67 | Whit Wyatt | 7.00 | 2.80 | .70 |
| ☐ 68 | Dolph Camilli | 6.00 | 2.40 | .60 |
| ☐ 69 | Cookie Lavagetto | 7.00 | 2.80 | .70 |
| ☐ 70 | Hot Potato Hamlin | 6.00 | 2.40 | .60 |
| ☐ 71 | Mel Almada | 6.00 | 2.40 | .60 |
| ☐ 72 | Chuck Dressen | 7.00 | 2.80 | .70 |
| ☐ 73 | Bucky Walters | 7.00 | 2.80 | .70 |
| ☐ 74 | Duke Derringer | 8.00 | 3.25 | .80 |
| ☐ 75 | Buck McCormick | 7.00 | 2.80 | .70 |
| ☐ 76 | Lonny Frey | 6.00 | 2.40 | .60 |
| ☐ 77 | Bill Hershberger | 6.00 | 2.40 | .60 |
| ☐ 78 | Lew Riggs | 6.00 | 2.40 | .60 |
| ☐ 79 | Harry Wildfire Craft | 6.00 | 2.40 | .60 |
| ☐ 80 | Billy Myers | 6.00 | 2.40 | .60 |
| ☐ 81 | Wally Berger | 7.00 | 2.80 | .70 |
| ☐ 82 | Hank Gowdy | 7.00 | 2.80 | .70 |
| ☐ 83 | Cliff Melton | 6.00 | 2.40 | .60 |
| ☐ 84 | Jo Jo Moore | 6.00 | 2.40 | .60 |
| ☐ 85 | Hal Schumacher | 6.00 | 2.40 | .60 |
| ☐ 86 | Harry Gumbert | 6.00 | 2.40 | .60 |
| ☐ 87 | Carl Hubbell | 45.00 | 18.00 | 4.50 |
| ☐ 88 | Mel Ott | 60.00 | 24.00 | 6.00 |

| | | | | |
|---|---|---|---|---|
| ☐ 89 | Bill Jurges | 6.00 | 2.40 | .60 |
| ☐ 90 | Frank Demaree | 6.00 | 2.40 | .60 |
| ☐ 91 | Suitcase Seeds | 6.00 | 2.40 | .60 |
| ☐ 92 | Whitey Whitehead | 6.00 | 2.40 | .60 |
| ☐ 93 | Harry Danning | 6.00 | 2.40 | .60 |
| ☐ 94 | Gus Suhr | 6.00 | 2.40 | .60 |
| ☐ 95 | Mul Mulcahy | 6.00 | 2.40 | .60 |
| ☐ 96 | Heinie Mueller | 6.00 | 2.40 | .60 |
| ☐ 97 | Morry Arnovich | 6.00 | 2.40 | .60 |
| ☐ 98 | Pinky May | 6.00 | 2.40 | .60 |
| ☐ 99 | Syl Johnson | 6.00 | 2.40 | .60 |
| ☐ 100 | Hersh Martin | 6.00 | 2.40 | .60 |
| ☐ 101 | Del Young | 6.00 | 2.40 | .60 |
| ☐ 102 | Chuck Klein | 35.00 | 14.00 | 3.50 |
| ☐ 103 | Elbie Fletcher | 6.00 | 2.40 | .60 |
| ☐ 104 | Big Poison Waner | 30.00 | 12.00 | 3.00 |
| ☐ 105 | Little Poison Waner | 25.00 | 10.00 | 2.50 |
| ☐ 106 | Pep Young | 6.00 | 2.40 | .60 |
| ☐ 107 | Arky Vaughan | 25.00 | 10.00 | 2.50 |
| ☐ 108 | Johnny Rizzo | 6.00 | 2.40 | .60 |
| ☐ 109 | Don Padgett | 6.00 | 2.40 | .60 |
| ☐ 110 | Tom Sunkell | 6.00 | 2.40 | .60 |
| ☐ 111 | Mickey Owen | 7.00 | 2.80 | .70 |
| ☐ 112 | Jimmy Brown | 6.00 | 2.40 | .60 |
| ☐ 113 | Mort Cooper | 7.00 | 2.80 | .70 |
| ☐ 114 | Lon Warneke | 6.00 | 2.40 | .60 |
| ☐ 115 | Mike Gonzales | 6.00 | 2.40 | .60 |
| ☐ 116 | Al Schacht | 7.00 | 2.80 | .70 |
| ☐ 117 | Dolly Stark | 7.00 | 2.80 | .70 |
| ☐ 118 | Schoolboy Hoyt | 30.00 | 12.00 | 3.00 |
| ☐ 119 | Ol Pete Alexander | 45.00 | 18.00 | 4.50 |
| ☐ 120 | Walter Johnson | 75.00 | 30.00 | 7.50 |
| ☐ 121 | Atley Donald | 7.00 | 2.80 | .70 |
| ☐ 122 | Sandy Sundra | 7.00 | 2.80 | .70 |
| ☐ 123 | Hildy Hildebrand | 7.00 | 2.80 | .70 |
| ☐ 124 | Colonel Earle Combs | 35.00 | 14.00 | 3.50 |
| ☐ 125 | Art Fletcher | 7.00 | 2.80 | .70 |
| ☐ 126 | Jake Solters | 7.00 | 2.80 | .70 |
| ☐ 127 | Muddy Ruel | 7.00 | 2.80 | .70 |
| ☐ 128 | Pete Appleton | 7.00 | 2.80 | .70 |
| ☐ 129 | Bucky Harris | 21.00 | 8.50 | 2.10 |
| ☐ 130 | Deerfoot Milan | 7.00 | 2.80 | .70 |
| ☐ 131 | Zeke Bonura | 7.00 | 2.80 | .70 |
| ☐ 132 | Connie Mack | 45.00 | 18.00 | 4.50 |
| ☐ 133 | Jimmie Foxx | 75.00 | 30.00 | 7.50 |
| ☐ 134 | Joe Cronin | 45.00 | 18.00 | 4.50 |
| ☐ 135 | Line Drive Nelson | 7.00 | 2.80 | .70 |
| ☐ 136 | Cotton Pippen | 7.00 | 2.80 | .70 |
| ☐ 137 | Bing Miller | 7.00 | 2.80 | .70 |
| ☐ 138 | Beau Bell | 7.00 | 2.80 | .70 |
| ☐ 139 | Elden Auker | 7.00 | 2.80 | .70 |
| ☐ 140 | Dick Coffman | 7.00 | 2.80 | .70 |
| ☐ 141 | Casey Stengel | 60.00 | 24.00 | 6.00 |
| ☐ 142 | Highpockets Kelly | 30.00 | 12.00 | 3.00 |
| ☐ 143 | Gene Moore | 7.00 | 2.80 | .70 |
| ☐ 144 | Joe Vosmik | 7.00 | 2.80 | .70 |
| ☐ 145 | Vito Tamulis | 7.00 | 2.80 | .70 |
| ☐ 146 | Tot Pressnell | 7.00 | 2.80 | .70 |
| ☐ 147 | Johnny Hudson | 7.00 | 2.80 | .70 |
| ☐ 148 | Hugh Casey | 7.00 | 2.80 | .70 |
| ☐ 149 | Pinky Shoffner | 7.00 | 2.80 | .70 |
| ☐ 150 | Whitey Moore | 7.00 | 2.80 | .70 |
| ☐ 151 | Edwin Joost | 7.00 | 2.80 | .70 |
| ☐ 152 | Jimmy Wilson | 7.00 | 2.80 | .70 |
| ☐ 153 | Bill McKechnie | 25.00 | 10.00 | 2.50 |
| ☐ 154 | Jumbo Brown | 7.00 | 2.80 | .70 |
| ☐ 155 | Ray Hayworth | 7.00 | 2.80 | .70 |
| ☐ 156 | Daffy Dean | 10.00 | 4.00 | 1.00 |
| ☐ 157 | Lou Chiozza | 7.00 | 2.80 | .70 |
| ☐ 158 | Travis Jackson | 25.00 | 10.00 | 2.50 |
| ☐ 159 | Pancho Snyder | 7.00 | 2.80 | .70 |
| ☐ 160 | Hans Lobert | 7.00 | 2.80 | .70 |
| ☐ 161 | Debs Garms | 7.00 | 2.80 | .70 |
| ☐ 162 | Joe Bowman | 7.00 | 2.80 | .70 |
| ☐ 163 | Spud Davis | 7.00 | 2.80 | .70 |
| ☐ 164 | Ray Berres | 7.00 | 2.80 | .70 |
| ☐ 165 | Bob Klinger | 7.00 | 2.80 | .70 |
| ☐ 166 | Bill Brubaker | 7.00 | 2.80 | .70 |
| ☐ 167 | Frankie Frisch | 40.00 | 16.00 | 4.00 |
| ☐ 168 | Honus Wagner | 75.00 | 30.00 | 7.50 |
| ☐ 169 | Gabby Street | 7.00 | 2.80 | .70 |
| ☐ 170 | Tris Speaker | 60.00 | 24.00 | 6.00 |
| ☐ 171 | Harry Heilmann | 40.00 | 16.00 | 4.00 |
| ☐ 172 | Chief Bender | 30.00 | 12.00 | 3.00 |
| ☐ 173 | Larry Lajoie | 60.00 | 24.00 | 6.00 |
| ☐ 174 | Johnny Evers | 35.00 | 14.00 | 3.50 |
| ☐ 175 | Christy Mathewson | 75.00 | 30.00 | 7.50 |
| ☐ 176 | Heinie Manush | 25.00 | 10.00 | 2.50 |
| ☐ 177 | Homerun Baker | 30.00 | 12.00 | 3.00 |
| ☐ 178 | Max Carey | 30.00 | 12.00 | 3.00 |
| ☐ 179 | George Sisler | 45.00 | 18.00 | 4.50 |
| ☐ 180 | Mickey Cochrane | 60.00 | 24.00 | 6.00 |
| ☐ 181 | Spud Chandler | 25.00 | 10.00 | 2.50 |

| | | | | |
|---|---|---|---|---|
| ☐ 182 | Knick Knickerbocker | 20.00 | 8.00 | 2.00 |
| ☐ 183 | Marvin Breuer | 20.00 | 8.00 | 2.00 |
| ☐ 184 | Mule Haas | 20.00 | 8.00 | 2.00 |
| ☐ 185 | Joe Kuhel | 20.00 | 8.00 | 2.00 |
| ☐ 186 | Taft Wright | 20.00 | 8.00 | 2.00 |
| ☐ 187 | Jimmy Dykes | 20.00 | 8.00 | 2.00 |
| ☐ 188 | Joe Krakauskas | 20.00 | 8.00 | 2.00 |
| ☐ 189 | Jim Bloodworth | 20.00 | 8.00 | 2.00 |
| ☐ 190 | Charley Berry | 20.00 | 8.00 | 2.00 |
| ☐ 191 | John Babich | 20.00 | 8.00 | 2.00 |
| ☐ 192 | Dick Siebert | 20.00 | 8.00 | 2.00 |
| ☐ 193 | Chubby Dean | 20.00 | 8.00 | 2.00 |
| ☐ 194 | Sam Chapman | 20.00 | 8.00 | 2.00 |
| ☐ 195 | Dee Miles | 20.00 | 8.00 | 2.00 |
| ☐ 196 | Noony Nonnenkamp | 20.00 | 8.00 | 2.00 |
| ☐ 197 | Lou Finney | 20.00 | 8.00 | 2.00 |
| ☐ 198 | Denny Galehouse | 20.00 | 8.00 | 2.00 |
| ☐ 199 | Pinky Higgins | 20.00 | 8.00 | 2.00 |
| ☐ 200 | Soup Campbell | 20.00 | 8.00 | 2.00 |
| ☐ 201 | Barney McCosky | 20.00 | 8.00 | 2.00 |
| ☐ 202 | Al Milnar | 20.00 | 8.00 | 2.00 |
| ☐ 203 | Bad News Hale | 20.00 | 8.00 | 2.00 |
| ☐ 204 | Harry Eisenstat | 20.00 | 8.00 | 2.00 |
| ☐ 205 | Rollie Hemsley | 20.00 | 8.00 | 2.00 |
| ☐ 206 | Chet Laabs | 20.00 | 8.00 | 2.00 |
| ☐ 207 | Gus Mancuso | 20.00 | 8.00 | 2.00 |
| ☐ 208 | Lee Gamble | 20.00 | 8.00 | 2.00 |
| ☐ 209 | Hy Vandenberg | 20.00 | 8.00 | 2.00 |
| ☐ 210 | Bill Lohrman | 20.00 | 8.00 | 2.00 |
| ☐ 211 | Pop Joiner | 20.00 | 8.00 | 2.00 |
| ☐ 212 | Babe Young | 20.00 | 8.00 | 2.00 |
| ☐ 213 | John Rucker | 20.00 | 8.00 | 2.00 |
| ☐ 214 | Ken O'Dea | 20.00 | 8.00 | 2.00 |
| ☐ 215 | Johnnie McCarthy | 20.00 | 8.00 | 2.00 |
| ☐ 216 | Joe Marty | 20.00 | 8.00 | 2.00 |
| ☐ 217 | Walter Beck | 20.00 | 8.00 | 2.00 |
| ☐ 218 | Wally Millies | 20.00 | 8.00 | 2.00 |
| ☐ 219 | Russ Bauers | 20.00 | 8.00 | 2.00 |
| ☐ 220 | Mace Brown | 20.00 | 8.00 | 2.00 |
| ☐ 221 | Lee Handley | 20.00 | 8.00 | 2.00 |
| ☐ 222 | Max Butcher | 20.00 | 8.00 | 2.00 |
| ☐ 223 | Hugh Jennings | 40.00 | 16.00 | 4.00 |
| ☐ 224 | Pie Traynor | 60.00 | 24.00 | 6.00 |
| ☐ 225 | Shoeless Joe Jackson | 275.00 | 110.00 | 27.00 |
| ☐ 226 | Harry Hooper | 50.00 | 20.00 | 5.00 |
| ☐ 227 | Pop Haines | 40.00 | 16.00 | 4.00 |
| ☐ 228 | Charley Grimm | 25.00 | 10.00 | 2.50 |
| ☐ 229 | Buck Herzog | 20.00 | 8.00 | 2.00 |
| ☐ 230 | Red Faber | 40.00 | 16.00 | 4.00 |
| ☐ 231 | Dolf Luque | 20.00 | 8.00 | 2.00 |
| ☐ 232 | Goose Goslin | 40.00 | 16.00 | 4.00 |
| ☐ 233 | Moose Earnshaw | 20.00 | 8.00 | 2.00 |
| ☐ 234 | Frank (Husk) Chance | 50.00 | 20.00 | 5.00 |
| ☐ 235 | John J. McGraw | 60.00 | 24.00 | 6.00 |
| ☐ 236 | Jim Bottomley | 40.00 | 16.00 | 4.00 |
| ☐ 237 | Wee Willie Keeler | 50.00 | 20.00 | 5.00 |
| ☐ 238 | Tony Lazzeri | 30.00 | 12.00 | 3.00 |
| ☐ 239 | George Uhle | 20.00 | 8.00 | 2.00 |
| ☐ 240 | Bill Atwood | 20.00 | 8.00 | 2.00 |

# 1941 Playball

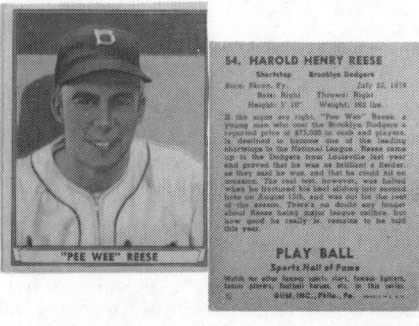

The cards in this 72 card set measure 2 1/2" by 3 1/8". Many of the cards in the 1941 Play Ball series are simply color versions of pictures appearing in the 1940 set. This was the only color baseball card set produced by Gum, Inc., and it carries the ACC designation R336. Card numbers 49-72 are slightly more difficult to obtain as they supposedly were not issued until 1942. The cards were also printed on paper without a cardboard backing; these are generally encountered in sheets or strips.

| | | MINT | VG-E | F-G |
|---|---|---|---|---|
| | COMPLETE SET | 2500.00 | 1000.00 | 250.00 |
| | COMMON PLAYER (1-48) | 15.00 | 6.00 | 1.50 |
| | COMMON PLAYER (49-72) | 21.00 | 8.50 | 2.10 |
| ☐ 1 | Eddie Miller | 50.00 | 8.00 | 1.50 |
| ☐ 2 | Max West | 15.00 | 6.00 | 1.50 |
| ☐ 3 | Bucky Walters | 18.00 | 7.25 | 1.80 |
| ☐ 4 | Paul Derringer | 18.00 | 7.25 | 1.80 |
| ☐ 5 | Buck McCormick | 18.00 | 7.25 | 1.80 |
| ☐ 6 | Carl Hubbell | 60.00 | 24.00 | 6.00 |
| ☐ 7 | Harry Danning | 15.00 | 6.00 | 1.50 |
| ☐ 8 | Mel Ott | 75.00 | 30.00 | 7.50 |
| ☐ 9 | Pinky May | 15.00 | 6.00 | 1.50 |
| ☐ 10 | Arky Vaughan | 35.00 | 14.00 | 3.50 |
| ☐ 11 | Debs Garms | 15.00 | 6.00 | 1.50 |
| ☐ 12 | Jimmy Brown | 15.00 | 6.00 | 1.50 |
| ☐ 13 | Jimmy Foxx | 90.00 | 36.00 | 9.00 |
| ☐ 14 | Ted Williams | 325.00 | 130.00 | 32.00 |
| ☐ 15 | Joe Cronin | 45.00 | 18.00 | 4.50 |
| ☐ 16 | Hal Trosky | 15.00 | 6.00 | 1.50 |
| ☐ 17 | Roy Weatherly | 15.00 | 6.00 | 1.50 |
| ☐ 18 | Hank Greenberg | 75.00 | 30.00 | 7.50 |
| ☐ 19 | Charlie Gehringer | 60.00 | 24.00 | 6.00 |
| ☐ 20 | Red Ruffing | 45.00 | 18.00 | 4.50 |
| ☐ 21 | Charlie Keller | 18.00 | 7.25 | 1.80 |
| ☐ 22 | Indian Bob Johnson | 18.00 | 7.25 | 1.80 |
| ☐ 23 | George McQuinn | 15.00 | 6.00 | 1.50 |
| ☐ 24 | Dutch Leonard | 18.00 | 7.25 | 1.80 |
| ☐ 25 | Gene Moore | 15.00 | 6.00 | 1.50 |
| ☐ 26 | Harry Gumpert | 15.00 | 6.00 | 1.50 |
| ☐ 27 | Babe Young | 15.00 | 6.00 | 1.50 |
| ☐ 28 | Joe Marty | 15.00 | 6.00 | 1.50 |
| ☐ 29 | Jack Wilson | 15.00 | 6.00 | 1.50 |
| ☐ 30 | Lou Finney | 15.00 | 6.00 | 1.50 |
| ☐ 31 | Joe Kuhel | 15.00 | 6.00 | 1.50 |
| ☐ 32 | Taft Wright | 15.00 | 6.00 | 1.50 |
| ☐ 33 | Al Milnar | 15.00 | 6.00 | 1.50 |
| ☐ 34 | Rollie Hemsley | 15.00 | 6.00 | 1.50 |
| ☐ 35 | Pinky Higgins | 15.00 | 6.00 | 1.50 |
| ☐ 36 | Barney McCosky | 15.00 | 6.00 | 1.50 |
| ☐ 37 | Bruce Campbell | 15.00 | 6.00 | 1.50 |
| ☐ 38 | Atley Donald | 15.00 | 6.00 | 1.50 |
| ☐ 39 | Tom Henrich | 18.00 | 7.25 | 1.80 |
| ☐ 40 | John Babich | 15.00 | 6.00 | 1.50 |
| ☐ 41 | Frank"Blimp" Hayes | 15.00 | 6.00 | 1.50 |
| ☐ 42 | Wally Moses | 15.00 | 6.00 | 1.50 |
| ☐ 43 | Al Brancato | 15.00 | 6.00 | 1.50 |
| ☐ 44 | Sam Chapman | 15.00 | 6.00 | 1.50 |
| ☐ 45 | Eldon Auker | 15.00 | 6.00 | 1.50 |
| ☐ 46 | Sid Hudson | 15.00 | 6.00 | 1.50 |
| ☐ 47 | Buddy Lewis | 15.00 | 6.00 | 1.50 |
| ☐ 48 | Cecil Travis | 15.00 | 6.00 | 1.50 |
| ☐ 49 | Babe Dahlgren | 21.00 | 8.50 | 2.10 |
| ☐ 50 | Johnny Cooney | 21.00 | 8.50 | 2.10 |
| ☐ 51 | Dolph Camilli | 21.00 | 8.50 | 2.10 |
| ☐ 52 | Kirby Higbe | 21.00 | 8.50 | 2.10 |
| ☐ 53 | Luke Hamlin | 21.00 | 8.50 | 2.10 |
| ☐ 54 | Pee Wee Reese | 150.00 | 60.00 | 15.00 |
| ☐ 55 | Whit Wyatt | 21.00 | 8.50 | 2.10 |
| ☐ 56 | Johnny VanderMeer | 30.00 | 12.00 | 3.00 |
| ☐ 57 | Moe Arnovich | 21.00 | 8.50 | 2.10 |
| ☐ 58 | Frank Demaree | 21.00 | 8.50 | 2.10 |
| ☐ 59 | Bill Jurges | 21.00 | 8.50 | 2.10 |
| ☐ 60 | Chuck Klein | 50.00 | 20.00 | 5.00 |
| ☐ 61 | Vince DiMaggio | 60.00 | 24.00 | 6.00 |
| ☐ 62 | Elbie Fletcher | 21.00 | 8.50 | 2.10 |
| ☐ 63 | Dom DiMaggio | 50.00 | 20.00 | 5.00 |
| ☐ 64 | Bobby Doerr | 50.00 | 20.00 | 5.00 |
| ☐ 65 | Tommy Bridges | 25.00 | 10.00 | 2.50 |
| ☐ 66 | Harland Clift | 21.00 | 8.50 | 2.10 |
| ☐ 67 | Walt Judnich | 21.00 | 8.50 | 2.10 |
| ☐ 68 | John Knott | 21.00 | 8.50 | 2.10 |
| ☐ 69 | George Case | 21.00 | 8.50 | 2.10 |
| ☐ 70 | Bill Dickey | 125.00 | 50.00 | 12.50 |
| ☐ 71 | Joe DiMaggio | 650.00 | 260.00 | 65.00 |
| ☐ 72 | Lefty Gomez | 125.00 | 50.00 | 12.50 |

## 1979 Police Giants

#44 Willie McCovey
Infielder

The cards in this 30 card set measure 2 5/8" by 4 1/8". The 1979 Police Giants set features cards numbered by the player's uniform number. This full color set features the player's photo, the Giants' logo, and the player's name, number and position on the front of the cards. A facsimile autograph in an attractive blue ink is also contained on the front. The backs, printed in orange and black, feature Tips from the Giants, the Giants' and sponsoring radio station, KNBR, logos and a line listing the Giants, KNBR, and the San Francisco Police Department as sponsors of the set. The 15 cards which are shown with an asterisk below were available only from the Police. The other 15 cards were given away at the ballpark on June 17, 1979.

| | | MINT | VG-E | F-G |
|---|---|---|---|---|
| | COMPLETE SET | 14.00 | 5.75 | 1.40 |
| | COMMON PLAYER | .30 | .12 | .03 |
| ☐ 1 | Dave Bristol MGR | .30 | .12 | .03 |
| ☐ 2 | Marc Hill | .30 | .12 | .03 |
| ☐ 3 | Mike Sadek * | .35 | .14 | .03 |
| ☐ 5 | Tom Haller | .30 | .12 | .03 |
| ☐ 6 | Joe Altobelli CO * | .35 | .14 | .03 |
| ☐ 8 | Larry Shepard CO * | .35 | .14 | .03 |
| ☐ 9 | Heity Cruz | .30 | .12 | .03 |
| ☐ 10 | Johnnie LeMaster | .30 | .12 | .03 |
| ☐ 12 | Jim Davenport | .50 | .20 | .05 |
| ☐ 14 | Vida Blue | .50 | .20 | .05 |
| ☐ 15 | Mike Ivie | .30 | .12 | .03 |
| ☐ 16 | Roger Metzger | .30 | .12 | .03 |
| ☐ 17 | Randy Moffitt | .30 | .12 | .03 |
| ☐ 18 | Bill Madlock | 1.00 | .40 | .10 |
| ☐ 21 | Rob Andrews * | .35 | .14 | .03 |
| ☐ 22 | Jack Clark * | 1.50 | .60 | .15 |
| ☐ 25 | Dave Roberts | .30 | .12 | .03 |
| ☐ 26 | John Montefusco | .35 | .14 | .03 |
| ☐ 28 | Ed Halicki * | .35 | .14 | .03 |
| ☐ 30 | John Tamargo | .30 | .12 | .03 |
| ☐ 31 | Larry Herndon | .35 | .14 | .03 |
| ☐ 36 | Bill North * | .35 | .14 | .03 |
| ☐ 39 | Bob Knepper * | .75 | .30 | .07 |
| ☐ 40 | John Curtis * | .35 | .14 | .03 |
| ☐ 41 | Darrell Evans * | 1.00 | .40 | .10 |
| ☐ 43 | Tom Griffin * | .35 | .14 | .03 |
| ☐ 44 | Willie McCovey * | 2.50 | 1.00 | .25 |
| ☐ 45 | Terry Whitfield * | .35 | .14 | .03 |
| ☐ 46 | Gary Lavelle * | .35 | .14 | .03 |
| ☐ 49 | Max Venable * | .35 | .14 | .03 |

## 1980 Police Dodgers

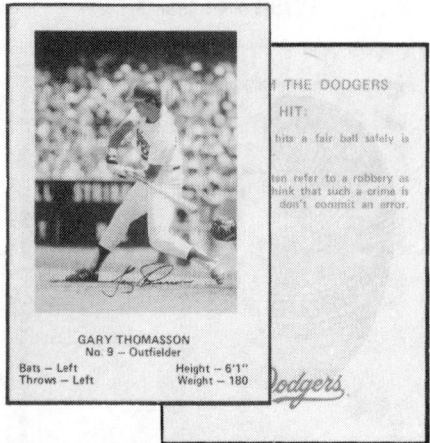

GARY THOMASSON
No. 9 — Outfielder

Bats — Left      Height — 6'1"
Throws — Left    Weight — 180

20   Joe Strain
Infielder

The cards in this 30 card set measure 2 13/16" by 4 1/8". The full color 1980 Police Los Angeles Dodgers set features the player's name, uniform number, position, and biographical data on the fronts in addition to the photo. The backs feature Tips from the Dodgers, the LAPD logo, and the Dodgers' logo. The cards are listed below according to uniform number.

|  | MINT | VG-E | F-G |
|---|---|---|---|
| COMPLETE SET | 8.00 | 3.25 | .80 |
| COMMON PLAYER | .25 | .10 | .02 |
| ☐ 5 Johnny Oates | .25 | .10 | .02 |
| ☐ 6 Steve Garvey | 1.00 | .40 | .10 |
| ☐ 7 Steve Yeager | .30 | .12 | .03 |
| ☐ 8 Reggie Smith | .40 | .16 | .04 |
| ☐ 9 Gary Thomasson | .25 | .10 | .02 |
| ☐ 10 Ron Cey | .45 | .18 | .04 |
| ☐ 12 Dusty Baker | .30 | .12 | .03 |
| ☐ 13 Joe Ferguson | .25 | .10 | .02 |
| ☐ 15 Davey Lopes | .35 | .14 | .03 |
| ☐ 16 Rick Monday | .30 | .12 | .03 |
| ☐ 18 Bill Russell | .35 | .14 | .03 |
| ☐ 20 Don Sutton | .75 | .30 | .07 |
| ☐ 21 Jay Johnstone | .30 | .12 | .03 |
| ☐ 23 Teddy Martinez | .25 | .10 | .02 |
| ☐ 27 Joe Beckwith | .25 | .10 | .02 |
| ☐ 28 Pedro Guerrero | 1.00 | .40 | .10 |
| ☐ 29 Don Stanhouse | .25 | .10 | .02 |
| ☐ 30 Derrel Thomas | .25 | .10 | .02 |
| ☐ 31 Doug Rau | .25 | .10 | .02 |
| ☐ 34 Ken Brett | .25 | .10 | .02 |
| ☐ 35 Bob Welch | .50 | .20 | .05 |
| ☐ 37 Robert Castillo | .25 | .10 | .02 |
| ☐ 38 Dave Goltz | .25 | .10 | .02 |
| ☐ 41 Jerry Reuss | .35 | .14 | .03 |
| ☐ 43 Rick Sutcliffe | .60 | .24 | .06 |
| ☐ 44 Mickey Hatcher | .30 | .12 | .03 |
| ☐ 46 Burt Hooton | .30 | .12 | .03 |
| ☐ 49 Charlie Hough | .40 | .16 | .04 |
| ☐ xx Team Card (unnumbered) | .30 | .12 | .03 |

## 1980 Police Giants

The cards in this 31 card set measure 2 5/8" by 4 1/8". The 1980 Police San Francisco Giants set features cards numbered by the player's uniform number. This full color set features the player's photo, the Giants' logo, and the player's name, number and position on the front of the cards. A facsimile autograph in an attractive blue ink is also contained on the front. The backs, printed in orange and black, feature Tips from the Giants, the Giants' and sponsoring radio station, KNBR, logos and a line listing the Giants, KNBR, and the San Francisco Police Department as sponsors of the set. The sets were given away at the ballpark on May 31, 1980.

|  | MINT | VG-E | F-G |
|---|---|---|---|
| COMPLETE SET | 9.00 | 3.75 | .90 |
| COMMON PLAYER | .25 | .10 | .02 |
| ☐ 1 Dave Bristol MGR | .25 | .10 | .02 |
| ☐ 2 Marc Hill | .25 | .10 | .02 |
| ☐ 3 Mike Sadek | .25 | .10 | .02 |
| ☐ 5 Jim Lefebvre | .25 | .10 | .02 |
| ☐ 6 Rennie Stennett | .25 | .10 | .02 |
| ☐ 7 Milt May | .25 | .10 | .02 |
| ☐ 8 Vern Benson CO | .25 | .10 | .02 |
| ☐ 9 Jim Wohlford | .25 | .10 | .02 |
| ☐ 10 Johnnie LeMaster | .25 | .10 | .02 |
| ☐ 12 Jim Davenport | .50 | .20 | .05 |
| ☐ 14 Vida Blue | .45 | .18 | .04 |
| ☐ 15 Mike Ivie | .25 | .10 | .02 |
| ☐ 16 Roger Metzger | .25 | .10 | .02 |
| ☐ 17 Randy Moffitt | .25 | .10 | .02 |
| ☐ 19 Al Holland | .35 | .14 | .03 |
| ☐ 20 Joe Strain | .25 | .10 | .02 |
| ☐ 22 Jack Clark | 1.00 | .40 | .10 |
| ☐ 26 John Montefusco | .35 | .14 | .03 |
| ☐ 28 Ed Halicki | .25 | .10 | .02 |
| ☐ 31 Larry Herndon | .35 | .14 | .03 |
| ☐ 32 Ed Whitson | .40 | .16 | .04 |
| ☐ 36 Bill North | .25 | .10 | .02 |
| ☐ 38 Greg Minton | .35 | .14 | .03 |
| ☐ 39 Bob Knepper | .60 | .24 | .06 |
| ☐ 41 Darrell Evans | .75 | .30 | .07 |
| ☐ 42 John Van Ornum | .25 | .10 | .02 |
| ☐ 43 Tom Griffin | .25 | .10 | .02 |
| ☐ 44 Willie McCovey | 1.50 | .60 | .15 |
| ☐ 45 Terry Whitfield | .25 | .10 | .02 |
| ☐ 46 Gary Lavelle | .35 | .14 | .03 |
| ☐ 47 Don McMahon CO | .25 | .10 | .02 |

## 1981 Police Braves

The cards in this 27 card set measure 2 5/8" by 4 1/8". This first Atlanta Police set features full color cards sponsored by the Braves, the Atlanta Police Department, Coca-Cola and Hostess. The cards are numbered by uniform number, which is contained on the front along with an Atlanta Police Athletic League logo, a black and white Braves logo, and a green bow in the upper right corner of the frameline. The backs feature brief player biographies, logos of

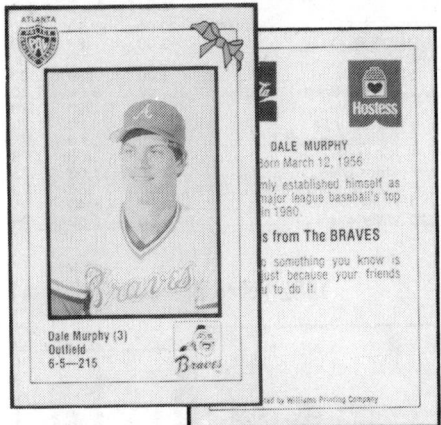

DALE MURPHY
orn March 12, 1956

nly established himself as
ajor league baseball's top
n 1980.

s from The BRAVES

something you know is
ust because your friends
to do it.

Dale Murphy (3)
Outfield
6-5—215

d by Williams Printing Company

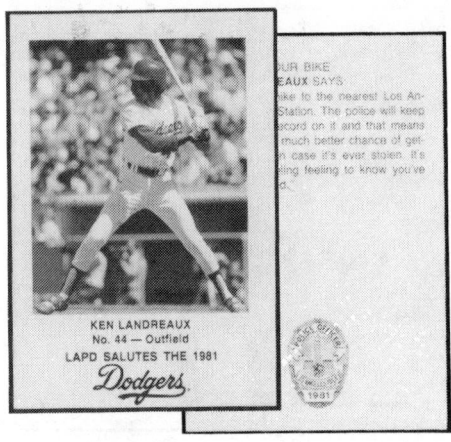

UR BIKE
EAUX SAYS

ike to the nearest Los An-
Station. The police will keep
cord on it and that means
much better chance of get-
n case it's ever stolen. It's
ing feeling to know you've
d.

KEN LANDREAUX
No. 44 — Outfield
LAPD SALUTES THE 1981
Dodgers

Coke and Hostess, and Tips from the Braves. It is reported that 33,000 of these sets were printed. The Terry Harper card is supposed to be more difficult to obtain than other cards in the set.

|  | | MINT | VG-E | F-G |
|---|---|---|---|---|
| COMPLETE SET | | 12.00 | 5.00 | 1.20 |
| COMMON PLAYER | | .30 | .12 | .03 |

| | | | MINT | VG-E | F-G |
|---|---|---|---|---|---|
| ☐ | 1 | Jerry Royster | .30 | .12 | .03 |
| ☐ | 3 | Dale Murphy | 3.50 | 1.40 | .35 |
| ☐ | 4 | Biff Pocoroba | .30 | .12 | .03 |
| ☐ | 5 | Bob Horner | 1.25 | .50 | .12 |
| ☐ | 6 | Bobby Cox MGR | .30 | .12 | .03 |
| ☐ | 9 | Luis Gomez | .30 | .12 | .03 |
| ☐ | 10 | Chris Chambliss | .40 | .16 | .04 |
| ☐ | 15 | Bill Nahorodny | .30 | .12 | .03 |
| ☐ | 16 | Rafael Ramirez | .40 | .16 | .04 |
| ☐ | 17 | Glenn Hubbard | .40 | .16 | .04 |
| ☐ | 18 | Claudell Washington | .50 | .20 | .05 |
| ☐ | 19 | Terry Harper | .75 | .30 | .07 |
| ☐ | 20 | Bruce Benedict | .30 | .12 | .03 |
| ☐ | 24 | John Montefusco | .40 | .16 | .04 |
| ☐ | 25 | Rufino Linares | .30 | .12 | .03 |
| ☐ | 26 | Gene Garber | .40 | .16 | .04 |
| ☐ | 30 | Brian Asselstine | .30 | .12 | .03 |
| ☐ | 34 | Larry Bradford | .30 | .12 | .03 |
| ☐ | 35 | Phil Niekro | 1.50 | .60 | .15 |
| ☐ | 37 | Rick Camp | .30 | .12 | .03 |
| ☐ | 39 | Al Hrabosky | .50 | .20 | .05 |
| ☐ | 40 | Tommy Boggs | .30 | .12 | .03 |
| ☐ | 42 | Rick Mahler | .40 | .16 | .04 |
| ☐ | 44 | Hank Aaron CO | 2.50 | 1.00 | .25 |
| ☐ | 45 | Ed Miller | .30 | .12 | .03 |
| ☐ | 46 | Gaylord Perry | 1.50 | .60 | .15 |
| ☐ | 49 | Preston Hanna | .30 | .12 | .03 |

## 1981 Police Dodgers

The cards in this 32 card set measure 2 13/16" by 4 1/8". The full color set of 1981 Los Angeles Dodgers features the player's name, number, position and a line stating that the LAPD salutes the 1981 Dodgers, in addition to the player's photo. The backs feature the LAPD logo and short narratives, attributable to the player on the front of the card, revealing police associated tips. The cards of Ken Landreaux and Dave Stewart are reported to be more difficult to obtain than other cards in this set due to the fact that they are replacements for Stanhouse (released 4/17/81) and Hatcher (traded for Landreaux 3/30/81). The complete set price below refers to all 32 cards, i.e., including the variations.

|  | | MINT | VG-E | F-G |
|---|---|---|---|---|
| COMPLETE SET (32) | | 10.00 | 4.00 | 1.00 |
| COMMON PLAYER | | .25 | .10 | .02 |

| | | | MINT | VG-E | F-G |
|---|---|---|---|---|---|
| ☐ | 2 | Tom Lasorda MGR | .40 | .16 | .04 |
| ☐ | 3 | Rudy Law | .25 | .10 | .02 |
| ☐ | 6 | Steve Garvey | 1.25 | .50 | .12 |
| ☐ | 7 | Steve Yeager | .30 | .12 | .03 |
| ☐ | 8 | Reggie Smith | .35 | .14 | .03 |
| ☐ | 10 | Ron Cey | .45 | .18 | .04 |
| ☐ | 12 | Dusty Baker | .35 | .14 | .03 |
| ☐ | 13 | Joe Ferguson | .25 | .10 | .02 |
| ☐ | 14 | Mike Scioscia | .25 | .10 | .02 |
| ☐ | 15 | Davey Lopes | .35 | .14 | .03 |
| ☐ | 16 | Rick Monday | .30 | .12 | .03 |
| ☐ | 18 | Bill Russell | .35 | .14 | .03 |
| ☐ | 21 | Jay Johnstone | .30 | .12 | .03 |
| ☐ | 26 | Don Stanhouse | .40 | .16 | .04 |
| ☐ | 27 | Joe Beckwith | .25 | .10 | .02 |
| ☐ | 28 | Pedro Guerrero | 1.00 | .40 | .10 |
| ☐ | 30 | Derrel Thomas | .25 | .10 | .02 |
| ☐ | 34 | Fernando Valenzuela | 2.50 | 1.00 | .25 |
| ☐ | 35 | Bob Welch | .40 | .16 | .04 |
| ☐ | 36 | Pepe Frias | .25 | .10 | .02 |
| ☐ | 37 | Robert Castillo | .25 | .10 | .02 |
| ☐ | 38 | Dave Goltz | .25 | .10 | .02 |
| ☐ | 41 | Jerry Reuss | .35 | .14 | .03 |
| ☐ | 43 | Rick Sutcliffe | .60 | .24 | .06 |
| ☐ | 44A | Mickey Hatcher | .35 | .14 | .03 |
| ☐ | 44B | Ken Landreaux | 1.00 | .40 | .10 |
| ☐ | 46 | Burt Hooton | .30 | .12 | .03 |
| ☐ | 48 | Dave Stewart | 1.00 | .40 | .10 |
| ☐ | 51 | Terry Forster | .45 | .18 | .04 |
| ☐ | 57 | Steve Howe | .30 | .12 | .03 |
| ☐ | xx | Team Photo (Checklist) .... (unnumbered) | .30 | .12 | .03 |
| ☐ | xx | Coaching Staff (unnumbered) | .25 | .10 | .02 |

## 1981 Police Mariners

The cards in this 16 card set measure 2 5/8" by 4 1/8". The full color Seattle Mariners Police set of this year was sponsored by the Washington State Crime Prevention Association, the Kiwanis Club, Coca-Cola and Ernst Home Centers. The fronts feature the player's name, his position, and the Seattle Mariners name in addition to the player's photo. The backs, in red and blue, feature Tips from the Mariners and the logos of the four sponsors of the set. The cards are numbered in the lower left corners of the backs.

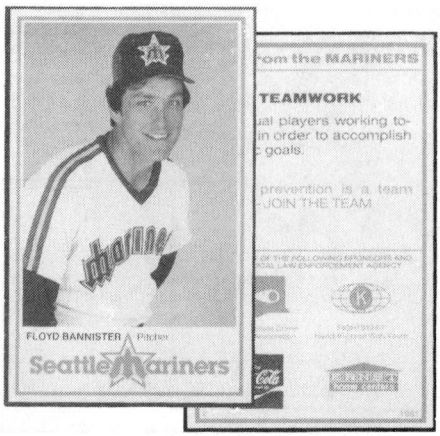

FLOYD BANNISTER / Pitcher

Seattle Mariners

| | MINT | VG-E | F-G |
|---|---|---|---|
| COMPLETE SET | 5.00 | 2.00 | .50 |
| COMMON PLAYER | .30 | .12 | .03 |
| ☐ 1 Jeff Burroughs | .40 | .16 | .04 |
| ☐ 2 Floyd Bannister | .40 | .16 | .04 |
| ☐ 3 Glenn Abbott | .30 | .12 | .03 |
| ☐ 4 Jim Anderson | .30 | .12 | .03 |
| ☐ 5 Danny Meyer | .30 | .12 | .03 |
| ☐ 6 Julio Cruz | .40 | .16 | .04 |
| ☐ 7 Dave Edler | .30 | .12 | .03 |
| ☐ 8 Kenny Clay | .30 | .12 | .03 |
| ☐ 9 Lenny Randle | .30 | .12 | .03 |
| ☐ 10 Mike Parrott | .30 | .12 | .03 |
| ☐ 11 Tom Paciorek | .40 | .16 | .04 |
| ☐ 12 Jerry Narron | .30 | .12 | .03 |
| ☐ 13 Richie Zisk | .40 | .16 | .04 |
| ☐ 14 Maury Wills MGR | .75 | .30 | .07 |
| ☐ 15 Joe Simpson | .30 | .12 | .03 |
| ☐ 16 Shane Rawley | .60 | .24 | .06 |

## 1981 Police Royals

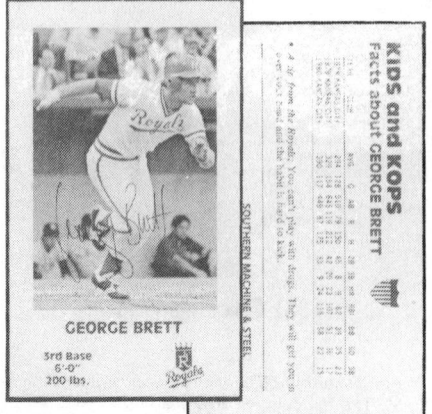

GEORGE BRETT

3rd Base
6'-0"
200 lbs.

The cards in this 10 card set measure 2 1/2" by 4 1/8". The 1981 Police Kansas City Royals set features full color cards of Royals players. The fronts feature the player's name, position, height and weight, and the Royals' logo in addition to the photo and facsimile autograph of the player. The backs feature player statistics, Tips from the Royals, and identification of the sponsoring organizations.

| | MINT | VG-E | F-G |
|---|---|---|---|
| COMPLETE SET | 30.00 | 12.00 | 3.00 |
| COMMON PLAYER | 2.00 | .80 | .20 |
| ☐ 1 Willie Aikens | 2.00 | .80 | .20 |
| ☐ 2 George Brett | 12.00 | 5.00 | 1.20 |
| ☐ 3 Rich Gale | 2.00 | .80 | .20 |
| ☐ 4 Clint Hurdle | 2.00 | .80 | .20 |
| ☐ 5 Dennis Leonard | 2.50 | 1.00 | .25 |
| ☐ 6 Hal McRae | 2.50 | 1.00 | .25 |
| ☐ 7 Amos Otis | 2.50 | 1.00 | .25 |
| ☐ 8 U.L. Washington | 2.00 | .80 | .20 |
| ☐ 9 Frank White | 3.50 | 1.40 | .35 |
| ☐ 10 Willie Wilson | 4.50 | 1.80 | .45 |

## 1982 Police Braves

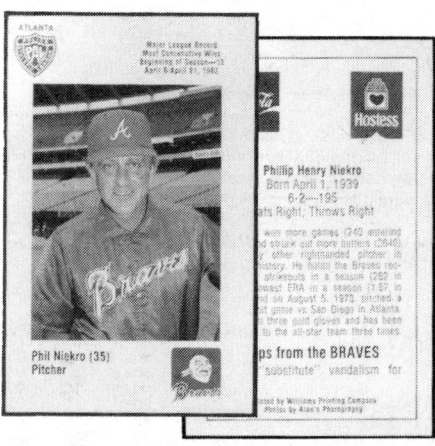

Phil Niekro (35)
Pitcher

The cards in this 30 card set measure 2 5/8" by 4 1/8". The Atlanta Police Department followed up on their successful 1981 safety set by publishing a new Braves set for 1982. Featured in excellent color photos are manager Joe Torre, 24 players, and 5 coaches. The cards are numbered, by uniform number, on the front only, while the backs contain a short biography of the individual and a Tips from the Braves section. The logos for the Atlanta PAL and the Braves appear on the front; those of Coca-Cola and Hostess are found on the back. A line commemorating Atlanta's record-shattering, season-beginning win streak is located in the upper right corner on every card obverse. The player list on the reverse of the Torre card is a roster list and not a checklist for the set. There were 8,000 sets reportedly printed. The Bob Watson card is supposedly more difficult to obtain than others in this set.

| | MINT | VG-E | F-G |
|---|---|---|---|
| COMPLETE SET | 18.00 | 7.25 | 1.80 |
| COMMON PLAYER | .35 | .14 | .03 |
| ☐ 1 Jerry Royster | .35 | .14 | .03 |
| ☐ 3 Dale Murphy | 5.00 | 2.00 | .50 |
| ☐ 4 Biff Pocoroba | .35 | .14 | .03 |
| ☐ 5 Bob Horner | 1.50 | .60 | .15 |
| ☐ 6 Randy Johnson | .35 | .14 | .03 |
| ☐ 8 Bob Watson | 1.50 | .60 | .15 |
| ☐ 9 Joe Torre MGR | .60 | .24 | .06 |
| ☐ 10 Chris Chambliss | .40 | .16 | .04 |
| ☐ 15 Claudell Washington | .50 | .20 | .05 |
| ☐ 16 Rafael Ramirez | .40 | .16 | .04 |
| ☐ 17 Glenn Hubbard | .40 | .16 | .04 |
| ☐ 20 Bruce Benedict | .35 | .14 | .03 |
| ☐ 22 Brett Butler | 1.00 | .40 | .10 |
| ☐ 23 Tommy Aaron CO | .45 | .18 | .04 |
| ☐ 25 Rufino Linares | .35 | .14 | .03 |

| | | MINT | VG-E | F-G |
|---|---|---|---|---|
| ☐ 26 | Gene Garber | .35 | .14 | .03 |
| ☐ 27 | Larry McWilliams | .50 | .20 | .05 |
| ☐ 28 | Larry Whisenton | .35 | .14 | .03 |
| ☐ 32 | Steve Bedrosian | .50 | .20 | .05 |
| ☐ 35 | Phil Niekro | 2.00 | .80 | .20 |
| ☐ 37 | Rick Camp | .35 | .14 | .03 |
| ☐ 38 | Joe Cowley | .45 | .18 | .04 |
| ☐ 39 | Al Hrabosky | .45 | .18 | .04 |
| ☐ 42 | Rick Mahler | .45 | .18 | .04 |
| ☐ 43 | Bob Walk | .35 | .14 | .03 |
| ☐ 45 | Bob Gibson CO | 1.50 | .60 | .15 |
| ☐ 49 | Preston Hanna | .35 | .14 | .03 |
| ☐ 52 | Joe Pignatano CO | .35 | .14 | .03 |
| ☐ 53 | Dal Maxvill CO | .35 | .14 | .03 |
| ☐ 54 | Rube Walker CO | .35 | .14 | .03 |

## 1982 Police Brewers

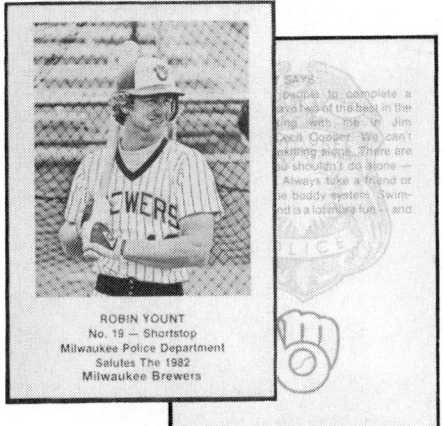

ROBIN YOUNT
No. 19 — Shortstop
Milwaukee Police Department
Salutes The 1982
Milwaukee Brewers

The cards in this 30 card set measure 2 13/16" by 4 1/8". The 1982 series of 30 Milwaukee Brewers baseball cards is noted for its excellent color photographs set upon a simple white background. The set was initially distributed at the stadium on May 5th, but was also handed out by several local police departments, and credit lines for the Wisconsin State Fair Park Police (no shield design on reverse), Milwaukee, Brookfield, and Wauwatosa PD's have already been found. The reverses feature advice concerning safety measures, social situations, and crime prevention (Romero card in both Spanish and English). The team card carries a checklist which lists the Brewer's coaches separately although they all appear on a single card; VP/GM Harry Dalton is not mentioned on this list but is included in the set.The prices below are for the basic set without regard to the Police Department listed on the backs. Cards from the more obscure corners and small towns of Wisconsin (where fewer cards were produced) will be valued higher.

| | | MINT | VG-E | F-G |
|---|---|---|---|---|
| | COMPLETE SET | 9.00 | 3.75 | .90 |
| | COMMON PLAYER | .25 | .10 | .02 |
| | | | | |
| ☐ 4 | Paul Molitor | .60 | .24 | .06 |
| ☐ 5 | Ned Yost | .25 | .10 | .02 |
| ☐ 7 | Don Money | .35 | .14 | .03 |
| ☐ 9 | Larry Hisle | .35 | .14 | .03 |
| ☐ 10 | Bob McClure | .25 | .10 | .02 |
| ☐ 11 | Ed Romero | .25 | .10 | .02 |
| ☐ 13 | Roy Howell | .25 | .10 | .02 |
| ☐ 15 | Cecil Cooper | .50 | .20 | .05 |
| ☐ 17 | Jim Gantner | .35 | .14 | .03 |

| | | MINT | VG-E | F-G |
|---|---|---|---|---|
| ☐ 19 | Robin Yount | 1.50 | .60 | .15 |
| ☐ 20 | Gorman Thomas | .50 | .20 | .05 |
| ☐ 22 | Charlie Moore | .30 | .12 | .03 |
| ☐ 23 | Ted Simmons | .50 | .20 | .05 |
| ☐ 24 | Ben Oglivie | .35 | .14 | .03 |
| ☐ 26 | Kevin Bass | .50 | .20 | .05 |
| ☐ 28 | Jamie Easterly | .25 | .10 | .02 |
| ☐ 29 | Mark Brouhard | .25 | .10 | .02 |
| ☐ 30 | Moose Haas | .35 | .14 | .03 |
| ☐ 34 | Rollie Fingers | .75 | .30 | .07 |
| ☐ 35 | Randy Lerch | .25 | .10 | .02 |
| ☐ 41 | Jim Slaton | .35 | .14 | .03 |
| ☐ 45 | Doug Jones | .25 | .10 | .02 |
| ☐ 46 | Jerry Augustine | .25 | .10 | .02 |
| ☐ 47 | Dwight Bernard | .25 | .10 | .02 |
| ☐ 48 | Mike Caldwell | .35 | .14 | .03 |
| ☐ 50 | Pete Vuckovich | .40 | .16 | .04 |
| ☐ xx | Team Card (unnumbered) | .25 | .10 | .02 |
| ☐ xx | Harry Dalton GM (unnumbered) | .25 | .10 | .02 |
| ☐ xx | Buck Rodgers MGR (unnumbered) | .25 | .10 | .02 |
| ☐ xx | Brewer Coaches (unnumbered) | .25 | .10 | .02 |

## 1982 Police Dodgers

STEVE GARVEY
No. 6 — FIRST BASE
The Los Angeles Police Department
presents the World Champion
*Dodgers*

The cards in this 30 card set measure 2 13/16" by 4 1/8". The 1982 Los Angeles Dodgers police set depicts the players and events of the 1981 season. There is a World Series trophy card, three cards commemorating the Division, League, and World Series wins, one manager card, and 25 player cards. The obverses have brilliant color photos set on white, and the player cards are numbered according to the uniform number of the individual. The reverses contain biographical material, information about stadium events, and a safety feature emphasizing "the team that wouldn't quit."

| | | MINT | VG-E | F-G |
|---|---|---|---|---|
| | COMPLETE SET | 6.00 | 2.40 | .60 |
| | COMMON PLAYER | .18 | .08 | .01 |
| | | | | |
| ☐ 2 | Tom Lasorda MGR | .25 | .10 | .02 |
| ☐ 6 | Steve Garvey | 1.00 | .40 | .10 |
| ☐ 7 | Steve Yeager | .25 | .10 | .02 |
| ☐ 8 | Mark Belanger | .25 | .10 | .02 |
| ☐ 10 | Ron Cey | .40 | .16 | .04 |
| ☐ 12 | Dusty Baker | .30 | .12 | .03 |
| ☐ 14 | Mike Scioscia | .18 | .08 | .01 |
| ☐ 16 | Rick Monday | .25 | .10 | .02 |
| ☐ 18 | Bill Russell | .25 | .10 | .02 |
| ☐ 21 | Jay Johnstone | .25 | .10 | .02 |
| ☐ 26 | Alejandro Pena | .35 | .14 | .03 |
| ☐ 28 | Pedro Guerrero | 1.00 | .40 | .10 |

| | | MINT | VG-E | F-G |
|---|---|---|---|---|
| ☐ 30 | Derrel Thomas | .18 | .08 | .01 |
| ☐ 31 | Jorge Orta | .18 | .08 | .01 |
| ☐ 34 | Fernando Valenzuela | 1.00 | .40 | .10 |
| ☐ 35 | Bob Welch | .35 | .14 | .03 |
| ☐ 38 | Dave Goltz | .18 | .08 | .01 |
| ☐ 40 | Ron Roenicke | .18 | .08 | .01 |
| ☐ 41 | Jerry Reuss | .30 | .12 | .03 |
| ☐ 44 | Ken Landreaux | .18 | .08 | .01 |
| ☐ 46 | Burt Hooton | .25 | .10 | .02 |
| ☐ 48 | Dave Stewart | .18 | .08 | .01 |
| ☐ 49 | Tom Niedenfuer | .35 | .14 | .03 |
| ☐ 51 | Terry Forster | .35 | .14 | .03 |
| ☐ 52 | Steve Sax | .75 | .30 | .07 |
| ☐ 57 | Steve Howe | .25 | .10 | .02 |
| ☐ xx | World Series Trophy (checklist back) (unnumbered) | .25 | .10 | .02 |
| ☐ xx | World Series Commemorative (unnumbered) | .25 | .10 | .02 |
| ☐ xx | NL Champions (unnumbered) | .25 | .10 | .02 |
| ☐ xx | Division Champs (unnumbered) | .25 | .10 | .02 |

| | | | | |
|---|---|---|---|---|
| ☐ 20 | Bruce Benedict | .35 | .14 | .03 |
| ☐ 22 | Brett Butler | .75 | .30 | .07 |
| ☐ 24 | Larry Owen | .35 | .14 | .03 |
| ☐ 26 | Gene Garber | .35 | .14 | .03 |
| ☐ 27 | Pascual Perez | .35 | .14 | .03 |
| ☐ 29 | Craig McMurtry | .35 | .14 | .03 |
| ☐ 32 | Steve Bedrosian | .50 | .20 | .05 |
| ☐ 33 | Pete Falcone | .35 | .14 | .03 |
| ☐ 35 | Phil Niekro | 1.50 | .60 | .15 |
| ☐ 36 | Sonny Jackson | .35 | .14 | .03 |
| ☐ 37 | Rick Camp | .35 | .14 | .03 |
| ☐ 45 | Bob Gibson CO | 1.50 | .60 | .15 |
| ☐ 49 | Rick Behenna | .35 | .14 | .03 |
| ☐ 51 | Terry Forster | .50 | .20 | .05 |
| ☐ 52 | Joe Pignatano CO | .35 | .14 | .03 |
| ☐ 53 | Dal Maxvill CO | .35 | .14 | .03 |
| ☐ 54 | Rube Walker CO | .35 | .14 | .03 |

## 1983 Police Braves

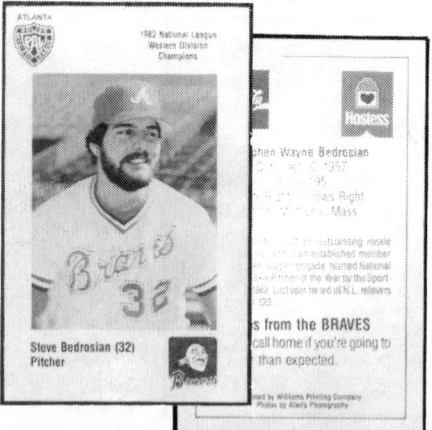

Steve Bedrosian (32)
Pitcher

The cards in this 30 card set measure 2 5/8" by 4 1/8". For the third year in a row, the Atlanta Braves, in cooperation with the Atlanta Police Department, Coca-Cola, and Hostess, issued a full color safety set. The set features Joe Torre, five coaches, and 24 of the Atlanta Braves. Numbered only by uniform number, the statement that the Braves were the 1982 National League Western Division Champions is included on the fronts along with the Braves and Police Athletic biographies, a short narrative on the player, Tips from the Braves, and the Coke and Hostess logos.

| | | MINT | VG-E | F-G |
|---|---|---|---|---|
| COMPLETE SET | | 14.00 | 5.75 | 1.40 |
| COMMON PLAYER | | .35 | .14 | .03 |
| ☐ 1 | Jerry Royster | .35 | .14 | .03 |
| ☐ 3 | Dale Murphy | 4.00 | 1.60 | .40 |
| ☐ 4 | Biff Pocoroba | .35 | .14 | .03 |
| ☐ 5 | Bob Horner | 1.25 | .50 | .12 |
| ☐ 6 | Randy Johnson | .35 | .14 | .03 |
| ☐ 8 | Bob Watson | .40 | .16 | .04 |
| ☐ 9 | Joe Torre MGR | .50 | .20 | .05 |
| ☐ 10 | Chris Chambliss | .40 | .16 | .04 |
| ☐ 11 | Ken Smith | .35 | .14 | .03 |
| ☐ 15 | Claudell Washington | .50 | .20 | .05 |
| ☐ 16 | Rafael Ramirez | .40 | .16 | .04 |
| ☐ 17 | Glenn Hubbard | .40 | .16 | .04 |
| ☐ 19 | Terry Harper | .35 | .14 | .03 |

## 1983 Police Brewers

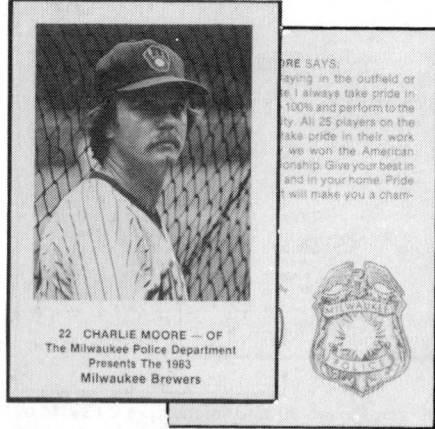

22 CHARLIE MOORE — OF
The Milwaukee Police Department
Presents The 1983
Milwaukee Brewers

The cards in this 30 card set measure 2 13/16" by 4 1/8". The 1983 Police Milwaukee Brewers set contains full color cards issued by the Milwaukee Police Department in conjunction with the Brewers. The cards are numbered on the fronts by the player uniform number and contain the line, "The Milwaukee Police Department Presents the 1983 Milwaukee Braves." The backs contain a brief narrative attributable to the player on the front, the Milwaukee Police logo, and a Milwaukee Brewers logo stating that they were the 1982 American League Champions. In all, 28 variations of these Police sets have been found to date. Prices below are for the basic set without regard to the Police Department listed on the backs of the cards; cards from the more obscure corners and small towns of Wisconsin (whose cards were produced in lesser quantities) will be valued higher.

| | | MINT | VG-E | F-G |
|---|---|---|---|---|
| COMPLETE SET | | 7.00 | 2.80 | .70 |
| COMMON PLAYER | | .20 | .08 | .02 |
| ☐ xx | Dave Garcia COACH | .20 | .08 | .02 |
| ☐ 4 | Paul Molitor | .50 | .20 | .05 |
| ☐ 5 | Ned Yost | .20 | .08 | .02 |
| ☐ 7 | Don Money | .25 | .10 | .02 |
| ☐ 8 | Rob Picciolo | .20 | .08 | .02 |
| ☐ 10 | Bob McClure | .20 | .08 | .02 |
| ☐ 11 | Ed Romero | .20 | .08 | .02 |
| ☐ 12 | Larry Haney COACH | .20 | .08 | .02 |
| ☐ 13 | Roy Howell | .20 | .08 | .02 |
| ☐ 15 | Cecil Cooper | .50 | .20 | .05 |
| ☐ 16 | Marshall Edwards | .20 | .08 | .02 |
| ☐ 17 | Jim Gantner | .30 | .12 | .03 |

| | | MINT | VG-E | F-G |
|---|---|---|---|---|
| ☐ 18 | Ron Hansen COACH | .20 | .08 | .02 |
| ☐ 19 | Robin Yount | 1.00 | .40 | .10 |
| ☐ 20 | Gorman Thomas | .40 | .16 | .04 |
| ☐ 21 | Don Sutton | .75 | .30 | .07 |
| ☐ 22 | Charlie Moore | .25 | .10 | .02 |
| ☐ 23 | Ted Simmons | .50 | .20 | .05 |
| ☐ 24 | Ben Oglivie | .40 | .16 | .04 |
| ☐ 26 | Bob Skube | .20 | .08 | .02 |
| ☐ 27 | Pete Ladd | .20 | .08 | .02 |
| ☐ 28 | Jamie Easterly | .20 | .08 | .02 |
| ☐ 30 | Moose Haas | .25 | .10 | .02 |
| ☐ 32 | Harvey Kuenn MGR | .35 | .14 | .03 |
| ☐ 34 | Rollie Fingers | .60 | .24 | .06 |
| ☐ 40 | Bob L. Gibson | .20 | .08 | .02 |
| ☐ 41 | Jim Slaton | .20 | .08 | .02 |
| ☐ 42 | Tom Tellmann | .20 | .08 | .02 |
| ☐ 45 | Pat Dobson COACH | .20 | .08 | .02 |
| ☐ 46 | Jerry Augustine | .20 | .08 | .02 |
| ☐ 48 | Mike Caldwell | .25 | .10 | .02 |
| ☐ 50 | Pete Vuckovich | .35 | .14 | .03 |
| ☐ xx | Team Photo | .25 | .10 | .02 |
| | (Checklist back) | | | |
| | (unnumbered) | | | |

| | | MINT | VG-E | F-G |
|---|---|---|---|---|
| ☐ 35 | Bob Welch | .20 | .08 | .02 |
| ☐ 38 | Pat Zachry | .15 | .06 | .01 |
| ☐ 40 | Ron Roenicke | .15 | .06 | .01 |
| ☐ 41 | Jerry Reuss | .20 | .08 | .02 |
| ☐ 43 | Jose Morales | .15 | .06 | .01 |
| ☐ 44 | Ken Landreaux | .15 | .06 | .01 |
| ☐ 46 | Burt Hooton | .15 | .06 | .01 |
| ☐ 47 | Larry White | .15 | .06 | .01 |
| ☐ 48 | Dave Stewart | .15 | .06 | .01 |
| ☐ 49 | Tom Niedenfuer | .25 | .10 | .02 |
| ☐ 57 | Steve Howe | .25 | .10 | .02 |
| ☐ xx | Coaching Staff | .15 | .06 | .01 |
| | (unnumbered) | | | |

## 1983 Police Dodgers

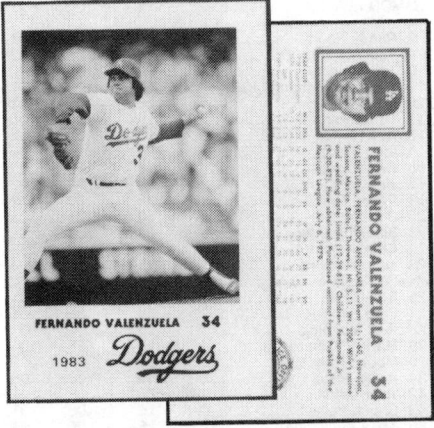

The cards in this 30 card set measure 2 13/16" by 4 1/8". The full color Police Los Angeles Dodgers set of 1983 features the player's name and uniform number on the front along with the Dodger's logo, the year, and the player's photo. The backs feature a small insert portrait picture of the player, player biographies, and career statistics. The logo of the Los Angeles Police Department, the sponsor of the set, is found on the backs of the cards.

| | | MINT | VG-E | F-G |
|---|---|---|---|---|
| COMPLETE SET | | 5.00 | 2.00 | .50 |
| COMMON PLAYER | | .15 | .06 | .01 |
| ☐ 2 | Tom Lasorda MGR | .20 | .08 | .02 |
| ☐ 3 | Steve Sax | .50 | .20 | .05 |
| ☐ 5 | Mike Marshall | .60 | .24 | .06 |
| ☐ 7 | Steve Yeager | .15 | .06 | .01 |
| ☐ 12 | Dusty Baker | .25 | .10 | .02 |
| ☐ 14 | Mike Scioscia | .15 | .06 | .01 |
| ☐ 16 | Rick Monday | .20 | .08 | .02 |
| ☐ 17 | Greg Brock | .30 | .12 | .03 |
| ☐ 18 | Bill Russell | .20 | .08 | .02 |
| ☐ 20 | Candy Maldonado | .25 | .10 | .02 |
| ☐ 21 | Ricky Wright | .15 | .06 | .01 |
| ☐ 22 | Mark Bradley | .20 | .08 | .02 |
| ☐ 23 | Dave Sax | .15 | .06 | .01 |
| ☐ 26 | Alejandro Pena | .20 | .08 | .02 |
| ☐ 27 | Joe Beckwith | .15 | .06 | .01 |
| ☐ 28 | Pedro Guerrero | .75 | .30 | .07 |
| ☐ 30 | Derrel Thomas | .15 | .06 | .01 |
| ☐ 34 | Fernando Valenzuela | .75 | .30 | .07 |

## 1983 Police Royals

The cards in this 10 card set measure 2 1/2" by 4 1/8". The 1983 Police Kansas City Royals set features full color cards of Royals players. The fronts feature the player's name, height and weight, and the Royals' logo in addition to the player's photo and a facsimile autograph. The backs feature Kids and Cops Facts about the players, Tips from the Royals, and identification of the sponsors of the set. The cards are unnumbered.

| | | MINT | VG-E | F-G |
|---|---|---|---|---|
| COMPLETE SET | | 25.00 | 10.00 | 2.50 |
| COMMON PLAYER | | 1.50 | .60 | .15 |
| ☐ 1 | Willie Aikens | 1.50 | .60 | .15 |
| ☐ 2 | George Brett | 10.00 | 4.00 | 1.00 |
| ☐ 3 | Dennis Leonard | 2.00 | .80 | .20 |
| ☐ 4 | Hal McRae | 2.00 | .80 | .20 |
| ☐ 5 | Amos Otis | 2.00 | .80 | .20 |
| ☐ 6 | Dan Quisenberry | 3.50 | 1.40 | .35 |
| ☐ 7 | U.L. Washington | 1.50 | .60 | .15 |
| ☐ 8 | John Wathan | 1.50 | .60 | .15 |
| ☐ 9 | Frank White | 3.00 | 1.20 | .30 |
| ☐ 10 | Willie Wilson | 3.50 | 1.40 | .35 |

## 1984 Police Braves

The cards in this 30 card set measure 2 5/8" by 4 1/8". For the fourth straight year, the Atlanta Police Department issued a full color set of Atlanta Braves. The cards were given out two per week by Atlanta police officers. In addition to the police department, the set was sponsored by Coke and Hostess. The backs of the cards of Perez and Ramirez are in Spanish. The Joe Torre card contains the checklist.

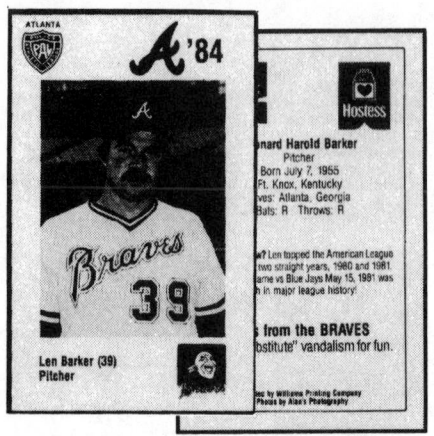

17 JIM GANTNER — IF
The Milwaukee Police Department
Presents The 1984
MILWAUKEE BREWERS

|  |  |  | MINT | VG-E | F-G |
|---|---|---|---|---|---|
|  | COMPLETE SET | | 12.00 | 5.00 | 1.20 |
|  | COMMON PLAYER | | .35 | .14 | .03 |
| ☐ | 1 | Jerry Royster | .35 | .14 | .03 |
| ☐ | 3 | Dale Murphy | 4.00 | 1.60 | .40 |
| ☐ | 5 | Bob Horner | 1.25 | .50 | .12 |
| ☐ | 6 | Randy Johnson | .35 | .14 | .03 |
| ☐ | 8 | Bob Watson | .40 | .16 | .04 |
| ☐ | 9 | Joe Torre MGR | .50 | .20 | .05 |
|  |  | (checklist back) |  |  |  |
| ☐ | 10 | Chris Chambliss | .40 | .16 | .04 |
| ☐ | 11 | Mike Jorgensen | .35 | .14 | .03 |
| ☐ | 15 | Claudell Washington | .50 | .20 | .05 |
| ☐ | 16 | Rafael Ramirez | .40 | .16 | .04 |
| ☐ | 17 | Glenn Hubbard | .40 | .16 | .04 |
| ☐ | 19 | Terry Harper | .35 | .14 | .03 |
| ☐ | 20 | Bruce Benedict | .35 | .14 | .03 |
| ☐ | 25 | Alex Trevino | .35 | .14 | .03 |
| ☐ | 26 | Gene Garber | .35 | .14 | .03 |
| ☐ | 27 | Pascual Perez | .35 | .14 | .03 |
| ☐ | 28 | Gerald Perry | .40 | .16 | .04 |
| ☐ | 29 | Craig McMurtry | .35 | .14 | .03 |
| ☐ | 31 | Donnie Moore | .50 | .20 | .05 |
| ☐ | 32 | Steve Bedrosian | .40 | .16 | .04 |
| ☐ | 33 | Pete Falcone | .35 | .14 | .03 |
| ☐ | 37 | Rick Camp | .35 | .14 | .03 |
| ☐ | 39 | Len Barker | .40 | .16 | .04 |
| ☐ | 42 | Rick Mahler | .40 | .16 | .04 |
| ☐ | 45 | Bob Gibson COACH | 1.25 | .50 | .12 |
| ☐ | 51 | Terry Forster | .50 | .20 | .05 |
| ☐ | 52 | Joe Pignatano COACH | .35 | .14 | .03 |
| ☐ | 53 | Dal Maxvill COACH | .35 | .14 | .03 |
| ☐ | 54 | Rube Walker COACH | .35 | .14 | .03 |
| ☐ | 55 | Luke Appling COACH | .50 | .20 | .05 |

|  |  |  | MINT | VG-E | F-G |
|---|---|---|---|---|---|
|  | COMPLETE SET | | 5.00 | 2.00 | .50 |
|  | COMMON PLAYER | | .15 | .06 | .01 |
| ☐ | 2 | Randy Ready | .15 | .06 | .01 |
| ☐ | 4 | Paul Molitor | .35 | .14 | .03 |
| ☐ | 8 | Jim Sundberg | .20 | .08 | .02 |
| ☐ | 9 | Rene Lachemann MGR | .15 | .06 | .01 |
| ☐ | 10 | Bob McClure | .15 | .06 | .01 |
| ☐ | 11 | Ed Romero | .15 | .06 | .01 |
| ☐ | 13 | Roy Howell | .15 | .06 | .01 |
| ☐ | 14 | Dion James | .25 | .10 | .02 |
| ☐ | 15 | Cecil Cooper | .50 | .20 | .05 |
| ☐ | 17 | Jim Gantner | .20 | .08 | .02 |
| ☐ | 19 | Robin Yount | .75 | .30 | .07 |
| ☐ | 20 | Don Sutton | .60 | .24 | .06 |
| ☐ | 21 | Bill Schroeder | .20 | .08 | .02 |
| ☐ | 22 | Charlie Moore | .20 | .08 | .02 |
| ☐ | 23 | Ted Simmons | .35 | .14 | .03 |
| ☐ | 24 | Ben Oglivie | .25 | .10 | .02 |
| ☐ | 25 | Bob Clark | .15 | .06 | .01 |
| ☐ | 27 | Pete Ladd | .15 | .06 | .01 |
| ☐ | 28 | Rick Manning | .15 | .06 | .01 |
| ☐ | 29 | Mark Brouhard | .15 | .06 | .01 |
| ☐ | 30 | Moose Haas | .20 | .08 | .02 |
| ☐ | 34 | Rollie Fingers | .50 | .20 | .05 |
| ☐ | 42 | Tom Tellmann | .15 | .06 | .01 |
| ☐ | 43 | Chuck Porter | .15 | .06 | .01 |
| ☐ | 46 | Jerry Augustine | .15 | .06 | .01 |
| ☐ | 47 | Jaime Cocanower | .15 | .06 | .01 |
| ☐ | 48 | Mike Caldwell | .20 | .08 | .02 |
| ☐ | 50 | Pete Vuckovich | .25 | .10 | .02 |
| ☐ | xx | Coaches Card | .20 | .08 | .02 |
|  |  | (unnumbered) |  |  |  |
| ☐ | xx | Team Photo | .20 | .08 | .02 |
|  |  | (Checklist back) |  |  |  |
|  |  | (unnumbered) |  |  |  |

## 1984 Police Brewers

The cards in this 30 card set measure 2 13/16" by 4 1/8". Again this year, the police departments in and around Milwaukee issued sets of the Milwaukee Brewers. Although each set contained the same players and numbers, the individual police departments placed their own name on the fronts of cards to show that they were the particular jurisdiction issuing the set. The backs contain the Brewers logo, a safety tip, and in some cases, a badge of the jurisdiction. To date, 59 variations of this set have been found. Prices below are for the basic set without regard to the Police Department issuing the cards; cards from the more obscure corners and small towns of Wisconsin will be valued higher. Cards are numbered by uniform number.

## 1984 Police Dodgers

The cards in this 30 card set measure 2 13/16" by 4 1/8". For the fifth straight year, the Los Angeles Police Department sponsored a set of Dodger baseball cards. The set is numbered by player uniform number, which is featured on both the fronts and backs of the cards. The Dodgers' logo appears on the front, and the LAPD logo is superimposed on the backs of the cards. The backs are printed in Dodger blue ink and contain a small photo of the player on the front. Player biographical data and "Dare to Say No" antidrug information are featured on the back.

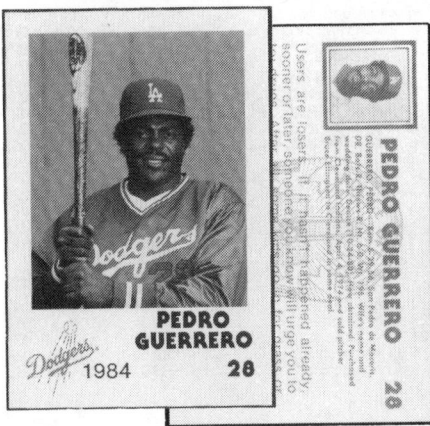

**Howard Bruce Sutter**
Pitcher
Born January 8, 1953
Lancaster, Pa.
Lives: Kennesaw, Ga.
Bats: R   Throws: R

**Did You Know?** With his devastating split-fingered fastball, Bruce has led the N.L. in saves every year but one since 1978! In fact, last season with the Cardinals, he set a new N.L. record with 45!

**Tips from the BRAVES**
Don't show off with your money. When you are going anywhere with money, don't flash your cash. Leave it in your pocket.

Printed by Williams Printing Company
Photos by Alan's Photography

Bruce Sutter (40)
Pitcher

|  |  | MINT | VG-E | F-G |
|---|---|---|---|---|
| COMPLETE SET | | 5.00 | 2.00 | .50 |
| COMMON PLAYER | | .15 | .06 | .01 |
| ☐ 2 | Tom Lasorda MGR | .20 | .08 | .02 |
| ☐ 3 | Steve Sax | .50 | .20 | .05 |
| ☐ 5 | Mike Marshall | .60 | .24 | .06 |
| ☐ 7 | Steve Yeager | .15 | .06 | .01 |
| ☐ 9 | Greg Brock | .25 | .10 | .02 |
| ☐ 10 | Dave Anderson | .20 | .08 | .02 |
| ☐ 14 | Mike Scioscia | .15 | .06 | .01 |
| ☐ 16 | Rick Monday | .20 | .08 | .02 |
| ☐ 17 | Rafael Landestoy | .15 | .06 | .01 |
| ☐ 18 | Bill Russell | .20 | .08 | .02 |
| ☐ 20 | Candy Maldonado | .25 | .10 | .02 |
| ☐ 21 | Bob Bailor | .15 | .06 | .01 |
| ☐ 25 | German Rivera | .20 | .08 | .02 |
| ☐ 26 | Alejandro Pena | .20 | .08 | .02 |
| ☐ 27 | Carlos Diaz | .20 | .08 | .02 |
| ☐ 28 | Pedro Guerrero | .75 | .30 | .07 |
| ☐ 31 | Jack Fimple | .15 | .06 | .01 |
| ☐ 34 | Fernando Valenzuela | .75 | .30 | .07 |
| ☐ 35 | Bob Welch | .25 | .10 | .02 |
| ☐ 38 | Pat Zachry | .15 | .06 | .01 |
| ☐ 40 | Rick Honeycutt | .20 | .08 | .02 |
| ☐ 41 | Jerry Reuss | .20 | .08 | .02 |
| ☐ 43 | Jose Morales | .15 | .06 | .01 |
| ☐ 44 | Ken Landreaux | .15 | .06 | .01 |
| ☐ 45 | Terry Whitfield | .15 | .06 | .01 |
| ☐ 46 | Burt Hooton | .15 | .06 | .01 |
| ☐ 49 | Tom Niedenfuer | .25 | .10 | .02 |
| ☐ 55 | Orel Hershiser | .75 | .30 | .07 |
| ☐ 56 | Richard Rodas | .15 | .06 | .01 |
| ☐ xx | Coaching Staff (unnumbered) | .15 | .06 | .01 |

| ☐ 11 | Bob Horner | 1.25 | .50 | .12 |
|---|---|---|---|---|
| ☐ 12 | Paul Runge | .40 | .16 | .04 |
| ☐ 15 | Claudell Washington | .50 | .20 | .05 |
| ☐ 16 | Rafael Ramirez | .40 | .16 | .04 |
| ☐ 17 | Glenn Hubbard | .40 | .16 | .04 |
| ☐ 18 | Paul Zuvella | .40 | .16 | .04 |
| ☐ 19 | Terry Harper | .30 | .12 | .03 |
| ☐ 20 | Bruce Benedict | .30 | .12 | .03 |
| ☐ 22 | Eddie Haas MGR | .30 | .12 | .03 |
| ☐ 24 | Ken Oberkfell | .30 | .12 | .03 |
| ☐ 26 | Gene Garber | .30 | .12 | .03 |
| ☐ 27 | Pascual Perez | .30 | .12 | .03 |
| ☐ 28 | Gerald Perry | .40 | .16 | .04 |
| ☐ 29 | Craig McMurtry | .30 | .12 | .03 |
| ☐ 32 | Steve Bedrosian | .40 | .16 | .04 |
| ☐ 33 | Johnny Sain CO | .50 | .20 | .05 |
| ☐ 34 | Zane Smith | .50 | .20 | .05 |
| ☐ 36 | Brad Komminsk | .40 | .16 | .04 |
| ☐ 37 | Rick Camp | .30 | .12 | .03 |
| ☐ 39 | Len Barker | .40 | .16 | .04 |
| ☐ 40 | Bruce Sutter | .60 | .24 | .06 |
| ☐ 42 | Rick Mahler | .40 | .16 | .04 |
| ☐ 51 | Terry Forster | .50 | .20 | .05 |
| ☐ 52 | Leo Mazzone CO | .30 | .12 | .03 |
| ☐ 53 | Bobby Dews CO | .30 | .12 | .03 |

## 1985 Police Brewers

y Burris says:

ur advance scouts are very important
. They check out opposing teams
re we play them and give us tips on
to play individual ballplayers. They act
ur eyes and ears. You, too, can be a
t for the police in your neighborhood.
and your friends can prevent crime by
g the eyes and ears of your local
e. Call them immediately to report
hing unusual or suspicious that you

h the Friday Milwaukee Journal
ts Weekend Section for the 2 players
red on next week's baseball cards. You
d win free tickets to a Brewer game!

48   **Ray Burris**   P
The Chilton Police Department and
The Chilton Local Merchants, Service Clubs
and Financial Institutions
present the 1985
**Milwaukee Brewers**

## 1985 Police Braves

The cards in this 30 card set measure 2 5/8" by 4 1/8". For the fifth straight year, the Atlanta Police Department issued a full color set of Atlanta Braves. The set was also sponsored by Coca Cola and Hostess. In the upper right of the obverse is a logo commemorating the 20th anniversary of the Braves in Atlanta. Cards are numbered by uniform number. Cards feature a safety tip on the back. Each card except for Manager Haas has an interesting "Did You Know" fact about the player.

|  |  | MINT | VG-E | F-G |
|---|---|---|---|---|
| COMPLETE SET | | 12.00 | 5.00 | 1.20 |
| COMMON PLAYER | | .30 | .12 | .03 |
| ☐ 2 | Albert Hall | .40 | .16 | .04 |
| ☐ 3 | Dale Murphy | 3.50 | 1.40 | .35 |
| ☐ 5 | Rick Cerone | .30 | .12 | .03 |
| ☐ 7 | Bobby Wine CO | .30 | .12 | .03 |
| ☐ 10 | Chris Chambliss | .40 | .16 | .04 |

The cards in this 30 card set measure 2 3/4" by 4 1/8". Again this year, the police departments in and around Milwaukee issued sets of the Milwaukee Brewers. The backs contain the Brewers logo, a safety tip, and in some cases, a badge of the jurisdiction. Prices below are for the basic set without regard to the Police Department issuing the cards; cards from the more obscure corners and small towns of Wisconsin (smaller production) will be valued higher. Cards are numbered by uniform number.

| | MINT | VG-E | F-G |
|---|---|---|---|
| COMPLETE SET | 5.00 | 2.00 | .50 |
| COMMON PLAYER | .15 | .06 | .01 |
| ☐ 2 Randy Ready | .15 | .06 | .01 |
| ☐ 4 Paul Molitor | .35 | .14 | .03 |
| ☐ 5 Doug Loman | .25 | .10 | .02 |
| ☐ 7 Paul Householder | .15 | .06 | .01 |
| ☐ 10 Bob McClure | .15 | .06 | .01 |
| ☐ 11 Ed Romero | .15 | .06 | .01 |
| ☐ 14 Dion James | .25 | .10 | .02 |
| ☐ 15 Cecil Cooper | .45 | .18 | .04 |
| ☐ 17 Jim Gantner | .25 | .10 | .02 |
| ☐ 18 Danny Darwin | .15 | .06 | .01 |
| ☐ 19 Robin Yount | .75 | .30 | .07 |
| ☐ 21 Bill Schroeder | .20 | .08 | .02 |
| ☐ 22 Charlie Moore | .15 | .06 | .01 |
| ☐ 23 Ted Simmons | .35 | .14 | .03 |
| ☐ 24 Ben Oglivie | .25 | .10 | .02 |
| ☐ 26 Brian Giles | .15 | .06 | .01 |
| ☐ 27 Pete Ladd | .15 | .06 | .01 |
| ☐ 28 Rick Manning | .15 | .06 | .01 |
| ☐ 29 Mark Brouhard | .15 | .06 | .01 |
| ☐ 30 Moose Haas | .20 | .08 | .02 |
| ☐ 31 George Bamberger MGR | .15 | .06 | .01 |
| ☐ 34 Rollie Fingers | .60 | .24 | .06 |
| ☐ 40 Bob L. Gibson | .15 | .06 | .01 |
| ☐ 41 Ray Searage | .15 | .06 | .01 |
| ☐ 47 Jaime Cocanower | .15 | .06 | .01 |
| ☐ 48 Ray Burris | .15 | .06 | .01 |
| ☐ 49 Ted Higuera | .60 | .24 | .06 |
| ☐ 50 Pete Vuckovich | .25 | .10 | .02 |
| ☐ xx Team Roster (unnumbered) | .15 | .06 | .01 |
| ☐ xx Coaches (unnumbered) | .15 | .06 | .01 |
| ☐ xx Newspaper Carrier (unnumbered) | .15 | .06 | .01 |

| | MINT | VG-E | F-G |
|---|---|---|---|
| ☐ 4 Kevin Bass | .50 | .20 | .05 |
| ☐ 5 Bill Doran | .50 | .20 | .05 |
| ☐ 6 Hal Lanier MGR | .25 | .10 | .02 |
| ☐ 7 Denny Walling | .10 | .04 | .01 |
| ☐ 8 Alan Ashby | .10 | .04 | .01 |
| ☐ 9 Phil Garner | .15 | .06 | .01 |
| ☐ 10 Charlie Kerfeld | .25 | .10 | .02 |
| ☐ 11 Dave Smith | .20 | .08 | .02 |
| ☐ 12 Jose Cruz | .50 | .20 | .05 |
| ☐ 13 Craig Reynolds | .10 | .04 | .01 |
| ☐ 14 Mark Bailey | .10 | .04 | .01 |
| ☐ 15 Bob Knepper | .25 | .10 | .02 |
| ☐ 16 Julio Solano | .10 | .04 | .01 |
| ☐ 17 Dickie Thon | .15 | .06 | .01 |
| ☐ 18 Mike Madden | .10 | .04 | .01 |
| ☐ 19 Jeff Calhoun | .15 | .06 | .01 |
| ☐ 20 Tony Walker | .20 | .08 | .02 |
| ☐ 21 Terry Puhl | .15 | .06 | .01 |
| ☐ 22 Glenn Davis | .90 | .36 | .09 |
| ☐ 23 Billy Hatcher | .15 | .06 | .01 |
| ☐ 24 Jim Deshaies | .30 | .12 | .03 |
| ☐ 25 Frank DiPino | .15 | .06 | .01 |
| ☐ 26 Coaching Staff | .10 | .04 | .01 |

## 1986 Police Astros

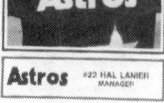
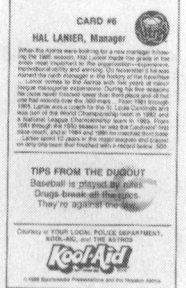

This 26 card safety set was also sponsored by Kool-Aid. The backs contain a biographical paragraph above a "Tip from the Dugout". The front features a full-color photo of the player, his name, and uniform number. The cards are numbered on the back and measure 2 5/8" by 4 1/8". The backs are printed in orange and blue on white card stock. Sets were distributed at the Astrodome on June 14th as well as given away throughout the summer by the Houston Police.

| | MINT | VG-E | F-G |
|---|---|---|---|
| COMPLETE SET | 5.00 | 2.00 | .40 |
| COMMON PLAYER | .10 | .04 | .01 |
| ☐ 1 Jim Pankovits | .10 | .04 | .01 |
| ☐ 2 Nolan Ryan | .90 | .36 | .09 |
| ☐ 3 Mike Scott | .60 | .24 | .06 |

## 1986 Police Braves

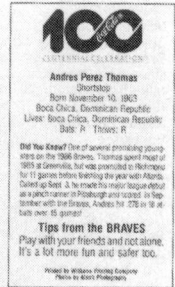

Andres Thomas (14)
Shortstop

This 30 card safety set was also sponsored by Coca-Cola. The backs contain the usual biographical info and safety tip. The front features a full-color photo of the player, his name, and uniform number. The cards measure 2 5/8" by 4 1/8". Cards were freely distributed throughout the summer by the Police Departments in the Atlanta area. Cards are numbered below by uniform number.

| | MINT | VG-E | F-G |
|---|---|---|---|
| COMPLETE SET | 9.00 | 3.75 | .90 |
| COMMON PLAYER | .20 | .08 | .02 |
| ☐ 2 Russ Nixon COA | .20 | .08 | .02 |
| ☐ 3 Dale Murphy | 2.00 | .80 | .20 |
| ☐ 4 Bob Skinner COA | .30 | .12 | .03 |
| ☐ 5 Billy Sample | .20 | .08 | .02 |
| ☐ 7 Chuck Tanner MGR | .30 | .12 | .03 |
| ☐ 8 Willie Stargell COA | .75 | .30 | .07 |
| ☐ 9 Ozzie Virgil | .30 | .12 | .03 |
| ☐ 10 Chris Chambliss | .30 | .12 | .03 |
| ☐ 11 Bob Horner | .75 | .30 | .07 |
| ☐ 14 Andres Thomas | .50 | .20 | .05 |
| ☐ 15 Claudell Washington | .30 | .12 | .03 |
| ☐ 16 Rafael Ramirez | .30 | .12 | .03 |
| ☐ 17 Glenn Hubbard | .30 | .12 | .03 |
| ☐ 18 Omar Moreno | .20 | .08 | .02 |
| ☐ 19 Terry Harper | .20 | .08 | .02 |
| ☐ 20 Bruce Benedict | .20 | .08 | .02 |
| ☐ 23 Ted Simmons | .40 | .16 | .04 |
| ☐ 24 Ken Oberkfell | .20 | .08 | .02 |
| ☐ 26 Gene Garber | .20 | .08 | .02 |
| ☐ 29 Craig McMurtry | .20 | .08 | .02 |
| ☐ 30 Paul Assenmacher | .20 | .08 | .02 |
| ☐ 33 Johnny Sain COA | .30 | .12 | .03 |
| ☐ 34 Zane Smith | .30 | .12 | .03 |
| ☐ 38 Joe Johnson | .30 | .12 | .03 |
| ☐ 40 Bruce Sutter | .40 | .16 | .04 |

| | | MINT | VG-E | F-G |
|---|---|---|---|---|
| ☐ 42 | Rick Mahler | .30 | .12 | .03 |
| ☐ 46 | David Palmer | .30 | .12 | .03 |
| ☐ 48 | Duane Ward | .30 | .12 | .03 |
| ☐ 49 | Jeff Dedmon | .20 | .08 | .02 |
| ☐ 52 | Al Monchak COA | .20 | .08 | .02 |

## 1986 Police Brewers

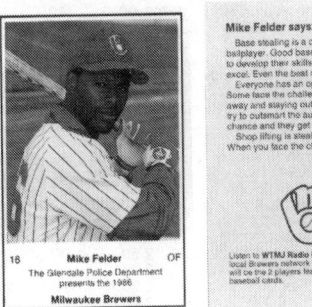
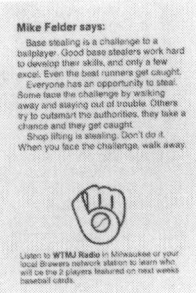

Mike Felder says:
Base stealing is a challenge to a ballplayer. Good base stealers work hard to develop their skills, and only a few excel. Even the best runners get caught. Everyone has an opportunity to steal. Some face the challenge by walking away and staying out of trouble. Others try to outsmart the authorities, they take a chance and they get caught. Shop lifting is stealing. Don't do it. When you face the challenge, walk away

18    Mike Felder    OF
The Glendale Police Department
presents the 1986
Milwaukee Brewers

Listen to WTMJ Radio in Milwaukee or your local Brewers network station to learn who will be the 2 players featured on next weeks baseball cards.

This 32 card safety set was also sponsored by WTMJ Radio and Kinney Shoes. The backs contain the usual biographical info and safety tip. The front features a full-color photo of the player, his name, position, and uniform number. The cards measure 2 5/8" by 4 1/8". Cards were freely distributed throughout the summer by the Police Departments in the Milwaukee area. Cards are numbered below by uniform number.

| | | MINT | VG-E | F-G |
|---|---|---|---|---|
| | COMPLETE SET | 6.00 | 2.40 | .60 |
| | COMMON PLAYER | .10 | .04 | .01 |
| ☐ 1 | Ernest Riles | .30 | .12 | .03 |
| ☐ 2 | Randy Ready | .10 | .04 | .01 |
| ☐ 3 | Juan Castillo | .15 | .06 | .01 |
| ☐ 4 | Paul Molitor | .40 | .16 | .04 |
| ☐ 7 | Paul Householder | .10 | .04 | .01 |
| ☐ 8 | Andy Etchebarren COA | .10 | .04 | .01 |
| ☐ 10 | Bob McClure | .15 | .06 | .01 |
| ☐ 11 | Rick Cerone | .15 | .06 | .01 |
| ☐ 12 | Larry Haney COA | .10 | .04 | .01 |
| ☐ 13 | Billy Jo Robidoux | .25 | .10 | .02 |
| ☐ 15 | Cecil Cooper | .40 | .16 | .04 |
| ☐ 16 | Mike Felder | .30 | .12 | .03 |
| ☐ 17 | Jim Gantner | .15 | .06 | .01 |
| ☐ 18 | Danny Darwin | .15 | .06 | .01 |
| ☐ 19 | Robin Yount | 1.00 | .40 | .10 |
| ☐ 20 | Juan Nieves | .25 | .10 | .02 |
| ☐ 21 | Bill Schroeder | .15 | .06 | .01 |
| ☐ 22 | Charlie Moore | .10 | .04 | .01 |
| ☐ 24 | Ben Oglivie | .20 | .08 | .02 |
| ☐ 25 | Mark Clear | .15 | .06 | .01 |
| ☐ 28 | Rick Manning | .10 | .04 | .01 |
| ☐ 31 | George Bamberger MGR | .20 | .08 | .02 |
| ☐ 33 | Frank Howard COA | .20 | .08 | .02 |
| ☐ 35 | Tony Muser COA | .10 | .04 | .01 |
| ☐ 37 | Dan Plesac | .25 | .10 | .02 |
| ☐ 38 | Herm Starrette COA | .10 | .04 | .01 |
| ☐ 39 | Tim Leary | .10 | .04 | .01 |
| ☐ 42 | Tom Trebelhorn COA | .20 | .08 | .02 |
| ☐ 45 | Rob Deer | .50 | .20 | .05 |
| ☐ 46 | Bill Wegman | .15 | .06 | .01 |
| ☐ 47 | Jaime Cocanower | .10 | .04 | .01 |
| ☐ 49 | Teddy Higuera | .75 | .30 | .07 |

**HELP WANTED:** Writers and artists, we're always looking for good material to publish in Beckett Monthly. Send us your best stuff. We pay on acceptance.

## 1986 Police Dodgers

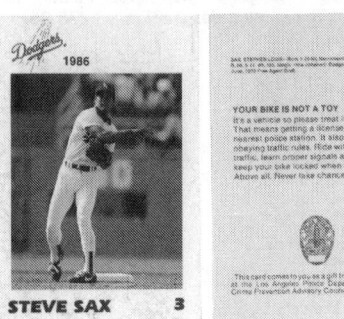

STEVE SAX    3

This 30 card set features full-color cards each measuring 2 13/16" by 4 1/8". The cards are unnumbered except for uniform numbers. The back give a safety tip as well as a short capsule biography. The sets were given away at Dodger Stadium on May 18th.

| | | MINT | VG-E | F-G |
|---|---|---|---|---|
| | COMPLETE SET | 5.00 | 2.00 | .40 |
| | COMMON PLAYER | .10 | .04 | .01 |
| ☐ 2 | Tom Lasorda MGR | .25 | .10 | .02 |
| ☐ 3 | Steve Sax | .75 | .30 | .07 |
| ☐ 5 | Mike Marshall | .50 | .20 | .05 |
| ☐ 9 | Greg Brock | .20 | .08 | .02 |
| ☐ 10 | Dave Anderson | .10 | .04 | .01 |
| ☐ 12 | Bill Madlock | .25 | .10 | .02 |
| ☐ 14 | Mike Scioscia | .15 | .06 | .01 |
| ☐ 17 | Len Matuszek | .10 | .04 | .01 |
| ☐ 18 | Bill Russell | .20 | .08 | .02 |
| ☐ 22 | Franklin Stubbs | .25 | .10 | .02 |
| ☐ 23 | Enos Cabell | .10 | .04 | .01 |
| ☐ 25 | Mariano Duncan | .20 | .08 | .02 |
| ☐ 26 | Alejandro Pena | .15 | .06 | .01 |
| ☐ 27 | Carlos Diaz | .10 | .04 | .01 |
| ☐ 28 | Pedro Guerrero | .75 | .30 | .07 |
| ☐ 29 | Alex Trevino | .10 | .04 | .01 |
| ☐ 31 | Ed VandeBerg | .10 | .04 | .01 |
| ☐ 34 | Fernando Valenzuela | .75 | .30 | .07 |
| ☐ 35 | Bob Welch | .25 | .10 | .02 |
| ☐ 40 | Rick Honeycutt | .15 | .06 | .01 |
| ☐ 41 | Jerry Reuss | .15 | .06 | .01 |
| ☐ 43 | Ken Howell | .15 | .06 | .01 |
| ☐ 44 | Ken Landreaux | .15 | .06 | .01 |
| ☐ 45 | Terry Whitfield | .10 | .04 | .01 |
| ☐ 48 | Dennis Powell | .15 | .06 | .01 |
| ☐ 49 | Tom Niedenfuer | .20 | .08 | .02 |
| ☐ 51 | Reggie Williams | .20 | .08 | .02 |
| ☐ 55 | Orel Hershiser | .25 | .10 | .02 |
| ☐ xx | Coaching Staff (unnumbered) Don McMahon Mark Cresse Ben Hines Ron Perranoski Monty Basgall Manny Mota Joe Amalfitano | .10 | .04 | .01 |
| ☐ xx | Team Photo (unnumbered) (checklist back) | .20 | .08 | .02 |

## 1960 Post Cereal

These large cards measure 7" by 8 3/4". The 1960 Post Cereal Sports Stars set contains nine cards depicting current baseball, football and basketball players. Each card comprised the entire back of a Grape Nuts Box and is blank backed. The color player photos are set on a colored background surrounded by a wooden frame design, and they are unnumbered (assigned numbers below for reference). The catalog designation is F278-26.

|  | MINT | VG-E | F-G |
|---|---|---|---|
| COMPLETE SET | 1650.00 | 750.00 | 175.00 |
| COMMON PLAYER (1-9) | 80.00 | 32.00 | 8.00 |
| □ 1 Bob Cousy (basketball) | 80.00 | 32.00 | 8.00 |
| □ 2 Don Drysdale (baseball) | 175.00 | 70.00 | 18.00 |
| □ 3 Frank Gifford (football) | 175.00 | 70.00 | 18.00 |
| □ 4 Al Kaline (baseball) | 225.00 | 90.00 | 22.00 |
| □ 5 Harmon Killebrew (baseball) | 175.00 | 70.00 | 18.00 |
| □ 6 Ed Mathews (baseball) | 175.00 | 70.00 | 18.00 |
| □ 7 Mickey Mantle (baseball) | 800.00 | 320.00 | 80.00 |
| □ 8 Bob Pettit (basketball) | 80.00 | 32.00 | 8.00 |
| □ 9 John Unitas (football) | 175.00 | 70.00 | 18.00 |

# 1961 Post Cereal

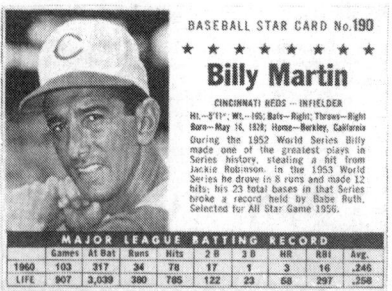

The cards in this 200 card set measure 2 1/2" by 3 1/2". The 1961 Post set was this company's first major set. The cards were available on thick cardbox stock, singly or in various panel sizes from cereal boxes (BOX), or in team sheets, printed on thinner cardboard stock, directly from the Post Cereal Company (COMP). Many variations exist and are noted in the checklist below. There are many cards which were produced in lesser quantities; the prices below reflect the relative scarcity of the cards. Cards 10, 23, 70, 73, 94, 113, 135, 163, and 183 are examples of cards printed in limited quantities and hence commanding premium prices. The cards are numbered essentially in team groups, i.e., New York Yankees (1-18), Chicago White Sox (19-34), Detroit (35-46), Boston (47-56), Cleveland (57-67), Baltimore (68-80), Kansas City (81-90), Minnesota (91-100), Milwaukee (101-114), Philadelphia (115-124), Pittsburgh (125-140), San Francisco (141-155), Los Angeles Dodgers (156-170), St. Louis (171-180), Cincinnati (181-190), and Chicago Cubs (191-200). The catalog number is F278-33. The complete set prices refer to both ways of collecting the set, all variations (357) or one of each player (200).

|  | MINT | VG-E | F-G |
|---|---|---|---|
| COMPLETE SET (357) | 1100.00 | 450.00 | 125.00 |
| COMPLETE SET (200) | 800.00 | 320.00 | 80.00 |
| COMMON PLAYER (1-200) | .80 | .32 | .08 |

| | | | | |
|---|---|---|---|---|
| □ | 1A Yogi Berra COMP | 7.50 | 3.00 | .75 |
| □ | 1B Yogi Berra BOX | 10.00 | 4.00 | 1.00 |
| □ | 2A Elston Howard COMP | 1.00 | .40 | .10 |
| □ | 2B Elston Howard BOX | 2.00 | .80 | .20 |
| □ | 3A Bill Skowron COMP | .80 | .32 | .08 |
| □ | 3B Bill Skowron BOX | .80 | .32 | .08 |
| □ | 4A Mickey Mantle COMP | 25.00 | 10.00 | 2.50 |
| □ | 4B Mickey Mantle BOX | 25.00 | 10.00 | 2.50 |
| □ | 5 Bob Turley COMP only | 7.50 | 3.00 | .75 |
| □ | 6A Whitey Ford COMP | 3.50 | 1.40 | .35 |
| □ | 6B Whitey Ford BOX | 3.50 | 1.40 | .35 |
| □ | 7A Roger Maris COMP | 6.00 | 2.40 | .60 |
| □ | 7B Roger Maris BOX | 6.00 | 2.40 | .60 |
| □ | 8A B.Richardson COMP | 1.00 | .40 | .10 |
| □ | 8B B.Richardson BOX | 1.00 | .40 | .10 |
| □ | 9A Tony Kubek COMP | 1.00 | .40 | .10 |
| □ | 9B Tony Kubek BOX | 1.00 | .40 | .10 |
| □ | 10 G.McDougald BOX only | 20.00 | 8.00 | 2.00 |
| □ | 11 Cletis Boyer BOX only | .80 | .32 | .08 |
| □ | 12A Hector Lopes COMP | .80 | .32 | .08 |
| □ | 12B Hector Lopes BOX | .80 | .32 | .08 |
| □ | 13 Bob Cerv BOX only | .80 | .32 | .08 |
| □ | 14 Ryne Duren BOX only | .80 | .32 | .08 |
| □ | 15 Bobby Shantz BOX only | .80 | .32 | .08 |
| □ | 16 Art Ditmar BOX only | .80 | .32 | .08 |
| □ | 17 Jim Coates BOX only | .80 | .32 | .08 |
| □ | 18 J.Blanchard BOX only | .80 | .32 | .08 |
| □ | 19A Luis Aparicio COMP | 2.50 | 1.00 | .25 |
| □ | 19B Luis Aparicio BOX | 2.50 | 1.00 | .25 |
| □ | 20A Nelson Fox COMP | 2.25 | .90 | .22 |
| □ | 20B Nelson Fox BOX | 2.25 | .90 | .22 |
| □ | 21A Bill Pierce COMP | 2.25 | .90 | .22 |
| □ | 21B Bill Pierce BOX | 4.00 | 1.60 | .40 |
| □ | 22A Early Wynn COMP | 4.00 | 1.60 | .40 |
| □ | 22B Early Wynn BOX | 8.00 | 3.25 | .80 |
| □ | 23 Bob Shaw BOX only | 60.00 | 24.00 | 6.00 |
| □ | 24A Al Smith COMP | .80 | .32 | .08 |
| □ | 24B Al Smith BOX | 2.50 | 1.00 | .25 |
| □ | 25A Minnie Minoso COMP | 1.00 | .40 | .10 |
| □ | 25B Minnie Minoso BOX | 1.00 | .40 | .10 |
| □ | 26A Roy Sievers COMP | .80 | .32 | .08 |
| □ | 26B Roy Sievers BOX | .80 | .32 | .08 |
| □ | 27A Jim Landis COMP | .80 | .32 | .08 |
| □ | 27B Jim Landis BOX | 1.50 | .60 | .15 |
| □ | 28A Sherm Lollar COMP | .80 | .32 | .08 |
| □ | 28B Sherm Lollar BOX | 2.00 | .80 | .20 |
| □ | 29 Gerry Staley BOX only | .80 | .32 | .08 |
| □ | 30A Gene Freese COMP (Reds) | 3.50 | 1.40 | .35 |
| □ | 30B Gene Freese BOX (White Sox) | .80 | .32 | .08 |
| □ | 31 T.Kluszewski BOX only | 1.00 | .40 | .10 |
| □ | 32 Turk Lown BOX only | .80 | .32 | .08 |
| □ | 33A Jim Rivera COMP | .80 | .32 | .08 |
| □ | 33B Jim Rivera BOX | .80 | .32 | .08 |
| □ | 34 F.Baumann BOX only | .80 | .32 | .08 |
| □ | 35A Al Kaline COMP | 5.00 | 2.00 | .50 |
| □ | 35B Al Kaline BOX | 8.00 | 3.25 | .80 |
| □ | 36A Rocky Colavito COMP | 2.75 | 1.10 | .27 |
| □ | 36B Rocky Colavito BOX | 4.00 | 1.60 | .40 |
| □ | 37A C.Maxwell COMP | .80 | .32 | .08 |
| □ | 37B C.Maxwell BOX | 2.50 | 1.00 | .25 |
| □ | 38A Frank Lary COMP | .80 | .32 | .08 |
| □ | 38B Frank Lary BOX | .80 | .32 | .08 |
| □ | 39A Jim Bunning COMP | 1.50 | .60 | .15 |
| □ | 39B Jim Bunning BOX | 1.50 | .60 | .15 |
| □ | 40A Norm Cash COMP | 1.00 | .40 | .10 |
| □ | 40B Norm Cash BOX | 1.00 | .40 | .10 |
| □ | 41B Frank Bolling COMP (Braves) | 2.50 | 1.00 | .25 |
| □ | 41A Frank Bolling BOX (Tigers) | 5.00 | 2.00 | .50 |
| □ | 42A Don Mossi COMP | .80 | .32 | .08 |
| □ | 42B Don Mossi BOX | .80 | .32 | .08 |
| □ | 43A Lou Berberet COMP | .80 | .32 | .08 |
| □ | 43B Lou Berberet BOX | .80 | .32 | .08 |
| □ | 44 Dave Sisler BOX only | .80 | .32 | .08 |
| □ | 45 Ed Yost BOX only | .80 | .32 | .08 |
| □ | 46 Pete Burnside BOX only | .80 | .32 | .08 |
| □ | 47A Pete Runnels COMP | 1.25 | .50 | .12 |
| □ | 47B Pete Runnels BOX | 2.50 | 1.00 | .25 |
| □ | 48A Frank Malzone COMP | .80 | .32 | .08 |
| □ | 48B Frank Malzone BOX | .80 | .32 | .08 |
| □ | 49A Vic Wertz COMP | 2.50 | 1.00 | .25 |
| □ | 49B Vic Wertz BOX | 4.00 | 1.60 | .40 |
| □ | 50A Tom Brewer COMP | .80 | .32 | .08 |
| □ | 50B Tom Brewer BOX | 2.00 | .80 | .20 |
| □ | 51A Willie Tasby COMP (Sold to Wash.) | 5.00 | 2.00 | .50 |
| □ | 51B Willie Tasby BOX (no sale mention) | .80 | .32 | .08 |
| □ | 52A Russ Nixon COMP | .80 | .32 | .08 |

| | | | | |
|---|---|---|---|---|
| ☐ 52B | Russ Nixon BOX | .80 | .32 | .08 |
| ☐ 53A | Don Buddin COMP | .80 | .32 | .08 |
| ☐ 53B | Don Buddin BOX | .80 | .32 | .08 |
| ☐ 54A | B.Monbouquette COMP | | .32 | .08 |
| ☐ 54B | B.Monbouquette BOX | .80 | .32 | .08 |
| ☐ 55A | Frank Sullivan COMP (Phillies) | 5.00 | 2.00 | .50 |
| ☐ 55B | Frank Sullivan BOX (Red Sox) | .80 | .32 | .08 |
| ☐ 56A | H.Sullivan COMP | .80 | .32 | .08 |
| ☐ 56B | H.Sullivan BOX | .80 | .32 | .08 |
| ☐ 57A | Harvey Kuenn COMP (Giants) | 3.50 | 1.40 | .35 |
| ☐ 57B | Harvey Kuenn BOX (Indians) | 2.50 | 1.00 | .25 |
| ☐ 58A | Gary Bell COMP | 1.50 | .60 | .15 |
| ☐ 58B | Gary Bell BOX | 3.50 | 1.40 | .35 |
| ☐ 59A | Jim Perry COMP | .80 | .32 | .08 |
| ☐ 59B | Jim Perry BOX | .80 | .32 | .08 |
| ☐ 60A | Jim Grant COMP | 1.50 | .60 | .15 |
| ☐ 60B | Jim Grant BOX | 2.50 | 1.00 | .25 |
| ☐ 61A | Johnny Temple COMP | .80 | .32 | .08 |
| ☐ 61B | Johnny Temple BOX | .80 | .32 | .08 |
| ☐ 62A | Paul Foytack COMP | .80 | .32 | .08 |
| ☐ 62B | Paul Foytack BOX | .80 | .32 | .08 |
| ☐ 63A | Vic Power COMP | .80 | .32 | .08 |
| ☐ 63B | Vic Power BOX | .80 | .32 | .08 |
| ☐ 64A | Tito Francona COMP | .80 | .32 | .08 |
| ☐ 64B | Tito Francona BOX | .80 | .32 | .08 |
| ☐ 65B | Ken Aspromonte COMP (Sold to L.A.) | 5.00 | 2.00 | .50 |
| ☐ 65A | Ken Aspromonte BOX (no sale mention) | 5.00 | 2.00 | .50 |
| ☐ 66 | Bob Wilson BOX only | .80 | .32 | .08 |
| ☐ 67A | John Romano COMP | .80 | .32 | .08 |
| ☐ 67B | John Romano BOX | .80 | .32 | .08 |
| ☐ 68A | Jim Gentile COMP | .80 | .32 | .08 |
| ☐ 68B | Jim Gentile BOX | 2.00 | .80 | .20 |
| ☐ 69A | Gus Triandos COMP | .80 | .32 | .08 |
| ☐ 69B | Gus Triandos BOX | 2.50 | 1.00 | .25 |
| ☐ 70 | G.Woodling BOX only | 20.00 | 8.00 | 2.00 |
| ☐ 71A | Milt Pappas COMP | .80 | .32 | .08 |
| ☐ 71B | Milt Pappas BOX | 2.50 | 1.00 | .25 |
| ☐ 72A | Ron Hansen COMP | .80 | .32 | .08 |
| ☐ 72B | Ron Hansen BOX | 2.00 | .80 | .20 |
| ☐ 73 | Chuck Estrada COMP only | 50.00 | 20.00 | 5.00 |
| ☐ 74A | Steve Barber COMP | .80 | .32 | .08 |
| ☐ 74B | Steve Barber BOX | .80 | .32 | .08 |
| ☐ 75A | B.Robinson COMP | 6.00 | 2.40 | .60 |
| ☐ 75B | B.Robinson BOX | 8.00 | 3.25 | .80 |
| ☐ 76A | Jackie Brandt COMP | .80 | .32 | .08 |
| ☐ 76B | Jackie Brandt BOX | .80 | .32 | .08 |
| ☐ 77A | Marv Breeding COMP | .80 | .32 | .08 |
| ☐ 77B | Marv Breeding BOX | .80 | .32 | .08 |
| ☐ 78 | Hal Brown BOX only | .80 | .32 | .08 |
| ☐ 79 | Billy Klaus BOX only | .80 | .32 | .08 |
| ☐ 80A | Hoyt Wilhelm COMP | 4.00 | 1.60 | .40 |
| ☐ 80B | Hoyt Wilhelm BOX | 3.00 | 1.20 | .30 |
| ☐ 81A | Jerry Lumpe COMP | 3.00 | 1.20 | .30 |
| ☐ 81B | Jerry Lumpe BOX | 4.00 | 1.60 | .40 |
| ☐ 82A | Norm Siebern COMP | .80 | .32 | .08 |
| ☐ 82B | Norm Siebern BOX | .90 | .32 | .08 |
| ☐ 83A | Bud Daley COMP | 2.00 | .80 | .20 |
| ☐ 83B | Bud Daley BOX | 1.50 | .60 | .15 |
| ☐ 84A | Bill Tuttle COMP | .80 | .32 | .08 |
| ☐ 84B | Bill Tuttle BOX | .80 | .32 | .08 |
| ☐ 85A | M.Throneberry COMP | 2.00 | .80 | .20 |
| ☐ 85B | M.Throneberry BOX | 2.00 | .80 | .20 |
| ☐ 86A | Dick Williams COMP | .80 | .32 | .08 |
| ☐ 86B | Dick Williams BOX | .80 | .32 | .08 |
| ☐ 87A | Ray Herbert COMP | .80 | .32 | .08 |
| ☐ 87B | Ray Herbert BOX | .80 | .32 | .08 |
| ☐ 88A | Whitey Herzog COMP | .80 | .32 | .08 |
| ☐ 88B | Whitey Herzog BOX | .80 | .32 | .08 |
| ☐ 89A | Ken Hamlin COMP (Sold to L.A.) | 6.00 | 2.40 | .60 |
| ☐ 89B | Ken Hamlin BOX (no sale mention) | .80 | .32 | .08 |
| ☐ 90A | Hank Bauer COMP | .80 | .32 | .08 |
| ☐ 90B | Hank Bauer BOX | .80 | .32 | .08 |
| ☐ 91A | Bob Allison COMP (Minnesota) | 3.00 | 1.20 | .30 |
| ☐ 91B | Bob Allison BOX (Minneapolis) | 3.00 | 1.20 | .30 |
| ☐ 92A | Harmon Killebrew (Minnesota) COMP | 7.00 | 2.80 | .70 |
| ☐ 92B | Harmon Killebrew (Minneapolis) BOX | 9.00 | 3.75 | .90 |
| ☐ 93A | Jim Lemon COMP (Minnesota) | 10.00 | 4.00 | 1.00 |
| ☐ 93B | Jim Lemon BOX (Minneapolis) | 20.00 | 8.00 | 2.00 |

| | | | | |
|---|---|---|---|---|
| ☐ 94A | Chuck Stobbs (Minnesota) COMP only | 80.00 | 32.00 | 8.00 |
| ☐ 95A | Reno Bertoia COMP (Minnesota) | 3.00 | 1.20 | .30 |
| ☐ 95B | Reno Bertoia BOX (Minneapolis) | .80 | .32 | .08 |
| ☐ 96A | Billy Gardner COMP (Minnesota) | 3.00 | 1.20 | .30 |
| ☐ 96B | Billy Gardner BOX (Minneapolis) | .80 | .32 | .08 |
| ☐ 97A | Earl Battey COMP (Minnesota) | 3.00 | 1.20 | .30 |
| ☐ 97B | Earl Battey BOX (Minneapolis) | .80 | .32 | .08 |
| ☐ 98A | Pedro Ramos COMP (Minnesota) | 3.00 | 1.20 | .30 |
| ☐ 98B | Pedro Ramos BOX (Minneapolis) | .80 | .32 | .08 |
| ☐ 99A | Camilo Pascual COMP (Minnesota) | 3.00 | 1.20 | .30 |
| ☐ 99B | Camilo Pascual BOX (Minneapolis) | .80 | .32 | .08 |
| ☐ 100A | Billy Consolo COMP (Minnesota) | 3.00 | 1.20 | .30 |
| ☐ 100B | Billy Consolo BOX (Minneapolis) | .80 | .32 | .08 |
| ☐ 101A | Warren Spahn COMP | 7.00 | 2.80 | .70 |
| ☐ 101B | Warren Spahn BOX | 10.00 | 4.00 | 1.00 |
| ☐ 102A | Lew Burdette COMP | 1.50 | .60 | .15 |
| ☐ 102B | Lew Burdette BOX | 1.50 | .60 | .15 |
| ☐ 103A | Bob Buhl COMP | .80 | .32 | .08 |
| ☐ 103B | Bob Buhl BOX | .80 | .32 | .08 |
| ☐ 104A | Joe Adcock COMP | 1.50 | .60 | .15 |
| ☐ 104B | Joe Adcock BOX | 3.00 | 1.20 | .30 |
| ☐ 105A | John Logan COMP | 1.50 | .60 | .15 |
| ☐ 105B | John Logan BOX | 3.00 | 1.20 | .30 |
| ☐ 106 | Ed Mathews COMP only | 15.00 | 6.00 | 1.50 |
| ☐ 107A | Hank Aaron COMP | 12.50 | 5.00 | 1.25 |
| ☐ 107B | Hank Aaron BOX | 12.50 | 5.00 | 1.25 |
| ☐ 108A | Wes Covington COMP | .80 | .32 | .08 |
| ☐ 108B | Wes Covington BOX | .80 | .32 | .08 |
| ☐ 109A | Bill Bruton COMP (Tigers) | 3.00 | 1.20 | .30 |
| ☐ 109B | Bill Bruton BOX (Braves) | 4.00 | 1.60 | .40 |
| ☐ 110A | Del Crandall COMP | .80 | .32 | .08 |
| ☐ 110B | Del Crandall BOX | 3.00 | 1.20 | .30 |
| ☐ 111 | Red Schoendienst BOX only | .80 | .32 | .08 |
| ☐ 112 | Juan Pizarro BOX only | .80 | .32 | .08 |
| ☐ 113 | Chuck Cottier BOX only | 6.00 | 2.40 | .60 |
| ☐ 114 | Al Spangler BOX only | .80 | .32 | .08 |
| ☐ 115A | Dick Farrell COMP | 3.00 | 1.20 | .30 |
| ☐ 115B | Dick Farrell BOX | 4.00 | 1.60 | .40 |
| ☐ 116A | Jim Owens COMP | 3.00 | 1.20 | .30 |
| ☐ 116B | Jim Owens BOX | 4.00 | 1.60 | .40 |
| ☐ 117A | Robin Roberts COMP | 4.00 | 1.60 | .40 |
| ☐ 117B | Robin Roberts BOX | 3.00 | 1.20 | .30 |
| ☐ 118A | Tony Taylor COMP | .80 | .32 | .08 |
| ☐ 118B | Tony Taylor BOX | .80 | .32 | .08 |
| ☐ 119A | Lee Walls COMP | .80 | .32 | .08 |
| ☐ 119B | Lee Walls BOX | .80 | .32 | .08 |
| ☐ 120A | Tony Curry COMP | .80 | .32 | .08 |
| ☐ 120B | Tony Curry BOX | .80 | .32 | .08 |
| ☐ 121A | Pancho Herrera COMP | .80 | .32 | .08 |
| ☐ 121B | Pancho Herrera BOX | .80 | .32 | .08 |
| ☐ 122A | Ken Walters COMP | .80 | .32 | .08 |
| ☐ 122B | Ken Walters BOX | .80 | .32 | .08 |
| ☐ 123A | John Callison COMP | .80 | .32 | .08 |
| ☐ 123B | John Callison BOX | .80 | .32 | .08 |
| ☐ 124A | Gene Conley COMP (Red Sox) | 5.00 | 2.00 | .50 |
| ☐ 124B | Gene Conley BOX (Phillies) | .80 | .32 | .08 |
| ☐ 125A | Bob Friend COMP | 1.25 | .50 | .12 |
| ☐ 125B | Bob Friend BOX | 3.00 | 1.20 | .30 |
| ☐ 126A | Vernon Law COMP | 1.25 | .50 | .12 |
| ☐ 126B | Vernon Law BOX | 3.00 | 1.20 | .30 |
| ☐ 127A | Dick Stuart COMP | .80 | .32 | .08 |
| ☐ 127B | Dick Stuart BOX | .80 | .32 | .08 |
| ☐ 128A | Bill Mazeroski COMP | 1.00 | .40 | .10 |
| ☐ 128B | Bill Mazeroski BOX | 1.00 | .40 | .10 |
| ☐ 129A | Dick Groat COMP | .80 | .32 | .08 |
| ☐ 129B | Dick Groat BOX | 2.00 | .80 | .20 |
| ☐ 130A | Don Hoak COMP | .80 | .32 | .08 |
| ☐ 130B | Don Hoak BOX | .80 | .32 | .08 |
| ☐ 131A | Bob Skinner COMP | .80 | .32 | .08 |
| ☐ 131B | Bob Skinner BOX | .80 | .32 | .08 |
| ☐ 132A | Bob Clemente COMP | 12.50 | 5.00 | 1.25 |
| ☐ 132B | Bob Clemente BOX | 16.00 | 6.50 | 1.60 |
| ☐ 133 | Roy Face BOX only | 2.50 | 1.00 | .25 |
| ☐ 134 | H.Haddix BOX only | .80 | .32 | .08 |

| | | | |
|---|---|---|---|
| ☐ 135 Bill Virdon BOX only ....... | 20.00 | 8.00 | 2.00 |
| ☐ 136A Gino Cimoli COMP ........ | .80 | .32 | .08 |
| ☐ 136B Gino Cimoli BOX .......... | .80 | .32 | .08 |
| ☐ 137 Rocky Nelson BOX only .. | .80 | .32 | .08 |
| ☐ 138A Smoky Burgess COMP ... | .80 | .32 | .08 |
| ☐ 138B Smoky Burgess BOX ..... | .80 | .32 | .08 |
| ☐ 139 Hal Smith BOX only ...... | .80 | .32 | .08 |
| ☐ 140 Wilmer Mizell BOX only ... | .80 | .32 | .08 |
| ☐ 141A M.McCormick COMP ...... | .80 | .32 | .08 |
| ☐ 141B M.McCormick BOX ........ | .80 | .32 | .08 |
| ☐ 142A John Antonelli COMP ... | 3.00 | 1.20 | .30 |
| (Cleveland) | | | |
| ☐ 142B John Antonelli BOX ...... | 2.50 | 1.00 | .25 |
| (San Francisco) | | | |
| ☐ 143A Sam Jones COMP ......... | 1.50 | .60 | .15 |
| ☐ 143B Sam Jones BOX ........... | 3.00 | 1.20 | .30 |
| ☐ 144A Orlando Cepeda COMP . | 3.00 | 1.20 | .30 |
| ☐ 144B Orlando Cepeda BOX .... | 4.00 | 1.60 | .40 |
| ☐ 145A Willie Mays COMP ........ | 12.50 | 5.00 | 1.25 |
| ☐ 145B Willie Mays BOX .......... | 12.50 | 5.00 | 1.25 |
| ☐ 146A Willie Kirkland .......... | 3.00 | 1.20 | .30 |
| (Cleve.) COMP | | | |
| ☐ 146B Willie Kirkland .......... | 3.00 | 1.20 | .30 |
| (San Fran.) BOX | | | |
| ☐ 147A Willie McCovey COMP .. | 5.00 | 2.00 | .50 |
| ☐ 147B Willie McCovey BOX .... | 3.50 | 1.40 | .35 |
| ☐ 148A Don Blasingame COMP . | .80 | .32 | .08 |
| ☐ 148B Don Blasingame BOX ... | .80 | .32 | .08 |
| ☐ 149A Jim Davenport COMP ... | .80 | .32 | .08 |
| ☐ 149B Jim Davenport BOX ...... | .80 | .32 | .08 |
| ☐ 150A Hobie Landrith COMP ... | .80 | .32 | .08 |
| ☐ 150B Hobie Landrith BOX ..... | .80 | .32 | .08 |
| ☐ 151 Bob Schmidt BOX only ... | .80 | .32 | .08 |
| ☐ 152A Ed Bressoud COMP ...... | .80 | .32 | .08 |
| ☐ 152B Ed Bressoud BOX ......... | .80 | .32 | .08 |
| ☐ 153A Andre Rodgers ........... | 7.50 | 3.00 | .75 |
| (no trade mention) BOX only | | | |
| ☐ 153B Andre Rodgers ............ | 1.50 | .60 | .15 |
| (Traded to Milw.) BOX only | | | |
| ☐ 154 Jack Sanford BOX only ... | .80 | .32 | .08 |
| ☐ 155 Billy O'Dell BOX only ...... | .80 | .32 | .08 |
| ☐ 156A Norm Larker COMP ...... | 2.00 | .80 | .20 |
| ☐ 156B Norm Larker BOX ........ | 2.00 | .80 | .20 |
| ☐ 157A Charlie Neal COMP ...... | .80 | .32 | .08 |
| ☐ 157B Charlie Neal BOX ........ | .80 | .32 | .08 |
| ☐ 158A Jim Gilliam COMP ........ | 1.25 | .50 | .12 |
| ☐ 158B Jim Gilliam BOX .......... | 3.00 | 1.20 | .30 |
| ☐ 159A Wally Moon COMP ........ | .80 | .32 | .08 |
| ☐ 159B Wally Moon BOX .......... | .80 | .32 | .08 |
| ☐ 160A Don Drysdale COMP ..... | 4.00 | 1.60 | .40 |
| ☐ 160B Don Drysdale BOX ....... | 4.00 | 1.60 | .40 |
| ☐ 161A Larry Sherry COMP ...... | .80 | .32 | .08 |
| ☐ 161B Larry Sherry BOX ......... | .80 | .32 | .08 |
| ☐ 162 Stan Williams BOX only .. | 4.00 | 1.60 | .40 |
| ☐ 163 Mel Roach BOX only ...... | 40.00 | 16.00 | 4.00 |
| ☐ 164A Maury Wills COMP ....... | 2.00 | .80 | .20 |
| ☐ 164B Maury Wills BOX .......... | 2.00 | .80 | .20 |
| ☐ 165 Tommy Davis BOX only .. | .80 | .32 | .08 |
| ☐ 166A John Roseboro COMP ... | .80 | .32 | .08 |
| ☐ 166B John Roseboro BOX ..... | .80 | .32 | .08 |
| ☐ 167A Duke Snider COMP ...... | 4.00 | 1.60 | .40 |
| ☐ 167B Duke Snider BOX ......... | 3.00 | 1.20 | .30 |
| ☐ 168A Gil Hodges COMP ........ | 4.00 | 1.60 | .40 |
| ☐ 168B Gil Hodges BOX .......... | 3.00 | 1.20 | .30 |
| ☐ 169 John Podres BOX only ... | 1.00 | .40 | .10 |
| ☐ 170 Ed Roebuck BOX only ..... | .80 | .32 | .08 |
| ☐ 171A Ken Boyer COMP ......... | 3.50 | 1.40 | .35 |
| ☐ 171B Ken Boyer BOX ........... | 4.00 | 1.60 | .40 |
| ☐ 172A J.Cunningham COMP .... | .80 | .32 | .08 |
| ☐ 172B J.Cunningham BOX ...... | .80 | .32 | .08 |
| ☐ 173A Daryl Spencer COMP ... | .80 | .32 | .08 |
| ☐ 173B Daryl Spencer BOX ...... | .80 | .32 | .08 |
| ☐ 174A Larry Jackson COMP .... | .80 | .32 | .08 |
| ☐ 174B Larry Jackson BOX ...... | .80 | .32 | .08 |
| ☐ 175A Lindy McDaniel COMP .. | .80 | .32 | .08 |
| ☐ 175B Lindy McDaniel BOX ..... | .80 | .32 | .08 |
| ☐ 176A Bill White COMP .......... | .80 | .32 | .08 |
| ☐ 176B Bill White BOX ............ | .80 | .32 | .08 |
| ☐ 177A Alex Grammas COMP .... | .80 | .32 | .08 |
| ☐ 177B Alex Grammas BOX ...... | .80 | .32 | .08 |
| ☐ 178A Curt Flood COMP ......... | 1.00 | .40 | .10 |
| ☐ 178B Curt Flood BOX ........... | 1.00 | .40 | .10 |
| ☐ 179A Ernie Broglio COMP ..... | .80 | .32 | .08 |
| ☐ 179B Ernie Broglio BOX ....... | .80 | .32 | .08 |
| ☐ 180A Hal Smith COMP .......... | .80 | .32 | .08 |
| ☐ 180B Hal Smith BOX ............ | .80 | .32 | .08 |
| ☐ 181A Vada Pinson COMP ...... | 1.00 | .40 | .10 |
| ☐ 181B Vada Pinson BOX ........ | 1.00 | .40 | .10 |
| ☐ 182A Frank Robinson COMP ... | 15.00 | 6.00 | 1.50 |
| ☐ 182B Frank Robinson BOX ... | 12.00 | 5.00 | 1.20 |
| ☐ 183 Roy McMillan BOX only .. | 40.00 | 16.00 | 4.00 |

| | | | |
|---|---|---|---|
| ☐ 184A Bob Purkey COMP ........ | .80 | .32 | .08 |
| ☐ 184B Bob Purkey BOX ........... | .80 | .32 | .08 |
| ☐ 185A Ed Kasko COMP ........... | .80 | .32 | .08 |
| ☐ 185B Ed Kasko BOX ............. | .80 | .32 | .08 |
| ☐ 186A Gus Bell COMP ............ | .80 | .32 | .08 |
| ☐ 186B Gus Bell BOX .............. | .80 | .32 | .08 |
| ☐ 187A Jerry Lynch COMP ........ | .80 | .32 | .08 |
| ☐ 187B Jerry Lynch BOX .......... | .80 | .32 | .08 |
| ☐ 188A Ed Bailey COMP ........... | .80 | .32 | .08 |
| ☐ 188B Ed Bailey BOX ............. | .80 | .32 | .08 |
| ☐ 189A Jim O'Toole COMP ....... | .80 | .32 | .08 |
| ☐ 189B Jim O'Toole BOX .......... | .80 | .32 | .08 |
| ☐ 190A Billy Martin COMP ....... | 3.00 | 1.20 | .30 |
| (Sold to Milw.) | | | |
| ☐ 190B Billy Martin BOX .......... | 1.00 | .40 | .10 |
| (no sale mention) | | | |
| ☐ 191A Ernie Banks COMP ...... | 5.00 | 2.00 | .50 |
| ☐ 191B Ernie Banks BOX ......... | 7.50 | 3.00 | .75 |
| ☐ 192A Richie Ashburn COMP .. | 1.50 | .60 | .15 |
| ☐ 192B Richie Ashburn BOX ..... | 1.50 | .60 | .15 |
| ☐ 193A Frank Thomas COMP ... | 6.00 | 2.40 | .60 |
| ☐ 193B Frank Thomas BOX ..... | 20.00 | 8.00 | 2.00 |
| ☐ 194A Don Cardwell COMP ... | .80 | .32 | .08 |
| ☐ 194B Don Cardwell BOX ..... | .80 | .32 | .08 |
| ☐ 195A George Altman COMP ... | .80 | .32 | .08 |
| ☐ 195B George Altman BOX ..... | .80 | .32 | .08 |
| ☐ 196A Ron Santo COMP ........ | 1.00 | .40 | .10 |
| ☐ 196B Ron Santo BOX ........... | 1.00 | .40 | .10 |
| ☐ 197A Glen Hobbie COMP ...... | .80 | .32 | .08 |
| ☐ 197B Glen Hobbie BOX ........ | .80 | .32 | .08 |
| ☐ 198A Sam Taylor COMP ....... | .80 | .32 | .08 |
| ☐ 198B Sam Taylor BOX ......... | .80 | .32 | .08 |
| ☐ 199A Jerry Kindall COMP ..... | .80 | .32 | .08 |
| ☐ 199B Jerry Kindall BOX ....... | .80 | .32 | .08 |
| ☐ 200A Don Elston COMP ........ | .80 | .32 | .08 |
| ☐ 200B Don Elston BOX ........... | .80 | .32 | .08 |

## 1962 Post Cereal

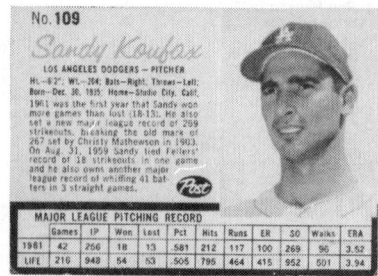

The cards in this 200 card series measure 2 1/2" by 3 1/2". The 1962 Post set is the easiest of the Post sets to complete. The cards are grouped numerically by team, for example, New York Yankees (1-13), Detroit (14-26), Baltimore (27-36), Cleveland (37-45), Chicago White Sox (46-55), Boston (56-64), Washington (65-73), Los Angeles Angels (74-82), Minnesota (83-91), Kansas City (92-100), Los Angeles Dodgers (101-115), Cincinnati (116-130), San Francisco (131-144), Milwaukee (145-157), St. Louis (158-168), Pittsburgh (169-181), Chicago Cubs (182-191), and Philadelphia (192-200). Cards 5B and 6B were printed on thin stock in a two card panel and distributed in a magazine promotion. The scarce cards are 55, 92, 101, 116, 121, and 140. The checklist for this set is the same as that of 1962 Jello and 1962 Post Canadian, but those sets are considered separate issues. The catalog number for this set is F278-37.

| | MINT | VG-E | F-G |
|---|---|---|---|
| COMPLETE SET ........................ | 650.00 | 260.00 | 65.00 |
| COMMON PLAYER (1-200) ........ | .70 | .28 | .07 |

| | # | Player | | | |
|---|---|---|---|---|---|
| ☐ | 1 | Bill Skowron | .80 | .32 | .08 |
| ☐ | 2 | Bobby Richardson | .90 | .36 | .09 |
| ☐ | 3 | Cletis Boyer | .80 | .32 | .08 |
| ☐ | 4 | Tony Kubek | .90 | .36 | .09 |
| ☐ | 5A | Mickey Mantle | 25.00 | 10.00 | 2.50 |
| ☐ | 5B | Mickey Mantle AD | 25.00 | 10.00 | 2.50 |
| ☐ | 6A | Roger Maris | 6.00 | 2.40 | .60 |
| ☐ | 6B | Roger Maris AD | 6.00 | 2.40 | .60 |
| ☐ | 7 | Yogi Berra | 5.00 | 2.00 | .50 |
| ☐ | 8 | Elston Howard | 1.00 | .40 | .10 |
| ☐ | 9 | Whitey Ford | 3.50 | 1.40 | .35 |
| ☐ | 10 | Ralph Terry | .80 | .32 | .08 |
| ☐ | 11 | John Blanchard | .70 | .28 | .07 |
| ☐ | 12 | Luis Arroyo | 1.25 | .50 | .12 |
| ☐ | 13 | Bill Stafford | .70 | .28 | .07 |
| ☐ | 14 | Norm Cash | .80 | .32 | .08 |
| ☐ | 15 | Jake Wood | .70 | .28 | .07 |
| ☐ | 16 | Steve Boros | .80 | .32 | .08 |
| ☐ | 17 | Chico Fernandez | .70 | .28 | .07 |
| ☐ | 18 | Bill Bruton | .70 | .28 | .07 |
| ☐ | 19 | Rocky Colavito | 1.25 | .50 | .12 |
| ☐ | 20 | Al Kaline | 4.00 | 1.60 | .40 |
| ☐ | 21 | Dick Brown | .70 | .28 | .07 |
| ☐ | 22 | Frank Lary | .90 | .36 | .09 |
| ☐ | 23 | Don Mossi | .80 | .32 | .08 |
| ☐ | 24 | Phil Regan | .70 | .28 | .07 |
| ☐ | 25 | Charley Maxwell | .70 | .28 | .07 |
| ☐ | 26 | Jim Bunning | 2.00 | .80 | .20 |
| ☐ | 27A | Jim Gentile | 1.00 | .40 | .10 |
| | | Home: Baltimore | | | |
| ☐ | 27B | Jim Gentile | 7.50 | 3.00 | .75 |
| | | Home: San Lorenzo | | | |
| ☐ | 28 | Marv Breeding | .70 | .28 | .07 |
| ☐ | 29 | Brooks Robinson | 6.00 | 2.40 | .60 |
| ☐ | 30 | Ron Hansen | .70 | .28 | .07 |
| ☐ | 31 | Jackie Brandt | .70 | .28 | .07 |
| ☐ | 32 | Dick Williams | .80 | .32 | .08 |
| ☐ | 33 | Gus Triandos | .70 | .28 | .07 |
| ☐ | 34 | Milt Pappas | .80 | .32 | .08 |
| ☐ | 35 | Hoyt Wilhelm | 3.50 | 1.40 | .35 |
| ☐ | 36 | Chuck Estrada | 1.50 | .60 | .15 |
| ☐ | 37 | Vic Power | .70 | .28 | .07 |
| ☐ | 38 | Johnny Temple | .70 | .28 | .07 |
| ☐ | 39 | Bubba Phillips | .70 | .28 | .07 |
| ☐ | 40 | Tito Francona | .80 | .32 | .08 |
| ☐ | 41 | Willie Kirkland | .70 | .28 | .07 |
| ☐ | 42 | John Romano | .80 | .32 | .08 |
| ☐ | 43 | Jim Perry | .80 | .32 | .08 |
| ☐ | 44 | Woodie Held | .70 | .28 | .07 |
| ☐ | 45 | Chuck Essegian | .70 | .28 | .07 |
| ☐ | 46 | Roy Sievers | .80 | .32 | .08 |
| ☐ | 47 | Nellie Fox | 1.25 | .50 | .12 |
| ☐ | 48 | Al Smith | .70 | .28 | .07 |
| ☐ | 49 | Luis Aparicio | 1.75 | .70 | .17 |
| ☐ | 50 | Jim Landis | .70 | .28 | .07 |
| ☐ | 51 | Minnie Minoso | 1.00 | .40 | .10 |
| ☐ | 52 | Andy Carey | .70 | .28 | .07 |
| ☐ | 53 | Sherman Lollar | .80 | .32 | .08 |
| ☐ | 54 | Bill Pierce | .90 | .36 | .09 |
| ☐ | 55 | Early Wynn | 15.00 | 6.00 | 1.50 |
| ☐ | 56 | Chuck Schilling | .70 | .28 | .07 |
| ☐ | 57 | Pete Runnels | .80 | .32 | .08 |
| ☐ | 58 | Frank Malzone | .80 | .32 | .08 |
| ☐ | 59 | Don Buddin | .70 | .28 | .07 |
| ☐ | 60 | Gary Geiger | 1.00 | .40 | .10 |
| ☐ | 61 | Carl Yastrzemski | 20.00 | 8.00 | 2.00 |
| ☐ | 62 | Jackie Jensen | .90 | .36 | .09 |
| ☐ | 63 | Jim Pagliaroni | .70 | .28 | .07 |
| ☐ | 64 | Don Schwall | .70 | .28 | .07 |
| ☐ | 65 | Dale Long | .70 | .28 | .07 |
| ☐ | 66 | Chuck Cottier | .80 | .32 | .08 |
| ☐ | 67 | Billy Klaus | .70 | .28 | .07 |
| ☐ | 68 | Coot Veal | .70 | .28 | .07 |
| ☐ | 69 | Marty Keough | 20.00 | 8.00 | 2.00 |
| ☐ | 70 | Willie Tasby | .70 | .28 | .07 |
| ☐ | 71 | Gene Woodling | .70 | .28 | .07 |
| ☐ | 72 | Gene Green | .70 | .28 | .07 |
| ☐ | 73 | Dick Donovan | .70 | .28 | .07 |
| ☐ | 74 | Steve Bilko | .70 | .28 | .07 |
| ☐ | 75 | Rocky Bridges | .70 | .28 | .07 |
| ☐ | 76 | Eddie Yost | .70 | .28 | .07 |
| ☐ | 77 | Leon Wagner | .70 | .28 | .07 |
| ☐ | 78 | Albie Pearson | .70 | .28 | .07 |
| ☐ | 79 | Ken Hunt | .70 | .28 | .07 |
| ☐ | 80 | Earl Averill Jr. | .70 | .28 | .07 |
| ☐ | 81 | Ryne Duren | .80 | .32 | .08 |
| ☐ | 82 | Ted Kluszewski | .90 | .36 | .09 |
| ☐ | 83 | Bob Allison | 10.00 | 4.00 | 1.00 |
| ☐ | 84 | Billy Martin | 1.50 | .60 | .15 |
| ☐ | 85 | Harmon Killebrew | 3.00 | 1.20 | .30 |
| ☐ | 86 | Zoilo Versalles | .70 | .28 | .07 |
| ☐ | 87 | Lenny Green | .70 | .28 | .07 |
| ☐ | 88 | Bill Tuttle | .70 | .28 | .07 |
| ☐ | 89 | Jim Lemon | .80 | .32 | .08 |
| ☐ | 90 | Earl Battey | .80 | .32 | .08 |
| ☐ | 91 | Camilo Pascual | .80 | .32 | .08 |
| ☐ | 92 | Norm Sieburn | 30.00 | 12.00 | 3.00 |
| ☐ | 93 | Jerry Lumpe | .70 | .28 | .07 |
| ☐ | 94 | Dick Howser | .90 | .36 | .09 |
| ☐ | 95A | Gene Stephens | 1.00 | .40 | .10 |
| | | Born: Jan. 5 | | | |
| ☐ | 95B | Gene Stephens | 7.50 | 3.00 | .75 |
| | | Born: Jan. 20 | | | |
| ☐ | 96 | Leo Posada | .70 | .28 | .07 |
| ☐ | 97 | Joe Pignatano | .70 | .28 | .07 |
| ☐ | 98 | Jim Archer | .70 | .28 | .07 |
| ☐ | 99 | Haywood Sullivan | .80 | .32 | .08 |
| ☐ | 100 | Art Ditmar | .70 | .28 | .07 |
| ☐ | 101 | Gil Hodges | 35.00 | 14.00 | 3.50 |
| ☐ | 102 | Charlie Neal | .70 | .28 | .07 |
| ☐ | 103 | Daryl Spencer | 12.00 | 5.00 | 1.20 |
| ☐ | 104 | Maury Wills | 2.00 | .80 | .20 |
| ☐ | 105 | Tommy Davis | .80 | .32 | .08 |
| ☐ | 106 | Willie Davis | .80 | .32 | .08 |
| ☐ | 107 | John Roseboro | .70 | .28 | .07 |
| ☐ | 108 | John Podres | 1.00 | .40 | .10 |
| ☐ | 109A | Sandy Koufax | 10.00 | 4.00 | 1.00 |
| ☐ | 109B | Sandy Koufax | 20.00 | 8.00 | 2.00 |
| | | (with blue lines) | | | |
| ☐ | 110 | Don Drysdale | 5.00 | 2.00 | .50 |
| ☐ | 111 | Larry Sherry | .70 | .28 | .07 |
| ☐ | 112 | Jim Gilliam | 1.00 | .40 | .10 |
| ☐ | 113 | Norm Larker | 20.00 | 8.00 | 2.00 |
| ☐ | 114 | Duke Snider | 3.00 | 1.20 | .30 |
| ☐ | 115 | Stan Williams | .70 | .28 | .07 |
| ☐ | 116 | Gordy Coleman | 50.00 | 20.00 | 5.00 |
| ☐ | 117 | Don Blasingame | .70 | .28 | .07 |
| ☐ | 118 | Gene Freese | .70 | .28 | .07 |
| ☐ | 119 | Ed Kasko | .70 | .28 | .07 |
| ☐ | 120 | Gus Bell | .80 | .32 | .08 |
| ☐ | 121 | Vada Pinson | 1.00 | .40 | .10 |
| ☐ | 122 | Frank Robinson | 12.00 | 5.00 | 1.20 |
| ☐ | 123 | Bob Purkey | .70 | .28 | .07 |
| ☐ | 124A | Joey Jay | .80 | .32 | .08 |
| ☐ | 124B | Joey Jay | 8.00 | 3.25 | .80 |
| | | (with blue lines) | | | |
| ☐ | 125 | Jim Brosnan | 20.00 | 8.00 | 2.00 |
| ☐ | 126 | Jim O'Toole | .70 | .28 | .07 |
| ☐ | 127 | Jerry Lynch | 30.00 | 12.00 | 3.00 |
| ☐ | 128 | Wally Post | .70 | .28 | .07 |
| ☐ | 129 | Ken Hunt | .70 | .28 | .07 |
| ☐ | 130 | Jerry Zimmerman | .70 | .28 | .07 |
| ☐ | 131 | Willie McCovey | 40.00 | 16.00 | 4.00 |
| ☐ | 132 | Jose Pagan | .70 | .28 | .07 |
| ☐ | 133 | Felipe Alou | .80 | .32 | .08 |
| ☐ | 134 | Jim Davenport | .80 | .32 | .08 |
| ☐ | 135 | Harvey Kuenn | 1.00 | .40 | .10 |
| ☐ | 136 | Orlando Cepeda | 1.50 | .60 | .15 |
| ☐ | 137 | Ed Bailey | .70 | .28 | .07 |
| ☐ | 138 | Sam Jones | .70 | .28 | .07 |
| ☐ | 139 | Mike McCormick | .80 | .32 | .08 |
| ☐ | 140 | Juan Marichal | 40.00 | 16.00 | 4.00 |
| ☐ | 141 | Jack Sanford | .70 | .28 | .07 |
| ☐ | 142 | Willie Mays | 15.00 | 6.00 | 1.50 |
| ☐ | 143 | Stu Miller | 2.50 | 1.00 | .25 |
| ☐ | 144 | Joe Amalfitano | 10.00 | 4.00 | 1.00 |
| ☐ | 145A | Joe Adcock | .80 | .32 | .08 |
| ☐ | 145B | Joe Adock (sic) ERR | 20.00 | 8.00 | 2.00 |
| ☐ | 146 | Frank Bolling | .70 | .28 | .07 |
| ☐ | 147 | Ed Mathews | 3.00 | 1.20 | .30 |
| ☐ | 148 | Roy McMillan | .70 | .28 | .07 |
| ☐ | 149 | Hank Aaron | 15.00 | 6.00 | 1.50 |
| ☐ | 150 | Gino Cimoli | .70 | .28 | .07 |
| ☐ | 151 | Frank Thomas | .80 | .32 | .08 |
| ☐ | 152 | Joe Torre | .90 | .36 | .09 |
| ☐ | 153 | Lew Burdette | .90 | .36 | .09 |
| ☐ | 154 | Bob Buhl | .70 | .28 | .07 |
| ☐ | 155 | Carlton Willey | .70 | .28 | .07 |
| ☐ | 156 | Lee Maye | .70 | .28 | .07 |
| ☐ | 157 | Al Spangler | .70 | .28 | .07 |
| ☐ | 158 | Bill White | 20.00 | 8.00 | 2.00 |
| ☐ | 159 | Ken Boyer | 1.50 | .60 | .15 |
| ☐ | 160 | Joe Cunningham | .70 | .28 | .07 |
| ☐ | 161 | Carl Warwick | .70 | .28 | .07 |
| ☐ | 162 | Carl Sawatski | .70 | .28 | .07 |
| ☐ | 163 | Lindy McDaniel | .70 | .28 | .07 |
| ☐ | 164 | Ernie Broglio | .70 | .28 | .07 |
| ☐ | 165 | Larry Jackson | .70 | .28 | .07 |
| ☐ | 166 | Curt Flood | .90 | .36 | .09 |
| ☐ | 167 | Curt Simmons | .80 | .32 | .08 |
| ☐ | 168 | Alex Grammas | .70 | .28 | .07 |
| ☐ | 169 | Dick Stuart | .80 | .32 | .08 |
| ☐ | 170 | Bill Mazeroski | .90 | .36 | .09 |
| ☐ | 171 | Don Hoak | .70 | .28 | .07 |
| ☐ | 172 | Dick Groat | 1.00 | .40 | .10 |
| ☐ | 173A | Roberto Clemente | 12.00 | 5.00 | 1.20 |

| ☐ 173B | Roberto Clemente ........<br>(with blue lines) | 20.00 | 8.00 | 2.00 |
|---|---|---|---|---|
| ☐ 174 | Bob Skinner ..................... | .70 | .28 | .07 |
| ☐ 175 | Bill Virdon ...................... | .90 | .36 | .09 |
| ☐ 176 | Smoky Burgess .............. | .80 | .32 | .08 |
| ☐ 177 | Elroy Face ...................... | .80 | .32 | .08 |
| ☐ 178 | Bob Friend ...................... | .80 | .32 | .08 |
| ☐ 179 | Vernon Law ..................... | .80 | .32 | .08 |
| ☐ 180 | Harvey Haddix ................ | .80 | .32 | .08 |
| ☐ 181 | Hal Smith ....................... | .70 | .28 | .07 |
| ☐ 182 | Ed Bouchee ..................... | .70 | .28 | .07 |
| ☐ 183 | Don Zimmer .................... | .80 | .32 | .08 |
| ☐ 184 | Ron Santo ....................... | .90 | .36 | .09 |
| ☐ 185 | Andre Rodgers ................ | .70 | .28 | .07 |
| ☐ 186 | Richie Ashburn ............... | 1.00 | .40 | .10 |
| ☐ 187 | George Altman ................ | .70 | .28 | .07 |
| ☐ 188 | Ernie Banks .................... | 5.00 | 2.00 | .50 |
| ☐ 189 | Sam Taylor ..................... | .90 | .36 | .09 |
| ☐ 190 | Don Elston ...................... | .70 | .28 | .07 |
| ☐ 191 | Jerry Kindall ................... | .70 | .28 | .07 |
| ☐ 192 | Pancho Herrera ............... | .70 | .28 | .07 |
| ☐ 193 | Tony Taylor ..................... | .70 | .28 | .07 |
| ☐ 194 | Ruben Amaro ................... | .70 | .28 | .07 |
| ☐ 195 | Don Demeter .................... | .70 | .28 | .07 |
| ☐ 196 | Bobby Gene Smith ......... | .70 | .28 | .07 |
| ☐ 197 | Clay Dalrymple ............... | .70 | .28 | .07 |
| ☐ 198 | Robin Roberts ................. | 3.00 | 1.20 | .30 |
| ☐ 199 | Art Mahaffey ................... | .70 | .28 | .07 |
| ☐ 200 | John Buzhardt ................. | .70 | .28 | .07 |

## 1963 Post Cereal

The cards in this 200 card set measure 2 1/2" by 3 1/2". The players are grouped by team with American Leaguers comprising 1-100 and National Leaguers 101-200. The ordering of teams is as follows: Minnesota (1-11), New York Yankees, Los Angeles Angels (24-34), Chicago White Sox (35-45), Detroit (46- 56), Baltimore (57-66), Cleveland (67-76), Boston (77-84), Kansas City (85-92), Washington (93-100), San Francisco (101-112), Los Angeles Dodgers (113-124), Cincinnati (125-136), Pittsburgh (137- 147), Milwaukee (148-157), St. Louis (158-168), Chicago Cubs (169-176), Philadelphia (177-184), Houston (185-192), and New York Mets (193-200). In contrast to the 1962 issue, the 1963 Post baseball card series is very difficult to complete. There are many card scarcities reflected in the price list below. Cards of the Post set are easily confused with those of the 1963 Jello set, which are 1/4" narrower (a difference which is often eliminated by bad cutting). The catalog designation is F278- 38.

| | | MINT | VG-E | F-G |
|---|---|---|---|---|
| COMPLETE SET | .......................... | 2100.00 | 900.00 | 225.00 |
| COMMON PLAYER (1-200) | ........ | 1.00 | .40 | .10 |

| ☐ 1 | Vic Power ....................... | 1.00 | .40 | .10 |
|---|---|---|---|---|
| ☐ 2 | Bernie Allen .................... | 1.00 | .40 | .10 |
| ☐ 3 | Zoilo Versalles ................ | 1.00 | .40 | .10 |
| ☐ 4 | Rich Rollins .................... | 1.00 | .40 | .10 |

| ☐ 5 | Harmon Killebrew .......... | 9.00 | 3.75 | .90 |
|---|---|---|---|---|
| ☐ 6 | Lenny Green ................... | 25.00 | 10.00 | 2.50 |
| ☐ 7 | Bob Allison .................... | 1.00 | .40 | .10 |
| ☐ 8 | Earl Battey .................... | 1.00 | .40 | .10 |
| ☐ 9 | Camilo Pascual .............. | 1.00 | .40 | .10 |
| ☐ 10 | Jim Kaat ........................ | 1.50 | .60 | .15 |
| ☐ 11 | Jack Kralick ................... | 1.00 | .40 | .10 |
| ☐ 12 | Bill Skowron .................. | 1.25 | .50 | .12 |
| ☐ 13 | Bobby Richardson .......... | 1.50 | .60 | .15 |
| ☐ 14 | Cletis Boyer ................... | 1.25 | .50 | .12 |
| ☐ 15 | Mickey Mantle ................ | 150.00 | 60.00 | 15.00 |
| ☐ 16 | Roger Maris .................... | 100.00 | 40.00 | 10.00 |
| ☐ 17 | Yogi Berra ...................... | 6.00 | 2.40 | .60 |
| ☐ 18 | Elston Howard ................ | 1.25 | .50 | .12 |
| ☐ 19 | Whitey Ford .................... | 4.00 | 1.60 | .40 |
| ☐ 20 | Ralph Terry .................... | 1.00 | .40 | .10 |
| ☐ 21 | John Blanchard ............... | 1.00 | .40 | .10 |
| ☐ 22 | Bill Stafford ................... | 1.00 | .40 | .10 |
| ☐ 23 | Tom Tresh ...................... | 1.00 | .40 | .10 |
| ☐ 24 | Steve Bilko .................... | 1.00 | .40 | .10 |
| ☐ 25 | Bill Moran ...................... | 1.00 | .40 | .10 |
| ☐ 26A | Joe Koppe ......................<br>BA: .277 | 1.25 | .50 | .12 |
| ☐ 26B | Joe Koppe ......................<br>BA: .227 | 4.00 | 1.60 | .40 |
| ☐ 27 | Felix Torres ................... | 1.00 | .40 | .10 |
| ☐ 28A | Leon Wagner ..................<br>BA: .278 | 1.25 | .50 | .12 |
| ☐ 28B | Leon Wagner ..................<br>BA: .272 | 4.00 | 1.60 | .40 |
| ☐ 29 | Albie Pearson ................. | 1.00 | .40 | .10 |
| ☐ 30 | Lee Thomas ....................<br>(photo actually<br>George Thomas) | 50.00 | 20.00 | 5.00 |
| ☐ 31 | Bob Rodgers ................... | 1.00 | .40 | .10 |
| ☐ 32 | Dean Chance ................... | 1.00 | .40 | .10 |
| ☐ 33 | Ken McBride .................... | 1.00 | .40 | .10 |
| ☐ 34 | George Thomas ...............<br>(photo actually<br>Lee Thomas) | 1.00 | .40 | .10 |
| ☐ 35 | Joe Cunningham .............. | 1.00 | .40 | .10 |
| ☐ 36 | Nelson Fox ...................... | 1.50 | .60 | .15 |
| ☐ 37 | Luis Aparicio .................. | 2.00 | .80 | .20 |
| ☐ 38 | Al Smith ........................ | 20.00 | 8.00 | 2.00 |
| ☐ 39 | Floyd Robinson ............... | 60.00 | 24.00 | 6.00 |
| ☐ 40 | Jim Landis ...................... | 1.00 | .40 | .10 |
| ☐ 41 | Charlie Maxwell .............. | 1.00 | .40 | .10 |
| ☐ 42 | Sherman Lollar ............... | 1.00 | .40 | .10 |
| ☐ 43 | Early Wynn ..................... | 2.50 | 1.00 | .25 |
| ☐ 44 | Juan Pizarro ................... | 1.00 | .40 | .10 |
| ☐ 45 | Ray Herbert .................... | 1.00 | .40 | .10 |
| ☐ 46 | Norm Cash ...................... | 1.25 | .50 | .12 |
| ☐ 47 | Steve Boros .................... | 1.00 | .40 | .10 |
| ☐ 48 | Dick McAuliffe ................ | 12.50 | 5.00 | 1.25 |
| ☐ 49 | Bill Bruton ..................... | 1.00 | .40 | .10 |
| ☐ 50 | Rocky Colavito ............... | 1.50 | .60 | .15 |
| ☐ 51 | Al Kaline ........................ | 6.00 | 2.40 | .60 |
| ☐ 52 | Dick Brown ..................... | 1.00 | .40 | .10 |
| ☐ 53 | Jim Bunning ................... | 75.00 | 30.00 | 7.50 |
| ☐ 54 | Hank Aguirre .................. | 1.00 | .40 | .10 |
| ☐ 55 | Frank Lary ..................... | 1.25 | .50 | .12 |
| ☐ 56 | Don Mossi ...................... | 1.25 | .50 | .12 |
| ☐ 57 | Jim Gentile ..................... | 1.25 | .50 | .12 |
| ☐ 58 | Jackie Brandt .................. | 1.00 | .40 | .10 |
| ☐ 59 | Brooks Robinson ............. | 6.00 | 2.40 | .60 |
| ☐ 60 | Ron Hanson ..................... | 1.00 | .40 | .10 |
| ☐ 61 | Jerry Adair ..................... | 100.00 | 40.00 | 10.00 |
| ☐ 62 | John (Boog) Powell ........ | 1.50 | .60 | .15 |
| ☐ 63 | Russ Snyder ................... | 1.00 | .40 | .10 |
| ☐ 64 | Steve Barber .................. | 1.00 | .40 | .10 |
| ☐ 65 | Milt Pappas .................... | 1.25 | .50 | .12 |
| ☐ 66 | Robin Roberts ................. | 2.50 | 1.00 | .25 |
| ☐ 67 | Tito Francona ................. | 1.00 | .40 | .10 |
| ☐ 68 | Jerry Kindall ................... | 1.00 | .40 | .10 |
| ☐ 69 | Woody Held ..................... | 1.00 | .40 | .10 |
| ☐ 70 | Bubba Phillips ................. | 10.00 | 4.00 | 1.00 |
| ☐ 71 | Chuck Essegian ............... | 1.00 | .40 | .10 |
| ☐ 72 | Willie Kirkland ................ | 1.00 | .40 | .10 |
| ☐ 73 | Al Luplow ....................... | 1.00 | .40 | .10 |
| ☐ 74 | Ty Cline ......................... | 1.00 | .40 | .10 |
| ☐ 75 | Dick Donovan .................. | 1.00 | .40 | .10 |
| ☐ 76 | John Romano ................... | 1.00 | .40 | .10 |
| ☐ 77 | Pete Runnels ................... | 1.25 | .50 | .12 |
| ☐ 78 | Ed Bressoud .................... | 1.00 | .40 | .10 |
| ☐ 79 | Frank Malzone ................. | 1.00 | .40 | .10 |
| ☐ 80 | Carl Yastrzemski ............ | 200.00 | 80.00 | 20.00 |
| ☐ 81 | Gary Geiger .................... | 1.00 | .40 | .10 |
| ☐ 82 | Lou Clinton ..................... | 1.00 | .40 | .10 |
| ☐ 83 | Earl Wilson ..................... | 1.00 | .40 | .10 |
| ☐ 84 | Bill Monbouquette ........... | 1.00 | .40 | .10 |
| ☐ 85 | Norm Sieburn .................. | 1.00 | .40 | .10 |
| ☐ 86 | Jerry Lumpe .................... | 50.00 | 20.00 | 5.00 |
| ☐ 87 | Manny Jimenez ............... | 50.00 | 20.00 | 5.00 |

| | | | | |
|---|---|---|---|---|
| ☐ 88 | Gino Cimoli | 1.00 | .40 | .10 |
| ☐ 89 | Ed Charles | 1.00 | .40 | .10 |
| ☐ 90 | Ed Rakow | 1.00 | .40 | .10 |
| ☐ 91 | Bob Del Greco | 1.00 | .40 | .10 |
| ☐ 92 | Haywood Sullivan | 1.00 | .40 | .10 |
| ☐ 93 | Chuck Hinton | 1.00 | .40 | .10 |
| ☐ 94 | Ken Retzer | 1.00 | .40 | .10 |
| ☐ 95 | Harry Bright | 1.00 | .40 | .10 |
| ☐ 96 | Bob Johnson | 1.00 | .40 | .10 |
| ☐ 97 | Dave Stenhouse | 8.00 | 3.25 | .80 |
| ☐ 98 | Chuck Cottier | 15.00 | 6.00 | 1.50 |
| ☐ 99 | Tom Cheney | 1.00 | .40 | .10 |
| ☐ 100 | Claude Osteen | 10.00 | 4.00 | 1.00 |
| ☐ 101 | Orlando Cepeda | 1.50 | .60 | .15 |
| ☐ 102 | Charley Hiller | 1.00 | .40 | .10 |
| ☐ 103 | Jose Pagan | 1.00 | .40 | .10 |
| ☐ 104 | Jim Davenport | 1.25 | .50 | .12 |
| ☐ 105 | Harvey Kuenn | 1.50 | .60 | .15 |
| ☐ 106 | Willie Mays | 16.00 | 6.50 | 1.60 |
| ☐ 107 | Felipe Alou | 1.25 | .50 | .12 |
| ☐ 108 | Tom Haller | 50.00 | 20.00 | 5.00 |
| ☐ 109 | Juan Marichal | 3.00 | 1.20 | .30 |
| ☐ 110 | Jack Sanford | 1.00 | .40 | .10 |
| ☐ 111 | Bill O'Dell | 1.00 | .40 | .10 |
| ☐ 112 | Willie McCovey | 3.50 | 1.40 | .35 |
| ☐ 113 | Lee Walls | 1.00 | .40 | .10 |
| ☐ 114 | Jim Gilliam | 1.25 | .50 | .12 |
| ☐ 115 | Maury Wills | 1.50 | .60 | .15 |
| ☐ 116 | Ron Fairly | 1.00 | .40 | .10 |
| ☐ 117 | Tommy Davis | 1.25 | .50 | .12 |
| ☐ 118 | Duke Snider | 3.50 | 1.40 | .35 |
| ☐ 119 | Willie Davis | 100.00 | 40.00 | 10.00 |
| ☐ 120 | John Roseboro | 1.00 | .40 | .10 |
| ☐ 121 | Sandy Koufax | 10.00 | 4.00 | 1.00 |
| ☐ 122 | Stan Williams | 1.00 | .40 | .10 |
| ☐ 123 | Don Drysdale | 3.50 | 1.40 | .35 |
| ☐ 124 | Daryl Spencer | 1.00 | .40 | .10 |
| ☐ 125 | Gordy Coleman | 1.00 | .40 | .10 |
| ☐ 126 | Don Blasingame | 1.00 | .40 | .10 |
| ☐ 127 | Leo Cardenas | 1.00 | .40 | .10 |
| ☐ 128 | Eddie Kasko | 100.00 | 40.00 | 10.00 |
| ☐ 129 | Jerry Lynch | 8.00 | 3.25 | .80 |
| ☐ 130 | Vada Pinson | 1.25 | .50 | .12 |
| ☐ 131A | Frank Robinson (no stripes) | 5.00 | 2.00 | .50 |
| ☐ 131B | Frank Robinson (stripes on hat) | 7.50 | 3.00 | .75 |
| ☐ 132 | John Edwards | 1.00 | .40 | .10 |
| ☐ 133 | Joey Jay | 1.00 | .40 | .10 |
| ☐ 134 | Bob Purkey | 1.00 | .40 | .10 |
| ☐ 135 | Marty Keough | 12.50 | 5.00 | 1.25 |
| ☐ 136 | Jim O'Toole | 1.00 | .40 | .10 |
| ☐ 137 | Dick Stuart | 1.25 | .50 | .12 |
| ☐ 138 | Bill Mazeroski | 1.50 | .60 | .15 |
| ☐ 139 | Dick Groat | 1.25 | .50 | .12 |
| ☐ 140 | Don Hoak | 20.00 | 8.00 | 2.00 |
| ☐ 141 | Bob Skinner | 10.00 | 4.00 | 1.00 |
| ☐ 142 | Bill Virdon | 1.25 | .50 | .12 |
| ☐ 143 | Roberto Clemente | 10.00 | 4.00 | 1.00 |
| ☐ 144 | Smoky Burgess | 1.25 | .50 | .12 |
| ☐ 145 | Bob Friend | 1.25 | .50 | .12 |
| ☐ 146 | Al McBean | 1.00 | .40 | .10 |
| ☐ 147 | Elroy Face | 1.25 | .50 | .12 |
| ☐ 148 | Joe Adcock | 1.25 | .50 | .12 |
| ☐ 149 | Frank Bolling | 1.00 | .40 | .10 |
| ☐ 150 | Roy McMillan | 1.00 | .40 | .10 |
| ☐ 151 | Eddie Mathews | 6.00 | 2.40 | .60 |
| ☐ 152 | Hank Aaron | 60.00 | 24.00 | 6.00 |
| ☐ 153 | Del Crandall | 25.00 | 10.00 | 2.50 |
| ☐ 154A | Bob Shaw COR | 1.25 | .50 | .12 |
| ☐ 154B | Bob Shaw ERR (two "in 1959" in same sentence) | 10.00 | 4.00 | 1.00 |
| ☐ 155 | Lew Burdette | 1.50 | .60 | .15 |
| ☐ 156 | Joe Torre | 1.50 | .60 | .15 |
| ☐ 157 | Tony Cloninger | 1.00 | .40 | .10 |
| ☐ 158 | Bill White | 1.25 | .50 | .12 |
| ☐ 159 | Julian Javier | 1.00 | .40 | .10 |
| ☐ 160 | Ken Boyer | 1.50 | .60 | .15 |
| ☐ 161 | Julio Gotay | 1.00 | .40 | .10 |
| ☐ 162 | Curt Flood | 75.00 | 30.00 | 7.50 |
| ☐ 163 | Charlie James | 1.00 | .40 | .10 |
| ☐ 164 | Gene Oliver | 1.00 | .40 | .10 |
| ☐ 165 | Ernie Broglio | 1.00 | .40 | .10 |
| ☐ 166 | Bob Gibson | 3.50 | 1.40 | .35 |
| ☐ 167A | Lindy McDaniel (no asterisk) | 4.00 | 1.60 | .40 |
| ☐ 167B | Lindy McDaniel (asterisk traded line) | 1.25 | .50 | .12 |
| ☐ 168 | Ray Washburn | 1.00 | .40 | .10 |
| ☐ 169 | Ernie Banks | 4.00 | 1.60 | .40 |
| ☐ 170 | Ron Santo | 1.50 | .60 | .15 |
| ☐ 171 | George Altman | 1.00 | .40 | .10 |
| ☐ 172 | Billy Williams | 75.00 | 30.00 | 7.50 |
| ☐ 173 | Andre Rodgers | 5.00 | 2.00 | .50 |
| ☐ 174 | Ken Hubbs | 12.50 | 5.00 | 1.25 |
| ☐ 175 | Don Landrum | 1.00 | .40 | .10 |
| ☐ 176 | Dick Bertell | 10.00 | 4.00 | 1.00 |
| ☐ 177 | Roy Sievers | 1.25 | .50 | .12 |
| ☐ 178 | Tony Taylor | 1.00 | .40 | .10 |
| ☐ 179 | John Callison | 1.25 | .50 | .12 |
| ☐ 180 | Don Demeter | 1.00 | .40 | .10 |
| ☐ 181 | Tony Gonzalez | 8.00 | 3.25 | .80 |
| ☐ 182 | Wes Covington | 12.50 | 5.00 | 1.25 |
| ☐ 183 | Art Mahaffey | 1.00 | .40 | .10 |
| ☐ 184 | Clay Dalrymple | 1.00 | .40 | .10 |
| ☐ 185 | Al Spangler | 1.00 | .40 | .10 |
| ☐ 186 | Roman Mejias | 1.00 | .40 | .10 |
| ☐ 187 | Bob Aspromonte | 200.00 | 80.00 | 20.00 |
| ☐ 188 | Norm Larker | 20.00 | 8.00 | 2.00 |
| ☐ 189 | Johnny Temple | 1.00 | .40 | .10 |
| ☐ 190 | Carl Warwick | 1.00 | .40 | .10 |
| ☐ 191 | Bob Lillis | 1.00 | .40 | .10 |
| ☐ 192 | Dick Farrell | 1.00 | .40 | .10 |
| ☐ 193 | Gil Hodges | 2.50 | 1.00 | .25 |
| ☐ 194 | Marv Throneberry | 1.25 | .50 | .12 |
| ☐ 195 | Charlie Neal | 5.00 | 2.00 | .50 |
| ☐ 196 | Frank Thomas | 100.00 | 40.00 | 10.00 |
| ☐ 197 | Richie Ashburn | 12.50 | 5.00 | 1.25 |
| ☐ 198 | Felix Mantilla | 1.00 | .40 | .10 |
| ☐ 199 | Rod Kanehl | 10.00 | 4.00 | 1.00 |
| ☐ 200 | Roger Craig | 1.50 | .60 | .15 |

# 1986 Quaker Granola

This set of 33 cards was available in packages of Quaker Oats Chewy Granola, three player cards plus a complete set offer card in each package. The set was also available through a mail-in offer where anyone sending in four UPC seals from Chewy Granola (before 12/31/86) would receive a complete set. The cards were produced by Topps for Quaker Oats and are 2 1/2" by 3 1/2". Card backs are printed in red and blue on gray card stock. The cards are numbered on the front and the back.

| | | MINT | VG-E | F-G |
|---|---|---|---|---|
| COMPLETE SET | | 6.00 | 2.40 | .60 |
| COMMON PLAYER | | .10 | .04 | .01 |
| ☐ 1 | Willie McGee | .20 | .08 | .02 |
| ☐ 2 | Dwight Gooden | .60 | .24 | .06 |
| ☐ 3 | Vince Coleman | .40 | .16 | .04 |
| ☐ 4 | Gary Carter | .30 | .12 | .03 |
| ☐ 5 | Jack Clark | .10 | .04 | .01 |
| ☐ 6 | Steve Garvey | .30 | .12 | .03 |
| ☐ 7 | Tony Gwynn | .30 | .12 | .03 |
| ☐ 8 | Dale Murphy | .50 | .20 | .05 |
| ☐ 9 | Dave Parker | .25 | .10 | .02 |
| ☐ 10 | Tim Raines | .60 | .24 | .06 |
| ☐ 11 | Pete Rose | .60 | .24 | .06 |
| ☐ 12 | Nolan Ryan | .40 | .16 | .04 |
| ☐ 13 | Ryne Sandberg | .30 | .12 | .03 |
| ☐ 14 | Mike Schmidt | .50 | .20 | .05 |
| ☐ 15 | Ozzie Smith | .15 | .06 | .01 |
| ☐ 16 | Darryl Strawberry | .50 | .20 | .05 |
| ☐ 17 | Fernando Valenzuela | .30 | .12 | .03 |

| | | | |
|---|---|---|---|
| ☐ 18 Don Mattingly | 1.00 | .40 | .10 |
| ☐ 19 Bret Saberhagen | .20 | .08 | .02 |
| ☐ 20 Ozzie Guillen | .20 | .08 | .02 |
| ☐ 21 Bert Blyleven | .15 | .06 | .01 |
| ☐ 22 Wade Boggs | .75 | .30 | .07 |
| ☐ 23 George Brett | .50 | .20 | .05 |
| ☐ 24 Darrell Evans | .10 | .04 | .01 |
| ☐ 25 Rickey Henderson | .50 | .20 | .05 |
| ☐ 26 Reggie Jackson | .50 | .20 | .05 |
| ☐ 27 Eddie Murray | .40 | .16 | .04 |
| ☐ 28 Phil Niekro | .20 | .08 | .02 |
| ☐ 29 Dan Quisenberry | .15 | .06 | .01 |
| ☐ 30 Jim Rice | .30 | .12 | .03 |
| ☐ 31 Cal Ripken | .35 | .14 | .03 |
| ☐ 32 Tom Seaver | .30 | .12 | .03 |
| ☐ 33 Dave Winfield | .30 | .12 | .03 |
| ☐ 34 Offer Card for | .03 | .01 | .00 |
| the complete set | | | |
| (unnumbered) | | | |

## 1984 Ralston Purina

 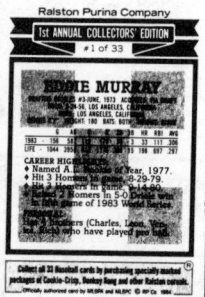

The cards in this 33 card set measure 2 1/2" by 3 1/2". In 1984 the Ralston Purina Company issued what it has entitled "The First Annual Collectors Edition of Baseball Cards." The cards feature portrait photos of the players rather than batting action shots. The Topps logo appears along with the Ralston logo on the front of the card. The backs are completely different from the Topps cards of this year; in fact, they contain neither a Topps logo nor a Topps copyright. Large quantities of these cards were obtained by card dealers for direct distribution into the organized hobby, hence the relatively low price of the set.

| | MINT | VG-E | F-G |
|---|---|---|---|
| COMPLETE SET | 3.00 | 1.20 | .30 |
| COMMON PLAYER | .05 | .02 | .00 |
| ☐ 1 Eddie Murray | .30 | .12 | .03 |
| ☐ 2 Ozzie Smith | .05 | .02 | .00 |
| ☐ 3 Ted Simmons | .05 | .02 | .00 |
| ☐ 4 Pete Rose | .50 | .20 | .05 |
| ☐ 5 Greg Luzinski | .05 | .02 | .00 |
| ☐ 6 Andre Dawson | .10 | .04 | .01 |
| ☐ 7 Dave Winfield | .20 | .08 | .02 |
| ☐ 8 Tom Seaver | .25 | .10 | .02 |
| ☐ 9 Jim Rice | .20 | .08 | .02 |
| ☐ 10 Fernando Valenzuela | .20 | .08 | .02 |
| ☐ 11 Wade Boggs | .50 | .20 | .05 |
| ☐ 12 Dale Murphy | .40 | .16 | .04 |
| ☐ 13 George Brett | .35 | .14 | .03 |
| ☐ 14 Nolan Ryan | .25 | .10 | .02 |
| ☐ 15 Rickey Henderson | .35 | .14 | .03 |
| ☐ 16 Steve Carlton | .20 | .08 | .02 |
| ☐ 17 Rod Carew | .25 | .10 | .02 |
| ☐ 18 Steve Garvey | .25 | .10 | .02 |
| ☐ 19 Reggie Jackson | .35 | .14 | .03 |
| ☐ 20 Dave Concepcion | .05 | .02 | .00 |
| ☐ 21 Robin Yount | .20 | .08 | .02 |
| ☐ 22 Mike Schmidt | .40 | .16 | .04 |
| ☐ 23 Jim Palmer | .20 | .08 | .02 |

| | | | |
|---|---|---|---|
| ☐ 24 Bruce Sutter | .10 | .04 | .01 |
| ☐ 25 Dan Quisenberry | .10 | .04 | .01 |
| ☐ 26 Bill Madlock | .10 | .04 | .01 |
| ☐ 27 Cecil Cooper | .05 | .02 | .00 |
| ☐ 28 Gary Carter | .25 | .10 | .02 |
| ☐ 29 Fred Lynn | .10 | .04 | .01 |
| ☐ 30 Pedro Guerrero | .15 | .06 | .01 |
| ☐ 31 Ron Guidry | .10 | .04 | .01 |
| ☐ 32 Keith Hernandez | .20 | .08 | .02 |
| ☐ 33 Carlton Fisk | .10 | .04 | .01 |

## 1983 Rangers Affiliated Food

The cards in this 28 card set measure 2 3/8" by 3 1/2". The Affiliated Food Stores chain of Arlington, Texas, produced this set of Texas Rangers late during the 1983 baseball season. Complete sets were given to children 13 and under at the September 3, 1983, Rangers game. The cards are numbered by uniform number and feature the player's name, card number, and the words "1983 Rangers" on the bottom front. The backs contain biographical data, career totals, a small black and white insert picture of the player, and the Affiliated Food Stores' logo. The coaches card is unnumbered.

| | MINT | VG-E | F-G |
|---|---|---|---|
| COMPLETE SET | 5.00 | 2.00 | .50 |
| COMMON PLAYER | .15 | .06 | .01 |
| ☐ 1 Bill Stein | .15 | .06 | .01 |
| ☐ 2 Mike Richardt | .15 | .06 | .01 |
| ☐ 3 Wayne Tolleson | .15 | .06 | .01 |
| ☐ 5 Billy Sample | .15 | .06 | .01 |
| ☐ 6 Bobby Jones | .15 | .06 | .01 |
| ☐ 7 Bucky Dent | .25 | .10 | .02 |
| ☐ 8 Bobby Johnson | .15 | .06 | .01 |
| ☐ 9 Pete O'Brien | .75 | .30 | .07 |
| ☐ 10 Jim Sundberg | .25 | .10 | .02 |
| ☐ 11 Doug Rader MGR | .25 | .10 | .02 |
| ☐ 12 Dave Hostetler | .20 | .08 | .02 |
| ☐ 14 Larry Biittner | .15 | .06 | .01 |
| ☐ 15 Larry Parrish | .35 | .14 | .03 |
| ☐ 17 Mickey Rivers | .20 | .08 | .02 |
| ☐ 21 Odell Jones | .15 | .06 | .01 |
| ☐ 24 Dave Schmidt | .15 | .06 | .01 |
| ☐ 25 Buddy Bell | .50 | .20 | .05 |
| ☐ 26 George Wright | .15 | .06 | .01 |
| ☐ 28 Frank Tanana | .25 | .10 | .02 |
| ☐ 29 John Butcher | .15 | .06 | .01 |
| ☐ 32 John Matlack | .20 | .08 | .02 |
| ☐ 40 Rick Honeycutt | .20 | .08 | .02 |
| ☐ 41 Dave Tobik | .15 | .06 | .01 |
| ☐ 44 Danny Darwin | .20 | .08 | .02 |
| ☐ 46 Jim Anderson | .15 | .06 | .01 |
| ☐ 48 Mike Smithson | .20 | .08 | .02 |
| ☐ 49 Charlie Hough | .35 | .14 | .03 |
| ☐ xx Rangers Coaches: | .15 | .06 | .01 |
| (unnumbered) | | | |
| Wayne Terwilliger 42 | | | |
| Merv Rettenmund 22 | | | |
| Dick Such 52 | | | |
| Glenn Ezell 18 | | | |
| Rich Donnelly 37 | | | |

## 1984 Rangers Jarvis Press

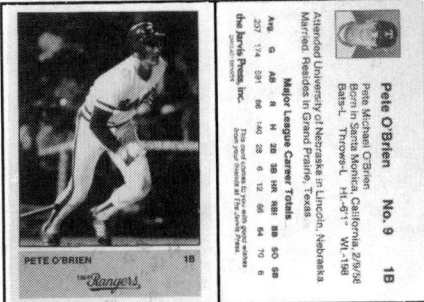

The cards in this 30 card set measure 2 1/2" by 3 1/2". The Jarvis Press of Dallas issued this full-color regional set of Texas Rangers. Cards are numbered on the front by the players uniform number. The cards were issued on an uncut sheet. Twenty-seven player cards, a manager card, a trainer card (unnumbered) and a coaches card (unnumbered) comprise this set. The backs are black and white and contain biographical information, statistics, and an additional photo of the player.

|  |  | MINT | VG-E | F-G |
|---|---|---|---|---|
| COMPLETE SET | | 5.00 | 2.00 | .50 |
| COMMON PLAYER | | .15 | .06 | .01 |
| ☐ 1 | Bill Stein | .15 | .06 | .01 |
| ☐ 2 | Alan Bannister | .15 | .06 | .01 |
| ☐ 3 | Wayne Tolleson | .15 | .06 | .01 |
| ☐ 5 | Billy Sample | .15 | .06 | .01 |
| ☐ 6 | Bobby Jones | .15 | .06 | .01 |
| ☐ 7 | Ned Yost | .15 | .06 | .01 |
| ☐ 9 | Pete O'Brien | .50 | .20 | .05 |
| ☐ 11 | Doug Rader MGR | .25 | .10 | .02 |
| ☐ 13 | Tommy Dunbar | .25 | .10 | .02 |
| ☐ 14 | Jim Anderson | .15 | .06 | .01 |
| ☐ 15 | Larry Parrish | .35 | .14 | .03 |
| ☐ 16 | Mike Mason | .25 | .10 | .02 |
| ☐ 17 | Mickey Rivers | .25 | .10 | .02 |
| ☐ 19 | Curtis Wilkerson | .20 | .08 | .02 |
| ☐ 20 | Jeff Kunkel | .20 | .08 | .02 |
| ☐ 21 | Odell Jones | .15 | .06 | .01 |
| ☐ 24 | Dave Schmidt | .15 | .06 | .01 |
| ☐ 25 | Buddy Bell | .50 | .20 | .05 |
| ☐ 26 | George Wright | .25 | .10 | .02 |
| ☐ 28 | Frank Tanana | .25 | .10 | .02 |
| ☐ 30 | Marv Foley | .15 | .06 | .01 |
| ☐ 31 | Dave Stewart | .20 | .08 | .02 |
| ☐ 32 | Gary Ward | .25 | .10 | .02 |
| ☐ 36 | Dickie Noles | .15 | .06 | .01 |
| ☐ 43 | Donnie Scott | .15 | .06 | .01 |
| ☐ 44 | Danny Darwin | .20 | .08 | .02 |
| ☐ 49 | Charlie Hough | .35 | .14 | .03 |
| ☐ 53 | Joey McLaughlin | .15 | .06 | .01 |
| ☐ xx | Bill Ziegler (Trainer) (unnumbered) | .15 | .06 | .01 |
| ☐ xx | Rangers Coaches: (unnumbered) | .15 | .06 | .01 |

Merv Rettenmund 22
Rich Donnelly 37
Glenn Ezell 18
Dick Such 52
Wayne Terwilliger 42

## 1985 Rangers Performance

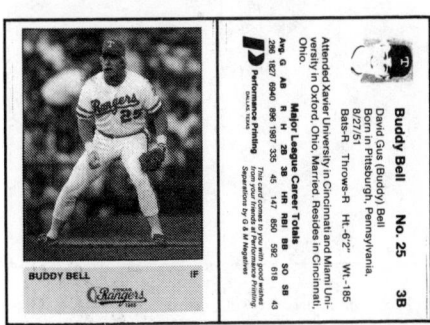

The cards in this 28 card set measure 2 3/8" by 3 1/2". Performance Printing sponsored this full-color regional set of Texas Rangers. Cards are numbered on the back by the players uniform number. The cards were also issued on an uncut sheet. Twenty-five player cards, a manager card, a trainer card (unnumbered) and a coaches card (unnumbered) comprise this set. The backs are black and white and contain biographical information, statistics, and an additional photo of the player.

|  |  | MINT | VG-E | F-G |
|---|---|---|---|---|
| COMPLETE SET | | 5.00 | 2.00 | .50 |
| COMMON PLAYER | | .15 | .06 | .01 |
| ☐ 0 | Oddibe McDowell | .75 | .30 | .07 |
| ☐ 1 | Bill Stein | .15 | .06 | .01 |
| ☐ 2 | Bobby Valentine MGR | .35 | .14 | .03 |
| ☐ 3 | Wayne Tolleson | .15 | .06 | .01 |
| ☐ 4 | Don Slaught | .25 | .10 | .02 |
| ☐ 5 | Alan Bannister | .15 | .06 | .01 |
| ☐ 6 | Bobby Jones | .15 | .06 | .01 |
| ☐ 7 | Glenn Brummer | .15 | .06 | .01 |
| ☐ 8 | Luis Pujols | .15 | .06 | .01 |
| ☐ 9 | Pete O'Brien | .50 | .20 | .05 |
| ☐ 11 | Toby Harrah | .30 | .12 | .03 |
| ☐ 13 | Tommy Dunbar | .20 | .08 | .02 |
| ☐ 15 | Larry Parrish | .35 | .14 | .03 |
| ☐ 16 | Mike Mason | .20 | .08 | .02 |
| ☐ 19 | Curtis Wilkerson | .20 | .08 | .02 |
| ☐ 24 | Dave Schmidt | .15 | .06 | .01 |
| ☐ 25 | Buddy Bell | .50 | .20 | .05 |
| ☐ 27 | Greg Harris | .30 | .12 | .03 |
| ☐ 30 | Dave Rozema | .20 | .08 | .02 |
| ☐ 32 | Gary Ward | .25 | .10 | .02 |
| ☐ 36 | Dickie Noles | .15 | .06 | .01 |
| ☐ 41 | Chris Welsh | .15 | .06 | .01 |
| ☐ 44 | Cliff Johnson | .15 | .06 | .01 |
| ☐ 46 | Burt Hooton | .20 | .08 | .02 |
| ☐ 48 | Dave Stewart | .20 | .08 | .02 |
| ☐ 49 | Charlie Hough | .35 | .14 | .03 |
| ☐ xx | Trainers: Bill Ziegler Danny Wheat (unnumbered) | .15 | .06 | .01 |
| ☐ xx | Rangers Coaches: (unnumbered) | .15 | .06 | .01 |

Art Howe 10
Rich Donnelly 37
Glenn Ezell 18
Tom House 35
Wayne Terwilliger 42

## 1986 Rangers Performance

Performance Printing of Dallas produced a 28 card set of Texas Rangers which were given out at the stadium on August 23rd. Cards measure 2 3/8" by

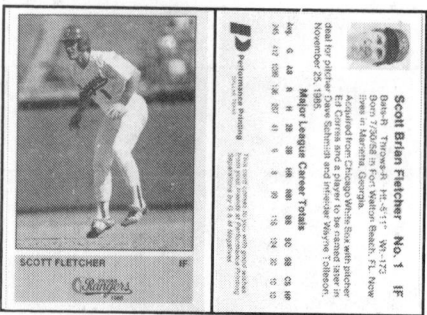

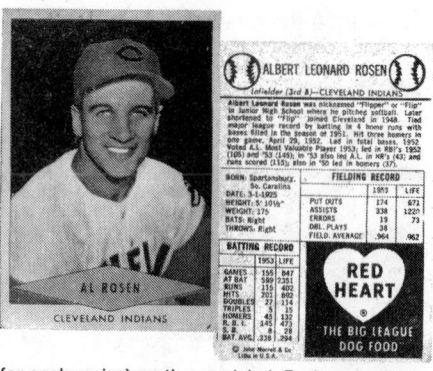

3 1/2" and are in full color. The cards are unnumbered except for uniform number which is given on the card back. Card backs feature black printing on white card stock with a small picture of the player's head in the upper left corner. The set seems to be more desirable than the previous Ranger sets due to the Rangers' 1986 success which was directly related to their outstanding rookie crop.

|  | | MINT | VG-E | F-G |
|---|---|---|---|---|
| COMPLETE SET | | 6.50 | 2.60 | .65 |
| COMMON PLAYER | | .10 | .04 | .01 |
| ☐ 0 | Oddibe McDowell | .50 | .20 | .05 |
| ☐ 1 | Scott Fletcher | .20 | .08 | .02 |
| ☐ 2 | Bobby Valentine MGR | .20 | .08 | .02 |
| ☐ 3 | Ruben Sierra | 1.00 | .40 | .10 |
| ☐ 4 | Don Slaught | .15 | .06 | .01 |
| ☐ 9 | Pete O'Brien | .40 | .16 | .04 |
| ☐ 11 | Toby Harrah | .15 | .06 | .01 |
| ☐ 12 | Geno Petralli | .10 | .04 | .01 |
| ☐ 15 | Larry Parrish | .20 | .08 | .02 |
| ☐ 16 | Mike Mason | .10 | .04 | .01 |
| ☐ 17 | Darrell Porter | .15 | .06 | .01 |
| ☐ 18 | Edwin Correa | .40 | .16 | .04 |
| ☐ 19 | Curtis Wilkerson | .10 | .04 | .01 |
| ☐ 22 | Steve Buechele | .20 | .08 | .02 |
| ☐ 23 | Jose Guzman | .30 | .12 | .03 |
| ☐ 24 | Ricky Wright | .10 | .04 | .01 |
| ☐ 27 | Greg Harris | .15 | .06 | .01 |
| ☐ 28 | Mitch Williams | .30 | .12 | .03 |
| ☐ 29 | Pete Incaviglia | 1.00 | .40 | .10 |
| ☐ 32 | Gary Ward | .20 | .08 | .02 |
| ☐ 34 | Dale Mohorcic | .20 | .08 | .02 |
| ☐ 40 | Jeff Russell | .10 | .04 | .01 |
| ☐ 44 | Tom Paciorek | .10 | .04 | .01 |
| ☐ 46 | Mike Loynd | .30 | .12 | .03 |
| ☐ 48 | Bobby Witt | .50 | .20 | .05 |
| ☐ 49 | Charlie Hough | .20 | .08 | .02 |
| ☐ xx | Coaching Staff: | .10 | .04 | .01 |
| | (unnumbered) | | | |
| | Art Howe 10 | | | |
| | Joe Ferguson 13 | | | |
| | Tim Foli 14 | | | |
| | Tom Robson 31 | | | |
| | Tom House 35 | | | |
| ☐ xx | Trainers: | .10 | .04 | .01 |
| | (unnumbered) | | | |
| | Bill Zeigler | | | |
| | Danny Wheat | | | |

## 1954 Red Heart

The cards in this 33 card set measure 2 5/8" by 3 3/4". The 1954 Red Heart baseball series was marketed by Red Heart dog food, which, incidentally, was a subsidiary of Morrell Meats. The set consists of three series of eleven unnumbered cards each of which could be ordered from the company via an offer (two can labels plus ten cents

for each series) on the can label. Each series has a specific color background (red, green or blue) behind the color player photo. Cards with red backgrounds are considered scarcer and are marked with an asterisk in the checklist (which has been alphabetized and numbered for reference). The ACC designation is F156.

|  | | MINT | VG-E | F-G |
|---|---|---|---|---|
| COMPLETE SET | | 550.00 | 220.00 | 55.00 |
| COMMON PLAYER (1-33) | | 12.00 | 5.00 | 1.20 |
| ☐ 1 | Richie Ashburn * | 21.00 | 8.50 | 2.10 |
| ☐ 2 | Frank Baumholtz * | 14.00 | 5.75 | 1.40 |
| ☐ 3 | Gus Bell | 12.00 | 5.00 | 1.20 |
| ☐ 4 | Billy Cox | 12.00 | 5.00 | 1.20 |
| ☐ 5 | Alvin Dark | 14.00 | 5.75 | 1.40 |
| ☐ 6 | Carl Erskine * | 16.00 | 6.50 | 1.60 |
| ☐ 7 | Ferris Fain | 12.00 | 5.00 | 1.20 |
| ☐ 8 | Dee Fondy | 12.00 | 5.00 | 1.20 |
| ☐ 9 | Nelson Fox | 16.00 | 6.50 | 1.60 |
| ☐ 10 | Jim Gilliam | 14.00 | 5.75 | 1.40 |
| ☐ 11 | Jim Hegan * | 14.00 | 5.75 | 1.40 |
| ☐ 12 | George Kell | 21.00 | 8.50 | 2.10 |
| ☐ 13 | Ralph Kiner * | 25.00 | 10.00 | 2.50 |
| ☐ 14 | Ted Kluszewski * | 18.00 | 7.25 | 1.80 |
| ☐ 15 | Harvey Kuenn | 14.00 | 5.75 | 1.40 |
| ☐ 16 | Bob Lemon * | 25.00 | 10.00 | 2.50 |
| ☐ 17 | Sherman Lollar | 12.00 | 5.00 | 1.20 |
| ☐ 18 | Mickey Mantle | 120.00 | 50.00 | 12.00 |
| ☐ 19 | Billy Martin | 20.00 | 8.00 | 2.00 |
| ☐ 20 | Gil McDougald * | 16.00 | 6.50 | 1.60 |
| ☐ 21 | Roy McMillan | 12.00 | 5.00 | 1.20 |
| ☐ 22 | Minnie Minoso | 14.00 | 5.75 | 1.40 |
| ☐ 23 | Stan Musial * | 90.00 | 36.00 | 9.00 |
| ☐ 24 | Billy Pierce | 14.00 | 5.75 | 1.40 |
| ☐ 25 | Al Rosen * | 16.00 | 6.50 | 1.60 |
| ☐ 26 | Hank Sauer | 12.00 | 5.00 | 1.20 |
| ☐ 27 | Red Schoendienst * | 16.00 | 6.50 | 1.60 |
| ☐ 28 | Enos Slaughter | 25.00 | 10.00 | 2.50 |
| ☐ 29 | Duke Snider | 45.00 | 18.00 | 4.50 |
| ☐ 30 | Warren Spahn | 25.00 | 10.00 | 2.50 |
| ☐ 31 | Sammy White | 12.00 | 5.00 | 1.20 |
| ☐ 32 | Eddie Yost | 12.00 | 5.00 | 1.20 |
| ☐ 33 | Gus Zernial | 12.00 | 5.00 | 1.20 |

## 1982 Red Lobster Cubs

The cards in this 28 card set measure 2 1/4" by 3 1/2". This set of Chicago Cubs players was co-produced by the Cubs and Chicago-area Red Lobster restaurants and was introduced as a promotional giveaway on August 20, 1982, at Wrigley Field. The cards contain borderless color photos of 25 players, manager Lee Elia, the coaching staff, and a team picture. A facsimile autograph appears on the front, and the cards run in sequence by uniform number. While the coaches have a short biographical sketch on back, the player cards simply list the individual's professional record.

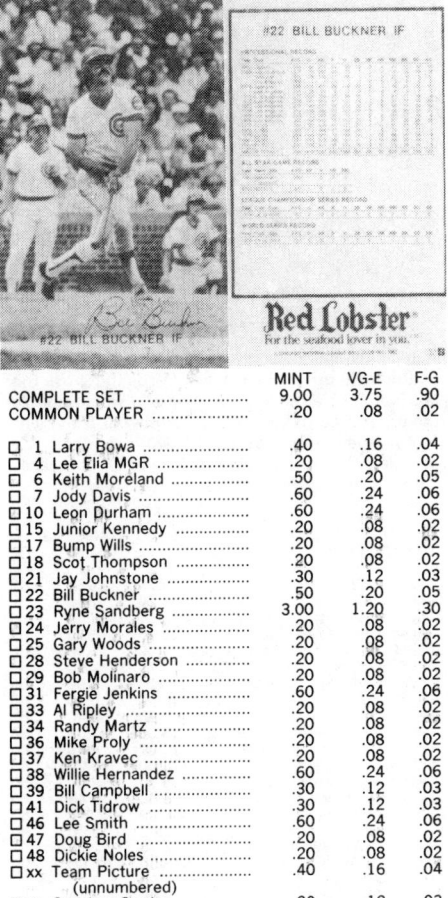

|                  | MINT | VG-E | F-G |
| ---------------- | ---- | ---- | --- |
| COMPLETE SET     | 9.00 | 3.75 | .90 |
| COMMON PLAYER    | .20  | .08  | .02 |

| | | MINT | VG-E | F-G |
| --- | --- | --- | --- | --- |
| ☐ | 1 Larry Bowa | .40 | .16 | .04 |
| ☐ | 4 Lee Elia MGR | .20 | .08 | .02 |
| ☐ | 6 Keith Moreland | .50 | .20 | .05 |
| ☐ | 7 Jody Davis | .60 | .24 | .06 |
| ☐ | 10 Leon Durham | .60 | .24 | .06 |
| ☐ | 15 Junior Kennedy | .20 | .08 | .02 |
| ☐ | 17 Bump Wills | .20 | .08 | .02 |
| ☐ | 18 Scot Thompson | .20 | .08 | .02 |
| ☐ | 21 Jay Johnstone | .30 | .12 | .03 |
| ☐ | 22 Bill Buckner | .50 | .20 | .05 |
| ☐ | 23 Ryne Sandberg | 3.00 | 1.20 | .30 |
| ☐ | 24 Jerry Morales | .20 | .08 | .02 |
| ☐ | 25 Gary Woods | .20 | .08 | .02 |
| ☐ | 28 Steve Henderson | .20 | .08 | .02 |
| ☐ | 29 Bob Molinaro | .20 | .08 | .02 |
| ☐ | 31 Fergie Jenkins | .60 | .24 | .06 |
| ☐ | 33 Al Ripley | .20 | .08 | .02 |
| ☐ | 34 Randy Martz | .20 | .08 | .02 |
| ☐ | 36 Mike Proly | .20 | .08 | .02 |
| ☐ | 37 Ken Kravec | .20 | .08 | .02 |
| ☐ | 38 Willie Hernandez | .60 | .24 | .06 |
| ☐ | 39 Bill Campbell | .30 | .12 | .03 |
| ☐ | 41 Dick Tidrow | .30 | .12 | .03 |
| ☐ | 46 Lee Smith | .60 | .24 | .06 |
| ☐ | 47 Doug Bird | .20 | .08 | .02 |
| ☐ | 48 Dickie Noles | .20 | .08 | .02 |
| ☐ | xx Team Picture (unnumbered) | .40 | .16 | .04 |
| ☐ | xx Coaches Card (unnumbered) | .30 | .12 | .03 |

## 1952 Red Man

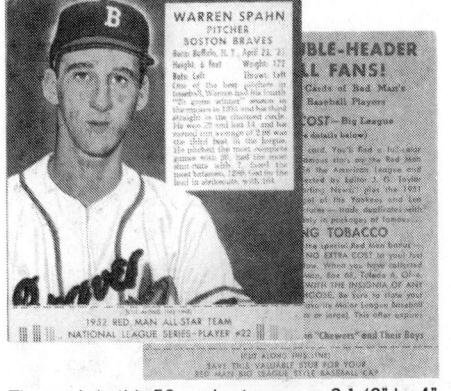

The cards in this 52 card set measure 3 1/2" by 4"
(or 3 1/2" by 3 5/8" without the tab). This Red Man
issue was the first nationally available tobacco issue

since the T cards of the teens early in this century.
This 52 card set contains 26 top players from each
league. Cards that have the tab (coupon) attached
are generally worth double the price of cards with
the tab removed. Card numbers are located on the
tabs. The prices listed below refer to cards without
tabs.

|                  | MINT  | VG-E   | F-G   |
| ---------------- | ----- | ------ | ----- |
| COMPLETE SET     | 325.00 | 130.00 | 32.00 |
| COMMON PLAYER    | 3.75  | 1.50   | .37   |

| | MINT | VG-E | F-G |
| --- | --- | --- | --- |
| ☐ AL1 Casey Stengel MGR | 15.00 | 6.00 | 1.50 |
| ☐ AL2 Roberto Avila | 3.75 | 1.50 | .37 |
| ☐ AL3 Yogi Berra | 18.00 | 7.25 | 1.80 |
| ☐ AL4 Gil Coan | 3.75 | 1.50 | .37 |
| ☐ AL5 Dom DiMaggio | 6.00 | 2.40 | .60 |
| ☐ AL6 Larry Doby | 5.00 | 2.00 | .50 |
| ☐ AL7 Ferris Fain | 3.75 | 1.50 | .37 |
| ☐ AL8 Bob Feller | 18.00 | 7.25 | 1.80 |
| ☐ AL9 Nelson Fox | 6.00 | 2.40 | .60 |
| ☐ AL10 Johnny Groth | 3.75 | 1.50 | .37 |
| ☐ AL11 Jim Hegan | 3.75 | 1.50 | .37 |
| ☐ AL12 Eddie Joost | 3.75 | 1.50 | .37 |
| ☐ AL13 George Kell | 10.00 | 4.00 | 1.00 |
| ☐ AL14 Gil McDougald | 6.00 | 2.40 | .60 |
| ☐ AL15 Minnie Minoso | 6.00 | 2.40 | .60 |
| ☐ AL16 Billy Pierce | 5.00 | 2.00 | .50 |
| ☐ AL17 Bob Porterfield | 3.75 | 1.50 | .37 |
| ☐ AL18 Eddie Robinson | 3.75 | 1.50 | .37 |
| ☐ AL19 Saul Rogovin | 3.75 | 1.50 | .37 |
| ☐ AL20 Bobby Shantz | 5.00 | 2.00 | .50 |
| ☐ AL21 Vern Stephens | 5.00 | 2.00 | .50 |
| ☐ AL22 Vic Wertz | 3.75 | 1.50 | .37 |
| ☐ AL23 Ted Williams | 60.00 | 24.00 | 6.00 |
| ☐ AL24 Early Wynn | 10.00 | 4.00 | 1.00 |
| ☐ AL25 Eddie Yost | 3.75 | 1.50 | .37 |
| ☐ AL26 Gus Zernial | 3.75 | 1.50 | .37 |
| ☐ NL1 Leo Durocher MGR | 8.00 | 3.25 | .80 |
| ☐ NL2 Richie Ashburn | 8.00 | 3.25 | .80 |
| ☐ NL3 Ewell Blackwell | 5.00 | 2.00 | .50 |
| ☐ NL4 Cliff Chambers | 3.75 | 1.50 | .37 |
| ☐ NL5 Murray Dickson | 3.75 | 1.50 | .37 |
| ☐ NL6 Sid Gordon | 3.75 | 1.50 | .37 |
| ☐ NL7 Granny Hamner | 3.75 | 1.50 | .37 |
| ☐ NL8 Jim Hearn | 3.75 | 1.50 | .37 |
| ☐ NL9 Monte Irvin | 10.00 | 4.00 | 1.00 |
| ☐ NL10 Larry Jansen | 3.75 | 1.50 | .37 |
| ☐ NL11 Willie Jones | 3.75 | 1.50 | .37 |
| ☐ NL12 Ralph Kiner | 10.00 | 4.00 | 1.00 |
| ☐ NL13 Whitey Lockman | 3.75 | 1.50 | .37 |
| ☐ NL14 Sal Maglie | 6.00 | 2.40 | .60 |
| ☐ NL15 Willie Mays | 40.00 | 16.00 | 4.00 |
| ☐ NL16 Stan Musial | 40.00 | 16.00 | 4.00 |
| ☐ NL17 Pee Wee Reese | 15.00 | 6.00 | 1.50 |
| ☐ NL18 Robin Roberts | 10.00 | 4.00 | 1.00 |
| ☐ NL19 Al Schoendienst | 6.00 | 2.40 | .60 |
| ☐ NL20 Enos Slaughter | 10.00 | 4.00 | 1.00 |
| ☐ NL21 Duke Snider | 25.00 | 10.00 | 2.50 |
| ☐ NL22 Warren Spahn | 12.00 | 5.00 | 1.20 |
| ☐ NL23 Ed Stanky | 5.00 | 2.00 | .50 |
| ☐ NL24 Bobby Thomson | 6.00 | 2.40 | .60 |
| ☐ NL25 Earl Torgeson | 3.75 | 1.50 | .37 |
| ☐ NL26 Wes Westrum | 3.75 | 1.50 | .37 |

## 1953 Red Man

The cards in this 52 card set measure 3 1/2" by 4"
(or 3 1/2" by 3 5/8" without the tab). The 1953 Red
Man set contains 26 National League stars and 26
American League stars. Card numbers are located
both on the write-up of the player and on the tab.
Cards that have the tab (coupon) attached are
generally worth double the price of cards with the
tab removed. The prices listed below refer to cards
without tabs.

|                  | MINT   | VG-E   | F-G   |
| ---------------- | ------ | ------ | ----- |
| COMPLETE SET     | 275.00 | 110.00 | 27.00 |
| COMMON PLAYER    | 3.75   | 1.50   | .37   |
| ☐ AL1 Casey Stengel MGR | 15.00 | 6.00 | 1.50 |

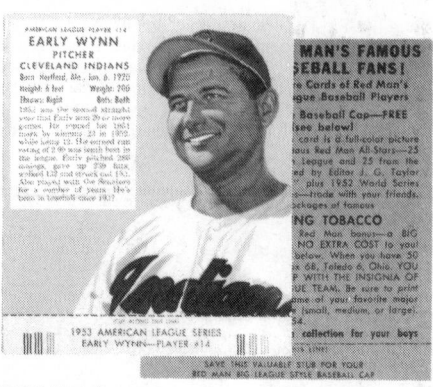

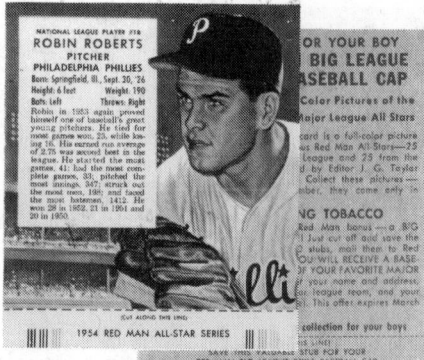

| | | | |
|---|---|---|---|
| ☐ AL2 Hank Bauer | 5.00 | 2.00 | .50 |
| ☐ AL3 Yogi Berra | 18.00 | 7.25 | 1.80 |
| ☐ AL4 Walt Dropo | 3.75 | 1.50 | .37 |
| ☐ AL5 Nelson Fox | 6.00 | 2.40 | .60 |
| ☐ AL6 Jackie Jensen | 5.00 | 2.00 | .50 |
| ☐ AL7 Eddie Joost | 3.75 | 1.50 | .37 |
| ☐ AL8 George Kell | 10.00 | 4.00 | 1.00 |
| ☐ AL9 Dale Mitchell | 5.00 | 2.00 | .50 |
| ☐ AL10 Phil Rizzuto | 12.00 | 5.00 | 1.20 |
| ☐ AL11 Eddie Robinson | 3.75 | 1.50 | .37 |
| ☐ AL12 Gene Woodling | 5.00 | 2.00 | .50 |
| ☐ AL13 Gus Zernial | 3.75 | 1.50 | .37 |
| ☐ AL14 Early Wynn | 10.00 | 4.00 | 1.00 |
| ☐ AL15 Joe Dobson | 3.75 | 1.50 | .37 |
| ☐ AL16 Billy Pierce | 5.00 | 2.00 | .50 |
| ☐ AL17 Bob Lemon | 10.00 | 4.00 | 1.00 |
| ☐ AL18 Johnny Mize | 10.00 | 4.00 | 1.00 |
| ☐ AL19 Bob Porterfield | 3.75 | 1.50 | .37 |
| ☐ AL20 Bobby Shantz | 5.00 | 2.00 | .50 |
| ☐ AL21 Mickey Vernon | 5.00 | 2.00 | .50 |
| ☐ AL22 Dom DiMaggio | 6.00 | 2.40 | .60 |
| ☐ AL23 Gil McDougald | 6.00 | 2.40 | .60 |
| ☐ AL24 Al Rosen | 6.00 | 2.40 | .60 |
| ☐ AL25 Mel Parnell | 5.00 | 2.00 | .50 |
| ☐ AL26 Bobby Avila | 3.75 | 1.50 | .37 |
| ☐ NL1 Charlie Dressen MGR | 5.00 | 2.00 | .50 |
| ☐ NL2 Bobby Adams | 3.75 | 1.50 | .37 |
| ☐ NL3 Richie Ashburn | 8.00 | 3.25 | .80 |
| ☐ NL4 Joe Black | 5.00 | 2.00 | .50 |
| ☐ NL5 Roy Campanella | 25.00 | 10.00 | 2.50 |
| ☐ NL6 Ted Kluszewski | 6.00 | 2.40 | .60 |
| ☐ NL7 Whitey Lockman | 3.75 | 1.50 | .37 |
| ☐ NL8 Sal Maglie | 6.00 | 2.40 | .60 |
| ☐ NL9 Andy Pafko | 3.75 | 1.50 | .37 |
| ☐ NL10 Pee Wee Reese | 15.00 | 6.00 | 1.50 |
| ☐ NL11 Robin Roberts | 10.00 | 4.00 | 1.00 |
| ☐ NL12 Al Schoendienst | 6.00 | 2.40 | .60 |
| ☐ NL13 Enos Slaughter | 10.00 | 4.00 | 1.00 |
| ☐ NL14 Duke Snider | 25.00 | 10.00 | 2.50 |
| ☐ NL15 Ralph Kiner | 10.00 | 4.00 | 1.00 |
| ☐ NL16 Hank Sauer | 5.00 | 2.00 | .50 |
| ☐ NL17 Del Ennis | 5.00 | 2.00 | .50 |
| ☐ NL18 Granny Hamner | 3.75 | 1.50 | .37 |
| ☐ NL19 Warren Spahn | 12.00 | 5.00 | 1.20 |
| ☐ NL20 Wes Westrum | 3.75 | 1.50 | .37 |
| ☐ NL21 Hoyt Wilhelm | 10.00 | 4.00 | 1.00 |
| ☐ NL22 Murray Dickson | 3.75 | 1.50 | .37 |
| ☐ NL23 Warren Hacker | 3.75 | 1.50 | .37 |
| ☐ NL24 Gerry Staley | 3.75 | 1.50 | .37 |
| ☐ NL25 Bobby Thomson | 6.00 | 2.40 | .60 |
| ☐ NL26 Stan Musial | 40.00 | 16.00 | 4.00 |

## 1954 Red Man

The cards in this 50 card set measure 3 1/2" by 4" (or 3 1/2" by 3 5/8" without the tab). The 1954 Red Man set witnessed a reduction to 25 players from each league. George Kell, Sam Mele, and Dave Philley are known to exist with two different teams. Card number 19 of the National League exists as Enos Slaughter and as Gus Bell. Card numbers are

on the write-ups of the players. Cards that have the tab (coupon) attached are generally worth double the price of cards with the tab removed. The prices listed below refer to cards without tabs. The complete set price below refers to all 54 cards including the four variations.

| | MINT | VG-E | F-G |
|---|---|---|---|
| COMPLETE SET (54) | 350.00 | 140.00 | 35.00 |
| COMMON PLAYERS | 3.75 | 1.50 | .37 |
| | | | |
| ☐ AL1 Bobby Avila | 3.75 | 1.50 | .37 |
| ☐ AL2 Jim Busby | 3.75 | 1.50 | .37 |
| ☐ AL3 Nelson Fox | 6.00 | 2.40 | .60 |
| ☐ AL4A George Kell (Boston) | 15.00 | 6.00 | 1.50 |
| ☐ AL4B George Kell (Chicago) | 25.00 | 10.00 | 2.50 |
| ☐ AL5 Sherman Lollar | 3.75 | 1.50 | .37 |
| ☐ AL6A Sam Mele (Baltimore) | 10.00 | 4.00 | 1.00 |
| ☐ AL6B Sam Mele (Chicago) | 15.00 | 6.00 | 1.50 |
| ☐ AL7 Minnie Minoso | 6.00 | 2.40 | .60 |
| ☐ AL8 Mel Parnell | 5.00 | 2.00 | .50 |
| ☐ AL9A Dave Philley (Cleve) | 10.00 | 4.00 | 1.00 |
| ☐ AL9B Dave Philley (Phila) | 15.00 | 6.00 | 1.50 |
| ☐ AL10 Billy Pierce | 5.00 | 2.00 | .50 |
| ☐ AL11 Jim Piersall | 6.00 | 2.40 | .60 |
| ☐ AL12 Al Rosen | 6.00 | 2.40 | .60 |
| ☐ AL13 Mickey Vernon | 5.00 | 2.00 | .50 |
| ☐ AL14 Sammy White | 3.75 | 1.50 | .37 |
| ☐ AL15 Gene Woodling | 5.00 | 2.00 | .50 |
| ☐ AL16 Whitey Ford | 12.00 | 5.00 | 1.20 |
| ☐ AL17 Phil Rizzuto | 12.00 | 5.00 | 1.20 |
| ☐ AL18 Bob Porterfield | 3.75 | 1.50 | .37 |
| ☐ AL19 Chico Carrasquel | 3.75 | 1.50 | .37 |
| ☐ AL20 Yogi Berra | 18.00 | 7.25 | 1.80 |
| ☐ AL21 Bob Lemon | 10.00 | 4.00 | 1.00 |
| ☐ AL22 Ferris Fain | 3.75 | 1.50 | .37 |
| ☐ AL23 Hank Bauer | 5.00 | 2.00 | .50 |
| ☐ AL24 Jim Delsing | 3.75 | 1.50 | .37 |
| ☐ AL25 Gil McDougald | 6.00 | 2.40 | .60 |
| ☐ NL1 Richie Ashburn | 8.00 | 3.25 | .80 |
| ☐ NL2 Billy Cox | 3.75 | 1.50 | .37 |
| ☐ NL3 Del Crandall | 3.75 | 1.50 | .37 |
| ☐ NL4 Carl Erskine | 5.00 | 2.00 | .50 |
| ☐ NL5 Monte Irvin | 10.00 | 4.00 | 1.00 |
| ☐ NL6 Ted Kluszewski | 6.00 | 2.40 | .60 |
| ☐ NL7 Don Mueller | 3.75 | 1.50 | .37 |
| ☐ NL8 Andy Pafko | 3.75 | 1.50 | .37 |
| ☐ NL9 Del Rice | 3.75 | 1.50 | .37 |
| ☐ NL10 Al Schoendienst | 6.00 | 2.40 | .60 |
| ☐ NL11 Warren Spahn | 12.00 | 5.00 | 1.20 |
| ☐ NL12 Curt Simmons | 5.00 | 2.00 | .50 |
| ☐ NL13 Roy Campanella | 25.00 | 10.00 | 2.50 |
| ☐ NL14 Jim Gilliam | 6.00 | 2.40 | .60 |
| ☐ NL15 Pee Wee Reese | 15.00 | 6.00 | 1.50 |
| ☐ NL16 Duke Snider | 25.00 | 10.00 | 2.50 |
| ☐ NL17 Rip Repulski | 3.75 | 1.50 | .37 |
| ☐ NL18 Robin Roberts | 10.00 | 4.00 | 1.00 |
| ☐ NL19A Enos Slaughter | 25.00 | 10.00 | 2.50 |
| ☐ NL19B Gus Bell | 20.00 | 8.00 | 2.00 |
| ☐ NL20 Johnny Logan | 3.75 | 1.50 | .37 |
| ☐ NL21 John Antonelli | 5.00 | 2.00 | .50 |
| ☐ NL22 Gil Hodges | 12.00 | 5.00 | 1.20 |
| ☐ NL23 Eddie Mathews | 12.00 | 5.00 | 1.20 |
| ☐ NL24 Lew Burdette | 5.00 | 2.00 | .50 |
| ☐ NL25 Willie Mays | 40.00 | 16.00 | 4.00 |

# 1955 Red Man

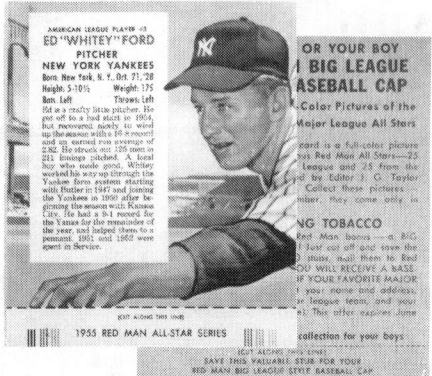

The cards in this 50 card set measure 3 1/2" by 4" (or 3 1/2" by 3 5/8" without the tab). The 1955 Red Man set contains 25 players from each league. Card numbers are on the write-ups of the players. Cards that have the tab (coupon) attached are generally worth double the price of cards with the tab removed. The prices listed below refer to cards without tabs.

|  | | MINT | VG-E | F-G |
|---|---|---|---|---|
| | COMPLETE SET | 275.00 | 110.00 | 27.00 |
| | COMMON PLAYER | 3.75 | 1.50 | .37 |
| ☐ AL1 | Ray Boone | 3.75 | 1.50 | .37 |
| ☐ AL2 | Jim Busby | 3.75 | 1.50 | .37 |
| ☐ AL3 | Whitey Ford | 12.00 | 5.00 | 1.20 |
| ☐ AL4 | Nelson Fox | 6.00 | 2.40 | .60 |
| ☐ AL5 | Bob Grim | 3.75 | 1.50 | .37 |
| ☐ AL6 | Jack Harshman | 3.75 | 1.50 | .37 |
| ☐ AL7 | Jim Hegan | 3.75 | 1.50 | .37 |
| ☐ AL8 | Bob Lemon | 10.00 | 4.00 | 1.00 |
| ☐ AL9 | Irv Noren | 3.75 | 1.50 | .37 |
| ☐ AL10 | Bob Porterfield | 3.75 | 1.50 | .37 |
| ☐ AL11 | Al Rosen | 6.00 | 2.40 | .60 |
| ☐ AL12 | Mickey Vernon | 5.00 | 2.00 | .50 |
| ☐ AL13 | Vic Wertz | 3.75 | 1.50 | .37 |
| ☐ AL14 | Early Wynn | 10.00 | 4.00 | 1.00 |
| ☐ AL15 | Bobby Avila | 3.75 | 1.50 | .37 |
| ☐ AL16 | Yogi Berra | 18.00 | 7.25 | 1.80 |
| ☐ AL17 | Joe Coleman | 3.75 | 1.50 | .37 |
| ☐ AL18 | Larry Doby | 6.00 | 2.40 | .60 |
| ☐ AL19 | Jackie Jensen | 5.00 | 2.00 | .50 |
| ☐ AL20 | Pete Runnels | 5.00 | 2.00 | .50 |
| ☐ AL21 | Jim Piersall | 6.00 | 2.40 | .60 |
| ☐ AL22 | Hank Bauer | 5.00 | 2.00 | .50 |
| ☐ AL23 | Chico Carrasquel | 3.75 | 1.50 | .37 |
| ☐ AL24 | Minnie Minoso | 6.00 | 2.40 | .60 |
| ☐ AL25 | Sandy Consuegra | 3.75 | 1.50 | .37 |
| ☐ NL1 | Richie Ashburn | 8.00 | 3.25 | .80 |
| ☐ NL2 | Del Crandall | 3.75 | 1.50 | .37 |
| ☐ NL3 | Gil Hodges | 12.00 | 5.00 | 1.20 |
| ☐ NL4 | Brooks Lawrence | 3.75 | 1.50 | .37 |
| ☐ NL5 | Johnny Logan | 3.75 | 1.50 | .37 |
| ☐ NL6 | Sal Maglie | 6.00 | 2.40 | .60 |
| ☐ NL7 | Willie Mays | 40.00 | 16.00 | 4.00 |
| ☐ NL8 | Don Mueller | 3.75 | 1.50 | .37 |
| ☐ NL9 | Bill Sarni | 3.75 | 1.50 | .37 |
| ☐ NL10 | Warren Spahn | 12.00 | 5.00 | 1.20 |
| ☐ NL11 | Hank Thompson | 3.75 | 1.50 | .37 |
| ☐ NL12 | Hoyt Wilhelm | 10.00 | 4.00 | 1.00 |
| ☐ NL13 | John Antonelli | 5.00 | 2.00 | .50 |
| ☐ NL14 | Carl Erskine | 5.00 | 2.00 | .50 |
| ☐ NL15 | Granny Hamner | 3.75 | 1.50 | .37 |
| ☐ NL16 | Ted Kluszewski | 6.00 | 2.40 | .60 |
| ☐ NL17 | Pee Wee Reese | 15.00 | 6.00 | 1.50 |
| ☐ NL18 | Al Schoendienst | 6.00 | 2.40 | .60 |
| ☐ NL19 | Duke Snider | 25.00 | 10.00 | 2.50 |
| ☐ NL20 | Frank Thomas | 3.75 | 1.50 | .37 |
| ☐ NL21 | Ray Jablonski | 3.75 | 1.50 | .37 |
| ☐ NL22 | Dusty Rhodes | 3.75 | 1.50 | .37 |
| ☐ NL23 | Gus Bell | 3.75 | 1.50 | .37 |
| ☐ NL24 | Curt Simmons | 5.00 | 2.00 | .50 |
| ☐ NL25 | Marv Grissom | 3.75 | 1.50 | .37 |

# 1955 Rodeo Meats

The cards in this 47 card set measure 2 1/2" by 3 1/2". The 1955 Rodeo Meats set contains unnumbered, color cards of the first Kansas City A's team. There are many background color variations noted in the checklist, and the card reverses carry a scrapbook offer. The Grimes and Kryhoski cards listed in the scrapbook album were apparently never issued. The ACC catalog number is F152-1. The cards have been arranged in alphabetical order and assigned numbers for reference.

|  | | MINT | VG-E | F-G |
|---|---|---|---|---|
| | COMPLETE SET | 2400.00 | 1000.00 | 250.00 |
| | COMMON PLAYER (1-47) | 40.00 | 16.00 | 4.00 |
| ☐ 1 | Joe Astroth | 40.00 | 16.00 | 4.00 |
| ☐ 2 | Harold Bevan | 60.00 | 24.00 | 6.00 |
| ☐ 3 | Charles Bishop | 60.00 | 24.00 | 6.00 |
| ☐ 4 | Don Bollweg | 60.00 | 24.00 | 6.00 |
| ☐ 5 | Lou Boudreau | 100.00 | 40.00 | 10.00 |
| ☐ 6 | Cloyd Boyer (salmon) | 40.00 | 16.00 | 4.00 |
| ☐ 7 | Cloyd Boyer (light blue) | 60.00 | 24.00 | 6.00 |
| ☐ 8 | Ed Burtschy | 100.00 | 40.00 | 10.00 |
| ☐ 9 | Art Ceccarelli | 60.00 | 24.00 | 6.00 |
| ☐ 10 | Joe DeMaestri (yellow) | 40.00 | 16.00 | 4.00 |
| ☐ 11 | Joe DeMaestri (green) | 40.00 | 16.00 | 4.00 |
| ☐ 12 | Art Ditmar | 40.00 | 16.00 | 4.00 |
| ☐ 13 | John Dixon | 60.00 | 24.00 | 6.00 |
| ☐ 14 | Jim Finigan | 40.00 | 16.00 | 4.00 |
| ☐ 15 | Marion Fricano | 60.00 | 24.00 | 6.00 |
| ☐ 16 | Tom Gorman | 40.00 | 16.00 | 4.00 |
| ☐ 17 | John Gray | 60.00 | 24.00 | 6.00 |
| ☐ 18 | Ray Herbert | 40.00 | 16.00 | 4.00 |
| ☐ 19 | Forest Jacobs | 100.00 | 40.00 | 10.00 |
| ☐ 20 | Alex Kellner | 40.00 | 16.00 | 4.00 |
| ☐ 21 | Harry Kraft | 40.00 | 16.00 | 4.00 |
| ☐ 22 | Jack Littrell | 40.00 | 16.00 | 4.00 |
| ☐ 23 | Hector Lopez | 40.00 | 16.00 | 4.00 |
| ☐ 24 | Oscar Melillo | 40.00 | 16.00 | 4.00 |
| ☐ 25 | Arnold Portocarrero (purple) | 60.00 | 24.00 | 6.00 |
| ☐ 26 | Arnold Portocarrero (gray) | 40.00 | 16.00 | 4.00 |
| ☐ 27 | Vic Power (yellow) | 40.00 | 16.00 | 4.00 |
| ☐ 28 | Vic Power (pink) | 60.00 | 24.00 | 6.00 |
| ☐ 29 | Vic Raschi | 60.00 | 24.00 | 6.00 |
| ☐ 30 | Bill Renna (lavender) | 40.00 | 16.00 | 4.00 |
| ☐ 31 | Bill Renna (dark pink) | 60.00 | 24.00 | 6.00 |
| ☐ 32 | Al Robertson | 60.00 | 24.00 | 6.00 |
| ☐ 33 | Johnny Sain | 75.00 | 30.00 | 7.50 |
| ☐ 34 | Bobby Shantz | 75.00 | 30.00 | 7.50 |
| ☐ 35 | Bobby Schantz (misspelling) | 100.00 | 40.00 | 10.00 |
| ☐ 36 | Wilmer Shantz (orange) | 40.00 | 16.00 | 4.00 |
| ☐ 37 | Wilmer Shantz (lavender) | 40.00 | 16.00 | 4.00 |
| ☐ 38 | Harry Simpson | 40.00 | 16.00 | 4.00 |
| ☐ 39 | Enos Slaughter | 125.00 | 50.00 | 12.50 |
| ☐ 40 | Lou Sleator | 40.00 | 16.00 | 4.00 |
| ☐ 41 | George Susce | 60.00 | 24.00 | 6.00 |
| ☐ 42 | Bob Trice | 60.00 | 24.00 | 6.00 |
| ☐ 43 | Elmer Valo (yellow) | 60.00 | 24.00 | 6.00 |
| ☐ 44 | Elmer Valo (green sky) | 40.00 | 16.00 | 4.00 |
| ☐ 45 | Bill Wilson (yellow) | 60.00 | 24.00 | 6.00 |

| | | | MINT | VG-E | F-G |
|---|---|---|---|---|---|
| ☐ 46 | Bill Wilson ........................ (lavender sky) | | 40.00 | 16.00 | 4.00 |
| ☐ 47 | Gus Zernial ...................... | | 40.00 | 16.00 | 4.00 |

## 1956 Rodeo Meats

Art Ditmar

The cards in this 13 card set measure 2 1/2" by 3 1/2". The unnumbered, color cards of the 1956 Rodeo baseball series are easily distinguished from their 1955 counterparts by the absence of the scrapbook offer on the reverse. They were available only in packages of Rodeo All-Meat Wieners. The ACC designation is F152-2, and the cards have been assigned numbers in alphabetical order in the checklist below.

| | | MINT | VG-E | F-G |
|---|---|---|---|---|
| COMPLETE SET ........................ | | 650.00 | 260.00 | 65.00 |
| COMMON PLAYER (1-12) .......... | | 40.00 | 16.00 | 4.00 |
| ☐ 1 | Joe Astroth ...................... | 40.00 | 16.00 | 4.00 |
| ☐ 2 | Lou Boudreau ................... | 125.00 | 50.00 | 12.50 |
| ☐ 3 | Joe DeMaestri ................. | 40.00 | 16.00 | 4.00 |
| ☐ 4 | Art Ditmar ....................... | 40.00 | 16.00 | 4.00 |
| ☐ 5 | Jim Finigan ..................... | 40.00 | 16.00 | 4.00 |
| ☐ 6 | Hector Lopez ................... | 40.00 | 16.00 | 4.00 |
| ☐ 7 | Vic Power ........................ | 40.00 | 16.00 | 4.00 |
| ☐ 9 | Harry Simpson ................ | 40.00 | 16.00 | 4.00 |
| ☐ 10 | Enos Slaughter ................ | 150.00 | 60.00 | 15.00 |
| ☐ 11 | Elmer Valo ....................... | 40.00 | 16.00 | 4.00 |
| ☐ 12 | Gus Zernial ...................... | 40.00 | 16.00 | 4.00 |

## 1958 SF Call-Bulletin

The cards in this 25 card set measure 2" by 4". The 1958 San Francisco Call-Bulletin set of unnumbered cards features black print on orange paper. These cards were given away as inserts in the San Francisco Call-Bulletin newspaper. The backs of the cards list the Giants home schedule and a radio station ad. The cards are entitled "Giant Payoff" and feature San Francisco Giant players only. The bottom part of the card (tab) could be detached as a ticket stub; hence, cards with the tab intact are worth approximately 50% more than the prices listed below. The ACC designation is M126. The Tom

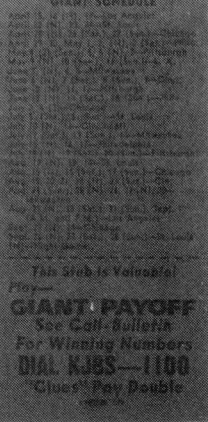

This 28-card set was distributed on August 14th at Wrigley Field for the game against the Expos. The cards measure 2 1/2" by 3 1/2" and were distributed wrapped in cellophane. The cards are unnumbered except for uniform number. The card backs are printed in black on white with a 7-Up logo in the upper right hand corner.

|  |  | MINT | VG-E | F-G |
|---|---|---|---|---|
| COMPLETE SET | | 5.00 | 2.00 | .50 |
| COMMON PLAYER | | .15 | .06 | .01 |
| ☐ 1 | Larry Bowa | .25 | .10 | .02 |
| ☐ 6 | Keith Moreland | .35 | .14 | .03 |
| ☐ 7 | Jody Davis | .35 | .14 | .03 |
| ☐ 10 | Leon Durham | .35 | .14 | .03 |
| ☐ 11 | Ron Cey | .25 | .10 | .02 |
| ☐ 15 | Davey Lopes | .25 | .10 | .02 |
| ☐ 16 | Steve Lake | .15 | .06 | .01 |
| ☐ 18 | Rich Hebner | .15 | .06 | .01 |
| ☐ 20 | Bob Dernier | .25 | .10 | .02 |
| ☐ 21 | Scott Sanderson | .15 | .06 | .01 |
| ☐ 22 | Billy Hatcher | .25 | .10 | .02 |
| ☐ 23 | Ryne Sandberg | 1.00 | .40 | .10 |
| ☐ 24 | Brian Dayett | .15 | .06 | .01 |
| ☐ 25 | Gary Woods | .15 | .06 | .01 |
| ☐ 27 | Thad Bosley | .15 | .06 | .01 |
| ☐ 28 | Chris Speier | .15 | .06 | .01 |
| ☐ 31 | Ray Fontenot | .15 | .06 | .01 |
| ☐ 34 | Steve Trout | .15 | .06 | .01 |
| ☐ 36 | Gary Matthews | .25 | .10 | .02 |
| ☐ 39 | George Frazier | .15 | .06 | .01 |
| ☐ 40 | Rick Sutcliffe | .35 | .14 | .03 |
| ☐ 41 | Warren Brusstar | .15 | .06 | .01 |
| ☐ 42 | Lary Sorensen | .15 | .06 | .01 |
| ☐ 43 | Dennis Eckersley | .25 | .10 | .02 |
| ☐ 44 | Dick Ruthven | .15 | .06 | .01 |
| ☐ 46 | Lee Smith | .35 | .14 | .03 |
| ☐ xx | Jim Frey MGR | .15 | .06 | .01 |
| | (unnumbered) | | | |
| ☐ xx | Cubs Coaching Staff | .15 | .06 | .01 |
| | Ruben Amaro | | | |
| | Billy Connors | | | |
| | Johnny Oates | | | |
| | John Vukovich | | | |
| | Don Zimmer | | | |
| | (unnumbered) | | | |

Bowers card was issued in very short supply; also Bressoud, Jablonski, and Kirkland are somewhat tougher to find than the others. All of these tougher cards are asterisked in the checklist below.

|  |  | MINT | VG-E | F-G |
|---|---|---|---|---|
| COMPLETE SET | | 600.00 | 240.00 | 60.00 |
| COMMON PLAYER (1-25) | | 10.00 | 4.00 | 1.00 |
| ☐ 1 | John Antonelli | 12.00 | 5.00 | 1.20 |
| ☐ 2 | Curt Barclay | 10.00 | 4.00 | 1.00 |
| ☐ 3 | Tom Bowers * | 150.00 | 60.00 | 15.00 |
| ☐ 4 | Ed Bressoud * | 40.00 | 16.00 | 4.00 |
| ☐ 5 | Orlando Cepeda | 40.00 | 16.00 | 4.00 |
| ☐ 6 | Ray Crone | 10.00 | 4.00 | 1.00 |
| ☐ 7 | Jim Davenport | 12.00 | 5.00 | 1.20 |
| ☐ 8 | Paul Giel | 10.00 | 4.00 | 1.00 |
| ☐ 9 | Ruben Gomez | 10.00 | 4.00 | 1.00 |
| ☐ 10 | Marv Grissom | 10.00 | 4.00 | 1.00 |
| ☐ 11 | Ray Jablonski * | 20.00 | 8.00 | 2.00 |
| ☐ 12 | Willie Kirkland * | 50.00 | 20.00 | 5.00 |
| ☐ 13 | Whitey Lockman | 10.00 | 4.00 | 1.00 |
| ☐ 14 | Willie Mays | 150.00 | 60.00 | 15.00 |
| ☐ 15 | Mike McCormick | 12.00 | 5.00 | 1.20 |
| ☐ 16 | Stu Miller | 10.00 | 4.00 | 1.00 |
| ☐ 17 | Ray Monzant | 10.00 | 4.00 | 1.00 |
| ☐ 18 | Danny O'Connell | 10.00 | 4.00 | 1.00 |
| ☐ 19 | Bill Rigney | 12.00 | 5.00 | 1.20 |
| ☐ 20 | Hank Sauer | 12.00 | 5.00 | 1.20 |
| ☐ 21 | Bob Schmidt | 10.00 | 4.00 | 1.00 |
| ☐ 22 | Daryl Spencer | 10.00 | 4.00 | 1.00 |
| ☐ 23 | Valmy Thomas | 10.00 | 4.00 | 1.00 |
| ☐ 24 | Bobby Thomson | 16.00 | 6.50 | 1.60 |
| ☐ 25 | Al Worthington | 10.00 | 4.00 | 1.00 |

## 1984 Smokey Angels

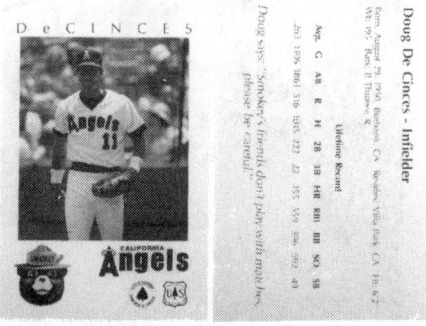

## 1985 Seven-Up Cubs

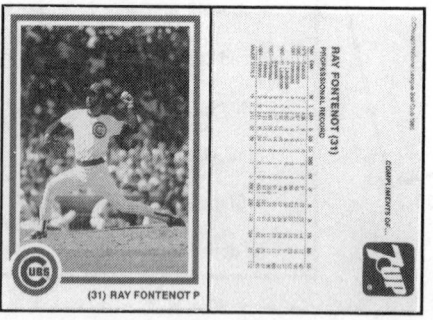

(31) RAY FONTENOT P

The cards in this 32 card set measure 2 1/2" by 3 3/4" and feature the California Angels in full color. Sets were given out to persons 15 and under attending the June 16th game against the Indians. Unlike the Padres set of this year, Smokey the Bear is not featured on these cards. The player's photo, the Angels' logo, and the Smokey the Bear logo appear on the front, in addition to the California Department of Forestry and the U.S. Forest Service logos. The abbreviated backs contain short biographical data, career statistics, and an anti-wildfire hint from the player on the front. Since the cards are unnumbered, they are ordered and numbered below alphabetically by the player's name.

| | | MINT | VG-E | F-G |
|---|---|---|---|---|
| COMPLETE SET (32) | | 7.50 | 3.00 | .75 |
| COMMON PLAYER | | .20 | .08 | .02 |
| ☐ 1 | Don Aase | .40 | .16 | .04 |
| ☐ 2 | Juan Beniquez | .25 | .10 | .02 |
| ☐ 3 | Bob Boone | .30 | .12 | .03 |
| ☐ 4 | Rick Burleson | .30 | .12 | .03 |
| ☐ 5 | Rod Carew | 1.00 | .40 | .10 |
| ☐ 6 | John Curtis | .20 | .08 | .02 |
| ☐ 7 | Doug DeCinces | .50 | .20 | .05 |
| ☐ 8 | Brian Downing | .30 | .12 | .03 |
| ☐ 9 | Ken Forsch | .20 | .08 | .02 |
| ☐ 10 | Bobby Grich | .30 | .12 | .03 |
| ☐ 11 | Reggie Jackson | 1.50 | .60 | .15 |
| ☐ 12 | Ron Jackson | .20 | .08 | .02 |
| ☐ 13 | Tommy John | .50 | .20 | .05 |
| ☐ 14 | Curt Kaufman | .30 | .12 | .03 |
| ☐ 15 | Bruce Kison | .20 | .08 | .02 |
| ☐ 16 | Frank LaCorte | .20 | .08 | .02 |
| ☐ 17 | Logo Card (Forestry Dept.) | .20 | .08 | .02 |
| ☐ 18 | Fred Lynn | .50 | .20 | .05 |
| ☐ 19 | John McNamara MGR | .20 | .08 | .02 |
| ☐ 20 | Jerry Narron | .20 | .08 | .02 |
| ☐ 21 | Gary Pettis | .50 | .20 | .05 |
| ☐ 22 | Rob Picciolo | .20 | .08 | .02 |
| ☐ 23 | Ron Romanick | .30 | .12 | .03 |
| ☐ 24 | Luis Sanchez | .20 | .08 | .02 |
| ☐ 25 | Dick Schofield | .30 | .12 | .03 |
| ☐ 26 | Daryl Sconiers | .20 | .08 | .02 |
| ☐ 27 | Jim Slaton | .20 | .08 | .02 |
| ☐ 28 | Smokey the Bear | .20 | .08 | .02 |
| ☐ 29 | Ellis Valentine | .20 | .08 | .02 |
| ☐ 30 | Rob Wilfong | .20 | .08 | .02 |
| ☐ 31 | Mike Witt | .60 | .24 | .06 |
| ☐ 32 | Geoff Zahn | .30 | .12 | .03 |

## 1984 Smokey Dodgers

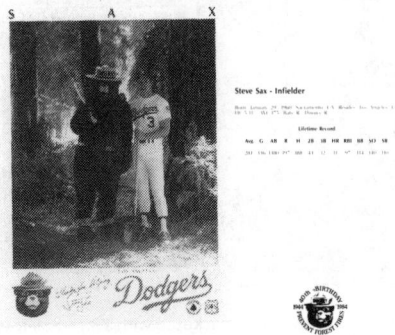

This four card set was not widely distributed and has not proven to be very popular with collectors. Cards were supposedly distributed by fire agencies in Southern California at fairs, mall displays, and special events. Cards are approximately 5" by 7" and feature a color picture of Smokey the Bear with a Dodger. The cards were printed on relatively thin card stock; printing on the back is black on white.

| | | MINT | VG-E | F-G |
|---|---|---|---|---|
| COMPLETE SET | | 6.00 | 2.40 | .60 |
| COMMON PLAYER | | .50 | .20 | .05 |
| ☐ 1 | Ken Landreaux with Smokey | 1.50 | .60 | .15 |
| ☐ 2 | Tom Niedenfuer with Smokey | 1.50 | .60 | .15 |

| | | MINT | VG-E | F-G |
|---|---|---|---|---|
| ☐ 3 | Steve Sax with Smokey | 3.00 | 1.20 | .30 |
| ☐ 4 | Smokey the Bear (batting pose) | .50 | .20 | .05 |

## 1984 Smokey Padres

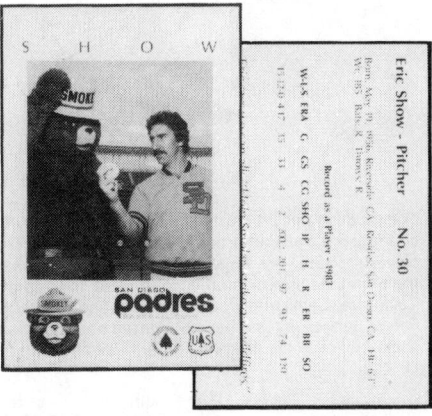

The cards in this 29 card set measure 2 1/2" by 3 3/4". This unnumbered, full color set features the Fire Prevention Bear and a Padres player, coach, manager, or associate on each card. The set was given out at the ballpark at the May 14th game against the Expos. Logos of the California Department of Forestry and the U.S. Forest Service appear in conjunction with a Smokey the Bear logo on the obverse. The set commemorates the 40th birthday of Smokey the Bear. The backs contain short biographical data, statistics and a fire prevention hint from the player pictured on the front.

| | | MINT | VG-E | F-G |
|---|---|---|---|---|
| COMPLETE SET | | 9.00 | 3.75 | .90 |
| COMMON PLAYER | | .25 | .10 | .02 |
| ☐ 1 | Kurt Bevacqua | .25 | .10 | .02 |
| ☐ 2 | Bobby Brown | .25 | .10 | .02 |
| ☐ 3 | Dave Campbell (Broadcast Team) | .25 | .10 | .02 |
| ☐ 4 | The Chicken (Mascot) | .40 | .16 | .04 |
| ☐ 5 | Jerry Coleman (Broadcast Team) | .25 | .10 | .02 |
| ☐ 6 | Luis DeLeon | .25 | .10 | .02 |
| ☐ 7 | Dave Dravecky | .35 | .14 | .03 |
| ☐ 8 | Harry Dunlop COACH | .25 | .10 | .02 |
| ☐ 9 | Tim Flannery | .25 | .10 | .02 |
| ☐ 10 | Steve Garvey | 1.25 | .50 | .12 |
| ☐ 11 | Doug Gwosdz | .25 | .10 | .02 |
| ☐ 12 | Tony Gwynn | 1.25 | .50 | .12 |
| ☐ 13 | Harold (Doug) Harvey (ex-UMP) | .25 | .10 | .02 |
| ☐ 14 | Terry Kennedy | .35 | .14 | .03 |
| ☐ 15 | Jack Krol COACH | .25 | .10 | .02 |
| ☐ 16 | Tim Lollar | .25 | .10 | .02 |
| ☐ 17 | Jack McKeon (VP for Baseball Operations) | .25 | .10 | .02 |
| ☐ 18 | Kevin McReynolds | .75 | .30 | .07 |
| ☐ 19 | Sid Monge | .25 | .10 | .02 |
| ☐ 20 | Luis Salazar | .25 | .10 | .02 |
| ☐ 21 | Norm Sherry COACH | .25 | .10 | .02 |
| ☐ 22 | Eric Show | .35 | .14 | .03 |
| ☐ 23 | Smokey the Bear | .25 | .10 | .02 |
| ☐ 24 | Garry Templeton | .35 | .14 | .03 |
| ☐ 25 | Mark Thurmond | .35 | .14 | .03 |
| ☐ 26 | Ozzie Virgil COACH | .25 | .10 | .02 |
| ☐ 27 | Ed Whitson | .35 | .14 | .03 |
| ☐ 28 | Alan Wiggins | .35 | .14 | .03 |
| ☐ 29 | Dick Williams MGR | .25 | .10 | .02 |

## 1985 Smokey Angels

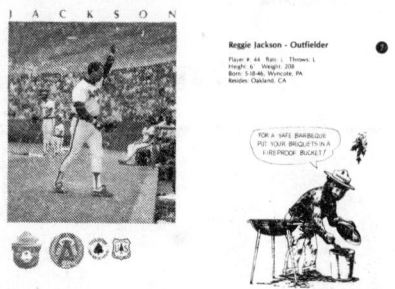

The cards in this 24 card set measure 4 1/4" by 6" and feature the California Angels in full color. The player's photo, the Angels' logo, and the Smokey the Bear logo appear on the front, in addition to the California Department of Forestry and the U.S. Forest Service logos. The abbreviated backs contain short biographical data and an anti-wildfire hint.

| | | MINT | VG-E | F-G |
|---|---|---|---|---|
| COMPLETE SET | | 6.00 | 2.40 | .60 |
| COMMON PLAYER | | .20 | .08 | .02 |
| ☐ 1 | Mike Witt | .60 | .24 | .06 |
| ☐ 2 | Reggie Jackson | 1.25 | .50 | .12 |
| ☐ 3 | Bob Boone | .30 | .12 | .03 |
| ☐ 4 | Mike Brown | .30 | .12 | .03 |
| ☐ 5 | Rod Carew | 1.00 | .40 | .10 |
| ☐ 6 | Doug DeCinces | .45 | .18 | .04 |
| ☐ 7 | Brian Downing | .30 | .12 | .03 |
| ☐ 8 | Ken Forsch | .20 | .08 | .02 |
| ☐ 9 | Gary Pettis | .40 | .16 | .04 |
| ☐ 10 | Jerry Narron | .20 | .08 | .02 |
| ☐ 11 | Ron Romanick | .30 | .12 | .03 |
| ☐ 12 | Bobby Grich | .30 | .12 | .03 |
| ☐ 13 | Dick Schofield | .30 | .12 | .03 |
| ☐ 14 | Juan Beniquez | .25 | .10 | .02 |
| ☐ 15 | Geoff Zahn | .20 | .08 | .02 |
| ☐ 16 | Luis Sanchez | .20 | .08 | .02 |
| ☐ 17 | Jim Slaton | .20 | .08 | .02 |
| ☐ 18 | Doug Corbett | .20 | .08 | .02 |
| ☐ 19 | Ruppert Jones | .25 | .10 | .02 |
| ☐ 20 | Rob Wilfong | .20 | .08 | .02 |
| ☐ 21 | Donnie Moore | .35 | .14 | .03 |
| ☐ 22 | Pat Clements | .25 | .10 | .02 |
| ☐ 23 | Tommy John | .35 | .14 | .03 |
| ☐ 24 | Gene Mauch MGR | .25 | .10 | .02 |

## 1986 Smokey Angels

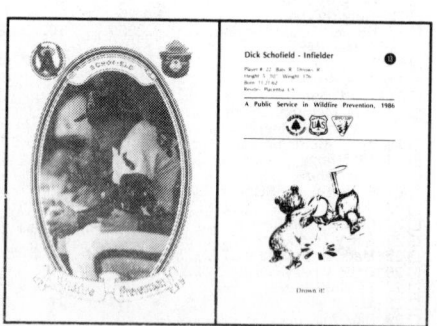

The Forestry Service (in conjunction with the California Angels) produced this large, attractive 24 card set. The cards feature Smokey the Bear pictured in the upper right corner of the card. The card backs give a fire safety tip. The set was given out free at Anaheim Stadium on August 9th. The cards measure 4 1/4" by 6" and are subtitled "Wildfire Prevention" on the front.

| | | MINT | VG-E | F-G |
|---|---|---|---|---|
| COMPLETE SET | | 7.00 | 2.80 | .70 |
| COMMON PLAYER | | .20 | .08 | .02 |
| ☐ 1 | Mike Witt | .50 | .20 | .05 |
| ☐ 2 | Reggie Jackson | .75 | .30 | .07 |
| ☐ 3 | Bob Boone | .30 | .12 | .03 |
| ☐ 4 | Don Sutton | .50 | .20 | .05 |
| ☐ 5 | Kirk McCaskill | .50 | .20 | .05 |
| ☐ 6 | Doug DeCinces | .40 | .16 | .04 |
| ☐ 7 | Brian Downing | .30 | .12 | .03 |
| ☐ 8 | Doug Corbett | .20 | .08 | .02 |
| ☐ 9 | Gary Pettis | .40 | .16 | .04 |
| ☐ 10 | Jerry Narron | .20 | .08 | .02 |
| ☐ 11 | Ron Romanick | .30 | .12 | .03 |
| ☐ 12 | Bobby Grich | .30 | .12 | .03 |
| ☐ 13 | Dick Schofield | .30 | .12 | .03 |
| ☐ 14 | George Hendrick | .30 | .12 | .03 |
| ☐ 15 | Rick Burleson | .30 | .12 | .03 |
| ☐ 16 | John Candelaria | .30 | .12 | .03 |
| ☐ 17 | Jim Slaton | .30 | .12 | .03 |
| ☐ 18 | Darrell Miller | .20 | .08 | .02 |
| ☐ 19 | Ruppert Jones | .20 | .08 | .02 |
| ☐ 20 | Rob Wilfong | .20 | .08 | .02 |
| ☐ 21 | Donnie Moore | .30 | .12 | .03 |
| ☐ 22 | Wally Joyner | 1.25 | .50 | .12 |
| ☐ 23 | Terry Forster | .30 | .12 | .03 |
| ☐ 24 | Gene Mauch MGR | .30 | .12 | .03 |

## 1986 Sportflics

This 200 card set was marketed with 133 small trivia cards. This inaugural set for Sportflics was well-received by the public. Sportflics was distributed by Major League Marketing; the company is also affiliated with Wrigley and Amurol. The set features 139 single player "magic motion" cards (which can be tilted to show three different pictures of the same player), 50 "Tri-Stars" (which show three different players), 10 "Big Six" cards (which show six players who share similar achievements), and one World Champs card featuring 12 members of the victorious Kansas City Royals. All cards measure 2 1/2" by 3 1/2".

| | | MINT | VG-E | F-G |
|---|---|---|---|---|
| COMPLETE SET | | 40.00 | 16.00 | 4.00 |
| COMMON PLAYER | | .15 | .06 | .01 |
| ☐ 1 | George Brett | 1.50 | .60 | .15 |
| ☐ 2 | Don Mattingly | 4.00 | 1.60 | .40 |
| ☐ 3 | Wade Boggs | 2.50 | 1.00 | .25 |

| ☐ | 4 Eddie Murray | 1.25 | .50 | .12 |
|---|---|---|---|---|
| ☐ | 5 Dale Murphy | 1.50 | .60 | .15 |
| ☐ | 6 Rickey Henderson | 1.25 | .50 | .12 |
| ☐ | 7 Harold Baines | .40 | .16 | .04 |
| ☐ | 8 Cal Ripken | 1.00 | .40 | .10 |
| ☐ | 9 Orel Hershiser | .50 | .20 | .05 |
| ☐ | 10 Bret Saberhagen | .40 | .16 | .04 |
| ☐ | 11 Tim Raines | .60 | .24 | .06 |
| ☐ | 12 Fernando Valenzuela | .50 | .20 | .05 |
| ☐ | 13 Tony Gwynn | .60 | .24 | .06 |
| ☐ | 14 Pedro Guerrero | .40 | .16 | .04 |
| ☐ | 15 Keith Hernandez | .40 | .16 | .04 |
| ☐ | 16 Ernie Riles | .35 | .14 | .03 |
| ☐ | 17 Jim Rice | .50 | .20 | .05 |
| ☐ | 18 Ron Guidry | .40 | .16 | .04 |
| ☐ | 19 Willie McGee | .50 | .20 | .05 |
| ☐ | 20 Ryne Sandberg | .75 | .30 | .07 |
| ☐ | 21 Kirk Gibson | .45 | .18 | .04 |
| ☐ | 22 Ozzie Guillen | .65 | .26 | .06 |
| ☐ | 23 Dave Parker | .45 | .18 | .04 |
| ☐ | 24 Vince Coleman | 2.00 | .80 | .20 |
| ☐ | 25 Tom Seaver | .75 | .30 | .07 |
| ☐ | 26 Brett Butler | .25 | .10 | .02 |
| ☐ | 27 Steve Carlton | .75 | .30 | .07 |
| ☐ | 28 Gary Carter | .75 | .30 | .07 |
| ☐ | 29 Cecil Cooper | .30 | .12 | .03 |
| ☐ | 30 Jose Cruz | .25 | .10 | .02 |
| ☐ | 31 Alvin Davis | .25 | .10 | .02 |
| ☐ | 32 Dwight Evans | .25 | .10 | .02 |
| ☐ | 33 Julio Franco | .25 | .10 | .02 |
| ☐ | 34 Damaso Garcia | .20 | .08 | .02 |
| ☐ | 35 Steve Garvey | 1.00 | .40 | .10 |
| ☐ | 36 Kent Hrbek | .40 | .16 | .04 |
| ☐ | 37 Reggie Jackson | 1.00 | .40 | .10 |
| ☐ | 38 Fred Lynn | .35 | .14 | .03 |
| ☐ | 39 Paul Molitor | .25 | .10 | .02 |
| ☐ | 40 Jim Presley | .50 | .20 | .05 |
| ☐ | 41 Dave Righetti | .35 | .14 | .03 |
| ☐ | 42 Robin Yount | .50 | .20 | .05 |
| ☐ | 43 Nolan Ryan | .75 | .30 | .07 |
| ☐ | 44 Mike Schmidt | 1.25 | .50 | .12 |
| ☐ | 45 Lee Smith | .25 | .10 | .02 |
| ☐ | 46 Rick Sutcliffe | .25 | .10 | .02 |
| ☐ | 47 Bruce Sutter | .30 | .12 | .03 |
| ☐ | 48 Lou Whitaker | .30 | .12 | .03 |
| ☐ | 49 Dave Winfield | .65 | .26 | .06 |
| ☐ | 50 Pete Rose | 2.50 | 1.00 | .25 |
| ☐ | 51 NL MVPs: | 1.00 | .40 | .10 |
| |   Ryne Sandberg | | | |
| |   Steve Garvey | | | |
| |   Pete Rose | | | |
| ☐ | 52 Slugging Stars: | .75 | .30 | .07 |
| |   George Brett | | | |
| |   Harold Baines | | | |
| |   Jim Rice | | | |
| ☐ | 53 No-Hitters: | .25 | .10 | .02 |
| |   Phil Niekro | | | |
| |   Jerry Reuss | | | |
| |   Mike Witt | | | |
| ☐ | 54 Big Hitters | 1.25 | .50 | .12 |
| |   Don Mattingly | | | |
| |   Cal Ripken | | | |
| |   Robin Yount | | | |
| ☐ | 55 Bullpen Aces: | .25 | .10 | .02 |
| |   Dan Quisenberry | | | |
| |   Goose Gossage | | | |
| |   Lee Smith | | | |
| ☐ | 56 Rookies of The Year: | 1.25 | .50 | .12 |
| |   Darryl Strawberry | | | |
| |   Steve Sax | | | |
| |   Pete Rose | | | |
| ☐ | 57 AL MVP's: | .60 | .24 | .06 |
| |   Cal Ripken | | | |
| |   Don Baylor | | | |
| |   Reggie Jackson | | | |
| ☐ | 58 Repeat Batting Champs: | 1.00 | .40 | .10 |
| |   Dave Parker | | | |
| |   Bill Madlock | | | |
| |   Pete Rose | | | |
| ☐ | 59 Cy Young Winners: | .25 | .10 | .02 |
| |   LaMarr Hoyt | | | |
| |   Mike Flanagan | | | |
| |   Ron Guidry | | | |
| ☐ | 60 Double Award Winners: | .35 | .14 | .03 |
| |   Fernando Valenzuela | | | |
| |   Rick Sutcliffe | | | |
| |   Tom Seaver | | | |
| ☐ | 61 Home Run Champs: | .75 | .30 | .07 |
| |   Reggie Jackson | | | |
| |   Jim Rice | | | |
| |   Tony Armas | | | |
| ☐ | 62 NL MVP's: | 1.00 | .40 | .10 |
| |   Keith Hernandez | | | |
| |   Dale Murphy | | | |
| |   Mike Schmidt | | | |
| ☐ | 63 AL MVP's: | .60 | .24 | .06 |
| |   Robin Yount | | | |
| |   George Brett | | | |
| |   Fred Lynn | | | |
| ☐ | 64 Comeback Players: | .20 | .08 | .02 |
| |   Bert Blyleven | | | |
| |   Jerry Koosman | | | |
| |   John Denny | | | |
| ☐ | 65 Cy Young Relievers: | .25 | .10 | .02 |
| |   Willie Hernandez | | | |
| |   Rollie Fingers | | | |
| |   Bruce Sutter | | | |
| ☐ | 66 Rookies of The Year: | .25 | .10 | .02 |
| |   Bob Horner | | | |
| |   Andre Dawson | | | |
| |   Gary Matthews | | | |
| ☐ | 67 Rookies of THe Year: | .35 | .14 | .03 |
| |   Ron Kittle | | | |
| |   Carlton Fisk | | | |
| |   Tom Seaver | | | |
| ☐ | 68 Home Run Champs: | .35 | .14 | .03 |
| |   Mike Schmidt | | | |
| |   George Foster | | | |
| |   Dave Kingman | | | |
| ☐ | 69 Double Award Winners: | 1.25 | .50 | .12 |
| |   Cal Ripken | | | |
| |   Rod Carew | | | |
| |   Pete Rose | | | |
| ☐ | 70 Cy Young Winners: | .45 | .18 | .04 |
| |   Rick Sutcliffe | | | |
| |   Steve Carlton | | | |
| |   Tom Seaver | | | |
| ☐ | 71 Top Sluggers: | .45 | .18 | .04 |
| |   Reggie Jackson | | | |
| |   Fred Lynn | | | |
| |   Robin Yount | | | |
| ☐ | 72 Rookies of The Year: | .35 | .14 | .03 |
| |   Dave Righetti | | | |
| |   Fernando Valenzuela | | | |
| |   Rick Sutcliffe | | | |
| ☐ | 73 Rookies of The Year: | .75 | .30 | .07 |
| |   Fred Lynn | | | |
| |   Eddie Murray | | | |
| |   Cal Ripken | | | |
| ☐ | 74 Rookies of The Year: | .35 | .14 | .03 |
| |   Alvin Davis | | | |
| |   Lou Whitaker | | | |
| |   Rod Carew | | | |
| ☐ | 75 Batting Champs: | 1.50 | .60 | .15 |
| |   Don Mattingly | | | |
| |   Wade Boggs | | | |
| |   Carney Lansford | | | |
| ☐ | 76 Jesse Barfield | .45 | .18 | .04 |
| ☐ | 77 Phil Bradley | .45 | .18 | .04 |
| ☐ | 78 Chris Brown | .75 | .30 | .07 |
| ☐ | 79 Tom Browning | .35 | .14 | .03 |
| ☐ | 80 Tom Brunansky | .25 | .10 | .02 |
| ☐ | 81 Bill Buckner | .20 | .08 | .02 |
| ☐ | 82 Chili Davis | .20 | .08 | .02 |
| ☐ | 83 Mike Davis | .20 | .08 | .02 |
| ☐ | 84 Rich Gedman | .25 | .10 | .02 |
| ☐ | 85 Willie Hernandez | .25 | .10 | .02 |
| ☐ | 86 Ron Kittle | .25 | .10 | .02 |
| ☐ | 87 Lee Lacy | .15 | .06 | .01 |
| ☐ | 88 Bill Madlock | .25 | .10 | .02 |
| ☐ | 89 Mike Marshall | .25 | .10 | .02 |
| ☐ | 90 Keith Moreland | .15 | .06 | .01 |
| ☐ | 91 Graig Nettles | .25 | .10 | .02 |
| ☐ | 92 Lance Parrish | .35 | .14 | .03 |
| ☐ | 93 Kirby Puckett | .75 | .30 | .07 |
| ☐ | 94 Juan Samuel | .25 | .10 | .02 |
| ☐ | 95 Steve Sax | .30 | .12 | .03 |
| ☐ | 96 Dave Stieb | .30 | .12 | .03 |
| ☐ | 97 Darryl Strawberry | 1.25 | .50 | .12 |
| ☐ | 98 Willie Upshaw | .20 | .08 | .02 |
| ☐ | 99 Frank Viola | .20 | .08 | .02 |
| ☐ | 100 Dwight Gooden | 3.50 | 1.40 | .35 |
| ☐ | 101 Joaquin Andujar | .25 | .10 | .02 |
| ☐ | 102 George Bell | .35 | .14 | .03 |
| ☐ | 103 Bert Blyleven | .20 | .08 | .02 |
| ☐ | 104 Mike Boddicker | .20 | .08 | .02 |
| ☐ | 105 Britt Burns | .20 | .08 | .02 |
| ☐ | 106 Rod Carew | .75 | .30 | .07 |
| ☐ | 107 Jack Clark | .30 | .12 | .03 |
| ☐ | 108 Danny Cox | .25 | .10 | .02 |
| ☐ | 109 Ron Darling | .50 | .20 | .05 |
| ☐ | 110 Andre Dawson | .45 | .18 | .04 |
| ☐ | 111 Leon Durham | .25 | .10 | .02 |
| ☐ | 112 Tony Fernandez | .30 | .12 | .03 |
| ☐ | 113 Tommy Herr | .20 | .08 | .02 |
| ☐ | 114 Teddy Higuera | .60 | .24 | .06 |

| | | | | |
|---|---|---|---|---|
| ☐ 115 Bob Horner | .35 | .14 | .03 |
| ☐ 116 Dave Kingman | .25 | .10 | .02 |
| ☐ 117 Jack Morris | .35 | .14 | .03 |
| ☐ 118 Dan Quisenberry | .35 | .14 | .03 |
| ☐ 119 Jeff Reardon | .25 | .10 | .02 |
| ☐ 120 Bryn Smith | .15 | .06 | .01 |
| ☐ 121 Ozzie Smith | .25 | .10 | .02 |
| ☐ 122 John Tudor | .25 | .10 | .02 |
| ☐ 123 Tim Wallach | .25 | .10 | .02 |
| ☐ 124 Willie Wilson | .30 | .12 | .03 |
| ☐ 125 Carlton Fisk | .35 | .14 | .03 |
| ☐ 126 RBI Sluggers: | .35 | .14 | .03 |

Gary Carter
Al Oliver
George Foster

| | | | | |
|---|---|---|---|---|
| ☐ 127 Run Scorers: | .60 | .24 | .06 |

Tim Raines
Ryne Sandberg
Keith Hernandez

| | | | | |
|---|---|---|---|---|
| ☐ 128 Run Scorers: | .60 | .24 | .06 |

Paul Molitor
Cal Ripken
Willie Wilson

| | | | | |
|---|---|---|---|---|
| ☐ 129 No-Hitters: | .20 | .08 | .02 |

John Candelaria
Dennis Eckersley
Bob Forsch

| | | | | |
|---|---|---|---|---|
| ☐ 130 World Series MVP's: | .75 | .30 | .07 |

Pete Rose
Ron Cey
Rollie Fingers

| | | | | |
|---|---|---|---|---|
| ☐ 131 All-Star Game MVPs: | .20 | .08 | .02 |

Dave Concepcion
George Foster
Bill Madlock

| | | | | |
|---|---|---|---|---|
| ☐ 132 Cy Young Winners: | .25 | .10 | .02 |

John Denny
Fernando Valenzuela
Vida Blue

| | | | | |
|---|---|---|---|---|
| ☐ 133 Comeback Players: | .20 | .08 | .02 |

Rich Dotson
Joaquin Andujar
Doyle Alexander

| | | | | |
|---|---|---|---|---|
| ☐ 134 Big Winners: | .45 | .18 | .04 |

Rick Sutcliffe
Tom Seaver
John Denny

| | | | | |
|---|---|---|---|---|
| ☐ 135 Veteran Pitchers: | .50 | .20 | .05 |

Tom Seaver
Phil Niekro
Don Sutton

| | | | | |
|---|---|---|---|---|
| ☐ 136 Rookies of The Year: | 1.50 | .60 | .15 |

Dwight Gooden
Vince Coleman
Alfredo Griffin

| | | | | |
|---|---|---|---|---|
| ☐ 137 All-Star Game MVPs: | .50 | .20 | .05 |

Gary Carter
Fred Lynn
Steve Garvey

| | | | | |
|---|---|---|---|---|
| ☐ 138 Veteran Hitters: | .75 | .30 | .07 |

Tony Perez
Rusty Staub
Pete Rose

| | | | | |
|---|---|---|---|---|
| ☐ 139 Power Hitters: | .60 | .24 | .06 |

Mike Schmidt
Jim Rice
George Foster

| | | | | |
|---|---|---|---|---|
| ☐ 140 Batting Champs: | .35 | .14 | .03 |

Tony Gwynn
Al Oliver
Bill Buckner

| | | | | |
|---|---|---|---|---|
| ☐ 141 No-Hitters: | .40 | .16 | .04 |

Nolan Ryan
Jack Morris
Dave Righetti

| | | | | |
|---|---|---|---|---|
| ☐ 142 No-Hitters: | .35 | .14 | .03 |

Tom Seaver
Bert Blyleven
Vida Blue

| | | | | |
|---|---|---|---|---|
| ☐ 143 Strikeout Kings: | 1.50 | .60 | .15 |

Nolan Ryan
Fernando Valenzuela
Dwight Gooden

| | | | | |
|---|---|---|---|---|
| ☐ 144 Base Stealers: | .45 | .18 | .04 |

Tim Raines
Willie Wilson
Davey Lopes

| | | | | |
|---|---|---|---|---|
| ☐ 145 RBI Sluggers: | .40 | .16 | .04 |

Tony Armas
Cecil Cooper
Eddie Murray

| | | | | |
|---|---|---|---|---|
| ☐ 146 AL MVP's: | .50 | .20 | .05 |

Rod Carew
Jim Rice
Rollie Fingers

| | | | | |
|---|---|---|---|---|
| ☐ 147 World Series MVP's: | .45 | .18 | .04 |

Alan Trammell
Rick Dempsey
Reggie Jackson

| | | | | |
|---|---|---|---|---|
| ☐ 148 World Series MVP's: | .45 | .18 | .04 |

Darrell Porter
Pedro Guerrero
Mike Schmidt

| | | | | |
|---|---|---|---|---|
| ☐ 149 ERA Leaders: | .25 | .10 | .02 |

Mike Boddicker
Rick Sutcliffe
Ron Guidry

| | | | | |
|---|---|---|---|---|
| ☐ 150 Comeback Players: | .45 | .18 | .04 |

Reggie Jackson
Dave Kingman
Fred Lynn

| | | | | |
|---|---|---|---|---|
| ☐ 151 Buddy Bell | .20 | .08 | .02 |
| ☐ 152 Dennis Boyd | .20 | .08 | .02 |
| ☐ 153 Dave Concepcion | .20 | .08 | .02 |
| ☐ 154 Brian Downing | .15 | .06 | .01 |
| ☐ 155 Shawon Dunston | .25 | .10 | .02 |
| ☐ 156 John Franco | .25 | .10 | .02 |
| ☐ 157 Scott Garrelts | .20 | .08 | .02 |
| ☐ 158 Bob James | .15 | .06 | .01 |
| ☐ 159 Charlie Leibrandt | .20 | .08 | .02 |
| ☐ 160 Oddibe McDowell | .75 | .30 | .07 |
| ☐ 161 Roger McDowell | .50 | .20 | .05 |
| ☐ 162 Mike Moore | .20 | .08 | .02 |
| ☐ 163 Phil Niekro | .50 | .20 | .05 |
| ☐ 164 Al Oliver | .25 | .10 | .02 |
| ☐ 165 Tony Pena | .25 | .10 | .02 |
| ☐ 166 Ted Power | .20 | .08 | .02 |
| ☐ 167 Mike Scioscia | .15 | .06 | .01 |
| ☐ 168 Mario Soto | .20 | .08 | .02 |
| ☐ 169 Bob Stanley | .20 | .08 | .02 |
| ☐ 170 Gary Templeton | .20 | .08 | .02 |
| ☐ 171 Andre Thornton | .20 | .08 | .02 |
| ☐ 172 Alan Trammell | .30 | .12 | .03 |
| ☐ 173 Doug DeCinces | .25 | .10 | .02 |
| ☐ 174 Greg Walker | .25 | .10 | .02 |
| ☐ 175 Don Sutton | .40 | .16 | .04 |
| ☐ 176 1985 Award Winners: | 1.50 | .60 | .15 |

Ozzie Guillen
Bret Saberhagen
Don Mattingly
Vince Coleman
Dwight Gooden
Willie McGee

| | | | | |
|---|---|---|---|---|
| ☐ 177 1985 Hot Rookies: | .50 | .20 | .05 |

Stew Cliburn
Brian Fisher
Joe Hesketh
Joe Orsulak
Mark Salas
Larry Sheets

| | | | | |
|---|---|---|---|---|
| ☐ 178 1986 Rookies To Watch: | 6.00 | 2.40 | .60 |

Jose Canseco
Mark Funderburk
Mike Greenwell
Steve Lombardozzi
Billy Joe Robidoux
Dan Tartabull

| | | | | |
|---|---|---|---|---|
| ☐ 179 1985 Gold Glovers: | 1.00 | .40 | .10 |

George Brett
Ron Guidry
Keith Hernandez
Don Mattingly
Willie McGee
Dale Murphy

| | | | | |
|---|---|---|---|---|
| ☐ 180 Active Lifetime .300 | 1.00 | .40 | .10 |

Wade Boggs
George Brett
Rod Carew
Cecil Cooper
Don Mattingly
Willie Wilson

| | | | | |
|---|---|---|---|---|
| ☐ 181 Active Lifetime .300 | 1.00 | .40 | .10 |

Tony Gwynn
Bill Madlock
Pedro Guerrero
Dave Parker
Pete Rose
Keith Hernandez

| | | | | |
|---|---|---|---|---|
| ☐ 182 1985 Milestones: | 1.00 | .40 | .10 |

Rod Carew
Phil Niekro
Pete Rose
Nolan Ryan
Tom Seaver
Matt Tallman (fan)

| | | | | |
|---|---|---|---|---|
| ☐ 183 1985 Triple Crown: | 1.00 | .40 | .10 |

|  | | | MINT | VG-E | F-G |
|---|---|---|---|---|---|
| | Wade Boggs | | | | |
| | Darrell Evans | | | | |
| | Don Mattingly | | | | |
| | Willie McGee | | | | |
| | Dale Murphy | | | | |
| | Dave Parker | | | | |
| ☐ 184 | 1985 Highlights: | | 2.00 | .80 | .20 |
| | Wade Boggs | | | | |
| | Dwight Gooden | | | | |
| | Rickey Henderson | | | | |
| | Don Mattingly | | | | |
| | Willie McGee | | | | |
| | John Tudor | | | | |
| ☐ 185 | 1985 20 Game Winners: | | 1.25 | .50 | .12 |
| | Dwight Gooden | | | | |
| | Ron Guidry | | | | |
| | John Tudor | | | | |
| | Joaquin Andujar | | | | |
| | Bret Saberhagen | | | | |
| | Tom Browning | | | | |
| ☐ 186 | World Series Champs | | .50 | .20 | .05 |
| | L. Smith, Dane Iorg | | | | |
| | W. Wilson, Leibrandt | | | | |
| | G. Brett, Saberhagen | | | | |
| | D. Motley, Quisenberry | | | | |
| | D. Jackson, Sundberg | | | | |
| | S. Balboni, F. White | | | | |
| ☐ 187 | Hubie Brooks | | .25 | .10 | .02 |
| ☐ 188 | Glenn Davis | | .75 | .30 | .07 |
| ☐ 189 | Darrell Evans | | .25 | .10 | .02 |
| ☐ 190 | Rich Gossage | | .35 | .14 | .03 |
| ☐ 191 | Andy Hawkins | | .20 | .08 | .02 |
| ☐ 192 | Jay Howell | | .20 | .08 | .02 |
| ☐ 193 | LaMarr Hoyt | | .25 | .10 | .02 |
| ☐ 194 | Davey Lopes | | .20 | .08 | .02 |
| ☐ 195 | Mike Scott | | .35 | .14 | .03 |
| ☐ 196 | Ted Simmons | | .25 | .10 | .02 |
| ☐ 197 | Gary Ward | | .15 | .06 | .01 |
| ☐ 198 | Bob Welch | | .20 | .08 | .02 |
| ☐ 199 | Mike Young | | .25 | .10 | .02 |
| ☐ 200 | Buddy Biancalana | | .15 | .06 | .01 |

## 1986 Sportflics Decade Greats

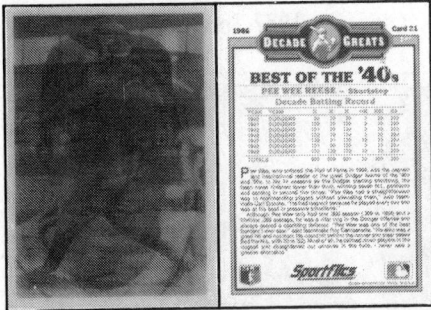

This set of 75 three-phase "animated" cards was produced by Sportflics and manufactured by Opti-Graphics of Arlington, Texas. Cards are standard size, 2 1/2" by 3 1/2", and feature both sepia (players of the '30s and '40s) and full color cards. The concept of the set was that the best players at each position for each decade (from the '30s to the '80s) were chosen. The bios were written by Les Woodcock. Also included with the set in the specially designed collector box are 51 trivia cards with historical questions about the six decades of All-Star games.

| | | MINT | VG-E | F-G |
|---|---|---|---|---|
| | COMPLETE SET | 16.00 | 6.50 | 1.60 |
| | COMMON PLAYER (1-75) | .15 | .06 | .01 |
| ☐ 1 | Babe Ruth | 2.00 | .80 | .20 |
| ☐ 2 | Jimmie Foxx | .35 | .14 | .03 |

| | | | MINT | VG-E | F-G |
|---|---|---|---|---|---|
| ☐ 3 | Lefty Grove | | .35 | .14 | .03 |
| ☐ 4 | Hank Greenberg | | .35 | .14 | .03 |
| ☐ 5 | Al Simmons | | .25 | .10 | .02 |
| ☐ 6 | Carl Hubbell | | .25 | .10 | .02 |
| ☐ 7 | Joe Cronin | | .25 | .10 | .02 |
| ☐ 8 | Mel Ott | | .25 | .10 | .02 |
| ☐ 9 | Lefty Gomez | | .25 | .10 | .02 |
| ☐ 10 | Lou Gehrig | | 1.00 | .40 | .10 |
| | (Best '30s Player) | | | | |
| ☐ 11 | Pie Traynor | | .25 | .10 | .02 |
| ☐ 12 | Charlie Gehringer | | .25 | .10 | .02 |
| ☐ 13 | Best '30s Catchers: | | .25 | .10 | .02 |
| | Bill Dickey | | | | |
| | Mickey Cochrane | | | | |
| | Gabby Hartnett | | | | |
| ☐ 14 | Best '30s Pitchers: | | .35 | .14 | .03 |
| | Dizzy Dean | | | | |
| | Red Ruffing | | | | |
| | Paul Derringer | | | | |
| ☐ 15 | Best '30s Outfielders: | | .25 | .10 | .02 |
| | Paul Waner | | | | |
| | Joe Medwick | | | | |
| | Earl Averill | | | | |
| ☐ 16 | Bob Feller | | .75 | .30 | .07 |
| ☐ 17 | Lou Boudreau | | .25 | .10 | .02 |
| ☐ 18 | Enos Slaughter | | .25 | .10 | .02 |
| ☐ 19 | Hal Newhouser | | .15 | .06 | .01 |
| ☐ 20 | Joe DiMaggio | | 1.25 | .50 | .12 |
| ☐ 21 | Pee Wee Reese | | .35 | .14 | .03 |
| ☐ 22 | Phil Rizzuto | | .25 | .10 | .02 |
| ☐ 23 | Ernie Lombardi | | .25 | .10 | .02 |
| ☐ 24 | Best '40s Infielders: | | .25 | .10 | .02 |
| | Johnny Mize | | | | |
| | Joe Gordon | | | | |
| | George Kell | | | | |
| ☐ 25 | Ted Williams | | 1.00 | .40 | .10 |
| | (Best '40s Player) | | | | |
| ☐ 26 | Mickey Mantle | | 2.00 | .80 | .20 |
| ☐ 27 | Warren Spahn | | .25 | .10 | .02 |
| ☐ 28 | Jackie Robinson | | .50 | .20 | .05 |
| ☐ 29 | Ernie Banks | | .35 | .14 | .03 |
| ☐ 30 | Stan Musial | | .50 | .20 | .05 |
| | (Best '50s Player) | | | | |
| ☐ 31 | Yogi Berra | | .50 | .20 | .05 |
| ☐ 32 | Duke Snider | | .75 | .30 | .07 |
| ☐ 33 | Roy Campanella | | .75 | .30 | .07 |
| ☐ 34 | Eddie Mathews | | .35 | .14 | .03 |
| ☐ 35 | Ralph Kiner | | .25 | .10 | .02 |
| ☐ 36 | Early Wynn | | .25 | .10 | .02 |
| ☐ 37 | Double Play Duo: | | .25 | .10 | .02 |
| | Nellie Fox | | | | |
| | Luis Aparicio | | | | |
| ☐ 38 | Best '50s First Base: | | .25 | .10 | .02 |
| | Gil Hodges | | | | |
| | Ted Kluszewski | | | | |
| | Mickey Vernon | | | | |
| ☐ 39 | Best '50s Pitchers: | | .25 | .10 | .02 |
| | Bob Lemon | | | | |
| | Don Newcombe | | | | |
| | Robin Roberts | | | | |
| ☐ 40 | Henry Aaron | | 1.00 | .40 | .10 |
| ☐ 41 | Frank Robinson | | .35 | .14 | .03 |
| ☐ 42 | Bob Gibson | | .35 | .14 | .03 |
| ☐ 43 | Roberto Clemente | | 1.00 | .40 | .10 |
| ☐ 44 | Whitey Ford | | .35 | .14 | .03 |
| ☐ 45 | Brooks Robinson | | .50 | .20 | .05 |
| ☐ 46 | Juan Marichal | | .35 | .14 | .03 |
| ☐ 47 | Carl Yastrzemski | | 1.00 | .40 | .10 |
| ☐ 48 | Best '60s First Base: | | .35 | .14 | .03 |
| | Willie McCovey | | | | |
| | Harmon Killebrew | | | | |
| | Orlando Cepeda | | | | |
| ☐ 49 | Best '60s Catchers: | | .15 | .06 | .01 |
| | Joe Torre | | | | |
| | Elston Howard | | | | |
| | Bill Freehan | | | | |
| ☐ 50 | Willie Mays | | 1.00 | .40 | .10 |
| | (Best '50s Player) | | | | |
| ☐ 51 | Best '60s Outfielders: | | .25 | .10 | .02 |
| | Al Kaline | | | | |
| | Tony Oliva | | | | |
| | Billy Williams | | | | |
| ☐ 52 | Tom Seaver | | .75 | .30 | .07 |
| ☐ 53 | Reggie Jackson | | 1.00 | .40 | .10 |
| ☐ 54 | Steve Carlton | | .75 | .30 | .07 |
| ☐ 55 | Mike Schmidt | | 1.00 | .40 | .10 |
| ☐ 56 | Joe Morgan | | .35 | .14 | .03 |
| ☐ 57 | Jim Rice | | .50 | .20 | .05 |
| ☐ 58 | Jim Palmer | | .35 | .14 | .03 |
| ☐ 59 | Lou Brock | | .35 | .14 | .03 |
| ☐ 60 | Pete Rose | | 1.25 | .50 | .12 |
| | (Best '70s Player) | | | | |
| ☐ 61 | Steve Garvey | | .75 | .30 | .07 |

| | | MINT | VG-E | F-G |
|---|---|---|---|---|
| ☐ 62 | Best '70s Catchers: .......... Thurman Munson Carlton Fisk Ted Simmons | .25 | .10 | .02 |
| ☐ 63 | Best '70s Pitchers: .......... Vida Blue Catfish Hunter Nolan Ryan | .25 | .10 | .02 |
| ☐ 64 | George Brett ..................... | 1.00 | .40 | .10 |
| ☐ 65 | Don Mattingly ................... | 2.00 | .80 | .20 |
| ☐ 66 | Fernando Valenzuela ........ | .35 | .14 | .03 |
| ☐ 67 | Dale Murphy ..................... | 1.00 | .40 | .10 |
| ☐ 68 | Wade Boggs ..................... | 1.25 | .50 | .12 |
| ☐ 69 | Rickey Henderson ............. | 1.00 | .40 | .10 |
| ☐ 70 | Eddie Murray ................... (Best '80s Player) | .75 | .30 | .07 |
| ☐ 71 | Ron Guidry ....................... | .25 | .10 | .02 |
| ☐ 72 | Best '80s Catchers: .......... Gary Carter Lance Parrish Tony Pena | .25 | .10 | .02 |
| ☐ 73 | Best '80s Infielders: .......... Cal Ripken Lou Whitaker Robin Yount | .25 | .10 | .02 |
| ☐ 74 | Best '80s Outfielders: ....... Pedro Guerrero Tim Raines Dave Winfield | .25 | .10 | .02 |
| ☐ 75 | Dwight Gooden ................. | 1.25 | .50 | .12 |

| | | MINT | VG-E | F-G |
|---|---|---|---|---|
| ☐ 18 | Cory Snyder ..................... | 1.25 | .50 | .12 |
| ☐ 19 | Reggie Williams ................ | .20 | .08 | .02 |
| ☐ 20 | Mitch Williams ................. | .30 | .12 | .03 |
| ☐ 21 | Glenn Braggs ................... | .60 | .24 | .06 |
| ☐ 22 | Danny Tartabull ............... | .50 | .20 | .05 |
| ☐ 23 | Charlie Kerfeld ................. | .30 | .12 | .03 |
| ☐ 24 | Paul Assenmacher ........... | .20 | .08 | .02 |
| ☐ 25 | Robby Thompson ............. | .50 | .20 | .05 |
| ☐ 26 | Bobby Bonilla .................. | .20 | .08 | .02 |
| ☐ 27 | Andres Galarraga ............. | .30 | .12 | .03 |
| ☐ 28 | Billy Jo Robidoux ............. | .20 | .08 | .02 |
| ☐ 29 | Bruce Ruffin .................... | .40 | .16 | .04 |
| ☐ 30 | Greg Swindell ................... | .60 | .24 | .06 |
| ☐ 31 | John Cangelosi ................ | .30 | .12 | .03 |
| ☐ 32 | Jim Traber ....................... | .20 | .08 | .02 |
| ☐ 33 | Russ Morman ................... | .35 | .14 | .03 |
| ☐ 34 | Barry Larkin ..................... | .60 | .24 | .06 |
| ☐ 35 | Todd Worrell .................... | .60 | .24 | .06 |
| ☐ 36 | John Cerutti .................... | .30 | .12 | .03 |
| ☐ 37 | Mike Kingery ................... | .25 | .10 | .02 |
| ☐ 38 | Mark Eichhorn ................. | .50 | .20 | .05 |
| ☐ 39 | Scott Bankhead ............... | .15 | .06 | .01 |
| ☐ 40 | Bo Jackson ...................... | 1.50 | .60 | .15 |
| ☐ 41 | Greg Mathews ................. | .40 | .16 | .04 |
| ☐ 42 | Eric King ......................... | .40 | .16 | .04 |
| ☐ 43 | Kal Daniels ...................... | .25 | .10 | .02 |
| ☐ 44 | Calvin Schiraldi ............... | .20 | .08 | .02 |
| ☐ 45 | Mickey Brantley ............... | .30 | .12 | .03 |
| ☐ 46 | Tri-Stars: ........................ Willie Mays Pete Rose Fred Lynn | .60 | .24 | .06 |
| ☐ 47 | Tri-Stars: ........................ Tom Seaver Fern. Valenzuela Dwight Gooden | .60 | .24 | .06 |
| ☐ 48 | Big Six: ........................... Eddie Murray Lou Whitaker Dave Righetti Steve Sax Cal Ripken Jr. Darryl Strawberry | .60 | .24 | .06 |
| ☐ 49 | Kevin Mitchell .................. | .50 | .20 | .05 |
| ☐ 50 | Mike Diaz ........................ | .40 | .16 | .04 |

# 1986 Sportflics Rookies

This set of 50 three-phase "animated" cards features top rookies of 1986 as well as a few outstanding rookies from the past. These "Magic Motion" cards are standard size 2 1/2" by 3 1/2" and feature a distinctive light blue border on the front of the card. Cards were distributed in a light blue box which also contained 34 trivia cards each measuring 1 3/4" by 2". There are 47 single player cards along with two Tri-Stars and one Big Six.

| | | MINT | VG-E | F-G |
|---|---|---|---|---|
| COMPLETE SET (50) ................. | | 15.00 | 6.00 | 1.50 |
| COMMON PLAYER (1-50) .......... | | .10 | .04 | .01 |
| ☐ 1 | John Kruk ........................ | .30 | .12 | .03 |
| ☐ 2 | Edwin Correa ................... | .40 | .16 | .04 |
| ☐ 3 | Pete Incaviglia ................. | 1.50 | .60 | .15 |
| ☐ 4 | Dale Sveum ..................... | .20 | .08 | .02 |
| ☐ 5 | Juan Nieves ..................... | .30 | .12 | .03 |
| ☐ 6 | Will Clark ........................ | .75 | .30 | .07 |
| ☐ 7 | Wally Joyner .................... | 3.00 | 1.20 | .30 |
| ☐ 8 | Lance McCullers .............. | .20 | .08 | .02 |
| ☐ 9 | Scott Bailes .................... | .20 | .08 | .02 |
| ☐ 10 | Dan Plesac ...................... | .20 | .08 | .02 |
| ☐ 11 | Jose Canseco .................. | 2.00 | .80 | .20 |
| ☐ 12 | Bobby Witt ...................... | .50 | .20 | .05 |
| ☐ 13 | Barry Bonds ..................... | .75 | .30 | .07 |
| ☐ 14 | Andres Thomas ................ | .40 | .16 | .04 |
| ☐ 15 | Jim Deshaies ................... | .50 | .20 | .05 |
| ☐ 16 | Ruben Sierra .................... | 1.50 | .60 | .15 |
| ☐ 17 | Steve Lombardozzi .......... | .10 | .04 | .01 |

# 1987 Sportflics

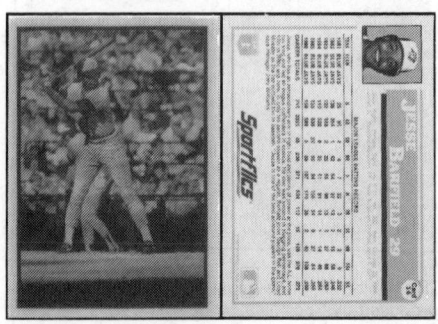

This 200 card set was produced by Sportflics and again features three sequence action pictures on each card. Cards measure 2 1/2" by 3 1/2" and are in full color. Also included with the cards were 136 small team logo and trivia cards. There are 165 individual players, 20 Tri-Stars (the top three players in each league at each position), and 15 other miscellaneous multi-player cards. The cards feature a red border on the front. A full-color face shot of the player is printed on the back of the card. Cards are numbered on the back in the upper right corner.

| | MINT | VG-E | F-G |
|---|---|---|---|
| COMPLETE SET ........................ | 35.00 | 14.00 | 3.50 |

| COMMON PLAYER | .15 | .06 | .01 |
|---|---|---|---|
| ☐ 1 Don Mattingly | 2.50 | 1.00 | .25 |
| ☐ 2 Wade Boggs | 1.25 | .50 | .12 |
| ☐ 3 Dale Murphy | .90 | .36 | .09 |
| ☐ 4 Rickey Henderson | .75 | .30 | .07 |
| ☐ 5 George Brett | .75 | .30 | .07 |
| ☐ 6 Eddie Murray | .60 | .24 | .06 |
| ☐ 7 Kirby Puckett | .50 | .20 | .05 |
| ☐ 8 Ryne Sandberg | .50 | .20 | .05 |
| ☐ 9 Cal Ripken Jr. | .50 | .20 | .05 |
| ☐ 10 Roger Clemens | 1.25 | .50 | .12 |
| ☐ 11 Ted Higuera | .25 | .10 | .02 |
| ☐ 12 Steve Sax | .25 | .10 | .02 |
| ☐ 13 Chris Brown | .25 | .10 | .02 |
| ☐ 14 Jesse Barfield | .35 | .14 | .03 |
| ☐ 15 Kent Hrbek | .25 | .10 | .02 |
| ☐ 16 Robin Yount | .45 | .18 | .04 |
| ☐ 17 Glenn Davis | .60 | .24 | .06 |
| ☐ 18 Hubie Brooks | .25 | .10 | .02 |
| ☐ 19 Mike Scott | .30 | .12 | .03 |
| ☐ 20 Darryl Strawberry | .75 | .30 | .07 |
| ☐ 21 Alvin Davis | .25 | .10 | .02 |
| ☐ 22 Eric Davis | .75 | .30 | .07 |
| ☐ 23 Danny Tartabull | .50 | .20 | .05 |
| ☐ 24 Cory Snyder | .75 | .30 | .07 |
| ☐ 25 Pete Rose | 1.25 | .50 | .12 |
| ☐ 26 Wally Joyner | 2.50 | 1.00 | .25 |
| ☐ 27 Pedro Guerrero | .35 | .14 | .03 |
| ☐ 28 Tom Seaver | .75 | .30 | .07 |
| ☐ 29 Bob Knepper | .20 | .08 | .02 |
| ☐ 30 Mike Schmidt | 1.00 | .40 | .10 |
| ☐ 31 Tony Gwynn | .60 | .24 | .06 |
| ☐ 32 Don Slaught | .15 | .06 | .01 |
| ☐ 33 Todd Worrell | .35 | .14 | .03 |
| ☐ 34 Tim Raines | .35 | .14 | .03 |
| ☐ 35 Dave Parker | .35 | .14 | .03 |
| ☐ 36 Bob Ojeda | .25 | .10 | .02 |
| ☐ 37 Pete Incaviglia | 1.00 | .40 | .10 |
| ☐ 38 Bruce Hurst | .25 | .10 | .02 |
| ☐ 39 Bobby Witt | .50 | .20 | .05 |
| ☐ 40 Steve Garvey | .60 | .24 | .06 |
| ☐ 41 Dave Winfield | .50 | .20 | .05 |
| ☐ 42 Jose Cruz | .20 | .08 | .02 |
| ☐ 43 Orel Hershiser | .25 | .10 | .02 |
| ☐ 44 Reggie Jackson | 1.00 | .40 | .10 |
| ☐ 45 Chili Davis | .20 | .08 | .02 |
| ☐ 46 Robby Thompson | .35 | .14 | .03 |
| ☐ 47 Dennis Boyd | .25 | .10 | .02 |
| ☐ 48 Kirk Gibson | .35 | .14 | .03 |
| ☐ 49 Fred Lynn | .25 | .10 | .02 |
| ☐ 50 Gary Carter | .60 | .24 | .06 |
| ☐ 51 George Bell | .30 | .12 | .03 |
| ☐ 52 Pete O'Brien | .25 | .10 | .02 |
| ☐ 53 Ron Darling | .35 | .14 | .03 |
| ☐ 54 Paul Molitor | .20 | .08 | .02 |
| ☐ 55 Mike Pagliarulo | .25 | .10 | .02 |
| ☐ 56 Mike Boddicker | .20 | .08 | .02 |
| ☐ 57 Dave Righetti | .25 | .10 | .02 |
| ☐ 58 Len Dykstra | .35 | .14 | .03 |
| ☐ 59 Mike Witt | .25 | .10 | .02 |
| ☐ 60 Tony Bernazard | .15 | .06 | .01 |
| ☐ 61 John Kruk | .30 | .12 | .03 |
| ☐ 62 Mike Krukow | .20 | .08 | .02 |
| ☐ 63 Sid Fernandez | .35 | .14 | .03 |
| ☐ 64 Gary Gaetti | .25 | .10 | .02 |
| ☐ 65 Vince Coleman | .60 | .24 | .06 |
| ☐ 66 Pat Tabler | .25 | .10 | .02 |
| ☐ 67 Mike Scioscia | .15 | .06 | .01 |
| ☐ 68 Scott Garrelts | .15 | .06 | .01 |
| ☐ 69 Brett Butler | .25 | .10 | .02 |
| ☐ 70 Bill Buckner | .20 | .08 | .02 |
| ☐ 71 Dennis Rasmussen | .20 | .08 | .02 |
| ☐ 72 Tim Wallach | .20 | .08 | .02 |
| ☐ 73 Bob Horner | .30 | .12 | .03 |
| ☐ 74 Willie McGee | .30 | .12 | .03 |
| ☐ 75 Tri-Stars: | 1.50 | .60 | .15 |
| Don Mattingly | | | |
| Wally Joyner | | | |
| Eddie Murray | | | |
| ☐ 76 Jesse Orosco | .15 | .06 | .01 |
| ☐ 77 Tri-Stars: | .25 | .10 | .02 |
| Todd Worrell | | | |
| Jeff Reardon | | | |
| Lee Smith | | | |
| ☐ 78 Candy Maldonado | .25 | .10 | .02 |
| ☐ 79 Tri-Stars: | .25 | .10 | .02 |
| Ozzie Smith | | | |
| Hubie Brooks | | | |
| Shawon Dunston | | | |
| ☐ 80 Tri-Stars: | 1.00 | .40 | .10 |
| George Bell | | | |
| Jose Canseco | | | |
| Jim Rice | | | |
| ☐ 81 Bert Blyleven | .25 | .10 | .02 |
| ☐ 82 Mike Marshall | .25 | .10 | .02 |
| ☐ 83 Ron Guidry | .25 | .10 | .02 |
| ☐ 84 Julio Franco | .20 | .08 | .02 |
| ☐ 85 Willie Wilson | .25 | .10 | .02 |
| ☐ 86 Lee Lacy | .15 | .06 | .01 |
| ☐ 87 Jack Morris | .30 | .12 | .03 |
| ☐ 88 Ray Knight | .25 | .10 | .02 |
| ☐ 89 Phil Bradley | .35 | .14 | .03 |
| ☐ 90 Jose Canseco | 2.00 | .80 | .20 |
| ☐ 91 Gary Ward | .20 | .08 | .02 |
| ☐ 92 Mike Easler | .20 | .08 | .02 |
| ☐ 93 Tony Pena | .25 | .10 | .02 |
| ☐ 94 Dave Smith | .20 | .08 | .02 |
| ☐ 95 Will Clark | .75 | .30 | .07 |
| ☐ 96 Lloyd Moseby | .20 | .08 | .02 |
| ☐ 97 Jim Rice | .50 | .20 | .05 |
| ☐ 98 Shawon Dunston | .25 | .10 | .02 |
| ☐ 99 Don Sutton | .35 | .14 | .03 |
| ☐ 100 Dwight Gooden | 1.25 | .50 | .12 |
| ☐ 101 Lance Parrish | .35 | .14 | .03 |
| ☐ 102 Mark Langston | .25 | .10 | .02 |
| ☐ 103 Floyd Youmans | .30 | .12 | .03 |
| ☐ 104 Lee Smith | .25 | .10 | .02 |
| ☐ 105 Willie Hernandez | .25 | .10 | .02 |
| ☐ 106 Doug DeCinces | .20 | .08 | .02 |
| ☐ 107 Ken Schrom | .15 | .06 | .01 |
| ☐ 108 Don Carman | .15 | .06 | .01 |
| ☐ 109 Brook Jacoby | .25 | .10 | .02 |
| ☐ 110 Steve Bedrosian | .15 | .06 | .01 |
| ☐ 111 Tri-Stars: | .75 | .30 | .07 |
| Roger Clemens | | | |
| Jack Morris | | | |
| Ted Higuera | | | |
| ☐ 112 Tri-Stars: | .20 | .08 | .02 |
| Marty Barrett | | | |
| Tony Bernazard | | | |
| Lou Whitaker | | | |
| ☐ 113 Tri-Stars: | .35 | .14 | .03 |
| Cal Ripken | | | |
| Scott Fletcher | | | |
| Tony Fernandez | | | |
| ☐ 114 Tri-Stars: | 1.00 | .40 | .10 |
| Wade Boggs | | | |
| George Brett | | | |
| Gary Gaetti | | | |
| ☐ 115 Tri-Stars: | .50 | .20 | .05 |
| Mike Schmidt | | | |
| Chris Brown | | | |
| Tim Wallach | | | |
| ☐ 116 Tri-Stars: | .35 | .14 | .03 |
| Ryne Sandberg | | | |
| Johnny Ray | | | |
| Bill Doran | | | |
| ☐ 117 Tri-Stars: | .35 | .14 | .03 |
| Dave Parker | | | |
| Tony Gwynn | | | |
| Kevin Bass | | | |
| ☐ 118 Big Six Rookies: | 2.00 | .80 | .20 |
| Ty Gainey | | | |
| Terry Steinbach | | | |
| David Clark | | | |
| Pat Dodson | | | |
| Phil Lombardi | | | |
| Benito Santiago | | | |
| ☐ 119 Hi-Lite Tri-Stars: | .50 | .20 | .05 |
| Dave Righetti | | | |
| Fernando Valenzuela | | | |
| Mike Scott | | | |
| ☐ 120 Tri-Stars: | 1.00 | .40 | .10 |
| Fernando Valenzuela | | | |
| Mike Scott | | | |
| Dwight Gooden | | | |
| ☐ 121 Johnny Ray | .20 | .08 | .02 |
| ☐ 122 Keith Moreland | .20 | .08 | .02 |
| ☐ 123 Juan Samuel | .25 | .10 | .02 |
| ☐ 124 Wally Backman | .20 | .08 | .02 |
| ☐ 125 Nolan Ryan | .60 | .24 | .06 |
| ☐ 126 Greg Harris | .20 | .08 | .02 |
| ☐ 127 Kirk McCaskill | .30 | .12 | .03 |
| ☐ 128 Dwight Evans | .25 | .10 | .02 |
| ☐ 129 Rick Rhoden | .20 | .08 | .02 |
| ☐ 130 Bill Madlock | .25 | .10 | .02 |
| ☐ 131 Oddibe McDowell | .35 | .14 | .03 |
| ☐ 132 Darrell Evans | .20 | .08 | .02 |
| ☐ 133 Keith Hernandez | .35 | .14 | .03 |
| ☐ 134 Tom Brunansky | .20 | .08 | .02 |
| ☐ 135 Kevin McReynolds | .30 | .12 | .03 |
| ☐ 136 Scott Fletcher | .20 | .08 | .02 |
| ☐ 137 Lou Whitaker | .25 | .10 | .02 |
| ☐ 138 Carney Lansford | .25 | .10 | .02 |
| ☐ 139 Andre Dawson | .30 | .12 | .03 |

| | | | | |
|---|---|---|---|---|
| ☐ 140 | Carlton Fisk | .25 | .10 | .02 |
| ☐ 141 | Buddy Bell | .20 | .08 | .02 |
| ☐ 142 | Ozzie Smith | .25 | .10 | .02 |
| ☐ 143 | Dan Pasqua | .30 | .12 | .03 |
| ☐ 144 | Kevin Mitchell | .35 | .14 | .03 |
| ☐ 145 | Bret Saberhagen | .25 | .10 | .02 |
| ☐ 146 | Charlie Kerfeld | .25 | .10 | .02 |
| ☐ 147 | Phil Niekro | .30 | .12 | .03 |
| ☐ 148 | John Candelaria | .20 | .08 | .02 |
| ☐ 149 | Rich Gedman | .25 | .10 | .02 |
| ☐ 150 | Fernando Valenzuela | .50 | .20 | .05 |
| ☐ 151 | Tri-Stars: | .35 | .14 | .03 |
| | Gary Carter | | | |
| | Mike Scioscia | | | |
| | Tony Pena | | | |
| ☐ 152 | Tri-Stars: | .60 | .24 | .06 |
| | Tim Raines | | | |
| | Jose Cruz | | | |
| | Vince Coleman | | | |
| ☐ 153 | Tri-Stars: | .35 | .14 | .03 |
| | Jesse Barfield | | | |
| | Harold Baines | | | |
| | Dave Winfield | | | |
| ☐ 154 | Tri-Stars: | .35 | .14 | .03 |
| | Lance Parrish | | | |
| | Don Slaught | | | |
| | Rich Gedman | | | |
| ☐ 155 | Tri-Stars: | .75 | .30 | .07 |
| | Dale Murphy | | | |
| | Kevin McReynolds | | | |
| | Eric Davis | | | |
| ☐ 156 | Hi-Lite Tri-Stars: | .50 | .20 | .05 |
| | Don Sutton | | | |
| | Mike Schmidt | | | |
| | Jim Deshaies | | | |
| ☐ 157 | Speedburners: | .45 | .18 | .04 |
| | Rickey Henderson | | | |
| | John Cangelosi | | | |
| | Gary Pettis | | | |
| ☐ 158 | Big Six Rookies: | 2.00 | .80 | .20 |
| | Randy Asadoor | | | |
| | Casey Candaele | | | |
| | Kevin Seitzer | | | |
| | Rafael Palmeiro | | | |
| | Tim Pyznarski | | | |
| | Dave Cochrane | | | |
| ☐ 159 | Big Six: | 2.50 | 1.00 | .25 |
| | Don Mattingly | | | |
| | Rickey Henderson | | | |
| | Roger Clemens | | | |
| | Dale Murphy | | | |
| | Eddie Murray | | | |
| | Dwight Gooden | | | |
| ☐ 160 | Roger McDowell | .25 | .10 | .02 |
| ☐ 161 | Brian Downing | .15 | .06 | .01 |
| ☐ 162 | Bill Doran | .25 | .10 | .02 |
| ☐ 163 | Don Baylor | .25 | .10 | .02 |
| ☐ 164 | Alfredo Griffin | .15 | .06 | .01 |
| ☐ 165 | Don Aase | .15 | .06 | .01 |
| ☐ 166 | Glenn Wilson | .25 | .10 | .02 |
| ☐ 167 | Dan Quisenberry | .25 | .10 | .02 |
| ☐ 168 | Frank White | .20 | .08 | .02 |
| ☐ 169 | Cecil Cooper | .25 | .10 | .02 |
| ☐ 170 | Jody Davis | .25 | .10 | .02 |
| ☐ 171 | Harold Baines | .35 | .14 | .03 |
| ☐ 172 | Rob Deer | .35 | .14 | .03 |
| ☐ 173 | John Tudor | .25 | .10 | .02 |
| ☐ 174 | Larry Parrish | .20 | .08 | .02 |
| ☐ 175 | Kevin Bass | .25 | .10 | .02 |
| ☐ 176 | Joe Carter | .45 | .18 | .04 |
| ☐ 177 | Mitch Webster | .25 | .10 | .02 |
| ☐ 178 | Dave Kingman | .30 | .12 | .03 |
| ☐ 179 | Jim Presley | .40 | .16 | .04 |
| ☐ 180 | Mel Hall | .25 | .10 | .02 |
| ☐ 181 | Shane Rawley | .20 | .08 | .02 |
| ☐ 182 | Marty Barrett | .30 | .12 | .03 |
| ☐ 183 | Damaso Garcia | .20 | .08 | .02 |
| ☐ 184 | Bobby Grich | .20 | .08 | .02 |
| ☐ 185 | Leon Durham | .20 | .08 | .02 |
| ☐ 186 | Ozzie Guillen | .25 | .10 | .02 |
| ☐ 187 | Tony Fernandez | .25 | .10 | .02 |
| ☐ 188 | Alan Trammell | .25 | .10 | .02 |
| ☐ 189 | Jim Clancy | .15 | .06 | .01 |
| ☐ 190 | Bo Jackson | 1.25 | .50 | .12 |
| ☐ 191 | Bob Forsch | .20 | .08 | .02 |
| ☐ 192 | John Franco | .25 | .10 | .02 |
| ☐ 193 | Von Hayes | .35 | .14 | .03 |
| ☐ 194 | Tri-Stars: | .25 | .10 | .02 |
| | Don Aase | | | |
| | Dave Righetti | | | |
| | Mark Eichhorn | | | |
| ☐ 195 | Tri-Stars: | .35 | .14 | .03 |
| | Keith Hernandez | | | |

| | | | | |
|---|---|---|---|---|
| | Jack Clark | | | |
| | Glenn Davis | | | |
| ☐ 196 | Hi-Lite Tri-Stars: | .75 | .30 | .07 |
| | Roger Clemens | | | |
| | Joe Cowley | | | |
| | Bob Horner | | | |
| ☐ 197 | Big Six: | 1.00 | .40 | .10 |
| | George Brett | | | |
| | Hubie Brooks | | | |
| | Tony Gwynn | | | |
| | Ryne Sandberg | | | |
| | Tim Raines | | | |
| | Wade Boggs | | | |
| ☐ 198 | Tri-Stars: | .50 | .20 | .05 |
| | Kirby Puckett | | | |
| | Rickey Henderson | | | |
| | Fred Lynn | | | |
| ☐ 199 | Speedburners: | 1.00 | .40 | .10 |
| | Tim Raines | | | |
| | Vince Coleman | | | |
| | Eric Davis | | | |
| ☐ 200 | Steve Carlton | .50 | .20 | .05 |

# 1933 Sport Kings

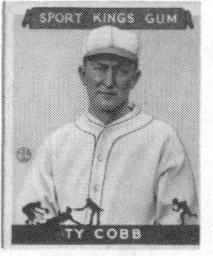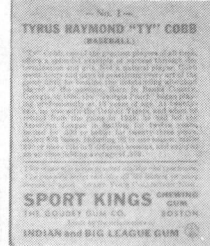

The cards in this 48 card set measure 2 3/8" by 2 7/8". The 1933 Sport Kings set, issued by the Goudey Gum Company, contains cards for the most famous athletic heroes of the times. No less than 18 different sports are represented in the set. The baseball cards of Cobb, Hubbell, and Ruth, and the football cards of Rockne and Thorpe command premium prices. The ACC designation for this set is R318.

| | | MINT | VG-E | F-G |
|---|---|---|---|---|
| COMPLETE SET | | 2250.00 | 1000.00 | 250.00 |
| COMMON PLAYER (1-24) | | 14.00 | 5.75 | 1.40 |
| COMMON PLAYER (25-36) | | 20.00 | 8.00 | 2.00 |
| COMMON PLAYER (37-48) | | 30.00 | 12.00 | 3.00 |
| | | | | |
| ☐ 1 | Ty Cobb: baseball | 450.00 | 125.00 | 25.00 |
| ☐ 2 | Babe Ruth: baseball | 600.00 | 240.00 | 60.00 |
| ☐ 3 | Nat Holman: basketball | 20.00 | 8.00 | 2.00 |
| ☐ 4 | Red Grange: football | 100.00 | 40.00 | 10.00 |
| ☐ 5 | Ed Wachter: basketball | 20.00 | 8.00 | 2.00 |
| ☐ 6 | Jim Thorpe: football | 125.00 | 50.00 | 12.50 |
| ☐ 7 | B. Walthour, Sr.: cycling | 14.00 | 5.75 | 1.40 |
| ☐ 8 | Walter Hagen: golf | 20.00 | 8.00 | 2.00 |
| ☐ 9 | Ed Blood: skiing | 14.00 | 5.75 | 1.40 |
| ☐ 10 | Anton Lekang: skiing | 14.00 | 5.75 | 1.40 |
| ☐ 11 | C. Jewtraw: ice skating | 14.00 | 5.75 | 1.40 |
| ☐ 12 | Bobby McLean: ice skating | 14.00 | 5.75 | 1.40 |
| ☐ 13 | Laverne Fator: jockey | 14.00 | 5.75 | 1.40 |
| ☐ 14 | Jim Londos: wrestling | 14.00 | 5.75 | 1.40 |
| ☐ 15 | Reggie McNamara: bicycling | 14.00 | 5.75 | 1.40 |
| ☐ 16 | Bill Tilden: tennis | 20.00 | 8.00 | 2.00 |
| ☐ 17 | Jack Dempsey: boxing | 60.00 | 24.00 | 6.00 |
| ☐ 18 | Gene Tunney: boxing | 50.00 | 20.00 | 5.00 |
| ☐ 19 | Eddie Shore: hockey | 50.00 | 20.00 | 5.00 |
| ☐ 20 | Duke Kahanamoku: swimming | 20.00 | 8.00 | 2.00 |

| | | MINT | VG-E | F-G |
|---|---|---|---|---|
| ☐ 21 | John Weissmuller: .............. swimming | 125.00 | 50.00 | 12.50 |
| ☐ 22 | Gene Sarazen: golf | 20.00 | 8.00 | 2.00 |
| ☐ 23 | Vincent Richards: .............. tennis | 14.00 | 5.75 | 1.40 |
| ☐ 24 | Howie Morenz: hockey ..... | 60.00 | 24.00 | 6.00 |
| ☐ 25 | Ralph Snoddy: ................... speedboat | 20.00 | 8.00 | 2.00 |
| ☐ 26 | James R. Wedell: .............. aviator | 20.00 | 8.00 | 2.00 |
| ☐ 27 | Col. R. Turner: .............. aviator | 20.00 | 8.00 | 2.00 |
| ☐ 28 | James Doolittle: ................ aviator | 24.00 | 10.00 | 2.40 |
| ☐ 29 | Ace Bailey: hockey .......... | 50.00 | 20.00 | 5.00 |
| ☐ 30 | Ching Johnson: hockey .... | 50.00 | 20.00 | 5.00 |
| ☐ 31 | B. Walthour, Jr.: .............. cycling | 20.00 | 8.00 | 2.00 |
| ☐ 32 | Joe Lopchick: ................... basketball | 40.00 | 16.00 | 4.00 |
| ☐ 33 | Eddie Burke: ..................... basketball | 30.00 | 12.00 | 3.00 |
| ☐ 34 | Irving Jaffee: ..................... ice skating | 20.00 | 8.00 | 2.00 |
| ☐ 35 | Knute Rockne: ................... football | 225.00 | 90.00 | 22.00 |
| ☐ 36 | Willie Hoppe: ..................... billiards | 20.00 | 8.00 | 2.00 |
| ☐ 37 | Helene Madison: ............... swimming | 30.00 | 12.00 | 3.00 |
| ☐ 38 | Bobby Jones: golf | 40.00 | 16.00 | 4.00 |
| ☐ 39 | Jack Westrope: jockey ...... | 30.00 | 12.00 | 3.00 |
| ☐ 40 | Don George: wrestling ...... | 30.00 | 12.00 | 3.00 |
| ☐ 41 | Jim Browning: .................... wrestling | 30.00 | 12.00 | 3.00 |
| ☐ 42 | Carl Hubbell: ..................... baseball | 125.00 | 50.00 | 12.50 |
| ☐ 43 | Primo Carnera: .................. boxing | 40.00 | 16.00 | 4.00 |
| ☐ 44 | Max Baer: boxing .............. | 40.00 | 16.00 | 4.00 |
| ☐ 45 | Babe Didrickson: .............. track | 150.00 | 60.00 | 15.00 |
| ☐ 46 | Ellsworth Vines: ............... tennis | 30.00 | 12.00 | 3.00 |
| ☐ 47 | J.H. Stevens: .................... bob-sled | 30.00 | 12.00 | 3.00 |
| ☐ 48 | L. Seppala: dog-sled ......... | 60.00 | 24.00 | 6.00 |

| | | MINT | VG-E | F-G |
|---|---|---|---|---|
| | COMPLETE SET ......................... | 400.00 | 160.00 | 40.00 |
| | COMMON PLAYER (1-20) .......... | 10.00 | 4.00 | 1.00 |
| ☐ 1 | Greatest Single Inning: ..... Athletics' 10 Run Rally | 10.00 | 4.00 | 1.00 |
| ☐ 2 | Amazing Record: .............. Reiser's Debut With Dodgers | 10.00 | 4.00 | 1.00 |
| ☐ 3 | Dramatic Debut: .............. Jackie Robinson ROY | 50.00 | 20.00 | 5.00 |
| ☐ 4 | Greatest Pitcher of .......... Them All: W.Johnson | 30.00 | 12.00 | 3.00 |
| ☐ 5 | Three Strikes Not Out: ..... Lost Third Strike Changes Tide of 1941 World Series | 10.00 | 4.00 | 1.00 |
| ☐ 6 | Home Run Wins Series: ..... Bill Dickey's Last Home Run | 16.00 | 6.50 | 1.60 |
| ☐ 7 | Never Say Die Pitcher: ..... Schumacher Pitching | 10.00 | 4.00 | 1.00 |
| ☐ 8 | Five Strikeouts: ................. Nationals Lose All Star Game (Hubbell) | 16.00 | 6.50 | 1.60 |
| ☐ 9 | Greatest Catch: Al ........... Gionfriddo's Catch | 16.00 | 6.50 | 1.60 |
| ☐ 10 | No Hits No Runs: .............. VanderMeer Comes Back | 12.50 | 5.00 | 1.25 |
| ☐ 11 | Bases Loaded: ................... Alexander The Great | 20.00 | 8.00 | 2.00 |
| ☐ 12 | Most Dramatic Homer: ..... Babe Ruth Points | 90.00 | 36.00 | 9.00 |
| ☐ 13 | Winning Run: Bridges' ....... Pitching and Goslin's Single Wins 1935 W.S. | 10.00 | 4.00 | 1.00 |
| ☐ 14 | Great Slugging: Lou ........... Gehrig's Four Homers | 75.00 | 30.00 | 7.50 |
| ☐ 15 | Four Men To Stop Him: ..... DiMaggio's Bat Streak | 25.00 | 10.00 | 2.50 |
| ☐ 16 | Three Run Homer in .......... Ninth: Williams' Homer | 60.00 | 24.00 | 6.00 |
| ☐ 17 | Football Block: ................... Lindell's Football Block Paves Way For Yank's Series Victory | 10.00 | 4.00 | 1.00 |
| ☐ 18 | Home Run To Fame: ........ Reese's Grand Slam | 20.00 | 8.00 | 2.00 |
| ☐ 19 | Strikeout Record: ............. Feller Whiffs Five | 20.00 | 8.00 | 2.00 |
| ☐ 20 | Rifle Arm: Furillo .............. | 30.00 | 12.00 | 3.00 |

## 1948 Sport Thrills

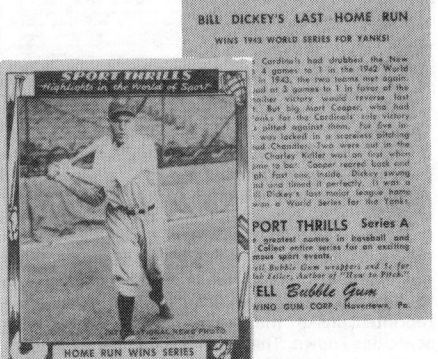

The cards in this 20 card set measure 2 1/2" by 3". The 1948 Swell Gum Sports Thrills set of black and white, numbered cards highlights events from baseball history. The cards have picture framed borders with the title "Sports Thrills Highlights in the World of Sport" on the front. The backs of the cards give the story of the event pictured on the front. Cards numbered 9, 11, 16, and 20 are more difficult to obtain than the other cards in this set. The ACC designation is R448.

## 1981 Squirt

The cards in this 22 panel set consist of 33 different individual cards, each measuring 2 1/2" by 3 1/2" while the panels measure 2 1/2" by 10 1/2" as the 1981 Squirt cards were issued individually as well as in two card panels. Cards numbered 1-11 appear twice, whereas cards 12-33 appear only once in the 22 panel set. The pattern for pairings was 1/12 and 1/23, 2/13 and 2/24, 3/14 and 3/25, and so forth on up to 11/22 and 11/33. Two card panels have a value equal to the sum of the individual cards on the panel. Supposedly panels 4/15, 5/27, and 6/28 are more difficult to find than the others.

| | MINT | VG-E | F-G |
|---|---|---|---|
| COMPLETE PANEL SET | 15.00 | 6.00 | 1.50 |
| COMPLETE IND. SET | 10.00 | 4.00 | 1.00 |
| COMMON PANEL | .40 | .16 | .04 |
| COMMON PLAYER (1-11) DP | .20 | .08 | .02 |
| COMMON PLAYER (12-33) | .20 | .08 | .02 |

| | | MINT | VG-E | F-G |
|---|---|---|---|---|
| ☐ 1 | George Brett DP | .60 | .24 | .06 |
| ☐ 2 | George Foster DP | .20 | .08 | .02 |
| ☐ 3 | Ben Oglivie DP | .20 | .08 | .02 |
| ☐ 4 | Steve Garvey DP | .60 | .24 | .06 |
| ☐ 5 | Reggie Jackson DP | .90 | .36 | .09 |
| ☐ 6 | Bill Buckner DP | .20 | .08 | .02 |
| ☐ 7 | Jim Rice DP | .35 | .14 | .03 |
| ☐ 8 | Mike Schmidt DP | .60 | .24 | .06 |
| ☐ 9 | Rod Carew DP | .50 | .20 | .05 |
| ☐ 10 | Dave Parker DP | .20 | .08 | .02 |
| ☐ 11 | Pete Rose DP | 1.00 | .40 | .10 |
| ☐ 12 | Garry Templeton | .30 | .12 | .03 |
| ☐ 13 | Rick Burleson | .20 | .08 | .02 |
| ☐ 14 | Dave Kingman | .20 | .08 | .02 |
| ☐ 15 | Eddie Murray | 2.00 | .80 | .20 |
| ☐ 16 | Don Sutton | .60 | .24 | .06 |
| ☐ 17 | Dusty Baker | .20 | .08 | .02 |
| ☐ 18 | Jack Clark | .30 | .12 | .03 |
| ☐ 19 | Dave Winfield | 1.00 | .40 | .10 |
| ☐ 20 | Johnny Bench | .80 | .32 | .08 |
| ☐ 21 | Lee Mazzilli | .20 | .08 | .02 |
| ☐ 22 | Al Oliver | .30 | .12 | .03 |
| ☐ 23 | Jerry Mumphrey | .20 | .08 | .02 |
| ☐ 24 | Tony Armas | .30 | .12 | .03 |
| ☐ 25 | Fred Lynn | .40 | .16 | .04 |
| ☐ 26 | Ron LeFlore | .40 | .16 | .04 |
| ☐ 27 | Steve Kemp | .75 | .30 | .07 |
| ☐ 28 | Rickey Henderson | 2.00 | .80 | .20 |
| ☐ 29 | John Castino | .20 | .08 | .02 |
| ☐ 30 | Cecil Cooper | .40 | .16 | .04 |
| ☐ 31 | Bruce Bochte | .20 | .08 | .02 |
| ☐ 32 | Joe Charboneau | .20 | .08 | .02 |
| ☐ 33 | Chet Lemon | .20 | .08 | .02 |

## 1982 Squirt

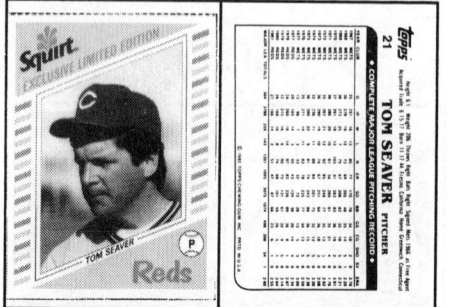

The cards in this 22 card set measure 2 1/2" by 3 1/2". Although the 1982 "Exclusive Limited Edition" was prepared for Squirt by Topps, the format and pictures are completely different from the regular Topps cards of this year. Each color picture is obliquely cut and the word Squirt is printed in red in the top left corner. The cards are numbered 1 through 22 and the reverses are yellow and black on white. The cards were issued on four types of panels: (1) yellow attachment card at top with picture card in center and scratch-off game at bottom; (2) yellow attachment card at top with scratch-off game in center and picture card at bottom; (3) white attachment card at top with "Collect all 22" panel in center and picture card at

bottom; (4) two card panel with attachment card at top. The two card panels have parallel cards; that is, numbers 1 and 12 together, numbers 2 and 13 together, etc. Two card panels have a value equal to the sum of the individual cards on the panel.

| | | MINT | VG-E | F-G |
|---|---|---|---|---|
| COMPLETE SET | | 5.00 | 2.00 | .50 |
| COMMON PLAYER | | .15 | .06 | .01 |

| | | MINT | VG-E | F-G |
|---|---|---|---|---|
| ☐ 1 | Cecil Cooper | .20 | .08 | .02 |
| ☐ 2 | Jerry Remy | .15 | .06 | .01 |
| ☐ 3 | George Brett | .75 | .30 | .07 |
| ☐ 4 | Alan Trammell | .25 | .10 | .02 |
| ☐ 5 | Reggie Jackson | .75 | .30 | .07 |
| ☐ 6 | Kirk Gibson | .35 | .14 | .03 |
| ☐ 7 | Dave Winfield | .45 | .18 | .04 |
| ☐ 8 | Carlton Fisk | .25 | .10 | .02 |
| ☐ 9 | Ron Guidry | .25 | .10 | .02 |
| ☐ 10 | Dennis Leonard | .15 | .06 | .01 |
| ☐ 11 | Rollie Fingers | .25 | .10 | .02 |
| ☐ 12 | Pete Rose | 1.00 | .40 | .10 |
| ☐ 13 | Phil Garner | .15 | .06 | .01 |
| ☐ 14 | Mike Schmidt | .75 | .30 | .07 |
| ☐ 15 | Dave Concepcion | .15 | .06 | .01 |
| ☐ 16 | George Hendrick | .15 | .06 | .01 |
| ☐ 17 | Andre Dawson | .25 | .10 | .02 |
| ☐ 18 | George Foster | .25 | .10 | .02 |
| ☐ 19 | Gary Carter | .45 | .18 | .04 |
| ☐ 20 | Fernando Valenzuela | .35 | .14 | .03 |
| ☐ 21 | Tom Seaver | .50 | .20 | .05 |
| ☐ 22 | Bruce Sutter | .25 | .10 | .02 |

## 1976 SSPC

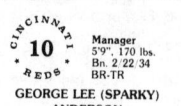

The cards in this 630 card set measure 2 1/2" by 3 1/2". The 1976 "Pure Card" set issued by TCMA derives its name from the lack of borders, logos, signatures, etc., which often clutter up the picture areas of some baseball sets. It differs from other sets produced by this company in that it cannot be re- issued due to an agreement entered into by the manufacturer. Thus, while not technically a legitimate issue, it is significant because it cannot be reprinted, unlike other collector issues. There are no scarcities known. The cards are numbered in team groups, i.e., Atlanta (1-21), Cincinnati (22-46), Houston (47- 65), Los Angeles (66-91), San Francisco (92-113), San Diego (114- 133), Chicago White Sox (134-158), Kansas City (159-195), California (186-204), Minnesota (205-225), Milwaukee (226-251), Texas (252-273), St. Louis (274-300), Chicago Cubs (301-321), Montreal (322-351), Detroit (352-373), Baltimore (374-401), Boston (402-424), New York Yankees (425-455), Philadelphia (456- 477), Oakland (478-503), Cleveland (504-532), New York Mets (533- 560), and Pittsburgh (561-586). The rest of the numbers are filled in with checklists (589-595), miscellaneous players, and a heavy dose of coaches.

| | | | MINT | VG-E | F-G |
|---|---|---|------|------|-----|
| | | COMPLETE SET | 60.00 | 24.00 | 6.00 |
| | | COMMON PLAYER (1-630) | .08 | .03 | .01 |

| | | | MINT | VG-E | F-G |
|---|---|---|------|------|-----|
| ☐ | 1 | Buzz Capra | .12 | .05 | .01 |
| ☐ | 2 | Tom House | .12 | .05 | .01 |
| ☐ | 3 | Max Leon | .08 | .03 | .01 |
| ☐ | 4 | Carl Morton | .08 | .03 | .01 |
| ☐ | 5 | Phil Niekro | 2.00 | .80 | .20 |
| ☐ | 6 | Mike Thompson | .08 | .03 | .01 |
| ☐ | 7 | Elias Sosa | .08 | .03 | .01 |
| ☐ | 8 | Larvell Blanks | .08 | .03 | .01 |
| ☐ | 9 | Darrell Evans | .25 | .10 | .02 |
| ☐ | 10 | Rod Gilbreath | .08 | .03 | .01 |
| ☐ | 11 | Mike Lum | .08 | .03 | .01 |
| ☐ | 12 | Craig Robinson | .08 | .03 | .01 |
| ☐ | 13 | Earl Williams | .08 | .03 | .01 |
| ☐ | 14 | Vic Correll | .08 | .03 | .01 |
| ☐ | 15 | Biff Pocoroba | .08 | .03 | .01 |
| ☐ | 16 | Dusty Baker | .25 | .10 | .02 |
| ☐ | 17 | Ralph Garr | .12 | .05 | .01 |
| ☐ | 18 | Cito Gaston | .08 | .03 | .01 |
| ☐ | 19 | Dave May | .08 | .03 | .01 |
| ☐ | 20 | Rowland Office | .08 | .03 | .01 |
| ☐ | 21 | Bob Beall | .08 | .03 | .01 |
| ☐ | 22 | Sparky Anderson MGR | .25 | .10 | .02 |
| ☐ | 23 | Jack Billingham | .08 | .03 | .01 |
| ☐ | 24 | Pedro Borbon | .08 | .03 | .01 |
| ☐ | 25 | Clay Carroll | .08 | .03 | .01 |
| ☐ | 26 | Pat Darcy | .08 | .03 | .01 |
| ☐ | 27 | Don Gullett | .12 | .05 | .01 |
| ☐ | 28 | Clay Kirby | .08 | .03 | .01 |
| ☐ | 29 | Gary Nolan | .08 | .03 | .01 |
| ☐ | 30 | Fred Norman | .08 | .03 | .01 |
| ☐ | 31 | Johnny Bench | 3.50 | 1.40 | .35 |
| ☐ | 32 | Bill Plummer | .08 | .03 | .01 |
| ☐ | 33 | Darrel Chaney | .08 | .03 | .01 |
| ☐ | 34 | Dave Concepcion | .25 | .10 | .02 |
| ☐ | 35 | Terry Crowley | .08 | .03 | .01 |
| ☐ | 36 | Dan Driessen | .12 | .05 | .01 |
| ☐ | 37 | Doug Flynn | .08 | .03 | .01 |
| ☐ | 38 | Joe Morgan | 2.00 | .80 | .20 |
| ☐ | 39 | Tony Perez | .60 | .24 | .06 |
| ☐ | 40 | Ken Griffey | .25 | .10 | .02 |
| ☐ | 41 | Pete Rose | 10.00 | 4.00 | 1.00 |
| ☐ | 42 | Ed Armbrister | .08 | .03 | .01 |
| ☐ | 43 | John Vukovich | .08 | .03 | .01 |
| ☐ | 44 | George Foster | 1.00 | .40 | .10 |
| ☐ | 45 | Cesar Geronimo | .08 | .03 | .01 |
| ☐ | 46 | Merv Rettenmund | .08 | .03 | .01 |
| ☐ | 47 | Jim Crawford | .08 | .03 | .01 |
| ☐ | 48 | Ken Forsch | .12 | .05 | .01 |
| ☐ | 49 | Doug Konieczny | .08 | .03 | .01 |
| ☐ | 50 | Joe Niekro | .25 | .10 | .02 |
| ☐ | 51 | Cliff Johnson | .08 | .03 | .01 |
| ☐ | 52 | Skip Jutze | .08 | .03 | .01 |
| ☐ | 53 | Milt May | .08 | .03 | .01 |
| ☐ | 54 | Rob Andrews | .08 | .03 | .01 |
| ☐ | 55 | Ken Boswell | .08 | .03 | .01 |
| ☐ | 56 | Tommy Helms | .08 | .03 | .01 |
| ☐ | 57 | Roger Metzger | .08 | .03 | .01 |
| ☐ | 58 | Larry Milbourne | .08 | .03 | .01 |
| ☐ | 59 | Doug Rader | .15 | .06 | .01 |
| ☐ | 60 | Bob Watson | .15 | .06 | .01 |
| ☐ | 61 | Enos Cabell | .08 | .03 | .01 |
| ☐ | 62 | Jose Cruz | .50 | .20 | .05 |
| ☐ | 63 | Cesar Cedeno | .25 | .10 | .02 |
| ☐ | 64 | Greg Gross | .08 | .03 | .01 |
| ☐ | 65 | Wilbur Howard | .08 | .03 | .01 |
| ☐ | 66 | Al Downing | .08 | .03 | .01 |
| ☐ | 67 | Burt Hooton | .12 | .05 | .01 |
| ☐ | 68 | Charlie Hough | .20 | .08 | .02 |
| ☐ | 69 | Tommy John | .75 | .30 | .07 |
| ☐ | 70 | Andy Messersmith | .12 | .05 | .01 |
| ☐ | 71 | Doug Rau | .08 | .03 | .01 |
| ☐ | 72 | Rick Rhoden | .15 | .06 | .01 |
| ☐ | 73 | Don Sutton | 1.25 | .50 | .12 |
| ☐ | 74 | Rick Auerbach | .08 | .03 | .01 |
| ☐ | 75 | Ron Cey | .60 | .24 | .06 |
| ☐ | 76 | Ivan DeJesus | .08 | .03 | .01 |
| ☐ | 77 | Steve Garvey | 3.50 | 1.40 | .35 |
| ☐ | 78 | Lee Lacy | .12 | .05 | .01 |
| ☐ | 79 | Dave Lopes | .25 | .10 | .02 |
| ☐ | 80 | Ken McMullen | .08 | .03 | .01 |
| ☐ | 81 | Joe Ferguson | .08 | .03 | .01 |
| ☐ | 82 | Paul Powell | .08 | .03 | .01 |
| ☐ | 83 | Steve Yeager | .12 | .05 | .01 |
| ☐ | 84 | Willie Crawford | .08 | .03 | .01 |
| ☐ | 85 | Henry Cruz | .08 | .03 | .01 |
| ☐ | 86 | Charlie Manuel | .08 | .03 | .01 |
| ☐ | 87 | Manny Mota | .12 | .05 | .01 |
| ☐ | 88 | Tom Paciorek | .12 | .05 | .01 |
| ☐ | 89 | Jim Wynn | .12 | .05 | .01 |
| ☐ | 90 | Walt Alston MGR | .50 | .20 | .05 |
| ☐ | 91 | Bill Buckner | .50 | .20 | .05 |
| ☐ | 92 | Jim Barr | .08 | .03 | .01 |
| ☐ | 93 | Mike Caldwell | .12 | .05 | .01 |
| ☐ | 94 | John D'Acquisto | .08 | .03 | .01 |
| ☐ | 95 | Dave Heaverlo | .08 | .03 | .01 |
| ☐ | 96 | Gary Lavelle | .12 | .05 | .01 |
| ☐ | 97 | John Montefusco | .12 | .05 | .01 |
| ☐ | 98 | Charlie Williams | .08 | .03 | .01 |
| ☐ | 99 | Chris Arnold | .08 | .03 | .01 |
| ☐ | 100 | Marc Hill | .08 | .03 | .01 |
| ☐ | 101 | Dave Rader | .08 | .03 | .01 |
| ☐ | 102 | Bruce Miller | .08 | .03 | .01 |
| ☐ | 103 | Willie Montanez | .12 | .05 | .01 |
| ☐ | 104 | Steve Ontiveros | .08 | .03 | .01 |
| ☐ | 105 | Chris Speier | .08 | .03 | .01 |
| ☐ | 106 | Derrel Thomas | .08 | .03 | .01 |
| ☐ | 107 | Gary Thomasson | .08 | .03 | .01 |
| ☐ | 108 | Glenn Adams | .08 | .03 | .01 |
| ☐ | 109 | Von Joshua | .08 | .03 | .01 |
| ☐ | 110 | Gary Matthews | .25 | .10 | .02 |
| ☐ | 111 | Bobby Murcer | .40 | .16 | .04 |
| ☐ | 112 | Horace Speed | .08 | .03 | .01 |
| ☐ | 113 | Wes Westrum MGR | .08 | .03 | .01 |
| ☐ | 114 | Rich Folkers | .08 | .03 | .01 |
| ☐ | 115 | Alan Foster | .08 | .03 | .01 |
| ☐ | 116 | Dave Freisleben | .08 | .03 | .01 |
| ☐ | 117 | Dan Frisella | .08 | .03 | .01 |
| ☐ | 118 | Randy Jones | .20 | .08 | .02 |
| ☐ | 119 | Dan Spillner | .12 | .05 | .01 |
| ☐ | 120 | Larry Hardy | .08 | .03 | .01 |
| ☐ | 121 | Randy Hundley | .08 | .03 | .01 |
| ☐ | 122 | Fred Kendall | .08 | .03 | .01 |
| ☐ | 123 | John McNamara MGR | .20 | .08 | .02 |
| ☐ | 124 | Tito Fuentes | .08 | .03 | .01 |
| ☐ | 125 | Enzo Hernandez | .08 | .03 | .01 |
| ☐ | 126 | Steve Huntz | .08 | .03 | .01 |
| ☐ | 127 | Mike Ivie | .08 | .03 | .01 |
| ☐ | 128 | Hector Torres | .08 | .03 | .01 |
| ☐ | 129 | Ted Kubiak | .08 | .03 | .01 |
| ☐ | 130 | John Grubb | .08 | .03 | .01 |
| ☐ | 131 | John Scott | .08 | .03 | .01 |
| ☐ | 132 | Bob Tolan | .08 | .03 | .01 |
| ☐ | 133 | Dave Winfield | 3.50 | 1.40 | .35 |
| ☐ | 134 | Bill Gogolewski | .08 | .03 | .01 |
| ☐ | 135 | Dan Osborn | .08 | .03 | .01 |
| ☐ | 136 | Jim Kaat | .50 | .20 | .05 |
| ☐ | 137 | Claude Osteen | .12 | .05 | .01 |
| ☐ | 138 | Cecil Upshaw | .08 | .03 | .01 |
| ☐ | 139 | Wilbur Wood | .12 | .05 | .01 |
| ☐ | 140 | Lloyd Allen | .08 | .03 | .01 |
| ☐ | 141 | Brian Downing | .16 | .07 | .01 |
| ☐ | 142 | Jim Essian | .08 | .03 | .01 |
| ☐ | 143 | Bucky Dent | .20 | .08 | .02 |
| ☐ | 144 | Jorge Orta | .08 | .03 | .01 |
| ☐ | 145 | Lee Richard | .08 | .03 | .01 |
| ☐ | 146 | Bill Stein | .08 | .03 | .01 |
| ☐ | 147 | Ken Henderson | .08 | .03 | .01 |
| ☐ | 148 | Carlos May | .08 | .03 | .01 |
| ☐ | 149 | Nyls Nyman | .08 | .03 | .01 |
| ☐ | 150 | Bob Coluccio | .08 | .03 | .01 |
| ☐ | 151 | Chuck Tanner MGR | .20 | .08 | .02 |
| ☐ | 152 | Pat Kelly | .08 | .03 | .01 |
| ☐ | 153 | Jerry Hairston | .08 | .03 | .01 |
| ☐ | 154 | Pete Varney | .08 | .03 | .01 |
| ☐ | 155 | Bill Melton | .08 | .03 | .01 |
| ☐ | 156 | Rich Gossage | 1.00 | .40 | .10 |
| ☐ | 157 | Terry Forster | .25 | .10 | .02 |
| ☐ | 158 | Rich Hinton | .08 | .03 | .01 |
| ☐ | 159 | Nelson Briles | .12 | .05 | .01 |
| ☐ | 160 | Al Fitzmorris | .08 | .03 | .01 |
| ☐ | 161 | Steve Mingori | .08 | .03 | .01 |
| ☐ | 162 | Marty Pattin | .08 | .03 | .01 |
| ☐ | 163 | Paul Splittorff | .12 | .05 | .01 |
| ☐ | 164 | Dennis Leonard | .20 | .08 | .02 |
| ☐ | 165 | Buck Martinez | .08 | .03 | .01 |
| ☐ | 166 | Bob Stinson | .08 | .03 | .01 |
| ☐ | 167 | George Brett | 6.00 | 2.40 | .60 |
| ☐ | 168 | Harmon Killebrew | 2.50 | 1.00 | .25 |
| ☐ | 169 | John Mayberry | .12 | .05 | .01 |
| ☐ | 170 | Fred Patek | .08 | .03 | .01 |
| ☐ | 171 | Cookie Rojas | .08 | .03 | .01 |
| ☐ | 172 | Rodney Scott | .08 | .03 | .01 |
| ☐ | 173 | Tony Solaita | .08 | .03 | .01 |
| ☐ | 174 | Frank White | .30 | .12 | .03 |
| ☐ | 175 | Al Cowens | .12 | .05 | .01 |
| ☐ | 176 | Hal McRae | .20 | .08 | .02 |
| ☐ | 177 | Amos Otis | .25 | .10 | .02 |
| ☐ | 178 | Vada Pinson | .30 | .12 | .03 |

| | | | | |
|---|---|---|---|---|
| ☐ 179 | Jim Wohlford | .08 | .03 | .01 |
| ☐ 180 | Doug Bird | .08 | .03 | .01 |
| ☐ 181 | Mark Littell | .08 | .03 | .01 |
| ☐ 182 | Bob McClure | .08 | .03 | .01 |
| ☐ 183 | Steve Busby | .12 | .05 | .01 |
| ☐ 184 | Fran Healy | .08 | .03 | .01 |
| ☐ 185 | Whitey Herzog MGR | .20 | .08 | .02 |
| ☐ 186 | Andy Hassler | .08 | .03 | .01 |
| ☐ 187 | Nolan Ryan | 3.50 | 1.40 | .35 |
| ☐ 188 | Bill Singer | .08 | .03 | .01 |
| ☐ 189 | Frank Tanana | .15 | .06 | .01 |
| ☐ 190 | Ed Figueroa | .08 | .03 | .01 |
| ☐ 191 | Dave Collins | .15 | .06 | .01 |
| ☐ 192 | Dick Williams | .12 | .05 | .01 |
| ☐ 193 | Ellie Rodriguez | .08 | .03 | .01 |
| ☐ 194 | Dave Chalk | .08 | .03 | .01 |
| ☐ 195 | Winston Llenas | .08 | .03 | .01 |
| ☐ 196 | Rudy Meoli | .08 | .03 | .01 |
| ☐ 197 | Orlando Ramirez | .08 | .03 | .01 |
| ☐ 198 | Jerry Remy | .12 | .05 | .01 |
| ☐ 199 | Billy Smith | .08 | .03 | .01 |
| ☐ 200 | Bruce Bochte | .12 | .05 | .01 |
| ☐ 201 | Joe Lahoud | .08 | .03 | .01 |
| ☐ 202 | Morris Nettles | .08 | .03 | .01 |
| ☐ 203 | Mickey Rivers | .25 | .10 | .02 |
| ☐ 204 | Leroy Stanton | .08 | .03 | .01 |
| ☐ 205 | Vic Albury | .08 | .03 | .01 |
| ☐ 206 | Tom Burgmeier | .08 | .03 | .01 |
| ☐ 207 | Bill Butler | .08 | .03 | .01 |
| ☐ 208 | Bill Campbell | .12 | .05 | .01 |
| ☐ 209 | Ray Corbin | .08 | .03 | .01 |
| ☐ 210 | Joe Decker | .08 | .03 | .01 |
| ☐ 211 | Jim Hughes | .08 | .03 | .01 |
| ☐ 212 | Ed Bane | .08 | .03 | .01 |
| | (photo actually Mike Pazik) | | | |
| ☐ 213 | Glenn Borgman | .08 | .03 | .01 |
| ☐ 214 | Rod Carew | 3.50 | 1.40 | .35 |
| ☐ 215 | Steve Brye | .08 | .03 | .01 |
| ☐ 216 | Dan Ford | .12 | .05 | .01 |
| ☐ 217 | Tony Oliva | .60 | .24 | .06 |
| ☐ 218 | Dave Goltz | .12 | .05 | .01 |
| ☐ 219 | Bert Blyleven | .40 | .16 | .04 |
| ☐ 220 | Larry Hisle | .12 | .05 | .01 |
| ☐ 221 | Steve Braun | .08 | .03 | .01 |
| ☐ 222 | Jerry Terrell | .08 | .03 | .01 |
| ☐ 223 | Eric Soderholm | .08 | .03 | .01 |
| ☐ 224 | Phil Roof | .08 | .03 | .01 |
| ☐ 225 | Danny Thompson | .08 | .03 | .01 |
| ☐ 226 | Jim Colborn | .08 | .03 | .01 |
| ☐ 227 | Tom Murphy | .08 | .03 | .01 |
| ☐ 228 | Ed Rodriquez | .08 | .03 | .01 |
| ☐ 229 | Jim Slaton | .12 | .05 | .01 |
| ☐ 230 | Ed Sprague | .08 | .03 | .01 |
| ☐ 231 | Charlie Moore | .12 | .05 | .01 |
| ☐ 232 | Darrell Porter | .20 | .08 | .02 |
| ☐ 233 | Kurt Bevacqua | .08 | .03 | .01 |
| ☐ 234 | Pedro Garcia | .08 | .03 | .01 |
| ☐ 235 | Mike Hegan | .08 | .03 | .01 |
| ☐ 236 | Don Money | .12 | .05 | .01 |
| ☐ 237 | George Scott | .12 | .05 | .01 |
| ☐ 238 | Robin Yount | 3.00 | 1.20 | .30 |
| ☐ 239 | Hank Aaron | 5.00 | 2.00 | .50 |
| ☐ 240 | Rob Ellis | .08 | .03 | .01 |
| ☐ 241 | Sixto Lezcano | .12 | .05 | .01 |
| ☐ 242 | Bob Mitchell | .08 | .03 | .01 |
| ☐ 243 | Gorman Thomas | .35 | .14 | .03 |
| ☐ 244 | Bill Travers | .08 | .03 | .01 |
| ☐ 245 | Pete Broberg | .08 | .03 | .01 |
| ☐ 246 | Bill Sharp | .08 | .03 | .01 |
| ☐ 247 | Bobby Darwin | .08 | .03 | .01 |
| ☐ 248 | Rick Austin | .08 | .03 | .01 |
| | (photo actually Larry Anderson) | | | |
| ☐ 249 | Larry Anderson | .08 | .03 | .01 |
| | (photo actually Rick Austin) | | | |
| ☐ 250 | Tom Bianco | .08 | .03 | .01 |
| ☐ 251 | L. Currence | .08 | .03 | .01 |
| ☐ 252 | Steve Foucault | .08 | .03 | .01 |
| ☐ 253 | Bill Hands | .08 | .03 | .01 |
| ☐ 254 | Steve Hargan | .08 | .03 | .01 |
| ☐ 255 | Fergie Jenkins | .50 | .20 | .05 |
| ☐ 256 | Bob Sheldon | .08 | .03 | .01 |
| ☐ 257 | Jim Umbarger | .08 | .03 | .01 |
| ☐ 258 | Clyde Wright | .08 | .03 | .01 |
| ☐ 259 | Bill Fahey | .08 | .03 | .01 |
| ☐ 260 | Jim Sundberg | .18 | .08 | .01 |
| ☐ 261 | Leo Cardenas | .08 | .03 | .01 |
| ☐ 262 | Jim Fregosi | .20 | .08 | .02 |
| ☐ 263 | Mike Hargrove | .12 | .05 | .01 |
| ☐ 264 | Toby Harrah | .20 | .08 | .02 |
| ☐ 265 | Roy Howell | .08 | .03 | .01 |
| ☐ 266 | Lenny Randle | .08 | .03 | .01 |
| ☐ 267 | Roy Smalley | .15 | .06 | .01 |
| ☐ 268 | Jim Spencer | .08 | .03 | .01 |
| ☐ 269 | Jeff Burroughs | .12 | .05 | .01 |
| ☐ 270 | Tom Grieve | .15 | .06 | .01 |
| ☐ 271 | Joe Lovitto | .08 | .03 | .01 |
| ☐ 272 | Frank Lucchesi MGR | .08 | .03 | .01 |
| ☐ 273 | Dave Nelson | .08 | .03 | .01 |
| ☐ 274 | Ted Simmons | .75 | .30 | .07 |
| ☐ 275 | Lou Brock | 3.00 | 1.20 | .30 |
| ☐ 276 | Ron Fairly | .12 | .05 | .01 |
| ☐ 277 | Bake McBride | .12 | .05 | .01 |
| ☐ 278 | Reggie Smith | .25 | .10 | .02 |
| ☐ 279 | Willie Davis | .12 | .05 | .01 |
| ☐ 280 | Ken Reitz | .08 | .03 | .01 |
| ☐ 281 | Buddy Bradford | .08 | .03 | .01 |
| ☐ 282 | Luis Melendez | .08 | .03 | .01 |
| ☐ 283 | Mike Tyson | .08 | .03 | .01 |
| ☐ 284 | Ted Sizemore | .08 | .03 | .01 |
| ☐ 285 | Mario Guerrero | .08 | .03 | .01 |
| ☐ 286 | Larry Lintz | .08 | .03 | .01 |
| ☐ 287 | Ken Rudolph | .08 | .03 | .01 |
| ☐ 288 | Dick Billings | .08 | .03 | .01 |
| ☐ 289 | Jerry Mumphrey | .12 | .05 | .01 |
| ☐ 290 | Mike Wallace | .08 | .03 | .01 |
| ☐ 291 | Al Hrabosky | .18 | .08 | .01 |
| ☐ 292 | Ken Reynolds | .08 | .03 | .01 |
| ☐ 293 | Mike Garman | .08 | .03 | .01 |
| ☐ 294 | Bob Forsch | .15 | .06 | .01 |
| ☐ 295 | John Denny | .20 | .08 | .02 |
| ☐ 296 | Harry Rasmussen | .08 | .03 | .01 |
| ☐ 297 | Lynn McGlothen | .08 | .03 | .01 |
| ☐ 298 | Mike Barlow | .08 | .03 | .01 |
| ☐ 299 | Greg Terlecky | .08 | .03 | .01 |
| ☐ 300 | Red Schoendienst MGR | .18 | .08 | .01 |
| ☐ 301 | Rick Reuschel | .20 | .08 | .02 |
| ☐ 302 | Steve Stone | .20 | .08 | .02 |
| ☐ 303 | Bill Bonham | .08 | .03 | .01 |
| ☐ 304 | Oscar Zamora | .08 | .03 | .01 |
| ☐ 305 | Ken Frailing | .08 | .03 | .01 |
| ☐ 306 | Milt Wilcox | .08 | .03 | .01 |
| ☐ 307 | Darold Knowles | .08 | .03 | .01 |
| ☐ 308 | Jim Marshall | .08 | .03 | .01 |
| ☐ 309 | Bill Madlock | 1.00 | .40 | .10 |
| ☐ 310 | Jose Cardenal | .08 | .03 | .01 |
| ☐ 311 | Rick Monday | .15 | .06 | .01 |
| ☐ 312 | Jerry Morales | .08 | .03 | .01 |
| ☐ 313 | Tim Hosley | .08 | .03 | .01 |
| ☐ 314 | Gene Hiser | .08 | .03 | .01 |
| ☐ 315 | Don Kessinger | .12 | .05 | .01 |
| ☐ 316 | Manny Trillo | .12 | .05 | .01 |
| ☐ 317 | Pete LaCock | .08 | .03 | .01 |
| ☐ 318 | George Mitterwald | .08 | .03 | .01 |
| ☐ 319 | Steve Swisher | .08 | .03 | .01 |
| ☐ 320 | Rob Sperring | .08 | .03 | .01 |
| ☐ 321 | Vic Harris | .08 | .03 | .01 |
| ☐ 322 | Ron Dunn | .08 | .03 | .01 |
| ☐ 323 | Jose Morales | .08 | .03 | .01 |
| ☐ 324 | Pete Mackanin | .08 | .03 | .01 |
| ☐ 325 | Jim Cox | .08 | .03 | .01 |
| ☐ 326 | Larry Parrish | .20 | .08 | .02 |
| ☐ 327 | Mike Jorgensen | .08 | .03 | .01 |
| ☐ 328 | Tim Foli | .08 | .03 | .01 |
| ☐ 329 | Hal Breeden | .08 | .03 | .01 |
| ☐ 330 | Nate Colbert | .08 | .03 | .01 |
| ☐ 331 | Pepe Frias | .08 | .03 | .01 |
| ☐ 332 | Pat Scanlon | .08 | .03 | .01 |
| ☐ 333 | Bob Bailey | .08 | .03 | .01 |
| ☐ 334 | Gary Carter | 4.00 | 1.60 | .40 |
| ☐ 335 | Pepe Mangual | .08 | .03 | .01 |
| ☐ 336 | Larry Biittner | .08 | .03 | .01 |
| ☐ 337 | Jim Lyttle | .08 | .03 | .01 |
| ☐ 338 | Gary Roenicke | .12 | .05 | .01 |
| ☐ 339 | Tony Scott | .08 | .03 | .01 |
| ☐ 340 | Jerry White | .08 | .03 | .01 |
| ☐ 341 | Jim Dwyer | .08 | .03 | .01 |
| ☐ 342 | Ellis Valentine | .12 | .05 | .01 |
| ☐ 343 | Fred Scherman | .08 | .03 | .01 |
| ☐ 344 | Dennis Blair | .08 | .03 | .01 |
| ☐ 345 | Woodie Fryman | .08 | .03 | .01 |
| ☐ 346 | Chuck Taylor | .08 | .03 | .01 |
| ☐ 347 | Dan Warthen | .08 | .03 | .01 |
| ☐ 348 | Dan Carrithers | .08 | .03 | .01 |
| ☐ 349 | Steve Rogers | .25 | .10 | .02 |
| ☐ 350 | Dale Murray | .08 | .03 | .01 |
| ☐ 351 | Duke Snider | 1.50 | .60 | .15 |
| ☐ 352 | Ralph Houk MGR | .12 | .05 | .01 |
| ☐ 353 | John Hiller | .15 | .06 | .01 |
| ☐ 354 | Mickey Lolich | .25 | .10 | .02 |
| ☐ 355 | Dave Lemancyzk | .08 | .03 | .01 |
| ☐ 356 | Lerrin LaGrow | .08 | .03 | .01 |
| ☐ 357 | Fred Arroyo | .08 | .03 | .01 |
| ☐ 358 | Joe Coleman | .08 | .03 | .01 |

| # | Name | | | | # | Name | | | |
|---|------|---|---|---|---|------|---|---|---|
| ☐ 359 | Ben Oglivie | .25 | .10 | .02 | ☐ 452 | Kerry Dineen | .08 | .03 | .01 |
| ☐ 360 | Willie Horton | .15 | .06 | .01 | ☐ 453 | Billy Martin MGR | .75 | .30 | .07 |
| ☐ 361 | John Knox | .08 | .03 | .01 | ☐ 454 | Dave Bergman | .08 | .03 | .01 |
| ☐ 362 | Leon Roberts | .08 | .03 | .01 | ☐ 455 | Otto Velez | .08 | .03 | .01 |
| ☐ 363 | Ron LeFlore | .15 | .06 | .01 | ☐ 456 | Joe Hoerner | .08 | .03 | .01 |
| ☐ 364 | G. Sutherland | .08 | .03 | .01 | ☐ 457 | Tug McGraw | .25 | .10 | .02 |
| ☐ 365 | Dan Meyer | .08 | .03 | .01 | ☐ 458 | Gene Garber | .12 | .05 | .01 |
| ☐ 366 | Aurelio Rodriguez | .12 | .05 | .01 | ☐ 459 | Steve Carlton | 3.00 | 1.20 | .30 |
| ☐ 367 | Tom Veryzer | .08 | .03 | .01 | ☐ 460 | Larry Christenson | .08 | .03 | .01 |
| ☐ 368 | Jack Pierce | .08 | .03 | .01 | ☐ 461 | Tom Underwood | .08 | .03 | .01 |
| ☐ 369 | Gene Michael | .12 | .05 | .01 | ☐ 462 | Jim Lonborg | .12 | .05 | .01 |
| ☐ 370 | Billy Baldwin | .08 | .03 | .01 | ☐ 463 | Jay Johnstone | .12 | .05 | .01 |
| ☐ 371 | Gates Brown | .12 | .05 | .01 | ☐ 464 | Larry Bowa | .35 | .14 | .03 |
| ☐ 372 | Mickey Stanley | .12 | .05 | .01 | ☐ 465 | Dave Cash | .08 | .03 | .01 |
| ☐ 373 | Terry Humphrey | .08 | .03 | .01 | ☐ 466 | Ollie Brown | .08 | .03 | .01 |
| ☐ 374 | Doyle Alexander | .16 | .07 | .01 | ☐ 467 | Greg Luzinski | .35 | .14 | .03 |
| ☐ 375 | Mike Cuellar | .12 | .05 | .01 | ☐ 468 | Johnny Oates | .08 | .03 | .01 |
| ☐ 376 | Wayne Garland | .08 | .03 | .01 | ☐ 469 | Mike Anderson | .08 | .03 | .01 |
| ☐ 377 | Ross Grimsley | .08 | .03 | .01 | ☐ 470 | Mike Schmidt | 6.00 | 2.40 | .60 |
| ☐ 378 | Grant Jackson | .08 | .03 | .01 | ☐ 471 | Bob Boone | .15 | .06 | .01 |
| ☐ 379 | Dyar Miller | .08 | .03 | .01 | ☐ 472 | Tom Hutton | .08 | .03 | .01 |
| ☐ 380 | Jim Palmer | 3.00 | 1.20 | .30 | ☐ 473 | Rich Allen | .35 | .14 | .03 |
| ☐ 381 | Mike Torrez | .12 | .05 | .01 | ☐ 474 | Tony Taylor | .08 | .03 | .01 |
| ☐ 382 | Mike Willis | .08 | .03 | .01 | ☐ 475 | Jerry Martin | .08 | .03 | .01 |
| ☐ 383 | Dave Duncan | .08 | .03 | .01 | ☐ 476 | Danny Ozark MGR | .08 | .03 | .01 |
| ☐ 384 | Ellie Hendricks | .08 | .03 | .01 | ☐ 477 | Dick Ruthven | .08 | .03 | .01 |
| ☐ 385 | Jim Hutto | .08 | .03 | .01 | ☐ 478 | Jim Todd | .08 | .03 | .01 |
| ☐ 386 | Bob Bailor | .08 | .03 | .01 | ☐ 479 | Paul Lindblad | .08 | .03 | .01 |
| ☐ 387 | Doug DeCinces | .40 | .16 | .04 | ☐ 480 | Rollie Fingers | 1.25 | .50 | .12 |
| ☐ 388 | Bob Grich | .30 | .12 | .03 | ☐ 481 | Vida Blue | .25 | .10 | .02 |
| ☐ 389 | Lee May | .20 | .08 | .02 | ☐ 482 | Ken Holtzman | .12 | .05 | .01 |
| ☐ 390 | Tony Muser | .08 | .03 | .01 | ☐ 483 | Dick Bosman | .08 | .03 | .01 |
| ☐ 391 | Tim Nordbrook | .08 | .03 | .01 | ☐ 484 | Sonny Siebert | .08 | .03 | .01 |
| ☐ 392 | Brooks Robinson | 3.00 | 1.20 | .30 | ☐ 485 | Glenn Abbott | .08 | .03 | .01 |
| ☐ 393 | Royle Stillman | .08 | .03 | .01 | ☐ 486 | Stan Bahnsen | .08 | .03 | .01 |
| ☐ 394 | Don Baylor | .40 | .16 | .04 | ☐ 487 | Mike Norris | .15 | .06 | .01 |
| ☐ 395 | Paul Blair | .12 | .05 | .01 | ☐ 488 | Alvin Dark MGR | .12 | .05 | .01 |
| ☐ 396 | Al Bumbry | .12 | .05 | .01 | ☐ 489 | Claudell Washington | .20 | .08 | .02 |
| ☐ 397 | Larry Harlow | .08 | .03 | .01 | ☐ 490 | Joe Rudi | .15 | .06 | .01 |
| ☐ 398 | Tommy Davis | .15 | .06 | .01 | ☐ 491 | Bill North | .08 | .03 | .01 |
| ☐ 399 | Jim Northrup | .12 | .05 | .01 | ☐ 492 | Bert Campaneris | .15 | .06 | .01 |
| ☐ 400 | Ken Singleton | .30 | .12 | .03 | ☐ 493 | Gene Tenace | .12 | .05 | .01 |
| ☐ 401 | Tom Shopay | .08 | .03 | .01 | ☐ 494 | Reggie Jackson | 5.00 | 2.00 | .50 |
| ☐ 402 | Fred Lynn | 1.50 | .60 | .15 | ☐ 495 | Phil Garner | .12 | .05 | .01 |
| ☐ 403 | Carlton Fisk | 1.00 | .40 | .10 | ☐ 496 | Billy Williams | 1.50 | .60 | .15 |
| ☐ 404 | Cecil Cooper | .75 | .30 | .07 | ☐ 497 | Sal Bando | .15 | .06 | .01 |
| ☐ 405 | Jim Rice | 3.00 | 1.20 | .30 | ☐ 498 | Jim Holt | .08 | .03 | .01 |
| ☐ 406 | Juan Beniquez | .12 | .05 | .01 | ☐ 499 | Ted Martinez | .08 | .03 | .01 |
| ☐ 407 | Denny Doyle | .08 | .03 | .01 | ☐ 500 | Ray Fosse | .08 | .03 | .01 |
| ☐ 408 | Dwight Evans | .50 | .20 | .05 | ☐ 501 | Matt Alexander | .08 | .03 | .01 |
| ☐ 409 | Carl Yastrzemski | 6.00 | 2.40 | .60 | ☐ 502 | Larry Haney | .08 | .03 | .01 |
| ☐ 410 | Rick Burleson | .15 | .06 | .01 | ☐ 503 | Angel Mangual | .08 | .03 | .01 |
| ☐ 411 | Bernie Carbo | .08 | .03 | .01 | ☐ 504 | Fred Beene | .08 | .03 | .01 |
| ☐ 412 | Doug Griffin | .08 | .03 | .01 | ☐ 505 | Tom Buskey | .08 | .03 | .01 |
| ☐ 413 | Rico Petrocelli | .12 | .05 | .01 | ☐ 506 | Dennis Eckersley | .20 | .08 | .02 |
| ☐ 414 | Bob Montgomery | .08 | .03 | .01 | ☐ 507 | Roric Harrison | .08 | .03 | .01 |
| ☐ 415 | Tim Blackwell | .08 | .03 | .01 | ☐ 508 | Don Hood | .08 | .03 | .01 |
| ☐ 416 | Rick Miller | .08 | .03 | .01 | ☐ 509 | Jim Kern | .12 | .05 | .01 |
| ☐ 417 | Darrell Johnson | .08 | .03 | .01 | ☐ 510 | Dave LaRoche | .08 | .03 | .01 |
| ☐ 418 | Jim Burton | .08 | .03 | .01 | ☐ 511 | Fritz Peterson | .08 | .03 | .01 |
| ☐ 419 | Jim Willoughby | .08 | .03 | .01 | ☐ 512 | Jim Strickland | .08 | .03 | .01 |
| ☐ 420 | Rogelio Moret | .08 | .03 | .01 | ☐ 513 | Rick Waits | .12 | .05 | .01 |
| ☐ 421 | Bill Lee | .12 | .05 | .01 | ☐ 514 | Alan Ashby | .08 | .03 | .01 |
| ☐ 422 | Dick Drago | .08 | .03 | .01 | ☐ 515 | John Ellis | .08 | .03 | .01 |
| ☐ 423 | Diego Segui | .08 | .03 | .01 | ☐ 516 | Rick Cerone | .12 | .05 | .01 |
| ☐ 424 | Luis Tiant | .25 | .10 | .02 | ☐ 517 | Buddy Bell | .35 | .14 | .03 |
| ☐ 425 | Jim Hunter | 2.00 | .80 | .20 | ☐ 518 | Jack Brohamer | .08 | .03 | .01 |
| ☐ 426 | Rick Sawyer | .08 | .03 | .01 | ☐ 519 | Rico Carty | .12 | .05 | .01 |
| ☐ 427 | Rudy May | .08 | .03 | .01 | ☐ 520 | Ed Crosby | .08 | .03 | .01 |
| ☐ 428 | Dick Tidrow | .08 | .03 | .01 | ☐ 521 | Frank Duffy | .08 | .03 | .01 |
| ☐ 429 | Sparky Lyle | .30 | .12 | .03 | ☐ 522 | Duane Kuiper | .08 | .03 | .01 |
| ☐ 430 | Doc Medich | .08 | .03 | .01 | | (photo actually | | | |
| ☐ 431 | Pat Dobson | .12 | .05 | .01 | | Rick Manning) | | | |
| ☐ 432 | Dave Pagan | .08 | .03 | .01 | ☐ 523 | Joe Lis | .08 | .03 | .01 |
| ☐ 433 | Thurman Munson | 3.00 | 1.20 | .30 | ☐ 524 | Boog Powell | .50 | .20 | .05 |
| ☐ 434 | Chris Chambliss | .15 | .06 | .01 | ☐ 525 | Frank Robinson | 2.00 | .80 | .20 |
| ☐ 435 | Roy White | .12 | .05 | .01 | ☐ 526 | Oscar Gamble | .18 | .08 | .01 |
| ☐ 436 | Walt Williams | .08 | .03 | .01 | ☐ 527 | George Hendrick | .20 | .08 | .02 |
| ☐ 437 | Graig Nettles | .75 | .30 | .07 | ☐ 528 | John Lowenstein | .08 | .03 | .01 |
| ☐ 438 | Rick Dempsey | .08 | .03 | .01 | ☐ 529 | Rick Manning | .08 | .03 | .01 |
| ☐ 439 | Bobby Bonds | .25 | .10 | .02 | | (photo actually | | | |
| ☐ 440 | Ed Herrmann | .08 | .03 | .01 | | Duane Kuiper) | | | |
| ☐ 441 | Sandy Alomar | .08 | .03 | .01 | ☐ 530 | Tommy Smith | .08 | .03 | .01 |
| ☐ 442 | Fred Stanley | .08 | .03 | .01 | ☐ 531 | Charlie Spikes | .08 | .03 | .01 |
| ☐ 443 | Terry Whitfield | .08 | .03 | .01 | ☐ 532 | Steve Kline | .08 | .03 | .01 |
| ☐ 444 | Rich Bladt | .08 | .03 | .01 | ☐ 533 | Ed Kranepool | .15 | .06 | .01 |
| ☐ 445 | Lou Piniella | .25 | .10 | .02 | ☐ 534 | Mike Vail | .08 | .03 | .01 |
| ☐ 446 | Rich Coggins | .08 | .03 | .01 | ☐ 535 | Del Unser | .08 | .03 | .01 |
| ☐ 447 | Ed Brinkman | .08 | .03 | .01 | ☐ 536 | Felix Millan | .08 | .03 | .01 |
| ☐ 448 | Jim Mason | .08 | .03 | .01 | ☐ 537 | Rusty Staub | .35 | .14 | .03 |
| ☐ 449 | Larry Murray | .08 | .03 | .01 | ☐ 538 | Jesus Alou | .08 | .03 | .01 |
| ☐ 450 | Ron Blomberg | .08 | .03 | .01 | ☐ 539 | Wayne Garrett | .08 | .03 | .01 |
| ☐ 451 | Elliott Maddox | .08 | .03 | .01 | ☐ 540 | Mike Phillips | .08 | .03 | .01 |

| | | | | |
|---|---|---|---|---|
| ☐ 541 | Joe Torre | .40 | .16 | .04 |
| ☐ 542 | Dave Kingman | .80 | .32 | .08 |
| ☐ 543 | Gene Clines | .08 | .03 | .01 |
| ☐ 544 | Jack Heidemann | .08 | .03 | .01 |
| ☐ 545 | Bud Harrelson | .08 | .03 | .01 |
| ☐ 546 | John Stearns | .12 | .05 | .01 |
| ☐ 547 | John Milner | .08 | .03 | .01 |
| ☐ 548 | Bob Apodaca | .08 | .03 | .01 |
| ☐ 549 | Skip Lockwood | .08 | .03 | .01 |
| ☐ 550 | Ken Sanders | .08 | .03 | .01 |
| ☐ 551 | Tom Seaver | 3.50 | 1.40 | .35 |
| ☐ 552 | Rick Baldwin | .08 | .03 | .01 |
| ☐ 553 | Hank Webb | .08 | .03 | .01 |
| ☐ 554 | Jon Matlack | .12 | .05 | .01 |
| ☐ 555 | Randy Tate | .08 | .03 | .01 |
| ☐ 556 | Tom Hall | .08 | .03 | .01 |
| ☐ 557 | George Stone | .08 | .03 | .01 |
| ☐ 558 | Craig Swan | .12 | .05 | .01 |
| ☐ 559 | Jerry Cram | .08 | .03 | .01 |
| ☐ 560 | Roy Staiger | .08 | .03 | .01 |
| ☐ 561 | Kent Tekulve | .15 | .06 | .01 |
| ☐ 562 | Jerry Reuss | .15 | .06 | .01 |
| ☐ 563 | John Candelaria | .20 | .08 | .02 |
| ☐ 564 | Larry Demery | .08 | .03 | .01 |
| ☐ 565 | Dave Giusti | .12 | .05 | .01 |
| ☐ 566 | Jim Rooker | .08 | .03 | .01 |
| ☐ 567 | Ramon Hernandez | .08 | .03 | .01 |
| ☐ 568 | Bruce Kison | .12 | .05 | .01 |
| ☐ 569 | Ken Brett | .08 | .03 | .01 |
| ☐ 570 | Bob Moose | .12 | .05 | .01 |
| ☐ 571 | Manny Sanguillen | .15 | .06 | .01 |
| ☐ 572 | Dave Parker | 2.00 | .80 | .20 |
| ☐ 573 | Willie Stargell | 2.00 | .80 | .20 |
| ☐ 574 | Richie Zisk | .15 | .06 | .01 |
| ☐ 575 | Rennie Stennett | .08 | .03 | .01 |
| ☐ 576 | Al Oliver | 1.00 | .40 | .10 |
| ☐ 577 | Bill Robinson | .08 | .03 | .01 |
| ☐ 578 | Bob Robertson | .08 | .03 | .01 |
| ☐ 579 | Rich Hebner | .08 | .03 | .01 |
| ☐ 580 | Ed Kirkpatrick | .08 | .03 | .01 |
| ☐ 581 | Duffy Dyer | .08 | .03 | .01 |
| ☐ 582 | Craig Reynolds | .08 | .03 | .01 |
| ☐ 583 | Frank Taveras | .08 | .03 | .01 |
| ☐ 584 | Willie Randolph | .60 | .24 | .06 |
| ☐ 585 | Art Howe | .08 | .03 | .01 |
| ☐ 586 | Dan Murtaugh MGR | .12 | .05 | .01 |
| ☐ 587 | Rick McKinney | .08 | .03 | .01 |
| ☐ 588 | Ed Goodson | .08 | .03 | .01 |
| ☐ 589 | Checklist 1<br>George Brett<br>Al Cowens | 1.00 | .10 | .02 |
| ☐ 590 | Checklist 2<br>Keith Hernandez<br>Lou Brock | 1.00 | .10 | .02 |
| ☐ 591 | Checklist 3<br>Jerry Koosman<br>Duke Snider | .50 | .05 | .01 |
| ☐ 592 | Checklist 4<br>Maury Wills<br>John Knox | .25 | .03 | .01 |
| ☐ 593 | Checklist 5<br>Jim Hunter<br>Nolan Ryan | 1.25 | .10 | .02 |
| ☐ 594 | Checklist 6<br>Ralph Branca<br>Carl Erskine<br>Pee Wee Reese | .30 | .04 | .01 |
| ☐ 595 | Checklist 7<br>Willie Mays<br>Herb Score | .75 | .07 | .01 |
| ☐ 596 | Larry Cox | .08 | .03 | .01 |
| ☐ 597 | Gene Mauch MGR | .12 | .05 | .01 |
| ☐ 598 | Whitey Wietelmann | .08 | .03 | .01 |
| ☐ 599 | Wayne Simpson | .08 | .03 | .01 |
| ☐ 600 | Mel Thomason | .08 | .03 | .01 |
| ☐ 601 | Ike Hampton | .08 | .03 | .01 |
| ☐ 602 | Ken Crosby | .08 | .03 | .01 |
| ☐ 603 | Ralph Rowe | .08 | .03 | .01 |
| ☐ 604 | Jim Tyrone | .08 | .03 | .01 |
| ☐ 605 | Mick Kelleher | .08 | .03 | .01 |
| ☐ 606 | Mario Mendoza | .08 | .03 | .01 |
| ☐ 607 | Mike Rogodzinski | .08 | .03 | .01 |
| ☐ 608 | Bob Gallagher | .08 | .03 | .01 |
| ☐ 609 | Jerry Koosman | .18 | .08 | .01 |
| ☐ 610 | Joe Frazier | .08 | .03 | .01 |
| ☐ 611 | Karl Kuehl | .08 | .03 | .01 |
| ☐ 612 | Frank LaCorte | .08 | .03 | .01 |
| ☐ 613 | Ray Bare | .08 | .03 | .01 |
| ☐ 614 | Billy Muffett | .08 | .03 | .01 |
| ☐ 615 | Bill Laxton | .08 | .03 | .01 |
| ☐ 616 | Willie Mays | 4.00 | 1.60 | .40 |
| ☐ 617 | Phil Cavarretta COA | .12 | .05 | .01 |
| ☐ 618 | Ted Kluszewski COA | .25 | .10 | .02 |

| | | | | |
|---|---|---|---|---|
| ☐ 619 | Elston Howard COA | .35 | .14 | .03 |
| ☐ 620 | Alex Grammas COA | .08 | .03 | .01 |
| ☐ 621 | Mickey Vernon COA | .12 | .05 | .01 |
| ☐ 622 | Dick Sisler COA | .08 | .03 | .01 |
| ☐ 623 | Harvey Haddix COA | .12 | .05 | .01 |
| ☐ 624 | Bobby Winkles COA | .08 | .03 | .01 |
| ☐ 625 | John Pesky COA | .08 | .03 | .01 |
| ☐ 626 | Jim Davenport COA | .15 | .06 | .01 |
| ☐ 627 | Dave Tomlin | .08 | .03 | .01 |
| ☐ 628 | Roger Craig COA | .15 | .06 | .01 |
| ☐ 629 | Joe Amalfitano COA | .08 | .03 | .01 |
| ☐ 630 | Jim Reese COA | .12 | .05 | .01 |

## 1953 Stahl Meyer

The cards in this 9 card set measure 3 1/4" by 4 1/2". The 1953 Stahl Meyer set of full color, unnumbered cards includes three players from each of the three New York teams. The cards have white borders. The Lockman card is the most plentiful of any card in the set. Some batting and fielding statistics and short biography are included on the back. The cards are ordered in the checklist below by alphabetical order without regard to team affiliation.

| | | MINT | VG-E | F-G |
|---|---|---|---|---|
| COMPLETE SET | | 2100.00 | 900.00 | 225.00 |
| COMMON PLAYER (1-9) | | 80.00 | 32.00 | 8.00 |
| ☐ 1 | Hank Bauer | 80.00 | 32.00 | 8.00 |
| ☐ 2 | Roy Campanella | 350.00 | 140.00 | 35.00 |
| ☐ 3 | Gil Hodges | 175.00 | 70.00 | 18.00 |
| ☐ 4 | Monte Irvin | 125.00 | 50.00 | 12.50 |
| ☐ 5 | Whitey Lockman | 80.00 | 32.00 | 8.00 |
| ☐ 6 | Mickey Mantle | 1000.00 | 400.00 | 125.00 |
| ☐ 7 | Phil Rizzuto | 175.00 | 70.00 | 18.00 |
| ☐ 8 | Duke Snider | 275.00 | 110.00 | 27.00 |
| ☐ 9 | Bobby Thomson | 80.00 | 32.00 | 8.00 |

## 1954 Stahl Meyer

The cards in this 12 card set measure 3 1/4" by 4 1/2". The 1954 Stahl Meyer set of full color, unnumbered cards includes four players from each of the three New York teams. The cards have yellow borders and the backs, oriented horizontally, include an ad for a baseball kit and the player's statistics. No player biography is included on the back. The cards are ordered in the checklist below by alphabetical order without regard to team affiliation.

| | | MINT | VG-E | F-G |
|---|---|---|---|---|
| COMPLETE SET | | 3200.00 | 1400.00 | 350.00 |
| COMMON PLAYER (1-12) | | 100.00 | 40.00 | 10.00 |
| ☐ 1 | Hank Bauer | 100.00 | 40.00 | 10.00 |
| ☐ 2 | Carl Erskine | 100.00 | 40.00 | 10.00 |
| ☐ 3 | Gil Hodges | 200.00 | 80.00 | 20.00 |
| ☐ 4 | Monte Irvin | 150.00 | 60.00 | 15.00 |
| ☐ 5 | Whitey Lockman | 100.00 | 40.00 | 10.00 |
| ☐ 6 | Mickey Mantle | 1250.00 | 500.00 | 150.00 |
| ☐ 7 | Willie Mays | 750.00 | 300.00 | 75.00 |
| ☐ 8 | Gil McDougald | 100.00 | 40.00 | 10.00 |
| ☐ 9 | Don Mueller | 100.00 | 40.00 | 10.00 |
| ☐ 10 | Don Newcombe | 125.00 | 50.00 | 12.50 |
| ☐ 11 | Phil Rizzuto | 200.00 | 80.00 | 20.00 |
| ☐ 12 | Duke Snider | 300.00 | 120.00 | 30.00 |

## 1955 Stahl Meyer

The cards in this 12 card set measure 3 1/4" by 4 1/2". The 1955 Stahl Meyer set of full color, unnumbered cards contains four players each from the three New York teams. As in the 1954 set, the cards have yellow borders; however, the back of the cards contain a sketch of Mickey Mantle with an ad for a baseball cap or a pennant. The cards are ordered in the checklist below by alphabetical order without regard to team affiliation.

|  | | MINT | VG-E | F-G |
|---|---|---|---|---|
| COMPLETE SET | | 2500.00 | 1000.00 | 275.00 |
| COMMON PLAYER (1-12) | | 100.00 | 40.00 | 10.00 |
| ☐ 1 | Hank Bauer | 100.00 | 40.00 | 10.00 |
| ☐ 2 | Carl Erskine | 100.00 | 40.00 | 10.00 |
| ☐ 3 | Gil Hodges | 200.00 | 80.00 | 20.00 |
| ☐ 4 | Monte Irvin | 150.00 | 60.00 | 15.00 |
| ☐ 5 | Whitey Lockman | 100.00 | 40.00 | 10.00 |
| ☐ 6 | Mickey Mantle | 1250.00 | 500.00 | 150.00 |
| ☐ 7 | Gil McDougald | 100.00 | 40.00 | 10.00 |
| ☐ 8 | Don Mueller | 100.00 | 40.00 | 10.00 |
| ☐ 9 | Don Newcombe | 125.00 | 50.00 | 12.50 |
| ☐ 10 | Dusty Rhodes | 100.00 | 40.00 | 10.00 |
| ☐ 11 | Phil Rizzuto | 200.00 | 80.00 | 20.00 |
| ☐ 12 | Duke Snider | 300.00 | 120.00 | 30.00 |

## 1962 Sugardale

The cards in this 22 card set measure 3 3/4" by 5 1/8". The 1962 Sugardale Meats set of black and white, numbered and lettered cards features the Cleveland Indians and the Pittsburgh Pirates. The Indians are numbered while the Pirates are lettered. The backs, in red print, give player tips. The Bob Nieman card was just recently discovered and is quite scarce. The catalog designation is F174-1.

|  | | MINT | VG-E | F-G |
|---|---|---|---|---|
| COMPLETE SET | | 900.00 | 360.00 | 90.00 |
| COMMON PLAYER (1-19) | | 30.00 | 12.00 | 3.00 |
| COMMON PLAYER (A-D) | | 40.00 | 16.00 | 4.00 |
| ☐ 1 | Barry Latman | 30.00 | 12.00 | 3.00 |
| ☐ 2 | Gary Bell | 30.00 | 12.00 | 3.00 |
| ☐ 3 | Dick Donovan | 30.00 | 12.00 | 3.00 |
| ☐ 4 | Frank Funk | 30.00 | 12.00 | 3.00 |
| ☐ 5 | Jim Perry | 40.00 | 16.00 | 4.00 |
| ☐ 6 | not issued | 0.00 | .00 | .00 |
| ☐ 7 | John Romano | 30.00 | 12.00 | 3.00 |
| ☐ 8 | Ty Cline | 30.00 | 12.00 | 3.00 |
| ☐ 9 | Tito Francona | 30.00 | 12.00 | 3.00 |
| ☐ 10 | Bob Nieman | 150.00 | 60.00 | 15.00 |
| ☐ 11 | Willie Kirkland | 30.00 | 12.00 | 3.00 |
| ☐ 12 | Woody Held | 30.00 | 12.00 | 3.00 |
| ☐ 13 | Jerry Kindall | 30.00 | 12.00 | 3.00 |
| ☐ 14 | Bubba Phillips | 30.00 | 12.00 | 3.00 |
| ☐ 15 | Mel Harder | 30.00 | 12.00 | 3.00 |
| ☐ 16 | Salty Parker | 30.00 | 12.00 | 3.00 |
| ☐ 17 | Ray Katt | 30.00 | 12.00 | 3.00 |
| ☐ 18 | Mel McGaha | 30.00 | 12.00 | 3.00 |
| ☐ 19 | Pedro Ramos | 30.00 | 12.00 | 3.00 |
| ☐ A | Dick Groat | 60.00 | 24.00 | 6.00 |
| ☐ B | Robert Clemente | 300.00 | 120.00 | 30.00 |
| ☐ C | Don Hoak | 40.00 | 16.00 | 4.00 |
| ☐ D | Dick Stuart | 45.00 | 18.00 | 4.50 |

## 1963 Sugardale

The cards in this 31 card set measure 3 3/4" by 5 1/8". The 1963 Sugardale Meats set of 31 black and white, numbered cards features the Cleveland Indians and Pittsburgh Pirates. The backs are printed in red and give player tips. The 1963 Sugardale set can be distinguished from the 1962 Sugardale set by examining the biographies on the card for mention of the 1962 season. The Perry and Skinner cards were withdrawn after June trades and are difficult to obtain.

|  | | MINT | VG-E | F-G |
|---|---|---|---|---|
| COMPLETE SET | | 950.00 | 400.00 | 100.00 |
| COMMON PLAYER (1-33) | | 30.00 | 12.00 | 3.00 |
| COMMON PLAYER (34-38) | | 35.00 | 14.00 | 3.50 |
| ☐ 1 | Barry Latman | 30.00 | 12.00 | 3.00 |
| ☐ 2 | Gary Bell | 30.00 | 12.00 | 3.00 |
| ☐ 3 | Dick Donovan | 30.00 | 12.00 | 3.00 |
| ☐ 4 | Joe Adcock | 40.00 | 16.00 | 4.00 |
| ☐ 5 | Jim Perry | 100.00 | 40.00 | 10.00 |
| ☐ 6 | Not issued | 0.00 | 0.00 | 0.00 |
| ☐ 7 | John Romano | 30.00 | 12.00 | 3.00 |
| ☐ 8 | Mike de la Hoz | 30.00 | 12.00 | 3.00 |
| ☐ 9 | Tito Francona | 30.00 | 12.00 | 3.00 |
| ☐ 10 | Gene Green | 30.00 | 12.00 | 3.00 |
| ☐ 11 | Willie Kirkland | 30.00 | 12.00 | 3.00 |
| ☐ 12 | Woody Held | 30.00 | 12.00 | 3.00 |
| ☐ 13 | Jerry Kindall | 30.00 | 12.00 | 3.00 |
| ☐ 14 | Max Alvis | 30.00 | 12.00 | 3.00 |
| ☐ 15 | Mel Harder | 30.00 | 12.00 | 3.00 |
| ☐ 16 | George Strickland | 30.00 | 12.00 | 3.00 |
| ☐ 17 | Elmer Valo | 30.00 | 12.00 | 3.00 |
| ☐ 18 | Birdie Tebbetts | 30.00 | 12.00 | 3.00 |
| ☐ 19 | Pedro Ramos | 30.00 | 12.00 | 3.00 |
| ☐ 20 | Al Luplow | 30.00 | 12.00 | 3.00 |
| ☐ 21 | Not issued | 0.00 | 0.00 | 0.00 |
| ☐ 22 | Not issued | 0.00 | 0.00 | 0.00 |
| ☐ 23 | Jim Grant | 30.00 | 12.00 | 3.00 |
| ☐ 24 | Victor Davalillo | 30.00 | 12.00 | 3.00 |
| ☐ 25 | Jerry Walker | 30.00 | 12.00 | 3.00 |
| ☐ 26 | Sam McDowell | 35.00 | 14.00 | 3.50 |
| ☐ 27 | Fred Whitfield | 30.00 | 12.00 | 3.00 |
| ☐ 28 | Jack Kralick | 30.00 | 12.00 | 3.00 |
| ☐ 29 | Not issued | 0.00 | 0.00 | 0.00 |
| ☐ 30 | Not issued | 0.00 | 0.00 | 0.00 |
| ☐ 31 | Not issued | 0.00 | 0.00 | 0.00 |
| ☐ 32 | Not issued | 0.00 | 0.00 | 0.00 |
| ☐ 33 | Bob Allen | 30.00 | 12.00 | 3.00 |
| ☐ 34 | Don Cardwell | 35.00 | 14.00 | 3.50 |
| ☐ 35 | Don Skinner | 100.00 | 40.00 | 10.00 |
| ☐ 36 | Don Schwall | 35.00 | 14.00 | 3.50 |
| ☐ 37 | Jim Pagliaroni | 35.00 | 14.00 | 3.50 |
| ☐ 38 | Dick Schofield | 35.00 | 14.00 | 3.50 |

## 1957 Swifts Franks

The cards in this 18 card set measure 3 1/2" by 4". These full color, numbered cards issued in 1957 by the Swift Company are die-cut. Each card consists of several pieces which can be punched out and assembled to form a stand-up model of the player. The cards and a game board were available directly from the company. The ACC designation is F162.

|  | | MINT | VG-E | F-G |
|---|---|---|---|---|
| COMPLETE SET (18) | | 900.00 | 360.00 | 90.00 |
| COMMON PLAYER (1-18) | | 30.00 | 12.00 | 3.00 |
| ☐ 1 | John Podres | 40.00 | 16.00 | 4.00 |
| ☐ 2 | Gus Triandos | 30.00 | 12.00 | 3.00 |
| ☐ 3 | Dale Long | 30.00 | 12.00 | 3.00 |
| ☐ 4 | Billy Pierce | 40.00 | 16.00 | 4.00 |
| ☐ 5 | Ed Bailey | 30.00 | 12.00 | 3.00 |
| ☐ 6 | Vic Wertz | 30.00 | 12.00 | 3.00 |
| ☐ 7 | Nelson Fox | 60.00 | 24.00 | 6.00 |
| ☐ 8 | Ken Boyer | 60.00 | 24.00 | 6.00 |

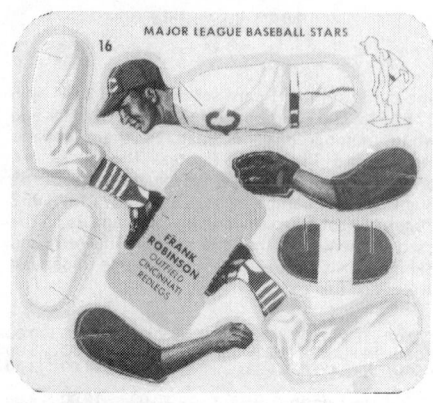

| | | | | |
|---|---|---|---|---|
| ☐ 9 | Gil McDougald | 40.00 | 16.00 | 4.00 |
| ☐ 10 | Junior Gilliam | 50.00 | 20.00 | 5.00 |
| ☐ 11 | Eddie Yost | 30.00 | 12.00 | 3.00 |
| ☐ 12 | Johnny Logan | 30.00 | 12.00 | 3.00 |
| ☐ 13 | Hank Aaron | 250.00 | 100.00 | 25.00 |
| ☐ 14 | Bill Tuttle | 30.00 | 12.00 | 3.00 |
| ☐ 15 | Jackie Jensen | 40.00 | 16.00 | 4.00 |
| ☐ 16 | Frank Robinson | 100.00 | 40.00 | 10.00 |
| ☐ 17 | Richie Ashburn | 75.00 | 30.00 | 7.50 |
| ☐ 18 | Rocky Colavito | 60.00 | 24.00 | 6.00 |

## 1933 Tatoo Orbit

The cards in this 60 card set measure 2" by 2 1/4". The 1933 Tatoo Orbit set contains unnumbered, color cards. Blaeholder and Hadley, and to a lesser degree Andrews and Hornsby are considered more difficult to obtain than the other cards in this set. The ACC designation is R305. The cards are ordered and numbered below alphabetically by the player's name.

| | | MINT | VG-E | F-G |
|---|---|---|---|---|
| COMPLETE SET | | 1650.00 | 750.00 | 175.00 |
| COMMON PLAYER (1-60) | | 20.00 | 8.00 | 2.00 |
| ☐ 1 | Dale Alexander | 20.00 | 8.00 | 2.00 |
| ☐ 2 | Ivy Andrews | 60.00 | 24.00 | 6.00 |
| ☐ 3 | Earl Averill | 35.00 | 14.00 | 3.50 |
| ☐ 4 | Dick Bartell | 20.00 | 8.00 | 2.00 |
| ☐ 5 | Wally Berger | 20.00 | 8.00 | 2.00 |
| ☐ 6 | George Blaeholder | 100.00 | 40.00 | 10.00 |
| ☐ 7 | Irving Burns | 20.00 | 8.00 | 2.00 |
| ☐ 8 | Guy Bush | 20.00 | 8.00 | 2.00 |
| ☐ 9 | Bruce Campbell | 20.00 | 8.00 | 2.00 |
| ☐ 10 | Chalmers Cissell | 20.00 | 8.00 | 2.00 |
| ☐ 11 | Watson Clark | 20.00 | 8.00 | 2.00 |
| ☐ 12 | Mickey Cochrane | 50.00 | 20.00 | 5.00 |
| ☐ 13 | Phil Collins | 20.00 | 8.00 | 2.00 |
| ☐ 14 | Kiki Cuyler | 35.00 | 14.00 | 3.50 |
| ☐ 15 | Dizzy Dean | 125.00 | 50.00 | 12.50 |
| ☐ 16 | Jimmy Dykes | 20.00 | 8.00 | 2.00 |

| | | | | |
|---|---|---|---|---|
| ☐ 17 | George Earnshaw | 20.00 | 8.00 | 2.00 |
| ☐ 18 | Woody English | 20.00 | 8.00 | 2.00 |
| ☐ 19 | Lou Fonseca | 20.00 | 8.00 | 2.00 |
| ☐ 20 | Jimmy Foxx | 75.00 | 30.00 | 7.50 |
| ☐ 21 | Burleigh Grimes | 35.00 | 14.00 | 3.50 |
| ☐ 22 | Charlie Grimm | 20.00 | 8.00 | 2.00 |
| ☐ 23 | Lefty Grove | 50.00 | 20.00 | 5.00 |
| ☐ 24 | Frank Grube | 20.00 | 8.00 | 2.00 |
| ☐ 25 | George Haas | 20.00 | 8.00 | 2.00 |
| ☐ 26 | Bump Hadley | 100.00 | 40.00 | 10.00 |
| ☐ 27 | Chick Hafey | 35.00 | 14.00 | 3.50 |
| ☐ 28 | Jess Haines | 35.00 | 14.00 | 3.50 |
| ☐ 29 | Bill Hallahan | 20.00 | 8.00 | 2.00 |
| ☐ 30 | Mel Harder | 20.00 | 8.00 | 2.00 |
| ☐ 31 | Gabby Hartnett | 35.00 | 14.00 | 3.50 |
| ☐ 32 | Babe Herman | 24.00 | 10.00 | 2.40 |
| ☐ 33 | Billy Herman | 35.00 | 14.00 | 3.50 |
| ☐ 34 | Rogers Hornsby | 150.00 | 60.00 | 15.00 |
| ☐ 35 | Roy Johnson | 20.00 | 8.00 | 2.00 |
| ☐ 36 | Smead Jolly | 20.00 | 8.00 | 2.00 |
| ☐ 37 | Billy Jurges | 20.00 | 8.00 | 2.00 |
| ☐ 38 | Willie Kamm | 20.00 | 8.00 | 2.00 |
| ☐ 39 | Mark Koenig | 20.00 | 8.00 | 2.00 |
| ☐ 40 | Jim Levey | 20.00 | 8.00 | 2.00 |
| ☐ 41 | Ernie Lombardi | 35.00 | 14.00 | 3.50 |
| ☐ 42 | Red Lucas | 20.00 | 8.00 | 2.00 |
| ☐ 43 | Ted Lyons | 35.00 | 14.00 | 3.50 |
| ☐ 44 | Connie Mack | 45.00 | 18.00 | 4.50 |
| ☐ 45 | Pat Malone | 20.00 | 8.00 | 2.00 |
| ☐ 46 | Pepper Martin | 24.00 | 10.00 | 2.40 |
| ☐ 47 | Marty McManus | 20.00 | 8.00 | 2.00 |
| ☐ 48 | Frank O'Doul | 24.00 | 10.00 | 2.40 |
| ☐ 49 | Dick Porter | 20.00 | 8.00 | 2.00 |
| ☐ 50 | Carl N. Reynolds | 20.00 | 8.00 | 2.00 |
| ☐ 51 | Charlie Root | 20.00 | 8.00 | 2.00 |
| ☐ 52 | Bob Seeds | 20.00 | 8.00 | 2.00 |
| ☐ 53 | Al Simmons | 35.00 | 14.00 | 3.50 |
| ☐ 54 | Riggs Stephenson | 24.00 | 10.00 | 2.40 |
| ☐ 55 | Lyle Tinning | 20.00 | 8.00 | 2.00 |
| ☐ 56 | Joe Vosmik | 20.00 | 8.00 | 2.00 |
| ☐ 57 | Rube Walberg | 20.00 | 8.00 | 2.00 |
| ☐ 58 | Paul Waner | 35.00 | 14.00 | 3.50 |
| ☐ 59 | Lon Warneke | 20.00 | 8.00 | 2.00 |
| ☐ 60 | Arthur Whitney | 20.00 | 8.00 | 2.00 |

## 1983 Thorn Apple Valley Cubs

This set of 28 Chicago Cubs features full-color action photos on the front and was sponsored by Thorn Apple Valley. The cards measure 2 1/4" by 3 1/2". The backs provide year-by-year statistics. The cards are unnumbered except for uniform number; they are listed below by uniform with the special cards listed at the end.

| | | MINT | VG-E | F-G |
|---|---|---|---|---|
| COMPLETE SET | | 8.00 | 3.25 | .80 |
| COMMON PLAYER | | .25 | .10 | .02 |
| ☐ 1 | Larry Bowa | .35 | .14 | .03 |
| ☐ 6 | Keith Moreland | .45 | .18 | .04 |
| ☐ 7 | Jody Davis | .55 | .22 | .05 |
| ☐ 10 | Leon Durham | .55 | .22 | .05 |
| ☐ 11 | Ron Cey | .45 | .18 | .04 |
| ☐ 16 | Steve Lake | .25 | .10 | .02 |

| | | MINT | VG-E | F-G |
|---|---|---|---|---|
| ☐ 20 | Thad Bosley | .25 | .10 | .02 |
| ☐ 21 | Jay Johnstone | .30 | .12 | .03 |
| ☐ 22 | Bill Buckner | .50 | .20 | .05 |
| ☐ 23 | Ryne Sandberg | 1.50 | .60 | .15 |
| ☐ 24 | Jerry Morales | .25 | .10 | .02 |
| ☐ 25 | Gary Woods | .25 | .10 | .02 |
| ☐ 27 | Mel Hall | .55 | .22 | .05 |
| ☐ 29 | Tom Veryzer | .25 | .10 | .02 |
| ☐ 30 | Chuck Rainey | .25 | .10 | .02 |
| ☐ 31 | Fergie Jenkins | .50 | .20 | .05 |
| ☐ 32 | Craig Lefferts | .30 | .12 | .03 |
| ☐ 33 | Joe Carter | .75 | .30 | .07 |
| ☐ 34 | Steve Trout | .30 | .12 | .03 |
| ☐ 36 | Mike Proly | .25 | .10 | .02 |
| ☐ 39 | Bill Campbell | .30 | .12 | .03 |
| ☐ 41 | Warren Brusstar | .25 | .10 | .02 |
| ☐ 44 | Dick Ruthven | .25 | .10 | .02 |
| ☐ 46 | Lee Smith | .45 | .18 | .04 |
| ☐ 48 | Dickie Noles | .25 | .10 | .02 |
| ☐ 26 | Manager/Coaches | .25 | .10 | .02 |
| | Lee Elia MGR | | | |
| | Ruben Amaro | | | |
| | Billy Connors | | | |
| | Duffy Dyer | | | |
| | Fred Koenig | | | |
| | John Vukovich | | | |
| | (unnumbered) | | | |
| ☐ 27 | Team Photo | .35 | .14 | .03 |
| | (unnumbered) | | | |

## 1947 Tip Top

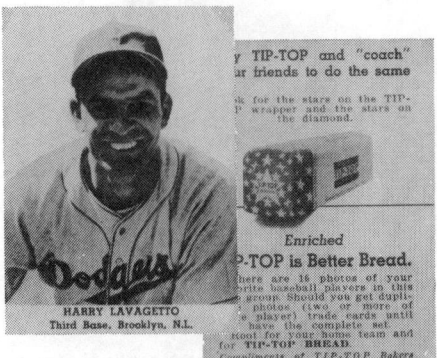

The cards in this 163 card set measure 2 1/4" by 3". The 1947 Tip Top Bread issue contains unnumbered cards with black and white player photos. The set is of interest to baseball historians in that it contains cards of many players not appearing in any other card sets. The cards were issued locally for the eleven following teams: Red Sox (1-15), White Sox (16- 30), Tigers (31-45), Yankees (46-60), Browns (61-75), Braves (76- 90), Dodgers (91-104), Cubs (105-119), Giants (120-135), Pirates (136-149), and Cardinals (150-164). Players of the Red Sox, Tigers, White Sox, Braves, and the Cubs are scarcer than those of the other teams. The ACC designation is D323.

| | | MINT | VG-E | F-G |
|---|---|---|---|---|
| COMPLETE SET | | 5000.00 | 2000.00 | 600.00 |
| COMMON PLAYER (1-164) | | 15.00 | 6.00 | 1.50 |
| | | | | |
| ☐ 1 | Leon Culberson | 45.00 | 18.00 | 4.50 |
| ☐ 2 | Dom DiMaggio | 75.00 | 30.00 | 7.50 |
| ☐ 3 | Joe Dobson | 45.00 | 18.00 | 4.50 |
| ☐ 4 | Bob Doerr | 90.00 | 36.00 | 9.00 |
| ☐ 5 | Dave (Boo) Ferris | 45.00 | 18.00 | 4.50 |
| ☐ 6 | Mickey Harris | 45.00 | 18.00 | 4.50 |
| ☐ 7 | Frank Hayes | 45.00 | 18.00 | 4.50 |
| ☐ 8 | Cecil Hughson | 45.00 | 18.00 | 4.50 |
| ☐ 9 | Earl Johnson | 45.00 | 18.00 | 4.50 |
| ☐ 10 | Roy Partee | 45.00 | 18.00 | 4.50 |

| | | MINT | VG-E | F-G |
|---|---|---|---|---|
| ☐ 11 | Johnny Pesky | 45.00 | 18.00 | 4.50 |
| ☐ 12 | Rip Russell | 45.00 | 18.00 | 4.50 |
| ☐ 13 | Hal Wagner | 45.00 | 18.00 | 4.50 |
| ☐ 14 | Rudy York | 45.00 | 18.00 | 4.50 |
| ☐ 15 | Bill Zuber | 45.00 | 18.00 | 4.50 |
| ☐ 16 | Floyd Baker | 45.00 | 18.00 | 4.50 |
| ☐ 17 | Earl Caldwell | 45.00 | 18.00 | 4.50 |
| ☐ 18 | Lloyd Christopher | 45.00 | 18.00 | 4.50 |
| ☐ 19 | George Dickey | 45.00 | 18.00 | 4.50 |
| ☐ 20 | Ralph Hodgin | 45.00 | 18.00 | 4.50 |
| ☐ 21 | Bob Kennedy | 45.00 | 18.00 | 4.50 |
| ☐ 22 | Joe Kuhel | 45.00 | 18.00 | 4.50 |
| ☐ 23 | Thornton Lee | 45.00 | 18.00 | 4.50 |
| ☐ 24 | Ed Lopat | 75.00 | 30.00 | 7.50 |
| ☐ 25 | Cass Michaels | 45.00 | 18.00 | 4.50 |
| ☐ 26 | John Rigney | 45.00 | 18.00 | 4.50 |
| ☐ 27 | Mike Tresh | 45.00 | 18.00 | 4.50 |
| ☐ 28 | Thurman Tucker | 45.00 | 18.00 | 4.50 |
| ☐ 29 | Jack Wallasca | 45.00 | 18.00 | 4.50 |
| ☐ 30 | Taft Wright | 45.00 | 18.00 | 4.50 |
| ☐ 31 | Walter (Hoot) Evers | 45.00 | 18.00 | 4.50 |
| ☐ 32 | John Gorsica | 45.00 | 18.00 | 4.50 |
| ☐ 33 | Fred Hutchinson | 60.00 | 24.00 | 6.00 |
| ☐ 34 | George Kell | 150.00 | 60.00 | 15.00 |
| ☐ 35 | Eddie Lake | 45.00 | 18.00 | 4.50 |
| ☐ 36 | Ed Mayo | 45.00 | 18.00 | 4.50 |
| ☐ 37 | Arthur Mills | 45.00 | 18.00 | 4.50 |
| ☐ 38 | Pat Mullin | 45.00 | 18.00 | 4.50 |
| ☐ 39 | James Outlaw | 45.00 | 18.00 | 4.50 |
| ☐ 40 | Frank (Stub) Overmire | 45.00 | 18.00 | 4.50 |
| ☐ 41 | Bob Swift | 45.00 | 18.00 | 4.50 |
| ☐ 42 | Geo. Birdie Tebbets | 45.00 | 18.00 | 4.50 |
| ☐ 43 | Paul (Diz) Trout | 45.00 | 18.00 | 4.50 |
| ☐ 44 | Virgil Trucks | 45.00 | 18.00 | 4.50 |
| ☐ 45 | Dick Wakefield | 45.00 | 18.00 | 4.50 |
| ☐ 46 | Larry Berra | 60.00 | 24.00 | 6.00 |
| ☐ 47 | Floyd (Bill) Bevans | 15.00 | 6.00 | 1.50 |
| ☐ 48 | Bobby Brown | 20.00 | 8.00 | 2.00 |
| ☐ 49 | Thomas Byrne | 15.00 | 6.00 | 1.50 |
| ☐ 50 | Frank Crosetti | 20.00 | 8.00 | 2.00 |
| ☐ 51 | Tom Henrich | 20.00 | 8.00 | 2.00 |
| ☐ 52 | Charlie Keller | 20.00 | 8.00 | 2.00 |
| ☐ 53 | Johnny Lindell | 15.00 | 6.00 | 1.50 |
| ☐ 54 | Joe Page | 15.00 | 6.00 | 1.50 |
| ☐ 55 | Mel Queen | 15.00 | 6.00 | 1.50 |
| ☐ 56 | Allie Reynolds | 20.00 | 8.00 | 2.00 |
| ☐ 57 | Phil Rizzuto | 50.00 | 20.00 | 5.00 |
| ☐ 58 | Aaron Robinson | 15.00 | 6.00 | 1.50 |
| ☐ 59 | George Stirnweiss | 20.00 | 8.00 | 2.00 |
| ☐ 60 | Charles Wensloff | 20.00 | 8.00 | 2.00 |
| ☐ 61 | John Berardino | 15.00 | 6.00 | 1.50 |
| ☐ 62 | Clifford Fannin | 15.00 | 6.00 | 1.50 |
| ☐ 63 | Dennis Galehouse | 15.00 | 6.00 | 1.50 |
| ☐ 64 | Jeff Heath | 15.00 | 6.00 | 1.50 |
| ☐ 65 | Walter Judnich | 15.00 | 6.00 | 1.50 |
| ☐ 66 | Jack Kramer | 15.00 | 6.00 | 1.50 |
| ☐ 67 | Paul Lehner | 15.00 | 6.00 | 1.50 |
| ☐ 68 | Lester Moss | 15.00 | 6.00 | 1.50 |
| ☐ 69 | Bob Muncrief | 15.00 | 6.00 | 1.50 |
| ☐ 70 | Nelson Potter | 15.00 | 6.00 | 1.50 |
| ☐ 71 | Fred Sanford | 15.00 | 6.00 | 1.50 |
| ☐ 72 | Joe Schultz | 15.00 | 6.00 | 1.50 |
| ☐ 73 | Vern Stephens | 15.00 | 6.00 | 1.50 |
| ☐ 74 | Jerry Witte | 15.00 | 6.00 | 1.50 |
| ☐ 75 | Al Zarilla | 15.00 | 6.00 | 1.50 |
| ☐ 76 | Charles Barrett | 45.00 | 18.00 | 4.50 |
| ☐ 77 | Hank Camelli | 45.00 | 18.00 | 4.50 |
| ☐ 78 | Dick Culler | 45.00 | 18.00 | 4.50 |
| ☐ 79 | Nanny Fernandez | 45.00 | 18.00 | 4.50 |
| ☐ 80 | Si Johnson | 45.00 | 18.00 | 4.50 |
| ☐ 81 | Danny Litwhiler | 45.00 | 18.00 | 4.50 |
| ☐ 82 | Phil Masi | 45.00 | 18.00 | 4.50 |
| ☐ 83 | Carvel Rowell | 45.00 | 18.00 | 4.50 |
| ☐ 84 | Connie Ryan | 45.00 | 18.00 | 4.50 |
| ☐ 85 | John Sain | 75.00 | 30.00 | 7.50 |
| ☐ 86 | Ray Sanders | 45.00 | 18.00 | 4.50 |
| ☐ 87 | Sibby Sisti | 45.00 | 18.00 | 4.50 |
| ☐ 88 | Billy Southworth | 45.00 | 18.00 | 4.50 |
| ☐ 89 | Warren Spahn | 150.00 | 60.00 | 15.00 |
| ☐ 90 | Ed Wright | 45.00 | 18.00 | 4.50 |
| ☐ 91 | Bob Bragan | 15.00 | 6.00 | 1.50 |
| ☐ 92 | Ralph Branca | 20.00 | 8.00 | 2.00 |
| ☐ 93 | Hugh Casey | 15.00 | 6.00 | 1.50 |
| ☐ 94 | Bruce Edwards | 15.00 | 6.00 | 1.50 |
| ☐ 95 | Hal Gregg | 15.00 | 6.00 | 1.50 |
| ☐ 96 | Joe Hatten | 15.00 | 6.00 | 1.50 |
| ☐ 97 | Gene Hermanski | 15.00 | 6.00 | 1.50 |
| ☐ 98 | John Jorgensen | 15.00 | 6.00 | 1.50 |
| ☐ 99 | Harry Lavagetto | 15.00 | 6.00 | 1.50 |
| ☐ 100 | Vic Lombardi | 15.00 | 6.00 | 1.50 |
| ☐ 101 | Frank Melton | 15.00 | 6.00 | 1.50 |
| ☐ 102 | Ed Miksis | 15.00 | 6.00 | 1.50 |
| ☐ 103 | Marv Rackley | 15.00 | 6.00 | 1.50 |

# FIRST BASE
## SPORTS NOSTALGIA SHOP

**231 Webb Chapel Village**
**Dallas, Texas 75229**
**(214) 243-5271**

OPEN:   MONDAY THROUGH SATURDAY
11 A.M. to 7 P.M.

N
I—35 (Stemmons)
Webb Chapel
Hwy 635 (LBJ)
Forest Lane
First Base
Hwy 75 →
N. Central
Expwy

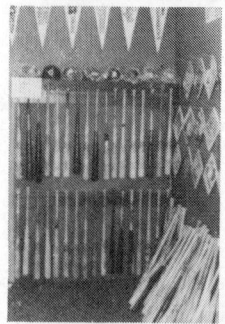

We are located on the Southeast corner of Webb Chapel and Forest just 15 minutes from the airport. Our large (1650 square foot showroom) store is convenient to all parts of Dallas being only one block south of the LBJ (635) Freeway at the Webb Chapel exit. Many collectors (and dealers) have told us that our store is the most complete they've ever seen. Just look on the opposite page for a few of our offers. We want you for a customer — please stop in and see for yourself.

Sincerely,

Wayne Grove
Gervise Ford

**FIRST
BASE**

P.S.   We are always interested in buying your cards — let us know what you have.

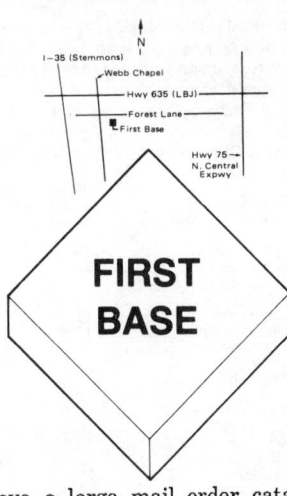

**FIRST BASE**

We have a large mail order catalog; just send us $2.00 for postage and handling for the catalog. Below is a partial list of special offers we have for sale. Include $2.00 for postage and handling per order. All inquiries require a self-addressed stamped envelope. We have most Topps, Donruss, Fleer, etc. Sets and Singles for sale. These are listed in our catalog that we will send you. Better yet, why don't you stop in some time and see for yourself.

## COMPLETE SETS

| | |
|---|---|
| 1986 Rangers Performance (28) | 6.95 |
| 1985 Rangers Performance (28) | 6.95 |
| 1984 Rangers Jarvis (28) | 5.95 |
| 1983 Rangers Affiliated (28) | 4.95 |
| 1984 Ralston Baseball (33) | 4.95 |
| 1983 Seven-Eleven 3D Coins (12) | 12.95 |
| 1983 Fleer Stamps (224) | 3.95 |
| 1983 Seven-Eleven 3D Coins (12) | 12.95 |
| 1982 K-Mart Baseball (33) | 1.50 |
| 1981 Topps 5x7 Dodgers/Angels (18) | 6.95 |
| 1978 Tucson Toros (24) | 3.95 |
| 1980 Tucson Toros (24) | 3.95 |
| 1983 Police Cowboys (28) | 9.95 |
| 1981 Police Cowboys (14) | 7.95 |
| 1980 Police Cowboys (14) | 9.95 |
| 1979 Police Cowboys (15) | 13.95 |
| 1986 McDonalds Cowboys (25) | 9.95 |
| 1986 McDonalds All-Stars (24) | 4.95 |

## BASEBALL CARD LOTS

| | |
|---|---|
| 1958 Topps 25 diff (f-vg) | 7.95 |
| 1959 Topps 25 diff (f-vg) | 6.95 |
| 1960 Topps 25 diff (f-vg) | 4.95 |
| 1961 Topps 25 diff (f-vg) | 4.50 |
| 1962 Topps 25 diff (f-vg) | 4.50 |
| 1963 Topps 25 diff (f-vg) | 3.95 |
| 1964 Topps 25 diff (f-vg) | 3.50 |
| 1965 Topps 25 diff (f-vg) | 3.50 |
| 1966 Topps 25 diff (f-vg) | 2.95 |
| 1967 Topps 25 diff (f-vg) | 2.95 |
| 1968 Topps 25 diff (f-vg) | 2.95 |
| 1969 Topps 25 diff (f-vg) | 2.95 |
| 1970 Topps 25 diff (f-vg) | 2.50 |
| 1971 Topps 25 diff (f-vg) | 2.25 |
| 1972 Topps 25 diff (f-vg) | 1.95 |
| 1973 Topps 25 diff (f-vg) | 1.75 |
| 1974 Topps 25 diff (f-vg) | 1.75 |

## SPECIAL OFFERS

**#1:** Type Set: One card from each year of Topps baseball 1952 through 1987, our choice of cards, 36 cards for 12.95.

**#2:** Baseball cigarette card from 1910, our choice 5.95.

**#3:** 500 assorted (mostly different) baseball cards from 1978 to 1984 in excellent condition for 19.95.

**#4:** Dallas Cowboy Weekly: 20 different back issues, our choice, for 14.95. We also have most single issues from 1977 to date available from 1.00 to 2.00 each. Send your want list. Some older issues also available.

**#5:** Poster: Robert Redford as "The Natural" plus free Bucky Dent poster, 6.95 postpaid.

**#6:** 1978 Topps baseball cards 50 different in excellent to mint condition, 3.95.

**#7:** 1979 Topps baseball cards 50 different in excellent to mint condition including some stars, 3.95.

**#8:** 1980 Topps baseball cards 50 different in excellent to mint condition including some stars, 3.95.

**#9:** 1981 Topps baseball cards 50 different in excellent to mint condition including some stars, 3.95.

**#10:** 89 different 1984-85 Topps hockey cards in excellent to mint condition including some stars, 2.95.

**#11:** 66 different 1981-82 Topps basketball cards in excellent to mint condition including stars, 3.95.

**#12:** 115 different 1983 Topps football cards in excellent to mint condition including many stars, 2.95.

**#13:** Super Bowl XX game program, 5.00.

**#14:** 1979 Scottsdale Dodge Arizona Convention postcard set of 9 including Jocko Conlon, Charlie Grimm, etc. for 3.50.

**#15:** Dallas Cowboy Media Guide (not issued to the public): 1986 edition 5.00, 1985 edition 5.00. Dallas Cowboy Bluebook: 1986 edition 13.95, 1985 edition 13.95.

## FIRST BASE

231 Webb Chapel Village

Dallas, Texas 75229

(214) 243-5271

| | | | | |
|---|---|---|---|---|
| ☐ 104 | Ed Stevens | 15.00 | 6.00 | 1.50 |
| ☐ 105 | Phil Cavarretta | 60.00 | 24.00 | 6.00 |
| ☐ 106 | Bob Chipman | 45.00 | 18.00 | 4.50 |
| ☐ 107 | Stanley Hack | 45.00 | 18.00 | 4.50 |
| ☐ 108 | Don Johnson | 45.00 | 18.00 | 4.50 |
| ☐ 109 | Emil Kush | 45.00 | 18.00 | 4.50 |
| ☐ 110 | Bill Lee | 45.00 | 18.00 | 4.50 |
| ☐ 111 | Mickey Livingston | 45.00 | 18.00 | 4.50 |
| ☐ 112 | Harry Lowrey | 45.00 | 18.00 | 4.50 |
| ☐ 113 | Clyde McCullough | 45.00 | 18.00 | 4.50 |
| ☐ 114 | Andy Pafko | 45.00 | 18.00 | 4.50 |
| ☐ 115 | Marv Rickert | 45.00 | 18.00 | 4.50 |
| ☐ 116 | John Schmitz | 45.00 | 18.00 | 4.50 |
| ☐ 117 | Bobby Sturgeon | 45.00 | 18.00 | 4.50 |
| ☐ 118 | Ed Waitkus | 45.00 | 18.00 | 4.50 |
| ☐ 119 | Henry Wyse | 45.00 | 18.00 | 4.50 |
| ☐ 120 | Bill Ayers | 15.00 | 6.00 | 1.50 |
| ☐ 121 | Robert Blattner | 15.00 | 6.00 | 1.50 |
| ☐ 122 | Mike Budnick | 15.00 | 6.00 | 1.50 |
| ☐ 123 | Sid Gordon | 15.00 | 6.00 | 1.50 |
| ☐ 124 | Clinton Hartung | 15.00 | 6.00 | 1.50 |
| ☐ 125 | Monte Kennedy | 15.00 | 6.00 | 1.50 |
| ☐ 126 | Dave Koslo | 15.00 | 6.00 | 1.50 |
| ☐ 127 | Carroll Lockman | 15.00 | 6.00 | 1.50 |
| ☐ 128 | Jack Lohrke | 15.00 | 6.00 | 1.50 |
| ☐ 129 | Ernie Lombardi | 25.00 | 10.00 | 2.50 |
| ☐ 130 | Willard Marshall | 15.00 | 6.00 | 1.50 |
| ☐ 131 | John Mize | 40.00 | 16.00 | 4.00 |
| ☐ 132 | Eugene Thompson (does not exist) | 0.00 | 0.00 | 0.00 |
| ☐ 133 | Ken Trinkle | 15.00 | 6.00 | 1.50 |
| ☐ 134 | Bill Voiselle | 15.00 | 6.00 | 1.50 |
| ☐ 135 | Mickey Witek | 15.00 | 6.00 | 1.50 |
| ☐ 136 | Eddie Basinski | 15.00 | 6.00 | 1.50 |
| ☐ 137 | Ernie Bonham | 15.00 | 6.00 | 1.50 |
| ☐ 138 | Bill Cox | 15.00 | 6.00 | 1.50 |
| ☐ 139 | Elbie Fletcher | 15.00 | 6.00 | 1.50 |
| ☐ 140 | Frank Gustine | 15.00 | 6.00 | 1.50 |
| ☐ 141 | Kirby Higbe | 15.00 | 6.00 | 1.50 |
| ☐ 142 | Leroy Jarvis | 15.00 | 6.00 | 1.50 |
| ☐ 143 | Ralph Kiner | 40.00 | 16.00 | 4.00 |
| ☐ 144 | Fred Ostermueller | 15.00 | 6.00 | 1.50 |
| ☐ 145 | Preacher Roe | 20.00 | 8.00 | 2.00 |
| ☐ 146 | Jim Russell | 15.00 | 6.00 | 1.50 |
| ☐ 147 | Rip Sewell | 15.00 | 6.00 | 1.50 |
| ☐ 148 | Nick Strincevich | 15.00 | 6.00 | 1.50 |
| ☐ 149 | Honus Wagner | 50.00 | 20.00 | 5.00 |
| ☐ 150 | Alpha Brazle | 15.00 | 6.00 | 1.50 |
| ☐ 151 | Ken Burkhart | 15.00 | 6.00 | 1.50 |
| ☐ 152 | Bernard Creger | 15.00 | 6.00 | 1.50 |
| ☐ 153 | Joffre Cross | 15.00 | 6.00 | 1.50 |
| ☐ 154 | Charles E. Diering | 15.00 | 6.00 | 1.50 |
| ☐ 155 | Ervin Dusak | 15.00 | 6.00 | 1.50 |
| ☐ 156 | Joe Garagiola | 40.00 | 16.00 | 4.00 |
| ☐ 157 | Tony Kaufmann | 15.00 | 6.00 | 1.50 |
| ☐ 158 | George Kurowski | 15.00 | 6.00 | 1.50 |
| ☐ 159 | Marty Marion | 20.00 | 8.00 | 2.00 |
| ☐ 160 | George Munger | 15.00 | 6.00 | 1.50 |
| ☐ 161 | Del Rice | 15.00 | 6.00 | 1.50 |
| ☐ 162 | Dick Sisler | 15.00 | 6.00 | 1.50 |
| ☐ 163 | Enos Slaughter | 40.00 | 16.00 | 4.00 |
| ☐ 164 | Ted Wilks | 15.00 | 6.00 | 1.50 |

## 1951 Topps Blue Backs

The cards in this 52 card set measure 2" by 2 5/8". The 1951 Topps series of blue backed baseball cards could be used to play a baseball game by shuffling the cards and drawing them from a pile. These cards

were marketed with a piece of caramel candy, which often melted or was squashed in such a way as to damage the card and wrapper (despite the fact that a paper shield was inserted between candy and card). Blue Backs are more difficult to obtain than the similarly styled Red Backs. Appropriately leading off the set is Eddie Yost.

| | | | MINT | VG-E | F-G |
|---|---|---|---|---|---|
| COMPLETE SET | | | 550.00 | 220.00 | 55.00 |
| COMMON PLAYER (1-52) | | | 10.00 | 4.00 | 1.00 |
| ☐ 1 | Eddie Yost | | 15.00 | 5.00 | 1.00 |
| ☐ 2 | Hank Majeski | | 10.00 | 4.00 | 1.00 |
| ☐ 3 | Richie Ashburn | | 20.00 | 8.00 | 2.00 |
| ☐ 4 | Del Ennis | | 11.00 | 4.50 | 1.10 |
| ☐ 5 | Johnny Pesky | | 11.00 | 4.50 | 1.10 |
| ☐ 6 | Al Schoendienst | | 15.00 | 6.00 | 1.50 |
| ☐ 7 | Gerry Staley | | 10.00 | 4.00 | 1.00 |
| ☐ 8 | Dick Sisler | | 10.00 | 4.00 | 1.00 |
| ☐ 9 | Johnny Sain | | 15.00 | 6.00 | 1.50 |
| ☐ 10 | Joe Page | | 12.00 | 5.00 | 1.20 |
| ☐ 11 | Johnny Groth | | 10.00 | 4.00 | 1.00 |
| ☐ 12 | Sam Jethroe | | 10.00 | 4.00 | 1.00 |
| ☐ 13 | Mickey Vernon | | 12.00 | 5.00 | 1.20 |
| ☐ 14 | Red Munger | | 10.00 | 4.00 | 1.00 |
| ☐ 15 | Eddie Joost | | 10.00 | 4.00 | 1.00 |
| ☐ 16 | Murry Dickson | | 10.00 | 4.00 | 1.00 |
| ☐ 17 | Roy Smalley | | 10.00 | 4.00 | 1.00 |
| ☐ 18 | Ned Garver | | 10.00 | 4.00 | 1.00 |
| ☐ 19 | Phil Masi | | 10.00 | 4.00 | 1.00 |
| ☐ 20 | Ralph Branca | | 12.00 | 5.00 | 1.20 |
| ☐ 21 | Billy Johnson | | 10.00 | 4.00 | 1.00 |
| ☐ 22 | Bob Kuzava | | 10.00 | 4.00 | 1.00 |
| ☐ 23 | Dizzy Trout | | 10.00 | 4.00 | 1.00 |
| ☐ 24 | Sherman Lollar | | 11.00 | 4.50 | 1.10 |
| ☐ 25 | Sam Mele | | 10.00 | 4.00 | 1.00 |
| ☐ 26 | Chico Carrasquel | | 10.00 | 4.00 | 1.00 |
| ☐ 27 | Andy Pafko | | 10.00 | 4.00 | 1.00 |
| ☐ 28 | Harry Brecheen | | 10.00 | 4.00 | 1.00 |
| ☐ 29 | Granville Hamner | | 10.00 | 4.00 | 1.00 |
| ☐ 30 | Enos Slaughter | | 25.00 | 10.00 | 2.50 |
| ☐ 31 | Lou Brissie | | 10.00 | 4.00 | 1.00 |
| ☐ 32 | Bob Elliott | | 12.00 | 5.00 | 1.20 |
| ☐ 33 | Don Lenhardt | | 10.00 | 4.00 | 1.00 |
| ☐ 34 | Earl Torgeson | | 10.00 | 4.00 | 1.00 |
| ☐ 35 | Tommy Byrne | | 11.00 | 4.50 | 1.10 |
| ☐ 36 | Cliff Fannin | | 10.00 | 4.00 | 1.00 |
| ☐ 37 | Bobby Doerr | | 20.00 | 8.00 | 2.00 |
| ☐ 38 | Irv Noren | | 10.00 | 4.00 | 1.00 |
| ☐ 39 | Ed Lopat | | 15.00 | 6.00 | 1.50 |
| ☐ 40 | Vic Wertz | | 10.00 | 4.00 | 1.00 |
| ☐ 41 | Johnny Schmitz | | 10.00 | 4.00 | 1.00 |
| ☐ 42 | Bruce Edwards | | 10.00 | 4.00 | 1.00 |
| ☐ 43 | Willie Jones | | 10.00 | 4.00 | 1.00 |
| ☐ 44 | Johnny Wyrostek | | 10.00 | 4.00 | 1.00 |
| ☐ 45 | Billy Pierce | | 12.00 | 5.00 | 1.20 |
| ☐ 46 | Gerry Priddy | | 10.00 | 4.00 | 1.00 |
| ☐ 47 | Herman Wehmeier | | 10.00 | 4.00 | 1.00 |
| ☐ 48 | Billy Cox | | 11.00 | 4.50 | 1.10 |
| ☐ 49 | Henry Sauer | | 11.00 | 4.50 | 1.10 |
| ☐ 50 | Johnny Mize | | 25.00 | 10.00 | 2.50 |
| ☐ 51 | Eddie Waitkus | | 10.00 | 4.00 | 1.00 |
| ☐ 52 | Sam Chapman | | 11.00 | 4.50 | 1.10 |

## 1951 Topps Red Backs

The cards in this 52 card set measure 2" by 2 5/8". The 1951 Topps Red Back set is identical in style to the Blue Back set of the same year. The cards have rounded corners and were designed to be used as a baseball game. Zernial, number 36, is listed with either the White Sox or Athletics, and Holmes, number 52, with either the Braves or Hartford.

| | | | MINT | VG-E | F-G |
|---|---|---|---|---|---|
| COMPLETE SET | | | 225.00 | 90.00 | 22.00 |
| COMMON PLAYER (1-52) | | | 2.50 | 1.00 | .25 |
| ☐ 1 | Yogi Berra | | 30.00 | 10.00 | 2.00 |
| ☐ 2 | Sid Gordon | | 2.50 | 1.00 | .25 |
| ☐ 3 | Ferris Fain | | 3.00 | 1.20 | .30 |
| ☐ 4 | Vern Stephens | | 2.50 | 1.00 | .25 |

| | MINT | VG-E | F-G |
|---|---|---|---|
| COMPLETE SET ........................ | 900.00 | 360.00 | 90.00 |
| COMMON PLAYER (1-9) ........... | 90.00 | 36.00 | 9.00 |
| ☐ 1 Boston Red Sox ................. | 150.00 | 60.00 | 15.00 |
| ☐ 2 Brooklyn Dodgers .............. | 125.00 | 50.00 | 12.50 |
| ☐ 3 Chicago White Sox ............. | 125.00 | 50.00 | 12.50 |
| ☐ 4 Cincinnati Reds ................. | 90.00 | 36.00 | 9.00 |
| ☐ 5 New York Giants ............... | 125.00 | 50.00 | 12.50 |
| ☐ 6 Philadelphia Athletics ......... | 90.00 | 36.00 | 9.00 |
| ☐ 7 Philadelphia Phillies ........... | 90.00 | 36.00 | 9.00 |
| ☐ 8 St. Louis Cardinals ............. | 150.00 | 60.00 | 15.00 |
| ☐ 9 Washington Senators .......... | 90.00 | 36.00 | 9.00 |

| | | | |
|---|---|---|---|
| ☐ 5 Phil Rizzuto ....................... | 12.00 | 5.00 | 1.20 |
| ☐ 6 Allie Reynolds ................... | 4.50 | 1.80 | .45 |
| ☐ 7 Howie Pollet ...................... | 2.50 | 1.00 | .25 |
| ☐ 8 Early Wynn ........................ | 8.00 | 3.25 | .80 |
| ☐ 9 Roy Sievers ....................... | 2.50 | 1.00 | .25 |
| ☐ 10 Mel Parnell ...................... | 2.50 | 1.00 | .25 |
| ☐ 11 Gene Hermanski ............... | 2.50 | 1.00 | .25 |
| ☐ 12 Jim Hegan ....................... | 2.50 | 1.00 | .25 |
| ☐ 13 Dale Mitchell .................... | 2.50 | 1.00 | .25 |
| ☐ 14 Wayne Terwilliger ............. | 2.50 | 1.00 | .25 |
| ☐ 15 Ralph Kiner ...................... | 9.00 | 3.75 | .90 |
| ☐ 16 Preacher Roe ................... | 4.50 | 1.80 | .45 |
| ☐ 17 Dave (Gus) Bell ............... | 3.50 | 1.40 | .35 |
| ☐ 18 Gerry Coleman ................. | 3.00 | 1.20 | .30 |
| ☐ 19 Dick Kokos ...................... | 2.50 | 1.00 | .25 |
| ☐ 20 Dom DiMaggio .................. | 4.50 | 1.80 | .45 |
| ☐ 21 Larry Jansen .................... | 2.50 | 1.00 | .25 |
| ☐ 22 Bob Feller ........................ | 14.00 | 5.75 | 1.40 |
| ☐ 23 Ray Boone ....................... | 3.00 | 1.20 | .30 |
| ☐ 24 Hank Bauer ...................... | 4.00 | 1.60 | .40 |
| ☐ 25 Cliff Chambers ................. | 2.50 | 1.00 | .25 |
| ☐ 26 Luke Easter ...................... | 3.00 | 1.20 | .30 |
| ☐ 27 Wally Westlake ................. | 2.50 | 1.00 | .25 |
| ☐ 28 Elmer Valo ....................... | 2.50 | 1.00 | .25 |
| ☐ 29 Bob Kennedy .................... | 2.50 | 1.00 | .25 |
| ☐ 30 Warren Spahn .................. | 12.00 | 5.00 | 1.20 |
| ☐ 31 Gil Hodges ....................... | 12.00 | 5.00 | 1.20 |
| ☐ 32 Henry Thompson .............. | 3.00 | 1.20 | .30 |
| ☐ 33 William Werle ................... | 2.50 | 1.00 | .25 |
| ☐ 34 Grady Hatton .................... | 2.50 | 1.00 | .25 |
| ☐ 35 Al Rosen ......................... | 4.50 | 1.80 | .45 |
| ☐ 36A Gus Zernial (Chicago) .... | 12.50 | 5.00 | 1.25 |
| ☐ 36B Gus Zernial (Phila.) ........ | 8.00 | 3.25 | .80 |
| ☐ 37 Wes Westrum .................. | 2.50 | 1.00 | .25 |
| ☐ 38 Duke Snider ..................... | 18.00 | 7.25 | 1.80 |
| ☐ 39 Ted Kluszewski ................ | 4.50 | 1.80 | .45 |
| ☐ 40 Mike Garcia ..................... | 3.00 | 1.20 | .30 |
| ☐ 41 Whitey Lockman ............... | 2.50 | 1.00 | .25 |
| ☐ 42 Ray Scarborough .............. | 2.50 | 1.00 | .25 |
| ☐ 43 Maurice McDermott ......... | 2.50 | 1.00 | .25 |
| ☐ 44 Sid Hudson ...................... | 2.50 | 1.00 | .25 |
| ☐ 45 Andy Seminick .................. | 2.50 | 1.00 | .25 |
| ☐ 46 Billy Goodman ................. | 2.50 | 1.00 | .25 |
| ☐ 47 Tommy Glaviano ............... | 2.50 | 1.00 | .25 |
| ☐ 48 Eddie Stanky .................... | 3.00 | 1.20 | .30 |
| ☐ 49 Al Zarilla ......................... | 2.50 | 1.00 | .25 |
| ☐ 50 Monte Irvin ...................... | 12.00 | 5.00 | 1.20 |
| ☐ 51 Eddie Robinson ................ | 2.50 | 1.00 | .25 |
| ☐ 52A Tommy Holmes ............... | 14.00 | 5.75 | 1.40 |
| (Boston) | | | |
| ☐ 52B Tommy Holmes ............... | 9.00 | 3.75 | .90 |
| (Hartford) | | | |

## 1951 Topps Teams

The cards in this 9 card set measure 2 1/16" by 5 1/4". These unnumbered team cards issued by Topps in 1951 carry black and white photographs framed by a yellow border. They are found with or without "1950" printed in the name panel before the team name (no difference in value for either variety). These cards were issued in the same 5 cent wrapper as the Connie Mack and Current All Stars. They have been assigned reference numbers in the checklist alphabetically by team city and name.

## 1951 Topps Connie Mack

The cards in this 11 card set measure 2 1/16" by 5 1/4". The series of die-cut cards which comprise the set entitled Connie Mack All-Stars was one of Topps' most distinctive and fragile card designs. Printed on thin cardboard, these elegant cards were protected in the wrapper by panels of accompanying Red Backs, but once removed were easily damaged (after all, they were intended to be folded and used as toy figures). Cards without tops have a value less than one-half of that listed below. The cards are unnumbered and are listed below in alphabetical order.

| | MINT | VG-E | F-G |
|---|---|---|---|
| COMPLETE SET ........................ | 2750.00 | 1200.00 | 300.00 |
| COMMON PLAYER (1-11) ......... | 90.00 | 36.00 | 9.00 |
| ☐ 1 Grover C. Alexander ........ | 300.00 | 120.00 | 30.00 |
| ☐ 2 Mickey Cochrane ............. | 200.00 | 80.00 | 20.00 |
| ☐ 3 Ed Collins ....................... | 120.00 | 50.00 | 12.00 |
| ☐ 4 Jimmy Collins .................. | 90.00 | 36.00 | 9.00 |
| ☐ 5 Lou Gehrig ...................... | 700.00 | 280.00 | 70.00 |
| ☐ 6 Walter Johnson ............... | 400.00 | 160.00 | 40.00 |
| ☐ 7 Connie Mack ................... | 200.00 | 80.00 | 20.00 |
| ☐ 8 Christy Mathewson .......... | 200.00 | 80.00 | 20.00 |
| ☐ 9 Babe Ruth ...................... | 700.00 | 280.00 | 70.00 |
| ☐ 10 Tris Speaker ................... | 120.00 | 50.00 | 12.00 |
| ☐ 11 Honus Wagner ................ | 200.00 | 80.00 | 20.00 |

## 1951 Topps Current AS

The cards in this 11 card set measure 2 1/16" by 5 1/4". The 1951 Topps Current All-Star series is probably the rarest of all legitimate, regularly issued, post war baseball issues. The set price listed below does not include the prices for the cards of Konstanty, Roberts and Stanky, which likely never were released to the public in gum packs. These three cards (asterisked in the checklist below) were probably obtained directly from the company and exist in extremely limited numbers. As with the Connie Mack set, cards without the die-cut background are worth half of the value listed below. The cards are unnumbered and are listed below in alphabetical order.

| | MINT | VG-E | F-G |
|---|---|---|---|
| COMPLETE SET (8) .................... | 2250.00 | 1000.00 | 250.00 |
| COMMON PLAYER (1-11) ......... | 150.00 | 60.00 | 15.00 |
| ☐ 1 Yogi Berra ....................... | 500.00 | 200.00 | 50.00 |
| ☐ 2 Larry Doby ...................... | 200.00 | 80.00 | 20.00 |
| ☐ 3 Walt Dropo ..................... | 250.00 | 100.00 | 25.00 |
| ☐ 4 Hoot Evers ...................... | 150.00 | 60.00 | 15.00 |

| | | | | | |
|---|---|---|---|---|---|
| ☐ | 5 | George Kell | 350.00 | 140.00 | 35.00 |
| ☐ | 6 | Ralph Kiner | 350.00 | 140.00 | 35.00 |
| ☐ | 7 | Jim Konstanty * | 4000.00 | 1600.00 | 400.00 |
| ☐ | 8 | Bob Lemon | 350.00 | 140.00 | 35.00 |
| ☐ | 9 | Phil Rizzuto | 350.00 | 140.00 | 35.00 |
| ☐ | 10 | Robin Roberts * | 4000.00 | 1600.00 | 400.00 |
| ☐ | 11 | Eddie Stanky * | 4000.00 | 1600.00 | 400.00 |

## 1952 Topps

 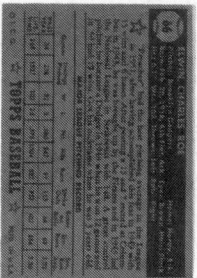

The cards in this 407 card set measure 2 5/8" by 3 3/4". The 1952 Topps set is Topps' first truly major set. Card numbers 1 to 80 were issued with red or black backs, both of which are less plentiful than card numbers 81 to 250. Card number 48 (Joe Page) and number 49 (Johnny Sain) can be found with each other's write-up on their back. Card numbers 251 to 310 are somewhat scarce and numbers 311 to 407 are quite scarce. Cards 281-300 were single printed compared to the other cards in the next to last series. Cards 311-313 were double printed on the last high number printing sheet. The key card in the set is obviously Mickey Mantle #311, Mickey's first of many Topps cards.

| | MINT | VG-E | F-G |
|---|---|---|---|
| COMPLETE SET | 18000.00 | 7500.00 | 2000. |
| COMMON PLAYER (1-80) | 14.00 | 6.50 | 1.60 |
| COMMON PLAYER (81-250) | 8.00 | 3.25 | .80 |
| COMMON PLAYER (251-280) | 16.00 | 6.50 | 1.60 |
| COMMON PLAYER (281-300) | 20.00 | 8.00 | 2.00 |
| COMMON PLAYER (301-310) | 16.00 | 6.50 | 1.60 |
| COMMON PLAYER (311-407) | 75.00 | 30.00 | 7.50 |

| | | | | | |
|---|---|---|---|---|---|
| ☐ | 1 | Andy Pafko | 350.00 | 15.00 | 3.00 |
| ☐ | 2 | James Pete Runnels | 17.00 | 7.25 | 1.80 |
| ☐ | 3 | Henry Thompson | 17.00 | 7.25 | 1.80 |
| ☐ | 4 | Don Lenhardt | 14.00 | 6.50 | 1.60 |
| ☐ | 5 | Larry Jansen | 14.00 | 6.50 | 1.60 |
| ☐ | 6 | Grady Hatton | 14.00 | 6.50 | 1.60 |
| ☐ | 7 | Wayne Terwilliger | 14.00 | 6.50 | 1.60 |
| ☐ | 8 | Fred Marsh | 14.00 | 6.50 | 1.60 |
| ☐ | 9 | Robert Hogue | 14.00 | 6.50 | 1.60 |
| ☐ | 10 | Al Rosen | 24.00 | 10.00 | 2.50 |
| ☐ | 11 | Phil Rizzuto | 60.00 | 24.00 | 6.00 |
| ☐ | 12 | Romanus Basgall | 14.00 | 6.50 | 1.60 |
| ☐ | 13 | Johnny Wyrostek | 14.00 | 6.50 | 1.60 |
| ☐ | 14 | Bob Elliott | 17.00 | 7.25 | 1.80 |
| ☐ | 15 | Johnny Pesky | 17.00 | 7.25 | 1.80 |
| ☐ | 16 | Gene Hermanski | 14.00 | 6.50 | 1.60 |
| ☐ | 17 | Jim Hegan | 17.00 | 6.50 | 1.60 |
| ☐ | 18 | Merrill Combs | 14.00 | 6.50 | 1.60 |
| ☐ | 19 | Johnny Bucha | 14.00 | 6.50 | 1.60 |
| ☐ | 20 | Billy Loes | 24.00 | 10.00 | 2.50 |
| ☐ | 21 | Ferris Fain | 17.00 | 7.25 | 1.80 |
| ☐ | 22 | Dom DiMaggio | 24.00 | 10.00 | 2.50 |
| ☐ | 23 | Billy Goodman | 17.00 | 7.25 | 1.80 |
| ☐ | 24 | Luke Easter | 17.00 | 7.25 | 1.80 |
| ☐ | 25 | John Groth | 14.00 | 6.50 | 1.60 |
| ☐ | 26 | Monte Irvin | 30.00 | 13.00 | 3.20 |
| ☐ | 27 | Sam Jethroe | 14.00 | 6.50 | 1.60 |

| | | | | | |
|---|---|---|---|---|---|
| ☐ | 28 | Jerry Priddy | 14.00 | 6.50 | 1.60 |
| ☐ | 29 | Ted Kluszewski | 24.00 | 10.00 | 2.50 |
| ☐ | 30 | Mel Parnell | 17.00 | 7.25 | 1.80 |
| ☐ | 31 | Gus Zernial | 17.00 | 7.25 | 1.80 |
| ☐ | 32 | Eddie Robinson | 14.00 | 6.50 | 1.60 |
| ☐ | 33 | Warren Spahn | 70.00 | 30.00 | 7.50 |
| ☐ | 34 | Elmer Valo | 14.00 | 6.50 | 1.60 |
| ☐ | 35 | Hank Sauer | 17.00 | 7.25 | 1.80 |
| ☐ | 36 | Gil Hodges | 50.00 | 20.00 | 5.00 |
| ☐ | 37 | Duke Snider | 90.00 | 36.00 | 9.00 |
| ☐ | 38 | Wally Westlake | 14.00 | 6.50 | 1.60 |
| ☐ | 39 | Dizzy Trout | 14.00 | 6.50 | 1.60 |
| ☐ | 40 | Irv Noren | 14.00 | 6.50 | 1.60 |
| ☐ | 41 | Bob Wellman | 14.00 | 6.50 | 1.60 |
| ☐ | 42 | Lou Kretlow | 14.00 | 6.50 | 1.60 |
| ☐ | 43 | Ray Scarborough | 14.00 | 6.50 | 1.60 |
| ☐ | 44 | Con Dempsey | 14.00 | 6.50 | 1.60 |
| ☐ | 45 | Eddie Joost | 14.00 | 6.50 | 1.60 |
| ☐ | 46 | Gordon Goldsberry | 14.00 | 6.50 | 1.60 |
| ☐ | 47 | Willie Jones | 14.00 | 6.50 | 1.60 |
| ☐ | 48A | Joe Page COR | 20.00 | 8.00 | 2.00 |
| ☐ | 48B | Joe Page ERR | 150.00 | 60.00 | 15.00 |
| ☐ | 49A | Johnny Sain COR | 20.00 | 8.00 | 2.00 |
| ☐ | 49B | Johnny Sain ERR | 150.00 | 60.00 | 15.00 |
| ☐ | 50 | Marv Rickert | 14.00 | 6.50 | 1.60 |
| ☐ | 51 | Jim Russell | 14.00 | 6.50 | 1.60 |
| ☐ | 52 | Don Mueller | 17.00 | 7.25 | 1.80 |
| ☐ | 53 | Chris Van Cuyk | 14.00 | 6.50 | 1.60 |
| ☐ | 54 | Leo Kiely | 14.00 | 6.50 | 1.60 |
| ☐ | 55 | Ray Boone | 17.00 | 7.25 | 1.80 |
| ☐ | 56 | Thomas Glaviano | 14.00 | 6.50 | 1.60 |
| ☐ | 57 | Ed Lopat | 24.00 | 10.00 | 2.50 |
| ☐ | 58 | Bob Mahoney | 14.00 | 6.50 | 1.60 |
| ☐ | 59 | Robin Roberts | 45.00 | 18.00 | 4.50 |
| ☐ | 60 | Sid Hudson | 14.00 | 6.50 | 1.60 |
| ☐ | 61 | Tookie Gilbert | 14.00 | 6.50 | 1.60 |
| ☐ | 62 | Chuck Stobbs | 14.00 | 6.50 | 1.60 |
| ☐ | 63 | Howie Pollet | 14.00 | 6.50 | 1.60 |
| ☐ | 64 | Roy Sievers | 17.00 | 7.25 | 1.80 |
| ☐ | 65 | Enos Slaughter | 40.00 | 16.00 | 4.00 |
| ☐ | 66 | Preacher Roe | 24.00 | 10.00 | 2.50 |
| ☐ | 67 | Allie Reynolds | 24.00 | 10.00 | 2.50 |
| ☐ | 68 | Cliff Chambers | 14.00 | 6.50 | 1.60 |
| ☐ | 69 | Virgil Stallcup | 14.00 | 6.50 | 1.60 |
| ☐ | 70 | Al Zarilla | 14.00 | 6.50 | 1.60 |
| ☐ | 71 | Tom Upton | 14.00 | 6.50 | 1.60 |
| ☐ | 72 | Karl Olson | 14.00 | 6.50 | 1.60 |
| ☐ | 73 | William Werle | 14.00 | 6.50 | 1.60 |
| ☐ | 74 | Andy Hansen | 14.00 | 6.50 | 1.60 |
| ☐ | 75 | Wes Westrum | 14.00 | 6.50 | 1.60 |
| ☐ | 76 | Eddie Stanky | 17.00 | 7.25 | 1.80 |
| ☐ | 77 | Bob Kennedy | 14.00 | 6.50 | 1.60 |
| ☐ | 78 | Ellis Kinder | 14.00 | 6.50 | 1.60 |
| ☐ | 79 | Gerald Staley | 14.00 | 6.50 | 1.60 |
| ☐ | 80 | Herman Wehmeier | 14.00 | 6.50 | 1.60 |
| ☐ | 81 | Vernon Law | 10.00 | 4.00 | 1.00 |
| ☐ | 82 | Duane Pillette | 8.00 | 3.25 | .80 |
| ☐ | 83 | Billy Johnson | 8.00 | 3.25 | .80 |
| ☐ | 84 | Vern Stephens | 9.00 | 3.75 | .90 |
| ☐ | 85 | Bob Kuzava | 8.00 | 3.25 | .80 |
| ☐ | 86 | Ted Gray | 8.00 | 3.25 | .80 |
| ☐ | 87 | Dale Coogan | 8.00 | 3.25 | .80 |
| ☐ | 88 | Bob Feller | 50.00 | 20.00 | 5.00 |
| ☐ | 89 | Johnny Lipon | 8.00 | 3.25 | .80 |
| ☐ | 90 | Mickey Grasso | 8.00 | 3.25 | .80 |
| ☐ | 91 | Red Schoendienst | 12.00 | 5.00 | 1.20 |
| ☐ | 92 | Dale Mitchell | 9.00 | 3.75 | .90 |
| ☐ | 93 | Al Sima | 8.00 | 3.25 | .80 |
| ☐ | 94 | Sam Mele | 8.00 | 3.25 | .80 |
| ☐ | 95 | Ken Holcombe | 8.00 | 3.25 | .80 |
| ☐ | 96 | Willard Marshall | 8.00 | 3.25 | .80 |
| ☐ | 97 | Earl Torgeson | 8.00 | 3.25 | .80 |
| ☐ | 98 | Billy Pierce | 10.00 | 4.00 | 1.00 |
| ☐ | 99 | Gene Woodling | 10.00 | 4.00 | 1.00 |
| ☐ | 100 | Del Rice | 8.00 | 3.25 | .80 |
| ☐ | 101 | Max Lanier | 8.00 | 3.25 | .80 |
| ☐ | 102 | Bill Kennedy | 8.00 | 3.25 | .80 |
| ☐ | 103 | Cliff Mapes | 8.00 | 3.25 | .80 |
| ☐ | 104 | Don Kolloway | 8.00 | 3.25 | .80 |
| ☐ | 105 | John Pramesa | 8.00 | 3.25 | .80 |
| ☐ | 106 | Mickey Vernon | 10.00 | 4.00 | 1.00 |
| ☐ | 107 | Connie Ryan | 8.00 | 3.25 | .80 |
| ☐ | 108 | Jim Konstanty | 10.00 | 4.00 | 1.00 |
| ☐ | 109 | Ted Wilks | 8.00 | 3.25 | .80 |
| ☐ | 110 | Dutch Leonard | 8.00 | 3.25 | .80 |
| ☐ | 111 | Peanuts Lowrey | 8.00 | 3.25 | .80 |
| ☐ | 112 | Henry Majeski | 8.00 | 3.25 | .80 |
| ☐ | 113 | Dick Sisler | 8.00 | 3.25 | .80 |
| ☐ | 114 | Willard Ramsdell | 8.00 | 3.25 | .80 |
| ☐ | 115 | Red Munger | 8.00 | 3.25 | .80 |
| ☐ | 116 | Carl Scheib | 8.00 | 3.25 | .80 |
| ☐ | 117 | Sherman Lollar | 9.00 | 3.75 | .90 |
| ☐ | 118 | Ken Raffensberger | 8.00 | 3.25 | .80 |

| | | | | | | | | | |
|---|---|---|---|---|---|---|---|---|---|
| ☐ 119 | Mickey McDermott | 8.00 | 3.25 | .80 | ☐ 212 | Ned Garver | 8.00 | 3.25 | .80 |
| ☐ 120 | Bob Chakales | 8.00 | 3.25 | .80 | ☐ 213 | Nippy Jones | 8.00 | 3.25 | .80 |
| ☐ 121 | Gus Niarhos | 8.00 | 3.25 | .80 | ☐ 214 | Johnny Hopp | 9.00 | 3.75 | .90 |
| ☐ 122 | Jackie Jensen | 18.00 | 7.25 | 1.80 | ☐ 215 | Hank Bauer | 16.00 | 6.50 | 1.60 |
| ☐ 123 | Eddie Yost | 9.00 | 3.75 | .90 | ☐ 216 | Richie Ashburn | 21.00 | 8.50 | 2.10 |
| ☐ 124 | Monte Kennedy | 8.00 | 3.25 | .80 | ☐ 217 | Snuffy Stirnweiss | 9.00 | 3.75 | .90 |
| ☐ 125 | Bill Rigney | 8.00 | 3.25 | .80 | ☐ 218 | Clyde McCullough | 8.00 | 3.25 | .80 |
| ☐ 126 | Fred Hutchinson | 10.00 | 4.00 | 1.00 | ☐ 219 | Bobby Shantz | 12.00 | 5.00 | 1.20 |
| ☐ 127 | Paul Minner | 8.00 | 3.25 | .80 | ☐ 220 | Joe Presko | 8.00 | 3.25 | .80 |
| ☐ 128 | Don Bollweg | 8.00 | 3.25 | .80 | ☐ 221 | Granny Hamner | 8.00 | 3.25 | .80 |
| ☐ 129 | Johnny Mize | 25.00 | 10.00 | 2.50 | ☐ 222 | Hoot Evers | 8.00 | 3.25 | .80 |
| ☐ 130 | Sheldon Jones | 8.00 | 3.25 | .80 | ☐ 223 | Del Ennis | 10.00 | 4.00 | 1.00 |
| ☐ 131 | Morris Martin | 8.00 | 3.25 | .80 | ☐ 224 | Bruce Edwards | 8.00 | 3.25 | .80 |
| ☐ 132 | Clyde Klutz | 8.00 | 3.25 | .80 | ☐ 225 | Frank Baumholtz | 8.00 | 3.25 | .80 |
| ☐ 133 | Al Widmar | 8.00 | 3.25 | .80 | ☐ 226 | Dave Philley | 8.00 | 3.25 | .80 |
| ☐ 134 | Joe Tipton | 8.00 | 3.25 | .80 | ☐ 227 | Joe Garagiola | 25.00 | 10.00 | 2.50 |
| ☐ 135 | Dixie Howell | 8.00 | 3.25 | .80 | ☐ 228 | Al Brazle | 8.00 | 3.25 | .80 |
| ☐ 136 | Johnny Schmitz | 8.00 | 3.25 | .80 | ☐ 229 | Gene Bearden | 8.00 | 3.25 | .80 |
| ☐ 137 | Roy McMillan | 8.00 | 3.25 | .80 | ☐ 230 | Matt Batts | 8.00 | 3.25 | .80 |
| ☐ 138 | Bill MacDonald | 8.00 | 3.25 | .80 | ☐ 231 | Sam Zoldak | 8.00 | 3.25 | .80 |
| ☐ 139 | Ken Wood | 8.00 | 3.25 | .80 | ☐ 232 | Billy Cox | 10.00 | 4.00 | 1.00 |
| ☐ 140 | Johnny Antonelli | 10.00 | 4.00 | 1.00 | ☐ 233 | Bob Friend | 10.00 | 4.00 | 1.00 |
| ☐ 141 | Clint Hartung | 8.00 | 3.25 | .80 | ☐ 234 | Steve Souchock | 8.00 | 3.25 | .80 |
| ☐ 142 | Harry Perkowski | 8.00 | 3.25 | .80 | ☐ 235 | Walt Dropo | 8.00 | 3.25 | .80 |
| ☐ 143 | Les Moss | 8.00 | 3.25 | .80 | ☐ 236 | Ed Fitzgerald | 8.00 | 3.25 | .80 |
| ☐ 144 | Ed Blake | 8.00 | 3.25 | .80 | ☐ 237 | Jerry Coleman | 10.00 | 4.00 | 1.00 |
| ☐ 145 | Joe Haynes | 8.00 | 3.25 | .80 | ☐ 238 | Art Houtteman | 8.00 | 3.25 | .80 |
| ☐ 146 | Frank House | 8.00 | 3.25 | .80 | ☐ 239 | Rocky Bridges | 8.00 | 3.25 | .80 |
| ☐ 147 | Bob Young | 8.00 | 3.25 | .80 | ☐ 240 | Jack Phillips | 8.00 | 3.25 | .80 |
| ☐ 148 | Johnny Klippstein | 8.00 | 3.25 | .80 | ☐ 241 | Tommy Byrne | 9.00 | 3.75 | .90 |
| ☐ 149 | Dick Kryhoski | 8.00 | 3.25 | .80 | ☐ 242 | Tom Poholsky | 8.00 | 3.25 | .80 |
| ☐ 150 | Ted Beard | 8.00 | 3.25 | .80 | ☐ 243 | Larry Doby | 15.00 | 6.00 | 1.50 |
| ☐ 151 | Wally Post | 8.00 | 3.25 | .80 | ☐ 244 | Vic Wertz | 10.00 | 4.00 | 1.00 |
| ☐ 152 | Al Evans | 8.00 | 3.25 | .80 | ☐ 245 | Sherry Robertson | 8.00 | 3.25 | .80 |
| ☐ 153 | Bob Rush | 8.00 | 3.25 | .80 | ☐ 246 | George Kell | 25.00 | 10.00 | 2.50 |
| ☐ 154 | Joe Muir | 8.00 | 3.25 | .80 | ☐ 247 | Randy Gumpert | 8.00 | 3.25 | .80 |
| ☐ 155 | Frank Overmire | 8.00 | 3.25 | .80 | ☐ 248 | Frank Shea | 8.00 | 3.25 | .80 |
| ☐ 156 | Frank Hiller | 8.00 | 3.25 | .80 | ☐ 249 | Bobby Adams | 8.00 | 3.25 | .80 |
| ☐ 157 | Bob Usher | 8.00 | 3.25 | .80 | ☐ 250 | Carl Erskine | 16.00 | 6.50 | 1.60 |
| ☐ 158 | Eddie Waitkus | 8.00 | 3.25 | .80 | ☐ 251 | Chico Carrasquel | 16.00 | 6.50 | 1.60 |
| ☐ 159 | Saul Rogovin | 8.00 | 3.25 | .80 | ☐ 252 | Vern Bickford | 16.00 | 6.50 | 1.60 |
| ☐ 160 | Owen Friend | 8.00 | 3.25 | .80 | ☐ 253 | Johnny Berardino | 18.00 | 7.25 | 1.80 |
| ☐ 161 | Bud Byerly | 8.00 | 3.25 | .80 | ☐ 254 | Joe Dobson | 16.00 | 6.50 | 1.60 |
| ☐ 162 | Del Crandall | 10.00 | 4.00 | 1.00 | ☐ 255 | Clyde Vollmer | 16.00 | 6.50 | 1.60 |
| ☐ 163 | Stan Rojek | 8.00 | 3.25 | .80 | ☐ 256 | Pete Suder | 16.00 | 6.50 | 1.60 |
| ☐ 164 | Walt Dubiel | 8.00 | 3.25 | .80 | ☐ 257 | Bobby Avila | 18.00 | 7.25 | 1.80 |
| ☐ 165 | Eddie Kazak | 8.00 | 3.25 | .80 | ☐ 258 | Steve Gromek | 16.00 | 6.50 | 1.60 |
| ☐ 166 | Paul LaPalme | 8.00 | 3.25 | .80 | ☐ 259 | Bob Addis | 16.00 | 6.50 | 1.60 |
| ☐ 167 | Bill Howerton | 8.00 | 3.25 | .80 | ☐ 260 | Pete Castiglione | 16.00 | 6.50 | 1.60 |
| ☐ 168 | Charlie Silvera | 8.00 | 3.25 | .80 | ☐ 261 | Willie Mays | 500.00 | 200.00 | 50.00 |
| ☐ 169 | Howie Judson | 8.00 | 3.25 | .80 | ☐ 262 | Virgil Trucks | 18.00 | 7.25 | 1.80 |
| ☐ 170 | Gus Bell | 9.00 | 3.75 | .90 | ☐ 263 | Harry Brecheen | 18.00 | 7.25 | 1.80 |
| ☐ 171 | Ed Erautt | 8.00 | 3.25 | .80 | ☐ 264 | Roy Hartsfield | 16.00 | 6.50 | 1.60 |
| ☐ 172 | Eddie Miksis | 8.00 | 3.25 | .80 | ☐ 265 | Chuck Diering | 16.00 | 6.50 | 1.60 |
| ☐ 173 | Roy Smalley | 8.00 | 3.25 | .80 | ☐ 266 | Murry Dickson | 16.00 | 6.50 | 1.60 |
| ☐ 174 | Clarence Marshall | 8.00 | 3.25 | .80 | ☐ 267 | Sid Gordon | 16.00 | 6.50 | 1.60 |
| ☐ 175 | Billy Martin | 75.00 | 30.00 | 7.50 | ☐ 268 | Bob Lemon | 75.00 | 30.00 | 7.50 |
| ☐ 176 | Hank Edwards | 8.00 | 3.25 | .80 | ☐ 269 | Willard Nixon | 16.00 | 6.50 | 1.60 |
| ☐ 177 | Bill Wight | 8.00 | 3.25 | .80 | ☐ 270 | Lou Brissie | 16.00 | 6.50 | 1.60 |
| ☐ 178 | Cass Michaels | 8.00 | 3.25 | .80 | ☐ 271 | Jim Delsing | 16.00 | 6.50 | 1.60 |
| ☐ 179 | Frank Smith | 8.00 | 3.25 | .80 | ☐ 272 | Mike Garcia | 18.00 | 7.25 | 1.80 |
| ☐ 180 | Charley Maxwell | 8.00 | 3.25 | .80 | ☐ 273 | Erv Palica | 16.00 | 6.50 | 1.60 |
| ☐ 181 | Bob Swift | 8.00 | 3.25 | .80 | ☐ 274 | Ralph Branca | 18.00 | 7.25 | 1.80 |
| ☐ 182 | Billy Hitchcock | 8.00 | 3.25 | .80 | ☐ 275 | Pat Mullin | 16.00 | 6.50 | 1.60 |
| ☐ 183 | Erv Dusak | 8.00 | 3.25 | .80 | ☐ 276 | Jim Wilson | 16.00 | 6.50 | 1.60 |
| ☐ 184 | Bob Ramazotti | 8.00 | 3.25 | .80 | ☐ 277 | Early Wynn | 75.00 | 30.00 | 7.50 |
| ☐ 185 | Bill Nicholson | 8.00 | 3.25 | .80 | ☐ 278 | Al Clark | 16.00 | 6.50 | 1.60 |
| ☐ 186 | Walt Masterson | 8.00 | 3.25 | .80 | ☐ 279 | Ed Stewart | 16.00 | 6.50 | 1.60 |
| ☐ 187 | Bob Miller | 8.00 | 3.25 | .80 | ☐ 280 | Cloyd Boyer | 18.00 | 7.25 | 1.80 |
| ☐ 188 | Clarence Podbielan | 8.00 | 3.25 | .80 | ☐ 281 | Tommy Brown SP | 20.00 | 8.00 | 2.00 |
| ☐ 189 | Pete Reiser | 10.00 | 4.00 | 1.00 | ☐ 282 | Birdie Tebbetts SP | 20.00 | 8.00 | 2.00 |
| ☐ 190 | Don Johnson | 8.00 | 3.25 | .80 | ☐ 283 | Philip Masi SP | 20.00 | 8.00 | 2.00 |
| ☐ 191 | Yogi Berra | 90.00 | 36.00 | 9.00 | ☐ 284 | Hank Arft SP | 20.00 | 8.00 | 2.00 |
| ☐ 192 | Myron Ginsberg | 8.00 | 3.25 | .80 | ☐ 285 | Cliff Fannin SP | 20.00 | 8.00 | 2.00 |
| ☐ 193 | Harry Simpson | 8.00 | 3.25 | .80 | ☐ 286 | Joe DeMaestri SP | 20.00 | 8.00 | 2.00 |
| ☐ 194 | Joe Hatton | 8.00 | 3.25 | .80 | ☐ 287 | Steve Bilko SP | 20.00 | 8.00 | 2.00 |
| ☐ 195 | Minnie Minoso | 18.00 | 7.25 | 1.80 | ☐ 288 | Chet Nichols SP | 20.00 | 8.00 | 2.00 |
| ☐ 196 | Solly Hemus | 8.00 | 3.25 | .80 | ☐ 289 | Tommy Holmes SP | 20.00 | 8.00 | 2.00 |
| ☐ 197 | George Strickland | 8.00 | 3.25 | .80 | ☐ 290 | Joe Astroth SP | 20.00 | 8.00 | 2.00 |
| ☐ 198 | Phil Haugstad | 8.00 | 3.25 | .80 | ☐ 291 | Gil Coan SP | 20.00 | 8.00 | 2.00 |
| ☐ 199 | George Zuverink | 8.00 | 3.25 | .80 | ☐ 292 | Floyd Baker SP | 20.00 | 8.00 | 2.00 |
| ☐ 200 | Ralph Houk | 18.00 | 7.25 | 1.80 | ☐ 293 | Sibby Sisti SP | 20.00 | 8.00 | 2.00 |
| ☐ 201 | Alex Kellner | 8.00 | 3.25 | .80 | ☐ 294 | Walker Cooper SP | 20.00 | 8.00 | 2.00 |
| ☐ 202 | Joe Collins | 9.00 | 3.75 | .90 | ☐ 295 | Phil Cavarretta SP | 20.00 | 8.00 | 2.00 |
| ☐ 203 | Curt Simmons | 10.00 | 4.00 | 1.00 | ☐ 296 | Red Rolfe SP | 20.00 | 8.00 | 2.00 |
| ☐ 204 | Ron Northey | 8.00 | 3.25 | .80 | ☐ 297 | Andy Seminick SP | 20.00 | 8.00 | 2.00 |
| ☐ 205 | Clyde King | 9.00 | 3.75 | .90 | ☐ 298 | Bob Ross SP | 20.00 | 8.00 | 2.00 |
| ☐ 206 | Joe Ostrowski | 8.00 | 3.25 | .80 | ☐ 299 | Ray Murray SP | 20.00 | 8.00 | 2.00 |
| ☐ 207 | Mickey Harris | 8.00 | 3.25 | .80 | ☐ 300 | Barney McCosky SP | 20.00 | 8.00 | 2.00 |
| ☐ 208 | Marlin Stuart | 8.00 | 3.25 | .80 | ☐ 301 | Bob Porterfield | 16.00 | 6.50 | 1.60 |
| ☐ 209 | Howie Fox | 8.00 | 3.25 | .80 | ☐ 302 | Max Surkont | 16.00 | 6.50 | 1.60 |
| ☐ 210 | Dick Fowler | 8.00 | 3.25 | .80 | ☐ 303 | Harry Dorish | 16.00 | 6.50 | 1.60 |
| ☐ 211 | Ray Coleman | 8.00 | 3.25 | .80 | ☐ 304 | Sam Dente | 16.00 | 6.50 | 1.60 |

| | | | | |
|---|---|---|---|---|
| ☐ 305 | Paul Richards | 18.00 | 7.25 | 1.80 |
| ☐ 306 | Lou Sleater | 16.00 | 6.50 | 1.60 |
| ☐ 307 | Frank Campos | 16.00 | 6.50 | 1.60 |
| ☐ 308 | Luis Aloma | 16.00 | 6.50 | 1.60 |
| ☐ 309 | Jim Busby | 16.00 | 6.50 | 1.60 |
| ☐ 310 | George Metkovich | 16.00 | 6.50 | 1.60 |
| ☐ 311 | Mickey Mantle DP | 3300.00 | 1100.00 | 200.00 |
| ☐ 312 | Jackie Robinson DP | 450.00 | 180.00 | 45.00 |
| ☐ 313 | Bobby Thomson DP | 90.00 | 36.00 | 9.00 |
| ☐ 314 | Roy Campanella | 650.00 | 260.00 | 65.00 |
| ☐ 315 | Leo Durocher | 150.00 | 60.00 | 15.00 |
| ☐ 316 | Dave Williams | 90.00 | 36.00 | 9.00 |
| ☐ 317 | Conrado Marrerro | 75.00 | 30.00 | 7.50 |
| ☐ 318 | Harold Gregg | 75.00 | 30.00 | 7.50 |
| ☐ 319 | Al Walker | 75.00 | 30.00 | 7.50 |
| ☐ 320 | John Rutherford | 75.00 | 30.00 | 7.50 |
| ☐ 321 | Joe Black | 90.00 | 36.00 | 9.00 |
| ☐ 322 | Randy Jackson | 75.00 | 30.00 | 7.50 |
| ☐ 323 | Bubba Church | 75.00 | 30.00 | 7.50 |
| ☐ 324 | Warren Hacker | 75.00 | 30.00 | 7.50 |
| ☐ 325 | Bill Serena | 75.00 | 30.00 | 7.50 |
| ☐ 326 | George Shuba | 75.00 | 30.00 | 7.50 |
| ☐ 327 | Al Wilson | 75.00 | 30.00 | 7.50 |
| ☐ 328 | Bob Borkowski | 75.00 | 30.00 | 7.50 |
| ☐ 329 | Ike Delock | 75.00 | 30.00 | 7.50 |
| ☐ 330 | Turk Lown | 75.00 | 30.00 | 7.50 |
| ☐ 331 | Tom Morgan | 75.00 | 30.00 | 7.50 |
| ☐ 332 | Anthony Bartirome | 75.00 | 30.00 | 7.50 |
| ☐ 333 | Pee Wee Reese | 350.00 | 140.00 | 35.00 |
| ☐ 334 | Wilmer Mizell | 75.00 | 30.00 | 7.50 |
| ☐ 335 | Ted Lepcio | 75.00 | 30.00 | 7.50 |
| ☐ 336 | Dave Koslo | 75.00 | 30.00 | 7.50 |
| ☐ 337 | Jim Hearn | 75.00 | 30.00 | 7.50 |
| ☐ 338 | Sal Yvars | 75.00 | 30.00 | 7.50 |
| ☐ 339 | Russ Meyer | 75.00 | 30.00 | 7.50 |
| ☐ 340 | Bob Hooper | 75.00 | 30.00 | 7.50 |
| ☐ 341 | Hal Jeffcoat | 75.00 | 30.00 | 7.50 |
| ☐ 342 | Clem Labine | 90.00 | 36.00 | 9.00 |
| ☐ 343 | Dick Gernert | 75.00 | 30.00 | 7.50 |
| ☐ 344 | Ewell Blackwell | 90.00 | 36.00 | 9.00 |
| ☐ 345 | Sammy White | 75.00 | 30.00 | 7.50 |
| ☐ 346 | George Spencer | 75.00 | 30.00 | 7.50 |
| ☐ 347 | Joe Adcock | 90.00 | 36.00 | 9.00 |
| ☐ 348 | Robert Kelly | 75.00 | 30.00 | 7.50 |
| ☐ 349 | Bob Cain | 75.00 | 30.00 | 7.50 |
| ☐ 350 | Cal Abrams | 75.00 | 30.00 | 7.50 |
| ☐ 351 | Alvin Dark | 90.00 | 36.00 | 9.00 |
| ☐ 352 | Karl Drews | 75.00 | 30.00 | 7.50 |
| ☐ 353 | Bobby Del Greco | 75.00 | 30.00 | 7.50 |
| ☐ 354 | Fred Hatfield | 75.00 | 30.00 | 7.50 |
| ☐ 355 | Bobby Morgan | 75.00 | 30.00 | 7.50 |
| ☐ 356 | Toby Atwell | 75.00 | 30.00 | 7.50 |
| ☐ 357 | Smoky Burgess | 90.00 | 36.00 | 9.00 |
| ☐ 358 | John Kucab | 75.00 | 30.00 | 7.50 |
| ☐ 359 | Dee Fondy | 75.00 | 30.00 | 7.50 |
| ☐ 360 | George Crowe | 75.00 | 30.00 | 7.50 |
| ☐ 361 | William Posedel | 75.00 | 30.00 | 7.50 |
| ☐ 362 | Ken Heintzelman | 75.00 | 30.00 | 7.50 |
| ☐ 363 | Dick Rozek | 75.00 | 30.00 | 7.50 |
| ☐ 364 | Clyde Sukeforth | 75.00 | 30.00 | 7.50 |
| ☐ 365 | Cookie Lavagetto | 75.00 | 30.00 | 7.50 |
| ☐ 366 | Dave Madison | 75.00 | 30.00 | 7.50 |
| ☐ 367 | Ben Thorpe | 75.00 | 30.00 | 7.50 |
| ☐ 368 | Ed Wright | 75.00 | 30.00 | 7.50 |
| ☐ 369 | Dick Groat | 150.00 | 60.00 | 15.00 |
| ☐ 370 | Billy Hoeft | 75.00 | 30.00 | 7.50 |
| ☐ 371 | Bobby Hofman | 75.00 | 30.00 | 7.50 |
| ☐ 372 | Gil McDougald | 150.00 | 60.00 | 15.00 |
| ☐ 373 | Jim Turner COA | 75.00 | 30.00 | 7.50 |
| ☐ 374 | John Benton | 75.00 | 30.00 | 7.50 |
| ☐ 375 | John Merson | 75.00 | 30.00 | 7.50 |
| ☐ 376 | Faye Throneberry | 75.00 | 30.00 | 7.50 |
| ☐ 377 | Chuck Dressen MGR | 90.00 | 36.00 | 9.00 |
| ☐ 378 | Leroy Fusselman | 75.00 | 30.00 | 7.50 |
| ☐ 379 | Joseph Rossi | 75.00 | 30.00 | 7.50 |
| ☐ 380 | Clem Koshorek | 75.00 | 30.00 | 7.50 |
| ☐ 381 | Milton Stock | 75.00 | 30.00 | 7.50 |
| ☐ 382 | Sam Jones | 75.00 | 30.00 | 7.50 |
| ☐ 383 | Del Wilber | 75.00 | 30.00 | 7.50 |
| ☐ 384 | Frank Crosetti COA | 150.00 | 60.00 | 15.00 |
| ☐ 385 | Herman Franks | 75.00 | 30.00 | 7.50 |
| ☐ 386 | John Yuhas | 75.00 | 30.00 | 7.50 |
| ☐ 387 | William Meyer | 75.00 | 30.00 | 7.50 |
| ☐ 388 | Bob Chipman | 75.00 | 30.00 | 7.50 |
| ☐ 389 | Ben Wade | 75.00 | 30.00 | 7.50 |
| ☐ 390 | Glenn Nelson | 75.00 | 30.00 | 7.50 |
| ☐ 391 | Ben Chapman (photo actually Sam Chapman) | 75.00 | 30.00 | 7.50 |
| ☐ 392 | Hoyt Wilhelm | 250.00 | 100.00 | 25.00 |
| ☐ 393 | Ebba St.Claire | 75.00 | 30.00 | 7.50 |
| ☐ 394 | Billy Herman COA | 120.00 | 50.00 | 12.00 |
| ☐ 395 | Jake Pitler COA | 75.00 | 30.00 | 7.50 |

| | | | | |
|---|---|---|---|---|
| ☐ 396 | Dick Williams | 90.00 | 36.00 | 9.00 |
| ☐ 397 | Forrest Main | 75.00 | 30.00 | 7.50 |
| ☐ 398 | Hal Rice | 75.00 | 30.00 | 7.50 |
| ☐ 399 | Jim Fridley | 75.00 | 30.00 | 7.50 |
| ☐ 400 | Bill Dickey COA | 300.00 | 120.00 | 30.00 |
| ☐ 401 | Bob Schultz | 75.00 | 30.00 | 7.50 |
| ☐ 402 | Earl Harrist | 75.00 | 30.00 | 7.50 |
| ☐ 403 | Bill Miller | 75.00 | 30.00 | 7.50 |
| ☐ 404 | Dick Brodowski | 75.00 | 30.00 | 7.50 |
| ☐ 405 | Ed Pellagrini | 75.00 | 30.00 | 7.50 |
| ☐ 406 | Joe Nuxhall | 90.00 | 36.00 | 9.00 |
| ☐ 407 | Eddie Mathews | 750.00 | 150.00 | 30.00 |

# 1953 Topps

 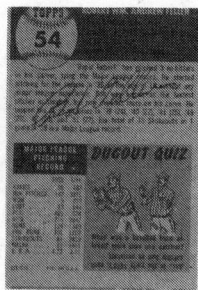

BOB FELLER
CLEVELAND INDIANS

The cards in this 274 card set measure 2 5/8" by 3/3/4". Although the last card is numbered 280, there are only 274 cards in the set since numbers 253, 261, 267, 268, 271, and 275 were never issued. The 1953 Topps series contains line drawings of players in full color. The name and team panel at the card base is easily damaged, making it very difficult to complete a Mint set. The high number series, 221 to 280, was produced in shorter supply late in the year and hence is more difficult to complete than the lower numbers. The key cards in the set are Mickey Mantle #82 and Willie Mays #244.

| | | MINT | VG-E | F-G |
|---|---|---|---|---|
| COMPLETE SET | | 3000.00 | 1000.00 | 300.00 |
| COMMON PLAYER (1-165) | | 5.00 | 2.00 | .50 |
| COMMON PLAYER (166-220) | | 3.50 | 1.40 | .35 |
| COMMON PLAYER (221-280) | | 17.00 | 7.00 | 1.70 |

| | | | | |
|---|---|---|---|---|
| ☐ 1 | Jackie Robinson | 150.00 | 30.00 | 6.00 |
| ☐ 2 | Luke Easter | 5.00 | 2.00 | .50 |
| ☐ 3 | George Crowe | 5.00 | 2.00 | .50 |
| ☐ 4 | Ben Wade | 5.00 | 2.00 | .50 |
| ☐ 5 | Joe Dobson | 5.00 | 2.00 | .50 |
| ☐ 6 | Sam Jones | 5.00 | 2.00 | .50 |
| ☐ 7 | Bob Borkowski | 5.00 | 2.00 | .50 |
| ☐ 8 | Clem Koshorek | 5.00 | 2.00 | .50 |
| ☐ 9 | Joe Collins | 5.00 | 2.00 | .50 |
| ☐ 10 | Smoky Burgess | 6.00 | 2.40 | .60 |
| ☐ 11 | Sal Yvars | 5.00 | 2.00 | .50 |
| ☐ 12 | Howie Judson | 5.00 | 2.00 | .50 |
| ☐ 13 | Connie Marrero | 5.00 | 2.00 | .50 |
| ☐ 14 | Clem Labine | 6.00 | 2.40 | .60 |
| ☐ 15 | Bobo Newsom | 6.00 | 2.40 | .60 |
| ☐ 16 | Peanuts Lowrey | 5.00 | 2.00 | .50 |
| ☐ 17 | Billy Hitchcock | 5.00 | 2.00 | .50 |
| ☐ 18 | Ted Lepcio | 5.00 | 2.00 | .50 |
| ☐ 19 | Mel Parnell | 6.00 | 2.40 | .60 |
| ☐ 20 | Hank Thompson | 6.00 | 2.40 | .60 |
| ☐ 21 | Billy Johnson | 5.00 | 2.00 | .50 |
| ☐ 22 | Howie Fox | 5.00 | 2.00 | .50 |
| ☐ 23 | Toby Atwell | 5.00 | 2.00 | .50 |
| ☐ 24 | Ferris Fain | 5.00 | 2.00 | .50 |
| ☐ 25 | Ray Boone | 5.00 | 2.00 | .50 |
| ☐ 26 | Dale Mitchell | 6.00 | 2.40 | .60 |
| ☐ 27 | Roy Campanella | 60.00 | 24.00 | 6.00 |
| ☐ 28 | Eddie Pellagrini | 5.00 | 2.00 | .50 |

| # | Player | | | |
|---|--------|------|------|------|
| 29 | Hal Jeffcoat | 5.00 | 2.00 | .50 |
| 30 | Willard Nixon | 5.00 | 2.00 | .50 |
| 31 | Ewell Blackwell | 6.00 | 2.40 | .60 |
| 32 | Clyde Vollmer | 5.00 | 2.00 | .50 |
| 33 | Bob Kennedy | 5.00 | 2.00 | .50 |
| 34 | George Shuba | 6.00 | 2.40 | .60 |
| 35 | Irv Noren | 5.00 | 2.00 | .50 |
| 36 | Johnny Groth | 5.00 | 2.00 | .50 |
| 37 | Ed Mathews | 21.00 | 8.50 | 2.10 |
| 38 | Jim Hearn | 5.00 | 2.00 | .50 |
| 39 | Eddie Miksis | 5.00 | 2.00 | .50 |
| 40 | John Lipon | 5.00 | 2.00 | .50 |
| 41 | Enos Slaughter | 12.50 | 5.00 | 1.25 |
| 42 | Gus Zernial | 5.00 | 2.00 | .50 |
| 43 | Gil McDougald | 7.50 | 3.00 | .75 |
| 44 | Ellis Kinder | 5.00 | 2.00 | .50 |
| 45 | Grady Hatton | 5.00 | 2.00 | .50 |
| 46 | Johnny Klippstein | 5.00 | 2.00 | .50 |
| 47 | Bubba Church | 5.00 | 2.00 | .50 |
| 48 | Bob Del Greco | 5.00 | 2.00 | .50 |
| 49 | Faye Throneberry | 5.00 | 2.00 | .50 |
| 50 | Chuck Dressen MGR | 6.00 | 2.40 | .60 |
| 51 | Frank Campos | 5.00 | 2.00 | .50 |
| 52 | Ted Gray | 5.00 | 2.00 | .50 |
| 53 | Sherman Lollar | 6.00 | 2.40 | .60 |
| 54 | Bob Feller | 32.00 | 13.00 | 3.20 |
| 55 | Maurice McDermott | 5.00 | 2.00 | .50 |
| 56 | Gerry Staley | 5.00 | 2.00 | .50 |
| 57 | Carl Scheib | 5.00 | 2.00 | .50 |
| 58 | George Metkovich | 5.00 | 2.00 | .50 |
| 59 | Karl Drews | 5.00 | 2.00 | .50 |
| 60 | Cloyd Boyer | 5.00 | 2.00 | .50 |
| 61 | Early Wynn | 12.50 | 5.00 | 1.25 |
| 62 | Monte Irvin | 10.00 | 4.00 | 1.00 |
| 63 | Gus Niarhos | 5.00 | 2.00 | .50 |
| 64 | Dave Philley | 5.00 | 2.00 | .50 |
| 65 | Earl Harrist | 5.00 | 2.00 | .50 |
| 66 | Minnie Minoso | 7.50 | 3.00 | .75 |
| 67 | Roy Sievers | 6.00 | 2.40 | .60 |
| 68 | Del Rice | 5.00 | 2.00 | .50 |
| 69 | Dick Brodowski | 5.00 | 2.00 | .50 |
| 70 | Ed Yuhas | 5.00 | 2.00 | .50 |
| 71 | Tony Bartirome | 5.00 | 2.00 | .50 |
| 72 | Fred Hutchinson | 6.00 | 2.40 | .60 |
| 73 | Eddie Robinson | 5.00 | 2.00 | .50 |
| 74 | Joe Rossi | 5.00 | 2.00 | .50 |
| 75 | Mike Garcia | 6.00 | 2.40 | .60 |
| 76 | Pee Wee Reese | 27.00 | 11.00 | 2.70 |
| 77 | Johnny Mize | 14.00 | 5.75 | 1.40 |
| 78 | Al (Red) Schoendienst | 7.50 | 3.00 | .75 |
| 79 | Johnny Wyrostek | 5.00 | 2.00 | .50 |
| 80 | Jim Hegan | 6.00 | 2.40 | .60 |
| 81 | Joe Black | 6.00 | 2.40 | .60 |
| 82 | Mickey Mantle | 600.00 | 240.00 | 60.00 |
| 83 | Howie Pollet | 5.00 | 2.00 | .50 |
| 84 | Bob Hooper | 5.00 | 2.00 | .50 |
| 85 | Bobby Morgan | 5.00 | 2.00 | .50 |
| 86 | Billy Martin | 27.00 | 11.00 | 2.70 |
| 87 | Ed Lopat | 9.00 | 3.75 | .90 |
| 88 | Willie Jones | 5.00 | 2.00 | .50 |
| 89 | Chuck Stobbs | 5.00 | 2.00 | .50 |
| 90 | Hank Edwards | 5.00 | 2.00 | .50 |
| 91 | Ebba St.Claire | 5.00 | 2.00 | .50 |
| 92 | Paul Minner | 5.00 | 2.00 | .50 |
| 93 | Hal Rice | 5.00 | 2.00 | .50 |
| 94 | Bill Kennedy | 5.00 | 2.00 | .50 |
| 95 | Willard Marshall | 5.00 | 2.00 | .50 |
| 96 | Virgil Trucks | 6.00 | 2.40 | .60 |
| 97 | Don Kolloway | 5.00 | 2.00 | .50 |
| 98 | Cal Abrams | 5.00 | 2.00 | .50 |
| 99 | Dave Madison | 5.00 | 2.00 | .50 |
| 100 | Bill Miller | 5.00 | 2.00 | .50 |
| 101 | Ted Wilks | 5.00 | 2.00 | .50 |
| 102 | Connie Ryan | 5.00 | 2.00 | .50 |
| 103 | Joe Astroth | 5.00 | 2.00 | .50 |
| 104 | Yogi Berra | 50.00 | 20.00 | 5.00 |
| 105 | Joe Nuxhall | 6.00 | 2.40 | .60 |
| 106 | Johnny Antonelli | 6.00 | 2.40 | .60 |
| 107 | Danny O'Connell | 5.00 | 2.00 | .50 |
| 108 | Bob Porterfield | 5.00 | 2.00 | .50 |
| 109 | Alvin Dark | 7.50 | 3.00 | .75 |
| 110 | Herman Wehmeier | 5.00 | 2.00 | .50 |
| 111 | Hank Sauer | 6.00 | 2.40 | .60 |
| 112 | Ned Garver | 5.00 | 2.00 | .50 |
| 113 | Jerry Priddy | 5.00 | 2.00 | .50 |
| 114 | Phil Rizzuto | 27.00 | 11.00 | 2.70 |
| 115 | George Spencer | 5.00 | 2.00 | .50 |
| 116 | Frank Smith | 5.00 | 2.00 | .50 |
| 117 | Sid Gordon | 5.00 | 2.00 | .50 |
| 118 | Gus Bell | 6.00 | 2.40 | .60 |
| 119 | John Sain | 9.00 | 3.75 | .90 |
| 120 | Davey Williams | 6.00 | 2.40 | .60 |
| 121 | Walter Dropo | 5.00 | 2.00 | .50 |
| 122 | Elmer Valo | 5.00 | 2.00 | .50 |
| 123 | Tommy Byrne | 5.00 | 2.00 | .50 |
| 124 | Sibby Sisti | 5.00 | 2.00 | .50 |
| 125 | Dick Williams | 7.50 | 3.00 | .75 |
| 126 | Bill Connelly | 5.00 | 2.00 | .50 |
| 127 | Clint Courtney | 5.00 | 2.00 | .50 |
| 128 | Wilmer Mizell | 6.00 | 2.40 | .60 |
| 129 | Keith Thomas | 5.00 | 2.00 | .50 |
| 130 | Turk Lown | 5.00 | 2.00 | .50 |
| 131 | Harry Byrd | 5.00 | 2.00 | .50 |
| 132 | Tom Morgan | 5.00 | 2.00 | .50 |
| 133 | Gil Coan | 5.00 | 2.00 | .50 |
| 134 | Rube Walker | 6.00 | 2.40 | .60 |
| 135 | Al Rosen | 10.00 | 4.00 | 1.00 |
| 136 | Ken Heintzelman | 5.00 | 2.00 | .50 |
| 137 | John Rutherford | 5.00 | 2.00 | .50 |
| 138 | George Kell | 12.50 | 5.00 | 1.25 |
| 139 | Sammy White | 5.00 | 2.00 | .50 |
| 140 | Tommy Glaviano | 5.00 | 2.00 | .50 |
| 141 | Allie Reynolds | 9.00 | 3.75 | .90 |
| 142 | Vic Wertz | 5.00 | 2.00 | .50 |
| 143 | Billy Pierce | 7.50 | 3.00 | .75 |
| 144 | Bob Schultz | 5.00 | 2.00 | .50 |
| 145 | Harry Dorish | 5.00 | 2.00 | .50 |
| 146 | Granny Hamner | 5.00 | 2.00 | .50 |
| 147 | Warren Spahn | 30.00 | 12.00 | 3.00 |
| 148 | Mickey Grasso | 5.00 | 2.00 | .50 |
| 149 | Dom DiMaggio | 10.00 | 4.00 | 1.00 |
| 150 | Harry Simpson | 5.00 | 2.00 | .50 |
| 151 | Hoyt Wilhelm | 18.00 | 7.25 | 1.80 |
| 152 | Bob Adams | 5.00 | 2.00 | .50 |
| 153 | Andy Seminick | 5.00 | 2.00 | .50 |
| 154 | Dick Groat | 7.50 | 3.00 | .75 |
| 155 | Dutch Leonard | 5.00 | 2.00 | .50 |
| 156 | Jim Rivera | 5.00 | 2.00 | .50 |
| 157 | Bob Addis | 5.00 | 2.00 | .50 |
| 158 | John Logan | 6.00 | 2.40 | .60 |
| 159 | Wayne Terwilliger | 5.00 | 2.00 | .50 |
| 160 | Bob Young | 5.00 | 2.00 | .50 |
| 161 | Vern Bickford | 5.00 | 2.00 | .50 |
| 162 | Ted Kluszewski | 9.00 | 3.75 | .90 |
| 163 | Fred Hatfield | 5.00 | 2.00 | .50 |
| 164 | Frank Shea | 5.00 | 2.00 | .50 |
| 165 | Billy Hoeft | 5.00 | 2.00 | .50 |
| 166 | Bill Hunter | 3.50 | 1.40 | .35 |
| 167 | Art Schult | 3.50 | 1.40 | .35 |
| 168 | Willard Schmidt | 3.50 | 1.40 | .35 |
| 169 | Dizzy Trout | 3.50 | 1.40 | .35 |
| 170 | Bill Werle | 3.50 | 1.40 | .35 |
| 171 | Bill Glynn | 3.50 | 1.40 | .35 |
| 172 | Rip Repulski | 3.50 | 1.40 | .35 |
| 173 | Preston Ward | 3.50 | 1.40 | .35 |
| 174 | Billy Loes | 3.50 | 1.40 | .35 |
| 175 | Ronnie Kline | 3.50 | 1.40 | .35 |
| 176 | Don Hoak | 4.50 | 1.80 | .45 |
| 177 | Jim Dyck | 3.50 | 1.40 | .35 |
| 178 | Jim Waugh | 3.50 | 1.40 | .35 |
| 179 | Gene Hermanski | 3.50 | 1.40 | .35 |
| 180 | Virgil Stallcup | 3.50 | 1.40 | .35 |
| 181 | Al Zarilla | 3.50 | 1.40 | .35 |
| 182 | Bobby Hofman | 3.50 | 1.40 | .35 |
| 183 | Stu Miller | 3.50 | 1.40 | .35 |
| 184 | Hal Brown | 3.50 | 1.40 | .35 |
| 185 | Jim Pendleton | 3.50 | 1.40 | .35 |
| 186 | Charlie Bishop | 3.50 | 1.40 | .35 |
| 187 | Jim Fridley | 3.50 | 1.40 | .35 |
| 188 | Andy Carey | 4.50 | 1.80 | .45 |
| 189 | Ray Jablonski | 3.50 | 1.40 | .35 |
| 190 | Dixie Walker | 3.50 | 1.40 | .35 |
| 191 | Ralph Kiner | 15.00 | 6.00 | 1.50 |
| 192 | Wally Westlake | 3.50 | 1.40 | .35 |
| 193 | Mike Clark | 3.50 | 1.40 | .35 |
| 194 | Eddie Kazak | 3.50 | 1.40 | .35 |
| 195 | Ed McGhee | 3.50 | 1.40 | .35 |
| 196 | Bob Keegan | 3.50 | 1.40 | .35 |
| 197 | Del Crandall | 4.50 | 1.80 | .45 |
| 198 | Forrest Main | 3.50 | 1.40 | .35 |
| 199 | Marion Fricano | 3.50 | 1.40 | .35 |
| 200 | Gordon Goldsberry | 3.50 | 1.40 | .35 |
| 201 | Paul LaPalme | 3.50 | 1.40 | .35 |
| 202 | Carl Sawatski | 3.50 | 1.40 | .35 |
| 203 | Cliff Fannin | 3.50 | 1.40 | .35 |
| 204 | Dick Bokelman | 3.50 | 1.40 | .35 |
| 205 | Vern Benson | 3.50 | 1.40 | .35 |
| 206 | Ed Bailey | 4.50 | 1.80 | .45 |
| 207 | Whitey Ford | 25.00 | 10.00 | 2.50 |
| 208 | Jim Wilson | 3.50 | 1.40 | .35 |
| 209 | Jim Greengrass | 3.50 | 1.40 | .35 |
| 210 | Bob Cerv | 4.50 | 1.80 | .45 |
| 211 | J.W. Porter | 3.50 | 1.40 | .35 |
| 212 | Jack Dittmer | 3.50 | 1.40 | .35 |
| 213 | Ray Scarborough | 3.50 | 1.40 | .35 |
| 214 | Bill Bruton | 4.50 | 1.80 | .45 |

| | | MINT | VG-E | F-G |
|---|---|---|---|---|
| ☐ 215 | Gene Conley | 4.50 | 1.80 | .45 |
| ☐ 216 | Jim Hughes | 3.50 | 1.40 | .35 |
| ☐ 217 | Murray Wall | 3.50 | 1.40 | .35 |
| ☐ 218 | Les Fusselman | 3.50 | 1.40 | .35 |
| ☐ 219 | Pete Runnels | 4.50 | 1.80 | .45 |
| | (Photo actually Don Johnson) | | | |
| ☐ 220 | Satchel Paige | 90.00 | 36.00 | 9.00 |
| ☐ 221 | Bob Milliken | 17.00 | 7.00 | 1.70 |
| ☐ 222 | Vic Janowicz | 20.00 | 8.00 | 2.00 |
| ☐ 223 | Johnny O'Brien | 17.00 | 7.00 | 1.70 |
| ☐ 224 | Lou Sleater | 17.00 | 7.00 | 1.70 |
| ☐ 225 | Bobby Shantz | 24.00 | 10.00 | 2.40 |
| ☐ 226 | Ed Erautt | 17.00 | 7.00 | 1.70 |
| ☐ 227 | Morris Martin | 17.00 | 7.00 | 1.70 |
| ☐ 228 | Hal Newhouser | 32.00 | 13.00 | 3.20 |
| ☐ 229 | Rockey Krsnich | 17.00 | 7.00 | 1.70 |
| ☐ 230 | Johnny Lindell | 17.00 | 7.00 | 1.70 |
| ☐ 231 | Solly Hemus | 17.00 | 7.00 | 1.70 |
| ☐ 232 | Dick Kokos | 17.00 | 7.00 | 1.70 |
| ☐ 233 | Al Aber | 17.00 | 7.00 | 1.70 |
| ☐ 234 | Ray Murray | 17.00 | 7.00 | 1.70 |
| ☐ 235 | John Hetki | 17.00 | 7.00 | 1.70 |
| ☐ 236 | Harry Perkowski | 17.00 | 7.00 | 1.70 |
| ☐ 237 | Bud Podbielan | 17.00 | 7.00 | 1.70 |
| ☐ 238 | Cal Hogue | 17.00 | 7.00 | 1.70 |
| ☐ 239 | Jim Delsing | 17.00 | 7.00 | 1.70 |
| ☐ 240 | Freddie Marsh | 17.00 | 7.00 | 1.70 |
| ☐ 241 | Al Sima | 17.00 | 7.00 | 1.70 |
| ☐ 242 | Charlie Silvera | 17.00 | 7.00 | 1.70 |
| ☐ 243 | Carlos Bernier | 17.00 | 7.00 | 1.70 |
| ☐ 244 | Willie Mays | 600.00 | 240.00 | 60.00 |
| ☐ 245 | Bill Norman | 17.00 | 7.00 | 1.70 |
| ☐ 246 | Roy Face | 32.00 | 13.00 | 3.20 |
| ☐ 247 | Mike Sandlock | 17.00 | 7.00 | 1.70 |
| ☐ 248 | Gene Stephens | 17.00 | 7.00 | 1.70 |
| ☐ 249 | Eddie O'Brien | 17.00 | 7.00 | 1.70 |
| ☐ 250 | Bob Wilson | 17.00 | 7.00 | 1.70 |
| ☐ 251 | Sid Hudson | 17.00 | 7.00 | 1.70 |
| ☐ 252 | Henry Foiles | 17.00 | 7.00 | 1.70 |
| ☐ 253 | Does not exist | 0.00 | 0.00 | 0.00 |
| ☐ 254 | Preacher Roe | 32.00 | 13.00 | 3.20 |
| ☐ 255 | Dixie Howell | 17.00 | 7.00 | 1.70 |
| ☐ 256 | Les Peden | 17.00 | 7.00 | 1.70 |
| ☐ 257 | Bob Boyd | 17.00 | 7.00 | 1.70 |
| ☐ 258 | Jim Gilliam | 90.00 | 36.00 | 9.00 |
| ☐ 259 | Roy McMillan | 17.00 | 7.00 | 1.70 |
| ☐ 260 | Sam Calderone | 17.00 | 7.00 | 1.70 |
| ☐ 261 | Does not exist | 0.00 | 0.00 | 0.00 |
| ☐ 262 | Bob Oldis | 17.00 | 7.00 | 1.70 |
| ☐ 263 | Johnny Podres | 75.00 | 30.00 | 7.50 |
| ☐ 264 | Gene Woodling | 32.00 | 13.00 | 3.20 |
| ☐ 265 | Jackie Jensen | 40.00 | 16.00 | 4.00 |
| ☐ 266 | Bob Cain | 17.00 | 7.00 | 1.70 |
| ☐ 267 | Does not exist | 0.00 | 0.00 | 0.00 |
| ☐ 268 | Does not exist | 0.00 | 0.00 | 0.00 |
| ☐ 269 | Duane Pillette | 17.00 | 7.00 | 1.70 |
| ☐ 270 | Vern Stephens | 20.00 | 8.00 | 2.00 |
| ☐ 271 | Does not exist | 0.00 | 0.00 | 0.00 |
| ☐ 272 | Bill Antonello | 17.00 | 7.00 | 1.70 |
| ☐ 273 | Harvey Haddix | 24.00 | 10.00 | 2.40 |
| ☐ 274 | John Riddle | 17.00 | 7.00 | 1.70 |
| ☐ 275 | Does not exist | 0.00 | 0.00 | 0.00 |
| ☐ 276 | Ken Raffensberger | 17.00 | 7.00 | 1.70 |
| ☐ 277 | Don Lund | 17.00 | 7.00 | 1.70 |
| ☐ 278 | Willie Miranda | 17.00 | 7.00 | 1.70 |
| ☐ 279 | Joe Coleman | 17.00 | 7.00 | 1.70 |
| ☐ 280 | Milt Bolling | 90.00 | 12.00 | 2.00 |

| | | MINT | VG-E | F-G |
|---|---|---|---|---|
| | COMPLETE SET | 1500.00 | 650.00 | 175.00 |
| | COMMON PLAYER (1-50) | 1.50 | .60 | .15 |
| | COMMON PLAYER (51-75) | 3.50 | 1.40 | .35 |
| | COMMON PLAYER (76-250) | 2.00 | .80 | .20 |
| ☐ 1 | Ted Williams | 125.00 | 25.00 | 5.00 |
| ☐ 2 | Gus Zernial | 1.50 | .60 | .15 |
| ☐ 3 | Monte Irvin | 6.50 | 2.60 | .65 |
| ☐ 4 | Hank Sauer | 2.00 | .80 | .20 |
| ☐ 5 | Ed Lopat | 4.00 | 1.60 | .40 |
| ☐ 6 | Pete Runnels | 2.00 | .80 | .20 |
| ☐ 7 | Ted Kluszewski | 4.00 | 1.60 | .40 |
| ☐ 8 | Bob Young | 1.50 | .60 | .15 |
| ☐ 9 | Harvey Haddix | 2.00 | .80 | .20 |
| ☐ 10 | Jackie Robinson | 60.00 | 24.00 | 6.00 |
| ☐ 11 | Paul Leslie Smith | 1.50 | .60 | .15 |
| ☐ 12 | Del Crandall | 2.00 | .80 | .20 |
| ☐ 13 | Billy Martin | 20.00 | 8.00 | 2.00 |
| ☐ 14 | Preacher Roe | 4.00 | 1.60 | .40 |
| ☐ 15 | Al Rosen | 5.00 | 2.00 | .50 |
| ☐ 16 | Vic Janowicz | 2.00 | .80 | .20 |
| ☐ 17 | Phil Rizzuto | 18.00 | 7.25 | 1.80 |
| ☐ 18 | Walt Dropo | 1.50 | .60 | .15 |
| ☐ 19 | Johnny Lipon | 1.50 | .60 | .15 |
| ☐ 20 | Warren Spahn | 20.00 | 8.00 | 2.00 |
| ☐ 21 | Bobby Shantz | 2.00 | .80 | .20 |
| ☐ 22 | Jim Greengrass | 1.50 | .60 | .15 |
| ☐ 23 | Luke Easter | 2.00 | .80 | .20 |
| ☐ 24 | Granny Hamner | 1.50 | .60 | .15 |
| ☐ 25 | Harvey Kuenn | 6.00 | 2.40 | .60 |
| ☐ 26 | Ray Jablonski | 1.50 | .60 | .15 |
| ☐ 27 | Ferris Fain | 2.00 | .80 | .20 |
| ☐ 28 | Paul Minner | 1.50 | .60 | .15 |
| ☐ 29 | Jim Hegan | 1.50 | .60 | .15 |
| ☐ 30 | Ed Mathews | 16.00 | 6.50 | 1.60 |
| ☐ 31 | Johnny Klippstein | 1.50 | .60 | .15 |
| ☐ 32 | Duke Snider | 40.00 | 16.00 | 4.00 |
| ☐ 33 | Johnny Schmitz | 1.50 | .60 | .15 |
| ☐ 34 | Jim Rivera | 1.50 | .60 | .15 |
| ☐ 35 | Jim Gilliam | 4.00 | 1.60 | .40 |
| ☐ 36 | Hoyt Wilhelm | 9.00 | 3.75 | .90 |
| ☐ 37 | Whitey Ford | 18.00 | 7.25 | 1.80 |
| ☐ 38 | Eddie Stanky | 2.00 | .80 | .20 |
| ☐ 39 | Sherm Lollar | 2.00 | .80 | .20 |
| ☐ 40 | Mel Parnell | 2.00 | .80 | .20 |
| ☐ 41 | Willie Jones | 1.50 | .60 | .15 |
| ☐ 42 | Don Mueller | 2.00 | .80 | .20 |
| ☐ 43 | Dick Groat | 3.50 | 1.40 | .35 |
| ☐ 44 | Ned Garver | 1.50 | .60 | .15 |
| ☐ 45 | Richie Ashburn | 5.00 | 2.00 | .50 |
| ☐ 46 | Ken Raffensberger | 1.50 | .60 | .15 |
| ☐ 47 | Ellis Kinder | 1.50 | .60 | .15 |
| ☐ 48 | William Hunter | 1.50 | .60 | .15 |
| ☐ 49 | Ray Murray | 1.50 | .60 | .15 |
| ☐ 50 | Yogi Berra | 35.00 | 14.00 | 3.50 |
| ☐ 51 | Johnny Lindell | 3.50 | 1.40 | .35 |
| ☐ 52 | Vic Power | 3.50 | 1.40 | .35 |
| ☐ 53 | Jack Dittmer | 3.50 | 1.40 | .35 |
| ☐ 54 | Vern Stephens | 4.00 | 1.60 | .40 |
| ☐ 55 | Phil Cavarretta | 4.00 | 1.60 | .40 |
| ☐ 56 | Willie Miranda | 3.50 | 1.40 | .35 |
| ☐ 57 | Luis Aloma | 3.50 | 1.40 | .35 |
| ☐ 58 | Bob Wilson | 3.50 | 1.40 | .35 |
| ☐ 59 | Gene Conley | 3.50 | 1.40 | .35 |
| ☐ 60 | Frank Baumholtz | 3.50 | 1.40 | .35 |
| ☐ 61 | Bob Cain | 3.50 | 1.40 | .35 |
| ☐ 62 | Eddie Robinson | 3.50 | 1.40 | .35 |
| ☐ 63 | Johnny Pesky | 4.00 | 1.60 | .40 |
| ☐ 64 | Hank Thompson | 4.00 | 1.60 | .40 |
| ☐ 65 | Bob Swift | 3.50 | 1.40 | .35 |
| ☐ 66 | Ted Lepcio | 3.50 | 1.40 | .35 |

# 1954 Topps

The cards in this 250 card set measure 2 5/8" by 3 3/4". Each of the cards in the 1954 Topps set contains a large "head" shot of the player in color plus a smaller full length photo in black and white set against a color background. This series contains the rookie cards of Hank Aaron, Ernie Banks, and Al Kaline and two separate cards of Ted Williams (number 1 and number 250). Conspicuous by his absence is Mickey Mantle who apparently was the exclusive property of Bowman during 1954 (and 1955).

| | | | | | | | | | | |
|---|---|---|---|---|---|---|---|---|---|---|
| ☐ | 67 | Jim Willis | 3.50 | 1.40 | .35 | ☐ | 158 | Peanuts Lowrey | 2.00 | .80 | .20 |

| | No. | Player | | | | | No. | Player | | | |
|---|---|---|---|---|---|---|---|---|---|---|---|
| ☐ | 67 | Jim Willis | 3.50 | 1.40 | .35 | ☐ | 158 | Peanuts Lowrey | 2.00 | .80 | .20 |
| ☐ | 68 | Sam Calderone | 3.50 | 1.40 | .35 | ☐ | 159 | Dave Philley | 2.00 | .80 | .20 |
| ☐ | 69 | Bud Podbielan | 3.50 | 1.40 | .35 | ☐ | 160 | Ralph Kress | 2.00 | .80 | .20 |
| ☐ | 70 | Larry Doby | 7.50 | 3.00 | .75 | ☐ | 161 | John Hetki | 2.00 | .80 | .20 |
| ☐ | 71 | Frank Smith | 3.50 | 1.40 | .35 | ☐ | 162 | Herman Wehmeier | 2.00 | .80 | .20 |
| ☐ | 72 | Preston Ward | 3.50 | 1.40 | .35 | ☐ | 163 | Frank House | 2.00 | .80 | .20 |
| ☐ | 73 | Wayne Terwilliger | 3.50 | 1.40 | .35 | ☐ | 164 | Stu Miller | 2.00 | .80 | .20 |
| ☐ | 74 | Bill Taylor | 3.50 | 1.40 | .35 | ☐ | 165 | Jim Pendleton | 2.00 | .80 | .20 |
| ☐ | 75 | Fred Haney | 3.50 | 1.40 | .35 | ☐ | 166 | Johnny Podres | 4.00 | 1.60 | .40 |
| ☐ | 76 | Bob Scheffing | 2.00 | .80 | .20 | ☐ | 167 | Don Lund | 2.00 | .80 | .20 |
| ☐ | 77 | Ray Boone | 2.50 | 1.00 | .25 | ☐ | 168 | Morrie Martin | 2.00 | .80 | .20 |
| ☐ | 78 | Ted Kazanski | 2.00 | .80 | .20 | ☐ | 169 | Jim Hughes | 2.00 | .80 | .20 |
| ☐ | 79 | Andy Pafko | 2.00 | .80 | .20 | ☐ | 170 | James (Dusty) Rhodes | 2.50 | 1.00 | .25 |
| ☐ | 80 | Jackie Jensen | 3.50 | 1.40 | .35 | ☐ | 171 | Leo Kiely | 2.00 | .80 | .20 |
| ☐ | 81 | Dave Hoskins | 2.00 | .80 | .20 | ☐ | 172 | Harold Brown | 2.00 | .80 | .20 |
| ☐ | 82 | Milt Bolling | 2.00 | .80 | .20 | ☐ | 173 | Jack Harshman | 2.00 | .80 | .20 |
| ☐ | 83 | Joe Collins | 2.50 | 1.00 | .25 | ☐ | 174 | Tom Qualters | 2.00 | .80 | .20 |
| ☐ | 84 | Dick Cole | 2.00 | .80 | .20 | ☐ | 175 | Frank Leja | 2.00 | .80 | .20 |
| ☐ | 85 | Bob Turley | 4.50 | 1.80 | .45 | ☐ | 176 | Robert Keeley | 2.00 | .80 | .20 |
| ☐ | 86 | Billy Herman | 3.50 | 1.40 | .35 | ☐ | 177 | Bob Milliken | 2.00 | .80 | .20 |
| ☐ | 87 | Roy Face | 2.50 | 1.00 | .25 | ☐ | 178 | Bill Glynn | 2.00 | .80 | .20 |
| ☐ | 88 | Matt Batts | 2.00 | .80 | .20 | ☐ | 179 | Gair Allie | 2.00 | .80 | .20 |
| ☐ | 89 | Howie Pollet | 2.00 | .80 | .20 | ☐ | 180 | Wes Westrum | 2.00 | .80 | .20 |
| ☐ | 90 | Willie Mays | 150.00 | 60.00 | 15.00 | ☐ | 181 | Mel Roach | 2.00 | .80 | .20 |
| ☐ | 91 | Bob Oldis | 2.00 | .80 | .20 | ☐ | 182 | Chuck Harmon | 2.00 | .80 | .20 |
| ☐ | 92 | Wally Westlake | 2.00 | .80 | .20 | ☐ | 183 | Earle Combs | 3.00 | 1.20 | .30 |
| ☐ | 93 | Sid Hudson | 2.00 | .80 | .20 | ☐ | 184 | Ed Bailey | 2.00 | .80 | .20 |
| ☐ | 94 | Ernie Banks | 100.00 | 40.00 | 10.00 | ☐ | 185 | Chuck Stobbs | 2.00 | .80 | .20 |
| ☐ | 95 | Hal Rice | 2.00 | .80 | .20 | ☐ | 186 | Karl Olson | 2.00 | .80 | .20 |
| ☐ | 96 | Charlie Silvera | 2.00 | .80 | .20 | ☐ | 187 | Henry Manush | 3.00 | 1.20 | .30 |
| ☐ | 97 | Jerald Hal Lane | 2.00 | .80 | .20 | ☐ | 188 | Dave Jolly | 2.00 | .80 | .20 |
| ☐ | 98 | Joe Black | 2.50 | 1.00 | .25 | ☐ | 189 | Floyd Ross | 2.00 | .80 | .20 |
| ☐ | 99 | Bobby Hofman | 2.00 | .80 | .20 | ☐ | 190 | Ray Herbert | 2.00 | .80 | .20 |
| ☐ | 100 | Bob Keegan | 2.00 | .80 | .20 | ☐ | 191 | John (Dick) Schofield | 2.50 | 1.00 | .25 |
| ☐ | 101 | Gene Woodling | 2.50 | 1.00 | .25 | ☐ | 192 | Ellis Deal | 2.00 | .80 | .20 |
| ☐ | 102 | Gil Hodges | 18.00 | 7.25 | 1.80 | ☐ | 193 | Johnny Hopp | 2.50 | 1.00 | .25 |
| ☐ | 103 | Jim Lemon | 2.50 | 1.00 | .25 | ☐ | 194 | Bill Sarni | 2.00 | .80 | .20 |
| ☐ | 104 | Mike Sandlock | 2.00 | .80 | .20 | ☐ | 195 | Bill Consolo | 2.00 | .80 | .20 |
| ☐ | 105 | Andy Carey | 2.50 | 1.00 | .25 | ☐ | 196 | Stanley Jok | 2.00 | .80 | .20 |
| ☐ | 106 | Dick Kokos | 2.00 | .80 | .20 | ☐ | 197 | Lynwood Rowe | 2.50 | 1.00 | .25 |
| ☐ | 107 | Duane Pillette | 2.00 | .80 | .20 | ☐ | 198 | Carl Sawatski | 2.00 | .80 | .20 |
| ☐ | 108 | Thornton Kipper | 2.00 | .80 | .20 | ☐ | 199 | Glenn (Rocky) Nelson | 2.00 | .80 | .20 |
| ☐ | 109 | Bill Bruton | 2.00 | .80 | .20 | ☐ | 200 | Larry Jansen | 2.00 | .80 | .20 |
| ☐ | 110 | Harry Dorish | 2.00 | .80 | .20 | ☐ | 201 | Al Kaline | 120.00 | 50.00 | 12.00 |
| ☐ | 111 | Jim Delsing | 2.00 | .80 | .20 | ☐ | 202 | Bob Purkey | 2.00 | .80 | .20 |
| ☐ | 112 | Bill Renna | 2.00 | .80 | .20 | ☐ | 203 | Harry Brecheen | 2.00 | .80 | .20 |
| ☐ | 113 | Bob Boyd | 2.00 | .80 | .20 | ☐ | 204 | Angel Scull | 2.00 | .80 | .20 |
| ☐ | 114 | Dean Stone | 2.00 | .80 | .20 | ☐ | 205 | Johnny Sain | 4.50 | 1.80 | .45 |
| ☐ | 115 | Rip Repulski | 2.00 | .80 | .20 | ☐ | 206 | Ray Crone | 2.00 | .80 | .20 |
| ☐ | 116 | Steve Bilko | 2.00 | .80 | .20 | ☐ | 207 | Tom Oliver | 2.00 | .80 | .20 |
| ☐ | 117 | Solly Hemus | 2.00 | .80 | .20 | ☐ | 208 | Grady Hatton | 2.00 | .80 | .20 |
| ☐ | 118 | Carl Scheib | 2.00 | .80 | .20 | ☐ | 209 | Chuck Thompson | 2.00 | .80 | .20 |
| ☐ | 119 | Johnny Antonelli | 2.50 | 1.00 | .25 | ☐ | 210 | Bob Buhl | 2.50 | 1.00 | .25 |
| ☐ | 120 | Roy McMillan | 2.00 | .80 | .20 | ☐ | 211 | Don Hoak | 2.00 | .80 | .20 |
| ☐ | 121 | Clem Labine | 2.50 | 1.00 | .25 | ☐ | 212 | Bob Micelotta | 2.00 | .80 | .20 |
| ☐ | 122 | Johnny Logan | 2.50 | 1.00 | .25 | ☐ | 213 | Johnny Fitzpatrick | 2.00 | .80 | .20 |
| ☐ | 123 | Bobby Adams | 2.00 | .80 | .20 | ☐ | 214 | Arnie Portocarrero | 2.00 | .80 | .20 |
| ☐ | 124 | Marion Fricano | 2.00 | .80 | .20 | ☐ | 215 | Warren McGhee | 2.00 | .80 | .20 |
| ☐ | 125 | Harry Perkowski | 2.00 | .80 | .20 | ☐ | 216 | Al Sima | 2.00 | .80 | .20 |
| ☐ | 126 | Ben Wade | 2.00 | .80 | .20 | ☐ | 217 | Paul Schreiber | 2.00 | .80 | .20 |
| ☐ | 127 | Steve O'Neill | 2.00 | .80 | .20 | ☐ | 218 | Fred Marsh | 2.00 | .80 | .20 |
| ☐ | 128 | Hank Aaron | 325.00 | 130.00 | 32.00 | ☐ | 219 | Chuck Kress | 2.00 | .80 | .20 |
| ☐ | 129 | Forrest Jacobs | 2.00 | .80 | .20 | ☐ | 220 | Ruben Gomez | 2.00 | .80 | .20 |
| ☐ | 130 | Hank Bauer | 4.00 | 1.60 | .40 | ☐ | 221 | Dick Brodowski | 2.00 | .80 | .20 |
| ☐ | 131 | Reno Bertoia | 2.00 | .80 | .20 | ☐ | 222 | Bill Wilson | 2.00 | .80 | .20 |
| ☐ | 132 | Tom Lasorda | 25.00 | 10.00 | 2.50 | ☐ | 223 | Joe Haynes | 2.00 | .80 | .20 |
| ☐ | 133 | Dave Baker | 2.00 | .80 | .20 | ☐ | 224 | Dick Weik | 2.00 | .80 | .20 |
| ☐ | 134 | Cal Hogue | 2.00 | .80 | .20 | ☐ | 225 | Don Liddle | 2.00 | .80 | .20 |
| ☐ | 135 | Joe Presko | 2.00 | .80 | .20 | ☐ | 226 | Jehosie Heard | 2.00 | .80 | .20 |
| ☐ | 136 | Connie Ryan | 2.00 | .80 | .20 | ☐ | 227 | Colonel Mills | 2.00 | .80 | .20 |
| ☐ | 137 | Wally Moon | 4.00 | 1.60 | .40 | ☐ | 228 | Gene Hermanski | 2.00 | .80 | .20 |
| ☐ | 138 | Bob Borkowski | 2.00 | .80 | .20 | ☐ | 229 | Robert Talbot | 2.00 | .80 | .20 |
| ☐ | 139 | The O'Brien's | 3.50 | 1.40 | .35 | ☐ | 230 | Bob Kuzava | 2.00 | .80 | .20 |
| | | Johnny O'Brien | | | | ☐ | 231 | Roy Smalley | 2.00 | .80 | .20 |
| | | Eddie O'Brien | | | | ☐ | 232 | Lou Limmer | 2.00 | .80 | .20 |
| ☐ | 140 | Tom Wright | 2.00 | .80 | .20 | ☐ | 233 | Augie Galan | 2.00 | .80 | .20 |
| ☐ | 141 | Joe Jay | 2.50 | 1.00 | .25 | ☐ | 234 | Jerry Lynch | 2.50 | 1.00 | .25 |
| ☐ | 142 | Tom Poholsky | 2.00 | .80 | .20 | ☐ | 235 | Vernon Law | 2.50 | 1.00 | .25 |
| ☐ | 143 | Ralston Hemsley | 2.00 | .80 | .20 | ☐ | 236 | Paul Penson | 2.00 | .80 | .20 |
| ☐ | 144 | Bill Werle | 2.00 | .80 | .20 | ☐ | 237 | Dominic Ryba | 2.00 | .80 | .20 |
| ☐ | 145 | Elmer Valo | 2.00 | .80 | .20 | ☐ | 238 | Al Aber | 2.00 | .80 | .20 |
| ☐ | 146 | Don Johnson | 2.00 | .80 | .20 | ☐ | 239 | Bill Skowron | 6.00 | 2.40 | .60 |
| ☐ | 147 | Johnny Riddle | 2.00 | .80 | .20 | ☐ | 240 | Sam Mele | 2.00 | .80 | .20 |
| ☐ | 148 | Bob Trice | 2.00 | .80 | .20 | ☐ | 241 | Robert Miller | 2.00 | .80 | .20 |
| ☐ | 149 | Al Robertson | 2.00 | .80 | .20 | ☐ | 242 | Curt Roberts | 2.00 | .80 | .20 |
| ☐ | 150 | Dick Kryhoski | 2.00 | .80 | .20 | ☐ | 243 | Ray Blades | 2.00 | .80 | .20 |
| ☐ | 151 | Alex Grammas | 2.00 | .80 | .20 | ☐ | 244 | Leroy Wheat | 2.00 | .80 | .20 |
| ☐ | 152 | Michael Blyzka | 2.00 | .80 | .20 | ☐ | 245 | Roy Sievers | 2.50 | 1.00 | .25 |
| ☐ | 153 | Al Walker | 2.00 | .80 | .20 | ☐ | 246 | Howie Fox | 2.00 | .80 | .20 |
| ☐ | 154 | Mike Fornieles | 2.00 | .80 | .20 | ☐ | 247 | Ed Mayo | 2.00 | .80 | .20 |
| ☐ | 155 | Bob Kennedy | 2.00 | .80 | .20 | ☐ | 248 | Alphonse Smith | 2.50 | 1.00 | .25 |
| ☐ | 156 | Joe Coleman | 2.00 | .80 | .20 | ☐ | 249 | Wilmer Mizell | 2.00 | .80 | .20 |
| ☐ | 157 | Don Lenhardt | 2.00 | .80 | .20 | ☐ | 250 | Ted Williams | 125.00 | 25.00 | 5.00 |

# 1955 Topps

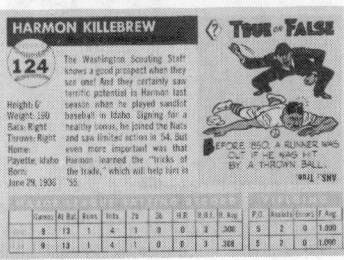

The cards in this 206 card set measure 2 5/8" by 3 3/4". Both the large "head" shot and the smaller full length photos used on each card of the 1955 Topps set are in color. The card fronts were designed horizontally for the first time in Topps' history. The first card features Dusty Rhodes, hitting star for the Giants 1954 World Series sweep over the Indians. A "high" series, 161 to 210, is more difficult to find than cards 1 to 160. Numbers 175, 186, 203, and 209 were never issued. To fill in for the four cards not issued in the high number series, Topps double printed four players, those appearing on cards 170, 172, 184, and 188.

|  | MINT | VG-E | F-G |
|---|---|---|---|
| COMPLETE SET | 1200.00 | 500.00 | 150.00 |
| COMMON PLAYER (1-150) | 1.50 | .60 | .15 |
| COMMON PLAYER (151-160) | 3.00 | 1.20 | .30 |
| COMMON PLAYER (161-210) | 4.25 | 1.70 | .42 |

| | | MINT | VG-E | F-G |
|---|---|---|---|---|
| ☐ | 1 Dusty Rhodes | 6.00 | 1.00 | .20 |
| ☐ | 2 Ted Williams | 60.00 | 24.00 | 6.00 |
| ☐ | 3 Art Fowler | 1.50 | .60 | .15 |
| ☐ | 4 Al Kaline | 22.00 | 9.00 | 2.20 |
| ☐ | 5 Jim Gilliam | 3.00 | 1.20 | .30 |
| ☐ | 6 Stan Hack | 1.50 | .60 | .15 |
| ☐ | 7 Jim Hegan | 1.50 | .60 | .15 |
| ☐ | 8 Harold Smith | 1.50 | .60 | .15 |
| ☐ | 9 Robert Miller | 1.50 | .60 | .15 |
| ☐ | 10 Bob Keegan | 1.50 | .60 | .15 |
| ☐ | 11 Ferris Fain | 1.50 | .60 | .15 |
| ☐ | 12 Vernon Thies | 1.50 | .60 | .15 |
| ☐ | 13 Fred Marsh | 1.50 | .60 | .15 |
| ☐ | 14 Jim Finigan | 1.50 | .60 | .15 |
| ☐ | 15 Jim Pendleton | 1.50 | .60 | .15 |
| ☐ | 16 Roy Sievers | 1.50 | .60 | .15 |
| ☐ | 17 Bobby Hofman | 1.50 | .60 | .15 |
| ☐ | 18 Russ Kemmerer | 1.50 | .60 | .15 |
| ☐ | 19 Billy Herman | 2.50 | 1.00 | .25 |
| ☐ | 20 Andy Carey | 1.50 | .60 | .15 |
| ☐ | 21 Alex Grammas | 1.50 | .60 | .15 |
| ☐ | 22 Bill Skowron | 3.00 | 1.20 | .30 |
| ☐ | 23 Jack Parks | 1.50 | .60 | .15 |
| ☐ | 24 Hal Newhouser | 3.00 | 1.20 | .30 |
| ☐ | 25 John Podres | 3.00 | 1.20 | .30 |
| ☐ | 26 Dick Groat | 2.50 | 1.00 | .25 |

| | | MINT | VG-E | F-G |
|---|---|---|---|---|
| ☐ | 27 Bill Gardner | 1.50 | .60 | .15 |
| ☐ | 28 Ernie Banks | 18.00 | 7.25 | 1.80 |
| ☐ | 29 Herman Wehmeier | 1.50 | .60 | .15 |
| ☐ | 30 Vic Power | 1.50 | .60 | .15 |
| ☐ | 31 Warren Spahn | 14.00 | 5.75 | 1.40 |
| ☐ | 32 Warren McGhee | 1.50 | .60 | .15 |
| ☐ | 33 Tom Qualters | 1.50 | .60 | .15 |
| ☐ | 34 Wayne Terwilliger | 1.50 | .60 | .15 |
| ☐ | 35 Dave Jolly | 1.50 | .60 | .15 |
| ☐ | 36 Leo Kiely | 1.50 | .60 | .15 |
| ☐ | 37 Joe Cunningham | 2.00 | .80 | .20 |
| ☐ | 38 Bob Turley | 2.50 | 1.00 | .25 |
| ☐ | 39 Bill Glynn | 1.50 | .60 | .15 |
| ☐ | 40 Don Hoak | 1.50 | .60 | .15 |
| ☐ | 41 Chuck Stobbs | 1.50 | .60 | .15 |
| ☐ | 42 John (Windy) McCall | 1.50 | .60 | .15 |
| ☐ | 43 Harvey Haddix | 2.00 | .80 | .20 |
| ☐ | 44 Harold Valentine | 1.50 | .60 | .15 |
| ☐ | 45 Hank Sauer | 2.00 | .80 | .20 |
| ☐ | 46 Ted Kazanski | 1.50 | .60 | .15 |
| ☐ | 47 Hank Aaron | 60.00 | 24.00 | 6.00 |
| ☐ | 48 Bob Kennedy | 1.50 | .60 | .15 |
| ☐ | 49 J.W. Porter | 1.50 | .60 | .15 |
| ☐ | 50 Jackie Robinson | 50.00 | 20.00 | 5.00 |
| ☐ | 51 Jim Hughes | 1.50 | .60 | .15 |
| ☐ | 52 Bill Tremel | 1.50 | .60 | .15 |
| ☐ | 53 Bill Taylor | 1.50 | .60 | .15 |
| ☐ | 54 Lou Limmer | 1.50 | .60 | .15 |
| ☐ | 55 Rip Repulski | 1.50 | .60 | .15 |
| ☐ | 56 Ray Jablonski | 1.50 | .60 | .15 |
| ☐ | 57 Billy O'Dell | 1.50 | .60 | .15 |
| ☐ | 58 Jim Rivera | 1.50 | .60 | .15 |
| ☐ | 59 Gair Allie | 1.50 | .60 | .15 |
| ☐ | 60 Dean Stone | 1.50 | .60 | .15 |
| ☐ | 61 Forrest Jacobs | 1.50 | .60 | .15 |
| ☐ | 62 Thornton Kipper | 1.50 | .60 | .15 |
| ☐ | 63 Joe Collins | 1.50 | .60 | .15 |
| ☐ | 64 Gus Triandos | 1.50 | .60 | .15 |
| ☐ | 65 Ray Boone | 1.50 | .60 | .15 |
| ☐ | 66 Ron Jackson | 1.50 | .60 | .15 |
| ☐ | 67 Wally Moon | 2.00 | .80 | .20 |
| ☐ | 68 Jim Davis | 1.50 | .60 | .15 |
| ☐ | 69 Ed Bailey | 1.50 | .60 | .15 |
| ☐ | 70 Al Rosen | 3.50 | 1.40 | .35 |
| ☐ | 71 Ruben Gomez | 1.50 | .60 | .15 |
| ☐ | 72 Karl Olson | 1.50 | .60 | .15 |
| ☐ | 73 Jack Shepard | 1.50 | .60 | .15 |
| ☐ | 74 Robert Borkowski | 1.50 | .60 | .15 |
| ☐ | 75 Sandy Amoros | 2.00 | .80 | .20 |
| ☐ | 76 Howie Pollet | 1.50 | .60 | .15 |
| ☐ | 77 Arnold Portocarrero | 1.50 | .60 | .15 |
| ☐ | 78 Gordon Jones | 1.50 | .60 | .15 |
| ☐ | 79 Clyde Schell | 1.50 | .60 | .15 |
| ☐ | 80 Bob Grim | 2.00 | .80 | .20 |
| ☐ | 81 Gene Conley | 1.50 | .60 | .15 |
| ☐ | 82 Chuck Harmon | 1.50 | .60 | .15 |
| ☐ | 83 Tom Brewer | 1.50 | .60 | .15 |
| ☐ | 84 Camilo Pascual | 2.00 | .80 | .20 |
| ☐ | 85 Don Mossi | 2.00 | .80 | .20 |
| ☐ | 86 Bill Wilson | 1.50 | .60 | .15 |
| ☐ | 87 Frank House | 1.50 | .60 | .15 |
| ☐ | 88 Bob Skinner | 2.00 | .80 | .20 |
| ☐ | 89 Joe Frazier | 1.50 | .60 | .15 |
| ☐ | 90 Karl Spooner | 1.50 | .60 | .15 |
| ☐ | 91 Milt Bolling | 1.50 | .60 | .15 |
| ☐ | 92 Don Zimmer | 3.00 | 1.20 | .30 |
| ☐ | 93 Steve Bilko | 1.50 | .60 | .15 |
| ☐ | 94 Reno Bertoia | 1.50 | .60 | .15 |
| ☐ | 95 Preston Ward | 1.50 | .60 | .15 |
| ☐ | 96 Chuck Bishop | 1.50 | .60 | .15 |
| ☐ | 97 Carlos Paula | 1.50 | .60 | .15 |
| ☐ | 98 John Riddle | 1.50 | .60 | .15 |
| ☐ | 99 Frank Leja | 1.50 | .60 | .15 |
| ☐ | 100 Monte Irvin | 5.00 | 2.00 | .50 |
| ☐ | 101 Johnny Gray | 1.50 | .60 | .15 |
| ☐ | 102 Wally Westlake | 1.50 | .60 | .15 |
| ☐ | 103 Chuck White | 1.50 | .60 | .15 |
| ☐ | 104 Jack Harshman | 1.50 | .60 | .15 |
| ☐ | 105 Chuck Diering | 1.50 | .60 | .15 |
| ☐ | 106 Frank Sullivan | 1.50 | .60 | .15 |
| ☐ | 107 Curt Roberts | 1.50 | .60 | .15 |
| ☐ | 108 Al Walker | 1.50 | .60 | .15 |
| ☐ | 109 Ed Lopat | 3.00 | 1.20 | .30 |
| ☐ | 110 Gus Zernial | 1.50 | .60 | .15 |
| ☐ | 111 Bob Milliken | 1.50 | .60 | .15 |
| ☐ | 112 Nelson King | 1.50 | .60 | .15 |
| ☐ | 113 Harry Brecheen | 1.50 | .60 | .15 |
| ☐ | 114 Louis Ortiz | 1.50 | .60 | .15 |
| ☐ | 115 Ellis Kinder | 1.50 | .60 | .15 |
| ☐ | 116 Tom Hurd | 1.50 | .60 | .15 |
| ☐ | 117 Mel Roach | 1.50 | .60 | .15 |
| ☐ | 118 Bob Purkey | 1.50 | .60 | .15 |
| ☐ | 119 Bob Lennon | 1.50 | .60 | .15 |

| □ 120 | Ted Kluszewski | 3.00 | 1.20 | .30 |
|---|---|---|---|---|
| □ 121 | Bill Renna | 1.50 | .60 | .15 |
| □ 122 | Carl Sawatski | 1.50 | .60 | .15 |
| □ 123 | Sandy Koufax | 125.00 | 50.00 | 12.50 |
| □ 124 | Harmon Killebrew | 60.00 | 24.00 | 6.00 |
| □ 125 | Ken Boyer | 6.00 | 2.40 | .60 |
| □ 126 | Dick Hall | 1.50 | .60 | .15 |
| □ 127 | Dale Long | 1.50 | .60 | .15 |
| □ 128 | Ted Lepcio | 1.50 | .60 | .15 |
| □ 129 | Elvin Tappe | 1.50 | .60 | .15 |
| □ 130 | Mayo Smith MGR | 1.50 | .60 | .15 |
| □ 131 | Grady Hatton | 1.50 | .60 | .15 |
| □ 132 | Bob Trice | 1.50 | .60 | .15 |
| □ 133 | Dave Hoskins | 1.50 | .60 | .15 |
| □ 134 | Joe Jay | 1.50 | .60 | .15 |
| □ 135 | Johnny O'Brien | 1.50 | .60 | .15 |
| □ 136 | Vernon Stewart | 1.50 | .60 | .15 |
| □ 137 | Harry Elliott | 1.50 | .60 | .15 |
| □ 138 | Ray Herbert | 1.50 | .60 | .15 |
| □ 139 | Steve Kraly | 1.50 | .60 | .15 |
| □ 140 | Mel Parnell | 2.00 | .80 | .20 |
| □ 141 | Tom Wright | 1.50 | .60 | .15 |
| □ 142 | Gerry Lynch | 1.50 | .60 | .15 |
| □ 143 | John (Dick) Schofield | 1.50 | .60 | .15 |
| □ 144 | John (Joe) Amalfitano | 1.50 | .60 | .15 |
| □ 145 | Elmer Valo | 1.50 | .60 | .15 |
| □ 146 | Dick Donovan | 1.50 | .60 | .15 |
| □ 147 | Hugh Pepper | 1.50 | .60 | .15 |
| □ 148 | Hector Brown | 1.50 | .60 | .15 |
| □ 149 | Ray Crone | 1.50 | .60 | .15 |
| □ 150 | Michael Higgins | 1.50 | .60 | .15 |
| □ 151 | Ralph Kress | 3.00 | 1.20 | .30 |
| □ 152 | Harry Agganis | 4.50 | 1.80 | .45 |
| □ 153 | Bud Podbielan | 3.00 | 1.20 | .30 |
| □ 154 | Willie Miranda | 3.00 | 1.20 | .30 |
| □ 155 | Eddie Mathews | 16.00 | 6.50 | 1.60 |
| □ 156 | Joe Black | 4.50 | 1.80 | .45 |
| □ 157 | Robert Miller | 3.00 | 1.20 | .30 |
| □ 158 | Tommy Carroll | 4.50 | 1.80 | .45 |
| □ 159 | Johnny Schmitz | 3.00 | 1.20 | .30 |
| □ 160 | Ray Narleski | 3.00 | 1.20 | .30 |
| □ 161 | Chuck Tanner | 5.00 | 2.00 | .50 |
| □ 162 | Joe Coleman | 4.25 | 1.70 | .42 |
| □ 163 | Faye Throneberry | 4.25 | 1.70 | .42 |
| □ 164 | Roberto Clemente | 200.00 | 80.00 | 20.00 |
| □ 165 | Don Johnson | 4.25 | 1.70 | .42 |
| □ 166 | Hank Bauer | 9.00 | 3.75 | .90 |
| □ 167 | Thomas Casagrande | 4.25 | 1.70 | .42 |
| □ 168 | Duane Pillette | 4.25 | 1.70 | .42 |
| □ 169 | Bob Oldis | 4.25 | 1.70 | .42 |
| □ 170 | Jim Pearce DP | 2.00 | .80 | .20 |
| □ 171 | Dick Brodowski | 4.25 | 1.70 | .42 |
| □ 172 | Frank Baumholtz DP | 2.00 | .80 | .20 |
| □ 173 | Johnny Kline | 4.25 | 1.70 | .42 |
| □ 174 | Rudy Minarcin | 4.25 | 1.70 | .42 |
| □ 175 | Does not exist | 0.00 | .00 | .00 |
| □ 176 | Norm Zauchin | 4.25 | 1.70 | .42 |
| □ 177 | Al Robertson | 4.25 | 1.70 | .42 |
| □ 178 | Bobby Adams | 4.25 | 1.70 | .42 |
| □ 179 | Jim Bolger | 4.25 | 1.70 | .42 |
| □ 180 | Clem Labine | 5.00 | 2.00 | .50 |
| □ 181 | Roy McMillan | 4.25 | 1.70 | .42 |
| □ 182 | Humberto Robinson | 4.25 | 1.70 | .42 |
| □ 183 | Anthony Jacobs | 4.25 | 1.70 | .42 |
| □ 184 | Harry Perkowski DP | 2.00 | .80 | .20 |
| □ 185 | Don Ferrarese | 4.25 | 1.70 | .42 |
| □ 186 | Does not exist | 0.00 | .00 | .00 |
| □ 187 | Gil Hodges | 40.00 | 16.00 | 4.00 |
| □ 188 | Charlie Silvera DP | 2.00 | .80 | .20 |
| □ 189 | Phil Rizzuto | 35.00 | 14.00 | 3.50 |
| □ 190 | Gene Woodling | 5.00 | 2.00 | .50 |
| □ 191 | Eddie Stanky | 5.00 | 2.00 | .50 |
| □ 192 | Jim Delsing | 4.25 | 1.70 | .42 |
| □ 193 | Johnny Sain | 6.00 | 2.40 | .60 |
| □ 194 | Willie Mays | 200.00 | 80.00 | 20.00 |
| □ 195 | Ed Roebuck | 5.00 | 2.00 | .50 |
| □ 196 | Gale Wade | 4.25 | 1.70 | .42 |
| □ 197 | Al Smith | 4.25 | 1.70 | .42 |
| □ 198 | Yogi Berra | 60.00 | 24.00 | 6.00 |
| □ 199 | Odbert Hamric | 4.25 | 1.70 | .42 |
| □ 200 | Jackie Jensen | 7.00 | 2.80 | .70 |
| □ 201 | Sherman Lollar | 5.00 | 2.00 | .50 |
| □ 202 | Jim Owens | 4.25 | 1.70 | .42 |
| □ 203 | Does not exist | 0.00 | .00 | .00 |
| □ 204 | Frank Smith | 4.25 | 1.70 | .42 |
| □ 205 | Gene Freese | 4.25 | 1.70 | .42 |
| □ 206 | Pete Daley | 4.25 | 1.70 | .42 |
| □ 207 | Bill Consolo | 4.25 | 1.70 | .42 |
| □ 208 | Ray Moore | 4.25 | 1.70 | .42 |
| □ 209 | Does not exist | 0.00 | .00 | .00 |
| □ 210 | Duke Snider | 175.00 | 50.00 | 10.00 |

## 1955 Topps Double Header

The cards in ths 66 card set measure 2 1/16" by 4 7/8". Borrowing a design from the T201 Mecca series, Topps issued a 132 player "Double Header" set in a separate wrapper in 1955. Each player is numbered in the biographical section on the reverse. When open, with perforated flap up, one player is revealed; when the flap is lowered, or closed, the player design on top incorporates a portion of the inside player artwork. When the cards are placed side by side, a continuous ballpark background is formed. Some cards have been found without perforations, and all players pictured appear in the low series of the 1955 regular issue.

| | | MINT | VG-E | F-G |
|---|---|---|---|---|
| | COMPLETE SET | 1400.00 | 600.00 | 150.00 |
| | COMMON PAIR | 15.00 | 6.00 | 1.50 |
| □ | 1 Al Rosen and<br>2 Chuck Diering | 18.00 | 7.25 | 1.80 |
| □ | 3 Monte Irvin and<br>4 Russ Kemmerer | 21.00 | 8.50 | 2.10 |
| □ | 5 Ted Kazanski and<br>6 Gordon Jones | 15.00 | 6.00 | 1.50 |
| □ | 7 Bill Taylor and<br>8 Billy O'Dell | 15.00 | 6.00 | 1.50 |
| □ | 9 J.W. Porter and<br>10 Thornton Kipper | 15.00 | 6.00 | 1.50 |
| □ | 11 Curt Roberts and<br>12 Arnie Portocarrero | 15.00 | 6.00 | 1.50 |
| □ | 13 Wally Westlake and<br>14 Frank House | 15.00 | 6.00 | 1.50 |
| □ | 15 Rube Walker and<br>16 Lou Limmer | 15.00 | 6.00 | 1.50 |
| □ | 17 Dean Stone and<br>18 Charlie White | 15.00 | 6.00 | 1.50 |
| □ | 19 Karl Spooner and<br>20 Jim Hughes | 15.00 | 6.00 | 1.50 |
| □ | 21 Bill Skowron and<br>22 Frank Sullivan | 18.00 | 7.25 | 1.80 |
| □ | 23 Jack Shepard and<br>24 Stan Hack | 15.00 | 6.00 | 1.50 |
| □ | 25 Jackie Robinson and<br>26 Don Hoak | 80.00 | 32.00 | 8.00 |
| □ | 27 Dusty Rhodes and<br>28 Jim Davis | 15.00 | 6.00 | 1.50 |
| □ | 29 Vic Power and<br>30 Ed Bailey | 15.00 | 6.00 | 1.50 |
| □ | 31 Howie Pollet and<br>32 Ernie Banks | 60.00 | 24.00 | 6.00 |
| □ | 33 Jim Pendleton and<br>34 Gene Conley | 15.00 | 6.00 | 1.50 |
| □ | 35 Karl Olson and<br>36 Andy Carey | 15.00 | 6.00 | 1.50 |

| | | | | |
|---|---|---|---|---|
| ☐ | 37 Wally Moon and ............... 38 Joe Cunningham | 15.00 | 6.00 | 1.50 |
| ☐ | 39 Freddie Marsh and ......... 40 Vernon Thies | 15.00 | 6.00 | 1.50 |
| ☐ | 41 Eddie Lopat and ............. 42 Harvey Haddix | 18.00 | 7.25 | 1.80 |
| ☐ | 43 Leo Kiely and .................. 44 Chuck Stobbs | 15.00 | 6.00 | 1.50 |
| ☐ | 45 Al Kaline and ................... 46 Harold Valentine | 70.00 | 28.00 | 7.00 |
| ☐ | 47 Forrest Jacobs and ......... 48 Johnny Gray | 15.00 | 6.00 | 1.50 |
| ☐ | 49 Ron Jackson and ............ 50 Jim Finigan | 15.00 | 6.00 | 1.50 |
| ☐ | 51 Ray Jablonski and .......... 52 Bob Keegan | 15.00 | 6.00 | 1.50 |
| ☐ | 53 Billy Herman and ........... 54 Sandy Amoros | 18.00 | 7.25 | 1.80 |
| ☐ | 55 Chuck Harmon and ......... 56 Bob Skinner | 15.00 | 6.00 | 1.50 |
| ☐ | 57 Dick Hall and ................. 58 Bob Grim | 15.00 | 6.00 | 1.50 |
| ☐ | 59 Billy Glynn and ............. 60 Bob Miller | 15.00 | 6.00 | 1.50 |
| ☐ | 61 Billy Gardner and ........... 62 John Hetki | 15.00 | 6.00 | 1.50 |
| ☐ | 63 Bob Borkowski and ........ 64 Bob Turley | 15.00 | 6.00 | 1.50 |
| ☐ | 65 Joe Collins and .............. 66 Jack Harshman | 15.00 | 6.00 | 1.50 |
| ☐ | 67 Jim Hegan and ............... 68 Jack Parks | 15.00 | 6.00 | 1.50 |
| ☐ | 69 Ted Williams and ............ 70 Mayo Smith | 125.00 | 50.00 | 12.50 |
| ☐ | 71 Gair Allie and ................. 72 Grady Hatton | 15.00 | 6.00 | 1.50 |
| ☐ | 73 Jerry Lynch and ............. 74 Harry Brecheen | 15.00 | 6.00 | 1.50 |
| ☐ | 75 Tom Wright and .............. 76 Vernon Stewart | 15.00 | 6.00 | 1.50 |
| ☐ | 77 Dave Hoskins and .......... 78 Warren McGhee | 15.00 | 6.00 | 1.50 |
| ☐ | 79 Roy Sievers and ............ 80 Art Fowler | 15.00 | 6.00 | 1.50 |
| ☐ | 81 Danny Schell and ........... 82 Gus Triandos | 15.00 | 6.00 | 1.50 |
| ☐ | 83 Joe Frazier and .............. 84 Don Mossi | 15.00 | 6.00 | 1.50 |
| ☐ | 85 Elmer Valo and .............. 86 Hector Brown | 15.00 | 6.00 | 1.50 |
| ☐ | 87 Bob Kennedy and ........... 88 Windy McCall | 15.00 | 6.00 | 1.50 |
| ☐ | 89 Ruben Gomez and .......... 90 Jim Rivera | 15.00 | 6.00 | 1.50 |
| ☐ | 91 Louis Ortiz and .............. 92 Milt Bolling | 15.00 | 6.00 | 1.50 |
| ☐ | 93 Carl Sawatski and .......... 94 El Tappe | 15.00 | 6.00 | 1.50 |
| ☐ | 95 Dave Jolly and ............... 96 Bobby Hofman | 15.00 | 6.00 | 1.50 |
| ☐ | 97 Preston Ward and .......... 98 Don Zimmer | 15.00 | 6.00 | 1.50 |
| ☐ | 99 Bill Renna and ............... 100 Dick Groat | 18.00 | 7.25 | 1.80 |
| ☐ 101 | Bill Wilson and ................ 102 Bill Tremel | 15.00 | 6.00 | 1.50 |
| ☐ 103 | Hank Sauer and .............. 104 Camilo Pascual | 18.00 | 7.25 | 1.80 |
| ☐ 105 | Hank Aaron and ............... 106 Ray Herbert | 150.00 | 60.00 | 15.00 |
| ☐ 107 | Alex Grammas and ......... 108 Tom Qualters | 15.00 | 6.00 | 1.50 |
| ☐ 109 | Hal Newhouser and ........ 110 Chuck Bishop | 18.00 | 7.25 | 1.80 |
| ☐ 111 | Harmon Killebrew ........... 112 and John Podres | 60.00 | 24.00 | 6.00 |
| ☐ 113 | Ray Boone and ............... 114 Bob Purkey | 15.00 | 6.00 | 1.50 |
| ☐ 115 | Dale Long and ................ 116 Ferris Fain | 15.00 | 6.00 | 1.50 |
| ☐ 117 | Steve Bilko and .............. 118 Bob Milliken | 15.00 | 6.00 | 1.50 |
| ☐ 119 | Mel Parnell and .............. 120 Tom Hurd | 15.00 | 6.00 | 1.50 |
| ☐ 121 | Ted Kluszewski and ........ 122 Jim Owens | 18.00 | 7.25 | 1.80 |
| ☐ 123 | Gus Zernial and ............. 124 Bob Trice | 15.00 | 6.00 | 1.50 |
| ☐ 125 | Rip Repulski and ............ 126 Ted Lepcio | 15.00 | 6.00 | 1.50 |
| ☐ 127 | Warren Spahn and .......... 128 Tom Brewer | 60.00 | 24.00 | 6.00 |
| ☐ 129 | Jim Gilliam and ............... | 18.00 | 7.25 | 1.80 |

| | | | |
|---|---|---|---|
| 130 Ellis Kinder | | | |
| ☐ 131 Herm Wehmeier and ....... 132 Wayne Terwilliger | 15.00 | 6.00 | 1.50 |

# 1956 Topps

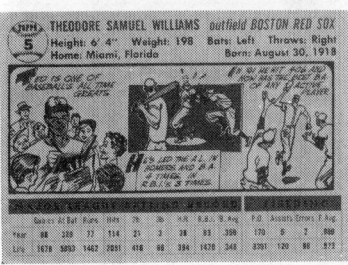

The cards in this 340 card set measure 2 5/8" by 3 3/4". Following up with another horizontally oriented card in 1956, Topps improved the format by layering the color "head" shot onto an actual action sequence involving the player. Cards 1 to 180 come with either white or gray backs: in the 1 to 100 sequence, gray backs are less common (worth about 10% more) and in the 101 to 180 sequence, white backs are less common (worth 30% more). The team cards used for the first time in a regular set by Topps, are found dated 1955, or undated, with the team name appearing on either side. The two unnumbered checklist cards are highly prized (must be unmarked to qualify as excellent or mint). The complete set price below does not include the unnumbered checklist cards or any of the variations.

| | | MINT | VG-E | F-G |
|---|---|---|---|---|
| COMPLETE SET (340) ................ | | 1250.00 | 550.00 | 150.00 |
| COMMON PLAYER (1-100) ........ | | 1.00 | .40 | .10 |
| COMMON PLAYER (101-180) .... | | 1.50 | .60 | .15 |
| COMMON PLAYER (181-260) .... | | 2.50 | 1.00 | .25 |
| COMMON PLAYER (261-340) .... | | 1.50 | .60 | .15 |
| ☐ | 1 William Harridge ............. (AL President) | 10.00 | 2.00 | .40 |
| ☐ | 2 Warren Giles ................. (NL President) | 2.50 | 1.00 | .25 |
| ☐ | 3 Elmer Valo ...................... | 1.00 | .40 | .10 |
| ☐ | 4 Carlos Paula .................. | 2.00 | .80 | .20 |
| ☐ | 5 Ted Williams .................... | 50.00 | 20.00 | 5.00 |
| ☐ | 6 Ray Boone ...................... | 1.00 | .40 | .10 |
| ☐ | 7 Ron Negray .................... | 1.00 | .40 | .10 |
| ☐ | 8 Walter Alston MGR ......... | 7.50 | 3.00 | .75 |
| ☐ | 9 Ruben Gomez ................. | 1.00 | .40 | .10 |
| ☐ | 10 Warren Spahn ................. | 12.50 | 5.00 | 1.25 |
| ☐ | 11A Chicago Cubs ............... (centered) | 3.00 | 1.20 | .30 |
| ☐ | 11B Cubs Team ................... (dated 1955) | 15.00 | 6.00 | 1.50 |

| | | | | |
|---|---|---|---|---|
| ☐ 11C | Cubs Team (name ........ at far left) | 3.00 | 1.20 | .30 |
| ☐ 12 | Andy Carey ..................... | 1.25 | .50 | .12 |
| ☐ 13 | Roy Face ........................ | 1.50 | .60 | .15 |
| ☐ 14 | Ken Boyer ...................... | 2.50 | 1.00 | .25 |
| ☐ 15 | Ernie Banks .................... | 14.00 | 5.75 | 1.40 |
| ☐ 16 | Hector Lopez ................... | 1.00 | .40 | .10 |
| ☐ 17 | Gene Conley ................... | 1.00 | .40 | .10 |
| ☐ 18 | Dick Donovan .................. | 1.00 | .40 | .10 |
| ☐ 19 | Chuck Diering ................. | 1.00 | .40 | .10 |
| ☐ 20 | Al Kaline ....................... | 16.00 | 6.50 | 1.60 |
| ☐ 21 | Joe Collins ..................... | 1.25 | .50 | .12 |
| ☐ 22 | Jim Finigan .................... | 1.00 | .40 | .10 |
| ☐ 23 | Freddie Marsh ................ | 1.00 | .40 | .10 |
| ☐ 24 | Dick Groat ..................... | 2.00 | .80 | .20 |
| ☐ 25 | Ted Kluszewski ............... | 3.00 | 1.20 | .30 |
| ☐ 26 | Grady Hatton .................. | 1.00 | .40 | .10 |
| ☐ 27 | Nelson Burbrink ............... | 1.00 | .40 | .10 |
| ☐ 28 | Bobby Hofman ................ | 1.00 | .40 | .10 |
| ☐ 29 | Jack Harshman ................ | 1.00 | .40 | .10 |
| ☐ 30 | Jackie Robinson ............. | 45.00 | 18.00 | 4.50 |
| ☐ 31 | Hank Aaron ..................... (small photo actually W.Mays) | 50.00 | 20.00 | 5.00 |
| ☐ 32 | Frank House ................... | 1.00 | .40 | .10 |
| ☐ 33 | Roberto Clemente .......... | 45.00 | 18.00 | 4.50 |
| ☐ 34 | Tom Brewer .................... | 1.00 | .40 | .10 |
| ☐ 35 | Al Rosen ........................ | 3.00 | 1.20 | .30 |
| ☐ 36 | Rudy Minarcin ................. | 1.00 | .40 | .10 |
| ☐ 37 | Alex Grammas ................. | 1.00 | .40 | .10 |
| ☐ 38 | Bob Kennedy ................... | 1.00 | .40 | .10 |
| ☐ 39 | Don Mossi ...................... | 1.50 | .60 | .15 |
| ☐ 40 | Bob Turley ..................... | 2.00 | .80 | .20 |
| ☐ 41 | Hank Sauer ..................... | 1.25 | .50 | .12 |
| ☐ 42 | Sandy Amoros ................. | 1.25 | .50 | .12 |
| ☐ 43 | Ray Moore ...................... | 1.00 | .40 | .10 |
| ☐ 44 | Windy McCall .................. | 1.00 | .40 | .10 |
| ☐ 45 | Gus Zernial .................... | 1.00 | .40 | .10 |
| ☐ 46 | Gene Freese ................... | 1.00 | .40 | .10 |
| ☐ 47 | Art Fowler ...................... | 1.00 | .40 | .10 |
| ☐ 48 | Jim Hegan ...................... | 1.00 | .40 | .10 |
| ☐ 49 | Pedro Ramos ................... | 1.00 | .40 | .10 |
| ☐ 50 | Dusty Rhodes .................. | 1.25 | .50 | .12 |
| ☐ 51 | Ernie Oravetz .................. | 1.00 | .40 | .10 |
| ☐ 52 | Bob Grim ....................... | 1.25 | .50 | .12 |
| ☐ 53 | Arnie Portocarrero .......... | 1.00 | .40 | .10 |
| ☐ 54 | Bob Keegan .................... | 1.00 | .40 | .10 |
| ☐ 55 | Wally Moon .................... | 1.25 | .50 | .12 |
| ☐ 56 | Dale Long ...................... | 1.00 | .40 | .10 |
| ☐ 57 | Duke Maas ..................... | 1.00 | .40 | .10 |
| ☐ 58 | Ed Roebuck .................... | 1.00 | .40 | .10 |
| ☐ 59 | Jose Santiago ................. | 1.00 | .40 | .10 |
| ☐ 60 | Mayo Smith MGR ........... | 1.00 | .40 | .10 |
| ☐ 61 | Bill Skowron ................... | 3.00 | 1.20 | .30 |
| ☐ 62 | Hal Smith ...................... | 1.00 | .40 | .10 |
| ☐ 63 | Roger Craig .................... | 3.00 | 1.20 | .30 |
| ☐ 64 | Luis Arroyo .................... | 1.25 | .50 | .12 |
| ☐ 65 | Johnny O'Brien ............... | 1.00 | .40 | .10 |
| ☐ 66 | Bob Speake .................... | 1.00 | .40 | .10 |
| ☐ 67 | Vic Power ...................... | 1.00 | .40 | .10 |
| ☐ 68 | Chuck Stobbs .................. | 1.00 | .40 | .10 |
| ☐ 69 | Chuck Tanner .................. | 1.25 | .50 | .12 |
| ☐ 70 | Jim Rivera ..................... | 1.00 | .40 | .10 |
| ☐ 71 | Frank Sullivan ................ | 1.00 | .40 | .10 |
| ☐ 72A | Phillies Team ................ (centered) | 3.00 | 1.20 | .30 |
| ☐ 72B | Phillies Team ................ (dated 1955) | 15.00 | 6.00 | 1.50 |
| ☐ 72C | Phillies Team ................ (name at far left) | 3.00 | 1.20 | .30 |
| ☐ 73 | Wayne Terwilliger ........... | 1.00 | .40 | .10 |
| ☐ 74 | Jim King ....................... | 1.00 | .40 | .10 |
| ☐ 75 | Roy Sievers ................... | 1.25 | .50 | .12 |
| ☐ 76 | Ray Crone ...................... | 1.00 | .40 | .10 |
| ☐ 77 | Harvey Haddix ................ | 1.25 | .50 | .12 |
| ☐ 78 | Herman Wehmeier ........... | 1.00 | .40 | .10 |
| ☐ 79 | Sandy Koufax ................. | 45.00 | 18.00 | 4.50 |
| ☐ 80 | Gus Triandos .................. | 1.25 | .50 | .12 |
| ☐ 81 | Wally Westlake ............... | 1.00 | .40 | .10 |
| ☐ 82 | Bill Renna ..................... | 1.00 | .40 | .10 |
| ☐ 83 | Karl Spooner .................. | 1.25 | .50 | .12 |
| ☐ 84 | Babe Birrer .................... | 1.00 | .40 | .10 |
| ☐ 85A | Cleveland Indians .......... (centered) | 3.00 | 1.20 | .30 |
| ☐ 85B | Indians Team ................ (dated 1955) | 15.00 | 6.00 | 1.50 |
| ☐ 85C | Indians Team ................ (name at far left) | 3.00 | 1.20 | .30 |
| ☐ 86 | Ray Jablonski ................. | 1.00 | .40 | .10 |
| ☐ 87 | Dean Stone .................... | 1.00 | .40 | .10 |
| ☐ 88 | Johnny Kucks .................. | 1.25 | .50 | .12 |
| ☐ 89 | Norm Zauchin ................. | 1.00 | .40 | .10 |
| ☐ 90A | Cincinnati Redlegs ......... | 3.00 | 1.20 | .30 |

| | | | | |
|---|---|---|---|---|
| | Team (centered) | | | |
| ☐ 90B | Reds Team ................... (dated 1955) | 15.00 | 6.00 | 1.50 |
| ☐ 90C | Reds Team (name ........ at far left) | 3.00 | 1.20 | .30 |
| ☐ 91 | Gail Harris ..................... | 1.00 | .40 | .10 |
| ☐ 92 | Bob (Red) Wilson ............ | 1.00 | .40 | .10 |
| ☐ 93 | George Susce ................. | 1.00 | .40 | .10 |
| ☐ 94 | Ronnie Kline .................. | 1.00 | .40 | .10 |
| ☐ 95A | Milwaukee Braves ........ Team (centered) | 3.00 | 1.20 | .30 |
| ☐ 95B | Braves Team ................ (dated 1955) | 15.00 | 6.00 | 1.50 |
| ☐ 95C | Braves Team (name ..... at far left) | 3.00 | 1.20 | .30 |
| ☐ 96 | Bill Tremel .................... | 1.00 | .40 | .10 |
| ☐ 97 | Jerry Lynch .................... | 1.00 | .40 | .10 |
| ☐ 98 | Camilo Pascual ............... | 1.25 | .50 | .12 |
| ☐ 99 | Don Zimmer ................... | 1.50 | .60 | .15 |
| ☐100A | Baltimore Orioles .......... Team (centered) | 3.00 | 1.20 | .30 |
| ☐100B | Orioles Team ................ (dated 1955) | 15.00 | 6.00 | 1.50 |
| ☐100C | Orioles Team ................ (name at far left) | 3.00 | 1.20 | .30 |
| ☐101 | Roy Campanella .............. | 36.00 | 15.00 | 3.60 |
| ☐102 | Jim Davis ...................... | 1.50 | .60 | .15 |
| ☐103 | Willie Miranda ................ | 1.50 | .60 | .15 |
| ☐104 | Bob Lennon ................... | 1.50 | .60 | .15 |
| ☐105 | Al Smith ....................... | 1.50 | .60 | .15 |
| ☐106 | Joe Astroth .................... | 1.50 | .60 | .15 |
| ☐107 | Ed Mathews ................... | 11.00 | 4.50 | 1.10 |
| ☐108 | Laurin Pepper ................ | 1.50 | .60 | .15 |
| ☐109 | Enos Slaughter ............... | 7.00 | 2.80 | .70 |
| ☐110 | Yogi Berra ..................... | 27.00 | 11.00 | 2.70 |
| ☐111 | Boston Red Sox Team .... | 4.50 | 1.80 | .45 |
| ☐112 | Dee Fondy ..................... | 1.50 | .60 | .15 |
| ☐113 | Phil Rizzuto ................... | 14.00 | 5.75 | 1.40 |
| ☐114 | Jim Owens ..................... | 1.50 | .60 | .15 |
| ☐115 | Jackie Jensen ................. | 2.50 | 1.00 | .25 |
| ☐116 | Eddie O'Brien ................. | 1.50 | .60 | .15 |
| ☐117 | Virgil Trucks .................. | 1.50 | .60 | .15 |
| ☐118 | Nelson Fox ..................... | 3.50 | 1.40 | .35 |
| ☐119 | Larry Jackson ................. | 1.50 | .60 | .15 |
| ☐120 | Richie Ashburn ............... | 4.00 | 1.60 | .40 |
| ☐121 | Pirates Team .................. | 3.50 | 1.40 | .35 |
| ☐122 | Willard Nixon ................. | 1.50 | .60 | .15 |
| ☐123 | Roy McMillan .................. | 1.50 | .60 | .15 |
| ☐124 | Don Kaiser ..................... | 1.50 | .60 | .15 |
| ☐125 | Minnie Minoso ................ | 3.00 | 1.20 | .30 |
| ☐126 | Jim Brady ...................... | 1.50 | .60 | .15 |
| ☐127 | Willie Jones ................... | 1.50 | .60 | .15 |
| ☐128 | Eddie Yost ..................... | 1.50 | .60 | .15 |
| ☐129 | Jake Martin .................... | 1.50 | .60 | .15 |
| ☐130 | Willie Mays .................... | 60.00 | 24.00 | 6.00 |
| ☐131 | Bob Roselli .................... | 1.50 | .60 | .15 |
| ☐132 | Bobby Avila .................... | 1.50 | .60 | .15 |
| ☐133 | Ray Narleski .................. | 1.50 | .60 | .15 |
| ☐134 | Cardinals Team ............... | 4.00 | 1.60 | .40 |
| ☐135 | Mickey Mantle ................ | 200.00 | 80.00 | 20.00 |
| ☐136 | Johnny Logan ................. | 2.00 | .80 | .20 |
| ☐137 | Al Silvera ...................... | 1.50 | .60 | .15 |
| ☐138 | Johnny Antonelli ............. | 2.00 | .80 | .20 |
| ☐139 | Tommy Carroll ................ | 1.50 | .60 | .15 |
| ☐140 | Herb Score ..................... | 3.50 | 1.40 | .35 |
| ☐141 | Joe Frazier .................... | 1.50 | .60 | .15 |
| ☐142 | Gene Baker .................... | 1.50 | .60 | .15 |
| ☐143 | Jim Piersall ................... | 2.50 | 1.00 | .25 |
| ☐144 | Leroy Powell .................. | 1.50 | .60 | .15 |
| ☐145 | Gil Hodges ..................... | 12.50 | 5.00 | 1.25 |
| ☐146 | Washington Team ............ | 3.00 | 1.20 | .30 |
| ☐147 | Earl Torgeson ................. | 1.50 | .60 | .15 |
| ☐148 | Al Dark ......................... | 2.00 | .80 | .20 |
| ☐149 | Dixie Howell .................. | 1.50 | .60 | .15 |
| ☐150 | Duke Snider ................... | 40.00 | 16.00 | 4.00 |
| ☐151 | Spook Jacobs ................. | 1.50 | .60 | .15 |
| ☐152 | Billy Hoeft .................... | 1.50 | .60 | .15 |
| ☐153 | Frank Thomas ................. | 1.50 | .60 | .15 |
| ☐154 | David Pope .................... | 1.50 | .60 | .15 |
| ☐155 | Harvey Kuenn ................. | 2.50 | 1.00 | .25 |
| ☐156 | Wes Westrum .................. | 1.50 | .60 | .15 |
| ☐157 | Dick Brodowski .............. | 1.50 | .60 | .15 |
| ☐158 | Wally Post ..................... | 1.50 | .60 | .15 |
| ☐159 | Clint Courtney ................ | 1.50 | .60 | .15 |
| ☐160 | Billy Pierce ................... | 2.00 | .80 | .20 |
| ☐161 | Joe DeMaestri ................ | 1.50 | .60 | .15 |
| ☐162 | Dave (Gus) Bell .............. | 2.00 | .80 | .20 |
| ☐163 | Gene Woodling ............... | 2.00 | .80 | .20 |
| ☐164 | Harmon Killebrew ........... | 18.00 | 7.25 | 1.80 |
| ☐165 | Red Schoendienst ........... | 2.50 | 1.00 | .25 |
| ☐166 | Brooklyn Dodgers ........... Team Card | 24.00 | 10.00 | 2.40 |
| ☐167 | Harry Dorish ................... | 1.50 | .60 | .15 |

| | | | | | | | | | |
|---|---|---|---|---|---|---|---|---|---|
| ☐ 168 | Sammy White | 1.50 | .60 | .15 | ☐ 259 | Sam Jones | 3.00 | 1.20 | .30 |
| ☐ 169 | Bob Nelson | 1.50 | .60 | .15 | ☐ 260 | Pee Wee Reese | 20.00 | 8.00 | 2.00 |
| ☐ 170 | Bill Virdon | 2.50 | 1.00 | .25 | ☐ 261 | Bobby Shantz | 2.00 | .80 | .20 |
| ☐ 171 | Jim Wilson | 1.50 | .60 | .15 | ☐ 262 | Howie Pollet | 1.50 | .60 | .15 |
| ☐ 172 | Frank Torre | 1.50 | .60 | .15 | ☐ 263 | Bob Miller | 1.50 | .60 | .15 |
| ☐ 173 | Johnny Podres | 2.50 | 1.00 | .25 | ☐ 264 | Ray Monzant | 1.50 | .60 | .15 |
| ☐ 174 | Glen Gorbous | 1.50 | .60 | .15 | ☐ 265 | Sandy Consuegra | 1.50 | .60 | .15 |
| ☐ 175 | Del Crandall | 2.00 | .80 | .20 | ☐ 266 | Don Ferrarese | 1.50 | .60 | .15 |
| ☐ 176 | Alex Kellner | 1.50 | .60 | .15 | ☐ 267 | Bob Nieman | 1.50 | .60 | .15 |
| ☐ 177 | Hank Bauer | 2.50 | 1.00 | .25 | ☐ 268 | Dale Mitchell | 2.00 | .80 | .20 |
| ☐ 178 | Joe Black | 2.00 | .80 | .20 | ☐ 269 | Jack Meyer | 1.50 | .60 | .15 |
| ☐ 179 | Harry Chiti | 1.50 | .60 | .15 | ☐ 270 | Billy Loes | 2.00 | .80 | .20 |
| ☐ 180 | Robin Roberts | 9.00 | 3.75 | .90 | ☐ 271 | Foster Castleman | 1.50 | .60 | .15 |
| ☐ 181 | Billy Martin | 16.00 | 6.50 | 1.60 | ☐ 272 | Danny O'Connell | 1.50 | .60 | .15 |
| ☐ 182 | Paul Minner | 2.50 | 1.00 | .25 | ☐ 273 | Walker Cooper | 1.50 | .60 | .15 |
| ☐ 183 | Stan Lopata | 2.50 | 1.00 | .25 | ☐ 274 | Frank Baumholtz | 1.50 | .60 | .15 |
| ☐ 184 | Don Bessent | 2.50 | 1.00 | .25 | ☐ 275 | Jim Greengrass | 1.50 | .60 | .15 |
| ☐ 185 | Bill Bruton | 2.50 | 1.00 | .25 | ☐ 276 | George Zuverink | 1.50 | .60 | .15 |
| ☐ 186 | Ron Jackson | 2.50 | 1.00 | .25 | ☐ 277 | Daryl Spencer | 1.50 | .60 | .15 |
| ☐ 187 | Early Wynn | 11.00 | 4.50 | 1.10 | ☐ 278 | Chet Nichols | 1.50 | .60 | .15 |
| ☐ 188 | White Sox Team | 4.50 | 1.80 | .45 | ☐ 279 | Johnny Groth | 1.50 | .60 | .15 |
| ☐ 189 | Ned Garver | 2.50 | 1.00 | .25 | ☐ 280 | Jim Gilliam | 3.50 | 1.40 | .35 |
| ☐ 190 | Carl Furillo | 5.00 | 2.00 | .50 | ☐ 281 | Art Houtteman | 1.50 | .60 | .15 |
| ☐ 191 | Frank Lary | 3.00 | 1.20 | .30 | ☐ 282 | Warren Hacker | 1.50 | .60 | .15 |
| ☐ 192 | Smoky Burgess | 3.00 | 1.20 | .30 | ☐ 283 | Hal Smith | 1.50 | .60 | .15 |
| ☐ 193 | Wilmer Mizell | 2.50 | 1.00 | .25 | ☐ 284 | Ike Delock | 1.50 | .60 | .15 |
| ☐ 194 | Monte Irvin | 9.00 | 3.75 | .90 | ☐ 285 | Eddie Miksis | 1.50 | .60 | .15 |
| ☐ 195 | George Kell | 10.00 | 4.00 | 1.00 | ☐ 286 | Bill Wight | 1.50 | .60 | .15 |
| ☐ 196 | Tom Poholsky | 2.50 | 1.00 | .25 | ☐ 287 | Bobby Adams | 1.50 | .60 | .15 |
| ☐ 197 | Granny Hamner | 2.50 | 1.00 | .25 | ☐ 288 | Bob Cerv | 2.00 | .80 | .20 |
| ☐ 198 | Ed Fitzgerald | 2.50 | 1.00 | .25 | ☐ 289 | Hal Jeffcoat | 1.50 | .60 | .15 |
| ☐ 199 | Hank Thompson | 3.00 | 1.20 | .30 | ☐ 290 | Curt Simmons | 2.00 | .80 | .20 |
| ☐ 200 | Bob Feller | 25.00 | 10.00 | 2.50 | ☐ 291 | Frank Kellert | 1.50 | .60 | .15 |
| ☐ 201 | Rip Repulski | 2.50 | 1.00 | .25 | ☐ 292 | Luis Aparicio | 24.00 | 10.00 | 2.40 |
| ☐ 202 | Jim Hearn | 2.50 | 1.00 | .25 | ☐ 293 | Stu Miller | 1.50 | .60 | .15 |
| ☐ 203 | Bill Tuttle | 2.50 | 1.00 | .25 | ☐ 294 | Ernie Johnson | 1.50 | .60 | .15 |
| ☐ 204 | Art Swanson | 2.50 | 1.00 | .25 | ☐ 295 | Clem Labine | 2.00 | .80 | .20 |
| ☐ 205 | Whitey Lockman | 2.50 | 1.00 | .25 | ☐ 296 | Andy Seminick | 1.50 | .60 | .15 |
| ☐ 206 | Erv Palica | 2.50 | 1.00 | .25 | ☐ 297 | Bob Skinner | 2.00 | .80 | .20 |
| ☐ 207 | Jim Small | 2.50 | 1.00 | .25 | ☐ 298 | Johnny Schmitz | 1.50 | .60 | .15 |
| ☐ 208 | Elston Howard | 7.00 | 2.80 | .70 | ☐ 299 | Charley Neal | 2.00 | .80 | .20 |
| ☐ 209 | Max Surkont | 2.50 | 1.00 | .25 | ☐ 300 | Vic Wertz | 2.00 | .80 | .20 |
| ☐ 210 | Mike Garcia | 3.00 | 1.20 | .30 | ☐ 301 | Marv Grissom | 1.50 | .60 | .15 |
| ☐ 211 | Murry Dickson | 2.50 | 1.00 | .25 | ☐ 302 | Eddie Robinson | 1.50 | .60 | .15 |
| ☐ 212 | Johnny Temple | 3.00 | 1.20 | .30 | ☐ 303 | Jim Dyck | 1.50 | .60 | .15 |
| ☐ 213 | Detroit Tigers Team | 7.50 | 3.00 | .75 | ☐ 304 | Frank Malzone | 2.00 | .80 | .20 |
| ☐ 214 | Bob Rush | 2.50 | 1.00 | .25 | ☐ 305 | Brooks Lawrence | 1.50 | .60 | .15 |
| ☐ 215 | Tommy Byrne | 2.50 | 1.00 | .25 | ☐ 306 | Curt Roberts | 1.50 | .60 | .15 |
| ☐ 216 | Jerry Schoonmaker | 2.50 | 1.00 | .25 | ☐ 307 | Hoyt Wilhelm | 10.00 | 4.00 | 1.00 |
| ☐ 217 | Billy Klaus | 2.50 | 1.00 | .25 | ☐ 308 | Chuck Harmon | 1.50 | .60 | .15 |
| ☐ 218 | Joe Nuxall | 3.00 | 1.20 | .30 | ☐ 309 | Don Blasingame | 2.00 | .80 | .20 |
| | (sic, Nuxhall) | | | | ☐ 310 | Steve Gromek | 1.50 | .60 | .15 |
| ☐ 219 | Lew Burdette | 4.50 | 1.80 | .45 | ☐ 311 | Hal Naragon | 1.50 | .60 | .15 |
| ☐ 220 | Del Ennis | 3.00 | 1.20 | .30 | ☐ 312 | Andy Pafko | 1.50 | .60 | .15 |
| ☐ 221 | Bob Friend | 3.00 | 1.20 | .30 | ☐ 313 | Gene Stephens | 1.50 | .60 | .15 |
| ☐ 222 | Dave Philley | 2.50 | 1.00 | .25 | ☐ 314 | Hobie Landrith | 1.50 | .60 | .15 |
| ☐ 223 | Randy Jackson | 2.50 | 1.00 | .25 | ☐ 315 | Milt Bolling | 1.50 | .60 | .15 |
| ☐ 224 | Bud Podbielan | 2.50 | 1.00 | .25 | ☐ 316 | Jerry Coleman | 2.00 | .80 | .20 |
| ☐ 225 | Gil McDougald | 6.00 | 2.40 | .60 | ☐ 317 | Al Aber | 1.50 | .60 | .15 |
| ☐ 226 | Giants Team | 10.00 | 4.00 | 1.00 | ☐ 318 | Fred Hatfield | 1.50 | .60 | .15 |
| ☐ 227 | Russ Meyer | 2.50 | 1.00 | .25 | ☐ 319 | Jack Crimian | 1.50 | .60 | .15 |
| ☐ 228 | Mickey Vernon | 3.00 | 1.20 | .30 | ☐ 320 | Joe Adcock | 2.50 | 1.00 | .25 |
| ☐ 229 | Harry Brecheen | 2.50 | 1.00 | .25 | ☐ 321 | Jim Konstanty | 2.00 | .80 | .20 |
| ☐ 230 | Chico Carrasquel | 2.50 | 1.00 | .25 | ☐ 322 | Karl Olson | 1.50 | .60 | .15 |
| ☐ 231 | Bob Hale | 2.50 | 1.00 | .25 | ☐ 323 | Willard Schmidt | 1.50 | .60 | .15 |
| ☐ 232 | Toby Atwell | 2.50 | 1.00 | .25 | ☐ 324 | Rocky Bridges | 1.50 | .60 | .15 |
| ☐ 233 | Carl Erskine | 6.00 | 2.40 | .60 | ☐ 325 | Don Liddle | 1.50 | .60 | .15 |
| ☐ 234 | Pete Runnels | 3.00 | 1.20 | .30 | ☐ 326 | Connie Johnson | 1.50 | .60 | .15 |
| ☐ 235 | Don Newcombe | 10.00 | 4.00 | 1.00 | ☐ 327 | Bob Wiesler | 1.50 | .60 | .15 |
| ☐ 236 | Athletics Team | 4.50 | 1.80 | .45 | ☐ 328 | Preston Ward | 1.50 | .60 | .15 |
| ☐ 237 | Jose Valdivielso | 2.50 | 1.00 | .25 | ☐ 329 | Lou Berberet | 1.50 | .60 | .15 |
| ☐ 238 | Walt Dropo | 2.50 | 1.00 | .25 | ☐ 330 | Jim Busby | 1.50 | .60 | .15 |
| ☐ 239 | Harry Simpson | 2.50 | 1.00 | .25 | ☐ 331 | Dick Hall | 1.50 | .60 | .15 |
| ☐ 240 | Whitey Ford | 20.00 | 8.00 | 2.00 | ☐ 332 | Don Larsen | 4.00 | 1.60 | .40 |
| ☐ 241 | Don Mueller | 3.00 | 1.20 | .30 | ☐ 333 | Rube Walker | 2.00 | .80 | .20 |
| ☐ 242 | Hershell Freeman | 2.50 | 1.00 | .25 | ☐ 334 | Bob Miller | 1.50 | .60 | .15 |
| ☐ 243 | Sherm Lollar | 3.00 | 1.20 | .30 | ☐ 335 | Don Hoak | 1.50 | .60 | .15 |
| ☐ 244 | Bob Buhl | 2.50 | 1.00 | .25 | ☐ 336 | Ellis Kinder | 1.50 | .60 | .15 |
| ☐ 245 | Billy Goodman | 3.00 | 1.20 | .30 | ☐ 337 | Bobby Morgan | 1.50 | .60 | .15 |
| ☐ 246 | Tom Gorman | 2.50 | 1.00 | .25 | ☐ 338 | Jim Delsing | 1.50 | .60 | .15 |
| ☐ 247 | Bill Sarni | 2.50 | 1.00 | .25 | ☐ 339 | Rance Pless | 1.50 | .60 | .15 |
| ☐ 248 | Bob Porterfield | 2.50 | 1.00 | .25 | ☐ 340 | Mickey McDermott | 4.00 | 1.00 | .20 |
| ☐ 249 | Johnny Klippstein | 2.50 | 1.00 | .25 | ☐ 341 | Checklist 1/3 | 90.00 | 15.00 | 3.00 |
| ☐ 250 | Larry Doby | 5.00 | 2.00 | .50 | | (unnumbered) | | | |
| ☐ 251 | New York Yankees | 32.00 | 13.00 | 3.20 | ☐ 342 | Checklist 2/4 | 90.00 | 15.00 | 3.00 |
| | Team Card | | | | | (unnumbered) | | | |
| ☐ 252 | Vernon Law | 3.00 | 1.20 | .30 | | | | | |
| ☐ 253 | Irv Noren | 2.50 | 1.00 | .25 | | | | | |
| ☐ 254 | George Crowe | 2.50 | 1.00 | .25 | | | | | |
| ☐ 255 | Bob Lemon | 11.00 | 4.50 | 1.10 | | | | | |
| ☐ 256 | Tom Hurd | 2.50 | 1.00 | .25 | | | | | |
| ☐ 257 | Bobby Thomson | 4.50 | 1.80 | .45 | | | | | |
| ☐ 258 | Art Ditmar | 2.50 | 1.00 | .25 | | | | | |

# 1957 Topps

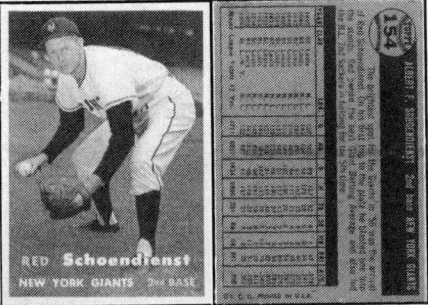

RED **Schoendienst**
NEW YORK GIANTS 2nd BASE

The cards in this 407 card set measure 2 1/2" by 3 1/2". In 1957, Topps returned to the vertical obverse, adopted what we now call the standard card size, and used a large, uncluttered color photo for the first time since 1952. Cards in the series 265 to 352 and the unnumbered checklist cards are scarcer than other cards in the set. The first star combination cards, #400 and #407, are quite popular with collectors. They feature the big stars of the previous season's World Series teams, the Dodgers (Furillo, Hodges, Campanella, and Snider) and Yankees (Berra and Mantle). The complete set price below does not include the unnumbered checklist cards.

|  | MINT | VG-E | F-G |
|---|---|---|---|
| COMPLETE SET (407) | 1600.00 | 700.00 | 175.00 |
| COMMON PLAYER (1-264) | .90 | .36 | .09 |
| COMMON PLAYER (265-352) | 5.00 | 2.00 | .50 |
| COMMON PLAYER (353-407) | 1.00 | .40 | .10 |

| | | MINT | VG-E | F-G |
|---|---|---|---|---|
| ☐ | 1 Ted Williams | 125.00 | 25.00 | 5.00 |
| ☐ | 2 Yogi Berra | 25.00 | 10.00 | 2.50 |
| ☐ | 3 Dale Long | .90 | .36 | .09 |
| ☐ | 4 Johnny Logan | 1.00 | .40 | .10 |
| ☐ | 5 Sal Maglie | 2.50 | 1.00 | .25 |
| ☐ | 6 Hector Lopez | .90 | .36 | .09 |
| ☐ | 7 Luis Aparicio | 6.00 | 2.40 | .60 |
| ☐ | 8 Don Mossi | 1.00 | .40 | .10 |
| ☐ | 9 Johnny Temple | 1.00 | .40 | .10 |
| ☐ | 10 Willie Mays | 45.00 | 18.00 | 4.50 |
| ☐ | 11 George Zuverink | .90 | .36 | .09 |
| ☐ | 12 Dick Groat | 1.50 | .60 | .15 |
| ☐ | 13 Wally Burnette | .90 | .36 | .09 |
| ☐ | 14 Bob Nieman | .90 | .36 | .09 |
| ☐ | 15 Robin Roberts | 7.00 | 2.80 | .70 |
| ☐ | 16 Walt Moryn | .90 | .36 | .09 |
| ☐ | 17 Billy Gardner | .90 | .36 | .09 |
| ☐ | 18 Don Drysdale | 40.00 | 16.00 | 4.00 |
| ☐ | 19 Bob Wilson | .90 | .36 | .09 |
| ☐ | 20 Hank Aaron | 50.00 | 20.00 | 5.00 |
| | (reverse negative photo on front) | | | |
| ☐ | 21 Frank Sullivan | .90 | .36 | .09 |
| ☐ | 22 Jerry Snyder | .90 | .36 | .09 |
| | (photo actually Ed Fitzgerald) | | | |
| ☐ | 23 Sherm Lollar | 1.00 | .40 | .10 |
| ☐ | 24 Bill Mazeroski | 6.00 | 2.40 | .60 |
| ☐ | 25 Whitey Ford | 12.00 | 5.00 | 1.20 |
| ☐ | 26 Bob Boyd | .90 | .36 | .09 |
| ☐ | 27 Ted Kazanski | .90 | .36 | .09 |
| ☐ | 28 Gene Conley | .90 | .36 | .09 |
| ☐ | 29 Whitey Herzog | 3.00 | 1.20 | .30 |
| ☐ | 30 Pee Wee Reese | 12.50 | 5.00 | 1.25 |
| ☐ | 31 Ron Northey | .90 | .36 | .09 |
| ☐ | 32 Hershell Freeman | .90 | .36 | .09 |
| ☐ | 33 Jim Small | .90 | .36 | .09 |
| ☐ | 34 Tom Sturdivant | .90 | .36 | .09 |
| ☐ | 35 Frank Robinson | 45.00 | 18.00 | 4.50 |
| ☐ | 36 Bob Grim | 1.00 | .40 | .10 |
| ☐ | 37 Frank Torre | 1.00 | .40 | .10 |
| ☐ | 38 Nelson Fox | 3.00 | 1.20 | .30 |
| ☐ | 39 Al Worthington | .90 | .36 | .09 |
| ☐ | 40 Early Wynn | 6.50 | 2.60 | .65 |
| ☐ | 41 Hal W. Smith | .90 | .36 | .09 |
| ☐ | 42 Dee Fondy | .90 | .36 | .09 |
| ☐ | 43 Connie Johnson | .90 | .36 | .09 |
| ☐ | 44 Joe DeMaestri | .90 | .36 | .09 |
| ☐ | 45 Carl Furillo | 3.00 | 1.20 | .30 |
| ☐ | 46 Robert J. Miller | .90 | .36 | .09 |
| ☐ | 47 Don Blasingame | .90 | .36 | .09 |
| ☐ | 48 Bill Bruton | 1.00 | .40 | .10 |
| ☐ | 49 Daryl Spencer | .90 | .36 | .09 |
| ☐ | 50 Herb Score | 1.50 | .60 | .15 |
| ☐ | 51 Clint Courtney | .90 | .36 | .09 |
| ☐ | 52 Lee Walls | .90 | .36 | .09 |
| ☐ | 53 Clem Labine | 1.25 | .50 | .12 |
| ☐ | 54 Elmer Valo | .90 | .36 | .09 |
| ☐ | 55 Ernie Banks | 13.00 | 5.25 | 1.30 |
| ☐ | 56 Dave Sisler | .90 | .36 | .09 |
| ☐ | 57 Jim Lemon | 1.00 | .40 | .10 |
| ☐ | 58 Ruben Gomez | .90 | .36 | .09 |
| ☐ | 59 Dick Williams | 1.25 | .50 | .12 |
| ☐ | 60 Billy Hoeft | .90 | .36 | .09 |
| ☐ | 61 James Rhodes | 1.00 | .40 | .10 |
| ☐ | 62 Billy Martin | 10.00 | 4.00 | 1.00 |
| ☐ | 63 Ike Delock | .90 | .36 | .09 |
| ☐ | 64 Pete Runnels | 1.00 | .40 | .10 |
| ☐ | 65 Wally Moon | 1.25 | .50 | .12 |
| ☐ | 66 Brooks Lawrence | .90 | .36 | .09 |
| ☐ | 67 Chico Carrasquel | .90 | .36 | .09 |
| ☐ | 68 Ray Crone | .90 | .36 | .09 |
| ☐ | 69 Roy McMillan | .90 | .36 | .09 |
| ☐ | 70 Richie Ashburn | 3.50 | 1.40 | .35 |
| ☐ | 71 Murry Dickson | .90 | .36 | .09 |
| ☐ | 72 Bill Tuttle | .90 | .36 | .09 |
| ☐ | 73 George Crowe | .90 | .36 | .09 |
| ☐ | 74 Vito Valentinetti | .90 | .36 | .09 |
| ☐ | 75 Jim Piersall | 1.75 | .70 | .17 |
| ☐ | 76 Roberto Clemente | 27.00 | 11.00 | 2.70 |
| ☐ | 77 Paul Foytack | .90 | .36 | .09 |
| ☐ | 78 Vic Wertz | 1.00 | .40 | .10 |
| ☐ | 79 Lindy McDaniel | 1.00 | .40 | .10 |
| ☐ | 80 Gil Hodges | 10.00 | 4.00 | 1.00 |
| ☐ | 81 Herman Wehmeier | .90 | .36 | .09 |
| ☐ | 82 Elston Howard | 3.00 | 1.20 | .30 |
| ☐ | 83 Lou Skizas | .90 | .36 | .09 |
| ☐ | 84 Moe Drabowsky | 1.00 | .40 | .10 |
| ☐ | 85 Larry Doby | 2.00 | .80 | .20 |
| ☐ | 86 Bill Sarni | .90 | .36 | .09 |
| ☐ | 87 Tom Gorman | .90 | .36 | .09 |
| ☐ | 88 Harvey Kuenn | 2.00 | .80 | .20 |
| ☐ | 89 Roy Sievers | 1.00 | .40 | .10 |
| ☐ | 90 Warren Spahn | 12.00 | 5.00 | 1.20 |
| ☐ | 91 Mack Burk | .90 | .36 | .09 |
| ☐ | 92 Mickey Vernon | 1.00 | .40 | .10 |
| ☐ | 93 Hal Jeffcoat | .90 | .36 | .09 |
| ☐ | 94 Bobby Del Greco | .90 | .36 | .09 |
| ☐ | 95 Mickey Mantle | 200.00 | 80.00 | 20.00 |
| ☐ | 96 Hank Aguirre | .90 | .36 | .09 |
| ☐ | 97 New York Yankees Team Card | 7.50 | 3.00 | .75 |
| ☐ | 98 Alvin Dark | 1.50 | .60 | .15 |
| ☐ | 99 Bob Keegan | .90 | .36 | .09 |
| ☐ | 100 Giles and Harridge League Presidents | 2.00 | .80 | .20 |
| ☐ | 101 Chuck Stobbs | .90 | .36 | .09 |
| ☐ | 102 Ray Boone | 1.00 | .40 | .10 |
| ☐ | 103 Joe Nuxhall | 1.00 | .40 | .10 |
| ☐ | 104 Hank Foiles | .90 | .36 | .09 |
| ☐ | 105 Johnny Antonelli | 1.25 | .50 | .12 |
| ☐ | 106 Ray Moore | .90 | .36 | .09 |
| ☐ | 107 Jim Rivera | .90 | .36 | .09 |
| ☐ | 108 Tommy Byrne | 1.00 | .40 | .10 |
| ☐ | 109 Hank Thompson | 1.00 | .40 | .10 |
| ☐ | 110 Bill Virdon | 1.75 | .70 | .17 |
| ☐ | 111 Hal R. Smith | .90 | .36 | .09 |
| ☐ | 112 Tom Brewer | .90 | .36 | .09 |
| ☐ | 113 Wilmer Mizell | .90 | .36 | .09 |
| ☐ | 114 Milwaukee Braves Team Card | 3.00 | 1.20 | .30 |
| ☐ | 115 Jim Gilliam | 2.50 | 1.00 | .25 |
| ☐ | 116 Mike Fornieles | .90 | .36 | .09 |
| ☐ | 117 Joe Adcock | 1.50 | .60 | .15 |
| ☐ | 118 Bob Porterfield | .90 | .36 | .09 |
| ☐ | 119 Stan Lopata | .90 | .36 | .09 |
| ☐ | 120 Bob Lemon | 6.00 | 2.40 | .60 |
| ☐ | 121 Cletis Boyer | 2.00 | .80 | .20 |
| ☐ | 122 Ken Boyer | 2.50 | 1.00 | .25 |
| ☐ | 123 Steve Ridzik | .90 | .36 | .09 |
| ☐ | 124 Dave Philley | .90 | .36 | .09 |
| ☐ | 125 Al Kaline | 12.50 | 5.00 | 1.25 |
| ☐ | 126 Bob Wiesler | .90 | .36 | .09 |
| ☐ | 127 Bob Buhl | .90 | .36 | .09 |
| ☐ | 128 Ed Bailey | .90 | .36 | .09 |
| ☐ | 129 Saul Rogovin | .90 | .36 | .09 |

| | | | | |
|---|---|---|---|---|
| ☐ 130 | Don Newcombe | 3.00 | 1.20 | .30 |
| ☐ 131 | Milt Bolling | .90 | .36 | .09 |
| ☐ 132 | Art Ditmar | .90 | .36 | .09 |
| ☐ 133 | Del Crandall | 1.00 | .40 | .10 |
| ☐ 134 | Don Kaiser | .90 | .36 | .09 |
| ☐ 135 | Bill Skowron | 2.50 | 1.00 | .25 |
| ☐ 136 | Jim Hegan | 1.00 | .40 | .10 |
| ☐ 137 | Bob Rush | .90 | .36 | .09 |
| ☐ 138 | Minnie Minoso | 2.50 | 1.00 | .25 |
| ☐ 139 | Lou Kretlow | .90 | .36 | .09 |
| ☐ 140 | Frank Thomas | 1.00 | .40 | .10 |
| ☐ 141 | Al Aber | .90 | .36 | .09 |
| ☐ 142 | Charley Thompson | .90 | .36 | .09 |
| ☐ 143 | Andy Pafko | .90 | .36 | .09 |
| ☐ 144 | Ray Narleski | .90 | .36 | .09 |
| ☐ 145 | Al Smith | .90 | .36 | .09 |
| ☐ 146 | Don Ferrarese | .90 | .36 | .09 |
| ☐ 147 | Al Walker | .90 | .36 | .09 |
| ☐ 148 | Don Mueller | 1.00 | .40 | .10 |
| ☐ 149 | Bob Kennedy | 1.00 | .40 | .10 |
| ☐ 150 | Bob Friend | 1.25 | .50 | .12 |
| ☐ 151 | Willie Miranda | .90 | .36 | .09 |
| ☐ 152 | Jack Harshman | .90 | .36 | .09 |
| ☐ 153 | Karl Olson | .90 | .36 | .09 |
| ☐ 154 | Red Schoendienst | 1.75 | .70 | .17 |
| ☐ 155 | Jim Brosnan | 1.00 | .40 | .10 |
| ☐ 156 | Gus Triandos | 1.00 | .40 | .10 |
| ☐ 157 | Wally Post | .90 | .36 | .09 |
| ☐ 158 | Curt Simmons | 1.25 | .50 | .12 |
| ☐ 159 | Solly Drake | .90 | .36 | .09 |
| ☐ 160 | Billy Pierce | 1.50 | .60 | .15 |
| ☐ 161 | Pirates Team | 2.00 | .80 | .20 |
| ☐ 162 | Jack Meyer | .90 | .36 | .09 |
| ☐ 163 | Sammy White | .90 | .36 | .09 |
| ☐ 164 | Tommy Carroll | .90 | .36 | .09 |
| ☐ 165 | Ted Kluszewski | 2.50 | 1.00 | .25 |
| ☐ 166 | Elroy Face | 1.50 | .60 | .15 |
| ☐ 167 | Vic Power | 1.00 | .40 | .10 |
| ☐ 168 | Frank Lary | 1.00 | .40 | .10 |
| ☐ 169 | Herb Plews | .90 | .36 | .09 |
| ☐ 170 | Duke Snider | 27.00 | 11.00 | 2.70 |
| ☐ 171 | Boston Red Sox Team Card | 2.00 | .80 | .20 |
| ☐ 172 | Gene Woodling | 1.25 | .50 | .12 |
| ☐ 173 | Roger Craig | 1.50 | .60 | .15 |
| ☐ 174 | Willie Jones | .90 | .36 | .09 |
| ☐ 175 | Don Larsen | 2.50 | 1.00 | .25 |
| ☐ 176 | Gene Baker | .90 | .36 | .09 |
| ☐ 177 | Eddie Yost | 1.00 | .40 | .10 |
| ☐ 178 | Don Bessent | .90 | .36 | .09 |
| ☐ 179 | Ernie Oravetz | .90 | .36 | .09 |
| ☐ 180 | Dave (Gus) Bell | 1.00 | .40 | .10 |
| ☐ 181 | Dick Donovan | .90 | .36 | .09 |
| ☐ 182 | Hobie Landrith | .90 | .36 | .09 |
| ☐ 183 | Chicago Cubs Team | 2.00 | .80 | .20 |
| ☐ 184 | Tito Francona | 1.00 | .40 | .10 |
| ☐ 185 | Johnny Kucks | 1.00 | .40 | .10 |
| ☐ 186 | Jim King | .90 | .36 | .09 |
| ☐ 187 | Virgil Trucks | 1.00 | .40 | .10 |
| ☐ 188 | Felix Mantilla | .90 | .36 | .09 |
| ☐ 189 | Willard Nixon | .90 | .36 | .09 |
| ☐ 190 | Randy Jackson | .90 | .36 | .09 |
| ☐ 191 | Joe Margoneri | .90 | .36 | .09 |
| ☐ 192 | Gerry Coleman | 1.00 | .40 | .10 |
| ☐ 193 | Del Rice | .90 | .36 | .09 |
| ☐ 194 | Hal Brown | .90 | .36 | .09 |
| ☐ 195 | Bobby Avila | .90 | .36 | .09 |
| ☐ 196 | Larry Jackson | .90 | .36 | .09 |
| ☐ 197 | Hank Sauer | 1.25 | .50 | .12 |
| ☐ 198 | Detroit Tigers Team | 3.00 | 1.20 | .30 |
| ☐ 199 | Vern Law | 1.25 | .50 | .12 |
| ☐ 200 | Gil McDougald | 2.50 | 1.00 | .25 |
| ☐ 201 | Sandy Amoros | 1.25 | .50 | .12 |
| ☐ 202 | Dick Gernert | .90 | .36 | .09 |
| ☐ 203 | Hoyt Wilhelm | 6.00 | 2.40 | .60 |
| ☐ 204 | Athletics Team | 2.00 | .80 | .20 |
| ☐ 205 | Charlie Maxwell | .90 | .36 | .09 |
| ☐ 206 | Willard Schmidt | .90 | .36 | .09 |
| ☐ 207 | Gordon (Billy) Hunter | .90 | .36 | .09 |
| ☐ 208 | Lou Burdette | 2.50 | 1.00 | .25 |
| ☐ 209 | Bob Skinner | 1.00 | .40 | .10 |
| ☐ 210 | Roy Campanella | 27.00 | 11.00 | 2.70 |
| ☐ 211 | Camilo Pascual | 1.00 | .40 | .10 |
| ☐ 212 | Rocco Colavito | 5.00 | 2.00 | .50 |
| ☐ 213 | Les Moss | .90 | .36 | .09 |
| ☐ 214 | Phillies Team | 2.00 | .80 | .20 |
| ☐ 215 | Enos Slaughter | 6.00 | 2.40 | .60 |
| ☐ 216 | Marv Grissom | .90 | .36 | .09 |
| ☐ 217 | Gene Stephens | .90 | .36 | .09 |
| ☐ 218 | Ray Jablonski | .90 | .36 | .09 |
| ☐ 219 | Tom Acker | .90 | .36 | .09 |
| ☐ 220 | Jackie Jensen | 1.75 | .70 | .17 |
| ☐ 221 | Dixie Howell | .90 | .36 | .09 |
| ☐ 222 | Alex Grammas | .90 | .36 | .09 |
| ☐ 223 | Frank House | .90 | .36 | .09 |
| ☐ 224 | Marv Blaylock | .90 | .36 | .09 |
| ☐ 225 | Harry Simpson | .90 | .36 | .09 |
| ☐ 226 | Preston Ward | .90 | .36 | .09 |
| ☐ 227 | Gerry Staley | .90 | .36 | .09 |
| ☐ 228 | Smoky Burgess | 1.00 | .40 | .10 |
| ☐ 229 | George Susce | .90 | .36 | .09 |
| ☐ 230 | George Kell | 6.00 | 2.40 | .60 |
| ☐ 231 | Solly Hemus | .90 | .36 | .09 |
| ☐ 232 | Whitey Lockman | 1.00 | .40 | .10 |
| ☐ 233 | Art Fowler | .90 | .36 | .09 |
| ☐ 234 | Dick Cole | .90 | .36 | .09 |
| ☐ 235 | Tom Poholsky | .90 | .36 | .09 |
| ☐ 236 | Joe Ginsberg | .90 | .36 | .09 |
| ☐ 237 | Foster Castleman | .90 | .36 | .09 |
| ☐ 238 | Eddie Robinson | .90 | .36 | .09 |
| ☐ 239 | Tom Morgan | .90 | .36 | .09 |
| ☐ 240 | Hank Bauer | 2.50 | 1.00 | .25 |
| ☐ 241 | Joe Lonnett | .90 | .36 | .09 |
| ☐ 242 | Charlie Neal | 1.00 | .40 | .10 |
| ☐ 243 | Cardinals Team | 2.50 | 1.00 | .25 |
| ☐ 244 | Billy Loes | 1.00 | .40 | .10 |
| ☐ 245 | Rip Repulski | .90 | .36 | .09 |
| ☐ 246 | Jose Valdivielso | .90 | .36 | .09 |
| ☐ 247 | Turk Lown | .90 | .36 | .09 |
| ☐ 248 | Jim Finigan | .90 | .36 | .09 |
| ☐ 249 | Dave Pope | .90 | .36 | .09 |
| ☐ 250 | Ed Mathews | 8.00 | 3.25 | .80 |
| ☐ 251 | Orioles Team | 2.50 | 1.00 | .25 |
| ☐ 252 | Carl Erskine | 2.50 | 1.00 | .25 |
| ☐ 253 | Gus Zernial | 1.00 | .40 | .10 |
| ☐ 254 | Ron Negray | .90 | .36 | .09 |
| ☐ 255 | Charlie Silvera | .90 | .36 | .09 |
| ☐ 256 | Ron Kline | .90 | .36 | .09 |
| ☐ 257 | Walt Dropo | .90 | .36 | .09 |
| ☐ 258 | Steve Gromek | .90 | .36 | .09 |
| ☐ 259 | Eddie O'Brien | .90 | .36 | .09 |
| ☐ 260 | Del Ennis | 1.00 | .40 | .10 |
| ☐ 261 | Bob Chakales | .90 | .36 | .09 |
| ☐ 262 | Bobby Thomson | 2.00 | .80 | .20 |
| ☐ 263 | George Strickland | .90 | .36 | .09 |
| ☐ 264 | Bob Turley | 2.00 | .80 | .20 |
| ☐ 265 | Harvey Haddix | 6.00 | 2.40 | .60 |
| ☐ 266 | Ken Kuhn | 5.00 | 2.00 | .50 |
| ☐ 267 | Danny Kravitz | 5.00 | 2.00 | .50 |
| ☐ 268 | Joe Collum | 5.00 | 2.00 | .50 |
| ☐ 269 | Bob Cerv | 6.00 | 2.40 | .60 |
| ☐ 270 | Washington Team | 8.00 | 3.25 | .80 |
| ☐ 271 | Danny O'Connell | 5.00 | 2.00 | .50 |
| ☐ 272 | Bobby Shantz | 11.00 | 4.50 | 1.10 |
| ☐ 273 | Jim Davis | 5.00 | 2.00 | .50 |
| ☐ 274 | Don Hoak | 5.00 | 2.00 | .50 |
| ☐ 275 | Indians Team | 8.00 | 3.25 | .80 |
| ☐ 276 | Jim Pyburn | 5.00 | 2.00 | .50 |
| ☐ 277 | Johnny Podres | 25.00 | 10.00 | 2.50 |
| ☐ 278 | Fred Hatfield | 5.00 | 2.00 | .50 |
| ☐ 279 | Bob Thurman | 5.00 | 2.00 | .50 |
| ☐ 280 | Alex Kellner | 5.00 | 2.00 | .50 |
| ☐ 281 | Gail Harris | 5.00 | 2.00 | .50 |
| ☐ 282 | Jack Dittmer | 5.00 | 2.00 | .50 |
| ☐ 283 | Wes Covington | 6.00 | 2.40 | .60 |
| ☐ 284 | Don Zimmer | 7.00 | 2.80 | .70 |
| ☐ 285 | Ned Garver | 5.00 | 2.00 | .50 |
| ☐ 286 | Bobby Richardson | 27.00 | 11.00 | 2.70 |
| ☐ 287 | Sam Jones | 6.00 | 2.40 | .60 |
| ☐ 288 | Ted Lepcio | 5.00 | 2.00 | .50 |
| ☐ 289 | Jim Bolger | 5.00 | 2.00 | .50 |
| ☐ 290 | Andy Carey | 6.00 | 2.40 | .60 |
| ☐ 291 | Windy McCall | 5.00 | 2.00 | .50 |
| ☐ 292 | Billy Klaus | 5.00 | 2.00 | .50 |
| ☐ 293 | Ted Abernathy | 5.00 | 2.00 | .50 |
| ☐ 294 | Rocky Bridges | 5.00 | 2.00 | .50 |
| ☐ 295 | Joe Collins | 6.00 | 2.40 | .60 |
| ☐ 296 | Johnny Klippstein | 5.00 | 2.00 | .50 |
| ☐ 297 | Jack Crimian | 5.00 | 2.00 | .50 |
| ☐ 298 | Irv Noren | 5.00 | 2.00 | .50 |
| ☐ 299 | Chuck Harmon | 5.00 | 2.00 | .50 |
| ☐ 300 | Mike Garcia | 7.00 | 2.80 | .70 |
| ☐ 301 | Sammy Esposito | 5.00 | 2.00 | .50 |
| ☐ 302 | Sandy Koufax | 125.00 | 50.00 | 12.50 |
| ☐ 303 | Billy Goodman | 6.00 | 2.40 | .60 |
| ☐ 304 | Joe Cunningham | 6.00 | 2.40 | .60 |
| ☐ 305 | Chico Fernandez | 5.00 | 2.00 | .50 |
| ☐ 306 | Darrell Johnson | 5.00 | 2.00 | .50 |
| ☐ 307 | J.D. (Bubba) Phillips | 5.00 | 2.00 | .50 |
| ☐ 308 | Richard Hall | 5.00 | 2.00 | .50 |
| ☐ 309 | Jim Busby | 5.00 | 2.00 | .50 |
| ☐ 310 | Max Surkont | 5.00 | 2.00 | .50 |
| ☐ 311 | Al Pilarcik | 5.00 | 2.00 | .50 |
| ☐ 312 | Tony Kubek | 35.00 | 14.00 | 3.50 |
| ☐ 313 | Mel Parnell | 6.00 | 2.40 | .60 |
| ☐ 314 | Ed Bouchee | 5.00 | 2.00 | .50 |

| | | | | |
|---|---|---|---|---|
| ☐ 315 | Lou Berberet | 5.00 | 2.00 | .50 |
| ☐ 316 | Billy O'Dell | 5.00 | 2.00 | .50 |
| ☐ 317 | New York Giants Team Card | 21.00 | 8.50 | 2.10 |
| ☐ 318 | Mickey McDermott | 5.00 | 2.00 | .50 |
| ☐ 319 | Gino Cimoli | 5.00 | 2.00 | .50 |
| ☐ 320 | Neil Chrisley | 5.00 | 2.00 | .50 |
| ☐ 321 | John (Red) Murff | 5.00 | 2.00 | .50 |
| ☐ 322 | Cincinnati Team | 18.00 | 7.25 | 1.80 |
| ☐ 323 | Wes Westrum | 5.00 | 2.00 | .50 |
| ☐ 324 | Brooklyn Dodgers Team Card | 32.00 | 13.00 | 3.20 |
| ☐ 325 | Frank Bolling | 5.00 | 2.00 | .50 |
| ☐ 326 | Pedro Ramos | 5.00 | 2.00 | .50 |
| ☐ 327 | Jim Pendleton | 5.00 | 2.00 | .50 |
| ☐ 328 | Brooks Robinson | 125.00 | 50.00 | 12.50 |
| ☐ 329 | White Sox Team | 12.00 | 5.00 | 1.20 |
| ☐ 330 | Jim Wilson | 5.00 | 2.00 | .50 |
| ☐ 331 | Ray Katt | 5.00 | 2.00 | .50 |
| ☐ 332 | Bob Bowman | 5.00 | 2.00 | .50 |
| ☐ 333 | Ernie Johnson | 5.00 | 2.00 | .50 |
| ☐ 334 | Jerry Schoonmaker | 5.00 | 2.00 | .50 |
| ☐ 335 | Granny Hamner | 5.00 | 2.00 | .50 |
| ☐ 336 | Haywood Sullivan | 6.00 | 2.40 | .60 |
| ☐ 337 | Rene Valdes | 5.00 | 2.00 | .50 |
| ☐ 338 | Jim Bunning | 30.00 | 12.00 | 3.00 |
| ☐ 339 | Bob Speake | 5.00 | 2.00 | .50 |
| ☐ 340 | Bill Wight | 5.00 | 2.00 | .50 |
| ☐ 341 | Don Gross | 5.00 | 2.00 | .50 |
| ☐ 342 | Gene Mauch | 8.00 | 3.25 | .80 |
| ☐ 343 | Taylor Phillips | 5.00 | 2.00 | .50 |
| ☐ 344 | Paul LaPalme | 5.00 | 2.00 | .50 |
| ☐ 345 | Paul Smith | 5.00 | 2.00 | .50 |
| ☐ 346 | Dick Littlefield | 5.00 | 2.00 | .50 |
| ☐ 347 | Hal Naragon | 5.00 | 2.00 | .50 |
| ☐ 348 | Jim Hearn | 5.00 | 2.00 | .50 |
| ☐ 349 | Nellie King | 5.00 | 2.00 | .50 |
| ☐ 350 | Eddie Miksis | 5.00 | 2.00 | .50 |
| ☐ 351 | Dave Hillman | 5.00 | 2.00 | .50 |
| ☐ 352 | Ellis Kinder | 5.00 | 2.00 | .50 |
| ☐ 353 | Cal Neeman | 1.00 | .40 | .10 |
| ☐ 354 | W. (Rip) Coleman | 1.00 | .40 | .10 |
| ☐ 355 | Frank Malzone | 1.50 | .60 | .15 |
| ☐ 356 | Faye Throneberry | 1.00 | .40 | .10 |
| ☐ 357 | Earl Torgeson | 1.00 | .40 | .10 |
| ☐ 358 | Gerry Lynch | 1.25 | .50 | .12 |
| ☐ 359 | Tom Cheney | 1.00 | .40 | .10 |
| ☐ 360 | Johnny Groth | 1.00 | .40 | .10 |
| ☐ 361 | Curt Barclay | 1.00 | .40 | .10 |
| ☐ 362 | Roman Mejias | 1.00 | .40 | .10 |
| ☐ 363 | Eddie Kasko | 1.00 | .40 | .10 |
| ☐ 364 | Cal McLish | 1.00 | .40 | .10 |
| ☐ 365 | Ozzie Virgil | 1.00 | .40 | .10 |
| ☐ 366 | Ken Lehman | 1.00 | .40 | .10 |
| ☐ 367 | Ed Fitzgerald | 1.00 | .40 | .10 |
| ☐ 368 | Bob Purkey | 1.00 | .40 | .10 |
| ☐ 369 | Milt Graff | 1.00 | .40 | .10 |
| ☐ 370 | Warren Hacker | 1.00 | .40 | .10 |
| ☐ 371 | Bob Lennon | 1.00 | .40 | .10 |
| ☐ 372 | Norm Zauchin | 1.00 | .40 | .10 |
| ☐ 373 | Pete Whisenant | 1.00 | .40 | .10 |
| ☐ 374 | Don Cardwell | 1.00 | .40 | .10 |
| ☐ 375 | Jim Landis | 1.00 | .40 | .10 |
| ☐ 376 | Don Elston | 1.00 | .40 | .10 |
| ☐ 377 | Andre Rodgers | 1.00 | .40 | .10 |
| ☐ 378 | Elmer Singleton | 1.00 | .40 | .10 |
| ☐ 379 | Don Lee | 1.00 | .40 | .10 |
| ☐ 380 | Walker Cooper | 1.00 | .40 | .10 |
| ☐ 381 | Dean Stone | 1.00 | .40 | .10 |
| ☐ 382 | Jim Brideweser | 1.00 | .40 | .10 |
| ☐ 383 | Juan Pizarro | 1.00 | .40 | .10 |
| ☐ 384 | Bobby G. Smith | 1.00 | .40 | .10 |
| ☐ 385 | Art Houtteman | 1.00 | .40 | .10 |
| ☐ 386 | Lyle Luttrell | 1.00 | .40 | .10 |
| ☐ 387 | Jack Sanford | 2.00 | .80 | .20 |
| ☐ 388 | Pete Daley | 1.00 | .40 | .10 |
| ☐ 389 | Dave Jolly | 1.00 | .40 | .10 |
| ☐ 390 | Reno Bertoia | 1.00 | .40 | .10 |
| ☐ 391 | Ralph Terry | 2.00 | .80 | .20 |
| ☐ 392 | Chuck Tanner | 1.50 | .60 | .15 |
| ☐ 393 | Raul Sanchez | 1.00 | .40 | .10 |
| ☐ 394 | Luis Arroyo | 1.25 | .50 | .12 |
| ☐ 395 | J.M. (Bubba) Phillips | 1.00 | .40 | .10 |
| ☐ 396 | K. (Casey) Wise | 1.00 | .40 | .10 |
| ☐ 397 | Roy Smalley | 1.00 | .40 | .10 |
| ☐ 398 | Al Cicotte | 1.00 | .40 | .10 |
| ☐ 399 | Bill Consolo | 1.00 | .40 | .10 |
| ☐ 400 | Dodgers' Sluggers: Carl Furillo Gil Hodges Roy Campanella Duke Snider | 45.00 | 18.00 | 4.50 |
| ☐ 401 | Earl Battey | 1.25 | .50 | .12 |

| | | | | |
|---|---|---|---|---|
| ☐ 402 | Jim Pisani | 1.00 | .40 | .10 |
| ☐ 403 | Richard Hyde | 1.00 | .40 | .10 |
| ☐ 404 | Harry Anderson | 1.00 | .40 | .10 |
| ☐ 405 | Duke Maas | 1.00 | .40 | .10 |
| ☐ 406 | Bob Hale | 1.00 | .40 | .10 |
| ☐ 407 | Yankee Power Hitters: Mickey Mantle Yogi Berra | 75.00 | 30.00 | 7.50 |
| ☐ 408 | Checklist 1/2 (unnumbered) | 35.00 | 6.00 | 1.00 |
| ☐ 409 | Checklist 2/3 (unnumbered) | 50.00 | 8.00 | 1.50 |
| ☐ 410 | Checklist 3/4 (unnumbered) | 100.00 | 18.00 | 3.00 |
| ☐ 411 | Checklist 4/5 (unnumbered) | 150.00 | 25.00 | 5.00 |

# 1958 Topps

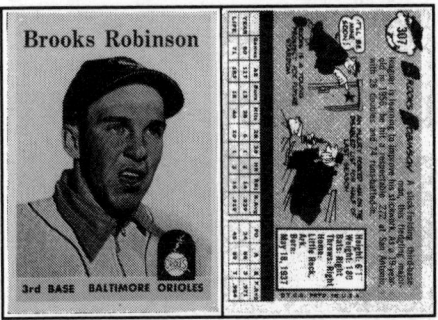

The cards in this 494 card set measure 2 1/2" by 3 1/2". Although the last card is numbered 495, number 145 was not issued, bringing the set total to 494 cards. The 1958 Topps set contains the first Sport Magazine All-Star selection series (475-495) and expanded use of combination cards. The team cards carried series checklists on back (Milwaukee, Detroit, Baltimore, and Cincinnati are also found with players listed alphabetically). Cards with the scarce yellow name (YL) or team (YT) lettering as opposed to the common white lettering are noted in the checklist. In the last series cards of Stan Musial and Mickey Mantle were triple printed; the cards they replaced (443, 446, 450, and 462) on the printing sheet were hence printed in shorter supply than other cards in the last series and are marked with an SP in the list below.

| | MINT | VG-E | F-G |
|---|---|---|---|
| COMPLETE SET (494) | 1000.00 | 400.00 | 125.00 |
| COMMON PLAYER (1-110) | .90 | .36 | .09 |
| COMMON PLAYER (111-198) | .70 | .28 | .07 |
| COMMON PLAYER (199-440) | .60 | .24 | .06 |
| COMMON PLAYER (441-474) | .50 | .20 | .05 |
| COMMON PLAYER (475-495) | .60 | .24 | .06 |

| | | | | |
|---|---|---|---|---|
| ☐ 1 | Ted Williams | 100.00 | 20.00 | 4.00 |
| ☐ 2A | Bob Lemon | 5.00 | 2.00 | .50 |
| ☐ 2B | Bob Lemon YT | 15.00 | 6.00 | 1.50 |
| ☐ 3 | Alex Kellner | .90 | .36 | .09 |
| ☐ 4 | Hank Foiles | .90 | .36 | .09 |
| ☐ 5 | Willie Mays | 36.00 | 15.00 | 3.60 |
| ☐ 6 | George Zuverink | .90 | .36 | .09 |
| ☐ 7 | Dale Long | .90 | .36 | .09 |
| ☐ 8A | Eddie Kasko | .90 | .36 | .09 |
| ☐ 8B | Eddie Kasko YL | 11.00 | 4.50 | 1.10 |
| ☐ 9 | Hank Bauer | 2.00 | .80 | .20 |
| ☐ 10 | Lou Burdette | 2.00 | .80 | .20 |
| ☐ 11A | Jim Rivera | .90 | .36 | .09 |
| ☐ 11B | Jim Rivera YT | 7.50 | 3.00 | .75 |
| ☐ 12 | George Crowe | .90 | .36 | .09 |
| ☐ 13A | Billy Hoeft | .90 | .36 | .09 |
| ☐ 13B | Billy Hoeft YL | 11.00 | 4.50 | 1.10 |

| No. | Player | | | |
|---|---|---|---|---|
| ☐ | 14 Rip Repulski | .90 | .36 | .09 |
| ☐ | 15 Jim Lemon | 1.00 | .40 | .10 |
| ☐ | 16 Charley Neal | 1.00 | .40 | .10 |
| ☐ | 17 Felix Mantilla | .90 | .36 | .09 |
| ☐ | 18 Frank Sullivan | .90 | .36 | .09 |
| ☐ | 19 New York Giants Team Card | 4.50 | .75 | .15 |
| ☐ | 20A Gil McDougald | 2.50 | 1.00 | .25 |
| ☐ | 20B Gil McDougald YL | 15.00 | 6.00 | 1.50 |
| ☐ | 21 Curt Barclay | .90 | .36 | .09 |
| ☐ | 22 Hal Naragon | .90 | .36 | .09 |
| ☐ | 23A Bill Tuttle | .90 | .36 | .09 |
| ☐ | 23B Bill Tuttle YL | 11.00 | 4.50 | 1.10 |
| ☐ | 24A Hobie Landrith | .90 | .36 | .09 |
| ☐ | 24B Hobie Landrith YL | 11.00 | 4.50 | 1.10 |
| ☐ | 25 Don Drysdale | 9.00 | 3.75 | .90 |
| ☐ | 26 Ron Jackson | .90 | .36 | .09 |
| ☐ | 27 Bud Freeman | .90 | .36 | .09 |
| ☐ | 28 Jim Busby | .90 | .36 | .09 |
| ☐ | 29 Ted Lepcio | .90 | .36 | .09 |
| ☐ | 30A Hank Aaron | 36.00 | 15.00 | 3.60 |
| ☐ | 30B Hank Aaron YL | 90.00 | 36.00 | 9.00 |
| ☐ | 31 Tex Clevenger | .90 | .36 | .09 |
| ☐ | 32A J.W. Porter | .90 | .36 | .09 |
| ☐ | 32B J.W. Porter YL | 11.00 | 4.50 | 1.10 |
| ☐ | 33A Cal Neeman | .90 | .36 | .09 |
| ☐ | 33B Cal Neeman YT | 7.50 | 3.00 | .75 |
| ☐ | 34 Bob Thurman | .90 | .36 | .09 |
| ☐ | 35A Don Mossi | 1.00 | .40 | .10 |
| ☐ | 35B Don Mossi YT | 8.50 | 3.50 | .85 |
| ☐ | 36 Ted Kazanski | .90 | .36 | .09 |
| ☐ | 37 Mike McCormick (photo actually Ray Monzant) | 1.50 | .60 | .15 |
| ☐ | 38 Dick Gernert | .90 | .36 | .09 |
| ☐ | 39 Bob Martyn | .90 | .36 | .09 |
| ☐ | 40 George Kell | 5.00 | 2.00 | .50 |
| ☐ | 41 Dave Hillman | .90 | .36 | .09 |
| ☐ | 42 John Roseboro | 2.00 | .80 | .20 |
| ☐ | 43 Sal Maglie | 1.75 | .70 | .17 |
| ☐ | 44 Washington Senators Team Card | 2.50 | .50 | .10 |
| ☐ | 45 Dick Groat | 1.50 | .60 | .15 |
| ☐ | 46A Lou Sleater | .90 | .36 | .09 |
| ☐ | 46B Lou Sleater YL | 11.00 | 4.50 | 1.10 |
| ☐ | 47 Roger Maris | 50.00 | 20.00 | 5.00 |
| ☐ | 48 Chuck Harmon | .90 | .36 | .09 |
| ☐ | 49 Smoky Burgess | 1.00 | .40 | .10 |
| ☐ | 50A Billy Pierce | 1.50 | .60 | .15 |
| ☐ | 50B Billy Pierce YT | 11.00 | 4.50 | 1.10 |
| ☐ | 51 Del Rice | .90 | .36 | .09 |
| ☐ | 52A Bob Clemente | 18.00 | 7.25 | 1.80 |
| ☐ | 52B Bob Clemente YT | 45.00 | 18.00 | 4.50 |
| ☐ | 53A Morrie Martin | .90 | .36 | .09 |
| ☐ | 53B Morrie Martin YL | 11.00 | 4.50 | 1.10 |
| ☐ | 54 Norm Siebern | .90 | .36 | .09 |
| ☐ | 55 Chico Carrasquel | .90 | .36 | .09 |
| ☐ | 56 Bill Fischer | .90 | .36 | .09 |
| ☐ | 57A Tim Thompson | .90 | .36 | .09 |
| ☐ | 57B Tim Thompson YL | 11.00 | 4.50 | 1.10 |
| ☐ | 58A Art Schult | .90 | .36 | .09 |
| ☐ | 58B Art Schult YT | 7.50 | 3.00 | .75 |
| ☐ | 59 Dave Sisler | .90 | .36 | .09 |
| ☐ | 60A Del Ennis | 1.00 | .40 | .10 |
| ☐ | 60B Del Ennis YL | 11.00 | 4.50 | 1.10 |
| ☐ | 61A Darrell Johnson | 1.00 | .40 | .10 |
| ☐ | 61B Darrell Johnson YL | 11.00 | 4.50 | 1.10 |
| ☐ | 62 Joe DeMaestri | .90 | .36 | .09 |
| ☐ | 63 Joe Nuxhall | 1.00 | .40 | .10 |
| ☐ | 64 Joe Lonnett | .90 | .36 | .09 |
| ☐ | 65A Von McDaniel | .90 | .36 | .09 |
| ☐ | 65B Von McDaniel YL | 11.00 | 4.50 | 1.10 |
| ☐ | 66 Lee Walls | .90 | .36 | .09 |
| ☐ | 67 Joe Ginsberg | .90 | .36 | .09 |
| ☐ | 68 Daryl Spencer | .90 | .36 | .09 |
| ☐ | 69 Wally Burnette | .90 | .36 | .09 |
| ☐ | 70A Al Kaline | 11.00 | 4.50 | 1.10 |
| ☐ | 70B Al Kaline YL | 40.00 | 16.00 | 4.00 |
| ☐ | 71 Dodgers Team | 6.50 | 1.00 | .20 |
| ☐ | 72 Bud Byerly | .90 | .36 | .09 |
| ☐ | 73 Pete Daley | .90 | .36 | .09 |
| ☐ | 74 Roy Face | 1.25 | .50 | .12 |
| ☐ | 75 Gus Bell | 1.00 | .40 | .10 |
| ☐ | 76A Dick Farrell | 1.00 | .40 | .10 |
| ☐ | 76B Dick Farrell YT | 7.50 | 3.00 | .75 |
| ☐ | 77A Don Zimmer | 1.25 | .50 | .12 |
| ☐ | 77B Don Zimmer YT | 8.50 | 3.50 | .85 |
| ☐ | 78A Ernie Johnson | .90 | .36 | .09 |
| ☐ | 78B Ernie Johnson YL | 11.00 | 4.50 | 1.10 |
| ☐ | 79A Dick Williams | 1.25 | .50 | .12 |
| ☐ | 79B Dick Williams YT | 8.50 | 3.50 | .85 |
| ☐ | 80 Dick Drott | .90 | .36 | .09 |
| ☐ | 81A Steve Boros | 1.00 | .40 | .10 |
| ☐ | 81B Steve Boros YT | 8.50 | 3.50 | .85 |
| ☐ | 82 Ronnie Kline | .90 | .36 | .09 |
| ☐ | 83 Bob Hazle | .90 | .36 | .09 |
| ☐ | 84 Billy O'Dell | .90 | .36 | .09 |
| ☐ | 85A Luis Aparicio | 5.00 | 2.00 | .50 |
| ☐ | 85B Luis Aparicio YT | 18.00 | 7.25 | 1.80 |
| ☐ | 86 Valmy Thomas | .90 | .36 | .09 |
| ☐ | 87 Johnny Kucks | .90 | .36 | .09 |
| ☐ | 88 Duke Snider | 18.00 | 7.25 | 1.80 |
| ☐ | 89 Billy Klaus | .90 | .36 | .09 |
| ☐ | 90 Robin Roberts | 6.00 | 2.40 | .60 |
| ☐ | 91 Chuck Tanner | 1.25 | .50 | .12 |
| ☐ | 92A Clint Courtney | .90 | .36 | .09 |
| ☐ | 92B Clint Courtney YL | 11.00 | 4.50 | 1.10 |
| ☐ | 93 Sandy Amoros | 1.25 | .50 | .12 |
| ☐ | 94 Bob Skinner | 1.00 | .40 | .10 |
| ☐ | 95 Frank Bolling | .90 | .36 | .09 |
| ☐ | 96 Joe Durham | .90 | .36 | .09 |
| ☐ | 97A Larry Jackson | .90 | .36 | .09 |
| ☐ | 97B Larry Jackson YL | 11.00 | 4.50 | 1.10 |
| ☐ | 98A Billy Hunter | .90 | .36 | .09 |
| ☐ | 98B Billy Hunter YL | 11.00 | 4.50 | 1.10 |
| ☐ | 99 Bobby Adams | .90 | .36 | .09 |
| ☐ | 100A Early Wynn | 5.00 | 2.00 | .50 |
| ☐ | 100B Early Wynn YT | 15.00 | 6.00 | 1.50 |
| ☐ | 101A Bobby Richardson | 3.00 | 1.20 | .30 |
| ☐ | 101B Bobby Richardson YL | 15.00 | 6.00 | 1.50 |
| ☐ | 102 George Strickland | .90 | .36 | .09 |
| ☐ | 103 Jerry Lynch | 1.00 | .40 | .10 |
| ☐ | 104 Jim Pendleton | .90 | .36 | .09 |
| ☐ | 105 Billy Gardner | 1.00 | .40 | .10 |
| ☐ | 106 Dick Schofield | .90 | .36 | .09 |
| ☐ | 107 Ossie Virgil | .90 | .36 | .09 |
| ☐ | 108A Jim Landis | .90 | .36 | .09 |
| ☐ | 108B Jim Landis YT | 7.50 | 3.00 | .75 |
| ☐ | 109 Herb Plews | .90 | .36 | .09 |
| ☐ | 110 Johnny Logan | 1.00 | .40 | .10 |
| ☐ | 111 Stu Miller | .70 | .28 | .07 |
| ☐ | 112 Gus Zernial | .80 | .32 | .08 |
| ☐ | 113 Jerry Walker | .70 | .28 | .07 |
| ☐ | 114 Irv Noren | .70 | .28 | .07 |
| ☐ | 115 Jim Bunning | 3.00 | 1.20 | .30 |
| ☐ | 116 Dave Philley | .70 | .28 | .07 |
| ☐ | 117 Frank Torre | .80 | .32 | .08 |
| ☐ | 118 Harvey Haddix | 1.00 | .40 | .10 |
| ☐ | 119 Harry Chiti | .70 | .28 | .07 |
| ☐ | 120 Johnny Podres | 2.00 | .80 | .20 |
| ☐ | 121 Eddie Miksis | .70 | .28 | .07 |
| ☐ | 122 Walt Moryn | .70 | .28 | .07 |
| ☐ | 123 Dick Tomanek | .70 | .28 | .07 |
| ☐ | 124 Bobby Usher | .70 | .28 | .07 |
| ☐ | 125 Al Dark | 1.25 | .50 | .12 |
| ☐ | 126 Stan Palys | .70 | .28 | .07 |
| ☐ | 127 Tom Sturdivant | .80 | .32 | .08 |
| ☐ | 128 Willie Kirkland | .80 | .32 | .08 |
| ☐ | 129 Jim Derrington | .70 | .28 | .07 |
| ☐ | 130 Jackie Jensen | 2.50 | 1.00 | .25 |
| ☐ | 131 Bob Henrich | .70 | .28 | .07 |
| ☐ | 132 Vernon Law | .90 | .36 | .09 |
| ☐ | 133 Russ Nixon | .70 | .28 | .07 |
| ☐ | 134 Phillies Team | 2.50 | .50 | .10 |
| ☐ | 135 Mike (Moe) Drabowsky | .70 | .28 | .07 |
| ☐ | 136 Jim Finigan | .70 | .28 | .07 |
| ☐ | 137 Russ Kemmerer | .70 | .28 | .07 |
| ☐ | 138 Earl Torgeson | .70 | .28 | .07 |
| ☐ | 139 George Brunet | .70 | .28 | .07 |
| ☐ | 140 Wes Covington | .80 | .32 | .08 |
| ☐ | 141 Ken Lehman | .70 | .28 | .07 |
| ☐ | 142 Enos Slaughter | 4.50 | 1.80 | .45 |
| ☐ | 143 Billy Muffett | .70 | .28 | .07 |
| ☐ | 144 Bobby Morgan | .70 | .28 | .07 |
| ☐ | 145 Never issued | .00 | .00 | .00 |
| ☐ | 146 Dick Gray | .70 | .28 | .07 |
| ☐ | 147 Don McMahon | .80 | .32 | .08 |
| ☐ | 148 Billy Consolo | .70 | .28 | .07 |
| ☐ | 149 Tom Acker | .70 | .28 | .07 |
| ☐ | 150 Mickey Mantle | 120.00 | 50.00 | 12.00 |
| ☐ | 151 Buddy Pritchard | .70 | .28 | .07 |
| ☐ | 152 Johnny Antonelli | .90 | .36 | .09 |
| ☐ | 153 Les Moss | .70 | .28 | .07 |
| ☐ | 154 Harry Byrd | .70 | .28 | .07 |
| ☐ | 155 Hector Lopez | .70 | .28 | .07 |
| ☐ | 156 Dick Hyde | .70 | .28 | .07 |
| ☐ | 157 Dee Fondy | .70 | .28 | .07 |
| ☐ | 158 Indians Team | 2.50 | .50 | .10 |
| ☐ | 159 Taylor Phillips | .70 | .28 | .07 |
| ☐ | 160 Don Hoak | .70 | .28 | .07 |
| ☐ | 161 Don Larsen | 2.00 | .80 | .20 |
| ☐ | 162 Gil Hodges | 8.00 | 3.25 | .80 |
| ☐ | 163 Jim Wilson | .70 | .28 | .07 |
| ☐ | 164 Bob Taylor | .70 | .28 | .07 |
| ☐ | 165 Bob Nieman | .70 | .28 | .07 |
| ☐ | 166 Danny O'Connell | .70 | .28 | .07 |

| # | Player | | | |
|---|---|---|---|---|
| ☐ 167 | Frank Baumann | .70 | .28 | .07 |
| ☐ 168 | Joe Cunningham | .80 | .32 | .08 |
| ☐ 169 | Ralph Terry | 1.00 | .40 | .10 |
| ☐ 170 | Vic Wertz | .80 | .32 | .08 |
| ☐ 171 | Harry Anderson | .70 | .28 | .07 |
| ☐ 172 | Don Gross | .70 | .28 | .07 |
| ☐ 173 | Eddie Yost | .70 | .28 | .07 |
| ☐ 174 | Athletics Team | 2.50 | .50 | .10 |
| ☐ 175 | Marv Throneberry | 3.00 | 1.20 | .30 |
| ☐ 176 | Bob Buhl | .70 | .28 | .07 |
| ☐ 177 | Al Smith | .70 | .28 | .07 |
| ☐ 178 | Ted Kluszewski | 2.00 | .80 | .20 |
| ☐ 179 | Willie Miranda | .70 | .28 | .07 |
| ☐ 180 | Lindy McDaniel | .80 | .32 | .08 |
| ☐ 181 | Willie Jones | .70 | .28 | .07 |
| ☐ 182 | Joe Caffie | .70 | .28 | .07 |
| ☐ 183 | Dave Jolly | .70 | .28 | .07 |
| ☐ 184 | Elvin Tappe | .70 | .28 | .07 |
| ☐ 185 | Ray Boone | .80 | .32 | .08 |
| ☐ 186 | Jack Meyer | .70 | .28 | .07 |
| ☐ 187 | Sandy Koufax | 27.00 | 11.00 | 2.70 |
| ☐ 188 | Milt Bolling (photo actually Lou Berberet) | .70 | .28 | .07 |
| ☐ 189 | George Susce | .70 | .28 | .07 |
| ☐ 190 | Red Schoendienst | 1.25 | .50 | .12 |
| ☐ 191 | Art Ceccarelli | .70 | .28 | .07 |
| ☐ 192 | Milt Graff | .70 | .28 | .07 |
| ☐ 193 | Jerry Lumpe | .80 | .32 | .08 |
| ☐ 194 | Roger Craig | 1.25 | .50 | .12 |
| ☐ 195 | Whitey Lockman | .80 | .32 | .08 |
| ☐ 196 | Mike Garcia | .90 | .36 | .09 |
| ☐ 197 | Haywood Sullivan | .80 | .32 | .08 |
| ☐ 198 | Bill Virdon | 1.25 | .50 | .12 |
| ☐ 199 | Don Blasingame | .60 | .24 | .06 |
| ☐ 200 | Bob Keegan | .60 | .24 | .06 |
| ☐ 201 | Jim Bolger | .60 | .24 | .06 |
| ☐ 202 | Woody Held | .60 | .24 | .06 |
| ☐ 203 | Al Walker | .60 | .24 | .06 |
| ☐ 204 | Leo Kiely | .60 | .24 | .06 |
| ☐ 205 | Johnny Temple | .70 | .28 | .07 |
| ☐ 206 | Bob Shaw | .60 | .24 | .06 |
| ☐ 207 | Solly Hemus | .60 | .24 | .06 |
| ☐ 208 | Cal McLish | .60 | .24 | .06 |
| ☐ 209 | Bob Anderson | .60 | .24 | .06 |
| ☐ 210 | Wally Moon | .80 | .32 | .08 |
| ☐ 211 | Pete Burnside | .60 | .24 | .06 |
| ☐ 212 | Bubba Phillips | .60 | .24 | .06 |
| ☐ 213 | Red Wilson | .60 | .24 | .06 |
| ☐ 214 | Willard Schmidt | .60 | .24 | .06 |
| ☐ 215 | Jim Gilliam | 2.00 | .80 | .20 |
| ☐ 216 | Cardinals Team | 2.50 | .50 | .10 |
| ☐ 217 | Jack Harshman | .60 | .24 | .06 |
| ☐ 218 | Dick Rand | .60 | .24 | .06 |
| ☐ 219 | Camilo Pascual | .70 | .28 | .07 |
| ☐ 220 | Tom Brewer | .60 | .24 | .06 |
| ☐ 221 | Jerry Kindall | .60 | .24 | .06 |
| ☐ 222 | Bud Daley | .60 | .24 | .06 |
| ☐ 223 | Andy Pafko | .80 | .32 | .08 |
| ☐ 224 | Bob Grim | .70 | .28 | .07 |
| ☐ 225 | Billy Goodman | .60 | .24 | .06 |
| ☐ 226 | Bob Smith | .60 | .24 | .06 |
| ☐ 227 | Gene Stephens | .60 | .24 | .06 |
| ☐ 228 | Duke Maas | .60 | .24 | .06 |
| ☐ 229 | Frank Zupo | .60 | .24 | .06 |
| ☐ 230 | Richie Ashburn | 3.00 | 1.20 | .30 |
| ☐ 231 | Lloyd Merritt | .60 | .24 | .06 |
| ☐ 232 | Reno Bertoia | .60 | .24 | .06 |
| ☐ 233 | Mickey Vernon | .80 | .32 | .08 |
| ☐ 234 | Carl Sawatski | .60 | .24 | .06 |
| ☐ 235 | Tom Gorman | .60 | .24 | .06 |
| ☐ 236 | Ed Fitzgerald | .60 | .24 | .06 |
| ☐ 237 | Bill Wight | .60 | .24 | .06 |
| ☐ 238 | Bill Mazeroski | 2.50 | 1.00 | .25 |
| ☐ 239 | Chuck Stobbs | .60 | .24 | .06 |
| ☐ 240 | Moose Skowron | 2.50 | 1.00 | .25 |
| ☐ 241 | Dick Littlefield | .60 | .24 | .06 |
| ☐ 242 | Johnny Klippstein | .60 | .24 | .06 |
| ☐ 243 | Larry Raines | .60 | .24 | .06 |
| ☐ 244 | Don Demeter | .80 | .32 | .08 |
| ☐ 245 | Frank Lary | .70 | .28 | .07 |
| ☐ 246 | Yankees Team | 9.00 | 1.50 | .30 |
| ☐ 247 | Casey Wise | .60 | .24 | .06 |
| ☐ 248 | Herm Wehmeier | .60 | .24 | .06 |
| ☐ 249 | Ray Moore | .60 | .24 | .06 |
| ☐ 250 | Roy Sievers | .80 | .32 | .08 |
| ☐ 251 | Warren Hacker | .60 | .24 | .06 |
| ☐ 252 | Bob Trowbridge | .60 | .24 | .06 |
| ☐ 253 | Don Mueller | .70 | .28 | .07 |
| ☐ 254 | Alex Grammas | .60 | .24 | .06 |
| ☐ 255 | Bob Turley | 2.25 | .90 | .22 |
| ☐ 256 | White Sox Team | 2.50 | .50 | .10 |
| ☐ 257 | Hal Smith | .60 | .24 | .06 |
| ☐ 258 | Carl Erskine | 2.00 | .80 | .20 |
| ☐ 259 | Al Pilarcik | .60 | .24 | .06 |
| ☐ 260 | Frank Malzone | .80 | .32 | .08 |
| ☐ 261 | Turk Lown | .60 | .24 | .06 |
| ☐ 262 | Johnny Groth | .60 | .24 | .06 |
| ☐ 263 | Eddie Bressoud | .60 | .24 | .06 |
| ☐ 264 | Jack Sanford | .70 | .28 | .07 |
| ☐ 265 | Pete Runnels | .70 | .28 | .07 |
| ☐ 266 | Connie Johnson | .60 | .24 | .06 |
| ☐ 267 | Sherm Lollar | .70 | .28 | .07 |
| ☐ 268 | Granny Hamner | .60 | .24 | .06 |
| ☐ 269 | Paul Smith | .60 | .24 | .06 |
| ☐ 270 | Warren Spahn | 8.00 | 3.25 | .80 |
| ☐ 271 | Billy Martin | 3.25 | 1.30 | .32 |
| ☐ 272 | Ray Crone | .60 | .24 | .06 |
| ☐ 273 | Hal Smith | .60 | .24 | .06 |
| ☐ 274 | Rocky Bridges | .60 | .24 | .06 |
| ☐ 275 | Elston Howard | 2.50 | 1.00 | .25 |
| ☐ 276 | Bobby Avila | .70 | .28 | .07 |
| ☐ 277 | Virgil Trucks | .70 | .28 | .07 |
| ☐ 278 | Mack Burk | .60 | .24 | .06 |
| ☐ 279 | Bob Boyd | .60 | .24 | .06 |
| ☐ 280 | Jim Piersall | 1.75 | .70 | .17 |
| ☐ 281 | Sam Taylor | .60 | .24 | .06 |
| ☐ 282 | Paul Foytack | .60 | .24 | .06 |
| ☐ 283 | Ray Shearer | .60 | .24 | .06 |
| ☐ 284 | Ray Katt | .60 | .24 | .06 |
| ☐ 285 | Frank Robinson | 11.00 | 4.50 | 1.10 |
| ☐ 286 | Gino Cimoli | .60 | .24 | .06 |
| ☐ 287 | Sam Jones | .70 | .28 | .07 |
| ☐ 288 | Harmon Killebrew | 11.00 | 4.50 | 1.10 |
| ☐ 289 | Series Hurling Rivals Lou Burdette Bobby Shantz | 1.50 | .60 | .15 |
| ☐ 290 | Dick Donovan | .60 | .24 | .06 |
| ☐ 291 | Don Landrum | .60 | .24 | .06 |
| ☐ 292 | Ned Garver | .60 | .24 | .06 |
| ☐ 293 | Gene Freese | .60 | .24 | .06 |
| ☐ 294 | Hal Jeffcoat | .60 | .24 | .06 |
| ☐ 295 | Minnie Minoso | 2.00 | .80 | .20 |
| ☐ 296 | Ryne Duren | 1.50 | .60 | .15 |
| ☐ 297 | Don Buddin | .60 | .24 | .06 |
| ☐ 298 | Jim Hearn | .60 | .24 | .06 |
| ☐ 299 | Harry Simpson | .60 | .24 | .06 |
| ☐ 300 | Harridge and Giles League Presidents | 2.00 | .80 | .20 |
| ☐ 301 | Randy Jackson | .60 | .24 | .06 |
| ☐ 302 | Mike Baxes | .60 | .24 | .06 |
| ☐ 303 | Neil Chrisley | .60 | .24 | .06 |
| ☐ 304 | Tigers' Big Bats: Harvey Kuenn Al Kaline | 3.50 | 1.40 | .35 |
| ☐ 305 | Clem Labine | .80 | .32 | .08 |
| ☐ 306 | Whammy Douglas | .60 | .24 | .06 |
| ☐ 307 | Brooks Robinson | 20.00 | 8.00 | 2.00 |
| ☐ 308 | Paul Giel | .60 | .24 | .06 |
| ☐ 309 | Gail Harris | .60 | .24 | .06 |
| ☐ 310 | Ernie Banks | 14.00 | 5.75 | 1.40 |
| ☐ 311 | Bob Purkey | .60 | .24 | .06 |
| ☐ 312 | Boston Red Sox Team | 3.00 | .60 | .10 |
| ☐ 313 | Bob Rush | .60 | .24 | .06 |
| ☐ 314 | Dodgers' Boss and Power: Duke Snider Walt Alston | 7.00 | 2.80 | .70 |
| ☐ 315 | Bob Friend | .80 | .32 | .08 |
| ☐ 316 | Tito Francona | .70 | .28 | .07 |
| ☐ 317 | Albie Pearson | .80 | .32 | .08 |
| ☐ 318 | Frank House | .60 | .24 | .06 |
| ☐ 319 | Lou Skizas | .60 | .24 | .06 |
| ☐ 320 | Whitey Ford | 10.00 | 4.00 | 1.00 |
| ☐ 321 | Sluggers Supreme: Ted Kluszewski Ted Williams | 9.00 | 3.75 | .90 |
| ☐ 322 | Harding Peterson | .70 | .28 | .07 |
| ☐ 323 | Elmer Valo | .60 | .24 | .06 |
| ☐ 324 | Hoyt Wilhelm | 4.50 | 1.80 | .45 |
| ☐ 325 | Joe Adcock | 1.25 | .50 | .12 |
| ☐ 326 | Bob Miller | .60 | .24 | .06 |
| ☐ 327 | Chicago Cubs Team | 2.50 | .50 | .10 |
| ☐ 328 | Ike Delock | .60 | .24 | .06 |
| ☐ 329 | Bob Cerv | .70 | .28 | .07 |
| ☐ 330 | Ed Bailey | .70 | .28 | .07 |
| ☐ 331 | Pedro Ramos | .60 | .24 | .06 |
| ☐ 332 | Jim King | .60 | .24 | .06 |
| ☐ 333 | Andy Carey | .70 | .28 | .07 |
| ☐ 334 | Mound Aces: Bob Friend Billy Pierce | 1.00 | .40 | .10 |
| ☐ 335 | Ruben Gomez | .60 | .24 | .06 |
| ☐ 336 | Bert Hamric | .60 | .24 | .06 |
| ☐ 337 | Hank Aguirre | .60 | .24 | .06 |
| ☐ 338 | Walt Dropo | .60 | .24 | .06 |
| ☐ 339 | Fred Hatfield | .60 | .24 | .06 |

| | | | | |
|---|---|---|---|---|
| ☐ 340 | Don Newcombe | 2.25 | .90 | .22 |
| ☐ 341 | Pirates Team | 2.50 | .50 | .10 |
| ☐ 342 | Jim Brosnan | .70 | .28 | .07 |
| ☐ 343 | Orlando Cepeda | 10.00 | 4.00 | 1.00 |
| ☐ 344 | Bob Porterfield | .60 | .24 | .06 |
| ☐ 345 | Jim Hegan | .70 | .28 | .07 |
| ☐ 346 | Steve Bilko | .60 | .24 | .06 |
| ☐ 347 | Don Rudolph | .60 | .24 | .06 |
| ☐ 348 | Chico Fernandez | .60 | .24 | .06 |
| ☐ 349 | Murry Dickson | .60 | .24 | .06 |
| ☐ 350 | Ken Boyer | 2.00 | .80 | .20 |
| ☐ 351 | Braves Fence Busters: Del Crandall Eddie Mathews Hank Aaron Joe Adcock | 9.00 | 3.75 | .90 |
| ☐ 352 | Herb Score | 1.25 | .50 | .12 |
| ☐ 353 | Stan Lopata | .60 | .24 | .06 |
| ☐ 354 | Art Ditmar | .70 | .28 | .07 |
| ☐ 355 | Bill Bruton | .70 | .28 | .07 |
| ☐ 356 | Bob Malkmus | .60 | .24 | .06 |
| ☐ 357 | Danny McDevitt | .60 | .24 | .06 |
| ☐ 358 | Gene Baker | .60 | .24 | .06 |
| ☐ 359 | Billy Loes | .70 | .28 | .07 |
| ☐ 360 | Roy McMillan | .60 | .24 | .06 |
| ☐ 361 | Mike Fornieles | .60 | .24 | .06 |
| ☐ 362 | Ray Jablonski | .60 | .24 | .06 |
| ☐ 363 | Don Elston | .60 | .24 | .06 |
| ☐ 364 | Earl Battey | .70 | .28 | .07 |
| ☐ 365 | Tom Morgan | .60 | .24 | .06 |
| ☐ 366 | Gene Green | .60 | .24 | .06 |
| ☐ 367 | Jack Urban | .60 | .24 | .06 |
| ☐ 368 | Rocky Colavito | 2.50 | 1.00 | .25 |
| ☐ 369 | Ralph Lumenti | .60 | .24 | .06 |
| ☐ 370 | Yogi Berra | 12.00 | 5.00 | 1.20 |
| ☐ 371 | Marty Keough | .60 | .24 | .06 |
| ☐ 372 | Don Cardwell | .60 | .24 | .06 |
| ☐ 373 | Joe Pignatano | .70 | .28 | .07 |
| ☐ 374 | Brooks Lawrence | .60 | .24 | .06 |
| ☐ 375 | Pee Wee Reese | 9.00 | 3.75 | .90 |
| ☐ 376 | Charley Rabe | .60 | .24 | .06 |
| ☐ 377A | Milwaukee Team alphabetical | 3.00 | 1.20 | .30 |
| ☐ 377B | Milwaukee Team numerical | 20.00 | 3.00 | .50 |
| ☐ 378 | Hank Sauer | .80 | .32 | .08 |
| ☐ 379 | Ray Herbert | .60 | .24 | .06 |
| ☐ 380 | Charley Maxwell | .60 | .24 | .06 |
| ☐ 381 | Hal Brown | .60 | .24 | .06 |
| ☐ 382 | Al Cicotte | .70 | .28 | .07 |
| ☐ 383 | Lou Berberet | .60 | .24 | .06 |
| ☐ 384 | John Goryl | .60 | .24 | .06 |
| ☐ 385 | Wilmer Mizell | .60 | .24 | .06 |
| ☐ 386 | Birdie's Sluggers: Ed Bailey Birdie Tebbetts Frank Robinson | 2.00 | .80 | .20 |
| ☐ 387 | Wally Post | .60 | .24 | .06 |
| ☐ 388 | Billy Moran | .60 | .24 | .06 |
| ☐ 389 | Bill Taylor | .60 | .24 | .06 |
| ☐ 390 | Del Crandall | .80 | .32 | .08 |
| ☐ 391 | Dave Melton | .60 | .24 | .06 |
| ☐ 392 | Bennie Daniels | .60 | .24 | .06 |
| ☐ 393 | Tony Kubek | 3.50 | 1.40 | .35 |
| ☐ 394 | Jim Grant | .60 | .24 | .06 |
| ☐ 395 | Willard Nixon | .60 | .24 | .06 |
| ☐ 396 | Dutch Dotterer | .60 | .24 | .06 |
| ☐ 397A | Detroit Team alphabetical | 3.00 | 1.20 | .30 |
| ☐ 397B | Detroit Team numerical | 20.00 | 3.00 | .50 |
| ☐ 398 | Gene Woodling | .80 | .32 | .08 |
| ☐ 399 | Marv Grissom | .60 | .24 | .06 |
| ☐ 400 | Nellie Fox | 2.50 | 1.00 | .25 |
| ☐ 401 | Don Bessent | .70 | .28 | .07 |
| ☐ 402 | Bobby Gene Smith | .60 | .24 | .06 |
| ☐ 403 | Steve Korcheck | .60 | .24 | .06 |
| ☐ 404 | Curt Simmons | .80 | .32 | .08 |
| ☐ 405 | Ken Aspromonte | .60 | .24 | .06 |
| ☐ 406 | Vic Power | .70 | .28 | .07 |
| ☐ 407 | Carlton Willey | .60 | .24 | .06 |
| ☐ 408A | Baltimore Team alphabetical | 3.00 | 1.20 | .30 |
| ☐ 408B | Baltimore Team numerical | 20.00 | 3.00 | .50 |
| ☐ 409 | Frank Thomas | .70 | .28 | .07 |
| ☐ 410 | Murray Wall | .60 | .24 | .06 |
| ☐ 411 | Tony Taylor | .60 | .24 | .06 |
| ☐ 412 | Jerry Staley | .60 | .24 | .06 |
| ☐ 413 | Jim Davenport | .80 | .32 | .08 |
| ☐ 414 | Sammy White | .60 | .24 | .06 |
| ☐ 415 | Bob Bowman | .60 | .24 | .06 |
| ☐ 416 | Foster Castleman | .60 | .24 | .06 |

| | | | | |
|---|---|---|---|---|
| ☐ 417 | Carl Furillo | 2.25 | .90 | .22 |
| ☐ 418 | World Series Batting Foes: Mickey Mantle Hank Aaron | 30.00 | 12.00 | 3.00 |
| ☐ 419 | Bobby Shantz | 1.25 | .50 | .12 |
| ☐ 420 | Vada Pinson | 4.00 | 1.60 | .40 |
| ☐ 421 | Dixie Howell | .60 | .24 | .06 |
| ☐ 422 | Norm Zauchin | .60 | .24 | .06 |
| ☐ 423 | Phil Clark | .60 | .24 | .06 |
| ☐ 424 | Larry Doby | 1.75 | .70 | .17 |
| ☐ 425 | Sam Esposito | .60 | .24 | .06 |
| ☐ 426 | Johnny O'Brien | .60 | .24 | .06 |
| ☐ 427 | Al Worthington | .60 | .24 | .06 |
| ☐ 428A | Cincinnati Team alphabetical | 3.00 | 1.20 | .30 |
| ☐ 428B | Cincinnati Team numerical | 20.00 | 3.00 | .50 |
| ☐ 429 | Gus Triandos | .80 | .32 | .08 |
| ☐ 430 | Bobby Thomson | 1.25 | .50 | .12 |
| ☐ 431 | Gene Conley | .70 | .28 | .07 |
| ☐ 432 | John Powers | .60 | .24 | .06 |
| ☐ 433A | Pancho Herrera COR | .70 | .28 | .07 |
| ☐ 433B | Pancho Herrer ERR | 20.00 | 8.00 | 2.00 |
| ☐ 434 | Harvey Kuenn | 1.75 | .70 | .17 |
| ☐ 435 | Ed Roebuck | .70 | .28 | .07 |
| ☐ 436 | Rival Fence Busters: Willie Mays Duke Snider | 18.00 | 7.25 | 1.80 |
| ☐ 437 | Bob Speake | .60 | .24 | .06 |
| ☐ 438 | Whitey Herzog | 1.25 | .50 | .12 |
| ☐ 439 | Ray Narleski | .60 | .24 | .06 |
| ☐ 440 | Ed Mathews | 7.50 | 3.00 | .75 |
| ☐ 441 | Jim Marshall | .50 | .20 | .05 |
| ☐ 442 | Phil Paine | .50 | .20 | .05 |
| ☐ 443 | Billy Harrell SP | 4.50 | 1.80 | .45 |
| ☐ 444 | Danny Kravitz | .50 | .20 | .05 |
| ☐ 445 | Bob Smith | .50 | .20 | .05 |
| ☐ 446 | Carroll Hardy SP | 4.50 | 1.80 | .45 |
| ☐ 447 | Ray Monzant | .50 | .20 | .05 |
| ☐ 448 | Charlie Lau | 1.00 | .40 | .10 |
| ☐ 449 | Gene Fodge | .50 | .20 | .05 |
| ☐ 450 | Preston Ward SP | 4.50 | 1.80 | .45 |
| ☐ 451 | Joe Taylor | .50 | .20 | .05 |
| ☐ 452 | Roman Mejias | .50 | .20 | .05 |
| ☐ 453 | Tom Qualters | .50 | .20 | .05 |
| ☐ 454 | Harry Hanebrink | .50 | .20 | .05 |
| ☐ 455 | Hal Griggs | .50 | .20 | .05 |
| ☐ 456 | Dick Brown | .50 | .20 | .05 |
| ☐ 457 | Milt Pappas | 1.25 | .50 | .12 |
| ☐ 458 | Julio Becquer | .50 | .20 | .05 |
| ☐ 459 | Ron Blackburn | .50 | .20 | .05 |
| ☐ 460 | Chuck Essegian | .50 | .20 | .05 |
| ☐ 461 | Ed Mayer | .50 | .20 | .05 |
| ☐ 462 | Gary Geiger SP | 4.50 | 1.80 | .45 |
| ☐ 463 | Vito Valentinetti | .50 | .20 | .05 |
| ☐ 464 | Curt Flood | 3.00 | 1.20 | .30 |
| ☐ 465 | Arnie Portocarrero | .50 | .20 | .05 |
| ☐ 466 | Pete Whisenant | .50 | .20 | .05 |
| ☐ 467 | Glen Hobbie | .50 | .20 | .05 |
| ☐ 468 | Bob Schmidt | .50 | .20 | .05 |
| ☐ 469 | Don Ferrarese | .50 | .20 | .05 |
| ☐ 470 | R.C. Stevens | .50 | .20 | .05 |
| ☐ 471 | Lenny Green | .50 | .20 | .05 |
| ☐ 472 | Joe Jay | .50 | .20 | .05 |
| ☐ 473 | Bill Renna | .50 | .20 | .05 |
| ☐ 474 | Roman Semproch | .50 | .20 | .05 |
| ☐ 475 | Haney/Stengel AS (checklist back) | 4.00 | 1.00 | .20 |
| ☐ 476 | Stan Musial AS TP | 6.00 | 2.40 | .60 |
| ☐ 477 | Bill Skowron AS | .80 | .32 | .08 |
| ☐ 478 | Johnny Temple AS | .60 | .24 | .06 |
| ☐ 479 | Nellie Fox AS | 1.50 | .60 | .15 |
| ☐ 480 | Eddie Mathews AS | 3.50 | 1.40 | .35 |
| ☐ 481 | Frank Malzone AS | .60 | .24 | .06 |
| ☐ 482 | Ernie Banks AS | 4.00 | 1.60 | .40 |
| ☐ 483 | Luis Aparicio AS | 3.00 | 1.20 | .30 |
| ☐ 484 | Frank Robinson AS | 3.50 | 1.40 | .35 |
| ☐ 485 | Ted Williams AS | 12.00 | 5.00 | 1.20 |
| ☐ 486 | Willie Mays AS | 9.00 | 3.75 | .90 |
| ☐ 487 | Mickey Mantle AS TP | 10.00 | 4.00 | 1.00 |
| ☐ 488 | Hank Aaron AS | 9.00 | 3.75 | .90 |
| ☐ 489 | Jackie Jensen AS | .70 | .28 | .07 |
| ☐ 490 | Ed Bailey AS | .60 | .24 | .06 |
| ☐ 491 | Sherm Lollar AS | .60 | .24 | .06 |
| ☐ 492 | Bob Friend AS | .60 | .24 | .06 |
| ☐ 493 | Bob Turley AS | .70 | .28 | .07 |
| ☐ 494 | Warren Spahn AS | 3.00 | 1.20 | .30 |
| ☐ 495 | Herb Score AS | 1.00 | .40 | .10 |

## 1959 Topps

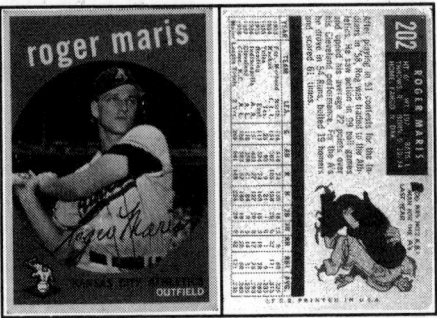

The cards in this 572 card set measure 2 1/2" by 3 1/2". The 1959 Topps set contains bust pictures of the players in a colored circle. Card numbers 551 to 572 are The Sporting News All-Star selections. High numbers 507 to 572 have the card number in a black background on the reverse rather than a green background as in the lower numbers. The high numbers are more difficult to obtain. Several cards in the 300's exist with or without an extra traded or option line on the back of the card. Cards 199 to 286 exist with either white or gray backs. Cards 461 to 470 contain "Highlights" while cards 116 to 146 give an alphabetically ordered listing of "Rookie Prospects." These Rookie Prospects (RP) were Topps' first organized inclusion of untested "Rookie" cards. Card 440 features Lew Burdette erroneously posing as a lefthanded pitcher.

|  | MINT | VG-E | F-G |
|---|---|---|---|
| COMPLETE SET | 850.00 | 340.00 | 85.00 |
| COMMON PLAYER (1-110) | .60 | .24 | .06 |
| COMMON PLAYER (111-506) | .50 | .20 | .05 |
| COMMON PLAYER (507-550) | 2.50 | 1.00 | .25 |
| COMMON PLAYER (551-572) | 3.00 | 1.20 | .30 |

| | | | MINT | VG-E | F-G |
|---|---|---|---|---|---|
| ☐ | 1 | Ford Frick | 4.00 | 1.00 | .20 |
| ☐ | 2 | Eddie Yost | .60 | .24 | .06 |
| ☐ | 3 | Don McMahon | .60 | .24 | .06 |
| ☐ | 4 | Albie Pearson | .60 | .24 | .06 |
| ☐ | 5 | Dick Donovan | .60 | .24 | .06 |
| ☐ | 6 | Alex Grammas | .60 | .24 | .06 |
| ☐ | 7 | Al Pilarcik | .60 | .24 | .06 |
| ☐ | 8 | Phillies Team | 2.25 | .50 | .10 |
| ☐ | 9 | Paul Giel | .60 | .24 | .06 |
| ☐ | 10 | Mickey Mantle | 90.00 | 36.00 | 9.00 |
| ☐ | 11 | Billy Hunter | .60 | .24 | .06 |
| ☐ | 12 | Vern Law | .75 | .30 | .07 |
| ☐ | 13 | Dick Gernert | .60 | .24 | .06 |
| ☐ | 14 | Pete Whisenant | .60 | .24 | .06 |
| ☐ | 15 | Dick Drott | .60 | .24 | .06 |
| ☐ | 16 | Joe Pignatano | .60 | .24 | .06 |
| ☐ | 17 | Danny's Stars<br>Frank Thomas<br>Danny Murtaugh<br>Ted Kluszewski | .90 | .36 | .09 |
| ☐ | 18 | Jack Urban | .60 | .24 | .06 |
| ☐ | 19 | Eddie Bressoud | .60 | .24 | .06 |
| ☐ | 20 | Duke Snider | 12.50 | 5.00 | 1.25 |
| ☐ | 21 | Connie Johnson | .60 | .24 | .06 |
| ☐ | 22 | Al Smith | .60 | .24 | .06 |
| ☐ | 23 | Murry Dickson | .60 | .24 | .06 |
| ☐ | 24 | Red Wilson | .60 | .24 | .06 |
| ☐ | 25 | Don Hoak | .60 | .24 | .06 |
| ☐ | 26 | Chuck Stobbs | .60 | .24 | .06 |
| ☐ | 27 | Andy Pafko | .60 | .24 | .06 |
| ☐ | 28 | Ray Worthington | .60 | .24 | .06 |
| ☐ | 29 | Jim Bolger | .60 | .24 | .06 |
| ☐ | 30 | Nellie Fox | 2.50 | 1.00 | .25 |
| ☐ | 31 | Ken Lehman | .60 | .24 | .06 |
| ☐ | 32 | Don Buddin | .60 | .24 | .06 |
| ☐ | 33 | Ed Fitzgerald | .60 | .24 | .06 |
| ☐ | 34 | Pitchers Beware<br>Al Kaline<br>Charley Maxwell | 2.25 | .90 | .22 |

| | | | | | |
|---|---|---|---|---|---|
| ☐ | 35 | Ted Kluszewski | 1.50 | .60 | .15 |
| ☐ | 36 | Hank Aguirre | .60 | .24 | .06 |
| ☐ | 37 | Gene Green | .60 | .24 | .06 |
| ☐ | 38 | Morrie Martin | .60 | .24 | .06 |
| ☐ | 39 | Ed Bouchee | .60 | .24 | .06 |
| ☐ | 40 | Warren Spahn | 8.50 | 3.50 | .85 |
| ☐ | 41 | Bob Martyn | .60 | .24 | .06 |
| ☐ | 42 | Murray Wall | .60 | .24 | .06 |
| ☐ | 43 | Steve Bilko | .60 | .24 | .06 |
| ☐ | 44 | Vito Valentinetti | .60 | .24 | .06 |
| ☐ | 45 | Andy Carey | .75 | .30 | .07 |
| ☐ | 46 | R. Henry | .60 | .24 | .06 |
| ☐ | 47 | Jim Finigan | .60 | .24 | .06 |
| ☐ | 48 | Orioles Team | 2.25 | .50 | .10 |
| ☐ | 49 | Bill Hall | .60 | .24 | .06 |
| ☐ | 50 | Willie Mays | 32.00 | 13.00 | 3.20 |
| ☐ | 51 | Rip Coleman | .60 | .24 | .06 |
| ☐ | 52 | Coot Veal | .60 | .24 | .06 |
| ☐ | 53 | Stan Williams | .60 | .24 | .06 |
| ☐ | 54 | Mel Roach | .60 | .24 | .06 |
| ☐ | 55 | Tom Brewer | .60 | .24 | .06 |
| ☐ | 56 | Carl Sawatski | .60 | .24 | .06 |
| ☐ | 57 | Al Cicotte | .60 | .24 | .06 |
| ☐ | 58 | Eddie Miksis | .60 | .24 | .06 |
| ☐ | 59 | Irv Noren | .60 | .24 | .06 |
| ☐ | 60 | Bob Turley | 1.50 | .60 | .15 |
| ☐ | 61 | Dick Brown | .60 | .24 | .06 |
| ☐ | 62 | Tony Taylor | .60 | .24 | .06 |
| ☐ | 63 | Jim Hearn | .60 | .24 | .06 |
| ☐ | 64 | Joe DeMaestri | .60 | .24 | .06 |
| ☐ | 65 | Frank Torre | .60 | .24 | .06 |
| ☐ | 66 | Joe Ginsberg | .60 | .24 | .06 |
| ☐ | 67 | Brooks Lawrence | .60 | .24 | .06 |
| ☐ | 68 | Dick Schofield | .60 | .24 | .06 |
| ☐ | 69 | Giants Team | 2.25 | .50 | .10 |
| ☐ | 70 | Harvey Kuenn | 1.50 | .60 | .15 |
| ☐ | 71 | Don Bessent | .60 | .24 | .06 |
| ☐ | 72 | Bill Renna | .60 | .24 | .06 |
| ☐ | 73 | Ron Jackson | .60 | .24 | .06 |
| ☐ | 74 | Directing Power<br>Jim Lemon<br>Cookie Lavagetto<br>Roy Sievers | .75 | .30 | .07 |
| ☐ | 75 | Sam Jones | .75 | .30 | .07 |
| ☐ | 76 | Bobby Richardson | 2.50 | 1.00 | .25 |
| ☐ | 77 | John Goryl | .60 | .24 | .06 |
| ☐ | 78 | Pedro Ramos | .60 | .24 | .06 |
| ☐ | 79 | Harry Chiti | .60 | .24 | .06 |
| ☐ | 80 | Minnie Minoso | 2.00 | .80 | .20 |
| ☐ | 81 | Hal Jeffcoat | .60 | .24 | .06 |
| ☐ | 82 | Bob Boyd | .60 | .24 | .06 |
| ☐ | 83 | Bob Smith | .60 | .24 | .06 |
| ☐ | 84 | Reno Bertoia | .60 | .24 | .06 |
| ☐ | 85 | Harry Anderson | .60 | .24 | .06 |
| ☐ | 86 | Bob Keegan | .60 | .24 | .06 |
| ☐ | 87 | Danny O'Connell | .60 | .24 | .06 |
| ☐ | 88 | Herb Score | 1.25 | .50 | .12 |
| ☐ | 89 | Billy Gardner | .75 | .30 | .07 |
| ☐ | 90 | Bill Skowron | 2.25 | .90 | .22 |
| ☐ | 91 | Herb Moford | .60 | .24 | .06 |
| ☐ | 92 | Dave Philley | .60 | .24 | .06 |
| ☐ | 93 | Julio Becquer | .60 | .24 | .06 |
| ☐ | 94 | White Sox Team | 2.50 | .50 | .10 |
| ☐ | 95 | Carl Willey | .60 | .24 | .06 |
| ☐ | 96 | Lou Berberet | .60 | .24 | .06 |
| ☐ | 97 | Jerry Lynch | .60 | .24 | .06 |
| ☐ | 98 | Arnie Portocarrero | .60 | .24 | .06 |
| ☐ | 99 | Ted Kazanski | .60 | .24 | .06 |
| ☐ | 100 | Bob Cerv | .75 | .30 | .07 |
| ☐ | 101 | Alex Kellner | .60 | .24 | .06 |
| ☐ | 102 | Felipe Alou | 2.00 | .80 | .20 |
| ☐ | 103 | Billy Goodman | .75 | .30 | .07 |
| ☐ | 104 | Del Rice | .60 | .24 | .06 |
| ☐ | 105 | Lee Walls | .60 | .24 | .06 |
| ☐ | 106 | Hal Woodeshick | .60 | .24 | .06 |
| ☐ | 107 | Norm Larker | .60 | .24 | .06 |
| ☐ | 108 | Zack Monroe | .60 | .24 | .06 |
| ☐ | 109 | Bob Schmidt | .60 | .24 | .06 |
| ☐ | 110 | George Witt | .60 | .24 | .06 |
| ☐ | 111 | Redlegs Team | 2.50 | .50 | .10 |
| ☐ | 112 | Billy Consolo | .50 | .20 | .05 |
| ☐ | 113 | Taylor Phillips | .50 | .20 | .05 |
| ☐ | 114 | Earl Battey | .60 | .24 | .06 |
| ☐ | 115 | Mickey Vernon | .60 | .24 | .06 |
| ☐ | 116 | Bob Allison RP | 2.50 | 1.00 | .25 |
| ☐ | 117 | John Blanchard RP | .75 | .30 | .07 |
| ☐ | 118 | John Buzhardt RP | .50 | .20 | .05 |
| ☐ | 119 | John Callison RP | 1.75 | .70 | .17 |
| ☐ | 120 | Chuck Coles RP | .50 | .20 | .05 |
| ☐ | 121 | Bob Conley RP | .50 | .20 | .05 |
| ☐ | 122 | Bennie Daniels RP | .50 | .20 | .05 |
| ☐ | 123 | Don Dillard RP | .50 | .20 | .05 |

| | | | | |
|---|---|---|---|---|
| ☐ 124 | Dan Dobbek RP | .50 | .20 | .05 |
| ☐ 125 | Ron Fairly RP | 1.50 | .60 | .15 |
| ☐ 126 | Ed Haas RP | .60 | .24 | .06 |
| ☐ 127 | Kent Hadley RP | .50 | .20 | .05 |
| ☐ 128 | Bob Hartman RP | .50 | .20 | .05 |
| ☐ 129 | Frank Herrera RP | .50 | .20 | .05 |
| ☐ 130 | Lou Jackson RP | .50 | .20 | .05 |
| ☐ 131 | Deron Johnson RP | .60 | .24 | .06 |
| ☐ 132 | Don Lee RP | .50 | .20 | .05 |
| ☐ 133 | Bob Lillis RP | .75 | .30 | .07 |
| ☐ 134 | Jim McDaniel RP | .50 | .20 | .05 |
| ☐ 135 | Gene Oliver RP | .50 | .20 | .05 |
| ☐ 136 | Jim O'Toole RP | .75 | .30 | .07 |
| ☐ 137 | Dick Ricketts RP | .50 | .20 | .05 |
| ☐ 138 | John Romano RP | .50 | .20 | .05 |
| ☐ 139 | Ed Sadowski RP | .50 | .20 | .05 |
| ☐ 140 | Charlie Secrest RP | .50 | .20 | .05 |
| ☐ 141 | Joe Shipley RP | .50 | .20 | .05 |
| ☐ 142 | Dick Stigman RP | .50 | .20 | .05 |
| ☐ 143 | Willie Tasby RP | .50 | .20 | .05 |
| ☐ 144 | Jerry Walker RP | .50 | .20 | .05 |
| ☐ 145 | Dom Zanni RP | .50 | .20 | .05 |
| ☐ 146 | Jerry Zimmerman RP | .50 | .20 | .05 |
| ☐ 147 | Cubs Clubbers: | 2.00 | .80 | .20 |
| | Dale Long | | | |
| | Ernie Banks | | | |
| | Walt Moryn | | | |
| ☐ 148 | Mike McCormick | .75 | .30 | .07 |
| ☐ 149 | Jim Bunning | 2.50 | 1.00 | .25 |
| ☐ 150 | Stan Musial | 30.00 | 12.00 | 3.00 |
| ☐ 151 | Bob Malkmus | .50 | .20 | .05 |
| ☐ 152 | John Klippstein | .50 | .20 | .05 |
| ☐ 153 | Jim Marshall | .50 | .20 | .05 |
| ☐ 154 | Ray Herbert | .50 | .20 | .05 |
| ☐ 155 | Enos Slaughter | 4.00 | 1.60 | .40 |
| ☐ 156 | Ace Hurlers | 1.50 | .60 | .15 |
| | Billy Pierce | | | |
| | Robin Roberts | | | |
| ☐ 157 | Felix Mantilla | .50 | .20 | .05 |
| ☐ 158 | Walt Dropo | .50 | .20 | .05 |
| ☐ 159 | Bob Shaw | .50 | .20 | .05 |
| ☐ 160 | Dick Groat | 1.25 | .50 | .12 |
| ☐ 161 | Frank Baumann | .50 | .20 | .05 |
| ☐ 162 | Bobby G. Smith | .50 | .20 | .05 |
| ☐ 163 | Sandy Koufax | 22.00 | 9.00 | 2.20 |
| ☐ 164 | Johnny Groth | .50 | .20 | .05 |
| ☐ 165 | Bill Bruton | .50 | .20 | .05 |
| ☐ 166 | Destruction Crew | 1.00 | .40 | .10 |
| | Minnie Minoso | | | |
| | Rocky Colavito | | | |
| | Larry Doby | | | |
| ☐ 167 | Duke Maas | .50 | .20 | .05 |
| ☐ 168 | Carroll Hardy | .50 | .20 | .05 |
| ☐ 169 | Ted Abernathy | .50 | .20 | .05 |
| ☐ 170 | Gene Woodling | .75 | .30 | .07 |
| ☐ 171 | Willard Schmidt | .50 | .20 | .05 |
| ☐ 172 | Athletics Team | 2.25 | .50 | .10 |
| ☐ 173 | Bill Monbouquette | .50 | .20 | .05 |
| ☐ 174 | Jim Pendleton | .50 | .20 | .05 |
| ☐ 175 | Dick Farrell | .50 | .20 | .05 |
| ☐ 176 | Preston Ward | .50 | .20 | .05 |
| ☐ 177 | John Briggs | .50 | .20 | .05 |
| ☐ 178 | Ruben Amaro | .50 | .20 | .05 |
| ☐ 179 | Don Rudolph | .50 | .20 | .05 |
| ☐ 180 | Yogi Berra | 11.00 | 4.50 | 1.10 |
| ☐ 181 | Bob Porterfield | .50 | .20 | .05 |
| ☐ 182 | Milt Graff | .50 | .20 | .05 |
| ☐ 183 | Stu Miller | .50 | .20 | .05 |
| ☐ 184 | Harvey Haddix | .75 | .30 | .07 |
| ☐ 185 | Jim Busby | .50 | .20 | .05 |
| ☐ 186 | Mudcat Grant | .50 | .20 | .05 |
| ☐ 187 | Bubba Phillips | .50 | .20 | .05 |
| ☐ 188 | Juan Pizarro | .50 | .20 | .05 |
| ☐ 189 | Neil Chrisley | .50 | .20 | .05 |
| ☐ 190 | Bill Virdon | 1.00 | .40 | .10 |
| ☐ 191 | Russ Kemmerer | .50 | .20 | .05 |
| ☐ 192 | Charlie Beamon | .50 | .20 | .05 |
| ☐ 193 | Sammy Taylor | .50 | .20 | .05 |
| ☐ 194 | Jim Brosnan | .60 | .24 | .06 |
| ☐ 195 | Rip Repulski | .50 | .20 | .05 |
| ☐ 196 | Billy Moran | .50 | .20 | .05 |
| ☐ 197 | Ray Semproch | .50 | .20 | .05 |
| ☐ 198 | Jim Davenport | .60 | .24 | .06 |
| ☐ 199 | Leo Kiely | .50 | .20 | .05 |
| ☐ 200 | Warren Giles | 1.50 | .60 | .15 |
| | (NL President) | | | |
| ☐ 201 | Tom Acker | .50 | .20 | .05 |
| ☐ 202 | Roger Maris | 9.00 | 3.75 | .90 |
| ☐ 203 | Ossie Virgil | .50 | .20 | .05 |
| ☐ 204 | Casey Wise | .50 | .20 | .05 |
| ☐ 205 | Don Larsen | 1.75 | .70 | .17 |
| ☐ 206 | Carl Furillo | 1.75 | .70 | .17 |
| ☐ 207 | George Strickland | .50 | .20 | .05 |
| ☐ 208 | Willie Jones | .50 | .20 | .05 |
| ☐ 209 | Lenny Green | .50 | .20 | .05 |
| ☐ 210 | Ed Bailey | .50 | .20 | .05 |
| ☐ 211 | Bob Blaylock | .50 | .20 | .05 |
| ☐ 212 | Fence Busters | 6.00 | 2.40 | .60 |
| | Hank Aaron | | | |
| | Eddie Mathews | | | |
| ☐ 213 | Jim Rivera | .50 | .20 | .05 |
| ☐ 214 | Marcelino Solis | .50 | .20 | .05 |
| ☐ 215 | Jim Lemon | .60 | .24 | .06 |
| ☐ 216 | Andre Rodgers | .50 | .20 | .05 |
| ☐ 217 | Carl Erskine | 1.50 | .60 | .15 |
| ☐ 218 | Roman Mejias | .50 | .20 | .05 |
| ☐ 219 | George Zuverink | .50 | .20 | .05 |
| ☐ 220 | Frank Malzone | .60 | .24 | .06 |
| ☐ 221 | Bob Bowman | .50 | .20 | .05 |
| ☐ 222 | Bobby Shantz | .75 | .30 | .07 |
| ☐ 223 | Cardinals Team | 2.25 | .50 | .10 |
| ☐ 224 | Claude Osteen | 1.00 | .40 | .10 |
| ☐ 225 | Johnny Logan | .60 | .24 | .06 |
| ☐ 226 | Art Ceccarelli | .50 | .20 | .05 |
| ☐ 227 | Hal W. Smith | .50 | .20 | .05 |
| ☐ 228 | Don Gross | .50 | .20 | .05 |
| ☐ 229 | Vic Power | .50 | .20 | .05 |
| ☐ 230 | Bill Fischer | .50 | .20 | .05 |
| ☐ 231 | Ellis Burton | .50 | .20 | .05 |
| ☐ 232 | Eddie Kasko | .50 | .20 | .05 |
| ☐ 233 | Paul Foytack | .50 | .20 | .05 |
| ☐ 234 | Chuck Tanner | .75 | .30 | .07 |
| ☐ 235 | Valmy Thomas | .50 | .20 | .05 |
| ☐ 236 | Ted Bowsfield | .50 | .20 | .05 |
| ☐ 237 | Run Preventers | 1.25 | .50 | .12 |
| | Gil McDougald | | | |
| | Bob Turley | | | |
| | Bobby Richardson | | | |
| ☐ 238 | Gene Baker | .50 | .20 | .05 |
| ☐ 239 | Bob Trowbridge | .50 | .20 | .05 |
| ☐ 240 | Hank Bauer | 1.25 | .50 | .12 |
| ☐ 241 | Billy Muffett | .50 | .20 | .05 |
| ☐ 242 | Ron Samford | .50 | .20 | .05 |
| ☐ 243 | Marv Grissom | .50 | .20 | .05 |
| ☐ 244 | Ted Gray | .50 | .20 | .05 |
| ☐ 245 | Ned Garver | .50 | .20 | .05 |
| ☐ 246 | J.W. Porter | .50 | .20 | .05 |
| ☐ 247 | Don Ferrarese | .50 | .20 | .05 |
| ☐ 248 | Red Sox Team | 2.50 | .50 | .10 |
| ☐ 249 | Bobby Adams | .50 | .20 | .05 |
| ☐ 250 | Billy O'Dell | .50 | .20 | .05 |
| ☐ 251 | Cletis Boyer | 1.00 | .40 | .10 |
| ☐ 252 | Ray Boone | .60 | .24 | .06 |
| ☐ 253 | Seth Morehead | .50 | .20 | .05 |
| ☐ 254 | Zeke Bella | .50 | .20 | .05 |
| ☐ 255 | Del Ennis | .60 | .24 | .06 |
| ☐ 256 | Jerry Davie | .50 | .20 | .05 |
| ☐ 257 | Leon Wagner | .50 | .20 | .05 |
| ☐ 258 | Fred Kipp | .50 | .20 | .05 |
| ☐ 259 | Jim Pisoni | .50 | .20 | .05 |
| ☐ 260 | Early Wynn | 4.00 | 1.60 | .40 |
| ☐ 261 | Gene Stephens | .50 | .20 | .05 |
| ☐ 262 | Hitters' Foes | 2.00 | .80 | .20 |
| | Johnny Podres | | | |
| | Clem Labine | | | |
| | Don Drysdale | | | |
| ☐ 263 | B. Daley | .50 | .20 | .05 |
| ☐ 264 | Chico Carrasquel | .50 | .20 | .05 |
| ☐ 265 | Ron Kline | .50 | .20 | .05 |
| ☐ 266 | Woody Held | .50 | .20 | .05 |
| ☐ 267 | John Romonosky | .50 | .20 | .05 |
| ☐ 268 | Tito Francona | .60 | .24 | .06 |
| ☐ 269 | Jack Mayer | .50 | .20 | .05 |
| ☐ 270 | Gil Hodges | 4.50 | 1.80 | .45 |
| ☐ 271 | Orlando Pena | .50 | .20 | .05 |
| ☐ 272 | Jerry Lumpe | .50 | .20 | .05 |
| ☐ 273 | Joey Jay | .60 | .24 | .06 |
| ☐ 274 | Jerry Kindall | .50 | .20 | .05 |
| ☐ 275 | Jack Sanford | .60 | .24 | .06 |
| ☐ 276 | Pete Daley | .50 | .20 | .05 |
| ☐ 277 | Turk Lown | .50 | .20 | .05 |
| ☐ 278 | Chuck Essegian | .50 | .20 | .05 |
| ☐ 279 | Ernie Johnson | .50 | .20 | .05 |
| ☐ 280 | Frank Bolling | .50 | .20 | .05 |
| ☐ 281 | Walt Craddock | .50 | .20 | .05 |
| ☐ 282 | R.C. Stevens | .50 | .20 | .05 |
| ☐ 283 | Russ Heman | .50 | .20 | .05 |
| ☐ 284 | Steve Korcheck | .50 | .20 | .05 |
| ☐ 285 | Joe Cunningham | .60 | .24 | .06 |
| ☐ 286 | Dean Stone | .50 | .20 | .05 |
| ☐ 287 | Don Zimmer | .75 | .30 | .07 |
| ☐ 288 | Dutch Dotterer | .50 | .20 | .05 |
| ☐ 289 | Johnny Kucks | .60 | .24 | .06 |
| ☐ 290 | Wes Covington | .60 | .24 | .06 |
| ☐ 291 | Pitching Partners: | .60 | .24 | .06 |
| | Pedro Ramos | | | |

Camilo Pascual

| | | | | |
|---|---|---|---|---|
| ☐ 292 | Dick Williams | .60 | .24 | .06 |
| ☐ 293 | Ray Moore | .50 | .20 | .05 |
| ☐ 294 | Hank Foiles | .50 | .20 | .05 |
| ☐ 295 | Billy Martin | 2.50 | 1.00 | .25 |
| ☐ 296 | Ernie Broglio | .60 | .24 | .06 |
| ☐ 297 | Jackie Brandt | .50 | .20 | .05 |
| ☐ 298 | Tex Clevenger | .50 | .20 | .05 |
| ☐ 299 | Billy Klaus | .50 | .20 | .05 |
| ☐ 300 | Richie Ashburn | 2.50 | 1.00 | .25 |
| ☐ 301 | Earl Averill | .50 | .20 | .05 |
| ☐ 302 | Don Mossi | .60 | .24 | .06 |
| ☐ 303 | Marty Keough | .50 | .20 | .05 |
| ☐ 304 | Cubs Team | 2.25 | .50 | .10 |
| ☐ 305 | Curt Raydon | .50 | .20 | .05 |
| ☐ 306 | Jim Gilliam | 1.75 | .70 | .17 |
| ☐ 307 | Curt Barclay | .50 | .20 | .05 |
| ☐ 308 | Norm Siebern | .50 | .20 | .05 |
| ☐ 309 | Sal Maglie | 1.25 | .50 | .12 |
| ☐ 310 | Luis Aparicio | 4.00 | 1.60 | .40 |
| ☐ 311 | Norm Zauchin | .50 | .20 | .05 |
| ☐ 312 | Don Newcombe | 1.25 | .50 | .12 |
| ☐ 313 | Frank House | .50 | .20 | .05 |
| ☐ 314 | Don Cardwell | .50 | .20 | .05 |
| ☐ 315 | Joe Adcock | 1.00 | .40 | .10 |
| ☐ 316A | Ralph Lumenti (Opt.) .... (photo actually Camilo Pascual) | .60 | .24 | .06 |
| ☐ 316B | Ralph Lumenti (No Option) (photo actually Camilo Pascual) | 40.00 | 16.00 | 4.00 |
| ☐ 317 | Hitting Kings: Willie Mays Richie Ashburn | 5.00 | 2.00 | .50 |
| ☐ 318 | Rocky Bridges | .50 | .20 | .05 |
| ☐ 319 | Dave Hillmann | .50 | .20 | .05 |
| ☐ 320 | Bob Skinner | .60 | .24 | .06 |
| ☐ 321A | Bob Giallombardo (Option) | .60 | .24 | .06 |
| ☐ 321B | Bob Giallombardo (No Option) | 40.00 | 16.00 | 4.00 |
| ☐ 322A | Harry Hanebrink (Traded) | .60 | .24 | .06 |
| ☐ 322B | Harry Hanebrink (No Trade) | 40.00 | 16.00 | 4.00 |
| ☐ 323 | Frank Sullivan | .50 | .20 | .05 |
| ☐ 324 | Don Demeter | .50 | .20 | .05 |
| ☐ 325 | Ken Boyer | 1.50 | .60 | .15 |
| ☐ 326 | Marv Throneberry | 1.50 | .60 | .15 |
| ☐ 327 | Gary Bell | .50 | .20 | .05 |
| ☐ 328 | Lou Skizas | .50 | .20 | .05 |
| ☐ 329 | Tigers Team | 2.50 | .50 | .10 |
| ☐ 330 | Gus Triandos | .60 | .24 | .06 |
| ☐ 331 | Steve Boros | .60 | .24 | .06 |
| ☐ 332 | Ray Monzant | .50 | .20 | .05 |
| ☐ 333 | Harry Simpson | .50 | .20 | .05 |
| ☐ 334 | Glen Hobbie | .50 | .20 | .05 |
| ☐ 335 | Johnny Temple | .60 | .24 | .06 |
| ☐ 336A | Billy Loes (with traded line) | .60 | .24 | .06 |
| ☐ 336B | Billy Loes (no trade) | 40.00 | 16.00 | 4.00 |
| ☐ 337 | George Crowe | .50 | .20 | .05 |
| ☐ 338 | Sparky Anderson | 3.00 | 1.20 | .30 |
| ☐ 339 | Roy Face | 1.00 | .40 | .10 |
| ☐ 340 | Roy Sievers | .60 | .24 | .06 |
| ☐ 341 | Tom Qualters | .50 | .20 | .05 |
| ☐ 342 | Ray Jablonski | .60 | .24 | .06 |
| ☐ 343 | Bill Hoeft | .50 | .20 | .05 |
| ☐ 344 | Russ Nixon | .50 | .20 | .05 |
| ☐ 345 | Gil McDougald | 1.50 | .60 | .15 |
| ☐ 346 | Batter Bafflers Dave Sisler Tom Brewer | .60 | .24 | .06 |
| ☐ 347 | Bob Buhl | .50 | .20 | .05 |
| ☐ 348 | Ted Lepcio | .50 | .20 | .05 |
| ☐ 349 | Hoyt Wilhelm | 4.00 | 1.60 | .40 |
| ☐ 350 | Ernie Banks | 11.00 | 4.50 | 1.10 |
| ☐ 351 | Earl Torgeson | .50 | .20 | .05 |
| ☐ 352 | Robin Roberts | 4.00 | 1.60 | .40 |
| ☐ 353 | Curt Flood | 1.25 | .50 | .12 |
| ☐ 354 | Pete Burnside | .50 | .20 | .05 |
| ☐ 355 | Jim Piersall | 1.25 | .50 | .12 |
| ☐ 356 | Bob Mabe | .50 | .20 | .05 |
| ☐ 357 | Dick Stuart | 1.00 | .40 | .10 |
| ☐ 358 | Ralph Terry | .75 | .30 | .07 |
| ☐ 359 | Bill White | 2.00 | .80 | .20 |
| ☐ 360 | Al Kaline | 9.00 | 3.75 | .90 |
| ☐ 361 | Willard Nixon | .50 | .20 | .05 |
| ☐ 362A | Dolan Nichols (with option line) | .60 | .24 | .06 |
| ☐ 362B | Dolan Nichols | 40.00 | 16.00 | 4.00 |

| | | | | |
|---|---|---|---|---|
| | (no option) | | | |
| ☐ 363 | Bobby Avila | .50 | .20 | .05 |
| ☐ 364 | Danny McDevitt | .50 | .20 | .05 |
| ☐ 365 | Gus Bell | .60 | .24 | .06 |
| ☐ 366 | Humberto Robinson | .50 | .20 | .05 |
| ☐ 367 | Cal Neeman | .50 | .20 | .05 |
| ☐ 368 | Don Mueller | .60 | .24 | .06 |
| ☐ 369 | Dick Tomanek | .50 | .20 | .05 |
| ☐ 370 | Pete Runnels | .60 | .24 | .06 |
| ☐ 371 | Dick Brodowski | .50 | .20 | .05 |
| ☐ 372 | Jim Hegan | .60 | .24 | .06 |
| ☐ 373 | Herb Plews | .50 | .20 | .05 |
| ☐ 374 | Art Ditmar | .60 | .24 | .06 |
| ☐ 375 | Bob Nieman | .50 | .20 | .05 |
| ☐ 376 | Hal Naragon | .50 | .20 | .05 |
| ☐ 377 | John Antonelli | .75 | .30 | .07 |
| ☐ 378 | Gail Harris | .50 | .20 | .05 |
| ☐ 379 | Bob Miller | .50 | .20 | .05 |
| ☐ 380 | Hank Aaron | 27.00 | 11.00 | 2.70 |
| ☐ 381 | Mike Baxes | .50 | .20 | .05 |
| ☐ 382 | Curt Simmons | .60 | .24 | .06 |
| ☐ 383 | Words of Wisdom Don Larsen Casey Stengel | 2.00 | .80 | .20 |
| ☐ 384 | Dave Sisler | .50 | .20 | .05 |
| ☐ 385 | Sherm Lollar | .60 | .24 | .06 |
| ☐ 386 | Jim Delsing | .50 | .20 | .05 |
| ☐ 387 | Don Drysdale | 6.50 | 2.60 | .65 |
| ☐ 388 | Bob Will | .50 | .20 | .05 |
| ☐ 389 | Joe Nuxhall | .60 | .24 | .06 |
| ☐ 390 | Orlando Cepeda | 2.25 | .90 | .22 |
| ☐ 391 | Milt Pappas | .60 | .24 | .06 |
| ☐ 392 | Whitey Herzog | 1.00 | .40 | .10 |
| ☐ 393 | Frank Lary | .60 | .24 | .06 |
| ☐ 394 | Randy Jackson | .50 | .20 | .05 |
| ☐ 395 | Elston Howard | 2.00 | .80 | .20 |
| ☐ 396 | Bob Rush | .50 | .20 | .05 |
| ☐ 397 | Senators Team | 2.25 | .50 | .10 |
| ☐ 398 | Wally Post | .50 | .20 | .05 |
| ☐ 399 | Larry Jackson | .50 | .20 | .05 |
| ☐ 400 | Jackie Jensen | 1.00 | .40 | .10 |
| ☐ 401 | Ron Blackburn | .50 | .20 | .05 |
| ☐ 402 | Hector Lopez | .50 | .20 | .05 |
| ☐ 403 | Clem Labine | .60 | .24 | .06 |
| ☐ 404 | Hank Sauer | .60 | .24 | .06 |
| ☐ 405 | Roy McMillan | .50 | .20 | .05 |
| ☐ 406 | Solly Drake | .50 | .20 | .05 |
| ☐ 407 | Moe Drabowsky | .60 | .24 | .06 |
| ☐ 408 | Keystone Combo Nellie Fox Luis Aparicio | 2.00 | .80 | .20 |
| ☐ 409 | Gus Zernial | .60 | .24 | .06 |
| ☐ 410 | Billy Pierce | .75 | .30 | .07 |
| ☐ 411 | Whitey Lockman | .60 | .24 | .06 |
| ☐ 412 | Stan Lopata | .50 | .20 | .05 |
| ☐ 413 | Camilo Pascual (listed as Camillo on front) | .60 | .24 | .06 |
| ☐ 414 | Dale Long | .50 | .20 | .05 |
| ☐ 415 | Bill Mazeroski | 1.75 | .70 | .17 |
| ☐ 416 | Haywood Sullivan | .60 | .24 | .06 |
| ☐ 417 | Virgil Trucks | .60 | .24 | .06 |
| ☐ 418 | Gino Cimoli | .50 | .20 | .05 |
| ☐ 419 | Braves Team | 2.50 | .50 | .10 |
| ☐ 420 | Rocky Colavito | 1.75 | .70 | .17 |
| ☐ 421 | Herm Wehmeier | .50 | .20 | .05 |
| ☐ 422 | Hobie Landrith | .50 | .20 | .05 |
| ☐ 423 | Bob Grim | .60 | .24 | .06 |
| ☐ 424 | Ken Aspromonte | .50 | .20 | .05 |
| ☐ 425 | Del Crandall | .60 | .24 | .06 |
| ☐ 426 | Jerry Staley | .50 | .20 | .05 |
| ☐ 427 | Charlie Neal | .60 | .24 | .06 |
| ☐ 428 | Buc Hill Aces Ron Kline Bob Friend Vernon Law Roy Face | .75 | .30 | .07 |
| ☐ 429 | Bobby Thomson | 1.00 | .40 | .10 |
| ☐ 430 | Whitey Ford | 9.00 | 3.75 | .90 |
| ☐ 431 | Whammy Douglas | .50 | .20 | .05 |
| ☐ 432 | Smoky Burgess | .60 | .24 | .06 |
| ☐ 433 | Billy Harrell | .50 | .20 | .05 |
| ☐ 434 | Hal Griggs | .50 | .20 | .05 |
| ☐ 435 | Frank Robinson | 9.00 | 3.75 | .90 |
| ☐ 436 | Granny Hamner | .50 | .20 | .05 |
| ☐ 437 | Ike Delock | .50 | .20 | .05 |
| ☐ 438 | Sam Esposito | .50 | .20 | .05 |
| ☐ 439 | Brooks Robinson | 11.00 | 4.50 | 1.10 |
| ☐ 440 | Lou Burdette (posing as if lefthanded) | 2.25 | .90 | .22 |
| ☐ 441 | John Roseboro | .75 | .30 | .07 |
| ☐ 442 | Ray Narleski | .50 | .20 | .05 |

| | | | | |
|---|---|---|---|---|
| ☐ 443 | Daryl Spencer | .50 | .20 | .05 |
| ☐ 444 | Ron Hansen | .75 | .30 | .07 |
| ☐ 445 | Cal McLish | .50 | .20 | .05 |
| ☐ 446 | Rocky Nelson | .50 | .20 | .05 |
| ☐ 447 | Bob Anderson | .50 | .20 | .05 |
| ☐ 448 | Vada Pinson | 1.50 | .60 | .15 |
| ☐ 449 | Tom Gorman | .50 | .20 | .05 |
| ☐ 450 | Ed Mathews | 5.00 | 2.00 | .50 |
| ☐ 451 | Jimmy Constable | .50 | .20 | .05 |
| ☐ 452 | Chico Fernandez | .50 | .20 | .05 |
| ☐ 453 | Les Moss | .50 | .20 | .05 |
| ☐ 454 | Phil Clark | .50 | .20 | .05 |
| ☐ 455 | Larry Doby | 1.25 | .50 | .12 |
| ☐ 456 | Jerry Casale | .50 | .20 | .05 |
| ☐ 457 | Dodgers Team | 5.00 | 1.00 | .20 |
| ☐ 458 | Gordon Jones | .50 | .20 | .05 |
| ☐ 459 | Bill Tuttle | .50 | .20 | .05 |
| ☐ 460 | Bob Friend | .60 | .24 | .06 |
| ☐ 461 | Mantle Hits Homer | 7.50 | 3.00 | .75 |
| ☐ 462 | Colavito's Catch | .90 | .36 | .09 |
| ☐ 463 | Kaline Batting Champ | 2.00 | .80 | .20 |
| ☐ 464 | Mays' Series Catch | 5.00 | 2.00 | .50 |
| ☐ 465 | Sievers Sets Mark | .60 | .24 | .06 |
| ☐ 466 | Pierce All-Star | .60 | .24 | .06 |
| ☐ 467 | Aaron Clubs Homer | 4.00 | 1.60 | .40 |
| ☐ 468 | Snider's Play | 3.00 | 1.20 | .30 |
| ☐ 469 | Hustler Banks | 2.00 | .80 | .20 |
| ☐ 470 | Musial's 3000 Hit | 3.50 | 1.40 | .35 |
| ☐ 471 | Tom Sturdivant | .50 | .20 | .05 |
| ☐ 472 | Gene Freese | .50 | .20 | .05 |
| ☐ 473 | Mike Fornieles | .50 | .20 | .05 |
| ☐ 474 | Moe Thacker | .50 | .20 | .05 |
| ☐ 475 | Jack Harshman | .50 | .20 | .05 |
| ☐ 476 | Indians Team | 2.25 | .50 | .10 |
| ☐ 477 | Barry Latman | .50 | .20 | .05 |
| ☐ 478 | Bob Clemente | 15.00 | 6.00 | 1.50 |
| ☐ 479 | Lindy McDaniel | .60 | .24 | .06 |
| ☐ 480 | Red Schoendienst | 1.25 | .50 | .12 |
| ☐ 481 | Charlie Maxwell | .50 | .20 | .05 |
| ☐ 482 | Russ Meyer | .50 | .20 | .05 |
| ☐ 483 | Clint Courtney | .50 | .20 | .05 |
| ☐ 484 | Willie Kirkland | .50 | .20 | .05 |
| ☐ 485 | Ryne Duren | .75 | .30 | .07 |
| ☐ 486 | Sammy White | .50 | .20 | .05 |
| ☐ 487 | Hal Brown | .50 | .20 | .05 |
| ☐ 488 | Walt Moryn | .50 | .20 | .05 |
| ☐ 489 | John Powers | .50 | .20 | .05 |
| ☐ 490 | Frank Thomas | .60 | .24 | .06 |
| ☐ 491 | Don Blasingame | .50 | .20 | .05 |
| ☐ 492 | Gene Conley | .50 | .20 | .05 |
| ☐ 493 | Jim Landis | .50 | .20 | .05 |
| ☐ 494 | Don Pavletich | .50 | .20 | .05 |
| ☐ 495 | John Podres | 1.25 | .50 | .12 |
| ☐ 496 | Wayne Terwilliger | .50 | .20 | .05 |
| ☐ 497 | Hal R. Smith | .50 | .20 | .05 |
| ☐ 498 | Dick Hyde | .50 | .20 | .05 |
| ☐ 499 | John O'Brien | .50 | .20 | .05 |
| ☐ 500 | Vic Wertz | .60 | .24 | .06 |
| ☐ 501 | Bob Tiefenauer | .50 | .20 | .05 |
| ☐ 502 | Alvin Dark | .75 | .30 | .07 |
| ☐ 503 | Jim Owens | .50 | .20 | .05 |
| ☐ 504 | Ossie Alvarez | .50 | .20 | .05 |
| ☐ 505 | Tony Kubek | 2.00 | .80 | .20 |
| ☐ 506 | Bob Purkey | .50 | .20 | .05 |
| ☐ 507 | Bob Hale | 2.50 | 1.00 | .25 |
| ☐ 508 | Art Fowler | 2.50 | 1.00 | .25 |
| ☐ 509 | Norm Cash | 5.00 | 2.00 | .50 |
| ☐ 510 | Yankees Team | 10.00 | 2.00 | .40 |
| ☐ 511 | George Susce | 2.50 | 1.00 | .25 |
| ☐ 512 | George Altman | 2.50 | 1.00 | .25 |
| ☐ 513 | Tommy Carroll | 2.50 | 1.00 | .25 |
| ☐ 514 | Bob Gibson | 50.00 | 20.00 | 5.00 |
| ☐ 515 | Harmon Killebrew | 20.00 | 8.00 | 2.00 |
| ☐ 516 | Mike Garcia | 3.00 | 1.20 | .30 |
| ☐ 517 | Joe Koppe | 2.50 | 1.00 | .25 |
| ☐ 518 | Mike Cueller (sic, Cuellar) | 3.50 | 1.40 | .35 |
| ☐ 519 | Infield Power Pete Runnels Dick Gernert Frank Malzone | 3.00 | 1.20 | .30 |
| ☐ 520 | Don Elston | 2.50 | 1.00 | .25 |
| ☐ 521 | Gary Geiger | 2.50 | 1.00 | .25 |
| ☐ 522 | Gene Snyder | 2.50 | 1.00 | .25 |
| ☐ 523 | Harry Bright | 2.50 | 1.00 | .25 |
| ☐ 524 | Larry Osborne | 2.50 | 1.00 | .25 |
| ☐ 525 | Jim Coates | 2.50 | 1.00 | .25 |
| ☐ 526 | Bob Speake | 2.50 | 1.00 | .25 |
| ☐ 527 | Solly Hemus | 2.50 | 1.00 | .25 |
| ☐ 528 | Pirates Team | 5.00 | 1.00 | .20 |
| ☐ 529 | George Bamberger | 4.50 | 1.80 | .45 |
| ☐ 530 | Wally Moon | 3.00 | 1.20 | .30 |
| ☐ 531 | Ray Webster | 2.50 | 1.00 | .25 |

| | | | | |
|---|---|---|---|---|
| ☐ 532 | Mark Freeman | 2.50 | 1.00 | .25 |
| ☐ 533 | Darrell Johnson | 2.50 | 1.00 | .25 |
| ☐ 534 | Faye Throneberry | 2.50 | 1.00 | .25 |
| ☐ 535 | Ruben Gomez | 2.50 | 1.00 | .25 |
| ☐ 536 | Danny Kravitz | 2.50 | 1.00 | .25 |
| ☐ 537 | Rudolph Arias | 2.50 | 1.00 | .25 |
| ☐ 538 | Chick King | 2.50 | 1.00 | .25 |
| ☐ 539 | Gary Blaylock | 2.50 | 1.00 | .25 |
| ☐ 540 | Willie Miranda | 2.50 | 1.00 | .25 |
| ☐ 541 | Bob Thurman | 2.50 | 1.00 | .25 |
| ☐ 542 | Jim Perry | 5.00 | 2.00 | .50 |
| ☐ 543 | Corsair Trio Bob Skinner Bill Virdon Roberto Clemente | 12.50 | 5.00 | 1.25 |
| ☐ 544 | Lee Tate | 2.50 | 1.00 | .25 |
| ☐ 545 | Tom Morgan | 2.50 | 1.00 | .25 |
| ☐ 546 | Al Schroll | 2.50 | 1.00 | .25 |
| ☐ 547 | Jim Baxes | 2.50 | 1.00 | .25 |
| ☐ 548 | Elmer Singleton | 2.50 | 1.00 | .25 |
| ☐ 549 | Howie Nunn | 2.50 | 1.00 | .25 |
| ☐ 550 | Roy Campanella (Symbol of Courage) | 30.00 | 12.00 | 3.00 |
| ☐ 551 | Fred Haney MGR AS | 3.00 | 1.20 | .30 |
| ☐ 552 | Casey Stengel MGR AS | 4.50 | 1.80 | .45 |
| ☐ 553 | Orlando Cepeda AS | 3.00 | 1.20 | .30 |
| ☐ 554 | Bill Skowron AS | 3.00 | 1.20 | .30 |
| ☐ 555 | Bill Mazeroski AS | 3.00 | 1.20 | .30 |
| ☐ 556 | Nellie Fox AS | 3.50 | 1.40 | .35 |
| ☐ 557 | Ken Boyer AS | 3.00 | 1.20 | .30 |
| ☐ 558 | Frank Malzone AS | 3.00 | 1.20 | .30 |
| ☐ 559 | Ernie Banks AS | 9.00 | 3.75 | .90 |
| ☐ 560 | Luis Aparicio AS | 6.00 | 2.40 | .60 |
| ☐ 561 | Hank Aaron AS | 20.00 | 8.00 | 2.00 |
| ☐ 562 | Al Kaline AS | 9.00 | 3.75 | .90 |
| ☐ 563 | Willie Mays AS | 20.00 | 8.00 | 2.00 |
| ☐ 564 | Mickey Mantle AS | 45.00 | 18.00 | 4.50 |
| ☐ 565 | Wes Covington AS | 3.00 | 1.20 | .30 |
| ☐ 566 | Roy Sievers AS | 3.00 | 1.20 | .30 |
| ☐ 567 | Del Crandall AS | 3.00 | 1.20 | .30 |
| ☐ 568 | Gus Triandos AS | 3.00 | 1.20 | .30 |
| ☐ 569 | Bob Friend AS | 3.00 | 1.20 | .30 |
| ☐ 570 | Bob Turley AS | 3.00 | 1.20 | .30 |
| ☐ 571 | Warren Spahn AS | 8.00 | 3.25 | .80 |
| ☐ 572 | Billy Pierce AS | 3.00 | 1.20 | .30 |

## 1960 Topps

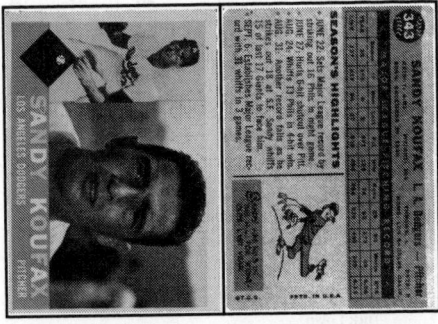

The cards in this 572 card set measure 2 1/2" by 3 1/2". The 1960 Topps set is the only Topps standard size issue to use a horizontally oriented front. World Series cards appeared for the first time (385 to 391), and there is a Rookie Prospect (RP) series (117-148), the most famous of which is Carl Yastrzemski, and a Sport Magazine All-Star Selection (AS) series (553-572). There are 16 manager cards listed alphabetically from 212 through 227. The coaching staff of each team was also afforded their own card in 16 card subset (455-470). Cards 375 to 440 come with either gray or white backs, and the high series (507-572) were printed on a more limited basis than the rest of the set. The team cards have series checklists on the reverse.

| | MINT | VG-E | F-G |
|---|---|---|---|
| COMPLETE SET ................. | 800.00 | 320.00 | 80.00 |
| COMMON PLAYER (1-286) ........ | .40 | .16 | .04 |
| COMMON PLAYER (287-440) .... | .50 | .20 | .05 |
| COMMON PLAYER (441-506) .... | .75 | .30 | .07 |
| COMMON PLAYER (507-552) .... | 2.25 | .90 | .22 |
| COMMON PLAYER (553-572) .... | 2.75 | 1.10 | .27 |

| | | | |
|---|---|---|---|
| ☐ 1 Early Wynn ..................... | 5.00 | 1.50 | .30 |
| ☐ 2 Roman Mejias ................. | .40 | .16 | .04 |
| ☐ 3 Joe Adcock ..................... | .80 | .32 | .08 |
| ☐ 4 Bob Purkey ..................... | .40 | .16 | .04 |
| ☐ 5 Wally Moon ..................... | .50 | .20 | .05 |
| ☐ 6 Lou Berberet ................... | .40 | .16 | .04 |
| ☐ 7 Master and Mentor: ........ | 4.00 | 1.60 | .40 |
|    Willie Mays | | | |
|    Bill Rigney | | | |
| ☐ 8 Bud Daley ...................... | .40 | .16 | .04 |
| ☐ 9 Faye Throneberry ........... | .40 | .16 | .04 |
| ☐ 10 Ernie Banks ................... | 6.50 | 2.60 | .65 |
| ☐ 11 Norm Siebern ................. | .40 | .16 | .04 |
| ☐ 12 Milt Pappas ................... | .50 | .20 | .05 |
| ☐ 13 Wally Post ..................... | .40 | .16 | .04 |
| ☐ 14 Jim Grant ...................... | .40 | .16 | .04 |
| ☐ 15 Pete Runnels ................. | .50 | .20 | .05 |
| ☐ 16 Ernie Broglio ................. | .50 | .20 | .05 |
| ☐ 17 Johnny Callison ............. | .60 | .24 | .06 |
| ☐ 18 Dodgers Team ............... | 3.50 | .75 | .15 |
| ☐ 19 Felix Mantilla ................ | .40 | .16 | .04 |
| ☐ 20 Roy Face ...................... | .80 | .32 | .08 |
| ☐ 21 Dutch Dotterer ............. | .40 | .16 | .04 |
| ☐ 22 Rocky Bridges ............... | .40 | .16 | .04 |
| ☐ 23 Eddie Fisher .................. | .40 | .16 | .04 |
| ☐ 24 Dick Gray ..................... | .40 | .16 | .04 |
| ☐ 25 Roy Sievers ................... | .50 | .20 | .05 |
| ☐ 26 Wayne Terwilliger .......... | .40 | .16 | .04 |
| ☐ 27 Dick Drott ..................... | .40 | .16 | .04 |
| ☐ 28 Brooks Robinson ........... | 10.00 | 4.00 | 1.00 |
| ☐ 29 Clem Labine .................. | .50 | .20 | .05 |
| ☐ 30 Tito Francona ................ | .50 | .20 | .05 |
| ☐ 31 Sammy Esposito ........... | .40 | .16 | .04 |
| ☐ 32 Sophomore Stalwarts: .... | .60 | .24 | .06 |
|    Jim O'Toole | | | |
|    Vada Pinson | | | |
| ☐ 33 Tom Morgan ................... | .40 | .16 | .04 |
| ☐ 34 George Anderson ............ | 1.25 | .50 | .12 |
| ☐ 35 Whitey Ford ................... | 6.50 | 2.60 | .65 |
| ☐ 36 Russ Nixon .................... | .40 | .16 | .04 |
| ☐ 37 Bill Bruton .................... | .40 | .16 | .04 |
| ☐ 38 Jerry Casale .................. | .40 | .16 | .04 |
| ☐ 39 Earl Averill .................... | .40 | .16 | .04 |
| ☐ 40 Joe Cunningham ............ | .50 | .20 | .05 |
| ☐ 41 Barry Latman ................. | .40 | .16 | .04 |
| ☐ 42 Hobie Landrith .............. | .40 | .16 | .04 |
| ☐ 43 Senators Team ............... | 2.00 | .40 | .08 |
| ☐ 44 Bob Locke .................... | .40 | .16 | .04 |
| ☐ 45 Roy McMillan ................ | .40 | .16 | .04 |
| ☐ 46 Jerry Fisher .................. | .40 | .16 | .04 |
| ☐ 47 Don Zimmer .................. | .60 | .24 | .06 |
| ☐ 48 Hal W. Smith ................ | .40 | .16 | .04 |
| ☐ 49 Curt Raydon .................. | .40 | .16 | .04 |
| ☐ 50 Al Kaline ...................... | 7.00 | 2.80 | .70 |
| ☐ 51 Jim Coates ................... | .40 | .16 | .04 |
| ☐ 52 Dave Philley .................. | .40 | .16 | .04 |
| ☐ 53 Jackie Brandt ................ | .40 | .16 | .04 |
| ☐ 54 Mike Fornieles .............. | .40 | .16 | .04 |
| ☐ 55 Bill Mazeroski ............... | 1.50 | .60 | .15 |
| ☐ 56 Steve Korcheck .............. | .40 | .16 | .04 |
| ☐ 57 Win Savers .................... | .50 | .20 | .05 |
|    Turk Lown | | | |
|    Jerry Staley | | | |
| ☐ 58 Gino Cimoli ................... | .40 | .16 | .04 |
| ☐ 59 Juan Pizarro ................. | .40 | .16 | .04 |
| ☐ 60 Gus Triandos ................ | .50 | .20 | .05 |
| ☐ 61 Eddie Kasko .................. | .40 | .16 | .04 |
| ☐ 62 Roger Craig ................... | .80 | .32 | .08 |
| ☐ 63 George Strickland .......... | .40 | .16 | .04 |
| ☐ 64 Jack Meyer .................... | .40 | .16 | .04 |
| ☐ 65 Elston Howard ............... | 1.75 | .70 | .17 |
| ☐ 66 Bob Trowbridge ............. | .40 | .16 | .04 |
| ☐ 67 Jose Pagan ................... | .40 | .16 | .04 |
| ☐ 68 Dave Hillman ................ | .40 | .16 | .04 |
| ☐ 69 Billy Goodman ............... | .50 | .20 | .05 |
| ☐ 70 Lew Burdette .................. | 1.25 | .50 | .12 |
| ☐ 71 Marty Keough ................ | .40 | .16 | .04 |
| ☐ 72 Tigers Team .................. | 2.25 | .50 | .10 |
| ☐ 73 Bob Gibson ................... | 7.50 | 3.00 | .75 |
| ☐ 74 Walt Moryn ................... | .40 | .16 | .04 |
| ☐ 75 Vic Power ..................... | .40 | .16 | .04 |

| | | | |
|---|---|---|---|
| ☐ 76 Bill Fischer ................... | .40 | .16 | .04 |
| ☐ 77 Hank Foiles ................... | .40 | .16 | .04 |
| ☐ 78 Bob Grim ...................... | .40 | .16 | .04 |
| ☐ 79 Walt Dropo .................... | .40 | .16 | .04 |
| ☐ 80 Johnny Antonelli ............ | .60 | .24 | .06 |
| ☐ 81 Russ Snyder .................. | .40 | .16 | .04 |
| ☐ 82 Ruben Gomez ................ | .40 | .16 | .04 |
| ☐ 83 Tony Kubek .................... | 1.75 | .70 | .17 |
| ☐ 84 Hal R. Smith ................. | .40 | .16 | .04 |
| ☐ 85 Frank Lary .................... | .50 | .20 | .05 |
| ☐ 86 Dick Gernert ................. | .40 | .16 | .04 |
| ☐ 87 John Romonosky ........... | .40 | .16 | .04 |
| ☐ 88 John Roseboro ............. | .50 | .20 | .05 |
| ☐ 89 Hal Brown .................... | .40 | .16 | .04 |
| ☐ 90 Bobby Avila ................... | .40 | .16 | .04 |
| ☐ 91 Bennie Daniels .............. | .40 | .16 | .04 |
| ☐ 92 Whitey Herzog ............... | 1.00 | .40 | .10 |
| ☐ 93 Art Schult .................... | .40 | .16 | .04 |
| ☐ 94 Leo Kiely ...................... | .40 | .16 | .04 |
| ☐ 95 Frank Thomas ............... | .50 | .20 | .05 |
| ☐ 96 Ralph Terry ................... | .60 | .24 | .06 |
| ☐ 97 Ted Lepcio .................... | .40 | .16 | .04 |
| ☐ 91 Gordon Jones ............... | .40 | .16 | .04 |
| ☐ 99 Lenny Green .................. | .40 | .16 | .04 |
| ☐ 100 Nellie Fox ................... | 1.75 | .70 | .17 |
| ☐ 101 Bob Miller ................... | .40 | .16 | .04 |
| ☐ 102 Kent Hadley ................. | .40 | .16 | .04 |
| ☐ 103 Dick Farrell ................. | .40 | .16 | .04 |
| ☐ 104 Dick Schofield ............ | .40 | .16 | .04 |
| ☐ 105 Larry Sherry ............... | .75 | .30 | .07 |
| ☐ 106 Billy Gardner ............... | .50 | .20 | .05 |
| ☐ 107 Carlton Willey .............. | .40 | .16 | .04 |
| ☐ 108 Pete Daley .................. | .40 | .16 | .04 |
| ☐ 109 Clete Boyer ................. | .75 | .30 | .07 |
| ☐ 110 Cal McLish .................. | .40 | .16 | .04 |
| ☐ 111 Vic Wertz .................... | .50 | .20 | .05 |
| ☐ 112 Jack Harshman ............ | .40 | .16 | .04 |
| ☐ 113 Bob Skinner ................ | .50 | .20 | .05 |
| ☐ 114 Ken Aspromonte .......... | .40 | .16 | .04 |
| ☐ 115 Fork and Knuckler: ........ | 1.50 | .60 | .15 |
|    Roy Face | | | |
|    Hoyt Wilhelm | | | |
| ☐ 116 Jim Rivera ................... | .40 | .16 | .04 |
| ☐ 117 Tom Borland RP ........... | .40 | .16 | .04 |
| ☐ 118 Bob Bruce RP .............. | .40 | .16 | .04 |
| ☐ 119 Chico Cardenas RP ........ | .50 | .20 | .05 |
| ☐ 120 Duke Carmel RP ........... | .40 | .16 | .04 |
| ☐ 121 Camilo Carreon RP ........ | .40 | .16 | .04 |
| ☐ 122 Don Dillard RP ............. | .40 | .16 | .04 |
| ☐ 123 Dan Dobbek RP ............ | .40 | .16 | .04 |
| ☐ 124 Jim Donohue RP ........... | .40 | .16 | .04 |
| ☐ 125 Dick Ellsworth RP ......... | .60 | .24 | .06 |
| ☐ 126 Chuck Estrada RP ......... | .75 | .30 | .07 |
| ☐ 127 Ron Hansen RP ............ | .50 | .20 | .05 |
| ☐ 128 Bill Harris RP .............. | .40 | .16 | .04 |
| ☐ 129 Bob Hartman RP ........... | .40 | .16 | .04 |
| ☐ 130 Frank Herrera RP .......... | .40 | .16 | .04 |
| ☐ 131 Ed Hobaugh RP ........... | .40 | .16 | .04 |
| ☐ 132 Frank Howard RP .......... | 3.00 | 1.20 | .30 |
| ☐ 133 Manuel Javier RP .......... | .50 | .20 | .05 |
|    (sic, Julian) | | | |
| ☐ 134 Deron Johnson RP ........ | .50 | .20 | .05 |
| ☐ 135 Ken Johnson RP ........... | .40 | .16 | .04 |
| ☐ 136 Jim Kaat RP ................ | 10.00 | 4.00 | 1.00 |
| ☐ 137 Lou Klimchock RP ......... | .40 | .16 | .04 |
| ☐ 138 Art Mahaffey RP ........... | .50 | .20 | .05 |
| ☐ 139 Carl Mathias RP ........... | .40 | .16 | .04 |
| ☐ 140 Julio Navarro RP ........... | .40 | .16 | .04 |
| ☐ 141 Jim Proctor RP ............. | .40 | .16 | .04 |
| ☐ 142 Bill Short RP ............... | .40 | .16 | .04 |
| ☐ 143 Al Spangler RP ............. | .40 | .16 | .04 |
| ☐ 144 Al Stieglitz RP .............. | .40 | .16 | .04 |
| ☐ 145 Jim Umbricht RP ........... | .40 | .16 | .04 |
| ☐ 146 Ted Wieand RP ............. | .40 | .16 | .04 |
| ☐ 147 Bob Will RP ................. | .40 | .16 | .04 |
| ☐ 148 Carl Yastrzemski RP ........ | 110.00 | 45.00 | 11.00 |
| ☐ 149 Bob Nieman ................ | .40 | .16 | .04 |
| ☐ 150 Billy Pierce .................. | .75 | .30 | .07 |
| ☐ 151 Giants Team ................ | 2.25 | .50 | .10 |
| ☐ 152 Gail Harris .................. | .40 | .16 | .04 |
| ☐ 153 Bobby Thomson ........... | .80 | .32 | .08 |
| ☐ 154 Jim Davenport .............. | .60 | .24 | .06 |
| ☐ 155 Charlie Neal ................ | .50 | .20 | .05 |
| ☐ 156 Art Ceccarelli .............. | .40 | .16 | .04 |
| ☐ 157 Rocky Nelson ............... | .40 | .16 | .04 |
| ☐ 158 Wes Covington ............. | .50 | .20 | .05 |
| ☐ 159 Jim Piersall ................. | 1.00 | .40 | .10 |
| ☐ 160 Rival All-Stars: ........... | 7.00 | 2.80 | .70 |
|    Mickey Mantle | | | |
|    Ken Boyer | | | |
| ☐ 161 Ray Narleski ................ | .40 | .16 | .04 |
| ☐ 162 Sammy Taylor .............. | .40 | .16 | .04 |
| ☐ 163 Hector Lopez ............... | .40 | .16 | .04 |

| | | | | |
|---|---|---|---|---|
| ☐ 164 | Reds Team | 2.25 | .50 | .10 |
| ☐ 165 | Jack Sanford | .50 | .20 | .05 |
| ☐ 166 | Chuck Essegian | .40 | .16 | .04 |
| ☐ 167 | Valmy Thomas | .40 | .16 | .04 |
| ☐ 168 | Alex Grammas | .40 | .16 | .04 |
| ☐ 169 | Jake Striker | .40 | .16 | .04 |
| ☐ 170 | Del Crandall | .50 | .20 | .05 |
| ☐ 171 | Johnny Groth | .40 | .16 | .04 |
| ☐ 172 | Willie Kirkland | .40 | .16 | .04 |
| ☐ 173 | Billy Martin | 2.00 | .80 | .20 |
| ☐ 174 | Indians Team | 2.00 | .40 | .08 |
| ☐ 175 | Pete Ramos | .40 | .16 | .04 |
| ☐ 176 | Vada Pinson | 1.25 | .50 | .12 |
| ☐ 177 | Johnny Kucks | .40 | .16 | .04 |
| ☐ 178 | Woody Held | .40 | .16 | .04 |
| ☐ 179 | Rip Coleman | .40 | .16 | .04 |
| ☐ 180 | Harry Simpson | .40 | .16 | .04 |
| ☐ 181 | Billy Loes | .40 | .16 | .04 |
| ☐ 182 | Glen Hobbie | .40 | .16 | .04 |
| ☐ 183 | Eli Grba | .40 | .16 | .04 |
| ☐ 184 | Gary Geiger | .40 | .16 | .04 |
| ☐ 185 | Jim Owens | .40 | .16 | .04 |
| ☐ 186 | Dave Sisler | .40 | .16 | .04 |
| ☐ 187 | Jay Hook | .60 | .24 | .06 |
| ☐ 188 | Dick Williams | .40 | .16 | .04 |
| ☐ 189 | Don McMahon | .60 | .24 | .06 |
| ☐ 190 | Gene Woodling | .40 | .16 | .04 |
| ☐ 191 | John Klippstein | .40 | .16 | .04 |
| ☐ 192 | Danny O'Connell | .40 | .16 | .04 |
| ☐ 193 | Dick Hyde | .40 | .16 | .04 |
| ☐ 194 | Bobby Gene Smith | .40 | .16 | .04 |
| ☐ 195 | Lindy McDaniel | .50 | .20 | .05 |
| ☐ 196 | Andy Carey | .50 | .20 | .05 |
| ☐ 197 | Ron Kline | .40 | .16 | .04 |
| ☐ 198 | Jerry Lynch | .40 | .16 | .04 |
| ☐ 199 | Dick Donovan | .40 | .16 | .04 |
| ☐ 200 | Willie Mays | 27.00 | 11.00 | 2.70 |
| ☐ 201 | Larry Osborne | .40 | .16 | .04 |
| ☐ 202 | Fred Kipp | .40 | .16 | .04 |
| ☐ 203 | Sammy White | .40 | .16 | .04 |
| ☐ 204 | Ryne Duren | .75 | .30 | .07 |
| ☐ 205 | John Logan | .50 | .20 | .05 |
| ☐ 206 | Claude Osteen | .50 | .20 | .05 |
| ☐ 207 | Bob Boyd | .40 | .16 | .04 |
| ☐ 208 | White Sox Team | 2.00 | .40 | .08 |
| ☐ 209 | Ron Blackburn | .40 | .16 | .04 |
| ☐ 210 | Harmon Killebrew | 5.50 | 2.20 | .55 |
| ☐ 211 | Taylor Phillips | .40 | .16 | .04 |
| ☐ 212 | Walt Alston MGR | 1.75 | .70 | .17 |
| ☐ 213 | Chuck Dressen MGR | .50 | .20 | .05 |
| ☐ 214 | Jimmy Dykes MGR | .50 | .20 | .05 |
| ☐ 215 | Bob Elliott MGR | .40 | .16 | .04 |
| ☐ 216 | Joe Gordon MGR | .50 | .20 | .05 |
| ☐ 217 | Charlie Grimm MGR | .50 | .20 | .05 |
| ☐ 218 | Solly Hemus MGR | .40 | .16 | .04 |
| ☐ 219 | Fred Hutchinson MGR | .60 | .24 | .06 |
| ☐ 220 | Billy Jurges MGR | .40 | .16 | .04 |
| ☐ 221 | Cookie Lavagetto MGR | .40 | .16 | .04 |
| ☐ 222 | Al Lopez MGR | 1.50 | .60 | .15 |
| ☐ 223 | Danny Murtaugh MGR | .50 | .20 | .05 |
| ☐ 224 | Paul Richards MGR | .50 | .20 | .05 |
| ☐ 225 | Bill Rigney MGR | .40 | .16 | .04 |
| ☐ 226 | Eddie Sawyer MGR | .40 | .16 | .04 |
| ☐ 227 | Casey Stengel MGR | 4.50 | 1.80 | .45 |
| ☐ 228 | Ernie Johnson | .40 | .16 | .04 |
| ☐ 229 | Joe M. Morgan | .40 | .16 | .04 |
| ☐ 230 | Mound Magicians: | 2.25 | .90 | .22 |
| | Lou Burdette | | | |
| | Warren Spahn | | | |
| | Bob Buhl | | | |
| ☐ 231 | Hal Naragon | .40 | .16 | .04 |
| ☐ 232 | Jim Busby | .40 | .16 | .04 |
| ☐ 233 | Don Elston | .40 | .16 | .04 |
| ☐ 234 | Don Demeter | .40 | .16 | .04 |
| ☐ 235 | Gus Bell | .50 | .20 | .05 |
| ☐ 236 | Dick Ricketts | .40 | .16 | .04 |
| ☐ 237 | Elmer Valo | .40 | .16 | .04 |
| ☐ 238 | Danny Kravitz | .40 | .16 | .04 |
| ☐ 239 | Joe Shipley | .40 | .16 | .04 |
| ☐ 240 | Luis Aparicio | 3.50 | 1.40 | .35 |
| ☐ 241 | Albie Pearson | .40 | .16 | .04 |
| ☐ 242 | Cardinals Team | 2.00 | .40 | .08 |
| ☐ 243 | Bubba Phillips | .40 | .16 | .04 |
| ☐ 244 | Hal Griggs | .40 | .16 | .04 |
| ☐ 245 | Ed Yost | .40 | .16 | .04 |
| ☐ 246 | Lee Maye | .40 | .16 | .04 |
| ☐ 247 | Gil McDougald | 1.50 | .60 | .15 |
| ☐ 248 | Del Rice | .40 | .16 | .04 |
| ☐ 249 | Earl Wilson | .50 | .20 | .05 |
| ☐ 250 | Stan Musial | 21.00 | 8.50 | 2.10 |
| ☐ 251 | Bob Malkmus | .40 | .16 | .04 |
| ☐ 252 | Ray Herbert | .40 | .16 | .04 |
| ☐ 253 | Eddie Bressoud | .40 | .16 | .04 |
| ☐ 254 | Arnie Portocarrero | .40 | .16 | .04 |
| ☐ 255 | Jim Gilliam | 1.50 | .60 | .15 |
| ☐ 256 | Dick Brown | .40 | .16 | .04 |
| ☐ 257 | Gordy Coleman | .50 | .20 | .05 |
| ☐ 258 | Dick Groat | 1.75 | .70 | .17 |
| ☐ 259 | George Altman | .40 | .16 | .04 |
| ☐ 260 | Power Plus | .50 | .20 | .05 |
| | Rocky Colavito | | | |
| | Tito Francona | | | |
| ☐ 261 | Pete Burnside | .40 | .16 | .04 |
| ☐ 262 | Hank Bauer | .75 | .30 | .07 |
| ☐ 263 | Darrell Johnson | .50 | .20 | .05 |
| ☐ 264 | Robin Roberts | 3.50 | 1.40 | .35 |
| ☐ 265 | Rip Repulski | .40 | .16 | .04 |
| ☐ 266 | Joe Jay | .40 | .16 | .04 |
| ☐ 267 | Jim Marshall | .40 | .16 | .04 |
| ☐ 268 | Al Worthington | .40 | .16 | .04 |
| ☐ 269 | Gene Green | .40 | .16 | .04 |
| ☐ 270 | Bob Turley | 1.00 | .40 | .10 |
| ☐ 271 | Julio Becquer | .40 | .16 | .04 |
| ☐ 272 | Fred Green | .40 | .16 | .04 |
| ☐ 273 | Neil Chrisley | .40 | .16 | .04 |
| ☐ 274 | Tom Acker | .40 | .16 | .04 |
| ☐ 275 | Curt Flood | 1.00 | .40 | .10 |
| ☐ 276 | Ken McBride | .40 | .16 | .04 |
| ☐ 277 | Harry Bright | .40 | .16 | .04 |
| ☐ 278 | Stan Williams | .50 | .20 | .05 |
| ☐ 279 | Chuck Tanner | .60 | .24 | .06 |
| ☐ 280 | Frank Sullivan | .40 | .16 | .04 |
| ☐ 281 | Ray Boone | .50 | .20 | .05 |
| ☐ 282 | Joe Nuxhall | .50 | .20 | .05 |
| ☐ 283 | John Blanchard | .50 | .20 | .05 |
| ☐ 284 | Don Gross | .40 | .16 | .04 |
| ☐ 285 | Harry Anderson | .40 | .16 | .04 |
| ☐ 286 | Ray Semproch | .40 | .16 | .04 |
| ☐ 287 | Felipe Alou | .75 | .30 | .07 |
| ☐ 288 | Bob Mabe | .50 | .20 | .05 |
| ☐ 289 | Willie Jones | .50 | .20 | .05 |
| ☐ 290 | Jerry Lumpe | .50 | .20 | .05 |
| ☐ 291 | Bob Keegan | .50 | .20 | .05 |
| ☐ 292 | Dodger Backstops | .60 | .24 | .06 |
| | Joe Pignatano | | | |
| | John Roseboro | | | |
| ☐ 293 | Gene Conley | .50 | .20 | .05 |
| ☐ 294 | Tony Taylor | .50 | .20 | .05 |
| ☐ 295 | Gil Hodges | 4.00 | 1.60 | .40 |
| ☐ 296 | Nelson Chittum | .50 | .20 | .05 |
| ☐ 297 | Reno Bertoia | .50 | .20 | .05 |
| ☐ 298 | George Witt | .50 | .20 | .05 |
| ☐ 299 | Earl Torgeson | .50 | .20 | .05 |
| ☐ 300 | Hank Aaron | 27.00 | 11.00 | 2.70 |
| ☐ 301 | Jerry Davie | .50 | .20 | .05 |
| ☐ 302 | Phillies Team | 2.00 | .40 | .08 |
| ☐ 303 | Billy O'Dell | .50 | .20 | .05 |
| ☐ 304 | Joe Ginsberg | .50 | .20 | .05 |
| ☐ 305 | Richie Ashburn | 2.00 | .80 | .20 |
| ☐ 306 | Frank Baumann | .50 | .20 | .05 |
| ☐ 307 | Gene Oliver | .50 | .20 | .05 |
| ☐ 308 | Dick Hall | .50 | .20 | .05 |
| ☐ 309 | Bob Hale | .50 | .20 | .05 |
| ☐ 310 | Frank Malzone | .60 | .24 | .06 |
| ☐ 311 | Raul Sanchez | .50 | .20 | .05 |
| ☐ 312 | Charley Lau | .60 | .24 | .06 |
| ☐ 313 | Turk Lown | .50 | .20 | .05 |
| ☐ 314 | Chico Fernandez | .50 | .20 | .05 |
| ☐ 315 | Bobby Shantz | .80 | .32 | .08 |
| ☐ 316 | Willie McCovey | 45.00 | 18.00 | 4.50 |
| ☐ 317 | Pumpsie Green | .50 | .20 | .05 |
| ☐ 318 | Jim Baxes | .50 | .20 | .05 |
| ☐ 319 | Joe Koppe | .50 | .20 | .05 |
| ☐ 320 | Bob Allison | .75 | .30 | .07 |
| ☐ 321 | Ron Fairly | .60 | .24 | .06 |
| ☐ 322 | Willie Tasby | .50 | .20 | .05 |
| ☐ 323 | John Romano | .50 | .20 | .05 |
| ☐ 324 | Jim Perry | .80 | .32 | .08 |
| ☐ 325 | Jim O'Toole | .60 | .24 | .06 |
| ☐ 326 | Bob Clemente | 16.00 | 6.50 | 1.60 |
| ☐ 327 | Ray Sadecki | .50 | .20 | .05 |
| ☐ 328 | Earl Battey | .60 | .24 | .06 |
| ☐ 329 | Zack Monroe | .50 | .20 | .05 |
| ☐ 330 | Harvey Kuenn | 1.25 | .50 | .12 |
| ☐ 331 | Henry Mason | .50 | .20 | .05 |
| ☐ 332 | Yankees Team | 6.50 | 1.00 | .20 |
| ☐ 333 | Danny McDevitt | .50 | .20 | .05 |
| ☐ 334 | Ted Abernathy | .50 | .20 | .05 |
| ☐ 335 | Red Schoendienst | 1.00 | .40 | .10 |
| ☐ 336 | Ike Delock | .50 | .20 | .05 |
| ☐ 337 | Cal Neeman | .50 | .20 | .05 |
| ☐ 338 | Ray Monzant | .50 | .20 | .05 |
| ☐ 339 | Harry Chiti | .50 | .20 | .05 |
| ☐ 340 | Harvey Haddix | .75 | .30 | .07 |
| ☐ 341 | Carroll Hardy | .50 | .20 | .05 |
| ☐ 342 | Casey Wise | .50 | .20 | .05 |

| | | | | |
|---|---|---|---|---|
| ☐ 343 | Sandy Koufax | 15.00 | 6.00 | 1.50 |
| ☐ 344 | Clint Courtney | .50 | .20 | .05 |
| ☐ 345 | Don Newcombe | .80 | .32 | .08 |
| ☐ 346 | J.C. Martin (face actually Gary Peters) | .60 | .24 | .06 |
| ☐ 347 | Ed Bouchee | .50 | .20 | .05 |
| ☐ 348 | Barry Shetrone | .50 | .20 | .05 |
| ☐ 349 | Moe Drabowsky | .50 | .20 | .05 |
| ☐ 350 | Mickey Mantle | 75.00 | 30.00 | 7.50 |
| ☐ 351 | Don Nottebart | .50 | .20 | .05 |
| ☐ 352 | Cincy Clouters Gus Bell Frank Robinson Jerry Lynch | 1.75 | .70 | .17 |
| ☐ 353 | Don Larsen | .80 | .32 | .08 |
| ☐ 354 | Bob Lillis | .60 | .24 | .06 |
| ☐ 355 | Bill White | .80 | .32 | .08 |
| ☐ 356 | Joe Amalfitano | .50 | .20 | .05 |
| ☐ 357 | Al Schroll | .50 | .20 | .05 |
| ☐ 358 | Joe DeMaestri | .50 | .20 | .05 |
| ☐ 359 | Buddy Gilbert | .50 | .20 | .05 |
| ☐ 360 | Herb Score | .80 | .32 | .08 |
| ☐ 361 | Bob Oldis | .50 | .20 | .05 |
| ☐ 362 | Russ Kemmerer | .50 | .20 | .05 |
| ☐ 363 | Gene Stephens | .50 | .20 | .05 |
| ☐ 364 | Paul Foytack | .50 | .20 | .05 |
| ☐ 365 | Minnie Minoso | 1.25 | .50 | .12 |
| ☐ 366 | Dallas Green | 1.50 | .60 | .15 |
| ☐ 367 | Bill Tuttle | .50 | .20 | .05 |
| ☐ 368 | Daryl Spencer | .50 | .20 | .05 |
| ☐ 369 | Billy Hoeft | .50 | .20 | .05 |
| ☐ 370 | Bill Skowron | 1.50 | .60 | .15 |
| ☐ 371 | Bud Byerly | .50 | .20 | .05 |
| ☐ 372 | Frank House | .50 | .20 | .05 |
| ☐ 373 | Don Hoak | .50 | .20 | .05 |
| ☐ 374 | Bob Buhl | .50 | .20 | .05 |
| ☐ 375 | Dale Long | .50 | .20 | .05 |
| ☐ 376 | John Briggs | .50 | .20 | .05 |
| ☐ 377 | Roger Maris | 16.00 | 6.50 | 1.60 |
| ☐ 378 | Stu Miller | .50 | .20 | .05 |
| ☐ 379 | Red Wilson | .50 | .20 | .05 |
| ☐ 380 | Bob Shaw | .50 | .20 | .05 |
| ☐ 381 | Braves Team | 2.00 | .40 | .08 |
| ☐ 382 | Ted Bowsfield | .50 | .20 | .05 |
| ☐ 383 | Leon Wagner | .50 | .20 | .05 |
| ☐ 384 | Don Cardwell | .50 | .20 | .05 |
| ☐ 385 | World Series Game 1 Neal Steals Second | 1.50 | .60 | .15 |
| ☐ 386 | World Series Game 2 Neal Belts 2nd Homer | 1.50 | .60 | .15 |
| ☐ 387 | World Series Game 3 Furillo Breaks Game | 1.50 | .60 | .15 |
| ☐ 388 | World Series Game 4 Hodges' Homer | 2.00 | .80 | .20 |
| ☐ 389 | World Series Game 5 Luis Swipes Base | 2.00 | .80 | .20 |
| ☐ 390 | World Series Game 6 Scrambling After Ball | 1.50 | .60 | .15 |
| ☐ 391 | World Series Summary The Champs Celebrate | 1.50 | .60 | .15 |
| ☐ 392 | Tex Clevenger | .50 | .20 | .05 |
| ☐ 393 | Smoky Burgess | .60 | .24 | .06 |
| ☐ 394 | Norm Larker | .50 | .20 | .05 |
| ☐ 395 | Hoyt Wilhelm | 3.50 | 1.40 | .35 |
| ☐ 396 | Steve Bilko | .50 | .20 | .05 |
| ☐ 397 | Don Blasingame | .50 | .20 | .05 |
| ☐ 398 | Mike Cuellar | .60 | .24 | .06 |
| ☐ 399 | Young Hill Stars Milt Pappas Jack Fisher Jerry Walker | .60 | .24 | .06 |
| ☐ 400 | Rocky Colavito | 1.25 | .50 | .12 |
| ☐ 401 | Bob Duliba | .50 | .20 | .05 |
| ☐ 402 | Dick Stuart | .60 | .24 | .06 |
| ☐ 403 | Ed Sadowski | .50 | .20 | .05 |
| ☐ 404 | Bob Rush | .50 | .20 | .05 |
| ☐ 405 | Bobby Richardson | 1.75 | .70 | .17 |
| ☐ 406 | Billy Klaus | .50 | .20 | .05 |
| ☐ 407 | Gary Peters (face actually J.C. Martin) | .80 | .32 | .08 |
| ☐ 408 | Carl Furillo | 1.50 | .60 | .15 |
| ☐ 409 | Ron Samford | .50 | .20 | .05 |
| ☐ 410 | Sam Jones | .60 | .24 | .06 |
| ☐ 411 | Ed Bailey | .50 | .20 | .05 |
| ☐ 412 | Bob Anderson | .50 | .20 | .05 |
| ☐ 413 | Athletics Team | 2.00 | .00 | .00 |
| ☐ 414 | Don Williams | .50 | .20 | .05 |
| ☐ 415 | Bob Cerv | .60 | .24 | .06 |
| ☐ 416 | Humberto Robinson | .50 | .20 | .05 |
| ☐ 417 | Chuck Cottier | .75 | .30 | .07 |
| ☐ 418 | Don Mossi | .60 | .24 | .06 |

| | | | | |
|---|---|---|---|---|
| ☐ 419 | George Crowe | .50 | .20 | .05 |
| ☐ 420 | Ed Mathews | 4.50 | 1.80 | .45 |
| ☐ 421 | Duke Maas | .50 | .20 | .05 |
| ☐ 422 | John Powers | .50 | .20 | .05 |
| ☐ 423 | Ed Fitzgerald | .50 | .20 | .05 |
| ☐ 424 | Pete Whisenant | .50 | .20 | .05 |
| ☐ 425 | John Podres | 1.25 | .50 | .12 |
| ☐ 426 | Ron Jackson | .50 | .20 | .05 |
| ☐ 427 | Al Grunwald | .50 | .20 | .05 |
| ☐ 428 | Al Smith | .50 | .20 | .05 |
| ☐ 429 | AL Kings Nellie Fox Harvey Kuenn | 1.25 | .50 | .12 |
| ☐ 430 | Art Ditmar | .60 | .24 | .06 |
| ☐ 431 | Andre Rodgers | .50 | .20 | .05 |
| ☐ 432 | Chuck Stobbs | .50 | .20 | .05 |
| ☐ 433 | Irv Noren | .50 | .20 | .05 |
| ☐ 434 | Brooks Lawrence | .50 | .20 | .05 |
| ☐ 435 | Gene Freese | .50 | .20 | .05 |
| ☐ 436 | Marv Throneberry | 1.25 | .50 | .12 |
| ☐ 437 | Bob Friend | .60 | .24 | .06 |
| ☐ 438 | Jim Coker | .50 | .20 | .05 |
| ☐ 439 | Tom Brewer | .50 | .20 | .05 |
| ☐ 440 | Jim Lemon | .60 | .24 | .06 |
| ☐ 441 | Gary Bell | .75 | .30 | .07 |
| ☐ 442 | Joe Pignatano | .75 | .30 | .07 |
| ☐ 443 | Charley Maxwell | .75 | .30 | .07 |
| ☐ 444 | Jerry Kindall | .75 | .30 | .07 |
| ☐ 445 | Warren Spahn | 7.00 | 2.80 | .70 |
| ☐ 446 | Ellis Burton | .75 | .30 | .07 |
| ☐ 447 | Ray Moore | .75 | .30 | .07 |
| ☐ 448 | Jim Gentile | 1.00 | .40 | .10 |
| ☐ 449 | Jim Brosnan | .90 | .36 | .09 |
| ☐ 450 | Orlando Cepeda | 2.25 | .90 | .22 |
| ☐ 451 | Curt Simmons | 1.00 | .40 | .10 |
| ☐ 452 | Ray Webster | .75 | .30 | .07 |
| ☐ 453 | Vern Law | 1.25 | .50 | .12 |
| ☐ 454 | Hal Woodeshick | .75 | .30 | .07 |
| ☐ 455 | Baltimore Coaches Eddie Robinson Harry Brecheen Luman Harris | 1.00 | .40 | .10 |
| ☐ 456 | Red Sox Coaches Rudy York Billy Herman Sal Maglie Del Baker | 1.25 | .50 | .12 |
| ☐ 457 | Cubs Coaches Charlie Root Lou Klein Elvin Tappe | 1.00 | .40 | .10 |
| ☐ 458 | White Sox Coaches Johnny Cooney Don Gutteridge Tony Cuccinello Ray Berres | 1.00 | .40 | .10 |
| ☐ 459 | Reds Coaches Reggie Otero Cot Deal Wally Moses | 1.00 | .40 | .10 |
| ☐ 460 | Indians Coaches: Mel Harder Jo-Jo White Bob Lemon Ralph (Red) Kress | 1.25 | .50 | .12 |
| ☐ 461 | Tigers Coaches: Tom Ferrick Luke Appling Billy Hitchcock | 1.25 | .50 | .12 |
| ☐ 462 | Athletics Coaches Fred Fitzsimmons Don Heffner Walker Cooper | 1.00 | .40 | .10 |
| ☐ 463 | Dodgers Coaches Bobby Bragan Pete Reiser Joe Becker Greg Mulleavy | 1.25 | .50 | .12 |
| ☐ 464 | Braves Coaches Bob Scheffing Whitlow Wyatt Andy Pafko George Myatt | 1.00 | .40 | .10 |
| ☐ 465 | Yankees Coaches Bill Dickey Ralph Houk Frank Crosetti Ed Lopat | 2.50 | 1.00 | .25 |
| ☐ 466 | Phillies Coaches Ken Silvestri Dick Carter Andy Cohen | 1.00 | .40 | .10 |
| ☐ 467 | Pirates Coaches | 1.00 | .40 | .10 |

| | | | | |
|---|---|---|---|---|
| | Mickey Vernon | | | |
| | Frank Oceak | | | |
| | Sam Narron | | | |
| | Bill Burwell | | | |
| ☐ 468 | Cardinals Coaches | 1.00 | .40 | .10 |
| | Johnny Keane | | | |
| | Howie Pollet | | | |
| | Ray Katt | | | |
| | Harry Walker | | | |
| ☐ 469 | Giants Coaches | 1.00 | .40 | .10 |
| | Wes Westrum | | | |
| | Salty Parker | | | |
| | Bill Posedel | | | |
| ☐ 470 | Senators Coaches | 1.00 | .40 | .10 |
| | Bob Swift | | | |
| | Ellis Clary | | | |
| | Sam Mele | | | |
| ☐ 471 | Ned Garver | .75 | .30 | .07 |
| ☐ 472 | Al Dark | 1.00 | .40 | .10 |
| ☐ 473 | Al Cicotte | .75 | .30 | .07 |
| ☐ 474 | Haywood Sullivan | .90 | .36 | .09 |
| ☐ 475 | Don Drysdale | 6.50 | 2.60 | .65 |
| ☐ 476 | Lou Johnson | .75 | .30 | .07 |
| ☐ 477 | Don Ferrarese | .75 | .30 | .07 |
| ☐ 478 | Frank Torre | .75 | .30 | .07 |
| ☐ 479 | Georges Maranda | .75 | .30 | .07 |
| ☐ 480 | Yogi Berra | 11.00 | 4.50 | 1.10 |
| ☐ 481 | Wes Stock | .90 | .36 | .09 |
| ☐ 482 | Frank Bolling | .75 | .30 | .07 |
| ☐ 483 | Camilo Pascual | 1.00 | .40 | .10 |
| ☐ 484 | Pirates Team | 5.00 | 1.00 | .20 |
| ☐ 485 | Ken Boyer | 1.75 | .70 | .17 |
| ☐ 486 | Bobby Del Greco | .75 | .30 | .07 |
| ☐ 487 | Tom Sturdivant | .75 | .30 | .07 |
| ☐ 488 | Norm Cash | 2.00 | .80 | .20 |
| ☐ 489 | Steve Ridzik | .75 | .30 | .07 |
| ☐ 490 | Frank Robinson | 8.50 | 3.50 | .85 |
| ☐ 491 | Mel Roach | .75 | .30 | .07 |
| ☐ 492 | Larry Jackson | .75 | .30 | .07 |
| ☐ 493 | Duke Snider | 11.00 | 4.50 | 1.10 |
| ☐ 494 | Orioles Team | 3.00 | .60 | .10 |
| ☐ 495 | Sherm Lollar | .90 | .36 | .09 |
| ☐ 496 | Bill Virdon | 1.25 | .50 | .12 |
| ☐ 497 | John Tsitouris | .75 | .30 | .07 |
| ☐ 498 | Al Pilarcik | .75 | .30 | .07 |
| ☐ 499 | Johnny James | .75 | .30 | .07 |
| ☐ 500 | Johnny Temple | .90 | .36 | .09 |
| ☐ 501 | Bob Schmidt | .75 | .30 | .07 |
| ☐ 502 | Jim Bunning | 2.50 | 1.00 | .25 |
| ☐ 503 | Don Lee | .75 | .30 | .07 |
| ☐ 504 | Seth Morehead | .75 | .30 | .07 |
| ☐ 505 | Ted Kluszewski | 1.50 | .60 | .15 |
| ☐ 506 | Lee Walls | .75 | .30 | .07 |
| ☐ 507 | Dick Stigman | 2.25 | .90 | .22 |
| ☐ 508 | Bill Consolo | 2.25 | .90 | .22 |
| ☐ 509 | Tommy Davis | 5.00 | 2.00 | .50 |
| ☐ 510 | Jerry Staley | 2.25 | .90 | .22 |
| ☐ 511 | Ken Walters | 2.25 | .90 | .22 |
| ☐ 512 | Joe Gibbon | 2.25 | .90 | .22 |
| ☐ 513 | Cubs Team | 5.00 | 1.00 | .20 |
| ☐ 514 | Steve Barber | 2.50 | 1.00 | .25 |
| ☐ 515 | Stan Lopata | 2.25 | .90 | .22 |
| ☐ 516 | Marty Kutyna | 2.25 | .90 | .22 |
| ☐ 517 | Charlie James | 2.25 | .90 | .22 |
| ☐ 518 | Tony Gonzales | 2.25 | .90 | .22 |
| ☐ 519 | Ed Roebuck | 2.25 | .90 | .22 |
| ☐ 520 | Don Buddin | 2.25 | .90 | .22 |
| ☐ 521 | Mike Lee | 2.25 | .90 | .22 |
| ☐ 522 | Ken Hunt | 2.25 | .90 | .22 |
| ☐ 523 | Clay Dalrymple | 2.25 | .90 | .22 |
| ☐ 524 | Bill Henry | 2.25 | .90 | .22 |
| ☐ 525 | Marv Breeding | 2.25 | .90 | .22 |
| ☐ 526 | Paul Giel | 2.25 | .90 | .22 |
| ☐ 527 | Jose Valdivielso | 2.25 | .90 | .22 |
| ☐ 528 | Ben Johnson | 2.25 | .90 | .22 |
| ☐ 529 | Norm Sherry | 2.50 | 1.00 | .25 |
| ☐ 530 | Mike McCormick | 2.50 | 1.00 | .25 |
| ☐ 531 | Sandy Amoros | 2.50 | 1.00 | .25 |
| ☐ 532 | Mike Garcia | 2.50 | 1.00 | .25 |
| ☐ 533 | Lou Clinton | 2.25 | .90 | .22 |
| ☐ 534 | Ken Mackenzie | 2.25 | .90 | .22 |
| ☐ 535 | Whitey Lockman | 2.50 | 1.00 | .25 |
| ☐ 536 | Wynn Hawkins | 2.25 | .90 | .22 |
| ☐ 537 | Red Sox Team | 5.00 | 1.00 | .20 |
| ☐ 538 | Frank Barnes | 2.25 | .90 | .22 |
| ☐ 539 | Gene Baker | 2.25 | .90 | .22 |
| ☐ 540 | Jerry Walker | 2.25 | .90 | .22 |
| ☐ 541 | Tony Curry | 2.25 | .90 | .22 |
| ☐ 542 | Ken Hamlin | 2.25 | .90 | .22 |
| ☐ 543 | Elio Chacon | 2.25 | .90 | .22 |
| ☐ 544 | Bill Monbouquette | 2.25 | .90 | .22 |
| ☐ 545 | Carl Sawatski | 2.25 | .90 | .22 |
| ☐ 546 | Hank Aguirre | 2.25 | .90 | .22 |

| | | | | |
|---|---|---|---|---|
| ☐ 547 | Bob Aspromonte | 2.25 | .90 | .22 |
| ☐ 548 | Don Mincher | 3.00 | 1.20 | .30 |
| ☐ 549 | John Buzhardt | 2.25 | .90 | .22 |
| ☐ 550 | Jim Landis | 2.25 | .90 | .22 |
| ☐ 551 | Ed Rakow | 2.25 | .90 | .22 |
| ☐ 552 | Walt Bond | 2.25 | .90 | .22 |
| ☐ 553 | Bill Skowron AS | 2.75 | 1.10 | .27 |
| ☐ 554 | Willie McCovey AS | 11.00 | 4.50 | 1.10 |
| ☐ 555 | Nellie Fox AS | 3.00 | 1.20 | .30 |
| ☐ 556 | Charlie Neal AS | 2.75 | 1.10 | .27 |
| ☐ 557 | Frank Malzone AS | 2.75 | 1.10 | .27 |
| ☐ 558 | Eddie Mathews AS | 7.00 | 2.80 | .70 |
| ☐ 559 | Luis Aparicio AS | 6.00 | 2.40 | .60 |
| ☐ 560 | Ernie Banks AS | 9.00 | 3.75 | .90 |
| ☐ 561 | Al Kaline AS | 9.00 | 3.75 | .90 |
| ☐ 562 | Joe Cunningham AS | 2.75 | 1.10 | .27 |
| ☐ 563 | Mickey Mantle AS | 45.00 | 18.00 | 4.50 |
| ☐ 564 | Willie Mays AS | 20.00 | 8.00 | 2.00 |
| ☐ 565 | Roger Maris AS | 9.00 | 3.75 | .90 |
| ☐ 566 | Hank Aaron AS | 20.00 | 8.00 | 2.00 |
| ☐ 567 | Sherm Lollar AS | 2.75 | 1.10 | .27 |
| ☐ 568 | Del Crandall AS | 2.75 | 1.10 | .27 |
| ☐ 569 | Camilo Pascual AS | 2.75 | 1.10 | .27 |
| ☐ 570 | Don Drysdale AS | 7.00 | 2.80 | .70 |
| ☐ 571 | Billy Pierce AS | 2.75 | 1.10 | .27 |
| ☐ 572 | Johnny Antonelli AS | 3.00 | 1.20 | .30 |

## 1961 Topps

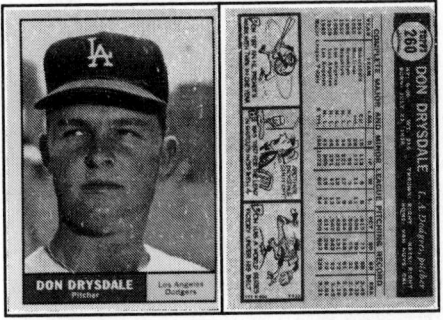

The cards in this 587 card set measure 2 1/2" by 3 1/2". In 1961, Topps returned to the vertical obverse format. Introduced for the first time were "League Leaders" (41 to 50) and separate, numbered checklist cards. Two number 463's exist: the Braves team card carrying that number was meant to be number 426. There are three versions of the second series checklist card #98; the variations are distinguished by the color of the "CHECKLIST" headline on the front of the card, the color of the printing of the card number on the bottom of the reverse, and the presence of the copyright notice running vertically on the card back. There are two groups of managers (131-139 and 219-226) as well as separate series of World Series cards (306-313), Baseball Thrills (401 to 410), previous MVP's (AL 471-478 and NL 479-486) and Sporting News All-Stars (566 to 589). The usual last series scarcity (523 to 589) exists. The set actually totals 587 cards since numbers 587 and 588 were never issued.

| | MINT | VG-E | F-G |
|---|---|---|---|
| COMPLETE SET | 1400.00 | 600.00 | 150.00 |
| COMMON PLAYER (1-370) | .35 | .14 | .03 |
| COMMON PLAYER (371-522) | .50 | .20 | .05 |
| COMMON PLAYER (523-565) | 7.00 | 2.80 | .70 |
| COMMON PLAYER (566-589) | 8.00 | 3.25 | .80 |
| ☐ 1 Dick Groat | 3.00 | .50 | .10 |
| ☐ 2 Roger Maris | 16.00 | 6.50 | 1.60 |

| | | | | |
|---|---|---|---|---|
| ☐ | 3 | John Buzhardt | .35 | .14 | .03 |

| ☐ | 3 | John Buzhardt | .35 | .14 | .03 |
|---|---|---|---|---|---|
| ☐ | 4 | Lenny Green | .35 | .14 | .03 |
| ☐ | 5 | John Romano | .35 | .14 | .03 |
| ☐ | 6 | Ed Roebuck | .35 | .14 | .03 |
| ☐ | 7 | White Sox Team | 1.00 | .40 | .10 |
| ☐ | 8 | Dick Williams | .50 | .20 | .05 |
| ☐ | 9 | Bob Purkey | .35 | .14 | .03 |
| ☐ | 10 | Brooks Robinson | 7.50 | 3.00 | .75 |
| ☐ | 11 | Curt Simmons | .50 | .20 | .05 |
| ☐ | 12 | Moe Thacker | .35 | .14 | .03 |
| ☐ | 13 | Chuck Cottier | .50 | .20 | .05 |
| ☐ | 14 | Don Mossi | .50 | .20 | .05 |
| ☐ | 15 | Willie Kirkland | .35 | .14 | .03 |
| ☐ | 16 | Billy Muffett | .35 | .14 | .03 |
| ☐ | 17 | Checklist 1 | 3.00 | .30 | .06 |
| ☐ | 18 | Jim Grant | .35 | .14 | .03 |
| ☐ | 19 | Cletis Boyer | .75 | .30 | .07 |
| ☐ | 20 | Robin Roberts | 3.50 | 1.40 | .35 |
| ☐ | 21 | Zorro Versalles | .50 | .20 | .05 |
| ☐ | 22 | Clem Labine | .50 | .20 | .05 |
| ☐ | 23 | Don Demeter | .35 | .14 | .03 |
| ☐ | 24 | Ken Johnson | .35 | .14 | .03 |
| ☐ | 25 | Reds' Heavy Artillery | 1.50 | .60 | .15 |
| | | Vada Pinson | | | |
| | | Gus Bell | | | |
| | | Frank Robinson | | | |
| ☐ | 26 | Wes Stock | .35 | .14 | .03 |
| ☐ | 27 | Jerry Kindall | .35 | .14 | .03 |
| ☐ | 28 | Hector Lopez | .35 | .14 | .03 |
| ☐ | 29 | Don Nottebart | .35 | .14 | .03 |
| ☐ | 30 | Nellie Fox | 1.75 | .70 | .17 |
| ☐ | 31 | Bob Schmidt | .35 | .14 | .03 |
| ☐ | 32 | Ray Sadecki | .35 | .14 | .03 |
| ☐ | 33 | Gary Geiger | .35 | .14 | .03 |
| ☐ | 34 | Wynn Hawkins | .35 | .14 | .03 |
| ☐ | 35 | Ron Santo | 2.50 | 1.00 | .25 |
| ☐ | 36 | Jack Kralick | .35 | .14 | .03 |
| ☐ | 37 | Charley Maxwell | .35 | .14 | .03 |
| ☐ | 38 | Bob Lillis | .50 | .20 | .05 |
| ☐ | 39 | Leo Posada | .35 | .14 | .03 |
| ☐ | 40 | Bob Turley | .75 | .30 | .07 |
| ☐ | 41 | NL Batting Leaders | 1.50 | .60 | .15 |
| | | Dick Groat | | | |
| | | Norm Larker | | | |
| | | Willie Mays | | | |
| | | Roberto Clemente | | | |
| ☐ | 42 | AL Batting Leaders | 1.00 | .40 | .10 |
| | | Pete Runnels | | | |
| | | Al Smith | | | |
| | | Minnie Minoso | | | |
| | | Bill Skowron | | | |
| ☐ | 43 | NL Home Run Leaders | 2.00 | .80 | .20 |
| | | Ernie Banks | | | |
| | | Hank Aaron | | | |
| | | Ed Mathews | | | |
| | | Ken Boyer | | | |
| ☐ | 44 | AL Home Run Leaders | 3.00 | 1.20 | .30 |
| | | Mickey Mantle | | | |
| | | Roger Maris | | | |
| | | Jim Lemon | | | |
| | | Rocky Colavito | | | |
| ☐ | 45 | NL ERA Leaders | 1.00 | .40 | .10 |
| | | Mike McCormick | | | |
| | | Ernie Broglio | | | |
| | | Don Drysdale | | | |
| | | Bob Friend | | | |
| | | Stan Williams | | | |
| ☐ | 46 | AL ERA Leaders | 1.00 | .40 | .10 |
| | | Frank Baumann | | | |
| | | Jim Bunning | | | |
| | | Art Ditmar | | | |
| | | H. Brown | | | |
| ☐ | 47 | NL Pitching Leaders | 1.00 | .40 | .10 |
| | | Ernie Broglio | | | |
| | | Warren Spahn | | | |
| | | Vern Law | | | |
| | | Lou Burdette | | | |
| ☐ | 48 | AL Pitching Leaders | 1.00 | .40 | .10 |
| | | Chuck Estrada | | | |
| | | Jim Perry | | | |
| | | Bud Daley | | | |
| | | Art Ditmar | | | |
| | | Frank Lary | | | |
| | | Milt Pappas | | | |
| ☐ | 49 | NL Strikeout Leaders | 1.50 | .60 | .15 |
| | | Don Drysdale | | | |
| | | Sandy Koufax | | | |
| | | Sam Jones | | | |
| | | Ernie Broglio | | | |
| ☐ | 50 | AL Strikeout Leaders | 1.00 | .40 | .10 |
| | | Jim Bunning | | | |
| | | Pedro Ramos | | | |
| | | Early Wynn | | | |
| | | Frank Lary | | | |
| ☐ | 51 | Tigers Team | 1.00 | .40 | .10 |
| ☐ | 52 | George Crowe | .35 | .14 | .03 |
| ☐ | 53 | Russ Nixon | .35 | .14 | .03 |
| ☐ | 54 | Earl Francis | .35 | .14 | .03 |
| ☐ | 55 | Jim Davenport | .50 | .20 | .05 |
| ☐ | 56 | Russ Kemmerer | .35 | .14 | .03 |
| ☐ | 57 | Marv Throneberry | 1.00 | .40 | .10 |
| ☐ | 58 | Joe Schaffernoth | .35 | .14 | .03 |
| ☐ | 59 | Jim Woods | .35 | .14 | .03 |
| ☐ | 60 | Woodie Held | .35 | .14 | .03 |
| ☐ | 61 | Ron Piche | .35 | .14 | .03 |
| ☐ | 62 | Al Pilarcik | .35 | .14 | .03 |
| ☐ | 63 | Jim Kaat | 2.50 | 1.00 | .25 |
| ☐ | 64 | Alex Grammas | .35 | .14 | .03 |
| ☐ | 65 | Ted Kluszewski | 1.25 | .50 | .12 |
| ☐ | 66 | Billy Henry | .35 | .14 | .03 |
| ☐ | 67 | Ossie Virgil | .35 | .14 | .03 |
| ☐ | 68 | Deron Johnson | .35 | .14 | .03 |
| ☐ | 69 | Earl Wilson | .35 | .14 | .03 |
| ☐ | 70 | Bill Virdon | .75 | .30 | .07 |
| ☐ | 71 | Jerry Adair | .35 | .14 | .03 |
| ☐ | 72 | Stu Miller | .35 | .14 | .03 |
| ☐ | 73 | Al Spangler | .35 | .14 | .03 |
| ☐ | 74 | Joe Pignatano | .35 | .14 | .03 |
| ☐ | 75 | Lindy Shows Larry | .50 | .20 | .05 |
| | | Lindy McDaniel | | | |
| | | Larry Jackson | | | |
| ☐ | 76 | Harry Anderson | .35 | .14 | .03 |
| ☐ | 77 | Dick Stigman | .35 | .14 | .03 |
| ☐ | 78 | Lee Walls | .35 | .14 | .03 |
| ☐ | 79 | Joe Ginsberg | .35 | .14 | .03 |
| ☐ | 80 | Harmon Killebrew | 4.50 | 1.80 | .45 |
| ☐ | 81 | Tracy Stallard | .35 | .14 | .03 |
| ☐ | 82 | Joe Christopher | .35 | .14 | .03 |
| ☐ | 83 | Bob Bruce | .35 | .14 | .03 |
| ☐ | 84 | Lee Maye | .35 | .14 | .03 |
| ☐ | 85 | Jerry Walker | .35 | .14 | .03 |
| ☐ | 86 | Dodgers Team | 1.50 | .60 | .15 |
| ☐ | 87 | Joe Amalfitano | .35 | .14 | .03 |
| ☐ | 88 | Richie Ashburn | 1.75 | .70 | .17 |
| ☐ | 89 | Billy Martin | 2.00 | .80 | .20 |
| ☐ | 90 | Jerry Staley | .35 | .14 | .03 |
| ☐ | 91 | Walt Moryn | .35 | .14 | .03 |
| ☐ | 92 | Hal Naragon | .35 | .14 | .03 |
| ☐ | 93 | Tony Gonzalez | .35 | .14 | .03 |
| ☐ | 94 | John Kucks | .35 | .14 | .03 |
| ☐ | 95 | Norm Cash | 1.25 | .50 | .12 |
| ☐ | 96 | Bill O'Dell | .35 | .14 | .03 |
| ☐ | 97 | Jerry Lynch | .35 | .14 | .03 |
| ☐ | 98A | Checklist 2 | 3.00 | .30 | .06 |
| | | (red "Checklist", | | | |
| | | 98 black on white) | | | |
| ☐ | 98B | Checklist 2 | 3.00 | .30 | .06 |
| | | (yellow "Checklist", | | | |
| | | 98 black on white) | | | |
| ☐ | 98C | Checklist 2 | 3.00 | .30 | .06 |
| | | (yellow "Checklist", | | | |
| | | 98 white on black, | | | |
| | | no copyright) | | | |
| ☐ | 99 | Don Buddin | .35 | .14 | .03 |
| ☐ | 100 | Harvey Haddix | .60 | .24 | .06 |
| ☐ | 101 | Bubba Phillips | .35 | .14 | .03 |
| ☐ | 102 | Gene Stephens | .35 | .14 | .03 |
| ☐ | 103 | Ruben Amaro | .35 | .14 | .03 |
| ☐ | 104 | John Blanchard | .50 | .20 | .05 |
| ☐ | 105 | Carl Willey | .35 | .14 | .03 |
| ☐ | 106 | Whitey Herzog | 1.00 | .40 | .10 |
| ☐ | 107 | Seth Morehead | .35 | .14 | .03 |
| ☐ | 108 | Dan Dobbek | .35 | .14 | .03 |
| ☐ | 109 | John Podres | 1.25 | .50 | .12 |
| ☐ | 110 | Vada Pinson | 1.25 | .50 | .12 |
| ☐ | 111 | Jack Meyer | .35 | .14 | .03 |
| ☐ | 112 | Chico Fernandez | .35 | .14 | .03 |
| ☐ | 113 | Mike Fornieles | .35 | .14 | .03 |
| ☐ | 114 | Hobie Landrith | .35 | .14 | .03 |
| ☐ | 115 | Johnny Antonelli | .50 | .20 | .05 |
| ☐ | 116 | Joe DeMaestri | .35 | .14 | .03 |
| ☐ | 117 | Dale Long | .35 | .14 | .03 |
| ☐ | 118 | Chris Cannizzaro | .35 | .14 | .03 |
| ☐ | 119 | A's Big Armor | .50 | .20 | .05 |
| | | Norm Siebern | | | |
| | | Hank Bauer | | | |
| | | Jerry Lumpe | | | |
| ☐ | 120 | Ed Mathews | 4.00 | 1.60 | .40 |
| ☐ | 121 | Eli Grba | .35 | .14 | .03 |
| ☐ | 122 | Cubs Team | 1.00 | .40 | .10 |
| ☐ | 123 | Billy Gardner | .50 | .20 | .05 |
| ☐ | 124 | J.C. Martin | .35 | .14 | .03 |
| ☐ | 125 | Steve Barber | .35 | .14 | .03 |
| ☐ | 126 | Dick Stuart | .50 | .20 | .05 |
| ☐ | 127 | Ron Kline | .35 | .14 | .03 |
| ☐ | 128 | Rip Repulski | .35 | .14 | .03 |

| | | | | |
|---|---|---|---|---|
| ☐ 129 | Ed Hobaugh | .35 | .14 | .03 |
| ☐ 130 | Norm Larker | .35 | .14 | .03 |
| ☐ 131 | Paul Richards MGR | .50 | .20 | .05 |
| ☐ 132 | Al Lopez MGR | 1.25 | .50 | .12 |
| ☐ 133 | Ralph Houk MGR | .75 | .30 | .07 |
| ☐ 134 | Mickey Vernon MGR | .50 | .20 | .05 |
| ☐ 135 | Fred Hutchinson MGR | .50 | .20 | .05 |
| ☐ 136 | Walt Alston MGR | 1.50 | .60 | .15 |
| ☐ 137 | Chuck Dressen MGR | .50 | .20 | .05 |
| ☐ 138 | Danny Murtaugh MGR | .50 | .20 | .05 |
| ☐ 139 | Solly Hemus MGR | .35 | .14 | .03 |
| ☐ 140 | Gus Triandos | .50 | .20 | .05 |
| ☐ 141 | Billy Williams | 18.00 | 7.25 | 1.80 |
| ☐ 142 | Luis Arroyo | .50 | .20 | .05 |
| ☐ 143 | Russ Snyder | .35 | .14 | .03 |
| ☐ 144 | Jim Coker | .35 | .14 | .03 |
| ☐ 145 | Bob Buhl | .35 | .14 | .03 |
| ☐ 146 | Marty Keough | .35 | .14 | .03 |
| ☐ 147 | Ed Rakow | .35 | .14 | .03 |
| ☐ 148 | Julian Javier | .35 | .14 | .03 |
| ☐ 149 | Bob Oldis | .35 | .14 | .03 |
| ☐ 150 | Willie Mays | 25.00 | 10.00 | 2.50 |
| ☐ 151 | Jim Donohue | .35 | .14 | .03 |
| ☐ 152 | Earl Torgeson | .35 | .14 | .03 |
| ☐ 153 | Don Lee | .35 | .14 | .03 |
| ☐ 154 | Bobby Del Greco | .35 | .14 | .03 |
| ☐ 155 | John Temple | .35 | .14 | .03 |
| ☐ 156 | Ken Hunt | .35 | .14 | .03 |
| ☐ 157 | Cal McLish | .35 | .14 | .03 |
| ☐ 158 | Pete Daley | .35 | .14 | .03 |
| ☐ 159 | Orioles Team | 1.00 | .40 | .10 |
| ☐ 160 | Whitey Ford | 8.00 | 3.25 | .80 |
| ☐ 161 | Sherman Jones (photo actually Eddie Fisher) | .50 | .20 | .05 |
| ☐ 162 | Jay Hook | .35 | .14 | .03 |
| ☐ 163 | Ed Sadowski | .35 | .14 | .03 |
| ☐ 164 | Felix Mantilla | .35 | .14 | .03 |
| ☐ 165 | Gino Cimoli | .35 | .14 | .03 |
| ☐ 166 | Danny Kravitz | .35 | .14 | .03 |
| ☐ 167 | Giants Team | 1.00 | .40 | .10 |
| ☐ 168 | Tommy Davis | 1.25 | .50 | .12 |
| ☐ 169 | Don Elston | .35 | .14 | .03 |
| ☐ 170 | Al Smith | .35 | .14 | .03 |
| ☐ 171 | Paul Foytack | .35 | .14 | .03 |
| ☐ 172 | Don Dillard | .35 | .14 | .03 |
| ☐ 173 | Beantown Bombers Frank Malzone Vic Wertz Jackie Jensen | .50 | .20 | .05 |
| ☐ 174 | Ray Semproch | .35 | .14 | .03 |
| ☐ 175 | Gene Freese | .35 | .14 | .03 |
| ☐ 176 | Ken Aspromonte | .35 | .14 | .03 |
| ☐ 177 | Don Larsen | .50 | .20 | .05 |
| ☐ 178 | Bob Nieman | .35 | .14 | .03 |
| ☐ 179 | Joe Koppe | .35 | .14 | .03 |
| ☐ 180 | Bobby Richardson | 1.75 | .70 | .17 |
| ☐ 181 | Fred Green | .35 | .14 | .03 |
| ☐ 182 | Dave Nicholson | .35 | .14 | .03 |
| ☐ 183 | Andre Rodgers | .35 | .14 | .03 |
| ☐ 184 | Steve Bilko | .35 | .14 | .03 |
| ☐ 185 | Herb Score | .60 | .24 | .06 |
| ☐ 186 | Elmer Valo | .35 | .14 | .03 |
| ☐ 187 | Billy Klaus | .35 | .14 | .03 |
| ☐ 188 | Jim Marshall | .35 | .14 | .03 |
| ☐ 189 | Checklist 3 | 3.00 | .30 | .06 |
| ☐ 190 | Stan Williams | .35 | .14 | .03 |
| ☐ 191 | Mike De La Hoz | .35 | .14 | .03 |
| ☐ 192 | Dick Brown | .35 | .14 | .03 |
| ☐ 193 | Gene Conley | .35 | .14 | .03 |
| ☐ 194 | Gordy Coleman | .35 | .14 | .03 |
| ☐ 195 | Jerry Casale | .35 | .14 | .03 |
| ☐ 196 | Ed Bouchee | .35 | .14 | .03 |
| ☐ 197 | Dick Hall | .35 | .14 | .03 |
| ☐ 198 | Carl Sawatski | .35 | .14 | .03 |
| ☐ 199 | Bob Boyd | .35 | .14 | .03 |
| ☐ 200 | Warren Spahn | 5.50 | 2.20 | .55 |
| ☐ 201 | Pete Whisenant | .35 | .14 | .03 |
| ☐ 202 | Al Neiger | .35 | .14 | .03 |
| ☐ 203 | Eddie Bressoud | .35 | .14 | .03 |
| ☐ 204 | Bob Skinner | .50 | .20 | .05 |
| ☐ 205 | Bill Pierce | .75 | .30 | .07 |
| ☐ 206 | Gene Green | .35 | .14 | .03 |
| ☐ 207 | Dodger Southpaws Sandy Koufax Johnny Podres | 2.50 | 1.00 | .25 |
| ☐ 208 | Larry Osborne | .35 | .14 | .03 |
| ☐ 209 | Ken McBride | .35 | .14 | .03 |
| ☐ 210 | Pete Runnels | .50 | .20 | .05 |
| ☐ 211 | Bob Gibson | 5.50 | 2.20 | .55 |
| ☐ 212 | Haywood Sullivan | .50 | .20 | .05 |
| ☐ 213 | Billy Stafford | .50 | .20 | .05 |
| ☐ 214 | Danny Murphy | .35 | .14 | .03 |
| ☐ 215 | Gus Bell | .50 | .20 | .05 |
| ☐ 216 | Ted Bowsfield | .35 | .14 | .03 |
| ☐ 217 | Mel Roach | .35 | .14 | .03 |
| ☐ 218 | Hal Brown | .35 | .14 | .03 |
| ☐ 219 | Gene Mauch MGR | .50 | .20 | .05 |
| ☐ 220 | Al Dark MGR | .50 | .20 | .05 |
| ☐ 221 | Mike Higgins MGR | .35 | .14 | .03 |
| ☐ 222 | Jimmie Dykes MGR | .35 | .14 | .03 |
| ☐ 223 | Bob Scheffing MGR | .35 | .14 | .03 |
| ☐ 224 | Joe Gordon MGR | .35 | .14 | .03 |
| ☐ 225 | Bill Rigney MGR | .35 | .14 | .03 |
| ☐ 226 | Harry Lavagetto MGR | .35 | .14 | .03 |
| ☐ 227 | Juan Pizarro | .35 | .14 | .03 |
| ☐ 228 | Yankees Team | 5.00 | 2.00 | .50 |
| ☐ 229 | Rudy Hernandez | .35 | .14 | .03 |
| ☐ 230 | Don Hoak | .35 | .14 | .03 |
| ☐ 231 | Dick Drott | .35 | .14 | .03 |
| ☐ 232 | Bill White | .60 | .24 | .06 |
| ☐ 233 | Joe Jay | .35 | .14 | .03 |
| ☐ 234 | Ted Lepcio | .35 | .14 | .03 |
| ☐ 235 | Camilo Pascual | .50 | .20 | .05 |
| ☐ 236 | Don Gile | .35 | .14 | .03 |
| ☐ 237 | Billy Loes | .35 | .14 | .03 |
| ☐ 238 | Jim Gilliam | 1.50 | .60 | .15 |
| ☐ 239 | Dave Sisler | .35 | .14 | .03 |
| ☐ 240 | Ron Hansen | .35 | .14 | .03 |
| ☐ 241 | Al Cicotte | .35 | .14 | .03 |
| ☐ 242 | Hal Smith | .35 | .14 | .03 |
| ☐ 243 | Frank Lary | .50 | .20 | .05 |
| ☐ 244 | Chico Cardenas | .35 | .14 | .03 |
| ☐ 245 | Joe Adcock | .80 | .32 | .08 |
| ☐ 246 | Bob Davis | .35 | .14 | .03 |
| ☐ 247 | Billy Goodman | .50 | .20 | .05 |
| ☐ 248 | Ed Keegan | .35 | .14 | .03 |
| ☐ 249 | Reds Team | 1.25 | .50 | .12 |
| ☐ 250 | Buc Hill Aces: Vern Law Roy Face | .60 | .24 | .06 |
| ☐ 251 | Bill Bruton | .35 | .14 | .03 |
| ☐ 252 | Bill Short | .35 | .14 | .03 |
| ☐ 253 | Sammy Taylor | .35 | .14 | .03 |
| ☐ 254 | Ted Sadowski | .35 | .14 | .03 |
| ☐ 255 | Vic Power | .35 | .14 | .03 |
| ☐ 256 | Billy Hoeft | .35 | .14 | .03 |
| ☐ 257 | Carroll Hardy | .35 | .14 | .03 |
| ☐ 258 | Jack Sanford | .35 | .14 | .03 |
| ☐ 259 | John Schaive | .35 | .14 | .03 |
| ☐ 260 | Don Drysdale | 4.50 | 1.80 | .45 |
| ☐ 261 | Charlie Lau | .60 | .24 | .06 |
| ☐ 262 | Tony Curry | .35 | .14 | .03 |
| ☐ 263 | Ken Hamlin | .35 | .14 | .03 |
| ☐ 264 | Glen Hobbie | .35 | .14 | .03 |
| ☐ 265 | Tony Kubek | 2.25 | .90 | .22 |
| ☐ 266 | Lindy McDaniel | .35 | .14 | .03 |
| ☐ 267 | Norm Siebern | .35 | .14 | .03 |
| ☐ 268 | Ike Delock | .35 | .14 | .03 |
| ☐ 269 | Harry Chiti | .35 | .14 | .03 |
| ☐ 270 | Bob Friend | .50 | .20 | .05 |
| ☐ 271 | Jim Landis | .35 | .14 | .03 |
| ☐ 272 | Tom Morgan | .35 | .14 | .03 |
| ☐ 273 | Checklist 4 | 3.00 | .30 | .06 |
| ☐ 274 | Gary Bell | .35 | .14 | .03 |
| ☐ 275 | Gene Woodling | .50 | .20 | .05 |
| ☐ 276 | Ray Rippelmeyer | .35 | .14 | .03 |
| ☐ 277 | Hank Foiles | .35 | .14 | .03 |
| ☐ 278 | Don McMahon | .35 | .14 | .03 |
| ☐ 279 | Jose Pagan | .35 | .14 | .03 |
| ☐ 280 | Frank Howard | 1.25 | .50 | .12 |
| ☐ 281 | Frank Sullivan | .35 | .14 | .03 |
| ☐ 282 | Faye Throneberry | .35 | .14 | .03 |
| ☐ 283 | Bob Anderson | .35 | .14 | .03 |
| ☐ 284 | Dick Gernert | .35 | .14 | .03 |
| ☐ 285 | Sherm Lollar | .50 | .20 | .05 |
| ☐ 286 | George Witt | .35 | .14 | .03 |
| ☐ 287 | Carl Yastrzemski | 65.00 | 26.00 | 6.50 |
| ☐ 288 | Albie Pearson | .35 | .14 | .03 |
| ☐ 289 | Ray Moore | .35 | .14 | .03 |
| ☐ 290 | Stan Musial | 20.00 | 8.00 | 2.00 |
| ☐ 291 | Tex Clevenger | .35 | .14 | .03 |
| ☐ 292 | Jim Baumer | .50 | .20 | .05 |
| ☐ 293 | Tom Sturdivant | .35 | .14 | .03 |
| ☐ 294 | Don Blasingame | .35 | .14 | .03 |
| ☐ 295 | Milt Pappas | .60 | .24 | .06 |
| ☐ 296 | Wes Covington | .50 | .20 | .05 |
| ☐ 297 | Athletics Team | 1.00 | .40 | .10 |
| ☐ 298 | Jim Golden | .35 | .14 | .03 |
| ☐ 299 | Clay Dalrymple | .35 | .14 | .03 |
| ☐ 300 | Mickey Mantle | 75.00 | 30.00 | 7.50 |
| ☐ 301 | Chet Nichols | .35 | .14 | .03 |
| ☐ 302 | Al Heist | .35 | .14 | .03 |
| ☐ 303 | Gary Peters | .50 | .20 | .05 |
| ☐ 304 | Rocky Nelson | .35 | .14 | .03 |
| ☐ 305 | Mike McCormick | .50 | .20 | .05 |

| | | | | |
|---|---|---|---|---|
| ☐ 306 | World Series Game 1 ...... Virdon Saves Game | 1.50 | .60 | .15 |
| ☐ 307 | World Series Game 2 ...... Mantle 2 Homers | 5.00 | 2.00 | .50 |
| ☐ 308 | World Series Game 3 ...... Richardson is Hero | 1.50 | .60 | .15 |
| ☐ 309 | World Series Game 4 ...... Cimoli Safe | 1.50 | .60 | .15 |
| ☐ 310 | World Series Game 5 ...... Face Saves the Day | 1.50 | .60 | .15 |
| ☐ 311 | World Series Game 6 ...... Ford Second Shutout | 2.00 | .80 | .20 |
| ☐ 312 | World Series Game 7 ...... Mazeroski's Homer | 2.00 | .80 | .20 |
| ☐ 313 | World Series Summary ... Pirates Celebrate | 1.50 | .60 | .15 |
| ☐ 314 | Bob Miller | .35 | .14 | .03 |
| ☐ 315 | Earl Battey | .35 | .14 | .03 |
| ☐ 316 | Bobby Gene Smith | .35 | .14 | .03 |
| ☐ 317 | Jim Brewer | .35 | .14 | .03 |
| ☐ 318 | Danny O'Connell | .35 | .14 | .03 |
| ☐ 319 | Valmy Thomas | .35 | .14 | .03 |
| ☐ 320 | Lou Burdette | 1.25 | .50 | .12 |
| ☐ 321 | Marv Breeding | .35 | .14 | .03 |
| ☐ 322 | Bill Kunkel | .50 | .20 | .05 |
| ☐ 323 | Sammy Esposito | .35 | .14 | .03 |
| ☐ 324 | Hank Aguirre | .35 | .14 | .03 |
| ☐ 325 | Wally Moon | .50 | .20 | .05 |
| ☐ 326 | Dave Hillman | .35 | .14 | .03 |
| ☐ 327 | Matty Alou | 1.25 | .50 | .12 |
| ☐ 328 | Jim O'Toole | .50 | .20 | .05 |
| ☐ 329 | Julio Becquer | .35 | .14 | .03 |
| ☐ 330 | Rocky Colavito | 1.25 | .50 | .12 |
| ☐ 331 | Ned Garver | .35 | .14 | .03 |
| ☐ 332 | Dutch Dotterer (photo actually Tommy Dotterer Dutch's brother) | .50 | .20 | .05 |
| ☐ 333 | Fritz Brickell | .35 | .14 | .03 |
| ☐ 334 | Walt Bond | .35 | .14 | .03 |
| ☐ 335 | Frank Bolling | .35 | .14 | .03 |
| ☐ 336 | Don Mincher | .50 | .20 | .05 |
| ☐ 337 | Al's Aces Early Wynn Al Lopez Herb Score | 1.50 | .60 | .15 |
| ☐ 338 | Don Landrum | .35 | .14 | .03 |
| ☐ 339 | Gene Baker | .35 | .14 | .03 |
| ☐ 340 | Vic Wertz | .50 | .20 | .05 |
| ☐ 341 | Jim Owens | .35 | .14 | .03 |
| ☐ 342 | Clint Courtney | .35 | .14 | .03 |
| ☐ 343 | Earl Robinson | .35 | .14 | .03 |
| ☐ 344 | Sandy Koufax | 15.00 | 6.00 | 1.50 |
| ☐ 345 | Jim Piersall | .80 | .32 | .08 |
| ☐ 346 | Howie Nunn | .35 | .14 | .03 |
| ☐ 347 | Cardinals Team | 1.00 | .40 | .10 |
| ☐ 348 | Steve Boros | .50 | .20 | .05 |
| ☐ 349 | Danny McDevitt | .35 | .14 | .03 |
| ☐ 350 | Ernie Banks | 6.00 | 2.40 | .60 |
| ☐ 351 | Jim King | .35 | .14 | .03 |
| ☐ 352 | Bob Shaw | .35 | .14 | .03 |
| ☐ 353 | Howie Bedell | .35 | .14 | .03 |
| ☐ 354 | Billy Harrell | .35 | .14 | .03 |
| ☐ 355 | Bob Allison | .60 | .24 | .06 |
| ☐ 356 | Ryne Duren | .75 | .30 | .07 |
| ☐ 357 | Daryl Spencer | .35 | .14 | .03 |
| ☐ 358 | Earl Averill | .35 | .14 | .03 |
| ☐ 359 | Dallas Green | .75 | .30 | .07 |
| ☐ 360 | Frank Robinson | 10.00 | 4.00 | 1.00 |
| ☐ 361A | Checklist 5 (no ad on back) | 3.00 | .30 | .06 |
| ☐ 361B | Checklist 5 (Special Feature ad on back) | 6.00 | .60 | .10 |
| ☐ 362 | Frank Funk | .35 | .14 | .03 |
| ☐ 363 | John Roseboro | .50 | .20 | .05 |
| ☐ 364 | Moe Drabowsky | .35 | .14 | .03 |
| ☐ 365 | Jerry Lumpe | .35 | .14 | .03 |
| ☐ 366 | Eddie Fisher | .35 | .14 | .03 |
| ☐ 367 | Jim Rivera | .35 | .14 | .03 |
| ☐ 368 | Bennie Daniels | .35 | .14 | .03 |
| ☐ 369 | Dave Philley | .35 | .14 | .03 |
| ☐ 370 | Roy Face | .80 | .32 | .08 |
| ☐ 371 | Bill Skowron | 2.00 | .80 | .20 |
| ☐ 372 | Bob Hendley | .50 | .20 | .05 |
| ☐ 373 | Red Sox Team | 1.25 | .50 | .12 |
| ☐ 374 | Paul Giel | .50 | .20 | .05 |
| ☐ 375 | Ken Boyer | 2.00 | .80 | .20 |
| ☐ 376 | Mike Roarke | .50 | .20 | .05 |
| ☐ 377 | Ruben Gomez | .50 | .20 | .05 |
| ☐ 378 | Wally Post | .50 | .20 | .05 |
| ☐ 379 | Bobby Shantz | 1.00 | .40 | .10 |
| ☐ 380 | Minnie Minoso | 1.25 | .50 | .12 |

| | | | | |
|---|---|---|---|---|
| ☐ 381 | Dave Wickersham | .50 | .20 | .05 |
| ☐ 382 | Frank Thomas | .60 | .24 | .06 |
| ☐ 383 | Frisco First Liners Mike McCormick Jack Sanford Billy O'Dell | .60 | .24 | .06 |
| ☐ 384 | Chuck Essegian | .50 | .20 | .05 |
| ☐ 385 | Jim Perry | .80 | .32 | .08 |
| ☐ 386 | Joe Hicks | .50 | .20 | .05 |
| ☐ 387 | Duke Maas | .50 | .20 | .05 |
| ☐ 388 | Bob Clemente | 15.00 | 6.00 | 1.50 |
| ☐ 389 | Ralph Terry | .80 | .32 | .08 |
| ☐ 390 | Del Crandall | .60 | .24 | .06 |
| ☐ 391 | Winston Brown | .50 | .20 | .05 |
| ☐ 392 | Reno Bertoia | .50 | .20 | .05 |
| ☐ 393 | Batter Bafflers Don Cardwell Glen Hobbie | .60 | .24 | .06 |
| ☐ 394 | Ken Walters | .50 | .20 | .05 |
| ☐ 395 | Chuck Estrada | .60 | .24 | .06 |
| ☐ 396 | Bob Aspromonte | .50 | .20 | .05 |
| ☐ 397 | Hal Woodeshick | .50 | .20 | .05 |
| ☐ 398 | Hank Bauer | .80 | .32 | .08 |
| ☐ 399 | Cliff Cook | .50 | .20 | .05 |
| ☐ 400 | Vern Law | .80 | .32 | .08 |
| ☐ 401 | Ruth 60th Homer | 6.00 | 2.40 | .60 |
| ☐ 402 | Perfect Game (Larsen) | 2.00 | .80 | .20 |
| ☐ 403 | 26 Inning Tie | .80 | .32 | .08 |
| ☐ 404 | Hornsby .424 Average | 1.50 | .60 | .15 |
| ☐ 405 | Gehrig's Streak | 4.00 | 1.60 | .40 |
| ☐ 406 | Mantle 565 Ft. Homer | 6.00 | 2.40 | .60 |
| ☐ 407 | Chesbro Wins 41 | .80 | .32 | .08 |
| ☐ 408 | Mathewson Fans 267 | 2.00 | .80 | .20 |
| ☐ 409 | Johnson Shutouts | 2.00 | .80 | .20 |
| ☐ 410 | Haddix 12 Perfect Innings | 1.00 | .40 | .10 |
| ☐ 411 | Tony Taylor | .50 | .20 | .05 |
| ☐ 412 | Larry Sherry | .75 | .30 | .07 |
| ☐ 413 | Eddie Yost | .50 | .20 | .05 |
| ☐ 414 | Dick Donovan | .50 | .20 | .05 |
| ☐ 415 | Hank Aaron | 30.00 | 12.00 | 3.00 |
| ☐ 416 | Dick Howser | 2.00 | .80 | .20 |
| ☐ 417 | Juan Marichal | 36.00 | 15.00 | 3.60 |
| ☐ 418 | Ed Bailey | .50 | .20 | .05 |
| ☐ 419 | Tom Borland | .50 | .20 | .05 |
| ☐ 420 | Ernie Broglio | .60 | .24 | .06 |
| ☐ 421 | Ty Cline | .50 | .20 | .05 |
| ☐ 422 | Bud Daley | .50 | .20 | .05 |
| ☐ 423 | Charlie Neal | .60 | .24 | .06 |
| ☐ 424 | Turk Lown | .50 | .20 | .05 |
| ☐ 425 | Yogi Berra | 10.00 | 4.00 | 1.00 |
| ☐ 426 | Braves Team (back numbered 463) | 4.00 | 1.60 | .40 |
| ☐ 427 | Dick Ellsworth | .75 | .30 | .07 |
| ☐ 428 | Ray Barker | .50 | .20 | .05 |
| ☐ 429 | Al Kaline | 8.00 | 3.25 | .80 |
| ☐ 430 | Bill Mazeroski | 1.75 | .70 | .17 |
| ☐ 431 | Chuck Stobbs | .50 | .20 | .05 |
| ☐ 432 | Coot Veal | .50 | .20 | .05 |
| ☐ 433 | Art Mahaffey | .50 | .20 | .05 |
| ☐ 434 | Tom Brewer | .50 | .20 | .05 |
| ☐ 435 | Orlando Cepeda | 2.00 | .80 | .20 |
| ☐ 436 | Jim Maloney | 1.25 | .50 | .12 |
| ☐ 437 | Checklist 6 | 3.00 | .60 | .10 |
| ☐ 438 | Curt Flood | 1.00 | .40 | .10 |
| ☐ 439 | Phil Regan | .60 | .24 | .06 |
| ☐ 440 | Luis Aparicio | 3.50 | 1.40 | .35 |
| ☐ 441 | Dick Bertell | .50 | .20 | .05 |
| ☐ 442 | Gordon Jones | .50 | .20 | .05 |
| ☐ 443 | Duke Snider | 9.00 | 3.75 | .90 |
| ☐ 444 | Joe Nuxhall | .60 | .24 | .06 |
| ☐ 445 | Frank Malzone | .60 | .24 | .06 |
| ☐ 446 | Bob Taylor | .50 | .20 | .05 |
| ☐ 447 | Harry Bright | .50 | .20 | .05 |
| ☐ 448 | Del Rice | .50 | .20 | .05 |
| ☐ 449 | Bob Bolin | .50 | .20 | .05 |
| ☐ 450 | Jim Lemon | .60 | .24 | .06 |
| ☐ 451 | Power for Ernie Daryl Spencer Bill White Ernie Broglio | .60 | .24 | .06 |
| ☐ 452 | Bob Allen | .50 | .20 | .05 |
| ☐ 453 | Dick Schofield | .50 | .20 | .05 |
| ☐ 454 | Pumpsie Green | .50 | .20 | .05 |
| ☐ 455 | Early Wynn | 3.50 | 1.40 | .35 |
| ☐ 456 | Hal Bevan | .50 | .20 | .05 |
| ☐ 457 | John James | .50 | .20 | .05 |
| ☐ 458 | Willie Tasby | .50 | .20 | .05 |
| ☐ 459 | Terry Fox | .50 | .20 | .05 |
| ☐ 460 | Gil Hodges | 4.00 | 1.60 | .40 |
| ☐ 461 | Smoky Burgess | .60 | .24 | .06 |
| ☐ 462 | Lou Klimchock | .50 | .20 | .05 |
| ☐ 463 | Jack Fisher | .60 | .24 | .06 |

# — SUPERSTAR SALE —

**ALL STAR CARDS VG CONDITION**      Please List Second Choices

| | 1959 | 1960 | 1961 | 1962 | 1963 | 1964 | 1965 | 1966 | 1967 | 1968 | 1969 | 1970 | 1971 | 1972 | 1973 |
|---|---|---|---|---|---|---|---|---|---|---|---|---|---|---|---|
| AARON | 12.00 | 9.00 | 10.00 | 12.00 | 20.00 | 9.00 | 9.00 | 9.00 | 7.00 | 6.00 | 6.00 | 5.50 | 5.00 | 4.00 | 4.00 |
| BANKS | 4.75 | 4.00 | 3.00 | 3.00 | 5.00 | 3.00 | 6.00 | 2.50 | 2.25 | 2.00 | 1.75 | 3.50 | 3.00 | | |
| BENCH | | | | | | | | | | 25.00 | 8.00 | 25.00 | 4.00 | 3.50 | 3.00 |
| BERRA | 6.50 | 6.00 | 4.75 | 4.50 | 6.50 | 4.50 | 5.00 | | | | | | | | |
| BROCK | | | | 17.00 | 22.00 | 5.00 | 5.50 | 2.75 | 2.50 | 3.00 | 2.75 | 2.50 | 3.00 | 1.50 | 1.25 |
| CAREW | | | | | | | | | 55.00 | 11.00 | 8.00 | 4.50 | 3.50 | 25.00 | 2.75 |
| CARLTON | | | | | | | 50.00 | | 13.00 | 10.00 | 10.00 | 5.00 | 4.50 | 3.50 | 3.50 |
| CLEMENTE | 8.50 | 6.00 | 6.00 | 5.00 | 23.00 | 5.50 | 4.50 | 4.25 | 4.75 | 3.75 | 3.50 | 4.00 | 4.00 | 3.00 | 2.75 |
| DRYSDALE | 3.50 | 3.00 | 2.75 | 3.50 | 4.00 | 2.50 | 2.50 | 2.50 | 1.75 | 1.75 | 1.75 | | | | |
| FORD | 3.25 | 2.75 | 2.75 | 2.75 | 3.75 | 2.75 | 2.00 | 2.00 | 1.50 | | | | 17.00 | 30.00 | 2.50 |
| GARVEY | | | | | | | | | | | | | | | |
| GIBSON | 20.00 | 2.75 | 2.50 | 14.50 | 4.50 | 3.00 | 2.25 | 2.25 | 2.00 | 2.00 | 1.50 | 1.50 | 1.60 | 1.25 | 1.25 |
| HODGES | 3.00 | 2.50 | 2.00 | 1.75 | 1.75 | 2.00 | | 1.50 | 1.50 | 1.25 | 1.25 | 1.25 | 1.00 | 1.00 | |
| HUNTER | | | | | | | 5.50 | 1.25 | 1.25 | 1.25 | | | | | |
| JACKSON | | | | | | | | | | | 40.00 | 8.50 | 5.50 | 4.75 | 3.75 |
| KALINE | 4.00 | 3.50 | 3.25 | 2.75 | 2.75 | 2.50 | 2.50 | 2.50 | 2.00 | 1.75 | 1.50 | 5.00 | 1.75 | 2.75 | 1.75 |
| KILLEBREW | 9.50 | 2.50 | 1.75 | 1.75 | 9.00 | 2.00 | 1.75 | 3.00 | 3.00 | 1.25 | 1.00 | 1.25 | 2.00 | 1.00 | .75 |
| KOUFAX | 10.00 | 6.50 | 6.50 | 6.50 | 11.50 | 8.00 | 9.00 | 6.00 | | | | | | | |
| MANTLE | 35.00 | 25.00 | 25.00 | 25.00 | 25.00 | 20.00 | 23.00 | 18.00 | 17.00 | 22.00 | 22.00 | | | | |
| MARIS | 6.00 | 6.50 | 7.00 | 9.50 | 3.75 | 3.50 | 3.50 | 3.50 | 2.50 | 2.50 | | | | | |
| MATHEWS | 3.25 | 2.25 | 2.00 | 1.75 | 2.00 | 1.75 | 2.00 | 2.00 | 1.75 | 1.75 | | | | | |
| MAYS | 12.00 | 9.50 | 8.50 | 12.00 | 16.00 | 9.00 | 10.00 | 10.00 | 7.50 | 6.00 | 6.00 | 6.50 | 3.50 | 3.50 | |
| McCOVEY | | 16.00 | 4.25 | 15.00 | 15.00 | 2.50 | 2.25 | 20.00 | 2.50 | 2.00 | 2.75 | 1.75 | 1.50 | 1.50 | .75 |
| MORGAN | | | | | | | 7.50 | 2.50 | 1.50 | 1.25 | 1.25 | 2.00 | 1.00 | 1.00 | |
| MUNSON | | | | | | | | | | | | 10.00 | 3.50 | 2.75 | 2.00 |
| MUSIAL | 9.00 | 7.00 | 7.00 | 7.00 | 7.25 | | | | | | | | | | |
| PALMER | | | | | | | 14.00 | | 3.75 | 3.75 | 3.75 | 2.00 | 2.00 | 1.25 | 1.00 |
| PERRY | | | | 14.00 | 3.50 | 3.50 | 2.00 | 25.00 | 2.00 | 1.50 | 2.00 | 1.75 | 1.30 | 1.00 | 1.00 |
| ROBERTS | 2.00 | 2.00 | 1.50 | 1.50 | 1.50 | 1.25 | 1.25 | 6.00 | | | | | | | |
| B. ROBINSON | 5.00 | 3.00 | 2.75 | 2.50 | 4.25 | 3.00 | 2.75 | 2.75 | 50.00 | 1.75 | 2.75 | 1.75 | 1.75 | 2.75 | 1.50 |
| F. ROBINSON | 5.00 | 3.00 | 3.00 | 2.75 | 4.50 | 2.75 | 3.00 | 2.75 | 2.50 | 3.00 | 3.00 | 5.00 | 2.75 | 1.50 | 1.50 |
| ROSE | | | | | P.O.R. | 60.00 | 50.00 | 19.00 | 22.00 | 16.00 | 15.00 | 25.00 | 11.00 | 20.00 | 7.50 |
| RYAN | | | | | | | | | | 30.00 | 8.00 | 8.50 | 4.00 | 4.25 | 2.25 |
| SEAVER | | | | | | | | | P.O.R. | 10.00 | 8.00 | 5.00 | 4.00 | 2.75 | |
| SNIDER | 5.00 | 4.50 | 3.50 | 4.00 | 10.00 | 3.25 | | | | | | | | | |
| SPAHN | 3.75 | 2.75 | 2.75 | 2.75 | 3.75 | 3.75 | 2.75 | | | | | | | | |
| STARGELL | | | | | P.O.R. | 4.50 | 2.75 | 2.25 | 2.00 | 2.00 | 2.25 | 1.50 | 1.50 | 1.25 | 1.25 |
| YASTRZEMSKI | | 45.00 | 25.00 | 50.00 | 14.00 | 14.00 | 14.00 | 12.50 | 12.00 | 7.50 | 7.50 | 5.00 | 6.00 | 4.00 | 3.50 |

**SportsCards Plus**

**14038M Beach Blvd.**
**Westminster, CA 92683**
**(714) 895-4401**

★★★★★★★★★★★
**FREE 1987 illustrated catalog is now available. Included in it is a variety of material, 1950s-1980s, including stars, complete sets, unopened material, rookie cards, Hartlands, bulk lots, etc. Please send two 22 cent stamps. Free with any order from this ad.**
★★★★★★★★★★★

AMERICAN EXPRESS CARDS   VISA   MasterCard

**PLACING ORDERS**
Please list second choices. All cards very good condition. Minimum order $5.00. You may telephone your order

8 a.m.–11 p.m., 7 days a week. We accept VISA, MasterCard, & American Express. Postage/handling $1.95. All orders fully guaranteed!

## BARGAIN SALE

For collectors who are not particularly concerned with condition, we offer the following groups of Topps baseball cards at prices substantially below market values. Condition varies from Good to Very Good or better. All cards are our choice.

### 100 ASSORTED

| | |
|---|---|
| 1959 | 17.00 |
| 1960 | 12.00 |
| 1961 | 12.00 |
| 1962 | 12.00 |
| 1963 | 12.00 |
| 1964 | 10.00 |
| 1965 | 10.00 |
| 1966 | 9.00 |
| 1967 | 9.00 |
| 1968 | 9.00 |
| 1969 | 7.00 |
| 1970 | 7.00 |
| 1971 | 7.00 |
| 1972 | 6.00 |
| 1973 | 6.00 |
| 1974 | 6.00 |
| 1975 | 6.00 |
| 1976 | 6.00 |
| 1977 | 5.00 |
| 1,000 assorted 1960-1969, G-VG | 95.00 |
| 700 assorted 1970-1976, G-VG | 38.00 |

### T-206 Tobacco Cards 1909-1911
All Cards G-VG or Better
(original over 75 years old)

| | |
|---|---|
| 1 Card | 5.00 |
| 5 diff. | 22.50 |
| 10 diff. | 40.00 |

## BUYING

We will pay cash for the following:

1. COLLECTIONS: This includes Topps and Bowman as well as pre-1950 cards, Goudeys, Diamond Stars, Leafs, tobacco cards, Play Balls, and regionals such as Kahn's and Red Hearts.

2. STAR CARDS: All cards of major stars, including Mantle, Berra, Rose, Aaron, Mays, Musial, Clemente, T. Williams, Garvey, Banks, Koufax, Snider, Yaz, etc. We buy cards in **EX-MT** and VG condition.

3. COMPLETE BASEBALL SETS: From 1948-1983 and any earlier issues. Topps, Bowman, regionals, etc. We will buy EX-MT sets in all years and VG-EX sets through 1972.

4. UNOPENED BOXES & CASES: All years and all sports.

5. FOOTBALL, BASKETBALL, HOCKEY SETS: 1950-1975.

6. ALL HARTLAND STATUES & PRESS PINS: EX-MT.

7. TOPPS, BOWMAN, FLEER, ETC. COMMONS & HIGH NUMBERS: Before 1970 in **EX-MT and also in VG-EX.**

We have ample cash on hand to finance any purchase. All transactions are held in strictest confidence. Please call (714) 895-4401 or write if you are interested in selling any cards. Bank credit, and hobby references always available.

*"Serving Collectors and Investors Since 1979"*

(See also 426)

| | | MINT | VG-E | F-G |
|---|---|---|---|---|
| ☐ 464 | Leroy Thomas | .50 | .20 | .05 |
| ☐ 465 | Roy McMillan | .50 | .20 | .05 |
| ☐ 466 | Ron Moeller | .50 | .20 | .05 |
| ☐ 467 | Indians Team | 1.00 | .40 | .10 |
| ☐ 468 | John Callison | .60 | .24 | .06 |
| ☐ 469 | Ralph Lumenti | .50 | .20 | .05 |
| ☐ 470 | Roy Sievers | .60 | .24 | .06 |
| ☐ 471 | Phil Rizzuto MVP | 4.00 | 1.60 | .40 |
| ☐ 472 | Yogi Berra MVP | 5.00 | 2.00 | .50 |
| ☐ 473 | Bob Shantz MVP | .80 | .32 | .08 |
| ☐ 474 | Al Rosen MVP | 1.00 | .40 | .10 |
| ☐ 475 | Mickey Mantle MVP | 15.00 | 6.00 | 1.50 |
| ☐ 476 | Jackie Jensen MVP | .80 | .32 | .08 |
| ☐ 477 | Nellie Fox MVP | 1.25 | .50 | .12 |
| ☐ 478 | Roger Maris MVP | 5.00 | 2.00 | .50 |
| ☐ 479 | Jim Konstanty MVP | .80 | .32 | .08 |
| ☐ 480 | Roy Campanella MVP | 8.00 | 3.25 | .80 |
| ☐ 481 | Hank Sauer MVP | .80 | .32 | .08 |
| ☐ 482 | Willie Mays MVP | 8.00 | 3.25 | .80 |
| ☐ 483 | Don Newcombe MVP | .80 | .32 | .08 |
| ☐ 484 | Hank Aaron MVP | 8.00 | 3.25 | .80 |
| ☐ 485 | Ernie Banks MVP | 4.00 | 1.60 | .40 |
| ☐ 486 | Dick Groat MVP | .80 | .32 | .08 |
| ☐ 487 | Gene Oliver | .50 | .20 | .05 |
| ☐ 488 | Joe McClain | .50 | .20 | .05 |
| ☐ 489 | Walt Dropo | .50 | .20 | .05 |
| ☐ 490 | Jim Bunning | 2.00 | .80 | .20 |
| ☐ 491 | Phillies Team | 1.00 | .40 | .10 |
| ☐ 492 | Ron Fairly | .60 | .24 | .06 |
| ☐ 493 | Don Zimmer | .75 | .30 | .07 |
| ☐ 494 | Tom Cheney | .50 | .20 | .05 |
| ☐ 495 | Elston Howard | 2.00 | .80 | .20 |
| ☐ 496 | Ken Mackenzie | .50 | .20 | .05 |
| ☐ 497 | Willie Jones | .50 | .20 | .05 |
| ☐ 498 | Ray Herbert | .50 | .20 | .05 |
| ☐ 499 | Chuck Schilling | .50 | .20 | .05 |
| ☐ 500 | Harvey Kuenn | 1.25 | .50 | .12 |
| ☐ 501 | John DeMerit | .50 | .20 | .05 |
| ☐ 502 | Clarence Coleman | .50 | .20 | .05 |
| ☐ 503 | Tito Francona | .60 | .24 | .06 |
| ☐ 504 | Billy Consolo | .50 | .20 | .05 |
| ☐ 505 | Red Schoendienst | 1.25 | .50 | .12 |
| ☐ 506 | Willie Davis | 2.00 | .80 | .20 |
| ☐ 507 | Pete Burnside | .50 | .20 | .05 |
| ☐ 508 | Rocky Bridges | .50 | .20 | .05 |
| ☐ 509 | Camilo Carreon | .50 | .20 | .05 |
| ☐ 510 | Art Ditmar | .50 | .20 | .05 |
| ☐ 511 | Joe Morgan | .50 | .20 | .05 |
| ☐ 512 | Bob Will | .50 | .20 | .05 |
| ☐ 513 | Jim Brosnan | .60 | .24 | .06 |
| ☐ 514 | Jake Wood | .50 | .20 | .05 |
| ☐ 515 | Jackie Brandt | .50 | .20 | .05 |
| ☐ 516 | Checklist 7 | 4.00 | .80 | .15 |
| ☐ 517 | Willie McCovey | 10.00 | 4.00 | 1.00 |
| ☐ 518 | Andy Carey | .50 | .20 | .05 |
| ☐ 519 | Jim Pagliaroni | .50 | .20 | .05 |
| ☐ 520 | Joe Cunningham | .60 | .24 | .06 |
| ☐ 521 | Brother Battery<br>Norm Sherry<br>Larry Sherry | .60 | .24 | .06 |
| ☐ 522 | Dick Farrell | .50 | .20 | .05 |
| ☐ 523 | Joe Gibbon | 7.00 | 2.80 | .70 |
| ☐ 524 | John Logan | 8.00 | 3.25 | .80 |
| ☐ 525 | Ron Perranoski | 8.00 | 3.25 | .80 |
| ☐ 526 | R.C. Stevens | 7.00 | 2.80 | .70 |
| ☐ 527 | Gene Leek | 7.00 | 2.80 | .70 |
| ☐ 528 | Pedro Ramos | 7.00 | 2.80 | .70 |
| ☐ 529 | Bob Roselli | 7.00 | 2.80 | .70 |
| ☐ 530 | Bob Malkmus | 7.00 | 2.80 | .70 |
| ☐ 531 | Jim Coates | 7.00 | 2.80 | .70 |
| ☐ 532 | Bob Hale | 7.00 | 2.80 | .70 |
| ☐ 533 | Jack Curtis | 7.00 | 2.80 | .70 |
| ☐ 534 | Eddie Kasko | 7.00 | 2.80 | .70 |
| ☐ 535 | Larry Jackson | 7.00 | 2.80 | .70 |
| ☐ 536 | Bill Tuttle | 7.00 | 2.80 | .70 |
| ☐ 537 | Bobby Locke | 7.00 | 2.80 | .70 |
| ☐ 538 | Chuck Hiller | 7.00 | 2.80 | .70 |
| ☐ 539 | John Klippstein | 7.00 | 2.80 | .70 |
| ☐ 540 | Jackie Jensen | 9.00 | 3.75 | .90 |
| ☐ 541 | Roland Sheldon | 7.00 | 2.80 | .70 |
| ☐ 542 | Minnesota Twins<br>Team Card | 12.00 | 5.00 | 1.20 |
| ☐ 543 | Roger Craig | 10.00 | 4.00 | 1.00 |
| ☐ 544 | George Thomas | 7.00 | 2.80 | .70 |
| ☐ 545 | Hoyt Wilhelm | 20.00 | 8.00 | 2.00 |
| ☐ 546 | Marty Kutyna | 7.00 | 2.80 | .70 |
| ☐ 547 | Leon Wagner | 7.00 | 2.80 | .70 |
| ☐ 548 | Ted Wills | 7.00 | 2.80 | .70 |
| ☐ 549 | Hal R. Smith | 7.00 | 2.80 | .70 |
| ☐ 550 | Frank Baumann | 7.00 | 2.80 | .70 |
| ☐ 551 | George Altman | 7.00 | 2.80 | .70 |
| ☐ 552 | Jim Archer | 7.00 | 2.80 | .70 |
| ☐ 553 | Bill Fischer | 7.00 | 2.80 | .70 |
| ☐ 554 | Pirates Team | 10.00 | 4.00 | 1.00 |
| ☐ 555 | Sam Jones | 8.00 | 3.25 | .80 |
| ☐ 556 | Ken R. Hunt | 7.00 | 2.80 | .70 |
| ☐ 557 | Jose Valdivielso | 7.00 | 2.80 | .70 |
| ☐ 558 | Don Ferrarese | 7.00 | 2.80 | .70 |
| ☐ 559 | Jim Gentile | 8.00 | 3.25 | .80 |
| ☐ 560 | Barry Latman | 7.00 | 2.80 | .70 |
| ☐ 561 | Charley James | 7.00 | 2.80 | .70 |
| ☐ 562 | Bill Monbouquette | 7.00 | 2.80 | .70 |
| ☐ 563 | Bob Cerv | 8.00 | 3.25 | .80 |
| ☐ 564 | Don Cardwell | 7.00 | 2.80 | .70 |
| ☐ 565 | Felipe Alou | 8.00 | 3.25 | .80 |
| ☐ 566 | Paul Richards MGR AS | 8.00 | 3.25 | .80 |
| ☐ 567 | Danny Murtaugh MGR AS | 8.00 | 3.25 | .80 |
| ☐ 568 | Bill Skowron AS | 8.00 | 3.25 | .80 |
| ☐ 569 | Frank Herrera AS | 8.00 | 3.25 | .80 |
| ☐ 570 | Nellie Fox AS | 10.00 | 4.00 | 1.00 |
| ☐ 571 | Bill Mazeroski AS | 9.00 | 3.75 | .90 |
| ☐ 572 | Brooks Robinson AS | 24.00 | 10.00 | 2.40 |
| ☐ 573 | Ken Boyer AS | 9.00 | 3.75 | .90 |
| ☐ 574 | Luis Aparicio AS | 18.00 | 7.25 | 1.80 |
| ☐ 575 | Ernie Banks AS | 24.00 | 10.00 | 2.40 |
| ☐ 576 | Roger Maris AS | 24.00 | 10.00 | 2.40 |
| ☐ 577 | Hank Aaron AS | 60.00 | 24.00 | 6.00 |
| ☐ 578 | Mickey Mantle AS | 120.00 | 50.00 | 12.00 |
| ☐ 579 | Willie Mays AS | 60.00 | 24.00 | 6.00 |
| ☐ 580 | Al Kaline AS | 24.00 | 10.00 | 2.40 |
| ☐ 581 | Frank Robinson AS | 24.00 | 10.00 | 2.40 |
| ☐ 582 | Earl Battey AS | 8.00 | 3.25 | .80 |
| ☐ 583 | Del Crandall AS | 8.00 | 3.25 | .80 |
| ☐ 584 | Jim Perry AS | 8.00 | 3.25 | .80 |
| ☐ 585 | Bob Friend AS | 8.00 | 3.25 | .80 |
| ☐ 586 | Whitey Ford AS | 24.00 | 10.00 | 2.40 |
| ☐ 587 | Does not exist | 0.00 | 0.00 | .00 |
| ☐ 588 | Does not exist | 0.00 | 0.00 | .00 |
| ☐ 589 | Warren Spahn AS | 24.00 | 10.00 | 2.40 |

## 1962 Topps

The cards in this 598 card set measure 2 1/2" by 3 1/2". The 1962 Topps set contains a mini-series spotlighting Babe Ruth (135 to 144). Other subsets in the set include League Leaders (51-60), World Series cards (232-237), In Action cards (311-319), NL All Stars (390-399), AL All Stars (466-475), and Rookie Prospects (591-598). The second series had two distinct printings which are distinguishable by numerous color and pose variations. Card number 139 exists as A: Babe Ruth Special card, B: Hal Reniff with arms over head, or C: Hal Reniff in the same pose as card number 159. In addition, two poses exist for players depicted on card numbers 129, 132, 134, 147, 174, 176, and 190. The high number series, 523 to 598, is somewhat more difficult to obtain than other cards in the set. The set price listed does not include the pose variations (see checklist below for individual values).

| | MINT | VG-E | F-G |
|---|---|---|---|
| COMPLETE SET | 950.00 | 400.00 | 120.00 |

| | | | | |
|---|---|---|---|---|
| COMMON PLAYER (1-370) ........ | .35 | .14 | .03 |
| COMMON PLAYER (371-522) .... | .55 | .22 | .05 |
| COMMON PLAYER (523-590) .... | 2.50 | 1.00 | .25 |
| COMMON PLAYER (591-598) .... | 5.00 | 2.00 | .50 |

| | | | | | |
|---|---|---|---|---|---|
| ☐ | 1 | Roger Maris ..................... | 35.00 | 5.00 | 1.00 |
| ☐ | 2 | Jim Brosnan .................... | .50 | .20 | .05 |
| ☐ | 3 | Pete Runnels ................... | .50 | .20 | .05 |
| ☐ | 4 | John DeMerit .................. | .35 | .14 | .03 |
| ☐ | 5 | Sandy Koufax ................. | 15.00 | 6.00 | 1.50 |
| ☐ | 6 | Marv Breeding ................ | .35 | .14 | .03 |
| ☐ | 7 | Frank Thomas ................ | .50 | .20 | .05 |
| ☐ | 8 | Ray Herbert .................... | .35 | .14 | .03 |
| ☐ | 9 | Jim Davenport ................ | .50 | .20 | .05 |
| ☐ | 10 | Bob Clemente ................ | 15.00 | 6.00 | 1.50 |
| ☐ | 11 | Tom Morgan ................... | .35 | .14 | .03 |
| ☐ | 12 | Harry Craft MGR .............. | .35 | .14 | .03 |
| ☐ | 13 | Dick Howser ................... | .60 | .24 | .06 |
| ☐ | 14 | Bill White ...................... | .60 | .24 | .06 |
| ☐ | 15 | Dick Donovan ................. | .35 | .14 | .03 |
| ☐ | 16 | Darrell Johnson .............. | .35 | .14 | .03 |
| ☐ | 17 | John Callison .................. | .50 | .20 | .05 |
| ☐ | 18 | Managers' Dream: | 20.00 | 8.00 | 2.00 |
| | | Mickey Mantle | | | |
| | | Willie Mays | | | |
| ☐ | 19 | Ray Washburn ................ | .35 | .14 | .03 |
| ☐ | 20 | Rocky Colavito ................ | 1.00 | .40 | .10 |
| ☐ | 21 | Jim Kaat ....................... | 1.50 | .60 | .15 |
| ☐ | 22A | Checklist 1 COR .............. | 2.50 | .25 | .05 |
| ☐ | 22B | Checklist 1 ERR .............. | 3.50 | .35 | .07 |
| | | (121-176 on back) | | | |
| ☐ | 23 | Norm Larker ................... | .35 | .14 | .03 |
| ☐ | 24 | Tigers Team ................... | 1.00 | .40 | .10 |
| ☐ | 25 | Ernie Banks ................... | 5.00 | 2.00 | .50 |
| ☐ | 26 | Chris Cannizzaro .............. | .35 | .14 | .03 |
| ☐ | 27 | Chuck Cottier ................. | .50 | .20 | .05 |
| ☐ | 28 | Minnie Minoso ................ | 1.00 | .40 | .10 |
| ☐ | 29 | Casey Stengel MGR ......... | 4.00 | 1.60 | .40 |
| ☐ | 30 | Ed Mathews ................... | 4.00 | 1.60 | .40 |
| ☐ | 31 | Tom Tresh ..................... | 2.50 | 1.00 | .25 |
| ☐ | 32 | John Roseboro ................ | .50 | .20 | .05 |
| ☐ | 33 | Don Larsen .................... | .60 | .24 | .06 |
| ☐ | 34 | Johnny Temple ............... | .35 | .14 | .03 |
| ☐ | 35 | Don Schwall ................... | .35 | .14 | .03 |
| ☐ | 36 | Don Leppert ................... | .35 | .14 | .03 |
| ☐ | 37 | Tribe Hill Trio .................. | .50 | .20 | .05 |
| | | Barry Latman | | | |
| | | Dick Stigman | | | |
| | | Jim Perry | | | |
| ☐ | 38 | Gene Stephens ................ | .35 | .14 | .03 |
| ☐ | 39 | Joe Koppe ..................... | .35 | .14 | .03 |
| ☐ | 40 | Orlando Cepeda .............. | 1.50 | .60 | .15 |
| ☐ | 41 | Cliff Cook ...................... | .35 | .14 | .03 |
| ☐ | 42 | Jim King ....................... | .35 | .14 | .03 |
| ☐ | 43 | Dodgers Team ................ | 1.25 | .50 | .12 |
| ☐ | 44 | Don Taussig ................... | .35 | .14 | .03 |
| ☐ | 45 | Brooks Robinson .............. | 7.50 | 3.00 | .75 |
| ☐ | 46 | Jack Baldschun ............... | .35 | .14 | .03 |
| ☐ | 47 | Bob Will ....................... | .35 | .14 | .03 |
| ☐ | 48 | Ralph Terry ................... | .60 | .24 | .06 |
| ☐ | 49 | Hal Jones ...................... | .35 | .14 | .03 |
| ☐ | 50 | Stan Musial .................... | 18.00 | 7.25 | 1.80 |
| ☐ | 51 | AL Batting Leaders ......... | .80 | .32 | .08 |
| | | Norm Cash | | | |
| | | Jim Piersall | | | |
| | | Al Kaline | | | |
| | | Elston Howard | | | |
| ☐ | 52 | NL Batting Leaders ......... | 1.00 | .40 | .10 |
| | | Bob Clemente | | | |
| | | Vada Pinson | | | |
| | | Ken Boyer | | | |
| | | Wally Moon | | | |
| ☐ | 53 | AL Home Run Leaders .... | 3.50 | 1.40 | .35 |
| | | Roger Maris | | | |
| | | Mickey Mantle | | | |
| | | Jim Gentile | | | |
| | | Harmon Killebrew | | | |
| ☐ | 54 | NL Home Run Leaders ... | 1.25 | .50 | .12 |
| | | Orlando Cepeda | | | |
| | | Willie Mays | | | |
| | | Frank Robinson | | | |
| ☐ | 55 | AL ERA Leaders .............. | .80 | .32 | .08 |
| | | Dick Donovan | | | |
| | | Bill Stafford | | | |
| | | Don Mossi | | | |
| | | Milt Pappas | | | |
| ☐ | 56 | NL ERA Leaders .............. | 1.00 | .40 | .10 |
| | | Warren Spahn | | | |
| | | Jim O'Toole | | | |
| | | Curt Simmons | | | |
| | | Mike McCormick | | | |
| ☐ | 57 | AL Wins Leaders ............. | 1.00 | .40 | .10 |
| | | Whitey Ford | | | |
| | | Frank Lary | | | |
| | | Steve Barber | | | |
| | | Jim Bunning | | | |
| ☐ | 58 | NL Wins Leaders ............. | 1.00 | .40 | .10 |
| | | Warren Spahn | | | |
| | | Joe Jay | | | |
| | | Jim O'Toole | | | |
| ☐ | 59 | AL Strikeout Leaders ...... | .80 | .32 | .08 |
| | | Camilo Pascual | | | |
| | | Whitey Ford | | | |
| | | Jim Bunning | | | |
| | | Juan Pizzaro | | | |
| ☐ | 60 | NL Strikeout Leaders ...... | 1.50 | .60 | .15 |
| | | Sandy Koufax | | | |
| | | Stan Williams | | | |
| | | Don Drysdale | | | |
| | | Jim O'Toole | | | |
| ☐ | 61 | Cardinals Team ............... | 1.00 | .40 | .10 |
| ☐ | 62 | Steve Boros ................... | .50 | .20 | .05 |
| ☐ | 63 | Tony Cloninger ............... | .35 | .14 | .03 |
| ☐ | 64 | Russ Snyder ................... | .35 | .14 | .03 |
| ☐ | 65 | Bobby Richardson .......... | 1.50 | .60 | .15 |
| ☐ | 66 | Cuno Barragon ............... | .35 | .14 | .03 |
| ☐ | 67 | Harvey Haddix ................ | .50 | .20 | .05 |
| ☐ | 68 | Ken Hunt ...................... | .35 | .14 | .03 |
| ☐ | 69 | Phil Ortega .................... | .35 | .14 | .03 |
| ☐ | 70 | Harmon Killebrew ........... | 4.00 | 1.60 | .40 |
| ☐ | 71 | Dick LeMay .................... | .35 | .14 | .03 |
| ☐ | 72 | Bob's Pupils .................. | .50 | .20 | .05 |
| | | Steve Boros | | | |
| | | Bob Scheffing | | | |
| | | Jake Wood | | | |
| ☐ | 73 | Nellie Fox ..................... | 1.50 | .60 | .15 |
| ☐ | 74 | Bob Lillis ...................... | .50 | .20 | .05 |
| ☐ | 75 | Milt Pappas ................... | .50 | .20 | .05 |
| ☐ | 76 | Howie Bedell .................. | .35 | .14 | .03 |
| ☐ | 77 | Tony Taylor ................... | .35 | .14 | .03 |
| ☐ | 78 | Gene Green .................... | .35 | .14 | .03 |
| ☐ | 79 | Ed Hobaugh ................... | .35 | .14 | .03 |
| ☐ | 80 | Vada Pinson ................... | 1.00 | .40 | .10 |
| ☐ | 81 | Jim Pagliaroni ................ | .35 | .14 | .03 |
| ☐ | 82 | Deron Johnson ............... | .35 | .14 | .03 |
| ☐ | 83 | Larry Jackson ................. | .35 | .14 | .03 |
| ☐ | 84 | Lenny Green .................. | .35 | .14 | .03 |
| ☐ | 85 | Gil Hodges .................... | 3.50 | 1.40 | .35 |
| ☐ | 86 | Donn Clendenon .............. | .75 | .30 | .07 |
| ☐ | 87 | Mike Roarke .................. | .35 | .14 | .03 |
| ☐ | 88 | Ralph Houk MGR ............. | .75 | .30 | .07 |
| ☐ | 89 | Barney Schultz ............... | .35 | .14 | .03 |
| ☐ | 90 | Jim Piersall ................... | .75 | .30 | .07 |
| ☐ | 91 | J.C. Martin .................... | .35 | .14 | .03 |
| ☐ | 92 | Sam Jones ..................... | .35 | .14 | .03 |
| ☐ | 93 | John Blanchard ............... | .50 | .20 | .05 |
| ☐ | 94 | Jay Hook ...................... | .35 | .14 | .03 |
| ☐ | 95 | Don Hoak ...................... | .35 | .14 | .03 |
| ☐ | 96 | Eli Grba ........................ | .35 | .14 | .03 |
| ☐ | 97 | Tito Francona ................. | .50 | .20 | .05 |
| ☐ | 98 | Checklist 2 .................... | 2.50 | .50 | .10 |
| ☐ | 99 | John (Boog) Powell ........ | 3.00 | 1.20 | .30 |
| ☐ | 100 | Warren Spahn ................ | 5.00 | 2.00 | .50 |
| ☐ | 101 | Carroll Hardy ................. | .35 | .14 | .03 |
| ☐ | 102 | Al Schroll ...................... | .35 | .14 | .03 |
| ☐ | 103 | Don Blasingame .............. | .35 | .14 | .03 |
| ☐ | 104 | Ted Savage .................... | .35 | .14 | .03 |
| ☐ | 105 | Don Mossi ..................... | .50 | .20 | .05 |
| ☐ | 106 | Carl Sawatski ................. | .35 | .14 | .03 |
| ☐ | 107 | Mike McCormick .............. | .50 | .20 | .05 |
| ☐ | 108 | Willie Davis .................... | .75 | .30 | .07 |
| ☐ | 109 | Bob Shaw ...................... | .35 | .14 | .03 |
| ☐ | 110 | Bill Skowron .................. | 1.50 | .60 | .15 |
| ☐ | 111 | Dallas Green .................. | .50 | .20 | .05 |
| ☐ | 112 | Hank Foiles ................... | .35 | .14 | .03 |
| ☐ | 113 | White Sox Team .............. | 1.00 | .40 | .10 |
| ☐ | 114 | Howie Koplitz ................. | .35 | .14 | .03 |
| ☐ | 115 | Bob Skinner ................... | .50 | .20 | .05 |
| ☐ | 116 | Herb Score .................... | .60 | .24 | .06 |
| ☐ | 117 | Gary Geiger ................... | .35 | .14 | .03 |
| ☐ | 118 | Julian Javier .................. | .35 | .14 | .03 |
| ☐ | 119 | Danny Murphy ................ | .35 | .14 | .03 |
| ☐ | 120 | Bob Purkey .................... | .35 | .14 | .03 |
| ☐ | 121 | Billy Hitchcock MGR ........ | .35 | .14 | .03 |
| ☐ | 122 | Norm Bass ..................... | .35 | .14 | .03 |
| ☐ | 123 | Mike De La Hoz .............. | .35 | .14 | .03 |
| ☐ | 124 | Bill Pleis ....................... | .35 | .14 | .03 |
| ☐ | 125 | Gene Woodling ............... | .50 | .20 | .05 |
| ☐ | 126 | Al Cicotte ...................... | .35 | .14 | .03 |
| ☐ | 127 | Pride of A's: .................. | .50 | .20 | .05 |
| | | Norm Siebern | | | |
| | | Hank Bauer | | | |
| | | Jerry Lumpe | | | |
| ☐ | 128 | Art Fowler ..................... | .35 | .14 | .03 |
| ☐ | 129A | Lee Walls ...................... | .60 | .24 | .06 |
| | | (facing right) | | | |

| | | | | |
|---|---|---|---|---|
| ☐ 129B | Lee Walls (face left) | 6.00 | 2.40 | .60 |
| ☐ 130 | Frank Bolling | .35 | .14 | .03 |
| ☐ 131 | Pete Richert | .35 | .14 | .03 |
| ☐ 132A | Angels Team (without photo) | 1.00 | .40 | .10 |
| ☐ 132B | Angels Team (with photo) | 6.00 | 2.40 | .60 |
| ☐ 133 | Felipe Alou | .60 | .24 | .06 |
| ☐ 134A | Billy Hoeft (facing right) | .60 | .24 | .06 |
| ☐ 134B | Billy Hoeft (facing straight) | 6.00 | 2.40 | .60 |
| ☐ 135 | Babe Ruth Special 1 Babe as a boy | 4.00 | 1.60 | .40 |
| ☐ 136 | Babe Ruth Special 2 Babe Joins Yanks | 4.00 | 1.60 | .40 |
| ☐ 137 | Babe Ruth Special 3 Babe with Huggins | 4.00 | 1.60 | .40 |
| ☐ 138 | Babe Ruth Special 4 Famous Slugger | 4.00 | 1.60 | .40 |
| ☐ 139A | Babe Ruth Special 5 | 6.00 | 2.40 | .60 |
| ☐ 139B | Hal Reniff PORT | 7.50 | 3.00 | .75 |
| ☐ 139C | Hal Reniff (pitching) | 25.00 | 10.00 | 2.50 |
| ☐ 140 | Babe Ruth Special 6 Gehrig and Ruth | 5.00 | 2.00 | .50 |
| ☐ 141 | Babe Ruth Special 7 Twilight Years | 4.00 | 1.60 | .40 |
| ☐ 142 | Babe Ruth Special 8 Coaching Dodgers | 4.00 | 1.60 | .40 |
| ☐ 143 | Babe Ruth Special 9 Greatest Sports Hero | 4.00 | 1.60 | .40 |
| ☐ 144 | Babe Ruth Special 10 Farewell Speech | 4.00 | 1.60 | .40 |
| ☐ 145 | Barry Latman | .35 | .14 | .03 |
| ☐ 146 | Don Demeter | .35 | .14 | .03 |
| ☐ 147A | Bill Kunkel PORT | .60 | .24 | .06 |
| ☐ 147B | Bill Kunkel (pitching pose) | 6.00 | 2.40 | .60 |
| ☐ 148 | Wally Post | .35 | .14 | .03 |
| ☐ 149 | Bob Duliba | .35 | .14 | .03 |
| ☐ 150 | Al Kaline | 5.50 | 2.20 | .55 |
| ☐ 151 | Johnny Klippstein | .35 | .14 | .03 |
| ☐ 152 | Mickey Vernon | .50 | .20 | .05 |
| ☐ 153 | Pumpsie Green | .35 | .14 | .03 |
| ☐ 154 | Lee Thomas | .35 | .14 | .03 |
| ☐ 155 | Stu Miller | .35 | .14 | .03 |
| ☐ 156 | Merritt Ranew | .35 | .14 | .03 |
| ☐ 157 | Wes Covington | .35 | .14 | .03 |
| ☐ 158 | Braves Team | 1.00 | .40 | .10 |
| ☐ 159 | Hal Reniff | .60 | .24 | .06 |
| ☐ 160 | Dick Stuart | .60 | .24 | .06 |
| ☐ 161 | Frank Baumann | .35 | .14 | .03 |
| ☐ 162 | Sammy Drake | .35 | .14 | .03 |
| ☐ 163 | Hot Corner Guard Billy Gardner Cletis Boyer | .60 | .24 | .06 |
| ☐ 164 | Hal Naragon | .35 | .14 | .03 |
| ☐ 165 | Jackie Brandt | .35 | .14 | .03 |
| ☐ 166 | Don Lee | .35 | .14 | .03 |
| ☐ 167 | Tim McCarver | 2.50 | 1.00 | .25 |
| ☐ 168 | Leo Posada | .35 | .14 | .03 |
| ☐ 169 | Bob Cerv | .50 | .20 | .05 |
| ☐ 170 | Ron Santo | 1.25 | .50 | .12 |
| ☐ 171 | Dave Sisler | .35 | .14 | .03 |
| ☐ 172 | Fred Hutchinson MGR | .50 | .20 | .05 |
| ☐ 173 | Chico Fernandez | .35 | .14 | .03 |
| ☐ 174A | Carl Willey (capless) | .60 | .24 | .06 |
| ☐ 174B | Carl Willey (with cap) | 6.00 | 2.40 | .60 |
| ☐ 175 | Frank Howard | 1.00 | .40 | .10 |
| ☐ 176A | Eddie Yost PORT | .60 | .24 | .06 |
| ☐ 176B | Eddie Yost BATTING | 6.00 | 2.40 | .60 |
| ☐ 177 | Bobby Shantz | .60 | .24 | .06 |
| ☐ 178 | Camilo Carreon | .35 | .14 | .03 |
| ☐ 179 | Tom Sturdivant | .35 | .14 | .03 |
| ☐ 180 | Bob Allison | .50 | .20 | .05 |
| ☐ 181 | Paul Brown | .35 | .14 | .03 |
| ☐ 182 | Bob Nieman | .35 | .14 | .03 |
| ☐ 183 | Roger Craig | .60 | .24 | .06 |
| ☐ 184 | Haywood Sullivan | .50 | .20 | .05 |
| ☐ 185 | Roland Sheldon | .35 | .14 | .03 |
| ☐ 186 | Mack Jones | .35 | .14 | .03 |
| ☐ 187 | Gene Conley | .35 | .14 | .03 |
| ☐ 188 | Chuck Hiller | .35 | .14 | .03 |
| ☐ 189 | Dick Hall | .35 | .14 | .03 |
| ☐ 190A | Wally Moon PORT | .60 | .24 | .06 |
| ☐ 190B | Wally Moon BATTING | 6.00 | 2.40 | .60 |
| ☐ 191 | Jim Brewer | .35 | .14 | .03 |
| ☐ 192A | Checklist 3 (without comma) | 2.50 | .25 | .05 |

| | | | | |
|---|---|---|---|---|
| ☐ 192B | Checklist 3 (comma after Checklist) | 3.50 | .35 | .07 |
| ☐ 193 | Eddie Kasko | .35 | .14 | .03 |
| ☐ 194 | Dean Chance | .75 | .30 | .07 |
| ☐ 195 | Joe Cunningham | .35 | .14 | .03 |
| ☐ 196 | Terry Fox | .35 | .14 | .03 |
| ☐ 197 | Daryl Spencer | .35 | .14 | .03 |
| ☐ 198 | Johnny Keane MGR | .50 | .20 | .05 |
| ☐ 199 | Gaylord Perry | 30.00 | 12.00 | 3.00 |
| ☐ 200 | Mickey Mantle | 90.00 | 36.00 | 9.00 |
| ☐ 201 | Ike Delock | .35 | .14 | .03 |
| ☐ 202 | Carl Warwick | .35 | .14 | .03 |
| ☐ 203 | Jack Fisher | .35 | .14 | .03 |
| ☐ 204 | Johnny Weekly | .35 | .14 | .03 |
| ☐ 205 | Gene Freese | .35 | .14 | .03 |
| ☐ 206 | Senators Team | .90 | .36 | .09 |
| ☐ 207 | Pete Burnside | .35 | .14 | .03 |
| ☐ 208 | Billy Martin | 2.00 | .80 | .20 |
| ☐ 209 | Jim Fregosi | 2.50 | 1.00 | .25 |
| ☐ 210 | Roy Face | .75 | .30 | .07 |
| ☐ 211 | Midway Masters: Frank Bolling Roy McMillan | .50 | .20 | .05 |
| ☐ 212 | Jim Owens | .35 | .14 | .03 |
| ☐ 213 | Richie Ashburn | 1.25 | .50 | .12 |
| ☐ 214 | Dom Zanni | .35 | .14 | .03 |
| ☐ 215 | Woody Held | .35 | .14 | .03 |
| ☐ 216 | Ron Kline | .35 | .14 | .03 |
| ☐ 217 | Walt Alston MGR | 1.25 | .50 | .12 |
| ☐ 218 | Joe Torre | 5.00 | 2.00 | .50 |
| ☐ 219 | Al Downing | .60 | .24 | .06 |
| ☐ 220 | Roy Sievers | .50 | .20 | .05 |
| ☐ 221 | Bill Short | .35 | .14 | .03 |
| ☐ 222 | Jerry Zimmerman | .35 | .14 | .03 |
| ☐ 223 | Alex Grammas | .35 | .14 | .03 |
| ☐ 224 | Don Rudolph | .35 | .14 | .03 |
| ☐ 225 | Frank Malzone | .50 | .20 | .05 |
| ☐ 226 | Giants Team | 1.00 | .40 | .10 |
| ☐ 227 | Bob Tiefenauer | .35 | .14 | .03 |
| ☐ 228 | Dale Long | .35 | .14 | .03 |
| ☐ 229 | Jesus McFarlane | .35 | .14 | .03 |
| ☐ 230 | Camilo Pascual | .50 | .20 | .05 |
| ☐ 231 | Ernie Bowman | .35 | .14 | .03 |
| ☐ 232 | World Series Game 1 Yanks win opener | 1.25 | .50 | .12 |
| ☐ 233 | World Series Game 2 Jay ties it up | 1.25 | .50 | .12 |
| ☐ 234 | World Series Game 3 Maris wins in 9th | 2.50 | 1.00 | .25 |
| ☐ 235 | World Series Game 4 Ford sets new mark | 2.50 | 1.00 | .25 |
| ☐ 236 | World Series Game 5 Yanks crush Reds | 1.25 | .50 | .12 |
| ☐ 237 | World Series Summary Yanks celebrate | 1.25 | .50 | .12 |
| ☐ 238 | Norm Sherry | .50 | .20 | .05 |
| ☐ 239 | Cecil Butler | .35 | .14 | .03 |
| ☐ 240 | George Altman | .35 | .14 | .03 |
| ☐ 241 | Johnny Kucks | .35 | .14 | .03 |
| ☐ 242 | Mel McGaha | .35 | .14 | .03 |
| ☐ 243 | Robin Roberts | 3.00 | 1.20 | .30 |
| ☐ 244 | Don Gile | .35 | .14 | .03 |
| ☐ 245 | Ron Hansen | .35 | .14 | .03 |
| ☐ 246 | Art Ditmar | .35 | .14 | .03 |
| ☐ 247 | Joe Pignatano | .35 | .14 | .03 |
| ☐ 248 | Bob Aspromonte | .35 | .14 | .03 |
| ☐ 249 | Ed Keegan | .35 | .14 | .03 |
| ☐ 250 | Norm Cash | 1.00 | .40 | .10 |
| ☐ 251 | New York Yankees Team Card | 4.00 | 1.60 | .40 |
| ☐ 252 | Earl Francis | .35 | .14 | .03 |
| ☐ 253 | Harry Chiti | .35 | .14 | .03 |
| ☐ 254 | Gordon Windhorn | .35 | .14 | .03 |
| ☐ 255 | Juan Pizarro | .35 | .14 | .03 |
| ☐ 256 | Elio Chacon | .35 | .14 | .03 |
| ☐ 257 | Jack Spring | .35 | .14 | .03 |
| ☐ 258 | Marty Keough | .35 | .14 | .03 |
| ☐ 259 | Lou Klimchock | .35 | .14 | .03 |
| ☐ 260 | Bill Pierce | .75 | .30 | .07 |
| ☐ 261 | George Alusik | .35 | .14 | .03 |
| ☐ 262 | Bob Schmidt | .35 | .14 | .03 |
| ☐ 263 | The Right Pitch Bob Purkey Jim Turner Joe Jay | .50 | .20 | .05 |
| ☐ 264 | Dick Ellsworth | .50 | .20 | .05 |
| ☐ 265 | Joe Adcock | .75 | .30 | .07 |
| ☐ 266 | John Anderson | .35 | .14 | .03 |
| ☐ 267 | Dan Dobbek | .35 | .14 | .03 |
| ☐ 268 | Ken McBride | .35 | .14 | .03 |
| ☐ 269 | Bob Oldis | .35 | .14 | .03 |
| ☐ 270 | Dick Groat | .90 | .36 | .09 |

| # | Player | | | |
|---|--------|------|------|------|
| ☐ 271 | Ray Rippelmeyer | .35 | .14 | .03 |
| ☐ 272 | Earl Robinson | .35 | .14 | .03 |
| ☐ 273 | Gary Bell | .35 | .14 | .03 |
| ☐ 274 | Sammy Taylor | .35 | .14 | .03 |
| ☐ 275 | Norm Siebern | .35 | .14 | .03 |
| ☐ 276 | Hal Kolstad | .35 | .14 | .03 |
| ☐ 277 | Checklist 4 | 2.50 | .25 | .05 |
| ☐ 278 | Ken Johnson | .35 | .14 | .03 |
| ☐ 279 | Hobie Landrith | .35 | .14 | .03 |
| ☐ 280 | Johnny Podres | 1.00 | .40 | .10 |
| ☐ 281 | Jake Gibbs | .50 | .20 | .05 |
| ☐ 282 | Dave Hillman | .35 | .14 | .03 |
| ☐ 283 | Charlie Smith | .35 | .14 | .03 |
| ☐ 284 | Ruben Amaro | .35 | .14 | .03 |
| ☐ 285 | Curt Simmons | .50 | .20 | .05 |
| ☐ 286 | Al Lopez MGR | 1.00 | .40 | .10 |
| ☐ 287 | George Witt | .35 | .14 | .03 |
| ☐ 288 | Billy Williams | 5.00 | 2.00 | .50 |
| ☐ 289 | Mike Krsnich | .35 | .14 | .03 |
| ☐ 290 | Jim Gentile | .50 | .20 | .05 |
| ☐ 291 | Hal Stowe | .35 | .14 | .03 |
| ☐ 292 | Jerry Kindall | .35 | .14 | .03 |
| ☐ 293 | Bob Miller | .35 | .14 | .03 |
| ☐ 294 | Phillies Team | 1.00 | .40 | .10 |
| ☐ 295 | Vern Law | .60 | .24 | .06 |
| ☐ 296 | Ken Hamlin | .35 | .14 | .03 |
| ☐ 297 | Ron Perranoski | .50 | .20 | .05 |
| ☐ 298 | Bill Tuttle | .35 | .14 | .03 |
| ☐ 299 | Don Wert | .35 | .14 | .03 |
| ☐ 300 | Willie Mays | 35.00 | 14.00 | 3.50 |
| ☐ 301 | Galen Cisco | .35 | .14 | .03 |
| ☐ 302 | John Edwards | .35 | .14 | .03 |
| ☐ 303 | Frank Torre | .35 | .14 | .03 |
| ☐ 304 | Dick Farrell | .35 | .14 | .03 |
| ☐ 305 | Jerry Lumpe | .35 | .14 | .03 |
| ☐ 306 | Redbird Rippers | .50 | .20 | .05 |
| | Lindy McDaniel | | | |
| | Larry Jackson | | | |
| ☐ 307 | Jim Grant | .35 | .14 | .03 |
| ☐ 308 | Neil Chrisley | .35 | .14 | .03 |
| ☐ 309 | Moe Morhardt | .35 | .14 | .03 |
| ☐ 310 | Whitey Ford | 6.00 | 2.40 | .60 |
| ☐ 311 | Tony Kubek IA | .90 | .36 | .09 |
| ☐ 312 | Warren Spahn IA | 2.00 | .80 | .20 |
| ☐ 313 | Roger Maris IA | 2.50 | 1.00 | .25 |
| ☐ 314 | Rocky Colavito IA | .90 | .36 | .09 |
| ☐ 315 | Whitey Ford IA | 2.00 | .80 | .20 |
| ☐ 316 | Harmon Killebrew IA | 2.00 | .80 | .20 |
| ☐ 317 | Stan Musial IA | 3.50 | 1.40 | .35 |
| ☐ 318 | Mickey Mantle IA | 7.00 | 2.80 | .70 |
| ☐ 319 | Mike McCormick IA | .60 | .24 | .06 |
| ☐ 320 | Hank Aaron | 35.00 | 14.00 | 3.50 |
| ☐ 321 | Lee Stange | .35 | .14 | .03 |
| ☐ 322 | Al Dark | .50 | .20 | .05 |
| ☐ 323 | Don Landrum | .35 | .14 | .03 |
| ☐ 324 | Joe McClain | .35 | .14 | .03 |
| ☐ 325 | Luis Aparicio | 3.50 | 1.40 | .35 |
| ☐ 326 | Tom Parsons | .35 | .14 | .03 |
| ☐ 327 | Ozzie Virgil | .35 | .14 | .03 |
| ☐ 328 | Ken Walters | .35 | .14 | .03 |
| ☐ 329 | Bob Bolin | .35 | .14 | .03 |
| ☐ 330 | John Romano | .35 | .14 | .03 |
| ☐ 331 | Moe Drabowsky | .35 | .14 | .03 |
| ☐ 332 | Don Buddin | .35 | .14 | .03 |
| ☐ 333 | Frank Cipriani | .35 | .14 | .03 |
| ☐ 334 | Red Sox Team | 1.00 | .40 | .10 |
| ☐ 335 | Bill Bruton | .35 | .14 | .03 |
| ☐ 336 | Billy Muffett | .35 | .14 | .03 |
| ☐ 337 | Jim Marshall | .35 | .14 | .03 |
| ☐ 338 | Billy Gardner | .35 | .14 | .03 |
| ☐ 339 | Jose Valdivielso | .35 | .14 | .03 |
| ☐ 340 | Don Drysdale | 6.50 | 2.60 | .65 |
| ☐ 341 | Mike Hershberger | .35 | .14 | .03 |
| ☐ 342 | Ed Rakow | .35 | .14 | .03 |
| ☐ 343 | Albie Pearson | .35 | .14 | .03 |
| ☐ 344 | Ed Bauta | .35 | .14 | .03 |
| ☐ 345 | Chuck Schilling | .35 | .14 | .03 |
| ☐ 346 | Jack Kralick | .35 | .14 | .03 |
| ☐ 347 | Chuck Hinton | .35 | .14 | .03 |
| ☐ 348 | Larry Burright | .35 | .14 | .03 |
| ☐ 349 | Paul Foytack | .35 | .14 | .03 |
| ☐ 350 | Frank Robinson | 7.00 | 2.80 | .70 |
| ☐ 351 | Braves' Backstops | .60 | .24 | .06 |
| | Joe Torre | | | |
| | Del Crandall | | | |
| ☐ 352 | Frank Sullivan | .35 | .14 | .03 |
| ☐ 353 | Bill Mazeroski | 1.00 | .40 | .10 |
| ☐ 354 | Roman Mejias | .35 | .14 | .03 |
| ☐ 355 | Steve Barber | .35 | .14 | .03 |
| ☐ 356 | Tom Haller | .35 | .14 | .03 |
| ☐ 357 | Jerry Walker | .35 | .14 | .03 |
| ☐ 358 | Tommy Davis | 1.00 | .40 | .10 |
| ☐ 359 | Bobby Locke | .35 | .14 | .03 |

| # | Player | | | |
|---|--------|------|------|------|
| ☐ 360 | Yogi Berra | 9.00 | 3.75 | .90 |
| ☐ 361 | Bob Hendley | .35 | .14 | .03 |
| ☐ 362 | Ty Cline | .35 | .14 | .03 |
| ☐ 363 | Bob Roselli | .35 | .14 | .03 |
| ☐ 364 | Ken Hunt | .35 | .14 | .03 |
| ☐ 365 | Charley Neal | .50 | .20 | .05 |
| ☐ 366 | Phil Regan | .50 | .20 | .05 |
| ☐ 367 | Checklist 5 | 2.50 | .25 | .05 |
| ☐ 368 | Bob Tillman | .35 | .14 | .03 |
| ☐ 369 | Ted Bowsfield | .35 | .14 | .03 |
| ☐ 370 | Ken Boyer | 1.50 | .60 | .15 |
| ☐ 371 | Earl Battey | .55 | .22 | .05 |
| ☐ 372 | Jack Curtis | .55 | .22 | .05 |
| ☐ 373 | Al Heist | .55 | .22 | .05 |
| ☐ 374 | Gene Mauch | .75 | .30 | .07 |
| ☐ 375 | Ron Fairly | .75 | .30 | .07 |
| ☐ 376 | Bud Daley | .55 | .22 | .05 |
| ☐ 377 | John Orsino | .55 | .22 | .05 |
| ☐ 378 | Bennie Daniels | .55 | .22 | .05 |
| ☐ 379 | Chuck Essegian | .55 | .22 | .05 |
| ☐ 380 | Lou Burdette | 1.00 | .40 | .10 |
| ☐ 381 | Chico Cardenas | .55 | .22 | .05 |
| ☐ 382 | Dick Williams | .75 | .30 | .07 |
| ☐ 383 | Ray Sadecki | .55 | .22 | .05 |
| ☐ 384 | K.C. Athletics | 1.00 | .40 | .10 |
| | Team Card | | | |
| ☐ 385 | Early Wynn | 3.50 | 1.40 | .35 |
| ☐ 386 | Don Mincher | .55 | .22 | .05 |
| ☐ 387 | Lou Brock | 45.00 | 18.00 | 4.50 |
| ☐ 388 | Ryne Duren | .75 | .30 | .07 |
| ☐ 389 | Smoky Burgess | .75 | .30 | .07 |
| ☐ 390 | Orlando Cepeda AS | 1.00 | .40 | .10 |
| ☐ 391 | Bill Mazeroski AS | .75 | .30 | .07 |
| ☐ 392 | Ken Boyer AS | .75 | .30 | .07 |
| ☐ 393 | Roy McMillan AS | .55 | .22 | .05 |
| ☐ 394 | Hank Aaron AS | 8.00 | 3.25 | .80 |
| ☐ 395 | Willie Mays AS | 8.00 | 3.25 | .80 |
| ☐ 396 | Frank Robinson AS | 3.50 | 1.40 | .35 |
| ☐ 397 | John Roseboro AS | .55 | .22 | .05 |
| ☐ 398 | Don Drysdale AS | 3.00 | 1.20 | .30 |
| ☐ 399 | Warren Spahn AS | 3.00 | 1.20 | .30 |
| ☐ 400 | Elston Howard | 1.75 | .70 | .17 |
| ☐ 401 | AL/NL Homer Kings | 6.00 | 2.40 | .60 |
| | Roger Maris | | | |
| | Orlando Cepeda | | | |
| ☐ 402 | Gino Cimoli | .55 | .22 | .05 |
| ☐ 403 | Chet Nichols | .55 | .22 | .05 |
| ☐ 404 | Tim Harkness | .55 | .22 | .05 |
| ☐ 405 | Jim Perry | .90 | .36 | .09 |
| ☐ 406 | Bob Taylor | .55 | .22 | .05 |
| ☐ 407 | Hank Aguirre | .55 | .22 | .05 |
| ☐ 408 | Gus Bell | .75 | .30 | .07 |
| ☐ 409 | Pirates Team | 1.00 | .40 | .10 |
| ☐ 410 | Al Smith | .55 | .22 | .05 |
| ☐ 411 | Danny O'Connell | .55 | .22 | .05 |
| ☐ 412 | Charlie James | .55 | .22 | .05 |
| ☐ 413 | Matty Alou | .75 | .30 | .07 |
| ☐ 414 | Joe Gaines | .55 | .22 | .05 |
| ☐ 415 | Bill Virdon | .90 | .36 | .09 |
| ☐ 416 | Bob Scheffing MGR | .55 | .22 | .05 |
| ☐ 417 | Joe Azcue | .55 | .22 | .05 |
| ☐ 418 | Andy Carey | .55 | .22 | .05 |
| ☐ 419 | Bob Bruce | .55 | .22 | .05 |
| ☐ 420 | Gus Triandos | .55 | .22 | .05 |
| ☐ 421 | Ken Mackenzie | .55 | .22 | .05 |
| ☐ 422 | Steve Bilko | .55 | .22 | .05 |
| ☐ 423 | Rival League | 1.50 | .60 | .15 |
| | Relief Aces: | | | |
| | Roy Face | | | |
| | Hoyt Wilhelm | | | |
| ☐ 424 | Al McBean | .55 | .22 | .05 |
| ☐ 425 | Carl Yastrzemski | 80.00 | 32.00 | 8.00 |
| ☐ 426 | Bob Farley | .55 | .22 | .05 |
| ☐ 427 | Jake Wood | .55 | .22 | .05 |
| ☐ 428 | Joe Hicks | .55 | .22 | .05 |
| ☐ 429 | Billy O'Dell | .55 | .22 | .05 |
| ☐ 430 | Tony Kubek | 3.00 | 1.20 | .30 |
| ☐ 431 | Bob Rodgers | .55 | .22 | .05 |
| ☐ 432 | Jim Pendleton | .55 | .22 | .05 |
| ☐ 433 | Jim Archer | .55 | .22 | .05 |
| ☐ 434 | Clay Dalrymple | .55 | .22 | .05 |
| ☐ 435 | Larry Sherry | .75 | .30 | .07 |
| ☐ 436 | Felix Mantilla | .55 | .22 | .05 |
| ☐ 437 | Ray Moore | .55 | .22 | .05 |
| ☐ 438 | Dick Brown | .55 | .22 | .05 |
| ☐ 439 | Jerry Buchek | .55 | .22 | .05 |
| ☐ 440 | Joe Jay | .55 | .22 | .05 |
| ☐ 441 | Checklist 6 | 3.00 | .30 | .06 |
| ☐ 442 | Wes Stock | .55 | .22 | .05 |
| ☐ 443 | Del Crandall | .75 | .30 | .07 |
| ☐ 444 | Ted Wills | .55 | .22 | .05 |
| ☐ 445 | Vic Power | .55 | .22 | .05 |
| ☐ 446 | Don Elston | .55 | .22 | .05 |

| | | | |
|---|---|---|---|
| ☐ 447 Willie Kirkland | .55 | .22 | .05 |
| ☐ 448 Joe Gibbon | .55 | .22 | .05 |
| ☐ 449 Jerry Adair | .55 | .22 | .05 |
| ☐ 450 Jim O'Toole | .55 | .22 | .05 |
| ☐ 451 Jose Tartabull | .55 | .22 | .05 |
| ☐ 452 Earl Averill | .55 | .22 | .05 |
| ☐ 453 Cal McLish | .55 | .22 | .05 |
| ☐ 454 Floyd Robinson | .55 | .22 | .05 |
| ☐ 455 Luis Arroyo | .55 | .22 | .05 |
| ☐ 456 Joe Amalfitano | .55 | .22 | .05 |
| ☐ 457 Lou Clinton | .55 | .22 | .05 |
| ☐ 458A Bob Buhl | .75 | .30 | .07 |
| (Braves cap emblem) | | | |
| ☐ 458B Bob Buhl | 15.00 | 6.00 | 1.50 |
| (no emblem on cap) | | | |
| ☐ 459 Ed Bailey | .55 | .22 | .05 |
| ☐ 460 Jim Bunning | 2.50 | 1.00 | .25 |
| ☐ 461 Ken Hubbs | 2.50 | 1.00 | .25 |
| ☐ 462A Willie Tasby | .75 | .30 | .07 |
| (Senators cap emblem) | | | |
| ☐ 462B Willie Tasby | 15.00 | 6.00 | 1.50 |
| (no emblem on cap) | | | |
| ☐ 463 Hank Bauer | .75 | .30 | .07 |
| ☐ 464 Al Jackson | .55 | .22 | .05 |
| ☐ 465 Reds Team | 1.25 | .50 | .12 |
| ☐ 466 Norm Cash AS | .75 | .30 | .07 |
| ☐ 467 Chuck Schilling AS | .55 | .22 | .05 |
| ☐ 468 Brooks Robinson AS | 4.50 | 1.80 | .45 |
| ☐ 469 Luis Aparicio AS | 2.00 | .80 | .20 |
| ☐ 470 Al Kaline AS | 4.50 | 1.80 | .45 |
| ☐ 471 Mickey Mantle AS | 20.00 | 8.00 | 2.00 |
| ☐ 472 Rocky Colavito AS | .90 | .36 | .09 |
| ☐ 473 Elston Howard AS | .90 | .36 | .09 |
| ☐ 474 Frank Lary AS | .55 | .22 | .05 |
| ☐ 475 Whitey Ford AS | 4.00 | 1.60 | .40 |
| ☐ 476 Orioles Team | 1.25 | .50 | .12 |
| ☐ 477 Andre Rodgers | .55 | .22 | .05 |
| ☐ 478 Don Zimmer | .75 | .30 | .07 |
| ☐ 479 Joel Horlen | .75 | .30 | .07 |
| ☐ 480 Harvey Kuenn | 1.00 | .40 | .10 |
| ☐ 481 Vic Wertz | .75 | .30 | .07 |
| ☐ 482 Sam Mele MGR | .55 | .22 | .05 |
| ☐ 483 Don McMahon | .55 | .22 | .05 |
| ☐ 484 Dick Schofield | .55 | .22 | .05 |
| ☐ 485 Pedro Ramos | .55 | .22 | .05 |
| ☐ 486 Jim Gilliam | 2.50 | 1.00 | .25 |
| ☐ 487 Jerry Lynch | .55 | .22 | .05 |
| ☐ 488 Hal Brown | .55 | .22 | .05 |
| ☐ 489 Julio Gotay | .55 | .22 | .05 |
| ☐ 490 Clete Boyer | 1.75 | .70 | .17 |
| ☐ 491 Leon Wagner | .55 | .22 | .05 |
| ☐ 492 Hal W. Smith | .55 | .22 | .05 |
| ☐ 493 Danny McDevitt | .55 | .22 | .05 |
| ☐ 494 Sammy White | .55 | .22 | .05 |
| ☐ 495 Don Cardwell | .55 | .22 | .05 |
| ☐ 496 Wayne Causey | .55 | .22 | .05 |
| ☐ 497 Ed Bouchee | .55 | .22 | .05 |
| ☐ 498 Jim Donohue | .55 | .22 | .05 |
| ☐ 499 Zoilo Versalles | .55 | .22 | .05 |
| ☐ 500 Duke Snider | 12.00 | 5.00 | 1.20 |
| ☐ 501 Claude Osteen | .75 | .30 | .07 |
| ☐ 502 Hector Lopez | .55 | .22 | .05 |
| ☐ 503 Danny Murtaugh MGR | .55 | .22 | .05 |
| ☐ 504 Eddie Bressoud | .55 | .22 | .05 |
| ☐ 505 Juan Marichal | 10.00 | 4.00 | 1.00 |
| ☐ 506 Charlie Maxwell | .55 | .22 | .05 |
| ☐ 507 Ernie Broglio | .55 | .22 | .05 |
| ☐ 508 Gordy Coleman | .55 | .22 | .05 |
| ☐ 509 Dave Giusti | .75 | .30 | .07 |
| ☐ 510 Jim Lemon | .55 | .22 | .05 |
| ☐ 511 Bubba Phillips | .55 | .22 | .05 |
| ☐ 512 Mike Fornieles | .55 | .22 | .05 |
| ☐ 513 Whitey Herzog | 1.00 | .40 | .10 |
| ☐ 514 Sherm Lollar | .55 | .22 | .05 |
| ☐ 515 Stan Williams | .55 | .22 | .05 |
| ☐ 516 Checklist 7 | 5.00 | .50 | .10 |
| ☐ 517 Dave Wickersham | .55 | .22 | .05 |
| ☐ 518 Lee Maye | .55 | .22 | .05 |
| ☐ 519 Bob Johnson | .55 | .22 | .05 |
| ☐ 520 Bob Friend | .75 | .30 | .07 |
| ☐ 521 Jacke Davis | .55 | .22 | .05 |
| ☐ 522 Lindy McDaniel | .55 | .22 | .05 |
| ☐ 523 Russ Nixon | 2.50 | 1.00 | .25 |
| ☐ 524 Howie Nunn | 2.50 | 1.00 | .25 |
| ☐ 525 George Thomas | 2.50 | 1.00 | .25 |
| ☐ 526 Hal Woodeshick | 2.50 | 1.00 | .25 |
| ☐ 527 Dick McAuliffe | 3.00 | 1.20 | .30 |
| ☐ 528 Turk Lown | 2.50 | 1.00 | .25 |
| ☐ 529 John Schaive | 2.50 | 1.00 | .25 |
| ☐ 530 Bob Gibson | 35.00 | 14.00 | 3.50 |
| ☐ 531 Bobby G. Smith | 2.50 | 1.00 | .25 |
| ☐ 532 Dick Stigman | 2.50 | 1.00 | .25 |
| ☐ 533 Charley Lau | 2.50 | 1.00 | .25 |

| | | | |
|---|---|---|---|
| ☐ 534 Tony Gonzalez | 2.50 | 1.00 | .25 |
| ☐ 535 Ed Roebuck | 2.50 | 1.00 | .25 |
| ☐ 536 Dick Gernert | 2.50 | 1.00 | .25 |
| ☐ 537 Indians Team | 4.50 | 1.80 | .45 |
| ☐ 538 Jack Sanford | 2.50 | 1.00 | .25 |
| ☐ 539 Billy Moran | 2.50 | 1.00 | .25 |
| ☐ 540 Jim Landis | 2.50 | 1.00 | .25 |
| ☐ 541 Don Nottebart | 2.50 | 1.00 | .25 |
| ☐ 542 Dave Philley | 2.50 | 1.00 | .25 |
| ☐ 543 Bob Allen | 2.50 | 1.00 | .25 |
| ☐ 544 Willie McCovey | 35.00 | 14.00 | 3.50 |
| ☐ 545 Hoyt Wilhelm | 15.00 | 6.00 | 1.50 |
| ☐ 546 Moe Thacker | 2.50 | 1.00 | .25 |
| ☐ 547 Don Ferrarese | 2.50 | 1.00 | .25 |
| ☐ 548 Bobby Del Greco | 2.50 | 1.00 | .25 |
| ☐ 549 Bill Rigney MGR | 2.50 | 1.00 | .25 |
| ☐ 550 Art Mahaffey | 2.50 | 1.00 | .25 |
| ☐ 551 Harry Bright | 2.50 | 1.00 | .25 |
| ☐ 552 Chicago Cubs Team | 4.50 | 1.80 | .45 |
| ☐ 553 Jim Coates | 2.50 | 1.00 | .25 |
| ☐ 554 Bubba Morton | 2.50 | 1.00 | .25 |
| ☐ 555 John Buzhardt | 2.50 | 1.00 | .25 |
| ☐ 556 Al Spangler | 2.50 | 1.00 | .25 |
| ☐ 557 Bob Anderson | 2.50 | 1.00 | .25 |
| ☐ 558 John Goryl | 2.50 | 1.00 | .25 |
| ☐ 559 Mike Higgins MGR | 2.50 | 1.00 | .25 |
| ☐ 560 Chuck Estrada | 2.50 | 1.00 | .25 |
| ☐ 561 Gene Oliver | 2.50 | 1.00 | .25 |
| ☐ 562 Bill Henry | 2.50 | 1.00 | .25 |
| ☐ 563 Ken Aspromonte | 2.50 | 1.00 | .25 |
| ☐ 564 Bob Grim | 2.50 | 1.00 | .25 |
| ☐ 565 Jose Pagan | 2.50 | 1.00 | .25 |
| ☐ 566 Marty Kutyna | 2.50 | 1.00 | .25 |
| ☐ 567 Tracy Stallard | 2.50 | 1.00 | .25 |
| ☐ 568 Jim Golden | 2.50 | 1.00 | .25 |
| ☐ 569 Ed Sadowski | 2.50 | 1.00 | .25 |
| ☐ 570 Bill Stafford | 2.50 | 1.00 | .25 |
| ☐ 571 Billy Klaus | 2.50 | 1.00 | .25 |
| ☐ 572 Bob G. Miller | 2.50 | 1.00 | .25 |
| ☐ 573 Johnny Logan | 2.50 | 1.00 | .25 |
| ☐ 574 Dean Stone | 2.50 | 1.00 | .25 |
| ☐ 575 Red Schoendienst | 3.00 | 1.20 | .30 |
| ☐ 576 Russ Kemmerer | 2.50 | 1.00 | .25 |
| ☐ 577 Dave Nicholson | 2.50 | 1.00 | .25 |
| ☐ 578 Jim Duffalo | 2.50 | 1.00 | .25 |
| ☐ 579 Jim Schaffer | 2.50 | 1.00 | .25 |
| ☐ 580 Bill Monbouquette | 2.50 | 1.00 | .25 |
| ☐ 581 Mel Roach | 2.50 | 1.00 | .25 |
| ☐ 582 Ron Piche | 2.50 | 1.00 | .25 |
| ☐ 583 Larry Osborne | 2.50 | 1.00 | .25 |
| ☐ 584 Minnesota Twins Team Card | 4.50 | 1.80 | .45 |
| ☐ 585 Glen Hobbie | 2.50 | 1.00 | .25 |
| ☐ 586 Sam Esposito | 2.50 | 1.00 | .25 |
| ☐ 587 Frank Funk | 2.50 | 1.00 | .25 |
| ☐ 588 Birdie Tebbetts MGR | 2.50 | 1.00 | .25 |
| ☐ 589 Bob Turley | 3.00 | 1.20 | .30 |
| ☐ 590 Curt Flood | 3.50 | 1.40 | .35 |
| ☐ 591 Rookie Pitchers | 9.00 | 3.75 | .90 |
| Sam McDowell | | | |
| Ron Taylor | | | |
| Ron Nischwitz | | | |
| Art Quirk | | | |
| Dick Radatz | | | |
| ☐ 592 Rookie Pitchers | 12.00 | 5.00 | 1.20 |
| Dan Pfister | | | |
| Bo Belinsky | | | |
| Dave Stenhouse | | | |
| Jim Bouton | | | |
| Joe Bonikowski | | | |
| ☐ 593 Rookie Pitchers | 6.00 | 2.40 | .60 |
| Jack Lamabe | | | |
| Craig Anderson | | | |
| Jack Hamilton | | | |
| Bob Moorhead | | | |
| Bob Veale | | | |
| ☐ 594 Rookie Catchers | 35.00 | 14.00 | 3.50 |
| Doc Edwards | | | |
| Ken Retzer | | | |
| Bob Uecker | | | |
| Doug Camilli | | | |
| Don Pavletich | | | |
| ☐ 595 Rookie Catchers | 5.00 | 2.00 | .50 |
| Bob Sadowski | | | |
| Felix Torres | | | |
| Marlan Coughtry | | | |
| Ed Charles | | | |
| ☐ 596 Rookie Infielders | 9.00 | 3.75 | .90 |
| Bernie Allen | | | |
| Joe Pepitone | | | |
| Phil Linz | | | |
| Rich Rollins | | | |
| ☐ 597 Rookie Infielders | 5.00 | 2.00 | .50 |

Jim McKnight
Rod Kanehl
Amado Samuel
Denis Menke
□ 598 Rookie Outfielders .......... 6.00 2.40 .60
Al Luplow
Manny Jimenez
Howie Goss
Jim Hickman
Ed Olivares

## 1963 Topps

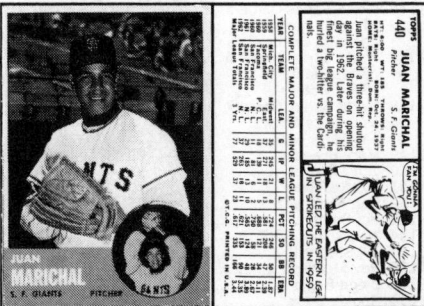

The cards in this 576 card set measure 2 1/2" by 3 1/2". The sharp color photographs of the 1963 set are a vivid contrast to the drab pictures of 1962. In addition to the "Leaders" series (1-10) and the World Series cards (142-148), the seventh and last series of cards (507-576) contains seven rookie cards (each depicting four players). This set has gained special prominence in recent years since it contains the rookie card of Pete Rose, #537.

|  | | MINT | VG-E | F-G |
|---|---|---|---|---|
| COMPLETE SET | ...................... | 1350.00 | 600.00 | 150.00 |
| COMMON PLAYER (1-196) | ........ | .25 | .10 | .02 |
| COMMON PLAYER (197-446) | .... | .35 | .14 | .03 |
| COMMON PLAYER (447-506) | .... | 2.50 | 1.00 | .25 |
| COMMON PLAYER (507-576) | .... | 2.00 | .80 | .20 |

□ 1 NL Batting Leaders ......... 3.00 .60 .12
　Tommy Davis
　Frank Robinson
　Stan Musial
　Hank Aaron
　Bill White
□ 2 AL Batting Leaders ......... 2.00 .80 .20
　Pete Runnels
　Mickey Mantle
　Floyd Robinson
　Norm Siebern
　Chuck Hinton
□ 3 NL Home Run Leaders ... 3.00 1.20 .30
　Willie Mays
　Hank Aaron
　Frank Robinson
　Orlando Cepeda
　Ernie Banks
□ 4 AL Home Run Leaders .... 1.25 .50 .12
　Harmon Killebrew
　Norm Cash
　Rocky Colavito
　Roger Maris
　Jim Gentile
　Leon Wagner
□ 5 NL ERA Leaders ............. 1.50 .60 .15
　Sandy Koufax
　Bob Shaw
　Bob Purkey
　Bob Gibson
　Don Drysdale
□ 6 AL ERA Leaders ............. 1.00 .40 .10
　Hank Aguirre
　Robin Roberts

　Whitey Ford
　Eddie Fisher
　Dean Chance
□ 7 AL Pitching Leaders ........ 1.00 .40 .10
　Don Drysdale
　Jack Sanford
　Bob Purkey
　Billy O'Dell
　Art Mahaffey
　Joe Jay
□ 8 AL Pitching Leaders ........ .80 .32 .08
　Ralph Terry
　Dick Donovan
　Ray Herbert
　Jim Bunning
　Camilo Pascual
□ 9 NL Strikeout Leaders ...... 2.00 .80 .20
　Don Drysdale
　Sandy Koufax
　Bob Gibson
　Billy O'Dell
　Dick Farrell
□ 10 AL Strikeout Leaders ........ .80 .32 .08
　Camilo Pascual
　Jim Bunning
　Ralph Terry
　Juan Pizarro
　Jim Kaat
□ 11 Lee Walls ....................... .25 .10 .02
□ 12 Steve Barber ................. .25 .10 .02
□ 13 Phillies Team ................. .70 .28 .07
□ 14 Pedro Ramos ................. .25 .10 .02
□ 15 Ken Hubbs ..................... 1.00 .40 .10
□ 16 Al Smith ....................... .25 .10 .02
□ 17 Ryne Duren ................... .35 .14 .03
□ 18 Buc Blasters ................. 2.00 .80 .20
　Smoky Burgess
　Dick Stuart
　Bob Clemente
　Bob Skinner
□ 19 Pete Burnside ................ .25 .10 .02
□ 20 Tony Kubek ................... 1.50 .60 .15
□ 21 Marty Keough ................ .25 .10 .02
□ 22 Curt Simmons ............... .35 .14 .03
□ 23 Ed Lopat MGR ............... .60 .24 .06
□ 24 Bob Bruce ..................... .25 .10 .02
□ 25 Al Kaline ....................... 5.00 2.00 .50
□ 26 Ray Moore ..................... .25 .10 .02
□ 27 Choo Choo Coleman ...... .25 .10 .02
□ 28 Mike Fornieles ............... .25 .10 .02
□ 29A 1963 Rookie Stars ........ .35 .14 .03
　Sammy Ellis
　Ray Culp
　John Boozer
　Jesse Gonder
□ 29B 1962 Rookie Stars ........ 2.00 .80 .20
　Sammy Ellis
　Ray Culp
　John Boozer
　Jesse Gonder
□ 30 Harvey Kuenn ................ .70 .28 .07
□ 31 Cal Koonce .................... .25 .10 .02
□ 32 Tony Gonzalez ............... .25 .10 .02
□ 33 Bo Belinsky ................... .35 .14 .03
□ 34 Dick Schofield ............... .25 .10 .02
□ 35 John Buzhardt ............... .25 .10 .02
□ 36 Jerry Kindall .................. .25 .10 .02
□ 37 Jerry Lynch .................... .25 .10 .02
□ 38 Bud Daley ..................... .25 .10 .02
□ 39 Angels Team .................. .70 .28 .07
□ 40 Vic Power ..................... .25 .10 .02
□ 41 Charley Lau ................... .35 .14 .03
□ 42 Stan Williams ................ .25 .10 .02
□ 43 Veteran Masters ............ 1.25 .50 .12
　Casey Stengel
　Gene Woodling
□ 44 Terry Fox ..................... .25 .10 .02
□ 45 Bob Aspromonte ............ .25 .10 .02
□ 46 Tommy Aaron ................ .35 .14 .03
□ 47 Don Lock ....................... .25 .10 .02
□ 48 Birdie Tebbetts MGR ...... .25 .10 .02
□ 49 Dal Maxvill .................... .25 .10 .02
□ 50 Billy Pierce ................... .60 .24 .06
□ 51 George Alusik ................ .25 .10 .02
□ 52 Chuck Schilling .............. .25 .10 .02
□ 53 Joe Moeller ................... .25 .10 .02
□ 54A 1963 Rookie Stars ........ 2.50 1.00 .25
　Nelson Mathews
　Harry Fanok
　Jack Cullen
　Dave DeBusschere
□ 54B 1962 Rookie Stars ........ 4.00 1.60 .40
　Nelson Mathews

|  |  |  | | |
|---|---|---|---|---|
| | Harry Fanok | | | |
| | Jack Cullen | | | |
| | Dave DeBusschere | | | |
| ☐ 55 | Bill Virdon | .80 | .32 | .08 |
| ☐ 56 | Dennis Bennett | .25 | .10 | .02 |
| ☐ 57 | Billy Moran | .25 | .10 | .02 |
| ☐ 58 | Bob Will | .25 | .10 | .02 |
| ☐ 59 | Craig Anderson | .25 | .10 | .02 |
| ☐ 60 | Elston Howard | 2.00 | .80 | .20 |
| ☐ 61 | Ernie Bowman | .25 | .10 | .02 |
| ☐ 62 | Bob Hendley | .25 | .10 | .02 |
| ☐ 63 | Reds Team | .70 | .28 | .07 |
| ☐ 64 | Dick McAuliffe | .25 | .10 | .02 |
| ☐ 65 | Jackie Brandt | .25 | .10 | .02 |
| ☐ 66 | Mike Joyce | .25 | .10 | .02 |
| ☐ 67 | Ed Charles | .25 | .10 | .02 |
| ☐ 68 | Friendly Foes | 3.00 | 1.20 | .30 |
| | Duke Snider | | | |
| | Gil Hodges | | | |
| ☐ 69 | Bud Zipfel | .25 | .10 | .02 |
| ☐ 70 | Jim O'Toole | .25 | .10 | .02 |
| ☐ 71 | Bobby Wine | .25 | .10 | .02 |
| ☐ 72 | Johnny Romano | .25 | .10 | .02 |
| ☐ 73 | Bob Bragan MGR | .25 | .10 | .02 |
| ☐ 74 | Denny Lemaster | .25 | .10 | .02 |
| ☐ 75 | Bob Allison | .35 | .14 | .03 |
| ☐ 76 | Earl Wilson | .25 | .10 | .02 |
| ☐ 77 | Al Spangler | .25 | .10 | .02 |
| ☐ 78 | Marv Throneberry | .80 | .32 | .08 |
| ☐ 79 | Checklist 1 | 2.50 | .25 | .05 |
| ☐ 80 | Jim Gilliam | 1.50 | .60 | .15 |
| ☐ 81 | Jim Schaffer | .25 | .10 | .02 |
| ☐ 82 | Ed Rakow | .25 | .10 | .02 |
| ☐ 83 | Charley James | .25 | .10 | .02 |
| ☐ 84 | Ron Kline | .25 | .10 | .02 |
| ☐ 85 | Tom Haller | .25 | .10 | .02 |
| ☐ 86 | Charley Maxwell | .25 | .10 | .02 |
| ☐ 87 | Bob Veale | .35 | .14 | .03 |
| ☐ 88 | Ron Hansen | .25 | .10 | .02 |
| ☐ 89 | Dick Stigman | .25 | .10 | .02 |
| ☐ 90 | Gordy Coleman | .25 | .10 | .02 |
| ☐ 91 | Dallas Green | .35 | .14 | .03 |
| ☐ 92 | Hector Lopez | .25 | .10 | .02 |
| ☐ 93 | Galen Cisco | .25 | .10 | .02 |
| ☐ 94 | Bob Schmidt | .25 | .10 | .02 |
| ☐ 95 | Larry Jackson | .25 | .10 | .02 |
| ☐ 96 | Lou Clinton | .25 | .10 | .02 |
| ☐ 97 | Bob Duliba | .25 | .10 | .02 |
| ☐ 98 | George Thomas | .25 | .10 | .02 |
| ☐ 99 | Jim Umbricht | .25 | .10 | .02 |
| ☐ 100 | Joe Cunningham | .35 | .14 | .03 |
| ☐ 101 | Joe Gibbon | .25 | .10 | .02 |
| ☐ 102A | Checklist 2 | 2.50 | .25 | .05 |
| | (red on yellow) | | | |
| ☐ 102B | Checklist 2 | 3.50 | .35 | .07 |
| | (white on red) | | | |
| ☐ 103 | Chuck Essegian | .25 | .10 | .02 |
| ☐ 104 | Lew Krausse | .25 | .10 | .02 |
| ☐ 105 | Ron Fairly | .35 | .14 | .03 |
| ☐ 106 | Bobby Bolin | .25 | .10 | .02 |
| ☐ 107 | Jim Hickman | .25 | .10 | .02 |
| ☐ 108 | Hoyt Wilhelm | 3.00 | 1.20 | .30 |
| ☐ 109 | Lee Maye | .25 | .10 | .02 |
| ☐ 110 | Rich Rollins | .25 | .10 | .02 |
| ☐ 111 | Al Jackson | .25 | .10 | .02 |
| ☐ 112 | Dick Brown | .25 | .10 | .02 |
| ☐ 113 | Don Landrum | .35 | .14 | .03 |
| | (photo actually | | | |
| | Ron Santo) | | | |
| ☐ 114 | Dan Osinski | .25 | .10 | .02 |
| ☐ 115 | Carl Yastrzemski | 35.00 | 14.00 | 3.50 |
| ☐ 116 | Jim Brosnan | .35 | .14 | .03 |
| ☐ 117 | Jacke Davis | .25 | .10 | .02 |
| ☐ 118 | Sherm Lollar | .35 | .14 | .03 |
| ☐ 119 | Bob Lillis | .35 | .14 | .03 |
| ☐ 120 | Roger Maris | 6.50 | 2.60 | .65 |
| ☐ 121 | Jim Hannan | .25 | .10 | .02 |
| ☐ 122 | Julio Gotay | .25 | .10 | .02 |
| ☐ 123 | Frank Howard | 1.00 | .40 | .10 |
| ☐ 124 | Dick Howser | .50 | .20 | .05 |
| ☐ 125 | Robin Roberts | 3.00 | 1.20 | .30 |
| ☐ 126 | Bob Uecker | 5.00 | 2.00 | .50 |
| ☐ 127 | Bill Tuttle | .25 | .10 | .02 |
| ☐ 128 | Matty Alou | .35 | .14 | .03 |
| ☐ 129 | Gary Bell | .25 | .10 | .02 |
| ☐ 130 | Dick Groat | .60 | .24 | .06 |
| ☐ 131 | Senators Team | .70 | .28 | .07 |
| ☐ 132 | Jack Hamilton | .25 | .10 | .02 |
| ☐ 133 | Gene Freese | .25 | .10 | .02 |
| ☐ 134 | Bob Scheffing MGR | .25 | .10 | .02 |
| ☐ 135 | Richie Ashburn | 1.50 | .60 | .15 |
| ☐ 136 | Ike Delock | .25 | .10 | .02 |
| ☐ 137 | Mack Jones | .25 | .10 | .02 |
| ☐ 138 | Pride Of N.L. | 7.50 | 3.00 | .75 |
| | Willie Mays | | | |
| | Stan Musial | | | |
| ☐ 139 | Earl Averill | .25 | .10 | .02 |
| ☐ 140 | Frank Lary | .35 | .14 | .03 |
| ☐ 141 | Manny Mota | 1.50 | .60 | .15 |
| ☐ 142 | World Series Game 1 | 2.25 | .90 | .22 |
| | Ford wins | | | |
| | series opener | | | |
| ☐ 143 | World Series Game 2 | 1.50 | .60 | .15 |
| | Sanford flashes | | | |
| | shutout magic | | | |
| ☐ 144 | World Series Game 3 | 2.25 | .90 | .22 |
| | Maris sparks | | | |
| | Yankee rally | | | |
| ☐ 145 | World Series Game 4 | 1.50 | .60 | .15 |
| | Hiller blasts | | | |
| | grand slammer | | | |
| ☐ 146 | World Series Game 5 | 1.50 | .60 | .15 |
| | Tresh's homer | | | |
| | defeats Giants | | | |
| ☐ 147 | World Series Game 6 | 1.50 | .60 | .15 |
| | Pierce stars in | | | |
| | 3 hit victory | | | |
| ☐ 148 | World Series Game 7 | 1.50 | .60 | .15 |
| | Yanks celebrate | | | |
| | as Terry wins | | | |
| ☐ 149 | Marv Breeding | .25 | .10 | .02 |
| ☐ 150 | John Podres | .90 | .36 | .09 |
| ☐ 151 | Pirates Team | .70 | .28 | .07 |
| ☐ 152 | Ron Nischwitz | .25 | .10 | .02 |
| ☐ 153 | Hal Smith | .25 | .10 | .02 |
| ☐ 154 | Walt Alston MGR | 1.00 | .40 | .10 |
| ☐ 155 | Bill Stafford | .25 | .10 | .02 |
| ☐ 156 | Roy McMillan | .25 | .10 | .02 |
| ☐ 157 | Diego Segui | .25 | .10 | .02 |
| ☐ 158 | Rookie Stars | .35 | .14 | .03 |
| | Rogelio Alvares | | | |
| | Dave Roberts | | | |
| | Tommy Harper | | | |
| | Bob Saverine | | | |
| ☐ 159 | Jim Pagliaroni | .25 | .10 | .02 |
| ☐ 160 | Juan Pizarro | .25 | .10 | .02 |
| ☐ 161 | Frank Torre | .25 | .10 | .02 |
| ☐ 162 | Twins Team | .70 | .28 | .07 |
| ☐ 163 | Don Larsen | .50 | .20 | .05 |
| ☐ 164 | Bubba Morton | .25 | .10 | .02 |
| ☐ 165 | Jim Kaat | 1.75 | .70 | .17 |
| ☐ 166 | Johnny Keane MGR | .35 | .14 | .03 |
| ☐ 167 | Jim Fregosi | .80 | .32 | .08 |
| ☐ 168 | Russ Nixon | .25 | .10 | .02 |
| ☐ 169 | Rookie Stars | 6.50 | 2.60 | .65 |
| | Dick Egan | | | |
| | Julio Navarro | | | |
| | Tommie Sisk | | | |
| | Gaylord Perry | | | |
| ☐ 170 | Joe Adcock | .50 | .20 | .05 |
| ☐ 171 | Steve Hamilton | .25 | .10 | .02 |
| ☐ 172 | Gene Oliver | .25 | .10 | .02 |
| ☐ 173 | Bombers' Best | 9.00 | 3.75 | .90 |
| | Tom Tresh | | | |
| | Mickey Mantle | | | |
| | Bobby Richardson | | | |
| ☐ 174 | Larry Burright | .25 | .10 | .02 |
| ☐ 175 | Bob Buhl | .25 | .10 | .02 |
| ☐ 176 | Jim King | .25 | .10 | .02 |
| ☐ 177 | Bubba Phillips | .25 | .10 | .02 |
| ☐ 178 | Johnny Edwards | .25 | .10 | .02 |
| ☐ 179 | Ron Piche | .25 | .10 | .02 |
| ☐ 180 | Bill Skowron | .80 | .32 | .08 |
| ☐ 181 | Sammy Esposito | .25 | .10 | .02 |
| ☐ 182 | Albie Pearson | .25 | .10 | .02 |
| ☐ 183 | Joe Pepitone | .60 | .24 | .06 |
| ☐ 184 | Vern Law | .35 | .14 | .03 |
| ☐ 185 | Chuck Hiller | .25 | .10 | .02 |
| ☐ 186 | Jerry Zimmerman | .25 | .10 | .02 |
| ☐ 187 | Willie Kirkland | .25 | .10 | .02 |
| ☐ 188 | Eddie Bressoud | .25 | .10 | .02 |
| ☐ 189 | Dave Giusti | .25 | .10 | .02 |
| ☐ 190 | Minnie Minoso | 1.00 | .40 | .10 |
| ☐ 191 | Checklist 3 | 2.50 | .25 | .05 |
| ☐ 192 | Clay Dalrymple | .25 | .10 | .02 |
| ☐ 193 | Andre Rodgers | .25 | .10 | .02 |
| ☐ 194 | Joe Nuxhall | .35 | .14 | .03 |
| ☐ 195 | Manny Jimenez | .25 | .10 | .02 |
| ☐ 196 | Doug Camilli | .25 | .10 | .02 |
| ☐ 197 | Roger Craig | .75 | .30 | .07 |
| ☐ 198 | Lenny Green | .35 | .14 | .03 |
| ☐ 199 | Joe Amalfitano | .35 | .14 | .03 |
| ☐ 200 | Mickey Mantle | 75.00 | 30.00 | 7.50 |
| ☐ 201 | Cecil Butler | .35 | .14 | .03 |
| ☐ 202 | Red Sox Team | 1.00 | .40 | .10 |
| ☐ 203 | Chico Cardenas | .35 | .14 | .03 |

| # | Player | | | |
|---|--------|------|------|------|
| 204 | Don Nottebart | .35 | .14 | .03 |
| 205 | Luis Aparicio | 3.50 | 1.40 | .35 |
| 206 | Ray Washburn | .35 | .14 | .03 |
| 207 | Ken Hunt | .35 | .14 | .03 |
| 208 | Rookie Stars | .35 | .14 | .03 |
| | Ron Herbel | | | |
| | John Miller | | | |
| | Wally Wolf | | | |
| | Ron Taylor | | | |
| 209 | Hobie Landrith | .35 | .14 | .03 |
| 210 | Sandy Koufax | 27.00 | 11.00 | 2.70 |
| 211 | Fred Whitfield | .35 | .14 | .03 |
| 212 | Glen Hobbie | .35 | .14 | .03 |
| 213 | Billy Hitchcock MGR | .35 | .14 | .03 |
| 214 | Orlando Pena | .35 | .14 | .03 |
| 215 | Bob Skinner | .35 | .14 | .03 |
| 216 | Gene Conley | .35 | .14 | .03 |
| 217 | Joe Christopher | .35 | .14 | .03 |
| 218 | Tiger Twirlers | .75 | .30 | .07 |
| | Frank Lary | | | |
| | Don Mossi | | | |
| | Jim Bunning | | | |
| 219 | Chuck Cottier | .35 | .14 | .03 |
| 220 | Camilo Pascual | .35 | .14 | .03 |
| 221 | Cookie Rojas | .35 | .14 | .03 |
| 222 | Cubs Team | 1.00 | .40 | .10 |
| 223 | Eddie Fisher | .35 | .14 | .03 |
| 224 | Mike Roarke | .35 | .14 | .03 |
| 225 | Joe Jay | .35 | .14 | .03 |
| 226 | Julian Javier | .35 | .14 | .03 |
| 227 | Jim Grant | .35 | .14 | .03 |
| 228 | Rookie Stars | 6.50 | 2.60 | .65 |
| | Max Alvis | | | |
| | Bob Bailey | | | |
| | Pedro Oliva | | | |
| | Ed Kranepool | | | |
| 229 | Willie Davis | .75 | .30 | .07 |
| 230 | Pete Runnels | .50 | .20 | .05 |
| 231 | Eli Grba | .50 | .20 | .05 |
| | (large photo is | | | |
| | Ryne Duren) | | | |
| 232 | Frank Malzone | .50 | .20 | .05 |
| 233 | Casey Stengel MGR | 4.00 | 1.60 | .40 |
| 234 | Dave Nicholson | .35 | .14 | .03 |
| 235 | Billy O'Dell | .35 | .14 | .03 |
| 236 | Bill Bryan | .35 | .14 | .03 |
| 237 | Jim Coates | .35 | .14 | .03 |
| 238 | Lou Johnson | .35 | .14 | .03 |
| 239 | Harvey Haddix | .50 | .20 | .05 |
| 240 | Rocky Colavito | 1.25 | .50 | .12 |
| 241 | Bob Smith | .35 | .14 | .03 |
| 242 | Power Plus | 4.50 | 1.80 | .45 |
| | Ernie Banks | | | |
| | Hank Aaron | | | |
| 243 | Don Leppert | .35 | .14 | .03 |
| 244 | John Tsitouris | .35 | .14 | .03 |
| 245 | Gil Hodges | 3.50 | 1.40 | .35 |
| 246 | Lee Stange | .35 | .14 | .03 |
| 247 | Yankees Team | 3.50 | 1.40 | .35 |
| 248 | Tito Francona | .35 | .14 | .03 |
| 249 | Leo Burke | .35 | .14 | .03 |
| 250 | Stan Musial | 20.00 | 8.00 | 2.00 |
| 251 | Jack Lamabe | .35 | .14 | .03 |
| 252 | Ron Santo | 1.25 | .50 | .12 |
| 253 | Rookie Stars | .35 | .14 | .03 |
| | Len Gabrielson | | | |
| | Pete Jernigan | | | |
| | John Wojcik | | | |
| | Deacon Jones | | | |
| 254 | Mike Hershberger | .35 | .14 | .03 |
| 255 | Bob Shaw | .35 | .14 | .03 |
| 256 | Jerry Lumpe | .35 | .14 | .03 |
| 257 | Hank Aguirre | .35 | .14 | .03 |
| 258 | Al Dark MGR | .60 | .24 | .06 |
| 259 | John Logan | .50 | .20 | .05 |
| 260 | Jim Gentile | .50 | .20 | .05 |
| 261 | Bob Miller | .35 | .14 | .03 |
| 262 | Ellis Burton | .35 | .14 | .03 |
| 263 | Dave Stenhouse | .35 | .14 | .03 |
| 264 | Phil Linz | .35 | .14 | .03 |
| 265 | Vada Pinson | 1.25 | .50 | .12 |
| 266 | Bob Allen | .35 | .14 | .03 |
| 267 | Carl Sawatski | .35 | .14 | .03 |
| 268 | Don Demeter | .35 | .14 | .03 |
| 269 | Don Mincher | .50 | .20 | .05 |
| 270 | Felipe Alou | .75 | .30 | .07 |
| 271 | Dean Stone | .35 | .14 | .03 |
| 272 | Danny Murphy | .35 | .14 | .03 |
| 273 | Sammy Taylor | .35 | .14 | .03 |
| 274 | Checklist 4 | 2.50 | .25 | .05 |
| 275 | Eddie Mathews | 4.50 | 1.80 | .45 |
| 276 | Barry Shetrone | .35 | .14 | .03 |
| 277 | Dick Farrell | .35 | .14 | .03 |
| 278 | Chico Fernandez | .35 | .14 | .03 |
| 279 | Wally Moon | .50 | .20 | .05 |
| 280 | Bob Rodgers | .35 | .14 | .03 |
| 281 | Tom Sturdivant | .35 | .14 | .03 |
| 282 | Bobby Del Greco | .35 | .14 | .03 |
| 283 | Roy Sievers | .50 | .20 | .05 |
| 284 | Dave Sisler | .35 | .14 | .03 |
| 285 | Dick Stuart | .50 | .20 | .05 |
| 286 | Stu Miller | .35 | .14 | .03 |
| 287 | Dick Bertell | .35 | .14 | .03 |
| 288 | White Sox Team | 1.00 | .40 | .10 |
| 289 | Hal Brown | .35 | .14 | .03 |
| 290 | Bill White | .50 | .20 | .05 |
| 291 | Don Rudolph | .35 | .14 | .03 |
| 292 | Pumpsie Green | .35 | .14 | .03 |
| 293 | Bill Pleis | .35 | .14 | .03 |
| 294 | Bill Rigney MGR | .35 | .14 | .03 |
| 295 | Ed Roebuck | .35 | .14 | .03 |
| 296 | Doc Edwards | .35 | .14 | .03 |
| 297 | Jim Golden | .35 | .14 | .03 |
| 298 | Don Dillard | .35 | .14 | .03 |
| 299 | Rookie Stars | .35 | .14 | .03 |
| | Dave Morehead | | | |
| | Bob Dustal | | | |
| | Tom Butters | | | |
| | Dan Schneider | | | |
| 300 | Willie Mays | 35.00 | 14.00 | 3.50 |
| 301 | Bill Fischer | .35 | .14 | .03 |
| 302 | Whitey Herzog | .75 | .30 | .07 |
| 303 | Earl Francis | .35 | .14 | .03 |
| 304 | Harry Bright | .35 | .14 | .03 |
| 305 | Don Hoak | .35 | .14 | .03 |
| 306 | Star Receivers | .80 | .32 | .08 |
| | Earl Battey | | | |
| | Elston Howard | | | |
| 307 | Chet Nichols | .35 | .14 | .03 |
| 308 | Camilo Carreon | .35 | .14 | .03 |
| 309 | Jim Brewer | .35 | .14 | .03 |
| 310 | Tommy Davis | 1.00 | .40 | .10 |
| 311 | Joe McClain | .35 | .14 | .03 |
| 312 | Houston Colts Team | 3.00 | 1.20 | .30 |
| 313 | Ernie Broglio | .50 | .20 | .05 |
| 314 | John Goryl | .35 | .14 | .03 |
| 315 | Ralph Terry | .50 | .20 | .05 |
| 316 | Norm Sherry | .50 | .20 | .05 |
| 317 | Sam McDowell | .75 | .30 | .07 |
| 318 | Gene Mauch MGR | .75 | .30 | .07 |
| 319 | Joe Gaines | .35 | .14 | .03 |
| 320 | Warren Spahn | 6.50 | 2.60 | .65 |
| 321 | Gino Cimoli | .35 | .14 | .03 |
| 322 | Bob Turley | .75 | .30 | .07 |
| 323 | Bill Mazeroski | 1.00 | .40 | .10 |
| 324 | Rookie Stars | .75 | .30 | .07 |
| | George Williams | | | |
| | Pete Ward | | | |
| | Phil Ward | | | |
| | Vic Davalillo | | | |
| 325 | Jack Sanford | .35 | .14 | .03 |
| 326 | Hank Foiles | .35 | .14 | .03 |
| 327 | Paul Foytack | .35 | .14 | .03 |
| 328 | Dick Williams MGR | .75 | .30 | .07 |
| 329 | Lindy McDaniel | .35 | .14 | .03 |
| 330 | Chuck Hinton | .35 | .14 | .03 |
| 331 | Series Foes | .50 | .20 | .05 |
| | Bill Stafford | | | |
| | Bill Pierce | | | |
| 332 | Joel Horlen | .50 | .20 | .05 |
| 333 | Carl Warwick | .35 | .14 | .03 |
| 334 | Wynn Hawkins | .35 | .14 | .03 |
| 335 | Leon Wagner | .35 | .14 | .03 |
| 336 | Ed Bauta | .35 | .14 | .03 |
| 337 | Dodgers Team | 3.00 | 1.20 | .30 |
| 338 | Russ Kemmerer | .35 | .14 | .03 |
| 339 | Ted Bowsfield | .35 | .14 | .03 |
| 340 | Yogi Berra | 12.00 | 5.00 | 1.20 |
| 341 | Jack Baldschun | .35 | .14 | .03 |
| 342 | Gene Woodling | .50 | .20 | .05 |
| 343 | Johnny Pesky MGR | .50 | .20 | .05 |
| 344 | Don Schwall | .35 | .14 | .03 |
| 345 | Brooks Robinson | 12.00 | 5.00 | 1.20 |
| 346 | Billy Hoeft | .35 | .14 | .03 |
| 347 | Joe Torre | 1.75 | .70 | .17 |
| 348 | Vic Wertz | .50 | .20 | .05 |
| 349 | Zoilo Versailles | .35 | .14 | .03 |
| 350 | Bob Purkey | .35 | .14 | .03 |
| 351 | Al Luplow | .35 | .14 | .03 |
| 352 | Ken Johnson | .35 | .14 | .03 |
| 353 | Billy Williams | 4.00 | 1.60 | .40 |
| 354 | Dom Zanni | .35 | .14 | .03 |
| 355 | Dean Chance | .50 | .20 | .05 |
| 356 | John Schaive | .35 | .14 | .03 |
| 357 | George Altman | .35 | .14 | .03 |
| 358 | Milt Pappas | .50 | .20 | .05 |

| | | | | |
|---|---|---|---|---|
| ☐ 359 | Haywood Sullivan | .50 | .20 | .05 |
| ☐ 360 | Don Drysdale | 5.50 | 2.20 | .55 |
| ☐ 361 | Cletis Boyer | .75 | .30 | .07 |
| ☐ 362 | Checklist 5 | 2.50 | .25 | .05 |
| ☐ 363 | Dick Radatz | .50 | .20 | .05 |
| ☐ 364 | Howie Goss | .35 | .14 | .03 |
| ☐ 365 | Jim Bunning | 2.25 | .90 | .22 |
| ☐ 366 | Tony Taylor | .35 | .14 | .03 |
| ☐ 367 | Tony Cloninger | .35 | .14 | .03 |
| ☐ 368 | Ed Bailey | .35 | .14 | .03 |
| ☐ 369 | Jim Lemon MGR | .35 | .14 | .03 |
| ☐ 370 | Dick Donovan | .35 | .14 | .03 |
| ☐ 371 | Rod Kanehl | .35 | .14 | .03 |
| ☐ 372 | Don Lee | .35 | .14 | .03 |
| ☐ 373 | Jim Campbell | .35 | .14 | .03 |
| ☐ 374 | Claude Osteen | .50 | .20 | .05 |
| ☐ 375 | Ken Boyer | 1.50 | .60 | .15 |
| ☐ 376 | John Wyatt | .35 | .14 | .03 |
| ☐ 377 | Orioles Team | 1.00 | .40 | .10 |
| ☐ 378 | Bill Henry | .35 | .14 | .03 |
| ☐ 379 | Bob Anderson | .35 | .14 | .03 |
| ☐ 380 | Ernie Banks | 12.50 | 5.00 | 1.25 |
| ☐ 381 | Frank Baumann | .35 | .14 | .03 |
| ☐ 382 | Ralph Houk MGR | .75 | .30 | .07 |
| ☐ 383 | Pete Richert | .35 | .14 | .03 |
| ☐ 384 | Bob Tillman | .35 | .14 | .03 |
| ☐ 385 | Art Mahaffey | .35 | .14 | .03 |
| ☐ 386 | Rookie Stars | .60 | .24 | .06 |
| | Ed Kirkpatrick | | | |
| | John Bateman | | | |
| | Larry Bearnarth | | | |
| | Garry Roggenburk | | | |
| ☐ 387 | Al McBean | .35 | .14 | .03 |
| ☐ 388 | Jim Davenport | .50 | .20 | .05 |
| ☐ 389 | Frank Sullivan | .35 | .14 | .03 |
| ☐ 390 | Hank Aaron | 35.00 | 14.00 | 3.50 |
| ☐ 391 | B. Dailey | .35 | .14 | .03 |
| ☐ 392 | Tribe Thumpers | .50 | .20 | .05 |
| | Johnny Romano | | | |
| | Tito Francona | | | |
| ☐ 393 | Ken MacKenzie | .35 | .14 | .03 |
| ☐ 394 | Tim McCarver | 1.00 | .40 | .10 |
| ☐ 395 | Don McMahon | .35 | .14 | .03 |
| ☐ 396 | Joe Koppe | .35 | .14 | .03 |
| ☐ 397 | K.C. Athletics Team | .90 | .36 | .09 |
| ☐ 398 | Boog Powell | 1.75 | .70 | .17 |
| ☐ 399 | Dick Ellsworth | .35 | .14 | .03 |
| ☐ 400 | Frank Robinson | 12.00 | 5.00 | 1.20 |
| ☐ 401 | Jim Bouton | 1.50 | .60 | .15 |
| ☐ 402 | Mickey Vernon | .50 | .20 | .05 |
| ☐ 403 | Ron Perranoski | .50 | .20 | .05 |
| ☐ 404 | Bob Oldis | .35 | .14 | .03 |
| ☐ 405 | Floyd Robinson | .35 | .14 | .03 |
| ☐ 406 | Howie Koplitz | .35 | .14 | .03 |
| ☐ 407 | Rookie Stars | .35 | .14 | .03 |
| | Frank Kostro | | | |
| | Chico Ruiz | | | |
| | Larry Elliot | | | |
| | Dick Simpson | | | |
| ☐ 408 | Billy Gardner | .35 | .14 | .03 |
| ☐ 409 | Roy Face | .75 | .30 | .07 |
| ☐ 410 | Earl Battey | .50 | .20 | .05 |
| ☐ 411 | Jim Constable | .35 | .14 | .03 |
| ☐ 412 | Dodger Big Three | 7.00 | 2.80 | .70 |
| | Johnny Podres | | | |
| | Don Drysdale | | | |
| | Sandy Koufax | | | |
| ☐ 413 | Jerry Walker | .35 | .14 | .03 |
| ☐ 414 | Ty Cline | .35 | .14 | .03 |
| ☐ 415 | Bob Gibson | 12.00 | 5.00 | 1.20 |
| ☐ 416 | Alex Grammas | .35 | .14 | .03 |
| ☐ 417 | Giants Team | 1.00 | .40 | .10 |
| ☐ 418 | John Orsino | .35 | .14 | .03 |
| ☐ 419 | Tracy Stallard | .35 | .14 | .03 |
| ☐ 420 | Bobby Richardson | 1.75 | .70 | .17 |
| ☐ 421 | Tom Morgan | .35 | .14 | .03 |
| ☐ 422 | Fred Hutchinson MGR | .60 | .24 | .06 |
| ☐ 423 | Ed Hobaugh | .35 | .14 | .03 |
| ☐ 424 | Charley Smith | .35 | .14 | .03 |
| ☐ 425 | Smoky Burgess | .50 | .20 | .05 |
| ☐ 426 | Barry Latman | .35 | .14 | .03 |
| ☐ 427 | Bernie Allen | .35 | .14 | .03 |
| ☐ 428 | Carl Boles | .35 | .14 | .03 |
| ☐ 429 | Lou Burdette | 1.00 | .40 | .10 |
| ☐ 430 | Norm Siebern | .35 | .14 | .03 |
| ☐ 431A | Checklist 6 | 2.50 | .25 | .05 |
| | (white on red) | | | |
| ☐ 431B | Checklist 6 | 5.00 | .50 | .10 |
| | (black on orange) | | | |
| ☐ 432 | Roman Mejias | .35 | .14 | .03 |
| ☐ 433 | Denis Menke | .35 | .14 | .03 |
| ☐ 434 | John Callison | .50 | .20 | .05 |
| ☐ 435 | Woody Held | .35 | .14 | .03 |
| ☐ 436 | Tim Harkness | .35 | .14 | .03 |
| ☐ 437 | Bill Bruton | .35 | .14 | .03 |
| ☐ 438 | Wes Stock | .35 | .14 | .03 |
| ☐ 439 | Don Zimmer | .50 | .20 | .05 |
| ☐ 440 | Juan Marichal | 7.50 | 3.00 | .75 |
| ☐ 441 | Lee Thomas | .35 | .14 | .03 |
| ☐ 442 | J.C. Hartman | .35 | .14 | .03 |
| ☐ 443 | Jim Piersall | .90 | .36 | .09 |
| ☐ 444 | Jim Maloney | .75 | .30 | .07 |
| ☐ 445 | Norm Cash | 1.50 | .60 | .15 |
| ☐ 446 | Whitey Ford | 12.00 | 5.00 | 1.20 |
| ☐ 447 | Felix Mantilla | 2.50 | 1.00 | .25 |
| ☐ 448 | Jack Kralick | 2.50 | 1.00 | .25 |
| ☐ 449 | Jose Tartabull | 2.50 | 1.00 | .25 |
| ☐ 450 | Bob Friend | 3.00 | 1.20 | .30 |
| ☐ 451 | Indians Team | 4.00 | 1.60 | .40 |
| ☐ 452 | Buddy Schultz | 2.50 | 1.00 | .25 |
| ☐ 453 | Jake Wood | 2.50 | 1.00 | .25 |
| ☐ 454A | Art Fowler | 2.50 | 1.00 | .25 |
| | (card number on white background) | | | |
| ☐ 454B | Art Fowler | 5.00 | 2.00 | .50 |
| | (card number on orange background) | | | |
| ☐ 455 | Ruben Amaro | 2.50 | 1.00 | .25 |
| ☐ 456 | Jim Coker | 2.50 | 1.00 | .25 |
| ☐ 457 | Tex Clevenger | 2.50 | 1.00 | .25 |
| ☐ 458 | Al Lopez MGR | 4.00 | 1.60 | .40 |
| ☐ 459 | Dick LeMay | 2.50 | 1.00 | .25 |
| ☐ 460 | Del Crandall | 3.00 | 1.20 | .30 |
| ☐ 461 | Norm Bass | 2.50 | 1.00 | .25 |
| ☐ 462 | Wally Post | 2.50 | 1.00 | .25 |
| ☐ 463 | Joe Schaffernoth | 2.50 | 1.00 | .25 |
| ☐ 464 | Ken Aspromonte | 2.50 | 1.00 | .25 |
| ☐ 465 | Chuck Estrada | 2.50 | 1.00 | .25 |
| ☐ 466 | Rookie Stars | 4.00 | 1.60 | .40 |
| | Nate Oliver | | | |
| | Tony Martinez | | | |
| | Bill Freehan | | | |
| | Jerry Robinson | | | |
| ☐ 467 | Phil Ortega | 2.50 | 1.00 | .25 |
| ☐ 468 | Carroll Hardy | 2.50 | 1.00 | .25 |
| ☐ 469 | Jay Hook | 2.50 | 1.00 | .25 |
| ☐ 470 | Tom Tresh | 10.00 | 4.00 | 1.00 |
| ☐ 471 | Ken Retzer | 2.50 | 1.00 | .25 |
| ☐ 472 | Lou Brock | 50.00 | 20.00 | 5.00 |
| ☐ 473 | Mets Team | 5.00 | 2.00 | .50 |
| ☐ 474 | Jack Fisher | 2.50 | 1.00 | .25 |
| ☐ 475 | Gus Triandos | 2.50 | 1.00 | .25 |
| ☐ 476 | Frank Funk | 2.50 | 1.00 | .25 |
| ☐ 477 | Donn Clendenon | 3.00 | 1.20 | .30 |
| ☐ 478 | Paul Brown | 2.50 | 1.00 | .25 |
| ☐ 479 | Ed Brinkman | 2.50 | 1.00 | .25 |
| ☐ 480 | Bill Monbouquette | 2.50 | 1.00 | .25 |
| ☐ 481 | Bill Taylor | 2.50 | 1.00 | .25 |
| ☐ 482 | Frank Torre | 2.50 | 1.00 | .25 |
| ☐ 483 | Jim Owens | 2.50 | 1.00 | .25 |
| ☐ 484 | Dale Long | 2.50 | 1.00 | .25 |
| ☐ 485 | Jim Landis | 2.50 | 1.00 | .25 |
| ☐ 486 | Ray Sadecki | 2.50 | 1.00 | .25 |
| ☐ 487 | John Roseboro | 2.50 | 1.00 | .25 |
| ☐ 488 | Jerry Adair | 2.50 | 1.00 | .25 |
| ☐ 489 | Paul Toth | 2.50 | 1.00 | .25 |
| ☐ 490 | Willie McCovey | 35.00 | 14.00 | 3.50 |
| ☐ 491 | Harry Craft MGR | 2.50 | 1.00 | .25 |
| ☐ 492 | Dave Wickersham | 2.50 | 1.00 | .25 |
| ☐ 493 | Walt Bond | 2.50 | 1.00 | .25 |
| ☐ 494 | Phil Regan | 2.50 | 1.00 | .25 |
| ☐ 495 | Frank Thomas | 2.50 | 1.00 | .25 |
| ☐ 496 | Rookie Stars | 2.50 | 1.00 | .25 |
| | Steve Dalkowski | | | |
| | Fred Newman | | | |
| | Jack Smith | | | |
| | Carl Bouldin | | | |
| ☐ 497 | Bennie Daniels | 2.50 | 1.00 | .25 |
| ☐ 498 | Ed Kasko | 2.50 | 1.00 | .25 |
| ☐ 499 | J.C. Martin | 2.50 | 1.00 | .25 |
| ☐ 500 | Harmon Killebrew | 21.00 | 8.50 | 2.10 |
| ☐ 501 | Joe Azcue | 2.50 | 1.00 | .25 |
| ☐ 502 | Daryl Spencer | 2.50 | 1.00 | .25 |
| ☐ 503 | Braves Team | 4.00 | 1.60 | .40 |
| ☐ 504 | Bob Johnson | 2.50 | 1.00 | .25 |
| ☐ 505 | Curt Flood | 5.00 | 2.00 | .50 |
| ☐ 506 | Gene Green | 2.50 | 1.00 | .25 |
| ☐ 507 | Rollie Sheldon | 2.00 | .80 | .20 |
| ☐ 508 | Ted Savage | 2.00 | .80 | .20 |
| ☐ 509 | Checklist 7 | 7.50 | .75 | .15 |
| ☐ 510 | Ken McBride | 2.00 | .80 | .20 |
| ☐ 511 | Charlie Neal | 2.00 | .80 | .20 |
| ☐ 512 | Cal McLish | 2.00 | .80 | .20 |
| ☐ 513 | Gary Geiger | 2.00 | .80 | .20 |
| ☐ 514 | Larry Osborne | 2.00 | .80 | .20 |
| ☐ 515 | Don Elston | 2.00 | .80 | .20 |

| □ 516 | Purnell Goldy | 2.00 | .80 | .20 |
|---|---|---|---|---|
| □ 517 | Hal Woodeshick | 2.00 | .80 | .20 |
| □ 518 | Don Blasingame | 2.00 | .80 | .20 |
| □ 519 | Claude Raymond | 2.00 | .80 | .20 |
| □ 520 | Orlando Cepeda | 5.00 | 2.00 | .50 |
| □ 521 | Dan Pfister | 2.00 | .80 | .20 |
| □ 522 | Rookie Stars | 2.50 | 1.00 | .25 |
| | Mel Nelson | | | |
| | Gary Peters | | | |
| | Jim Roland | | | |
| | Art Quirk | | | |
| □ 523 | Bill Kunkel | 2.00 | .80 | .20 |
| □ 524 | Cardinals Team | 4.00 | 1.60 | .40 |
| □ 525 | Nellie Fox | 4.00 | 1.60 | .40 |
| □ 526 | Dick Hall | 2.00 | .80 | .20 |
| □ 527 | Ed Sadowski | 2.00 | .80 | .20 |
| □ 528 | Carl Willey | 2.00 | .80 | .20 |
| □ 529 | Wes Covington | 2.00 | .80 | .20 |
| □ 530 | Don Mossi | 2.50 | 1.00 | .25 |
| □ 531 | Sam Mele MGR | 2.00 | .80 | .20 |
| □ 532 | Steve Boros | 2.00 | .80 | .20 |
| □ 533 | Bobby Shantz | 2.50 | 1.00 | .25 |
| □ 534 | Ken Walters | 2.00 | .80 | .20 |
| □ 535 | Jim Perry | 3.00 | 1.20 | .30 |
| □ 536 | Norm Larker | 2.00 | .80 | .20 |
| □ 537 | Rookie Stars | 500.00 | 200.00 | 50.00 |
| | Pedro Gonzales | | | |
| | Ken McMullen | | | |
| | Al Weis | | | |
| | Pete Rose | | | |
| □ 538 | George Brunet | 2.00 | .80 | .20 |
| □ 539 | Wayne Causey | 2.00 | .80 | .20 |
| □ 540 | Bob Clemente | 60.00 | 24.00 | 6.00 |
| □ 541 | Ron Moeller | 2.00 | .80 | .20 |
| □ 542 | Lou Klimchock | 2.00 | .80 | .20 |
| □ 543 | Russ Snyder | 2.00 | .80 | .20 |
| □ 544 | Rookie Stars | 12.00 | 5.00 | 1.20 |
| | Duke Carmel | | | |
| | Bill Haas | | | |
| | Rusty Staub | | | |
| | Dick Phillips | | | |
| □ 545 | Jose Pagan | 2.00 | .80 | .20 |
| □ 546 | Hal Reniff | 2.00 | .80 | .20 |
| □ 547 | Gus Bell | 2.00 | .80 | .20 |
| □ 548 | Tom Satriano | 2.00 | .80 | .20 |
| □ 549 | Rookie Stars | 2.00 | .80 | .20 |
| | Marcelino Lopez | | | |
| | Pete Lovrich | | | |
| | Paul Ratliff | | | |
| | Elmo Plaskett | | | |
| □ 550 | Duke Snider | 25.00 | 10.00 | 2.50 |
| □ 551 | Billy Klaus | 2.00 | .80 | .20 |
| □ 552 | Tigers Team | 6.00 | 2.40 | .60 |
| □ 553 | Rookie Stars | 60.00 | 24.00 | 6.00 |
| | Brock Davis | | | |
| | Jim Gosger | | | |
| | Willie Stargell | | | |
| | John Herrnstein | | | |
| □ 554 | Hank Fischer | 2.00 | .80 | .20 |
| □ 555 | John Blanchard | 2.00 | .80 | .20 |
| □ 556 | Al Worthington | 2.00 | .80 | .20 |
| □ 557 | Cuno Barragan | 2.00 | .80 | .20 |
| □ 558 | Rookie Stars | 2.00 | .80 | .20 |
| | Bill Faul | | | |
| | Ron Hunt | | | |
| | Al Moran | | | |
| | Bob Lipski | | | |
| □ 559 | Danny Murtaugh MGR | 2.00 | .80 | .20 |
| □ 560 | Ray Herbert | 2.00 | .80 | .20 |
| □ 561 | Mike De La Hoz | 2.00 | .80 | .20 |
| □ 562 | Rookie Stars | 4.00 | 1.60 | .40 |
| | Randy Cardinal | | | |
| | Dave McNally | | | |
| | Ken Rowe | | | |
| | Don Rowe | | | |
| □ 563 | Mike McCormick | 2.50 | 1.00 | .25 |
| □ 564 | George Banks | 2.00 | .80 | .20 |
| □ 565 | Larry Sherry | 2.50 | 1.00 | .25 |
| □ 566 | Cliff Cook | 2.00 | .80 | .20 |
| □ 567 | Jim Duffalo | 2.00 | .80 | .20 |
| □ 568 | Bob Sadowski | 2.00 | .80 | .20 |
| □ 569 | Luis Arroyo | 2.00 | .80 | .20 |
| □ 570 | Frank Bolling | 2.00 | .80 | .20 |
| □ 571 | John Klippstein | 2.00 | .80 | .20 |
| □ 572 | Jack Spring | 2.00 | .80 | .20 |
| □ 573 | Coot Veal | 2.00 | .80 | .20 |
| □ 574 | Hal Kolstad | 2.00 | .80 | .20 |
| □ 575 | Don Cardwell | 2.00 | .80 | .20 |
| □ 576 | Johnny Temple | 3.50 | 1.40 | .35 |

# 1964 Topps

The cards in this 587 Card set measure 2 1/2" by 3 1/2". Players in the 1964 Topps baseball series were easy to sort by team due to the giant block lettering found at the top of each card. The name and position of the player are found underneath the picture and the card is numbered in a ball design on the orange-colored back. The usual last series scarcity holds for this set (523 to 587). Subsets within this set include League Leaders (1-12) and World Series cards (136-140).

| | | MINT | VG-E | F-G |
|---|---|---|---|---|
| | COMPLETE SET | 725.00 | 325.00 | 80.00 |
| | COMMON PLAYER (1-370) | .25 | .10 | .02 |
| | COMMON PLAYER (371-522) | .40 | .16 | .04 |
| | COMMON PLAYER (523-587) | .90 | .36 | .09 |
| □ 1 | NL ERA Leaders | 3.00 | .75 | .15 |
| | Sandy Koufax | | | |
| | Dick Ellsworth | | | |
| | Bob Friend | | | |
| □ 2 | AL ERA Leaders | .80 | .32 | .08 |
| | Gary Peters | | | |
| | Juan Pizarro | | | |
| | Camilo Pascual | | | |
| □ 3 | NL Pitching Leaders | 2.50 | 1.00 | .25 |
| | Sandy Koufax | | | |
| | Juan Marichal | | | |
| | Warren Spahn | | | |
| | Jim Maloney | | | |
| □ 4 | AL Pitching Leaders | 1.25 | .50 | .12 |
| | Whitey Ford | | | |
| | Camilo Pascual | | | |
| | Jim Bouton | | | |
| □ 5 | NL Strikeout Leaders | 2.00 | .80 | .20 |
| | Sandy Koufax | | | |
| | Jim Maloney | | | |
| | Don Drysdale | | | |
| □ 6 | AL Strikeout Leaders | .80 | .32 | .08 |
| | Camilo Pascual | | | |
| | Jim Bunning | | | |
| | Dick Stigman | | | |
| □ 7 | NL Batting Leaders | 1.50 | .60 | .15 |
| | Tommy Davis | | | |
| | Bob Clemente | | | |
| | Dick Groat | | | |
| | Hank Aaron | | | |
| □ 8 | AL Batting Leaders | 2.00 | .80 | .20 |
| | Carl Yastrzemski | | | |
| | Al Kaline | | | |
| | Rich Rollins | | | |
| □ 9 | NL Home Run Leaders | 3.00 | 1.20 | .30 |
| | Hank Aaron | | | |
| | Willie McCovey | | | |
| | Willie Mays | | | |
| | Orlando Cepeda | | | |
| □ 10 | AL Home Run Leaders | 1.00 | .40 | .10 |
| | Harmon Killebrew | | | |
| | Dick Stuart | | | |
| | Bob Allison | | | |
| □ 11 | NL RBI Leaders | 1.00 | .40 | .10 |
| | Hank Aaron | | | |
| | Ken Boyer | | | |
| | Bill White | | | |
| □ 12 | AL RBI Leaders | 1.00 | .40 | .10 |

| | | | | |
|---|---|---|---|---|
| | Dick Stuart | | | |
| | Al Kaline | | | |
| | Harmon Killebrew | | | |
| ☐ 13 | Hoyt Wilhelm | 3.00 | 1.20 | .30 |
| ☐ 14 | Dodgers Rookies: | .25 | .10 | .02 |
| | Dick Nen | | | |
| | Nick Willhite | | | |
| ☐ 15 | Zoilo Versalles | .25 | .10 | .02 |
| ☐ 16 | John Boozer | .25 | .10 | .02 |
| ☐ 17 | Willie Kirkland | .25 | .10 | .02 |
| ☐ 18 | Billy O'Dell | .25 | .10 | .02 |
| ☐ 19 | Don Wert | .25 | .10 | .02 |
| ☐ 20 | Bob Friend | .35 | .14 | .03 |
| ☐ 21 | Yogi Berra | 8.00 | 3.25 | .80 |
| ☐ 22 | Jerry Adair | .25 | .10 | .02 |
| ☐ 23 | Chris Zachary | .25 | .10 | .02 |
| ☐ 24 | Carl Sawatski | .25 | .10 | .02 |
| ☐ 25 | Bill Monbouquette | .25 | .10 | .02 |
| ☐ 26 | Gino Cimoli | .25 | .10 | .02 |
| ☐ 27 | Mets Team | 1.00 | .40 | .10 |
| ☐ 28 | Claude Osteen | .35 | .14 | .03 |
| ☐ 29 | Lou Brock | 10.00 | 4.00 | 1.00 |
| ☐ 30 | Ron Perranoski | .35 | .14 | .03 |
| ☐ 31 | Dave Nicholson | .25 | .10 | .02 |
| ☐ 32 | Dean Chance | .35 | .14 | .03 |
| ☐ 33 | Reds Rookies: | .35 | .14 | .03 |
| | Sammy Ellis | | | |
| | Mel Queen | | | |
| ☐ 34 | Jim Perry | .35 | .14 | .03 |
| ☐ 35 | Ed Mathews | 3.50 | 1.40 | .35 |
| ☐ 36 | Hal Reniff | .25 | .10 | .02 |
| ☐ 37 | Smoky Burgess | .35 | .14 | .03 |
| ☐ 38 | Jim Wynn | .75 | .30 | .07 |
| ☐ 39 | Hank Aguirre | .25 | .10 | .02 |
| ☐ 40 | Dick Groat | .60 | .24 | .06 |
| ☐ 41 | Friendly Foes | 1.25 | .50 | .12 |
| | Willie McCovey | | | |
| | Leon Wagner | | | |
| ☐ 42 | Moe Drabowsky | .25 | .10 | .02 |
| ☐ 43 | Roy Sievers | .35 | .14 | .03 |
| ☐ 44 | Duke Carmel | .25 | .10 | .02 |
| ☐ 45 | Milt Pappas | .35 | .14 | .03 |
| ☐ 46 | Ed Brinkman | .25 | .10 | .02 |
| ☐ 47 | Giants Rookies: | .50 | .20 | .05 |
| | Jesus Alou | | | |
| | Ron Herbel | | | |
| ☐ 48 | Bob Perry | .25 | .10 | .02 |
| ☐ 49 | Bill Henry | .25 | .10 | .02 |
| ☐ 50 | Mickey Mantle | 60.00 | 24.00 | 6.00 |
| ☐ 51 | Pete Richert | .25 | .10 | .02 |
| ☐ 52 | Chuck Hinton | .25 | .10 | .02 |
| ☐ 53 | Denis Menke | .25 | .10 | .02 |
| ☐ 54 | Sam Mele MGR | .25 | .10 | .02 |
| ☐ 55 | Ernie Banks | 5.00 | 2.00 | .50 |
| ☐ 56 | Hal Brown | .25 | .10 | .02 |
| ☐ 57 | Tim Harkness | .25 | .10 | .02 |
| ☐ 58 | Don Demeter | .25 | .10 | .02 |
| ☐ 59 | Ernie Broglio | .35 | .14 | .03 |
| ☐ 60 | Frank Malzone | .35 | .14 | .03 |
| ☐ 61 | Angel Backstops | .35 | .14 | .03 |
| | Bob Rodgers | | | |
| | Ed Sadowski | | | |
| ☐ 62 | Ted Savage | .25 | .10 | .02 |
| ☐ 63 | Johnny Orsino | .25 | .10 | .02 |
| ☐ 64 | Ted Abernathy | .25 | .10 | .02 |
| ☐ 65 | Felipe Alou | .50 | .20 | .05 |
| ☐ 66 | Eddie Fisher | .25 | .10 | .02 |
| ☐ 67 | Tigers Team | .85 | .34 | .08 |
| ☐ 68 | Willie Davis | .60 | .24 | .06 |
| ☐ 69 | Clete Boyer | .35 | .14 | .03 |
| ☐ 70 | Joe Torre | 1.00 | .40 | .10 |
| ☐ 71 | Jack Spring | .25 | .10 | .02 |
| ☐ 72 | Chico Cardenas | .25 | .10 | .02 |
| ☐ 73 | Jimmie Hall | .25 | .10 | .02 |
| ☐ 74 | Pirates Rookies: | .25 | .10 | .02 |
| | Bob Priddy | | | |
| | Tom Butters | | | |
| ☐ 75 | Wayne Causey | .25 | .10 | .02 |
| ☐ 76 | Checklist 1 | 2.25 | .20 | .04 |
| ☐ 77 | Jerry Walker | .25 | .10 | .02 |
| ☐ 78 | Merritt Ranew | .25 | .10 | .02 |
| ☐ 79 | Bob Heffner | .25 | .10 | .02 |
| ☐ 80 | Vada Pinson | 1.00 | .40 | .10 |
| ☐ 81 | All-Star Vets | 2.50 | 1.00 | .25 |
| | Nellie Fox | | | |
| | Harmon Killebrew | | | |
| ☐ 82 | Jim Davenport | .35 | .14 | .03 |
| ☐ 83 | Gus Triandos | .35 | .14 | .03 |
| ☐ 84 | Carl Willey | .25 | .10 | .02 |
| ☐ 85 | Pete Ward | .25 | .10 | .02 |
| ☐ 86 | Al Downing | .35 | .14 | .03 |
| ☐ 87 | Cardinals Team | 1.00 | .40 | .10 |
| ☐ 88 | John Roseboro | .35 | .14 | .03 |

| | | | | |
|---|---|---|---|---|
| ☐ 89 | Boog Powell | 1.25 | .50 | .12 |
| ☐ 90 | Earl Battey | .35 | .14 | .03 |
| ☐ 91 | Bob Bailey | .25 | .10 | .02 |
| ☐ 92 | Steve Ridzik | .25 | .10 | .02 |
| ☐ 93 | Gary Geiger | .25 | .10 | .02 |
| ☐ 94 | Braves Rookies: | .25 | .10 | .02 |
| | Jim Britton | | | |
| | Larry Maxie | | | |
| ☐ 95 | George Altman | .25 | .10 | .02 |
| ☐ 96 | Bob Buhl | .25 | .10 | .02 |
| ☐ 97 | Jim Fregosi | .50 | .20 | .05 |
| ☐ 98 | Bill Bruton | .25 | .10 | .02 |
| ☐ 99 | Al Stanek | .25 | .10 | .02 |
| ☐ 100 | Elston Howard | 1.25 | .50 | .12 |
| ☐ 101 | Walt Alston MGR | 1.00 | .40 | .10 |
| ☐ 102 | Checklist 2 | 2.25 | .20 | .04 |
| ☐ 103 | Curt Flood | .80 | .32 | .08 |
| ☐ 104 | Art Mahaffey | .25 | .10 | .02 |
| ☐ 105 | Woody Held | .25 | .10 | .02 |
| ☐ 106 | Joe Nuxhall | .35 | .14 | .03 |
| ☐ 107 | White Sox Rookies | .25 | .10 | .02 |
| | Bruce Howard | | | |
| | Frank Kreutzer | | | |
| ☐ 108 | John Wyatt | .25 | .10 | .02 |
| ☐ 109 | Rusty Staub | 2.00 | .80 | .20 |
| ☐ 110 | Albie Pearson | .25 | .10 | .02 |
| ☐ 111 | Don Elston | .25 | .10 | .02 |
| ☐ 112 | Bob Tillman | .25 | .10 | .02 |
| ☐ 113 | Grover Powell | .25 | .10 | .02 |
| ☐ 114 | Don Lock | .25 | .10 | .02 |
| ☐ 115 | Frank Bolling | .25 | .10 | .02 |
| ☐ 116 | Twins Rookies: | 3.00 | 1.20 | .30 |
| | Jay Ward | | | |
| | Tony Oliva | | | |
| ☐ 117 | Earl Francis | .25 | .10 | .02 |
| ☐ 118 | John Blanchard | .25 | .10 | .02 |
| ☐ 119 | Gary Kolb | .25 | .10 | .02 |
| ☐ 120 | Don Drysdale | 4.50 | 1.80 | .45 |
| ☐ 121 | Pete Runnels | .35 | .14 | .03 |
| ☐ 122 | Don McMahon | .25 | .10 | .02 |
| ☐ 123 | Jose Pagan | .25 | .10 | .02 |
| ☐ 124 | Orlando Pena | .25 | .10 | .02 |
| ☐ 125 | Pete Rose | 120.00 | 50.00 | 12.00 |
| ☐ 126 | Russ Snyder | .25 | .10 | .02 |
| ☐ 127 | Angels Rookies: | .25 | .10 | .02 |
| | Aubrey Gatewood | | | |
| | Dick Simpson | | | |
| ☐ 128 | Mickey Lolich | 3.00 | 1.20 | .30 |
| ☐ 129 | Amado Samuel | .25 | .10 | .02 |
| ☐ 130 | Gary Peters | .35 | .14 | .03 |
| ☐ 131 | Steve Boros | .35 | .14 | .03 |
| ☐ 132 | Braves Team | .85 | .34 | .08 |
| ☐ 133 | Jim Grant | .25 | .10 | .02 |
| ☐ 134 | Don Zimmer | .50 | .20 | .05 |
| ☐ 135 | Johnny Callison | .35 | .14 | .03 |
| ☐ 136 | World Series Game 1 | 3.00 | 1.20 | .30 |
| | Koufax strikes out 15 | | | |
| ☐ 137 | World Series Game 2 | 1.50 | .60 | .15 |
| | Davis sparks rally | | | |
| ☐ 138 | World Series Game 3 | 1.50 | .60 | .15 |
| | LA 3 straight | | | |
| ☐ 139 | World Series Game 4 | 1.50 | .60 | .15 |
| | Sealing Yanks doom | | | |
| ☐ 140 | World Series Summary | 1.50 | .60 | .15 |
| | Dodgers celebrate | | | |
| ☐ 141 | Danny Murtaugh MGR | .25 | .10 | .02 |
| ☐ 142 | John Bateman | .25 | .10 | .02 |
| ☐ 143 | Bubba Phillips | .25 | .10 | .02 |
| ☐ 144 | Al Worthington | .25 | .10 | .02 |
| ☐ 145 | Norm Siebern | .25 | .10 | .02 |
| ☐ 146 | Indians Rookies | 8.00 | 3.25 | .80 |
| | Tommy John | | | |
| | Bob Chance | | | |
| ☐ 147 | Ray Sadecki | .25 | .10 | .02 |
| ☐ 148 | J.C. Martin | .25 | .10 | .02 |
| ☐ 149 | Paul Foytack | .25 | .10 | .02 |
| ☐ 150 | Willie Mays | 22.00 | 9.00 | 2.20 |
| ☐ 151 | Athletics Team | .80 | .32 | .08 |
| ☐ 152 | Denver Lemaster | .25 | .10 | .02 |
| ☐ 153 | Dick Williams MGR | .35 | .14 | .03 |
| ☐ 154 | Dick Tracewski | .25 | .10 | .02 |
| ☐ 155 | Duke Snider | 6.50 | 2.60 | .65 |
| ☐ 156 | Bill Dailey | .25 | .10 | .02 |
| ☐ 157 | Gene Mauch MGR | .35 | .14 | .03 |
| ☐ 158 | Ken Johnson | .25 | .10 | .02 |
| ☐ 159 | Charlie Dees | .25 | .10 | .02 |
| ☐ 160 | Ken Boyer | 2.00 | .80 | .20 |
| ☐ 161 | Dave McNally | .75 | .30 | .07 |
| ☐ 162 | Hitting Area | .35 | .14 | .03 |
| | Dick Sisler | | | |
| | Vada Pinson | | | |
| ☐ 163 | Donn Clendenon | .35 | .14 | .03 |
| ☐ 164 | Bud Daley | .25 | .10 | .02 |

| | | | | |
|---|---|---|---|---|
| ☐ 165 | Jerry Lumpe | .25 | .10 | .02 |
| ☐ 166 | Marty Keough | .25 | .10 | .02 |
| ☐ 167 | Senators Rookies | 7.50 | 3.00 | .75 |
| | Mike Brumley | | | |
| | Lou Piniella | | | |
| ☐ 168 | Al Weis | .25 | .10 | .02 |
| ☐ 169 | Del Crandall | .35 | .14 | .03 |
| ☐ 170 | Dick Radatz | .35 | .14 | .03 |
| ☐ 171 | Ty Cline | .25 | .10 | .02 |
| ☐ 172 | Indians Team | .85 | .34 | .08 |
| ☐ 173 | Ryne Duren | .35 | .14 | .03 |
| ☐ 174 | Doc Edwards | .25 | .10 | .02 |
| ☐ 175 | Billy Williams | 3.50 | 1.40 | .35 |
| ☐ 176 | Tracy Stallard | .25 | .10 | .02 |
| ☐ 177 | Harmon Killebrew | 4.50 | 1.80 | .45 |
| ☐ 178 | Hank Bauer MGR | .35 | .14 | .03 |
| ☐ 179 | Carl Warwick | .25 | .10 | .02 |
| ☐ 180 | Tommy Davis | .65 | .26 | .06 |
| ☐ 181 | Dave Wickersham | .25 | .10 | .02 |
| ☐ 182 | Sox Sockers | 3.00 | 1.20 | .30 |
| | Carl Yastrzemski | | | |
| | Chuck Schilling | | | |
| ☐ 183 | Ron Taylor | .25 | .10 | .02 |
| ☐ 184 | Al Luplow | .25 | .10 | .02 |
| ☐ 185 | Jim O'Toole | .25 | .10 | .02 |
| ☐ 186 | Roman Mejias | .25 | .10 | .02 |
| ☐ 187 | Ed Roebuck | .25 | .10 | .02 |
| ☐ 188 | Checklist 3 | 2.25 | .20 | .04 |
| ☐ 189 | Bob Hendley | .25 | .10 | .02 |
| ☐ 190 | Bobby Richardson | 1.25 | .50 | .12 |
| ☐ 191 | Clay Dalrymple | .25 | .10 | .02 |
| ☐ 192 | Cubs Rookies: | .25 | .10 | .02 |
| | John Boccabella | | | |
| | Billy Cowan | | | |
| ☐ 193 | Jerry Lynch | .25 | .10 | .02 |
| ☐ 194 | John Goryl | .25 | .10 | .02 |
| ☐ 195 | Floyd Robinson | .25 | .10 | .02 |
| ☐ 196 | Jim Gentile | .35 | .14 | .03 |
| ☐ 197 | Frank Lary | .35 | .14 | .03 |
| ☐ 198 | Len Gabrielson | .25 | .10 | .02 |
| ☐ 199 | Joe Azcue | .25 | .10 | .02 |
| ☐ 200 | Sandy Koufax | 16.00 | 6.50 | 1.60 |
| ☐ 201 | Orioles Rookies: | .35 | .14 | .03 |
| | Sam Bowens | | | |
| | Wally Bunker | | | |
| ☐ 202 | Galen Cisco | .25 | .10 | .02 |
| ☐ 203 | John Kennedy | .25 | .10 | .02 |
| ☐ 204 | Matty Alou | .35 | .14 | .03 |
| ☐ 205 | Nellie Fox | 1.50 | .60 | .15 |
| ☐ 206 | Steve Hamilton | .25 | .10 | .02 |
| ☐ 207 | Fred Hutchinson MGR | .35 | .14 | .03 |
| ☐ 208 | Wes Covington | .35 | .14 | .03 |
| ☐ 209 | Bob Allen | .25 | .10 | .02 |
| ☐ 210 | Carl Yastrzemski | 32.00 | 13.00 | 3.20 |
| ☐ 211 | Jim Coker | .25 | .10 | .02 |
| ☐ 212 | Pete Lovrich | .25 | .10 | .02 |
| ☐ 213 | Angels Team | .80 | .32 | .08 |
| ☐ 214 | Ken McMullen | .35 | .14 | .03 |
| ☐ 215 | Ray Herbert | .25 | .10 | .02 |
| ☐ 216 | Mike De La Hoz | .25 | .10 | .02 |
| ☐ 217 | Jim King | .25 | .10 | .02 |
| ☐ 218 | Hank Fischer | .25 | .10 | .02 |
| ☐ 219 | Young Aces | .75 | .30 | .07 |
| | Al Downing | | | |
| | Jim Bouton | | | |
| ☐ 220 | Dick Ellsworth | .35 | .14 | .03 |
| ☐ 221 | Bob Saverine | .25 | .10 | .02 |
| ☐ 222 | Billy Pierce | .60 | .24 | .06 |
| ☐ 223 | George Banks | .25 | .10 | .02 |
| ☐ 224 | Tommie Sisk | .25 | .10 | .02 |
| ☐ 225 | Roger Maris | 6.00 | 2.40 | .60 |
| ☐ 226 | Colts Rookies: | .35 | .14 | .03 |
| | Gerald Grote | | | |
| | Larry Yellen | | | |
| ☐ 227 | Barry Latman | .25 | .10 | .02 |
| ☐ 228 | Felix Mantilla | .25 | .10 | .02 |
| ☐ 229 | Charley Lau | .35 | .14 | .03 |
| ☐ 230 | Brooks Robinson | 9.00 | 3.75 | .90 |
| ☐ 231 | Dick Calmus | .25 | .10 | .02 |
| ☐ 232 | Al Lopez MGR | 1.25 | .50 | .12 |
| ☐ 233 | Hal Smith | .25 | .10 | .02 |
| ☐ 234 | Gary Bell | .25 | .10 | .02 |
| ☐ 235 | Ron Hunt | .25 | .10 | .02 |
| ☐ 236 | Bill Faul | .25 | .10 | .02 |
| ☐ 237 | Cubs Team | .80 | .32 | .08 |
| ☐ 238 | Roy McMillan | .25 | .10 | .02 |
| ☐ 239 | Herm Starrette | .25 | .10 | .02 |
| ☐ 240 | Bill White | .35 | .14 | .03 |
| ☐ 241 | Jim Owens | .25 | .10 | .02 |
| ☐ 242 | Harvey Kuenn | .65 | .26 | .06 |
| ☐ 243 | Phillies Rookies: | 4.50 | 1.80 | .45 |
| | Richie Allen | | | |
| | John Herrnstein | | | |
| ☐ 244 | Tony LaRussa | 1.25 | .50 | .12 |
| ☐ 245 | Dick Stigman | .25 | .10 | .02 |
| ☐ 246 | Manny Mota | .60 | .24 | .06 |
| ☐ 247 | Dave DeBusschere | 1.50 | .60 | .15 |
| ☐ 248 | Johnny Pesky MGR | .35 | .14 | .03 |
| ☐ 249 | Doug Camilli | .25 | .10 | .02 |
| ☐ 250 | Al Kaline | 5.50 | 2.20 | .55 |
| ☐ 251 | Choo Choo Coleman | .25 | .10 | .02 |
| ☐ 252 | Ken Aspromonte | .25 | .10 | .02 |
| ☐ 253 | Wally Post | .25 | .10 | .02 |
| ☐ 254 | Don Hoak | .25 | .10 | .02 |
| ☐ 255 | Lee Thomas | .25 | .10 | .02 |
| ☐ 256 | Johnny Weekly | .25 | .10 | .02 |
| ☐ 257 | Giants Team | .80 | .32 | .08 |
| ☐ 258 | Garry Roggenburk | .25 | .10 | .02 |
| ☐ 259 | Harry Bright | .25 | .10 | .02 |
| ☐ 260 | Frank Robinson | 4.50 | 1.80 | .45 |
| ☐ 261 | Jim Hannan | .25 | .10 | .02 |
| ☐ 262 | Cards Rookies: | 1.00 | .40 | .10 |
| | Mike Shannon | | | |
| | Harry Fanok | | | |
| ☐ 263 | Chuck Estrada | .35 | .14 | .03 |
| ☐ 264 | Jim Landis | .25 | .10 | .02 |
| ☐ 265 | Jim Bunning | 1.50 | .60 | .15 |
| ☐ 266 | Gene Freese | .25 | .10 | .02 |
| ☐ 267 | Wilbur Wood | .60 | .24 | .06 |
| ☐ 268 | Bill's Got It | .35 | .14 | .03 |
| | Danny Murtaugh | | | |
| | Bill Virdon | | | |
| ☐ 269 | Ellis Burton | .25 | .10 | .02 |
| ☐ 270 | Rich Rollins | .25 | .10 | .02 |
| ☐ 271 | Bob Sadowski | .25 | .10 | .02 |
| ☐ 272 | Jake Wood | .25 | .10 | .02 |
| ☐ 273 | Mel Nelson | .25 | .10 | .02 |
| ☐ 274 | Checklist 4 | 2.25 | .20 | .04 |
| ☐ 275 | John Tsitouris | .25 | .10 | .02 |
| ☐ 276 | Jose Tartabull | .25 | .10 | .02 |
| ☐ 277 | Ken Retzer | .25 | .10 | .02 |
| ☐ 278 | Bobby Shantz | .35 | .14 | .03 |
| ☐ 279 | Joe Koppe (glove | .35 | .14 | .03 |
| | on wrong hand) | | | |
| ☐ 280 | Juan Marichal | 4.00 | 1.60 | .40 |
| ☐ 281 | Yankees Rookies: | .35 | .14 | .03 |
| | Jake Gibbs | | | |
| | Tom Metcalf | | | |
| ☐ 282 | Bob Bruce | .25 | .10 | .02 |
| ☐ 283 | Tommy McCraw | .25 | .10 | .02 |
| ☐ 284 | Dick Schofield | .25 | .10 | .02 |
| ☐ 285 | Robin Roberts | 3.00 | 1.20 | .30 |
| ☐ 286 | Don Landrum | .25 | .10 | .02 |
| ☐ 287 | Red Sox Rookies | 2.50 | 1.00 | .25 |
| | Tony Conigliaro | | | |
| | Bill Spanswick | | | |
| ☐ 288 | Al Moran | .25 | .10 | .02 |
| ☐ 289 | Frank Funk | .25 | .10 | .02 |
| ☐ 290 | Bob Allison | .35 | .14 | .03 |
| ☐ 291 | Phil Ortega | .25 | .10 | .02 |
| ☐ 292 | Mike Roarke | .25 | .10 | .02 |
| ☐ 293 | Phillies Team | .80 | .32 | .08 |
| ☐ 294 | Kent Hunt | .25 | .10 | .02 |
| ☐ 295 | Roger Craig | .60 | .24 | .06 |
| ☐ 296 | Ed Kirkpatrick | .25 | .10 | .02 |
| ☐ 297 | Ken MacKenzie | .25 | .10 | .02 |
| ☐ 298 | Harry Craft | .25 | .10 | .02 |
| ☐ 299 | Bill Stafford | .25 | .10 | .02 |
| ☐ 300 | Hank Aaron | 22.00 | 9.00 | 2.20 |
| ☐ 301 | Larry Brown | .25 | .10 | .02 |
| ☐ 302 | Dan Pfister | .25 | .10 | .02 |
| ☐ 303 | Jim Campbell | .25 | .10 | .02 |
| ☐ 304 | Bob Johnson | .25 | .10 | .02 |
| ☐ 305 | Jack Lamabe | .25 | .10 | .02 |
| ☐ 306 | Giant Gunners | 5.00 | 2.00 | .50 |
| | Willie Mays | | | |
| | Orlando Cepeda | | | |
| ☐ 307 | Joe Gibbon | .25 | .10 | .02 |
| ☐ 308 | Gene Stephens | .25 | .10 | .02 |
| ☐ 309 | Paul Toth | .25 | .10 | .02 |
| ☐ 310 | Jim Gilliam | 1.25 | .50 | .12 |
| ☐ 311 | Tom Brown | .25 | .10 | .02 |
| ☐ 312 | Tigers Rookies: | .25 | .10 | .02 |
| | Fritz Fisher | | | |
| | Fred Gladding | | | |
| ☐ 313 | Chuck Hiller | .25 | .10 | .02 |
| ☐ 314 | Jerry Buchek | .25 | .10 | .02 |
| ☐ 315 | Bo Belinsky | .35 | .14 | .03 |
| ☐ 316 | Gene Oliver | .25 | .10 | .02 |
| ☐ 317 | Al Smith | .25 | .10 | .02 |
| ☐ 318 | Twins Team | .80 | .32 | .08 |
| ☐ 319 | Paul Brown | .25 | .10 | .02 |
| ☐ 320 | Rocky Colavito | 1.25 | .50 | .12 |
| ☐ 321 | Bob Lillis | .35 | .14 | .03 |
| ☐ 322 | George Brunet | .25 | .10 | .02 |
| ☐ 323 | John Buzhardt | .25 | .10 | .02 |

| | | | | |
|---|---|---|---|---|
| ☐ 324 | Casey Stengel MGR | 4.00 | 1.60 | .40 |
| ☐ 325 | Hector Lopez | .25 | .10 | .02 |
| ☐ 326 | Ron Brand | .25 | .10 | .02 |
| ☐ 327 | Don Blasingame | .25 | .10 | .02 |
| ☐ 328 | Bob Shaw | .25 | .10 | .02 |
| ☐ 329 | Russ Nixon | .25 | .10 | .02 |
| ☐ 330 | Tommy Harper | .35 | .14 | .03 |
| ☐ 331 | AL Bombers: | 15.00 | 6.00 | 1.50 |
| | Roger Maris | | | |
| | Norm Cash | | | |
| | Mickey Mantle | | | |
| | Al Kaline | | | |
| ☐ 332 | Ray Washburn | .25 | .10 | .02 |
| ☐ 333 | Billy Moran | .25 | .10 | .02 |
| ☐ 334 | Lew Krausse | .25 | .10 | .02 |
| ☐ 335 | Don Mossi | .35 | .14 | .03 |
| ☐ 336 | Andre Rodgers | .25 | .10 | .02 |
| ☐ 337 | Dodgers Rookies: | .50 | .20 | .05 |
| | Al Ferrara | | | |
| | Jeff Torborg | | | |
| ☐ 338 | Jack Kralick | .25 | .10 | .02 |
| ☐ 339 | Walt Bond | .25 | .10 | .02 |
| ☐ 340 | Joe Cunningham | .25 | .10 | .02 |
| ☐ 341 | Jim Roland | .25 | .10 | .02 |
| ☐ 342 | Willie Stargell | 7.50 | 3.00 | .75 |
| ☐ 343 | Senators Team | .80 | .32 | .08 |
| ☐ 344 | Phil Linz | .25 | .10 | .02 |
| ☐ 345 | Frank Thomas | .25 | .10 | .02 |
| ☐ 346 | Joe Jay | .25 | .10 | .02 |
| ☐ 347 | Bobby Wine | .25 | .10 | .02 |
| ☐ 348 | Ed Lopat MGR | .50 | .20 | .05 |
| ☐ 349 | Art Fowler | .25 | .10 | .02 |
| ☐ 350 | Willie McCovey | 6.50 | 2.60 | .65 |
| ☐ 351 | Dan Schneider | .25 | .10 | .02 |
| ☐ 352 | Eddie Bressoud | .25 | .10 | .02 |
| ☐ 353 | Wally Moon | .35 | .14 | .03 |
| ☐ 354 | Dave Giusti | .35 | .14 | .03 |
| ☐ 355 | Vic Power | .25 | .10 | .02 |
| ☐ 356 | Reds Rookies: | .35 | .14 | .03 |
| | Bill McCool | | | |
| | Chico Ruiz | | | |
| ☐ 357 | Charley James | .25 | .10 | .02 |
| ☐ 358 | Ron Kline | .25 | .10 | .02 |
| ☐ 359 | Jim Schaffer | .25 | .10 | .02 |
| ☐ 360 | Joe Pepitone | .60 | .24 | .06 |
| ☐ 361 | Jay Hook | .25 | .10 | .02 |
| ☐ 362 | Checklist 5 | 2.25 | .20 | .04 |
| ☐ 363 | Dick McAuliffe | .25 | .10 | .02 |
| ☐ 364 | Joe Gaines | .25 | .10 | .02 |
| ☐ 365 | Cal McLish | .25 | .10 | .02 |
| ☐ 366 | Nelson Mathews | .25 | .10 | .02 |
| ☐ 367 | Fred Whitfield | .25 | .10 | .02 |
| ☐ 368 | White Sox Rookies | .35 | .14 | .03 |
| | Fritz Ackley | | | |
| | Don Buford | | | |
| ☐ 369 | Jerry Zimmerman | .25 | .10 | .02 |
| ☐ 370 | Hal Woodeshick | .25 | .10 | .02 |
| ☐ 371 | Frank Howard | 1.25 | .50 | .12 |
| ☐ 372 | Howie Koplitz | .40 | .16 | .04 |
| ☐ 373 | Pirates Team | 1.00 | .40 | .10 |
| ☐ 374 | Bobby Bolin | .40 | .16 | .04 |
| ☐ 375 | Ron Santo | 1.00 | .40 | .10 |
| ☐ 376 | Dave Morehead | .40 | .16 | .04 |
| ☐ 377 | Bob Skinner | .50 | .20 | .05 |
| ☐ 378 | Braves Rookies: | .50 | .20 | .05 |
| | Woody Woodward | | | |
| | Jack Smith | | | |
| ☐ 379 | Tony Gonzalez | .40 | .16 | .04 |
| ☐ 380 | Whitey Ford | 7.00 | 2.80 | .70 |
| ☐ 381 | Bob Taylor | .40 | .16 | .04 |
| ☐ 382 | Wes Stock | .40 | .16 | .04 |
| ☐ 383 | Bill Rigney MGR | .40 | .16 | .04 |
| ☐ 384 | Ron Hansen | .40 | .16 | .04 |
| ☐ 385 | Curt Simmons | .50 | .20 | .05 |
| ☐ 386 | Lenny Green | .40 | .16 | .04 |
| ☐ 387 | Terry Fox | .40 | .16 | .04 |
| ☐ 388 | A's Rookies | .40 | .16 | |
| | John O'Donoghue | | | |
| | George Williams | | | |
| ☐ 389 | Jim Umbricht | .40 | .16 | .04 |
| ☐ 390 | Orlando Cepeda | 2.00 | .80 | .20 |
| ☐ 391 | Sam McDowell | .75 | .30 | .07 |
| ☐ 392 | Jim Pagliaroni | .40 | .16 | .04 |
| ☐ 393 | Casey Teaches | 2.00 | .80 | .20 |
| | Casey Stengel | | | |
| | Ed Kranepool | | | |
| ☐ 394 | Bob Miller | .40 | .16 | .04 |
| ☐ 395 | Tom Tresh | 1.00 | .40 | .10 |
| ☐ 396 | Dennis Bennett | .40 | .16 | .04 |
| ☐ 397 | Chuck Cottier | .50 | .20 | .05 |
| ☐ 398 | Mets Rookies: | .40 | .16 | .04 |
| | Bill Haas | | | |
| | Dick Smith | | | |
| ☐ 399 | Jackie Brandt | .40 | .16 | .04 |
| ☐ 400 | Warren Spahn | 7.00 | 2.80 | .70 |
| ☐ 401 | Charlie Maxwell | .40 | .16 | .04 |
| ☐ 402 | Tom Sturdivant | .40 | .16 | .04 |
| ☐ 403 | Reds Team | 1.00 | .40 | .10 |
| ☐ 404 | Tony Martinez | .40 | .16 | .04 |
| ☐ 405 | Ken McBride | .40 | .16 | .04 |
| ☐ 406 | Al Spangler | .40 | .16 | .04 |
| ☐ 407 | Bill Freehan | 1.50 | .60 | .15 |
| ☐ 408 | Cubs Rookies: | .40 | .16 | .04 |
| | Jim Stewart | | | |
| | Fred Burdette | | | |
| ☐ 409 | Bill Fischer | .40 | .16 | .04 |
| ☐ 410 | Dick Stuart | .60 | .24 | .06 |
| ☐ 411 | Lee Walls | .40 | .16 | .04 |
| ☐ 412 | Ray Culp | .40 | .16 | .04 |
| ☐ 413 | Johnny Keane MGR | .50 | .20 | .05 |
| ☐ 414 | Jack Sanford | .50 | .20 | .05 |
| ☐ 415 | Tony Kubek | 2.25 | .90 | .22 |
| ☐ 416 | Lee Maye | .40 | .16 | .04 |
| ☐ 417 | Don Cardwell | .40 | .16 | .04 |
| ☐ 418 | Orioles Rookies: | .60 | .24 | .06 |
| | Darold Knowles | | | |
| | Les Narum | | | |
| ☐ 419 | Ken Harrelson | 2.50 | 1.00 | .25 |
| ☐ 420 | Jim Maloney | .75 | .30 | .07 |
| ☐ 421 | Camilo Carreon | .40 | .16 | .04 |
| ☐ 422 | Jack Fisher | .40 | .16 | .04 |
| ☐ 423 | Tops in N.L. | 12.00 | 5.00 | 1.20 |
| | Hank Aaron | | | |
| | Willie Mays | | | |
| ☐ 424 | Dick Bertell | .40 | .16 | .04 |
| ☐ 425 | Norm Cash | 1.00 | .40 | .10 |
| ☐ 426 | Bob Rodgers | .40 | .16 | .04 |
| ☐ 427 | Don Rudolph | .40 | .16 | .04 |
| ☐ 428 | Red Sox Rookies: | .40 | .16 | .04 |
| | Archie Skeen | | | |
| | Pete Smith | | | |
| ☐ 429 | Tim McCarver | 1.00 | .40 | .10 |
| ☐ 430 | Juan Pizarro | .40 | .16 | .04 |
| ☐ 431 | George Alusik | .40 | .16 | .04 |
| ☐ 432 | Ruben Amaro | .40 | .16 | .04 |
| ☐ 433 | Yankees Team | 2.50 | 1.00 | .25 |
| ☐ 434 | Don Nottebart | .40 | .16 | .04 |
| ☐ 435 | Vic Davalillo | .50 | .20 | .05 |
| ☐ 436 | Charlie Neal | .50 | .20 | .05 |
| ☐ 437 | Ed Bailey | .40 | .16 | .04 |
| ☐ 438 | Checklist 6 | 2.50 | .25 | .05 |
| ☐ 439 | Harvey Haddix | .60 | .24 | .06 |
| ☐ 440 | Bob Clemente | 16.00 | 6.50 | 1.60 |
| ☐ 441 | Bob Duliba | .40 | .16 | .04 |
| ☐ 442 | Pumpsie Green | .40 | .16 | .04 |
| ☐ 443 | Chuck Dressen MGR | .40 | .16 | .04 |
| ☐ 444 | Larry Jackson | .40 | .16 | .04 |
| ☐ 445 | Bill Skowron | 1.00 | .40 | .10 |
| ☐ 446 | Julian Javier | .40 | .16 | .04 |
| ☐ 447 | Ted Bowsfield | .40 | .16 | .04 |
| ☐ 448 | Cookie Rojas | .40 | .16 | .04 |
| ☐ 449 | Deron Johnson | .40 | .16 | .04 |
| ☐ 450 | Steve Barber | .40 | .16 | .04 |
| ☐ 451 | Joe Amalfitano | .40 | .16 | .04 |
| ☐ 452 | Giants Rookies | 1.00 | .40 | .10 |
| | Gil Garrido | | | |
| | Jim Ray Hart | | | |
| ☐ 453 | Frank Baumann | .40 | .16 | .04 |
| ☐ 454 | Tommie Aaron | .60 | .24 | .06 |
| ☐ 455 | Bernie Allen | .40 | .16 | .04 |
| ☐ 456 | Dodgers Rookies | 1.25 | .50 | .12 |
| | Wes Parker | | | |
| | John Werhas | | | |
| ☐ 457 | Jesse Gonder | .40 | .16 | .04 |
| ☐ 458 | Ralph Terry | .60 | .24 | .06 |
| ☐ 459 | Red Sox Rookies | .40 | .16 | .04 |
| | Pete Charton | | | |
| | Dalton Jones | | | |
| ☐ 460 | Bob Gibson | 7.50 | 3.00 | .75 |
| ☐ 461 | George Thomas | .40 | .16 | .04 |
| ☐ 462 | Birdie Tebbetts MGR | .40 | .16 | .04 |
| ☐ 463 | Don Leppert | .40 | .16 | .04 |
| ☐ 464 | Dallas Green | .75 | .30 | .07 |
| ☐ 465 | Mike Hershberger | .40 | .16 | .04 |
| ☐ 466 | A's Rookies | .40 | .16 | .04 |
| | Dick Green | | | |
| | Aurelio Monteagudo | | | |
| ☐ 467 | Bob Aspromonte | .40 | .16 | .04 |
| ☐ 468 | Gaylord Perry | 7.00 | 2.80 | .70 |
| ☐ 469 | Cubs Rookies | .60 | .24 | .06 |
| | Fred Norman | | | |
| | Sterling Slaughter | | | |
| ☐ 470 | Jim Bouton | 1.25 | .50 | .12 |
| ☐ 471 | Gates Brown | 1.00 | .40 | .10 |
| ☐ 472 | Vern Law | .65 | .26 | .06 |
| ☐ 473 | Orioles Team | 1.00 | .40 | .10 |

| | | | | |
|---|---|---|---|---|
| ☐ 474 | Larry Sherry | .50 | .20 | .05 |
| ☐ 475 | Ed Charles | .40 | .16 | .04 |
| ☐ 476 | Braves Rookies: | 2.25 | .90 | .22 |
| | Rico Carty | | | |
| | Dick Kelley | | | |
| ☐ 477 | Mike Joyce | .40 | .16 | .04 |
| ☐ 478 | Dick Howser | .75 | .30 | .07 |
| ☐ 479 | Cardinals Rookies: | .40 | .16 | .04 |
| | Dave Bakenhaster | | | |
| | Johnny Lewis | | | |
| ☐ 480 | Bob Purkey | .40 | .16 | .04 |
| ☐ 481 | Chuck Schilling | .40 | .16 | .04 |
| ☐ 482 | Phillies Rookies | .60 | .24 | .06 |
| | John Briggs | | | |
| | Danny Cater | | | |
| ☐ 483 | Fred Valentine | .40 | .16 | .04 |
| ☐ 484 | Bill Pleis | .40 | .16 | .04 |
| ☐ 485 | Tom Haller | .40 | .16 | .04 |
| ☐ 486 | Bob Kennedy MGR | .40 | .16 | .04 |
| ☐ 487 | Mike McCormick | .50 | .20 | .05 |
| ☐ 488 | Yankees Rookies | .40 | .16 | .04 |
| | Pete Mikkelsen | | | |
| | Bob Meyer | | | |
| ☐ 489 | Julio Navarro | .40 | .16 | .04 |
| ☐ 490 | Ron Fairly | .50 | .20 | .05 |
| ☐ 491 | Ed Rakow | .40 | .16 | .04 |
| ☐ 492 | Colts Rookies | .40 | .16 | .04 |
| | Jim Beauchamp | | | |
| | Mike White | | | |
| ☐ 493 | Don Lee | .40 | .16 | .04 |
| ☐ 494 | Al Jackson | .40 | .16 | .04 |
| ☐ 495 | Bill Virdon | 1.00 | .40 | .10 |
| ☐ 496 | White Sox Team | 1.00 | .40 | .10 |
| ☐ 497 | Jeoff Long | .40 | .16 | .04 |
| ☐ 498 | Dave Stenhouse | .40 | .16 | .04 |
| ☐ 499 | Indians Rookies | .40 | .16 | .04 |
| | Chico Salmon | | | |
| | Gordon Seyfried | | | |
| ☐ 500 | Camilo Pascual | .50 | .20 | .05 |
| ☐ 501 | Bob Veale | .50 | .20 | .05 |
| ☐ 502 | Angels Rookies: | .50 | .20 | .05 |
| | Bobby Knoop | | | |
| | Bob Lee | | | |
| ☐ 503 | Earl Wilson | .40 | .16 | .04 |
| ☐ 504 | Claude Raymond | .40 | .16 | .04 |
| ☐ 505 | Stan Williams | .40 | .16 | .04 |
| ☐ 506 | Bobby Bragan MGR | .40 | .16 | .04 |
| ☐ 507 | John Edwards | .40 | .16 | .04 |
| ☐ 508 | Diego Segui | .40 | .16 | .04 |
| ☐ 509 | Pirates Rookies: | .80 | .32 | .08 |
| | Gene Alley | | | |
| | Orlando McFarlane | | | |
| ☐ 510 | Lindy McDaniel | .50 | .20 | .05 |
| ☐ 511 | Lou Jackson | .40 | .16 | .04 |
| ☐ 512 | Tigers Rookies: | 2.25 | .90 | .22 |
| | Willie Horton | | | |
| | Joe Sparma | | | |
| ☐ 513 | Don Larsen | .60 | .24 | .06 |
| ☐ 514 | Jim Hickman | .40 | .16 | .04 |
| ☐ 515 | Johnny Romano | .40 | .16 | .04 |
| ☐ 516 | Twins Rookies: | .40 | .16 | .04 |
| | Jerry Arrigo | | | |
| | Dwight Siebler | | | |
| ☐ 517A | Checklist 7 COR | 3.00 | .30 | .06 |
| | (correct numbering on back) | | | |
| ☐ 517B | Checklist 7 ERR | 6.00 | .60 | .10 |
| | (incorrect numbering sequence on back) | | | |
| ☐ 518 | Carl Bouldin | .40 | .16 | .04 |
| ☐ 519 | Charlie Smith | .40 | .16 | .04 |
| ☐ 520 | Jack Baldschun | .40 | .16 | .04 |
| ☐ 521 | Tom Satriano | .40 | .16 | .04 |
| ☐ 522 | Bob Tiefenauer | .40 | .16 | .04 |
| ☐ 523 | Lou Burdette | 2.00 | .80 | .20 |
| | (pitching lefty) | | | |
| ☐ 524 | Reds Rookies: | .90 | .36 | .09 |
| | Jim Dickson | | | |
| | Bobby Klaus | | | |
| ☐ 525 | Al McBean | .90 | .36 | .09 |
| ☐ 526 | Lou Clinton | .90 | .36 | .09 |
| ☐ 527 | Larry Bearnarth | .90 | .36 | .09 |
| ☐ 528 | A's Rookies: | 1.00 | .40 | .10 |
| | Dave Duncan | | | |
| | Tom Reynolds | | | |
| ☐ 529 | Al Dark MGR | 1.00 | .40 | .10 |
| ☐ 530 | Leon Wagner | .90 | .36 | .09 |
| ☐ 531 | Dodgers Team | 2.50 | 1.00 | .25 |
| ☐ 532 | Twins Rookies | .90 | .36 | .09 |
| | Bud Bloomfield | | | |
| | (Bloomfield photo actually Jay Ward) | | | |
| | Joe Nossek | | | |

| | | | | |
|---|---|---|---|---|
| ☐ 533 | John Klippstein | .90 | .36 | .09 |
| ☐ 534 | Gus Bell | 1.00 | .40 | .10 |
| ☐ 535 | Phil Regan | 1.00 | .40 | .10 |
| ☐ 536 | Mets Rookies: | .90 | .36 | .09 |
| | Larry Elliot | | | |
| | John Stephenson | | | |
| ☐ 537 | Dan Osinski | .90 | .36 | .09 |
| ☐ 538 | Minnie Minoso | 2.00 | .80 | .20 |
| ☐ 539 | Roy Face | 1.50 | .60 | .15 |
| ☐ 540 | Luis Aparicio | 5.50 | 2.20 | .55 |
| ☐ 541 | Braves Rookies: | 35.00 | 14.00 | 3.50 |
| | Phil Roof | | | |
| | Phil Niekro | | | |
| ☐ 542 | Don Mincher | 1.00 | .40 | .10 |
| ☐ 543 | Bob Uecker | 9.00 | 3.75 | .90 |
| ☐ 544 | Colts Rookies: | .90 | .36 | .09 |
| | Steve Hertz | | | |
| | Joe Hoerner | | | |
| ☐ 545 | Max Alvis | .90 | .36 | .09 |
| ☐ 546 | Joe Christopher | .90 | .36 | .09 |
| ☐ 547 | Gil Hodges | 4.00 | 1.60 | .40 |
| ☐ 548 | NL Rookies | .90 | .36 | .09 |
| | Wayne Schurr | | | |
| | Paul Speckenbach | | | |
| ☐ 549 | Joe Moeller | .90 | .36 | .09 |
| ☐ 550 | Ken Hubbs | 3.00 | 1.20 | .30 |
| | (in memoriam) | | | |
| ☐ 551 | Billy Hoeft | .90 | .36 | .09 |
| ☐ 552 | Indians Rookies | 1.00 | .40 | .10 |
| | Tom Kelley | | | |
| | Sonny Siebert | | | |
| ☐ 553 | Jim Brewer | .90 | .36 | .09 |
| ☐ 554 | Hank Foiles | .90 | .36 | .09 |
| ☐ 555 | Lee Stange | .90 | .36 | .09 |
| ☐ 556 | Mets Rookies | .90 | .36 | .09 |
| | Steve Dillon | | | |
| | Ron Locke | | | |
| ☐ 557 | Leo Burke | .90 | .36 | .09 |
| ☐ 558 | Don Schwall | .90 | .36 | .09 |
| ☐ 559 | Dick Phillips | .90 | .36 | .09 |
| ☐ 560 | Dick Farrell | .90 | .36 | .09 |
| ☐ 561 | Phillies Rookies | 2.00 | .80 | .20 |
| | Dave Bennett | | | |
| | (19 ... is 18) | | | |
| | Rick Wise | | | |
| ☐ 562 | Pedro Ramos | .90 | .36 | .09 |
| ☐ 563 | Dal Maxvill | .90 | .36 | .09 |
| ☐ 564 | AL Rookies | .90 | .36 | .09 |
| | Joe McCabe | | | |
| | Jerry McNertney | | | |
| ☐ 565 | Stu Miller | .90 | .36 | .09 |
| ☐ 566 | Ed Kranepool | 1.25 | .50 | .12 |
| ☐ 567 | Jim Kaat | 4.00 | 1.60 | .40 |
| ☐ 568 | NL Rookies | .90 | .36 | .09 |
| | Phil Gagliano | | | |
| | Cap Peterson | | | |
| ☐ 569 | Fred Newman | .90 | .36 | .09 |
| ☐ 570 | Bill Mazeroski | 2.00 | .80 | .20 |
| ☐ 571 | Gene Conley | .90 | .36 | .09 |
| ☐ 572 | AL Rookies | .90 | .36 | .09 |
| | Dave Gray | | | |
| | Dick Egan | | | |
| ☐ 573 | Jim Duffalo | .90 | .36 | .09 |
| ☐ 574 | Manny Jimenez | .90 | .36 | .09 |
| ☐ 575 | Tony Cloninger | .90 | .36 | .09 |
| ☐ 576 | Mets Rookies: | .90 | .36 | .09 |
| | Jerry Hinsley | | | |
| | Bill Wakefield | | | |
| ☐ 577 | Gordy Coleman | .90 | .36 | .09 |
| ☐ 578 | Glen Hobbie | .90 | .36 | .09 |
| ☐ 579 | Red Sox Team | 2.00 | .80 | .20 |
| ☐ 580 | Johnny Podres | 1.75 | .70 | .17 |
| ☐ 581 | Yankees Rookies | .90 | .36 | .09 |
| | Pedro Gonzales | | | |
| | Archie Moore | | | |
| ☐ 582 | Rod Kanehl | .90 | .36 | .09 |
| ☐ 583 | Tito Francona | 1.00 | .40 | .10 |
| ☐ 584 | Joel Horlen | 1.00 | .40 | .10 |
| ☐ 585 | Tony Taylor | .90 | .36 | .09 |
| ☐ 586 | Jim Piersall | 1.50 | .60 | .15 |
| ☐ 587 | Bennie Daniels | 1.50 | .50 | .10 |

## 1964 Topps Giants

The cards in this 60 card set measure 3 1/8" by 5 1/4". The 1964 Topps Giants are postcard size cards containing color player photographs. They are numbered on the backs, which also contain biographical information presented in a newspaper format. These "giant size" cards were distributed in both cellophane and waxed gum packs apart from the Topps regular issue of 1964. Cards 3, 28, 42, 45, 47, 51 and 60 slightly more difficult to find and are indicated by SP in the checklist below.

|  | MINT | VG-E | F-G |
|---|---|---|---|
| COMPLETE SET | 45.00 | 18.00 | 4.50 |
| COMMON PLAYER (1-60) | .10 | .04 | .01 |
| □ 1 Gary Peters | .10 | .04 | .01 |
| □ 2 Ken Johnson | .10 | .04 | .01 |
| □ 3 Sandy Koufax SP | 8.00 | 3.25 | .80 |
| □ 4 Bob Bailey | .10 | .04 | .01 |
| □ 5 Milt Pappas | .10 | .04 | .01 |
| □ 6 Ron Hunt | .10 | .04 | .01 |
| □ 7 Whitey Ford | 1.00 | .40 | .10 |
| □ 8 Roy McMillan | .10 | .04 | .01 |
| □ 9 Rocky Colavito | .25 | .10 | .02 |
| □ 10 Jim Bunning | .40 | .16 | .04 |
| □ 11 Bob Clemente | 2.25 | .90 | .22 |
| □ 12 Al Kaline | 1.50 | .60 | .15 |
| □ 13 Nellie Fox | .25 | .10 | .02 |
| □ 14 Tony Gonzalez | .10 | .04 | .01 |
| □ 15 Jim Gentile | .10 | .04 | .01 |
| □ 16 Dean Chance | .10 | .04 | .01 |
| □ 17 Dick Ellsworth | .10 | .04 | .01 |
| □ 18 Jim Fregosi | .15 | .06 | .01 |
| □ 19 Dick Groat | .15 | .06 | .01 |
| □ 20 Chuck Hinton | .10 | .04 | .01 |
| □ 21 Elston Howard | .25 | .10 | .02 |
| □ 22 Dick Farrell | .10 | .04 | .01 |
| □ 23 Albie Pearson | .10 | .04 | .01 |
| □ 24 Frank Howard | .20 | .08 | .02 |
| □ 25 Mickey Mantle | 4.50 | 1.80 | .45 |
| □ 26 Joe Torre | .20 | .08 | .02 |
| □ 27 Eddie Brinkman | .10 | .04 | .01 |
| □ 28 Bob Friend SP | 2.25 | .90 | .22 |
| □ 29 Frank Robinson | 1.25 | .50 | .12 |
| □ 30 Bill Freehan | .15 | .06 | .01 |
| □ 31 Warren Spahn | 1.25 | .50 | .12 |
| □ 32 Camilo Pascual | .10 | .04 | .01 |
| □ 33 Pete Ward | .10 | .04 | .01 |
| □ 34 Jim Maloney | .10 | .04 | .01 |
| □ 35 Dave Wickersham | .10 | .04 | .01 |
| □ 36 Johnny Callison | .10 | .04 | .01 |
| □ 37 Juan Marichal | 1.00 | .40 | .10 |
| □ 38 Harmon Killebrew | 1.00 | .40 | .10 |
| □ 39 Luis Aparicio | 1.00 | .40 | .10 |
| □ 40 Dick Radatz | .10 | .04 | .01 |
| □ 41 Bob Gibson | 1.00 | .40 | .10 |
| □ 42 Dick Stuart SP | 2.25 | .90 | .22 |
| □ 43 Tommy Davis | .15 | .06 | .01 |
| □ 44 Tony Oliva | .20 | .08 | .02 |
| □ 45 Wayne Causey SP | 2.25 | .90 | .22 |
| □ 46 Max Alvis | .10 | .04 | .01 |
| □ 47 Galen Cisco SP | 2.25 | .90 | .22 |
| □ 48 Carl Yastrzemski | 2.50 | 1.00 | .25 |
| □ 49 Hank Aaron | 2.50 | 1.00 | .25 |
| □ 50 Brooks Robinson | 1.50 | .60 | .15 |
| □ 51 Willie Mays SP | 9.00 | 3.75 | .90 |
| □ 52 Billy Williams | 1.00 | .40 | .10 |
| □ 53 Juan Pizarro | .10 | .04 | .01 |
| □ 54 Leon Wagner | .10 | .04 | .01 |
| □ 55 Orlando Cepeda | .25 | .10 | .02 |
| □ 56 Vada Pinson | .15 | .06 | .01 |
| □ 57 Ken Boyer | .20 | .08 | .02 |
| □ 58 Ron Santo | .15 | .06 | .01 |
| □ 59 John Romano | .10 | .04 | .01 |
| □ 60 Bill Skowron SP | 3.00 | 1.20 | .30 |

## 1964 Topps Stand Ups

In 1964 Topps produced a die-cut "Stand-Up" card design for the first time since their Connie Mack and Current All Stars of 1951. The cards have full length, color player photos set against a green and yellow background. Of the 77 cards in the set, 22 were single printed and these are marked in the checklist below with an SP. These unnumbered cards are standard sized (2 1/2" by 3 1/2"), blank backed, and have been numbered here for reference in alphabetical order of players.

|  | MINT | VG-E | F-G |
|---|---|---|---|
| COMPLETE SET | 800.00 | 320.00 | 80.00 |
| COMMON PLAYER (1-77) | 2.00 | .80 | .20 |
| COMMON PLAYER SP | 12.00 | 5.00 | 1.20 |
| □ 1 Hank Aaron | 40.00 | 16.00 | 4.00 |
| □ 2 Hank Aguirre | 2.00 | .80 | .20 |
| □ 3 George Altman | 2.00 | .80 | .20 |
| □ 4 Max Alvis | 2.00 | .80 | .20 |
| □ 5 Bob Aspromonte | 2.00 | .80 | .20 |
| □ 6 Jack Baldschun SP | 12.00 | 5.00 | 1.20 |
| □ 7 Ernie Banks | 18.00 | 7.25 | 1.80 |
| □ 8 Steve Barber | 2.00 | .80 | .20 |
| □ 9 Earl Battey | 2.00 | .80 | .20 |
| □ 10 Ken Boyer | 3.50 | 1.40 | .35 |
| □ 11 Ernie Broglio | 2.00 | .80 | .20 |
| □ 12 John Callison | 2.00 | .80 | .20 |
| □ 13 Norm Cash SP | 14.00 | 5.75 | 1.40 |
| □ 14 Wayne Causey | 2.00 | .80 | .20 |
| □ 15 Orlando Cepeda | 3.50 | 1.40 | .35 |
| □ 16 Ed Charles | 2.00 | .80 | .20 |
| □ 17 Bob Clemente | 32.00 | 13.00 | 3.20 |
| □ 18 Donn Clendenon SP | 12.00 | 5.00 | 1.20 |
| □ 19 Rocky Colavito | 3.50 | 1.40 | .35 |
| □ 20 Ray Culp SP | 12.00 | 5.00 | 1.20 |
| □ 21 Tommy Davis | 2.50 | 1.00 | .25 |
| □ 22 Don Drysdale SP | 40.00 | 16.00 | 4.00 |
| □ 23 Dick Ellsworth | 2.00 | .80 | .20 |
| □ 24 Dick Farrell | 2.00 | .80 | .20 |
| □ 25 Jim Fregosi | 2.50 | 1.00 | .25 |
| □ 26 Bob Friend | 2.00 | .80 | .20 |

| | | MINT | VG-E | F-G |
|---|---|---|---|---|
| ☐ 27 | Jim Gentile | 2.00 | .80 | .20 |
| ☐ 28 | Jesse Gonder SP | 12.00 | 5.00 | 1.20 |
| ☐ 29 | Tony Gonzalez SP | 12.00 | 5.00 | 1.20 |
| ☐ 30 | Dick Groat | 2.50 | 1.00 | .25 |
| ☐ 31 | Woody Held | 2.00 | .80 | .20 |
| ☐ 32 | Chuck Hinton | 2.00 | .80 | .20 |
| ☐ 33 | Elston Howard | 3.50 | 1.40 | .35 |
| ☐ 34 | Frank Howard SP | 14.00 | 5.75 | 1.40 |
| ☐ 35 | Ron Hunt | 2.00 | .80 | .20 |
| ☐ 36 | Al Jackson | 2.00 | .80 | .20 |
| ☐ 37 | Ken Johnson | 2.00 | .80 | .20 |
| ☐ 38 | Al Kaline | 20.00 | 8.00 | 2.00 |
| ☐ 39 | Harmon Killebrew | 15.00 | 6.00 | 1.50 |
| ☐ 40 | Sandy Koufax | 27.00 | 11.00 | 2.70 |
| ☐ 41 | Don Lock SP | 12.00 | 5.00 | 1.20 |
| ☐ 42 | Jerry Lumpe SP | 12.00 | 5.00 | 1.20 |
| ☐ 43 | Jim Maloney | 2.00 | .80 | .20 |
| ☐ 44 | Frank Malzone | 2.00 | .80 | .20 |
| ☐ 45 | Mickey Mantle | 90.00 | 36.00 | 9.00 |
| ☐ 46 | Juan Marichal SP | 40.00 | 16.00 | 4.00 |
| ☐ 47 | Eddie Mathews SP | 40.00 | 16.00 | 4.00 |
| ☐ 48 | Willie Mays | 40.00 | 16.00 | 4.00 |
| ☐ 49 | Bill Mazeroski | 2.50 | 1.00 | .25 |
| ☐ 50 | Ken McBride | 2.00 | .80 | .20 |
| ☐ 51 | Willie McCovey SP | 40.00 | 16.00 | 4.00 |
| ☐ 52 | Claude Osteen | 2.00 | .80 | .20 |
| ☐ 53 | Jim O'Toole | 2.00 | .80 | .20 |
| ☐ 54 | Camilo Pascual | 2.00 | .80 | .20 |
| ☐ 55 | Albie Pearson SP | 12.00 | 5.00 | 1.20 |
| ☐ 56 | Gary Peters | 2.00 | .80 | .20 |
| ☐ 57 | Vada Pinson | 2.50 | 1.00 | .25 |
| ☐ 58 | Juan Pizarro | 2.00 | .80 | .20 |
| ☐ 59 | Boog Powell | 2.50 | 1.00 | .25 |
| ☐ 60 | Bobby Richardson | 2.50 | 1.00 | .25 |
| ☐ 61 | Brooks Robinson | 24.00 | 10.00 | 2.40 |
| ☐ 62 | Floyd Robinson | 2.00 | .80 | .20 |
| ☐ 63 | Frank Robinson | 18.00 | 7.25 | 1.80 |
| ☐ 64 | Ed Roebuck SP | 12.00 | 5.00 | 1.20 |
| ☐ 65 | Rich Rollins | 2.00 | .80 | .20 |
| ☐ 66 | John Romano | 2.00 | .80 | .20 |
| ☐ 67 | Ron Santo SP | 14.00 | 5.75 | 1.40 |
| ☐ 68 | Norm Siebern | 2.00 | .80 | .20 |
| ☐ 69 | Warren Spahn SP | 40.00 | 16.00 | 4.00 |
| ☐ 70 | Dick Stuart SP | 12.00 | 5.00 | 1.20 |
| ☐ 71 | Lee Thomas | 2.00 | .80 | .20 |
| ☐ 72 | Joe Torre | 3.50 | 1.40 | .35 |
| ☐ 73 | Pete Ward | 2.00 | .80 | .20 |
| ☐ 74 | Bill White SP | 14.00 | 5.75 | 1.40 |
| ☐ 75 | Billy Williams SP | 35.00 | 14.00 | 3.50 |
| ☐ 76 | Hal Woodeshick SP | 12.00 | 5.00 | 1.20 |
| ☐ 77 | Carl Yastrzemski SP | 150.00 | 60.00 | 15.00 |

## 1965 Topps

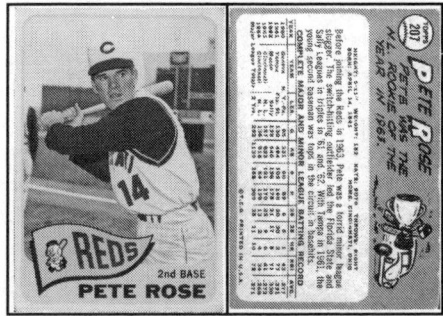

2nd BASE
PETE ROSE

The cards in this 598 card set measure 2 1/2" by 3 1/2". The cards comprising the 1965 Topps set have team names located within a distinctive pennant design below the picture. The cards have blue borders on the reverse and were issued by series. Cards 523 to 598 are more difficult to obtain than all other series. In addition, the sixth series (447-522) is more difficult to obtain than series one through five. Featured subsets within this set include League Leaders (1-12) and World Series

cards (132-139). Key cards in this set include Steve Carlton's rookie and Pete Rose.

| | | MINT | VG-E | F-G |
|---|---|---|---|---|
| COMPLETE SET | | 750.00 | 300.00 | 75.00 |
| COMMON PLAYER (1-198) | | .21 | .09 | .02 |
| COMMON PLAYER (199-446) | | .30 | .12 | .03 |
| COMMON PLAYER (447-522) | | .55 | .22 | .05 |
| COMMON PLAYER (523-598) | | .85 | .34 | .08 |
| ☐ 1 | AL Batting Leaders<br>Tony Oliva<br>Elston Howard<br>Brooks Robinson | 2.25 | .50 | .10 |
| ☐ 2 | NL Batting Leaders<br>Bob Clemente<br>Hank Aaron<br>Rico Carty | 2.00 | .80 | .20 |
| ☐ 3 | AL Home Run Leaders<br>Harmon Killebrew<br>Mickey Mantle<br>Boog Powell | 2.00 | .80 | .20 |
| ☐ 4 | NL Home Run Leaders<br>Willie Mays<br>Billy Williams<br>Jim Ray Hart<br>Orlando Cepeda<br>Johnny Callison | 2.00 | .80 | .20 |
| ☐ 5 | AL RBI Leaders<br>Brooks Robinson<br>Harmon Killebrew<br>Mickey Mantle<br>Dick Stuart | 2.00 | .80 | .20 |
| ☐ 6 | NL RBI Leaders<br>Ken Boyer<br>Willie Mays<br>Ron Santo | 1.00 | .40 | .10 |
| ☐ 7 | AL ERA Leaders<br>Dean Chance<br>Joel Horlen | .75 | .30 | .07 |
| ☐ 8 | NL ERA Leaders<br>Sandy Koufax<br>Don Drysdale | 3.00 | 1.20 | .30 |
| ☐ 9 | AL Pitching Leaders<br>Dean Chance<br>Gary Peters<br>Dave Wickersham<br>Juan Pizarro<br>Wally Bunker | .75 | .30 | .07 |
| ☐ 10 | NL Pitching Leaders<br>Larry Jackson<br>Ray Sadecki<br>Juan Marichal | .75 | .30 | .07 |
| ☐ 11 | AL Strikeout Leaders<br>Al Downing<br>Dean Chance<br>Camilo Pascual | .75 | .30 | .07 |
| ☐ 12 | NL Strikeout Leaders<br>Bob Veale<br>Don Drysdale<br>Bob Gibson | 1.00 | .40 | .10 |
| ☐ 13 | Pedro Ramos | .21 | .09 | .02 |
| ☐ 14 | Len Gabrielson | .21 | .09 | .02 |
| ☐ 15 | Robin Roberts | 3.00 | 1.20 | .30 |
| ☐ 16 | Houston Rookies:<br>Joe Morgan<br>Sonny Jackson | 18.00 | 7.25 | 1.80 |
| ☐ 17 | John Romano | .21 | .09 | .02 |
| ☐ 18 | Bill McCool | .21 | .09 | .02 |
| ☐ 19 | Gates Brown | .30 | .12 | .03 |
| ☐ 20 | Jim Bunning | 1.50 | .60 | .15 |
| ☐ 21 | Don Blasingame | .21 | .09 | .02 |
| ☐ 22 | Charlie Smith | .21 | .09 | .02 |
| ☐ 23 | Bob Tiefenauer | .21 | .09 | .02 |
| ☐ 24 | Twins Team | 1.00 | .40 | .10 |
| ☐ 25 | Al McBean | .21 | .09 | .02 |
| ☐ 26 | Bob Knoop | .21 | .09 | .02 |
| ☐ 27 | Dick Bertell | .21 | .09 | .02 |
| ☐ 28 | Barney Schultz | .21 | .09 | .02 |
| ☐ 29 | Felix Mantilla | .21 | .09 | .02 |
| ☐ 30 | Jim Bouton | .75 | .30 | .07 |
| ☐ 31 | Mike White | .21 | .09 | .02 |
| ☐ 32 | Herman Franks MGR | .21 | .09 | .02 |
| ☐ 33 | Jackie Brandt | .21 | .09 | .02 |
| ☐ 34 | Cal Koonce | .21 | .09 | .02 |
| ☐ 35 | Ed Charles | .21 | .09 | .02 |
| ☐ 36 | Bob Wine | .21 | .09 | .02 |
| ☐ 37 | Fred Gladding | .21 | .09 | .02 |
| ☐ 38 | Jim King | .21 | .09 | .02 |
| ☐ 39 | Gerry Arrigo | .21 | .09 | .02 |
| ☐ 40 | Frank Howard | .90 | .36 | .09 |
| ☐ 41 | White Sox Rookies | .21 | .09 | .02 |

| | | | | | |
|---|---|---|---|---|---|
| | Bruce Howard | | | | |
| | Marv Staehle | | | | |
| ☐ 42 | Earl Wilson | .21 | .09 | .02 |
| ☐ 43 | Mike Shannon | .40 | .16 | .04 |
| ☐ 44 | Wade Blasingame | .21 | .09 | .02 |
| ☐ 45 | Roy McMillan | .21 | .09 | .02 |
| ☐ 46 | Bob Lee | .21 | .09 | .02 |
| ☐ 47 | Tom Harper | .30 | .12 | .03 |
| ☐ 48 | Claude Raymond | .21 | .09 | .02 |
| ☐ 49 | Orioles Rookies | .50 | .20 | .05 |
| | Curt Blefary | | | | |
| | John Miller | | | | |
| ☐ 50 | Juan Marichal | 3.50 | 1.40 | .35 |
| ☐ 51 | Bill Bryan | .21 | .09 | .02 |
| ☐ 52 | Ed Roebuck | .21 | .09 | .02 |
| ☐ 53 | Dick McAuliffe | .21 | .09 | .02 |
| ☐ 54 | Joe Gibbon | .21 | .09 | .02 |
| ☐ 55 | Tony Conigliaro | .90 | .36 | .09 |
| ☐ 56 | Ron Kline | .21 | .09 | .02 |
| ☐ 57 | Cardinals Team | .80 | .32 | .08 |
| ☐ 58 | Fred Talbot | .21 | .09 | .02 |
| ☐ 59 | Nate Oliver | .21 | .09 | .02 |
| ☐ 60 | Jim O'Toole | .21 | .09 | .02 |
| ☐ 61 | Chris Cannizzaro | .21 | .09 | .02 |
| ☐ 62 | Jim Katt (sic, Kaat) | 2.00 | .80 | .20 |
| ☐ 63 | Ty Cline | .21 | .09 | .02 |
| ☐ 64 | Lou Burdette | .65 | .26 | .06 |
| ☐ 65 | Tony Kubek | 1.25 | .50 | .12 |
| ☐ 66 | Bill Rigney MGR | .21 | .09 | .02 |
| ☐ 67 | Harvey Haddix | .35 | .14 | .03 |
| ☐ 68 | Del Crandall | .30 | .12 | .03 |
| ☐ 69 | Bill Virdon | .60 | .24 | .06 |
| ☐ 70 | Bill Skowron | .60 | .24 | .06 |
| ☐ 71 | John O'Donoghue | .21 | .09 | .02 |
| ☐ 72 | Tony Gonzalez | .21 | .09 | .02 |
| ☐ 73 | Dennis Ribant | .21 | .09 | .02 |
| ☐ 74 | Red Sox Rookies | 1.00 | .40 | .10 |
| | Rico Petrocelli | | | | |
| | Jerry Stephenson | | | | |
| ☐ 75 | Deron Johnson | .25 | .10 | .02 |
| ☐ 76 | Sam McDowell | .35 | .14 | .03 |
| ☐ 77 | Doug Camilli | .21 | .09 | .02 |
| ☐ 78 | Dal Maxvill | .21 | .09 | .02 |
| ☐ 79 | Checklist 1 | 2.00 | .20 | .04 |
| ☐ 80 | Turk Farrell | .21 | .09 | .02 |
| ☐ 81 | Don Buford | .21 | .09 | .02 |
| ☐ 82 | Braves Rookies: | .30 | .12 | .03 |
| | Santos Alomar | | | | |
| | John Braun | | | | |
| ☐ 83 | George Thomas | .21 | .09 | .02 |
| ☐ 84 | Ron Herbel | .21 | .09 | .02 |
| ☐ 85 | Willie Smith | .21 | .09 | .02 |
| ☐ 86 | Les Narum | .21 | .09 | .02 |
| ☐ 87 | Nelson Mathews | .21 | .09 | .02 |
| ☐ 88 | Jack Lamabe | .21 | .09 | .02 |
| ☐ 89 | Mike Hershberger | .21 | .09 | .02 |
| ☐ 90 | Rich Rollins | .21 | .09 | .02 |
| ☐ 91 | Cubs Team | .75 | .30 | .07 |
| ☐ 92 | Dick Howser | .50 | .20 | .05 |
| ☐ 93 | Jack Fisher | .21 | .09 | .02 |
| ☐ 94 | Charlie Lau | .30 | .12 | .03 |
| ☐ 95 | Bill Mazeroski | 1.00 | .40 | .10 |
| ☐ 96 | Sonny Siebert | .25 | .10 | .02 |
| ☐ 97 | Pedro Gonzalez | .21 | .09 | .02 |
| ☐ 98 | Bob Miller | .21 | .09 | .02 |
| ☐ 99 | Gil Hodges MGR | 3.00 | 1.20 | .30 |
| ☐ 100 | Ken Boyer | 1.25 | .50 | .12 |
| ☐ 101 | Fred Newman | .21 | .09 | .02 |
| ☐ 102 | Steve Boros | .30 | .12 | .03 |
| ☐ 103 | Harvey Kuenn | .55 | .22 | .05 |
| ☐ 104 | Checklist 2 | 2.00 | .20 | .04 |
| ☐ 105 | Chico Salmon | .21 | .09 | .02 |
| ☐ 106 | Gene Oliver | .21 | .09 | .02 |
| ☐ 107 | Phillies Rookies | .75 | .30 | .07 |
| | Pat Corrales | | | | |
| | Costen Shockley | | | | |
| ☐ 108 | Don Mincher | .25 | .10 | .02 |
| ☐ 109 | Walt Bond | .21 | .09 | .02 |
| ☐ 110 | Ron Santo | .80 | .32 | .08 |
| ☐ 111 | Lee Thomas | .21 | .09 | .02 |
| ☐ 112 | Derrell Griffith | .21 | .09 | .02 |
| ☐ 113 | Steve Barber | .21 | .09 | .02 |
| ☐ 114 | Jim Hickman | .21 | .09 | .02 |
| ☐ 115 | Bobby Richardson | 1.00 | .40 | .10 |
| ☐ 116 | Cardinals Rookies: | .40 | .16 | .04 |
| | Dave Dowling | | | | |
| | Bob Tolan | | | | |
| ☐ 117 | Wes Stock | .25 | .10 | .02 |
| ☐ 118 | Hal Lanier | .50 | .20 | .05 |
| ☐ 119 | John Kennedy | .21 | .09 | .02 |
| ☐ 120 | Frank Robinson | 4.50 | 1.80 | .45 |
| ☐ 121 | Gene Alley | .25 | .10 | .02 |
| ☐ 122 | Bill Pleis | .21 | .09 | .02 |

| | | | | | |
|---|---|---|---|---|---|
| ☐ 123 | Frank Thomas | .21 | .09 | .02 |
| ☐ 124 | Tom Satriano | .21 | .09 | .02 |
| ☐ 125 | Juan Pizarro | .21 | .09 | .02 |
| ☐ 126 | Dodgers Team | 1.50 | .60 | .15 |
| ☐ 127 | Frank Lary | .25 | .10 | .02 |
| ☐ 128 | Vic Davalillo | .25 | .10 | .02 |
| ☐ 129 | Bennie Daniels | .21 | .09 | .02 |
| ☐ 130 | Al Kaline | 4.50 | 1.80 | .45 |
| ☐ 131 | Johnny Keane MGR | .30 | .12 | .03 |
| ☐ 132 | World Series Game 1 | 1.00 | .40 | .10 |
| | Cards take opener | | | | |
| ☐ 133 | World Series Game 2 | 1.00 | .40 | .10 |
| | Stottlemyre wins | | | | |
| ☐ 134 | World Series Game 3 | 4.50 | 1.80 | .45 |
| | Mantle's homer | | | | |
| ☐ 135 | World Series Game 4 | 1.25 | .50 | .12 |
| | Boyer's grand-slam | | | | |
| ☐ 136 | World Series Game 5 | 1.00 | .40 | .10 |
| | 10th inning triumph | | | | |
| ☐ 137 | World Series Game 6 | 1.25 | .50 | .12 |
| | Bouton wins again | | | | |
| ☐ 138 | World Series Game 7 | 2.25 | .90 | .22 |
| | Gibson wins finale | | | | |
| ☐ 139 | World Series Summary | 1.00 | .40 | .10 |
| | Cards celebrate | | | | |
| ☐ 140 | Dean Chance | .25 | .10 | .02 |
| ☐ 141 | Charlie James | .21 | .09 | .02 |
| ☐ 142 | Bill Monbouquette | .21 | .09 | .02 |
| ☐ 143 | Pirates Rookies: | .21 | .09 | .02 |
| | John Gelnar | | | | |
| | Jerry May | | | | |
| ☐ 144 | Ed Kranepool | .30 | .12 | .03 |
| ☐ 145 | Luis Tiant | 2.50 | 1.00 | .25 |
| ☐ 146 | Ron Hansen | .21 | .09 | .02 |
| ☐ 147 | Dennis Bennett | .21 | .09 | .02 |
| ☐ 148 | Willie Kirkland | .21 | .09 | .02 |
| ☐ 149 | Wayne Schurr | .21 | .09 | .02 |
| ☐ 150 | Brooks Robinson | 5.00 | 2.00 | .50 |
| ☐ 151 | Athletics Team | .75 | .30 | .07 |
| ☐ 152 | Phil Ortega | .21 | .09 | .02 |
| ☐ 153 | Norm Cash | .90 | .36 | .09 |
| ☐ 154 | Bob Humphreys | .21 | .09 | .02 |
| ☐ 155 | Roger Maris | 5.00 | 2.00 | .50 |
| ☐ 156 | Bob Sadowski | .21 | .09 | .02 |
| ☐ 157 | Zoilo Versalles | .50 | .20 | .05 |
| ☐ 158 | Dick Sisler | .21 | .09 | .02 |
| ☐ 159 | Jim Duffalo | .21 | .09 | .02 |
| ☐ 160 | Bob Clemente | 12.00 | 5.00 | 1.20 |
| ☐ 161 | Frank Baumann | .21 | .09 | .02 |
| ☐ 162 | Russ Nixon | .21 | .09 | .02 |
| ☐ 163 | John Briggs | .21 | .09 | .02 |
| ☐ 164 | Al Spangler | .21 | .09 | .02 |
| ☐ 165 | Dick Ellsworth | .25 | .10 | .02 |
| ☐ 166 | Indians Rookies | .50 | .20 | .05 |
| | George Culver | | | | |
| | Tommie Agee | | | | |
| ☐ 167 | Bill Wakefield | .21 | .09 | .02 |
| ☐ 168 | Dick Green | .21 | .09 | .02 |
| ☐ 169 | Dave Vineyard | .21 | .09 | .02 |
| ☐ 170 | Hank Aaron | 20.00 | 8.00 | 2.00 |
| ☐ 171 | Jim Roland | .21 | .09 | .02 |
| ☐ 172 | Jim Piersall | .65 | .26 | .06 |
| ☐ 173 | Tigers Team | .85 | .34 | .08 |
| ☐ 174 | Joe Jay | .21 | .09 | .02 |
| ☐ 175 | Bob Aspromonte | .21 | .09 | .02 |
| ☐ 176 | Willie McCovey | 5.00 | 2.00 | .50 |
| ☐ 177 | Pete Mikkelsen | .21 | .09 | .02 |
| ☐ 178 | Dalton Jones | .21 | .09 | .02 |
| ☐ 179 | Hal Woodeshick | .21 | .09 | .02 |
| ☐ 180 | Bob Allison | .35 | .14 | .03 |
| ☐ 181 | Senators Rookies | .21 | .09 | .02 |
| | Don Loun | | | | |
| | Joe McCabe | | | | |
| ☐ 182 | Mike De La Hoz | .21 | .09 | .02 |
| ☐ 183 | Dave Nicholson | .21 | .09 | .02 |
| ☐ 184 | John Boozer | .21 | .09 | .02 |
| ☐ 185 | Max Alvis | .21 | .09 | .02 |
| ☐ 186 | Bill Cowan | .21 | .09 | .02 |
| ☐ 187 | Casey Stengel MGR | 3.50 | 1.40 | .35 |
| ☐ 188 | Sam Bowens | .21 | .09 | .02 |
| ☐ 189 | Checklist 3 | 2.00 | .20 | .04 |
| ☐ 190 | Bill White | .40 | .16 | .04 |
| ☐ 191 | Phil Regan | .25 | .10 | .02 |
| ☐ 192 | Jim Coker | .21 | .09 | .02 |
| ☐ 193 | Gaylord Perry | 3.50 | 1.40 | .35 |
| ☐ 194 | Rookie Stars | .25 | .10 | .02 |
| | Bill Kelso | | | | |
| | Rick Reichardt | | | | |
| ☐ 195 | Bob Veale | .30 | .12 | .03 |
| ☐ 196 | Ron Fairly | .30 | .12 | .03 |
| ☐ 197 | Diego Segui | .21 | .09 | .02 |
| ☐ 198 | Smoky Burgess | .30 | .12 | .03 |
| ☐ 199 | Bob Heffner | .30 | .12 | .03 |

| | | | |
|---|---|---|---|
| ☐ 200 Joe Torre | 1.00 | .40 | .10 |
| ☐ 201 Twins Rookies | .40 | .16 | .04 |
| Sandy Valdespino | | | |
| Cesar Tovar | | | |
| ☐ 202 Leo Burke | .30 | .12 | .03 |
| ☐ 203 Dallas Green | .40 | .16 | .04 |
| ☐ 204 Russ Snyder | .30 | .12 | .03 |
| ☐ 205 Warren Spahn | 4.50 | 1.80 | .45 |
| ☐ 206 Willie Horton | .75 | .30 | .07 |
| ☐ 207 Pete Rose | 110.00 | 45.00 | 11.00 |
| ☐ 208 Tommy John | 2.25 | .90 | .22 |
| ☐ 209 Pirates Team | .85 | .34 | .08 |
| ☐ 210 Jim Fregosi | .50 | .20 | .05 |
| ☐ 211 Steve Ridzik | .30 | .12 | .03 |
| ☐ 212 Ron Brand | .30 | .12 | .03 |
| ☐ 213 Jim Davenport | .40 | .16 | .04 |
| ☐ 214 Bob Purkey | .30 | .12 | .03 |
| ☐ 215 Pete Ward | .30 | .12 | .03 |
| ☐ 216 Al Worthington | .30 | .12 | .03 |
| ☐ 217 Walt Alston MGR | 1.00 | .40 | .10 |
| ☐ 218 Dick Schofield | .30 | .12 | .03 |
| ☐ 219 Bob Meyer | .30 | .12 | .03 |
| ☐ 220 Billy Williams | 3.50 | 1.40 | .35 |
| ☐ 221 John Tsitouris | .30 | .12 | .03 |
| ☐ 222 Bob Tillman | .30 | .12 | .03 |
| ☐ 223 Dan Osinski | .30 | .12 | .03 |
| ☐ 224 Bob Chance | .30 | .12 | .03 |
| ☐ 225 Bo Belinsky | .40 | .16 | .04 |
| ☐ 226 Yankees Rookies | .40 | .16 | .04 |
| Elvio Jimenez | | | |
| Jake Gibbs | | | |
| ☐ 227 Bob Klaus | .30 | .12 | .03 |
| ☐ 228 Jack Sanford | .40 | .16 | .04 |
| ☐ 229 Lou Clinton | .30 | .12 | .03 |
| ☐ 230 Ray Sadecki | .30 | .12 | .03 |
| ☐ 231 Jerry Adair | .30 | .12 | .03 |
| ☐ 232 Steve Blass | .60 | .24 | .06 |
| ☐ 233 Don Zimmer | .50 | .20 | .05 |
| ☐ 234 White Sox Team | .85 | .34 | .08 |
| ☐ 235 Chuck Hinton | .30 | .12 | .03 |
| ☐ 236 Dennis McLain | 2.50 | 1.00 | .25 |
| ☐ 237 Bernie Allen | .30 | .12 | .03 |
| ☐ 238 Joe Moeller | .30 | .12 | .03 |
| ☐ 239 Doc Edwards | .30 | .12 | .03 |
| ☐ 240 Bob Bruce | .30 | .12 | .03 |
| ☐ 241 Mack Jones | .30 | .12 | .03 |
| ☐ 242 George Brunet | .30 | .12 | .03 |
| ☐ 243 Reds Rookies | .50 | .20 | .05 |
| Ted Davidson | | | |
| Tommy Helms | | | |
| ☐ 244 Lindy McDaniel | .30 | .12 | .03 |
| ☐ 245 Joe Pepitone | .50 | .20 | .05 |
| ☐ 246 Tom Butters | .30 | .12 | .03 |
| ☐ 247 Wally Moon | .40 | .16 | .04 |
| ☐ 248 Gus Triandos | .40 | .16 | .04 |
| ☐ 249 Dave McNally | .75 | .30 | .07 |
| ☐ 250 Willie Mays | 22.00 | 9.00 | 2.20 |
| ☐ 251 Billy Herman MGR | 1.00 | .40 | .10 |
| ☐ 252 Pete Richert | .30 | .12 | .03 |
| ☐ 253 Danny Cater | .30 | .12 | .03 |
| ☐ 254 Roland Sheldon | .30 | .12 | .03 |
| ☐ 255 Camilo Pascual | .40 | .16 | .04 |
| ☐ 256 Tito Francona | .40 | .16 | .04 |
| ☐ 257 Jim Wynn | .60 | .24 | .06 |
| ☐ 258 Larry Bearnarth | .30 | .12 | .03 |
| ☐ 259 Tigers Rookies | .50 | .20 | .05 |
| Jim Northrup | | | |
| Ray Oyler | | | |
| ☐ 260 Don Drysdale | 4.00 | 1.60 | .40 |
| ☐ 261 Duke Carmel | .30 | .12 | .03 |
| ☐ 262 Bud Daley | .30 | .12 | .03 |
| ☐ 263 Marty Keough | .30 | .12 | .03 |
| ☐ 264 Bob Buhl | .30 | .12 | .03 |
| ☐ 265 Jim Pagliaroni | .30 | .12 | .03 |
| ☐ 266 Bert Campaneris | 1.25 | .50 | .12 |
| ☐ 267 Senators Team | .75 | .30 | .07 |
| ☐ 268 Ken McBride | .30 | .12 | .03 |
| ☐ 269 Frank Bolling | .30 | .12 | .03 |
| ☐ 270 Milt Pappas | .40 | .16 | .04 |
| ☐ 271 Don Wert | .30 | .12 | .03 |
| ☐ 272 Chuck Schilling | .30 | .12 | .03 |
| ☐ 273 Checklist 4 | 2.00 | .20 | .04 |
| ☐ 274 Lum Harris MGR | .30 | .12 | .03 |
| ☐ 275 Dick Groat | .60 | .24 | .06 |
| ☐ 276 Hoyt Wilhelm | 3.00 | 1.20 | .30 |
| ☐ 277 John Lewis | .30 | .12 | .03 |
| ☐ 278 Ken Retzer | .30 | .12 | .03 |
| ☐ 279 Dick Tracewski | .30 | .12 | .03 |
| ☐ 280 Dick Stuart | .40 | .16 | .04 |
| ☐ 281 Bill Stafford | .30 | .12 | .03 |
| ☐ 282 Giants Rookies | .60 | .24 | .06 |
| Dick Estelle | | | |
| Masanori Murakami | | | |
| ☐ 283 Fred Whitfield | .30 | .12 | .03 |
| ☐ 284 Nick Willhite | .30 | .12 | .03 |
| ☐ 285 Ron Hunt | .30 | .12 | .03 |
| ☐ 286 Athletics Rookies | .30 | .12 | .03 |
| Jim Dickson | | | |
| Aurelio Monteagudo | | | |
| ☐ 287 Gary Kolb | .30 | .12 | .03 |
| ☐ 288 Jack Hamilton | .30 | .12 | .03 |
| ☐ 289 Gordy Coleman | .30 | .12 | .03 |
| ☐ 290 Wally Bunker | .30 | .12 | .03 |
| ☐ 291 Jerry Lynch | .30 | .12 | .03 |
| ☐ 292 Larry Yellen | .30 | .12 | .03 |
| ☐ 293 Angels Team | .75 | .30 | .07 |
| ☐ 294 Tim McCarver | .85 | .34 | .08 |
| ☐ 295 Dick Radatz | .40 | .16 | .04 |
| ☐ 296 Tony Taylor | .30 | .12 | .03 |
| ☐ 297 Dave Debusschere | 1.50 | .60 | .15 |
| ☐ 298 Jim Stewart | .30 | .12 | .03 |
| ☐ 299 Jerry Zimmerman | .30 | .12 | .03 |
| ☐ 300 Sandy Koufax | 20.00 | 8.00 | 2.00 |
| ☐ 301 Birdie Tebbetts MGR | .30 | .12 | .03 |
| ☐ 302 Al Stanek | .30 | .12 | .03 |
| ☐ 303 John Orsino | .30 | .12 | .03 |
| ☐ 304 Dave Stenhouse | .30 | .12 | .03 |
| ☐ 305 Rico Carty | .75 | .30 | .07 |
| ☐ 306 Bubba Phillips | .30 | .12 | .03 |
| ☐ 307 Barry Latman | .30 | .12 | .03 |
| ☐ 308 Mets Rookies | .40 | .16 | .04 |
| Cleon Jones | | | |
| Tom Parsons | | | |
| ☐ 309 Steve Hamilton | .30 | .12 | .03 |
| ☐ 310 John Callison | .40 | .16 | .04 |
| ☐ 311 Orlando Pena | .30 | .12 | .03 |
| ☐ 312 Joe Nuxhall | .40 | .16 | .04 |
| ☐ 313 Jim Schaffer | .30 | .12 | .03 |
| ☐ 314 Sterling Slaughter | .30 | .12 | .03 |
| ☐ 315 Frank Malzone | .40 | .16 | .04 |
| ☐ 316 Reds Team | .85 | .34 | .08 |
| ☐ 317 Don McMahon | .30 | .12 | .03 |
| ☐ 318 Matty Alou | .40 | .16 | .04 |
| ☐ 319 Ken McMullen | .30 | .12 | .03 |
| ☐ 320 Bob Gibson | 4.00 | 1.60 | .40 |
| ☐ 321 Rusty Staub | 1.75 | .70 | .17 |
| ☐ 322 Rick Wise | .50 | .20 | .05 |
| ☐ 323 Hank Bauer MGR | .40 | .16 | .04 |
| ☐ 324 Bob Locke | .30 | .12 | .03 |
| ☐ 325 Donn Clendenon | .40 | .16 | .04 |
| ☐ 326 Dwight Siebler | .30 | .12 | .03 |
| ☐ 327 Denis Menke | .30 | .12 | .03 |
| ☐ 328 Eddie Fisher | .30 | .12 | .03 |
| ☐ 329 Hawk Taylor | .30 | .12 | .03 |
| ☐ 330 Whitey Ford | 5.50 | 2.20 | .55 |
| ☐ 331 Dodgers Rookies | .40 | .16 | .04 |
| Al Ferrara | | | |
| John Purdin | | | |
| ☐ 332 Ted Abernathy | .30 | .12 | .03 |
| ☐ 333 Tom Reynolds | .30 | .12 | .03 |
| ☐ 334 Vic Roznovsky | .30 | .12 | .03 |
| ☐ 335 Mickey Lolich | 1.50 | .60 | .15 |
| ☐ 336 Woody Held | .30 | .12 | .03 |
| ☐ 337 Mike Cuellar | .50 | .20 | .05 |
| ☐ 338 Phillies Team | .80 | .32 | .08 |
| ☐ 339 Ryne Duren | .40 | .16 | .04 |
| ☐ 340 Tony Oliva | 2.00 | .80 | .20 |
| ☐ 341 Bob Bolin | .30 | .12 | .03 |
| ☐ 342 Bob Rodgers | .30 | .12 | .03 |
| ☐ 343 Mike McCormick | .40 | .16 | .04 |
| ☐ 344 Wes Parker | .50 | .20 | .05 |
| ☐ 345 Floyd Robinson | .30 | .12 | .03 |
| ☐ 346 Bob Bragan MGR | .30 | .12 | .03 |
| ☐ 347 Roy Face | .60 | .24 | .06 |
| ☐ 348 George Banks | .30 | .12 | .03 |
| ☐ 349 Larry Miller | .30 | .12 | .03 |
| ☐ 350 Mickey Mantle | 75.00 | 30.00 | 7.50 |
| ☐ 351 Jim Perry | .50 | .20 | .05 |
| ☐ 352 Alex Johnson | .40 | .16 | .04 |
| ☐ 353 Jerry Lumpe | .30 | .12 | .03 |
| ☐ 354 Cubs Rookies | .30 | .12 | .03 |
| Billy Ott | | | |
| Jack Warner | | | |
| ☐ 355 Vada Pinson | 1.00 | .40 | .10 |
| ☐ 356 Bill Spanswick | .30 | .12 | .03 |
| ☐ 357 Carl Warwick | .30 | .12 | .03 |
| ☐ 358 Albie Pearson | .30 | .12 | .03 |
| ☐ 359 Ken Johnson | .30 | .12 | .03 |
| ☐ 360 Orlando Cepeda | 1.75 | .70 | .17 |
| ☐ 361 Checklist 5 | 2.00 | .20 | .04 |
| ☐ 362 Don Schwall | .30 | .12 | .03 |
| ☐ 363 Bob Johnson | .30 | .12 | .03 |
| ☐ 364 Galen Cisco | .30 | .12 | .03 |
| ☐ 365 Jim Gentile | .40 | .16 | .04 |
| ☐ 366 Dan Schneider | .30 | .12 | .03 |
| ☐ 367 Leon Wagner | .30 | .12 | .03 |

| | | | |
|---|---|---|---|
| □ 368 White Sox Rookies .......... | .40 | .16 | .04 |
| Ken Berry | | | |
| Joel Gibson | | | |
| □ 369 Phil Linz ......................... | .40 | .16 | .04 |
| □ 370 Tommy Davis ................. | .65 | .26 | .06 |
| □ 371 Frank Kreutzer ............... | .30 | .12 | .03 |
| □ 372 Clay Dalrymple ............. | .30 | .12 | .03 |
| □ 373 Curt Simmons ............... | .40 | .16 | .04 |
| □ 374 Angels Rookies .............. | .50 | .20 | .05 |
| Jose Cardenal | | | |
| Dick Simpson | | | |
| □ 375 Dave Wickersham .......... | .30 | .12 | .03 |
| □ 376 Jim Landis .................... | .30 | .12 | .03 |
| □ 377 Willie Stargell .............. | 4.50 | 1.80 | .45 |
| □ 378 Chuck Estrada ............... | .40 | .16 | .04 |
| □ 379 Giants Team ................. | .85 | .34 | .08 |
| □ 380 Rocky Colavito .............. | 1.25 | .50 | .12 |
| □ 381 Al Jackson ................... | .30 | .12 | .03 |
| □ 382 J.C. Martin .................. | .30 | .12 | .03 |
| □ 383 Felipe Alou .................. | .40 | .16 | .04 |
| □ 384 John Klippstein ............. | .30 | .12 | .03 |
| □ 385 Carl Yastrzemski ........... | 35.00 | 14.00 | 3.50 |
| □ 386 Cubs Rookies ................ | .40 | .16 | .04 |
| Paul Jaeckel | | | |
| Fred Norman | | | |
| □ 387 John Podres ................. | .90 | .36 | .09 |
| □ 388 John Blanchard ............. | .40 | .16 | .04 |
| □ 389 Don Larsen .................. | .50 | .20 | .05 |
| □ 390 Bill Freehan ................. | .90 | .36 | .09 |
| □ 391 Mel McGaha MGR .......... | .30 | .12 | .03 |
| □ 392 Bob Friend ................... | .40 | .16 | .04 |
| □ 393 Ed Kirkpatrick .............. | .30 | .12 | .03 |
| □ 394 Jim Hannan .................. | .30 | .12 | .03 |
| □ 395 Jim Ray Hart ............... | .40 | .16 | .04 |
| □ 396 Frank Bertaina ............. | .30 | .12 | .03 |
| □ 397 Jerry Buchek ................ | .30 | .12 | .03 |
| □ 398 Reds Rookies ................ | .30 | .12 | .03 |
| Dan Neville | | | |
| Art Shamsky | | | |
| □ 399 Ray Herbert ................. | .30 | .12 | .03 |
| □ 400 Harmon Killebrew .......... | 4.50 | 1.80 | .45 |
| □ 401 Carl Willey .................. | .30 | .12 | .03 |
| □ 402 Joe Amalfitano ............. | .30 | .12 | .03 |
| □ 403 Red Sox Team ............. | .85 | .34 | .08 |
| □ 404 Stan Williams .............. | .30 | .12 | .03 |
| □ 405 John Roseboro .............. | .40 | .16 | .04 |
| □ 406 Ralph Terry .................. | .40 | .16 | .04 |
| □ 407 Lee Maye .................... | .30 | .12 | .03 |
| □ 408 Larry Sherry ................ | .40 | .16 | .04 |
| □ 409 Astros Rookies .............. | .50 | .20 | .05 |
| Jim Beauchamp | | | |
| Larry Dierker | | | |
| □ 410 Luis Aparicio ............... | 3.00 | 1.20 | .30 |
| □ 411 Roger Craig ................. | .50 | .20 | .05 |
| □ 412 Bob Bailey ................... | .30 | .12 | .03 |
| □ 413 Hal Reniff ................... | .30 | .12 | .03 |
| □ 414 Al Lopez MGR ............... | 1.25 | .50 | .12 |
| □ 415 Curt Flood .................. | .75 | .30 | .07 |
| □ 416 Jim Brewer .................. | .30 | .12 | .03 |
| □ 417 Ed Brinkman ................ | .30 | .12 | .03 |
| □ 418 John Edwards ............... | .30 | .12 | .03 |
| □ 419 Ruben Amaro ............... | .30 | .12 | .03 |
| □ 420 Larry Jackson .............. | .30 | .12 | .03 |
| □ 421 Twins Rookies ............... | .30 | .12 | .03 |
| Gary Dotter | | | |
| Jay Ward | | | |
| □ 422 Aubrey Gatewood .......... | .30 | .12 | .03 |
| □ 423 Jesse Gonder ............... | .30 | .12 | .03 |
| □ 424 Gary Bell .................... | .30 | .12 | .03 |
| □ 425 Wayne Causey .............. | .30 | .12 | .03 |
| □ 426 Braves Team ................ | .85 | .34 | .08 |
| □ 427 Bob Saverine ............... | .30 | .12 | .03 |
| □ 428 Bob Shaw .................... | .30 | .12 | .03 |
| □ 429 Don Demeter ............... | .30 | .12 | .03 |
| □ 430 Gary Peters .................. | .40 | .16 | .04 |
| □ 431 Cards Rookies .............. | .50 | .20 | .05 |
| Nelson Briles | | | |
| Wayne Spiezio | | | |
| □ 432 Jim Grant .................... | .30 | .12 | .03 |
| □ 433 John Bateman ............... | .30 | .12 | .03 |
| □ 434 Dave Morehead ............. | .30 | .12 | .03 |
| □ 435 Willie Davis ................. | .60 | .24 | .06 |
| □ 436 Don Elston .................. | .30 | .12 | .03 |
| □ 437 Chico Cardenas ............. | .30 | .12 | .03 |
| □ 438 Harry Walker MGR ......... | .30 | .12 | .03 |
| □ 439 Moe Drabowsky ............ | .30 | .12 | .03 |
| □ 440 Tom Tresh .................. | .70 | .28 | .07 |
| □ 441 Denny Lemaster ............ | .30 | .12 | .03 |
| □ 442 Vic Power .................... | .30 | .12 | .03 |
| □ 443 Checklist 6 .................. | 2.25 | .20 | .04 |
| □ 444 Bob Hendley ................ | .30 | .12 | .03 |
| □ 445 Don Lock .................... | .30 | .12 | .03 |
| □ 446 Art Mahaffey ............... | .30 | .12 | .03 |

| | | | |
|---|---|---|---|
| □ 447 Julian Javier ................. | .55 | .22 | .05 |
| □ 448 Lee Stange .................. | .55 | .22 | .05 |
| □ 449 Mets Rookies ................ | .55 | .22 | .05 |
| Jerry Hinsley | | | |
| Gary Kroll | | | |
| □ 450 Elston Howard .............. | 1.75 | .70 | .17 |
| □ 451 Jim Owens ................... | .55 | .22 | .05 |
| □ 452 Gary Geiger ................. | .55 | .22 | .05 |
| □ 453 Dodgers Rookies ........... | .65 | .26 | .06 |
| Willie Crawford | | | |
| John Werhas | | | |
| □ 454 Ed Rakow .................... | .55 | .22 | .05 |
| □ 455 Norm Siebern ............... | .55 | .22 | .05 |
| □ 456 Bill Henry ................... | .55 | .22 | .05 |
| □ 457 Bob Kennedy MGR ......... | .55 | .22 | .05 |
| □ 458 John Buzhardt .............. | .55 | .22 | .05 |
| □ 459 Frank Kostro ................ | .55 | .22 | .05 |
| □ 460 Richie Allen ................. | 2.00 | .80 | .20 |
| □ 461 Braves Rookies ............. | 9.00 | 3.75 | .90 |
| Clay Carroll | | | |
| Phil Niekro | | | |
| □ 462 Lew Krausse ................. | .55 | .22 | .05 |
| (photo actually | | | |
| Pete Lovrich) | | | |
| □ 463 Manny Mota ................. | .75 | .30 | .07 |
| □ 464 Ron Piche .................... | .55 | .22 | .05 |
| □ 465 Tom Haller ................... | .55 | .22 | .05 |
| □ 466 Senators Rookies ........... | .55 | .22 | .05 |
| Pete Craig | | | |
| Dick Nen | | | |
| □ 467 Ray Washburn .............. | .55 | .22 | .05 |
| □ 468 Larry Brown ................. | .55 | .22 | .05 |
| □ 469 Don Nottebart .............. | .55 | .22 | .05 |
| □ 470 Yogi Berra MGR ............ | 10.00 | 4.00 | 1.00 |
| □ 471 Bill Hoeft .................... | .55 | .22 | .05 |
| □ 472 Don Pavletich .............. | .55 | .22 | .05 |
| □ 473 Orioles Rookies ............ | 4.00 | 1.60 | .40 |
| Paul Blair | | | |
| Dave Johnson | | | |
| □ 474 Cookie Rojas ................ | .55 | .22 | .05 |
| □ 475 Clete Boyer ................. | 1.00 | .40 | .10 |
| □ 476 Billy O'Dell ................. | .55 | .22 | .05 |
| □ 477 Cards Rookies .............. | 110.00 | 45.00 | 11.00 |
| Fritz Ackley | | | |
| Steve Carlton | | | |
| □ 478 Wilbur Wood ................ | .75 | .30 | .07 |
| □ 479 Ken Harrelson .............. | 1.50 | .60 | .15 |
| □ 480 Joel Horlen .................. | .65 | .26 | .06 |
| □ 481 Indians Team ............... | 1.25 | .50 | .12 |
| □ 482 Bob Priddy .................. | .55 | .22 | .05 |
| □ 483 George Smith ............... | .55 | .22 | .05 |
| □ 484 Ron Perranoski ............. | .75 | .30 | .07 |
| □ 485 Nellie Fox ................... | 1.75 | .70 | .17 |
| □ 486 Angels Rookies ............. | .55 | .22 | .05 |
| Tom Egan | | | |
| Pat Rogan | | | |
| □ 487 Woody Woodward .......... | .55 | .22 | .05 |
| □ 488 Ted Wills .................... | .55 | .22 | .05 |
| □ 489 Gene Mauch MGR .......... | .75 | .30 | .07 |
| □ 490 Earl Battey .................. | .55 | .22 | .05 |
| □ 491 Tracy Stallard .............. | .55 | .22 | .05 |
| □ 492 Gene Freese ................ | .55 | .22 | .05 |
| □ 493 Tigers Rookies .............. | .55 | .22 | .05 |
| Bill Roman | | | |
| Bruce Brubaker | | | |
| □ 494 Jay Ritchie .................. | .55 | .22 | .05 |
| □ 495 Joe Christopher ............ | .55 | .22 | .05 |
| □ 496 Joe Cunningham ........... | .55 | .22 | .05 |
| □ 497 Giants Rookies ............. | .65 | .26 | .06 |
| Ken Henderson | | | |
| Jack Hiatt | | | |
| □ 498 Gene Stephens ............. | .55 | .22 | .05 |
| □ 499 Stu Miller ................... | .55 | .22 | .05 |
| □ 500 Ed Mathews ................. | 6.00 | 2.40 | .60 |
| □ 501 Indians Rookies ............ | .55 | .22 | .05 |
| Ralph Gagliano | | | |
| Jim Rittwage | | | |
| □ 502 Don Cardwell ............... | .55 | .22 | .05 |
| □ 503 Phil Gagliano ............... | .55 | .22 | .05 |
| □ 504 Jerry Grote .................. | .55 | .22 | .05 |
| □ 505 Ray Culp .................... | .55 | .22 | .05 |
| □ 506 Sam Mele MGR ............. | .55 | .22 | .05 |
| □ 507 Sam Ellis .................... | .55 | .22 | .05 |
| □ 508 Checklist 7 .................. | 3.50 | .35 | .07 |
| □ 509 Red Sox Rookies ........... | .55 | .22 | .05 |
| Bob Guindon | | | |
| Gerry Vezendy | | | |
| □ 510 Ernie Banks ................. | 14.00 | 5.75 | 1.40 |
| □ 511 Ron Locke ................... | .55 | .22 | .05 |
| □ 512 Cap Peterson ............... | .55 | .22 | .05 |
| □ 513 Yankees Team .............. | 2.50 | 1.00 | .25 |
| □ 514 Joe Azcue ................... | .55 | .22 | .05 |
| □ 515 Vern Law .................... | .75 | .30 | .07 |

| □ 516 | Al Weis | .55 | .22 | .05 |
|---|---|---|---|---|
| □ 517 | Angels Rookies | .55 | .22 | .05 |
| | Paul Schaal | | | |
| | Jack Warner | | | |
| □ 518 | Ken Rowe | .55 | .22 | .05 |
| □ 519 | Bob Uecker | 8.00 | 3.25 | .80 |
| □ 520 | Tony Cloninger | .55 | .22 | .05 |
| □ 521 | Phillies Rookies | .55 | .22 | .05 |
| | Dave Bennett | | | |
| | Morrie Stevens | | | |
| □ 522 | Hank Aguirre | .55 | .22 | .05 |
| □ 523 | Mike Brumley | .85 | .34 | .08 |
| □ 524 | Dave Giusti | .85 | .34 | .08 |
| □ 525 | Ed Bressoud | .85 | .34 | .08 |
| □ 526 | Athletics Rookies | 25.00 | 10.00 | 2.50 |
| | Rene Lachemann | | | |
| | Johnny Odom | | | |
| | Jim Hunter | | | |
| | Skip Lockwood | | | |
| □ 527 | Jeff Torborg | 1.00 | .40 | .10 |
| □ 528 | George Altman | .85 | .34 | .08 |
| □ 529 | Jerry Fosnow | .85 | .34 | .08 |
| □ 530 | Jim Maloney | 1.00 | .40 | .10 |
| □ 531 | Chuck Hiller | .85 | .34 | .08 |
| □ 532 | Hector Lopez | .85 | .34 | .08 |
| □ 533 | Mets Rookies | 4.50 | 1.80 | .45 |
| | Dan Napoleon | | | |
| | Ron Swoboda | | | |
| | Tug McGraw | | | |
| | Jim Bethke | | | |
| □ 534 | John Herrnstein | .85 | .34 | .08 |
| □ 535 | Jack Kralick | .85 | .34 | .08 |
| □ 536 | Andre Rodgers | .85 | .34 | .08 |
| □ 537 | Angels Rookies | 1.00 | .40 | .10 |
| | Marcelino Lopes | | | |
| | Phil Roof | | | |
| | Rudy May | | | |
| □ 538 | Chuck Dressen MGR | .85 | .34 | .08 |
| □ 539 | Herm Starrette | .85 | .34 | .08 |
| □ 540 | Lou Brock | 14.00 | 5.75 | 1.40 |
| □ 541 | White Sox Rookies | .85 | .34 | .08 |
| | Greg Bollo | | | |
| | Bob Locker | | | |
| □ 542 | Lou Klimchock | .85 | .34 | .08 |
| □ 543 | Ed Connolly | .85 | .34 | .08 |
| □ 544 | Howie Reed | .85 | .34 | .08 |
| □ 545 | Jesus Alou | .85 | .34 | .08 |
| □ 546 | Indians Rookies | .85 | .34 | .08 |
| | Bill Davis | | | |
| | Mike Hedlund | | | |
| | Ray Barker | | | |
| | Floyd Weaver | | | |
| □ 547 | Jake Wood | .85 | .34 | .08 |
| □ 548 | Dick Stigman | .85 | .34 | .08 |
| □ 549 | Cubs Rookies | 1.50 | .60 | .15 |
| | Roberto Pena | | | |
| | Glenn Beckert | | | |
| □ 550 | Mel Stottlemyre | 4.00 | 1.60 | .40 |
| □ 551 | Mets Team | 2.50 | 1.00 | .25 |
| □ 552 | Julio Gotay | .85 | .34 | .08 |
| □ 553 | Astros Rookies | .85 | .34 | .08 |
| | Gene Ratliff | | | |
| | Jack McClure | | | |
| □ 554 | Chico Ruiz | .85 | .34 | .08 |
| □ 555 | Jack Baldschun | .85 | .34 | .08 |
| □ 556 | Red Schoendienst MGR | 1.50 | .60 | .15 |
| □ 557 | Jose Santiago | .85 | .34 | .08 |
| □ 558 | Tom Sisk | .85 | .34 | .08 |
| □ 559 | Ed Bailey | .85 | .34 | .08 |
| □ 560 | Boog Powell | 1.75 | .70 | .17 |
| □ 561 | Dodgers Rookies | 1.75 | .70 | .17 |
| | Dennis Daboll | | | |
| | Mike Kekich | | | |
| | Hector Valle | | | |
| | Jim Lefebvre | | | |
| □ 562 | Bill Moran | .85 | .34 | .08 |
| □ 563 | Julio Navarro | .85 | .34 | .08 |
| □ 564 | Mel Nelson | .85 | .34 | .08 |
| □ 565 | Ernie Broglio | .85 | .34 | .08 |
| □ 566 | Yankees Rookies | .85 | .34 | .08 |
| | Gil Blanco | | | |
| | Ross Moschitto | | | |
| | Art Lopez | | | |
| □ 567 | Tommie Aaron | 1.00 | .40 | .10 |
| □ 568 | Ron Taylor | .85 | .34 | .08 |
| □ 569 | Gino Cimoli | .85 | .34 | .08 |
| □ 570 | Claude Osteen | 1.00 | .40 | .10 |
| □ 571 | Ossie Virgil | .85 | .34 | .08 |
| □ 572 | Orioles Team | 1.75 | .70 | .17 |
| □ 573 | Red Sox Rookies | 2.00 | .80 | .20 |
| | Jim Lonborg | | | |
| | Gerry Moses | | | |
| | Bill Schlesinger | | | |
| | Mike Ryan | | | |

| □ 574 | Roy Sievers | 1.00 | .40 | .10 |
|---|---|---|---|---|
| □ 575 | Jose Pagan | .85 | .34 | .08 |
| □ 576 | Terry Fox | .85 | .34 | .08 |
| □ 577 | AL Rookie Stars | .85 | .34 | .08 |
| | Darold Knowles | | | |
| | Don Buschhorn | | | |
| | Richie Scheinblum | | | |
| □ 578 | Camilo Carreon | .85 | .34 | .08 |
| □ 579 | Dick Smith | .85 | .34 | .08 |
| □ 580 | Jim Hall | .85 | .34 | .08 |
| □ 581 | NL Rookie Stars | 18.00 | 7.25 | 1.80 |
| | Tony Perez | | | |
| | Dave Ricketts | | | |
| | Kevin Collins | | | |
| □ 582 | Bob Schmidt | .85 | .34 | .08 |
| □ 583 | Wes Covington | .85 | .34 | .08 |
| □ 584 | Harry Bright | .85 | .34 | .08 |
| □ 585 | Hank Fischer | .85 | .34 | .08 |
| □ 586 | Tom McCraw | .85 | .34 | .08 |
| □ 587 | Joe Sparma | .85 | .34 | .08 |
| □ 588 | Len Green | .85 | .34 | .08 |
| □ 589 | Giants Rookies | .85 | .34 | .08 |
| | Frank Linzy | | | |
| | B. Schroder | | | |
| □ 590 | John Wyatt | .85 | .34 | .08 |
| □ 591 | Bob Skinner | 1.00 | .40 | .10 |
| □ 592 | Frank Bork | .85 | .34 | .08 |
| □ 593 | Tigers Rookies | 1.00 | .40 | .10 |
| | Jackie Moore | | | |
| | John Sullivan | | | |
| □ 594 | Joe Gaines | .85 | .34 | .08 |
| □ 595 | Don Lee | .85 | .34 | .08 |
| □ 596 | Don Landrum | .85 | .34 | .08 |
| □ 597 | Twins Rookies | .85 | .34 | .08 |
| | Joe Nossek | | | |
| | John Sevcik | | | |
| | Dick Reese | | | |
| □ 598 | Al Downing | 1.50 | .50 | .10 |

## 1965 Topps Embossed

The cards in this 72 card set measure 2 1/8" by 3 1/2". The 1965 Topps Embossed set contains gold foil cameo player portraits. Each league had 36 representatives set on blue backgrounds for the AL and red backgrounds for the NL. The Topps embossed set was distributed as inserts in packages of the regular 1965 baseball series.

| | | MINT | VG-E | F-G |
|---|---|---|---|---|
| COMPLETE SET | | 45.00 | 18.00 | 4.50 |
| COMMON PLAYER (1-72) | | .40 | .16 | .04 |
| □ 1 | Carl Yastrzemski | 6.00 | 2.40 | .60 |
| □ 2 | Ron Fairly | .40 | .16 | .04 |
| □ 3 | Max Alvis | .40 | .16 | .04 |
| □ 4 | Jim Ray Hart | .40 | .16 | .04 |
| □ 5 | Bill Skowron | .50 | .20 | .05 |
| □ 6 | Ed Kranepool | .40 | .16 | .04 |
| □ 7 | Tim McCarver | .50 | .20 | .05 |
| □ 8 | Sandy Koufax | 3.50 | 1.40 | .35 |
| □ 9 | Donn Clendenon | .40 | .16 | .04 |

| | | | | |
|---|---|---|---|---|
| ☐ 10 | John Romano | .40 | .16 | .04 |
| ☐ 11 | Mickey Mantle | 8.00 | 3.25 | .80 |
| ☐ 12 | Joe Torre | .60 | .24 | .06 |
| ☐ 13 | Al Kaline | 2.25 | .90 | .22 |
| ☐ 14 | Al McBean | .40 | .16 | .04 |
| ☐ 15 | Don Drysdale | 1.75 | .70 | .17 |
| ☐ 16 | Brooks Robinson | 2.25 | .90 | .22 |
| ☐ 17 | Jim Bunning | .80 | .32 | .08 |
| ☐ 18 | Gary Peters | .40 | .16 | .04 |
| ☐ 19 | Bob Clemente | 3.50 | 1.40 | .35 |
| ☐ 20 | Milt Pappas | .40 | .16 | .04 |
| ☐ 21 | Wayne Causey | .40 | .16 | .04 |
| ☐ 22 | Frank Robinson | 2.25 | .90 | .22 |
| ☐ 23 | Bill Mazeroski | .50 | .20 | .05 |
| ☐ 24 | Diego Segui | .40 | .16 | .04 |
| ☐ 25 | Jim Bouton | .50 | .20 | .05 |
| ☐ 26 | Ed Mathews | 1.75 | .70 | .17 |
| ☐ 27 | Willie Mays | 4.50 | 1.80 | .45 |
| ☐ 28 | Ron Santo | .50 | .20 | .05 |
| ☐ 29 | Boog Powell | .50 | .20 | .05 |
| ☐ 30 | Ken McBride | .40 | .16 | .04 |
| ☐ 31 | Leon Wagner | .40 | .16 | .04 |
| ☐ 32 | John Callison | .40 | .16 | .04 |
| ☐ 33 | Zoilo Versalles | .40 | .16 | .04 |
| ☐ 34 | Jack Baldschun | .40 | .16 | .04 |
| ☐ 35 | Ron Hunt | .40 | .16 | .04 |
| ☐ 36 | Richie Allen | .50 | .20 | .05 |
| ☐ 37 | Frank Malzone | .40 | .16 | .04 |
| ☐ 38 | Bob Allison | .40 | .16 | .04 |
| ☐ 39 | Jim Fregosi | .50 | .20 | .05 |
| ☐ 40 | Billy Williams | 1.50 | .60 | .15 |
| ☐ 41 | Bill Freehan | .50 | .20 | .05 |
| ☐ 42 | Vada Pinson | .60 | .24 | .06 |
| ☐ 43 | Bill White | .50 | .20 | .05 |
| ☐ 44 | Roy McMillan | .40 | .16 | .04 |
| ☐ 45 | Orlando Cepeda | .75 | .30 | .07 |
| ☐ 46 | Rocky Colavito | .60 | .24 | .06 |
| ☐ 47 | Ken Boyer | .65 | .26 | .06 |
| ☐ 48 | Dick Radatz | .40 | .16 | .04 |
| ☐ 49 | Tommy Davis | .50 | .20 | .05 |
| ☐ 50 | Walt Bond | .40 | .16 | .04 |
| ☐ 51 | John Orsino | .40 | .16 | .04 |
| ☐ 52 | Joe Christopher | .40 | .16 | .04 |
| ☐ 53 | Al Spangler | .40 | .16 | .04 |
| ☐ 54 | Jim King | .40 | .16 | .04 |
| ☐ 55 | Mickey Lolich | .60 | .24 | .06 |
| ☐ 56 | Harmon Killebrew | 1.75 | .70 | .17 |
| ☐ 57 | Bob Shaw | .40 | .16 | .04 |
| ☐ 58 | Ernie Banks | 2.25 | .90 | .22 |
| ☐ 59 | Hank Aaron | 4.50 | 1.80 | .45 |
| ☐ 60 | Chuck Hinton | .40 | .16 | .04 |
| ☐ 61 | Bob Aspromonte | .40 | .16 | .04 |
| ☐ 62 | Lee Maye | .40 | .16 | .04 |
| ☐ 63 | Joe Cunningham | .40 | .16 | .04 |
| ☐ 64 | Pete Ward | .40 | .16 | .04 |
| ☐ 65 | Bobby Richardson | .60 | .24 | .06 |
| ☐ 66 | Dean Chance | .40 | .16 | .04 |
| ☐ 67 | Dick Ellsworth | .40 | .16 | .04 |
| ☐ 68 | Jim Maloney | .40 | .16 | .04 |
| ☐ 69 | Bob Gibson | 1.75 | .70 | .17 |
| ☐ 70 | Earl Battey | .40 | .16 | .04 |
| ☐ 71 | Tony Kubek | .80 | .32 | .08 |
| ☐ 72 | Jack Kralick | .40 | .16 | .04 |

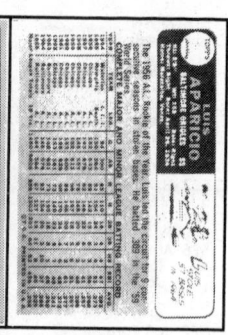

# 1966 Topps

The cards in this 598 card set measure 2 1/2" by 3 1/2". There are the same number of cards as in the 1965 set. Once again, the seventh series cards (523 to 598) are considered more difficult to obtain than any other series' cards in the set. The only featured subset within this set is League Leaders (215- 226). Noteworthy rookie cards in the set include Jim Palmer (126) and Don Sutton (288).

| | | MINT | VG-E | F-G |
|---|---|---|---|---|
| COMPLETE SET | | 950.00 | 400.00 | 100.00 |
| COMMON PLAYER (1-110) | | .21 | .09 | .02 |
| COMMON PLAYER (111-446) | | .27 | .11 | .03 |
| COMMON PLAYER (447-522) | | .65 | .26 | .06 |
| COMMON PLAYER (523-598) | | 4.25 | 1.70 | .42 |
| ☐ 1 | Willie Mays | 40.00 | 12.00 | 2.00 |
| ☐ 2 | Ted Abernathy | .21 | .09 | .02 |
| ☐ 3 | Sam Mele MGR | .21 | .09 | .02 |

| | | | | |
|---|---|---|---|---|
| ☐ 4 | Ray Culp | .21 | .09 | .02 |
| ☐ 5 | Jim Fregosi | .40 | .16 | .04 |
| ☐ 6 | Chuck Schilling | .21 | .09 | .02 |
| ☐ 7 | Tracy Stallard | .21 | .09 | .02 |
| ☐ 8 | Floyd Robinson | .21 | .09 | .02 |
| ☐ 9 | Clete Boyer | .35 | .14 | .03 |
| ☐ 10 | Tony Cloninger | .21 | .09 | .02 |
| ☐ 11 | Senators Rookies | .21 | .09 | .02 |
| | Brant Alyea | | | |
| | Pete Craig | | | |
| ☐ 12 | John Tsitouris | .21 | .09 | .02 |
| ☐ 13 | Lou Johnson | .21 | .09 | .02 |
| ☐ 14 | Norm Siebern | .21 | .09 | .02 |
| ☐ 15 | Vern Law | .30 | .12 | .03 |
| ☐ 16 | Larry Brown | .21 | .09 | .02 |
| ☐ 17 | John Stephenson | .21 | .09 | .02 |
| ☐ 18 | Roland Sheldon | .21 | .09 | .02 |
| ☐ 19 | Giants Team | .65 | .26 | .06 |
| ☐ 20 | Willie Horton | .50 | .20 | .05 |
| ☐ 21 | Don Nottebart | .21 | .09 | .02 |
| ☐ 22 | Joe Nossek | .21 | .09 | .02 |
| ☐ 23 | Jack Sanford | .21 | .09 | .02 |
| ☐ 24 | Don Kessinger | .65 | .26 | .06 |
| ☐ 25 | Pete Ward | .21 | .09 | .02 |
| ☐ 26 | Ray Sadecki | .21 | .09 | .02 |
| ☐ 27 | Orioles Rookies | .30 | .12 | .03 |
| | Darold Knowles | | | |
| | Andy Etchebarren | | | |
| ☐ 28 | Phil Niekro | 5.00 | 2.00 | .50 |
| ☐ 29 | Mike Brumley | .21 | .09 | .02 |
| ☐ 30 | Pete Rose | 40.00 | 16.00 | 4.00 |
| ☐ 31 | Jack Cullen | .21 | .09 | .02 |
| ☐ 32 | Adolfo Phillips | .21 | .09 | .02 |
| ☐ 33 | Jim Pagliaroni | .21 | .09 | .02 |
| ☐ 34 | Checklist 1 | 2.00 | .20 | .04 |
| ☐ 35 | Ron Swoboda | .21 | .09 | .02 |
| ☐ 36 | Jim Hunter | 5.00 | 2.00 | .50 |
| ☐ 37 | Billy Herman MGR | .80 | .32 | .08 |
| ☐ 38 | Ron Nischwitz | .21 | .09 | .02 |
| ☐ 39 | Ken Henderson | .21 | .09 | .02 |
| ☐ 40 | Jim Grant | .21 | .09 | .02 |
| ☐ 41 | Don LeJohn | .21 | .09 | .02 |
| ☐ 42 | Aubrey Gatewood | .21 | .09 | .02 |
| ☐ 43 | Don Landrum | .21 | .09 | .02 |
| ☐ 44 | Indians Rookies | .21 | .09 | .02 |
| | Bill Davis | | | |
| | Tom Kelley | | | |
| ☐ 45 | Jim Gentile | .30 | .12 | .03 |
| ☐ 46 | Howie Koplitz | .21 | .09 | .02 |
| ☐ 47 | J.C. Martin | .21 | .09 | .02 |
| ☐ 48 | Paul Blair | .30 | .12 | .03 |
| ☐ 49 | Woody Woodward | .21 | .09 | .02 |
| ☐ 50 | Mickey Mantle | 50.00 | 20.00 | 5.00 |
| ☐ 51 | Gordon Richardson | .21 | .09 | .02 |
| ☐ 52 | Power Plus | .25 | .10 | .02 |
| | Wes Covington | | | |
| | Johnny Callison | | | |
| ☐ 53 | Bob Duliba | .21 | .09 | .02 |
| ☐ 54 | Jose Pagan | .21 | .09 | .02 |
| ☐ 55 | Ken Harrelson | .80 | .32 | .08 |
| ☐ 56 | Sandy Valdespino | .21 | .09 | .02 |
| ☐ 57 | Jim Lefebvre | .30 | .12 | .03 |
| ☐ 58 | Dave Wickersham | .21 | .09 | .02 |
| ☐ 59 | Reds Team | .75 | .30 | .07 |
| ☐ 60 | Curt Flood | .60 | .24 | .06 |
| ☐ 61 | Bob Bolin | .21 | .09 | .02 |
| ☐ 62A | Merritt Ranew | .25 | .10 | .02 |
| | (with sold line) | | | |
| ☐ 62B | Merritt Ranew | 12.00 | 5.00 | 1.20 |
| | (without sold line) | | | |
| ☐ 63 | Jim Stewart | .21 | .09 | .02 |
| ☐ 64 | Bob Bruce | .21 | .09 | .02 |

| | | | |
|---|---|---|---|
| ☐ 65 | Leon Wagner | .21 | .09 | .02 |
| ☐ 66 | Al Weis | .21 | .09 | .02 |
| ☐ 67 | Mets Rookies | .30 | .12 | .03 |
| | Cleon Jones | | | |
| | Dick Selma | | | |
| ☐ 68 | Hal Reniff | .21 | .09 | .02 |
| ☐ 69 | Ken Hamlin | .21 | .09 | .02 |
| ☐ 70 | Carl Yastrzemski | 27.00 | 11.00 | 2.70 |
| ☐ 71 | Frank Carpin | .21 | .09 | .02 |
| ☐ 72 | Tony Perez | 3.50 | 1.40 | .35 |
| ☐ 73 | Jerry Zimmerman | .21 | .09 | .02 |
| ☐ 74 | Don Mossi | .30 | .12 | .03 |
| ☐ 75 | Tommy Davis | .50 | .20 | .05 |
| ☐ 76 | Red Schoendienst MGR | .50 | .20 | .05 |
| ☐ 77 | Johnny Orsino | .21 | .09 | .02 |
| ☐ 78 | Frank Linzy | .21 | .09 | .02 |
| ☐ 79 | Joe Pepitone | .50 | .20 | .05 |
| ☐ 80 | Richie Allen | 1.25 | .50 | .12 |
| ☐ 81 | Ray Oyler | .21 | .09 | .02 |
| ☐ 82 | Bob Hendley | .21 | .09 | .02 |
| ☐ 83 | Albie Pearson | .21 | .09 | .02 |
| ☐ 84 | Braves Rookies | .21 | .09 | .02 |
| | Jim Beauchamp | | | |
| | Dick Kelley | | | |
| ☐ 85 | Eddie Fisher | .21 | .09 | .02 |
| ☐ 86 | John Bateman | .21 | .09 | .02 |
| ☐ 87 | Dan Napoleon | .21 | .09 | .02 |
| ☐ 88 | Fred Whitfield | .21 | .09 | .02 |
| ☐ 89 | Ted Davidson | .21 | .09 | .02 |
| ☐ 90 | Luis Aparicio | 3.00 | 1.20 | .30 |
| ☐ 91A | Bob Uecker | 4.00 | 1.60 | .40 |
| | (with traded line) | | | |
| ☐ 91B | Bob Uecker | 20.00 | 8.00 | 2.00 |
| | (no traded line) | | | |
| ☐ 92 | Yankees Team | 1.25 | .50 | .12 |
| ☐ 93 | Jim Lonborg | .50 | .20 | .05 |
| ☐ 94 | Matty Alou | .30 | .12 | .03 |
| ☐ 95 | Pete Richert | .21 | .09 | .02 |
| ☐ 96 | Felipe Alou | .30 | .12 | .03 |
| ☐ 97 | Jim Merritt | .21 | .09 | .02 |
| ☐ 98 | Don Demeter | .21 | .09 | .02 |
| ☐ 99 | Buc Belters | 1.25 | .50 | .12 |
| | Willie Stargell | | | |
| | Donn Clendenon | | | |
| ☐ 100 | Sandy Koufax | 14.00 | 5.75 | 1.40 |
| ☐ 101A | Checklist 2 | 2.50 | .25 | .05 |
| | (115 Bill Henry) | | | |
| ☐ 101B | Checklist 2 | 6.00 | .60 | .10 |
| | (115 W. Spahn) | | | |
| ☐ 102 | Ed Kirkpatrick | .21 | .09 | .02 |
| ☐ 103A | Dick Groat | .50 | .20 | .05 |
| | (with traded line) | | | |
| ☐ 103B | Dick Groat | 15.00 | 6.00 | 1.50 |
| | (no traded line) | | | |
| ☐ 104A | Alex Johnson | .40 | .16 | .04 |
| | (with traded line) | | | |
| ☐ 104B | Alex Johnson | 15.00 | 6.00 | 1.50 |
| | (no traded line) | | | |
| ☐ 105 | Milt Pappas | .30 | .12 | .03 |
| ☐ 106 | Rusty Staub | 1.25 | .50 | .12 |
| ☐ 107 | A's Rookies | .21 | .09 | .02 |
| | Larry Stahl | | | |
| | Ron Tompkins | | | |
| ☐ 108 | Bobby Klaus | .21 | .09 | .02 |
| ☐ 109 | Ralph Terry | .30 | .12 | .03 |
| ☐ 110 | Ernie Banks | 4.00 | 1.60 | .40 |
| ☐ 111 | Gary Peters | .35 | .14 | .03 |
| ☐ 112 | Manny Mota | .35 | .14 | .03 |
| ☐ 113 | Hank Aguirre | .27 | .11 | .03 |
| ☐ 114 | Jim Gosger | .27 | .11 | .03 |
| ☐ 115 | Bill Henry | .27 | .11 | .03 |
| ☐ 116 | Walt Alston MGR | .90 | .36 | .09 |
| ☐ 117 | Jake Gibbs | .27 | .11 | .03 |
| ☐ 118 | Mike McCormick | .35 | .14 | .03 |
| ☐ 119 | Art Shamsky | .27 | .11 | .03 |
| ☐ 120 | Harmon Killebrew | 4.00 | 1.60 | .40 |
| ☐ 121 | Ray Herbert | .27 | .11 | .03 |
| ☐ 122 | Joe Gaines | .27 | .11 | .03 |
| ☐ 123 | Pirates Rookies | .27 | .11 | .03 |
| | Frank Bork | | | |
| | Jerry May | | | |
| ☐ 124 | Tug McGraw | 1.25 | .50 | .12 |
| ☐ 125 | Lou Brock | 5.50 | 2.20 | .55 |
| ☐ 126 | Jim Palmer | 36.00 | 15.00 | 3.60 |
| ☐ 127 | Ken Berry | .27 | .11 | .03 |
| ☐ 128 | Jim Landis | .27 | .11 | .03 |
| ☐ 129 | Jack Kralick | .27 | .11 | .03 |
| ☐ 130 | Joe Torre | .80 | .32 | .08 |
| ☐ 131 | Angels Team | .75 | .30 | .07 |
| ☐ 132 | Orlando Cepeda | 1.50 | .60 | .15 |
| ☐ 133 | Don McMahon | .27 | .11 | .03 |
| ☐ 134 | Wes Parker | .40 | .16 | .04 |
| ☐ 135 | Dave Morehead | .27 | .11 | .03 |

| | | | |
|---|---|---|---|
| ☐ 136 | Woody Held | .27 | .11 | .03 |
| ☐ 137 | Pat Corrales | .40 | .16 | .04 |
| ☐ 138 | Roger Repoz | .27 | .11 | .03 |
| ☐ 139 | Cubs Rookies | .27 | .11 | .03 |
| | Byron Browne | | | |
| | Don Young | | | |
| ☐ 140 | Jim Maloney | .35 | .14 | .03 |
| ☐ 141 | Tom McCraw | .27 | .11 | .03 |
| ☐ 142 | Don Dennis | .27 | .11 | .03 |
| ☐ 143 | Jose Tartabull | .27 | .11 | .03 |
| ☐ 144 | Don Schwall | .27 | .11 | .03 |
| ☐ 145 | Bill Freehan | .60 | .24 | .06 |
| ☐ 146 | George Altman | .27 | .11 | .03 |
| ☐ 147 | Lum Harris MGR | .27 | .11 | .03 |
| ☐ 148 | Bob Johnson | .27 | .11 | .03 |
| ☐ 149 | Dick Nen | .27 | .11 | .03 |
| ☐ 150 | Rocky Colavito | 1.00 | .40 | .10 |
| ☐ 151 | Gary Wagner | .27 | .11 | .03 |
| ☐ 152 | Frank Malzone | .35 | .14 | .03 |
| ☐ 153 | Rico Carty | .65 | .26 | .06 |
| ☐ 154 | Chuck Hiller | .27 | .11 | .03 |
| ☐ 155 | Marcelino Lopez | .27 | .11 | .03 |
| ☐ 156 | Double Play Combo | .40 | .16 | .04 |
| | Dick Schofield | | | |
| | Hal Lanier | | | |
| ☐ 157 | Rene Lachemann | .40 | .16 | .04 |
| ☐ 158 | Jim Brewer | .27 | .11 | .03 |
| ☐ 159 | Chico Ruiz | .27 | .11 | .03 |
| ☐ 160 | Whitey Ford | 5.00 | 2.00 | .50 |
| ☐ 161 | Jerry Lumpe | .27 | .11 | .03 |
| ☐ 162 | Lee Maye | .27 | .11 | .03 |
| ☐ 163 | Tito Francona | .35 | .14 | .03 |
| ☐ 164 | White Sox Rookies | .45 | .18 | .04 |
| | Tommie Agee | | | |
| | Marv Staehle | | | |
| ☐ 165 | Don Lock | .27 | .11 | .03 |
| ☐ 166 | Chris Krug | .27 | .11 | .03 |
| ☐ 167 | Boog Powell | 1.00 | .40 | .10 |
| ☐ 168 | Dan Osinski | .27 | .11 | .03 |
| ☐ 169 | Duke Sims | .27 | .11 | .03 |
| ☐ 170 | Cookie Rojas | .27 | .11 | .03 |
| ☐ 171 | Nick Willhite | .27 | .11 | .03 |
| ☐ 172 | Mets Team | .85 | .34 | .08 |
| ☐ 173 | Al Spangler | .27 | .11 | .03 |
| ☐ 174 | Ron Taylor | .27 | .11 | .03 |
| ☐ 175 | Bert Campaneris | .60 | .24 | .06 |
| ☐ 176 | Jim Davenport | .35 | .14 | .03 |
| ☐ 177 | Hector Lopez | .27 | .11 | .03 |
| ☐ 178 | Bob Tillman | .27 | .11 | .03 |
| ☐ 179 | Cards Rookies | .35 | .14 | .03 |
| | Dennis Aust | | | |
| | Bob Tolan | | | |
| ☐ 180 | Vada Pinson | .90 | .36 | .09 |
| ☐ 181 | Al Worthington | .27 | .11 | .03 |
| ☐ 182 | Jerry Lynch | .27 | .11 | .03 |
| ☐ 183 | Checklist 3 | 2.00 | .20 | .04 |
| ☐ 184 | Denis Menke | .27 | .11 | .03 |
| ☐ 185 | Bob Buhl | .27 | .11 | .03 |
| ☐ 186 | Ruben Amaro | .27 | .11 | .03 |
| ☐ 187 | Chuck Dressen MGR | .27 | .11 | .03 |
| ☐ 188 | Al Luplow | .27 | .11 | .03 |
| ☐ 189 | John Roseboro | .35 | .14 | .03 |
| ☐ 190 | Jimmie Hall | .27 | .11 | .03 |
| ☐ 191 | Darrell Sutherland | .27 | .11 | .03 |
| ☐ 192 | Vic Power | .27 | .11 | .03 |
| ☐ 193 | Dave McNally | .50 | .20 | .05 |
| ☐ 194 | Senators Team | .75 | .30 | .07 |
| ☐ 195 | Joe Morgan | 5.00 | 2.00 | .50 |
| ☐ 196 | Don Pavletich | .27 | .11 | .03 |
| ☐ 197 | Sonny Siebert | .35 | .14 | .03 |
| ☐ 198 | Mickey Stanley | .60 | .24 | .06 |
| ☐ 199 | Chisox Clubbers | .35 | .14 | .03 |
| | Bill Skowron | | | |
| | Johnny Romano | | | |
| | Floyd Robinson | | | |
| ☐ 200 | Eddie Mathews | 3.50 | 1.40 | .35 |
| ☐ 201 | Jim Dickson | .27 | .11 | .03 |
| ☐ 202 | Clay Dalrymple | .27 | .11 | .03 |
| ☐ 203 | Jose Santiago | .27 | .11 | .03 |
| ☐ 204 | Cubs Team | .75 | .30 | .07 |
| ☐ 205 | Tom Tresh | .65 | .26 | .06 |
| ☐ 206 | Alvin Jackson | .27 | .11 | .03 |
| ☐ 207 | Frank Quilici | .27 | .11 | .03 |
| ☐ 208 | Bob Miller | .27 | .11 | .03 |
| ☐ 209 | Tigers Rookies | .75 | .30 | .07 |
| | Fritz Fisher | | | |
| | John Hiller | | | |
| ☐ 210 | Bill Mazeroski | .90 | .36 | .09 |
| ☐ 211 | Frank Kreutzer | .27 | .11 | .03 |
| ☐ 212 | Ed Kranepool | .40 | .16 | .04 |
| ☐ 213 | Fred Newman | .27 | .11 | .03 |
| ☐ 214 | Tommy Harper | .35 | .14 | .03 |
| ☐ 215 | NL Batting Leaders: | 5.00 | 2.00 | .50 |

|  |  |  |  |  |
|---|---|---|---|---|
| | Bob Clemente | | | |
| | Hank Aaron | | | |
| | Willie Mays | | | |
| ☐ 216 | AL Batting Leaders: | 1.50 | .60 | .15 |
| | Tony Oliva | | | |
| | Carl Yastrzemski | | | |
| | Vic Davalillo | | | |
| ☐ 217 | NL Home Run Leaders: | 3.50 | 1.40 | .35 |
| | Willie Mays | | | |
| | Willie McCovey | | | |
| | Billy Williams | | | |
| ☐ 218 | AL Home Run Leaders: | .80 | .32 | .08 |
| | Tony Conigliaro | | | |
| | Norm Cash | | | |
| | Willie Horton | | | |
| ☐ 219 | NL RBI Leaders: | 1.50 | .60 | .15 |
| | Deron Johnson | | | |
| | Frank Robinson | | | |
| | Willie Mays | | | |
| ☐ 220 | AL RBI Leaders: | .80 | .32 | .08 |
| | Rocky Colavito | | | |
| | Willie Horton | | | |
| | Tony Oliva | | | |
| ☐ 221 | NL ERA Leaders: | 1.75 | .70 | .17 |
| | Sandy Koufax | | | |
| | Juan Marichal | | | |
| | Vern Law | | | |
| ☐ 222 | AL ERA Leaders: | .80 | .32 | .08 |
| | Sam McDowell | | | |
| | Eddie Fisher | | | |
| | Sonny Siebert | | | |
| ☐ 223 | NL Pitching Leaders: | 1.75 | .70 | .17 |
| | Sandy Koufax | | | |
| | Tony Cloninger | | | |
| | Don Drysdale | | | |
| ☐ 224 | AL Pitching Leaders: | .80 | .32 | .08 |
| | Jim Grant | | | |
| | Mel Stottlemyre | | | |
| | Jim Kaat | | | |
| ☐ 225 | NL Strikeout Leaders: | 1.75 | .70 | .17 |
| | Sandy Koufax | | | |
| | Bob Veale | | | |
| | Bob Gibson | | | |
| ☐ 226 | AL Strikeout Leaders: | .80 | .32 | .08 |
| | Sam McDowell | | | |
| | Mickey Lolich | | | |
| | Dennis McLain | | | |
| | Sonny Siebert | | | |
| ☐ 227 | Russ Nixon | .27 | .11 | .03 |
| ☐ 228 | Larry Dierker | .27 | .11 | .03 |
| ☐ 229 | Hank Bauer MGR | .35 | .14 | .03 |
| ☐ 230 | John Callison | .35 | .14 | .03 |
| ☐ 231 | Floyd Weaver | .27 | .11 | .03 |
| ☐ 232 | Glenn Beckert | .35 | .14 | .03 |
| ☐ 233 | Dom Zanni | .27 | .11 | .03 |
| ☐ 234 | Yankees Rookies | 1.50 | .60 | .15 |
| | Rich Beck | | | |
| | Roy White | | | |
| ☐ 235 | Don Cardwell | .27 | .11 | .03 |
| ☐ 236 | Mike Hershberger | .27 | .11 | .03 |
| ☐ 237 | Billy O'Dell | .27 | .11 | .03 |
| ☐ 238 | Dodgers Team | 1.00 | .40 | .10 |
| ☐ 239 | Orlando Pena | .27 | .11 | .03 |
| ☐ 240 | Earl Battey | .27 | .11 | .03 |
| ☐ 241 | Dennis Ribant | .27 | .11 | .03 |
| ☐ 242 | Jesus Alou | .27 | .11 | .03 |
| ☐ 243 | Nelson Briles | .35 | .14 | .03 |
| ☐ 244 | Astros Rookies | .27 | .11 | .03 |
| | Chuck Harrison | | | |
| | Sonny Jackson | | | |
| ☐ 245 | John Buzhardt | .27 | .11 | .03 |
| ☐ 246 | Ed Bailey | .27 | .11 | .03 |
| ☐ 247 | Carl Warwick | .27 | .11 | .03 |
| ☐ 248 | Pete Mikkelsen | .27 | .11 | .03 |
| ☐ 249 | Bill Rigney MGR | .27 | .11 | .03 |
| ☐ 250 | Sam Ellis | .27 | .11 | .03 |
| ☐ 251 | Ed Brinkman | .27 | .11 | .03 |
| ☐ 252 | Denny Lemaster | .27 | .11 | .03 |
| ☐ 253 | Don Wert | .27 | .11 | .03 |
| ☐ 254 | Phillies Rookies | 12.00 | 5.00 | 1.20 |
| | Ferguson Jenkins | | | |
| | Bill Sorrell | | | |
| ☐ 255 | Willie Stargell | 4.50 | 1.80 | .45 |
| ☐ 256 | Lew Krausse | .27 | .11 | .03 |
| ☐ 257 | Jeff Torborg | .35 | .14 | .03 |
| ☐ 258 | Dave Giusti | .27 | .11 | .03 |
| ☐ 259 | Red Sox Team | .75 | .30 | .07 |
| ☐ 260 | Bob Shaw | .27 | .11 | .03 |
| ☐ 261 | Ron Hansen | .27 | .11 | .03 |
| ☐ 262 | Jack Hamilton | .27 | .11 | .03 |
| ☐ 263 | Tom Egan | .27 | .11 | .03 |
| ☐ 264 | Twins Rookies | .27 | .11 | .03 |
| | Andy Kosco | | | |

|  |  |  |  |  |
|---|---|---|---|---|
| | Ted Uhlaender | | | |
| ☐ 265 | Stu Miller | .27 | .11 | .03 |
| ☐ 266 | Pedro Gonzalez | .27 | .11 | .03 |
| ☐ 267 | Joe Sparma | .27 | .11 | .03 |
| ☐ 268 | John Blanchard | .27 | .11 | .03 |
| ☐ 269 | Don Heffner MGR | .27 | .11 | .03 |
| ☐ 270 | Claude Osteen | .35 | .14 | .03 |
| ☐ 271 | Hal Lanier | .50 | .20 | .05 |
| ☐ 272 | Jack Baldschun | .27 | .11 | .03 |
| ☐ 273 | Astro Aces | .50 | .20 | .05 |
| | Bob Aspromonte | | | |
| | Rusty Staub | | | |
| ☐ 274 | Buster Narum | .27 | .11 | .03 |
| ☐ 275 | Tim McCarver | .75 | .30 | .07 |
| ☐ 276 | Jim Bouton | .75 | .30 | .07 |
| ☐ 277 | George Thomas | .27 | .11 | .03 |
| ☐ 278 | Calvin Koonce | .27 | .11 | .03 |
| ☐ 279 | Checklist 4 | 2.00 | .20 | .04 |
| ☐ 280 | Bobby Knoop | .27 | .11 | .03 |
| ☐ 281 | Bruce Howard | .27 | .11 | .03 |
| ☐ 282 | Johnny Lewis | .27 | .11 | .03 |
| ☐ 283 | Jim Perry | .40 | .16 | .04 |
| ☐ 284 | Bobby Wine | .27 | .11 | .03 |
| ☐ 285 | Luis Tiant | 1.00 | .40 | .10 |
| ☐ 286 | Gary Geiger | .27 | .11 | .03 |
| ☐ 287 | Jack Aker | .27 | .11 | .03 |
| ☐ 288 | Dodgers Rookies | 27.00 | 11.00 | 2.70 |
| | Bill Singer | | | |
| | Don Sutton | | | |
| ☐ 289 | Larry Sherry | .35 | .14 | .03 |
| ☐ 290 | Ron Santo | .75 | .30 | .07 |
| ☐ 291 | Moe Drabowsky | .27 | .11 | .03 |
| ☐ 292 | Jim Coker | .27 | .11 | .03 |
| ☐ 293 | Mike Shannon | .50 | .20 | .05 |
| ☐ 294 | Steve Ridzik | .27 | .11 | .03 |
| ☐ 295 | Jim Ray Hart | .35 | .14 | .03 |
| ☐ 296 | Johnny Keane MGR | .35 | .14 | .03 |
| ☐ 297 | Jim Owens | .27 | .11 | .03 |
| ☐ 298 | Rico Petrocelli | .35 | .14 | .03 |
| ☐ 299 | Lou Burdette | .55 | .22 | .05 |
| ☐ 300 | Bob Clemente | 20.00 | 8.00 | 2.00 |
| ☐ 301 | Greg Bollo | .27 | .11 | .03 |
| ☐ 302 | Ernie Bowman | .27 | .11 | .03 |
| ☐ 303 | Indians Team | .75 | .30 | .07 |
| ☐ 304 | John Herrnstein | .27 | .11 | .03 |
| ☐ 305 | Camilo Pascual | .35 | .14 | .03 |
| ☐ 306 | Ty Cline | .27 | .11 | .03 |
| ☐ 307 | Clay Carroll | .27 | .11 | .03 |
| ☐ 308 | Tom Haller | .27 | .11 | .03 |
| ☐ 309 | Diego Segui | .27 | .11 | .03 |
| ☐ 310 | Frank Robinson | 10.00 | 4.00 | 1.00 |
| ☐ 311 | Reds Rookies | .40 | .16 | .04 |
| | Tommy Helms | | | |
| | Dick Simpson | | | |
| ☐ 312 | Bob Saverine | .27 | .11 | .03 |
| ☐ 313 | Chris Zachary | .27 | .11 | .03 |
| ☐ 314 | Hector Valle | .27 | .11 | .03 |
| ☐ 315 | Norm Cash | .90 | .36 | .09 |
| ☐ 316 | Jack Fisher | .27 | .11 | .03 |
| ☐ 317 | Dalton Jones | .27 | .11 | .03 |
| ☐ 318 | Harry Walker MGR | .27 | .11 | .03 |
| ☐ 319 | Gene Freese | .27 | .11 | .03 |
| ☐ 320 | Bob Gibson | 4.50 | 1.80 | .45 |
| ☐ 321 | Rick Reichardt | .27 | .11 | .03 |
| ☐ 322 | Bill Faul | .27 | .11 | .03 |
| ☐ 323 | Ray Barker | .27 | .11 | .03 |
| ☐ 324 | John Boozer | .27 | .11 | .03 |
| ☐ 325 | Vic Davalillo | .27 | .11 | .03 |
| ☐ 326 | Braves Team | .75 | .30 | .07 |
| ☐ 327 | Bernie Allen | .27 | .11 | .03 |
| ☐ 328 | Jerry Grote | .27 | .11 | .03 |
| ☐ 329 | Pete Charton | .27 | .11 | .03 |
| ☐ 330 | Ron Fairly | .35 | .14 | .03 |
| ☐ 331 | Ron Herbel | .27 | .11 | .03 |
| ☐ 332 | Billy Bryan | .27 | .11 | .03 |
| ☐ 333 | Senators Rookies | .27 | .11 | .03 |
| | Joe Coleman | | | |
| | Jim French | | | |
| ☐ 334 | Marty Keough | .27 | .11 | .03 |
| ☐ 335 | Juan Pizarro | .27 | .11 | .03 |
| ☐ 336 | Gene Alley | .40 | .16 | .04 |
| ☐ 337 | Fred Gladding | .27 | .11 | .03 |
| ☐ 338 | Dal Maxvill | .27 | .11 | .03 |
| ☐ 339 | Del Crandall | .35 | .14 | .03 |
| ☐ 340 | Dean Chance | .35 | .14 | .03 |
| ☐ 341 | Wes Westrum MGR | .27 | .11 | .03 |
| ☐ 342 | Bob Humphreys | .27 | .11 | .03 |
| ☐ 343 | Joe Christopher | .27 | .11 | .03 |
| ☐ 344 | Steve Blass | .35 | .14 | .03 |
| ☐ 345 | Bob Allison | .35 | .14 | .03 |
| ☐ 346 | Mike De La Hoz | .27 | .11 | .03 |
| ☐ 347 | Phil Regan | .35 | .14 | .03 |
| ☐ 348 | Orioles Team | .75 | .30 | .07 |

| | | | | |
|---|---|---|---|---|
| ☐ 349 | Cap Peterson | .27 | .11 | .03 |
| ☐ 350 | Mel Stottlemyre | .75 | .30 | .07 |
| ☐ 351 | Fred Valentine | .27 | .11 | .03 |
| ☐ 352 | Bob Aspromonte | .27 | .11 | .03 |
| ☐ 353 | Al McBean | .27 | .11 | .03 |
| ☐ 354 | Smoky Burgess | .35 | .14 | .03 |
| ☐ 355 | Wade Blasingame | .27 | .11 | .03 |
| ☐ 356 | Red Sox Rookies | .27 | .11 | .03 |
| | Owen Johnson | | | |
| | Ken Sanders | | | |
| ☐ 357 | Gerry Arrigo | .27 | .11 | .03 |
| ☐ 358 | Charlie Smith | .27 | .11 | .03 |
| ☐ 359 | Johnny Briggs | .27 | .11 | .03 |
| ☐ 360 | Ron Hunt | .27 | .11 | .03 |
| ☐ 361 | Tom Satriano | .27 | .11 | .03 |
| ☐ 362 | Gates Brown | .35 | .14 | .03 |
| ☐ 363 | Checklist 5 | 2.00 | .20 | .04 |
| ☐ 364 | Nate Oliver | .27 | .11 | .03 |
| ☐ 365 | Roger Maris | 5.00 | 2.00 | .50 |
| ☐ 366 | Wayne Causey | .27 | .11 | .03 |
| ☐ 367 | Mel Nelson | .27 | .11 | .03 |
| ☐ 368 | Charlie Lau | .35 | .14 | .03 |
| ☐ 369 | Jim King | .27 | .11 | .03 |
| ☐ 370 | Chico Cardenas | .27 | .11 | .03 |
| ☐ 371 | Lee Stange | .27 | .11 | .03 |
| ☐ 372 | Harvey Kuenn | .50 | .20 | .05 |
| ☐ 373 | Giants Rookies | .27 | .11 | .03 |
| | Jack Hiatt | | | |
| | Dick Estelle | | | |
| ☐ 374 | Bob Locker | .27 | .11 | .03 |
| ☐ 375 | Donn Clendenon | .35 | .14 | .03 |
| ☐ 376 | Paul Schaal | .27 | .11 | .03 |
| ☐ 377 | Turk Farrell | .27 | .11 | .03 |
| ☐ 378 | Dick Tracewski | .27 | .11 | .03 |
| ☐ 379 | Cardinal Team | .75 | .30 | .07 |
| ☐ 380 | Tony Conigliaro | .80 | .32 | .08 |
| ☐ 381 | Hank Fischer | .27 | .11 | .03 |
| ☐ 382 | Phil Roof | .27 | .11 | .03 |
| ☐ 383 | Jack Brandt | .27 | .11 | .03 |
| ☐ 384 | Al Downing | .35 | .14 | .03 |
| ☐ 385 | Ken Boyer | 1.25 | .50 | .12 |
| ☐ 386 | Gil Hodges MGR | 2.50 | 1.00 | .25 |
| ☐ 387 | Howie Reed | .27 | .11 | .03 |
| ☐ 388 | Don Mincher | .35 | .14 | .03 |
| ☐ 389 | Jim O'Toole | .27 | .11 | .03 |
| ☐ 390 | Brooks Robinson | 5.00 | 2.00 | .50 |
| ☐ 391 | Chuck Hinton | .27 | .11 | .03 |
| ☐ 392 | Cubs Rookies | .40 | .16 | .04 |
| | Bill Hands | | | |
| | Randy Hundley | | | |
| ☐ 393 | George Brunet | .27 | .11 | .03 |
| ☐ 394 | Ron Brand | .27 | .11 | .03 |
| ☐ 395 | Len Gabrielson | .27 | .11 | .03 |
| ☐ 396 | J. Stephenson | .27 | .11 | .03 |
| ☐ 397 | Bill White | .40 | .16 | .04 |
| ☐ 398 | Danny Cater | .27 | .11 | .03 |
| ☐ 399 | Ray Washburn | .27 | .11 | .03 |
| ☐ 400 | Zoilo Versalles | .35 | .14 | .03 |
| ☐ 401 | Ken McMullen | .27 | .11 | .03 |
| ☐ 402 | Jim Hickman | .27 | .11 | .03 |
| ☐ 403 | Fred Talbot | .27 | .11 | .03 |
| ☐ 404 | Pirates Team | .75 | .30 | .07 |
| ☐ 405 | Elston Howard | 1.25 | .50 | .12 |
| ☐ 406 | Joe Jay | .27 | .11 | .03 |
| ☐ 407 | John Kennedy | .27 | .11 | .03 |
| ☐ 408 | Lee Thomas | .27 | .11 | .03 |
| ☐ 409 | Billy Hoeft | .27 | .11 | .03 |
| ☐ 410 | Al Kaline | 4.50 | 1.80 | .45 |
| ☐ 411 | Gene Mauch MGR | .40 | .16 | .04 |
| ☐ 412 | Sam Bowens | .27 | .11 | .03 |
| ☐ 413 | John Romano | .27 | .11 | .03 |
| ☐ 414 | Dan Coombs | .27 | .11 | .03 |
| ☐ 415 | Max Alvis | .27 | .11 | .03 |
| ☐ 416 | Phil Ortega | .27 | .11 | .03 |
| ☐ 417 | Angels Rookies | .35 | .14 | .03 |
| | Jim McGlothlin | | | |
| | Ed Sukla | | | |
| ☐ 418 | Phil Gagliano | .27 | .11 | .03 |
| ☐ 419 | Mike Ryan | .27 | .11 | .03 |
| ☐ 420 | Juan Marichal | 3.50 | 1.40 | .35 |
| ☐ 421 | Roy McMillan | .27 | .11 | .03 |
| ☐ 422 | Ed Charles | .27 | .11 | .03 |
| ☐ 423 | Ernie Broglio | .27 | .11 | .03 |
| ☐ 424 | Reds Rookies | 1.25 | .50 | .12 |
| | Lee May | | | |
| | Darrell Osteen | | | |
| ☐ 425 | Bob Veale | .35 | .14 | .03 |
| ☐ 426 | White Sox Team | .75 | .30 | .07 |
| ☐ 427 | John Miller | .27 | .11 | .03 |
| ☐ 428 | Sandy Alomar | .27 | .11 | .03 |
| ☐ 429 | Bill Monbouquette | .27 | .11 | .03 |
| ☐ 430 | Don Drysdale | 4.00 | 1.60 | .40 |
| ☐ 431 | Walt Bond | .27 | .11 | .03 |
| ☐ 432 | Bob Heffner | .27 | .11 | .03 |
| ☐ 433 | Alvin Dark MGR | .35 | .14 | .03 |
| ☐ 434 | Willie Kirkland | .27 | .11 | .03 |
| ☐ 435 | Jim Bunning | 1.50 | .60 | .15 |
| ☐ 436 | Julian Javier | .35 | .14 | .03 |
| ☐ 437 | Al Stanek | .27 | .11 | .03 |
| ☐ 438 | Willie Smith | .27 | .11 | .03 |
| ☐ 439 | Pedro Ramos | .27 | .11 | .03 |
| ☐ 440 | Deron Johnson | .27 | .11 | .03 |
| ☐ 441 | Tommie Sisk | .27 | .11 | .03 |
| ☐ 442 | Orioles Rookies | .27 | .11 | .03 |
| | Ed Barnowski | | | |
| | Eddie Watt | | | |
| ☐ 443 | Bill Wakefield | .27 | .11 | .03 |
| ☐ 444 | Checklist 6 | 2.50 | .25 | .05 |
| ☐ 445 | Jim Kaat | 2.00 | .80 | .20 |
| ☐ 446 | Mack Jones | .27 | .11 | .03 |
| ☐ 447 | Dick Ellsworth | .75 | .30 | .07 |
| | (photo actually | | | |
| | Ken Hubbs) | | | |
| ☐ 448 | Eddie Stanky MGR | .75 | .30 | .07 |
| ☐ 449 | Joe Moeller | .65 | .26 | .06 |
| ☐ 450 | Tony Oliva | 1.75 | .70 | .17 |
| ☐ 451 | Barry Latman | .65 | .26 | .06 |
| ☐ 452 | Joe Azcue | .65 | .26 | .06 |
| ☐ 453 | Ron Kline | .65 | .26 | .06 |
| ☐ 454 | Jerry Buchek | .65 | .26 | .06 |
| ☐ 455 | Mickey Lolich | 1.25 | .50 | .12 |
| ☐ 456 | Red Sox Rookies | .65 | .26 | .06 |
| | Darrell Brandon | | | |
| | Joe Foy | | | |
| ☐ 457 | Joe Gibbon | .65 | .26 | .06 |
| ☐ 458 | Manny Jiminez | .65 | .26 | .06 |
| ☐ 459 | Bill McCool | .65 | .26 | .06 |
| ☐ 460 | Curt Blefary | .75 | .30 | .07 |
| ☐ 461 | Roy Face | .90 | .36 | .09 |
| ☐ 462 | Bob Rodgers | .65 | .26 | .06 |
| ☐ 463 | Phillies Team | 1.00 | .40 | .10 |
| ☐ 464 | Larry Bearnarth | .65 | .26 | .06 |
| ☐ 465 | Don Buford | .65 | .26 | .06 |
| ☐ 466 | Ken Johnson | .65 | .26 | .06 |
| ☐ 467 | Vic Roznovsky | .65 | .26 | .06 |
| ☐ 468 | Johnny Podres | 1.25 | .50 | .12 |
| ☐ 469 | Yankees Rookies | 4.50 | 1.80 | .45 |
| | Bobby Murcer | | | |
| | Dooley Womack | | | |
| ☐ 470 | Sam McDowell | .75 | .30 | .07 |
| ☐ 471 | Bob Skinner | .75 | .30 | .07 |
| ☐ 472 | Terry Fox | .65 | .26 | .06 |
| ☐ 473 | Rich Rollins | .65 | .26 | .06 |
| ☐ 474 | Dick Schofield | .65 | .26 | .06 |
| ☐ 475 | Dick Radatz | .75 | .30 | .07 |
| ☐ 476 | Bobby Bragan MGR | .65 | .26 | .06 |
| ☐ 477 | Steve Barber | .65 | .26 | .06 |
| ☐ 478 | Tony Gonzalez | .65 | .26 | .06 |
| ☐ 479 | Jim Hannan | .65 | .26 | .06 |
| ☐ 480 | Dick Stuart | .75 | .30 | .07 |
| ☐ 481 | Bob Lee | .65 | .26 | .06 |
| ☐ 482 | Cubs Rookies | .65 | .26 | .06 |
| | John Boccabella | | | |
| | Dave Dowling | | | |
| ☐ 483 | Joe Nuxhall | .75 | .30 | .07 |
| ☐ 484 | Wes Covington | .75 | .30 | .07 |
| ☐ 485 | Bob Bailey | .65 | .26 | .06 |
| ☐ 486 | Tommy John | 2.50 | 1.00 | .25 |
| ☐ 487 | Al Ferrara | .65 | .26 | .06 |
| ☐ 488 | George Banks | .75 | .30 | .07 |
| ☐ 489 | Curt Simmons | .65 | .26 | .06 |
| ☐ 490 | Bobby Richardson | 2.50 | 1.00 | .25 |
| ☐ 491 | Dennis Bennett | .65 | .26 | .06 |
| ☐ 492 | Athletics Team | 1.00 | .40 | .10 |
| ☐ 493 | John Klippstein | .65 | .26 | .06 |
| ☐ 494 | Gordon Coleman | .65 | .26 | .06 |
| ☐ 495 | Dick McAuliffe | .75 | .30 | .07 |
| ☐ 496 | Lindy McDaniel | .75 | .30 | .07 |
| ☐ 497 | Chris Cannizzaro | .65 | .26 | .06 |
| ☐ 498 | Pirates Rookies | .75 | .30 | .07 |
| | Luke Walker | | | |
| | Woody Fryman | | | |
| ☐ 499 | Wally Bunker | .65 | .26 | .06 |
| ☐ 500 | Hank Aaron | 25.00 | 10.00 | 2.50 |
| ☐ 501 | John O'Donoghue | .65 | .26 | .06 |
| ☐ 502 | Lenny Green | .65 | .26 | .06 |
| ☐ 503 | Steve Hamilton | .65 | .26 | .06 |
| ☐ 504 | Grady Hatton MGR | .65 | .26 | .06 |
| ☐ 505 | Jose Cardenal | .65 | .26 | .06 |
| ☐ 506 | Bo Belinsky | .75 | .30 | .07 |
| ☐ 507 | John Edwards | .65 | .26 | .06 |
| ☐ 508 | Steve Hargan | .65 | .26 | .06 |
| ☐ 509 | Jake Wood | .65 | .26 | .06 |
| ☐ 510 | Hoyt Wilhelm | 4.00 | 1.60 | .40 |
| ☐ 511 | Giants Rookies | .65 | .26 | .06 |
| | Bob Barton | | | |
| | Tito Fuentes | | | |

| □ 512 | Dick Stigman | .65 | .26 | .06 |
|---|---|---|---|---|
| □ 513 | Camilo Carreon | .65 | .26 | .06 |
| □ 514 | Hal Woodeshick | .65 | .26 | .06 |
| □ 515 | Frank Howard | 1.50 | .60 | .15 |
| □ 516 | Eddie Bressoud | .65 | .26 | .06 |
| □ 517 | Checklist 7 | 5.00 | .50 | .10 |
| □ 518 | Braves Rookies | .65 | .26 | .06 |
|  | Herb Hippauf |  |  |  |
|  | Arnie Umbach |  |  |  |
| □ 519 | Bob Friend | .75 | .30 | .07 |
| □ 520 | Jim Wynn | .75 | .30 | .07 |
| □ 521 | John Wyatt | .65 | .26 | .06 |
| □ 522 | Phil Linz | .75 | .30 | .07 |
| □ 523 | Bob Sadowski | 4.25 | 1.70 | .42 |
| □ 524 | Giants Rookies | 4.25 | 1.70 | .42 |
|  | Ollie Brown |  |  |  |
|  | Don Mason |  |  |  |
| □ 525 | Gary Bell | 4.25 | 1.70 | .42 |
| □ 526 | Twins Team | 8.00 | 3.25 | .80 |
| □ 527 | Julio Navarro | 4.25 | 1.70 | .42 |
| □ 528 | Jesse Gonder | 4.25 | 1.70 | .42 |
| □ 529 | White Sox Rookies | 5.00 | 2.00 | .50 |
|  | Lee Elia |  |  |  |
|  | Dennis Higgins |  |  |  |
|  | Bill Voss |  |  |  |
| □ 530 | Robin Roberts | 14.00 | 5.75 | 1.40 |
| □ 531 | Joe Cunningham | 4.25 | 1.70 | .42 |
| □ 532 | Aurelio Monteagudo | 4.25 | 1.70 | .42 |
| □ 533 | Jerry Adair | 4.25 | 1.70 | .42 |
| □ 534 | Mets Rookies | 4.25 | 1.70 | .42 |
|  | Dave Eilers |  |  |  |
|  | Rob Gardner |  |  |  |
| □ 535 | Willie Davis | 6.00 | 2.40 | .60 |
| □ 536 | Dick Egan | 4.25 | 1.70 | .42 |
| □ 537 | Herman Franks MGR | 4.25 | 1.70 | .42 |
| □ 538 | Bob Allen | 4.25 | 1.70 | .42 |
| □ 539 | Astros Rookies | 4.25 | 1.70 | .42 |
|  | Bill Heath |  |  |  |
|  | Carroll Sembera |  |  |  |
| □ 540 | Denny McLain | 12.00 | 5.00 | 1.20 |
| □ 541 | Gene Oliver | 4.25 | 1.70 | .42 |
| □ 542 | George Smith | 4.25 | 1.70 | .42 |
| □ 543 | Roger Craig | 6.00 | 2.40 | .60 |
| □ 544 | Cardinals Rookies | 4.25 | 1.70 | .42 |
|  | Joe Hoerner |  |  |  |
|  | George Kernek |  |  |  |
|  | Jimmy Williams |  |  |  |
| □ 545 | Dick Green | 4.25 | 1.70 | .42 |
| □ 546 | Dwight Siebler | 4.25 | 1.70 | .42 |
| □ 547 | Horace Clarke | 5.00 | 2.00 | .50 |
| □ 548 | Gary Kroll | 4.25 | 1.70 | .42 |
| □ 549 | Senators Rookies | 4.25 | 1.70 | .42 |
|  | Al Closter |  |  |  |
|  | Casey Cox |  |  |  |
| □ 550 | Willie McCovey | 50.00 | 20.00 | 5.00 |
| □ 551 | Bob Purkey | 4.25 | 1.70 | .42 |
| □ 552 | Birdie Tebbetts MGR | 4.25 | 1.70 | .42 |
| □ 553 | Rookie Stars | 4.25 | 1.70 | .42 |
|  | Pat Garrett |  |  |  |
|  | Jackie Warner |  |  |  |
| □ 554 | Jim Northrup | 5.00 | 2.00 | .50 |
| □ 555 | Ron Perranoski | 5.00 | 2.00 | .50 |
| □ 556 | Mel Queen | 4.25 | 1.70 | .42 |
| □ 557 | Felix Mantilla | 4.25 | 1.70 | .42 |
| □ 558 | Red Sox Rookies | 7.50 | 3.00 | .75 |
|  | Guido Grilli |  |  |  |
|  | Pete Magrini |  |  |  |
|  | George Scott |  |  |  |
| □ 559 | Roberto Pena | 4.25 | 1.70 | .42 |
| □ 560 | Joel Horlen | 5.00 | 2.00 | .50 |
| □ 561 | Choo Choo Coleman | 4.25 | 1.70 | .42 |
| □ 562 | Russ Snyder | 4.25 | 1.70 | .42 |
| □ 563 | Twins Rookies | 5.00 | 2.00 | .50 |
|  | Pete Cimino |  |  |  |
|  | Cesar Tovar |  |  |  |
| □ 564 | Bob Chance | 4.25 | 1.70 | .42 |
| □ 565 | Jimmy Piersall | 6.50 | 2.60 | .65 |
| □ 566 | Mike Cuellar | 5.00 | 2.00 | .50 |
| □ 567 | Dick Howser | 6.00 | 2.40 | .60 |
| □ 568 | Athletics Rookies | 5.00 | 2.00 | .50 |
|  | Paul Lindblad |  |  |  |
|  | Rod Stone |  |  |  |
| □ 569 | Orlando McFarlane | 4.25 | 1.70 | .42 |
| □ 570 | Art Mahaffey | 4.25 | 1.70 | .42 |
| □ 571 | Dave Roberts | 4.25 | 1.70 | .42 |
| □ 572 | Bob Priddy | 4.25 | 1.70 | .42 |
| □ 573 | Derrell Griffith | 4.25 | 1.70 | .42 |
| □ 574 | Mets Rookies | 4.25 | 1.70 | .42 |
|  | Bill Hepler |  |  |  |
|  | Bill Murphy |  |  |  |
| □ 575 | Earl Wilson | 4.25 | 1.70 | .42 |
| □ 576 | Dave Nicholson | 4.25 | 1.70 | .42 |

| □ 577 | Jack Lamabe | 4.25 | 1.70 | .42 |
|---|---|---|---|---|
| □ 578 | Chi Chi Olivo | 4.25 | 1.70 | .42 |
| □ 579 | Orioles Rookies | 6.00 | 2.40 | .60 |
|  | Frank Bertaina |  |  |  |
|  | Gene Brabender |  |  |  |
|  | Dave Johnson |  |  |  |
| □ 580 | Billy Williams | 20.00 | 8.00 | 2.00 |
| □ 581 | Tony Martinez | 4.25 | 1.70 | .42 |
| □ 582 | Garry Roggenburk | 4.25 | 1.70 | .42 |
| □ 583 | Tigers Team | 12.00 | 5.00 | 1.20 |
| □ 584 | Yankees Rookies | 5.00 | 2.00 | .50 |
|  | Frank Fernandez |  |  |  |
|  | Fritz Peterson |  |  |  |
| □ 585 | Tony Taylor | 4.25 | 1.70 | .42 |
| □ 586 | Claude Raymond | 4.25 | 1.70 | .42 |
| □ 587 | Dick Bertell | 4.25 | 1.70 | .42 |
| □ 588 | Athletics Rookies | 4.25 | 1.70 | .42 |
|  | Chuck Dobson |  |  |  |
|  | Ken Suarez |  |  |  |
| □ 589 | Lou Klimchock | 4.25 | 1.70 | .42 |
| □ 590 | Bill Skowron | 6.00 | 2.40 | .60 |
| □ 591 | N.L. Rookies | 5.00 | 2.00 | .50 |
|  | Bart Shirley |  |  |  |
|  | Grant Jackson |  |  |  |
| □ 592 | Andre Rodgers | 4.25 | 1.70 | .42 |
| □ 593 | Doug Camilli | 4.25 | 1.70 | .42 |
| □ 594 | Chico Salmon | 4.25 | 1.70 | .42 |
| □ 595 | Larry Jackson | 4.25 | 1.70 | .42 |
| □ 596 | Astros Rookies | 5.00 | 2.00 | .50 |
|  | Nate Colbert |  |  |  |
|  | Greg Sims |  |  |  |
| □ 597 | John Sullivan | 4.25 | 1.70 | .42 |
| □ 598 | Gaylord Perry | 90.00 | 25.00 | 5.00 |

## 1967 Topps

The cards in this 609 card set measure 2 1/2" by 3 1/2". The 1967 Topps series is considered by some collectors to be one of the company's finest accomplishments in baseball card production. Excellent color photographs are combined with easy to read backs. Cards 458 to 533 are slightly harder to find than numbers 1 to 457, and the inevitable (difficult to find) high series (534 to 609) exists. Each checklist card features a small circular picture of a popular player included in that series. Printing discrepancies resulted in some high series cards being in short supply. Featured subsets within this set include World series cards (151-155) and League Leaders (233-244). Although there are several relatively expensive card in this popular set, the key cards in the set are undoubtedly the Tom Seaver rookie card (581) and the Rod Carew rookie card (569).

|  | MINT | VG-E | F-G |
|---|---|---|---|
| COMPLETE SET | 1250.00 | 550.00 | 150.00 |
| COMMON PLAYER (1-370) | .25 | .10 | .02 |
| COMMON PLAYER (371-457) | .35 | .14 | .03 |
| COMMON PLAYER (458-533) | .75 | .30 | .07 |
| COMMON PLAYER (534-609) | 2.25 | .90 | .22 |

| | | | | |
|---|---|---|---|---|
| ☐ | 1 | The Champs: .................. | 3.50 | 1.40 | .35 |

| ☐ | 1 | The Champs: .................. | 3.50 | 1.40 | .35 |
|---|---|---|---|---|---|
| | | Frank Robinson | | | |
| | | Hank Bauer | | | |
| | | Brooks Robinson | | | |
| ☐ | 2 | Jack Hamilton ................ | .25 | .10 | .02 |
| ☐ | 3 | Duke Sims ..................... | .25 | .10 | .02 |
| ☐ | 4 | Hal Lanier ..................... | .40 | .16 | .04 |
| ☐ | 5 | Whitey Ford ................... | 4.50 | 1.80 | .45 |
| ☐ | 6 | Dick Simpson ................. | .25 | .10 | .02 |
| ☐ | 7 | Don McMahon ................ | .25 | .10 | .02 |
| ☐ | 8 | Chuck Harrison ............... | .25 | .10 | .02 |
| ☐ | 9 | Ron Hansen .................... | .25 | .10 | .02 |
| ☐ | 10 | Matty Alou ..................... | .35 | .14 | .03 |
| ☐ | 11 | Barry Moore ................... | .25 | .10 | .02 |
| ☐ | 12 | Dodgers Rookies ............. | .35 | .14 | .03 |
| | | Jim Campanis | | | |
| | | Bill Singer | | | |
| ☐ | 13 | Joe Sparma .................... | .25 | .10 | .02 |
| ☐ | 14 | Phil Linz ....................... | .25 | .10 | .02 |
| ☐ | 15 | Earl Battey .................... | .25 | .10 | .02 |
| ☐ | 16 | Bill Hands ..................... | .25 | .10 | .02 |
| ☐ | 17 | Jim Gosger .................... | .25 | .10 | .02 |
| ☐ | 18 | Gene Oliver ................... | .25 | .10 | .02 |
| ☐ | 19 | Jim McGlothlin ............... | .25 | .10 | .02 |
| ☐ | 20 | Orlando Cepeda .............. | 2.00 | .80 | .20 |
| ☐ | 21 | Dave Bristol MGR ............ | .25 | .10 | .02 |
| ☐ | 22 | Gene Brabender .............. | .25 | .10 | .02 |
| ☐ | 23 | Larry Elliot ................... | .25 | .10 | .02 |
| ☐ | 24 | Bob Allen ...................... | .25 | .10 | .02 |
| ☐ | 25 | Elston Howard ................ | 1.25 | .50 | .12 |
| ☐ | 26A | Bob Priddy .................... | .25 | .10 | .02 |
| | | (with traded line) | | | |
| ☐ | 26B | Bob Priddy .................... | 10.00 | 4.00 | 1.00 |
| | | (no traded line) | | | |
| ☐ | 27 | Bob Saverine .................. | .25 | .10 | .02 |
| ☐ | 28 | Barry Latman .................. | .25 | .10 | .02 |
| ☐ | 29 | Tommy McCraw ............... | .25 | .10 | .02 |
| ☐ | 30 | Al Kaline ....................... | 4.00 | 1.60 | .40 |
| ☐ | 31 | Jim Brewer .................... | .25 | .10 | .02 |
| ☐ | 32 | Bob Bailey ..................... | .25 | .10 | .02 |
| ☐ | 33 | Athletic Rookies .............. | 1.00 | .40 | .10 |
| | | Sal Bando | | | |
| | | Randy Schwartz | | | |
| ☐ | 34 | Pete Cimino ................... | .25 | .10 | .02 |
| ☐ | 35 | Rico Carty ..................... | .55 | .22 | .05 |
| ☐ | 36 | Bob Tillman ................... | .25 | .10 | .02 |
| ☐ | 37 | Rick Wise ...................... | .35 | .14 | .03 |
| ☐ | 38 | Bob Johnson .................. | .25 | .10 | .02 |
| ☐ | 39 | Curt Simmons ................ | .35 | .14 | .03 |
| ☐ | 40 | Rick Reichardt ............... | .25 | .10 | .02 |
| ☐ | 41 | Joe Hoerner ................... | .25 | .10 | .02 |
| ☐ | 42 | Mets Team .................... | .85 | .34 | .08 |
| ☐ | 43 | Chico Salmon ................. | .25 | .10 | .02 |
| ☐ | 44 | Joe Nuxhall ................... | .35 | .14 | .03 |
| ☐ | 45 | Roger Maris ................... | 4.50 | 1.80 | .45 |
| ☐ | 46 | Lindy McDaniel ............... | .25 | .10 | .02 |
| ☐ | 47 | Ken McMullen ................ | .25 | .10 | .02 |
| ☐ | 48 | Bill Freehan ................... | .60 | .24 | .06 |
| ☐ | 49 | Roy Face ....................... | .45 | .18 | .04 |
| ☐ | 50 | Tony Oliva ..................... | 1.25 | .50 | .12 |
| ☐ | 51 | Astros Rookies ............... | .25 | .10 | .02 |
| | | Dave Adlesh | | | |
| | | Wes Bales | | | |
| ☐ | 52 | Dennis Higgins ............... | .25 | .10 | .02 |
| ☐ | 53 | Clay Dalrymple ............... | .25 | .10 | .02 |
| ☐ | 54 | Dick Green ..................... | .25 | .10 | .02 |
| ☐ | 55 | Don Drysdale .................. | 3.50 | 1.40 | .35 |
| ☐ | 56 | Jose Tartabull ................ | .25 | .10 | .02 |
| ☐ | 57 | Pat Jarvis ..................... | .25 | .10 | .02 |
| ☐ | 58 | Paul Schaal ................... | .25 | .10 | .02 |
| ☐ | 59 | Ralph Terry .................... | .35 | .14 | .03 |
| ☐ | 60 | Luis Aparicio .................. | 2.75 | 1.10 | .27 |
| ☐ | 61 | Gordy Coleman ............... | .25 | .10 | .02 |
| ☐ | 62 | Checklist 1 .................... | 1.75 | .15 | .03 |
| | | Frank Robinson | | | |
| ☐ | 63 | Cards' Clubbers .............. | 1.50 | .60 | .15 |
| | | Lou Brock | | | |
| | | Curt Flood | | | |
| ☐ | 64 | Fred Valentine ............... | .25 | .10 | .02 |
| ☐ | 65 | Tom Haller .................... | .25 | .10 | .02 |
| ☐ | 66 | Manny Mota .................. | .35 | .14 | .03 |
| ☐ | 67 | Ken Berry ...................... | .25 | .10 | .02 |
| ☐ | 68 | Bob Buhl ....................... | .25 | .10 | .02 |
| ☐ | 69 | Vic Davalillo .................. | .65 | .26 | .06 |
| ☐ | 70 | Ron Santo ..................... | .65 | .26 | .06 |
| ☐ | 71 | Camilo Pascual ............... | .35 | .14 | .03 |
| ☐ | 72 | Tigers Rookies ............... | .35 | .14 | .03 |
| | | George Korince (Photo | | | |
| | | actually John Brown) | | | |
| | | John (Tom) Matchick | | | |
| ☐ | 73 | Rusty Staub ................... | 1.25 | .50 | .12 |
| ☐ | 74 | Wes Stock ..................... | .25 | .10 | .02 |
| ☐ | 75 | George Scott .................. | .35 | .14 | .03 |

| ☐ | 76 | Jim Barbieri ................... | .25 | .10 | .02 |
|---|---|---|---|---|---|
| ☐ | 77 | Dooley Womack ............... | .25 | .10 | .02 |
| ☐ | 78 | Pat Corrales ................... | .35 | .14 | .03 |
| ☐ | 79 | Bubba Morton ................. | .25 | .10 | .02 |
| ☐ | 80 | Jim Maloney ................... | .35 | .14 | .03 |
| ☐ | 81 | Eddie Stanky MGR .......... | .35 | .14 | .03 |
| ☐ | 82 | Steve Barber .................. | .25 | .10 | .02 |
| ☐ | 83 | Ollie Brown .................... | .25 | .10 | .02 |
| ☐ | 84 | Tommie Sisk .................. | .25 | .10 | .02 |
| ☐ | 85 | Johnny Callison .............. | .35 | .14 | .03 |
| ☐ | 86A | Mike McCormick ............. | .35 | .14 | .03 |
| | | (with traded line) | | | |
| ☐ | 86B | Mike McCormick .......... | 10.00 | 4.00 | 1.00 |
| | | (no traded line) | | | |
| ☐ | 87 | George Altman ................ | .25 | .10 | .02 |
| ☐ | 88 | Mickey Lolich ................. | .80 | .32 | .08 |
| ☐ | 89 | Felix Millan ................... | .35 | .14 | .03 |
| ☐ | 90 | Jim Nash ...................... | .25 | .10 | .02 |
| ☐ | 91 | Johnny Lewis ................. | .25 | .10 | .02 |
| ☐ | 92 | Ray Washburn ................ | .25 | .10 | .02 |
| ☐ | 93 | Yankees Rookies ............. | 1.25 | .50 | .12 |
| | | Stan Bahnsen | | | |
| | | Bobby Murcer | | | |
| ☐ | 94 | Ron Fairly ..................... | .35 | .14 | .03 |
| ☐ | 95 | Sonny Siebert ................ | .35 | .14 | .03 |
| ☐ | 96 | Art Shamsky .................. | .25 | .10 | .02 |
| ☐ | 97 | Mike Cuellar .................. | .35 | .14 | .03 |
| ☐ | 98 | Rich Rollins ................... | .25 | .10 | .02 |
| ☐ | 99 | Lee Stange .................... | .25 | .10 | .02 |
| ☐ | 100 | Frank Robinson ............... | 3.75 | 1.50 | .37 |
| ☐ | 101 | Ken Johnson .................. | .25 | .10 | .02 |
| ☐ | 102 | Phillies Team ................. | .75 | .30 | .07 |
| ☐ | 103 | Checklist 2 .................... | 2.50 | .25 | .05 |
| | | Mickey Mantle | | | |
| ☐ | 104 | Minnie Rojas .................. | .25 | .10 | .02 |
| ☐ | 105 | Ken Boyer ..................... | .80 | .32 | .08 |
| ☐ | 106 | Randy Hundley ............... | .35 | .14 | .03 |
| ☐ | 107 | Joel Horlen ................... | .35 | .14 | .03 |
| ☐ | 108 | Alex Johnson ................. | .35 | .14 | .03 |
| ☐ | 109 | Tribe Thumpers .............. | .40 | .16 | .04 |
| | | Rocky Colavito | | | |
| | | Leon Wagner | | | |
| ☐ | 110 | Jack Aker ...................... | .25 | .10 | .02 |
| ☐ | 111 | John Kennedy ................. | .25 | .10 | .02 |
| ☐ | 112 | Dave Wickersham ........... | .25 | .10 | .02 |
| ☐ | 113 | Dave Nicholson ............... | .25 | .10 | .02 |
| ☐ | 114 | Jack Baldschun ............... | .25 | .10 | .02 |
| ☐ | 115 | Paul Casanova ................ | .25 | .10 | .02 |
| ☐ | 116 | Herman Franks MGR ....... | .25 | .10 | .02 |
| ☐ | 117 | Darrell Brandon .............. | .25 | .10 | .02 |
| ☐ | 118 | Bernie Allen ................... | .25 | .10 | .02 |
| ☐ | 119 | Wade Blasingame ............ | .25 | .10 | .02 |
| ☐ | 120 | Floyd Robinson ............... | .25 | .10 | .02 |
| ☐ | 121 | Ed Bressoud ................... | .25 | .10 | .02 |
| ☐ | 122 | George Brunet ................ | .25 | .10 | .02 |
| ☐ | 123 | Pirates Rookies .............. | .25 | .10 | .02 |
| | | Jim Price | | | |
| | | Luke Walker | | | |
| ☐ | 124 | Jim Stewart ................... | .25 | .10 | .02 |
| ☐ | 125 | Moe Drabowsky ............... | .25 | .10 | .02 |
| ☐ | 126 | Tony Taylor ................... | .25 | .10 | .02 |
| ☐ | 127 | John O'Donoghue ............ | .25 | .10 | .02 |
| ☐ | 128 | Ed Spiezio ..................... | .25 | .10 | .02 |
| ☐ | 129 | Phil Roof ...................... | .25 | .10 | .02 |
| ☐ | 130 | Phil Regan .................... | .35 | .14 | .03 |
| ☐ | 131 | Yankees Team ................ | .90 | .36 | .09 |
| ☐ | 132 | Ozzie Virgil ................... | .25 | .10 | .02 |
| ☐ | 133 | Ron Kline ...................... | .25 | .10 | .02 |
| ☐ | 134 | Gates Brown .................. | .35 | .14 | .03 |
| ☐ | 135 | Deron Johnson ............... | .25 | .10 | .02 |
| ☐ | 136 | Carroll Sembera ............. | .25 | .10 | .02 |
| ☐ | 137 | Twins Rookies ................ | .25 | .10 | .02 |
| | | Ron Clark | | | |
| | | Jim Ollum | | | |
| ☐ | 138 | Dick Kelley .................... | .25 | .10 | .02 |
| ☐ | 139 | Dalton Jones .................. | .25 | .10 | .02 |
| ☐ | 140 | Willie Stargell ................ | 4.00 | 1.60 | .40 |
| ☐ | 141 | John Miller .................... | .25 | .10 | .02 |
| ☐ | 142 | Jackie Brandt ................. | .25 | .10 | .02 |
| ☐ | 143 | Sox Sockers ................... | .35 | .14 | .03 |
| | | Pete Ward | | | |
| | | Don Buford | | | |
| ☐ | 144 | Bill Hepler ..................... | .25 | .10 | .02 |
| ☐ | 145 | Larry Brown ................... | .25 | .10 | .02 |
| ☐ | 146 | Steve Carlton ................. | 36.00 | 15.00 | 3.60 |
| ☐ | 147 | Tom Egan ...................... | .25 | .10 | .02 |
| ☐ | 148 | Adolfo Phillips ............... | .25 | .10 | .02 |
| ☐ | 149 | Joe Moeller .................... | .25 | .10 | .02 |
| ☐ | 150 | Mickey Mantle ................ | 50.00 | 20.00 | 5.00 |
| ☐ | 151 | World Series Game 1 ...... | 1.00 | .40 | .10 |
| | | Moe mows down 11 | | | |
| ☐ | 152 | World Series Game 2 ...... | 2.00 | .80 | .20 |
| | | Palmer blanks Dodgers | | | |

| | | | | |
|---|---|---|---|---|
| ☐ 153 | World Series Game 3 ...... Blair's homer defeats L.A. | 1.00 | .40 | .10 |
| ☐ 154 | World Series Game 4 ...... Orioles 4 straight | 1.00 | .40 | .10 |
| ☐ 155 | World Series Summary ... Winners celebrate | 1.25 | .50 | .12 |
| ☐ 156 | Ron Herbel ...................... | .25 | .10 | .02 |
| ☐ 157 | Danny Cater .................... | .25 | .10 | .02 |
| ☐ 158 | Jimmie Coker .................. | .25 | .10 | .02 |
| ☐ 159 | Bruce Howard ................. | .25 | .10 | .02 |
| ☐ 160 | Willie Davis .................... | .50 | .20 | .05 |
| ☐ 161 | Dick Williams MGR .......... | .35 | .14 | .03 |
| ☐ 162 | Billy O'Dell .................... | .25 | .10 | .02 |
| ☐ 163 | Vic Roznovsky ................. | .25 | .10 | .02 |
| ☐ 164 | Dwight Siebler ................ | .25 | .10 | .02 |
| ☐ 165 | Cleon Jones ................... | .25 | .10 | .02 |
| ☐ 166 | Ed Mathews .................... | 3.00 | 1.20 | .30 |
| ☐ 167 | Senators Rookies ............ Joe Coleman Tim Cullen | .25 | .10 | .02 |
| ☐ 168 | Ray Culp ........................ | .25 | .10 | .02 |
| ☐ 169 | Horace Clarke ................. | .25 | .10 | .02 |
| ☐ 170 | Dick McAuliffe ................ | .35 | .14 | .03 |
| ☐ 171 | Calvin Koonce ................. | .25 | .10 | .02 |
| ☐ 172 | Bill Heath ...................... | .25 | .10 | .02 |
| ☐ 173 | Cardinals Team ............... | .85 | .34 | .08 |
| ☐ 174 | Dick Radatz ................... | .35 | .14 | .03 |
| ☐ 175 | Bobby Knoop ................... | .25 | .10 | .02 |
| ☐ 176 | Sammy Ellis .................... | .25 | .10 | .02 |
| ☐ 177 | Tito Fuentes ................... | .25 | .10 | .02 |
| ☐ 178 | John Buzhardt ................ | .25 | .10 | .02 |
| ☐ 179 | Braves Rookies ............... Charles Vaughan Cecil Upshaw | .25 | .10 | .02 |
| ☐ 180 | Curt Blefary .................... | .35 | .14 | .03 |
| ☐ 181 | Terry Fox ...................... | .25 | .10 | .02 |
| ☐ 182 | Ed Charles ..................... | .25 | .10 | .02 |
| ☐ 183 | Jim Pagliaroni ................ | .25 | .10 | .02 |
| ☐ 184 | George Thomas ............... | .25 | .10 | .02 |
| ☐ 185 | Ken Holtzman ................. | .75 | .30 | .07 |
| ☐ 186 | Mets Maulers .................. Ed Kranepool Ron Swoboda | .40 | .16 | .04 |
| ☐ 187 | Pedro Ramos ................... | .25 | .10 | .02 |
| ☐ 188 | Ken Harrelson ................. | .75 | .30 | .07 |
| ☐ 189 | Chuck Hinton .................. | .25 | .10 | .02 |
| ☐ 190 | Turk Farrell .................... | .25 | .10 | .02 |
| ☐ 191A | Checklist 3 .................... (214 Tom Kelley) (Willie Mays) | 2.00 | .20 | .04 |
| ☐ 191B | Checklist 3 .................... (214 Dick Kelley) (Willie Mays) | 5.00 | .50 | .10 |
| ☐ 192 | Fred Gladding ................. | .25 | .10 | .02 |
| ☐ 193 | Jose Cardenal ................. | .25 | .10 | .02 |
| ☐ 194 | Bob Allison .................... | .35 | .14 | .03 |
| ☐ 195 | Al Jackson ..................... | .25 | .10 | .02 |
| ☐ 196 | Johnny Romano ............... | .25 | .10 | .02 |
| ☐ 197 | Ron Perranoski ............... | .35 | .14 | .03 |
| ☐ 198 | Chuck Hiller .................... | .25 | .10 | .02 |
| ☐ 199 | Billy Hitchcock MGR ........ | .25 | .10 | .02 |
| ☐ 200 | Willie Mays .................... | 21.00 | 8.50 | 2.10 |
| ☐ 201 | Hal Reniff ...................... | .25 | .10 | .02 |
| ☐ 202 | Johnny Edwards ............... | .25 | .10 | .02 |
| ☐ 203 | Al McBean ...................... | .25 | .10 | .02 |
| ☐ 204 | Orioles Rookies ............... Mike Epstein Tom Phoebus | .35 | .14 | .03 |
| ☐ 205 | Dick Groat ..................... | .50 | .20 | .05 |
| ☐ 206 | Dennis Bennett ............... | .25 | .10 | .02 |
| ☐ 207 | John Orsino .................... | .25 | .10 | .02 |
| ☐ 208 | Jack Lamabe ................... | .25 | .10 | .02 |
| ☐ 209 | Joe Nossek ..................... | .25 | .10 | .02 |
| ☐ 210 | Bob Gibson ..................... | 3.75 | 1.50 | .37 |
| ☐ 211 | Twins Team ..................... | .75 | .30 | .07 |
| ☐ 212 | Chris Zachary ................. | .25 | .10 | .02 |
| ☐ 213 | Jay Johnstone ................. | .35 | .14 | .03 |
| ☐ 214 | Dick Kelley .................... | .25 | .10 | .02 |
| ☐ 215 | Ernie Banks .................... | 3.75 | 1.50 | .37 |
| ☐ 216 | Bengal Belters ................ Norm Cash Al Kaline | 1.75 | .70 | .17 |
| ☐ 217 | Rob Gardner ................... | .25 | .10 | .02 |
| ☐ 218 | Wes Parker .................... | .35 | .14 | .03 |
| ☐ 219 | Clay Carroll ................... | .25 | .10 | .02 |
| ☐ 220 | Jim Ray Hart .................. | .35 | .14 | .03 |
| ☐ 221 | Woody Fryman ................. | .25 | .10 | .02 |
| ☐ 222 | Reds Rookies .................. Darrell Osteen Lee May | .45 | .18 | .04 |
| ☐ 223 | Mike Ryan ...................... | .25 | .10 | .02 |
| ☐ 224 | Walt Bond ...................... | .25 | .10 | .02 |
| ☐ 225 | Mel Stottlemyre .............. | .65 | .26 | .06 |
| ☐ 226 | Julian Javier .................. | .35 | .14 | .03 |
| ☐ 227 | Paul Lindblad ................. | .25 | .10 | .02 |
| ☐ 228 | Gil Hodges MGR .............. | 2.25 | .90 | .22 |
| ☐ 229 | Larry Jackson ................. | .25 | .10 | .02 |
| ☐ 230 | Boog Powell ................... | 1.00 | .40 | .10 |
| ☐ 231 | John Bateman ................. | .25 | .10 | .02 |
| ☐ 232 | Don Buford ..................... | .25 | .10 | .02 |
| ☐ 233 | AL ERA Leaders: ............ Gary Peters Joel Horlen Steve Hargan | .80 | .32 | .08 |
| ☐ 234 | NL ERA Leaders: ............. Sandy Koufax Mike Cuellar Juan Marichal | 2.50 | 1.00 | .25 |
| ☐ 235 | AL Pitching Leaders: ....... Jim Kaat Denny McLain Earl Wilson | .80 | .32 | .08 |
| ☐ 236 | NL Pitching Leaders: ...... Sandy Koufax Juan Marichal Bob Gibson Gaylord Perry | 3.50 | 1.40 | .35 |
| ☐ 237 | AL Strikeout Leaders: ..... Sam McDowell Jim Kaat Earl Wilson | .80 | .32 | .08 |
| ☐ 238 | NL Strikeout Leaders: ..... Sandy Koufax Jim Bunning Bob Veale | 1.50 | .60 | .15 |
| ☐ 239 | AL Batting Leaders: ......... Frank Robinson Tony Oliva Al Kaline | 1.75 | .70 | .17 |
| ☐ 240 | NL Batting Leaders: ........ Matty Alou Felipe Alou Rico Carty | .80 | .32 | .08 |
| ☐ 241 | AL RBI Leaders: .............. Frank Robinson Harmon Killebrew Boog Powell | 1.50 | .60 | .15 |
| ☐ 242 | NL RBI Leaders: ............. Hank Aaron Bob Clemente Richie Allen | 2.00 | .80 | .20 |
| ☐ 243 | AL Home Run Leaders: ... Frank Robinson Harmon Killebrew Boog Powell | 1.50 | .60 | .15 |
| ☐ 244 | NL Home Run Leaders: .. Hank Aaron Richie Allen Willie Mays | 2.00 | .80 | .20 |
| ☐ 245 | Curt Flood ..................... | .55 | .22 | .05 |
| ☐ 246 | Jim Perry ...................... | .45 | .18 | .04 |
| ☐ 247 | Jerry Lumpe ................... | .25 | .10 | .02 |
| ☐ 248 | Gene Mauch MGR ............ | .35 | .14 | .03 |
| ☐ 249 | Nick Willhite .................. | .25 | .10 | .02 |
| ☐ 250 | Hank Aaron .................... | 21.00 | 8.50 | 2.10 |
| ☐ 251 | Woody Held .................... | .25 | .10 | .02 |
| ☐ 252 | Bob Bolin ...................... | .25 | .10 | .02 |
| ☐ 253 | Indians Rookies .............. Bill Davis Gus Gil | .25 | .10 | .02 |
| ☐ 254 | Milt Pappas ................... | .35 | .14 | .03 |
| ☐ 255 | Frank Howard ................. | .80 | .32 | .08 |
| ☐ 256 | Bob Hendley ................... | .25 | .10 | .02 |
| ☐ 257 | Charlie Smith ................. | .25 | .10 | .02 |
| ☐ 258 | Lee Maye ...................... | .25 | .10 | .02 |
| ☐ 259 | Don Dennis ..................... | .25 | .10 | .02 |
| ☐ 260 | Jim Lefebvre .................. | .35 | .14 | .03 |
| ☐ 261 | John Wyatt ..................... | .25 | .10 | .02 |
| ☐ 262 | Athletics Team ............... | .75 | .30 | .07 |
| ☐ 263 | Hank Aguirre .................. | .25 | .10 | .02 |
| ☐ 264 | Ron Swoboda .................. | .35 | .14 | .03 |
| ☐ 265 | Lou Burdette ................... | .60 | .24 | .06 |
| ☐ 266 | Pitt Power ..................... Willie Stargell Donn Clendenon | 1.25 | .50 | .12 |
| ☐ 267 | Don Schwall ................... | .25 | .10 | .02 |
| ☐ 268 | John Briggs .................... | .25 | .10 | .02 |
| ☐ 269 | Don Nottebart ................ | .25 | .10 | .02 |
| ☐ 270 | Zoilo Versalles ............... | .25 | .10 | .02 |
| ☐ 271 | Eddie Watt ..................... | .25 | .10 | .02 |
| ☐ 272 | Cubs Rookies .................. Bill Connors Dave Dowling | .25 | .10 | .02 |
| ☐ 273 | Dick Lines ...................... | .25 | .10 | .02 |

| | | | | |
|---|---|---|---|---|
| ☐ 274 | Bob Aspromonte | .25 | .10 | .02 |
| ☐ 275 | Fred Whitfield | .25 | .10 | .02 |
| ☐ 276 | Bruce Brubaker | .25 | .10 | .02 |
| ☐ 277 | Steve Whitaker | .25 | .10 | .02 |
| ☐ 278 | Checklist 4 | 1.75 | .15 | .03 |
| | Jim Kaat | | | |
| ☐ 279 | Frank Linzy | .25 | .10 | .02 |
| ☐ 280 | Tony Conigliaro | .75 | .30 | .07 |
| ☐ 281 | Bob Rodgers | .25 | .10 | .02 |
| ☐ 282 | Johnny Odom | .25 | .10 | .02 |
| ☐ 283 | Gene Alley | .35 | .14 | .03 |
| ☐ 284 | Johnny Podres | .60 | .24 | .06 |
| ☐ 285 | Lou Brock | 5.00 | 2.00 | .50 |
| ☐ 286 | Wayne Causey | .25 | .10 | .02 |
| ☐ 287 | Mets Rookies | .25 | .10 | .02 |
| | Greg Goossen | | | |
| | Bart Shirley | | | |
| ☐ 288 | Denny Lemaster | .25 | .10 | .02 |
| ☐ 289 | Tom Tresh | .45 | .18 | .04 |
| ☐ 290 | Bill White | .45 | .18 | .04 |
| ☐ 291 | Jim Hannan | .25 | .10 | .02 |
| ☐ 292 | Don Pavletich | .25 | .10 | .02 |
| ☐ 293 | Ed Kirkpatrick | .25 | .10 | .02 |
| ☐ 294 | Walt Alston MGR | .90 | .36 | .09 |
| ☐ 295 | Sam McDowell | .45 | .18 | .04 |
| ☐ 296 | Glenn Beckert | .40 | .16 | .04 |
| ☐ 297 | Dave Morehead | .25 | .10 | .02 |
| ☐ 298 | Ron Davis | .25 | .10 | .02 |
| ☐ 299 | Norm Siebern | .25 | | |
| ☐ 300 | Jim Kaat | 1.25 | .50 | .12 |
| ☐ 301 | Jesse Gonder | .25 | .10 | .02 |
| ☐ 302 | Orioles Team | .75 | .30 | .07 |
| ☐ 303 | Gil Blanco | .25 | .10 | .02 |
| ☐ 304 | Phil Gagliano | .25 | .10 | .02 |
| ☐ 305 | Earl Wilson | .25 | .10 | .02 |
| ☐ 306 | Bud Harrelson | .35 | .14 | .03 |
| ☐ 307 | Jim Beauchamp | .25 | .10 | .02 |
| ☐ 308 | Al Downing | .35 | .14 | .03 |
| ☐ 309 | Hurlers Beware | .45 | .18 | .04 |
| | Johnny Callison | | | |
| | Richie Allen | | | |
| ☐ 310 | Gary Peters | .35 | .14 | .03 |
| ☐ 311 | Ed Brinkman | .25 | .10 | .02 |
| ☐ 312 | Don Mincher | .25 | .10 | .02 |
| ☐ 313 | Bob Lee | .25 | .10 | .02 |
| ☐ 314 | Red Sox Rookies | 1.50 | .60 | .15 |
| | Mike Andrews | | | |
| | Reggie Smith | | | |
| ☐ 315 | Billy Williams | 3.50 | 1.40 | .35 |
| ☐ 316 | Jack Kralick | .25 | .10 | .02 |
| ☐ 317 | Cesar Tovar | .25 | .10 | .02 |
| ☐ 318 | Dave Giusti | .25 | .10 | .02 |
| ☐ 319 | Paul Blair | .35 | .14 | .03 |
| ☐ 320 | Gaylord Perry | 3.00 | 1.20 | .30 |
| ☐ 321 | Mayo Smith MGR | .25 | .10 | .02 |
| ☐ 322 | Jose Pagan | .25 | .10 | .02 |
| ☐ 323 | Mike Hershberger | .25 | .10 | .02 |
| ☐ 324 | Hal Woodeshick | .25 | .10 | .02 |
| ☐ 325 | Chico Cardenas | .25 | .10 | .02 |
| ☐ 326 | Bob Uecker | 3.50 | 1.40 | .35 |
| ☐ 327 | Angels Team | .75 | .30 | .07 |
| ☐ 328 | Clete Boyer | .45 | .18 | .04 |
| ☐ 329 | Charlie Lau | .35 | .14 | .03 |
| ☐ 330 | Claude Osteen | .35 | .14 | .03 |
| ☐ 331 | Joe Foy | .25 | .10 | .02 |
| ☐ 332 | Jesus Alou | .25 | .10 | .02 |
| ☐ 333 | Fergie Jenkins | 2.00 | .80 | .20 |
| ☐ 334 | Twin Terrors | 1.75 | .70 | .17 |
| | Bob Allison | | | |
| | Harmon Killebrew | | | |
| ☐ 335 | Bob Veale | .35 | .14 | .03 |
| ☐ 336 | Joe Azcue | .25 | .10 | .02 |
| ☐ 337 | Joe Morgan | 3.00 | 1.20 | .30 |
| ☐ 338 | Bob Locker | .25 | .10 | .02 |
| ☐ 339 | Chico Ruiz | .25 | .10 | .02 |
| ☐ 340 | Joe Pepitone | .45 | .18 | .04 |
| ☐ 341 | Giants Rookies | .25 | .10 | .02 |
| | Dick Dietz | | | |
| | Bill Sorrell | | | |
| ☐ 342 | Hank Fischer | .25 | .10 | .02 |
| ☐ 343 | Tom Satriano | .25 | .10 | .02 |
| ☐ 344 | Ossie Chavarria | .25 | .10 | .02 |
| ☐ 345 | Stu Miller | .25 | .10 | .02 |
| ☐ 346 | Jim Hickman | .25 | .10 | .02 |
| ☐ 347 | Grady Hatton MGR | .25 | .10 | .02 |
| ☐ 348 | Tug McGraw | .75 | .30 | .07 |
| ☐ 349 | Bob Chance | .25 | .10 | .02 |
| ☐ 350 | Joe Torre | .75 | .30 | .07 |
| ☐ 351 | Vern Law | .35 | .14 | .03 |
| ☐ 352 | Ray Oyler | .25 | .10 | .02 |
| ☐ 353 | Bill McCool | .25 | .10 | .02 |
| ☐ 354 | Cubs Team | .75 | .30 | .07 |
| ☐ 355 | Carl Yastrzemski | 45.00 | 18.00 | 4.50 |

| | | | | |
|---|---|---|---|---|
| ☐ 356 | Larry Jaster | .25 | .10 | .02 |
| ☐ 357 | Bill Skowron | .50 | .20 | .05 |
| ☐ 358 | Ruben Amaro | .25 | .10 | .02 |
| ☐ 359 | Dick Ellsworth | .35 | .14 | .03 |
| ☐ 360 | Leon Wagner | .25 | .10 | .02 |
| ☐ 361 | Checklist 5 | 2.00 | .20 | .04 |
| | Roberto Clemente | | | |
| ☐ 362 | Darold Knowles | .25 | .10 | .02 |
| ☐ 363 | Dave Johnson | .75 | .30 | .07 |
| ☐ 364 | Claude Raymond | .25 | .10 | .02 |
| ☐ 365 | John Roseboro | .35 | .14 | .03 |
| ☐ 366 | Andy Kosco | .25 | .10 | .02 |
| ☐ 367 | Angels Rookies | .25 | .10 | .02 |
| | Bill Kelso | | | |
| | Don Wallace | | | |
| ☐ 368 | Jack Hiatt | .25 | .10 | .02 |
| ☐ 369 | Jim Hunter | 3.50 | 1.40 | .35 |
| ☐ 370 | Tommy Davis | .50 | .20 | .05 |
| ☐ 371 | Jim Lonborg | .80 | .32 | .08 |
| ☐ 372 | Mike De La Hoz | .35 | .14 | .03 |
| ☐ 373 | White Sox Rookies | .35 | .14 | .03 |
| | Duane Josephson | | | |
| | Fred Klages | | | |
| ☐ 374 | Mel Queen | .35 | .14 | .03 |
| ☐ 375 | Jake Gibbs | .35 | .14 | .03 |
| ☐ 376 | Don Lock | .35 | .14 | .03 |
| ☐ 377 | Luis Tiant | .90 | .36 | .09 |
| ☐ 378 | Tigers Team | .90 | .36 | .09 |
| ☐ 379 | Jerry May | .35 | .14 | .03 |
| ☐ 380 | Dean Chance | .35 | .14 | .03 |
| ☐ 381 | Dick Schofield | .35 | .14 | .03 |
| ☐ 382 | Dave McNally | .75 | .30 | .07 |
| ☐ 383 | Ken Henderson | .35 | .14 | .03 |
| ☐ 384 | Cardinals Rookies | .35 | .14 | .03 |
| | Jim Cosman | | | |
| | Dick Hughes | | | |
| ☐ 385 | Jim Fregosi | .65 | .26 | .06 |
| | (batting wrong) | | | |
| ☐ 386 | Dick Selma | .35 | .14 | .03 |
| ☐ 387 | Cap Peterson | .35 | .14 | .03 |
| ☐ 388 | Arnold Earley | .35 | .14 | .03 |
| ☐ 389 | Al Dark MGR | .45 | .18 | .04 |
| ☐ 390 | Jim Wynn | .60 | .24 | .06 |
| ☐ 391 | Wilbur Wood | .50 | .20 | .05 |
| ☐ 392 | Tommy Harper | .45 | .18 | .04 |
| ☐ 393 | Jim Bouton | .90 | .36 | .09 |
| ☐ 394 | Jake Wood | .35 | .14 | .03 |
| ☐ 395 | Chris Short | .35 | .14 | .03 |
| ☐ 396 | Atlanta Aces | .40 | .16 | .04 |
| | Denis Menke | | | |
| | Tony Cloninger | | | |
| ☐ 397 | Willie Smith | .35 | .14 | .03 |
| ☐ 398 | Jeff Torborg | .40 | .16 | .04 |
| ☐ 399 | Al Worthington | .35 | .14 | .03 |
| ☐ 400 | Bob Clemente | 15.00 | 6.00 | 1.50 |
| ☐ 401 | Jim Coates | .35 | .14 | .03 |
| ☐ 402 | Phillies Rookies | .40 | .16 | .04 |
| | Grant Jackson | | | |
| | Billy Wilson | | | |
| ☐ 403 | Dick Nen | .35 | .14 | .03 |
| ☐ 404 | Nelson Briles | .45 | .18 | .04 |
| ☐ 405 | Russ Snyder | .35 | .14 | .03 |
| ☐ 406 | Lee Elia | .35 | .14 | .03 |
| ☐ 407 | Reds Team | .90 | .36 | .09 |
| ☐ 408 | Jim Northrup | .45 | .18 | .04 |
| ☐ 409 | Ray Sadecki | .35 | .14 | .03 |
| ☐ 410 | Lou Johnson | .35 | .14 | .03 |
| ☐ 411 | Dick Howser | .60 | .24 | .06 |
| ☐ 412 | Astros Rookies | .75 | .30 | .07 |
| | Norm Miller | | | |
| | Doug Rader | | | |
| ☐ 413 | Jerry Grote | .35 | .14 | .03 |
| ☐ 414 | Casey Cox | .35 | .14 | .03 |
| ☐ 415 | Sonny Jackson | .35 | .14 | .03 |
| ☐ 416 | Roger Repoz | .35 | .14 | .03 |
| ☐ 417 | Bob Bruce | .35 | .14 | .03 |
| ☐ 418 | Sam Mele MGR | .35 | .14 | .03 |
| ☐ 419 | Don Kessinger | .50 | .20 | .05 |
| ☐ 420 | Denny McLain | 1.25 | .50 | .12 |
| ☐ 421 | Dal Maxvill | .35 | .14 | .03 |
| ☐ 422 | Hoyt Wilhelm | 3.00 | 1.20 | .30 |
| ☐ 423 | Fence Busters | 5.00 | 2.00 | .50 |
| | Willie Mays | | | |
| | Willie McCovey | | | |
| ☐ 424 | Pedro Gonzales | .35 | .14 | .03 |
| ☐ 425 | Pete Mikkelsen | .35 | .14 | .03 |
| ☐ 426 | Lou Clinton | .35 | .14 | .03 |
| ☐ 427 | Ruben Gomez | .35 | .14 | .03 |
| ☐ 428 | Dodgers Rookies | .60 | .24 | .06 |
| | Tom Hutton | | | |
| | Gene Michael | | | |
| ☐ 429 | Garry Roggenburk | .35 | .14 | .03 |
| ☐ 430 | Pete Rose | 50.00 | 20.00 | 5.00 |

| | | | | |
|---|---|---|---|---|
| ☐ 431 | Ted Uhlaender | .35 | .14 | .03 |
| ☐ 432 | Jimmie Hall | .35 | .14 | .03 |
| ☐ 433 | Al Luplow | .35 | .14 | .03 |
| ☐ 434 | Eddie Fisher | .35 | .14 | .03 |
| ☐ 435 | Mack Jones | .35 | .14 | .03 |
| ☐ 436 | Pete Ward | .35 | .14 | .03 |
| ☐ 437 | Senators Team | .75 | .30 | .07 |
| ☐ 438 | Chuck Dobson | .35 | .14 | .03 |
| ☐ 439 | Byron Browne | .35 | .14 | .03 |
| ☐ 440 | Steve Hargan | .35 | .14 | .03 |
| ☐ 441 | Jim Davenport | .50 | .20 | .05 |
| ☐ 442 | Yankees Rookies | .50 | .20 | .05 |
| | Bill Robinson | | | |
| | Joe Verbanic | | | |
| ☐ 443 | Tito Francona | .40 | .16 | .04 |
| ☐ 444 | George Smith | .35 | .14 | .03 |
| ☐ 445 | Don Sutton | 4.50 | 1.80 | .45 |
| ☐ 446 | Russ Nixon | .35 | .14 | .03 |
| ☐ 447 | Bo Belinsky | .40 | .16 | .04 |
| ☐ 448 | Harry Walker MGR | .35 | .14 | .03 |
| ☐ 449 | Orlando Pena | .35 | .14 | .03 |
| ☐ 450 | Richie Allen | 1.25 | .50 | .12 |
| ☐ 451 | Fred Newman | .35 | .14 | .03 |
| ☐ 452 | Ed Kranepool | .50 | .20 | .05 |
| ☐ 453 | Aurelio Monteagudo | .35 | .14 | .03 |
| ☐ 454A | Checklist 6 | 2.50 | .25 | .05 |
| | Juan Marichal | | | |
| | (missing left ear) | | | |
| ☐ 454B | Checklist 6 | 5.00 | .50 | .10 |
| | Juan Marichal | | | |
| | (left ear showing) | | | |
| ☐ 455 | Tommy Agee | .40 | .16 | .04 |
| ☐ 456 | Phil Niekro | 3.50 | 1.40 | .35 |
| ☐ 457 | Andy Etchebarren | .35 | .14 | .03 |
| ☐ 458 | Lee Thomas | .75 | .30 | .07 |
| ☐ 459 | Senators Rookies | .75 | .30 | .07 |
| | Dick Bosman | | | |
| | Pete Craig | | | |
| ☐ 460 | Harmon Killebrew | 6.00 | 2.40 | .60 |
| ☐ 461 | Bob Miller | .75 | .30 | .07 |
| ☐ 462 | Bob Barton | .75 | .30 | .07 |
| ☐ 463 | Hill Aces | .90 | .36 | .09 |
| | Sam McDowell | | | |
| | Sonny Siebert | | | |
| ☐ 464 | Dan Coombs | .75 | .30 | .07 |
| ☐ 465 | Willie Horton | .90 | .36 | .09 |
| ☐ 466 | Bobby Wine | .75 | .30 | .07 |
| ☐ 467 | Jim O'Toole | .75 | .30 | .07 |
| ☐ 468 | Ralph Houk MGR | .90 | .36 | .09 |
| ☐ 469 | Len Gabrielson | .75 | .30 | .07 |
| ☐ 470 | Bob Shaw | .75 | .30 | .07 |
| ☐ 471 | Rene Lachemann | .90 | .36 | .09 |
| ☐ 472 | Rookies Pirates | .75 | .30 | .07 |
| | John Gelnar | | | |
| | George Spriggs | | | |
| ☐ 473 | Jose Santiago | .75 | .30 | .07 |
| ☐ 474 | Bob Tolan | .90 | .36 | .09 |
| ☐ 475 | Jim Palmer | 11.00 | 4.50 | 1.10 |
| ☐ 476 | Tony Perez SP | 12.50 | 5.00 | 1.25 |
| ☐ 477 | Braves Team | 1.25 | .50 | .12 |
| ☐ 478 | Bob Humphreys | .75 | .30 | .07 |
| ☐ 479 | Gary Bell | .75 | .30 | .07 |
| ☐ 480 | Willie McCovey | 7.50 | 3.00 | .75 |
| ☐ 481 | Leo Durocher MGR | 1.25 | .50 | .12 |
| ☐ 482 | Bill Monbouquette | .75 | .30 | .07 |
| ☐ 483 | Jim Landis | .75 | .30 | .07 |
| ☐ 484 | Jerry Adair | .75 | .30 | .07 |
| ☐ 485 | Tim McCarver | 1.25 | .50 | .12 |
| ☐ 486 | Twins Rookies | .75 | .30 | .07 |
| | Rich Reese | | | |
| | Bill Whitby | | | |
| ☐ 487 | Tommie Reynolds | .75 | .30 | .07 |
| ☐ 488 | Gerry Arrigo | .75 | .30 | .07 |
| ☐ 489 | Doug Clemens | .75 | .30 | .07 |
| ☐ 490 | Tony Cloninger | .75 | .30 | .07 |
| ☐ 491 | Sam Bowens | .75 | .30 | .07 |
| ☐ 492 | Pirates Team | 1.25 | .50 | .12 |
| ☐ 493 | Phil Ortega | .75 | .30 | .07 |
| ☐ 494 | Bill Rigney MGR | .75 | .30 | .07 |
| ☐ 495 | Fritz Peterson | .75 | .30 | .07 |
| ☐ 496 | Orlando McFarlane | .75 | .30 | .07 |
| ☐ 497 | Ron Campbell | .75 | .30 | .07 |
| ☐ 498 | Larry Dierker | .90 | .36 | .09 |
| ☐ 499 | Indians Rookies | .75 | .30 | .07 |
| | George Culver | | | |
| | Jose Vidal | | | |
| ☐ 500 | Juan Marichal | 5.00 | 2.00 | .50 |
| ☐ 501 | Jerry Zimmerman | .75 | .30 | .07 |
| ☐ 502 | Derrell Griffith | .75 | .30 | .07 |
| ☐ 503 | Dodgers Team | 2.00 | .80 | .20 |
| ☐ 504 | Orlando Martinez | .75 | .30 | .07 |
| ☐ 505 | Tommy Helms | .90 | .36 | .09 |
| ☐ 506 | Smoky Burgess | .90 | .36 | .09 |
| ☐ 507 | Orioles Rookies | .75 | .30 | .07 |
| | Ed Barnowski | | | |
| | Larry Haney | | | |
| ☐ 508 | Dick Hall | .75 | .30 | .07 |
| ☐ 509 | Jim King | .75 | .30 | .07 |
| ☐ 510 | Bill Mazeroski | 1.50 | .60 | .15 |
| ☐ 511 | Don Wert | .75 | .30 | .07 |
| ☐ 512 | Red Schoendienst MGR | 1.00 | .40 | .10 |
| ☐ 513 | Marcelino Lopez | .75 | .30 | .07 |
| ☐ 514 | John Werhas | .75 | .30 | .07 |
| ☐ 515 | Bert Campaneris | 1.00 | .40 | .10 |
| ☐ 516 | Giants Team | 1.25 | .50 | .12 |
| ☐ 517 | Fred Talbot | .75 | .30 | .07 |
| ☐ 518 | Denis Menke | .75 | .30 | .07 |
| ☐ 519 | Ted Davidson | .75 | .30 | .07 |
| ☐ 520 | Max Alvis | .75 | .30 | .07 |
| ☐ 521 | Bird Bombers | .90 | .36 | .09 |
| | Boog Powell | | | |
| | Curt Blefary | | | |
| ☐ 522 | John Stephenson | .75 | .30 | .07 |
| ☐ 523 | Jim Merritt | .75 | .30 | .07 |
| ☐ 524 | Felix Mantilla | .75 | .30 | .07 |
| ☐ 525 | Ron Hunt | .75 | .30 | .07 |
| ☐ 526 | Tigers Rookies | 1.25 | .50 | .12 |
| | Pat Dobson | | | |
| | George Korince | | | |
| | (See 67T-72) | | | |
| ☐ 527 | Dennis Ribant | .75 | .30 | .07 |
| ☐ 528 | Rico Petrocelli | 1.00 | .40 | .10 |
| ☐ 529 | Gary Wagner | .75 | .30 | .07 |
| ☐ 530 | Felipe Alou | 1.00 | .40 | .10 |
| ☐ 531 | Checklist 7 | 3.50 | .35 | .07 |
| | Brooks Robinson | | | |
| ☐ 532 | Jim Hicks | .75 | .30 | .07 |
| ☐ 533 | Jack Fisher | .75 | .30 | .07 |
| ☐ 534 | Hank Bauer | 3.00 | 1.20 | .30 |
| ☐ 535 | Donn Clendenon | 3.00 | 1.20 | .30 |
| ☐ 536 | Cubs Rookies | 4.50 | 1.80 | .45 |
| | Joe Niekro | | | |
| | Paul Popovich | | | |
| ☐ 537 | Chuck Estrada | 2.25 | .90 | .22 |
| ☐ 538 | J.C. Martin | 2.25 | .90 | .22 |
| ☐ 539 | Dick Egan | 2.25 | .90 | .22 |
| ☐ 540 | Norm Cash | 8.00 | 3.25 | .80 |
| ☐ 541 | Joe Gibbon | 2.25 | .90 | .22 |
| ☐ 542 | Athletics Rookies | 3.50 | 1.40 | .35 |
| | Rick Monday | | | |
| | Tony Pierce | | | |
| ☐ 543 | Dan Schneider | 2.25 | .90 | .22 |
| ☐ 544 | Indians Team | 4.50 | 1.80 | .45 |
| ☐ 545 | Jim Grant | 2.25 | .90 | .22 |
| ☐ 546 | Woody Woodward | 2.25 | .90 | .22 |
| ☐ 547 | Red Sox Rookies | 2.25 | .90 | .22 |
| | Russ Gibson | | | |
| | Bill Rohr | | | |
| ☐ 548 | Tony Gonzalez | 2.25 | .90 | .22 |
| ☐ 549 | Jack Sanford | 2.25 | .90 | .22 |
| ☐ 550 | Vada Pinson | 3.00 | 1.20 | .30 |
| ☐ 551 | Doug Camilli | 2.25 | .90 | .22 |
| ☐ 552 | Ted Savage | 2.25 | .90 | .22 |
| ☐ 553 | Yankees Rookies | 4.50 | 1.80 | .45 |
| | Mike Hegan | | | |
| | Thad Tillotson | | | |
| ☐ 554 | Andre Rodgers | 2.25 | .90 | .22 |
| ☐ 555 | Don Cardwell | 2.25 | .90 | .22 |
| ☐ 556 | Al Weis | 2.25 | .90 | .22 |
| ☐ 557 | Al Ferrara | 2.25 | .90 | .22 |
| ☐ 558 | Orioles Rookies | 7.50 | 3.00 | .75 |
| | Mark Belanger | | | |
| | Bill Dillman | | | |
| ☐ 559 | Dick Tracewski | 2.25 | .90 | .22 |
| ☐ 560 | Jim Bunning | 12.50 | 5.00 | 1.25 |
| ☐ 561 | Sandy Alomar | 2.25 | .90 | .22 |
| ☐ 562 | Steve Blass | 2.25 | .90 | .22 |
| ☐ 563 | Joe Adcock | 7.50 | 3.00 | .75 |
| ☐ 564 | Astros Rookies | 2.25 | .90 | .22 |
| | Alonzo Harris | | | |
| | Aaron Pointer | | | |
| ☐ 565 | Lew Krausse | 2.25 | .90 | .22 |
| ☐ 566 | Gary Geiger | 2.25 | .90 | .22 |
| ☐ 567 | Steve Hamilton | 2.25 | .90 | .22 |
| ☐ 568 | John Sullivan | 2.25 | .90 | .22 |
| ☐ 569 | A.L. Rookies | 120.00 | 50.00 | 12.00 |
| | Rod Carew | | | |
| | Hank Allen | | | |
| ☐ 570 | Maury Wills | 50.00 | 20.00 | 5.00 |
| ☐ 571 | Larry Sherry | 2.25 | .90 | .22 |
| ☐ 572 | Don Demeter | 2.25 | .90 | .22 |
| ☐ 573 | White Sox Team | 4.50 | 1.80 | .45 |
| ☐ 574 | Jerry Buchek | 2.25 | .90 | .22 |
| ☐ 575 | Dave Boswell | 2.25 | .90 | .22 |
| ☐ 576 | N.L. Rookies | 2.25 | .90 | .22 |
| | Ramon Hernandez | | | |
| | Norm Gigon | | | |

| | | | |
|---|---|---|---|
| ☐ 577 | Bill Short ........................ | 2.25 | .90 | .22 |
| ☐ 578 | John Boccabella ............. | 2.25 | .90 | .22 |
| ☐ 579 | Bill Henry ...................... | 2.25 | .90 | .22 |
| ☐ 580 | Rocky Colavito ............... | 9.00 | 3.75 | .90 |
| ☐ 581 | Mets Rookies ................. | 250.00 | 100.00 | 25.00 |
| | Bill Denehy | | | |
| | Tom Seaver | | | |
| ☐ 582 | Jim Owens ..................... | 2.25 | .90 | .22 |
| ☐ 583 | Ray Barker ..................... | 2.25 | .90 | .22 |
| ☐ 584 | Jim Piersall ................... | 6.00 | 2.40 | .60 |
| ☐ 585 | Wally Bunker .................. | 2.25 | .90 | .22 |
| ☐ 586 | Manny Jimenez ............... | 2.25 | .90 | .22 |
| ☐ 587 | N.L. Rookies .................. | 2.25 | .90 | .22 |
| | Don Shaw | | | |
| | Gary Sutherland | | | |
| ☐ 588 | Johnny Klippstein ........... | 2.25 | .90 | .22 |
| ☐ 589 | Dave Ricketts ................. | 2.25 | .90 | .22 |
| ☐ 590 | Pete Richert ................... | 2.25 | .90 | .22 |
| ☐ 591 | Ty Cline ........................ | 2.25 | .90 | .22 |
| ☐ 592 | N.L. Rookies .................. | 2.25 | .90 | .22 |
| | Jim Shellenback | | | |
| | Ron Willis | | | |
| ☐ 593 | Wes Westrum MGR ......... | 2.25 | .90 | .22 |
| ☐ 594 | Dan Osinski ................... | 2.25 | .90 | .22 |
| ☐ 595 | Cookie Rojas .................. | 2.25 | .90 | .22 |
| ☐ 596 | Galen Cisco ................... | 2.25 | .90 | .22 |
| ☐ 597 | Ted Abernathy ................ | 2.25 | .90 | .22 |
| ☐ 598 | White Sox Rookies .......... | 2.25 | .90 | .22 |
| | Walt Williams | | | |
| | Ed Stroud | | | |
| ☐ 599 | Bob Duliba ..................... | 2.25 | .90 | .22 |
| ☐ 600 | Brooks Robinson ............ | 100.00 | 40.00 | 10.00 |
| ☐ 601 | Bill Bryan ...................... | 2.25 | .90 | .22 |
| ☐ 602 | Juan Pizarro .................. | 2.25 | .90 | .22 |
| ☐ 603 | Athletics Rookies ............ | 2.25 | .90 | .22 |
| | Tim Talton | | | |
| | Ramon Webster | | | |
| ☐ 604 | Red Sox Team ................ | 8.00 | 3.25 | .80 |
| ☐ 605 | Mike Shannon ................ | 3.00 | 1.20 | .30 |
| ☐ 606 | Ron Taylor ..................... | 2.25 | .90 | .22 |
| ☐ 607 | Mickey Stanley ............... | 3.00 | 1.20 | .30 |
| ☐ 608 | Cubs Rookies ................. | 2.25 | .90 | .22 |
| | Rich Nye | | | |
| | John Upham | | | |
| ☐ 609 | Tommy John ................... | 30.00 | 12.00 | 3.00 |

## 1968 Topps

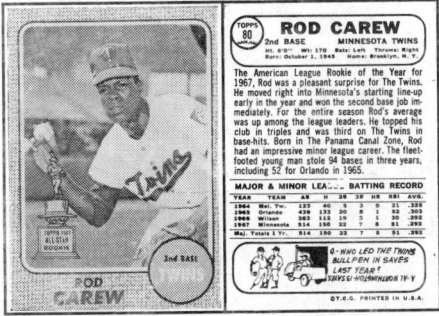

The cards in this 598 card set measure 2 1/2" by 3 1/2". The 1968 Topps set includes The Sporting News All-Star selections as card numbers 361 to 380. Other subsets in the set include League Leaders (1-12) and World Series cards (151-158). The front of each checklist card features a picture of a popular player inside a circle. High numbers 534 to 598 are slightly more difficult to obtain. The first series looks different from the other series as it has a lighter, wider mesh background on the card front. The later series all had a much darker, finer mesh pattern. Key cards in the set are the rookie cards of Johnny Bench (247) and Nolan Ryan (177).

| | | MINT | VG-E | F-G |
|---|---|---|---|---|
| | COMPLETE SET ..................... | 600.00 | 240.00 | 60.00 |
| | COMMON PLAYER (1-457) ........ | .21 | .09 | .02 |
| | COMMON PLAYER (458-533) .... | .30 | .12 | .03 |
| | COMMON PLAYER (534-598) .... | .30 | .12 | .03 |
| ☐ 1 | NL Batting Leaders ......... | 2.50 | .60 | .12 |
| | Bob Clemente | | | |
| | Tony Gonzales | | | |
| | Matty Alou | | | |
| ☐ 2 | AL Batting Leaders ......... | 2.50 | 1.00 | .25 |
| | Carl Yastrzemski | | | |
| | Frank Robinson | | | |
| | Al Kaline | | | |
| ☐ 3 | NL RBI Leaders .............. | 2.00 | .80 | .20 |
| | Orlando Cepeda | | | |
| | Bob Clemente | | | |
| | Hank Aaron | | | |
| ☐ 4 | AL RBI Leaders .............. | 2.50 | 1.00 | .25 |
| | Carl Yastrzemski | | | |
| | Harmon Killebrew | | | |
| | Frank Robinson | | | |
| ☐ 5 | NL Home Run Leaders ... | 1.50 | .60 | .15 |
| | Hank Aaron | | | |
| | Jim Wynn | | | |
| | Ron Santo | | | |
| | Willie McCovey | | | |
| ☐ 6 | NL Home Run Leaders ... | 2.00 | .80 | .20 |
| | Carl Yastrzemski | | | |
| | Harmon Killebrew | | | |
| | Frank Howard | | | |
| ☐ 7 | NL ERA Leaders ............. | .80 | .32 | .08 |
| | Phil Niekro | | | |
| | Jim Bunning | | | |
| | Chris Short | | | |
| ☐ 8 | AL ERA Leaders ............. | .60 | .24 | .06 |
| | Joe Horlen | | | |
| | Gary Peters | | | |
| | Sonny Siebert | | | |
| ☐ 9 | NL Pitching Leaders ....... | .80 | .32 | .08 |
| | Mike McCormick | | | |
| | Ferguson Jenkins | | | |
| | Jim Bunning | | | |
| | Claude Osteen | | | |
| ☐ 10 | AL Pitching Leaders ........ | .60 | .24 | .06 |
| | Jim Lonborg | | | |
| | Earl Wilson | | | |
| | Dean Chance | | | |
| ☐ 11 | NL Strikeout Leaders ...... | 1.25 | .50 | .12 |
| | Jim Bunning | | | |
| | Ferguson Jenkins | | | |
| | Gaylord Perry | | | |
| ☐ 12 | AL Strikeout Leaders ...... | .60 | .24 | .06 |
| | Jim Lonborg | | | |
| | Sam McDowell | | | |
| | Dean Chance | | | |
| ☐ 13 | Chuck Hartenstein .......... | .21 | .09 | .02 |
| ☐ 14 | Jerry McNertney ............. | .21 | .09 | .02 |
| ☐ 15 | Ron Hunt ........................ | .21 | .09 | .02 |
| ☐ 16 | Indians Rookies .............. | 1.00 | .40 | .10 |
| | Lou Piniella | | | |
| | Richie Scheinblum | | | |
| ☐ 17 | Dick Hall ....................... | .21 | .09 | .02 |
| ☐ 18 | Mike Hershberger ........... | .21 | .09 | .02 |
| ☐ 19 | Juan Pizarro .................. | .21 | .09 | .02 |
| ☐ 20 | Brooks Robinson ............ | 4.25 | 1.70 | .42 |
| ☐ 21 | Ron Davis ...................... | .21 | .09 | .02 |
| ☐ 22 | Pat Dobson .................... | .30 | .12 | .03 |
| ☐ 23 | Chico Cardenas .............. | .21 | .09 | .02 |
| ☐ 24 | Bobby Locke ................... | .21 | .09 | .02 |
| ☐ 25 | Julian Javier .................. | .21 | .09 | .02 |
| ☐ 26 | Darrell Brandon .............. | .21 | .09 | .02 |
| ☐ 27 | Gil Hodges MGR ............ | 2.00 | .80 | .20 |
| ☐ 28 | Ted Uhlaender ................ | .21 | .09 | .02 |
| ☐ 29 | Joe Verbanic .................. | .21 | .09 | .02 |
| ☐ 30 | Joe Torre ....................... | .75 | .30 | .07 |
| ☐ 31 | Ed Stroud ...................... | .21 | .09 | .02 |
| ☐ 32 | Joe Gibbon .................... | .21 | .09 | .02 |
| ☐ 33 | Pete Ward ...................... | .21 | .09 | .02 |
| ☐ 34 | Al Ferrara ...................... | .21 | .09 | .02 |
| ☐ 35 | Steve Hargan ................. | .21 | .09 | .02 |
| ☐ 36 | Pirates Rookies .............. | .30 | .12 | .03 |
| | Bob Moose | | | |
| | Bob Robertson | | | |
| ☐ 37 | Billy Williams ................. | 3.00 | 1.20 | .30 |
| ☐ 38 | Tony Pierce .................... | .21 | .09 | .02 |
| ☐ 39 | Cookie Rojas .................. | .21 | .09 | .02 |
| ☐ 40 | Denny McLain ................. | 1.50 | .60 | .15 |
| ☐ 41 | Julio Gotay .................... | .21 | .09 | .02 |
| ☐ 42 | Larry Haney ................... | .21 | .09 | .02 |
| ☐ 43 | Gary Bell ....................... | .21 | .09 | .02 |

| | | | | |
|---|---|---|---|---|
| ☐ 44 | Frank Kostro | .21 | .09 | .02 |
| ☐ 45 | Tom Seaver | 30.00 | 12.00 | 3.00 |
| ☐ 46 | Dave Ricketts | .21 | .09 | .02 |
| ☐ 47 | Ralph Houk MGR | .35 | .14 | .03 |
| ☐ 48 | Ted Davidson | .21 | .09 | .02 |
| ☐ 49A | Eddie Brinkman (white team name) | .30 | .12 | .03 |
| ☐ 49B | Eddie Brinkman (yellow team name) | 10.00 | 4.00 | 1.00 |
| ☐ 50 | Willie Mays | 15.00 | 6.00 | 1.50 |
| ☐ 51 | Bob Locker | .21 | .09 | .02 |
| ☐ 52 | Hawk Taylor | .21 | .09 | .02 |
| ☐ 53 | Gene Alley | .30 | .12 | .03 |
| ☐ 54 | Stan Williams | .21 | .09 | .02 |
| ☐ 55 | Felipe Alou | .30 | .12 | .03 |
| ☐ 56 | Orioles Rookies Dave Leonhard Dave May | .21 | .09 | .02 |
| ☐ 57 | Dan Schneider | .21 | .09 | .02 |
| ☐ 58 | Eddie Mathews | 3.00 | 1.20 | .30 |
| ☐ 59 | Don Lock | .21 | .09 | .02 |
| ☐ 60 | Ken Holtzman | .35 | .14 | .03 |
| ☐ 61 | Reggie Smith | .75 | .30 | .07 |
| ☐ 62 | Chuck Dobson | .21 | .09 | .02 |
| ☐ 63 | Dick Kenworthy | .21 | .09 | .02 |
| ☐ 64 | Jim Merritt | .21 | .09 | .02 |
| ☐ 65 | John Roseboro | .30 | .12 | .03 |
| ☐ 66A | Casey Cox (white team name) | .30 | .12 | .03 |
| ☐ 66B | Casey Cox (yellow team name) | 10.00 | 4.00 | 1.00 |
| ☐ 67 | Checklist 1 Jim Kaat | 1.50 | .15 | .03 |
| ☐ 68 | Ron Willis | .21 | .09 | .02 |
| ☐ 69 | Tom Tresh | .40 | .16 | .04 |
| ☐ 70 | Bob Veale | .30 | .12 | .03 |
| ☐ 71 | Vern Fuller | .21 | .09 | .02 |
| ☐ 72 | Tommy John | 1.50 | .60 | .15 |
| ☐ 73 | Jim Ray Hart | .30 | .12 | .03 |
| ☐ 74 | Milt Pappas | .30 | .12 | .03 |
| ☐ 75 | Don Mincher | .21 | .09 | .02 |
| ☐ 76 | Braves Rookies Jim Britton Ron Reed | .30 | .12 | .03 |
| ☐ 77 | Don Wilson | .21 | .09 | .02 |
| ☐ 78 | Jim Northrup | .30 | .12 | .03 |
| ☐ 79 | Ted Kubiak | .21 | .09 | .02 |
| ☐ 80 | Rod Carew | 21.00 | 8.50 | 2.10 |
| ☐ 81 | Larry Jackson | .21 | .09 | .02 |
| ☐ 82 | Sam Bowens | .21 | .09 | .02 |
| ☐ 83 | John Stephenson | .21 | .09 | .02 |
| ☐ 84 | Bob Tolan | .21 | .09 | .02 |
| ☐ 85 | Gaylord Perry | 2.50 | 1.00 | .25 |
| ☐ 86 | Willie Stargell | 3.50 | 1.40 | .35 |
| ☐ 87 | Dick Williams MGR | .30 | .12 | .03 |
| ☐ 88 | Phil Regan | .30 | .12 | .03 |
| ☐ 89 | Jake Gibbs | .21 | .09 | .02 |
| ☐ 90 | Vada Pinson | .75 | .30 | .07 |
| ☐ 91 | Jim Ollom | .21 | .09 | .02 |
| ☐ 92 | Ed Kranepool | .30 | .12 | .03 |
| ☐ 93 | Tony Cloninger | .21 | .09 | .02 |
| ☐ 94 | Lee Maye | .21 | .09 | .02 |
| ☐ 95 | Bob Aspromonte | .21 | .09 | .02 |
| ☐ 96 | Senator Rookies Frank Coggins Dick Nold | .21 | .09 | .02 |
| ☐ 97 | Tom Phoebus | .21 | .09 | .02 |
| ☐ 98 | Gary Sutherland | .21 | .09 | .02 |
| ☐ 99 | Rocky Colavito | .75 | .30 | .07 |
| ☐ 100 | Bob Gibson | 4.00 | 1.60 | .40 |
| ☐ 101 | Glenn Beckert | .30 | .12 | .03 |
| ☐ 102 | Jose Cardenal | .21 | .09 | .02 |
| ☐ 103 | Don Sutton | 2.50 | 1.00 | .25 |
| ☐ 104 | Dick Dietz | .21 | .09 | .02 |
| ☐ 105 | Al Downing | .21 | .09 | .02 |
| ☐ 106 | Dalton Jones | .21 | .09 | .02 |
| ☐ 107A | Checklist 2 Juan Marichal (tan wide mesh) | 1.50 | .15 | .03 |
| ☐ 107B | Checklist 2 Juan Marichal (brown fine mesh) | 2.00 | .20 | .04 |
| ☐ 108 | Don Pavletich | .21 | .09 | .02 |
| ☐ 109 | Bert Campaneris | .35 | .14 | .03 |
| ☐ 110 | Hank Aaron | 15.00 | 6.00 | 1.50 |
| ☐ 111 | Rich Reese | .21 | .09 | .02 |
| ☐ 112 | Woody Fryman | .21 | .09 | .02 |
| ☐ 113 | Tigers Rookies Tom Matchick Daryl Patterson | .21 | .09 | .02 |
| ☐ 114 | Ron Swoboda | .30 | .12 | .03 |
| ☐ 115 | Sam McDowell | .35 | .14 | .03 |
| ☐ 116 | Ken McMullen | .21 | .09 | .02 |
| ☐ 117 | Larry Jaster | .21 | .09 | .02 |
| ☐ 118 | Mark Belanger | .50 | .20 | .05 |
| ☐ 119 | Ted Savage | .21 | .09 | .02 |
| ☐ 120 | Mel Stottlemyre | .35 | .14 | .03 |
| ☐ 121 | Jimmie Hall | .21 | .09 | .02 |
| ☐ 122 | Gene Mauch MGR | .30 | .12 | .03 |
| ☐ 123 | Jose Santiago | .21 | .09 | .02 |
| ☐ 124 | Nate Oliver | .21 | .09 | .02 |
| ☐ 125 | Joe Horlen | .30 | .12 | .03 |
| ☐ 126 | Bob Etheridge | .21 | .09 | .02 |
| ☐ 127 | Paul Lindblad | .21 | .09 | .02 |
| ☐ 128 | Astros Rookies Tom Dukes Alonzo Harris | .21 | .09 | .02 |
| ☐ 129 | Mickey Stanley | .30 | .12 | .03 |
| ☐ 130 | Tony Perez | 2.00 | .80 | .20 |
| ☐ 131 | Frank Bertaina | .21 | .09 | .02 |
| ☐ 132 | Bud Harrelson | .30 | .12 | .03 |
| ☐ 133 | Fred Whitfield | .21 | .09 | .02 |
| ☐ 134 | Pat Jarvis | .21 | .09 | .02 |
| ☐ 135 | Paul Blair | .30 | .12 | .03 |
| ☐ 136 | Randy Hundley | .21 | .09 | .02 |
| ☐ 137 | Twins Team | .55 | .22 | .05 |
| ☐ 138 | Ruben Amaro | .21 | .09 | .02 |
| ☐ 139 | Chris Short | .21 | .09 | .02 |
| ☐ 140 | Tony Conigliaro | .65 | .26 | .06 |
| ☐ 141 | Dal Maxvill | .21 | .09 | .02 |
| ☐ 142 | White Sox Rookies Buddy Bradford Bill Voss | .21 | .09 | .02 |
| ☐ 143 | Pete Cimino | .21 | .09 | .02 |
| ☐ 144 | Joe Morgan | 2.50 | 1.00 | .25 |
| ☐ 145 | Don Drysdale | 3.00 | 1.20 | .30 |
| ☐ 146 | Sal Bando | .50 | .20 | .05 |
| ☐ 147 | Frank Linzy | .21 | .09 | .02 |
| ☐ 148 | Dave Bristol MGR | .21 | .09 | .02 |
| ☐ 149 | Bob Saverine | .21 | .09 | .02 |
| ☐ 150 | Bob Clemente | 11.00 | 4.50 | 1.10 |
| ☐ 151 | World Series Game 1: Brock socks 4 hits in opener | 2.00 | .80 | .20 |
| ☐ 152 | World Series Game 2: Yaz smashes 2 homers | 2.50 | 1.00 | .25 |
| ☐ 153 | World Series Game 3: Briles cools off Boston | 1.00 | .40 | .10 |
| ☐ 154 | World Series Game 4: Gibson hurls shutout | 2.00 | .80 | .20 |
| ☐ 155 | World Series Game 5: Lonborg wins again | 1.00 | .40 | .10 |
| ☐ 156 | World Series Game 6: Petrocelli 2 homers | 1.00 | .40 | .10 |
| ☐ 157 | World Series Game 7: St. Louis wins it | 1.00 | .40 | .10 |
| ☐ 158 | World Series Summary Cardinal celebrate | 1.00 | .40 | .10 |
| ☐ 159 | Don Kessinger | .35 | .14 | .03 |
| ☐ 160 | Earl Wilson | .21 | .09 | .02 |
| ☐ 161 | Norm Miller | .21 | .09 | .02 |
| ☐ 162 | Cards Rookies Hal Gilson Mike Torrez | .60 | .24 | .06 |
| ☐ 163 | Gene Brabender | .21 | .09 | .02 |
| ☐ 164 | Ramon Webster | .21 | .09 | .02 |
| ☐ 165 | Tony Oliva | 1.00 | .40 | .10 |
| ☐ 166 | Claude Raymond | .21 | .09 | .02 |
| ☐ 167 | Elston Howard | 1.00 | .40 | .10 |
| ☐ 168 | Dodgers Team | .80 | .32 | .08 |
| ☐ 169 | Bob Bolin | .21 | .09 | .02 |
| ☐ 170 | Jim Fregosi | .40 | .16 | .04 |
| ☐ 171 | Don Nottebart | .21 | .09 | .02 |
| ☐ 172 | Walt Williams | .21 | .09 | .02 |
| ☐ 173 | John Boozer | .21 | .09 | .02 |
| ☐ 174 | Bob Tillman | .21 | .09 | .02 |
| ☐ 175 | Maury Wills | 1.25 | .50 | .12 |
| ☐ 176 | Bob Allen | .21 | .09 | .02 |
| ☐ 177 | Mets Rookies Jerry Koosman Nolan Ryan | 80.00 | 32.00 | 8.00 |
| ☐ 178 | Don Wert | .21 | .09 | .02 |
| ☐ 179 | Bill Stoneman | .21 | .09 | .02 |
| ☐ 180 | Curt Flood | .55 | .22 | .05 |
| ☐ 181 | Jerry Zimmerman | .21 | .09 | .02 |
| ☐ 182 | Dave Giusti | .21 | .09 | .02 |
| ☐ 183 | Bob Kennedy MGR | .21 | .09 | .02 |
| ☐ 184 | Lou Johnson | .21 | .09 | .02 |
| ☐ 185 | Tom Haller | .21 | .09 | .02 |
| ☐ 186 | Eddie Watt | .21 | .09 | .02 |
| ☐ 187 | Sonny Jackson | .21 | .09 | .02 |
| ☐ 188 | Cap Peterson | .21 | .09 | .02 |
| ☐ 189 | Bill Landis | .21 | .09 | .02 |
| ☐ 190 | Bill White | .35 | .14 | .03 |
| ☐ 191 | Dan Frisella | .21 | .09 | .02 |

| | | | |
|---|---|---|---|
| ☐ 192 Checklist 3 | 1.75 | .15 | .03 |
| Carl Yastrzemski | | | |
| ☐ 193 Jack Hamilton | .21 | .09 | .02 |
| ☐ 194 Don Buford | .21 | .09 | .02 |
| ☐ 195 Joe Pepitone | .35 | .14 | .03 |
| ☐ 196 Gary Nolan | .21 | .09 | .02 |
| ☐ 197 Larry Brown | .21 | .09 | .02 |
| ☐ 198 Roy Face | .40 | .16 | .04 |
| ☐ 199 A's Rookies | .21 | .09 | .02 |
| Roberto Rodriquez | | | |
| Darrell Osteen | | | |
| ☐ 200 Orlando Cepeda | 1.50 | .60 | .15 |
| ☐ 201 Mike Marshall | .75 | .30 | .07 |
| ☐ 202 Adolfo Phillips | .21 | .09 | .02 |
| ☐ 203 Dick Kelley | .21 | .09 | .02 |
| ☐ 204 Andy Etchebarren | .21 | .09 | .02 |
| ☐ 205 Juan Marichal | 3.00 | 1.20 | .30 |
| ☐ 206 Cal Ermer MGR | .21 | .09 | .02 |
| ☐ 207 Carroll Sembera | .21 | .09 | .02 |
| ☐ 208 Willie Davis | .45 | .18 | .04 |
| ☐ 209 Tim Cullen | .21 | .09 | .02 |
| ☐ 210 Gary Peters | .30 | .12 | .03 |
| ☐ 211 J.C. Martin | .21 | .09 | .02 |
| ☐ 212 Dave Morehead | .21 | .09 | .02 |
| ☐ 213 Chico Ruiz | .21 | .09 | .02 |
| ☐ 214 Yankees Rookies | .40 | .16 | .04 |
| Stan Bahnsen | | | |
| Frank Fernandez | | | |
| ☐ 215 Jim Bunning | 1.50 | .60 | .15 |
| ☐ 216 Bubba Morton | .21 | .09 | .02 |
| ☐ 217 Turk Farrell | .21 | .09 | .02 |
| ☐ 218 Ken Suarez | .21 | .09 | .02 |
| ☐ 219 Rob Gardner | .21 | .09 | .02 |
| ☐ 220 Harmon Killebrew | 3.50 | 1.40 | .35 |
| ☐ 221 Braves Team | .60 | .24 | .06 |
| ☐ 222 Jim Hardin | .21 | .09 | .02 |
| ☐ 223 Ollie Brown | .21 | .09 | .02 |
| ☐ 224 Jack Aker | .21 | .09 | .02 |
| ☐ 225 Richie Allen | .80 | .32 | .08 |
| ☐ 226 Jimmie Price | .21 | .09 | .02 |
| ☐ 227 Joe Hoerner | .21 | .09 | .02 |
| ☐ 228 Dodgers Rookies | .30 | .12 | .03 |
| Jack Billingham | | | |
| Jim Fairey | | | |
| ☐ 229 Fred Klages | .21 | .09 | .02 |
| ☐ 230 Pete Rose | 36.00 | 15.00 | 3.60 |
| ☐ 231 Dave Baldwin | .21 | .09 | .02 |
| ☐ 232 Denis Menke | .21 | .09 | .02 |
| ☐ 233 George Scott | .30 | .12 | .03 |
| ☐ 234 Bill Monbouquette | .21 | .09 | .02 |
| ☐ 235 Ron Santo | .60 | .24 | .06 |
| ☐ 236 Tug McGraw | .75 | .30 | .07 |
| ☐ 237 Alvin Dark MGR | .30 | .12 | .03 |
| ☐ 238 Tom Satriano | .21 | .09 | .02 |
| ☐ 239 Bill Henry | .21 | .09 | .02 |
| ☐ 240 Al Kaline | 4.00 | 1.60 | .40 |
| ☐ 241 Felix Millan | .21 | .09 | .02 |
| ☐ 242 Moe Drabowsky | .21 | .09 | .02 |
| ☐ 243 Rich Rollins | .21 | .09 | .02 |
| ☐ 244 John Donaldson | .21 | .09 | .02 |
| ☐ 245 Tony Gonzalez | .21 | .09 | .02 |
| ☐ 246 Fritz Peterson | .21 | .09 | .02 |
| ☐ 247 Reds Rookies | 70.00 | 28.00 | 7.00 |
| Johnny Bench | | | |
| Ron Tompkins | | | |
| ☐ 248 Fred Valentine | .21 | .09 | .02 |
| ☐ 249 Bill Singer | .21 | .09 | .02 |
| ☐ 250 Carl Yastrzemski | 18.00 | 7.25 | 1.80 |
| ☐ 251 Manny Sanguillen | .75 | .30 | .07 |
| ☐ 252 Angels Team | .55 | .22 | .05 |
| ☐ 253 Dick Hughes | .21 | .09 | .02 |
| ☐ 254 Cleon Jones | .21 | .09 | .02 |
| ☐ 255 Dean Chance | .30 | .12 | .03 |
| ☐ 256 Norm Cash | .75 | .30 | .07 |
| ☐ 257 Phil Niekro | 2.50 | 1.00 | .25 |
| ☐ 258 Cubs Rookies | .21 | .09 | .02 |
| Jose Arcia | | | |
| Bill Schlesinger | | | |
| ☐ 259 Ken Boyer | .75 | .30 | .07 |
| ☐ 260 Jim Wynn | .50 | .20 | .05 |
| ☐ 261 Dave Duncan | .21 | .09 | .02 |
| ☐ 262 Rick Wise | .30 | .12 | .03 |
| ☐ 263 Horace Clarke | .21 | .09 | .02 |
| ☐ 264 Ted Abernathy | .21 | .09 | .02 |
| ☐ 265 Tommy Davis | .40 | .16 | .04 |
| ☐ 266 Paul Popovich | .21 | .09 | .02 |
| ☐ 267 Herman Franks MGR | .21 | .09 | .02 |
| ☐ 268 Bob Humphreys | .21 | .09 | .02 |
| ☐ 269 Bob Tiefenauer | .21 | .09 | .02 |
| ☐ 270 Matty Alou | .30 | .12 | .03 |
| ☐ 271 Bobby Knoop | .21 | .09 | .02 |
| ☐ 272 Ray Culp | .21 | .09 | .02 |
| ☐ 273 Dave Johnson | .50 | .20 | .05 |

| | | | |
|---|---|---|---|
| ☐ 274 Mike Cuellar | .35 | .14 | .03 |
| ☐ 275 Tim McCarver | .50 | .20 | .05 |
| ☐ 276 Jim Roland | .21 | .09 | .02 |
| ☐ 277 Jerry Buchek | .21 | .09 | .02 |
| ☐ 278 Checklist 4 | 1.50 | .15 | .03 |
| Orlando Cepeda | | | |
| ☐ 279 Bill Hands | .21 | .09 | .02 |
| ☐ 280 Mickey Mantle | 45.00 | 18.00 | 4.50 |
| ☐ 281 Jim Campanis | .21 | .09 | .02 |
| ☐ 282 Rick Monday | .40 | .16 | .04 |
| ☐ 283 Mel Queen | .21 | .09 | .02 |
| ☐ 284 John Briggs | .21 | .09 | .02 |
| ☐ 285 Dick McAuliffe | .21 | .09 | .02 |
| ☐ 286 Cecil Upshaw | .21 | .09 | .02 |
| ☐ 287 White Sox Rookies | .21 | .09 | .02 |
| Mickey Abarbanel | | | |
| Cisco Carlos | | | |
| ☐ 288 Dave Wickersham | .21 | .09 | .02 |
| ☐ 289 Woody Held | .21 | .09 | .02 |
| ☐ 290 Willie McCovey | 3.50 | 1.40 | .35 |
| ☐ 291 Dick Lines | .21 | .09 | .02 |
| ☐ 292 Art Shamsky | .21 | .09 | .02 |
| ☐ 293 Bruce Howard | .21 | .09 | .02 |
| ☐ 294 Red Schoendienst MGR | .40 | .16 | .04 |
| ☐ 295 Sonny Siebert | .30 | .12 | .03 |
| ☐ 296 Byron Browne | .21 | .09 | .02 |
| ☐ 297 Russ Gibson | .21 | .09 | .02 |
| ☐ 298 Jim Brewer | .21 | .09 | .02 |
| ☐ 299 Gene Michael | .35 | .14 | .03 |
| ☐ 300 Rusty Staub | .75 | .30 | .07 |
| ☐ 301 Twins Rookies | .21 | .09 | .02 |
| George Mitterwald | | | |
| Rick Renick | | | |
| ☐ 302 Gerry Arrigo | .21 | .09 | .02 |
| ☐ 303 Dick Green | .21 | .09 | .02 |
| ☐ 304 Sandy Valdespino | .21 | .09 | .02 |
| ☐ 305 Minnie Rojas | .21 | .09 | .02 |
| ☐ 306 Mike Ryan | .21 | .09 | .02 |
| ☐ 307 John Hiller | .35 | .14 | .03 |
| ☐ 308 Pirates Team | .55 | .22 | .05 |
| ☐ 309 Ken Henderson | .21 | .09 | .02 |
| ☐ 310 Luis Aparicio | 2.50 | 1.00 | .25 |
| ☐ 311 Jack Lamabe | .21 | .09 | .02 |
| ☐ 312 Curt Blefary | .30 | .12 | .03 |
| ☐ 313 Al Weis | .21 | .09 | .02 |
| ☐ 314 Red Sox Rookies | .21 | .09 | .02 |
| Bill Rohr | | | |
| George Spriggs | | | |
| ☐ 315 Zoilo Versalles | .21 | .09 | .02 |
| ☐ 316 Steve Barber | .21 | .09 | .02 |
| ☐ 317 Ron Brand | .21 | .09 | .02 |
| ☐ 318 Chico Salmon | .21 | .09 | .02 |
| ☐ 319 George Culver | .21 | .09 | .02 |
| ☐ 320 Frank Howard | .75 | .30 | .07 |
| ☐ 321 Leo Durocher MGR | .75 | .30 | .07 |
| ☐ 322 Dave Boswell | .21 | .09 | .02 |
| ☐ 323 Deron Johnson | .21 | .09 | .02 |
| ☐ 324 Jim Nash | .21 | .09 | .02 |
| ☐ 325 Manny Mota | .30 | .12 | .03 |
| ☐ 326 Denny Ribant | .21 | .09 | .02 |
| ☐ 327 Tony Taylor | .21 | .09 | .02 |
| ☐ 328 Angels Rookies | .21 | .09 | .02 |
| Chuck Vinson | | | |
| Jim Weaver | | | |
| ☐ 329 Duane Josephson | .21 | .09 | .02 |
| ☐ 330 Roger Maris | 3.50 | 1.40 | .35 |
| ☐ 331 Dan Osinski | .21 | .09 | .02 |
| ☐ 332 Doug Rader | .30 | .12 | .03 |
| ☐ 333 Ron Herbel | .21 | .09 | .02 |
| ☐ 334 Orioles Team | .55 | .22 | .05 |
| ☐ 335 Bob Allison | .35 | .14 | .03 |
| ☐ 336 John Purdin | .21 | .09 | .02 |
| ☐ 337 Bill Robinson | .21 | .09 | .02 |
| ☐ 338 Bob Johnson | .21 | .09 | .02 |
| ☐ 339 Rich Nye | .21 | .09 | .02 |
| ☐ 340 Max Alvis | .21 | .09 | .02 |
| ☐ 341 Jim Lemon MGR | .21 | .09 | .02 |
| ☐ 342 Ken Johnson | .21 | .09 | .02 |
| ☐ 343 Jim Gosger | .21 | .09 | .02 |
| ☐ 344 Donn Clendenon | .30 | .12 | .03 |
| ☐ 345 Bob Hendley | .21 | .09 | .02 |
| ☐ 346 Jerry Adair | .21 | .09 | .02 |
| ☐ 347 George Brunet | .21 | .09 | .02 |
| ☐ 348 Phillies Rookies | .21 | .09 | .02 |
| Larry Colton | | | |
| Dick Thoenen | | | |
| ☐ 349 Ed Spiezio | .21 | .09 | .02 |
| ☐ 350 Hoyt Wilhelm | 2.50 | 1.00 | .25 |
| ☐ 351 Bob Barton | .21 | .09 | .02 |
| ☐ 352 Jackie Hernandez | .21 | .09 | .02 |
| ☐ 353 Mack Jones | .21 | .09 | .02 |
| ☐ 354 Pete Richert | .21 | .09 | .02 |
| ☐ 355 Ernie Banks | 3.50 | 1.40 | .35 |

| | | | | |
|---|---|---|---|---|
| ☐ 356A | Checklist 5<br>Ken Holtzman<br>(head centered<br>within circle) | 1.50 | .15 | .03 |
| ☐ 356B | Checklist 5<br>Ken Holtzman<br>(head shifted right<br>within circle) | 1.50 | .15 | .03 |
| ☐ 357 | Len Gabrielson | .21 | .09 | .02 |
| ☐ 358 | Mike Epstein | .21 | .09 | .02 |
| ☐ 359 | Joe Moeller | .21 | .09 | .02 |
| ☐ 360 | Willie Horton | .45 | .18 | .04 |
| ☐ 361 | Harmon Killebrew AS | 1.75 | .70 | .17 |
| ☐ 362 | Orlando Cepeda AS | .75 | .30 | .07 |
| ☐ 363 | Rod Carew AS | 3.50 | 1.40 | .35 |
| ☐ 364 | Joe Morgan AS | 1.50 | .60 | .15 |
| ☐ 365 | Brooks Robinson AS | 2.50 | 1.00 | .25 |
| ☐ 366 | Ron Santo AS | .40 | .16 | .04 |
| ☐ 367 | Jim Fregosi AS | .35 | .14 | .03 |
| ☐ 368 | Gene Alley AS | .35 | .14 | .03 |
| ☐ 369 | Carl Yastrzemski AS | 3.75 | 1.50 | .37 |
| ☐ 370 | Hank Aaron AS | 3.75 | 1.50 | .37 |
| ☐ 371 | Tony Oliva AS | .45 | .18 | .04 |
| ☐ 372 | Lou Brock AS | 2.50 | 1.00 | .25 |
| ☐ 373 | Frank Robinson AS | 2.50 | 1.00 | .25 |
| ☐ 374 | Bob Clemente AS | 3.25 | 1.30 | .32 |
| ☐ 375 | Bill Freehan AS | .35 | .14 | .03 |
| ☐ 376 | Tim McCarver AS | .35 | .14 | .03 |
| ☐ 377 | Joe Horlen AS | .35 | .14 | .03 |
| ☐ 378 | Bob Gibson AS | 2.25 | .90 | .22 |
| ☐ 379 | Gary Peters AS | .35 | .14 | .03 |
| ☐ 380 | Ken Holtzman AS | .35 | .14 | .03 |
| ☐ 381 | Boog Powell | .75 | .30 | .07 |
| ☐ 382 | Ramon Hernandez | .21 | .09 | .02 |
| ☐ 383 | Steve Whitaker | .21 | .09 | .02 |
| ☐ 384 | Reds Rookies<br>Bill Henry<br>Hal McRae | 2.00 | .80 | .20 |
| ☐ 385 | Jim Hunter | 2.75 | 1.10 | .27 |
| ☐ 386 | Greg Goossen | .21 | .09 | .02 |
| ☐ 387 | Joe Foy | .21 | .09 | .02 |
| ☐ 388 | Ray Washburn | .21 | .09 | .02 |
| ☐ 389 | Jay Johnstone | .30 | .12 | .03 |
| ☐ 390 | Bill Mazeroski | .60 | .24 | .06 |
| ☐ 391 | Bob Priddy | .21 | .09 | .02 |
| ☐ 392 | Grady Hatton MGR | .21 | .09 | .02 |
| ☐ 393 | Jim Perry | .40 | .16 | .04 |
| ☐ 394 | Tommie Aaron | .30 | .12 | .03 |
| ☐ 395 | Camilo Pascual | .30 | .12 | .03 |
| ☐ 396 | Bobby Wine | .21 | .09 | .02 |
| ☐ 397 | Vic Davalillo | .21 | .09 | .02 |
| ☐ 398 | Jim Grant | .21 | .09 | .02 |
| ☐ 399 | Ray Oyler | .21 | .09 | .02 |
| ☐ 400 | Mike McCormick | .30 | .12 | .03 |
| ☐ 401 | Mets Team | .75 | .30 | .07 |
| ☐ 402 | Mike Hegan | .21 | .09 | .02 |
| ☐ 403 | John Buzhardt | .21 | .09 | .02 |
| ☐ 404 | Floyd Robinson | .21 | .09 | .02 |
| ☐ 405 | Tommy Helms | .30 | .12 | .03 |
| ☐ 406 | Dick Ellsworth | .30 | .12 | .03 |
| ☐ 407 | Gary Kolb | .21 | .09 | .02 |
| ☐ 408 | Steve Carlton | 25.00 | 10.00 | 2.50 |
| ☐ 409 | Orioles Rookies<br>Frank Peters<br>Don Stone | .21 | .09 | .02 |
| ☐ 410 | Ferguson Jenkins | 1.50 | .60 | .15 |
| ☐ 411 | Ron Hansen | .21 | .09 | .02 |
| ☐ 412 | Clay Carroll | .21 | .09 | .02 |
| ☐ 413 | Tommy McCraw | .21 | .09 | .02 |
| ☐ 414 | Mickey Lolich | 1.00 | .40 | .10 |
| ☐ 415 | Johnny Callison | .30 | .12 | .03 |
| ☐ 416 | Bill Rigney MGR | .21 | .09 | .02 |
| ☐ 417 | Willie Crawford | .21 | .09 | .02 |
| ☐ 418 | Eddie Fisher | .21 | .09 | .02 |
| ☐ 419 | Jack Hiatt | .21 | .09 | .02 |
| ☐ 420 | Cesar Tovar | .21 | .09 | .02 |
| ☐ 421 | Ron Taylor | .21 | .09 | .02 |
| ☐ 422 | Rene Lachemann | .30 | .12 | .03 |
| ☐ 423 | Fred Gladding | .21 | .09 | .02 |
| ☐ 424 | White Sox Team | .55 | .22 | .05 |
| ☐ 425 | Jim Maloney | .35 | .14 | .03 |
| ☐ 426 | Hank Allen | .21 | .09 | .02 |
| ☐ 427 | Dick Calmus | .21 | .09 | .02 |
| ☐ 428 | Vic Roznovsky | .21 | .09 | .02 |
| ☐ 429 | Tommie Sisk | .21 | .09 | .02 |
| ☐ 430 | Rico Petrocelli | .35 | .14 | .03 |
| ☐ 431 | Dooley Womack | .21 | .09 | .02 |
| ☐ 432 | Indians Rookies<br>Bill Davis<br>Jose Vidal | .21 | .09 | .02 |
| ☐ 433 | Bob Rodgers | .21 | .09 | .02 |
| ☐ 434 | Ricardo Joseph | .21 | .09 | .02 |
| ☐ 435 | Ron Perranoski | .30 | .12 | .03 |
| ☐ 436 | Hal Lanier | .40 | .16 | .04 |
| ☐ 437 | Don Cardwell | .21 | .09 | .02 |
| ☐ 438 | Lee Thomas | .21 | .09 | .02 |
| ☐ 439 | Luman Harris MGR | .21 | .09 | .02 |
| ☐ 440 | Claude Osteen | .35 | .14 | .03 |
| ☐ 441 | Alex Johnson | .30 | .12 | .03 |
| ☐ 442 | Dick Bosman | .21 | .09 | .02 |
| ☐ 443 | Joe Azcue | .21 | .09 | .02 |
| ☐ 444 | Jack Fisher | .21 | .09 | .02 |
| ☐ 445 | Mike Shannon | .35 | .14 | .03 |
| ☐ 446 | Ron Kline | .21 | .09 | .02 |
| ☐ 447 | Tigers Rookies<br>George Korince<br>Fred Lasher | .21 | .09 | .02 |
| ☐ 448 | Gary Wagner | .21 | .09 | .02 |
| ☐ 449 | Gene Oliver | .21 | .09 | .02 |
| ☐ 450 | Jim Kaat | 1.25 | .50 | .12 |
| ☐ 451 | Al Spangler | .21 | .09 | .02 |
| ☐ 452 | Jesus Alou | .21 | .09 | .02 |
| ☐ 453 | Sammy Ellis | .21 | .09 | .02 |
| ☐ 454A | Checklist 6<br>Frank Robinson<br>(cap complete<br>within circle) | 1.50 | .15 | .03 |
| ☐ 454B | Checklist 6<br>Frank Robinson<br>(cap partially<br>within circle) | 1.50 | .15 | .03 |
| ☐ 455 | Rico Carty | .50 | .20 | .05 |
| ☐ 456 | John O'Donoghue | .21 | .09 | .02 |
| ☐ 457 | Jim Lefebvre | .30 | .12 | .03 |
| ☐ 458 | Lew Krausse | .30 | .12 | .03 |
| ☐ 459 | Dick Simpson | .30 | .12 | .03 |
| ☐ 460 | Jim Lonborg | .50 | .20 | .05 |
| ☐ 461 | Chuck Hiller | .30 | .12 | .03 |
| ☐ 462 | Barry Moore | .30 | .12 | .03 |
| ☐ 463 | Jim Schaffer | .30 | .12 | .03 |
| ☐ 464 | Don McMahon | .30 | .12 | .03 |
| ☐ 465 | Tommie Agee | .40 | .16 | .04 |
| ☐ 466 | Bill Dillman | .30 | .12 | .03 |
| ☐ 467 | Dick Howser | .50 | .20 | .05 |
| ☐ 468 | Larry Sherry | .40 | .16 | .04 |
| ☐ 469 | Ty Cline | .30 | .12 | .03 |
| ☐ 470 | Bill Freehan | .60 | .24 | .06 |
| ☐ 471 | Orlando Pena | .30 | .12 | .03 |
| ☐ 472 | Walt Alston MGR | .90 | .36 | .09 |
| ☐ 473 | Al Worthington | .30 | .12 | .03 |
| ☐ 474 | Paul Schaal | .30 | .12 | .03 |
| ☐ 475 | Joe Niekro | 1.00 | .40 | .10 |
| ☐ 476 | Woody Woodward | .30 | .12 | .03 |
| ☐ 477 | Phillies Team | .65 | .26 | .06 |
| ☐ 478 | Dave McNally | .65 | .26 | .06 |
| ☐ 479 | Phil Gagliano | .30 | .12 | .03 |
| ☐ 480 | Manager's Dream<br>Tony Oliva<br>Chico Cardenas<br>Bob Clemente | 5.00 | 2.00 | .50 |
| ☐ 481 | John Wyatt | .30 | .12 | .03 |
| ☐ 482 | Jose Pagan | .30 | .12 | .03 |
| ☐ 483 | Darold Knowles | .30 | .12 | .03 |
| ☐ 484 | Phil Roof | .30 | .12 | .03 |
| ☐ 485 | Ken Berry | .30 | .12 | .03 |
| ☐ 486 | Cal Koonce | .30 | .12 | .03 |
| ☐ 487 | Lee May | .50 | .20 | .05 |
| ☐ 488 | Dick Tracewski | .30 | .12 | .03 |
| ☐ 489 | Wally Bunker | .40 | .16 | .04 |
| ☐ 490 | Super Stars:<br>Harmon Killebrew<br>Willie Mays<br>Mickey Mantle | 12.50 | 5.00 | 1.25 |
| ☐ 491 | Denny Lemaster | .30 | .12 | .03 |
| ☐ 492 | Jeff Torborg | .30 | .12 | .03 |
| ☐ 493 | Jim McGlothlin | .30 | .12 | .03 |
| ☐ 494 | Ray Sadecki | .30 | .12 | .03 |
| ☐ 495 | Leon Wagner | .30 | .12 | .03 |
| ☐ 496 | Steve Hamilton | .30 | .12 | .03 |
| ☐ 497 | Cards Team | .85 | .34 | .08 |
| ☐ 498 | Bill Bryan | .30 | .12 | .03 |
| ☐ 499 | Steve Blass | .40 | .16 | .04 |
| ☐ 500 | Frank Robinson | 4.50 | 1.80 | .45 |
| ☐ 501 | John Odom | .30 | .12 | .03 |
| ☐ 502 | Mike Andrews | .30 | .12 | .03 |
| ☐ 503 | Al Jackson | .30 | .12 | .03 |
| ☐ 504 | Russ Snyder | .30 | .12 | .03 |
| ☐ 505 | Joe Sparma | .30 | .12 | .03 |
| ☐ 506 | Clarence Jones | .30 | .12 | .03 |
| ☐ 507 | Wade Blasingame | .30 | .12 | .03 |
| ☐ 508 | Duke Sims | .30 | .12 | .03 |
| ☐ 509 | Dennis Higgins | .30 | .12 | .03 |
| ☐ 510 | Ron Fairly | .40 | .16 | .04 |
| ☐ 511 | Bill Kelso | .30 | .12 | .03 |
| ☐ 512 | Grant Jackson | .30 | .12 | .03 |
| ☐ 513 | Hank Bauer MGR | .40 | .16 | .04 |

| | | | |
|---|---|---|---|
| ☐ 514 | Al McBean | .30 .12 | .03 |
| ☐ 515 | Russ Nixon | .30 .12 | .03 |
| ☐ 516 | Pete Mikkelsen | .30 .12 | .03 |
| ☐ 517 | Diego Segui | .30 .12 | .03 |
| ☐ 518A | Checklist 7 | 1.50 .15 | .03 |
| | (539 ML Rookies) | | |
| | (Clete Boyer) | | |
| ☐ 518B | Checklist 7 | 5.00 .50 | .10 |
| | (539 AL Rookies) | | |
| | (Clete Boyer) | | |
| ☐ 519 | Jerry Stephenson | .30 .12 | .03 |
| ☐ 520 | Lou Brock | 5.50 2.20 | .55 |
| ☐ 521 | Don Shaw | .30 .12 | .03 |
| ☐ 522 | Wayne Causey | .30 .12 | .03 |
| ☐ 523 | John Tsitouris | .30 .12 | .03 |
| ☐ 524 | Andy Kosco | .30 .12 | .03 |
| ☐ 525 | Jim Davenport | .40 .16 | .04 |
| ☐ 526 | Bill Denehy | .30 .12 | .03 |
| ☐ 527 | Tito Francona | .40 .16 | .04 |
| ☐ 528 | Tigers Team | 2.50 1.00 | .25 |
| ☐ 529 | Bruce Von Hoff | .30 .12 | .03 |
| ☐ 530 | Bird Belters: | 3.50 1.40 | .35 |
| | Brooks Robinson | | |
| | Frank Robinson | | |
| ☐ 531 | Chuck Hinton | .30 .12 | .03 |
| ☐ 532 | Luis Tiant | .75 .30 | .07 |
| ☐ 533 | Wes Parker | .45 .18 | .04 |
| ☐ 534 | Bob Miller | .30 .12 | .03 |
| ☐ 535 | Danny Cater | .30 .12 | .03 |
| ☐ 536 | Bill Short | .30 .12 | .03 |
| ☐ 537 | Norm Siebern | .30 .12 | .03 |
| ☐ 538 | Manny Jimenez | .30 .12 | .03 |
| ☐ 539 | Major League Rookies | .60 .24 | .06 |
| | Jim Ray | | |
| | Mike Ferraro | | |
| ☐ 540 | Nelson Briles | .40 .16 | .04 |
| ☐ 541 | Sandy Alomar | .30 .12 | .03 |
| ☐ 542 | John Boccabella | .30 .12 | .03 |
| ☐ 543 | Bob Lee | .30 .12 | .03 |
| ☐ 544 | Mayo Smith MGR | .30 .12 | .03 |
| ☐ 545 | Lindy McDaniel | .30 .12 | .03 |
| ☐ 546 | Roy White | .45 .18 | .04 |
| ☐ 547 | Dan Coombs | .30 .12 | .03 |
| ☐ 548 | Bernie Allen | .30 .12 | .03 |
| ☐ 549 | Orioles Rookies | .30 .12 | .03 |
| | Curt Motton | | |
| | Roger Nelson | | |
| ☐ 550 | Clete Boyer | .50 .20 | .05 |
| ☐ 551 | Darrell Sutherland | .30 .12 | .03 |
| ☐ 552 | Ed Kirkpatrick | .30 .12 | .03 |
| ☐ 553 | Hank Aguirre | .30 .12 | .03 |
| ☐ 554 | A's Team | .85 .34 | .08 |
| ☐ 555 | Jose Tartabull | .30 .12 | .03 |
| ☐ 556 | Dick Selma | .30 .12 | .03 |
| ☐ 557 | Frank Quilici | .30 .12 | .03 |
| ☐ 558 | John Edwards | .30 .12 | .03 |
| ☐ 559 | Pirates Rookies | .30 .12 | .03 |
| | Carl Taylor | | |
| | Luke Walker | | |
| ☐ 560 | Paul Casanova | .30 .12 | .03 |
| ☐ 561 | Lee Elia | .30 .12 | .03 |
| ☐ 562 | Jim Bouton | .80 .32 | .08 |
| ☐ 563 | Ed Charles | .30 .12 | .03 |
| ☐ 564 | Ed Stanky MGR | .40 .16 | .04 |
| ☐ 565 | Larry Dierker | .40 .16 | .04 |
| ☐ 566 | Ken Harrelson | .75 .30 | .07 |
| ☐ 567 | Clay Dalrymple | .30 .12 | .03 |
| ☐ 568 | Willie Smith | .30 .12 | .03 |
| ☐ 569 | N.L. Rookies | .30 .12 | .03 |
| | Ivan Murrell | | |
| | Les Rohr | | |
| ☐ 570 | Rick Reichardt | .30 .12 | .03 |
| ☐ 571 | Tony LaRussa | .50 .20 | .05 |
| ☐ 572 | Don Bosch | .30 .12 | .03 |
| ☐ 573 | Joe Coleman | .30 .12 | .03 |
| ☐ 574 | Reds Team | .85 .34 | .08 |
| ☐ 575 | Jim Palmer | 7.00 2.80 | .70 |
| ☐ 576 | Dave Adlesh | .30 .12 | .03 |
| ☐ 577 | Fred Talbot | .30 .12 | .03 |
| ☐ 578 | Orlando Martinez | .30 .12 | .03 |
| ☐ 579 | N.L. Rookies | .70 .28 | .07 |
| | Larry Hisle | | |
| | Mike Lum | | |
| ☐ 580 | Bob Bailey | .30 .12 | .03 |
| ☐ 581 | Garry Roggenburk | .30 .12 | .03 |
| ☐ 582 | Jerry Grote | .30 .12 | .03 |
| ☐ 583 | Gates Brown | .45 .18 | .04 |
| ☐ 584 | Larry Shepard MGR | .30 .12 | .03 |
| ☐ 585 | Wilbur Wood | .40 .16 | .04 |
| ☐ 586 | Jim Pagliaroni | .30 .12 | .03 |
| ☐ 587 | Roger Repoz | .30 .12 | .03 |
| ☐ 588 | Dick Schofield | .30 .12 | .03 |
| ☐ 589 | Twins Rookies | .30 .12 | .03 |

| | | | |
|---|---|---|---|
| | Ron Clark | | |
| | Moe Ogier | | |
| ☐ 590 | Tommy Harper | .40 .16 | .04 |
| ☐ 591 | Dick Nen | .30 .12 | .03 |
| ☐ 592 | John Bateman | .30 .12 | .03 |
| ☐ 593 | Lee Stange | .30 .12 | .03 |
| ☐ 594 | Phil Linz | .30 .12 | .03 |
| ☐ 595 | Phil Ortega | .30 .12 | .03 |
| ☐ 596 | Charlie Smith | .30 .12 | .03 |
| ☐ 597 | Bill McCool | .30 .12 | .03 |
| ☐ 598 | Jerry May | .75 .15 | .03 |

## 1968 Topps 3-D

The cards in this 12 card set measure 2 1/4" by 3 1/2". Topps' experiment with "3-D" cards came two years before Kellogg's inaugural set. Only 12 unnumbered cards are known to exist and they are rare. This was a "test set" sold in a plain white wrapper with a sticker attached as a design, a device used by Topps for limited marketing. The cards employ a sharp foreground picture set against an indistinct background, covered by a layer of plastic, to produce the "3-D" effect. The checklist below is ordered alphabetically.

| | | MINT | VG-E | F-G |
|---|---|---|---|---|
| | COMPLETE SET | 4500.00 | 200.00 | 50.00 |
| | COMMON PLAYER (1-12) | 300.00 | 120.00 | 30.00 |
| ☐ 1 | Bob Clemente | 1100.00 | 450.00 | 100.00 |
| ☐ 2 | Willie Davis | 350.00 | 140.00 | 35.00 |
| ☐ 3 | Ron Fairly | 300.00 | 120.00 | 30.00 |
| ☐ 4 | Curt Flood | 350.00 | 140.00 | 35.00 |
| ☐ 5 | Jim Lonborg | 350.00 | 140.00 | 35.00 |
| ☐ 6 | Jim Maloney | 350.00 | 140.00 | 35.00 |
| ☐ 7 | Tony Perez | 500.00 | 200.00 | 50.00 |
| ☐ 8 | Boog Powell | 400.00 | 160.00 | 40.00 |
| ☐ 9 | Bill Robinson | 300.00 | 120.00 | 30.00 |
| ☐ 10 | Rusty Staub | 400.00 | 160.00 | 40.00 |
| ☐ 11 | Mel Stottlemyre | 350.00 | 140.00 | 35.00 |
| ☐ 12 | Ron Swoboda | 300.00 | 120.00 | 30.00 |

## 1968 Topps Game

The cards in this 33 card set measure 2 1/4" by 3 1/4". This "Game" card set of players, issued as inserts with the regular 1968 Topps baseball series, was patterned directly after the Red Back and Blue Back sets of 1951. Each card has a color player photo set upon a pure white background, with a

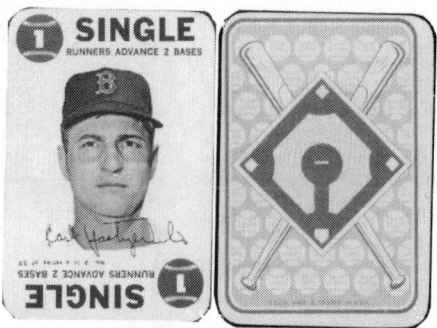

facsimile autograph underneath the picture. The cards have blue backs, and were also sold in boxed sets on a limited basis.

|  | MINT | VG-E | F-G |
|---|---|---|---|
| COMPLETE SET | 40.00 | 16.00 | 4.00 |
| COMMON PLAYER (1-33) | .30 | .12 | .03 |

| | | MINT | VG-E | F-G |
|---|---|---|---|---|
| ☐ 1 | Matty Alou | .30 | .12 | .03 |
| ☐ 2 | Mickey Mantle | 8.00 | 3.25 | .80 |
| ☐ 3 | Carl Yastrzemski | 4.00 | 1.60 | .40 |
| ☐ 4 | Hank Aaron | 3.50 | 1.40 | .35 |
| ☐ 5 | Harmon Killebrew | 1.50 | .60 | .15 |
| ☐ 6 | Roberto Clemente | 3.00 | 1.20 | .30 |
| ☐ 7 | Frank Robinson | 2.00 | .80 | .20 |
| ☐ 8 | Willie Mays | 3.50 | 1.40 | .35 |
| ☐ 9 | Brooks Robinson | 2.00 | .80 | .20 |
| ☐ 10 | Tommy Davis | .35 | .14 | .03 |
| ☐ 11 | Bill Freehan | .40 | .16 | .04 |
| ☐ 12 | Claude Osteen | .30 | .12 | .03 |
| ☐ 13 | Gary Peters | .30 | .12 | .03 |
| ☐ 14 | Jim Lonborg | .30 | .12 | .03 |
| ☐ 15 | Steve Hargan | .30 | .12 | .03 |
| ☐ 16 | Dean Chance | .30 | .12 | .03 |
| ☐ 17 | Mike McCormick | .30 | .12 | .03 |
| ☐ 18 | Tim McCarver | .35 | .14 | .03 |
| ☐ 19 | Ron Santo | .40 | .16 | .04 |
| ☐ 20 | Tony Gonzalez | .30 | .12 | .03 |
| ☐ 21 | Frank Howard | .40 | .16 | .04 |
| ☐ 22 | George Scott | .30 | .12 | .03 |
| ☐ 23 | Rich Allen | .40 | .16 | .04 |
| ☐ 24 | Jim Wynn | .30 | .12 | .03 |
| ☐ 25 | Gene Alley | .30 | .12 | .03 |
| ☐ 26 | Rick Monday | .30 | .12 | .03 |
| ☐ 27 | Al Kaline | 2.50 | 1.00 | .25 |
| ☐ 28 | Rusty Staub | .40 | .16 | .04 |
| ☐ 29 | Rod Carew | 3.00 | 1.20 | .30 |
| ☐ 30 | Pete Rose | 8.00 | 3.25 | .80 |
| ☐ 31 | Joe Torre | .50 | .20 | .05 |
| ☐ 32 | Orlando Cepeda | .50 | .20 | .05 |
| ☐ 33 | Jim Fregosi | .35 | .14 | .03 |

## 1969 Topps

The cards in this 664 card set measure 2 1/2" by 3 1/2". The 1969 Topps set includes The Sporting News All-Star selections as card numbers 416 to 435. Other popular subsets within this set include League Leaders (1-12) and World Series cards (162-169). The fifth series contains several variations; the more difficult variety consists of cards with the player's whole name in white letters, which are designated in the checklist below by WL. Each checklist card features a different popular player's picture inside a circle on the front of the checklist card. Two different poses of Clay Dalrymple and Donn Clendenon exist as indicated in the checklist.

|  | MINT | VG-E | F-G |
|---|---|---|---|
| COMPLETE SET | 600.00 | 240.00 | 60.00 |

| | MINT | VG-E | F-G |
|---|---|---|---|
| COMMON PLAYER (1-218) | .21 | .09 | .02 |
| COMMON PLAYER (219-327) | .35 | .14 | .03 |
| COMMON PLAYER (328-512) | .21 | .09 | .02 |
| COMMON PLAYER (513-664) | .25 | .10 | .02 |

| | | MINT | VG-E | F-G |
|---|---|---|---|---|
| ☐ 1 | AL Batting Leaders<br>Carl Yastrzemski<br>Danny Cater<br>Tony Oliva | 2.50 | .60 | .10 |
| ☐ 2 | NL Batting Leaders<br>Pete Rose<br>Matty Alou<br>Felipe Alou | 2.00 | .80 | .20 |
| ☐ 3 | AL RBI Leaders<br>Ken Harrelson<br>Frank Howard<br>Jim Northrup | .70 | .28 | .07 |
| ☐ 4 | NL RBI Leaders<br>Willie McCovey<br>Ron Santo<br>Billy Williams | 1.00 | .40 | .10 |
| ☐ 5 | AL Home Run Leaders<br>Frank Howard<br>Willie Horton<br>Ken Harrelson | .70 | .28 | .07 |
| ☐ 6 | NL Home Run Leaders<br>Willie McCovey<br>Richie Allen<br>Ernie Banks | 1.25 | .50 | .12 |
| ☐ 7 | AL ERA Leaders<br>Luis Tiant<br>Sam McDowell<br>Dave McNally | .60 | .24 | .06 |
| ☐ 8 | NL ERA Leaders<br>Bob Gibson<br>Bobby Bolin<br>Bob Veale | .75 | .30 | .07 |
| ☐ 9 | AL Pitching Leaders<br>Denny McLain<br>Dave McNally<br>Luis Tiant<br>Mel Stottlemyre | .60 | .24 | .06 |
| ☐ 10 | NL Pitching Leaders<br>Juan Marichal<br>Bob Gibson<br>Fergie Jenkins | 1.50 | .60 | .15 |
| ☐ 11 | AL Strikeout Leaders<br>Sam McDowell<br>Denny McLain<br>Luis Tiant | .60 | .24 | .06 |
| ☐ 12 | NL Strikeout Leaders<br>Bob Gibson<br>Fergie Jenkins<br>Bill Singer | .80 | .32 | .08 |
| ☐ 13 | Mickey Stanley | .30 | .12 | .03 |
| ☐ 14 | Al McBean | .21 | .09 | .02 |
| ☐ 15 | Boog Powell | .75 | .30 | .07 |
| ☐ 16 | Giants Rookies<br>Cesar Gutierrez<br>Rich Robertson | .21 | .09 | .02 |
| ☐ 17 | Mike Marshall | .45 | .18 | .04 |
| ☐ 18 | Dick Schofield | .21 | .09 | .02 |
| ☐ 19 | Ken Suarez | .21 | .09 | .02 |
| ☐ 20 | Ernie Banks | 3.25 | 1.30 | .32 |
| ☐ 21 | Jose Santiago | .21 | .09 | .02 |
| ☐ 22 | Jesus Alou | .21 | .09 | .02 |
| ☐ 23 | Lew Krausse | .21 | .09 | .02 |
| ☐ 24 | Walt Alston MGR | .80 | .32 | .08 |
| ☐ 25 | Roy White | .30 | .12 | .03 |
| ☐ 26 | Clay Carroll | .21 | .09 | .02 |
| ☐ 27 | Bernie Allen | .21 | .09 | .02 |
| ☐ 28 | Mike Ryan | .21 | .09 | .02 |

| | | | |
|---|---|---|---|
| ☐ 29 Dave Morehead ............... | .21 | .09 | .02 |
| ☐ 30 Bob Allison ..................... | .35 | .14 | .03 |
| ☐ 31 Mets Rookies .................. | .85 | .34 | .08 |
|     Gary Gentry | | | |
|     Amos Otis | | | |
| ☐ 32 Sammy Ellis .................... | .21 | .09 | .02 |
| ☐ 33 Wayne Causey ................ | .21 | .09 | .02 |
| ☐ 34 Gary Peters .................... | .30 | .12 | .03 |
| ☐ 35 Joe Morgan .................... | 2.50 | 1.00 | .25 |
| ☐ 36 Luke Walker ................... | .21 | .09 | .02 |
| ☐ 37 Curt Motton ................... | .21 | .09 | .02 |
| ☐ 38 Zoilo Versalles ............... | .21 | .09 | .02 |
| ☐ 39 Dick Hughes .................. | .21 | .09 | .02 |
| ☐ 40 Mayo Smith MGR .......... | .21 | .09 | .02 |
| ☐ 41 Bob Barton .................... | .21 | .09 | .02 |
| ☐ 42 Tommy Harper ............... | .30 | .12 | .03 |
| ☐ 43 Joe Niekro ..................... | .60 | .24 | .06 |
| ☐ 44 Danny Cater ................... | .21 | .09 | .02 |
| ☐ 45 Maury Wills ................... | 1.00 | .40 | .10 |
| ☐ 46 Fritz Peterson ................ | .21 | .09 | .02 |
| ☐ 47A Paul Popovich .............. | .30 | .12 | .03 |
|     (no helmet emblem) | | | |
| ☐ 47B Paul Popovich .............. | 10.00 | 4.00 | 1.00 |
|     (C emblem on helmet) | | | |
| ☐ 48 Brant Alyea .................... | .21 | .09 | .02 |
| ☐ 49A Royals Rookies ............. | .30 | .12 | .03 |
|     Steve Jones | | | |
|     E. Rodriguez "g" | | | |
| ☐ 49B Royals Rookies ............. | 10.00 | 4.00 | 1.00 |
|     Steve Jones | | | |
|     E. Rodriquez "q" | | | |
| ☐ 50 Bob Clemente ................ | 9.00 | 3.75 | .90 |
| ☐ 51 Woody Fryman ............... | .21 | .09 | .02 |
| ☐ 52 Mike Andrews ................ | .21 | .09 | .02 |
| ☐ 53 Sonny Jackson ............... | .21 | .09 | .02 |
| ☐ 54 Cisco Carlos .................. | .21 | .09 | .02 |
| ☐ 55 Jerry Grote .................... | .21 | .09 | .02 |
| ☐ 56 Rich Reese .................... | .21 | .09 | .02 |
| ☐ 57 Checklist 1 .................... | 1.50 | .15 | .03 |
|     Denny McLain | | | |
| ☐ 58 Fred Gladding ................ | .21 | .09 | .02 |
| ☐ 59 Jay Johnstone ............... | .30 | .12 | .03 |
| ☐ 60 Nelson Briles ................. | .30 | .12 | .03 |
| ☐ 61 Jimmie Hall .................... | .21 | .09 | .02 |
| ☐ 62 Chico Salmon ................ | .30 | .12 | .03 |
| ☐ 63 Jim Hickman .................. | .21 | .09 | .02 |
| ☐ 64 Bill Monbouquette ......... | .21 | .09 | .02 |
| ☐ 65 Willie Davis ................... | .45 | .18 | .04 |
| ☐ 66 Orioles Rookies .............. | .30 | .12 | .03 |
|     Mike Adamson | | | |
|     Merv Rettenmund | | | |
| ☐ 67 Bill Stoneman ................ | .21 | .09 | .02 |
| ☐ 68 Dave Duncan ................. | .21 | .09 | .02 |
| ☐ 69 Steve Hamilton .............. | .21 | .09 | .02 |
| ☐ 70 Tommy Helms ................ | .30 | .12 | .03 |
| ☐ 71 Steve Whitaker ............... | .21 | .09 | .02 |
| ☐ 72 Ron Taylor .................... | .21 | .09 | .02 |
| ☐ 73 Johnny Briggs ................ | .21 | .09 | .02 |
| ☐ 74 Preston Gomez MGR ..... | .21 | .09 | .02 |
| ☐ 75 Luis Aparicio ................. | 2.50 | 1.00 | .25 |
| ☐ 76 Norm Miller ................... | .21 | .09 | .02 |
| ☐ 77A Ron Perranoski ............ | .30 | .12 | .03 |
|     (no emblem on cap) | | | |
| ☐ 77B Ron Perranoski ............ | 10.00 | 4.00 | 1.00 |
|     (LA on cap) | | | |
| ☐ 78 Tom Satriano ................. | .21 | .09 | .02 |
| ☐ 79 Milt Pappas ................... | .30 | .12 | .03 |
| ☐ 80 Norm Cash .................... | .75 | .30 | .07 |
| ☐ 81 Mel Queen ..................... | .21 | .09 | .02 |
| ☐ 82 Pirates Rookies .............. | 7.00 | 2.80 | .70 |
|     Rich Hebner | | | |
|     Al Oliver | | | |
| ☐ 83 Mike Ferraro .................. | .35 | .14 | .03 |
| ☐ 84 Bob Humphreys .............. | .21 | .09 | .02 |
| ☐ 85 Lou Brock ..................... | 4.00 | 1.60 | .40 |
| ☐ 86 Pete Richert ................... | .21 | .09 | .02 |
| ☐ 87 Horace Clarke ............... | .21 | .09 | .02 |
| ☐ 88 Rich Nye ...................... | .21 | .09 | .02 |
| ☐ 89 Russ Gibson .................. | .21 | .09 | .02 |
| ☐ 90 Jerry Koosman ............... | .90 | .36 | .09 |
| ☐ 91 Al Dark MGR .................. | .30 | .12 | .03 |
| ☐ 92 Jack Billingham .............. | .21 | .09 | .02 |
| ☐ 93 Joe Foy ........................ | .21 | .09 | .02 |
| ☐ 94 Hank Aguirre .................. | .21 | .09 | .02 |
| ☐ 95 Johnny Bench ................ | 30.00 | 12.00 | 3.00 |
| ☐ 96 Denver Lemaster ............ | .21 | .09 | .02 |
| ☐ 97 Buddy Bradford .............. | .21 | .09 | .02 |
| ☐ 98 Dave Giusti ................... | .21 | .09 | .02 |
| ☐ 99A Twins Rookies .............. | 8.00 | 3.25 | .80 |
|     Danny Morris | | | |
|     Graig Nettles | | | |
|     (no loop) | | | |
| ☐ 99B Twins Rookies .............. | 16.00 | 6.50 | 1.60 |

| | | | |
|---|---|---|---|
|     Danny Morris | | | |
|     Graig Nettles | | | |
|     (errant loop in | | | |
|     upper left corner | | | |
|     of obverse) | | | |
| ☐ 100 Hank Aaron ................... | 12.50 | 5.00 | 1.25 |
| ☐ 101 Daryl Patterson .............. | .21 | .09 | .02 |
| ☐ 102 Jim Davenport ............... | .30 | .12 | .03 |
| ☐ 103 Roger Repoz ................. | .21 | .09 | .02 |
| ☐ 104 Steve Blass ................... | .30 | .12 | .03 |
| ☐ 105 Rick Monday ................. | .30 | .12 | .03 |
| ☐ 106 Jim Hannan ................... | .21 | .09 | .02 |
| ☐ 107A Checklist 2 .................. | 1.50 | .15 | .03 |
|     (161 Jim Purdin) | | | |
|     (Bob Gibson) | | | |
| ☐ 107B Checklist 2 .................. | 4.00 | .40 | .08 |
|     (161 John Purdin) | | | |
|     (Bob Gibson) | | | |
| ☐ 108 Tony Taylor ................... | .21 | .09 | .02 |
| ☐ 109 Jim Lonborg ................. | .35 | .14 | .03 |
| ☐ 110 Mike Shannon ............... | .35 | .14 | .03 |
| ☐ 111 Johnny Morris ............... | .30 | .12 | .03 |
| ☐ 112 J.C. Martin ................... | .21 | .09 | .02 |
| ☐ 113 Dave May ..................... | .21 | .09 | .02 |
| ☐ 114 Yankees Rookies ............ | .21 | .09 | .02 |
|     Alan Closter | | | |
|     John Cumberland | | | |
| ☐ 115 Bill Hands .................... | .21 | .09 | .02 |
| ☐ 116 Chuck Harrison .............. | .21 | .09 | .02 |
| ☐ 117 Jim Fairey .................... | .21 | .09 | .02 |
| ☐ 118 Stan Williams ................ | .21 | .09 | .02 |
| ☐ 119 Doug Rader .................. | .30 | .12 | .03 |
| ☐ 120 Pete Rose .................... | 25.00 | 10.00 | 2.50 |
| ☐ 121 Joe Grzenda ................. | .21 | .09 | .02 |
| ☐ 122 Ron Fairly .................... | .30 | .12 | .03 |
| ☐ 123 Wilbur Wood ................. | .30 | .12 | .03 |
| ☐ 124 Hank Bauer MGR ........... | .30 | .12 | .03 |
| ☐ 125 Ray Sadecki ................. | .21 | .09 | .02 |
| ☐ 126 Dick Tracewski .............. | .21 | .09 | .02 |
| ☐ 127 Kevin Collins ................. | .21 | .09 | .02 |
| ☐ 128 Tommie Aaron ............... | .30 | .12 | .03 |
| ☐ 129 Bill McCool .................. | .21 | .09 | .02 |
| ☐ 130 Carl Yastrzemski ............ | 16.00 | 6.50 | 1.60 |
| ☐ 131 Chris Cannizzaro ........... | .21 | .09 | .02 |
| ☐ 132 Dave Baldwin ................ | .21 | .09 | .02 |
| ☐ 133 Johnny Callison ............. | .30 | .12 | .03 |
| ☐ 134 Jim Weaver ................... | .21 | .09 | .02 |
| ☐ 135 Tommy Davis ................ | .45 | .18 | .04 |
| ☐ 136 Cards Rookies ............... | .30 | .12 | .03 |
|     Steve Huntz | | | |
|     Mike Torrez | | | |
| ☐ 137 Wally Bunker ................. | .21 | .09 | .02 |
| ☐ 138 John Bateman ............... | .21 | .09 | .02 |
| ☐ 139 Andy Kosco .................. | .21 | .09 | .02 |
| ☐ 140 Jim Lefebvre ................. | .21 | .09 | .02 |
| ☐ 141 Bill Dillman ................... | .21 | .09 | .02 |
| ☐ 142 Woody Woodward .......... | .21 | .09 | .02 |
| ☐ 143 Joe Nossek ................... | .21 | .09 | .02 |
| ☐ 144 Bob Hendley ................. | .21 | .09 | .02 |
| ☐ 145 Max Alvis ..................... | .21 | .09 | .02 |
| ☐ 146 Jim Perry ..................... | .40 | .16 | .04 |
| ☐ 147 Leo Durocher MGR ......... | .75 | .30 | .07 |
| ☐ 148 Lee Stange ................... | .21 | .09 | .02 |
| ☐ 149 Ollie Brown .................. | .21 | .09 | .02 |
| ☐ 150 Denny McLain ............... | 1.00 | .40 | .10 |
| ☐ 151A Clay Dalrymple ............ | .30 | .12 | .03 |
|     (Portrait) (Orioles) | | | |
| ☐ 151B Clay Dalrymple ............ | 10.00 | 4.00 | 1.00 |
|     (Catching) (Phillies) | | | |
| ☐ 152 Tommie Sisk .................. | .21 | .09 | .02 |
| ☐ 153 Ed Brinkman ................. | .21 | .09 | .02 |
| ☐ 154 Jim Britton ................... | .21 | .09 | .02 |
| ☐ 155 Pete Ward .................... | .21 | .09 | .02 |
| ☐ 156 Houston Rookies ............ | .21 | .09 | .02 |
|     Hal Gilson | | | |
|     Leon McFadden | | | |
| ☐ 157 Bob Rodgers ................. | .21 | .09 | .02 |
| ☐ 158 Joe Gibbon .................. | .21 | .09 | .02 |
| ☐ 159 Jerry Adair ................... | .21 | .09 | .02 |
| ☐ 160 Vada Pinson ................. | .75 | .30 | .07 |
| ☐ 161 John Purdin .................. | .21 | .09 | .02 |
| ☐ 162 World Series Game 1 ...... | 2.25 | .90 | .22 |
|     Gibson fans 17 | | | |
| ☐ 163 World Series Game 2 ...... | 1.00 | .40 | .10 |
|     Tiger homers | | | |
|     deck the Cards | | | |
| ☐ 164 World Series Game 3 ...... | 1.25 | .50 | .12 |
|     McCarver's homer | | | |
| ☐ 165 World Series Game 4 ...... | 2.25 | .90 | .22 |
|     Brock lead-off homer | | | |
| ☐ 166 World Series Game 5 ...... | 2.50 | 1.00 | .25 |
|     Kaline's key hit | | | |
| ☐ 167 World Series Game 6 ...... | 1.00 | .40 | .10 |

| | | | |
|---|---|---|---|
| Northrup grandslam | | | |
| ☐ 168 World Series Game 7 ...... | 2.00 | .80 | .20 |
| Lolich outduels | | | |
| Bob Gibson | | | |
| ☐ 169 World Series Summary ... | 1.00 | .40 | .10 |
| Tigers celebrate | | | |
| ☐ 170 Frank Howard ................. | .70 | .28 | .07 |
| ☐ 171 Glenn Beckert ................ | .30 | .12 | .03 |
| ☐ 172 Jerry Stephenson .......... | .21 | .09 | .02 |
| ☐ 173 White Sox Rookies ......... | .21 | .09 | .02 |
| Bob Christian | | | |
| Gerry Nyman | | | |
| ☐ 174 Grant Jackson ............... | .21 | .09 | .02 |
| ☐ 175 Jim Bunning .................. | 1.00 | .40 | .10 |
| ☐ 176 Joe Azcue .................... | .21 | .09 | .02 |
| ☐ 177 Ron Reed ..................... | .21 | .09 | .02 |
| ☐ 178 Ray Oyler .................... | .21 | .09 | .02 |
| ☐ 179 Don Pavletich ............... | .21 | .09 | .02 |
| ☐ 180 Willie Horton ................ | .35 | .14 | .03 |
| ☐ 181 Mel Nelson .................. | .21 | .09 | .02 |
| ☐ 182 Bill Rigney MGR ............ | .21 | .09 | .02 |
| ☐ 183 Don Shaw ................... | .21 | .09 | .02 |
| ☐ 184 Roberto Pena ............... | .21 | .09 | .02 |
| ☐ 185 Tom Phoebus ............... | .21 | .09 | .02 |
| ☐ 186 John Edwards ............... | .21 | .09 | .02 |
| ☐ 187 Leon Wagner ............... | .21 | .09 | .02 |
| ☐ 188 Rick Wise ................... | .30 | .12 | .03 |
| ☐ 189 Red Sox Rookies ........... | .21 | .09 | .02 |
| Joe Lahoud | | | |
| John Thibodeau | | | |
| ☐ 190 Willie Mays ................. | 12.50 | 5.00 | 1.25 |
| ☐ 191 Lindy McDaniel ............. | .21 | .09 | .02 |
| ☐ 192 Jose Pagan ................. | .21 | .09 | .02 |
| ☐ 193 Don Cardwell .............. | .21 | .09 | .02 |
| ☐ 194 Ted Uhlaender ............. | .21 | .09 | .02 |
| ☐ 195 John Odom ................. | .21 | .09 | .02 |
| ☐ 196 Lum Harris MGR ........... | .21 | .09 | .02 |
| ☐ 197 Dick Selma ................. | .21 | .09 | .02 |
| ☐ 198 Willie Smith ................ | .21 | .09 | .02 |
| ☐ 199 Jim French ................. | .21 | .09 | .02 |
| ☐ 200 Bob Gibson ................. | 3.00 | 1.20 | .30 |
| ☐ 201 Russ Snyder ............... | .21 | .09 | .02 |
| ☐ 202 Don Wilson ................. | .21 | .09 | .02 |
| ☐ 203 Dave Johnson .............. | .50 | .20 | .05 |
| ☐ 204 Jack Hiatt .................. | .21 | .09 | .02 |
| ☐ 205 Rick Reichardt ............. | .21 | .09 | .02 |
| ☐ 206 Phillies Rookies ........... | .30 | .12 | .03 |
| Larry Hisle | | | |
| Barry Lersch | | | |
| ☐ 207 Roy Face ................... | .35 | .14 | .03 |
| ☐ 208A Donn Clendenon .......... | .30 | .12 | .03 |
| (Houston) | | | |
| ☐ 208B Donn Clendenon .......... | 10.00 | 4.00 | 1.00 |
| (Expos) | | | |
| ☐ 209 Larry Haney ................ | .30 | .12 | .03 |
| (reverse negative) | | | |
| ☐ 210 Felix Millan ................ | .21 | .09 | .02 |
| ☐ 211 Galen Cisco ................ | .21 | .09 | .02 |
| ☐ 212 Tom Tresh .................. | .35 | .14 | .03 |
| ☐ 213 Gerry Arrigo ............... | .21 | .09 | .02 |
| ☐ 214 Checklist 3 ................. | 1.50 | .15 | .03 |
| With 69T deckle CL | | | |
| on back (no player) | | | |
| ☐ 215 Rico Petrocelli ............. | .30 | .12 | .03 |
| ☐ 216 Don Sutton ................. | 2.00 | .80 | .20 |
| ☐ 217 John Donaldson ........... | .21 | .09 | .02 |
| ☐ 218 John Roseboro ............. | .30 | .12 | .03 |
| ☐ 219 Freddie Patek .............. | .35 | .14 | .03 |
| ☐ 220 Sam McDowell ............ | .50 | .20 | .05 |
| ☐ 221 Art Shamsky ............... | .35 | .14 | .03 |
| ☐ 222 Duane Josephson ......... | .35 | .14 | .03 |
| ☐ 223 Tom Dukes ................. | .35 | .14 | .03 |
| ☐ 224 Angels Rookies ............ | .35 | .14 | .03 |
| Bill Harrelson | | | |
| Steve Kealey | | | |
| ☐ 225 Don Kessinger ............. | .50 | .20 | .05 |
| ☐ 226 Bruce Howard .............. | .35 | .14 | .03 |
| ☐ 227 Frank Johnson ............. | .35 | .14 | .03 |
| ☐ 228 Dave Leonhard ............ | .35 | .14 | .03 |
| ☐ 229 Don Lock .................... | .35 | .14 | .03 |
| ☐ 230 Rusty Staub ............... | .80 | .32 | .08 |
| ☐ 231 Pat Dobson ................ | .50 | .20 | .05 |
| ☐ 232 Dave Ricketts ............. | .35 | .14 | .03 |
| ☐ 233 Steve Barber .............. | .35 | .14 | .03 |
| ☐ 234 Dave Bristol MGR ......... | .35 | .14 | .03 |
| ☐ 235 Jim Hunter ................. | 3.00 | 1.20 | .30 |
| ☐ 236 Manny Mota ............... | .50 | .20 | .05 |
| ☐ 237 Bobby Cox MGR ........... | .50 | .20 | .05 |
| ☐ 238 Ken Johnson .............. | .35 | .14 | .03 |
| ☐ 239 Bob Taylor ................. | .35 | .14 | .03 |
| ☐ 240 Ken Harrelson ............. | .75 | .30 | .07 |
| ☐ 241 Jim Brewer ................ | .35 | .14 | .03 |
| ☐ 242 Frank Kostro .............. | .35 | .14 | .03 |
| ☐ 243 Ron Kline ................... | .35 | .14 | .03 |
| ☐ 244 Indians Rookies ........... | .50 | .20 | .05 |
| Ray Fosse | | | |
| George Woodson | | | |
| ☐ 245 Ed Charles ................. | .35 | .14 | .03 |
| ☐ 246 Joe Coleman .............. | .35 | .14 | .03 |
| ☐ 247 Gene Oliver ................ | .35 | .14 | .03 |
| ☐ 248 Bob Priddy ................. | .35 | .14 | .03 |
| ☐ 249 Ed Spiezio ................. | .35 | .14 | .03 |
| ☐ 250 Frank Robinson ........... | 6.50 | 2.60 | .65 |
| ☐ 251 Ron Herbel ................. | .35 | .14 | .03 |
| ☐ 252 Chuck Cottier ............. | .35 | .14 | .03 |
| ☐ 253 Jerry Johnson ............. | .35 | .14 | .03 |
| ☐ 254 Joe Schultz ................ | .35 | .14 | .03 |
| ☐ 255 Steve Carlton ............. | 25.00 | 10.00 | 2.50 |
| ☐ 256 Gates Brown ............... | .45 | .18 | .04 |
| ☐ 257 Jim Ray .................... | .35 | .14 | .03 |
| ☐ 258 Jackie Hernandez ......... | .35 | .14 | .03 |
| ☐ 259 Bill Short ................... | .35 | .14 | .03 |
| ☐ 260 Reggie Jackson ........... | 100.00 | 40.00 | 10.00 |
| ☐ 261 Bob Johnson .............. | .35 | .14 | .03 |
| ☐ 262 Mike Kekich ............... | .35 | .14 | .03 |
| ☐ 263 Jerry May .................. | .35 | .14 | .03 |
| ☐ 264 Bill Landis .................. | .35 | .14 | .03 |
| ☐ 265 Chico Cardenas ........... | .35 | .14 | .03 |
| ☐ 266 Dodger Rookies ........... | .35 | .14 | .03 |
| Tom Hutton | | | |
| Alan Foster | | | |
| ☐ 267 Vicente Romo .............. | .35 | .14 | .03 |
| ☐ 268 Al Spangler ................ | .35 | .14 | .03 |
| ☐ 269 Al Weis .................... | .35 | .14 | .03 |
| ☐ 270 Mickey Lolich .............. | 1.00 | .40 | .10 |
| ☐ 271 Larry Stahl ................ | .35 | .14 | .03 |
| ☐ 272 Ed Stroud ................. | .35 | .14 | .03 |
| ☐ 273 Ron Willis .................. | .35 | .14 | .03 |
| ☐ 274 Clyde King MGR ........... | .35 | .14 | .03 |
| ☐ 275 Vic Davalillo ............... | .35 | .14 | .03 |
| ☐ 276 Gary Wagner .............. | .35 | .14 | .03 |
| ☐ 277 Rod Hendricks ............ | .35 | .14 | .03 |
| ☐ 278 Gary Geiger ............... | .45 | .18 | .04 |
| (Batting wrong) | | | |
| ☐ 279 Roger Nelson .............. | .35 | .14 | .03 |
| ☐ 280 Alex Johnson .............. | .45 | .18 | .04 |
| ☐ 281 Ted Kubiak ................ | .35 | .14 | .03 |
| ☐ 282 Pat Jarvis .................. | .35 | .14 | .03 |
| ☐ 283 Sandy Alomar ............. | .35 | .14 | .03 |
| ☐ 284 Expos Rookies ............. | .35 | .14 | .03 |
| Jerry Robertson | | | |
| Mike Wegener | | | |
| ☐ 285 Don Mincher .............. | .45 | .18 | .04 |
| ☐ 286 Dock Ellis ................. | .35 | .14 | .03 |
| ☐ 287 Jose Tartabull ............ | .35 | .14 | .03 |
| ☐ 288 Ken Holtzman ............. | .55 | .22 | .05 |
| ☐ 289 Bart Shirley ............... | .35 | .14 | .03 |
| ☐ 290 Jim Kaat ................... | 1.75 | .70 | .17 |
| ☐ 291 Vern Fuller ................ | .35 | .14 | .03 |
| ☐ 292 Al Downing ................ | .35 | .14 | .03 |
| ☐ 293 Dick Dietz ................. | .35 | .14 | .03 |
| ☐ 294 Jim Lemon MGR ........... | .35 | .14 | .03 |
| ☐ 295 Tony Perez ................ | 2.25 | .90 | .22 |
| ☐ 296 Andy Messersmith ........ | .75 | .30 | .07 |
| ☐ 297 Deron Johnson ........... | .35 | .14 | .03 |
| ☐ 298 Dave Nicholson ........... | .35 | .14 | .03 |
| ☐ 299 Mark Belanger ............ | .50 | .20 | .05 |
| ☐ 300 Felipe Alou ................ | .50 | .20 | .05 |
| ☐ 301 Darrell Brandon ........... | .45 | .18 | .04 |
| ☐ 302 Jim Pagliaroni ............ | .35 | .14 | .03 |
| ☐ 303 Cal Koonce ................ | .35 | .14 | .03 |
| ☐ 304 Padres Rookies ........... | .35 | .14 | .03 |
| Bill Davis | | | |
| Clarence Gaston | | | |
| ☐ 305 Dick McAuliffe ............ | .35 | .14 | .03 |
| ☐ 306 Jim Grant .................. | .35 | .14 | .03 |
| ☐ 307 Gary Kolb .................. | .35 | .14 | .03 |
| ☐ 308 Wade Blasingame ........ | .35 | .14 | .03 |
| ☐ 309 Walt Williams ............. | .35 | .14 | .03 |
| ☐ 310 Tom Haller ................ | .35 | .14 | .03 |
| ☐ 311 Sparky Lyle ............... | 1.50 | .60 | .15 |
| ☐ 312 Lee Elia ................... | .45 | .18 | .04 |
| ☐ 313 Bill Robinson ............. | .35 | .14 | .03 |
| ☐ 314 Checklist 4 ................ | 1.50 | .15 | .03 |
| Don Drysdale | | | |
| ☐ 315 Eddie Fisher .............. | .35 | .14 | .03 |
| ☐ 316 Hal Lanier ................. | .50 | .20 | .05 |
| ☐ 317 Bruce Look ................ | .35 | .14 | .03 |
| ☐ 318 Jack Fisher ................ | .35 | .14 | .03 |
| ☐ 319 Ken McMullen ............. | .35 | .14 | .03 |
| ☐ 320 Dal Maxvill ................ | .35 | .14 | .03 |
| ☐ 321 Jim McAndrew ............ | .35 | .14 | .03 |
| ☐ 322 Jose Vidal ................. | .45 | .18 | .04 |
| ☐ 323 Larry Miller ............... | .35 | .14 | .03 |
| ☐ 324 Tiger Rookies ............. | .35 | .14 | .03 |
| Les Cain | | | |

# San Diego Sports Collectibles

## THE WEST COAST'S LARGEST BASEBALL CARD STORE

**TOPPS HALL OF FAMER LOTS** Over the years we have built a large inventory of these popular **regular issue** Topps cards. All cards are in very good condition or better and are **guaranteed** originals. All cards are our choice but we will do our best to send your **three** preferences.

| PLAYER | YEARS | 3 DIFF. |
|---|---|---|
| Henry Aaron | 1962-1967 | $21.95 |
| Henry Aaron | 1968-1972 | 14.95 |
| Henry Aaron | 1973-1976 | 9.95 |
| Ernie Banks | 1966-1971 | 8.95 |
| Johnny Bench | 1973-1976 | 6.50 |
| Johnny Bench | 1977-1980 | 3.25 |
| Lou Brock | 1966-1971 | 8.00 |
| Lou Brock | 1972-1977 | 3.00 |
| Rod Carew | 1968-1971 | 14.95 |
| Rod Carew | 1973-1977 | 6.50 |
| Rod Carew | 1978-1980 | 3.00 |
| Steve Carlton | 1967-1970 | 24.95 |
| Steve Carlton | 1971-1976 | 8.25 |
| Steve Carlton | 1977-1980 | 2.75 |
| Roberto Clemente | 1965-1968 | 18.25 |
| Roberto Clemente | 1968-1973 | 12.95 |
| Don Drysdale | 1959-1964 | 9.95 |
| Don Drysdale | 1965-1969 | 7.25 |
| Steve Garvey | 1973-1976 | 7.95 |
| Steve Garvey | 1977-1980 | 4.50 |
| Bob Gibson | 1965-1969 | 6.25 |
| Bob Gibson | 1970-1975 | 3.95 |
| Gil Hodges | 1959-1966 | 6.25 |
| Gil Hodges | 1967-1972 | 2.95 |
| Catfish Hunter | 1966-1970 | 3.95 |
| Catfish Hunter | 1971-1975 | 1.95 |
| Catfish Hunter | 1976-1979 | 1.00 |
| Reggie Jackson | 1971-1975 | 9.50 |
| Reggie Jackson | 1976-1980 | 3.70 |

| PLAYER | YEARS | 3 DIFF. |
|---|---|---|
| Al Kaline | 1964-1969 | 6.00 |
| Al Kaline | 1971-1975 | 3.75 |
| Harmon Killebrew | 1960-1965 | 8.25 |
| Harmon Killebrew | 1966-1971 | 5.95 |
| Harmon Killebrew | 1972-1975 | 2.20 |
| Sandy Koufax | 1959-1966 | 24.95 |
| Fred Lynn | 1976-1980 | 2.25 |
| Mickey Mantle | 1959-1963 | 99.00 |
| Mickey Mantle | 1964-1969 | 75.00 |
| Juan Marichal | 1962-1966 | 6.50 |
| Juan Marichal | 1971-1974 | 5.50 |
| Juan Marichal | 1967-1970 | 2.75 |
| Ed Mathews | 1959-1964 | 6.95 |
| Ed Mathews | 1965-1968 | 5.50 |
| Willie Mays | 1959-1963 | 29.75 |
| Willie Mays | 1964-1968 | 24.50 |
| Willie Mays | 1969-1973 | 14.95 |
| Willie McCovey | 1967-1971 | 6.95 |
| Willie McCovey | 1972-1976 | 2.95 |
| Willie McCovey | 1977-1980 | 1.95 |
| Joe Morgan | 1966-1970 | 5.75 |
| Joe Morgan | 1971-1975 | 2.50 |
| Joe Morgan | 1976-1980 | 1.50 |
| Thurman Munson | 1976-1979 | 2.50 |
| Jim Palmer | 1967-1971 | 8.95 |
| Jim Palmer | 1972-1976 | 2.25 |
| Jim Palmer | 1977-1980 | 1.75 |
| Gaylord Perry | 1967-1971 | 5.75 |
| Gaylord Perry | 1972-1976 | 2.75 |

| PLAYER | YEARS | 3 DIFF. |
|---|---|---|
| Gaylord Perry | 1977-1980 | 1.45 |
| Robin Roberts | 1959-1965 | 4.75 |
| Brooks Robinson | 1964-1969 | 7.50 |
| Brooks Robinson | 1970-1973 | 5.95 |
| Brooks Robinson | 1974-1977 | 2.50 |
| Frank Robinson | 1959-1964 | 10.50 |
| Frank Robinson | 1965-1971 | 8.50 |
| Frank Robinson | 1972-1975 | 3.25 |
| Pete Rose | 1966-1969 | 59.00 |
| Pete Rose | 1977-1980 | 8.25 |
| Nolan Ryan | 1973-1976 | 3.75 |
| Nolan Ryan | 1977-1980 | 1.95 |
| Mike Schmidt | 1977-1980 | 5.50 |
| Mike Schmidt | 1981-1986 | 1.45 |
| Tom Seaver | 1968-1970 | 19.95 |
| Tom Seaver | 1976-1980 | 2.95 |
| Willie Stargell | 1964-1969 | 7.95 |
| Willie Stargell | 1970-1975 | 2.95 |
| Willie Stargell | 1976-1980 | 1.75 |
| Dave Winfield | 1975-1977 | 4.95 |
| Dave Winfield | 1978-1980 | 2.95 |
| Dave Winfield | 1981-1986 | 1.45 |
| Early Wynn | 1959-1962 | 6.25 |
| Carl Yastrzemski | 1964-1969 | 34.50 |
| Carl Yastrzemski | 1970-1973 | 12.95 |
| Carl Yastrzemski | 1974-1977 | 7.75 |
| Carl Yastrzemski | 1978-1980 | 2.95 |
| Robin Yount | 1976-1980 | 2.75 |

## SUPER CARD LOTS

We have good quantities of all lots listed below. This is an excellent way of obtaining major portions of sets at low prices.

### 1. TOPPS 1959-1965

1500 different cards, approximately 80 each year, including: Aaron, Allen, Alston, Aparicio, Banks, Bauer, Boyer, Brock, Bunning, Burdette, Carew, Cash, Cepeda, Clemente, Dark, Davis, Drysdale, Face, Flood, Ford, Gibson, Gilliam, Groat, Hodges, Houk, E. Howard, F. Howard, Jenkins, John, Kaat, Kaline, Killebrew, Koufax, Kubek, Kuenn, Larsen, Lopez, Mantle, Maris, Martin, Mathews, Mays, Mazeroski, McCovey, McGraw, McLain, Minoso, Moon, Morgan, Murcer, Niekro, Oliva, Perez, Perry, Pierce, Piniella, Piersall, Pinson, Podres, Powell, B. Robby, F. Robby, Rose, Santo, Schoendienst, Score, Shantz, Skowron, Spahn, Stargell, Staub, Sutton, Tiant, Torre, Turley, Virdon, Wilhelm, Wills, Zimmer and Yaz. Very Good to Excellent condition.**$295.00**

### 2. TOPPS 1959-1965

150 different cards including Clemente, Mays, Aaron, Drysdale, Ford, Killebrew, Wynn, Hodges, Spahn, Banks, Mathews, Roberts, Aparicio, Fox, Minoso and many more. Very Good to Excellent condition.**$89.00**

### 3. TOPPS 1964-1974

150 different cards including: Aaron, Banks, Clemente, Drysdale, Ford, Gibson, Hodges, Kaline, Killebrew, Koufax, Mathews, Mays, McCovey, Morgan, Roberts, F. Robby, Aparicio, Hunter and many more. Very Good to Excellent condition. **$89.00**

### 4. TOPPS 1976-1983

200 different, including Rose, Henderson, Bench, Carlton, Schmidt, Lynn, Rice, Winfield, Garvey, Palmer, Brett, Seaver, Jackson, Carew, Murphy, Murray, Guerrero, Perry, Hunter, Stargell, Parker, Foster, Jenkins, McCovey, Sutton, Bowa, Tiant, Cooper, Blue. Excellent to Mint condition. **$39.00**

### 5. TOPPS/FLEER/ DONRUSS 1981-1987

800 assorted including Valenzuela, Rose, Henderson, Schmidt, Carlton, Seaver, Bench, Murphy, Carew, Ripken, Palmer, Brett, Winfield, Rice, Jackson, Guerrero, Garvey, Carter, Murray, Perry, Dawson, Murray, Lynn, Strawberry, and Yaz. Excellent to Mint condition. **$19.95**

San Diego Sports Collectibles Catalogue

NEW REVISED 1987 CATALOGUE

## FREE!

Please send 3 stamps to receive a listing of thousands of old baseball cards from the early 1900's to present. Includes Topps Sets, Singles and Stars as well as Bowman, Fleer, Donruss, Goudey, Tobacco, Leaf and many other regional and miscellaneous issues. Also featured are Football Cards and Sports Collectibles of all types. Issued 3 times yearly.

**MAIL ORDER INSTRUCTIONS**
Credit card holders for instant service Mon.-Sat. call toll free 1-800-621-0852 ext. 561 orders only. All other inquiries call (619) 282-0143.

**SHIPPING & INSURANCE**

| | | | |
|---|---|---|---|
| 1-25 cards | $1.95 | 101-800 cards | 4.95 |
| 26-100 cards | 2.50 | 801 or more | 9.95 |

California residents please add 6% sales tax.

**Send Payment To:**
**S.D. Sports Collectibles**
5043 Westminster Terr., Dept. D-1,
San Diego, CA 92116

| | | | | |
|---|---|---|---|---|
| | Dave Campbell | | | |
| ☐ 325 | Jose Cardenal | .35 | .14 | .03 |
| ☐ 326 | Gary Sutherland | .35 | .14 | .03 |
| ☐ 327 | Willie Crawford | .35 | .14 | .03 |
| ☐ 328 | Joe Horlen | .30 | .12 | .03 |
| ☐ 329 | Rick Joseph | .21 | .09 | .02 |
| ☐ 330 | Tony Conigliaro | .60 | .24 | .06 |
| ☐ 331 | Braves Rookies | .35 | .14 | .03 |
| | Gil Garrido | | | |
| | Tom House | | | |
| ☐ 332 | Fred Talbot | .21 | .09 | .02 |
| ☐ 333 | Ivan Murrell | .21 | .09 | .02 |
| ☐ 334 | Phil Roof | .21 | .09 | .02 |
| ☐ 335 | Bill Mazeroski | .60 | .24 | .06 |
| ☐ 336 | Jim Roland | .21 | .09 | .02 |
| ☐ 337 | Marty Martinez | .21 | .09 | .02 |
| ☐ 338 | Del Unser | .21 | .09 | .02 |
| ☐ 339 | Reds Rookies | .21 | .09 | .02 |
| | Steve Mingori | | | |
| | Jose Pena | | | |
| ☐ 340 | Dave McNally | .40 | .16 | .04 |
| ☐ 341 | Dave Adlesh | .21 | .09 | .02 |
| ☐ 342 | Bubba Morton | .21 | .09 | .02 |
| ☐ 343 | Dan Frisella | .21 | .09 | .02 |
| ☐ 344 | Tom Matchick | .21 | .09 | .02 |
| ☐ 345 | Frank Linzy | .21 | .09 | .02 |
| ☐ 346 | Wayne Comer | .30 | .12 | .03 |
| ☐ 347 | Randy Hundley | .21 | .09 | .02 |
| ☐ 348 | Steve Hargan | .21 | .09 | .02 |
| ☐ 349 | Dick Williams MGR | .30 | .12 | .03 |
| ☐ 350 | Richie Allen | .75 | .30 | .07 |
| ☐ 351 | Carroll Sembera | .21 | .09 | .02 |
| ☐ 352 | Paul Schaal | .21 | .09 | .02 |
| ☐ 353 | Jeff Torborg | .21 | .09 | .02 |
| ☐ 354 | Nate Oliver | .21 | .09 | .02 |
| ☐ 355 | Phil Niekro | 2.50 | 1.00 | .25 |
| ☐ 356 | Frank Quilici MGR | .21 | .09 | .02 |
| ☐ 357 | Carl Taylor | .21 | .09 | .02 |
| ☐ 358 | Athletics Rookies | .21 | .09 | .02 |
| | George Lauzerique | | | |
| | Roberto Rodriquez | | | |
| ☐ 359 | Dick Kelley | .21 | .09 | .02 |
| ☐ 360 | Jim Wynn | .35 | .14 | .03 |
| ☐ 361 | Gary Holman | .21 | .09 | .02 |
| ☐ 362 | Jim Maloney | .30 | .12 | .03 |
| ☐ 363 | Russ Nixon | .21 | .09 | .02 |
| ☐ 364 | Tommie Agee | .30 | .12 | .03 |
| ☐ 365 | Jim Fregosi | .40 | .16 | .04 |
| ☐ 366 | Bo Belinsky | .30 | .12 | .03 |
| ☐ 367 | Lou Johnson | .21 | .09 | .02 |
| ☐ 368 | Vic Roznovsky | .21 | .09 | .02 |
| ☐ 369 | Bob Skinner | .30 | .12 | .03 |
| ☐ 370 | Juan Marichal | 2.75 | 1.10 | .27 |
| ☐ 371 | Sal Bando | .50 | .20 | .05 |
| ☐ 372 | Adolfo Phillips | .21 | .09 | .02 |
| ☐ 373 | Fred Lasher | .21 | .09 | .02 |
| ☐ 374 | Bob Tillman | .21 | .09 | .02 |
| ☐ 375 | Harmon Killebrew | 5.00 | 2.00 | .50 |
| ☐ 376 | Royals Rookies | .21 | .09 | .02 |
| | Mike Fiore | | | |
| | Jim Rooker | | | |
| ☐ 377 | Gary Bell | .30 | .12 | .03 |
| ☐ 378 | Jose Herrera | .21 | .09 | .02 |
| ☐ 379 | Ken Boyer | .75 | .30 | .07 |
| ☐ 380 | Stan Bahnsen | .21 | .09 | .02 |
| ☐ 381 | Ed Kranepool | .30 | .12 | .03 |
| ☐ 382 | Pat Corrales | .30 | .12 | .03 |
| ☐ 383 | Casey Cox | .21 | .09 | .02 |
| ☐ 384 | Larry Shepard MGR | .21 | .09 | .02 |
| ☐ 385 | Orlando Cepeda | 1.25 | .50 | .12 |
| ☐ 386 | Jim McGlothlin | .21 | .09 | .02 |
| ☐ 387 | Bobby Klaus | .21 | .09 | .02 |
| ☐ 388 | Tom McCraw | .21 | .09 | .02 |
| ☐ 389 | Dan Coombs | .21 | .09 | .02 |
| ☐ 390 | Bill Freehan | .50 | .20 | .05 |
| ☐ 391 | Ray Culp | .21 | .09 | .02 |
| ☐ 392 | Bob Burda | .21 | .09 | .02 |
| ☐ 393 | Gene Brabender | .21 | .09 | .02 |
| ☐ 394 | Pilots Rookies | 1.25 | .50 | .12 |
| | Lou Piniella | | | |
| | Marv Staehle | | | |
| ☐ 395 | Chris Short | .21 | .09 | .02 |
| ☐ 396 | Jim Campanis | .21 | .09 | .02 |
| ☐ 397 | Chuck Dobson | .21 | .09 | .02 |
| ☐ 398 | Tito Francona | .21 | .09 | .02 |
| ☐ 399 | Bob Bailey | .21 | .09 | .02 |
| ☐ 400 | Don Drysdale | 3.00 | 1.20 | .30 |
| ☐ 401 | Jake Gibbs | .21 | .09 | .02 |
| ☐ 402 | Ken Boswell | .21 | .09 | .02 |
| ☐ 403 | Bob Miller | .21 | .09 | .02 |
| ☐ 404 | Cubs Rookies | .21 | .09 | .02 |
| | Vic LaRose | | | |
| | Gary Ross | | | |

| | | | | |
|---|---|---|---|---|
| ☐ 405 | Lee May | .40 | .16 | .04 |
| ☐ 406 | Phil Ortega | .21 | .09 | .02 |
| ☐ 407 | Tom Egan | .21 | .09 | .02 |
| ☐ 408 | Nate Colbert | .21 | .09 | .02 |
| ☐ 409 | Bob Moose | .21 | .09 | .02 |
| ☐ 410 | Al Kaline | 3.50 | 1.40 | .35 |
| ☐ 411 | Larry Dierker | .30 | .12 | .03 |
| ☐ 412 | Checklist 5 | 2.50 | .25 | .05 |
| | Mickey Mantle | | | |
| ☐ 413 | Roland Sheldon | .30 | .12 | .03 |
| ☐ 414 | Duke Sims | .21 | .09 | .02 |
| ☐ 415 | Ray Washburn | .21 | .09 | .02 |
| ☐ 416 | Willie McCovey AS | 2.00 | .80 | .20 |
| ☐ 417 | Ken Harrelson AS | .30 | .12 | .03 |
| ☐ 418 | Tommy Helms AS | .30 | .12 | .03 |
| ☐ 419 | Rod Carew AS | 3.00 | 1.20 | .30 |
| ☐ 420 | Ron Santo AS | .30 | .12 | .03 |
| ☐ 421 | Brooks Robinson AS | 2.50 | 1.00 | .25 |
| ☐ 422 | Don Kessinger AS | .30 | .12 | .03 |
| ☐ 423 | Bert Campaneris AS | .30 | .12 | .03 |
| ☐ 424 | Pete Rose AS | 6.50 | 2.60 | .65 |
| ☐ 425 | Carl Yastrzemski AS | 4.00 | 1.60 | .40 |
| ☐ 426 | Curt Flood AS | .30 | .12 | .03 |
| ☐ 427 | Tony Oliva AS | .45 | .18 | .04 |
| ☐ 428 | Lou Brock AS | 2.25 | .90 | .22 |
| ☐ 429 | Willie Horton AS | .30 | .12 | .03 |
| ☐ 430 | Johnny Bench AS | 4.00 | 1.60 | .40 |
| ☐ 431 | Bill Freehan AS | .30 | .12 | .03 |
| ☐ 432 | Bob Gibson AS | 2.00 | .80 | .20 |
| ☐ 433 | Denny McLain AS | .40 | .16 | .04 |
| ☐ 434 | Jerry Koosman AS | .30 | .12 | .03 |
| ☐ 435 | Sam McDowell AS | .30 | .12 | .03 |
| ☐ 436 | Gene Alley | .30 | .12 | .03 |
| ☐ 437 | Luis Alcaraz | .21 | .09 | .02 |
| ☐ 438 | Gary Waslewski | .21 | .09 | .02 |
| ☐ 439 | White Sox Rookies | .21 | .09 | .02 |
| | Ed Herrmann | | | |
| | Dan Lazar | | | |
| ☐ 440A | Willie McCovey | 7.50 | 3.00 | .75 |
| ☐ 440B | Willie McCovey WL | 50.00 | 20.00 | 5.00 |
| ☐ 441A | Dennis Higgins | .25 | .10 | .02 |
| ☐ 441B | Dennis Higgins WL | 6.50 | 2.40 | .60 |
| ☐ 442 | Ty Cline | .21 | .09 | .02 |
| ☐ 443 | Don Wert | .21 | .09 | .02 |
| ☐ 444A | Joe Moeller | .25 | .10 | .02 |
| ☐ 444B | Joe Moeller WL | 6.50 | 2.40 | .60 |
| ☐ 445 | Bobby Knoop | .21 | .09 | .02 |
| ☐ 446 | Claude Raymond | .21 | .09 | .02 |
| ☐ 447A | Ralph Houk MGR | .40 | .16 | .04 |
| ☐ 447B | Ralph Houk WL MGR | 7.50 | 2.80 | .70 |
| ☐ 448 | Bob Tolan | .21 | .09 | .02 |
| ☐ 449 | Paul Lindblad | .21 | .09 | .02 |
| ☐ 450 | Billy Williams | 3.00 | 1.20 | .30 |
| ☐ 451A | Rich Rollins | .25 | .10 | .02 |
| ☐ 451B | Rich Rollins WL | 6.50 | 2.40 | .60 |
| ☐ 452A | Al Ferrara | .25 | .10 | .02 |
| ☐ 452B | Al Ferrara WL | 6.50 | 2.40 | .60 |
| ☐ 453 | Mike Cuellar | .50 | .20 | .05 |
| ☐ 454A | Phillies Rookies | .35 | .14 | .03 |
| | Larry Colton | | | |
| | Don Money | | | |
| ☐ 454B | Phillies Rookies WL | 7.50 | 2.80 | .70 |
| | Larry Colton | | | |
| | Don Money | | | |
| ☐ 455 | Sonny Siebert | .30 | .12 | .03 |
| ☐ 456 | Bud Harrelson | .30 | .12 | .03 |
| ☐ 457 | Dalton Jones | .21 | .09 | .02 |
| ☐ 458 | Curt Blefary | .21 | .09 | .02 |
| ☐ 459 | Dave Boswell | .21 | .09 | .02 |
| ☐ 460 | Joe Torre | .70 | .28 | .07 |
| ☐ 461A | Mike Epstein | .25 | .10 | .02 |
| ☐ 461B | Mike Epstein WL | 6.50 | 2.40 | .60 |
| ☐ 462 | Red Schoendienst MGR | .45 | .18 | .04 |
| ☐ 463 | Dennis Ribant | .21 | .09 | .02 |
| ☐ 464A | Dave Marshall | .25 | .10 | .02 |
| ☐ 464B | Dave Marshall WL | 6.50 | 2.40 | .60 |
| ☐ 465 | Tommy John | 1.25 | .50 | .12 |
| ☐ 466 | John Boccabella | .21 | .09 | .02 |
| ☐ 467 | Tom Reynolds | .21 | .09 | .02 |
| ☐ 468A | Pirates Rookies | .25 | .10 | .02 |
| | Bruce Dal Canton | | | |
| | Bob Robertson | | | |
| ☐ 468B | Pirates Rookies WL | 6.50 | 2.40 | .60 |
| | Bruce Dal Canton | | | |
| | Bob Robertson | | | |
| ☐ 469 | Chico Ruiz | .21 | .09 | .02 |
| ☐ 470A | Mel Stottlemyre | .50 | .20 | .05 |
| ☐ 470B | Mel Stottlemyre WL | 7.50 | 2.80 | .70 |
| ☐ 471A | Ted Savage | .25 | .10 | .02 |
| ☐ 471B | Ted Savage WL | 6.50 | 2.40 | .60 |
| ☐ 472 | Jim Price | .21 | .09 | .02 |
| ☐ 473A | Jose Arcia | .25 | .10 | .02 |
| ☐ 473B | Jose Arcia WL | 6.50 | 2.40 | .60 |

| | | | | |
|---|---|---|---|---|
| ☐ 474 | Tom Murphy | .21 | .09 | .02 |
| ☐ 475 | Tim McCarver | .35 | .14 | .03 |
| ☐ 476A | Boston Rookies | .30 | .12 | .03 |
| | Ken Brett | | | |
| | Gerry Moses | | | |
| ☐ 476B | Boston Rookies WL | 6.50 | 2.40 | .60 |
| | Ken Brett | | | |
| | Gerry Moses | | | |
| ☐ 477 | Jeff James | .21 | .09 | .02 |
| ☐ 478 | Don Buford | .21 | .09 | .02 |
| ☐ 479 | Richie Scheinblum | .21 | .09 | .02 |
| ☐ 480 | Tom Seaver | 25.00 | 10.00 | 2.50 |
| ☐ 481 | Bill Melton | .21 | .09 | .02 |
| ☐ 482A | Jim Gosger | .25 | .10 | .02 |
| ☐ 482B | Jim Gosger WL | 6.50 | 2.40 | .60 |
| ☐ 483 | Ted Abernathy | .21 | .09 | .02 |
| ☐ 484 | Joe Gordon MGR | .30 | .12 | .03 |
| ☐ 485A | Gaylord Perry | 3.00 | 1.20 | .30 |
| ☐ 485B | Gaylord Perry WL | 25.00 | 10.00 | 2.50 |
| ☐ 486A | Paul Casanova | .25 | .10 | .02 |
| ☐ 486B | Paul Casanova WL | 6.50 | 2.40 | .60 |
| ☐ 487 | Denis Menke | .30 | .12 | .03 |
| ☐ 488 | Joe Sparma | .21 | .09 | .02 |
| ☐ 489 | Clete Boyer | .40 | .16 | .04 |
| ☐ 490 | Matty Alou | .30 | .12 | .03 |
| ☐ 491A | Twins Rookies | .30 | .12 | .03 |
| | Jerry Crider | | | |
| | George Mitterwald | | | |
| ☐ 491B | Twins Rookies WL | 6.50 | 2.40 | .60 |
| | Jerry Crider | | | |
| | George Mitterwald | | | |
| ☐ 492 | Tony Cloninger | .21 | .09 | .02 |
| ☐ 493A | Wes Parker | .40 | .16 | .04 |
| ☐ 493B | Wes Parker WL | 7.50 | 2.80 | .70 |
| ☐ 494 | Ken Berry | .21 | .09 | .02 |
| ☐ 495 | Bert Campaneris | .40 | .16 | .04 |
| ☐ 496 | Larry Jaster | .21 | .09 | .02 |
| ☐ 497 | Julian Javier | .30 | .12 | .03 |
| ☐ 498 | Juan Pizarro | .21 | .09 | .02 |
| ☐ 499 | Astro Rookies | .21 | .09 | .02 |
| | Don Bryant | | | |
| | Steve Shea | | | |
| ☐ 500A | Mickey Mantle | 50.00 | 20.00 | 5.00 |
| ☐ 500B | Mickey Mantle WL | 125.00 | 50.00 | 12.50 |
| ☐ 501A | Tony Gonzalez | .30 | .12 | .03 |
| ☐ 501B | Tony Gonzalez WL | 6.50 | 2.40 | .60 |
| ☐ 502 | Minnie Rojas | .21 | .09 | .02 |
| ☐ 503 | Larry Brown | .21 | .09 | .02 |
| ☐ 504 | Checklist 6 | 1.50 | .15 | .03 |
| | Brooks Robinson | | | |
| ☐ 505A | Bobby Bolin | .25 | .10 | .02 |
| ☐ 505B | Bobby Bolin WL | 6.50 | 2.40 | .60 |
| ☐ 506 | Paul Blair | .30 | .12 | .03 |
| ☐ 507 | Cookie Rojas | .21 | .09 | .02 |
| ☐ 508 | Moe Drabowsky | .21 | .09 | .02 |
| ☐ 509 | Manny Sanguillen | .35 | .14 | .03 |
| ☐ 510 | Rod Carew | 20.00 | 8.00 | 2.00 |
| ☐ 511A | Diego Segui | .35 | .14 | .03 |
| ☐ 511B | Diego Segui WL | 6.50 | 2.40 | .60 |
| ☐ 512 | Cleon Jones | .21 | .09 | .02 |
| ☐ 513 | Camilo Pascual | .30 | .12 | .03 |
| ☐ 514 | Mike Lum | .25 | .10 | .02 |
| ☐ 515 | Dick Green | .25 | .10 | .02 |
| ☐ 516 | Earl Weaver MGR | 2.00 | .80 | .20 |
| ☐ 517 | Mike McCormick | .35 | .14 | .03 |
| ☐ 518 | Fred Whitfield | .25 | .10 | .02 |
| ☐ 519 | Yankees Rookies | .25 | .10 | .02 |
| | Gerry Kenney | | | |
| | Len Boehmer | | | |
| ☐ 520 | Bob Veale | .35 | .14 | .03 |
| ☐ 521 | George Thomas | .25 | .10 | .02 |
| ☐ 522 | Joe Hoerner | .25 | .10 | .02 |
| ☐ 523 | Bob Chance | .25 | .10 | .02 |
| ☐ 524 | Expos Rookies | .25 | .10 | .02 |
| | Jose Laboy | | | |
| | Floyd Wicker | | | |
| ☐ 525 | Earl Wilson | .25 | .10 | .02 |
| ☐ 526 | Hector Torres | .25 | .10 | .02 |
| ☐ 527 | Al Lopez MGR | 1.00 | .40 | .10 |
| ☐ 528 | Claude Osteen | .35 | .14 | .03 |
| ☐ 529 | Ed Kirkpatrick | .25 | .10 | .02 |
| ☐ 530 | Cesar Tovar | .25 | .10 | .02 |
| ☐ 531 | Dick Farrell | .25 | .10 | .02 |
| ☐ 532 | Bird Hill Aces | .45 | .18 | .04 |
| | Tom Phoebus | | | |
| | Jim Hardin | | | |
| | Dave McNally | | | |
| | Mike Cuellar | | | |
| ☐ 533 | Nolan Ryan | 25.00 | 10.00 | 2.50 |
| ☐ 534 | Jerry McNertney | .30 | .12 | .03 |
| ☐ 535 | Phil Regan | .35 | .14 | .03 |
| ☐ 536 | Padres Rookies | .25 | .10 | .02 |
| | Danny Breeden | | | |
| | Dave Roberts | | | |
| ☐ 537 | Mike Paul | .25 | .10 | .02 |
| ☐ 538 | Charlie Smith | .25 | .10 | .02 |
| ☐ 539 | Ted Shows How | 2.00 | .80 | .20 |
| | Mike Epstein | | | |
| | Ted Williams | | | |
| ☐ 540 | Curt Flood | .50 | .20 | .05 |
| ☐ 541 | Joe Verbanic | .25 | .10 | .02 |
| ☐ 542 | Bob Aspromonte | .25 | .10 | .02 |
| ☐ 543 | Fred Newman | .25 | .10 | .02 |
| ☐ 544 | Tigers Rookies | .25 | .10 | .02 |
| | Mike Kilkenny | | | |
| | Ron Woods | | | |
| ☐ 545 | Willie Stargell | 3.50 | 1.40 | .35 |
| ☐ 546 | Jim Nash | .25 | .10 | .02 |
| ☐ 547 | Billy Martin MGR | 1.00 | .40 | .10 |
| ☐ 548 | Bob Locker | .25 | .10 | .02 |
| ☐ 549 | Ron Brand | .25 | .10 | .02 |
| ☐ 550 | Brooks Robinson | 6.50 | 2.60 | .65 |
| ☐ 551 | Wayne Granger | .25 | .10 | .02 |
| ☐ 552 | Dodgers Rookies | .40 | .16 | .04 |
| | Ted Sizemore | | | |
| | Bill Sudakis | | | |
| ☐ 553 | Ron Davis | .25 | .10 | .02 |
| ☐ 554 | Frank Bertaina | .25 | .10 | .02 |
| ☐ 555 | Jim Ray Hart | .35 | .14 | .03 |
| ☐ 556 | A's Stars | .45 | .18 | .04 |
| | Sal Bando | | | |
| | Bert Campaneris | | | |
| | Danny Cater | | | |
| ☐ 557 | Frank Fernandez | .25 | .10 | .02 |
| ☐ 558 | Tom Burgmeier | .35 | .14 | .03 |
| ☐ 559 | Cardinals Rookies | .25 | .10 | .02 |
| | Joe Hague | | | |
| | Jim Hicks | | | |
| ☐ 560 | Luis Tiant | .75 | .30 | .07 |
| ☐ 561 | Ron Clark | .25 | .10 | .02 |
| ☐ 562 | Bob Watson | 1.00 | .40 | .10 |
| ☐ 563 | Martin Pattin | .35 | .14 | .03 |
| ☐ 564 | Gil Hodges MGR | 2.50 | 1.00 | .25 |
| ☐ 565 | Hoyt Wilhelm | 3.00 | 1.20 | .30 |
| ☐ 566 | Ron Hansen | .25 | .10 | .02 |
| ☐ 567 | Pirates Rookies | .25 | .10 | .02 |
| | Elvio Jimenez | | | |
| | Jim Shellenback | | | |
| ☐ 568 | Cecil Upshaw | .25 | .10 | .02 |
| ☐ 569 | Billy Harris | .25 | .10 | .02 |
| ☐ 570 | Ron Santo | .65 | .26 | .06 |
| ☐ 571 | Cap Peterson | .25 | .10 | .02 |
| ☐ 572 | Giants Heroes | 4.00 | 1.60 | .40 |
| | Willie McCovey | | | |
| | Juan Marichal | | | |
| ☐ 573 | Jim Palmer | 6.50 | 2.60 | .65 |
| ☐ 574 | George Scott | .35 | .14 | .03 |
| ☐ 575 | Bill Singer | .25 | .10 | .02 |
| ☐ 576 | Phillies Rookies | .25 | .10 | .02 |
| | Ron Stone | | | |
| | Bill Wilson | | | |
| ☐ 577 | Mike Hegan | .30 | .12 | .03 |
| ☐ 578 | Don Bosch | .25 | .10 | .02 |
| ☐ 579 | Dave Nelson | .25 | .10 | .02 |
| ☐ 580 | Jim Northrup | .35 | .14 | .03 |
| ☐ 581 | Gary Nolan | .25 | .10 | .02 |
| ☐ 582A | Checklist 7 | 1.75 | .15 | .03 |
| | (White circle on back) | | | |
| | (Tony Oliva) | | | |
| ☐ 582B | Checklist 7 | 3.50 | .35 | .07 |
| | (Red circle on back) | | | |
| | (Tony Oliva) | | | |
| ☐ 583 | Clyde Wright | .25 | .10 | .02 |
| ☐ 584 | Don Mason | .25 | .10 | .02 |
| ☐ 585 | Ron Swoboda | .35 | .14 | .03 |
| ☐ 586 | Tim Cullen | .25 | .10 | .02 |
| ☐ 587 | Joe Rudi | .75 | .30 | .07 |
| ☐ 588 | Bill White | .45 | .18 | .04 |
| ☐ 589 | Joe Pepitone | .45 | .18 | .04 |
| ☐ 590 | Rico Carty | .45 | .18 | .04 |
| ☐ 591 | Mike Hedlund | .25 | .10 | .02 |
| ☐ 592 | Padres Rookies | .25 | .10 | .02 |
| | Rafael Robles | | | |
| | Al Santorini | | | |
| ☐ 593 | Don Nottebart | .25 | .10 | .02 |
| ☐ 594 | Dooley Womack | .25 | .10 | .02 |
| ☐ 595 | Lee Maye | .25 | .10 | .02 |
| ☐ 596 | Chuck Hartenstein | .25 | .10 | .02 |
| ☐ 597 | A.L. Rookies | 10.00 | 4.00 | 1.00 |
| | Bob Floyd | | | |
| | Larry Burchart | | | |
| | Rollie Fingers | | | |
| ☐ 598 | Ruben Amaro | .25 | .10 | .02 |
| ☐ 599 | John Boozer | .25 | .10 | .02 |
| ☐ 600 | Tony Oliva | 1.00 | .40 | .10 |
| ☐ 601 | Tug McGraw | 1.00 | .40 | .10 |

| | | | | |
|---|---|---|---|---|
| ☐ 602 | Cubs Rookies .................. | .25 | .10 | .02 |
| | Alec Distaso | | | |
| | Don Young | | | |
| | Jim Qualls | | | |
| ☐ 603 | Joe Keough .................. | .25 | .10 | .02 |
| ☐ 604 | Bobby Etheridge ............. | .25 | .10 | .02 |
| ☐ 605 | Dick Ellsworth .............. | .25 | .10 | .02 |
| ☐ 606 | Gene Mauch MGR .......... | .35 | .14 | .03 |
| ☐ 607 | Dick Bosman ................ | .25 | .10 | .02 |
| ☐ 608 | Dick Simpson ................ | .25 | .10 | .02 |
| ☐ 609 | Phil Gagliano ................ | .25 | .10 | .02 |
| ☐ 610 | Jim Hardin .................. | .25 | .10 | .02 |
| ☐ 611 | Braves Rookies ............. | .25 | .10 | .02 |
| | Bob Didier | | | |
| | Walt Hriniak | | | |
| | Gary Neibauer | | | |
| ☐ 612 | Jack Aker ................... | .35 | .14 | .03 |
| ☐ 613 | Jim Beauchamp .............. | .25 | .10 | .02 |
| ☐ 614 | Houston Rookies ............ | .25 | .10 | .02 |
| | Tom Griffin | | | |
| | Skip Guinn | | | |
| ☐ 615 | Len Gabrielson .............. | .25 | .10 | .02 |
| ☐ 616 | Don McMahon ................ | .25 | .10 | .02 |
| ☐ 617 | Jesse Gonder ................ | .25 | .10 | .02 |
| ☐ 618 | Ramon Webster ............. | .25 | .10 | .02 |
| ☐ 619 | Royals Rookies .............. | .40 | .16 | .04 |
| | Bill Butler | | | |
| | Pat Kelly | | | |
| | Juan Rios | | | |
| ☐ 620 | Dean Chance ................ | .35 | .14 | .03 |
| ☐ 621 | Bill Voss ................... | .25 | .10 | .02 |
| ☐ 622 | Dan Osinski ................. | .25 | .10 | .02 |
| ☐ 623 | Hank Allen .................. | .25 | .10 | .02 |
| ☐ 624 | N.L. Rookies ................ | .35 | .14 | .03 |
| | Darrel Chaney | | | |
| | Duffy Dyer | | | |
| | Terry Harmon | | | |
| ☐ 625 | Mack Jones ................. | .35 | .14 | .03 |
| | (Batting wrong) | | | |
| ☐ 626 | Gene Michael ................ | .35 | .14 | .03 |
| ☐ 627 | George Stone ............... | .25 | .10 | .02 |
| ☐ 628 | Red Sox Rookies ............ | .35 | .14 | .03 |
| | Bill Conigliaro | | | |
| | Syd O'Brien | | | |
| | Fred Wenz | | | |
| ☐ 629 | Jack Hamilton ............... | .25 | .10 | .02 |
| ☐ 630 | Bobby Bonds ................ | 2.00 | .80 | .20 |
| ☐ 631 | John Kennedy ............... | .30 | .12 | .03 |
| ☐ 632 | Jon Warden ................. | .25 | .10 | .02 |
| ☐ 633 | Harry Walker MGR .......... | .25 | .10 | .02 |
| ☐ 634 | Andy Etchebarren .......... | .25 | .10 | .02 |
| ☐ 635 | George Culver ............... | .25 | .10 | .02 |
| ☐ 636 | Woodie Held ................ | .25 | .10 | .02 |
| ☐ 637 | Padres Rookies .............. | .25 | .10 | .02 |
| | Jerry DaVanon | | | |
| | Frank Reberger | | | |
| | Clay Kirby | | | |
| ☐ 638 | Ed Sprague ................. | .25 | .10 | .02 |
| ☐ 639 | Barry Moore ................. | .25 | .10 | .02 |
| ☐ 640 | Fergie Jenkins .............. | 1.50 | .60 | .15 |
| ☐ 641 | N.L. Rookies ................ | .25 | .10 | .02 |
| | Bobby Darwin | | | |
| | John Miller | | | |
| | Tommy Dean | | | |
| ☐ 642 | John Hiller ................. | .35 | .14 | .03 |
| ☐ 643 | Billy Cowan ................. | .25 | .10 | .02 |
| ☐ 644 | Chuck Hinton ............... | .25 | .10 | .02 |
| ☐ 645 | George Brunet ............... | .25 | .10 | .02 |
| ☐ 646 | Expos Rookies .............. | .25 | .10 | .02 |
| | Dan McGinn | | | |
| | Carl Morton | | | |
| ☐ 647 | Dave Wickersham .......... | .25 | .10 | .02 |
| ☐ 648 | Bobby Wine ................. | .25 | .10 | .02 |
| ☐ 649 | Al Jackson .................. | .25 | .10 | .02 |
| ☐ 650 | Ted Williams MGR .......... | 3.50 | 1.40 | .35 |
| ☐ 651 | Gus Gil .................... | .30 | .12 | .03 |
| ☐ 652 | Eddie Watt .................. | .25 | .10 | .02 |
| ☐ 653 | Aurelio Rodriguez .......... | 1.25 | .50 | .12 |
| | (photo actually | | | |
| | Angels' batboy) | | | |
| ☐ 654 | White Sox Rookies .......... | .45 | .18 | .04 |
| | Carlos May | | | |
| | Don Secrist | | | |
| | Rich Morales | | | |
| ☐ 655 | Mike Hershberger ........... | .25 | .10 | .02 |
| ☐ 656 | Dan Schneider .............. | .25 | .10 | .02 |
| ☐ 657 | Bobby Murcer ............... | .80 | .32 | .08 |
| ☐ 658 | A.L. Rookies ................ | .25 | .10 | .02 |
| | Tom Hall | | | |
| | Bill Burbach | | | |
| | Jim Miles | | | |
| ☐ 659 | Johnny Podres .............. | .55 | .22 | .05 |
| ☐ 660 | Reggie Smith ................ | .85 | .34 | .08 |

| | | | | |
|---|---|---|---|---|
| ☐ 661 | Jim Merritt .................. | .25 | .10 | .02 |
| ☐ 662 | Royals Rookies .............. | .35 | .14 | .03 |
| | Dick Drago | | | |
| | George Spriggs | | | |
| | Bob Oliver | | | |
| ☐ 663 | Dick Radatz ................. | .35 | .14 | .03 |
| ☐ 664 | Ron Hunt .................... | .60 | .24 | .06 |

# 1969 Topps Deckle

The cards in this 33 card set measure 2 1/4" by 3 1/4". This unusual black and white insert set derives its name from the serrated border, or edge, of the cards. The cards were included as inserts in the regularly issued Topps baseball series of 1969. Card number 11 is found with either Hoyt Wilhelm or Jim Wynn, and number 22 with either Rusty Staub or Joe Foy. The set price below does include all variations.

| | | MINT | VG-E | F-G |
|---|---|---|---|---|
| | COMPLETE SET (35) ................ | 45.00 | 18.00 | 4.50 |
| | COMMON PLAYER .................... | .30 | .12 | .03 |
| ☐ 1 | Brooks Robinson ............. | 2.50 | 1.00 | .25 |
| ☐ 2 | Boog Powell ................. | .45 | .18 | .04 |
| ☐ 3 | Ken Harrelson ............... | .40 | .16 | .04 |
| ☐ 4 | Carl Yastrzemski ............ | 4.00 | 1.60 | .40 |
| ☐ 5 | Jim Fregosi ................. | .30 | .12 | .03 |
| ☐ 6 | Luis Aparicio ............... | 1.00 | .40 | .10 |
| ☐ 7 | Luis Tiant .................. | .40 | .16 | .04 |
| ☐ 8 | Denny McLain ............... | .40 | .16 | .04 |
| ☐ 9 | Willie Horton ............... | .30 | .12 | .03 |
| ☐ 10 | Bill Freehan ................ | .30 | .12 | .03 |
| ☐ 11A | Hoyt Wilhelm ................ | 5.00 | 2.00 | .50 |
| ☐ 11B | Jim Wynn ................... | 6.00 | 2.40 | .60 |
| ☐ 12 | Rod Carew .................. | 3.00 | 1.20 | .30 |
| ☐ 13 | Mel Stottlemyre ............. | .30 | .12 | .03 |
| ☐ 14 | Rick Monday ................ | .30 | .12 | .03 |
| ☐ 15 | Tommy Davis ................ | .30 | .12 | .03 |
| ☐ 16 | Frank Howard ............... | .40 | .16 | .04 |
| ☐ 17 | Felipe Alou ................. | .30 | .12 | .03 |
| ☐ 18 | Don Kessinger ............... | .30 | .12 | .03 |
| ☐ 19 | Ron Santo .................. | .40 | .16 | .04 |
| ☐ 20 | Tommy Helms ............... | .30 | .12 | .03 |
| ☐ 21 | Pete Rose .................. | 7.00 | 2.80 | .70 |
| ☐ 22A | Rusty Staub ................ | 3.00 | 1.20 | .30 |
| ☐ 22B | Joe Foy .................... | 6.00 | 2.40 | .60 |
| ☐ 23 | Tom Haller .................. | .30 | .12 | .03 |
| ☐ 24 | Maury Wills ................. | .60 | .24 | .06 |
| ☐ 25 | Jerry Koosman .............. | .40 | .16 | .04 |
| ☐ 26 | Richie Allen ................. | .40 | .16 | .04 |
| ☐ 27 | Bob Clemente ............... | 3.00 | 1.20 | .30 |
| ☐ 28 | Curt Flood ................. | .40 | .16 | .04 |
| ☐ 29 | Bob Gibson ................. | 1.75 | .70 | .17 |
| ☐ 30 | Al Ferrara .................. | .30 | .12 | .03 |
| ☐ 31 | Willie McCovey ............. | 2.00 | .80 | .20 |
| ☐ 32 | Juan Marichal ............... | 1.75 | .70 | .17 |
| ☐ 33 | Willie Mays ................. | 3.50 | 1.40 | .35 |

## 1969 Topps Super

| | | MINT | VG-E | F-G |
|---|---|---|---|---|
| ☐ 53 | Richie Allen | 11.00 | 4.50 | 1.10 |
| ☐ 54 | Chris Short | 8.00 | 3.25 | .80 |
| ☐ 55 | Cookie Rojas | 8.00 | 3.25 | .80 |
| ☐ 56 | Matty Alou | 8.00 | 3.25 | .80 |
| ☐ 57 | Steve Blass | 8.00 | 3.25 | .80 |
| ☐ 58 | Bob Clemente | 150.00 | 60.00 | 15.00 |
| ☐ 59 | Curt Flood | 12.00 | 5.00 | 1.20 |
| ☐ 60 | Bob Gibson | 60.00 | 24.00 | 6.00 |
| ☐ 61 | Tim McCarver | 9.00 | 3.75 | .90 |
| ☐ 62 | Dick Selma | 8.00 | 3.25 | .80 |
| ☐ 63 | Ollie Brown | 8.00 | 3.25 | .80 |
| ☐ 64 | Juan Marichal | 60.00 | 24.00 | 6.00 |
| ☐ 65 | Willie Mays | 200.00 | 80.00 | 20.00 |
| ☐ 66 | Willie McCovey | 75.00 | 30.00 | 7.50 |

## 1970 Topps

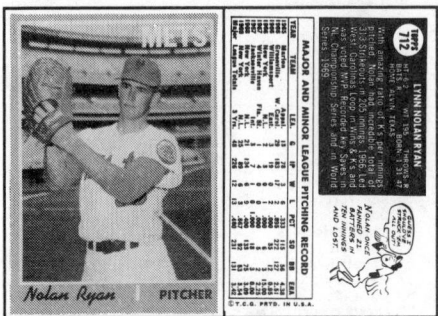

The cards in this 66 card set measure 2 1/4" by 3 1/4". This beautiful Topps set was released independently of the regular baseball series of 1969. It is referred to as "Super Baseball" on the back of the card, a title which was also used for the postcard size cards issued in 1970 and 1971. Complete sheets, and cards with square corners cut from these sheets, are sometimes encountered.

| | | MINT | VG-E | F-G |
|---|---|---|---|---|
| COMPLETE SET | | 2400.00 | 900.00 | 250.00 |
| COMMON PLAYER (1-66) | | 8.00 | 3.25 | .80 |
| ☐ 1 | Dave McNally | 10.00 | 4.00 | 1.00 |
| ☐ 2 | Frank Robinson | 100.00 | 40.00 | 10.00 |
| ☐ 3 | Brooks Robinson | 125.00 | 50.00 | 12.50 |
| ☐ 4 | Ken Harrelson | 10.00 | 4.00 | 1.00 |
| ☐ 5 | Carl Yastrzemski | 250.00 | 100.00 | 25.00 |
| ☐ 6 | Ray Culp | 8.00 | 3.25 | .80 |
| ☐ 7 | Jim Fregosi | 10.00 | 4.00 | 1.00 |
| ☐ 8 | Rick Reichardt | 8.00 | 3.25 | .80 |
| ☐ 9 | Vic Davalillo | 8.00 | 3.25 | .80 |
| ☐ 10 | Luis Aparicio | 35.00 | 14.00 | 3.50 |
| ☐ 11 | Pete Ward | 8.00 | 3.25 | .80 |
| ☐ 12 | Joe Horlen | 8.00 | 3.25 | .80 |
| ☐ 13 | Luis Tiant | 11.00 | 4.50 | 1.10 |
| ☐ 14 | Sam McDowell | 9.00 | 3.75 | .90 |
| ☐ 15 | Jose Cardenal | 8.00 | 3.25 | .80 |
| ☐ 16 | Willie Horton | 8.00 | 3.25 | .80 |
| ☐ 17 | Denny McLain | 12.00 | 5.00 | 1.20 |
| ☐ 18 | Bill Freehan | 9.00 | 3.75 | .90 |
| ☐ 19 | Harmon Killebrew | 60.00 | 24.00 | 6.00 |
| ☐ 20 | Tony Oliva | 14.00 | 5.75 | 1.40 |
| ☐ 21 | Dean Chance | 8.00 | 3.25 | .80 |
| ☐ 22 | Joe Foy | 8.00 | 3.25 | .80 |
| ☐ 23 | Roger Nelson | 8.00 | 3.25 | .80 |
| ☐ 24 | Mickey Mantle | 450.00 | 180.00 | 45.00 |
| ☐ 25 | Mel Stottlemyre | 9.00 | 3.75 | .90 |
| ☐ 26 | Roy White | 9.00 | 3.75 | .90 |
| ☐ 27 | Rick Monday | 9.00 | 3.75 | .90 |
| ☐ 28 | Reggie Jackson | 275.00 | 110.00 | 27.00 |
| ☐ 29 | Bert Campaneris | 9.00 | 3.75 | .90 |
| ☐ 30 | Frank Howard | 11.00 | 4.50 | 1.10 |
| ☐ 31 | Camilo Pascual | 8.00 | 3.25 | .80 |
| ☐ 32 | Tommy Davis | 9.00 | 3.75 | .90 |
| ☐ 33 | Don Mincher | 8.00 | 3.25 | .80 |
| ☐ 34 | Hank Aaron | 200.00 | 80.00 | 20.00 |
| ☐ 35 | Felipe Alou | 8.00 | 3.25 | .80 |
| ☐ 36 | Joe Torre | 12.00 | 5.00 | 1.20 |
| ☐ 37 | Fergie Jenkins | 15.00 | 6.00 | 1.50 |
| ☐ 38 | Ron Santo | 11.00 | 4.50 | 1.10 |
| ☐ 39 | Billy Williams | 35.00 | 14.00 | 3.50 |
| ☐ 40 | Tommy Helms | 8.00 | 3.25 | .80 |
| ☐ 41 | Pete Rose | 400.00 | 160.00 | 40.00 |
| ☐ 42 | Joe Morgan | 40.00 | 16.00 | 4.00 |
| ☐ 43 | Jim Wynn | 8.00 | 3.25 | .80 |
| ☐ 44 | Curt Blefary | 8.00 | 3.25 | .80 |
| ☐ 45 | Willie Davis | 9.00 | 3.75 | .90 |
| ☐ 46 | Don Drysdale | 40.00 | 16.00 | 4.00 |
| ☐ 47 | Tom Haller | 8.00 | 3.25 | .80 |
| ☐ 48 | Rusty Staub | 12.00 | 5.00 | 1.20 |
| ☐ 49 | Maury Wills | 14.00 | 5.75 | 1.40 |
| ☐ 50 | Cleon Jones | 8.00 | 3.25 | .80 |
| ☐ 51 | Jerry Koosman | 10.00 | 4.00 | 1.00 |
| ☐ 52 | Tom Seaver | 125.00 | 50.00 | 12.50 |

The cards in this 720 card set measure 2 1/2" by 3 1/2". The Topps set for 1970 has color photos surrounded by white frame lines and gray borders. The backs have a blue biographical section and a yellow record section. All Star selections are featured on cards 450 to 469. Other topical subsets within this set include League Leaders (61-72), Playoffs cards (195-202), and World Series cards (305-310). There are graduations of scarcity, terminating in the high series (634-720), which are outlined in the value summary.

| | | MINT | VG-E | F-G |
|---|---|---|---|---|
| COMPLETE SET | | 600.00 | 240.00 | 60.00 |
| COMMON PLAYER (1-132) | | .16 | .07 | .01 |
| COMMON PLAYER (133-459) | | .20 | .08 | .02 |
| COMMON PLAYER (460-546) | | .25 | .10 | .02 |
| COMMON PLAYER (547-633) | | .40 | .16 | .04 |
| COMMON PLAYER (634-720) | | 1.00 | .40 | .10 |
| ☐ 1 | New York Mets Team Card | 2.50 | .50 | .10 |
| ☐ 2 | Diego Segui | .20 | .08 | .02 |
| ☐ 3 | Darrel Chaney | .16 | .07 | .01 |
| ☐ 4 | Tom Egan | .16 | .07 | .01 |
| ☐ 5 | Wes Parker | .25 | .10 | .02 |
| ☐ 6 | Grant Jackson | .16 | .07 | .01 |
| ☐ 7 | Indians Rookies Gary Boyd Russ Nagelson | .16 | .07 | .01 |
| ☐ 8 | Jose Martinez | .16 | .07 | .01 |
| ☐ 9 | Checklist 1 | 1.25 | .12 | .02 |
| ☐ 10 | Carl Yastrzemski | 15.00 | 6.00 | 1.50 |
| ☐ 11 | Nate Colbert | .16 | .07 | .01 |
| ☐ 12 | John Hiller | .20 | .08 | .02 |
| ☐ 13 | Jack Hiatt | .16 | .07 | .01 |
| ☐ 14 | Hank Allen | .16 | .07 | .01 |
| ☐ 15 | Larry Dierker | .20 | .08 | .02 |
| ☐ 16 | Charlie Metro MGR | .16 | .07 | .01 |
| ☐ 17 | Hoyt Wilhelm | 2.25 | .90 | .22 |
| ☐ 18 | Carlos May | .20 | .08 | .02 |
| ☐ 19 | John Boccabella | .16 | .07 | .01 |
| ☐ 20 | Dave McNally | .30 | .12 | .03 |
| ☐ 21 | A's Rookies Vida Blue Gene Tenace | 1.75 | .70 | .17 |
| ☐ 22 | Ray Washburn | .16 | .07 | .01 |

| | | | | | |
|---|---|---|---|---|---|
| ☐ | 23 | Bill Robinson | .16 | .07 | .01 |
| ☐ | 24 | Dick Selma | .16 | .07 | .01 |
| ☐ | 25 | Cesar Tovar | .16 | .07 | .01 |
| ☐ | 26 | Tug McGraw | .60 | .24 | .06 |
| ☐ | 27 | Chuck Hinton | .16 | .07 | .01 |
| ☐ | 28 | Billy Wilson | .16 | .07 | .01 |
| ☐ | 29 | Sandy Alomar | .16 | .07 | .01 |
| ☐ | 30 | Matty Alou | .25 | .10 | .02 |
| ☐ | 31 | Marty Pattin | .20 | .08 | .02 |
| ☐ | 32 | Harry Walker MGR | .16 | .07 | .01 |
| ☐ | 33 | Don Wert | .16 | .07 | .01 |
| ☐ | 34 | Willie Crawford | .16 | .07 | .01 |
| ☐ | 35 | Joe Horlen | .16 | .07 | .01 |
| ☐ | 36 | Red Rookies | .16 | .07 | .01 |
| | | Danny Breeden | | | |
| | | Bernie Carbo | | | |
| ☐ | 37 | Dick Drago | .16 | .07 | .01 |
| ☐ | 38 | Mack Jones | .16 | .07 | .01 |
| ☐ | 39 | Mike Nagy | .16 | .07 | .01 |
| ☐ | 40 | Rich Allen | .60 | .24 | .06 |
| ☐ | 41 | George Lauzerique | .16 | .07 | .01 |
| ☐ | 42 | Tito Fuentes | .16 | .07 | .01 |
| ☐ | 43 | Jack Aker | .16 | .07 | .01 |
| ☐ | 44 | Roberto Pena | .16 | .07 | .01 |
| ☐ | 45 | Dave Johnson | .35 | .14 | .03 |
| ☐ | 46 | Ken Rudolph | .16 | .07 | .01 |
| ☐ | 47 | Bob Miller | .16 | .07 | .01 |
| ☐ | 48 | Gil Garrido | .16 | .07 | .01 |
| ☐ | 49 | Tim Cullen | .16 | .07 | .01 |
| ☐ | 50 | Tommie Agee | .20 | .08 | .02 |
| ☐ | 51 | Bob Christian | .16 | .07 | .01 |
| ☐ | 52 | Bruce Dal Canton | .16 | .07 | .01 |
| ☐ | 53 | John Kennedy | .20 | .08 | .02 |
| ☐ | 54 | Jeff Torborg | .16 | .07 | .01 |
| ☐ | 55 | John Odom | .16 | .07 | .01 |
| ☐ | 56 | Phillies Rookies | .16 | .07 | .01 |
| | | Joe Lis | | | |
| | | Scott Reid | | | |
| ☐ | 57 | Pat Kelly | .16 | .07 | .01 |
| ☐ | 58 | Dave Marshall | .16 | .07 | .01 |
| ☐ | 59 | Dick Ellsworth | .16 | .07 | .01 |
| ☐ | 60 | Jim Wynn | .25 | .10 | .02 |
| ☐ | 61 | NL Batting Leaders | 2.00 | .80 | .20 |
| | | Pete Rose | | | |
| | | Bob Clemente | | | |
| | | Cleon Jones | | | |
| ☐ | 62 | AL Batting Leaders | 1.00 | .40 | .10 |
| | | Rod Carew | | | |
| | | Reggie Smith | | | |
| | | Tony Oliva | | | |
| ☐ | 63 | NL RBI Leaders | .80 | .32 | .08 |
| | | Willie McCovey | | | |
| | | Ron Santo | | | |
| | | Tony Perez | | | |
| ☐ | 64 | AL RBI Leaders | 1.00 | .40 | .10 |
| | | Harmon Killebrew | | | |
| | | Boog Powell | | | |
| | | Reggie Jackson | | | |
| ☐ | 65 | NL Home Run Leaders | 1.25 | .50 | .12 |
| | | Willie McCovey | | | |
| | | Hank Aaron | | | |
| | | Lee May | | | |
| ☐ | 66 | AL Home Run Leaders | 1.25 | .50 | .12 |
| | | Harmon Killebrew | | | |
| | | Frank Howard | | | |
| | | Reggie Jackson | | | |
| ☐ | 67 | NL ERA Leaders | 2.00 | .80 | .20 |
| | | Juan Marichal | | | |
| | | Steve Carlton | | | |
| | | Bob Gibson | | | |
| ☐ | 68 | AL ERA Leaders | .70 | .28 | .07 |
| | | Dick Bosman | | | |
| | | Jim Palmer | | | |
| | | Mike Cuellar | | | |
| ☐ | 69 | NL Pitching Leaders | 2.00 | .80 | .20 |
| | | Tom Seaver | | | |
| | | Phil Niekro | | | |
| | | Fergie Jenkins | | | |
| | | Juan Marichal | | | |
| ☐ | 70 | AL Pitching Leaders | .50 | .20 | .05 |
| | | Dennis McLain | | | |
| | | Mike Cuellar | | | |
| | | Dave Boswell | | | |
| | | Dave McNally | | | |
| | | Jim Perry | | | |
| | | Mel Stottlemyre | | | |
| ☐ | 71 | NL Strikeout Leaders | .75 | .30 | .07 |
| | | Fergie Jenkins | | | |
| | | Bob Gibson | | | |
| | | Bill Singer | | | |
| ☐ | 72 | AL Strikeout Leaders | .50 | .20 | .05 |
| | | Sam McDowell | | | |
| | | Mickey Lolich | | | |

| | | | | | |
|---|---|---|---|---|---|
| | | Andy Messersmith | | | |
| ☐ | 73 | Wayne Granger | .16 | .07 | .01 |
| ☐ | 74 | Angels Rookies | .16 | .07 | .01 |
| | | Greg Washburn | | | |
| | | Wally Wolf | | | |
| ☐ | 75 | Jim Kaat | 1.00 | .40 | .10 |
| ☐ | 76 | Carl Taylor | .16 | .07 | .01 |
| ☐ | 77 | Frank Linzy | .16 | .07 | .01 |
| ☐ | 78 | Joe Lahoud | .16 | .07 | .01 |
| ☐ | 79 | Clay Kirby | .16 | .07 | .01 |
| ☐ | 80 | Don Kessinger | .25 | .10 | .02 |
| ☐ | 81 | Dave May | .16 | .07 | .01 |
| ☐ | 82 | Frank Fernandez | .16 | .07 | .01 |
| ☐ | 83 | Don Cardwell | .16 | .07 | .01 |
| ☐ | 84 | Paul Casanova | .16 | .07 | .01 |
| ☐ | 85 | Max Alvis | .16 | .07 | .01 |
| ☐ | 86 | Lum Harris MGR | .16 | .07 | .01 |
| ☐ | 87 | Steve Renko | .16 | .07 | .01 |
| ☐ | 88 | Pilots Rookies | .20 | .08 | .02 |
| | | Miguel Fuentes | | | |
| | | Dick Baney | | | |
| ☐ | 89 | Juan Rios | .16 | .07 | .01 |
| ☐ | 90 | Tim McCarver | .35 | .14 | .03 |
| ☐ | 91 | Rich Morales | .16 | .07 | .01 |
| ☐ | 92 | George Culver | .16 | .07 | .01 |
| ☐ | 93 | Rick Renick | .16 | .07 | .01 |
| ☐ | 94 | Fred Patek | .20 | .08 | .02 |
| ☐ | 95 | Earl Wilson | .16 | .07 | .01 |
| ☐ | 96 | Cardinals Rookies | 1.50 | .60 | .15 |
| | | Leron Lee | | | |
| | | Jerry Reuss | | | |
| ☐ | 97 | Joe Moeller | .16 | .07 | .01 |
| ☐ | 98 | Gates Brown | .20 | .08 | .02 |
| ☐ | 99 | Bobby Pfeil | .16 | .07 | .01 |
| ☐ | 100 | Mel Stottlemyre | .25 | .10 | .02 |
| ☐ | 101 | Bobby Floyd | .16 | .07 | .01 |
| ☐ | 102 | Joe Rudi | .30 | .12 | .03 |
| ☐ | 103 | Frank Reberger | .16 | .07 | .01 |
| ☐ | 104 | Gerry Moses | .16 | .07 | .01 |
| ☐ | 105 | Tony Gonzalez | .16 | .07 | .01 |
| ☐ | 106 | Darold Knowles | .16 | .07 | .01 |
| ☐ | 107 | Bobby Etheridge | .16 | .07 | .01 |
| ☐ | 108 | Tom Burgmeier | .20 | .08 | .02 |
| ☐ | 109 | Expos Rookies | .25 | .10 | .02 |
| | | Garry Jestadt | | | |
| | | Carl Morton | | | |
| ☐ | 110 | Bob Moose | .16 | .07 | .01 |
| ☐ | 111 | Mike Hegan | .20 | .08 | .02 |
| ☐ | 112 | Dave Nelson | .16 | .07 | .01 |
| ☐ | 113 | Jim Ray | .16 | .07 | .01 |
| ☐ | 114 | Gene Michael | .25 | .10 | .02 |
| ☐ | 115 | Alex Johnson | .20 | .08 | .02 |
| ☐ | 116 | Sparky Lyle | .55 | .22 | .05 |
| ☐ | 117 | Don Young | .16 | .07 | .01 |
| ☐ | 118 | George Mitterwald | .16 | .07 | .01 |
| ☐ | 119 | Chuck Taylor | .16 | .07 | .01 |
| ☐ | 120 | Sal Bando | .40 | .16 | .04 |
| ☐ | 121 | Orioles Rookies | .20 | .08 | .02 |
| | | Fred Beene | | | |
| | | Terry Crowley | | | |
| ☐ | 122 | George Stone | .16 | .07 | .01 |
| ☐ | 123 | Don Gutteridge | .16 | .07 | .01 |
| ☐ | 124 | Larry Jaster | .16 | .07 | .01 |
| ☐ | 125 | Deron Johnson | .16 | .07 | .01 |
| ☐ | 126 | Marty Martinez | .16 | .07 | .01 |
| ☐ | 127 | Joe Coleman | .16 | .07 | .01 |
| ☐ | 128 | Checklist 2 | 1.25 | .12 | .02 |
| ☐ | 129 | Jimmie Price | .16 | .07 | .01 |
| ☐ | 130 | Ollie Brown | .16 | .07 | .01 |
| ☐ | 131 | Dodgers Rookies | .16 | .07 | .01 |
| | | Ray Lamb | | | |
| | | Bob Stinson | | | |
| ☐ | 132 | Jim McGlothlin | .16 | .07 | .01 |
| ☐ | 133 | Clay Carroll | .20 | .08 | .02 |
| ☐ | 134 | Danny Walton | .25 | .10 | .02 |
| ☐ | 135 | Dick Dietz | .20 | .08 | .02 |
| ☐ | 136 | Steve Hargan | .20 | .08 | .02 |
| ☐ | 137 | Art Shamsky | .20 | .08 | .02 |
| ☐ | 138 | Joe Foy | .20 | .08 | .02 |
| ☐ | 139 | Rich Nye | .20 | .08 | .02 |
| ☐ | 140 | Reggie Jackson | 25.00 | 10.00 | 2.50 |
| ☐ | 141 | Pirates Rookies | .30 | .12 | .03 |
| | | Dave Cash | | | |
| | | Johnny Jeter | | | |
| ☐ | 142 | Fritz Peterson | .20 | .08 | .02 |
| ☐ | 143 | Phil Gagliano | .20 | .08 | .02 |
| ☐ | 144 | Ray Culp | .20 | .08 | .02 |
| ☐ | 145 | Rico Carty | .40 | .16 | .04 |
| ☐ | 146 | Danny Murphy | .20 | .08 | .02 |
| ☐ | 147 | Angel Hermoso | .20 | .08 | .02 |
| ☐ | 148 | Earl Weaver MGR | .75 | .30 | .07 |
| ☐ | 149 | Billy Champion | .20 | .08 | .02 |
| ☐ | 150 | Harmon Killebrew | 3.25 | 1.30 | .32 |

| | | | | |
|---|---|---|---|---|
| ☐ 151 | Dave Roberts | .20 | .08 | .02 |
| ☐ 152 | Ike Brown | .20 | .08 | .02 |
| ☐ 153 | Gary Gentry | .20 | .08 | .02 |
| ☐ 154 | Senators Rookies | .20 | .08 | .02 |
| | Jim Miles | | | |
| | Jan Dukes | | | |
| ☐ 155 | Denis Menke | .20 | .08 | .02 |
| ☐ 156 | Eddie Fisher | .20 | .08 | .02 |
| ☐ 157 | Manny Mota | .30 | .12 | .03 |
| ☐ 158 | Jerry McNertney | .25 | .10 | .02 |
| ☐ 159 | Tommy Helms | .25 | .10 | .02 |
| ☐ 160 | Phil Niekro | 2.00 | .80 | .20 |
| ☐ 161 | Richie Scheinblum | .20 | .08 | .02 |
| ☐ 162 | Jerry Johnson | .20 | .08 | .02 |
| ☐ 163 | Syd O'Brien | .20 | .08 | .02 |
| ☐ 164 | Ty Cline | .20 | .08 | .02 |
| ☐ 165 | Ed Kirkpatrick | .20 | .08 | .02 |
| ☐ 166 | Al Oliver | 1.50 | .60 | .15 |
| ☐ 167 | Bill Burbach | .20 | .08 | .02 |
| ☐ 168 | Dave Watkins | .20 | .08 | .02 |
| ☐ 169 | Tom Hall | .20 | .08 | .02 |
| ☐ 170 | Billy Williams | 2.50 | 1.00 | .25 |
| ☐ 171 | Jim Nash | .20 | .08 | .02 |
| ☐ 172 | Braves Rookies | .75 | .30 | .07 |
| | Garry Hill | | | |
| | Ralph Garr | | | |
| ☐ 173 | Jim Hicks | .20 | .08 | .02 |
| ☐ 174 | Ted Sizemore | .20 | .08 | .02 |
| ☐ 175 | Dick Bosman | .20 | .08 | .02 |
| ☐ 176 | Jim Ray Hart | .25 | .10 | .02 |
| ☐ 177 | Jim Northrup | .25 | .10 | .02 |
| ☐ 178 | Denny Lemaster | .20 | .08 | .02 |
| ☐ 179 | Ivan Murrell | .20 | .08 | .02 |
| ☐ 180 | Tommy John | 1.25 | .50 | .12 |
| ☐ 181 | Sparky Anderson MGR | .50 | .20 | .05 |
| ☐ 182 | Dick Hall | .20 | .08 | .02 |
| ☐ 183 | Jerry Grote | .20 | .08 | .02 |
| ☐ 184 | Ray Fosse | .20 | .08 | .02 |
| ☐ 185 | Don Mincher | .25 | .10 | .02 |
| ☐ 186 | Rick Joseph | .20 | .08 | .02 |
| ☐ 187 | Mike Hedlund | .20 | .08 | .02 |
| ☐ 188 | Manny Sanguillen | .35 | .14 | .03 |
| ☐ 189 | Yankees Rookies | 21.00 | 8.50 | 2.10 |
| | Thurman Munson | | | |
| | Dave McDonald | | | |
| ☐ 190 | Joe Torre | .60 | .24 | .06 |
| ☐ 191 | Vicente Romo | .20 | .08 | .02 |
| ☐ 192 | Jim Qualls | .20 | .08 | .02 |
| ☐ 193 | Mike Wegener | .20 | .08 | .02 |
| ☐ 194 | Chuck Manuel | .20 | .08 | .02 |
| ☐ 195 | NL Playoff Game 1 | 1.50 | .60 | .15 |
| | Seaver wins opener | | | |
| ☐ 196 | NL Playoff Game 2 | .75 | .30 | .07 |
| | Mets show muscle | | | |
| ☐ 197 | NL Playoff Game 3 | 1.50 | .60 | .15 |
| | Ryan saves the day | | | |
| ☐ 198 | NL Playoff Summary | .75 | .30 | .07 |
| | Mets celebrate | | | |
| ☐ 199 | AL Playoff Game 1 | .75 | .30 | .07 |
| | Orioles win | | | |
| | squeaker (Cuellar) | | | |
| ☐ 200 | AL Playoff Game 2 | .75 | .30 | .07 |
| | Powell scores | | | |
| | winning run | | | |
| ☐ 201 | AL Playoff Game 3 | .75 | .30 | .07 |
| | Birds wrap it up | | | |
| ☐ 202 | AL Playoff Summary | .75 | .30 | .07 |
| | Orioles celebrate | | | |
| ☐ 203 | Rudy May | .20 | .08 | .02 |
| ☐ 204 | Len Gabrielson | .20 | .08 | .02 |
| ☐ 205 | Bert Campaneris | .35 | .14 | .03 |
| ☐ 206 | Clete Boyer | .35 | .14 | .03 |
| ☐ 207 | Tigers Rookies | .20 | .08 | .02 |
| | Norman McRae | | | |
| | Bob Reed | | | |
| ☐ 208 | Fred Gladding | .20 | .08 | .02 |
| ☐ 209 | Ken Suarez | .20 | .08 | .02 |
| ☐ 210 | Juan Marichal | 2.50 | 1.00 | .25 |
| ☐ 211 | Ted Williams MGR | 3.00 | 1.20 | .30 |
| ☐ 212 | Al Santorini | .20 | .08 | .02 |
| ☐ 213 | Andy Etchebarren | .20 | .08 | .02 |
| ☐ 214 | Ken Boswell | .20 | .08 | .02 |
| ☐ 215 | Reggie Smith | .75 | .30 | .07 |
| ☐ 216 | Chuck Hartenstein | .20 | .08 | .02 |
| ☐ 217 | Ron Hansen | .20 | .08 | .02 |
| ☐ 218 | Ron Stone | .20 | .08 | .02 |
| ☐ 219 | Jerry Kenney | .20 | .08 | .02 |
| ☐ 220 | Steve Carlton | 10.00 | 4.00 | 1.00 |
| ☐ 221 | Ron Brand | .20 | .08 | .02 |
| ☐ 222 | Jim Rooker | .20 | .08 | .02 |
| ☐ 223 | Nate Oliver | .20 | .08 | .02 |
| ☐ 224 | Steve Barber | .25 | .10 | .02 |
| ☐ 225 | Lee May | .35 | .14 | .03 |

| | | | | |
|---|---|---|---|---|
| ☐ 226 | Ron Perranoski | .30 | .12 | .03 |
| ☐ 227 | Astros Rookies | .60 | .24 | .06 |
| | John Mayberry | | | |
| | Bob Watkins | | | |
| ☐ 228 | Aurelio Rodriguez | .25 | .10 | .02 |
| ☐ 229 | Rich Robertson | .20 | .08 | .02 |
| ☐ 230 | Brooks Robinson | 4.00 | 1.60 | .40 |
| ☐ 231 | Luis Tiant | .55 | .22 | .05 |
| ☐ 232 | Bob Didier | .20 | .08 | .02 |
| ☐ 233 | Lew Krausse | .20 | .08 | .02 |
| ☐ 234 | Tommy Dean | .20 | .08 | .02 |
| ☐ 235 | Mike Epstein | .20 | .08 | .02 |
| ☐ 236 | Bob Veale | .25 | .10 | .02 |
| ☐ 237 | Russ Gibson | .20 | .08 | .02 |
| ☐ 238 | Jose Laboy | .20 | .08 | .02 |
| ☐ 239 | Ken Berry | .20 | .08 | .02 |
| ☐ 240 | Fergie Jenkins | 1.00 | .40 | .10 |
| ☐ 241 | Royals Rookies | .20 | .08 | .02 |
| | Al Fitzmorris | | | |
| | Scott Northey | | | |
| ☐ 242 | Walter Alston MGR | .75 | .30 | .07 |
| ☐ 243 | Joe Sparma | .20 | .08 | .02 |
| ☐ 244A | Checklist 3 | 1.25 | .12 | .02 |
| | (red bat on front) | | | |
| ☐ 244B | Checklist 3 | 1.50 | .15 | .03 |
| | (brown bat on front) | | | |
| ☐ 245 | Leo Cardenas | .20 | .08 | .02 |
| ☐ 246 | Jim McAndrew | .20 | .08 | .02 |
| ☐ 247 | Lou Klimchock | .20 | .08 | .02 |
| ☐ 248 | Jesus Alou | .20 | .08 | .02 |
| ☐ 249 | Bob Locker | .25 | .10 | .02 |
| ☐ 250 | Willie McCovey | 3.50 | 1.40 | .35 |
| ☐ 251 | Dick Schofield | .20 | .08 | .02 |
| ☐ 252 | Lowell Palmer | .20 | .08 | .02 |
| ☐ 253 | Ron Woods | .20 | .08 | .02 |
| ☐ 254 | Camilo Pascual | .25 | .10 | .02 |
| ☐ 255 | Jim Spencer | .20 | .08 | .02 |
| ☐ 256 | Vic Davalillo | .20 | .08 | .02 |
| ☐ 257 | Dennis Higgins | .20 | .08 | .02 |
| ☐ 258 | Paul Popovich | .20 | .08 | .02 |
| ☐ 259 | Tommie Reynolds | .20 | .08 | .02 |
| ☐ 260 | Claude Osteen | .25 | .10 | .02 |
| ☐ 261 | Curt Motton | .20 | .08 | .02 |
| ☐ 262 | Twins Rookies | .20 | .08 | .02 |
| | Jerry Morales | | | |
| | Jim Williams | | | |
| ☐ 263 | Duane Josephson | .20 | .08 | .02 |
| ☐ 264 | Rich Hebner | .25 | .10 | .02 |
| ☐ 265 | Randy Hundley | .25 | .10 | .02 |
| ☐ 266 | Wally Bunker | .20 | .08 | .02 |
| ☐ 267 | Twins Rookies | .20 | .08 | .02 |
| | Herman Hill | | | |
| | Paul Ratliff | | | |
| ☐ 268 | Claude Raymond | .20 | .08 | .02 |
| ☐ 269 | Cesar Gutierrez | .20 | .08 | .02 |
| ☐ 270 | Chris Short | .20 | .08 | .02 |
| ☐ 271 | Greg Goossen | .25 | .10 | .02 |
| ☐ 272 | Hector Torres | .20 | .08 | .02 |
| ☐ 273 | Ralph Houk MGR | .35 | .14 | .03 |
| ☐ 274 | Gerry Arrigo | .20 | .08 | .02 |
| ☐ 275 | Duke Sims | .20 | .08 | .02 |
| ☐ 276 | Ron Hunt | .20 | .08 | .02 |
| ☐ 277 | Paul Doyle | .20 | .08 | .02 |
| ☐ 278 | Tommie Aaron | .30 | .12 | .03 |
| ☐ 279 | Bill Lee | .30 | .12 | .03 |
| ☐ 280 | Donn Clendenon | .30 | .12 | .03 |
| ☐ 281 | Casey Cox | .20 | .08 | .02 |
| ☐ 282 | Steve Huntz | .20 | .08 | .02 |
| ☐ 283 | Angel Bravo | .20 | .08 | .02 |
| ☐ 284 | Jack Baldschun | .20 | .08 | .02 |
| ☐ 285 | Paul Blair | .25 | .10 | .02 |
| ☐ 286 | Dodgers Rookies | 5.00 | 2.00 | .50 |
| | Jack Jenkins | | | |
| | Bill Buckner | | | |
| ☐ 287 | Fred Talbot | .20 | .08 | .02 |
| ☐ 288 | Larry Hisle | .30 | .12 | .03 |
| ☐ 289 | Gene Brabender | .25 | .10 | .02 |
| ☐ 290 | Rod Carew | 11.00 | 4.50 | 1.10 |
| ☐ 291 | Leo Durocher MGR | .60 | .24 | .06 |
| ☐ 292 | Eddie Leon | .20 | .08 | .02 |
| ☐ 293 | Bob Bailey | .20 | .08 | .02 |
| ☐ 294 | Jose Azcue | .20 | .08 | .02 |
| ☐ 295 | Cecil Upshaw | .20 | .08 | .02 |
| ☐ 296 | Woody Woodward | .20 | .08 | .02 |
| ☐ 297 | Curt Blefary | .20 | .08 | .02 |
| ☐ 298 | Ken Henderson | .20 | .08 | .02 |
| ☐ 299 | Buddy Bradford | .20 | .08 | .02 |
| ☐ 300 | Tom Seaver | 15.00 | 6.00 | 1.50 |
| ☐ 301 | Chico Salmon | .20 | .08 | .02 |
| ☐ 302 | Jeff James | .20 | .08 | .02 |
| ☐ 303 | Brant Alyea | .20 | .08 | .02 |
| ☐ 304 | Bill Russell | 1.50 | .60 | .15 |
| ☐ 305 | World Series Game 1 | .75 | .30 | .07 |

|  |  | | |
|---|---|---|---|
| | Buford leadoff homer | | |
| ☐ 306 | World Series Game 2 ...... .75 | .30 | .07 |
| | Clendenon's homer | | |
| | breaks ice | | |
| ☐ 307 | World Series Game 3 ...... .75 | .30 | .07 |
| | Agee's catch | | |
| | saves the day | | |
| ☐ 308 | World Series Game 4 ...... .75 | .30 | .07 |
| | Martin's bunt | | |
| | ends deadlock | | |
| ☐ 309 | World Series Game 5 ...... .75 | .30 | .07 |
| | Koosman shuts door | | |
| ☐ 310 | World Series Summary ... .75 | .30 | .07 |
| | Mets whoop it up | | |
| ☐ 311 | Dick Green ...... .20 | .08 | .02 |
| ☐ 312 | Mike Torrez ...... .35 | .14 | .03 |
| ☐ 313 | Mayo Smith MGR ...... .20 | .08 | .02 |
| ☐ 314 | Bill McCool ...... .20 | .08 | .02 |
| ☐ 315 | Luis Aparicio ...... 2.25 | .90 | .22 |
| ☐ 316 | Skip Guinn ...... .20 | .08 | .02 |
| ☐ 317 | Red Sox Rookies ...... .30 | .12 | .03 |
| | Billy Conigliaro | | |
| | Luis Alvarado | | |
| ☐ 318 | Willie Smith ...... .20 | .08 | .02 |
| ☐ 319 | Clay Dalrymple ...... .20 | .08 | .02 |
| ☐ 320 | Jim Maloney ...... .25 | .10 | .02 |
| ☐ 321 | Lou Piniella ...... .80 | .32 | .08 |
| ☐ 322 | Luke Walker ...... .20 | .08 | .02 |
| ☐ 323 | Wayne Comer ...... .25 | .10 | .02 |
| ☐ 324 | Tony Taylor ...... .20 | .08 | .02 |
| ☐ 325 | Dave Boswell ...... .20 | .08 | .02 |
| ☐ 326 | Bill Voss ...... .20 | .08 | .02 |
| ☐ 327 | Hal King ...... .20 | .08 | .02 |
| ☐ 328 | George Brunet ...... .20 | .08 | .02 |
| ☐ 329 | Chris Cannizzaro ...... .20 | .08 | .02 |
| ☐ 330 | Lou Brock ...... 3.50 | 1.40 | .35 |
| ☐ 331 | Chuck Dobson ...... .20 | .08 | .02 |
| ☐ 332 | Bobby Wine ...... .20 | .08 | .02 |
| ☐ 333 | Bobby Murcer ...... .70 | .28 | .07 |
| ☐ 334 | Phil Regan ...... .25 | .10 | .02 |
| ☐ 335 | Bill Freehan ...... .40 | .16 | .04 |
| ☐ 336 | Del Unser ...... .20 | .08 | .02 |
| ☐ 337 | Mike McCormick ...... .30 | .12 | .03 |
| ☐ 338 | Paul Schaal ...... .20 | .08 | .02 |
| ☐ 339 | Johnny Edwards ...... .20 | .08 | .02 |
| ☐ 340 | Tony Conigliaro ...... .45 | .18 | .04 |
| ☐ 341 | Bill Sudakis ...... .20 | .08 | .02 |
| ☐ 342 | Wilbur Wood ...... .25 | .10 | .02 |
| ☐ 343A | Checklist 4 ...... 1.25 | .12 | .02 |
| | (red bat on front) | | |
| ☐ 343B | Checklist 4 ...... 1.50 | .15 | .03 |
| | (brown bat on front) | | |
| ☐ 344 | Marcelino Lopez ...... .20 | .08 | .02 |
| ☐ 345 | Al Ferrara ...... .20 | .08 | .02 |
| ☐ 346 | Red Schoendienst MGR .. .40 | .16 | .04 |
| ☐ 347 | Russ Snyder ...... .20 | .08 | .02 |
| ☐ 348 | Mets Rookies ...... .25 | .10 | .02 |
| | Mike Jorgensen | | |
| | Jesse Hudson | | |
| ☐ 349 | Steve Hamilton ...... .20 | .08 | .02 |
| ☐ 350 | Roberto Clemente ...... 12.00 | 5.00 | 1.20 |
| ☐ 351 | Tom Murphy ...... .20 | .08 | .02 |
| ☐ 352 | Bob Barton ...... .20 | .08 | .02 |
| ☐ 353 | Stan Williams ...... .20 | .08 | .02 |
| ☐ 354 | Amos Otis ...... .35 | .14 | .03 |
| ☐ 355 | Doug Rader ...... .30 | .12 | .03 |
| ☐ 356 | Fred Lasher ...... .20 | .08 | .02 |
| ☐ 357 | Bob Burda ...... .20 | .08 | .02 |
| ☐ 358 | Pedro Borbon ...... .20 | .08 | .02 |
| ☐ 359 | Phil Roof ...... .25 | .10 | .02 |
| ☐ 360 | Curt Flood ...... .40 | .16 | .04 |
| ☐ 361 | Ray Jarvis ...... .20 | .08 | .02 |
| ☐ 362 | Joe Hague ...... .20 | .08 | .02 |
| ☐ 363 | Tom Shopay ...... .20 | .08 | .02 |
| ☐ 364 | Dan McGinn ...... .20 | .08 | .02 |
| ☐ 365 | Zoilo Versalles ...... .20 | .08 | .02 |
| ☐ 366 | Barry Moore ...... .20 | .08 | .02 |
| ☐ 367 | Mike Lum ...... .20 | .08 | .02 |
| ☐ 368 | Ed Herrmann ...... .20 | .08 | .02 |
| ☐ 369 | Alan Foster ...... .20 | .08 | .02 |
| ☐ 370 | Tommy Harper ...... .25 | .10 | .02 |
| ☐ 371 | Rod Gaspar ...... .20 | .08 | .02 |
| ☐ 372 | Dave Giusti ...... .20 | .08 | .02 |
| ☐ 373 | Roy White ...... .30 | .12 | .03 |
| ☐ 374 | Tommie Sisk ...... .20 | .08 | .02 |
| ☐ 375 | Johnny Callison ...... .25 | .10 | .02 |
| ☐ 376 | Lefty Phillips MGR ...... .20 | .08 | .02 |
| ☐ 377 | Bill Butler ...... .20 | .08 | .02 |
| ☐ 378 | Jim Davenport ...... .30 | .12 | .03 |
| ☐ 379 | Tom Tischinski ...... .20 | .08 | .02 |
| ☐ 380 | Tony Perez ...... 1.25 | .50 | .12 |
| ☐ 381 | Athletics Rookies ...... .20 | .08 | .02 |
| | Bobby Brooks | | |

|  |  | | |
|---|---|---|---|
| | Mike Olivo | | |
| ☐ 382 | Jack DiLauro ...... .20 | .08 | .02 |
| ☐ 383 | Mickey Stanley ...... .25 | .10 | .02 |
| ☐ 384 | Gary Neibauer ...... .20 | .08 | .02 |
| ☐ 385 | George Scott ...... .25 | .10 | .02 |
| ☐ 386 | Bill Dillman ...... .20 | .08 | .02 |
| ☐ 387 | Orioles Team ...... .70 | .28 | .07 |
| ☐ 388 | Byron Browne ...... .20 | .08 | .02 |
| ☐ 389 | Jim Shellenback ...... .20 | .08 | .02 |
| ☐ 390 | Willie Davis ...... .40 | .16 | .04 |
| ☐ 391 | Larry Brown ...... .20 | .08 | .02 |
| ☐ 392 | Walt Hriniak ...... .20 | .08 | .02 |
| ☐ 393 | John Gelnar ...... .25 | .10 | .02 |
| ☐ 394 | Gil Hodges MGR ...... 2.00 | .80 | .20 |
| ☐ 395 | Walt Williams ...... .20 | .08 | .02 |
| ☐ 396 | Steve Blass ...... .25 | .10 | .02 |
| ☐ 397 | Roger Repoz ...... .20 | .08 | .02 |
| ☐ 398 | Bill Stoneman ...... .20 | .08 | .02 |
| ☐ 399 | Yankees Team ...... .75 | .30 | .07 |
| ☐ 400 | Denny McLain ...... .65 | .26 | .06 |
| ☐ 401 | Giants Rookies ...... .20 | .08 | .02 |
| | John Harrell | | |
| | Bernie Williams | | |
| ☐ 402 | Ellie Rodriguez ...... .20 | .08 | .02 |
| ☐ 403 | Jim Bunning ...... 1.00 | .40 | .10 |
| ☐ 404 | Rich Reese ...... .20 | .08 | .02 |
| ☐ 405 | Bill Hands ...... .20 | .08 | .02 |
| ☐ 406 | Mike Andrews ...... .20 | .08 | .02 |
| ☐ 407 | Bob Watson ...... .40 | .16 | .04 |
| ☐ 408 | Paul Lindblad ...... .20 | .08 | .02 |
| ☐ 409 | Bob Tolan ...... .20 | .08 | .02 |
| ☐ 410 | Boog Powell ...... 1.25 | .50 | .12 |
| ☐ 411 | Dodgers Team ...... .75 | .30 | .07 |
| ☐ 412 | Larry Burchart ...... .20 | .08 | .02 |
| ☐ 413 | Sonny Jackson ...... .20 | .08 | .02 |
| ☐ 414 | Paul Edmondson ...... .20 | .08 | .02 |
| ☐ 415 | Julian Javier ...... .20 | .08 | .02 |
| ☐ 416 | Joe Verbanic ...... .20 | .08 | .02 |
| ☐ 417 | John Bateman ...... .20 | .08 | .02 |
| ☐ 418 | John Donaldson ...... .25 | .10 | .02 |
| ☐ 419 | Ron Taylor ...... .20 | .08 | .02 |
| ☐ 420 | Ken McMullen ...... .20 | .08 | .02 |
| ☐ 421 | Pat Dobson ...... .25 | .10 | .02 |
| ☐ 422 | Royals Team ...... .55 | .22 | .05 |
| ☐ 423 | Jerry May ...... .20 | .08 | .02 |
| ☐ 424 | Mike Kilkenny ...... .20 | .08 | .02 |
| ☐ 425 | Bobby Bonds ...... .75 | .30 | .07 |
| ☐ 426 | Bill Rigney MGR ...... .20 | .08 | .02 |
| ☐ 427 | Fred Norman ...... .20 | .08 | .02 |
| ☐ 428 | Don Buford ...... .20 | .08 | .02 |
| ☐ 429 | Cubs Rookies ...... .20 | .08 | .02 |
| | Randy Bobb | | |
| | Jim Cosman | | |
| ☐ 430 | Andy Messersmith ...... .45 | .18 | .04 |
| ☐ 431 | Ron Swoboda ...... .25 | .10 | .02 |
| ☐ 432A | Checklist 5 ...... 1.25 | .12 | .02 |
| | ("Baseball" in | | |
| | yellow letters) | | |
| ☐ 432B | Checklist 5 ...... 1.50 | .15 | .03 |
| | ("Baseball" in | | |
| | white letters) | | |
| ☐ 433 | Ron Bryant ...... .20 | .08 | .02 |
| ☐ 434 | Felipe Alou ...... .25 | .10 | .02 |
| ☐ 435 | Nelson Briles ...... .25 | .10 | .02 |
| ☐ 436 | Phillies Team ...... .55 | .22 | .05 |
| ☐ 437 | Danny Cater ...... .20 | .08 | .02 |
| ☐ 438 | Pat Jarvis ...... .20 | .08 | .02 |
| ☐ 439 | Lee Maye ...... .20 | .08 | .02 |
| ☐ 440 | Bill Mazeroski ...... .50 | .20 | .05 |
| ☐ 441 | John O'Donoghue ...... .25 | .10 | .02 |
| ☐ 442 | Gene Mauch MGR ...... .30 | .12 | .03 |
| ☐ 443 | Al Jackson ...... .20 | .08 | .02 |
| ☐ 444 | White Sox Rookies ...... .20 | .08 | .02 |
| | Billy Farmer | | |
| | John Matias | | |
| ☐ 445 | Vada Pinson ...... .60 | .24 | .06 |
| ☐ 446 | Billy Grabarkewitz ...... .20 | .08 | .02 |
| ☐ 447 | Lee Stange ...... .20 | .08 | .02 |
| ☐ 448 | Astros Team ...... .55 | .22 | .05 |
| ☐ 449 | Jim Palmer ...... 6.00 | 2.40 | .60 |
| ☐ 450 | Willie McCovey AS ...... 2.00 | .80 | .20 |
| ☐ 451 | Boog Powell AS ...... .45 | .18 | .04 |
| ☐ 452 | Felix Millan AS ...... .25 | .10 | .02 |
| ☐ 453 | Rod Carew AS ...... 3.00 | 1.20 | .30 |
| ☐ 454 | Ron Santo AS ...... .25 | .10 | .02 |
| ☐ 455 | Brooks Robinson AS ...... 2.25 | .90 | .22 |
| ☐ 456 | Don Kessinger AS ...... .25 | .10 | .02 |
| ☐ 457 | Rico Petrocelli AS ...... .25 | .10 | .02 |
| ☐ 458 | Pete Rose AS ...... 6.50 | 2.60 | .65 |
| ☐ 459 | Reggie Jackson AS ...... 4.50 | 1.80 | .45 |
| ☐ 460 | Matty Alou AS ...... .25 | .10 | .02 |
| ☐ 461 | Carl Yastrzemski AS ...... 3.50 | 1.40 | .35 |
| ☐ 462 | Hank Aaron AS ...... 3.50 | 1.40 | .35 |

| | | | | |
|---|---|---:|---:|---:|
| ☐ 463 | Frank Robinson AS | 2.00 | .80 | .20 |
| ☐ 464 | Johnny Bench AS | 3.25 | 1.30 | .32 |
| ☐ 465 | Bill Freehan AS | .25 | .10 | .02 |
| ☐ 466 | Juan Marichal AS | 1.75 | .70 | .17 |
| ☐ 467 | Denny McLain AS | .35 | .14 | .03 |
| ☐ 468 | Jerry Koosman AS | .25 | .10 | .02 |
| ☐ 469 | Sam McDowell AS | .25 | .10 | .02 |
| ☐ 470 | Willie Stargell | 3.00 | 1.20 | .30 |
| ☐ 471 | Chris Zachary | .45 | .18 | .04 |
| ☐ 472 | Braves Team | .60 | .24 | .06 |
| ☐ 473 | Don Bryant | .25 | .10 | .02 |
| ☐ 474 | Dick Kelley | .25 | .10 | .02 |
| ☐ 475 | Dick McAuliffe | .25 | .10 | .02 |
| ☐ 476 | Don Shaw | .25 | .10 | .02 |
| ☐ 477 | Orioles Rookies | .25 | .10 | .02 |
| | Al Severinsen | | | |
| | Roger Freed | | | |
| ☐ 478 | Bob Heise | .25 | .10 | .02 |
| ☐ 479 | Dick Woodson | .25 | .10 | .02 |
| ☐ 480 | Glen Beckert | .35 | .14 | .03 |
| ☐ 481 | Jose Tartabull | .25 | .10 | .02 |
| ☐ 482 | Tom Hilgendorf | .25 | .10 | .02 |
| ☐ 483 | Gail Hopkins | .25 | .10 | .02 |
| ☐ 484 | Gary Nolan | .25 | .10 | .02 |
| ☐ 485 | Jay Johnstone | .35 | .14 | .03 |
| ☐ 486 | Terry Harmon | .25 | .10 | .02 |
| ☐ 487 | Cisco Carlos | .25 | .10 | .02 |
| ☐ 488 | J.C. Martin | .25 | .10 | .02 |
| ☐ 489 | Eddie Kasko MGR | .25 | .10 | .02 |
| ☐ 490 | Bill Singer | .25 | .10 | .02 |
| ☐ 491 | Graig Nettles | 2.25 | .90 | .22 |
| ☐ 492 | Astros Rookies | .25 | .10 | .02 |
| | Keith Lampard | | | |
| | Scipio Spinks | | | |
| ☐ 493 | Lindy McDaniel | .25 | .10 | .02 |
| ☐ 494 | Larry Stahl | .25 | .10 | .02 |
| ☐ 495 | Dave Morehead | .25 | .10 | .02 |
| ☐ 496 | Steve Whitaker | .25 | .10 | .02 |
| ☐ 497 | Eddie Watt | .25 | .10 | .02 |
| ☐ 498 | Al Weis | .25 | .10 | .02 |
| ☐ 499 | Skip Lockwood | .25 | .10 | .02 |
| ☐ 500 | Hank Aaron | 14.00 | 5.75 | 1.40 |
| ☐ 501 | White Sox Team | .60 | .24 | .06 |
| ☐ 502 | Rollie Fingers | 2.50 | 1.00 | .25 |
| ☐ 503 | Dal Maxvill | .25 | .10 | .02 |
| ☐ 504 | Don Pavletich | .25 | .10 | .02 |
| ☐ 505 | Ken Holtzman | .35 | .14 | .03 |
| ☐ 506 | Ed Stroud | .25 | .10 | .02 |
| ☐ 507 | Pat Corrales | .35 | .14 | .03 |
| ☐ 508 | Joe Niekro | .45 | .18 | .04 |
| ☐ 509 | Expos Team | .60 | .24 | .06 |
| ☐ 510 | Tony Oliva | 1.00 | .40 | .10 |
| ☐ 511 | Joe Hoerner | .25 | .10 | .02 |
| ☐ 512 | Billy Harris | .25 | .10 | .02 |
| ☐ 513 | Preston Gomez MGR | .25 | .10 | .02 |
| ☐ 514 | Steve Hovley | .25 | .10 | .02 |
| ☐ 515 | Don Wilson | .25 | .10 | .02 |
| ☐ 516 | Yankees Rookies | .25 | .10 | .02 |
| | John Ellis | | | |
| | Jim Lyttle | | | |
| ☐ 517 | Joe Gibbon | .25 | .10 | .02 |
| ☐ 518 | Bill Melton | .25 | .10 | .02 |
| ☐ 519 | Don McMahon | .25 | .10 | .02 |
| ☐ 520 | Willie Horton | .50 | .20 | .05 |
| ☐ 521 | Cal Koonce | .25 | .10 | .02 |
| ☐ 522 | Angels Team | .60 | .24 | .06 |
| ☐ 523 | Jose Pena | .25 | .10 | .02 |
| ☐ 524 | Alvin Dark MGR | .25 | .10 | .02 |
| ☐ 525 | Jerry Adair | .25 | .10 | .02 |
| ☐ 526 | Ron Herbel | .25 | .10 | .02 |
| ☐ 527 | Don Bosch | .25 | .10 | .02 |
| ☐ 528 | Elrod Hendricks | .25 | .10 | .02 |
| ☐ 529 | Bob Aspromonte | .25 | .10 | .02 |
| ☐ 530 | Bob Gibson | 3.50 | 1.40 | .35 |
| ☐ 531 | Ron Clark | .25 | .10 | .02 |
| ☐ 532 | Danny Murtaugh MGR | .25 | .10 | .02 |
| ☐ 533 | Buzz Stephen | .25 | .10 | .02 |
| ☐ 534 | Twins Team | .60 | .24 | .06 |
| ☐ 535 | Andy Kosco | .25 | .10 | .02 |
| ☐ 536 | Mike Kekich | .25 | .10 | .02 |
| ☐ 537 | Joe Morgan | 2.25 | .90 | .22 |
| ☐ 538 | Bob Humphreys | .25 | .10 | .02 |
| ☐ 539 | Phillies Rookies | 2.50 | 1.00 | .25 |
| | Dennis Doyle | | | |
| | Larry Bowa | | | |
| ☐ 540 | Gary Peters | .35 | .14 | .03 |
| ☐ 541 | Bill Heath | .25 | .10 | .02 |
| ☐ 542 | Checklist 6 | 1.50 | .15 | .03 |
| ☐ 543 | Clyde Wright | .25 | .10 | .02 |
| ☐ 544 | Reds Team | .80 | .32 | .08 |
| ☐ 545 | Ken Harrelson | .75 | .30 | .07 |
| ☐ 546 | Ron Reed | .25 | .10 | .02 |
| ☐ 547 | Rick Monday | .60 | .24 | .06 |
| ☐ 548 | Howie Reed | .40 | .16 | .04 |
| ☐ 549 | Cardinals Team | .90 | .36 | .09 |
| ☐ 550 | Frank Howard | .85 | .34 | .08 |
| ☐ 551 | Dock Ellis | .40 | .16 | .04 |
| ☐ 552 | Royals Rookies | .40 | .16 | .04 |
| | Don O'Riley | | | |
| | Dennis Paepke | | | |
| | Fred Rico | | | |
| ☐ 553 | Jim Lefebvre | .40 | .16 | .04 |
| ☐ 554 | Tom Timmermann | .40 | .16 | .04 |
| ☐ 555 | Orlando Cepeda | 1.75 | .70 | .17 |
| ☐ 556 | Dave Bristol MGR | .40 | .16 | .04 |
| ☐ 557 | Ed Kranepool | .50 | .20 | .05 |
| ☐ 558 | Vern Fuller | .40 | .16 | .04 |
| ☐ 559 | Tommy Davis | .60 | .24 | .06 |
| ☐ 560 | Gaylord Perry | 3.50 | 1.40 | .35 |
| ☐ 561 | Tom McCraw | .40 | .16 | .04 |
| ☐ 562 | Ted Abernathy | .40 | .16 | .04 |
| ☐ 563 | Red Sox Team | .80 | .32 | .08 |
| ☐ 564 | Johnny Briggs | .40 | .16 | .04 |
| ☐ 565 | Jim Hunter | 3.50 | 1.40 | .35 |
| ☐ 566 | Gene Alley | .50 | .20 | .05 |
| ☐ 567 | Bob Oliver | .40 | .16 | .04 |
| ☐ 568 | Stan Bahnsen | .40 | .16 | .04 |
| ☐ 569 | Cookie Rojas | .40 | .16 | .04 |
| ☐ 570 | Jim Fregosi | .60 | .24 | .06 |
| ☐ 571 | Jim Brewer | .40 | .16 | .04 |
| ☐ 572 | Frank Quilici MGR | .40 | .16 | .04 |
| ☐ 573 | Padres Rookies | .40 | .16 | .04 |
| | Mike Corkins | | | |
| | Rafael Robles | | | |
| | Ron Slocum | | | |
| ☐ 574 | Bobby Bolin | .40 | .16 | .04 |
| ☐ 575 | Cleon Jones | .40 | .16 | .04 |
| ☐ 576 | Milt Pappas | .50 | .20 | .05 |
| ☐ 577 | Bernie Allen | .40 | .16 | .04 |
| ☐ 578 | Tom Griffin | .40 | .16 | .04 |
| ☐ 579 | Tigers Team | .90 | .36 | .09 |
| ☐ 580 | Pete Rose | 55.00 | 22.00 | 5.50 |
| ☐ 581 | Tom Satriano | .40 | .16 | .04 |
| ☐ 582 | Mike Paul | .40 | .16 | .04 |
| ☐ 583 | Hal Lanier | .60 | .24 | .06 |
| ☐ 584 | Al Downing | .50 | .20 | .05 |
| ☐ 585 | Rusty Staub | 1.00 | .40 | .10 |
| ☐ 586 | Rickey Clark | .40 | .16 | .04 |
| ☐ 587 | Jose Arcia | .40 | .16 | .04 |
| ☐ 588A | Checklist 7 | 1.75 | .15 | .03 |
| | (666 Adolpho) | | | |
| ☐ 588B | Checklist 7 | 3.50 | .35 | .07 |
| | (666 Adolfo) | | | |
| ☐ 589 | Joe Keough | .40 | .16 | .04 |
| ☐ 590 | Mike Cuellar | .60 | .24 | .06 |
| ☐ 591 | Mike Ryan | .40 | .16 | .04 |
| ☐ 592 | Daryl Patterson | .40 | .16 | .04 |
| ☐ 593 | Cubs Team | .80 | .32 | .08 |
| ☐ 594 | Jake Gibbs | .40 | .16 | .04 |
| ☐ 595 | Maury Wills | 1.00 | .40 | .10 |
| ☐ 596 | Mike Hershberger | .40 | .16 | .04 |
| ☐ 597 | Sonny Siebert | .50 | .20 | .05 |
| ☐ 598 | Joe Pepitone | .50 | .20 | .05 |
| ☐ 599 | Senators Rookies | .40 | .16 | .04 |
| | Dick Stelmaszek | | | |
| | Gene Martin | | | |
| | Dick Such | | | |
| ☐ 600 | Willie Mays | 15.00 | 6.00 | 1.50 |
| ☐ 601 | Pete Richert | .40 | .16 | .04 |
| ☐ 602 | Ted Savage | .40 | .16 | .04 |
| ☐ 603 | Ray Oyler | .40 | .16 | .04 |
| ☐ 604 | Clarence Gaston | .40 | .16 | .04 |
| ☐ 605 | Rick Wise | .50 | .20 | .05 |
| ☐ 606 | Chico Ruiz | .40 | .16 | .04 |
| ☐ 607 | Gary Waslewski | .40 | .16 | .04 |
| ☐ 608 | Pirates Team | .80 | .32 | .08 |
| ☐ 609 | Buck Martinez | .40 | .16 | .04 |
| ☐ 610 | Jerry Koosman | .80 | .32 | .08 |
| ☐ 611 | Norm Cash | .80 | .32 | .08 |
| ☐ 612 | Jim Hickman | .40 | .16 | .04 |
| ☐ 613 | Dave Baldwin | .40 | .16 | .04 |
| ☐ 614 | Mike Shannon | .60 | .24 | .06 |
| ☐ 615 | Mark Belanger | .60 | .24 | .06 |
| ☐ 616 | Jim Merritt | .40 | .16 | .04 |
| ☐ 617 | Jim French | .40 | .16 | .04 |
| ☐ 618 | Billy Wynne | .40 | .16 | .04 |
| ☐ 619 | Norm Miller | .40 | .16 | .04 |
| ☐ 620 | Jim Perry | .90 | .36 | .09 |
| ☐ 621 | Braves Rookies | 3.50 | 1.40 | .35 |
| | Mike McQueen | | | |
| | Darrell Evans | | | |
| | Rick Kester | | | |
| ☐ 622 | Don Sutton | 2.50 | 1.00 | .25 |
| ☐ 623 | Horace Clarke | .40 | .16 | .04 |
| ☐ 624 | Clyde King MGR | .40 | .16 | .04 |
| ☐ 625 | Dean Chance | .50 | .20 | .05 |

| | | | | |
|---|---|---|---|---|
| ☐ 626 | Dave Ricketts | .40 | .16 | .04 |
| ☐ 627 | Gary Wagner | .40 | .16 | .04 |
| ☐ 628 | Wayne Garrett | .40 | .16 | .04 |
| ☐ 629 | Merv Rettenmund | .40 | .16 | .04 |
| ☐ 630 | Ernie Banks | 8.00 | 3.25 | .80 |
| ☐ 631 | Athletics Team | .80 | .32 | .08 |
| ☐ 632 | Gary Sutherland | .40 | .16 | .04 |
| ☐ 633 | Roger Nelson | .35 | .14 | .03 |
| ☐ 634 | Bud Harrelson | 1.25 | .50 | .12 |
| ☐ 635 | Bob Allison | 1.25 | .50 | .12 |
| ☐ 636 | Jim Stewart | 1.00 | .40 | .10 |
| ☐ 637 | Indians Team | 1.75 | .70 | .17 |
| ☐ 638 | Frank Bertaina | 1.00 | .40 | .10 |
| ☐ 639 | Dave Campbell | 1.00 | .40 | .10 |
| ☐ 640 | Al Kaline | 12.00 | 5.00 | 1.20 |
| ☐ 641 | Al McBean | 1.00 | .40 | .10 |
| ☐ 642 | Angels Rookies | 1.00 | .40 | .10 |
| | Greg Garrett | | | |
| | Gordon Lund | | | |
| | Jarvis Tatum | | | |
| ☐ 643 | Jose Pagan | 1.00 | .40 | .10 |
| ☐ 644 | Gerry Nyman | 1.00 | .40 | .10 |
| ☐ 645 | Don Money | 1.25 | .50 | .12 |
| ☐ 646 | Jim Britton | 1.00 | .40 | .10 |
| ☐ 647 | Tom Matchick | 1.00 | .40 | .10 |
| ☐ 648 | Larry Haney | 1.00 | .40 | .10 |
| ☐ 649 | Jimmie Hall | 1.00 | .40 | .10 |
| ☐ 650 | Sam McDowell | 1.25 | .50 | .12 |
| ☐ 651 | Jim Gosger | 1.00 | .40 | .10 |
| ☐ 652 | Rich Rollins | 1.00 | .40 | .10 |
| ☐ 653 | Moe Drabowsky | 1.00 | .40 | .10 |
| ☐ 654 | N.L. Rookies | 2.00 | .80 | .20 |
| | Oscar Gamble | | | |
| | Boots Day | | | |
| | Angel Mangual | | | |
| ☐ 655 | John Roseboro | 1.25 | .50 | .12 |
| ☐ 656 | Jim Hardin | 1.00 | .40 | .10 |
| ☐ 657 | Padres Team | 2.50 | 1.00 | .25 |
| ☐ 658 | Ken Tatum | 1.00 | .40 | .10 |
| ☐ 659 | Pete Ward | 1.00 | .40 | .10 |
| ☐ 660 | Johnny Bench | 60.00 | 24.00 | 6.00 |
| ☐ 661 | Jerry Robertson | 1.00 | .40 | .10 |
| ☐ 662 | Frank Lucchesi MGR | 1.00 | .40 | .10 |
| ☐ 663 | Tito Francona | 1.00 | .40 | .10 |
| ☐ 664 | Bob Robertson | 1.00 | .40 | .10 |
| ☐ 665 | Jim Lonborg | 1.25 | .50 | .12 |
| ☐ 666 | Adolpho Phillips | 1.00 | .40 | .10 |
| ☐ 667 | Bob Meyer | 1.00 | .40 | .10 |
| ☐ 668 | Bob Tillman | 1.00 | .40 | .10 |
| ☐ 669 | White Sox Rookies | 1.00 | .40 | .10 |
| | Bart Johnson | | | |
| | Dan Lazar | | | |
| | Mickey Scott | | | |
| ☐ 670 | Ron Santo | 1.75 | .70 | .17 |
| ☐ 671 | Jim Campanis | 1.00 | .40 | .10 |
| ☐ 672 | Leon McFadden | 1.00 | .40 | .10 |
| ☐ 673 | Ted Uhlaender | 1.00 | .40 | .10 |
| ☐ 674 | Dave Leonhard | 1.00 | .40 | .10 |
| ☐ 675 | Jose Cardenal | 1.25 | .50 | .12 |
| ☐ 676 | Senators Team | 1.75 | .70 | .17 |
| ☐ 677 | Woodie Fryman | 1.25 | .50 | .12 |
| ☐ 678 | Dave Duncan | 1.00 | .40 | .10 |
| ☐ 679 | Ray Sadecki | 1.00 | .40 | .10 |
| ☐ 680 | Rico Petrocelli | 1.25 | .50 | .12 |
| ☐ 681 | Bob Garibaldi | 1.00 | .40 | .10 |
| ☐ 682 | Dalton Jones | 1.00 | .40 | .10 |
| ☐ 683 | Reds Rookies | 2.00 | .80 | .20 |
| | Vern Geishert | | | |
| | Hal McRae | | | |
| | Wayne Simpson | | | |
| ☐ 684 | Jack Fisher | 1.00 | .40 | .10 |
| ☐ 685 | Tom Haller | 1.00 | .40 | .10 |
| ☐ 686 | Jackie Hernandez | 1.00 | .40 | .10 |
| ☐ 687 | Bob Priddy | 1.00 | .40 | .10 |
| ☐ 688 | Ted Kubiak | 1.00 | .40 | .10 |
| ☐ 689 | Frank Tepedino | 1.00 | .40 | .10 |
| ☐ 690 | Ron Fairly | 1.25 | .50 | .12 |
| ☐ 691 | Joe Grzenda | 1.00 | .40 | .10 |
| ☐ 692 | Duffy Dyer | 1.00 | .40 | .10 |
| ☐ 693 | Bob Johnson | 1.00 | .40 | .10 |
| ☐ 694 | Gary Ross | 1.00 | .40 | .10 |
| ☐ 695 | Bobby Knoop | 1.00 | .40 | .10 |
| ☐ 696 | Giants Team | 1.75 | .70 | .17 |
| ☐ 697 | Jim Hannan | 1.00 | .40 | .10 |
| ☐ 698 | Tom Tresh | 1.50 | .60 | .15 |
| ☐ 699 | Hank Aguirre | 1.00 | .40 | .10 |
| ☐ 700 | Frank Robinson | 12.00 | 5.00 | 1.20 |
| ☐ 701 | Jack Billingham | 1.00 | .40 | .10 |
| ☐ 702 | AL Rookies | 1.00 | .40 | .10 |
| | Bob Johnson | | | |
| | Ron Klimkowski | | | |
| | Bill Zepp | | | |
| ☐ 703 | Lou Marone | 1.00 | .40 | .10 |

| | | | | |
|---|---|---|---|---|
| ☐ 704 | Frank Baker | 1.00 | .40 | .10 |
| ☐ 705 | Tony Cloninger | 1.00 | .40 | .10 |
| ☐ 706 | John McNamara MGR | 2.25 | .90 | .22 |
| ☐ 707 | Kevin Collins | 1.00 | .40 | .10 |
| ☐ 708 | Jose Santiago | 1.00 | .40 | .10 |
| ☐ 709 | Mike Fiore | 1.00 | .40 | .10 |
| ☐ 710 | Felix Millan | 1.00 | .40 | .10 |
| ☐ 711 | Ed Brinkman | 1.00 | .40 | .10 |
| ☐ 712 | Nolan Ryan | 25.00 | 10.00 | 2.50 |
| ☐ 713 | Pilots Team | 6.00 | 2.40 | .60 |
| ☐ 714 | Al Spangler | 1.00 | .40 | .10 |
| ☐ 715 | Mickey Lolich | 2.00 | .80 | .20 |
| ☐ 716 | Cardinals Rookies | 1.00 | .40 | .10 |
| | Sal Campisi | | | |
| | Reggie Cleveland | | | |
| | Santiago Guzman | | | |
| ☐ 717 | Tom Phoebus | 1.00 | .40 | .10 |
| ☐ 718 | Ed Spiezio | 1.00 | .40 | .10 |
| ☐ 719 | Jim Roland | 1.00 | .40 | .10 |
| ☐ 720 | Rick Reichardt | 1.50 | .50 | .10 |

## 1970 Topps Super

The cards in this 42 card set measure 3 1/8" by 5 1/4". The 1970 Topps Super set was a separate Topps issue printed on heavy stock and marketed in its own wrapper with gum. The blue and yellow backs are identical to the respective player's backs in the 1970 Topps regular issue. Cards 38, Boog Powell, is the key card of the set; other short print run cards are listed in the checklist with SP. The obverse pictures are borderless and contain a facsimile autograph.

| | | MINT | VG-E | F-G |
|---|---|---|---|---|
| COMPLETE SET | | 150.00 | 60.00 | 15.00 |
| COMMON PLAYER (1-42) | | .75 | .30 | .07 |
| ☐ 1 | Claude Osteen SP | 1.50 | .60 | .15 |
| ☐ 2 | Sal Bando SP | 1.50 | .60 | .15 |
| ☐ 3 | Luis Aparicio | 2.00 | .80 | .20 |
| ☐ 4 | Harmon Killebrew | 3.00 | 1.20 | .30 |
| ☐ 5 | Tom Seaver SP | 10.00 | 4.00 | 1.00 |
| ☐ 6 | Larry Dierker | .75 | .30 | .07 |
| ☐ 7 | Bill Freehan | .75 | .30 | .07 |
| ☐ 8 | Johnny Bench | 7.50 | 3.00 | .75 |
| ☐ 9 | Tommy Harper | .75 | .30 | .07 |
| ☐ 10 | Sam McDowell | .75 | .30 | .07 |
| ☐ 11 | Lou Brock | 3.50 | 1.40 | .35 |
| ☐ 12 | Bob Clemente | 8.00 | 3.25 | .80 |
| ☐ 13 | Willie McCovey | 3.50 | 1.40 | .35 |
| ☐ 14 | Rico Petrocelli | .75 | .30 | .07 |
| ☐ 15 | Phil Niekro | 2.00 | .80 | .20 |
| ☐ 16 | Frank Howard | .75 | .30 | .07 |
| ☐ 17 | Denny McLain | .75 | .30 | .07 |
| ☐ 18 | Willie Mays | 9.00 | 3.75 | .90 |
| ☐ 19 | Willie Stargell | 3.00 | 1.20 | .30 |
| ☐ 20 | Joel Horlen | .75 | .30 | .07 |

| | | MINT | VG-E | F-G |
|---|---|---|---|---|
| ☐ 21 | Ron Santo | .75 | .30 | .07 |
| ☐ 22 | Dick Bosman | .75 | .30 | .07 |
| ☐ 23 | Tim McCarver | .75 | .30 | .07 |
| ☐ 24 | Hank Aaron | 9.00 | 3.75 | .90 |
| ☐ 25 | Andy Messersmith | .75 | .30 | .07 |
| ☐ 26 | Tony Oliva | 1.00 | .40 | .10 |
| ☐ 27 | Mel Stottlemyre | .75 | .30 | .07 |
| ☐ 28 | Reggie Jackson | 14.00 | 5.75 | 1.40 |
| ☐ 29 | Carl Yastrzemski | 14.00 | 5.75 | 1.40 |
| ☐ 30 | Jim Fregosi | .75 | .30 | .07 |
| ☐ 31 | Vada Pinson | .75 | .30 | .07 |
| ☐ 32 | Lou Piniella | .75 | .30 | .07 |
| ☐ 33 | Bob Gibson | 3.00 | 1.20 | .30 |
| ☐ 34 | Pete Rose | 24.00 | 10.00 | 2.40 |
| ☐ 35 | Jim Wynn | .75 | .30 | .07 |
| ☐ 36 | Ollie Brown SP | 4.00 | 1.60 | .40 |
| ☐ 37 | Frank Robinson SP | 12.00 | 5.00 | 1.20 |
| ☐ 38 | Boog Powell SP | 45.00 | 18.00 | 4.50 |
| ☐ 39 | Willie Davis SP | 1.50 | .60 | .15 |
| ☐ 40 | Billy Williams SP | 6.00 | 2.40 | .60 |
| ☐ 41 | Rusty Staub | 1.00 | .40 | .10 |
| ☐ 42 | Tommie Agee | .75 | .30 | .07 |

## 1971 Topps

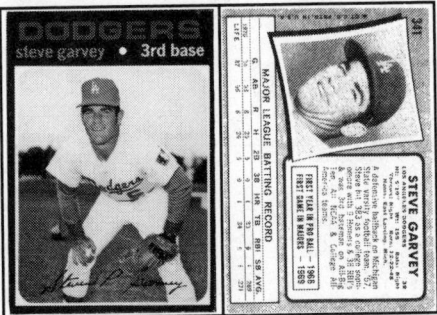

The cards in this 752 card set measure 2 1/2" by 3 1/2". The 1971 Topps set is a challenge to complete in "mint" condition because the black obverse border is easily scratched and damaged. An unusual feature of this set is that the player is also pictured in black and white on the back of the card. Featured subsets within this set include League Leaders (61-72), Playoffs cards (195-202), and World Series cards (327-332). Cards 524-643 and the last series (644-752) are somewhat scarce.

| | | MINT | VG-E | F-G |
|---|---|---|---|---|
| COMPLETE SET | | 650.00 | 260.00 | 65.00 |
| COMMON PLAYER (1-523) | | .23 | .10 | .02 |
| COMMON PLAYER (524-643) | | .45 | .18 | .04 |
| COMMON PLAYER (644-752) | | 1.00 | .40 | .10 |
| ☐ 1 | Orioles Team | 2.00 | .80 | .20 |
| ☐ 2 | Dock Ellis | .23 | .10 | .02 |
| ☐ 3 | Dick McAuliffe | .23 | .10 | .02 |
| ☐ 4 | Vic Davalillo | .23 | .10 | .02 |
| ☐ 5 | Thurman Munson | 10.00 | 4.00 | 1.00 |
| ☐ 6 | Ed Spiezio | .23 | .10 | .02 |
| ☐ 7 | Jim Holt | .23 | .10 | .02 |
| ☐ 8 | Mike McQueen | .23 | .10 | .02 |
| ☐ 9 | George Scott | .30 | .12 | .03 |
| ☐ 10 | Claude Osteen | .30 | .12 | .03 |
| ☐ 11 | Elliott Maddox | .23 | .10 | .02 |
| ☐ 12 | Johnny Callison | .30 | .12 | .03 |
| ☐ 13 | White Sox Rookies<br>Charlie Brinkman<br>Dick Moloney | .23 | .10 | .02 |
| ☐ 14 | Dave Concepcion | 4.00 | 1.60 | .40 |
| ☐ 15 | Andy Messersmith | .35 | .14 | .03 |
| ☐ 16 | Ken Singleton | 1.50 | .60 | .15 |
| ☐ 17 | Billy Sorrell | .23 | .10 | .02 |
| ☐ 18 | Norm Miller | .23 | .10 | .02 |
| ☐ 19 | Skip Pitlock | .23 | .10 | .02 |
| ☐ 20 | Reggie Jackson | 14.00 | 5.75 | 1.40 |

| | | | | |
|---|---|---|---|---|
| ☐ 21 | Dan McGinn | .23 | .10 | .02 |
| ☐ 22 | Phil Roof | .23 | .10 | .02 |
| ☐ 23 | Oscar Gamble | .40 | .16 | .04 |
| ☐ 24 | Rich Hand | .23 | .10 | .02 |
| ☐ 25 | Clarence Gaston | .23 | .10 | .02 |
| ☐ 26 | Bert Blyleven | 8.00 | 3.25 | .80 |
| ☐ 27 | Pirates Rookies<br>Fred Cambria<br>Gene Clines | .23 | .10 | .02 |
| ☐ 28 | Ron Klimkowski | .23 | .10 | .02 |
| ☐ 29 | Don Buford | .23 | .10 | .02 |
| ☐ 30 | Phil Niekro | 2.00 | .80 | .20 |
| ☐ 31 | Eddie Kasko MGR | .23 | .10 | .02 |
| ☐ 32 | Jerry DaVanon | .23 | .10 | .02 |
| ☐ 33 | Del Unser | .23 | .10 | .02 |
| ☐ 34 | Sandy Vance | .23 | .10 | .02 |
| ☐ 35 | Lou Piniella | .65 | .26 | .06 |
| ☐ 36 | Dean Chance | .30 | .12 | .03 |
| ☐ 37 | Rich McKinney | .23 | .10 | .02 |
| ☐ 38 | Jim Colborn | .23 | .10 | .02 |
| ☐ 39 | Tiger Rookies<br>Lerrin LaGrow<br>Gene Lamont | .23 | .10 | .02 |
| ☐ 40 | Lee May | .35 | .14 | .03 |
| ☐ 41 | Rick Austin | .23 | .10 | .02 |
| ☐ 42 | Boots Day | .23 | .10 | .02 |
| ☐ 43 | Steve Kealey | .23 | .10 | .02 |
| ☐ 44 | Johnny Edwards | .23 | .10 | .02 |
| ☐ 45 | Jim Hunter | 2.50 | 1.00 | .25 |
| ☐ 46 | Dave Campbell | .23 | .10 | .02 |
| ☐ 47 | Johnny Jeter | .23 | .10 | .02 |
| ☐ 48 | Dave Baldwin | .23 | .10 | .02 |
| ☐ 49 | Don Money | .30 | .12 | .03 |
| ☐ 50 | Willie McCovey | 3.00 | 1.20 | .30 |
| ☐ 51 | Steve Kline | .23 | .10 | .02 |
| ☐ 52 | Braves Rookies<br>Oscar Brown<br>Earl Williams | .35 | .14 | .03 |
| ☐ 53 | Paul Blair | .30 | .12 | .03 |
| ☐ 54 | Checklist 1 | 1.00 | .10 | .02 |
| ☐ 55 | Steve Carlton | 10.00 | 4.00 | 1.00 |
| ☐ 56 | Duane Josephson | .23 | .10 | .02 |
| ☐ 57 | Von Joshua | .23 | .10 | .02 |
| ☐ 58 | Bill Lee | .30 | .12 | .03 |
| ☐ 59 | Gene Mauch MGR | .30 | .12 | .03 |
| ☐ 60 | Dick Bosman | .23 | .10 | .02 |
| ☐ 61 | AL Batting Leaders<br>Alex Johnson<br>Carl Yastrzemski<br>Tony Oliva | 1.00 | .40 | .10 |
| ☐ 62 | NL Batting Leaders<br>Rico Carty<br>Joe Torre<br>Manny Sanguillen | .50 | .20 | .05 |
| ☐ 63 | AL RBI Leaders<br>Frank Robinson<br>Tony Conigliaro<br>Boog Powell | .75 | .30 | .07 |
| ☐ 64 | NL RBI Leaders<br>Johnny Bench<br>Tony Perez<br>Billy Williams | 1.00 | .40 | .10 |
| ☐ 65 | AL HR Leaders<br>Frank Howard<br>Harmon Killebrew<br>Carl Yastrzemski | 1.00 | .40 | .10 |
| ☐ 66 | NL HR Leaders<br>Johnny Bench<br>Billy Williams<br>Tony Perez | 1.00 | .40 | .10 |
| ☐ 67 | AL ERA Leaders<br>Diego Segui<br>Jim Palmer<br>Clyde Wright | .50 | .20 | .05 |
| ☐ 68 | NL ERA Leaders<br>Tom Seaver<br>Wayne Simpson<br>Luke Walker | .75 | .30 | .07 |
| ☐ 69 | AL Pitching Leaders<br>Mike Cuellar<br>Dave McNally<br>Jim Perry | .50 | .20 | .05 |
| ☐ 70 | NL Pitching Leaders<br>Bob Gibson<br>Gaylord Perry<br>Fergie Jenkins | 1.25 | .50 | .12 |
| ☐ 71 | AL Strikeout Leaders<br>Sam McDowell<br>Mickey Lolich<br>Bob Johnson | .50 | .20 | .05 |
| ☐ 72 | NL Strikeout Leaders<br>Tom Seaver<br>Bob Gibson | 1.25 | .50 | .12 |

|  |  |  |  |  |
|---|---|---|---|---|
|  | Fergie Jenkins |  |  |  |
| ☐ 73 | George Brunet | .23 | .10 | .02 |
| ☐ 74 | Twins Rookies | .23 | .10 | .02 |
|  | Pete Hamm |  |  |  |
|  | Jim Nettles |  |  |  |
| ☐ 75 | Gary Nolan | .23 | .10 | .02 |
| ☐ 76 | Ted Savage | .23 | .10 | .02 |
| ☐ 77 | Mike Compton | .23 | .10 | .02 |
| ☐ 78 | Jim Spencer | .23 | .10 | .02 |
| ☐ 79 | Wade Blasingame | .23 | .10 | .02 |
| ☐ 80 | Bill Melton | .23 | .10 | .02 |
| ☐ 81 | Felix Millan | .23 | .10 | .02 |
| ☐ 82 | Casey Cox | .23 | .10 | .02 |
| ☐ 83 | Met Rookies | .35 | .14 | .03 |
|  | Tim Foli |  |  |  |
|  | Randy Bobb |  |  |  |
| ☐ 84 | Marcel Lachemann | .23 | .10 | .02 |
| ☐ 85 | Bill Grabarkewitz | .23 | .10 | .02 |
| ☐ 86 | Mike Kilkenny | .23 | .10 | .02 |
| ☐ 87 | Jack Heidemann | .23 | .10 | .02 |
| ☐ 88 | Hal King | .23 | .10 | .02 |
| ☐ 89 | Ken Brett | .23 | .10 | .02 |
| ☐ 90 | Joe Pepitone | .35 | .14 | .03 |
| ☐ 91 | Bob Lemon MGR | .75 | .30 | .07 |
| ☐ 92 | Fred Wenz | .23 | .10 | .02 |
| ☐ 93 | Senators Rookies | .23 | .10 | .02 |
|  | Norm McRae |  |  |  |
|  | Denny Riddleberger |  |  |  |
| ☐ 94 | Don Hahn | .23 | .10 | .02 |
| ☐ 95 | Luis Tiant | .60 | .24 | .06 |
| ☐ 96 | Joe Hague | .23 | .10 | .02 |
| ☐ 97 | Floyd Wicker | .23 | .10 | .02 |
| ☐ 98 | Joe Decker | .23 | .10 | .02 |
| ☐ 99 | Mark Belanger | .35 | .14 | .03 |
| ☐ 100 | Pete Rose | 33.00 | 12.50 | 3.00 |
| ☐ 101 | Les Cain | .23 | .10 | .02 |
| ☐ 102 | Astros Rookies | .40 | .16 | .04 |
|  | Ken Forsch |  |  |  |
|  | Larry Howard |  |  |  |
| ☐ 103 | Rich Severinson | .23 | .10 | .02 |
| ☐ 104 | Dan Frisella | .23 | .10 | .02 |
| ☐ 105 | Tony Conigliaro | .40 | .16 | .04 |
| ☐ 106 | Tom Dukes | .23 | .10 | .02 |
| ☐ 107 | Roy Foster | .23 | .10 | .02 |
| ☐ 108 | John Cumberland | .23 | .10 | .02 |
| ☐ 109 | Steve Hovley | .23 | .10 | .02 |
| ☐ 110 | Bill Mazeroski | .50 | .20 | .05 |
| ☐ 111 | Yankee Rookies | .23 | .10 | .02 |
|  | Loyd Colson |  |  |  |
|  | Bobby Mitchell |  |  |  |
| ☐ 112 | Manny Mota | .35 | .14 | .03 |
| ☐ 113 | Jerry Crider | .23 | .10 | .02 |
| ☐ 114 | Billy Conigliaro | .23 | .10 | .02 |
| ☐ 115 | Donn Clendenon | .30 | .12 | .03 |
| ☐ 116 | Ken Sanders | .23 | .10 | .02 |
| ☐ 117 | Ted Simmons | 5.00 | 2.00 | .50 |
| ☐ 118 | Cookie Rojas | .23 | .10 | .02 |
| ☐ 119 | Frank Lucchesi MGR | .23 | .10 | .02 |
| ☐ 120 | Willie Horton | .35 | .14 | .03 |
| ☐ 121 | Cubs Rookies | .23 | .10 | .02 |
|  | Jim Dunegan |  |  |  |
|  | Roe Skidmore |  |  |  |
| ☐ 122 | Eddie Watt | .23 | .10 | .02 |
| ☐ 123A | Checklist 2 | 1.25 | .12 | .02 |
|  | (card number |  |  |  |
|  | at bottom right) |  |  |  |
| ☐ 123B | Checklist 2 | 1.50 | .15 | .03 |
|  | (card number |  |  |  |
|  | centered) |  |  |  |
| ☐ 124 | Don Gullett | .35 | .14 | .03 |
| ☐ 125 | Ray Fosse | .23 | .10 | .02 |
| ☐ 126 | Danny Coombs | .23 | .10 | .02 |
| ☐ 127 | Danny Thompson | .23 | .10 | .02 |
| ☐ 128 | Frank Johnson | .23 | .10 | .02 |
| ☐ 129 | Aurelio Monteagudo | .23 | .10 | .02 |
| ☐ 130 | Denis Menke | .23 | .10 | .02 |
| ☐ 131 | Curt Blefary | .23 | .10 | .02 |
| ☐ 132 | Jose Laboy | .23 | .10 | .02 |
| ☐ 133 | Mickey Lolich | .60 | .24 | .06 |
| ☐ 134 | Jose Arcia | .23 | .10 | .02 |
| ☐ 135 | Rick Monday | .35 | .14 | .03 |
| ☐ 136 | Duffy Dyer | .23 | .10 | .02 |
| ☐ 137 | Marcelino Lopez | .23 | .10 | .02 |
| ☐ 138 | Phillies Rookies | .35 | .14 | .03 |
|  | Joe Lis |  |  |  |
|  | Willie Montanez |  |  |  |
| ☐ 139 | Paul Casanova | .23 | .10 | .02 |
| ☐ 140 | Gaylord Perry | 3.00 | 1.20 | .30 |
| ☐ 141 | Frank Quilici MGR | .23 | .10 | .02 |
| ☐ 142 | Mack Jones | .23 | .10 | .02 |
| ☐ 143 | Steve Blass | .30 | .12 | .03 |
| ☐ 144 | Jackie Hernandez | .23 | .10 | .02 |
| ☐ 145 | Bill Singer | .23 | .10 | .02 |

|  |  |  |  |  |
|---|---|---|---|---|
| ☐ 146 | Ralph Houk MGR | .30 | .12 | .03 |
| ☐ 147 | Bob Priddy | .23 | .10 | .02 |
| ☐ 148 | John Mayberry | .30 | .12 | .03 |
| ☐ 149 | Mike Hershberger | .23 | .10 | .02 |
| ☐ 150 | Sam McDowell | .35 | .14 | .03 |
| ☐ 151 | Tommy Davis | .40 | .16 | .04 |
| ☐ 152 | Angels Rookies | .23 | .10 | .02 |
|  | Lloyd Allen |  |  |  |
|  | Winston Llenas |  |  |  |
| ☐ 153 | Gary Ross | .23 | .10 | .02 |
| ☐ 154 | Cesar Gutierrez | .23 | .10 | .02 |
| ☐ 155 | Ken Henderson | .23 | .10 | .02 |
| ☐ 156 | Bart Johnson | .23 | .10 | .02 |
| ☐ 157 | Bob Bailey | .23 | .10 | .02 |
| ☐ 158 | Jerry Reuss | .60 | .24 | .06 |
| ☐ 159 | Jarvis Tatum | .23 | .10 | .02 |
| ☐ 160 | Tom Seaver | 11.00 | 4.50 | 1.10 |
| ☐ 161 | Coin Checklist | 1.00 | .10 | .02 |
| ☐ 162 | Jack Billingham | .23 | .10 | .02 |
| ☐ 163 | Buck Martinez | .23 | .10 | .02 |
| ☐ 164 | Reds Rookies: | .45 | .18 | .04 |
|  | Frank Duffy |  |  |  |
|  | Milt Wilcox |  |  |  |
| ☐ 165 | Cesar Tovar | .23 | .10 | .02 |
| ☐ 166 | Joe Hoerner | .23 | .10 | .02 |
| ☐ 167 | Tom Grieve | .35 | .14 | .03 |
| ☐ 168 | Bruce Dal Canton | .23 | .10 | .02 |
| ☐ 169 | Ed Herrmann | .23 | .10 | .02 |
| ☐ 170 | Mike Cuellar | .35 | .14 | .03 |
| ☐ 171 | Bobby Wine | .23 | .10 | .02 |
| ☐ 172 | Duke Sims | .23 | .10 | .02 |
| ☐ 173 | Gil Garrido | .23 | .10 | .02 |
| ☐ 174 | Dave LaRoche | .23 | .10 | .02 |
| ☐ 175 | Jim Hickman | .23 | .10 | .02 |
| ☐ 176 | Red Sox Rookies | .23 | .10 | .02 |
|  | Bob Montgomery |  |  |  |
|  | Doug Griffin |  |  |  |
| ☐ 177 | Hal McRae | .40 | .16 | .04 |
| ☐ 178 | Dave Duncan | .23 | .10 | .02 |
| ☐ 179 | Mike Corkins | .23 | .10 | .02 |
| ☐ 180 | Al Kaline | 3.25 | 1.30 | .32 |
| ☐ 181 | Hal Lanier | .40 | .16 | .04 |
| ☐ 182 | Al Downing | .23 | .10 | .02 |
| ☐ 183 | Gil Hodges MGR | 1.75 | .70 | .17 |
| ☐ 184 | Stan Bahnsen | .23 | .10 | .02 |
| ☐ 185 | Julian Javier | .23 | .10 | .02 |
| ☐ 186 | Bob Spence | .23 | .10 | .02 |
| ☐ 187 | Ted Abernathy | .23 | .10 | .02 |
| ☐ 188 | Dodgers Rookies | 1.00 | .40 | .10 |
|  | Bob Valentine |  |  |  |
|  | Mike Strahler |  |  |  |
| ☐ 189 | George Mitterwald | .23 | .10 | .02 |
| ☐ 190 | Bob Tolan | .23 | .10 | .02 |
| ☐ 191 | Mike Andrews | .23 | .10 | .02 |
| ☐ 192 | Billy Wilson | .23 | .10 | .02 |
| ☐ 193 | Bob Grich | 1.50 | .60 | .15 |
| ☐ 194 | Mike Lum | .23 | .10 | .02 |
| ☐ 195 | AL Playoff Game 1 | .75 | .30 | .07 |
|  | Powell muscles Twins |  |  |  |
| ☐ 196 | AL Playoff Game 2 | .75 | .30 | .07 |
|  | McNally makes it |  |  |  |
|  | two straight |  |  |  |
| ☐ 197 | AL Playoff Game 3 | 1.25 | .50 | .12 |
|  | Palmer mows'em down |  |  |  |
| ☐ 198 | AL Playoff Summary | .75 | .30 | .07 |
|  | Orioles Celebrate |  |  |  |
| ☐ 199 | NL Playoff Game 1 | .75 | .30 | .07 |
|  | Cline pinch-triple |  |  |  |
|  | decides it |  |  |  |
| ☐ 200 | NL Playoff Game 2 | .75 | .30 | .07 |
|  | Tolan scores for |  |  |  |
|  | third time |  |  |  |
| ☐ 201 | NL Playoff Game 3 | .75 | .30 | .07 |
|  | Cline scores |  |  |  |
|  | winning run |  |  |  |
| ☐ 202 | NL Playoff Summary | .75 | .30 | .07 |
|  | Reds Celebrate |  |  |  |
| ☐ 203 | Larry Gura | .75 | .30 | .07 |
| ☐ 204 | Brewers Rookies | .23 | .10 | .02 |
|  | Bernie Smith |  |  |  |
|  | George Kopacz |  |  |  |
| ☐ 205 | Gerry Moses | .23 | .10 | .02 |
| ☐ 206 | Checklist 3 | 1.00 | .10 | .02 |
| ☐ 207 | Alan Foster | .23 | .10 | .02 |
| ☐ 208 | Billy Martin MGR | 1.00 | .40 | .10 |
| ☐ 209 | Steve Renko | .23 | .10 | .02 |
| ☐ 210 | Rod Carew | 10.00 | 4.00 | 1.00 |
| ☐ 211 | Phil Hennigan | .23 | .10 | .02 |
| ☐ 212 | Rich Hebner | .30 | .12 | .03 |
| ☐ 213 | Frank Baker | .23 | .10 | .02 |
| ☐ 214 | Al Ferrara | .23 | .10 | .02 |
| ☐ 215 | Diego Segui | .23 | .10 | .02 |
| ☐ 216 | Cards Rookies | .23 | .10 | .02 |

| | | | | |
|---|---|---|---|---|
| | Reggie Cleveland | | | |
| | Luis Melendez | | | |
| ☐ 217 | Ed Stroud | .23 | .10 | .02 |
| ☐ 218 | Tony Cloninger | .23 | .10 | .02 |
| ☐ 219 | Elrod Hendricks | .23 | .10 | .02 |
| ☐ 220 | Ron Santo | .50 | .20 | .05 |
| ☐ 221 | Dave Morehead | .23 | .10 | .02 |
| ☐ 222 | Bob Watson | .40 | .16 | .04 |
| ☐ 223 | Cecil Upshaw | .23 | .10 | .02 |
| ☐ 224 | Alan Gallagher | .23 | .10 | .02 |
| ☐ 225 | Gary Peters | .30 | .12 | .03 |
| ☐ 226 | Bill Russell | .35 | .14 | .03 |
| ☐ 227 | Floyd Weaver | .23 | .10 | .02 |
| ☐ 228 | Wayne Garrett | .23 | .10 | .02 |
| ☐ 229 | Jim Hannan | .23 | .10 | .02 |
| ☐ 230 | Willie Stargell | 3.00 | 1.20 | .30 |
| ☐ 231 | Indians Rookies | .35 | .14 | .03 |
| | Vince Colbert | | | |
| | John Lowenstein | | | |
| ☐ 232 | John Strohmayer | .23 | .10 | .02 |
| ☐ 233 | Larry Bowa | 1.00 | .40 | .10 |
| ☐ 234 | Jim Lyttle | .23 | .10 | .02 |
| ☐ 235 | Nate Colbert | .23 | .10 | .02 |
| ☐ 236 | Bob Humphreys | .23 | .10 | .02 |
| ☐ 237 | Cesar Cedeno | 1.25 | .50 | .12 |
| ☐ 238 | Chuck Dobson | .23 | .10 | .02 |
| ☐ 239 | Red Schoendienst MGR | .40 | .16 | .04 |
| ☐ 240 | Clyde Wright | .23 | .10 | .02 |
| ☐ 241 | Dave Nelson | .23 | .10 | .02 |
| ☐ 242 | Jim Ray | .23 | .10 | .02 |
| ☐ 243 | Carlos May | .30 | .12 | .03 |
| ☐ 244 | Bob Tillman | .23 | .10 | .02 |
| ☐ 245 | Jim Kaat | 1.00 | .40 | .10 |
| ☐ 246 | Tony Taylor | .23 | .10 | .02 |
| ☐ 247 | Royals Rookies | .40 | .16 | .04 |
| | Jerry Cram | | | |
| | Paul Splittorff | | | |
| ☐ 248 | Hoyt Wilhelm | 2.00 | .80 | .20 |
| ☐ 249 | Chico Salmon | .23 | .10 | .02 |
| ☐ 250 | Johnny Bench | 11.00 | 4.50 | 1.10 |
| ☐ 251 | Frank Reberger | .23 | .10 | .02 |
| ☐ 252 | Eddie Leon | .23 | .10 | .02 |
| ☐ 253 | Bill Sudakis | .23 | .10 | .02 |
| ☐ 254 | Cal Koonce | .23 | .10 | .02 |
| ☐ 255 | Bob Robertson | .23 | .10 | .02 |
| ☐ 256 | Tony Gonzalez | .23 | .10 | .02 |
| ☐ 257 | Nelson Briles | .30 | .12 | .03 |
| ☐ 258 | Dick Green | .23 | .10 | .02 |
| ☐ 259 | Dave Marshall | .23 | .10 | .02 |
| ☐ 260 | Tommy Harper | .30 | .12 | .03 |
| ☐ 261 | Darold Knowles | .23 | .10 | .02 |
| ☐ 262 | Padres Rookies | .23 | .10 | .02 |
| | Jim Williams | | | |
| | Dave Robinson | | | |
| ☐ 263 | John Ellis | .23 | .10 | .02 |
| ☐ 264 | Joe Morgan | 2.25 | .90 | .22 |
| ☐ 265 | Jim Northrup | .30 | .12 | .03 |
| ☐ 266 | Bill Stoneman | .23 | .10 | .02 |
| ☐ 267 | Rich Morales | .23 | .10 | .02 |
| ☐ 268 | Phillies Team | .55 | .22 | .05 |
| ☐ 269 | Gail Hopkins | .23 | .10 | .02 |
| ☐ 270 | Rico Carty | .45 | .18 | .04 |
| ☐ 271 | Bill Zepp | .23 | .10 | .02 |
| ☐ 272 | Tommy Helms | .30 | .12 | .03 |
| ☐ 273 | Pete Richert | .23 | .10 | .02 |
| ☐ 274 | Ron Slocum | .23 | .10 | .02 |
| ☐ 275 | Vada Pinson | .60 | .24 | .06 |
| ☐ 276 | Giants Rookies | 4.50 | 1.80 | .45 |
| | Mike Davison | | | |
| | George Foster | | | |
| ☐ 277 | Gary Waslewski | .23 | .10 | .02 |
| ☐ 278 | Jerry Grote | .23 | .10 | .02 |
| ☐ 279 | Lefty Phillips MGR | .23 | .10 | .02 |
| ☐ 280 | Fergie Jenkins | 1.25 | .50 | .12 |
| ☐ 281 | Danny Walton | .23 | .10 | .02 |
| ☐ 282 | Jose Pagan | .23 | .10 | .02 |
| ☐ 283 | Dick Such | .23 | .10 | .02 |
| ☐ 284 | Jim Gosger | .23 | .10 | .02 |
| ☐ 285 | Sal Bando | .35 | .14 | .03 |
| ☐ 286 | Jerry McNertney | .23 | .10 | .02 |
| ☐ 287 | Mike Fiore | .23 | .10 | .02 |
| ☐ 288 | Joe Moeller | .23 | .10 | .02 |
| ☐ 289 | White Sox Team | .55 | .22 | .05 |
| ☐ 290 | Tony Oliva | .90 | .36 | .09 |
| ☐ 291 | George Culver | .23 | .10 | .02 |
| ☐ 292 | Jay Johnstone | .35 | .14 | .03 |
| ☐ 293 | Pat Corrales | .35 | .14 | .03 |
| ☐ 294 | Steve Dunning | .23 | .10 | .02 |
| ☐ 295 | Bobby Bonds | .65 | .26 | .06 |
| ☐ 296 | Tom Timmermann | .23 | .10 | .02 |
| ☐ 297 | Johnny Briggs | .23 | .10 | .02 |
| ☐ 298 | Jim Nelson | .23 | .10 | .02 |
| ☐ 299 | Ed Kirkpatrick | .23 | .10 | .02 |

| | | | | |
|---|---|---|---|---|
| ☐ 300 | Brooks Robinson | 4.50 | 1.80 | .45 |
| ☐ 301 | Earl Wilson | .23 | .10 | .02 |
| ☐ 302 | Phil Gagliano | .23 | .10 | .02 |
| ☐ 303 | Lindy McDaniel | .23 | .10 | .02 |
| ☐ 304 | Ron Brand | .23 | .10 | .02 |
| ☐ 305 | Reggie Smith | .60 | .24 | .06 |
| ☐ 306 | Jim Nash | .23 | .10 | .02 |
| ☐ 307 | Don Wert | .23 | .10 | .02 |
| ☐ 308 | Cardinals Team | .55 | .22 | .05 |
| ☐ 309 | Dick Ellsworth | .23 | .10 | .02 |
| ☐ 310 | Tommie Agee | .30 | .12 | .03 |
| ☐ 311 | Lee Stange | .23 | .10 | .02 |
| ☐ 312 | Harry Walker MGR | .23 | .10 | .02 |
| ☐ 313 | Tom Hall | .23 | .10 | .02 |
| ☐ 314 | Jeff Torborg | .23 | .10 | .02 |
| ☐ 315 | Ron Fairly | .30 | .12 | .03 |
| ☐ 316 | Fred Scherman | .23 | .10 | .02 |
| ☐ 317 | Athletic Rookies | .23 | .10 | .02 |
| | Jim Driscoll | | | |
| | Angel Mangual | | | |
| ☐ 318 | Rudy May | .23 | .10 | .02 |
| ☐ 319 | Ty Cline | .23 | .10 | .02 |
| ☐ 320 | Dave McNally | .35 | .14 | .03 |
| ☐ 321 | Tom Matchick | .23 | .10 | .02 |
| ☐ 322 | Jim Beauchamp | .23 | .10 | .02 |
| ☐ 323 | Billy Champion | .23 | .10 | .02 |
| ☐ 324 | Graig Nettles | 2.00 | .80 | .20 |
| ☐ 325 | Juan Marichal | 2.50 | 1.00 | .25 |
| ☐ 326 | Richie Scheinblum | .23 | .10 | .02 |
| ☐ 327 | World Series Game 1 | .75 | .30 | .07 |
| | Powell homers to | | | |
| | opposite field | | | |
| ☐ 328 | World Series Game 2 | .75 | .30 | .07 |
| | Don Buford | | | |
| ☐ 329 | World Series Game 3 | 1.50 | .60 | .15 |
| | Frank Robinson | | | |
| | shows muscle | | | |
| ☐ 330 | World Series Game 4 | .75 | .30 | .07 |
| | Reds stay alive | | | |
| ☐ 331 | World Series Game 5 | 1.50 | .60 | .15 |
| | Brooks Robinson | | | |
| | commits robbery | | | |
| ☐ 332 | World Series Summary | .75 | .30 | .07 |
| | Orioles Celebrate | | | |
| ☐ 333 | Clay Kirby | .23 | .10 | .02 |
| ☐ 334 | Roberto Pena | .23 | .10 | .02 |
| ☐ 335 | Jerry Koosman | .50 | .20 | .05 |
| ☐ 336 | Tigers Team | .60 | .24 | .06 |
| ☐ 337 | Jesus Alou | .23 | .10 | .02 |
| ☐ 338 | Gene Tenace | .35 | .14 | .03 |
| ☐ 339 | Wayne Simpson | .23 | .10 | .02 |
| ☐ 340 | Rico Petrocelli | .35 | .14 | .03 |
| ☐ 341 | Steve Garvey | 45.00 | 18.00 | 4.50 |
| ☐ 342 | Frank Tepedino | .23 | .10 | .02 |
| ☐ 343 | Pirates Rookies | .23 | .10 | .02 |
| | Ed Acosta | | | |
| | Milt May | | | |
| ☐ 344 | Ellie Rodriguez | .23 | .10 | .02 |
| ☐ 345 | Joe Horlen | .30 | .12 | .03 |
| ☐ 346 | Lum Harris MGR | .23 | .10 | .02 |
| ☐ 347 | Ted Uhlaender | .23 | .10 | .02 |
| ☐ 348 | Fred Norman | .23 | .10 | .02 |
| ☐ 349 | Rich Reese | .23 | .10 | .02 |
| ☐ 350 | Billy Williams | 2.50 | 1.00 | .25 |
| ☐ 351 | Jim Shellenback | .23 | .10 | .02 |
| ☐ 352 | Denny Doyle | .23 | .10 | .02 |
| ☐ 353 | Carl Taylor | .23 | .10 | .02 |
| ☐ 354 | Don McMahon | .23 | .10 | .02 |
| ☐ 355 | Bud Harrelson | .30 | .12 | .03 |
| ☐ 356 | Bob Locker | .23 | .10 | .02 |
| ☐ 357 | Reds Team | .75 | .30 | .07 |
| ☐ 358 | Danny Cater | .23 | .10 | .02 |
| ☐ 359 | Ron Reed | .23 | .10 | .02 |
| ☐ 360 | Jim Fregosi | .40 | .16 | .04 |
| ☐ 361 | Don Sutton | 1.75 | .70 | .17 |
| ☐ 362 | Orioles Rookies | .23 | .10 | .02 |
| | Mike Adamson | | | |
| | Roger Freed | | | |
| ☐ 363 | Mike Nagy | .23 | .10 | .02 |
| ☐ 364 | Tommy Dean | .23 | .10 | .02 |
| ☐ 365 | Bob Johnson | .23 | .10 | .02 |
| ☐ 366 | Ron Stone | .23 | .10 | .02 |
| ☐ 367 | Dalton Jones | .23 | .10 | .02 |
| ☐ 368 | Bob Veale | .30 | .12 | .03 |
| ☐ 369 | Checklist 4 | 1.00 | .10 | .02 |
| ☐ 370 | Joe Torre | 1.25 | .50 | .12 |
| ☐ 371 | Jack Hiatt | .23 | .10 | .02 |
| ☐ 372 | Lew Krausse | .23 | .10 | .02 |
| ☐ 373 | Tom McCraw | .23 | .10 | .02 |
| ☐ 374 | Clete Boyer | .35 | .14 | .03 |
| ☐ 375 | Steve Hargan | .23 | .10 | .02 |
| ☐ 376 | Expos Rookies | .23 | .10 | .02 |
| | Clyde Mashore | | | |

| # | Player | | | |
|---|---|---|---|---|
| | Ernie McAnally | | | |
| ☐ 377 | Greg Garrett | .23 | .10 | .02 |
| ☐ 378 | Tito Fuentes | .23 | .10 | .02 |
| ☐ 379 | Wayne Granger | .23 | .10 | .02 |
| ☐ 380 | Ted Williams MGR | 3.00 | 1.20 | .30 |
| ☐ 381 | Fred Gladding | .23 | .10 | .02 |
| ☐ 382 | Jake Gibbs | .23 | .10 | .02 |
| ☐ 383 | Rod Gaspar | .23 | .10 | .02 |
| ☐ 384 | Rollie Fingers | 2.00 | .80 | .20 |
| ☐ 385 | Maury Wills | .90 | .36 | .09 |
| ☐ 386 | Red Sox Team | .75 | .30 | .07 |
| ☐ 387 | Ron Herbel | .23 | .10 | .02 |
| ☐ 388 | Al Oliver | 1.75 | .70 | .17 |
| ☐ 389 | Ed Brinkman | .23 | .10 | .02 |
| ☐ 390 | Glenn Beckert | .35 | .14 | .03 |
| ☐ 391 | Twins Rookies | .35 | .14 | .03 |
| | Steve Brye | | | |
| | Cotton Nash | | | |
| ☐ 392 | Grant Jackson | .23 | .10 | .02 |
| ☐ 393 | Merv Rettenmund | .23 | .10 | .02 |
| ☐ 394 | Clay Carroll | .23 | .10 | .02 |
| ☐ 395 | Roy White | .35 | .14 | .03 |
| ☐ 396 | Dick Schofield | .23 | .10 | .02 |
| ☐ 397 | Alvin Dark MGR | .35 | .14 | .03 |
| ☐ 398 | Howie Reed | .23 | .10 | .02 |
| ☐ 399 | Jim French | .23 | .10 | .02 |
| ☐ 400 | Hank Aaron | 12.00 | 5.00 | 1.20 |
| ☐ 401 | Tom Murphy | .23 | .10 | .02 |
| ☐ 402 | Dodgers Team | .75 | .30 | .07 |
| ☐ 403 | Joe Coleman | .23 | .10 | .02 |
| ☐ 404 | Astros Rookies | .23 | .10 | .02 |
| | Buddy Harris | | | |
| | Roger Metzger | | | |
| ☐ 405 | Leo Cardenas | .23 | .10 | .02 |
| ☐ 406 | Ray Sadecki | .23 | .10 | .02 |
| ☐ 407 | Joe Rudi | .35 | .14 | .03 |
| ☐ 408 | Rafael Robles | .23 | .10 | .02 |
| ☐ 409 | Don Pavletich | .23 | .10 | .02 |
| ☐ 410 | Ken Holtzman | .35 | .14 | .03 |
| ☐ 411 | George Spriggs | .23 | .10 | .02 |
| ☐ 412 | Jerry Johnson | .23 | .10 | .02 |
| ☐ 413 | Pat Kelly | .23 | .10 | .02 |
| ☐ 414 | Woodie Fryman | .23 | .10 | .02 |
| ☐ 415 | Mike Hegan | .23 | .10 | .02 |
| ☐ 416 | Gene Alley | .30 | .12 | .03 |
| ☐ 417 | Dick Hall | .23 | .10 | .02 |
| ☐ 418 | Adolfo Phillips | .23 | .10 | .02 |
| ☐ 419 | Ron Hansen | .23 | .10 | .02 |
| ☐ 420 | Jim Merritt | .23 | .10 | .02 |
| ☐ 421 | John Stephenson | .23 | .10 | .02 |
| ☐ 422 | Frank Bertaina | .23 | .10 | .02 |
| ☐ 423 | Tigers Rookies | .23 | .10 | .02 |
| | Dennis Saunders | | | |
| | Tim Marting | | | |
| ☐ 424 | R. Rodriquez | .23 | .10 | .02 |
| ☐ 425 | Doug Rader | .35 | .14 | .03 |
| ☐ 426 | Chris Cannizzaro | .23 | .10 | .02 |
| ☐ 427 | Bernie Allen | .23 | .10 | .02 |
| ☐ 428 | Jim McAndrew | .23 | .10 | .02 |
| ☐ 429 | Chuck Hinton | .23 | .10 | .02 |
| ☐ 430 | Wes Parker | .35 | .14 | .03 |
| ☐ 431 | Tom Burgmeier | .23 | .10 | .02 |
| ☐ 432 | Bob Didier | .23 | .10 | .02 |
| ☐ 433 | Skip Lockwood | .23 | .10 | .02 |
| ☐ 434 | Gary Sutherland | .23 | .10 | .02 |
| ☐ 435 | Jose Cardenal | .23 | .10 | .02 |
| ☐ 436 | Wilbur Wood | .35 | .14 | .03 |
| ☐ 437 | Danny Murtaugh MGR | .23 | .10 | .02 |
| ☐ 438 | Mike McCormick | .35 | .14 | .03 |
| ☐ 439 | Phillies Rookies | 1.75 | .70 | .17 |
| | Greg Luzinski | | | |
| | Scott Reid | | | |
| ☐ 440 | Bert Campaneris | .35 | .14 | .03 |
| ☐ 441 | Milt Pappas | .35 | .14 | .03 |
| ☐ 442 | Angels Team | .55 | .22 | .05 |
| ☐ 443 | Rich Robertson | .23 | .10 | .02 |
| ☐ 444 | Jimmie Price | .23 | .10 | .02 |
| ☐ 445 | Art Shamsky | .23 | .10 | .02 |
| ☐ 446 | Bobby Bolin | .23 | .10 | .02 |
| ☐ 447 | Cesar Geronimo | .23 | .10 | .02 |
| ☐ 448 | Dave Roberts | .23 | .10 | .02 |
| ☐ 449 | Brant Alyea | .23 | .10 | .02 |
| ☐ 450 | Bob Gibson | 3.50 | 1.40 | .35 |
| ☐ 451 | Joe Keough | .23 | .10 | .02 |
| ☐ 452 | John Boccabella | .23 | .10 | .02 |
| ☐ 453 | Terry Crowley | .23 | .10 | .02 |
| ☐ 454 | Mike Paul | .23 | .10 | .02 |
| ☐ 455 | Don Kessinger | .35 | .14 | .03 |
| ☐ 456 | Bob Meyer | .23 | .10 | .02 |
| ☐ 457 | Willie Smith | .23 | .10 | .02 |
| ☐ 458 | White Sox Rookies | .23 | .10 | .02 |
| | Ron Lolich | | | |
| | Dave Lemonds | | | |
| ☐ 459 | Jim Lefebvre | .23 | .10 | .02 |
| ☐ 460 | Fritz Peterson | .23 | .10 | .02 |
| ☐ 461 | Jim Ray Hart | .35 | .14 | .03 |
| ☐ 462 | Senators Team | .55 | .22 | .05 |
| ☐ 463 | Tom Kelley | .23 | .10 | .02 |
| ☐ 464 | Aurelio Rodriguez | .23 | .10 | .02 |
| ☐ 465 | Tim McCarver | .45 | .18 | .04 |
| ☐ 466 | Ken Berry | .23 | .10 | .02 |
| ☐ 467 | Al Santorini | .23 | .10 | .02 |
| ☐ 468 | Frank Fernandez | .23 | .10 | .02 |
| ☐ 469 | Bob Aspromonte | .23 | .10 | .02 |
| ☐ 470 | Bob Oliver | .23 | .10 | .02 |
| ☐ 471 | Tom Griffin | .23 | .10 | .02 |
| ☐ 472 | Ken Rudolph | .23 | .10 | .02 |
| ☐ 473 | Gary Wagner | .23 | .10 | .02 |
| ☐ 474 | Jim Fairey | .23 | .10 | .02 |
| ☐ 475 | Ron Perranoski | .35 | .14 | .03 |
| ☐ 476 | Dal Maxvill | .23 | .10 | .02 |
| ☐ 477 | Earl Weaver MGR | .75 | .30 | .07 |
| ☐ 478 | Bernie Carbo | .23 | .10 | .02 |
| ☐ 479 | Dennis Higgins | .23 | .10 | .02 |
| ☐ 480 | Manny Sanguillen | .35 | .14 | .03 |
| ☐ 481 | Daryl Patterson | .23 | .10 | .02 |
| ☐ 482 | Padres Team | .55 | .22 | .05 |
| ☐ 483 | Gene Michael | .35 | .14 | .03 |
| ☐ 484 | Don Wilson | .23 | .10 | .02 |
| ☐ 485 | Ken McMullen | .23 | .10 | .02 |
| ☐ 486 | Steve Huntz | .23 | .10 | .02 |
| ☐ 487 | Paul Schaal | .23 | .10 | .02 |
| ☐ 488 | Jerry Stephenson | .23 | .10 | .02 |
| ☐ 489 | Luis Alvarado | .23 | .10 | .02 |
| ☐ 490 | Deron Johnson | .23 | .10 | .02 |
| ☐ 491 | Jim Hardin | .23 | .10 | .02 |
| ☐ 492 | Ken Boswell | .23 | .10 | .02 |
| ☐ 493 | Dave May | .23 | .10 | .02 |
| ☐ 494 | Braves Rookies | .35 | .14 | .03 |
| | Ralph Garr | | | |
| | Rick Kester | | | |
| ☐ 495 | Felipe Alou | .35 | .14 | .03 |
| ☐ 496 | Woody Woodward | .23 | .10 | .02 |
| ☐ 497 | Horacio Pina | .23 | .10 | .02 |
| ☐ 498 | John Kennedy | .23 | .10 | .02 |
| ☐ 499 | Checklist 5 | 1.00 | .10 | .02 |
| ☐ 500 | Jim Perry | .50 | .20 | .05 |
| ☐ 501 | Andy Etchebarren | .23 | .10 | .02 |
| ☐ 502 | Cubs Team | .55 | .22 | .05 |
| ☐ 503 | Gates Brown | .30 | .12 | .03 |
| ☐ 504 | Ken Wright | .23 | .10 | .02 |
| ☐ 505 | Ollie Brown | .23 | .10 | .02 |
| ☐ 506 | Bobby Knoop | .23 | .10 | .02 |
| ☐ 507 | George Stone | .23 | .10 | .02 |
| ☐ 508 | Roger Repoz | .23 | .10 | .02 |
| ☐ 509 | Jim Grant | .23 | .10 | .02 |
| ☐ 510 | Ken Harrelson | .65 | .26 | .06 |
| ☐ 511 | Chris Short | .23 | .10 | .02 |
| ☐ 512 | Red Sox Rookies | .23 | .10 | .02 |
| | Dick Mills | | | |
| | Mike Garman | | | |
| ☐ 513 | Nolan Ryan | 11.00 | 4.50 | 1.10 |
| ☐ 514 | Ron Woods | .23 | .10 | .02 |
| ☐ 515 | Carl Morton | .23 | .10 | .02 |
| ☐ 516 | Ted Kubiak | .23 | .10 | .02 |
| ☐ 517 | Charlie Fox MGR | .23 | .10 | .02 |
| ☐ 518 | Joe Grzenda | .23 | .10 | .02 |
| ☐ 519 | Willie Crawford | .23 | .10 | .02 |
| ☐ 520 | Tommy John | 1.50 | .60 | .15 |
| ☐ 521 | Leron Lee | .23 | .10 | .02 |
| ☐ 522 | Twins Team | .55 | .22 | .05 |
| ☐ 523 | John Odom | .23 | .10 | .02 |
| ☐ 524 | Mickey Stanley | .60 | .24 | .06 |
| ☐ 525 | Ernie Banks | 5.50 | 2.20 | .55 |
| ☐ 526 | Ray Jarvis | .45 | .18 | .04 |
| ☐ 527 | Cleon Jones | .45 | .18 | .04 |
| ☐ 528 | Wally Bunker | .45 | .18 | .04 |
| ☐ 529 | NL Rookie Infielders | 2.50 | 1.00 | .25 |
| | Enzo Hernandez | | | |
| | Bill Buckner | | | |
| | Marty Perez | | | |
| ☐ 530 | Carl Yastrzemski | 15.00 | 6.00 | 1.50 |
| ☐ 531 | Mike Torrez | .60 | .24 | .06 |
| ☐ 532 | Bill Rigney MGR | .45 | .18 | .04 |
| ☐ 533 | Mike Ryan | .45 | .18 | .04 |
| ☐ 534 | Luke Walker | .45 | .18 | .04 |
| ☐ 535 | Curt Flood | .65 | .26 | .06 |
| ☐ 536 | Claude Raymond | .45 | .18 | .04 |
| ☐ 537 | Tom Egan | .45 | .18 | .04 |
| ☐ 538 | Angel Bravo | .45 | .18 | .04 |
| ☐ 539 | Larry Brown | .45 | .18 | .04 |
| ☐ 540 | Larry Dierker | .60 | .24 | .06 |
| ☐ 541 | Bob Burda | .45 | .18 | .04 |
| ☐ 542 | Bob Miller | .45 | .18 | .04 |
| ☐ 543 | Yankees Team | 1.00 | .40 | .10 |
| ☐ 544 | Vida Blue | 2.25 | .90 | .22 |

| | | | | |
|---|---|---|---|---|
| ☐ 545 | Dick Dietz | .45 | .18 | .04 |
| ☐ 546 | John Matias | .45 | .18 | .04 |
| ☐ 547 | Pat Dobson | .60 | .24 | .06 |
| ☐ 548 | Don Mason | .45 | .18 | .04 |
| ☐ 549 | Jim Brewer | .45 | .18 | .04 |
| ☐ 550 | Harmon Killebrew | 4.50 | 1.80 | .45 |
| ☐ 551 | Frank Linzy | .45 | .18 | .04 |
| ☐ 552 | Buddy Bradford | .45 | .18 | .04 |
| ☐ 553 | Kevin Collins | .45 | .18 | .04 |
| ☐ 554 | Lowell Palmer | .45 | .18 | .04 |
| ☐ 555 | Walt Williams | .45 | .18 | .04 |
| ☐ 556 | Jim McGlothlin | .45 | .18 | .04 |
| ☐ 557 | Tom Satriano | .45 | .18 | .04 |
| ☐ 558 | Hector Torres | .45 | .18 | .04 |
| ☐ 559 | AL Rookie Pitchers | .45 | .18 | .04 |
| | Terry Cox | | | |
| | Bill Gogolewski | | | |
| | Gary Jones | | | |
| ☐ 560 | Rusty Staub | 1.00 | .40 | .10 |
| ☐ 561 | Syd O'Brien | .45 | .18 | .04 |
| ☐ 562 | Dave Giusti | .45 | .18 | .04 |
| ☐ 563 | Giants Team | 1.00 | .40 | .10 |
| ☐ 564 | Al Fitzmorris | .45 | .18 | .04 |
| ☐ 565 | Jim Wynn | .65 | .26 | .06 |
| ☐ 566 | Tim Cullen | .45 | .18 | .04 |
| ☐ 567 | Walt Alston MGR | 1.25 | .50 | .12 |
| ☐ 568 | Sal Campisi | .45 | .18 | .04 |
| ☐ 569 | Ivan Murrell | .45 | .18 | .04 |
| ☐ 570 | Jim Palmer | 6.00 | 2.40 | .60 |
| ☐ 571 | Ted Sizemore | .45 | .18 | .04 |
| ☐ 572 | Jerry Kenney | .45 | .18 | .04 |
| ☐ 573 | Ed Kranepool | .60 | .24 | .06 |
| ☐ 574 | Jim Bunning | 1.25 | .50 | .12 |
| ☐ 575 | Bill Freehan | .75 | .30 | .07 |
| ☐ 576 | Cubs Rookies | .45 | .18 | .04 |
| | Adrian Garrett | | | |
| | Brock Davis | | | |
| | Garry Jestadt | | | |
| ☐ 577 | Jim Lonborg | .60 | .24 | .06 |
| ☐ 578 | Ron Hunt | .45 | .18 | .04 |
| ☐ 579 | Marty Pattin | .45 | .18 | .04 |
| ☐ 580 | Tony Perez | 1.50 | .60 | .15 |
| ☐ 581 | Roger Nelson | .45 | .18 | .04 |
| ☐ 582 | Dave Cash | .60 | .24 | .06 |
| ☐ 583 | Ron Cook | .45 | .18 | .04 |
| ☐ 584 | Indians Team | 1.00 | .40 | .10 |
| ☐ 585 | Willie Davis | .65 | .26 | .06 |
| ☐ 586 | Dick Woodson | .45 | .18 | .04 |
| ☐ 587 | Sonny Jackson | .45 | .18 | .04 |
| ☐ 588 | Tom Bradley | .45 | .18 | .04 |
| ☐ 589 | Bob Barton | .45 | .18 | .04 |
| ☐ 590 | Alex Johnson | .60 | .24 | .06 |
| ☐ 591 | Jackie Brown | .60 | .24 | .06 |
| ☐ 592 | Randy Hundley | .45 | .18 | .04 |
| ☐ 593 | Jack Aker | .45 | .18 | .04 |
| ☐ 594 | Cards Rookies | .90 | .36 | .09 |
| | Bob Chlupsa | | | |
| | Bob Stinson | | | |
| | Al Hrabosky | | | |
| ☐ 595 | Dave Johnson | 1.25 | .50 | .12 |
| ☐ 596 | Mike Jorgensen | .45 | .18 | .04 |
| ☐ 597 | Ken Suarez | .45 | .18 | .04 |
| ☐ 598 | Rick Wise | .60 | .24 | .06 |
| ☐ 599 | Norm Cash | 1.00 | .40 | .10 |
| ☐ 600 | Willie Mays | 16.00 | 6.50 | 1.60 |
| ☐ 601 | Ken Tatum | .45 | .18 | .04 |
| ☐ 602 | Marty Martinez | .45 | .18 | .04 |
| ☐ 603 | Pirates Team | 1.00 | .40 | .10 |
| ☐ 604 | John Gelnar | .45 | .18 | .04 |
| ☐ 605 | Orlando Cepeda | 1.50 | .60 | .15 |
| ☐ 606 | Chuck Taylor | .45 | .18 | .04 |
| ☐ 607 | Paul Ratliff | .45 | .18 | .04 |
| ☐ 608 | Mike Wegener | .45 | .18 | .04 |
| ☐ 609 | Leo Durocher MGR | .80 | .32 | .08 |
| ☐ 610 | Amos Otis | .75 | .30 | .07 |
| ☐ 611 | Tom Phoebus | .45 | .18 | .04 |
| ☐ 612 | Indians Rookies | .45 | .18 | .04 |
| | Lou Camilli | | | |
| | Ted Ford | | | |
| | Steve Mingori | | | |
| ☐ 613 | Pedro Borbon | .45 | .18 | .04 |
| ☐ 614 | Billy Cowan | .45 | .18 | .04 |
| ☐ 615 | Mel Stottlemyre | .75 | .30 | .07 |
| ☐ 616 | Larry Hisle | .60 | .24 | .06 |
| ☐ 617 | Clay Dalrymple | .45 | .18 | .04 |
| ☐ 618 | Tug McGraw | 1.00 | .40 | .10 |
| ☐ 619A | Checklist 6 | 1.50 | .15 | .03 |
| | (copyright on back) | | | |
| ☐ 619B | Checklist 6 | 2.00 | .20 | .04 |
| | (no copyright) | | | |
| ☐ 620 | Frank Howard | 1.00 | .40 | .10 |
| ☐ 621 | Ron Bryant | .45 | .18 | .04 |
| ☐ 622 | Joe Lahoud | .45 | .18 | .04 |

| | | | | |
|---|---|---|---|---|
| ☐ 623 | Pat Jarvis | .45 | .18 | .04 |
| ☐ 624 | Athletics Team | 1.00 | .40 | .10 |
| ☐ 625 | Lou Brock | 6.50 | 2.60 | .65 |
| ☐ 626 | Freddie Patek | .60 | .24 | .06 |
| ☐ 627 | Steve Hamilton | .45 | .18 | .04 |
| ☐ 628 | John Bateman | .45 | .18 | .04 |
| ☐ 629 | John Hiller | .60 | .24 | .06 |
| ☐ 630 | Roberto Clemente | 15.00 | 6.00 | 1.50 |
| ☐ 631 | Eddie Fisher | .45 | .18 | .04 |
| ☐ 632 | Darrel Chaney | .45 | .18 | .04 |
| ☐ 633 | AL Rookie Outfielders | .45 | .18 | .04 |
| | Bobby Brooks | | | |
| | Pete Koegel | | | |
| | Scott Northey | | | |
| ☐ 634 | Phil Regan | .60 | .24 | .06 |
| ☐ 635 | Bobby Murcer | 1.00 | .40 | .10 |
| ☐ 636 | Denny Lemaster | .45 | .18 | .04 |
| ☐ 637 | Dave Bristol MGR | .45 | .18 | .04 |
| ☐ 638 | Stan Williams | .45 | .18 | .04 |
| ☐ 639 | Tom Haller | .45 | .18 | .04 |
| ☐ 640 | Frank Robinson | 7.50 | 3.00 | .75 |
| ☐ 641 | Mets Team | 1.50 | .60 | .15 |
| ☐ 642 | Jim Roland | .45 | .18 | .04 |
| ☐ 643 | Rick Reichardt | .45 | .18 | .04 |
| ☐ 644 | Jim Stewart | 1.00 | .40 | .10 |
| ☐ 645 | Jim Maloney | 1.25 | .50 | .12 |
| ☐ 646 | Bobby Floyd | 1.00 | .40 | .10 |
| ☐ 647 | Juan Pizarro | 1.00 | .40 | .10 |
| ☐ 648 | Mets Rookies | 3.00 | 1.20 | .30 |
| | Rich Folkers | | | |
| | Ted Martinez | | | |
| | John Matlack | | | |
| ☐ 649 | Sparky Lyle | 2.00 | .80 | .20 |
| ☐ 650 | Rich Allen | 5.00 | 2.00 | .50 |
| ☐ 651 | Jerry Robertson | 1.00 | .40 | .10 |
| ☐ 652 | Braves Team | 2.00 | .80 | .20 |
| ☐ 653 | Russ Snyder | 1.00 | .40 | .10 |
| ☐ 654 | Don Shaw | 1.00 | .40 | .10 |
| ☐ 655 | Mike Epstein | 1.00 | .40 | .10 |
| ☐ 656 | Gerry Nyman | 1.00 | .40 | .10 |
| ☐ 657 | Jose Azcue | 1.00 | .40 | .10 |
| ☐ 658 | Paul Lindblad | 1.00 | .40 | .10 |
| ☐ 659 | Byron Browne | 1.00 | .40 | .10 |
| ☐ 660 | Ray Culp | 1.00 | .40 | .10 |
| ☐ 661 | Chuck Tanner MGR | 1.75 | .70 | .17 |
| ☐ 662 | Mike Hedlund | 1.00 | .40 | .10 |
| ☐ 663 | Marv Staehle | 1.00 | .40 | .10 |
| ☐ 664 | Rookie Pitchers | 1.25 | .50 | .12 |
| | Archie Reynolds | | | |
| | Bob Reynolds | | | |
| | Ken Reynolds | | | |
| ☐ 665 | Ron Swoboda | 1.25 | .50 | .12 |
| ☐ 666 | Gene Brabender | 1.00 | .40 | .10 |
| ☐ 667 | Pete Ward | 1.00 | .40 | .10 |
| ☐ 668 | Gary Neibauer | 1.00 | .40 | .10 |
| ☐ 669 | Ike Brown | 1.00 | .40 | .10 |
| ☐ 670 | Bill Hands | 1.00 | .40 | .10 |
| ☐ 671 | Bill Voss | 1.00 | .40 | .10 |
| ☐ 672 | Ed Crosby | 1.00 | .40 | .10 |
| ☐ 673 | Gerry Janeski | 1.00 | .40 | .10 |
| ☐ 674 | Expos Team | 2.25 | .90 | .22 |
| ☐ 675 | Dave Boswell | 1.00 | .40 | .10 |
| ☐ 676 | Tommie Reynolds | 1.00 | .40 | .10 |
| ☐ 677 | Jack DiLauro | 1.00 | .40 | .10 |
| ☐ 678 | George Thomas | 1.00 | .40 | .10 |
| ☐ 679 | Don O'Riley | 1.00 | .40 | .10 |
| ☐ 680 | Don Mincher | 1.25 | .50 | .12 |
| ☐ 681 | Bill Butler | 1.00 | .40 | .10 |
| ☐ 682 | Terry Harmon | 1.00 | .40 | .10 |
| ☐ 683 | Bill Burbach | 1.00 | .40 | .10 |
| ☐ 684 | Curt Motton | 1.00 | .40 | .10 |
| ☐ 685 | Moe Drabowsky | 1.00 | .40 | .10 |
| ☐ 686 | Chico Ruiz | 1.00 | .40 | .10 |
| ☐ 687 | Ron Taylor | 1.00 | .40 | .10 |
| ☐ 688 | Sparky Anderson MGR | 2.25 | .90 | .22 |
| ☐ 689 | Frank Baker | 1.00 | .40 | .10 |
| ☐ 690 | Bob Moose | 1.00 | .40 | .10 |
| ☐ 691 | Bob Heise | 1.00 | .40 | .10 |
| ☐ 692 | AL Rookie Pitchers | 1.00 | .40 | .10 |
| | Hal Haydel | | | |
| | Rogelio Moret | | | |
| | Wayne Twitchell | | | |
| ☐ 693 | Jose Pena | 1.00 | .40 | .10 |
| ☐ 694 | Rick Renick | 1.00 | .40 | .10 |
| ☐ 695 | Joe Niekro | 2.00 | .80 | .20 |
| ☐ 696 | Jerry Morales | 1.00 | .40 | .10 |
| ☐ 697 | Rickey Clark | 1.00 | .40 | .10 |
| ☐ 698 | Brewers Team | 2.25 | .90 | .22 |
| ☐ 699 | Jim Britton | 1.00 | .40 | .10 |
| ☐ 700 | Boog Powell | 2.25 | .90 | .22 |
| ☐ 701 | Bob Garibaldi | 1.00 | .40 | .10 |
| ☐ 702 | Milt Ramirez | 1.00 | .40 | .10 |
| ☐ 703 | Mike Kekich | 1.00 | .40 | .10 |

| | | | | |
|---|---|---|---|---|
| ☐ 704 | J.C. Martin | 1.00 | .40 | .10 |
| ☐ 705 | Dick Selma | 1.00 | .40 | .10 |
| ☐ 706 | Joe Foy | 1.00 | .40 | .10 |
| ☐ 707 | Fred Lasher | 1.00 | .40 | .10 |
| ☐ 708 | Russ Nagelson | 1.00 | .40 | .10 |
| ☐ 709 | Rookie Outfielders | 18.00 | 7.25 | 1.80 |
| | Dusty Baker | | | |
| | Don Baylor | | | |
| | Tom Paciorek | | | |
| ☐ 710 | Sonny Siebert | 1.25 | .50 | .12 |
| ☐ 711 | Larry Stahl | 1.00 | .40 | .10 |
| ☐ 712 | Jose Martinez | 1.00 | .40 | .10 |
| ☐ 713 | Mike Marshall | 1.50 | .60 | .15 |
| ☐ 714 | Dick Williams MGR | 1.25 | .50 | .12 |
| ☐ 715 | Horace Clarke | 1.00 | .40 | .10 |
| ☐ 716 | Dave Leonhard | 1.00 | .40 | .10 |
| ☐ 717 | Tommie Aaron | 1.25 | .50 | .12 |
| ☐ 718 | Billy Wynne | 1.00 | .40 | .10 |
| ☐ 719 | Jerry May | 1.00 | .40 | .10 |
| ☐ 720 | Matty Alou | 1.25 | .50 | .12 |
| ☐ 721 | John Morris | 1.00 | .40 | .10 |
| ☐ 722 | Astros Team | 2.00 | .80 | .20 |
| ☐ 723 | Vicente Romo | 1.00 | .40 | .10 |
| ☐ 724 | Tom Tischinski | 1.00 | .40 | .10 |
| ☐ 725 | Gary Gentry | 1.00 | .40 | .10 |
| ☐ 726 | Paul Popovich | 1.00 | .40 | .10 |
| ☐ 727 | Ray Lamb | 1.00 | .40 | .10 |
| ☐ 728 | NL Rookie Outfielders | 1.00 | .40 | .10 |
| | Wayne Redmond | | | |
| | Keith Lampard | | | |
| | Bernie Williams | | | |
| ☐ 729 | Dick Billings | 1.00 | .40 | .10 |
| ☐ 730 | Jim Rooker | 1.00 | .40 | .10 |
| ☐ 731 | Jim Qualls | 1.00 | .40 | .10 |
| ☐ 732 | Bob Reed | 1.00 | .40 | .10 |
| ☐ 733 | Lee Maye | 1.00 | .40 | .10 |
| ☐ 734 | Rob Gardner | 1.00 | .40 | .10 |
| ☐ 735 | Mike Shannon | 1.50 | .60 | .15 |
| ☐ 736 | Mel Queen | 1.00 | .40 | .10 |
| ☐ 737 | Preston Gomez MGR | 1.00 | .40 | .10 |
| ☐ 738 | Russ Gibson | 1.00 | .40 | .10 |
| ☐ 739 | Barry Lersch | 1.00 | .40 | .10 |
| ☐ 740 | Luis Aparicio | 6.00 | 2.40 | .60 |
| ☐ 741 | Skip Guinn | 1.00 | .40 | .10 |
| ☐ 742 | Royals Team | 2.25 | .90 | .22 |
| ☐ 743 | John O'Donoghue | 1.00 | .40 | .10 |
| ☐ 744 | Chuck Manuel | 1.00 | .40 | .10 |
| ☐ 745 | Sandy Alomar | 1.00 | .40 | .10 |
| ☐ 746 | Andy Kosco | 1.00 | .40 | .10 |
| ☐ 747 | NL Rookie Pitchers | 1.00 | .40 | .10 |
| | Al Severinsen | | | |
| | Scipio Spinks | | | |
| | Balor Moore | | | |
| ☐ 748 | John Purdin | 1.00 | .40 | .10 |
| ☐ 749 | Ken Szotkiewicz | 1.00 | .40 | .10 |
| ☐ 750 | Denny McLain | 2.25 | .90 | .22 |
| ☐ 751 | Al Weis | 1.50 | .60 | .15 |
| ☐ 752 | Dick Drago | 1.50 | .50 | .10 |

## 1971 Topps Greatest Moments

The cards in this 55 card set measure 2 1/2" by 4 3/4". The 1971 Topps Greatest Moments set contains numbered cards depicting specific career highlights of current players. The obverses are black bordered and contain a small cameo picture of the left side; a deckle bordered black and white action photo dominates the rest of the card. The backs are designed in newspaper style. Sometimes found in uncut sheets, this test set was retailed in gum packs on a very limited basis. Double prints (DP) are listed in the checklist below; there were 22 double prints and 33 single prints.

| | MINT | VG-E | F-G |
|---|---|---|---|
| COMPLETE SET | 900.00 | 360.00 | 90.00 |
| COMMON CARD | 12.00 | 5.00 | 1.20 |
| COMMON CARD (DP) | 3.00 | 1.20 | .30 |

| | | | | |
|---|---|---|---|---|
| ☐ 1 | Thurman Munson: 1970 AL ROY DP | 20.00 | 8.00 | 2.00 |
| ☐ 2 | Hoyt Wilhelm: Hurls 1000th Game | 25.00 | 10.00 | 2.50 |

| | | | | |
|---|---|---|---|---|
| ☐ 3 | Rico Carty: Leads ML .366 in 1970 | 12.00 | 5.00 | 1.20 |
| ☐ 4 | Carl Morton: 1970 NL ROY DP | 3.00 | 1.20 | .30 |
| ☐ 5 | Sal Bando: Plays All A's Games 1st 2 years DP | 3.00 | 1.20 | .30 |
| ☐ 6 | Bert Campaneris: Hits 2 HRs in First ML Game DP | 3.00 | 1.20 | .30 |
| ☐ 7 | Jim Kaat: Gold Glove 9 Straight Years | 15.00 | 6.00 | 1.50 |
| ☐ 8 | Harmon Killebrew: Tops 40 Homers 8th Time | 35.00 | 14.00 | 3.50 |
| ☐ 9 | Brooks Robinson: MVP 1970 W.S. | 60.00 | 24.00 | 6.00 |
| ☐ 10 | Jim Perry: AL Cy Young 1970 | 12.00 | 5.00 | 1.20 |
| ☐ 11 | Tony Oliva: Leads AL in Batting 1st 2 Full Years | 15.00 | 6.00 | 1.50 |
| ☐ 12 | Vada Pinson: Tops 200 Hits 1st Full Year in ML | 15.00 | 6.00 | 1.50 |
| ☐ 13 | Johnny Bench: 1970 ML Player of the Year. | 125.00 | 50.00 | 12.50 |
| ☐ 14 | Tony Perez: 15th Inning Homer Wins A-S Game | 15.00 | 6.00 | 1.50 |
| ☐ 15 | Pete Rose: Leads ML Batting 2nd Cons. year. DP | 100.00 | 40.00 | 10.00 |
| ☐ 16 | Jim Fregosi: Hits for cycle twice DP | 3.00 | 1.20 | .30 |
| ☐ 17 | Alex Johnson: Leads AL batting 1st year in league DP | 3.00 | 1.20 | .30 |
| ☐ 18 | Clyde Wright: No-Hitter vs. A's DP | 3.00 | 1.20 | .30 |
| ☐ 19 | Al Kaline: Youngest player to win AL batting crown DP | 20.00 | 8.00 | 2.00 |
| ☐ 20 | Denny McLain: 1st AL Pitcher to win 30 in 37 years | 15.00 | 6.00 | 1.50 |
| ☐ 21 | Jim Northrup: Hits Three Grand-Slams in One Week | 12.00 | 5.00 | 1.20 |
| ☐ 22 | Bill Freehan: Leads AL Catchers in fielding 6 cons. years | 12.00 | 5.00 | 1.20 |
| ☐ 23 | Mickey Lolich: Wins 3 in 1968 W.S. | 15.00 | 6.00 | 1.50 |
| ☐ 24 | Bob Gibson: Lowest ERA ever 300 or more innings DP | 12.00 | 5.00 | 1.20 |
| ☐ 25 | Tim McCarver: 1st catcher to lead ML in triples DP | 3.00 | 1.20 | .30 |

| | | MINT | VG-E | F-G |
|---|---|---|---|---|
| ☐ 26 | Orlando Cepeda: ...............<br>1967 NL player<br>of the year DP | 4.00 | 1.60 | .40 |
| ☐ 27 | Lou Brock: 50 SB's 6th ....<br>straight year DP | 15.00 | 6.00 | 1.50 |
| ☐ 28 | Nate Colbert: New Club ....<br>Mark with 38 HR's DP | 3.00 | 1.20 | .30 |
| ☐ 29 | Maury Wills: ......................<br>Sets Modern Mark<br>with 104 SB's | 15.00 | 6.00 | 1.50 |
| ☐ 30 | Wes Parker: Leads ...........<br>ML with 47 Doubles | 12.00 | 5.00 | 1.20 |
| ☐ 31 | Jim Wynn: 1 of 2 Astro .....<br>Grand Slams<br>Same Inning | 12.00 | 5.00 | 1.20 |
| ☐ 32 | Larry Dierker: ...................<br>Makes ML Debut<br>on 18th Birthday | 12.00 | 5.00 | 1.20 |
| ☐ 33 | Bill Melton: .......................<br>1st Chisox<br>to Hit 30 HR's | 12.00 | 5.00 | 1.20 |
| ☐ 34 | Joe Morgan: ......................<br>Ties Record<br>6 Hits in 6 AB's | 25.00 | 10.00 | 2.50 |
| ☐ 35 | Rusty Staub: .....................<br>Leads ML 44 2B's. | 15.00 | 6.00 | 1.50 |
| ☐ 36 | Ernie Banks: Sets ML ........<br>Record with 5<br>Grand Slams. DP | 20.00 | 8.00 | 2.00 |
| ☐ 37 | Billy Williams: 1117 ..........<br>Cons. Games | 25.00 | 10.00 | 2.50 |
| ☐ 38 | Lou Piniella: 1969 ............<br>AL ROY | 15.00 | 6.00 | 1.50 |
| ☐ 39 | Rico Petrocelli: AL HR ......<br>Mark for SS's DP | 3.00 | 1.20 | .30 |
| ☐ 40 | Carl Yastrzemski: AL .........<br>Triple Crown DP | 60.00 | 24.00 | 6.00 |
| ☐ 41 | Willie Mays: 3000th ..........<br>Career Hit DP | 40.00 | 16.00 | 4.00 |
| ☐ 42 | Tommy Harper: .................<br>Leads ML 73 SB's | 12.00 | 5.00 | 1.20 |
| ☐ 43 | Jim Bunning: No-Hitter .....<br>Both AL and NL DP | 5.00 | 2.00 | .50 |
| ☐ 44 | Fritz Peterson: ..................<br>Wins 20th on<br>Last Day of 1970 | 12.00 | 5.00 | 1.20 |
| ☐ 45 | Roy White: Hits HR's ........<br>Lefty and Righty | 12.00 | 5.00 | 1.20 |
| ☐ 46 | Bobby Murcer: ..................<br>Hits 4 Cons. HR's<br>in a Twinbill | 12.00 | 5.00 | 1.20 |
| ☐ 47 | Reggie Jackson: ...............<br>10 RBI's One Game | 125.00 | 50.00 | 12.50 |
| ☐ 48 | Frank Howard: ..................<br>New Record, 10<br>HR's in One Week | 12.00 | 5.00 | 1.20 |
| ☐ 49 | Dick Bosman: ...................<br>Leads AL in ERA | 12.00 | 5.00 | 1.20 |
| ☐ 50 | Sam McDowell: .................<br>Hurls Two Cons.<br>One-Hitters DP | 3.00 | 1.20 | .30 |
| ☐ 51 | Luis Aparicio: ...................<br>Leads AL SB's 9<br>cons. years DP | 10.00 | 4.00 | 1.00 |
| ☐ 52 | Willie McCovey: ................<br>Four Hits in<br>His First Game DP | 12.00 | 5.00 | 1.20 |
| ☐ 53 | Joe Pepitone: ...................<br>2 HR's One Inning | 12.00 | 5.00 | 1.20 |
| ☐ 54 | Jerry Grote: 20 PO's .........<br>in 9 Inning Game | 12.00 | 5.00 | 1.20 |
| ☐ 55 | Bud Harrelson: .................<br>54 Consecutive<br>Errorless Games SS | 12.00 | 5.00 | 1.20 |

## 1971 Topps Super

The cards in this 63 card set measure 3 1/8" by 5 1/4". The obverse format of the Topps Super set of 1971 is identical to that of the 1970 set, that is, a borderless color photograph with a facsimile autograph printed on it. The backs are enlargements of the respective player's cards of the 1971 regular baseball issue. There are no reported scarcities in the set.

| | | MINT | VG-E | F-G |
|---|---|---|---|---|
| | COMPLETE SET ........................ | 140.00 | 56.00 | 14.00 |
| | COMMON PLAYER (1-63) .......... | .75 | .30 | .07 |
| ☐ 1 | Reggie Smith ..................... | .90 | .36 | .09 |
| ☐ 2 | Gaylord Perry ..................... | 2.75 | 1.10 | .27 |
| ☐ 3 | Ted Savage ........................ | .75 | .30 | .07 |
| ☐ 4 | Donn Clendenon ................. | .75 | .30 | .07 |
| ☐ 5 | Boog Powell ....................... | .90 | .36 | .09 |
| ☐ 6 | Tony Perez ......................... | 1.25 | .50 | .12 |
| ☐ 7 | Dick Bosman ...................... | .75 | .30 | .07 |
| ☐ 8 | Alex Johnson ...................... | .75 | .30 | .07 |
| ☐ 9 | Rusty Staub ....................... | 1.00 | .40 | .10 |
| ☐ 10 | Mel Stottlemyre .................. | .75 | .30 | .07 |
| ☐ 11 | Tony Oliva ......................... | 1.00 | .40 | .10 |
| ☐ 12 | Bill Freehan ....................... | .75 | .30 | .07 |
| ☐ 13 | Fritz Peterson .................... | .75 | .30 | .07 |
| ☐ 14 | Wes Parker ........................ | .75 | .30 | .07 |
| ☐ 15 | Cesar Cedeno ..................... | .75 | .30 | .07 |
| ☐ 16 | Sam McDowell .................... | .75 | .30 | .07 |
| ☐ 17 | Frank Howard ..................... | .75 | .30 | .07 |
| ☐ 18 | Dave McNally ...................... | .75 | .30 | .07 |
| ☐ 19 | Rico Petrocelli ................... | .75 | .30 | .07 |
| ☐ 20 | Pete Rose .......................... | 24.00 | 10.00 | 2.40 |
| ☐ 21 | Luke Walker ....................... | .75 | .30 | .07 |
| ☐ 22 | Nate Colbert ...................... | .75 | .30 | .07 |
| ☐ 23 | Luis Aparicio ...................... | 2.00 | .80 | .20 |
| ☐ 24 | Jim Perry .......................... | .90 | .36 | .09 |
| ☐ 25 | Lou Brock .......................... | 3.50 | 1.40 | .35 |
| ☐ 26 | Roy White .......................... | .75 | .30 | .07 |
| ☐ 27 | Claude Osteen .................... | .75 | .30 | .07 |
| ☐ 28 | Carl Morton ....................... | .75 | .30 | .07 |
| ☐ 29 | Rico Carty ......................... | .90 | .36 | .09 |
| ☐ 30 | Larry Dierker ..................... | .75 | .30 | .07 |
| ☐ 31 | Bert Campaneris ................. | .75 | .30 | .07 |
| ☐ 32 | Johnny Bench ..................... | 7.50 | 3.00 | .75 |
| ☐ 33 | Felix Millan ....................... | .75 | .30 | .07 |
| ☐ 34 | Tim McCarver ..................... | .90 | .36 | .09 |
| ☐ 35 | Ron Santo ......................... | .90 | .36 | .09 |
| ☐ 36 | Tommie Agee ...................... | .75 | .30 | .07 |
| ☐ 37 | Bob Clemente ..................... | 9.00 | 3.75 | .90 |
| ☐ 38 | Reggie Jackson ................... | 12.00 | 5.00 | 1.20 |
| ☐ 39 | Clyde Wright ...................... | .75 | .30 | .07 |
| ☐ 40 | Rich Allen ......................... | .90 | .36 | .09 |
| ☐ 41 | Curt Flood ......................... | .90 | .36 | .09 |
| ☐ 42 | Fergie Jenkins ................... | 1.25 | .50 | .12 |
| ☐ 43 | Willie Stargell .................... | 3.00 | 1.20 | .30 |
| ☐ 44 | Hank Aaron ........................ | 10.00 | 4.00 | 1.00 |
| ☐ 45 | Amos Otis .......................... | .75 | .30 | .07 |
| ☐ 46 | Willie McCovey .................... | 3.50 | 1.40 | .35 |
| ☐ 47 | Bill Melton ........................ | .75 | .30 | .07 |
| ☐ 48 | Bob Gibson ........................ | 3.00 | 1.20 | .30 |
| ☐ 49 | Carl Yastremski .................. | 12.00 | 5.00 | 1.20 |
| ☐ 50 | Glenn Beckert ..................... | .75 | .30 | .07 |
| ☐ 51 | Ray Fosse ......................... | .75 | .30 | .07 |
| ☐ 52 | Cito Gaston ....................... | .75 | .30 | .07 |
| ☐ 53 | Tom Seaver ........................ | 9.00 | 3.75 | .90 |
| ☐ 54 | Al Kaline .......................... | 6.00 | 2.40 | .60 |
| ☐ 55 | Jim Northup ....................... | .75 | .30 | .07 |
| ☐ 56 | Willie Mays ........................ | 10.00 | 4.00 | 1.00 |
| ☐ 57 | Sal Bando .......................... | .75 | .30 | .07 |
| ☐ 58 | Deron Johnson ................... | .75 | .30 | .07 |
| ☐ 59 | Brooks Robinson ................. | 6.50 | 2.60 | .65 |

| | | | MINT | VG-E | F-G |
|---|---|---|---|---|---|
| ☐ | 60 | Harmon Killebrew ............ | 3.00 | 1.20 | .30 |
| ☐ | 61 | Joe Torre ......................... | 1.00 | .40 | .10 |
| ☐ | 62 | Lou Piniella ..................... | .90 | .36 | .09 |
| ☐ | 63 | Tommy Harper ................. | .75 | .30 | .07 |

# 1972 Topps

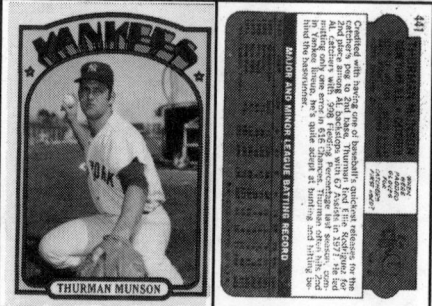

The cards in this 787 card set measure 2 1/2" by 3 1/2". The 1972 Topps set contained the most cards ever for a Topps set to that point in time. Features appearing for the first time were "Boyhood Photos" (KP: 341-348 and 491-498), Awards and Trophy cards (621-626), "In Action" (distributed throughout the set) and "Traded Cards" (TR: 751-757). Other subsets included League Leaders (85-96), Playoffs cards (221-222), and World Series cards (223-230). The curved lines of the color picture are a departure from the rectangular designs of other years. There is a series of intermediate scarcity (526-656) and the usual high numbers (657-787).

| | | MINT | VG-E | F-G |
|---|---|---|---|---|
| COMPLETE SET ........................ | | 675.00 | 300.00 | 75.00 |
| COMMON PLAYER (1-132) ........ | | .15 | .06 | .01 |
| COMMON PLAYER (133-394) .... | | .18 | .08 | .01 |
| COMMON PLAYER (395-525) .... | | .22 | .10 | .02 |
| COMMON PLAYER (526-656) .... | | .40 | .16 | .04 |
| COMMON PLAYER (657-787) .... | | 1.20 | .50 | .12 |

| | | | MINT | VG-E | F-G |
|---|---|---|---|---|---|
| ☐ | 1 | Pirates Team .................. | 1.75 | .35 | .05 |
| ☐ | 2 | Ray Culp ........................ | .15 | .06 | .01 |
| ☐ | 3 | Bob Tolan ...................... | .15 | .06 | .01 |
| ☐ | 4 | Checklist 1 ..................... | .90 | .10 | .02 |
| ☐ | 5 | John Bateman ................. | .15 | .06 | .01 |
| ☐ | 6 | Fred Scherman ............... | .15 | .06 | .01 |
| ☐ | 7 | Enzo Hernandez ............. | .15 | .06 | .01 |
| ☐ | 8 | Ron Swoboda ................. | .20 | .08 | .02 |
| ☐ | 9 | Stan Williams ................. | .15 | .06 | .01 |
| ☐ | 10 | Amos Otis ...................... | .30 | .12 | .03 |
| ☐ | 11 | Bobby Valentine ............. | .50 | .20 | .05 |
| ☐ | 12 | Jose Cardenal ................. | .15 | .06 | .01 |
| ☐ | 13 | Joe Grzenda ................... | .15 | .06 | .01 |
| ☐ | 14 | Phillies Rookies .............. | .15 | .06 | .01 |
| | | Pete Koegel | | | |
| | | Mike Anderson | | | |
| | | Wayne Twitchell | | | |
| ☐ | 15 | Walt Williams ................. | .15 | .06 | .01 |
| ☐ | 16 | Mike Jorgensen .............. | .15 | .06 | .01 |
| ☐ | 17 | Dave Duncan .................. | .15 | .06 | .01 |
| ☐ | 18A | Juan Pizarro ................... | .20 | .08 | .02 |
| | | (yellow underline | | | |
| | | C and S of Cubs) | | | |
| ☐ | 18B | Juan Pizarro ................... | 4.00 | 1.60 | .40 |
| | | (green underline | | | |
| | | C and S of Cubs) | | | |
| ☐ | 19 | Billy Cowan .................... | .15 | .06 | .01 |
| ☐ | 20 | Don Wilson ..................... | .15 | .06 | .01 |
| ☐ | 21 | Braves Team .................. | .50 | .20 | .05 |
| ☐ | 22 | Rob Gardner ................... | .15 | .06 | .01 |
| ☐ | 23 | Ted Kubiak ..................... | .15 | .06 | .01 |
| ☐ | 24 | Ted Ford ........................ | .15 | .06 | .01 |
| ☐ | 25 | Bill Singer ...................... | .15 | .06 | .01 |

| | | | MINT | VG-E | F-G |
|---|---|---|---|---|---|
| ☐ | 26 | Andy Etchebarren ........... | .15 | .06 | .01 |
| ☐ | 27 | Bob Johnson .................. | .15 | .06 | .01 |
| ☐ | 28 | Twins Rookies ................. | .15 | .06 | .01 |
| | | Bob Gebhard | | | |
| | | Steve Brye | | | |
| | | Hal Haydel | | | |
| ☐ | 29A | Bill Bonham ................... | .20 | .08 | .02 |
| | | (yellow underline | | | |
| | | C and S of Cubs) | | | |
| ☐ | 29B | Bill Bonham ................... | 4.00 | 1.60 | .40 |
| | | (green underline | | | |
| | | C and S of Cubs) | | | |
| ☐ | 30 | Rico Petrocelli ............... | .25 | .10 | .02 |
| ☐ | 31 | Cleon Jones ................... | .15 | .06 | .01 |
| ☐ | 32 | Jones In Action .............. | .15 | .06 | .01 |
| ☐ | 33 | Billy Martin MGR ............ | .90 | .36 | .09 |
| ☐ | 34 | Martin In Action ............. | .50 | .20 | .05 |
| ☐ | 35 | Jerry Johnson ................. | .15 | .06 | .01 |
| ☐ | 36 | Johnson In Action ........... | .15 | .06 | .01 |
| ☐ | 37 | Carl Yastrzemski ............ | 9.00 | 3.75 | .90 |
| ☐ | 38 | Yastrzemski In Action ..... | 4.50 | 1.80 | .45 |
| ☐ | 39 | Bob Barton ..................... | .15 | .06 | .01 |
| ☐ | 40 | Barton In Action ............. | .15 | .06 | .01 |
| ☐ | 41 | Tommy Davis ................. | .25 | .10 | .02 |
| ☐ | 42 | Davis In Action ............... | .20 | .08 | .02 |
| ☐ | 43 | Rick Wise ...................... | .15 | .06 | .01 |
| ☐ | 44 | Wise In Action ............... | .15 | .06 | .01 |
| ☐ | 45A | Glenn Beckert ................ | .30 | .12 | .03 |
| | | (yellow underline | | | |
| | | C and S of Cubs) | | | |
| ☐ | 45B | Glenn Beckert ............... | 4.50 | 1.80 | .45 |
| | | (green underline | | | |
| | | C and S of Cubs) | | | |
| ☐ | 46 | Beckert In Action ........... | .20 | .08 | .02 |
| ☐ | 47 | John Ellis ....................... | .15 | .06 | .01 |
| ☐ | 48 | Ellis In Action ................ | .15 | .06 | .01 |
| ☐ | 49 | Willie Mays .................... | 9.00 | 3.75 | .90 |
| ☐ | 50 | Mays In Action ............... | 4.50 | 1.80 | .45 |
| ☐ | 51 | Harmon Killebrew ........... | 2.00 | .80 | .20 |
| ☐ | 52 | Killebrew In Action ......... | 1.00 | .40 | .10 |
| ☐ | 53 | Bud Harrelson ................ | .15 | .06 | .01 |
| ☐ | 54 | Harrelson In Action ........ | .15 | .06 | .01 |
| ☐ | 55 | Clyde Wright .................. | .15 | .06 | .01 |
| ☐ | 56 | Rich Chiles .................... | .15 | .06 | .01 |
| ☐ | 57 | Bob Oliver ..................... | .15 | .06 | .01 |
| ☐ | 58 | Ernie McAnally ............... | .15 | .06 | .01 |
| ☐ | 59 | Fred Stanley ................... | .15 | .06 | .01 |
| ☐ | 60 | Manny Sanguillen ........... | .25 | .10 | .02 |
| ☐ | 61 | Cubs Rookies ................. | .60 | .24 | .06 |
| | | Burt Hooton | | | |
| | | Gene Hiser | | | |
| | | Earl Stephenson | | | |
| ☐ | 62 | Angel Mangual ................ | .15 | .06 | .01 |
| ☐ | 63 | Duke Sims ...................... | .15 | .06 | .01 |
| ☐ | 64 | Pete Broberg .................. | .15 | .06 | .01 |
| ☐ | 65 | Cesar Cedeno ................. | .60 | .24 | .06 |
| ☐ | 66 | Ray Corbin ..................... | .15 | .06 | .01 |
| ☐ | 67 | Red Schoendienst MGR .. | .30 | .12 | .03 |
| ☐ | 68 | Jim York ......................... | .15 | .06 | .01 |
| ☐ | 69 | Roger Freed ................... | .15 | .06 | .01 |
| ☐ | 70 | Mike Cuellar ................... | .25 | .10 | .02 |
| ☐ | 71 | Angels Team .................. | .45 | .18 | .04 |
| ☐ | 72 | Bruce Kison ................... | .50 | .20 | .05 |
| ☐ | 73 | Steve Huntz ................... | .15 | .06 | .01 |
| ☐ | 74 | Cecil Upshaw ................. | .15 | .06 | .01 |
| ☐ | 75 | Bert Campaneris ............ | .30 | .12 | .03 |
| ☐ | 76 | Don Carrithers ............... | .15 | .06 | .01 |
| ☐ | 77 | Ron Theobald ................. | .15 | .06 | .01 |
| ☐ | 78 | Steve Arlin .................... | .15 | .06 | .01 |
| ☐ | 79 | Red Sox Rookies ............ | 18.00 | 7.25 | 1.80 |
| | | Mike Garman | | | |
| | | Cecil Cooper | | | |
| | | Carlton Fisk | | | |
| ☐ | 80 | Tony Perez ..................... | 1.00 | .40 | .10 |
| ☐ | 81 | Mike Hedlund .................. | .15 | .06 | .01 |
| ☐ | 82 | Ron Woods ..................... | .15 | .06 | .01 |
| ☐ | 83 | Dalton Jones .................. | .15 | .06 | .01 |
| ☐ | 84 | Vince Colbert ................. | .15 | .06 | .01 |
| ☐ | 85 | NL Batting Leaders: ........ | .50 | .20 | .05 |
| | | Joe Torre | | | |
| | | Ralph Garr | | | |
| | | Glenn Beckert | | | |
| ☐ | 86 | AL Batting Leaders: ........ | .50 | .20 | .05 |
| | | Tony Oliva | | | |
| | | Bobby Murcer | | | |
| | | Merv Rettenmund | | | |
| ☐ | 87 | NL RBI Leaders: ............. | 1.00 | .40 | .10 |
| | | Joe Torre | | | |
| | | Willie Stargell | | | |
| | | Hank Aaron | | | |
| ☐ | 88 | AL RBI Leaders: ............. | .75 | .30 | .07 |
| | | Harmon Killebrew | | | |
| | | Frank Robinson | | | |

|  |  |  |  |  |
|---|---|---|---|---|
| | Reggie Smith | | | |
| ☐ 89 | NL Home Run Leaders: .. | 1.00 | .40 | .10 |
| | Willie Stargell | | | |
| | Hank Aaron | | | |
| | Lee May | | | |
| ☐ 90 | AL Home Run Leaders: ... | .75 | .30 | .07 |
| | Bill Melton | | | |
| | Norm Cash | | | |
| | Reggie Jackson | | | |
| ☐ 91 | NL ERA Leaders: ............. | .75 | .30 | .07 |
| | Tom Seaver | | | |
| | Dave Roberts | | | |
| | (photo actually | | | |
| | Danny Coombs) | | | |
| | Don Wilson | | | |
| ☐ 92 | AL ERA Leaders: ............. | .65 | .26 | .06 |
| | Vida Blue | | | |
| | Wilbur Wood | | | |
| | Jim Palmer | | | |
| ☐ 93 | NL Pitching Leaders: ...... | 1.00 | .40 | .10 |
| | Fergie Jenkins | | | |
| | Steve Carlton | | | |
| | Al Downing | | | |
| | Tom Seaver | | | |
| ☐ 94 | AL Pitching Leaders: ....... | .50 | .20 | .05 |
| | Mickey Lolich | | | |
| | Vida Blue | | | |
| | Wilbur Wood | | | |
| ☐ 95 | NL Strikeout Leaders: ..... | .75 | .30 | .07 |
| | Tom Seaver | | | |
| | Fergie Jenkins | | | |
| | Bill Stoneman | | | |
| ☐ 96 | AL Strikeout Leaders: ..... | .50 | .20 | .05 |
| | Mickey Lolich | | | |
| | Vida Blue | | | |
| | Joe Coleman | | | |
| ☐ 97 | Tom Kelley | .15 | .06 | .01 |
| ☐ 98 | Chuck Tanner MGR | .25 | .10 | .02 |
| ☐ 99 | Ross Grimsley | .15 | .06 | .01 |
| ☐ 100 | Frank Robinson | 2.50 | 1.00 | .25 |
| ☐ 101 | Astros Rookies | 1.25 | .50 | .12 |
| | Bill Greif | | | |
| | J.R. Richard | | | |
| | Ray Busse | | | |
| ☐ 102 | Lloyd Allen | .15 | .06 | .01 |
| ☐ 103 | Checklist 2 | .90 | .10 | .02 |
| ☐ 104 | Toby Harrah | 1.50 | .60 | .15 |
| ☐ 105 | Gary Gentry | .15 | .06 | .01 |
| ☐ 106 | Brewers Team | .50 | .20 | .05 |
| ☐ 107 | Jose Cruz | 2.50 | 1.00 | .25 |
| ☐ 108 | Gary Waslewski | .15 | .06 | .01 |
| ☐ 109 | Jerry May | .15 | .06 | .01 |
| ☐ 110 | Ron Hunt | .15 | .06 | .01 |
| ☐ 111 | Jim Grant | .15 | .06 | .01 |
| ☐ 112 | Greg Luzinski | .85 | .34 | .08 |
| ☐ 113 | Rogelio Moret | .15 | .06 | .01 |
| ☐ 114 | Bill Buckner | 1.50 | .60 | .15 |
| ☐ 115 | Jim Fregosi | .30 | .12 | .03 |
| ☐ 116 | Ed Farmer | .25 | .10 | .02 |
| ☐ 117A | Cleo James | .20 | .08 | .02 |
| | (yellow underline | | | |
| | C and S of Cubs) | | | |
| ☐ 117B | Cleo James | 4.00 | 1.60 | .40 |
| | (green underline | | | |
| | C and S of Cubs) | | | |
| ☐ 118 | Skip Lockwood | .15 | .06 | .01 |
| ☐ 119 | Marty Perez | .15 | .06 | .01 |
| ☐ 120 | Bill Freehan | .30 | .12 | .03 |
| ☐ 121 | Ed Sprague | .15 | .06 | .01 |
| ☐ 122 | Larry Biittner | .15 | .06 | .01 |
| ☐ 123 | Ed Acosta | .15 | .06 | .01 |
| ☐ 124 | Yankees Rookies | .15 | .06 | .01 |
| | Alan Closter | | | |
| | Rusty Torres | | | |
| | Roger Hambright | | | |
| ☐ 125 | Dave Cash | .15 | .06 | .01 |
| ☐ 126 | Bart Johnson | .15 | .06 | .01 |
| ☐ 127 | Duffy Dyer | .15 | .06 | .01 |
| ☐ 128 | Eddie Watt | .15 | .06 | .01 |
| ☐ 129 | Charlie Fox MGR | .15 | .06 | .01 |
| ☐ 130 | Bob Gibson | 2.50 | 1.00 | .25 |
| ☐ 131 | Jim Nettles | .15 | .06 | .01 |
| ☐ 132 | Joe Morgan | 2.00 | .80 | .20 |
| ☐ 133 | Joe Keough | .18 | .08 | .01 |
| ☐ 134 | Carl Morton | .18 | .08 | .01 |
| ☐ 135 | Vada Pinson | .35 | .14 | .03 |
| ☐ 136 | Darrell Chaney | .18 | .08 | .01 |
| ☐ 137 | Dick Williams MGR | .25 | .10 | .02 |
| ☐ 138 | Mike Kekich | .18 | .08 | .01 |
| ☐ 139 | Tim McCarver | .35 | .14 | .03 |
| ☐ 140 | Pat Dobson | .25 | .10 | .02 |
| ☐ 141 | Mets Rookies | .40 | .16 | .04 |
| | Buzz Capra | | | |

|  |  |  |  |  |
|---|---|---|---|---|
| | Leroy Stanton | | | |
| | Jon Matlack | | | |
| ☐ 142 | Chris Chambliss | 1.75 | .70 | .17 |
| ☐ 143 | Garry Jestadt | .18 | .08 | .01 |
| ☐ 144 | Marty Pattin | .18 | .08 | .01 |
| ☐ 145 | Don Kessinger | .25 | .10 | .02 |
| ☐ 146 | Steve Kealey | .18 | .08 | .01 |
| ☐ 147 | Dave Kingman | 4.00 | 1.60 | .40 |
| ☐ 148 | Dick Billings | .18 | .08 | .01 |
| ☐ 149 | Gary Neibauer | .18 | .08 | .01 |
| ☐ 150 | Norm Cash | .40 | .16 | .04 |
| ☐ 151 | Jim Brewer | .18 | .08 | .01 |
| ☐ 152 | Gene Clines | .18 | .08 | .01 |
| ☐ 153 | Rick Auerbach | .18 | .08 | .01 |
| ☐ 154 | Ted Simmons | 1.25 | .50 | .12 |
| ☐ 155 | Larry Dierker | .25 | .10 | .02 |
| ☐ 156 | Twins Team | .45 | .18 | .04 |
| ☐ 157 | Don Gullett | .25 | .10 | .02 |
| ☐ 158 | Jerry Kenney | .18 | .08 | .01 |
| ☐ 159 | John Boccabella | .18 | .08 | .01 |
| ☐ 160 | Andy Messersmith | .35 | .14 | .03 |
| ☐ 161 | Brock Davis | .18 | .08 | .01 |
| ☐ 162 | Brewers Rookies | 1.00 | .40 | .10 |
| | Jerry Bell | | | |
| | Darrell Porter | | | |
| | Bob Reynolds | | | |
| | (Porter and Bell | | | |
| | photos switched) | | | |
| ☐ 163 | Tug McGraw | .50 | .20 | .05 |
| ☐ 164 | McGraw In Action | .25 | .10 | .02 |
| ☐ 165 | Chris Speier | .18 | .08 | .01 |
| ☐ 166 | Speier In Action | .18 | .08 | .01 |
| ☐ 167 | Deron Johnson | .18 | .08 | .01 |
| ☐ 168 | Johnson In Action | .18 | .08 | .01 |
| ☐ 169 | Vida Blue | .65 | .26 | .06 |
| ☐ 170 | Blue In Action | .65 | .26 | .06 |
| ☐ 171 | Darrell Evans | .35 | .14 | .03 |
| ☐ 172 | Evans In Action | .35 | .14 | .03 |
| ☐ 173 | Clay Kirby | .18 | .08 | .01 |
| ☐ 174 | Kirby In Action | .18 | .08 | .01 |
| ☐ 175 | Tom Haller | .18 | .08 | .01 |
| ☐ 176 | Haller In Action | .18 | .08 | .01 |
| ☐ 177 | Paul Schaal | .18 | .08 | .01 |
| ☐ 178 | Schaal In Action | .18 | .08 | .01 |
| ☐ 179 | Dock Ellis | .18 | .08 | .01 |
| ☐ 180 | Ellis In Action | .18 | .08 | .01 |
| ☐ 181 | Ed Kranepool | .25 | .10 | .02 |
| ☐ 182 | Kranepool In Action | .25 | .10 | .02 |
| ☐ 183 | Bill Melton | .18 | .08 | .01 |
| ☐ 184 | Melton In Action | .18 | .08 | .01 |
| ☐ 185 | Ron Bryant | .18 | .08 | .01 |
| ☐ 186 | Bryant In Action | .18 | .08 | .01 |
| ☐ 187 | Gates Brown | .25 | .10 | .02 |
| ☐ 188 | Frank Lucchesi MGR | .18 | .08 | .01 |
| ☐ 189 | Gene Tenace | .25 | .10 | .02 |
| ☐ 190 | Dave Giusti | .18 | .08 | .01 |
| ☐ 191 | Jeff Burroughs | .50 | .20 | .05 |
| ☐ 192 | Cubs Team | .50 | .20 | .05 |
| ☐ 193 | Kurt Bevacqua | .18 | .08 | .01 |
| ☐ 194 | Fred Norman | .18 | .08 | .01 |
| ☐ 195 | Orlando Cepeda | 1.00 | .40 | .10 |
| ☐ 196 | Mel Queen | .18 | .08 | .01 |
| ☐ 197 | Johnny Briggs | .18 | .08 | .01 |
| ☐ 198 | Dodgers Rookies | .75 | .30 | .07 |
| | Charlie Hough | | | |
| | Bob O'Brien | | | |
| | Mike Strahler | | | |
| ☐ 199 | Mike Fiore | .18 | .08 | .01 |
| ☐ 200 | Lou Brock | 2.75 | 1.10 | .27 |
| ☐ 201 | Phil Roof | .18 | .08 | .01 |
| ☐ 202 | Scipio Spinks | .18 | .08 | .01 |
| ☐ 203 | Ron Blomberg | .25 | .10 | .02 |
| ☐ 204 | Tommy Helms | .25 | .10 | .02 |
| ☐ 205 | Dick Drago | .18 | .08 | .01 |
| ☐ 206 | Dal Maxvill | .18 | .08 | .01 |
| ☐ 207 | Tom Egan | .18 | .08 | .01 |
| ☐ 208 | Milt Pappas | .25 | .10 | .02 |
| ☐ 209 | Joe Rudi | .30 | .12 | .03 |
| ☐ 210 | Denny McLain | .60 | .24 | .06 |
| ☐ 211 | Gary Sutherland | .18 | .08 | .01 |
| ☐ 212 | Grant Jackson | .18 | .08 | .01 |
| ☐ 213 | Angels Rookies | .18 | .08 | .01 |
| | Billy Parker | | | |
| | Art Kusnyer | | | |
| | Tom Silverio | | | |
| ☐ 214 | Mike McQueen | .18 | .08 | .01 |
| ☐ 215 | Alex Johnson | .25 | .10 | .02 |
| ☐ 216 | Joe Niekro | .35 | .14 | .03 |
| ☐ 217 | Roger Metzger | .18 | .08 | .01 |
| ☐ 218 | Eddie Kasko MGR | .18 | .08 | .01 |
| ☐ 219 | Rennie Stennett | .25 | .10 | .02 |
| ☐ 220 | Jim Perry | .30 | .12 | .03 |
| ☐ 221 | NL Playoffs: | .60 | .24 | .06 |

| | | | |
|---|---|---|---|
| Bucs champs | | | |
| ☐ 222 AL Playoffs: ...................... | .90 | .36 | .09 |
| Orioles champs | | | |
| (Brooks Robinson) | | | |
| ☐ 223 World Series Game 1 ...... | .60 | .24 | .06 |
| (McNally pitching) | | | |
| ☐ 224 World Series Game 2 ...... | .60 | .24 | .06 |
| (B. Robinson and | | | |
| Belanger | | | |
| ☐ 225 World Series Game 3 ...... | .60 | .24 | .06 |
| (Sanguillen scoring) | | | |
| ☐ 226 World Series Game 4 ...... | 1.50 | .60 | .15 |
| (Clemente on 2nd) | | | |
| ☐ 227 World Series Game 5 ...... | .60 | .24 | .06 |
| (Briles pitching) | | | |
| ☐ 228 World Series Game 6 ...... | .75 | .30 | .07 |
| (Frank Robinson and | | | |
| Manny Sanguillen) | | | |
| ☐ 229 World Series Game 7 ...... | .60 | .24 | .06 |
| (Blass pitching) | | | |
| ☐ 230 World Series Summary ... | .60 | .24 | .06 |
| Pirates celebrate | | | |
| ☐ 231 Casey Cox ...................... | .18 | .08 | .01 |
| ☐ 232 Giants Rookies ................ | .18 | .08 | .01 |
| Chris Arnold | | | |
| Jim Barr | | | |
| Dave Rader | | | |
| ☐ 233 Jay Johnstone ................ | .25 | .10 | .02 |
| ☐ 234 Ron Taylor ...................... | .18 | .08 | .01 |
| ☐ 235 Merv Rettenmund ........... | .18 | .08 | .01 |
| ☐ 236 Jim McGlothlin ................ | .18 | .08 | .01 |
| ☐ 237 Yankees Team ................ | .65 | .26 | .06 |
| ☐ 238 Leron Lee ...................... | .18 | .08 | .01 |
| ☐ 239 Tom Timmermann ........... | .18 | .08 | .01 |
| ☐ 240 Rich Allen ...................... | 1.00 | .40 | .10 |
| ☐ 241 Rollie Fingers ................. | 1.50 | .60 | .15 |
| ☐ 242 Don Mincher .................. | .18 | .08 | .01 |
| ☐ 243 Frank Linzy .................... | .18 | .08 | .01 |
| ☐ 244 Steve Braun ................... | .18 | .08 | .01 |
| ☐ 245 Tommie Agee ................. | .18 | .08 | .01 |
| ☐ 246 Tom Burgmeier ............... | .18 | .08 | .01 |
| ☐ 247 Milt May ........................ | .18 | .08 | .01 |
| ☐ 248 Tom Bradley ................... | .18 | .08 | .01 |
| ☐ 249 Harry Walker MGR .......... | .18 | .08 | .01 |
| ☐ 250 Boog Powell ................... | .60 | .24 | .06 |
| ☐ 251 Checklist 3 .................... | .90 | .10 | .02 |
| ☐ 252 Ken Reynolds ................. | .18 | .08 | .01 |
| ☐ 253 Sandy Alomar ................ | .18 | .08 | .01 |
| ☐ 254 Boots Day ...................... | .18 | .08 | .01 |
| ☐ 255 Jim Lonborg ................... | .25 | .10 | .02 |
| ☐ 256 George Foster ................ | 1.50 | .60 | .15 |
| ☐ 257 Tigers Rookies ................ | .18 | .08 | .01 |
| Jim Foor | | | |
| Tim Hosley | | | |
| Paul Jata | | | |
| ☐ 258 Randy Hundley ............... | .18 | .08 | .01 |
| ☐ 259 Sparky Lyle .................... | .35 | .14 | .03 |
| ☐ 260 Ralph Garr ..................... | .25 | .10 | .02 |
| ☐ 261 Steve Mingori ................ | .18 | .08 | .01 |
| ☐ 262 Padres Team .................. | .45 | .18 | .04 |
| ☐ 263 Felipe Alou .................... | .25 | .10 | .02 |
| ☐ 264 Tommy John ................... | 1.25 | .50 | .12 |
| ☐ 265 Wes Parker .................... | .25 | .10 | .02 |
| ☐ 266 Bobby Bolin ................... | .18 | .08 | .01 |
| ☐ 267 Dave Concepcion ........... | 1.25 | .50 | .12 |
| ☐ 268 A's Rookies .................... | .18 | .08 | .01 |
| Dwain Anderson | | | |
| Chris Floethe | | | |
| ☐ 269 Don Hahn ...................... | .18 | .08 | .01 |
| ☐ 270 Jim Palmer ..................... | 3.25 | 1.30 | .32 |
| ☐ 271 Ken Rudolph ................... | .18 | .08 | .01 |
| ☐ 272 Mickey Rivers ................ | .90 | .36 | .09 |
| ☐ 273 Bobby Floyd ................... | .18 | .08 | .01 |
| ☐ 274 Al Severinsen ................. | .18 | .08 | .01 |
| ☐ 275 Cesar Tovar ................... | .18 | .08 | .01 |
| ☐ 276 Gene Mauch MGR .......... | .25 | .10 | .02 |
| ☐ 277 Elliot Maddox ................. | .18 | .08 | .01 |
| ☐ 278 Dennis Higgins ............... | .18 | .08 | .01 |
| ☐ 279 Larry Brown ................... | .18 | .08 | .01 |
| ☐ 280 Willie McCovey ............... | 3.00 | 1.20 | .30 |
| ☐ 281 Bill Parsons ................... | .18 | .08 | .01 |
| ☐ 282 Astros Team ................... | .45 | .18 | .04 |
| ☐ 283 Darrell Brandon .............. | .18 | .08 | .01 |
| ☐ 284 Ike Brown ...................... | .18 | .08 | .01 |
| ☐ 285 Gaylord Perry ................. | 2.75 | 1.10 | .27 |
| ☐ 286 Gene Alley ..................... | .25 | .10 | .02 |
| ☐ 287 Jim Hardin ..................... | .18 | .08 | .01 |
| ☐ 288 Johnny Jeter .................. | .18 | .08 | .01 |
| ☐ 289 Syd O'Brien ................... | .18 | .08 | .01 |
| ☐ 290 Sonny Siebert ................ | .25 | .10 | .02 |
| ☐ 291 Hal McRae ..................... | .35 | .14 | .03 |
| ☐ 292 McRae In Action ............. | .18 | .08 | .01 |
| ☐ 293 Danny Frisella ................ | .18 | .08 | .01 |

| | | | |
|---|---|---|---|
| ☐ 294 Frisella In Action ............. | .18 | .08 | .01 |
| ☐ 295 Dick Dietz ...................... | .18 | .08 | .01 |
| ☐ 296 Dietz In Action ................ | .18 | .08 | .01 |
| ☐ 297 Claude Osteen ............... | .25 | .10 | .02 |
| ☐ 298 Osteen In Action ............ | .18 | .08 | .01 |
| ☐ 299 Hank Aaron .................... | 9.00 | 3.75 | .90 |
| ☐ 300 Aaron In Action .............. | 4.50 | 1.80 | .45 |
| ☐ 301 George Mitterwald ......... | .18 | .08 | .01 |
| ☐ 302 Mitterwald In Action ....... | .18 | .08 | .01 |
| ☐ 303 Joe Pepitone .................. | .25 | .10 | .02 |
| ☐ 304 Pepitone In Action .......... | .18 | .08 | .01 |
| ☐ 305 Ken Boswell .................... | .18 | .08 | .01 |
| ☐ 306 Boswell In Action ............ | .18 | .08 | .01 |
| ☐ 307 Steve Renko ................... | .18 | .08 | .01 |
| ☐ 308 Renko In Action .............. | .18 | .08 | .01 |
| ☐ 309 Roberto Clemente .......... | 7.50 | 3.00 | .75 |
| ☐ 310 Clemente In Action ......... | 3.75 | 1.50 | .37 |
| ☐ 311 Clay Carroll ................... | .18 | .08 | .01 |
| ☐ 312 Carroll In Action ............. | .18 | .08 | .01 |
| ☐ 313 Luis Aparicio .................. | 2.00 | .80 | .20 |
| ☐ 314 Aparicio In Action ........... | 1.00 | .40 | .10 |
| ☐ 315 Paul Splittorff ................. | .25 | .10 | .02 |
| ☐ 316 Cardinals Rookies ........... | .30 | .12 | .03 |
| Jim Bibby | | | |
| Jorge Roque | | | |
| Santiago Guzman | | | |
| ☐ 317 Rich Hand ...................... | .18 | .08 | .01 |
| ☐ 318 Sonny Jackson ............... | .18 | .08 | .01 |
| ☐ 319 Aurelio Rodriguez ........... | .18 | .08 | .01 |
| ☐ 320 Steve Blass .................... | .25 | .10 | .02 |
| ☐ 321 Joe Lahoud .................... | .18 | .08 | .01 |
| ☐ 322 Jose Pena ...................... | .18 | .08 | .01 |
| ☐ 323 Earl Weaver MGR ........... | .35 | .14 | .03 |
| ☐ 324 Mike Ryan ...................... | .18 | .08 | .01 |
| ☐ 325 Mel Stottlemyre ............. | .25 | .10 | .02 |
| ☐ 326 Pat Kelly ....................... | .18 | .08 | .01 |
| ☐ 327 Steve Stone .................... | .65 | .26 | .06 |
| ☐ 328 Red Sox Team ................ | .60 | .24 | .06 |
| ☐ 329 Roy Foster ..................... | .18 | .08 | .01 |
| ☐ 330 Jim Hunter ..................... | 2.50 | 1.00 | .25 |
| ☐ 331 Stan Swanson ................ | .18 | .08 | .01 |
| ☐ 332 Buck Martinez ................ | .18 | .08 | .01 |
| ☐ 333 Steve Barber .................. | .18 | .08 | .01 |
| ☐ 334 Rangers Rookies ............. | .18 | .08 | .01 |
| Bill Fahey | | | |
| Jim Mason | | | |
| Tom Ragland | | | |
| ☐ 335 Bill Hands ...................... | .18 | .08 | .01 |
| ☐ 336 Marty Martinez ............... | .18 | .08 | .01 |
| ☐ 337 Mike Kilkenny ................ | .18 | .08 | .01 |
| ☐ 338 Bob Grich ...................... | .50 | .20 | .05 |
| ☐ 339 Ron Cook ...................... | .18 | .08 | .01 |
| ☐ 340 Roy White ..................... | .25 | .10 | .02 |
| ☐ 341 KP: Joe Torre ................. | .30 | .12 | .03 |
| ☐ 342 KP: Wilbur Wood ............ | .18 | .08 | .01 |
| ☐ 343 KP: Willie Stargell .......... | .50 | .20 | .05 |
| ☐ 344 KP: Dave McNally ........... | .18 | .08 | .01 |
| ☐ 345 KP: Rick Wise ................ | .18 | .08 | .01 |
| ☐ 346 KP: Jim Fregosi .............. | .25 | .10 | .02 |
| ☐ 347 KP: Tom Seaver ............. | 1.00 | .40 | .10 |
| ☐ 348 KP: Sal Bando ................ | .18 | .08 | .01 |
| ☐ 349 Al Fitzmorris .................. | .18 | .08 | .01 |
| ☐ 350 Frank Howard ................ | .50 | .20 | .05 |
| ☐ 351 Braves Rookies ............... | .25 | .10 | .02 |
| Tom House | | | |
| Rick Kester | | | |
| Jimmy Britton | | | |
| ☐ 352 Dave LaRoche ................ | .18 | .08 | .01 |
| ☐ 353 Art Shamsky ................... | .18 | .08 | .01 |
| ☐ 354 Tom Murphy ................... | .18 | .08 | .01 |
| ☐ 355 Bob Watson .................... | .30 | .12 | .03 |
| ☐ 356 Gerry Moses ................... | .18 | .08 | .01 |
| ☐ 357 Woodie Fryman ............... | .18 | .08 | .01 |
| ☐ 358 Sparky Anderson MGR .... | .35 | .14 | .03 |
| ☐ 359 Don Pavletich ................. | .18 | .08 | .01 |
| ☐ 360 Dave Roberts .................. | .18 | .08 | .01 |
| ☐ 361 Mike Andrews .................. | .18 | .08 | .01 |
| ☐ 362 Mets Team ..................... | .60 | .24 | .06 |
| ☐ 363 Ron Klimkowski .............. | .18 | .08 | .01 |
| ☐ 364 Johnny Callison ............... | .25 | .10 | .02 |
| ☐ 365 Dick Bosman ................... | .18 | .08 | .01 |
| ☐ 366 Jimmy Rosario ............... | .18 | .08 | .01 |
| ☐ 367 Ron Perranoski ............... | .25 | .10 | .02 |
| ☐ 368 Danny Thompson ............ | .18 | .08 | .01 |
| ☐ 369 Jim Lefebvre .................. | .18 | .08 | .01 |
| ☐ 370 Don Buford .................... | .18 | .08 | .01 |
| ☐ 371 Denny Lemaster ............. | .18 | .08 | .01 |
| ☐ 372 Royals Rookies ............... | .18 | .08 | .01 |
| Lance Clemons | | | |
| Monty Montgomery | | | |
| ☐ 373 John Mayberry ............... | .25 | .10 | .02 |
| ☐ 374 Jack Heidemann ............. | .18 | .08 | .01 |
| ☐ 375 Reggie Cleveland ............ | .18 | .08 | .01 |

| | | | | |
|---|---|---|---|---|
| ☐ 376 | Andy Kosco | .18 | .08 | .01 |
| ☐ 377 | Terry Harmon | .18 | .08 | .01 |
| ☐ 378 | Checklist 4 | .90 | .10 | .02 |
| ☐ 379 | Ken Berry | .18 | .08 | .01 |
| ☐ 380 | Earl Williams | .18 | .08 | .01 |
| ☐ 381 | White Sox Team | .50 | .20 | .05 |
| ☐ 382 | Joe Gibbon | .18 | .08 | .01 |
| ☐ 383 | Brant Alyea | .18 | .08 | .01 |
| ☐ 384 | Dave Campbell | .18 | .08 | .01 |
| ☐ 385 | Mickey Stanley | .25 | .10 | .02 |
| ☐ 386 | Jim Colborn | .18 | .08 | .01 |
| ☐ 387 | Horace Clarke | .18 | .08 | .01 |
| ☐ 388 | Charlie Williams | .18 | .08 | .01 |
| ☐ 389 | Bill Rigney MGR | .18 | .08 | .01 |
| ☐ 390 | Willie Davis | .30 | .12 | .01 |
| ☐ 391 | Ken Sanders | .18 | .08 | .01 |
| ☐ 392 | Pirates Rookies | .75 | .30 | .07 |
| | Fred Cambria | | | |
| | Richie Zisk | | | |
| ☐ 393 | Curt Motton | .18 | .08 | .01 |
| ☐ 394 | Ken Forsch | .25 | .10 | .02 |
| ☐ 395 | Matty Alou | .30 | .12 | .03 |
| ☐ 396 | Paul Lindblad | .22 | .10 | .02 |
| ☐ 397 | Phillies Team | .60 | .24 | .06 |
| ☐ 398 | Larry Hisle | .35 | .14 | .03 |
| ☐ 399 | Milt Wilcox | .30 | .12 | .03 |
| ☐ 400 | Tony Oliva | 1.00 | .40 | .10 |
| ☐ 401 | Jim Nash | .22 | .10 | .02 |
| ☐ 402 | Bobby Heise | .22 | .10 | .02 |
| ☐ 403 | John Cumberland | .22 | .10 | .02 |
| ☐ 404 | Jeff Torborg | .22 | .10 | .02 |
| ☐ 405 | Ron Fairly | .30 | .12 | .03 |
| ☐ 406 | George Hendrick | 1.00 | .40 | .10 |
| ☐ 407 | Chuck Taylor | .22 | .10 | .02 |
| ☐ 408 | Jim Northrup | .30 | .12 | .03 |
| ☐ 409 | Frank Baker | .22 | .10 | .02 |
| ☐ 410 | Fergie Jenkins | 1.00 | .40 | .10 |
| ☐ 411 | Bob Montgomery | .22 | .10 | .02 |
| ☐ 412 | Dick Kelley | .22 | .10 | .02 |
| ☐ 413 | White Sox Rookies | .22 | .10 | .02 |
| | Don Eddy | | | |
| | Dave Lemonds | | | |
| ☐ 414 | Bob Miller | .22 | .10 | .02 |
| ☐ 415 | Cookie Rojas | .22 | .10 | .02 |
| ☐ 416 | Johnny Edwards | .22 | .10 | .02 |
| ☐ 417 | Tom Hall | .22 | .10 | .02 |
| ☐ 418 | Tom Shopay | .22 | .10 | .02 |
| ☐ 419 | Jim Spencer | .22 | .10 | .02 |
| ☐ 420 | Steve Carlton | 10.00 | 4.00 | 1.00 |
| ☐ 421 | Ellie Rodriguez | .22 | .10 | .02 |
| ☐ 422 | Ray Lamb | .22 | .10 | .02 |
| ☐ 423 | Oscar Gamble | .30 | .12 | .03 |
| ☐ 424 | Bill Gogolewski | .22 | .10 | .02 |
| ☐ 425 | Ken Singleton | .60 | .24 | .06 |
| ☐ 426 | Singleton In Action | .30 | .12 | .03 |
| ☐ 427 | Tito Fuentes | .22 | .10 | .02 |
| ☐ 428 | Fuentes In Action | .22 | .10 | .02 |
| ☐ 429 | Bob Robertson | .22 | .10 | .02 |
| ☐ 430 | Robertson In Action | .22 | .10 | .02 |
| ☐ 431 | Clarence Gaston | .22 | .10 | .02 |
| ☐ 432 | Gaston In Action | .22 | .10 | .02 |
| ☐ 433 | Johnny Bench | 11.00 | 4.50 | 1.10 |
| ☐ 434 | Bench In Action | 5.50 | 2.20 | .55 |
| ☐ 435 | Reggie Jackson | 11.00 | 4.50 | 1.10 |
| ☐ 436 | Jackson In Action | 5.50 | 2.20 | .55 |
| ☐ 437 | Maury Wills | .90 | .36 | .09 |
| ☐ 438 | Wills In Action | .50 | .20 | .05 |
| ☐ 439 | Billy Williams | 2.00 | .80 | .20 |
| ☐ 440 | Williams In Action | 1.00 | .40 | .10 |
| ☐ 441 | Thurman Munson | 6.50 | 2.60 | .65 |
| ☐ 442 | Munson In Action | 3.25 | 1.30 | .32 |
| ☐ 443 | Ken Henderson | .22 | .10 | .02 |
| ☐ 444 | Henderson In Action | .22 | .10 | .02 |
| ☐ 445 | Tom Seaver | 9.00 | 3.75 | .90 |
| ☐ 446 | Seaver In Action | 4.50 | 1.80 | .45 |
| ☐ 447 | Willie Stargell | 2.50 | 1.00 | .25 |
| ☐ 448 | Stargell In Action | 1.25 | .50 | .12 |
| ☐ 449 | Bob Lemon MGR | .60 | .24 | .06 |
| ☐ 450 | Mickey Lolich | .60 | .24 | .06 |
| ☐ 451 | Tony LaRussa | .35 | .14 | .03 |
| ☐ 452 | Ed Herrmann | .22 | .10 | .02 |
| ☐ 453 | Barry Lerch | .22 | .10 | .02 |
| ☐ 454 | A's Team | .70 | .28 | .07 |
| ☐ 455 | Tommy Harper | .30 | .12 | .03 |
| ☐ 456 | Mark Belanger | .35 | .14 | .03 |
| ☐ 457 | Padres Rookies | .30 | .12 | .03 |
| | Darcy Fast | | | |
| | Derrel Thomas | | | |
| | Mike Ivie | | | |
| ☐ 458 | Aurelio Monteagudo | .22 | .10 | .02 |
| ☐ 459 | Rick Renick | .22 | .10 | .02 |
| ☐ 460 | Al Downing | .30 | .12 | .03 |
| ☐ 461 | Tim Cullen | .22 | .10 | .02 |

| | | | | |
|---|---|---|---|---|
| ☐ 462 | Rickey Clark | .22 | .10 | .02 |
| ☐ 463 | Bernie Carbo | .22 | .10 | .02 |
| ☐ 464 | Jim Roland | .22 | .10 | .02 |
| ☐ 465 | Gil Hodges MGR | 1.50 | .60 | .15 |
| ☐ 466 | Norm Miller | .22 | .10 | .02 |
| ☐ 467 | Steve Kline | .22 | .10 | .02 |
| ☐ 468 | Richie Scheinblum | .22 | .10 | .02 |
| ☐ 469 | Ron Herbel | .22 | .10 | .02 |
| ☐ 470 | Ray Fosse | .22 | .10 | .02 |
| ☐ 471 | Luke Walker | .22 | .10 | .02 |
| ☐ 472 | Phil Gagliano | .22 | .10 | .02 |
| ☐ 473 | Dan McGinn | .22 | .10 | .02 |
| ☐ 474 | Orioles Rookies | 2.00 | .80 | .20 |
| | Don Baylor | | | |
| | Roric Harrison | | | |
| | Johnny Oates | | | |
| ☐ 475 | Gary Nolan | .22 | .10 | .02 |
| ☐ 476 | Lee Richard | .22 | .10 | .02 |
| ☐ 477 | Tom Phoebus | .22 | .10 | .02 |
| ☐ 478 | Checklist 5 | .90 | .10 | .02 |
| ☐ 479 | Don Shaw | .22 | .10 | .02 |
| ☐ 480 | Lee May | .35 | .14 | .03 |
| ☐ 481 | Billy Conigliaro | .30 | .12 | .03 |
| ☐ 482 | Joe Hoerner | .22 | .10 | .02 |
| ☐ 483 | Ken Suarez | .22 | .10 | .02 |
| ☐ 484 | Lum Harris MGR | .22 | .10 | .02 |
| ☐ 485 | Phil Regan | .30 | .12 | .03 |
| ☐ 486 | John Lowenstein | .30 | .12 | .03 |
| ☐ 487 | Tigers Team | .75 | .30 | .07 |
| ☐ 488 | Mike Nagy | .22 | .10 | .02 |
| ☐ 489 | Expos Rookies | .22 | .10 | .02 |
| | Terry Humphrey | | | |
| | Keith Lampard | | | |
| ☐ 490 | Dave McNally | .35 | .14 | .03 |
| ☐ 491 | KP: Lou Piniella | .35 | .14 | .03 |
| ☐ 492 | KP: Mel Stottlemyre | .30 | .12 | .03 |
| ☐ 493 | KP: Bob Bailey | .22 | .10 | .02 |
| ☐ 494 | KP: Willie Horton | .30 | .12 | .03 |
| ☐ 495 | KP: Bill Melton | .22 | .10 | .02 |
| ☐ 496 | KP: Bud Harrelson | .22 | .10 | .02 |
| ☐ 497 | KP: Jim Perry | .30 | .12 | .03 |
| ☐ 498 | KP: Brooks Robinson | 1.00 | .40 | .10 |
| ☐ 499 | Vicente Romo | .22 | .10 | .02 |
| ☐ 500 | Joe Torre | .60 | .24 | .06 |
| ☐ 501 | Pete Hamm | .22 | .10 | .02 |
| ☐ 502 | Jackie Hernandez | .22 | .10 | .02 |
| ☐ 503 | Gary Peters | .30 | .12 | .03 |
| ☐ 504 | Ed Spiezio | .22 | .10 | .02 |
| ☐ 505 | Mike Marshall | .35 | .14 | .03 |
| ☐ 506 | Indians Rookies | .35 | .14 | .03 |
| | Terry Ley | | | |
| | Jim Moyer | | | |
| | Dick Tidrow | | | |
| ☐ 507 | Fred Gladding | .22 | .10 | .02 |
| ☐ 508 | Ellie Hendricks | .22 | .10 | .02 |
| ☐ 509 | Don McMahon | .22 | .10 | .02 |
| ☐ 510 | Ted Williams MGR | 3.50 | 1.40 | .35 |
| ☐ 511 | Tony Taylor | .22 | .10 | .02 |
| ☐ 512 | Paul Popovich | .22 | .10 | .02 |
| ☐ 513 | Lindy McDaniel | .22 | .10 | .02 |
| ☐ 514 | Ted Sizemore | .22 | .10 | .02 |
| ☐ 515 | Bert Blyleven | 2.00 | .80 | .20 |
| ☐ 516 | Oscar Brown | .22 | .10 | .02 |
| ☐ 517 | Ken Brett | .22 | .10 | .02 |
| ☐ 518 | Wayne Garrett | .22 | .10 | .02 |
| ☐ 519 | Ted Abernathy | .22 | .10 | .02 |
| ☐ 520 | Larry Bowa | 1.00 | .40 | .10 |
| ☐ 521 | Alan Foster | .22 | .10 | .02 |
| ☐ 522 | Dodgers Team | .90 | .36 | .09 |
| ☐ 523 | Chuck Dobson | .22 | .10 | .02 |
| ☐ 524 | Reds Rookies | .22 | .10 | .02 |
| | Ed Armbrister | | | |
| | Mel Behney | | | |
| ☐ 525 | Carlos May | .22 | .10 | .02 |
| ☐ 526 | Bob Bailey | .40 | .16 | .04 |
| ☐ 527 | Dave Leonhard | .40 | .16 | .04 |
| ☐ 528 | Ron Stone | .40 | .16 | .04 |
| ☐ 529 | Dave Nelson | .40 | .16 | .04 |
| ☐ 530 | Don Sutton | 2.25 | .90 | .22 |
| ☐ 531 | Freddie Patek | .50 | .20 | .05 |
| ☐ 532 | Fred Kendall | .40 | .16 | .04 |
| ☐ 533 | Ralph Houk MGR | .60 | .24 | .06 |
| ☐ 534 | Jim Hickman | .40 | .16 | .04 |
| ☐ 535 | Ed Brinkman | .40 | .16 | .04 |
| ☐ 536 | Doug Rader | .50 | .20 | .05 |
| ☐ 537 | Bob Locker | .40 | .16 | .04 |
| ☐ 538 | Charlie Sands | .40 | .16 | .04 |
| ☐ 539 | Terry Forster | 1.50 | .60 | .15 |
| ☐ 540 | Felix Millan | .40 | .16 | .04 |
| ☐ 541 | Roger Repoz | .40 | .16 | .04 |
| ☐ 542 | Jack Billingham | .40 | .16 | .04 |
| ☐ 543 | Duane Josephson | .40 | .16 | .04 |
| ☐ 544 | Ted Martinez | .40 | .16 | .04 |

| | | | | |
|---|---|---|---|---|
| ☐ 545 | Wayne Granger | .40 | .16 | .04 |
| ☐ 546 | Joe Hague | .40 | .16 | .04 |
| ☐ 547 | Indians Team | .75 | .30 | .07 |
| ☐ 548 | Frank Reberger | .40 | .16 | .04 |
| ☐ 549 | Dave May | .40 | .16 | .04 |
| ☐ 550 | Brooks Robinson | 5.50 | 2.20 | .55 |
| ☐ 551 | Ollie Brown | .40 | .16 | .04 |
| ☐ 552 | Brown In Action | .40 | .16 | .04 |
| ☐ 553 | Wilbur Wood | .50 | .20 | .05 |
| ☐ 554 | Wood In Action | .40 | .16 | .04 |
| ☐ 555 | Ron Santo | .75 | .30 | .07 |
| ☐ 556 | Santo In Action | .50 | .20 | .05 |
| ☐ 557 | John Odom | .40 | .16 | .04 |
| ☐ 558 | Odom In Action | .40 | .16 | .04 |
| ☐ 559 | Pete Rose | 45.00 | 18.00 | 4.50 |
| ☐ 560 | Rose In Action | 15.00 | 6.00 | 1.50 |
| ☐ 561 | Leo Cardenas | .40 | .16 | .04 |
| ☐ 562 | Cardenas In Action | .40 | .16 | .04 |
| ☐ 563 | Ray Sadecki | .40 | .16 | .04 |
| ☐ 564 | Sadecki In Action | .40 | .16 | .04 |
| ☐ 565 | Reggie Smith | .75 | .30 | .07 |
| ☐ 566 | Smith In Action | .50 | .20 | .05 |
| ☐ 567 | Juan Marichal | 2.50 | 1.00 | .25 |
| ☐ 568 | Marichal In Action | 1.25 | .50 | .12 |
| ☐ 569 | Ed Kirkpatrick | .40 | .16 | .04 |
| ☐ 570 | Kirkpatrick In Action | .40 | .16 | .04 |
| ☐ 571 | Nate Colbert | .40 | .16 | .04 |
| ☐ 572 | Colbert In Action | .40 | .16 | .04 |
| ☐ 573 | Fritz Peterson | .40 | .16 | .04 |
| ☐ 574 | Peterson In Action | .40 | .16 | .04 |
| ☐ 575 | Al Oliver | 1.50 | .60 | .15 |
| ☐ 576 | Leo Durocher MGR | .75 | .30 | .07 |
| ☐ 577 | Mike Paul | .40 | .16 | .04 |
| ☐ 578 | Billy Grabarkewitz | .40 | .16 | .04 |
| ☐ 579 | Doyle Alexander | 1.00 | .40 | .10 |
| ☐ 580 | Lou Piniella | 1.50 | .60 | .15 |
| ☐ 581 | Wade Blasingame | .40 | .16 | .04 |
| ☐ 582 | Expos Team | .75 | .30 | .07 |
| ☐ 583 | Darold Knowles | .40 | .16 | .04 |
| ☐ 584 | Jerry McNertney | .40 | .16 | .04 |
| ☐ 585 | George Scott | .50 | .20 | .05 |
| ☐ 586 | Denis Menke | .40 | .16 | .04 |
| ☐ 587 | Billy Wilson | .40 | .16 | .04 |
| ☐ 588 | Jim Holt | .40 | .16 | .04 |
| ☐ 589 | Hal Lanier | .60 | .24 | .06 |
| ☐ 590 | Graig Nettles | 1.75 | .70 | .17 |
| ☐ 591 | Paul Casanova | .40 | .16 | .04 |
| ☐ 592 | Lew Krausse | .40 | .16 | .04 |
| ☐ 593 | Rich Morales | .40 | .16 | .04 |
| ☐ 594 | Jim Beauchamp | .40 | .16 | .04 |
| ☐ 595 | Nolan Ryan | 11.00 | 4.50 | 1.10 |
| ☐ 596 | Manny Mota | .60 | .24 | .06 |
| ☐ 597 | Jim Magnuson | .40 | .16 | .04 |
| ☐ 598 | Hal King | .40 | .16 | .04 |
| ☐ 599 | Billy Champion | .40 | .16 | .04 |
| ☐ 600 | Al Kaline | 6.00 | 2.40 | .60 |
| ☐ 601 | George Stone | .40 | .16 | .04 |
| ☐ 602 | Dave Bristol MGR | .40 | .16 | .04 |
| ☐ 603 | Jim Ray | .40 | .16 | .04 |
| ☐ 604A | Checklist 6 (copyright on back bottom right) | 2.00 | .20 | .04 |
| ☐ 604B | Checklist 6 (copyright on back bottom left) | 4.00 | .40 | .08 |
| ☐ 605 | Nelson Briles | .50 | .20 | .05 |
| ☐ 606 | Luis Melendez | .40 | .16 | .04 |
| ☐ 607 | Frank Duffy | .40 | .16 | .04 |
| ☐ 608 | Mike Corkins | .40 | .16 | .04 |
| ☐ 609 | Tom Grieve | .60 | .24 | .06 |
| ☐ 610 | Bill Stoneman | .40 | .16 | .04 |
| ☐ 611 | Rich Reese | .40 | .16 | .04 |
| ☐ 612 | Joe Decker | .40 | .16 | .04 |
| ☐ 613 | Mike Ferraro | .50 | .20 | .05 |
| ☐ 614 | Ted Uhlaender | .40 | .16 | .04 |
| ☐ 615 | Steve Hargan | .40 | .16 | .04 |
| ☐ 616 | Joe Ferguson | .60 | .24 | .06 |
| ☐ 617 | Royals Team | .75 | .30 | .07 |
| ☐ 618 | Rich Robertson | .40 | .16 | .04 |
| ☐ 619 | Rich McKinney | .40 | .16 | .04 |
| ☐ 620 | Phil Niekro | 2.00 | .80 | .20 |
| ☐ 621 | Commissioners Award | .60 | .24 | .06 |
| ☐ 622 | MVP Award | .60 | .24 | .06 |
| ☐ 623 | Cy Young Award | .60 | .24 | .06 |
| ☐ 624 | Minor League Player | .60 | .24 | .06 |
| ☐ 625 | Rookie of the Year | .60 | .24 | .06 |
| ☐ 626 | Babe Ruth Award | .90 | .36 | .09 |
| ☐ 627 | Moe Drabowsky | .40 | .16 | .04 |
| ☐ 628 | Terry Crowley | .40 | .16 | .04 |
| ☐ 629 | Paul Doyle | .40 | .16 | .04 |
| ☐ 630 | Rich Hebner | .40 | .16 | .04 |
| ☐ 631 | John Strohmayer | .40 | .16 | .04 |
| ☐ 632 | Mike Hegan | .40 | .16 | .04 |

| | | | | |
|---|---|---|---|---|
| ☐ 633 | Jack Hiatt | .40 | .16 | .04 |
| ☐ 634 | Dick Woodson | .40 | .16 | .04 |
| ☐ 635 | Don Money | .50 | .20 | .05 |
| ☐ 636 | Bill Lee | .50 | .20 | .05 |
| ☐ 637 | Preston Gomez MGR | .40 | .16 | .04 |
| ☐ 638 | Ken Wright | .40 | .16 | .04 |
| ☐ 639 | J.C. Martin | .40 | .16 | .04 |
| ☐ 640 | Joe Coleman | .40 | .16 | .04 |
| ☐ 641 | Mike Lum | .40 | .16 | .04 |
| ☐ 642 | Dennis Riddleberger | .40 | .16 | .04 |
| ☐ 643 | Russ Gibson | .40 | .16 | .04 |
| ☐ 644 | Bernie Allen | .40 | .16 | .04 |
| ☐ 645 | Jim Maloney | .50 | .20 | .05 |
| ☐ 646 | Chico Salmon | .40 | .16 | .04 |
| ☐ 647 | Bob Moose | .40 | .16 | .04 |
| ☐ 648 | Jim Lyttle | .40 | .16 | .04 |
| ☐ 649 | Pete Richert | .40 | .16 | .04 |
| ☐ 650 | Sal Bando | .60 | .24 | .06 |
| ☐ 651 | Reds Team | .90 | .36 | .09 |
| ☐ 652 | Marcelino Lopez | .40 | .16 | .04 |
| ☐ 653 | Jim Fairey | .40 | .16 | .04 |
| ☐ 654 | Horacio Pina | .40 | .16 | .04 |
| ☐ 655 | Jerry Grote | .40 | .16 | .04 |
| ☐ 656 | Rudy May | .40 | .16 | .04 |
| ☐ 657 | Bobby Wine | 1.20 | .50 | .12 |
| ☐ 658 | Steve Dunning | 1.20 | .50 | .12 |
| ☐ 659 | Bob Aspromonte | 1.20 | .50 | .12 |
| ☐ 660 | Paul Blair | 1.50 | .60 | .15 |
| ☐ 661 | Bill Virdon | 1.75 | .70 | .17 |
| ☐ 662 | Stan Bahnsen | 1.20 | .50 | .12 |
| ☐ 663 | Fran Healy | 1.20 | .50 | .12 |
| ☐ 664 | Bobby Knoop | 1.20 | .50 | .12 |
| ☐ 665 | Chris Short | 1.20 | .50 | .12 |
| ☐ 666 | Hector Torres | 1.20 | .50 | .12 |
| ☐ 667 | Ray Newman | 1.20 | .50 | .12 |
| ☐ 668 | Rangers Team | 3.00 | 1.20 | .30 |
| ☐ 669 | Willie Crawford | 1.20 | .50 | .12 |
| ☐ 670 | Ken Holtzman | 1.50 | .60 | .15 |
| ☐ 671 | Donn Clendenon | 1.50 | .60 | .15 |
| ☐ 672 | Archie Reynolds | 1.20 | .50 | .12 |
| ☐ 673 | Dave Marshall | 1.20 | .50 | .12 |
| ☐ 674 | John Kennedy | 1.20 | .50 | .12 |
| ☐ 675 | Pat Jarvis | 1.20 | .50 | .12 |
| ☐ 676 | Danny Cater | 1.20 | .50 | .12 |
| ☐ 677 | Ivan Murrell | 1.20 | .50 | .12 |
| ☐ 678 | Steve Luebber | 1.20 | .50 | .12 |
| ☐ 679 | Astros Rookies Bob Fenwick Bob Stinson | 1.20 | .50 | .12 |
| ☐ 680 | Dave Johnson | 2.50 | 1.00 | .25 |
| ☐ 681 | Bobby Pfeil | 1.20 | .50 | .12 |
| ☐ 682 | Mike McCormick | 1.50 | .60 | .15 |
| ☐ 683 | Steve Hovley | 1.20 | .50 | .12 |
| ☐ 684 | Hal Breeden | 1.20 | .50 | .12 |
| ☐ 685 | Joe Horlen | 1.50 | .60 | .15 |
| ☐ 686 | Steve Garvey | 55.00 | 22.00 | 5.50 |
| ☐ 687 | Del Unser | 1.20 | .50 | .12 |
| ☐ 688 | Cardinals Team | 2.25 | .90 | .22 |
| ☐ 689 | Eddie Fisher | 1.20 | .50 | .12 |
| ☐ 690 | Willie Montanez | 1.20 | .50 | .12 |
| ☐ 691 | Curt Blefary | 1.20 | .50 | .12 |
| ☐ 692 | Blefary In Action | 1.20 | .50 | .12 |
| ☐ 693 | Alan Gallagher | 1.20 | .50 | .12 |
| ☐ 694 | Gallagher In Action | 1.20 | .50 | .12 |
| ☐ 695 | Rod Carew | 55.00 | 22.00 | 5.50 |
| ☐ 696 | Carew In Action | 20.00 | 8.00 | 2.00 |
| ☐ 697 | Jerry Koosman | 4.00 | 1.60 | .40 |
| ☐ 698 | Koosman In Action | 2.00 | .80 | .20 |
| ☐ 699 | Bobby Murcer | 4.00 | 1.60 | .40 |
| ☐ 700 | Murcer In Action | 2.00 | .80 | .20 |
| ☐ 701 | Jose Pagan | 1.20 | .50 | .12 |
| ☐ 702 | Pagan In Action | 1.20 | .50 | .12 |
| ☐ 703 | Doug Griffin | 1.20 | .50 | .12 |
| ☐ 704 | Griffin In Action | 1.20 | .50 | .12 |
| ☐ 705 | Pat Corrales | 1.75 | .70 | .17 |
| ☐ 706 | Corrales In Action | 1.50 | .60 | .15 |
| ☐ 707 | Tim Foli | 1.20 | .50 | .12 |
| ☐ 708 | Foli In Action | 1.20 | .50 | .12 |
| ☐ 709 | Jim Kaat | 4.00 | 1.60 | .40 |
| ☐ 710 | Kaat In Action | 2.00 | .80 | .20 |
| ☐ 711 | Bobby Bonds | 3.50 | 1.40 | .35 |
| ☐ 712 | Bonds In Action | 1.75 | .70 | .17 |
| ☐ 713 | Gene Michael | 1.75 | .70 | .17 |
| ☐ 714 | Michael In Action | 1.50 | .60 | .15 |
| ☐ 715 | Mike Epstein | 1.20 | .50 | .12 |
| ☐ 716 | Jesus Alou | 1.20 | .50 | .12 |
| ☐ 717 | Bruce Dal Canton | 1.20 | .50 | .12 |
| ☐ 718 | Del Rice MGR | 1.20 | .50 | .12 |
| ☐ 719 | Cesar Geronimo | 1.20 | .50 | .12 |
| ☐ 720 | Sam McDowell | 1.50 | .60 | .15 |
| ☐ 721 | Eddie Leon | 1.20 | .50 | .12 |
| ☐ 722 | Bill Sudakis | 1.20 | .50 | .12 |
| ☐ 723 | Al Santorini | 1.20 | .50 | .12 |

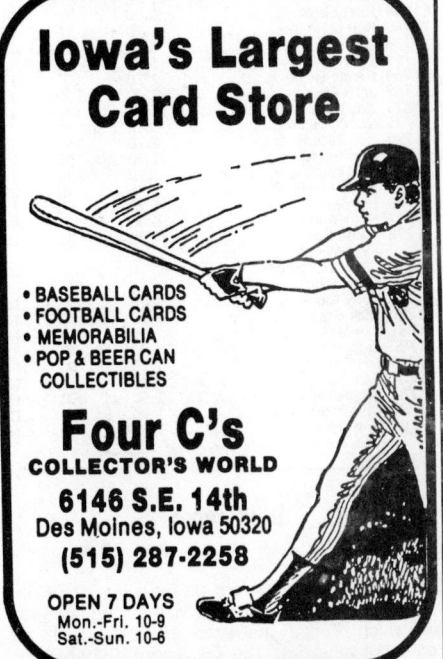

| | | | | |
|---|---|---|---|---|
| ☐ 724 | AL Rookie Pitchers ......... | 1.50 | .60 | .15 |
| | John Curtis | | | |
| | Rich Hinton | | | |
| | Mickey Scott | | | |
| ☐ 725 | Dick McAuliffe .................. | 1.20 | .50 | .12 |
| ☐ 726 | Dick Selma ...................... | 1.20 | .50 | .12 |
| ☐ 727 | Jose LaBoy ...................... | 1.20 | .50 | .12 |
| ☐ 728 | Gail Hopkins .................... | 1.20 | .50 | .12 |
| ☐ 729 | Bob Veale ........................ | 1.50 | .60 | .15 |
| ☐ 730 | Rick Monday .................... | 1.75 | .70 | .17 |
| ☐ 731 | Orioles Team .................... | 2.25 | .90 | .22 |
| ☐ 732 | George Culver .................. | 1.20 | .50 | .12 |
| ☐ 733 | Jim Ray Hart .................... | 1.50 | .60 | .15 |
| ☐ 734 | Bob Burda ........................ | 1.20 | .50 | .12 |
| ☐ 735 | Diego Segui ...................... | 1.20 | .50 | .12 |
| ☐ 736 | Bill Russell ...................... | 2.50 | 1.00 | .25 |
| ☐ 737 | Lenny Randle .................... | 1.20 | .50 | .12 |
| ☐ 738 | Jim Merritt ...................... | 1.20 | .50 | .12 |
| ☐ 739 | Don Mason ...................... | 1.20 | .50 | .12 |
| ☐ 740 | Rico Carty ........................ | 1.75 | .70 | .17 |
| ☐ 741 | Rookie First Basemen ..... | 1.75 | .70 | .17 |
| | Tom Hutton | | | |
| | John Milner | | | |
| | Rick Miller | | | |
| ☐ 742 | Jim Rooker ...................... | 1.50 | .60 | .15 |
| ☐ 743 | Cesar Gutierrez .............. | 1.20 | .50 | .12 |
| ☐ 744 | Jim Slaton ...................... | 1.50 | .60 | .15 |
| ☐ 745 | Julian Javier .................... | 1.20 | .50 | .12 |
| ☐ 746 | Lowell Palmer .................. | 1.20 | .50 | .12 |
| ☐ 747 | Jim Stewart ...................... | 1.20 | .50 | .12 |
| ☐ 748 | Phil Hennigan .................. | 1.20 | .50 | .12 |
| ☐ 749 | Walter Alston MGR ......... | 3.00 | 1.20 | .30 |
| ☐ 750 | Willie Horton .................... | 1.75 | .70 | .17 |
| ☐ 751 | Steve Carlton TR ............. | 30.00 | 12.00 | 3.00 |
| ☐ 752 | Joe Morgan TR ................ | 9.00 | 3.75 | .90 |
| ☐ 753 | Denny McLain TR ............. | 2.50 | 1.00 | .25 |
| ☐ 754 | Frank Robinson TR ........... | 9.00 | 3.75 | .90 |
| ☐ 755 | Jim Fregosi TR ................ | 2.00 | .80 | .20 |
| ☐ 756 | Rick Wise TR .................... | 1.50 | .60 | .15 |
| ☐ 757 | Jose Cardenal TR ............. | 1.50 | .60 | .15 |
| ☐ 758 | Gil Garrido ...................... | 1.20 | .50 | .12 |
| ☐ 759 | Chris Cannizzaro .............. | 1.20 | .50 | .12 |
| ☐ 760 | Bill Mazeroski .................. | 2.00 | .80 | .20 |
| ☐ 761 | Rookie Outfielders .......... | 10.00 | 4.00 | 1.00 |
| | Ben Oglivie | | | |
| | Ron Cey | | | |
| | Bernie Williams | | | |
| ☐ 762 | Wayne Simpson .............. | 1.20 | .50 | .12 |
| ☐ 763 | Ron Hansen ...................... | 1.20 | .50 | .12 |
| ☐ 764 | Dusty Baker ...................... | 3.00 | 1.20 | .30 |
| ☐ 765 | Ken McMullen .................. | 1.20 | .50 | .12 |
| ☐ 766 | Steve Hamilton ................ | 1.20 | .50 | .12 |
| ☐ 767 | Tom McCraw .................... | 1.20 | .50 | .12 |
| ☐ 768 | Denny Doyle .................... | 1.20 | .50 | .12 |
| ☐ 769 | Jack Aker ........................ | 1.20 | .50 | .12 |
| ☐ 770 | Jim Wynn ........................ | 1.75 | .70 | .17 |
| ☐ 771 | Giants Team .................... | 2.25 | .90 | .22 |
| ☐ 772 | Ken Tatum ........................ | 1.20 | .50 | .12 |
| ☐ 773 | Ron Brand ........................ | 1.20 | .50 | .12 |
| ☐ 774 | Luis Alvarado .................. | 1.20 | .50 | .12 |
| ☐ 775 | Jerry Reuss ...................... | 2.25 | .90 | .22 |
| ☐ 776 | Bill Voss ........................ | 1.20 | .50 | .12 |
| ☐ 777 | Hoyt Wilhelm .................. | 6.00 | 2.40 | .60 |
| ☐ 778 | Twins Rookies .................. | 2.00 | .80 | .20 |
| | Vic Albury | | | |
| | Rick Dempsey | | | |
| | Jim Strickland | | | |
| ☐ 779 | Tony Cloninger ................ | 1.20 | .50 | .12 |
| ☐ 780 | Dick Green ...................... | 1.20 | .50 | .12 |
| ☐ 781 | Jim McAndrew .................. | 1.20 | .50 | .12 |
| ☐ 782 | Larry Stahl ...................... | 1.20 | .50 | .12 |
| ☐ 783 | Les Cain ........................ | 1.20 | .50 | .12 |
| ☐ 784 | Ken Aspromonte .............. | 1.20 | .50 | .12 |
| ☐ 785 | Vic Davalillo .................... | 1.50 | .60 | .15 |
| ☐ 786 | Chuck Brinkman ................ | 1.20 | .50 | .12 |
| ☐ 787 | Ron Reed ........................ | 1.50 | .60 | .15 |

## 1973 Topps

The cards in this 660 card set measure 2 1/2" by 3 1/2". The 1973 Topps set marked the last year in which Topps marketed baseball cards in consecutive series. The last series (529-660) is more difficult to obtain. Beginning in 1974, all Topps cards were printed at the same time, thus

eliminating the "high number" factor. The set features team leader cards featuring small individual pictures of the coaching staff members with a larger picture of the manager. The "background" variations below with respect to these leader cards are subtle and are best understood after a side-by-side comparison of the two varieties. An "All-Time Leaders" series (471-478) appeared for the first time in this set. Kid pictures appeared again for the second year in a row (341-346). Other topical subsets within the set included League Leaders (61-68), Playoffs cards (201-202), World Series cards (203-210), and Rookie prospects (601-616).

| | | MINT | VG-E | F-G |
|---|---|---|---|---|
| COMPLETE SET ........................ | | 350.00 | 140.00 | 35.00 |
| COMMON PLAYER (1-264) ........ | | .14 | .06 | .01 |
| COMMON PLAYER (265-396) .... | | .17 | .07 | .01 |
| COMMON PLAYER (397-528) .... | | .22 | .10 | .02 |
| COMMON PLAYER (529-660) .... | | .75 | .30 | .07 |
| ☐ | 1 All-Time HR Leaders: ...... | 6.00 | 2.40 | .60 |
| | 714 Babe Ruth | | | |
| | 673 Hank Aaron | | | |
| | 654 Willie Mays | | | |
| ☐ | 2 Rich Hebner .................. | .14 | .06 | .01 |
| ☐ | 3 Jim Lonborg .................. | .20 | .08 | .02 |
| ☐ | 4 John Milner .................. | .14 | .06 | .01 |
| ☐ | 5 Ed Brinkman .................. | .14 | .06 | .01 |
| ☐ | 6 Mac Scarce .................. | .14 | .06 | .01 |
| ☐ | 7 Texas Rangers Team ...... | .40 | .16 | .04 |
| ☐ | 8 Tom Hall ........................ | .14 | .06 | .01 |
| ☐ | 9 Johnny Oates ................ | .14 | .06 | .01 |
| ☐ | 10 Don Sutton .................. | 1.50 | .60 | .15 |
| ☐ | 11 Chris Chambliss ............ | .35 | .14 | .03 |
| ☐ | 12A Padres Leaders: .......... | .30 | .12 | .03 |
| | Don Zimmer MGR | | | |
| | Dave Garcia CO | | | |
| | Johnny Podres CO | | | |
| | Bob Skinner CO | | | |
| | Whitey Wietelmann CO | | | |
| | (Podres no right ear) | | | |
| ☐ | 12B Padres Leaders: .......... | .60 | .24 | .06 |
| | (Podres has right ear) | | | |
| ☐ | 13 George Hendrick ............ | .50 | .20 | .05 |
| ☐ | 14 Sonny Siebert .............. | .20 | .08 | .02 |
| ☐ | 15 Ralph Garr .................. | .20 | .08 | .02 |
| ☐ | 16 Steve Braun .................. | .14 | .06 | .01 |
| ☐ | 17 Fred Gladding .............. | .14 | .06 | .01 |
| ☐ | 18 Leroy Stanton .............. | .14 | .06 | .01 |
| ☐ | 19 Tim Foli ...................... | .14 | .06 | .01 |
| ☐ | 20 Stan Bahnsen .............. | .14 | .06 | .01 |
| ☐ | 21 Randy Hundley .............. | .14 | .06 | .01 |
| ☐ | 22 Ted Abernathy .............. | .14 | .06 | .01 |
| ☐ | 23 Dave Kingman .............. | 1.25 | .50 | .12 |
| ☐ | 24 Al Santorini .................. | .14 | .06 | .01 |
| ☐ | 25 Roy White .................... | .20 | .08 | .02 |
| ☐ | 26 Pirates Team ................ | .40 | .16 | .04 |
| ☐ | 27 Bill Gogolewski ............ | .14 | .06 | .01 |
| ☐ | 28 Hal McRae .................... | .35 | .14 | .03 |
| ☐ | 29 Tony Taylor .................. | .14 | .06 | .01 |
| ☐ | 30 Tug McGraw .................. | .50 | .20 | .05 |
| ☐ | 31 Buddy Bell .................... | 3.00 | 1.20 | .30 |
| ☐ | 32 Fred Norman ................ | .14 | .06 | .01 |
| ☐ | 33 Jim Breazeale .............. | .14 | .06 | .01 |
| ☐ | 34 Pat Dobson .................. | .20 | .08 | .02 |
| ☐ | 35 Willie Davis .................. | .30 | .12 | .03 |
| ☐ | 36 Steve Barber ................ | .14 | .06 | .01 |

| # | Player | | | |
|---|---|---|---|---|
| 37 | Bill Robinson | .14 | .06 | .01 |
| 38 | Mike Epstein | .14 | .06 | .01 |
| 39 | Dave Roberts | .14 | .06 | .01 |
| 40 | Reggie Smith | .50 | .20 | .05 |
| 41 | Tom Walker | .14 | .06 | .01 |
| 42 | Mike Andrews | .14 | .06 | .01 |
| 43 | Randy Moffitt | .14 | .06 | .01 |
| 44 | Rick Monday | .25 | .10 | .02 |
| 45 | Ellie Rodriguez | .20 | .08 | .02 |
| | (photo actually John Felske) | | | |
| 46 | Lindy McDaniel | .14 | .06 | .01 |
| 47 | Luis Melendez | .14 | .06 | .01 |
| 48 | Paul Splittorff | .25 | .10 | .02 |
| 49A | Twins Leaders: | .30 | .12 | .03 |
| | Frank Quilici MGR | | | |
| | Vern Morgan CO | | | |
| | Bob Rodgers CO | | | |
| | Ralph Rowe CO | | | |
| | Al Worthington CO | | | |
| | (solid backgrounds) | | | |
| 49B | Twins Leaders: | .60 | .24 | .06 |
| | (natural backgrounds) | | | |
| 50 | Roberto Clemente | 8.00 | 3.25 | .80 |
| 51 | Chuck Seelbach | .14 | .06 | .01 |
| 52 | Denis Menke | .14 | .06 | .01 |
| 53 | Steve Dunning | .14 | .06 | .01 |
| 54 | Checklist 1 | .80 | .08 | .01 |
| 55 | Jon Matlack | .25 | .10 | .02 |
| 56 | Merv Rettenmund | .14 | .06 | .01 |
| 57 | Derrel Thomas | .14 | .06 | .01 |
| 58 | Mike Paul | .14 | .06 | .01 |
| 59 | Steve Yeager | .45 | .18 | .04 |
| 60 | Ken Holtzman | .25 | .10 | .02 |
| 61 | Batting Leaders | 1.00 | .40 | .10 |
| | Billy Williams | | | |
| | Rod Carew | | | |
| 62 | Home Run Leaders | .90 | .36 | .09 |
| | Johnny Bench | | | |
| | Dick Allen | | | |
| 63 | RBI Leaders | .90 | .36 | .09 |
| | Johnny Bench | | | |
| | Dick Allen | | | |
| 64 | Stolen Base Leaders | .60 | .24 | .06 |
| | Lou Brock | | | |
| | Bert Campaneris | | | |
| 65 | ERA Leaders | .75 | .30 | .07 |
| | Steve Carlton | | | |
| | Luis Tiant | | | |
| 66 | Victory Leaders | .90 | .36 | .09 |
| | Steve Carlton | | | |
| | Gaylord Perry | | | |
| | Wilbur Wood | | | |
| 67 | Strikeout Leaders | 2.00 | .80 | .20 |
| | Steve Carlton | | | |
| | Nolan Ryan | | | |
| 68 | Leading Firemen | .30 | .12 | .03 |
| | Clay Carroll | | | |
| | Sparky Lyle | | | |
| 69 | Phil Gagliano | .14 | .06 | .01 |
| 70 | Milt Pappas | .20 | .08 | .02 |
| 71 | Johnny Briggs | .14 | .06 | .01 |
| 72 | Ron Reed | .14 | .06 | .01 |
| 73 | Ed Herrmann | .14 | .06 | .01 |
| 74 | Billy Champion | .14 | .06 | .01 |
| 75 | Vada Pinson | .35 | .14 | .03 |
| 76 | Doug Rader | .25 | .10 | .02 |
| 77 | Mike Torrez | .25 | .10 | .02 |
| 78 | Richie Scheinblum | .14 | .06 | .01 |
| 79 | Jim Willoughby | .14 | .06 | .01 |
| 80 | Tony Oliva | .65 | .26 | .06 |
| 81A | Cubs Leaders: | .35 | .14 | .03 |
| | Whitey Lockman MGR | | | |
| | Hank Aguirre CO | | | |
| | Ernie Banks CO | | | |
| | Larry Jansen CO | | | |
| | Pete Reiser CO | | | |
| | (solid backgrounds) | | | |
| 81B | Cubs Leaders: | .70 | .28 | .07 |
| | (natural backgrounds) | | | |
| 82 | Fritz Peterson | .14 | .06 | .01 |
| 83 | Leron Lee | .14 | .06 | .01 |
| 84 | Rollie Fingers | 1.25 | .50 | .12 |
| 85 | Ted Simmons | 1.00 | .40 | .10 |
| 86 | Tom McCraw | .14 | .06 | .01 |
| 87 | Ken Boswell | .14 | .06 | .01 |
| 88 | Mickey Stanley | .20 | .08 | .02 |
| 89 | Jack Billingham | .14 | .06 | .01 |
| 90 | Brooks Robinson | 3.00 | 1.20 | .30 |
| 91 | Dodgers Team | .60 | .24 | .06 |
| 92 | Jerry Bell | .14 | .06 | .01 |
| 93 | Jesus Alou | .14 | .06 | .01 |
| 94 | Dick Billings | .14 | .06 | .01 |
| 95 | Steve Blass | .14 | .06 | .01 |
| 96 | Doug Griffin | .14 | .06 | .01 |
| 97 | Willie Montanez | .14 | .06 | .01 |
| 98 | Dick Woodson | .14 | .06 | .01 |
| 99 | Carl Taylor | .14 | .06 | .01 |
| 100 | Hank Aaron | 9.00 | 3.75 | .90 |
| 101 | Ken Henderson | .14 | .06 | .01 |
| 102 | Rudy May | .14 | .06 | .01 |
| 103 | Celerino Sanchez | .14 | .06 | .01 |
| 104 | Reggie Cleveland | .14 | .06 | .01 |
| 105 | Carlos May | .14 | .06 | .01 |
| 106 | Terry Humphrey | .14 | .06 | .01 |
| 107 | Phil Hennigan | .14 | .06 | .01 |
| 108 | Bill Russell | .25 | .10 | .02 |
| 109 | Doyle Alexander | .25 | .10 | .02 |
| 110 | Bob Watson | .25 | .10 | .02 |
| 111 | Dave Nelson | .14 | .06 | .01 |
| 112 | Gary Ross | .14 | .06 | .01 |
| 113 | Jerry Grote | .14 | .06 | .01 |
| 114 | Lynn McGlothen | .14 | .06 | .01 |
| 115 | Ron Santo | .35 | .14 | .03 |
| 116A | Yankees Leaders: | .40 | .16 | .04 |
| | Ralph Houk MGR | | | |
| | Jim Hegan CO | | | |
| | Elston Howard CO | | | |
| | Dick Howser CO | | | |
| | Jim Turner CO | | | |
| | (solid backgrounds) | | | |
| 116B | Yankees Leaders: | .75 | .30 | .07 |
| | (natural backgrounds) | | | |
| 117 | Ramon Hernandez | .14 | .06 | .01 |
| 118 | John Mayberry | .25 | .10 | .02 |
| 119 | Larry Bowa | .60 | .24 | .06 |
| 120 | Joe Coleman | .14 | .06 | .01 |
| 121 | Dave Rader | .14 | .06 | .01 |
| 122 | Jim Strickland | .14 | .06 | .01 |
| 123 | Sandy Alomar | .14 | .06 | .01 |
| 124 | Jim Hardin | .14 | .06 | .01 |
| 125 | Ron Fairly | .20 | .08 | .02 |
| 126 | Jim Brewer | .14 | .06 | .01 |
| 127 | Brewers Team | .40 | .16 | .04 |
| 128 | Ted Sizemore | .14 | .06 | .01 |
| 129 | Terry Forster | .35 | .14 | .03 |
| 130 | Pete Rose | 15.00 | 6.00 | 1.50 |
| 131A | Red Sox Leaders: | .25 | .10 | .02 |
| | Eddie Kasko MGR | | | |
| | Doug Camilli CO | | | |
| | Don Lenhardt CO | | | |
| | Eddie Popowski CO | | | |
| | Lee Stange CO | | | |
| | (Popowski no right ear) | | | |
| 131B | Red Sox Leaders: | .50 | .20 | .05 |
| | (Popowski has right ear) | | | |
| 132 | Matty Alou | .20 | .08 | .02 |
| 133 | Dave Roberts | .14 | .06 | .01 |
| 134 | Milt Wilcox | .20 | .08 | .02 |
| 135 | Lee May | .25 | .10 | .02 |
| 136A | Orioles Leaders: | .50 | .20 | .05 |
| | Earl Weaver MGR | | | |
| | George Bamberger CO | | | |
| | Jim Frey CO | | | |
| | Billy Hunter CO | | | |
| | George Staller CO | | | |
| | (orange backgrounds) | | | |
| 136B | Orioles Leaders: | .90 | .36 | .09 |
| | (dark pale backgrounds) | | | |
| 137 | Jim Beauchamp | .14 | .06 | .01 |
| 138 | Horacio Pina | .14 | .06 | .01 |
| 139 | Carmen Fanzone | .14 | .06 | .01 |
| 140 | Lou Piniella | .50 | .20 | .05 |
| 141 | Bruce Kison | .25 | .10 | .02 |
| 142 | Thurman Munson | 4.00 | 1.60 | .40 |
| 143 | John Curtis | .14 | .06 | .01 |
| 144 | Marty Perez | .14 | .06 | .01 |
| 145 | Bobby Bonds | .35 | .14 | .03 |
| 146 | Woodie Fryman | .14 | .06 | .01 |
| 147 | Mike Anderson | .14 | .06 | .01 |
| 148 | Dave Goltz | .20 | .08 | .02 |
| 149 | Ron Hunt | .14 | .06 | .01 |
| 150 | Wilbur Wood | .20 | .08 | .02 |
| 151 | Wes Parker | .25 | .10 | .02 |
| 152 | Dave May | .14 | .06 | .01 |
| 153 | Al Hrabosky | .25 | .10 | .02 |
| 154 | Jeff Torborg | .14 | .06 | .01 |
| 155 | Sal Bando | .30 | .12 | .03 |
| 156 | Cesar Geronimo | .14 | .06 | .01 |
| 157 | Denny Riddleberger | .14 | .06 | .01 |
| 158 | Astros Team | .40 | .16 | .04 |
| 159 | Clarence Gaston | .14 | .06 | .01 |
| 160 | Jim Palmer | 3.00 | 1.20 | .30 |
| 161 | Ted Martinez | .14 | .06 | .01 |
| 162 | Pete Broberg | .14 | .06 | .01 |
| 163 | Vic Davalillo | .14 | .06 | .01 |

| | | | | |
|---|---|---|---|---|
| ☐ 164 | Monty Montgomery | .14 | .06 | .01 |
| ☐ 165 | Luis Aparicio | 1.75 | .70 | .17 |
| ☐ 166 | Terry Harmon | .14 | .06 | .01 |
| ☐ 167 | Steve Stone | .30 | .12 | .03 |
| ☐ 168 | Jim Northrup | .20 | .08 | .02 |
| ☐ 169 | Ron Schueler | .14 | .06 | .01 |
| ☐ 170 | Harmon Killebrew | 2.25 | .90 | .22 |
| ☐ 171 | Bernie Carbo | .14 | .06 | .01 |
| ☐ 172 | Steve Kline | .14 | .06 | .01 |
| ☐ 173 | Hal Breeden | .14 | .06 | .01 |
| ☐ 174 | Rich Gossage | 6.00 | 2.40 | .60 |
| ☐ 175 | Frank Robinson | 2.75 | 1.10 | .27 |
| ☐ 176 | Chuck Taylor | .14 | .06 | .01 |
| ☐ 177 | Bill Plummer | .14 | .06 | .01 |
| ☐ 178 | Don Rose | .14 | .06 | .01 |
| ☐ 179A | A's Leaders: | .30 | .12 | .03 |
| | Dick Williams MGR | | | |
| | Jerry Adair CO | | | |
| | Vern Hoscheit CO | | | |
| | Irv Noren CO | | | |
| | Wes Stock CO | | | |
| | (orange backgrounds) | | | |
| ☐ 179B | A's Leaders: | .60 | .24 | .06 |
| | (dark pale backgrounds) | | | |
| ☐ 180 | Fergie Jenkins | .90 | .36 | .09 |
| ☐ 181 | Jack Brohamer | .14 | .06 | .01 |
| ☐ 182 | Mike Caldwell | .45 | .18 | .04 |
| ☐ 183 | Don Buford | .14 | .06 | .01 |
| ☐ 184 | Jerry Koosman | .35 | .14 | .03 |
| ☐ 185 | Jim Wynn | .30 | .12 | .03 |
| ☐ 186 | Bill Fahey | .14 | .06 | .01 |
| ☐ 187 | Luke Walker | .14 | .06 | .01 |
| ☐ 188 | Cookie Rojas | .14 | .06 | .01 |
| ☐ 189 | Greg Luzinski | .75 | .30 | .07 |
| ☐ 190 | Bob Gibson | 2.50 | 1.00 | .25 |
| ☐ 191 | Tigers Team | .50 | .20 | .05 |
| ☐ 192 | Pat Jarvis | .14 | .06 | .01 |
| ☐ 193 | Carlton Fisk | 2.50 | 1.00 | .25 |
| ☐ 194 | Jorge Orta | .14 | .06 | .01 |
| ☐ 195 | Clay Carroll | .14 | .06 | .01 |
| ☐ 196 | Ken McMullen | .14 | .06 | .01 |
| ☐ 197 | Ed Goodson | .14 | .06 | .01 |
| ☐ 198 | Horace Clarke | .14 | .06 | .01 |
| ☐ 199 | Bert Blyleven | .80 | .32 | .08 |
| ☐ 200 | Billy Williams | 1.75 | .70 | .17 |
| ☐ 201 | A.L. Playoffs | .60 | .24 | .06 |
| | A's over Tigers; | | | |
| | Hendrick scores | | | |
| | winning run | | | |
| ☐ 202 | N.L. Playoffs | .60 | .24 | .06 |
| | Reds over Pirates | | | |
| | Foster's run decides | | | |
| ☐ 203 | World Series Game 1 | .60 | .24 | .06 |
| | Tenace the Menace | | | |
| ☐ 204 | World Series Game 2 | .60 | .24 | .06 |
| | A's two straight | | | |
| ☐ 205 | World Series Game 3 | .60 | .24 | .06 |
| | Reds win squeeker | | | |
| ☐ 206 | World Series Game 4 | .60 | .24 | .06 |
| | Tenace singles | | | |
| | in ninth | | | |
| ☐ 207 | World Series Game 5 | .60 | .24 | .06 |
| | Odom out at plate | | | |
| ☐ 208 | World Series Game 6 | .60 | .24 | .06 |
| | Red's slugging | | | |
| | ties series | | | |
| ☐ 209 | World Series Game 7 | .60 | .24 | .06 |
| | Campy stars | | | |
| | winning rally | | | |
| ☐ 210 | World Series Summary | .60 | .24 | .06 |
| | World champions: | | | |
| | A's Win | | | |
| ☐ 211 | Balor Moore | .14 | .06 | .01 |
| ☐ 212 | Joe Lahoud | .14 | .06 | .01 |
| ☐ 213 | Steve Garvey | 8.00 | 3.25 | .80 |
| ☐ 214 | Steve Hamilton | .14 | .06 | .01 |
| ☐ 215 | Dusty Baker | .70 | .28 | .07 |
| ☐ 216 | Toby Harrah | .35 | .14 | .03 |
| ☐ 217 | Don Wilson | .14 | .06 | .01 |
| ☐ 218 | Aurelio Rodriguez | .14 | .06 | .01 |
| ☐ 219 | Cardinals Team | .40 | .16 | .04 |
| ☐ 220 | Nolan Ryan | 5.00 | 2.00 | .50 |
| ☐ 221 | Fred Kendall | .14 | .06 | .01 |
| ☐ 222 | Rob Gardner | .14 | .06 | .01 |
| ☐ 223 | Bud Harrelson | .20 | .08 | .02 |
| ☐ 224 | Bill Lee | .20 | .08 | .02 |
| ☐ 225 | Al Oliver | 1.00 | .40 | .10 |
| ☐ 226 | Ray Fosse | .14 | .06 | .01 |
| ☐ 227 | Wayne Twitchell | .14 | .06 | .01 |
| ☐ 228 | Bobby Darwin | .14 | .06 | .01 |
| ☐ 229 | Roric Harrison | .14 | .06 | .01 |
| ☐ 230 | Joe Morgan | 2.00 | .80 | .20 |
| ☐ 231 | Bill Parsons | .14 | .06 | .01 |
| ☐ 232 | Ken Singleton | .35 | .14 | .03 |
| ☐ 233 | Ed Kirkpatrick | .14 | .06 | .01 |
| ☐ 234 | Bill North | .20 | .08 | .02 |
| ☐ 235 | Jim Hunter | 1.75 | .70 | .17 |
| ☐ 236 | Tito Fuentes | .14 | .06 | .01 |
| ☐ 237A | Braves Leaders: | .50 | .20 | .05 |
| | Eddie Mathews MGR | | | |
| | Lew Burdette CO | | | |
| | Jim Busby CO | | | |
| | Roy Hartsfield CO | | | |
| | Ken Silvestri CO | | | |
| | (orange backgrounds) | | | |
| ☐ 237B | Braves Leaders: | .90 | .36 | .09 |
| | (dark pale backgrounds) | | | |
| ☐ 238 | Tony Muser | .14 | .06 | .01 |
| ☐ 239 | Pete Richert | .14 | .06 | .01 |
| ☐ 240 | Bobby Murcer | .50 | .20 | .05 |
| ☐ 241 | Dwain Anderson | .14 | .06 | .01 |
| ☐ 242 | George Culver | .14 | .06 | .01 |
| ☐ 243 | Angels Team | .40 | .16 | .04 |
| ☐ 244 | Ed Acosta | .14 | .06 | .01 |
| ☐ 245 | Carl Yastrzemski | 8.00 | 3.25 | .80 |
| ☐ 246 | Ken Sanders | .14 | .06 | .01 |
| ☐ 247 | Del Unser | .14 | .06 | .01 |
| ☐ 248 | Jerry Johnson | .14 | .06 | .01 |
| ☐ 249 | Larry Biittner | .14 | .06 | .01 |
| ☐ 250 | Manny Sanguillen | .25 | .10 | .02 |
| ☐ 251 | Roger Nelson | .14 | .06 | .01 |
| ☐ 252A | Giants Leaders: | .25 | .10 | .02 |
| | Charlie Fox MGR | | | |
| | Joe Amalfitano CO | | | |
| | Andy Gilbert CO | | | |
| | Don McMahon CO | | | |
| | John McNamara CO | | | |
| | (orange backgrounds) | | | |
| ☐ 252B | Giants Leaders: | .50 | .20 | .05 |
| | (dark pale backgrounds) | | | |
| ☐ 253 | Mark Belanger | .25 | .10 | .02 |
| ☐ 254 | Bill Stoneman | .14 | .06 | .01 |
| ☐ 255 | Reggie Jackson | 10.00 | 4.00 | 1.00 |
| ☐ 256 | Chris Zachary | .14 | .06 | .01 |
| ☐ 257A | Mets Leaders: | .50 | .20 | .05 |
| | Yogi Berra MGR | | | |
| | Roy McMillan CO | | | |
| | Joe Pignatano CO | | | |
| | Rube Walker CO | | | |
| | Eddie Yost CO | | | |
| | (orange backgrounds) | | | |
| ☐ 257B | Mets Leaders: | .90 | .36 | .09 |
| | (dark pale backgrounds) | | | |
| ☐ 258 | Tommy John | .90 | .36 | .09 |
| ☐ 259 | Jim Holt | .14 | .06 | .01 |
| ☐ 260 | Gary Nolan | .14 | .06 | .01 |
| ☐ 261 | Pat Kelly | .14 | .06 | .01 |
| ☐ 262 | Jack Aker | .14 | .06 | .01 |
| ☐ 263 | George Scott | .20 | .08 | .02 |
| ☐ 264 | Checklist 2 | .80 | .08 | .01 |
| ☐ 265 | Gene Michael | .25 | .10 | .02 |
| ☐ 266 | Mike Lum | .17 | .07 | .01 |
| ☐ 267 | Lloyd Allen | .17 | .07 | .01 |
| ☐ 268 | Jerry Morales | .17 | .07 | .01 |
| ☐ 269 | Tim McCarver | .30 | .12 | .03 |
| ☐ 270 | Luis Tiant | .35 | .14 | .03 |
| ☐ 271 | Tom Hutton | .17 | .07 | .01 |
| ☐ 272 | Ed Farmer | .17 | .07 | .01 |
| ☐ 273 | Chris Speier | .17 | .07 | .01 |
| ☐ 274 | Darold Knowles | .17 | .07 | .01 |
| ☐ 275 | Tony Perez | .75 | .30 | .07 |
| ☐ 276 | Joe Lovitto | .17 | .07 | .01 |
| ☐ 277 | Bob Miller | .17 | .07 | .01 |
| ☐ 278 | Orioles Team | .45 | .18 | .04 |
| ☐ 279 | Mike Strahler | .17 | .07 | .01 |
| ☐ 280 | Al Kaline | 2.75 | 1.10 | .27 |
| ☐ 281 | Mike Jorgensen | .17 | .07 | .01 |
| ☐ 282 | Steve Hovley | .17 | .07 | .01 |
| ☐ 283 | Ray Sadecki | .17 | .07 | .01 |
| ☐ 284 | Glenn Borgmann | .17 | .07 | .01 |
| ☐ 285 | Don Kessinger | .25 | .10 | .02 |
| ☐ 286 | Frank Linzy | .17 | .07 | .01 |
| ☐ 287 | Eddie Leon | .17 | .07 | .01 |
| ☐ 288 | Gary Gentry | .17 | .07 | .01 |
| ☐ 289 | Bob Oliver | .17 | .07 | .01 |
| ☐ 290 | Cesar Cedeno | .35 | .14 | .03 |
| ☐ 291 | Rogelio Moret | .17 | .07 | .01 |
| ☐ 292 | Jose Cruz | .65 | .26 | .06 |
| ☐ 293 | Bernie Allen | .17 | .07 | .01 |
| ☐ 294 | Steve Arlin | .17 | .07 | .01 |
| ☐ 295 | Bert Campaneris | .30 | .12 | .03 |
| ☐ 296 | Reds Leaders: | .35 | .14 | .03 |
| | Sparky Anderson MGR | | | |
| | Alex Grammas CO | | | |
| | Ted Kluszewski CO | | | |
| | George Scherger CO | | | |

| | | | | |
|---|---|---|---|---|
| | Larry Shepard CO | | | |
| ☐ 297 | Walt Williams | .17 | .07 | .01 |
| ☐ 298 | Ron Bryant | .17 | .07 | .01 |
| ☐ 299 | Ted Ford | .17 | .07 | .01 |
| ☐ 300 | Steve Carlton | 6.50 | 2.60 | .65 |
| ☐ 301 | Billy Grabarkewitz | .17 | .07 | .01 |
| ☐ 302 | Terry Crowley | .17 | .07 | .01 |
| ☐ 303 | Nelson Briles | .25 | .10 | .02 |
| ☐ 304 | Duke Sims | .17 | .07 | .01 |
| ☐ 305 | Willie Mays | 9.00 | 3.75 | .90 |
| ☐ 306 | Tom Burgmeier | .17 | .07 | .01 |
| ☐ 307 | Boots Day | .17 | .07 | .01 |
| ☐ 308 | Skip Lockwood | .17 | .07 | .01 |
| ☐ 309 | Paul Popovich | .17 | .07 | .01 |
| ☐ 310 | Dick Allen | .40 | .16 | .04 |
| ☐ 311 | Joe Decker | .17 | .07 | .01 |
| ☐ 312 | Oscar Brown | .17 | .07 | .01 |
| ☐ 313 | Jim Ray | .17 | .07 | .01 |
| ☐ 314 | Ron Swoboda | .25 | .10 | .02 |
| ☐ 315 | John Odom | .17 | .07 | .01 |
| ☐ 316 | Padres Team | .45 | .18 | .04 |
| ☐ 317 | Danny Cater | .17 | .07 | .01 |
| ☐ 318 | Jim McGlothlin | .17 | .07 | .01 |
| ☐ 319 | Jim Spencer | .17 | .07 | .01 |
| ☐ 320 | Lou Brock | 2.50 | 1.00 | .25 |
| ☐ 321 | Rich Hinton | .17 | .07 | .01 |
| ☐ 322 | Garry Maddox | .50 | .20 | .05 |
| ☐ 323 | Tigers Leaders: | .50 | .20 | .05 |
| | Billy Martin MGR | | | |
| | Art Fowler CO | | | |
| | Charlie Silvera CO | | | |
| | Dick Tracewski CO | | | |
| ☐ 324 | Al Downing | .17 | .07 | .01 |
| ☐ 325 | Boog Powell | .50 | .20 | .05 |
| ☐ 326 | Darrell Brandon | .17 | .07 | .01 |
| ☐ 327 | John Lowenstein | .17 | .07 | .01 |
| ☐ 328 | Bill Bonham | .17 | .07 | .01 |
| ☐ 329 | Ed Kranepool | .17 | .07 | .01 |
| ☐ 330 | Rod Carew | 6.00 | 2.40 | .60 |
| ☐ 331 | Carl Morton | .17 | .07 | .01 |
| ☐ 332 | John Felske | .17 | .07 | .01 |
| ☐ 333 | Gene Clines | .17 | .07 | .01 |
| ☐ 334 | Freddie Patek | .17 | .07 | .01 |
| ☐ 335 | Bob Tolan | .17 | .07 | .01 |
| ☐ 336 | Tom Bradley | .17 | .07 | .01 |
| ☐ 337 | Dave Duncan | .17 | .07 | .01 |
| ☐ 338 | Checklist 3 | .80 | .08 | .01 |
| ☐ 339 | Dick Tidrow | .17 | .07 | .01 |
| ☐ 340 | Nate Colbert | .17 | .07 | .01 |
| ☐ 341 | KP: Jim Palmer | .90 | .36 | .09 |
| ☐ 342 | KP: Sam McDowell | .17 | .07 | .01 |
| ☐ 343 | KP: Bobby Murcer | .25 | .10 | .02 |
| ☐ 344 | KP: Jim Hunter | .75 | .30 | .07 |
| ☐ 345 | KP: Chris Speier | .17 | .07 | .01 |
| ☐ 346 | KP: Gaylord Perry | .60 | .24 | .06 |
| ☐ 347 | Royals Team | .45 | .18 | .04 |
| ☐ 348 | Rennie Stennett | .17 | .07 | .01 |
| ☐ 349 | Dick McAuliffe | .17 | .07 | .01 |
| ☐ 350 | Tom Seaver | 6.00 | 2.40 | .60 |
| ☐ 351 | Jimmy Stewart | .17 | .07 | .01 |
| ☐ 352 | Don Stanhouse | .17 | .07 | .01 |
| ☐ 353 | Steve Brye | .17 | .07 | .01 |
| ☐ 354 | Billy Parker | .17 | .07 | .01 |
| ☐ 355 | Mike Marshall | .35 | .14 | .03 |
| ☐ 356 | White Sox Leaders: | .30 | .12 | .03 |
| | Chuck Tanner MGR | | | |
| | Joe Lonnett CO | | | |
| | Jim Mahoney CO | | | |
| | Al Monchak CO | | | |
| | Johnny Sain CO | | | |
| ☐ 357 | Ross Grimsley | .17 | .07 | .01 |
| ☐ 358 | Jim Nettles | .17 | .07 | .01 |
| ☐ 359 | Cecil Upshaw | .17 | .07 | .01 |
| ☐ 360 | Joe Rudi | .35 | .14 | .03 |
| | (photo actually | | | |
| | Gene Tenace) | | | |
| ☐ 361 | Fran Healy | .17 | .07 | .01 |
| ☐ 362 | Eddie Watt | .17 | .07 | .01 |
| ☐ 363 | Jackie Hernandez | .17 | .07 | .01 |
| ☐ 364 | Rick Wise | .17 | .07 | .01 |
| ☐ 365 | Rico Petrocelli | .25 | .10 | .02 |
| ☐ 366 | Brock Davis | .17 | .07 | .01 |
| ☐ 367 | Burt Hooton | .25 | .10 | .02 |
| ☐ 368 | Bill Buckner | .70 | .28 | .07 |
| ☐ 369 | Lerrin LaGrow | .17 | .07 | .01 |
| ☐ 370 | Willie Stargell | 2.25 | .90 | .22 |
| ☐ 371 | Mike Kekich | .17 | .07 | .01 |
| ☐ 372 | Oscar Gamble | .25 | .10 | .02 |
| ☐ 373 | Clyde Wright | .17 | .07 | .01 |
| ☐ 374 | Darrell Evans | .50 | .20 | .05 |
| ☐ 375 | Larry Dierker | .17 | .07 | .01 |
| ☐ 376 | Frank Duffy | .17 | .07 | .01 |
| ☐ 377 | Expos Leaders: | .30 | .12 | .03 |

| | | | | |
|---|---|---|---|---|
| | Gene Mauch MGR | | | |
| | Dave Bristol CO | | | |
| | Larry Doby CO | | | |
| | Cal McLish CO | | | |
| | Jerry Zimmerman CO | | | |
| ☐ 378 | Lenny Randle | .17 | .07 | .01 |
| ☐ 379 | Cy Acosta | .17 | .07 | .01 |
| ☐ 380 | Johnny Bench | 6.50 | 2.60 | .65 |
| ☐ 381 | Vicente Romo | .17 | .07 | .01 |
| ☐ 382 | Mike Hegan | .17 | .07 | .01 |
| ☐ 383 | Diego Segui | .17 | .07 | .01 |
| ☐ 384 | Don Baylor | 1.00 | .40 | .10 |
| ☐ 385 | Jim Perry | .35 | .14 | .03 |
| ☐ 386 | Don Money | .17 | .07 | .01 |
| ☐ 387 | Jim Barr | .17 | .07 | .01 |
| ☐ 388 | Ben Oglivie | .50 | .20 | .05 |
| ☐ 389 | Mets Team | .90 | .36 | .09 |
| ☐ 390 | Mickey Lolich | .50 | .20 | .05 |
| ☐ 391 | Lee Lacy | .80 | .32 | .08 |
| ☐ 392 | Dick Drago | .17 | .07 | .01 |
| ☐ 393 | Jose Cardenal | .17 | .07 | .01 |
| ☐ 394 | Sparky Lyle | .40 | .16 | .04 |
| ☐ 395 | Roger Metzger | .17 | .07 | .01 |
| ☐ 396 | Grant Jackson | .17 | .07 | .01 |
| ☐ 397 | Dave Cash | .22 | .10 | .02 |
| ☐ 398 | Rich Hand | .22 | .10 | .02 |
| ☐ 399 | George Foster | 1.25 | .50 | .12 |
| ☐ 400 | Gaylord Perry | 1.75 | .70 | .17 |
| ☐ 401 | Clyde Mashore | .22 | .10 | .02 |
| ☐ 402 | Jack Hiatt | .22 | .10 | .02 |
| ☐ 403 | Sonny Jackson | .22 | .10 | .02 |
| ☐ 404 | Chuck Brinkman | .22 | .10 | .02 |
| ☐ 405 | Cesar Tovar | .22 | .10 | .02 |
| ☐ 406 | Paul Lindblad | .22 | .10 | .02 |
| ☐ 407 | Felix Millan | .22 | .10 | .02 |
| ☐ 408 | Jim Colborn | .22 | .10 | .02 |
| ☐ 409 | Ivan Murrell | .22 | .10 | .02 |
| ☐ 410 | Willie McCovey | 2.50 | 1.00 | .25 |
| ☐ 411 | Ray Corbin | .22 | .10 | .02 |
| ☐ 412 | Manny Mota | .30 | .12 | .03 |
| ☐ 413 | Tom Timmerman | .22 | .10 | .02 |
| ☐ 414 | Ken Rudolph | .22 | .10 | .02 |
| ☐ 415 | Marty Pattin | .22 | .10 | .02 |
| ☐ 416 | Paul Schaal | .22 | .10 | .02 |
| ☐ 417 | Scipio Spinks | .22 | .10 | .02 |
| ☐ 418 | Bobby Grich | .40 | .16 | .04 |
| ☐ 419 | Casey Cox | .22 | .10 | .02 |
| ☐ 420 | Tommie Agee | .22 | .10 | .02 |
| ☐ 421A | Angels Leaders: | .30 | .12 | .03 |
| | Bobby Winkles MGR | | | |
| | Tom Morgan CO | | | |
| | Salty Parker CO | | | |
| | Jimmie Reese CO | | | |
| | John Roseboro CO | | | |
| | (orange backgrounds) | | | |
| ☐ 421B | Angels Leaders: | .60 | .24 | .06 |
| | (dark pale backgrounds) | | | |
| ☐ 422 | Bob Robertson | .22 | .10 | .02 |
| ☐ 423 | Johnny Jeter | .22 | .10 | .02 |
| ☐ 424 | Denny Doyle | .22 | .10 | .02 |
| ☐ 425 | Alex Johnson | .30 | .12 | .03 |
| ☐ 426 | Dave LaRoche | .22 | .10 | .02 |
| ☐ 427 | Rick Auerbach | .22 | .10 | .02 |
| ☐ 428 | Wayne Simpson | .22 | .10 | .02 |
| ☐ 429 | Jim Fairey | .22 | .10 | .02 |
| ☐ 430 | Vida Blue | .45 | .18 | .04 |
| ☐ 431 | Gerry Moses | .22 | .10 | .02 |
| ☐ 432 | Dan Frisella | .22 | .10 | .02 |
| ☐ 433 | Willie Horton | .30 | .12 | .03 |
| ☐ 434 | Giants Team | .50 | .20 | .05 |
| ☐ 435 | Rico Carty | .40 | .16 | .04 |
| ☐ 436 | Jim McAndrew | .22 | .10 | .02 |
| ☐ 437 | John Kennedy | .22 | .10 | .02 |
| ☐ 438 | Enzo Hernandez | .22 | .10 | .02 |
| ☐ 439 | Eddie Fisher | .22 | .10 | .02 |
| ☐ 440 | Glenn Beckert | .22 | .10 | .02 |
| ☐ 441 | Gail Hopkins | .22 | .10 | .02 |
| ☐ 442 | Dick Dietz | .22 | .10 | .02 |
| ☐ 443 | Danny Thompson | .22 | .10 | .02 |
| ☐ 444 | Ken Brett | .22 | .10 | .02 |
| ☐ 445 | Ken Berry | .22 | .10 | .02 |
| ☐ 446 | Jerry Reuss | .40 | .16 | .04 |
| ☐ 447 | Joe Hague | .22 | .10 | .02 |
| ☐ 448 | John Hiller | .30 | .12 | .03 |
| ☐ 449A | Indians Leaders: | .35 | .14 | .03 |
| | Ken Aspromonte MGR | | | |
| | Rocky Colavito CO | | | |
| | Joe Lutz CO | | | |
| | Warren Spahn CO | | | |
| | (Spahn's right | | | |
| | ear pointed) | | | |
| ☐ 449B | Indians Leaders: | .75 | .30 | .07 |
| | (Spahn's right | | | |

| | | | |
|---|---|---|---|
| ☐ 450 Joe Torre | .60 | .24 | .06 |
| ☐ 451 John Vuckovich | .22 | .10 | .02 |
| ☐ 452 Paul Casanova | .22 | .10 | .02 |
| ☐ 453 Checklist 4 | 1.00 | .10 | .02 |
| ☐ 454 Tom Haller | .22 | .10 | .02 |
| ☐ 455 Bill Melton | .22 | .10 | .02 |
| ☐ 456 Dick Green | .22 | .10 | .02 |
| ☐ 457 John Strohmayer | .22 | .10 | .02 |
| ☐ 458 Jim Mason | .22 | .10 | .02 |
| ☐ 459 Jimmy Howarth | .22 | .10 | .02 |
| ☐ 460 Bill Freehan | .35 | .14 | .03 |
| ☐ 461 Mike Corkins | .22 | .10 | .02 |
| ☐ 462 Ron Blomberg | .22 | .10 | .02 |
| ☐ 463 Ken Tatum | .22 | .10 | .02 |
| ☐ 464 Chicago Cubs Team | .50 | .20 | .05 |
| ☐ 465 Dave Giusti | .22 | .10 | .02 |
| ☐ 466 Jose Arcia | .22 | .10 | .02 |
| ☐ 467 Mike Ryan | .22 | .10 | .02 |
| ☐ 468 Tom Griffin | .22 | .10 | .02 |
| ☐ 469 Dan Monzon | .22 | .10 | .02 |
| ☐ 470 Mike Cuellar | .35 | .14 | .03 |
| ☐ 471 Hits Leaders | 2.00 | .80 | .20 |
|     Ty Cobb 4191 | | | |
| ☐ 472 Grand Slam Leaders | 2.00 | .80 | .20 |
|     Lou Gehrig 23 | | | |
| ☐ 473 Total Bases Leaders | 2.00 | .80 | .20 |
|     Hank Aaron 6172 | | | |
| ☐ 474 RBI Leaders | 3.00 | 1.20 | .30 |
|     Babe Ruth 2209 | | | |
| ☐ 475 Batting Leaders | 2.00 | .80 | .20 |
|     Ty Cobb .367 | | | |
| ☐ 476 Shutout Leaders | 1.00 | .40 | .10 |
|     Walter Johnson 113 | | | |
| ☐ 477 Victory Leaders | 1.00 | .40 | .10 |
|     Cy Young 511 | | | |
| ☐ 478 Strikeout Leaders | 1.00 | .40 | .10 |
|     Walter Johnson 3508 | | | |
| ☐ 479 Hal Lanier | .40 | .16 | .04 |
| ☐ 480 Juan Marichal | 2.25 | .90 | .22 |
| ☐ 481 White Sox Team | .45 | .18 | .04 |
| ☐ 482 Rick Reuschel | .75 | .30 | .07 |
| ☐ 483 Dal Maxvill | .22 | .10 | .02 |
| ☐ 484 Ernie McAnally | .22 | .10 | .02 |
| ☐ 485 Norm Cash | .40 | .16 | .04 |
| ☐ 486A Phillies Leaders: | .35 | .14 | .03 |
|     Danny Ozark MGR | | | |
|     Carroll Beringer CO | | | |
|     Billy DeMars CO | | | |
|     Ray Rippelmeyer CO | | | |
|     Bobby Wine CO | | | |
|     (orange backgrounds) | | | |
| ☐ 486B Phillies Leaders: | .70 | .28 | .07 |
|     (dark pale backgrounds) | | | |
| ☐ 487 Bruce Dal Canton | .22 | .10 | .02 |
| ☐ 488 Dave Campbell | .22 | .10 | .02 |
| ☐ 489 Jeff Burroughs | .35 | .14 | .03 |
| ☐ 490 Claude Osteen | .30 | .12 | .03 |
| ☐ 491 Bob Montgomery | .22 | .10 | .02 |
| ☐ 492 Pedro Borbon | .22 | .10 | .02 |
| ☐ 493 Duffy Dyer | .22 | .10 | .02 |
| ☐ 494 Rich Morales | .22 | .10 | .02 |
| ☐ 495 Tommy Helms | .30 | .12 | .03 |
| ☐ 496 Ray Lamb | .22 | .10 | .02 |
| ☐ 497A Cardinals Leaders: | .35 | .14 | .03 |
|     Red Schoendienst MGR | | | |
|     Vern Benson CO | | | |
|     George Kissell CO | | | |
|     Barney Schultz CO | | | |
|     (orange backgrounds) | | | |
| ☐ 497B Cardinals Leaders: | .70 | .28 | .07 |
|     (dark pale backgrounds) | | | |
| ☐ 498 Graig Nettles | 1.75 | .70 | .17 |
| ☐ 499 Bob Moose | .22 | .10 | .02 |
| ☐ 500 Oakland A's Team | .65 | .26 | .06 |
| ☐ 501 Larry Gura | .35 | .14 | .03 |
| ☐ 502 Bobby Valentine | .45 | .18 | .04 |
| ☐ 503 Phil Niekro | 1.75 | .70 | .17 |
| ☐ 504 Earl Williams | .22 | .10 | .02 |
| ☐ 505 Bob Bailey | .22 | .10 | .02 |
| ☐ 506 Bart Johnson | .22 | .10 | .02 |
| ☐ 507 Darrel Chaney | .22 | .10 | .02 |
| ☐ 508 Gates Brown | .30 | .12 | .03 |
| ☐ 509 Jim Nash | .22 | .10 | .02 |
| ☐ 510 Amos Otis | .35 | .14 | .03 |
| ☐ 511 Sam McDowell | .30 | .12 | .03 |
| ☐ 512 Dalton Jones | .22 | .10 | .02 |
| ☐ 513 Dave Marshall | .22 | .10 | .02 |
| ☐ 514 Jerry Kenney | .22 | .10 | .02 |
| ☐ 515 Andy Messersmith | .35 | .14 | .03 |
| ☐ 516 Danny Walton | .22 | .10 | .02 |
| ☐ 517A Pirates Leaders: | .30 | .12 | .03 |
|     Bill Virdon MGR | | | |

| | | | |
|---|---|---|---|
|     Don Leppert CO | | | |
|     Bill Mazeroski CO | | | |
|     Dave Ricketts CO | | | |
|     Mel Wright CO | | | |
|     (Mazeroski has | | | |
|     no right ear) | | | |
| ☐ 517B Pirates Leaders: | .60 | .24 | .06 |
|     (Mazeroski has | | | |
|     right ear) | | | |
| ☐ 518 Bob Veale | .30 | .12 | .03 |
| ☐ 519 John Edwards | .22 | .10 | .02 |
| ☐ 520 Mel Stottlemyre | .35 | .14 | .03 |
| ☐ 521 Atlanta Braves Team | .45 | .18 | .04 |
| ☐ 522 Leo Cardenas | .22 | .10 | .02 |
| ☐ 523 Wayne Granger | .22 | .10 | .02 |
| ☐ 524 Gene Tenace | .30 | .12 | .03 |
| ☐ 525 Jim Fregosi | .40 | .16 | .04 |
| ☐ 526 Ollie Brown | .22 | .10 | .02 |
| ☐ 527 Dan McGinn | .22 | .10 | .02 |
| ☐ 528 Paul Blair | .30 | .12 | .03 |
| ☐ 529 Milt May | .75 | .30 | .07 |
| ☐ 530 Jim Kaat | 2.00 | .80 | .20 |
| ☐ 531 Ron Woods | .75 | .30 | .07 |
| ☐ 532 Steve Mingori | .75 | .30 | .07 |
| ☐ 533 Larry Stahl | .75 | .30 | .07 |
| ☐ 534 Dave Lemonds | .75 | .30 | .07 |
| ☐ 535 John Callison | .90 | .36 | .09 |
| ☐ 536 Phillies Team | 1.25 | .50 | .12 |
| ☐ 537 Bill Slayback | .75 | .30 | .07 |
| ☐ 538 Jim Ray Hart | .90 | .36 | .09 |
| ☐ 539 Tom Murphy | .75 | .30 | .07 |
| ☐ 540 Cleon Jones | .75 | .30 | .07 |
| ☐ 541 Bob Bolin | .75 | .30 | .07 |
| ☐ 542 Pat Corrales | .90 | .36 | .09 |
| ☐ 543 Alan Foster | .75 | .30 | .07 |
| ☐ 544 Von Joshua | .75 | .30 | .07 |
| ☐ 545 Orlando Cepeda | 2.00 | .80 | .20 |
| ☐ 546 Jim York | .75 | .30 | .07 |
| ☐ 547 Bobby Heise | .75 | .30 | .07 |
| ☐ 548 Don Durham | .75 | .30 | .07 |
| ☐ 549 Rangers Leaders: | 1.50 | .60 | .15 |
|     Whitey Herzog MGR | | | |
|     Chuck Estrada CO | | | |
|     Chuck Hiller CO | | | |
|     Jackie Moore CO | | | |
| ☐ 550 Dave Johnson | 2.25 | .90 | .22 |
| ☐ 551 Mike Kilkenny | .75 | .30 | .07 |
| ☐ 552 J.C. Martin | .75 | .30 | .07 |
| ☐ 553 Mickey Scott | .75 | .30 | .07 |
| ☐ 554 Dave Concepcion | 2.00 | .80 | .20 |
| ☐ 555 Bill Hands | .75 | .30 | .07 |
| ☐ 556 Yankees Team | 2.00 | .80 | .20 |
| ☐ 557 Bernie Williams | .75 | .30 | .07 |
| ☐ 558 Jerry May | .75 | .30 | .07 |
| ☐ 559 Barry Lersch | .75 | .30 | .07 |
| ☐ 560 Frank Howard | 1.75 | .70 | .17 |
| ☐ 561 Jim Geddes | .75 | .30 | .07 |
| ☐ 562 Wayne Garrett | .75 | .30 | .07 |
| ☐ 563 Larry Haney | .75 | .30 | .07 |
| ☐ 564 Mike Thompson | .75 | .30 | .07 |
| ☐ 565 Jim Hickman | .75 | .30 | .07 |
| ☐ 566 Lew Krausse | .75 | .30 | .07 |
| ☐ 567 Bob Fenwick | .75 | .30 | .07 |
| ☐ 568 Ray Newman | .75 | .30 | .07 |
| ☐ 569 Dodgers Leaders: | 1.75 | .70 | .17 |
|     Walt Alston MGR | | | |
|     Red Adams CO | | | |
|     Monty Basgall CO | | | |
|     Jim Gilliam CO | | | |
|     Tom Lasorda CO | | | |
| ☐ 570 Bill Singer | .75 | .30 | .07 |
| ☐ 571 Rusty Torres | .75 | .30 | .07 |
| ☐ 572 Gary Sutherland | .75 | .30 | .07 |
| ☐ 573 Fred Beene | .75 | .30 | .07 |
| ☐ 574 Bob Didier | .75 | .30 | .07 |
| ☐ 575 Dock Ellis | .75 | .30 | .07 |
| ☐ 576 Expos Team | 1.50 | .60 | .15 |
| ☐ 577 Eric Soderholm | .75 | .30 | .07 |
| ☐ 578 Ken Wright | .75 | .30 | .07 |
| ☐ 579 Tom Grieve | 1.00 | .40 | .10 |
| ☐ 580 Joe Pepitone | 1.00 | .40 | .10 |
| ☐ 581 Steve Kealey | .75 | .30 | .07 |
| ☐ 582 Darrell Porter | 1.25 | .50 | .12 |
| ☐ 583 Bill Grief | .75 | .30 | .07 |
| ☐ 584 Chris Arnold | .75 | .30 | .07 |
| ☐ 585 Joe Niekro | 1.50 | .60 | .15 |
| ☐ 586 Bill Sudakis | .75 | .30 | .07 |
| ☐ 587 Rich McKinney | .75 | .30 | .07 |
| ☐ 588 Checklist 5 | 10.00 | 1.00 | .20 |
| ☐ 589 Ken Forsch | .90 | .36 | .09 |
| ☐ 590 Deron Johnson | .75 | .30 | .07 |
| ☐ 591 Mike Hedlund | .75 | .30 | .07 |
| ☐ 592 John Boccabella | .75 | .30 | .07 |

| | | | | |
|---|---|---|---|---|
| ☐ 593 | Royals Leaders: .............. | 1.00 | .40 | .10 |
| | Jack McKeon MGR | | | |
| | Galen Cisco CO | | | |
| | Harry Dunlop CO | | | |
| | Charlie Lau CO | | | |
| ☐ 594 | Vic Harris ...................... | .75 | .30 | .07 |
| ☐ 595 | Don Gullett ..................... | .90 | .36 | .09 |
| ☐ 596 | Red Sox Team ................. | 1.50 | .60 | .15 |
| ☐ 597 | Mickey Rivers ................. | 1.50 | .60 | .15 |
| ☐ 598 | Phil Roof ......................... | .75 | .30 | .07 |
| ☐ 599 | Ed Crosby ...................... | .75 | .30 | .07 |
| ☐ 600 | Dave McNally .................. | 1.25 | .50 | .12 |
| ☐ 601 | Rookie Catchers ............. | .75 | .30 | .07 |
| | Sergio Robles | | | |
| | George Pena | | | |
| | Rick Stelmaszek | | | |
| ☐ 602 | Rookie Pitchers .............. | .75 | .30 | .07 |
| | Mel Behney | | | |
| | Ralph Garcia | | | |
| | Doug Rau | | | |
| ☐ 603 | Rookie 3rd Basemen ...... | .75 | .30 | .07 |
| | Terry Hughes | | | |
| | Bill McNulty | | | |
| | Ken Reitz | | | |
| ☐ 604 | Rookie Pitchers .............. | .75 | .30 | .07 |
| | Jesse Jefferson | | | |
| | Dennis O'Toole | | | |
| | Bob Strampe | | | |
| ☐ 605 | Rookie 1st Basemen ...... | 1.00 | .40 | .10 |
| | Enos Cabell | | | |
| | Pat Bourque | | | |
| | Gonzalo Marquez | | | |
| ☐ 606 | Rookie Outfielders .......... | 2.50 | 1.00 | .25 |
| | Gary Matthews | | | |
| | Tom Paciorek | | | |
| | Jorge Roque | | | |
| ☐ 607 | Rookie Shortstops .......... | .75 | .30 | .07 |
| | Pepe Frias | | | |
| | Ray Busse | | | |
| | Mario Guerrero | | | |
| ☐ 608 | Rookie Pitchers .............. | 1.00 | .40 | .10 |
| | Steve Busby | | | |
| | Dick Colpaert | | | |
| | George Medich | | | |
| ☐ 609 | Rookie 2nd Basemen ...... | 2.50 | 1.00 | .25 |
| | Larvell Blanks | | | |
| | Pedro Garcia | | | |
| | Dave Lopes | | | |
| ☐ 610 | Rookie Pitchers .............. | 1.50 | .60 | .15 |
| | Jimmy Freeman | | | |
| | Charlie Hough | | | |
| | Hank Webb | | | |
| ☐ 611 | Rookie Outfielders .......... | 1.50 | .60 | .15 |
| | Rich Coggins | | | |
| | Jim Wohlford | | | |
| | Richie Zisk | | | |
| ☐ 612 | Rookie Pitchers .............. | .75 | .30 | .07 |
| | Steve Lawson | | | |
| | Bob Reynolds | | | |
| | Brent Strom | | | |
| ☐ 613 | Rookie Catchers ............. | 2.00 | .80 | .20 |
| | Bob Boone | | | |
| | Skip Jutze | | | |
| | Mike Ivie | | | |
| ☐ 614 | Rookie Outfielders .......... | 7.50 | 3.00 | .75 |
| | Alonza Bumbry | | | |
| | Dwight Evans | | | |
| | Charlie Spikes | | | |
| ☐ 615 | Rookie 3rd Basemen ...... | 125.00 | 50.00 | 12.50 |
| | Ron Cey | | | |
| | John Hilton | | | |
| | Mike Schmidt | | | |
| ☐ 616 | Rookie Pitchers .............. | .75 | .30 | .07 |
| | Norm Angelini | | | |
| | Steve Blateric | | | |
| | Mike Garman | | | |
| ☐ 617 | Rich Chiles ..................... | .75 | .30 | .07 |
| ☐ 618 | Andy Etchebarren ........... | .75 | .30 | .07 |
| ☐ 619 | Billy Wilson .................... | .75 | .30 | .07 |
| ☐ 620 | Tommy Harper ................ | .90 | .36 | .09 |
| ☐ 621 | Joe Ferguson ................. | .90 | .36 | .09 |
| ☐ 622 | Larry Hisle ..................... | .90 | .36 | .09 |
| ☐ 623 | Steve Renko ................... | .75 | .30 | .07 |
| ☐ 624 | Astros Leaders: .............. | 1.50 | .60 | .15 |
| | Leo Durocher MGR | | | |
| | Preston Gomez CO | | | |
| | Grady Hatton CO | | | |
| | Hub Kittle CO | | | |
| | Jim Owens CO | | | |
| ☐ 625 | Angel Mangual ................ | .75 | .30 | .07 |
| ☐ 626 | Bob Barton .................... | .75 | .30 | .07 |
| ☐ 627 | Luis Alvarado ................. | .75 | .30 | .07 |
| ☐ 628 | Jim Slaton ..................... | .90 | .36 | .09 |

| | | | | |
|---|---|---|---|---|
| ☐ 629 | Indians Team ................. | 1.50 | .60 | .15 |
| ☐ 630 | Denny McLain ................ | 1.75 | .70 | .17 |
| ☐ 631 | Tom Matchick ................ | .75 | .30 | .07 |
| ☐ 632 | Dick Selma .................... | .75 | .30 | .07 |
| ☐ 633 | Ike Brown ...................... | .75 | .30 | .07 |
| ☐ 634 | Alan Closter .................. | .75 | .30 | .07 |
| ☐ 635 | Gene Alley ..................... | .90 | .36 | .09 |
| ☐ 636 | Rickey Clark .................. | .75 | .30 | .07 |
| ☐ 637 | Norm Miller .................... | .75 | .30 | .07 |
| ☐ 638 | Ken Reynolds ................. | .75 | .30 | .07 |
| ☐ 639 | Willie Crawford .............. | .75 | .30 | .07 |
| ☐ 640 | Dick Bosman .................. | .75 | .30 | .07 |
| ☐ 641 | Reds Team ..................... | 1.75 | .70 | .17 |
| ☐ 642 | Jose LaBoy .................... | .75 | .30 | .07 |
| ☐ 643 | Al Fitzmorris .................. | .75 | .30 | .07 |
| ☐ 644 | Jack Heidemann ............. | .75 | .30 | .07 |
| ☐ 645 | Bob Locker ..................... | .75 | .30 | .07 |
| ☐ 646 | Brewers Leaders: ........... | 1.25 | .50 | .12 |
| | Del Crandall MGR | | | |
| | Harvey Kuenn CO | | | |
| | Joe Nossek CO | | | |
| | Bob Shaw CO | | | |
| | Jim Walton CO | | | |
| ☐ 647 | George Stone ................. | .75 | .30 | .07 |
| ☐ 648 | Tom Egan ...................... | .75 | .30 | .07 |
| ☐ 649 | Rich Folkers .................. | .75 | .30 | .07 |
| ☐ 650 | Felipe Alou .................... | .90 | .36 | .09 |
| ☐ 651 | Don Carrithers ............... | .75 | .30 | .07 |
| ☐ 652 | Ted Kubiak .................... | .75 | .30 | .07 |
| ☐ 653 | Joe Hoerner ................... | .75 | .30 | .07 |
| ☐ 654 | Twins Team .................... | 1.50 | .60 | .15 |
| ☐ 655 | Clay Kirby ..................... | .75 | .30 | .07 |
| ☐ 656 | John Ellis ...................... | .75 | .30 | .07 |
| ☐ 657 | Bob Johnson .................. | .75 | .30 | .07 |
| ☐ 658 | Elliott Maddox ................ | .75 | .30 | .07 |
| ☐ 659 | Jose Pagan .................... | .75 | .30 | .07 |
| ☐ 660 | Fred Scherman ............... | 1.25 | .50 | .12 |

# 1974 Topps

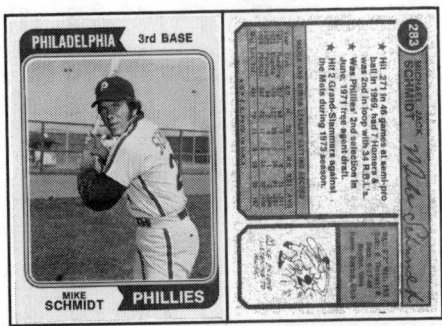

The cards in this 660 card set measure 2 1/2" by 3 1/2". This year marked the first time Topps issued all the cards of its baseball set at the same time rather than in series. Some interesting variations were created by the rumored move of the San Diego Padres to Washington. Fifteen cards (13 players, the team card, and the rookie card #599) of the Padres were printed either as "San Diego" (SD) or "Washington". The latter are the scarcer variety and are denoted in the checklist below by WASH. Each team's manager and his coaches again have a combined card with small pictures of each coach below the larger photo of the team's manager. The first six cards in the set (1-6) feature Hank Aaron and his illustrious career. Other topical subsets included in the set are League Leaders (201-208), All Star selections (331-339), Playoffs cards (470-471), World Series cards (472-479), and Rookie prospects (596-608).

| | | MINT | VG-E | F-G |
|---|---|---|---|---|
| | COMPLETE SET | 250.00 | 100.00 | 25.00 |
| | COMMON PLAYER (1-660) | .15 | .06 | .01 |
| ☐ 1 | Hank Aaron | 9.00 | 3.75 | .90 |
| | Complete ML record | | | |
| ☐ 2 | Aaron Special 54-57 | 2.25 | .90 | .22 |
| | Records on back | | | |
| ☐ 3 | Aaron Special 58-61 | 2.25 | .90 | .22 |
| | Memorable homers | | | |
| ☐ 4 | Aaron Special 62-65 | 2.25 | .90 | .22 |
| | Life in ML's 1954-63 | | | |
| ☐ 5 | Aaron Special 66-69 | 2.25 | .90 | .22 |
| | Life in ML's 1964-73 | | | |
| ☐ 6 | Aaron Special 70-73 | 2.25 | .90 | .22 |
| | Milestone homers | | | |
| ☐ 7 | Jim Hunter | 1.75 | .70 | .17 |
| ☐ 8 | George Theodore | .15 | .06 | .01 |
| ☐ 9 | Mickey Lolich | .35 | .14 | .03 |
| ☐ 10 | Johnny Bench | 5.00 | 2.00 | .50 |
| ☐ 11 | Jim Bibby | .20 | .08 | .02 |
| ☐ 12 | Dave May | .15 | .06 | .01 |
| ☐ 13 | Tom Hilgendorf | .15 | .06 | .01 |
| ☐ 14 | Paul Popovich | .15 | .06 | .01 |
| ☐ 15 | Joe Torre | .50 | .20 | .05 |
| ☐ 16 | Orioles Team | .40 | .16 | .04 |
| ☐ 17 | Doug Bird | .15 | .06 | .01 |
| ☐ 18 | Gary Thomasson | .15 | .06 | .01 |
| ☐ 19 | Gerry Moses | .15 | .06 | .01 |
| ☐ 20 | Nolan Ryan | 4.50 | 1.80 | .45 |
| ☐ 21 | Bob Gallagher | .15 | .06 | .01 |
| ☐ 22 | Cy Acosta | .15 | .06 | .01 |
| ☐ 23 | Craig Robinson | .15 | .06 | .01 |
| ☐ 24 | John Hiller | .20 | .08 | .02 |
| ☐ 25 | Ken Singleton | .30 | .12 | .03 |
| ☐ 26 | Bill Campbell | .25 | .10 | .02 |
| ☐ 27 | George Scott | .20 | .08 | .02 |
| ☐ 28 | Manny Sanguillen | .20 | .08 | .02 |
| ☐ 29 | Phil Niekro | 1.25 | .50 | .12 |
| ☐ 30 | Bobby Bonds | .30 | .12 | .03 |
| ☐ 31 | Astros Leaders: | .25 | .10 | .02 |
| | Preston Gomez MGR | | | |
| | Roger Craig CO | | | |
| | Hub Kittle CO | | | |
| | Grady Hatton CO | | | |
| | Bob Lillis CO | | | |
| ☐ 32A | Johnny Grubb SD | .30 | .12 | .03 |
| ☐ 32B | Johnny Grubb WASH | 3.00 | 1.20 | .30 |
| ☐ 33 | Don Newhauser | .15 | .06 | .01 |
| ☐ 34 | Andy Kosco | .15 | .06 | .01 |
| ☐ 35 | Gaylord Perry | 1.75 | .70 | .17 |
| ☐ 36 | Cardinals Team | .40 | .16 | .04 |
| ☐ 37 | Dave Sells | .15 | .06 | .01 |
| ☐ 38 | Don Kessinger | .20 | .08 | .02 |
| ☐ 39 | Ken Suarez | .15 | .06 | .01 |
| ☐ 40 | Jim Palmer | 2.75 | 1.10 | .27 |
| ☐ 41 | Bobby Floyd | .15 | .06 | .01 |
| ☐ 42 | Claude Osteen | .20 | .08 | .02 |
| ☐ 43 | Jim Wynn | .25 | .10 | .02 |
| ☐ 44 | Mel Stottlemyre | .25 | .10 | .02 |
| ☐ 45 | Dave Johnson | .35 | .14 | .03 |
| ☐ 46 | Pat Kelly | .15 | .06 | .01 |
| ☐ 47 | Dick Ruthven | .15 | .06 | .01 |
| ☐ 48 | Dick Sharon | .15 | .06 | .01 |
| ☐ 49 | Steve Renko | .15 | .06 | .01 |
| ☐ 50 | Rod Carew | 4.50 | 1.80 | .45 |
| ☐ 51 | Bob Heise | .15 | .06 | .01 |
| ☐ 52 | Al Oliver | .90 | .36 | .09 |
| ☐ 53A | Fred Kendall SD | .30 | .12 | .03 |
| ☐ 53B | Fred Kendall WASH | 3.00 | 1.20 | .30 |
| ☐ 54 | Elias Sosa | .15 | .06 | .01 |
| ☐ 55 | Frank Robinson | 2.25 | .90 | .22 |
| ☐ 56 | New York Mets Team | .60 | .24 | .06 |
| ☐ 57 | Darold Knowles | .15 | .06 | .01 |
| ☐ 58 | Charlie Spikes | .15 | .06 | .01 |
| ☐ 59 | Ross Grimsley | .15 | .06 | .01 |
| ☐ 60 | Lou Brock | 2.25 | .90 | .22 |
| ☐ 61 | Luis Aparicio | 1.75 | .70 | .17 |
| ☐ 62 | Bob Locker | .15 | .06 | .01 |
| ☐ 63 | Bill Sudakis | .15 | .06 | .01 |
| ☐ 64 | Doug Rau | .15 | .06 | .01 |
| ☐ 65 | Amos Otis | .30 | .12 | .03 |
| ☐ 66 | Sparky Lyle | .30 | .12 | .03 |
| ☐ 67 | Tommy Helms | .20 | .08 | .02 |
| ☐ 68 | Grant Jackson | .15 | .06 | .01 |
| ☐ 69 | Del Unser | .15 | .06 | .01 |
| ☐ 70 | Dick Allen | .40 | .16 | .04 |
| ☐ 71 | Dan Frisella | .15 | .06 | .01 |
| ☐ 72 | Aurelio Rodriguez | .15 | .06 | .01 |
| ☐ 73 | Mike Marshall | .45 | .18 | .04 |
| ☐ 74 | Twins Team | .40 | .16 | .04 |
| ☐ 75 | Jim Colborn | .15 | .06 | .01 |
| ☐ 76 | Mickey Rivers | .30 | .12 | .03 |
| ☐ 77A | Rich Troedson SD | .30 | .12 | .03 |
| ☐ 77B | Rich Troedson WASH | 3.00 | 1.20 | .30 |
| ☐ 78 | Giants Leaders: | .25 | .10 | .02 |
| | Charlie Fox MGR | | | |
| | John McNamara CO | | | |
| | Joe Amalfitano CO | | | |
| | Andy Gilbert CO | | | |
| | Don McMahon CO | | | |
| ☐ 79 | Gene Tenace | .20 | .08 | .02 |
| ☐ 80 | Tom Seaver | 5.00 | 2.00 | .50 |
| ☐ 81 | Frank Duffy | .15 | .06 | .01 |
| ☐ 82 | Dave Giusti | .15 | .06 | .01 |
| ☐ 83 | Orlando Cepeda | .55 | .22 | .05 |
| ☐ 84 | Rick Wise | .20 | .08 | .02 |
| ☐ 85 | Joe Morgan | 1.75 | .70 | .17 |
| ☐ 86 | Joe Ferguson | .20 | .08 | .02 |
| ☐ 87 | Fergie Jenkins | .80 | .32 | .08 |
| ☐ 88 | Fred Patek | .15 | .06 | .01 |
| ☐ 89 | Jackie Brown | .15 | .06 | .01 |
| ☐ 90 | Bobby Murcer | .45 | .18 | .04 |
| ☐ 91 | Ken Forsch | .20 | .08 | .02 |
| ☐ 92 | Paul Blair | .20 | .08 | .02 |
| ☐ 93 | Rod Gilbreath | .15 | .06 | .01 |
| ☐ 94 | Tigers Team | .40 | .16 | .04 |
| ☐ 95 | Steve Carlton | 5.00 | 2.00 | .50 |
| ☐ 96 | Jerry Hairston | .15 | .06 | .01 |
| ☐ 97 | Bob Bailey | .15 | .06 | .01 |
| ☐ 98 | Bert Blyleven | .60 | .24 | .06 |
| ☐ 99 | Brewers Leaders: | .30 | .12 | .03 |
| | Del Crandall MGR | | | |
| | Harvey Kuenn CO | | | |
| | Joe Nossek CO | | | |
| | Jim Walton CO | | | |
| | Al Widmar CO | | | |
| ☐ 100 | Willie Stargell | 2.00 | .80 | .20 |
| ☐ 101 | Bobby Valentine | .35 | .14 | .03 |
| ☐ 102A | Bill Greif SD | .30 | .12 | .03 |
| ☐ 102B | Bill Greif WASH | 3.00 | 1.20 | .30 |
| ☐ 103 | Sal Bando | .30 | .12 | .03 |
| ☐ 104 | Ron Bryant | .15 | .06 | .01 |
| ☐ 105 | Carlton Fisk | 1.25 | .50 | .12 |
| ☐ 106 | Harry Parker | .15 | .06 | .01 |
| ☐ 107 | Alex Johnson | .20 | .08 | .02 |
| ☐ 108 | Al Hrabosky | .20 | .08 | .02 |
| ☐ 109 | Bobby Grich | .30 | .12 | .03 |
| ☐ 110 | Billy Williams | 1.50 | .60 | .15 |
| ☐ 111 | Clay Carroll | .15 | .06 | .01 |
| ☐ 112 | Dave Lopes | .30 | .12 | .03 |
| ☐ 113 | Dick Drago | .15 | .06 | .01 |
| ☐ 114 | Angels Team | .40 | .16 | .04 |
| ☐ 115 | Willie Horton | .25 | .10 | .02 |
| ☐ 116 | Jerry Reuss | .30 | .12 | .03 |
| ☐ 117 | Ron Blomberg | .15 | .06 | .01 |
| ☐ 118 | Bill Lee | .20 | .08 | .02 |
| ☐ 119 | Phillies Leaders: | .25 | .10 | .02 |
| | Danny Ozark MGR | | | |
| | Ray Ripplemeyer CO | | | |
| | Bobby Wine CO | | | |
| | Carroll Beringer CO | | | |
| | Billy DeMars CO | | | |
| ☐ 120 | Wilbur Wood | .20 | .08 | .02 |
| ☐ 121 | Larry Lintz | .15 | .06 | .01 |
| ☐ 122 | Jim Holt | .15 | .06 | .01 |
| ☐ 123 | Nellie Briles | .20 | .08 | .02 |
| ☐ 124 | Bobby Coluccio | .15 | .06 | .01 |
| ☐ 125A | Nate Colbert SD | .30 | .12 | .03 |
| ☐ 125B | Nate Colbert WASH | 3.00 | 1.20 | .30 |
| ☐ 126 | Checklist 1 | .75 | .07 | .01 |
| ☐ 127 | Tom Paciorek | .20 | .08 | .02 |
| ☐ 128 | John Ellis | .15 | .06 | .01 |
| ☐ 129 | Chris Speier | .15 | .06 | .01 |
| ☐ 130 | Reggie Jackson | 6.00 | 2.40 | .60 |
| ☐ 131 | Bob Boone | .35 | .14 | .03 |
| ☐ 132 | Felix Millan | .15 | .06 | .01 |
| ☐ 133 | David Clyde | .20 | .08 | .02 |
| ☐ 134 | Denis Menke | .15 | .06 | .01 |
| ☐ 135 | Roy White | .20 | .08 | .02 |
| ☐ 136 | Rick Reuschel | .25 | .10 | .02 |
| ☐ 137 | Al Bumbry | .15 | .06 | .01 |
| ☐ 138 | Eddie Brinkman | .15 | .06 | .01 |
| ☐ 139 | Aurelio Monteagudo | .15 | .06 | .01 |
| ☐ 140 | Darrell Evans | .35 | .14 | .03 |
| ☐ 141 | Pat Bourque | .15 | .06 | .01 |
| ☐ 142 | Pedro Garcia | .15 | .06 | .01 |
| ☐ 143 | Dick Woodson | .15 | .06 | .01 |
| ☐ 144 | Dodgers Leaders: | .55 | .22 | .05 |
| | Walter Alston MGR | | | |
| | Tom Lasorda CO | | | |
| | Jim Gilliam CO | | | |
| | Red Adams CO | | | |
| | Monty Basgall CO | | | |
| ☐ 145 | Dock Ellis | .15 | .06 | .01 |
| ☐ 146 | Ron Fairly | .20 | .08 | .02 |
| ☐ 147 | Bart Johnson | .15 | .06 | .01 |

| | | | | |
|---|---|---|---|---|
| ☐ 148A | Dave Hilton SD | .30 | .12 | .03 |
| ☐ 148B | Dave Hilton WASH | 3.00 | 1.20 | .30 |
| ☐ 149 | Mac Scarce | .15 | .06 | .01 |
| ☐ 150 | John Mayberry | .20 | .08 | .02 |
| ☐ 151 | Diego Segui | .15 | .06 | .01 |
| ☐ 152 | Oscar Gamble | .25 | .10 | .02 |
| ☐ 153 | Jon Matlack | .25 | .10 | .02 |
| ☐ 154 | Astros Team | .40 | .16 | .04 |
| ☐ 155 | Bert Campaneris | .30 | .12 | .03 |
| ☐ 156 | Randy Moffitt | .15 | .06 | .01 |
| ☐ 157 | Vic Harris | .15 | .06 | .01 |
| ☐ 158 | Jack Billingham | .15 | .06 | .01 |
| ☐ 159 | Jim Ray Hart | .20 | .08 | .02 |
| ☐ 160 | Brooks Robinson | 2.50 | 1.00 | .25 |
| ☐ 161 | Ray Burris | .50 | .20 | .05 |
| ☐ 162 | Bill Freehan | .30 | .12 | .03 |
| ☐ 163 | Ken Berry | .15 | .06 | .01 |
| ☐ 164 | Tom House | .20 | .08 | .02 |
| ☐ 165 | Willie Davis | .25 | .10 | .02 |
| ☐ 166 | Royals Leaders:<br>Jack McKeon MGR<br>Charlie Lau CO<br>Harry Dunlop CO<br>Galen Cisco CO | .25 | .10 | .02 |
| ☐ 167 | Luis Tiant | .35 | .14 | .03 |
| ☐ 168 | Danny Thompson | .15 | .06 | .01 |
| ☐ 169 | Steve Rogers | .90 | .36 | .09 |
| ☐ 170 | Bill Melton | .15 | .06 | .01 |
| ☐ 171 | Eduardo Rodriguez | .15 | .06 | .01 |
| ☐ 172 | Gene Clines | .15 | .06 | .01 |
| ☐ 173A | Randy Jones SD | .45 | .18 | .04 |
| ☐ 173B | Randy Jones WASH | 3.50 | 1.40 | .35 |
| ☐ 174 | Bill Robinson | .15 | .06 | .01 |
| ☐ 175 | Reggie Cleveland | .15 | .06 | .01 |
| ☐ 176 | John Lowenstein | .15 | .06 | .01 |
| ☐ 177 | Dave Roberts | .15 | .06 | .01 |
| ☐ 178 | Garry Maddox | .20 | .08 | .02 |
| ☐ 179 | Mets Leaders:<br>Yogi Berra MGR<br>Rube Walker CO<br>Eddie Yost CO<br>Roy McMillan CO<br>Joe Pignatano CO | .65 | .26 | .06 |
| ☐ 180 | Ken Holtzman | .25 | .10 | .02 |
| ☐ 181 | Cesar Geronimo | .15 | .06 | .01 |
| ☐ 182 | Lindy McDaniel | .15 | .06 | .01 |
| ☐ 183 | Johnny Oates | .15 | .06 | .01 |
| ☐ 184 | Rangers Team | .40 | .16 | .04 |
| ☐ 185 | Jose Cardenal | .15 | .06 | .01 |
| ☐ 186 | Fred Scherman | .15 | .06 | .01 |
| ☐ 187 | Don Baylor | .70 | .28 | .07 |
| ☐ 188 | Rudy Meoli | .15 | .06 | .01 |
| ☐ 189 | Jim Brewer | .15 | .06 | .01 |
| ☐ 190 | Tony Oliva | .50 | .20 | .05 |
| ☐ 191 | Al Fitzmorris | .15 | .06 | .01 |
| ☐ 192 | Mario Guerrero | .15 | .06 | .01 |
| ☐ 193 | Tom Walker | .15 | .06 | .01 |
| ☐ 194 | Darrell Porter | .25 | .10 | .02 |
| ☐ 195 | Carlos May | .15 | .06 | .01 |
| ☐ 196 | Jim Fregosi | .30 | .12 | .03 |
| ☐ 197A | Vicente Romo SD | .30 | .12 | .03 |
| ☐ 197B | Vicente Romo WASH | 3.00 | 1.20 | .30 |
| ☐ 198 | Dave Cash | .20 | .08 | .02 |
| ☐ 199 | Mike Kekich | .15 | .06 | .01 |
| ☐ 200 | Cesar Cedeno | .30 | .12 | .03 |
| ☐ 201 | Batting Leaders:<br>Rod Carew<br>Pete Rose | 2.50 | 1.00 | .25 |
| ☐ 202 | Home Run Leaders:<br>Reggie Jackson<br>Willie Stargell | 1.25 | .50 | .12 |
| ☐ 203 | RBI Leaders:<br>Reggie Jackson<br>Willie Stargell | 1.25 | .50 | .12 |
| ☐ 204 | Stolen Base Leaders:<br>Tommy Harper<br>Lou Brock | .60 | .24 | .06 |
| ☐ 205 | Victory Leaders:<br>Wilbur Wood<br>Ron Bryant | .30 | .12 | .03 |
| ☐ 206 | ERA Leaders:<br>Jim Palmer<br>Tom Seaver | 1.50 | .60 | .15 |
| ☐ 207 | Strikeout Leaders:<br>Nolan Ryan<br>Tom Seaver | 1.50 | .60 | .15 |
| ☐ 208 | Leading Firemen:<br>John Hiller<br>Mike Marshall | .30 | .12 | .03 |
| ☐ 209 | Ted Sizemore | .15 | .06 | .01 |
| ☐ 210 | Bill Singer | .15 | .06 | .01 |
| ☐ 211 | Chicago Cubs Team | .40 | .16 | .04 |
| ☐ 212 | Rollie Fingers | 1.00 | .40 | .10 |
| ☐ 213 | Dave Rader | .15 | .06 | .01 |
| ☐ 214 | Bill Grabarkewitz | .15 | .06 | .01 |
| ☐ 215 | Al Kaline | 2.25 | .90 | .22 |
| ☐ 216 | Ray Sadecki | .15 | .06 | .01 |
| ☐ 217 | Tim Foli | .15 | .06 | .01 |
| ☐ 218 | John Briggs | .15 | .06 | .01 |
| ☐ 219 | Doug Griffin | .15 | .06 | .01 |
| ☐ 220 | Don Sutton | 1.50 | .60 | .15 |
| ☐ 221 | White Sox Leaders:<br>Chuck Tanner MGR<br>Jim Mahoney CO<br>Alex Monchak CO<br>Johnny Sain CO<br>Joe Lonnett CO | .25 | .10 | .02 |
| ☐ 222 | Ramon Hernandez | .15 | .06 | .01 |
| ☐ 223 | Jeff Burroughs | .40 | .16 | .04 |
| ☐ 224 | Roger Metzger | .15 | .06 | .01 |
| ☐ 225 | Paul Splittorff | .20 | .08 | .02 |
| ☐ 226A | Padres Team SD | .60 | .24 | .06 |
| ☐ 226B | Padres Team WASH | 5.00 | 2.00 | .50 |
| ☐ 227 | Mike Lum | .15 | .06 | .01 |
| ☐ 228 | Ted Kubiak | .15 | .06 | .01 |
| ☐ 229 | Fritz Peterson | .15 | .06 | .01 |
| ☐ 230 | Tony Perez | .65 | .26 | .06 |
| ☐ 231 | Dick Tidrow | .15 | .06 | .01 |
| ☐ 232 | Steve Brye | .15 | .06 | .01 |
| ☐ 233 | Jim Barr | .15 | .06 | .01 |
| ☐ 234 | John Milner | .15 | .06 | .01 |
| ☐ 235 | Dave McNally | .25 | .10 | .02 |
| ☐ 236 | Cardinals Leaders:<br>Red Schoendienst MGR<br>Barney Schultz CO<br>George Kissell CO<br>Johnny Lewis CO<br>Vern Benson CO | .30 | .12 | .03 |
| ☐ 237 | Ken Brett | .15 | .06 | .01 |
| ☐ 238 | Fran Healy | .15 | .06 | .01 |
| ☐ 239 | Bill Russell | .25 | .10 | .02 |
| ☐ 240 | Joe Coleman | .15 | .06 | .01 |
| ☐ 241A | Glenn Beckert SD | .30 | .12 | .03 |
| ☐ 241B | Glenn Beckert WASH | 3.00 | 1.20 | .30 |
| ☐ 242 | Bill Gogolewski | .15 | .06 | .01 |
| ☐ 243 | Bob Oliver | .15 | .06 | .01 |
| ☐ 244 | Carl Morton | .15 | .06 | .01 |
| ☐ 245 | Cleon Jones | .15 | .06 | .01 |
| ☐ 246 | Athletics Team | .45 | .18 | .04 |
| ☐ 247 | Rick Miller | .15 | .06 | .01 |
| ☐ 248 | Tom Hall | .15 | .06 | .01 |
| ☐ 249 | George Mitterwald | .15 | .06 | .01 |
| ☐ 250A | Willie McCovey SD | 3.00 | 1.20 | .30 |
| ☐ 250B | Willie McCovey WASH | 16.00 | 6.50 | 1.60 |
| ☐ 251 | Graig Nettles | 1.50 | .60 | .15 |
| ☐ 252 | Dave Parker | 14.00 | 5.75 | 1.40 |
| ☐ 253 | John Boccabella | .15 | .06 | .01 |
| ☐ 254 | Stan Bahnsen | .15 | .06 | .01 |
| ☐ 255 | Larry Bowa | .45 | .18 | .04 |
| ☐ 256 | Tom Griffin | .15 | .06 | .01 |
| ☐ 257 | Buddy Bell | .80 | .32 | .08 |
| ☐ 258 | Jerry Morales | .15 | .06 | .01 |
| ☐ 259 | Bob Reynolds | .15 | .06 | .01 |
| ☐ 260 | Ted Simmons | .80 | .32 | .08 |
| ☐ 261 | Jerry Bell | .15 | .06 | .01 |
| ☐ 262 | Ed Kirkpatrick | .15 | .06 | .01 |
| ☐ 263 | Checklist 2 | .75 | .07 | .01 |
| ☐ 264 | Joe Rudi | .25 | .10 | .02 |
| ☐ 265 | Tug McGraw | .35 | .14 | .03 |
| ☐ 266 | Jim Northrup | .20 | .08 | .02 |
| ☐ 267 | Andy Messersmith | .25 | .10 | .02 |
| ☐ 268 | Tom Grieve | .25 | .10 | .02 |
| ☐ 269 | Bob Johnson | .15 | .06 | .01 |
| ☐ 270 | Ron Santo | .35 | .14 | .03 |
| ☐ 271 | Bill Hands | .15 | .06 | .01 |
| ☐ 272 | Paul Casanova | .15 | .06 | .01 |
| ☐ 273 | Checklist 3 | .75 | .07 | .01 |
| ☐ 274 | Fred Beene | .15 | .06 | .01 |
| ☐ 275 | Ron Hunt | .15 | .06 | .01 |
| ☐ 276 | Angels Leaders:<br>Bobby Winkles MGR<br>John Roseboro CO<br>Tom Morgan CO<br>Jimmie Reese CO<br>Salty Parker CO | .25 | .10 | .02 |
| ☐ 277 | Gary Nolan | .15 | .06 | .01 |
| ☐ 278 | Cookie Rojas | .15 | .06 | .01 |
| ☐ 279 | Jim Crawford | .15 | .06 | .01 |
| ☐ 280 | Carl Yastrzemski | 6.50 | 2.60 | .65 |
| ☐ 281 | Giants Team | .40 | .16 | .04 |
| ☐ 282 | Doyle Alexander | .20 | .08 | .02 |
| ☐ 283 | Mike Schmidt | 20.00 | 8.00 | 2.00 |
| ☐ 284 | Dave Duncan | .15 | .06 | .01 |
| ☐ 285 | Reggie Smith | .35 | .14 | .03 |
| ☐ 286 | Tony Muser | .15 | .06 | .01 |
| ☐ 287 | Clay Kirby | .15 | .06 | .01 |

| | | | | |
|---|---|---|---|---|
| ☐ 288 | Gorman Thomas | 1.50 | .60 | .15 |
| ☐ 289 | Rick Auerbach | .15 | .06 | .01 |
| ☐ 290 | Vida Blue | .35 | .14 | .03 |
| ☐ 291 | Don Hahn | .15 | .06 | .01 |
| ☐ 292 | Chuck Seelbach | .15 | .06 | .01 |
| ☐ 293 | Milt May | .15 | .06 | .01 |
| ☐ 294 | Steve Foucault | .15 | .06 | .01 |
| ☐ 295 | Rick Monday | .20 | .08 | .02 |
| ☐ 296 | Ray Corbin | .15 | .06 | .01 |
| ☐ 297 | Hal Breeden | .15 | .06 | .01 |
| ☐ 298 | Roric Harrison | .15 | .06 | .01 |
| ☐ 299 | Gene Michael | .25 | .10 | .02 |
| ☐ 300 | Pete Rose | 13.00 | 5.25 | 1.30 |
| ☐ 301 | Bob Montgomery | .15 | .06 | .01 |
| ☐ 302 | Rudy May | .15 | .06 | .01 |
| ☐ 303 | George Hendrick | .35 | .14 | .03 |
| ☐ 304 | Don Wilson | .15 | .06 | .01 |
| ☐ 305 | Tito Fuentes | .15 | .06 | .01 |
| ☐ 306 | Orioles Leaders: | .45 | .18 | .04 |
| | Earl Weaver MGR | | | |
| | Jim Frey CO | | | |
| | George Bamberger CO | | | |
| | Billy Hunter CO | | | |
| | George Staller CO | | | |
| ☐ 307 | Luis Melendez | .15 | .06 | .01 |
| ☐ 308 | Bruce Dal Canton | .15 | .06 | .01 |
| ☐ 309A | Dave Roberts SD | .30 | .12 | .03 |
| ☐ 309B | Dave Roberts WASH | 3.75 | 1.50 | .37 |
| ☐ 310 | Terry Forster | .30 | .12 | .03 |
| ☐ 311 | Jerry Grote | .15 | .06 | .01 |
| ☐ 312 | Deron Johnson | .15 | .06 | .01 |
| ☐ 313 | Barry Lersch | .15 | .06 | .01 |
| ☐ 314 | Brewers Team | .40 | .16 | .04 |
| ☐ 315 | Ron Cey | 1.00 | .40 | .10 |
| ☐ 316 | Jim Perry | .25 | .10 | .02 |
| ☐ 317 | Richie Zisk | .25 | .10 | .02 |
| ☐ 318 | Jim Merritt | .15 | .06 | .01 |
| ☐ 319 | Randy Hundley | .15 | .06 | .01 |
| ☐ 320 | Dusty Baker | .40 | .16 | .04 |
| ☐ 321 | Steve Braun | .15 | .06 | .01 |
| ☐ 322 | Ernie McAnally | .15 | .06 | .01 |
| ☐ 323 | Richie Scheinblum | .15 | .06 | .01 |
| ☐ 324 | Steve Kline | .15 | .06 | .01 |
| ☐ 325 | Tommy Harper | .20 | .08 | .02 |
| ☐ 326 | Reds Leaders: | .30 | .12 | .03 |
| | Sparky Anderson MGR | | | |
| | Larry Shephard CO | | | |
| | George Scherger CO | | | |
| | Alex Grammas CO | | | |
| | Ted Kluszewski CO | | | |
| ☐ 327 | Tom Timmermann | .15 | .06 | .01 |
| ☐ 328 | Skip Jutze | .15 | .06 | .01 |
| ☐ 329 | Mark Belanger | .25 | .10 | .02 |
| ☐ 330 | Juan Marichal | 2.00 | .80 | .20 |
| ☐ 331 | All-Star Catchers: | 1.25 | .50 | .12 |
| | Carlton Fisk | | | |
| | Johnny Bench | | | |
| ☐ 332 | All-Star 1B: | 1.25 | .50 | .12 |
| | Dick Allen | | | |
| | Hank Aaron | | | |
| ☐ 333 | All-Star 2B: | 1.25 | .50 | .12 |
| | Rod Carew | | | |
| | Joe Morgan | | | |
| ☐ 334 | All-Star 3B: | .90 | .36 | .09 |
| | Brooks Robinson | | | |
| | Ron Santo | | | |
| ☐ 335 | All-Star SS: | .25 | .10 | .02 |
| | Bert Campaneris | | | |
| | Chris Speier | | | |
| ☐ 336 | All-Star LF: | 2.25 | .90 | .22 |
| | Bobby Murcer | | | |
| | Pete Rose | | | |
| ☐ 337 | All-Star CF: | .25 | .10 | .02 |
| | Amos Otis | | | |
| | Cesar Cedeno | | | |
| ☐ 338 | All-Star RF: | 1.50 | .60 | .15 |
| | Reggie Jackson | | | |
| | Billy Williams | | | |
| ☐ 339 | All-Star Pitchers: | .40 | .16 | .04 |
| | Jim Hunter | | | |
| | Rick Wise | | | |
| ☐ 340 | Thurman Munson | 3.50 | 1.40 | .35 |
| ☐ 341 | Dan Driessen | .35 | .14 | .03 |
| ☐ 342 | Jim Lonborg | .20 | .08 | .02 |
| ☐ 343 | Royals Team | .40 | .16 | .04 |
| ☐ 344 | Mike Caldwell | .20 | .08 | .02 |
| ☐ 345 | Bill North | .15 | .06 | .01 |
| ☐ 346 | Ron Reed | .15 | .06 | .01 |
| ☐ 347 | Sandy Alomar | .15 | .06 | .01 |
| ☐ 348 | Pete Richert | .15 | .06 | .01 |
| ☐ 349 | John Vukovich | .15 | .06 | .01 |
| ☐ 350 | Bob Gibson | 2.25 | .90 | .22 |
| ☐ 351 | Dwight Evans | 1.25 | .50 | .12 |

| | | | | |
|---|---|---|---|---|
| ☐ 352 | Bill Stoneman | .15 | .06 | .01 |
| ☐ 353 | Rich Coggins | .15 | .06 | .01 |
| ☐ 354 | Cubs Leaders: | .25 | .10 | .02 |
| | Whitey Lockman MGR | | | |
| | J.C. Martin CO | | | |
| | Hank Aguirre CO | | | |
| | Al Spangler CO | | | |
| | Jim Marshall CO | | | |
| ☐ 355 | Dave Nelson | .15 | .06 | .01 |
| ☐ 356 | Jerry Koosman | .30 | .12 | .03 |
| ☐ 357 | Buddy Bradford | .15 | .06 | .01 |
| ☐ 358 | Dal Maxvill | .15 | .06 | .01 |
| ☐ 359 | Brent Strom | .15 | .06 | .01 |
| ☐ 360 | Greg Luzinski | .70 | .28 | .07 |
| ☐ 361 | Don Carrithers | .15 | .06 | .01 |
| ☐ 362 | Hal King | .15 | .06 | .01 |
| ☐ 363 | Yankees Team | .55 | .22 | .05 |
| ☐ 364A | Cito Gaston SD | .30 | .12 | .03 |
| ☐ 364B | Cito Gaston WASH | 3.75 | 1.50 | .37 |
| ☐ 365 | Steve Busby | .25 | .10 | .02 |
| ☐ 366 | Larry Hisle | .25 | .10 | .02 |
| ☐ 367 | Norm Cash | .35 | .14 | .03 |
| ☐ 368 | Manny Mota | .25 | .10 | .02 |
| ☐ 369 | Paul Lindblad | .15 | .06 | .01 |
| ☐ 370 | Bob Watson | .30 | .12 | .03 |
| ☐ 371 | Jim Slaton | .15 | .06 | .01 |
| ☐ 372 | Ken Reitz | .15 | .06 | .01 |
| ☐ 373 | John Curtis | .15 | .06 | .01 |
| ☐ 374 | Marty Perez | .15 | .06 | .01 |
| ☐ 375 | Earl Williams | .15 | .06 | .01 |
| ☐ 376 | Jorge Orta | .15 | .06 | .01 |
| ☐ 377 | Ron Woods | .15 | .06 | .01 |
| ☐ 378 | Burt Hooton | .20 | .08 | .02 |
| ☐ 379 | Rangers Leaders: | .55 | .22 | .05 |
| | Billy Martin MGR | | | |
| | Frank Lucchesi CO | | | |
| | Art Fowler CO | | | |
| | Charlie Silvera CO | | | |
| | Jackie Moore CO | | | |
| ☐ 380 | Bud Harrelson | .15 | .06 | .01 |
| ☐ 381 | Charlie Sands | .15 | .06 | .01 |
| ☐ 382 | Bob Moose | .15 | .06 | .01 |
| ☐ 383 | Phillies Team | .40 | .16 | .04 |
| ☐ 384 | Chris Chambliss | .30 | .12 | .03 |
| ☐ 385 | Don Gullett | .20 | .08 | .02 |
| ☐ 386 | Gary Matthews | .45 | .18 | .04 |
| ☐ 387A | Rich Morales SD | .30 | .12 | .03 |
| ☐ 387B | Rich Morales WASH | 3.75 | 1.50 | .37 |
| ☐ 388 | Phil Roof | .15 | .06 | .01 |
| ☐ 389 | Gates Brown | .20 | .08 | .02 |
| ☐ 390 | Lou Piniella | .45 | .18 | .04 |
| ☐ 391 | Billy Champion | .15 | .06 | .01 |
| ☐ 392 | Dick Green | .15 | .06 | .01 |
| ☐ 393 | Orlando Pena | .15 | .06 | .01 |
| ☐ 394 | Ken Henderson | .15 | .06 | .01 |
| ☐ 395 | Doug Rader | .20 | .08 | .02 |
| ☐ 396 | Tommy Davis | .25 | .10 | .02 |
| ☐ 397 | George Stone | .15 | .06 | .01 |
| ☐ 398 | Duke Sims | .15 | .06 | .01 |
| ☐ 399 | Mike Paul | .15 | .06 | .01 |
| ☐ 400 | Harmon Killebrew | 2.25 | .90 | .22 |
| ☐ 401 | Elliott Maddox | .15 | .06 | .01 |
| ☐ 402 | Jim Rooker | .15 | .06 | .01 |
| ☐ 403 | Red Sox Leaders: | .25 | .10 | .02 |
| | Darrell Johnson MGR | | | |
| | Eddie Popowski CO | | | |
| | Lee Stange CO | | | |
| | Don Zimmer CO | | | |
| | Don Bryant CO | | | |
| ☐ 404 | Jim Howarth | .15 | .06 | .01 |
| ☐ 405 | Ellie Rodriguez | .15 | .06 | .01 |
| ☐ 406 | Steve Arlin | .15 | .06 | .01 |
| ☐ 407 | Jim Wohlford | .15 | .06 | .01 |
| ☐ 408 | Charlie Hough | .30 | .12 | .03 |
| ☐ 409 | Ike Brown | .15 | .06 | .01 |
| ☐ 410 | Pedro Borbon | .15 | .06 | .01 |
| ☐ 411 | Frank Baker | .15 | .06 | .01 |
| ☐ 412 | Chuck Taylor | .15 | .06 | .01 |
| ☐ 413 | Don Money | .20 | .08 | .02 |
| ☐ 414 | Checklist 4 | .75 | .07 | .01 |
| ☐ 415 | Gary Gentry | .15 | .06 | .01 |
| ☐ 416 | White Sox Team | .40 | .16 | .04 |
| ☐ 417 | Rich Folkers | .15 | .06 | .01 |
| ☐ 418 | Walt Williams | .15 | .06 | .01 |
| ☐ 419 | Wayne Twitchell | .15 | .06 | .01 |
| ☐ 420 | Ray Fosse | .15 | .06 | .01 |
| ☐ 421 | Dan Fife | .15 | .06 | .01 |
| ☐ 422 | Gonzalo Marquez | .15 | .06 | .01 |
| ☐ 423 | Fred Stanley | .15 | .06 | .01 |
| ☐ 424 | Jim Beauchamp | .15 | .06 | .01 |
| ☐ 425 | Pete Broberg | .15 | .06 | .01 |
| ☐ 426 | Rennie Stennett | .15 | .06 | .01 |
| ☐ 427 | Bobby Bolin | .15 | .06 | .01 |

| | | | | | | | | | |
|---|---|---|---|---|---|---|---|---|---|
| ☐ 428 | Gary Sutherland | .15 | .06 | .01 | ☐ 498 | Pat Corrales | .25 | .10 | .02 |
| ☐ 429 | Dick Lange | .15 | .06 | .01 | ☐ 499 | Rusty Torres | .15 | .06 | .01 |
| ☐ 430 | Matty Alou | .20 | .08 | .02 | ☐ 500 | Lee May | .25 | .10 | .02 |
| ☐ 431 | Gene Garber | .20 | .08 | .02 | ☐ 501 | Eddie Leon | .15 | .06 | .01 |
| ☐ 432 | Chris Arnold | .15 | .06 | .01 | ☐ 502 | Dave LaRoche | .15 | .06 | .01 |
| ☐ 433 | Lerrin LaGrow | .15 | .06 | .01 | ☐ 503 | Eric Soderholm | .15 | .06 | .01 |
| ☐ 434 | Ken McMullen | .15 | .06 | .01 | ☐ 504 | Joe Niekro | .30 | .12 | .03 |
| ☐ 435 | Dave Concepcion | .50 | .20 | .05 | ☐ 505 | Bill Buckner | .50 | .20 | .05 |
| ☐ 436 | Don Hood | .15 | .06 | .01 | ☐ 506 | Ed Farmer | .15 | .06 | .01 |
| ☐ 437 | Jim Lyttle | .15 | .06 | .01 | ☐ 507 | Larry Stahl | .15 | .06 | .01 |
| ☐ 438 | Ed Herrmann | .15 | .06 | .01 | ☐ 508 | Expos Team | .40 | .16 | .04 |
| ☐ 439 | Norm Miller | .15 | .06 | .01 | ☐ 509 | Jesse Jefferson | .15 | .06 | .01 |
| ☐ 440 | Jim Kaat | .75 | .30 | .07 | ☐ 510 | Wayne Garrett | .15 | .06 | .01 |
| ☐ 441 | Tom Ragland | .15 | .06 | .01 | ☐ 511 | Toby Harrah | .25 | .10 | .02 |
| ☐ 442 | Alan Foster | .15 | .06 | .01 | ☐ 512 | Joe Lahoud | .15 | .06 | .01 |
| ☐ 443 | Tom Hutton | .15 | .06 | .01 | ☐ 513 | Jim Campanis | .15 | .06 | .01 |
| ☐ 444 | Vic Davalillo | .15 | .06 | .01 | ☐ 514 | Paul Schaal | .15 | .06 | .01 |
| ☐ 445 | George Medich | .20 | .08 | .02 | ☐ 515 | Willie Montanez | .15 | .06 | .01 |
| ☐ 446 | Len Randle | .15 | .06 | .01 | ☐ 516 | Horacio Pina | .15 | .06 | .01 |
| ☐ 447 | Twins Leaders: | .25 | .10 | .02 | ☐ 517 | Mike Hegan | .15 | .06 | .01 |
| | Frank Quilici MGR | | | | ☐ 518 | Derrel Thomas | .15 | .06 | .01 |
| | Ralph Rowe CO | | | | ☐ 519 | Bill Sharp | .15 | .06 | .01 |
| | Bob Rodgers CO | | | | ☐ 520 | Tim McCarver | .30 | .12 | .03 |
| | Vern Morgan CO | | | | ☐ 521 | Indians Leaders: | .25 | .10 | .02 |
| ☐ 448 | Ron Hodges | .15 | .06 | .01 | | Ken Aspromonte MGR | | | |
| ☐ 449 | Tom McCraw | .15 | .06 | .01 | | Clay Bryant CO | | | |
| ☐ 450 | Rich Hebner | .15 | .06 | .01 | | Tony Pacheco CO | | | |
| ☐ 451 | Tommy John | .85 | .34 | .08 | ☐ 522 | J.R. Richard | .40 | .16 | .04 |
| ☐ 452 | Gene Hiser | .15 | .06 | .01 | ☐ 523 | Cecil Cooper | 1.50 | .60 | .15 |
| ☐ 453 | Balor Moore | .15 | .06 | .01 | ☐ 524 | Bill Plummer | .15 | .06 | .01 |
| ☐ 454 | Kurt Bevacqua | .15 | .06 | .01 | ☐ 525 | Clyde Wright | .15 | .06 | .01 |
| ☐ 455 | Tom Bradley | .15 | .06 | .01 | ☐ 526 | Frank Tepedino | .15 | .06 | .01 |
| ☐ 456 | Dave Winfield | 18.00 | 7.25 | 1.80 | ☐ 527 | Bobby Darwin | .15 | .06 | .01 |
| ☐ 457 | Chuck Goggin | .15 | .06 | .01 | ☐ 528 | Bill Bonham | .15 | .06 | .01 |
| ☐ 458 | Jim Ray | .15 | .06 | .01 | ☐ 529 | Horace Clarke | .15 | .06 | .01 |
| ☐ 459 | Reds Team | .45 | .18 | .04 | ☐ 530 | Mickey Stanley | .15 | .06 | .01 |
| ☐ 460 | Boog Powell | .50 | .20 | .05 | ☐ 531 | Expos Leaders: | .25 | .10 | .02 |
| ☐ 461 | John Odom | .15 | .06 | .01 | | Gene Mauch MGR | | | |
| ☐ 462 | Luis Alvarado | .15 | .06 | .01 | | Dave Bristol CO | | | |
| ☐ 463 | Pat Dobson | .20 | .08 | .02 | | Cal McLish CO | | | |
| ☐ 464 | Jose Cruz | .50 | .20 | .05 | | Larry Doby CO | | | |
| ☐ 465 | Dick Bosman | .15 | .06 | .01 | | Jerry Zimmerman CO | | | |
| ☐ 466 | Dick Billings | .15 | .06 | .01 | ☐ 532 | Skip Lockwood | .15 | .06 | .01 |
| ☐ 467 | Winston Llenas | .15 | .06 | .01 | ☐ 533 | Mike Phillips | .15 | .06 | .01 |
| ☐ 468 | Pepe Frias | .15 | .06 | .01 | ☐ 534 | Eddie Watt | .15 | .06 | .01 |
| ☐ 469 | Joe Decker | .15 | .06 | .01 | ☐ 535 | Bob Tolan | .15 | .06 | .01 |
| ☐ 470 | A.L. Playoffs: | 1.50 | .60 | .15 | ☐ 536 | Duffy Dyer | .15 | .06 | .01 |
| | A's over Orioles | | | | ☐ 537 | Steve Mingori | .15 | .06 | .01 |
| | (Reggie Jackson) | | | | ☐ 538 | Cesar Tovar | .15 | .06 | .01 |
| ☐ 471 | N.L. Playoffs: | .50 | .20 | .05 | ☐ 539 | Lloyd Allen | .15 | .06 | .01 |
| | Mets over Reds | | | | ☐ 540 | Bob Robertson | .15 | .06 | .01 |
| | (Matlack pitching) | | | | ☐ 541 | Indians Team | .40 | .16 | .04 |
| ☐ 472 | World Series Game 1: | .50 | .20 | .05 | ☐ 542 | Rich Gossage | 1.50 | .60 | .15 |
| | (Knowles pitching) | | | | ☐ 543 | Danny Cater | .15 | .06 | .01 |
| ☐ 473 | World Series Game 2: | 1.50 | .60 | .15 | ☐ 544 | Ron Schueler | .15 | .06 | .01 |
| | (Willie Mays batting) | | | | ☐ 545 | Billy Conigliaro | .15 | .06 | .01 |
| ☐ 474 | World Series Game 3: | .50 | .20 | .05 | ☐ 546 | Mike Corkins | .15 | .06 | .01 |
| | (Campaneris stealing) | | | | ☐ 547 | Glenn Borgmann | .15 | .06 | .01 |
| ☐ 475 | World Series Game 4: | .50 | .20 | .05 | ☐ 548 | Sonny Siebert | .20 | .08 | .02 |
| | (Staub batting) | | | | ☐ 549 | Mike Jorgensen | .15 | .06 | .01 |
| ☐ 476 | World Series Game 5: | .50 | .20 | .05 | ☐ 550 | Sam McDowell | .20 | .08 | .02 |
| | (Cleon Jones scoring) | | | | ☐ 551 | Von Joshua | .15 | .06 | .01 |
| ☐ 477 | World Series Game 6: | 1.50 | .60 | .15 | ☐ 552 | Denny Doyle | .15 | .06 | .01 |
| | (Reggie Jackson) | | | | ☐ 553 | Jim Willoughby | .15 | .06 | .01 |
| ☐ 478 | World Series Game 7: | .50 | .20 | .05 | ☐ 554 | Tim Johnson | .15 | .06 | .01 |
| | (Campaneris batting) | | | | ☐ 555 | Woody Fryman | .15 | .06 | .01 |
| ☐ 479 | World Series Summary: | .50 | .20 | .05 | ☐ 556 | Dave Campbell | .15 | .06 | .01 |
| | A's Celebrate; Win | | | | ☐ 557 | Jim McGlothlin | .15 | .06 | .01 |
| | 2nd Consecutive | | | | ☐ 558 | Bill Fahey | .15 | .06 | .01 |
| | Championship | | | | ☐ 559 | Darrell Chaney | .15 | .06 | .01 |
| ☐ 480 | Willie Crawford | .15 | .06 | .01 | ☐ 560 | Mike Cuellar | .25 | .10 | .02 |
| ☐ 481 | Jerry Terrell | .15 | .06 | .01 | ☐ 561 | Ed Kranepool | .20 | .08 | .02 |
| ☐ 482 | Bob Didier | .15 | .06 | .01 | ☐ 562 | Jack Aker | .15 | .06 | .01 |
| ☐ 483 | Braves Team | .40 | .16 | .04 | ☐ 563 | Hal McRae | .30 | .12 | .03 |
| ☐ 484 | Carmen Fanzone | .15 | .06 | .01 | ☐ 564 | Mike Ryan | .15 | .06 | .01 |
| ☐ 485 | Felipe Alou | .25 | .10 | .02 | ☐ 565 | Milt Wilcox | .20 | .08 | .02 |
| ☐ 486 | Steve Stone | .25 | .10 | .02 | ☐ 566 | Jackie Hernandez | .15 | .06 | .01 |
| ☐ 487 | Ted Martinez | .15 | .06 | .01 | ☐ 567 | Red Sox Team | .40 | .16 | .04 |
| ☐ 488 | Andy Etchebarren | .15 | .06 | .01 | ☐ 568 | Mike Torrez | .25 | .10 | .02 |
| ☐ 489 | Pirates Leaders: | .25 | .10 | .02 | ☐ 569 | Rick Dempsey | .25 | .10 | .02 |
| | Danny Murtaugh MGR | | | | ☐ 570 | Ralph Garr | .25 | .10 | .02 |
| | Don Osborn CO | | | | ☐ 571 | Rich Hand | .15 | .06 | .01 |
| | Don Leppert CO | | | | ☐ 572 | Enzo Hernandez | .15 | .06 | .01 |
| | Bill Mazeroski CO | | | | ☐ 573 | Mike Adams | .15 | .06 | .01 |
| | Bob Skinner CO | | | | ☐ 574 | Bill Parsons | .15 | .06 | .01 |
| ☐ 490 | Vada Pinson | .35 | .14 | .03 | ☐ 575 | Steve Garvey | 6.50 | 2.60 | .65 |
| ☐ 491 | Roger Nelson | .15 | .06 | .01 | ☐ 576 | Scipio Spinks | .15 | .06 | .01 |
| ☐ 492 | Mike Rogodzinski | .15 | .06 | .01 | ☐ 577 | Mike Sadek | .15 | .06 | .01 |
| ☐ 493 | Joe Hoerner | .15 | .06 | .01 | ☐ 578 | Ralph Houk MGR | .25 | .10 | .02 |
| ☐ 494 | Ed Goodson | .15 | .06 | .01 | ☐ 579 | Cecil Upshaw | .15 | .06 | .01 |
| ☐ 495 | Dick McAuliffe | .15 | .06 | .01 | ☐ 580 | Jim Spencer | .15 | .06 | .01 |
| ☐ 496 | Tom Murphy | .15 | .06 | .01 | ☐ 581 | Fred Norman | .15 | .06 | .01 |
| ☐ 497 | Bobby Mitchell | .15 | .06 | .01 | ☐ 582 | Bucky Dent | .50 | .20 | .05 |

| | | | | |
|---|---|---|---|---|
| ☐ 583 | Marty Pattin | .15 | .06 | .01 |
| ☐ 584 | Ken Rudolph | .15 | .06 | .01 |
| ☐ 585 | Merv Rettenmund | .15 | .06 | .01 |
| ☐ 586 | Jack Brohamer | .15 | .06 | .01 |
| ☐ 587 | Larry Christenson | .15 | .06 | .01 |
| ☐ 588 | Hal Lanier | .30 | .12 | .03 |
| ☐ 589 | Boots Day | .15 | .06 | .01 |
| ☐ 590 | Roger Moret | .15 | .06 | .01 |
| ☐ 591 | Sonny Jackson | .15 | .06 | .01 |
| ☐ 592 | Ed Bane | .15 | .06 | .01 |
| ☐ 593 | Steve Yeager | .20 | .08 | .02 |
| ☐ 594 | Lee Stanton | .15 | .06 | .01 |
| ☐ 595 | Steve Blass | .15 | .06 | .01 |
| ☐ 596 | Rookie Pitchers: | .30 | .12 | .03 |
| | Wayne Garland | | | |
| | Fred Holdsworth | | | |
| | Mark Littell | | | |
| | Dick Pole | | | |
| ☐ 597 | Rookie Shortstops: | .75 | .30 | .07 |
| | Dave Chalk | | | |
| | John Gamble | | | |
| | Pete MacKanin | | | |
| | Manny Trillo | | | |
| ☐ 598 | Rookie Outfielders: | 1.75 | .70 | .17 |
| | Dave Augustine | | | |
| | Ken Griffey | | | |
| | Steve Ontiveros | | | |
| | Jim Tyrone | | | |
| ☐ 599A | Rookie Pitchers WASH: | .75 | .30 | .07 |
| | Ron Diorio | | | |
| | Dave Freisleben | | | |
| | Frank Riccelli | | | |
| | Greg Shanahan | | | |
| ☐ 599B | Rookie Pitchers SD: | 2.50 | 1.00 | .25 |
| | (SD in large print) | | | |
| ☐ 599C | Rookie Pitchers SD: | 6.00 | 2.40 | .60 |
| | (SD in small print) | | | |
| ☐ 600 | Rookie Infielders: | 6.00 | 2.40 | .60 |
| | Ron Cash | | | |
| | Jim Cox | | | |
| | Bill Madlock | | | |
| | Reggie Sanders | | | |
| ☐ 601 | Rookie Outfielders: | 1.00 | .40 | .10 |
| | Ed Armbrister | | | |
| | Rich Bladt | | | |
| | Brian Downing | | | |
| | Bake McBride | | | |
| ☐ 602 | Rookie Pitchers: | .40 | .16 | .04 |
| | Glen Abbott | | | |
| | Rick Henninger | | | |
| | Craig Swan | | | |
| | Dan Vossler | | | |
| ☐ 603 | Rookie Catchers: | .30 | .12 | .03 |
| | Barry Foote | | | |
| | Tom Lundstedt | | | |
| | Charlie Moore | | | |
| | Sergio Robles | | | |
| ☐ 604 | Rookie Infielders: | 2.25 | .90 | .22 |
| | Terry Hughes | | | |
| | John Knox | | | |
| | Andy Thornton | | | |
| | Frank White | | | |
| ☐ 605 | Rookie Pitchers: | .60 | .24 | .06 |
| | Vic Albury | | | |
| | Ken Frailing | | | |
| | Kevin Kobel | | | |
| | Frank Tanana | | | |
| ☐ 606 | Rookie Outfielders: | .20 | .08 | .02 |
| | Jim Fuller | | | |
| | Wilbur Howard | | | |
| | Tommy Smith | | | |
| | Otto Velez | | | |
| ☐ 607 | Rookie Shortstops: | .20 | .08 | .02 |
| | Leo Foster | | | |
| | Tom Heintzelman | | | |
| | Dave Rosello | | | |
| | Frank Taveras | | | |
| ☐ 608A | Rookie Pitchers: ERR | 2.25 | .90 | .22 |
| | Bob Apodaco (sic) | | | |
| | Dick Baney | | | |
| | John D'Acquisto | | | |
| | Mike Wallace | | | |
| ☐ 608B | Rookie Pitchers: COR | .30 | .12 | .03 |
| | Bob Apodaca | | | |
| | Dick Baney | | | |
| | John D'Acquisto | | | |
| | Mike Wallace | | | |
| ☐ 609 | Rico Petrocelli | .25 | .10 | .02 |
| ☐ 610 | Dave Kingman | .80 | .32 | .08 |
| ☐ 611 | Rich Stelmaszek | .15 | .06 | .01 |
| ☐ 612 | Luke Walker | .15 | .06 | .01 |
| ☐ 613 | Dan Monzon | .15 | .06 | .01 |
| ☐ 614 | Adrian Devine | .15 | .06 | .01 |

| | | | | |
|---|---|---|---|---|
| ☐ 615 | John Jeter | .15 | .06 | .01 |
| ☐ 616 | Larry Gura | .25 | .10 | .02 |
| ☐ 617 | Ted Ford | .15 | .06 | .01 |
| ☐ 618 | Jim Mason | .15 | .06 | .01 |
| ☐ 619 | Mike Anderson | .15 | .06 | .01 |
| ☐ 620 | Al Downing | .15 | .06 | .01 |
| ☐ 621 | Bernie Carbo | .15 | .06 | .01 |
| ☐ 622 | Phil Gagliano | .15 | .06 | .01 |
| ☐ 623 | Celerino Sanchez | .15 | .06 | .01 |
| ☐ 624 | Bob Miller | .15 | .06 | .01 |
| ☐ 625 | Ollie Brown | .15 | .06 | .01 |
| ☐ 626 | Pirates Team | .40 | .16 | .04 |
| ☐ 627 | Carl Taylor | .15 | .06 | .01 |
| ☐ 628 | Ivan Murrell | .15 | .06 | .01 |
| ☐ 629 | Rusty Staub | .50 | .20 | .05 |
| ☐ 630 | Tommy Agee | .15 | .06 | .01 |
| ☐ 631 | Steve Barber | .15 | .06 | .01 |
| ☐ 632 | George Culver | .15 | .06 | .01 |
| ☐ 633 | Dave Hamilton | .15 | .06 | .01 |
| ☐ 634 | Braves Leaders: | .55 | .22 | .05 |
| | Eddie Mathews MGR | | | |
| | Herm Starrette CO | | | |
| | Connie Ryan CO | | | |
| | Jim Busby CO | | | |
| | Ken Silvestri CO | | | |
| ☐ 635 | John Edwards | .15 | .06 | .01 |
| ☐ 636 | Dave Goltz | .20 | .08 | .02 |
| ☐ 637 | Checklist 5 | .75 | .07 | .01 |
| ☐ 638 | Ken Sanders | .15 | .06 | .01 |
| ☐ 639 | Joe Lovitto | .15 | .06 | .01 |
| ☐ 640 | Milt Pappas | .25 | .10 | .02 |
| ☐ 641 | Chuck Brinkman | .15 | .06 | .01 |
| ☐ 642 | Terry Harmon | .15 | .06 | .01 |
| ☐ 643 | Dodgers Team | .60 | .24 | .06 |
| ☐ 644 | Wayne Granger | .15 | .06 | .01 |
| ☐ 645 | Ken Boswell | .15 | .06 | .01 |
| ☐ 646 | George Foster | .90 | .36 | .09 |
| ☐ 647 | Juan Beniquez | .60 | .24 | .06 |
| ☐ 648 | Terry Crowley | .15 | .06 | .01 |
| ☐ 649 | Fernando Gonzalez | .15 | .06 | .01 |
| ☐ 650 | Mike Epstein | .15 | .06 | .01 |
| ☐ 651 | Leron Lee | .15 | .06 | .01 |
| ☐ 652 | Gail Hopkins | .15 | .06 | .01 |
| ☐ 653 | Bob Stinson | .15 | .06 | .01 |
| ☐ 654A | Jesus Alou (outfield) | .35 | .14 | .03 |
| ☐ 654B | Jesus Alou | 6.00 | 2.40 | .60 |
| | (no position) | | | |
| ☐ 655 | Mike Tyson | .15 | .06 | .01 |
| ☐ 656 | Adrian Garrett | .15 | .06 | .01 |
| ☐ 657 | Jim Shellenback | .15 | .06 | .01 |
| ☐ 658 | Lee Lacy | .25 | .10 | .02 |
| ☐ 659 | Joe Lis | .15 | .06 | .01 |
| ☐ 660 | Larry Dierker | .30 | .12 | .03 |

## 1974 Topps Traded

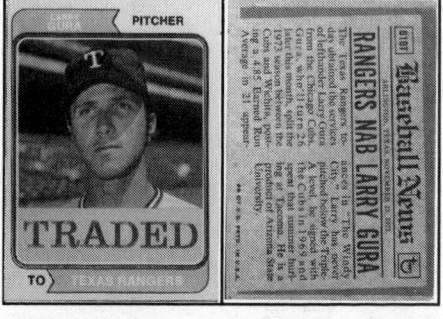

The cards in this 44 card set measure 2 1/2" by 3 1/2". The 1974 Topps Traded set contains 43 player cards and one unnumbered checklist card. The obverses have the word "traded" in block letters and the backs are designed in newspaper style. Card numbers are the same as in the regular set except they are followed by a "T". No known scarcities exist for this set.

|  | MINT | VG-E | F-G |
|---|---|---|---|
| COMPLETE SET ...................... | 5.50 | 2.20 | .55 |
| COMMON PLAYER ...................... | .10 | .04 | .01 |

| | | MINT | VG-E | F-G |
|---|---|---|---|---|
| ☐ | 23T Craig Robinson .............. | .10 | .04 | .01 |
| ☐ | 42T Claude Osteen .............. | .15 | .06 | .01 |
| ☐ | 43T Jim Wynn ..................... | .20 | .08 | .02 |
| ☐ | 51T Bobby Heise .................. | .10 | .04 | .01 |
| ☐ | 59T Ross Grimsley ............... | .10 | .04 | .01 |
| ☐ | 62T Bob Locker ................... | .10 | .04 | .01 |
| ☐ | 63T Bill Sudakis ................. | .10 | .04 | .01 |
| ☐ | 73T Mike Marshall ............... | .25 | .10 | .02 |
| ☐ | 123T Nelson Briles ............... | .15 | .06 | .01 |
| ☐ | 139T Aurelio Monteagudo ...... | .10 | .04 | .01 |
| ☐ | 151T Diego Segui ................. | .10 | .04 | .01 |
| ☐ | 165T Willie Davis ................ | .25 | .10 | .02 |
| ☐ | 175T Reggie Cleveland .......... | .10 | .04 | .01 |
| ☐ | 182T Lindy McDaniel ............ | .15 | .06 | .01 |
| ☐ | 186T Fred Scherman ............. | .10 | .04 | .01 |
| ☐ | 249T George Mitterwald ........ | .10 | .04 | .01 |
| ☐ | 262T Ed Kirkpatrick ............. | .10 | .04 | .01 |
| ☐ | 269T Bob Johnson ................ | .10 | .04 | .01 |
| ☐ | 270T Ron Santo ................... | .35 | .14 | .03 |
| ☐ | 313T Barry Lersch ............... | .10 | .04 | .01 |
| ☐ | 319T Randy Hundley ............. | .15 | .06 | .01 |
| ☐ | 330T Juan Marichal .............. | 1.50 | .60 | .15 |
| ☐ | 348T Pete Richert ................ | .10 | .04 | .01 |
| ☐ | 373T John Curtis ................. | .10 | .04 | .01 |
| ☐ | 390T Lou Piniella ................ | .35 | .14 | .03 |
| ☐ | 428T Gary Sutherland ........... | .10 | .04 | .01 |
| ☐ | 454T Kurt Bevacqua ............. | .10 | .04 | .01 |
| ☐ | 458T Jim Ray ..................... | .10 | .04 | .01 |
| ☐ | 485T Felipe Alou ................. | .15 | .06 | .01 |
| ☐ | 486T Steve Stone ................ | .15 | .06 | .01 |
| ☐ | 496T Tom Murphy ................ | .10 | .04 | .01 |
| ☐ | 516T Horacio Pina ............... | .10 | .04 | .01 |
| ☐ | 534T Eddie Watt ................. | .10 | .04 | .01 |
| ☐ | 538T Cesar Tovar ................ | .10 | .04 | .01 |
| ☐ | 544T Ron Schueler .............. | .10 | .04 | .01 |
| ☐ | 579T Cecil Upshaw .............. | .10 | .04 | .01 |
| ☐ | 585T Merv Rettenmund ......... | .10 | .04 | .01 |
| ☐ | 612T Luke Walker ................ | .10 | .04 | .01 |
| ☐ | 616T Larry Gura ................. | .20 | .08 | .02 |
| ☐ | 618T Jim Mason .................. | .10 | .04 | .01 |
| ☐ | 630T Tommie Agee ............... | .15 | .06 | .01 |
| ☐ | 648T Terry Crowley .............. | .10 | .04 | .01 |
| ☐ | 649T Fernando Gonzalez ....... | .10 | .04 | .01 |
| ☐ | xxxx Traded Checklist ........... (unnumbered) | .50 | .05 | .01 |

## 1974 Topps Team Checklists

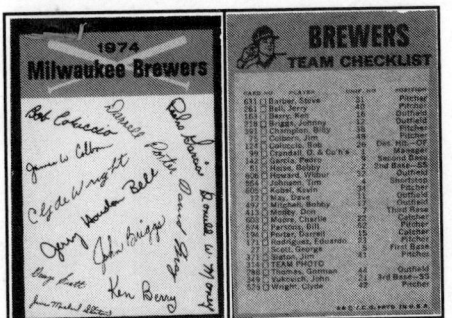

The cards in ths 24 card set measure 2 1/2" by 3 1/2". The 1974 series of checklists was issued in packs with the regular cards for that year. The cards are unnumbered (arbitrarily numbered below alphabetically by team name) and have bright red borders. The year and team name appear in a green panel decorated by a crossed bats design, below which is a white area containing facsimile autographs of various players. The mustard-yellow and gray-colored backs list team members

alphabetically, along with their card number, uniform number and position.

| | | MINT | VG-E | F-G |
|---|---|---|---|---|
| COMPLETE SET ......................... | | 7.50 | 2.00 | .40 |
| COMMON TEAM ......................... | | .40 | .10 | .02 |

| | | MINT | VG-E | F-G |
|---|---|---|---|---|
| ☐ | 1 Atlanta Braves .................. | .40 | .10 | .02 |
| ☐ | 2 Baltimore Orioles ............. | .40 | .10 | .02 |
| ☐ | 3 Boston Red Sox .............. | .40 | .10 | .02 |
| ☐ | 4 California Angels ............. | .40 | .10 | .02 |
| ☐ | 5 Chicago Cubs ................. | .40 | .10 | .02 |
| ☐ | 6 Chicago White Sox .......... | .40 | .10 | .02 |
| ☐ | 7 Cincinnati Reds .............. | .40 | .10 | .02 |
| ☐ | 8 Cleveland Indians ........... | .40 | .10 | .02 |
| ☐ | 9 Detroit Tigers ................. | .40 | .10 | .02 |
| ☐ | 10 Houston Astros ............... | .40 | .10 | .02 |
| ☐ | 11 Kansas City Royals .......... | .40 | .10 | .02 |
| ☐ | 12 Los Angeles Dodgers ........ | .40 | .10 | .02 |
| ☐ | 13 Milwaukee Brewers .......... | .40 | .10 | .02 |
| ☐ | 14 Minnesota Twins ............. | .40 | .10 | .02 |
| ☐ | 15 Montreal Expos ............... | .40 | .10 | .02 |
| ☐ | 16 New York Mets ................ | .40 | .10 | .02 |
| ☐ | 17 New York Yankees ........... | .40 | .10 | .02 |
| ☐ | 18 Oakland A's ................... | .40 | .10 | .02 |
| ☐ | 19 Philadelphia Phillies ........ | .40 | .10 | .02 |
| ☐ | 20 Pittsburgh Pirates ............ | .40 | .10 | .02 |
| ☐ | 21 San Diego Padres ............ | .40 | .10 | .02 |
| ☐ | 22 San Francisco Giants ........ | .40 | .10 | .02 |
| ☐ | 23 St. Louis Cardinals ........... | .40 | .10 | .02 |
| ☐ | 24 Texas Rangers ................. | .40 | .10 | .02 |

## 1974 Topps Deckle Edge

The cards in this 72 card set measure 2 7/8" by 5". Returning to a format first used in 1969, Topps produced a set of black and white photo cards in 1974 bearing an unusual serrated or "deckle" border. A facsimile autograph appears on the obverse while the backs contain the card number and a "newspaper-clipping" design detailing a milestone in the player's career. This was a test set, and uncut sheets are sometimes found. Card backs are either white or gray; the white back cards are slightly tougher to obtain.

| | MINT | VG-E | F-G |
|---|---|---|---|
| COMPLETE SET ........................ | 1000.00 | 400.00 | 100.00 |
| COMMON PLAYER (1-72) .......... | 8.00 | 3.25 | .80 |
| ☐ 1 Amos Otis ....................... | 9.00 | 3.75 | .90 |

| | | | | |
|---|---|---|---|---|
| ☐ | 2 | Darrell Evans | 9.00 | 3.75 | .90 |
| ☐ | 3 | Bob Gibson | 35.00 | 14.00 | 3.50 |
| ☐ | 4 | Dave Nelson | 8.00 | 3.25 | .80 |
| ☐ | 5 | Steve Carlton | 60.00 | 24.00 | 6.00 |
| ☐ | 6 | Jim Hunter | 35.00 | 14.00 | 3.50 |
| ☐ | 7 | Thurman Munson | 50.00 | 20.00 | 5.00 |
| ☐ | 8 | Bob Grich | 8.00 | 3.25 | .80 |
| ☐ | 9 | Tom Seaver | 75.00 | 30.00 | 7.50 |
| ☐ | 10 | Ted Simmons | 10.00 | 4.00 | 1.00 |
| ☐ | 11 | Bobby Valentine | 9.00 | 3.75 | .90 |
| ☐ | 12 | Don Sutton | 20.00 | 8.00 | 2.00 |
| ☐ | 13 | Wilbur Wood | 8.00 | 3.25 | .80 |
| ☐ | 14 | Doug Rader | 8.00 | 3.25 | .80 |
| ☐ | 15 | Chris Chambliss | 8.00 | 3.25 | .80 |
| ☐ | 16 | Pete Rose | 225.00 | 90.00 | 22.00 |
| ☐ | 17 | John Hiller | 8.00 | 3.25 | .80 |
| ☐ | 18 | Burt Hooton | 8.00 | 3.25 | .80 |
| ☐ | 19 | Tim Foli | 8.00 | 3.25 | .80 |
| ☐ | 20 | Lou Brock | 50.00 | 20.00 | 5.00 |
| ☐ | 21 | Ron Bryant | 8.00 | 3.25 | .80 |
| ☐ | 22 | Manny Sanguillen | 8.00 | 3.25 | .80 |
| ☐ | 23 | Bob Tolan | 8.00 | 3.25 | .80 |
| ☐ | 24 | Greg Luzinski | 10.00 | 4.00 | 1.00 |
| ☐ | 25 | Brooks Robinson | 50.00 | 20.00 | 5.00 |
| ☐ | 26 | Felix Millan | 8.00 | 3.25 | .80 |
| ☐ | 27 | Luis Tiant | 9.00 | 3.75 | .90 |
| ☐ | 28 | Willie McCovey | 40.00 | 16.00 | 4.00 |
| ☐ | 29 | Chris Speier | 8.00 | 3.25 | .80 |
| ☐ | 30 | George Scott | 8.00 | 3.25 | .80 |
| ☐ | 31 | Willie Stargell | 30.00 | 12.00 | 3.00 |
| ☐ | 32 | Rod Carew | 50.00 | 20.00 | 5.00 |
| ☐ | 33 | Charlie Spikes | 8.00 | 3.25 | .80 |
| ☐ | 34 | Nate Colbert | 8.00 | 3.25 | .80 |
| ☐ | 35 | Rich Hebner | 8.00 | 3.25 | .80 |
| ☐ | 36 | Bobby Bonds | 10.00 | 4.00 | 1.00 |
| ☐ | 37 | Buddy Bell | 9.00 | 3.75 | .90 |
| ☐ | 38 | Claude Osteen | 8.00 | 3.25 | .80 |
| ☐ | 39 | Dick Allen | 10.00 | 4.00 | 1.00 |
| ☐ | 40 | Bill Russell | 8.00 | 3.25 | .80 |
| ☐ | 41 | Nolan Ryan | 60.00 | 24.00 | 6.00 |
| ☐ | 42 | Willie Davis | 8.00 | 3.25 | .80 |
| ☐ | 43 | Carl Yastrzemski | 150.00 | 60.00 | 15.00 |
| ☐ | 44 | Jon Matlack | 8.00 | 3.25 | .80 |
| ☐ | 45 | Jim Palmer | 30.00 | 12.00 | 3.00 |
| ☐ | 46 | Bert Campaneris | 8.00 | 3.25 | .80 |
| ☐ | 47 | Bert Blyleven | 10.00 | 4.00 | 1.00 |
| ☐ | 48 | Jeff Burroughs | 8.00 | 3.25 | .80 |
| ☐ | 49 | Jim Colborn | 8.00 | 3.25 | .80 |
| ☐ | 50 | Dave Johnson | 9.00 | 3.75 | .90 |
| ☐ | 51 | John Mayberry | 8.00 | 3.25 | .80 |
| ☐ | 52 | Don Kessinger | 8.00 | 3.25 | .80 |
| ☐ | 53 | Joe Coleman | 8.00 | 3.25 | .80 |
| ☐ | 54 | Tony Perez | 12.00 | 5.00 | 1.20 |
| ☐ | 55 | Jose Cardenal | 8.00 | 3.25 | .80 |
| ☐ | 56 | Paul Splittorff | 8.00 | 3.25 | .80 |
| ☐ | 57 | Hank Aaron | 100.00 | 40.00 | 10.00 |
| ☐ | 58 | Dave May | 8.00 | 3.25 | .80 |
| ☐ | 59 | Fergie Jenkins | 12.00 | 5.00 | 1.20 |
| ☐ | 60 | Ron Blomberg | 8.00 | 3.25 | .80 |
| ☐ | 61 | Reggie Jackson | 125.00 | 50.00 | 12.50 |
| ☐ | 62 | Tony Oliva | 12.00 | 5.00 | 1.20 |
| ☐ | 63 | Bobby Murcer | 10.00 | 4.00 | 1.00 |
| ☐ | 64 | Carlton Fisk | 12.00 | 5.00 | 1.20 |
| ☐ | 65 | Steve Rogers | 8.00 | 3.25 | .80 |
| ☐ | 66 | Frank Robinson | 35.00 | 14.00 | 3.50 |
| ☐ | 67 | Joe Ferguson | 8.00 | 3.25 | .80 |
| ☐ | 68 | Bill Melton | 8.00 | 3.25 | .80 |
| ☐ | 69 | Bob Watson | 8.00 | 3.25 | .80 |
| ☐ | 70 | Larry Bowa | 10.00 | 4.00 | 1.00 |
| ☐ | 71 | Johnny Bench | 75.00 | 30.00 | 7.50 |
| ☐ | 72 | Willie Horton | 8.00 | 3.25 | .80 |

# 1975 Topps

The cards in the 1975 Topps set were issued in two different sizes: a regular standard size and a mini size which was issued as a test in certain areas of the country. The standard size cards measure 2 1/2" by 3 1/2" versus 2 1/4" by 3 1/8" for the minis. The 660 card Topps baseball set for 1975 was radically different in appearance from sets of the preceding years. The most prominent change was the use of a two-color frame surrounding the picture area rather than a single, subdued color. A facsimile

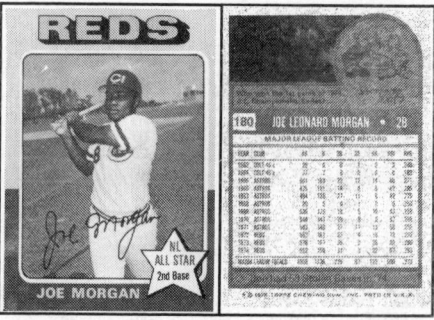

autograph appears on the picture, and the backs are printed in red and green on gray. Cards 189-212 depict the MVP's of both leagues from 1951 through 1974. The first seven cards (1- 7) feature players breaking records or achieving milestones during the previous season. Cards 306-313 picture league leaders in various statistical categories. Cards 459-466 depict the results of post-season action. Team cards feature a checklist back for players on that team and show a small inset photo of the manager on the front. This set is quite popular with collectors, at least in part due to the fact that the rookie cards of Robin Yount, George Brett, Jim Rice, Gary Carter, Fred Lynn, and Keith Hernandez are all in the set. Topps mini's have the same checklist and are worth approximately double the prices listed below.

| | | | MINT | VG-E | F-G |
|---|---|---|---|---|---|
| | | COMPLETE SET | 350.00 | 140.00 | 35.00 |
| | | COMMON PLAYER (1-132) | .18 | .08 | .01 |
| | | COMMON PLAYER (133-660) | .15 | .06 | .01 |
| ☐ | 1 | RB: Hank Aaron Sets Homer Mark | 6.50 | 2.00 | .40 |
| ☐ | 2 | RB: Lou Brock 118 Stolen Bases | 1.25 | .50 | .12 |
| ☐ | 3 | RB: Bob Gibson 3000th Strikeout | 1.25 | .50 | .12 |
| ☐ | 4 | RB: Al Kaline 3000 Hit Club | 1.25 | .50 | .12 |
| ☐ | 5 | RB: Nolan Ryan Fans 300 for 3rd Year in a Row | 1.50 | .60 | .15 |
| ☐ | 6 | RB: Mike Marshall Hurls 106 Games | .30 | .12 | .03 |
| ☐ | 7 | No Hitters: Steve Busby Dick Bosman Nolan Ryan | .50 | .20 | .05 |
| ☐ | 8 | Rogelio Moret | .18 | .08 | .01 |
| ☐ | 9 | Frank Tepedino | .18 | .08 | .01 |
| ☐ | 10 | Willie Davis | .25 | .10 | .02 |
| ☐ | 11 | Bill Melton | .18 | .08 | .01 |
| ☐ | 12 | David Clyde | .18 | .08 | .01 |
| ☐ | 13 | Gene Locklear | .18 | .08 | .01 |
| ☐ | 14 | Milt Wilcox | .18 | .08 | .01 |
| ☐ | 15 | Jose Cardenal | .18 | .08 | .01 |
| ☐ | 16 | Frank Tanana | .30 | .12 | .03 |
| ☐ | 17 | Dave Concepcion | .50 | .20 | .05 |
| ☐ | 18 | Tigers: Team/Mgr. Ralph Houk (checklist back) | .40 | .08 | .01 |
| ☐ | 19 | Jerry Koosman | .30 | .12 | .03 |
| ☐ | 20 | Thurman Munson | 3.50 | 1.40 | .35 |
| ☐ | 21 | Rollie Fingers | .90 | .36 | .09 |
| ☐ | 22 | Dave Cash | .18 | .08 | .01 |
| ☐ | 23 | Bill Russell | .25 | .10 | .02 |
| ☐ | 24 | Al Fitzmorris | .18 | .08 | .01 |
| ☐ | 25 | Lee May | .25 | .10 | .02 |
| ☐ | 26 | Dave McNally | .25 | .10 | .02 |
| ☐ | 27 | Ken Reitz | .18 | .08 | .01 |
| ☐ | 28 | Tom Murphy | .18 | .08 | .01 |
| ☐ | 29 | Dave Parker | 3.50 | 1.40 | .35 |
| ☐ | 30 | Bert Blyleven | .60 | .24 | .06 |
| ☐ | 31 | Dave Rader | .18 | .08 | .01 |
| ☐ | 32 | Reggie Cleveland | .18 | .08 | .01 |
| ☐ | 33 | Dusty Baker | .40 | .16 | .04 |

| | | | | | |
|---|---|---|---|---|---|
| ☐ 34 | Steve Renko | .18 | .08 | .01 |
| ☐ 35 | Ron Santo | .35 | .14 | .03 |
| ☐ 36 | Joe Lovitto | .18 | .08 | .01 |
| ☐ 37 | Dave Freisleben | .18 | .08 | .01 |
| ☐ 38 | Buddy Bell | .75 | .30 | .07 |
| ☐ 39 | Andy Thornton | .60 | .24 | .06 |
| ☐ 40 | Bill Singer | .18 | .08 | .01 |
| ☐ 41 | Cesar Geronimo | .18 | .08 | .01 |
| ☐ 42 | Joe Coleman | .18 | .08 | .01 |
| ☐ 43 | Cleon Jones | .18 | .08 | .01 |
| ☐ 44 | Pat Dobson | .18 | .08 | .01 |
| ☐ 45 | Joe Rudi | .25 | .10 | .02 |
| ☐ 46 | Phillies: Team/Mgr. | .40 | .08 | .01 |
| | Danny Ozark | | | |
| | (checklist back) | | | |
| ☐ 47 | Tommy John | .80 | .32 | .08 |
| ☐ 48 | Freddie Patek | .18 | .08 | .01 |
| ☐ 49 | Larry Dierker | .25 | .10 | .02 |
| ☐ 50 | Brooks Robinson | 2.50 | 1.00 | .25 |
| ☐ 51 | Bob Forsch | .75 | .30 | .07 |
| ☐ 52 | Darrell Porter | .25 | .10 | .02 |
| ☐ 53 | Dave Giusti | .18 | .08 | .01 |
| ☐ 54 | Eric Soderholm | .18 | .08 | .01 |
| ☐ 55 | Bobby Bonds | .35 | .14 | .03 |
| ☐ 56 | Rick Wise | .25 | .10 | .02 |
| ☐ 57 | Dave Johnson | .35 | .14 | .03 |
| ☐ 58 | Chuck Taylor | .18 | .08 | .01 |
| ☐ 59 | Ken Henderson | .18 | .08 | .01 |
| ☐ 60 | Fergie Jenkins | .75 | .30 | .07 |
| ☐ 61 | Dave Winfield | 5.00 | 2.00 | .50 |
| ☐ 62 | Fritz Peterson | .18 | .08 | .01 |
| ☐ 63 | Steve Swisher | .18 | .08 | .01 |
| ☐ 64 | Dave Chalk | .18 | .08 | .01 |
| ☐ 65 | Don Gullett | .25 | .10 | .02 |
| ☐ 66 | Willie Horton | .25 | .10 | .02 |
| ☐ 67 | Tug McGraw | .35 | .14 | .03 |
| ☐ 68 | Ron Blomberg | .18 | .08 | .01 |
| ☐ 69 | John Odom | .18 | .08 | .01 |
| ☐ 70 | Mike Schmidt | 15.00 | 6.00 | 1.50 |
| ☐ 71 | Charlie Hough | .30 | .12 | .03 |
| ☐ 72 | Royals: Team/Mgr. | .40 | .08 | .01 |
| | Jack McKeon | | | |
| | (checklist back) | | | |
| ☐ 73 | J.R. Richard | .30 | .12 | .03 |
| ☐ 74 | Mark Belanger | .25 | .10 | .02 |
| ☐ 75 | Ted Simmons | .75 | .30 | .07 |
| ☐ 76 | Ed Sprague | .18 | .08 | .01 |
| ☐ 77 | Richie Zisk | .25 | .10 | .02 |
| ☐ 78 | Ray Corbin | .18 | .08 | .01 |
| ☐ 79 | Gary Matthews | .35 | .14 | .03 |
| ☐ 80 | Carlton Fisk | 1.00 | .40 | .10 |
| ☐ 81 | Ron Reed | .18 | .08 | .01 |
| ☐ 82 | Pat Kelly | .18 | .08 | .01 |
| ☐ 83 | Jim Merritt | .18 | .08 | .01 |
| ☐ 84 | Enzo Hernandez | .18 | .08 | .01 |
| ☐ 85 | Bill Bonham | .18 | .08 | .01 |
| ☐ 86 | Joe Lis | .18 | .08 | .01 |
| ☐ 87 | George Foster | .90 | .36 | .09 |
| ☐ 88 | Tom Egan | .18 | .08 | .01 |
| ☐ 89 | Jim Ray | .18 | .08 | .01 |
| ☐ 90 | Rusty Staub | .35 | .14 | .03 |
| ☐ 91 | Dick Green | .18 | .08 | .01 |
| ☐ 92 | Cecil Upshaw | .18 | .08 | .01 |
| ☐ 93 | Dave Lopes | .35 | .14 | .03 |
| ☐ 94 | Jim Lonborg | .25 | .10 | .02 |
| ☐ 95 | John Mayberry | .25 | .10 | .02 |
| ☐ 96 | Mike Cosgrove | .18 | .08 | .01 |
| ☐ 97 | Earl Williams | .18 | .08 | .01 |
| ☐ 98 | Rich Folkers | .18 | .08 | .01 |
| ☐ 99 | Mike Hegan | .18 | .08 | .01 |
| ☐ 100 | Willie Stargell | 2.00 | .80 | .20 |
| ☐ 101 | Expos: Team/Mgr. | .40 | .08 | .01 |
| | Gene Mauch | | | |
| | (checklist back) | | | |
| ☐ 102 | Joe Decker | .18 | .08 | .01 |
| ☐ 103 | Rick Miller | .18 | .08 | .01 |
| ☐ 104 | Bill Madlock | 1.50 | .60 | .15 |
| ☐ 105 | Buzz Capra | .18 | .08 | .01 |
| ☐ 106 | Mike Hargrove | .50 | .20 | .05 |
| ☐ 107 | Jim Barr | .18 | .08 | .01 |
| ☐ 108 | Tom Hall | .18 | .08 | .01 |
| ☐ 109 | George Hendrick | .30 | .12 | .03 |
| ☐ 110 | Wilbur Wood | .25 | .10 | .02 |
| ☐ 111 | Wayne Garrett | .18 | .08 | .01 |
| ☐ 112 | Larry Hardy | .18 | .08 | .01 |
| ☐ 113 | Elliott Maddox | .18 | .08 | .01 |
| ☐ 114 | Dick Lange | .18 | .08 | .01 |
| ☐ 115 | Joe Ferguson | .25 | .10 | .02 |
| ☐ 116 | Lerrin LaGrow | .18 | .08 | .01 |
| ☐ 117 | Orioles: Team/Mgr. | .50 | .10 | .02 |
| | Earl Weaver | | | |
| | (checklist back) | | | |
| ☐ 118 | Mike Anderson | .18 | .08 | .01 |

| | | | | | |
|---|---|---|---|---|---|
| ☐ 119 | Tommy Helms | .18 | .08 | .01 |
| ☐ 120 | Steve Busby | .25 | .10 | .02 |
| | (photo actually | | | |
| | Fran Healy) | | | |
| ☐ 121 | Bill North | .18 | .08 | .01 |
| ☐ 122 | Al Hrabosky | .25 | .10 | .02 |
| ☐ 123 | Johnny Briggs | .18 | .08 | .01 |
| ☐ 124 | Jerry Reuss | .35 | .14 | .03 |
| ☐ 125 | Ken Singleton | .35 | .14 | .03 |
| ☐ 126 | Checklist 1-132 | .75 | .07 | .01 |
| ☐ 127 | Glenn Borgmann | .18 | .08 | .01 |
| ☐ 128 | Bill Lee | .25 | .10 | .02 |
| ☐ 129 | Rick Monday | .25 | .10 | .02 |
| ☐ 130 | Phil Niekro | 1.25 | .50 | .12 |
| ☐ 131 | Toby Harrah | .25 | .10 | .02 |
| ☐ 132 | Randy Moffitt | .18 | .08 | .01 |
| ☐ 133 | Dan Driessen | .20 | .08 | .02 |
| ☐ 134 | Ron Hodges | .15 | .06 | .01 |
| ☐ 135 | Charlie Spikes | .15 | .06 | .01 |
| ☐ 136 | Jim Mason | .15 | .06 | .01 |
| ☐ 137 | Terry Forster | .25 | .10 | .02 |
| ☐ 138 | Del Unser | .15 | .06 | .01 |
| ☐ 139 | Horacio Pina | .15 | .06 | .01 |
| ☐ 140 | Steve Garvey | 4.50 | 1.80 | .45 |
| ☐ 141 | Mickey Stanley | .15 | .06 | .01 |
| ☐ 142 | Bob Reynolds | .15 | .06 | .01 |
| ☐ 143 | Cliff Johnson | .20 | .08 | .01 |
| ☐ 144 | Jim Wohlford | .15 | .06 | .01 |
| ☐ 145 | Ken Holtzman | .20 | .08 | .01 |
| ☐ 146 | Padres: Team/Mgr. | .40 | .08 | .01 |
| | John McNamara | | | |
| | (checklist back) | | | |
| ☐ 147 | Pedro Garcia | .15 | .06 | .01 |
| ☐ 148 | Jim Rooker | .15 | .06 | .01 |
| ☐ 149 | Tim Foli | .15 | .06 | .01 |
| ☐ 150 | Bob Gibson | 1.75 | .70 | .17 |
| ☐ 151 | Steve Brye | .15 | .06 | .01 |
| ☐ 152 | Mario Guerrero | .15 | .06 | .01 |
| ☐ 153 | Rick Reuschel | .25 | .10 | .02 |
| ☐ 154 | Mike Lum | .15 | .06 | .01 |
| ☐ 155 | Jim Bibby | .20 | .08 | .02 |
| ☐ 156 | Dave Kingman | .90 | .36 | .09 |
| ☐ 157 | Pedro Borbon | .15 | .06 | .01 |
| ☐ 158 | Jerry Grote | .15 | .06 | .01 |
| ☐ 159 | Steve Arlin | .15 | .06 | .01 |
| ☐ 160 | Graig Nettles | 1.25 | .50 | .12 |
| ☐ 161 | Stan Bahnsen | .15 | .06 | .01 |
| ☐ 162 | Willie Montanez | .15 | .06 | .01 |
| ☐ 163 | Jim Brewer | .15 | .06 | .01 |
| ☐ 164 | Mickey Rivers | .20 | .08 | .02 |
| ☐ 165 | Doug Rader | .20 | .08 | .02 |
| ☐ 166 | Woodie Fryman | .15 | .06 | .01 |
| ☐ 167 | Rich Coggins | .15 | .06 | .01 |
| ☐ 168 | Bill Greif | .15 | .06 | .01 |
| ☐ 169 | Cookie Rojas | .25 | .10 | .02 |
| ☐ 170 | Bert Campaneris | .25 | .10 | .02 |
| ☐ 171 | Ed Kirkpatrick | .15 | .06 | .01 |
| ☐ 172 | Red Sox: Team/Mgr. | .40 | .08 | .01 |
| | Darrell Johnson | | | |
| | (checklist back) | | | |
| ☐ 173 | Steve Rogers | .30 | .12 | .03 |
| ☐ 174 | Bake McBride | .20 | .08 | .02 |
| ☐ 175 | Don Money | .20 | .08 | .02 |
| ☐ 176 | Burt Hooton | .20 | .08 | .02 |
| ☐ 177 | Vic Correll | .15 | .06 | .01 |
| ☐ 178 | Cesar Tovar | .15 | .06 | .01 |
| ☐ 179 | Tom Bradley | .15 | .06 | .01 |
| ☐ 180 | Joe Morgan | 2.25 | .90 | .22 |
| ☐ 181 | Fred Beene | .15 | .06 | .01 |
| ☐ 182 | Don Hahn | .15 | .06 | .01 |
| ☐ 183 | Mel Stottlemyre | .25 | .10 | .02 |
| ☐ 184 | Jorge Orta | .15 | .06 | .01 |
| ☐ 185 | Steve Carlton | 4.50 | 1.80 | .45 |
| ☐ 186 | Willie Crawford | .15 | .06 | .01 |
| ☐ 187 | Denny Doyle | .15 | .06 | .01 |
| ☐ 188 | Tom Griffin | .15 | .06 | .01 |
| ☐ 189 | 1951 MVP's: | 1.00 | .40 | .10 |
| | Larry (Yogi) Berra | | | |
| | Roy Campanella | | | |
| | (Campy never issued) | | | |
| ☐ 190 | 1952 MVP's: | .30 | .12 | .03 |
| | Bobby Shantz | | | |
| | Hank Bauer | | | |
| ☐ 191 | 1953 MVP's: | .55 | .22 | .05 |
| | Al Rosen | | | |
| | Roy Campanella | | | |
| ☐ 192 | 1954 MVP's: | 1.00 | .40 | .10 |
| | Yogi Berra | | | |
| | Willie Mays | | | |
| ☐ 193 | 1955 MVP's: | 1.25 | .50 | .12 |
| | Yogi Berra | | | |
| | Roy Campanella | | | |
| | (Campy never issued) | | | |

| | Card | .60 | .30 | .12 |
|---|---|---|---|---|
| ☐ 194 | 1956 MVP's: | 1.25 | .50 | .12 |
| | Mickey Mantle | | | |
| | Don Newcombe | | | |
| ☐ 195 | 1957 MVP's: | 2.25 | .90 | .22 |
| | Mickey Mantle | | | |
| | Hank Aaron | | | |
| ☐ 196 | 1958 MVP's: | .55 | .22 | .05 |
| | Jackie Jensen | | | |
| | Ernie Banks | | | |
| ☐ 197 | 1959 MVP's: | .55 | .22 | .05 |
| | Nellie Fox | | | |
| | Ernie Banks | | | |
| ☐ 198 | 1960 MVP's: | .55 | .22 | .05 |
| | Roger Maris | | | |
| | Dick Groat | | | |
| ☐ 199 | 1961 MVP's: | .75 | .30 | .07 |
| | Roger Maris | | | |
| | Frank Robinson | | | |
| ☐ 200 | 1962 MVP's: | 1.75 | .70 | .17 |
| | Mickey Mantle | | | |
| | Maury Wills | | | |
| | (Wills never issued) | | | |
| ☐ 201 | 1963 MVP's: | .55 | .22 | .05 |
| | Elston Howard | | | |
| | Sandy Koufax | | | |
| ☐ 202 | 1964 MVP's: | .55 | .22 | .05 |
| | Brooks Robinson | | | |
| | Ken Boyer | | | |
| ☐ 203 | 1965 MVP's: | .55 | .22 | .05 |
| | Zoilo Versalles | | | |
| | Willie Mays | | | |
| ☐ 204 | 1966 MVP's: | .75 | .30 | .07 |
| | Frank Robinson | | | |
| | Bob Clemente | | | |
| ☐ 205 | 1967 MVP's: | .75 | .30 | .07 |
| | Carl Yastrzemski | | | |
| | Orlando Cepeda | | | |
| ☐ 206 | 1968 MVP's: | .55 | .22 | .05 |
| | Denny McLain | | | |
| | Bob Gibson | | | |
| ☐ 207 | 1969 MVP's: | .65 | .26 | .06 |
| | Harmon Killebrew | | | |
| | Willie McCovey | | | |
| ☐ 208 | 1970 MVP's: | .55 | .22 | .05 |
| | Boog Powell | | | |
| | Johnny Bench | | | |
| ☐ 209 | 1971 MVP's: | .45 | .18 | .04 |
| | Vida Blue | | | |
| | Joe Torre | | | |
| ☐ 210 | 1972 MVP's: | .55 | .22 | .05 |
| | Rich Allen | | | |
| | Johnny Bench | | | |
| ☐ 211 | 1973 MVP's: | 2.25 | .90 | .22 |
| | Reggie Jackson | | | |
| | Pete Rose | | | |
| ☐ 212 | 1974 MVP's: | .55 | .22 | .05 |
| | Jeff Burroughs | | | |
| | Steve Garvey | | | |
| ☐ 213 | Oscar Gamble | .25 | .10 | .02 |
| ☐ 214 | Harry Parker | .15 | .06 | .01 |
| ☐ 215 | Bobby Valentine | .30 | .12 | .03 |
| ☐ 216 | Giants: Team/Mgr. | .40 | .08 | .01 |
| | Wes Westrum | | | |
| | (checklist back) | | | |
| ☐ 217 | Lou Piniella | .35 | .14 | .03 |
| ☐ 218 | Jerry Johnson | .15 | .06 | .01 |
| ☐ 219 | Ed Herrmann | .15 | .06 | .01 |
| ☐ 220 | Don Sutton | 1.25 | .50 | .12 |
| ☐ 221 | Aurelio Rodriguez | .15 | .06 | .01 |
| ☐ 222 | Dan Spillner | .25 | .10 | .02 |
| ☐ 223 | Robin Yount | 25.00 | 10.00 | 2.50 |
| ☐ 224 | Ramon Hernandez | .15 | .06 | .01 |
| ☐ 225 | Bob Grich | .30 | .12 | .03 |
| ☐ 226 | Bill Campbell | .20 | .08 | .02 |
| ☐ 227 | Bob Watson | .25 | .10 | .02 |
| ☐ 228 | George Brett | 37.50 | 14.00 | 2.50 |
| ☐ 229 | Barry Foote | .15 | .06 | .01 |
| ☐ 230 | Jim Hunter | 1.50 | .60 | .15 |
| ☐ 231 | Mike Tyson | .15 | .06 | .01 |
| ☐ 232 | Diego Segui | .15 | .06 | .01 |
| ☐ 233 | Billy Grabarkewitz | .15 | .06 | .01 |
| ☐ 234 | Tom Grieve | .25 | .10 | .02 |
| ☐ 235 | Jack Billingham | .15 | .06 | .01 |
| ☐ 236 | Angels: Team/Mgr. | .40 | .08 | .01 |
| | Dick Williams | | | |
| | (checklist back) | | | |
| ☐ 237 | Carl Morton | .15 | .06 | .01 |
| ☐ 238 | Dave Duncan | .15 | .06 | .01 |
| ☐ 239 | George Stone | .15 | .06 | .01 |
| ☐ 240 | Garry Maddox | .20 | .08 | .02 |
| ☐ 241 | Dick Tidrow | .15 | .06 | .01 |
| ☐ 242 | Jay Johnstone | .25 | .10 | .02 |
| ☐ 243 | Jim Kaat | .65 | .26 | .06 |

| |  | | | |
|---|---|---|---|---|
| ☐ 244 | Bill Buckner | .50 | .20 | .05 |
| ☐ 245 | Mickey Lolich | .30 | .12 | .03 |
| ☐ 246 | Cardinals: Team/Mgr. | .40 | .08 | .01 |
| | Red Schoendienst | | | |
| | (checklist back) | | | |
| ☐ 247 | Enos Cabell | .20 | .08 | .02 |
| ☐ 248 | Randy Jones | .20 | .08 | .02 |
| ☐ 249 | Danny Thompson | .15 | .06 | .01 |
| ☐ 250 | Ken Brett | .15 | .06 | .01 |
| ☐ 251 | Fran Healy | .15 | .06 | .01 |
| ☐ 252 | Fred Scherman | .15 | .06 | .01 |
| ☐ 253 | Jesus Alou | .15 | .06 | .01 |
| ☐ 254 | Mike Torrez | .20 | .08 | .02 |
| ☐ 255 | Dwight Evans | .75 | .30 | .07 |
| ☐ 256 | Billy Champion | .15 | .06 | .01 |
| ☐ 257 | Checklist: 133-264 | .60 | .06 | .01 |
| ☐ 258 | Dave LaRoche | .15 | .06 | .01 |
| ☐ 259 | Len Randle | .15 | .06 | .01 |
| ☐ 260 | Johnny Bench | 4.50 | 1.80 | .45 |
| ☐ 261 | Andy Hassler | .15 | .06 | .01 |
| ☐ 262 | Rowland Office | .15 | .06 | .01 |
| ☐ 263 | Jim Perry | .25 | .10 | .02 |
| ☐ 264 | John Milner | .15 | .06 | .01 |
| ☐ 265 | Ron Bryant | .15 | .06 | .01 |
| ☐ 266 | Sandy Alomar | .15 | .06 | .01 |
| ☐ 267 | Dick Ruthven | .15 | .06 | .01 |
| ☐ 268 | Hal McRae | .30 | .12 | .03 |
| ☐ 269 | Doug Rau | .15 | .06 | .01 |
| ☐ 270 | Ron Fairly | .20 | .08 | .02 |
| ☐ 271 | Jerry Moses | .15 | .06 | .01 |
| ☐ 272 | Lynn McGlothen | .15 | .06 | .01 |
| ☐ 273 | Steve Braun | .15 | .06 | .01 |
| ☐ 274 | Vincente Romo | .15 | .06 | .01 |
| ☐ 275 | Paul Blair | .20 | .08 | .02 |
| ☐ 276 | White Sox Team/Mgr. | .40 | .08 | .01 |
| | Chuck Tanner | | | |
| | (checklist back) | | | |
| ☐ 277 | Frank Taveras | .15 | .06 | .01 |
| ☐ 278 | Paul Lindblad | .15 | .06 | .01 |
| ☐ 279 | Milt May | .15 | .06 | .01 |
| ☐ 280 | Carl Yastrzemski | 5.50 | 2.20 | .55 |
| ☐ 281 | Jim Slaton | .15 | .06 | .01 |
| ☐ 282 | Jerry Morales | .15 | .06 | .01 |
| ☐ 283 | Steve Foucault | .15 | .06 | .01 |
| ☐ 284 | Ken Griffey | .55 | .22 | .05 |
| ☐ 285 | Ellie Rodriguez | .15 | .06 | .01 |
| ☐ 286 | Mike Jorgensen | .15 | .06 | .01 |
| ☐ 287 | Roric Harrison | .15 | .06 | .01 |
| ☐ 288 | Bruce Ellingsen | .15 | .06 | .01 |
| ☐ 289 | Ken Rudolph | .15 | .06 | .01 |
| ☐ 290 | Jon Matlack | .25 | .10 | .02 |
| ☐ 291 | Bill Sudakis | .15 | .06 | .01 |
| ☐ 292 | Ron Schueler | .15 | .06 | .01 |
| ☐ 293 | Dick Sharon | .15 | .06 | .01 |
| ☐ 294 | Geoff Zahn | .25 | .10 | .02 |
| ☐ 295 | Vada Pinson | .35 | .14 | .03 |
| ☐ 296 | Alan Foster | .15 | .06 | .01 |
| ☐ 297 | Craig Kusick | .15 | .06 | .01 |
| ☐ 298 | Johnny Grubb | .15 | .06 | .01 |
| ☐ 299 | Bucky Dent | .30 | .12 | .03 |
| ☐ 300 | Reggie Jackson | 6.00 | 2.40 | .60 |
| ☐ 301 | Dave Roberts | .15 | .06 | .01 |
| ☐ 302 | Rick Burleson | .75 | .30 | .07 |
| ☐ 303 | Grant Jackson | .15 | .06 | .01 |
| ☐ 304 | Pirates: Team/Mgr. | .40 | .08 | .01 |
| | Danny Murtaugh | | | |
| | (checklist back) | | | |
| ☐ 305 | Jim Colborn | .15 | .06 | .01 |
| ☐ 306 | Batting Leaders: | .55 | .22 | .05 |
| | Rod Carew | | | |
| | Ralph Garr | | | |
| ☐ 307 | Home Run Leaders: | .75 | .30 | .07 |
| | Dick Allen | | | |
| | Mike Schmidt | | | |
| ☐ 308 | RBI Leaders: | .55 | .22 | .05 |
| | Jeff Burroughs | | | |
| | Johnny Bench | | | |
| ☐ 309 | Stolen Base Leaders: | .55 | .22 | .05 |
| | Bill North | | | |
| | Lou Brock | | | |
| ☐ 310 | Victory Leaders: | .65 | .26 | .06 |
| | Jim Hunter | | | |
| | Fergie Jenkins | | | |
| | Andy Messersmith | | | |
| | Phil Niekro | | | |
| ☐ 311 | ERA Leaders: | .35 | .14 | .03 |
| | Jim Hunter | | | |
| | Buzz Capra | | | |
| ☐ 312 | Strikeout Leaders: | 1.75 | .70 | .17 |
| | Nolan Ryan | | | |
| | Steve Carlton | | | |
| ☐ 313 | Leading Firemen: | .30 | .12 | .03 |
| | Terry Forster | | | |

Mike Marshall

| | | | | |
|---|---|---|---|---|
| ☐ 314 | Buck Martinez | .15 | .06 | .01 |
| ☐ 315 | Don Kessinger | .20 | .08 | .02 |
| ☐ 316 | Jackie Brown | .15 | .06 | .01 |
| ☐ 317 | Joe Lahoud | .15 | .06 | .01 |
| ☐ 318 | Ernie McAnally | .15 | .06 | .01 |
| ☐ 319 | Johnny Oates | .15 | .06 | .01 |
| ☐ 320 | Pete Rose | 13.00 | 5.25 | 1.30 |
| ☐ 321 | Rudy May | .15 | .06 | .01 |
| ☐ 322 | Ed Goodson | .15 | .06 | .01 |
| ☐ 323 | Fred Holdsworth | .15 | .06 | .01 |
| ☐ 324 | Ed Kranepool | .20 | .08 | .02 |
| ☐ 325 | Tony Oliva | .50 | .20 | .05 |
| ☐ 326 | Wayne Twitchell | .15 | .06 | .01 |
| ☐ 327 | Jerry Hairston | .15 | .06 | .01 |
| ☐ 328 | Sonny Siebert | .20 | .08 | .02 |
| ☐ 329 | Ted Kubiak | .15 | .06 | .01 |
| ☐ 330 | Mike Marshall | .25 | .10 | .02 |
| ☐ 331 | Indians: Team/Mgr. | .50 | .10 | .02 |

Frank Robinson
(checklist back)

| | | | | |
|---|---|---|---|---|
| ☐ 332 | Fred Kendall | .15 | .06 | .01 |
| ☐ 333 | Dick Drago | .15 | .06 | .01 |
| ☐ 334 | Greg Gross | .15 | .06 | .01 |
| ☐ 335 | Jim Palmer | 2.75 | 1.10 | .27 |
| ☐ 336 | Rennie Stennett | .15 | .06 | .01 |
| ☐ 337 | Kevin Kobel | .15 | .06 | .01 |
| ☐ 338 | Rick Stelmaszek | .15 | .06 | .01 |
| ☐ 339 | Jim Fregosi | .30 | .12 | .03 |
| ☐ 340 | Paul Splittorff | .20 | .08 | .02 |
| ☐ 341 | Hal Breeden | .15 | .06 | .01 |
| ☐ 342 | Leroy Stanton | .15 | .06 | .01 |
| ☐ 343 | Danny Frisella | .15 | .06 | .01 |
| ☐ 344 | Ben Oglivie | .30 | .12 | .03 |
| ☐ 345 | Clay Carroll | .15 | .06 | .01 |
| ☐ 346 | Bobby Darwin | .15 | .06 | .01 |
| ☐ 347 | Mike Caldwell | .20 | .08 | .02 |
| ☐ 348 | Tony Muser | .15 | .06 | .01 |
| ☐ 349 | Ray Sadecki | .15 | .06 | .01 |
| ☐ 350 | Bobby Murcer | .45 | .18 | .04 |
| ☐ 351 | Bob Boone | .25 | .10 | .02 |
| ☐ 352 | Darold Knowles | .15 | .06 | .01 |
| ☐ 353 | Luis Melendez | .15 | .06 | .01 |
| ☐ 354 | Dick Bosman | .15 | .06 | .01 |
| ☐ 355 | Chris Cannizzaro | .15 | .06 | .01 |
| ☐ 356 | Rico Petrocelli | .20 | .08 | .02 |
| ☐ 357 | Ken Forsch | .20 | .08 | .02 |
| ☐ 358 | Al Bumbry | .15 | .06 | .01 |
| ☐ 359 | Paul Popovich | .15 | .06 | .01 |
| ☐ 360 | George Scott | .20 | .08 | .02 |
| ☐ 361 | Dodgers: Team/Mgr. | .50 | .10 | .02 |

Walter Alston
(checklist back)

| | | | | |
|---|---|---|---|---|
| ☐ 362 | Steve Hargan | .15 | .06 | .01 |
| ☐ 363 | Carmen Fanzone | .15 | .06 | .01 |
| ☐ 364 | Doug Bird | .15 | .06 | .01 |
| ☐ 365 | Bob Bailey | .15 | .06 | .01 |
| ☐ 366 | Ken Sanders | .15 | .06 | .01 |
| ☐ 367 | Craig Robinson | .15 | .06 | .01 |
| ☐ 368 | Vic Albury | .15 | .06 | .01 |
| ☐ 369 | Merv Rettenmund | .15 | .06 | .01 |
| ☐ 370 | Tom Seaver | 4.50 | 1.80 | .45 |
| ☐ 371 | Gates Brown | .20 | .08 | .02 |
| ☐ 372 | John D'Acquisto | .15 | .06 | .01 |
| ☐ 373 | Bill Sharp | .15 | .06 | .01 |
| ☐ 374 | Eddie Watt | .15 | .06 | .01 |
| ☐ 375 | Roy White | .20 | .08 | .02 |
| ☐ 376 | Steve Yeager | .20 | .08 | .02 |
| ☐ 377 | Tom Hilgendorf | .15 | .06 | .01 |
| ☐ 378 | Derrel Thomas | .15 | .06 | .01 |
| ☐ 379 | Bernie Carbo | .15 | .06 | .01 |
| ☐ 380 | Sal Bando | .25 | .10 | .02 |
| ☐ 381 | John Curtis | .15 | .06 | .01 |
| ☐ 382 | Don Baylor | .80 | .32 | .08 |
| ☐ 383 | Jim York | .15 | .06 | .01 |
| ☐ 384 | Brewers: Team/Mgr. | .40 | .08 | .01 |

Del Crandall
(checklist back)

| | | | | |
|---|---|---|---|---|
| ☐ 385 | Dock Ellis | .15 | .06 | .01 |
| ☐ 386 | Checklist: 265-396 | .60 | .06 | .01 |
| ☐ 387 | Jim Spencer | .15 | .06 | .01 |
| ☐ 388 | Steve Stone | .25 | .10 | .02 |
| ☐ 389 | Tony Solaita | .15 | .06 | .01 |
| ☐ 390 | Ron Cey | .70 | .28 | .07 |
| ☐ 391 | Don DeMola | .15 | .06 | .01 |
| ☐ 392 | Bruce Bochte | .55 | .22 | .05 |
| ☐ 393 | Gary Gentry | .15 | .06 | .01 |
| ☐ 394 | Larvell Blanks | .15 | .06 | .01 |
| ☐ 395 | Bud Harrelson | .20 | .08 | .02 |
| ☐ 396 | Fred Norman | .15 | .06 | .01 |
| ☐ 397 | Bill Freehan | .25 | .10 | .02 |
| ☐ 398 | Elias Sosa | .15 | .06 | .01 |
| ☐ 399 | Terry Harmon | .15 | .06 | .01 |

| | | | | |
|---|---|---|---|---|
| ☐ 400 | Dick Allen | .40 | .16 | .04 |
| ☐ 401 | Mike Wallace | .15 | .06 | .01 |
| ☐ 402 | Bob Tolan | .15 | .06 | .01 |
| ☐ 403 | Tom Buskey | .15 | .06 | .01 |
| ☐ 404 | Ted Sizemore | .15 | .06 | .01 |
| ☐ 405 | John Montague | .15 | .06 | .01 |
| ☐ 406 | Bob Gallagher | .15 | .06 | .01 |
| ☐ 407 | Herb Washington | .15 | .06 | .01 |
| ☐ 408 | Clyde Wright | .15 | .06 | .01 |
| ☐ 409 | Bob Robertson | .15 | .06 | .01 |
| ☐ 410 | Mike Cueller | .25 | .10 | .02 |

(sic, Cuellar)

| | | | | |
|---|---|---|---|---|
| ☐ 411 | George Mitterwald | .15 | .06 | .01 |
| ☐ 412 | Bill Hands | .15 | .06 | .01 |
| ☐ 413 | Marty Pattin | .15 | .06 | .01 |
| ☐ 414 | Manny Mota | .25 | .10 | .02 |
| ☐ 415 | John Hiller | .25 | .10 | .02 |
| ☐ 416 | Larry Lintz | .15 | .06 | .01 |
| ☐ 417 | Skip Lockwood | .15 | .06 | .01 |
| ☐ 418 | Leo Foster | .15 | .06 | .01 |
| ☐ 419 | Dave Goltz | .20 | .08 | .02 |
| ☐ 420 | Larry Bowa | .35 | .14 | .03 |
| ☐ 421 | Mets: Team/Mgr. | .50 | .10 | .02 |

Yogi Berra
(checklist back)

| | | | | |
|---|---|---|---|---|
| ☐ 422 | Brian Downing | .25 | .10 | .02 |
| ☐ 423 | Clay Kirby | .15 | .06 | .01 |
| ☐ 424 | John Lowenstein | .15 | .06 | .01 |
| ☐ 425 | Tito Fuentes | .15 | .06 | .01 |
| ☐ 426 | George Medich | .20 | .08 | .02 |
| ☐ 427 | Clarence Gaston | .15 | .06 | .01 |
| ☐ 428 | Dave Hamilton | .15 | .06 | .01 |
| ☐ 429 | Jim Dwyer | .15 | .06 | .01 |
| ☐ 430 | Luis Tiant | .35 | .14 | .03 |
| ☐ 431 | Rod Gilbreath | .15 | .06 | .01 |
| ☐ 432 | Ken Berry | .15 | .06 | .01 |
| ☐ 433 | Larry Demery | .15 | .06 | .01 |
| ☐ 434 | Bob Locker | .15 | .06 | .01 |
| ☐ 435 | Dave Nelson | .15 | .06 | .01 |
| ☐ 436 | Ken Frailing | .15 | .06 | .01 |
| ☐ 437 | Al Cowens | .40 | .16 | .04 |
| ☐ 438 | Don Carrithers | .15 | .06 | .01 |
| ☐ 439 | Ed Brinkman | .15 | .06 | .01 |
| ☐ 440 | Andy Messersmith | .25 | .10 | .02 |
| ☐ 441 | Bobby Heise | .15 | .06 | .01 |
| ☐ 442 | Maximino Leon | .15 | .06 | .01 |
| ☐ 443 | Twins: Team/Mgr. | .40 | .08 | .01 |

Frank Quilici
(checklist back)

| | | | | |
|---|---|---|---|---|
| ☐ 444 | Gene Garber | .20 | .08 | .02 |
| ☐ 445 | Felix Millan | .15 | .06 | .01 |
| ☐ 446 | Bart Johnson | .15 | .06 | .01 |
| ☐ 447 | Terry Crowley | .15 | .06 | .01 |
| ☐ 448 | Frank Duffy | .15 | .06 | .01 |
| ☐ 449 | Charlie Williams | .15 | .06 | .01 |
| ☐ 450 | Willie McCovey | 2.50 | 1.00 | .25 |
| ☐ 451 | Rick Dempsey | .25 | .10 | .02 |
| ☐ 452 | Angel Mangual | .15 | .06 | .01 |
| ☐ 453 | Claude Osteen | .25 | .10 | .02 |
| ☐ 454 | Doug Griffin | .15 | .06 | .01 |
| ☐ 455 | Don Wilson | .15 | .06 | .01 |
| ☐ 456 | Bob Coluccio | .15 | .06 | .01 |
| ☐ 457 | Mario Mendoza | .15 | .06 | .01 |
| ☐ 458 | Ross Grimsley | .15 | .06 | .01 |
| ☐ 459 | 1974 AL Champs: | .30 | .12 | .03 |

A's over Orioles
(Second base
action pictured)

| | | | | |
|---|---|---|---|---|
| ☐ 460 | 1974 NL Champs: | .50 | .20 | .05 |

Dodgers over Pirates
(Taveras and Garvey
at second base)

| | | | | |
|---|---|---|---|---|
| ☐ 461 | World Series Game 1 | 1.25 | .50 | .12 |

(Reggie Jackson)

| | | | | |
|---|---|---|---|---|
| ☐ 462 | World Series Game 2 | .30 | .12 | .03 |

(Dodger dugout)

| | | | | |
|---|---|---|---|---|
| ☐ 463 | World Series Game 3 | .50 | .20 | .05 |

(Fingers pitching)

| | | | | |
|---|---|---|---|---|
| ☐ 464 | World Series Game 4 | .30 | .12 | .03 |

(A's batter)

| | | | | |
|---|---|---|---|---|
| ☐ 465 | World Series Game 5 | .30 | .12 | .03 |

(Rudi rounding third)

| | | | | |
|---|---|---|---|---|
| ☐ 466 | World Series Summary: | .30 | .12 | .03 |

A's do it again
Win 3rd straight
(A's group)

| | | | | |
|---|---|---|---|---|
| ☐ 467 | Ed Halicki | .15 | .06 | .01 |
| ☐ 468 | Bobby Mitchell | .15 | .06 | .01 |
| ☐ 469 | Tom Dettore | .15 | .06 | .01 |
| ☐ 470 | Jeff Burroughs | .20 | .08 | .02 |
| ☐ 471 | Bob Stinson | .15 | .06 | .01 |
| ☐ 472 | Bruce Dal Canton | .15 | .06 | .01 |
| ☐ 473 | Ken McMullen | .15 | .06 | .01 |

| # | Name | | | |
|---|------|---|---|---|
| ☐ 474 | Luke Walker | .15 | .06 | .01 |
| ☐ 475 | Darrell Evans | .40 | .16 | .04 |
| ☐ 476 | Eduardo Figueroa | .20 | .08 | .02 |
| ☐ 477 | Tom Hutton | .15 | .06 | .01 |
| ☐ 478 | Tom Burgmeier | .15 | .06 | .01 |
| ☐ 479 | Ken Boswell | .15 | .06 | .01 |
| ☐ 480 | Carlos May | .20 | .08 | .02 |
| ☐ 481 | Will McEnaney | .15 | .06 | .01 |
| ☐ 482 | Tom McCraw | .15 | .06 | .01 |
| ☐ 483 | Steve Ontiveros | .15 | .06 | .01 |
| ☐ 484 | Glenn Beckert | .20 | .08 | .02 |
| ☐ 485 | Sparky Lyle | .35 | .14 | .03 |
| ☐ 486 | Ray Fosse | .15 | .06 | .01 |
| ☐ 487 | Astros: Team/Mgr. Preston Gomez (checklist back) | .40 | .08 | .01 |
| ☐ 488 | Bill Travers | .15 | .06 | .01 |
| ☐ 489 | Cecil Cooper | 1.00 | .40 | .10 |
| ☐ 490 | Reggie Smith | .30 | .12 | .03 |
| ☐ 491 | Doyle Alexander | .25 | .10 | .02 |
| ☐ 492 | Rich Hebner | .15 | .06 | .01 |
| ☐ 493 | Don Stanhouse | .15 | .06 | .01 |
| ☐ 494 | Pete LaCock | .20 | .08 | .02 |
| ☐ 495 | Nelson Briles | .20 | .08 | .02 |
| ☐ 496 | Pepe Frias | .15 | .06 | .01 |
| ☐ 497 | Jim Nettles | .15 | .06 | .01 |
| ☐ 498 | Al Downing | .15 | .06 | .01 |
| ☐ 499 | Marty Perez | .15 | .06 | .01 |
| ☐ 500 | Nolan Ryan | 4.25 | 1.70 | .42 |
| ☐ 501 | Bill Robinson | .15 | .06 | .01 |
| ☐ 502 | Pat Bourque | .15 | .06 | .01 |
| ☐ 503 | Fred Stanley | .15 | .06 | .01 |
| ☐ 504 | Buddy Bradford | .15 | .06 | .01 |
| ☐ 505 | Chris Speier | .15 | .06 | .01 |
| ☐ 506 | Leron Lee | .15 | .06 | .01 |
| ☐ 507 | Tom Carroll | .15 | .06 | .01 |
| ☐ 508 | Bob Hansen | .15 | .06 | .01 |
| ☐ 509 | Dave Hilton | .15 | .06 | .01 |
| ☐ 510 | Vida Blue | .35 | .14 | .03 |
| ☐ 511 | Rangers: Team/Mgr. Billy Martin (checklist back) | .50 | .10 | .02 |
| ☐ 512 | Larry Milbourne | .15 | .06 | .01 |
| ☐ 513 | Dick Pole | .15 | .06 | .01 |
| ☐ 514 | Jose Cruz | .50 | .20 | .05 |
| ☐ 515 | Manny Sanguillen | .25 | .10 | .02 |
| ☐ 516 | Don Hood | .15 | .06 | .01 |
| ☐ 517 | Checklist: 397-528 | .60 | .06 | .01 |
| ☐ 518 | Leo Cardenas | .15 | .06 | .01 |
| ☐ 519 | Jim Todd | .15 | .06 | .01 |
| ☐ 520 | Amos Otis | .30 | .12 | .03 |
| ☐ 521 | Dennis Blair | .15 | .06 | .01 |
| ☐ 522 | Gary Sutherland | .15 | .06 | .01 |
| ☐ 523 | Tom Paciorek | .15 | .06 | .01 |
| ☐ 524 | John Doherty | .15 | .06 | .01 |
| ☐ 525 | Tom House | .15 | .06 | .01 |
| ☐ 526 | Larry Hisle | .20 | .08 | .02 |
| ☐ 527 | Mac Scarce | .15 | .06 | .01 |
| ☐ 528 | Eddie Leon | .15 | .06 | .01 |
| ☐ 529 | Gary Thomasson | .15 | .06 | .01 |
| ☐ 530 | Gaylord Perry | 1.75 | .70 | .17 |
| ☐ 531 | Reds: Team/Mgr. Sparky Anderson (checklist back) | .50 | .10 | .02 |
| ☐ 532 | Gorman Thomas | .75 | .30 | .07 |
| ☐ 533 | Rudy Meoli | .15 | .06 | .01 |
| ☐ 534 | Alex Johnson | .20 | .08 | .02 |
| ☐ 535 | Gene Tenace | .20 | .08 | .02 |
| ☐ 536 | Bob Moose | .15 | .06 | .01 |
| ☐ 537 | Tommy Harper | .20 | .08 | .02 |
| ☐ 538 | Duffy Dyer | .15 | .06 | .01 |
| ☐ 539 | Jesse Jefferson | .15 | .06 | .01 |
| ☐ 540 | Lou Brock | 2.00 | .80 | .20 |
| ☐ 541 | Roger Metzger | .15 | .06 | .01 |
| ☐ 542 | Pete Broberg | .15 | .06 | .01 |
| ☐ 543 | Larry Biittner | .15 | .06 | .01 |
| ☐ 544 | Steve Mingori | .15 | .06 | .01 |
| ☐ 545 | Billy Williams | 1.25 | .50 | .12 |
| ☐ 546 | John Knox | .15 | .06 | .01 |
| ☐ 547 | Von Joshua | .15 | .06 | .01 |
| ☐ 548 | Charlie Sands | .15 | .06 | .01 |
| ☐ 549 | Bill Butler | .15 | .06 | .01 |
| ☐ 550 | Ralph Garr | .20 | .08 | .02 |
| ☐ 551 | Larry Christenson | .15 | .06 | .01 |
| ☐ 552 | Jack Brohamer | .15 | .06 | .01 |
| ☐ 553 | John Boccabella | .15 | .06 | .01 |
| ☐ 554 | Rich Gossage | 1.00 | .40 | .10 |
| ☐ 555 | Al Oliver | .75 | .30 | .07 |
| ☐ 556 | Tim Johnson | .15 | .06 | .01 |
| ☐ 557 | Larry Gura | .25 | .10 | .02 |
| ☐ 558 | Dave Roberts | .15 | .06 | .01 |
| ☐ 559 | Bob Montgomery | .15 | .06 | .01 |
| ☐ 560 | Tony Perez | .75 | .30 | .07 |
| ☐ 561 | A's: Team/Mgr. Alvin Dark (checklist back) | .40 | .08 | .01 |
| ☐ 562 | Gary Nolan | .15 | .06 | .01 |
| ☐ 563 | Wilbur Howard | .15 | .06 | .01 |
| ☐ 564 | Tommy Davis | .25 | .10 | .02 |
| ☐ 565 | Joe Torre | .50 | .20 | .05 |
| ☐ 566 | Ray Burris | .20 | .08 | .02 |
| ☐ 567 | Jim Sundberg | .75 | .30 | .07 |
| ☐ 568 | Dale Murray | .15 | .06 | .01 |
| ☐ 569 | Frank White | .50 | .20 | .05 |
| ☐ 570 | Jim Wynn | .25 | .10 | .02 |
| ☐ 571 | Dave Lemanczyk | .15 | .06 | .01 |
| ☐ 572 | Roger Nelson | .15 | .06 | .01 |
| ☐ 573 | Orlando Pena | .15 | .06 | .01 |
| ☐ 574 | Tony Taylor | .15 | .06 | .01 |
| ☐ 575 | Gene Clines | .15 | .06 | .01 |
| ☐ 576 | Phil Roof | .15 | .06 | .01 |
| ☐ 577 | John Morris | .15 | .06 | .01 |
| ☐ 578 | Dave Tomlin | .15 | .06 | .01 |
| ☐ 579 | Skip Pitlock | .15 | .06 | .01 |
| ☐ 580 | Frank Robinson | 2.00 | .80 | .20 |
| ☐ 581 | Darrel Chaney | .15 | .06 | .01 |
| ☐ 582 | Eduardo Rodriguez | .15 | .06 | .01 |
| ☐ 583 | Andy Etchebarren | .15 | .06 | .01 |
| ☐ 584 | Mike Garman | .15 | .06 | .01 |
| ☐ 585 | Chris Chambliss | .30 | .12 | .03 |
| ☐ 586 | Tim McCarver | .30 | .12 | .03 |
| ☐ 587 | Chris Ward | .15 | .06 | .01 |
| ☐ 588 | Rick Auerbach | .15 | .06 | .01 |
| ☐ 589 | Braves: Team/Mgr. Clyde King (checklist back) | .40 | .08 | .01 |
| ☐ 590 | Cesar Cedeno | .30 | .12 | .03 |
| ☐ 591 | Glenn Abbott | .15 | .06 | .01 |
| ☐ 592 | Balor Moore | .15 | .06 | .01 |
| ☐ 593 | Gene Lamont | .15 | .06 | .01 |
| ☐ 594 | Jim Fuller | .15 | .06 | .01 |
| ☐ 595 | Joe Niekro | .30 | .12 | .03 |
| ☐ 596 | Ollie Brown | .15 | .06 | .01 |
| ☐ 597 | Winston Llenas | .15 | .06 | .01 |
| ☐ 598 | Bruce Kison | .15 | .06 | .01 |
| ☐ 599 | Nate Colbert | .15 | .06 | .01 |
| ☐ 600 | Rod Carew | 4.50 | 1.80 | .45 |
| ☐ 601 | Juan Beniquez | .25 | .10 | .02 |
| ☐ 602 | John Vukovich | .15 | .06 | .01 |
| ☐ 603 | Lew Krausse | .15 | .06 | .01 |
| ☐ 604 | Oscar Zamora | .15 | .06 | .01 |
| ☐ 605 | John Ellis | .15 | .06 | .01 |
| ☐ 606 | Bruce Miller | .15 | .06 | .01 |
| ☐ 607 | Jim Holt | .15 | .06 | .01 |
| ☐ 608 | Gene Michael | .20 | .08 | .02 |
| ☐ 609 | Ellie Hendricks | .15 | .06 | .01 |
| ☐ 610 | Ron Hunt | .15 | .06 | .01 |
| ☐ 611 | Yankees: Team/Mgr. Bill Virdon (checklist back) | .50 | .10 | .02 |
| ☐ 612 | Terry Hughes | .15 | .06 | .01 |
| ☐ 613 | Bill Parsons | .15 | .06 | .01 |
| ☐ 614 | Rookie Pitchers: Jack Kucek Dyar Miller Vern Ruhle Paul Siebert | .25 | .10 | .02 |
| ☐ 615 | Rookie Pitchers: Pat Darcy Dennis Leonard Tom Underwood Hank Webb | 1.00 | .40 | .10 |
| ☐ 616 | Rookie Outfielders: Dave Augustine Pepe Mangual Jim Rice John Scott | 35.00 | 14.00 | 3.50 |
| ☐ 617 | Rookie Infielders: Mike Cubbage Doug DeCinces Reggie Sanders Manny Trillo | 2.50 | 1.00 | .25 |
| ☐ 618 | Rookie Pitchers: Jamie Easterly Tom Johnson Scott McGregor Rick Rhoden | 2.00 | .80 | .20 |
| ☐ 619 | Rookie Outfielders: Benny Ayala Nyls Nyman Tommy Smith Jerry Turner | .25 | .10 | .02 |
| ☐ 620 | Rookie Catcher/OF: Gary Carter Marc Hill Danny Meyer | 35.00 | 14.00 | 3.50 |

|   |   |   |   |   |
|---|---|---|---|---|
| | Leon Roberts | | | |
| ☐ 621 | Rookie Pitchers: ............. | 1.50 | .60 | .15 |
| | John Denny | | | |
| | Rawly Eastwick | | | |
| | Jim Kern | | | |
| | Juan Veintidos | | | |
| ☐ 622 | Rookie Outfielders: ......... | 10.00 | 4.00 | 1.00 |
| | Ed Armbrister | | | |
| | Fred Lynn | | | |
| | Tom Poquette | | | |
| | Terry Whitfield | | | |
| ☐ 623 | Rookie Infielders: ............. | 20.00 | 8.00 | 2.00 |
| | Phil Garner | | | |
| | Keith Hernandez | | | |
| | Bob Sheldon | | | |
| | Tom Veryzer | | | |
| ☐ 624 | Rookie Pitchers: ............. | .30 | .12 | .03 |
| | Doug Konieczny | | | |
| | Gary Lavelle | | | |
| | Jim Otten | | | |
| | Eddie Solomon | | | |
| ☐ 625 | Boog Powell ..................... | .45 | .18 | .04 |
| ☐ 626 | Larry Haney ..................... | .25 | .10 | .02 |
| | (photo actually | | | |
| | Dave Duncan) | | | |
| ☐ 627 | Tom Walker ..................... | .15 | .06 | .01 |
| ☐ 628 | Ron LeFlore ..................... | .50 | .20 | .05 |
| ☐ 629 | Joe Hoerner ..................... | .15 | .06 | .01 |
| ☐ 630 | Greg Luzinski .................. | .60 | .24 | .06 |
| ☐ 631 | Lee Lacy ........................ | .25 | .10 | .02 |
| ☐ 632 | Morris Nettles ................. | .15 | .06 | .01 |
| ☐ 633 | Paul Casanova ................ | .15 | .06 | .01 |
| ☐ 634 | Cy Acosta ...................... | .15 | .06 | .01 |
| ☐ 635 | Chuck Dobson ................ | .15 | .06 | .01 |
| ☐ 636 | Charlie Moore ................. | .15 | .06 | .01 |
| ☐ 637 | Ted Martinez .................. | .15 | .06 | .01 |
| ☐ 638 | Cubs: Team/Mgr. ........... | .40 | .08 | .01 |
| | Jim Marshall | | | |
| | (checklist back) | | | |
| ☐ 639 | Steve Kline ..................... | .15 | .06 | .01 |
| ☐ 640 | Harmon Killebrew .......... | 1.75 | .70 | .17 |
| ☐ 641 | Jim Northrup .................. | .20 | .08 | .02 |
| ☐ 642 | Mike Phillips .................. | .15 | .06 | .01 |
| ☐ 643 | Brent Strom ................... | .15 | .06 | .01 |
| ☐ 644 | Bill Fahey ...................... | .15 | .06 | .01 |
| ☐ 645 | Danny Cater ................... | .15 | .06 | .01 |
| ☐ 646 | Checklist: 529-660 ......... | .60 | .06 | .01 |
| ☐ 647 | Claudell Washington ....... | 1.00 | .40 | .10 |
| ☐ 648 | Dave Pagan .................... | .15 | .06 | .01 |
| ☐ 649 | Jack Heidemann ............. | .15 | .06 | .01 |
| ☐ 650 | Dave May ....................... | .15 | .06 | .01 |
| ☐ 651 | John Morlan ................... | .15 | .06 | .01 |
| ☐ 652 | Lindy McDaniel ............... | .15 | .06 | .01 |
| ☐ 653 | Lee Richard ................... | .15 | .06 | .01 |
| ☐ 654 | Jerry Terrell .................. | .15 | .06 | .01 |
| ☐ 655 | Rico Carty ..................... | .25 | .10 | .02 |
| ☐ 656 | Bill Plummer ................... | .15 | .06 | .01 |
| ☐ 657 | Bob Oliver ..................... | .15 | .06 | .01 |
| ☐ 658 | Vic Harris ...................... | .15 | .06 | .01 |
| ☐ 659 | Bob Apodaca .................. | .15 | .06 | .01 |
| ☐ 660 | Hank Aaron ..................... | 7.50 | 3.00 | .75 |

# 1976 Topps

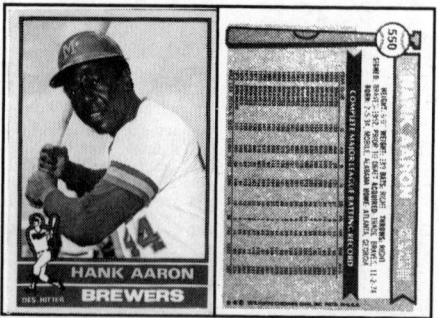

The 1976 Topps set of 660 cards (measuring 2 1/2"
by 3 1/2") is known for its sharp color photographs

and interesting presentation of subjects. Team
cards feature a checklist back for players on that
team and show a small inset photo of the manager
on the front. A "Father and Son" series (66-70)
spotlights five Major Leaguers whose fathers also
made the "Big Show". Other sub-series include "All
Time All Stars" (341-350), "Record Breakers" from
the previous season (1-6), League Leaders (191-
205), Post-season cards (461-462), and Rookie
prospects (589-599).

|   |   |   | MINT | VG-E | F-G |
|---|---|---|---|---|---|
| | COMPLETE SET ....................... | | 180.00 | 75.00 | 18.00 |
| | COMMON PLAYER (1-660) ........ | | .13 | .05 | .01 |
| ☐ | 1 | RB: Hank Aaron .............. | 5.00 | 1.50 | .30 |
| | | Most RBI's 2262 | | | |
| ☐ | 2 | RB: Bobby Bonds ........... | .25 | .10 | .02 |
| | | Most leadoff HR's 32; | | | |
| | | Plus 3 Seasons of | | | |
| | | 30 HR's and 30 SB's | | | |
| ☐ | 3 | RB: Mickey Lolich .......... | .25 | .10 | .02 |
| | | Lefthander Most | | | |
| | | Strikeouts 2679 | | | |
| ☐ | 4 | RB: Dave Lopes .............. | .25 | .10 | .02 |
| | | Most consecutive | | | |
| | | SB attempts, 38 | | | |
| ☐ | 5 | RB: Tom Seaver ............. | 1.25 | .50 | .12 |
| | | Most cons. seasons | | | |
| | | with 200 SO's, 8 | | | |
| ☐ | 6 | RB: Rennie Stennett ....... | .20 | .08 | .02 |
| | | Most hits in a 9 | | | |
| | | inning game, 7 | | | |
| ☐ | 7 | Jim Umbarger ................ | .13 | .05 | .01 |
| ☐ | 8 | Tito Fuentes .................. | .13 | .05 | .01 |
| ☐ | 9 | Paul Lindblad ................. | .13 | .05 | .01 |
| ☐ | 10 | Lou Brock ...................... | 1.75 | .70 | .17 |
| ☐ | 11 | Jim Hughes .................... | .13 | .05 | .01 |
| ☐ | 12 | Richie Zisk ..................... | .20 | .08 | .02 |
| ☐ | 13 | John Wockenfuss ........... | .13 | .05 | .01 |
| ☐ | 14 | Gene Garber ................... | .13 | .05 | .01 |
| ☐ | 15 | George Scott .................. | .20 | .08 | .02 |
| ☐ | 16 | Bob Apodaca .................. | .13 | .05 | .01 |
| ☐ | 17 | New York Yankees .......... | .50 | .10 | .02 |
| | | Team Card | | | |
| | | (checklist back) | | | |
| ☐ | 18 | Dale Murray .................... | .13 | .05 | .01 |
| ☐ | 19 | George Brett ................... | 10.00 | 4.00 | 1.00 |
| ☐ | 20 | Bob Watson .................... | .20 | .08 | .02 |
| ☐ | 21 | Dave LaRoche ................ | .13 | .05 | .01 |
| ☐ | 22 | Bill Russell .................... | .20 | .08 | .02 |
| ☐ | 23 | Brian Downing ................ | .20 | .08 | .02 |
| ☐ | 24 | Cesar Geronimo ............. | .13 | .05 | .01 |
| ☐ | 25 | Mike Torrez .................... | .20 | .08 | .02 |
| ☐ | 26 | Andy Thornton ................ | .25 | .10 | .02 |
| ☐ | 27 | Ed Figueroa ................... | .13 | .05 | .01 |
| ☐ | 28 | Dusty Baker .................... | .30 | .12 | .03 |
| ☐ | 29 | Rick Burleson ................. | .25 | .10 | .02 |
| ☐ | 30 | John Montefusco ............ | .30 | .12 | .03 |
| ☐ | 31 | Len Randle ..................... | .13 | .05 | .01 |
| ☐ | 32 | Danny Frisella ................ | .13 | .05 | .01 |
| ☐ | 33 | Bill North ....................... | .13 | .05 | .01 |
| ☐ | 34 | Mike Garman ................... | .13 | .05 | .01 |
| ☐ | 35 | Tony Oliva ...................... | .40 | .16 | .04 |
| ☐ | 36 | Frank Taveras ................. | .13 | .05 | .01 |
| ☐ | 37 | John Hiller ...................... | .20 | .08 | .02 |
| ☐ | 38 | Garry Maddox ................. | .20 | .08 | .02 |
| ☐ | 39 | Pete Broberg ................... | .13 | .05 | .01 |
| ☐ | 40 | Dave Kingman ................. | .60 | .24 | .06 |
| ☐ | 41 | Tippy Martinez ................ | .50 | .20 | .05 |
| ☐ | 42 | Barry Foote ..................... | .13 | .05 | .01 |
| ☐ | 43 | Paul Splittorff ................. | .13 | .05 | .01 |
| ☐ | 44 | Doug Rader ..................... | .20 | .08 | .02 |
| ☐ | 45 | Boog Powell ................... | .35 | .14 | .03 |
| ☐ | 46 | Dodgers Team ................ | .50 | .10 | .02 |
| | | (checklist back) | | | |
| ☐ | 47 | Jesse Jefferson .............. | .13 | .05 | .01 |
| ☐ | 48 | Dave Concepcion ............ | .35 | .14 | .03 |
| ☐ | 49 | Dave Duncan ................... | .13 | .05 | .01 |
| ☐ | 50 | Fred Lynn ....................... | 2.00 | .80 | .20 |
| ☐ | 51 | Ray Burris ...................... | .13 | .05 | .01 |
| ☐ | 52 | Dave Chalk ..................... | .13 | .05 | .01 |
| ☐ | 53 | Mike Beard ..................... | .13 | .05 | .01 |
| ☐ | 54 | Dave Radar ..................... | .13 | .05 | .01 |
| ☐ | 55 | Gaylord Perry ................. | 1.25 | .50 | .12 |
| ☐ | 56 | Bob Tolan ....................... | .13 | .05 | .01 |
| ☐ | 57 | Phil Garner ..................... | .25 | .10 | .02 |
| ☐ | 58 | Ron Reed ....................... | .13 | .05 | .01 |
| ☐ | 59 | Larry Hisle ...................... | .20 | .08 | .02 |
| ☐ | 60 | Jerry Reuss .................... | .25 | .10 | .02 |

| | | | | |
|---|---|---|---|---|
| □ 61 | Ron LeFlore | .25 | .10 | .02 |
| □ 62 | Johnny Oates | .13 | .05 | .01 |
| □ 63 | Bobby Darwin | .13 | .05 | .01 |
| □ 64 | Jerry Koosman | .30 | .12 | .03 |
| □ 65 | Chris Chambliss | .25 | .10 | .02 |
| □ 66 | Father and Son: | .35 | .14 | .03 |
| | Gus Bell | | | |
| | Buddy Bell | | | |
| □ 67 | Father and Son: | .20 | .08 | .02 |
| | Ray Boone | | | |
| | Bob Boone | | | |
| □ 68 | Father and Son: | .20 | .08 | .02 |
| | Joe Coleman | | | |
| | Joe Coleman Jr. | | | |
| □ 69 | Father and Son: | .20 | .08 | .02 |
| | Jim Hegan | | | |
| | Mike Hegan | | | |
| □ 70 | Father and Son: | .20 | .08 | .02 |
| | Roy Smalley | | | |
| | Roy Smalley Jr. | | | |
| □ 71 | Steve Rogers | .25 | .10 | .02 |
| □ 72 | Hal McRae | .25 | .10 | .02 |
| □ 73 | Orioles Team | .50 | .10 | .02 |
| | (checklist back) | | | |
| □ 74 | Oscar Gamble | .20 | .08 | .02 |
| □ 75 | Larry Dierker | .20 | .08 | .02 |
| □ 76 | Willie Crawford | .13 | .05 | .01 |
| □ 77 | Pedro Borbon | .13 | .05 | .01 |
| □ 78 | Cecil Cooper | .75 | .30 | .07 |
| □ 79 | Jerry Morales | .13 | .05 | .01 |
| □ 80 | Jim Kaat | .50 | .20 | .05 |
| □ 81 | Darrell Evans | .35 | .14 | .03 |
| □ 82 | Von Joshua | .13 | .05 | .01 |
| □ 83 | Jim Spencer | .13 | .05 | .01 |
| □ 84 | Brent Strom | .13 | .05 | .01 |
| □ 85 | Mickey Rivers | .25 | .10 | .02 |
| □ 86 | Mike Tyson | .13 | .05 | .01 |
| □ 87 | Tom Burgmeier | .13 | .05 | .01 |
| □ 88 | Duffy Dyer | .13 | .05 | .01 |
| □ 89 | Vern Ruhle | .13 | .05 | .01 |
| □ 90 | Sal Bando | .25 | .10 | .02 |
| □ 91 | Tom Hutton | .13 | .05 | .01 |
| □ 92 | Eduardo Rodriguez | .13 | .05 | .01 |
| □ 93 | Mike Phillips | .13 | .05 | .01 |
| □ 94 | Jim Dwyer | .13 | .05 | .01 |
| □ 95 | Brooks Robinson | 1.75 | .70 | .17 |
| □ 96 | Doug Bird | .13 | .05 | .01 |
| □ 97 | Wilbur Howard | .13 | .05 | .01 |
| □ 98 | Dennis Eckersley | 1.00 | .40 | .10 |
| □ 99 | Lee Lacy | .25 | .10 | .02 |
| □ 100 | Jim Hunter | 1.25 | .50 | .12 |
| □ 101 | Pete LaCock | .13 | .05 | .01 |
| □ 102 | Jim Willoughby | .13 | .05 | .01 |
| □ 103 | Biff Pocoroba | .13 | .05 | .01 |
| □ 104 | Reds Team | .50 | .10 | .02 |
| | (checklist back) | | | |
| □ 105 | Gary Lavelle | .20 | .08 | .02 |
| □ 106 | Tom Grieve | .20 | .08 | .02 |
| □ 107 | Dave Roberts | .13 | .05 | .01 |
| □ 108 | Don Kirkwood | .13 | .05 | .01 |
| □ 109 | Larry Lintz | .13 | .05 | .01 |
| □ 110 | Carlos May | .13 | .05 | .01 |
| □ 111 | Danny Thompson | .13 | .05 | .01 |
| □ 112 | Kent Tekulve | .75 | .30 | .07 |
| □ 113 | Gary Sutherland | .13 | .05 | .01 |
| □ 114 | Jay Johnstone | .20 | .08 | .02 |
| □ 115 | Ken Holtzman | .20 | .08 | .02 |
| □ 116 | Charlie Moore | .13 | .05 | .01 |
| □ 117 | Mike Jorgensen | .13 | .05 | .01 |
| □ 118 | Red Sox Team | .50 | .10 | .02 |
| | (checklist back) | | | |
| □ 119 | Checklist 1-132 | .50 | .05 | .01 |
| □ 120 | Rusty Staub | .35 | .14 | .03 |
| □ 121 | Tony Solaita | .13 | .05 | .01 |
| □ 122 | Mike Cosgrove | .13 | .05 | .01 |
| □ 123 | Walt Williams | .13 | .05 | .01 |
| □ 124 | Doug Rau | .13 | .05 | .01 |
| □ 125 | Don Baylor | .65 | .26 | .06 |
| □ 126 | Tom Dettore | .13 | .05 | .01 |
| □ 127 | Larvell Blanks | .13 | .05 | .01 |
| □ 128 | Ken Griffey | .35 | .14 | .03 |
| □ 129 | Andy Etchebarren | .13 | .05 | .01 |
| □ 130 | Luis Tiant | .30 | .12 | .03 |
| □ 131 | Bill Stein | .13 | .05 | .01 |
| □ 132 | Don Hood | .13 | .05 | .01 |
| □ 133 | Gary Matthews | .30 | .12 | .03 |
| □ 134 | Mike Ivie | .13 | .05 | .01 |
| □ 135 | Bake McBride | .20 | .08 | .02 |
| □ 136 | Dave Goltz | .20 | .08 | .02 |
| □ 137 | Bill Robinson | .13 | .05 | .01 |
| □ 138 | Lerrin LaGrow | .13 | .05 | .01 |
| □ 139 | Gorman Thomas | .45 | .18 | .04 |
| □ 140 | Vida Blue | .30 | .12 | .03 |
| □ 141 | Larry Parrish | 1.25 | .50 | .12 |
| □ 142 | Dick Drago | .13 | .05 | .01 |
| □ 143 | Jerry Grote | .13 | .05 | .01 |
| □ 144 | Al Fitzmorris | .13 | .05 | .01 |
| □ 145 | Larry Bowa | .40 | .16 | .04 |
| □ 146 | George Medich | .20 | .08 | .02 |
| □ 147 | Astros Team | .40 | .08 | .01 |
| | (checklist back) | | | |
| □ 148 | Stan Thomas | .13 | .05 | .01 |
| □ 149 | Tommy Davis | .20 | .08 | .02 |
| □ 150 | Steve Garvey | 3.75 | 1.50 | .37 |
| □ 151 | Bill Bonham | .13 | .05 | .01 |
| □ 152 | Leroy Stanton | .13 | .05 | .01 |
| □ 153 | Buzz Capra | .13 | .05 | .01 |
| □ 154 | Bucky Dent | .25 | .10 | .02 |
| □ 155 | Jack Billingham | .13 | .05 | .01 |
| □ 156 | Rico Carty | .25 | .10 | .02 |
| □ 157 | Mike Caldwell | .20 | .08 | .02 |
| □ 158 | Ken Reitz | .13 | .05 | .01 |
| □ 159 | Jerry Terrell | .13 | .05 | .01 |
| □ 160 | Dave Winfield | 3.50 | 1.40 | .35 |
| □ 161 | Bruce Kison | .13 | .05 | .01 |
| □ 162 | Jack Pierce | .13 | .05 | .01 |
| □ 163 | Jim Slaton | .13 | .05 | .01 |
| □ 164 | Pepe Mangual | .13 | .05 | .01 |
| □ 165 | Gene Tenace | .13 | .05 | .01 |
| □ 166 | Skip Lockwood | .13 | .05 | .01 |
| □ 167 | Freddie Patek | .13 | .05 | .01 |
| □ 168 | Tom Hilgendorf | .13 | .05 | .01 |
| □ 169 | Graig Nettles | 1.00 | .40 | .10 |
| □ 170 | Rick Wise | .20 | .08 | .02 |
| □ 171 | Greg Gross | .13 | .05 | .01 |
| □ 172 | Rangers Team | .40 | .08 | .01 |
| | (checklist back) | | | |
| □ 173 | Steve Swisher | .13 | .05 | .01 |
| □ 174 | Charlie Hough | .25 | .10 | .02 |
| □ 175 | Ken Singleton | .35 | .14 | .03 |
| □ 176 | Dick Lange | .13 | .05 | .01 |
| □ 177 | Marty Perez | .13 | .05 | .01 |
| □ 178 | Tom Buskey | .13 | .05 | .01 |
| □ 179 | George Foster | .85 | .34 | .08 |
| □ 180 | Rich Gossage | 1.00 | .40 | .10 |
| □ 181 | Willie Montanez | .13 | .05 | .01 |
| □ 182 | Harry Rasmussen | .13 | .05 | .01 |
| □ 183 | Steve Braun | .13 | .05 | .01 |
| □ 184 | Bill Greif | .13 | .05 | .01 |
| □ 185 | Dave Parker | 2.25 | .90 | .22 |
| □ 186 | Tom Walker | .13 | .05 | .01 |
| □ 187 | Pedro Garcia | .13 | .05 | .01 |
| □ 188 | Fred Scherman | .13 | .05 | .01 |
| □ 189 | Claudell Washington | .35 | .14 | .03 |
| □ 190 | Jon Matlack | .20 | .08 | .02 |
| □ 191 | NL Batting Leaders: | .40 | .16 | .04 |
| | Bill Madlock | | | |
| | Ted Simmons | | | |
| | Manny Sanguillen | | | |
| □ 192 | AL Batting Leaders: | 1.25 | .50 | .12 |
| | Rod Carew | | | |
| | Fred Lynn | | | |
| | Thurman Munson | | | |
| □ 193 | NL Home Run Leaders: | .65 | .26 | .06 |
| | Mike Schmidt | | | |
| | Dave Kingman | | | |
| | Greg Luzinski | | | |
| □ 194 | AL Home Run Leaders: | .65 | .26 | .06 |
| | Reggie Jackson | | | |
| | George Scott | | | |
| | John Mayberry | | | |
| □ 195 | NL RBI Leaders: | .45 | .18 | .04 |
| | Greg Luzinski | | | |
| | Johnny Bench | | | |
| | Tony Perez | | | |
| □ 196 | AL RBI Leaders: | .40 | .16 | .04 |
| | George Scott | | | |
| | John Mayberry | | | |
| | Fred Lynn | | | |
| □ 197 | NL Steals Leaders: | .75 | .30 | .07 |
| | Dave Lopes | | | |
| | Joe Morgan | | | |
| | Lou Brock | | | |
| □ 198 | AL Steals Leaders: | .25 | .10 | .02 |
| | Mickey Rivers | | | |
| | Claudell Washington | | | |
| | Amos Otis | | | |
| □ 199 | NL Victory Leaders: | .45 | .18 | .04 |
| | Tom Seaver | | | |
| | Randy Jones | | | |
| | Andy Messersmith | | | |
| □ 200 | AL Victory Leaders: | .65 | .26 | .06 |
| | Jim Hunter | | | |
| | Jim Palmer | | | |
| | Vida Blue | | | |
| □ 201 | NL ERA Leaders: | .45 | .18 | .04 |

Randy Jones
Andy Messersmith
Tom Seaver

| | | | | |
|---|---|---|---|---|
| ☐ 202 | AL ERA Leaders: ............. | .55 | .22 | .05 |
| | Jim Palmer | | | |
| | Jim Hunter | | | |
| | Dennis Eckersley | | | |
| ☐ 203 | NL Strikeout Leaders: ..... | .45 | .18 | .04 |
| | Tom Seaver | | | |
| | John Montefusco | | | |
| | Andy Messersmith | | | |
| ☐ 204 | AL Strikeout Leaders: ..... | .40 | .16 | .04 |
| | Frank Tanana | | | |
| | Bert Blyleven | | | |
| | Gaylord Perry | | | |
| ☐ 205 | Leading Firemen: | .25 | .10 | .02 |
| | Al Hrabosky | | | |
| | Rich Gossage | | | |
| ☐ 206 | Manny Trillo .................... | .25 | .10 | .02 |
| ☐ 207 | Andy Hassler .................. | .13 | .05 | .01 |
| ☐ 208 | Mike Lum ...................... | .13 | .05 | .01 |
| ☐ 209 | Alan Ashby ................... | .25 | .10 | .02 |
| ☐ 210 | Lee May ....................... | .25 | .10 | .02 |
| ☐ 211 | Clay Carroll .................. | .13 | .05 | .01 |
| ☐ 212 | Pat Kelly ..................... | .13 | .05 | .01 |
| ☐ 213 | Dave Heaverlo ............... | .13 | .05 | .01 |
| ☐ 214 | Eric Soderholm ............... | .13 | .05 | .01 |
| ☐ 215 | Reggie Smith ................. | .35 | .14 | .03 |
| ☐ 216 | Expos Team .................. | .40 | .08 | .01 |
| | (checklist back) | | | |
| ☐ 217 | Dave Freisleben .............. | .13 | .05 | .01 |
| ☐ 218 | John Knox ..................... | .13 | .05 | .01 |
| ☐ 219 | Tom Murphy ................... | .13 | .05 | .01 |
| ☐ 220 | Manny Sanguillen ............ | .20 | .08 | .02 |
| ☐ 221 | Jim Todd ...................... | .13 | .05 | .01 |
| ☐ 222 | Wayne Garrett ................ | .13 | .05 | .01 |
| ☐ 223 | Ollie Brown ................... | .13 | .05 | .01 |
| ☐ 224 | Jim York ...................... | .13 | .05 | .01 |
| ☐ 225 | Roy White .................... | .20 | .08 | .02 |
| ☐ 226 | Jim Sundberg ................. | .20 | .08 | .02 |
| ☐ 227 | Oscar Zamora ................ | .13 | .05 | .01 |
| ☐ 228 | John Hale ..................... | .13 | .05 | .01 |
| ☐ 229 | Jerry Remy ................... | .30 | .12 | .03 |
| ☐ 230 | Carl Yastrzemski ............ | 4.50 | 1.80 | .45 |
| ☐ 231 | Tom House .................... | .20 | .08 | .02 |
| ☐ 232 | Frank Duffy ................... | .13 | .05 | .01 |
| ☐ 233 | Grant Jackson ................ | .13 | .05 | .01 |
| ☐ 234 | Mike Sadek ................... | .13 | .05 | .01 |
| ☐ 235 | Bert Blyleven ................. | .50 | .20 | .05 |
| ☐ 236 | Royals Team .................. | .40 | .08 | .01 |
| | (checklist back) | | | |
| ☐ 237 | Dave Hamilton ................ | .13 | .05 | .01 |
| ☐ 238 | Larry Biittner ................. | .13 | .05 | .01 |
| ☐ 239 | John Curtis ................... | .13 | .05 | .01 |
| ☐ 240 | Pete Rose .................... | 12.00 | 5.00 | 1.20 |
| ☐ 241 | Hector Torres ................. | .13 | .05 | .01 |
| ☐ 242 | Dan Meyer .................... | .13 | .05 | .01 |
| ☐ 243 | Jim Rooker ................... | .13 | .05 | .01 |
| ☐ 244 | Bill Sharp .................... | .13 | .05 | .01 |
| ☐ 245 | Felix Millan .................. | .13 | .05 | .01 |
| ☐ 246 | Cesar Tovar .................. | .13 | .05 | .01 |
| ☐ 247 | Terry Harmon ................. | .13 | .05 | .01 |
| ☐ 248 | Dick Tidrow .................. | .13 | .05 | .01 |
| ☐ 249 | Cliff Johnson ................. | .13 | .05 | .01 |
| ☐ 250 | Fergie Jenkins ............... | .45 | .18 | .04 |
| ☐ 251 | Rick Monday .................. | .20 | .08 | .02 |
| ☐ 252 | Tim Nordbrook ................ | .13 | .05 | .01 |
| ☐ 253 | Bill Buckner .................. | .45 | .18 | .04 |
| ☐ 254 | Rudy Meoli ................... | .13 | .05 | .01 |
| ☐ 255 | Fritz Peterson ................ | .13 | .05 | .01 |
| ☐ 256 | Rowland Office ............... | .13 | .05 | .01 |
| ☐ 257 | Ross Grimsley ................ | .13 | .05 | .01 |
| ☐ 258 | Nyls Nyman ................... | .13 | .05 | .01 |
| ☐ 259 | Darrel Chaney ................ | .13 | .05 | .01 |
| ☐ 260 | Steve Busby .................. | .20 | .08 | .02 |
| ☐ 261 | Gary Thomasson .............. | .13 | .05 | .01 |
| ☐ 262 | Checklist 133-264 .......... | .50 | .05 | .01 |
| ☐ 263 | Lyman Bostock ............... | .60 | .24 | .06 |
| ☐ 264 | Steve Renko .................. | .13 | .05 | .01 |
| ☐ 265 | Willie Davis .................. | .20 | .08 | .02 |
| ☐ 266 | Alan Foster .................. | .13 | .05 | .01 |
| ☐ 267 | Aurelio Rodriguez ............ | .13 | .05 | .01 |
| ☐ 268 | Del Unser .................... | .13 | .05 | .01 |
| ☐ 269 | Rick Austin .................. | .13 | .05 | .01 |
| ☐ 270 | Willie Stargell ............... | 1.75 | .70 | .17 |
| ☐ 271 | Jim Lonborg .................. | .20 | .08 | .02 |
| ☐ 272 | Rick Dempsey ................ | .20 | .08 | .02 |
| ☐ 273 | Joe Niekro ................... | .25 | .10 | .02 |
| ☐ 274 | Tommy Harper ................ | .20 | .08 | .02 |
| ☐ 275 | Rick Manning ................. | .25 | .10 | .02 |
| ☐ 276 | Mickey Scott ................. | .13 | .05 | .01 |
| ☐ 277 | Cubs Team ................... | .40 | .08 | .01 |
| | (checklist back) | | | |

| | | | | |
|---|---|---|---|---|
| ☐ 278 | Bernie Carbo ................. | .13 | .05 | .01 |
| ☐ 279 | Roy Howell ................... | .13 | .05 | .01 |
| ☐ 280 | Burt Hooton .................. | .20 | .08 | .02 |
| ☐ 281 | Dave May ..................... | .13 | .05 | .01 |
| ☐ 282 | Dan Osborn .................. | .13 | .05 | .01 |
| ☐ 283 | Merv Rettenmund ........... | .13 | .05 | .01 |
| ☐ 284 | Steve Ontiveros .............. | .13 | .05 | .01 |
| ☐ 285 | Mike Cuellar ................. | .20 | .08 | .02 |
| ☐ 286 | Jim Wohlford ................. | .13 | .05 | .01 |
| ☐ 287 | Pete Mackanin ............... | .13 | .05 | .01 |
| ☐ 288 | Bill Campbell ................. | .13 | .05 | .01 |
| ☐ 289 | Enzo Hernandez .............. | .13 | .05 | .01 |
| ☐ 290 | Ted Simmons ................. | .65 | .26 | .06 |
| ☐ 291 | Ken Sanders ................. | .13 | .05 | .01 |
| ☐ 292 | Leon Roberts ................. | .13 | .05 | .01 |
| ☐ 293 | Bill Castro ................... | .13 | .05 | .01 |
| ☐ 294 | Ed Kirkpatrick ............... | .13 | .05 | .01 |
| ☐ 295 | Dave Cash .................... | .13 | .05 | .01 |
| ☐ 296 | Pat Dobson .................. | .20 | .08 | .02 |
| ☐ 297 | Roger Metzger ................ | .13 | .05 | .01 |
| ☐ 298 | Dick Bosman ................. | .13 | .05 | .01 |
| ☐ 299 | Champ Summers .............. | .13 | .05 | .01 |
| ☐ 300 | Johnny Bench ................. | 3.50 | 1.40 | .35 |
| ☐ 301 | Jackie Brown ................. | .13 | .05 | .01 |
| ☐ 302 | Rick Miller ................... | .13 | .05 | .01 |
| ☐ 303 | Steve Foucault ............... | .13 | .05 | .01 |
| ☐ 304 | Angels Team .................. | .40 | .08 | .01 |
| | (checklist back) | | | |
| ☐ 305 | Andy Messersmith .......... | .25 | .10 | .02 |
| ☐ 306 | Rod Gilbreath ................ | .13 | .05 | .01 |
| ☐ 307 | Al Bumbry .................... | .13 | .05 | .01 |
| ☐ 308 | Jim Barr ...................... | .13 | .05 | .01 |
| ☐ 309 | Bill Melton ................... | .13 | .05 | .01 |
| ☐ 310 | Randy Jones .................. | .25 | .10 | .02 |
| ☐ 311 | Cookie Rojas ................. | .13 | .05 | .01 |
| ☐ 312 | Don Carrithers ............... | .13 | .05 | .01 |
| ☐ 313 | Dan Ford ..................... | .25 | .10 | .02 |
| ☐ 314 | Ed Kranepool ................. | .20 | .08 | .02 |
| ☐ 315 | Al Hrabosky .................. | .20 | .08 | .02 |
| ☐ 316 | Robin Yount .................. | 5.00 | 2.00 | .50 |
| ☐ 317 | John Candelaria .............. | 2.00 | .80 | .20 |
| ☐ 318 | Bob Boone .................... | .25 | .10 | .02 |
| ☐ 319 | Larry Gura ................... | .20 | .08 | .02 |
| ☐ 320 | Willie Horton ................. | .20 | .08 | .02 |
| ☐ 321 | Jose Cruz .................... | .40 | .16 | .04 |
| ☐ 322 | Glenn Abbott ................. | .13 | .05 | .01 |
| ☐ 323 | Rob Sperring ................. | .13 | .05 | .01 |
| ☐ 324 | Jim Bibby .................... | .20 | .08 | .02 |
| ☐ 325 | Tony Perez ................... | .50 | .20 | .05 |
| ☐ 326 | Dick Pole .................... | .13 | .05 | .01 |
| ☐ 327 | Dave Moates ................. | .13 | .05 | .01 |
| ☐ 328 | Carl Morton .................. | .13 | .05 | .01 |
| ☐ 329 | Joe Ferguson ................. | .20 | .08 | .02 |
| ☐ 330 | Nolan Ryan ................... | 3.50 | 1.40 | .35 |
| ☐ 331 | Padres Team .................. | .40 | .08 | .01 |
| | (checklist back) | | | |
| ☐ 332 | Charlie Williams .............. | .13 | .05 | .01 |
| ☐ 333 | Bob Coluccio ................. | .13 | .05 | .01 |
| ☐ 334 | Dennis Leonard .............. | .30 | .12 | .03 |
| ☐ 335 | Bob Grich .................... | .25 | .10 | .02 |
| ☐ 336 | Vic Albury ................... | .13 | .05 | .01 |
| ☐ 337 | Bud Harrelson ................ | .20 | .08 | .02 |
| ☐ 338 | Bob Bailey ................... | .13 | .05 | .01 |
| ☐ 339 | John Denny ................... | .40 | .16 | .04 |
| ☐ 340 | Jim Rice ...................... | 10.00 | 4.00 | 1.00 |
| ☐ 341 | All-Time 1B: .................. | 1.75 | .70 | .17 |
| | Lou Gehrig | | | |
| ☐ 342 | All-Time 2B: .................. | 1.00 | .40 | .10 |
| | Rogers Hornsby | | | |
| ☐ 343 | All-Time 3B: .................. | .60 | .24 | .06 |
| | Pie Traynor | | | |
| ☐ 344 | All-Time SS: .................. | 1.00 | .40 | .10 |
| | Honus Wagner | | | |
| ☐ 345 | All-Time OF: .................. | 2.75 | 1.10 | .27 |
| | Babe Ruth | | | |
| ☐ 346 | All-Time OF: .................. | 1.75 | .70 | .17 |
| | Ty Cobb | | | |
| ☐ 347 | All-Time OF: .................. | 1.75 | .70 | .17 |
| | Ted Williams | | | |
| ☐ 348 | All-Time C: ................... | .60 | .24 | .06 |
| | Mickey Cochrane | | | |
| ☐ 349 | All-Time RHP: ................ | 1.00 | .40 | .10 |
| | Walter Johnson | | | |
| ☐ 350 | All-Time LHP: ................ | .75 | .30 | .07 |
| | Lefty Grove | | | |
| ☐ 351 | Randy Hundley ................ | .13 | .05 | .01 |
| ☐ 352 | Dave Giusti .................. | .13 | .05 | .01 |
| ☐ 353 | Sixto Lezcano ................ | .25 | .10 | .02 |
| ☐ 354 | Ron Blomberg ................ | .13 | .05 | .01 |
| ☐ 355 | Steve Carlton ................ | 4.00 | 1.60 | .40 |
| ☐ 356 | Ted Martinez ................. | .13 | .05 | .01 |
| ☐ 357 | Ken Forsch ................... | .20 | .08 | .02 |
| ☐ 358 | Buddy Bell ................... | .35 | .14 | .03 |

| | | | | |
|---|---|---|---|---|
| ☐ 359 | Rick Reuschel | .20 | .08 | .02 |
| ☐ 360 | Jeff Burroughs | .20 | .08 | .02 |
| ☐ 361 | Tigers Team | .50 | .10 | .02 |
| | (checklist back) | | | |
| ☐ 362 | Will McEnaney | .13 | .05 | .01 |
| ☐ 363 | Dave Collins | .90 | .36 | .09 |
| ☐ 364 | Elias Sosa | .13 | .05 | .01 |
| ☐ 365 | Carlton Fisk | .90 | .36 | .09 |
| ☐ 366 | Bobby Valentine | .30 | .12 | .03 |
| ☐ 367 | Bruce Miller | .13 | .05 | .01 |
| ☐ 368 | Wilbur Wood | .20 | .08 | .02 |
| ☐ 369 | Frank White | .40 | .16 | .04 |
| ☐ 370 | Ron Cey | .60 | .24 | .06 |
| ☐ 371 | Ellie Hendricks | .13 | .05 | .01 |
| ☐ 372 | Rick Baldwin | .13 | .05 | .01 |
| ☐ 373 | Johnny Briggs | .13 | .05 | .01 |
| ☐ 374 | Dan Warthen | .13 | .05 | .01 |
| ☐ 375 | Ron Fairly | .20 | .08 | .02 |
| ☐ 376 | Rich Hebner | .13 | .05 | .01 |
| ☐ 377 | Mike Hegan | .13 | .05 | .01 |
| ☐ 378 | Steve Stone | .20 | .08 | .02 |
| ☐ 379 | Ken Boswell | .13 | .05 | .01 |
| ☐ 380 | Bobby Bonds | .30 | .12 | .03 |
| ☐ 381 | Denny Doyle | .13 | .05 | .01 |
| ☐ 382 | Matt Alexander | .13 | .05 | .01 |
| ☐ 383 | John Ellis | .13 | .05 | .01 |
| ☐ 384 | Phillies Team | .40 | .08 | .01 |
| | (checklist back) | | | |
| ☐ 385 | Mickey Lolich | .30 | .12 | .03 |
| ☐ 386 | Ed Goodson | .13 | .05 | .01 |
| ☐ 387 | Mike Miley | .13 | .05 | .01 |
| ☐ 388 | Stan Perzanowski | .13 | .05 | .01 |
| ☐ 389 | Glenn Adams | .13 | .05 | .01 |
| ☐ 390 | Don Gullett | .20 | .08 | .02 |
| ☐ 391 | Jerry Hairston | .13 | .05 | .01 |
| ☐ 392 | Checklist 265-396 | .50 | .05 | .01 |
| ☐ 393 | Paul Mitchell | .13 | .05 | .01 |
| ☐ 394 | Fran Healy | .13 | .05 | .01 |
| ☐ 395 | Jim Wynn | .20 | .08 | .02 |
| ☐ 396 | Bill Lee | .20 | .08 | .02 |
| ☐ 397 | Tim Foli | .13 | .05 | .01 |
| ☐ 398 | Dave Tomlin | .13 | .05 | .01 |
| ☐ 399 | Luis Melendez | .13 | .05 | .01 |
| ☐ 400 | Rod Carew | 3.50 | 1.40 | .35 |
| ☐ 401 | Ken Brett | .13 | .05 | .01 |
| ☐ 402 | Don Money | .13 | .05 | .01 |
| ☐ 403 | Geoff Zahn | .13 | .05 | .01 |
| ☐ 404 | Enos Cabell | .13 | .05 | .01 |
| ☐ 405 | Rollie Fingers | .75 | .30 | .07 |
| ☐ 406 | Ed Herrmann | .13 | .05 | .01 |
| ☐ 407 | Tom Underwood | .13 | .05 | .01 |
| ☐ 408 | Charlie Spikes | .13 | .05 | .01 |
| ☐ 409 | Dave Lemanczyk | .13 | .05 | .01 |
| ☐ 410 | Ralph Garr | .13 | .05 | .01 |
| ☐ 411 | Bill Singer | .13 | .05 | .01 |
| ☐ 412 | Toby Harrah | .20 | .08 | .02 |
| ☐ 413 | Pete Varney | .13 | .05 | .01 |
| ☐ 414 | Wayne Garland | .13 | .05 | .01 |
| ☐ 415 | Vada Pinson | .25 | .10 | .02 |
| ☐ 416 | Tommy John | .65 | .26 | .06 |
| ☐ 417 | Gene Clines | .13 | .05 | .01 |
| ☐ 418 | Jose Morales | .13 | .05 | .01 |
| ☐ 419 | Reggie Cleveland | .13 | .05 | .01 |
| ☐ 420 | Joe Morgan | 2.25 | .90 | .22 |
| ☐ 421 | A's Team | .40 | .08 | .01 |
| | (checklist back) | | | |
| ☐ 422 | Johnny Grubb | .13 | .05 | .01 |
| ☐ 423 | Ed Halicki | .13 | .05 | .01 |
| ☐ 424 | Phil Roof | .13 | .05 | .01 |
| ☐ 425 | Rennie Stennett | .13 | .05 | .01 |
| ☐ 426 | Bob Forsch | .25 | .10 | .02 |
| ☐ 427 | Kurt Bevacqua | .13 | .05 | .01 |
| ☐ 428 | Jim Crawford | .13 | .05 | .01 |
| ☐ 429 | Fred Stanley | .13 | .05 | .01 |
| ☐ 430 | Jose Cardenal | .13 | .05 | .01 |
| ☐ 431 | Dick Ruthven | .13 | .05 | .01 |
| ☐ 432 | Tom Veryzer | .13 | .05 | .01 |
| ☐ 433 | Rick Waits | .20 | .08 | .02 |
| ☐ 434 | Morris Nettles | .13 | .05 | .01 |
| ☐ 435 | Phil Niekro | 1.25 | .50 | .12 |
| ☐ 436 | Bill Fahey | .13 | .05 | .01 |
| ☐ 437 | Terry Forster | .25 | .10 | .02 |
| ☐ 438 | Doug DeCinces | .65 | .26 | .06 |
| ☐ 439 | Rick Rhoden | .50 | .20 | .05 |
| ☐ 440 | John Mayberry | .20 | .08 | .02 |
| ☐ 441 | Gary Carter | 10.00 | 4.00 | 1.00 |
| ☐ 442 | Hank Webb | .13 | .05 | .01 |
| ☐ 443 | Giants Team | .40 | .08 | .01 |
| | (checklist back) | | | |
| ☐ 444 | Gary Nolan | .13 | .05 | .01 |
| ☐ 445 | Rico Petrocelli | .20 | .08 | .02 |
| ☐ 446 | Larry Haney | .13 | .05 | .01 |
| ☐ 447 | Gene Locklear | .13 | .05 | .01 |
| ☐ 448 | Tom Johnson | .13 | .05 | .01 |
| ☐ 449 | Bob Robertson | .13 | .05 | .01 |
| ☐ 450 | Jim Palmer | 2.50 | 1.00 | .25 |
| ☐ 451 | Buddy Bradford | .13 | .05 | .01 |
| ☐ 452 | Tom Hausman | .13 | .05 | .01 |
| ☐ 453 | Lou Piniella | .30 | .12 | .03 |
| ☐ 454 | Tom Griffin | .13 | .05 | .01 |
| ☐ 455 | Dick Allen | .35 | .14 | .03 |
| ☐ 456 | Joe Coleman | .13 | .05 | .01 |
| ☐ 457 | Ed Crosby | .13 | .05 | .01 |
| ☐ 458 | Earl Williams | .13 | .05 | .01 |
| ☐ 459 | Jim Brewer | .13 | .05 | .01 |
| ☐ 460 | Cesar Cedeno | .25 | .10 | .02 |
| ☐ 461 | NL and AL Champs: | .40 | .16 | .04 |
| | Reds sweep Bucs | | | |
| | Bosox surprise A's | | | |
| ☐ 462 | '75 World Series: | .40 | .16 | .04 |
| | Reds Champs | | | |
| ☐ 463 | Steve Hargan | .13 | .05 | .01 |
| ☐ 464 | Ken Henderson | .13 | .05 | .01 |
| ☐ 465 | Mike Marshall | .20 | .08 | .02 |
| ☐ 466 | Bob Stinson | .13 | .05 | .01 |
| ☐ 467 | Woodie Fryman | .13 | .05 | .01 |
| ☐ 468 | Jesus Alou | .13 | .05 | .01 |
| ☐ 469 | Rawley Eastwick | .13 | .05 | .01 |
| ☐ 470 | Bobby Murcer | .35 | .14 | .03 |
| ☐ 471 | Jim Burton | .13 | .05 | .01 |
| ☐ 472 | Bob Davis | .13 | .05 | .01 |
| ☐ 473 | Paul Blair | .20 | .08 | .02 |
| ☐ 474 | Ray Corbin | .13 | .05 | .01 |
| ☐ 475 | Joe Rudi | .20 | .08 | .02 |
| ☐ 476 | Bob Moose | .13 | .05 | .01 |
| ☐ 477 | Indians Team | .40 | .08 | .01 |
| | (checklist back) | | | |
| ☐ 478 | Lynn McGlothen | .13 | .05 | .01 |
| ☐ 479 | Bobby Mitchell | .13 | .05 | .01 |
| ☐ 480 | Mike Schmidt | 9.00 | 3.75 | .90 |
| ☐ 481 | Rudy May | .13 | .05 | .01 |
| ☐ 482 | Tim Hosley | .13 | .05 | .01 |
| ☐ 483 | Mickey Stanley | .13 | .05 | .01 |
| ☐ 484 | Eric Raich | .13 | .05 | .01 |
| ☐ 485 | Mike Hargrove | .20 | .08 | .02 |
| ☐ 486 | Bruce Dal Canton | .13 | .05 | .01 |
| ☐ 487 | Leron Lee | .13 | .05 | .01 |
| ☐ 488 | Claude Osteen | .20 | .08 | .02 |
| ☐ 489 | Skip Jutze | .13 | .05 | .01 |
| ☐ 490 | Frank Tanana | .25 | .10 | .02 |
| ☐ 491 | Terry Crowley | .13 | .05 | .01 |
| ☐ 492 | Martin Pattin | .13 | .05 | .01 |
| ☐ 493 | Derrel Thomas | .13 | .05 | .01 |
| ☐ 494 | Craig Swan | .20 | .08 | .02 |
| ☐ 495 | Nate Colbert | .13 | .05 | .01 |
| ☐ 496 | Juan Beniquez | .20 | .08 | .02 |
| ☐ 497 | Joe McIntosh | .13 | .05 | .01 |
| ☐ 498 | Glenn Borgmann | .13 | .05 | .01 |
| ☐ 499 | Mario Guerrero | .13 | .05 | .01 |
| ☐ 500 | Reggie Jackson | 6.00 | 2.40 | .60 |
| ☐ 501 | Billy Champion | .13 | .05 | .01 |
| ☐ 502 | Tim McCarver | .25 | .10 | .02 |
| ☐ 503 | Elliott Maddox | .13 | .05 | .01 |
| ☐ 504 | Pirates Team | .40 | .08 | .01 |
| | (checklist back) | | | |
| ☐ 505 | Mark Belanger | .25 | .10 | .02 |
| ☐ 506 | George Mitterwald | .13 | .05 | .01 |
| ☐ 507 | Ray Bare | .13 | .05 | .01 |
| ☐ 508 | Duane Kuiper | .13 | .05 | .01 |
| ☐ 509 | Bill Hands | .13 | .05 | .01 |
| ☐ 510 | Amos Otis | .25 | .10 | .02 |
| ☐ 511 | Jamie Easterly | .13 | .05 | .01 |
| ☐ 512 | Ellie Rodriguez | .13 | .05 | .01 |
| ☐ 513 | Bart Johnson | .13 | .05 | .01 |
| ☐ 514 | Dan Driessen | .20 | .08 | .02 |
| ☐ 515 | Steve Yeager | .20 | .08 | .02 |
| ☐ 516 | Wayne Granger | .13 | .05 | .01 |
| ☐ 517 | John Milner | .13 | .05 | .01 |
| ☐ 518 | Doug Flynn | .13 | .05 | .01 |
| ☐ 519 | Steve Brye | .13 | .05 | .01 |
| ☐ 520 | Willie McCovey | 1.75 | .70 | .17 |
| ☐ 521 | Jim Colborn | .13 | .05 | .01 |
| ☐ 522 | Ted Sizemore | .13 | .05 | .01 |
| ☐ 523 | Bob Montgomery | .13 | .05 | .01 |
| ☐ 524 | Pete Falcone | .13 | .05 | .01 |
| ☐ 525 | Billy Williams | 1.25 | .50 | .12 |
| ☐ 526 | Checklist 397-528 | .50 | .05 | .01 |
| ☐ 527 | Mike Anderson | .13 | .05 | .01 |
| ☐ 528 | Dock Ellis | .13 | .05 | .01 |
| ☐ 529 | Deron Johnson | .13 | .05 | .01 |
| ☐ 530 | Don Sutton | 1.25 | .50 | .12 |
| ☐ 531 | New York Mets Team | .50 | .10 | .02 |
| | (checklist back) | | | |
| ☐ 532 | Milt May | .13 | .05 | .01 |
| ☐ 533 | Lee Richard | .13 | .05 | .01 |
| ☐ 534 | Stan Bahnsen | .13 | .05 | .01 |

| | | | | |
|---|---|---|---|---|
| ☐ 535 | Dave Nelson | .13 | .05 | .01 |
| ☐ 536 | Mike Thompson | .13 | .05 | .01 |
| ☐ 537 | Tony Muser | .13 | .05 | .01 |
| ☐ 538 | Pat Darcy | .13 | .05 | .01 |
| ☐ 539 | John Balaz | .13 | .05 | .01 |
| ☐ 540 | Bill Freehan | .25 | .10 | .02 |
| ☐ 541 | Steve Mingori | .13 | .05 | .01 |
| ☐ 542 | Keith Hernandez | 5.00 | 2.00 | .50 |
| ☐ 543 | Wayne Twitchell | .13 | .05 | .01 |
| ☐ 544 | Pepe Frias | .13 | .05 | .01 |
| ☐ 545 | Sparky Lyle | .30 | .12 | .03 |
| ☐ 546 | Dave Rosello | .13 | .05 | .01 |
| ☐ 547 | Roric Harrison | .13 | .05 | .01 |
| ☐ 548 | Manny Mota | .20 | .08 | .02 |
| ☐ 549 | Randy Tate | .13 | .05 | .01 |
| ☐ 550 | Hank Aaron | 5.00 | 2.00 | .50 |
| ☐ 551 | Jerry DaVanon | .13 | .05 | .01 |
| ☐ 552 | Terry Humphrey | .13 | .05 | .01 |
| ☐ 553 | Randy Moffitt | .13 | .05 | .01 |
| ☐ 554 | Ray Fosse | .13 | .05 | .01 |
| ☐ 555 | Dyar Miller | .13 | .05 | .01 |
| ☐ 556 | Twins Team (checklist back) | .40 | .08 | .01 |
| ☐ 557 | Dan Spillner | .13 | .05 | .01 |
| ☐ 558 | Clarence Gaston | .13 | .05 | .01 |
| ☐ 559 | Clyde Wright | .13 | .05 | .01 |
| ☐ 560 | Jorge Orta | .13 | .05 | .01 |
| ☐ 561 | Tom Carroll | .13 | .05 | .01 |
| ☐ 562 | Adrian Garrett | .13 | .05 | .01 |
| ☐ 563 | Larry Demery | .13 | .05 | .01 |
| ☐ 564 | Bubble Gum Champ: Kurt Bevacqua | .20 | .08 | .02 |
| ☐ 565 | Tug McGraw | .30 | .12 | .03 |
| ☐ 566 | Ken McMullen | .13 | .05 | .01 |
| ☐ 567 | George Stone | .13 | .05 | .01 |
| ☐ 568 | Rob Andrews | .13 | .05 | .01 |
| ☐ 569 | Nelson Briles | .20 | .08 | .02 |
| ☐ 570 | George Hendrick | .25 | .10 | .02 |
| ☐ 571 | Don DeMola | .13 | .05 | .01 |
| ☐ 572 | Rich Coggins | .13 | .05 | .01 |
| ☐ 573 | Bill Travers | .13 | .05 | .01 |
| ☐ 574 | Don Kessinger | .20 | .08 | .02 |
| ☐ 575 | Dwight Evans | .50 | .20 | .05 |
| ☐ 576 | Maximino Leon | .13 | .05 | .01 |
| ☐ 577 | Marc Hill | .13 | .05 | .01 |
| ☐ 578 | Ted Kubiak | .13 | .05 | .01 |
| ☐ 579 | Clay Kirby | .13 | .05 | .01 |
| ☐ 580 | Bert Campaneris | .25 | .10 | .02 |
| ☐ 581 | Cardinals Team (checklist back) | .50 | .10 | .02 |
| ☐ 582 | Mike Kekich | .13 | .05 | .01 |
| ☐ 583 | Tommy Helms | .13 | .05 | .01 |
| ☐ 584 | Stan Wall | .13 | .05 | .01 |
| ☐ 585 | Joe Torre | .40 | .16 | .04 |
| ☐ 586 | Ron Schueler | .13 | .05 | .01 |
| ☐ 587 | Leo Cardenas | .13 | .05 | .01 |
| ☐ 588 | Kevin Kobel | .13 | .05 | .01 |
| ☐ 589 | Rookie Pitchers: Santo Alcala, Mike Flanagan, Joe Pactwa, Pablo Torrealba | 1.25 | .50 | .12 |
| ☐ 590 | Rookie Outfielders: Henry Cruz, Chet Lemon, Ellis Valentine, Terry Whitfield | 1.25 | .50 | .12 |
| ☐ 591 | Rookie Pitchers: Steve Grilli, Craig Mitchell, Jose Sosa, George Throop | .20 | .08 | .02 |
| ☐ 592 | Rookie Infielders: Willie Randolph, Dave McKay, Jerry Royster, Roy Staiger | 1.25 | .50 | .12 |
| ☐ 593 | Rookie Pitchers: Larry Anderson, Ken Crosby, Mark Littell, Butch Metzger | .25 | .10 | .02 |
| ☐ 594 | Rookie Catchers/OF: Andy Merchant, Ed Ott, Royle Stillman, Jerry White | .20 | .08 | .02 |
| ☐ 595 | Rookie Pitchers: Art DeFillipis, Randy Lerch, Sid Monge, Steve Barr | .20 | .08 | .02 |
| ☐ 596 | Rookie Infielders: | .35 | .14 | .03 |
| | Craig Reynolds, Lamar Johnson, Johnnie LeMaster, Jerry Manuel | | | |
| ☐ 597 | Rookie Pitchers: Don Aase, Jack Kucek, Frank LaCorte, Mike Pazik | .75 | .30 | .07 |
| ☐ 598 | Rookie Outfielders: Hector Cruz, Jamie Quirk, Jerry Turner, Joe Wallis | .20 | .08 | .02 |
| ☐ 599 | Rookie Pitchers: Rob Dressler, Ron Guidry, Bob McClure, Pat Zachry | 10.00 | 4.00 | 1.00 |
| ☐ 600 | Tom Seaver | 3.50 | 1.40 | .35 |
| ☐ 601 | Ken Rudolph | .13 | .05 | .01 |
| ☐ 602 | Doug Konieczny | .13 | .05 | .01 |
| ☐ 603 | Jim Holt | .13 | .05 | .01 |
| ☐ 604 | Joe Lovitto | .13 | .05 | .01 |
| ☐ 605 | Al Downing | .13 | .05 | .01 |
| ☐ 606 | Brewers Team (checklist back) | .40 | .08 | .01 |
| ☐ 607 | Rich Hinton | .13 | .05 | .01 |
| ☐ 608 | Vic Correll | .13 | .05 | .01 |
| ☐ 609 | Fred Norman | .13 | .05 | .01 |
| ☐ 610 | Greg Luzinski | .40 | .16 | .04 |
| ☐ 611 | Rich Folkers | .13 | .05 | .01 |
| ☐ 612 | Joe Lahoud | .13 | .05 | .01 |
| ☐ 613 | Tim Johnson | .13 | .05 | .01 |
| ☐ 614 | Fernando Arroyo | .13 | .05 | .01 |
| ☐ 615 | Mike Cubbage | .13 | .05 | .01 |
| ☐ 616 | Buck Martinez | .13 | .05 | .01 |
| ☐ 617 | Darold Knowles | .13 | .05 | .01 |
| ☐ 618 | Jack Brohamer | .13 | .05 | .01 |
| ☐ 619 | Bill Butler | .13 | .05 | .01 |
| ☐ 620 | Al Oliver | .60 | .24 | .06 |
| ☐ 621 | Tom Hall | .13 | .05 | .01 |
| ☐ 622 | Rick Auerbach | .13 | .05 | .01 |
| ☐ 623 | Bob Allietta | .13 | .05 | .01 |
| ☐ 624 | Tony Taylor | .13 | .05 | .01 |
| ☐ 625 | J.R. Richard | .25 | .10 | .02 |
| ☐ 626 | Bob Sheldon | .13 | .05 | .01 |
| ☐ 627 | Bill Plummer | .13 | .05 | .01 |
| ☐ 628 | John D'Acquisto | .13 | .05 | .01 |
| ☐ 629 | Sandy Alomar | .13 | .05 | .01 |
| ☐ 630 | Chris Speier | .13 | .05 | .01 |
| ☐ 631 | Braves Team (checklist back) | .40 | .08 | .01 |
| ☐ 632 | Rogelio Moret | .13 | .05 | .01 |
| ☐ 633 | John Stearns | .25 | .10 | .02 |
| ☐ 634 | Larry Christenson | .13 | .05 | .01 |
| ☐ 635 | Jim Fregosi | .25 | .10 | .02 |
| ☐ 636 | Joe Decker | .13 | .05 | .01 |
| ☐ 637 | Bruce Bochte | .20 | .08 | .02 |
| ☐ 638 | Doyle Alexander | .20 | .08 | .02 |
| ☐ 639 | Fred Kendall | .13 | .05 | .01 |
| ☐ 640 | Bill Madlock | .75 | .30 | .07 |
| ☐ 641 | Tom Paciorek | .13 | .05 | .01 |
| ☐ 642 | Dennis Blair | .13 | .05 | .01 |
| ☐ 643 | Checklist 529-660 | .50 | .05 | .01 |
| ☐ 644 | Tom Bradley | .13 | .05 | .01 |
| ☐ 645 | Darrell Porter | .20 | .08 | .02 |
| ☐ 646 | John Lowenstein | .13 | .05 | .01 |
| ☐ 647 | Ramon Hernandez | .13 | .05 | .01 |
| ☐ 648 | Al Cowens | .20 | .08 | .02 |
| ☐ 649 | Dave Roberts | .13 | .05 | .01 |
| ☐ 650 | Thurman Munson | 3.50 | 1.40 | .35 |
| ☐ 651 | John Odom | .13 | .05 | .01 |
| ☐ 652 | Ed Armbrister | .13 | .05 | .01 |
| ☐ 653 | Mike Norris | .25 | .10 | .02 |
| ☐ 654 | Doug Griffin | .13 | .05 | .01 |
| ☐ 655 | Mike Vail | .13 | .05 | .01 |
| ☐ 656 | White Sox Team (checklist back) | .40 | .08 | .01 |
| ☐ 657 | Roy Smalley | .45 | .18 | .04 |
| ☐ 658 | Jerry Johnson | .13 | .05 | .01 |
| ☐ 659 | Ben Oglivie | .25 | .10 | .02 |
| ☐ 660 | Dave Lopes | .60 | .24 | .06 |

## 1976 Topps Traded

The cards in this 44 card set measure 2 1/2" by 3 1/2". The 1976 Topps Traded set contains 43 players and one unnumbered checklist card. The individuals pictured were traded after the Topps regular set was printed. A "Sports Extra" heading design is found on each picture and is also used to introduce the biographical section of the reverse. Each card is numbered according to the player's regular 1976 card with the addition of "T" to indicate his new status.

| | | MINT | VG-E | F-G |
|---|---|---|---|---|
| COMPLETE SET | | 5.00 | 2.00 | .50 |
| COMMON PLAYER | | .10 | .04 | .01 |
| | | | | |
| ☐ 27T | Ed Figueroa | .10 | .04 | .01 |
| ☐ 28T | Dusty Baker | .30 | .12 | .03 |
| ☐ 44T | Doug Rader | .15 | .06 | .01 |
| ☐ 58T | Ron Reed | .15 | .06 | .01 |
| ☐ 74T | Oscar Gamble | .20 | .08 | .02 |
| ☐ 80T | Jim Kaat | .50 | .20 | .05 |
| ☐ 83T | Jim Spencer | .10 | .04 | .01 |
| ☐ 85T | Mickey Rivers | .15 | .06 | .01 |
| ☐ 99T | Lee Lacy | .20 | .08 | .02 |
| ☐ 120T | Rusty Staub | .35 | .14 | .03 |
| ☐ 127T | Larvell Blanks | .10 | .04 | .01 |
| ☐ 146T | George Medich | .15 | .06 | .01 |
| ☐ 158T | Ken Reitz | .10 | .04 | .01 |
| ☐ 208T | Mike Lum | .10 | .04 | .01 |
| ☐ 211T | Clay Carroll | .10 | .04 | .01 |
| ☐ 231T | Tom House | .15 | .06 | .01 |
| ☐ 250T | Fergie Jenkins | .50 | .20 | .05 |
| ☐ 259T | Darrel Chaney | .10 | .04 | .01 |
| ☐ 292T | Leon Roberts | .10 | .04 | .01 |
| ☐ 296T | Pat Dobson | .15 | .06 | .01 |
| ☐ 309T | Bill Melton | .10 | .04 | .01 |
| ☐ 338T | Bob Bailey | .10 | .04 | .01 |
| ☐ 380T | Bobby Bonds | .25 | .10 | .02 |
| ☐ 383T | John Ellis | .10 | .04 | .01 |
| ☐ 385T | Mickey Lolich | .25 | .10 | .02 |
| ☐ 401T | Ken Brett | .15 | .06 | .01 |
| ☐ 410T | Ralph Garr | .15 | .06 | .01 |
| ☐ 411T | Bill Singer | .10 | .04 | .01 |
| ☐ 428T | Jim Crawford | .10 | .04 | .01 |
| ☐ 434T | Morris Nettles | .10 | .04 | .01 |
| ☐ 464T | Ken Henderson | .10 | .04 | .01 |
| ☐ 497T | Joe McIntosh | .10 | .04 | .01 |
| ☐ 524T | Pete Falcone | .10 | .04 | .01 |
| ☐ 527T | Mike Anderson | .10 | .04 | .01 |
| ☐ 528T | Dock Ellis | .10 | .04 | .01 |
| ☐ 532T | Milt May | .10 | .04 | .01 |
| ☐ 554T | Ray Fosse | .10 | .04 | .01 |
| ☐ 579T | Clay Kirby | .10 | .04 | .01 |
| ☐ 583T | Tommy Helms | .10 | .04 | .01 |
| ☐ 592T | Willie Randolph | .50 | .20 | .05 |
| ☐ 618T | Jack Brohamer | .10 | .04 | .01 |
| ☐ 632T | Rogelio Moret | .10 | .04 | .01 |
| ☐ 649T | Dave Roberts | .10 | .04 | .01 |
| ☐ xxxx | Traded Checklist (unnumbered) | .40 | .04 | .00 |

## 1977 Topps

The cards in this 660 card set measure 2 1/2" by 3 1/2". In 1977, for the fifth consecutive year, Topps produced a 660 card baseball set. The player's name, team affiliation and his position are compactly arranged over the picture area and a facsimile autograph apears on the photo. Team cards feature a checklist of that team's players in the set and a small picture of the manager on the front of the card. Appearing for the first time are the series "Brothers" (631-634) and "Turn Back The Clock" (433-437). Other sub-series in the set are League Leaders (1-8), Record breakers (231-234), Playoffs cards (276-277), World Series cards (411-413), and Rookie prospects (472-479 and 487-494). The key card in the set is the rookie card of Dale Murphy (476).

| | | | MINT | VG-E | F-G |
|---|---|---|---|---|---|
| COMPLETE SET | | | 180.00 | 75.00 | 18.00 |
| COMMON PLAYER (1-660) | | | .11 | .05 | .01 |
| | | | | | |
| ☐ 1 | Batting Leaders: George Brett Bill Madlock | | 1.25 | .25 | .05 |
| ☐ 2 | Home Run Leaders: Graig Nettles Mike Schmidt | | .60 | .24 | .06 |
| ☐ 3 | RBI Leaders: Lee May George Foster | | .30 | .12 | .03 |
| ☐ 4 | Stolen Base Leaders: Bill North Dave Lopes | | .20 | .08 | .02 |
| ☐ 5 | Victory Leaders: Jim Palmer Randy Jones | | .35 | .14 | .03 |
| ☐ 6 | Strikeout Leaders: Nolan Ryan Tom Seaver | | 1.25 | .50 | .12 |
| ☐ 7 | ERA Leaders: Mark Fidrych John Denny | | .20 | .08 | .02 |
| ☐ 8 | Leading Firemen: Bill Campbell Rawly Eastwick | | .15 | .06 | .01 |
| ☐ 9 | Doug Rader | | .15 | .06 | .01 |
| ☐ 10 | Reggie Jackson | | 5.50 | 2.20 | .55 |
| ☐ 11 | Rob Dressler | | .11 | .05 | .01 |
| ☐ 12 | Larry Haney | | .11 | .05 | .01 |
| ☐ 13 | Luis Gomez | | .11 | .05 | .01 |
| ☐ 14 | Tommy Smith | | .15 | .06 | .01 |
| ☐ 15 | Don Gullett | | .15 | .06 | .01 |
| ☐ 16 | Bob Jones | | .11 | .05 | .01 |
| ☐ 17 | Steve Stone | | .15 | .06 | .01 |
| ☐ 18 | Indians Team/Mgr. Frank Robinson (checklist back) | | .50 | .10 | .02 |
| ☐ 19 | John D'Acquisto | | .11 | .05 | .01 |
| ☐ 20 | Graig Nettles | | .80 | .32 | .08 |
| ☐ 21 | Ken Forsch | | .15 | .06 | .01 |
| ☐ 22 | Bill Freehan | | .20 | .08 | .02 |
| ☐ 23 | Dan Driessen | | .15 | .06 | .01 |
| ☐ 24 | Carl Morton | | .11 | .05 | .01 |

| | | | | |
|---|---|---|---|---|
| ☐ 25 | Dwight Evans | .40 | .16 | .04 |
| ☐ 26 | Ray Sadecki | .11 | .05 | .01 |
| ☐ 27 | Bill Buckner | .35 | .14 | .03 |
| ☐ 28 | Woodie Fryman | .11 | .05 | .01 |
| ☐ 29 | Bucky Dent | .20 | .08 | .02 |
| ☐ 30 | Greg Luzinski | .35 | .14 | .03 |
| ☐ 31 | Jim Todd | .11 | .05 | .01 |
| ☐ 32 | Checklist 1 | .50 | .05 | .01 |
| ☐ 33 | Wayne Garland | .11 | .05 | .01 |
| ☐ 34 | Angels Team/Mgr. | .40 | .08 | .01 |
| | Norm Sherry | | | |
| | (checklist back) | | | |
| ☐ 35 | Rennie Stennett | .11 | .05 | .01 |
| ☐ 36 | John Ellis | .11 | .05 | .01 |
| ☐ 37 | Steve Hargan | .11 | .05 | .01 |
| ☐ 38 | Craig Kusick | .11 | .05 | .01 |
| ☐ 39 | Tom Griffin | .11 | .05 | .01 |
| ☐ 40 | Bobby Murcer | .30 | .12 | .03 |
| ☐ 41 | Jim Kern | .11 | .05 | .01 |
| ☐ 42 | Jose Cruz | .35 | .14 | .03 |
| ☐ 43 | Ray Bare | .11 | .05 | .01 |
| ☐ 44 | Bud Harrelson | .15 | .06 | .01 |
| ☐ 45 | Rawly Eastwick | .11 | .05 | .01 |
| ☐ 46 | Buck Martinez | .11 | .05 | .01 |
| ☐ 47 | Lynn McGlothen | .11 | .05 | .01 |
| ☐ 48 | Tom Paciorek | .11 | .05 | .01 |
| ☐ 49 | Grant Jackson | .11 | .05 | .01 |
| ☐ 50 | Ron Cey | .40 | .16 | .04 |
| ☐ 51 | Brewers Team/Mgr. | .40 | .08 | .01 |
| | Alex Grammas | | | |
| | (checklist back) | | | |
| ☐ 52 | Ellis Valentine | .15 | .06 | .01 |
| ☐ 53 | Paul Mitchell | .11 | .05 | .01 |
| ☐ 54 | Sandy Alomar | .11 | .05 | .01 |
| ☐ 55 | Jeff Burroughs | .15 | .06 | .01 |
| ☐ 56 | Rudy May | .11 | .05 | .01 |
| ☐ 57 | Marc Hill | .11 | .05 | .01 |
| ☐ 58 | Chet Lemon | .30 | .12 | .03 |
| ☐ 59 | Larry Christenson | .11 | .05 | .01 |
| ☐ 60 | Jim Rice | 6.00 | 2.40 | .60 |
| ☐ 61 | Manny Sanguillen | .15 | .06 | .01 |
| ☐ 62 | Eric Raich | .11 | .05 | .01 |
| ☐ 63 | Tito Fuentes | .11 | .05 | .01 |
| ☐ 64 | Larry Biittner | .11 | .05 | .01 |
| ☐ 65 | Skip Lockwood | .11 | .05 | .01 |
| ☐ 66 | Roy Smalley | .15 | .06 | .01 |
| ☐ 67 | Joaquin Andujar | 1.25 | .50 | .12 |
| ☐ 68 | Bruce Bochte | .15 | .06 | .01 |
| ☐ 69 | Jim Crawford | .11 | .05 | .01 |
| ☐ 70 | Johnny Bench | 2.75 | 1.10 | .27 |
| ☐ 71 | Dock Ellis | .11 | .05 | .01 |
| ☐ 72 | Mike Anderson | .11 | .05 | .01 |
| ☐ 73 | Charles Williams | .11 | .05 | .01 |
| ☐ 74 | A's Team/Mgr. | .40 | .08 | .01 |
| | Jack McKeon | | | |
| | (checklist back) | | | |
| ☐ 75 | Dennis Leonard | .20 | .08 | .02 |
| ☐ 76 | Tim Foli | .11 | .05 | .01 |
| ☐ 77 | Dyar Miller | .11 | .05 | .01 |
| ☐ 78 | Bob Davis | .11 | .05 | .01 |
| ☐ 79 | Don Money | .11 | .05 | .01 |
| ☐ 80 | Andy Messersmith | .15 | .06 | .01 |
| ☐ 81 | Juan Beniquez | .15 | .06 | .01 |
| ☐ 82 | Jim Rooker | .11 | .05 | .01 |
| ☐ 83 | Kevin Bell | .11 | .05 | .01 |
| ☐ 84 | Ollie Brown | .11 | .05 | .01 |
| ☐ 85 | Duane Kuiper | .11 | .05 | .01 |
| ☐ 86 | Pat Zachry | .11 | .05 | .01 |
| ☐ 87 | Glenn Borgmann | .11 | .05 | .01 |
| ☐ 88 | Stan Wall | .11 | .05 | .01 |
| ☐ 89 | Butch Hobson | .11 | .05 | .01 |
| ☐ 90 | Cesar Cedeno | .20 | .08 | .02 |
| ☐ 91 | John Verhoeven | .11 | .05 | .01 |
| ☐ 92 | Dave Rosello | .11 | .05 | .01 |
| ☐ 93 | Tom Poquette | .11 | .05 | .01 |
| ☐ 94 | Craig Swan | .15 | .06 | .01 |
| ☐ 95 | Keith Hernandez | 2.50 | 1.00 | .25 |
| ☐ 96 | Lou Piniella | .25 | .10 | .02 |
| ☐ 97 | Dave Heaverlo | .11 | .05 | .01 |
| ☐ 98 | Milt May | .11 | .05 | .01 |
| ☐ 99 | Tom Hausman | .11 | .05 | .01 |
| ☐ 100 | Joe Morgan | 1.25 | .50 | .12 |
| ☐ 101 | Dick Bosman | .11 | .05 | .01 |
| ☐ 102 | Jose Morales | .11 | .05 | .01 |
| ☐ 103 | Mike Bacsik | .11 | .05 | .01 |
| ☐ 104 | Omar Moreno | .25 | .10 | .02 |
| ☐ 105 | Steve Yeager | .15 | .06 | .01 |
| ☐ 106 | Mike Flanagan | .25 | .10 | .02 |
| ☐ 107 | Bill Melton | .11 | .05 | .01 |
| ☐ 108 | Alan Foster | .11 | .05 | .01 |
| ☐ 109 | Jorge Orta | .11 | .05 | .01 |
| ☐ 110 | Steve Carlton | 3.50 | 1.40 | .35 |
| ☐ 111 | Rico Petrocelli | .15 | .06 | .01 |

| | | | | |
|---|---|---|---|---|
| ☐ 112 | Bill Greif | .11 | .05 | .01 |
| ☐ 113 | Blue Jays Leaders: | .30 | .06 | .01 |
| | Roy Hartsfield MGR | | | |
| | Don Leppert CO | | | |
| | Bob Miller CO | | | |
| | Jackie Moore CO | | | |
| | Harry Warner CO | | | |
| | (checklist back) | | | |
| ☐ 114 | Bruce Dal Canton | .11 | .05 | .01 |
| ☐ 115 | Rick Manning | .15 | .06 | .01 |
| ☐ 116 | Joe Niekro | .25 | .10 | .02 |
| ☐ 117 | Frank White | .25 | .10 | .02 |
| ☐ 118 | Rick Jones | .11 | .05 | .01 |
| ☐ 119 | John Stearns | .15 | .06 | .01 |
| ☐ 120 | Rod Carew | 3.50 | 1.40 | .35 |
| ☐ 121 | Gary Nolan | .11 | .05 | .01 |
| ☐ 122 | Ben Oglivie | .20 | .08 | .02 |
| ☐ 123 | Fred Stanley | .11 | .05 | .01 |
| ☐ 124 | George Mitterwald | .11 | .05 | .01 |
| ☐ 125 | Bill Travers | .11 | .05 | .01 |
| ☐ 126 | Rod Gilbreath | .11 | .05 | .01 |
| ☐ 127 | Ron Fairly | .15 | .06 | .01 |
| ☐ 128 | Tommy John | .55 | .22 | .05 |
| ☐ 129 | Mike Sadek | .11 | .05 | .01 |
| ☐ 130 | Al Oliver | .55 | .22 | .05 |
| ☐ 131 | Orlando Ramirez | .11 | .05 | .01 |
| ☐ 132 | Chip Lang | .11 | .05 | .01 |
| ☐ 133 | Ralph Garr | .15 | .06 | .01 |
| ☐ 134 | Padres Team/Mgr. | .40 | .08 | .01 |
| | John McNamara | | | |
| | (checklist back) | | | |
| ☐ 135 | Mark Belanger | .15 | .06 | .01 |
| ☐ 136 | Jerry Mumphrey | .35 | .14 | .03 |
| ☐ 137 | Jeff Terpko | .11 | .05 | .01 |
| ☐ 138 | Bob Stinson | .11 | .05 | .01 |
| ☐ 139 | Fred Norman | .11 | .05 | .01 |
| ☐ 140 | Mike Schmidt | 7.00 | 2.80 | .70 |
| ☐ 141 | Mark Littell | .11 | .05 | .01 |
| ☐ 142 | Steve Dillard | .11 | .05 | .01 |
| ☐ 143 | Ed Herrmann | .11 | .05 | .01 |
| ☐ 144 | Bruce Sutter | 3.00 | 1.20 | .30 |
| ☐ 145 | Tom Veryzer | .11 | .05 | .01 |
| ☐ 146 | Dusty Baker | .25 | .10 | .02 |
| ☐ 147 | Jackie Brown | .11 | .05 | .01 |
| ☐ 148 | Fran Healy | .11 | .05 | .01 |
| ☐ 149 | Mike Cubbage | .11 | .05 | .01 |
| ☐ 150 | Tom Seaver | 3.00 | 1.20 | .30 |
| ☐ 151 | Johnny LeMaster | .11 | .05 | .01 |
| ☐ 152 | Gaylord Perry | 1.25 | .50 | .12 |
| ☐ 153 | Ron Jackson | .11 | .05 | .01 |
| ☐ 154 | Dave Giusti | .11 | .05 | .01 |
| ☐ 155 | Joe Rudi | .15 | .06 | .01 |
| ☐ 156 | Pete Mackanin | .11 | .05 | .01 |
| ☐ 157 | Ken Brett | .11 | .05 | .01 |
| ☐ 158 | Ted Kubiak | .11 | .05 | .01 |
| ☐ 159 | Bernie Carbo | .11 | .05 | .01 |
| ☐ 160 | Will McEnaney | .11 | .05 | .01 |
| ☐ 161 | Garry Templeton | 1.25 | .50 | .12 |
| ☐ 162 | Mike Cuellar | .15 | .06 | .01 |
| ☐ 163 | Dave Hilton | .11 | .05 | .01 |
| ☐ 164 | Tug McGraw | .25 | .10 | .02 |
| ☐ 165 | Jim Wynn | .15 | .06 | .01 |
| ☐ 166 | Bill Campbell | .15 | .06 | .01 |
| ☐ 167 | Rich Hebner | .11 | .05 | .01 |
| ☐ 168 | Charlie Spikes | .11 | .05 | .01 |
| ☐ 169 | Darold Knowles | .11 | .05 | .01 |
| ☐ 170 | Thurman Munson | 2.75 | 1.10 | .27 |
| ☐ 171 | Ken Sanders | .11 | .05 | .01 |
| ☐ 172 | John Milner | .11 | .05 | .01 |
| ☐ 173 | Chuck Scrivener | .11 | .05 | .01 |
| ☐ 174 | Nelson Briles | .15 | .06 | .01 |
| ☐ 175 | Butch Wynegar | .65 | .26 | .06 |
| ☐ 176 | Bob Robertson | .11 | .05 | .01 |
| ☐ 177 | Bart Johnson | .11 | .05 | .01 |
| ☐ 178 | Bombo Rivera | .11 | .05 | .01 |
| ☐ 179 | Paul Hartzell | .11 | .05 | .01 |
| ☐ 180 | Dave Lopes | .25 | .10 | .02 |
| ☐ 181 | Ken McMullen | .11 | .05 | .01 |
| ☐ 182 | Dan Spillner | .11 | .05 | .01 |
| ☐ 183 | Cardinals Team/Mgr. | .40 | .08 | .01 |
| | Vern Rapp | | | |
| | (checklist back) | | | |
| ☐ 184 | Bo McLaughlin | .11 | .05 | .01 |
| ☐ 185 | Sixto Lezcano | .15 | .06 | .01 |
| ☐ 186 | Doug Flynn | .11 | .05 | .01 |
| ☐ 187 | Dick Pole | .11 | .05 | .01 |
| ☐ 188 | Bob Tolan | .11 | .05 | .01 |
| ☐ 189 | Rick Dempsey | .15 | .06 | .01 |
| ☐ 190 | Ray Burris | .11 | .05 | .01 |
| ☐ 191 | Doug Griffin | .11 | .05 | .01 |
| ☐ 192 | Clarence Gaston | .11 | .05 | .01 |
| ☐ 193 | Larry Gura | .15 | .06 | .01 |
| ☐ 194 | Gary Matthews | .25 | .10 | .02 |

| | | | | |
|---|---|---|---|---|
| ☐ 195 | Ed Figueroa | .11 | .05 | .01 |
| ☐ 196 | Len Randle | .11 | .05 | .01 |
| ☐ 197 | Ed Ott | .11 | .05 | .01 |
| ☐ 198 | Wilbur Wood | .15 | .06 | .01 |
| ☐ 199 | Pepe Frias | .11 | .05 | .01 |
| ☐ 200 | Frank Tanana | .20 | .08 | .02 |
| ☐ 201 | Ed Kranepool | .15 | .06 | .01 |
| ☐ 202 | Tom Johnson | .11 | .05 | .01 |
| ☐ 203 | Ed Armbrister | .11 | .05 | .01 |
| ☐ 204 | Jeff Newman | .11 | .05 | .01 |
| ☐ 205 | Pete Falcone | .11 | .05 | .01 |
| ☐ 206 | Boog Powell | .30 | .12 | .03 |
| ☐ 207 | Glenn Abbott | .11 | .05 | .01 |
| ☐ 208 | Checklist 2 | .50 | .05 | .01 |
| ☐ 209 | Rob Andrews | .11 | .05 | .01 |
| ☐ 210 | Fred Lynn | 1.50 | .60 | .15 |
| ☐ 211 | Giants Team/Mgr. | .40 | .08 | .01 |
| | Joe Altobelli | | | |
| | (checklist back) | | | |
| ☐ 212 | Jim Mason | .11 | .05 | .01 |
| ☐ 213 | Maximino Leon | .11 | .05 | .01 |
| ☐ 214 | Darrell Porter | .15 | .06 | .01 |
| ☐ 215 | Butch Metzger | .11 | .05 | .01 |
| ☐ 216 | Doug DeCinces | .35 | .14 | .03 |
| ☐ 217 | Tom Underwood | .11 | .05 | .01 |
| ☐ 218 | John Wathan | .25 | .10 | .02 |
| ☐ 219 | Joe Coleman | .11 | .05 | .01 |
| ☐ 220 | Chris Chambliss | .20 | .08 | .02 |
| ☐ 221 | Bob Bailey | .11 | .05 | .01 |
| ☐ 222 | Fran Barrios | .11 | .05 | .01 |
| ☐ 223 | Earl Williams | .11 | .05 | .01 |
| ☐ 224 | Rusty Torres | .11 | .05 | .01 |
| ☐ 225 | Bob Apodaca | .11 | .05 | .01 |
| ☐ 226 | Leroy Stanton | .11 | .05 | .01 |
| ☐ 227 | Joe Sambito | .30 | .12 | .03 |
| ☐ 228 | Twins Team/Mgr. | .40 | .08 | .01 |
| | Gene Mauch | | | |
| | (checklist back) | | | |
| ☐ 229 | Don Kessinger | .15 | .06 | .01 |
| ☐ 230 | Vida Blue | .25 | .10 | .02 |
| ☐ 231 | RB: George Brett | 1.50 | .60 | .15 |
| | Most cons. games | | | |
| | with 3 or more hits | | | |
| ☐ 232 | RB: Minnie Minoso | .20 | .08 | .02 |
| | Oldest to Hit Safely | | | |
| ☐ 233 | RB: Jose Morales, Most | .15 | .06 | .01 |
| | pinch-hits, Season | | | |
| ☐ 234 | RB: Nolan Ryan | 1.00 | .40 | .10 |
| | Most seasons 300 | | | |
| | or more Strikouts | | | |
| ☐ 235 | Cecil Cooper | .65 | .26 | .06 |
| ☐ 236 | Tom Buskey | .11 | .05 | .01 |
| ☐ 237 | Gene Clines | .11 | .05 | .01 |
| ☐ 238 | Tippy Martinez | .15 | .06 | .01 |
| ☐ 239 | Bill Plummer | .11 | .05 | .01 |
| ☐ 240 | Ron LeFlore | .20 | .08 | .02 |
| ☐ 241 | Dave Tomlin | .11 | .05 | .01 |
| ☐ 242 | Ken Henderson | .11 | .05 | .01 |
| ☐ 243 | Ron Reed | .11 | .05 | .01 |
| ☐ 244 | John Mayberry | .25 | .10 | .02 |
| | (cartoon mentions | | | |
| | T206 Wagner) | | | |
| ☐ 245 | Rick Rhoden | .25 | .10 | .02 |
| ☐ 246 | Mike Vail | .11 | .05 | .01 |
| ☐ 247 | Chris Knapp | .11 | .05 | .01 |
| ☐ 248 | Wilbur Howard | .11 | .05 | .01 |
| ☐ 249 | Pete Redfern | .11 | .05 | .01 |
| ☐ 250 | Bill Madlock | .75 | .30 | .07 |
| ☐ 251 | Tony Muser | .11 | .05 | .01 |
| ☐ 252 | Dale Murray | .11 | .05 | .01 |
| ☐ 253 | John Hale | .11 | .05 | .01 |
| ☐ 254 | Doyle Alexander | .15 | .06 | .01 |
| ☐ 255 | George Scott | .15 | .06 | .01 |
| ☐ 256 | Joe Hoerner | .11 | .05 | .01 |
| ☐ 257 | Mike Miley | .11 | .05 | .01 |
| ☐ 258 | Luis Tiant | .25 | .10 | .02 |
| ☐ 259 | Mets Team/Mgr. | .50 | .10 | .02 |
| | Joe Frazier | | | |
| | (checklist back) | | | |
| ☐ 260 | J.R. Richard | .25 | .10 | .02 |
| ☐ 261 | Phil Garner | .15 | .06 | .01 |
| ☐ 262 | Al Cowens | .15 | .06 | .01 |
| ☐ 263 | Mike Marshall | .15 | .06 | .01 |
| ☐ 264 | Tom Hutton | .11 | .05 | .01 |
| ☐ 265 | Mark Fidrych | .50 | .20 | .05 |
| ☐ 266 | Derrel Thomas | .11 | .05 | .01 |
| ☐ 267 | Ray Fosse | .11 | .05 | .01 |
| ☐ 268 | Rick Sawyer | .11 | .05 | .01 |
| ☐ 269 | Joe Lis | .11 | .05 | .01 |
| ☐ 270 | Dave Parker | 1.75 | .70 | .17 |
| ☐ 271 | Terry Forster | .25 | .10 | .02 |
| ☐ 272 | Lee Lacy | .20 | .08 | .02 |
| ☐ 273 | Eric Soderholm | .11 | .05 | .01 |

| | | | | |
|---|---|---|---|---|
| ☐ 274 | Don Stanhouse | .11 | .05 | .01 |
| ☐ 275 | Mike Hargrove | .15 | .06 | .01 |
| ☐ 276 | A.L. Champs: | .35 | .14 | .03 |
| | Chambliss' homer | | | |
| | decides it | | | |
| ☐ 277 | N.L. Champs: | .35 | .14 | .03 |
| | Reds sweep Phillies | | | |
| ☐ 278 | Danny Frisella | .11 | .05 | .01 |
| ☐ 279 | Joe Wallis | .11 | .05 | .01 |
| ☐ 280 | Jim Hunter | 1.00 | .40 | .10 |
| ☐ 281 | Roy Staiger | .11 | .05 | .01 |
| ☐ 282 | Sid Monge | .11 | .05 | .01 |
| ☐ 283 | Jerry DaVanon | .11 | .05 | .01 |
| ☐ 284 | Mike Norris | .15 | .06 | .01 |
| ☐ 285 | Brooks Robinson | 1.75 | .70 | .17 |
| ☐ 286 | Johnny Grubb | .11 | .05 | .01 |
| ☐ 287 | Reds Team/Mgr. | .50 | .10 | .02 |
| | Sparky Anderson | | | |
| | (checklist back) | | | |
| ☐ 288 | Bob Montgomery | .11 | .05 | .01 |
| ☐ 289 | Gene Garber | .15 | .06 | .01 |
| ☐ 290 | Amos Otis | .20 | .08 | .02 |
| ☐ 291 | Jason Thompson | .60 | .24 | .06 |
| ☐ 292 | Rogelio Moret | .11 | .05 | .01 |
| ☐ 293 | Jack Brohamer | .11 | .05 | .01 |
| ☐ 294 | George Medich | .15 | .06 | .01 |
| ☐ 295 | Gary Carter | 6.00 | 2.40 | .60 |
| ☐ 296 | Don Hood | .11 | .05 | .01 |
| ☐ 297 | Ken Reitz | .11 | .05 | .01 |
| ☐ 298 | Charlie Hough | .25 | .10 | .02 |
| ☐ 299 | Otto Velez | .11 | .05 | .01 |
| ☐ 300 | Jerry Koosman | .25 | .10 | .02 |
| ☐ 301 | Toby Harrah | .15 | .06 | .01 |
| ☐ 302 | Mike Garman | .11 | .05 | .01 |
| ☐ 303 | Gene Tenace | .15 | .06 | .01 |
| ☐ 304 | Jim Hughes | .11 | .05 | .01 |
| ☐ 305 | Mickey Rivers | .15 | .06 | .01 |
| ☐ 306 | Rick Waits | .11 | .05 | .01 |
| ☐ 307 | Gary Sutherland | .11 | .05 | .01 |
| ☐ 308 | Gene Pentz | .11 | .05 | .01 |
| ☐ 309 | Red Sox Team/Mgr. | .40 | .08 | .01 |
| | Don Zimmer | | | |
| | (checklist back) | | | |
| ☐ 310 | Larry Bowa | .35 | .14 | .03 |
| ☐ 311 | Vern Ruhle | .11 | .05 | .01 |
| ☐ 312 | Rob Belloir | .11 | .05 | .01 |
| ☐ 313 | Paul Blair | .15 | .06 | .01 |
| ☐ 314 | Steve Mingori | .11 | .05 | .01 |
| ☐ 315 | Dave Chalk | .11 | .05 | .01 |
| ☐ 316 | Steve Rogers | .20 | .08 | .02 |
| ☐ 317 | Kurt Bevacqua | .11 | .05 | .01 |
| ☐ 318 | Duffy Dyer | .11 | .05 | .01 |
| ☐ 319 | Rich Gossage | .70 | .28 | .07 |
| ☐ 320 | Ken Griffey | .25 | .10 | .02 |
| ☐ 321 | Dave Goltz | .15 | .06 | .01 |
| ☐ 322 | Bill Russell | .15 | .06 | .01 |
| ☐ 323 | Larry Lintz | .11 | .05 | .01 |
| ☐ 324 | John Curtis | .11 | .05 | .01 |
| ☐ 325 | Mike Ivie | .11 | .05 | .01 |
| ☐ 326 | Jesse Jefferson | .11 | .05 | .01 |
| ☐ 327 | Astros Team/Mgr. | .40 | .08 | .01 |
| | Bill Virdon | | | |
| | (checklist back) | | | |
| ☐ 328 | Tommy Boggs | .11 | .05 | .01 |
| ☐ 329 | Ron Hodges | .11 | .05 | .01 |
| ☐ 330 | George Hendrick | .25 | .10 | .02 |
| ☐ 331 | Jim Colborn | .11 | .05 | .01 |
| ☐ 332 | Elliott Maddox | .11 | .05 | .01 |
| ☐ 333 | Paul Reuschel | .11 | .05 | .01 |
| ☐ 334 | Bill Stein | .11 | .05 | .01 |
| ☐ 335 | Bill Robinson | .11 | .05 | .01 |
| ☐ 336 | Denny Doyle | .11 | .05 | .01 |
| ☐ 337 | Ron Schueler | .11 | .05 | .01 |
| ☐ 338 | Dave Duncan | .11 | .05 | .01 |
| ☐ 339 | Adrian Devine | .11 | .05 | .01 |
| ☐ 340 | Hal McRae | .20 | .08 | .02 |
| ☐ 341 | Joe Kerrigan | .11 | .05 | .01 |
| ☐ 342 | Jerry Remy | .15 | .06 | .01 |
| ☐ 343 | Ed Halicki | .11 | .05 | .01 |
| ☐ 344 | Brian Downing | .15 | .06 | .01 |
| ☐ 345 | Reggie Smith | .25 | .10 | .02 |
| ☐ 346 | Bill Singer | .11 | .05 | .01 |
| ☐ 347 | George Foster | .90 | .36 | .09 |
| ☐ 348 | Brent Strom | .11 | .05 | .01 |
| ☐ 349 | Jim Holt | .11 | .05 | .01 |
| ☐ 350 | Larry Dierker | .15 | .06 | .01 |
| ☐ 351 | Jim Sundberg | .15 | .06 | .01 |
| ☐ 352 | Mike Phillips | .11 | .05 | .01 |
| ☐ 353 | Stan Thomas | .11 | .05 | .01 |
| ☐ 354 | Pirates Team/Mgr. | .40 | .08 | .01 |
| | Chuck Tanner | | | |
| | (checklist back) | | | |
| ☐ 355 | Lou Brock | 1.50 | .60 | .15 |

| | | | | |
|---|---|---|---|---|
| ☐ 356 | Checklist 3 | .50 | .05 | .01 |
| ☐ 357 | Tim McCarver | .20 | .08 | .02 |
| ☐ 358 | Tom House | .15 | .06 | .01 |
| ☐ 359 | Willie Randolph | .35 | .14 | .03 |
| ☐ 360 | Rick Monday | .15 | .06 | .01 |
| ☐ 361 | Ed Rodriguez | .11 | .05 | .01 |
| ☐ 362 | Tommy Davis | .20 | .08 | .02 |
| ☐ 363 | Dave Roberts | .11 | .05 | .01 |
| ☐ 364 | Vic Correll | .11 | .05 | .01 |
| ☐ 365 | Mike Torrez | .15 | .06 | .01 |
| ☐ 366 | Ted Sizemore | .11 | .05 | .01 |
| ☐ 367 | Dave Hamilton | .11 | .05 | .01 |
| ☐ 368 | Mike Jorgensen | .11 | .05 | .01 |
| ☐ 369 | Terry Humphrey | .11 | .05 | .01 |
| ☐ 370 | John Montefusco | .15 | .06 | .01 |
| ☐ 371 | Royals Team/Mgr. Whitey Herzog (checklist back) | .40 | .08 | .01 |
| ☐ 372 | Rich Folkers | .11 | .05 | .01 |
| ☐ 373 | Bert Campaneris | .20 | .08 | .02 |
| ☐ 374 | Kent Tekulve | .20 | .08 | .02 |
| ☐ 375 | Larry Hisle | .15 | .06 | .01 |
| ☐ 376 | Nino Espinosa | .11 | .05 | .01 |
| ☐ 377 | Dave McKay | .11 | .05 | .01 |
| ☐ 378 | Jim Umbarger | .11 | .05 | .01 |
| ☐ 379 | Larry Cox | .11 | .05 | .01 |
| ☐ 380 | Lee May | .20 | .08 | .02 |
| ☐ 381 | Bob Forsch | .20 | .08 | .02 |
| ☐ 382 | Charlie Moore | .11 | .05 | .01 |
| ☐ 383 | Stan Bahnsen | .11 | .05 | .01 |
| ☐ 384 | Darrel Chaney | .11 | .05 | .01 |
| ☐ 385 | Dave LaRoche | .11 | .05 | .01 |
| ☐ 386 | Manny Mota | .15 | .06 | .01 |
| ☐ 387 | Yankees Team | .50 | .20 | .05 |
| ☐ 388 | Terry Harmon | .11 | .05 | .01 |
| ☐ 389 | Ken Kravec | .11 | .05 | .01 |
| ☐ 390 | Dave Winfield | 2.75 | 1.10 | .27 |
| ☐ 391 | Dan Warthen | .11 | .05 | .01 |
| ☐ 392 | Phil Roof | .11 | .05 | .01 |
| ☐ 393 | John Lowenstein | .11 | .05 | .01 |
| ☐ 394 | Bill Laxton | .11 | .05 | .01 |
| ☐ 395 | Manny Trillo | .15 | .06 | .01 |
| ☐ 396 | Tom Murphy | .11 | .05 | .01 |
| ☐ 397 | Larry Herndon | .45 | .18 | .04 |
| ☐ 398 | Tom Burgmeier | .11 | .05 | .01 |
| ☐ 399 | Bruce Boisclair | .11 | .05 | .01 |
| ☐ 400 | Steve Garvey | 3.00 | 1.20 | .30 |
| ☐ 401 | Mickey Scott | .11 | .05 | .01 |
| ☐ 402 | Tommy Helms | .11 | .05 | .01 |
| ☐ 403 | Tom Grieve | .15 | .06 | .01 |
| ☐ 404 | Eric Rasmussen | .11 | .05 | .01 |
| ☐ 405 | Claudell Washington | .20 | .08 | .02 |
| ☐ 406 | Tim Johnson | .11 | .05 | .01 |
| ☐ 407 | Dave Freisleben | .11 | .05 | .01 |
| ☐ 408 | Cesar Tovar | .11 | .05 | .01 |
| ☐ 409 | Pete Broberg | .11 | .05 | .01 |
| ☐ 410 | Willie Montanez | .11 | .05 | .01 |
| ☐ 411 | W.S. Games 1 and 2 Morgan homers opener; Bench stars as Reds take 2nd game | .40 | .16 | .04 |
| ☐ 412 | W.S. Games 3 and 4 Reds' stop Yankees; Bench's two homers wrap it up | .40 | .16 | .04 |
| ☐ 413 | World Series Summary Cincy wins 2nd straight series | .40 | .16 | .04 |
| ☐ 414 | Tommy Harper | .15 | .06 | .01 |
| ☐ 415 | Jay Johnstone | .15 | .06 | .01 |
| ☐ 416 | Chuck Hartenstein | .11 | .05 | .01 |
| ☐ 417 | Wayne Garrett | .11 | .05 | .01 |
| ☐ 418 | White Sox Team/Mgr. Bob Lemon (checklist back) | .50 | .10 | .02 |
| ☐ 419 | Steve Swisher | .11 | .05 | .01 |
| ☐ 420 | Rusty Staub | .25 | .10 | .02 |
| ☐ 421 | Doug Rau | .11 | .05 | .01 |
| ☐ 422 | Freddie Patek | .11 | .05 | .01 |
| ☐ 423 | Gary Lavelle | .15 | .06 | .01 |
| ☐ 424 | Steve Brye | .11 | .05 | .01 |
| ☐ 425 | Joe Torre | .35 | .14 | .03 |
| ☐ 426 | Dick Drago | .11 | .05 | .01 |
| ☐ 427 | Dave Rader | .11 | .05 | .01 |
| ☐ 428 | Rangers Team/Mgr. Frank Lucchesi (checklist back) | .40 | .08 | .01 |
| ☐ 429 | Ken Boswell | .11 | .05 | .01 |
| ☐ 430 | Fergie Jenkins | .40 | .16 | .04 |
| ☐ 431 | Dave Collins (photo actually Bobby Jones) | .25 | .10 | .02 |
| ☐ 432 | Buzz Capra | .11 | .05 | .01 |

| | | | | |
|---|---|---|---|---|
| ☐ 433 | Turn Back Clock 1972 Nate Colbert | .15 | .06 | .01 |
| ☐ 434 | Turn Back Clock 1967 Yaz Triple Crown | 1.50 | .60 | .15 |
| ☐ 435 | Turn Back Clock 1962 Wills 104 Steals | .40 | .16 | .04 |
| ☐ 436 | Turn Back Clock 1957 Keegan hurls Majors' only No-Hitter | .15 | .06 | .01 |
| ☐ 437 | Turn Back Clock 1952 Kiner leads NL HR's 7th straight year | .40 | .16 | .04 |
| ☐ 438 | Marty Perez | .11 | .05 | .01 |
| ☐ 439 | Gorman Thomas | .35 | .14 | .03 |
| ☐ 440 | Jon Matlack | .15 | .06 | .01 |
| ☐ 441 | Larvell Blanks | .11 | .05 | .01 |
| ☐ 442 | Braves Team/Mgr. Dave Bristol (checklist back) | .40 | .08 | .01 |
| ☐ 443 | Lamar Johnson | .11 | .05 | .01 |
| ☐ 444 | Wayne Twitchell | .11 | .05 | .01 |
| ☐ 445 | Ken Singleton | .30 | .12 | .03 |
| ☐ 446 | Bill Bonham | .11 | .05 | .01 |
| ☐ 447 | Jerry Turner | .11 | .05 | .01 |
| ☐ 448 | Ellie Rodriguez | .11 | .05 | .01 |
| ☐ 449 | Al Fitzmorris | .11 | .05 | .01 |
| ☐ 450 | Pete Rose | 7.50 | 3.00 | .75 |
| ☐ 451 | Checklist 4 | .50 | .05 | .01 |
| ☐ 452 | Mike Caldwell | .15 | .06 | .01 |
| ☐ 453 | Pedro Garcia | .11 | .05 | .01 |
| ☐ 454 | Andy Etchebarren | .11 | .05 | .01 |
| ☐ 455 | Rick Wise | .15 | .06 | .01 |
| ☐ 456 | Leon Roberts | .11 | .05 | .01 |
| ☐ 457 | Steve Luebber | .11 | .05 | .01 |
| ☐ 458 | Leo Foster | .11 | .05 | .01 |
| ☐ 459 | Steve Foucault | .11 | .05 | .01 |
| ☐ 460 | Willie Stargell | 1.50 | .60 | .15 |
| ☐ 461 | Dick Tidrow | .11 | .05 | .01 |
| ☐ 462 | Don Baylor | .55 | .22 | .05 |
| ☐ 463 | Jamie Quirk | .11 | .05 | .01 |
| ☐ 464 | Randy Moffitt | .11 | .05 | .01 |
| ☐ 465 | Rico Carty | .20 | .08 | .02 |
| ☐ 466 | Fred Holdsworth | .11 | .05 | .01 |
| ☐ 467 | Phillies Team/Mgr. Danny Ozark (checklist back) | .40 | .08 | .01 |
| ☐ 468 | Ramon Hernandez | .11 | .05 | .01 |
| ☐ 469 | Pat Kelly | .11 | .05 | .01 |
| ☐ 470 | Ted Simmons | .45 | .18 | .04 |
| ☐ 471 | Del Unser | .11 | .05 | .01 |
| ☐ 472 | Rookie Pitchers: Don Aase Bob McClure Gil Patterson Dave Wehrmeister | .50 | .20 | .05 |
| ☐ 473 | Rookie Outfielders: Andre Dawson Gene Richards John Scott Denny Walling | 6.00 | 2.40 | .60 |
| ☐ 474 | Rookie Shortstops: Bob Bailor Kiko Garcia Craig Reynolds Alex Taveras | .20 | .08 | .02 |
| ☐ 475 | Rookie Pitchers: Chris Batton Rick Camp Scott McGregor Manny Sarmiento | .45 | .18 | .04 |
| ☐ 476 | Rookie Catchers: Gary Alexander Rick Cerone Dale Murphy Kevin Pasley | 48.00 | 18.00 | 4.00 |
| ☐ 477 | Rookie Infielders: Doug Ault Rich Dauer Orlando Gonzalez Phil Mankowski | .20 | .08 | .02 |
| ☐ 478 | Rookie Pitchers: Jim Gideon Leon Hooten Dave Johnson Mark Lemongello | .20 | .08 | .02 |
| ☐ 479 | Rookie Outfielders: Brian Asselstine Wayne Gross Sam Mejias Alvis Woods | .20 | .08 | .02 |
| ☐ 480 | Carl Yastrzemski | 3.50 | 1.40 | .35 |
| ☐ 481 | Roger Metzger | .11 | .05 | .01 |
| ☐ 482 | Tony Solaita | .11 | .05 | .01 |

| | | | | |
|---|---|---|---|---|
| ☐ 483 | Richie Zisk | .15 | .06 | .01 |
| ☐ 484 | Burt Hooton | .15 | .06 | .01 |
| ☐ 485 | Roy White | .15 | .06 | .01 |
| ☐ 486 | Ed Bane | .11 | .05 | .01 |
| ☐ 487 | Rookie Pitchers: Larry Anderson Ed Glynn Joe Henderson Greg Terlecky | .20 | .08 | .02 |
| ☐ 488 | Rookie Outfielders: Jack Clark Ruppert Jones Lee Mazzilli Dan Thomas | 5.00 | 2.00 | .50 |
| ☐ 489 | Rookie Pitchers: Len Barker Randy Lerch Greg Minton Mike Overy | .60 | .24 | .06 |
| ☐ 490 | Rookie Shortstops: Billy Almon Mickey Klutts Tommy McMillan Mark Wagner | .30 | .12 | .03 |
| ☐ 491 | Rookie Pitchers: Mike Dupree Denny Martinez Craig Mitchell Bob Sykes | .30 | .12 | .03 |
| ☐ 492 | Rookie Outfielders: Tony Armas Steve Kemp Carlos Lopez Gary Woods | 2.50 | 1.00 | .25 |
| ☐ 493 | Rookie Pitchers: Mike Krukow Jim Otten Gary Wheelock Mike Willis | 1.25 | .50 | .12 |
| ☐ 494 | Rookie Infielders: Juan Bernhardt Mike Champion Jim Gantner Bump Wills | .50 | .20 | .05 |
| ☐ 495 | Al Hrabosky | .15 | .06 | .01 |
| ☐ 496 | Gary Thomasson | .11 | .05 | .01 |
| ☐ 497 | Clay Carroll | .11 | .05 | .01 |
| ☐ 498 | Sal Bando | .20 | .08 | .02 |
| ☐ 499 | Pablo Torrealba | .11 | .05 | .01 |
| ☐ 500 | Dave Kingman | .50 | .20 | .05 |
| ☐ 501 | Jim Bibby | .15 | .06 | .01 |
| ☐ 502 | Randy Hundley | .11 | .05 | .01 |
| ☐ 503 | Bill Lee | .15 | .06 | .01 |
| ☐ 504 | Dodgers Team/Mgr. Tom Lasorda (checklist back) | .50 | .10 | .02 |
| ☐ 505 | Oscar Gamble | .20 | .08 | .02 |
| ☐ 506 | Steve Grilli | .11 | .05 | .01 |
| ☐ 507 | Mike Hegan | .11 | .05 | .01 |
| ☐ 508 | Dave Pagan | .11 | .05 | .01 |
| ☐ 509 | Cookie Rojas | .11 | .05 | .01 |
| ☐ 510 | John Candelaria | .25 | .10 | .02 |
| ☐ 511 | Bill Fahey | .11 | .05 | .01 |
| ☐ 512 | Jack Billingham | .11 | .05 | .01 |
| ☐ 513 | Jerry Terrell | .11 | .05 | .01 |
| ☐ 514 | Cliff Johnson | .11 | .05 | .01 |
| ☐ 515 | Chris Speier | .11 | .05 | .01 |
| ☐ 516 | Bake McBride | .15 | .06 | .01 |
| ☐ 517 | Pete Vuckovich | .50 | .20 | .05 |
| ☐ 518 | Cubs Team/Mgr. Herman Franks (checklist back) | .40 | .08 | .01 |
| ☐ 519 | Don Kirkwood | .11 | .05 | .01 |
| ☐ 520 | Garry Maddox | .15 | .06 | .01 |
| ☐ 521 | Bob Grich | .20 | .08 | .02 |
| ☐ 522 | Enzo Hernandez | .11 | .05 | .01 |
| ☐ 523 | Rollie Fingers | .60 | .24 | .06 |
| ☐ 524 | Rowland Office | .11 | .05 | .01 |
| ☐ 525 | Dennis Eckersley | .20 | .08 | .02 |
| ☐ 526 | Larry Parrish | .25 | .10 | .02 |
| ☐ 527 | Dan Meyer | .11 | .05 | .01 |
| ☐ 528 | Bill Castro | .11 | .05 | .01 |
| ☐ 529 | Jim Essian | .11 | .05 | .01 |
| ☐ 530 | Rick Reuschel | .20 | .08 | .02 |
| ☐ 531 | Lyman Bostock | .25 | .10 | .02 |
| ☐ 532 | Jim Willoughby | .11 | .05 | .01 |
| ☐ 533 | Mickey Stanley | .11 | .05 | .01 |
| ☐ 534 | Paul Splittorff | .15 | .06 | .01 |
| ☐ 535 | Cesar Geronimo | .11 | .05 | .01 |
| ☐ 536 | Vic Albury | .11 | .05 | .01 |
| ☐ 537 | Dave Roberts | .11 | .05 | .01 |
| ☐ 538 | Frank Taveras | .11 | .05 | .01 |
| ☐ 539 | Mike Wallace | .11 | .05 | .01 |
| ☐ 540 | Bob Watson | .15 | .06 | .01 |
| ☐ 541 | John Denny | .25 | .10 | .02 |
| ☐ 542 | Frank Duffy | .11 | .05 | .01 |
| ☐ 543 | Ron Blomberg | .11 | .05 | .01 |
| ☐ 544 | Gary Ross | .11 | .05 | .01 |
| ☐ 545 | Bob Boone | .20 | .08 | .02 |
| ☐ 546 | Orioles Team/Mgr. Earl Weaver (checklist back) | .50 | .10 | .02 |
| ☐ 547 | Willie McCovey | 1.50 | .60 | .15 |
| ☐ 548 | Joel Youngblood | .11 | .05 | .01 |
| ☐ 549 | Jerry Royster | .11 | .05 | .01 |
| ☐ 550 | Randy Jones | .15 | .06 | .01 |
| ☐ 551 | Bill North | .11 | .05 | .01 |
| ☐ 552 | Pepe Mangual | .11 | .05 | .01 |
| ☐ 553 | Jack Heidemann | .11 | .05 | .01 |
| ☐ 554 | Bruce Kimm | .11 | .05 | .01 |
| ☐ 555 | Dan Ford | .15 | .06 | .01 |
| ☐ 556 | Doug Bird | .11 | .05 | .01 |
| ☐ 557 | Jerry White | .11 | .05 | .01 |
| ☐ 558 | Elias Sosa | .11 | .05 | .01 |
| ☐ 559 | Alan Bannister | .11 | .05 | .01 |
| ☐ 560 | Dave Concepcion | .35 | .14 | .03 |
| ☐ 561 | Pete LaCock | .11 | .05 | .01 |
| ☐ 562 | Checklist 5 | .50 | .05 | .01 |
| ☐ 563 | Bruce Kison | .11 | .05 | .01 |
| ☐ 564 | Alan Ashby | .15 | .06 | .01 |
| ☐ 565 | Mickey Lolich | .25 | .10 | .02 |
| ☐ 566 | Rick Miller | .11 | .05 | .01 |
| ☐ 567 | Enos Cabell | .11 | .05 | .01 |
| ☐ 568 | Carlos May | .11 | .05 | .01 |
| ☐ 569 | Jim Lonborg | .15 | .06 | .01 |
| ☐ 570 | Bobby Bonds | .25 | .10 | .02 |
| ☐ 571 | Darrell Evans | .30 | .12 | .03 |
| ☐ 572 | Ross Grimsley | .11 | .05 | .01 |
| ☐ 573 | Joe Ferguson | .15 | .06 | .01 |
| ☐ 574 | Aurelio Rodriguez | .11 | .05 | .01 |
| ☐ 575 | Dick Ruthven | .11 | .05 | .01 |
| ☐ 576 | Fred Kendall | .11 | .05 | .01 |
| ☐ 577 | Jerry Augustine | .11 | .05 | .01 |
| ☐ 578 | Bob Randall | .11 | .05 | .01 |
| ☐ 579 | Don Carrithers | .11 | .05 | .01 |
| ☐ 580 | George Brett | 6.00 | 2.40 | .60 |
| ☐ 581 | Pedro Borbon | .11 | .05 | .01 |
| ☐ 582 | Ed Kirkpatrick | .11 | .05 | .01 |
| ☐ 583 | Paul Lindblad | .11 | .05 | .01 |
| ☐ 584 | Ed Goodson | .11 | .05 | .01 |
| ☐ 585 | Rick Burleson | .15 | .06 | .01 |
| ☐ 586 | Steve Renko | .11 | .05 | .01 |
| ☐ 587 | Rick Baldwin | .11 | .05 | .01 |
| ☐ 588 | Dave Moates | .11 | .05 | .01 |
| ☐ 589 | Mike Cosgrove | .11 | .05 | .01 |
| ☐ 590 | Buddy Bell | .35 | .14 | .03 |
| ☐ 591 | Chris Arnold | .11 | .05 | .01 |
| ☐ 592 | Dan Briggs | .11 | .05 | .01 |
| ☐ 593 | Dennis Blair | .11 | .05 | .01 |
| ☐ 594 | Biff Pocoroba | .11 | .05 | .01 |
| ☐ 595 | John Hiller | .15 | .06 | .01 |
| ☐ 596 | Jerry Martin | .11 | .05 | .01 |
| ☐ 597 | Mariners Leaders: Darrell Johnson MGR Don Bryant CO Jim Busby CO Vada Pinson CO Wes Stock CO (checklist back) | .30 | .06 | .01 |
| ☐ 598 | Sparky Lyle | .35 | .14 | .03 |
| ☐ 599 | Mike Tyson | .11 | .05 | .01 |
| ☐ 600 | Jim Palmer | 1.75 | .70 | .17 |
| ☐ 601 | Mike Lum | .11 | .05 | .01 |
| ☐ 602 | Andy Hassler | .11 | .05 | .01 |
| ☐ 603 | Willie Davis | .15 | .06 | .01 |
| ☐ 604 | Jim Slaton | .11 | .05 | .01 |
| ☐ 605 | Felix Millan | .11 | .05 | .01 |
| ☐ 606 | Steve Braun | .11 | .05 | .01 |
| ☐ 607 | Larry Demery | .11 | .05 | .01 |
| ☐ 608 | Roy Howell | .11 | .05 | .01 |
| ☐ 609 | Jim Barr | .11 | .05 | .01 |
| ☐ 610 | Jose Cardenal | .11 | .05 | .01 |
| ☐ 611 | Dave Lemanczyk | .11 | .05 | .01 |
| ☐ 612 | Barry Foote | .11 | .05 | .01 |
| ☐ 613 | Reggie Cleveland | .11 | .05 | .01 |
| ☐ 614 | Greg Gross | .11 | .05 | .01 |
| ☐ 615 | Phil Niekro | 1.00 | .40 | .10 |
| ☐ 616 | Tommy Sandt | .11 | .05 | .01 |
| ☐ 617 | Bobby Darwin | .11 | .05 | .01 |
| ☐ 618 | Pat Dobson | .15 | .06 | .01 |
| ☐ 619 | Johnny Oates | .11 | .05 | .01 |
| ☐ 620 | Don Sutton | 1.00 | .40 | .10 |
| ☐ 621 | Tigers Team/Mgr. Ralph Houk (checklist back) | .50 | .10 | .02 |
| ☐ 622 | Jim Wohlford | .11 | .05 | .01 |

| | | | | |
|---|---|---|---|---|
| ☐ 623 | Jack Kucek | .11 | .05 | .01 |
| ☐ 624 | Hector Cruz | .11 | .05 | .01 |
| ☐ 625 | Ken Holtzman | .15 | .06 | .01 |
| ☐ 626 | Al Bumbry | .11 | .05 | .01 |
| ☐ 627 | Bob Myrick | .11 | .05 | .01 |
| ☐ 628 | Mario Guerrero | .11 | .05 | .01 |
| ☐ 629 | Bob Valentine | .25 | .10 | .02 |
| ☐ 630 | Bert Blyleven | .40 | .16 | .04 |
| ☐ 631 | Big League Brothers: George Brett Ken Brett | 1.25 | .50 | .12 |
| ☐ 632 | Big League Brothers: Bob Forsch Ken Forsch | .25 | .10 | .02 |
| ☐ 633 | Big League Brothers: Lee May Carlos May | .25 | .10 | .02 |
| ☐ 634 | Big League Brothers: Paul Reuschel Rick Reuschel (photos switched) | .25 | .10 | .02 |
| ☐ 635 | Robin Yount | 3.50 | 1.40 | .35 |
| ☐ 636 | Santo Alcala | .11 | .05 | .01 |
| ☐ 637 | Alex Johnson | .15 | .06 | .01 |
| ☐ 638 | Jim Kaat | .40 | .16 | .04 |
| ☐ 639 | Jerry Morales | .11 | .05 | .01 |
| ☐ 640 | Carlton Fisk | .65 | .26 | .06 |
| ☐ 641 | Dan Larson | .11 | .05 | .01 |
| ☐ 642 | Willie Crawford | .11 | .05 | .01 |
| ☐ 643 | Mike Pazik | .11 | .05 | .01 |
| ☐ 644 | Matt Alexander | .11 | .05 | .01 |
| ☐ 645 | Jerry Reuss | .20 | .08 | .02 |
| ☐ 646 | Andres Mora | .11 | .05 | .01 |
| ☐ 647 | Expos Team/Mgr. Dick Williams (checklist back) | .40 | .08 | .01 |
| ☐ 648 | Jim Spencer | .11 | .05 | .01 |
| ☐ 649 | Dave Cash | .11 | .05 | .01 |
| ☐ 650 | Nolan Ryan | 2.75 | 1.10 | .27 |
| ☐ 651 | Von Joshua | .11 | .05 | .01 |
| ☐ 652 | Tom Walker | .11 | .05 | .01 |
| ☐ 653 | Diego Segui | .11 | .05 | .01 |
| ☐ 654 | Ron Pruitt | .11 | .05 | .01 |
| ☐ 655 | Tony Perez | .45 | .18 | .04 |
| ☐ 656 | Ron Guidry | 2.25 | .90 | .22 |
| ☐ 657 | Mick Kelleher | .11 | .05 | .01 |
| ☐ 658 | Marty Pattin | .11 | .05 | .01 |
| ☐ 659 | Merv Rettenmund | .11 | .05 | .01 |
| ☐ 660 | Willie Horton | .20 | .08 | .02 |

## 1977 Topps Cloth Sticker

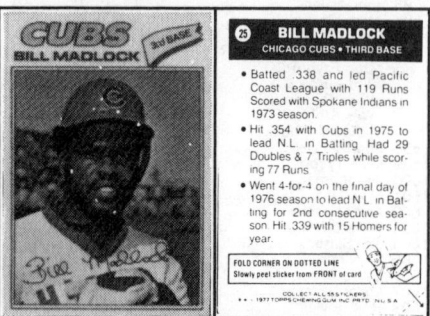

The "cards" in this 73 card set measure 2 1/2" by 3 1/2". The 1977 Cloth Stickers series was issued as a test set separately from the regular baseball series of that year. The obverse pictures are identical to those appearing in the regular set, but the backs are completely different. There are 55 player cards and 18 unnumbered checklists, the latter bearing the title "Baseball Patches". The checklists are puzzle pieces which, when properly arranged, form pictures of the A.L. and N.L. All-Star teams. Puzzle pieces are coded below by U (Upper),

M (Middle), B (Bottom), L (left), C (Center), and R (Right). Cards marked with an SP in the checklist are in shorter supply than all others in the set.

| | | MINT | VG-E | F-G |
|---|---|---|---|---|
| COMPLETE SET | | 50.00 | 20.00 | 5.00 |
| COMMON PLAYER (1-55) | | .30 | .12 | .03 |
| COMMON PUZZLE (56-73) | | .03 | .01 | .00 |
| ☐ 1 | Alan Ashby | .30 | .12 | .03 |
| ☐ 2 | Buddy Bell SP | .75 | .30 | .07 |
| ☐ 3 | Johnny Bench | 3.00 | 1.20 | .30 |
| ☐ 4 | Vida Blue | .50 | .20 | .05 |
| ☐ 5 | Bert Blyleven | .50 | .20 | .05 |
| ☐ 6 | Steve Braun SP | .50 | .20 | .05 |
| ☐ 7 | George Brett | 4.00 | 1.60 | .40 |
| ☐ 8 | Lou Brock | 2.00 | .80 | .20 |
| ☐ 9 | Jose Cardenal | .30 | .12 | .03 |
| ☐ 10 | Rod Carew SP | 3.50 | 1.40 | .35 |
| ☐ 11 | Steve Carlton | 2.50 | 1.00 | .25 |
| ☐ 12 | Dave Cash | .30 | .12 | .03 |
| ☐ 13 | Cesar Cedeno SP | .50 | .20 | .05 |
| ☐ 14 | Ron Cey | .40 | .16 | .04 |
| ☐ 15 | Mark Fidrych | .40 | .16 | .04 |
| ☐ 16 | Dan Ford | .30 | .12 | .03 |
| ☐ 17 | Wayne Garland | .30 | .12 | .03 |
| ☐ 18 | Ralph Garr | .30 | .12 | .03 |
| ☐ 19 | Steve Garvey | 3.00 | 1.20 | .30 |
| ☐ 20 | Mike Hargrove | .30 | .12 | .03 |
| ☐ 21 | Jim Hunter | .75 | .30 | .07 |
| ☐ 22 | Reggie Jackson | 4.00 | 1.60 | .40 |
| ☐ 23 | Randy Jones | .30 | .12 | .03 |
| ☐ 24 | Dave Kingman SP | 1.00 | .40 | .10 |
| ☐ 25 | Bill Madlock | .75 | .30 | .07 |
| ☐ 26 | Lee May SP | .50 | .20 | .05 |
| ☐ 27 | John Mayberry | .30 | .12 | .03 |
| ☐ 28 | John (Andy) Messersmith | .30 | .12 | .03 |
| ☐ 29 | Willie Montanez | .30 | .12 | .03 |
| ☐ 30 | John Montefusco SP | .50 | .20 | .05 |
| ☐ 31 | Joe Morgan | 1.50 | .60 | .15 |
| ☐ 32 | Thurman Munson | 2.00 | .80 | .20 |
| ☐ 33 | Bobby Murcer | .40 | .16 | .04 |
| ☐ 34 | Al Oliver SP | .75 | .30 | .07 |
| ☐ 35 | Dave Pagan | .30 | .12 | .03 |
| ☐ 36 | Jim Palmer SP | 3.00 | 1.20 | .30 |
| ☐ 37 | Tony Perez | .50 | .20 | .05 |
| ☐ 38 | Pete Rose SP | 10.00 | 4.00 | 1.00 |
| ☐ 39 | Joe Rudi | .30 | .12 | .03 |
| ☐ 40 | Nolan Ryan SP | 4.00 | 1.60 | .40 |
| ☐ 41 | Mike Schmidt | 4.00 | 1.60 | .40 |
| ☐ 42 | Tom Seaver | 3.00 | 1.20 | .30 |
| ☐ 43 | Ted Simmons | .50 | .20 | .05 |
| ☐ 44 | Bill Singer | .30 | .12 | .03 |
| ☐ 45 | Willie Stargell | 1.50 | .60 | .15 |
| ☐ 46 | Rusty Staub | .40 | .16 | .04 |
| ☐ 47 | Don Sutton | 1.00 | .40 | .10 |
| ☐ 48 | Luis Tiant | .40 | .16 | .04 |
| ☐ 49 | Bill Travers | .30 | .12 | .03 |
| ☐ 50 | Claudell Washington | .30 | .12 | .03 |
| ☐ 51 | Bob Watson | .30 | .12 | .03 |
| ☐ 52 | Dave Winfield | 2.50 | 1.00 | .25 |
| ☐ 53 | Carl Yastrzemski | 3.50 | 1.40 | .35 |
| ☐ 54 | Robin Yount | 3.00 | 1.20 | .30 |
| ☐ 55 | Richie Zisk | .30 | .12 | .03 |
| ☐ 56 | AL Puzzle UL (unnumbered) | .03 | .01 | .00 |
| ☐ 57 | AL Puzzle UC (unnumbered) | .03 | .01 | .00 |
| ☐ 58 | AL Puzzle UR (unnumbered) | .03 | .01 | .00 |
| ☐ 59 | AL Puzzle ML (unnumbered) | .03 | .01 | .00 |
| ☐ 60 | AL Puzzle MC (unnumbered) | .03 | .01 | .00 |
| ☐ 61 | AL Puzzle MR (unnumbered) | .03 | .01 | .00 |
| ☐ 62 | AL Puzzle BL SP (unnumbered) | .15 | .06 | .01 |
| ☐ 63 | AL Puzzle BC SP (unnumbered) | .15 | .06 | .01 |
| ☐ 64 | AL Puzzle BR SP (unnumbered) | .15 | .06 | .01 |
| ☐ 65 | NL Puzzle UL (unnumbered) | .03 | .01 | .00 |
| ☐ 66 | NL Puzzle UC (unnumbered) | .03 | .01 | .00 |
| ☐ 67 | NL Puzzle UR (unnumbered) | .03 | .01 | .00 |
| ☐ 68 | NL Puzzle ML (unnumbered) | .03 | .01 | .00 |
| ☐ 69 | NL Puzzle MC (unnumbered) | .03 | .01 | .00 |

| | | MINT | VG-E | F-G |
|---|---|---|---|---|
| ☐ 70 | NL Puzzle MR ................... (unnumbered) | .03 | .01 | .00 |
| ☐ 71 | NL Puzzle BL ................... (unnumbered) | .03 | .01 | .00 |
| ☐ 72 | NL Puzzle BC ................... (unnumbered) | .03 | .01 | .00 |
| ☐ 73 | NL Puzzle BR ................... (unnumbered) | .03 | .01 | .00 |

## 1978 Topps

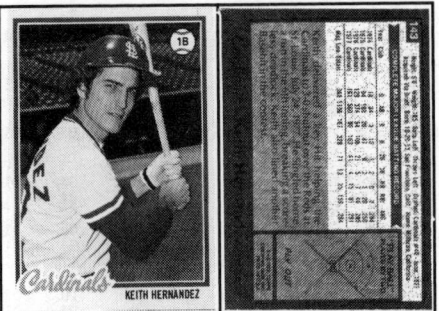

KEITH HERNANDEZ

The cards in this 726 card set measure 2 1/2" by 3 1/2". The 1978 Topps set experienced an increase in number of cards from the previous five regular issue sets of 660. Cards 1 through 7 feature record breakers (RB) of the 1977 season. Other subsets within this set include League Leaders (201-208), Post- season cards (411-413), and Rookie prospects (701-711). While no scarcities exist, 66 of the cards are more abundant in supply as they were "double printed." These 66 double printed cards are noted in the checklist by DP. Team cards again feature a checklist of that team's players in the set on the back.

| | | MINT | VG-E | F-G |
|---|---|---|---|---|
| | COMPLETE SET ........................ | 140.00 | 55.00 | 15.00 |
| | COMMON PLAYER (1-726) ........ | .09 | .04 | .01 |
| | COMMON DP's (1-726) .............. | .04 | .02 | .00 |
| ☐ 1 | RB: Lou Brock ................. Most Steals, Lifetime | 1.25 | .50 | .12 |
| ☐ 2 | RB: Sparky Lyle ................. Most Games Pure Relief, Lifetime | .15 | .06 | .01 |
| ☐ 3 | RB: Willie McCovey ......... Most times 2 HR's in inning, Lifetime | .50 | .20 | .05 |
| ☐ 4 | RB: Brooks Robinson ...... Most consecutive Seasons with one club | .75 | .30 | .07 |
| ☐ 5 | RB: Pete Rose ................. Most Hits Switch Hitter, Lifetime | 1.75 | .70 | .17 |
| ☐ 6 | RB: Nolan Ryan ............... Most Games with 10 or more Strikeouts, Lifetime | .90 | .36 | .09 |
| ☐ 7 | RB: Reggie Jackson ........ Most Homers One World Series | 1.25 | .50 | .12 |
| ☐ 8 | Mike Sadek ..................... | .09 | .04 | .01 |
| ☐ 9 | Doug DeCinces ................ | .25 | .10 | .02 |
| ☐ 10 | Phil Niekro .................... | .85 | .34 | .08 |
| ☐ 11 | Rick Manning .................. | .09 | .04 | .01 |
| ☐ 12 | Don Aase ....................... | .15 | .06 | .01 |
| ☐ 13 | Art Howe ....................... | .09 | .04 | .01 |
| ☐ 14 | Lerrin LaGrow ................. | .09 | .04 | .01 |
| ☐ 15 | Tony Perez DP ................ | .15 | .06 | .01 |
| ☐ 16 | Roy White ...................... | .12 | .05 | .01 |
| ☐ 17 | Mike Krukow ................... | .25 | .10 | .02 |
| ☐ 18 | Bob Grich ...................... | .15 | .06 | .01 |
| ☐ 19 | Darrell Porter ................. | .15 | .06 | .01 |

| | | MINT | VG-E | F-G |
|---|---|---|---|---|
| ☐ 20 | Pete Rose DP ................. | 3.25 | 1.30 | .32 |
| ☐ 21 | Steve Kemp ..................... | .25 | .10 | .02 |
| ☐ 22 | Charlie Hough ................ | .15 | .06 | .01 |
| ☐ 23 | Bump Wills ..................... | .09 | .04 | .01 |
| ☐ 24 | Don Money DP ................ | .04 | .02 | .00 |
| ☐ 25 | Jon Matlack .................... | .12 | .05 | .01 |
| ☐ 26 | Rich Hebner ................... | .09 | .04 | .01 |
| ☐ 27 | Geoff Zahn ..................... | .09 | .04 | .01 |
| ☐ 28 | Ed Ott .......................... | .09 | .04 | .01 |
| ☐ 29 | Bob Lacey ...................... | .09 | .04 | .01 |
| ☐ 30 | George Hendrick ............. | .15 | .06 | .01 |
| ☐ 31 | Glenn Abbott .................. | .09 | .04 | .01 |
| ☐ 32 | Garry Templeton ............. | .35 | .14 | .03 |
| ☐ 33 | Dave Lemanczyk ............. | .09 | .04 | .01 |
| ☐ 34 | Willie McCovey ................ | 1.50 | .60 | .15 |
| ☐ 35 | Sparky Lyle .................... | .20 | .08 | .02 |
| ☐ 36 | Eddie Murray .................. | 27.00 | 11.00 | 2.70 |
| ☐ 37 | Rick Waits ...................... | .09 | .04 | .01 |
| ☐ 38 | Willie Montanez .............. | .09 | .04 | .01 |
| ☐ 39 | Floyd Bannister .............. | .75 | .30 | .07 |
| ☐ 40 | Carl Yastrzemski ............ | 2.25 | .90 | .22 |
| ☐ 41 | Burt Hooton ................... | .09 | .04 | .01 |
| ☐ 42 | Jorge Orta ..................... | .09 | .04 | .01 |
| ☐ 43 | Bill Atkinson .................. | .09 | .04 | .01 |
| ☐ 44 | Toby Harrah ................... | .12 | .05 | .01 |
| ☐ 45 | Mark Fidrych .................. | .20 | .08 | .02 |
| ☐ 46 | Al Cowens ...................... | .12 | .05 | .01 |
| ☐ 47 | Jack Billingham .............. | .09 | .04 | .01 |
| ☐ 48 | Don Baylor ..................... | .45 | .18 | .04 |
| ☐ 49 | Ed Kranepool .................. | .12 | .05 | .01 |
| ☐ 50 | Rick Reuschel ................. | .15 | .06 | .01 |
| ☐ 51 | Charlie Moore DP .......... | .04 | .02 | .00 |
| ☐ 52 | Jim Lonborg ................... | .12 | .05 | .01 |
| ☐ 53 | Phil Garner DP ............... | .04 | .02 | .00 |
| ☐ 54 | Tom Johnson ................... | .09 | .04 | .01 |
| ☐ 55 | Mitchell Page ................. | .12 | .05 | .01 |
| ☐ 56 | Randy Jones ................... | .12 | .05 | .01 |
| ☐ 57 | Dan Meyer ...................... | .09 | .04 | .01 |
| ☐ 58 | Bob Forsch ..................... | .15 | .06 | .01 |
| ☐ 59 | Otto Velez ..................... | .09 | .04 | .01 |
| ☐ 60 | Thurman Munson ............ | 1.75 | .70 | .17 |
| ☐ 61 | Larvell Blanks ................ | .09 | .04 | .01 |
| ☐ 62 | Jim Barr ....................... | .09 | .04 | .01 |
| ☐ 63 | Don Zimmer .................... | .09 | .04 | .01 |
| ☐ 64 | Gene Pentz ..................... | .09 | .04 | .01 |
| ☐ 65 | Ken Singleton ................. | .20 | .08 | .02 |
| ☐ 66 | White Sox Team ............. (checklist back) | .35 | .07 | .01 |
| ☐ 67 | Claudell Washington ....... | .15 | .06 | .01 |
| ☐ 68 | Steve Foucault DP ......... | .04 | .02 | .00 |
| ☐ 69 | Mike Vail ....................... | .09 | .04 | .01 |
| ☐ 70 | Rich Gossage .................. | .60 | .24 | .06 |
| ☐ 71 | Terry Humphrey .............. | .09 | .04 | .01 |
| ☐ 72 | Andre Dawson ................. | 1.00 | .40 | .10 |
| ☐ 73 | Andy Hassler .................. | .09 | .04 | .01 |
| ☐ 74 | Checklist 1 .................... | .30 | .03 | .00 |
| ☐ 75 | Dick Ruthven .................. | .09 | .04 | .01 |
| ☐ 76 | Steve Ontiveros ............. | .09 | .04 | .01 |
| ☐ 77 | Ed Kirkpatrick ................ | .09 | .04 | .01 |
| ☐ 78 | Pablo Torrealba .............. | .09 | .04 | .01 |
| ☐ 79 | Darrell Johnson DP ......... | .04 | .02 | .00 |
| ☐ 80 | Ken Griffey .................... | .20 | .08 | .02 |
| ☐ 81 | Pete Redfern .................. | .09 | .04 | .01 |
| ☐ 82 | Giants Team ................... (checklist back) | .35 | .07 | .01 |
| ☐ 83 | Bob Montgomery ............. | .09 | .04 | .01 |
| ☐ 84 | Kent Tekulve ................... | .15 | .06 | .01 |
| ☐ 85 | Ron Fairly ...................... | .12 | .05 | .01 |
| ☐ 86 | Dave Tomlin ................... | .09 | .04 | .01 |
| ☐ 87 | John Lowenstein ............. | .09 | .04 | .01 |
| ☐ 88 | Mike Phillips .................. | .09 | .04 | .01 |
| ☐ 89 | Ken Clay ....................... | .09 | .04 | .01 |
| ☐ 90 | Larry Bowa ..................... | .25 | .10 | .02 |
| ☐ 91 | Oscar Zamora ................. | .09 | .04 | .01 |
| ☐ 92 | Adrian Devine ................. | .09 | .04 | .01 |
| ☐ 93 | Bobby Cox DP ................ | .04 | .02 | .00 |
| ☐ 94 | Chuck Scrivener ............. | .09 | .04 | .01 |
| ☐ 95 | Jamie Quirk ................... | .09 | .04 | .01 |
| ☐ 96 | Orioles Team .................. (checklist back) | .35 | .07 | .01 |
| ☐ 97 | Stan Bahnsen ................. | .09 | .04 | .01 |
| ☐ 98 | Jim Essian ..................... | .09 | .04 | .01 |
| ☐ 99 | Willie Hernandez ............ | 1.25 | .50 | .12 |
| ☐ 100 | George Brett .................. | 3.50 | 1.40 | .35 |
| ☐ 101 | Sid Monge ...................... | .09 | .04 | .01 |
| ☐ 102 | Matt Alexander ............... | .09 | .04 | .01 |
| ☐ 103 | Tom Murphy .................... | .09 | .04 | .01 |
| ☐ 104 | Lee Lacy ....................... | .15 | .06 | .01 |
| ☐ 105 | Reggie Cleveland ............ | .09 | .04 | .01 |
| ☐ 106 | Bill Plummer ................... | .09 | .04 | .01 |
| ☐ 107 | Ed Halicki ...................... | .09 | .04 | .01 |
| ☐ 108 | Von Joshua .................... | .09 | .04 | .01 |
| ☐ 109 | Joe Torre ....................... | .20 | .08 | .02 |

| # | Player | | | |
|---|--------|---|---|---|
| 110 | Richie Zisk | .12 | .05 | .01 |
| 111 | Mike Tyson | .09 | .04 | .01 |
| 112 | Astros Team (checklist back) | .35 | .07 | .01 |
| 113 | Don Carrithers | .09 | .04 | .01 |
| 114 | Paul Blair | .12 | .05 | .01 |
| 115 | Gary Nolan | .09 | .04 | .01 |
| 116 | Tucker Ashford | .09 | .04 | .01 |
| 117 | John Montague | .09 | .04 | .01 |
| 118 | Terry Harmon | .09 | .04 | .01 |
| 119 | Denny Martinez | .12 | .05 | .01 |
| 120 | Gary Carter | 3.00 | 1.20 | .30 |
| 121 | Alvis Woods | .09 | .04 | .01 |
| 122 | Dennis Eckersley | .12 | .05 | .01 |
| 123 | Manny Trillo | .12 | .05 | .01 |
| 124 | Dave Rozema | .12 | .05 | .01 |
| 125 | George Scott | .12 | .05 | .01 |
| 126 | Paul Moskau | .09 | .04 | .01 |
| 127 | Chet Lemon | .15 | .06 | .01 |
| 128 | Bill Russell | .12 | .05 | .01 |
| 129 | Jim Colborn | .09 | .04 | .01 |
| 130 | Jeff Burroughs | .12 | .05 | .01 |
| 131 | Bert Blyleven | .30 | .12 | .03 |
| 132 | Enos Cabell | .09 | .04 | .01 |
| 133 | Jerry Augustine | .09 | .04 | .01 |
| 134 | Steve Henderson | .12 | .05 | .01 |
| 135 | Ron Guidry DP | .70 | .28 | .07 |
| 136 | Ted Sizemore | .09 | .04 | .01 |
| 137 | Craig Kusick | .09 | .04 | .01 |
| 138 | Larry Demery | .09 | .04 | .01 |
| 139 | Wayne Gross | .09 | .04 | .01 |
| 140 | Rollie Fingers | .50 | .20 | .05 |
| 141 | Ruppert Jones | .15 | .06 | .01 |
| 142 | John Montefusco | .12 | .05 | .01 |
| 143 | Keith Hernandez | 2.00 | .80 | .20 |
| 144 | Jesse Jefferson | .09 | .04 | .01 |
| 145 | Rick Monday | .12 | .05 | .01 |
| 146 | Doyle Alexander | .12 | .05 | .01 |
| 147 | Lee Mazzilli | .15 | .06 | .01 |
| 148 | Andre Thornton | .20 | .08 | .02 |
| 149 | Dale Murray | .09 | .04 | .01 |
| 150 | Bobby Bonds | .20 | .08 | .02 |
| 151 | Milt Wilcox | .12 | .05 | .01 |
| 152 | Ivan DeJesus | .09 | .04 | .01 |
| 153 | Steve Stone | .12 | .05 | .01 |
| 154 | Cecil Cooper DP | .20 | .08 | .02 |
| 155 | Butch Hobson | .09 | .04 | .01 |
| 156 | Andy Messersmith | .15 | .06 | .01 |
| 157 | Pete LaCock DP | .04 | .02 | .00 |
| 158 | Joaquin Andujar | .30 | .12 | .03 |
| 159 | Lou Piniella | .25 | .10 | .02 |
| 160 | Jim Palmer | 1.50 | .60 | .15 |
| 161 | Bob Boone | .15 | .06 | .01 |
| 162 | Paul Thormodsgard | .09 | .04 | .01 |
| 163 | Bill North | .09 | .04 | .01 |
| 164 | Bob Owchinko | .09 | .04 | .01 |
| 165 | Rennie Stennett | .09 | .04 | .01 |
| 166 | Carlos Lopez | .09 | .04 | .01 |
| 167 | Tim Foli | .09 | .04 | .01 |
| 168 | Reggie Smith | .25 | .10 | .02 |
| 169 | Jerry Johnson | .09 | .04 | .01 |
| 170 | Lou Brock | 1.50 | .60 | .15 |
| 171 | Pat Zachry | .09 | .04 | .01 |
| 172 | Mike Hargrove | .12 | .05 | .01 |
| 173 | Robin Yount | 2.25 | .90 | .22 |
| 174 | Wayne Garland | .09 | .04 | .01 |
| 175 | Jerry Morales | .09 | .04 | .01 |
| 176 | Milt May | .09 | .04 | .01 |
| 177 | Gene Garber DP | .04 | .02 | .00 |
| 178 | Dave Chalk | .09 | .04 | .01 |
| 179 | Dick Tidrow | .09 | .04 | .01 |
| 180 | Dave Concepcion | .25 | .10 | .02 |
| 181 | Ken Forsch | .12 | .05 | .01 |
| 182 | Jim Spencer | .09 | .04 | .01 |
| 183 | Doug Bird | .09 | .04 | .01 |
| 184 | Checklist 2 | .30 | .03 | .00 |
| 185 | Ellis Valentine | .12 | .05 | .01 |
| 186 | Bob Stanley DP | .25 | .10 | .02 |
| 187 | Jerry Royster DP | .04 | .02 | .00 |
| 188 | Al Bumbry | .09 | .04 | .01 |
| 189 | Tom Lasorda MGR | .15 | .06 | .01 |
| 190 | John Candelaria | .18 | .08 | .01 |
| 191 | Rodney Scott | .09 | .04 | .01 |
| 192 | Padres Team (checklist back) | .35 | .07 | .01 |
| 193 | Rich Chiles | .09 | .04 | .01 |
| 194 | Derrel Thomas | .09 | .04 | .01 |
| 195 | Larry Dierker | .12 | .05 | .01 |
| 196 | Bob Bailor | .09 | .04 | .01 |
| 197 | Nino Espinosa | .09 | .04 | .01 |
| 198 | Ron Pruitt | .09 | .04 | .01 |
| 199 | Craig Reynolds | .09 | .04 | .01 |
| 200 | Reggie Jackson | 2.50 | 1.00 | .25 |
| 201 | Batting Leaders: Dave Parker Rod Carew | .50 | .20 | .05 |
| 202 | Home Run Leaders DP: George Foster Jim Rice | .12 | .05 | .01 |
| 203 | RBI Leaders: George Foster Larry Hisle | .20 | .08 | .02 |
| 204 | Steals Leaders DP: Frank Taveras Freddie Patek | .09 | .04 | .01 |
| 205 | Victory Leaders: Steve Carlton Dave Goltz Dennis Leonard Jim Palmer | .45 | .18 | .04 |
| 206 | Strikeout Leaders DP: Phil Niekro Nolan Ryan | .12 | .05 | .01 |
| 207 | ERA Leaders DP: John Candelaria Frank Tanana | .09 | .04 | .01 |
| 208 | Top Firemen: Rollie Fingers Bill Campbell | .18 | .08 | .01 |
| 209 | Dock Ellis | .09 | .04 | .01 |
| 210 | Jose Cardenal | .09 | .04 | .01 |
| 211 | Earl Weaver MGR DP | .09 | .04 | .01 |
| 212 | Mike Caldwell | .12 | .05 | .01 |
| 213 | Alan Bannister | .09 | .04 | .01 |
| 214 | Angels Team (checklist back) | .35 | .07 | .01 |
| 215 | Darrell Evans | .25 | .10 | .02 |
| 216 | Mike Paxton | .09 | .04 | .01 |
| 217 | Rod Gilbreath | .09 | .04 | .01 |
| 218 | Marty Pattin | .09 | .04 | .01 |
| 219 | Mike Cubbage | .09 | .04 | .01 |
| 220 | Pedro Borbon | .09 | .04 | .01 |
| 221 | Chris Speier | .09 | .04 | .01 |
| 222 | Jerry Martin | .09 | .04 | .01 |
| 223 | Bruce Kison | .09 | .04 | .01 |
| 224 | Jerry Tabb | .09 | .04 | .01 |
| 225 | Don Gullett DP | .04 | .02 | .00 |
| 226 | Joe Ferguson | .12 | .05 | .01 |
| 227 | Al Fitzmorris | .09 | .04 | .01 |
| 228 | Manny Mota DP | .09 | .04 | .01 |
| 229 | Leo Foster | .09 | .04 | .01 |
| 230 | Al Hrabosky | .12 | .05 | .01 |
| 231 | Wayne Nordhagen | .09 | .04 | .01 |
| 232 | Mickey Stanley | .09 | .04 | .01 |
| 233 | Dick Pole | .09 | .04 | .01 |
| 234 | Herman Franks MGR | .09 | .04 | .01 |
| 235 | Tim McCarver | .15 | .06 | .01 |
| 236 | Terry Whitfield | .09 | .04 | .01 |
| 237 | Rich Dauer | .09 | .04 | .01 |
| 238 | Juan Beniquez | .12 | .05 | .01 |
| 239 | Dyar Miller | .09 | .04 | .01 |
| 240 | Gene Tenace | .09 | .04 | .01 |
| 241 | Pete Vuckovich | .18 | .08 | .01 |
| 242 | Barry Bonnell DP | .09 | .04 | .01 |
| 243 | Bob McClure | .09 | .04 | .01 |
| 244 | Expos Team DP (checklist back) | .15 | .03 | .00 |
| 245 | Rick Burleson | .15 | .06 | .01 |
| 246 | Dan Driessen | .12 | .05 | .01 |
| 247 | Larry Christenson | .09 | .04 | .01 |
| 248 | Frank White DP | .09 | .04 | .01 |
| 249 | Dave Goltz DP | .04 | .02 | .00 |
| 250 | Graig Nettles DP | .18 | .08 | .01 |
| 251 | Don Kirkwood | .09 | .04 | .01 |
| 252 | Steve Swisher DP | .04 | .02 | .00 |
| 253 | Jim Kern | .09 | .04 | .01 |
| 254 | Dave Collins | .15 | .06 | .01 |
| 255 | Jerry Reuss | .18 | .08 | .01 |
| 256 | Joe Altobelli MGR | .09 | .04 | .01 |
| 257 | Hector Cruz | .09 | .04 | .01 |
| 258 | John Hiller | .12 | .05 | .01 |
| 259 | Dodgers Team (checklist back) | .40 | .08 | .01 |
| 260 | Bert Campaneris | .15 | .06 | .01 |
| 261 | Tim Hosley | .09 | .04 | .01 |
| 262 | Rudy May | .09 | .04 | .01 |
| 263 | Danny Walton | .09 | .04 | .01 |
| 264 | Jamie Easterly | .09 | .04 | .01 |
| 265 | Sal Bando DP | .09 | .04 | .01 |
| 266 | Bob Shirley | .09 | .04 | .01 |
| 267 | Doug Ault | .09 | .04 | .01 |
| 268 | Gil Flores | .09 | .04 | .01 |
| 269 | Wayne Twitchell | .09 | .04 | .01 |
| 270 | Carlton Fisk | .60 | .24 | .06 |
| 271 | Randy Lerch DP | .04 | .02 | .00 |
| 272 | Royle Stillman | .09 | .04 | .01 |

| | | | | |
|---|---|---|---|---|
| ☐ 273 | Fred Norman | .09 | .04 | .01 |
| ☐ 274 | Freddie Patek | .09 | .04 | .01 |
| ☐ 275 | Dan Ford | .12 | .05 | .01 |
| ☐ 276 | Bill Bonham DP | .04 | .02 | .00 |
| ☐ 277 | Bruce Boisclair | .09 | .04 | .01 |
| ☐ 278 | Enrique Romo | .09 | .04 | .01 |
| ☐ 279 | Bill Virdon MGR | .12 | .05 | .01 |
| ☐ 280 | Buddy Bell | .25 | .10 | .02 |
| ☐ 281 | Eric Rasmussen DP | .04 | .02 | .00 |
| ☐ 282 | Yankees Team | .50 | .10 | .02 |
| | (checklist back) | | | |
| ☐ 283 | Omar Moreno | .12 | .05 | .01 |
| ☐ 284 | Randy Moffitt | .09 | .04 | .01 |
| ☐ 285 | Steve Yeager DP | .04 | .02 | .00 |
| ☐ 286 | Ben Oglivie | .15 | .06 | .01 |
| ☐ 287 | Kiko Garcia | .09 | .04 | .01 |
| ☐ 288 | Dave Hamilton | .09 | .04 | .01 |
| ☐ 289 | Checklist 3 | .30 | .03 | .00 |
| ☐ 290 | Willie Horton | .12 | .05 | .01 |
| ☐ 291 | Gary Ross | .09 | .04 | .01 |
| ☐ 292 | Gene Richards | .09 | .04 | .01 |
| ☐ 293 | Mike Willis | .09 | .04 | .01 |
| ☐ 294 | Larry Parrish | .20 | .08 | .02 |
| ☐ 295 | Bill Lee | .12 | .05 | .01 |
| ☐ 296 | Biff Pocoroba | .09 | .04 | .01 |
| ☐ 297 | Warren Brusstar DP | .04 | .02 | .00 |
| ☐ 298 | Tony Armas | .40 | .16 | .04 |
| ☐ 299 | Whitey Herzog MGR | .12 | .05 | .01 |
| ☐ 300 | Joe Morgan | 1.00 | .40 | .10 |
| ☐ 301 | Buddy Schultz | .09 | .04 | .01 |
| ☐ 302 | Cubs Team | .35 | .07 | .01 |
| | (checklist back) | | | |
| ☐ 303 | Sam Hinds | .09 | .04 | .01 |
| ☐ 304 | John Milner | .09 | .04 | .01 |
| ☐ 305 | Rico Carty | .15 | .06 | .01 |
| ☐ 306 | Joe Niekro | .20 | .08 | .02 |
| ☐ 307 | Glenn Borgmann | .09 | .04 | .01 |
| ☐ 308 | Jim Rooker | .09 | .04 | .01 |
| ☐ 309 | Cliff Johnson | .09 | .04 | .01 |
| ☐ 310 | Don Sutton | .85 | .34 | .08 |
| ☐ 311 | Jose Baez DP | .04 | .02 | .00 |
| ☐ 312 | Greg Minton | .18 | .08 | .01 |
| ☐ 313 | Andy Etchebarren | .09 | .04 | .01 |
| ☐ 314 | Paul Lindblad | .09 | .04 | .01 |
| ☐ 315 | Mark Belanger | .15 | .06 | .01 |
| ☐ 316 | Henry Cruz DP | .04 | .02 | .00 |
| ☐ 317 | Dave Johnson | .20 | .08 | .02 |
| ☐ 318 | Tom Griffin | .09 | .04 | .01 |
| ☐ 319 | Alan Ashby | .09 | .04 | .01 |
| ☐ 320 | Fred Lynn | .90 | .36 | .09 |
| ☐ 321 | Santo Alcala | .09 | .04 | .01 |
| ☐ 322 | Tom Paciorek | .09 | .04 | .01 |
| ☐ 323 | Jim Fregosi DP | .09 | .04 | .01 |
| ☐ 324 | Vern Rapp MGR | .09 | .04 | .01 |
| ☐ 325 | Bruce Sutter | .80 | .32 | .08 |
| ☐ 326 | Mike Lum DP | .04 | .02 | .00 |
| ☐ 327 | Rick Langford DP | .04 | .02 | .00 |
| ☐ 328 | Milwaukee Brewers | .35 | .07 | .01 |
| | Team Card | | | |
| | (checklist back) | | | |
| ☐ 329 | John Verhoeven | .09 | .04 | .01 |
| ☐ 330 | Bob Watson | .12 | .05 | .01 |
| ☐ 331 | Mark Littell | .09 | .04 | .01 |
| ☐ 332 | Duane Kuiper | .09 | .04 | .01 |
| ☐ 333 | Jim Todd | .09 | .04 | .01 |
| ☐ 334 | John Stearns | .09 | .04 | .01 |
| ☐ 335 | Bucky Dent | .18 | .08 | .01 |
| ☐ 336 | Steve Busby | .12 | .05 | .01 |
| ☐ 337 | Tom Grieve | .12 | .05 | .01 |
| ☐ 338 | Dave Heaverlo | .09 | .04 | .01 |
| ☐ 339 | Mario Guerrero | .09 | .04 | .01 |
| ☐ 340 | Bake McBride | .12 | .05 | .01 |
| ☐ 341 | Mike Flanagan | .18 | .08 | .01 |
| ☐ 342 | Aurelio Rodriguez | .09 | .04 | .01 |
| ☐ 343 | John Wathan DP | .04 | .02 | .00 |
| ☐ 344 | Sam Ewing | .09 | .04 | .01 |
| ☐ 345 | Luis Tiant | .18 | .08 | .01 |
| ☐ 346 | Larry Biittner | .09 | .04 | .01 |
| ☐ 347 | Terry Forster | .18 | .08 | .01 |
| ☐ 348 | Del Unser | .09 | .04 | .01 |
| ☐ 349 | Rick Camp DP | .04 | .02 | .00 |
| ☐ 350 | Steve Garvey | 2.50 | 1.00 | .25 |
| ☐ 351 | Jeff Torborg | .09 | .04 | .01 |
| ☐ 352 | Tony Scott | .09 | .04 | .01 |
| ☐ 353 | Doug Bair | .12 | .05 | .01 |
| ☐ 354 | Cesar Geronimo | .09 | .04 | .01 |
| ☐ 355 | Bill Travers | .09 | .04 | .01 |
| ☐ 356 | Mets Team | .40 | .08 | .01 |
| | (checklist back) | | | |
| ☐ 357 | Tom Poquette | .09 | .04 | .01 |
| ☐ 358 | Mark Lemongello | .09 | .04 | .01 |
| ☐ 359 | Marc Hill | .09 | .04 | .01 |
| ☐ 360 | Mike Schmidt | 4.00 | 1.60 | .40 |

| | | | | |
|---|---|---|---|---|
| ☐ 361 | Chris Knapp | .09 | .04 | .01 |
| ☐ 362 | Dave May | .09 | .04 | .01 |
| ☐ 363 | Bob Randall | .09 | .04 | .01 |
| ☐ 364 | Jerry Turner | .09 | .04 | .01 |
| ☐ 365 | Ed Figueroa | .09 | .04 | .01 |
| ☐ 366 | Larry Milbourne DP | .04 | .02 | .00 |
| ☐ 367 | Rick Dempsey | .12 | .05 | .01 |
| ☐ 368 | Balor Moore | .09 | .04 | .01 |
| ☐ 369 | Tim Nordbrook | .09 | .04 | .01 |
| ☐ 370 | Rusty Staub | .20 | .08 | .02 |
| ☐ 371 | Ray Burris | .09 | .04 | .01 |
| ☐ 372 | Brian Asselstine | .09 | .04 | .01 |
| ☐ 373 | Jim Willoughby | .09 | .04 | .01 |
| ☐ 374 | Jose Morales | .09 | .04 | .01 |
| ☐ 375 | Tommy John | .45 | .18 | .04 |
| ☐ 376 | Jim Wohlford | .09 | .04 | .01 |
| ☐ 377 | Manny Sarmiento | .09 | .04 | .01 |
| ☐ 378 | Bobby Winkles MGR | .09 | .04 | .01 |
| ☐ 379 | Skip Lockwood | .09 | .04 | .01 |
| ☐ 380 | Ted Simmons | .35 | .14 | .03 |
| ☐ 381 | Phillies Team | .35 | .07 | .01 |
| | (checklist back) | | | |
| ☐ 382 | Joe Lahoud | .09 | .04 | .01 |
| ☐ 383 | Mario Mendoza | .09 | .04 | .01 |
| ☐ 384 | Jack Clark | .90 | .36 | .09 |
| ☐ 385 | Tito Fuentes | .09 | .04 | .01 |
| ☐ 386 | Bob Gorinski | .09 | .04 | .01 |
| ☐ 387 | Ken Holtzman | .12 | .05 | .01 |
| ☐ 388 | Bill Fahey DP | .04 | .02 | .00 |
| ☐ 389 | Julio Gonzalez | .09 | .04 | .01 |
| ☐ 390 | Oscar Gamble | .12 | .05 | .01 |
| ☐ 391 | Larry Haney | .09 | .04 | .01 |
| ☐ 392 | Billy Almon | .12 | .05 | .01 |
| ☐ 393 | Tippy Martinez | .12 | .05 | .01 |
| ☐ 394 | Roy Howell DP | .04 | .02 | .00 |
| ☐ 395 | Jim Hughes | .09 | .04 | .01 |
| ☐ 396 | Bob Stinson DP | .04 | .02 | .00 |
| ☐ 397 | Greg Gross | .09 | .04 | .01 |
| ☐ 398 | Don Hood | .09 | .04 | .01 |
| ☐ 399 | Pete Mackanin | .09 | .04 | .01 |
| ☐ 400 | Nolan Ryan | 2.00 | .80 | .20 |
| ☐ 401 | Sparky Anderson MGR | .15 | .06 | .01 |
| ☐ 402 | Dave Campbell | .09 | .04 | .01 |
| ☐ 403 | Bud Harrelson | .12 | .05 | .01 |
| ☐ 404 | Tigers Team | .40 | .08 | .01 |
| | (checklist back) | | | |
| ☐ 405 | Rawly Eastwick | .09 | .04 | .01 |
| ☐ 406 | Mike Jorgensen | .09 | .04 | .01 |
| ☐ 407 | Odell Jones | .09 | .04 | .01 |
| ☐ 408 | Joe Zdeb | .09 | .04 | .01 |
| ☐ 409 | Ron Schueler | .09 | .04 | .01 |
| ☐ 410 | Bill Madlock | .50 | .20 | .05 |
| ☐ 411 | AL Champs: | .45 | .18 | .04 |
| | Yankees rally to | | | |
| | defeat Royals | | | |
| ☐ 412 | NL Champs: | .45 | .18 | .04 |
| | Dodgers overpower | | | |
| | Phillies in four | | | |
| ☐ 413 | World Series: | 1.00 | .40 | .10 |
| | Reggie and Yankees | | | |
| | reign supreme | | | |
| ☐ 414 | Darold Knowles DP | .04 | .02 | .00 |
| ☐ 415 | Ray Fosse | .09 | .04 | .01 |
| ☐ 416 | Jack Brohamer | .09 | .04 | .01 |
| ☐ 417 | Mike Garman DP | .04 | .02 | .00 |
| ☐ 418 | Tony Muser | .09 | .04 | .01 |
| ☐ 419 | Jerry Garvin | .09 | .04 | .01 |
| ☐ 420 | Greg Luzinski | .25 | .10 | .02 |
| ☐ 421 | Junior Moore | .09 | .04 | .01 |
| ☐ 422 | Steve Braun | .09 | .04 | .01 |
| ☐ 423 | Dave Rosello | .09 | .04 | .01 |
| ☐ 424 | Red Sox Team | .35 | .07 | .01 |
| | (checklist back) | | | |
| ☐ 425 | Steve Rogers DP | .09 | .04 | .01 |
| ☐ 426 | Fred Kendall | .09 | .04 | .01 |
| ☐ 427 | Mario Soto | 1.00 | .40 | .10 |
| ☐ 428 | Joel Youngblood | .09 | .04 | .01 |
| ☐ 429 | Mike Barlow | .09 | .04 | .01 |
| ☐ 430 | Al Oliver | .40 | .16 | .04 |
| ☐ 431 | Butch Metzger | .12 | .05 | .01 |
| ☐ 432 | Terry Bulling | .09 | .04 | .01 |
| ☐ 433 | Fernando Gonzalez | .09 | .04 | .01 |
| ☐ 434 | Mike Norris | .12 | .05 | .01 |
| ☐ 435 | Checklist 4 | .30 | .03 | .00 |
| ☐ 436 | Vic Harris DP | .04 | .02 | .00 |
| ☐ 437 | Bo McLaughlin | .09 | .04 | .01 |
| ☐ 438 | John Ellis | .09 | .04 | .01 |
| ☐ 439 | Ken Kravec | .09 | .04 | .01 |
| ☐ 440 | Dave Lopes | .20 | .08 | .02 |
| ☐ 441 | Larry Gura | .15 | .06 | .01 |
| ☐ 442 | Elliott Maddox | .09 | .04 | .01 |
| ☐ 443 | Darrel Chaney | .09 | .04 | .01 |
| ☐ 444 | Roy Hartsfield MGR | .09 | .04 | .01 |

| | | | | |
|---|---|---|---|---|
| ☐ 445 | Mike Ivie | .09 | .04 | .01 |
| ☐ 446 | Tug McGraw | .20 | .08 | .02 |
| ☐ 447 | Leroy Stanton | .09 | .04 | .01 |
| ☐ 448 | Bill Castro | .09 | .04 | .01 |
| ☐ 449 | Tim Blackwell DP | .04 | .02 | .00 |
| ☐ 450 | Tom Seaver | 2.00 | .80 | .20 |
| ☐ 451 | Twins Team | .35 | .07 | .01 |
| | (checklist back) | | | |
| ☐ 452 | Jerry Mumphrey | .15 | .06 | .01 |
| ☐ 453 | Doug Flynn | .09 | .04 | .01 |
| ☐ 454 | Dave LaRoche | .09 | .04 | .01 |
| ☐ 455 | Bill Robinson | .09 | .04 | .01 |
| ☐ 456 | Vern Ruhle | .09 | .04 | .01 |
| ☐ 457 | Bob Bailey | .09 | .04 | .01 |
| ☐ 458 | Jeff Newman | .09 | .04 | .01 |
| ☐ 459 | Charlie Spikes | .09 | .04 | .01 |
| ☐ 460 | Jim Hunter | .90 | .36 | .09 |
| ☐ 461 | Rob Andrews DP | .04 | .02 | .00 |
| ☐ 462 | Rogelio Moret | .09 | .04 | .01 |
| ☐ 463 | Kevin Bell | .09 | .04 | .01 |
| ☐ 464 | Jerry Grote | .09 | .04 | .01 |
| ☐ 465 | Hal McRae | .18 | .08 | .01 |
| ☐ 466 | Dennis Blair | .09 | .04 | .01 |
| ☐ 467 | Alvin Dark MGR | .12 | .05 | .01 |
| ☐ 468 | Warren Cromartie | .15 | .06 | .01 |
| ☐ 469 | Rick Cerone | .12 | .05 | .01 |
| ☐ 470 | J.R. Richard | .18 | .08 | .01 |
| ☐ 471 | Roy Smalley | .12 | .05 | .01 |
| ☐ 472 | Ron Reed | .09 | .04 | .01 |
| ☐ 473 | Bill Buckner | .25 | .10 | .02 |
| ☐ 474 | Jim Slaton | .09 | .04 | .01 |
| ☐ 475 | Gary Matthews | .18 | .08 | .01 |
| ☐ 476 | Bill Stein | .09 | .04 | .01 |
| ☐ 477 | Doug Capilla | .09 | .04 | .01 |
| ☐ 478 | Jerry Remy | .12 | .05 | .01 |
| ☐ 479 | Cardinals Team | .35 | .07 | .01 |
| | (checklist back) | | | |
| ☐ 480 | Ron LeFlore | .15 | .06 | .01 |
| ☐ 481 | Jackson Todd | .09 | .04 | .01 |
| ☐ 482 | Rick Miller | .09 | .04 | .01 |
| ☐ 483 | Ken Macha | .09 | .04 | .01 |
| ☐ 484 | Jim Norris | .09 | .04 | .01 |
| ☐ 485 | Chris Chambliss | .15 | .06 | .01 |
| ☐ 486 | John Curtis | .09 | .04 | .01 |
| ☐ 487 | Jim Tyrone | .09 | .04 | .01 |
| ☐ 488 | Dan Spillner | .09 | .04 | .01 |
| ☐ 489 | Rudy Meoli | .09 | .04 | .01 |
| ☐ 490 | Amos Otis | .18 | .08 | .01 |
| ☐ 491 | Scott McGregor | .18 | .08 | .01 |
| ☐ 492 | Jim Sundberg | .12 | .05 | .01 |
| ☐ 493 | Steve Renko | .09 | .04 | .01 |
| ☐ 494 | Chuck Tanner MGR | .12 | .05 | .01 |
| ☐ 495 | Dave Cash | .09 | .04 | .01 |
| ☐ 496 | Jim Clancy DP | .12 | .05 | .01 |
| ☐ 497 | Glenn Adams | .09 | .04 | .01 |
| ☐ 498 | Joe Sambito | .12 | .05 | .01 |
| ☐ 499 | Seattle Mariners Team | .30 | .06 | .01 |
| | (checklist back) | | | |
| ☐ 500 | George Foster | .70 | .28 | .07 |
| ☐ 501 | Dave Roberts | .09 | .04 | .01 |
| ☐ 502 | Pat Rockett | .09 | .04 | .01 |
| ☐ 503 | Ike Hampton | .09 | .04 | .01 |
| ☐ 504 | Roger Freed | .09 | .04 | .01 |
| ☐ 505 | Felix Millan | .09 | .04 | .01 |
| ☐ 506 | Ron Blomberg | .09 | .04 | .01 |
| ☐ 507 | Willie Crawford | .09 | .04 | .01 |
| ☐ 508 | Johnny Oates | .09 | .04 | .01 |
| ☐ 509 | Brent Strom | .09 | .04 | .01 |
| ☐ 510 | Willie Stargell | 1.25 | .50 | .12 |
| ☐ 511 | Frank Duffy | .09 | .04 | .01 |
| ☐ 512 | Larry Herndon | .15 | .06 | .01 |
| ☐ 513 | Barry Foote | .09 | .04 | .01 |
| ☐ 514 | Rob Sperring | .09 | .04 | .01 |
| ☐ 515 | Tim Corcoran | .09 | .04 | .01 |
| ☐ 516 | Gary Beare | .09 | .04 | .01 |
| ☐ 517 | Andres Mora | .09 | .04 | .01 |
| ☐ 518 | Tommy Boggs DP | .04 | .02 | .00 |
| ☐ 519 | Brian Downing | .12 | .05 | .01 |
| ☐ 520 | Larry Hisle | .12 | .05 | .01 |
| ☐ 521 | Steve Staggs | .09 | .04 | .01 |
| ☐ 522 | Dick Williams MGR | .12 | .05 | .01 |
| ☐ 523 | Donnie Moore | .50 | .20 | .05 |
| ☐ 524 | Bernie Carbo | .09 | .04 | .01 |
| ☐ 525 | Jerry Terrell | .09 | .04 | .01 |
| ☐ 526 | Reds Team | .40 | .08 | .01 |
| | (checklist back) | | | |
| ☐ 527 | Vic Correll | .09 | .04 | .01 |
| ☐ 528 | Rob Picciolo | .09 | .04 | .01 |
| ☐ 529 | Paul Hartzell | .09 | .04 | .01 |
| ☐ 530 | Dave Winfield | 1.75 | .70 | .17 |
| ☐ 531 | Tom Underwood | .09 | .04 | .01 |
| ☐ 532 | Skip Jutze | .09 | .04 | .01 |
| ☐ 533 | Sandy Alomar | .09 | .04 | .01 |
| ☐ 534 | Wilbur Howard | .09 | .04 | .01 |
| ☐ 535 | Checklist 5 | .30 | .03 | .00 |
| ☐ 536 | Roric Harrison | .09 | .04 | .01 |
| ☐ 537 | Bruce Bochte | .12 | .05 | .01 |
| ☐ 538 | Johnny LeMaster | .09 | .04 | .01 |
| ☐ 539 | Vic Davalillo DP | .04 | .02 | .00 |
| ☐ 540 | Steve Carlton | 2.00 | .80 | .20 |
| ☐ 541 | Larry Cox | .09 | .04 | .01 |
| ☐ 542 | Tim Johnson | .09 | .04 | .01 |
| ☐ 543 | Larry Harlow DP | .04 | .02 | .00 |
| ☐ 544 | Len Randle DP | .04 | .02 | .00 |
| ☐ 545 | Bill Campbell | .12 | .05 | .01 |
| ☐ 546 | Ted Martinez | .09 | .04 | .01 |
| ☐ 547 | John Scott | .09 | .04 | .01 |
| ☐ 548 | Billy Hunter MGR DP | .04 | .02 | .00 |
| ☐ 549 | Joe Kerrigan | .09 | .04 | .01 |
| ☐ 550 | John Mayberry | .12 | .05 | .01 |
| ☐ 551 | Atlanta Braves Team | .35 | .07 | .01 |
| | (checklist back) | | | |
| ☐ 552 | Francisco Barrios | .09 | .04 | .01 |
| ☐ 553 | Terry Puhl | .35 | .14 | .03 |
| ☐ 554 | Joe Coleman | .09 | .04 | .01 |
| ☐ 555 | Butch Wynegar | .15 | .06 | .01 |
| ☐ 556 | Ed Armbrister | .09 | .04 | .01 |
| ☐ 557 | Tony Solaita | .09 | .04 | .01 |
| ☐ 558 | Paul Mitchell | .09 | .04 | .01 |
| ☐ 559 | Phil Mankowski | .09 | .04 | .01 |
| ☐ 560 | Dave Parker | 1.50 | .60 | .15 |
| ☐ 561 | Charlie Williams | .09 | .04 | .01 |
| ☐ 562 | Glenn Burke | .09 | .04 | .01 |
| ☐ 563 | Dave Rader | .09 | .04 | .01 |
| ☐ 564 | Mick Kelleher | .09 | .04 | .01 |
| ☐ 565 | Jerry Koosman | .20 | .08 | .02 |
| ☐ 566 | Merv Rettenmund | .09 | .04 | .01 |
| ☐ 567 | Dick Drago | .09 | .04 | .01 |
| ☐ 568 | Tom Hutton | .09 | .04 | .01 |
| ☐ 569 | Lary Sorensen | .09 | .04 | .01 |
| ☐ 570 | Dave Kingman | .50 | .20 | .05 |
| ☐ 571 | Buck Martinez | .09 | .04 | .01 |
| ☐ 572 | Rick Wise | .12 | .05 | .01 |
| ☐ 573 | Luis Gomez | .09 | .04 | .01 |
| ☐ 574 | Bob Lemon MGR | .18 | .08 | .01 |
| ☐ 575 | Pat Dobson | .12 | .05 | .01 |
| ☐ 576 | Sam Mejias | .09 | .04 | .01 |
| ☐ 577 | Oakland A's Team | .35 | .07 | .01 |
| | (checklist back) | | | |
| ☐ 578 | Buzz Capra | .09 | .04 | .01 |
| ☐ 579 | Rance Mulliniks | .15 | .06 | .01 |
| ☐ 580 | Rod Carew | 1.75 | .70 | .17 |
| ☐ 581 | Lynn McGlothen | .09 | .04 | .01 |
| ☐ 582 | Fran Healy | .09 | .04 | .01 |
| ☐ 583 | George Medich | .12 | .05 | .01 |
| ☐ 584 | John Hale | .09 | .04 | .01 |
| ☐ 585 | Woodie Fryman DP | .04 | .02 | .00 |
| ☐ 586 | Ed Goodson | .09 | .04 | .01 |
| ☐ 587 | John Urrea | .09 | .04 | .01 |
| ☐ 588 | Jim Mason | .09 | .04 | .01 |
| ☐ 589 | Bob Knepper | 1.50 | .60 | .15 |
| ☐ 590 | Bobby Murcer | .25 | .10 | .02 |
| ☐ 591 | George Zeber | .09 | .04 | .01 |
| ☐ 592 | Bob Apodaca | .09 | .04 | .01 |
| ☐ 593 | Dave Skaggs | .09 | .04 | .01 |
| ☐ 594 | Dave Freisleben | .09 | .04 | .01 |
| ☐ 595 | Sixto Lezcano | .12 | .05 | .01 |
| ☐ 596 | Gary Wheelock | .09 | .04 | .01 |
| ☐ 597 | Steve Dillard | .09 | .04 | .01 |
| ☐ 598 | Eddie Solomon | .09 | .04 | .01 |
| ☐ 599 | Gary Woods | .09 | .04 | .01 |
| ☐ 600 | Frank Tanana | .15 | .06 | .01 |
| ☐ 601 | Gene Mauch MGR | .12 | .05 | .01 |
| ☐ 602 | Eric Soderholm | .09 | .04 | .01 |
| ☐ 603 | Will McEnaney | .09 | .04 | .01 |
| ☐ 604 | Earl Williams | .09 | .04 | .01 |
| ☐ 605 | Rick Rhoden | .20 | .08 | .02 |
| ☐ 606 | Pirates Team | .35 | .07 | .01 |
| | (checklist back) | | | |
| ☐ 607 | Fernando Arroyo | .09 | .04 | .01 |
| ☐ 608 | Johnny Grubb | .09 | .04 | .01 |
| ☐ 609 | John Denny | .20 | .08 | .02 |
| ☐ 610 | Garry Maddox | .12 | .05 | .01 |
| ☐ 611 | Pat Scanlon | .09 | .04 | .01 |
| ☐ 612 | Ken Henderson | .09 | .04 | .01 |
| ☐ 613 | Marty Perez | .09 | .04 | .01 |
| ☐ 614 | Joe Wallis | .09 | .04 | .01 |
| ☐ 615 | Clay Carroll | .09 | .04 | .01 |
| ☐ 616 | Pat Kelly | .09 | .04 | .01 |
| ☐ 617 | Joe Nolan | .09 | .04 | .01 |
| ☐ 618 | Tommy Helms | .09 | .04 | .01 |
| ☐ 619 | Thad Bosley DP | .09 | .04 | .01 |
| ☐ 620 | Willie Randolph | .20 | .08 | .02 |
| ☐ 621 | Craig Swan DP | .09 | .04 | .01 |
| ☐ 622 | Champ Summers | .09 | .04 | .01 |
| ☐ 623 | Ed Rodriquez | .09 | .04 | .01 |

| | | | | |
|---|---|---|---|---|
| ☐ 624 | Gary Alexander DP | .04 | .02 | .00 |
| ☐ 625 | Jose Cruz | .30 | .12 | .03 |
| ☐ 626 | Blue Jays Team DP (checklist back) | .15 | .03 | .00 |
| ☐ 627 | David Johnson | .09 | .04 | .01 |
| ☐ 628 | Ralph Garr | .12 | .05 | .01 |
| ☐ 629 | Don Stanhouse | .09 | .04 | .01 |
| ☐ 630 | Ron Cey | .30 | .12 | .03 |
| ☐ 631 | Danny Ozark MGR | .09 | .04 | .01 |
| ☐ 632 | Rowland Office | .09 | .04 | .01 |
| ☐ 633 | Tom Veryzer | .09 | .04 | .01 |
| ☐ 634 | Len Barker | .15 | .06 | .01 |
| ☐ 635 | Joe Rudi | .12 | .05 | .01 |
| ☐ 636 | Jim Bibby | .12 | .05 | .01 |
| ☐ 637 | Duffy Dyer | .09 | .04 | .01 |
| ☐ 638 | Paul Splittorff | .12 | .05 | .01 |
| ☐ 639 | Gene Clines | .09 | .04 | .01 |
| ☐ 640 | Lee May DP | .09 | .04 | .01 |
| ☐ 641 | Doug Rau | .09 | .04 | .01 |
| ☐ 642 | Denny Doyle | .09 | .04 | .01 |
| ☐ 643 | Tom House | .09 | .04 | .01 |
| ☐ 644 | Jim Dwyer | .09 | .04 | .01 |
| ☐ 645 | Mike Torrez | .12 | .05 | .01 |
| ☐ 646 | Rick Auerbach DP | .04 | .02 | .00 |
| ☐ 647 | Steve Dunning | .09 | .04 | .01 |
| ☐ 648 | Gary Thomasson | .09 | .04 | .01 |
| ☐ 649 | Moose Haas | .45 | .18 | .04 |
| ☐ 650 | Cesar Cedeno | .20 | .08 | .02 |
| ☐ 651 | Doug Rader | .12 | .05 | .01 |
| ☐ 652 | Checklist 6 | .30 | .03 | .00 |
| ☐ 653 | Ron Hodges DP | .04 | .02 | .00 |
| ☐ 654 | Pepe Frias | .09 | .04 | .01 |
| ☐ 655 | Lyman Bostock | .18 | .08 | .01 |
| ☐ 656 | Dave Garcia MGR | .09 | .04 | .01 |
| ☐ 657 | Bombo Rivera | .09 | .04 | .01 |
| ☐ 658 | Manny Sanguillen | .12 | .05 | .01 |
| ☐ 659 | Rangers Team (checklist back) | .35 | .07 | .01 |
| ☐ 660 | Jason Thompson | .18 | .08 | .01 |
| ☐ 661 | Grant Jackson | .09 | .04 | .01 |
| ☐ 662 | Paul Dade | .09 | .04 | .01 |
| ☐ 663 | Paul Reuschel | .09 | .04 | .01 |
| ☐ 664 | Fred Stanley | .09 | .04 | .01 |
| ☐ 665 | Dennis Leonard | .15 | .06 | .01 |
| ☐ 666 | Billy Smith | .09 | .04 | .01 |
| ☐ 667 | Jeff Byrd | .09 | .04 | .01 |
| ☐ 668 | Dusty Baker | .18 | .08 | .01 |
| ☐ 669 | Pete Falcone | .09 | .04 | .01 |
| ☐ 670 | Jim Rice | 3.50 | 1.40 | .35 |
| ☐ 671 | Gary Lavelle | .12 | .05 | .01 |
| ☐ 672 | Don Kessinger | .12 | .05 | .01 |
| ☐ 673 | Steve Brye | .09 | .04 | .01 |
| ☐ 674 | Ray Knight | 1.00 | .40 | .10 |
| ☐ 675 | Jay Johnstone | .12 | .05 | .01 |
| ☐ 676 | Bob Myrick | .09 | .04 | .01 |
| ☐ 677 | Ed Herrmann | .09 | .04 | .01 |
| ☐ 678 | Tom Burgmeier | .09 | .04 | .01 |
| ☐ 679 | Wayne Garrett | .09 | .04 | .01 |
| ☐ 680 | Vida Blue | .18 | .08 | .01 |
| ☐ 681 | Rob Belloir | .09 | .04 | .01 |
| ☐ 682 | Ken Brett | .12 | .05 | .01 |
| ☐ 683 | Mike Champion | .09 | .04 | .01 |
| ☐ 684 | Ralph Houk MGR | .12 | .05 | .01 |
| ☐ 685 | Frank Taveras | .09 | .04 | .01 |
| ☐ 586 | Gaylord Perry | 1.25 | .50 | .12 |
| ☐ 687 | Julio Cruz | .25 | .10 | .02 |
| ☐ 688 | George Mitterwald | .09 | .04 | .01 |
| ☐ 689 | Indians Team (checklist back) | .35 | .07 | .01 |
| ☐ 690 | Mickey Rivers | .15 | .06 | .01 |
| ☐ 691 | Ross Grimsley | .09 | .04 | .01 |
| ☐ 692 | Ken Reitz | .09 | .04 | .01 |
| ☐ 693 | Lamar Johnson | .09 | .04 | .01 |
| ☐ 694 | Elias Sosa | .09 | .04 | .01 |
| ☐ 695 | Dwight Evans | .35 | .14 | .03 |
| ☐ 696 | Steve Mingori | .09 | .04 | .01 |
| ☐ 697 | Roger Metzger | .09 | .04 | .01 |
| ☐ 698 | Juan Bernhardt | .09 | .04 | .01 |
| ☐ 699 | Jackie Brown | .09 | .04 | .01 |
| ☐ 700 | Johnny Bench | 1.75 | .70 | .17 |
| ☐ 701 | Rookie Pitchers: Tom Hume Larry Landreth Steve McCatty Bruce Taylor | .30 | .12 | .03 |
| ☐ 702 | Rookie Catchers: Bill Nahordony Kevin Pasley Rick Sweet Don Werner | .12 | .05 | .01 |
| ☐ 703 | Rookie Pitchers DP: Larry Andersen Tim Jones | 4.50 | 1.80 | .45 |

| | | | | |
|---|---|---|---|---|
| | Mickey Mahler Jack Morris | | | |
| ☐ 704 | Rookie 2nd Basemen: Garth Iorg Dave Oliver Sam Perlozzo Lou Whitaker | 6.00 | 2.40 | .60 |
| ☐ 705 | Rookie Outfielders: Dave Bergman Miguel Dilone Clint Hurdle Willie Norwood | .30 | .12 | .03 |
| ☐ 706 | Rookie 1st Basemen: Wayne Cage Ted Cox Pat Putnam Dave Revering | .20 | .08 | .02 |
| ☐ 707 | Rookie Shortstops: Mickey Klutts Paul Molitor Alan Trammell U.L. Washington | 9.00 | 3.75 | .90 |
| ☐ 708 | Rookie Catchers: Bo Diaz Dale Murphy Lance Parrish Ernie Whitt | 24.00 | 10.00 | 2.40 |
| ☐ 709 | Rookie Pitchers: Steve Burke Matt Keough Lance Rautzhan Dan Schatzeder | .20 | .08 | .02 |
| ☐ 710 | Rookie Outfielders: Dell Alston Rick Bosetti Mike Easler Keith Smith | 1.50 | .60 | .15 |
| ☐ 711 | Rookie Pitchers DP: Cardell Camper Dennis Lamp Craig Mitchell Roy Thomas | .12 | .05 | .01 |
| ☐ 712 | Bobby Valentine | .18 | .08 | .01 |
| ☐ 713 | Bob Davis | .09 | .04 | .01 |
| ☐ 714 | Mike Anderson | .09 | .04 | .01 |
| ☐ 715 | Jim Kaat | .30 | .12 | .03 |
| ☐ 716 | Clarence Gaston | .09 | .04 | .01 |
| ☐ 717 | Nelson Briles | .12 | .05 | .01 |
| ☐ 718 | Ron Jackson | .09 | .04 | .01 |
| ☐ 719 | Randy Elliott | .09 | .04 | .01 |
| ☐ 720 | Fergie Jenkins | .30 | .12 | .03 |
| ☐ 721 | Billy Martin MGR | .25 | .10 | .02 |
| ☐ 722 | Pete Broberg | .09 | .04 | .01 |
| ☐ 723 | John Wockenfuss | .09 | .04 | .01 |
| ☐ 724 | K.C. Royals Team (checklist back) | .35 | .07 | .01 |
| ☐ 725 | Kurt Bevacqua | .09 | .04 | .01 |
| ☐ 726 | Wilbur Wood | .15 | .06 | .01 |

## 1979 Topps

The cards in this 726 set measure 2 1/2" by 3 1/2". Topps continued with the same number of cards as in 1978. Various series spotlight League Leaders (1-8), "Season and Career Record Holders" (411-418), "Record Breakers of 1978" (201-206) and one

"Prospects" card for each team (701-726). Team cards feature a checklist on back of that team's players in the set and a small picture of the manager on the front of the card. There are 66 cards that were double-printed and these are noted in the checklist by the abbreviation DP. Bump Wills was initially depicted in a Ranger uniform but with a Blue Jays affiliation; later printings correctly labeled him with Texas. The set price listed does not include the scarcer Wills (Rangers) card.

|  | MINT | VG-E | F-G |
|---|---|---|---|
| COMPLETE SET | 100.00 | 40.00 | 10.00 |
| COMMON PLAYER (1-726) | .08 | .03 | .01 |
| COMMON DP's (1-726) | .03 | .01 | .00 |

| | | MINT | VG-E | F-G |
|---|---|---|---|---|
| ☐ | 1 Batting Leaders:<br>Rod Carew<br>Dave Parker | .75 | .15 | .03 |
| ☐ | 2 Home Run Leaders:<br>Jim Rice<br>George Foster | .35 | .14 | .03 |
| ☐ | 3 RBI Leaders:<br>Jim Rice<br>George Foster | .35 | .14 | .03 |
| ☐ | 4 Stolen Base Leaders:<br>Ron LeFlore<br>Omar Moreno | .12 | .05 | .01 |
| ☐ | 5 Victory Leaders:<br>Ron Guidry<br>Gaylord Perry | .25 | .10 | .02 |
| ☐ | 6 Strikeout Leaders:<br>Nolan Ryan<br>J.R. Richard | .25 | .10 | .02 |
| ☐ | 7 ERA Leaders:<br>Ron Guidry<br>Craig Swan | .15 | .06 | .01 |
| ☐ | 8 Leading Firemen:<br>Rich Gossage<br>Rollie Fingers | .20 | .08 | .02 |
| ☐ | 9 Dave Campbell | .08 | .03 | .01 |
| ☐ | 10 Lee May | .12 | .05 | .01 |
| ☐ | 11 Marc Hill | .08 | .03 | .01 |
| ☐ | 12 Dick Drago | .08 | .03 | .01 |
| ☐ | 13 Paul Dade | .08 | .03 | .01 |
| ☐ | 14 Rafael Landestoy | .08 | .03 | .01 |
| ☐ | 15 Ross Grimsley | .08 | .03 | .01 |
| ☐ | 16 Fred Stanley | .08 | .03 | .01 |
| ☐ | 17 Donnie Moore | .12 | .05 | .01 |
| ☐ | 18 Tony Solaita | .08 | .03 | .01 |
| ☐ | 19 Larry Gura DP | .08 | .03 | .01 |
| ☐ | 20 Joe Morgan DP | .20 | .08 | .02 |
| ☐ | 21 Kevin Kobel | .08 | .03 | .01 |
| ☐ | 22 Mike Jorgensen | .08 | .03 | .01 |
| ☐ | 23 Terry Forster | .15 | .06 | .01 |
| ☐ | 24 Paul Molitor | .65 | .26 | .06 |
| ☐ | 25 Steve Carlton | 1.75 | .70 | .17 |
| ☐ | 26 Jamie Quirk | .08 | .03 | .01 |
| ☐ | 27 Dave Goltz | .12 | .05 | .01 |
| ☐ | 28 Steve Brye | .08 | .03 | .01 |
| ☐ | 29 Rick Langford | .08 | .03 | .01 |
| ☐ | 30 Dave Winfield | 1.75 | .70 | .17 |
| ☐ | 31 Tom House DP | .03 | .01 | .00 |
| ☐ | 32 Jerry Mumphrey | .12 | .05 | .01 |
| ☐ | 33 Dave Rozema | .08 | .03 | .01 |
| ☐ | 34 Rob Andrews | .08 | .03 | .01 |
| ☐ | 35 Ed Figueroa | .08 | .03 | .01 |
| ☐ | 36 Alan Ashby | .08 | .03 | .01 |
| ☐ | 37 Joe Kerrigan DP | .03 | .01 | .00 |
| ☐ | 38 Bernie Carbo | .08 | .03 | .01 |
| ☐ | 39 Dale Murphy | 6.00 | 2.40 | .60 |
| ☐ | 40 Dennis Eckersley | .12 | .05 | .01 |
| ☐ | 41 Twins Team/Mgr.<br>Gene Mauch<br>(checklist back) | .30 | .06 | .01 |
| ☐ | 42 Ron Blomberg | .08 | .03 | .01 |
| ☐ | 43 Wayne Twitchell | .08 | .03 | .01 |
| ☐ | 44 Kurt Bevacqua | .08 | .03 | .01 |
| ☐ | 45 Al Hrabosky | .12 | .05 | .01 |
| ☐ | 46 Ron Hodges | .08 | .03 | .01 |
| ☐ | 47 Fred Norman | .08 | .03 | .01 |
| ☐ | 48 Merv Rettenmund | .08 | .03 | .01 |
| ☐ | 49 Vern Ruhle | .08 | .03 | .01 |
| ☐ | 50 Steve Garvey DP | .80 | .32 | .08 |
| ☐ | 51 Ray Fosse DP | .03 | .01 | .00 |
| ☐ | 52 Randy Lerch | .08 | .03 | .01 |
| ☐ | 53 Mick Kelleher | .08 | .03 | .01 |
| ☐ | 54 Dell Alston DP | .03 | .01 | .00 |
| ☐ | 55 Willie Stargell | 1.25 | .50 | .12 |
| ☐ | 56 John Hale | .08 | .03 | .01 |
| ☐ | 57 Eric Rasmussen | .08 | .03 | .01 |
| ☐ | 58 Bob Randall DP | .03 | .01 | .00 |
| ☐ | 59 John Denny DP | .08 | .03 | .01 |
| ☐ | 60 Mickey Rivers | .12 | .05 | .01 |
| ☐ | 61 Bo Diaz | .20 | .08 | .02 |
| ☐ | 62 Randy Moffitt | .08 | .03 | .01 |
| ☐ | 63 Jack Brohamer | .08 | .03 | .01 |
| ☐ | 64 Tom Underwood | .08 | .03 | .01 |
| ☐ | 65 Mark Belanger | .15 | .06 | .01 |
| ☐ | 66 Tigers Team/Mgr.<br>Les Moss<br>(checklist back) | .30 | .06 | .01 |
| ☐ | 67 Jim Mason DP | .03 | .01 | .00 |
| ☐ | 68 Joe Niekro DP | .08 | .03 | .01 |
| ☐ | 69 Elliott Maddox | .08 | .03 | .01 |
| ☐ | 70 John Candelaria | .15 | .06 | .01 |
| ☐ | 71 Brian Downing | .12 | .05 | .01 |
| ☐ | 72 Steve Mingori | .08 | .03 | .01 |
| ☐ | 73 Ken Henderson | .08 | .03 | .01 |
| ☐ | 74 Shane Rawley | .75 | .30 | .07 |
| ☐ | 75 Steve Yeager | .12 | .05 | .01 |
| ☐ | 76 Warren Cromartie | .08 | .03 | .01 |
| ☐ | 77 Dan Briggs DP | .03 | .01 | .00 |
| ☐ | 78 Elias Sosa | .08 | .03 | .01 |
| ☐ | 79 Ted Cox | .08 | .03 | .01 |
| ☐ | 80 Jason Thompson | .12 | .05 | .01 |
| ☐ | 81 Roger Erickson | .12 | .05 | .01 |
| ☐ | 82 Mets Team/Mgr.<br>Joe Torre<br>(checklist back) | .30 | .06 | .01 |
| ☐ | 83 Fred Kendall | .08 | .03 | .01 |
| ☐ | 84 Greg Minton | .12 | .05 | .01 |
| ☐ | 85 Gary Matthews | .18 | .08 | .01 |
| ☐ | 86 Rodney Scott | .08 | .03 | .01 |
| ☐ | 87 Pete Falcone | .08 | .03 | .01 |
| ☐ | 88 Bob Molinaro | .08 | .03 | .01 |
| ☐ | 89 Dick Tidrow | .08 | .03 | .01 |
| ☐ | 90 Bob Boone | .12 | .05 | .01 |
| ☐ | 91 Terry Crowley | .08 | .03 | .01 |
| ☐ | 92 Jim Bibby | .12 | .05 | .01 |
| ☐ | 93 Phil Mankowski | .08 | .03 | .01 |
| ☐ | 94 Len Barker | .15 | .06 | .01 |
| ☐ | 95 Robin Yount | 1.75 | .70 | .17 |
| ☐ | 96 Indians Team/Mgr.<br>Jeff Torborg<br>(checklist back) | .30 | .06 | .01 |
| ☐ | 97 Sam Mejias | .08 | .03 | .01 |
| ☐ | 98 Ray Burris | .08 | .03 | .01 |
| ☐ | 99 John Wathan | .08 | .03 | .01 |
| ☐ | 100 Tom Seaver DP | .80 | .32 | .08 |
| ☐ | 101 Roy Howell | .08 | .03 | .01 |
| ☐ | 102 Mike Anderson | .08 | .03 | .01 |
| ☐ | 103 Jim Todd | .08 | .03 | .01 |
| ☐ | 104 Johnny Oates DP | .03 | .01 | .00 |
| ☐ | 105 Rick Camp DP | .03 | .01 | .00 |
| ☐ | 106 Frank Duffy | .08 | .03 | .01 |
| ☐ | 107 Jesus Alou DP | .03 | .01 | .00 |
| ☐ | 108 Eduardo Rodriguez | .08 | .03 | .01 |
| ☐ | 109 Joel Youngblood | .08 | .03 | .01 |
| ☐ | 110 Vida Blue | .15 | .06 | .01 |
| ☐ | 111 Roger Freed | .08 | .03 | .01 |
| ☐ | 112 Phillies Team/Mgr.<br>Danny Ozark<br>(checklist back) | .30 | .06 | .01 |
| ☐ | 113 Pete Redfern | .08 | .03 | .01 |
| ☐ | 114 Cliff Johnson | .08 | .03 | .01 |
| ☐ | 115 Nolan Ryan | 1.75 | .70 | .17 |
| ☐ | 116 Ozzie Smith | 4.50 | 1.80 | .45 |
| ☐ | 117 Grant Jackson | .08 | .03 | .01 |
| ☐ | 118 Bud Harrelson | .12 | .05 | .01 |
| ☐ | 119 Don Stanhouse | .08 | .03 | .01 |
| ☐ | 120 Jim Sundberg | .12 | .05 | .01 |
| ☐ | 121 Checklist 1 DP | .10 | .01 | .00 |
| ☐ | 122 Mike Paxton | .08 | .03 | .01 |
| ☐ | 123 Lou Whitaker | 1.50 | .60 | .15 |
| ☐ | 124 Dan Schatzeder | .08 | .03 | .01 |
| ☐ | 125 Rick Burleson | .12 | .05 | .01 |
| ☐ | 126 Doug Bair | .08 | .03 | .01 |
| ☐ | 127 Thad Bosley | .08 | .03 | .01 |
| ☐ | 128 Ted Martinez | .08 | .03 | .01 |
| ☐ | 129 Marty Pattin DP | .03 | .01 | .00 |
| ☐ | 130 Bob Watson DP | .08 | .03 | .01 |
| ☐ | 131 Jim Clancy | .12 | .05 | .01 |
| ☐ | 132 Rowland Office | .08 | .03 | .01 |
| ☐ | 133 Bill Castro | .08 | .03 | .01 |
| ☐ | 134 Alan Bannister | .08 | .03 | .01 |
| ☐ | 135 Bobby Murcer | .18 | .08 | .01 |
| ☐ | 136 Jim Kaat | .30 | .12 | .03 |
| ☐ | 137 Larry Wolfe DP | .03 | .01 | .00 |
| ☐ | 138 Mark Lee | .08 | .03 | .01 |
| ☐ | 139 Luis Pujols | .08 | .03 | .01 |
| ☐ | 140 Don Gullett | .12 | .05 | .01 |
| ☐ | 141 Tom Paciorek | .08 | .03 | .01 |

| No. | Player | | | |
|-----|--------|------|------|------|
| ☐ 142 | Charlie Williams | .08 | .03 | .01 |
| ☐ 143 | Tony Scott | .08 | .03 | .01 |
| ☐ 144 | Sandy Alomar | .08 | .03 | .01 |
| ☐ 145 | Rick Rhoden | .18 | .08 | .01 |
| ☐ 146 | Duane Kuiper | .08 | .03 | .01 |
| ☐ 147 | Dave Hamilton | .08 | .03 | .01 |
| ☐ 148 | Bruce Boisclair | .08 | .03 | .01 |
| ☐ 149 | Manny Sarmiento | .08 | .03 | .01 |
| ☐ 150 | Wayne Cage | .08 | .03 | .01 |
| ☐ 151 | John Hiller | .12 | .05 | .01 |
| ☐ 152 | Rick Cerone | .12 | .05 | .01 |
| ☐ 153 | Dennis Lamp | .08 | .03 | .01 |
| ☐ 154 | Jim Gantner DP | .08 | .03 | .01 |
| ☐ 155 | Dwight Evans | .30 | .12 | .03 |
| ☐ 156 | Buddy Solomon | .08 | .03 | .01 |
| ☐ 157 | U.L. Washington | .08 | .03 | .01 |
| ☐ 158 | Joe Sambito | .12 | .05 | .01 |
| ☐ 159 | Roy White | .12 | .05 | .01 |
| ☐ 160 | Mike Flanagan | .18 | .08 | .01 |
| ☐ 161 | Barry Foote | .08 | .03 | .01 |
| ☐ 162 | Tom Johnson | .08 | .03 | .01 |
| ☐ 163 | Glenn Burke | .08 | .03 | .01 |
| ☐ 164 | Mickey Lolich | .18 | .08 | .01 |
| ☐ 165 | Frank Taveras | .08 | .03 | .01 |
| ☐ 166 | Leon Roberts | .08 | .03 | .01 |
| ☐ 167 | Roger Metzger DP | .03 | .01 | .00 |
| ☐ 168 | Dave Freisleben | .08 | .03 | .01 |
| ☐ 169 | Bill Nahorodny | .08 | .03 | .01 |
| ☐ 170 | Don Sutton | .75 | .30 | .07 |
| ☐ 171 | Gene Clines | .08 | .03 | .01 |
| ☐ 172 | Mike Bruhert | .08 | .03 | .01 |
| ☐ 173 | John Lowenstein | .08 | .03 | .01 |
| ☐ 174 | Rick Auerbach | .08 | .03 | .01 |
| ☐ 175 | George Hendrick | .15 | .06 | .01 |
| ☐ 176 | Aurelio Rodriguez | .08 | .03 | .01 |
| ☐ 177 | Ron Reed | .08 | .03 | .01 |
| ☐ 178 | Alvis Woods | .08 | .03 | .01 |
| ☐ 179 | Jim Beattie DP | .08 | .03 | .01 |
| ☐ 180 | Larry Hisle | .12 | .05 | .01 |
| ☐ 181 | Mike Garman | .08 | .03 | .01 |
| ☐ 182 | Tim Johnson | .08 | .03 | .01 |
| ☐ 183 | Paul Splittorff | .12 | .05 | .01 |
| ☐ 184 | Darrel Chaney | .08 | .03 | .01 |
| ☐ 185 | Mike Torrez | .12 | .05 | .01 |
| ☐ 186 | Eric Soderholm | .08 | .03 | .01 |
| ☐ 187 | Mark Lemongello | .08 | .03 | .01 |
| ☐ 188 | Pat Kelly | .08 | .03 | .01 |
| ☐ 189 | Eddie Whitson | .35 | .14 | .03 |
| ☐ 190 | Ron Cey | .30 | .12 | .03 |
| ☐ 191 | Mike Norris | .12 | .05 | .01 |
| ☐ 192 | Cardinals Team/Mgr. Ken Boyer (checklist back) | .30 | .06 | .01 |
| ☐ 193 | Glenn Adams | .08 | .03 | .01 |
| ☐ 194 | Randy Jones | .12 | .05 | .01 |
| ☐ 195 | Bill Madlock | .35 | .14 | .03 |
| ☐ 196 | Steve Kemp DP | .08 | .03 | .01 |
| ☐ 197 | Bob Apodaca | .08 | .03 | .01 |
| ☐ 198 | Johnny Grubb | .08 | .03 | .01 |
| ☐ 199 | Larry Milbourne | .08 | .03 | .01 |
| ☐ 200 | Johnny Bench DP | .75 | .30 | .07 |
| ☐ 201 | RB: Mike Edwards Most unassisted 2nd basemen DP's | .08 | .03 | .01 |
| ☐ 202 | RB: Ron Guidry, Most Strikeouts, Lefthander 9 inning game | .30 | .12 | .03 |
| ☐ 203 | RB: J.R. Richard Most Strikeouts Season, Righthander | .15 | .06 | .01 |
| ☐ 204 | RB: Pete Rose Most consecutive games batting safe | 1.25 | .50 | .12 |
| ☐ 205 | RB: John Stearns Most SB's by Catcher, Season | .08 | .03 | .01 |
| ☐ 206 | RB: Sammy Stewart 7 straight SO's First ML Game | .12 | .05 | .01 |
| ☐ 207 | Dave Lemanczyk | .08 | .03 | .01 |
| ☐ 208 | Clarence Gaston | .08 | .03 | .01 |
| ☐ 209 | Reggie Cleveland | .08 | .03 | .01 |
| ☐ 210 | Larry Bowa | .20 | .08 | .02 |
| ☐ 211 | Denny Martinez | .12 | .05 | .01 |
| ☐ 212 | Carney Lansford | 1.50 | .60 | .15 |
| ☐ 213 | Bill Travers | .08 | .03 | .01 |
| ☐ 214 | Red Sox Team/Mgr. Don Zimmer (checklist back) | .30 | .06 | .01 |
| ☐ 215 | Willie McCovey | 1.25 | .50 | .12 |
| ☐ 216 | Wilbur Wood | .12 | .05 | .01 |
| ☐ 217 | Steve Dillard | .08 | .03 | .01 |
| ☐ 218 | Dennis Leonard | .15 | .06 | .01 |
| ☐ 219 | Roy Smalley | .12 | .05 | .01 |
| ☐ 220 | Cesar Geronimo | .08 | .03 | .01 |
| ☐ 221 | Jesse Jefferson | .08 | .03 | .01 |
| ☐ 222 | Bob Beall | .08 | .03 | .01 |
| ☐ 223 | Kent Tekulve | .15 | .06 | .01 |
| ☐ 224 | Dave Revering | .08 | .03 | .01 |
| ☐ 225 | Rich Gossage | .50 | .20 | .05 |
| ☐ 226 | Ron Pruitt | .08 | .03 | .01 |
| ☐ 227 | Steve Stone | .12 | .05 | .01 |
| ☐ 228 | Vic Davalillo | .08 | .03 | .01 |
| ☐ 229 | Doug Flynn | .08 | .03 | .01 |
| ☐ 230 | Bob Forsch | .15 | .06 | .01 |
| ☐ 231 | Johnny Wockenfuss | .08 | .03 | .01 |
| ☐ 232 | Jimmy Sexton | .08 | .03 | .01 |
| ☐ 233 | Paul Mitchell | .08 | .03 | .01 |
| ☐ 234 | Toby Harrah | .12 | .05 | .01 |
| ☐ 235 | Steve Rogers | .15 | .06 | .01 |
| ☐ 236 | Jim Dwyer | .08 | .03 | .01 |
| ☐ 237 | Billy Smith | .08 | .03 | .01 |
| ☐ 238 | Balor Moore | .08 | .03 | .01 |
| ☐ 239 | Willie Horton | .12 | .05 | .01 |
| ☐ 240 | Rick Reuschel | .12 | .05 | .01 |
| ☐ 241 | Checklist 2 DP | .10 | .01 | .00 |
| ☐ 242 | Pablo Torrealba | .08 | .03 | .01 |
| ☐ 243 | Buck Martinez DP | .03 | .01 | .00 |
| ☐ 244 | Pirates Team/Mgr. Chuck Tanner (checklist back) | .30 | .06 | .01 |
| ☐ 245 | Jeff Burroughs | .12 | .05 | .01 |
| ☐ 246 | Darrell Jackson | .08 | .03 | .01 |
| ☐ 247 | Tucker Ashford DP | .03 | .01 | .00 |
| ☐ 248 | Pete LaCock | .08 | .03 | .01 |
| ☐ 249 | Paul Thormodsgard | .08 | .03 | .01 |
| ☐ 250 | Willie Randolph | .15 | .06 | .01 |
| ☐ 251 | Jack Morris | 1.50 | .60 | .15 |
| ☐ 252 | Bob Stinson | .08 | .03 | .01 |
| ☐ 253 | Rick Wise | .12 | .05 | .01 |
| ☐ 254 | Luis Gomez | .08 | .03 | .01 |
| ☐ 255 | Tommy John | .35 | .14 | .03 |
| ☐ 256 | Mike Sadek | .08 | .03 | .01 |
| ☐ 257 | Adrian Devine | .08 | .03 | .01 |
| ☐ 258 | Mike Phillips | .08 | .03 | .01 |
| ☐ 259 | Reds Team/Mgr. Sparky Anderson (checklist back) | .30 | .06 | .01 |
| ☐ 260 | Richie Zisk | .12 | .05 | .01 |
| ☐ 261 | Mario Guerrero | .08 | .03 | .01 |
| ☐ 262 | Nelson Briles | .12 | .05 | .01 |
| ☐ 263 | Oscar Gamble | .12 | .05 | .01 |
| ☐ 264 | Don Robinson | .35 | .14 | .03 |
| ☐ 265 | Don Money | .12 | .05 | .01 |
| ☐ 266 | Jim Willoughby | .08 | .03 | .01 |
| ☐ 267 | Joe Rudi | .12 | .05 | .01 |
| ☐ 268 | Julio Gonzalez | .08 | .03 | .01 |
| ☐ 269 | Woodie Fryman | .08 | .03 | .01 |
| ☐ 270 | Butch Hobson | .08 | .03 | .01 |
| ☐ 271 | Rawly Eastwick | .08 | .03 | .01 |
| ☐ 272 | Tim Corcoran | .08 | .03 | .01 |
| ☐ 273 | Jerry Terrell | .08 | .03 | .01 |
| ☐ 274 | Willie Norwood | .08 | .03 | .01 |
| ☐ 275 | Junior Moore | .08 | .03 | .01 |
| ☐ 276 | Jim Colborn | .08 | .03 | .01 |
| ☐ 277 | Tom Grieve | .12 | .05 | .01 |
| ☐ 278 | Andy Messersmith | .15 | .06 | .01 |
| ☐ 279 | Jerry Grote DP | .03 | .01 | .00 |
| ☐ 280 | Andre Thornton | .15 | .06 | .01 |
| ☐ 281 | Vic Correll DP | .03 | .01 | .00 |
| ☐ 282 | Blue Jays Team/Mgr Roy Hartsfield (checklist back) | .25 | .05 | .01 |
| ☐ 283 | Ken Kravec | .08 | .03 | .01 |
| ☐ 284 | Johnnie LeMaster | .08 | .03 | .01 |
| ☐ 285 | Bobby Bonds | .18 | .08 | .01 |
| ☐ 286 | Duffy Dyer | .08 | .03 | .01 |
| ☐ 287 | Andres Mora | .08 | .03 | .01 |
| ☐ 288 | Milt Wilcox | .12 | .05 | .01 |
| ☐ 289 | Jose Cruz | .25 | .10 | .02 |
| ☐ 290 | Dave Lopes | .20 | .08 | .02 |
| ☐ 291 | Tom Griffin | .08 | .03 | .01 |
| ☐ 292 | Don Reynolds | .08 | .03 | .01 |
| ☐ 293 | Jerry Garvin | .08 | .03 | .01 |
| ☐ 294 | Pepe Frias | .08 | .03 | .01 |
| ☐ 295 | Mitchell Page | .08 | .03 | .01 |
| ☐ 296 | Preston Hanna | .08 | .03 | .01 |
| ☐ 297 | Ted Sizemore | .08 | .03 | .01 |
| ☐ 298 | Rich Gale | .08 | .03 | .01 |
| ☐ 299 | Steve Ontiveros | .08 | .03 | .01 |
| ☐ 300 | Rod Carew | 1.50 | .60 | .15 |
| ☐ 301 | Tom Hume | .08 | .03 | .01 |
| ☐ 302 | Braves Team/Mgr. Bobby Cox (checklist back) | .30 | .06 | .01 |
| ☐ 303 | Lary Sorensen | .08 | .03 | .01 |

| # | Player | | | |
|---|---|---|---|---|
| 304 | Steve Swisher | .08 | .03 | .01 |
| 305 | Willie Montanez | .08 | .03 | .01 |
| 306 | Floyd Bannister | .15 | .06 | .01 |
| 307 | Larvell Blanks | .08 | .03 | .01 |
| 308 | Bert Blyleven | .30 | .12 | .03 |
| 309 | Ralph Garr | .12 | .05 | .01 |
| 310 | Thurman Munson | 1.50 | .60 | .15 |
| 311 | Gary Lavelle | .12 | .05 | .01 |
| 312 | Bob Robertson | .08 | .03 | .01 |
| 313 | Dyar Miller | .08 | .03 | .01 |
| 314 | Larry Harlow | .08 | .03 | .01 |
| 315 | Jon Matlack | .12 | .05 | .01 |
| 316 | Milt May | .08 | .03 | .01 |
| 317 | Jose Cardenal | .08 | .03 | .01 |
| 318 | Bob Welch | 1.00 | .40 | .10 |
| 319 | Wayne Garrett | .08 | .03 | .01 |
| 320 | Carl Yastrzemski | 2.00 | .80 | .20 |
| 321 | Gaylord Perry | .85 | .34 | .08 |
| 322 | Danny Goodwin | .08 | .03 | .01 |
| 323 | Lynn McGlothen | .08 | .03 | .01 |
| 324 | Mike Tyson | .08 | .03 | .01 |
| 325 | Cecil Cooper | .40 | .16 | .04 |
| 326 | Pedro Borbon | .08 | .03 | .01 |
| 327 | Art Howe | .08 | .03 | .01 |
| 328 | Oakland A's Team/Mgr. Jack McKeon (checklist back) | .25 | .05 | .01 |
| 329 | Joe Coleman | .08 | .03 | .01 |
| 330 | George Brett | 2.50 | 1.00 | .25 |
| 331 | Mickey Mahler | .08 | .03 | .01 |
| 332 | Gary Alexander | .08 | .03 | .01 |
| 333 | Chet Lemon | .15 | .06 | .01 |
| 334 | Craig Swan | .12 | .05 | .01 |
| 335 | Chris Chambliss | .15 | .06 | .01 |
| 336 | Bobby Thompson | .08 | .03 | .01 |
| 337 | John Montague | .08 | .03 | .01 |
| 338 | Vic Harris | .08 | .03 | .01 |
| 339 | Ron Jackson | .08 | .03 | .01 |
| 340 | Jim Palmer | 1.00 | .40 | .10 |
| 341 | Willie Upshaw | 1.00 | .40 | .10 |
| 342 | Dave Roberts | .08 | .03 | .01 |
| 343 | Ed Glynn | .08 | .03 | .01 |
| 344 | Jerry Royster | .08 | .03 | .01 |
| 345 | Tug McGraw | .18 | .08 | .01 |
| 346 | Bill Buckner | .20 | .08 | .02 |
| 347 | Doug Rau | .08 | .03 | .01 |
| 348 | Andre Dawson | .85 | .34 | .08 |
| 349 | Jim Wright | .08 | .03 | .01 |
| 350 | Garry Templeton | .25 | .10 | .02 |
| 351 | Wayne Nordhagen | .08 | .03 | .01 |
| 352 | Steve Renko | .08 | .03 | .01 |
| 353 | Checklist 3 | .30 | .03 | .00 |
| 354 | Bill Bonham | .08 | .03 | .01 |
| 355 | Lee Mazzilli | .12 | .05 | .01 |
| 356 | Giants Team/Mgr. Joe Altobelli (checklist back) | .30 | .06 | .01 |
| 357 | Jerry Augustine | .08 | .03 | .01 |
| 358 | Alan Trammell | 1.50 | .60 | .15 |
| 359 | Dan Spillner DP | .08 | .03 | .01 |
| 360 | Amos Otis | .15 | .06 | .01 |
| 361 | Tom Dixon | .08 | .03 | .01 |
| 362 | Mike Cubbage | .08 | .03 | .01 |
| 363 | Craig Skok | .08 | .03 | .01 |
| 364 | Gene Richards | .08 | .03 | .01 |
| 365 | Sparky Lyle | .18 | .08 | .01 |
| 366 | Juan Bernhardt | .08 | .03 | .01 |
| 367 | Dave Skaggs | .08 | .03 | .01 |
| 368 | Don Aase | .15 | .06 | .01 |
| 369A | Bump Wills ERR (Blue Jays) | 3.00 | 1.20 | .30 |
| 369B | Bump Wills COR (Rangers) | 4.00 | 1.60 | .40 |
| 370 | Dave Kingman | .40 | .16 | .04 |
| 371 | Jeff Holly | .08 | .03 | .01 |
| 372 | Lamar Johnson | .08 | .03 | .01 |
| 373 | Lance Rautzhan | .08 | .03 | .01 |
| 374 | Ed Herrmann | .08 | .03 | .01 |
| 375 | Bill Campbell | .12 | .05 | .01 |
| 376 | Gorman Thomas | .25 | .10 | .02 |
| 377 | Paul Moskau | .08 | .03 | .01 |
| 378 | Rob Picciolo DP | .03 | .01 | .00 |
| 379 | Dale Murray | .08 | .03 | .01 |
| 380 | John Mayberry | .12 | .05 | .01 |
| 381 | Astros Team/Mgr. Bill Virdon (checklist back) | .30 | .06 | .01 |
| 382 | Jerry Martin | .08 | .03 | .01 |
| 383 | Phil Garner | .12 | .05 | .01 |
| 384 | Tommy Boggs | .08 | .03 | .01 |
| 385 | Dan Ford | .12 | .05 | .01 |
| 386 | Francisco Barrios | .08 | .03 | .01 |
| 387 | Gary Thomasson | .08 | .03 | .01 |
| 388 | Jack Billingham | .08 | .03 | .01 |
| 389 | Joe Zdeb | .08 | .03 | .01 |
| 390 | Rollie Fingers | .35 | .14 | .03 |
| 391 | Al Oliver | .30 | .12 | .03 |
| 392 | Doug Ault | .08 | .03 | .01 |
| 393 | Scott McGregor | .15 | .06 | .01 |
| 394 | Randy Stein | .08 | .03 | .01 |
| 395 | Dave Cash | .08 | .03 | .01 |
| 396 | Bill Plummer | .08 | .03 | .01 |
| 397 | Sergio Ferrer | .08 | .03 | .01 |
| 398 | Ivan DeJesus | .08 | .03 | .01 |
| 399 | David Clyde | .08 | .03 | .01 |
| 400 | Jim Rice | 2.50 | 1.00 | .25 |
| 401 | Ray Knight | .25 | .10 | .02 |
| 402 | Paul Hartzell | .08 | .03 | .01 |
| 403 | Tim Foli | .08 | .03 | .01 |
| 404 | White Sox Team/Mgr Don Kessinger (checklist back) | .30 | .06 | .01 |
| 405 | Butch Wynegar DP | .08 | .03 | .01 |
| 406 | Joe Wallis DP | .03 | .01 | .00 |
| 407 | Pete Vuckovich | .12 | .05 | .01 |
| 408 | Charlie Moore DP | .03 | .01 | .00 |
| 409 | Willie Wilson | 1.50 | .60 | .15 |
| 410 | Darrell Evans | .25 | .10 | .02 |
| 411 | Hits Record: Season:George Sisler Career:Ty Cobb | .40 | .16 | .04 |
| 412 | RBI Record: Season:Hack Wilson Career:Hank Aaron | .40 | .16 | .04 |
| 413 | Home Run Record: Season:Roger Maris Career:Hank Aaron | .40 | .16 | .04 |
| 414 | Batting Record: Season:R.Hornsby Career:Ty Cobb | .40 | .16 | .04 |
| 415 | Steals Record: Season:Lou Brock Career:Lou Brock | .40 | .16 | .04 |
| 416 | Wins Record: Season:Jack Chesbro Career:Cy Young | .20 | .08 | .02 |
| 417 | Strikeout Record DP: Season:Nolan Ryan Career:Walter Johnson | .10 | .04 | .01 |
| 418 | ERA Record DP: Season:Dutch Leonard Career:Walter Johnson | .08 | .03 | .01 |
| 419 | Dick Ruthven | .08 | .03 | .01 |
| 420 | Ken Griffey | .15 | .06 | .01 |
| 421 | Doug DeCinces | .18 | .08 | .01 |
| 422 | Ruppert Jones | .12 | .05 | .01 |
| 423 | Bob Montgomery | .08 | .03 | .01 |
| 424 | Angels Team/Mgr. Jim Fregosi (checklist back) | .30 | .06 | .01 |
| 425 | Rick Manning | .08 | .03 | .01 |
| 426 | Chris Speier | .08 | .03 | .01 |
| 427 | Andy Replogle | .08 | .03 | .01 |
| 428 | Bobby Valentine | .18 | .08 | .01 |
| 429 | John Urrea DP | .03 | .01 | .00 |
| 430 | Dave Parker | 1.00 | .40 | .10 |
| 431 | Glenn Borgmann | .08 | .03 | .01 |
| 432 | Dave Heaverlo | .08 | .03 | .01 |
| 433 | Larry Biittner | .08 | .03 | .01 |
| 434 | Ken Clay | .08 | .03 | .01 |
| 435 | Gene Tenace | .12 | .05 | .01 |
| 436 | Hector Cruz | .08 | .03 | .01 |
| 437 | Rick Williams | .08 | .03 | .01 |
| 438 | Horace Speed | .08 | .03 | .01 |
| 439 | Frank White | .20 | .08 | .02 |
| 440 | Rusty Staub | .20 | .08 | .02 |
| 441 | Lee Lacy | .15 | .06 | .01 |
| 442 | Doyle Alexander | .12 | .05 | .01 |
| 443 | Bruce Bochte | .12 | .05 | .01 |
| 444 | Aurelio Lopez | .25 | .10 | .02 |
| 445 | Steve Henderson | .12 | .05 | .01 |
| 446 | Jim Lonborg | .12 | .05 | .01 |
| 447 | Manny Sanguillen | .12 | .05 | .01 |
| 448 | Moose Haas | .12 | .05 | .01 |
| 449 | Bombo Rivera | .08 | .03 | .01 |
| 450 | Dave Concepcion | .20 | .08 | .02 |
| 451 | Royals Team/Mgr. Whitey Herzog (checklist back) | .30 | .06 | .01 |
| 452 | Jerry Morales | .08 | .03 | .01 |
| 453 | Chris Knapp | .08 | .03 | .01 |
| 454 | Len Randle | .08 | .03 | .01 |
| 455 | Bill Lee DP | .08 | .03 | .01 |
| 456 | Chuck Baker | .08 | .03 | .01 |
| 457 | Bruce Sutter | .65 | .26 | .06 |
| 458 | Jim Essian | .08 | .03 | .01 |

| | | | | |
|---|---|---|---|---|
| ☐ 459 | Sid Monge | .08 | .03 | .01 |
| ☐ 460 | Graig Nettles | .35 | .14 | .03 |
| ☐ 461 | Jim Barr DP | .03 | .01 | .00 |
| ☐ 462 | Otto Velez | .08 | .03 | .01 |
| ☐ 463 | Steve Comer | .08 | .03 | .01 |
| ☐ 464 | Joe Nolan | .08 | .03 | .01 |
| ☐ 465 | Reggie Smith | .18 | .08 | .01 |
| ☐ 466 | Mark Littell | .08 | .03 | .01 |
| ☐ 467 | Don Kessinger DP | .08 | .03 | .01 |
| ☐ 468 | Stan Bahnsen DP | .03 | .01 | .00 |
| ☐ 469 | Lance Parrish | 3.50 | 1.40 | .35 |
| ☐ 470 | Garry Maddox DP | .08 | .03 | .01 |
| ☐ 471 | Joaquin Andujar | .25 | .10 | .02 |
| ☐ 472 | Craig Kusick | .08 | .03 | .01 |
| ☐ 473 | Dave Roberts | .08 | .03 | .01 |
| ☐ 474 | Dick Davis | .08 | .03 | .01 |
| ☐ 475 | Dan Driessen | .12 | .05 | .01 |
| ☐ 476 | Tom Poquette | .08 | .03 | .01 |
| ☐ 477 | Bob Grich | .15 | .06 | .01 |
| ☐ 478 | Juan Beniquez | .12 | .05 | .01 |
| ☐ 479 | Padres Team/Mgr. Roger Craig (checklist back) | .30 | .06 | .01 |
| ☐ 480 | Fred Lynn | .75 | .30 | .07 |
| ☐ 481 | Skip Lockwood | .08 | .03 | .01 |
| ☐ 482 | Craig Reynolds | .08 | .03 | .01 |
| ☐ 483 | Checklist 4 DP | .10 | .01 | .00 |
| ☐ 484 | Rick Waits | .08 | .03 | .01 |
| ☐ 485 | Bucky Dent | .15 | .06 | .01 |
| ☐ 486 | Bob Knepper | .40 | .16 | .04 |
| ☐ 487 | Miguel Dilone | .12 | .05 | .01 |
| ☐ 488 | Bob Owchinko | .08 | .03 | .01 |
| ☐ 489 | Larry Cox (photo actually Dave Rader) | .12 | .05 | .01 |
| ☐ 490 | Al Cowens | .12 | .05 | .01 |
| ☐ 491 | Tippy Martinez | .12 | .05 | .01 |
| ☐ 492 | Bob Bailor | .08 | .03 | .01 |
| ☐ 493 | Larry Christenson | .08 | .03 | .01 |
| ☐ 494 | Jerry White | .08 | .03 | .01 |
| ☐ 495 | Tony Perez | .35 | .14 | .03 |
| ☐ 496 | Barry Bonnell DP | .03 | .01 | .00 |
| ☐ 497 | Glenn Abbott | .08 | .03 | .01 |
| ☐ 498 | Rich Chiles | .08 | .03 | .01 |
| ☐ 499 | Rangers Team/Mgr. Pat Corrales (checklist back) | .30 | .06 | .01 |
| ☐ 500 | Ron Guidry | .90 | .36 | .09 |
| ☐ 501 | Junior Kennedy | .08 | .03 | .01 |
| ☐ 502 | Steve Braun | .08 | .03 | .01 |
| ☐ 503 | Terry Humphrey | .08 | .03 | .01 |
| ☐ 504 | Larry McWilliams | .40 | .16 | .04 |
| ☐ 505 | Ed Kranepool | .12 | .05 | .01 |
| ☐ 506 | John D'Acquisto | .08 | .03 | .01 |
| ☐ 507 | Tony Armas | .30 | .12 | .03 |
| ☐ 508 | Charlie Hough | .15 | .06 | .01 |
| ☐ 509 | Mario Mendoza | .08 | .03 | .01 |
| ☐ 510 | Ted Simmons | .35 | .14 | .03 |
| ☐ 511 | Paul Reuschel DP | .03 | .01 | .00 |
| ☐ 512 | Jack Clark | .50 | .20 | .05 |
| ☐ 513 | Dave Johnson | .18 | .08 | .01 |
| ☐ 514 | Mike Proly | .08 | .03 | .01 |
| ☐ 515 | Enos Cabell | .08 | .03 | .01 |
| ☐ 516 | Champ Summers DP | .03 | .01 | .00 |
| ☐ 517 | Al Bumbry | .08 | .03 | .01 |
| ☐ 518 | Jim Umbarger | .08 | .03 | .01 |
| ☐ 519 | Ben Oglivie | .15 | .06 | .01 |
| ☐ 520 | Gary Carter | 2.50 | 1.00 | .25 |
| ☐ 521 | Sam Ewing | .08 | .03 | .01 |
| ☐ 522 | Ken Holtzman | .12 | .05 | .01 |
| ☐ 523 | John Milner | .08 | .03 | .01 |
| ☐ 524 | Tom Burgmeier | .08 | .03 | .01 |
| ☐ 525 | Freddie Patek | .08 | .03 | .01 |
| ☐ 526 | Dodgers Team/Mgr. Tom Lasorda (checklist back) | .35 | .07 | .01 |
| ☐ 527 | Lerrin LaGrow | .08 | .03 | .01 |
| ☐ 528 | Wayne Gross DP | .03 | .01 | .00 |
| ☐ 529 | Brian Asselstine | .08 | .03 | .01 |
| ☐ 530 | Frank Tanana | .15 | .06 | .01 |
| ☐ 531 | Fernando Gonzalez | .08 | .03 | .01 |
| ☐ 532 | Buddy Schultz | .08 | .03 | .01 |
| ☐ 533 | Leroy Stanton | .08 | .03 | .01 |
| ☐ 534 | Ken Forsch | .12 | .05 | .01 |
| ☐ 535 | Ellis Valentine | .15 | .06 | .01 |
| ☐ 536 | Jerry Reuss | .15 | .06 | .01 |
| ☐ 537 | Tom Veryzer | .08 | .03 | .01 |
| ☐ 538 | Mike Ivie DP | .03 | .01 | .00 |
| ☐ 539 | John Ellis | .08 | .03 | .01 |
| ☐ 540 | Greg Luzinski | .20 | .08 | .02 |
| ☐ 541 | Jim Slaton | .08 | .03 | .01 |
| ☐ 542 | Rick Bosetti | .08 | .03 | .01 |
| ☐ 543 | Kiko Garcia | .08 | .03 | .01 |
| ☐ 544 | Fergie Jenkins | .30 | .12 | .03 |
| ☐ 545 | John Stearns | .08 | .03 | .01 |
| ☐ 546 | Bill Russell | .12 | .05 | .01 |
| ☐ 547 | Clint Hurdle | .08 | .03 | .01 |
| ☐ 548 | Enrique Romo | .08 | .03 | .01 |
| ☐ 549 | Bob Bailey | .08 | .03 | .01 |
| ☐ 550 | Sal Bando | .15 | .06 | .01 |
| ☐ 551 | Cubs Team/Mgr. Herman Franks (checklist back) | .30 | .06 | .01 |
| ☐ 552 | Jose Morales | .08 | .03 | .01 |
| ☐ 553 | Denny Walling | .08 | .03 | .01 |
| ☐ 554 | Matt Keough | .12 | .05 | .01 |
| ☐ 555 | Biff Pocoroba | .08 | .03 | .01 |
| ☐ 556 | Mike Lum | .08 | .03 | .01 |
| ☐ 557 | Ken Brett | .12 | .05 | .01 |
| ☐ 558 | Jay Johnstone | .12 | .05 | .01 |
| ☐ 559 | Greg Pryor | .08 | .03 | .01 |
| ☐ 560 | John Montefusco | .12 | .05 | .01 |
| ☐ 561 | Ed Ott | .08 | .03 | .01 |
| ☐ 562 | Dusty Baker | .18 | .08 | .01 |
| ☐ 563 | Roy Thomas | .08 | .03 | .01 |
| ☐ 564 | Jerry Turner | .08 | .03 | .01 |
| ☐ 565 | Rico Carty | .15 | .06 | .01 |
| ☐ 566 | Nino Espinosa | .08 | .03 | .01 |
| ☐ 567 | Rich Hebner | .08 | .03 | .01 |
| ☐ 568 | Carlos Lopez | .08 | .03 | .01 |
| ☐ 569 | Bob Sykes | .08 | .03 | .01 |
| ☐ 570 | Cesar Cedeno | .18 | .08 | .01 |
| ☐ 571 | Darrell Porter | .12 | .05 | .01 |
| ☐ 572 | Rod Gilbreath | .08 | .03 | .01 |
| ☐ 573 | Jim Kern | .08 | .03 | .01 |
| ☐ 574 | Claudell Washington | .15 | .06 | .01 |
| ☐ 575 | Luis Tiant | .18 | .08 | .01 |
| ☐ 576 | Mike Parrott | .08 | .03 | .01 |
| ☐ 577 | Brewers Team/Mgr. George Bamberger (checklist back) | .30 | .06 | .01 |
| ☐ 578 | Pete Broberg | .08 | .03 | .01 |
| ☐ 579 | Greg Gross | .08 | .03 | .01 |
| ☐ 580 | Ron Fairly | .12 | .05 | .01 |
| ☐ 581 | Darold Knowles | .08 | .03 | .01 |
| ☐ 582 | Paul Blair | .12 | .05 | .01 |
| ☐ 583 | Julio Cruz | .12 | .05 | .01 |
| ☐ 584 | Jim Rooker | .08 | .03 | .01 |
| ☐ 585 | Hal McRae | .15 | .06 | .01 |
| ☐ 586 | Bob Horner | 4.00 | 1.60 | .40 |
| ☐ 587 | Ken Reitz | .08 | .03 | .01 |
| ☐ 588 | Tom Murphy | .08 | .03 | .01 |
| ☐ 589 | Terry Whitfield | .08 | .03 | .01 |
| ☐ 590 | J.R. Richard | .18 | .08 | .01 |
| ☐ 591 | Mike Hargrove | .12 | .05 | .01 |
| ☐ 592 | Mike Krukow | .20 | .08 | .02 |
| ☐ 593 | Rick Dempsey | .12 | .05 | .01 |
| ☐ 594 | Bob Shirley | .08 | .03 | .01 |
| ☐ 595 | Phil Niekro | .75 | .30 | .07 |
| ☐ 596 | Jim Wohlford | .08 | .03 | .01 |
| ☐ 597 | Bob Stanley | .15 | .06 | .01 |
| ☐ 598 | Mark Wagner | .08 | .03 | .01 |
| ☐ 599 | Jim Spencer | .08 | .03 | .01 |
| ☐ 600 | George Foster | .65 | .26 | .06 |
| ☐ 601 | Dave LaRoche | .08 | .03 | .01 |
| ☐ 602 | Checklist 5 | .30 | .03 | .00 |
| ☐ 603 | Rudy May | .08 | .03 | .01 |
| ☐ 604 | Jeff Newman | .08 | .03 | .01 |
| ☐ 605 | Rick Monday DP | .08 | .03 | .01 |
| ☐ 606 | Expos Team/Mgr. Dick Williams (checklist back) | .30 | .06 | .01 |
| ☐ 607 | Omar Moreno | .12 | .05 | .01 |
| ☐ 608 | Dave McKay | .08 | .03 | .01 |
| ☐ 609 | Silvio Martinez | .08 | .03 | .01 |
| ☐ 610 | Mike Schmidt | 2.75 | 1.10 | .27 |
| ☐ 611 | Jim Norris | .08 | .03 | .01 |
| ☐ 612 | Rick Honeycutt | .75 | .30 | .07 |
| ☐ 613 | Mike Edwards | .08 | .03 | .01 |
| ☐ 614 | Willie Hernandez | .50 | .20 | .05 |
| ☐ 615 | Ken Singleton | .20 | .08 | .02 |
| ☐ 616 | Billy Almon | .08 | .03 | .01 |
| ☐ 617 | Terry Puhl | .12 | .05 | .01 |
| ☐ 618 | Jerry Remy | .12 | .05 | .01 |
| ☐ 619 | Ken Landreaux | .30 | .12 | .03 |
| ☐ 620 | Bert Campaneris | .12 | .05 | .01 |
| ☐ 621 | Pat Zachry | .08 | .03 | .01 |
| ☐ 622 | Dave Collins | .15 | .06 | .01 |
| ☐ 623 | Bob McClure | .08 | .03 | .01 |
| ☐ 624 | Larry Herndon | .12 | .05 | .01 |
| ☐ 625 | Mark Fidrych | .15 | .06 | .01 |
| ☐ 626 | Yankees Team/Mgr. Bob Lemon (checklist back) | .35 | .07 | .01 |
| ☐ 627 | Gary Serum | .08 | .03 | .01 |
| ☐ 628 | Del Unser | .08 | .03 | .01 |

| | | | | |
|---|---|---|---|---|
| ☐ 629 | Gene Garber | .12 | .05 | .01 |
| ☐ 630 | Bake McBride | .12 | .05 | .01 |
| ☐ 631 | Jorge Orta | .08 | .03 | .01 |
| ☐ 632 | Don Kirkwood | .08 | .03 | .01 |
| ☐ 633 | Rob Wilfong DP | .03 | .01 | .00 |
| ☐ 634 | Paul Lindblad | .08 | .03 | .01 |
| ☐ 635 | Don Baylor | .75 | .30 | .07 |
| ☐ 636 | Wayne Garland | .08 | .03 | .01 |
| ☐ 637 | Bill Robinson | .08 | .03 | .01 |
| ☐ 638 | Al Fitzmorris | .08 | .03 | .01 |
| ☐ 639 | Manny Trillo | .12 | .05 | .01 |
| ☐ 640 | Eddie Murray | 4.50 | 1.80 | .45 |
| ☐ 641 | Bobby Castillo | .08 | .03 | .01 |
| ☐ 642 | Wilbur Howard DP | .03 | .01 | .00 |
| ☐ 643 | Tom Hausman | .08 | .03 | .01 |
| ☐ 644 | Manny Mota | .12 | .05 | .01 |
| ☐ 645 | George Scott DP | .08 | .03 | .01 |
| ☐ 646 | Rick Sweet | .08 | .03 | .01 |
| ☐ 647 | Bob Lacey | .08 | .03 | .01 |
| ☐ 648 | Lou Piniella | .20 | .08 | .02 |
| ☐ 649 | John Curtis | .08 | .03 | .01 |
| ☐ 650 | Pete Rose | 4.00 | 1.60 | .40 |
| ☐ 651 | Mike Caldwell | .12 | .05 | .01 |
| ☐ 652 | Stan Papi | .08 | .03 | .01 |
| ☐ 653 | Warren Brusstar DP | .03 | .01 | .00 |
| ☐ 654 | Rick Miller | .08 | .03 | .01 |
| ☐ 655 | Jerry Koosman | .15 | .06 | .01 |
| ☐ 656 | Hosken Powell | .08 | .03 | .01 |
| ☐ 657 | George Medich | .12 | .05 | .01 |
| ☐ 658 | Taylor Duncan | .08 | .03 | .01 |
| ☐ 659 | Mariners Team/Mgr. Darrell Johnson (checklist back) | .25 | .05 | .01 |
| ☐ 660 | Ron LeFlore DP | .08 | .03 | .01 |
| ☐ 661 | Bruce Kison | .08 | .03 | .01 |
| ☐ 662 | Kevin Bell | .08 | .03 | .01 |
| ☐ 663 | Mike Vail | .08 | .03 | .01 |
| ☐ 664 | Doug Bird | .08 | .03 | .01 |
| ☐ 665 | Lou Brock | 1.25 | .50 | .12 |
| ☐ 666 | Rich Dauer | .08 | .03 | .01 |
| ☐ 667 | Don Hood | .08 | .03 | .01 |
| ☐ 668 | Bill North | .08 | .03 | .01 |
| ☐ 669 | Checklist 6 | .30 | .03 | .00 |
| ☐ 670 | Jim Hunter DP | .25 | .10 | .02 |
| ☐ 671 | Joe Ferguson DP | .03 | .01 | .00 |
| ☐ 672 | Ed Halicki | .08 | .03 | .01 |
| ☐ 673 | Tom Hutton | .08 | .03 | .01 |
| ☐ 674 | Dave Tomlin | .08 | .03 | .01 |
| ☐ 675 | Tim McCarver | .15 | .06 | .01 |
| ☐ 676 | Johnny Sutton | .08 | .03 | .01 |
| ☐ 677 | Larry Parrish | .15 | .06 | .01 |
| ☐ 678 | Geoff Zahn | .08 | .03 | .01 |
| ☐ 679 | Derrel Thomas | .08 | .03 | .01 |
| ☐ 680 | Carlton Fisk | .50 | .20 | .05 |
| ☐ 681 | John Henry Johnson | .08 | .03 | .01 |
| ☐ 682 | Dave Chalk | .08 | .03 | .01 |
| ☐ 683 | Dan Meyer DP | .03 | .01 | .00 |
| ☐ 684 | Jamie Easterly DP | .03 | .01 | .00 |
| ☐ 685 | Sixto Lezcano | .12 | .05 | .01 |
| ☐ 686 | Ron Schueler DP | .03 | .01 | .00 |
| ☐ 687 | Rennie Stennett | .08 | .03 | .01 |
| ☐ 688 | Mike Willis | .08 | .03 | .01 |
| ☐ 689 | Orioles Team/Mgr. Earl Weaver (checklist back) | .35 | .07 | .01 |
| ☐ 690 | Buddy Bell | .10 | .04 | .01 |
| ☐ 691 | Dock Ellis DP | .03 | .01 | .00 |
| ☐ 692 | Mickey Stanley | .08 | .03 | .01 |
| ☐ 693 | Dave Rader | .08 | .03 | .01 |
| ☐ 694 | Burt Hooton | .12 | .05 | .01 |
| ☐ 695 | Keith Hernandez | 1.50 | .60 | .15 |
| ☐ 696 | Andy Hassler | .08 | .03 | .01 |
| ☐ 697 | Dave Bergman | .08 | .03 | .01 |
| ☐ 698 | Bill Stein | .08 | .03 | .01 |
| ☐ 699 | Hal Dues | .08 | .03 | .01 |
| ☐ 700 | Reggie Jackson DP | .90 | .36 | .09 |
| ☐ 701 | Orioles Prospects: Mark Corey John Flinn Sammy Stewart | .25 | .10 | .02 |
| ☐ 702 | Red Sox Prospects: Joel Finch Garry Hancock Allen Ripley | .12 | .05 | .01 |
| ☐ 703 | Angels Prospects: Jim Anderson Dave Frost Bob Slater | .12 | .05 | .01 |
| ☐ 704 | White Sox Prospects: Ross Baumgarten Mike Colbern Mike Squires | .12 | .05 | .01 |
| ☐ 705 | Indians Prospects: | .60 | .24 | .06 |
| | Alfredo Griffin | | | |
| | Tim Norrid | | | |
| | Dave Oliver | | | |
| ☐ 706 | Tigers Prospects: Dave Stegman Dave Tobik Kip Young | .12 | .05 | .01 |
| ☐ 707 | Royals Prospects: Randy Bass Jim Gaudet Randy McGilberry | .12 | .05 | .01 |
| ☐ 708 | Brewers Prospects: Kevin Bass Eddie Romero Ned Yost | 1.25 | .50 | .12 |
| ☐ 709 | Twins Prospects: Sam Perlozzo Rick Sofield Kevin Stanfield | .12 | .05 | .01 |
| ☐ 710 | Yankees Prospects: Brian Doyle Mike Heath Dave Rajsich | .25 | .10 | .02 |
| ☐ 711 | A's Prospects: Dwayne Murphy Bruce Robinson Alan Wirth | .80 | .32 | .08 |
| ☐ 712 | Mariners Prospects: Bud Anderson Greg Biercevicz Byron McLaughlin | .12 | .05 | .01 |
| ☐ 713 | Rangers Prospects: Danny Darwin Pat Putnam Billy Sample | .40 | .16 | .04 |
| ☐ 714 | Blue Jays Prospects: Victor Cruz Pat Kelly Ernie Whitt | .12 | .05 | .01 |
| ☐ 715 | Braves Prospects: Bruce Benedict Glenn Hubbard Larry Whisenton | .40 | .16 | .04 |
| ☐ 716 | Cubs Prospects: Dave Geisel Karl Pagel Scot Thompson | .12 | .05 | .01 |
| ☐ 717 | Reds Prospects: Mike LaCoss Ron Oester Harry Spilman | .40 | .16 | .04 |
| ☐ 718 | Astros Prospects: Bruce Bochy Mike Fischlin Don Pisker | .12 | .05 | .01 |
| ☐ 719 | Dodgers Prospects: Pedro Guerrero Rudy Law Joe Simpson | 4.00 | 1.60 | .40 |
| ☐ 720 | Expos Prospects: Jerry Fry Jerry Pirtle Scott Sanderson | .25 | .10 | .02 |
| ☐ 721 | Mets Prospects: Juan Berenguer Dwight Bernard Dan Norman | .15 | .06 | .01 |
| ☐ 722 | Phillies Prospects: Jim Morrison Lonnie Smith Jim Wright | .90 | .36 | .09 |
| ☐ 723 | Pirates Prospects: Dale Berra Eugenio Cotes Ben Wiltbank | .30 | .12 | .03 |
| ☐ 724 | Cardinals Prospects: Tom Bruno George Frazier Terry Kennedy | .90 | .36 | .09 |
| ☐ 725 | Padres Prospects: Jim Beswick Steve Mura Broderick Perkins | .12 | .05 | .01 |
| ☐ 726 | Giants Prospects: Greg Johnston Joe Strain John Tamargo | .12 | .05 | .01 |

# 1980 Topps

The cards in this 726 Card set measure 2 1/2" by 3 1/2". In 1980 Topps released another set of the same size and number of cards as the previous two years. As with those sets, Topps again has produced 66 double printed cards in the set; they are noted by DP in the checklist below. The player's name appears over the picture and his position and team are found in pennant design. Every card carries a facsimile autograph. Team cards feature a team checklist of players in the set on the back and the manager's name on the front. Cards 1-6 show Highlights (HL) of the 1979 season, cards 201-207 are League Leaders, and cards 661-686 feature American and National League rookie "Future Stars," one card for each team showing three young prospects.

|  | MINT | VG-E | F-G |
|---|---|---|---|
| COMPLETE SET | 90.00 | 36.00 | 9.00 |
| COMMON PLAYER (1-726) | .07 | .03 | .01 |
| COMMON DP's (1-726) | .03 | .01 | .00 |

| | | | MINT | VG-E | F-G |
|---|---|---|---|---|---|
| ☐ | 1 | HL: Brock and Yaz, Enter 3000 hit circle | 1.00 | .20 | .04 |
| ☐ | 2 | HL: Willie McCovey, 512th homer sets new mark for NL lefties | .50 | .20 | .05 |
| ☐ | 3 | HL: Manny Mota, All-time pinch-hits, 145 | .12 | .05 | .01 |
| ☐ | 4 | HL: Pete Rose, Career Record 10th season with 200 or more hits | 1.50 | .60 | .15 |
| ☐ | 5 | HL: Garry Templeton, 1st with 100 hits from each side of plate | .18 | .08 | .01 |
| ☐ | 6 | HL: Del Unser, 3rd cons. pinch homer sets new ML standard | .10 | .04 | .01 |
| ☐ | 7 | Mike Lum | .07 | .03 | .01 |
| ☐ | 8 | Craig Swan | .10 | .04 | .01 |
| ☐ | 9 | Steve Braun | .07 | .03 | .01 |
| ☐ | 10 | Denny Martinez | .10 | .04 | .01 |
| ☐ | 11 | Jimmy Sexton | .07 | .03 | .01 |
| ☐ | 12 | John Curtis DP | .03 | .01 | .00 |
| ☐ | 13 | Ron Pruitt | .07 | .03 | .01 |
| ☐ | 14 | Dave Cash | .10 | .04 | .01 |
| ☐ | 15 | Bill Campbell | .10 | .04 | .01 |
| ☐ | 16 | Jerry Narron | .07 | .03 | .01 |
| ☐ | 17 | Bruce Sutter | .40 | .16 | .04 |
| ☐ | 18 | Ron Jackson | .07 | .03 | .01 |
| ☐ | 19 | Balor Moore | .07 | .03 | .01 |
| ☐ | 20 | Dan Ford | .07 | .03 | .01 |
| ☐ | 21 | Manny Sarmiento | .07 | .03 | .01 |
| ☐ | 22 | Pat Putnam | .07 | .03 | .01 |
| ☐ | 23 | Derrel Thomas | .07 | .03 | .01 |
| ☐ | 24 | Jim Slaton | .10 | .04 | .01 |
| ☐ | 25 | Lee Mazzilli | .12 | .05 | .01 |
| ☐ | 26 | Marty Pattin | .07 | .03 | .01 |
| ☐ | 27 | Del Unser | .07 | .03 | .01 |
| ☐ | 28 | Bruce Kison | .07 | .03 | .01 |
| ☐ | 29 | Mark Wagner | .07 | .03 | .01 |
| ☐ | 30 | Vida Blue | .18 | .08 | .01 |
| ☐ | 31 | Jay Johnstone | .10 | .04 | .01 |

| | | | MINT | VG-E | F-G |
|---|---|---|---|---|---|
| ☐ | 32 | Julio Cruz DP | .07 | .03 | .01 |
| ☐ | 33 | Tony Scott | .07 | .03 | .01 |
| ☐ | 34 | Jeff Newman DP | .03 | .01 | .00 |
| ☐ | 35 | Luis Tiant | .18 | .08 | .01 |
| ☐ | 36 | Rusty Torres | .07 | .03 | .01 |
| ☐ | 37 | Kiko Garcia | .07 | .03 | .01 |
| ☐ | 38 | Dan Spillner DP | .03 | .01 | .00 |
| ☐ | 39 | Rowland Office | .07 | .03 | .01 |
| ☐ | 40 | Carlton Fisk | .35 | .14 | .03 |
| ☐ | 41 | Rangers Team/Mgr. Pat Corrales (checklist back) | .25 | .05 | .01 |
| ☐ | 42 | David Palmer | .45 | .18 | .04 |
| ☐ | 43 | Bombo Rivera | .07 | .03 | .01 |
| ☐ | 44 | Bill Fahey | .07 | .03 | .01 |
| ☐ | 45 | Frank White | .15 | .06 | .01 |
| ☐ | 46 | Rico Carty | .10 | .04 | .01 |
| ☐ | 47 | Bill Bonham DP | .03 | .01 | .00 |
| ☐ | 48 | Rick Miller | .07 | .03 | .01 |
| ☐ | 49 | Mario Guerrero | .07 | .03 | .01 |
| ☐ | 50 | J.R. Richard | .18 | .08 | .01 |
| ☐ | 51 | Joe Ferguson DP | .03 | .01 | .00 |
| ☐ | 52 | Warren Brusstar | .07 | .03 | .01 |
| ☐ | 53 | Ben Oglivie | .15 | .06 | .01 |
| ☐ | 54 | Dennis Lamp | .07 | .03 | .01 |
| ☐ | 55 | Bill Madlock | .35 | .14 | .03 |
| ☐ | 56 | Bobby Valentine | .15 | .06 | .01 |
| ☐ | 57 | Pete Vuckovich | .12 | .05 | .01 |
| ☐ | 58 | Doug Flynn | .07 | .03 | .01 |
| ☐ | 59 | Eddy Putman | .07 | .03 | .01 |
| ☐ | 60 | Bucky Dent | .12 | .05 | .01 |
| ☐ | 61 | Gary Serum | .07 | .03 | .01 |
| ☐ | 62 | Mike Ivie | .07 | .03 | .01 |
| ☐ | 63 | Bob Stanley | .12 | .05 | .01 |
| ☐ | 64 | Joe Nolan | .07 | .03 | .01 |
| ☐ | 65 | Al Bumbry | .07 | .03 | .01 |
| ☐ | 66 | Royals Team/Mgr. Jim Frey (checklist back) | .25 | .05 | .01 |
| ☐ | 67 | Doyle Alexander | .10 | .04 | .01 |
| ☐ | 68 | Larry Harlow | .07 | .03 | .01 |
| ☐ | 69 | Rick Williams | .07 | .03 | .01 |
| ☐ | 70 | Gary Carter | 2.00 | .80 | .20 |
| ☐ | 71 | John Milner DP | .03 | .01 | .00 |
| ☐ | 72 | Fred Howard DP | .03 | .01 | .00 |
| ☐ | 73 | Dave Collins | .10 | .04 | .01 |
| ☐ | 74 | Sid Monge | .07 | .03 | .01 |
| ☐ | 75 | Bill Russell | .10 | .04 | .01 |
| ☐ | 76 | John Stearns | .07 | .03 | .01 |
| ☐ | 77 | Dave Stieb | 1.50 | .60 | .15 |
| ☐ | 78 | Ruppert Jones | .10 | .04 | .01 |
| ☐ | 79 | Bob Owchinko | .07 | .03 | .01 |
| ☐ | 80 | Ron LeFlore | .10 | .04 | .01 |
| ☐ | 81 | Ted Sizemore | .07 | .03 | .01 |
| ☐ | 82 | Astros Team/Mgr. Bill Virdon (checklist back) | .25 | .05 | .01 |
| ☐ | 83 | Steve Trout | .35 | .14 | .03 |
| ☐ | 84 | Gary Lavelle | .10 | .04 | .01 |
| ☐ | 85 | Ted Simmons | .35 | .14 | .03 |
| ☐ | 86 | Dave Hamilton | .07 | .03 | .01 |
| ☐ | 87 | Pepe Frias | .07 | .03 | .01 |
| ☐ | 88 | Ken Landreaux | .10 | .04 | .01 |
| ☐ | 89 | Don Hood | .07 | .03 | .01 |
| ☐ | 90 | Manny Trillo | .10 | .04 | .01 |
| ☐ | 91 | Rick Dempsey | .10 | .04 | .01 |
| ☐ | 92 | Rick Rhoden | .15 | .06 | .01 |
| ☐ | 93 | Dave Roberts DP | .03 | .01 | .00 |
| ☐ | 94 | Neil Allen | .35 | .14 | .03 |
| ☐ | 95 | Cecil Cooper | .30 | .12 | .03 |
| ☐ | 96 | A's Team/Mgr. Jim Marshall (checklist back) | .25 | .05 | .01 |
| ☐ | 97 | Bill Lee | .10 | .04 | .01 |
| ☐ | 98 | Jerry Terrell | .07 | .03 | .01 |
| ☐ | 99 | Victor Cruz | .07 | .03 | .01 |
| ☐ | 100 | Johnny Bench | 1.50 | .60 | .15 |
| ☐ | 101 | Aurelio Lopez | .07 | .03 | .01 |
| ☐ | 102 | Rich Dauer | .07 | .03 | .01 |
| ☐ | 103 | Bill Caudill | .35 | .14 | .03 |
| ☐ | 104 | Manny Mota | .10 | .04 | .01 |
| ☐ | 105 | Frank Tanana | .12 | .05 | .01 |
| ☐ | 106 | Jeff Leonard | .75 | .30 | .07 |
| ☐ | 107 | Francisco Barrios | .07 | .03 | .01 |
| ☐ | 108 | Bob Horner | 1.00 | .40 | .10 |
| ☐ | 109 | Bill Travers | .07 | .03 | .01 |
| ☐ | 110 | Fred Lynn DP | .25 | .10 | .02 |
| ☐ | 111 | Bob Knepper | .20 | .08 | .02 |
| ☐ | 112 | White Sox Team/Mgr. Tony LaRussa (checklist back) | .25 | .05 | .01 |
| ☐ | 113 | Geoff Zahn | .07 | .03 | .01 |
| ☐ | 114 | Juan Beniquez | .10 | .04 | .01 |

| | | | | |
|---|---|---|---|---|
| ☐ 115 | Sparky Lyle | .15 | .06 | .01 |
| ☐ 116 | Larry Cox | .07 | .03 | .01 |
| ☐ 117 | Dock Ellis | .07 | .03 | .01 |
| ☐ 118 | Phil Garner | .10 | .04 | .01 |
| ☐ 119 | Sammy Stewart | .10 | .04 | .01 |
| ☐ 120 | Greg Luzinski | .20 | .08 | .02 |
| ☐ 121 | Checklist 1 | .20 | .02 | .00 |
| ☐ 122 | Dave Rosello DP | .03 | .01 | .00 |
| ☐ 123 | Lynn Jones | .07 | .03 | .01 |
| ☐ 124 | Dave Lemanczyk | .07 | .03 | .01 |
| ☐ 125 | Tony Perez | .25 | .10 | .02 |
| ☐ 126 | Dave Tomlin | .07 | .03 | .01 |
| ☐ 127 | Gary Thomasson | .07 | .03 | .01 |
| ☐ 128 | Tom Burgmeier | .07 | .03 | .01 |
| ☐ 129 | Craig Reynolds | .07 | .03 | .01 |
| ☐ 130 | Amos Otis | .12 | .05 | .01 |
| ☐ 131 | Paul Mitchell | .07 | .03 | .01 |
| ☐ 132 | Biff Pocoroba | .07 | .03 | .01 |
| ☐ 133 | Jerry Turner | .07 | .03 | .01 |
| ☐ 134 | Matt Keough | .07 | .03 | .01 |
| ☐ 135 | Bill Buckner | .20 | .08 | .02 |
| ☐ 136 | Dick Ruthven | .07 | .03 | .01 |
| ☐ 137 | John Castino | .20 | .08 | .02 |
| ☐ 138 | Ross Baumgarten | .07 | .03 | .01 |
| ☐ 139 | Dane Iorg | .15 | .06 | .01 |
| ☐ 140 | Rich Gossage | .40 | .16 | .04 |
| ☐ 141 | Gary Alexander | .07 | .03 | .01 |
| ☐ 142 | Phil Huffman | .07 | .03 | .01 |
| ☐ 143 | Bruce Bochte DP | .07 | .03 | .01 |
| ☐ 144 | Steve Comer | .07 | .03 | .01 |
| ☐ 145 | Darrell Evans | .18 | .08 | .01 |
| ☐ 146 | Bob Welch | .18 | .08 | .01 |
| ☐ 147 | Terry Puhl | .10 | .04 | .01 |
| ☐ 148 | Manny Sanguillen | .10 | .04 | .01 |
| ☐ 149 | Tom Hume | .07 | .03 | .01 |
| ☐ 150 | Jason Thompson | .15 | .06 | .01 |
| ☐ 151 | Tom Hausman DP | .03 | .01 | .00 |
| ☐ 152 | John Fulgham | .07 | .03 | .01 |
| ☐ 153 | Tim Blackwell | .07 | .03 | .01 |
| ☐ 154 | Lary Sorensen | .07 | .03 | .01 |
| ☐ 155 | Jerry Remy | .10 | .04 | .01 |
| ☐ 156 | Tony Brizzolara | .07 | .03 | .01 |
| ☐ 157 | Willie Wilson DP | .18 | .08 | .01 |
| ☐ 158 | Rob Picciolo DP | .03 | .01 | .00 |
| ☐ 159 | Ken Clay | .07 | .03 | .01 |
| ☐ 160 | Eddie Murray | 2.75 | 1.10 | .27 |
| ☐ 161 | Larry Christenson | .07 | .03 | .01 |
| ☐ 162 | Bob Randall | .07 | .03 | .01 |
| ☐ 163 | Steve Swisher | .07 | .03 | .01 |
| ☐ 164 | Greg Pryor | .07 | .03 | .01 |
| ☐ 165 | Omar Moreno | .07 | .03 | .01 |
| ☐ 166 | Glenn Abbott | .07 | .03 | .01 |
| ☐ 167 | Jack Clark | .40 | .16 | .04 |
| ☐ 168 | Rick Waits | .07 | .03 | .01 |
| ☐ 169 | Luis Gomez | .07 | .03 | .01 |
| ☐ 170 | Burt Hooton | .07 | .03 | .01 |
| ☐ 171 | Fernando Gonzalez | .07 | .03 | .01 |
| ☐ 172 | Ron Hodges | .07 | .03 | .01 |
| ☐ 173 | John Henry Johnson | .07 | .03 | .01 |
| ☐ 174 | Ray Knight | .15 | .06 | .01 |
| ☐ 175 | Rick Reuschel | .12 | .05 | .01 |
| ☐ 176 | Champ Summers | .07 | .03 | .01 |
| ☐ 177 | Dave Heaverlo | .07 | .03 | .01 |
| ☐ 178 | Tim McCarver | .15 | .06 | .01 |
| ☐ 179 | Ron Davis | .25 | .10 | .02 |
| ☐ 180 | Warren Cromartie | .07 | .03 | .01 |
| ☐ 181 | Moose Haas | .10 | .04 | .01 |
| ☐ 182 | Ken Reitz | .07 | .03 | .01 |
| ☐ 183 | Jim Anderson DP | .03 | .01 | .00 |
| ☐ 184 | Steve Renko DP | .03 | .01 | .00 |
| ☐ 185 | Hal McRae | .12 | .05 | .01 |
| ☐ 186 | Junior Moore | .07 | .03 | .01 |
| ☐ 187 | Alan Ashby | .07 | .03 | .01 |
| ☐ 188 | Terry Crowley | .07 | .03 | .01 |
| ☐ 189 | Kevin Kobel | .07 | .03 | .01 |
| ☐ 190 | Buddy Bell | .18 | .08 | .01 |
| ☐ 191 | Ted Martinez | .07 | .03 | .01 |
| ☐ 192 | Braves Team/Mgr. | .25 | .05 | .01 |
| | Bobby Cox | | | |
| | (checklist back) | | | |
| ☐ 193 | Dave Goltz | .10 | .04 | .01 |
| ☐ 194 | Mike Easler | .20 | .08 | .02 |
| ☐ 195 | John Montefusco | .10 | .04 | .01 |
| ☐ 196 | Lance Parrish | 1.50 | .60 | .15 |
| ☐ 197 | Byron McLaughlin | .07 | .03 | .01 |
| ☐ 198 | Dell Alston DP | .03 | .01 | .00 |
| ☐ 199 | Mike LaCoss | .07 | .03 | .01 |
| ☐ 200 | Jim Rice | 2.00 | .80 | .20 |
| ☐ 201 | Batting Leaders: | .20 | .08 | .02 |
| | Keith Hernandez | | | |
| | Fred Lynn | | | |
| ☐ 202 | Home Run Leaders: | .15 | .06 | .01 |
| | Dave Kingman | | | |

| | | | | |
|---|---|---|---|---|
| | Gorman Thomas | | | |
| ☐ 203 | RBI Leaders: | .20 | .08 | .02 |
| | Dave Winfield | | | |
| | Don Baylor | | | |
| ☐ 204 | Stolen Base Leaders: | .12 | .05 | .01 |
| | Omar Moreno | | | |
| | Willie Wilson | | | |
| ☐ 205 | Victory Leaders: | .20 | .08 | .02 |
| | Joe Niekro | | | |
| | Phil Niekro | | | |
| | Mike Flanagan | | | |
| ☐ 206 | Strikeout Leaders: | .20 | .08 | .02 |
| | J.R. Richard | | | |
| | Nolan Ryan | | | |
| ☐ 207 | ERA Leaders: | .15 | .06 | .01 |
| | J.R. Richard | | | |
| | Ron Guidry | | | |
| ☐ 208 | Wayne Cage | .07 | .03 | .01 |
| ☐ 209 | Von Joshua | .07 | .03 | .01 |
| ☐ 210 | Steve Carlton | 1.75 | .70 | .17 |
| ☐ 211 | Dave Skaggs DP | .03 | .01 | .00 |
| ☐ 212 | Dave Roberts | .07 | .03 | .01 |
| ☐ 213 | Mike Jorgensen DP | .03 | .01 | .00 |
| ☐ 214 | Angels Team/Mgr. | .25 | .05 | .01 |
| | Jim Fregosi | | | |
| | (checklist back) | | | |
| ☐ 215 | Sixto Lezcano | .07 | .03 | .01 |
| ☐ 216 | Phil Mankowski | .07 | .03 | .01 |
| ☐ 217 | Ed Halicki | .07 | .03 | .01 |
| ☐ 218 | Jose Morales | .07 | .03 | .01 |
| ☐ 219 | Steve Mingori | .07 | .03 | .01 |
| ☐ 220 | Dave Concepcion | .20 | .08 | .02 |
| ☐ 221 | Joe Cannon | .07 | .03 | .01 |
| ☐ 222 | Ron Hassey | .10 | .04 | .01 |
| ☐ 223 | Bob Sykes | .07 | .03 | .01 |
| ☐ 224 | Willie Montanez | .10 | .04 | .01 |
| ☐ 225 | Lou Piniella | .18 | .08 | .01 |
| ☐ 226 | Bill Stein | .07 | .03 | .01 |
| ☐ 227 | Len Barker | .12 | .05 | .01 |
| ☐ 228 | Johnny Oates | .07 | .03 | .01 |
| ☐ 229 | Jim Bibby | .10 | .04 | .01 |
| ☐ 230 | Dave Winfield | 1.50 | .60 | .15 |
| ☐ 231 | Steve McCatty | .07 | .03 | .01 |
| ☐ 232 | Alan Trammell | .90 | .36 | .09 |
| ☐ 233 | LaRue Washington | .07 | .03 | .01 |
| ☐ 234 | Vern Ruhle | .07 | .03 | .01 |
| ☐ 235 | Andre Dawson | .90 | .36 | .09 |
| ☐ 236 | Marc Hill | .07 | .03 | .01 |
| ☐ 237 | Scott McGregor | .12 | .05 | .01 |
| ☐ 238 | Rob Wilfong | .07 | .03 | .01 |
| ☐ 239 | Don Aase | .12 | .05 | .01 |
| ☐ 240 | Dave Kingman | .35 | .14 | .03 |
| ☐ 241 | Checklist 2 | .20 | .02 | .00 |
| ☐ 242 | Lamar Johnson | .07 | .03 | .01 |
| ☐ 243 | Jerry Augustine | .07 | .03 | .01 |
| ☐ 244 | Cardinals Team/Mgr. | .25 | .05 | .01 |
| | Ken Boyer | | | |
| | (checklist back) | | | |
| ☐ 245 | Phil Niekro | .50 | .20 | .05 |
| ☐ 246 | Tim Foli DP | .03 | .01 | .00 |
| ☐ 247 | Frank Riccelli | .07 | .03 | .01 |
| ☐ 248 | Jamie Quirk | .07 | .03 | .01 |
| ☐ 249 | Jim Clancy | .10 | .04 | .01 |
| ☐ 250 | Jim Kaat | .30 | .12 | .03 |
| ☐ 251 | Kip Young | .07 | .03 | .01 |
| ☐ 252 | Ted Cox | .07 | .03 | .01 |
| ☐ 253 | John Montague | .07 | .03 | .01 |
| ☐ 254 | Paul Dade DP | .03 | .01 | .00 |
| ☐ 255 | Dusty Baker DP | .07 | .03 | .01 |
| ☐ 256 | Roger Erickson | .07 | .03 | .01 |
| ☐ 257 | Larry Herndon | .10 | .04 | .01 |
| ☐ 258 | Paul Moskau | .07 | .03 | .01 |
| ☐ 259 | Mets Team/Mgr. | .30 | .06 | .01 |
| | Joe Torre | | | |
| | (checklist back) | | | |
| ☐ 260 | Al Oliver | .25 | .10 | .02 |
| ☐ 261 | Dave Chalk | .07 | .03 | .01 |
| ☐ 262 | Benny Ayala | .07 | .03 | .01 |
| ☐ 263 | Dave LaRoche DP | .03 | .01 | .00 |
| ☐ 264 | Bill Robinson | .07 | .03 | .01 |
| ☐ 265 | Robin Yount | 1.50 | .60 | .15 |
| ☐ 266 | Bernie Carbo | .07 | .03 | .01 |
| ☐ 267 | Dan Schatzeder | .07 | .03 | .01 |
| ☐ 268 | Rafael Landestoy | .07 | .03 | .01 |
| ☐ 269 | Dave Tobik | .07 | .03 | .01 |
| ☐ 270 | Mike Schmidt DP | 1.00 | .40 | .10 |
| ☐ 271 | Dick Drago DP | .03 | .01 | .00 |
| ☐ 272 | Ralph Garr | .10 | .04 | .01 |
| ☐ 273 | Eduardo Rodriguez | .07 | .03 | .01 |
| ☐ 274 | Dale Murphy | 4.00 | 1.60 | .40 |
| ☐ 275 | Jerry Koosman | .15 | .06 | .01 |
| ☐ 276 | Tom Veryzer | .07 | .03 | .01 |
| ☐ 277 | Rick Bosetti | .07 | .03 | .01 |

| | | | |
|---|---|---|---|
| ☐ 278 Jim Spencer | .07 | .03 | .01 |
| ☐ 279 Rob Andrews | .07 | .03 | .01 |
| ☐ 280 Gaylord Perry | .55 | .22 | .05 |
| ☐ 281 Paul Blair | .10 | .04 | .01 |
| ☐ 282 Mariners Team/Mgr. Darrell Johnson (checklist back) | .20 | .04 | .01 |
| ☐ 283 John Ellis | .07 | .03 | .01 |
| ☐ 284 Larry Murray DP | .03 | .01 | .00 |
| ☐ 285 Don Baylor | .35 | .14 | .03 |
| ☐ 286 Darold Knowles DP | .03 | .01 | .00 |
| ☐ 287 John Lowenstein | .07 | .03 | .01 |
| ☐ 288 Dave Rozema | .07 | .03 | .01 |
| ☐ 289 Bruce Bochy | .07 | .03 | .01 |
| ☐ 290 Steve Garvey | 1.50 | .60 | .15 |
| ☐ 291 Randy Scarberry | .07 | .03 | .01 |
| ☐ 292 Dale Berra | .10 | .04 | .01 |
| ☐ 293 Elias Sosa | .07 | .03 | .01 |
| ☐ 294 Charlie Spikes | .07 | .03 | .01 |
| ☐ 295 Larry Gura | .10 | .04 | .01 |
| ☐ 296 Dave Rader | .07 | .03 | .01 |
| ☐ 297 Tim Johnson | .07 | .03 | .01 |
| ☐ 298 Ken Holtzman | .10 | .04 | .01 |
| ☐ 299 Steve Henderson | .07 | .03 | .01 |
| ☐ 300 Ron Guidry | .75 | .30 | .07 |
| ☐ 301 Mike Edwards | .07 | .03 | .01 |
| ☐ 302 Dodgers Team/Mgr. Tom Lasorda (checklist back) | .30 | .06 | .01 |
| ☐ 303 Bill Castro | .07 | .03 | .01 |
| ☐ 304 Butch Wynegar | .10 | .04 | .01 |
| ☐ 305 Randy Jones | .10 | .04 | .01 |
| ☐ 306 Denny Walling | .07 | .03 | .01 |
| ☐ 307 Rick Honeycutt | .15 | .06 | .01 |
| ☐ 308 Mike Hargrove | .10 | .04 | .01 |
| ☐ 309 Larry McWilliams | .10 | .04 | .01 |
| ☐ 310 Dave Parker | .85 | .34 | .08 |
| ☐ 311 Roger Metzger | .07 | .03 | .01 |
| ☐ 312 Mike Barlow | .07 | .03 | .01 |
| ☐ 313 Johnny Grubb | .07 | .03 | .01 |
| ☐ 314 Tim Stoddard | .20 | .08 | .02 |
| ☐ 315 Steve Kemp | .15 | .06 | .01 |
| ☐ 316 Bob Lacey | .07 | .03 | .01 |
| ☐ 317 Mike Anderson DP | .03 | .01 | .00 |
| ☐ 318 Jerry Reuss | .12 | .05 | .01 |
| ☐ 319 Chris Speier | .07 | .03 | .01 |
| ☐ 320 Dennis Eckersley | .10 | .04 | .01 |
| ☐ 321 Keith Hernandez | 1.00 | .40 | .10 |
| ☐ 322 Claudell Washington | .12 | .05 | .01 |
| ☐ 323 Mick Kelleher | .07 | .03 | .01 |
| ☐ 324 Tom Underwood | .07 | .03 | .01 |
| ☐ 325 Dan Driessen | .10 | .04 | .01 |
| ☐ 326 Bo McLaughlin | .07 | .03 | .01 |
| ☐ 327 Ray Fosse DP | .03 | .01 | .00 |
| ☐ 328 Twins Team/Mgr. Gene Mauch (checklist back) | .25 | .05 | .01 |
| ☐ 329 Bert Roberge | .07 | .03 | .01 |
| ☐ 330 Al Cowens | .10 | .04 | .01 |
| ☐ 331 Rich Hebner | .07 | .03 | .01 |
| ☐ 332 Enrique Romo | .07 | .03 | .01 |
| ☐ 333 Jim Norris DP | .03 | .01 | .00 |
| ☐ 334 Jim Beattie | .07 | .03 | .01 |
| ☐ 335 Willie McCovey | 1.25 | .50 | .12 |
| ☐ 336 George Medich | .07 | .03 | .01 |
| ☐ 337 Carney Lansford | .35 | .14 | .03 |
| ☐ 338 Johnny Wockenfuss | .07 | .03 | .01 |
| ☐ 339 John D'Acquisto | .07 | .03 | .01 |
| ☐ 340 Ken Singleton | .18 | .08 | .01 |
| ☐ 341 Jim Essian | .07 | .03 | .01 |
| ☐ 342 Odell Jones | .07 | .03 | .01 |
| ☐ 343 Mike Vail | .07 | .03 | .01 |
| ☐ 344 Randy Lerch | .07 | .03 | .01 |
| ☐ 345 Larry Parrish | .12 | .05 | .01 |
| ☐ 346 Buddy Solomon | .07 | .03 | .01 |
| ☐ 347 Harry Chappas | .07 | .03 | .01 |
| ☐ 348 Checklist 3 | .20 | .02 | .00 |
| ☐ 349 Jack Brohamer | .07 | .03 | .01 |
| ☐ 350 George Hendrick | .15 | .06 | .01 |
| ☐ 351 Bob Davis | .07 | .03 | .01 |
| ☐ 352 Dan Briggs | .07 | .03 | .01 |
| ☐ 353 Andy Hassler | .07 | .03 | .01 |
| ☐ 354 Rick Auerbach | .07 | .03 | .01 |
| ☐ 355 Gary Matthews | .18 | .08 | .01 |
| ☐ 356 Padres Team/Mgr. Jerry Coleman (checklist back) | .25 | .05 | .01 |
| ☐ 357 Bob McClure | .10 | .04 | .01 |
| ☐ 358 Lou Whitaker | .90 | .36 | .09 |
| ☐ 359 Randy Moffitt | .07 | .03 | .01 |
| ☐ 360 Darrell Porter DP | .07 | .03 | .01 |
| ☐ 361 Wayne Garland | .07 | .03 | .01 |
| ☐ 362 Danny Goodwin | .07 | .03 | .01 |
| ☐ 363 Wayne Gross | .07 | .03 | .01 |
| ☐ 364 Ray Burris | .07 | .03 | .01 |
| ☐ 365 Bobby Murcer | .18 | .08 | .01 |
| ☐ 366 Rob Dressler | .07 | .03 | .01 |
| ☐ 367 Billy Smith | .07 | .03 | .01 |
| ☐ 368 Willie Aikens | .20 | .08 | .02 |
| ☐ 369 Jim Kern | .07 | .03 | .01 |
| ☐ 370 Cesar Cedeno | .15 | .06 | .01 |
| ☐ 371 Jack Morris | 1.25 | .50 | .12 |
| ☐ 372 Joel Youngblood | .07 | .03 | .01 |
| ☐ 373 Dan Petry DP | 1.00 | .40 | .10 |
| ☐ 374 Jim Gantner | .10 | .04 | .01 |
| ☐ 375 Ross Grimsley | .07 | .03 | .01 |
| ☐ 376 Gary Allenson | .10 | .04 | .01 |
| ☐ 377 Junior Kennedy | .07 | .03 | .01 |
| ☐ 378 Jerry Mumphrey | .10 | .04 | .01 |
| ☐ 379 Kevin Bell | .07 | .03 | .01 |
| ☐ 380 Garry Maddox | .10 | .04 | .01 |
| ☐ 381 Cubs Team/Mgr. Preston Gomez (checklist back) | .25 | .05 | .01 |
| ☐ 382 Dave Freisleben | .07 | .03 | .01 |
| ☐ 383 Ed Ott | .07 | .03 | .01 |
| ☐ 384 Joey McLaughlin | .07 | .03 | .01 |
| ☐ 385 Enos Cabell | .07 | .03 | .01 |
| ☐ 386 Darrell Jackson | .07 | .03 | .01 |
| ☐ 387 Fred Stanley | .07 | .03 | .01 |
| ☐ 388 Mike Paxton | .07 | .03 | .01 |
| ☐ 389 Pete LaCock | .07 | .03 | .01 |
| ☐ 390 Fergie Jenkins | .35 | .14 | .03 |
| ☐ 391 Tony Armas DP | .10 | .04 | .01 |
| ☐ 392 Milt Wilcox | .10 | .04 | .01 |
| ☐ 393 Ozzie Smith | .80 | .32 | .08 |
| ☐ 394 Reggie Cleveland | .07 | .03 | .01 |
| ☐ 395 Ellis Valentine | .10 | .04 | .01 |
| ☐ 396 Dan Meyer | .07 | .03 | .01 |
| ☐ 397 Roy Thomas DP | .03 | .01 | .00 |
| ☐ 398 Barry Foote | .07 | .03 | .01 |
| ☐ 399 Mike Proly DP | .03 | .01 | .00 |
| ☐ 400 George Foster | .40 | .16 | .04 |
| ☐ 401 Pete Falcone | .07 | .03 | .01 |
| ☐ 402 Merv Rettenmund | .07 | .03 | .01 |
| ☐ 403 Pete Redfern DP | .03 | .01 | .00 |
| ☐ 404 Orioles Team/Mgr. Earl Weaver (checklist back) | .30 | .06 | .01 |
| ☐ 405 Dwight Evans | .35 | .14 | .03 |
| ☐ 406 Paul Molitor | .35 | .14 | .03 |
| ☐ 407 Tony Solaita | .07 | .03 | .01 |
| ☐ 408 Bill North | .07 | .03 | .01 |
| ☐ 409 Paul Splittorff | .10 | .04 | .01 |
| ☐ 410 Bobby Bonds | .18 | .08 | .01 |
| ☐ 411 Frank LaCorte | .07 | .03 | .01 |
| ☐ 412 Thad Bosley | .07 | .03 | .01 |
| ☐ 413 Allen Ripley | .07 | .03 | .01 |
| ☐ 414 George Scott | .10 | .04 | .01 |
| ☐ 415 Bill Atkinson | .07 | .03 | .01 |
| ☐ 416 Tom Brookens | .07 | .03 | .01 |
| ☐ 417 Craig Chamberlain DP | .03 | .01 | .00 |
| ☐ 418 Roger Freed DP | .03 | .01 | .00 |
| ☐ 419 Vic Correll | .07 | .03 | .01 |
| ☐ 420 Butch Hobson | .07 | .03 | .01 |
| ☐ 421 Doug Bird | .07 | .03 | .01 |
| ☐ 422 Larry Milbourne | .07 | .03 | .01 |
| ☐ 423 Dave Frost | .07 | .03 | .01 |
| ☐ 424 Yankees Team/Mgr. Dick Howser (checklist back) | .30 | .06 | .01 |
| ☐ 425 Mark Belanger | .12 | .05 | .01 |
| ☐ 426 Grant Jackson | .07 | .03 | .01 |
| ☐ 427 Tom Hutton DP | .03 | .01 | .00 |
| ☐ 428 Pat Zachry | .07 | .03 | .01 |
| ☐ 429 Duane Kuiper | .07 | .03 | .01 |
| ☐ 430 Larry Hisle DP | .07 | .03 | .01 |
| ☐ 431 Mike Krukow | .15 | .06 | .01 |
| ☐ 432 Willie Norwood | .07 | .03 | .01 |
| ☐ 433 Rich Gale | .07 | .03 | .01 |
| ☐ 434 Johnnie LeMaster | .07 | .03 | .01 |
| ☐ 435 Don Gullett | .10 | .04 | .01 |
| ☐ 436 Billy Almon | .07 | .03 | .01 |
| ☐ 437 Joe Niekro | .15 | .06 | .01 |
| ☐ 438 Dave Revering | .07 | .03 | .01 |
| ☐ 439 Mike Phillips | .07 | .03 | .01 |
| ☐ 440 Don Sutton | .60 | .24 | .06 |
| ☐ 441 Eric Soderholm | .07 | .03 | .01 |
| ☐ 442 Jorge Orta | .07 | .03 | .01 |
| ☐ 443 Mike Parrott | .07 | .03 | .01 |
| ☐ 444 Alvis Woods | .07 | .03 | .01 |
| ☐ 445 Mark Fidrych | .15 | .06 | .01 |
| ☐ 446 Duffy Dyer | .07 | .03 | .01 |
| ☐ 447 Nino Espinosa | .07 | .03 | .01 |
| ☐ 448 Jim Wohlford | .07 | .03 | .01 |
| ☐ 449 Doug Bair | .07 | .03 | .01 |

| | | | | |
|---|---|---|---|---|
| ☐ 450 | George Brett | 2.75 | 1.10 | .27 |
| ☐ 451 | Indians Team/Mgr. | .25 | .05 | .01 |
| | Dave Garcia | | | |
| | (checklist back) | | | |
| ☐ 452 | Steve Dillard | .07 | .03 | .01 |
| ☐ 453 | Mike Bacsik | .07 | .03 | .01 |
| ☐ 454 | Tom Donohue | .07 | .03 | .01 |
| ☐ 455 | Mike Torrez | .10 | .04 | .01 |
| ☐ 456 | Frank Taveras | .07 | .03 | .01 |
| ☐ 457 | Bert Blyleven | .30 | .12 | .03 |
| ☐ 458 | Billy Sample | .07 | .03 | .01 |
| ☐ 459 | Mickey Lolich DP | .07 | .03 | .01 |
| ☐ 460 | Willie Randolph | .12 | .05 | .01 |
| ☐ 461 | Dwayne Murphy | .15 | .06 | .01 |
| ☐ 462 | Mike Sadek DP | .03 | .01 | .00 |
| ☐ 463 | Jerry Royster | .07 | .03 | .01 |
| ☐ 464 | John Denny | .15 | .06 | .01 |
| ☐ 465 | Rick Monday | .10 | .04 | .01 |
| ☐ 466 | Mike Squires | .07 | .03 | .01 |
| ☐ 467 | Jesse Jefferson | .07 | .03 | .01 |
| ☐ 468 | Aurelio Rodriguez | .07 | .03 | .01 |
| ☐ 469 | Randy Niemann DP | .03 | .01 | .00 |
| ☐ 470 | Bob Boone | .10 | .04 | .01 |
| ☐ 471 | Hosken Powell DP | .03 | .01 | .00 |
| ☐ 472 | Willie Hernandez | .40 | .16 | .04 |
| ☐ 473 | Bump Wills | .07 | .03 | .01 |
| ☐ 474 | Steve Busby | .10 | .04 | .01 |
| ☐ 475 | Cesar Geronimo | .07 | .03 | .01 |
| ☐ 476 | Bob Shirley | .07 | .03 | .01 |
| ☐ 477 | Buck Martinez | .07 | .03 | .01 |
| ☐ 478 | Gil Flores | .07 | .03 | .01 |
| ☐ 479 | Expos Team/Mgr. | .25 | .05 | .01 |
| | Dick Williams | | | |
| | (checklist back) | | | |
| ☐ 480 | Bob Watson | .10 | .04 | .01 |
| ☐ 481 | Tom Paciorek | .07 | .03 | .01 |
| ☐ 482 | Rickey Henderson | 22.00 | 9.00 | 2.00 |
| ☐ 483 | Bo Diaz | .10 | .04 | .01 |
| ☐ 484 | Checklist 4 | .20 | .02 | .00 |
| ☐ 485 | Mickey Rivers | .10 | .04 | .01 |
| ☐ 486 | Mike Tyson DP | .03 | .01 | .00 |
| ☐ 487 | Wayne Nordhagen | .07 | .03 | .01 |
| ☐ 488 | Roy Howell | .07 | .03 | .01 |
| ☐ 489 | Preston Hanna DP | .03 | .01 | .00 |
| ☐ 490 | Lee May | .10 | .04 | .01 |
| ☐ 491 | Steve Mura DP | .03 | .01 | .00 |
| ☐ 492 | Todd Cruz | .10 | .04 | .01 |
| ☐ 493 | Jerry Martin | .07 | .03 | .01 |
| ☐ 494 | Craig Minetto | .07 | .03 | .01 |
| ☐ 495 | Bake McBride | .10 | .04 | .01 |
| ☐ 496 | Silvio Martinez | .07 | .03 | .01 |
| ☐ 497 | Jim Mason | .07 | .03 | .01 |
| ☐ 498 | Danny Darwin | .10 | .04 | .01 |
| ☐ 499 | Giants Team/Mgr. | .25 | .05 | .01 |
| | Dave Bristol | | | |
| ☐ 500 | Tom Seaver | 1.25 | .50 | .12 |
| ☐ 501 | Rennie Stennett | .07 | .03 | .01 |
| ☐ 502 | Rich Wortham DP | .03 | .01 | .00 |
| ☐ 503 | Mike Cubbage | .07 | .03 | .01 |
| ☐ 504 | Gene Garber | .07 | .03 | .01 |
| ☐ 505 | Bert Campaneris | .12 | .05 | .01 |
| ☐ 506 | Tom Buskey | .07 | .03 | .01 |
| ☐ 507 | Leon Roberts | .07 | .03 | .01 |
| ☐ 508 | U.L. Washington | .07 | .03 | .01 |
| ☐ 509 | Ed Glynn | .07 | .03 | .01 |
| ☐ 510 | Ron Cey | .30 | .12 | .03 |
| ☐ 511 | Eric Wilkins | .07 | .03 | .01 |
| ☐ 512 | Jose Cardenal | .07 | .03 | .01 |
| ☐ 513 | Tom Dixon DP | .03 | .01 | .00 |
| ☐ 514 | Steve Ontiveros | .07 | .03 | .01 |
| ☐ 515 | Mike Caldwell | .10 | .04 | .01 |
| ☐ 516 | Hector Cruz | .07 | .03 | .01 |
| ☐ 517 | Don Stanhouse | .07 | .03 | .01 |
| ☐ 518 | Nelson Norman | .07 | .03 | .01 |
| ☐ 519 | Steve Nicosia | .07 | .03 | .01 |
| ☐ 520 | Steve Rogers | .15 | .06 | .01 |
| ☐ 521 | Ken Brett | .10 | .04 | .01 |
| ☐ 522 | Jim Morrison | .10 | .04 | .01 |
| ☐ 523 | Ken Henderson | .07 | .03 | .01 |
| ☐ 524 | Jim Wright DP | .03 | .01 | .00 |
| ☐ 525 | Clint Hurdle | .07 | .03 | .01 |
| ☐ 526 | Phillies Team/Mgr. | .25 | .05 | .01 |
| | Dallas Green | | | |
| | (checklist back) | | | |
| ☐ 527 | Doug Rau DP | .03 | .01 | .00 |
| ☐ 528 | Adrian Devine | .07 | .03 | .01 |
| ☐ 529 | Jim Barr | .07 | .03 | .01 |
| ☐ 530 | Jim Sundberg DP | .07 | .03 | .01 |
| ☐ 531 | Eric Rasmussen | .07 | .03 | .01 |
| ☐ 532 | Willie Horton | .10 | .04 | .01 |
| ☐ 533 | Checklist 5 | .20 | .02 | .00 |
| ☐ 534 | Andre Thornton | .18 | .08 | .01 |
| ☐ 535 | Bob Forsch | .12 | .05 | .01 |

| | | | | |
|---|---|---|---|---|
| ☐ 536 | Lee Lacy | .15 | .06 | .01 |
| ☐ 537 | Alex Trevino | .12 | .05 | .01 |
| ☐ 538 | Joe Strain | .07 | .03 | .01 |
| ☐ 539 | Rudy May | .07 | .03 | .01 |
| ☐ 540 | Pete Rose | 3.50 | 1.40 | .35 |
| ☐ 541 | Miguel Dilone | .07 | .03 | .01 |
| ☐ 542 | Joe Coleman | .07 | .03 | .01 |
| ☐ 543 | Pat Kelly | .07 | .03 | .01 |
| ☐ 544 | Rick Sutcliffe | 1.25 | .50 | .12 |
| ☐ 545 | Jeff Burroughs | .10 | .04 | .01 |
| ☐ 546 | Rick Langford | .07 | .03 | .01 |
| ☐ 547 | John Wathan | .07 | .03 | .01 |
| ☐ 548 | Dave Rajsich | .07 | .03 | .01 |
| ☐ 549 | Larry Wolfe | .07 | .03 | .01 |
| ☐ 550 | Ken Griffey | .12 | .05 | .01 |
| ☐ 551 | Pirates Team/Mgr. | .25 | .05 | .01 |
| | Chuck Tanner | | | |
| | (checklist back) | | | |
| ☐ 552 | Bill Nahorodny | .07 | .03 | .01 |
| ☐ 553 | Dick Davis | .07 | .03 | .01 |
| ☐ 554 | Art Howe | .07 | .03 | .01 |
| ☐ 555 | Ed Figueroa | .07 | .03 | .01 |
| ☐ 556 | Joe Rudi | .10 | .04 | .01 |
| ☐ 557 | Mark Lee | .07 | .03 | .01 |
| ☐ 558 | Alfredo Griffin | .15 | .06 | .01 |
| ☐ 559 | Dale Murray | .07 | .03 | .01 |
| ☐ 560 | Dave Lopes | .15 | .06 | .01 |
| ☐ 561 | Eddie Whitson | .12 | .05 | .01 |
| ☐ 562 | Joe Wallis | .07 | .03 | .01 |
| ☐ 563 | Will McEnaney | .07 | .03 | .01 |
| ☐ 564 | Rick Manning | .07 | .03 | .01 |
| ☐ 565 | Dennis Leonard | .12 | .05 | .01 |
| ☐ 566 | Bud Harrelson | .10 | .04 | .01 |
| ☐ 567 | Skip Lockwood | .07 | .03 | .01 |
| ☐ 568 | Gary Roenicke | .30 | .12 | .03 |
| ☐ 569 | Terry Kennedy | .25 | .10 | .02 |
| ☐ 570 | Roy Smalley | .10 | .04 | .01 |
| ☐ 571 | Joe Sambito | .10 | .04 | .01 |
| ☐ 572 | Jerry Morales DP | .03 | .01 | .00 |
| ☐ 573 | Kent Tekulve | .12 | .05 | .01 |
| ☐ 574 | Scot Thompson | .07 | .03 | .01 |
| ☐ 575 | Ken Kravec | .07 | .03 | .01 |
| ☐ 576 | Jim Dwyer | .07 | .03 | .01 |
| ☐ 577 | Blue Jays Team/Mgr. | .20 | .04 | .01 |
| | Bobby Mattick | | | |
| | (checklist back) | | | |
| ☐ 578 | Scott Sanderson | .10 | .04 | .01 |
| ☐ 579 | Charlie Moore | .07 | .03 | .01 |
| ☐ 580 | Nolan Ryan | 1.25 | .50 | .12 |
| ☐ 581 | Bob Bailor | .07 | .03 | .01 |
| ☐ 582 | Brian Doyle | .07 | .03 | .01 |
| ☐ 583 | Bob Stinson | .07 | .03 | .01 |
| ☐ 584 | Kurt Bevacqua | .07 | .03 | .01 |
| ☐ 585 | Al Hrabosky | .10 | .04 | .01 |
| ☐ 586 | Mitchell Page | .07 | .03 | .01 |
| ☐ 587 | Garry Templeton | .18 | .08 | .01 |
| ☐ 588 | Greg Minton | .10 | .04 | .01 |
| ☐ 589 | Chet Lemon | .12 | .05 | .01 |
| ☐ 590 | Jim Palmer | 1.00 | .40 | .10 |
| ☐ 591 | Rick Cerone | .10 | .04 | .01 |
| ☐ 592 | Jon Matlack | .10 | .04 | .01 |
| ☐ 593 | Jesus Alou | .07 | .03 | .01 |
| ☐ 594 | Dick Tidrow | .07 | .03 | .01 |
| ☐ 595 | Don Money | .07 | .03 | .01 |
| ☐ 596 | Rick Matula | .07 | .03 | .01 |
| ☐ 597 | Tom Poquette | .07 | .03 | .01 |
| ☐ 598 | Fred Kendall DP | .03 | .01 | .00 |
| ☐ 599 | Mike Norris | .10 | .04 | .01 |
| ☐ 600 | Reggie Jackson | 1.75 | .70 | .17 |
| ☐ 601 | Buddy Schultz | .07 | .03 | .01 |
| ☐ 602 | Brian Downing | .10 | .04 | .01 |
| ☐ 603 | Jack Billingham DP | .03 | .01 | .00 |
| ☐ 604 | Glenn Adams | .07 | .03 | .01 |
| ☐ 605 | Terry Forster | .15 | .06 | .01 |
| ☐ 606 | Reds Team/Mgr. | .25 | .05 | .01 |
| | John McNamara | | | |
| | (checklist back) | | | |
| ☐ 607 | Woodie Fryman | .07 | .03 | .01 |
| ☐ 608 | Alan Bannister | .07 | .03 | .01 |
| ☐ 609 | Ron Reed | .07 | .03 | .01 |
| ☐ 610 | Willie Stargell | .90 | .36 | .09 |
| ☐ 611 | Jerry Garvin DP | .03 | .01 | .00 |
| ☐ 612 | Cliff Johnson | .07 | .03 | .01 |
| ☐ 613 | Randy Stein | .07 | .03 | .01 |
| ☐ 614 | John Hiller | .10 | .04 | .01 |
| ☐ 615 | Doug DeCinces | .18 | .08 | .01 |
| ☐ 616 | Gene Richards | .07 | .03 | .01 |
| ☐ 617 | Joaquin Andujar | .18 | .08 | .01 |
| ☐ 618 | Bob Montgomery DP | .03 | .01 | .00 |
| ☐ 619 | Sergio Ferrer | .07 | .03 | .01 |
| ☐ 620 | Richie Zisk | .10 | .04 | .01 |
| ☐ 621 | Bob Grich | .15 | .06 | .01 |
| ☐ 622 | Mario Soto | .15 | .06 | .01 |

| | | | | |
|---|---|---|---|---|
| ☐ 623 | Gorman Thomas | .18 | .08 | .01 |
| ☐ 624 | Lerrin LaGrow | .07 | .03 | .01 |
| ☐ 625 | Chris Chambliss | .12 | .05 | .01 |
| ☐ 626 | Tigers Team/Mgr. | .30 | .06 | .01 |
| | Sparky Anderson | | | |
| | (checklist back) | | | |
| ☐ 627 | Pedro Borbon | .07 | .03 | .01 |
| ☐ 628 | Doug Capilla | .07 | .03 | .01 |
| ☐ 629 | Jim Todd | .07 | .03 | .01 |
| ☐ 630 | Larry Bowa | .20 | .08 | .02 |
| ☐ 631 | Mark Littell | .07 | .03 | .01 |
| ☐ 632 | Barry Bonnell | .10 | .04 | .01 |
| ☐ 633 | Bob Apodaca | .07 | .03 | .01 |
| ☐ 634 | Glenn Borgmann DP | .03 | .01 | .00 |
| ☐ 635 | John Candelaria | .15 | .06 | .01 |
| ☐ 636 | Toby Harrah | .10 | .04 | .01 |
| ☐ 637 | Joe Simpson | .07 | .03 | .01 |
| ☐ 638 | Mark Clear | .35 | .14 | .03 |
| ☐ 639 | Larry Biittner | .07 | .03 | .01 |
| ☐ 640 | Mike Flanagan | .12 | .05 | .01 |
| ☐ 641 | Ed Kranepool | .10 | .04 | .01 |
| ☐ 642 | Ken Forsch DP | .07 | .03 | .01 |
| ☐ 643 | John Mayberry | .10 | .04 | .01 |
| ☐ 644 | Charlie Hough | .15 | .06 | .01 |
| ☐ 645 | Rick Burleson | .12 | .05 | .01 |
| ☐ 646 | Checklist 6 | .20 | .02 | .00 |
| ☐ 647 | Milt May | .07 | .03 | .01 |
| ☐ 648 | Roy White | .10 | .04 | .01 |
| ☐ 649 | Tom Griffin | .07 | .03 | .01 |
| ☐ 650 | Joe Morgan | .75 | .30 | .07 |
| ☐ 651 | Rollie Fingers | .35 | .14 | .03 |
| ☐ 652 | Mario Mendoza | .07 | .03 | .01 |
| ☐ 653 | Stan Bahnsen | .07 | .03 | .01 |
| ☐ 654 | Bruce Boisclair DP | .03 | .01 | .00 |
| ☐ 655 | Tug McGraw | .18 | .08 | .01 |
| ☐ 656 | Larvell Blanks | .07 | .03 | .01 |
| ☐ 657 | Dave Edwards | .07 | .03 | .01 |
| ☐ 658 | Chris Knapp | .07 | .03 | .01 |
| ☐ 659 | Brewers Team/Mgr. | .25 | .05 | .01 |
| | George Bamberger | | | |
| | (checklist back) | | | |
| ☐ 660 | Rusty Staub | .18 | .08 | .01 |
| ☐ 661 | Orioles Rookies: | .12 | .05 | .01 |
| | Mark Corey | | | |
| | Dave Ford | | | |
| | Wayne Krenchicki | | | |
| ☐ 662 | Red Sox Rookies: | .12 | .05 | .01 |
| | Joel Finch | | | |
| | Mike O'Berry | | | |
| | Chuck Rainey | | | |
| ☐ 663 | Angels Rookies: | .50 | .20 | .05 |
| | Ralph Botting | | | |
| | Bob Clark | | | |
| | Dickie Thon | | | |
| ☐ 664 | White Sox Rookies: | .12 | .05 | .01 |
| | Mike Colbern | | | |
| | Guy Hoffman | | | |
| | Dewey Robinson | | | |
| ☐ 665 | Indians Rookies: | .12 | .05 | .01 |
| | Larry Anderson | | | |
| | Bobby Cuellar | | | |
| | Randy Wihtol | | | |
| ☐ 666 | Tigers Rookies: | .12 | .05 | .01 |
| | Mike Chris | | | |
| | Al Greene | | | |
| | Bruce Robbins | | | |
| ☐ 667 | Royals Rookies: | 2.50 | 1.00 | .25 |
| | Renie Martin | | | |
| | Bill Paschall | | | |
| | Dan Quisenberry | | | |
| ☐ 668 | Brewers Rookies: | .12 | .05 | .01 |
| | Danny Boitano | | | |
| | Willie Mueller | | | |
| | Lenn Sakata | | | |
| ☐ 669 | Twins Rookies: | .75 | .30 | .07 |
| | Dan Graham | | | |
| | Rick Sofield | | | |
| | Gary Ward | | | |
| ☐ 670 | Yankees Rookies: | .12 | .05 | .01 |
| | Bobby Brown | | | |
| | Brad Gulden | | | |
| | Darryl Jones | | | |
| ☐ 671 | A's Rookies: | .25 | .10 | .02 |
| | Derek Bryant | | | |
| | Brian Kingman | | | |
| | Mike Morgan | | | |
| ☐ 672 | Mariners Rookies: | .12 | .05 | .01 |
| | Charlie Beamon | | | |
| | Rodney Craig | | | |
| | Rafael Vasquez | | | |
| ☐ 673 | Rangers Rookies: | .12 | .05 | .01 |
| | Brian Allard | | | |
| | Jerry Don Gleaton | | | |
| | Greg Mahlberg | | | |
| ☐ 674 | Blue Jays Rookies: | .12 | .05 | .01 |
| | Butch Edge | | | |
| | Pat Kelly | | | |
| | Ted Wilborn | | | |
| ☐ 675 | Braves Rookies: | .20 | .08 | .02 |
| | Bruce Benedict | | | |
| | Larry Bradford | | | |
| | Eddie Miller | | | |
| ☐ 676 | Cubs Rookies: | .12 | .05 | .01 |
| | Dave Geisel | | | |
| | Steve Macko | | | |
| | Karl Pagel | | | |
| ☐ 677 | Reds Rookies: | .12 | .05 | .01 |
| | Art DeFreites | | | |
| | Frank Pastore | | | |
| | Harry Spilman | | | |
| ☐ 678 | Astros Rookies: | .20 | .08 | .02 |
| | Reggie Baldwin | | | |
| | Alan Knicely | | | |
| | Pete Ladd | | | |
| ☐ 679 | Dodgers Rookies: | .30 | .12 | .03 |
| | Joe Beckwith | | | |
| | Mickey Hatcher | | | |
| | Dave Patterson | | | |
| ☐ 680 | Expos Rookies: | .60 | .24 | .06 |
| | Tony Bernazard | | | |
| | Randy Miller | | | |
| | John Tamargo | | | |
| ☐ 681 | Mets Rookies: | 5.00 | 2.00 | .50 |
| | Dan Norman | | | |
| | Jesse Orosco | | | |
| | Mike Scott | | | |
| ☐ 682 | Phillies Rookies: | .20 | .08 | .02 |
| | Ramon Aviles | | | |
| | Dickie Noles | | | |
| | Kevin Saucier | | | |
| ☐ 683 | Pirates Rookies: | .12 | .05 | .01 |
| | Dorian Boyland | | | |
| | Alberto Lois | | | |
| | Harry Saferight | | | |
| ☐ 684 | Cardinals Rookies: | .75 | .30 | .07 |
| | George Frazier | | | |
| | Tom Herr | | | |
| | Dan O'Brien | | | |
| ☐ 685 | Padres Rookies: | .12 | .05 | .01 |
| | Tim Flannery | | | |
| | Brian Greer | | | |
| | Jim Wilhelm | | | |
| ☐ 686 | Giants Rookies: | .12 | .05 | .01 |
| | Greg Johnston | | | |
| | Dennis Littlejohn | | | |
| | Phil Nastu | | | |
| ☐ 687 | Mike Heath DP | .03 | .01 | .00 |
| ☐ 688 | Steve Stone | .12 | .05 | .01 |
| ☐ 689 | Red Sox Team/Mgr. | .25 | .05 | .01 |
| | Don Zimmer | | | |
| | (checklist back) | | | |
| ☐ 690 | Tommy John | .25 | .10 | .02 |
| ☐ 691 | Ivan DeJesus | .07 | .03 | .01 |
| ☐ 692 | Rawly Eastwick DP | .03 | .01 | .00 |
| ☐ 693 | Craig Kusick | .07 | .03 | .01 |
| ☐ 694 | Jim Rooker | .07 | .03 | .01 |
| ☐ 695 | Reggie Smith | .15 | .06 | .01 |
| ☐ 696 | Julio Gonzalez | .07 | .03 | .01 |
| ☐ 697 | David Clyde | .07 | .03 | .01 |
| ☐ 698 | Oscar Gamble | .10 | .04 | .01 |
| ☐ 699 | Floyd Bannister | .10 | .04 | .01 |
| ☐ 700 | Rod Carew DP | .65 | .26 | .06 |
| ☐ 701 | Ken Oberkfell | .35 | .14 | .03 |
| ☐ 702 | Ed Farmer | .07 | .03 | .01 |
| ☐ 703 | Otto Velez | .07 | .03 | .01 |
| ☐ 704 | Gene Tenace | .07 | .03 | .01 |
| ☐ 705 | Freddie Patek | .07 | .03 | .01 |
| ☐ 706 | Tippy Martinez | .10 | .04 | .01 |
| ☐ 707 | Elliott Maddox | .07 | .03 | .01 |
| ☐ 708 | Bob Tolan | .07 | .03 | .01 |
| ☐ 709 | Pat Underwood | .07 | .03 | .01 |
| ☐ 710 | Graig Nettles | .30 | .12 | .03 |
| ☐ 711 | Bob Galasso | .07 | .03 | .01 |
| ☐ 712 | Rodney Scott | .07 | .03 | .01 |
| ☐ 713 | Terry Whitfield | .07 | .03 | .01 |
| ☐ 714 | Fred Norman | .07 | .03 | .01 |
| ☐ 715 | Sal Bando | .10 | .04 | .01 |
| ☐ 716 | Lynn McGlothen | .07 | .03 | .01 |
| ☐ 717 | Mickey Klutts DP | .03 | .01 | .00 |
| ☐ 718 | Greg Gross | .07 | .03 | .01 |
| ☐ 719 | Don Robinson | .10 | .04 | .01 |
| ☐ 720 | Carl Yastrzemski DP | .85 | .34 | .08 |
| ☐ 721 | Paul Hartzell | .07 | .03 | .01 |
| ☐ 722 | Jose Cruz | .20 | .08 | .02 |
| ☐ 723 | Shane Rawley | .15 | .06 | .01 |
| ☐ 724 | Jerry White | .07 | .03 | .01 |

| | | MINT | VG-E | F-G |
|---|---|---|---|---|
| ☐ 725 | Rick Wise | .10 | .04 | .01 |
| ☐ 726 | Steve Yeager | .15 | .06 | .01 |

| | | | | |
|---|---|---|---|---|
| ☐ 59 | Vida Blue | .10 | .04 | .01 |
| ☐ 60 | Davey Lopes | .10 | .04 | .01 |

## 1980 Topps Super

The cards in this 60 card set measure 4 7/8" by 6 7/8". The 1980 Topps Superstar Photo set was issued in two different varieties. Both have identical fronts, but one is printed on thick cardboard with white backs, while the other is printed on thin stock with gray backs. Cards of the "white back" variety were issued first in three-card cellophane packages. To meet demand for the set, Topps then issued the gray back set via a variety of promotions. Cards 2, 6, 12, 13, 14 and 17 of the gray back set are triple-printed. The prices listed below are for gray backs (which have a Topps logo centered on the back); white backs are worth two and a half times (2.5X) the listed prices below.

| | | MINT | VG-E | F-G |
|---|---|---|---|---|
| COMPLETE SET | | 6.00 | 2.40 | .60 |
| COMMON PLAYER (1-60) | | .07 | .03 | .01 |
| ☐ 1 | Willie Stargell | .30 | .12 | .03 |
| ☐ 2 | Mike Schmidt TP | .35 | .14 | .03 |
| ☐ 3 | Johnny Bench | .50 | .20 | .05 |
| ☐ 4 | Jim Palmer | .35 | .14 | .03 |
| ☐ 5 | Jim Rice | .50 | .20 | .05 |
| ☐ 6 | Reggie Jackson TP | .30 | .12 | .03 |
| ☐ 7 | Ron Guidry | .25 | .10 | .02 |
| ☐ 8 | Lee Mazzilli | .10 | .04 | .01 |
| ☐ 9 | Don Baylor | .12 | .05 | .01 |
| ☐ 10 | Fred Lynn | .20 | .08 | .02 |
| ☐ 11 | Ken Singleton | .10 | .04 | .01 |
| ☐ 12 | Rod Carew TP | .25 | .10 | .02 |
| ☐ 13 | Steve Garvey TP | .30 | .12 | .03 |
| ☐ 14 | George Brett TP | .35 | .14 | .03 |
| ☐ 15 | Tom Seaver | .35 | .14 | .03 |
| ☐ 16 | Dave Kingman | .15 | .06 | .01 |
| ☐ 17 | Dave Parker TP | .15 | .06 | .01 |
| ☐ 18 | Dave Winfield | .40 | .16 | .04 |
| ☐ 19 | Pete Rose | 1.00 | .40 | .10 |
| ☐ 20 | Nolan Ryan | .35 | .14 | .03 |
| ☐ 21 | Graig Nettles | .15 | .06 | .01 |
| ☐ 22 | Carl Yastrzemski | .65 | .26 | .06 |
| ☐ 23 | Tommy John | .15 | .06 | .01 |
| ☐ 24 | George Foster | .15 | .06 | .01 |
| ☐ 25 | J.R. Richard | .10 | .04 | .01 |
| ☐ 26 | Keith Hernandez | .25 | .10 | .02 |
| ☐ 27 | Bob Horner | .25 | .10 | .02 |
| ☐ 28 | Eddie Murray | .60 | .24 | .06 |
| ☐ 29 | Steve Kemp | .10 | .04 | .01 |
| ☐ 30 | Gorman Thomas | .10 | .04 | .01 |
| ☐ 31 | Sixto Lezcano | .07 | .03 | .01 |
| ☐ 32 | Bruce Sutter | .15 | .06 | .01 |
| ☐ 33 | Cecil Cooper | .15 | .06 | .01 |
| ☐ 34 | Larry Bowa | .12 | .05 | .01 |
| ☐ 35 | Al Oliver | .15 | .06 | .01 |
| ☐ 36 | Ted Simmons | .15 | .06 | .01 |
| ☐ 37 | Garry Templeton | .10 | .04 | .01 |
| ☐ 38 | Jerry Koosman | .10 | .04 | .01 |
| ☐ 39 | Darrell Porter | .07 | .03 | .01 |
| ☐ 40 | Roy Smalley | .07 | .03 | .01 |
| ☐ 41 | Craig Swan | .07 | .03 | .01 |
| ☐ 42 | Jason Thompson | .10 | .04 | .01 |
| ☐ 43 | Andre Thornton | .10 | .04 | .01 |
| ☐ 44 | Rick Manning | .07 | .03 | .01 |
| ☐ 45 | Kent Tekulve | .10 | .04 | .01 |
| ☐ 46 | Phil Niekro | .20 | .08 | .02 |
| ☐ 47 | Buddy Bell | .15 | .06 | .01 |
| ☐ 48 | Randy Jones | .07 | .03 | .01 |
| ☐ 49 | Brian Downing | .07 | .03 | .01 |
| ☐ 50 | Amos Otis | .10 | .04 | .01 |
| ☐ 51 | Rick Bosetti | .07 | .03 | .01 |
| ☐ 52 | Gary Carter | .50 | .20 | .05 |
| ☐ 53 | Larry Parrish | .10 | .04 | .01 |
| ☐ 54 | Jack Clark | .15 | .06 | .01 |
| ☐ 55 | Bruce Bochte | .07 | .03 | .01 |
| ☐ 56 | Cesar Cedeno | .10 | .04 | .01 |
| ☐ 57 | Chet Lemon | .10 | .04 | .01 |
| ☐ 58 | Dave Revering | .07 | .03 | .01 |

## 1981 Topps

The cards in this 726 card set measure 2 1/2" by 3 1/2". League Leaders (1-8), Record Breakers (201-208), and Post-season cards (401-404) are topical subsets found in this set marketed by Topps in 1981. The team cards are all grouped together (661-686) and feature team checklist backs and a very small photo of the team's manager in the upper right corner of the obverse. The obverses carry the player's position and team in a baseball cap design, and the company name is printed in a small baseball. The backs are red and gray. The 66 double printed cards are noted in the checklist by DP. The set is quite popular with collectors partly due to the presence of rookie cards of Fernando Valenzuela, Tim Raines, Kirk Gibson, Harold Baines, John Tudor, Lloyd Moseby, Hubie Brooks, Mike Boddicker, and Tony Pena.

| | | MINT | VG-E | F-G |
|---|---|---|---|---|
| COMPLETE SET | | 60.00 | 24.00 | 6.00 |
| COMMON PLAYER (1-726) | | .05 | .02 | .00 |
| COMMON DP's (1-726) | | .02 | .01 | .00 |
| ☐ 1 | Batting Leaders: George Brett Bill Buckner | .50 | .20 | .05 |
| ☐ 2 | Home Run Leaders: Reggie Jackson Ben Oglivie Mike Schmidt | .30 | .12 | .03 |
| ☐ 3 | RBI Leaders: Cecil Cooper Mike Schmidt | .20 | .08 | .02 |
| ☐ 4 | Stolen Base Leaders: Rickey Henderson Ron LeFlore | .18 | .08 | .01 |
| ☐ 5 | Victory Leaders: Steve Stone Steve Carlton | .15 | .06 | .01 |
| ☐ 6 | Strikeout Leaders: Len Barker Steve Carlton | .15 | .06 | .01 |
| ☐ 7 | ERA Leaders: Rudy May Don Sutton | .10 | .04 | .01 |
| ☐ 8 | Leading Firemen: Dan Quisenberry Rollie Fingers Tom Hume | .15 | .06 | .01 |
| ☐ 9 | Pete LaCock DP | .02 | .01 | .00 |
| ☐ 10 | Mike Flanagan | .10 | .04 | .01 |
| ☐ 11 | Jim Wohlford DP | .02 | .01 | .00 |
| ☐ 12 | Mark Clear | .05 | .02 | .00 |
| ☐ 13 | Joe Charboneau | .15 | .06 | .01 |
| ☐ 14 | John Tudor | 1.50 | .60 | .15 |
| ☐ 15 | Larry Parrish | .10 | .04 | .01 |
| ☐ 16 | Ron Davis | .10 | .04 | .01 |
| ☐ 17 | Cliff Johnson | .05 | .02 | .00 |

| | | | | |
|---|---|---|---|---|
| ☐ 18 | Glenn Adams | .05 | .02 | .00 |
| ☐ 19 | Jim Clancy | .08 | .03 | .01 |
| ☐ 20 | Jeff Burroughs | .08 | .03 | .01 |
| ☐ 21 | Ron Oester | .08 | .03 | .01 |
| ☐ 22 | Danny Darwin | .05 | .02 | .00 |
| ☐ 23 | Alex Trevino | .05 | .02 | .00 |
| ☐ 24 | Don Stanhouse | .05 | .02 | .00 |
| ☐ 25 | Sixto Lezcano | .05 | .02 | .00 |
| ☐ 26 | U.L. Washington | .05 | .02 | .00 |
| ☐ 27 | Champ Summers DP | .02 | .01 | .00 |
| ☐ 28 | Enrique Romo | .05 | .02 | .00 |
| ☐ 29 | Gene Tenace | .05 | .02 | .00 |
| ☐ 30 | Jack Clark | .25 | .10 | .02 |
| ☐ 31 | Checklist 1-121 DP | .07 | .01 | .00 |
| ☐ 32 | Ken Oberkfell | .05 | .02 | .00 |
| ☐ 33 | Rick Honeycutt | .08 | .03 | .01 |
| ☐ 34 | Aurelio Rodriguez | .05 | .02 | .00 |
| ☐ 35 | Mitchell Page | .05 | .02 | .00 |
| ☐ 36 | Ed Farmer | .05 | .02 | .00 |
| ☐ 37 | Gary Roenicke | .08 | .03 | .01 |
| ☐ 38 | Win Remmerswaal | .05 | .02 | .00 |
| ☐ 39 | Tom Veryzer | .05 | .02 | .00 |
| ☐ 40 | Tug McGraw | .15 | .06 | .01 |
| ☐ 41 | Ranger Rookies | .20 | .08 | .02 |
| | Bob Babcock | | | |
| | John Butcher | | | |
| | Jerry Don Gleaton | | | |
| ☐ 42 | Jerry White DP | .02 | .01 | .00 |
| ☐ 43 | Jose Morales | .05 | .02 | .00 |
| ☐ 44 | Larry McWilliams | .08 | .03 | .01 |
| ☐ 45 | Enos Cabell | .05 | .02 | .00 |
| ☐ 46 | Rick Bosetti | .05 | .02 | .00 |
| ☐ 47 | Ken Brett | .08 | .03 | .01 |
| ☐ 48 | Dave Skaggs | .05 | .02 | .00 |
| ☐ 49 | Bob Shirley | .05 | .02 | .00 |
| ☐ 50 | Dave Lopes | .12 | .05 | .01 |
| ☐ 51 | Bill Robinson DP | .02 | .01 | .00 |
| ☐ 52 | Hector Cruz | .05 | .02 | .00 |
| ☐ 53 | Kevin Saucier | .05 | .02 | .00 |
| ☐ 54 | Ivan DeJesus | .05 | .02 | .00 |
| ☐ 55 | Mike Norris | .08 | .03 | .01 |
| ☐ 56 | Buck Martinez | .05 | .02 | .00 |
| ☐ 57 | Dave Roberts | .05 | .02 | .00 |
| ☐ 58 | Joel Youngblood | .05 | .02 | .00 |
| ☐ 59 | Dan Petry | .35 | .14 | .03 |
| ☐ 60 | Willie Randolph | .12 | .05 | .01 |
| ☐ 61 | Butch Wynegar | .08 | .03 | .01 |
| ☐ 62 | Joe Pettini | .05 | .02 | .00 |
| ☐ 63 | Steve Renko DP | .02 | .01 | .00 |
| ☐ 64 | Brian Asselstine | .05 | .02 | .00 |
| ☐ 65 | Scott McGregor | .12 | .05 | .01 |
| ☐ 66 | Royals Rookies | .10 | .04 | .01 |
| | Manny Castillo | | | |
| | Tim Ireland | | | |
| | Mike Jones | | | |
| ☐ 67 | Ken Kravec | .05 | .02 | .00 |
| ☐ 68 | Matt Alexander DP | .02 | .01 | .00 |
| ☐ 69 | Ed Halicki | .05 | .02 | .00 |
| ☐ 70 | Al Oliver DP | .10 | .04 | .01 |
| ☐ 71 | Hal Dues | .05 | .02 | .00 |
| ☐ 72 | Barry Evans DP | .02 | .01 | .00 |
| ☐ 73 | Doug Bair | .05 | .02 | .00 |
| ☐ 74 | Mike Hargrove | .08 | .03 | .01 |
| ☐ 75 | Reggie Smith | .12 | .05 | .01 |
| ☐ 76 | Mario Mendoza | .05 | .02 | .00 |
| ☐ 77 | Mike Barlow | .05 | .02 | .00 |
| ☐ 78 | Steve Dillard | .05 | .02 | .00 |
| ☐ 79 | Bruce Robbins | .05 | .02 | .00 |
| ☐ 80 | Rusty Staub | .15 | .06 | .01 |
| ☐ 81 | Dave Stapleton | .10 | .04 | .01 |
| ☐ 82 | Astros Rookies DP | .10 | .04 | .01 |
| | Danny Heep | | | |
| | Alan Knicely | | | |
| | Bobby Sprowl | | | |
| ☐ 83 | Mike Proly | .05 | .02 | .00 |
| ☐ 84 | Johnnie LeMaster | .05 | .02 | .00 |
| ☐ 85 | Mike Caldwell | .08 | .03 | .01 |
| ☐ 86 | Wayne Gross | .05 | .02 | .00 |
| ☐ 87 | Rick Camp | .05 | .02 | .00 |
| ☐ 88 | Joe LeFebvre | .10 | .04 | .01 |
| ☐ 89 | Darrell Jackson | .05 | .02 | .00 |
| ☐ 90 | Bake McBride | .08 | .03 | .01 |
| ☐ 91 | Tim Stoddard DP | .05 | .02 | .00 |
| ☐ 92 | Mike Easler | .12 | .05 | .01 |
| ☐ 93 | Ed Glynn DP | .02 | .01 | .00 |
| ☐ 94 | Harry Spilman DP | .02 | .01 | .00 |
| ☐ 95 | Jim Sundberg | .08 | .03 | .01 |
| ☐ 96 | A's Rookies | .12 | .05 | .01 |
| | Dave Beard | | | |
| | Ernie Camacho | | | |
| | Pat Dempsey | | | |
| ☐ 97 | Chris Speier | .05 | .02 | .00 |
| ☐ 98 | Clint Hurdle | .05 | .02 | .00 |

| | | | | |
|---|---|---|---|---|
| ☐ 99 | Eric Wilkins | .05 | .02 | .00 |
| ☐ 100 | Rod Carew | 1.25 | .50 | .12 |
| ☐ 101 | Benny Ayala | .05 | .02 | .00 |
| ☐ 102 | Dave Tobik | .05 | .02 | .00 |
| ☐ 103 | Jerry Martin | .05 | .02 | .00 |
| ☐ 104 | Terry Forster | .12 | .05 | .01 |
| ☐ 105 | Jose Cruz | .20 | .08 | .02 |
| ☐ 106 | Don Money | .05 | .02 | .00 |
| ☐ 107 | Rich Wortham | .05 | .02 | .00 |
| ☐ 108 | Bruce Benedict | .08 | .03 | .01 |
| ☐ 109 | Mike Scott | .75 | .30 | .07 |
| ☐ 110 | Carl Yastrzemski | 1.25 | .50 | .12 |
| ☐ 111 | Greg Minton | .08 | .03 | .01 |
| ☐ 112 | White Sox Rookies | .10 | .04 | .01 |
| | Rusty Kuntz | | | |
| | Fran Mullin | | | |
| | Leo Sutherland | | | |
| ☐ 113 | Mike Phillips | .05 | .02 | .00 |
| ☐ 114 | Tom Underwood | .05 | .02 | .00 |
| ☐ 115 | Roy Smalley | .08 | .03 | .01 |
| ☐ 116 | Joe Simpson | .05 | .02 | .00 |
| ☐ 117 | Pete Falcone | .05 | .02 | .00 |
| ☐ 118 | Kurt Bevacqua | .05 | .02 | .00 |
| ☐ 119 | Tippy Martinez | .08 | .03 | .01 |
| ☐ 120 | Larry Bowa | .15 | .06 | .01 |
| ☐ 121 | Larry Harlow | .05 | .02 | .00 |
| ☐ 122 | John Denny | .12 | .05 | .01 |
| ☐ 123 | Al Cowens | .08 | .03 | .01 |
| ☐ 124 | Jerry Garvin | .05 | .02 | .00 |
| ☐ 125 | Andre Dawson | .50 | .20 | .05 |
| ☐ 126 | Charlie Leibrandt | .50 | .20 | .05 |
| ☐ 127 | Rudy Law | .05 | .02 | .00 |
| ☐ 128 | Garry Allenson DP | .02 | .01 | .00 |
| ☐ 129 | Art Howe | .05 | .02 | .00 |
| ☐ 130 | Larry Gura | .08 | .03 | .01 |
| ☐ 131 | Keith Moreland | .75 | .30 | .07 |
| ☐ 132 | Tommy Boggs | .05 | .02 | .00 |
| ☐ 133 | Jeff Cox | .05 | .02 | .00 |
| ☐ 134 | Steve Mura | .05 | .02 | .00 |
| ☐ 135 | Gorman Thomas | .18 | .08 | .01 |
| ☐ 136 | Doug Capilla | .05 | .02 | .00 |
| ☐ 137 | Hosken Powell | .05 | .02 | .00 |
| ☐ 138 | Rich Dotson DP | .30 | .12 | .03 |
| ☐ 139 | Oscar Gamble | .10 | .04 | .01 |
| ☐ 140 | Bob Forsch | .10 | .04 | .01 |
| ☐ 141 | Miguel Dilone | .05 | .02 | .00 |
| ☐ 142 | Jackson Todd | .05 | .02 | .00 |
| ☐ 143 | Dan Meyer | .05 | .02 | .00 |
| ☐ 144 | Allen Ripley | .05 | .02 | .00 |
| ☐ 145 | Mickey Rivers | .10 | .04 | .01 |
| ☐ 146 | Bobby Castillo | .05 | .02 | .00 |
| ☐ 147 | Dale Berra | .08 | .03 | .01 |
| ☐ 148 | Randy Niemann | .05 | .02 | .00 |
| ☐ 149 | Joe Nolan | .05 | .02 | .00 |
| ☐ 150 | Mark Fidrych | .10 | .04 | .01 |
| ☐ 151 | Claudell Washington | .12 | .05 | .01 |
| ☐ 152 | John Urrea | .05 | .02 | .00 |
| ☐ 153 | Tom Poquette | .05 | .02 | .00 |
| ☐ 154 | Rick Langford | .05 | .02 | .00 |
| ☐ 155 | Chris Chambliss | .10 | .04 | .01 |
| ☐ 156 | Bob McClure | .05 | .02 | .00 |
| ☐ 157 | John Wathan | .05 | .02 | .00 |
| ☐ 158 | Fergie Jenkins | .25 | .10 | .02 |
| ☐ 159 | Brian Doyle | .05 | .02 | .00 |
| ☐ 160 | Garry Maddox | .08 | .03 | .01 |
| ☐ 161 | Dan Graham | .05 | .02 | .00 |
| ☐ 162 | Doug Corbett | .15 | .06 | .01 |
| ☐ 163 | Billy Almon | .05 | .02 | .00 |
| ☐ 164 | LaMarr Hoyt | .50 | .20 | .05 |
| ☐ 165 | Tony Scott | .05 | .02 | .00 |
| ☐ 166 | Floyd Bannister | .10 | .04 | .01 |
| ☐ 167 | Terry Whitfield | .05 | .02 | .00 |
| ☐ 168 | Don Robinson DP | .02 | .01 | .00 |
| ☐ 169 | John Mayberry | .08 | .03 | .01 |
| ☐ 170 | Ross Grimsley | .05 | .02 | .00 |
| ☐ 171 | Gene Richards | .05 | .02 | .00 |
| ☐ 172 | Gary Woods | .05 | .02 | .00 |
| ☐ 173 | Bump Wills | .05 | .02 | .00 |
| ☐ 174 | Doug Rau | .05 | .02 | .00 |
| ☐ 175 | Dave Collins | .08 | .03 | .01 |
| ☐ 176 | Mike Krukow | .15 | .06 | .01 |
| ☐ 177 | Rick Peters | .05 | .02 | .00 |
| ☐ 178 | Jim Essian DP | .02 | .01 | .00 |
| ☐ 179 | Rudy May | .05 | .02 | .00 |
| ☐ 180 | Pete Rose | 3.25 | 1.30 | .32 |
| ☐ 181 | Elias Sosa | .05 | .02 | .00 |
| ☐ 182 | Bob Grich | .12 | .05 | .01 |
| ☐ 183 | Dick Davis DP | .02 | .01 | .00 |
| ☐ 184 | Jim Dwyer | .05 | .02 | .00 |
| ☐ 185 | Dennis Leonard | .10 | .04 | .01 |
| ☐ 186 | Wayne Nordhagen | .05 | .02 | .00 |
| ☐ 187 | Mike Parrott | .05 | .02 | .00 |
| ☐ 188 | Doug DeCinces | .15 | .06 | .01 |

| | | | |
|---|---|---|---|
| ☐ 189 Craig Swan | .08 | .03 | .01 |
| ☐ 190 Cesar Cedeno | .12 | .05 | .01 |
| ☐ 191 Rick Sutcliffe | .35 | .14 | .03 |
| ☐ 192 Braves Rookies | .25 | .10 | .02 |
|     Terry Harper | | | |
|     Ed Miller | | | |
|     Rafael Ramirez | | | |
| ☐ 193 Pete Vuckovich | .12 | .05 | .01 |
| ☐ 194 Rod Scurry | .12 | .05 | .01 |
| ☐ 195 Rich Murray | .05 | .02 | .00 |
| ☐ 196 Duffy Dyer | .05 | .02 | .00 |
| ☐ 197 Jim Kern | .05 | .02 | .00 |
| ☐ 198 Jerry Dybzinski | .05 | .02 | .00 |
| ☐ 199 Chuck Rainey | .05 | .02 | .00 |
| ☐ 200 George Foster | .25 | .10 | .02 |
| ☐ 201 RB: Johnny Bench | .30 | .12 | .03 |
|     Most HR's | | | |
|     lifetime catcher | | | |
| ☐ 202 RB: Steve Carlton | .30 | .12 | .03 |
|     Most Strikeouts, | | | |
|     Lefthander, Lifetime | | | |
| ☐ 203 RB: Bill Gullickson | .10 | .04 | .01 |
|     Most Strikeouts | | | |
|     Game, Rookie | | | |
| ☐ 204 RB: Ron LeFlore and | .08 | .03 | .01 |
|     Rodney Scott | | | |
|     Most Stolen Bases | | | |
|     Teammates, Season | | | |
| ☐ 205 RB: Pete Rose | .75 | .30 | .07 |
|     Most Cons. Seasons | | | |
|     600 or More At-Bats | | | |
| ☐ 206 RB: Mike Schmidt | .40 | .16 | .04 |
|     Most Homers, Third | | | |
|     Baseman, Season | | | |
| ☐ 207 RB: Ozzie Smith | .12 | .05 | .01 |
|     Most Assists | | | |
|     Season, SS | | | |
| ☐ 208 RB: Willie Wilson | .12 | .05 | .01 |
|     Most At-Bats, Season | | | |
| ☐ 209 Dickie Thon DP | .08 | .03 | .01 |
| ☐ 210 Jim Palmer | .75 | .30 | .07 |
| ☐ 211 Derrel Thomas | .05 | .02 | .00 |
| ☐ 212 Steve Nicosia | .05 | .02 | .00 |
| ☐ 213 Al Holland | .25 | .10 | .02 |
| ☐ 214 Angels Rookies | .10 | .04 | .01 |
|     Ralph Botting | | | |
|     Jim Dorsey | | | |
|     John Harris | | | |
| ☐ 215 Larry Hisle | .08 | .03 | .01 |
| ☐ 216 John Henry Johnson | .05 | .02 | .00 |
| ☐ 217 Rich Hebner | .05 | .02 | .00 |
| ☐ 218 Paul Splittorff | .08 | .03 | .01 |
| ☐ 219 Ken Landreaux | .08 | .03 | .01 |
| ☐ 220 Tom Seaver | 1.25 | .50 | .12 |
| ☐ 221 Bob Davis | .05 | .02 | .00 |
| ☐ 222 Jorge Orta | .05 | .02 | .00 |
| ☐ 223 Roy Lee Jackson | .08 | .03 | .01 |
| ☐ 224 Pat Zachry | .05 | .02 | .00 |
| ☐ 225 Ruppert Jones | .08 | .03 | .01 |
| ☐ 226 Manny Sanguillen DP | .05 | .02 | .00 |
| ☐ 227 Fred Martinez | .05 | .02 | .00 |
| ☐ 228 Tom Paciorek | .05 | .02 | .00 |
| ☐ 229 Rollie Fingers | .40 | .16 | .04 |
| ☐ 230 George Hendrick | .12 | .05 | .01 |
| ☐ 231 Joe Beckwith | .05 | .02 | .00 |
| ☐ 232 Mickey Klutts | .05 | .02 | .00 |
| ☐ 233 Skip Lockwood | .05 | .02 | .00 |
| ☐ 234 Lou Whitaker | .50 | .20 | .05 |
| ☐ 235 Scott Sanderson | .08 | .03 | .01 |
| ☐ 236 Mike Ivie | .05 | .02 | .00 |
| ☐ 237 Charlie Moore | .05 | .02 | .00 |
| ☐ 238 Willie Hernandez | .25 | .10 | .02 |
| ☐ 239 Rick Miller DP | .02 | .01 | .00 |
| ☐ 240 Nolan Ryan | 1.25 | .50 | .12 |
| ☐ 241 Checklist 122-242 DP | .07 | .01 | .00 |
| ☐ 242 Chet Lemon | .10 | .04 | .01 |
| ☐ 243 Sal Butera | .05 | .02 | .00 |
| ☐ 244 Cardinals Rookies | .15 | .06 | .01 |
|     Tito Landrum | | | |
|     Al Olmsted | | | |
|     Andy Rincon | | | |
| ☐ 245 Ed Figueroa | .05 | .02 | .00 |
| ☐ 246 Ed Ott DP | .02 | .01 | .00 |
| ☐ 247 Glen Hubbard DP | .02 | .01 | .00 |
| ☐ 248 Joey McLaughlin | .05 | .02 | .00 |
| ☐ 249 Larry Cox | .05 | .02 | .00 |
| ☐ 250 Ron Guidry | .45 | .18 | .04 |
| ☐ 251 Tom Brookens | .05 | .02 | .00 |
| ☐ 252 Victor Cruz | .05 | .02 | .00 |
| ☐ 253 Dave Bergman | .05 | .02 | .00 |
| ☐ 254 Ozzie Smith | .50 | .20 | .05 |
| ☐ 255 Mark Littell | .05 | .02 | .00 |
| ☐ 256 Bombo Rivera | .05 | .02 | .00 |

| | | | |
|---|---|---|---|
| ☐ 257 Rennie Stennett | .05 | .02 | .00 |
| ☐ 258 Joe Price | .08 | .03 | .01 |
| ☐ 259 Mets Rookies | 2.25 | .90 | .22 |
|     Juan Berenguer | | | |
|     Hubie Brooks | | | |
|     Mookie Wilson | | | |
| ☐ 260 Ron Cey | .20 | .08 | .02 |
| ☐ 261 Rickey Henderson | 3.00 | 1.20 | .30 |
| ☐ 262 Sammy Stewart | .05 | .02 | .00 |
| ☐ 263 Brian Downing | .08 | .03 | .01 |
| ☐ 264 Jim Norris | .05 | .02 | .00 |
| ☐ 265 John Candelaria | .12 | .05 | .01 |
| ☐ 266 Tom Herr | .20 | .08 | .02 |
| ☐ 267 Stan Bahnsen | .05 | .02 | .00 |
| ☐ 268 Jerry Royster | .05 | .02 | .00 |
| ☐ 269 Ken Forsch | .08 | .03 | .01 |
| ☐ 270 Greg Luzinski | .15 | .06 | .01 |
| ☐ 271 Bill Castro | .05 | .02 | .00 |
| ☐ 272 Bruce Kimm | .05 | .02 | .00 |
| ☐ 273 Stan Papi | .05 | .02 | .00 |
| ☐ 274 Craig Chamberlain | .05 | .02 | .00 |
| ☐ 275 Dwight Evans | .25 | .10 | .02 |
| ☐ 276 Dan Spillner | .05 | .02 | .00 |
| ☐ 277 Alfredo Griffin | .10 | .04 | .01 |
| ☐ 278 Rick Sofield | .05 | .02 | .00 |
| ☐ 279 Bob Knepper | .15 | .06 | .01 |
| ☐ 280 Ken Griffey | .12 | .05 | .01 |
| ☐ 281 Fred Stanley | .05 | .02 | .00 |
| ☐ 282 Mariners Rookies | .08 | .03 | .01 |
|     Rick Anderson | | | |
|     Greg Biercevicz | | | |
|     Rodney Craig | | | |
| ☐ 283 Billy Sample | .05 | .02 | .00 |
| ☐ 284 Brian Kingman | .05 | .02 | .00 |
| ☐ 285 Jerry Turner | .05 | .02 | .00 |
| ☐ 286 Dave Frost | .05 | .02 | .00 |
| ☐ 287 Lenn Sakata | .05 | .02 | .00 |
| ☐ 288 Bob Clark | .05 | .02 | .00 |
| ☐ 289 Mickey Hatcher | .08 | .03 | .01 |
| ☐ 290 Bob Boone DP | .05 | .02 | .00 |
| ☐ 291 Aurelio Lopez | .05 | .02 | .00 |
| ☐ 292 Mike Squires | .05 | .02 | .00 |
| ☐ 293 Charlie Lea | .25 | .10 | .02 |
| ☐ 294 Mike Tyson DP | .02 | .01 | .00 |
| ☐ 295 Hal McRae | .10 | .04 | .01 |
| ☐ 296 Bill Nahorodny DP | .02 | .01 | .00 |
| ☐ 297 Bob Bailor | .05 | .02 | .00 |
| ☐ 298 Buddy Solomon | .05 | .02 | .00 |
| ☐ 299 Elliott Maddox | .05 | .02 | .00 |
| ☐ 300 Paul Molitor | .20 | .08 | .02 |
| ☐ 301 Matt Keough | .05 | .02 | .00 |
| ☐ 302 Dodgers Rookies | 7.50 | 3.00 | .75 |
|     Jack Perconte | | | |
|     Mike Scioscia | | | |
|     Fernando Valenzuela | | | |
| ☐ 303 Johnny Oates | .05 | .02 | .00 |
| ☐ 304 John Castino | .05 | .02 | .00 |
| ☐ 305 Ken Clay | .05 | .02 | .00 |
| ☐ 306 Juan Beniquez DP | .05 | .02 | .00 |
| ☐ 307 Gene Garber | .05 | .02 | .00 |
| ☐ 308 Rick Manning | .05 | .02 | .00 |
| ☐ 309 Luis Salazar | .10 | .04 | .01 |
| ☐ 310 Vida Blue DP | .08 | .03 | .01 |
| ☐ 311 Freddie Patek | .05 | .02 | .00 |
| ☐ 312 Rick Rhoden | .15 | .06 | .01 |
| ☐ 313 Luis Pujols | .05 | .02 | .00 |
| ☐ 314 Rich Dauer | .05 | .02 | .00 |
| ☐ 315 Kirk Gibson | 4.00 | 1.60 | .40 |
| ☐ 316 Craig Minetto | .05 | .02 | .00 |
| ☐ 317 Lonnie Smith | .12 | .05 | .01 |
| ☐ 318 Steve Yeager | .08 | .03 | .01 |
| ☐ 319 Rowland Office | .05 | .02 | .00 |
| ☐ 320 Tom Burgmeier | .05 | .02 | .00 |
| ☐ 321 Leon Durham | .90 | .36 | .09 |
| ☐ 322 Neil Allen | .08 | .03 | .01 |
| ☐ 323 Jim Morrison DP | .05 | .02 | .00 |
| ☐ 324 Mike Willis | .05 | .02 | .00 |
| ☐ 325 Ray Knight | .15 | .06 | .01 |
| ☐ 326 Biff Pocoroba | .05 | .02 | .00 |
| ☐ 327 Moose Haas | .08 | .03 | .01 |
| ☐ 328 Twins Rookies | .30 | .12 | .03 |
|     Dave Engle | | | |
|     Greg Johnston | | | |
|     Gary Ward | | | |
| ☐ 329 Joaquin Andujar | .18 | .08 | .01 |
| ☐ 330 Frank White | .15 | .06 | .01 |
| ☐ 331 Dennis Lamp | .05 | .02 | .00 |
| ☐ 332 Lee Lacy DP | .05 | .02 | .00 |
| ☐ 333 Sid Monge | .05 | .02 | .00 |
| ☐ 334 Dane Iorg | .05 | .02 | .00 |
| ☐ 335 Rick Cerone | .08 | .03 | .01 |
| ☐ 336 Eddie Whitson | .10 | .04 | .01 |
| ☐ 337 Lynn Jones | .05 | .02 | .00 |

| | | | | |
|---|---|---|---|---|
| ☐ 338 | Checklist 243-363 | .15 | .02 | .00 |
| ☐ 339 | John Ellis | .05 | .02 | .00 |
| ☐ 340 | Bruce Kison | .05 | .02 | .00 |
| ☐ 341 | Dwayne Murphy | .12 | .05 | .01 |
| ☐ 342 | Eric Rasmussen DP | .02 | .01 | .00 |
| ☐ 343 | Frank Taveras | .05 | .02 | .00 |
| ☐ 344 | Byron McLaughlin | .05 | .02 | .00 |
| ☐ 345 | Warren Cromartie | .05 | .02 | .00 |
| ☐ 346 | Larry Christenson DP | .02 | .01 | .00 |
| ☐ 347 | Harold Baines | 4.50 | 1.80 | .45 |
| ☐ 348 | Bob Sykes | .05 | .02 | .00 |
| ☐ 349 | Glenn Hoffman | .10 | .04 | .01 |
| ☐ 350 | J.R. Richard | .15 | .06 | .01 |
| ☐ 351 | Otto Velez | .05 | .02 | .00 |
| ☐ 352 | Dick Tidrow DP | .02 | .01 | .00 |
| ☐ 353 | Terry Kennedy | .15 | .06 | .01 |
| ☐ 354 | Mario Soto | .12 | .05 | .01 |
| ☐ 355 | Bob Horner | .40 | .16 | .04 |
| ☐ 356 | Padres Rookies | .10 | .04 | .01 |
| | George Stablein | | | |
| | Craig Stimac | | | |
| | Tom Tellmann | | | |
| ☐ 357 | Jim Slaton | .05 | .02 | .00 |
| ☐ 358 | Mark Wagner | .05 | .02 | .00 |
| ☐ 359 | Tom Hausman | .05 | .02 | .00 |
| ☐ 360 | Willie Wilson | .25 | .10 | .02 |
| ☐ 361 | Joe Strain | .05 | .02 | .00 |
| ☐ 362 | Bo Diaz | .08 | .03 | .01 |
| ☐ 363 | Geoff Zahn | .08 | .03 | .01 |
| ☐ 364 | Mike Davis | .50 | .20 | .05 |
| ☐ 365 | Graig Nettles DP | .08 | .03 | .01 |
| ☐ 366 | Mike Ramsey | .05 | .02 | .00 |
| ☐ 367 | Denny Martinez | .08 | .03 | .01 |
| ☐ 368 | Leon Roberts | .05 | .02 | .00 |
| ☐ 369 | Frank Tanana | .10 | .04 | .01 |
| ☐ 370 | Dave Winfield | .80 | .32 | .08 |
| ☐ 371 | Charlie Hough | .12 | .05 | .01 |
| ☐ 372 | Jay Johnstone | .08 | .03 | .01 |
| ☐ 373 | Pat Underwood | .05 | .02 | .00 |
| ☐ 374 | Tom Hutton | .05 | .02 | .00 |
| ☐ 375 | Dave Concepcion | .15 | .06 | .01 |
| ☐ 376 | Ron Reed | .05 | .02 | .00 |
| ☐ 377 | Jerry Morales | .05 | .02 | .00 |
| ☐ 378 | Dave Rader | .05 | .02 | .00 |
| ☐ 379 | Lary Sorensen | .05 | .02 | .00 |
| ☐ 380 | Willie Stargell | .80 | .32 | .08 |
| ☐ 381 | Cubs Rookies | .10 | .04 | .01 |
| | Carlos Lezcano | | | |
| | Steve Macko | | | |
| | Randy Martz | | | |
| ☐ 382 | Paul Mirabella | .05 | .02 | .00 |
| ☐ 383 | Eric Soderholm DP | .02 | .01 | .00 |
| ☐ 384 | Mike Sadek | .05 | .02 | .00 |
| ☐ 385 | Joe Sambito | .08 | .03 | .01 |
| ☐ 386 | Dave Edwards | .05 | .02 | .00 |
| ☐ 387 | Phil Niekro | .65 | .26 | .06 |
| ☐ 388 | Andre Thornton | .15 | .06 | .01 |
| ☐ 389 | Marty Pattin | .05 | .02 | .00 |
| ☐ 390 | Cesar Geronimo | .05 | .02 | .00 |
| ☐ 391 | Dave Lemanczyk DP | .02 | .01 | .00 |
| ☐ 392 | Lance Parrish | .80 | .32 | .08 |
| ☐ 393 | Broderick Perkins | .05 | .02 | .00 |
| ☐ 394 | Woodie Fryman | .05 | .02 | .00 |
| ☐ 395 | Scot Thompson | .05 | .02 | .00 |
| ☐ 396 | Bill Campbell | .08 | .03 | .01 |
| ☐ 397 | Julio Cruz | .05 | .02 | .00 |
| ☐ 398 | Ross Baumgarten | .05 | .02 | .00 |
| ☐ 399 | Orioles Rookies | 2.00 | .80 | .20 |
| | Mike Boddicker | | | |
| | Mark Corey | | | |
| | Floyd Rayford | | | |
| ☐ 400 | Reggie Jackson | 1.50 | .60 | .15 |
| ☐ 401 | A.L. Champs: | .40 | .16 | .04 |
| | Royals sweep Yanks | | | |
| | (Brett swinging) | | | |
| ☐ 402 | N.L. Champs: | .20 | .08 | .02 |
| | Phillies squeak | | | |
| | past Astros | | | |
| ☐ 403 | 1980 World Series: | .20 | .08 | .02 |
| | Phillies beat | | | |
| | Royals in 6 | | | |
| ☐ 404 | 1980 World Series: | .20 | .08 | .02 |
| | Phillies win first | | | |
| | World Series | | | |
| ☐ 405 | Nino Espinosa | .05 | .02 | .00 |
| ☐ 406 | Dickie Noles | .05 | .02 | .00 |
| ☐ 407 | Ernie Whitt | .05 | .02 | .00 |
| ☐ 408 | Fernando Arroyo | .05 | .02 | .00 |
| ☐ 409 | Larry Herndon | .08 | .03 | .01 |
| ☐ 410 | Bert Campaneris | .10 | .04 | .01 |
| ☐ 411 | Terry Puhl | .08 | .03 | .01 |
| ☐ 412 | Britt Burns | .35 | .14 | .03 |
| ☐ 413 | Tony Bernazard | .10 | .04 | .01 |

| | | | | |
|---|---|---|---|---|
| ☐ 414 | John Pacella DP | .02 | .01 | .00 |
| ☐ 415 | Ben Oglivie | .12 | .05 | .01 |
| ☐ 416 | Gary Alexander | .05 | .02 | .00 |
| ☐ 417 | Dan Schatzeder | .05 | .02 | .00 |
| ☐ 418 | Bobby Brown | .05 | .02 | .00 |
| ☐ 419 | Tom Hume | .05 | .02 | .00 |
| ☐ 420 | Keith Hernandez | .75 | .30 | .07 |
| ☐ 421 | Bob Stanley | .10 | .04 | .01 |
| ☐ 422 | Dan Ford | .08 | .03 | .01 |
| ☐ 423 | Shane Rawley | .12 | .05 | .01 |
| ☐ 424 | Yankees Rookies | .15 | .06 | .01 |
| | Tim Lollar | | | |
| | Bruce Robinson | | | |
| | Dennis Werth | | | |
| ☐ 425 | Al Bumbry | .05 | .02 | .00 |
| ☐ 426 | Warren Brusstar | .05 | .02 | .00 |
| ☐ 427 | John D'Acquisto | .05 | .02 | .00 |
| ☐ 428 | John Stearns | .05 | .02 | .00 |
| ☐ 429 | Mick Kelleher | .05 | .02 | .00 |
| ☐ 430 | Jim Bibby | .08 | .03 | .01 |
| ☐ 431 | Dave Roberts | .05 | .02 | .00 |
| ☐ 432 | Len Barker | .10 | .04 | .01 |
| ☐ 433 | Rance Mulliniks | .08 | .03 | .01 |
| ☐ 434 | Roger Erickson | .05 | .02 | .00 |
| ☐ 435 | Jim Spencer | .05 | .02 | .00 |
| ☐ 436 | Gary Lucas | .10 | .04 | .01 |
| ☐ 437 | Mike Heath DP | .02 | .01 | .00 |
| ☐ 438 | John Montefusco | .08 | .03 | .01 |
| ☐ 439 | Denny Walling | .05 | .02 | .00 |
| ☐ 440 | Jerry Reuss | .12 | .05 | .01 |
| ☐ 441 | Ken Reitz | .05 | .02 | .00 |
| ☐ 442 | Ron Pruitt | .05 | .02 | .00 |
| ☐ 443 | Jim Beattie DP | .02 | .01 | .00 |
| ☐ 444 | Garth Iorg | .05 | .02 | .00 |
| ☐ 445 | Ellis Valentine | .08 | .03 | .01 |
| ☐ 446 | Checklist 364-484 | .15 | .02 | .00 |
| ☐ 447 | Junior Kennedy DP | .02 | .01 | .00 |
| ☐ 448 | Tim Corcoran | .05 | .02 | .00 |
| ☐ 449 | Paul Mitchell | .05 | .02 | .00 |
| ☐ 450 | Dave Kingman DP | .10 | .04 | .01 |
| ☐ 451 | Indians Rookies | .15 | .06 | .01 |
| | Chris Bando | | | |
| | Tom Brennan | | | |
| | Sandy Wihtol | | | |
| ☐ 452 | Renie Martin | .05 | .02 | .00 |
| ☐ 453 | Rob Wilfong DP | .02 | .01 | .00 |
| ☐ 454 | Andy Hassler | .05 | .02 | .00 |
| ☐ 455 | Rick Burleson | .08 | .03 | .01 |
| ☐ 456 | Jeff Reardon | .60 | .24 | .06 |
| ☐ 457 | Mike Lum | .05 | .02 | .00 |
| ☐ 458 | Randy Jones | .08 | .03 | .01 |
| ☐ 459 | Greg Gross | .05 | .02 | .00 |
| ☐ 460 | Rich Gossage | .30 | .12 | .03 |
| ☐ 461 | Dave McKay | .05 | .02 | .00 |
| ☐ 462 | Jack Brohamer | .05 | .02 | .00 |
| ☐ 463 | Milt May | .05 | .02 | .00 |
| ☐ 464 | Adrian Devine | .05 | .02 | .00 |
| ☐ 465 | Bill Russell | .08 | .03 | .01 |
| ☐ 466 | Bob Molinaro | .05 | .02 | .00 |
| ☐ 467 | Dave Stieb | .40 | .16 | .04 |
| ☐ 468 | Johnny Wockenfuss | .05 | .02 | .00 |
| ☐ 469 | Jeff Leonard | .12 | .05 | .01 |
| ☐ 470 | Manny Trillo | .08 | .03 | .01 |
| ☐ 471 | Mike Vail | .05 | .02 | .00 |
| ☐ 472 | Dyar Miller DP | .02 | .01 | .00 |
| ☐ 473 | Jose Cardenal | .05 | .02 | .00 |
| ☐ 474 | Mike LaCoss | .05 | .02 | .00 |
| ☐ 475 | Buddy Bell | .18 | .08 | .01 |
| ☐ 476 | Jerry Koosman | .15 | .06 | .01 |
| ☐ 477 | Luis Gomez | .05 | .02 | .00 |
| ☐ 478 | Juan Eichelberger | .08 | .03 | .01 |
| ☐ 479 | Expos Rookies | 6.50 | 2.60 | .65 |
| | Tim Raines | | | |
| | Roberto Ramos | | | |
| | Bobby Pate | | | |
| ☐ 480 | Carlton Fisk | .30 | .12 | .03 |
| ☐ 481 | Bob Lacey DP | .02 | .01 | .00 |
| ☐ 482 | Jim Gantner | .08 | .03 | .01 |
| ☐ 483 | Mike Griffin | .05 | .02 | .00 |
| ☐ 484 | Max Venable DP | .02 | .01 | .00 |
| ☐ 485 | Garry Templeton | .15 | .06 | .01 |
| ☐ 486 | Marc Hill | .05 | .02 | .00 |
| ☐ 487 | Dewey Robinson | .05 | .02 | .00 |
| ☐ 488 | Damaso Garcia | .65 | .26 | .06 |
| ☐ 489 | John Littlefield | .07 | .03 | .01 |
| ☐ 490 | Eddie Murray | 1.50 | .60 | .15 |
| ☐ 491 | Gordy Pladson | .08 | .03 | .01 |
| ☐ 492 | Barry Foote | .05 | .02 | .00 |
| ☐ 493 | Dan Quisenberry | .45 | .18 | .04 |
| ☐ 494 | Bob Walk | .07 | .03 | .01 |
| ☐ 495 | Dusty Baker | .12 | .05 | .01 |
| ☐ 496 | Paul Dade | .05 | .02 | .00 |
| ☐ 497 | Fred Norman | .05 | .02 | .00 |

| | | | | | | | | |
|---|---|---|---|---|---|---|---|---|
| ☐ 498 | Pat Putnam | .05 | .02 | .00 | ☐ 579 Tim Flannery | .05 | .02 | .00 |
| ☐ 499 | Frank Pastore | .05 | .02 | .00 | ☐ 580 Don Baylor | .30 | .12 | .03 |
| ☐ 500 | Jim Rice | 1.25 | .50 | .12 | ☐ 581 Roy Howell | .05 | .02 | .00 |
| ☐ 501 | Tim Foli DP | .02 | .01 | .00 | ☐ 582 Gaylord Perry | .50 | .20 | .05 |
| ☐ 502 | Giants Rookies | .08 | .03 | .01 | ☐ 583 Larry Milbourne | .05 | .02 | .00 |
| | Chris Bourjos | | | | ☐ 584 Randy Lerch | .05 | .02 | .00 |
| | Al Hargesheimer | | | | ☐ 585 Amos Otis | .12 | .05 | .01 |
| | Mike Rowland | | | | ☐ 586 Silvio Martinez | .05 | .02 | .00 |
| ☐ 503 | Steve McCatty | .05 | .02 | .00 | ☐ 587 Jeff Newman | .05 | .02 | .00 |
| ☐ 504 | Dale Murphy | 2.50 | 1.00 | .25 | ☐ 588 Gary Lavelle | .08 | .03 | .01 |
| ☐ 505 | Jason Thompson | .10 | .04 | .01 | ☐ 589 Lamar Johnson | .05 | .02 | .00 |
| ☐ 506 | Phil Huffman | .05 | .02 | .00 | ☐ 590 Bruce Sutter | .35 | .14 | .03 |
| ☐ 507 | Jamie Quirk | .05 | .02 | .00 | ☐ 591 John Lowenstein | .05 | .02 | .00 |
| ☐ 508 | Rob Dressler | .05 | .02 | .00 | ☐ 592 Steve Comer | .05 | .02 | .00 |
| ☐ 509 | Pete Mackanin | .05 | .02 | .00 | ☐ 593 Steve Kemp | .12 | .05 | .01 |
| ☐ 510 | Lee Mazzilli | .08 | .03 | .01 | ☐ 594 Preston Hanna DP | .02 | .01 | .00 |
| ☐ 511 | Wayne Garland | .05 | .02 | .00 | ☐ 595 Butch Hobson | .05 | .02 | .00 |
| ☐ 512 | Gary Thomasson | .05 | .02 | .00 | ☐ 596 Jerry Augustine | .05 | .02 | .00 |
| ☐ 513 | Frank LaCorte | .05 | .02 | .00 | ☐ 597 Rafael Landestoy | .05 | .02 | .00 |
| ☐ 514 | George Riley | .08 | .03 | .01 | ☐ 598 George Vukovich DP | .02 | .01 | .00 |
| ☐ 515 | Robin Yount | 1.00 | .40 | .10 | ☐ 599 Dennis Kinney | .05 | .02 | .00 |
| ☐ 516 | Doug Bird | .05 | .02 | .00 | ☐ 600 Johnny Bench | 1.25 | .50 | .12 |
| ☐ 517 | Richie Zisk | .08 | .03 | .01 | ☐ 601 Don Aase | .10 | .04 | .01 |
| ☐ 518 | Grant Jackson | .05 | .02 | .00 | ☐ 602 Bobby Murcer | .15 | .06 | .01 |
| ☐ 519 | John Tamargo DP | .02 | .01 | .00 | ☐ 603 John Verhoeven | .05 | .02 | .00 |
| ☐ 520 | Steve Stone | .10 | .04 | .01 | ☐ 604 Rob Picciolo | .05 | .02 | .00 |
| ☐ 521 | Sam Mejias | .05 | .02 | .00 | ☐ 605 Don Sutton | .60 | .24 | .06 |
| ☐ 522 | Mike Colbern | .05 | .02 | .00 | ☐ 606 Reds Rookies DP | .08 | .03 | .01 |
| ☐ 523 | John Fulgham | .05 | .02 | .00 | | Bruce Berenyi | | | |
| ☐ 524 | Willie Aikens | .10 | .04 | .01 | | Geoff Combe | | | |
| ☐ 525 | Mike Torrez | .08 | .03 | .01 | | Paul Householder | | | |
| ☐ 526 | Phillies Rookies | .18 | .08 | .01 | ☐ 607 Dave Palmer | .10 | .04 | .01 |
| | Marty Bystrom | | | | ☐ 608 Greg Pryor | .05 | .02 | .00 |
| | Jay Loviglio | | | | ☐ 609 Lynn McGlothen | .05 | .02 | .00 |
| | Jim Wright | | | | ☐ 610 Darrell Porter | .08 | .03 | .01 |
| ☐ 527 | Danny Goodwin | .05 | .02 | .00 | ☐ 611 Rick Matula DP | .02 | .01 | .00 |
| ☐ 528 | Gary Matthews | .12 | .05 | .01 | ☐ 612 Duane Kuiper | .05 | .02 | .00 |
| ☐ 529 | Dave LaRoche | .05 | .02 | .00 | ☐ 613 Jim Anderson | .05 | .02 | .00 |
| ☐ 530 | Steve Garvey | 1.25 | .50 | .12 | ☐ 614 Dave Rozema | .05 | .02 | .00 |
| ☐ 531 | John Curtis | .05 | .02 | .00 | ☐ 615 Rick Dempsey | .08 | .03 | .01 |
| ☐ 532 | Bill Stein | .05 | .02 | .00 | ☐ 616 Rick Wise | .08 | .03 | .01 |
| ☐ 533 | Jesus Figueroa | .05 | .02 | .00 | ☐ 617 Craig Reynolds | .05 | .02 | .00 |
| ☐ 534 | Dave Smith | .35 | .14 | .03 | ☐ 618 John Milner | .05 | .02 | .00 |
| ☐ 535 | Omar Moreno | .08 | .03 | .01 | ☐ 619 Steve Henderson | .08 | .03 | .01 |
| ☐ 536 | Bob Owchinko DP | .02 | .01 | .00 | ☐ 620 Dennis Eckersley | .08 | .03 | .01 |
| ☐ 537 | Ron Hodges | .05 | .02 | .00 | ☐ 621 Tom Donohue | .05 | .02 | .00 |
| ☐ 538 | Tom Griffin | .05 | .02 | .00 | ☐ 622 Randy Moffitt | .05 | .02 | .00 |
| ☐ 539 | Rodney Scott | .05 | .02 | .00 | ☐ 623 Sal Bando | .08 | .03 | .01 |
| ☐ 540 | Mike Schmidt DP | .85 | .34 | .08 | ☐ 624 Bob Welch | .15 | .06 | .01 |
| ☐ 541 | Steve Swisher | .05 | .02 | .00 | ☐ 625 Bill Buckner | .15 | .06 | .01 |
| ☐ 542 | Larry Bradford DP | .02 | .01 | .00 | ☐ 626 Tigers Rookies | .10 | .04 | .01 |
| ☐ 543 | Terry Crowley | .05 | .02 | .00 | | Dave Steffen | | | |
| ☐ 544 | Rich Gale | .05 | .02 | .00 | | Jerry Ujdur | | | |
| ☐ 545 | Johnny Grubb | .05 | .02 | .00 | | Roger Weaver | | | |
| ☐ 546 | Paul Moskau | .05 | .02 | .00 | ☐ 627 Luis Tiant | .12 | .05 | .01 |
| ☐ 547 | Mario Guerrero | .05 | .02 | .00 | ☐ 628 Vic Correll | .05 | .02 | .00 |
| ☐ 548 | Dave Goltz | .05 | .02 | .00 | ☐ 629 Tony Armas | .15 | .06 | .01 |
| ☐ 549 | Jerry Remy | .08 | .03 | .01 | ☐ 630 Steve Carlton | 1.00 | .40 | .10 |
| ☐ 550 | Tommy John | .25 | .10 | .02 | ☐ 631 Ron Jackson | .05 | .02 | .00 |
| ☐ 551 | Pirates Rookies | 1.75 | .70 | .17 | ☐ 632 Alan Bannister | .05 | .02 | .00 |
| | Vance Law | | | | ☐ 633 Bill Lee | .08 | .03 | .01 |
| | Tony Pena | | | | ☐ 634 Doug Flynn | .05 | .02 | .00 |
| | Pascual Perez | | | | ☐ 635 Bobby Bonds | .12 | .05 | .01 |
| ☐ 552 | Steve Trout | .08 | .03 | .01 | ☐ 636 Al Hrabosky | .08 | .03 | .01 |
| ☐ 553 | Tim Blackwell | .05 | .02 | .00 | ☐ 637 Jerry Narron | .05 | .02 | .00 |
| ☐ 554 | Bert Blyleven | .25 | .10 | .02 | ☐ 638 Checklist 606-726 | .15 | .02 | .00 |
| ☐ 555 | Cecil Cooper | .25 | .10 | .02 | ☐ 639 Carney Lansford | .20 | .08 | .02 |
| ☐ 556 | Jerry Mumphrey | .08 | .03 | .01 | ☐ 640 Dave Parker | .70 | .28 | .07 |
| ☐ 557 | Chris Knapp | .05 | .02 | .00 | ☐ 641 Mark Belanger | .08 | .03 | .01 |
| ☐ 558 | Barry Bonnell | .08 | .03 | .01 | ☐ 642 Vern Ruhle | .05 | .02 | .00 |
| ☐ 559 | Willie Montanez | .05 | .02 | .00 | ☐ 643 Lloyd Moseby | 1.75 | .70 | .17 |
| ☐ 560 | Joe Morgan | .60 | .24 | .06 | ☐ 644 Ramon Aviles DP | .02 | .01 | .00 |
| ☐ 561 | Dennis Littlejohn | .05 | .02 | .00 | ☐ 645 Rick Reuschel | .08 | .03 | .01 |
| ☐ 562 | Checklist 485-605 | .15 | .02 | .00 | ☐ 646 Marvis Foley | .05 | .02 | .00 |
| ☐ 563 | Jim Kaat | .25 | .10 | .02 | ☐ 647 Dick Drago | .05 | .02 | .00 |
| ☐ 564 | Ron Hassey DP | .02 | .01 | .00 | ☐ 648 Darrell Evans | .18 | .08 | .01 |
| ☐ 565 | Burt Hooton | .05 | .02 | .00 | ☐ 649 Manny Sarmiento | .05 | .02 | .00 |
| ☐ 566 | Del Unser | .05 | .02 | .00 | ☐ 650 Bucky Dent | .12 | .05 | .01 |
| ☐ 567 | Mark Bomback | .05 | .02 | .00 | ☐ 651 Pedro Guerrero | 1.00 | .40 | .10 |
| ☐ 568 | Dave Revering | .05 | .02 | .00 | ☐ 652 John Montague | .05 | .02 | .00 |
| ☐ 569 | Al Williams DP | .02 | .01 | .00 | ☐ 653 Bill Fahey | .05 | .02 | .00 |
| ☐ 570 | Ken Singleton | .15 | .06 | .01 | ☐ 654 Ray Burris | .05 | .02 | .00 |
| ☐ 571 | Todd Cruz | .05 | .02 | .00 | ☐ 655 Dan Driessen | .08 | .03 | .01 |
| ☐ 572 | Jack Morris | .60 | .24 | .06 | ☐ 656 Jon Matlack | .08 | .03 | .01 |
| ☐ 573 | Phil Garner | .08 | .03 | .01 | ☐ 657 Mike Cubbage DP | .02 | .01 | .00 |
| ☐ 574 | Bill Caudill | .10 | .04 | .01 | ☐ 658 Milt Wilcox | .05 | .02 | .00 |
| ☐ 575 | Tony Perez | .20 | .08 | .02 | ☐ 659 Brewers Rookies: | .08 | .03 | .01 |
| ☐ 576 | Reggie Cleveland | .05 | .02 | .00 | | John Flinn | | | |
| ☐ 577 | Blue Jays Rookies | .20 | .08 | .02 | | Ed Romero | | | |
| | Luis Leal | | | | | Ned Yost | | | |
| | Brian Milner | | | | ☐ 660 Gary Carter | 1.50 | .60 | .15 |
| | Ken Schrom | | | | ☐ 661 Orioles Team/Mgr. | .20 | .04 | .01 |
| ☐ 578 | Bill Gullickson | .50 | .20 | .05 | | Earl Weaver | | | |

| | | | | |
|---|---|---|---|---|
| ☐ 662 | Red Sox Team/Mgr. ....... Ralph Houk | .18 | .04 | .01 |
| ☐ 663 | Angels Team/Mgr. .......... Jim Fregosi | .18 | .04 | .01 |
| ☐ 664 | White Sox Team/Mgr. .... Tony LaRussa | .18 | .04 | .01 |
| ☐ 665 | Indians Team/Mgr. ......... Dave Garcia | .18 | .04 | .01 |
| ☐ 666 | Tigers Team/Mgr. .......... Sparky Anderson | .20 | .04 | .01 |
| ☐ 667 | Royals Team/Mgr. ......... Jim Frey | .18 | .04 | .01 |
| ☐ 668 | Brewers Team/Mgr. ........ Bob Rodgers | .18 | .04 | .01 |
| ☐ 669 | Twins Team/Mgr. ........... John Goryl | .15 | .03 | .01 |
| ☐ 670 | Yankees Team/Mgr. ....... Gene Michael | .20 | .04 | .01 |
| ☐ 671 | A's Team/Mgr. ............... Billy Martin | .20 | .04 | .01 |
| ☐ 672 | Mariners Team/Mgr. ...... Maury Wills | .15 | .03 | .01 |
| ☐ 673 | Rangers Team/Mgr. ........ Don Zimmer | .15 | .03 | .01 |
| ☐ 674 | Blue Jays Team/Mgr. ..... Bobby Mattick | .15 | .03 | .01 |
| ☐ 675 | Braves Team/Mgr. ......... Bobby Cox | .18 | .04 | .01 |
| ☐ 676 | Cubs Team/Mgr. ........... Joe Amalfitano | .18 | .04 | .01 |
| ☐ 677 | Reds Team/Mgr. ........... John McNamara | .18 | .04 | .01 |
| ☐ 678 | Astros Team/Mgr. ......... Bill Virdon | .18 | .04 | .01 |
| ☐ 679 | Dodgers Team/Mgr. ....... Tom Lasorda | .20 | .04 | .01 |
| ☐ 680 | Expos Team/Mgr. .......... Dick Williams | .18 | .04 | .01 |
| ☐ 681 | Mets Team/Mgr. ............ Joe Torre | .20 | .04 | .01 |
| ☐ 682 | Phillies Team/Mgr. ........ Dallas Green | .18 | .04 | .01 |
| ☐ 683 | Pirates Team/Mgr. ......... Chuck Tanner | .18 | .04 | .01 |
| ☐ 684 | Cardinals Team/Mgr. ..... Whitey Herzog | .18 | .04 | .01 |
| ☐ 685 | Padres Team/Mgr. ......... Frank Howard | .15 | .03 | .01 |
| ☐ 686 | Giants Team/Mgr. ......... Dave Bristol | .18 | .04 | .01 |
| ☐ 687 | Jeff Jones ...................... | .10 | .04 | .01 |
| ☐ 688 | Kiko Garcia .................... | .05 | .02 | .00 |
| ☐ 689 | Red Sox Rookies: .......... Bruce Hurst Keith MacWhorter Reid Nichols | 1.00 | .40 | .10 |
| ☐ 690 | Bob Watson .................... | .08 | .03 | .01 |
| ☐ 691 | Dick Ruthven .................. | .05 | .02 | .00 |
| ☐ 692 | Lenny Randle ................. | .05 | .02 | .00 |
| ☐ 693 | Steve Howe ................... | .20 | .08 | .02 |
| ☐ 694 | Bud Harrelson DP .......... | .02 | .01 | .00 |
| ☐ 695 | Kent Tekulve .................. | .08 | .03 | .01 |
| ☐ 696 | Alan Ashby .................... | .05 | .02 | .00 |
| ☐ 697 | Rick Waits ..................... | .05 | .02 | .00 |
| ☐ 698 | Mike Jorgensen .............. | .05 | .02 | .00 |
| ☐ 699 | Glen Abbott ................... | .05 | .02 | .00 |
| ☐ 700 | George Brett .................. | 1.75 | .70 | .17 |
| ☐ 701 | Joe Rudi ....................... | .08 | .03 | .01 |
| ☐ 702 | George Medich ............... | .05 | .02 | .00 |
| ☐ 703 | Alvis Woods ................... | .05 | .02 | .00 |
| ☐ 704 | Bill Travers DP .............. | .02 | .01 | .00 |
| ☐ 705 | Ted Simmons .................. | .18 | .08 | .01 |
| ☐ 706 | Dave Ford ..................... | .05 | .02 | .00 |
| ☐ 707 | Dave Cash ..................... | .05 | .02 | .00 |
| ☐ 708 | Doyle Alexander ............. | .08 | .03 | .01 |
| ☐ 709 | Alan Trammell DP ........... | .10 | .04 | .01 |
| ☐ 710 | Ron LeFlore DP .............. | .05 | .02 | .00 |
| ☐ 711 | Joe Ferguson ................. | .08 | .03 | .01 |
| ☐ 712 | Bill Bonham ................... | .05 | .02 | .00 |
| ☐ 713 | Bill North ...................... | .05 | .02 | .00 |
| ☐ 714 | Pete Redfern .................. | .05 | .02 | .00 |
| ☐ 715 | Bill Madlock ................... | .25 | .10 | .02 |
| ☐ 716 | Glenn Borgmann ............. | .05 | .02 | .00 |
| ☐ 717 | Jim Barr DP ................... | .02 | .01 | .00 |
| ☐ 718 | Larry Biittner ................. | .05 | .02 | .00 |
| ☐ 719 | Sparky Lyle ................... | .15 | .06 | .01 |
| ☐ 720 | Fred Lynn ...................... | .35 | .14 | .03 |
| ☐ 721 | Toby Harrah ................... | .08 | .03 | .01 |
| ☐ 722 | Joe Niekro .................... | .12 | .05 | .01 |
| ☐ 723 | Bruce Bochte ................. | .08 | .03 | .01 |
| ☐ 724 | Lou Piniella ................... | .12 | .05 | .01 |
| ☐ 725 | Steve Rogers ................. | .12 | .05 | .01 |
| ☐ 726 | Rick Monday .................. | .10 | .04 | .01 |

# 1981 Topps Traded

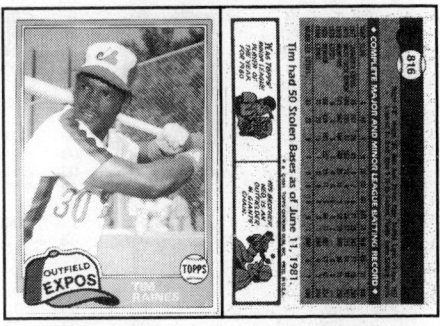

The cards in this 132 card set measure 2 1/2" by 3 1/2". For the first time since 1976, Topps issued a "Traded Set" in 1981. Unlike the small traded sets of 1974 and 1976, this set contains a larger number of cards and was sequentially numbered, alphabetically, from 727 to 858. Thus, this set gives the impression it is a continuation of their regular issue of this year. The sets were issued only through hobby card dealers and were boxed in complete sets of 132 cards.

| | | MINT | VG-E | F-G |
|---|---|---|---|---|
| COMPLETE SET | ........................ | 21.00 | 8.50 | 2.10 |
| COMMON PLAYER | ................. | .08 | .03 | .01 |
| ☐ 727 | Danny Ainge ................... | .45 | .18 | .04 |
| ☐ 728 | Doyle Alexander ............... | .12 | .05 | .01 |
| ☐ 729 | Gary Alexander ............... | .08 | .03 | .01 |
| ☐ 730 | Billy Almon ..................... | .08 | .03 | .01 |
| ☐ 731 | Joaquin Andujar .............. | .20 | .08 | .02 |
| ☐ 732 | Bob Bailor ..................... | .08 | .03 | .01 |
| ☐ 733 | Juan Beniquez ................. | .12 | .05 | .01 |
| ☐ 734 | Dave Bergman ................. | .08 | .03 | .01 |
| ☐ 735 | Tony Bernazard ............... | .12 | .05 | .01 |
| ☐ 736 | Larry Biittner ................. | .08 | .03 | .01 |
| ☐ 737 | Doug Bird ...................... | .08 | .03 | .01 |
| ☐ 738 | Bert Blyleven .................. | .40 | .16 | .04 |
| ☐ 739 | Mark Bomback ................ | .08 | .03 | .01 |
| ☐ 740 | Bobby Bonds .................. | .15 | .06 | .01 |
| ☐ 741 | Rick Bosetti ................... | .08 | .03 | .01 |
| ☐ 742 | Hubie Brooks ................. | 1.50 | .60 | .15 |
| ☐ 743 | Rick Burleson ................. | .12 | .05 | .01 |
| ☐ 744 | Ray Burris ..................... | .08 | .03 | .01 |
| ☐ 745 | Jeff Burroughs ............... | .12 | .05 | .01 |
| ☐ 746 | Enos Cabell ................... | .08 | .03 | .01 |
| ☐ 747 | Ken Clay ....................... | .08 | .03 | .01 |
| ☐ 748 | Mark Clear ..................... | .12 | .05 | .01 |
| ☐ 749 | Larry Cox ...................... | .08 | .03 | .01 |
| ☐ 750 | Hector Cruz ................... | .08 | .03 | .01 |
| ☐ 751 | Victor Cruz .................... | .08 | .03 | .01 |
| ☐ 752 | Mike Cubbage ................. | .08 | .03 | .01 |
| ☐ 753 | Dick Davis ..................... | .08 | .03 | .01 |
| ☐ 754 | Brian Doyle .................... | .08 | .03 | .01 |
| ☐ 755 | Dick Drago ..................... | .08 | .03 | .01 |
| ☐ 756 | Leon Durham .................. | .75 | .30 | .07 |
| ☐ 757 | Jim Dwyer ..................... | .08 | .03 | .01 |
| ☐ 758 | Dave Edwards ................. | .08 | .03 | .01 |
| ☐ 759 | Jim Essian ..................... | .08 | .03 | .01 |
| ☐ 760 | Bill Fahey ...................... | .08 | .03 | .01 |
| ☐ 761 | Rollie Fingers ................. | .75 | .30 | .07 |
| ☐ 762 | Carlton Fisk ................... | .60 | .24 | .06 |
| ☐ 763 | Barry Foote .................... | .08 | .03 | .01 |
| ☐ 764 | Ken Forsch .................... | .12 | .05 | .01 |
| ☐ 765 | Kiko Garcia .................... | .08 | .03 | .01 |
| ☐ 766 | Cesar Geronimo .............. | .08 | .03 | .01 |
| ☐ 767 | Gary Gray ...................... | .12 | .05 | .01 |
| ☐ 768 | Mickey Hatcher ............... | .12 | .05 | .01 |
| ☐ 769 | Steve Henderson ............. | .12 | .05 | .01 |
| ☐ 770 | Marc Hill ....................... | .08 | .03 | .01 |
| ☐ 771 | Butch Hobson ................. | .08 | .03 | .01 |
| ☐ 772 | Rick Honeycutt ............... | .12 | .05 | .01 |

| | | | | |
|---|---|---|---|---|
| ☐ 773 | Roy Howell | .08 | .03 | .01 |
| ☐ 774 | Mike Ivie | .08 | .03 | .01 |
| ☐ 775 | Roy Lee Jackson | .08 | .03 | .01 |
| ☐ 776 | Cliff Johnson | .08 | .03 | .01 |
| ☐ 777 | Randy Jones | .12 | .05 | .01 |
| ☐ 778 | Ruppert Jones | .12 | .05 | .01 |
| ☐ 779 | Mick Kelleher | .08 | .03 | .01 |
| ☐ 780 | Terry Kennedy | .20 | .08 | .02 |
| ☐ 781 | Dave Kingman | .35 | .14 | .03 |
| ☐ 782 | Bob Knepper | .20 | .08 | .02 |
| ☐ 783 | Ken Kravec | .08 | .03 | .01 |
| ☐ 784 | Bob Lacey | .08 | .03 | .01 |
| ☐ 785 | Dennis Lamp | .08 | .03 | .01 |
| ☐ 786 | Rafael Landestoy | .08 | .03 | .01 |
| ☐ 787 | Ken Landreaux | .12 | .05 | .01 |
| ☐ 788 | Carney Lansford | .40 | .16 | .04 |
| ☐ 789 | Dave LaRoche | .08 | .03 | .01 |
| ☐ 790 | Joe Lefebvre | .08 | .03 | .01 |
| ☐ 791 | Ron LeFlore | .12 | .05 | .01 |
| ☐ 792 | Randy Lerch | .08 | .03 | .01 |
| ☐ 793 | Sixto Lezcano | .12 | .05 | .01 |
| ☐ 794 | John Littlefield | .08 | .03 | .01 |
| ☐ 795 | Mike Lum | .08 | .03 | .01 |
| ☐ 796 | Greg Luzinski | .30 | .12 | .03 |
| ☐ 797 | Fred Lynn | .70 | .28 | .07 |
| ☐ 798 | Jerry Martin | .08 | .03 | .01 |
| ☐ 799 | Buck Martinez | .08 | .03 | .01 |
| ☐ 800 | Gary Matthews | .15 | .06 | .01 |
| ☐ 801 | Mario Mendoza | .08 | .03 | .01 |
| ☐ 802 | Larry Milbourne | .08 | .03 | .01 |
| ☐ 803 | Rick Miller | .08 | .03 | .01 |
| ☐ 804 | John Montefusco | .12 | .05 | .01 |
| ☐ 805 | Jerry Morales | .08 | .03 | .01 |
| ☐ 806 | Jose Morales | .08 | .03 | .01 |
| ☐ 807 | Joe Morgan | 1.25 | .50 | .12 |
| ☐ 808 | Jerry Mumphrey | .12 | .05 | .01 |
| ☐ 809 | Gene Nelson | .20 | .08 | .02 |
| ☐ 810 | Ed Ott | .08 | .03 | .01 |
| ☐ 811 | Bob Owchinko | .08 | .03 | .01 |
| ☐ 812 | Gaylord Perry | 1.25 | .50 | .12 |
| ☐ 813 | Mike Phillips | .08 | .03 | .01 |
| ☐ 814 | Darrell Porter | .12 | .05 | .01 |
| ☐ 815 | Mike Proly | .08 | .03 | .01 |
| ☐ 816 | Tim Raines | 4.50 | 1.80 | .45 |
| ☐ 817 | Len Randle | .08 | .03 | .01 |
| ☐ 818 | Doug Rau | .08 | .03 | .01 |
| ☐ 819 | Jeff Reardon | .35 | .14 | .03 |
| ☐ 820 | Ken Reitz | .08 | .03 | .01 |
| ☐ 821 | Steve Renko | .08 | .03 | .01 |
| ☐ 822 | Rick Reuschel | .15 | .06 | .01 |
| ☐ 823 | Dave Revering | .08 | .03 | .01 |
| ☐ 824 | Dave Roberts | .08 | .03 | .01 |
| ☐ 825 | Leon Roberts | .08 | .03 | .01 |
| ☐ 826 | Joe Rudi | .12 | .05 | .01 |
| ☐ 827 | Kevin Saucier | .08 | .03 | .01 |
| ☐ 828 | Tony Scott | .08 | .03 | .01 |
| ☐ 829 | Bob Shirley | .08 | .03 | .01 |
| ☐ 830 | Ted Simmons | .40 | .16 | .04 |
| ☐ 831 | Lary Sorensen | .08 | .03 | .01 |
| ☐ 832 | Jim Spencer | .08 | .03 | .01 |
| ☐ 833 | Harry Spilman | .08 | .03 | .01 |
| ☐ 834 | Fred Stanley | .08 | .03 | .01 |
| ☐ 835 | Rusty Staub | .25 | .10 | .02 |
| ☐ 836 | Bill Stein | .08 | .03 | .01 |
| ☐ 837 | Joe Strain | .08 | .03 | .01 |
| ☐ 838 | Bruce Sutter | .65 | .26 | .06 |
| ☐ 839 | Don Sutton | 1.00 | .40 | .10 |
| ☐ 840 | Steve Swisher | .08 | .03 | .01 |
| ☐ 841 | Frank Tanana | .12 | .05 | .01 |
| ☐ 842 | Gene Tenace | .08 | .03 | .01 |
| ☐ 843 | Jason Thompson | .12 | .05 | .01 |
| ☐ 844 | Dickie Thon | .20 | .08 | .02 |
| ☐ 845 | Bill Travers | .08 | .03 | .01 |
| ☐ 846 | Tom Underwood | .08 | .03 | .01 |
| ☐ 847 | John Urrea | .08 | .03 | .01 |
| ☐ 848 | Mike Vail | .08 | .03 | .01 |
| ☐ 849 | Ellis Valentine | .12 | .05 | .01 |
| ☐ 850 | Fernando Valenzuela | 5.00 | 2.00 | .50 |
| ☐ 851 | Pete Vuckovich | .15 | .06 | .01 |
| ☐ 852 | Mark Wagner | .08 | .03 | .01 |
| ☐ 853 | Bob Walk | .08 | .03 | .01 |
| ☐ 854 | Claudell Washington | .15 | .06 | .01 |
| ☐ 855 | Dave Winfield | 1.75 | .70 | .17 |
| ☐ 856 | Geoff Zahn | .12 | .05 | .01 |
| ☐ 857 | Richie Zisk | .12 | .05 | .01 |
| ☐ 858 | Checklist 727-858 | .20 | .02 | .00 |

# 1981 Topps Super Home Team

The cards in this 102 card set measure 4 7/8" by 6 7/8". In 1981 Topps issued an attractive series of photos of players from eleven AL and NL teams. The Phillies, Red Sox and Reds each were marketed in twelve-player subsets. Eighteen-player subsets were issued for the following areas: Chicago (nine White Sox and nine Cubs); New York (twelve Yankees and six Mets); Los Angeles (twelve Dodgers and six Angels); and Texas (six Rangers and six Astros). The cards of each subset contain a subset checklist on the reverse. Team sets could be obtained via a mail offer printed on the wrapper. These cards are often sold by the team or team pair.

| | MINT | VG-E | F-G |
|---|---|---|---|
| COMPLETE (1-102) | 30.00 | 12.00 | 3.00 |
| BOSTON SET (1-12) | 4.25 | 1.70 | .42 |
| CHICAGO SET (13-30) | 4.50 | 1.80 | .45 |
| CINCINNATI SET (31-42) | 4.25 | 1.70 | .42 |
| LOS ANGELES SET (43-60) | 5.00 | 2.00 | .50 |
| NEW YORK SET (61-78) | 5.00 | 2.00 | .50 |
| PHILLIES SET (79-90) | 4.25 | 1.70 | .42 |
| TEXAS SET (91-102) | 3.25 | 1.30 | .32 |
| COMMON PLAYER | .20 | .08 | .02 |

| | | | | | |
|---|---|---|---|---|---|
| ☐ | 1 | Tom Burgmeier | .20 | .08 | .02 |
| ☐ | 2 | Dennis Eckersley | .25 | .10 | .02 |
| ☐ | 3 | Dwight Evans | .40 | .16 | .04 |
| ☐ | 4 | Carlton Fisk | .50 | .20 | .05 |
| ☐ | 5 | Glenn Hoffman | .20 | .08 | .02 |
| ☐ | 6 | Carney Lansford | .30 | .12 | .03 |
| ☐ | 7 | Tony Perez | .40 | .16 | .04 |
| ☐ | 8 | Jim Rice | 1.00 | .40 | .10 |
| ☐ | 9 | Bob Stanley | .30 | .12 | .03 |
| ☐ | 10 | Dave Stapleton | .20 | .08 | .02 |
| ☐ | 11 | Frank Tanana | .25 | .10 | .02 |
| ☐ | 12 | Carl Yastrzemski | 1.25 | .50 | .12 |
| ☐ | 13 | Britt Burns | .30 | .12 | .03 |
| ☐ | 14 | Rich Dotson | .25 | .10 | .02 |
| ☐ | 15 | Ed Farmer | .20 | .08 | .02 |
| ☐ | 16 | Lamar Johnson | .20 | .08 | .02 |
| ☐ | 17 | Ron LeFlore | .25 | .10 | .02 |
| ☐ | 18 | Chet Lemon | .25 | .10 | .02 |
| ☐ | 19 | Bob Molinaro | .20 | .08 | .02 |
| ☐ | 20 | Jim Morrison | .25 | .10 | .02 |
| ☐ | 21 | Wayne Nordhagen | .20 | .08 | .02 |
| ☐ | 22 | Tim Blackwell | .20 | .08 | .02 |
| ☐ | 23 | Bill Buckner | .40 | .16 | .04 |
| ☐ | 24 | Ivan DeJesus | .20 | .08 | .02 |
| ☐ | 25 | Leon Durham | .50 | .20 | .05 |
| ☐ | 26 | Dave Kingman | .50 | .20 | .05 |
| ☐ | 27 | Mike Krukow | .40 | .16 | .04 |
| ☐ | 28 | Ken Reitz | .20 | .08 | .02 |
| ☐ | 29 | Rick Reuschel | .30 | .12 | .03 |
| ☐ | 30 | Mike Tyson | .20 | .08 | .02 |
| ☐ | 31 | Johnny Bench | 1.00 | .40 | .10 |
| ☐ | 32 | Dave Collins | .30 | .12 | .03 |
| ☐ | 33 | Dave Concepcion | .35 | .14 | .03 |
| ☐ | 34 | Dan Driessen | .25 | .10 | .02 |
| ☐ | 35 | George Foster | .40 | .16 | .04 |
| ☐ | 36 | Ken Griffey | .30 | .12 | .03 |
| ☐ | 37 | Tom Hume | .20 | .08 | .02 |
| ☐ | 38 | Ray Knight | .30 | .12 | .03 |
| ☐ | 39 | Joe Nolan | .20 | .08 | .02 |
| ☐ | 40 | Ron Oester | .25 | .10 | .02 |
| ☐ | 41 | Tom Seaver | 1.00 | .40 | .10 |
| ☐ | 42 | Mario Soto | .35 | .14 | .03 |
| ☐ | 43 | Dusty Baker | .25 | .10 | .02 |
| ☐ | 44 | Ron Cey | .40 | .16 | .04 |
| ☐ | 45 | Steve Garvey | 1.00 | .40 | .10 |
| ☐ | 46 | Burt Hooton | .20 | .08 | .02 |
| ☐ | 47 | Steve Howe | .25 | .10 | .02 |
| ☐ | 48 | Davey Lopes | .30 | .12 | .03 |
| ☐ | 49 | Rick Monday | .20 | .08 | .02 |
| ☐ | 50 | Jerry Reuss | .25 | .10 | .02 |
| ☐ | 51 | Bill Russell | .25 | .10 | .02 |
| ☐ | 52 | Reggie Smith | .30 | .12 | .03 |
| ☐ | 53 | Bob Welch | .35 | .14 | .03 |
| ☐ | 54 | Steve Yeager | .20 | .08 | .02 |
| ☐ | 55 | Don Baylor | .35 | .14 | .03 |
| ☐ | 56 | Rick Burleson | .25 | .10 | .02 |
| ☐ | 57 | Rod Carew | 1.00 | .40 | .10 |
| ☐ | 58 | Bobby Grich | .35 | .14 | .03 |
| ☐ | 59 | Butch Hobson | .20 | .08 | .02 |

| | | | MINT | VG-E | F-G |
|---|---|---|---|---|---|
| ☐ | 60 | Fred Lynn | .50 | .20 | .05 |
| ☐ | 61 | Rick Cerone | .20 | .08 | .02 |
| ☐ | 62 | Bucky Dent | .25 | .10 | .02 |
| ☐ | 63 | Rich Gossage | .50 | .20 | .05 |
| ☐ | 64 | Ron Guidry | .60 | .24 | .06 |
| ☐ | 65 | Reggie Jackson | 1.25 | .50 | .12 |
| ☐ | 66 | Tommy John | .45 | .18 | .04 |
| ☐ | 67 | Ruppert Jones | .25 | .10 | .02 |
| ☐ | 68 | Rudy May | .20 | .08 | .02 |
| ☐ | 69 | Graig Nettles | .40 | .16 | .04 |
| ☐ | 70 | Willie Randolph | .30 | .12 | .03 |
| ☐ | 71 | Bob Watson | .25 | .10 | .02 |
| ☐ | 72 | Dave Winfield | 1.00 | .40 | .10 |
| ☐ | 73 | Neil Allen | .25 | .10 | .02 |
| ☐ | 74 | Doug Flynn | .20 | .08 | .02 |
| ☐ | 75 | Lee Mazzilli | .25 | .10 | .02 |
| ☐ | 76 | Rusty Staub | .35 | .14 | .03 |
| ☐ | 77 | Frank Taveras | .20 | .08 | .02 |
| ☐ | 78 | Alex Trevino | .20 | .08 | .02 |
| ☐ | 79 | Bob Boone | .25 | .10 | .02 |
| ☐ | 80 | Larry Bowa | .35 | .14 | .03 |
| ☐ | 81 | Steve Carlton | 1.00 | .40 | .10 |
| ☐ | 82 | Greg Luzinski | .30 | .12 | .03 |
| ☐ | 83 | Garry Maddox | .20 | .08 | .02 |
| ☐ | 84 | Bake McBride | .20 | .08 | .02 |
| ☐ | 85 | Tug McGraw | .30 | .12 | .03 |
| ☐ | 86 | Pete Rose | 1.50 | .60 | .15 |
| ☐ | 87 | Dick Ruthven | .20 | .08 | .02 |
| ☐ | 88 | Mike Schmidt | 1.25 | .50 | .12 |
| ☐ | 89 | Manny Trillo | .20 | .08 | .02 |
| ☐ | 90 | Del Unser | .20 | .08 | .02 |
| ☐ | 91 | Buddy Bell | .50 | .20 | .05 |
| ☐ | 92 | Jon Matlack | .25 | .10 | .02 |
| ☐ | 93 | Al Oliver | .50 | .20 | .05 |
| ☐ | 94 | Mickey Rivers | .25 | .10 | .02 |
| ☐ | 95 | Jim Sundberg | .25 | .10 | .02 |
| ☐ | 96 | Bump Wills | .20 | .08 | .02 |
| ☐ | 97 | Cesar Cedeno | .30 | .12 | .03 |
| ☐ | 98 | Jose Cruz | .40 | .16 | .04 |
| ☐ | 99 | Art Howe | .20 | .08 | .02 |
| ☐ | 100 | Terry Puhl | .25 | .10 | .02 |
| ☐ | 101 | Nolan Ryan | 1.00 | .40 | .10 |
| ☐ | 102 | Don Sutton | .75 | .30 | .07 |

## 1981 Topps National Super

The cards in this 15 card set measure 4 7/8" by 6 7/8". In a format similar to the Home Team series of 1981 and the Super Star Photo set of 1980, these cards feature excellent photos of the top stars of 1981. The pictures of players appearing in both the regional Home Team and National sets are identical, but Brett, Cooper, Palmer, Parker, and Simmons are unique to the latter and are indicated in the checklist below with an asterisk. The backs of the cards contain the player's name, team and position, and a single copyright line.

| | | | MINT | VG-E | F-G |
|---|---|---|---|---|---|
| | COMPLETE SET | | 4.00 | 1.60 | .40 |
| | COMMON PLAYER | | .15 | .06 | .01 |
| ☐ | 1 | Buddy Bell | .15 | .06 | .01 |
| ☐ | 2 | Johnny Bench | .50 | .20 | .05 |
| ☐ | 3 | George Brett * | 1.00 | .40 | .10 |
| ☐ | 4 | Rod Carew | .50 | .20 | .05 |
| ☐ | 5 | Cecil Cooper * | .20 | .08 | .02 |
| ☐ | 6 | Steve Garvey | .60 | .24 | .06 |
| ☐ | 7 | Rich Gossage | .25 | .10 | .02 |
| ☐ | 8 | Reggie Jackson | .75 | .30 | .07 |
| ☐ | 9 | Jim Palmer * | .35 | .14 | .03 |
| ☐ | 10 | Dave Parker * | .35 | .14 | .03 |
| ☐ | 11 | Jim Rice | .35 | .14 | .03 |
| ☐ | 12 | Pete Rose | 1.00 | .40 | .10 |
| ☐ | 13 | Mike Schmidt | .75 | .30 | .07 |
| ☐ | 14 | Tom Seaver | .50 | .20 | .05 |
| ☐ | 15 | Ted Simmons * | .20 | .08 | .02 |

## 1982 Topps

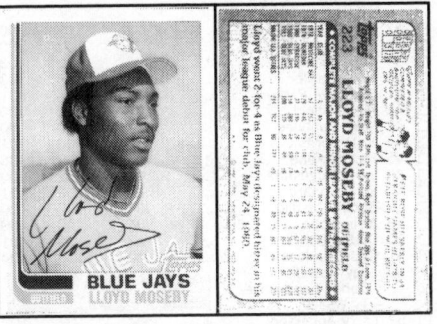

The cards in this 792 card set measure 2 1/2" by 3 1/2". The 1982 baseball series is the largest set Topps has ever issued at one printing. The 66 card increase from the previous year's total eliminated the "double print" practice which had occurred in every regular issue since 1978. Cards 1-6 depict Highlights (HL) of the 1981 season, cards 161-168 picture League Leaders, and there are mini-series of A.L. (547-557) and N.L. (337-347) All Stars (AS). The abbreviation "SA" in the checklist is given for the 40 "Super Action" cards introduced in this set. The team cards are actually Team Leader (TL) cards picturing the batting and pitching leader for that team with a checklist back.

| | | | MINT | VG-E | F-G |
|---|---|---|---|---|---|
| | COMPLETE SET | | 55.00 | 20.00 | 5.00 |
| | COMMON PLAYER (1-792) | | .04 | .02 | .00 |
| ☐ | 1 | HL: Steve Carlton, Sets New NL Strikeout Record | .40 | .10 | .02 |
| ☐ | 2 | HL: Ron Davis, Fans 8 Straight in Relief | .06 | .02 | .00 |
| ☐ | 3 | HL: Tim Raines, Swipes 71 Bases as Rookie | .25 | .10 | .02 |
| ☐ | 4 | HL: Pete Rose, Sets NL Career Hits Mark | .75 | .30 | .07 |
| ☐ | 5 | HL: Nolan Ryan, Pitches 5th Career No-Hitter | .30 | .12 | .03 |
| ☐ | 6 | HL: Fern. Valenzuela, 8 Shutouts as Rookie | .30 | .12 | .03 |
| ☐ | 7 | Scott Sanderson | .04 | .02 | .00 |
| ☐ | 8 | Rich Dauer | .04 | .02 | .00 |
| ☐ | 9 | Ron Guidry | .30 | .12 | .03 |
| ☐ | 10 | SA: Ron Guidry | .15 | .06 | .01 |
| ☐ | 11 | Gary Alexander | .04 | .02 | .00 |
| ☐ | 12 | Moose Haas | .06 | .02 | .00 |
| ☐ | 13 | Lamar Johnson | .04 | .02 | .00 |
| ☐ | 14 | Steve Howe | .06 | .02 | .00 |
| ☐ | 15 | Ellis Valentine | .04 | .02 | .00 |
| ☐ | 16 | Steve Comer | .04 | .02 | .00 |
| ☐ | 17 | Darrell Evans | .12 | .05 | .01 |
| ☐ | 18 | Fernando Arroyo | .04 | .02 | .00 |
| ☐ | 19 | Ernie Whitt | .04 | .02 | .00 |
| ☐ | 20 | Garry Maddox | .06 | .02 | .00 |
| ☐ | 21 | Orioles Rookies: Bob Bonner Cal Ripken Jeff Schneider | 9.00 | 3.75 | .90 |
| ☐ | 22 | Jim Beattie | .04 | .02 | .00 |
| ☐ | 23 | Willie Hernandez | .20 | .08 | .02 |
| ☐ | 24 | Dave Frost | .04 | .02 | .00 |
| ☐ | 25 | Jerry Remy | .04 | .02 | .00 |
| ☐ | 26 | Jorge Orta | .04 | .02 | .00 |
| ☐ | 27 | Tom Herr | .12 | .05 | .01 |
| ☐ | 28 | John Urrea | .04 | .02 | .00 |
| ☐ | 29 | Dwayne Murphy | .06 | .02 | .00 |
| ☐ | 30 | Tom Seaver | .65 | .26 | .06 |
| ☐ | 31 | SA: Tom Seaver | .30 | .12 | .03 |
| ☐ | 32 | Gene Garber | .04 | .02 | .00 |
| ☐ | 33 | Jerry Morales | .04 | .02 | .00 |
| ☐ | 34 | Joe Sambito | .06 | .02 | .00 |

| | | | | | |
|---|---|---|---|---|---|
| ☐ | 35 | Willie Aikens | .06 | .02 | .00 |
| ☐ | 36 | Rangers TL: | .10 | .02 | .00 |
| | | Mgr. Don Zimmer | | | |
| | | Batting: Al Oliver | | | |
| | | Pitching: Doc Medich | | | |
| ☐ | 37 | Dan Graham | .04 | .02 | .00 |
| ☐ | 38 | Charlie Lea | .06 | .02 | .00 |
| ☐ | 39 | Lou Whitaker | .30 | .12 | .03 |
| ☐ | 40 | Dave Parker | .35 | .14 | .03 |
| ☐ | 41 | SA: Dave Parker | .15 | .06 | .01 |
| ☐ | 42 | Rick Sofield | .04 | .02 | .00 |
| ☐ | 43 | Mike Cubbage | .04 | .02 | .00 |
| ☐ | 44 | Britt Burns | .08 | .03 | .01 |
| ☐ | 45 | Rick Cerone | .04 | .02 | .00 |
| ☐ | 46 | Jerry Augustine | .04 | .02 | .00 |
| ☐ | 47 | Jeff Leonard | .08 | .03 | .01 |
| ☐ | 48 | Bobby Castillo | .04 | .02 | .00 |
| ☐ | 49 | Alvis Woods | .04 | .02 | .00 |
| ☐ | 50 | Buddy Bell | .12 | .05 | .01 |
| ☐ | 51 | Cubs Rookies: | .40 | .16 | .04 |
| | | Jay Howell | | | |
| | | Carlos Lezcano | | | |
| | | Ty Waller | | | |
| ☐ | 52 | Larry Andersen | .04 | .02 | .00 |
| ☐ | 53 | Greg Gross | .04 | .02 | .00 |
| ☐ | 54 | Ron Hassey | .04 | .02 | .00 |
| ☐ | 55 | Rick Burleson | .06 | .02 | .00 |
| ☐ | 56 | Mark Littell | .04 | .02 | .00 |
| ☐ | 57 | Craig Reynolds | .04 | .02 | .00 |
| ☐ | 58 | John D'Acquisto | .04 | .02 | .00 |
| ☐ | 59 | Rich Gedman | 1.50 | .60 | .15 |
| ☐ | 60 | Tony Armas | .15 | .06 | .01 |
| ☐ | 61 | Tommy Boggs | .04 | .02 | .00 |
| ☐ | 62 | Mike Tyson | .04 | .02 | .00 |
| ☐ | 63 | Mario Soto | .10 | .04 | .01 |
| ☐ | 64 | Lynn Jones | .04 | .02 | .00 |
| ☐ | 65 | Terry Kennedy | .10 | .04 | .01 |
| ☐ | 66 | Astros TL: | .15 | .03 | .00 |
| | | Mgr. Bill Virdon | | | |
| | | Batting: Art Howe | | | |
| | | Pitching: Nolan Ryan | | | |
| ☐ | 67 | Rich Gale | .04 | .02 | .00 |
| ☐ | 68 | Roy Howell | .04 | .02 | .00 |
| ☐ | 69 | Al Williams | .04 | .02 | .00 |
| ☐ | 70 | Tim Raines | 1.25 | .50 | .12 |
| ☐ | 71 | Roy Lee Jackson | .04 | .02 | .00 |
| ☐ | 72 | Rick Auerbach | .04 | .02 | .00 |
| ☐ | 73 | Buddy Solomon | .04 | .02 | .00 |
| ☐ | 74 | Bob Clark | .04 | .02 | .00 |
| ☐ | 75 | Tommy John | .20 | .08 | .02 |
| ☐ | 76 | Greg Pryor | .04 | .02 | .00 |
| ☐ | 77 | Miguel Dilone | .04 | .02 | .00 |
| ☐ | 78 | George Medich | .04 | .02 | .00 |
| ☐ | 79 | Bob Bailor | .04 | .02 | .00 |
| ☐ | 80 | Jim Palmer | .45 | .18 | .04 |
| ☐ | 81 | SA: Jim Palmer | .20 | .08 | .02 |
| ☐ | 82 | Bob Welch | .08 | .03 | .01 |
| ☐ | 83 | Yankees Rookies: | .60 | .24 | .06 |
| | | Steve Balboni | | | |
| | | Andy McGaffigan | | | |
| | | Andre Robertson | | | |
| ☐ | 84 | Rennie Stennett | .04 | .02 | .00 |
| ☐ | 85 | Lynn McGlothen | .04 | .02 | .00 |
| ☐ | 86 | Dane Iorg | .04 | .02 | .00 |
| ☐ | 87 | Matt Keough | .04 | .02 | .00 |
| ☐ | 88 | Biff Pocoroba | .04 | .02 | .00 |
| ☐ | 89 | Steve Henderson | .04 | .02 | .00 |
| ☐ | 90 | Nolan Ryan | .65 | .26 | .06 |
| ☐ | 91 | Carney Lansford | .15 | .06 | .01 |
| ☐ | 92 | Brad Havens | .06 | .02 | .00 |
| ☐ | 93 | Larry Hisle | .06 | .02 | .00 |
| ☐ | 94 | Andy Hassler | .04 | .02 | .00 |
| ☐ | 95 | Ozzie Smith | .25 | .10 | .02 |
| ☐ | 96 | Royals TL: | .15 | .03 | .00 |
| | | Mgr. Jim Frey | | | |
| | | Batting: George Brett | | | |
| | | Pitching: Larry Gura | | | |
| ☐ | 97 | Paul Moskau | .04 | .02 | .00 |
| ☐ | 98 | Terry Bulling | .04 | .02 | .00 |
| ☐ | 99 | Barry Bonnell | .04 | .02 | .00 |
| ☐ | 100 | Mike Schmidt | 1.25 | .50 | .12 |
| ☐ | 101 | SA: Mike Schmidt | .50 | .20 | .05 |
| ☐ | 102 | Dan Briggs | .04 | .02 | .00 |
| ☐ | 103 | Bob Lacey | .04 | .02 | .00 |
| ☐ | 104 | Rance Mulliniks | .04 | .02 | .00 |
| ☐ | 105 | Kirk Gibson | .75 | .30 | .07 |
| ☐ | 106 | Enrique Romo | .04 | .02 | .00 |
| ☐ | 107 | Wayne Krenchicki | .04 | .02 | .00 |
| ☐ | 108 | Bob Sykes | .04 | .02 | .00 |
| ☐ | 109 | Dave Revering | .04 | .02 | .00 |
| ☐ | 110 | Carlton Fisk | .25 | .10 | .02 |
| ☐ | 111 | SA: Carlton Fisk | .15 | .06 | .01 |
| ☐ | 112 | Billy Sample | .04 | .02 | .00 |
| ☐ | 113 | Steve McCatty | .04 | .02 | .00 |
| ☐ | 114 | Ken Landreaux | .06 | .02 | .00 |
| ☐ | 115 | Gaylord Perry | .25 | .10 | .02 |
| ☐ | 116 | Jim Wohlford | .04 | .02 | .00 |
| ☐ | 117 | Rawly Eastwick | .04 | .02 | .00 |
| ☐ | 118 | Expos Rookies: | .25 | .10 | .02 |
| | | Terry Francona | | | |
| | | Brad Mills | | | |
| | | Bryn Smith | | | |
| ☐ | 119 | Joe Pittman | .04 | .02 | .00 |
| ☐ | 120 | Gary Lucas | .04 | .02 | .00 |
| ☐ | 121 | Ed Lynch | .12 | .05 | .01 |
| ☐ | 122 | Jamie Easterly | .06 | .02 | .00 |
| | | (photo actually | | | |
| | | Reggie Cleveland) | | | |
| ☐ | 123 | Danny Goodwin | .04 | .02 | .00 |
| ☐ | 124 | Reid Nichols | .04 | .02 | .00 |
| ☐ | 125 | Danny Ainge | .10 | .04 | .01 |
| ☐ | 126 | Braves TL: | .10 | .02 | .00 |
| | | Mgr. Bobby Cox | | | |
| | | Batting: C.Washington | | | |
| | | Pitching: Rick Mahler | | | |
| ☐ | 127 | Lonnie Smith | .10 | .04 | .01 |
| ☐ | 128 | Frank Pastore | .04 | .02 | .00 |
| ☐ | 129 | Checklist 1-132 | .10 | .01 | .00 |
| ☐ | 130 | Julio Cruz | .04 | .02 | .00 |
| ☐ | 131 | Stan Bahnsen | .04 | .02 | .00 |
| ☐ | 132 | Lee May | .06 | .02 | .00 |
| ☐ | 133 | Pat Underwood | .04 | .02 | .00 |
| ☐ | 134 | Dan Ford | .04 | .02 | .00 |
| ☐ | 135 | Andy Rincon | .04 | .02 | .00 |
| ☐ | 136 | Lenn Sakata | .04 | .02 | .00 |
| ☐ | 137 | George Cappuzzello | .04 | .02 | .00 |
| ☐ | 138 | Tony Pena | .30 | .12 | .03 |
| ☐ | 139 | Jeff Jones | .04 | .02 | .00 |
| ☐ | 140 | Ron LeFlore | .06 | .02 | .00 |
| ☐ | 141 | Indians Rookies | 2.00 | .80 | .20 |
| | | Chris Bando | | | |
| | | Tom Brennan | | | |
| | | Von Hayes | | | |
| ☐ | 142 | Dave LaRoche | .04 | .02 | .00 |
| ☐ | 143 | Mookie Wilson | .10 | .04 | .01 |
| ☐ | 144 | Fred Breining | .12 | .05 | .01 |
| ☐ | 145 | Bob Horner | .35 | .14 | .03 |
| ☐ | 146 | Mike Griffin | .04 | .02 | .00 |
| ☐ | 147 | Denny Walling | .04 | .02 | .00 |
| ☐ | 148 | Mickey Klutts | .04 | .02 | .00 |
| ☐ | 149 | Pat Putnam | .04 | .02 | .00 |
| ☐ | 150 | Ted Simmons | .15 | .06 | .01 |
| ☐ | 151 | Dave Edwards | .04 | .02 | .00 |
| ☐ | 152 | Ramon Aviles | .04 | .02 | .00 |
| ☐ | 153 | Roger Erickson | .04 | .02 | .00 |
| ☐ | 154 | Dennis Werth | .04 | .02 | .00 |
| ☐ | 155 | Otto Velez | .04 | .02 | .00 |
| ☐ | 156 | Oakland A's TL: | .15 | .03 | .00 |
| | | Mgr. Billy Martin | | | |
| | | Batting: R.Henderson | | | |
| | | Pitching: S. McCatty | | | |
| ☐ | 157 | Steve Crawford | .08 | .03 | .01 |
| ☐ | 158 | Brian Downing | .06 | .02 | .00 |
| ☐ | 159 | Larry Biittner | .04 | .02 | .00 |
| ☐ | 160 | Luis Tiant | .10 | .04 | .01 |
| ☐ | 161 | Batting Leaders: | .15 | .06 | .01 |
| | | Bill Madlock | | | |
| | | Carney Lansford | | | |
| ☐ | 162 | Home Run Leaders: | .20 | .08 | .02 |
| | | Mike Schmidt | | | |
| | | Tony Armas | | | |
| | | Dwight Evans | | | |
| | | Bobby Grich | | | |
| | | Eddie Murray | | | |
| ☐ | 163 | RBI Leaders: | .30 | .12 | .03 |
| | | Mike Schmidt | | | |
| | | Eddie Murray | | | |
| ☐ | 164 | Stolen Base Leaders | .30 | .12 | .03 |
| | | Tim Raines | | | |
| | | Rickey Henderson | | | |
| ☐ | 165 | Victory Leaders | .15 | .06 | .01 |
| | | Tom Seaver | | | |
| | | Denny Martinez | | | |
| | | Steve McCatty | | | |
| | | Jack Morris | | | |
| | | Pete Vuckovich | | | |
| ☐ | 166 | Strikeout Leaders | .15 | .06 | .01 |
| | | Fernando Valenzuela | | | |
| | | Len Barker | | | |
| ☐ | 167 | ERA Leaders: | .15 | .06 | .01 |
| | | Nolan Ryan | | | |
| | | Steve McCatty | | | |
| ☐ | 168 | Leading Firemen: | .15 | .06 | .01 |
| | | Bruce Sutter | | | |
| | | Rollie Fingers | | | |
| ☐ | 169 | Charlie Leibrandt | .08 | .03 | .01 |

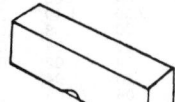
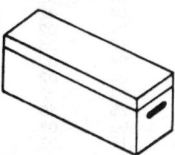

| | | | | |
|---|---|---|---|---|
| ☐ 170 | Jim Bibby | .06 | .02 | .00 |
| ☐ 171 | Giants Rookies | 1.25 | .50 | .12 |
| | Bob Brenly | | | |
| | Chili Davis | | | |
| | Bob Tufts | | | |
| ☐ 172 | Bill Gullickson | .06 | .02 | .00 |
| ☐ 173 | Jamie Quirk | .04 | .02 | .00 |
| ☐ 174 | Dave Ford | .04 | .02 | .00 |
| ☐ 175 | Jerry Mumphrey | .06 | .02 | .00 |
| ☐ 176 | Dewey Robinson | .04 | .02 | .00 |
| ☐ 177 | John Ellis | .04 | .02 | .00 |
| ☐ 178 | Dyar Miller | .04 | .02 | .00 |
| ☐ 179 | Steve Garvey | .80 | .32 | .08 |
| ☐ 180 | SA: Steve Garvey | .40 | .16 | .04 |
| ☐ 181 | Silvio Martinez | .04 | .02 | .00 |
| ☐ 182 | Larry Herndon | .06 | .02 | .00 |
| ☐ 183 | Mike Proly | .04 | .02 | .00 |
| ☐ 184 | Mick Kelleher | .04 | .02 | .00 |
| ☐ 185 | Phil Niekro | .40 | .16 | .04 |
| ☐ 186 | Cardinals TL: | .15 | .03 | .00 |
| | Mgr. Whitey Herzog | | | |
| | Batting K. Hernandez | | | |
| | Pitching Bob Forsch | | | |
| ☐ 187 | Jeff Newman | .04 | .02 | .00 |
| ☐ 188 | Randy Martz | .04 | .02 | .00 |
| ☐ 189 | Glenn Hoffman | .04 | .02 | .00 |
| ☐ 190 | J.R. Richard | .10 | .04 | .01 |
| ☐ 191 | Tim Wallach | .60 | .24 | .06 |
| ☐ 192 | Broderick Perkins | .04 | .02 | .00 |
| ☐ 193 | Darrell Jackson | .04 | .02 | .00 |
| ☐ 194 | Mike Vail | .04 | .02 | .00 |
| ☐ 195 | Paul Molitor | .15 | .06 | .01 |
| ☐ 196 | Willie Upshaw | .12 | .05 | .01 |
| ☐ 197 | Shane Rawley | .08 | .03 | .01 |
| ☐ 198 | Chris Speier | .04 | .02 | .00 |
| ☐ 199 | Don Aase | .06 | .02 | .00 |
| ☐ 200 | George Brett | 1.50 | .60 | .15 |
| ☐ 201 | SA: George Brett | .60 | .24 | .06 |
| ☐ 202 | Rick Manning | .03 | .01 | .00 |
| ☐ 203 | Blue Jays Rookies | 4.00 | 1.60 | .40 |
| | Jesse Barfield | | | |
| | Brian Milner | | | |
| | Boomer Wells | | | |
| ☐ 204 | Gary Roenicke | .06 | .02 | .00 |
| ☐ 205 | Neil Allen | .06 | .02 | .00 |
| ☐ 206 | Tony Bernazard | .06 | .02 | .00 |
| ☐ 207 | Rod Scurry | .04 | .02 | .00 |
| ☐ 208 | Bobby Murcer | .12 | .05 | .01 |
| ☐ 209 | Gary Lavelle | .06 | .02 | .00 |
| ☐ 210 | Keith Hernandez | .50 | .20 | .05 |
| ☐ 211 | Dan Petry | .20 | .08 | .02 |
| ☐ 212 | Mario Mendoza | .04 | .02 | .00 |
| ☐ 213 | Dave Stewart | .25 | .10 | .02 |
| ☐ 214 | Brian Asselstine | .04 | .02 | .00 |
| ☐ 215 | Mike Krukow | .12 | .05 | .01 |
| ☐ 216 | White Sox TL: | .10 | .02 | .00 |
| | Mgr. Tony LaRussa | | | |
| | Batting: Chet Lemon | | | |
| | Pitching: Dennis Lamp | | | |
| ☐ 217 | Bo McLaughlin | .04 | .02 | .00 |
| ☐ 218 | Dave Roberts | .04 | .02 | .00 |
| ☐ 219 | John Curtis | .04 | .02 | .00 |
| ☐ 220 | Manny Trillo | .06 | .02 | .00 |
| ☐ 221 | Jim Slaton | .04 | .02 | .00 |
| ☐ 222 | Butch Wynegar | .06 | .02 | .00 |
| ☐ 223 | Lloyd Moseby | .30 | .12 | .03 |
| ☐ 224 | Bruce Bochte | .06 | .02 | .00 |
| ☐ 225 | Mike Torrez | .06 | .02 | .00 |
| ☐ 226 | Checklist 133-264 | .10 | .01 | .00 |
| ☐ 227 | Ray Burris | .04 | .02 | .00 |
| ☐ 228 | Sam Mejias | .04 | .02 | .00 |
| ☐ 229 | Geoff Zahn | .04 | .02 | .00 |
| ☐ 230 | Willie Wilson | .25 | .10 | .02 |
| ☐ 231 | Phillies Rookies | .40 | .16 | .04 |
| | Mark Davis | | | |
| | Bob Dernier | | | |
| | Ozzie Virgil | | | |
| ☐ 232 | Terry Crowley | .04 | .02 | .00 |
| ☐ 233 | Duane Kuiper | .04 | .02 | .00 |
| ☐ 234 | Ron Hodges | .04 | .02 | .00 |
| ☐ 235 | Mike Easler | .10 | .04 | .01 |
| ☐ 236 | John Martin | .04 | .02 | .00 |
| ☐ 237 | Rusty Kuntz | .04 | .02 | .00 |
| ☐ 238 | Kevin Saucier | .04 | .02 | .00 |
| ☐ 239 | Jon Matlack | .06 | .02 | .00 |
| ☐ 240 | Bucky Dent | .08 | .03 | .01 |
| ☐ 241 | SA: Bucky Dent | .06 | .02 | .00 |
| ☐ 242 | Milt May | .04 | .02 | .00 |
| ☐ 243 | Bob Owchinko | .04 | .02 | .00 |
| ☐ 244 | Rufino Linares | .04 | .02 | .00 |
| ☐ 245 | Ken Reitz | .04 | .02 | .00 |
| ☐ 246 | New York Mets TL: | .15 | .03 | .00 |
| | Mgr. Joe Torre | | | |
| | Batting: Hubie Brooks | | | |
| | Pitching: Mike Scott | | | |
| ☐ 247 | Pedro Guerrero | .60 | .24 | .06 |
| ☐ 248 | Frank LaCorte | .04 | .02 | .00 |
| ☐ 249 | Tim Flannery | .04 | .02 | .00 |
| ☐ 250 | Tug McGraw | .10 | .04 | .01 |
| ☐ 251 | Fred Lynn | .30 | .12 | .03 |
| ☐ 252 | SA: Fred Lynn | .15 | .06 | .01 |
| ☐ 253 | Chuck Baker | .04 | .02 | .00 |
| ☐ 254 | Jorge Bell | 3.50 | 1.40 | .35 |
| ☐ 255 | Tony Perez | .20 | .08 | .02 |
| ☐ 256 | SA: Tony Perez | .10 | .04 | .01 |
| ☐ 257 | Larry Harlow | .04 | .02 | .00 |
| ☐ 258 | Bo Diaz | .10 | .04 | .01 |
| ☐ 259 | Rodney Scott | .04 | .02 | .00 |
| ☐ 260 | Bruce Sutter | .30 | .12 | .03 |
| ☐ 261 | Tigers Rookies: | .10 | .04 | .01 |
| | Howard Bailey | | | |
| | Marty Castillo | | | |
| | Dave Rucker | | | |
| ☐ 262 | Doug Bair | .04 | .02 | .00 |
| ☐ 263 | Victor Cruz | .04 | .02 | .00 |
| ☐ 264 | Dan Quisenberry | .25 | .10 | .02 |
| ☐ 265 | Al Bumbry | .04 | .02 | .00 |
| ☐ 266 | Rick Leach | .06 | .02 | .00 |
| ☐ 267 | Kurt Bevacqua | .04 | .02 | .00 |
| ☐ 268 | Rickey Keeton | .04 | .02 | .00 |
| ☐ 269 | Jim Essian | .04 | .02 | .00 |
| ☐ 270 | Rusty Staub | .12 | .05 | .01 |
| ☐ 271 | Larry Bradford | .04 | .02 | .00 |
| ☐ 272 | Bump Wills | .04 | .02 | .00 |
| ☐ 273 | Doug Bird | .04 | .02 | .00 |
| ☐ 274 | Bob Ojeda | 1.25 | .50 | .12 |
| ☐ 275 | Bob Watson | .06 | .02 | .00 |
| ☐ 276 | Angels TL: | .15 | .03 | .00 |
| | Mgr. Gene Mauch | | | |
| | Batting: Rod Carew | | | |
| | Pitching: Ken Forsch | | | |
| ☐ 277 | Terry Puhl | .06 | .02 | .00 |
| ☐ 278 | John Littlefield | .04 | .02 | .00 |
| ☐ 279 | Bill Russell | .06 | .02 | .00 |
| ☐ 280 | Ben Oglivie | .08 | .03 | .01 |
| ☐ 281 | John Verhoeven | .04 | .02 | .00 |
| ☐ 282 | Ken Macha | .04 | .02 | .00 |
| ☐ 283 | Brian Allard | .04 | .02 | .00 |
| ☐ 284 | Bob Grich | .08 | .03 | .01 |
| ☐ 285 | Sparky Lyle | .12 | .05 | .01 |
| ☐ 286 | Bill Fahey | .04 | .02 | .00 |
| ☐ 287 | Alan Bannister | .04 | .02 | .00 |
| ☐ 288 | Garry Templeton | .12 | .05 | .01 |
| ☐ 289 | Bob Stanley | .06 | .02 | .00 |
| ☐ 290 | Ken Singleton | .12 | .05 | .01 |
| ☐ 291 | Pirates Rookies | 1.25 | .50 | .12 |
| | Vance Law | | | |
| | Bob Long | | | |
| | Johnny Ray | | | |
| ☐ 292 | David Palmer | .06 | .02 | .00 |
| ☐ 293 | Rob Picciolo | .04 | .02 | .00 |
| ☐ 294 | Mike LaCoss | .04 | .02 | .00 |
| ☐ 295 | Jason Thompson | .08 | .03 | .01 |
| ☐ 296 | Bob Walk | .04 | .02 | .00 |
| ☐ 297 | Clint Hurdle | .04 | .02 | .00 |
| ☐ 298 | Danny Darwin | .04 | .02 | .00 |
| ☐ 299 | Steve Trout | .06 | .02 | .00 |
| ☐ 300 | Reggie Jackson | 1.25 | .50 | .12 |
| ☐ 301 | SA: Reggie Jackson | .50 | .20 | .05 |
| ☐ 302 | Doug Flynn | .04 | .02 | .00 |
| ☐ 303 | Bill Caudill | .06 | .02 | .00 |
| ☐ 304 | Johnnie LeMaster | .04 | .02 | .00 |
| ☐ 305 | Don Sutton | .40 | .16 | .04 |
| ☐ 306 | SA: Don Sutton | .20 | .08 | .02 |
| ☐ 307 | Randy Bass | .04 | .02 | .00 |
| ☐ 308 | Charlie Moore | .04 | .02 | .00 |
| ☐ 309 | Pete Redfern | .04 | .02 | .00 |
| ☐ 310 | Mike Hargrove | .06 | .02 | .00 |
| ☐ 311 | Dodgers TL: | .10 | .02 | .00 |
| | Mgr. Tom Lasorda | | | |
| | Batting: Dusty Baker | | | |
| | Pitching: Burt Hooton | | | |
| ☐ 312 | Lenny Randle | .04 | .02 | .00 |
| ☐ 313 | John Harris | .04 | .02 | .00 |
| ☐ 314 | Buck Martinez | .04 | .02 | .00 |
| ☐ 315 | Burt Hooton | .04 | .02 | .00 |
| ☐ 316 | Steve Braun | .04 | .02 | .00 |
| ☐ 317 | Dick Ruthven | .04 | .02 | .00 |
| ☐ 318 | Mike Heath | .04 | .02 | .00 |
| ☐ 319 | Dave Rozema | .04 | .02 | .00 |
| ☐ 320 | Chris Chambliss | .06 | .02 | .00 |
| ☐ 321 | SA: Chris Chambliss | .06 | .02 | .00 |
| ☐ 322 | Garry Hancock | .04 | .02 | .00 |
| ☐ 323 | Bill Lee | .06 | .02 | .00 |
| ☐ 324 | Steve Dillard | .04 | .02 | .00 |
| ☐ 325 | Jose Cruz | .15 | .06 | .01 |

| | | | | |
|---|---|---|---|---|
| ☐ 326 Pete Falcone | .04 | .02 | .00 |
| ☐ 327 Joe Nolan | .04 | .02 | .00 |
| ☐ 328 Ed Farmer | .04 | .02 | .00 |
| ☐ 329 U.L. Washington | .04 | .02 | .00 |
| ☐ 330 Rick Wise | .06 | .02 | .00 |
| ☐ 331 Benny Ayala | .04 | .02 | .00 |
| ☐ 332 Don Robinson | .06 | .02 | .00 |
| ☐ 333 Brewers Rookies | .15 | .06 | .01 |
|     Frank DiPino | | | |
|     Marshall Edwards | | | |
|     Chuck Porter | | | |
| ☐ 334 Aurelio Rodriguez | .04 | .02 | .00 |
| ☐ 335 Jim Sundberg | .06 | .02 | .00 |
| ☐ 336 Mariners TL: | .10 | .02 | .00 |
|     Mgr. Rene Lachemann | | | |
|     Batting: Tom Paciorek | | | |
|     Pitching: Glenn Abbott | | | |
| ☐ 337 Pete Rose AS | .75 | .30 | .07 |
| ☐ 338 Dave Lopes AS | .06 | .02 | .00 |
| ☐ 339 Mike Schmidt AS | .40 | .16 | .04 |
| ☐ 340 Dave Concepcion AS | .08 | .03 | .01 |
| ☐ 341 Andre Dawson AS | .15 | .06 | .01 |
| ☐ 342A George Foster AS | .35 | .14 | .03 |
|     (with autograph) | | | |
| ☐ 342B George Foster AS | 2.50 | 1.00 | .25 |
|     (w/o autograph) | | | |
| ☐ 343 Dave Parker AS | .15 | .06 | .01 |
| ☐ 344 Gary Carter AS | .30 | .12 | .03 |
| ☐ 345 Fern. Valenzuela AS | .25 | .10 | .02 |
| ☐ 346 Tom Seaver AS | .25 | .10 | .02 |
| ☐ 347 Bruce Sutter AS | .15 | .06 | .01 |
| ☐ 348 Derrel Thomas | .04 | .02 | .00 |
| ☐ 349 George Frazier | .04 | .02 | .00 |
| ☐ 350 Thad Bosley | .04 | .02 | .00 |
| ☐ 351 Reds Rookies: | .08 | .03 | .01 |
|     Scott Brown | | | |
|     Geoff Coumbe | | | |
|     Paul Householder | | | |
| ☐ 352 Dick Davis | .04 | .02 | .00 |
| ☐ 353 Jack O'Connor | .04 | .02 | .00 |
| ☐ 354 Roberto Ramos | .04 | .02 | .00 |
| ☐ 355 Dwight Evans | .15 | .06 | .01 |
| ☐ 356 Denny Lewallyn | .08 | .03 | .01 |
| ☐ 357 Butch Hobson | .04 | .02 | .00 |
| ☐ 358 Mike Parrott | .04 | .02 | .00 |
| ☐ 359 Jim Dwyer | .04 | .02 | .00 |
| ☐ 360 Len Barker | .08 | .03 | .01 |
| ☐ 361 Rafael Landestoy | .04 | .02 | .00 |
| ☐ 362 Jim Wright | .04 | .02 | .00 |
| ☐ 363 Bob Molinaro | .04 | .02 | .00 |
| ☐ 364 Doyle Alexander | .06 | .02 | .00 |
| ☐ 365 Bill Madlock | .20 | .08 | .02 |
| ☐ 366 Padres TL: | .10 | .02 | .00 |
|     Mgr. Frank Howard | | | |
|     Batting: Luis Salazar | | | |
|     Pitching: Eichelberger | | | |
| ☐ 367 Jim Kaat | .15 | .06 | .01 |
| ☐ 368 Alex Trevino | .04 | .02 | .00 |
| ☐ 369 Champ Summers | .04 | .02 | .00 |
| ☐ 370 Mike Norris | .06 | .02 | .00 |
| ☐ 371 Jerry Don Gleaton | .04 | .02 | .00 |
| ☐ 372 Luis Gomez | .04 | .02 | .00 |
| ☐ 373 Gene Nelson | .12 | .05 | .01 |
| ☐ 374 Tim Blackwell | .04 | .02 | .00 |
| ☐ 375 Dusty Baker | .08 | .03 | .01 |
| ☐ 376 Chris Welsh | .06 | .02 | .00 |
| ☐ 377 Kiko Garcia | .04 | .02 | .00 |
| ☐ 378 Mike Caldwell | .06 | .02 | .00 |
| ☐ 379 Rob Wilfong | .04 | .02 | .00 |
| ☐ 380 Dave Stieb | .30 | .12 | .03 |
| ☐ 381 Red Sox Rookies: | .25 | .10 | .02 |
|     Bruce Hurst | | | |
|     Dave Schmidt | | | |
|     Julio Valdez | | | |
| ☐ 382 Joe Simpson | .04 | .02 | .00 |
| ☐ 383A Pascual Perez ERR | 35.00 | 14.00 | 3.50 |
|     (no position | | | |
|     on front) | | | |
| ☐ 383B Pascual Perez COR | .10 | .04 | .01 |
| ☐ 384 Keith Moreland | .08 | .03 | .01 |
| ☐ 385 Ken Forsch | .04 | .02 | .00 |
| ☐ 386 Jerry White | .04 | .02 | .00 |
| ☐ 387 Tom Veryzer | .04 | .02 | .00 |
| ☐ 388 Joe Rudi | .06 | .02 | .00 |
| ☐ 389 George Vukovich | .04 | .02 | .00 |
| ☐ 390 Eddie Murray | 1.25 | .50 | .12 |
| ☐ 391 Dave Tobik | .04 | .02 | .00 |
| ☐ 392 Rick Bosetti | .04 | .02 | .00 |
| ☐ 393 Al Hrabosky | .06 | .02 | .00 |
| ☐ 394 Checklist 265-396 | .10 | .01 | .00 |
| ☐ 395 Omar Moreno | .04 | .02 | .00 |
| ☐ 396 Twins TL: | .10 | .02 | .00 |
|     Mgr. Billy Gardner | | | |

| | | | | |
|---|---|---|---|---|
|     Batting: John Castino | | | |
|     Pitching: F. Arroyo | | | |
| ☐ 397 Ken Brett | .04 | .02 | .00 |
| ☐ 398 Mike Squires | .04 | .02 | .00 |
| ☐ 399 Pat Zachry | .04 | .02 | .00 |
| ☐ 400 Johnny Bench | .75 | .30 | .07 |
| ☐ 401 SA: Johnny Bench | .35 | .14 | .03 |
| ☐ 402 Bill Stein | .04 | .02 | .00 |
| ☐ 403 Jim Tracy | .04 | .02 | .00 |
| ☐ 404 Dickie Thon | .10 | .04 | .01 |
| ☐ 405 Rick Reuschel | .06 | .02 | .00 |
| ☐ 406 Al Holland | .06 | .02 | .00 |
| ☐ 407 Danny Boone | .04 | .02 | .00 |
| ☐ 408 Ed Romero | .04 | .02 | .00 |
| ☐ 409 Don Cooper | .04 | .02 | .00 |
| ☐ 410 Ron Cey | .15 | .06 | .01 |
| ☐ 411 SA: Ron Cey | .08 | .03 | .01 |
| ☐ 412 Luis Leal | .04 | .02 | .00 |
| ☐ 413 Dan Meyer | .04 | .02 | .00 |
| ☐ 414 Elias Sosa | .04 | .02 | .00 |
| ☐ 415 Don Baylor | .15 | .06 | .01 |
| ☐ 416 Marty Bystrom | .04 | .02 | .00 |
| ☐ 417 Pat Kelly | .04 | .02 | .00 |
| ☐ 418 Rangers Rookies: | .08 | .03 | .01 |
|     John Butcher | | | |
|     Bobby Johnson | | | |
|     Dave Schmidt | | | |
| ☐ 419 Steve Stone | .08 | .03 | .01 |
| ☐ 420 George Hendrick | .10 | .04 | .01 |
| ☐ 421 Mark Clear | .04 | .02 | .00 |
| ☐ 422 Cliff Johnson | .04 | .02 | .00 |
| ☐ 423 Stan Papi | .04 | .02 | .00 |
| ☐ 424 Bruce Benedict | .04 | .02 | .00 |
| ☐ 425 John Candelaria | .10 | .04 | .01 |
| ☐ 426 Orioles TL: | .15 | .03 | .00 |
|     Mgr. Earl Weaver | | | |
|     Batting: Eddie Murray | | | |
|     Pitching: Sam Stewart | | | |
| ☐ 427 Ron Oester | .06 | .02 | .00 |
| ☐ 428 LaMarr Hoyt | .12 | .05 | .01 |
| ☐ 429 John Wathan | .04 | .02 | .00 |
| ☐ 430 Vida Blue | .10 | .04 | .01 |
| ☐ 431 SA: Vida Blue | .06 | .02 | .00 |
| ☐ 432 Mike Scott | .35 | .14 | .03 |
| ☐ 433 Alan Ashby | .04 | .02 | .00 |
| ☐ 434 Joe Lefebvre | .04 | .02 | .00 |
| ☐ 435 Robin Yount | .75 | .30 | .07 |
| ☐ 436 Joe Strain | .04 | .02 | .00 |
| ☐ 437 Juan Berenguer | .04 | .02 | .00 |
| ☐ 438 Pete Mackanin | .04 | .02 | .00 |
| ☐ 439 Dave Righetti | 2.00 | .80 | .20 |
| ☐ 440 Jeff Burroughs | .06 | .02 | .00 |
| ☐ 441 Astros Rookies | .08 | .03 | .01 |
|     Danny Heep | | | |
|     Billy Smith | | | |
|     Bobby Sprowl | | | |
| ☐ 442 Bruce Kison | .04 | .02 | .00 |
| ☐ 443 Mark Wagner | .04 | .02 | .00 |
| ☐ 444 Terry Forster | .10 | .04 | .01 |
| ☐ 445 Larry Parrish | .08 | .03 | .01 |
| ☐ 446 Wayne Garland | .04 | .02 | .00 |
| ☐ 447 Darrell Porter | .08 | .03 | .01 |
| ☐ 448 SA: Darrell Porter | .06 | .02 | .00 |
| ☐ 449 Luis Aguayo | .06 | .02 | .00 |
| ☐ 450 Jack Morris | .50 | .20 | .05 |
| ☐ 451 Ed Miller | .04 | .02 | .00 |
| ☐ 452 Lee Smith | .75 | .30 | .07 |
| ☐ 453 Art Howe | .04 | .02 | .00 |
| ☐ 454 Rick Langford | .04 | .02 | .00 |
| ☐ 455 Tom Burgmeier | .04 | .02 | .00 |
| ☐ 456 Chicago Cubs TL: | .10 | .02 | .00 |
|     Mgr. Joe Amalfitano | | | |
|     Batting: Bill Buckner | | | |
|     Pitching: Randy Martz | | | |
| ☐ 457 Tim Stoddard | .04 | .02 | .00 |
| ☐ 458 Willie Montanez | .04 | .02 | .00 |
| ☐ 459 Bruce Berenyi | .06 | .02 | .00 |
| ☐ 460 Jack Clark | .25 | .10 | .02 |
| ☐ 461 Rich Dotson | .08 | .03 | .01 |
| ☐ 462 Dave Chalk | .04 | .02 | .00 |
| ☐ 463 Jim Kern | .04 | .02 | .00 |
| ☐ 464 Juan Bonilla | .06 | .02 | .00 |
| ☐ 465 Lee Mazzilli | .06 | .02 | .00 |
| ☐ 466 Randy Lerch | .04 | .02 | .00 |
| ☐ 467 Mickey Hatcher | .06 | .02 | .00 |
| ☐ 468 Floyd Bannister | .08 | .03 | .01 |
| ☐ 469 Ed Ott | .04 | .02 | .00 |
| ☐ 470 John Mayberry | .06 | .02 | .00 |
| ☐ 471 Royals Rookies | .25 | .10 | .02 |
|     Atlee Hammaker | | | |
|     Mike Jones | | | |
|     Darryl Motley | | | |
| ☐ 472 Oscar Gamble | .06 | .02 | .00 |

| | | | | |
|---|---|---|---|---|
| ☐ 473 | Mike Stanton | .04 | .02 | .00 |
| ☐ 474 | Ken Oberkfell | .06 | .02 | .00 |
| ☐ 475 | Alan Trammell | .35 | .14 | .03 |
| ☐ 476 | Brian Kingman | .04 | .02 | .00 |
| ☐ 477 | Steve Yeager | .06 | .02 | .00 |
| ☐ 478 | Ray Searage | .12 | .05 | .01 |
| ☐ 479 | Rowland Office | .04 | .02 | .00 |
| ☐ 480 | Steve Carlton | 1.00 | .40 | .10 |
| ☐ 481 | SA: Steve Carlton | .40 | .16 | .04 |
| ☐ 482 | Glenn Hubbard | .04 | .02 | .00 |
| ☐ 483 | Gary Woods | .04 | .02 | .00 |
| ☐ 484 | Ivan DeJesus | .04 | .02 | .00 |
| ☐ 485 | Kent Tekulve | .08 | .03 | .01 |
| ☐ 486 | Yankees TL: | .10 | .02 | .00 |
| | Mgr. Bob Lemon | | | |
| | Batting: J. Mumphrey | | | |
| | Pitching: Tommy John | | | |
| ☐ 487 | Bob McClure | .04 | .02 | .00 |
| ☐ 488 | Ron Jackson | .04 | .02 | .00 |
| ☐ 489 | Rick Dempsey | .06 | .02 | .00 |
| ☐ 490 | Dennis Eckersley | .06 | .02 | .00 |
| ☐ 491 | Checklist 397-528 | .10 | .01 | .00 |
| ☐ 492 | Joe Price | .04 | .02 | .00 |
| ☐ 493 | Chet Lemon | .08 | .03 | .01 |
| ☐ 494 | Hubie Brooks | .25 | .10 | .02 |
| ☐ 495 | Dennis Leonard | .06 | .02 | .00 |
| ☐ 496 | Johnny Grubb | .04 | .02 | .00 |
| ☐ 497 | Jim Anderson | .04 | .02 | .00 |
| ☐ 498 | Dave Bergman | .04 | .02 | .00 |
| ☐ 499 | Paul Mirabella | .04 | .02 | .00 |
| ☐ 500 | Rod Carew | 1.00 | .40 | .10 |
| ☐ 501 | SA: Rod Carew | .40 | .16 | .04 |
| ☐ 502 | Braves Rookies: | 1.00 | .40 | .10 |
| | Steve Bedrosian | | | |
| | Brett Butler | | | |
| | Larry Owen | | | |
| ☐ 503 | Julio Gonzalez | .04 | .02 | .00 |
| ☐ 504 | Rick Peters | .04 | .02 | .00 |
| ☐ 505 | Graig Nettles | .20 | .08 | .02 |
| ☐ 506 | SA: Graig Nettles | .10 | .04 | .01 |
| ☐ 507 | Terry Harper | .04 | .02 | .00 |
| ☐ 508 | Jody Davis | .75 | .30 | .07 |
| ☐ 509 | Harry Spilman | .04 | .02 | .00 |
| ☐ 510 | Fernando Valenzuela | 1.50 | .60 | .15 |
| ☐ 511 | Ruppert Jones | .04 | .02 | .00 |
| ☐ 512 | Jerry Dybzinski | .04 | .02 | .00 |
| ☐ 513 | Rick Rhoden | .10 | .04 | .01 |
| ☐ 514 | Joe Ferguson | .06 | .02 | .00 |
| ☐ 515 | Larry Bowa | .12 | .05 | .01 |
| ☐ 516 | SA: Larry Bowa | .06 | .02 | .00 |
| ☐ 517 | Mark Brouhard | .06 | .02 | .00 |
| ☐ 518 | Garth Iorg | .04 | .02 | .00 |
| ☐ 519 | Glenn Adams | .04 | .02 | .00 |
| ☐ 520 | Mike Flanagan | .10 | .04 | .01 |
| ☐ 521 | Billy Almon | .04 | .02 | .00 |
| ☐ 522 | Chuck Rainey | .04 | .02 | .00 |
| ☐ 523 | Gary Gray | .06 | .02 | .00 |
| ☐ 524 | Tom Hausman | .04 | .02 | .00 |
| ☐ 525 | Ray Knight | .10 | .04 | .01 |
| ☐ 526 | Expos TL: | .10 | .02 | .00 |
| | Mgr. Jim Fanning | | | |
| | Batting: W.Cromartie | | | |
| | Pitching: B.Gullickson | | | |
| ☐ 527 | John Henry Johnson | .04 | .02 | .00 |
| ☐ 528 | Matt Alexander | .04 | .02 | .00 |
| ☐ 529 | Allen Ripley | .04 | .02 | .00 |
| ☐ 530 | Dickie Noles | .04 | .02 | .00 |
| ☐ 531 | A's Rookies: | .08 | .03 | .01 |
| | Rich Bordi | | | |
| | Mark Budaska | | | |
| | Kelvin Moore | | | |
| ☐ 532 | Toby Harrah | .06 | .02 | .00 |
| ☐ 533 | Joaquin Andujar | .15 | .06 | .01 |
| ☐ 534 | Dave McKay | .04 | .02 | .00 |
| ☐ 535 | Lance Parrish | .45 | .18 | .04 |
| ☐ 536 | Rafael Ramirez | .06 | .02 | .00 |
| ☐ 537 | Doug Capilla | .04 | .02 | .00 |
| ☐ 538 | Lou Piniella | .10 | .04 | .01 |
| ☐ 539 | Vern Ruhle | .04 | .02 | .00 |
| ☐ 540 | Andre Dawson | .30 | .12 | .03 |
| ☐ 541 | Barry Evans | .04 | .02 | .00 |
| ☐ 542 | Ned Yost | .04 | .02 | .00 |
| ☐ 543 | Bill Robinson | .04 | .02 | .00 |
| ☐ 544 | Larry Christenson | .04 | .02 | .00 |
| ☐ 545 | Reggie Smith | .10 | .04 | .01 |
| ☐ 546 | SA: Reggie Smith | .06 | .02 | .00 |
| ☐ 547 | Rod Carew AS | .25 | .10 | .02 |
| ☐ 548 | Willie Randolph AS | .06 | .02 | .00 |
| ☐ 549 | George Brett AS | .40 | .16 | .04 |
| ☐ 550 | Bucky Dent AS | .06 | .02 | .00 |
| ☐ 551 | Reggie Jackson AS | .35 | .14 | .03 |
| ☐ 552 | Ken Singleton AS | .08 | .03 | .01 |
| ☐ 553 | Dave Winfield AS | .30 | .12 | .03 |

| | | | | |
|---|---|---|---|---|
| ☐ 554 | Carlton Fisk AS | .15 | .06 | .01 |
| ☐ 555 | Scott McGregor AS | .06 | .02 | .00 |
| ☐ 556 | Jack Morris AS | .15 | .06 | .01 |
| ☐ 557 | Rich Gossage AS | .15 | .06 | .01 |
| ☐ 558 | John Tudor | .35 | .14 | .03 |
| ☐ 559 | Indians TL: | .10 | .02 | .00 |
| | Mgr. Dave Garcia | | | |
| | Batting: Mike Hargrove | | | |
| | Pitching: Bert Blyleven | | | |
| ☐ 560 | Doug Corbett | .04 | .02 | .00 |
| ☐ 561 | Cardinals Rookies: | .15 | .06 | .01 |
| | Glenn Brummer | | | |
| | Luis DeLeon | | | |
| | Gene Roof | | | |
| ☐ 562 | Mike O'Berry | .04 | .02 | .00 |
| ☐ 563 | Ross Baumgarten | .04 | .02 | .00 |
| ☐ 564 | Doug DeCinces | .12 | .05 | .01 |
| ☐ 565 | Jackson Todd | .04 | .02 | .00 |
| ☐ 566 | Mike Jorgensen | .04 | .02 | .00 |
| ☐ 567 | Bob Babcock | .04 | .02 | .00 |
| ☐ 568 | Joe Pettini | .04 | .02 | .00 |
| ☐ 569 | Willie Randolph | .08 | .03 | .01 |
| ☐ 570 | SA: Willie Randolph | .04 | .02 | .00 |
| ☐ 571 | Glenn Abbott | .04 | .02 | .00 |
| ☐ 572 | Juan Beniquez | .06 | .02 | .00 |
| ☐ 573 | Rick Waits | .04 | .02 | .00 |
| ☐ 574 | Mike Ramsey | .04 | .02 | .00 |
| ☐ 575 | Al Cowens | .06 | .02 | .00 |
| ☐ 576 | Giants TL: | .10 | .02 | .00 |
| | Mgr. Frank Robinson | | | |
| | Batting: Milt May | | | |
| | Pitching: Vida Blue | | | |
| ☐ 577 | Rick Monday | .06 | .02 | .00 |
| ☐ 578 | Shooty Babitt | .04 | .02 | .00 |
| ☐ 579 | Rick Mahler | .25 | .10 | .02 |
| ☐ 580 | Bobby Bonds | .10 | .04 | .01 |
| ☐ 581 | Ron Reed | .04 | .02 | .00 |
| ☐ 582 | Luis Pujols | .04 | .02 | .00 |
| ☐ 583 | Tippy Martinez | .04 | .02 | .00 |
| ☐ 584 | Hosken Powell | .04 | .02 | .00 |
| ☐ 585 | Rollie Fingers | .25 | .10 | .02 |
| ☐ 586 | SA: Rollie Fingers | .15 | .06 | .01 |
| ☐ 587 | Tim Lollar | .04 | .02 | .00 |
| ☐ 588 | Dale Berra | .06 | .02 | .00 |
| ☐ 589 | Dave Stapleton | .04 | .02 | .00 |
| ☐ 590 | Al Oliver | .20 | .08 | .02 |
| ☐ 591 | SA: Al Oliver | .10 | .04 | .01 |
| ☐ 592 | Craig Swan | .04 | .02 | .00 |
| ☐ 593 | Billy Smith | .04 | .02 | .00 |
| ☐ 594 | Renie Martin | .04 | .02 | .00 |
| ☐ 595 | Dave Collins | .06 | .02 | .00 |
| ☐ 596 | Damaso Garcia | .15 | .06 | .01 |
| ☐ 597 | Wayne Nordhagen | .04 | .02 | .00 |
| ☐ 598 | Bob Galasso | .04 | .02 | .00 |
| ☐ 599 | White Sox Rookies | .08 | .03 | .01 |
| | Jay Loviglio | | | |
| | Reggie Patterson | | | |
| | Leo Sutherland | | | |
| ☐ 600 | Dave Winfield | .50 | .20 | .05 |
| ☐ 601 | Sid Monge | .04 | .02 | .00 |
| ☐ 602 | Freddie Patek | .04 | .02 | .00 |
| ☐ 603 | Rich Hebner | .04 | .02 | .00 |
| ☐ 604 | Orlando Sanchez | .04 | .02 | .00 |
| ☐ 605 | Steve Rogers | .08 | .03 | .01 |
| ☐ 606 | Blue Jays TL: | .10 | .02 | .00 |
| | Mgr. Bobby Mattick | | | |
| | Batting: J.Mayberry | | | |
| | Pitching: Dave Stieb | | | |
| ☐ 607 | Leon Durham | .20 | .08 | .02 |
| ☐ 608 | Jerry Royster | .04 | .02 | .00 |
| ☐ 609 | Rick Sutcliffe | .20 | .08 | .02 |
| ☐ 610 | Rickey Henderson | 1.50 | .60 | .15 |
| ☐ 611 | Joe Niekro | .12 | .05 | .01 |
| ☐ 612 | Gary Ward | .06 | .02 | .00 |
| ☐ 613 | Jim Gantner | .06 | .02 | .00 |
| ☐ 614 | Juan Eichelberger | .04 | .02 | .00 |
| ☐ 615 | Bob Boone | .06 | .02 | .00 |
| ☐ 616 | SA: Bob Boone | .06 | .02 | .00 |
| ☐ 617 | Scott McGregor | .10 | .04 | .01 |
| ☐ 618 | Tim Foli | .04 | .02 | .00 |
| ☐ 619 | Bill Campbell | .06 | .02 | .00 |
| ☐ 620 | Ken Griffey | .10 | .04 | .01 |
| ☐ 621 | SA: Ken Griffey | .06 | .02 | .00 |
| ☐ 622 | Dennis Lamp | .04 | .02 | .00 |
| ☐ 623 | Mets Rookies: | .15 | .06 | .01 |
| | Ron Gardenhire | | | |
| | Terry Leach | | | |
| | Tim Leary | | | |
| ☐ 624 | Fergie Jenkins | .20 | .08 | .02 |
| ☐ 625 | Hal McRae | .08 | .03 | .01 |
| ☐ 626 | Randy Jones | .06 | .02 | .00 |
| ☐ 627 | Enos Cabell | .04 | .02 | .00 |
| ☐ 628 | Bill Travers | .04 | .02 | .00 |

| | | | | |
|---|---|---|---|---|
| ☐ 629 | Johnny Wockenfuss | .04 | .02 | .00 |
| ☐ 630 | Joe Charboneau | .06 | .02 | .00 |
| ☐ 631 | Gene Tenace | .04 | .02 | .00 |
| ☐ 632 | Bryan Clark | .04 | .02 | .00 |
| ☐ 633 | Mitchell Page | .04 | .02 | .00 |
| ☐ 634 | Checklist 529-660 | .10 | .01 | .00 |
| ☐ 635 | Ron Davis | .04 | .02 | .00 |
| ☐ 636 | Phillies TL: | .30 | .06 | .01 |

Mgr. Dallas Green
Batting: Pete Rose
Pitching: Steve Carlton

| | | | | |
|---|---|---|---|---|
| ☐ 637 | Rick Camp | .04 | .02 | .00 |
| ☐ 638 | John Milner | .04 | .02 | .00 |
| ☐ 639 | Ken Kravec | .04 | .02 | .00 |
| ☐ 640 | Cesar Cedeno | .10 | .04 | .01 |
| ☐ 641 | Steve Mura | .04 | .02 | .00 |
| ☐ 642 | Mike Scioscia | .08 | .03 | .01 |
| ☐ 643 | Pete Vuckovich | .12 | .05 | .01 |
| ☐ 644 | John Castino | .04 | .02 | .00 |
| ☐ 645 | Frank White | .08 | .03 | .01 |
| ☐ 646 | SA: Frank White | .06 | .02 | .00 |
| ☐ 647 | Warren Brusstar | .04 | .02 | .00 |
| ☐ 648 | Jose Morales | .04 | .02 | .00 |
| ☐ 649 | Ken Clay | .04 | .02 | .00 |
| ☐ 650 | Carl Yastrzemski | 1.25 | .50 | .12 |
| ☐ 651 | SA: Carl Yastrzemski | .50 | .20 | .05 |
| ☐ 652 | Steve Nicosia | .04 | .02 | .00 |
| ☐ 653 | Angels Rookies | 2.25 | .90 | .22 |

Tom Brunansky
Luis Sanchez
Daryl Sconiers

| | | | | |
|---|---|---|---|---|
| ☐ 654 | Jim Morrison | .06 | .02 | .00 |
| ☐ 655 | Joel Youngblood | .04 | .02 | .00 |
| ☐ 656 | Eddie Whitson | .06 | .02 | .00 |
| ☐ 657 | Tom Poquette | .04 | .02 | .00 |
| ☐ 658 | Tito Landrum | .04 | .02 | .00 |
| ☐ 659 | Fred Martinez | .04 | .02 | .00 |
| ☐ 660 | Dave Concepcion | .12 | .05 | .01 |
| ☐ 661 | SA: Dave Concepcion | .08 | .03 | .01 |
| ☐ 662 | Luis Salazar | .04 | .02 | .00 |
| ☐ 663 | Hector Cruz | .04 | .02 | .00 |
| ☐ 664 | Dan Spillner | .04 | .02 | .00 |
| ☐ 665 | Jim Clancy | .06 | .02 | .00 |
| ☐ 666 | Tigers TL: | .10 | .02 | .00 |

Mgr. Sparky Anderson
Batting: Steve Kemp
Pitching: Dan Petry

| | | | | |
|---|---|---|---|---|
| ☐ 667 | Jeff Reardon | .10 | .04 | .01 |
| ☐ 668 | Dale Murphy | 2.00 | .80 | .20 |
| ☐ 669 | Larry Milbourne | .04 | .02 | .00 |
| ☐ 670 | Steve Kemp | .08 | .03 | .01 |
| ☐ 671 | Mike Davis | .15 | .06 | .01 |
| ☐ 672 | Bob Knepper | .10 | .04 | .01 |
| ☐ 673 | Keith Drumright | .04 | .02 | .00 |
| ☐ 674 | Dave Goltz | .04 | .02 | .00 |
| ☐ 675 | Cecil Cooper | .20 | .08 | .02 |
| ☐ 676 | Sal Butera | .04 | .02 | .00 |
| ☐ 677 | Alfredo Griffin | .08 | .03 | .01 |
| ☐ 678 | Tom Paciorek | .04 | .02 | .00 |
| ☐ 679 | Sammy Stewart | .04 | .02 | .00 |
| ☐ 680 | Gary Matthews | .10 | .04 | .01 |
| ☐ 681 | Dodgers Rookies: | 4.00 | 1.60 | .40 |

Mike Marshall
Ron Roenicke
Steve Sax

| | | | | |
|---|---|---|---|---|
| ☐ 682 | Jesse Jefferson | .04 | .02 | .00 |
| ☐ 683 | Phil Garner | .06 | .02 | .00 |
| ☐ 684 | Harold Baines | .75 | .30 | .07 |
| ☐ 685 | Bert Blyleven | .20 | .08 | .02 |
| ☐ 686 | Gary Allenson | .04 | .02 | .00 |
| ☐ 687 | Greg Minton | .06 | .02 | .00 |
| ☐ 688 | Leon Roberts | .04 | .02 | .00 |
| ☐ 689 | Lary Sorensen | .04 | .02 | .00 |
| ☐ 690 | Dave Kingman | .20 | .08 | .02 |
| ☐ 691 | Dan Schatzeder | .04 | .02 | .00 |
| ☐ 692 | Wayne Gross | .04 | .02 | .00 |
| ☐ 693 | Cesar Geronimo | .04 | .02 | .00 |
| ☐ 694 | Dave Wehrmeister | .04 | .02 | .00 |
| ☐ 695 | Warren Cromartie | .04 | .02 | .00 |
| ☐ 696 | Pirates TL: | .10 | .02 | .00 |

Mgr. Chuck Tanner
Batting: Bill Madlock
Pitching:Eddie Solomon

| | | | | |
|---|---|---|---|---|
| ☐ 697 | John Montefusco | .06 | .02 | .00 |
| ☐ 698 | Tony Scott | .04 | .02 | .00 |
| ☐ 699 | Dick Tidrow | .04 | .02 | .00 |
| ☐ 700 | George Foster | .25 | .10 | .02 |
| ☐ 701 | SA: George Foster | .12 | .05 | .01 |
| ☐ 702 | Steve Renko | .04 | .02 | .00 |
| ☐ 703 | Brewers TL: | .10 | .02 | .00 |

Mgr. Bob Rodgers
Batting: Cecil Cooper
Pitching: P.Vuckovich

| | | | | |
|---|---|---|---|---|
| ☐ 704 | Mickey Rivers | .06 | .02 | .00 |
| ☐ 705 | SA: Mickey Rivers | .06 | .02 | .00 |
| ☐ 706 | Barry Foote | .04 | .02 | .00 |
| ☐ 707 | Mark Bomback | .04 | .02 | .00 |
| ☐ 708 | Gene Richards | .04 | .02 | .00 |
| ☐ 709 | Don Money | .04 | .02 | .00 |
| ☐ 710 | Jerry Reuss | .08 | .03 | .01 |
| ☐ 711 | Mariners Rookies: | .75 | .30 | .07 |

Dave Edler
Dave Henderson
Reggie Walton

| | | | | |
|---|---|---|---|---|
| ☐ 712 | Denny Martinez | .04 | .02 | .00 |
| ☐ 713 | Del Unser | .04 | .02 | .00 |
| ☐ 714 | Jerry Koosman | .10 | .04 | .01 |
| ☐ 715 | Willie Stargell | .50 | .20 | .05 |
| ☐ 716 | SA: Willie Stargell | .20 | .08 | .02 |
| ☐ 717 | Rick Miller | .04 | .02 | .00 |
| ☐ 718 | Charlie Hough | .08 | .03 | .01 |
| ☐ 719 | Jerry Narron | .04 | .02 | .00 |
| ☐ 720 | Greg Luzinski | .15 | .06 | .01 |
| ☐ 721 | SA: Greg Luzinski | .10 | .04 | .01 |
| ☐ 722 | Jerry Martin | .04 | .02 | .00 |
| ☐ 723 | Junior Kennedy | .04 | .02 | .00 |
| ☐ 724 | Dave Rosello | .04 | .02 | .00 |
| ☐ 725 | Amos Otis | .08 | .03 | .01 |
| ☐ 726 | SA: Amos Otis | .06 | .02 | .00 |
| ☐ 727 | Sixto Lezcano | .04 | .02 | .00 |
| ☐ 728 | Aurelio Lopez | .04 | .02 | .00 |
| ☐ 729 | Jim Spencer | .04 | .02 | .00 |
| ☐ 730 | Gary Carter | 1.00 | .40 | .10 |
| ☐ 731 | Padres Rookies: | .10 | .04 | .01 |

Mike Armstrong
Doug Gwosdz
Fred Kuhaulua

| | | | | |
|---|---|---|---|---|
| ☐ 732 | Mike Lum | .04 | .02 | .00 |
| ☐ 733 | Larry McWilliams | .04 | .02 | .00 |
| ☐ 734 | Mike Ivie | .04 | .02 | .00 |
| ☐ 735 | Rudy May | .04 | .02 | .00 |
| ☐ 736 | Jerry Turner | .04 | .02 | .00 |
| ☐ 737 | Reggie Cleveland | .04 | .02 | .00 |
| ☐ 738 | Dave Engle | .04 | .02 | .00 |
| ☐ 739 | Joey McLaughlin | .04 | .02 | .00 |
| ☐ 740 | Dave Lopes | .08 | .03 | .01 |
| ☐ 741 | SA: Dave Lopes | .06 | .02 | .00 |
| ☐ 742 | Dick Drago | .04 | .02 | .00 |
| ☐ 743 | John Stearns | .04 | .02 | .00 |
| ☐ 744 | Mike Witt | 2.00 | .80 | .20 |
| ☐ 745 | Bake McBride | .06 | .02 | .00 |
| ☐ 746 | Andre Thornton | .10 | .04 | .01 |
| ☐ 747 | John Lowenstein | .04 | .02 | .00 |
| ☐ 748 | Marc Hill | .04 | .02 | .00 |
| ☐ 749 | Bob Shirley | .04 | .02 | .00 |
| ☐ 750 | Jim Rice | 1.00 | .40 | .10 |
| ☐ 751 | Rick Honeycutt | .06 | .02 | .00 |
| ☐ 752 | Lee Lacy | .08 | .03 | .01 |
| ☐ 753 | Tom Brookens | .04 | .02 | .00 |
| ☐ 754 | Joe Morgan | .40 | .16 | .04 |
| ☐ 755 | SA: Joe Morgan | .20 | .08 | .02 |
| ☐ 756 | Reds TL: | .15 | .03 | .00 |

Mgr. John McNamara
Batting: Ken Griffey
Pitching: Tom Seaver

| | | | | |
|---|---|---|---|---|
| ☐ 757 | Tom Underwood | .04 | .02 | .00 |
| ☐ 758 | Claudell Washington | .10 | .04 | .01 |
| ☐ 759 | Paul Splittorff | .06 | .02 | .00 |
| ☐ 760 | Bill Buckner | .15 | .06 | .01 |
| ☐ 761 | Dave Smith | .10 | .04 | .01 |
| ☐ 762 | Mike Phillips | .04 | .02 | .00 |
| ☐ 763 | Tom Hume | .04 | .02 | .00 |
| ☐ 764 | Steve Swisher | .04 | .02 | .00 |
| ☐ 765 | Gorman Thomas | .12 | .05 | .01 |
| ☐ 766 | Twins Rookies: | 3.50 | 1.40 | .35 |

Lenny Faedo
Kent Hrbek
Tim Laudner

| | | | | |
|---|---|---|---|---|
| ☐ 767 | Roy Smalley | .06 | .02 | .00 |
| ☐ 768 | Jerry Garvin | .04 | .02 | .00 |
| ☐ 769 | Richie Zisk | .06 | .02 | .00 |
| ☐ 770 | Rich Gossage | .25 | .10 | .02 |
| ☐ 771 | SA: Rich Gossage | .15 | .06 | .01 |
| ☐ 772 | Bert Campaneris | .08 | .03 | .01 |
| ☐ 773 | John Denny | .10 | .04 | .01 |
| ☐ 774 | Jay Johnstone | .06 | .02 | .00 |
| ☐ 775 | Bob Forsch | .08 | .03 | .01 |
| ☐ 776 | Mark Belanger | .06 | .02 | .00 |
| ☐ 777 | Tom Griffin | .04 | .02 | .00 |
| ☐ 778 | Kevin Hickey | .08 | .03 | .01 |
| ☐ 779 | Grant Jackson | .04 | .02 | .00 |
| ☐ 780 | Pete Rose | 2.25 | .90 | .22 |
| ☐ 781 | SA: Pete Rose | .75 | .30 | .07 |
| ☐ 782 | Frank Taveras | .04 | .02 | .00 |
| ☐ 783 | Greg Harris | .25 | .10 | .02 |
| ☐ 784 | Milt Wilcox | .04 | .02 | .00 |

| | | MINT | VG-E | F-G |
|---|---|---|---|---|
| ☐ 785 | Dan Driessen | .06 | .02 | .00 |
| ☐ 786 | Red Sox TL: | .10 | .02 | .00 |
| | Mgr. Ralph Houk | | | |
| | Batting: C.Lansford | | | |
| | Pitching: Mike Torrez | | | |
| ☐ 787 | Fred Stanley | .04 | .02 | .00 |
| ☐ 788 | Woodie Fryman | .04 | .02 | .00 |
| ☐ 789 | Checklist 661-792 | .10 | .01 | .00 |
| ☐ 790 | Larry Gura | .06 | .02 | .00 |
| ☐ 791 | Bobby Brown | .04 | .02 | .00 |
| ☐ 792 | Frank Tanana | .10 | .04 | .01 |

## 1982 Topps Traded

The cards in this 132 card set measure 2 1/2" by 3 1/2". The Topps "Traded" or extended series for 1982 is distinguished by a "T" printed after the number (located on the reverse). Of the total cards, 70 players represent the American League and 61 represent the National League, with the remaining card a numbered checklist (132T). The Cubs lead the pack with 12 changes while the Red Sox are the only team in either league to have no new additions. All 131 player photos used in the set are completely new. Of this total, 112 individuals are seen in the uniform of their new team, 11 others have been elevated to single card status from "Future Stars" cards, and 8 more are entirely new to the 1982 Topps lineup. The backs are almost completely red in color with black print.

| | | MINT | VG-E | F-G |
|---|---|---|---|---|
| COMPLETE SET | | 20.00 | 8.00 | 2.00 |
| COMMON PLAYER | | .08 | .03 | .01 |
| ☐ 1T | Doyle Alexander | .12 | .05 | .01 |
| ☐ 2T | Jesse Barfield | 3.00 | 1.20 | .30 |
| ☐ 3T | Ross Baumgarten | .08 | .03 | .01 |
| ☐ 4T | Steve Bedrosian | .20 | .08 | .02 |
| ☐ 5T | Mark Belanger | .12 | .05 | .01 |
| ☐ 6T | Kurt Bevacqua | .08 | .03 | .01 |
| ☐ 7T | Tim Blackwell | .08 | .03 | .01 |
| ☐ 8T | Vida Blue | .16 | .07 | .01 |
| ☐ 9T | Bob Boone | .12 | .05 | .01 |
| ☐ 10T | Larry Bowa | .20 | .08 | .02 |
| ☐ 11T | Dan Briggs | .08 | .03 | .01 |
| ☐ 12T | Bobby Brown | .08 | .03 | .01 |
| ☐ 13T | Tom Brunansky | 1.50 | .60 | .15 |
| ☐ 14T | Jeff Burroughs | .12 | .05 | .01 |
| ☐ 15T | Enos Cabell | .08 | .03 | .01 |
| ☐ 16T | Bill Campbell | .08 | .03 | .01 |
| ☐ 17T | Bobby Castillo | .08 | .03 | .01 |
| ☐ 18T | Bill Caudill | .12 | .05 | .01 |
| ☐ 19T | Cesar Cedeno | .15 | .06 | .01 |
| ☐ 20T | Dave Collins | .15 | .06 | .01 |
| ☐ 21T | Doug Corbett | .12 | .05 | .01 |
| ☐ 22T | Al Cowens | .12 | .05 | .01 |
| ☐ 23T | Chili Davis | 1.00 | .40 | .10 |
| ☐ 24T | Dick Davis | .08 | .03 | .01 |
| ☐ 25T | Ron Davis | .12 | .05 | .01 |
| ☐ 26T | Doug DeCinces | .25 | .10 | .02 |
| ☐ 27T | Ivan DeJesus | .08 | .03 | .01 |

| | | | | |
|---|---|---|---|---|
| ☐ 28T | Bob Dernier | .25 | .10 | .02 |
| ☐ 29T | Bo Diaz | .12 | .05 | .01 |
| ☐ 30T | Roger Erickson | .08 | .03 | .01 |
| ☐ 31T | Jim Essian | .08 | .03 | .01 |
| ☐ 32T | Ed Farmer | .08 | .03 | .01 |
| ☐ 33T | Doug Flynn | .08 | .03 | .01 |
| ☐ 34T | Tim Foli | .08 | .03 | .01 |
| ☐ 35T | Dan Ford | .12 | .05 | .01 |
| ☐ 36T | George Foster | .40 | .16 | .04 |
| ☐ 37T | Dave Frost | .08 | .03 | .01 |
| ☐ 38T | Rich Gale | .08 | .03 | .01 |
| ☐ 39T | Ron Gardenhire | .12 | .05 | .01 |
| ☐ 40T | Ken Griffey | .15 | .06 | .01 |
| ☐ 41T | Greg Harris | .15 | .06 | .01 |
| ☐ 42T | Von Hayes | 2.00 | .80 | .20 |
| ☐ 43T | Larry Herndon | .12 | .05 | .01 |
| ☐ 44T | Kent Hrbek | 3.00 | 1.20 | .30 |
| ☐ 45T | Mike Ivie | .08 | .03 | .01 |
| ☐ 46T | Grant Jackson | .08 | .03 | .01 |
| ☐ 47T | Reggie Jackson | 2.50 | 1.00 | .25 |
| ☐ 48T | Ron Jackson | .08 | .03 | .01 |
| ☐ 49T | Fergie Jenkins | .35 | .14 | .03 |
| ☐ 50T | Lamar Johnson | .08 | .03 | .01 |
| ☐ 51T | Randy Johnson | .08 | .03 | .01 |
| ☐ 52T | Jay Johnstone | .15 | .06 | .01 |
| ☐ 53T | Mick Kelleher | .08 | .03 | .01 |
| ☐ 54T | Steve Kemp | .15 | .06 | .01 |
| ☐ 55T | Junior Kennedy | .08 | .03 | .01 |
| ☐ 56T | Jim Kern | .08 | .03 | .01 |
| ☐ 57T | Ray Knight | .25 | .10 | .02 |
| ☐ 58T | Wayne Krenchicki | .08 | .03 | .01 |
| ☐ 59T | Mike Krukow | .20 | .08 | .02 |
| ☐ 60T | Duane Kuiper | .08 | .03 | .01 |
| ☐ 61T | Mike LaCoss | .08 | .03 | .01 |
| ☐ 62T | Chet Lemon | .15 | .06 | .01 |
| ☐ 63T | Sixto Lezcano | .12 | .05 | .01 |
| ☐ 64T | Dave Lopes | .15 | .06 | .01 |
| ☐ 65T | Jerry Martin | .08 | .03 | .01 |
| ☐ 66T | Renie Martin | .08 | .03 | .01 |
| ☐ 67T | John Mayberry | .12 | .05 | .01 |
| ☐ 68T | Lee Mazzilli | .12 | .05 | .01 |
| ☐ 69T | Bake McBride | .12 | .05 | .01 |
| ☐ 70T | Dan Meyer | .08 | .03 | .01 |
| ☐ 71T | Larry Milbourne | .08 | .03 | .01 |
| ☐ 72T | Eddie Milner | .25 | .10 | .02 |
| ☐ 73T | Sid Monge | .08 | .03 | .01 |
| ☐ 74T | John Montefusco | .12 | .05 | .01 |
| ☐ 75T | Jose Morales | .08 | .03 | .01 |
| ☐ 76T | Keith Moreland | .25 | .10 | .02 |
| ☐ 77T | Jim Morrison | .12 | .05 | .01 |
| ☐ 78T | Rance Mulliniks | .08 | .03 | .01 |
| ☐ 79T | Steve Mura | .08 | .03 | .01 |
| ☐ 80T | Gene Nelson | .12 | .05 | .01 |
| ☐ 81T | Joe Nolan | .08 | .03 | .01 |
| ☐ 82T | Dickie Noles | .08 | .03 | .01 |
| ☐ 83T | Al Oliver | .40 | .16 | .04 |
| ☐ 84T | Jorge Orta | .08 | .03 | .01 |
| ☐ 85T | Tom Paciorek | .12 | .05 | .01 |
| ☐ 86T | Larry Parrish | .16 | .07 | .01 |
| ☐ 87T | Jack Perconte | .08 | .03 | .01 |
| ☐ 88T | Gaylord Perry | 1.00 | .40 | .10 |
| ☐ 89T | Rob Picciolo | .08 | .03 | .01 |
| ☐ 90T | Joe Pittman | .08 | .03 | .01 |
| ☐ 91T | Hosken Powell | .08 | .03 | .01 |
| ☐ 92T | Mike Proly | .08 | .03 | .01 |
| ☐ 93T | Greg Pryor | .08 | .03 | .01 |
| ☐ 94T | Charlie Puleo | .12 | .05 | .01 |
| ☐ 95T | Shane Rawley | .20 | .08 | .02 |
| ☐ 96T | Johnny Ray | 1.00 | .40 | .10 |
| ☐ 97T | Dave Revering | .08 | .03 | .01 |
| ☐ 98T | Cal Ripken | 7.50 | 3.00 | .75 |
| ☐ 99T | Allen Ripley | .08 | .03 | .01 |
| ☐ 100T | Bill Robinson | .08 | .03 | .01 |
| ☐ 101T | Aurelio Rodriguez | .08 | .03 | .01 |
| ☐ 102T | Joe Rudi | .12 | .05 | .01 |
| ☐ 103T | Steve Sax | 2.00 | .80 | .20 |
| ☐ 104T | Dan Schatzeder | .08 | .03 | .01 |
| ☐ 105T | Bob Shirley | .08 | .03 | .01 |
| ☐ 106T | Eric Show | .40 | .16 | .04 |
| ☐ 107T | Roy Smalley | .12 | .05 | .01 |
| ☐ 108T | Lonnie Smith | .20 | .08 | .02 |
| ☐ 109T | Ozzie Smith | .75 | .30 | .07 |
| ☐ 110T | Reggie Smith | .20 | .08 | .02 |
| ☐ 111T | Lary Sorensen | .08 | .03 | .01 |
| ☐ 112T | Elias Sosa | .08 | .03 | .01 |
| ☐ 113T | Mike Stanton | .08 | .03 | .01 |
| ☐ 114T | Steve Strougher | .12 | .05 | .01 |
| ☐ 115T | Champ Summers | .08 | .03 | .01 |
| ☐ 116T | Rick Sutcliffe | .40 | .16 | .04 |
| ☐ 117T | Frank Tanana | .15 | .06 | .01 |
| ☐ 118T | Frank Taveras | .08 | .03 | .01 |
| ☐ 119T | Garry Templeton | .20 | .08 | .02 |
| ☐ 120T | Alex Trevino | .08 | .03 | .01 |

| | | | | |
|---|---|---|---|---|
| ☐ 121T | Jerry Turner | .08 | .03 | .01 |
| ☐ 122T | Ed VandeBerg | .25 | .10 | .02 |
| ☐ 123T | Tom Veryzer | .08 | .03 | .01 |
| ☐ 124T | Ron Washington | .12 | .05 | .01 |
| ☐ 125T | Bob Watson | .12 | .05 | .01 |
| ☐ 126T | Dennis Werth | .08 | .03 | .01 |
| ☐ 127T | Eddie Whitson | .12 | .05 | .01 |
| ☐ 128T | Rob Wilfong | .08 | .03 | .01 |
| ☐ 129T | Bump Wills | .08 | .03 | .01 |
| ☐ 130T | Gary Woods | .08 | .03 | .01 |
| ☐ 131T | Butch Wynegar | .12 | .05 | .01 |
| ☐ 132T | Checklist: 1-132 | .20 | .02 | .00 |

## 1983 Topps

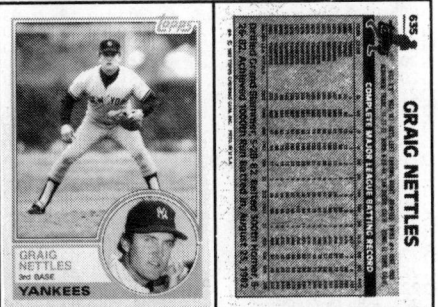

The cards in this 792 card set measure 2 1/2" by 3 1/2". Each regular card of the Topps set for 1983 features a large action shot of a player with a small cameo portrait at bottom right. There are special series for A.L. and N.L. All Stars (386-407), League Leaders (701-708) and Record Breakers (1- 6). In addition, there are 34 "Super Veteran" (SV) cards and 6 numbered checklist cards. The Super Veteran cards are oriented horizontally and show two pictures of the featured player, a recent picture and a picture showing the player as a rookie when he broke in. The cards are numbered on the reverse at the upper left corner. The team cards are actually Team Leader (TL) cards picturing the batting and pitching leader for that team with a checklist back.

| | | MINT | VG-E | F-G |
|---|---|---|---|---|
| | COMPLETE SET | 60.00 | 24.00 | 6.00 |
| | COMMON PLAYER (1-792) | .04 | .02 | .00 |
| ☐ 1 | RB: Tony Armas<br>11 Putouts by<br>Rightfielder | .12 | .04 | .01 |
| ☐ 2 | RB: Rickey Henderson<br>Sets modern record<br>for steals, season | .25 | .10 | .02 |
| ☐ 3 | RB: Greg Minton<br>269 1/3 homerless<br>innings streak | .06 | .02 | .00 |
| ☐ 4 | RB: Lance Parrish<br>Threw out three<br>Baserunners in<br>All Star game | .15 | .06 | .01 |
| ☐ 5 | RB: Manny Trillo<br>479 consecutive<br>errorless chances,<br>second baseman | .06 | .02 | .00 |
| ☐ 6 | RB: John Wathan<br>ML steals-record<br>for catchers, 31 | .06 | .02 | .00 |
| ☐ 7 | Gene Richards | .04 | .02 | .00 |
| ☐ 8 | Steve Balboni | .10 | .04 | .01 |
| ☐ 9 | Joey McLaughlin | .04 | .02 | .00 |
| ☐ 10 | Gorman Thomas | .12 | .05 | .01 |
| ☐ 11 | Billy Gardner MGR | .04 | .02 | .00 |
| ☐ 12 | Paul Mirabella | .04 | .02 | .00 |
| ☐ 13 | Larry Herndon | .04 | .02 | .00 |

| | | | | |
|---|---|---|---|---|
| ☐ 14 | Frank LaCorte | .04 | .02 | .00 |
| ☐ 15 | Ron Cey | .15 | .06 | .01 |
| ☐ 16 | George Vukovich | .04 | .02 | .00 |
| ☐ 17 | Kent Tekulve | .08 | .03 | .01 |
| ☐ 18 | SV: Kent Tekulve | .06 | .02 | .00 |
| ☐ 19 | Oscar Gamble | .06 | .02 | .00 |
| ☐ 20 | Carlton Fisk | .20 | .08 | .02 |
| ☐ 21 | Baltimore Orioles TL:<br>BA: Eddie Murray<br>ERA: Jim Palmer | .20 | .04 | .01 |
| ☐ 22 | Randy Martz | .04 | .02 | .00 |
| ☐ 23 | Mike Heath | .04 | .02 | .00 |
| ☐ 24 | Steve Mura | .04 | .02 | .00 |
| ☐ 25 | Hal McRae | .08 | .03 | .01 |
| ☐ 26 | Jerry Royster | .04 | .02 | .00 |
| ☐ 27 | Doug Corbett | .04 | .02 | .00 |
| ☐ 28 | Bruce Bochte | .06 | .02 | .00 |
| ☐ 29 | Randy Jones | .06 | .02 | .00 |
| ☐ 30 | Jim Rice | .75 | .30 | .07 |
| ☐ 31 | Bill Gullickson | .06 | .02 | .00 |
| ☐ 32 | Dave Bergman | .04 | .02 | .00 |
| ☐ 33 | Jack O'Connor | .04 | .02 | .00 |
| ☐ 34 | Paul Householder | .04 | .02 | .00 |
| ☐ 35 | Rollie Fingers | .25 | .10 | .02 |
| ☐ 36 | SV: Rollie Fingers | .12 | .05 | .01 |
| ☐ 37 | Darrell Johnson MGR | .04 | .02 | .00 |
| ☐ 38 | Tim Flannery | .04 | .02 | .00 |
| ☐ 39 | Terry Puhl | .06 | .02 | .00 |
| ☐ 40 | Fernando Valenzuela | .60 | .24 | .06 |
| ☐ 41 | Jerry Turner | .04 | .02 | .00 |
| ☐ 42 | Dale Murray | .04 | .02 | .00 |
| ☐ 43 | Bob Dernier | .08 | .03 | .01 |
| ☐ 44 | Don Robinson | .06 | .02 | .00 |
| ☐ 45 | John Mayberry | .06 | .02 | .00 |
| ☐ 46 | Richard Dotson | .08 | .03 | .01 |
| ☐ 47 | Dave McKay | .04 | .02 | .00 |
| ☐ 48 | Lary Sorensen | .04 | .02 | .00 |
| ☐ 49 | Willie McGee | 2.25 | .90 | .22 |
| ☐ 50 | Bob Horner<br>('82 RBI total 7) | .35 | .14 | .03 |
| ☐ 51 | Chicago Cubs TL:<br>BA: Leon Durham<br>ERA: Fergie Jenkins | .10 | .02 | .00 |
| ☐ 52 | Onix Concepcion | .08 | .03 | .01 |
| ☐ 53 | Mike Witt | .25 | .10 | .02 |
| ☐ 54 | Jim Maler | .06 | .02 | .00 |
| ☐ 55 | Mookie Wilson | .08 | .03 | .01 |
| ☐ 56 | Chuck Rainey | .04 | .02 | .00 |
| ☐ 57 | Tim Blackwell | .04 | .02 | .00 |
| ☐ 58 | Al Holland | .04 | .02 | .00 |
| ☐ 59 | Benny Ayala | .04 | .02 | .00 |
| ☐ 60 | Johnny Bench | .60 | .24 | .06 |
| ☐ 61 | SV: Johnny Bench | .25 | .10 | .02 |
| ☐ 62 | Bob McClure | .04 | .02 | .00 |
| ☐ 63 | Rick Monday | .06 | .02 | .00 |
| ☐ 64 | Bill Stein | .04 | .02 | .00 |
| ☐ 65 | Jack Morris | .30 | .12 | .03 |
| ☐ 66 | Bob Lillis MGR | .04 | .02 | .00 |
| ☐ 67 | Sal Butera | .04 | .02 | .00 |
| ☐ 68 | Eric Show | .20 | .08 | .02 |
| ☐ 69 | Lee Lacy | .06 | .02 | .00 |
| ☐ 70 | Steve Carlton | .60 | .24 | .06 |
| ☐ 71 | SV: Steve Carlton | .25 | .10 | .02 |
| ☐ 72 | Tom Paciorek | .04 | .02 | .00 |
| ☐ 73 | Allen Ripley | .04 | .02 | .00 |
| ☐ 74 | Julio Gonzalez | .04 | .02 | .00 |
| ☐ 75 | Amos Otis | .08 | .03 | .01 |
| ☐ 76 | Rick Mahler | .06 | .02 | .00 |
| ☐ 77 | Hosken Powell | .04 | .02 | .00 |
| ☐ 78 | Bill Caudill | .06 | .02 | .00 |
| ☐ 79 | Mick Kelleher | .04 | .02 | .00 |
| ☐ 80 | George Foster | .20 | .08 | .02 |
| ☐ 81 | Yankees TL:<br>BA: Jerry Mumphrey<br>ERA: Dave Righetti | .10 | .02 | .00 |
| ☐ 82 | Bruce Hurst | .12 | .05 | .01 |
| ☐ 83 | Ryne Sandberg | 5.00 | 2.00 | .50 |
| ☐ 84 | Milt May | .04 | .02 | .00 |
| ☐ 85 | Ken Singleton | .10 | .04 | .01 |
| ☐ 86 | Tom Hume | .04 | .02 | .00 |
| ☐ 87 | Joe Rudi | .06 | .02 | .00 |
| ☐ 88 | Jim Gantner | .06 | .02 | .00 |
| ☐ 89 | Leon Roberts | .04 | .02 | .00 |
| ☐ 90 | Jerry Reuss | .08 | .03 | .01 |
| ☐ 91 | Larry Milbourne | .04 | .02 | .00 |
| ☐ 92 | Mike LaCoss | .04 | .02 | .00 |
| ☐ 93 | John Castino | .04 | .02 | .00 |
| ☐ 94 | Dave Edwards | .04 | .02 | .00 |
| ☐ 95 | Alan Trammell | .30 | .12 | .03 |
| ☐ 96 | Dick Howser MGR | .06 | .02 | .00 |
| ☐ 97 | Ross Baumgarten | .04 | .02 | .00 |
| ☐ 98 | Vance Law | .04 | .02 | .00 |
| ☐ 99 | Dickie Noles | .04 | .02 | .00 |

| | | | | |
|---|---|---|---|---|
| ☐ 100 | Pete Rose | 2.00 | .80 | .20 |
| ☐ 101 | SV: Pete Rose | .75 | .30 | .07 |
| ☐ 102 | Dave Beard | .04 | .02 | .00 |
| ☐ 103 | Darrell Porter | .06 | .02 | .00 |
| ☐ 104 | Bob Walk | .04 | .02 | .00 |
| ☐ 105 | Don Baylor | .15 | .06 | .01 |
| ☐ 106 | Gene Nelson | .04 | .02 | .00 |
| ☐ 107 | Mike Jorgensen | .04 | .02 | .00 |
| ☐ 108 | Glenn Hoffman | .04 | .02 | .00 |
| ☐ 109 | Luis Leal | .04 | .02 | .00 |
| ☐ 110 | Ken Griffey | .10 | .04 | .01 |
| ☐ 111 | Montreal Expos TL: | .10 | .02 | .00 |
| | BA: Al Oliver | | | |
| | ERA: Steve Rogers | | | |
| ☐ 112 | Bob Shirley | .04 | .02 | .00 |
| ☐ 113 | Ron Roenicke | .04 | .02 | .00 |
| ☐ 114 | Jim Slaton | .04 | .02 | .00 |
| ☐ 115 | Chili Davis | .15 | .06 | .01 |
| ☐ 116 | Dave Schmidt | .04 | .02 | .00 |
| ☐ 117 | Alan Knicely | .04 | .02 | .00 |
| ☐ 118 | Chris Welsh | .04 | .02 | .00 |
| ☐ 119 | Tom Brookens | .04 | .02 | .00 |
| ☐ 120 | Len Barker | .06 | .02 | .00 |
| ☐ 121 | Mickey Hatcher | .04 | .02 | .00 |
| ☐ 122 | Jimmy Smith | .04 | .02 | .00 |
| ☐ 123 | George Frazier | .04 | .02 | .00 |
| ☐ 124 | Marc Hill | .04 | .02 | .00 |
| ☐ 125 | Leon Durham | .12 | .05 | .01 |
| ☐ 126 | Joe Torre MGR | .08 | .03 | .01 |
| ☐ 127 | Preston Hanna | .04 | .02 | .00 |
| ☐ 128 | Mike Ramsey | .04 | .02 | .00 |
| ☐ 129 | Checklist: 1-132 | .10 | .01 | .00 |
| ☐ 130 | Dave Stieb | .20 | .08 | .02 |
| ☐ 131 | Ed Ott | .04 | .02 | .00 |
| ☐ 132 | Todd Cruz | .04 | .02 | .00 |
| ☐ 133 | Jim Barr | .04 | .02 | .00 |
| ☐ 134 | Hubie Brooks | .20 | .08 | .02 |
| ☐ 135 | Dwight Evans | .15 | .06 | .01 |
| ☐ 136 | Willie Aikens | .06 | .02 | .00 |
| ☐ 137 | Woodie Fryman | .04 | .02 | .00 |
| ☐ 138 | Rick Dempsey | .06 | .02 | .00 |
| ☐ 139 | Bruce Berenyi | .04 | .02 | .00 |
| ☐ 140 | Willie Randolph | .08 | .03 | .01 |
| ☐ 141 | Indians TL: | .10 | .02 | .02 |
| | BA: Toby Harrah | | | |
| | ERA: Rick Sutcliffe | | | |
| ☐ 142 | Mike Caldwell | .06 | .02 | .00 |
| ☐ 143 | Joe Pettini | .04 | .02 | .00 |
| ☐ 144 | Mark Wagner | .04 | .02 | .00 |
| ☐ 145 | Don Sutton | .30 | .12 | .03 |
| ☐ 146 | SV: Don Sutton | .15 | .06 | .01 |
| ☐ 147 | Rick Leach | .04 | .02 | .00 |
| ☐ 148 | Dave Roberts | .04 | .02 | .00 |
| ☐ 149 | Johnny Ray | .20 | .08 | .02 |
| ☐ 150 | Bruce Sutter | .20 | .08 | .02 |
| ☐ 151 | SV: Bruce Sutter | .12 | .05 | .01 |
| ☐ 152 | Jay Johnstone | .06 | .02 | .00 |
| ☐ 153 | Jerry Koosman | .08 | .03 | .01 |
| ☐ 154 | Johnnie LeMaster | .04 | .02 | .00 |
| ☐ 155 | Dan Quisenberry | .20 | .08 | .02 |
| ☐ 156 | Billy Martin MGR | .12 | .05 | .01 |
| ☐ 157 | Steve Bedrosian | .08 | .03 | .01 |
| ☐ 158 | Rob Wilfong | .04 | .02 | .00 |
| ☐ 159 | Mike Stanton | .04 | .02 | .00 |
| ☐ 160 | Dave Kingman | .15 | .06 | .01 |
| ☐ 161 | SV: Dave Kingman | .10 | .04 | .01 |
| ☐ 162 | Mark Clear | .04 | .02 | .00 |
| ☐ 163 | Cal Ripken | 1.50 | .60 | .15 |
| ☐ 164 | David Palmer | .06 | .02 | .00 |
| ☐ 165 | Dan Driessen | .04 | .02 | .00 |
| ☐ 166 | John Pacella | .04 | .02 | .00 |
| ☐ 167 | Mark Brouhard | .04 | .02 | .00 |
| ☐ 168 | Juan Eichelberger | .04 | .02 | .00 |
| ☐ 169 | Doug Flynn | .04 | .02 | .00 |
| ☐ 170 | Steve Howe | .06 | .02 | .00 |
| ☐ 171 | Giants TL: | .10 | .02 | .00 |
| | BA: Joe Morgan | | | |
| | ERA: Bill Laskey | | | |
| ☐ 172 | Vern Ruhle | .04 | .02 | .00 |
| ☐ 173 | Jim Morrison | .06 | .02 | .00 |
| ☐ 174 | Jerry Ujdur | .04 | .02 | .00 |
| ☐ 175 | Bo Diaz | .06 | .02 | .00 |
| ☐ 176 | Dave Righetti | .30 | .12 | .03 |
| ☐ 177 | Harold Baines | .30 | .12 | .03 |
| ☐ 178 | Luis Tiant | .10 | .04 | .01 |
| ☐ 179 | SV: Luis Tiant | .06 | .02 | .00 |
| ☐ 180 | Rickey Henderson | .75 | .30 | .07 |
| ☐ 181 | Terry Felton | .06 | .02 | .00 |
| ☐ 182 | Mike Fischlin | .04 | .02 | .00 |
| ☐ 183 | Ed VandeBerg | .15 | .06 | .01 |
| ☐ 184 | Bob Clark | .04 | .02 | .00 |
| ☐ 185 | Tim Lollar | .04 | .02 | .00 |
| ☐ 186 | Whitey Herzog MGR | .06 | .02 | .00 |

| | | | | |
|---|---|---|---|---|
| ☐ 187 | Terry Leach | .04 | .02 | .00 |
| ☐ 188 | Rick Miller | .04 | .02 | .00 |
| ☐ 189 | Dan Schatzeder | .04 | .02 | .00 |
| ☐ 190 | Cecil Cooper | .15 | .06 | .01 |
| ☐ 191 | Joe Price | .04 | .02 | .00 |
| ☐ 192 | Floyd Rayford | .04 | .02 | .00 |
| ☐ 193 | Harry Spilman | .04 | .02 | .00 |
| ☐ 194 | Cesar Geronimo | .04 | .02 | .00 |
| ☐ 195 | Bob Stoddard | .06 | .02 | .00 |
| ☐ 196 | Bill Fahey | .04 | .02 | .00 |
| ☐ 197 | Jim Eisenreich | .08 | .03 | .01 |
| ☐ 198 | Kiko Garcia | .04 | .02 | .00 |
| ☐ 199 | Marty Bystrom | .04 | .02 | .00 |
| ☐ 200 | Rod Carew | .75 | .30 | .07 |
| ☐ 201 | SV: Rod Carew | .30 | .12 | .03 |
| ☐ 202 | Blue Jays TL: | .10 | .02 | .00 |
| | BA: Damaso Garcia | | | |
| | ERA: Dave Stieb | | | |
| ☐ 203 | Mike Morgan | .06 | .02 | .00 |
| ☐ 204 | Junior Kennedy | .04 | .02 | .00 |
| ☐ 205 | Dave Parker | .30 | .12 | .03 |
| ☐ 206 | Ken Oberkfell | .04 | .02 | .00 |
| ☐ 207 | Rick Camp | .04 | .02 | .00 |
| ☐ 208 | Dan Meyer | .04 | .02 | .00 |
| ☐ 209 | Mike Moore | .35 | .14 | .03 |
| ☐ 210 | Jack Clark | .20 | .08 | .02 |
| ☐ 211 | John Denny | .12 | .05 | .01 |
| ☐ 212 | John Stearns | .04 | .02 | .00 |
| ☐ 213 | Tom Burgmeier | .04 | .02 | .00 |
| ☐ 214 | Jerry White | .04 | .02 | .00 |
| ☐ 215 | Mario Soto | .10 | .04 | .01 |
| ☐ 216 | Tony LaRussa MGR | .06 | .02 | .00 |
| ☐ 217 | Tim Stoddard | .04 | .02 | .00 |
| ☐ 218 | Roy Howell | .04 | .02 | .00 |
| ☐ 219 | Mike Armstrong | .04 | .02 | .00 |
| ☐ 220 | Dusty Baker | .08 | .03 | .01 |
| ☐ 221 | Joe Niekro | .10 | .04 | .01 |
| ☐ 222 | Damaso Garcia | .15 | .06 | .01 |
| ☐ 223 | John Montefusco | .06 | .02 | .00 |
| ☐ 224 | Mickey Rivers | .06 | .02 | .00 |
| ☐ 225 | Enos Cabell | .04 | .02 | .00 |
| ☐ 226 | Enrique Romo | .04 | .02 | .00 |
| ☐ 227 | Chris Bando | .04 | .02 | .00 |
| ☐ 228 | Joaquin Andujar | .15 | .06 | .01 |
| ☐ 229 | Phillies TL: | .12 | .02 | .00 |
| | BA: Bo Diaz | | | |
| | ERA: Steve Carlton | | | |
| ☐ 230 | Fergie Jenkins | .15 | .06 | .01 |
| ☐ 231 | SV: Fergie Jenkins | .10 | .04 | .01 |
| ☐ 232 | Tom Brunansky | .25 | .10 | .02 |
| ☐ 233 | Wayne Gross | .04 | .02 | .00 |
| ☐ 234 | Larry Andersen | .04 | .02 | .00 |
| ☐ 235 | Claudell Washington | .08 | .03 | .01 |
| ☐ 236 | Steve Renko | .04 | .02 | .00 |
| ☐ 237 | Dan Norman | .04 | .02 | .00 |
| ☐ 238 | Bud Black | .25 | .10 | .02 |
| ☐ 239 | Dave Stapleton | .04 | .02 | .00 |
| ☐ 240 | Rich Gossage | .25 | .10 | .02 |
| ☐ 241 | SV: Rich Gossage | .12 | .05 | .01 |
| ☐ 242 | Joe Nolan | .04 | .02 | .00 |
| ☐ 243 | Duane Walker | .08 | .03 | .01 |
| ☐ 244 | Dwight Bernard | .04 | .02 | .00 |
| ☐ 245 | Steve Sax | .30 | .12 | .03 |
| ☐ 246 | George Bamberger MGR | | .02 | .00 |
| ☐ 247 | Dave Smith | .06 | .02 | .00 |
| ☐ 248 | Bake McBride | .06 | .02 | .00 |
| ☐ 249 | Checklist: 133-264 | .10 | .01 | .00 |
| ☐ 250 | Bill Buckner | .15 | .06 | .01 |
| ☐ 251 | Alan Wiggins | .25 | .10 | .02 |
| ☐ 252 | Luis Aguayo | .04 | .02 | .00 |
| ☐ 253 | Larry McWilliams | .06 | .02 | .00 |
| ☐ 254 | Rick Cerone | .04 | .02 | .00 |
| ☐ 255 | Gene Garber | .04 | .02 | .00 |
| ☐ 256 | SV: Gene Garber | .04 | .02 | .00 |
| ☐ 257 | Jesse Barfield | .40 | .16 | .04 |
| ☐ 258 | Manny Castillo | .04 | .02 | .00 |
| ☐ 259 | Jeff Jones | .04 | .02 | .00 |
| ☐ 260 | Steve Kemp | .10 | .04 | .01 |
| ☐ 261 | Tigers TL: | .10 | .02 | .00 |
| | BA: Larry Herndon | | | |
| | ERA: Dan Petry | | | |
| ☐ 262 | Ron Jackson | .04 | .02 | .00 |
| ☐ 263 | Renie Martin | .04 | .02 | .00 |
| ☐ 264 | Jamie Quirk | .04 | .02 | .00 |
| ☐ 265 | Joel Youngblood | .04 | .02 | .00 |
| ☐ 266 | Paul Boris | .04 | .02 | .00 |
| ☐ 267 | Terry Francona | .04 | .02 | .00 |
| ☐ 268 | Storm Davis | .75 | .30 | .07 |
| ☐ 269 | Ron Oester | .06 | .02 | .00 |
| ☐ 270 | Dennis Eckersley | .06 | .02 | .00 |
| ☐ 271 | Ed Romero | .04 | .02 | .00 |
| ☐ 272 | Frank Tanana | .06 | .02 | .00 |
| ☐ 273 | Mark Belanger | .06 | .02 | .00 |

| | | | | |
|---|---|---|---|---|
| ☐ 274 | Terry Kennedy | .10 | .04 | .01 |
| ☐ 275 | Ray Knight | .10 | .04 | .01 |
| ☐ 276 | Gene Mauch MGR | .06 | .02 | .00 |
| ☐ 277 | Rance Mulliniks | .04 | .02 | .00 |
| ☐ 278 | Kevin Hickey | .04 | .02 | .00 |
| ☐ 279 | Greg Gross | .04 | .02 | .00 |
| ☐ 280 | Bert Blyleven | .15 | .06 | .01 |
| ☐ 281 | Andre Robertson | .04 | .02 | .00 |
| ☐ 282 | Reggie Smith | .10 | .04 | .01 |
| ☐ 283 | SV: Reggie Smith | .06 | .02 | .00 |
| ☐ 284 | Jeff Lahti | .10 | .04 | .01 |
| ☐ 285 | Lance Parrish | .35 | .14 | .03 |
| ☐ 286 | Rick Langford | .04 | .02 | .00 |
| ☐ 287 | Bobby Brown | .04 | .02 | .00 |
| ☐ 288 | Joe Cowley | .40 | .16 | .04 |
| ☐ 289 | Jerry Dybzinski | .04 | .02 | .00 |
| ☐ 290 | Jeff Reardon | .08 | .03 | .01 |
| ☐ 291 | Pirates TL: | .10 | .02 | .00 |
| | BA: Bill Madlock | | | |
| | ERA: John Candelaria | | | |
| ☐ 292 | Craig Swan | .04 | .02 | .00 |
| ☐ 293 | Glenn Gulliver | .04 | .02 | .00 |
| ☐ 294 | Dave Engle | .04 | .02 | .00 |
| ☐ 295 | Jerry Remy | .04 | .02 | .00 |
| ☐ 296 | Greg Harris | .06 | .02 | .00 |
| ☐ 297 | Ned Yost | .04 | .02 | .00 |
| ☐ 298 | Floyd Chiffer | .04 | .02 | .00 |
| ☐ 299 | George Wright | .10 | .04 | .01 |
| ☐ 300 | Mike Schmidt | .75 | .30 | .07 |
| ☐ 301 | SV: Mike Schmidt | .30 | .12 | .03 |
| ☐ 302 | Ernie Whitt | .04 | .02 | .00 |
| ☐ 303 | Miguel Dilone | .04 | .02 | .00 |
| ☐ 304 | Dave Rucker | .04 | .02 | .00 |
| ☐ 305 | Larry Bowa | .10 | .04 | .01 |
| ☐ 306 | Tom Lasorda MGR | .08 | .03 | .01 |
| ☐ 307 | Lou Piniella | .10 | .04 | .01 |
| ☐ 308 | Jesus Vega | .04 | .02 | .00 |
| ☐ 309 | Jeff Leonard | .06 | .02 | .00 |
| ☐ 310 | Greg Luzinski | .12 | .05 | .01 |
| ☐ 311 | Glenn Brummer | .04 | .02 | .00 |
| ☐ 312 | Brian Kingman | .04 | .02 | .00 |
| ☐ 313 | Gary Gray | .04 | .02 | .00 |
| ☐ 314 | Ken Dayley | .06 | .02 | .00 |
| ☐ 315 | Rick Burleson | .06 | .02 | .00 |
| ☐ 316 | Paul Splittorff | .06 | .02 | .00 |
| ☐ 317 | Gary Rajsich | .06 | .02 | .00 |
| ☐ 318 | John Tudor | .30 | .12 | .03 |
| ☐ 319 | Lenn Sakata | .04 | .02 | .00 |
| ☐ 320 | Steve Rogers | .08 | .03 | .01 |
| ☐ 321 | Brewers TL: | .15 | .03 | .00 |
| | BA: Robin Yount | | | |
| | ERA: Pete Vuckovich | | | |
| ☐ 322 | Dave Van Gorder | .04 | .02 | .00 |
| ☐ 323 | Luis DeLeon | .04 | .02 | .00 |
| ☐ 324 | Mike Marshall | .30 | .12 | .03 |
| ☐ 325 | Von Hayes | .30 | .12 | .03 |
| ☐ 326 | Garth Iorg | .04 | .02 | .00 |
| ☐ 327 | Bobby Castillo | .04 | .02 | .00 |
| ☐ 328 | Craig Reynolds | .04 | .02 | .00 |
| ☐ 329 | Randy Niemann | .04 | .02 | .00 |
| ☐ 330 | Buddy Bell | .15 | .06 | .01 |
| ☐ 331 | Mike Krukow | .10 | .04 | .01 |
| ☐ 332 | Glenn Wilson | .80 | .32 | .08 |
| ☐ 333 | Dave LaRoche | .04 | .02 | .00 |
| ☐ 334 | SV: Dave LaRoche | .04 | .02 | .00 |
| ☐ 335 | Steve Henderson | .04 | .02 | .00 |
| ☐ 336 | Rene Lachemann MGR | .04 | .02 | .00 |
| ☐ 337 | Tito Landrum | .04 | .02 | .00 |
| ☐ 338 | Bob Owchinko | .04 | .02 | .00 |
| ☐ 339 | Terry Harper | .04 | .02 | .00 |
| ☐ 340 | Larry Gura | .06 | .02 | .00 |
| ☐ 341 | Doug DeCinces | .12 | .05 | .01 |
| ☐ 342 | Atlee Hammaker | .08 | .03 | .01 |
| ☐ 343 | Bob Bailor | .04 | .02 | .00 |
| ☐ 344 | Roger LaFrancois | .06 | .02 | .00 |
| ☐ 345 | Jim Clancy | .04 | .02 | .00 |
| ☐ 346 | Joe Pittman | .04 | .02 | .00 |
| ☐ 347 | Sammy Stewart | .04 | .02 | .00 |
| ☐ 348 | Alan Bannister | .04 | .02 | .00 |
| ☐ 349 | Checklist: 265-396 | .10 | .01 | .00 |
| ☐ 350 | Robin Yount | .45 | .18 | .04 |
| ☐ 351 | Reds TL: | .10 | .02 | .00 |
| | BA: Cesar Cedeno | | | |
| | ERA: Mario Soto | | | |
| ☐ 352 | Mike Scioscia | .06 | .02 | .00 |
| ☐ 353 | Steve Comer | .04 | .02 | .00 |
| ☐ 354 | Randy Johnson | .04 | .02 | .00 |
| ☐ 355 | Jim Bibby | .06 | .02 | .00 |
| ☐ 356 | Gary Woods | .04 | .02 | .00 |
| ☐ 357 | Len Matuszek | .10 | .04 | .01 |
| ☐ 358 | Jerry Garvin | .04 | .02 | .00 |
| ☐ 359 | Dave Collins | .06 | .02 | .00 |
| ☐ 360 | Nolan Ryan | .50 | .20 | .05 |
| ☐ 361 | SV: Nolan Ryan | .20 | .08 | .02 |
| ☐ 362 | Billy Almon | .04 | .02 | .00 |
| ☐ 363 | John Stuper | .10 | .04 | .01 |
| ☐ 364 | Bret Butler | .15 | .06 | .01 |
| ☐ 365 | Dave Lopes | .08 | .03 | .01 |
| ☐ 366 | Dick Williams MGR | .06 | .02 | .00 |
| ☐ 367 | Bud Anderson | .04 | .02 | .00 |
| ☐ 368 | Richie Zisk | .06 | .02 | .00 |
| ☐ 369 | Jesse Orosco | .10 | .04 | .01 |
| ☐ 370 | Gary Carter | .60 | .24 | .06 |
| ☐ 371 | Mike Richardt | .06 | .02 | .00 |
| ☐ 372 | Terry Crowley | .04 | .02 | .00 |
| ☐ 373 | Kevin Saucier | .04 | .02 | .00 |
| ☐ 374 | Wayne Krenchicki | .04 | .02 | .00 |
| ☐ 375 | Pete Vuckovich | .06 | .02 | .00 |
| ☐ 376 | Ken Landreaux | .06 | .02 | .00 |
| ☐ 377 | Lee May | .06 | .02 | .00 |
| ☐ 378 | SV: Lee May | .06 | .02 | .00 |
| ☐ 379 | Guy Sularz | .04 | .02 | .00 |
| ☐ 380 | Ron Davis | .04 | .02 | .00 |
| ☐ 381 | Red Sox TL: | .15 | .03 | .00 |
| | BA: Jim Rice | | | |
| | ERA: Bob Stanley | | | |
| ☐ 382 | Bob Knepper | .12 | .05 | .01 |
| ☐ 383 | Ozzie Virgil | .08 | .03 | .01 |
| ☐ 384 | Dave Dravecky | .50 | .20 | .05 |
| ☐ 385 | Mike Easler | .08 | .03 | .01 |
| ☐ 386 | Rod Carew AS | .25 | .10 | .02 |
| ☐ 387 | Bob Grich AS | .06 | .02 | .00 |
| ☐ 388 | George Brett AS | .35 | .14 | .03 |
| ☐ 389 | Robin Yount AS | .25 | .10 | .02 |
| ☐ 390 | Reggie Jackson AS | .30 | .12 | .03 |
| ☐ 391 | Rickey Henderson AS | .35 | .14 | .03 |
| ☐ 392 | Fred Lynn AS | .15 | .06 | .01 |
| ☐ 393 | Carlton Fisk AS | .12 | .05 | .01 |
| ☐ 394 | Pete Vuckovich AS | .06 | .02 | .00 |
| ☐ 395 | Larry Gura AS | .06 | .02 | .00 |
| ☐ 396 | Dan Quisenberry AS | .10 | .04 | .01 |
| ☐ 397 | Pete Rose AS | .60 | .24 | .06 |
| ☐ 398 | Manny Trillo AS | .06 | .02 | .00 |
| ☐ 399 | Mike Schmidt AS | .40 | .16 | .04 |
| ☐ 400 | Dave Concepcion AS | .06 | .02 | .00 |
| ☐ 401 | Dale Murphy AS | .45 | .18 | .04 |
| ☐ 402 | Andre Dawson AS | .15 | .06 | .01 |
| ☐ 403 | Tim Raines AS | .20 | .08 | .02 |
| ☐ 404 | Gary Carter AS | .30 | .12 | .03 |
| ☐ 405 | Steve Rogers AS | .06 | .02 | .00 |
| ☐ 406 | Steve Carlton AS | .25 | .10 | .02 |
| ☐ 407 | Bruce Sutter AS | .10 | .04 | .01 |
| ☐ 408 | Rudy May | .04 | .02 | .00 |
| ☐ 409 | Marvis Foley | .04 | .02 | .00 |
| ☐ 410 | Phil Niekro | .30 | .12 | .03 |
| ☐ 411 | SV: Phil Niekro | .15 | .06 | .01 |
| ☐ 412 | Rangers TL: | .10 | .02 | .00 |
| | BA: Buddy Bell | | | |
| | ERA: Charlie Hough | | | |
| ☐ 413 | Matt Keough | .04 | .02 | .00 |
| ☐ 414 | Julio Cruz | .04 | .02 | .00 |
| ☐ 415 | Bob Forsch | .06 | .02 | .00 |
| ☐ 416 | Joe Ferguson | .04 | .02 | .00 |
| ☐ 417 | Tom Hausman | .04 | .02 | .00 |
| ☐ 418 | Greg Pryor | .04 | .02 | .00 |
| ☐ 419 | Steve Crawford | .04 | .02 | .00 |
| ☐ 420 | Al Oliver | .15 | .06 | .01 |
| ☐ 421 | SV: Al Oliver | .10 | .04 | .01 |
| ☐ 422 | George Cappuzzello | .04 | .02 | .00 |
| ☐ 423 | Tom Lawless | .04 | .02 | .00 |
| ☐ 424 | Jerry Augustine | .04 | .02 | .00 |
| ☐ 425 | Pedro Guerrero | .45 | .18 | .04 |
| ☐ 426 | Earl Weaver MGR | .10 | .04 | .01 |
| ☐ 427 | Roy Lee Jackson | .04 | .02 | .00 |
| ☐ 428 | Champ Summers | .04 | .02 | .00 |
| ☐ 429 | Eddie Whitson | .06 | .02 | .00 |
| ☐ 430 | Kirk Gibson | .35 | .14 | .03 |
| ☐ 431 | Gary Gaetti | 1.00 | .40 | .10 |
| ☐ 432 | Porfirio Altamirano | .04 | .02 | .00 |
| ☐ 433 | Dale Berra | .06 | .02 | .00 |
| ☐ 434 | Dennis Lamp | .04 | .02 | .00 |
| ☐ 435 | Tony Armas | .15 | .06 | .01 |
| ☐ 436 | Bill Campbell | .06 | .02 | .00 |
| ☐ 437 | Rick Sweet | .04 | .02 | .00 |
| ☐ 438 | Dave LaPoint | .15 | .06 | .01 |
| ☐ 439 | Rafael Ramirez | .04 | .02 | .00 |
| ☐ 440 | Ron Guidry | .25 | .10 | .02 |
| ☐ 441 | Astros TL: | .10 | .02 | .00 |
| | BA: Ray Knight | | | |
| | ERA: Joe Niekro | | | |
| ☐ 442 | Brian Downing | .06 | .02 | .00 |
| ☐ 443 | Don Hood | .04 | .02 | .00 |
| ☐ 444 | Wally Backman | .10 | .04 | .01 |
| ☐ 445 | Mike Flanagan | .08 | .03 | .01 |
| ☐ 446 | Reid Nichols | .04 | .02 | .00 |
| ☐ 447 | Bryn Smith | .06 | .02 | .00 |

| | | | | |
|---|---|---|---|---|
| ☐ 448 | Darrell Evans | .12 | .05 | .01 |
| ☐ 449 | Eddie Milner | .15 | .06 | .01 |
| ☐ 450 | Ted Simmons | .15 | .06 | .01 |
| ☐ 451 | SV: Ted Simmons | .10 | .04 | .01 |
| ☐ 452 | Lloyd Moseby | .15 | .06 | .01 |
| ☐ 453 | Lamar Johnson | .04 | .02 | .00 |
| ☐ 454 | Bob Welch | .08 | .03 | .01 |
| ☐ 455 | Sixto Lezcano | .04 | .02 | .00 |
| ☐ 456 | Lee Elia MGR | .04 | .02 | .00 |
| ☐ 457 | Milt Wilcox | .04 | .02 | .00 |
| ☐ 458 | Ron Washington | .06 | .02 | .00 |
| ☐ 459 | Ed Farmer | .04 | .02 | .00 |
| ☐ 460 | Roy Smalley | .06 | .02 | .00 |
| ☐ 461 | Steve Trout | .06 | .02 | .00 |
| ☐ 462 | Steve Nicosia | .04 | .02 | .00 |
| ☐ 463 | Gaylord Perry | .25 | .10 | .02 |
| ☐ 464 | SV: Gaylord Perry | .12 | .05 | .01 |
| ☐ 465 | Lonnie Smith | .10 | .04 | .01 |
| ☐ 466 | Tom Underwood | .04 | .02 | .00 |
| ☐ 467 | Rufino Linares | .04 | .02 | .00 |
| ☐ 468 | Dave Goltz | .04 | .02 | .00 |
| ☐ 469 | Ron Gardenhire | .04 | .02 | .00 |
| ☐ 470 | Greg Minton | .06 | .02 | .00 |
| ☐ 471 | K.C. Royals TL: | .10 | .02 | .00 |
| | BA: Willie Wilson | | | |
| | ERA: Vida Blue | | | |
| ☐ 472 | Gary Allenson | .04 | .02 | .00 |
| ☐ 473 | John Lowenstein | .04 | .02 | .00 |
| ☐ 474 | Ray Burris | .04 | .02 | .00 |
| ☐ 475 | Cesar Cedeno | .10 | .04 | .01 |
| ☐ 476 | Rob Picciolo | .04 | .02 | .00 |
| ☐ 477 | Tom Niedenfuer | .12 | .05 | .01 |
| ☐ 478 | Phil Garner | .06 | .02 | .00 |
| ☐ 479 | Charlie Hough | .08 | .03 | .01 |
| ☐ 480 | Toby Harrah | .06 | .02 | .00 |
| ☐ 481 | Scot Thompson | .04 | .02 | .00 |
| ☐ 482 | Tony Gwynn | 8.00 | 3.25 | .80 |
| ☐ 483 | Lynn Jones | .04 | .02 | .00 |
| ☐ 484 | Dick Ruthven | .04 | .02 | .00 |
| ☐ 485 | Omar Moreno | .04 | .02 | .00 |
| ☐ 486 | Clyde King MGR | .04 | .02 | .00 |
| ☐ 487 | Jerry Hairston | .04 | .02 | .00 |
| ☐ 488 | Alfredo Griffin | .04 | .02 | .00 |
| ☐ 489 | Tom Herr | .12 | .05 | .01 |
| ☐ 490 | Jim Palmer | .35 | .14 | .03 |
| ☐ 491 | SV: Jim Palmer | .15 | .06 | .01 |
| ☐ 492 | Paul Serna | .04 | .02 | .00 |
| ☐ 493 | Steve McCatty | .04 | .02 | .00 |
| ☐ 494 | Bob Brenly | .08 | .03 | .01 |
| ☐ 495 | Warren Cromartie | .04 | .02 | .00 |
| ☐ 496 | Tom Veryzer | .04 | .02 | .00 |
| ☐ 497 | Rick Sutcliffe | .20 | .08 | .02 |
| ☐ 498 | Wade Boggs | 22.00 | 9.00 | 2.20 |
| ☐ 499 | Jeff Little | .04 | .02 | .00 |
| ☐ 500 | Reggie Jackson | .90 | .36 | .09 |
| ☐ 501 | SV: Reggie Jackson | .35 | .14 | .03 |
| ☐ 502 | Atlanta Braves TL: | .25 | .05 | .01 |
| | BA: Dale Murphy | | | |
| | ERA: Phil Niekro | | | |
| ☐ 503 | Moose Haas | .06 | .02 | .00 |
| ☐ 504 | Don Werner | .04 | .02 | .00 |
| ☐ 505 | Garry Templeton | .12 | .05 | .01 |
| ☐ 506 | Jim Gott | .10 | .04 | .01 |
| ☐ 507 | Tony Scott | .04 | .02 | .00 |
| ☐ 508 | Tom Filer | .15 | .06 | .01 |
| ☐ 509 | Lou Whitaker | .25 | .10 | .02 |
| ☐ 510 | Tug McGraw | .10 | .04 | .01 |
| ☐ 511 | SV: Tug McGraw | .06 | .02 | .00 |
| ☐ 512 | Doyle Alexander | .06 | .02 | .00 |
| ☐ 513 | Fred Stanley | .04 | .02 | .00 |
| ☐ 514 | Rudy Law | .04 | .02 | .00 |
| ☐ 515 | Gene Tenace | .04 | .02 | .00 |
| ☐ 516 | Bill Virdon MGR | .06 | .02 | .00 |
| ☐ 517 | Gary Ward | .06 | .02 | .00 |
| ☐ 518 | Bill Laskey | .12 | .05 | .01 |
| ☐ 519 | Terry Bulling | .04 | .02 | .00 |
| ☐ 520 | Fred Lynn | .25 | .10 | .02 |
| ☐ 521 | Bruce Benedict | .04 | .02 | .00 |
| ☐ 522 | Pat Zachry | .04 | .02 | .00 |
| ☐ 523 | Carney Lansford | .12 | .05 | .01 |
| ☐ 524 | Tom Brennan | .04 | .02 | .00 |
| ☐ 525 | Frank White | .08 | .03 | .01 |
| ☐ 526 | Checklist: 397-528 | .10 | .01 | .00 |
| ☐ 527 | Larry Biittner | .04 | .02 | .00 |
| ☐ 528 | Jamie Easterly | .04 | .02 | .00 |
| ☐ 529 | Tim Laudner | .04 | .02 | .00 |
| ☐ 530 | Eddie Murray | .75 | .30 | .07 |
| ☐ 531 | Oakland A's TL: | .15 | .03 | .00 |
| | BA: Rickey Henderson | | | |
| | ERA: Rick Langford | | | |
| ☐ 532 | Dave Stewart | .04 | .02 | .00 |
| ☐ 533 | Luis Salazar | .04 | .02 | .00 |
| ☐ 534 | John Butcher | .04 | .02 | .00 |

| | | | | |
|---|---|---|---|---|
| ☐ 535 | Manny Trillo | .06 | .02 | .00 |
| ☐ 536 | Johnny Wockenfuss | .04 | .02 | .00 |
| ☐ 537 | Rod Scurry | .04 | .02 | .00 |
| ☐ 538 | Danny Heep | .04 | .02 | .00 |
| ☐ 539 | Roger Erickson | .04 | .02 | .00 |
| ☐ 540 | Ozzie Smith | .25 | .10 | .02 |
| ☐ 541 | Britt Burns | .08 | .03 | .01 |
| ☐ 542 | Jody Davis | .10 | .04 | .01 |
| ☐ 543 | Alan Fowlkes | .04 | .02 | .00 |
| ☐ 544 | Larry Whisenton | .04 | .02 | .00 |
| ☐ 545 | Floyd Bannister | .06 | .02 | .00 |
| ☐ 546 | Dave Garcia MGR | .04 | .02 | .00 |
| ☐ 547 | Geoff Zahn | .04 | .02 | .00 |
| ☐ 548 | Brian Giles | .04 | .02 | .00 |
| ☐ 549 | Charlie Puleo | .04 | .02 | .00 |
| ☐ 550 | Carl Yastrzemski | 1.00 | .40 | .10 |
| ☐ 551 | SV: Carl Yastrzemski | .40 | .16 | .04 |
| ☐ 552 | Tim Wallach | .10 | .04 | .01 |
| ☐ 553 | Denny Martinez | .04 | .02 | .00 |
| ☐ 554 | Mike Vail | .04 | .02 | .00 |
| ☐ 555 | Steve Yeager | .06 | .02 | .00 |
| ☐ 556 | Willie Upshaw | .08 | .03 | .01 |
| ☐ 557 | Rick Honeycutt | .06 | .02 | .00 |
| ☐ 558 | Dickie Thon | .08 | .03 | .01 |
| ☐ 559 | Pete Redfern | .04 | .02 | .00 |
| ☐ 560 | Ron LeFlore | .06 | .02 | .00 |
| ☐ 561 | Cardinals TL: | .10 | .02 | .00 |
| | BA: Lonnie Smith | | | |
| | ERA: Joaquin Andujar | | | |
| ☐ 562 | Dave Rozema | .04 | .02 | .00 |
| ☐ 563 | Juan Bonilla | .04 | .02 | .00 |
| ☐ 564 | Sid Monge | .04 | .02 | .00 |
| ☐ 565 | Bucky Dent | .06 | .02 | .00 |
| ☐ 566 | Manny Sarmiento | .04 | .02 | .00 |
| ☐ 567 | Joe Simpson | .04 | .02 | .00 |
| ☐ 568 | Willie Hernandez | .15 | .06 | .01 |
| ☐ 569 | Jack Perconte | .04 | .02 | .00 |
| ☐ 570 | Vida Blue | .10 | .04 | .01 |
| ☐ 571 | Mickey Klutts | .04 | .02 | .00 |
| ☐ 572 | Bob Watson | .06 | .02 | .00 |
| ☐ 573 | Andy Hassler | .04 | .02 | .00 |
| ☐ 574 | Glenn Adams | .04 | .02 | .00 |
| ☐ 575 | Neil Allen | .06 | .02 | .00 |
| ☐ 576 | Frank Robinson MGR | .15 | .06 | .01 |
| ☐ 577 | Luis Aponte | .06 | .02 | .00 |
| ☐ 578 | David Green | .12 | .05 | .01 |
| ☐ 579 | Rich Dauer | .04 | .02 | .00 |
| ☐ 580 | Tom Seaver | .60 | .24 | .06 |
| ☐ 581 | SV: Tom Seaver | .25 | .10 | .02 |
| ☐ 582 | Marshall Edwards | .04 | .02 | .00 |
| ☐ 583 | Terry Forster | .08 | .03 | .01 |
| ☐ 584 | Dave Hostetler | .06 | .02 | .00 |
| ☐ 585 | Jose Cruz | .12 | .05 | .01 |
| ☐ 586 | Frank Viola | .90 | .36 | .09 |
| ☐ 587 | Ivan DeJesus | .04 | .02 | .00 |
| ☐ 588 | Pat Underwood | .04 | .02 | .00 |
| ☐ 589 | Alvis Woods | .04 | .02 | .00 |
| ☐ 590 | Tony Pena | .20 | .08 | .02 |
| ☐ 591 | White Sox TL: | .10 | .02 | .00 |
| | BA: Greg Luzinski | | | |
| | ERA: LaMarr Hoyt | | | |
| ☐ 592 | Shane Rawley | .08 | .03 | .01 |
| ☐ 593 | Broderick Perkins | .04 | .02 | .00 |
| ☐ 594 | Eric Rasmussen | .04 | .02 | .00 |
| ☐ 595 | Tim Raines | .40 | .16 | .04 |
| ☐ 596 | Randy Johnson | .04 | .02 | .00 |
| ☐ 597 | Mike Proly | .04 | .02 | .00 |
| ☐ 598 | Dwayne Murphy | .06 | .02 | .00 |
| ☐ 599 | Don Aase | .06 | .02 | .00 |
| ☐ 600 | George Brett | 1.00 | .40 | .10 |
| ☐ 601 | Ed Lynch | .04 | .02 | .00 |
| ☐ 602 | Rich Gedman | .25 | .10 | .02 |
| ☐ 603 | Joe Morgan | .30 | .12 | .03 |
| ☐ 604 | SV: Joe Morgan | .15 | .06 | .01 |
| ☐ 605 | Gary Roenicke | .06 | .02 | .00 |
| ☐ 606 | Bobby Cox MGR | .04 | .02 | .00 |
| ☐ 607 | Charlie Leibrandt | .06 | .02 | .00 |
| ☐ 608 | Don Money | .04 | .02 | .00 |
| ☐ 609 | Danny Darwin | .04 | .02 | .00 |
| ☐ 610 | Steve Garvey | .75 | .30 | .07 |
| ☐ 611 | Bert Roberge | .04 | .02 | .00 |
| ☐ 612 | Steve Swisher | .04 | .02 | .00 |
| ☐ 613 | Mike Ivie | .04 | .02 | .00 |
| ☐ 614 | Ed Glynn | .04 | .02 | .00 |
| ☐ 615 | Garry Maddox | .06 | .02 | .00 |
| ☐ 616 | Bill Nahorodny | .04 | .02 | .00 |
| ☐ 617 | Butch Wynegar | .06 | .02 | .00 |
| ☐ 618 | LaMarr Hoyt | .10 | .04 | .01 |
| ☐ 619 | Keith Moreland | .10 | .04 | .01 |
| ☐ 620 | Mike Norris | .06 | .02 | .00 |
| ☐ 621 | New York Mets TL: | .10 | .02 | .00 |
| | BA: Mookie Wilson | | | |
| | ERA: Craig Swan | | | |

| No. | Player | | | |
|---|---|---|---|---|
| ☐ 622 | Dave Edler | .04 | .02 | .00 |
| ☐ 623 | Luis Sanchez | .04 | .02 | .00 |
| ☐ 624 | Glenn Hubbard | .04 | .02 | .00 |
| ☐ 625 | Ken Forsch | .04 | .02 | .00 |
| ☐ 626 | Jerry Martin | .04 | .02 | .00 |
| ☐ 627 | Doug Bair | .04 | .02 | .00 |
| ☐ 628 | Julio Valdez | .04 | .02 | .00 |
| ☐ 629 | Charlie Lea | .06 | .02 | .00 |
| ☐ 630 | Paul Molitor | .15 | .06 | .01 |
| ☐ 631 | Tippy Martinez | .04 | .02 | .00 |
| ☐ 632 | Alex Trevino | .04 | .02 | .00 |
| ☐ 633 | Vicente Romo | .04 | .02 | .00 |
| ☐ 634 | Max Venable | .04 | .02 | .00 |
| ☐ 635 | Graig Nettles | .15 | .06 | .01 |
| ☐ 636 | SV: Graig Nettles | .10 | .04 | .01 |
| ☐ 637 | Pat Corrales MGR | .04 | .02 | .00 |
| ☐ 638 | Dan Petry | .15 | .06 | .01 |
| ☐ 639 | Art Howe | .04 | .02 | .00 |
| ☐ 640 | Andre Thornton | .10 | .04 | .01 |
| ☐ 641 | Billy Sample | .04 | .02 | .00 |
| ☐ 642 | Checklist: 529-660 | .10 | .01 | .00 |
| ☐ 643 | Bump Wills | .04 | .02 | .00 |
| ☐ 644 | Joe Lefebvre | .04 | .02 | .00 |
| ☐ 645 | Bill Madlock | .15 | .06 | .01 |
| ☐ 646 | Jim Essian | .04 | .02 | .00 |
| ☐ 647 | Bobby Mitchell | .04 | .02 | .00 |
| ☐ 648 | Jeff Burroughs | .06 | .02 | .00 |
| ☐ 649 | Tommy Boggs | .04 | .02 | .00 |
| ☐ 650 | George Hendrick | .08 | .03 | .01 |
| ☐ 651 | Angels TL: | .15 | .03 | .00 |
| | BA: Rod Carew | | | |
| | ERA: Mike Witt | | | |
| ☐ 652 | Butch Hobson | .04 | .02 | .00 |
| ☐ 653 | Ellis Valentine | .04 | .02 | .00 |
| ☐ 654 | Bob Ojeda | .15 | .06 | .01 |
| ☐ 655 | Al Bumbry | .04 | .02 | .00 |
| ☐ 656 | Dave Frost | .04 | .02 | .00 |
| ☐ 657 | Mike Gates | .04 | .02 | .00 |
| ☐ 658 | Frank Pastore | .04 | .02 | .00 |
| ☐ 659 | Charlie Moore | .04 | .02 | .00 |
| ☐ 660 | Mike Hargrove | .06 | .02 | .00 |
| ☐ 661 | Bill Russell | .06 | .02 | .00 |
| ☐ 662 | Joe Sambito | .06 | .02 | .00 |
| ☐ 663 | Tom O'Malley | .06 | .02 | .00 |
| ☐ 664 | Bob Molinaro | .04 | .02 | .00 |
| ☐ 665 | Jim Sundberg | .06 | .02 | .00 |
| ☐ 666 | Sparky Anderson MGR | .08 | .03 | .01 |
| ☐ 667 | Dick Davis | .04 | .02 | .00 |
| ☐ 668 | Larry Christenson | .04 | .02 | .00 |
| ☐ 669 | Mike Squires | .04 | .02 | .00 |
| ☐ 670 | Jerry Mumphrey | .06 | .02 | .00 |
| ☐ 671 | Lenny Faedo | .04 | .02 | .00 |
| ☐ 672 | Jim Kaat | .15 | .06 | .01 |
| ☐ 673 | SV: Jim Kaat | .08 | .03 | .01 |
| ☐ 674 | Kurt Bevacqua | .04 | .02 | .00 |
| ☐ 675 | Jim Beattie | .04 | .02 | .00 |
| ☐ 676 | Biff Pocoroba | .04 | .02 | .00 |
| ☐ 677 | Dave Revering | .04 | .02 | .00 |
| ☐ 678 | Juan Beniquez | .06 | .02 | .00 |
| ☐ 679 | Mike Scott | .30 | .12 | .03 |
| ☐ 680 | Andre Dawson | .30 | .12 | .03 |
| ☐ 681 | Dodgers Leaders: | .20 | .04 | .01 |
| | BA: Pedro Guerrero | | | |
| | ERA: Fern.Valenzuela | | | |
| ☐ 682 | Bob Stanley | .06 | .02 | .00 |
| ☐ 683 | Dan Ford | .04 | .02 | .00 |
| ☐ 684 | Rafael Landestoy | .04 | .02 | .00 |
| ☐ 685 | Lee Mazzilli | .06 | .02 | .00 |
| ☐ 686 | Randy Lerch | .04 | .02 | .00 |
| ☐ 687 | U.L. Washington | .04 | .02 | .00 |
| ☐ 688 | Jim Wohlford | .04 | .02 | .00 |
| ☐ 689 | Ron Hassey | .04 | .02 | .00 |
| ☐ 690 | Kent Hrbek | .50 | .20 | .05 |
| ☐ 691 | Dave Tobik | .04 | .02 | .00 |
| ☐ 692 | Denny Walling | .04 | .02 | .00 |
| ☐ 693 | Sparky Lyle | .10 | .04 | .01 |
| ☐ 694 | SV: Sparky Lyle | .06 | .02 | .00 |
| ☐ 695 | Ruppert Jones | .04 | .02 | .00 |
| ☐ 696 | Chuck Tanner MGR | .06 | .02 | .00 |
| ☐ 697 | Barry Foote | .04 | .02 | .00 |
| ☐ 698 | Tony Bernazard | .06 | .02 | .00 |
| ☐ 699 | Lee Smith | .12 | .05 | .01 |
| ☐ 700 | Keith Hernandez | .45 | .18 | .04 |
| ☐ 701 | Batting Leaders: | .15 | .06 | .01 |
| | AL: Willie Wilson | | | |
| | NL: Al Oliver | | | |
| ☐ 702 | Home Run Leaders: | .15 | .06 | .01 |
| | AL: Reggie Jackson | | | |
| | AL: Gorman Thomas | | | |
| | NL: Dave Kingman | | | |
| ☐ 703 | RBI Leaders: | .15 | .06 | .01 |
| | AL: Hal McRae | | | |
| | NL: Dale Murphy | | | |
| | NL: Al Oliver | | | |
| ☐ 704 | SB Leaders: | .25 | .10 | .02 |
| | AL: Rickey Henderson | | | |
| | NL: Tim Raines | | | |
| ☐ 705 | Victory Leaders: | .15 | .06 | .01 |
| | AL: LaMarr Hoyt | | | |
| | NL: Steve Carlton | | | |
| ☐ 706 | Strikeout Leaders: | .15 | .06 | .01 |
| | AL: Floyd Bannister | | | |
| | NL: Steve Carlton | | | |
| ☐ 707 | ERA Leaders: | .08 | .03 | .01 |
| | AL: Rick Sutcliffe | | | |
| | NL: Steve Rogers | | | |
| ☐ 708 | Leading Firemen: | .10 | .04 | .01 |
| | AL: Dan Quisenberry | | | |
| | NL: Bruce Sutter | | | |
| ☐ 709 | Jimmy Sexton | .04 | .02 | .00 |
| ☐ 710 | Willie Wilson | .25 | .10 | .02 |
| ☐ 711 | Mariners TL: | .08 | .02 | .00 |
| | BA: Bruce Bochte | | | |
| | ERA: Jim Beattie | | | |
| ☐ 712 | Bruce Kison | .04 | .02 | .00 |
| ☐ 713 | Ron Hodges | .04 | .02 | .00 |
| ☐ 714 | Wayne Nordhagen | .04 | .02 | .00 |
| ☐ 715 | Tony Perez | .15 | .06 | .01 |
| ☐ 716 | SV: Tony Perez | .10 | .04 | .01 |
| ☐ 717 | Scott Sanderson | .04 | .02 | .00 |
| ☐ 718 | Jim Dwyer | .04 | .02 | .00 |
| ☐ 719 | Rich Gale | .04 | .02 | .00 |
| ☐ 720 | Dave Concepcion | .10 | .04 | .01 |
| ☐ 721 | John Martin | .04 | .02 | .00 |
| ☐ 722 | Jorge Orta | .04 | .02 | .00 |
| ☐ 723 | Randy Moffitt | .04 | .02 | .00 |
| ☐ 724 | Johnny Grubb | .04 | .02 | .00 |
| ☐ 725 | Dan Spillner | .04 | .02 | .00 |
| ☐ 726 | Harvey Kuenn MGR | .06 | .02 | .00 |
| ☐ 727 | Chet Lemon | .06 | .02 | .00 |
| ☐ 728 | Ron Reed | .04 | .02 | .00 |
| ☐ 729 | Jerry Morales | .04 | .02 | .00 |
| ☐ 730 | Jason Thompson | .06 | .02 | .00 |
| ☐ 731 | Al Williams | .04 | .02 | .00 |
| ☐ 732 | Dave Henderson | .10 | .04 | .01 |
| ☐ 733 | Buck Martinez | .04 | .02 | .00 |
| ☐ 734 | Steve Braun | .04 | .02 | .00 |
| ☐ 735 | Tommy John | .15 | .06 | .01 |
| ☐ 736 | SV: Tommy John | .10 | .04 | .01 |
| ☐ 737 | Mitchell Page | .04 | .02 | .00 |
| ☐ 738 | Tim Foli | .04 | .02 | .00 |
| ☐ 739 | Rick Ownbey | .06 | .02 | .00 |
| ☐ 740 | Rusty Staub | .12 | .05 | .01 |
| ☐ 741 | SV: Rusty Staub | .08 | .03 | .01 |
| ☐ 742 | Padres TL: | .08 | .02 | .00 |
| | BA: Terry Kennedy | | | |
| | ERA: Tim Lollar | | | |
| ☐ 743 | Mike Torrez | .06 | .02 | .00 |
| ☐ 744 | Brad Mills | .04 | .02 | .00 |
| ☐ 745 | Scott McGregor | .10 | .04 | .01 |
| ☐ 746 | John Wathan | .04 | .02 | .00 |
| ☐ 747 | Fred Breining | .04 | .02 | .00 |
| ☐ 748 | Derrel Thomas | .04 | .02 | .00 |
| ☐ 749 | Jon Matlack | .06 | .02 | .00 |
| ☐ 750 | Ben Oglivie | .08 | .03 | .01 |
| ☐ 751 | Brad Havens | .04 | .02 | .00 |
| ☐ 752 | Luis Pujols | .04 | .02 | .00 |
| ☐ 753 | Elias Sosa | .04 | .02 | .00 |
| ☐ 754 | Bill Robinson | .04 | .02 | .00 |
| ☐ 755 | John Candelaria | .08 | .03 | .01 |
| ☐ 756 | Russ Nixon MGR | .04 | .02 | .00 |
| ☐ 757 | Rick Manning | .04 | .02 | .00 |
| ☐ 758 | Aurelio Rodriguez | .04 | .02 | .00 |
| ☐ 759 | Doug Bird | .04 | .02 | .00 |
| ☐ 760 | Dale Murphy | 1.50 | .60 | .15 |
| ☐ 761 | Gary Lucas | .04 | .02 | .00 |
| ☐ 762 | Cliff Johnson | .04 | .02 | .00 |
| ☐ 763 | Al Cowens | .06 | .02 | .00 |
| ☐ 764 | Pete Falcone | .04 | .02 | .00 |
| ☐ 765 | Bob Boone | .06 | .02 | .00 |
| ☐ 766 | Barry Bonnell | .04 | .02 | .00 |
| ☐ 767 | Duane Kuiper | .04 | .02 | .00 |
| ☐ 768 | Chris Speier | .04 | .02 | .00 |
| ☐ 769 | Checklist: 661-792 | .10 | .01 | .00 |
| ☐ 770 | Dave Winfield | .45 | .18 | .04 |
| ☐ 771 | Twins TL: | .10 | .02 | .00 |
| | BA: Kent Hrbek | | | |
| | ERA: Bobby Castillo | | | |
| ☐ 772 | Jim Kern | .04 | .02 | .00 |
| ☐ 773 | Larry Hisle | .06 | .02 | .00 |
| ☐ 774 | Alan Ashby | .04 | .02 | .00 |
| ☐ 775 | Burt Hooton | .04 | .02 | .00 |
| ☐ 776 | Larry Parrish | .06 | .02 | .00 |
| ☐ 777 | John Curtis | .04 | .02 | .00 |
| ☐ 778 | Rich Hebner | .04 | .02 | .00 |
| ☐ 779 | Rick Waits | .04 | .02 | .00 |

| | | | | |
|---|---|---|---|---|
| ☐ 780 | Gary Matthews | .08 | .03 | .01 |
| ☐ 781 | Rick Rhoden | .10 | .04 | .01 |
| ☐ 782 | Bobby Murcer | .10 | .04 | .01 |
| ☐ 783 | SV: Bobby Murcer | .06 | .02 | .00 |
| ☐ 784 | Jeff Newman | .04 | .02 | .00 |
| ☐ 785 | Dennis Leonard | .06 | .02 | .00 |
| ☐ 786 | Ralph Houk MGR | .06 | .02 | .00 |
| ☐ 787 | Dick Tidrow | .04 | .02 | .00 |
| ☐ 788 | Dane Iorg | .04 | .02 | .00 |
| ☐ 789 | Bryan Clark | .04 | .02 | .00 |
| ☐ 790 | Bob Grich | .08 | .03 | .01 |
| ☐ 791 | Gary Lavelle | .06 | .02 | .00 |
| ☐ 792 | Chris Chambliss | .08 | .03 | .01 |

## 1983 Topps Traded

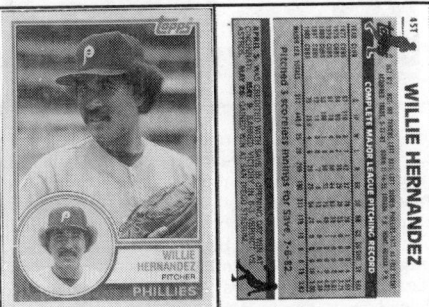

The cards in this 132 card set measure 2 1/2" by 3 1/2". For the third year in a row, Topps issued a 132 card Traded (or extended) set featuring some of the year's top rookies and players who had changed teams during the year, but were featured with their old team in the Topps regular issue of 1983. The cards were available through hobby dealers only and were printed in Ireland by the Topps affiliate in that country. The set is numbered alphabetically by the last name of the player of the card.

| | | MINT | VG-E | F-G |
|---|---|---|---|---|
| COMPLETE SET | | 32.00 | 13.00 | 3.20 |
| COMMON PLAYER | | .08 | .03 | .01 |

| | | | | |
|---|---|---|---|---|
| ☐ 1T | Neil Allen | .12 | .05 | .01 |
| ☐ 2T | Bill Almon | .08 | .03 | .01 |
| ☐ 3T | Joe Altobelli MGR | .08 | .03 | .01 |
| ☐ 4T | Tony Armas | .20 | .08 | .02 |
| ☐ 5T | Doug Bair | .08 | .03 | .01 |
| ☐ 6T | Steve Baker | .12 | .05 | .01 |
| ☐ 7T | Floyd Bannister | .12 | .05 | .01 |
| ☐ 8T | Don Baylor | .25 | .10 | .02 |
| ☐ 9T | Tony Bernazard | .12 | .05 | .01 |
| ☐ 10T | Larry Biittner | .08 | .03 | .01 |
| ☐ 11T | Dann Bilardello | .12 | .05 | .01 |
| ☐ 12T | Doug Bird | .08 | .03 | .01 |
| ☐ 13T | Steve Boros MGR | .08 | .03 | .01 |
| ☐ 14T | Greg Brock | .35 | .14 | .03 |
| ☐ 15T | Mike Brown | .15 | .06 | .01 |
| ☐ 16T | Tom Burgmeier | .08 | .03 | .01 |
| ☐ 17T | Randy Bush | .12 | .05 | .01 |
| ☐ 18T | Bert Campaneris | .15 | .06 | .01 |
| ☐ 19T | Ron Cey | .25 | .10 | .02 |
| ☐ 20T | Chris Codiroli | .12 | .05 | .01 |
| ☐ 21T | Dave Collins | .12 | .05 | .01 |
| ☐ 22T | Terry Crowley | .08 | .03 | .01 |
| ☐ 23T | Julio Cruz | .08 | .03 | .01 |
| ☐ 24T | Mike Davis | .25 | .10 | .02 |
| ☐ 25T | Frank DiPino | .12 | .05 | .01 |
| ☐ 26T | Bill Doran | 1.25 | .50 | .12 |
| ☐ 27T | Jerry Dybzinski | .08 | .03 | .01 |
| ☐ 28T | Jamie Easterly | .08 | .03 | .01 |
| ☐ 29T | Juan Eichelberger | .08 | .03 | .01 |
| ☐ 30T | Jim Essian | .08 | .03 | .01 |
| ☐ 31T | Pete Falcone | .08 | .03 | .01 |
| ☐ 32T | Mike Ferraro MGR | .08 | .03 | .01 |
| ☐ 33T | Terry Forster | .20 | .08 | .02 |
| ☐ 34T | Julio Franco | 1.25 | .50 | .12 |
| ☐ 35T | Rich Gale | .08 | .03 | .01 |
| ☐ 36T | Kiko Garcia | .08 | .03 | .01 |
| ☐ 37T | Steve Garvey | 1.25 | .50 | .12 |
| ☐ 38T | Johnny Grubb | .08 | .03 | .01 |
| ☐ 39T | Mel Hall | 1.00 | .40 | .10 |
| ☐ 40T | Von Hayes | 1.00 | .40 | .10 |
| ☐ 41T | Danny Heep | .12 | .05 | .01 |
| ☐ 42T | Steve Henderson | .08 | .03 | .01 |
| ☐ 43T | Keith Hernandez | 1.00 | .40 | .10 |
| ☐ 44T | Leo Hernandez | .15 | .06 | .01 |
| ☐ 45T | Willie Hernandez | .35 | .14 | .03 |
| ☐ 46T | Al Holland | .12 | .05 | .01 |
| ☐ 47T | Frank Howard MGR | .12 | .05 | .01 |
| ☐ 48T | Bobby Johnson | .08 | .03 | .01 |
| ☐ 49T | Cliff Johnson | .08 | .03 | .01 |
| ☐ 50T | Odell Jones | .08 | .03 | .01 |
| ☐ 51T | Mike Jorgensen | .08 | .03 | .01 |
| ☐ 52T | Bob Kearney | .08 | .03 | .01 |
| ☐ 53T | Steve Kemp | .15 | .06 | .01 |
| ☐ 54T | Matt Keough | .08 | .03 | .01 |
| ☐ 55T | Ron Kittle | .60 | .24 | .06 |
| ☐ 56T | Mickey Klutts | .08 | .03 | .01 |
| ☐ 57T | Alan Knicely | .08 | .03 | .01 |
| ☐ 58T | Mike Krukow | .20 | .08 | .02 |
| ☐ 59T | Rafael Landestoy | .08 | .03 | .01 |
| ☐ 60T | Carney Lansford | .25 | .10 | .02 |
| ☐ 61T | Joe Lefebvre | .08 | .03 | .01 |
| ☐ 62T | Bryan Little | .12 | .05 | .01 |
| ☐ 63T | Aurelio Lopez | .08 | .03 | .01 |
| ☐ 64T | Mike Madden | .15 | .06 | .01 |
| ☐ 65T | Rick Manning | .08 | .03 | .01 |
| ☐ 66T | Billy Martin MGR | .20 | .08 | .02 |
| ☐ 67T | Lee Mazzilli | .12 | .05 | .01 |
| ☐ 68T | Andy McGaffigan | .08 | .03 | .01 |
| ☐ 69T | Craig McMurtry | .20 | .08 | .02 |
| ☐ 70T | John McNamara MGR | .12 | .05 | .01 |
| ☐ 71T | Orlando Mercado | .12 | .05 | .01 |
| ☐ 72T | Larry Milbourne | .08 | .03 | .01 |
| ☐ 73T | Randy Moffitt | .08 | .03 | .01 |
| ☐ 74T | Sid Monge | .08 | .03 | .01 |
| ☐ 75T | Jose Morales | .08 | .03 | .01 |
| ☐ 76T | Omar Moreno | .12 | .05 | .01 |
| ☐ 77T | Joe Morgan | 1.00 | .40 | .10 |
| ☐ 78T | Mike Morgan | .08 | .03 | .01 |
| ☐ 79T | Dale Murray | .08 | .03 | .01 |
| ☐ 80T | Jeff Newman | .08 | .03 | .01 |
| ☐ 81T | Pete O'Brien | 1.25 | .50 | .12 |
| ☐ 82T | Jorge Orta | .08 | .03 | .01 |
| ☐ 83T | Alejandro Pena | .40 | .16 | .04 |
| ☐ 84T | Pascual Perez | .12 | .05 | .01 |
| ☐ 85T | Tony Perez | .35 | .14 | .03 |
| ☐ 86T | Broderick Perkins | .08 | .03 | .01 |
| ☐ 87T | Tony Phillips | .12 | .05 | .01 |
| ☐ 88T | Charlie Puleo | .08 | .03 | .01 |
| ☐ 89T | Pat Putnam | .08 | .03 | .01 |
| ☐ 90T | Jamie Quirk | .08 | .03 | .01 |
| ☐ 91T | Doug Rader MGR | .12 | .05 | .01 |
| ☐ 92T | Chuck Rainey | .08 | .03 | .01 |
| ☐ 93T | Bobby Ramos | .08 | .03 | .01 |
| ☐ 94T | Gary Redus | .75 | .30 | .07 |
| ☐ 95T | Steve Renko | .08 | .03 | .01 |
| ☐ 96T | Leon Roberts | .08 | .03 | .01 |
| ☐ 97T | Aurelio Rodriguez | .08 | .03 | .01 |
| ☐ 98T | Dick Ruthven | .08 | .03 | .01 |
| ☐ 99T | Daryl Sconiers | .12 | .05 | .01 |
| ☐ 100T | Mike Scott | 1.00 | .40 | .10 |
| ☐ 101T | Tom Seaver | 1.25 | .50 | .12 |
| ☐ 102T | John Shelby | .15 | .06 | .01 |
| ☐ 103T | Bob Shirley | .08 | .03 | .01 |
| ☐ 104T | Joe Simpson | .08 | .03 | .01 |
| ☐ 105T | Doug Sisk | .15 | .06 | .01 |
| ☐ 106T | Mike Smithson | .20 | .08 | .02 |
| ☐ 107T | Elias Sosa | .08 | .03 | .01 |
| ☐ 108T | Darryl Strawberry | 18.00 | 7.25 | 1.80 |
| ☐ 109T | Tom Tellmann | .08 | .03 | .01 |
| ☐ 110T | Gene Tenace | .08 | .03 | .01 |
| ☐ 111T | Gorman Thomas | .20 | .08 | .02 |
| ☐ 112T | Dick Tidrow | .08 | .03 | .01 |
| ☐ 113T | Dave Tobik | .08 | .03 | .01 |
| ☐ 114T | Wayne Tolleson | .12 | .05 | .01 |
| ☐ 115T | Mike Torrez | .12 | .05 | .01 |
| ☐ 116T | Manny Trillo | .12 | .05 | .01 |
| ☐ 117T | Steve Trout | .12 | .05 | .01 |
| ☐ 118T | Lee Tunnell | .15 | .06 | .01 |
| ☐ 119T | Mike Vail | .08 | .03 | .01 |
| ☐ 120T | Ellis Valentine | .12 | .05 | .01 |
| ☐ 121T | Tom Veryzer | .08 | .03 | .01 |
| ☐ 122T | George Vukovich | .08 | .03 | .01 |
| ☐ 123T | Rick Waits | .08 | .03 | .01 |
| ☐ 124T | Greg Walker | 2.00 | .80 | .20 |
| ☐ 125T | Chris Welsh | .08 | .03 | .01 |

| | | | | |
|---|---|---|---|---|
| ☐ 126T | Len Whitehouse | .12 | .05 | .01 |
| ☐ 127T | Eddie Whitson | .12 | .05 | .01 |
| ☐ 128T | Jim Wohlford | .08 | .03 | .01 |
| ☐ 129T | Matt Young | .25 | .10 | .02 |
| ☐ 130T | Joel Youngblood | .08 | .03 | .01 |
| ☐ 131T | Pat Zachry | .08 | .03 | .01 |
| ☐ 132T | Checklist 1T-132T | .20 | .02 | .00 |

## 1983 Topps Glossy 40

The cards in this 40 card set measure 2 1/2" by 3 1/2". The 1983 Topps "Collector's Edition" or "All Star Set" (popularly known as "Glossies") consists of color ballplayer picture cards with shiny, glazed surfaces. The player's name appears in small print outside the frame line at bottom left. The backs contain no biography or record and list only the set titles, the player's name, team and position and the card number.

| | | MINT | VG-E | F-G |
|---|---|---|---|---|
| COMPLETE SET | | 12.00 | 5.00 | 1.20 |
| COMMON PLAYER | | .15 | .06 | .01 |
| ☐ 1 | Carl Yastrzemski | 1.00 | .40 | .10 |
| ☐ 2 | Mookie Wilson | .15 | .06 | .01 |
| ☐ 3 | Andre Thornton | .15 | .06 | .01 |
| ☐ 4 | Keith Hernandez | .40 | .16 | .04 |
| ☐ 5 | Robin Yount | .50 | .20 | .05 |
| ☐ 6 | Terry Kennedy | .15 | .06 | .01 |
| ☐ 7 | Dave Winfield | .60 | .24 | .06 |
| ☐ 8 | Mike Schmidt | 1.00 | .40 | .10 |
| ☐ 9 | Buddy Bell | .20 | .08 | .02 |
| ☐ 10 | Fernando Valenzuela | .60 | .24 | .06 |
| ☐ 11 | Rich Gossage | .30 | .12 | .03 |
| ☐ 12 | Bob Horner | .30 | .12 | .03 |
| ☐ 13 | Toby Harrah | .15 | .06 | .01 |
| ☐ 14 | Pete Rose | 1.50 | .60 | .15 |
| ☐ 15 | Cecil Cooper | .25 | .10 | .02 |
| ☐ 16 | Dale Murphy | 1.25 | .50 | .12 |
| ☐ 17 | Carlton Fisk | .30 | .12 | .03 |
| ☐ 18 | Ray Knight | .15 | .06 | .01 |
| ☐ 19 | Jim Palmer | .45 | .18 | .04 |
| ☐ 20 | Gary Carter | .60 | .24 | .06 |
| ☐ 21 | Richie Zisk | .15 | .06 | .01 |
| ☐ 22 | Dusty Baker | .15 | .06 | .01 |
| ☐ 23 | Willie Wilson | .25 | .10 | .02 |
| ☐ 24 | Bill Buckner | .15 | .06 | .01 |
| ☐ 25 | Dave Stieb | .20 | .08 | .02 |
| ☐ 26 | Bill Madlock | .20 | .08 | .02 |
| ☐ 27 | Lance Parrish | .40 | .16 | .04 |
| ☐ 28 | Nolan Ryan | .60 | .24 | .06 |
| ☐ 29 | Rod Carew | .60 | .24 | .06 |
| ☐ 30 | Al Oliver | .25 | .10 | .02 |
| ☐ 31 | George Brett | 1.00 | .40 | .10 |
| ☐ 32 | Jack Clark | .25 | .10 | .02 |
| ☐ 33 | Ricky Henderson | 1.00 | .40 | .10 |
| ☐ 34 | Dave Concepcion | .15 | .06 | .01 |
| ☐ 35 | Kent Hrbek | .45 | .18 | .04 |
| ☐ 36 | Steve Carlton | .60 | .24 | .06 |
| ☐ 37 | Eddie Murray | 1.00 | .40 | .10 |
| ☐ 38 | Ruppert Jones | .15 | .06 | .01 |
| ☐ 39 | Reggie Jackson | 1.00 | .40 | .10 |
| ☐ 40 | Bruce Sutter | .30 | .12 | .03 |

## 1984 Topps

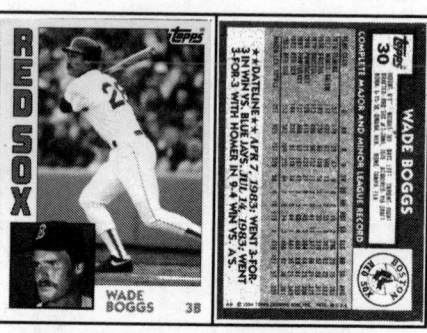

The cards in this 792 card set measure 2 1/2" by 3 1/2". For the second year in a row, Topps utilized a dual picture on the front of the card. A portrait is shown in a square insert and an action shot is featured in the main photo. Card numbers 1-6 feature 1983 Highlights (HL), cards 131-138 depict League Leaders, card numbers 386-407 feature All Stars and card numbers 701-718 feature active Major League career leaders in various statistical categories. Each team leader (TL) card features the team's leading hitter and pitcher pictured on the front with a team checklist back. There are six numerical checklist cards in the set. The player cards feature team logos in the upper right corner of the reverse.

| | | MINT | VG-E | F-G |
|---|---|---|---|---|
| COMPLETE SET | | 55.00 | 22.00 | 5.50 |
| COMMON PLAYER (1-792) | | .03 | .01 | .00 |
| ☐ 1 | HL: Steve Carlton 300th Win and All Time SO King | .25 | .07 | .01 |
| ☐ 2 | HL: Rickey Henderson 100 Stolen Bases Three Times | .20 | .08 | .02 |
| ☐ 3 | HL: Dan Quisenberry Sets Save Record | .10 | .04 | .01 |
| ☐ 4 | HL: Nolan Ryan, Steve Carlton, and Gaylord Perry (All Surpass Johnson) | .25 | .10 | .02 |
| ☐ 5 | HL: Dave Righetti, Bob Forsch, and Mike Warren (All Pitch No-Hitters) | .10 | .04 | .01 |
| ☐ 6 | HL: Johnny Bench Gaylord Perry, and Carl Yastrzemski (Superstars Retire) | .25 | .10 | .02 |
| ☐ 7 | Gary Lucas | .03 | .01 | .00 |
| ☐ 8 | Don Mattingly | 35.00 | 14.00 | 3.50 |
| ☐ 9 | Jim Gott | .03 | .01 | .00 |
| ☐ 10 | Robin Yount | .35 | .14 | .03 |
| ☐ 11 | Minnesota Twins TL: Kent Hrbek Ken Schrom | .10 | .02 | .00 |
| ☐ 12 | Billy Sample | .03 | .01 | .00 |
| ☐ 13 | Scott Holman | .03 | .01 | .00 |
| ☐ 14 | Tom Brookens | .03 | .01 | .00 |
| ☐ 15 | Burt Hooton | .03 | .01 | .00 |
| ☐ 16 | Omar Moreno | .03 | .01 | .00 |
| ☐ 17 | John Denny | .06 | .02 | .00 |
| ☐ 18 | Dale Berra | .05 | .02 | .00 |
| ☐ 19 | Ray Fontenot | .08 | .03 | .01 |
| ☐ 20 | Greg Luzinski | .10 | .04 | .01 |
| ☐ 21 | Joe Altobelli MGR | .03 | .01 | .00 |
| ☐ 22 | Bryan Clark | .03 | .01 | .00 |
| ☐ 23 | Keith Moreland | .06 | .02 | .00 |

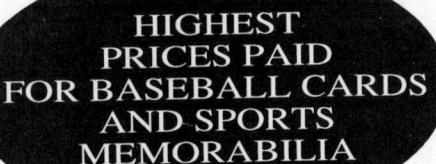

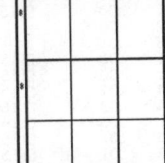

| | | | | |
|---|---|---|---|---|
| ☐ 24 | John Martin | .03 | .01 | .00 |
| ☐ 25 | Glenn Hubbard | .03 | .01 | .00 |
| ☐ 26 | Bud Black | .03 | .01 | .00 |
| ☐ 27 | Daryl Sconiers | .03 | .01 | .00 |
| ☐ 28 | Frank Viola | .07 | .03 | .01 |
| ☐ 29 | Danny Heep | .03 | .01 | .00 |
| ☐ 30 | Wade Boggs | 4.50 | 1.80 | .45 |
| ☐ 31 | Andy McGaffigan | .03 | .01 | .00 |
| ☐ 32 | Bobby Ramos | .03 | .01 | .00 |
| ☐ 33 | Tom Burgmeier | .03 | .01 | .00 |
| ☐ 34 | Eddie Milner | .03 | .01 | .00 |
| ☐ 35 | Don Sutton | .20 | .08 | .02 |
| ☐ 36 | Denny Walling | .03 | .01 | .00 |
| ☐ 37 | Texas Rangers TL:<br>Buddy Bell<br>Rick Honeycutt | .08 | .02 | .00 |
| ☐ 38 | Luis DeLeon | .03 | .01 | .00 |
| ☐ 39 | Garth Iorg | .03 | .01 | .00 |
| ☐ 40 | Dusty Baker | .07 | .03 | .01 |
| ☐ 41 | Tony Bernazard | .05 | .02 | .00 |
| ☐ 42 | Johnny Grubb | .03 | .01 | .00 |
| ☐ 43 | Ron Reed | .03 | .01 | .00 |
| ☐ 44 | Jim Morrison | .03 | .01 | .00 |
| ☐ 45 | Jerry Mumphrey | .05 | .02 | .00 |
| ☐ 46 | Ray Smith | .03 | .01 | .00 |
| ☐ 47 | Rudy Law | .03 | .01 | .00 |
| ☐ 48 | Julio Franco | .25 | .10 | .02 |
| ☐ 49 | John Stuper | .03 | .01 | .00 |
| ☐ 50 | Chris Chambliss | .05 | .02 | .00 |
| ☐ 51 | Jim Frey MGR | .03 | .01 | .00 |
| ☐ 52 | Paul Splittorff | .05 | .02 | .00 |
| ☐ 53 | Juan Beniquez | .05 | .02 | .00 |
| ☐ 54 | Jesse Orosco | .06 | .02 | .00 |
| ☐ 55 | Dave Concepcion | .09 | .04 | .01 |
| ☐ 56 | Gary Allenson | .03 | .01 | .00 |
| ☐ 57 | Dan Schatzeder | .03 | .01 | .00 |
| ☐ 58 | Max Venable | .03 | .01 | .00 |
| ☐ 59 | Sammy Stewart | .03 | .01 | .00 |
| ☐ 60 | Paul Molitor | .10 | .04 | .01 |
| ☐ 61 | Chris Codiroli | .07 | .03 | .01 |
| ☐ 62 | Dave Hostetler | .03 | .01 | .00 |
| ☐ 63 | Ed VandeBerg | .05 | .02 | .00 |
| ☐ 64 | Mike Scioscia | .05 | .02 | .00 |
| ☐ 65 | Kirk Gibson | .25 | .10 | .02 |
| ☐ 66 | Houston Astros TL:<br>Jose Cruz<br>Nolan Ryan | .12 | .02 | .00 |
| ☐ 67 | Gary Ward | .06 | .02 | .00 |
| ☐ 68 | Luis Salazar | .03 | .01 | .00 |
| ☐ 69 | Rod Scurry | .03 | .01 | .00 |
| ☐ 70 | Gary Matthews | .07 | .03 | .01 |
| ☐ 71 | Leo Hernandez | .09 | .04 | .01 |
| ☐ 72 | Mike Squires | .03 | .01 | .00 |
| ☐ 73 | Jody Davis | .09 | .04 | .01 |
| ☐ 74 | Jerry Martin | .03 | .01 | .00 |
| ☐ 75 | Bob Forsch | .06 | .02 | .00 |
| ☐ 76 | Alfredo Griffin | .05 | .02 | .00 |
| ☐ 77 | Brett Butler | .08 | .03 | .01 |
| ☐ 78 | Mike Torrez | .05 | .02 | .00 |
| ☐ 79 | Rob Wilfong | .03 | .01 | .00 |
| ☐ 80 | Steve Rogers | .07 | .03 | .01 |
| ☐ 81 | Billy Martin MGR | .12 | .05 | .01 |
| ☐ 82 | Doug Bird | .03 | .01 | .00 |
| ☐ 83 | Richie Zisk | .05 | .02 | .00 |
| ☐ 84 | Lenny Faedo | .03 | .01 | .00 |
| ☐ 85 | Atlee Hammaker | .05 | .02 | .00 |
| ☐ 86 | John Shelby | .08 | .03 | .01 |
| ☐ 87 | Frank Pastore | .03 | .01 | .00 |
| ☐ 88 | Rob Picciolo | .03 | .01 | .00 |
| ☐ 89 | Mike Smithson | .10 | .04 | .01 |
| ☐ 90 | Pedro Guerrero | .35 | .14 | .03 |
| ☐ 91 | Dan Spillner | .03 | .01 | .00 |
| ☐ 92 | Lloyd Moseby | .12 | .05 | .01 |
| ☐ 93 | Bob Knepper | .08 | .03 | .01 |
| ☐ 94 | Mario Ramirez | .05 | .02 | .00 |
| ☐ 95 | Aurelio Lopez | .03 | .01 | .00 |
| ☐ 96 | K.C. Royals TL:<br>Hal McRae<br>Larry Gura | .08 | .02 | .00 |
| ☐ 97 | LaMarr Hoyt | .08 | .03 | .01 |
| ☐ 98 | Steve Nicosia | .03 | .01 | .00 |
| ☐ 99 | Craig Lefferts | .12 | .05 | .01 |
| ☐ 100 | Reggie Jackson | .50 | .20 | .05 |
| ☐ 101 | Porfirio Altamirano | .03 | .01 | .00 |
| ☐ 102 | Ken Oberkfell | .03 | .01 | .00 |
| ☐ 103 | Dwayne Murphy | .06 | .02 | .00 |
| ☐ 104 | Ken Dayley | .03 | .01 | .00 |
| ☐ 105 | Tony Armas | .09 | .04 | .01 |
| ☐ 106 | Tim Stoddard | .03 | .01 | .00 |
| ☐ 107 | Ned Yost | .03 | .01 | .00 |
| ☐ 108 | Randy Moffitt | .03 | .01 | .00 |
| ☐ 109 | Brad Wellman | .05 | .02 | .00 |
| ☐ 110 | Ron Guidry | .20 | .08 | .02 |
| ☐ 111 | Bill Virdon MGR | .05 | .02 | .00 |
| ☐ 112 | Tom Niedenfuer | .07 | .03 | .01 |
| ☐ 113 | Kelly Paris | .09 | .04 | .01 |
| ☐ 114 | Checklist 1-132 | .08 | .01 | .00 |
| ☐ 115 | Andre Thornton | .07 | .03 | .01 |
| ☐ 116 | George Bjorkman | .03 | .01 | .00 |
| ☐ 117 | Tom Veryzer | .03 | .01 | .00 |
| ☐ 118 | Charlie Hough | .06 | .02 | .00 |
| ☐ 119 | Johnny Wockenfuss | .03 | .01 | .00 |
| ☐ 120 | Keith Hernandez | .35 | .14 | .03 |
| ☐ 121 | Pat Sheridan | .12 | .05 | .01 |
| ☐ 122 | Cecilio Guante | .05 | .02 | .00 |
| ☐ 123 | Butch Wynegar | .05 | .02 | .00 |
| ☐ 124 | Damaso Garcia | .09 | .04 | .01 |
| ☐ 125 | Britt Burns | .07 | .03 | .01 |
| ☐ 126 | Atlanta Braves TL:<br>Dale Murphy<br>Craig McMurtry | .15 | .03 | .00 |
| ☐ 127 | Mike Madden | .09 | .04 | .01 |
| ☐ 128 | Rick Manning | .03 | .01 | .00 |
| ☐ 129 | Bill Laskey | .03 | .01 | .00 |
| ☐ 130 | Ozzie Smith | .15 | .06 | .01 |
| ☐ 131 | Batting Leaders:<br>Bill Madlock<br>Wade Boggs | .25 | .10 | .02 |
| ☐ 132 | Home Run Leaders:<br>Mike Schmidt<br>Jim Rice | .25 | .10 | .02 |
| ☐ 133 | RBI Leaders:<br>Dale Murphy<br>Cecil Cooper<br>Jim Rice | .25 | .10 | .02 |
| ☐ 134 | Stolen Base Leaders:<br>Tim Raines<br>Rickey Henderson | .25 | .10 | .02 |
| ☐ 135 | Victory Leaders:<br>John Denny<br>LaMarr Hoyt | .07 | .03 | .01 |
| ☐ 136 | Strikeout Leaders:<br>Steve Carlton<br>Jack Morris | .15 | .06 | .01 |
| ☐ 137 | ERA Leaders:<br>Atlee Hammaker<br>Rick Honeycutt | .06 | .02 | .00 |
| ☐ 138 | Leading Firemen:<br>Al Holland<br>Dan Quisenberry | .07 | .03 | .01 |
| ☐ 139 | Bert Campaneris | .06 | .02 | .00 |
| ☐ 140 | Storm Davis | .08 | .03 | .01 |
| ☐ 141 | Pat Corrales MGR | .03 | .01 | .00 |
| ☐ 142 | Rich Gale | .03 | .01 | .00 |
| ☐ 143 | Jose Morales | .03 | .01 | .00 |
| ☐ 144 | Brian Harper | .07 | .03 | .01 |
| ☐ 145 | Gary Lavelle | .05 | .02 | .00 |
| ☐ 146 | Ed Romero | .03 | .01 | .00 |
| ☐ 147 | Dan Petry | .14 | .06 | .01 |
| ☐ 148 | Joe Lefebvre | .03 | .01 | .00 |
| ☐ 149 | Jon Matlack | .05 | .02 | .00 |
| ☐ 150 | Dale Murphy | .75 | .30 | .07 |
| ☐ 151 | Steve Trout | .05 | .02 | .00 |
| ☐ 152 | Glenn Brummer | .03 | .01 | .00 |
| ☐ 153 | Dick Tidrow | .03 | .01 | .00 |
| ☐ 154 | Dave Henderson | .07 | .03 | .01 |
| ☐ 155 | Frank White | .07 | .03 | .01 |
| ☐ 156 | Oakland A's TL:<br>Rickey Henderson<br>Tim Conroy | .12 | .02 | .00 |
| ☐ 157 | Gary Gaetti | .09 | .04 | .01 |
| ☐ 158 | John Curtis | .03 | .01 | .00 |
| ☐ 159 | Darryl Cias | .05 | .02 | .00 |
| ☐ 160 | Mario Soto | .08 | .03 | .01 |
| ☐ 161 | Junior Ortiz | .05 | .02 | .00 |
| ☐ 162 | Bob Ojeda | .09 | .04 | .01 |
| ☐ 163 | Lorenzo Gray | .05 | .02 | .00 |
| ☐ 164 | Scott Sanderson | .03 | .01 | .00 |
| ☐ 165 | Ken Singleton | .08 | .03 | .01 |
| ☐ 166 | Jamie Nelson | .08 | .03 | .01 |
| ☐ 167 | Marshall Edwards | .03 | .01 | .00 |
| ☐ 168 | Juan Bonilla | .03 | .01 | .00 |
| ☐ 169 | Larry Parrish | .06 | .02 | .00 |
| ☐ 170 | Jerry Reuss | .07 | .03 | .01 |
| ☐ 171 | Frank Robinson MGR | .14 | .06 | .01 |
| ☐ 172 | Frank DiPino | .05 | .02 | .00 |
| ☐ 173 | Marvell Wynne | .10 | .04 | .01 |
| ☐ 174 | Juan Berenguer | .03 | .01 | .00 |
| ☐ 175 | Graig Nettles | .12 | .05 | .01 |
| ☐ 176 | Lee Smith | .10 | .04 | .01 |
| ☐ 177 | Jerry Hairston | .03 | .01 | .00 |
| ☐ 178 | Bill Krueger | .07 | .03 | .01 |
| ☐ 179 | Buck Martinez | .03 | .01 | .00 |
| ☐ 180 | Manny Trillo | .05 | .02 | .00 |
| ☐ 181 | Roy Thomas | .03 | .01 | .00 |
| ☐ 182 | Darryl Strawberry | 7.50 | 3.00 | .75 |

| # | Name | | | |
|---|---|---|---|---|
| 183 | Al Williams | .03 | .01 | .00 |
| 184 | Mike O'Berry | .03 | .01 | .00 |
| 185 | Sixto Lezcano | .03 | .01 | .00 |
| 186 | Cardinal TL: | .08 | .02 | .00 |
| | Lonnie Smith | | | |
| | John Stuper | | | |
| 187 | Luis Aponte | .03 | .01 | .00 |
| 188 | Bryan Little | .03 | .01 | .00 |
| 189 | Tim Conroy | .06 | .02 | .00 |
| 190 | Ben Oglivie | .06 | .02 | .00 |
| 191 | Mike Boddicker | .09 | .04 | .01 |
| 192 | Nick Esasky | .25 | .10 | .02 |
| 193 | Darrell Brown | .05 | .02 | .00 |
| 194 | Domingo Ramos | .03 | .01 | .00 |
| 195 | Jack Morris | .20 | .08 | .02 |
| 196 | Don Slaught | .05 | .02 | .00 |
| 197 | Garry Hancock | .03 | .01 | .00 |
| 198 | Bill Doran | .65 | .26 | .06 |
| 199 | Willie Hernandez | .25 | .10 | .02 |
| 200 | Andre Dawson | .25 | .10 | .02 |
| 201 | Bruce Kison | .03 | .01 | .00 |
| 202 | Bobby Cox MGR | .03 | .01 | .00 |
| 203 | Matt Keough | .03 | .01 | .00 |
| 204 | Bobby Meacham | .20 | .08 | .02 |
| 205 | Greg Minton | .05 | .02 | .00 |
| 206 | Andy Van Slyke | .50 | .20 | .05 |
| 207 | Donnie Moore | .06 | .02 | .00 |
| 208 | Jose Oquendo | .06 | .02 | .00 |
| 209 | Manny Sarmiento | .03 | .01 | .00 |
| 210 | Joe Morgan | .18 | .08 | .01 |
| 211 | Rick Sweet | .03 | .01 | .00 |
| 212 | Broderick Perkins | .03 | .01 | .00 |
| 213 | Bruce Hurst | .08 | .03 | .01 |
| 214 | Paul Householder | .03 | .01 | .00 |
| 215 | Tippy Martinez | .03 | .01 | .00 |
| 216 | White Sox TL: | .08 | .02 | .00 |
| | Carlton Fisk | | | |
| | Richard Dotson | | | |
| 217 | Alan Ashby | .03 | .01 | .00 |
| 218 | Rick Waits | .03 | .01 | .00 |
| 219 | Joe Simpson | .03 | .01 | .00 |
| 220 | Fernando Valenzuela | .35 | .14 | .03 |
| 221 | Cliff Johnson | .03 | .01 | .00 |
| 222 | Rick Honeycutt | .05 | .02 | .00 |
| 223 | Wayne Krenchicki | .03 | .01 | .00 |
| 224 | Sid Monge | .03 | .01 | .00 |
| 225 | Lee Mazzilli | .05 | .02 | .00 |
| 226 | Juan Eichelberger | .03 | .01 | .00 |
| 227 | Steve Braun | .03 | .01 | .00 |
| 228 | John Rabb | .10 | .04 | .01 |
| 229 | Paul Owens MGR | .03 | .01 | .00 |
| 230 | Rickey Henderson | .50 | .20 | .05 |
| 231 | Gary Woods | .03 | .01 | .00 |
| 232 | Tim Wallach | .09 | .04 | .01 |
| 233 | Checklist 133-264 | .08 | .01 | .00 |
| 234 | Rafael Ramirez | .03 | .01 | .00 |
| 235 | Matt Young | .09 | .04 | .01 |
| 236 | Ellis Valentine | .03 | .01 | .00 |
| 237 | John Castino | .03 | .01 | .00 |
| 238 | Reid Nichols | .03 | .01 | .00 |
| 239 | Jay Howell | .06 | .02 | .00 |
| 240 | Eddie Murray | .55 | .22 | .05 |
| 241 | Billy Almon | .03 | .01 | .00 |
| 242 | Alex Trevino | .03 | .01 | .00 |
| 243 | Pete Ladd | .03 | .01 | .00 |
| 244 | Candy Maldonado | .09 | .04 | .01 |
| 245 | Rick Sutcliffe | .18 | .08 | .01 |
| 246 | New York Mets TL: | .12 | .02 | .00 |
| | Mookie Wilson | | | |
| | Tom Seaver | | | |
| 247 | Onix Concepcion | .03 | .01 | .00 |
| 248 | Bill Dawley | .15 | .06 | .01 |
| 249 | Jay Johnstone | .05 | .02 | .00 |
| 250 | Bill Madlock | .14 | .06 | .01 |
| 251 | Tony Gwynn | 1.25 | .50 | .12 |
| 252 | Larry Christenson | .03 | .01 | .00 |
| 253 | Jim Wohlford | .03 | .01 | .00 |
| 254 | Shane Rawley | .07 | .03 | .01 |
| 255 | Bruce Benedict | .03 | .01 | .00 |
| 256 | Dave Geisel | .03 | .01 | .00 |
| 257 | Julio Cruz | .03 | .01 | .00 |
| 258 | Luis Sanchez | .03 | .01 | .00 |
| 259 | Sparky Anderson MGR | .06 | .02 | .00 |
| 260 | Scott McGregor | .08 | .03 | .00 |
| 261 | Bobby Brown | .03 | .01 | .00 |
| 262 | Tom Candiotti | .15 | .06 | .01 |
| 263 | Jack Fimple | .05 | .02 | .00 |
| 264 | Doug Frobel | .07 | .03 | .01 |
| 265 | Donnie Hill | .08 | .03 | .01 |
| 266 | Steve Lubratich | .05 | .02 | .00 |
| 267 | Carmelo Martinez | .25 | .10 | .02 |
| 268 | Jack O'Connor | .03 | .01 | .00 |
| 269 | Aurelio Rodriguez | .03 | .01 | .00 |
| 270 | Jeff Russell | .06 | .02 | .00 |
| 271 | Moose Haas | .05 | .02 | .00 |
| 272 | Rick Dempsey | .05 | .02 | .00 |
| 273 | Charlie Puleo | .03 | .01 | .00 |
| 274 | Rick Monday | .05 | .02 | .00 |
| 275 | Len Matuszek | .03 | .01 | .00 |
| 276 | Angels TL: | .12 | .02 | .00 |
| | Rod Carew | | | |
| | Geoff Zahn | | | |
| 277 | Eddie Whitson | .06 | .02 | .00 |
| 278 | Jorge Bell | .15 | .06 | .01 |
| 279 | Ivan DeJesus | .03 | .01 | .00 |
| 280 | Floyd Bannister | .07 | .03 | .01 |
| 281 | Larry Milbourne | .03 | .01 | .00 |
| 282 | Jim Barr | .03 | .01 | .00 |
| 283 | Larry Biittner | .03 | .01 | .00 |
| 284 | Howard Bailey | .03 | .01 | .00 |
| 285 | Darrell Porter | .05 | .02 | .00 |
| 286 | Lary Sorensen | .03 | .01 | .00 |
| 287 | Warren Cromartie | .03 | .01 | .00 |
| 288 | Jim Beattie | .03 | .01 | .00 |
| 289 | Randy Johnson | .03 | .01 | .00 |
| 290 | Dave Dravecky | .07 | .03 | .01 |
| 291 | Chuck Tanner MGR | .05 | .02 | .00 |
| 292 | Tony Scott | .03 | .01 | .00 |
| 293 | Ed Lynch | .03 | .01 | .00 |
| 294 | U.L. Washington | .03 | .01 | .00 |
| 295 | Mike Flanagan | .07 | .03 | .01 |
| 296 | Jeff Newman | .03 | .01 | .00 |
| 297 | Bruce Berenyi | .03 | .01 | .00 |
| 298 | Jim Gantner | .05 | .02 | .00 |
| 299 | John Butcher | .03 | .01 | .00 |
| 300 | Pete Rose | 1.25 | .50 | .12 |
| 301 | Frank LaCorte | .03 | .01 | .00 |
| 302 | Barry Bonnell | .03 | .01 | .00 |
| 303 | Marty Castillo | .03 | .01 | .00 |
| 304 | Warren Brusstar | .03 | .01 | .00 |
| 305 | Roy Smalley | .05 | .02 | .00 |
| 306 | Dodgers TL: | .10 | .02 | .00 |
| | Pedro Guerrero | | | |
| | Bob Welch | | | |
| 307 | Bobby Mitchell | .03 | .01 | .00 |
| 308 | Ron Hassey | .03 | .01 | .00 |
| 309 | Tony Phillips | .06 | .02 | .00 |
| 310 | Willie McGee | .30 | .12 | .03 |
| 311 | Jerry Koosman | .08 | .03 | .01 |
| 312 | Jorge Orta | .03 | .01 | .00 |
| 313 | Mike Jorgensen | .03 | .01 | .00 |
| 314 | Orlando Mercado | .05 | .02 | .00 |
| 315 | Bob Grich | .07 | .03 | .01 |
| 316 | Mark Bradley | .09 | .04 | .01 |
| 317 | Greg Pryor | .03 | .01 | .00 |
| 318 | Bill Gullickson | .05 | .02 | .00 |
| 319 | Al Bumbry | .03 | .01 | .00 |
| 320 | Bob Stanley | .05 | .02 | .00 |
| 321 | Harvey Kuenn MGR | .05 | .02 | .00 |
| 322 | Ken Schrom | .05 | .02 | .00 |
| 323 | Alan Knicely | .03 | .01 | .00 |
| 324 | Alejandro Pena | .20 | .08 | .02 |
| 325 | Darrell Evans | .10 | .04 | .01 |
| 326 | Bob Kearney | .03 | .01 | .00 |
| 327 | Ruppert Jones | .03 | .01 | .00 |
| 328 | Vern Ruhle | .03 | .01 | .00 |
| 329 | Pat Tabler | .09 | .04 | .01 |
| 330 | John Candelaria | .08 | .03 | .01 |
| 331 | Bucky Dent | .06 | .02 | .00 |
| 332 | Kevin Gross | .20 | .08 | .02 |
| 333 | Larry Herndon | .05 | .02 | .00 |
| 334 | Chuck Rainey | .03 | .01 | .00 |
| 335 | Don Baylor | .12 | .05 | .01 |
| 336 | Seattle Mariners TL: | .08 | .02 | .00 |
| | Pat Putnam | | | |
| | Matt Young | | | |
| 337 | Kevin Hagen | .07 | .03 | .01 |
| 338 | Mike Warren | .10 | .04 | .01 |
| 339 | Roy Lee Jackson | .03 | .01 | .00 |
| 340 | Hal McRae | .06 | .02 | .00 |
| 341 | Dave Tobik | .03 | .01 | .00 |
| 342 | Tim Foli | .03 | .01 | .00 |
| 343 | Mark Davis | .03 | .01 | .00 |
| 344 | Rick Miller | .03 | .01 | .00 |
| 345 | Kent Hrbek | .35 | .14 | .03 |
| 346 | Kurt Bevacqua | .03 | .01 | .00 |
| 347 | Allan Ramirez | .03 | .01 | .00 |
| 348 | Toby Harrah | .05 | .02 | .00 |
| 349 | Bob L. Gibson | .06 | .02 | .00 |
| | (Brewers Pitcher) | | | |
| 350 | George Foster | .14 | .06 | .01 |
| 351 | Russ Nixon MGR | .03 | .01 | .00 |
| 352 | Dave Stewart | .03 | .01 | .00 |
| 353 | Jim Anderson | .03 | .01 | .00 |
| 354 | Jeff Burroughs | .05 | .02 | .00 |
| 355 | Jason Thompson | .07 | .03 | .01 |

| # | Player | | | |
|---|--------|----|----|----|
| ☐ 356 | Glenn Abbott | .03 | .01 | .00 |
| ☐ 357 | Ron Cey | .10 | .04 | .01 |
| ☐ 358 | Bob Dernier | .07 | .03 | .01 |
| ☐ 359 | Jim Acker | .12 | .05 | .01 |
| ☐ 360 | Willie Randolph | .06 | .02 | .00 |
| ☐ 361 | Dave Smith | .07 | .03 | .01 |
| ☐ 362 | David Green | .05 | .02 | .00 |
| ☐ 363 | Tim Laudner | .03 | .01 | .00 |
| ☐ 364 | Scott Fletcher | .05 | .02 | .00 |
| ☐ 365 | Steve Bedrosian | .06 | .02 | .00 |
| ☐ 366 | Padres TL: <br> Terry Kennedy <br> Dave Dravecky | .08 | .02 | .00 |
| ☐ 367 | Jamie Easterly | .03 | .01 | .00 |
| ☐ 368 | Hubie Brooks | .10 | .04 | .01 |
| ☐ 369 | Steve McCatty | .03 | .01 | .00 |
| ☐ 370 | Tim Raines | .35 | .14 | .03 |
| ☐ 371 | Dave Gumpert | .03 | .01 | .00 |
| ☐ 372 | Gary Roenicke | .05 | .02 | .00 |
| ☐ 373 | Bill Scherrer | .06 | .02 | .00 |
| ☐ 374 | Don Money | .03 | .01 | .00 |
| ☐ 375 | Dennis Leonard | .06 | .02 | .00 |
| ☐ 376 | Dave Anderson | .09 | .04 | .01 |
| ☐ 377 | Danny Darwin | .03 | .01 | .00 |
| ☐ 378 | Bob Brenly | .07 | .03 | .01 |
| ☐ 379 | Checklist 265-396 | .08 | .01 | .00 |
| ☐ 380 | Steve Garvey | .45 | .18 | .04 |
| ☐ 381 | Ralph Houk MGR | .06 | .02 | .00 |
| ☐ 382 | Chris Nyman | .05 | .02 | .00 |
| ☐ 383 | Terry Puhl | .05 | .02 | .00 |
| ☐ 384 | Lee Tunnell | .07 | .03 | .01 |
| ☐ 385 | Tony Perez | .12 | .05 | .01 |
| ☐ 386 | George Hendrick AS | .06 | .02 | .00 |
| ☐ 387 | Johnny Ray AS | .07 | .03 | .01 |
| ☐ 388 | Mike Schmidt AS | .30 | .12 | .03 |
| ☐ 389 | Ozzie Smith AS | .08 | .03 | .01 |
| ☐ 390 | Tim Raines AS | .20 | .08 | .02 |
| ☐ 391 | Dale Murphy AS | .35 | .14 | .03 |
| ☐ 392 | Andre Dawson AS | .15 | .06 | .01 |
| ☐ 393 | Gary Carter AS | .25 | .10 | .02 |
| ☐ 394 | Steve Rogers AS | .06 | .02 | .00 |
| ☐ 395 | Steve Carlton AS | .30 | .12 | .03 |
| ☐ 396 | Jesse Orosco AS | .06 | .02 | .00 |
| ☐ 397 | Eddie Murray AS | .35 | .14 | .03 |
| ☐ 398 | Lou Whitaker AS | .10 | .04 | .01 |
| ☐ 399 | George Brett AS | .35 | .14 | .03 |
| ☐ 400 | Cal Ripken AS | .35 | .14 | .03 |
| ☐ 401 | Jim Rice AS | .25 | .10 | .02 |
| ☐ 402 | Dave Winfield AS | .25 | .10 | .02 |
| ☐ 403 | Lloyd Moseby AS | .10 | .04 | .01 |
| ☐ 404 | Ted Simmons AS | .08 | .03 | .01 |
| ☐ 405 | LaMarr Hoyt AS | .06 | .02 | .00 |
| ☐ 406 | Ron Guidry AS | .12 | .05 | .01 |
| ☐ 407 | Dan Quisenberry AS | .12 | .05 | .01 |
| ☐ 408 | Lou Piniella | .08 | .03 | .01 |
| ☐ 409 | Juan Agosto | .05 | .02 | .00 |
| ☐ 410 | Claudell Washington | .06 | .02 | .00 |
| ☐ 411 | Houston Jimenez | .07 | .03 | .01 |
| ☐ 412 | Doug Rader MGR | .05 | .02 | .00 |
| ☐ 413 | Spike Owen | .25 | .10 | .02 |
| ☐ 414 | Mitchell Page | .03 | .01 | .00 |
| ☐ 415 | Tommy John | .14 | .06 | .01 |
| ☐ 416 | Dane Iorg | .03 | .01 | .00 |
| ☐ 417 | Mike Armstrong | .03 | .01 | .00 |
| ☐ 418 | Ron Hodges | .03 | .01 | .00 |
| ☐ 419 | John Henry Johnson | .03 | .01 | .00 |
| ☐ 420 | Cecil Cooper | .14 | .06 | .01 |
| ☐ 421 | Charlie Lea | .05 | .02 | .00 |
| ☐ 422 | Jose Cruz | .10 | .04 | .01 |
| ☐ 423 | Mike Morgan | .03 | .01 | .00 |
| ☐ 424 | Dann Bilardello | .03 | .01 | .00 |
| ☐ 425 | Steve Howe | .05 | .02 | .00 |
| ☐ 426 | Orioles TL: <br> Cal Ripken <br> Mike Boddicker | .15 | .03 | .00 |
| ☐ 427 | Rick Leach | .03 | .01 | .00 |
| ☐ 428 | Fred Breining | .03 | .01 | .00 |
| ☐ 429 | Randy Bush | .05 | .02 | .00 |
| ☐ 430 | Rusty Staub | .09 | .04 | .01 |
| ☐ 431 | Chris Bando | .03 | .01 | .00 |
| ☐ 432 | Charlie Hudson | .15 | .06 | .01 |
| ☐ 433 | Rich Hebner | .03 | .01 | .00 |
| ☐ 434 | Harold Baines | .25 | .10 | .02 |
| ☐ 435 | Neil Allen | .06 | .02 | .00 |
| ☐ 436 | Rick Peters | .03 | .01 | .00 |
| ☐ 437 | Mike Proly | .03 | .01 | .00 |
| ☐ 438 | Biff Pocoroba | .03 | .01 | .00 |
| ☐ 439 | Bob Stoddard | .03 | .01 | .00 |
| ☐ 440 | Steve Kemp | .08 | .03 | .01 |
| ☐ 441 | Bob Lillis MGR | .03 | .01 | .00 |
| ☐ 442 | Byron McLaughlin | .03 | .01 | .00 |
| ☐ 443 | Benny Ayala | .03 | .01 | .00 |
| ☐ 444 | Steve Renko | .03 | .01 | .00 |
| ☐ 445 | Jerry Remy | .03 | .01 | .00 |
| ☐ 446 | Luis Pujols | .03 | .01 | .00 |
| ☐ 447 | Tom Brunansky | .15 | .06 | .01 |
| ☐ 448 | Ben Hayes | .03 | .01 | .00 |
| ☐ 449 | Joe Pettini | .03 | .01 | .00 |
| ☐ 450 | Gary Carter | .35 | .14 | .03 |
| ☐ 451 | Bob Jones | .03 | .01 | .00 |
| ☐ 452 | Chuck Porter | .03 | .01 | .00 |
| ☐ 453 | Willie Upshaw | .08 | .03 | .01 |
| ☐ 454 | Joe Beckwith | .03 | .01 | .00 |
| ☐ 455 | Terry Kennedy | .08 | .03 | .01 |
| ☐ 456 | Chicago Cubs TL: <br> Keith Moreland <br> Fergie Jenkins | .10 | .02 | .00 |
| ☐ 457 | Dave Rozema | .03 | .01 | .00 |
| ☐ 458 | Kiko Garcia | .03 | .01 | .00 |
| ☐ 459 | Kevin Hickey | .03 | .01 | .00 |
| ☐ 460 | Dave Winfield | .40 | .16 | .04 |
| ☐ 461 | Jim Maler | .03 | .01 | .00 |
| ☐ 462 | Lee Lacy | .05 | .02 | .00 |
| ☐ 463 | Dave Engle | .03 | .01 | .00 |
| ☐ 464 | Jeff A. Jones <br> (A's Pitcher) | .05 | .02 | .00 |
| ☐ 465 | Mookie Wilson | .07 | .03 | .01 |
| ☐ 466 | Gene Garber | .03 | .01 | .00 |
| ☐ 467 | Mike Ramsey | .03 | .01 | .00 |
| ☐ 468 | Geoff Zahn | .03 | .01 | .00 |
| ☐ 469 | Tom O'Malley | .03 | .01 | .00 |
| ☐ 470 | Nolan Ryan | .30 | .12 | .03 |
| ☐ 471 | Dick Howser MGR | .05 | .02 | .00 |
| ☐ 472 | Mike Brown <br> (Red Sox Pitcher) | .06 | .02 | .00 |
| ☐ 473 | Jim Dwyer | .03 | .01 | .00 |
| ☐ 474 | Greg Bargar | .05 | .02 | .00 |
| ☐ 475 | Gary Redus | .35 | .14 | .03 |
| ☐ 476 | Tom Tellmann | .03 | .01 | .00 |
| ☐ 477 | Rafael Landestoy | .03 | .01 | .00 |
| ☐ 478 | Alan Bannister | .03 | .01 | .00 |
| ☐ 479 | Frank Tanana | .05 | .02 | .00 |
| ☐ 480 | Ron Kittle | .25 | .10 | .02 |
| ☐ 481 | Mark Thurmond | .20 | .08 | .02 |
| ☐ 482 | Enos Cabell | .03 | .01 | .00 |
| ☐ 483 | Fergie Jenkins | .12 | .05 | .01 |
| ☐ 484 | Ozzie Virgil | .06 | .02 | .00 |
| ☐ 485 | Rick Rhoden | .08 | .03 | .01 |
| ☐ 486 | N.Y. Yankees TL: <br> Don Baylor <br> Ron Guidry | .10 | .02 | .00 |
| ☐ 487 | Ricky Adams | .08 | .03 | .01 |
| ☐ 488 | Jesse Barfield | .18 | .08 | .01 |
| ☐ 489 | Dave Von Ohlen | .05 | .02 | .00 |
| ☐ 490 | Cal Ripken | .65 | .26 | .06 |
| ☐ 491 | Bobby Castillo | .03 | .01 | .00 |
| ☐ 492 | Tucker Ashford | .03 | .01 | .00 |
| ☐ 493 | Mike Norris | .05 | .02 | .00 |
| ☐ 494 | Chili Davis | .09 | .04 | .01 |
| ☐ 495 | Rollie Fingers | .18 | .08 | .01 |
| ☐ 496 | Terry Francona | .05 | .02 | .00 |
| ☐ 497 | Bud Anderson | .03 | .01 | .00 |
| ☐ 498 | Rich Gedman | .10 | .04 | .01 |
| ☐ 499 | Mike Witt | .10 | .04 | .01 |
| ☐ 500 | George Brett | .55 | .22 | .05 |
| ☐ 501 | Steve Henderson | .03 | .01 | .00 |
| ☐ 502 | Joe Torre MGR | .07 | .03 | .01 |
| ☐ 503 | Elias Sosa | .03 | .01 | .00 |
| ☐ 504 | Mickey Rivers | .05 | .02 | .00 |
| ☐ 505 | Pete Vuckovich | .07 | .03 | .01 |
| ☐ 506 | Ernie Whitt | .03 | .01 | .00 |
| ☐ 507 | Mike LaCoss | .03 | .01 | .00 |
| ☐ 508 | Mel Hall | .12 | .05 | .01 |
| ☐ 509 | Brad Havens | .03 | .01 | .00 |
| ☐ 510 | Alan Trammell | .20 | .08 | .02 |
| ☐ 511 | Marty Bystrom | .03 | .01 | .00 |
| ☐ 512 | Oscar Gamble | .05 | .02 | .00 |
| ☐ 513 | Dave Beard | .03 | .01 | .00 |
| ☐ 514 | Floyd Rayford | .03 | .01 | .00 |
| ☐ 515 | Gorman Thomas | .09 | .04 | .01 |
| ☐ 516 | Montreal Expos TL: <br> Al Oliver <br> Charlie Lea | .10 | .02 | .00 |
| ☐ 517 | John Moses | .07 | .03 | .01 |
| ☐ 518 | Greg Walker | .70 | .28 | .07 |
| ☐ 519 | Ron Davis | .03 | .01 | .00 |
| ☐ 520 | Bob Boone | .06 | .02 | .00 |
| ☐ 521 | Pete Falcone | .03 | .01 | .00 |
| ☐ 522 | Dave Bergman | .03 | .01 | .00 |
| ☐ 523 | Glenn Hoffman | .03 | .01 | .00 |
| ☐ 524 | Carlos Diaz | .03 | .01 | .00 |
| ☐ 525 | Willie Wilson | .18 | .08 | .01 |
| ☐ 526 | Ron Oester | .05 | .02 | .00 |
| ☐ 527 | Checklist 397-528 | .08 | .01 | .00 |
| ☐ 528 | Mark Brouhard | .03 | .01 | .00 |
| ☐ 529 | Keith Atherton | .06 | .02 | .00 |

| No. | Player | | | |
|---|---|---|---|---|
| ☐ 530 | Dan Ford | .03 | .01 | .00 |
| ☐ 531 | Steve Boros MGR | .03 | .01 | .00 |
| ☐ 532 | Eric Show | .03 | .01 | .00 |
| ☐ 533 | Ken Landreaux | .05 | .02 | .00 |
| ☐ 534 | Pete O'Brien | .75 | .30 | .07 |
| ☐ 535 | Bo Diaz | .05 | .02 | .00 |
| ☐ 536 | Doug Bair | .03 | .01 | .00 |
| ☐ 537 | Johnny Ray | .10 | .04 | .01 |
| ☐ 538 | Kevin Bass | .09 | .04 | .01 |
| ☐ 539 | George Frazier | .03 | .01 | .00 |
| ☐ 540 | George Hendrick | .08 | .03 | .01 |
| ☐ 541 | Dennis Lamp | .03 | .01 | .00 |
| ☐ 542 | Duane Kuiper | .03 | .01 | .00 |
| ☐ 543 | Craig McMurtry | .09 | .04 | .01 |
| ☐ 544 | Cesar Geronimo | .03 | .01 | .00 |
| ☐ 545 | Bill Buckner | .09 | .04 | .01 |
| ☐ 546 | Indians TL:<br>Mike Hargrove<br>Lary Sorensen | .08 | .02 | .00 |
| ☐ 547 | Mike Moore | .07 | .03 | .01 |
| ☐ 548 | Ron Jackson | .03 | .01 | .00 |
| ☐ 549 | Walt Terrell | .30 | .12 | .03 |
| ☐ 550 | Jim Rice | .35 | .14 | .03 |
| ☐ 551 | Scott Ullger | .05 | .02 | .00 |
| ☐ 552 | Ray Burris | .03 | .01 | .00 |
| ☐ 553 | Joe Nolan | .03 | .01 | .00 |
| ☐ 554 | Ted Power | .07 | .03 | .01 |
| ☐ 555 | Greg Brock | .08 | .03 | .01 |
| ☐ 556 | Joey McLaughlin | .03 | .01 | .00 |
| ☐ 557 | Wayne Tolleson | .05 | .02 | .00 |
| ☐ 558 | Mike Davis | .07 | .03 | .01 |
| ☐ 559 | Mike Scott | .15 | .06 | .01 |
| ☐ 560 | Carlton Fisk | .14 | .06 | .01 |
| ☐ 561 | Whitey Herzog MGR | .06 | .02 | .00 |
| ☐ 562 | Manny Castillo | .03 | .01 | .00 |
| ☐ 563 | Glenn Wilson | .10 | .04 | .01 |
| ☐ 564 | Al Holland | .05 | .02 | .00 |
| ☐ 565 | Leon Durham | .09 | .04 | .01 |
| ☐ 566 | Jim Bibby | .05 | .02 | .00 |
| ☐ 567 | Mike Heath | .03 | .01 | .00 |
| ☐ 568 | Pete Filson | .05 | .02 | .00 |
| ☐ 569 | Bake McBride | .03 | .01 | .00 |
| ☐ 570 | Dan Quisenberry | .18 | .08 | .01 |
| ☐ 571 | Bruce Bochy | .03 | .01 | .00 |
| ☐ 572 | Jerry Royster | .03 | .01 | .00 |
| ☐ 573 | Dave Kingman | .14 | .06 | .01 |
| ☐ 574 | Brian Downing | .05 | .02 | .00 |
| ☐ 575 | Jim Clancy | .05 | .02 | .00 |
| ☐ 576 | Giants TL:<br>Jeff Leonard<br>Atlee Hammaker | .08 | .02 | .00 |
| ☐ 577 | Mark Clear | .03 | .01 | .00 |
| ☐ 578 | Lenn Sakata | .03 | .01 | .00 |
| ☐ 579 | Bob James | .15 | .06 | .01 |
| ☐ 580 | Lonnie Smith | .07 | .03 | .01 |
| ☐ 581 | Jose DeLeon | .25 | .10 | .02 |
| ☐ 582 | Bob McClure | .03 | .01 | .00 |
| ☐ 583 | Derrel Thomas | .03 | .01 | .00 |
| ☐ 584 | Dave Schmidt | .03 | .01 | .00 |
| ☐ 585 | Dan Driessen | .05 | .02 | .00 |
| ☐ 586 | Joe Niekro | .08 | .03 | .01 |
| ☐ 587 | Von Hayes | .15 | .06 | .01 |
| ☐ 588 | Milt Wilcox | .03 | .01 | .00 |
| ☐ 589 | Mike Easler | .07 | .03 | .01 |
| ☐ 590 | Dave Stieb | .18 | .08 | .01 |
| ☐ 591 | Tony LaRussa MGR | .05 | .02 | .00 |
| ☐ 592 | Andre Robertson | .03 | .01 | .00 |
| ☐ 593 | Jeff Lahti | .03 | .01 | .00 |
| ☐ 594 | Gene Richards | .03 | .01 | .00 |
| ☐ 595 | Jeff Reardon | .07 | .03 | .01 |
| ☐ 596 | Ryne Sandberg | 1.00 | .40 | .10 |
| ☐ 597 | Rick Camp | .03 | .01 | .00 |
| ☐ 598 | Rusty Kuntz | .03 | .01 | .00 |
| ☐ 599 | Doug Sisk | .12 | .05 | .01 |
| ☐ 600 | Rod Carew | .35 | .14 | .03 |
| ☐ 601 | John Tudor | .20 | .08 | .02 |
| ☐ 602 | John Wathan | .03 | .01 | .00 |
| ☐ 603 | Renie Martin | .03 | .01 | .00 |
| ☐ 604 | John Lowenstein | .03 | .01 | .00 |
| ☐ 605 | Mike Caldwell | .05 | .02 | .00 |
| ☐ 606 | Blue Jays TL:<br>Lloyd Moseby<br>Dave Stieb | .10 | .02 | .00 |
| ☐ 607 | Tom Hume | .03 | .01 | .00 |
| ☐ 608 | Bobby Johnson | .03 | .01 | .00 |
| ☐ 609 | Dan Meyer | .03 | .01 | .00 |
| ☐ 610 | Steve Sax | .18 | .08 | .01 |
| ☐ 611 | Chet Lemon | .06 | .02 | .00 |
| ☐ 612 | Harry Spilman | .03 | .01 | .00 |
| ☐ 613 | Greg Gross | .03 | .01 | .00 |
| ☐ 614 | Len Barker | .05 | .02 | .00 |
| ☐ 615 | Garry Templeton | .09 | .04 | .01 |
| ☐ 616 | Don Robinson | .03 | .01 | .00 |
| ☐ 617 | Rick Cerone | .03 | .01 | .00 |
| ☐ 618 | Dickie Noles | .03 | .01 | .00 |
| ☐ 619 | Jerry Dybzinski | .03 | .01 | .00 |
| ☐ 620 | Al Oliver | .12 | .05 | .01 |
| ☐ 621 | Frank Howard MGR | .05 | .02 | .00 |
| ☐ 622 | Al Cowens | .05 | .02 | .00 |
| ☐ 623 | Ron Washington | .03 | .01 | .00 |
| ☐ 624 | Terry Harper | .03 | .01 | .00 |
| ☐ 625 | Larry Gura | .05 | .02 | .00 |
| ☐ 626 | Bob Clark | .03 | .01 | .00 |
| ☐ 627 | Dave LaPoint | .05 | .02 | .00 |
| ☐ 628 | Ed Jurak | .03 | .01 | .00 |
| ☐ 629 | Rick Langford | .03 | .01 | .00 |
| ☐ 630 | Ted Simmons | .10 | .04 | .01 |
| ☐ 631 | Denny Martinez | .03 | .01 | .00 |
| ☐ 632 | Tom Foley | .05 | .02 | .00 |
| ☐ 633 | Mike Krukow | .07 | .03 | .01 |
| ☐ 634 | Mike Marshall | .15 | .06 | .01 |
| ☐ 635 | Dave Righetti | .15 | .06 | .01 |
| ☐ 636 | Pat Putnam | .03 | .01 | .00 |
| ☐ 637 | Phillies TL:<br>Gary Matthews<br>John Denny | .08 | .02 | .00 |
| ☐ 638 | George Vukovich | .03 | .01 | .00 |
| ☐ 639 | Rick Lysander | .05 | .02 | .00 |
| ☐ 640 | Lance Parrish | .25 | .10 | .02 |
| ☐ 641 | Mike Richardt | .03 | .01 | .00 |
| ☐ 642 | Tom Underwood | .03 | .01 | .00 |
| ☐ 643 | Mike Brown<br>(Angels OF) | .25 | .10 | .02 |
| ☐ 644 | Tim Lollar | .03 | .01 | .00 |
| ☐ 645 | Tony Pena | .12 | .05 | .01 |
| ☐ 646 | Checklist 529-660 | .08 | .01 | .00 |
| ☐ 647 | Ron Roenicke | .03 | .01 | .00 |
| ☐ 648 | Len Whitehouse | .03 | .01 | .00 |
| ☐ 649 | Tom Herr | .09 | .04 | .01 |
| ☐ 650 | Phil Niekro | .18 | .08 | .01 |
| ☐ 651 | John McNamara MGR | .05 | .02 | .00 |
| ☐ 652 | Rudy May | .03 | .01 | .00 |
| ☐ 653 | Dave Stapleton | .03 | .01 | .00 |
| ☐ 654 | Bob Bailor | .03 | .01 | .00 |
| ☐ 655 | Amos Otis | .06 | .02 | .00 |
| ☐ 656 | Bryn Smith | .05 | .02 | .00 |
| ☐ 657 | Thad Bosley | .03 | .01 | .00 |
| ☐ 658 | Jerry Augustine | .03 | .01 | .00 |
| ☐ 659 | Duane Walker | .03 | .01 | .00 |
| ☐ 660 | Ray Knight | .08 | .03 | .01 |
| ☐ 661 | Steve Yeager | .05 | .02 | .00 |
| ☐ 662 | Tom Brennan | .03 | .01 | .00 |
| ☐ 663 | Johnnie LeMaster | .03 | .01 | .00 |
| ☐ 664 | Dave Stegman | .03 | .01 | .00 |
| ☐ 665 | Buddy Bell | .10 | .04 | .01 |
| ☐ 666 | Detroit Tigers TL:<br>Lou Whitaker<br>Jack Morris | .12 | .02 | .00 |
| ☐ 667 | Vance Law | .03 | .01 | .00 |
| ☐ 668 | Larry McWilliams | .05 | .02 | .00 |
| ☐ 669 | Dave Lopes | .07 | .03 | .01 |
| ☐ 670 | Rich Gossage | .18 | .08 | .01 |
| ☐ 671 | Jamie Quirk | .03 | .01 | .00 |
| ☐ 672 | Ricky Nelson | .08 | .03 | .01 |
| ☐ 673 | Mike Walters | .08 | .03 | .01 |
| ☐ 674 | Tim Flannery | .03 | .01 | .00 |
| ☐ 675 | Pascual Perez | .05 | .02 | .00 |
| ☐ 676 | Brian Giles | .03 | .01 | .00 |
| ☐ 677 | Doyle Alexander | .05 | .02 | .00 |
| ☐ 678 | Chris Speier | .03 | .01 | .00 |
| ☐ 679 | Art Howe | .03 | .01 | .00 |
| ☐ 680 | Fred Lynn | .20 | .08 | .02 |
| ☐ 681 | Tom Lasorda MGR | .06 | .02 | .00 |
| ☐ 682 | Dan Morogiello | .05 | .02 | .00 |
| ☐ 683 | Marty Barrett | 1.25 | .50 | .12 |
| ☐ 684 | Bob Shirley | .03 | .01 | .00 |
| ☐ 685 | Willie Aikens | .05 | .02 | .00 |
| ☐ 686 | Joe Price | .03 | .01 | .00 |
| ☐ 687 | Roy Howell | .03 | .01 | .00 |
| ☐ 688 | George Wright | .03 | .01 | .00 |
| ☐ 689 | Mike Fischlin | .03 | .01 | .00 |
| ☐ 690 | Jack Clark | .12 | .05 | .01 |
| ☐ 691 | Steve Lake | .05 | .02 | .00 |
| ☐ 692 | Dickie Thon | .05 | .02 | .00 |
| ☐ 693 | Alan Wiggins | .06 | .02 | .00 |
| ☐ 694 | Mike Stanton | .03 | .01 | .00 |
| ☐ 695 | Lou Whitaker | .15 | .06 | .01 |
| ☐ 696 | Pirates TL:<br>Bill Madlock<br>Rick Rhoden | .10 | .02 | .00 |
| ☐ 697 | Dale Murray | .03 | .01 | .00 |
| ☐ 698 | Marc Hill | .03 | .01 | .00 |
| ☐ 699 | Dave Rucker | .03 | .01 | .00 |
| ☐ 700 | Mike Schmidt | .45 | .18 | .04 |
| ☐ 701 | NL Active Batting:<br>Bill Madlock | .20 | .08 | .02 |

|  | | | |
|---|---|---|---|
| Pete Rose | | | |
| Dave Parker | | | |
| ☐ 702 NL Active Hits: | .20 | .08 | .02 |
| Pete Rose | | | |
| Rusty Staub | | | |
| Tony Perez | | | |
| ☐ 703 NL Active Home Run: | .18 | .08 | .01 |
| Mike Schmidt | | | |
| Tony Perez | | | |
| Dave Kingman | | | |
| ☐ 704 NL Active RBI: | .10 | .04 | .01 |
| Tony Perez | | | |
| Rusty Staub | | | |
| Al Oliver | | | |
| ☐ 705 NL Active Steals: | .10 | .04 | .01 |
| Joe Morgan | | | |
| Cesar Cedeno | | | |
| Larry Bowa | | | |
| ☐ 706 NL Active Victory: | .20 | .08 | .02 |
| Steve Carlton | | | |
| Fergie Jenkins | | | |
| Tom Seaver | | | |
| ☐ 707 NL Active Strikeout: | .20 | .08 | .02 |
| Steve Carlton | | | |
| Nolan Ryan | | | |
| Tom Seaver | | | |
| ☐ 708 NL Active ERA: | .18 | .08 | .01 |
| Tom Seaver | | | |
| Steve Carlton | | | |
| Steve Rogers | | | |
| ☐ 709 NL Active Save: | .08 | .03 | .01 |
| Bruce Sutter | | | |
| Tug McGraw | | | |
| Gene Garber | | | |
| ☐ 710 AL Active Batting: | .20 | .08 | .02 |
| Rod Carew | | | |
| George Brett | | | |
| Cecil Cooper | | | |
| ☐ 711 AL Active Hits: | .18 | .08 | .01 |
| Rod Carew | | | |
| Bert Campaneris | | | |
| Reggie Jackson | | | |
| ☐ 712 AL Active Home Run: | .18 | .08 | .01 |
| Reggie Jackson | | | |
| Graig Nettles | | | |
| Greg Luzinski | | | |
| ☐ 713 AL Active RBI: | .18 | .08 | .01 |
| Reggie Jackson | | | |
| Ted Simmons | | | |
| Graig Nettles | | | |
| ☐ 714 AL Active Steals: | .07 | .03 | .01 |
| Bert Campaneris | | | |
| Dave Lopes | | | |
| Omar Moreno | | | |
| ☐ 715 AL Active Victory: | .18 | .08 | .01 |
| Jim Palmer | | | |
| Don Sutton | | | |
| Tommy John | | | |
| ☐ 716 AL Active Strikeout: | .09 | .04 | .01 |
| Don Sutton | | | |
| Bert Blyleven | | | |
| Jerry Koosman | | | |
| ☐ 717 AL Active ERA: | .15 | .06 | .01 |
| Jim Palmer | | | |
| Rollie Fingers | | | |
| Ron Guidry | | | |
| ☐ 718 AL Active Save: | .15 | .06 | .01 |
| Rollie Fingers | | | |
| Rich Gossage | | | |
| Dan Quisenberry | | | |
| ☐ 719 Andy Hassler | .03 | .01 | .00 |
| ☐ 720 Dwight Evans | .10 | .04 | .01 |
| ☐ 721 Del Crandall MGR | .03 | .01 | .00 |
| ☐ 722 Bob Welch | .06 | .02 | .00 |
| ☐ 723 Rich Dauer | .03 | .01 | .00 |
| ☐ 724 Eric Rasmussen | .03 | .01 | .00 |
| ☐ 725 Cesar Cedeno | .06 | .02 | .00 |
| ☐ 726 Brewers TL: | .08 | .02 | .00 |
| Ted Simmons | | | |
| Moose Haas | | | |
| ☐ 727 Joel Youngblood | .03 | .01 | .00 |
| ☐ 728 Tug McGraw | .09 | .04 | .01 |
| ☐ 729 Gene Tenace | .03 | .01 | .00 |
| ☐ 730 Bruce Sutter | .15 | .06 | .01 |
| ☐ 731 Lynn Jones | .03 | .01 | .00 |
| ☐ 732 Terry Crowley | .03 | .01 | .00 |
| ☐ 733 Dave Collins | .05 | .02 | .00 |
| ☐ 734 Odell Jones | .03 | .01 | .00 |
| ☐ 735 Rick Burleson | .05 | .02 | .00 |
| ☐ 736 Dick Ruthven | .03 | .01 | .00 |
| ☐ 737 Jim Essian | .03 | .01 | .00 |
| ☐ 738 Bill Schroeder | .20 | .08 | .02 |
| ☐ 739 Bob Watson | .05 | .02 | .00 |
| ☐ 740 Tom Seaver | .40 | .16 | .04 |
| ☐ 741 Wayne Gross | .03 | .01 | .00 |
| ☐ 742 Dick Williams MGR | .03 | .01 | .00 |
| ☐ 743 Don Hood | .03 | .01 | .00 |
| ☐ 744 Jamie Allen | .10 | .04 | .01 |
| ☐ 745 Dennis Eckersley | .06 | .02 | .00 |
| ☐ 746 Mickey Hatcher | .03 | .01 | .00 |
| ☐ 747 Pat Zachry | .03 | .01 | .00 |
| ☐ 748 Jeff Leonard | .06 | .02 | .00 |
| ☐ 749 Doug Flynn | .03 | .01 | .00 |
| ☐ 750 Jim Palmer | .25 | .10 | .02 |
| ☐ 751 Charlie Moore | .03 | .01 | .00 |
| ☐ 752 Phil Garner | .05 | .02 | .00 |
| ☐ 753 Doug Gwosdz | .03 | .01 | .00 |
| ☐ 754 Kent Tekulve | .07 | .03 | .01 |
| ☐ 755 Garry Maddox | .05 | .02 | .00 |
| ☐ 756 Reds TL: | .08 | .02 | .00 |
| Ron Oester | | | |
| Mario Soto | | | |
| ☐ 757 Larry Bowa | .09 | .04 | .01 |
| ☐ 758 Bill Stein | .03 | .01 | .00 |
| ☐ 759 Richard Dotson | .07 | .03 | .01 |
| ☐ 760 Bob Horner | .25 | .10 | .02 |
| ☐ 761 John Montefusco | .05 | .02 | .00 |
| ☐ 762 Rance Mulliniks | .03 | .01 | .00 |
| ☐ 763 Craig Swan | .03 | .01 | .00 |
| ☐ 764 Mike Hargrove | .05 | .02 | .00 |
| ☐ 765 Ken Forsch | .03 | .01 | .00 |
| ☐ 766 Mike Vail | .03 | .01 | .00 |
| ☐ 767 Carney Lansford | .09 | .04 | .01 |
| ☐ 768 Champ Summers | .03 | .01 | .00 |
| ☐ 769 Bill Caudill | .06 | .02 | .00 |
| ☐ 770 Ken Griffey | .07 | .03 | .01 |
| ☐ 771 Billy Gardner MGR | .03 | .01 | .00 |
| ☐ 772 Jim Slaton | .03 | .01 | .00 |
| ☐ 773 Todd Cruz | .03 | .01 | .00 |
| ☐ 774 Tom Gorman | .10 | .04 | .01 |
| ☐ 775 Dave Parker | .20 | .08 | .02 |
| ☐ 776 Craig Reynolds | .03 | .01 | .00 |
| ☐ 777 Tom Paciorek | .03 | .01 | .00 |
| ☐ 778 Andy Hawkins | .20 | .08 | .02 |
| ☐ 779 Jim Sundberg | .05 | .02 | .00 |
| ☐ 780 Steve Carlton | .35 | .14 | .03 |
| ☐ 781 Checklist 661-792 | .08 | .01 | .00 |
| ☐ 782 Steve Balboni | .07 | .03 | .01 |
| ☐ 783 Luis Leal | .03 | .01 | .00 |
| ☐ 784 Leon Roberts | .03 | .01 | .00 |
| ☐ 785 Joaquin Andujar | .12 | .05 | .01 |
| ☐ 786 Red Sox TL: | .25 | .05 | .01 |
| Wade Boggs | | | |
| Bob Ojeda | | | |
| ☐ 787 Bill Campbell | .03 | .01 | .00 |
| ☐ 788 Milt May | .03 | .01 | .00 |
| ☐ 789 Bert Blyleven | .12 | .05 | .01 |
| ☐ 790 Doug DeCinces | .09 | .04 | .01 |
| ☐ 791 Terry Forster | .08 | .03 | .01 |
| ☐ 792 Bill Russell | .06 | .02 | .00 |

# 1984 Topps Traded

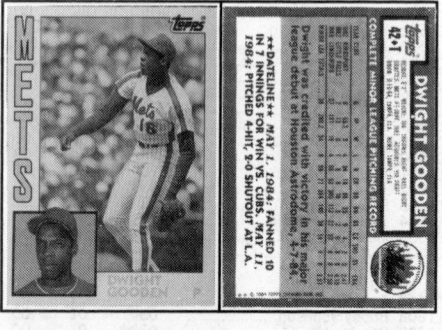

The cards in this 132 card set measure 2 1/2" by 3 1/2". In its now standard procedure, Topps issued its traded (or extended) set for the fourth year in a row. Because all photos and statistics of its regular set for the year were developed during the fall and winter months of the preceding year, players who changed teams during the fall, winter and spring months are portrayed with the teams they were with in 1983. The Traded set amends the shortcomings of the regular set by presenting the players with their proper teams for the current year. Rookies not contained in the regular set are also picked up in the Traded set. Again this year, the Topps affiliate in Ireland printed the cards, and the cards were available through hobby channels only.

|  |  | MINT | VG-E | F-G |
|---|---|---|---|---|
| COMPLETE SET | | 75.00 | 30.00 | 7.50 |
| COMMON PLAYER | | .10 | .04 | .01 |

| | | MINT | VG-E | F-G |
|---|---|---|---|---|
| ☐ | 1T Willie Aikens | .15 | .06 | .01 |
| ☐ | 2T Luis Aponte | .10 | .04 | .01 |
| ☐ | 3T Mike Armstrong | .10 | .04 | .01 |
| ☐ | 4T Bob Bailor | .10 | .04 | .01 |
| ☐ | 5T Dusty Baker | .15 | .06 | .01 |
| ☐ | 6T Steve Balboni | .20 | .08 | .02 |
| ☐ | 7T Alan Bannister | .10 | .04 | .01 |
| ☐ | 8T Dave Beard | .10 | .04 | .01 |
| ☐ | 9T Joe Beckwith | .10 | .04 | .01 |
| ☐ | 10T Bruce Berenyi | .15 | .06 | .01 |
| ☐ | 11T Dave Bergman | .10 | .04 | .01 |
| ☐ | 12T Tony Bernazard | .15 | .06 | .01 |
| ☐ | 13T Yogi Berra | .30 | .12 | .03 |
| ☐ | 14T Barry Bonnell | .10 | .04 | .01 |
| ☐ | 15T Phil Bradley | 4.00 | 1.60 | .40 |
| ☐ | 16T Fred Breining | .10 | .04 | .01 |
| ☐ | 17T Bill Buckner | .35 | .14 | .03 |
| ☐ | 18T Ray Burris | .10 | .04 | .01 |
| ☐ | 19T John Butcher | .10 | .04 | .01 |
| ☐ | 20T Brett Butler | .35 | .14 | .03 |
| ☐ | 21T Enos Cabell | .10 | .04 | .01 |
| ☐ | 22T Bill Campbell | .15 | .06 | .01 |
| ☐ | 23T Bill Caudill | .15 | .06 | .01 |
| ☐ | 24T Bob Clark | .10 | .04 | .01 |
| ☐ | 25T Bryan Clark | .10 | .04 | .01 |
| ☐ | 26T Jaime Cocanower | .15 | .06 | .01 |
| ☐ | 27T Ron Darling | 6.00 | 2.40 | .60 |
| ☐ | 28T Alvin Davis | 4.00 | 1.60 | .40 |
| ☐ | 29T Ken Dayley | .15 | .06 | .01 |
| ☐ | 30T Jeff Dedmon | .15 | .06 | .01 |
| ☐ | 31T Bob Dernier | .15 | .06 | .01 |
| ☐ | 32T Carlos Diaz | .10 | .04 | .01 |
| ☐ | 33T Mike Easler | .15 | .06 | .01 |
| ☐ | 34T Dennis Eckersley | .15 | .06 | .01 |
| ☐ | 35T Jim Essian | .10 | .04 | .01 |
| ☐ | 36T Darrell Evans | .25 | .10 | .02 |
| ☐ | 37T Mike Fitzgerald | .15 | .06 | .01 |
| ☐ | 38T Tim Foli | .10 | .04 | .01 |
| ☐ | 39T George Frazier | .10 | .04 | .01 |
| ☐ | 40T Rich Gale | .10 | .04 | .01 |
| ☐ | 41T Barbaro Garbey | .20 | .08 | .02 |
| ☐ | 42T Dwight Gooden | 40.00 | 16.00 | 4.00 |
| ☐ | 43T Rich Gossage | .35 | .14 | .03 |
| ☐ | 44T Wayne Gross | .10 | .04 | .01 |
| ☐ | 45T Mark Gubicza | .60 | .24 | .06 |
| ☐ | 46T Jackie Gutierrez | .25 | .10 | .02 |
| ☐ | 47T Mel Hall | .25 | .10 | .02 |
| ☐ | 48T Toby Harrah | .15 | .06 | .01 |
| ☐ | 49T Ron Hassey | .10 | .04 | .01 |
| ☐ | 50T Rich Hebner | .10 | .04 | .01 |
| ☐ | 51T Willie Hernandez | .35 | .14 | .03 |
| ☐ | 52T Ricky Horton | .35 | .14 | .03 |
| ☐ | 53T Art Howe | .10 | .04 | .01 |
| ☐ | 54T Dane Iorg | .10 | .04 | .01 |
| ☐ | 55T Brook Jacoby | 1.50 | .60 | .15 |
| ☐ | 56T Mike Jeffcoat | .20 | .08 | .02 |
| ☐ | 57T Dave Johnson MGR | .20 | .08 | .02 |
| ☐ | 58T Lynn Jones | .10 | .04 | .01 |
| ☐ | 59T Ruppert Jones | .15 | .06 | .01 |
| ☐ | 60T Mike Jorgensen | .10 | .04 | .01 |
| ☐ | 61T Bob Kearney | .10 | .04 | .01 |
| ☐ | 62T Jimmy Key | 1.00 | .40 | .10 |
| ☐ | 63T Dave Kingman | .50 | .20 | .05 |
| ☐ | 64T Jerry Koosman | .30 | .12 | .03 |
| ☐ | 65T Wayne Krenchicki | .10 | .04 | .01 |
| ☐ | 66T Rusty Kuntz | .10 | .04 | .01 |
| ☐ | 67T Rene Lachemann MGR | .10 | .04 | .01 |
| ☐ | 68T Frank LaCorte | .10 | .04 | .01 |
| ☐ | 69T Dennis Lamp | .10 | .04 | .01 |
| ☐ | 70T Mark Langston | 1.50 | .60 | .15 |
| ☐ | 71T Rick Leach | .10 | .04 | .01 |
| ☐ | 72T Craig Lefferts | .10 | .04 | .01 |
| ☐ | 73T Gary Lucas | .10 | .04 | .01 |
| ☐ | 74T Jerry Martin | .10 | .04 | .01 |
| ☐ | 75T Carmelo Martinez | .30 | .12 | .03 |
| ☐ | 76T Mike Mason | .30 | .12 | .03 |
| ☐ | 77T Gary Matthews | .20 | .08 | .02 |
| ☐ | 78T Andy McGaffigan | .10 | .04 | .01 |
| ☐ | 79T Larry Milbourne | .10 | .04 | .01 |
| ☐ | 80T Sid Monge | .10 | .04 | .01 |
| ☐ | 81T Jackie Moore MGR | .10 | .04 | .01 |
| ☐ | 82T Joe Morgan | 1.00 | .40 | .10 |
| ☐ | 83T Graig Nettles | .50 | .20 | .05 |
| ☐ | 84T Phil Niekro | 1.00 | .40 | .10 |
| ☐ | 85T Ken Oberkfell | .15 | .06 | .01 |
| ☐ | 86T Mike O'Berry | .10 | .04 | .01 |
| ☐ | 87T Al Oliver | .25 | .10 | .02 |
| ☐ | 88T Jorge Orta | .10 | .04 | .01 |
| ☐ | 89T Amos Otis | .20 | .08 | .02 |
| ☐ | 90T Dave Parker | 1.00 | .40 | .10 |
| ☐ | 91T Tony Perez | .45 | .18 | .04 |
| ☐ | 92T Gerald Perry | .35 | .14 | .03 |
| ☐ | 93T Gary Pettis | .60 | .24 | .06 |
| ☐ | 94T Rob Picciolo | .10 | .04 | .01 |
| ☐ | 95T Vern Rapp MGR | .10 | .04 | .01 |
| ☐ | 96T Floyd Rayford | .10 | .04 | .01 |
| ☐ | 97T Randy Ready | .25 | .10 | .02 |
| ☐ | 98T Ron Reed | .10 | .04 | .01 |
| ☐ | 99T Gene Richards | .10 | .04 | .01 |
| ☐ | 100T Jose Rijo | .60 | .24 | .06 |
| ☐ | 101T Jeff Robinson | .25 | .10 | .02 |
| ☐ | 102T Ron Romanick | .75 | .30 | .07 |
| ☐ | 103T Pete Rose | 6.00 | 2.40 | .60 |
| ☐ | 104T Bret Saberhagen | 3.00 | 1.20 | .30 |
| ☐ | 105T Juan Samuel | 1.50 | .60 | .15 |
| ☐ | 106T Scott Sanderson | .15 | .06 | .01 |
| ☐ | 107T Dick Schofield | .75 | .30 | .07 |
| ☐ | 108T Tom Seaver | 1.25 | .50 | .12 |
| ☐ | 109T Jim Slaton | .10 | .04 | .01 |
| ☐ | 110T Mike Smithson | .10 | .04 | .01 |
| ☐ | 111T Lary Sorensen | .10 | .04 | .01 |
| ☐ | 112T Tim Stoddard | .10 | .04 | .01 |
| ☐ | 113T Champ Summers | .10 | .04 | .01 |
| ☐ | 114T Jim Sundberg | .15 | .06 | .01 |
| ☐ | 115T Rick Sutcliffe | .50 | .20 | .05 |
| ☐ | 116T Craig Swan | .10 | .04 | .01 |
| ☐ | 117T Tim Teufel | .50 | .20 | .05 |
| ☐ | 118T Derrel Thomas | .10 | .04 | .01 |
| ☐ | 119T Gorman Thomas | .25 | .10 | .02 |
| ☐ | 120T Alex Trevino | .10 | .04 | .01 |
| ☐ | 121T Manny Trillo | .15 | .06 | .01 |
| ☐ | 122T John Tudor | .40 | .16 | .04 |
| ☐ | 123T Tom Underwood | .10 | .04 | .01 |
| ☐ | 124T Mike Vail | .10 | .04 | .01 |
| ☐ | 125T Tom Waddell | .25 | .10 | .02 |
| ☐ | 126T Gary Ward | .15 | .06 | .01 |
| ☐ | 127T Curt Wilkerson | .15 | .06 | .01 |
| ☐ | 128T Frank Williams | .20 | .08 | .02 |
| ☐ | 129T Glenn Wilson | .30 | .12 | .03 |
| ☐ | 130T Johnny Wockenfuss | .10 | .04 | .01 |
| ☐ | 131T Ned Yost | .10 | .04 | .01 |
| ☐ | 132T Checklist: 1-132 | .20 | .02 | .00 |

# 1984 Topps Glossy 22

The cards in this 22 card set measure 2 1/2" by 3 1/2". Unlike the 1983 Topps Glossy set which was not distributed with its regular baseball cards, the 1984 Topps Glossy set was distributed as inserts in Topps Rak-Paks. The set features the nine American and National League All Stars who started in the 1983 All Star game in Chicago. The managers and team captains (Yastrzemski and Bench) complete the set. The cards are numbered on the back and are ordered by position within league (AL: 1-11 and NL: 12-22).

|  | | MINT | VG-E | F-G |
|---|---|---|---|---|
| COMPLETE SET | | 3.75 | 1.25 | .30 |
| COMMON PLAYER | | .10 | .04 | .01 |
| ☐ 1 | Harvey Kuenn MGR | .10 | .04 | .01 |
| ☐ 2 | Rod Carew | .50 | .20 | .05 |
| ☐ 3 | Manny Trillo | .10 | .04 | .01 |
| ☐ 4 | George Brett | .75 | .30 | .07 |
| ☐ 5 | Robin Yount | .40 | .16 | .04 |
| ☐ 6 | Jim Rice | .45 | .18 | .04 |
| ☐ 7 | Fred Lynn | .25 | .10 | .02 |
| ☐ 8 | Dave Winfield | .40 | .16 | .04 |
| ☐ 9 | Ted Simmons | .15 | .06 | .01 |
| ☐ 10 | Dave Stieb | .20 | .08 | .02 |
| ☐ 11 | Carl Yastrzemski CAPT | .60 | .24 | .06 |
| ☐ 12 | Whitey Herzog MGR | .10 | .04 | .01 |
| ☐ 13 | Al Oliver | .20 | .08 | .02 |
| ☐ 14 | Steve Sax | .30 | .12 | .03 |
| ☐ 15 | Mike Schmidt | .75 | .30 | .07 |
| ☐ 16 | Ozzie Smith | .25 | .10 | .02 |
| ☐ 17 | Tim Raines | .50 | .20 | .05 |
| ☐ 18 | Andre Dawson | .30 | .12 | .03 |
| ☐ 19 | Dale Murphy | .75 | .30 | .07 |
| ☐ 20 | Gary Carter | .40 | .16 | .04 |
| ☐ 21 | Mario Soto | .10 | .04 | .01 |
| ☐ 22 | Johnny Bench CAPT | .35 | .14 | .03 |

## 1984 Topps Glossy 40

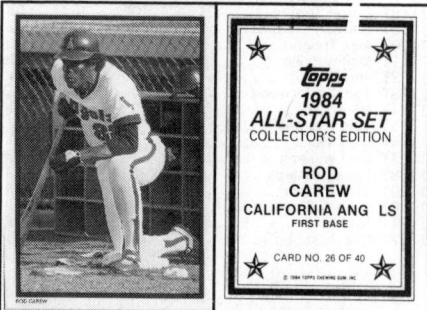

The cards in this 40 card set measure 2 1/2" by 3 1/2". Similar to last year's glossy set, this set was issued as a bonus prize to Topps All-Star Baseball Game cards found in wax packs. Twenty-five bonus runs from the game cards were necessary to obtain a five card subset of the series. There were eight different subsets of five cards. The cards are numbered and contain 20 stars from each league.

|  | | MINT | VG-E | F-G |
|---|---|---|---|---|
| COMPLETE SET | | 12.00 | 5.00 | 1.20 |
| COMMON PLAYER | | .15 | .06 | .01 |
| ☐ 1 | Pete Rose | 1.50 | .60 | .15 |
| ☐ 2 | Lance Parrish | .40 | .16 | .04 |
| ☐ 3 | Steve Rogers | .15 | .06 | .01 |
| ☐ 4 | Eddie Murray | 1.00 | .40 | .10 |
| ☐ 5 | Johnny Ray | .20 | .08 | .02 |
| ☐ 6 | Rickey Henderson | 1.00 | .40 | .10 |
| ☐ 7 | Atlee Hammaker | .15 | .06 | .01 |
| ☐ 8 | Wade Boggs | 2.00 | .80 | .20 |
| ☐ 9 | Gary Carter | .60 | .24 | .06 |
| ☐ 10 | Jack Morris | .35 | .14 | .03 |
| ☐ 11 | Darrell Evans | .20 | .08 | .02 |
| ☐ 12 | George Brett | 1.00 | .40 | .10 |
| ☐ 13 | Bob Horner | .35 | .14 | .03 |
| ☐ 14 | Ron Guidry | .35 | .14 | .03 |

| ☐ 15 | Nolan Ryan | .60 | .24 | .06 |
|---|---|---|---|---|
| ☐ 16 | Dave Winfield | .60 | .24 | .06 |
| ☐ 17 | Ozzie Smith | .15 | .06 | .01 |
| ☐ 18 | Ted Simmons | .20 | .08 | .02 |
| ☐ 19 | Bill Madlock | .25 | .10 | .02 |
| ☐ 20 | Tony Armas | .20 | .08 | .02 |
| ☐ 21 | Al Oliver | .25 | .10 | .02 |
| ☐ 22 | Jim Rice | .75 | .30 | .07 |
| ☐ 23 | George Hendrick | .15 | .06 | .01 |
| ☐ 24 | Dave Stieb | .25 | .10 | .02 |
| ☐ 25 | Pedro Guerrero | .35 | .14 | .03 |
| ☐ 26 | Rod Carew | .60 | .24 | .06 |
| ☐ 27 | Steve Carlton | .60 | .24 | .06 |
| ☐ 28 | Dave Righetti | .25 | .10 | .02 |
| ☐ 29 | Darryl Strawberry | 1.25 | .50 | .12 |
| ☐ 30 | Lou Whitaker | .25 | .10 | .02 |
| ☐ 31 | Dale Murphy | 1.25 | .50 | .12 |
| ☐ 32 | LaMarr Hoyt | .15 | .06 | .01 |
| ☐ 33 | Jesse Orosco | .15 | .06 | .01 |
| ☐ 34 | Cecil Cooper | .25 | .10 | .02 |
| ☐ 35 | Andre Dawson | .30 | .12 | .03 |
| ☐ 36 | Robin Yount | .50 | .20 | .05 |
| ☐ 37 | Tim Raines | .45 | .18 | .04 |
| ☐ 38 | Dan Quisenberry | .25 | .10 | .02 |
| ☐ 39 | Mike Schmidt | 1.00 | .40 | .10 |
| ☐ 40 | Carlton Fisk | .30 | .12 | .03 |

## 1984 Topps Supers 5x7

The cards in this 30 card set measure 4 7/8" by 6 7/8". The 1984 Topps Supers feature enlargements from the 1984 regular set. The cards differ from the corresponding cards of the regular set in size and number only. As one would expect, only those considered stars and superstars appear in this set.

|  | | MINT | VG-E | F-G |
|---|---|---|---|---|
| COMPLETE SET | | 9.00 | 3.75 | .90 |
| COMMON PLAYER | | .20 | .08 | .02 |
| ☐ 1 | Cal Ripken | 1.00 | .40 | .10 |
| ☐ 2 | Dale Murphy | 1.25 | .50 | .12 |
| ☐ 3 | LaMarr Hoyt | .20 | .08 | .02 |
| ☐ 4 | John Denny | .20 | .08 | .02 |
| ☐ 5 | Jim Rice | .60 | .24 | .06 |
| ☐ 6 | Mike Schmidt | 1.00 | .40 | .10 |
| ☐ 7 | Wade Boggs | 2.00 | .80 | .20 |
| ☐ 8 | Bill Madlock | .20 | .08 | .02 |
| ☐ 9 | Dan Quisenberry | .30 | .12 | .03 |
| ☐ 10 | Al Holland | .20 | .08 | .02 |
| ☐ 11 | Ron Kittle | .30 | .12 | .03 |
| ☐ 12 | Darryl Strawberry | 1.25 | .50 | .12 |
| ☐ 13 | George Brett | 1.00 | .40 | .10 |
| ☐ 14 | Bill Buckner | .20 | .08 | .02 |
| ☐ 15 | Carlton Fisk | .30 | .12 | .03 |
| ☐ 16 | Steve Carlton | .50 | .20 | .05 |
| ☐ 17 | Ron Guidry | .35 | .14 | .03 |
| ☐ 18 | Gary Carter | .60 | .24 | .06 |
| ☐ 19 | Rickey Henderson | 1.00 | .40 | .10 |
| ☐ 20 | Andre Dawson | .35 | .14 | .03 |
| ☐ 21 | Reggie Jackson | 1.00 | .40 | .10 |
| ☐ 22 | Steve Garvey | .75 | .30 | .07 |
| ☐ 23 | Fred Lynn | .30 | .12 | .03 |
| ☐ 24 | Pedro Guerrero | .35 | .14 | .03 |
| ☐ 25 | Eddie Murray | 1.00 | .40 | .10 |
| ☐ 26 | Keith Hernandez | .50 | .20 | .05 |
| ☐ 27 | Dave Winfield | .50 | .20 | .05 |
| ☐ 28 | Nolan Ryan | .60 | .24 | .06 |
| ☐ 29 | Robin Yount | .45 | .18 | .04 |
| ☐ 30 | Fernando Valenzuela | .50 | .20 | .05 |

## 1984 Topps Cereal

The cards in this 33 card set measure 2 1/2" by 3 1/2". The cards are numbered both on the front and the back. The 1984 Topps Cereal Series is exactly the same as the Ralston-Purina issue of this year except for a Topps logo and the words "Cereal

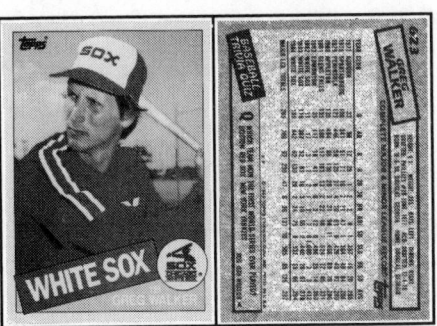

Series" on the tops of the fronts of the cards in place of the Ralston checkerboard background. The checkerboard background is absent from the reverse, and a Topps logo is on the reverse of the cereal cards. These cards were distributed in unmarked boxes of Ralston-Purina cereal with a pack of four cards (three players and a checklist) being inside random cereal boxes. The back of the checklist details an offer to obtain any twelve cards direct from the issuer for only 1.50.

|  | | MINT | VG-E | F-G |
|---|---|---|---|---|
| | COMPLETE SET | 12.00 | 5.00 | 1.20 |
| | COMMON PLAYER | .20 | .08 | .02 |
| ☐ 1 | Eddie Murray | 1.00 | .40 | .10 |
| ☐ 2 | Ozzie Smith | .25 | .10 | .02 |
| ☐ 3 | Ted Simmons | .25 | .10 | .02 |
| ☐ 4 | Pete Rose | 1.25 | .50 | .12 |
| ☐ 5 | Greg Luzinski | .20 | .08 | .02 |
| ☐ 6 | Andre Dawson | .25 | .10 | .02 |
| ☐ 7 | Dave Winfield | .50 | .20 | .05 |
| ☐ 8 | Tom Seaver | .50 | .20 | .05 |
| ☐ 9 | Jim Rice | .60 | .24 | .06 |
| ☐ 10 | Fernando Valenzuela | .50 | .20 | .05 |
| ☐ 11 | Wade Boggs | 2.00 | .80 | .20 |
| ☐ 12 | Dale Murphy | 1.25 | .50 | .12 |
| ☐ 13 | George Brett | 1.00 | .40 | .10 |
| ☐ 14 | Nolan Ryan | .60 | .24 | .06 |
| ☐ 15 | Rickey Henderson | 1.00 | .40 | .10 |
| ☐ 16 | Steve Carlton | .60 | .24 | .06 |
| ☐ 17 | Rod Carew | .60 | .24 | .06 |
| ☐ 18 | Steve Garvey | .60 | .24 | .06 |
| ☐ 19 | Reggie Jackson | 1.00 | .40 | .10 |
| ☐ 20 | Dave Concepcion | .20 | .08 | .02 |
| ☐ 21 | Robin Yount | .50 | .20 | .05 |
| ☐ 22 | Mike Schmidt | 1.00 | .40 | .10 |
| ☐ 23 | Jim Palmer | .40 | .16 | .04 |
| ☐ 24 | Bruce Sutter | .25 | .10 | .02 |
| ☐ 25 | Dan Quisenberry | .25 | .10 | .02 |
| ☐ 26 | Bill Madlock | .20 | .08 | .02 |
| ☐ 27 | Cecil Cooper | .20 | .08 | .02 |
| ☐ 28 | Gary Carter | .60 | .24 | .06 |
| ☐ 29 | Fred Lynn | .25 | .10 | .02 |
| ☐ 30 | Pedro Guerrero | .25 | .10 | .02 |
| ☐ 31 | Ron Guidry | .25 | .10 | .02 |
| ☐ 32 | Keith Hernandez | .35 | .14 | .03 |
| ☐ 33 | Carlton Fisk | .25 | .10 | .02 |
| ☐ 34 | Checklist card | .25 | .02 | .00 |
| | (unnumbered) | | | |

# 1985 Topps

The cards in this 792 card set measure 2 1/2" by 3 1/2". The 1985 Topps set contains full color cards. The fronts feature both the Topps and team logos along with the team name, player's name and his position. The backs feature player statistics with ink colors of light green and maroon on a gray stock. A trivia quiz is included on the lower portion of the

backs. The first ten cards (1-10) are Record Breakers (RB), cards 131-143 are Father and Son (FS) cards, and cards 701 to 722 portray all star selections (AS). Cards 271 to 282 represent "First Draft Picks" still active in the Major Leagues and cards 389-404 feature the coach and players on the 1984 U.S. Olympic Baseball Team. The manager cards in the set are important in that they contain the checklist of that team's players on the back.

|  | | MINT | VG-E | F-G |
|---|---|---|---|---|
| | COMPLETE SET | 55.00 | 20.00 | 5.00 |
| | COMMON PLAYER | .03 | .01 | .00 |
| ☐ 1 | Carlton Fisk RB Longest Game by Catcher | .15 | .04 | .01 |
| ☐ 2 | Steve Garvey RB Consecutive Error-less Games, 1B | .15 | .06 | .01 |
| ☐ 3 | Dwight Gooden RB Most Strikeouts, Rookie, Season | 1.00 | .40 | .10 |
| ☐ 4 | Cliff Johnson RB Most Pinch Homers, Lifetime | .05 | .02 | .00 |
| ☐ 5 | Joe Morgan RB Most Homers, 2B, Lifetime | .10 | .04 | .01 |
| ☐ 6 | Pete Rose RB Most Singles, Lifetime | .40 | .16 | .04 |
| ☐ 7 | Nolan Ryan RB Most Strikeouts, Lifetime | .15 | .06 | .01 |
| ☐ 8 | Juan Samuel RB Most Stolen Bases, Rookie, Season | .10 | .04 | .01 |
| ☐ 9 | Bruce Sutter RB Most Saves, Season, NL | .08 | .03 | .01 |
| ☐ 10 | Don Sutton RB Most Seasons, 100 or more K's | .08 | .03 | .01 |
| ☐ 11 | Ralph Houk MGR (checklist back) | .05 | .02 | .00 |
| ☐ 12 | Dave Lopes | .06 | .02 | .00 |
| ☐ 13 | Tim Lollar | .03 | .01 | .00 |
| ☐ 14 | Chris Bando | .03 | .01 | .00 |
| ☐ 15 | Jerry Koosman | .07 | .03 | .01 |
| ☐ 16 | Bobby Meacham | .03 | .01 | .00 |
| ☐ 17 | Mike Scott | .15 | .06 | .01 |
| ☐ 18 | Mickey Hatcher | .03 | .01 | .00 |
| ☐ 19 | George Frazier | .03 | .01 | .00 |
| ☐ 20 | Chet Lemon | .05 | .02 | .00 |
| ☐ 21 | Lee Tunnell | .03 | .01 | .00 |
| ☐ 22 | Duane Kuiper | .03 | .01 | .00 |
| ☐ 23 | Bret Saberhagen | 1.25 | .50 | .12 |
| ☐ 24 | Jesse Barfield | .15 | .06 | .01 |
| ☐ 25 | Steve Bedrosian | .06 | .02 | .00 |
| ☐ 26 | Roy Smalley | .05 | .02 | .00 |
| ☐ 27 | Bruce Berenyi | .03 | .01 | .00 |
| ☐ 28 | Dann Bilardello | .03 | .01 | .00 |
| ☐ 29 | Odell Jones | .03 | .01 | .00 |
| ☐ 30 | Cal Ripken | .45 | .18 | .04 |
| ☐ 31 | Terry Whitfield | .03 | .01 | .00 |
| ☐ 32 | Chuck Porter | .03 | .01 | .00 |
| ☐ 33 | Tito Landrum | .03 | .01 | .00 |
| ☐ 34 | Ed Nunez | .08 | .03 | .01 |

| # | Player | | | |
|---|---|---|---|---|
| ☐ 35 | Graig Nettles | .10 | .04 | .01 |
| ☐ 36 | Fred Breining | .03 | .01 | .00 |
| ☐ 37 | Reid Nichols | .03 | .01 | .00 |
| ☐ 38 | Jackie Moore MGR (checklist back) | .05 | .01 | .00 |
| ☐ 39 | John Wockenfuss | .03 | .01 | .00 |
| ☐ 40 | Phil Niekro | .15 | .06 | .01 |
| ☐ 41 | Mike Fischlin | .03 | .01 | .00 |
| ☐ 42 | Luis Sanchez | .03 | .01 | .00 |
| ☐ 43 | Andre David | .09 | .04 | .01 |
| ☐ 44 | Dickie Thon | .06 | .02 | .00 |
| ☐ 45 | Greg Minton | .05 | .02 | .00 |
| ☐ 46 | Gary Woods | .03 | .01 | .00 |
| ☐ 47 | Dave Rozema | .03 | .01 | .00 |
| ☐ 48 | Tony Fernandez | .35 | .14 | .03 |
| ☐ 49 | Butch Davis | .06 | .02 | .00 |
| ☐ 50 | John Candelaria | .07 | .03 | .01 |
| ☐ 51 | Bob Watson | .05 | .02 | .00 |
| ☐ 52 | Jerry Dybzinski | .03 | .01 | .00 |
| ☐ 53 | Tom Gorman | .03 | .01 | .00 |
| ☐ 54 | Cesar Cedeno | .06 | .02 | .00 |
| ☐ 55 | Frank Tanana | .05 | .02 | .00 |
| ☐ 56 | Jim Dwyer | .03 | .01 | .00 |
| ☐ 57 | Pat Zachry | .03 | .01 | .00 |
| ☐ 58 | Orlando Mercado | .03 | .01 | .00 |
| ☐ 59 | Rick Waits | .03 | .01 | .00 |
| ☐ 60 | George Hendrick | .06 | .02 | .00 |
| ☐ 61 | Curt Kaufman | .08 | .03 | .01 |
| ☐ 62 | Mike Ramsey | .03 | .01 | .00 |
| ☐ 63 | Steve McCatty | .03 | .01 | .00 |
| ☐ 64 | Mark Bailey | .09 | .04 | .01 |
| ☐ 65 | Bill Buckner | .08 | .03 | .01 |
| ☐ 66 | Dick Williams MGR (checklist back) | .05 | .01 | .00 |
| ☐ 67 | Rafael Santana | .09 | .04 | .01 |
| ☐ 68 | Von Hayes | .12 | .05 | .01 |
| ☐ 69 | Jim Winn | .07 | .03 | .01 |
| ☐ 70 | Don Baylor | .10 | .04 | .01 |
| ☐ 71 | Tim Laudner | .03 | .01 | .00 |
| ☐ 72 | Rick Sutcliffe | .10 | .04 | .01 |
| ☐ 73 | Rusty Kuntz | .03 | .01 | .00 |
| ☐ 74 | Mike Krukow | .07 | .03 | .01 |
| ☐ 75 | Willie Upshaw | .08 | .03 | .01 |
| ☐ 76 | Alan Bannister | .03 | .01 | .00 |
| ☐ 77 | Joe Beckwith | .03 | .01 | .00 |
| ☐ 78 | Scott Fletcher | .05 | .02 | .00 |
| ☐ 79 | Rick Mahler | .03 | .01 | .00 |
| ☐ 80 | Keith Hernandez | .25 | .10 | .02 |
| ☐ 81 | Lenn Sakata | .03 | .01 | .00 |
| ☐ 82 | Joe Price | .03 | .01 | .00 |
| ☐ 83 | Charlie Moore | .03 | .01 | .00 |
| ☐ 84 | Spike Owen | .06 | .02 | .00 |
| ☐ 85 | Mike Marshall | .12 | .05 | .01 |
| ☐ 86 | Don Aase | .05 | .02 | .00 |
| ☐ 87 | David Green | .05 | .02 | .00 |
| ☐ 88 | Bryn Smith | .03 | .01 | .00 |
| ☐ 89 | Jackie Gutierrez | .08 | .03 | .01 |
| ☐ 90 | Rich Gossage | .12 | .05 | .01 |
| ☐ 91 | Jeff Burroughs | .03 | .01 | .00 |
| ☐ 92 | Paul Owens MGR (checklist back) | .05 | .01 | .00 |
| ☐ 93 | Don Schulze | .07 | .03 | .01 |
| ☐ 94 | Toby Harrah | .05 | .02 | .00 |
| ☐ 95 | Jose Cruz | .09 | .04 | .01 |
| ☐ 96 | Johnny Ray | .09 | .04 | .01 |
| ☐ 97 | Pete Filson | .03 | .01 | .00 |
| ☐ 98 | Steve Lake | .03 | .01 | .00 |
| ☐ 99 | Milt Wilcox | .03 | .01 | .00 |
| ☐ 100 | George Brett | .45 | .18 | .04 |
| ☐ 101 | Jim Acker | .03 | .01 | .00 |
| ☐ 102 | Tommy Dunbar | .05 | .02 | .00 |
| ☐ 103 | Randy Lerch | .03 | .01 | .00 |
| ☐ 104 | Mike Fitzgerald | .05 | .02 | .00 |
| ☐ 105 | Ron Kittle | .12 | .05 | .01 |
| ☐ 106 | Pascual Perez | .03 | .01 | .00 |
| ☐ 107 | Tom Foley | .03 | .01 | .00 |
| ☐ 108 | Darnell Coles | .15 | .06 | .01 |
| ☐ 109 | Gary Roenicke | .05 | .02 | .00 |
| ☐ 110 | Alejandro Pena | .05 | .02 | .00 |
| ☐ 111 | Doug DeCinces | .08 | .03 | .01 |
| ☐ 112 | Tom Tellmann | .03 | .01 | .00 |
| ☐ 113 | Tom Herr | .08 | .03 | .01 |
| ☐ 114 | Bob James | .05 | .02 | .00 |
| ☐ 115 | Rickey Henderson | .40 | .16 | .04 |
| ☐ 116 | Dennis Boyd | .25 | .10 | .02 |
| ☐ 117 | Greg Gross | .03 | .01 | .00 |
| ☐ 118 | Eric Show | .05 | .02 | .00 |
| ☐ 119 | Pat Corrales MGR (checklist back) | .05 | .01 | .00 |
| ☐ 120 | Steve Kemp | .07 | .03 | .01 |
| ☐ 121 | Checklist: 1-132 | .07 | .01 | .00 |
| ☐ 122 | Tom Brunansky | .12 | .05 | .01 |
| ☐ 123 | Dave Smith | .07 | .03 | .01 |
| ☐ 124 | Rich Hebner | .03 | .01 | .00 |
| ☐ 125 | Kent Tekulve | .06 | .02 | .00 |
| ☐ 126 | Ruppert Jones | .03 | .01 | .00 |
| ☐ 127 | Mark Gubicza | .25 | .10 | .02 |
| ☐ 128 | Ernie Whitt | .03 | .01 | .00 |
| ☐ 129 | Gene Garber | .03 | .01 | .00 |
| ☐ 130 | Al Oliver | .09 | .04 | .01 |
| ☐ 131 | Buddy/Gus Bell FS | .07 | .03 | .01 |
| ☐ 132 | Dale/Yogi Berra FS | .07 | .03 | .01 |
| ☐ 133 | Bob/Ray Boone FS | .05 | .02 | .00 |
| ☐ 134 | Terry/Tito Francona FS | .07 | .03 | .01 |
| ☐ 135 | Terry/Bob Kennedy FS | .05 | .02 | .00 |
| ☐ 136 | Jeff/Jim Kunkel FS | .05 | .02 | .00 |
| ☐ 137 | Vance/Vern Law FS | .05 | .02 | .00 |
| ☐ 138 | Dick/Dick Schofield FS | .05 | .02 | .00 |
| ☐ 139 | Joel/Bob Skinner FS | .05 | .02 | .00 |
| ☐ 140 | Roy/Roy Smalley FS | .05 | .02 | .00 |
| ☐ 141 | Mike/D.Stenhouse FS | .05 | .02 | .00 |
| ☐ 142 | Steve/Dizzy Trout FS | .05 | .02 | .00 |
| ☐ 143 | Ozzie/Ozzie Virgil FS | .05 | .02 | .00 |
| ☐ 144 | Ron Gardenhire | .03 | .01 | .00 |
| ☐ 145 | Alvin Davis | 1.50 | .60 | .15 |
| ☐ 146 | Gary Redus | .06 | .02 | .00 |
| ☐ 147 | Bill Swaggerty | .09 | .04 | .01 |
| ☐ 148 | Steve Yeager | .05 | .02 | .00 |
| ☐ 149 | Dickie Noles | .03 | .01 | .00 |
| ☐ 150 | Jim Rice | .30 | .12 | .03 |
| ☐ 151 | Moose Haas | .05 | .02 | .00 |
| ☐ 152 | Steve Braun | .03 | .01 | .00 |
| ☐ 153 | Frank LaCorte | .03 | .01 | .00 |
| ☐ 154 | Argenis Salazar | .08 | .03 | .01 |
| ☐ 155 | Yogi Berra MGR (checklist back) | .10 | .03 | .00 |
| ☐ 156 | Craig Reynolds | .03 | .01 | .00 |
| ☐ 157 | Tug McGraw | .07 | .03 | .01 |
| ☐ 158 | Pat Tabler | .08 | .03 | .01 |
| ☐ 159 | Carlos Diaz | .03 | .01 | .00 |
| ☐ 160 | Lance Parrish | .20 | .08 | .02 |
| ☐ 161 | Ken Schrom | .05 | .02 | .00 |
| ☐ 162 | Benny Distefano | .10 | .04 | .01 |
| ☐ 163 | Dennis Eckersley | .05 | .02 | .00 |
| ☐ 164 | Jorge Orta | .03 | .01 | .00 |
| ☐ 165 | Dusty Baker | .06 | .02 | .00 |
| ☐ 166 | Keith Atherton | .03 | .01 | .00 |
| ☐ 167 | Rufino Linares | .03 | .01 | .00 |
| ☐ 168 | Garth Iorg | .03 | .01 | .00 |
| ☐ 169 | Dan Spillner | .03 | .01 | .00 |
| ☐ 170 | George Foster | .12 | .05 | .01 |
| ☐ 171 | Bill Stein | .03 | .01 | .00 |
| ☐ 172 | Jack Perconte | .03 | .01 | .00 |
| ☐ 173 | Mike Young | .15 | .06 | .01 |
| ☐ 174 | Rick Honeycutt | .05 | .02 | .00 |
| ☐ 175 | Dave Parker | .15 | .06 | .01 |
| ☐ 176 | Bill Schroeder | .03 | .01 | .00 |
| ☐ 177 | Dave Von Ohlen | .03 | .01 | .00 |
| ☐ 178 | Miguel Dilone | .03 | .01 | .00 |
| ☐ 179 | Tommy John | .10 | .04 | .01 |
| ☐ 180 | Dave Winfield | .30 | .12 | .03 |
| ☐ 181 | Roger Clemens | 8.00 | 3.25 | .80 |
| ☐ 182 | Tim Flannery | .03 | .01 | .00 |
| ☐ 183 | Larry McWilliams | .05 | .02 | .00 |
| ☐ 184 | Carmen Castillo | .03 | .01 | .00 |
| ☐ 185 | Al Holland | .03 | .01 | .00 |
| ☐ 186 | Bob Lillis MGR (checklist back) | .05 | .01 | .00 |
| ☐ 187 | Mike Walters | .05 | .02 | .00 |
| ☐ 188 | Greg Pryor | .03 | .01 | .00 |
| ☐ 189 | Warren Brusstar | .03 | .01 | .00 |
| ☐ 190 | Rusty Staub | .08 | .03 | .01 |
| ☐ 191 | Steve Nicosia | .03 | .01 | .00 |
| ☐ 192 | Howard Johnson | .03 | .01 | .00 |
| ☐ 193 | Jimmy Key | .35 | .14 | .03 |
| ☐ 194 | Dave Stegman | .03 | .01 | .00 |
| ☐ 195 | Glenn Hubbard | .03 | .01 | .00 |
| ☐ 196 | Pete O'Brien | .08 | .03 | .01 |
| ☐ 197 | Mike Warren | .03 | .01 | .00 |
| ☐ 198 | Eddie Milner | .03 | .01 | .00 |
| ☐ 199 | Denny Martinez | .03 | .01 | .00 |
| ☐ 200 | Reggie Jackson | .35 | .14 | .03 |
| ☐ 201 | Burt Hooton | .03 | .01 | .00 |
| ☐ 202 | Gorman Thomas | .07 | .03 | .01 |
| ☐ 203 | Bob McClure | .03 | .01 | .00 |
| ☐ 204 | Art Howe | .03 | .01 | .00 |
| ☐ 205 | Steve Rogers | .06 | .02 | .00 |
| ☐ 206 | Phil Garner | .05 | .02 | .00 |
| ☐ 207 | Mark Clear | .03 | .01 | .00 |
| ☐ 208 | Champ Summers | .03 | .01 | .00 |
| ☐ 209 | Bill Campbell | .03 | .01 | .00 |
| ☐ 210 | Gary Matthews | .06 | .02 | .00 |
| ☐ 211 | Clay Christiansen | .09 | .04 | .01 |
| ☐ 212 | George Vukovich | .03 | .01 | .00 |
| ☐ 213 | Billy Gardner MGR (checklist back) | .05 | .01 | .00 |

| | | | | |
|---|---|---|---|---|
| ☐ 214 | John Tudor | .10 | .04 | .01 |
| ☐ 215 | Bob Brenly | .07 | .03 | .01 |
| ☐ 216 | Jerry Don Gleaton | .03 | .01 | .00 |
| ☐ 217 | Leon Roberts | .03 | .01 | .00 |
| ☐ 218 | Doyle Alexander | .05 | .02 | .00 |
| ☐ 219 | Gerald Perry | .05 | .02 | .00 |
| ☐ 220 | Fred Lynn | .15 | .06 | .01 |
| ☐ 221 | Ron Reed | .03 | .01 | .00 |
| ☐ 222 | Hubie Brooks | .09 | .04 | .01 |
| ☐ 223 | Tom Hume | .03 | .01 | .00 |
| ☐ 224 | Al Cowens | .03 | .01 | .00 |
| ☐ 225 | Mike Boddicker | .09 | .04 | .01 |
| ☐ 226 | Juan Beniquez | .05 | .02 | .00 |
| ☐ 227 | Danny Darwin | .03 | .01 | .00 |
| ☐ 228 | Dion James | .09 | .04 | .01 |
| ☐ 229 | Dave LaPoint | .03 | .01 | .00 |
| ☐ 230 | Gary Carter | .30 | .12 | .03 |
| ☐ 231 | Dwayne Murphy | .06 | .02 | .00 |
| ☐ 232 | Dave Beard | .03 | .01 | .00 |
| ☐ 233 | Ed Jurak | .03 | .01 | .00 |
| ☐ 234 | Jerry Narron | .03 | .01 | .00 |
| ☐ 235 | Garry Maddox | .05 | .02 | .00 |
| ☐ 236 | Mark Thurmond | .05 | .02 | .00 |
| ☐ 237 | Julio Franco | .10 | .04 | .01 |
| ☐ 238 | Jose Rijo | .25 | .10 | .02 |
| ☐ 239 | Tim Teufel | .10 | .04 | .01 |
| ☐ 240 | Dave Stieb | .12 | .05 | .01 |
| ☐ 241 | Jim Frey MGR | .05 | .01 | .00 |
| | (checklist back) | | | |
| ☐ 242 | Greg Harris | .05 | .02 | .00 |
| ☐ 243 | Barbaro Garbey | .08 | .03 | .01 |
| ☐ 244 | Mike Jones | .05 | .02 | .00 |
| ☐ 245 | Chili Davis | .07 | .03 | .01 |
| ☐ 246 | Mike Norris | .03 | .01 | .00 |
| ☐ 247 | Wayne Tolleson | .03 | .01 | .00 |
| ☐ 248 | Terry Forster | .06 | .02 | .00 |
| ☐ 249 | Harold Baines | .15 | .06 | .01 |
| ☐ 250 | Jesse Orosco | .06 | .02 | .00 |
| ☐ 251 | Brad Gulden | .03 | .01 | .00 |
| ☐ 252 | Dan Ford | .03 | .01 | .00 |
| ☐ 253 | Sid Bream | .35 | .14 | .03 |
| ☐ 254 | Pete Vuckovich | .06 | .02 | .00 |
| ☐ 255 | Lonnie Smith | .06 | .02 | .00 |
| ☐ 256 | Mike Stanton | .03 | .01 | .00 |
| ☐ 257 | Bryan Little | .03 | .01 | .00 |
| ☐ 258 | Mike Brown | .05 | .02 | .00 |
| | (Angels OF) | | | |
| ☐ 259 | Gary Allenson | .03 | .01 | .00 |
| ☐ 260 | Dave Righetti | .12 | .05 | .01 |
| ☐ 261 | Checklist: 133-264 | .07 | .01 | .00 |
| ☐ 262 | Greg Booker | .06 | .02 | .00 |
| ☐ 263 | Mel Hall | .09 | .04 | .01 |
| ☐ 264 | Joe Sambito | .05 | .02 | .00 |
| ☐ 265 | Juan Samuel | .35 | .14 | .03 |
| ☐ 266 | Frank Viola | .07 | .03 | .01 |
| ☐ 267 | Henry Cotto | .08 | .03 | .01 |
| ☐ 268 | Chuck Tanner MGR | .05 | .01 | .00 |
| | (checklist back) | | | |
| ☐ 269 | Doug Baker | .06 | .02 | .00 |
| ☐ 270 | Dan Quisenberry | .12 | .05 | .01 |
| ☐ 271 | Tim Foli FDP68 | .03 | .01 | .00 |
| ☐ 272 | Jeff Burroughs FDP69 | .03 | .01 | .00 |
| ☐ 273 | Bill Almon FDP74 | .03 | .01 | .00 |
| ☐ 274 | Floyd Bannister FDP76 | .05 | .02 | .00 |
| ☐ 275 | Harold Baines FDP77 | .10 | .04 | .01 |
| ☐ 276 | Bob Horner FDP78 | .12 | .05 | .01 |
| ☐ 277 | Al Chambers FDP79 | .05 | .02 | .00 |
| ☐ 278 | D.Strawberry FDP80 | .35 | .14 | .03 |
| ☐ 279 | Mike Moore FDP81 | .06 | .02 | .00 |
| ☐ 280 | Shawon Dunston FDP82 | .50 | .20 | .05 |
| ☐ 281 | Tim Belcher FDP83 | .10 | .04 | .01 |
| ☐ 282 | Shawn Abner FDP84 | .35 | .14 | .03 |
| ☐ 283 | Fran Mullins | .03 | .01 | .00 |
| ☐ 284 | Marty Bystrom | .03 | .01 | .00 |
| ☐ 285 | Dan Driessen | .03 | .01 | .00 |
| ☐ 286 | Rudy Law | .03 | .01 | .00 |
| ☐ 287 | Walt Terrell | .03 | .01 | .00 |
| ☐ 288 | Jeff Kunkel | .08 | .03 | .01 |
| ☐ 289 | Tom Underwood | .03 | .01 | .00 |
| ☐ 290 | Cecil Cooper | .10 | .04 | .01 |
| ☐ 291 | Bob Welch | .06 | .02 | .00 |
| ☐ 292 | Brad Komminsk | .06 | .02 | .00 |
| ☐ 293 | Curt Young | .08 | .03 | .01 |
| ☐ 294 | Tom Nieto | .05 | .02 | .00 |
| ☐ 295 | Joe Niekro | .07 | .03 | .01 |
| ☐ 296 | Ricky Nelson | .05 | .02 | .00 |
| ☐ 297 | Gary Lucas | .03 | .01 | .00 |
| ☐ 298 | Marty Barrett | .09 | .04 | .01 |
| ☐ 299 | Andy Hawkins | .06 | .02 | .00 |
| ☐ 300 | Rod Carew | .35 | .14 | .03 |
| ☐ 301 | John Montefusco | .05 | .02 | .00 |
| ☐ 302 | Tim Corcoran | .03 | .01 | .00 |
| ☐ 303 | Mike Jeffcoat | .05 | .02 | .00 |
| ☐ 304 | Gary Gaetti | .08 | .03 | .01 |
| ☐ 305 | Dale Berra | .05 | .02 | .00 |
| ☐ 306 | Rick Reuschel | .05 | .02 | .00 |
| ☐ 307 | Sparky Anderson MGR | .07 | .02 | .00 |
| | (checklist back) | | | |
| ☐ 308 | John Wathan | .03 | .01 | .00 |
| ☐ 309 | Mike Witt | .10 | .04 | .01 |
| ☐ 310 | Manny Trillo | .05 | .02 | .00 |
| ☐ 311 | Jim Gott | .03 | .01 | .00 |
| ☐ 312 | Marc Hill | .03 | .01 | .00 |
| ☐ 313 | Dave Schmidt | .03 | .01 | .00 |
| ☐ 314 | Ron Oester | .05 | .02 | .00 |
| ☐ 315 | Doug Sisk | .05 | .02 | .00 |
| ☐ 316 | John Lowenstein | .03 | .01 | .00 |
| ☐ 317 | Jack Lazorko | .07 | .03 | .01 |
| ☐ 318 | Ted Simmons | .09 | .04 | .01 |
| ☐ 319 | Jeff Jones | .03 | .01 | .00 |
| ☐ 320 | Dale Murphy | .50 | .20 | .05 |
| ☐ 321 | Ricky Horton | .20 | .08 | .02 |
| ☐ 322 | Dave Stapleton | .03 | .01 | .00 |
| ☐ 323 | Andy McGaffigan | .03 | .01 | .00 |
| ☐ 324 | Bruce Bochy | .03 | .01 | .00 |
| ☐ 325 | John Denny | .06 | .02 | .00 |
| ☐ 326 | Kevin Bass | .07 | .03 | .01 |
| ☐ 327 | Brook Jacoby | .25 | .10 | .02 |
| ☐ 328 | Bob Shirley | .03 | .01 | .00 |
| ☐ 329 | Ron Washington | .03 | .01 | .00 |
| ☐ 330 | Leon Durham | .08 | .03 | .01 |
| ☐ 331 | Bill Laskey | .03 | .01 | .00 |
| ☐ 332 | Brian Harper | .03 | .01 | .00 |
| ☐ 333 | Willie Hernandez | .12 | .05 | .01 |
| ☐ 334 | Dick Howser MGR | .05 | .01 | .00 |
| | (checklist back) | | | |
| ☐ 335 | Bruce Benedict | .03 | .01 | .00 |
| ☐ 336 | Rance Mulliniks | .03 | .01 | .00 |
| ☐ 337 | Billy Sample | .03 | .01 | .00 |
| ☐ 338 | Britt Burns | .06 | .02 | .00 |
| ☐ 339 | Danny Heep | .03 | .01 | .00 |
| ☐ 340 | Robin Yount | .30 | .12 | .03 |
| ☐ 341 | Floyd Rayford | .03 | .01 | .00 |
| ☐ 342 | Ted Power | .07 | .03 | .01 |
| ☐ 343 | Bill Russell | .05 | .02 | .00 |
| ☐ 344 | Dave Henderson | .05 | .02 | .00 |
| ☐ 345 | Charlie Lea | .05 | .02 | .00 |
| ☐ 346 | Terry Pendleton | .25 | .10 | .02 |
| ☐ 347 | Rick Langford | .03 | .01 | .00 |
| ☐ 348 | Bob Boone | .05 | .02 | .00 |
| ☐ 349 | Domingo Ramos | .03 | .01 | .00 |
| ☐ 350 | Wade Boggs | 3.00 | 1.20 | .30 |
| ☐ 351 | Juan Agosto | .03 | .01 | .00 |
| ☐ 352 | Joe Morgan | .15 | .06 | .01 |
| ☐ 353 | Julio Solano | .07 | .03 | .01 |
| ☐ 354 | Andre Robertson | .03 | .01 | .00 |
| ☐ 355 | Bert Blyleven | .08 | .03 | .01 |
| ☐ 356 | Dave Meier | .09 | .04 | .01 |
| ☐ 357 | Rich Bordi | .03 | .01 | .00 |
| ☐ 358 | Tony Pena | .09 | .04 | .01 |
| ☐ 359 | Pat Sheridan | .03 | .01 | .00 |
| ☐ 360 | Steve Carlton | .30 | .12 | .03 |
| ☐ 361 | Alfredo Griffin | .05 | .02 | .00 |
| ☐ 362 | Craig McMurtry | .03 | .01 | .00 |
| ☐ 363 | Ron Hodges | .03 | .01 | .00 |
| ☐ 364 | Richard Dotson | .05 | .02 | .00 |
| ☐ 365 | Danny Ozark MGR | .05 | .01 | .00 |
| | (checklist back) | | | |
| ☐ 366 | Todd Cruz | .03 | .01 | .00 |
| ☐ 367 | Keefe Cato | .06 | .02 | .00 |
| ☐ 368 | Dave Bergman | .03 | .01 | .00 |
| ☐ 369 | R.J. Reynolds | .30 | .12 | .03 |
| ☐ 370 | Bruce Sutter | .12 | .05 | .01 |
| ☐ 371 | Mickey Rivers | .05 | .02 | .00 |
| ☐ 372 | Roy Howell | .03 | .01 | .00 |
| ☐ 373 | Mike Moore | .06 | .02 | .00 |
| ☐ 374 | Brian Downing | .05 | .02 | .00 |
| ☐ 375 | Jeff Reardon | .07 | .03 | .01 |
| ☐ 376 | Jeff Newman | .03 | .01 | .00 |
| ☐ 377 | Checklist: 265-396 | .07 | .01 | .00 |
| ☐ 378 | Alan Wiggins | .06 | .02 | .00 |
| ☐ 379 | Charles Hudson | .05 | .02 | .00 |
| ☐ 380 | Ken Griffey | .07 | .03 | .01 |
| ☐ 381 | Roy Smith | .06 | .02 | .00 |
| ☐ 382 | Denny Walling | .03 | .01 | .00 |
| ☐ 383 | Rick Lysander | .03 | .01 | .00 |
| ☐ 384 | Jody Davis | .08 | .03 | .01 |
| ☐ 385 | Jose DeLeon | .05 | .02 | .00 |
| ☐ 386 | Dan Gladden | .25 | .10 | .02 |
| ☐ 387 | Buddy Biancalana | .08 | .03 | .01 |
| ☐ 388 | Bert Roberge | .03 | .01 | .00 |
| ☐ 389 | Rod Dedeaux OLY COA | .03 | .01 | .00 |
| ☐ 390 | Sid Akins OLY | .07 | .03 | .01 |
| ☐ 391 | Flavio Alfaro OLY | .07 | .03 | .01 |
| ☐ 392 | Don August OLY | .07 | .03 | .01 |
| ☐ 393 | Scott Bankhead OLY | .15 | .06 | .01 |

| # | Name | | | |
|---|------|----|----|----|
| 394 | Bob Caffrey OLY | .07 | .03 | .01 |
| 395 | Mike Dunne OLY | .07 | .03 | .01 |
| 396 | Gary Green OLY | .07 | .03 | .01 |
| 397 | John Hoover OLY | .07 | .03 | .01 |
| 398 | Shane Mack OLY | .25 | .10 | .02 |
| 399 | John Marzano OLY | .10 | .04 | .01 |
| 400 | Oddibe McDowell OLY | 1.50 | .60 | .15 |
| 401 | Mark McGwire OLY | .50 | .20 | .05 |
| 402 | Pat Pacillo OLY | .10 | .04 | .01 |
| 403 | Cory Snyder OLY | 6.00 | 2.40 | .60 |
| 404 | Billy Swift OLY | .15 | .06 | .01 |
| 405 | Tom Veryzer | .03 | .01 | .00 |
| 406 | Len Whitehouse | .03 | .01 | .00 |
| 407 | Bobby Ramos | .03 | .01 | .00 |
| 408 | Sid Monge | .03 | .01 | .00 |
| 409 | Brad Wellman | .03 | .01 | .00 |
| 410 | Bob Horner | .15 | .06 | .01 |
| 411 | Bobby Cox MGR | .05 | .01 | .00 |
| | (checklist back) | | | |
| 412 | Bud Black | .03 | .01 | .00 |
| 413 | Vance Law | .03 | .01 | .00 |
| 414 | Gary Ward | .05 | .02 | .00 |
| 415 | Ron Darling | 1.00 | .40 | .10 |
| 416 | Wayne Gross | .03 | .01 | .00 |
| 417 | John Franco | .35 | .14 | .03 |
| 418 | Ken Landreaux | .05 | .02 | .00 |
| 419 | Mike Caldwell | .05 | .02 | .00 |
| 420 | Andre Dawson | .20 | .08 | .02 |
| 421 | Dave Rucker | .03 | .01 | .00 |
| 422 | Carney Lansford | .08 | .03 | .01 |
| 423 | Barry Bonnell | .03 | .01 | .00 |
| 424 | Al Nipper | .20 | .08 | .02 |
| 425 | Mike Hargrove | .05 | .02 | .00 |
| 426 | Vern Ruhle | .03 | .01 | .00 |
| 427 | Mario Ramirez | .03 | .01 | .00 |
| 428 | Larry Andersen | .03 | .01 | .00 |
| 429 | Rick Cerone | .03 | .01 | .00 |
| 430 | Ron Davis | .03 | .01 | .00 |
| 431 | U.L. Washington | .03 | .01 | .00 |
| 432 | Thad Bosley | .03 | .01 | .00 |
| 433 | Jim Morrison | .03 | .01 | .00 |
| 434 | Gene Richards | .03 | .01 | .00 |
| 435 | Dan Petry | .09 | .04 | .01 |
| 436 | Willie Aikens | .05 | .02 | .00 |
| 437 | Al Jones | .07 | .03 | .01 |
| 438 | Joe Torre MGR | .07 | .02 | .00 |
| | (checklist back) | | | |
| 439 | Junior Ortiz | .03 | .01 | .00 |
| 440 | Fernando Valenzuela | .30 | .12 | .03 |
| 441 | Duane Walker | .03 | .01 | .00 |
| 442 | Ken Forsch | .03 | .01 | .00 |
| 443 | George Wright | .03 | .01 | .00 |
| 444 | Tony Phillips | .03 | .01 | .00 |
| 445 | Tippy Martinez | .03 | .01 | .00 |
| 446 | Jim Sundberg | .05 | .02 | .00 |
| 447 | Jeff Lahti | .03 | .01 | .00 |
| 448 | Derrel Thomas | .03 | .01 | .00 |
| 449 | Phil Bradley | 1.25 | .50 | .12 |
| 450 | Steve Garvey | .35 | .14 | .03 |
| 451 | Bruce Hurst | .07 | .03 | .01 |
| 452 | John Castino | .03 | .01 | .00 |
| 453 | Tom Waddell | .12 | .05 | .01 |
| 454 | Glenn Wilson | .10 | .04 | .01 |
| 455 | Bob Knepper | .08 | .03 | .01 |
| 456 | Tim Foli | .03 | .01 | .00 |
| 457 | Cecilio Guante | .03 | .01 | .00 |
| 458 | Randy Johnson | .03 | .01 | .00 |
| 459 | Charlie Leibrandt | .06 | .02 | .00 |
| 460 | Ryne Sandberg | .45 | .18 | .04 |
| 461 | Marty Castillo | .03 | .01 | .00 |
| 462 | Gary Lavelle | .05 | .02 | .00 |
| 463 | Dave Collins | .05 | .02 | .00 |
| 464 | Mike Mason | .10 | .04 | .01 |
| 465 | Bob Grich | .06 | .02 | .00 |
| 466 | Tony LaRussa MGR | .05 | .01 | .00 |
| | (checklist back) | | | |
| 467 | Ed Lynch | .03 | .01 | .00 |
| 468 | Wayne Krenchicki | .03 | .01 | .00 |
| 469 | Sammy Stewart | .03 | .01 | .00 |
| 470 | Steve Sax | .12 | .05 | .01 |
| 471 | Pete Ladd | .03 | .01 | .00 |
| 472 | Jim Essian | .03 | .01 | .00 |
| 473 | Tim Wallach | .07 | .03 | .01 |
| 474 | Kurt Kepshire | .08 | .03 | .01 |
| 475 | Andre Thornton | .07 | .03 | .01 |
| 476 | Jeff Stone | .15 | .06 | .01 |
| 477 | Bob Ojeda | .09 | .04 | .01 |
| 478 | Kurt Bevacqua | .03 | .01 | .00 |
| 479 | Mike Madden | .03 | .01 | .00 |
| 480 | Lou Whitaker | .12 | .05 | .01 |
| 481 | Dale Murray | .03 | .01 | .00 |
| 482 | Harry Spilman | .03 | .01 | .00 |
| 483 | Mike Smithson | .05 | .02 | .00 |
| 484 | Larry Bowa | .08 | .03 | .01 |
| 485 | Matt Young | .05 | .02 | .00 |
| 486 | Steve Balboni | .05 | .02 | .00 |
| 487 | Frank Williams | .10 | .04 | .01 |
| 488 | Joel Skinner | .07 | .03 | .01 |
| 489 | Bryan Clark | .03 | .01 | .00 |
| 490 | Jason Thompson | .05 | .02 | .00 |
| 491 | Rick Camp | .03 | .01 | .00 |
| 492 | Dave Johnson MGR | .07 | .02 | .00 |
| | (checklist back) | | | |
| 493 | Orel Hershiser | 2.00 | .80 | .20 |
| 494 | Rich Dauer | .03 | .01 | .00 |
| 495 | Mario Soto | .07 | .03 | .01 |
| 496 | Donnie Scott | .05 | .02 | .00 |
| 497 | Gary Pettis | .35 | .14 | .03 |
| | (photo actually Gary's little brother, Lynn) | | | |
| 498 | Ed Romero | .03 | .01 | .00 |
| 499 | Danny Cox | .15 | .06 | .01 |
| 500 | Mike Schmidt | .35 | .14 | .03 |
| 501 | Dan Schatzeder | .03 | .01 | .00 |
| 502 | Rick Miller | .03 | .01 | .00 |
| 503 | Tim Conroy | .03 | .01 | .00 |
| 504 | Jerry Willard | .05 | .02 | .00 |
| 505 | Jim Beattie | .03 | .01 | .00 |
| 506 | Franklin Stubbs | 1.00 | .40 | .10 |
| 507 | Ray Fontenot | .03 | .01 | .00 |
| 508 | John Shelby | .03 | .01 | .00 |
| 509 | Milt May | .03 | .01 | .00 |
| 510 | Kent Hrbek | .30 | .12 | .03 |
| 511 | Lee Smith | .08 | .03 | .01 |
| 512 | Tom Brookens | .03 | .01 | .00 |
| 513 | Lynn Jones | .03 | .01 | .00 |
| 514 | Jeff Cornell | .07 | .03 | .01 |
| 515 | Dave Concepcion | .07 | .03 | .01 |
| 516 | Roy Lee Jackson | .03 | .01 | .00 |
| 517 | Jerry Martin | .03 | .01 | .00 |
| 518 | Chris Chambliss | .05 | .02 | .00 |
| 519 | Doug Rader MGR | .05 | .01 | .00 |
| | (checklist back) | | | |
| 520 | LaMarr Hoyt | .07 | .03 | .01 |
| 521 | Rick Dempsey | .05 | .02 | .00 |
| 522 | Paul Molitor | .09 | .04 | .01 |
| 523 | Candy Maldonado | .07 | .03 | .01 |
| 524 | Rob Wilfong | .03 | .01 | .00 |
| 525 | Darrell Porter | .05 | .02 | .00 |
| 526 | Dave Palmer | .05 | .02 | .00 |
| 527 | Checklist: 397-528 | .07 | .01 | .00 |
| 528 | Bill Krueger | .03 | .01 | .00 |
| 529 | Rich Gedman | .08 | .03 | .01 |
| 530 | Dave Dravecky | .05 | .02 | .00 |
| 531 | Joe Lefebvre | .03 | .01 | .00 |
| 532 | Frank DiPino | .03 | .01 | .00 |
| 533 | Tony Bernazard | .05 | .02 | .00 |
| 534 | Brian Dayett | .06 | .02 | .00 |
| 535 | Pat Putnam | .03 | .01 | .00 |
| 536 | Kirby Puckett | 6.00 | 2.40 | .60 |
| 537 | Don Robinson | .05 | .02 | .00 |
| 538 | Keith Moreland | .06 | .02 | .00 |
| 539 | Aurelio Lopez | .03 | .01 | .00 |
| 540 | Claudell Washington | .06 | .02 | .00 |
| 541 | Mark Davis | .03 | .01 | .00 |
| 542 | Don Slaught | .03 | .01 | .00 |
| 543 | Mike Squires | .03 | .01 | .00 |
| 544 | Bruce Kison | .03 | .01 | .00 |
| 545 | Lloyd Moseby | .10 | .04 | .01 |
| 546 | Brent Gaff | .03 | .01 | .00 |
| 547 | Pete Rose MGR | .45 | .15 | .03 |
| | (checklist back) | | | |
| 548 | Larry Parrish | .06 | .02 | .00 |
| 549 | Mike Scioscia | .05 | .02 | .00 |
| 550 | Scott McGregor | .06 | .02 | .00 |
| 551 | Andy Van Slyke | .06 | .02 | .00 |
| 552 | Chris Codiroli | .03 | .01 | .00 |
| 553 | Bob Clark | .03 | .01 | .00 |
| 554 | Doug Flynn | .03 | .01 | .00 |
| 555 | Bob Stanley | .05 | .02 | .00 |
| 556 | Sixto Lezcano | .03 | .01 | .00 |
| 557 | Len Barker | .05 | .02 | .00 |
| 558 | Carmelo Martinez | .07 | .03 | .01 |
| 559 | Jay Howell | .06 | .02 | .00 |
| 560 | Bill Madlock | .10 | .04 | .01 |
| 561 | Darryl Motley | .03 | .01 | .00 |
| 562 | Houston Jimenez | .03 | .01 | .00 |
| 563 | Dick Ruthven | .03 | .01 | .00 |
| 564 | Alan Ashby | .03 | .01 | .00 |
| 565 | Kirk Gibson | .20 | .08 | .02 |
| 566 | Ed VandeBerg | .03 | .01 | .00 |
| 567 | Joel Youngblood | .03 | .01 | .00 |
| 568 | Cliff Johnson | .03 | .01 | .00 |
| 569 | Ken Oberkfell | .03 | .01 | .00 |
| 570 | Darryl Strawberry | 1.00 | .40 | .10 |

| | | | | |
|---|---|---|---|---|
| ☐ 571 Charlie Hough | .06 | .02 | .00 | |
| ☐ 572 Tom Paciorek | .03 | .01 | .00 | |
| ☐ 573 Jay Tibbs | .20 | .08 | .02 | |
| ☐ 574 Joe Altobelli MGR | .05 | .01 | .00 | |
| (checklist back) | | | | |
| ☐ 575 Pedro Guerrero | .20 | .08 | .02 | |
| ☐ 576 Jaime Cocanower | .07 | .03 | .01 | |
| ☐ 577 Chris Speier | .03 | .01 | .00 | |
| ☐ 578 Terry Francona | .05 | .02 | .00 | |
| ☐ 579 Ron Romanick | .25 | .10 | .02 | |
| ☐ 580 Dwight Evans | .10 | .04 | .01 | |
| ☐ 581 Mark Wagner | .03 | .01 | .00 | |
| ☐ 582 Ken Phelps | .05 | .02 | .00 | |
| ☐ 583 Bobby Brown | .03 | .01 | .00 | |
| ☐ 584 Kevin Gross | .03 | .01 | .00 | |
| ☐ 585 Butch Wynegar | .05 | .02 | .00 | |
| ☐ 586 Bill Scherrer | .03 | .01 | .00 | |
| ☐ 587 Doug Frobel | .05 | .02 | .00 | |
| ☐ 588 Bobby Castillo | .03 | .01 | .00 | |
| ☐ 589 Bob Dernier | .05 | .02 | .00 | |
| ☐ 590 Ray Knight | .07 | .03 | .01 | |
| ☐ 591 Larry Herndon | .05 | .02 | .00 | |
| ☐ 592 Jeff Robinson | .10 | .04 | .01 | |
| ☐ 593 Rick Leach | .03 | .01 | .00 | |
| ☐ 594 Curt Wilkerson | .05 | .02 | .00 | |
| ☐ 595 Larry Gura | .05 | .02 | .00 | |
| ☐ 596 Jerry Hairston | .03 | .01 | .00 | |
| ☐ 597 Brad Lesley | .03 | .01 | .00 | |
| ☐ 598 Jose Oquendo | .03 | .01 | .00 | |
| ☐ 599 Storm Davis | .06 | .02 | .00 | |
| ☐ 600 Pete Rose | 1.00 | .40 | .10 | |
| ☐ 601 Tom Lasorda MGR | .07 | .02 | .00 | |
| (checklist back) | | | | |
| ☐ 602 Jeff Dedmon | .08 | .03 | .01 | |
| ☐ 603 Rick Manning | .03 | .01 | .00 | |
| ☐ 604 Daryl Sconiers | .03 | .01 | .00 | |
| ☐ 605 Ozzie Smith | .10 | .04 | .01 | |
| ☐ 606 Rich Gale | .03 | .01 | .00 | |
| ☐ 607 Bill Almon | .03 | .01 | .00 | |
| ☐ 608 Craig Lefferts | .03 | .01 | .00 | |
| ☐ 609 Broderick Perkins | .03 | .01 | .00 | |
| ☐ 610 Jack Morris | .15 | .06 | .01 | |
| ☐ 611 Ozzie Virgil | .06 | .02 | .00 | |
| ☐ 612 Mike Armstrong | .05 | .02 | .00 | |
| ☐ 613 Terry Puhl | .05 | .02 | .00 | |
| ☐ 614 Al Williams | .03 | .01 | .00 | |
| ☐ 615 Marvell Wynne | .03 | .01 | .00 | |
| ☐ 616 Scott Sanderson | .03 | .01 | .00 | |
| ☐ 617 Willie Wilson | .15 | .06 | .01 | |
| ☐ 618 Pete Falcone | .03 | .01 | .00 | |
| ☐ 619 Jeff Leonard | .06 | .02 | .00 | |
| ☐ 620 Dwight Gooden | 8.00 | 3.25 | .80 | |
| ☐ 621 Marvis Foley | .03 | .01 | .00 | |
| ☐ 622 Luis Leal | .03 | .01 | .00 | |
| ☐ 623 Greg Walker | .10 | .04 | .01 | |
| ☐ 624 Benny Ayala | .03 | .01 | .00 | |
| ☐ 625 Mark Langston | .40 | .16 | .04 | |
| ☐ 626 German Rivera | .10 | .04 | .01 | |
| ☐ 627 Eric Davis | 7.00 | 2.80 | .70 | |
| ☐ 628 Rene Lachemann MGR | .05 | .01 | .00 | |
| (checklist back) | | | | |
| ☐ 629 Dick Schofield | .10 | .04 | .01 | |
| ☐ 630 Tim Raines | .20 | .08 | .02 | |
| ☐ 631 Bob Forsch | .06 | .02 | .00 | |
| ☐ 632 Bruce Bochte | .05 | .02 | .00 | |
| ☐ 633 Glenn Hoffman | .03 | .01 | .00 | |
| ☐ 634 Bill Dawley | .03 | .01 | .00 | |
| ☐ 635 Terry Kennedy | .07 | .03 | .01 | |
| ☐ 636 Shane Rawley | .06 | .02 | .00 | |
| ☐ 637 Brett Butler | .08 | .03 | .01 | |
| ☐ 638 Mike Pagliarulo | 1.50 | .60 | .15 | |
| ☐ 639 Ed Hodge | .06 | .02 | .00 | |
| ☐ 640 Steve Henderson | .03 | .01 | .00 | |
| ☐ 641 Rod Scurry | .03 | .01 | .00 | |
| ☐ 642 Dave Owen | .06 | .02 | .00 | |
| ☐ 643 Johnny Grubb | .03 | .01 | .00 | |
| ☐ 644 Mark Huismann | .06 | .02 | .00 | |
| ☐ 645 Damaso Garcia | .07 | .03 | .01 | |
| ☐ 646 Scot Thompson | .03 | .01 | .00 | |
| ☐ 647 Rafael Ramirez | .03 | .01 | .00 | |
| ☐ 648 Bob Jones | .03 | .01 | .00 | |
| ☐ 649 Sid Fernandez | 1.00 | .40 | .10 | |
| ☐ 650 Greg Luzinski | .09 | .04 | .01 | |
| ☐ 651 Jeff Russell | .03 | .01 | .00 | |
| ☐ 652 Joe Nolan | .03 | .01 | .00 | |
| ☐ 653 Mark Brouhard | .03 | .01 | .00 | |
| ☐ 654 Dave Anderson | .03 | .01 | .00 | |
| ☐ 655 Joaquin Andujar | .08 | .03 | .01 | |
| ☐ 656 Chuck Cottier MGR | .05 | .01 | .00 | |
| (checklist back) | | | | |
| ☐ 657 Jim Slaton | .03 | .01 | .00 | |
| ☐ 658 Mike Stenhouse | .05 | .02 | .00 | |
| ☐ 659 Checklist: 529-660 | .07 | .01 | .00 | |
| ☐ 660 Tony Gwynn | .40 | .16 | .04 | |
| ☐ 661 Steve Crawford | .03 | .01 | .00 | |
| ☐ 662 Mike Heath | .03 | .01 | .00 | |
| ☐ 663 Luis Aguayo | .03 | .01 | .00 | |
| ☐ 664 Steve Farr | .09 | .04 | .01 | |
| ☐ 665 Don Mattingly | 8.00 | 3.25 | .80 | |
| ☐ 666 Mike LaCoss | .03 | .01 | .00 | |
| ☐ 667 Dave Engle | .03 | .01 | .00 | |
| ☐ 668 Steve Trout | .03 | .01 | .00 | |
| ☐ 669 Lee Lacy | .05 | .02 | .00 | |
| ☐ 670 Tom Seaver | .25 | .10 | .02 | |
| ☐ 671 Dane Iorg | .03 | .01 | .00 | |
| ☐ 672 Juan Berenguer | .03 | .01 | .00 | |
| ☐ 673 Buck Martinez | .03 | .01 | .00 | |
| ☐ 674 Atlee Hammaker | .03 | .01 | .00 | |
| ☐ 675 Tony Perez | .10 | .04 | .01 | |
| ☐ 676 Albert Hall | .08 | .03 | .01 | |
| ☐ 677 Wally Backman | .06 | .02 | .00 | |
| ☐ 678 Joe McLaughlin | .03 | .01 | .00 | |
| ☐ 679 Bob Kearney | .03 | .01 | .00 | |
| ☐ 680 Jerry Reuss | .05 | .02 | .00 | |
| ☐ 681 Ben Oglivie | .05 | .02 | .00 | |
| ☐ 682 Doug Corbett | .03 | .01 | .00 | |
| ☐ 683 Whitey Herzog MGR | .05 | .01 | .00 | |
| (checklist back) | | | | |
| ☐ 684 Bill Doran | .08 | .03 | .01 | |
| ☐ 685 Bill Caudill | .05 | .02 | .00 | |
| ☐ 686 Mike Easler | .06 | .02 | .00 | |
| ☐ 687 Bill Gullickson | .05 | .02 | .00 | |
| ☐ 688 Len Matuszek | .03 | .01 | .00 | |
| ☐ 689 Luis DeLeon | .03 | .01 | .00 | |
| ☐ 690 Alan Trammell | .15 | .06 | .01 | |
| ☐ 691 Dennis Rasmussen | .20 | .08 | .02 | |
| ☐ 692 Randy Bush | .03 | .01 | .00 | |
| ☐ 693 Tim Stoddard | .03 | .01 | .00 | |
| ☐ 694 Joe Carter | 1.25 | .50 | .12 | |
| ☐ 695 Rick Rhoden | .07 | .03 | .01 | |
| ☐ 696 John Rabb | .03 | .01 | .00 | |
| ☐ 697 Onix Concepcion | .03 | .01 | .00 | |
| ☐ 698 Jorge Bell | .12 | .05 | .01 | |
| ☐ 699 Donnie Moore | .05 | .02 | .00 | |
| ☐ 700 Eddie Murray | .40 | .16 | .04 | |
| ☐ 701 Eddie Murray AS | .25 | .10 | .02 | |
| ☐ 702 Damaso Garcia AS | .05 | .02 | .00 | |
| ☐ 703 George Brett AS | .25 | .10 | .02 | |
| ☐ 704 Cal Ripken AS | .25 | .10 | .02 | |
| ☐ 705 Dave Winfield AS | .20 | .08 | .02 | |
| ☐ 706 Rickey Henderson AS | .25 | .10 | .02 | |
| ☐ 707 Tony Armas AS | .06 | .02 | .00 | |
| ☐ 708 Lance Parrish AS | .12 | .05 | .01 | |
| ☐ 709 Mike Boddicker AS | .06 | .02 | .00 | |
| ☐ 710 Frank Viola AS | .06 | .02 | .00 | |
| ☐ 711 Dan Quisenberry AS | .12 | .05 | .01 | |
| ☐ 712 Keith Hernandez AS | .15 | .06 | .01 | |
| ☐ 713 Ryne Sandberg AS | .20 | .08 | .02 | |
| ☐ 714 Mike Schmidt AS | .25 | .10 | .02 | |
| ☐ 715 Ozzie Smith AS | .07 | .03 | .01 | |
| ☐ 716 Dale Murphy AS | .25 | .10 | .02 | |
| ☐ 717 Tony Gwynn AS | .20 | .08 | .02 | |
| ☐ 718 Jeff Leonard AS | .06 | .02 | .00 | |
| ☐ 719 Gary Carter AS | .20 | .08 | .02 | |
| ☐ 720 Rick Sutcliffe AS | .08 | .03 | .01 | |
| ☐ 721 Bob Knepper AS | .06 | .02 | .00 | |
| ☐ 722 Bruce Sutter AS | .09 | .04 | .01 | |
| ☐ 723 Dave Stewart | .03 | .01 | .00 | |
| ☐ 724 Oscar Gamble | .03 | .01 | .00 | |
| ☐ 725 Floyd Bannister | .05 | .02 | .00 | |
| ☐ 726 Al Bumbry | .03 | .01 | .00 | |
| ☐ 727 Frank Pastore | .03 | .01 | .00 | |
| ☐ 728 Bob Bailor | .03 | .01 | .00 | |
| ☐ 729 Don Sutton | .15 | .06 | .01 | |
| ☐ 730 Dave Kingman | .12 | .05 | .01 | |
| ☐ 731 Neil Allen | .05 | .02 | .00 | |
| ☐ 732 John McNamara MGR | .05 | .01 | .00 | |
| (checklist back) | | | | |
| ☐ 733 Tony Scott | .03 | .01 | .00 | |
| ☐ 734 John Henry Johnson | .03 | .01 | .00 | |
| ☐ 735 Garry Templeton | .08 | .03 | .01 | |
| ☐ 736 Jerry Mumphrey | .05 | .02 | .00 | |
| ☐ 737 Bo Diaz | .05 | .02 | .00 | |
| ☐ 738 Omar Moreno | .03 | .01 | .00 | |
| ☐ 739 Ernie Camacho | .03 | .01 | .00 | |
| ☐ 740 Jack Clark | .10 | .04 | .01 | |
| ☐ 741 John Butcher | .03 | .01 | .00 | |
| ☐ 742 Ron Hassey | .03 | .01 | .00 | |
| ☐ 743 Frank White | .06 | .02 | .00 | |
| ☐ 744 Doug Bair | .03 | .01 | .00 | |
| ☐ 745 Buddy Bell | .09 | .04 | .01 | |
| ☐ 746 Jim Clancy | .03 | .01 | .00 | |
| ☐ 747 Alex Trevino | .03 | .01 | .00 | |
| ☐ 748 Lee Mazzilli | .05 | .02 | .00 | |
| ☐ 749 Julio Cruz | .03 | .01 | .00 | |
| ☐ 750 Rollie Fingers | .15 | .06 | .01 | |

| | | | | | |
|---|---|---|---|---|---|
| ☐ 751 | Kelvin Chapman | .08 | .03 | .01 |
| ☐ 752 | Bob Owchinko | .03 | .01 | .00 |
| ☐ 753 | Greg Brock | .06 | .02 | .00 |
| ☐ 754 | Larry Milbourne | .03 | .01 | .00 |
| ☐ 755 | Ken Singleton | .08 | .03 | .01 |
| ☐ 756 | Rob Picciolo | .03 | .01 | .00 |
| ☐ 757 | Willie McGee | .35 | .14 | .03 |
| ☐ 758 | Ray Burris | .03 | .01 | .00 |
| ☐ 759 | Jim Fanning MGR (checklist back) | .05 | .01 | .00 |
| ☐ 760 | Nolan Ryan | .35 | .14 | .03 |
| ☐ 761 | Jerry Remy | .03 | .01 | .00 |
| ☐ 762 | Eddie Whitson | .05 | .02 | .00 |
| ☐ 763 | Kiko Garcia | .03 | .01 | .00 |
| ☐ 764 | Jamie Easterly | .03 | .01 | .00 |
| ☐ 765 | Willie Randolph | .05 | .02 | .00 |
| ☐ 766 | Paul Mirabella | .03 | .01 | .00 |
| ☐ 767 | Darrell Brown | .03 | .01 | .00 |
| ☐ 768 | Ron Cey | .08 | .03 | .01 |
| ☐ 769 | Joe Cowley | .05 | .02 | .00 |
| ☐ 770 | Carlton Fisk | .12 | .05 | .01 |
| ☐ 771 | Geoff Zahn | .03 | .01 | .00 |
| ☐ 772 | Johnnie LeMaster | .03 | .01 | .00 |
| ☐ 773 | Hal McRae | .05 | .02 | .00 |
| ☐ 774 | Dennis Lamp | .03 | .01 | .00 |
| ☐ 775 | Mookie Wilson | .06 | .02 | .00 |
| ☐ 776 | Jerry Royster | .03 | .01 | .00 |
| ☐ 777 | Ned Yost | .03 | .01 | .00 |
| ☐ 778 | Mike Davis | .06 | .02 | .00 |
| ☐ 779 | Nick Esasky | .06 | .02 | .00 |
| ☐ 780 | Mike Flanagan | .07 | .03 | .01 |
| ☐ 781 | Jim Gantner | .05 | .02 | .00 |
| ☐ 782 | Tom Niedenfuer | .06 | .02 | .00 |
| ☐ 783 | Mike Jorgensen | .03 | .01 | .00 |
| ☐ 784 | Checklist: 661-792 | .07 | .01 | .00 |
| ☐ 785 | Tony Armas | .09 | .04 | .01 |
| ☐ 786 | Enos Cabell | .03 | .01 | .00 |
| ☐ 787 | Jim Wohlford | .03 | .01 | .00 |
| ☐ 788 | Steve Comer | .03 | .01 | .00 |
| ☐ 789 | Luis Salazar | .03 | .01 | .00 |
| ☐ 790 | Ron Guidry | .15 | .06 | .01 |
| ☐ 791 | Ivan DeJesus | .03 | .01 | .00 |
| ☐ 792 | Darrell Evans | .12 | .05 | .01 |

| | | | | | |
|---|---|---|---|---|---|
| ☐ 23 | Nolan Ryan | .50 | .20 | .05 |
| ☐ 24 | Steve Carlton | .60 | .24 | .06 |
| ☐ 25 | Alan Trammell | .15 | .06 | .01 |
| ☐ 26 | Steve Garvey | .75 | .30 | .07 |
| ☐ 27 | Kirk Gibson | .35 | .14 | .03 |
| ☐ 28 | Juan Samuel | .15 | .06 | .01 |
| ☐ 29 | Reggie Jackson | .90 | .36 | .09 |
| ☐ 30 | Darryl Strawberry | 1.00 | .40 | .10 |
| ☐ 31 | Tom Seaver | .60 | .24 | .06 |
| ☐ 32 | Pete Rose | 1.50 | .60 | .15 |
| ☐ 33 | Dwight Evans | .10 | .04 | .01 |
| ☐ 34 | Jose Cruz | .10 | .04 | .01 |
| ☐ 35 | Bert Blyleven | .10 | .04 | .01 |
| ☐ 36 | Keith Hernandez | .25 | .10 | .02 |
| ☐ 37 | Robin Yount | .50 | .20 | .05 |
| ☐ 38 | Joaquin Andujar | .10 | .04 | .01 |
| ☐ 39 | Lloyd Moseby | .15 | .06 | .01 |
| ☐ 40 | Chili Davis | .10 | .04 | .01 |
| ☐ 41 | Kent Hrbek | .25 | .10 | .02 |
| ☐ 42 | Dave Parker | .30 | .12 | .03 |
| ☐ 43 | Jack Morris | .20 | .08 | .02 |
| ☐ 44 | Pedro Guerrero | .30 | .12 | .03 |
| ☐ 45 | Mike Witt | .15 | .06 | .01 |
| ☐ 46 | George Brett | .90 | .36 | .09 |
| ☐ 47 | Ozzie Smith | .15 | .06 | .01 |
| ☐ 48 | Cal Ripken | .75 | .30 | .07 |
| ☐ 49 | Rich Gossage | .20 | .08 | .02 |
| ☐ 50 | Jim Rice | .60 | .24 | .06 |
| ☐ 51 | Harold Baines | .40 | .16 | .04 |
| ☐ 52 | Fernando Valenzuela | .50 | .20 | .05 |
| ☐ 53 | Buddy Bell | .10 | .04 | .01 |
| ☐ 54 | Jesse Orosco | .10 | .04 | .01 |
| ☐ 55 | Lance Parrish | .30 | .12 | .03 |
| ☐ 56 | Jason Thompson | .10 | .04 | .01 |
| ☐ 57 | Tom Brunansky | .15 | .06 | .01 |
| ☐ 58 | Dave Righetti | .20 | .08 | .02 |
| ☐ 59 | Dave Kingman | .15 | .06 | .01 |
| ☐ 60 | Dave Winfield | .50 | .20 | .05 |

## 1985 Topps Super

This 60 card set was issued in packs of three. These large cards measure 4 7/8" by 6 7/8". The fronts of the cards are merely a blow-up of the Topps regular issue. In fact, the cards differ from the corresponding cards of the regular set in size and number only. As one would expect, only those considered stars and superstars appear in this set. Backs are green with maroon printing. A checklist for the set is contained on the back of the wrapper. The back of the wrapper also gives details of Topps' offer to send your "missing" cards.

| | | MINT | VG-E | F-G |
|---|---|---|---|---|
| COMPLETE SET | | 13.50 | 5.00 | 1.00 |
| COMMON PLAYER | | .10 | .04 | .01 |
| ☐ 1 | Ryne Sandberg | .60 | .24 | .06 |
| ☐ 2 | Willie Hernandez | .15 | .06 | .01 |
| ☐ 3 | Rick Sutcliffe | .15 | .06 | .01 |
| ☐ 4 | Don Mattingly | 2.50 | 1.00 | .25 |
| ☐ 5 | Tony Gwynn | .75 | .30 | .07 |
| ☐ 6 | Alvin Davis | .50 | .20 | .05 |
| ☐ 7 | Dwight Gooden | 2.00 | .80 | .20 |
| ☐ 8 | Dan Quisenberry | .15 | .06 | .01 |
| ☐ 9 | Bruce Sutter | .15 | .06 | .01 |
| ☐ 10 | Tony Armas | .10 | .04 | .01 |
| ☐ 11 | Dale Murphy | 1.00 | .40 | .10 |
| ☐ 12 | Mike Schmidt | .90 | .36 | .09 |
| ☐ 13 | Gary Carter | .60 | .24 | .06 |
| ☐ 14 | Rickey Henderson | .75 | .30 | .07 |
| ☐ 15 | Tim Raines | .50 | .20 | .05 |
| ☐ 16 | Mike Boddicker | .10 | .04 | .01 |
| ☐ 17 | Alejandro Pena | .10 | .04 | .01 |
| ☐ 18 | Eddie Murray | .90 | .36 | .09 |
| ☐ 19 | Gary Matthews | .10 | .04 | .01 |
| ☐ 20 | Mark Langston | .20 | .08 | .02 |
| ☐ 21 | Mario Soto | .10 | .04 | .01 |
| ☐ 22 | Dave Stieb | .15 | .06 | .01 |

## 1985 Topps 3-D

This innovative 30 card set was issued in packs of one. These large cards are very difficult to store (due to the 3-D effect) as they are not really stackable and are crumpled if placed in an album using plastic sheets. The cards are blank-backed except for two covered adhesive strips and measure approximately 4 1/4" by 5 7/8". Cards are numbered on the front and feature a prominent team logo on the front as well.

| | | MINT | VG-E | F-G |
|---|---|---|---|---|
| COMPLETE SET | | 12.50 | 5.00 | 1.25 |
| COMMON PLAYER | | .20 | .08 | .02 |
| ☐ 1 | Mike Schmidt | 1.00 | .40 | .10 |
| ☐ 2 | Eddie Murray | .90 | .36 | .09 |
| ☐ 3 | Dale Murphy | 1.25 | .50 | .12 |
| ☐ 4 | George Brett | .90 | .36 | .09 |
| ☐ 5 | Gary Carter | .60 | .24 | .06 |
| ☐ 6 | Jim Rice | .50 | .20 | .05 |
| ☐ 7 | Ryne Sandberg | .60 | .24 | .06 |
| ☐ 8 | Don Mattingly | 2.00 | .80 | .20 |
| ☐ 9 | Darryl Strawberry | 1.00 | .40 | .10 |
| ☐ 10 | Rickey Henderson | .90 | .36 | .09 |
| ☐ 11 | Keith Hernandez | .40 | .16 | .04 |
| ☐ 12 | Dave Kingman | .20 | .08 | .02 |
| ☐ 13 | Tony Gwynn | .50 | .20 | .05 |
| ☐ 14 | Reggie Jackson | 1.00 | .40 | .10 |
| ☐ 15 | Pete Rose | 1.50 | .60 | .15 |
| ☐ 16 | Cal Ripken | .75 | .30 | .07 |
| ☐ 17 | Tim Raines | .50 | .20 | .05 |
| ☐ 18 | Dave Winfield | .50 | .20 | .05 |
| ☐ 19 | Dwight Gooden | 1.50 | .60 | .15 |
| ☐ 20 | Dave Stieb | .20 | .08 | .02 |
| ☐ 21 | Fernando Valenzuela | .40 | .16 | .04 |
| ☐ 22 | Mark Langston | .20 | .08 | .02 |
| ☐ 23 | Bruce Sutter | .20 | .08 | .02 |
| ☐ 24 | Dan Quisenberry | .20 | .08 | .02 |
| ☐ 25 | Steve Carlton | .50 | .20 | .05 |
| ☐ 26 | Mike Boddicker | .20 | .08 | .02 |
| ☐ 27 | Rich Gossage | .25 | .10 | .02 |
| ☐ 28 | Jack Morris | .25 | .10 | .02 |
| ☐ 29 | Rick Sutcliffe | .20 | .08 | .02 |

☐ 30 Tom Seaver ...................... .50 .20 .05

## 1985 Topps Glossy 22

The cards in this 22 card set measure 2 1/2" by 3 1/2". Similar in design, both front and back, to last year's Glossy set, this edition features the managers, starting nine players and honorary captains of the National and American League teams in the 1984 All-Star game. The set is numbered on the reverse with plyers essentially ordered by position within league, NL: 1-11 and AL: 12-22.

|  | MINT | VG-E | F-G |
|---|---|---|---|
| COMPLETE SET ...................... | 3.75 | 1.25 | .30 |
| COMMON PLAYER ................... | .10 | .04 | .01 |
| ☐ 1 Paul Owens MGR ............... | .10 | .04 | .01 |
| ☐ 2 Steve Garvey ..................... | .45 | .18 | .04 |
| ☐ 3 Ryne Sandberg ................. | .65 | .26 | .06 |
| ☐ 4 Mike Schmidt .................... | .75 | .30 | .07 |
| ☐ 5 Ozzie Smith ...................... | .15 | .06 | .01 |
| ☐ 6 Tony Gwynn ...................... | .45 | .18 | .04 |
| ☐ 7 Dale Murphy ..................... | .75 | .30 | .07 |
| ☐ 8 Darryl Strawberry ............. | .75 | .30 | .07 |
| ☐ 9 Gary Carter ...................... | .40 | .16 | .04 |
| ☐ 10 Charlie Lea ....................... | .10 | .04 | .01 |
| ☐ 11 Willie McCovey CAPT ........ | .25 | .10 | .02 |
| ☐ 12 Joe Altobelli MGR ............ | .10 | .04 | .01 |
| ☐ 13 Rod Carew ....................... | .45 | .18 | .04 |
| ☐ 14 Lou Whitaker ................... | .20 | .08 | .02 |
| ☐ 15 George Brett .................... | .75 | .30 | .07 |
| ☐ 16 Cal Ripken ....................... | .65 | .26 | .06 |
| ☐ 17 Dave Winfield ................... | .45 | .18 | .04 |
| ☐ 18 Chet Lemon ...................... | .10 | .04 | .01 |
| ☐ 19 Reggie Jackson ................ | .60 | .24 | .06 |
| ☐ 20 Lance Parrish ................... | .30 | .12 | .03 |
| ☐ 21 Dave Stieb ....................... | .20 | .08 | .02 |
| ☐ 22 Hank Greenberg CAPT ...... | .15 | .06 | .01 |

## 1985 Topps Glossy 40

The cards in this 40 card set measure 2 1/2" by 3 1/2". Similar to last year's glossy set, this set was issued as a bonus prize to Topps All-Star Baseball Game cards found in wax packs. The set could be obtained by sending in the "Bonus Runs" from the "Winning Pitch" game insert cards. For 25 runs and 75 cents, a collector could send in for one of the eight different five card series plus automatically be entered in the Grand Prize Sweepstakes for a chance at a free trip to the All-Star game. The cards are numbered and contain 20 stars from each league.

|  | MINT | VG-E | F-G |
|---|---|---|---|
| COMPLETE SET ...................... | 12.00 | 5.00 | 1.20 |
| COMMON PLAYER ................... | .15 | .06 | .01 |
| ☐ 1 Dale Murphy ..................... | 1.25 | .50 | .12 |
| ☐ 2 Jesse Orosco ................... | .15 | .06 | .01 |
| ☐ 3 Bob Brenly ....................... | .15 | .06 | .01 |
| ☐ 4 Mike Boddicker ................ | .15 | .06 | .01 |
| ☐ 5 Dave Kingman ................. | .20 | .08 | .02 |
| ☐ 6 Jim Rice ........................... | .45 | .18 | .04 |
| ☐ 7 Frank Viola ....................... | .15 | .06 | .01 |
| ☐ 8 Alvin Davis ....................... | .25 | .10 | .02 |
| ☐ 9 Rick Sutcliffe ................... | .20 | .08 | .02 |
| ☐ 10 Pete Rose ........................ | 1.50 | .60 | .15 |
| ☐ 11 Leon Durham ................... | .15 | .06 | .01 |
| ☐ 12 Joaquin Andujar .............. | .15 | .06 | .01 |
| ☐ 13 Keith Hernandez .............. | .45 | .18 | .04 |
| ☐ 14 Dave Winfield ................... | .60 | .24 | .06 |
| ☐ 15 Reggie Jackson ................ | 1.00 | .40 | .10 |
| ☐ 16 Allan Trammell ................. | .25 | .10 | .02 |
| ☐ 17 Bert Blyleven ................... | .20 | .08 | .02 |
| ☐ 18 Tony Armas ..................... | .15 | .06 | .01 |
| ☐ 19 Rich Gossage ................... | .20 | .08 | .02 |
| ☐ 20 Jose Cruz ........................ | .15 | .06 | .01 |
| ☐ 21 Ryne Sandberg ................ | .60 | .24 | .06 |
| ☐ 22 Bruce Sutter .................... | .20 | .08 | .02 |
| ☐ 23 Mike Schmidt .................. | 1.00 | .40 | .10 |
| ☐ 24 Cal Ripken ...................... | 1.00 | .40 | .10 |
| ☐ 25 Dan Petry ....................... | .15 | .06 | .01 |
| ☐ 26 Jack Morris ..................... | .25 | .10 | .02 |
| ☐ 27 Don Mattingly .................. | 2.50 | 1.00 | .25 |
| ☐ 28 Eddie Murray ................... | 1.00 | .40 | .10 |
| ☐ 29 Tony Gwynn ..................... | .50 | .20 | .05 |
| ☐ 30 Charlie Lea ...................... | .15 | .06 | .01 |
| ☐ 31 Juan Samuel .................... | .20 | .08 | .02 |
| ☐ 32 Phil Niekro ...................... | .30 | .12 | .03 |
| ☐ 33 Alejandro Pena ................ | .15 | .06 | .01 |
| ☐ 34 Harold Baines .................. | .35 | .14 | .03 |
| ☐ 35 Dan Quisenberry .............. | .25 | .10 | .02 |
| ☐ 36 Gary Carter ..................... | .75 | .30 | .07 |
| ☐ 37 Mario Soto ...................... | .15 | .06 | .01 |
| ☐ 38 Dwight Gooden ................ | 2.00 | .80 | .20 |
| ☐ 39 Tom Brunansky ................ | .15 | .06 | .01 |
| ☐ 40 Dave Stieb ...................... | .20 | .08 | .02 |

## 1985 Topps Traded

The cards in this 132 card set measure 2 1/2" by 3 1/2". In its now standard procedure, Topps issued its traded (or extended) set for the fifth year in a row. Because all photos and statistics of its regular set for the year were developed during the fall and winter months of the preceding year, players who changed teams during the fall, winter and spring months are portrayed in the 1985 regular issue set with the teams they were with in 1984. The Traded set amends the shortcomings of the regular set by presenting the players with their proper teams for the current year. Rookies not contained in the regular set are also picked up in the Traded set.

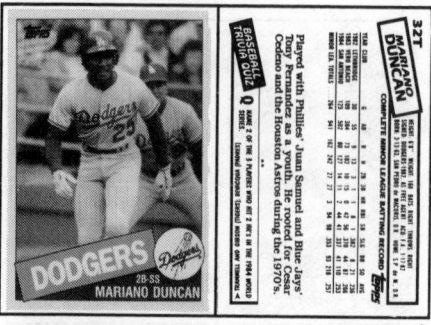

Again this year, the Topps affiliate in Ireland printed the cards, and the cards were available through hobby channels only.

|  | MINT | VG-E | F-G |
|---|---|---|---|
| COMPLETE SET | 14.00 | 5.75 | 1.40 |
| COMMON PLAYER | .06 | .02 | .00 |

| | | | MINT | VG-E | F-G |
|---|---|---|---|---|---|
| ☐ | 1T | Don Aase | .10 | .04 | .01 |
| ☐ | 2T | Bill Almon | .06 | .02 | .00 |
| ☐ | 3T | Benny Ayala | .06 | .02 | .00 |
| ☐ | 4T | Dusty Baker | .10 | .04 | .01 |
| ☐ | 5T | G.Bamberger MGR | .10 | .04 | .01 |
| ☐ | 6T | Dale Berra | .10 | .04 | .01 |
| ☐ | 7T | Rich Bordi | .06 | .02 | .00 |
| ☐ | 8T | Daryl Boston | .25 | .10 | .02 |
| ☐ | 9T | Hubie Brooks | .25 | .10 | .02 |
| ☐ | 10T | Chris Brown | 2.25 | .90 | .22 |
| ☐ | 11T | Tom Browning | .75 | .30 | .07 |
| ☐ | 12T | Al Bumbry | .06 | .02 | .00 |
| ☐ | 13T | Ray Burris | .06 | .02 | .00 |
| ☐ | 14T | Jeff Burroughs | .06 | .02 | .00 |
| ☐ | 15T | Bill Campbell | .06 | .02 | .00 |
| ☐ | 16T | Don Carman | .35 | .14 | .03 |
| ☐ | 17T | Gary Carter | .75 | .30 | .07 |
| ☐ | 18T | Bobby Castillo | .06 | .02 | .00 |
| ☐ | 19T | Bill Caudill | .10 | .04 | .01 |
| ☐ | 20T | Rick Cerone | .06 | .02 | .00 |
| ☐ | 21T | Bryan Clark | .06 | .02 | .00 |
| ☐ | 22T | Jack Clark | .25 | .10 | .02 |
| ☐ | 23T | Pat Clements | .25 | .10 | .02 |
| ☐ | 24T | Vince Coleman | 4.50 | 1.80 | .45 |
| ☐ | 25T | Dave Collins | .10 | .04 | .01 |
| ☐ | 26T | Danny Darwin | .06 | .02 | .00 |
| ☐ | 27T | Jim Davenport MGR | .06 | .02 | .00 |
| ☐ | 28T | Jerry Davis | .15 | .06 | .01 |
| ☐ | 29T | Brian Dayett | .06 | .02 | .00 |
| ☐ | 30T | Ivan DeJesus | .06 | .02 | .00 |
| ☐ | 31T | Ken Dixon | .25 | .10 | .02 |
| ☐ | 32T | Mariano Duncan | .75 | .30 | .07 |
| ☐ | 33T | John Felske MGR | .06 | .02 | .00 |
| ☐ | 34T | Mike Fitzgerald | .06 | .02 | .00 |
| ☐ | 35T | Ray Fontenot | .06 | .02 | .00 |
| ☐ | 36T | Greg Gagne | .20 | .08 | .02 |
| ☐ | 37T | Oscar Gamble | .10 | .04 | .01 |
| ☐ | 38T | Scott Garrelts | .35 | .14 | .03 |
| ☐ | 39T | Bob L. Gibson | .06 | .02 | .00 |
| ☐ | 40T | Jim Gott | .06 | .02 | .00 |
| ☐ | 41T | David Green | .10 | .04 | .01 |
| ☐ | 42T | Alfredo Griffin | .10 | .04 | .01 |
| ☐ | 43T | Ozzie Guillen | .75 | .30 | .07 |
| ☐ | 44T | Eddie Haas MGR | .06 | .02 | .00 |
| ☐ | 45T | Terry Harper | .06 | .02 | .00 |
| ☐ | 46T | Toby Harrah | .10 | .04 | .01 |
| ☐ | 47T | Greg Harris | .10 | .04 | .01 |
| ☐ | 48T | Ron Hassey | .06 | .02 | .00 |
| ☐ | 49T | Rickey Henderson | 1.00 | .40 | .10 |
| ☐ | 50T | Steve Henderson | .06 | .02 | .00 |
| ☐ | 51T | George Hendrick | .10 | .04 | .01 |
| ☐ | 52T | Joe Hesketh | .30 | .12 | .03 |
| ☐ | 53T | Teddy Higuera | 2.00 | .80 | .20 |
| ☐ | 54T | Donnie Hill | .10 | .04 | .01 |
| ☐ | 55T | Al Holland | .10 | .04 | .01 |
| ☐ | 56T | Burt Hooton | .06 | .02 | .00 |
| ☐ | 57T | Jay Howell | .10 | .04 | .01 |
| ☐ | 58T | Ken Howell | .25 | .10 | .02 |
| ☐ | 59T | LaMarr Hoyt | .15 | .06 | .01 |
| ☐ | 60T | Tim Hulett | .20 | .08 | .02 |
| ☐ | 61T | Bob James | .10 | .04 | .01 |
| ☐ | 62T | Steve Jeltz | .15 | .06 | .01 |
| ☐ | 63T | Cliff Johnson | .06 | .02 | .00 |
| ☐ | 64T | Howard Johnson | .10 | .04 | .01 |
| ☐ | 65T | Ruppert Jones | .10 | .04 | .01 |
| ☐ | 66T | Steve Kemp | .10 | .04 | .01 |
| ☐ | 67T | Bruce Kison | .06 | .02 | .00 |
| ☐ | 68T | Alan Knicely | .06 | .02 | .00 |
| ☐ | 69T | Mike LaCoss | .06 | .02 | .00 |
| ☐ | 70T | Lee Lacy | .10 | .04 | .01 |
| ☐ | 71T | Dave LaPoint | .06 | .02 | .00 |
| ☐ | 72T | Gary Lavelle | .10 | .04 | .01 |
| ☐ | 73T | Vance Law | .06 | .02 | .00 |
| ☐ | 74T | Johnnie LeMaster | .06 | .02 | .00 |
| ☐ | 75T | Sixto Lezcano | .06 | .02 | .00 |
| ☐ | 76T | Tim Lollar | .06 | .02 | .00 |
| ☐ | 77T | Fred Lynn | .25 | .10 | .02 |
| ☐ | 78T | Billy Martin MGR | .15 | .06 | .01 |
| ☐ | 79T | Ron Mathis | .15 | .06 | .01 |
| ☐ | 80T | Len Matuszek | .06 | .02 | .00 |
| ☐ | 81T | Gene Mauch MGR | .10 | .04 | .01 |
| ☐ | 82T | Oddibe McDowell | 1.00 | .40 | .10 |
| ☐ | 83T | Roger McDowell | 1.00 | .40 | .10 |
| ☐ | 84T | John McNamara MGR | .10 | .04 | .01 |
| ☐ | 85T | Donnie Moore | .10 | .04 | .01 |
| ☐ | 86T | Gene Nelson | .06 | .02 | .00 |
| ☐ | 87T | Steve Nicosia | .06 | .02 | .00 |
| ☐ | 88T | Al Oliver | .20 | .08 | .02 |
| ☐ | 89T | Joe Orsulak | .30 | .12 | .03 |
| ☐ | 90T | Rob Picciolo | .06 | .02 | .00 |
| ☐ | 91T | Chris Pittaro | .15 | .06 | .01 |
| ☐ | 92T | Jim Presley | 2.00 | .80 | .20 |
| ☐ | 93T | Rick Reuschel | .10 | .04 | .01 |
| ☐ | 94T | Bert Roberge | .06 | .02 | .00 |
| ☐ | 95T | Bob Rodgers MGR | .06 | .02 | .00 |
| ☐ | 96T | Jerry Royster | .06 | .02 | .00 |
| ☐ | 97T | Dave Rozema | .06 | .02 | .00 |
| ☐ | 98T | Dave Rucker | .06 | .02 | .00 |
| ☐ | 99T | Vern Ruhle | .06 | .02 | .00 |
| ☐ | 100T | Paul Runge | .15 | .06 | .01 |
| ☐ | 101T | Mark Salas | .30 | .12 | .03 |
| ☐ | 102T | Luis Salazar | .06 | .02 | .00 |
| ☐ | 103T | Joe Sambito | .10 | .04 | .01 |
| ☐ | 104T | Rick Schu | .25 | .10 | .02 |
| ☐ | 105T | Donnie Scott | .06 | .02 | .00 |
| ☐ | 106T | Larry Sheets | .50 | .20 | .05 |
| ☐ | 107T | Don Slaught | .10 | .04 | .01 |
| ☐ | 108T | Roy Smalley | .10 | .04 | .01 |
| ☐ | 109T | Lonnie Smith | .10 | .04 | .01 |
| ☐ | 110T | Nate Snell | .15 | .06 | .01 |
| ☐ | 111T | Chris Speier | .06 | .02 | .00 |
| ☐ | 112T | Mike Stenhouse | .10 | .04 | .01 |
| ☐ | 113T | Tim Stoddard | .06 | .02 | .00 |
| ☐ | 114T | Jim Sundberg | .10 | .04 | .01 |
| ☐ | 115T | Bruce Sutter | .25 | .10 | .02 |
| ☐ | 116T | Don Sutton | .50 | .20 | .05 |
| ☐ | 117T | Kent Tekulve | .10 | .04 | .01 |
| ☐ | 118T | Tom Tellman | .06 | .02 | .00 |
| ☐ | 119T | Walt Terrell | .10 | .04 | .01 |
| ☐ | 120T | Mickey Tettleton | .10 | .04 | .01 |
| ☐ | 121T | Derrel Thomas | .06 | .02 | .00 |
| ☐ | 122T | Rich Thompson | .10 | .04 | .01 |
| ☐ | 123T | Alex Trevino | .06 | .02 | .00 |
| ☐ | 124T | John Tudor | .20 | .08 | .02 |
| ☐ | 125T | Jose Uribe | .10 | .04 | .01 |
| ☐ | 126T | Bobby Valentine MGR | .15 | .06 | .01 |
| ☐ | 127T | Dave Von Ohlen | .06 | .02 | .00 |
| ☐ | 128T | U.L. Washington | .06 | .02 | .00 |
| ☐ | 129T | Earl Weaver MGR | .15 | .06 | .01 |
| ☐ | 130T | Eddie Whitson | .10 | .04 | .01 |
| ☐ | 131T | Herm Winningham | .20 | .08 | .02 |
| ☐ | 132T | Checklist 1-132 | .10 | .02 | .00 |

## 1986 Topps

The cards in this 792 card set are standard sized (2 1/2" by 3 1/2"). The first seven cards are a tribute to Pete Rose and his career. Cards 2-7 show small photos of Pete's Topps cards of the given years on the front with biographical information pertaining to those years on the back. The team leader cards were done differently with a simple player action shot on a white background; the player pictured is dubbed the "Dean" of the that team, i.e., the player with the longest continuous service with that team. Topps again features a "Turn Back the Clock" series

WADE BOGGS

(401-405). Record breakers of the previous year are acknowledged on cards 201 to 207. Cards 701-722 feature all star selections from each league. Manager cards feature the team checklist on the reverse. Ryne Sandberg (#690) is the only player card in the set without a Topps logo on the front of the card; this omission was never corrected by Topps. There are two other uncorrected errors involving misnumbered cards; see card numbers 51, 57, 141, and 171 in the checklist below. The backs of all the cards have a distinctive red background. Topps also printed cards on the bottoms of their wax pack boxes; there are four different boxes, each with four cards. These sixteen cards ("numbered" A through P) are listed at the end of the checklist below but are not considered an integral part of the set and are not included in the complete set price below.

|  | | MINT | VG-E | F-G |
|---|---|---|---|---|
|  | COMPLETE SET | 24.00 | 10.00 | 2.40 |
|  | COMMON PLAYER | .03 | .01 | .00 |
| ☐ | 1 Pete Rose | .85 | .20 | .04 |
| ☐ | 2 Rose Special: '63-'66 | .25 | .10 | .02 |
| ☐ | 3 Rose Special: '67-'70 | .25 | .10 | .02 |
| ☐ | 4 Rose Special: '71-'74 | .25 | .10 | .02 |
| ☐ | 5 Rose Special: '75-'78 | .25 | .10 | .02 |
| ☐ | 6 Rose Special: '79-'82 | .25 | .10 | .02 |
| ☐ | 7 Rose Special: '83-'85 | .25 | .10 | .02 |
| ☐ | 8 Dwayne Murphy | .05 | .02 | .00 |
| ☐ | 9 Roy Smith | .03 | .01 | .00 |
| ☐ | 10 Tony Gwynn | .25 | .10 | .02 |
| ☐ | 11 Bob Ojeda | .08 | .03 | .01 |
| ☐ | 12 Jose Uribe | .08 | .03 | .01 |
| ☐ | 13 Bob Kearney | .03 | .01 | .00 |
| ☐ | 14 Julio Cruz | .03 | .01 | .00 |
| ☐ | 15 Eddie Whitson | .05 | .02 | .00 |
| ☐ | 16 Rick Schu | .06 | .02 | .00 |
| ☐ | 17 Mike Stenhouse | .03 | .01 | .00 |
| ☐ | 18 Brent Gaff | .03 | .01 | .00 |
| ☐ | 19 Rich Hebner | .03 | .01 | .00 |
| ☐ | 20 Lou Whitaker | .12 | .05 | .01 |
| ☐ | 21 G.Bamberger MGR | .05 | .01 | .00 |
|  | (checklist back) | | | |
| ☐ | 22 Duane Walker | .03 | .01 | .00 |
| ☐ | 23 Manny Lee | .10 | .04 | .01 |
| ☐ | 24 Len Barker | .05 | .02 | .00 |
| ☐ | 25 Willie Wilson | .15 | .06 | .01 |
| ☐ | 26 Frank DiPino | .03 | .01 | .00 |
| ☐ | 27 Ray Knight | .08 | .03 | .01 |
| ☐ | 28 Eric Davis | 1.00 | .40 | .10 |
| ☐ | 29 Tony Phillips | .03 | .01 | .00 |
| ☐ | 30 Eddie Murray | .35 | .14 | .03 |
| ☐ | 31 Jamie Easterly | .03 | .01 | .00 |
| ☐ | 32 Steve Yeager | .05 | .02 | .00 |
| ☐ | 33 Jeff Lahti | .03 | .01 | .00 |
| ☐ | 34 Ken Phelps | .03 | .01 | .00 |
| ☐ | 35 Jeff Reardon | .06 | .02 | .00 |
| ☐ | 36 Tigers Leaders | .12 | .05 | .01 |
|  | Lance Parrish | | | |
| ☐ | 37 Mark Thurmond | .05 | .02 | .00 |
| ☐ | 38 Glenn Hoffman | .03 | .01 | .00 |
| ☐ | 39 Dave Rucker | .03 | .01 | .00 |
| ☐ | 40 Ken Griffey | .06 | .02 | .00 |
| ☐ | 41 Brad Wellman | .03 | .01 | .00 |
| ☐ | 42 Geoff Zahn | .03 | .01 | .00 |
| ☐ | 43 Dave Engle | .03 | .01 | .00 |
| ☐ | 44 Lance McCullers | .25 | .10 | .02 |
| ☐ | 45 Damaso Garcia | .07 | .03 | .01 |
| ☐ | 46 Billy Hatcher | .06 | .02 | .00 |
| ☐ | 47 Juan Berenguer | .03 | .01 | .00 |
| ☐ | 48 Bill Almon | .03 | .01 | .00 |
| ☐ | 49 Rick Manning | .03 | .01 | .00 |
| ☐ | 50 Dan Quisenberry | .14 | .06 | .01 |
| ☐ | 51 Bobby Wine MGR ERR | .08 | .02 | .00 |
|  | (checklist back) | | | |
|  | (number of card on | | | |
|  | back is actually 57) | | | |
| ☐ | 52 Chris Welsh | .03 | .01 | .00 |
| ☐ | 53 Len Dykstra | 1.50 | .60 | .15 |
| ☐ | 54 John Franco | .09 | .04 | .01 |
| ☐ | 55 Fred Lynn | .15 | .06 | .01 |
| ☐ | 56 Tom Niedenfuer | .06 | .02 | .00 |
| ☐ | 57 Bill Doran | .10 | .04 | .01 |
|  | (see also 51) | | | |
| ☐ | 58 Bill Krueger | .03 | .01 | .00 |
| ☐ | 59 Andre Thornton | .06 | .02 | .00 |
| ☐ | 60 Dwight Evans | .10 | .04 | .01 |
| ☐ | 61 Karl Best | .10 | .04 | .01 |
| ☐ | 62 Bob Boone | .05 | .02 | .00 |
| ☐ | 63 Ron Roenicke | .03 | .01 | .00 |
| ☐ | 64 Floyd Bannister | .05 | .02 | .00 |
| ☐ | 65 Dan Driessen | .03 | .01 | .00 |
| ☐ | 66 Cardinals Leaders | .05 | .02 | .00 |
|  | Bob Forsch | | | |
| ☐ | 67 Carmelo Martinez | .05 | .02 | .00 |
| ☐ | 68 Ed Lynch | .03 | .01 | .00 |
| ☐ | 69 Luis Aguayo | .03 | .01 | .00 |
| ☐ | 70 Dave Winfield | .30 | .12 | .03 |
| ☐ | 71 Ken Schrom | .05 | .02 | .00 |
| ☐ | 72 Shawon Dunston | .10 | .04 | .01 |
| ☐ | 73 Randy O'Neal | .05 | .02 | .00 |
| ☐ | 74 Rance Mulliniks | .03 | .01 | .00 |
| ☐ | 75 Jose DeLeon | .05 | .02 | .00 |
| ☐ | 76 Dion James | .05 | .02 | .00 |
| ☐ | 77 Charlie Leibrandt | .06 | .02 | .00 |
| ☐ | 78 Bruce Benedict | .03 | .01 | .00 |
| ☐ | 79 Dave Schmidt | .03 | .01 | .00 |
| ☐ | 80 Darryl Strawberry | .40 | .16 | .04 |
| ☐ | 81 Gene Mauch MGR | .05 | .01 | .00 |
|  | (checklist back) | | | |
| ☐ | 82 Tippy Martinez | .03 | .01 | .00 |
| ☐ | 83 Phil Garner | .05 | .02 | .00 |
| ☐ | 84 Curt Young | .03 | .01 | .00 |
| ☐ | 85 Tony Perez | .10 | .04 | .01 |
| ☐ | 86 Tom Waddell | .03 | .01 | .00 |
| ☐ | 87 Candy Maldonado | .07 | .03 | .01 |
| ☐ | 88 Tom Nieto | .03 | .01 | .00 |
| ☐ | 89 Randy St.Claire | .05 | .02 | .00 |
| ☐ | 90 Garry Templeton | .08 | .03 | .01 |
| ☐ | 91 Steve Crawford | .03 | .01 | .00 |
| ☐ | 92 Al Cowens | .05 | .02 | .00 |
| ☐ | 93 Scot Thompson | .03 | .01 | .00 |
| ☐ | 94 Rich Bordi | .03 | .01 | .00 |
| ☐ | 95 Ozzie Virgil | .05 | .02 | .00 |
| ☐ | 96 Blue Jays Leaders | .05 | .02 | .00 |
|  | Jim Clancy | | | |
| ☐ | 97 Gary Gaetti | .08 | .03 | .01 |
| ☐ | 98 Dick Ruthven | .03 | .01 | .00 |
| ☐ | 99 Buddy Biancalana | .03 | .01 | .00 |
| ☐ | 100 Nolan Ryan | .35 | .14 | .03 |
| ☐ | 101 Dave Bergman | .03 | .01 | .00 |
| ☐ | 102 Joe Orsulak | .25 | .10 | .02 |
| ☐ | 103 Luis Salazar | .03 | .01 | .00 |
| ☐ | 104 Sid Fernandez | .20 | .08 | .02 |
| ☐ | 105 Gary Ward | .03 | .01 | .00 |
| ☐ | 106 Ray Burris | .03 | .01 | .00 |
| ☐ | 107 Rafael Ramirez | .03 | .01 | .00 |
| ☐ | 108 Ted Power | .07 | .03 | .01 |
| ☐ | 109 Len Matuszek | .03 | .01 | .00 |
| ☐ | 110 Scott McGregor | .07 | .03 | .01 |
| ☐ | 111 Roger Craig MGR | .05 | .01 | .00 |
|  | (checklist back) | | | |
| ☐ | 112 Bill Campbell | .03 | .01 | .00 |
| ☐ | 113 U.L. Washington | .03 | .01 | .00 |
| ☐ | 114 Mike Brown | .03 | .01 | .00 |
| ☐ | 115 Jay Howell | .05 | .02 | .00 |
| ☐ | 116 Brook Jacoby | .10 | .04 | .01 |
| ☐ | 117 Bruce Kison | .03 | .01 | .00 |
| ☐ | 118 Jerry Royster | .03 | .01 | .00 |
| ☐ | 119 Barry Bonnell | .03 | .01 | .00 |
| ☐ | 120 Steve Carlton | .30 | .12 | .03 |
| ☐ | 121 Nelson Simmons | .15 | .06 | .01 |
| ☐ | 122 Pete Filson | .03 | .01 | .00 |
| ☐ | 123 Greg Walker | .10 | .04 | .01 |
| ☐ | 124 Luis Sanchez | .03 | .01 | .00 |
| ☐ | 125 Dave Lopes | .06 | .02 | .00 |
| ☐ | 126 Mets Leaders | .05 | .02 | .00 |

| | | | | |
|---|---|---|---|---|
| | Mookie Wilson | | | |
| ☐ 127 | Jack Howell | .35 | .14 | .03 |
| ☐ 128 | John Wathan | .03 | .01 | .00 |
| ☐ 129 | Jeff Dedmon | .03 | .01 | .00 |
| ☐ 130 | Alan Trammell | .15 | .06 | .01 |
| ☐ 131 | Checklist: 1-132 | .06 | .01 | .00 |
| ☐ 132 | Razor Shines | .06 | .02 | .00 |
| ☐ 133 | Andy McGaffigan | .03 | .01 | .00 |
| ☐ 134 | Carney Lansford | .09 | .04 | .01 |
| ☐ 135 | Joe Niekro | .07 | .03 | .01 |
| ☐ 136 | Mike Hargrove | .05 | .02 | .00 |
| ☐ 137 | Charlie Moore | .03 | .01 | .00 |
| ☐ 138 | Mark Davis | .03 | .01 | .00 |
| ☐ 139 | Daryl Boston | .08 | .03 | .01 |
| ☐ 140 | John Candelaria | .07 | .03 | .01 |
| ☐ 141 | Chuck Cottier MGR | .08 | .02 | .00 |
| | (checklist back) | | | |
| | (see also 171) | | | |
| ☐ 142 | Bob Jones | .03 | .01 | .00 |
| ☐ 143 | Dave Van Gorder | .03 | .01 | .00 |
| ☐ 144 | Doug Sisk | .03 | .01 | .00 |
| ☐ 145 | Pedro Guerrero | .20 | .08 | .02 |
| ☐ 146 | Jack Perconte | .03 | .01 | .00 |
| ☐ 147 | Larry Sheets | .10 | .04 | .01 |
| ☐ 148 | Mike Heath | .03 | .01 | .00 |
| ☐ 149 | Brett Butler | .09 | .04 | .01 |
| ☐ 150 | Joaquin Andujar | .08 | .03 | .01 |
| ☐ 151 | Dave Stapleton | .03 | .01 | .00 |
| ☐ 152 | Mike Morgan | .03 | .01 | .00 |
| ☐ 153 | Ricky Adams | .03 | .01 | .00 |
| ☐ 154 | Bert Roberge | .03 | .01 | .00 |
| ☐ 155 | Bob Grich | .06 | .02 | .00 |
| ☐ 156 | White Sox Leaders | .05 | .02 | .00 |
| | Richard Dotson | | | |
| ☐ 157 | Ron Hassey | .03 | .01 | .00 |
| ☐ 158 | Derrel Thomas | .03 | .01 | .00 |
| ☐ 159 | Orel Hershiser | .35 | .14 | .03 |
| ☐ 160 | Chet Lemon | .05 | .02 | .00 |
| ☐ 161 | Lee Tunnell | .03 | .01 | .00 |
| ☐ 162 | Greg Gagne | .05 | .02 | .00 |
| ☐ 163 | Pete Ladd | .03 | .01 | .00 |
| ☐ 164 | Steve Balboni | .06 | .02 | .00 |
| ☐ 165 | Mike Davis | .06 | .02 | .00 |
| ☐ 166 | Dickie Thon | .05 | .02 | .00 |
| ☐ 167 | Zane Smith | .06 | .02 | .00 |
| ☐ 168 | Jeff Burroughs | .03 | .01 | .00 |
| ☐ 169 | George Wright | .03 | .01 | .00 |
| ☐ 170 | Gary Carter | .30 | .12 | .03 |
| ☐ 171 | Bob Rodgers MGR ERR | .10 | .02 | .00 |
| | (checklist back) | | | |
| | (number of card on | | | |
| | back actually 141) | | | |
| ☐ 172 | Jerry Reed | .09 | .04 | .01 |
| ☐ 173 | Wayne Gross | .03 | .01 | .00 |
| ☐ 174 | Brian Snyder | .10 | .04 | .01 |
| ☐ 175 | Steve Sax | .12 | .05 | .01 |
| ☐ 176 | Jay Tibbs | .03 | .01 | .00 |
| ☐ 177 | Joel Youngblood | .03 | .01 | .00 |
| ☐ 178 | Ivan DeJesus | .03 | .01 | .00 |
| ☐ 179 | Stu Cliburn | .15 | .06 | .01 |
| ☐ 180 | Don Mattingly | 3.50 | 1.50 | .30 |
| ☐ 181 | Al Nipper | .03 | .01 | .00 |
| ☐ 182 | Bobby Brown | .03 | .01 | .00 |
| ☐ 183 | Larry Andersen | .03 | .01 | .00 |
| ☐ 184 | Tim Laudner | .03 | .01 | .00 |
| ☐ 185 | Rollie Fingers | .15 | .06 | .01 |
| ☐ 186 | Astros Leaders | .07 | .03 | .01 |
| | Jose Cruz | | | |
| ☐ 187 | Scott Fletcher | .05 | .02 | .00 |
| ☐ 188 | Bob Dernier | .03 | .01 | .00 |
| ☐ 189 | Mike Mason | .03 | .01 | .00 |
| ☐ 190 | George Hendrick | .06 | .02 | .00 |
| ☐ 191 | Wally Backman | .06 | .02 | .00 |
| ☐ 192 | Milt Wilcox | .03 | .01 | .00 |
| ☐ 193 | Daryl Sconiers | .03 | .01 | .00 |
| ☐ 194 | Craig McMurtry | .03 | .01 | .00 |
| ☐ 195 | Dave Concepcion | .07 | .03 | .01 |
| ☐ 196 | Doyle Alexander | .05 | .02 | .00 |
| ☐ 197 | Enos Cabell | .03 | .01 | .00 |
| ☐ 198 | Ken Dixon | .06 | .02 | .00 |
| ☐ 199 | Dick Howser MGR | .05 | .01 | .00 |
| | (checklist back) | | | |
| ☐ 200 | Mike Schmidt | .40 | .16 | .04 |
| ☐ 201 | RB: Vince Coleman | .25 | .10 | .02 |
| | Most Stolen Bases, | | | |
| | Season, Rookie | | | |
| ☐ 202 | RB: Dwight Gooden | .50 | .20 | .05 |
| | Youngest 20 Game | | | |
| | Winner | | | |
| ☐ 203 | RB: Keith Hernandez | .15 | .06 | .01 |
| | Most Game Winning | | | |
| | RBI's | | | |
| ☐ 204 | RB: Phil Niekro | .12 | .05 | .01 |

| | | | | |
|---|---|---|---|---|
| | Oldest Shutout | | | |
| | Pitcher | | | |
| ☐ 205 | RB: Tony Perez | .08 | .03 | .01 |
| | Oldest Grand Slammer | | | |
| ☐ 206 | RB: Pete Rose | .40 | .16 | .04 |
| | Most Hits, Lifetime | | | |
| ☐ 207 | RB: Fern.Valenzuela | .15 | .06 | .01 |
| | Most Cons. Innings, | | | |
| | Start of Season, | | | |
| | No Earned Runs | | | |
| ☐ 208 | Ramon Romero | .08 | .03 | .01 |
| ☐ 209 | Randy Ready | .06 | .02 | .00 |
| ☐ 210 | Calvin Schiraldi | .15 | .06 | .01 |
| ☐ 211 | Ed Wojna | .10 | .04 | .01 |
| ☐ 212 | Chris Speier | .03 | .01 | .00 |
| ☐ 213 | Bob Shirley | .03 | .01 | .00 |
| ☐ 214 | Randy Bush | .03 | .01 | .00 |
| ☐ 215 | Frank White | .06 | .02 | .00 |
| ☐ 216 | A's Leaders | .05 | .02 | .00 |
| | Dwayne Murphy | | | |
| ☐ 217 | Bill Scherrer | .03 | .01 | .00 |
| ☐ 218 | Randy Hunt | .08 | .03 | .01 |
| ☐ 219 | Dennis Lamp | .03 | .01 | .00 |
| ☐ 220 | Bob Horner | .15 | .06 | .01 |
| ☐ 221 | Dave Henderson | .06 | .02 | .00 |
| ☐ 222 | Craig Gerber | .08 | .03 | .01 |
| ☐ 223 | Atlee Hammaker | .05 | .02 | .00 |
| ☐ 224 | Cesar Cedeno | .06 | .02 | .00 |
| ☐ 225 | Ron Darling | .20 | .08 | .02 |
| ☐ 226 | Lee Lacy | .06 | .02 | .00 |
| ☐ 227 | Al Jones | .03 | .01 | .00 |
| ☐ 228 | Tom Lawless | .03 | .01 | .00 |
| ☐ 229 | Bill Gullickson | .05 | .02 | .00 |
| ☐ 230 | Terry Kennedy | .06 | .02 | .00 |
| ☐ 231 | Jim Frey MGR | .05 | .01 | .00 |
| | (checklist back) | | | |
| ☐ 232 | Rick Rhoden | .07 | .03 | .01 |
| ☐ 233 | Steve Lyons | .07 | .03 | .01 |
| ☐ 234 | Doug Corbett | .03 | .01 | .00 |
| ☐ 235 | Butch Wynegar | .05 | .02 | .00 |
| ☐ 236 | Frank Eufemia | .08 | .03 | .01 |
| ☐ 237 | Ted Simmons | .10 | .04 | .01 |
| ☐ 238 | Larry Parrish | .06 | .02 | .00 |
| ☐ 239 | Joel Skinner | .05 | .02 | .00 |
| ☐ 240 | Tommy John | .10 | .04 | .01 |
| ☐ 241 | Tony Fernandez | .10 | .04 | .01 |
| ☐ 242 | Rich Thompson | .08 | .03 | .01 |
| ☐ 243 | Johnny Grubb | .03 | .01 | .00 |
| ☐ 244 | Craig Lefferts | .03 | .01 | .00 |
| ☐ 245 | Jim Sundberg | .05 | .02 | .00 |
| ☐ 246 | Phillies Leaders | .15 | .06 | .01 |
| | Steve Carlton | | | |
| ☐ 247 | Terry Harper | .03 | .01 | .00 |
| ☐ 248 | Spike Owen | .05 | .02 | .00 |
| ☐ 249 | Rob Deer | .45 | .18 | .04 |
| ☐ 250 | Dwight Gooden | 2.50 | 1.00 | .25 |
| ☐ 251 | Rich Dauer | .03 | .01 | .00 |
| ☐ 252 | Bobby Castillo | .03 | .01 | .00 |
| ☐ 253 | Dann Bilardello | .03 | .01 | .00 |
| ☐ 254 | Ozzie Guillen | .45 | .18 | .04 |
| ☐ 255 | Tony Armas | .09 | .04 | .01 |
| ☐ 256 | Kurt Kepshire | .03 | .01 | .00 |
| ☐ 257 | Doug DeCinces | .08 | .03 | .01 |
| ☐ 258 | Tim Burke | .20 | .08 | .02 |
| ☐ 259 | Dan Pasqua | .50 | .20 | .05 |
| ☐ 260 | Tony Pena | .10 | .04 | .01 |
| ☐ 261 | Bobby Valentine MGR | .05 | .01 | .00 |
| | (checklist back) | | | |
| ☐ 262 | Mario Ramirez | .03 | .01 | .00 |
| ☐ 263 | Checklist: 133-264 | .06 | .01 | .00 |
| ☐ 264 | Darren Daulton | .20 | .08 | .02 |
| ☐ 265 | Ron Davis | .03 | .01 | .00 |
| ☐ 266 | Keith Moreland | .06 | .02 | .00 |
| ☐ 267 | Paul Molitor | .09 | .04 | .01 |
| ☐ 268 | Mike Scott | .25 | .10 | .02 |
| ☐ 269 | Dane Iorg | .03 | .01 | .00 |
| ☐ 270 | Jack Morris | .15 | .06 | .01 |
| ☐ 271 | Dave Collins | .05 | .02 | .00 |
| ☐ 272 | Tim Tolman | .08 | .03 | .01 |
| ☐ 273 | Jerry Willard | .03 | .01 | .00 |
| ☐ 274 | Ron Gardenhire | .03 | .01 | .00 |
| ☐ 275 | Charlie Hough | .06 | .02 | .00 |
| ☐ 276 | Yankees Leaders | .06 | .02 | .00 |
| | Willie Randolph | | | |
| ☐ 277 | Jaime Cocanower | .03 | .01 | .00 |
| ☐ 278 | Sixto Lezcano | .03 | .01 | .00 |
| ☐ 279 | Al Pardo | .10 | .04 | .01 |
| ☐ 280 | Tim Raines | .20 | .08 | .02 |
| ☐ 281 | Steve Mura | .03 | .01 | .00 |
| ☐ 282 | Jerry Mumphrey | .05 | .02 | .00 |
| ☐ 283 | Mike Fischlin | .03 | .01 | .00 |
| ☐ 284 | Brian Dayett | .03 | .01 | .00 |
| ☐ 285 | Buddy Bell | .09 | .04 | .01 |

| | | | | |
|---|---|---|---|---|
| ☐ 286 | Luis DeLeon | .03 | .01 | .00 |
| ☐ 287 | John Christensen | .07 | .03 | .01 |
| ☐ 288 | Don Aase | .05 | .02 | .00 |
| ☐ 289 | Johnnie LeMaster | .03 | .01 | .00 |
| ☐ 290 | Carlton Fisk | .12 | .05 | .01 |
| ☐ 291 | Tom Lasorda MGR (checklist back) | .10 | .02 | .00 |
| ☐ 292 | Chuck Porter | .03 | .01 | .00 |
| ☐ 293 | Chris Chambliss | .05 | .02 | .00 |
| ☐ 294 | Danny Cox | .09 | .04 | .01 |
| ☐ 295 | Kirk Gibson | .20 | .08 | .02 |
| ☐ 296 | Geno Petralli | .03 | .01 | .00 |
| ☐ 297 | Tim Lollar | .03 | .01 | .00 |
| ☐ 298 | Craig Reynolds | .03 | .01 | .00 |
| ☐ 299 | Bryn Smith | .05 | .02 | .00 |
| ☐ 300 | George Brett | .40 | .16 | .04 |
| ☐ 301 | Dennis Rasmussen | .08 | .03 | .01 |
| ☐ 302 | Greg Gross | .03 | .01 | .00 |
| ☐ 303 | Curt Wardle | .08 | .03 | .01 |
| ☐ 304 | Mike Gallego | .08 | .03 | .01 |
| ☐ 305 | Phil Bradley | .20 | .08 | .02 |
| ☐ 306 | Padres Leaders Terry Kennedy | .05 | .02 | .00 |
| ☐ 307 | Dave Sax | .03 | .01 | .00 |
| ☐ 308 | Ray Fontenot | .03 | .01 | .00 |
| ☐ 309 | John Shelby | .03 | .01 | .00 |
| ☐ 310 | Greg Minton | .05 | .02 | .00 |
| ☐ 311 | Dick Schofield | .06 | .02 | .00 |
| ☐ 312 | Tom Filer | .05 | .02 | .00 |
| ☐ 313 | Joe DeSa | .06 | .02 | .00 |
| ☐ 314 | Frank Pastore | .03 | .01 | .00 |
| ☐ 315 | Mookie Wilson | .06 | .02 | .00 |
| ☐ 316 | Sammy Khalifa | .10 | .04 | .01 |
| ☐ 317 | Ed Romero | .03 | .01 | .00 |
| ☐ 318 | Terry Whitfield | .03 | .01 | .00 |
| ☐ 319 | Rick Camp | .03 | .01 | .00 |
| ☐ 320 | Jim Rice | .30 | .12 | .03 |
| ☐ 321 | Earl Weaver MGR (checklist back) | .08 | .02 | .00 |
| ☐ 322 | Bob Forsch | .06 | .02 | .00 |
| ☐ 323 | Jerry Davis | .06 | .02 | .00 |
| ☐ 324 | Dan Schatzeder | .03 | .01 | .00 |
| ☐ 325 | Juan Beniquez | .05 | .02 | .00 |
| ☐ 326 | Kent Tekulve | .05 | .02 | .00 |
| ☐ 327 | Mike Pagliarulo | .25 | .10 | .02 |
| ☐ 328 | Pete O'Brien | .09 | .04 | .01 |
| ☐ 329 | Kirby Puckett | .40 | .16 | .04 |
| ☐ 330 | Rick Sutcliffe | .10 | .04 | .01 |
| ☐ 331 | Alan Ashby | .03 | .01 | .00 |
| ☐ 332 | Darryl Motley | .03 | .01 | .00 |
| ☐ 333 | Tom Henke | .06 | .02 | .00 |
| ☐ 334 | Ken Oberkfell | .03 | .01 | .00 |
| ☐ 335 | Don Sutton | .15 | .06 | .01 |
| ☐ 336 | Indians Leaders Andre Thornton | .05 | .02 | .00 |
| ☐ 337 | Darnell Coles | .08 | .03 | .01 |
| ☐ 338 | Jorge Bell | .15 | .06 | .01 |
| ☐ 339 | Bruce Berenyi | .03 | .01 | .00 |
| ☐ 340 | Cal Ripken | .40 | .16 | .04 |
| ☐ 341 | Frank Williams | .03 | .01 | .00 |
| ☐ 342 | Gary Redus | .05 | .02 | .00 |
| ☐ 343 | Carlos Diaz | .03 | .01 | .00 |
| ☐ 344 | Jim Wohlford | .03 | .01 | .00 |
| ☐ 345 | Donnie Moore | .05 | .02 | .00 |
| ☐ 346 | Bryan Little | .03 | .01 | .00 |
| ☐ 347 | Teddy Higuera | .90 | .36 | .09 |
| ☐ 348 | Cliff Johnson | .03 | .01 | .00 |
| ☐ 349 | Mark Clear | .03 | .01 | .00 |
| ☐ 350 | Jack Clark | .12 | .05 | .01 |
| ☐ 351 | Chuck Tanner MGR (checklist back) | .05 | .01 | .00 |
| ☐ 352 | Harry Spilman | .03 | .01 | .00 |
| ☐ 353 | Keith Atherton | .03 | .01 | .00 |
| ☐ 354 | Tony Bernazard | .05 | .02 | .00 |
| ☐ 355 | Lee Smith | .07 | .03 | .01 |
| ☐ 356 | Mickey Hatcher | .03 | .01 | .00 |
| ☐ 357 | Ed VandeBerg | .03 | .01 | .00 |
| ☐ 358 | Rick Dempsey | .05 | .02 | .00 |
| ☐ 359 | Mike LaCoss | .03 | .01 | .00 |
| ☐ 360 | Lloyd Moseby | .12 | .05 | .01 |
| ☐ 361 | Shane Rawley | .07 | .03 | .01 |
| ☐ 362 | Tom Paciorek | .03 | .01 | .00 |
| ☐ 363 | Terry Forster | .07 | .03 | .01 |
| ☐ 364 | Reid Nichols | .03 | .01 | .00 |
| ☐ 365 | Mike Flanagan | .07 | .03 | .01 |
| ☐ 366 | Reds Leaders Dave Concepcion | .06 | .02 | .00 |
| ☐ 367 | Aurelio Lopez | .03 | .01 | .00 |
| ☐ 368 | Greg Brock | .06 | .02 | .00 |
| ☐ 369 | Al Holland | .03 | .01 | .00 |
| ☐ 370 | Vince Coleman | 2.00 | .80 | .20 |
| ☐ 371 | Bill Stein | .03 | .01 | .00 |
| ☐ 372 | Ben Oglivie | .06 | .02 | .00 |
| ☐ 373 | Urbano Lugo | .08 | .03 | .01 |
| ☐ 374 | Terry Francona | .05 | .02 | .00 |
| ☐ 375 | Rich Gedman | .08 | .03 | .01 |
| ☐ 376 | Bill Dawley | .03 | .01 | .00 |
| ☐ 377 | Joe Carter | .25 | .10 | .02 |
| ☐ 378 | Bruce Bochte | .05 | .02 | .00 |
| ☐ 379 | Bobby Meacham | .03 | .01 | .00 |
| ☐ 380 | LaMarr Hoyt | .07 | .03 | .01 |
| ☐ 381 | Ray Miller MGR (checklist back) | .05 | .01 | .00 |
| ☐ 382 | Ivan Calderon | .25 | .10 | .02 |
| ☐ 383 | Chris Brown | 1.25 | .50 | .12 |
| ☐ 384 | Steve Trout | .03 | .01 | .00 |
| ☐ 385 | Cecil Cooper | .10 | .04 | .01 |
| ☐ 386 | Cecil Fielder | .25 | .10 | .02 |
| ☐ 387 | Steve Kemp | .07 | .03 | .01 |
| ☐ 388 | Dickie Noles | .03 | .01 | .00 |
| ☐ 389 | Glenn Davis | 1.50 | .60 | .15 |
| ☐ 390 | Tom Seaver | .30 | .12 | .03 |
| ☐ 391 | Julio Franco | .09 | .04 | .01 |
| ☐ 392 | John Russell | .05 | .02 | .00 |
| ☐ 393 | Chris Pittaro | .08 | .03 | .01 |
| ☐ 394 | Checklist: 265-396 | .06 | .01 | .00 |
| ☐ 395 | Scott Garrelts | .05 | .02 | .00 |
| ☐ 396 | Red Sox Leaders Dwight Evans | .07 | .03 | .01 |
| ☐ 397 | Steve Buechele | .25 | .10 | .02 |
| ☐ 398 | Earnie Riles | .40 | .16 | .04 |
| ☐ 399 | Bill Swift | .05 | .02 | .00 |
| ☐ 400 | Rod Carew | .30 | .12 | .03 |
| ☐ 401 | Turn Back 5 Years Fern.Valenzuela '81 | .15 | .06 | .01 |
| ☐ 402 | Turn Back 10 Years Tom Seaver '76 | .15 | .06 | .01 |
| ☐ 403 | Turn Back 15 Years Willie Mays '71 | .15 | .06 | .01 |
| ☐ 404 | Turn Back 20 Years Frank Robinson '66 | .10 | .04 | .01 |
| ☐ 405 | Turn Back 25 Years Roger Maris '61 | .15 | .06 | .01 |
| ☐ 406 | Scott Sanderson | .03 | .01 | .00 |
| ☐ 407 | Sal Butera | .03 | .01 | .00 |
| ☐ 408 | Dave Smith | .06 | .02 | .00 |
| ☐ 409 | Paul Runge | .09 | .04 | .01 |
| ☐ 410 | Dave Kingman | .10 | .04 | .01 |
| ☐ 411 | Sparky Anderson MGR (checklist back) | .08 | .02 | .00 |
| ☐ 412 | Jim Clancy | .03 | .01 | .00 |
| ☐ 413 | Tim Flannery | .03 | .01 | .00 |
| ☐ 414 | Tom Gorman | .03 | .01 | .00 |
| ☐ 415 | Hal McRae | .05 | .02 | .00 |
| ☐ 416 | Denny Martinez | .03 | .01 | .00 |
| ☐ 417 | R.J. Reynolds | .05 | .02 | .00 |
| ☐ 418 | Alan Knicely | .03 | .01 | .00 |
| ☐ 419 | Frank Wills | .08 | .03 | .01 |
| ☐ 420 | Von Hayes | .10 | .04 | .01 |
| ☐ 421 | Dave Palmer | .05 | .02 | .00 |
| ☐ 422 | Mike Jorgensen | .03 | .01 | .00 |
| ☐ 423 | Dan Spillner | .03 | .01 | .00 |
| ☐ 424 | Rick Miller | .03 | .01 | .00 |
| ☐ 425 | Larry McWilliams | .03 | .01 | .00 |
| ☐ 426 | Brewers Leaders Charlie Moore | .05 | .02 | .00 |
| ☐ 427 | Joe Cowley | .05 | .02 | .00 |
| ☐ 428 | Max Venable | .03 | .01 | .00 |
| ☐ 429 | Greg Booker | .03 | .01 | .00 |
| ☐ 430 | Kent Hrbek | .15 | .06 | .01 |
| ☐ 431 | George Frazier | .03 | .01 | .00 |
| ☐ 432 | Mark Bailey | .03 | .01 | .00 |
| ☐ 433 | Chris Codiroli | .03 | .01 | .00 |
| ☐ 434 | Curt Wilkerson | .03 | .01 | .00 |
| ☐ 435 | Bill Caudill | .05 | .02 | .00 |
| ☐ 436 | Doug Flynn | .03 | .01 | .00 |
| ☐ 437 | Rick Mahler | .03 | .01 | .00 |
| ☐ 438 | Clint Hurdle | .03 | .01 | .00 |
| ☐ 439 | Rick Honeycutt | .05 | .02 | .00 |
| ☐ 440 | Alvin Davis | .20 | .08 | .02 |
| ☐ 441 | Whitey Herzog MGR (checklist back) | .07 | .01 | .00 |
| ☐ 442 | Ron Robinson | .03 | .01 | .00 |
| ☐ 443 | Bill Buckner | .08 | .03 | .01 |
| ☐ 444 | Alex Trevino | .03 | .01 | .00 |
| ☐ 445 | Bert Blyleven | .09 | .04 | .01 |
| ☐ 446 | Lenn Sakata | .03 | .01 | .00 |
| ☐ 447 | Jerry Don Gleaton | .03 | .01 | .00 |
| ☐ 448 | Herm Winningham | .15 | .06 | .01 |
| ☐ 449 | Rod Scurry | .03 | .01 | .00 |
| ☐ 450 | Graig Nettles | .12 | .05 | .01 |
| ☐ 451 | Mark Brown | .08 | .03 | .01 |
| ☐ 452 | Bob Clark | .03 | .01 | .00 |
| ☐ 453 | Steve Jeltz | .06 | .02 | .00 |
| ☐ 454 | Burt Hooton | .03 | .01 | .00 |
| ☐ 455 | Willie Randolph | .06 | .02 | .00 |

| | | | | |
|---|---|---|---|---|
| ☐ 456 | Braves Leaders | .25 | .10 | .02 |
| | Dale Murphy | | | |
| ☐ 457 | Mickey Tettleton | .09 | .04 | .01 |
| ☐ 458 | Kevin Bass | .07 | .03 | .01 |
| ☐ 459 | Luis Leal | .03 | .01 | .00 |
| ☐ 460 | Leon Durham | .08 | .03 | .01 |
| ☐ 461 | Walt Terrell | .03 | .01 | .00 |
| ☐ 462 | Domingo Ramos | .03 | .01 | .00 |
| ☐ 463 | Jim Gott | .03 | .01 | .00 |
| ☐ 464 | Ruppert Jones | .03 | .01 | .00 |
| ☐ 465 | Jesse Orosco | .05 | .02 | .00 |
| ☐ 466 | Tom Foley | .03 | .01 | .00 |
| ☐ 467 | Bob James | .05 | .02 | .00 |
| ☐ 468 | Mike Scioscia | .05 | .02 | .00 |
| ☐ 469 | Storm Davis | .07 | .03 | .01 |
| ☐ 470 | Bill Madlock | .10 | .04 | .01 |
| ☐ 471 | Bobby Cox MGR | .05 | .01 | .00 |
| | (checklist back) | | | |
| ☐ 472 | Joe Hesketh | .10 | .04 | .01 |
| ☐ 473 | Mark Brouhard | .03 | .01 | .00 |
| ☐ 474 | John Tudor | .10 | .04 | .01 |
| ☐ 475 | Juan Samuel | .12 | .05 | .01 |
| ☐ 476 | Ron Mathis | .10 | .04 | .01 |
| ☐ 477 | Mike Easler | .06 | .02 | .00 |
| ☐ 478 | Andy Hawkins | .06 | .02 | .00 |
| ☐ 479 | Bob Melvin | .09 | .04 | .01 |
| ☐ 480 | Oddibe McDowell | .35 | .14 | .03 |
| ☐ 481 | Scott Bradley | .10 | .04 | .01 |
| ☐ 482 | Rick Lysander | .03 | .01 | .00 |
| ☐ 483 | George Vukovich | .03 | .01 | .00 |
| ☐ 484 | Donnie Hill | .03 | .01 | .00 |
| ☐ 485 | Gary Matthews | .06 | .02 | .00 |
| ☐ 486 | Angels Leaders | .05 | .02 | .00 |
| | Bobby Grich | | | |
| ☐ 487 | Bret Saberhagen | .25 | .10 | .02 |
| ☐ 488 | Lou Thornton | .10 | .04 | .01 |
| ☐ 489 | Jim Winn | .03 | .01 | .00 |
| ☐ 490 | Jeff Leonard | .06 | .02 | .00 |
| ☐ 491 | Pascual Perez | .03 | .01 | .00 |
| ☐ 492 | Kelvin Chapman | .03 | .01 | .00 |
| ☐ 493 | Gene Nelson | .03 | .01 | .00 |
| ☐ 494 | Gary Roenicke | .05 | .02 | .00 |
| ☐ 495 | Mark Langston | .06 | .02 | .00 |
| ☐ 496 | Jay Johnstone | .05 | .02 | .00 |
| ☐ 497 | John Stuper | .03 | .01 | .00 |
| ☐ 498 | Tito Landrum | .03 | .01 | .00 |
| ☐ 499 | Bob L. Gibson | .03 | .01 | .00 |
| ☐ 500 | Rickey Henderson | .35 | .14 | .03 |
| ☐ 501 | Dave Johnson MGR | .08 | .02 | .00 |
| | (checklist back) | | | |
| ☐ 502 | Glen Cook | .10 | .04 | .01 |
| ☐ 503 | Mike Fitzgerald | .03 | .01 | .00 |
| ☐ 504 | Denny Walling | .03 | .01 | .00 |
| ☐ 505 | Jerry Koosman | .07 | .03 | .01 |
| ☐ 506 | Bill Russell | .05 | .02 | .00 |
| ☐ 507 | Steve Ontiveros | .20 | .08 | .02 |
| ☐ 508 | Alan Wiggins | .06 | .02 | .00 |
| ☐ 509 | Ernie Camacho | .03 | .01 | .00 |
| ☐ 510 | Wade Boggs | 1.50 | .60 | .15 |
| ☐ 511 | Ed Nunez | .05 | .02 | .00 |
| ☐ 512 | Thad Bosley | .03 | .01 | .00 |
| ☐ 513 | Ron Washington | .03 | .01 | .00 |
| ☐ 514 | Mike Jones | .03 | .01 | .00 |
| ☐ 515 | Darrell Evans | .08 | .03 | .01 |
| ☐ 516 | Giants Leaders | .05 | .02 | .00 |
| | Greg Minton | | | |
| ☐ 517 | Milt Thompson | .20 | .08 | .02 |
| ☐ 518 | Buck Martinez | .03 | .01 | .00 |
| ☐ 519 | Danny Darwin | .03 | .01 | .00 |
| ☐ 520 | Keith Hernandez | .25 | .10 | .02 |
| ☐ 521 | Nate Snell | .10 | .04 | .01 |
| ☐ 522 | Bob Bailor | .03 | .01 | .00 |
| ☐ 523 | Joe Price | .03 | .01 | .00 |
| ☐ 524 | Darrell Miller | .07 | .03 | .01 |
| ☐ 525 | Marvell Wynne | .03 | .01 | .00 |
| ☐ 526 | Charlie Lea | .05 | .02 | .00 |
| ☐ 527 | Checklist: 397-528 | .06 | .01 | .00 |
| ☐ 528 | Terry Pendleton | .05 | .02 | .00 |
| ☐ 529 | Marc Sullivan | .08 | .03 | .01 |
| ☐ 530 | Rich Gossage | .12 | .05 | .01 |
| ☐ 531 | Tony LaRussa MGR | .05 | .01 | .00 |
| | (checklist back) | | | |
| ☐ 532 | Don Carman | .25 | .10 | .02 |
| ☐ 533 | Billy Sample | .03 | .01 | .00 |
| ☐ 534 | Jeff Calhoun | .08 | .03 | .01 |
| ☐ 535 | Toby Harrah | .05 | .02 | .00 |
| ☐ 536 | Jose Rijo | .07 | .03 | .01 |
| ☐ 537 | Mark Salas | .06 | .02 | .00 |
| ☐ 538 | Dennis Eckersley | .06 | .02 | .00 |
| ☐ 539 | Glenn Hubbard | .03 | .01 | .00 |
| ☐ 540 | Dan Petry | .10 | .04 | .01 |
| ☐ 541 | Jorge Orta | .03 | .01 | .00 |
| ☐ 542 | Don Schulze | .03 | .01 | .00 |
| ☐ 543 | Jerry Narron | .03 | .01 | .00 |
| ☐ 544 | Eddie Milner | .05 | .02 | .00 |
| ☐ 545 | Jimmy Key | .10 | .04 | .01 |
| ☐ 546 | Mariners Leaders | .05 | .02 | .00 |
| | Dave Henderson | | | |
| ☐ 547 | Roger McDowell | .40 | .16 | .04 |
| ☐ 548 | Mike Young | .10 | .04 | .01 |
| ☐ 549 | Bob Welch | .06 | .02 | .00 |
| ☐ 550 | Tom Herr | .08 | .03 | .01 |
| ☐ 551 | Dave LaPoint | .03 | .01 | .00 |
| ☐ 552 | Marc Hill | .03 | .01 | .00 |
| ☐ 553 | Jim Morrison | .03 | .01 | .00 |
| ☐ 554 | Paul Householder | .03 | .01 | .00 |
| ☐ 555 | Hubie Brooks | .10 | .04 | .01 |
| ☐ 556 | John Denny | .07 | .03 | .01 |
| ☐ 557 | Gerald Perry | .05 | .02 | .00 |
| ☐ 558 | Tim Stoddard | .03 | .01 | .00 |
| ☐ 559 | Tommy Dunbar | .03 | .01 | .00 |
| ☐ 560 | Dave Righetti | .14 | .06 | .01 |
| ☐ 561 | Bob Lillis MGR | .05 | .01 | .00 |
| | (checklist back) | | | |
| ☐ 562 | Joe Beckwith | .03 | .01 | .00 |
| ☐ 563 | Alejandro Sanchez | .05 | .02 | .00 |
| ☐ 564 | Warren Brusstar | .03 | .01 | .00 |
| ☐ 565 | Tom Brunansky | .10 | .04 | .01 |
| ☐ 566 | Alfredo Griffin | .05 | .02 | .00 |
| ☐ 567 | Jeff Barkley | .08 | .03 | .01 |
| ☐ 568 | Donnie Scott | .03 | .01 | .00 |
| ☐ 569 | Jim Acker | .03 | .01 | .00 |
| ☐ 570 | Rusty Staub | .08 | .03 | .01 |
| ☐ 571 | Mike Jeffcoat | .03 | .01 | .00 |
| ☐ 572 | Paul Zuvella | .07 | .03 | .01 |
| ☐ 573 | Tom Hume | .03 | .01 | .00 |
| ☐ 574 | Ron Kittle | .10 | .04 | .01 |
| ☐ 575 | Mike Boddicker | .09 | .04 | .01 |
| ☐ 576 | Expos Leaders | .12 | .05 | .01 |
| | Andre Dawson | | | |
| ☐ 577 | Jerry Reuss | .06 | .02 | .00 |
| ☐ 578 | Lee Mazzilli | .05 | .02 | .00 |
| ☐ 579 | Jim Slaton | .03 | .01 | .00 |
| ☐ 580 | Willie McGee | .20 | .08 | .02 |
| ☐ 581 | Bruce Hurst | .07 | .03 | .01 |
| ☐ 582 | Jim Gantner | .05 | .02 | .00 |
| ☐ 583 | Al Bumbry | .03 | .01 | .00 |
| ☐ 584 | Brian Fisher | .25 | .10 | .02 |
| ☐ 585 | Garry Maddox | .05 | .02 | .00 |
| ☐ 586 | Greg Harris | .05 | .02 | .00 |
| ☐ 587 | Rafael Santana | .03 | .01 | .00 |
| ☐ 588 | Steve Lake | .03 | .01 | .00 |
| ☐ 589 | Sid Bream | .06 | .02 | .00 |
| ☐ 590 | Bob Knepper | .07 | .03 | .01 |
| ☐ 591 | Jackie Moore MGR | .05 | .01 | .00 |
| | (checklist back) | | | |
| ☐ 592 | Frank Tanana | .05 | .02 | .00 |
| ☐ 593 | Jesse Barfield | .15 | .06 | .01 |
| ☐ 594 | Chris Bando | .03 | .01 | .00 |
| ☐ 595 | Dave Parker | .20 | .08 | .02 |
| ☐ 596 | Onix Concepcion | .03 | .01 | .00 |
| ☐ 597 | Sammy Stewart | .03 | .01 | .00 |
| ☐ 598 | Jim Presley | .75 | .30 | .07 |
| ☐ 599 | Rick Aguilera | .30 | .12 | .03 |
| ☐ 600 | Dale Murphy | .45 | .18 | .04 |
| ☐ 601 | Gary Lucas | .03 | .01 | .00 |
| ☐ 602 | Mariano Duncan | .45 | .18 | .04 |
| ☐ 603 | Bill Laskey | .03 | .01 | .00 |
| ☐ 604 | Gary Pettis | .08 | .03 | .01 |
| ☐ 605 | Dennis Boyd | .08 | .03 | .01 |
| ☐ 606 | Royals Leaders | .05 | .02 | .00 |
| | Hal McRae | | | |
| ☐ 607 | Ken Dayley | .03 | .01 | .00 |
| ☐ 608 | Bruce Bochy | .03 | .01 | .00 |
| ☐ 609 | Barbaro Garbey | .03 | .01 | .00 |
| ☐ 610 | Ron Guidry | .15 | .06 | .01 |
| ☐ 611 | Gary Woods | .03 | .01 | .00 |
| ☐ 612 | Richard Dotson | .06 | .02 | .00 |
| ☐ 613 | Roy Smalley | .05 | .02 | .00 |
| ☐ 614 | Rick Waits | .03 | .01 | .00 |
| ☐ 615 | Johnny Ray | .09 | .04 | .01 |
| ☐ 616 | Glenn Brummer | .03 | .01 | .00 |
| ☐ 617 | Lonnie Smith | .06 | .02 | .00 |
| ☐ 618 | Jim Pankovits | .05 | .02 | .00 |
| ☐ 619 | Danny Heep | .03 | .01 | .00 |
| ☐ 620 | Bruce Sutter | .12 | .05 | .01 |
| ☐ 621 | John Felske MGR | .05 | .01 | .00 |
| | (checklist back) | | | |
| ☐ 622 | Gary Lavelle | .05 | .02 | .00 |
| ☐ 623 | Floyd Rayford | .03 | .01 | .00 |
| ☐ 624 | Steve McCatty | .03 | .01 | .00 |
| ☐ 625 | Bob Brenly | .05 | .02 | .00 |
| ☐ 626 | Roy Thomas | .03 | .01 | .00 |
| ☐ 627 | Ron Oester | .05 | .02 | .00 |
| ☐ 628 | Kirk McCaskill | .75 | .30 | .07 |
| ☐ 629 | Mitch Webster | .75 | .30 | .07 |

# THE CARD KING

*An Institution in Quality Sportscards All Items Excellent To Mint or Better*

**1987 BASEBALL SETS! IN STOCK NOW.**

| | |
|---|---|
| TOPPS (792) | 17.00 |
| FLEER (660 + 12 World Series Cards) | 29.00 |
| DONRUSS (660) | 29.00 |

**SPECIAL -- Buy all 3 at 72.00 and Receive the 1987 TOPPS and FLEER Updates in October for just 10.00 ea. Please Request. This offer good only as a package deal.**

**OTHER REGULAR ISSUE BASEBALL SETS**

| | |
|---|---|
| 1986 Topps (792) | 24.00 |
| 1986 Topps Traded | 18.00 |
| 1986 Fleer (660) | 45.00 |
| 1986 Fleer Update (132) | 29.00 |
| 1985 Fleer Update (132) | 20.00 |
| 1986 Donruss Hi-Lites (56) | 15.00 |
| 1985 Donruss Hi-Lites (56) | 40.00 |
| 1986 Sportsflicks Rookies | 18.00 |

**DONRUSS ACTION ALL-STARS**

1983 - 8.00  1985 - 8.00
1984 - 8.00  1986 - 8.00

*SPECIAL - All 4 Sets 25.00!*

**MORE BASEBALL SETS**

| | |
|---|---|
| 1986 Fleer Star Sticker | 28.00 |
| 1986 Fleer Classic Minis | 14.00 |
| 1986 Donruss/Leaf Canadian Set | 17.00 |
| 1986 Pop-Ups Donruss | 9.00 |

**TOPPS STICKER SETS. ALL MINT**

Sorry No Albums. Just Sets.
1981 - 16.00  1982 - 10.00
1983 - 10.00  1984 - 10.00
1985 - 10.00  1986 - 10.00

*SPECIAL - All 6 Sets 60.00!*

**UNOPENED BOXES! GUARANTEED**

| | |
|---|---|
| 1987 Topps Rac Pac Box (1152 Cards) | 21.00 |
| 1987 Topps Vendor Box (500 Cards) | 11.00 |
| 1986 Topps Wax Box (540 Cards) | 22.00 |
| 1986 Fleer Wax Box (540 Cards) | 50.00 |

| | |
|---|---|
| (10) Packs of 1986 Fleer Rac Pacs (450 Cards) | 40.00 |

**WE STOCK FOOTBALL ITEMS, TOO!**

**COMPLETE MINT TOPPS FOOTBALL SETS**

| | |
|---|---|
| 1985 Topps (396) | 12.00 |
| 1984 Topps (396) | 16.00 |
| 1983 Topps (396) | 13.00 |
| 1982 Topps (528) | 18.00 |
| 1981 Topps (528) | 22.00 |

*SPECIAL - All 5 Football Sets 70.00!*

**WE ALSO STOCK HOCKEY SETS**

| | |
|---|---|
| 1984/5 Topps (198) | 15.00 |
| 1983/4 OPC | 15.00 |
| 1984/5 OPC | 14.00 |
| 1986/7 OPC (264) | 15.00 |

*SPECIAL - All 4 Hockey Sets 50.00!*

**Terms:**

(1) Your Satisfaction is Guaranteed.
(2) Please Add $1.00 for Shipping and Handling.
(3) MASTERCARD/VISA Welcome - Please Add 2% Service Charge.
(4) Cash Only C.O.D.'s Welcome - Please Add $2.50 for Service Charge
(5) Money Orders Receive Same Day Service. Personal Checks Must Clear.
(6) Canada, Hawaii, Alaska, Foreign - Please Add 20% for Postage.
(7) PA Residents Must Include 6% Tax.

## The Card King

**Dept. B**
211 Mac Dade Blvd.
Collingdale, PA 19023
(215) 461-4781 Feel Welcome to
Call to Discuss Any Transaction.

**Owners**
**Dan Bruner - John McNichol**
**Diane Bruner**

| | | | |
|---|---|---|---|
| ☐ 630 Fernando Valenzuela | .30 | .12 | .03 |
| ☐ 631 Steve Braun | .03 | .01 | .00 |
| ☐ 632 Dave Von Ohlen | .03 | .01 | .00 |
| ☐ 633 Jackie Gutierrez | .03 | .01 | .00 |
| ☐ 634 Roy Lee Jackson | .03 | .01 | .00 |
| ☐ 635 Jason Thompson | .06 | .02 | .00 |
| ☐ 636 Cubs Leaders | .06 | .02 | .00 |
| Lee Smith | | | |
| ☐ 637 Rudy Law | .03 | .01 | .00 |
| ☐ 638 John Butcher | .03 | .01 | .00 |
| ☐ 639 Bo Diaz | .05 | .02 | .00 |
| ☐ 640 Jose Cruz | .09 | .04 | .01 |
| ☐ 641 Wayne Tolleson | .03 | .01 | .00 |
| ☐ 642 Ray Searage | .03 | .01 | .00 |
| ☐ 643 Tom Brookens | .03 | .01 | .00 |
| ☐ 644 Mark Gubicza | .07 | .03 | .01 |
| ☐ 645 Dusty Baker | .06 | .02 | .00 |
| ☐ 646 Mike Moore | .05 | .02 | .00 |
| ☐ 647 Mel Hall | .08 | .03 | .01 |
| ☐ 648 Steve Bedrosian | .06 | .02 | .00 |
| ☐ 649 Ronn Reynolds | .08 | .03 | .01 |
| ☐ 650 Dave Stieb | .12 | .05 | .01 |
| ☐ 651 Billy Martin MGR | .08 | .02 | .00 |
| (checklist back) | | | |
| ☐ 652 Tom Browning | .25 | .10 | .02 |
| ☐ 653 Jim Dwyer | .03 | .01 | .00 |
| ☐ 654 Ken Howell | .08 | .03 | .01 |
| ☐ 655 Manny Trillo | .05 | .02 | .00 |
| ☐ 656 Brian Harper | .03 | .01 | .00 |
| ☐ 657 Juan Agosto | .03 | .01 | .00 |
| ☐ 658 Rob Wilfong | .03 | .01 | .00 |
| ☐ 659 Checklist: 529-660 | .06 | .01 | .00 |
| ☐ 660 Steve Garvey | .35 | .14 | .03 |
| ☐ 661 Roger Clemens | 2.00 | .80 | .20 |
| ☐ 662 Bill Schroeder | .03 | .01 | .00 |
| ☐ 663 Neil Allen | .05 | .02 | .00 |
| ☐ 664 Tim Corcoran | .03 | .01 | .00 |
| ☐ 665 Alejandro Pena | .06 | .02 | .00 |
| ☐ 666 Rangers Leaders | .05 | .02 | .00 |
| Charlie Hough | | | |
| ☐ 667 Tim Teufel | .07 | .03 | .01 |
| ☐ 668 Cecilio Guante | .03 | .01 | .00 |
| ☐ 669 Ron Cey | .09 | .04 | .01 |
| ☐ 670 Willie Hernandez | .10 | .04 | .01 |
| ☐ 671 Lynn Jones | .03 | .01 | .00 |
| ☐ 672 Rob Picciolo | .03 | .01 | .00 |
| ☐ 673 Ernie Whitt | .03 | .01 | .00 |
| ☐ 674 Pat Tabler | .08 | .03 | .01 |
| ☐ 675 Claudell Washington | .06 | .02 | .00 |
| ☐ 676 Matt Young | .05 | .02 | .00 |
| ☐ 677 Nick Esasky | .05 | .02 | .00 |
| ☐ 678 Dan Gladden | .05 | .02 | .00 |
| ☐ 679 Britt Burns | .06 | .02 | .00 |
| ☐ 680 George Foster | .12 | .05 | .01 |
| ☐ 681 Dick Williams MGR | .05 | .01 | .00 |
| (checklist back) | | | |
| ☐ 682 Junior Ortiz | .03 | .01 | .00 |
| ☐ 683 Andy Van Slyke | .06 | .02 | .00 |
| ☐ 684 Bob McClure | .03 | .01 | .00 |
| ☐ 685 Tim Wallach | .07 | .03 | .01 |
| ☐ 686 Jeff Stone | .06 | .02 | .00 |
| ☐ 687 Mike Trujillo | .08 | .03 | .01 |
| ☐ 688 Larry Herndon | .03 | .01 | .00 |
| ☐ 689 Dave Stewart | .03 | .01 | .00 |
| ☐ 690 Ryne Sandberg | .45 | .18 | .04 |
| (no Topps logo | | | |
| on front) | | | |
| ☐ 691 Mike Madden | .03 | .01 | .00 |
| ☐ 692 Dale Berra | .03 | .01 | .00 |
| ☐ 693 Tom Tellmann | .03 | .01 | .00 |
| ☐ 694 Garth Iorg | .03 | .01 | .00 |
| ☐ 695 Mike Smithson | .03 | .01 | .00 |
| ☐ 696 Dodgers Leaders | .05 | .02 | .00 |
| Bill Russell | | | |
| ☐ 697 Bud Black | .03 | .01 | .00 |
| ☐ 698 Brad Komminsk | .06 | .02 | .00 |
| ☐ 699 Pat Corrales MGR | .05 | .01 | .00 |
| (checklist back) | | | |
| ☐ 700 Reggie Jackson | .35 | .14 | .03 |
| ☐ 701 Keith Hernandez AS | .15 | .06 | .01 |
| ☐ 702 Tom Herr AS | .06 | .02 | .00 |
| ☐ 703 Tim Wallach AS | .06 | .02 | .00 |
| ☐ 704 Ozzie Smith AS | .08 | .03 | .01 |
| ☐ 705 Dale Murphy AS | .25 | .10 | .02 |
| ☐ 706 Pedro Guerrero AS | .15 | .06 | .01 |
| ☐ 707 Willie McGee AS | .12 | .05 | .01 |
| ☐ 708 Gary Carter AS | .20 | .08 | .02 |
| ☐ 709 Dwight Gooden AS | .50 | .20 | .05 |
| ☐ 710 John Tudor AS | .06 | .02 | .00 |
| ☐ 711 Jeff Reardon AS | .06 | .02 | .00 |
| ☐ 712 Don Mattingly AS | .50 | .20 | .05 |
| ☐ 713 Damaso Garcia AS | .06 | .02 | .00 |
| ☐ 714 George Brett AS | .30 | .12 | .03 |

| | | | |
|---|---|---|---|
| ☐ 715 Cal Ripken AS | .25 | .10 | .02 |
| ☐ 716 Rickey Henderson AS | .25 | .10 | .02 |
| ☐ 717 Dave Winfield AS | .20 | .08 | .02 |
| ☐ 718 Jorge Bell AS | .10 | .04 | .01 |
| ☐ 719 Carlton Fisk AS | .10 | .04 | .01 |
| ☐ 720 Bret Saberhagen AS | .12 | .05 | .01 |
| ☐ 721 Ron Guidry AS | .12 | .05 | .01 |
| ☐ 722 Dan Quisenberry AS | .10 | .04 | .01 |
| ☐ 723 Marty Bystrom | .03 | .01 | .00 |
| ☐ 724 Tim Hulett | .07 | .03 | .01 |
| ☐ 725 Mario Soto | .08 | .03 | .01 |
| ☐ 726 Orioles Leaders | .05 | .02 | .00 |
| Rick Dempsey | | | |
| ☐ 727 David Green | .03 | .01 | .00 |
| ☐ 728 Mike Marshall | .12 | .05 | .01 |
| ☐ 729 Jim Beattie | .03 | .01 | .00 |
| ☐ 730 Ozzie Smith | .10 | .04 | .01 |
| ☐ 731 Don Robinson | .03 | .01 | .00 |
| ☐ 732 Floyd Youmans | 1.00 | .40 | .10 |
| ☐ 733 Ron Romanick | .05 | .02 | .00 |
| ☐ 734 Marty Barrett | .10 | .04 | .01 |
| ☐ 735 Dave Dravecky | .06 | .02 | .00 |
| ☐ 736 Glenn Wilson | .09 | .04 | .01 |
| ☐ 737 Pete Vuckovich | .05 | .02 | .00 |
| ☐ 738 Andre Robertson | .03 | .01 | .00 |
| ☐ 739 Dave Rozema | .03 | .01 | .00 |
| ☐ 740 Lance Parrish | .20 | .08 | .02 |
| ☐ 741 Pete Rose MGR | .35 | .10 | .02 |
| (checklist back) | | | |
| ☐ 742 Frank Viola | .05 | .02 | .00 |
| ☐ 743 Pat Sheridan | .03 | .01 | .00 |
| ☐ 744 Lary Sorensen | .03 | .01 | .00 |
| ☐ 745 Willie Upshaw | .07 | .03 | .01 |
| ☐ 746 Denny Gonzalez | .07 | .03 | .01 |
| ☐ 747 Rick Cerone | .03 | .01 | .00 |
| ☐ 748 Steve Henderson | .03 | .01 | .00 |
| ☐ 749 Ed Jurak | .03 | .01 | .00 |
| ☐ 750 Gorman Thomas | .07 | .03 | .01 |
| ☐ 751 Howard Johnson | .03 | .01 | .00 |
| ☐ 752 Mike Krukow | .07 | .03 | .01 |
| ☐ 753 Dan Ford | .03 | .01 | .00 |
| ☐ 754 Pat Clements | .20 | .08 | .02 |
| ☐ 755 Harold Baines | .20 | .08 | .02 |
| ☐ 756 Pirates Leaders | .05 | .02 | .00 |
| Rick Rhoden | | | |
| ☐ 757 Darrell Porter | .05 | .02 | .00 |
| ☐ 758 Dave Anderson | .03 | .01 | .00 |
| ☐ 759 Moose Haas | .05 | .02 | .00 |
| ☐ 760 Andre Dawson | .20 | .08 | .02 |
| ☐ 761 Don Slaught | .03 | .01 | .00 |
| ☐ 762 Eric Show | .03 | .01 | .00 |
| ☐ 763 Terry Puhl | .05 | .02 | .00 |
| ☐ 764 Kevin Gross | .03 | .01 | .00 |
| ☐ 765 Don Baylor | .10 | .04 | .01 |
| ☐ 766 Rick Langford | .03 | .01 | .00 |
| ☐ 767 Jody Davis | .08 | .03 | .01 |
| ☐ 768 Vern Ruhle | .03 | .01 | .00 |
| ☐ 769 Harold Reynolds | .12 | .05 | .01 |
| ☐ 770 Vida Blue | .08 | .03 | .01 |
| ☐ 771 John McNamara MGR | .05 | .01 | .00 |
| (checklist back) | | | |
| ☐ 772 Brian Downing | .05 | .02 | .00 |
| ☐ 773 Greg Pryor | .03 | .01 | .00 |
| ☐ 774 Terry Leach | .03 | .01 | .00 |
| ☐ 775 Al Oliver | .10 | .04 | .01 |
| ☐ 776 Gene Garber | .03 | .01 | .00 |
| ☐ 777 Wayne Krenchicki | .03 | .01 | .00 |
| ☐ 778 Jerry Hairston | .03 | .01 | .00 |
| ☐ 779 Rick Reuschel | .05 | .02 | .00 |
| ☐ 780 Robin Yount | .25 | .10 | .02 |
| ☐ 781 Joe Nolan | .03 | .01 | .00 |
| ☐ 782 Ken Landreaux | .05 | .02 | .00 |
| ☐ 783 Ricky Horton | .03 | .01 | .00 |
| ☐ 784 Alan Bannister | .03 | .01 | .00 |
| ☐ 785 Bob Stanley | .05 | .02 | .00 |
| ☐ 786 Twins Leaders | .05 | .02 | .00 |
| Mickey Hatcher | | | |
| ☐ 787 Vance Law | .03 | .01 | .00 |
| ☐ 788 Marty Castillo | .03 | .01 | .00 |
| ☐ 789 Kurt Bevacqua | .03 | .01 | .00 |
| ☐ 790 Phil Niekro | .15 | .06 | .01 |
| ☐ 791 Checklist: 661-792 | .06 | .01 | .00 |
| ☐ 792 Charles Hudson | .06 | .02 | .00 |
| ☐ A Jorge Bell | .15 | .06 | .01 |
| (wax pack box card) | | | |
| ☐ B Wade Boggs | 1.50 | .60 | .15 |
| (wax pack box card) | | | |
| ☐ C George Brett | .75 | .30 | .07 |
| (wax pack box card) | | | |
| ☐ D Vince Coleman | 1.00 | .40 | .10 |
| (wax pack box card) | | | |
| ☐ E Carlton Fisk | .15 | .06 | .01 |
| (wax pack box card) | | | |

| | | MINT | VG-E | F-G |
|---|---|---|---|---|
| ☐ F | Dwight Gooden | 1.50 | .60 | .15 |
| | (wax pack box card) | | | |
| ☐ G | Pedro Guerrero | .25 | .10 | .02 |
| | (wax pack box card) | | | |
| ☐ H | Ron Guidry | .20 | .08 | .02 |
| | (wax pack box card) | | | |
| ☐ I | Reggie Jackson | .60 | .24 | .06 |
| | (wax pack box card) | | | |
| ☐ J | Don Mattingly | 2.00 | .80 | .20 |
| | (wax pack box card) | | | |
| ☐ K | Oddibe McDowell | .35 | .14 | .03 |
| | (wax pack box card) | | | |
| ☐ L | Willie McGee | .25 | .10 | .02 |
| | (wax pack box card) | | | |
| ☐ M | Dale Murphy | 1.00 | .40 | .10 |
| | (wax pack box card) | | | |
| ☐ N | Pete Rose | 1.25 | .50 | .12 |
| | (wax pack box card) | | | |
| ☐ O | Bret Saberhagen | .25 | .10 | .02 |
| | (wax pack box card) | | | |
| ☐ P | Fernando Valenzuela | .25 | .10 | .02 |
| | (wax pack box card) | | | |

## 1986 Topps Glossy 22

This 22 card set was distributed as an insert, one card per rak pack. The players featured are the starting lineups of the 1985 All-Star Game played in Minnesota. Cards are very colorful with a high gloss finish and are standard size, 2 1/2" by 3 1/2". Cards are numbered on the back.

| | | MINT | VG-E | F-G |
|---|---|---|---|---|
| | COMPLETE SET (22) | 3.75 | 1.25 | .30 |
| | COMMON PLAYER (1-22) | .10 | .04 | .01 |
| ☐ 1 | Sparky Anderson MGR | .10 | .04 | .01 |
| ☐ 2 | Eddie Murray | .30 | .12 | .03 |
| ☐ 3 | Lou Whitaker | .15 | .06 | .01 |
| ☐ 4 | George Brett | .40 | .16 | .04 |
| ☐ 5 | Cal Ripken | .30 | .12 | .03 |
| ☐ 6 | Jim Rice | .30 | .12 | .03 |
| ☐ 7 | Rickey Henderson | .40 | .16 | .04 |
| ☐ 8 | Dave Winfield | .30 | .12 | .03 |
| ☐ 9 | Carlton Fisk | .20 | .08 | .02 |
| ☐ 10 | Jack Morris | .20 | .08 | .02 |
| ☐ 11 | AL Team Photo | .10 | .04 | .01 |
| ☐ 12 | Dick Williams MGR | .10 | .04 | .01 |
| ☐ 13 | Steve Garvey | .30 | .12 | .03 |
| ☐ 14 | Tom Herr | .10 | .04 | .01 |
| ☐ 15 | Graig Nettles | .15 | .06 | .01 |
| ☐ 16 | Ozzie Smith | .15 | .06 | .01 |
| ☐ 17 | Tony Gwynn | .30 | .12 | .03 |
| ☐ 18 | Dale Murphy | .50 | .20 | .05 |
| ☐ 19 | Darryl Strawberry | .40 | .16 | .04 |
| ☐ 20 | Terry Kennedy | .10 | .04 | .01 |
| ☐ 21 | LaMarr Hoyt | .10 | .04 | .01 |
| ☐ 22 | NL Team Photo | .10 | .04 | .01 |

> **FAMILY FUN:** Take along a family member with you to a sports show.

## 1986 Topps Glossy 60

This 60 card glossy set was produced by Topps and distributed ten cards at a time based on the offer found on the wax packs. Cards measure the standard 2 1/2" by 3 1/2". Each series of ten cards was available by sending in 1.00 plus six "special offer" cards inserted one per wax pack. The card backs are printed in red and blue on white card stock. The card fronts feature a white border and a green frame surrounding a full-color photo of the player.

| | | MINT | VG-E | F-G |
|---|---|---|---|---|
| | COMPLETE SET (60) | 10.00 | 4.00 | 1.00 |
| | COMMON PLAYER (1-60) | .10 | .04 | .01 |
| ☐ 1 | Oddibe McDowell | .25 | .10 | .02 |
| ☐ 2 | Reggie Jackson | .50 | .20 | .05 |
| ☐ 3 | Fernando Valenzuela | .25 | .10 | .02 |
| ☐ 4 | Jack Clark | .15 | .06 | .01 |
| ☐ 5 | Rickey Henderson | .50 | .20 | .05 |
| ☐ 6 | Steve Balboni | .10 | .04 | .01 |
| ☐ 7 | Keith Hernandez | .20 | .08 | .02 |
| ☐ 8 | Lance Parrish | .20 | .08 | .02 |
| ☐ 9 | Willie McGee | .20 | .08 | .02 |
| ☐ 10 | Chris Brown | .25 | .10 | .02 |
| ☐ 11 | Darryl Strawberry | .50 | .20 | .05 |
| ☐ 12 | Ron Guidry | .15 | .06 | .01 |
| ☐ 13 | Dave Parker | .20 | .08 | .02 |
| ☐ 14 | Cal Ripken | .30 | .12 | .03 |
| ☐ 15 | Tim Raines | .25 | .10 | .02 |
| ☐ 16 | Rod Carew | .30 | .12 | .03 |
| ☐ 17 | Mike Schmidt | .50 | .20 | .05 |
| ☐ 18 | George Brett | .50 | .20 | .05 |
| ☐ 19 | Joe Hesketh | .10 | .04 | .01 |
| ☐ 20 | Dan Pasqua | .20 | .08 | .02 |
| ☐ 21 | Vince Coleman | .40 | .16 | .04 |
| ☐ 22 | Tom Seaver | .30 | .12 | .03 |
| ☐ 23 | Gary Carter | .30 | .12 | .03 |
| ☐ 24 | Orel Hershiser | .20 | .08 | .02 |
| ☐ 25 | Pedro Guerrero | .20 | .08 | .02 |
| ☐ 26 | Wade Boggs | .75 | .30 | .07 |
| ☐ 27 | Bret Saberhagen | .20 | .08 | .02 |
| ☐ 28 | Carlton Fisk | .20 | .08 | .02 |
| ☐ 29 | Kirk Gibson | .25 | .10 | .02 |
| ☐ 30 | Brian Fisher | .10 | .04 | .01 |
| ☐ 31 | Don Mattingly | 1.25 | .50 | .12 |
| ☐ 32 | Tom Herr | .10 | .04 | .01 |
| ☐ 33 | Eddie Murray | .35 | .14 | .03 |
| ☐ 34 | Ryne Sandberg | .30 | .12 | .03 |
| ☐ 35 | Dan Quisenberry | .15 | .06 | .01 |
| ☐ 36 | Jim Rice | .30 | .12 | .03 |
| ☐ 37 | Dale Murphy | .50 | .20 | .05 |
| ☐ 38 | Steve Garvey | .35 | .14 | .03 |
| ☐ 39 | Roger McDowell | .20 | .08 | .02 |
| ☐ 40 | Earnie Riles | .15 | .06 | .01 |
| ☐ 41 | Dwight Gooden | .75 | .30 | .07 |
| ☐ 42 | Dave Winfield | .30 | .12 | .03 |
| ☐ 43 | Dave Stieb | .15 | .06 | .01 |
| ☐ 44 | Bob Horner | .20 | .08 | .02 |
| ☐ 45 | Nolan Ryan | .30 | .12 | .03 |
| ☐ 46 | Ozzie Smith | .15 | .06 | .01 |
| ☐ 47 | Jorge Bell | .15 | .06 | .01 |
| ☐ 48 | Gorman Thomas | .15 | .06 | .01 |
| ☐ 49 | Tom Browning | .15 | .06 | .01 |
| ☐ 50 | Larry Sheets | .15 | .06 | .01 |

| | | | | |
|---|---|---|---|---|
| ☐ 51 | Pete Rose | .75 | .30 | .07 |
| ☐ 52 | Brett Butler | .15 | .06 | .01 |
| ☐ 53 | John Tudor | .15 | .06 | .01 |
| ☐ 54 | Phil Bradley | .20 | .08 | .02 |
| ☐ 55 | Jeff Reardon | .10 | .04 | .01 |
| ☐ 56 | Rich Gossage | .15 | .06 | .01 |
| ☐ 57 | Tony Gwynn | .30 | .12 | .03 |
| ☐ 58 | Ozzie Guillen | .20 | .08 | .02 |
| ☐ 59 | Glenn Davis | .30 | .12 | .03 |
| ☐ 60 | Darrell Evans | .10 | .04 | .01 |

## 1986 Topps Super

This 60 card set actually consists of giant sized versions of the Topps regular issue of some of the most popular players. The cards measure 4 7/8" by 6 7/8". Cards are very similar to the Topps regular issue; two exceptions are that on the back they are numbered differently and an additional line of type is printed at the bottom of the back noting an accomplishment of that player at the end of the 1986 season.

| | | MINT | VG-E | F-G |
|---|---|---|---|---|
| COMPLETE SET (60) | | 12.00 | 5.00 | 1.20 |
| COMMON PLAYER (1-60) | | .10 | .04 | .01 |
| ☐ 1 | Don Mattingly | 1.50 | .60 | .15 |
| ☐ 2 | Willie McGee | .20 | .08 | .02 |
| ☐ 3 | Bret Saberhagen | .20 | .08 | .02 |
| ☐ 4 | Dwight Gooden | 1.00 | .40 | .10 |
| ☐ 5 | Dan Quisenberry | .15 | .06 | .01 |
| ☐ 6 | Jeff Reardon | .10 | .04 | .01 |
| ☐ 7 | Ozzie Guillen | .20 | .08 | .02 |
| ☐ 8 | Vince Coleman | .50 | .20 | .05 |
| ☐ 9 | Harold Baines | .25 | .10 | .02 |
| ☐ 10 | Jorge Bell | .20 | .08 | .02 |
| ☐ 11 | Bert Blyleven | .15 | .06 | .01 |
| ☐ 12 | Wade Boggs | 1.00 | .40 | .10 |
| ☐ 13 | Phil Bradley | .25 | .10 | .02 |
| ☐ 14 | George Brett | .50 | .20 | .05 |
| ☐ 15 | Hubie Brooks | .15 | .06 | .01 |
| ☐ 16 | Tom Browning | .15 | .06 | .01 |
| ☐ 17 | Bill Buckner | .15 | .06 | .01 |
| ☐ 18 | Brett Butler | .15 | .06 | .01 |
| ☐ 19 | Gary Carter | .30 | .12 | .03 |
| ☐ 20 | Cecil Cooper | .15 | .06 | .01 |
| ☐ 21 | Darrell Evans | .10 | .04 | .01 |
| ☐ 22 | Dwight Evans | .10 | .04 | .01 |
| ☐ 23 | Carlton Fisk | .20 | .08 | .02 |
| ☐ 24 | Steve Garvey | .35 | .14 | .03 |
| ☐ 25 | Kirk Gibson | .25 | .10 | .02 |
| ☐ 26 | Rich Gossage | .15 | .06 | .01 |
| ☐ 27 | Pedro Guerrero | .20 | .08 | .02 |
| ☐ 28 | Ron Guidry | .15 | .06 | .01 |
| ☐ 29 | Tony Gwynn | .35 | .14 | .03 |
| ☐ 30 | Rickey Henderson | .50 | .20 | .05 |
| ☐ 31 | Keith Hernandez | .25 | .10 | .02 |
| ☐ 32 | Tom Herr | .10 | .04 | .01 |
| ☐ 33 | Orel Hershiser | .20 | .08 | .02 |
| ☐ 34 | Jay Howell | .10 | .04 | .01 |
| ☐ 35 | Reggie Jackson | .50 | .20 | .05 |
| ☐ 36 | Bob James | .10 | .04 | .01 |
| ☐ 37 | Charlie Leibrandt | .10 | .04 | .01 |
| ☐ 38 | Jack Morris | .20 | .08 | .02 |
| ☐ 39 | Dale Murphy | .60 | .24 | .06 |
| ☐ 40 | Eddie Murray | .40 | .16 | .04 |
| ☐ 41 | Dave Parker | .25 | .10 | .02 |
| ☐ 42 | Tim Raines | .25 | .10 | .02 |
| ☐ 43 | Jim Rice | .30 | .12 | .03 |
| ☐ 44 | Dave Righetti | .20 | .08 | .02 |
| ☐ 45 | Cal Ripken | .35 | .14 | .03 |
| ☐ 46 | Pete Rose | 1.00 | .40 | .10 |
| ☐ 47 | Nolan Ryan | .40 | .16 | .04 |
| ☐ 48 | Ryne Sandberg | .40 | .16 | .04 |
| ☐ 49 | Mike Schmidt | .60 | .24 | .06 |
| ☐ 50 | Tom Seaver | .40 | .16 | .04 |
| ☐ 51 | Bryn Smith | .10 | .04 | .01 |
| ☐ 52 | Lee Smith | .10 | .04 | .01 |
| ☐ 53 | Ozzie Smith | .20 | .08 | .02 |
| ☐ 54 | Dave Stieb | .15 | .06 | .01 |
| ☐ 55 | Darryl Strawberry | .50 | .20 | .05 |
| ☐ 56 | Gorman Thomas | .10 | .04 | .01 |
| ☐ 57 | John Tudor | .15 | .06 | .01 |

| | | | | |
|---|---|---|---|---|
| ☐ 58 | Fernando Valenzuela | .30 | .12 | .03 |
| ☐ 59 | Willie Wilson | .20 | .08 | .02 |
| ☐ 60 | Dave Winfield | .30 | .12 | .03 |

## 1986 Topps Mini Leaders

The 1986 Topps Mini set of Major League Leaders features leaders of the various statistical categories for the 1985 season. The cards are numbered on the back and measure 2 1/8" by 2 15/16". They are very similar in design to the Team Leader "Dean" cards in the 1986 Topps regular issue.

| | | MINT | VG-E | F-G |
|---|---|---|---|---|
| COMPLETE SET | | 5.00 | 2.00 | .50 |
| COMMON PLAYER | | .05 | .02 | .00 |
| ☐ 1 | Eddie Murray | .25 | .10 | .02 |
| ☐ 2 | Cal Ripken | .25 | .10 | .02 |
| ☐ 3 | Wade Boggs | .50 | .20 | .05 |
| ☐ 4 | Dennis Boyd | .10 | .04 | .01 |
| ☐ 5 | Dwight Evans | .10 | .04 | .01 |
| ☐ 6 | Bruce Hurst | .10 | .04 | .01 |
| ☐ 7 | Gary Pettis | .10 | .04 | .01 |
| ☐ 8 | Harold Baines | .15 | .06 | .01 |
| ☐ 9 | Floyd Bannister | .05 | .02 | .00 |
| ☐ 10 | Britt Burns | .05 | .02 | .00 |
| ☐ 11 | Carlton Fisk | .10 | .04 | .01 |
| ☐ 12 | Brett Butler | .10 | .04 | .01 |
| ☐ 13 | Darrell Evans | .05 | .02 | .00 |
| ☐ 14 | Jack Morris | .15 | .06 | .01 |
| ☐ 15 | Lance Parrish | .15 | .06 | .01 |
| ☐ 16 | Walt Terrell | .05 | .02 | .00 |
| ☐ 17 | Steve Balboni | .05 | .02 | .00 |
| ☐ 18 | George Brett | .25 | .10 | .02 |
| ☐ 19 | Charlie Leibrandt | .05 | .02 | .00 |
| ☐ 20 | Bret Saberhagen | .15 | .06 | .01 |
| ☐ 21 | Lonnie Smith | .05 | .02 | .00 |
| ☐ 22 | Willie Wilson | .10 | .04 | .01 |
| ☐ 23 | Bert Blyleven | .10 | .04 | .01 |
| ☐ 24 | Mike Smithson | .05 | .02 | .00 |
| ☐ 25 | Frank Viola | .05 | .02 | .00 |
| ☐ 26 | Ron Guidry | .10 | .04 | .01 |
| ☐ 27 | Rickey Henderson | .25 | .10 | .02 |
| ☐ 28 | Don Mattingly | 1.00 | .40 | .10 |
| ☐ 29 | Dave Winfield | .25 | .10 | .02 |
| ☐ 30 | Mike Moore | .05 | .02 | .00 |
| ☐ 31 | Gorman Thomas | .10 | .04 | .01 |
| ☐ 32 | Toby Harrah | .05 | .02 | .00 |
| ☐ 33 | Charlie Hough | .05 | .02 | .00 |
| ☐ 34 | Doyle Alexander | .05 | .02 | .00 |
| ☐ 35 | Jimmy Key | .10 | .04 | .01 |
| ☐ 36 | Dave Stieb | .10 | .04 | .01 |
| ☐ 37 | Dale Murphy | .35 | .14 | .03 |
| ☐ 38 | Keith Moreland | .05 | .02 | .00 |
| ☐ 39 | Ryne Sandberg | .25 | .10 | .02 |
| ☐ 40 | Tom Browning | .10 | .04 | .01 |
| ☐ 41 | Dave Parker | .15 | .06 | .01 |
| ☐ 42 | Mario Soto | .05 | .02 | .00 |
| ☐ 43 | Nolan Ryan | .25 | .10 | .02 |
| ☐ 44 | Pedro Guerrero | .15 | .06 | .01 |
| ☐ 45 | Orel Hershiser | .15 | .06 | .01 |
| ☐ 46 | Mike Scioscia | .05 | .02 | .00 |
| ☐ 47 | Fernando Valenzuela | .20 | .08 | .02 |
| ☐ 48 | Bob Welch | .10 | .04 | .01 |
| ☐ 49 | Tim Raines | .20 | .08 | .02 |
| ☐ 50 | Gary Carter | .25 | .10 | .02 |

| | | | | |
|---|---|---|---|---|
| ☐ 51 | Sid Fernandez | .15 | .06 | .01 |
| ☐ 52 | Dwight Gooden | .75 | .30 | .07 |
| ☐ 53 | Keith Hernandez | .20 | .08 | .02 |
| ☐ 54 | Juan Samuel | .10 | .04 | .01 |
| ☐ 55 | Mike Schmidt | .35 | .14 | .03 |
| ☐ 56 | Glenn Wilson | .10 | .04 | .01 |
| ☐ 57 | Rick Reuschel | .05 | .02 | .00 |
| ☐ 58 | Joaquin Andujar | .10 | .04 | .01 |
| ☐ 59 | Jack Clark | .10 | .04 | .01 |
| ☐ 60 | Vince Coleman | .35 | .14 | .03 |
| ☐ 61 | Danny Cox | .05 | .02 | .00 |
| ☐ 62 | Tom Herr | .05 | .02 | .00 |
| ☐ 63 | Willie McGee | .15 | .06 | .01 |
| ☐ 64 | John Tudor | .10 | .04 | .01 |
| ☐ 65 | Tony Gwynn | .25 | .10 | .02 |
| ☐ 66 | Checklist card | .05 | .00 | .00 |

KEVIN MITCHELL

## 1986 Topps Super 3-D

This set consists of 30 plastic sculpted "cards" each measuring 4 3/8" by 6". Each card was individually wrapped in a red paper wrapper. The card back is blank except for two adhesive strips which could used for mounting the card. Cards are numbered on the front.

| | MINT | VG-E | F-G |
|---|---|---|---|
| COMPLETE SET (30) | 12.00 | 5.00 | 1.20 |
| COMMON PLAYER (1-30) | .20 | .08 | .02 |

| | | | | |
|---|---|---|---|---|
| ☐ 1 | Bert Blyleven | .20 | .08 | .02 |
| ☐ 2 | Gary Carter | .40 | .16 | .04 |
| ☐ 3 | Wade Boggs | 1.00 | .40 | .10 |
| ☐ 4 | Dwight Gooden | .75 | .30 | .07 |
| ☐ 5 | George Brett | .60 | .24 | .06 |
| ☐ 6 | Rich Gossage | .25 | .10 | .02 |
| ☐ 7 | Darrell Evans | .20 | .08 | .02 |
| ☐ 8 | Pedro Guerrero | .30 | .12 | .03 |
| ☐ 9 | Ron Guidry | .30 | .12 | .03 |
| ☐ 10 | Keith Hernandez | .30 | .12 | .03 |
| ☐ 11 | Rickey Henderson | .60 | .24 | .06 |
| ☐ 12 | Orel Hershiser | .30 | .12 | .03 |
| ☐ 13 | Reggie Jackson | .60 | .24 | .06 |
| ☐ 14 | Willie McGee | .30 | .12 | .03 |
| ☐ 15 | Don Mattingly | 1.50 | .60 | .15 |
| ☐ 16 | Dale Murphy | .60 | .24 | .06 |
| ☐ 17 | Jack Morris | .30 | .12 | .03 |
| ☐ 18 | Dave Parker | .30 | .12 | .03 |
| ☐ 19 | Eddie Murray | .40 | .16 | .04 |
| ☐ 20 | Jeff Reardon | .20 | .08 | .02 |
| ☐ 21 | Dan Quisenberry | .25 | .10 | .02 |
| ☐ 22 | Pete Rose | 1.00 | .40 | .10 |
| ☐ 23 | Jim Rice | .40 | .16 | .04 |
| ☐ 24 | Mike Schmidt | .60 | .24 | .06 |
| ☐ 25 | Bret Saberhagen | .30 | .12 | .03 |
| ☐ 26 | Darryl Strawberry | .60 | .24 | .06 |
| ☐ 27 | Dave Stieb | .25 | .10 | .02 |
| ☐ 28 | John Tudor | .20 | .08 | .02 |
| ☐ 29 | Dave Winfield | .40 | .16 | .04 |
| ☐ 30 | Fernando Valenzuela | .30 | .12 | .03 |

## 1986 Topps Traded

This 132 card extended set was distributed by Topps to dealers in a special red and white box as a complete set. The card fronts are identical in style to the Topps regular issue and are also 2 1/2" by 3 1/2". The backs are printed in red and black on white card stock. Cards are numbered (with a T suffix) alphabetically according to the name of the player.

| | MINT | VG-E | F-G |
|---|---|---|---|
| COMPLETE SET | 13.00 | 5.00 | 1.00 |
| COMMON PLAYER | .06 | .02 | .00 |

| | | | | |
|---|---|---|---|---|
| ☐ 1T | Andy Allanson | .20 | .08 | .02 |
| ☐ 2T | Neil Allen | .06 | .02 | .00 |
| ☐ 3T | Joaquin Andujar | .10 | .04 | .01 |
| ☐ 4T | Paul Assenmacher | .20 | .08 | .02 |
| ☐ 5T | Scott Bailes | .20 | .08 | .02 |
| ☐ 6T | Don Baylor | .15 | .06 | .01 |
| ☐ 7T | Steve Bedrosian | .10 | .04 | .01 |
| ☐ 8T | Juan Beniquez | .10 | .04 | .01 |
| ☐ 9T | Juan Berenguer | .06 | .02 | .00 |
| ☐ 10T | Mike Bielecki | .10 | .04 | .01 |
| ☐ 11T | Barry Bonds | .75 | .30 | .07 |
| ☐ 12T | Bobby Bonilla | .20 | .08 | .02 |
| ☐ 13T | Juan Bonilla | .06 | .02 | .00 |
| ☐ 14T | Rich Bordi | .06 | .02 | .00 |
| ☐ 15T | Steve Boros MGR | .06 | .02 | .00 |
| ☐ 16T | Rick Burleson | .10 | .04 | .01 |
| ☐ 17T | Bill Campbell | .06 | .02 | .00 |
| ☐ 18T | Tom Candiotti | .10 | .04 | .01 |
| ☐ 19T | John Cangelosi | .35 | .14 | .03 |
| ☐ 20T | Jose Canseco | 3.50 | 1.40 | .35 |
| ☐ 21T | Carmen Castillo | .10 | .04 | .01 |
| ☐ 22T | Rick Cerone | .06 | .02 | .00 |
| ☐ 23T | John Cerutti | .35 | .14 | .03 |
| ☐ 24T | Will Clark | 1.25 | .50 | .12 |
| ☐ 25T | Mark Clear | .06 | .02 | .00 |
| ☐ 26T | Darnell Coles | .15 | .06 | .01 |
| ☐ 27T | Dave Collins | .10 | .04 | .01 |
| ☐ 28T | Tim Conroy | .06 | .02 | .00 |
| ☐ 29T | Joe Cowley | .10 | .04 | .01 |
| ☐ 30T | Joel Davis | .20 | .08 | .02 |
| ☐ 31T | Rob Deer | .40 | .16 | .04 |
| ☐ 32T | John Denny | .10 | .04 | .01 |
| ☐ 33T | Mike Easler | .10 | .04 | .01 |
| ☐ 34T | Mark Eichhorn | .50 | .20 | .05 |
| ☐ 35T | Steve Farr | .06 | .02 | .00 |
| ☐ 36T | Scott Fletcher | .10 | .04 | .01 |
| ☐ 37T | Terry Forster | .10 | .04 | .01 |
| ☐ 38T | Terry Francona | .06 | .02 | .00 |
| ☐ 39T | Jim Fregosi MGR | .10 | .04 | .01 |
| ☐ 40T | Andres Galarraga | .25 | .10 | .02 |
| ☐ 41T | Ken Griffey | .10 | .04 | .01 |
| ☐ 42T | Bill Gullickson | .10 | .04 | .01 |
| ☐ 43T | Jose Guzman | .20 | .08 | .02 |
| ☐ 44T | Moose Haas | .10 | .04 | .01 |
| ☐ 45T | Billy Hatcher | .10 | .04 | .01 |
| ☐ 46T | Mike Heath | .06 | .02 | .00 |
| ☐ 47T | Tom Hume | .06 | .02 | .00 |
| ☐ 48T | Pete Incaviglia | 2.00 | .80 | .20 |
| ☐ 49T | Dane Iorg | .06 | .02 | .00 |
| ☐ 50T | Bo Jackson | 2.00 | .80 | .20 |
| ☐ 51T | Wally Joyner | 3.50 | 1.40 | .35 |
| ☐ 52T | Charlie Kerfeld | .35 | .14 | .03 |
| ☐ 53T | Eric King | .35 | .14 | .03 |
| ☐ 54T | Bob Kipper | .06 | .02 | .00 |
| ☐ 55T | Wayne Krenchicki | .06 | .02 | .00 |
| ☐ 56T | John Kruk | .30 | .12 | .03 |
| ☐ 57T | Mike LaCoss | .06 | .02 | .00 |
| ☐ 58T | Pete Ladd | .06 | .02 | .00 |
| ☐ 59T | Mike Laga | .10 | .04 | .01 |
| ☐ 60T | Hal Lanier MGR | .10 | .04 | .01 |
| ☐ 61T | Dave LaPoint | .06 | .02 | .00 |
| ☐ 62T | Rudy Law | .06 | .02 | .00 |
| ☐ 63T | Rick Leach | .06 | .02 | .00 |
| ☐ 64T | Tim Leary | .06 | .02 | .00 |
| ☐ 65T | Dennis Leonard | .10 | .04 | .01 |
| ☐ 66T | Jim Leyland MGR | .06 | .02 | .00 |
| ☐ 67T | Steve Lyons | .06 | .02 | .00 |
| ☐ 68T | Mickey Mahler | .06 | .02 | .00 |
| ☐ 69T | Candy Maldonado | .10 | .04 | .01 |
| ☐ 70T | Roger Mason | .15 | .06 | .01 |
| ☐ 71T | Bob McClure | .06 | .02 | .00 |
| ☐ 72T | Andy McGaffigan | .06 | .02 | .00 |
| ☐ 73T | Gene Michael MGR | .06 | .02 | .00 |

| | | | | |
|---|---|---|---|---|
| ☐ | 74T | Kevin Mitchell ............... | .75 | .30 | .07 |
| ☐ | 75T | Omar Moreno ............... | .06 | .02 | .00 |
| ☐ | 76T | Jerry Mumphrey ........... | .06 | .02 | .00 |
| ☐ | 77T | Phil Niekro ................... | .25 | .10 | .02 |
| ☐ | 78T | Randy Niemann ........... | .06 | .02 | .00 |
| ☐ | 79T | Juan Nieves ................ | .20 | .08 | .02 |
| ☐ | 80T | Otis Nixon .................. | .15 | .06 | .01 |
| ☐ | 81T | Bob Ojeda .................. | .15 | .06 | .01 |
| ☐ | 82T | Jose Oquendo .............. | .06 | .02 | .00 |
| ☐ | 83T | Tom Paciorek .............. | .06 | .02 | .00 |
| ☐ | 84T | Dave Palmer ............... | .06 | .02 | .00 |
| ☐ | 85T | Frank Pastore .............. | .06 | .02 | .00 |
| ☐ | 86T | Lou Piniella MGR ......... | .10 | .04 | .01 |
| ☐ | 87T | Dan Plesac .................. | .20 | .08 | .02 |
| ☐ | 88T | Darrell Porter .............. | .10 | .04 | .01 |
| ☐ | 89T | Rey Quinones .............. | .20 | .08 | .02 |
| ☐ | 90T | Gary Redus .................. | .10 | .04 | .01 |
| ☐ | 91T | Bip Roberts ................. | .15 | .06 | .01 |
| ☐ | 92T | Billy Jo Robidoux ......... | .35 | .14 | .03 |
| ☐ | 93T | Jeff Robinson .............. | .10 | .04 | .01 |
| ☐ | 94T | Gary Roenicke ............. | .10 | .04 | .01 |
| ☐ | 95T | Ed Romero ................... | .06 | .02 | .00 |
| ☐ | 96T | Argenis Salazar ........... | .06 | .02 | .00 |
| ☐ | 97T | Joe Sambito ................ | .10 | .04 | .01 |
| ☐ | 98T | Billy Sample ................ | .06 | .02 | .00 |
| ☐ | 99T | Dave Schmidt ............. | .06 | .02 | .00 |
| ☐ | 100T | Ken Schrom ................. | .10 | .04 | .01 |
| ☐ | 101T | Tom Seaver ................. | .45 | .18 | .04 |
| ☐ | 102T | Ted Simmons ............... | .15 | .06 | .01 |
| ☐ | 103T | Sammy Stewart ........... | .06 | .02 | .00 |
| ☐ | 104T | Kurt Stillwell .............. | .15 | .06 | .01 |
| ☐ | 105T | Franklin Stubbs ........... | .15 | .06 | .01 |
| ☐ | 106T | Dale Sveum ................. | .20 | .08 | .02 |
| ☐ | 107T | Chuck Tanner MGR ....... | .10 | .04 | .01 |
| ☐ | 108T | Danny Tartabull ........... | .75 | .30 | .07 |
| ☐ | 109T | Tim Teufel .................. | .10 | .04 | .01 |
| ☐ | 110T | Bob Tewksbury ............ | .35 | .14 | .03 |
| ☐ | 111T | Andres Thomas ........... | .35 | .14 | .03 |
| ☐ | 112T | Milt Thompson ............ | .10 | .04 | .01 |
| ☐ | 113T | Robby Thompson ......... | .40 | .16 | .04 |
| ☐ | 114T | Jay Tibbs ................... | .06 | .02 | .00 |
| ☐ | 115T | Wayne Tolleson ........... | .06 | .02 | .00 |
| ☐ | 116T | Alex Trevino ............... | .06 | .02 | .00 |
| ☐ | 117T | Manny Trillo ............... | .06 | .02 | .00 |
| ☐ | 118T | Ed VandeBerg ............. | .06 | .02 | .00 |
| ☐ | 119T | Ozzie Virgil ................ | .06 | .02 | .00 |
| ☐ | 120T | Bob Walk .................... | .06 | .02 | .00 |
| ☐ | 121T | Gene Walter ................ | .15 | .06 | .01 |
| ☐ | 122T | Claudell Washington ...... | .10 | .04 | .01 |
| ☐ | 123T | Bill Wegman ............... | .20 | .08 | .02 |
| ☐ | 124T | Dick Williams MGR ........ | .06 | .02 | .00 |
| ☐ | 125T | Mitch Williams ............ | .30 | .12 | .03 |
| ☐ | 126T | Bobby Witt ................. | .50 | .20 | .05 |
| ☐ | 127T | Todd Worrell ............... | 1.00 | .40 | .10 |
| ☐ | 128T | George Wright .............. | .06 | .02 | .00 |
| ☐ | 129T | Ricky Wright ............... | .06 | .02 | .00 |
| ☐ | 130T | Steve Yeager ............... | .06 | .02 | .00 |
| ☐ | 131T | Paul Zuvella ................ | .06 | .02 | .00 |
| ☐ | 132T | Checklist card ............. | .10 | .01 | .00 |

## 1987 Topps

This 792 card set is reminiscent of the 1962 Topps baseball cards with their simulated wood grain borders. The backs are printed in yellow and blue on gray card stock. The manager cards contain a checklist of the respective team's players on the back. Subsets in the set include Record Breakers (1-7), Turn Back the Clock (311-315), and All-Star selections (595-616). The Team Leader cards typically show players conferring on the mound inside a white cloud. The wax pack wrapper gives details of "Spring Fever Baseball" where a lucky collector can win a trip for four to Spring Training. Four different sets of two smaller (2 1/8" by 3") cards were printed on the side of the wax pack box; these eight cards are lettered A through H and listed at the end of the checklist below.

| | | | MINT | VG-E | F-G |
|---|---|---|---|---|---|
| | COMPLETE SET ......................... | | 22.00 | 9.00 | 2.20 |
| | COMMON PLAYER ..................... | | .03 | .01 | .00 |
| ☐ | 1 | RB: Roger Clemens ........ Most Strikeouts, 9 Inning Game | .35 | .14 | .03 |
| ☐ | 2 | RB: Jim Deshaies ............ Most Cons. K's, Start of Game | .10 | .04 | .01 |
| ☐ | 3 | RB: Dwight Evans ........... Earliest Home Run, Season | .08 | .03 | .01 |
| ☐ | 4 | RB: Davey Lopes ............. Most Steals, Season 40-year-old | .06 | .02 | .00 |
| ☐ | 5 | RB: Dave Righetti ........... Most Saves, Season | .10 | .04 | .01 |
| ☐ | 6 | RB: Ruben Sierra ............ Youngest Player to Switch Hit Homers in Game | .15 | .06 | .01 |
| ☐ | 7 | RB: Todd Worrell ............ Most Saves, Season, Rookie | .15 | .06 | .01 |
| ☐ | 8 | Terry Pendleton .............. | .05 | .02 | .00 |
| ☐ | 9 | Jay Tibbs ....................... | .03 | .01 | .00 |
| ☐ | 10 | Cecil Cooper ................... | .09 | .04 | .01 |
| ☐ | 11 | Indians Team ................... (mound conference) | .03 | .01 | .00 |
| ☐ | 12 | Jeff Sellers .................... | .12 | .05 | .01 |
| ☐ | 13 | Nick Esasky .................... | .03 | .01 | .00 |
| ☐ | 14 | Dave Stewart .................. | .03 | .01 | .00 |
| ☐ | 15 | Claudell Washington ....... | .05 | .02 | .00 |
| ☐ | 16 | Pat Clements .................. | .05 | .02 | .00 |
| ☐ | 17 | Pete O'Brien .................. | .08 | .03 | .01 |
| ☐ | 18 | Dick Howser MGR .......... (checklist back) | .06 | .01 | .00 |
| ☐ | 19 | Matt Young ..................... | .03 | .01 | .00 |
| ☐ | 20 | Gary Carter .................... | .25 | .10 | .02 |
| ☐ | 21 | Mark Davis ..................... | .03 | .01 | .00 |
| ☐ | 22 | Doug DeCinces ............... | .07 | .03 | .01 |
| ☐ | 23 | Lee Smith ...................... | .07 | .03 | .01 |
| ☐ | 24 | Tony Walker .................... | .12 | .05 | .01 |
| ☐ | 25 | Bert Blyleven .................. | .09 | .04 | .01 |
| ☐ | 26 | Greg Brock ..................... | .05 | .02 | .00 |
| ☐ | 27 | Joe Cowley ..................... | .05 | .02 | .00 |
| ☐ | 28 | Rick Dempsey .................. | .05 | .02 | .00 |
| ☐ | 29 | Jimmy Key ..................... | .07 | .03 | .01 |
| ☐ | 30 | Tim Raines ..................... | .25 | .10 | .02 |
| ☐ | 31 | Braves Team ................... (Hubbard/Ramirez) | .03 | .01 | .00 |
| ☐ | 32 | Tim Leary ...................... | .03 | .01 | .00 |
| ☐ | 33 | Andy Van Slyke ............... | .05 | .02 | .00 |
| ☐ | 34 | Jose Rijo ....................... | .05 | .02 | .00 |
| ☐ | 35 | Sid Bream ...................... | .05 | .02 | .00 |
| ☐ | 36 | Eric King ....................... | .25 | .10 | .02 |
| ☐ | 37 | Marvell Wynne ................ | .03 | .01 | .00 |
| ☐ | 38 | Dennis Leonard ............... | .05 | .02 | .00 |
| ☐ | 39 | Marty Barrett ................. | .10 | .04 | .01 |
| ☐ | 40 | Dave Righetti .................. | .12 | .05 | .01 |
| ☐ | 41 | Bo Diaz ......................... | .05 | .02 | .00 |
| ☐ | 42 | Gary Redus ..................... | .05 | .02 | .00 |
| ☐ | 43 | Gene Michael MGR .......... (checklist back) | .06 | .01 | .00 |
| ☐ | 44 | Greg Harris .................... | .05 | .02 | .00 |
| ☐ | 45 | Jim Presley .................... | .20 | .08 | .02 |
| ☐ | 46 | Dan Gladden ................... | .05 | .02 | .00 |
| ☐ | 47 | Dennis Powell ................. | .08 | .03 | .01 |
| ☐ | 48 | Wally Backman ............... | .07 | .03 | .01 |
| ☐ | 49 | Terry Harper ................... | .03 | .01 | .00 |
| ☐ | 50 | Dave Smith ..................... | .06 | .02 | .00 |
| ☐ | 51 | Mel Hall ........................ | .07 | .03 | .01 |
| ☐ | 52 | Keith Atherton ................ | .03 | .01 | .00 |
| ☐ | 53 | Ruppert Jones ................ | .03 | .01 | .00 |
| ☐ | 54 | Bill Dawley ..................... | .03 | .01 | .00 |

**GEORGIA MUSIC & SPORTS**
**Dick DeCourcy**
**1867 Flat Shoals Rd.**
**Riverdale, GA 30296**

**404-996-3385**

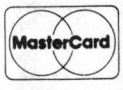 

# A PERSONAL MESSAGE
# TO THE DEALERS OF THE HOBBY

## *Baseball Cards have been good to us.*

Georgia Music & Sports has been a regular advertiser in hobby publications since 1983. We have set up at 40 shows in 1986, 31 shows in 1985 and 34 shows in 1984. Both through our ads and the shows we have met many regular customers - for this we are very thankful.

Most of our customers and dealers order from four to six times a month. We try to cultivate repeat business. It is far more important for us to obtain a customer for the long term than ever to think of a quick buck on one deal.

It is not possible to inventory every item in the hobby, but we always try to have on hand Mint sets from the last 10 years as well as unopened, unsearched products from the last 10 years.

We have at present 166 dealers that order from us every month. We work on the average of 15% profit on most items. Some of our prices may be high and some may be low, but we do try and have the major products always on hand at all times.

We pride ourselves on service . . . we spell service S-P-E-E-D. If you are a regular account and you call in an order today before 2 p.m., we ship it today. Also, 99% of our accounts pay us just as quickly as we ship, the same day they get their product. The rest pay interest.

We will soon be entering our 11th year of business. To those customers who have kept us going for all these years, we give thanks and trust that this union will continue for many years to come. To those new and honorable dealers and store owners who are entering this fast-paced, exciting and growing baseball card hobby, we welcome your business. We have a staff of 11 people to help serve your needs.

Please write or call for our current price list.

Sincerely,

*Dick*

Dick DeCourcy, President
Georgia Music & Sports

# MEMBER

Atlanta Area Chamber of Commerce    Atlanta Area Sports Collectors Association
Atlanta Area Better Business Bureau    National Association of Music Merchants

| | | | | |
|---|---|---|---|---|
| ☐ 55 | Tim Wallach | .07 | .03 | .01 |
| ☐ 56 | Brewers Team | .03 | .01 | .00 |
| | (mound cnference) | | | |
| ☐ 57 | Scott Nielsen | .15 | .06 | .01 |
| ☐ 58 | Thad Bosley | .03 | .01 | .00 |
| ☐ 59 | Ken Dayley | .03 | .01 | .00 |
| ☐ 60 | Tony Pena | .10 | .04 | .01 |
| ☐ 61 | Bobby Thigpen | .20 | .08 | .02 |
| ☐ 62 | Bobby Meacham | .03 | .01 | .00 |
| ☐ 63 | Fred Toliver | .05 | .02 | .00 |
| ☐ 64 | Harry Spilman | .03 | .01 | .00 |
| ☐ 65 | Tom Browning | .08 | .03 | .01 |
| ☐ 66 | Marc Sullivan | .03 | .01 | .00 |
| ☐ 67 | Bill Swift | .03 | .01 | .00 |
| ☐ 68 | Tony LaRussa MGR | .06 | .01 | .00 |
| | (checklist back) | | | |
| ☐ 69 | Lonnie Smith | .05 | .02 | .00 |
| ☐ 70 | Charlie Hough | .05 | .02 | .00 |
| ☐ 71 | Mike Aldrete | .12 | .05 | .01 |
| ☐ 72 | Walt Terrell | .03 | .01 | .00 |
| ☐ 73 | Dave Anderson | .03 | .01 | .00 |
| ☐ 74 | Dan Pasqua | .15 | .06 | .01 |
| ☐ 75 | Ron Darling | .20 | .08 | .02 |
| ☐ 76 | Rafael Ramirez | .03 | .01 | .00 |
| ☐ 77 | Bryan Oelkers | .03 | .01 | .00 |
| ☐ 78 | Tom Foley | .03 | .01 | .00 |
| ☐ 79 | Juan Nieves | .06 | .02 | .00 |
| ☐ 80 | Wally Joyner | 2.00 | .80 | .20 |
| ☐ 81 | Padres Team | .03 | .01 | .00 |
| | (Hawkins/Kennedy) | | | |
| ☐ 82 | Rob Murphy | .15 | .06 | .01 |
| ☐ 83 | Mike Davis | .05 | .02 | .00 |
| ☐ 84 | Steve Lake | .03 | .01 | .00 |
| ☐ 85 | Kevin Bass | .07 | .03 | .01 |
| ☐ 86 | Nate Snell | .03 | .01 | .00 |
| ☐ 87 | Mark Salas | .03 | .01 | .00 |
| ☐ 88 | Ed Wojna | .03 | .01 | .00 |
| ☐ 89 | Ozzie Guillen | .10 | .04 | .01 |
| ☐ 90 | Dave Stieb | .10 | .04 | .01 |
| ☐ 91 | Harold Reynolds | .03 | .01 | .00 |
| ☐ 92 | Urbano Lugo | .03 | .01 | .00 |
| ☐ 93 | Jim Leyland MGR | .06 | .01 | .00 |
| | (checklist back) | | | |
| ☐ 94 | Calvin Schiraldi | .09 | .04 | .01 |
| ☐ 95 | Oddibe McDowell | .20 | .08 | .02 |
| ☐ 96 | Frank Williams | .03 | .01 | .00 |
| ☐ 97 | Glenn Wilson | .08 | .03 | .01 |
| ☐ 98 | Bill Scherrer | .03 | .01 | .00 |
| ☐ 99 | Darryl Motley | .03 | .01 | .00 |
| ☐ 100 | Steve Garvey | .30 | .12 | .03 |
| ☐ 101 | Carl Willis | .10 | .04 | .01 |
| ☐ 102 | Paul Zuvella | .03 | .01 | .00 |
| ☐ 103 | Rick Aguilera | .05 | .02 | .00 |
| ☐ 104 | Billy Sample | .03 | .01 | .00 |
| ☐ 105 | Floyd Youmans | .10 | .04 | .01 |
| ☐ 106 | Blue Jays Team | .10 | .04 | .01 |
| | (Bell/Barfield) | | | |
| ☐ 107 | John Butcher | .03 | .01 | .00 |
| ☐ 108 | Jim Gantner | .03 | .01 | .00 |
| | (Brewers logo reversed) | | | |
| ☐ 109 | R.J. Reynolds | .05 | .02 | .00 |
| ☐ 110 | John Tudor | .09 | .04 | .01 |
| ☐ 111 | Alfredo Griffin | .05 | .02 | .00 |
| ☐ 112 | Alan Ashby | .03 | .01 | .00 |
| ☐ 113 | Neil Allen | .05 | .02 | .00 |
| ☐ 114 | Billy Beane | .05 | .02 | .00 |
| ☐ 115 | Donnie Moore | .05 | .02 | .00 |
| ☐ 116 | Bill Russell | .05 | .02 | .00 |
| ☐ 117 | Jim Beattie | .03 | .01 | .00 |
| ☐ 118 | Bobby Valentine MGR | .06 | .01 | .00 |
| | (checklist back) | | | |
| ☐ 119 | Ron Robinson | .05 | .02 | .00 |
| ☐ 120 | Eddie Murray | .30 | .12 | .03 |
| ☐ 121 | Kevin Romine | .12 | .05 | .01 |
| ☐ 122 | Jim Clancy | .03 | .01 | .00 |
| ☐ 123 | John Kruk | .25 | .10 | .02 |
| ☐ 124 | Ray Fontenot | .03 | .01 | .00 |
| ☐ 125 | Bob Brenly | .05 | .02 | .00 |
| ☐ 126 | Mike Loynd | .25 | .10 | .02 |
| ☐ 127 | Vance Law | .03 | .01 | .00 |
| ☐ 128 | Checklist 1-132 | .06 | .01 | .00 |
| ☐ 129 | Rick Cerone | .03 | .01 | .00 |
| ☐ 130 | Dwight Gooden | 1.00 | .40 | .10 |
| ☐ 131 | Pirates Team | .05 | .02 | .00 |
| | (Bream/Pena) | | | |
| ☐ 132 | Paul Assenmacher | .10 | .04 | .01 |
| ☐ 133 | Jose Oquendo | .03 | .01 | .00 |
| ☐ 134 | Rich Yett | .05 | .02 | .00 |
| ☐ 135 | Mike Easler | .06 | .02 | .00 |
| ☐ 136 | Ron Romanick | .05 | .02 | .00 |
| ☐ 137 | Jerry Willard | .03 | .01 | .00 |
| ☐ 138 | Roy Lee Jackson | .03 | .01 | .00 |

| | | | | |
|---|---|---|---|---|
| ☐ 139 | Devon White | .30 | .12 | .03 |
| ☐ 140 | Bret Saberhagen | .15 | .06 | .01 |
| ☐ 141 | Herm Winningham | .03 | .01 | .00 |
| ☐ 142 | Rick Sutcliffe | .10 | .04 | .01 |
| ☐ 143 | Steve Boros MGR | .06 | .01 | .00 |
| | (checklist back) | | | |
| ☐ 144 | Mike Scioscia | .05 | .02 | .00 |
| ☐ 145 | Charlie Kerfeld | .10 | .04 | .01 |
| ☐ 146 | Tracy Jones | .25 | .10 | .02 |
| ☐ 147 | Randy Niemann | .03 | .01 | .00 |
| ☐ 148 | Dave Collins | .05 | .02 | .00 |
| ☐ 149 | Ray Searage | .03 | .01 | .00 |
| ☐ 150 | Wade Boggs | 1.00 | .40 | .10 |
| ☐ 151 | Mike LaCoss | .03 | .01 | .00 |
| ☐ 152 | Toby Harrah | .03 | .01 | .00 |
| ☐ 153 | Duane Ward | .12 | .05 | .01 |
| ☐ 154 | Tom O'Malley | .03 | .01 | .00 |
| ☐ 155 | Eddie Whitson | .05 | .02 | .00 |
| ☐ 156 | Mariners Team | .03 | .01 | .00 |
| | (mound conference) | | | |
| ☐ 157 | Danny Darwin | .03 | .01 | .00 |
| ☐ 158 | Tim Teufel | .05 | .02 | .00 |
| ☐ 159 | Ed Olwine | .12 | .05 | .01 |
| ☐ 160 | Julio Franco | .09 | .04 | .01 |
| ☐ 161 | Steve Ontiveros | .03 | .01 | .00 |
| ☐ 162 | Mike Lavalliere | .09 | .04 | .01 |
| ☐ 163 | Kevin Gross | .03 | .01 | .00 |
| ☐ 164 | Sammy Khalifa | .03 | .01 | .00 |
| ☐ 165 | Jeff Reardon | .06 | .02 | .00 |
| ☐ 166 | Bob Boone | .05 | .02 | .00 |
| ☐ 167 | Jim Deshaies | .25 | .10 | .02 |
| ☐ 168 | Lou Piniella MGR | .07 | .01 | .00 |
| | (checklist back) | | | |
| ☐ 169 | Ron Washington | .03 | .01 | .00 |
| ☐ 170 | Bo Jackson | 1.00 | .40 | .10 |
| ☐ 171 | Chuck Cary | .15 | .06 | .01 |
| ☐ 172 | Ron Oester | .03 | .01 | .00 |
| ☐ 173 | Alex Trevino | .03 | .01 | .00 |
| ☐ 174 | Henry Cotto | .03 | .01 | .00 |
| ☐ 175 | Bob Stanley | .05 | .02 | .00 |
| ☐ 176 | Steve Buechele | .03 | .01 | .00 |
| ☐ 177 | Keith Moreland | .05 | .02 | .00 |
| ☐ 178 | Cecil Fielder | .07 | .03 | .01 |
| ☐ 179 | Bill Wegman | .07 | .03 | .01 |
| ☐ 180 | Chris Brown | .15 | .06 | .01 |
| ☐ 181 | Cardinals Team | .03 | .01 | .00 |
| | (mound conference) | | | |
| ☐ 182 | Lee Lacy | .03 | .01 | .00 |
| ☐ 183 | Andy Hawkins | .03 | .01 | .00 |
| ☐ 184 | Bobby Bonilla | .15 | .06 | .01 |
| ☐ 185 | Roger McDowell | .10 | .04 | .01 |
| ☐ 186 | Bruce Benedict | .03 | .01 | .00 |
| ☐ 187 | Mark Huismann | .03 | .01 | .00 |
| ☐ 188 | Tony Phillips | .03 | .01 | .00 |
| ☐ 189 | Joe Hesketh | .05 | .02 | .00 |
| ☐ 190 | Jim Sundberg | .05 | .02 | .00 |
| ☐ 191 | Charles Hudson | .05 | .02 | .00 |
| ☐ 192 | Cory Snyder | .60 | .24 | .06 |
| ☐ 193 | Roger Craig MGR | .06 | .01 | .00 |
| | (checklist back) | | | |
| ☐ 194 | Kirk McCaskill | .10 | .04 | .01 |
| ☐ 195 | Mike Pagliarulo | .15 | .06 | .01 |
| ☐ 196 | Randy O'Neal | .03 | .01 | .00 |
| ☐ 197 | Mark Bailey | .03 | .01 | .00 |
| ☐ 198 | Lee Mazzilli | .03 | .01 | .00 |
| ☐ 199 | Mariano Duncan | .08 | .03 | .01 |
| ☐ 200 | Pete Rose | .60 | .24 | .06 |
| ☐ 201 | John Cangelosi | .25 | .10 | .02 |
| ☐ 202 | Ricky Wright | .03 | .01 | .00 |
| ☐ 203 | Mike Kingery | .20 | .08 | .02 |
| ☐ 204 | Sammy Stewart | .03 | .01 | .00 |
| ☐ 205 | Graig Nettles | .10 | .04 | .01 |
| ☐ 206 | Twins Team | .03 | .01 | .00 |
| | (mound conference) | | | |
| ☐ 207 | George Frazier | .03 | .01 | .00 |
| ☐ 208 | John Shelby | .03 | .01 | .00 |
| ☐ 209 | Rick Schu | .03 | .01 | .00 |
| ☐ 210 | Lloyd Moseby | .10 | .04 | .01 |
| ☐ 211 | John Morris | .03 | .01 | .00 |
| ☐ 212 | Mike Fitzgerald | .03 | .01 | .00 |
| ☐ 213 | Randy Myers | .45 | .18 | .04 |
| ☐ 214 | Omar Moreno | .03 | .01 | .00 |
| ☐ 215 | Mark Langston | .06 | .02 | .00 |
| ☐ 216 | B.J. Surhoff | .50 | .20 | .05 |
| ☐ 217 | Chris Codiroli | .03 | .01 | .00 |
| ☐ 218 | Sparky Anderson MGR | .06 | .01 | .00 |
| | (checklist back) | | | |
| ☐ 219 | Cecilio Guante | .03 | .01 | .00 |
| ☐ 220 | Joe Carter | .20 | .08 | .02 |
| ☐ 221 | Vern Ruhle | .03 | .01 | .00 |
| ☐ 222 | Denny Walling | .03 | .01 | .00 |
| ☐ 223 | Charlie Leibrandt | .05 | .02 | .00 |
| ☐ 224 | Wayne Tolleson | .03 | .01 | .00 |

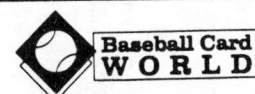

| | | | | |
|---|---|---|---|---|
| ☐ 225 | Mike Smithson | .03 | .01 | .00 |
| ☐ 226 | Max Venable | .03 | .01 | .00 |
| ☐ 227 | Jamie Moyer | .15 | .06 | .01 |
| ☐ 228 | Curt Wilkerson | .03 | .01 | .00 |
| ☐ 229 | Mike Birkbeck | .12 | .05 | .01 |
| ☐ 230 | Don Baylor | .10 | .04 | .01 |
| ☐ 231 | Giants Team (mound conference) | .03 | .01 | .00 |
| ☐ 232 | Reggie Williams | .15 | .06 | .01 |
| ☐ 233 | Russ Morman | .20 | .08 | .02 |
| ☐ 234 | Pat Sheridan | .03 | .01 | .00 |
| ☐ 235 | Alvin Davis | .12 | .05 | .01 |
| ☐ 236 | Tommy John | .10 | .04 | .01 |
| ☐ 237 | Jim Morrison | .03 | .01 | .00 |
| ☐ 238 | Bill Krueger | .03 | .01 | .00 |
| ☐ 239 | Juan Espino | .03 | .01 | .00 |
| ☐ 240 | Steve Balboni | .05 | .02 | .00 |
| ☐ 241 | Danny Heep | .03 | .01 | .00 |
| ☐ 242 | Rick Mahler | .03 | .01 | .00 |
| ☐ 243 | Whitey Herzog MGR (checklist back) | .06 | .01 | .00 |
| ☐ 244 | Dickie Noles | .03 | .01 | .00 |
| ☐ 245 | Willie Upshaw | .07 | .03 | .01 |
| ☐ 246 | Jim Dwyer | .03 | .01 | .00 |
| ☐ 247 | Jeff Reed | .03 | .01 | .00 |
| ☐ 248 | Gene Walter | .05 | .02 | .00 |
| ☐ 249 | Jim Pankovits | .03 | .01 | .00 |
| ☐ 250 | Teddy Higuera | .15 | .06 | .01 |
| ☐ 251 | Rob Wilfong | .03 | .01 | .00 |
| ☐ 252 | Denny Martinez | .03 | .01 | .00 |
| ☐ 253 | Eddie Milner | .05 | .02 | .00 |
| ☐ 254 | Bob Tewksbury | .20 | .08 | .02 |
| ☐ 255 | Juan Samuel | .10 | .04 | .01 |
| ☐ 256 | Royals Team (Brett/F.White) | .10 | .04 | .01 |
| ☐ 257 | Bob Forsch | .05 | .02 | .00 |
| ☐ 258 | Steve Yeager | .05 | .02 | .00 |
| ☐ 259 | Mike Greenwell | .15 | .06 | .01 |
| ☐ 260 | Vida Blue | .07 | .03 | .01 |
| ☐ 261 | Ruben Sierra | 1.00 | .40 | .10 |
| ☐ 262 | Jim Winn | .03 | .01 | .00 |
| ☐ 263 | Stan Javier | .07 | .03 | .01 |
| ☐ 264 | Checklist 133-264 | .06 | .01 | .00 |
| ☐ 265 | Darrell Evans | .07 | .03 | .01 |
| ☐ 266 | Jeff Hamilton | .15 | .06 | .01 |
| ☐ 267 | Howard Johnson | .03 | .01 | .00 |
| ☐ 268 | Pat Corrales MGR (checklist back) | .06 | .01 | .00 |
| ☐ 269 | Cliff Speck | .08 | .03 | .01 |
| ☐ 270 | Jody Davis | .07 | .03 | .01 |
| ☐ 271 | Mike Brown (Mariners P) | .03 | .01 | .00 |
| ☐ 272 | Andres Galarraga | .08 | .03 | .01 |
| ☐ 273 | Gene Nelson | .03 | .01 | .00 |
| ☐ 274 | Jeff Hearron | .10 | .04 | .01 |
| ☐ 275 | LaMarr Hoyt | .06 | .02 | .00 |
| ☐ 276 | Jackie Gutierrez | .03 | .01 | .00 |
| ☐ 277 | Juan Agosto | .03 | .01 | .00 |
| ☐ 278 | Gary Pettis | .07 | .03 | .01 |
| ☐ 279 | Dan Plesac | .20 | .08 | .02 |
| ☐ 280 | Jeff Leonard | .06 | .02 | .00 |
| ☐ 281 | Reds Team (Rose conference) | .10 | .04 | .01 |
| ☐ 282 | Jeff Calhoun | .09 | .04 | .01 |
| ☐ 283 | Doug Drabek | .15 | .06 | .01 |
| ☐ 284 | John Moses | .15 | .06 | .01 |
| ☐ 285 | Dennis Boyd | .08 | .03 | .01 |
| ☐ 286 | Mike Woodard | .05 | .02 | .00 |
| ☐ 287 | Dave Von Ohlen | .03 | .01 | .00 |
| ☐ 288 | Tito Landrum | .03 | .01 | .00 |
| ☐ 289 | Bob Kipper | .03 | .01 | .00 |
| ☐ 290 | Leon Durham | .07 | .03 | .01 |
| ☐ 291 | Mitch Williams | .20 | .08 | .02 |
| ☐ 292 | Franklin Stubbs | .10 | .04 | .01 |
| ☐ 293 | Bob Rodgers MGR (checklist back) | .06 | .01 | .00 |
| ☐ 294 | Steve Jeltz | .03 | .01 | .00 |
| ☐ 295 | Len Dykstra | .20 | .08 | .02 |
| ☐ 296 | Andres Thomas | .25 | .10 | .02 |
| ☐ 297 | Don Schulze | .03 | .01 | .00 |
| ☐ 298 | Larry Herndon | .03 | .01 | .00 |
| ☐ 299 | Joel Davis | .10 | .04 | .01 |
| ☐ 300 | Reggie Jackson | .30 | .12 | .03 |
| ☐ 301 | Luis Aquino | .09 | .04 | .01 |
| ☐ 302 | Bill Schroeder | .03 | .01 | .00 |
| ☐ 303 | Juan Berenguer | .03 | .01 | .00 |
| ☐ 304 | Phil Garner | .05 | .02 | .00 |
| ☐ 305 | John Franco | .08 | .03 | .01 |
| ☐ 306 | Red Sox Team (mound conference) | .05 | .02 | .00 |
| ☐ 307 | Lee Guetterman | .12 | .05 | .01 |
| ☐ 308 | Don Slaught | .03 | .01 | .00 |
| ☐ 309 | Mike Young | .07 | .03 | .01 |
| ☐ 310 | Frank Viola | .05 | .02 | .00 |
| ☐ 311 | Turn Back 1982 Rickey Henderson | .12 | .05 | .01 |
| ☐ 312 | Turn Back 1977 Reggie Jackson | .12 | .05 | .01 |
| ☐ 313 | Turn Back 1972 Roberto Clemente | .12 | .05 | .01 |
| ☐ 314 | Turn Back 1967 Carl Yastrzemski | .12 | .05 | .01 |
| ☐ 315 | Turn Back 1962 Maury Wills | .06 | .02 | .00 |
| ☐ 316 | Brian Fisher | .05 | .02 | .00 |
| ☐ 317 | Clint Hurdle | .03 | .01 | .00 |
| ☐ 318 | Jim Fregosi MGR (checklist back) | .06 | .01 | .00 |
| ☐ 319 | Greg Swindell | .45 | .18 | .04 |
| ☐ 320 | Barry Bonds | .35 | .14 | .03 |
| ☐ 321 | Mike Laga | .03 | .01 | .00 |
| ☐ 322 | Chris Bando | .03 | .01 | .00 |
| ☐ 323 | Al Newman | .10 | .04 | .01 |
| ☐ 324 | Dave Palmer | .05 | .02 | .00 |
| ☐ 325 | Garry Templeton | .07 | .03 | .01 |
| ☐ 326 | Mark Gubicza | .06 | .02 | .00 |
| ☐ 327 | Dale Sveum | .15 | .06 | .01 |
| ☐ 328 | Bob Welch | .06 | .02 | .00 |
| ☐ 329 | Ron Roenicke | .03 | .01 | .00 |
| ☐ 330 | Mike Scott | .15 | .06 | .01 |
| ☐ 331 | Mets Team (Carter/Strawberry) | .12 | .05 | .01 |
| ☐ 332 | Joe Price | .03 | .01 | .00 |
| ☐ 333 | Ken Phelps | .03 | .01 | .00 |
| ☐ 334 | Ed Correa | .35 | .14 | .03 |
| ☐ 335 | Candy Maldonado | .08 | .03 | .01 |
| ☐ 336 | Allan Anderson | .15 | .06 | .01 |
| ☐ 337 | Darrell Miller | .03 | .01 | .00 |
| ☐ 338 | Tim Conroy | .03 | .01 | .00 |
| ☐ 339 | Donnie Hill | .03 | .01 | .00 |
| ☐ 340 | Roger Clemens | 1.00 | .40 | .10 |
| ☐ 341 | Mike Brown (Pirates OF) | .03 | .01 | .00 |
| ☐ 342 | Bob James | .03 | .01 | .00 |
| ☐ 343 | Hal Lanier MGR (checklist back) | .06 | .01 | .00 |
| ☐ 344 | Joe Niekro | .07 | .03 | .01 |
| ☐ 345 | Andre Dawson | .16 | .07 | .01 |
| ☐ 346 | Shawon Dunston | .10 | .04 | .01 |
| ☐ 347 | Mickey Brantley | .10 | .04 | .01 |
| ☐ 348 | Carmelo Martinez | .05 | .02 | .00 |
| ☐ 349 | Storm Davis | .07 | .03 | .01 |
| ☐ 350 | Keith Hernandez | .20 | .08 | .02 |
| ☐ 351 | Gene Garber | .03 | .01 | .00 |
| ☐ 352 | Mike Felder | .10 | .04 | .01 |
| ☐ 353 | Ernie Camacho | .03 | .01 | .00 |
| ☐ 354 | Jamie Quirk | .03 | .01 | .00 |
| ☐ 355 | Don Carman | .05 | .02 | .00 |
| ☐ 356 | White Sox Team (mound conference) | .03 | .01 | .00 |
| ☐ 357 | Steve Fireovid | .10 | .04 | .01 |
| ☐ 358 | Sal Butera | .03 | .01 | .00 |
| ☐ 359 | Doug Corbett | .03 | .01 | .00 |
| ☐ 360 | Pedro Guerrero | .20 | .08 | .02 |
| ☐ 361 | Mark Thurmond | .03 | .01 | .00 |
| ☐ 362 | Luis Quinones | .10 | .04 | .01 |
| ☐ 363 | Jose Guzman | .10 | .04 | .01 |
| ☐ 364 | Randy Bush | .03 | .01 | .00 |
| ☐ 365 | Rick Rhoden | .05 | .02 | .00 |
| ☐ 366 | Mark McGwire | .10 | .04 | .01 |
| ☐ 367 | Jeff Lahti | .03 | .01 | .00 |
| ☐ 368 | John McNamara MGR (checklist back) | .06 | .01 | .00 |
| ☐ 369 | Brian Dayett | .03 | .01 | .00 |
| ☐ 370 | Fred Lynn | .15 | .06 | .01 |
| ☐ 371 | Mark Eichhorn | .35 | .14 | .03 |
| ☐ 372 | Jerry Mumphrey | .05 | .02 | .00 |
| ☐ 373 | Jeff Dedmon | .03 | .01 | .00 |
| ☐ 374 | Glenn Hoffman | .03 | .01 | .00 |
| ☐ 375 | Ron Guidry | .15 | .06 | .01 |
| ☐ 376 | Scott Bradley | .05 | .02 | .00 |
| ☐ 377 | John Henry Johnson | .03 | .01 | .00 |
| ☐ 378 | Rafael Santana | .03 | .01 | .00 |
| ☐ 379 | John Russell | .03 | .01 | .00 |
| ☐ 380 | Rich Gossage | .12 | .05 | .01 |
| ☐ 381 | Expos Team (mound conference) | .03 | .01 | .00 |
| ☐ 382 | Rudy Law | .03 | .01 | .00 |
| ☐ 383 | Ron Davis | .03 | .01 | .00 |
| ☐ 384 | Johnny Grubb | .03 | .01 | .00 |
| ☐ 385 | Orel Hershiser | .15 | .06 | .01 |
| ☐ 386 | Dickie Thon | .05 | .02 | .00 |
| ☐ 387 | T.R. Bryden | .12 | .05 | .01 |
| ☐ 388 | Geno Petralli | .03 | .01 | .00 |
| ☐ 389 | Jeff Robinson | .03 | .01 | .00 |
| ☐ 390 | Gary Matthews | .05 | .02 | .00 |

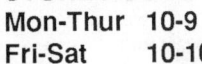

| No. | Player | | | |
|-----|--------|-----|-----|-----|
| ☐ 391 | Jay Howell | .05 | .02 | .00 |
| ☐ 392 | Checklist 265-396 | .06 | .01 | .00 |
| ☐ 393 | Pete Rose MGR | .35 | .10 | .02 |
| | (checklist back) | | | |
| ☐ 394 | Mike Bielecki | .06 | .02 | .00 |
| ☐ 395 | Damaso Garcia | .07 | .03 | .01 |
| ☐ 396 | Tim Lollar | .03 | .01 | .00 |
| ☐ 397 | Greg Walker | .10 | .04 | .01 |
| ☐ 398 | Brad Havens | .03 | .01 | .00 |
| ☐ 399 | Curt Ford | .20 | .08 | .02 |
| ☐ 400 | George Brett | .30 | .12 | .03 |
| ☐ 401 | Billy Jo Robidoux | .10 | .04 | .01 |
| ☐ 402 | Mike Trujillo | .03 | .01 | .00 |
| ☐ 403 | Jerry Royster | .03 | .01 | .00 |
| ☐ 404 | Doug Sisk | .03 | .01 | .00 |
| ☐ 405 | Brook Jacoby | .09 | .04 | .01 |
| ☐ 406 | Yankees Team | .25 | .10 | .02 |
| | (Henderson/Mattingly) | | | |
| ☐ 407 | Jim Acker | .03 | .01 | .00 |
| ☐ 408 | John Mizerock | .03 | .01 | .00 |
| ☐ 409 | Milt Thompson | .03 | .01 | .00 |
| ☐ 410 | Fernando Valenzuela | .25 | .10 | .02 |
| ☐ 411 | Darnell Coles | .09 | .04 | .01 |
| ☐ 412 | Eric Davis | .50 | .20 | .05 |
| ☐ 413 | Moose Haas | .05 | .02 | .00 |
| ☐ 414 | Joe Orsulak | .05 | .02 | .00 |
| ☐ 415 | Bobby Witt | .40 | .16 | .04 |
| ☐ 416 | Tom Nieto | .03 | .01 | .00 |
| ☐ 417 | Pat Perry | .07 | .03 | .01 |
| ☐ 418 | Dick Williams MGR | .06 | .01 | .00 |
| | (checklist back) | | | |
| ☐ 419 | Mark Portugal | .10 | .04 | .01 |
| ☐ 420 | Will Clark | .60 | .24 | .06 |
| ☐ 421 | Jose DeLeon | .05 | .02 | .00 |
| ☐ 422 | Jack Howell | .05 | .02 | .00 |
| ☐ 423 | Jaime Cocanower | .03 | .01 | .00 |
| ☐ 424 | Chris Speier | .03 | .01 | .00 |
| ☐ 425 | Tom Seaver | .25 | .10 | .02 |
| ☐ 426 | Floyd Rayford | .03 | .01 | .00 |
| ☐ 427 | Ed Nunez | .03 | .01 | .00 |
| ☐ 428 | Bruce Bochy | .03 | .01 | .00 |
| ☐ 429 | Tim Pyznarski | .15 | .06 | .01 |
| ☐ 430 | Mike Schmidt | .30 | .12 | .03 |
| ☐ 431 | Dodgers Team | .05 | .02 | .00 |
| | (mound conference) | | | |
| ☐ 432 | Jim Slaton | .03 | .01 | .00 |
| ☐ 433 | Ed Hearn | .10 | .04 | .01 |
| ☐ 434 | Mike Fischlin | .03 | .01 | .00 |
| ☐ 435 | Bruce Sutter | .12 | .05 | .01 |
| ☐ 436 | Andy Allanson | .15 | .06 | .01 |
| ☐ 437 | Ted Power | .06 | .02 | .00 |
| ☐ 438 | Kelly Downs | .12 | .05 | .01 |
| ☐ 439 | Karl Best | .03 | .01 | .00 |
| ☐ 440 | Willie McGee | .15 | .06 | .01 |
| ☐ 441 | Dave Leiper | .10 | .04 | .01 |
| ☐ 442 | Mitch Webster | .09 | .04 | .01 |
| ☐ 443 | John Felske MGR | .06 | .01 | .00 |
| | (checklist back) | | | |
| ☐ 444 | Jeff Russell | .03 | .01 | .00 |
| ☐ 445 | Dave Lopes | .06 | .02 | .00 |
| ☐ 446 | Chuck Finley | .12 | .05 | .01 |
| ☐ 447 | Bill Almon | .03 | .01 | .00 |
| ☐ 448 | Chris Bosio | .10 | .04 | .01 |
| ☐ 449 | Pat Dodson | .20 | .08 | .02 |
| ☐ 450 | Kirby Puckett | .30 | .12 | .03 |
| ☐ 451 | Joe Sambito | .05 | .02 | .00 |
| ☐ 452 | Dave Henderson | .05 | .02 | .00 |
| ☐ 453 | Scott Terry | .10 | .04 | .01 |
| ☐ 454 | Luis Salazar | .03 | .01 | .00 |
| ☐ 455 | Mike Boddicker | .07 | .03 | .01 |
| ☐ 456 | A's Team | .03 | .01 | .00 |
| | (mound conference) | | | |
| ☐ 457 | Len Matuszek | .03 | .01 | .00 |
| ☐ 458 | Kelly Gruber | .03 | .01 | .00 |
| ☐ 459 | Dennis Eckersley | .05 | .02 | .00 |
| ☐ 460 | Darryl Strawberry | .30 | .12 | .03 |
| ☐ 461 | Craig McMurtry | .03 | .01 | .00 |
| ☐ 462 | Scott Fletcher | .05 | .02 | .00 |
| ☐ 463 | Tom Candiotti | .05 | .02 | .00 |
| ☐ 464 | Butch Wynegar | .05 | .02 | .00 |
| ☐ 465 | Todd Worrell | .35 | .14 | .03 |
| ☐ 466 | Kal Daniels | .15 | .06 | .01 |
| ☐ 467 | Randy St.Claire | .03 | .01 | .00 |
| ☐ 468 | George Bamberger MGR | | .01 | .00 |
| | (checklist back) | | | |
| ☐ 469 | Mike Diaz | .20 | .08 | .02 |
| ☐ 470 | Dave Dravecky | .06 | .02 | .00 |
| ☐ 471 | Ronn Reynolds | .03 | .01 | .00 |
| ☐ 472 | Bill Doran | .09 | .04 | .01 |
| ☐ 473 | Steve Farr | .03 | .01 | .00 |
| ☐ 474 | Jerry Narron | .03 | .01 | .00 |
| ☐ 475 | Scott Garrelts | .05 | .02 | .00 |
| ☐ 476 | Danny Tartabull | .25 | .10 | .02 |
| ☐ 477 | Ken Howell | .05 | .02 | .00 |
| ☐ 478 | Tim Laudner | .03 | .01 | .00 |
| ☐ 479 | Bob Sebra | .10 | .04 | .01 |
| ☐ 480 | Jim Rice | .25 | .10 | .02 |
| ☐ 481 | Phillies Team | .05 | .02 | .00 |
| | (cage conference) | | | |
| ☐ 482 | Daryl Boston | .05 | .02 | .00 |
| ☐ 483 | Dwight Lowry | .15 | .06 | .01 |
| ☐ 484 | Jim Traber | .09 | .04 | .01 |
| ☐ 485 | Tony Fernandez | .09 | .04 | .01 |
| ☐ 486 | Otis Nixon | .15 | .06 | .01 |
| ☐ 487 | Dave Gumpert | .03 | .01 | .00 |
| ☐ 488 | Ray Knight | .07 | .03 | .01 |
| ☐ 489 | Bill Gullickson | .05 | .02 | .00 |
| ☐ 490 | Dale Murphy | .35 | .14 | .03 |
| ☐ 491 | Ron Karkovice | .25 | .10 | .02 |
| ☐ 492 | Mike Heath | .03 | .01 | .00 |
| ☐ 493 | Tom Lasorda MGR | .07 | .01 | .00 |
| | (checklist back) | | | |
| ☐ 494 | Barry Jones | .10 | .04 | .01 |
| ☐ 495 | Gorman Thomas | .08 | .03 | .01 |
| ☐ 496 | Bruce Bochte | .05 | .02 | .00 |
| ☐ 497 | Dale Mohorcic | .15 | .06 | .00 |
| ☐ 498 | Bob Kearney | .03 | .01 | .00 |
| ☐ 499 | Bruce Ruffin | .30 | .12 | .03 |
| ☐ 500 | Don Mattingly | 2.00 | .80 | .20 |
| ☐ 501 | Craig Lefferts | .03 | .01 | .00 |
| ☐ 502 | Dick Schofield | .05 | .02 | .00 |
| ☐ 503 | Larry Andersen | .03 | .01 | .00 |
| ☐ 504 | Mickey Hatcher | .03 | .01 | .00 |
| ☐ 505 | Bryn Smith | .03 | .01 | .00 |
| ☐ 506 | Orioles Team | .05 | .02 | .00 |
| | (mound conference) | | | |
| ☐ 507 | Dave Stapleton | .03 | .01 | .00 |
| ☐ 508 | Scott Bankhead | .05 | .02 | .00 |
| ☐ 509 | Enos Cabell | .03 | .01 | .00 |
| ☐ 510 | Tom Henke | .06 | .02 | .00 |
| ☐ 511 | Steve Lyons | .03 | .01 | .00 |
| ☐ 512 | Dave Magadan | .60 | .24 | .06 |
| ☐ 513 | Carmen Castillo | .03 | .01 | .00 |
| ☐ 514 | Orlando Mercado | .03 | .01 | .00 |
| ☐ 515 | Willie Hernandez | .09 | .04 | .01 |
| ☐ 516 | Ted Simmons | .09 | .04 | .01 |
| ☐ 517 | Mario Soto | .07 | .03 | .01 |
| ☐ 518 | Gene Mauch MGR | .06 | .01 | .00 |
| | (checklist back) | | | |
| ☐ 519 | Curt Young | .03 | .01 | .00 |
| ☐ 520 | Jack Clark | .10 | .04 | .01 |
| ☐ 521 | Rick Reuschel | .05 | .02 | .00 |
| ☐ 522 | Checklist 397-528 | .06 | .01 | .00 |
| ☐ 523 | Earnie Riles | .07 | .03 | .01 |
| ☐ 524 | Bob Shirley | .03 | .01 | .00 |
| ☐ 525 | Phil Bradley | .18 | .08 | .01 |
| ☐ 526 | Roger Mason | .07 | .03 | .01 |
| ☐ 527 | Jim Wohlford | .03 | .01 | .00 |
| ☐ 528 | Ken Dixon | .05 | .02 | .00 |
| ☐ 529 | Alvaro Espinoza | .09 | .04 | .01 |
| ☐ 530 | Tony Gwynn | .30 | .12 | .03 |
| ☐ 531 | Astros Team | .07 | .03 | .01 |
| | (Y.Berra conference) | | | |
| ☐ 532 | Jeff Stone | .05 | .02 | .00 |
| ☐ 533 | Argenis Salazar | .03 | .01 | .00 |
| ☐ 534 | Scott Sanderson | .03 | .01 | .00 |
| ☐ 535 | Tony Armas | .09 | .04 | .01 |
| ☐ 536 | Terry Mulholland | .10 | .04 | .01 |
| ☐ 537 | Rance Mulliniks | .03 | .01 | .00 |
| ☐ 538 | Tom Niedenfuer | .06 | .02 | .00 |
| ☐ 539 | Reid Nichols | .03 | .01 | .00 |
| ☐ 540 | Terry Kennedy | .06 | .02 | .00 |
| ☐ 541 | Rafael Belliard | .10 | .04 | .01 |
| ☐ 542 | Ricky Horton | .03 | .01 | .00 |
| ☐ 543 | Dave Johnson MGR | .08 | .01 | .00 |
| | (checklist back) | | | |
| ☐ 544 | Zane Smith | .03 | .01 | .00 |
| ☐ 545 | Buddy Bell | .09 | .04 | .01 |
| ☐ 546 | Mike Morgan | .03 | .01 | .00 |
| ☐ 547 | Rob Deer | .15 | .06 | .01 |
| ☐ 548 | Bill Mooneyham | .10 | .04 | .01 |
| ☐ 549 | Bob Melvin | .03 | .01 | .00 |
| ☐ 550 | Pete Incaviglia | 1.00 | .40 | .10 |
| ☐ 551 | Frank Wills | .03 | .01 | .00 |
| ☐ 552 | Larry Sheets | .05 | .02 | .00 |
| ☐ 553 | Mike Maddux | .10 | .04 | .01 |
| ☐ 554 | Buddy Biancalana | .03 | .01 | .00 |
| ☐ 555 | Dennis Rasmussen | .06 | .02 | .00 |
| ☐ 556 | Angels Team | .05 | .02 | .00 |
| | (mound conference) | | | |
| ☐ 557 | John Cerutti | .20 | .08 | .02 |
| ☐ 558 | Greg Gagne | .05 | .02 | .00 |
| ☐ 559 | Lance McCullers | .05 | .02 | .00 |
| ☐ 560 | Glenn Davis | .30 | .12 | .03 |
| ☐ 561 | Rey Quinones | .10 | .04 | .01 |
| ☐ 562 | Bryan Clutterbuck | .10 | .04 | .01 |

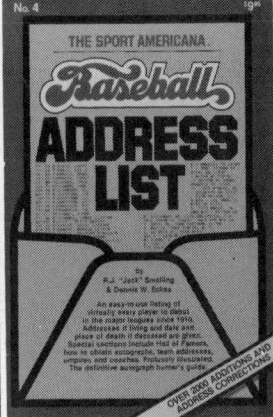

| | | | | |
|---|---|---|---|---|
| ☐ 563 | John Stefero | .03 | .01 | .00 |
| ☐ 564 | Larry McWilliams | .03 | .01 | .00 |
| ☐ 565 | Dusty Baker | .06 | .02 | .00 |
| ☐ 566 | Tim Hulett | .05 | .02 | .00 |
| ☐ 567 | Greg Mathews | .25 | .10 | .02 |
| ☐ 568 | Earl Weaver MGR (checklist back) | .08 | .01 | .00 |
| ☐ 569 | Wade Rowdon | .10 | .04 | .01 |
| ☐ 570 | Sid Fernandez | .20 | .08 | .02 |
| ☐ 571 | Ozzie Virgil | .05 | .02 | .00 |
| ☐ 572 | Pete Ladd | .03 | .01 | .00 |
| ☐ 573 | Hal McRae | .05 | .02 | .00 |
| ☐ 574 | Manny Lee | .05 | .02 | .00 |
| ☐ 575 | Pat Tabler | .07 | .03 | .01 |
| ☐ 576 | Frank Pastore | .03 | .01 | .00 |
| ☐ 577 | Dann Bilardello | .03 | .01 | .00 |
| ☐ 578 | Billy Hatcher | .05 | .02 | .00 |
| ☐ 579 | Rick Burleson | .06 | .02 | .00 |
| ☐ 580 | Mike Krukow | .07 | .03 | .01 |
| ☐ 581 | Cubs Team (Cey/Trout) | .05 | .02 | .00 |
| ☐ 582 | Bruce Berenyi | .03 | .01 | .00 |
| ☐ 583 | Junior Ortiz | .03 | .01 | .00 |
| ☐ 584 | Ron Kittle | .09 | .04 | .01 |
| ☐ 585 | Scott Bailes | .10 | .04 | .01 |
| ☐ 586 | Ben Oglivie | .06 | .02 | .00 |
| ☐ 587 | Eric Plunk | .08 | .03 | .01 |
| ☐ 588 | Wallace Johnson | .03 | .01 | .00 |
| ☐ 589 | Steve Crawford | .03 | .01 | .00 |
| ☐ 590 | Vince Coleman | .35 | .14 | .03 |
| ☐ 591 | Spike Owen | .05 | .02 | .00 |
| ☐ 592 | Chris Welsh | .03 | .01 | .00 |
| ☐ 593 | Chuck Tanner MGR (checklist back) | .06 | .01 | .00 |
| ☐ 594 | Rick Anderson | .03 | .01 | .00 |
| ☐ 595 | Keith Hernandez AS | .10 | .04 | .01 |
| ☐ 596 | Steve Sax AS | .07 | .03 | .01 |
| ☐ 597 | Mike Schmidt AS | .20 | .08 | .02 |
| ☐ 598 | Ozzie Smith AS | .07 | .03 | .01 |
| ☐ 599 | Tony Gwynn AS | .12 | .05 | .01 |
| ☐ 600 | Dave Parker AS | .09 | .04 | .01 |
| ☐ 601 | Darryl Strawberry AS | .15 | .06 | .01 |
| ☐ 602 | Gary Carter AS | .12 | .05 | .01 |
| ☐ 603 | Dwight Gooden AS | .25 | .10 | .02 |
| ☐ 604 | Fern. Valenzuela AS | .12 | .05 | .01 |
| ☐ 605 | Todd Worrell AS | .09 | .04 | .01 |
| ☐ 606 | Don Mattingly AS | .35 | .14 | .03 |
| ☐ 607 | Tony Bernazard AS | .05 | .02 | .00 |
| ☐ 608 | Wade Boggs AS | .25 | .10 | .02 |
| ☐ 609 | Cal Ripken AS | .12 | .05 | .01 |
| ☐ 610 | Jim Rice AS | .12 | .05 | .01 |
| ☐ 611 | Kirby Puckett AS | .12 | .05 | .01 |
| ☐ 612 | George Bell AS | .08 | .03 | .01 |
| ☐ 613 | Lance Parrish AS | .08 | .03 | .01 |
| ☐ 614 | Roger Clemens AS | .25 | .10 | .02 |
| ☐ 615 | Teddy Higuera AS | .07 | .03 | .01 |
| ☐ 616 | Dave Righetti AS | .07 | .03 | .01 |
| ☐ 617 | Al Nipper | .03 | .01 | .00 |
| ☐ 618 | Tom Kelly MGR (checklist back) | .06 | .01 | .00 |
| ☐ 619 | Jerry Reed | .03 | .01 | .00 |
| ☐ 620 | Jose Canseco | 2.00 | .80 | .20 |
| ☐ 621 | Danny Cox | .05 | .02 | .00 |
| ☐ 622 | Glenn Braggs | .40 | .16 | .04 |
| ☐ 623 | Kurt Stillwell | .15 | .06 | .01 |
| ☐ 624 | Tim Burke | .05 | .02 | .00 |
| ☐ 625 | Mookie Wilson | .05 | .02 | .00 |
| ☐ 626 | Joel Skinner | .05 | .02 | .00 |
| ☐ 627 | Ken Oberkfell | .03 | .01 | .00 |
| ☐ 628 | Bob Walk | .03 | .01 | .00 |
| ☐ 629 | Larry Parrish | .05 | .02 | .00 |
| ☐ 630 | John Candelaria | .07 | .03 | .01 |
| ☐ 631 | Tigers Team (mound conference) | .05 | .02 | .00 |
| ☐ 632 | Rob Woodward | .10 | .04 | .01 |
| ☐ 633 | Jose Uribe | .03 | .01 | .00 |
| ☐ 634 | Rafael Palmeiro | .30 | .12 | .03 |
| ☐ 635 | Ken Schrom | .05 | .02 | .00 |
| ☐ 636 | Darren Daulton | .03 | .01 | .00 |
| ☐ 637 | Bip Roberts | .09 | .04 | .01 |
| ☐ 638 | Rich Bordi | .03 | .01 | .00 |
| ☐ 639 | Gerald Perry | .03 | .01 | .00 |
| ☐ 640 | Mark Clear | .03 | .01 | .00 |
| ☐ 641 | Domingo Ramos | .03 | .01 | .00 |
| ☐ 642 | Al Pulido | .03 | .01 | .00 |
| ☐ 643 | Ron Shepherd | .05 | .02 | .00 |
| ☐ 644 | John Denny | .06 | .02 | .00 |
| ☐ 645 | Dwight Evans | .09 | .04 | .01 |
| ☐ 646 | Mike Mason | .03 | .01 | .00 |
| ☐ 647 | Tom Lawless | .03 | .01 | .00 |
| ☐ 648 | Barry Larkin | .45 | .18 | .04 |
| ☐ 649 | Mickey Tettleton | .03 | .01 | .00 |
| ☐ 650 | Hubie Brooks | .09 | .04 | .01 |
| ☐ 651 | Benny Distefano | .05 | .02 | .00 |
| ☐ 652 | Terry Forster | .05 | .02 | .00 |
| ☐ 653 | Kevin Mitchell | .35 | .14 | .03 |
| ☐ 654 | Checklist 529-660 | .06 | .01 | .00 |
| ☐ 655 | Jesse Barfield | .15 | .06 | .01 |
| ☐ 656 | Rangers Team (Valentine/R.Wright) | .05 | .02 | .00 |
| ☐ 657 | Tom Waddell | .03 | .01 | .00 |
| ☐ 658 | Robby Thompson | .30 | .12 | .03 |
| ☐ 659 | Aurelio Lopez | .03 | .01 | .00 |
| ☐ 660 | Bob Horner | .15 | .06 | .01 |
| ☐ 661 | Lou Whitaker | .10 | .04 | .01 |
| ☐ 662 | Frank DiPino | .03 | .01 | .00 |
| ☐ 663 | Cliff Johnson | .03 | .01 | .00 |
| ☐ 664 | Mike Marshall | .10 | .04 | .01 |
| ☐ 665 | Rod Scurry | .03 | .01 | .00 |
| ☐ 666 | Von Hayes | .12 | .05 | .01 |
| ☐ 667 | Ron Hassey | .03 | .01 | .00 |
| ☐ 668 | Juan Bonilla | .03 | .01 | .00 |
| ☐ 669 | Bud Black | .03 | .01 | .00 |
| ☐ 670 | Jose Cruz | .09 | .04 | .01 |
| ☐ 671 | Ray Soff | .09 | .04 | .01 |
| ☐ 672 | Chili Davis | .07 | .03 | .01 |
| ☐ 673 | Don Sutton | .12 | .05 | .01 |
| ☐ 674 | Bill Campbell | .03 | .01 | .00 |
| ☐ 675 | Ed Romero | .03 | .01 | .00 |
| ☐ 676 | Charlie Moore | .03 | .01 | .00 |
| ☐ 677 | Bob Grich | .05 | .02 | .00 |
| ☐ 678 | Carney Lansford | .07 | .03 | .01 |
| ☐ 679 | Kent Hrbek | .15 | .06 | .01 |
| ☐ 680 | Ryne Sandberg | .25 | .10 | .02 |
| ☐ 681 | George Bell | .15 | .06 | .01 |
| ☐ 682 | Jerry Reuss | .05 | .02 | .00 |
| ☐ 683 | Gary Roenicke | .05 | .02 | .00 |
| ☐ 684 | Kent Tekulve | .05 | .02 | .00 |
| ☐ 685 | Jerry Hairston | .03 | .01 | .00 |
| ☐ 686 | Doyle Alexander | .05 | .02 | .00 |
| ☐ 687 | Alan Trammell | .12 | .05 | .01 |
| ☐ 688 | Juan Beniquez | .05 | .02 | .00 |
| ☐ 689 | Darrell Porter | .05 | .02 | .00 |
| ☐ 690 | Dane Iorg | .03 | .01 | .00 |
| ☐ 691 | Dave Parker | .15 | .06 | .01 |
| ☐ 692 | Frank White | .06 | .02 | .00 |
| ☐ 693 | Terry Puhl | .05 | .02 | .00 |
| ☐ 694 | Phil Niekro | .15 | .06 | .01 |
| ☐ 695 | Chico Walker | .15 | .06 | .01 |
| ☐ 696 | Gary Lucas | .03 | .01 | .00 |
| ☐ 697 | Ed Lynch | .03 | .01 | .00 |
| ☐ 698 | Ernie Whitt | .03 | .01 | .00 |
| ☐ 699 | Ken Landreaux | .05 | .02 | .00 |
| ☐ 700 | Dave Bergman | .03 | .01 | .00 |
| ☐ 701 | Willie Randolph | .06 | .02 | .00 |
| ☐ 702 | Greg Gross | .03 | .01 | .00 |
| ☐ 703 | Dave Schmidt | .03 | .01 | .00 |
| ☐ 704 | Jesse Orosco | .05 | .02 | .00 |
| ☐ 705 | Bruce Hurst | .07 | .03 | .01 |
| ☐ 706 | Rick Manning | .03 | .01 | .00 |
| ☐ 707 | Bob McClure | .03 | .01 | .00 |
| ☐ 708 | Scott McGregor | .07 | .03 | .01 |
| ☐ 709 | Dave Kingman | .10 | .04 | .01 |
| ☐ 710 | Gary Gaetti | .09 | .04 | .01 |
| ☐ 711 | Ken Griffey | .06 | .02 | .00 |
| ☐ 712 | Don Robinson | .03 | .01 | .00 |
| ☐ 713 | Tom Brookens | .03 | .01 | .00 |
| ☐ 714 | Dan Quisenberry | .10 | .04 | .01 |
| ☐ 715 | Bob Dernier | .05 | .02 | .00 |
| ☐ 716 | Rick Leach | .03 | .01 | .00 |
| ☐ 717 | Ed VandeBerg | .03 | .01 | .00 |
| ☐ 718 | Steve Carlton | .25 | .10 | .02 |
| ☐ 719 | Tom Hume | .03 | .01 | .00 |
| ☐ 720 | Richard Dotson | .05 | .02 | .00 |
| ☐ 721 | Tom Herr | .07 | .03 | .01 |
| ☐ 722 | Bob Knepper | .07 | .03 | .01 |
| ☐ 723 | Brett Butler | .08 | .03 | .01 |
| ☐ 724 | Greg Minton | .05 | .02 | .00 |
| ☐ 725 | George Hendrick | .05 | .02 | .00 |
| ☐ 726 | Frank Tanana | .05 | .02 | .00 |
| ☐ 727 | Mike Moore | .05 | .02 | .00 |
| ☐ 728 | Tippy Martinez | .03 | .01 | .00 |
| ☐ 729 | Tom Paciorek | .03 | .01 | .00 |
| ☐ 730 | Eric Show | .03 | .01 | .00 |
| ☐ 731 | Dave Concepcion | .08 | .03 | .01 |
| ☐ 732 | Manny Trillo | .05 | .02 | .00 |
| ☐ 733 | Bill Caudill | .05 | .02 | .00 |
| ☐ 734 | Bill Madlock | .10 | .04 | .01 |
| ☐ 735 | Rickey Henderson | .30 | .12 | .03 |
| ☐ 736 | Steve Bedrosian | .05 | .02 | .00 |
| ☐ 737 | Floyd Bannister | .05 | .02 | .00 |
| ☐ 738 | Jorge Orta | .03 | .01 | .00 |
| ☐ 739 | Chet Lemon | .05 | .02 | .00 |
| ☐ 740 | Rich Gedman | .08 | .03 | .01 |
| ☐ 741 | Paul Molitor | .08 | .03 | .01 |
| ☐ 742 | Andy McGaffigan | .03 | .01 | .00 |

| | | MINT | VG-E | F-G |
|---|---|---|---|---|
| ☐ 743 | Dwayne Murphy | .05 | .02 | .00 |
| ☐ 744 | Roy Smalley | .05 | .02 | .00 |
| ☐ 745 | Glenn Hubbard | .03 | .01 | .00 |
| ☐ 746 | Bob Ojeda | .08 | .03 | .01 |
| ☐ 747 | Johnny Ray | .08 | .03 | .01 |
| ☐ 748 | Mike Flanagan | .07 | .03 | .01 |
| ☐ 749 | Ozzie Smith | .12 | .05 | .01 |
| ☐ 750 | Steve Trout | .05 | .02 | .00 |
| ☐ 751 | Garth Iorg | .03 | .01 | .00 |
| ☐ 752 | Dan Petry | .09 | .04 | .01 |
| ☐ 753 | Rick Honeycutt | .05 | .02 | .00 |
| ☐ 754 | Dave LaPoint | .03 | .01 | .00 |
| ☐ 755 | Luis Aguayo | .03 | .01 | .00 |
| ☐ 756 | Carlton Fisk | .12 | .05 | .01 |
| ☐ 757 | Nolan Ryan | .30 | .12 | .03 |
| ☐ 758 | Tony Bernazard | .05 | .02 | .00 |
| ☐ 759 | Joel Youngblood | .03 | .01 | .00 |
| ☐ 760 | Mike Witt | .10 | .04 | .01 |
| ☐ 761 | Greg Pryor | .03 | .01 | .00 |
| ☐ 762 | Gary Ward | .05 | .02 | .00 |
| ☐ 763 | Tim Flannery | .03 | .01 | .00 |
| ☐ 764 | Bill Buckner | .08 | .03 | .01 |
| ☐ 765 | Kirk Gibson | .20 | .08 | .02 |
| ☐ 766 | Don Aase | .05 | .02 | .00 |
| ☐ 767 | Ron Cey | .07 | .03 | .01 |
| ☐ 768 | Dennis Lamp | .03 | .01 | .00 |
| ☐ 769 | Steve Sax | .12 | .05 | .01 |
| ☐ 770 | Dave Winfield | .25 | .10 | .02 |
| ☐ 771 | Shane Rawley | .07 | .03 | .01 |
| ☐ 772 | Harold Baines | .15 | .06 | .01 |
| ☐ 773 | Robin Yount | .25 | .10 | .02 |
| ☐ 774 | Wayne Krenchicki | .03 | .01 | .00 |
| ☐ 775 | Joaquin Andujar | .08 | .03 | .01 |
| ☐ 776 | Tom Brunansky | .09 | .04 | .01 |
| ☐ 777 | Chris Chambliss | .05 | .02 | .00 |
| ☐ 778 | Jack Morris | .15 | .06 | .01 |
| ☐ 779 | Craig Reynolds | .03 | .01 | .00 |
| ☐ 780 | Andre Thornton | .05 | .02 | .00 |
| ☐ 781 | Atlee Hammaker | .05 | .02 | .00 |
| ☐ 782 | Brian Downing | .05 | .02 | .00 |
| ☐ 783 | Willie Wilson | .12 | .05 | .01 |
| ☐ 784 | Cal Ripken | .25 | .10 | .02 |
| ☐ 785 | Terry Francona | .03 | .01 | .00 |
| ☐ 786 | Jimy Williams MGR (checklist back) | .06 | .01 | .00 |
| ☐ 787 | Alejandro Pena | .05 | .02 | .00 |
| ☐ 788 | Tim Stoddard | .03 | .01 | .00 |
| ☐ 789 | Dan Schatzeder | .03 | .01 | .00 |
| ☐ 790 | Julio Cruz | .03 | .01 | .00 |
| ☐ 791 | Lance Parrish | .20 | .08 | .02 |
| ☐ 792 | Checklist 661-792 | .06 | .01 | .00 |
| ☐ A | Don Baylor (wax pack box card) | .15 | .06 | .01 |
| ☐ B | Steve Carlton (wax pack box card) | .30 | .12 | .03 |
| ☐ C | Ron Cey (wax pack box card) | .10 | .04 | .01 |
| ☐ D | Cecil Cooper (wax pack box card) | .10 | .04 | .01 |
| ☐ E | Rickey Henderson (wax pack box card) | .50 | .20 | .05 |
| ☐ F | Jim Rice (wax pack box card) | .30 | .12 | .03 |
| ☐ G | Don Sutton (wax pack box card) | .20 | .08 | .02 |
| ☐ H | Dave Winfield (wax pack box card) | .30 | .12 | .03 |

## 1987 Topps Glossy 22

This set of 22 glossy cards was inserted one per rack pack. Players selected for the set are the starting players (plus manager and two pitchers) in the 1986 All-Star Game in Houston. Cards measure standard size, 2 1/2" by 3 1/2" and the backs feature red and blue printing on a white card stock.

| | | MINT | VG-E | F-G |
|---|---|---|---|---|
| COMPLETE SET (22) | | 3.75 | 1.25 | .30 |
| COMMON PLAYER (1-22) | | .10 | .04 | .01 |
| ☐ 1 | Whitey Herzog MGR | .10 | .04 | .01 |
| ☐ 2 | Keith Hernandez | .20 | .08 | .02 |
| ☐ 3 | Ryne Sandberg | .30 | .12 | .03 |
| ☐ 4 | Mike Schmidt | .40 | .16 | .04 |

| | | MINT | VG-E | F-G |
|---|---|---|---|---|
| ☐ 5 | Ozzie Smith | .15 | .06 | .01 |
| ☐ 6 | Tony Gwynn | .30 | .12 | .03 |
| ☐ 7 | Dale Murphy | .50 | .20 | .05 |
| ☐ 8 | Darryl Strawberry | .40 | .16 | .04 |
| ☐ 9 | Gary Carter | .30 | .12 | .03 |
| ☐ 10 | Dwight Gooden | .60 | .24 | .06 |
| ☐ 11 | Fernando Valenzuela | .30 | .12 | .03 |
| ☐ 12 | Dick Howser MGR | .10 | .04 | .01 |
| ☐ 13 | Wally Joyner | .90 | .36 | .09 |
| ☐ 14 | Lou Whitaker | .15 | .06 | .01 |
| ☐ 15 | Wade Boggs | .75 | .30 | .07 |
| ☐ 16 | Cal Ripken | .30 | .12 | .03 |
| ☐ 17 | Dave Winfield | .30 | .12 | .03 |
| ☐ 18 | Rickey Henderson | .40 | .16 | .04 |
| ☐ 19 | Kirby Puckett | .30 | .12 | .03 |
| ☐ 20 | Lance Parrish | .20 | .08 | .02 |
| ☐ 21 | Roger Clemens | .75 | .30 | .07 |
| ☐ 22 | Teddy Higuera | .20 | .08 | .02 |

## 1986 True Value

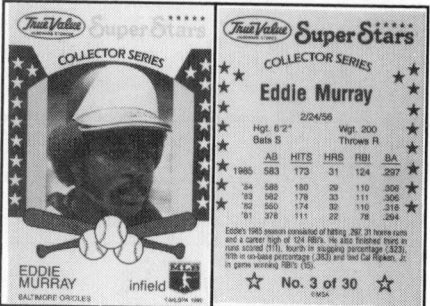

The 1986 True Value set consists of 30 cards each 2 1/2" by 3 1/2" which were printed as panels of four although one of the cards in the panel only pictures a featured product. The complete panel measures 10 3/8" by 3 1/2". The True Value logo is in the upper left corner of the obverse of each card. Supposedly the cards were distributed to customers purchasing 5.00 or more at the store. Cards are frequently found with perforations intact and still in the closed form where only the top card in the folded panel is visible. The card number appears at the bottom of the reverse. Team logos have been surgically removed (airbrushed) from the photos.

|  | | MINT | VG-E | F-G |
|---|---|---|---|---|
| COMPLETE SET (30) | | 6.00 | 2.40 | .60 |
| COMMON PLAYER (1-30) | | .10 | .04 | .01 |
| ☐ 1 | Pedro Guerrero | .20 | .08 | .02 |
| ☐ 2 | Steve Garvey | .30 | .12 | .03 |
| ☐ 3 | Eddie Murray | .30 | .12 | .03 |
| ☐ 4 | Pete Rose | .50 | .20 | .05 |
| ☐ 5 | Don Mattingly | .75 | .30 | .07 |
| ☐ 6 | Fernando Valenzuela | .30 | .12 | .03 |
| ☐ 7 | Jim Rice | .30 | .12 | .03 |
| ☐ 8 | Kirk Gibson | .20 | .08 | .02 |
| ☐ 9 | Ozzie Smith | .15 | .06 | .01 |
| ☐ 10 | Dale Murphy | .50 | .20 | .05 |
| ☐ 11 | Robin Yount | .30 | .12 | .03 |
| ☐ 12 | Tom Seaver | .30 | .12 | .03 |
| ☐ 13 | Reggie Jackson | .40 | .16 | .04 |
| ☐ 14 | Ryne Sandberg | .30 | .12 | .03 |
| ☐ 15 | Bruce Sutter | .15 | .06 | .01 |
| ☐ 16 | Gary Carter | .30 | .12 | .03 |
| ☐ 17 | George Brett | .40 | .16 | .04 |
| ☐ 18 | Rick Sutcliffe | .10 | .04 | .01 |
| ☐ 19 | Dave Stieb | .10 | .04 | .01 |
| ☐ 20 | Buddy Bell | .10 | .04 | .01 |
| ☐ 21 | Alvin Davis | .15 | .06 | .01 |
| ☐ 22 | Cal Ripken | .30 | .12 | .03 |
| ☐ 23 | Bill Madlock | .10 | .04 | .01 |
| ☐ 24 | Kent Hrbek | .15 | .06 | .01 |
| ☐ 25 | Lou Whitaker | .15 | .06 | .01 |
| ☐ 26 | Nolan Ryan | .30 | .12 | .03 |
| ☐ 27 | Dwayne Murphy | .10 | .04 | .01 |
| ☐ 28 | Mike Schmidt | .50 | .20 | .05 |
| ☐ 29 | Andre Dawson | .20 | .08 | .02 |
| ☐ 30 | Wade Boggs | .60 | .24 | .06 |

## T3 Turkey Red

The cards in this 126 card set measure 5 3/4" by 8". The 1911 "Turkey Red" set of color cabinet style cards, designated T3 in the American Card Catalog, is named after the brand of cigarettes with which it was offered as a premium. Cards 1-50 and 77-126

depict baseball players while the middle series (51-76) portrays boxers. The cards themselves are not numbered but were assigned numbers for ordering purposes by the manufacturer. This list appears on the backs of cards in the 77-126 sub-series and has been used in the checklist below. The boxers (51-76) were formerly assigned a separate catalog number (T9) but have now been returned to the classification to which they properly belong and are indicated in the checklist below by BOX.

|  | | MINT | VG-E | F-G |
|---|---|---|---|---|
| COMPLETE SET | | 17500.00 | 7500.00 | 2000. |
| COMMON BASEBALL (1-50) | | 110.00 | 45.00 | 11.00 |
| COMMON BOXERS (51-76) | | 60.00 | 24.00 | 6.00 |
| COMMON BASEBALL (77-126) | | 125.00 | 50.00 | 12.50 |
| ☐ 1 | M. Brown: Chicago NL | 200.00 | 80.00 | 20.00 |
| ☐ 2 | Bergen: Brooklyn | 110.00 | 45.00 | 11.00 |
| ☐ 3 | Leach: Pittsburgh | 110.00 | 45.00 | 11.00 |
| ☐ 4 | Bresnahan: St.L. NL | 160.00 | 65.00 | 16.00 |
| ☐ 5 | Crawford: Detroit | 175.00 | 70.00 | 18.00 |
| ☐ 6 | Chase: New York AL | 125.00 | 50.00 | 12.50 |
| ☐ 7 | Camnitz: Pittsburgh | 110.00 | 45.00 | 11.00 |
| ☐ 8 | Clarke: Pittsburgh | 175.00 | 70.00 | 18.00 |
| ☐ 9 | Cobb: Detroit | 2000.00 | 800.00 | 200.00 |
| ☐ 10 | Devlin: New York NL | 110.00 | 45.00 | 11.00 |
| ☐ 11 | Dahlen: Brooklyn | 110.00 | 45.00 | 11.00 |
| ☐ 12 | Donovan: Detroit | 110.00 | 45.00 | 11.00 |
| ☐ 13 | Doyle: New York NL | 110.00 | 45.00 | 11.00 |
| ☐ 14 | Dooin: Phila. NL | 110.00 | 45.00 | 11.00 |
| ☐ 15 | Elberfeld: Wash | 110.00 | 45.00 | 11.00 |
| ☐ 16 | Evers: Chicago NL | 200.00 | 80.00 | 20.00 |
| ☐ 17 | Griffith: Cinc. | 160.00 | 65.00 | 16.00 |
| ☐ 18 | Jennings: Detroit | 160.00 | 65.00 | 16.00 |
| ☐ 19 | Joss: Cleveland | 225.00 | 90.00 | 22.00 |
| ☐ 20 | Jordan: Brooklyn | 110.00 | 45.00 | 11.00 |
| ☐ 21 | Kleinow: New York NL | 110.00 | 45.00 | 11.00 |
| ☐ 22 | Krause: Phila. AL | 110.00 | 45.00 | 11.00 |
| ☐ 23 | Lajoie: Cleveland | 450.00 | 180.00 | 45.00 |
| ☐ 24 | Mitchell: Cincinnati | 110.00 | 45.00 | 11.00 |
| ☐ 25 | M. McIntyre: Detroit | 110.00 | 45.00 | 11.00 |
| ☐ 26 | McGraw: New York NL | 250.00 | 100.00 | 25.00 |
| ☐ 27 | Mathewson: N.Y. NL | 600.00 | 240.00 | 60.00 |
| ☐ 28 | H. McIntyre: Brk | 110.00 | 45.00 | 11.00 |
| ☐ 29 | McConnell: Boston AL | 110.00 | 45.00 | 11.00 |
| ☐ 30 | Mullin: Detroit | 110.00 | 45.00 | 11.00 |
| ☐ 31 | Magee: Phila. NL | 110.00 | 45.00 | 11.00 |
| ☐ 32 | Overall: Chicago NL | 110.00 | 45.00 | 11.00 |
| ☐ 33 | Pfeister: Chicago NL | 110.00 | 45.00 | 11.00 |
| ☐ 34 | Rucker: Brooklyn | 110.00 | 45.00 | 11.00 |
| ☐ 35 | Tinker: Chicago NL | 175.00 | 70.00 | 18.00 |
| ☐ 36 | Speaker: Boston AL | 450.00 | 180.00 | 45.00 |
| ☐ 37 | Sallee: St. Louis NL | 110.00 | 45.00 | 11.00 |
| ☐ 38 | Stahl: Boston AL | 110.00 | 45.00 | 11.00 |
| ☐ 39 | Waddell: St.Louis AL | 225.00 | 90.00 | 22.00 |
| ☐ 40 | Willis: St.Louis NL | 110.00 | 45.00 | 11.00 |
| ☐ 41 | Wiltse: New York NL | 110.00 | 45.00 | 11.00 |
| ☐ 42 | Young: Cleveland | 500.00 | 200.00 | 50.00 |
| ☐ 43 | Out At Third | 110.00 | 45.00 | 11.00 |
| ☐ 44 | Trying to Catch Him Napping | 110.00 | 45.00 | 11.00 |
| ☐ 45 | Jordan and Herzog at First | 110.00 | 45.00 | 11.00 |
| ☐ 46 | Safe At Third | 110.00 | 45.00 | 11.00 |
| ☐ 47 | Frank Chance At Bat | 175.00 | 70.00 | 18.00 |
| ☐ 48 | Jack Murray At Bat | 110.00 | 45.00 | 11.00 |
| ☐ 49 | Close Play At Second | 110.00 | 45.00 | 11.00 |
| ☐ 50 | Chief Myers At Bat | 110.00 | 45.00 | 11.00 |
| ☐ 51 | Jim Driscoll BOX | 60.00 | 24.00 | 6.00 |
| ☐ 52 | Abe Attell BOX | 60.00 | 24.00 | 6.00 |
| ☐ 53 | Ad. Walgast BOX | 60.00 | 24.00 | 6.00 |
| ☐ 54 | Johnny Coulon BOX | 60.00 | 24.00 | 6.00 |
| ☐ 55 | James Jeffries BOX | 110.00 | 45.00 | 11.00 |
| ☐ 56 | Jack Sullivan BOX (Twin) | 75.00 | 30.00 | 7.50 |
| ☐ 57 | Battling Nelson BOX | 75.00 | 30.00 | 7.50 |
| ☐ 58 | Packey McFarland BOX | 60.00 | 24.00 | 6.00 |
| ☐ 59 | Tommy Murphy BOX | 60.00 | 24.00 | 6.00 |
| ☐ 60 | Owen Moran BOX | 60.00 | 24.00 | 6.00 |
| ☐ 61 | Johnny Marto BOX | 60.00 | 24.00 | 6.00 |
| ☐ 62 | Jimmie Gardner BOX | 60.00 | 24.00 | 6.00 |
| ☐ 63 | Harry Lewis BOX | 60.00 | 24.00 | 6.00 |
| ☐ 64 | Wm. Papke BOX | 60.00 | 24.00 | 6.00 |
| ☐ 65 | Sam Langford BOX | 60.00 | 24.00 | 6.00 |
| ☐ 66 | Knock-out Brown BOX | 60.00 | 24.00 | 6.00 |
| ☐ 67 | Stanley Ketchel BOX | 90.00 | 36.00 | 9.00 |
| ☐ 68 | Joe Jeannette BOX | 60.00 | 24.00 | 6.00 |
| ☐ 69 | Leach Cross BOX | 60.00 | 24.00 | 6.00 |
| ☐ 70 | Phil. McGovern BOX | 60.00 | 24.00 | 6.00 |

| | | MINT | VG-E | F-G |
|---|---|---|---|---|
| ☐ 71 | Battling Hurley BOX | 60.00 | 24.00 | 6.00 |
| ☐ 72 | Honey Mellody BOX | 60.00 | 24.00 | 6.00 |
| ☐ 73 | Al Kaufman BOX | 60.00 | 24.00 | 6.00 |
| ☐ 74 | Willie Lewis BOX | 60.00 | 24.00 | 6.00 |
| ☐ 75 | Jack O'Brien BOX "Philadelphia" | 75.00 | 30.00 | 7.50 |
| ☐ 76 | Jack Johnson BOX | 125.00 | 50.00 | 12.50 |
| ☐ 77 | Ames: New York NL | 125.00 | 50.00 | 12.50 |
| ☐ 78 | Baker: Phila. AL | 225.00 | 90.00 | 22.00 |
| ☐ 79 | Bell: Brooklyn | 125.00 | 50.00 | 12.50 |
| ☐ 80 | Bender: Phila. AL | 175.00 | 70.00 | 18.00 |
| ☐ 81 | Bescher: Cincinnati | 125.00 | 50.00 | 12.50 |
| ☐ 82 | Bransfield: Phila. NL | 125.00 | 50.00 | 12.50 |
| ☐ 83 | Bridwell: Phila. NL | 125.00 | 50.00 | 12.50 |
| ☐ 84 | Browne: Wash and Chi | 125.00 | 50.00 | 12.50 |
| ☐ 85 | Burns: Chi. and Cin. | 125.00 | 50.00 | 12.50 |
| ☐ 86 | Carrigan: Boston AL | 125.00 | 50.00 | 12.50 |
| ☐ 87 | Collins: Phila. AL | 225.00 | 90.00 | 22.00 |
| ☐ 88 | Coveleski: Cinc. | 125.00 | 50.00 | 12.50 |
| ☐ 89 | Criger: New York AL | 125.00 | 50.00 | 12.50 |
| ☐ 90 | Doolan: Phila. NL | 125.00 | 50.00 | 12.50 |
| ☐ 91 | Downey: Cincinnati | 125.00 | 50.00 | 12.50 |
| ☐ 92 | Dygert: Phila. AL | 125.00 | 50.00 | 12.50 |
| ☐ 93 | Fromme: Cincinnati | 125.00 | 50.00 | 12.50 |
| ☐ 94 | Gibson: Pittsburgh | 125.00 | 50.00 | 12.50 |
| ☐ 95 | Graham: Boston NL | 125.00 | 50.00 | 12.50 |
| ☐ 96 | Groom: Washington | 125.00 | 50.00 | 12.50 |
| ☐ 97 | Hoblitzell: Cinc. | 125.00 | 50.00 | 12.50 |
| ☐ 98 | Hofman: Chicago NL | 125.00 | 50.00 | 12.50 |
| ☐ 99 | Johnson: Washington | 750.00 | 300.00 | 75.00 |
| ☐ 100 | D. Jones: Detroit | 125.00 | 50.00 | 12.50 |
| ☐ 101 | Keeler: New York NL | 300.00 | 120.00 | 30.00 |
| ☐ 102 | Kling: Chicago NL | 125.00 | 50.00 | 12.50 |
| ☐ 103 | Konetchy: St.Louis NL | 125.00 | 50.00 | 12.50 |
| ☐ 104 | Lennox: Brooklyn | 125.00 | 50.00 | 12.50 |
| ☐ 105 | Lobert: Cincinnati | 125.00 | 50.00 | 12.50 |
| ☐ 106 | Lord: Bos. and Chi. | 125.00 | 50.00 | 12.50 |
| ☐ 107 | Manning: N.Y. AL | 125.00 | 50.00 | 12.50 |
| ☐ 108 | Merkle: New York NL | 125.00 | 50.00 | 12.50 |
| ☐ 109 | Moran: Chi. and Phil. | 125.00 | 50.00 | 12.50 |
| ☐ 110 | McBride: Washington | 125.00 | 50.00 | 12.50 |
| ☐ 111 | Niles: Bos. and Cleve | 125.00 | 50.00 | 12.50 |
| ☐ 112 | Paskert: Cincinnati | 125.00 | 50.00 | 12.50 |
| ☐ 113 | Raymond: N.Y. NL | 125.00 | 50.00 | 12.50 |
| ☐ 114 | Rhoades: Cleveland | 160.00 | 65.00 | 16.00 |
| ☐ 115 | Schlei: New York NL | 125.00 | 50.00 | 12.50 |
| ☐ 116 | Schmidt: Detroit | 125.00 | 50.00 | 12.50 |
| ☐ 117 | Schulte: Chicago NL | 125.00 | 50.00 | 12.50 |
| ☐ 118 | Smith: Chi. and Bos. | 125.00 | 50.00 | 12.50 |
| ☐ 119 | Stone: St.L. AL | 125.00 | 50.00 | 12.50 |
| ☐ 120 | Street: Washington | 125.00 | 50.00 | 12.50 |
| ☐ 121 | Sullivan: Chi. AL | 125.00 | 50.00 | 12.50 |
| ☐ 122 | Tenney: New York NL | 125.00 | 50.00 | 12.50 |
| ☐ 123 | Thomas: Phila. AL | 125.00 | 50.00 | 12.50 |
| ☐ 124 | Wallace: St.Louis AL | 175.00 | 70.00 | 18.00 |
| ☐ 125 | Walsh: Chicago AL | 200.00 | 80.00 | 20.00 |
| ☐ 126 | Wilson: Pittsburgh | 125.00 | 50.00 | 12.50 |

## T200 Fatima

The cards in this 16 card set measure 2 5/8" by 5 13/16". The 1913 Fatima Cigarettes issue contains unnumbered glossy surface team cards. Both St. Louis team cards are considered difficult to obtain. A large 13" by 21" unnumbered, heavy cardboard premium issue is also known to exist and is quite scarce. These unnumbered team cards are ordered below by team alphabetical order within league.

| | | MINT | VG-E | F-G |
|---|---|---|---|---|
| | COMPLETE SET | 2000.00 | 800.00 | 200.00 |
| | COMMON TEAM | 100.00 | 40.00 | 10.00 |
| ☐ 1 | Boston AL | 150.00 | 60.00 | 15.00 |
| ☐ 2 | Chicago AL | 100.00 | 40.00 | 10.00 |
| ☐ 3 | Cleveland AL | 100.00 | 40.00 | 10.00 |
| ☐ 4 | Detroit AL | 175.00 | 70.00 | 18.00 |
| ☐ 5 | New York AL | 300.00 | 120.00 | 30.00 |
| ☐ 6 | Philadelphia AL | 100.00 | 40.00 | 10.00 |
| ☐ 7 | St. Louis AL | 250.00 | 100.00 | 25.00 |
| ☐ 8 | Washington AL | 100.00 | 40.00 | 10.00 |
| ☐ 9 | Boston NL | 175.00 | 70.00 | 18.00 |
| ☐ 10 | Brooklyn NL | 100.00 | 40.00 | 10.00 |
| ☐ 11 | Chicago NL | 100.00 | 40.00 | 10.00 |
| ☐ 12 | Cincinnati NL | 100.00 | 40.00 | 10.00 |
| ☐ 13 | New York NL | 100.00 | 40.00 | 10.00 |
| ☐ 14 | Philadelphia NL | 100.00 | 40.00 | 10.00 |
| ☐ 15 | Pittsburg NL | 100.00 | 40.00 | 10.00 |
| ☐ 16 | St. Louis NL | 175.00 | 70.00 | 18.00 |

## T201 Mecca

The cards in this 50 card set measure 2 1/4" by 4 11/16". The 1911 Mecca Double Folder issue contains unnumbered cards. This issue was one of the first to list statistics of players portrayed on the cards. Each card portrays two players, one when the card is folded, another when the card is unfolded. The card of Dougherty and Lord is considered scarce.

| | | MINT | VG-E | F-G |
|---|---|---|---|---|
| | COMPLETE SET | 1600.00 | 700.00 | 175.00 |
| | COMMON PAIR | 18.00 | 7.25 | 1.80 |
| ☐ 1 | F.Baker and Collins | 60.00 | 24.00 | 6.00 |
| ☐ 2 | Barry and Lapp | 18.00 | 7.25 | 1.80 |
| ☐ 3 | Bergen and Z.Wheat | 30.00 | 12.00 | 3.00 |
| ☐ 4 | Blair and Hartzell | 18.00 | 7.25 | 1.80 |
| ☐ 5 | Bresnahan and Huggins | 60.00 | 24.00 | 6.00 |
| ☐ 6 | Bridwell and Mathewson | 100.00 | 40.00 | 10.00 |
| ☐ 7 | Butler and Abstein | 18.00 | 7.25 | 1.80 |
| ☐ 8 | Byrne and F.Clarke | 30.00 | 12.00 | 3.00 |
| ☐ 9 | Chance and Evers | 60.00 | 24.00 | 6.00 |
| ☐ 10 | Clark and Gaspar | 18.00 | 7.25 | 1.80 |
| ☐ 11 | Cobb and S.Crawford | 275.00 | 100.00 | 30.00 |
| ☐ 12 | Cole and Kling | 18.00 | 7.25 | 1.80 |
| ☐ 13 | Coombs and Thomas | 18.00 | 7.25 | 1.80 |
| ☐ 14 | Daubert and Rucker | 18.00 | 7.25 | 1.80 |
| ☐ 15 | Dougherty and Lord | 175.00 | 70.00 | 18.00 |
| ☐ 16 | Dooin and Titus | 18.00 | 7.25 | 1.80 |
| ☐ 17 | Downie and Baker | 18.00 | 7.25 | 1.80 |
| ☐ 18 | Dygert and Seymour | 18.00 | 7.25 | 1.80 |
| ☐ 19 | Elberfeld and McBride | 18.00 | 7.25 | 1.80 |
| ☐ 20 | Falkenberg and Lajoie | 50.00 | 20.00 | 5.00 |
| ☐ 21 | Fitzpatrick , Killian | 18.00 | 7.25 | 1.80 |
| ☐ 22 | Gardner and Speaker | 50.00 | 20.00 | 5.00 |
| ☐ 23 | Gibson and Leach | 18.00 | 7.25 | 1.80 |
| ☐ 24 | Graham and Mattern | 18.00 | 7.25 | 1.80 |
| ☐ 25 | Hauser and Lush | 18.00 | 7.25 | 1.80 |
| ☐ 26 | Herzog and Miller | 18.00 | 7.25 | 1.80 |
| ☐ 27 | Hinchman and Hickman | 18.00 | 7.25 | 1.80 |
| ☐ 28 | Hofman and M.Brown | 30.00 | 12.00 | 3.00 |
| ☐ 29 | Jennings and Summers | 30.00 | 12.00 | 3.00 |
| ☐ 30 | Johnson and Ford | 18.00 | 7.25 | 1.80 |
| ☐ 31 | McCarty and McGinnity | 30.00 | 12.00 | 3.00 |
| ☐ 32 | McGlyn and Barrett | 18.00 | 7.25 | 1.80 |
| ☐ 33 | McLean and Grant | 18.00 | 7.25 | 1.80 |
| ☐ 34 | Merkle and Wiltse | 18.00 | 7.25 | 1.80 |
| ☐ 35 | Meyers and Doyle | 18.00 | 7.25 | 1.80 |
| ☐ 36 | Moore and Lobert | 18.00 | 7.25 | 1.80 |
| ☐ 37 | Odwell and Downs | 18.00 | 7.25 | 1.80 |
| ☐ 38 | Oldring and Bender | 30.00 | 12.00 | 3.00 |
| ☐ 39 | Payne and Walsh | 30.00 | 12.00 | 3.00 |
| ☐ 40 | Simon and Leifield | 18.00 | 7.25 | 1.80 |
| ☐ 41 | Starr and McCabe | 18.00 | 7.25 | 1.80 |
| ☐ 42 | Stephens and LaPorte | 18.00 | 7.25 | 1.80 |
| ☐ 43 | Stovall and Turner | 18.00 | 7.25 | 1.80 |
| ☐ 44 | Street and W.Johnson | 100.00 | 40.00 | 10.00 |
| ☐ 45 | Stroud and Donovan | 18.00 | 7.25 | 1.80 |
| ☐ 46 | Sweeney and Chase | 18.00 | 7.25 | 1.80 |
| ☐ 47 | Thoney and Cicotte | 18.00 | 7.25 | 1.80 |
| ☐ 48 | Wallace and Lake | 30.00 | 12.00 | 3.00 |
| ☐ 49 | Ward and Foster | 18.00 | 7.25 | 1.80 |
| ☐ 50 | Williams and Woodruff | 18.00 | 7.25 | 1.80 |

## T202 Triple Folders

The cards in this 134 card set measure 2 1/4" by 5 1/4". The 1912 T202 Hassan Triple Folder issue is perhaps the most ingenious baseball card ever issued. The two end cards of each panel are full color, T205-like individual cards whereas the black and white center panel pictures an action photo or portrait. The end cards can be folded across the center panel and stored in this manner. Seventy-six different center panels are known to exist; however, many of the center panels contain more than one combination of end cards. The center panel titles are listed below in alphabetical order while the different combinations of end cards are listed below each center panel as they appear left to right on the front of the card. A total of 132 different card fronts exist. The set price below includes all panel and player combinations listed in the checklist. Back color variations (red or black) also exist. The Birmingham's Home Run card is difficult to obtain as are other cards whose center panel exists with but one combination of end cards. The Devlin with Mathewson end panels on numbers 29A and 74C picture Devlin as a Giant. Devlin is pictured as a Rustler on 29B and 74D.

| | | MINT | VG-E | F-G |
|---|---|---|---|---|
| | COMPLETE SET | 9000.00 | 3750.00 | 900.00 |
| | COMMON PANEL | 50.00 | 20.00 | 5.00 |
| ☐ 1A | A Close Play at Home: Wallace-LaPorte | 60.00 | 24.00 | 6.00 |
| ☐ 1B | A Close Play at Home: Wallace-Pelty | 60.00 | 24.00 | 6.00 |
| ☐ 2 | A Desperate Slide: O'Leary-Cobb | 275.00 | 110.00 | 27.00 |
| ☐ 3A | A Great Batsman: Barger-Bergen | 50.00 | 20.00 | 5.00 |
| ☐ 3B | A Great Batsman: Rucker-Bergen | 50.00 | 20.00 | 5.00 |
| ☐ 4 | Ambrose McConnell at Bat: Blair-Quinn | 50.00 | 20.00 | 5.00 |
| ☐ 5 | A Wide Throw Saves Crawford: Mullin-Stanage | 60.00 | 24.00 | 6.00 |
| ☐ 6 | Baker Gets His Man: Collins-Baker | 90.00 | 36.00 | 9.00 |
| ☐ 7 | Birmingham Gets to Third: Johnson-Street | 120.00 | 50.00 | 12.00 |
| ☐ 8 | Birmingham's Home Run: Birmingham-Turner | 175.00 | 70.00 | 18.00 |
| ☐ 9 | Bush Just Misses Austin: Moran-Magee | 50.00 | 20.00 | 5.00 |
| ☐ 10A | Carrigan Blocks His Man: Gaspar-McLean | 50.00 | 20.00 | 5.00 |
| ☐ 10B | Carrigan Blocks His Man: Wagner-Carrigan | 50.00 | 20.00 | 5.00 |
| ☐ 11 | Catching Him Napping: Oakes-Bresnahan | 60.00 | 24.00 | 6.00 |
| ☐ 12 | Caught Asleep Off First: Bresnahan-Harmon | 60.00 | 24.00 | 6.00 |
| ☐ 13A | Chance Beats Out a Hit: Chance-Foxen | 75.00 | 30.00 | 7.50 |
| ☐ 13B | Chance Beats Out a Hit: McIntire-Archer | 60.00 | 24.00 | 6.00 |
| ☐ 13C | Chance Beats Out a Hit: Overall-Archer | 60.00 | 24.00 | 6.00 |
| ☐ 13D | Chance Beats Out a Hit: Rowan-Archer | 60.00 | 24.00 | 6.00 |
| ☐ 13E | Chance Beats Out a Hit: Shean-Chance | 75.00 | 30.00 | 7.50 |
| ☐ 14A | Chase Dives into Third: Chase-Wolter | 50.00 | 20.00 | 5.00 |
| ☐ 14B | Chase Dives into Third: Gibson-Clarke | 60.00 | 24.00 | 6.00 |
| ☐ 14C | Chase Dives into Third: Phillippe-Gibson | 50.00 | 20.00 | 5.00 |
| ☐ 15A | Chase Gets Ball Too Late: Egan-Mitchell | 50.00 | 20.00 | 5.00 |
| ☐ 15B | Chase Gets Ball Too Late: Wolter-Chase | 50.00 | 20.00 | 5.00 |
| ☐ 16A | Chase Guarding First: Chase-Wolter | 50.00 | 20.00 | 5.00 |
| ☐ 16B | Chase Guarding First: Gibson-Clarke | 60.00 | 24.00 | 6.00 |
| ☐ 16C | Chase Guarding First: Leifield-Gibson | 50.00 | 20.00 | 5.00 |
| ☐ 17 | Chase Ready Squeeze | 50.00 | 20.00 | 5.00 |

| | | MINT | VG-E | F-G |
|---|---|---|---|---|
| | Play: Paskert-Magee | | | |
| ☐ 18 | Chase Safe at Third: Barry-Baker | 60.00 | 24.00 | 6.00 |
| ☐ 19 | Chief Bender Waiting: Bender-Thomas | 60.00 | 24.00 | 6.00 |
| ☐ 20 | Clarke Hikes for Home: Bridwell-Kling | 60.00 | 24.00 | 6.00 |
| ☐ 21 | Close at First: Ball-Stovall | 50.00 | 20.00 | 5.00 |
| ☐ 22A | Close at the Plate: Walsh-Payne | 60.00 | 24.00 | 6.00 |
| ☐ 22B | Close at the Plate: White-Payne | 50.00 | 20.00 | 5.00 |
| ☐ 23 | Close at Third (Speaker): Wood-Speaker | 100.00 | 40.00 | 10.00 |
| ☐ 24 | Close at Third (Wagner): Wagner-Carrigan | 60.00 | 24.00 | 6.00 |
| ☐ 25A | Collins Easily Safe: Byrne-Clarke | 75.00 | 30.00 | 7.50 |
| ☐ 25B | Collins Easily Safe: Collins-Baker | 90.00 | 36.00 | 9.00 |
| ☐ 25C | Collins Easily Safe: Collins-Murphy | 75.00 | 30.00 | 7.50 |
| ☐ 26 | Crawford About to Smash: Stanage-Summers | 60.00 | 24.00 | 6.00 |
| ☐ 27 | Cree Rolls Home: Daubert-Hummell | 50.00 | 20.00 | 5.00 |
| ☐ 28 | Davy Jones' Great Slide: Delahanty-Jones | 50.00 | 20.00 | 5.00 |
| ☐ 29A | Devlin Gets His Man: Devlin (Giants)-Mathewson | 175.00 | 70.00 | 18.00 |
| ☐ 29B | Devlin Gets His Man: Devlin (Rustlers)-Mathewson | 90.00 | 36.00 | 9.00 |
| ☐ 29C | Devlin Gets His Man: Fletcher-Mathewson | 90.00 | 36.00 | 9.00 |
| ☐ 29D | Devlin Gets His Man: Meyers-Mathewson | 90.00 | 36.00 | 9.00 |
| ☐ 30A | Donlin Out at First: Camnitz-Gibson | 50.00 | 20.00 | 5.00 |
| ☐ 30B | Donlin Out at First: Doyle-Merkle | 50.00 | 20.00 | 5.00 |
| ☐ 30C | Donlin Out at First: Leach-Wilson | 50.00 | 20.00 | 5.00 |
| ☐ 30D | Donlin Out at First: Magee-Dooin | 50.00 | 20.00 | 5.00 |
| ☐ 30E | Donlin Out at First: Phillippe-Gibson | 50.00 | 20.00 | 5.00 |
| ☐ 31A | Dooin Gets His Man: Dooin-Doolan | 50.00 | 20.00 | 5.00 |
| ☐ 31B | Dooin Gets His Man: Lobert-Dooin | 50.00 | 20.00 | 5.00 |
| ☐ 31C | Dooin Gets His Man: Titus-Dooin | 50.00 | 20.00 | 5.00 |
| ☐ 32 | Easy for Larry: Doyle-Merkle | 50.00 | 20.00 | 5.00 |
| ☐ 33 | Elberfeld Beats: Milan-Elberfeld | 50.00 | 20.00 | 5.00 |
| ☐ 34 | Elberfeld Gets His Man: Milan-Elberfeld | 50.00 | 20.00 | 5.00 |
| ☐ 35 | Engle in a Close Play: Speaker-Engle | 75.00 | 30.00 | 7.50 |
| ☐ 36A | Evers Makes Safe Slide: Archer-Evers | 75.00 | 30.00 | 7.50 |
| ☐ 36B | Evers Makes Safe Slide: Evers-Chance | 90.00 | 36.00 | 9.00 |
| ☐ 36C | Evers Makes Safe Slide: Overall-Archer | 60.00 | 24.00 | 6.00 |
| ☐ 36D | Evers Makes Safe Slide: Reulbach-Archer | 60.00 | 24.00 | 6.00 |
| ☐ 36E | Evers Makes Safe Slide: Tinker-Chance | 125.00 | 50.00 | 12.50 |
| ☐ 37 | Fast Work at Third: O'Leary-Cobb | 275.00 | 110.00 | 27.00 |
| ☐ 38A | Ford Putting Over Spitter: Ford-Vaughn | 50.00 | 20.00 | 5.00 |
| ☐ 38B | Ford Putting Over Spitter: Sweeney-Ford | 50.00 | 20.00 | 5.00 |
| ☐ 39 | Good Play at Third: Moriarty-Cobb | 275.00 | 110.00 | 27.00 |
| ☐ 40 | Grant Gets His Man: Hoblitzel-Grant | 50.00 | 20.00 | 5.00 |

| | | | |
|---|---|---|---|
| ☐ 41A | Hal Chase Too Late: ....... McIntyre-McConnell | 50.00 | 20.00 | 5.00 |
| ☐ 41B | Hal Chase Too Late: ....... Suggs-McLean | 50.00 | 20.00 | 5.00 |
| ☐ 42 | Harry Lord at Third: ......... Lennox-Tinker | 60.00 | 24.00 | 6.00 |
| ☐ 43 | Hartzell Covering: ............. Scanlon-Dahlen | 50.00 | 20.00 | 5.00 |
| ☐ 44 | Hartzell Strikes Out: ......... Groom-Gray | 50.00 | 20.00 | 5.00 |
| ☐ 45 | Held at Third: .................... Tannehill-Lord | 50.00 | 20.00 | 5.00 |
| ☐ 46 | Jake Stahl Guarding: ........ Cicotte-Stahl | 50.00 | 20.00 | 5.00 |
| ☐ 47 | Jim Delahanty at Bat: ....... Delahanty-Jones | 50.00 | 20.00 | 5.00 |
| ☐ 48A | Just Before the ............... Battle: Ames-Meyers | 50.00 | 20.00 | 5.00 |
| ☐ 48B | Just Before the .............. Battle: Bresnahan-McGraw | 90.00 | 36.00 | 9.00 |
| ☐ 48C | Just Before the ............... Battle: Crandall-Meyers | 50.00 | 20.00 | 5.00 |
| ☐ 48D | Just Before the .............. Battle: Devore-Becker | 50.00 | 20.00 | 5.00 |
| ☐ 48E | Just Before the .............. Battle: Fletcher-Mathewson | 90.00 | 36.00 | 9.00 |
| ☐ 48F | Just Before the ............... Battle: Marquard-Meyers | 60.00 | 24.00 | 6.00 |
| ☐ 48G | Just Before the .............. Battle: McGraw-Jennings | 90.00 | 36.00 | 9.00 |
| ☐ 48H | Just Before the .............. Battle: Meyers-Mathewson | 90.00 | 36.00 | 9.00 |
| ☐ 48I | Just Before the ................ Battle: Snodgrass-Murray | 50.00 | 20.00 | 5.00 |
| ☐ 48J | Just Before the ............... Battle: Wiltse-Meyers | 50.00 | 20.00 | 5.00 |
| ☐ 49 | Knight Catches Runner: .... Knight-Johnson | 100.00 | 40.00 | 10.00 |
| ☐ 50A | Lobert Almost Caught: ... Bridwell-Kling | 50.00 | 20.00 | 5.00 |
| ☐ 50B | Lobert Almost Caught: ... Kling-Young | 60.00 | 24.00 | 6.00 |
| ☐ 50C | Lobert Almost Caught: ... Mattern-Kling | 50.00 | 20.00 | 5.00 |
| ☐ 50D | Lobert Almost Caught: ... Steinfeldt-Kling | 50.00 | 20.00 | 5.00 |
| ☐ 51 | Lobert Gets Tenney: ......... Lobert-Dooin | 50.00 | 20.00 | 5.00 |
| ☐ 52 | Lord Catches His Man: ... Tannehill-Lord | 50.00 | 20.00 | 5.00 |
| ☐ 53 | McConnell Caught: ........... Richie-Needham | 50.00 | 20.00 | 5.00 |
| ☐ 54 | McIntyre at Bat: .............. McIntrye-McConnell | 50.00 | 20.00 | 5.00 |
| ☐ 55 | Moriarty Spiked: .............. Willett-Stanage | 50.00 | 20.00 | 5.00 |
| ☐ 56 | Nearly Caught: ................. Bates-Bescher | 60.00 | 24.00 | 6.00 |
| ☐ 57 | Oldring Almost Home: ...... Lord-Oldring | 50.00 | 20.00 | 5.00 |
| ☐ 58 | Schaefer on First: ............ McBride-Milan | 50.00 | 20.00 | 5.00 |
| ☐ 59 | Schaefer Steals ............... Second: McBride-Griffith | 60.00 | 24.00 | 6.00 |
| ☐ 60 | Scoring from Second: ....... Lord-Oldring | 50.00 | 20.00 | 5.00 |
| ☐ 61A | Scrambling Back: ........... Barger-Bergen | 50.00 | 20.00 | 5.00 |
| ☐ 61B | Scrambling Back: ........... Wolter-Chase | 50.00 | 20.00 | 5.00 |
| ☐ 62 | Speaker Almost Caught: ... Miller-Clarke | 100.00 | 40.00 | 10.00 |
| ☐ 63 | Speaker Rounding ............ Third: Wood-Speaker | 100.00 | 40.00 | 10.00 |
| ☐ 64 | Speaker Scores: ............... Speaker-Engle | 100.00 | 40.00 | 10.00 |
| ☐ 65 | Stahl Safe: ....................... Stovall-Austin | 50.00 | 20.00 | 5.00 |
| ☐ 66 | Stone About to Swing: ..... Sheckard-Schulte | 50.00 | 20.00 | 5.00 |
| ☐ 67A | Sullivan Puts Up High ..... One: Evans-Huggins | 60.00 | 24.00 | 6.00 |

| | | | |
|---|---|---|---|
| ☐ 67B | Sullivan Puts Up High ..... One: Sweeney-Ford | 50.00 | 20.00 | 5.00 |
| ☐ 68A | Sweeney Gets Stahl: ....... Ford-Vaughn | 50.00 | 20.00 | 5.00 |
| ☐ 68B | Sweeney Gets Stahl: ...... Sweeney-Ford | 50.00 | 20.00 | 5.00 |
| ☐ 69 | Tenney Lands Safely: ........ Raymond-Latham | 50.00 | 20.00 | 5.00 |
| ☐ 70A | The Athletic Infield: ......... Barry-Baker | 60.00 | 24.00 | 6.00 |
| ☐ 70B | The Athletic Infield: ......... Brown-Graham | 50.00 | 20.00 | 5.00 |
| ☐ 70C | The Athletic Infield: ......... Hauser-Konetchy | 50.00 | 20.00 | 5.00 |
| ☐ 70D | The Athletic Infield: ......... Krause-Thomas | 50.00 | 20.00 | 5.00 |
| ☐ 71 | The Pinch Hitter: ............. Hoblitzel-Egan | 50.00 | 20.00 | 5.00 |
| ☐ 72 | The Scissors Slide: ........... Birmingham-Turner | 50.00 | 20.00 | 5.00 |
| ☐ 73A | Tom Jones at Bat: .......... Fromme-McLean | 50.00 | 20.00 | 5.00 |
| ☐ 73B | Tom Jones at Bat: .......... Gaspar-McLean | 50.00 | 20.00 | 5.00 |
| ☐ 74A | Too Late for Devlin: ........ Ames-Meyers | 50.00 | 20.00 | 5.00 |
| ☐ 74B | Too Late for Devlin: ........ Crandall-Meyers | 50.00 | 20.00 | 5.00 |
| ☐ 74C | Too Late for Devlin: ........ Devlin (Giants)-Mathewson | 175.00 | 70.00 | 18.00 |
| ☐ 74D | Too Late for Devlin: ........ Devlin (Rustlers)-Mathewson | 90.00 | 36.00 | 9.00 |
| ☐ 74E | Too Late for Devlin: ........ Marquard-Meyers | 60.00 | 24.00 | 6.00 |
| ☐ 74F | Too Late for Devlin: ........ Wiltse-Meyers | 50.00 | 20.00 | 5.00 |
| ☐ 75A | Ty Cobb Steals Third: ..... Jennings-Cobb | 450.00 | 180.00 | 45.00 |
| ☐ 75B | Ty Cobb Steals Third: ..... Moriarty-Cobb | 350.00 | 140.00 | 35.00 |
| ☐ 75C | Ty Cobb Steals Third: ..... Stovall-Austin | 275.00 | 110.00 | 27.00 |
| ☐ 76 | Wheat Strikes Out: .......... Dahlen-Wheat | 75.00 | 30.00 | 7.50 |

## T204 Ramly

The cards in this 121 card set measure 2" by 2 1/2". The Ramly baseball series, designated T204 in the ACC, contains unnumbered cards. This set is one of the most distinguished ever produced, containing ornate gold borders around a black and white portrait of each player. There are spelling errors, and two distinct backs, "Ramly" and "TT", are known. Much of the obverse card detail is actually embossed. The players have been alphabetized and numbered for reference in the checklist below.

| | | MINT | VG-E | F-G |
|---|---|---|---|---|
| COMPLETE SET | ........................ | 11000.00 | 4500.00 | 1250. |
| COMMON PLAYER | ..................... | 80.00 | 32.00 | 8.00 |
| ☐ 1 | Whitey Alperman ............ | 80.00 | 32.00 | 8.00 |
| ☐ 2 | John J. Anderson ............ | 80.00 | 32.00 | 8.00 |

| | | | | |
|---|---|---|---|---|
| ☐ | 3 Jimmy Archer | 80.00 | 32.00 | 8.00 |
| ☐ | 4 Frank Arellanes | 80.00 | 32.00 | 8.00 |
| ☐ | 5 Jim Ball (Boston NL) | 80.00 | 32.00 | 8.00 |
| ☐ | 6 Neal Ball (N.Y. AL) | 80.00 | 32.00 | 8.00 |
| ☐ | 7 Dave Bancroft | 160.00 | 65.00 | 16.00 |
| ☐ | 8 Johnny Bates | 80.00 | 32.00 | 8.00 |
| ☐ | 9 Fred Beebe | 80.00 | 32.00 | 8.00 |
| ☐ | 10 George Bell | 80.00 | 32.00 | 8.00 |
| ☐ | 11 Chief Bender | 160.00 | 65.00 | 16.00 |
| ☐ | 12 Walter Blair | 80.00 | 32.00 | 8.00 |
| ☐ | 13 Cliff Blankenship | 80.00 | 32.00 | 8.00 |
| ☐ | 14 Frank Bowerman | 80.00 | 32.00 | 8.00 |
| ☐ | 15 Kitty Bransfield | 80.00 | 32.00 | 8.00 |
| ☐ | 16 Roger Bresnahan | 160.00 | 65.00 | 16.00 |
| ☐ | 17 Al Bridwell | 80.00 | 32.00 | 8.00 |
| ☐ | 18 Mordecai Brown | 160.00 | 65.00 | 16.00 |
| ☐ | 19 Fred Burchell | 80.00 | 32.00 | 8.00 |
| ☐ | 20 Jesse Burkett | 225.00 | 90.00 | 22.00 |
| ☐ | 21 Robert Byrne | 80.00 | 32.00 | 8.00 |
| ☐ | 22 Bill Carrigan | 80.00 | 32.00 | 8.00 |
| ☐ | 23 Frank Chance | 200.00 | 80.00 | 20.00 |
| ☐ | 24 Charles Chech | 80.00 | 32.00 | 8.00 |
| ☐ | 25 Eddie Cicotte | 90.00 | 36.00 | 9.00 |
| ☐ | 26 Otis Clymer | 80.00 | 32.00 | 8.00 |
| ☐ | 27 Andrew Coakley | 80.00 | 32.00 | 8.00 |
| ☐ | 28 Eddie Collins | 200.00 | 80.00 | 20.00 |
| ☐ | 29 Jimmy Collins | 200.00 | 80.00 | 20.00 |
| ☐ | 30 Wid Conroy | 80.00 | 32.00 | 8.00 |
| ☐ | 31 Jack Coombs | 90.00 | 36.00 | 9.00 |
| ☐ | 32 Doc Crandall | 80.00 | 32.00 | 8.00 |
| ☐ | 33 Lou Criger | 80.00 | 32.00 | 8.00 |
| ☐ | 34 Harry (Jasper) Davis | 80.00 | 32.00 | 8.00 |
| ☐ | 35 Art Devlin | 80.00 | 32.00 | 8.00 |
| ☐ | 36 Bill Dineen | 80.00 | 32.00 | 8.00 |
| ☐ | 37 Pat Donahue | 80.00 | 32.00 | 8.00 |
| ☐ | 38 Mike Donlin | 80.00 | 32.00 | 8.00 |
| ☐ | 39 Wild Bill Donovan | 80.00 | 32.00 | 8.00 |
| ☐ | 40 Gus Dorner | 80.00 | 32.00 | 8.00 |
| ☐ | 41 Joe Dunn | 80.00 | 32.00 | 8.00 |
| ☐ | 42 Norman Elberfield | 80.00 | 32.00 | 8.00 |
| | (sic) Elberfeld | | | |
| ☐ | 43 Johnny Evers | 200.00 | 80.00 | 20.00 |
| ☐ | 44 George L. Ewing | 80.00 | 32.00 | 8.00 |
| ☐ | 45 George Ferguson | 80.00 | 32.00 | 8.00 |
| ☐ | 46 Hobe Ferris | 80.00 | 32.00 | 8.00 |
| ☐ | 47 James J. Freeman | 80.00 | 32.00 | 8.00 |
| ☐ | 48 Art Fromme | 80.00 | 32.00 | 8.00 |
| ☐ | 49 Bob Ganley | 80.00 | 32.00 | 8.00 |
| ☐ | 50 Harry (Doc) Gessler | 80.00 | 32.00 | 8.00 |
| ☐ | 51 George Graham | 80.00 | 32.00 | 8.00 |
| ☐ | 52 Clark Griffith | 160.00 | 65.00 | 16.00 |
| ☐ | 53 Roy Hartzell | 80.00 | 32.00 | 8.00 |
| ☐ | 54 Charlie Hemphill | 80.00 | 32.00 | 8.00 |
| ☐ | 55 Dick Hoblitzell | 80.00 | 32.00 | 8.00 |
| ☐ | 56 George (Del) Howard | 80.00 | 32.00 | 8.00 |
| ☐ | 57 Harry Howell | 80.00 | 32.00 | 8.00 |
| ☐ | 58 Miller Huggins | 200.00 | 80.00 | 20.00 |
| ☐ | 59 John Hummel | 80.00 | 32.00 | 8.00 |
| ☐ | 60 Walter Johnson | 550.00 | 220.00 | 55.00 |
| ☐ | 61 Charles Jones | 80.00 | 32.00 | 8.00 |
| ☐ | 62 Michael Kahoe | 80.00 | 32.00 | 8.00 |
| ☐ | 63 Ed Karger | 80.00 | 32.00 | 8.00 |
| ☐ | 64 Willie Keeler | 250.00 | 100.00 | 25.00 |
| ☐ | 65 Ed Kenotchey | 80.00 | 32.00 | 8.00 |
| | (sic) Konetchy | | | |
| ☐ | 66 John (Red) Kleinow | 80.00 | 32.00 | 8.00 |
| ☐ | 67 John Knight | 80.00 | 32.00 | 8.00 |
| ☐ | 68 Vive Lindeman | 80.00 | 32.00 | 8.00 |
| ☐ | 69 Hans Loebert | 80.00 | 32.00 | 8.00 |
| | (sic) Lobert | | | |
| ☐ | 70 Harry Lord | 80.00 | 32.00 | 8.00 |
| ☐ | 71 Harry Lumley | 80.00 | 32.00 | 8.00 |
| ☐ | 72 Ernie Lush | 80.00 | 32.00 | 8.00 |
| ☐ | 73 Rube Manning | 80.00 | 32.00 | 8.00 |
| ☐ | 74 James McAleer | 80.00 | 32.00 | 8.00 |
| ☐ | 75 Amby McConnell | 80.00 | 32.00 | 8.00 |
| ☐ | 76 Moose McCormick | 80.00 | 32.00 | 8.00 |
| ☐ | 77 Matthew McIntyre | 80.00 | 32.00 | 8.00 |
| ☐ | 78 Larry McLean | 80.00 | 32.00 | 8.00 |
| ☐ | 79 Fred Merkle | 90.00 | 36.00 | 9.00 |
| ☐ | 80 Clyde Milan | 80.00 | 32.00 | 8.00 |
| ☐ | 81 Michael Mitchell | 80.00 | 32.00 | 8.00 |
| ☐ | 82 Pat Moran | 80.00 | 32.00 | 8.00 |
| ☐ | 83 Harry (Cy) Morgan | 80.00 | 32.00 | 8.00 |
| ☐ | 84 Tim Murnane | 80.00 | 32.00 | 8.00 |
| ☐ | 85 Danny Murphy | 80.00 | 32.00 | 8.00 |
| ☐ | 86 Red Murray | 80.00 | 32.00 | 8.00 |
| ☐ | 87 Eustace (Doc) Newton | 80.00 | 32.00 | 8.00 |
| ☐ | 88 Simon Nichols | 80.00 | 32.00 | 8.00 |
| | (sic) Nicholls | | | |
| ☐ | 89 Harry Niles | 80.00 | 32.00 | 8.00 |
| ☐ | 90 Bill O'Hara | 80.00 | 32.00 | 8.00 |
| ☐ | 91 Charley O'Leary | 80.00 | 32.00 | 8.00 |

| | | | | |
|---|---|---|---|---|
| ☐ | 92 Dode Paskert | 80.00 | 32.00 | 8.00 |
| ☐ | 93 Barney Pelty | 80.00 | 32.00 | 8.00 |
| ☐ | 94 Jack Pfeister | 80.00 | 32.00 | 8.00 |
| ☐ | 95 Eddie Plank | 250.00 | 100.00 | 25.00 |
| ☐ | 96 Jack Powell | 80.00 | 32.00 | 8.00 |
| ☐ | 97 Bugs Raymond | 80.00 | 32.00 | 8.00 |
| ☐ | 98 Thomas Reilly | 80.00 | 32.00 | 8.00 |
| ☐ | 99 Lewis Ritchie | 80.00 | 32.00 | 8.00 |
| | (sic) Richie | | | |
| ☐ | 100 Nap Rucker | 80.00 | 32.00 | 8.00 |
| ☐ | 101 Ed Ruelbach | 80.00 | 32.00 | 8.00 |
| | (sic) Reulbach | | | |
| ☐ | 102 Slim Sallee | 80.00 | 32.00 | 8.00 |
| ☐ | 103 Germany Schaefer | 80.00 | 32.00 | 8.00 |
| ☐ | 104 Jimmy Schekard | 80.00 | 32.00 | 8.00 |
| | (sic) Sheckard | | | |
| ☐ | 105 Admiral Schlei | 80.00 | 32.00 | 8.00 |
| ☐ | 106 Frank Schulte | 80.00 | 32.00 | 8.00 |
| ☐ | 107 James Sebring | 80.00 | 32.00 | 8.00 |
| ☐ | 108 Bill Shipke | 80.00 | 32.00 | 8.00 |
| ☐ | 109 Anthony Smith | 80.00 | 32.00 | 8.00 |
| ☐ | 110 Tubby Spencer | 80.00 | 32.00 | 8.00 |
| ☐ | 111 Jake Stahl | 80.00 | 32.00 | 8.00 |
| ☐ | 112 Harry Steinfeldt | 80.00 | 32.00 | 8.00 |
| ☐ | 113 Jim Stephens | 80.00 | 32.00 | 8.00 |
| ☐ | 114 Gabby Street | 80.00 | 32.00 | 8.00 |
| ☐ | 115 William Sweeney | 80.00 | 32.00 | 8.00 |
| ☐ | 116 Fred Tenney | 80.00 | 32.00 | 8.00 |
| ☐ | 117 Ira Thomas | 80.00 | 32.00 | 8.00 |
| ☐ | 118 Joe Tinker | 160.00 | 65.00 | 16.00 |
| ☐ | 119 Bob Unglaub | 80.00 | 32.00 | 8.00 |
| ☐ | 120 Heine Wagner | 80.00 | 32.00 | 8.00 |
| ☐ | 121 Bobby Wallace | 160.00 | 65.00 | 16.00 |

## T205 Gold Border

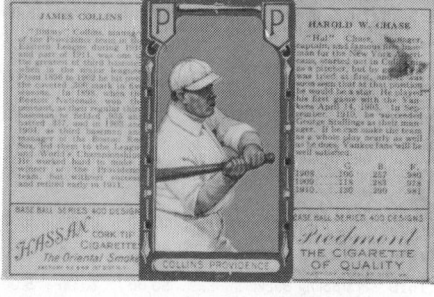

The cards in this 208 card set measure 1 1/2" by 2 5/8". The T205 set (ACC designation), also known as the "Gold Border" set, was issued in 1911 in packages of the following cigarette brands: American Beauty, Broadleaf, Cycle, Drum, Hassan, Honest Long Cut, Piedmont, Polar Bear, Sovereign and Sweet Caporal. All the above were products of the American Tobacco Company, and the ads for the various brands appear below the biographical section on the back of each card. There are pose variations noted in the checklist (which is alphabetized and numbered for reference) and there are 12 minor league cards of a more ornate design which are somewhat scarce. The numbers below correspond to alphabetical order within each team by team nickname, i.e., Philadelphia Athletics AL (1-13), St. Louis Browns (14-20), St. Louis Cardinals (21-32), Chicago Cubs (33- 51), New York Giants (52-72), Cleveland Naps (73-78), Philadelphia Phillies (79-90), Pittsburgh Pirates (91-103), Cincinnati Reds (104-114), Boston Red Sox (115-122), Boston Rustlers (123-131), Washington Senators (132-139), Detroit Tigers (154-167), Chicago White Sox (168-182), New York Yankees (183-196), and Minor Leaguers (197- 208). The gold borders of T205 cards chip easily and they are hard to find in ''Mint'' condition.

|  | | MINT | VG-E | F-G |
|---|---|---|---|---|
| | COMPLETE SET | 9000.00 | 3750.00 | 900.00 |
| | COMMON PLAYERS | 25.00 | 10.00 | 2.50 |
| ☐ 1 | Frank Baker | 75.00 | 30.00 | 7.50 |
| ☐ 2 | John J. Barry | 25.00 | 10.00 | 2.50 |
| ☐ 3 | Charles A. Bender | 75.00 | 30.00 | 7.50 |
| ☐ 4 | Edward T. Collins (mouth closed) | 75.00 | 30.00 | 7.50 |
| ☐ 5 | Edward T. Collins (mouth open) | 150.00 | 60.00 | 15.00 |
| ☐ 6 | James H. Dygert | 25.00 | 10.00 | 2.50 |
| ☐ 7 | Frederick T. Hartsel | 25.00 | 10.00 | 2.50 |
| ☐ 8 | Harry Krause | 25.00 | 10.00 | 2.50 |
| ☐ 9 | Pat'k J. Livingston | 25.00 | 10.00 | 2.50 |
| ☐ 10 | Briscoe Lord | 25.00 | 10.00 | 2.50 |
| ☐ 11 | Daniel Murphy | 25.00 | 10.00 | 2.50 |
| ☐ 12 | Reuben N. Oldring | 25.00 | 10.00 | 2.50 |
| ☐ 13 | Ira Thomas | 25.00 | 10.00 | 2.50 |
| ☐ 14 | William Bailey | 25.00 | 10.00 | 2.50 |
| ☐ 15 | Daniel J. Hoffman | 25.00 | 10.00 | 2.50 |
| ☐ 16 | Frank LaPorte | 25.00 | 10.00 | 2.50 |
| ☐ 17 | B. Pelty | 25.00 | 10.00 | 2.50 |
| ☐ 18 | George Stone | 25.00 | 10.00 | 2.50 |
| ☐ 19 | Roderick J. Wallace (with cap) | 75.00 | 30.00 | 7.50 |
| ☐ 20 | Roderick J. Wallace (without cap) | 150.00 | 60.00 | 15.00 |
| ☐ 21 | Roger Bresnahan (mouth closed) | 75.00 | 30.00 | 7.50 |
| ☐ 22 | Roger Bresnahan (mouth open) | 150.00 | 60.00 | 15.00 |
| ☐ 23 | Frank J. Corridon | 25.00 | 10.00 | 2.50 |
| ☐ 24 | Louis Evans | 25.00 | 10.00 | 2.50 |
| ☐ 25 | Robert Harmon (both ears) | 25.00 | 10.00 | 2.50 |
| ☐ 26 | Robert Harmon (left ear only) | 120.00 | 50.00 | 12.00 |
| ☐ 27 | Arnold J. Hauser | 25.00 | 10.00 | 2.50 |
| ☐ 28 | Miller Huggins | 75.00 | 30.00 | 7.50 |
| ☐ 29 | Edward Konetchy | 25.00 | 10.00 | 2.50 |
| ☐ 30 | John Lush | 25.00 | 10.00 | 2.50 |
| ☐ 31 | Rebel Oakes | 25.00 | 10.00 | 2.50 |
| ☐ 32 | Edward Phelps | 25.00 | 10.00 | 2.50 |
| ☐ 33 | James P. Archer | 25.00 | 10.00 | 2.50 |
| ☐ 34 | Mordecai Brown | 75.00 | 30.00 | 7.50 |
| ☐ 35 | Frank L. Chance | 75.00 | 30.00 | 7.50 |
| ☐ 36 | John J. Evers | 75.00 | 30.00 | 7.50 |
| ☐ 37 | William A. Foxen | 25.00 | 10.00 | 2.50 |
| ☐ 38 | George F. Graham | 175.00 | 70.00 | 18.00 |
| ☐ 39 | John Kling | 25.00 | 10.00 | 2.50 |
| ☐ 40 | Floyd M. Kroh | 25.00 | 10.00 | 2.50 |
| ☐ 41 | Harry McIntire | 25.00 | 10.00 | 2.50 |
| ☐ 42 | Thomas J. Needham | 25.00 | 10.00 | 2.50 |
| ☐ 43 | Orval Overall | 25.00 | 10.00 | 2.50 |
| ☐ 44 | John A. Pfiester | 25.00 | 10.00 | 2.50 |
| ☐ 45 | Edward M. Reulbach | 25.00 | 10.00 | 2.50 |
| ☐ 46 | Lewis Richie | 25.00 | 10.00 | 2.50 |
| ☐ 47 | Frank M. Schulte | 25.00 | 10.00 | 2.50 |
| ☐ 48 | David Shean (Cubs) | 200.00 | 80.00 | 20.00 |
| ☐ 49 | James T. Sheckard | 25.00 | 10.00 | 2.50 |
| ☐ 50 | Harry Steinfeldt | 25.00 | 10.00 | 2.50 |
| ☐ 51 | Joseph B. Tinker | 75.00 | 30.00 | 7.50 |
| ☐ 52 | Leon Ames | 25.00 | 10.00 | 2.50 |
| ☐ 53 | Beals Becker | 25.00 | 10.00 | 2.50 |
| ☐ 54 | Albert Bridwell | 25.00 | 10.00 | 2.50 |
| ☐ 55 | Otis Crandall | 25.00 | 10.00 | 2.50 |
| ☐ 56 | Arthur Devlin | 25.00 | 10.00 | 2.50 |
| ☐ 57 | Joshua Devore | 25.00 | 10.00 | 2.50 |
| ☐ 58 | W.R. Dickson | 25.00 | 10.00 | 2.50 |
| ☐ 59 | Lawrence Doyle | 25.00 | 10.00 | 2.50 |
| ☐ 60 | Arthur Fletcher | 25.00 | 10.00 | 2.50 |
| ☐ 61 | W.A. Latham | 25.00 | 10.00 | 2.50 |
| ☐ 62 | Richard Marquard | 75.00 | 30.00 | 7.50 |
| ☐ 63 | Christy Mathewson | 200.00 | 80.00 | 20.00 |
| ☐ 64 | John J. McGraw | 100.00 | 40.00 | 10.00 |
| ☐ 65 | Fred Merkle | 30.00 | 12.00 | 3.00 |
| ☐ 66 | John T. Meyers | 25.00 | 10.00 | 2.50 |
| ☐ 67 | John J. Murray | 25.00 | 10.00 | 2.50 |
| ☐ 68 | Arthur L. Raymond | 120.00 | 50.00 | 12.00 |
| ☐ 69 | George H. Schlei | 25.00 | 10.00 | 2.50 |
| ☐ 70 | Fred C. Snodgrass | 25.00 | 10.00 | 2.50 |
| ☐ 71 | George Wiltse (both ears) | 25.00 | 10.00 | 2.50 |
| ☐ 72 | George Wiltse (right ear only) | 120.00 | 50.00 | 12.00 |
| ☐ 73 | Neal Ball | 25.00 | 10.00 | 2.50 |
| ☐ 74 | Joseph Birmingham | 25.00 | 10.00 | 2.50 |
| ☐ 75 | Addie Joss | 175.00 | 70.00 | 18.00 |
| ☐ 76 | George T. Stovall | 25.00 | 10.00 | 2.50 |
| ☐ 77 | Terence Turner | 120.00 | 50.00 | 12.00 |
| ☐ 78 | Denton T. Young | 150.00 | 60.00 | 15.00 |
| ☐ 79 | John W. Bates | 25.00 | 10.00 | 2.50 |
| ☐ 80 | Wm. E. Bransfield | 25.00 | 10.00 | 2.50 |
| ☐ 81 | Charles S. Dooin | 25.00 | 10.00 | 2.50 |
| ☐ 82 | Michael Doolan | 25.00 | 10.00 | 2.50 |
| ☐ 83 | Robert Ewing | 25.00 | 10.00 | 2.50 |
| ☐ 84 | Fred Jacklitsch | 25.00 | 10.00 | 2.50 |
| ☐ 85 | John Lobert | 25.00 | 10.00 | 2.50 |
| ☐ 86 | Sherwood R. Magee | 25.00 | 10.00 | 2.50 |
| ☐ 87 | Patrick J. Moran | 25.00 | 10.00 | 2.50 |
| ☐ 88 | George Paskert | 25.00 | 10.00 | 2.50 |
| ☐ 89 | John A. Rowan | 100.00 | 40.00 | 10.00 |
| ☐ 90 | John Titus | 25.00 | 10.00 | 2.50 |
| ☐ 91 | Robert Byrne | 25.00 | 10.00 | 2.50 |
| ☐ 92 | Howard Camnitz | 25.00 | 10.00 | 2.50 |
| ☐ 93 | Fred Clarke | 75.00 | 30.00 | 7.50 |
| ☐ 94 | John Flynn | 25.00 | 10.00 | 2.50 |
| ☐ 95 | George Gibson | 25.00 | 10.00 | 2.50 |
| ☐ 96 | Thomas W. Leach | 25.00 | 10.00 | 2.50 |
| ☐ 97 | Sam Leever | 25.00 | 10.00 | 2.50 |
| ☐ 98 | Albert P. Leifield | 25.00 | 10.00 | 2.50 |
| ☐ 99 | Nicholas Maddox | 25.00 | 10.00 | 2.50 |
| ☐ 100 | John D. Miller | 25.00 | 10.00 | 2.50 |
| ☐ 101 | Charles Phillippe | 25.00 | 10.00 | 2.50 |
| ☐ 102 | Kirb White | 120.00 | 50.00 | 12.00 |
| ☐ 103 | J. Owen Wilson | 25.00 | 10.00 | 2.50 |
| ☐ 104 | Robert H. Bescher | 25.00 | 10.00 | 2.50 |
| ☐ 105 | Thomas W. Downey | 25.00 | 10.00 | 2.50 |
| ☐ 106 | Richard J. Egan | 25.00 | 10.00 | 2.50 |
| ☐ 107 | Arthur Fromme | 25.00 | 10.00 | 2.50 |
| ☐ 108 | Harry L. Gaspar | 25.00 | 10.00 | 2.50 |
| ☐ 109 | Edward L. Grant | 120.00 | 50.00 | 12.00 |
| ☐ 110 | Clark Griffith | 75.00 | 30.00 | 7.50 |
| ☐ 111 | Richard Hoblitzell | 25.00 | 10.00 | 2.50 |
| ☐ 112 | John B. McLean | 25.00 | 10.00 | 2.50 |
| ☐ 113 | Michael Mitchell | 25.00 | 10.00 | 2.50 |
| ☐ 114 | George Suggs | 100.00 | 40.00 | 10.00 |
| ☐ 115 | William Carrigan | 25.00 | 10.00 | 2.50 |
| ☐ 116 | Edward V. Cicotte | 30.00 | 12.00 | 3.00 |
| ☐ 117 | Clyde Engle | 25.00 | 10.00 | 2.50 |
| ☐ 118 | Edward Karger | 100.00 | 40.00 | 10.00 |
| ☐ 119 | John Kleinow | 100.00 | 40.00 | 10.00 |
| ☐ 120 | Tris Speaker | 175.00 | 70.00 | 18.00 |
| ☐ 121 | Jacob G. Stahl | 30.00 | 12.00 | 3.00 |
| ☐ 122 | Charles Wagner | 75.00 | 30.00 | 7.50 |
| ☐ 123 | Edward J. Abbaticchio | 25.00 | 10.00 | 2.50 |
| ☐ 124 | Frederick T. Beck | 25.00 | 10.00 | 2.50 |
| ☐ 125 | G.C. Ferguson | 25.00 | 10.00 | 2.50 |
| ☐ 126 | Wilbur Good | 25.00 | 10.00 | 2.50 |
| ☐ 127 | George F. Graham | 25.00 | 10.00 | 2.50 |
| ☐ 128 | Charles L. Herzog | 25.00 | 10.00 | 2.50 |
| ☐ 129 | A.A. Mattern | 25.00 | 10.00 | 2.50 |
| ☐ 130 | Bayard H. Sharpe | 25.00 | 10.00 | 2.50 |
| ☐ 131 | David Shean (Boston) | 25.00 | 10.00 | 2.50 |
| ☐ 132 | Norman Elberfeld | 25.00 | 10.00 | 2.50 |
| ☐ 133 | Gray | 25.00 | 10.00 | 2.50 |
| ☐ 134 | Robert Groom | 25.00 | 10.00 | 2.50 |
| ☐ 135 | Walter Johnson | 250.00 | 100.00 | 25.00 |
| ☐ 136 | George F. McBride | 25.00 | 10.00 | 2.50 |
| ☐ 137 | J. Clyde Milan | 25.00 | 10.00 | 2.50 |
| ☐ 138 | Herman Schaefer | 25.00 | 10.00 | 2.50 |
| ☐ 139 | Charles E. Street | 25.00 | 10.00 | 2.50 |
| ☐ 140 | Edward B. Barger (full B) | 25.00 | 10.00 | 2.50 |
| ☐ 141 | Edward B. Barger (part B) | 120.00 | 50.00 | 12.00 |
| ☐ 142 | George G. Bell | 25.00 | 10.00 | 2.50 |
| ☐ 143 | William Bergen | 25.00 | 10.00 | 2.50 |
| ☐ 144 | William Dahlen | 100.00 | 40.00 | 10.00 |
| ☐ 145 | Jacob Daubert | 30.00 | 12.00 | 3.00 |

| | | | |
|---|---|---|---|
| ☐ 146 | John E. Hummell | 25.00 | 10.00 2.50 |
| ☐ 147 | Edgar Lennox | 25.00 | 10.00 2.50 |
| ☐ 148 | Pryor McElveen | 25.00 | 10.00 2.50 |
| ☐ 149 | G.N. Rucker | 25.00 | 10.00 2.50 |
| ☐ 150 | W.D. Scanlan | 100.00 | 40.00 10.00 |
| ☐ 151 | Tony Smith | 25.00 | 10.00 2.50 |
| ☐ 152 | Zach D. Wheat | 75.00 | 30.00 7.50 |
| ☐ 153 | Irvin K. Wilhelm | 100.00 | 40.00 10.00 |
| ☐ 154 | Tyrus Raymond Cobb | 600.00 | 240.00 60.00 |
| ☐ 155 | James Delahanty | 25.00 | 10.00 2.50 |
| ☐ 156 | Hugh Jennings | 75.00 | 30.00 7.50 |
| ☐ 157 | David Jones | 25.00 | 10.00 2.50 |
| ☐ 158 | Thomas Jones | 25.00 | 10.00 2.50 |
| ☐ 159 | Edward Killian | 25.00 | 10.00 2.50 |
| ☐ 160 | George Moriarity | 25.00 | 10.00 2.50 |
| ☐ 161 | George J. Mullin | 25.00 | 10.00 2.50 |
| ☐ 162 | Charles O'Leary | 25.00 | 10.00 2.50 |
| ☐ 163 | Charles Schmidt | 25.00 | 10.00 2.50 |
| ☐ 164 | George Simmons | 25.00 | 10.00 2.50 |
| ☐ 165 | Oscar Stanage | 25.00 | 10.00 2.50 |
| ☐ 166 | Edgar Summers | 25.00 | 10.00 2.50 |
| ☐ 167 | Edgar Willett | 25.00 | 10.00 2.50 |
| ☐ 168 | Russell Blackburne | 25.00 | 10.00 2.50 |
| ☐ 169 | J. Donohue | 75.00 | 30.00 7.50 |
| ☐ 170A | Patsy Dougherty (white stocking) | 75.00 | 30.00 7.50 |
| ☐ 170B | Patsy Dougherty (red stocking) | 50.00 | 20.00 5.00 |
| ☐ 171 | Hugh Duffy | 100.00 | 40.00 10.00 |
| ☐ 172 | Frank Lang | 25.00 | 10.00 2.50 |
| ☐ 173 | Harry D. Lord | 25.00 | 10.00 2.50 |
| ☐ 174 | Ambrose McConnell | 25.00 | 10.00 2.50 |
| ☐ 175 | Matthew McIntyre | 25.00 | 10.00 2.50 |
| ☐ 176 | Frederick Olmstead | 25.00 | 10.00 2.50 |
| ☐ 177 | F. Parent | 25.00 | 10.00 2.50 |
| ☐ 178 | Fred Payne | 25.00 | 10.00 2.50 |
| ☐ 179 | James Scott | 25.00 | 10.00 2.50 |
| ☐ 180 | Lee Ford Tannehill | 25.00 | 10.00 2.50 |
| ☐ 181 | Edward Walsh | 150.00 | 60.00 15.00 |
| ☐ 182 | G.H. White | 25.00 | 10.00 2.50 |
| ☐ 183 | James Austin | 25.00 | 10.00 2.50 |
| ☐ 184 | Harold W. Chase (Chase only) | 150.00 | 60.00 15.00 |
| ☐ 185 | Harold W. Chase (Hal Chase) | 35.00 | 14.00 3.50 |
| ☐ 186 | Louis Criger | 25.00 | 10.00 2.50 |
| ☐ 187 | Ray Fisher | 100.00 | 40.00 10.00 |
| ☐ 188 | Russell Ford (dark cap) | 25.00 | 10.00 2.50 |
| ☐ 189 | Russell Ford (light cap) | 100.00 | 40.00 10.00 |
| ☐ 190 | Earl Gardner | 25.00 | 10.00 2.50 |
| ☐ 191 | Charles Hemphill | 25.00 | 10.00 2.50 |
| ☐ 192 | Jack Knight | 25.00 | 10.00 2.50 |
| ☐ 193 | John Quinn | 25.00 | 10.00 2.50 |
| ☐ 194 | Edward Sweeney | 100.00 | 40.00 10.00 |
| ☐ 195 | James Vaughn | 100.00 | 40.00 10.00 |
| ☐ 196 | Harry Wolter | 25.00 | 10.00 2.50 |
| ☐ 197 | Dr. Merle T. Adkins: Baltimore | 100.00 | 40.00 10.00 |
| ☐ 198 | John Dunn: Baltimore | 100.00 | 40.00 10.00 |
| ☐ 199 | George Merritt: Buffalo | 100.00 | 40.00 10.00 |
| ☐ 200 | Charles Hanford: Jersey City | 100.00 | 40.00 10.00 |
| ☐ 201 | Forrest D. Cady: Newark | 100.00 | 40.00 10.00 |
| ☐ 202 | James Frick: Newark | 100.00 | 40.00 10.00 |
| ☐ 203 | Wyatt Lee: Newark | 100.00 | 40.00 10.00 |
| ☐ 204 | Lewis McAllister: Newark | 100.00 | 40.00 10.00 |
| ☐ 205 | John Nee: Newark | 100.00 | 40.00 10.00 |
| ☐ 206 | James Collins: Providence | 150.00 | 60.00 15.00 |
| ☐ 207 | James Phelan: Providence | 100.00 | 40.00 10.00 |
| ☐ 208 | Henry Batch: Rochester | 100.00 | 40.00 10.00 |

## T206 White Border

The cards in this 523 card set measure 1 1/2" by 2 5/8". The T206 set was and is the most popular of all the tobacco issues. The set was issued from 1909 to 1911 with sixteen different brands of cigarettes: American Beauty, Broadleaf, Cycle,

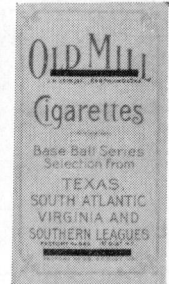

Carolina Brights, Drum, El Principe de Gales, Hindu, Lenox, Old Mill, Piedmont, Polar Bear, Sovereign, Sweet Caporal, Tolstoi, Ty Cobb and Uzit. The Ty Cobb brand back is very scarce. The minor league cards are supposedly slightly more difficult to obtain than the cards of the major leaguers, with the Southern League player cards being the most difficult. Minor League players were obtained from the American Association and the Eastern league. Southern League players were obtained from a variety of leagues including the following: South Atlantic League, Southern League, Texas League, and Virginia League. The set price below does not include ultra-expensive Wagner, Plank or Magie.

| | | MINT | VG-E | F-G |
|---|---|---|---|---|
| COMPLETE SET (520) | | 17000.00 | 7500.00 | 2250.00 |
| MAJOR LEAGUERS (1-389) | | 18.00 | 7.25 | 1.80 |
| MINOR LEAGUERS (390-475) | | 18.00 | 7.25 | 1.80 |
| SOUTHERN LEAG. (476-523) | | 50.00 | 20.00 | 5.00 |
| ☐ 1 | Abbaticchio: Pitt. Batting follow thru | 18.00 | 7.25 | 1.80 |
| ☐ 2 | Abbaticchio: Pitt. Batting waiting pitch | 25.00 | 10.00 | 2.50 |
| ☐ 3 | Abstein: Pitt. | 18.00 | 7.25 | 1.80 |
| ☐ 4 | Alperman: Brooklyn | 25.00 | 10.00 | 2.50 |
| ☐ 5 | Ames: Giants, Port. | 25.00 | 10.00 | 2.50 |
| ☐ 6 | Ames: Giants, Hands over head | 18.00 | 7.25 | 1.80 |
| ☐ 7 | Ames: Giants, Hands in front of chest | 25.00 | 10.00 | 2.50 |
| ☐ 8 | Arellanes: Boston AL | 18.00 | 7.25 | 1.80 |
| ☐ 9 | Atz: Chicago AL | 18.00 | 7.25 | 1.80 |
| ☐ 10 | Baker: Phila. AL | 60.00 | 24.00 | 6.00 |
| ☐ 11 | Ball: Cleveland | 18.00 | 7.25 | 1.80 |
| ☐ 12 | Ball: N.Y. AL | 25.00 | 10.00 | 2.50 |
| ☐ 13 | Barbeau: St.L. NL | 18.00 | 7.25 | 1.80 |
| ☐ 14 | Barry: Phila. AL | 18.00 | 7.25 | 1.80 |
| ☐ 15 | Bates: Boston NL | 25.00 | 10.00 | 2.50 |
| ☐ 16 | Beaumont: Boston NL | 25.00 | 10.00 | 2.50 |
| ☐ 17 | Beck: Boston NL | 18.00 | 7.25 | 1.80 |
| ☐ 18 | Becker: Boston NL | 18.00 | 7.25 | 1.80 |
| ☐ 19 | Bell: Brooklyn, pitching follow thru) | 18.00 | 7.25 | 1.80 |
| ☐ 20 | Bell: Brooklyn, Hands over head | 25.00 | 10.00 | 2.50 |
| ☐ 21 | Bender: Phila. AL Portrait | 80.00 | 32.00 | 8.00 |
| ☐ 22 | Bender: Phila. AL | 60.00 | 24.00 | 6.00 |

# WANTED

## BASEBALL MEMORABILIA

- CARDS (1869 - 1981)
  issued with Candy,
  Tobacco, Food, Gum
  or by Newspapers or
  from Vending machines

  No one will pay more
  for 19th Century Cards

- BOOKS
- GUIDES
- AUTOGRAPHS

- PINS
- CIGAR LABELS
- PHOTOGRAPHS
- SHEET MUSIC
- PRESS PINS
- SCORECARDS
- PRINTS
- ADVERTISING
- JACKIE ROBINSON
  ITEMS

We'll pay 75% and more for most of the items listed in this Price Guide. Also, will pay premium prices for desirable items. Send cards, description or list for immediate quote.

# FOR SALE

## THE ENCYCLOPEDIA OF BASEBALL CARDS

Vol. 1 — 19th Century Cards        SOLD OUT
        (Being revised and should be available in September)

Vol. 2 — Early Gum and Candy Cards        $10.95

Vol. 3 — Twentieth Century Tobacco Cards        12.95

        Add $2.00 for UPS Shipping

## THE OLD JUDGE

A Newsletter for the serious collector. Issued 6 times a year and containing price guides and articles on all forms of baseball memorabilia and hobby matters.
One Year — $8.00    Two Years — $15.00    Sample — $2.00

Detailed Price List for T205, T206, T207. Free on request.

# LEW LIPSET

Box 137P
Centereach, N.Y. 11720
(516) 981-3286

| | | | | |
|---|---|---|---|---|
| ☐ | 23 | Bender: Phila. AL ............ (pitching) trees | 60.00 | 24.00 | 6.00 |

| | | | | | |
|---|---|---|---|---|---|
| ☐ | 23 | Bender: Phila. AL ............ (pitching) trees | 60.00 | 24.00 | 6.00 |
| ☐ | 24 | Bergen: Brooklyn, .......... Catching | 18.00 | 7.25 | 1.80 |
| ☐ | 25 | Bergen: Brooklyn, .......... Batting | 25.00 | 10.00 | 2.50 |
| ☐ | 26 | Berger: Cleveland .......... | 18.00 | 7.25 | 1.80 |
| ☐ | 27 | Bescher: Cinc., .......... Catching fly ball | 18.00 | 7.25 | 1.80 |
| ☐ | 28 | Bescher: Cinc. ............... Portrait | 18.00 | 7.25 | 1.80 |
| ☐ | 29 | Birmingham: Cleve. ....... | 25.00 | 10.00 | 2.50 |
| ☐ | 30 | Bliss: St.L. NL .............. | 18.00 | 7.25 | 1.80 |
| ☐ | 31 | Bowerman: Bost. NL ..... | 25.00 | 10.00 | 2.50 |
| ☐ | 32 | Bradley: Cleveland, ......... Portrait | 25.00 | 10.00 | 2.50 |
| ☐ | 33 | Bradley: Cleveland, ......... Batting | 18.00 | 7.25 | 1.80 |
| ☐ | 34 | Bransfield: Phila. NL ...... | 25.00 | 10.00 | 2.50 |
| ☐ | 35 | Bresnahan: St.L. NL, ...... Portrait | 80.00 | 32.00 | 8.00 |
| ☐ | 36 | Bresnahan: St.L. NL, ...... Batting | 60.00 | 24.00 | 6.00 |
| ☐ | 37 | Bridwell: N.Y. NL, .......... Portrait | 25.00 | 10.00 | 2.50 |
| ☐ | 38 | Bridwell: N.Y. NL, .......... Wearing sweater | 18.00 | 7.25 | 1.80 |
| ☐ | 39 | G. Brown (sic): ............. Chicago NL | 40.00 | 16.00 | 4.00 |
| ☐ | 40 | G. Brown (sic): ............. Washington | 250.00 | 100.00 | 25.00 |
| ☐ | 41 | M. Brown: Chicago NL .... Portrait | 80.00 | 32.00 | 8.00 |
| ☐ | 42 | M. Brown: Chicago NL .... Chicago down front of shirt | 60.00 | 24.00 | 6.00 |
| ☐ | 43 | M. Brown: Chicago NL, ... Cubs across chest | 100.00 | 40.00 | 10.00 |
| ☐ | 44 | Burch: Brooklyn, ............ Fielding | 18.00 | 7.25 | 1.80 |
| ☐ | 45 | Burch: Brooklyn, ............ Batting | 40.00 | 16.00 | 4.00 |
| ☐ | 46 | Burns: Chicago AL .......... | 18.00 | 7.25 | 1.80 |
| ☐ | 47 | Bush: Detroit ................. | 18.00 | 7.25 | 1.80 |
| ☐ | 48 | Byrne: St.L. NL ............. | 18.00 | 7.25 | 1.80 |
| ☐ | 49 | Camnitz: Pitt., Arms ...... folded over chest | 25.00 | 10.00 | 2.50 |
| ☐ | 50 | Camnitz: Pitt., ............. Hands over head | 18.00 | 7.25 | 1.80 |
| ☐ | 51 | Camnitz: Pitt., ............. Throwing | 18.00 | 7.25 | 1.80 |
| ☐ | 52 | Campbell: Cinc. ............. | 18.00 | 7.25 | 1.80 |
| ☐ | 53 | Carrigan: Boston AL ....... | 18.00 | 7.25 | 1.80 |
| ☐ | 54 | Chance: Chicago NL, ...... Cubs across chest | 80.00 | 32.00 | 8.00 |
| ☐ | 55 | Chance: Chicago NL, ...... Chicago down front of shirt | 60.00 | 24.00 | 6.00 |
| ☐ | 56 | Chance: Chicago NL, ...... Batting | 60.00 | 24.00 | 6.00 |
| ☐ | 57 | Charles: St.L. NL ........... | 18.00 | 7.25 | 1.80 |
| ☐ | 58 | Chase: N.Y. AL, ............. Port. blue bkgd. | 25.00 | 10.00 | 2.50 |
| ☐ | 59 | Chase: N.Y. AL, ............. Port., pink bkgd. | 40.00 | 16.00 | 4.00 |
| ☐ | 60 | Chase: N.Y. AL, ............. Holding cup | 25.00 | 10.00 | 2.50 |
| ☐ | 61 | Chase: N.Y. AL, ............. Throwing, dark cap | 25.00 | 10.00 | 2.50 |
| ☐ | 62 | Chase: N.Y. AL, ............. Throwing, white cap | 80.00 | 32.00 | 8.00 |
| ☐ | 63 | Chesbro: N.Y. AL .......... | 100.00 | 40.00 | 10.00 |
| ☐ | 64 | Cicotte: Boston AL ......... | 30.00 | 12.00 | 3.00 |
| ☐ | 65 | Clarke: Pitt., ................ Portrait | 80.00 | 32.00 | 8.00 |
| ☐ | 66 | F. Clarke: Pitt. .............. | 80.00 | 32.00 | 8.00 |
| ☐ | 67 | J.J. Clarke: Cleve. .......... | 25.00 | 10.00 | 2.50 |
| ☐ | 68 | Cobb: Detroit, ............... Port., red bkgd. | 450.00 | 180.00 | 45.00 |
| ☐ | 69 | Cobb: Detroit, Port. ........ green background | 800.00 | 320.00 | 80.00 |
| ☐ | 70 | Cobb: Detroit, Bat ......... on shoulder | 650.00 | 260.00 | 65.00 |
| ☐ | 71 | Cobb: Detroit, Bat ......... away from shoulder | 500.00 | 200.00 | 50.00 |
| ☐ | 72 | Collins: Phila. AL ........... | 60.00 | 24.00 | 6.00 |
| ☐ | 73 | Conroy: Washington, ...... Fielding | 25.00 | 10.00 | 2.50 |
| ☐ | 74 | Conroy: Wash., Bat ........ on shoulder | 18.00 | 7.25 | 1.80 |
| ☐ | 75 | Covaleski: Phil. NL ......... (Harry) | 25.00 | 10.00 | 2.50 |

| | | | | | |
|---|---|---|---|---|---|
| ☐ | 76 | Crandall: N.Y. NL, .......... without cap | 25.00 | 10.00 | 2.50 |
| ☐ | 77 | Crandall: N.Y. NL, .......... sweater and cap | 18.00 | 7.25 | 1.80 |
| ☐ | 78 | Crawford: Detroit, ......... Batting | 60.00 | 24.00 | 6.00 |
| ☐ | 79 | Crawford: Detroit, ......... Throwing | 80.00 | 32.00 | 8.00 |
| ☐ | 80 | Cree: N.Y. AL ............... | 18.00 | 7.25 | 1.80 |
| ☐ | 81 | Criger: St.L. AL .............. | 25.00 | 10.00 | 2.50 |
| ☐ | 82 | Criss: St.L. AL .............. | 25.00 | 10.00 | 2.50 |
| ☐ | 83 | Dahlen: Brooklyn ........... | 100.00 | 40.00 | 10.00 |
| ☐ | 84 | Dahlen: Bost. NL ........... | 25.00 | 10.00 | 2.50 |
| ☐ | 85 | Davis: Phila. AL ............. | 18.00 | 7.25 | 1.80 |
| ☐ | 86 | G. Davis: Chicago AL ...... | 25.00 | 10.00 | 2.50 |
| ☐ | 87 | H. Davis: Phila. AL ......... | 25.00 | 10.00 | 2.50 |
| ☐ | 88 | Delehanty: Wash. .......... | 25.00 | 10.00 | 2.50 |
| ☐ | 89 | Demmitt: St.L. AL .......... | 1500.00 | 650.00 | 150.00 |
| ☐ | 90 | Demmitt: N.Y. AL .......... | 18.00 | 7.25 | 1.80 |
| ☐ | 91 | Devlin: N.Y. NL ............. | 25.00 | 10.00 | 2.50 |
| ☐ | 92 | Devore: N.Y. NL. ........... | 18.00 | 7.25 | 1.80 |
| ☐ | 93 | Dineen: St.L. AL ............ | 18.00 | 7.25 | 1.80 |
| ☐ | 94 | Donlin: N.Y. NL, ............ Fielding | 40.00 | 16.00 | 4.00 |
| ☐ | 95 | Donlin: N.Y. NL, ............ Sitting | 25.00 | 10.00 | 2.50 |
| ☐ | 96 | Donlin: N.Y. NL, ............ Batting | 18.00 | 7.25 | 1.80 |
| ☐ | 97 | Donohue: Chicago AL ..... | 25.00 | 10.00 | 2.50 |
| ☐ | 98 | Donovan: Detroit, .......... Portrait | 25.00 | 10.00 | 2.50 |
| ☐ | 99 | Donovan: Detroit, .......... Throwing | 18.00 | 7.25 | 1.80 |
| ☐ | 100 | Dooin: Phila. NL ............ | 25.00 | 10.00 | 2.50 |
| ☐ | 101 | Doolan: Phila. NL, .......... Fielding | 18.00 | 7.25 | 1.80 |
| ☐ | 102 | Doolan: Phila. NL, .......... Batting | 18.00 | 7.25 | 1.80 |
| ☐ | 103 | Doolin (sic, Dooin): ....... Phila. NL, | 25.00 | 10.00 | 2.50 |
| ☐ | 104 | Dougherty: Chic. AL, ..... Portrait | 25.00 | 10.00 | 2.50 |
| ☐ | 105 | Dougherty: Chic. AL, ..... Fielding | 18.00 | 7.25 | 1.80 |
| ☐ | 106 | Downey: Cinc., ............. Batting | 18.00 | 7.25 | 1.80 |
| ☐ | 107 | Downey: Cinc., ............. Fielding | 18.00 | 7.25 | 1.80 |
| ☐ | 108 | Doyle: N.Y. AL .............. | 18.00 | 7.25 | 1.80 |
| ☐ | 109 | Doyle: N.Y. NL, ............. Sweater | 18.00 | 7.25 | 1.80 |
| ☐ | 110 | Doyle: N.Y. NL, ............. Throwing | 25.00 | 10.00 | 2.50 |
| ☐ | 111 | Doyle: N.Y. NL, ............. Bat on shoulder | 18.00 | 7.25 | 1.80 |
| ☐ | 112 | Dubuc: Cin. .................. | 18.00 | 7.25 | 1.80 |
| ☐ | 113 | Duffy: Chicago AL .......... | 60.00 | 24.00 | 6.00 |
| ☐ | 114 | Dunn: Brooklyn .............. | 18.00 | 7.25 | 1.80 |
| ☐ | 115 | Durham: N.Y. NL. .......... | 25.00 | 10.00 | 2.50 |
| ☐ | 116 | Dygert: Phila. AL ........... | 18.00 | 7.25 | 1.80 |
| ☐ | 117 | Easterly: Cleveland ........ | 18.00 | 7.25 | 1.80 |
| ☐ | 118 | Egan: Cinc. .................. | 18.00 | 7.25 | 1.80 |
| ☐ | 119 | Elberfeld: Wash., ........... Fielding | 18.00 | 7.25 | 1.80 |
| ☐ | 120 | Elberfeld: Wash., ........... Portrait | 500.00 | 200.00 | 50.00 |
| ☐ | 121 | Elberfeld: N.Y. AL, ......... Portrait | 25.00 | 10.00 | 2.50 |
| ☐ | 122 | Engle: N.Y. AL .............. Portrait | 18.00 | 7.25 | 1.80 |
| ☐ | 123 | Evans: St.L. NL ............. | 18.00 | 7.25 | 1.80 |
| ☐ | 124 | Evers: Chicago NL, ......... Portrait | 80.00 | 32.00 | 8.00 |
| ☐ | 125 | Evers: Chicago NL, ......... Cubs across chest | 100.00 | 40.00 | 10.00 |
| ☐ | 126 | Evers: Chicago NL, ......... Chicago down front of shirt | 60.00 | 24.00 | 6.00 |
| ☐ | 127 | Ewing: Cinc. ................. | 25.00 | 10.00 | 2.50 |
| ☐ | 128 | Ferguson: Boston NL ...... | 18.00 | 7.25 | 1.80 |
| ☐ | 129 | Ferris: St.L. AL .............. | 25.00 | 10.00 | 2.50 |
| ☐ | 130 | Fiene: Chicago AL, ......... Portrait | 18.00 | 7.25 | 1.80 |
| ☐ | 131 | Fiene: Chicago AL, ......... Throwing | 18.00 | 7.25 | 1.80 |
| ☐ | 132 | Fletcher: N.Y. NL .......... | 18.00 | 7.25 | 1.80 |
| ☐ | 133 | Flick: Cleveland .............. | 80.00 | 32.00 | 8.00 |
| ☐ | 134 | Ford: N.Y. AL ............... | 18.00 | 7.25 | 1.80 |
| ☐ | 135 | Frill: N.Y. AL ................ | 18.00 | 7.25 | 1.80 |
| ☐ | 136 | Fromme: Cinc. .............. | 18.00 | 7.25 | 1.80 |
| ☐ | 137 | Gandil: Chicago AL ......... | 18.00 | 7.25 | 1.80 |
| ☐ | 138 | Ganley: Washington ........ | 25.00 | 10.00 | 2.50 |
| ☐ | 139 | Gasper: Cinc. ................ | 18.00 | 7.25 | 1.80 |
| ☐ | 140 | Geyer: St.L. NL .............. | 18.00 | 7.25 | 1.80 |

| | # | Name | | | |
|---|---|---|---|---|---|
| ☐ | 141 | Gibson: Pitt. | 25.00 | 10.00 | 2.50 |
| ☐ | 142 | Gilbert: St.L. NL | 25.00 | 10.00 | 2.50 |
| ☐ | 143 | Goode (sic): Cleve. | 25.00 | 10.00 | 2.50 |
| ☐ | 144 | Graham: Boston NL | 18.00 | 7.25 | 1.80 |
| ☐ | 145 | Graham: St.L. AL | 18.00 | 7.25 | 1.80 |
| ☐ | 146 | Gray: Washington | 18.00 | 7.25 | 1.80 |
| ☐ | 147 | Griffith: Cinc., Portrait | 80.00 | 32.00 | 8.00 |
| ☐ | 148 | Griffith: Cinc., Batting | 60.00 | 24.00 | 6.00 |
| ☐ | 149 | Groom: Washington | 18.00 | 7.25 | 1.80 |
| ☐ | 150 | Hahn: Chicago AL | 25.00 | 10.00 | 2.50 |
| ☐ | 151 | Hartsel: Phila. AL | 18.00 | 7.25 | 1.80 |
| ☐ | 152 | Hemphill: N.Y. AL | 25.00 | 10.00 | 2.50 |
| ☐ | 153 | Herzog : N.Y. NL | 25.00 | 10.00 | 2.50 |
| ☐ | 154 | Herzog: Boston NL | 18.00 | 7.25 | 1.80 |
| ☐ | 155 | Hinchman: Cleveland | 25.00 | 10.00 | 2.50 |
| ☐ | 156 | Hoblitzell: Cinc. | 18.00 | 7.25 | 1.80 |
| ☐ | 157 | Hoffman: St.L. AL | 18.00 | 7.25 | 1.80 |
| ☐ | 158 | Hofman: Chicago NL | 18.00 | 7.25 | 1.80 |
| ☐ | 159 | Howard: Chicago NL | 18.00 | 7.25 | 1.80 |
| ☐ | 160 | Howell: St.L. AL, Portrait | 18.00 | 7.25 | 1.80 |
| ☐ | 161 | Howell: St.L. AL, Left hand on hip | 18.00 | 7.25 | 1.80 |
| ☐ | 162 | Huggins: Cinc., Portrait | 80.00 | 32.00 | 8.00 |
| ☐ | 163 | Huggins: Cinc., Hands to mouth | 60.00 | 24.00 | 6.00 |
| ☐ | 164 | Hulswitt: St.L. NL | 18.00 | 7.25 | 1.80 |
| ☐ | 165 | Hummel: Brooklyn | 18.00 | 7.25 | 1.80 |
| ☐ | 166 | Hunter: Brooklyn | 18.00 | 7.25 | 1.80 |
| ☐ | 167 | Isbell: Chicago AL | 25.00 | 10.00 | 2.50 |
| ☐ | 168 | Jacklitsch: Phila.NL | 25.00 | 10.00 | 2.50 |
| ☐ | 169 | Jennings: Detroit, Portrait | 80.00 | 32.00 | 8.00 |
| ☐ | 170 | Jennings: Detroit, Yelling | 60.00 | 24.00 | 6.00 |
| ☐ | 171 | Jennings: Detroit, Dancing for joy | 60.00 | 24.00 | 6.00 |
| ☐ | 172 | Johnson: Washington, Portrait | 250.00 | 100.00 | 25.00 |
| ☐ | 173 | Johnson: Washington, Ready to pitch | 200.00 | 80.00 | 20.00 |
| ☐ | 174 | Jones: St.L. AL | 25.00 | 10.00 | 2.50 |
| ☐ | 175 | Jones: Detroit | 18.00 | 7.25 | 1.80 |
| ☐ | 176 | F. Jones: Chic. AL, Portrait | 25.00 | 10.00 | 2.50 |
| ☐ | 177 | F. Jones: Chic. AL, Hands on hips | 25.00 | 10.00 | 2.50 |
| ☐ | 178 | Jordan: Brooklyn, Portrait | 25.00 | 10.00 | 2.50 |
| ☐ | 179 | Jordan: Brooklyn, Batting | 18.00 | 7.25 | 1.80 |
| ☐ | 180 | Joss: Cleveland, Portrait | 100.00 | 40.00 | 10.00 |
| ☐ | 181 | Joss: Cleveland, Ready to pitch | 60.00 | 24.00 | 6.00 |
| ☐ | 182 | Karger: Cinc. | 25.00 | 10.00 | 2.50 |
| ☐ | 183 | Keeler: N.Y. AL, Portrait | 100.00 | 40.00 | 10.00 |
| ☐ | 184 | Keeler: N.Y. AL, Batting | 100.00 | 40.00 | 10.00 |
| ☐ | 185 | Killian: Detroit, Portrait | 25.00 | 10.00 | 2.50 |
| ☐ | 186 | Killian: Detroit, Pitching | 18.00 | 7.25 | 1.80 |
| ☐ | 187 | Kleinow: N.Y. AL, Batting | 25.00 | 10.00 | 2.50 |
| ☐ | 188 | Kleinow: N.Y. AL, Catching | 18.00 | 7.25 | 1.80 |
| ☐ | 189 | Kleinow: Bost. AL, Catching | 150.00 | 60.00 | 15.00 |
| ☐ | 190 | Kling: Chicago NL | 25.00 | 10.00 | 2.50 |
| ☐ | 191 | Knabe: Phila. NL | 18.00 | 7.25 | 1.80 |
| ☐ | 192 | Knight: N.Y. AL, Portrait | 18.00 | 7.25 | 1.80 |
| ☐ | 193 | Knight: N.Y. AL, Batting | 18.00 | 7.25 | 1.80 |
| ☐ | 194 | Konetchy: St.L. NL, Awaiting low ball | 18.00 | 7.25 | 1.80 |
| ☐ | 195 | Konetchy: St.L. NL, Glove above head | 25.00 | 10.00 | 2.50 |
| ☐ | 196 | Krause: Phila. AL, Portrait | 18.00 | 7.25 | 1.80 |
| ☐ | 197 | Krause: Phila. AL, Pitching | 18.00 | 7.25 | 1.80 |
| ☐ | 198 | Kroh: Chicago NL | 18.00 | 7.25 | 1.80 |
| ☐ | 199 | Lajoie: Cleveland, Portrait | 125.00 | 50.00 | 12.50 |
| ☐ | 200 | Lajoie: Cleveland, Batting | 100.00 | 40.00 | 10.00 |
| ☐ | 201 | Lajoie: Cleveland, Throwing | 125.00 | 50.00 | 12.50 |
| ☐ | 202 | Lake: N.Y. AL | 25.00 | 10.00 | 2.50 |
| ☐ | 203 | Lake: St.L. AL, Hands over head | 18.00 | 7.25 | 1.80 |
| ☐ | 204 | Lake: St.L. AL, Throwing | 18.00 | 7.25 | 1.80 |
| ☐ | 205 | LaPorte: N.Y. AL | 18.00 | 7.25 | 1.80 |
| ☐ | 206 | Latham: N.Y. NL | 18.00 | 7.25 | 1.80 |
| ☐ | 207 | Leach: Pitt., Portrait | 25.00 | 10.00 | 2.50 |
| ☐ | 208 | Leach: Pitt., In fielding position | 18.00 | 7.25 | 1.80 |
| ☐ | 209 | Leifield: Pitt., Batting | 18.00 | 7.25 | 1.80 |
| ☐ | 210 | Leifield: Pitt., Hands behind head | 25.00 | 10.00 | 2.50 |
| ☐ | 211 | Lennox: Brooklyn | 18.00 | 7.25 | 1.80 |
| ☐ | 212 | Liebhardt: Cleve. | 25.00 | 10.00 | 2.50 |
| ☐ | 213 | Lindaman: Boston NL | 25.00 | 10.00 | 2.50 |
| ☐ | 214 | Livingstone: Phila.AL | 18.00 | 7.25 | 1.80 |
| ☐ | 215 | Lobert: Cinc. | 25.00 | 10.00 | 2.50 |
| ☐ | 216 | Lord: Bost. AL | 18.00 | 7.25 | 1.80 |
| ☐ | 217 | Lumley: Brooklyn | 25.00 | 10.00 | 2.50 |
| ☐ | 218 | Lundgren: Chicago NL | 175.00 | 70.00 | 18.00 |
| ☐ | 219 | Maddox: Pitt. | 18.00 | 7.25 | 1.80 |
| ☐ | 220 | Magee: Phila. NL, Portrait | 25.00 | 10.00 | 2.50 |
| ☐ | 221 | Magee: Phila. NL, Batting | 18.00 | 7.25 | 1.80 |
| ☐ | 222 | Magie: Phila. NL (sic) Portrait, name misspelled | 4500.00 | 2000.00 | 500.00 |
| ☐ | 223 | Manning: N.Y. AL, Batting | 25.00 | 10.00 | 2.50 |
| ☐ | 224 | Manning: N.Y. AL, Hands over head | 18.00 | 7.25 | 1.80 |
| ☐ | 225 | Marquard: N.Y. NL, Portrait | 60.00 | 24.00 | 6.00 |
| ☐ | 226 | Marquard: N.Y. NL, Pitching | 60.00 | 24.00 | 6.00 |
| ☐ | 227 | Marquard: N.Y. NL, Standing | 80.00 | 32.00 | 8.00 |
| ☐ | 228 | Marshall: Brooklyn | 18.00 | 7.25 | 1.80 |
| ☐ | 229 | Mathewson: N.Y. NL, Portrait | 200.00 | 80.00 | 20.00 |
| ☐ | 230 | Mathewson: N.Y. NL, Pitching, white cap | 200.00 | 80.00 | 20.00 |
| ☐ | 231 | Mathewson: N.Y. NL, Pitching, dark cap | 150.00 | 60.00 | 15.00 |
| ☐ | 232 | Mattern: Boston NL | 18.00 | 7.25 | 1.80 |
| ☐ | 233 | McAleese: St.L. AL | 18.00 | 7.25 | 1.80 |
| ☐ | 234 | McBride: Washington | 18.00 | 7.25 | 1.80 |
| ☐ | 235 | McCormick: N.Y. NL | 18.00 | 7.25 | 1.80 |
| ☐ | 236 | McElveen: Brooklyn | 18.00 | 7.25 | 1.80 |
| ☐ | 237 | McGraw: N.Y. NL, Portrait, no cap | 100.00 | 40.00 | 10.00 |
| ☐ | 238 | McGraw: N.Y. NL, Wearing sweater | 80.00 | 32.00 | 8.00 |
| ☐ | 239 | McGraw: N.Y. NL, pointing | 100.00 | 40.00 | 10.00 |
| ☐ | 240 | McGraw: N.Y. NL, Glove on hip | 80.00 | 32.00 | 8.00 |
| ☐ | 241 | McIntyre: Detroit | 18.00 | 7.25 | 1.80 |
| ☐ | 242 | McIntyre: Brooklyn | 25.00 | 10.00 | 2.50 |
| ☐ | 243 | McIntyre: Brooklyn and Chicago NL | 18.00 | 7.25 | 1.80 |
| ☐ | 244 | McLean: Cinc. | 18.00 | 7.25 | 1.80 |
| ☐ | 245 | McQuillan: Phila. NL, Throwing | 25.00 | 10.00 | 2.50 |
| ☐ | 246 | McQuillan: Phila. NL, Batting | 18.00 | 7.25 | 1.80 |
| ☐ | 247 | Merkle: N.Y. NL, Portrait | 25.00 | 10.00 | 2.50 |
| ☐ | 248 | Merkle: N.Y. NL, Throwing | 18.00 | 7.25 | 1.80 |
| ☐ | 249 | Meyers: N.Y. NL | 18.00 | 7.25 | 1.80 |
| ☐ | 250 | Milan: Washington | 18.00 | 7.25 | 1.80 |
| ☐ | 251 | Miller: Pitt. | 18.00 | 7.25 | 1.80 |
| ☐ | 252 | Mitchell: Cinc. | 18.00 | 7.25 | 1.80 |
| ☐ | 253 | Moran: Chicago NL | 18.00 | 7.25 | 1.80 |
| ☐ | 254 | Moriarty: Detroit | 18.00 | 7.25 | 1.80 |
| ☐ | 255 | Mowrey: Cinc. | 18.00 | 7.25 | 1.80 |
| ☐ | 256 | Mullen: Detroit | 18.00 | 7.25 | 1.80 |
| ☐ | 257 | Mullin: Detroit, Throwing | 25.00 | 10.00 | 2.50 |
| ☐ | 258 | Mullin: Detroit, Batting | 18.00 | 7.25 | 1.80 |
| ☐ | 259 | Murphy: Phila. AL, Throwing | 25.00 | 10.00 | 2.50 |
| ☐ | 260 | Murphy: Phila. AL, Bat on shoulder | 18.00 | 7.25 | 1.80 |
| ☐ | 261 | Murray: N.Y. NL, Sweater | 18.00 | 7.25 | 1.80 |

| | | | | |
|---|---|---|---|---|
| ☐ 262 | Murray: N.Y. NL, .............. Bat on shoulder | 18.00 | 7.25 | 1.80 |
| ☐ 263 | Myers (sic): N.Y. NL, ...... Fielding | 18.00 | 7.25 | 1.80 |
| ☐ 264 | Myers (sic): N.Y. NL, ...... Batting | 18.00 | 7.25 | 1.80 |
| ☐ 265 | Needham: Chicago NL .... | 18.00 | 7.25 | 1.80 |
| ☐ 266 | Nicholls: Phila. AL .......... | 25.00 | 10.00 | 2.50 |
| ☐ 267 | Nichols(sic): Phila.AL ...... | 18.00 | 7.25 | 1.80 |
| ☐ 268 | Niles: Boston AL .............. | 25.00 | 10.00 | 2.50 |
| ☐ 269 | Oakes: Cinc. .................... | 18.00 | 7.25 | 1.80 |
| ☐ 270 | O'Hara: St.L. NL ............ | 1000.00 | 400.00 | 100.00 |
| ☐ 271 | O'Hara: N.Y. NL ............ | 18.00 | 7.25 | 1.80 |
| ☐ 272 | Oldring: Phila. AL, .......... Fielding | 25.00 | 10.00 | 2.50 |
| ☐ 273 | Oldring: Phila. AL, .......... Bat on shoulder | 18.00 | 7.25 | 1.80 |
| ☐ 274 | O'Leary: Detroit, ............ Portrait | 25.00 | 10.00 | 2.50 |
| ☐ 275 | O'Leary: Detroit, ............ Hands on knees | 18.00 | 7.25 | 1.80 |
| ☐ 276 | Overall: Chicago NL, ...... Portrait | 25.00 | 10.00 | 2.50 |
| ☐ 277 | Overall: Chicago NL, ...... Pitching, follow thru | 18.00 | 7.25 | 1.80 |
| ☐ 278 | Overall: Chicago NL, ...... Pitching hiding ball in glove | 18.00 | 7.25 | 1.80 |
| ☐ 279 | Owen: Chicago AL .......... | 25.00 | 10.00 | 2.50 |
| ☐ 280 | Parent: Chicago AL ........ | 25.00 | 10.00 | 2.50 |
| ☐ 281 | Paskert: Cinc. ................ | 18.00 | 7.25 | 1.80 |
| ☐ 282 | Pastorius: Brooklyn ........ | 25.00 | 10.00 | 2.50 |
| ☐ 283 | Pattee: Brooklyn ............ | 40.00 | 16.00 | 4.00 |
| ☐ 284 | Payne: Chicago AL .......... | 18.00 | 7.25 | 1.80 |
| ☐ 285 | Pelty: St.L. AL, HOR ...... | 40.00 | 16.00 | 4.00 |
| ☐ 286 | Pelty: St.L. AL, VERT ...... | 18.00 | 7.25 | 1.80 |
| ☐ 287 | Perring: Cleveland .......... | 18.00 | 7.25 | 1.80 |
| ☐ 288 | Pfeffer: Chicago NL ........ | 18.00 | 7.25 | 1.80 |
| ☐ 289 | Pfeister: Chic. NL, .......... Sitting | 18.00 | 7.25 | 1.80 |
| ☐ 290 | Pfeister: Chic. NL, .......... Pitching | 18.00 | 7.25 | 1.80 |
| ☐ 291 | Phelps: St.L. NL ............ | 18.00 | 7.25 | 1.80 |
| ☐ 292 | Phillippe: Pitt. ................ | 18.00 | 7.25 | 1.80 |
| ☐ 293 | Plank: Phila. AL .............. | 6000.00 | 2500.00 | 600.00 |
| ☐ 294 | Powell: St.L. AL .............. | 25.00 | 10.00 | 2.50 |
| ☐ 295 | Powers: Phil. AL .............. | 40.00 | 16.00 | 4.00 |
| ☐ 296 | Furtell: Chicago AL ........ | 18.00 | 7.25 | 1.80 |
| ☐ 297 | Quinn: N.Y. AL ................ | 18.00 | 7.25 | 1.80 |
| ☐ 298 | Raymond: N.Y. NL .......... | 18.00 | 7.25 | 1.80 |
| ☐ 299 | Reulbach: Chicago NL, ... Pitching | 18.00 | 7.25 | 1.80 |
| ☐ 300 | Reulbach: Chicago NL, ... Hands at side | 40.00 | 16.00 | 4.00 |
| ☐ 301 | Rhoades: Cleveland, ...... Hand in air | 18.00 | 7.25 | 1.80 |
| ☐ 302 | Rhoades: Cleveland, ...... Ready to pitch | 18.00 | 7.25 | 1.80 |
| ☐ 303 | Rhodes: St.L. NL ............ | 18.00 | 7.25 | 1.80 |
| ☐ 304 | Ritchey: Boston NL ........ | 25.00 | 10.00 | 2.50 |
| ☐ 305 | Rossman: Detroit ............ | 18.00 | 7.25 | 1.80 |
| ☐ 306 | Rucker: Brooklyn, .......... Portrait | 25.00 | 10.00 | 2.50 |
| ☐ 307 | Rucker: Brooklyn, .......... Pitching | 18.00 | 7.25 | 1.80 |
| ☐ 308 | Schaefer: Washington ..... | 18.00 | 7.25 | 1.80 |
| ☐ 309 | Schaefer: Detroit ............ | 25.00 | 10.00 | 2.50 |
| ☐ 310 | Schlei: N.Y. NL, ............ Sweater | 18.00 | 7.25 | 1.80 |
| ☐ 311 | Schlei: N.Y. NL, .............. Batting | 18.00 | 7.25 | 1.80 |
| ☐ 312 | Schlei: N.Y. NL, .............. Fielding | 25.00 | 10.00 | 2.50 |
| ☐ 313 | Schmidt: Detroit, ............ Portrait | 18.00 | 7.25 | 1.80 |
| ☐ 314 | Schmidt: Detroit, ............ Throwing | 25.00 | 10.00 | 2.50 |
| ☐ 315 | Schulte: Chicago NL, ...... Batting, back turned | 18.00 | 7.25 | 1.80 |
| ☐ 316 | Schulte: Chicago NL, ...... Batting, front pose | 25.00 | 10.00 | 2.50 |
| ☐ 317 | Scott: Chicago AL .......... | 18.00 | 7.25 | 1.80 |
| ☐ 318 | Seymour: N.Y. NL, .......... Portrait | 18.00 | 7.25 | 1.80 |
| ☐ 319 | Seymour: N.Y. NL, .......... Throwing | 18.00 | 7.25 | 1.80 |
| ☐ 320 | Seymour: N.Y. NL, .......... Batting | 25.00 | 10.00 | 2.50 |
| ☐ 321 | Shaw: St.L. NL ................ | 25.00 | 10.00 | 2.50 |
| ☐ 322 | Sheckard: Chic. NL, ........ Throwing | 18.00 | 7.25 | 1.80 |
| ☐ 323 | Sheckard: Chic. NL, ........ Side view | 25.00 | 10.00 | 2.50 |
| ☐ 324 | Shipke: Washington ........ | 25.00 | 10.00 | 2.50 |
| ☐ 325 | Smith: Chicago AL .......... | 18.00 | 7.25 | 1.80 |
| ☐ 326 | Smith: Chicago and ........ Boston AL | 200.00 | 80.00 | 20.00 |
| ☐ 327 | F. Smith: Chicago AL ...... | 25.00 | 10.00 | 2.50 |
| ☐ 328 | Happy Smith: Brk. .......... | 18.00 | 7.25 | 1.80 |
| ☐ 329 | Snodgrass: N.Y. NL, ........ Batting | 18.00 | 7.25 | 1.80 |
| ☐ 330 | Snodgrass: N.Y. NL, ........ Catching | 18.00 | 7.25 | 1.80 |
| ☐ 331 | Spade: Cinc. .................... | 25.00 | 10.00 | 2.50 |
| ☐ 332 | Speaker: Boston AL ........ | 125.00 | 50.00 | 12.50 |
| ☐ 333 | Spencer: Boston AL ........ | 25.00 | 10.00 | 2.50 |
| ☐ 334 | Stahl: Boston AL, ............ Catching fly ball | 18.00 | 7.25 | 1.80 |
| ☐ 335 | Stahl: Boston AL, ............ Standing, arms down | 25.00 | 10.00 | 2.50 |
| ☐ 336 | Stanage: Detroit ............ | 18.00 | 7.25 | 1.80 |
| ☐ 337 | Starr: Boston NL ............ | 18.00 | 7.25 | 1.80 |
| ☐ 338 | Steinfeldt: Chic. NL, ...... Portrait | 25.00 | 10.00 | 2.50 |
| ☐ 339 | Steinfeldt: Chic. NL, ...... Batting | 18.00 | 7.25 | 1.80 |
| ☐ 340 | Stephens: St.L. AL .......... | 18.00 | 7.25 | 1.80 |
| ☐ 341 | Stone: St.L. AL ................ | 25.00 | 10.00 | 2.50 |
| ☐ 342 | Stovall: Cleveland, .......... Portrait | 25.00 | 10.00 | 2.50 |
| ☐ 343 | Stovall: Cleveland, .......... Batting | 18.00 | 7.25 | 1.80 |
| ☐ 344 | Street: Washington, ........ Portrait | 18.00 | 7.25 | 1.80 |
| ☐ 345 | Street: Washington, ........ Catching | 18.00 | 7.25 | 1.80 |
| ☐ 346 | Sullivan: Chicago AL ...... | 25.00 | 10.00 | 2.50 |
| ☐ 347 | Summers: Detroit .......... | 18.00 | 7.25 | 1.80 |
| ☐ 348 | Sweeney: N.Y. AL .......... | 18.00 | 7.25 | 1.80 |
| ☐ 349 | Sweeney: Bost. NL .......... | 18.00 | 7.25 | 1.80 |
| ☐ 350 | L. Tannehill: Chic. AL .... | 25.00 | 10.00 | 2.50 |
| ☐ 351 | Tannehill: Chicago AL .... | 18.00 | 7.25 | 1.80 |
| ☐ 352 | Tannehill: Wash. ............ | 18.00 | 7.25 | 1.80 |
| ☐ 353 | Tenney: N.Y. NL. ............ | 25.00 | 10.00 | 2.50 |
| ☐ 354 | Thomas: Phila. AL .......... | 18.00 | 7.25 | 1.80 |
| ☐ 355 | Tinker: Chicago NL, ........ Ready to hit | 60.00 | 24.00 | 6.00 |
| ☐ 356 | Tinker: Chicago NL, ........ Bat on shoulder | 60.00 | 24.00 | 6.00 |
| ☐ 357 | Tinker: Chicago NL, ........ Portrait | 80.00 | 32.00 | 8.00 |
| ☐ 358 | Tinker: Chicago NL, ........ Hands on knees | 80.00 | 32.00 | 8.00 |
| ☐ 359 | Titus: Phila. NL .............. | 18.00 | 7.25 | 1.80 |
| ☐ 360 | Turner: Cleveland .......... | 25.00 | 10.00 | 2.50 |
| ☐ 361 | Unglaub: Washington ...... | 18.00 | 7.25 | 1.80 |
| ☐ 362 | Waddell: St.L. AL, .......... Portrait | 80.00 | 32.00 | 8.00 |
| ☐ 363 | Waddell: St.L. AL, .......... Pitching | 80.00 | 32.00 | 8.00 |
| ☐ 364 | Wagner: Boston AL, ........ Bat on left shoulder | 40.00 | 16.00 | 4.00 |
| ☐ 365 | Wagner: Boston AL, ........ Bat on right shoulder | 25.00 | 10.00 | 2.50 |
| ☐ 366 | Wagner: Pitt. ................ | 36000. | 15000. | 4000. |
| ☐ 367 | Wallace: St.L. AL ............ | 80.00 | 32.00 | 8.00 |
| ☐ 368 | Walsh: Chicago AL .......... | 80.00 | 32.00 | 8.00 |
| ☐ 369 | Warhop: N.Y. AL ............ | 18.00 | 7.25 | 1.80 |
| ☐ 370 | Weimer: N.Y. NL. ............ | 25.00 | 10.00 | 2.50 |
| ☐ 371 | Wheat: Brooklyn ............ | 60.00 | 24.00 | 6.00 |
| ☐ 372 | White: Chicago AL, ........ Portrait | 25.00 | 10.00 | 2.50 |
| ☐ 373 | White: Chicago AL, ........ Pitching | 18.00 | 7.25 | 1.80 |
| ☐ 374 | Wilhelm: Brooklyn, .......... Batting | 18.00 | 7.25 | 1.80 |
| ☐ 375 | Wilhelm: Brooklyn, .......... Hands to chest | 25.00 | 10.00 | 2.50 |
| ☐ 376 | Willett: Detroit, .............. Batting | 18.00 | 7.25 | 1.80 |
| ☐ 377 | Willetts (sic): .................. Detroit, Pitching | 18.00 | 7.25 | 1.80 |
| ☐ 378 | Williams: St.L. AL ............ | 25.00 | 10.00 | 2.50 |
| ☐ 379 | Willis: Pitt. .................... | 40.00 | 16.00 | 4.00 |
| ☐ 380 | Willis: St.L. NL, .............. Pitching | 25.00 | 10.00 | 2.50 |
| ☐ 381 | Willis: St.L. NL, .............. Batting | 25.00 | 10.00 | 2.50 |
| ☐ 382 | Wilson: Pitt. .................... | 18.00 | 7.25 | 1.80 |
| ☐ 383 | Wiltse: N.Y. NL, .............. Portrait | 25.00 | 10.00 | 2.50 |
| ☐ 384 | Wiltse: N.Y. NL, .............. Sweater | 18.00 | 7.25 | 1.80 |
| ☐ 385 | Wiltse: N.Y. NL, .............. Pitching | 18.00 | 7.25 | 1.80 |
| ☐ 386 | Young: Cleveland, .......... | 125.00 | 50.00 | 12.50 |

Portrait
- □ 387 Young: Cleveland, ........... 100.00  40.00  10.00
  Pitch, front view
- □ 388 Young: Cleveland, .......... 125.00  50.00  12.50
  Pitch, side view
- □ 389 Zimmerman: ................. 18.00  7.25  1.80
  Chicago NL
- □ 390 Fred Abbott: Toledo ........ 18.00  7.25  1.80
- □ 391 Merle (Doc) Adkins: ........ 18.00  7.25  1.80
  Baltimore
- □ 392 John Anderson: Prov. ..... 18.00  7.25  1.80
- □ 393 Herman Armbruster: ...... 18.00  7.25  1.80
  St. Paul
- □ 394 Harry Arndt: Prov. ......... 18.00  7.25  1.80
- □ 395 Cy Barger: Rochester ..... 18.00  7.25  1.80
- □ 396 John Barry: Milwaukee ... 18.00  7.25  1.80
- □ 397 Emil H. Batch: Roch. ...... 18.00  7.25  1.80
- □ 398 Jake Beckley: K.C. ......... 80.00  32.00  8.00
- □ 399 Russell Blackburne ......... 18.00  7.25  1.80
  (Lena): Providence
- □ 400 David Brain: Buffalo ........ 18.00  7.25  1.80
- □ 401 Roy Brashear: K.C. ......... 18.00  7.25  1.80
- □ 402 Fred Burchell: Buffalo ...... 18.00  7.25  1.80
- □ 403 Jimmy Burke: Ind. .......... 18.00  7.25  1.80
- □ 404 John Butler: Roch. .......... 18.00  7.25  1.80
- □ 405 Charles Carr: Ind. .......... 18.00  7.25  1.80
- □ 406 James Peter Casey ......... 18.00  7.25  1.80
  (Doc): Montreal
- □ 407 Peter Cassidy: Balt. ........ 18.00  7.25  1.80
- □ 408 Wm. Chappelle: Roch. ..... 18.00  7.25  1.80
- □ 409 Wm. Clancy: Buffalo ....... 18.00  7.25  1.80
- □ 410 Joshua Clark: Col. .......... 18.00  7.25  1.80
- □ 411 William Clymer: Col. ....... 18.00  7.25  1.80
- □ 412 Jimmy Collins: Minn. ...... 80.00  32.00  8.00
- □ 413 Bunk Congalton: ............ 18.00  7.25  1.80
  Columbus
- □ 414 Gavvy Cravath: Minn. ..... 25.00  10.00  2.50
- □ 415 Monte Cross: Ind. .......... 18.00  7.25  1.80
- □ 416 Paul Davidson: Ind. ......... 18.00  7.25  1.80
- □ 417 Frank Delehanty: ............ 18.00  7.25  1.80
  Louisville
- □ 418 Rube Dessau: Balt. ......... 18.00  7.25  1.80
- □ 419 Gus Dorner: K.C. ............ 18.00  7.25  1.80
- □ 420 Jerome Downs: Minn. ...... 18.00  7.25  1.80
- □ 421 Jack Dunn: Baltimore ...... 18.00  7.25  1.80
- □ 422 James Flanagan: Buff. .... 18.00  7.25  1.80
- □ 423 James Freeman: Tol. ...... 18.00  7.25  1.80
- □ 424 John Ganzel: Roch. ........ 18.00  7.25  1.80
- □ 425 Myron Grimshaw: Tor. .... 18.00  7.25  1.80
- □ 426 Robert Hall: Balt. ........... 18.00  7.25  1.80
- □ 427 William Hallman: K.C. ..... 18.00  7.25  1.80
- □ 428 John Hannifan: J.C. ........ 18.00  7.25  1.80
- □ 429 Jack Hayden: Ind. .......... 18.00  7.25  1.80
- □ 430 Harry Hinchman: Tol. ...... 18.00  7.25  1.80
- □ 431 Harry C. Hoffman ........... 18.00  7.25  1.80
  (Izzy): Providence
- □ 432 James B. Jackson: ......... 18.00  7.25  1.80
  Baltimore
- □ 433 Joe Kelley: Tor. ............. 80.00  32.00  8.00
- □ 434 Rube Kisinger: Buff. ........ 18.00  7.25  1.80
  (sic) Kissinger
- □ 435 Otto Kruger: Col. ............ 18.00  7.25  1.80
  (sic) Krueger
- □ 436 Wm. Lattimore: Tol. ........ 18.00  7.25  1.80
- □ 437 James Lavender: Prov. .... 18.00  7.25  1.80
- □ 438 Carl Lundgren: K.C. ........ 18.00  7.25  1.80
- □ 439 Wm. Malarkey: Buff. ....... 18.00  7.25  1.80
- □ 440 Wm. Maloney: Roch. ....... 18.00  7.25  1.80
- □ 441 Dennis McGann: Milw. ..... 18.00  7.25  1.80
- □ 442 James McGinley: Tor. ...... 18.00  7.25  1.80
- □ 443 Joe McGinnity: New. ....... 80.00  32.00  8.00
- □ 444 Ulysses McGlynn: Mil. ..... 18.00  7.25  1.80
- □ 445 George Merritt: J.C. ........ 18.00  7.25  1.80
- □ 446 Wm. Milligan: J.C. .......... 18.00  7.25  1.80
- □ 447 Fred Mitchell: Tor. .......... 18.00  7.25  1.80
- □ 448 Dan Moeller: J.C. ........... 18.00  7.25  1.80
- □ 449 Joseph Herbert Moran: .. 18.00  7.25  1.80
  Prov.
- □ 450 Wm. Nattress: Buffalo ..... 18.00  7.25  1.80
- □ 451 Frank Oberlin: Minn. ....... 18.00  7.25  1.80
- □ 452 Peter O'Brien: ............... 18.00  7.25  1.80
  St. Paul
- □ 453 Wm. O'Neil: Minn. .......... 18.00  7.25  1.80
- □ 454 James Phelan: Prov. ....... 18.00  7.25  1.80
- □ 455 Oliver Pickering: ............ 18.00  7.25  1.80
  Minneapolis.
- □ 456 Philip Poland: Balt. ......... 18.00  7.25  1.80
- □ 457 Ambrose Puttman: .......... 18.00  7.25  1.80
  Louisville
- □ 458 Lee Quillen: Minn. ........... 18.00  7.25  1.80
- □ 459 Newton Randall: Milw. .... 18.00  7.25  1.80
- □ 460 Louis Ritter: K.C. ........... 18.00  7.25  1.80
- □ 461 Dick Rudolph: Tor. .......... 18.00  7.25  1.80

- □ 462 George Schirm: Buff. ...... 18.00  7.25  1.80
- □ 463 Larry Schlafly: Newark ... 18.00  7.25  1.80
- □ 464 Ossie Schreck: Col. ........ 18.00  7.25  1.80
  (sic) Schreckengost
- □ 465 William Shannon: K.C. .... 18.00  7.25  1.80
- □ 466 Bayard Sharpe: Newark .. 18.00  7.25  1.80
- □ 467 Royal Shaw: Prov. .......... 18.00  7.25  1.80
- □ 468 James Slagle: Balt. ........ 18.00  7.25  1.80
- □ 469 George Henry Smith: ..... 18.00  7.25  1.80
  Buffalo
- □ 470 Samuel Strang: Balt. ....... 18.00  7.25  1.80
- □ 471 Luther(Dummy) Taylor: .. 18.00  7.25  1.80
  Buffalo
- □ 472 John Thielman: .............. 18.00  7.25  1.80
  Louisville
- □ 473 John F. White: Buff. ....... 18.00  7.25  1.80
- □ 474 William Wright: Tol. ........ 18.00  7.25  1.80
- □ 475 Irving M. Young: ............ 18.00  7.25  1.80
  Minneapolis
- □ 476 Jack Bastian: ................ 50.00  20.00  5.00
  San Antonio
- □ 477 Harry Bay: Nashv. .......... 50.00  20.00  5.00
- □ 478 Wm. Bernhard: Nashv. .... 50.00  20.00  5.00
- □ 479 Ted Breitenstein: ........... 50.00  20.00  5.00
  New Orleans
- □ 480 George(Scoops) Carey: .. 50.00  20.00  5.00
  Memphis
- □ 481 Cad Coles: Augusta ......... 50.00  20.00  5.00
- □ 482 Wm. Cranston: Memph. ... 50.00  20.00  5.00
- □ 483 Roy Ellam: Nashville ....... 50.00  20.00  5.00
- □ 484 Edward Foster: .............. 50.00  20.00  5.00
  Charleston
- □ 485 Charles Fritz: N.O. ......... 50.00  20.00  5.00
- □ 486 Ed Greminger: Montg. ..... 50.00  20.00  5.00
- □ 487 Guiheen: Portsmouth ..... 50.00  20.00  5.00
- □ 488 William F. Hart .............. 50.00  20.00  5.00
  Little Rock
- □ 489 James Henry Hart: ........ 50.00  20.00  5.00
  Montgomery
- □ 490 J.R. Helm: Columbus ...... 50.00  20.00  5.00
  (Georgia)
- □ 491 Gordon Hickman: ............ 50.00  20.00  5.00
  Mobile
- □ 492 Buck Hooker: ................ 50.00  20.00  5.00
  Lynchburg
- □ 493 Ernie Howard: Sav. ........ 50.00  20.00  5.00
- □ 494 A.O. Jordan: Atlanta ....... 50.00  20.00  5.00
- □ 495 J.F. Kiernan: ................. 50.00  20.00  5.00
  Columbia
- □ 496 Frank King: Danville ....... 50.00  20.00  5.00
- □ 497 James LaFitte: Macon .... 50.00  20.00  5.00
- □ 498 Harry Lentz: Little .......... 50.00  20.00  5.00
  Rock (sic) Sentz
- □ 499 Perry Lipe: Richmond ..... 50.00  20.00  5.00
- □ 500 George Manion: ............. 50.00  20.00  5.00
  Columbia
- □ 501 McCauley: Portsmouth ... 50.00  20.00  5.00
- □ 502 Charles B. Miller: ............ 50.00  20.00  5.00
  Dallas
- □ 503 Carlton Molesworth: ....... 50.00  20.00  5.00
  Birmingham
- □ 504 Dominic Mullaney: ........... 50.00  20.00  5.00
  Jacksonville
- □ 505 Albert Orth: Lynchb. ....... 50.00  20.00  5.00
- □ 506 William Otey: Norf. ......... 50.00  20.00  5.00
- □ 507 George Paige: ............... 50.00  20.00  5.00
  Charleston
- □ 508 Hub Perdue: Nashv. ....... 50.00  20.00  5.00
- □ 509 Archie Persons: ............. 50.00  20.00  5.00
  Montgomery
- □ 510 Edward Reagan: N.O. ..... 50.00  20.00  5.00
- □ 511 R.H. Revelle: Richm. ...... 50.00  20.00  5.00
- □ 512 Isaac Rockenfeld: ........... 50.00  20.00  5.00
  Montgomery
- □ 513 Ray Ryan: Roanoke ........ 50.00  20.00  5.00
- □ 514 Charles Seitz: Norf. ........ 50.00  20.00  5.00
- □ 515 Frank (Shag) Shaughn- .. 50.00  20.00  5.00
  essy: Roanoke
- □ 516 Carlos Smith: Shreve. ..... 50.00  20.00  5.00
- □ 517 Sid Smith: Atlanta .......... 50.00  20.00  5.00
- □ 518 M.R. (Dolly) Stark: .......... 50.00  20.00  5.00
  San Antonio
- □ 519 Tony Thebo: Waco .......... 50.00  20.00  5.00
- □ 520 Woodie Thornton: .......... 50.00  20.00  5.00
  Mobile
- □ 521 Juan Violat: Jackson- ..... 50.00  20.00  5.00
  ville: (sic) Viola
- □ 522 James Westlake: ............ 50.00  20.00  5.00
  Danville
- □ 523 Foley White: Houston ..... 50.00  20.00  5.00

# T207 Brown Background

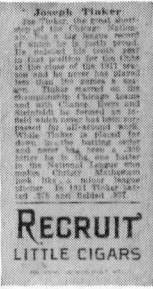

The cards in this 207 card set measure 1 1/2" by 2 5/8". The T207 set, also known as the "Brown Background" set was issued with Broadleaf, Cycle, Napoleon, Recruit and anonymous (Factories no. 2, 3 or 25) backs in 1912. Broadleaf, Cycle and anonymous backs are difficult to obtain. Although many scarcities and cards with varying degrees of difficulty to obtain exist (see prices below), the Loudermilk, Lewis (Boston NL) and Miller (Chicago NL) cards are the rarest, followed by Saier and Tyler. The cards are numbered below for reference in alphabetical order by player's name. The complete set price below does not include the Lewis variation missing the Braves patch on the sleeve.

|  |  |  | MINT | VG-E | F-G |
|---|---|---|---|---|---|
|  | COMPLETE SET | | 11500.00 | 4750.00 | 1250. |
|  | COMMON PLAYER | | 25.00 | 10.00 | 2.50 |
| ☐ | 1 | Adams: Cleve AL | 50.00 | 20.00 | 5.00 |
| ☐ | 2 | Ainsmith: Wash AL | 25.00 | 10.00 | 2.50 |
| ☐ | 3 | Almeida: Cinc AL | 50.00 | 20.00 | 5.00 |
| ☐ | 4 | Austin: StL AL with StL on shirt | 25.00 | 10.00 | 2.50 |
| ☐ | 5 | Austin: StL AL without StL on shirt | 75.00 | 30.00 | 7.50 |
| ☐ | 6 | Ball: Cleve AL | 25.00 | 10.00 | 2.50 |
| ☐ | 7 | Barger: Brk NL | 25.00 | 10.00 | 2.50 |
| ☐ | 8 | Barry: Phil AL | 25.00 | 10.00 | 2.50 |
| ☐ | 9 | Bauman: Det AL | 75.00 | 30.00 | 7.50 |
| ☐ | 10 | Becker: NY NL | 25.00 | 10.00 | 2.50 |
| ☐ | 11 | Bender: Phil AL | 75.00 | 30.00 | 7.50 |
| ☐ | 12 | Benz: Chi AL | 50.00 | 20.00 | 5.00 |
| ☐ | 13 | Bescher: Cinc NL | 25.00 | 10.00 | 2.50 |
| ☐ | 14 | Birmingham: Cleve AL | 50.00 | 20.00 | 5.00 |
| ☐ | 15 | Blackburne: Chi AL | 50.00 | 20.00 | 5.00 |
| ☐ | 16 | Blanding: Cleve AL | 50.00 | 20.00 | 5.00 |
| ☐ | 17 | Block: Chi AL | 25.00 | 10.00 | 2.50 |
| ☐ | 18 | Bodie: Chi AL | 25.00 | 10.00 | 2.50 |
| ☐ | 19 | Bradley: Bos AL | 25.00 | 10.00 | 2.50 |
| ☐ | 20 | Bresnahan: StL NL | 60.00 | 24.00 | 6.00 |
| ☐ | 21 | Bushelman: Bos AL | 50.00 | 20.00 | 5.00 |
| ☐ | 22 | Butcher: Cleve AL | 50.00 | 20.00 | 5.00 |
| ☐ | 23 | Byrne: Pitt NL | 25.00 | 10.00 | 2.50 |
| ☐ | 24 | Callahan: Chi AL | 25.00 | 10.00 | 2.50 |
| ☐ | 25 | Camnitz: Pitt NL | 25.00 | 10.00 | 2.50 |
| ☐ | 26 | Carey: Pitt NL | 75.00 | 30.00 | 7.50 |
| ☐ | 27 | Carrigan: Bos AL correct back | 25.00 | 10.00 | 2.50 |
| ☐ | 28 | Carrigan: Bos AL Wagner back | 100.00 | 40.00 | 10.00 |
| ☐ | 29 | Chalmers: Phil NL | 25.00 | 10.00 | 2.50 |
| ☐ | 30 | Chance: Chi NL | 90.00 | 36.00 | 9.00 |
| ☐ | 31 | Cicotte: Bos AL | 30.00 | 12.00 | 3.00 |
| ☐ | 32 | Clarke: Cinc NL | 25.00 | 10.00 | 2.50 |
| ☐ | 33 | Cole: Chi AL | 25.00 | 10.00 | 2.50 |
| ☐ | 34 | Collins: Chi AL | 150.00 | 60.00 | 15.00 |
| ☐ | 35 | Coulson: Brk NL | 25.00 | 10.00 | 2.50 |
| ☐ | 36 | Covington: Det AL | 25.00 | 10.00 | 2.50 |
| ☐ | 37 | Crandall: NY NL | 25.00 | 10.00 | 2.50 |
| ☐ | 38 | Cunningham: Wash AL | 50.00 | 20.00 | 5.00 |
| ☐ | 39 | Danforth: Phil AL | 25.00 | 10.00 | 2.50 |
| ☐ | 40 | Daniels: NY AL | 25.00 | 10.00 | 2.50 |
| ☐ | 41 | Daubert: Brk NL | 30.00 | 12.00 | 3.00 |
| ☐ | 42 | Davis: Cleve AL | 25.00 | 10.00 | 2.50 |
| ☐ | 43 | Delahanty: Det AL | 25.00 | 10.00 | 2.50 |
| ☐ | 44 | Derrick: Phil AL | 25.00 | 10.00 | 2.50 |
| ☐ | 45 | Devlin: Bos NL | 25.00 | 10.00 | 2.50 |
| ☐ | 46 | Devore: NY NL | 25.00 | 10.00 | 2.50 |
| ☐ | 47 | Donlin: Pitt NL | 50.00 | 20.00 | 5.00 |
| ☐ | 48 | Donnelly: Bos NL | 50.00 | 20.00 | 5.00 |
| ☐ | 49 | Dooin: Phil AL | 25.00 | 10.00 | 2.50 |
| ☐ | 50 | Downey: Phil NL | 50.00 | 20.00 | 5.00 |
| ☐ | 51 | Doyle: NY NL | 25.00 | 10.00 | 2.50 |
| ☐ | 52 | Drake: Det AL | 25.00 | 10.00 | 2.50 |
| ☐ | 53 | Easterly: Cleve AL | 25.00 | 10.00 | 2.50 |
| ☐ | 54 | Ellis: StL NL | 25.00 | 10.00 | 2.50 |
| ☐ | 55 | Engle: Bos AL | 25.00 | 10.00 | 2.50 |
| ☐ | 56 | Erwin: Brk NL | 25.00 | 10.00 | 2.50 |
| ☐ | 57 | Evans: StL NL | 25.00 | 10.00 | 2.50 |
| ☐ | 58 | Ferry: Pitt NL | 25.00 | 10.00 | 2.50 |
| ☐ | 59 | Fisher: NY AL white cap | 60.00 | 24.00 | 6.00 |
| ☐ | 60 | Fisher: NY AL blue cap | 35.00 | 14.00 | 3.50 |
| ☐ | 61 | Fletcher: NY NL | 25.00 | 10.00 | 2.50 |
| ☐ | 62 | Fournier: Chi AL | 50.00 | 20.00 | 5.00 |
| ☐ | 63 | Fromme: Cinc NL | 25.00 | 10.00 | 2.50 |
| ☐ | 64 | Gainor: Det AL | 25.00 | 10.00 | 2.50 |
| ☐ | 65 | Gardner: Bos AL | 25.00 | 10.00 | 2.50 |
| ☐ | 66 | George: Cleve AL | 25.00 | 10.00 | 2.50 |
| ☐ | 67 | Golden: StL NL | 25.00 | 10.00 | 2.50 |
| ☐ | 68 | Gowdy: Bos NL | 25.00 | 10.00 | 2.50 |
| ☐ | 69 | Graham: Phil NL | 35.00 | 14.00 | 3.50 |
| ☐ | 70 | Graney: Cleve AL | 25.00 | 10.00 | 2.50 |
| ☐ | 71 | Gregg: Cleve AL | 50.00 | 20.00 | 5.00 |
| ☐ | 72 | Hageman: Bos AL | 25.00 | 10.00 | 2.50 |
| ☐ | 73 | Hall: Bos AL | 25.00 | 10.00 | 2.50 |
| ☐ | 74 | Hallinan: St.L. AL | 25.00 | 10.00 | 2.50 |
| ☐ | 75 | E. Hamilton: St.L. AL | 25.00 | 10.00 | 2.50 |
| ☐ | 76 | Harmon: St.L. NL | 25.00 | 10.00 | 2.50 |
| ☐ | 77 | Hartley: NY NL | 50.00 | 20.00 | 5.00 |
| ☐ | 78 | Henriksen, Bos AL | 25.00 | 10.00 | 2.50 |
| ☐ | 79 | Henry: Wash AL | 35.00 | 14.00 | 3.50 |
| ☐ | 80 | Herzog: NY NL | 50.00 | 20.00 | 5.00 |
| ☐ | 81 | Higgins: Brk NL | 25.00 | 10.00 | 2.50 |
| ☐ | 82 | Hoff: NY AL | 50.00 | 20.00 | 5.00 |
| ☐ | 83 | Hogan: StL AL | 25.00 | 10.00 | 2.50 |
| ☐ | 84 | Hooper: Bos AL | 175.00 | 70.00 | 18.00 |
| ☐ | 85 | Houser: Bos NL | 50.00 | 20.00 | 5.00 |
| ☐ | 86 | Hyatt: Pitt NL | 50.00 | 20.00 | 5.00 |
| ☐ | 87 | Johnson: Wash AL | 250.00 | 100.00 | 25.00 |
| ☐ | 88 | Kaler: Cleve AL | 25.00 | 10.00 | 2.50 |
| ☐ | 89 | Kelly: Pitt NL | 50.00 | 20.00 | 5.00 |
| ☐ | 90 | Kirke: Bos NL | 50.00 | 20.00 | 5.00 |
| ☐ | 91 | Kling: Bos NL | 25.00 | 10.00 | 2.50 |
| ☐ | 92 | Knabe: Phil NL | 25.00 | 10.00 | 2.50 |
| ☐ | 93 | Knetzer: Brk NL | 25.00 | 10.00 | 2.50 |
| ☐ | 94 | Konetchy: StL NL | 25.00 | 10.00 | 2.50 |
| ☐ | 95 | Krause: Phil AL | 25.00 | 10.00 | 2.50 |
| ☐ | 96 | Kuhn: Chi AL | 50.00 | 20.00 | 5.00 |
| ☐ | 97 | Kutina: StL AL | 50.00 | 20.00 | 5.00 |
| ☐ | 98 | Lange: Chi AL | 50.00 | 20.00 | 5.00 |
| ☐ | 99 | Lapp: Phil AL | 25.00 | 10.00 | 2.50 |
| ☐ | 100 | Latham: NY NL | 25.00 | 10.00 | 2.50 |
| ☐ | 101 | Leach: Pitt NL | 25.00 | 10.00 | 2.50 |
| ☐ | 102 | Leifield: Pitt NL | 25.00 | 10.00 | 2.50 |
| ☐ | 103 | Lennox: Chi NL | 25.00 | 10.00 | 2.50 |
| ☐ | 104 | Lewis: Bos AL | 25.00 | 10.00 | 2.50 |
| ☐ | 105A | Lewis: Bos NL (Braves patch on sleeve) | 1200.00 | 500.00 | 125.00 |
| ☐ | 105B | Lewis: Bos NL (nothing on sleeve) | 1500.00 | 600.00 | 150.00 |
| ☐ | 106 | Lively: Det AL | 25.00 | 10.00 | 2.50 |
| ☐ | 107 | Livingston: Cleve AL "A" shirt | 100.00 | 40.00 | 10.00 |
| ☐ | 108 | Livingston: Cleve AL "C" shirt | 100.00 | 40.00 | 10.00 |
| ☐ | 109 | Livingston: Cleve AL "c" shirt | 35.00 | 14.00 | 3.50 |
| ☐ | 110 | Lord: Phil AL | 25.00 | 10.00 | 2.50 |
| ☐ | 111 | Lord: Chi AL | 25.00 | 10.00 | 2.50 |
| ☐ | 112 | Loudermilk: StL NL | 1200.00 | 500.00 | 125.00 |
| ☐ | 113 | Marquard: NY NL | 75.00 | 30.00 | 7.50 |
| ☐ | 114 | Marsans: Cinc NL | 25.00 | 10.00 | 2.50 |
| ☐ | 115 | McBride: Wash AL | 25.00 | 10.00 | 2.50 |
| ☐ | 116 | McCarthy: Pitt NL | 100.00 | 40.00 | 10.00 |
| ☐ | 117 | McDonald: Bos NL | 25.00 | 10.00 | 2.50 |
| ☐ | 118 | McGraw: NY NL | 100.00 | 40.00 | 10.00 |
| ☐ | 119 | McIntire: Chi NL | 25.00 | 10.00 | 2.50 |
| ☐ | 120 | McIntyre: Chi AL | 25.00 | 10.00 | 2.50 |
| ☐ | 121 | McKechnie: Pitt NL | 125.00 | 50.00 | 12.50 |
| ☐ | 122 | McLean: Cinc NL | 25.00 | 10.00 | 2.50 |
| ☐ | 123 | Milan: Wash AL | 25.00 | 10.00 | 2.50 |
| ☐ | 124 | Miller: Pitt NL | 25.00 | 10.00 | 2.50 |
| ☐ | 125 | Miller: Chi NL | 1200.00 | 500.00 | 125.00 |
| ☐ | 126 | Miller: Brk NL | 50.00 | 20.00 | 5.00 |

| | | | | |
|---|---|---|---|---|
| ☐ 127 | Miller: Bos NL | 50.00 | 20.00 | 5.00 |
| ☐ 128 | Mitchell: Cinc NL | 25.00 | 10.00 | 2.50 |
| ☐ 129 | Mitchell: Cleve AL | 35.00 | 14.00 | 3.50 |
| ☐ 130 | Mogridge: Chi AL | 50.00 | 20.00 | 5.00 |
| ☐ 131 | Moore: Phil NL | 50.00 | 20.00 | 5.00 |
| ☐ 132 | Moran: Phil NL | 25.00 | 10.00 | 2.50 |
| ☐ 133 | Morgan: Phil AL | 25.00 | 10.00 | 2.50 |
| ☐ 134 | Morgan: Wash AL | 25.00 | 10.00 | 2.50 |
| ☐ 135 | Moriarity: Det AL | 50.00 | 20.00 | 5.00 |
| ☐ 136 | Mullin: Det AL with "D" on cap | 25.00 | 10.00 | 2.50 |
| ☐ 137 | Mullin: Det AL without "D" on cap | 100.00 | 40.00 | 10.00 |
| ☐ 138 | Needham: Chi NL | 25.00 | 10.00 | 2.50 |
| ☐ 139 | Nelson: StL AL | 50.00 | 20.00 | 5.00 |
| ☐ 140 | Northen: Brk NL | 25.00 | 10.00 | 2.50 |
| ☐ 141 | Nunamaker: Bos AL | 25.00 | 10.00 | 2.50 |
| ☐ 142 | Oakes: StL NL | 25.00 | 10.00 | 2.50 |
| ☐ 143 | O'Brien: Bos AL | 25.00 | 10.00 | 2.50 |
| ☐ 144 | Oldring: Phil AL | 25.00 | 10.00 | 2.50 |
| ☐ 145 | Olson: Cleve AL | 25.00 | 10.00 | 2.50 |
| ☐ 146 | O'Toole: Pitt NL | 25.00 | 10.00 | 2.50 |
| ☐ 147 | Paskert: Phil NL | 25.00 | 10.00 | 2.50 |
| ☐ 148 | Pelty: StL AL | 50.00 | 20.00 | 5.00 |
| ☐ 149 | Perdue: Bos NL | 25.00 | 10.00 | 2.50 |
| ☐ 150 | Peters: Chi AL | 50.00 | 20.00 | 5.00 |
| ☐ 151 | Phelan: Cinc NL | 50.00 | 20.00 | 5.00 |
| ☐ 152 | Quinn: NY AL | 25.00 | 10.00 | 2.50 |
| ☐ 153 | Ragan: Brk NL | 300.00 | 120.00 | 30.00 |
| ☐ 154 | Rasmussen: Phil NL | 225.00 | 90.00 | 22.00 |
| ☐ 155 | Rath: Chi AL | 50.00 | 20.00 | 5.00 |
| ☐ 156 | Reulbach: Chi NL | 25.00 | 10.00 | 2.50 |
| ☐ 157 | Rucker: Brk NL | 25.00 | 10.00 | 2.50 |
| ☐ 158 | Ryan: Cleve AL | 50.00 | 20.00 | 5.00 |
| ☐ 159 | Saier: Chi NL | 400.00 | 160.00 | 40.00 |
| ☐ 160 | Scanlon: Phil NL | 25.00 | 10.00 | 2.50 |
| ☐ 161 | Schaefer: Wash AL | 25.00 | 10.00 | 2.50 |
| ☐ 162 | Schardt: Brk NL | 25.00 | 10.00 | 2.50 |
| ☐ 163 | Schulte: Chi NL | 25.00 | 10.00 | 2.50 |
| ☐ 164 | Scott: Chi AL | 25.00 | 10.00 | 2.50 |
| ☐ 165 | Severeid: Cinc NL | 25.00 | 10.00 | 2.50 |
| ☐ 166 | Simon: Pitt NL | 25.00 | 10.00 | 2.50 |
| ☐ 167 | Smith: StL NL | 25.00 | 10.00 | 2.50 |
| ☐ 168 | Smith: Cinc NL | 25.00 | 10.00 | 2.50 |
| ☐ 169 | Snodgrass: NY NL | 25.00 | 10.00 | 2.50 |
| ☐ 170 | Speaker: Bos AL | 350.00 | 140.00 | 35.00 |

| | | | | |
|---|---|---|---|---|
| ☐ 171 | Spratt: Bos NL | 25.00 | 10.00 | 2.50 |
| ☐ 172 | Stack: Brk NL | 25.00 | 10.00 | 2.50 |
| ☐ 173 | Stanage: Det AL | 25.00 | 10.00 | 2.50 |
| ☐ 174 | Steele: StL NL | 25.00 | 10.00 | 2.50 |
| ☐ 175 | Steinfeldt: StL NL | 25.00 | 10.00 | 2.50 |
| ☐ 176 | Stovall: StL AL | 25.00 | 10.00 | 2.50 |
| ☐ 177 | Street: NY AL | 25.00 | 10.00 | 2.50 |
| ☐ 178 | Strunk: Phil AL | 25.00 | 10.00 | 2.50 |
| ☐ 179 | Sullivan: Chi AL | 25.00 | 10.00 | 2.50 |
| ☐ 180 | Sweeney: Bos NL | 60.00 | 24.00 | 6.00 |
| ☐ 181 | Tannehill: Chi AL | 25.00 | 10.00 | 2.50 |
| ☐ 182 | Thomas: Bos AL | 25.00 | 10.00 | 2.50 |
| ☐ 183 | Tinker: Chi NL | 75.00 | 30.00 | 7.50 |
| ☐ 184 | Tooley: Brk NL | 25.00 | 10.00 | 2.50 |
| ☐ 185 | Turner: Cleve AL | 25.00 | 10.00 | 2.50 |
| ☐ 186 | Tyler: Bos NL | 400.00 | 160.00 | 40.00 |
| ☐ 187 | Vaughn: NY AL | 25.00 | 10.00 | 2.50 |
| ☐ 188 | Wagner: Bos AL correct back | 30.00 | 12.00 | 3.00 |
| ☐ 189 | Wagner: Bos AL Carrigan back | 120.00 | 50.00 | 12.00 |
| ☐ 190 | Walker: Wash AL | 25.00 | 10.00 | 2.50 |
| ☐ 191 | Wallace: St.L. AL | 75.00 | 30.00 | 7.50 |
| ☐ 192 | Warhop: NY AL | 25.00 | 10.00 | 2.50 |
| ☐ 193 | Weaver: Chi AL | 50.00 | 20.00 | 5.00 |
| ☐ 194 | Wheat: Brk NL | 75.00 | 30.00 | 7.50 |
| ☐ 195 | White: Chi AL | 50.00 | 20.00 | 5.00 |
| ☐ 196 | Wilie: St.L. NL | 35.00 | 14.00 | 3.50 |
| ☐ 197 | Williams: NY AL | 25.00 | 10.00 | 2.50 |
| ☐ 198 | Wilson: NY NL | 50.00 | 20.00 | 5.00 |
| ☐ 199 | Wilson: Pitt NL | 25.00 | 10.00 | 2.50 |
| ☐ 200 | Wiltse: NY NL | 25.00 | 10.00 | 2.50 |
| ☐ 201 | Wingo: StL NL | 25.00 | 10.00 | 2.50 |
| ☐ 202 | Wolverton: NY AL | 25.00 | 10.00 | 2.50 |
| ☐ 203 | Wood: Bos AL | 40.00 | 16.00 | 4.00 |
| ☐ 204 | Woodburn: StL NL | 50.00 | 20.00 | 5.00 |
| ☐ 205 | Works: Det AL | 150.00 | 60.00 | 15.00 |
| ☐ 206 | Yerkes: Bos AL | 25.00 | 10.00 | 2.50 |
| ☐ 207 | Zeider: Chi AL | 50.00 | 20.00 | 5.00 |

## 1932 U.S. Caramel

JOSEPH (JOE) CRONIN

The cards in this 32 card set measure 2 1/2" by 3". The U.S. Caramel set of "Famous Athletes" was issued in 1932. The cards contain black and white bust shots set against an attractive red background. The existence of card number 16, Joe Kuhel, has never been verified, which would make the mail-in premium offer described on the card backs "impossible." The ACC designation for this set is R328.

| | | MINT | VG-E | F-G |
|---|---|---|---|---|
| | COMPLETE SET (31) | 7500.00 | 3000.00 | 750.00 |
| | COMMON BASEBALL PLAYER | 150.00 | 60.00 | 15.00 |
| | COMMON BOXER | 75.00 | 30.00 | 7.50 |
| | COMMON GOLFER | 60.00 | 24.00 | 6.00 |
| ☐ 1 | Eddie Collins | 225.00 | 90.00 | 22.00 |
| ☐ 2 | Paul Waner | 200.00 | 80.00 | 20.00 |
| ☐ 3 | Bobby Jones GOLF | 60.00 | 24.00 | 6.00 |
| ☐ 4 | William Terry | 300.00 | 120.00 | 30.00 |
| ☐ 5 | Earl B. Combs | 200.00 | 80.00 | 20.00 |
| ☐ 6 | Bill Dickey | 350.00 | 140.00 | 35.00 |
| ☐ 7 | Joseph Cronin | 250.00 | 100.00 | 25.00 |
| ☐ 8 | Charles Hafey | 200.00 | 80.00 | 20.00 |
| ☐ 9 | Gene Sarazen GOLF | 60.00 | 24.00 | 6.00 |

| | | MINT | VG-E | F-G |
|---|---|---|---|---|
| ☐ 10 | Rabbit Maranville | 200.00 | 80.00 | 20.00 |
| ☐ 11 | Rogers Hornsby | 400.00 | 160.00 | 40.00 |
| ☐ 12 | Mickey Cochrane | 300.00 | 120.00 | 30.00 |
| ☐ 13 | Lloyd Waner | 200.00 | 80.00 | 20.00 |
| ☐ 14 | Ty Cobb | 900.00 | 360.00 | 90.00 |
| ☐ 15 | Gene Tunney BOXER | 150.00 | 60.00 | 15.00 |
| ☐ 16 | Joe Kuhel | 00.00 | 00.00 | 0.00 |
| | (does not exist) | | | |
| ☐ 17 | Al Simmons | 200.00 | 80.00 | 20.00 |
| ☐ 18 | Anthony Lazzeri | 175.00 | 70.00 | 18.00 |
| ☐ 19 | Wally Berger | 150.00 | 60.00 | 15.00 |
| ☐ 20 | Charles Ruffing | 200.00 | 80.00 | 20.00 |
| ☐ 21 | Chuck Klein | 250.00 | 100.00 | 25.00 |
| ☐ 22 | Jack Dempsey BOXER | 150.00 | 60.00 | 15.00 |
| ☐ 23 | Jimmy Foxx | 350.00 | 140.00 | 35.00 |
| ☐ 24 | Lefty O'Doul | 150.00 | 60.00 | 15.00 |
| ☐ 25 | Jack Sharkey BOXER | 60.00 | 24.00 | 6.00 |
| ☐ 26 | Henry Louis Gehrig | 900.00 | 360.00 | 90.00 |
| ☐ 27 | Robert (Lefty) Grove | 350.00 | 140.00 | 35.00 |
| ☐ 28 | Edward Brandt | 150.00 | 60.00 | 15.00 |
| ☐ 29 | George Earnshaw | 150.00 | 60.00 | 15.00 |
| ☐ 30 | Frank Frisch | 250.00 | 100.00 | 25.00 |
| ☐ 31 | Vernon (Lefty) Gomez | 300.00 | 120.00 | 30.00 |
| ☐ 32 | Babe Ruth | 1000.00 | 400.00 | 100.00 |

## 1985 Wendy's Tigers

This 22 card set features Detroit Tigers; cards measure 2 1/2" by 3 1/2". The set was co-sponsored by Wendy's and Coca-Cola and was distributed in the Detroit metropolitian area. Coca-Cola purchasers were given a pack which contained three Tiger cards plus a header card. The orange-bordered player photos are different from those used by Topps in their regular set. The cards were produced by Topps as evidenced by the similarity of the card backs with the Topps regular set backs. The set is numbered on the back; the order corresponds to the alphabetical order of the player's names.

| | | MINT | VG-E | F-G |
|---|---|---|---|---|
| COMPLETE SET | | 7.00 | 2.80 | .70 |
| COMMON PLAYER (1-22) | | .15 | .06 | .01 |
| ☐ 1 | Sparky Anderson MGR | .20 | .08 | .02 |
| | (checklist back) | | | |
| ☐ 2 | Doug Bair | .15 | .06 | .01 |
| ☐ 3 | Juan Berenguer | .15 | .06 | .01 |
| ☐ 4 | Dave Bergman | .15 | .06 | .01 |
| ☐ 5 | Tom Brookens | .15 | .06 | .01 |
| ☐ 6 | Marty Castillo | .15 | .06 | .01 |
| ☐ 7 | Darrell Evans | .30 | .12 | .03 |
| ☐ 8 | Barbaro Garbey | .15 | .06 | .01 |
| ☐ 9 | Kirk Gibson | 1.00 | .40 | .10 |
| ☐ 10 | Johnny Grubb | .15 | .06 | .01 |
| ☐ 11 | Willie Hernandez | .25 | .10 | .02 |
| ☐ 12 | Larry Herndon | .15 | .06 | .01 |
| ☐ 13 | Rusty Kuntz | .15 | .06 | .01 |
| ☐ 14 | Chet Lemon | .20 | .08 | .02 |
| ☐ 15 | Aurelio Lopez | .15 | .06 | .01 |
| ☐ 16 | Jack Morris | 1.00 | .40 | .10 |
| ☐ 17 | Lance Parrish | 1.00 | .40 | .10 |
| ☐ 18 | Dan Petry | .40 | .16 | .04 |
| ☐ 19 | Bill Scherrer | .15 | .06 | .01 |
| ☐ 20 | Alan Trammell | .75 | .30 | .07 |
| ☐ 21 | Lou Whitaker | .75 | .30 | .07 |
| ☐ 22 | Milt Wilcox | .15 | .06 | .01 |

## 1951 Wheaties

The cards in this 6 card set measure 2 1/2" by 3 1/4". Cards of the 1951 Wheaties set are actually the backs of small individual boxes of Wheaties. The cards are waxed and depict three baseball players, one football player, one basketball player and one golfer. They are occasionally found as complete boxes, which are worth 50% more than the prices listed below. The ACC designation for this set is F272-3. The cards are blank-backed and unnumbered; they are numbered below in alphabetical order for convenience.

| | | MINT | VG-E | F-G |
|---|---|---|---|---|
| COMPLETE SET | | 225.00 | 90.00 | 22.00 |
| COMMON PLAYER (1-6) | | 15.00 | 6.00 | 1.50 |
| ☐ 1 | Bob Feller (baseball) | 40.00 | 16.00 | 4.00 |
| ☐ 2 | Johnny Lujack (football) | 25.00 | 10.00 | 2.50 |
| ☐ 3 | George Mikan (basketball) | 25.00 | 10.00 | 2.50 |
| ☐ 4 | Stan Musial (baseball) | 75.00 | 30.00 | 7.50 |
| ☐ 5 | Sam Snead (golfer) | 15.00 | 6.00 | 1.50 |
| ☐ 6 | Ted Williams (baseball) | 100.00 | 40.00 | 10.00 |

## 1952 Wheaties

The cards in this 60 card set measure 2" by 2 3/4". The 1952 Wheaties set of orange, blue and white, unnumbered cards was issued in panels of eight or ten cards on the backs of Wheaties cereal boxes. Each player appears in an action pose, designated in the checklist with an "A", and as a portrait, listed in the checklist with a "B". The ACC designation is F272- 4. The cards are blank-backed and unnumbered; they are numbered below in alphabetical order for convenience.

| | MINT | VG-E | F-G |
|---|---|---|---|
| COMPLETE SET ....................... | 400.00 | 160.00 | 40.00 |
| COMMON BASEBALL ............... | 5.00 | 2.00 | .50 |
| COMMON FOOTBALL ............... | 5.00 | 2.00 | .50 |
| COMMON NON-BASEBALL ........ | 2.00 | .80 | .20 |
| ☐ 1A Alice Bauer ..................... | 2.00 | .80 | .20 |
| ☐ 1B Alice Bauer ..................... | 2.00 | .80 | .20 |
| ☐ 2A Marlene Bauer ................ | 2.00 | .80 | .20 |
| ☐ 2B Marlene Bauer ................ | 2.00 | .80 | .20 |
| ☐ 3A Patty Berg ..................... | 2.00 | .80 | .20 |
| ☐ 3B Patty Berg ..................... | 2.00 | .80 | .20 |
| ☐ 4A Larry (Yogi) Berra .......... | 14.00 | 5.75 | 1.40 |
| ☐ 4B Larry (Yogi) Berra .......... | 14.00 | 5.75 | 1.40 |
| ☐ 5A Roy Campanella ............. | 18.00 | 7.25 | 1.80 |
| ☐ 5B Roy Campanella ............. | 18.00 | 7.25 | 1.80 |
| ☐ 6A Bob Davies .................... | 2.50 | 1.00 | .25 |
| ☐ 6B Bob Davies .................... | 2.50 | 1.00 | .25 |
| ☐ 7A Glenn Davis ................... | 5.00 | 2.00 | .50 |
| ☐ 7B Glenn Davis ................... | 5.00 | 2.00 | .50 |
| ☐ 8A Ned Day ....................... | 2.00 | .80 | .20 |
| ☐ 8B Ned Day ....................... | 2.00 | .80 | .20 |
| ☐ 9A Charles Diehl ................. | 2.00 | .80 | .20 |
| ☐ 9B Charles Diehl ................. | 2.00 | .80 | .20 |
| ☐ 10A Tom Fears ..................... | 5.00 | 2.00 | .50 |
| ☐ 10B Tom Fears ..................... | 5.00 | 2.00 | .50 |
| ☐ 11A Bob Feller ..................... | 14.00 | 5.75 | 1.40 |
| ☐ 11B Bob Feller ..................... | 14.00 | 5.75 | 1.40 |
| ☐ 12A Gretchen Fraser ............ | 2.00 | .80 | .20 |
| ☐ 12B Gretchen Fraser ............ | 2.00 | .80 | .20 |
| ☐ 13A Otto Graham ................. | 9.00 | 3.75 | .90 |
| ☐ 13B Otto Graham ................. | 9.00 | 3.75 | .90 |
| ☐ 14A Ben Hogan .................... | 4.00 | 1.60 | .40 |
| ☐ 14B Ben Hogan .................... | 4.00 | 1.60 | .40 |
| ☐ 15A George Kell .................. | 9.00 | 3.75 | .90 |
| ☐ 15B George Kell .................. | 9.00 | 3.75 | .90 |
| ☐ 16A Ralph Kiner ................... | 9.00 | 3.75 | .90 |
| ☐ 16B Ralph Kiner ................... | 9.00 | 3.75 | .90 |
| ☐ 17A Jack Kramer .................. | 3.00 | 1.20 | .30 |
| ☐ 17B Jack Kramer .................. | 3.00 | 1.20 | .30 |
| ☐ 18A Bob Lemon .................... | 9.00 | 3.75 | .90 |
| ☐ 18B Bob Lemon .................... | 9.00 | 3.75 | .90 |
| ☐ 19A Johnny Lujack ............... | 5.00 | 2.00 | .50 |
| ☐ 19B Johnny Lujack ............... | 5.00 | 2.00 | .50 |
| ☐ 20A Lloyd Mangrum .............. | 2.00 | .80 | .20 |
| ☐ 20B Lloyd Mangrum .............. | 2.00 | .80 | .20 |
| ☐ 21A George Mikan ................ | 8.00 | 3.25 | .80 |
| ☐ 21B George Mikan ................ | 8.00 | 3.25 | .80 |
| ☐ 22A Stan Musial ................... | 25.00 | 10.00 | 2.50 |
| ☐ 22B Stan Musial ................... | 25.00 | 10.00 | 2.50 |
| ☐ 23A Jimmy Patterson ............ | 2.00 | .80 | .20 |
| ☐ 23B Jimmy Patterson ............ | 2.00 | .80 | .20 |
| ☐ 24A Jim Pollard ................... | 3.00 | 1.20 | .30 |
| ☐ 24B Jim Pollard ................... | 3.00 | 1.20 | .30 |
| ☐ 25A Phil Rizzuto .................. | 10.00 | 4.00 | 1.00 |
| ☐ 25B Phil Rizzuto .................. | 10.00 | 4.00 | 1.00 |
| ☐ 26A Elwin (Preacher) Roe ...... | 5.00 | 2.00 | .50 |
| ☐ 26B Elwin (Preacher) Roe ..... | 5.00 | 2.00 | .50 |
| ☐ 27A Sam Snead ................... | 4.00 | 1.60 | .40 |
| ☐ 27B Sam Snead ................... | 4.00 | 1.60 | .40 |
| ☐ 28A Doak Walker .................. | 7.50 | 3.00 | .75 |
| ☐ 28B Doak Walker .................. | 7.50 | 3.00 | .75 |
| ☐ 29A Bob Waterfield .............. | 6.00 | 2.40 | .60 |
| ☐ 29B Bob Waterfield .............. | 6.00 | 2.40 | .60 |
| ☐ 30A Ted Williams ................. | 30.00 | 12.00 | 3.00 |
| ☐ 30B Ted Williams ................. | 30.00 | 12.00 | 3.00 |

THE WHEATIES
...ble, irresistible ...ispy, crunchy ...at taste of

LEN BARKER
Pitcher

WHEATIES

...TIES.

of Champions.

color picture, player name and position. The cards are not numbered and the backs contain a Wheaties ad. The set was later sold at the Cleveland Indians gift shop. The cards are ordered below alphabetically within groups of ten as they were issued.

| | MINT | VG-E | F-G |
|---|---|---|---|
| COMPLETE SET ......................... | 6.00 | 2.40 | .60 |
| COMMON PLAYER ...................... | .15 | .06 | .01 |
| ☐ 1 Bert Blyleven ................... | .60 | .24 | .06 |
| ☐ 2 Joe Charboneau ............... | .25 | .10 | .02 |
| ☐ 3 Jerry Dybzinski ................ | .15 | .06 | .01 |
| ☐ 4 Dave Garcia MGR ............ | .15 | .06 | .01 |
| ☐ 5 Toby Harrah ................... | .35 | .14 | .03 |
| ☐ 6 Ron Hassey .................... | .15 | .06 | .01 |
| ☐ 7 Dennis Lewallyn .............. | .15 | .06 | .01 |
| ☐ 8 Rick Manning .................. | .20 | .08 | .02 |
| ☐ 9 Tommy McCraw COACH ... | .15 | .06 | .01 |
| ☐ 10 Rick Waits ..................... | .20 | .08 | .02 |
| ☐ 11 Chris Bando ................... | .20 | .08 | .02 |
| ☐ 12 Len Barker .................... | .25 | .10 | .02 |
| ☐ 13 Tom Brennan ................. | .15 | .06 | .01 |
| ☐ 14 Rodney Craig ................. | .15 | .06 | .01 |
| ☐ 15 Mike Fischlin .................. | .15 | .06 | .01 |
| ☐ 16 Johnny Goryl COACH ...... | .15 | .06 | .01 |
| ☐ 17 Mel Queen COACH .......... | .15 | .06 | .01 |
| ☐ 18 Lary Sorensen ................ | .20 | .08 | .02 |
| ☐ 19 Andre Thornton .............. | .50 | .20 | .05 |
| ☐ 20 Eddie Whitson ................ | .25 | .10 | .02 |
| ☐ 21 Alan Bannister ............... | .15 | .06 | .01 |
| ☐ 22 John Denny ................... | .35 | .14 | .03 |
| ☐ 23 Miguel Dilone ................ | .15 | .06 | .01 |
| ☐ 24 Mike Hargrove ............... | .25 | .10 | .02 |
| ☐ 25 Von Hayes .................... | .75 | .30 | .07 |
| ☐ 26 Bake McBride ................ | .20 | .08 | .02 |
| ☐ 27 Jack Perconte ................ | .15 | .06 | .01 |
| ☐ 28 Dennis Sommers COACH .. | .15 | .06 | .01 |
| ☐ 29 Dan Spillner .................. | .20 | .08 | .02 |
| ☐ 30 Rick Sutcliffe ................. | .40 | .16 | .04 |

## 1982 Wheaties Indians

The cards in this 30 card set measure 2 13/16" by 4 1/8". This set of Cleveland Indians baseball players was co- produced by the Indians baseball club and Wheaties, whose respective logos appear on the front of every card. The cards were given away in groups of 10 as a promotion during games on May 30 (1-10), June 19 (11-20) and July 16, 1982 (21-30). The manager (MGR), four coaches (CO), and 25 players are featured in a simple format of a

## 1983 Wheaties Indians

The cards in this 32 card set measure 2 13/16" by 4 1/8". The full color set of 1983 Wheaties Indians is quite similar to the Wheaties set of 1982. The backs, however, are significantly different. They contain complete career playing records of the players. The complete sets were given away at the ball park on May 15, 1983. The set was later made available at the Indians Gift Shop. The manager

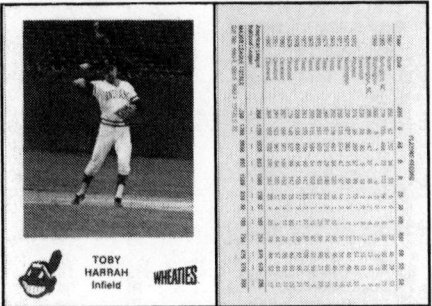

TOBY HARRAH
Infield WHEATIES

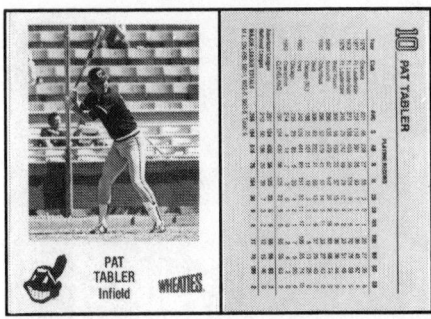

PAT TABLER
Infield WHEATIES

(MGR) and several coaches (CO) are included in the set. The cards below are ordered alphabetically by the subject's name.

| | MINT | VG-E | F-G |
|---|---|---|---|
| COMPLETE SET | 6.00 | 2.40 | .60 |
| COMMON PLAYER | .15 | .06 | .01 |

| | | MINT | VG-E | F-G |
|---|---|---|---|---|
| ☐ 1 | Bud Anderson | .15 | .06 | .01 |
| ☐ 2 | Jay Baller | .20 | .08 | .02 |
| ☐ 3 | Chris Bando | .15 | .06 | .01 |
| ☐ 4 | Alan Bannister | .15 | .06 | .01 |
| ☐ 5 | Len Barker | .25 | .10 | .02 |
| ☐ 6 | Bert Blyleven | .50 | .20 | .05 |
| ☐ 7 | Wil Culmer | .20 | .08 | .02 |
| ☐ 8 | Miguel Dilone | .15 | .06 | .01 |
| ☐ 9 | Juan Eichelberger | .15 | .06 | .01 |
| ☐ 10 | Jim Essian | .15 | .06 | .01 |
| ☐ 11 | Mike Ferraro MGR | .15 | .06 | .01 |
| ☐ 12 | Mike Fischlin | .15 | .06 | .01 |
| ☐ 13 | Julio Franco | .75 | .30 | .07 |
| ☐ 14 | Ed Glynn | .15 | .06 | .01 |
| ☐ 15 | Johnny Goryl COACH | .15 | .06 | .01 |
| ☐ 16 | Mike Hargrove | .25 | .10 | .02 |
| ☐ 17 | Toby Harrah | .30 | .12 | .03 |
| ☐ 18 | Ron Hassey | .15 | .06 | .01 |
| ☐ 19 | Neal Heaton | .20 | .08 | .02 |
| ☐ 20 | Rick Manning | .20 | .08 | .02 |
| ☐ 21 | Bake McBride | .20 | .08 | .02 |
| ☐ 22 | Don McMahon COACH | .15 | .06 | .01 |
| ☐ 23 | Ed Napoleon COACH | .15 | .06 | .01 |
| ☐ 24 | Broderick Perkins | .15 | .06 | .01 |
| ☐ 25 | Dennis Sommers COACH | .15 | .06 | .01 |
| ☐ 26 | Lary Sorensen | .20 | .08 | .02 |
| ☐ 27 | Dan Spillner | .20 | .08 | .02 |
| ☐ 28 | Rick Sutcliffe | .40 | .16 | .04 |
| ☐ 29 | Andre Thornton | .40 | .16 | .04 |
| ☐ 30 | Manny Trillo | .20 | .08 | .02 |
| ☐ 31 | George Vukovich | .15 | .06 | .01 |
| ☐ 32 | Rick Waits | .20 | .08 | .02 |

| | | MINT | VG-E | F-G |
|---|---|---|---|---|
| COMMON PLAYER | | .15 | .06 | .01 |
| ☐ 2 | Brett Butler | .50 | .20 | .05 |
| ☐ 4 | Tony Bernazard | .25 | .10 | .02 |
| ☐ 8 | Carmelo Castillo | .15 | .06 | .01 |
| ☐ 10 | Pat Tabler | .45 | .18 | .04 |
| ☐ 13 | Ernie Camacho | .25 | .10 | .02 |
| ☐ 14 | Julio Franco | .50 | .20 | .05 |
| ☐ 15 | Broderick Perkins | .15 | .06 | .01 |
| ☐ 16 | Jerry Willard | .20 | .08 | .02 |
| ☐ 18 | Pat Corrales MGR | .15 | .06 | .01 |
| ☐ 21 | Mike Hargrove | .25 | .10 | .02 |
| ☐ 22 | Mike Fischlin | .15 | .06 | .01 |
| ☐ 23 | Chris Bando | .15 | .06 | .01 |
| ☐ 24 | George Vukovich | .15 | .06 | .01 |
| ☐ 26 | Brook Jacoby | .50 | .20 | .05 |
| ☐ 27 | Steve Farr | .20 | .08 | .02 |
| ☐ 28 | Bert Blyleven | .45 | .18 | .04 |
| ☐ 29 | Andre Thornton | .35 | .14 | .03 |
| ☐ 30 | Joe Carter | .75 | .30 | .07 |
| ☐ 31 | Steve Comer | .15 | .06 | .01 |
| ☐ 33 | Roy Smith | .20 | .08 | .02 |
| ☐ 34 | Mel Hall | .45 | .18 | .04 |
| ☐ 37 | Don Schulze | .20 | .08 | .02 |
| ☐ 38 | Luis Aponte | .15 | .06 | .01 |
| ☐ 44 | Neal Heaton | .20 | .08 | .02 |
| ☐ 46 | Mike Jeffcoat | .20 | .08 | .02 |
| ☐ 54 | Tom Waddell | .20 | .08 | .02 |
| ☐ xx | Indians Coaches: (unnumbered) John Goryl Dennis Sommers Ed Napoleon Bobby Bonds Don McMahon | .15 | .06 | .01 |
| ☐ xx | Tom-E-Hawk (Mascot) (unnumbered) | .15 | .06 | .01 |

## 1954 Wilson

The cards in this 20 card set measure 2 5/8" by 3 3/4". The 1954 "Wilson Weiners" set contains 20 full color, unnumbered cards. The obverse design of a package of hot dogs appearing to fly through the air is a distinctive feature of this set. Uncut sheets have been seen. Cards are numbered below alphabetically by player's name.

| | | MINT | VG-E | F-G |
|---|---|---|---|---|
| COMPLETE SET | | 2500.00 | 1000.00 | 250.00 |
| COMMON PLAYER (1-20) | | 75.00 | 30.00 | 7.50 |
| ☐ 1 | Roy Campanella | 300.00 | 120.00 | 30.00 |
| ☐ 2 | Del Ennis | 75.00 | 30.00 | 7.50 |
| ☐ 3 | Carl Erskine | 90.00 | 36.00 | 9.00 |
| ☐ 4 | Ferris Fain | 75.00 | 30.00 | 7.50 |
| ☐ 5 | Bob Feller | 250.00 | 100.00 | 25.00 |
| ☐ 6 | Nelson Fox | 125.00 | 50.00 | 12.50 |

## 1984 Wheaties Indians

The cards in this 29 card set measure 2 13/16" by 4 1/8". For the third straight year, Wheaties distributed a set of Cleveland Indians baseball cards. These over-sized cards were passed out at a Baseball Card Day at the Cleveland Stadium. Similar in appearance to the cards of the past two years, both the Indians and the Wheaties logos appear on the obverse, along with the name, team and position. Cards are numbered on the back by the player's uniform number.

| | MINT | VG-E | F-G |
|---|---|---|---|
| COMPLETE SET | 6.00 | 2.40 | .60 |

| | | | | |
|---|---|---|---|---|
| ☐ 7 | Johnny Groth | 75.00 | 30.00 | 7.50 |
| ☐ 8 | Stan Hack | 75.00 | 30.00 | 7.50 |
| ☐ 9 | Gil Hodges | 175.00 | 70.00 | 18.00 |
| ☐ 10 | Ray Jablonski | 75.00 | 30.00 | 7.50 |
| ☐ 11 | Harvey Kuenn | 100.00 | 40.00 | 10.00 |
| ☐ 12 | Roy McMillan | 75.00 | 30.00 | 7.50 |
| ☐ 13 | Andy Pafko | 75.00 | 30.00 | 7.50 |
| ☐ 14 | Paul Richards MGR | 75.00 | 30.00 | 7.50 |
| ☐ 15 | Hank Sauer | 75.00 | 30.00 | 7.50 |
| ☐ 16 | Red Schoendienst | 90.00 | 36.00 | 9.00 |
| ☐ 17 | Enos Slaughter | 175.00 | 70.00 | 18.00 |
| ☐ 18 | Vern Stephens | 75.00 | 30.00 | 7.50 |
| ☐ 19 | Sammy White | 75.00 | 30.00 | 7.50 |
| ☐ 20 | Ted Williams | 1000.00 | 400.00 | 100.00 |

| | | | | |
|---|---|---|---|---|
| ☐ 7 | Jack Chesbro | .05 | .02 | .00 |
| ☐ 8 | Ty Cobb | .25 | .10 | .02 |
| ☐ 9 | Sam Crawford | .05 | .02 | .00 |
| ☐ 10 | Rollie Fingers | .05 | .02 | .00 |
| ☐ 11 | Whitey Ford | .07 | .03 | .01 |
| ☐ 12 | John Frederick | .05 | .02 | .00 |
| ☐ 13 | Frankie Frisch | .05 | .02 | .00 |
| ☐ 14 | Lou Gehrig | .20 | .08 | .02 |
| ☐ 15 | Jim Gentile | .05 | .02 | .00 |
| ☐ 16 | Dwight Gooden | .30 | .12 | .03 |
| ☐ 17 | Rickey Henderson | .15 | .06 | .01 |
| ☐ 18 | Rogers Hornsby | .10 | .04 | .01 |
| ☐ 19 | Frank Howard | .05 | .02 | .00 |
| ☐ 20 | Cliff Johnson | .05 | .02 | .00 |
| ☐ 21 | Walter Johnson | .15 | .06 | .01 |
| ☐ 22 | Hub Leonard | .05 | .02 | .00 |
| ☐ 23 | Mickey Mantle | .35 | .14 | .03 |
| ☐ 24 | Roger Maris | .10 | .04 | .01 |
| ☐ 25 | Christy Mathewson | .10 | .04 | .01 |
| ☐ 26 | Willie Mays | .10 | .04 | .01 |
| ☐ 27 | Stan Musial | .10 | .04 | .01 |
| ☐ 28 | Don Quisenberry | .05 | .02 | .00 |
| ☐ 29 | Frank Robinson | .07 | .03 | .01 |
| ☐ 30 | Pete Rose | .35 | .14 | .03 |
| ☐ 31 | Babe Ruth | .35 | .14 | .03 |
| ☐ 32 | Nolan Ryan | .15 | .06 | .01 |
| ☐ 33 | George Sisler | .05 | .02 | .00 |
| ☐ 34 | Tris Speaker | .10 | .04 | .01 |
| ☐ 35 | Ed Walsh | .05 | .02 | .00 |
| ☐ 36 | Lloyd Waner | .05 | .02 | .00 |
| ☐ 37 | Earl Webb | .05 | .02 | .00 |
| ☐ 38 | Ted Williams | .15 | .06 | .01 |
| ☐ 39 | Maury Wills | .05 | .02 | .00 |
| ☐ 40 | Hack Wilson | .07 | .03 | .01 |
| ☐ 41 | Owen Wilson | .05 | .02 | .00 |
| ☐ 42 | Willie Wilson | .05 | .02 | .00 |
| ☐ 43 | Rudy York | .05 | .02 | .00 |
| ☐ 44 | Cy Young | .10 | .04 | .01 |

## 1985 Woolworth's

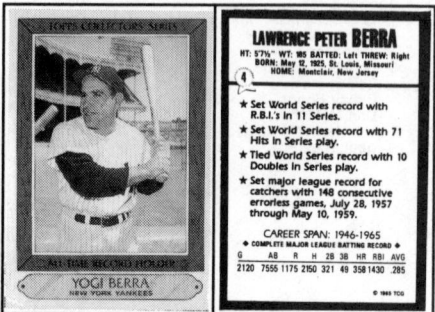

This 44 card set features color as well as black and white cards of All Time Record Holders. The cards are standard size (2 1/2" by 3 1/2") and are printed with blue ink on an orange and white back. The set was produced for Woolworth's by Topps and was packaged in a colorful box which contained a checklist of the cards in the set on the back panel. The numerical order of the cards coincides alphabetically with player's name.

| | | MINT | VG-E | F-G |
|---|---|---|---|---|
| COMPLETE SET | | 3.75 | 1.25 | .30 |
| COMMON PLAYER | | .05 | .02 | .00 |
| ☐ 1 | Hank Aaron | .12 | .05 | .01 |
| ☐ 2 | Grover C. Alexander | .05 | .02 | .00 |
| ☐ 3 | Ernie Banks | .10 | .04 | .01 |
| ☐ 4 | Yogi Berra | .10 | .04 | .01 |
| ☐ 5 | Lou Brock | .07 | .03 | .01 |
| ☐ 6 | Steve Carlton | .07 | .03 | .01 |

## 1986 Woolworth's

This boxed set of 33 cards was produced by Topps for Woolworth's variety stores. The set features players who hold or have held hitting, home run or RBI titles. Cards are the standard 2 1/2" by 3 1/2" and have a glossy finish. The card fronts are bordered in yellow with the subtitle "Topps Collectors' Series" across the top. The card backs are printed in green and blue ink on white card stock. The custom box gives the set checklist on the back.

| | | MINT | VG-E | F-G |
|---|---|---|---|---|
| COMPLETE SET | | 3.75 | 1.25 | .30 |
| COMMON PLAYER | | .10 | .04 | .01 |
| ☐ 1 | Tony Armas | .10 | .04 | .01 |
| ☐ 2 | Don Baylor | .15 | .06 | .01 |
| ☐ 3 | Wade Boggs | .60 | .24 | .06 |
| ☐ 4 | George Brett | .40 | .16 | .04 |
| ☐ 5 | Bill Buckner | .10 | .04 | .01 |
| ☐ 6 | Rod Carew | .30 | .12 | .03 |
| ☐ 7 | Gary Carter | .30 | .12 | .03 |
| ☐ 8 | Cecil Cooper | .15 | .06 | .01 |
| ☐ 9 | Darrell Evans | .10 | .04 | .01 |

| | | MINT | VG-E | F-G |
|---|---|---|---|---|
| ☐ 10 | Dwight Evans | .10 | .04 | .01 |
| ☐ 11 | George Foster | .15 | .06 | .01 |
| ☐ 12 | Bob Grich | .10 | .04 | .01 |
| ☐ 13 | Tony Gwynn | .30 | .12 | .03 |
| ☐ 14 | Keith Hernandez | .20 | .08 | .02 |
| ☐ 15 | Reggie Jackson | .40 | .16 | .04 |
| ☐ 16 | Dave Kingman | .15 | .06 | .01 |
| ☐ 17 | Carney Lansford | .15 | .06 | .01 |
| ☐ 18 | Fred Lynn | .15 | .06 | .01 |
| ☐ 19 | Bill Madlock | .15 | .06 | .01 |
| ☐ 20 | Don Mattingly | .75 | .30 | .07 |
| ☐ 21 | Willie McGee | .20 | .08 | .02 |
| ☐ 22 | Hal McRae | .10 | .04 | .01 |
| ☐ 23 | Dale Murphy | .50 | .20 | .05 |
| ☐ 24 | Eddie Murray | .35 | .14 | .03 |
| ☐ 25 | Ben Oglivie | .10 | .04 | .01 |
| ☐ 26 | Al Oliver | .15 | .06 | .01 |
| ☐ 27 | Dave Parker | .20 | .08 | .02 |
| ☐ 28 | Jim Rice | .30 | .12 | .03 |
| ☐ 29 | Pete Rose | .50 | .20 | .05 |
| ☐ 30 | Mike Schmidt | .40 | .16 | .04 |
| ☐ 31 | Gorman Thomas | .15 | .06 | .01 |
| ☐ 32 | Willie Wilson | .15 | .06 | .01 |
| ☐ 33 | Dave Winfield | .30 | .12 | .03 |

## 1931 W517

The cards in this 54 card set measure 3" by 4". This 1931 set of numbered, blank backed cards was placed in the "W" category in the ACC because (1) its producer was unknown and (2) it was issued in strips of three. The photo is black and white but the entire obverse of each card is generally found tinted in tones of sepia, blue, green, yellow, rose, black or gray. The cards are numbered in a small circle on the front. A solid dark line at one end of a card entitled the purchaser to another piece of candy as a prize. There are two different cards of both Babe Ruth and Mickey Cochrane.

| | | MINT | VG-E | F-G |
|---|---|---|---|---|
| COMPLETE SET | | 2000.00 | 800.00 | 200.00 |
| COMMON PLAYER (1-54) | | 16.00 | 6.50 | 1.60 |
| ☐ 1 | Earl Combs | 30.00 | 12.00 | 3.00 |
| ☐ 2 | Pie Traynor | 35.00 | 14.00 | 3.50 |
| ☐ 3 | Eddie Rousch | 35.00 | 14.00 | 3.50 |
| ☐ 4 | Babe Ruth | 350.00 | 140.00 | 35.00 |
| ☐ 5 | Chalmer Cissell | 16.00 | 6.50 | 1.60 |
| ☐ 6 | Bill Sherdel | 16.00 | 6.50 | 1.60 |
| ☐ 7 | Bill Shore | 16.00 | 6.50 | 1.60 |
| ☐ 8 | George Earnshaw | 16.00 | 6.50 | 1.60 |
| ☐ 9 | Bucky Harris | 30.00 | 12.00 | 3.00 |
| ☐ 10 | Charlie Klein | 35.00 | 14.00 | 3.50 |
| ☐ 11 | George Kelly | 30.00 | 12.00 | 3.00 |
| ☐ 12 | Travis Jackson | 30.00 | 12.00 | 3.00 |

| | | MINT | VG-E | F-G |
|---|---|---|---|---|
| ☐ 13 | Willie Kamm | 16.00 | 6.50 | 1.60 |
| ☐ 14 | Harry Heilman | 35.00 | 14.00 | 3.50 |
| ☐ 15 | Grover Alexander | 45.00 | 18.00 | 4.50 |
| ☐ 16 | Frank Frisch | 40.00 | 16.00 | 4.00 |
| ☐ 17 | Jack Quinn | 16.00 | 6.50 | 1.60 |
| ☐ 18 | Cy Williams | 16.00 | 6.50 | 1.60 |
| ☐ 19 | Kiki Cuyler | 30.00 | 12.00 | 3.00 |
| ☐ 20 | Babe Ruth | 400.00 | 160.00 | 40.00 |
| ☐ 21 | Jimmy Foxx | 90.00 | 36.00 | 9.00 |
| ☐ 22 | Jimmy Dykes | 16.00 | 6.50 | 1.60 |
| ☐ 23 | Bill Terry | 40.00 | 16.00 | 4.00 |
| ☐ 24 | Freddy Lindstrom | 30.00 | 12.00 | 3.00 |
| ☐ 25 | Hugh Critz | 16.00 | 6.50 | 1.60 |
| ☐ 26 | Pete Donahue | 16.00 | 6.50 | 1.60 |
| ☐ 27 | Tony Lazzeri | 20.00 | 8.00 | 2.00 |
| ☐ 28 | Heine Manush | 30.00 | 12.00 | 3.00 |
| ☐ 29 | Chick Hafey | 30.00 | 12.00 | 3.00 |
| ☐ 30 | Melvin Ott | 50.00 | 20.00 | 5.00 |
| ☐ 31 | Bing Miller | 16.00 | 6.50 | 1.60 |
| ☐ 32 | George Haas | 16.00 | 6.50 | 1.60 |
| ☐ 33 | Lefty O'Doul | 20.00 | 8.00 | 2.00 |
| ☐ 34 | Paul Waner | 30.00 | 12.00 | 3.00 |
| ☐ 35 | Lou Gehrig | 225.00 | 90.00 | 22.00 |
| ☐ 36 | Dazzy Vance | 30.00 | 12.00 | 3.00 |
| ☐ 37 | Mickey Cochrane | 45.00 | 18.00 | 4.50 |
| ☐ 38 | Rogers Hornsby | 90.00 | 36.00 | 9.00 |
| ☐ 39 | Lefty Grove | 60.00 | 24.00 | 6.00 |
| ☐ 40 | Al Simmons | 40.00 | 16.00 | 4.00 |
| ☐ 41 | Rube Walberg | 16.00 | 6.50 | 1.60 |
| ☐ 42 | Hack Wilson | 50.00 | 20.00 | 5.00 |
| ☐ 43 | Art Shires | 16.00 | 6.50 | 1.60 |
| ☐ 44 | Sammy Hale | 16.00 | 6.50 | 1.60 |
| ☐ 45 | Ted Lyons | 30.00 | 12.00 | 3.00 |
| ☐ 46 | Joe Sewell | 30.00 | 12.00 | 3.00 |
| ☐ 47 | Goose Goslin | 30.00 | 12.00 | 3.00 |
| ☐ 48 | Lou Fonseca | 16.00 | 6.50 | 1.60 |
| ☐ 49 | Bob Meusel | 16.00 | 6.50 | 1.60 |
| ☐ 50 | Lu Blue | 16.00 | 6.50 | 1.60 |
| ☐ 51 | Earl Averill | 30.00 | 12.00 | 3.00 |
| ☐ 52 | Eddy Collins | 35.00 | 14.00 | 3.50 |
| ☐ 53 | Joe Judge | 16.00 | 6.50 | 1.60 |
| ☐ 54 | Mickey Cochrane | 45.00 | 18.00 | 4.50 |

## 1938-39 W711-1

**EDDIE JOOST**
*Infielder*

Reserve infielder of the Reds, made the All-Star team of the American Association last season. Came to the Reds as a shortstop three years ago, but is now a second baseman. He can also play third. Joost is one of the many players who learned the rudiments of baseball around San Francisco.

The cards in this 32 card set measure 2" by 3". The 1938-39 Cincinnati Reds Baseball player set was printed in orange and gray tones. Many back variations exist and there are two poses of Vander Meer, portrait (PORT) and an action (ACT) poses. The set was sold at the ballpark and was printed on thin cardboard stock. The cards are unnumbered but have been alphabetized and numbered in the checklist below.

| | | MINT | VG-E | F-G |
|---|---|---|---|---|
| COMPLETE SET | | 300.00 | 120.00 | 30.00 |
| COMMON PLAYER (1-32) | | 7.00 | 2.80 | .70 |
| ☐ 1 | Wally Berger (2) | 8.00 | 3.25 | .80 |
| ☐ 2 | Nino Bongiovanni (39) | 30.00 | 12.00 | 3.00 |
| ☐ 3 | Stanley Bordagaray Frenchy (39) | 30.00 | 12.00 | 3.00 |

| | | MINT | VG-E | F-G |
|---|---|---|---|---|
| ☐ 4 | Joe Cascarella (38) | 7.00 | 2.80 | .70 |
| ☐ 5 | Allen Dusty Cooke (38) | 7.00 | 2.80 | .70 |
| ☐ 6 | Harry Craft | 7.00 | 2.80 | .70 |
| ☐ 7 | Ray (Peaches) Davis | 7.00 | 2.80 | .70 |
| ☐ 8 | Paul Derringer (2) | 10.00 | 4.00 | 1.00 |
| ☐ 9 | Linus Frey (2) | 7.00 | 2.80 | .70 |
| ☐ 10 | Lee Gamble (2) | 7.00 | 2.80 | .70 |
| ☐ 11 | Ival Goodman (2) | 7.00 | 2.80 | .70 |
| ☐ 12 | Hank Gowdy (2) | 7.00 | 2.80 | .70 |
| ☐ 13 | Lee Grissom (2) | 7.00 | 2.80 | .70 |
| ☐ 14 | Willard Hershberger (2) | 8.00 | 3.25 | .80 |
| ☐ 15 | Eddie Joost (39) | 7.00 | 2.80 | .70 |
| ☐ 16 | Wes Livengood (39) | 50.00 | 20.00 | 5.00 |
| ☐ 17 | Ernie Lombardi (2) | 20.00 | 8.00 | 2.00 |
| ☐ 18 | Frank McCormick | 9.00 | 3.75 | .90 |
| ☐ 19 | Bill McKechnie (2) | 15.00 | 6.00 | 1.50 |
| ☐ 20 | Lloyd Whitey Moore (2) | 7.00 | 2.80 | .70 |
| ☐ 21 | Billy Myers (2) | 7.00 | 2.80 | .70 |
| ☐ 22 | Lew Riggs (2) | 7.00 | 2.80 | .70 |
| ☐ 23 | Eddie Roush COA (38) | 20.00 | 8.00 | 2.00 |
| ☐ 24 | Les Scarsella (39) | 7.00 | 2.80 | .70 |
| ☐ 25 | Gene Schott (38) | 7.00 | 2.80 | .70 |
| ☐ 26 | Eugene Thompson | 7.00 | 2.80 | .70 |
| ☐ 27 | Johnny VanderMeer PORT | 15.00 | 6.00 | 1.50 |
| ☐ 28 | Johnny VanderMeer ACT | 15.00 | 6.00 | 1.50 |
| ☐ 29 | Wm.(Bucky) Walters (2) | 9.00 | 3.75 | .90 |
| ☐ 30 | Jim Weaver | 7.00 | 2.80 | .70 |
| ☐ 31 | Bill Werber (39) | 7.00 | 2.80 | .70 |
| ☐ 32 | Jimmy Wilson (39) | 7.00 | 2.80 | .70 |

| | | MINT | VG-E | F-G |
|---|---|---|---|---|
| ☐ 20 | Lewis Riggs | 8.00 | 3.25 | .80 |
| ☐ 21 | James A. Ripple | 8.00 | 3.25 | .80 |
| ☐ 22 | Milburn Shoffner | 8.00 | 3.25 | .80 |
| ☐ 23 | Eugene Thompson | 8.00 | 3.25 | .80 |
| ☐ 24 | James Turner | 8.00 | 3.25 | .80 |
| ☐ 25 | John VanderMeer | 15.00 | 6.00 | 1.50 |
| ☐ 26 | Bucky Walters | 10.00 | 4.00 | 1.00 |
| ☐ 27 | Bill Werber | 8.00 | 3.25 | .80 |
| ☐ 28 | James Wilson | 8.00 | 3.25 | .80 |
| ☐ 29 | Results 1940 World Series | 5.00 | 2.00 | .50 |
| ☐ 30 | The Cincinati Reds (Title Card) | 5.00 | 2.00 | .50 |
| ☐ 31 | The Cincinnati Reds World's Champions (Title Card) | 5.00 | 2.00 | .50 |
| ☐ 32 | Debt of Gratitude to Wm. Koehl Co. | 5.00 | 2.00 | .50 |
| ☐ 33 | Tell the World About Our Reds | 5.00 | 2.00 | .50 |
| ☐ 34 | Harry Hartman | 5.00 | 2.00 | .50 |

# 1941 W753 Browns

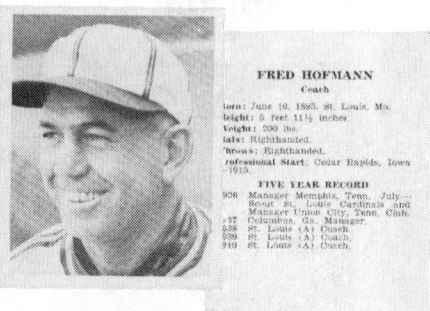

The cards in this 30 card set measure 2 1/8" by 2 5/8". The 1941 W753 set features unnumbered cards of the St. Louis Browns. The cards are numbered below alphabetically by player's name.

| | | MINT | VG-E | F-G |
|---|---|---|---|---|
| COMPLETE SET | | 275.00 | 110.00 | 27.00 |
| COMMON PLAYER (1-30) | | 9.00 | 3.75 | .90 |
| ☐ 1 | Johnny Allen | 9.00 | 3.75 | .90 |
| ☐ 2 | Elden Auker | 9.00 | 3.75 | .90 |
| ☐ 3 | Donald L. Barnes | 9.00 | 3.75 | .90 |
| ☐ 4 | Johnny Beradino | 10.00 | 4.00 | 1.00 |
| ☐ 5 | George Caster | 9.00 | 3.75 | .90 |
| ☐ 6 | Harland Clift | 9.00 | 3.75 | .90 |
| ☐ 7 | Roy J. Cullenbine | 9.00 | 3.75 | .90 |
| ☐ 8 | William O. DeWitt | 9.00 | 3.75 | .90 |
| ☐ 9 | Robert Estalella | 9.00 | 3.75 | .90 |
| ☐ 10 | Rick Ferrell | 25.00 | 10.00 | 2.50 |
| ☐ 11 | Dennis W. Galehouse | 9.00 | 3.75 | .90 |
| ☐ 12 | Joseph L. Grace | 9.00 | 3.75 | .90 |
| ☐ 13 | Frank Grube | 9.00 | 3.75 | .90 |
| ☐ 14 | Robert A. Harris | 9.00 | 3.75 | .90 |
| ☐ 15 | Donald Heffner | 9.00 | 3.75 | .90 |
| ☐ 16 | Fred Hofmann | 9.00 | 3.75 | .90 |
| ☐ 17 | Walter F. Judnich | 9.00 | 3.75 | .90 |
| ☐ 18 | Jack Kramer | 9.00 | 3.75 | .90 |
| ☐ 19 | Chester (Chet) Laabs | 9.00 | 3.75 | .90 |
| ☐ 20 | John Lucadello | 9.00 | 3.75 | .90 |
| ☐ 21 | George Hartley | 9.00 | 3.75 | .90 |
| ☐ 22 | George McQuinn | 9.00 | 3.75 | .90 |
| ☐ 23 | Robert Muncrief Jr. | 9.00 | 3.75 | .90 |
| ☐ 24 | John Niggeling | 9.00 | 3.75 | .90 |
| ☐ 25 | Fritz Ostermueller | 9.00 | 3.75 | .90 |
| ☐ 26 | James (Luke) Sewell | 12.00 | 5.00 | 1.20 |
| ☐ 27 | Alan C. Strange | 9.00 | 3.75 | .90 |
| ☐ 28 | Bob Swift | 9.00 | 3.75 | .90 |
| ☐ 29 | James (Zack) Taylor | 9.00 | 3.75 | .90 |
| ☐ 30 | Bill Trotter | 9.00 | 3.75 | .90 |

# 1941 W711-2

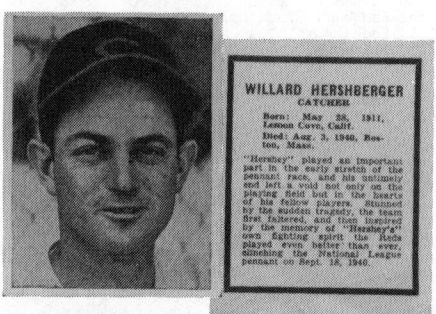

The cards in this 34 card set measure 2 1/8" by 2 5/8". The W711-2 Cincinnati Reds set contains unnumbered, black and white cards. This issue is sometimes called the "Harry Hartman" set. The cards are numbered below in alphabetical order by player's name with non-player cards listed at the end.

| | | MINT | VG-E | F-G |
|---|---|---|---|---|
| COMPLETE SET | | 275.00 | 110.00 | 27.00 |
| COMMON PLAYER (1-28) | | 8.00 | 3.25 | .80 |
| COMMON NON-PLAYER (29-34) | | | | |
| ☐ 1 | Morris Arnovich | 8.00 | 3.25 | .80 |
| ☐ 2 | William (Bill) Baker | 8.00 | 3.25 | .80 |
| ☐ 3 | Joseph Beggs | 8.00 | 3.25 | .80 |
| ☐ 4 | Harry Craft | 8.00 | 3.25 | .80 |
| ☐ 5 | Paul Derringer | 12.00 | 5.00 | 1.20 |
| ☐ 6 | Linus Frey | 8.00 | 3.25 | .80 |
| ☐ 7 | Ival Goodman | 8.00 | 3.25 | .80 |
| ☐ 8 | Hank Gowdy | 8.00 | 3.25 | .80 |
| ☐ 9 | Witt Guise | 8.00 | 3.25 | .80 |
| ☐ 10 | Willard Hershberger | 9.00 | 3.75 | .90 |
| ☐ 11 | John Hutchings | 8.00 | 3.25 | .80 |
| ☐ 12 | Edwin Joost | 8.00 | 3.25 | .80 |
| ☐ 13 | Ernie Lombardi | 25.00 | 10.00 | 2.50 |
| ☐ 14 | Frank McCormick | 10.00 | 4.00 | 1.00 |
| ☐ 15 | Myron McCormick | 8.00 | 3.25 | .80 |
| ☐ 16 | William McKechnie | 15.00 | 6.00 | 1.50 |
| ☐ 17 | Whitey Moore | 8.00 | 3.25 | .80 |
| ☐ 18 | William (Bill) Myers | 8.00 | 3.25 | .80 |
| ☐ 19 | Elmer Riddle | 8.00 | 3.25 | .80 |

## 1941 W754 Cardinals

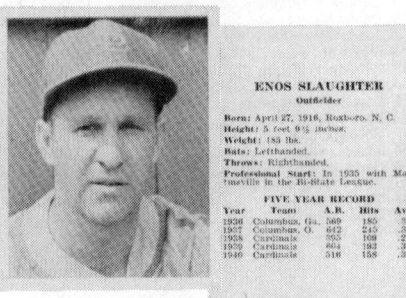

The cards in this 29 card set measure 2 1/8" by 2 5/8". The 1941 W754 set of unnumbered cards features St. Louis Cardinals. The cards are numbered below alphabetically by player's name.

|  | MINT | VG-E | F-G |
|---|---|---|---|
| COMPLETE SET | 275.00 | 110.00 | 27.00 |
| COMMON PLAYER (1-29) | 8.00 | 3.25 | .80 |

| | | MINT | VG-E | F-G |
|---|---|---|---|---|
| ☐ 1 | Sam Breadon | 8.00 | 3.25 | .80 |
| ☐ 2 | Jimmy Brown | 8.00 | 3.25 | .80 |
| ☐ 3 | Mort Cooper | 8.00 | 3.25 | .80 |
| ☐ 4 | Walker Cooper | 8.00 | 3.25 | .80 |
| ☐ 5 | Estel Crabtree | 8.00 | 3.25 | .80 |
| ☐ 6 | Frank Crespi | 8.00 | 3.25 | .80 |
| ☐ 7 | Bill Crouch | 8.00 | 3.25 | .80 |
| ☐ 8 | Mike Gonzalez | 8.00 | 3.25 | .80 |
| ☐ 9 | Harry Gumpert | 8.00 | 3.25 | .80 |
| ☐ 10 | John Hopp | 8.00 | 3.25 | .80 |
| ☐ 11 | Ira Hutchinson | 8.00 | 3.25 | .80 |
| ☐ 12 | Howie Krist | 8.00 | 3.25 | .80 |
| ☐ 13 | Eddie Lake | 8.00 | 3.25 | .80 |
| ☐ 14 | Max Lanier | 8.00 | 3.25 | .80 |
| ☐ 15 | Gus Mancuso | 8.00 | 3.25 | .80 |
| ☐ 16 | Marty Marion | 12.00 | 5.00 | 1.20 |
| ☐ 17 | Steve Mesner | 8.00 | 3.25 | .80 |
| ☐ 18 | John Mize | 25.00 | 10.00 | 2.50 |
| ☐ 19 | Terry Moore | 12.00 | 5.00 | 1.20 |
| ☐ 20 | Sam Nahem | 8.00 | 3.25 | .80 |
| ☐ 21 | Don Padgett | 8.00 | 3.25 | .80 |
| ☐ 22 | Branch Rickey | 20.00 | 8.00 | 2.00 |
| ☐ 23 | Clyde Shoun | 8.00 | 3.25 | .80 |
| ☐ 24 | Enos Slaughter | 25.00 | 10.00 | 2.50 |
| ☐ 25 | Billy Southworth | 8.00 | 3.25 | .80 |
| ☐ 26 | Coaker Triplett | 8.00 | 3.25 | .80 |
| ☐ 27 | Buzzy Wares | 8.00 | 3.25 | .80 |
| ☐ 28 | Lon Warneke | 8.00 | 3.25 | .80 |
| ☐ 29 | Ernie White | 8.00 | 3.25 | .80 |

## 1928 Yuenglings

The cards in this 60 card set measure 1 3/8" by 2 9/16". This black and white, numbered set contains many Hall of Famers. The obverses are the same as those found in sets of E210 and W502. The Paul Waner card, number 45, actually contains a picture of Clyde Barnhardt. Each back contains an offer to redeem pictures of Babe Ruth for ice cream. The ACC designation for this set is F50.

|  | MINT | VG-E | F-G |
|---|---|---|---|
| COMPLETE SET | 850.00 | 340.00 | 85.00 |
| COMMON PLAYER (1-60) | 8.00 | 3.25 | .80 |

| | | MINT | VG-E | F-G |
|---|---|---|---|---|
| ☐ 1 | Burleigh Grimes | 16.00 | 6.50 | 1.60 |
| ☐ 2 | Walter Reuther | 8.00 | 3.25 | .80 |
| ☐ 3 | Joe Dugan | 8.00 | 3.25 | .80 |
| ☐ 4 | Red Faber | 16.00 | 6.50 | 1.60 |
| ☐ 5 | Gabby Hartnett | 16.00 | 6.50 | 1.60 |

| | | MINT | VG-E | F-G |
|---|---|---|---|---|
| ☐ 6 | Babe Ruth | 125.00 | 50.00 | 12.50 |
| ☐ 7 | Bob Meusel | 8.00 | 3.25 | .80 |
| ☐ 8 | Herb Pennock | 16.00 | 6.50 | 1.60 |
| ☐ 9 | George Burns | 8.00 | 3.25 | .80 |
| ☐ 10 | Joe Sewell | 16.00 | 6.50 | 1.60 |
| ☐ 11 | George Uhle | 8.00 | 3.25 | .80 |
| ☐ 12 | Bob O'Farrell | 8.00 | 3.25 | .80 |
| ☐ 13 | Rogers Hornsby | 40.00 | 16.00 | 4.00 |
| ☐ 14 | Pie Traynor | 20.00 | 8.00 | 2.00 |
| ☐ 15 | Clarence Mitchell | 8.00 | 3.25 | .80 |
| ☐ 16 | Eppa Rixey | 16.00 | 6.50 | 1.60 |
| ☐ 17 | Carl Mays | 8.00 | 3.25 | .80 |
| ☐ 18 | Adolfo Luque | 8.00 | 3.25 | .80 |
| ☐ 19 | Dave Bancroft | 16.00 | 6.50 | 1.60 |
| ☐ 20 | George Kelly | 16.00 | 6.50 | 1.60 |
| ☐ 21 | Earl Combs | 16.00 | 6.50 | 1.60 |
| ☐ 22 | Harry Heilmann | 16.00 | 6.50 | 1.60 |
| ☐ 23 | Ray Schalk | 16.00 | 6.50 | 1.60 |
| ☐ 24 | John Mostil | 8.00 | 3.25 | .80 |
| ☐ 25 | Hack Wilson | 20.00 | 8.00 | 2.00 |
| ☐ 26 | Lou Gehrig | 75.00 | 30.00 | 7.50 |
| ☐ 27 | Ty Cobb | 75.00 | 30.00 | 7.50 |
| ☐ 28 | Tris Speaker | 30.00 | 12.00 | 3.00 |
| ☐ 29 | Tony Lazzeri | 10.00 | 4.00 | 1.00 |
| ☐ 30 | Waite Hoyt | 16.00 | 6.50 | 1.60 |
| ☐ 31 | Sherwood Smith | 8.00 | 3.25 | .80 |
| ☐ 32 | Max Carey | 16.00 | 6.50 | 1.60 |
| ☐ 33 | Gene Hargrave | 8.00 | 3.25 | .80 |
| ☐ 34 | Miguel Gonzalez | 8.00 | 3.25 | .80 |
| ☐ 35 | Joe Judge | 8.00 | 3.25 | .80 |
| ☐ 36 | Sam Rice | 16.00 | 6.50 | 1.60 |
| ☐ 37 | Earl Sheely | 8.00 | 3.25 | .80 |
| ☐ 38 | Sam Jones | 8.00 | 3.25 | .80 |
| ☐ 39 | Bibb Falk | 8.00 | 3.25 | .80 |
| ☐ 40 | Willie Kamm | 8.00 | 3.25 | .80 |
| ☐ 41 | Stan (Bucky) Harris | 16.00 | 6.50 | 1.60 |
| ☐ 42 | John McGraw | 20.00 | 8.00 | 2.00 |
| ☐ 43 | Art Nehf | 8.00 | 3.25 | .80 |
| ☐ 44 | Grover C. Alexander | 30.00 | 12.00 | 3.00 |
| ☐ 45 | Paul Waner | 16.00 | 6.50 | 1.60 |
| ☐ 46 | Bill Terry | 20.00 | 8.00 | 2.00 |
| ☐ 47 | Glenn Wright | 8.00 | 3.25 | .80 |
| ☐ 48 | Earl Smith | 8.00 | 3.25 | .80 |
| ☐ 49 | Goose Goslin | 16.00 | 6.50 | 1.60 |
| ☐ 50 | Frank Frisch | 20.00 | 8.00 | 2.00 |
| ☐ 51 | Joe Harris | 8.00 | 3.25 | .80 |
| ☐ 52 | Cy Williams | 8.00 | 3.25 | .80 |
| ☐ 53 | Eddie Roush | 16.00 | 6.50 | 1.60 |
| ☐ 54 | George Sisler | 20.00 | 8.00 | 2.00 |
| ☐ 55 | Ed Rommel | 8.00 | 3.25 | .80 |
| ☐ 56 | Roger Peckinpaugh | 8.00 | 3.25 | .80 |
| ☐ 57 | Stanley Coveleskie | 16.00 | 6.50 | 1.60 |
| ☐ 58 | Lester Bell | 8.00 | 3.25 | .80 |
| ☐ 59 | Lloyd Waner | 16.00 | 6.50 | 1.60 |
| ☐ 60 | John McInnis | 8.00 | 3.25 | .80 |

## C46

The cards in this 90 card set measure 1 1/2" by 2 3/4". The 1912 C46 Canadian set features numbered cards which were issued with an unidentified brand of cigarettes. The set features International League players.

|  | MINT | VG-E | F-G |
|---|---|---|---|
| COMPLETE SET | 2700.00 | 1100.00 | 275.00 |

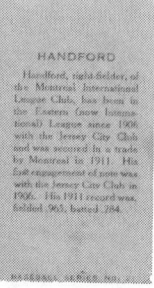

HANDFORD

Handford, right-fielder, of the Montreal International League Club, has been in the Eastern (now International) League since 1906, with the Jersey City Club and was secured in a trade by Montreal in 1911. His last engagement of note was with the Jersey City Club in 1906. His 1911 record was, fielded .965, batted .284.

BASEBALL SERIES NO.

| COMMON PLAYER (1-90) | 30.00 | 12.00 | 3.00 |
|---|---|---|---|
| ☐ 1 William O'Hara | 30.00 | 12.00 | 3.00 |
| ☐ 2 James McGinley | 30.00 | 12.00 | 3.00 |
| ☐ 3 Geo. Frenchy LeClaire | 30.00 | 12.00 | 3.00 |
| ☐ 4 John White | 30.00 | 12.00 | 3.00 |
| ☐ 5 James Murray | 30.00 | 12.00 | 3.00 |
| ☐ 6 Joe Ward | 30.00 | 12.00 | 3.00 |
| ☐ 7 Whitey Alperman | 30.00 | 12.00 | 3.00 |
| ☐ 8 Natty Nattress | 30.00 | 12.00 | 3.00 |
| ☐ 9 Fred Sline | 30.00 | 12.00 | 3.00 |
| ☐ 10 Royal Rock | 30.00 | 12.00 | 3.00 |
| ☐ 11 Ray Demmitt | 30.00 | 12.00 | 3.00 |
| ☐ 12 Butcher Boy Schmidt | 30.00 | 12.00 | 3.00 |
| ☐ 13 Samuel Frock | 30.00 | 12.00 | 3.00 |
| ☐ 14 Fred Burchell | 30.00 | 12.00 | 3.00 |
| ☐ 15 Jack Kelley | 30.00 | 12.00 | 3.00 |
| ☐ 16 Frank Barberich | 30.00 | 12.00 | 3.00 |
| ☐ 17 Frank Corridon | 30.00 | 12.00 | 3.00 |
| ☐ 18 Doc Adkins | 30.00 | 12.00 | 3.00 |
| ☐ 19 Jack Dunn | 30.00 | 12.00 | 3.00 |
| ☐ 20 James Walsh | 30.00 | 12.00 | 3.00 |
| ☐ 21 Charles Handford | 30.00 | 12.00 | 3.00 |
| ☐ 22 Dick Rudolph | 30.00 | 12.00 | 3.00 |
| ☐ 23 Curt Elston | 30.00 | 12.00 | 3.00 |
| ☐ 24 Silton | 30.00 | 12.00 | 3.00 |
| ☐ 25 Charlie French | 30.00 | 12.00 | 3.00 |
| ☐ 26 John Ganzel | 30.00 | 12.00 | 3.00 |
| ☐ 27 Joe Kelley | 100.00 | 40.00 | 10.00 |
| ☐ 28 Benny Meyers | 30.00 | 12.00 | 3.00 |
| ☐ 29 George Schirm | 30.00 | 12.00 | 3.00 |
| ☐ 30 William Purtell | 30.00 | 12.00 | 3.00 |
| ☐ 31 Bayard Sharpe | 30.00 | 12.00 | 3.00 |
| ☐ 32 Tony Smith | 30.00 | 12.00 | 3.00 |
| ☐ 33 John Lush | 30.00 | 12.00 | 3.00 |
| ☐ 34 William Collins | 30.00 | 12.00 | 3.00 |
| ☐ 35 Art Phelan | 30.00 | 12.00 | 3.00 |
| ☐ 36 Edward Phelps | 30.00 | 12.00 | 3.00 |
| ☐ 37 Rube Vickers | 30.00 | 12.00 | 3.00 |
| ☐ 38 Cy Seymour | 30.00 | 12.00 | 3.00 |
| ☐ 39 Shadow Carroll | 30.00 | 12.00 | 3.00 |
| ☐ 40 Jake Gettman | 30.00 | 12.00 | 3.00 |
| ☐ 41 Luther Taylor | 30.00 | 12.00 | 3.00 |
| ☐ 42 Walter Justis | 30.00 | 12.00 | 3.00 |
| ☐ 43 Robert Fisher | 30.00 | 12.00 | 3.00 |
| ☐ 44 Fred Parent | 30.00 | 12.00 | 3.00 |
| ☐ 45 James Dygert | 30.00 | 12.00 | 3.00 |
| ☐ 46 Johnnie Butler | 30.00 | 12.00 | 3.00 |
| ☐ 47 Fred Mitchell | 30.00 | 12.00 | 3.00 |
| ☐ 48 Heine Batch | 30.00 | 12.00 | 3.00 |
| ☐ 49 Michael Corcoran | 30.00 | 12.00 | 3.00 |
| ☐ 50 Edward Doescher | 30.00 | 12.00 | 3.00 |
| ☐ 51 Wheeler | 30.00 | 12.00 | 3.00 |
| ☐ 52 Elijah Jones | 30.00 | 12.00 | 3.00 |
| ☐ 53 Fred Truesdale | 30.00 | 12.00 | 3.00 |
| ☐ 54 Fred Beebe | 30.00 | 12.00 | 3.00 |
| ☐ 55 Louis Brockett | 30.00 | 12.00 | 3.00 |
| ☐ 56 Wells | 30.00 | 12.00 | 3.00 |
| ☐ 57 Lew McAllister | 30.00 | 12.00 | 3.00 |
| ☐ 58 Ralph Stroud | 30.00 | 12.00 | 3.00 |
| ☐ 59 Manser | 30.00 | 12.00 | 3.00 |
| ☐ 60 Ducky Holmes | 30.00 | 12.00 | 3.00 |
| ☐ 61 Rube Dessau | 30.00 | 12.00 | 3.00 |
| ☐ 62 Fred Jacklitsch | 30.00 | 12.00 | 3.00 |
| ☐ 63 Graham | 30.00 | 12.00 | 3.00 |
| ☐ 64 Noah Henline | 30.00 | 12.00 | 3.00 |
| ☐ 65 Chick Gandil | 30.00 | 12.00 | 3.00 |
| ☐ 66 Tom Hughes | 30.00 | 12.00 | 3.00 |
| ☐ 67 Joseph Delehanty | 30.00 | 12.00 | 3.00 |
| ☐ 68 Pierce | 30.00 | 12.00 | 3.00 |
| ☐ 69 Gaunt | 30.00 | 12.00 | 3.00 |
| ☐ 70 Edward Fitzpatrick | 30.00 | 12.00 | 3.00 |
| ☐ 71 Wyatt Lee | 30.00 | 12.00 | 3.00 |
| ☐ 72 John Kissinger | 30.00 | 12.00 | 3.00 |
| ☐ 73 William Malarkey | 30.00 | 12.00 | 3.00 |
| ☐ 74 William Byers | 30.00 | 12.00 | 3.00 |
| ☐ 75 George Simmons | 30.00 | 12.00 | 3.00 |
| ☐ 76 Daniel Moeller | 30.00 | 12.00 | 3.00 |
| ☐ 77 Joseph McGinnity | 100.00 | 40.00 | 10.00 |
| ☐ 78 Alex Hardy | 30.00 | 12.00 | 3.00 |
| ☐ 79 Bob Holmes | 30.00 | 12.00 | 3.00 |
| ☐ 80 William Baxter | 30.00 | 12.00 | 3.00 |
| ☐ 81 Edward Spencer | 30.00 | 12.00 | 3.00 |
| ☐ 82 Bradley Kocher | 30.00 | 12.00 | 3.00 |
| ☐ 83 Robert Shaw | 30.00 | 12.00 | 3.00 |
| ☐ 84 Joseph Yeager | 30.00 | 12.00 | 3.00 |
| ☐ 85 Carlo | 30.00 | 12.00 | 3.00 |
| ☐ 86 William Abstein | 30.00 | 12.00 | 3.00 |
| ☐ 87 Tim Jordan | 30.00 | 12.00 | 3.00 |
| ☐ 88 Dick Breen | 30.00 | 12.00 | 3.00 |
| ☐ 89 Tom McCarty | 30.00 | 12.00 | 3.00 |
| ☐ 90 Ed Curtis | 30.00 | 12.00 | 3.00 |

# V61

GROVER C. ALEXANDER
PITCHER, CHICAGO NATIONALS

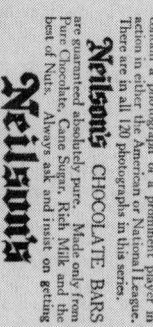

JAKE DAUBERT
FIRST BASE, CINCINNATI NATIONALS

The 1921 Neilson's Chocolate set entitled Big League Baseball Stars contains 120 cards and is essentially a reproduction of the E120 set. There are two versions of this set: a numbered paper issue and an unnumbered cardboard issue. Cards of the unnumbered cardboard issue are worth approximately 50% more than the values listed in the checklist below. The ACC designation is V61.

| | | MINT | VG-E | F-G |
|---|---|---|---|---|
| COMPLETE SET | | 2500.00 | 1000.00 | 250.00 |
| COMMON PLAYER (1-120) | | 16.00 | 6.50 | 1.60 |
| ☐ 1 | George Burns | 16.00 | 6.50 | 1.60 |
| ☐ 2 | John Tobin | 16.00 | 6.50 | 1.60 |
| ☐ 3 | Tom Zachary | 16.00 | 6.50 | 1.60 |
| ☐ 4 | Bullet Joe Bush | 16.00 | 6.50 | 1.60 |

| | | | | |
|---|---|---|---|---|
| ☐ | 5 Lu Blue | 16.00 | 6.50 | 1.60 |
| ☐ | 6 Tillie Walker | 16.00 | 6.50 | 1.60 |
| ☐ | 7 Carl Mays | 16.00 | 6.50 | 1.60 |
| ☐ | 8 Leon Goslin | 30.00 | 12.00 | 3.00 |
| ☐ | 9 Ed Rommel | 16.00 | 6.50 | 1.60 |
| ☐ | 10 Charles Robertson | 16.00 | 6.50 | 1.60 |
| ☐ | 11 Ralph Perkins | 16.00 | 6.50 | 1.60 |
| ☐ | 12 Joe Sewell | 30.00 | 12.00 | 3.00 |
| ☐ | 13 Harry Hooper | 30.00 | 12.00 | 3.00 |
| ☐ | 14 Urban Faber | 30.00 | 12.00 | 3.00 |
| ☐ | 15 Bibb Falk | 16.00 | 6.50 | 1.60 |
| ☐ | 16 George Uhle | 16.00 | 6.50 | 1.60 |
| ☐ | 17 Emory Rigney | 16.00 | 6.50 | 1.60 |
| ☐ | 18 George Dauss | 16.00 | 6.50 | 1.60 |
| ☐ | 19 Herman Pillette | 16.00 | 6.50 | 1.60 |
| ☐ | 20 Wallie Schang | 16.00 | 6.50 | 1.60 |
| ☐ | 21 Lawrence Woodall | 16.00 | 6.50 | 1.60 |
| ☐ | 22 Steve O'Neill | 16.00 | 6.50 | 1.60 |
| ☐ | 23 Edmund Miller | 16.00 | 6.50 | 1.60 |
| ☐ | 24 Sylvester Johnson | 16.00 | 6.50 | 1.60 |
| ☐ | 25 Henry Severeid | 16.00 | 6.50 | 1.60 |
| ☐ | 26 Dave Danforth | 16.00 | 6.50 | 1.60 |
| ☐ | 27 Harry Heilmann | 35.00 | 14.00 | 3.50 |
| ☐ | 28 Bert Cole | 16.00 | 6.50 | 1.60 |
| ☐ | 29 Eddie Collins | 35.00 | 14.00 | 3.50 |
| ☐ | 30 Ty Cobb | 300.00 | 120.00 | 30.00 |
| ☐ | 31 Bill Wambsganss | 16.00 | 6.50 | 1.60 |
| ☐ | 32 George Sisler | 40.00 | 16.00 | 4.00 |
| ☐ | 33 Bob Veach | 16.00 | 6.50 | 1.60 |
| ☐ | 34 Earl Sheely | 16.00 | 6.50 | 1.60 |
| ☐ | 35 Pat Collins | 16.00 | 6.50 | 1.60 |
| ☐ | 36 Frank Davis | 16.00 | 6.50 | 1.60 |
| ☐ | 37 Babe Ruth | 450.00 | 180.00 | 45.00 |
| ☐ | 38 Bryan Harris | 16.00 | 6.50 | 1.60 |
| ☐ | 39 Bob Shawkey | 16.00 | 6.50 | 1.60 |
| ☐ | 40 Urban Shocker | 16.00 | 6.50 | 1.60 |
| ☐ | 41 Martin McManus | 16.00 | 6.50 | 1.60 |
| ☐ | 42 Clark Pittenger | 16.00 | 6.50 | 1.60 |
| ☐ | 43 Sam Jones | 16.00 | 6.50 | 1.60 |
| ☐ | 44 Waite Hoyt | 30.00 | 12.00 | 3.00 |
| ☐ | 45 Johnny Mostil | 16.00 | 6.50 | 1.60 |
| ☐ | 46 Mike Menosky | 16.00 | 6.50 | 1.60 |
| ☐ | 47 Walter Johnson | 125.00 | 50.00 | 12.50 |
| ☐ | 48 Wallie Pipp | 20.00 | 8.00 | 2.00 |
| ☐ | 49 Walter Gerber | 16.00 | 6.50 | 1.60 |
| ☐ | 50 Ed Gharrity | 16.00 | 6.50 | 1.60 |
| ☐ | 51 Frank Ellerbe | 16.00 | 6.50 | 1.60 |
| ☐ | 52 Kenneth Williams | 16.00 | 6.50 | 1.60 |
| ☐ | 53 Joe Hauser | 16.00 | 6.50 | 1.60 |
| ☐ | 54 Carson Bigbee | 16.00 | 6.50 | 1.60 |
| ☐ | 55 Irish Meusel | 16.00 | 6.50 | 1.60 |
| ☐ | 56 Milton Stock | 16.00 | 6.50 | 1.60 |
| ☐ | 57 Wilbur Cooper | 16.00 | 6.50 | 1.60 |
| ☐ | 58 Tom Griffith | 16.00 | 6.50 | 1.60 |
| ☐ | 59 Butch Henline | 16.00 | 6.50 | 1.60 |
| ☐ | 60 Bubbles Hargrave | 16.00 | 6.50 | 1.60 |
| ☐ | 61 Russel Wrightstone | 16.00 | 6.50 | 1.60 |
| ☐ | 62 Frank Frisch | 35.00 | 14.00 | 3.50 |
| ☐ | 63 Jack Peters | 16.00 | 6.50 | 1.60 |
| ☐ | 64 Walter Ruether | 16.00 | 6.50 | 1.60 |
| ☐ | 65 Bill Doak | 16.00 | 6.50 | 1.60 |
| ☐ | 66 Marty Callaghan | 16.00 | 6.50 | 1.60 |
| ☐ | 67 Sammy Bohne | 16.00 | 6.50 | 1.60 |
| ☐ | 68 Earl Hamilton | 16.00 | 6.50 | 1.60 |
| ☐ | 69 Grover Alexander | 50.00 | 20.00 | 5.00 |
| ☐ | 70 George Burns | 16.00 | 6.50 | 1.60 |
| ☐ | 71 Max Carey | 30.00 | 12.00 | 3.00 |
| ☐ | 72 Adolph Luque | 16.00 | 6.50 | 1.60 |
| ☐ | 73 Dave Bancroft | 30.00 | 12.00 | 3.00 |
| ☐ | 74 Vic Aldridge | 16.00 | 6.50 | 1.60 |
| ☐ | 75 Jack Smith | 16.00 | 6.50 | 1.60 |
| ☐ | 76 Bob O'Farrell | 16.00 | 6.50 | 1.60 |
| ☐ | 77 Pete Donohue | 16.00 | 6.50 | 1.60 |
| ☐ | 78 Ralph Pinelli | 16.00 | 6.50 | 1.60 |
| ☐ | 79 Eddie Roush | 35.00 | 14.00 | 3.50 |
| ☐ | 80 Norman Boeckel | 16.00 | 6.50 | 1.60 |
| ☐ | 81 Rogers Hornsby | 90.00 | 36.00 | 9.00 |
| ☐ | 82 George Toporcer | 16.00 | 6.50 | 1.60 |
| ☐ | 83 Ivy Wingo | 16.00 | 6.50 | 1.60 |
| ☐ | 84 Virgil Cheeves | 16.00 | 6.50 | 1.60 |
| ☐ | 85 Vern Clemons | 16.00 | 6.50 | 1.60 |
| ☐ | 86 Lawrence Miller | 16.00 | 6.50 | 1.60 |
| ☐ | 87 Johnny Kelleher | 16.00 | 6.50 | 1.60 |
| ☐ | 88 Heinie Groh | 20.00 | 8.00 | 2.00 |
| ☐ | 89 Burleigh Grimes | 30.00 | 12.00 | 3.00 |
| ☐ | 90 Rabbit Maranville | 30.00 | 12.00 | 3.00 |
| ☐ | 91 Babe Adams | 16.00 | 6.50 | 1.60 |
| ☐ | 92 Lee King | 16.00 | 6.50 | 1.60 |
| ☐ | 93 Art Nehf | 16.00 | 6.50 | 1.60 |
| ☐ | 94 Frank Snyder | 16.00 | 6.50 | 1.60 |
| ☐ | 95 Raymond Powell | 16.00 | 6.50 | 1.60 |
| ☐ | 96 Wilbur Hubbell | 16.00 | 6.50 | 1.60 |
| ☐ | 97 Leon Cadore | 16.00 | 6.50 | 1.60 |

| | | | | |
|---|---|---|---|---|
| ☐ | 98 Joe Oeschger | 16.00 | 6.50 | 1.60 |
| ☐ | 99 Jake Daubert | 20.00 | 8.00 | 2.00 |
| ☐ | 100 Will Sherdel | 16.00 | 6.50 | 1.60 |
| ☐ | 101 Hank DeBerry | 16.00 | 6.50 | 1.60 |
| ☐ | 102 Johnny Lavan | 16.00 | 6.50 | 1.60 |
| ☐ | 103 Jesse Haines | 30.00 | 12.00 | 3.00 |
| ☐ | 104 Joe (Goldie) Rapp | 16.00 | 6.50 | 1.60 |
| ☐ | 105 Oscar Ray Grimes | 16.00 | 6.50 | 1.60 |
| ☐ | 106 Ross Youngs | 40.00 | 16.00 | 4.00 |
| ☐ | 107 Art Fletcher | 16.00 | 6.50 | 1.60 |
| ☐ | 108 Clyde Barnhart | 16.00 | 6.50 | 1.60 |
| ☐ | 109 Louis (Pat) Duncan | 16.00 | 6.50 | 1.60 |
| ☐ | 110 Charlie Hollacher | 16.00 | 6.50 | 1.60 |
| ☐ | 111 Horace Ford | 16.00 | 6.50 | 1.60 |
| ☐ | 112 Bill Cunningham | 16.00 | 6.50 | 1.60 |
| ☐ | 113 Walter Schmidt | 16.00 | 6.50 | 1.60 |
| ☐ | 114 Joe Schultz | 16.00 | 6.50 | 1.60 |
| ☐ | 115 John Morrison | 16.00 | 6.50 | 1.60 |
| ☐ | 116 Jimmy Caveney | 16.00 | 6.50 | 1.60 |
| ☐ | 117 Zach Wheat | 30.00 | 12.00 | 3.00 |
| ☐ | 118 Fred (Cy) Williams | 16.00 | 6.50 | 1.60 |
| ☐ | 119 George Kelly | 30.00 | 12.00 | 3.00 |
| ☐ | 120 Jimmy Ring | 16.00 | 6.50 | 1.60 |

## V100 Willards

_RICKEY_

The cards in this 180 card set measure 2" by 3 1/4". The 1923 Willards Chocolates set was issued in Canada and contains unnumbered cards. The ACC designation is V100. Cards are numbered below alphabetically by player's name.

| | | MINT | VG-E | F-G |
|---|---|---|---|---|
| COMPLETE SET | | 3750.00 | 1600.00 | 400.00 |
| COMMON PLAYER (1-180) | | 16.00 | 6.50 | 1.60 |
| ☐ | 1 Charles B. Adams | 16.00 | 6.50 | 1.60 |
| ☐ | 2 Grover C. Alexander | 45.00 | 18.00 | 4.50 |
| ☐ | 3 J.P. Austin | 16.00 | 6.50 | 1.60 |
| ☐ | 4 Jim Bagby | 16.00 | 6.50 | 1.60 |
| ☐ | 5 J. Franklin Baker | 30.00 | 12.00 | 3.00 |
| ☐ | 6 Dave Bancroft | 30.00 | 12.00 | 3.00 |
| ☐ | 7 Turner Barber | 16.00 | 6.50 | 1.60 |
| ☐ | 8 Jesse L. Barnes | 16.00 | 6.50 | 1.60 |
| ☐ | 9 John Bassler | 16.00 | 6.50 | 1.60 |
| ☐ | 10 Lu Blue | 16.00 | 6.50 | 1.60 |
| ☐ | 11 Norman Boekel | 16.00 | 6.50 | 1.60 |
| ☐ | 12 F.L. Brazil | 16.00 | 6.50 | 1.60 |
| ☐ | 13 G.H. Burns | 16.00 | 6.50 | 1.60 |
| ☐ | 14 G.J. Burns | 16.00 | 6.50 | 1.60 |
| ☐ | 15 Leon Cadore | 16.00 | 6.50 | 1.60 |
| ☐ | 16 Max Carey | 30.00 | 12.00 | 3.00 |
| ☐ | 17 Harold G. Carlson | 16.00 | 6.50 | 1.60 |
| ☐ | 18 Lloyd Christenberry | 16.00 | 6.50 | 1.60 |
| ☐ | 19 Vernon J. Clemons | 16.00 | 6.50 | 1.60 |
| ☐ | 20 Ty Cobb | 300.00 | 120.00 | 30.00 |
| ☐ | 21 Bert Cole | 16.00 | 6.50 | 1.60 |
| ☐ | 22 John F. Collins | 16.00 | 6.50 | 1.60 |
| ☐ | 23 Stan Coveleski | 30.00 | 12.00 | 3.00 |
| ☐ | 24 Walton E. Cruise | 16.00 | 6.50 | 1.60 |
| ☐ | 25 George W. Cutshaw | 16.00 | 6.50 | 1.60 |
| ☐ | 26 Jake Daubert | 20.00 | 8.00 | 2.00 |

| | | | | |
|---|---|---|---|---|
| ☐ 27 | George Dauss | 16.00 | 6.50 | 1.60 |
| ☐ 28 | F.T. Davis | 16.00 | 6.50 | 1.60 |
| ☐ 29 | Charles A. Deal | 16.00 | 6.50 | 1.60 |
| ☐ 30 | William L. Doak | 16.00 | 6.50 | 1.60 |
| ☐ 31 | Wild Bill Donovan | 16.00 | 6.50 | 1.60 |
| ☐ 32 | Hugh Duffy | 40.00 | 16.00 | 4.00 |
| ☐ 33 | Joe Dugan | 16.00 | 6.50 | 1.60 |
| ☐ 34 | Louis B. Duncan | 16.00 | 6.50 | 1.60 |
| ☐ 35 | Jimmy Dykes | 16.00 | 6.50 | 1.60 |
| ☐ 36 | Howard Ehmke | 16.00 | 6.50 | 1.60 |
| ☐ 37 | Francis R. Ellerbe | 16.00 | 6.50 | 1.60 |
| ☐ 38 | E.G. Erickson | 16.00 | 6.50 | 1.60 |
| ☐ 39 | Johnny Evers | 35.00 | 14.00 | 3.50 |
| ☐ 40 | Urban Faber | 30.00 | 12.00 | 3.00 |
| ☐ 41 | Bibb Falk | 16.00 | 6.50 | 1.60 |
| ☐ 42 | Max Flack | 16.00 | 6.50 | 1.60 |
| ☐ 43 | Lee Fohl | 16.00 | 6.50 | 1.60 |
| ☐ 44 | Jack Fournier | 16.00 | 6.50 | 1.60 |
| ☐ 45 | Frank Frisch | 40.00 | 16.00 | 4.00 |
| ☐ 46 | C.E. Galloway | 16.00 | 6.50 | 1.60 |
| ☐ 47 | W.C. Gardner | 16.00 | 6.50 | 1.60 |
| ☐ 48 | Edward Gharrity | 16.00 | 6.50 | 1.60 |
| ☐ 49 | George Gibson | 16.00 | 6.50 | 1.60 |
| ☐ 50 | Wm. Gleason | 16.00 | 6.50 | 1.60 |
| ☐ 51 | William Gleason | 16.00 | 6.50 | 1.60 |
| ☐ 52 | Hank Gowdy | 16.00 | 6.50 | 1.60 |
| ☐ 53 | I.M. Griffin | 16.00 | 6.50 | 1.60 |
| ☐ 54 | Griffith | 16.00 | 6.50 | 1.60 |
| ☐ 55 | Burleigh Grimes | 30.00 | 12.00 | 3.00 |
| ☐ 56 | Charlie Grimm | 20.00 | 8.00 | 2.00 |
| ☐ 57 | Jesse Haines | 30.00 | 12.00 | 3.00 |
| ☐ 58 | S. Harris | 30.00 | 12.00 | 3.00 |
| ☐ 59 | W. Harris | 16.00 | 6.50 | 1.60 |
| ☐ 60 | Robert Hasty | 16.00 | 6.50 | 1.60 |
| ☐ 61 | Harry Heilmann | 40.00 | 16.00 | 4.00 |
| ☐ 62 | Walter Henline | 16.00 | 6.50 | 1.60 |
| ☐ 63 | Walter Holke | 16.00 | 6.50 | 1.60 |
| ☐ 64 | Charles Hollocher | 16.00 | 6.50 | 1.60 |
| ☐ 65 | Harry Hooper | 35.00 | 14.00 | 3.50 |
| ☐ 66 | Roger Hornsby | 90.00 | 36.00 | 9.00 |
| ☐ 67 | Waite Hoyt | 30.00 | 12.00 | 3.00 |
| ☐ 68 | Miller Huggins | 30.00 | 12.00 | 3.00 |
| ☐ 69 | W.C. Jacobson | 16.00 | 6.50 | 1.60 |
| ☐ 70 | Charlie Jamieson | 16.00 | 6.50 | 1.60 |
| ☐ 71 | E. Johnson | 16.00 | 6.50 | 1.60 |
| ☐ 72 | W. Johnson | 125.00 | 50.00 | 12.50 |
| ☐ 73 | James H. Johnston | 16.00 | 6.50 | 1.60 |
| ☐ 74 | R. Jones | 16.00 | 6.50 | 1.60 |
| ☐ 75 | S. Jones | 16.00 | 6.50 | 1.60 |
| ☐ 76 | J.I. Judge | 16.00 | 6.50 | 1.60 |
| ☐ 77 | James W. Keenan | 16.00 | 6.50 | 1.60 |
| ☐ 78 | Geo. L. Kelly | 30.00 | 12.00 | 3.00 |
| ☐ 79 | Peter J. Kilduff | 16.00 | 6.50 | 1.60 |
| ☐ 80 | William Killefer | 16.00 | 6.50 | 1.60 |
| ☐ 81 | Lee King | 16.00 | 6.50 | 1.60 |
| ☐ 82 | Ray Kolp | 16.00 | 6.50 | 1.60 |
| ☐ 83 | John Lavan | 16.00 | 6.50 | 1.60 |
| ☐ 84 | H.L. Leibold | 16.00 | 6.50 | 1.60 |
| ☐ 85 | Connie Mack | 40.00 | 16.00 | 4.00 |
| ☐ 86 | J.W. Mails | 16.00 | 6.50 | 1.60 |
| ☐ 87 | Walter Maranville | 30.00 | 12.00 | 3.00 |
| ☐ 88 | Richard W Marquard | 35.00 | 14.00 | 3.50 |
| ☐ 89 | Carl W. Mays | 16.00 | 6.50 | 1.60 |
| ☐ 90 | Geo. F. McBride | 16.00 | 6.50 | 1.60 |
| ☐ 91 | H.M. McClellan | 16.00 | 6.50 | 1.60 |
| ☐ 92 | John J. McGraw | 40.00 | 16.00 | 4.00 |
| ☐ 93 | Austin B. McHenry | 16.00 | 6.50 | 1.60 |
| ☐ 94 | J. McInnis | 16.00 | 6.50 | 1.60 |
| ☐ 95 | Douglas McWeeny | 16.00 | 6.50 | 1.60 |
| ☐ 96 | M. Menosky | 16.00 | 6.50 | 1.60 |
| ☐ 97 | Emil F. Meusel | 16.00 | 6.50 | 1.60 |
| ☐ 98 | R. Meusel | 16.00 | 6.50 | 1.60 |
| ☐ 99 | Henry W. Meyers | 16.00 | 6.50 | 1.60 |
| ☐ 100 | J.C. Milan | 16.00 | 6.50 | 1.60 |
| ☐ 101 | John K. Miljus | 16.00 | 6.50 | 1.60 |
| ☐ 102 | Edmund J. Miller | 16.00 | 6.50 | 1.60 |
| ☐ 103 | Elmer Miller | 16.00 | 6.50 | 1.60 |
| ☐ 104 | Otto L. Miller | 16.00 | 6.50 | 1.60 |
| ☐ 105 | Fred Mitchell | 16.00 | 6.50 | 1.60 |
| ☐ 106 | Geo. Mogridge | 16.00 | 6.50 | 1.60 |
| ☐ 107 | Patrick J. Moran | 16.00 | 6.50 | 1.60 |
| ☐ 108 | John D. Morrison | 16.00 | 6.50 | 1.60 |
| ☐ 109 | J.A. Mostil | 16.00 | 6.50 | 1.60 |
| ☐ 110 | Clarence F. Mueller | 16.00 | 6.50 | 1.60 |
| ☐ 111 | A. Earle Neale | 20.00 | 8.00 | 2.00 |
| ☐ 112 | Joseph Oeschger | 16.00 | 6.50 | 1.60 |
| ☐ 113 | Robert J. O'Farrell | 16.00 | 6.50 | 1.60 |
| ☐ 114 | J.C. Oldham | 16.00 | 6.50 | 1.60 |
| ☐ 115 | I.M. Olson | 16.00 | 6.50 | 1.60 |
| ☐ 116 | Geo. M. O'Neil | 16.00 | 6.50 | 1.60 |
| ☐ 117 | S.F. O'Neill | 16.00 | 6.50 | 1.60 |
| ☐ 118 | Frank J. Parkinson | 16.00 | 6.50 | 1.60 |
| ☐ 119 | Geo. H. Paskert | 16.00 | 6.50 | 1.60 |

| | | | | |
|---|---|---|---|---|
| ☐ 120 | R.T. Peckinpaugh | 16.00 | 6.50 | 1.60 |
| ☐ 121 | H.J. Pennock | 30.00 | 12.00 | 3.00 |
| ☐ 122 | Ralph Perkins | 16.00 | 6.50 | 1.60 |
| ☐ 123 | Edw. J. Pfeffer | 16.00 | 6.50 | 1.60 |
| ☐ 124 | W.C. Pipp | 20.00 | 8.00 | 2.00 |
| ☐ 125 | Charles Ponder | 16.00 | 6.50 | 1.60 |
| ☐ 126 | Raymond R. Powell | 16.00 | 6.50 | 1.60 |
| ☐ 127 | D.B. Pratt | 16.00 | 6.50 | 1.60 |
| ☐ 128 | Joseph Rapp | 16.00 | 6.50 | 1.60 |
| ☐ 129 | John H. Rawlings | 16.00 | 6.50 | 1.60 |
| ☐ 130 | E.S. Rice | 30.00 | 12.00 | 3.00 |
| ☐ 131 | Branch Rickey | 40.00 | 16.00 | 4.00 |
| ☐ 132 | James J. Ring | 16.00 | 6.50 | 1.60 |
| ☐ 133 | Eppa J. Rixey | 30.00 | 12.00 | 3.00 |
| ☐ 134 | Davis A. Robertson | 16.00 | 6.50 | 1.60 |
| ☐ 135 | Edwin Rommel | 16.00 | 6.50 | 1.60 |
| ☐ 136 | Ed J. Roush | 35.00 | 14.00 | 3.50 |
| ☐ 137 | Harold Ruel | 16.00 | 6.50 | 1.60 |
| ☐ 138 | Allen Russell | 16.00 | 6.50 | 1.60 |
| ☐ 139 | G.H. Ruth | 400.00 | 160.00 | 40.00 |
| ☐ 140 | Wilfred D. Ryan | 16.00 | 6.50 | 1.60 |
| ☐ 141 | Henry F. Sallee | 16.00 | 6.50 | 1.60 |
| ☐ 142 | W.H. Schang | 16.00 | 6.50 | 1.60 |
| ☐ 143 | Raymond H. Schmandt | 16.00 | 6.50 | 1.60 |
| ☐ 144 | Everett Scott | 16.00 | 6.50 | 1.60 |
| ☐ 145 | Henry Severeid | 16.00 | 6.50 | 1.60 |
| ☐ 146 | Joseph W. Sewell | 30.00 | 12.00 | 3.00 |
| ☐ 147 | Howard S. Shanks | 16.00 | 6.50 | 1.60 |
| ☐ 148 | E.H. Sheely | 16.00 | 6.50 | 1.60 |
| ☐ 149 | Ralph Shinners | 16.00 | 6.50 | 1.60 |
| ☐ 150 | Urban J. Shocker | 16.00 | 6.50 | 1.60 |
| ☐ 151 | George H. Sisler | 40.00 | 16.00 | 4.00 |
| ☐ 152 | Earl L. Smith | 16.00 | 6.50 | 1.60 |
| ☐ 153 | Earl S. Smith | 16.00 | 6.50 | 1.60 |
| ☐ 154 | George A. Smith | 16.00 | 6.50 | 1.60 |
| ☐ 155 | J.W. Smith | 16.00 | 6.50 | 1.60 |
| ☐ 156 | Tris Speaker | 65.00 | 26.00 | 6.50 |
| ☐ 157 | Arnold Staatz | 16.00 | 6.50 | 1.60 |
| ☐ 158 | J.R. Stephenson | 20.00 | 8.00 | 2.00 |
| ☐ 159 | Milton J. Stock | 16.00 | 6.50 | 1.60 |
| ☐ 160 | John L. Sullivan | 16.00 | 6.50 | 1.60 |
| ☐ 161 | H.F. Thormahlen | 16.00 | 6.50 | 1.60 |
| ☐ 162 | James A. Tierney | 16.00 | 6.50 | 1.60 |
| ☐ 163 | J.T. Tobin | 16.00 | 6.50 | 1.60 |
| ☐ 164 | James L. Vaughn | 16.00 | 6.50 | 1.60 |
| ☐ 165 | R.H. Veach | 16.00 | 6.50 | 1.60 |
| ☐ 166 | C.W. Walker | 16.00 | 6.50 | 1.60 |
| ☐ 167 | A.L. Ward | 16.00 | 6.50 | 1.60 |
| ☐ 168 | Zack D. Wheat | 30.00 | 12.00 | 3.00 |
| ☐ 169 | George B. Whitted | 16.00 | 6.50 | 1.60 |
| ☐ 170 | Irvin K. Wilhelm | 16.00 | 6.50 | 1.60 |
| ☐ 171 | Roy H. Wilkinson | 16.00 | 6.50 | 1.60 |
| ☐ 172 | Fred C. Williams | 16.00 | 6.50 | 1.60 |
| ☐ 173 | K.R. Williams | 16.00 | 6.50 | 1.60 |
| ☐ 174 | Samuel W. Wilson | 16.00 | 6.50 | 1.60 |
| ☐ 175 | Ivy B. Wingo | 16.00 | 6.50 | 1.60 |
| ☐ 176 | L.W. Witt | 16.00 | 6.50 | 1.60 |
| ☐ 177 | Joseph Wood | 20.00 | 8.00 | 2.00 |
| ☐ 178 | E. Yaryan | 16.00 | 6.50 | 1.60 |
| ☐ 179 | R.S. Young | 16.00 | 6.50 | 1.60 |
| ☐ 180 | Ross Youngs | 40.00 | 16.00 | 4.00 |

## V300 Canadian Batter Ups

The cards in this 40 card set measure 2 1/2" by 3". The 1937 O-Pee-Chee Batter Up set contains unnumbered, die- cut cards. The set is peculiar in that it begins with No. 101. The back biographies are printed in both French and English, and the small ballplayer designs on the obverses are similar to those used on the 1934 American Goudey cards. Cards without tops have greatly reduced value.

| | | MINT | VG-E | F-G |
|---|---|---|---|---|
| COMPLETE SET | | 2500.00 | 1000.00 | 250.00 |
| COMMON PLAYER (101-140) | | 40.00 | 16.00 | 4.00 |
| ☐ 101 | John Lewis | 40.00 | 16.00 | 4.00 |
| ☐ 102 | Jack Hayes | 40.00 | 16.00 | 4.00 |
| ☐ 103 | Earl Averill | 60.00 | 24.00 | 6.00 |
| ☐ 104 | Harland Clift | 40.00 | 16.00 | 4.00 |
| ☐ 105 | Beau Bell | 40.00 | 16.00 | 4.00 |
| ☐ 106 | Jimmy Foxx | 150.00 | 60.00 | 15.00 |
| ☐ 107 | Hank Greenberg | 100.00 | 40.00 | 10.00 |
| ☐ 108 | George Selkirk | 40.00 | 16.00 | 4.00 |

ODELL HALE
Third base, Cleveland Indians

| | | | MINT | VG-E | F-G |
|---|---|---|---|---|---|
| ☐ 16 | George Blaeholder | | 20.00 | 8.00 | 2.00 |
| ☐ 17 | Watson Clark | | 20.00 | 8.00 | 2.00 |
| ☐ 18 | Muddy Ruel | | 20.00 | 8.00 | 2.00 |
| ☐ 19 | Bill Dickey | | 60.00 | 24.00 | 6.00 |
| ☐ 20 | Bill Terry | | 45.00 | 18.00 | 4.50 |
| ☐ 21 | Phil Collins | | 20.00 | 8.00 | 2.00 |
| ☐ 22 | Pie Traynor | | 40.00 | 16.00 | 4.00 |
| ☐ 23 | Kiki Cuyler | | 35.00 | 14.00 | 3.50 |
| ☐ 24 | Horace Ford | | 20.00 | 8.00 | 2.00 |
| ☐ 25 | Paul Waner | | 35.00 | 14.00 | 3.50 |
| ☐ 26 | Chalmer Cissell | | 20.00 | 8.00 | 2.00 |
| ☐ 27 | George Connally | | 20.00 | 8.00 | 2.00 |
| ☐ 28 | Dick Bartell | | 20.00 | 8.00 | 2.00 |
| ☐ 29 | Jimmy Foxx | | 90.00 | 36.00 | 9.00 |
| ☐ 30 | Frank Hogan | | 20.00 | 8.00 | 2.00 |
| ☐ 31 | Tony Lazzeri | | 25.00 | 10.00 | 2.50 |
| ☐ 32 | Bud Clancy | | 20.00 | 8.00 | 2.00 |
| ☐ 33 | Ralph Kress | | 20.00 | 8.00 | 2.00 |
| ☐ 34 | Bob O'Farrell | | 20.00 | 8.00 | 2.00 |
| ☐ 35 | Al Simmons | | 40.00 | 16.00 | 4.00 |
| ☐ 36 | Tommy Thevenow | | 20.00 | 8.00 | 2.00 |
| ☐ 37 | Jimmy Wilson | | 20.00 | 8.00 | 2.00 |
| ☐ 38 | Fred Bickell | | 20.00 | 8.00 | 2.00 |
| ☐ 39 | Mark Koenig | | 20.00 | 8.00 | 2.00 |
| ☐ 40 | Taylor Douthit | | 20.00 | 8.00 | 2.00 |
| ☐ 41 | Gus Mancuso | | 20.00 | 8.00 | 2.00 |
| ☐ 42 | Eddie Collins | | 35.00 | 14.00 | 3.50 |
| ☐ 43 | Lew Fonseca | | 20.00 | 8.00 | 2.00 |
| ☐ 44 | Jim Bottomley | | 35.00 | 14.00 | 3.50 |
| ☐ 45 | Larry Benton | | 20.00 | 8.00 | 2.00 |
| ☐ 46 | Ethan Allen | | 20.00 | 8.00 | 2.00 |
| ☐ 47 | Heine Manush | | 35.00 | 14.00 | 3.50 |
| ☐ 48 | Marty McManus | | 20.00 | 8.00 | 2.00 |
| ☐ 49 | Frank Frisch | | 45.00 | 18.00 | 4.50 |
| ☐ 50 | Ed Brandt | | 20.00 | 8.00 | 2.00 |
| ☐ 51 | Charlie Grimm | | 25.00 | 10.00 | 2.50 |
| ☐ 52 | Andy Cohen | | 20.00 | 8.00 | 2.00 |
| ☐ 53 | Jack Quinn | | 20.00 | 8.00 | 2.00 |
| ☐ 54 | Urban Faber | | 35.00 | 14.00 | 3.50 |
| ☐ 55 | Lou Gehrig | | 400.00 | 160.00 | 40.00 |
| ☐ 56 | John Welch | | 20.00 | 8.00 | 2.00 |
| ☐ 57 | Bill Walker | | 20.00 | 8.00 | 2.00 |
| ☐ 58 | Lefty O'Doul | | 25.00 | 10.00 | 2.50 |
| ☐ 59 | Bing Miller | | 20.00 | 8.00 | 2.00 |
| ☐ 60 | Waite Hoyt | | 35.00 | 14.00 | 3.50 |
| ☐ 61 | Max Bishop | | 20.00 | 8.00 | 2.00 |
| ☐ 62 | Pepper Martin | | 25.00 | 10.00 | 2.50 |
| ☐ 63 | Joe Cronin | | 40.00 | 16.00 | 4.00 |
| ☐ 64 | Burleigh Grimes | | 35.00 | 14.00 | 3.50 |
| ☐ 65 | Milt Gaston | | 20.00 | 8.00 | 2.00 |
| ☐ 66 | George Grantham | | 20.00 | 8.00 | 2.00 |
| ☐ 67 | Guy Bush | | 20.00 | 8.00 | 2.00 |
| ☐ 68 | Willie Kamm | | 20.00 | 8.00 | 2.00 |
| ☐ 69 | Mickey Cochrane | | 45.00 | 18.00 | 4.50 |
| ☐ 70 | Adam Comorosky | | 20.00 | 8.00 | 2.00 |
| ☐ 71 | Alvin Crowder | | 20.00 | 8.00 | 2.00 |
| ☐ 72 | Willis Hudlin | | 20.00 | 8.00 | 2.00 |
| ☐ 73 | Eddie Farrell | | 20.00 | 8.00 | 2.00 |
| ☐ 74 | Leo Durocher | | 35.00 | 14.00 | 3.50 |
| ☐ 75 | Walter Stewart | | 20.00 | 8.00 | 2.00 |
| ☐ 76 | George Walberg | | 20.00 | 8.00 | 2.00 |
| ☐ 77 | Glenn Wright | | 20.00 | 8.00 | 2.00 |
| ☐ 78 | Charles (Buddy) Myer | | 20.00 | 8.00 | 2.00 |
| ☐ 79 | James (Zack) Taylor | | 20.00 | 8.00 | 2.00 |
| ☐ 80 | George H. (Babe) Ruth | | 700.00 | 280.00 | 70.00 |
| ☐ 81 | D'Arcy (Jake) Flowers | | 20.00 | 8.00 | 2.00 |
| ☐ 82 | Ray Kolp | | 20.00 | 8.00 | 2.00 |
| ☐ 83 | Oswald Bluege | | 20.00 | 8.00 | 2.00 |
| ☐ 84 | Morris (Moe) Berg | | 25.00 | 10.00 | 2.50 |
| ☐ 85 | Jimmy Foxx | | 90.00 | 36.00 | 9.00 |
| ☐ 86 | Sam Byrd | | 20.00 | 8.00 | 2.00 |
| ☐ 87 | Danny MacFayden | | 20.00 | 8.00 | 2.00 |
| ☐ 88 | Joe Judge | | 20.00 | 8.00 | 2.00 |
| ☐ 89 | Joe Sewell | | 35.00 | 14.00 | 3.50 |
| ☐ 90 | Lloyd Waner | | 35.00 | 14.00 | 3.50 |
| ☐ 91 | Luke Sewell | | 25.00 | 10.00 | 2.50 |
| ☐ 92 | Leo Mangum | | 20.00 | 8.00 | 2.00 |
| ☐ 93 | George H. (Babe) Ruth | | 700.00 | 280.00 | 70.00 |
| ☐ 94 | Al Spohrer | | 20.00 | 8.00 | 2.00 |

| | | | MINT | VG-E | F-G |
|---|---|---|---|---|---|
| ☐ 109 | Wally Moses | | 40.00 | 16.00 | 4.00 |
| ☐ 110 | Gerry Walker | | 40.00 | 16.00 | 4.00 |
| ☐ 111 | Goose Goslin | | 60.00 | 24.00 | 6.00 |
| ☐ 112 | Charlie Gehringer | | 80.00 | 32.00 | 8.00 |
| ☐ 113 | Hal Trosky | | 40.00 | 16.00 | 4.00 |
| ☐ 114 | Buddy Myer | | 40.00 | 16.00 | 4.00 |
| ☐ 115 | Luke Appling | | 60.00 | 24.00 | 6.00 |
| ☐ 116 | Zeke Bonura | | 40.00 | 16.00 | 4.00 |
| ☐ 117 | Tony Lazzeri | | 50.00 | 20.00 | 5.00 |
| ☐ 118 | Joe DiMaggio | | 650.00 | 260.00 | 65.00 |
| ☐ 119 | Bill Dickey | | 125.00 | 50.00 | 12.50 |
| ☐ 120 | Bob Feller | | 200.00 | 80.00 | 20.00 |
| ☐ 121 | Harry Kelley | | 40.00 | 16.00 | 4.00 |
| ☐ 122 | Johnny Allen | | 40.00 | 16.00 | 4.00 |
| ☐ 123 | Bob Johnson | | 40.00 | 16.00 | 4.00 |
| ☐ 124 | Joe Cronin | | 80.00 | 32.00 | 8.00 |
| ☐ 125 | Rip Radcliff | | 40.00 | 16.00 | 4.00 |
| ☐ 126 | Cecil Travis | | 40.00 | 16.00 | 4.00 |
| ☐ 127 | Joe Kuhel | | 40.00 | 16.00 | 4.00 |
| ☐ 128 | Odell Hale | | 40.00 | 16.00 | 4.00 |
| ☐ 129 | Sam West | | 40.00 | 16.00 | 4.00 |
| ☐ 130 | Ben Chapman | | 40.00 | 16.00 | 4.00 |
| ☐ 131 | Monte Pearson | | 40.00 | 16.00 | 4.00 |
| ☐ 132 | Rick Ferrell | | 60.00 | 24.00 | 6.00 |
| ☐ 133 | Tommy Bridges | | 40.00 | 16.00 | 4.00 |
| ☐ 134 | Schoolboy Rowe | | 40.00 | 16.00 | 4.00 |
| ☐ 135 | Vernon Kennedy | | 40.00 | 16.00 | 4.00 |
| ☐ 136 | Red Ruffing | | 80.00 | 32.00 | 8.00 |
| ☐ 137 | Lefty Grove | | 125.00 | 50.00 | 12.50 |
| ☐ 138 | Wes Ferrell | | 40.00 | 16.00 | 4.00 |
| ☐ 139 | Buck Newsom | | 40.00 | 16.00 | 4.00 |
| ☐ 140 | Rogers Hornsby | | 150.00 | 60.00 | 15.00 |

## V353 Canadian Goudey

The cards in this 94 card set measure 2 3/8" by 2 7/8". World Wide Gum, the Canadian subsidiary of Goudey, issued this set of numbered color cards in 1933. Cards 1 to 52 contain obverses identical to the American issue, but cards 53 to 94 have a slightly different order. Backs are found printed in English only, or in French and English (the former are slightly harder to find).

| | MINT | VG-E | F-G |
|---|---|---|---|
| COMPLETE SET | 3250.00 | 1400.00 | 350.00 |
| COMMON PLAYER (1-94) | 20.00 | 8.00 | 2.00 |

| | | | MINT | VG-E | F-G |
|---|---|---|---|---|---|
| ☐ 1 | Benny Bengough | | 40.00 | 10.00 | 2.00 |
| ☐ 2 | Dazzy Vance | | 35.00 | 14.00 | 3.50 |
| ☐ 3 | Hugh Critz | | 20.00 | 8.00 | 2.00 |
| ☐ 4 | Heine Schuble | | 20.00 | 8.00 | 2.00 |
| ☐ 5 | Babe Herman | | 25.00 | 10.00 | 2.50 |
| ☐ 6 | Jimmy Dykes | | 25.00 | 10.00 | 2.50 |
| ☐ 7 | Ted Lyons | | 35.00 | 14.00 | 3.50 |
| ☐ 8 | Roy Johnson | | 20.00 | 8.00 | 2.00 |
| ☐ 9 | Dave Harris | | 20.00 | 8.00 | 2.00 |
| ☐ 10 | Glenn Myatt | | 20.00 | 8.00 | 2.00 |
| ☐ 11 | Billy Rogell | | 20.00 | 8.00 | 2.00 |
| ☐ 12 | George Pipgras | | 20.00 | 8.00 | 2.00 |
| ☐ 13 | Lafayette Thompson | | 20.00 | 8.00 | 2.00 |
| ☐ 14 | Henry Johnson | | 20.00 | 8.00 | 2.00 |
| ☐ 15 | Victor Sorrell | | 20.00 | 8.00 | 2.00 |

## V354 Canadian Goudey

The cards in this 96 card set measure 2 3/8" by 2 7/8". The 1934 Canadian Goudey set was issued by World Wide Gum Company. Cards 1 to 48 have the same format as the 1933 American Goudey issue while cards 49 to 96 have the same format as the 1934 American Goudey issue. Cards numbers 49 to 96 all have the "Lou Gehrig Says" endorsement on the front of the cards. No Chuck Klein endorsement exists as it does in the 1934 American issue. The backs are either in English or in English and French. The ACC designation is V354.

|  | MINT | VG-E | F-G |
|---|---|---|---|
| COMPLETE SET | 2900.00 | 1200.00 | 300.00 |
| COMMON PLAYER (1-96) | 20.00 | 8.00 | 2.00 |

| | | MINT | VG-E | F-G |
|---|---|---|---|---|
| ☐ 1 | Rogers Hornsby | 100.00 | 35.00 | 7.00 |
| ☐ 2 | Eddie Morgan | 20.00 | 8.00 | 2.00 |
| ☐ 3 | Valentine Picinich | 20.00 | 8.00 | 2.00 |
| ☐ 4 | Rabbit Maranville | 35.00 | 14.00 | 3.50 |
| ☐ 5 | Flint Rhem | 20.00 | 8.00 | 2.00 |
| ☐ 6 | Jim Elliott | 20.00 | 8.00 | 2.00 |
| ☐ 7 | Fred (Red) Lucas | 20.00 | 8.00 | 2.00 |
| ☐ 8 | Fred Marberry | 20.00 | 8.00 | 2.00 |
| ☐ 9 | Clifton Heathcote | 20.00 | 8.00 | 2.00 |
| ☐ 10 | Bernie Friberg | 20.00 | 8.00 | 2.00 |
| ☐ 11 | Elwood English | 20.00 | 8.00 | 2.00 |
| ☐ 12 | Carl Reynolds | 20.00 | 8.00 | 2.00 |
| ☐ 13 | Ray Benge | 20.00 | 8.00 | 2.00 |
| ☐ 14 | Ben Cantwell | 20.00 | 8.00 | 2.00 |
| ☐ 15 | Bump Hadley | 20.00 | 8.00 | 2.00 |
| ☐ 16 | Herb Pennock | 35.00 | 14.00 | 3.50 |
| ☐ 17 | Fred Lindstrom | 35.00 | 14.00 | 3.50 |
| ☐ 18 | Edgar (Sam) Rice | 35.00 | 14.00 | 3.50 |
| ☐ 19 | Fred Frankhouse | 20.00 | 8.00 | 2.00 |
| ☐ 20 | Fred Fitzsimmons | 20.00 | 8.00 | 2.00 |
| ☐ 21 | Earl Coombs | 35.00 | 14.00 | 3.50 |
| ☐ 22 | George Uhle | 20.00 | 8.00 | 2.00 |
| ☐ 23 | Richard Coffman | 20.00 | 8.00 | 2.00 |
| ☐ 24 | Travis C. Jackson | 35.00 | 14.00 | 3.50 |
| ☐ 25 | Robert J. Burke | 20.00 | 8.00 | 2.00 |
| ☐ 26 | Randy Moore | 20.00 | 8.00 | 2.00 |
| ☐ 27 | Heinie Sand | 20.00 | 8.00 | 2.00 |
| ☐ 28 | George (Babe) Ruth | 700.00 | 280.00 | 70.00 |
| ☐ 29 | Tris Speaker | 75.00 | 30.00 | 7.50 |
| ☐ 30 | Perce (Pat) Malone | 20.00 | 8.00 | 2.00 |
| ☐ 31 | Sam Jones | 20.00 | 8.00 | 2.00 |
| ☐ 32 | Eppa Rixey | 35.00 | 14.00 | 3.50 |
| ☐ 33 | Floyd (Pete) Scott | 20.00 | 8.00 | 2.00 |
| ☐ 34 | Pete Jablonowski | 20.00 | 8.00 | 2.00 |
| ☐ 35 | Clyde Manion | 20.00 | 8.00 | 2.00 |
| ☐ 36 | Dibrell Williams | 20.00 | 8.00 | 2.00 |
| ☐ 37 | Glenn Spencer | 20.00 | 8.00 | 2.00 |
| ☐ 38 | Ray Kremer | 20.00 | 8.00 | 2.00 |
| ☐ 39 | Phil Todt | 20.00 | 8.00 | 2.00 |
| ☐ 40 | Russell Rollings | 20.00 | 8.00 | 2.00 |
| ☐ 41 | Earl Clark | 20.00 | 8.00 | 2.00 |
| ☐ 42 | Jess Petty | 20.00 | 8.00 | 2.00 |
| ☐ 43 | Frank O'Rourke | 20.00 | 8.00 | 2.00 |
| ☐ 44 | Jesse Haines | 35.00 | 14.00 | 3.50 |
| ☐ 45 | Horace Lisenbee | 20.00 | 8.00 | 2.00 |
| ☐ 46 | Owen Carroll | 20.00 | 8.00 | 2.00 |
| ☐ 47 | Tom Zachary | 20.00 | 8.00 | 2.00 |
| ☐ 48 | Charlie Ruffing | 40.00 | 16.00 | 4.00 |
| ☐ 49 | Ray Benge | 20.00 | 8.00 | 2.00 |
| ☐ 50 | Woody English | 20.00 | 8.00 | 2.00 |
| ☐ 51 | Ben Chapman | 20.00 | 8.00 | 2.00 |
| ☐ 52 | Joe Kuhel | 20.00 | 8.00 | 2.00 |
| ☐ 53 | Bill Terry | 45.00 | 18.00 | 4.50 |
| ☐ 54 | Robert (Lefty) Grove | 75.00 | 30.00 | 7.50 |
| ☐ 55 | Jerome (Dizzy) Dean | 150.00 | 60.00 | 15.00 |
| ☐ 56 | Chuck Klein | 40.00 | 16.00 | 4.00 |
| ☐ 57 | Charley Gehringer | 45.00 | 18.00 | 4.50 |
| ☐ 58 | Jimmy Foxx | 100.00 | 40.00 | 10.00 |
| ☐ 59 | Mickey Cochrane | 50.00 | 20.00 | 5.00 |
| ☐ 60 | Willie Kamm | 20.00 | 8.00 | 2.00 |
| ☐ 61 | Charlie Grimm | 25.00 | 10.00 | 2.50 |
| ☐ 62 | Ed Brandt | 20.00 | 8.00 | 2.00 |
| ☐ 63 | Tony Piet | 20.00 | 8.00 | 2.00 |
| ☐ 64 | Frank Frisch | 45.00 | 18.00 | 4.50 |
| ☐ 65 | Alvin Crowder | 20.00 | 8.00 | 2.00 |
| ☐ 66 | Frank Hogan | 20.00 | 8.00 | 2.00 |
| ☐ 67 | Paul Waner | 35.00 | 14.00 | 3.50 |
| ☐ 68 | Heinie Manush | 35.00 | 14.00 | 3.50 |
| ☐ 69 | Leo Durocher | 35.00 | 14.00 | 3.50 |
| ☐ 70 | Floyd Vaughan | 35.00 | 14.00 | 3.50 |
| ☐ 71 | Carl Hubbell | 45.00 | 18.00 | 4.50 |
| ☐ 72 | Hugh Critz | 20.00 | 8.00 | 2.00 |
| ☐ 73 | John (Blondy) Ryan | 20.00 | 8.00 | 2.00 |
| ☐ 74 | Roger Cramer | 25.00 | 10.00 | 2.50 |
| ☐ 75 | Baxter Jordan | 20.00 | 8.00 | 2.00 |
| ☐ 76 | Ed Coleman | 20.00 | 8.00 | 2.00 |
| ☐ 77 | Julius Solters | 20.00 | 8.00 | 2.00 |
| ☐ 78 | Chick Hafey | 35.00 | 14.00 | 3.50 |
| ☐ 79 | Larry French | 20.00 | 8.00 | 2.00 |
| ☐ 80 | Frank (Don) Hurst | 20.00 | 8.00 | 2.00 |
| ☐ 81 | Gerald Walker | 20.00 | 8.00 | 2.00 |
| ☐ 82 | Ernie Lombardi | 35.00 | 14.00 | 3.50 |
| ☐ 83 | Walter (Huck) Betts | 20.00 | 8.00 | 2.00 |
| ☐ 84 | Luke Appling | 35.00 | 14.00 | 3.50 |
| ☐ 85 | John Frederick | 20.00 | 8.00 | 2.00 |
| ☐ 86 | Fred Walker | 20.00 | 8.00 | 2.00 |
| ☐ 87 | Tom Bridges | 25.00 | 10.00 | 2.50 |
| ☐ 88 | Dick Porter | 20.00 | 8.00 | 2.00 |
| ☐ 89 | John Stone | 20.00 | 8.00 | 2.00 |
| ☐ 90 | James (Tex) Carleton | 20.00 | 8.00 | 2.00 |
| ☐ 91 | Joe Stripp | 20.00 | 8.00 | 2.00 |
| ☐ 92 | Lou Gehrig | 400.00 | 160.00 | 40.00 |
| ☐ 93 | George Earnshaw | 20.00 | 8.00 | 2.00 |
| ☐ 94 | Oscar Melillo | 20.00 | 8.00 | 2.00 |
| ☐ 95 | Oral Hildebrand | 20.00 | 8.00 | 2.00 |
| ☐ 96 | John Allen | 20.00 | 8.00 | 2.00 |

# V362 World Wide Gum

The cards in this 48 card set measure 2 1/2" by 3 1/4". In 1950, long after its former parent company had disappeared from the card market, the World Wide Gum Company issued a set of blue printed cards depicting players from the International League. The cards are blank backed, with card numbers and French/English biographies appearing on front. The series was entitled "Big League Stars".

|  | MINT | VG-E | F-G |
|---|---|---|---|
| COMPLETE SET | 1500.00 | 600.00 | 150.00 |
| COMMON PLAYER (1-48) | 30.00 | 12.00 | 3.00 |

| | | MINT | VG-E | F-G |
|---|---|---|---|---|
| ☐ 1 | Rocky Bridges | 35.00 | 14.00 | 3.50 |
| ☐ 2 | Chuck Connors | 150.00 | 60.00 | 15.00 |
| ☐ 3 | Jake Wade | 30.00 | 12.00 | 3.00 |
| ☐ 4 | Al Cihocki | 30.00 | 12.00 | 3.00 |
| ☐ 5 | John Simmons | 30.00 | 12.00 | 3.00 |
| ☐ 6 | Frank Trechock | 30.00 | 12.00 | 3.00 |
| ☐ 7 | Steve Lembo | 30.00 | 12.00 | 3.00 |
| ☐ 8 | Johnny Welaj | 30.00 | 12.00 | 3.00 |
| ☐ 9 | Seymour Block | 30.00 | 12.00 | 3.00 |
| ☐ 10 | Pat McGlothlin | 30.00 | 12.00 | 3.00 |
| ☐ 11 | Bryan Stephans | 30.00 | 12.00 | 3.00 |
| ☐ 12 | Clarence Podbielan | 30.00 | 12.00 | 3.00 |
| ☐ 13 | Clem Hausmann | 30.00 | 12.00 | 3.00 |
| ☐ 14 | Turk Lown | 30.00 | 12.00 | 3.00 |
| ☐ 15 | Joe Payne | 30.00 | 12.00 | 3.00 |
| ☐ 16 | Coaker Triplett | 30.00 | 12.00 | 3.00 |
| ☐ 17 | Nick Strincevich | 30.00 | 12.00 | 3.00 |
| ☐ 18 | Charlie Thompson | 30.00 | 12.00 | 3.00 |
| ☐ 19 | Erick Silverman | 30.00 | 12.00 | 3.00 |
| ☐ 20 | George Schmees | 30.00 | 12.00 | 3.00 |
| ☐ 21 | George Binks | 30.00 | 12.00 | 3.00 |
| ☐ 22 | Gino Cimoli | 35.00 | 14.00 | 3.50 |
| ☐ 23 | Marty Tabacheck | 30.00 | 12.00 | 3.00 |
| ☐ 24 | Al Gionfriddo | 35.00 | 14.00 | 3.50 |
| ☐ 25 | Ronnie Lee | 30.00 | 12.00 | 3.00 |
| ☐ 26 | Clyde King | 35.00 | 14.00 | 3.50 |
| ☐ 27 | Harry Heslet | 30.00 | 12.00 | 3.00 |
| ☐ 28 | Jerry Scala | 30.00 | 12.00 | 3.00 |
| ☐ 29 | Boris Woyt | 30.00 | 12.00 | 3.00 |
| ☐ 30 | Jack Collum | 30.00 | 12.00 | 3.00 |
| ☐ 31 | Chet Laabs | 30.00 | 12.00 | 3.00 |
| ☐ 32 | Carden Gillenwater | 30.00 | 12.00 | 3.00 |
| ☐ 33 | Irving Medlinger | 30.00 | 12.00 | 3.00 |
| ☐ 34 | Toby Atwell | 30.00 | 12.00 | 3.00 |
| ☐ 35 | Charlie Marshall | 30.00 | 12.00 | 3.00 |
| ☐ 36 | Johnny Mayo | 30.00 | 12.00 | 3.00 |
| ☐ 37 | Gene Markland | 30.00 | 12.00 | 3.00 |
| ☐ 38 | Russ Kerns | 30.00 | 12.00 | 3.00 |
| ☐ 39 | Jim Prendergast | 30.00 | 12.00 | 3.00 |
| ☐ 40 | Lou Welaj | 30.00 | 12.00 | 3.00 |
| ☐ 41 | Clyde Kluttz | 30.00 | 12.00 | 3.00 |
| ☐ 42 | Bill Glynn | 30.00 | 12.00 | 3.00 |
| ☐ 43 | Don Richmond | 30.00 | 12.00 | 3.00 |
| ☐ 44 | Hank Biasatti | 30.00 | 12.00 | 3.00 |
| ☐ 45 | Tom Lasorda | 125.00 | 50.00 | 12.50 |
| ☐ 46 | Al Anderson | 30.00 | 12.00 | 3.00 |
| ☐ 47 | George Byam | 30.00 | 12.00 | 3.00 |
| ☐ 48 | Dutch Mele | 30.00 | 12.00 | 3.00 |

# Press Pins

*The following section is essentially the contribution of advanced pin collector/dealer Jim Johnston; although we have edited and added to his draft, we have tried to preserve his original flavor. His laborious undertaking in finding something informative and interesting to say about each and every pin is greatly appreciated. Undoubtedly, the following section is the definitive work on press pins. We hope you enjoy it.*

*The values listed for each pin were researched to include not just the opinions of Jim Johnston, but to consider as well prices from several of the leading collector/dealers of these attractive pieces.*

The first press pin dates to the 1911 World Series where the press box, then as now, was intended to be a limited-access area. Nevertheless the forceful Giant manager, John McGraw, had a history of violating that domain with his entourage of Irish cronies. According to collector cum laude Joe L. Brown, the ex-Pirate G.M., the Athletics anticipated the problem. The club ordered and dispensed a very visible lapel pin to writers with legitimate credentials.

The idea was adopted by subsequent Series participants, and with the exception of the 1918 Cubs, each host in the World Series since 1912 has issued a press badge. Though early on distribution of press pins was a requisite encumbrance, their intent today has become a symbolic gesture of welcome to the media.

Implicitly World Series pins have also helped to harmonize the sometimes strained relations between a team and the media. Especially in the early years of the Series, the majority of writers in attendance were local, and their prevailing role in projecting the image of the hometown club was a perennial source of challenge.

The first run of pins from 1911 through about the 1923 New York is very rare. The meager quantity available defies precise values, since the demand for any of them typically greatly exceeds the supply.

A misconception exists among collectors that the availability of a press pin is proportional to the number produced. Numbers available to collectors perhaps are governed more by the host team's disposition of the originally undistributed pieces. The likelihood is strong, for example, that residual All Star pins from 1974 in Pittsburgh were discarded, while the New York pins for the 1964 Series were virtually all distributed to the extensive media present with few left-overs.

There are other obvious factors that determine the scarcity of particular pins. As with any relic, press pins have fought a losing war of attrition against time. Coverage for All Star games is not as extensive as that for the World Series, so generally, the former are in shorter supply than the latter.

The pins pictured below are not all reduced at the same percentage as especially large or wide pins were further reduced to fit the column width. Identifying a particular pin is typically not a matter of measuring or sizing as most are about the same size, i.e., a little bigger than the size of a quarter.

Hosting franchises for World Series or All Star events frequently order supplemental pins that are struck from the standard mold, but bear variations in the fastener. These non-standard fasteners are typically ordered in lesser quantities, perhaps 25% of the standard pin quantity. These variations may appear in three forms: charms, clasps, and brooches. As a general rule, charms are valued at about 40% of the corresponding pin, clasps are valued at 60%, and brooches 80%. In some instances (noted below), needle posts or threaded posts were not made for a given pin; the value listed refers to a pin in its most desirable form.

Press pins are frequently found in lesser condition, for example, pins with chipped enamel or altered pins. Defects visible on routine inspection can reduce the value by 50%. Clearly visible, offensive, or distracting damage to the pin can put the value to around 10% of the normal mint condition value. Pins that have been converted to charms, cuff links, etc. but are otherwise undamaged would be valued less than an original issue charm. Attempts to re-convert a pin to a more desirable or valuable form are almost never fruitful.

Most collectibles as popular as these pins have fallen prey to the odious reproduction. To date, however, these "restrikes" can be readily detected by an intermediate collector. The narrative below mentions such instances. The value of restrikes (as with most reproductions) is related to the duplication cost rather than being related to the value of the original. What is the value of a forged or stamped autograph? What is the value of a fake diamond? Restrikes are generally worth between $5 and $10 depending on the detail on the reproduction. Furthermore, purchasing restrikes at any price encourages further illegal reproduction. The emphasis in the narrative below is to educate the reader so that restrikes can be recognized for what they are.

The last sentence of each paragraph description below gives the manufacturer, type of fastener(s), color(s), and value for that particular pin.

The **1986 New York** Mets design signals their supremacy in the Big Apple as well as on the ballfield. The team's logo, and baseball stitches are superimposed over the impressive Gotham skyline. The pin is actually a phantom from the near miss-Mets of 1985, and the comeback Series victory in '86's Classic proves the Met's third time was indeed a charm. A dated network (NBC) variation pin was also produced by Balfour; its value $80. Balfour; needle post and charms; blue and orange; value $200.

The **1986 Boston** pin is a striking design, featuring the Sox logo, surmounting a portion of a globe, and surrounded by laurel leaves and dual pennants, symbols of victory that was not to be. A dated network (NBC) variation pin was also produced by Balfour; its value $90. Balfour; needle post and charms; red, blue, and white; value $125.

The **1985 St. Louis** pin is a return to normalcy for the Cardinals considering their overly common 1982 issue. Struck in their familiar red and gold, the 1985 is actually a 1983 phantom. Balfour; needle post and charms; red and black; value $70.

The **1985 Kansas City** pin is reminiscent of their 1980 pin. It differs from the former in its asymmetry. Green Co.; needle post and charms; blue and white; value $65.

The **1984 San Diego** pin was produced in the team's traditional light brown and white enamel. Limited numbers of this pin and the counterpart Detroit pin were ordered by the NBC network and bear its logo at the bottom of the pieces. The Padre pin was illicitly reproduced. The "fake" version can be spotted by its uneven surface and criss-cross back design. A network (NBC) variation pin was also produced by Balfour; its value $75. Balfour; needle post and charms; brown and white; value $60.

The **1984 Detroit** was originally ordered in 1972, and quantities of this rather pedestrian design were reasonably available throughout the 12-year interim. A network (NBC) variation pin was also produced by Balfour; its value $75. Balfour; needle post and charms; blue; value $60.

The **1983 Philadelphia** marked the abandonment of a viable 1981 phantom. A very convincing reproduction appeared recently. The restrike can be distinguished from the original (which has a soft satin finish on its back) by its shiny back. Balfour; needle post and charms; red, white, and green; value $30.

The **1983 Baltimore** is typical of most recent World Series pins, announcing the club's participation in ordinal terms. This procedure is becoming fairly universal among the franchises in order to avert producing a functionally-useless, dated phantom. In this case, the pin was actually produced in the club's optimistic 1982 season. Balfour; needle post, brooch, and charms; orange, white, and black; value $50.

The **1982 St. Louis** is without a doubt the most common World Series pin of the 1980s. This issue had languished "on the shelf" since 1974 when the Cards finished a game and a half out in the N.L. East. Balfour; needle post and charms; red; value $20.

The **1982 Milwaukee** is nothing more than a carbon copy of the club's standard logo, notwithstanding the plaudits Sports Illustrated gave it shortly after its issue. A scarcer variation of the pin exists which bears the inscription "American League Champions 1982" on the reverse. Balfour; needle post and charms; blue; value $60.

The **1981 Los Angeles** is one of the more attractive Dodger pins. It continues to be available, while its popularity remains strong. Balfour; needle post and charms; red, white and blue; value $65.

The **1981 New York** Yankee pin is noticeably more abundant than its Dodger counterpart. Still the legions of Yankee fans have diluted the available supply. Balfour; needle post and charms; blue; value $50.

The **1980 Philadelphia** represents weakest press pin design of the decade. Although the Phillie Phanatic plays an important role in the marketing efforts of the franchise, most collectors consider his appearance on the reverse of the medallion inappropriate. Balfour; needle post; gold; value $45.

The **1980 Kansas City** is rather nondescript, but it is gaining respect with collectors as the most difficult standard Series pin of this decade to acquire. Green Co.; needle post and charms; blue and white; value $125.

The **1979 Pittsburgh** is a study in contrasts. Presenting a rather plain obverse, its beauty lies with its reverse which lists the Pirates' championship seasons beneath a likeness of the World Series trophy rendered in sharp relief. Balfour; needle post; gold; value $50.

The **1979 Baltimore** is arguably the Orioles' most attractive World Series pin, however it frequently comes with distracting manufacturing blemishes of uneven enameling. Balfour; needle post, brooch, clasp, and charms; white, black, and orange; value $70.

The **1978 Los Angeles** represents a step backward from the previous year. Furthermore a restrike has appeared, which can be detected by dull plating and light blue features. Balfour; needle post and charms; blue and white; value $90.

The **1978 New York** depicts the colonnade unique to Yankee Stadium's outfield. This is a colorful, popular piece. The adjunct charm is surprisingly common. Balfour; needle post and charms; red, white, and blue; value $65.

The **1977 Los Angeles** is a striking departure from the other Dodger pins. Featuring a classic, soaring baseball, this design is simple, yet majestic. The pin's vulnerability to scratches, however, is a liability. Balfour; needle post and charms; red, white, and blue; value $100.

The **1977 New York** was once considered the most common World Series pin of the Seventies. Availability of this popular pin, however, is steadily shrinking. Its appeal stems from its likeness to a ring. Balfour; needle post and charms; blue; value $55.

The **1976 Cincinnati**, which features the World Series trophy, reflects that franchise's resolute self-confidence. Though the dynasty was in its twilight, this pin embodies the epoch that belonged to the Reds. Balfour; needle post and charms; red; value $130.

The **1976 New York**, not unlike an anniversary pronouncement, proclaims the Yankee's "thirtieth!" World Series appearance. But after a 12-year hiatus from Series competition, the Yankees returned unimaginatively to the franchise's monotonous top hat logo for its press pin. Balfour; needle post; red, white, and blue; value $100.

The **1975 Cincinnati** and its companion Boston issue are as colorful as that series was, itself. The "Big Red Machine" is represented by an aerial view of its stadium surrounded by the big red "C". Balfour; needle post and charms; red; value $150.

The **1975 Boston** simply features the team's logo in red superimposed on the pure white field of a baseball. The seams of the ball are, of course, gold plated. Balfour; needle post and charms; red and white; value $275.

The **1974 Los Angeles** is typical of most Dodger pins. Although aesthetically lacking, vigorous collector interest persists because of its relative scarcity. This pin suffered an identity mixup when it was labeled in the previous Guide as the 1966 pin. Balfour; needle post and charms; blue; value $150.

The **1974 Oakland** is celebrated as the gem of the decade. It has been conjectured that the scarcity of the pin is a function of that franchise's alleged practice of thrift. In the final analysis, however, this exquisite piece is difficult but possible to obtain. Josten; needle post; green and white; value $325.

The **1973 New York** Mets pin is influenced mildly by their Series loss. Though collector enthusiasm for the '73 Mets is sustained, it pales behind the glory of the 1969 Mets. Balfour; needle post and charms; orange and blue; value $125.

The **1973 Oakland** is nearly a clone of the Balfour 1972 Oakland. Both are artistic disappointments, but the former, purely from the standpoint of scarcity, is proving as difficult to locate as the much heralded 1974 Oakland. Josten; needle post and charms; green and white; value $225.

The **1972 Cincinnati** attracts collectors with its thematic reprise of the legendary 1948 All Star piece. The Reds pin, however, typically has subtle manufacturing discolorations in the red enamel. Balfour; needle post and charms; red and white; value $100.

The **1972 Oakland** is the most common of the A's standard World Series pins. Nevertheless it commands respect from collectors because of its association with its pricier siblings, the 1973 and 1974 Oakland pins. Balfour; needle post and charms; green and white; value **$175**.

The **1971 Pittsburgh**, doubtless a phantom from 1970, highlights the new Three Rivers Stadium. After the Series, the mold for the pin was used to create a clasp celebrating the Pirate victory; it simply states "World Champs Pirates". Balfour; needle post; black; value **$150**.

The **1971 Baltimore** pin is currently enjoying accelerated respect in its needle post back form. The spring-loaded clasp back is quite common. Balfour; needle post, brooch and clasp; black, white, and orange; value **$100**.

The **1970 Cincinnati** was misidentified as the 1976 Cincinnati in the previous Guide. It is moderately common for its vintage. It was designed with the appearance of wear in its lower corners, which has aroused concern and criticism among collectors. G.B. Miller; needle post and charms; red, white, and black; value **$100**.

The **1970 Baltimore**, an asymmetrical pin, is unique with its generic MLBB logo. Demand for the pin is strong since it is marginally the most difficult of the Oriole pins for their three consecutive pennant winning years. Jenkins; needle post, clasp, charm, and brooch; black, white, and orange; value **$125**.

The **1969 New York** Mets became the new apple of The Big Apple's eyes as the Yankees became mired in mediocrity. These new heroes were immortalized as the "Amazin' Mets" for their heroics. The value of this pin is sustained by such demand with little regard for the pin's relative abundance. Balfour; needle post and charm; blue and orange; value **$225**.

The **1969 Baltimore** is a must on the shopping list of most Oriole collectors, although such enthusiasm is not manifested among pin collectors generally. The piece is conservative, and in the pin form, bears annoying impurities in the bill of the cap. Balfour; needle post, charms, clasp and brooch; black, white, and orange; value **$100**.

The **1968 St. Louis** is the most common World Series pin of its decade. Notwithstanding, it is a colorful entry. The baseball near the pin's center is unplated and usually tarnished. Balfour; needle post and charms; black, white, and red; value **$55**.

The **1968 Detroit** pin signals the end to two mediocre decades of Tiger baseball. It was originally ordered for the club's near (one game) miss a season earlier. Despite its rather unstimulating appearance, the pin continues to be locally pursued. Balfour; needle post and charms; blue; value **$150**.

The **1967 St. Louis** would enjoy a niche among the great press pins of the decade if it were not so available. Outside the circle of Cardinal collectors, the pin's appeal is driven by its electrifying colors. Balfour; needle post and charms; red, white and black; value **$90**.

The **1967 Boston** has an enigmatic lineage that can be traced to the Chicago All Star pin of 1950, which in turn, seems fashioned from the 1949 Boston phantom. The 1967 pin has become a "second tier" priority for Red Sox collectors whose priorities lie with the coveted 1975 World Series and 1961 All Star pins. Balfour; needle post; red, white, and blue; value **$125**.

The **1966 Los Angeles** is often mistaken for the 1965 Dodger. This is subjectively the most attractive of all Dodger pins since their relocation. The dates on the pin merely commemorate their World Series winning seasons. Balfour; needle post and charms; blue and white; value **$125**.

The **1966 Baltimore** is a reminder of a championship season for the heirs of the hapless St. Louis Browns. Of the six pennant winners produced in Baltimore, the 1966 Oriole represents its weakest won/lost percentage, but fans and collectors still embrace fond memories of this team. This is reflected in the pin's desirability. Balfour; needle post, clasp, charm, and brooch; black, white, and orange; value **$225**.

The **1965 Los Angeles** is the prototype of all that is boring in Dodger pins. It seems to be a last minute, unstudied production effort. This pin was erroneously depicted in the previous Guide as the 1977 Los Angeles. Balfour; needle post and charm; blue; value **$125**.

The **1965 Minnesota** pin has struggled to maintain standing among collectors. Representing the only World Series appearance by a somewhat provincial franchise, the Twins produced a somewhat common pin. Its motif is echoed by the 1965 All Star, the 1967 phantom, and the 1969 phantom. Balfour; needle post; red, white, and blue; value **$125**.

The **1964 St. Louis** Cardinals returned to the Series following an 18-year absence and the pin is pursued with commensurate verve. Like citizens of ancient Sparta trained their youth for lives of hardened warfare, modern St. Louis residents seem to prepare their youth for lives of uncompromising Red Bird loyalty. Josten; threaded post, needle post, and brooch; red; value **$150**.

The **1964 New York** pin brings the end of the third Yankee dynasty. The pin is moderately common, but actively sought by collectors who experienced the era of Mantle. Balfour; needle post; red, white, and blue, value **$125**.

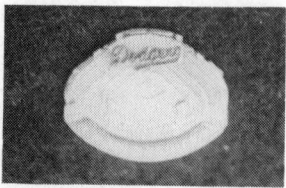

The **1963 Los Angeles**, mistaken for the 1974 Dodger in the first Memorabilia Guide, is likely a phantom from 1962, or possibly 1961. Consistent with the design of most Dodger pins, it is relatively featureless, but in contrast, this piece is discernably scarce. Balfour; threaded post; blue; value **$175**.

The **1963 New York** is yet another top hat. This time the execution is enhanced by its two-piece design which casts an attractive three-dimensional effect to the familiar theme. Balfour; needle post; red, white, and blue; value **$150**.

The **1962 San Francisco** Giant is one of the top pins of its decade, a diminutive, but artistic design triumph. Depicting wood grain in its bats and bridge detail, this pin is praised by collectors as a model of excellence. Balfour; threaded post; white; value **$225**.

The **1962 New York** Yankee occupies a place in history as the last press pin to mention the word "press". In the evolution of World Series news coverage, the electronic media has usurped much of the attention that was once visited exclusively upon the print media. And properly, these badges today should be termed "media pins". Balfour; threaded post and brooch; red, white, and blue; value **$150**.

The **1961 Cincinnati** Reds have lost a fond place in collectors' reminiscences over the years. The team was clearly led by Frank Robinson, whose subsequent dealing to the Orioles split his regional loyalty. As a result, interest in the otherwise appealing pin is lukewarm. Balfour; threaded post and charm; red, white, and blue; value **$125**.

The **1961 New York** pin symbolizes the legendary omnipotence of the team, and is a consistent favorite with Yankee collectors. Its design, similar to the cut out 1957 piece, further enhances its desirability. Balfour; threaded post and brooch; red, white, and blue; value **$150**.

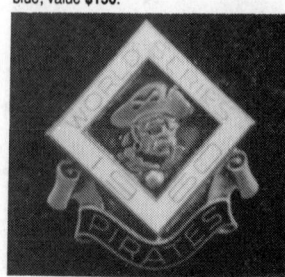

The **1960 Pittsburgh** marks an encore of David versus Goliath. The 1960 Pirates, and their representative pin, hold out the eternal hope of the meek. On that sole premise, this piece would command respect, but it is also of splendid composition, and scarcer than its contemporaries. Josten; threaded post; black and white; value **$200**.

The **1960 New York** Yankee is a bold and refreshing departure from the top hat. Paying homage to the team's folk hero manager, the two-piece pin presents Casey with a Mona Lisa smile in golden relief. There is a cruel irony to the pin, however; the Yankees lost the Series, and Casey was not invited to return in 1961. Balfour; threaded post and brooch; blue and white; value **$175**.

The **1959 Los Angeles** Dodgers reached the Series the year after they moved to the West Coast. They produced this gold-plated view of City Hall, an advanced rendition of Sgt. Joe Friday's badge. Unwittingly, the Dodgers also produced an inexpensive sheet metal stamping of this design the same year. The latter pin is identical to the press pin in color and dimension, but is little more than a concession trinket. Balfour; threaded post, charm, brooch; blue and white; value **$200**.

The **1959 Chicago** White Sox ended 40 years of frustration during World Series time by finally winning a pennant, and unveiling the consummate press pin. Complete with Mercury's wing and Mercator's projection, this pin is among the best to appear in the decade. Balfour; threaded post and brooch; blue and white; value **$225**.

The **1958 Milwaukee** pin is more sedate and also slightly more difficult to locate than its predecessor. This two-piece pin portrays the Brave in copper, and is vulnerable to oxidation. Balfour; threaded post; black and white; value **$175**.

The **1958 New York** is the antithesis of traditionally ornate Yankee pins. Symmetrical, innovative and simple in color scheme, it is a breath of fresh air in the bespangled history of Yankee press pins. Balfour; threaded post and brooch; blue and white; value **$175**.

The **1957 Milwaukee** Braves had a predominantly copper pin with a symbolic crown which is susceptible to irreparable oxidation. The Braves later ordered championship pins from the same mold, and these are easily differentiated by the white feather, and legend in the crown which appropriately says "World Champions". Balfour; threaded post; copper and red; value **$150**.

The **1957 New York** gets good marks from collectors, despite the all too familiar Yankee top hat, due in no small part to its appealing cut out design. Balfour; threaded post and brooch; red, white, and blue, value **$175**.

The **1956 Brooklyn** is the premier World Series pin of the 1950s. Apparently in accord with the unusual thrift in the Dodger front office, this pin was most likely ordered in limited numbers because its design necessitated a cumbersome and costly clasp. Futhermore, many may have been summarily discarded by media recipients because they weren't pins, but less desirable clasps. Dieges & Clust; clasps; blue, white, and silver, value **$450**.

In **1956 New York** designers were apparently pressed for an innovation. Whereupon the Yankees simply superimposed the top hat on a note pad. This pin was recently reproduced illegally; these can be readily identified by the erroneous needle post on the back. The stars on the original piece are smaller than the width of the hatband, while the stars on the bogus pin fully span the hatband. Balfour; threaded post and brooch; red, white, and blue; value **$200**.

The **1955 Brooklyn** Dodger is a rare instance of demand for a press pin being influenced by the team's performance. The Bums' World Series victory hopes had been dashed five times in recent memory, but 1955 belonged to the Dodgers. The pin is not particularly difficult to obtain, but demands a premium as Brooklyn's only World Series victory. Dieges & Clust; threaded post and brooch; blue, white, and silver; value **$300**.

The **1955 New York** is no exception to the monopoly the symbol of Uncle Sam's hat had on Yankee pins from 1947 to 1978. Adding a touch of freshness to the hat with each successive pennant may well have been a persistent problem, but in nearly every instance designers were equal to the task of producing aesthetically pleasing pins. Balfour; threaded post and brooch; red, white, and blue; value **$200**.

The **1954 New York** Giant is the most common World Series pin of the decade. In addition, it is generally agreed that the pin is unseemly, due in no small measure to its lack of plating, which in turn invites irreversible oxidation. Dieges & Clust; threaded post; black and white; value **$100**.

The **1954 Cleveland** Indian motif lends itself well to creative artistry. The popularity of this pin is for the most part a function of its colorful design. Balfour; threaded post; red, white, blue, and black; value **$175**.

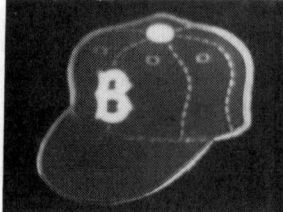

The **1953 Brooklyn** Dodger, the archetype of simplicity, is not for compulsive readers. With imposing Dodger blue enamel, trimmed in high-polished silver plating, this piece demonstrates that a quality pin need not be opulently complex. Dieges & Clust; threaded post and brooch; blue and white; value **$250**.

The **1953 New York** pin featured the multi-purpose "V". Perhaps "V" was to symbolize qualified victory in Korea; perhaps a portent of victory in the 1953 Series; but most likely it is a Roman numeral indicating New York's fifth consecutive World Series. Balfour; the threaded post and brooch; red, white, and blue; value **$250**.

The **1952 Brooklyn** Dodger is noticeably in stronger demand even though of comparable scarcity to other pins of the same vintage. This is due, in all likelihood, to the rendering of Willard Mullin's beloved Bum. With the bitterest of irony the Bum announces, "This is next year," but once again the cold-blooded nemesis from the Bronx prevailed. Dieges & Clust; threaded post and brooch; red and blue; value **$300**.

The **1952 New York** pin would be held in reverence if the Yankees had won but a single pennant since WWII. Collectors would view the imposing top hat admiringly. Despite the perennial monotony of that motif, the 1952 New York is aesthetically impressive. Its only liability is the manufacturer's difficulty in maintaining color purity in the red enamel. Balfour; threaded post and brooch; red, white, and blue; value **$250**.

The **1951 New York** Giant is relatively abundant. It is a somber reminder to most collectors of the 1954 Giant pin. Dieges & Clust; threaded post; black and white; value **$125**.

The **1951 New York** Yankees were systematically wrapping up another flag in the American League, while headlines of pennant drama were monopolized by the senior circuit. The Yanks rather unassuming pin for 1951 seems to reflect that aplomb. The pin has been another victim of unauthorized reproduction, and this recent pretender can be identified by its needle post and absence of manufacturer's credit on the back. Dieges & Clust; threaded post and brooch; red, white, and blue; value **$225**.

The **1950 Philadelphia** Phillies pin truly embodies the spirit of the "Whiz Kids." The character doffs his hat to an audience that has to love this team. The composition of the pin, however, is not above reproach. It was the first to employ a needle post and the clutch is materially inferior. Further, because the pin is sterling silver, it is usually seen heavily tarnished. Martin; needle post; red and silver; value **$250**.

The **1950 New York** pin is physically larger than most press pins. Somehow this conveys the irresistible and overpowering might that was synonymous with the Yankees of this period. Dieges & Clust; threaded post and brooch; red, white, and blue; value **$250**.

The **1949 Brooklyn** pin depicting the Temple of the Bums, embroidered with regal garland, rounds out the heritage of the franchise. Collectors of Dodger artifacts esteem this pin as the ultimate expression of the frustrated glory that was Brooklyn's. Dieges & Clust; threaded post and brooch; blue; value **$300**.

The **1949 New York** Yankee pin was coincidentally similar in embellishment to its Dodger counterpart. The royal garnishment was more appropriate in this case, since this tilt marked the first of five consecutive World Series victories by the Bombers. Dieges & Clust; threaded post and brooch; red, white, and blue; value **$275**.

The **1948 Boston** Braves pin was a colorful yet mature portrayal of its namesake. It is one of the few reminders left of the old National League franchise. The piece is moderately scarce and gaining in admiration from collectors. Balfour; threaded post; red, white, and copper; value **$275**.

The **1948 Cleveland** Indian design in conjunction with the beautiful 1954 piece should reverse the trendy, abusive humor aimed at this lake city. The colorful and innovative imagery that adorns this piece is a hallmark in post-war pins. Balfour; threaded post; red, white, and black; value **$250**.

The **1947 Brooklyn** could be the post-war "sleeper." Commemorating the Brooklyn Bridge, this unobtrusive yet engaging piece is usually categorized under "have not" by most collectors. Unfortunately this pin has been illegally reproduced. The fake is identified by the threaded post which is pointed at the top. The legitimate pin has a convex surface. Dieges & Clust; threaded post and brooch; blue; value **$400**.

The **1947 New York** is the first Yankee pin to utilize the top hat theme. At first glance the 1947 Yankee could be mistaken for a "Banana Republic's" pilot wings. An abnormally large piece, it remains popular with collectors, despite a design that stands on the threshold separating creative from outrageous. Dieges & Clust; threaded post; red, white, and blue; value **$275**.

The **1946 St. Louis** is a modest pin remembered principally as an engineering failure. The silver alloy plating ultimately did not adhere to its copper base. An example of this pin has yet to be found with the plating fully intact. St. Louis Button; threaded post; red, white, and silver; value **$300**.

The **1946 Boston** is Balfour's first World Series pin and a model of excellence. It possesses an alluring three dimensional translucence that unfortunately has been abandoned in more recent press pin manufacturing. Balfour; threaded post; red and white; value **$275**.

The **1945 Chicago** is probably the most common of Cubs' pins relative to their respective vintages. Press pins were intended to celebrate an event rather than be created for posterity. Although modern collectors grumble about the absence of the Cub logo, the American mood in the autumn of 1945 was joyously absorbed by victory in the war. Unknown; threaded post; red, white, and blue, value **$400**.

The **1945 Detroit** Tiger straddles that ill-defined demarcation in the lineage of World Series pins between the old to the new. Although it is chronologically a post-war pin, it conveys the mystique of "old." In the marketplace, this 1945 piece appears less frequently than the 1934 or 1935 Detroit pins, but more often than many others on the modern side of the threshold. Unknown; threaded post; red and blue; value **$350**.

The **1944 St. Louis** Cardinal is emerging as one of the easier pins in the decade. It was the only World Series pin to be gold plated during the war years. A substantial premium is realized for this piece when fully plated. St. Louis Button; threaded post; red and blue; value **$400**.

The **1944 St. Louis** Browns produced a "Guest" pin for this intra-city tilt, which suggests their utter inexperience in Series competition. There is a healthy demand for the copper-forged Browns' pin, but its dull features and primitive workmanship of the post attachment distress collectors. St. Louis Button; threaded post; copper; value **$375**.

The **1943 St. Louis** is dimensionally and materially identical to the 1942 Cardinal. An engineering miscalculation in the 1943 pin created distracting ripples in the paper insert. St. Louis Button; safety brooch; red, black, and white; value **$375**.

The **1943 New York** Yankee pin is another sterling silver war-era pin. Collectors who have advanced to this period don't pursue this pin to a great degree, citing its ungainly appearance. From the standpoint of scarcity, however, this piece should not be taken lightly. This pin has been reproduced. The original is sterling silver with a convex surface. The restrike has a flat surface and flat gold color. Dieges & Clust; threaded post and brooch; silver; value **$250**.

The **1942 St. Louis** pin shows the influence of wartime scarcity. Our country was not only engaged in full fury of battle, but our position seemed perilous. Conservation of most metals was imperative to the war effort. The 1942 Cardinal pin, a clear product of ingenuity in the face of such restrictions, is engineered in four parts. The colorful image is nothing more than a piece of paper. A sturdy piece of cardboard provides rigidity, and its face is protected by a transparent plastic-like material. The fastener, a crude excuse for a brooch, is a household safety pin. St. Louis Button; safety brooch; red, white, and black; value **$325**.

The **1942 New York** Yankee, although produced in roughly the same quantity as its contemporaries, has obviously survived the years in greater numbers. Again indicative of the war restrictions on most heavy metals, it is a common and rather lifeless sterling silver piece. Dieges & Clust; threaded post and brooch; silver; value **$225**.

The **1941 Brooklyn** pin is a second priority piece for Dodger collectors. It has even less favor with press pin collectors in general. Its unpretentiousness seemed to presage the team's humility in the Series. The striking similarity between this pin and Brooklyn's 1946 phantom reinforces the notion of Rickey's eye for calculated economy. This pin has been reproduced. The original is enameled. Its pin surface is convex, and it has a convex surface atop its threaded post. The restrikes are either not enameled, with a flat pin surface or enameled, but its red is bright and flat, having a threaded post with a sharp point. Dieges & Clust; threaded post; red, white, and blue; value **$275**.

The **1941 New York** is the last of the genre of patriotic expression. The 1941 and 1942 Yankees are the most plentiful press pins of the decade. Dieges & Clust; threaded post; red, white, and blue; value **$175**.

The **1940 Cincinnati** Reds copped the Series with an exemplary pitching staff supported by a line up renowned for its moderation. This press pin isn't an emotionally stirring piece. Its engineering faux pas mounts the female post over the manufacturer's credit. Bastian Bros.; threaded post and brooch; red, white, and blue; value **$250**.

The **1940 Detroit** is a listless rendition of the 1934 and 1935 Tiger pins, devoid of enamel and shallow in spirit. The Tiger's face has evolved to the likeness of a medieval gargoyle. Neutralizing its design distractions, however, the 1940 Tiger is not easily located and demands respect among collectors as the scarcest Detroit World Series pin. Unknown; threaded post; gold; value **$350**.

The **1939 Cincinnati** is measurably more popular with collectors than its 1940 companion. The pin contrasts an ideal composition of white prismatic with red enamel. Bastian Bros.; threaded post and brooch; red, white, and blue; value **$300**.

The **1939 New York** Yankee pin is as characteristic of its era as the pins corresponding to the top hat of Mantle's years are to theirs. Press pins from the "Age of DiMaggio" presented ornate compositions highlighted by red, white and blue. The Yankees early on projected their image in patriotic colors suggestive of their victorious Civil War namesakes. Appropriately red, white and blue came to represent unconditional mastery on the ballfield as well as on the battlefield. Dieges & Clust; threaded post; red, white, and blue; value **$300**.

The **1938 Chicago** Cubs press pin fills collectors' idle hours with thoughts of sweet contemplation. Here is a mere bauble that can be held in the palm, yet radiates visual splendor. Press pin collectors, who are also Cubs' fans and don't have this pin, have been known to go to extremes to fill their longing for this gem. The enchantment of this piece transcends the fraternity of Cub pins collectors, and it is a cruel injustice to mankind that these glorious pins are so scarce. Unknown; brooch; red, white, and blue, value **$750**.

The **1938 New York** Yankee dates from the glory years when the Bronx Bombers took four straight world championships in quick measure, losing only three Series games in four years. Individually, the Yankee pins from these years are beautiful productions, but collectively they lack imaginative variety. That is the case here. There is a very convincing restrike of the 1938. This illegally reproduced pin can be detected by its flat red enamel as opposed to the darker red in the original. Dieges & Clust; threaded post; red, white, and blue; value **$275**.

The **1937 New York** Giant pin is artistically the best in the history of that team's pins. Though the 1937 Giant has long languished in obscurity among collectors, it has more recently enjoyed a new vitality as its availability seems diminished. This pin has been reproduced. The original has a convex surface at the top of its threaded post. The restrike has a sharp point at top of its threaded post. Dieges & Clust; threaded post; black and orange; value **$275.**

The **1937 New York** Yankee is another of its dynasty's attractive, yet undistinguished pins. The balanced composition and patriotic colors from one year blend in collectors' minds with the designs and colors of the other years. Dieges & Clust; threaded post; red, white, and blue; value **$325.**

The **1936 New York** Giant is the most common pin of the 1930s. Dressed in gloomy earth colors, its appeal in modern circles is further reduced by the Giants' relocation two decades later. There is a curious paradox about the two erstwhile franchises from New York: the Dodgers reap a legacy of endearment from the fans, while the Giants have become forsaken refugees. This duality is noticable in the marketplace for collectibles. This pin has been reproduced. The original has a convex surface at top of the threaded post. The restrike has poor workmanship in post soldering, with a sharp point at the top of its threaded post. Dieges & Clust; threaded post; black, white, and orange; value **$250.**

The **1936 New York** Yankee is about as desirable as its 1937 counterpart. Worthy of note among these pins is the abnormally long post. Dieges & Clust; threaded post; red, white, and blue; value **$325.**

The **1935 Chicago** Cubs pin is no exception to the rule that short supply prevails from their pennant winning years. A credible suspicion has been advanced that the Wrigley owners, in their steadfast conservatism, ordered limited numbers of press pins. At any rate, their pins seem unbearably elusive to collectors. S.D. Childs; brooch; red, white, and blue; value **$750.**

The **1935 Detroit** is similar to its larger predecessor from 1934, and enjoys a comparable popularity. The detail of the tiger's face is sharply delivered through the simple medium of gold plate and black enamel. Unknown; threaded post; black; value **$350.**

The **1934 St. Louis** reflects a happy dilemma for the Cardinals. It was the team's fifth World Series in eight years, and it faced the problem of diversifying its pin design. Fortunately, a red bird in any of several different poses is dependably appealing, and the subtle shift to a scalloped perimeter furnished the 1934 Cardinal pin its individuality. St. Louis Button; threaded post; red and white; value **$450.**

The **1934 Detroit** pin's intricate, formidable, and ferocious countenance places it among the classics. The workmanship of this piece, as well as the 1935 Tiger, is worthy of note. The fasteners on both pins employ sophisticated two-pronged fabric grabs while the corresponding nut, by its relief design, assures that the pin is safely affixed to the lapel. Dieges & Clust; threaded post; black and white; value **$350.**

The **1933 New York** Giant was cast from a modified mold for the 1932 Yankee. Produced at the depth of the Great Depression, it is probably an attempt to forego engineering costs. The pin is unique in its peculiar clashing of colors. Dieges & Clust; threaded post; red, green, and blue, value **$300.**

The **1933 Washington** is the worst of the three boring Senators World Series pins. It is devoid of enamel and reads like the cornerstone of a stuffy government edifice. Dieges & Clust; threaded post; gold; value **$425.**

The **1932 Chicago** may prove to be the most difficult of the magnificent Cubs pins. A distraction prevalent in most exam-ples of this pin is the slightly incomplete enameling around the perimeter. Dieges & Clust; threaded post; black and white; value **$800.**

The **1932 New York** typifies all the Yankee pins of that era. A peculiarity about the piece is the enameled ball protruding in relief which is frequently damaged. Dieges & Clust; threaded post; red, white, blue; value **$450**.

The **1931 St. Louis** is a weak attempt to improve on the 1930 St. Louis issue. The Cardinals merely changed the date and transformed a round pin into a hexagon. Fortunately, the Series itself was memorable; Pepper Martin, for his superlative performance, became a household name. St. Louis Button; threaded post; red, white, and blue; value **$500**.

The **1931 Philadelphia** Athletics produced an attractive design which linked the club's historic elephant logo with the city's even more famous Liberty Bell motif. Unknown; threaded post; blue and white; value **$500**.

The **1930 St. Louis** press pin would approach the stature of a masterpiece of Americana if the Cardinals had won only a single pennant in this era. Currently, there are indications that this is also the scarcest of the Cardinal pins. St. Louis Button; threaded post; red, white, and blue; value **$575**.

The **1930 Philadelphia** Athletics was delivered up as a cold and impersonal pin. Due to its plain appearance, this piece has heretofore gone relatively unheralded by collectors, but its availability in the hobby market is very limited. The 1930 Philadelphia may one day be regarded as the rarest of post-WWI pins. Unknown; threaded post; blue and white; value **$750**.

The **1929 Chicago** depicts the Cub brandishing a bat. This primitive caricature also seems to be swinging a banner, which defines the perimeter of the pin. As are most Cub pins, this pin is colorful, energetic, rare, and revered by collectors. Hipp & Coburn; threaded post; red and white; value **$750**.

The **1929 Philadelphia** is fashioned in the shape of Pennsylvania's nickname. For no apparent reason, this was the first undated press pin. This practice prevailed in 1930 and 1931, too. Perhaps Mack was the first realist to contemplate defeat in a pennant race, despite his 1929 team's 18-game bulge over the second place Yankees. Unknown; threaded post; blue and white; value **$500**.

The **1928 St. Louis** pin launched a thematic statement fundamental to the team's press pin style during the era which lasted until 1934. As the masterpieces of Gauguin are similar to one another, so are the pins produced by the Cardinals during baseball's "Golden Age." The medium was consistent, yet each remains a dynamic and invigorating reiteration. St. Louis Button; threaded post; red, white, and blue; value **$550**.

The **1928 New York** Yankees dealt a second four-game sweep in as many years with vengeful impunity. Oddly, neither the 1927 nor the 1928 New York pins specifically state "New York," nor "Yankees." The peculiar absence is unexplainable in 1927 since New York took the pennant by 19 games. In 1928 however, the Athletics of Connie Mack finished a tense two and a half out. The resultant Yankee pin, without the franchise's identity, may have been the first attempt by a manufacturer to remedy the possibility of a phantom. Dieges & Clust; threaded post; red, white, and blue; value **$600**.

In **1927 Pittsburgh** was all dressed up, but may have wished they didn't have to go. The Pirates won the senior circuit with adequate pitching and impressive hitting, but the Bucs were ingloriously dispatched by the terrifying Yankees. With little else to salvage from this Series, the city can be proud of its superlative 1927 Pirate pin. Whitehead & Hoag; threaded post; black and white; value **$650**.

The **1927 New York** Yankee pin is not a particularly scarce piece for the decade. Nonetheless this pin stands among the hallowed collectibles in the hobby. A team's legacy affecting the value of a press pin is not a common phenomenon, but nowhere is it more readily apparent than in the demand for the 1927 New York pin. Dimensionally peculiar, the piece bears likeness to a police badge; in a sense the 1927 Yankee team indeed wrested control from all would-be adversaries. This piece has been reproduced. On the original, the threaded post has pronounced fabric grab, and the red enamel is dark and translucent. The restrike has a brooch back, and its red enamel is bright and flat. Dieges & Clust; threaded post; red, white, and blue; value **$800**.

The **1926 St. Louis** pin understates the drama of that series. The seventh game is memorable for Pete Alexander crushing the Yankees' threat in the seventh. The 1926 Cardinal pin is a tranquil statement against the backdrop of swashbuckling performances by Thevenow, Bottomley, and Southworth. Unknown; threaded post; red; value **$650**.

In **1926 New York** Yankees' slugger Babe Ruth would have gladly exchanged his four Series homers for the chance to reassess his prowess as a baserunner. The Cardinals won the seventh game by one run when the "invincible" Babe registered the final out trying to steal second. On that note, some of Gotham's media doubtless gazed upon their 1926 Yankee press badge and found solace in the red, white and blue -- the Series belonged to the Cardinals; the Yankees still belonged to America. This piece has been reproduced. On the original, the threaded post has pronounced fabric grab. The restrike has a brooch back; its red enamel, bright and flat. Dieges & Clust; threaded post; red, white, and blue; value **$600**.

The **1925 Pittsburgh** Pirate press pin may plausibly be the antecedent for the plaudit, "Black is beautiful." This imaginatively produced, miniature keystone with its striking contrast of a white baseball is among the finest of the decade. Whitehead & Hoag; threaded post; black and white; value **$650**.

The **1925 Washington** pin is a mellow, cheerless understatement for a team that rostered the likes of Johnson, Harris, Coveleski, Rice and Goslin. All three of the Washington World Series pins deny possessors esprit de corps by never mentioning the "Senators," and never risking an impropriety in color. Dieges & Clust; threaded post; blue; value **$700**.

The **1924 New York** Giant pin perhaps best exemplifies retrenchment after the excesses of the pre-WWI ribbons. It is one of several pins in the early to mid-1920s that seem restrained in comparison. It delivers the obligatory information without frivolity. Dieges & Clust; threaded post; blue; value **$650**.

The **1924 Washington**, in terms of color, represents the best this franchise ever created. If the pin were plucked from history, it would be celebrated as the team's premier contribution to the arts. Unfortunately, it is enmeshed in history, and following shortly on the heels of the previous year's New York pin, reeks with the specter of plagiarism. Dieges & Clust; threaded post; red, white, and blue; value **$650**.

The **1923 New York** is clearly the progenitor of all Yankee pins forward up to 1941. The 1923 Series was held exclusively in the new Yankee Stadium. Pins were produced solely by the hosting franchise. Dieges & Clust; threaded post; red, white, blue; value **$850**.

The **1922 New York** pins for this Polo Grounds' Series, like the previous year, are noted primarily for the delicate finery of their perimeters, and their shallow and fragile enameling. Whitehead & Hoag; brooches; white and blue; value **$1,200**.

The **1921 New York** pin reminds us that New York's Polo Grounds played host to the entire series between McGraw's Giants and Huggins' Yankees. The Giant's George Kelly led the senior circuit with 23 homers, while the Yankees boasted the incomparable "Babe" with his 59 clouts, but to no avail. The Giants prevailed in the last best of nine Series classic. Whitehead & Hoag; brooches; blue and white; value **$1,200**.

In **1920 Cleveland** left several press mementos. But, the 1920 World Series is remembered first for its unassisted triple play, second for Elmer Smith's grand slam, and a distant third for Cleveland's press pin(s). The 1920 Cleveland shown here is generally accepted to be the pertinent lapel pin for the event, but a larger celluloid piece was also dispensed to the media. The manufacturer of either piece is unknown; the enameled pin has threaded post; green and white; value **$1,300**. For the celluloid button, a safety brooch; black and white; value **$1,200**.

The **1920 Brooklyn** is undistinguished, seemingly a modest restatement of the more vibrant 1916 Brooklyn. To date these Dodger pins have surfaced more frequently than most others of this period. Unknown; threaded post; red; value **$1,300**.

The **1919 Cincinnati** reflects the provocative testament of that series which is well remembered by hobbyists and baseball enthusiasts alike. The pins issued in 1919 are appropriate ironies to the occasion. The 1919 Reds, despite their pennant victory in the senior circuit, were thought to be no match for the invincible White Sox, and Cincinnati's pin resembles an apology of implicit submission. Gustave Fox; threaded post; golden; value **$1,200**.

The **1919 Chicago** White Sox pin seems to announce surrender with its white banner. The pin may be considered rare, yet even less often seen is the white silk ribbon. These silk ribbons were not permanently affixed to the pins. Most have been lost to time, and as a supplemental hobby commodity may be regarded as virtually extinct. The same mold was used to make the metallic pin for both this and the 1917 issue. Since the ribbons are normally missing, the differences between the pins are critical to collectors. The blue enamel used to outline the 1919 pin is discernably a lighter than in 1917. Also in this year, the manufacturer's name, Greenduck, is lettered on an arc. threaded post; blue; value **$1,500**.

The **1918 Boston** Red Sox dwarf pin and its predecessors run chronologically juxtaposed with the eloquently ribboned pins of the period. They provide overtones that the economic foundation of the franchise was faulty. The 1915 and 1918 pins are without enamel and pathetically identical, which generally means a conscious effort to economize. Bent & Bush; threaded post; golden; value **$1,500**.

The **1917 New York** Giant is memorable chiefly for its large yellow and blue, bicolored ribbon, suspended from its fastener which announces "Press." Unknown; brooch; golden; value **$1,600**.

The **1917 Chicago** White Sox pins are rare, and those with purple banners rarer still (see description for 1919). This was the original use for the mold reemployed two years later. Distinctives for the pins of 1917 include a darker shade of blue near the periphery. Also, the manufacturer's name, Greenduck, on the back of this pin is in a straight line. threaded post; blue; value **$1,600**.

The **1916 Brooklyn** Dodger with its sculpted baseball and balanced design is better than the miniature Red Sox pins of its time, but not nearly so classy as the ribboned pieces of some of the other franchises. Dieges & Clust; threaded post; blue and white; value **$1,500**.

**1916 Boston** Red Sox issue is another of the Beantown franchise's miniature pins of the Teens. To be sure, this is one of the better of this peculiar species, indicating a somewhat meaningful expenditure on its production. This pin provides the basic data; but it gives nothing more than that. Bent & Bush; threaded post; red and blue; value **$1,800**.

The **1915 Philadelphia** is (one of) the cream of the (pin) crop. It is like a military medal, with a clasp molded in relief, a boldly colored, red suspending ribbon, and an attractive pendant. J.E.Caldwell; brooch; red; value **$2,000**.

The **1915 Boston** Red Sox is another diminutive reminder of this franchise's pre-war glory period. But the press pin does not reflect those winning years. This piece has been reproduced. The original has a threaded post. The restrike has a needle post, and is stamped "Josten". Bent & Bush; threaded post; golden; value **$1,500**.

**1914 Boston** Braves' pin is one of the better representatives of the non-ribboned visitors to the annual Series classic. The Indian head design recalls the nickel which also circulated at that time, although this Brave is a much more elaborate chieftain. It's bold legend is set off by its blue enameling. Having said that, it seems a miscarriage of justice that such a humble pin should represent the victor, while the A's magnificent production must represent the vanquished. Bent & Bush; threaded post; blue; value **$1,500**.

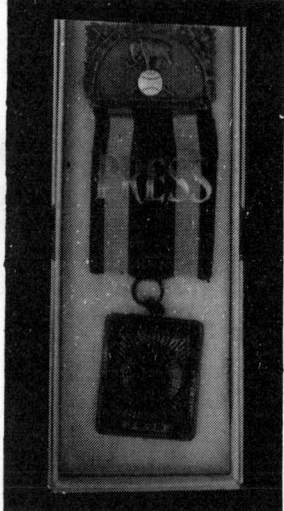

The **1914 Philadelphia** is the pinnacle from this "Age of Grandeur" in press pin design. It is opulent. The pin portion is embellished in Victorian flora and the centerpiece is, of course, the team's elephant balanced above a white-enameled baseball. The medallion features a radiant globe with the orthodox green-enameled logo of the Baseball Writer's Association, with the print detail about the edges is set in blue enamel. The silk ribbons are the accoutrements that isolate this genre from the mainstream of World Series pins, and the 1914 Philadelphia constitute the elite in press pin design. J.E. Caldwell; brooch; blue, white, and green; value **$2,000**.

The **1913 New York** Giant pin is another that pales by comparison to the ribbon pins in the "Age of Silk." It's balanced design is chiefly interesting for its rendition of a catcher's mask in its upper hemisphere and its freeform, irregular shape. Whitehead & Hoag; threaded post; blue; value **$1,500**.

The **1912 Boston** Red Sox possesses a certain engaging quality, but unfortunately will habitually be linked in collectors' minds to the inferior Red Sox pins of its era. Its scalloped design, and textured red enameling are not unattractive, but the pin's miniature design in its center is overly complex for its size. Unknown; threaded post; red; value **$1,500**.

The **1986 Houston** is qualitatively inferior to the norm, but the pin is proving to be the least attainable in the 1980s. With the influx of new press pin collectors, the strain of demand for current pins eclipses their availability. Balfour; needle post and charms; red, white, blue, and silver; value **$70**.

The **1913 Philadelphia** would be exceptional but for the high standards of its era. It seems artistic justice that Mack's celebrated team took this Series handily against McGraw's nine. The Baseball Writers' Association logo appears on the pin, while the familiar Athletics logo dominates the medallion, suspended by a silk ribbon. J.E. Caldwell; brooch; blue and green; value **$2,000**.

The **1911 Philadelphia** was the first press pin and is now the most valuable. A black and white illustration does not do this historic piece justice. The flourishes on the pin are ornate and are consistent with the antiquarian look of the Athletics' symbols. The legend on the ribbon stands out boldly, just the kind of credential to attract a gatekeeper's attention and preclude unwanted visitors from the press area. Allen A. Kerr; brooch; blue; value **$3,250**.

The **1985 Minnesota** has aroused more confusion than any other press pin. The day before the game, the public was admitted to the stadium for a "workout" exhibition. A cheap concession piece (value about $5) was distributed for this event which is nearly identical to the media's pin. The latter is most readily distinguished by its features, which stand in relief as opposed to the smooth surface of the former. Peter David; needle post and charms; red, white, and blue; value **$50**.

The **1912 New York** Giants' pin is efficiently designed. Its pin says "Press;" the dark blue ribbon gives the necessary historical details; and the suspended medallion makes a visual pun. It shows a batter and a catcher; the "Giant" batter towers over the pygmy Red Sox backstop. But it was not to be so as Boston triumphed narrowly. Whitehead & Hoag; brooch; blue; value **$2,500**.

# All-Star Press Pins

By 1933 the tradition of World Series pins was well entrenched in the proceedings of the event, and the arrival of baseball's All Star game would seem to have warranted a press pin. However it wasn't until five years later that the first All Star game pin arrived on the scene for the 1938 game in Cincinnati. A tradition of annual issues was slow in building. Pins were again furnished for 1941's and 1943's encounters, but their annual appearance did not begin until 1946.

The **1984 San Francisco** appeared in large numbers in the hobby marketplace in the months following the game. A very limited number of pins were ordered by the ABC network and are so designated; value **$50**. Unfortunately this variation was mass produced illegally, and the collector should be cautioned that distinguishing one from the other is difficult. Balfour; needle post and charm; orange, black, and white; value **$10**.

The **1983 Chicago** celebrates the 50th anniversary of mid-summer's stellar attraction, which was played a half century to the day and on the same Comiskey Park diamond as the first All Star game. Fittingly, the Junior Circuit prevailed and won what originally had been an annual American League feast. The stars are all out here, encircling an idealized Chicago skyline. A network (ABC) variation pin was also produced by Balfour; its value **$80**. Balfour; needle post and charms; red and blue; value **$25**.

The **1982 Montreal** is somewhat understated and causes little excitement in the hobby. Aside from the standard needle post back, the pin was also issued with a disconcerting straight-pin back. Unlike a brooch, the needle is awkwardly longer than the diameter of the face of the pin. A multi-colored novelty pin (valued at about $5) was sold at this game which has generated confusion among collectors. Balfour; needle post and straight pin; golden; value **$30**.

The **1981 Cleveland** was compromised as a collectible recently by an authorized second order. Similar in availability to the 1984 All Star, it is usually among the first pieces acquired by the novice collector. Balfour; needle post and charms; red, white, and blue; value **$15**.

The **1980 Los Angeles** is another chapter in the undistinguished saga of Dodger pins. Collectors resist purchasing this unenameled, rough-hewn piece, and its relative abundance in the hobby further stigmatizes it. Balfour; needle post and charms; golden; value **$50**.

The **1979 Seattle** pin commemorated the 50th All Star game, and its legend went unheralded in collector circles until the 1983 Chicago pin highlighted the 50th anniversary of All Star competition. Since two games were played for four years (1959-1962) while none was played in 1945, each respective pin is accurate. Balfour; needle post, charms and brooch; blue and white; value **$75**.

The **1978 San Diego** pin is flamboyant; its relief, detail, and freewheeling shape are harmonized by colors of gold and Franciscan brown. This pin has been reproduced. The original has thorough coloration with its relief surfaces highly polished. On the restrike, surfaces in relief are not polished, and coloration lacks brilliance at the pin's bottom. Balfour; needle post, brooch, and charms; brown and blue; value **$75**.

The **1977 New York** is affectionately known in the hobby as the "Big Apple." Actually, it is a small charm. The size limitations of the piece compromise the detail in the stadium and league logo. Balfour; charms; golden; value **$25**.

The **1976 Philadelphia** faces a difficulty similar to the 1985 All Star. In the game program, the Phillies advertised a commemorative piece for sale in which the medallion was virtually identical to the press pin, but was distinguished by a star at the top (similar to that used on the 1974 All Star). Balfour; needle post; golden; value **$125**.

The **1975 Milwaukee** is an aberration among All Star pins. Unadorned and visually somewhat offensive, it is also materially inferior. Unconfirmed reports of this moderately difficult pin indicate that it was ordered and coordinated by the city of Milwaukee rather than the Brewers. Unknown; brooch; golden; value **$125**.

The **1974 Pittsburgh** is a masterpiece in single medium artistry. Relief features on both sides of the medallion have ground surfaces, and the recessed areas of the pin exhibit a soft satin effect. There is a well-founded desire for this pin based on its pronounced scarcity. Balfour; needle post; golden; value **$225**.

The **1973 Kansas City** is a pin busy with confusion. In a medium of blue paint, the pin trumpets its hosting of the game while superimposing the team's logo over a representation of the centerfield water cascade, which is in turn superimposed over a barely perceptible rendering of the stadium. Ultimately the designer's grand vision was thwarted by the dimensional limitations of a press pin. Balfour; needle post and charms; blue; value **$150.**

The **1972 Atlanta** is an anomaly. Press pins are made for and dispensed to adults, so it is uncommon that they sustain damage or deteriorate from use. However, this piece's mirrorlike, silver finish is very sensitive to handling, and too frequently the pin is seen with disheartening scratches. The piece is striking in its pristine state, despite the witless caption "It's an All-Star Year." Balfour; needle post and charms; red and blue; value **$125.**

The **1971 Detroit** demands the admiration of collectors with its intricate texture. Hosting its third All Star game in 30 years, Detroit boldly depicted an American Flag in an age of doubt and protest. Balfour; needle post and charms; red, white, and blue; value **$175.**

The **1970 Cincinnati** game is remembered principally for Rose's "encounter" with Ray Fosse, but the game also marked the return of balloting to the fans. The pin is pleasant but predictable. The plating often fails to thoroughly adhere to the pin, especially in the recessed surfaces. Balfour; needle post and charms; red, white, and black; value **$100.**

The **1969 Washington** site was picked out of rotation, i.e., only seven years had passed since Washington had hosted the mid-season classic, in deference to baseball's 100th anniversary celebration. The spirit of the moment was perhaps dampened with the unveiling of the 1969 All Star press pin, however, since it projects a certain bureaucratic detachment. Balfour; needle post and clasp; blue; value **$75.**

The **1968 Houston** is the model of superlative moderation. Its fashionable cutout design seems neutralized by its pedestrian blue perimeter. It is likely the scarcest pin issued between 1966 and 1970, but not markedly enough to excite the envy of collectors. Balfour; needle post and charms; blue and white; value **$125.**

The **1967 California** is another generic rendition of "round pin with blue perimeter." Fortunately its now-retired Angels logo is a redeeming quality. Once considered unnaturally common, it is gradually returning to respectability. Balfour; needle post and charms; blue and white; value **$100.**

The **1966 St. Louis** pin was allegedly ordered in quantities large enough for liberal distribution beyond the nucleus of the media. The franchise was proud of its new Busch Stadium, and evidently wished to share its enthusiasm broadly. The pin is adequately pleasing to the eye, but stands unequivocally as the most plentiful of All Stars in its decade. Balfour; needle post; red; value **$35.**

The **1965 Minnesota** All Star marks its first press pin, one of the most attractive of the 1960s. Since the inception of All Star press pins, no fewer than eight times has the host team also hosted the World Series in the same season. In 1965 the Twins enjoyed one of these remarkable coincidences. However, its subsequent World Series pins, the 1965 and phantoms of 1967 and 1969, are merely shiftless standardizations. Balfour; needle post; red, white, and blue; value **$175.**

The **1964 New York** (Shea Stadium pin) illustrates that the desire for a pin is a function of its artistic merits, while the quality of the game itself is of no vital consequence to collectors. Callison's dramatic three-run blast with two out in the ninth snatched a victory for the Nationals. The pin, on the other hand, has inspired relatively little interest within the hobby. Balfour; needle post and charms; blue and orange; value **$200.**

In **1963 Cleveland** hosted the return of the mid-summer classic to a single event after both leagues had extended their schedules the previous year, and the serious business of regular season play could ill-afford two All Star breaks. The pin issued for the 1963 game is light-hearted and its cutout design tantalizes collectors. Balfour; threaded post; red, white, blue, and black; value **$90.**

The **1962 Washington**, the last year of tandem All Star games, witnessed release of two pins. This Washington piece has been somewhat ignored in comparison to its companion from Chicago. The pin is aesthetically worthy, and its future may well demonstrate a reputable scarcity. Balfour; threaded post and clasp; white and blue; value **$200**.

The **1962 Chicago** is calculably the premier All Star pin of the 1960s based on its scarcity and collector demand. It shares in the prestige of the family of Cubs' pins, yet in its own right this piece is uncommon for its vintage. Balfour; needle post; red, white, and blue; value **$375**.

The **1961 Boston**, with its companion piece from this year, is becoming recognized for its scarcity by collectors who had previously overlooked it's quaint design. Balfour; needle post; red, white, and blue; value **$375**.

The **1961 San Francisco** pin mirrors its companion of that year in an increasing desire exhibited by collectors. In the brief period of accelerated enthusiasm for press pins, these two pieces have lingered in the shadows. Their unqualified scarcity, however, has recently become more than just a sobering rumor. Balfour; threaded post; white; value **$400**.

The **1960 New York** can be forgiven its redundant Top Hat, since it is an ingenious creation which delivers to its audience the three-dimensional exclamation of a star. Atypical of Yankee-hosted pins in general, the 1960 All Star is noticeably in short supply. Balfour; threaded post; red, white, and blue; value **$250**.

The **1960 Kansas City** pin marks the sole contribution this franchise made (pre-Royals) to the body of press pins. Although the ball is easily scratched, the viewer's attention is directed to the majestic elephant. Balfour; threaded post; red; value **$275**.

In **1959 Pittsburgh** shared a revised All Star format when a second game was added in order to generate additional funds for retired players and the players' pension fund. The 1959 Pittsburgh Pirates' pin represents the first of these dual games, and equal to its principled cause this pin abounds in color and detail. Balfour; threaded post; red, white, and black; value **$225**.

The **1959 Los Angeles** is the most plentiful All Star pin in the decade by a full measure. The piece is a clever upbeat adaptation of Brooklyn's 1951 phantom. Balfour; threaded post and brooch; blue and white; value **$75**.

The **1958 Baltimore** pin is scarce and one of this franchise's treasures since its arrival in 1954. The Orioles presence in Baltimore has remained a novelty. Demand for early relics of the team appear insatiable, and this pin is no exception. Balfour; threaded post; black, white, and orange; value **$350**.

The **1957 St. Louis** is a prime example of an attractive pin being dear to hobbyists even though it represents an event of substandard achievement. Similar to the game in 1956 the National League roster was stacked with Cincinnati Reds, a pretentious affront to the National Pastime. Balfour; threaded post and brooch; black and red; value **$300**.

The **1956 Washington** is an energetic detour from this franchise's earlier World Series pins. With its Senator's cap irreverently draped over the Capitol dome, this piece was once regarded as the rarest of All Star pins in its decade, but time has demonstrated that it shares that designation with several others. Balfour; threaded post and clasp; red, white, and blue; value **$275**.

The **1955 Milwaukee** is a startling exception to the dismal failures in depicting aerial views of stadia in the history of either World Series or All Star press pins. This singular success is unenameled, delivering a sensitive and articulate rendering of County Stadium. Balfour; brooch; golden; value **$225**.

The **1954 Cleveland** is a pageant of color and detail. Collectors are fortunate that the design for this released pin was drawn from the prototype 1951 phantom. Balfour; threaded post; red, white, and black; value **$225**.

The **1953 Cincinnati** marks the first of four pin portrayals of the delightfully extroverted Little Red." While not readily attainable, the pin is available with limited frequency. In the previous Guide's pictorial, the 1953 All Star's absence created a nearly mythical illusion of its scarcity. Robbins; threaded post; red, white, and black; value **$350**.

The **1952 Philadelphia** pin has a predictable theme, but the execution of its admirable detailing is beyond the expected. The woodgrain of the beam and the painted recesses of the inscription qualify the pin as a thorough triumph. Martin; needle post; red, white, and blue; value **$350**.

The **1951 Detroit** is devoid of character except for its miniature crest with an Anglican lion (sic, Tiger). It is about as available to collectors as is its contemporary neighbor from Chicago. Unknown; threaded post; red, white, and blue; value **$225**.

The **1950 Chicago** is the clearest illustration that the scarcity of a pin is not directly proportional to its vintage. Though it deserves a measure of respect, the pin is usually acquired soon by the more advanced collectors. Balfour; threaded post; red and white; value **$200**.

The **1949 Brooklyn** and 1946 Boston are available with much greater frequency than other All Star pins of the decade preceding 1950. Even though there is a sustained interest for these in the hobby, their numbers continue to make them among the easiest of their vintage for collectors to acquire. Balfour; threaded post and brooch; blue; value **$325**.

The **1948 St. Louis** is the utter expression of an anti-hero. The unending plight of the St. Louis Browns was an enduring melodrama, and any tangible treasures they produced have become the stuff of legend. This pin is rare and beautiful, and has emerged as the standard of excellence in All Star press pins. St. Louis Button; threaded post; brown and white; value **$900**.

The **1947 Chicago** is an elusive pin. Though a member of the family of Cubs pins, it is not without its detractors. The piece spontaneously sheds its silver plating, and it bears neither a Cub Logo nor mention of Wrigley Field. Despite these complaints, this All Star piece is still "high profile." Unknown; threaded post; red, white, and blue; value **$700**.

The **1946 Boston** is, like the Brooklyn pin from three years later, one of the most frequently encountered of the pre-1950 All Star press pins. Collector interest is sustained despite a rather unattractive and static design, which seems to copy everything but color scheme from the 1941 All Star pin. Balfour; threaded post; red; value **$325**.

The **1943 Philadelphia** was the only All Star pin produced during World War II. Showing the war scarcity of certain necessary metals, the pin is sterling silver. It is unusually small and equally nondescript. Shibe Park hosted this contest, the first All Star game under the lights, and Yankee manager Joe McCarthy led the Americans to victory without the aid of a single Bronx Bomber in his lineup. Unknown; threaded post; silver; value **$500**.

The **1941 Detroit** pin has begun to warm collectors hearts as the grim realization of its actual scarcity has become evident. This simple and unadorned pin is not widely represented in advanced collections. Dodge; threaded post; blue; value **$550**.

The **1938 Cincinnati** is the first known All Star press pin. A celluloid production which does not particularly stir the senses, there is however sufficient reason to believe that it is the rarest of the All Star pins. Logically many would have been discarded after the game because its material composition does not connote the notion of "keepsake." Bastian Brothers; fastener is safety pin; red, white, and blue; value **$800**.

# Phantoms

A team's decision to produce an order of press pins must be made prior to the end of the season in order to give the pin producer sufficient time to deliver the full order of pins before the start of the World Series. The public relations department of an optimistic franchise works in consultation with the design engineer of a selected manufacturer to produce a painted rendering of the final product. This original art is then recreated into a three-dimensional manufacturing mold. Full-scale production begins only after the team gives final approval.

Baseball's front office personnel historically have provided token gratuities to the media, i.e. press pins. Traditionally such items should be fashionable and enduring, and should logically include the year of the host's participation in the Series. The 1952 New York Giants produced such a pin (ironically citing the eleventh-hour drama of the race), but the Giants finished four and a half games out and hence were stuck with a now-impractical press pin order.

A cost-effective solution had to be found to deal with the thorny problems presented by such dated pins. As early as 1945, the Cardinals discovered that reengineering costs could be significantly reduced by altering a single character in the mold, thus returning to serviceability what would become their "new" 1946 World Series pin. Other teams have followed this compromise, including Milwaukee 1956 (1957), Red Sox 1949 (1967), Cardinals 1963 (1964), and Oakland 1971 (1972).

This method was not universally successful, though, since several franchises directed modifications to an existing mold only to see their additional costs expended in vain. San Francisco dated a pin in 1965 and failed to capture the flag, redated it 1966 but failing again finally gave up that design upon what would become its 1969 phantom. Minnesota dated a pin in 1967, but smarting from its defeat, simply removed the date to produce what is now considered its 1969 phantom. Hope springs eternal for this pin. It was poised for release in the club's optimistic 1970 and 1984 seasons, and currently remains available for duty.

Perhaps the worst practitioner of date changing on phantoms was the Chicago White Sox. In 1960 Chicago was in the hunt until the Yankees reeled off 15 victories at the end of the season. They had confirmed the engineering design work, but declined production. The mold was resurrected and appropriately altered in 1964 as they went to the wire before finishing one game behind New York. Again in 1967, Chicago was a viable contender, and had the mold changed. Ultimately the year was removed, probably in 1972 when they finished a respectable five and a half out. Throughout the ordeal the White Sox tinkered with enamel variations, and finally, possibly out of superstition, abandoned the design to arrive at what is today considered its 1983 phantom.

Another remedy for the phantom problem is to eliminate a date altogether. Such a breach

in tradition was resisted by most franchises. The first undated pins were the Philadelphia issues for 1929, 1930 and 1931, but their respective finishes for these three years leave doubt that they consciously intended to avert a phantom.

In all likelihood the first instance of a pin's premeditated absence of a year came with the 1953 Dodger pin. Despite its 13 game finish in front of the Braves that year, Brooklyn had lost engineering costs to Balfour in 1950, and in 1951 lost the costs of both engineering and production to Dieges and Clust. Dated and unusable phantoms were the result both years. In 1955 Dodger management exercised a unique option by dating the back of the pin, ostensibly to permit defacing the date should they lose the pennant. Finally, in 1956 they ceased dating their press pins, thus ensuring against the recurrence of an unusable phantom.

In 1969 expansion in both leagues, and a reorganization into divisions, necessitating League Championship Series made the risk of dated phantoms nearly prohibitive. Virtually every team winning its division or finishing withing reach of victory were compelled to finalize at least an engineered prototype press pin. Then despite the outcome of the playoff Championship Series, teams were induced to order World Series pins. After 1969 the calculated risk of producing a dated phantom was waged and lost by the 1969 Giants, who abandoned the design after its defeat; the 1970 Cubs; the 1971 Giants; the 1971 A's, who salvaged the pin for 1972; the 1972 Pirates, who used the medallion in 1979; and the 75 A's. And conversely, those who gambled to date their pins and actually won the pennant since 1969 include the 1969 Mets, 1971 Orioles, 1972-1974 A's, and the 1983 Phillies.

Without exception every team in the major leagues has presently conformed to the use of undated pins, and the dynamics are fairly workable. By illustration, the Tigers in 1972 won the A.L. East, which stimulated an order for pins. Unfortunately for Detroit, Oakland beat them in the Championship Series, but the pin order could be stored for a sunnier day. In 1984 the Tigers won the pennant, went on to the Series, and drew its undated 1972 phantoms from the vault for distribution to the media.

The majority of major league franchises have pin orders completed and waiting for their next encounter with pennant victory. Following are those teams likely to have pins that may be considered current as of the end of the 1985 season: (probable production years in parentheses) A's (1981), Angels (1986), Astros (1986), Blue Jays (1985), Braves (1969), Brewers (1983), Cubs (1984), Dodgers (1982), Expos (1979), Giants (1978), Pirates (1983), Reds (1978), Twins (1969), and White Sox (1983).

It cannot be unconditionally assured that all of these phantoms will one day be released as bona fide press pins. The Pirates, as a case in point, may win a pennant several years following a design change in their uniform cap. The 1983 Pittsburgh pin would therefore be inappropriate. For that matter, abandoning undated pins is not uncommon. The design of the 1970 California pin was

simply not conducive to the team's projected logo by 1979 when the team was again nearing a pennant. The 1979 Houston was dropped because of unsolvable manufacturing problems in its characters, and the 1976 Philadelphia design was dismantled to use the stadium portion of the pin for their 1980 World Series design.

Phantoms can generally be categorized in four groups: (a) Those ordered in their full complement, then liberally distributed on request. Typical of these are the 1946 Brooklyn, 1963 St. Louis, 1964 Phillies, and 1971 Oakland to mention a few. (b) Those probably ordered complete then sparsely distributed. This group is the most difficult to evaluate for scarcity, because it is evident that large numbers were discarded. Examples here include the 1975 Oakland, 1966 Pittsburgh, 1949 Cardinal, and 1959 Milwaukee. (c) Examples of the third group are likely extant as prototypes only. These are extremely rare and their values on the market are volatile and hopelessly arbitrary. Included are the 1960 White Sox, 1951 Cleveland, 1950 Brooklyn and 1966 Giants. (d) The fourth group is peculiar because specimens probably exist in great numbers within the various franchises. They are considered inviolable by their respective teams, and are in most instances virtually unattainable in the hobby. These include the 1985 Blue Jays, 1984 Cubs, 1982 Dodgers, and 1983 Pittsburgh. From the collector's standpoint, the inherent danger with these is that presently they are suspended for release, but their numbers in the hobby will likely and suddenly swell.

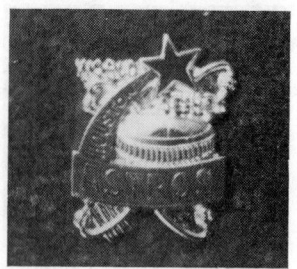

The **1986 Houston** phantom; Balfour; needle post and charm; red and blue; value **$100**. An NBC variation was produced by Balfour.

The **1986 California** phantom; Gem Peddler; needle post and charm; no color; value **$100**. An NBC variation was produced by Balfour.

The **1985 Toronto** phantom; Balfour; needle post and charm; red, white, blue; value $100.

The **1984 Chicago Cubs** phantom; Balfour; needle post and charm; red and black; value $150. A network (NBC) variation pin was also produced by Balfour; its value $80.

The **1983 Chicago White Sox** phantom; Balfour; needle post; red and blue; value $50.

The **1983 Milwaukee** phantom; Balfour; needle post; white and black; value $75.

The **1983 Pittsburgh** phantom; Balfour; needle post; colors is black; value $200.

The **1982 Los Angeles** phantom; Balfour; needle post and charm; red, white, and blue; value $75.

The **1981 Oakland** phantom; Balfour; needle post and charm; green; value $50.

The **1981 Philadelphia** phantom; Balfour; needle post; red and white; value $20.

The **1981 Chicago Cubs** phantom; Balfour; needle post; red, white, and blue; value $225.

The **1980 Houston** phantom; Balfour; needle post and charm; blue and orange; value $55.

The **1979 Houston** phantom; Balfour; needle post; white and blue; value $350.

The **1979 California** phantom; Balfour; needle post; red, white, and blue; value $125.

The **1979 Montreal** phantom; Balfour; needle post; no color; value $50.

The **1978 Cincinnati** phantom; Balfour; needle post and charm; red; value $60.

The **1978 San Francisco** phantom; Balfour; needle post; orange and black; value $20.

The **1977 Boston** phantom; Balfour; needle post and charm; red and blue; value **$60**.

The **1976 Philadelphia** phantom; Balfour; needle post; no color; value **$40**.

The 1975 **Oakland** phantom; Josten; needle post; green and white; value **$250**.

The 1972 **Pittsburgh** phantom; Balfour; needle post; no color; value **$300**.

The **1972 Chicago White Sox** phantom; Balfour; needle post; red, white, and blue; value **$200**.

The **1971 Oakland** phantoms; larger pin unknown; needle post; green and white; value **$300**. Smaller pin Balfour; needle post and charm; green and white; value **$75**.

The **1971 San Francisco** phantom; Balfour; needle post; black; value **$100**.

The 1970 **Chicago Cubs** phantom; Balfour; needle post; blue and white; value **$400**.

The 1970 **California** phantom; Balfour; needle post; red, white, and blue; value **$250**.

The 1969 **San Francisco** phantom; Balfour; needle post; white and black; value **$75**.

The 1969 **Minnesota** phantom; Balfour; needle post; red, white, and blue; value **$20**.

The 1969 **Atlanta** phantom; Josten; needle post and charm; blue; value **$75**.

The 1967 **Minnesota** phantom; Balfour; needle post; red, white, and blue; value **$50**.

The 1967 **Chicago White Sox** phantom; Balfour; needle post; red, white, and blue; value **$75**.

The **1966 San Francisco** phantom; Balfour; threaded post; white and black; value **$700**.

The **1964 Baltimore** phantoms (home plate or square); both Balfour; needle post; white, orange, and black; value **$300** each.

The **1959 San Francisco** phantom; Balfour; threaded post; white and black; value **$300**.

The **1966 Pittsburgh** phantom; Balfour; needle post; black; value **$200**.

The **1964 Cincinnati** phantom; Balfour; needle post and brooch; red, white, and black; value **$80**.

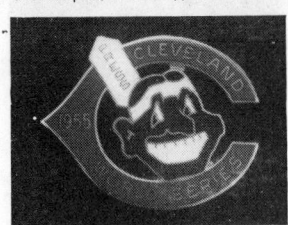

The **1959 Milwaukee** phantom; Balfour; threaded post and charm; red, white, and black; value **$400**.

The **1965 San Francisco** phantom; Balfour; threaded post; white and black; value **$75**.

The **1963 St. Louis** phantom; Josten; threaded post; red; value **$80**.

The **1956 Milwaukee** phantom; Balfour; threaded post; red and copper; value **$70**.

The **1964 Philadelphia** phantom; Martin; needle post; red and blue; value **$15**.

The **1960 Baltimore** phantom; Balfour; threaded post; red, green, black; value **$400**.

The **1955 Cleveland** phantom; Balfour; threaded post; red, white, blue, and black; value **$300**.

The **1964 Chicago White Sox** phantom; Balfour; needle post; red, white, and blue; value **$400**.

The **1960 Chicago White Sox** phantom; Balfour; threaded post; red, white; value **$700**.

The **1955 Chicago White Sox** phantom; unknown manufacturer; threaded post; red, white, and blue; value **$300**.

The **1952 New York Giants** phantom; Dieges & Clust; threaded post and brooch; white and black; value $175.

The **1951 Brooklyn** phantom; Dieges & Clust; threaded post and brooch; red, white, and blue; value **$225**. The 1951 Brooklyn phantom has been reproduced. On the original, the red enamel is dark and translucent, with a convex surface at the top of its threaded post. The restrike is stamped "H.J." on back. Its red enamel is bright and flat with unenameled surfaces flanking the ball's seams, and a sharp point atop its threaded post.

The **1951 Cleveland** phantom, Balfour; threaded post; red, white, and black; value $1,000.

The **1950 Brooklyn** phantom; Balfour; threaded post; red, white, and blue; value $1,500.

The **1949 St. Louis Cardinals** phantom; unknown manufacturer; threaded post; red, white, and black; value $300.

The **1949 Boston Red Sox** phantom; Balfour; threaded post; red, white, and blue; value **$1,000**.

The **1948 New York Yankees** phantom; Dieges & Clust; threaded post; red, white, and blue; value **$1,000**.

The **1948 Boston Red Sox** phantom; Balfour; threaded post; red, white, and blue; value **$1,000**.

The **1946 Brooklyn** phantom; Dieges & Clust; threaded post and brooch; no color; value $125. The 1946 Brooklyn phantom has been reproduced. The original has a convex surface; the restrike, a flat surface.

The **1945 St. Louis Cardinals** phantom; St. Louis Button; threaded post; red and white; value $200.

The **1944 Detroit** phantom; unknown manufacturer; threaded post; red, white, and blue; value $300.

The **1938 Pittsburgh** phantom; Whitehead & Hoag; threaded post; red, white, and black; value $400.

# BUYING PRESS PINS

### World Series Pins
### Buying Prices

| | |
|---|---|
| 1911 Phila. | 2,600. |
| 1912 Giants | 1,800. |
| 1912 Boston | 1,050. |
| 1913 Giants | 1,200. |
| 1913 Phila. | 1,800. |
| 1914 Boston | 1,300. |
| 1914 Phila. | 1,500. |
| 1915 Boston | 1,050. |
| 1915 Phila. | 1,700. |
| 1916 Boston | 1,500. |
| 1916 Brooklyn | 1,050. |
| 1917 Chicago | 1,550. |
| 1917 Giants | 1,300. |
| 1918 Boston | 1,050. |
| 1919 Chicago | 1,250. |
| 1919 Cincinnati | 1,050. |
| 1920 Cleveland | 950. |
| 1920 Brooklyn | 1,000. |
| 1921 New York | 1,050. |
| 1922 New York | 1,050. |
| 1923 New York | 800. |
| 1924 Giants | 600. |
| 1924 Washington | 600. |
| 1925 Pirates | 600. |
| 1925 Washington | 650. |
| 1926 St.Louis | 625. |
| 1926 New York | 550. |
| 1927 New York | 700. |
| 1927 Pirates | 600. |
| 1928 New York | 575. |
| 1928 St.Louis | 500. |
| 1929 Phila. | 450. |
| 1929 Chicago | 675. |
| 1930 St.Louis | 500. |
| 1930 Phila. | 600. |
| 1931 St.Louis | 450. |
| 1931 Phila. | 425. |
| 1932 Chicago | 750. |
| 1932 New York | 400. |
| 1933 Giants | 250. |
| 1933 Washington | 375. |
| 1934 St.Louis | 400. |
| 1934 Detroit | 300. |
| 1935 Chicago | 750. |
| 1935 Detroit | 300. |
| 1936 Giants | 200. |
| 1936 New York | 275. |
| 1937 Giants | 225. |
| 1937 New York | 275. |
| 1938 Chicago | 650. |
| 1938 New York | 225. |

| | |
|---|---|
| 1939 Cincinnati | 250. |
| 1939 New York | 240. |
| 1940 Cincinnati | 220. |
| 1940 Detroit | 250. |
| 1941 Brooklyn | 250. |
| 1941 New York | 130. |
| 1942 St.Louis | 275. |
| 1942 New York | 200. |
| 1943 St.Louis | 325. |
| 1943 New York | 225. |
| 1944 St.Louis | 350. |
| 1944 Browns | 300. |
| 1945 Chicago | 375. |
| 1945 Detroit | 300. |
| 1946 St.Louis | 275. |
| 1946 Boston | 250. |
| 1947 Brooklyn | 350. |
| 1947 New York | 225. |
| 1948 Boston | 225. |
| 1948 Cleveland | 200. |
| 1949 Brooklyn | 275. |
| 1949 New York | 250. |
| 1950 Phila. | 225. |
| 1950 New York | 225. |
| 1951 Giants | 75. |
| 1951 New York | 165. |
| 1952 Brooklyn | 225. |
| 1952 New York | 210. |
| 1953 Brooklyn | 225. |
| 1953 New York | 200. |
| 1954 Giants | 75. |
| 1954 Cleveland | 150. |
| 1955 Brooklyn | 260. |
| 1955 New York | 175. |
| 1956 Brooklyn | 350. |
| 1956 New York | 160. |
| 1957 Milwaukee | 110. |
| 1957 New York | 150. |
| 1958 Milwaukee | 150. |
| 1958 New York | 115. |
| 1959 Dodgers | 175. |
| 1959 Chicago | 225. |
| 1960 Pirates | 175. |
| 1960 New York | 150. |
| 1961 Cincinnati | 85. |
| 1961 New York | 110. |
| 1962 Giants | 200. |
| 1962 New York | 110. |
| 1963 Dodgers | 150. |
| 1963 New York | 135. |
| 1964 St.Louis | 125. |
| 1964 New York | 85. |
| 1965 Minnesota | 75. |
| 1965 Dodgers | 95. |
| 1966 Dodgers | 85. |

| | |
|---|---|
| 1966 Baltimore | 200. |
| 1967 St.Louis | 85. |
| 1967 Boston | 110. |
| 1968 St.Louis | 30. |
| 1968 Detroit | 135. |
| 1969 NY Mets | 200. |
| 1969 Baltimore | 75. |
| 1970 Cincinnati | 85. |
| 1970 Baltimore | 85. |
| 1971 Pirates | 125. |
| 1971 Baltimore | 75. |
| 1972 Cincinnati | 70. |
| 1972 Oakland | 175. |
| 1973 NY Mets | 110. |
| 1973 Oakland | 200. |
| 1974 Dodgers | 110. |
| 1974 Oakland | 300. |
| 1975 Boston | 250. |
| 1975 Cincinnati | 120. |
| 1976 Cincinnati | 110. |
| 1976 New York | 75. |
| 1977 Dodgers | 75. |
| 1977 New York | 50. |
| 1978 Dodgers | 60. |
| 1978 New York | 55. |
| 1979 Pirates | 30. |
| 1979 Baltimore | 40. |
| 1980 Phila. | 30. |
| 1980 Royals | 100. |
| 1981 Dodgers | 50. |
| 1981 New York | 40. |
| 1982 St.Louis | 20. |
| 1982 Milwaukee | 45. |
| 1983 Phila. | 20. |
| 1983 Baltimore | 35. |
| 1984 San Diego | 40. |
| 1984 Detroit | 40. |
| 1985 St.Louis | 60. |
| 1985 Royals | 50. |
| 1986 NY Mets | 125. |
| 1986 Boston | 75. |

### Hall of Fame
### Press Pins
### Buying Prices

| | |
|---|---|
| 1982 H.O.F. | 250. |
| 1983 H.O.F. | 300. |
| 1984 H.O.F. | 250. |
| 1985 H.O.F. | 250. |
| 1986 H.O.F. | 250. |

### All-Star Game
### Press Pins
### Buying Prices

| | |
|---|---|
| 1938 Cincinnati | 600. |
| 1941 Detroit | 500. |
| 1943 Phila. | 450. |
| 1946 Boston | 300. |
| 1947 Chicago | 450. |
| 1948 St.Louis | 650. |
| 1949 Brooklyn | 300. |
| 1950 Chicago | 150. |
| 1951 Detroit | 175. |
| 1952 Phila. | 275. |
| 1953 Cincinnati | 300. |
| 1954 Cleveland | 165. |
| 1955 Milwaukee | 175. |
| 1956 Washington | 225. |
| 1957 St.Louis | 250. |
| 1958 Baltimore | 300. |
| 1959 Dodgers | 55. |
| 1959 Pirates | 200. |
| 1960 Royals | 250. |
| 1960 New York | 200. |
| 1961 Boston | 275. |
| 1961 Giants | 300. |
| 1962 Washington | 125. |
| 1962 Chicago | 300. |
| 1963 Cleveland | 65. |
| 1964 New York | 175. |
| 1965 Minnesota | 120. |
| 1966 St.Louis | 25. |
| 1967 California | 60. |
| 1968 Houston | 100. |
| 1969 Washington | 50. |
| 1970 Cincinnati | 90. |
| 1971 Detroit | 150. |
| 1972 Atlanta | 100. |
| 1973 Royals | 95. |
| 1974 Pirates | 200. |
| 1975 Milwaukee | 100. |
| 1976 Phila. | 100. |
| 1977 New York | 25. |
| 1978 San Diego | 55. |
| 1979 Seattle | 55. |
| 1980 Dodgers | 25. |
| 1981 Cleveland | 15. |
| 1982 Montreal | 20. |
| 1983 Chicago | 15. |
| 1984 Giants | 10. |
| 1985 Minnesota | 40. |
| 1986 Houston | 45. |

WARREN SPAHN
MILWAUKEE BRAVES   pitcher
NO. 19 OF 36 CARDS

HARMON KILLEBREW
WASH. SENATORS   3rd base
NO. 20 OF 36 CARDS

JACKIE JENSEN
BOSTON RED SOX   outfield
NO. 21 OF 36 CARDS

*1960 Bazooka*

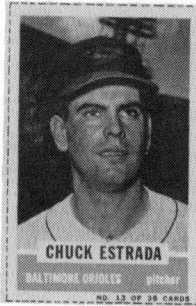

CHUCK ESTRADA
BALTIMORE ORIOLES   pitcher
NO. 13 OF 36 CARDS

KEN BOYER
ST. LOUIS CARDINALS   3rd base
NO. 14 OF 36 CARDS

HARVEY KUENN
SAN FRANCISCO GIANTS   outfield
NO. 15 OF 36 CARDS

*1961 Bazooka*

JOHNNY ROMANO

ERNIE BANKS

NORM SIEBERN
KANSAS CITY ATHLETICS   1b-of

*1962 Bazooka*

NORM SIEBERN
K. C. ATHLETICS   1B
NO. 4 OF 36 CARDS

WARREN SPAHN
MIL. BRAVES   PITCHER
NO. 5 OF 36 CARDS

BILL MAZEROSKI
PITTS. PIRATES   2B
NO. 6 OF 36 CARDS

*1963 Bazooka*

**1964 Bazooka**

**1965 Bazooka**

**1966 Bazooka**

**1967 Bazooka**

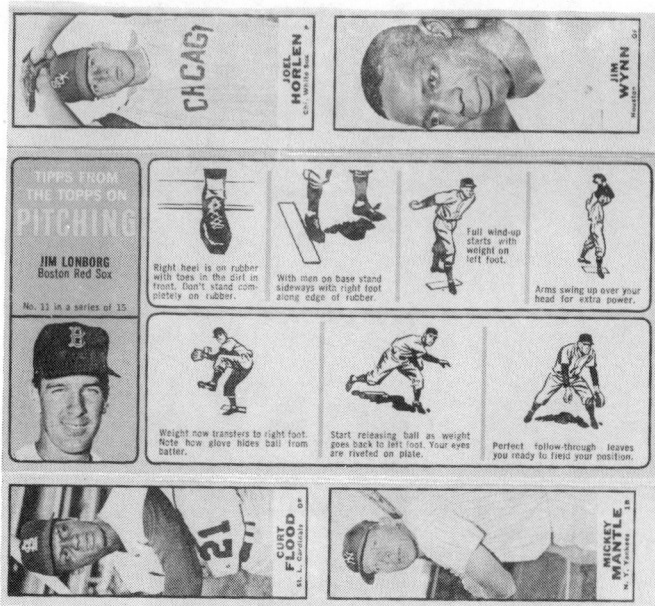

*1968 Bazooka*

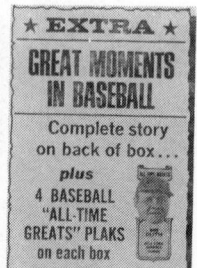

*1969-70 Bazooka*

**1971 Bazooka**

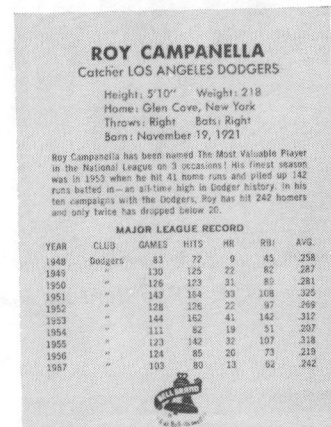

**1958 Bell Brand**

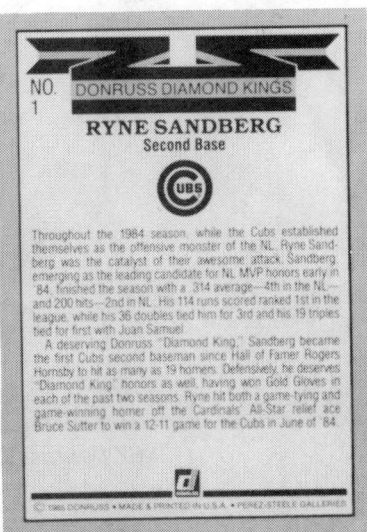

**1985 Donruss Diamond King Supers**

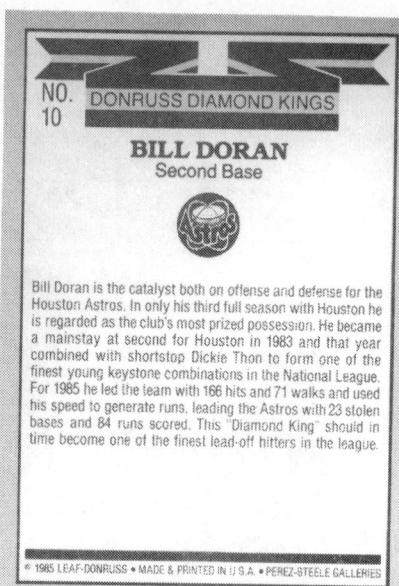

### DONRUSS DIAMOND KINGS

NO. 10

**BILL DORAN**
Second Base

Bill Doran is the catalyst both on offense and defense for the Houston Astros. In only his third full season with Houston he is regarded as the club's most prized possession. He became a mainstay at second for Houston in 1983 and that year combined with shortstop Dickie Thon to form one of the finest young keystone combinations in the National League. For 1985 he led the team with 166 hits and 71 walks and used his speed to generate runs, leading the Astros with 23 stolen bases and 84 runs scored. This "Diamond King" should in time become one of the finest lead-off hitters in the league.

© 1985 LEAF-DONRUSS • MADE & PRINTED IN U.S.A. • PEREZ-STEELE GALLERIES

*1986 Donruss Diamond King Supers*

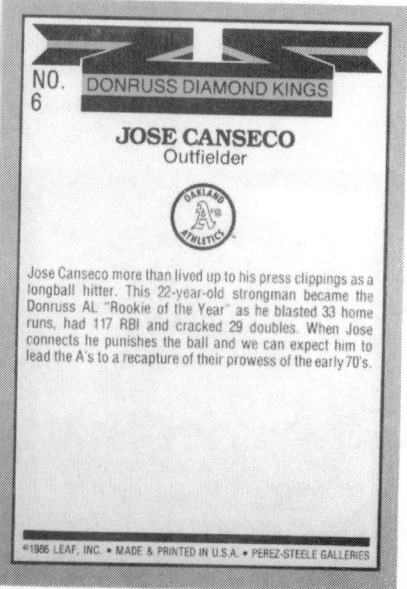

### DONRUSS DIAMOND KINGS

NO. 6

**JOSE CANSECO**
Outfielder

Jose Canseco more than lived up to his press clippings as a longball hitter. This 22-year-old strongman became the Donruss AL "Rookie of the Year" as he blasted 33 home runs, had 117 RBI and cracked 29 doubles. When Jose connects he punishes the ball and we can expect him to lead the A's to a recapture of their prowess of the early 70's.

© 1986 LEAF, INC. • MADE & PRINTED IN U.S.A. • PEREZ-STEELE GALLERIES

*1987 Donruss Diamond King Supers*

1953 Hunters                    1954 Hunters

1955 Hunters

1959 Morrell

1960 Morrell

1961 Morrell

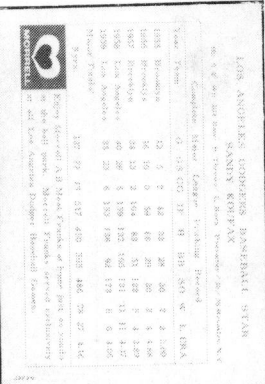

**MICKEY MANTLE**
New York Yankees

*Mickey Mantle*

**1960 Post**

#10—Al Rosen    Save these tabs. When you have completed the entire set (pictures 1 to 20) return the set of 20 tabs to NUM NUM Foods, and you will get an official American League Baseball—autographed by your favorite Cleveland Indian player. (Cut tab along the dotted line.) OFFER EXPIRES SEPTEMBER 14, 1952.

**#10—Al Rosen**

Born in Spartanburg, South Carolina, March 1, 1925. Bats and throws right handed. Height: 5'11". Weight: 185 lbs. Black hair and blue eyes. Jewish ancestry. Single. Winter home: Miami Beach, Florida.

A graduate of University of Miami, he starred in basketball and football as well as baseball . . . also was once Florida State middleweight boxing champion . . . spends off season as good will ambassador for nationally known brewery . . . plays golf as often as possible . . . one of most aggressive ball players, he's also considered one of keenest students of the game . . . earned host of minor league honors before reaching majors . . . chosen Rookie of the Year by SPORT Magazine in 1950, but was ineligible for other similar awards . . . is excellent speaker and has great future in radio and television . . . played against his present manager as member of Kansas City club in 1948 . . . first American League rookie to lead circuit in homers since 1915, he also set all-time record for right handed Cleveland batter.

NUM NUM FOODS, INC., 4180 Lorain, Cleveland 13, Ohio
Gentlemen: I am enclosing a complete set of tabs (1 to 20).
Send official league ball autographed by
                                        (insert name of player)
NAME
ADDRESS
CITY

**1952 Num Num**

**1953 Stahl Meyer**

**1954 Stahl Meyer**

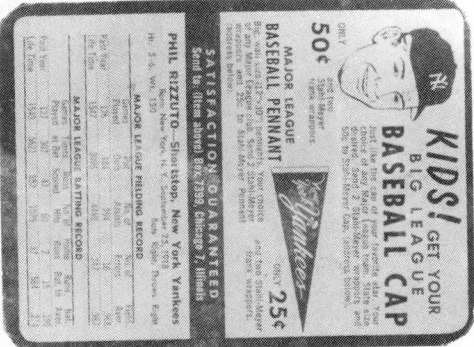

**1955 Stahl Meyer**

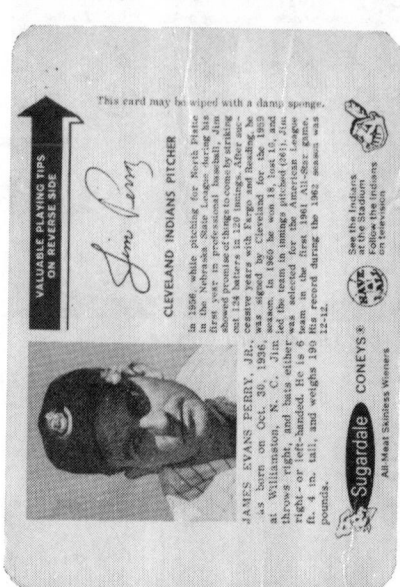

**1962 Sugardale**

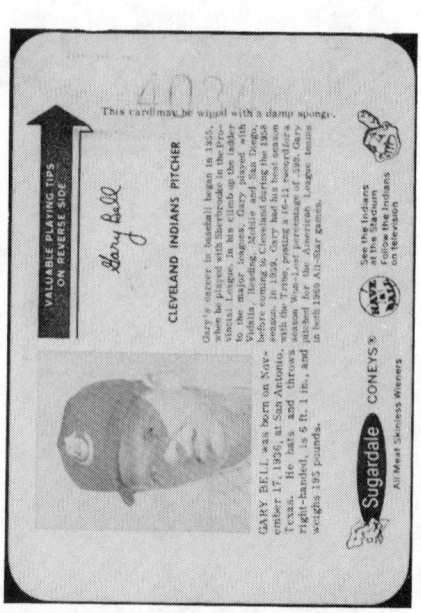

**1963 Sugardale**

### BROOKLYN DODGERS

TOP ROW (left to right): Billy Cox, Bobby Morgan, Carl Erskine, Erv Palica, Tommy Brown, Preacher Roe, Joe Hatten, Steve Lembo, Carl Furillo, Eddie Miksis, Rex Barney.

THIRD ROW (left to right): Traveling Secretary Harold Parrott, Trainer Harold E .Wendler, Dan Bankhead, Gil Hodges, Chris Van Cuyk, Don Newcombe, Mal Mallette, Billy Loes, Duke Snider, Pee Wee Reese, Bruce Edwards, Clubhouse Custodian John Griffin, Jackie Robinson.

SECOND ROW (left to right): Roy Campanella, Jim Russell, Ralph Branca, Coach Clyde Sukeforth, Coach Jake Pitler, Manager B. E. Shotton, Coach Milt Stock, Bullpen Catcher Sam Narron, Cal Abrams, Gene Hermanski, Wayne Belardi.

BOTTOM ROW (left to right): Ball Boy Marvin Parshall, Bat Boy Stanley Strull.

## 1951 Topps Teams

### CINCINNATI REDS

FRONT ROW (left to right): Ed Erautt, Sammy Meeks, Hobie Landrith, Coach Gus Mancuso, Ass't to President Gabriel Paul, Manager Luke Sewell, Coach Tony Cuccinello, Coach Phil Page, Bobby Adams, Kent Peterson, Danny Litwhiler.

SECOND ROW (left to right): Equipment Manager Larry McManus, Ken Raffensberger, Bud Byerly, John Hetki, Bobby Usher, Lloyd Merriman, Joe Adcock, Herman Wehmeier, John Pramesa, Harry Perkowski, Howard Fox, Ewell Blackwell, Trainer Wilbur Bohm.

TOP ROW (left to right): Grady Hatton, Homer Howell, Willard Ramsdell, Connie Ryan, John Wyrostek, Ted Kluszewski, Virgil Stallcup, Edgar Bailey, Ted Tappe, Frank Smith.

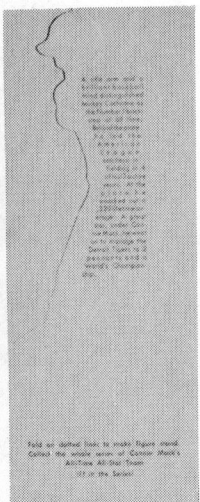

## 1951 Topps Current All-Stars     1951 Topps Connie Mack All-Stars

**1980 Topps Super**

**1981 Topps Super Home Team**

**1981 Topps Super National**

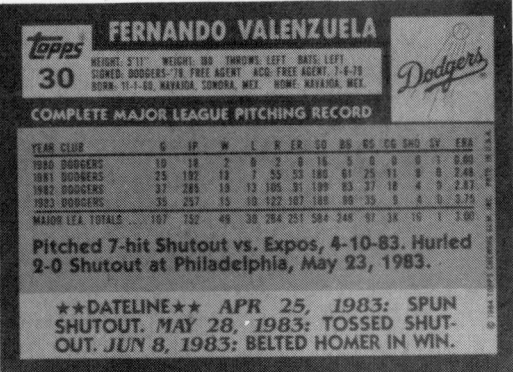

*1984 Topps Super*

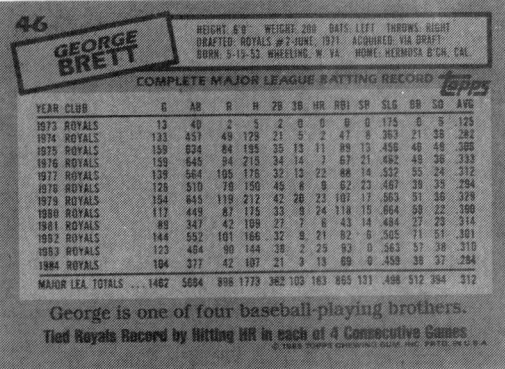

*1985 Topps Super*

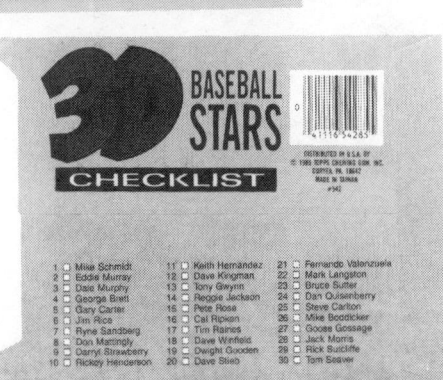

*1985 Topps Super 3D*

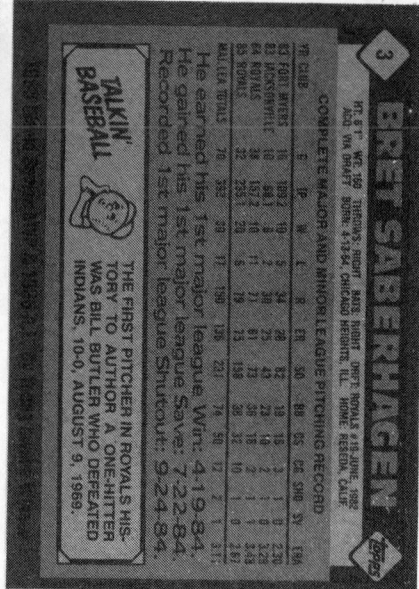

*1986 Topps Super*

*1986 Topps Super 3D*

**ED KRANEPOOL**

| 1st BASE | | | N.Y. METS |
|---|---|---|---|
| Ht: 6'3" | Wt: 210 | Bats: Left | Throws: Left |
| Born: Nov. 8, 1944 | | | Home: Bronx, N.Y. |

**AL WEIS**

| 2nd BASE | | | N.Y. METS |
|---|---|---|---|
| Ht: 6' | Wt: 165 | Bats: Right | Throws: Right |
| Born: April 2, 1938 | | | Home: Franklin Sq., N.Y. |

**TOM SEAVER**

| PITCHER | | | N.Y. METS |
|---|---|---|---|
| Ht: 6'1" | Wt: 200 | Bats: Right | Throws: Right |
| Born: Nov. 17, 1944 | | | Home: Fresno, Cal. |

*1970 Transogram Mets*

*T3 Turkey Reds*

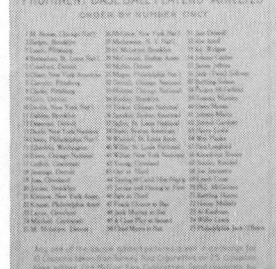

**T200 Fatima Teams**

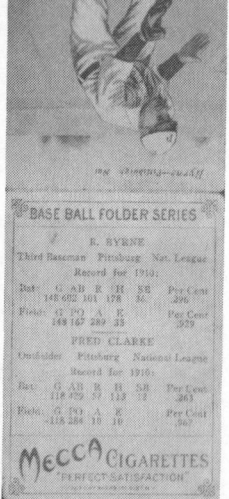

**T201 Mecca Doublefolders**

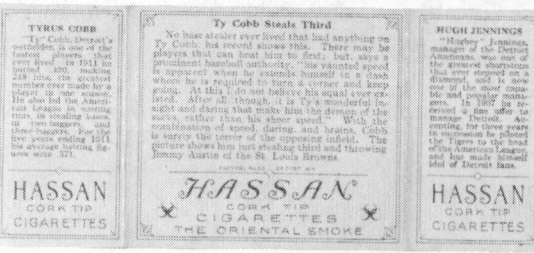

**T202 Hassan Trplefolders**

**1933 Goudey Canadian**

**1934 Goudey Canadian**

**Steve Rogers**
Pitching Stance
Utilisation de la plaque

**Steve Rogers**
Pitching Stance
Utilisation de la plaque

**Steve Rogers**
Pitching Stance
Utilisation de la plaque

The rubber allows you to develop power by thrusting forward with the back leg against a firm support. The rubber also allows you to have better balance which is important for proper delivery techniques.

Remember not to step on the rubber! Place the front part of your foot in front of the rubber, using it to push off and generate power. Placing your foot directly on the rubber will either cause your foot to slip off, or create poor balance.

The most important thing for a pitcher to learn in the development of speed and momentum on the mound is proper use of the pitching rubber. Use the rubber as a base and position your foot at either corner or along the front.

STEVE ROGERS

STEVE ROGERS

STEVE ROGERS

Ayant un support solide, votre jambe vous propulse vers l'avant et vous permet de développer plus de puissance. De plus, la plaque vous donne plus d'équilibre lors du lancer.

A retenir qu'il faut appuyer l'orteil ou le pied devant la plaque et non sur celle-ci. Ainsi vous utilisez la plaque pour votre impulsion et pour engendrer de la puissance. En plaçant le pied sur la plaque, vous glisserez.

Pour développer vitesse et momentum au monticule, l'utilisation de la plaque est primordiale. Vous devez utiliser la plaque comme support en plaçant votre pied à l'un des coins ou devant celle-ci.

**1982 Zellers Expos**

# CLASSIFIED ADVERTISING

# CLASSIFIED ADVERTISING

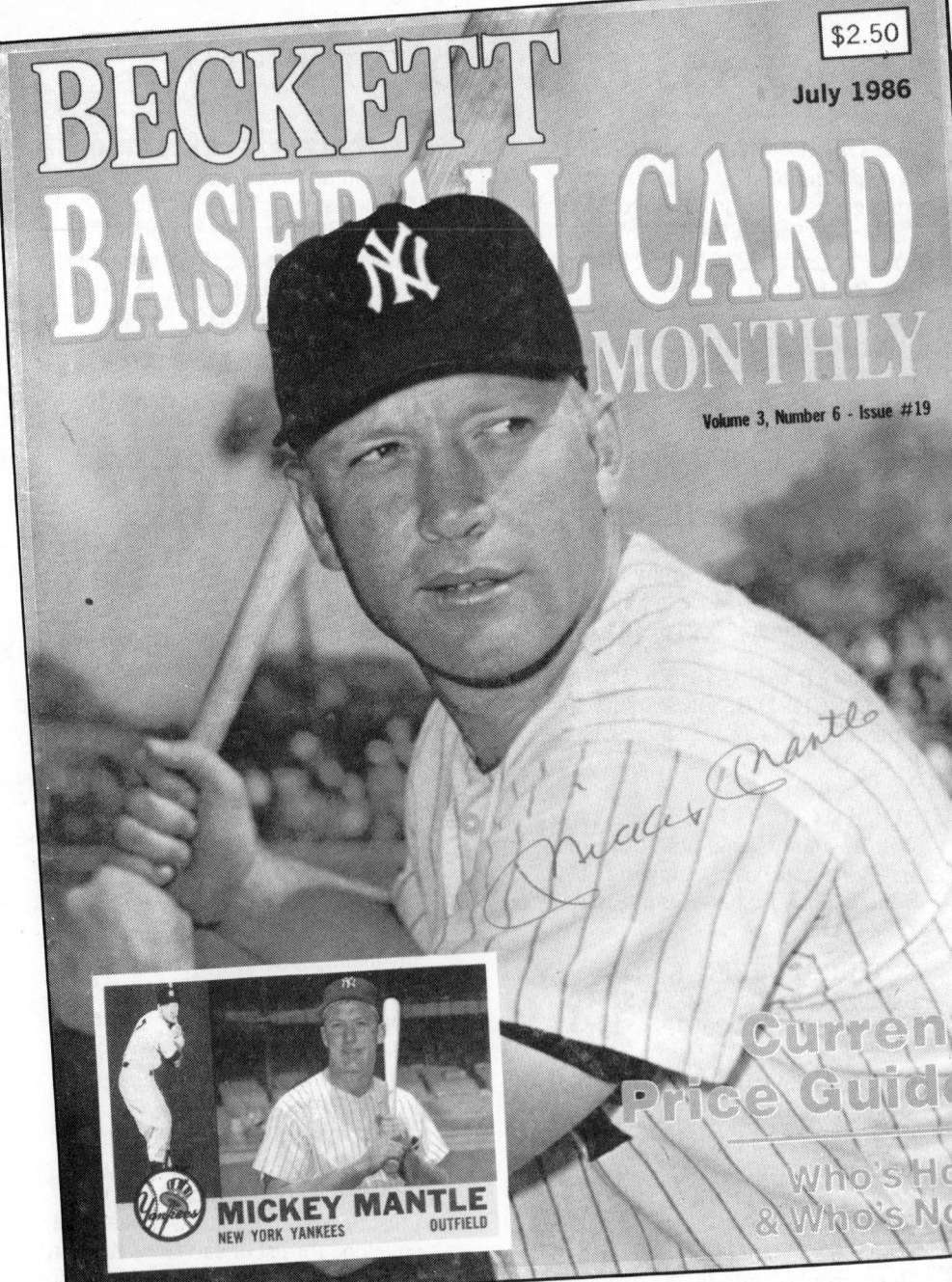

# BECKETT
## BASEBALL CARD
### MONTHLY

$2.50

July 1986

Volume 3, Number 6 - Issue #19

Current
Price Guide

Who's Ho
& Who's No

**MICKEY MANTLE**
NEW YORK YANKEES   OUTFIELD

# Subscribe Now.

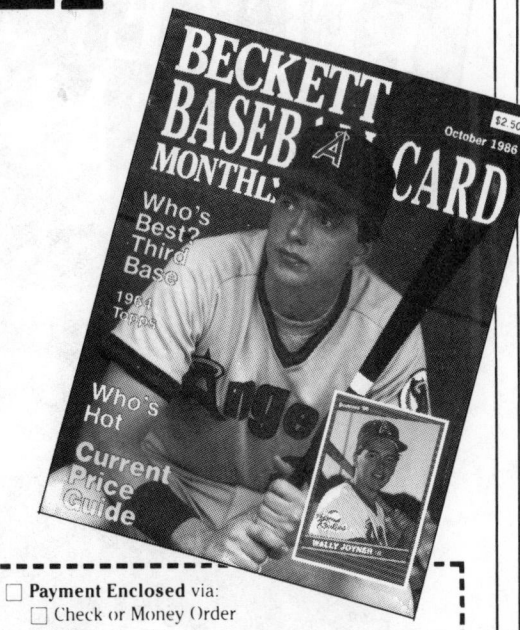